Contemporary Authors

Contemporary Authors

A BIO-BIBLIOGRAPHICAL GUIDE TO
CURRENT AUTHORS AND THEIR WORKS

CHRISTINE NASSO

Editor

 volumes 21-24

first revision

GALE RESEARCH COMPANY • BOOK TOWER • DETROIT, MICHIGAN 48226

CONTEMPORARY AUTHORS

Published by
Gale Research Company, Book Tower, Detroit, Michigan 48226
Each Year's Volumes Are Cumulated and Revised About Five Years Later

Frederick G. Ruffner, *Publisher*   James M. Ethridge, *Editorial Director*

Christine Nasso, *Editor*
Ann Evory, Robin Farbman, Frances Carol Locher,
Margaret Mazurkiewicz, Larry J. Moore, and Nancy M. Rusin, *Assistant Editors*
Ellen Koral, Norma Sawaya, and Shirley Seip, *Editorial Assistants*
Michaeline Nowinski, *Production Manager*

PREFACE

VOLUME 21-24, FIRST REVISION

This volume represents a complete revision and a consolidation into one alphabet of biographical material which originally appeared in *Contemporary Authors,* volume 21-22, published in 1969, and volume 23-24, published in 1970. The revision is up-to-date, in most cases, through late 1976.

In preparing the revision, the following major steps have been taken:

1) *Every sketch has been submitted to the authors concerned,* if still living, and all requested changes within the scope and purpose of *Contemporary Authors* have been made.

2) *The editors have attempted to verify present address, present position, and the bibliography* if authors have failed to submit changes or to approve sketches as still correct. Symbols have been used to indicate that (†) research yielded new information, or (††) research yielded no new information for those sketches appearing in this revision which have not been personally verified by their subjects.

3) *Additional research has been done on the bibliographies of many authors,* both to pick up publications which were not included in the previous versions of their sketches and to assure that all recent works have been included.

All sketches, therefore, should be regarded as "revised," even if they contain no changes, since the material in them has been approved as currently correct, or *CA* editors have made any possible changes in the absence of word from the authors.

4) *"Sidelights" have been added to many listings* for prominent authors whose sketches did not include this material previously, and *"Sidelights"* for numerous other authors have been revised substantially.

As a result of these editorial procedures, the amount of new material in this volume is substantial, and, even after the deletions described below, the revised volume contains approximately the same number of pages as the two original volumes.

Series of Permanent Volumes Established
For Retired and Deceased Authors

A series of Permanent Volumes, serving the same purpose as *Who Was Who* and similar compilations, has been established as an adjunct to *Contemporary Authors,* in order to avoid reprinting in revisions the sketches of authors which will normally not require further change.

Therefore, two classes of authors are omitted from this revision—first, persons now deceased, and second, persons approaching or past normal retirement age who have not published books recently and do not expect to do so in the future. This publication information has been verified either by the authors or through research if the authors failed to submit changes.

Cumulative Index Should Always be Consulted

As always, the cumulative index published in alternate volumes of *CA* will continue to be the user's guide to the location of an individual author's listing. Authors not included in this revision will be indicated in the cumulative index as having appeared in specific original volumes of *CA* (for the benefit of those who do not hold Permanent Volumes), *and* as having their finally revised sketches listed in a specific Permanent Volume.

The editors believe that this revision plan will prove to be not only convenient but also financially advantageous to libraries. Because the plan removes from the revision cycle material which no longer needs periodic review and reprinting, many expenses which would have to be reflected in selling prices will be avoided.

As always, suggestions from users on revision or any other aspect of *CA* will be welcomed.

CONTEMPORARY AUTHORS

† Indicates that informational changes and/or additions have been made on the basis of reliable secondary sources, but the author has not personally verified the entry in this edition.

†† Indicates that research in secondary sources revealed no informational changes or additions, but the author has not personally verified the entry in this edition.

AARON, Benjamin 1915-

PERSONAL: Born September 2, 1915, in Chicago, Ill.; son of Henry J. (a lawyer) and Rose (Weinstein) Aaron; married Eleanor M. Opsahl, May 24, 1941; children: Judith, Louise. *Education:* University of Michigan, A.B., 1937; Harvard University, LL.B., 1940; University of Chicago, graduate study, 1940-41. *Home:* 316 18th St., Santa Monica, Calif. 90402. *Office:* School of Law, University of California, Los Angeles, Calif. 90024.

CAREER: National War Labor Board, staff member, 1942-45; University of California, Los Angeles, research associate, Institute of Industrial Relations, 1946-57, associate director of Institute, 1957-60, director, 1960—, professor of law, 1960—. Member of faculty of Salzburg Seminar in American Studies, 1958, 1967; visiting professor at Cornell University, 1964-65, University of Washington, Seattle, 1965, Stanford University, 1967, and Harvard University, 1972; resident fellow, Center for Advanced Study in the Behavioral Sciences, 1966-67; visiting fellow, Cambridge University, 1973. U.S. Government posts include public member and vice-chairman of Wage Stabilization Board, 1951-52, member of National Commission on Technology, Automation and Economic Progress, 1965-66, and member of Advisory Council of Employee Welfare and Pension Benefit Plans, 1966-68. Member of numerous governmental arbitration boards; private arbitrator, principally in aerospace, nonferrous mining, rubber, steel, airline, and motion picture industries, 1946—.

MEMBER: National Academy of Arbitrators (president, 1962), American Arbitration Association, American Bar Association, Industrial Relations Research Association (president, 1972), International Society for Labor Law and Social Legislation (chairman of American national committee).

WRITINGS: (Cooperating editor) *Labor Relations and the Law,* Little, Brown, 1953, 3rd edition, 1965; (principal editor) *The Employment Relation and the Law,* Little, Brown, 1957; *Legal Status of Employee Benefit Rights Under Private Pension Plans,* Irwin, 1961; (editor) *Labor Courts and Grievance Settlement in Western Europe: Essays by Xavier Blanc Jouvan (and others),* University of California Press, 1971; (editor with K. W. Wedderburn) *Industrial Conflict: A Comparative Legal Survey,* Crane,

Russak, 1972. Contributor of articles on labor law, legislation, and industrial relations to journals.

WORK IN PROGRESS: Editing *Discrimination in Employment: A Six Country Survey.*

* * *

AARON, Chester 1923-

PERSONAL: Born May 9, 1923, in Butler, Pa.; son of Albert (a grocer and farmer) and Celia (Charleson) Aaron; married Margaurite Kelly (a self-employed jeweler), April 17, 1954; stepchildren: Louis Daniel Segal. *Education:* Attended University of California, Los Angeles; University of California, Berkeley, B.A., 1966. *Home:* 2927 Deakin St., Berkeley, Calif. 94705. *Agent:* Curtis Brown Ltd., 60 East 56th St., New York, N.Y. 10022. *Office:* Department of English, St. Mary's College of California, Moraga, Calif. 94575.

CAREER: St. Mary's College of California, Moraga, assistant professor of English. *Military service:* U.S. Army, 1943-46. *Member:* East Bay Association of X-Ray Technicians (president). *Awards, honors:* Chapelbrook Foundation grant.

WRITINGS: About Us (novel), McGraw, 1967; *Better Than Laughter* (juvenile novel), Harcourt, 1972; *An American Ghost,* Harcourt, 1973; *Hello to Bodega,* Atheneum, 1976. Author of play produced at University of California, Berkeley, 1955. Contributor of short stories to *Coastlines* and *North American Review.*

WORK IN PROGRESS: Two novels; a book of short stories.

SIDELIGHTS: Chester Aaron said that the writing style he likes "is almost archaic. I insist upon simplicity. I do not philosophize but engage my characters in action. I am uncomfortable with complicated story lines. My themes are unorthodox but not intellectually pretentious. I do tend toward exotic characters."

* * *

AARON, James Ethridge 1927-

PERSONAL: Born October 8, 1927, in Eldorado, Ill.; son of Ranzzie Orval (a miner) and Beulah (Boyd) Aaron; married Melba Runyon, August 21, 1951; children: Britt Le,

Brian Ethridge. *Education:* University of Illinois, B.S., 1950, M.S., 1951, graduate study, 1951-55; Purdue University, graduate study, 1955; New York University, Ed.D., 1960. *Religion:* Protestant. *Home:* R.R. 4, Carbondale, Ill. 62901. *Office:* Safety Center, Southern Illinois University, Carbondale, Ill. 62901.

CAREER: High school teacher in Illinois, 1950-56; New York University, New York, N.Y., teacher of driver education, 1956-57; Southern Illinois University, Carbondale, assistant professor of driver and safety education, 1960—, coordinator of Safety Center, 1960—. Delegate to President's Safety Conference, 1956, 1958, 1963; member of National Safety Advisory Commission, 1970-73; member, Illinois Governor's Official Traffic Safety Coordinating Committee. *Member:* National Safety Council (chairman of higher education section, 1961-62), American Driver and Traffic Safety Education Association (president, 1967-68), American Academy of Safety Education (honorary member), National Education Association, Association for Higher Education, Illinois High School and College Driver Education Association (president, 1956), Illinois Association of Chiefs of Police, Illinois Police Association, Phi Delta Kappa.

WRITINGS: (With Albert J. Shafter) *The Police Officer and Alcoholism,* C. C Thomas, 1963; (with Marland K. Strasser, J. Ralph Bohn, and John Eales) *Fundamentals of Safety Education,* Macmillan, 1964, 2nd edition, edited by Lloyd C. Chilton, Macmillan, 1973; (with Strasser) *Driver and Traffic Safety Education: Content, Methods and Organization,* Macmillan, 1966; (with Strasser) *Driver Education for Learning to Drive Defensively,* Laidlaw Brothers, 1969; (with A. Frank Bridges and Dale O. Ritzel) *First Aid and Emergency Care: Prevention and Protection of Injuries,* Macmillan, 1972; (with Strasser) *Driving Task Instruction: Dual Control, Simulation, and Multiple-Car,* Macmillan, 1974. Contributor to *Federal Bureau of Investigation Police Training Manual;* contributor to safety, educational, and medical periodicals.

WORK IN PROGRESS: In collaboration with A. Shafter and T. Leffler, *Introduction to the Police Function,* for C. C Thomas.

* * *

AARSLEFF, Hans 1925-

PERSONAL: Born July 19, 1925, in Rungsted, Denmark; son of Einar Faber and Inger (Lotz) Aarsleff. *Education:* University of Copenhagen, B.A., 1945, graduate study 1945-48; University of Minnesota, M.A., 1954, Ph.D., 1960. *Office:* English Department, 22 McCosh, Princeton University, Princeton, N.J. 08540.

CAREER: University of Minnesota, Minneapolis, instructor in English, 1952-56; Princeton University, Princeton, N.J., instructor, 1956-60, assistant professor, 1960-65, associate professor of English, 1965—. *Member:* Modern Language Association of America, Lardomshistoriska Samfundet (Uppsala), American Association of University Professors, Gottfried-Whilhelm-Leibniz-Gesellschaft. *Awards, honors:* Council of the Humanities junior fellow, 1962; American Council of Learned Societies fellow, 1964-65, 1972-73; National Endowment for the Humanities fellow, 1975-76.

WRITINGS: The Study of Language in England, 1780-1860, Princeton University Press, 1967; (contributor) John W. Yolton, editor, *John Locke: Problems and Perspectives,* Cambridge University Press, 1969; (contributor) Dell

Hymes, editor, *Studies in the History of Linguistics,* Indiana University Press, 1974. Contributor to *Dictionary of Scientific Biography,* Contributor of articles to *Language, Monist, Language Sciences,* and other professional journals. Associate editor, *Current Trends in Linguistics.*

WORK IN PROGRESS: The study and philosophy of language, 1600-1800; an edition of a Leibniz manuscript on etymology.

* * *

ABEL, Theodore 1896-

PERSONAL: Born November 24, 1896, in Lodz, Poland; son of Theodore and Jadwiga (Lorenz) Abel; married Theodora Mead (a psychotherapist), September 9, 1923; children: Peter, Caroline, Zita. *Education:* Columbia University, M.A., 1925, Ph.D., 1929. *Politics:* Democrat. *Religion:* Roman Catholic. *Home:* 4200 Sunningdale Ave. N.E., Albuquerque, N.M. 87110.

CAREER: University of Illinois, Urbana, assistant professor of sociology, 1925-29; Columbia University, New York, N.Y., associate professor of sociology, 1929-50; Hunter College of the City University of New York, New York, N.Y., professor of sociology, 1950-67. *Member:* Eastern Sociological Society (president, 1957).

WRITINGS: Protestant Home Missions to Catholic Immigrants, Harper, 1933; (editor) *Freedom and Control in Modern Society,* Van Nostrand, 1954; *Systematic Sociology in Germany,* Octagon, 1966; *The Nazi Movement,* Atherton, 1967; *The Foundation of Sociological Theory,* Random House, 1970.

WORK IN PROGRESS: The Charismatic Movement.

SIDELIGHTS: Abel is fluent in German, Russian, and French.

* * *

ABEL-SMITH, Brian 1926-

PERSONAL: Born November 6, 1926, in London, England; son of Lionel Abel (an army officer) and Genevieve (Walsh) Abel-Smith. *Education:* Clare College, Cambridge, B.A., 1951, M.A. and Ph.D., 1955. *Politics:* Labour Party. *Office:* London School of Economics and Political Science, Houghton St., London W.C. 2, England.

CAREER: National Institute of Social and Economic Research, London, England, research fellow, 1953-55; University of London, London School of Economics and Political Science, London, England, lecturer, 1955-61, reader, 1961-65, professor of social administration, 1965—. British Ministry of Health, member of Saintsbury Committee and Long-Term Study Group, both concerned with the British National Health Service. Consultant to World Health Organization, 1957—, Social Affairs Division of United Nations, 1959, 1961, and Organization for Economic Co-operation and Development. Associate professor, Yale University, 1961. Member, South West Regional Hospital Board, 1956-63; governor of St. Thomas's Hospital, 1957—, chairman of finance committee, 1963—; chairman of Chelsea and Kensington Hospital Management Committee, 1961-62; governor of Maudsley Hospital and the Institute of Psychiatry, 1963-67. Senior advisor to British Secretary of State for Health and Social Security, 1968-70, 1974—. *Military service:* British Army, 1945-48; became captain. *Member:* Fabian Society (chairman, 1964-65; treasurer, 1965-68).

WRITINGS: (With R. M. Titmuss) *The Cost of the National Health Service in England and Wales,* Cambridge University Press, 1956; *A History of the Nursing Profession,* Heinemann, 1960; (with Titmuss) *Social Policy and Population Growth in Mauritius,* Methuen, 1961; *Paying for Health Services,* World Health Organization, 1963; *The Hospitals, 1800-1948,* Heinemann, 1964; (with Titmuss and others) *The Health Services of Tanganyika,* Pitman, 1964; (with Kathleen Gales) *British Doctors at Home and Abroad,* Codicote Press, 1964; (with Peter Townsend) *The Poor and the Poorest,* G. Bell, 1965; (with Robert Stevens) *Lawyers and the Courts,* Harvard University Press, 1967; *An International Study of World Health Expenditure,* World Health Organization, 1967; (with Stevens) *In Search of Justice: Society and the Legal System,* Penguin, 1968; (with Hilary Rose) *Doctors, Patients, and Pathology,* G. Bell, 1972; (with M. Zander and R. Brooke) *Legal Problems and the Citizen: A Study in Three London Boroughs,* Heinemann, 1973. Author of pamphlets published by Fabian Society, 1953-66. Also author of reports: *Accounting for Health,* King Edward's Hospital Fund for London, 1973; *People Without Choice,* International Planned Parenthood Federation, 1973.

Contributor: *Conviction,* MacGibbon & Kee, 1958; M. Ginsberg, editor, *Law and Opinion in England in the Twentieth Century,* Stevens & Sons, 1959; *Aging and Social Health in the United States and Europe,* [Michigan], 1959; Clark Tibbitts and Wilma Donahue, editors, *Social and Psychological Aspects of Aging,* Columbia University Press, 1962; *The Changing Role of the Hospitals in a Changing World,* International Hospital Federation, 1963; Richard H. Williams, Tibbitts, and Donahue, editors, *Processes of Aging,* Volume II, Atherton, 1963; Peter Hall, editor, *Labour's New Frontiers,* Deutsch, 1964. Contributor of some twenty-five articles to *New Statesman, New Society, Guardian, Times, Lancet, Medical World,* and other publications in Britain and abroad.

WORK IN PROGRESS: Research on the economics of health services.

SIDELIGHTS: As World Health Organization consultant on the costs of medical care, Abel-Smith has traveled in Ceylon, Congo, Kenya, and other countries of Africa and Europe.

*   *   *

ABERG, Sherrill E. 1924-

PERSONAL: Born April 11, 1924, in Warren, Pa.; son of Stuart Edward (an insurance agent) and Rose (Brady) Aberg; married Phyllis E. Brenneman. *Education:* University of Missouri, B.S. in Ed., 1949, M.A., 1950; further study at Yale University, 1963, and Lehigh University, 1965. *Home:* 55 Oakland, Huntington, N.Y. 11743.

CAREER: Cold Spring Harbour (N.Y.) High School District 2, teacher of advanced placement classes in history, 1966—. Reader, College Entrance Examination Board, Princeton, N.J. *Military service:* U.S. Navy, foreign-language translator, 1943-46. *Member:* Organization of American Historians, New York Council of the Social Studies, New York Education Association.

WRITINGS: (Editor with Edward Fenton) *Thirty-two Problems in World History,* Scott, Foresman, 1965; (contributor) *The New Social Studies,* Holt, 1966; *Woodrow Wilson and the League of Nations: Why Was a Just Cause Defeated?,* Scholastic Book Services, 1967.

ABERLE, David F(riend) 1918-

PERSONAL: Born November 23, 1918, in St. Paul, Minn.; son of David Winfield (a candy manufacturer) and Lisette (Friend) Aberle; married Eleanor Kathleen Gough (an anthropologist), September 5, 1955; children: Stephen Daniel. *Education:* Harvard University, A.B., 1940, graduate study, 1946-47; Columbia University, Ph.D., 1950; also studied at University of New Mexico, summers, 1938-40, and University of Northern Arizona, summers, 1971, 1973. *Religion:* Jewish. *Office:* Department of Anthropology and Sociology, University of British Columbia, Vancouver, British Columbia, Canada.

CAREER: Harvard University, Cambridge, Mass., instructor in social anthropology, 1947-50, research associate, School of Public Health, 1948-50; Johns Hopkins University, Page School of International Relations, Baltimore, Md., visiting associate professor, 1950-52; University of Michigan, Ann Arbor, associate professor, 1952-58, professor in departments of sociology and anthropology, 1958-60; Brandeis University, Waltham, Mass., professor of anthropology and chairman of department, 1961-63; University of Oregon, Eugene, professor of anthropology, 1963-67; University of British Columbia, Vancouver, professor of anthropology, 1967—. Fellow, Center for Advanced Study in the Behavioral Sciences, Stanford, Calif., 1955-56; Simon Visiting Professor and honorary fellow, University of Manchester, 1960-61. Member of Behavioral Sciences Study section of National Institute of Mental Health, 1957-60. *Military service:* U.S. Army, 1942-46; technical sergeant; received Commendation Ribbon.

MEMBER: American Anthropological Association (fellow; member of executive board, 1968-71), American Sociological Association (fellow), Royal Anthropological Institute of Great Britain and Ireland (fellow), American Ethnological Society, Society for Applied Anthropology, Phi Beta Kappa. *Awards, honors:* Social Science Research Council demobilization award, 1946-47.

WRITINGS: *The Psychosocial Analysis of a Hopi Life-History,* Comparative Psychology Monographs, 1951; *The Kinship System of the Kalmuk Mongols,* University of New Mexico Publications in Anthropology, 1953; (with O. C. Stewart) *Navaho and Ute Peyotism: A Chronological and Distributional Study,* University of Colorado Studies, 1957; *Chahar and Dagor Mongol Bureaucratic Administration: 1912-1945,* Human Relations Area File Press, 1962; *The Peyote Religion Among the Navaho,* Aldine and Viking Fund Publications in Anthropology, 1966; (with Isidore Dyen) *Lexical Reconstruction: The Case of the Proto-Athapaskan Kinship System,* Cambridge University Press, 1974.

Contributor: Marvin B. Sussman, editor, *Sourcebook in Marriage and the Family,* Houghton, 1954; Gertrude E. Dole and Robert L. Carneiro, editors, *Essays in the Science of Culture in Honor of Leslie A. White,* Crowell, 1960; Francis L. K. Hsu, editor, *Psychological Anthropology: Approaches to Culture and Personality,* Dorsey, 1961; wife, Kathleen Gough and David M. Schneider, editors, *Matrilineal Kinship,* University of California Press, 1961; Yehudi A. Cohen, editor, *Social Structure and Personality: A Casebook,* Holt, 1961; Sylvia L. Thrupp, editor, *Millenial Dreams in Action: Essays in Comparative Study,* Mouton & Co., 1962; William J. Goode, editor, *Readings on the Family,* Prentice-Hall, 1964; Dell H. Hymes and William E. Bittle, editors, *Studies in Southwestern Ethnolinguistics,* Mouton & Co., 1967; *Toward*

Economic Development for Native American Communities, U.S. Government Printing Office, 1969; Joseph G. Jorgensen, editor, *Comparative Studies by Harold E. Driver and Essays in His Honor*, Human Relations Area File Press, 1974. Contributor of articles to *Journal of American Folklore, Ethics, Human Organization, American Sociological Review*, and anthropology journals. Review editor, *American Anthropologist*, 1952-55.

WORK IN PROGRESS: Research on Navajo kinship and economy.

* * *

ABERNETHY, Francis Edward 1925-

PERSONAL: Born December 3, 1925, in Altus, Okla.; son of Talbot and Aileen (Cherry) Abernethy; married Hazel Shelton, May 20, 1948; children: Luanna, Robert, Sarah, Margaret, Benjamin. *Education:* Stephen F. Austin State College (now University), B.A., 1949; Louisiana State University, M.A., 1951, Ph.D., 1956. *Politics:* Democrat. *Religion:* Methodist. *Home:* 210 South Lanana St., Nacogdoches, Tex. 75961. *Office:* Stephen F. Austin State University, Nacogdoches, Tex.

CAREER: High school teacher, Woodville, Tex., 1951-53; Lamar State College of Technology (now Lamar University), Beaumont, Tex., assistant professor, 1956-59, associate professor of English, 1959-65; Stephen F. Austin State University, Nacogdoches, Tex., professor of English, 1965—. *Military service:* U.S. Navy, 1943-46. *Member:* American Folklore Society, College Conference of Teachers of English, South Central Renaissance Society, South Central Modern Language Association, Texas Herpetological Society, Texas Folklore Society (secretary-editor; president), Texas Institute of Letters, East Texas Historical Association, Association of Mexican Cave Studies.

WRITINGS: (With Nossen and Emmons) *How to Write a Theme*, McCutchan, 1961; (contributor) *The Golden Log*, Southern Methodist University Press, 1962; *Tales from the Big Thicket*, University of Texas Press, 1966; *J. Frank Dobie*, Steck, 1967; (editor) *Observations and Reflections on Texas Folklore*, Encino Press, 1972; *The Folklore of Texan Cultures*, Encino Press, 1974; *Some Still Do*, Encino Press, 1975. Contributor to *Modern Drama, Sing Out, Studies in English Renaissance*, publications of Texas Folklore Society, and other journals.

WORK IN PROGRESS: Folklore, Mostly Modern, for Encino Press.

AVOCATIONAL INTERESTS: Speleology, herpetology, playing guitar, raising horses, hunting, fishing.

* * *

ABERNETHY, Robert G(ordon) 1927-

PERSONAL: Born November 5, 1927, in Geneva, Switzerland; son of Robert William (a teacher) and Lois (Jones) Abernethy; married Jean Montgomery, April 30, 1955; children: Jane Montgomery. *Education:* Princeton University, A.B., 1950, M.P.A., 1952. *Religion:* Congregationalist. *Office:* National Broadcasting Co., 3000 West Alameda Ave., Burbank, Calif. 91503.

CAREER: National Broadcasting Co., correspondent in Washington, D.C., 1953-55, London, England, 1955-58, Washington, D.C., 1958-66, and Los Angeles, Calif., 1966—, writer and narrator of "Update," news report for young people, 1961-63, science editor, 1965-66. *Military service:* U.S. Army, 1946-47. *Awards, honors:* Thomas

Alva Edison Foundation Award for best history for young people, 1966, for *Introduction to Tomorrow*.

WRITINGS: Introduction to Tomorrow, Harcourt, 1966.

* * *

ABISCH, Roslyn Kroop 1927-
(Roz Abisch; pseudonyms: Mr. McGillicuddy, Mr. Sniff; joint pseudonym: A. K. Roche)

PERSONAL: Born April 2, 1927, in Brooklyn, N.Y.; daughter of Benjamin and Frieda (Steinberg) Kroop; married Howard R. Abisch (a construction supervisor), December 25, 1946; children: Janet, Ellen, Susan. *Education:* Brooklyn College (now Brooklyn College of the City University of New York), B.A., 1948. *Home and office:* 1095 Verbena Ave., North Merrick, N.Y. 11566.

CAREER: Advertising copywriter, 1944-48; teacher in New York (N.Y.) public schools, 1948-49; Kalle Studio, New York, N.Y., advertising copywriter, 1949-50; United Cerebral Palsy of Queens, N.Y., teacher-therapist assistant, 1954-56; Union Free School District 29, North Merrick, N.Y., administrator and curriculum coordinator for enrichment workshop program, 1959-61; lecturer on juvenile literature. Developed learning programs and prepared teacher's manuals for various audio-visual purposes; designed and prepared an exhibit on the development of a children's book. *Member:* Child Study Association (member of speakers' bureau, 1964—), Authors Guild.

WRITINGS—With Boche Kaplan as illustrator, except as noted; all children's literature: Under name Roz Abisch: *Open Your Eyes*, Parents' Magazine Press, 1964; *Anywhere in the World*, McKay, 1966; *Art Is for You*, McKay, 1967; *Do You Know What Time It Is?*, Prentice-Hall, 1969; *'Twas in the Moon of Wintertime*, Prentice-Hall, 1969; *Mai-Ling and the Mirror* (adapted from a Chinese folk tale), Prentice-Hall, 1969; *The Shoe for Your Left Foot Won't Fit on the Right*, McCall Publishing, 1970; *Sweet Betsy from Pike*, McCall Publishing, 1970; *If I Could, I Would*, F. Watts, 1971; *Silly Street*, F. Watts, 1971; *Smile If You Meet a Crocodile*, F. Watts, 1971; *Blast Off!*, F. Watts, 1971; *Out in the Woods*, F. Watts, 1971; *Under the Ocean, Under the Sea*, F. Watts, 1971; *Let's Find Out about Butterflies*, F. Watts, 1972; *Around the House that Jack Built*, Parents' Magazine Press, 1972; *Easy to Make Holiday Fun Things*, Xerox Education Publications, 1973; *Mixed Bag of Magic Tricks*, Xerox Education Publications, 1973, hard cover edition, Walker & Co., 1975; *What's the Good Word?*, Urban Media Materials, 1973; *Star Books for Learning*, New Dimensions in Education, Series I, 1973, Series II, in press; *The Make-It, Play-It Game Book*, Walker & Co., 1974; (compiler) *Textiles*, F. Watts, 1974; *The Reading Works*, New Dimensions in Education, 1975; *Word Builders*, two volumes, Urban Media Materials, 1975.

Under pseudonym Mr. Sniff: *Wishes, Whiffs, and Birthday Gifts*, F. Watts, 1971; *Circus Tents and Circus Scents*, F. Watts, 1971; *Scented Rhymes for Story Times*, F. Watts, 1971; *Scents and Sun and Picnic Fun*, F. Watts, 1971.

With Boche Kaplan under joint pseudonym A. K. Roche: *I Can Be*, Prentice-Hall, 1967; (self-illustrated) *The Pumpkin Heads*, Prentice-Hall, 1968; (self-illustrated) *The Onion Maidens*, Prentice-Hall, 1968; (self-illustrated) *The Clever Turtle* (adapted from an African folk tale), Prentice-Hall, 1969; *Even the Promise of Freedom*, Prentice-Hall, 1970; (compiler) *The City . . . in Haiku*, Prentice-Hall, 1970.

Also author of, under pseudonym Mr. McGillicuddy, *Spring, Summer, Fall, Winter,* 1970, and, under pseudonym Mr. Sniff, *Big, Little, Tall, Short,* 1974.

SIDELIGHTS: Roslyn Abisch and Boche Kaplan's preliminary manuscripts and art work from *The Clever Turtle,* *'Twas in the Moon of Wintertime,* and *Sweet Betsy from Pike* have been included as part of the Kerlan Collection, Walter Library, at University of Minnesota. Preliminary and finished art from *Sweet Betsy from Pike* and *Around the House that Jack Built* are part of an exhibit on children's literature at the Portland Museum of Art in Oregon.

BIOGRAPHICAL/CRITICAL SOURCES: See also **KAPLAN, Boche.**

* * *

ABRAHAM, Claude K(urt) 1931-

PERSONAL: Born December 13, 1931, in Lorsch, Germany; son of Siegmund and Johanna (Wachenheimer) Abraham; married Marcia Phillips, June 3, 1956; children: Susan, Stephen, Catherine, Linda. *Education:* University of Cincinnati, B.A., 1953, M.A., 1956; Indiana University, Ph.D., 1959. *Home:* 677 Equador Pl., Davis, Calif. 95616. *Office:* Department of French and Italian, University of California, Davis, Calif. 95616.

CAREER: University of Illinois, Urbana, instructor, 1959-61, assistant professor of French, 1961-64; University of Florida, Gainesville, associate professor, 1964-70, professor of French, 1970-75, assistant dean of graduate school, 1972-73; University of California, Davis, professor of French, 1975—. *Military service:* U.S. Army, 1953-55. *Member:* Modern Language Association of America, American Association of Teachers of French (Florida chapter president, 1971-73), South Atlantic Modern Language Association (section chairman, 1969). *Awards, honors:* Research grants from University of Illinois, 1961, 1962, and University of Florida, 1965, 1967, 1969; National Endowment for Humanities grant, 1969; South Atlantic Modern Language Association studies award, 1970, for *Enfin Malherbe.*

WRITINGS: Gaston d'Orleans et sa cour, University of North Carolina Press, 1963; (editor) Moliere, *Le Bourgeois gentilhomme,* Prentice-Hall, 1966; *The Strangers: The Tragic World of Tristan L'Hermite,* University of Florida Press, 1966; (translator with wife, Marcia Abraham) J. Mesnard, *Pascal,* University of Alabama Press, 1969; *Enfin Malherbe: The Influence of Malherbe on French Lyric Prosody, 1605-1674,* University Press of Kentucky, 1971; *Pierre Corneille,* Twayne, 1972; (editor with J. Schweitzer and J. V. Baelen) *Theatre de Tristan L'Hermite,* University of Alabama Press, 1975. Contributor to *Modern Drama, Drama Critique, French Review,* and other language journals.

WORK IN PROGRESS: A monograph on Norman satirists; a book on Racine.

* * *

ABRAMS, Sam(uel) 1935-
(Frank Newman)

PERSONAL: Born November 18, 1935, in New York, N.Y.; son of Moe (a lawyer) and Miriam (Rosenthal) Abrams; married; wife's name Barbara; children: Ezra, Joshua. *Education:* Brooklyn College (now Brooklyn College of the City University of New York), A.B., 1958; University of Illinois, M.A., 1959, currently a Ph.D. candidate.

CAREER: Drew University, Madison, N.J., head of classics department (until 1969) with academic rank of instructor. Conducted a poetry project at St. Mark's-in-the-Bouwerie, 1967.

WRITINGS: (Under pseudonym Frank Newman) *Barbara* (poems), Ferry Press, (London), 1966; *Book of Days* (poems), [Madison, Wis.], 1967; *The Post-American Cultural Congress* (poems), Bobbs-Merrill, 1974.†

* * *

ABRASH, Merritt 1930-

PERSONAL: Born April 3, 1930, in Peterson, N.J.; married Barbara Blackman, 1952; children: Michael, Victoria. *Education:* Washington and Lee University, B.A., 1951; Columbia University, M.I.A. and Certificate of Russian Institute, 1958, Ph.D., 1961. *Home:* Van Winkle Dr., R.D. 1, Rensselaer, N.Y. 12144. *Office:* Rennselaer Polytechnic Institute, Troy, N.Y. 12181.

CAREER: Clark University, Worcester, Mass., instructor, 1960-61, assistant professor of history, 1961-62; Rensselaer Polytechnic Institute, Troy, N.Y., assistant professor, 1962-65, associate professor of history, 1965—, director of Institute on Industrial Archaeology, 1974, 1976. *Military Service:* U.S. Army, 1954-56. *Member:* Society for Industrial Archeology, College Art Association of America. *Awards, honors:* O'Neill Playwriting fellow of National Playwrights Conference, 1970.

WRITINGS: (Co-author) *Russian Diplomacy and Eastern Europe, 1914-1917,* King's Crown Press, 1963; ''Postscript'' (one-act play), produced at Yale Drama Festival, 1967, and at Berkshire Theatre Festival, 1970.

WORK IN PROGRESS: Articles on art history, especially Gustave Courbet, George Stubbs, and S. Spencer.

AVOCATIONAL INTERESTS: The theater.

* * *

ABSHIRE, David M. 1926-

PERSONAL: Born April 11, 1926, in Chattanooga, Tenn.; son of James Ernest (a businessman) and Edith (Patten) Abshire; married Carolyn Lamar Sample (an importer), September 7, 1957; children: Lupton, Anna Lamar, Mary Lee, Phyllis. *Education:* U.S. Military Academy, B.S., 1951; Georgetown University, Ph.D., 1959. *Politics:* Republican. *Religion:* Episcopalian. *Home:* 311 S. St. Asaph St., Alexandria, Va. 22314.

CAREER: U.S. Army, cadet, 1946-51, regular officer, 1951-55, leaving service with rank of first lieutenant; became captain, U.S. Army Reserve; U.S. House of Representatives, Washington, D.C., staff, 1959-60; American Enterprise Institute for Public Policy Research, Washington, D.C., staff, 1961-62; Georgetown University, Center for Strategic Studies, Washington, D.C., executive secretary and chairman of research committee, beginning 1962; assistant secretary of state for congressional relations, 1970-73. Presidential appointee to the Congressional Commission on the Organization of Government for Conduct of Foreign Policy, beginning 1973. Consultant to *Reader's Digest* and American International Group, Inc. *Member:* Foreign Policy Association, Academy of Political and Social Science, Gold Key Society, Chevy Chase, International Army and Navy Club, Phi Alpha Theta. *Awards, honors*—Military: Bronze Star Medal (twice), Commendation Ribbon, Combat Infantryman Badge (all for service in Korea).

WRITINGS: (Editor with Richard Allen) *National Security: Political, Military and Economic Strategies in the Decade Ahead,* Praeger, 1963; (contributor) *Detente: Cold War Strategies in Transition,* Praeger, 1965; *The South Rejects a Prophet: The Life of Senator D. M. Key, 1824-1900,* Praeger, 1967; (editor with M. Samuels) *Portuguese Africa: A Handbook,* Praeger, 1969. Contributor to *U.S. Navel Institute Proceedings, Army, New York Times, Annals of the American Academy of Political and Social Science, American Political Science Review.*†

* * *

ABU JABER, Kamel S. 1932-

PERSONAL: Born March 8, 1932, in Amman, Jordon; married Loretta Pacifico (a teacher), October 5, 1957; children: Linda, Nyla. *Education:* Syracuse University, B.A., 1960, Ph.D., 1965; Princeton University, graduate study, 1962-63. *Religion:* Greek Orthodox. *Office:* Smith College, Northampton, Mass.

CAREER: Jordan Ministry of Interior, Amman, clerical worker and translator, 1952-54; Syracuse University, Syracuse, N.Y., lecturer, 1965; University of Tennessee, Knoxville, assistant professor, 1965-67; Smith College, Northampton, Mass., associate professor, beginning 1967. *Military service:* U.S. Army, 1955-57. *Member:* American Political Science Association, Middle East Institute, Southern Political Science Association, Pi Sigma Alpha. *Awards, honors:* Woodrow Wilson fellowship; Ford Foundation Foreign Area fellowship for research in Lebanon, Syria, and Jordan, 1963-64.

WRITINGS: (Editor) *Judhur al-Ishtirakiyyah* (title means "Roots of Socialism"), Tal'ah Publishing House, 1964; *The Arab Ba'th Socialist Party: History, Ideology and Organization,* Syracuse University Press, 1966. Contributor to *Middle East Journal, Muslim World, Redaktion Bustan,* and *Revista Mexicana de Orientacion.*

WORK IN PROGRESS: The Arab Labor Movement, a study of the Arab trade union movement and its role in an emerging region of the world; editing *The Legislator in Transitional Societies.*††

* * *

ADAM, Ruth (Augusta) 1907-

PERSONAL: Born December 14, 1907, in Nottingham, England; daughter of Rupert William (a clergyman, Church of England) and Annie (Wearing) King; married Kenneth Adam (former director of television, British Broadcasting Corp.), May 24, 1932; children: Corinna (Mrs. Neal Ascherson), Clive, Piers, Nicolas. *Education:* Attended St. Elphin's School for Daughters of the Clergy, Matlock, Derbyshire, England, 1919-26. *Religion:* Church of England. *Home:* 19 Old Court House, Old Court Place, London W. 8, England. *Agent:* David Higham Associates Ltd., 5 Lower John St., London W. 1, England; and Harold Ober Associates, Inc., 40 East 49th St., New York, N.Y. 10017.

CAREER: Teacher in primary schools, Nottingham, England, 1926-32; writer, British Ministry of Information, London, England, 1940-45; author. Broadcaster on radio; occasional participant in television panels. Member of Police Dependent's Trust Committee, Fisher (children's welfare) Committee, and Hospital Management Committee. *Member:* Society of Authors, P.E.N., Fabian Society.

WRITINGS: Safety First (juvenile play), Macmillan, 1934; *War on Saturday Week* (novel), Lippincott, 1937; *I'm Not Complaining* (novel), Lippincott, 1938; *There Needs No Ghost* (novel), Chapman & Hall, 1940; *Murder in the Home Guard* (novel), Chapman & Hall, 1943; *They Built a Nation* (American history textbook), Methuen, 1944; *Set to Partners* (novel), Chapman & Hall, 1947; *Fetch Her Away* (novel), Chapman & Hall, 1954; *So Sweet a Changeling* (novel), Chapman & Hall, 1955; *House in the Country* (autobiographical), Muller, 1957; *Susan of St. Bride's* (juvenile novel), Longacre Press, 1958; *Susan and the Wrong Baby* (juvenile novel), Longacre Press, 1959; *Look Who's Talking* (novel), Muller, 1960; *Careers in Child Care,* H. M. Home Office, 1961; *Careers in Approved Schools,* H. M. Home Office, 1961; *What Shaw Really Said,* MacDonald & Co., 1966, Schocken, 1967; (with Kitty Muggeridge) *Beatrice Webb: A Life, 1858-1943,* Secker & Warburg, 1967, Knopf, 1968; *A Woman's Place* (social history), Chatto & Windus, 1975.

BIOGRAPHICAL/CRITICAL SOURCES: New Republic, June 22, 1968; *Best Sellers,* July 1, 1968; *New Yorker,* July 13, 1968; *Newsweek,* July 17, 1968; *Esquire,* August, 1968; *Commentary,* August, 1968; *Book World,* August 4, 1968.

* * *

ADAMEC, Ludwig W(arren) 1924-

PERSONAL: Born March 10, 1924, in Vienna, Austria; U.S. citizen; son of Ludwig and Emma (Kubitschek) Adamec; married Ena Vargas, June 9, 1962; children: Eric. *Education:* University of California, Los Angeles, B.A., 1960, M.A., 1961, Ph.D., 1966. *Home:* 5601 East Hawthorne, Tucson, Ariz. 85711. *Office:* Department of Oriental Studies, University of Arizona, Tucson, Ariz. 85721.

CAREER: University of California, Los Angeles, postdoctoral fellow, 1966, lecturer in history, 1966-67; University of Arizona, Tucson, assistant professor, 1967-69, associate professor, 1969-74, professor of Near Eastern Studies, 1974—. Research associate at University of Michigan, summer, 1967, and University of California, Los Angeles, 1968. *Member:* Middle East Studies Association of North America (fellow), Middle East Institute, American Association of University Professors. *Awards, honors:* Fulbright-Hays award for research in India and Afghanistan, 1964-65; Social Science Research Council grant, summer, 1968; Fulbright Professor in Iran, 1973-74.

WRITINGS: Afghanistan 1900-1923: A Diplomatic History, University of California Press, 1967; (editor with George L. Grassmuck and contributor) *Afghanistan: Some New Approaches,* Center for Near Eastern and North African Studies, University of Michigan, 1969; (editor) *Political and Historical Gazetteer of Afghanistan,* Akademische Druck- und Verlagsanstalt (Graz), Volume I: *Badakhshan and Northeastern Afghanistan,* 1972, Volume II: *Farah and Southwestern Afghanistan,* 1973, Volume III: *Herat and Northwestern Afghanistan,* 1975; *Afghanistan's Foreign Affairs in the 20th Century: Relations with Russia, Germany, and Britain,* University of Arizona Press, 1974; (editor) *Who's Who in Afghanistan,* Akademische Druck- und Verlagsanstalt, 1975.

WORK IN PROGRESS: Editing *Historical Gazetteer of Iran,* for Akademische Druck- und Verlagsanstalt; *A History of United States-Afghan Relations.*

SIDELIGHTS: Adamec has lived for periods in Afghanistan, India, Arab Middle East, Iran, and Europe; he is competent in German, French, Spanish, Persian, Arabic, and cognate languages.

ADAMS, Ansel (Easton) 1902-

PERSONAL: Born February 20, 1902, in San Francisco, Calif.; son of Charles Hitchcock (a businessman) and Olive (Bray) Adams; married Virginia Best, January 2, 1928; children: Michael, Anne (Mrs. Charles Mayhew). *Education:* "Erratic. Trained as musician." *Politics:* Democrat. *Religion:* "No formal religion." *Home and studio address:* Route 1, Box 181, Carmel, Calif. 93921.

CAREER: Professional pianist and teacher, 1920-30; professional photographer, 1932—. Instructor in photography, Art Center School, Los Angeles, Calif., 1939-42; director of photography department for Golden Gate International Exposition, 1940; vice-chairman of photography department, San Francisco Museum of Modern Art, 1940-42; director of photography department, California School of Fine Arts, 1946-49; consultant to Polaroid Corp., 1952—; faculty member, Idyllwild Arts Foundation, 1958-60; trustee of Foundation for Environmental Design and Trustees for Conservation, San Francisco.

MEMBER: American Academy of Arts and Sciences (fellow), Photographic Society of America (fellow), Royal Photographic Society (England; fellow), Sierra Club (San Francisco; director, 1934-71), Old Capital Club (Monterey). *Awards, honors:* Guggenheim fellowships, 1946-47, 1948-49, 1959-61; D.F.A., University of California, Berkeley, 1961, Yale University, 1973, University of Massachusetts, 1974, University of Arizona, 1975; D.H., Occidental College, 1967; Conservation Service Award, U.S. Department of the Interior, 1968.

WRITINGS: Making a Photograph: An Introduction to Photography, Studio, 1935, 2nd edition, 1949; *The Four Seasons in Yosemite National Park: A Photographic Story of Yosemite's Spectacular Scenery,* Times Mirror, 1936, 2nd edition, Yosemite Park & Curry Co., 1937; *Sierra Nevada: The John Muir Trail,* The Illustrator, 1938; (with wife, Virginia Adams) *Illustrated Guide to Yosemite Valley,* Crocker, 1940, 5th edition, Stanford University Press, 1952; (with Virginia Adams) *Michael and Anne in the Yosemite Valley,* Studio, 1941; *Born Free and Equal: Photographs of Loyal Japanese-Americans at Manzanar Relocation Center, Inyo County, California,* U.S. Camera, 1944; *My Camera in Yosemite Valley: 24 Photographs and an Essay on Mountain Photography,* Houghton, 1949; *My Camera in the National Parks: 30 Photographs with Interpretative Text and Informative Material on the Parks and Monuments, and Photographic Data,* Houghton, 1950; *Yosemite Valley,* 5 Associates, 1959, 2nd edition, 1963.

(With Nancy Newhall) *This is the American Earth,* Sierra Club, 1960; *These We Inherit: The Parklands of America,* Sierra Club, 1962; *Polaroid Land Photography Manual: A Technical Handbook,* Morgan & Morgan, 1963; (with Virginia Adams) *Illustrated Guide to Yosemite: The Valley, the Rim, and the Central Yosemite Sierra, and Mountain Photography,* Sierra Club, 1963; (with Newhall) *Fiat Lux: The University of California,* McGraw, 1967; (with Newhall) *The Tetons and the Yellowstone,* 5 Associates, 1970; *Ansel Adams: Images 1923-1974,* New York Graphic Society, 1974. Also author of "Basic Photo Series" for Morgan & Morgan, 1948—.

Portfolios: Portfolio I, National Parks and Monuments, 1948; *Portfolio II,* National Parks and Monuments, 1950; *Portfolio III: Yosemite Valley,* Sierra Club, 1960; *Portfolio IV,* Varian Foundation, 1961; *Portfolio V,* Parasol Press, 1971; *Portfolio VI,* Parasol Press, 1973.

Illustrator: Mary Hunter Austin, *Taos Pueblo,* [San Francisco], 1930; Austin, *The Land of Little Rain,* Houghton, 1950; Nancy Newhall, *The Pageant of History in Northern California,* [San Francisco], 1954; Newhall, *Death Valley,* 5 Associates, 1954, 4th edition, 1970; Newhall, *Mission San Xavier del Bac,* 5 Associates, 1954; Edward Joesting, *The Islands of Hawaii,* 1958; Edwin Corle, *Death Valley and the Creek Called Furnace,* Ritchie, 1962; Joesting, *An Introduction to Hawaii,* 5 Associates, 1964; (with others) David Ross Brower, editor, *Not Man Apart: Lines from Robinson Jeffers,* Sierra Club, 1965; (with others) Harvey Manning, *The Wild Cascades: Forgotten Parkland,* Sierra Club, 1965.

AVOCATIONAL INTERESTS: Conservation and music.

BIOGRAPHICAL/CRITICAL SOURCES: N. W. Newhall, *The Eloquent Light: Ansel Adams,* Sierra Club, 1964.

* * *

ADAMS, Cindy

PERSONAL: Born in New York, N.Y.; daughter of Harry (an insurance agent) and Jessica (Sugar) Heller; married Joey Adams (a comedian since the 1930's and writer), February 14, 1952. *Home:* 1050 Fifth Ave., New York, N.Y. 10028. *Agent:* (Literary) Mrs. Carleton Cole, Waldorf Astoria Hotel, New York, N.Y.; (lectures) Keedick Lecture Bureau, 475 Fifth Ave., New York, N.Y.

CAREER: Former model and cover girl; former war correspondent in Vietnam; WABC-TV, New York, N.Y., newscaster, 1966-68. Correspondent for North American Newspaper Alliance and Womens News Service; professional lecturer and fashion show commentator; conductor with husband of tours to the Orient for Northwest Orient Airlines, 1969—. *Member:* American Federation of Television and Radio Artists, American Guild of Variety Artists, Screen Actors Guild, Actors' Equity Association. *Awards, honors:* Named professional woman of the year by Yeshiva University and woman of the year by Troupers (theatrical organization), both 1967.

WRITINGS: Sukarno: An Autobiography As Told to Cindy Adams, Bobbs-Merrill, 1965; (editor) *The West Point Thayer Papers, 1808-1872,* Association of Graduates, 1965. *My Friend the Dictator,* Bobbs-Merrill, 1968; *Jolie Gabor: An Autobiography As Told to Cindy Adams,* Mason/Charter, 1975. Writer of syndicated column, "Cindy Says." Regular contributor to popular magazines, and contributor of feature articles to *Christian Science Monitor.*

WORK IN PROGRESS: How to Housebreak a Husband, for Bobbs-Merrill.

SIDELIGHTS: Cindy Adams lived in Indonesia for five years; she speaks some Indonesian, but better French, Spanish, and German. She told *CA* that her style of interviewing famous people has been called "sassy, brassy and irreverent." *Avocational interests:* Collecting Ming, Sung, and other Oriental objects of art.

* * *

ADAMS, Henry H(itch) 1917-
(Henry Allen, a joint pseudonym)

PERSONAL: Born March 26, 1917, in Ann Arbor, Mich.; son of Henry Foster (a professor) and Susan (Hitch) Adams; married Catherine Sanders, August 22, 1943; children: Catherine S., Henry Arthur Sanders. *Education:* University of Michigan, A.B., 1939; Columbia University, M.A., 1940, Ph.D., 1942. *Religion:* Episcopalian. *Home:* Ferry Farms, Annapolis, Md. 21402. *Agent:* Bill Berger

Associates, Inc., 444 East 58th St., New York, N.Y. 10022.

CAREER: Cornell University, Ithaca, N.Y., instructor in English, 1945-51; U.S. Naval Academy, Annapolis, Md., assistant professor, 1951-58, associate professor, 1958-63, professor of English and History, 1963-68; Illinois State University, Normal, professor of English and head of department, 1968-73; writer, 1973—. *Military service:* U.S. Naval Reserve, 1943—; now captain; commanding officer of Naval Reserve Officers School, Baltimore, Md., 1965-68. *Member:* College English Association (board of directors, 1961-64; vice-president, 1965-66; president, 1967-69), American Historical Association, Modern Language Association of America, U.S. Naval Institute.

WRITINGS: English Domestic or Homiletic Tragedy, 1575-1642, Columbia University Press, 1943; *Dramatic Essays of the Neoclassic Age,* Columbia University Press, 1950; *Techniques of Revision,* Ronald, 1951; (with E. B. Potter and others) *United States and World Sea Power,* Prentice-Hall, 1955; (with Potter and Fleet Admiral C. W. Nimitz) *Sea Power,* Prentice-Hall, 1960; *1942: The Year That Doomed the Axis,* McKay, 1967; *Years of Deadly Peril,* McKay, 1969; *Years of Expectation: Guadalcanal to Normandy,* McKay, 1973; *Years to Victory,* McKay, 1973. With Allen B. Cook, former contributor of "Acrosticklers" to *Reporter,* and *Harper's* under joint pseudonym Henry Allen.

WORK IN PROGRESS: The Man in Lincoln's Study; The Life of Harry L. Hopkins, for Putnam.

SIDELIGHTS: Henry Adams reads French, German, Italian. *Avocational interests:* Photography.

* * *

ADAMSON, William Robert 1927-

PERSONAL: Born December 14, 1927, in Maclean, Saskatchewan, Canada; son of Joseph (a farmer) and Edith (Miller) Adamson; married Louise Kruger, July 3, 1951; children: Bruce, Shelley, Susan, Michael. *Education:* University of Saskatchewan, B.A., 1948; St. Andrew's Theological College, Saskatoon, Saskatchewan, B.D., 1953; Pacific School of Religion, S.T.M., 1955, Th.D., 1960. *Home:* 805 Acadia Dr., Saskatoon, Saskatchewan, Canada 57H 3W2. *Office:* St. Andrew's Theological College, 1121 College Dr., Saskatoon, Saskatchewan, Canada 57N 0W3.

CAREER: Clergyman of United Church of Canada. Pastor in Esterhazy, Saskatchewan, 1951-57, and Regina, Saskatchewan, 1959-64; Naramata Centre for Continuing Education, Naramata, British Columbia, staff associate, 1964-67; United Church of Canada, Head Office, Toronto, Ontario, associate secretary of leadership development committee, 1968-73; St. Andrew's Theological College, Saskatoon, Saskatchewan, professor of Christian ministry, 1973—.

WRITINGS: Bushnell Rediscovered, United Church (Philadelphia), 1966.

* * *

ADDY, George M(ilton) 1927-

PERSONAL: Born July 6, 1927, in Salt Lake City, Utah; married Caroline Stucki, 1951; children: one daughter. *Education:* Brigham Young University, B.A., 1948, M.A., 1950; Duke University, Ph.D., 1957. *Office:* Brigham Young University, Provo, Utah 84601.

CAREER: Brigham Young University, Provo, Utah, instructor, 1957-58, assistant professor, 1958-63, associate professor, 1963-67, professor of history, beginning 1967. *Military service:* U.S. Army, 1951-52. *Member:* American Historical Association, Conference on Latin American History, Latin American Studies Association, Society of Spanish and Portuguese History Studies, American Association of University Professors, Phi Beta Kappa, Phi Alpha Theta. *Awards, honors:* Fulbright research scholar in Spain, 1964-65; National Endowment for the Humanities grant, 1972-74.

WRITINGS: The Enlightenment in the University of Salamanca, Duke University Press, 1966. Contributor to *Hispanic American Historical Review* and *BYU Studies.*

WORK IN PROGRESS: Further research in the Spanish enlightenment.†

* * *

ADELMAN, Irving 1926-

PERSONAL: Born February 22, 1926, in New London, Conn.; son of Joseph (a machinist) and Yetta (Broady) Adelman; married Florence Less, September 6, 1953; children: Steven, Marc. *Education:* Northeastern University, B.A., 1948; Columbia University, M.A., 1951, M.S. in L.S., 1954. *Politics:* Democrat. *Religion:* Jewish. *Home:* 73 Autumn Lane, Hicksville, N.Y. 11801.

CAREER: Long Beach (Calif.) Public Library, junior librarian, 1954-56; Brooklyn (N.Y.) Public Library, junior librarian, later senior librarian, 1956-58; East Meadow (N.Y.) Public Library, head of reference department, 1958—. Member of index committee, H. W. Wilson Co., 1973-74.

WRITINGS: (With Rita Dworkin) *Modern Drama: A Checklist of Critical Literature on 20th Century Plays,* Scarecrow, 1967; (with Rita Dworkin) *The Contemporary Novel: A Checklist of Critical Literature on the British and American Novel Since 1945,* Scarecrow, 1972. Member of national advisory committee, *Encyclopedia of World Biography,* 1966-75.

WORK IN PROGRESS: With Rita Dworkin, *Poetry Criticism: A Checklist of Critical Literature on British and American Poetry,* completion expected in 1978.

* * *

AFFRON, Charles 1935-

PERSONAL: Born October 16, 1935, in Brooklyn, N.Y.; son of Maurice B. (a salesman) and Toby (Lebow) Affron; married Mirella Jona (a university teacher), September 3, 1961; children: Matthew, Beatrice. *Education:* Brandeis University, B.A., 1957; Yale University, Ph.D., 1963. *Home:* 180 Park Row, New York, N.Y. 10038. *Office:* Department of French and Italian, New York University, New York, N.Y. 10003.

CAREER: Brandeis University, Waltham, Mass., assistant professor of French, 1962-65; New York University, New York, N.Y., 1965—, began as assistant professor, became professor of French. Director of Italian branch, Classrooms Abroad. *Member:* Modern Language Association of America.

WRITINGS: Patterns of Failure in "La Comedie humaine," Yale University Press, 1966; *A Stage for Poets: Studies in the Theatre of Hugo and Musset,* Princeton University Press, 1971; *Continuous Showings: Gish,*

Garbo, Davis and the Perception of Screen Acting, Dutton, 1976.

AVOCATIONAL INTERESTS: Opera, theater, and films.

* * *

AGARWALA, Amar N. 1917-

PERSONAL: Born July 18, 1917, in Firozabad, Uttar Pradesh, India; son of Girwardhari Lal and Bhagwandem Agarwala; married June 22, 1940, wife's name Rajeshwari; children: Kamlesh, Umesh, Rekha Agarwala Ashok, Sadhana, Shubhanjali. *Education:* K.P. Intermediate College, Allahabad, India, student, 1933-35; Allahabad University, B.Com., 1937, M.A., 1939, D.Litt., 1957. *Politics:* None. *Religion:* Hinduism. *Home:* 5 Balrampur House, Allahabad 2, Uttar Pradesh, India. *Office:* Allahabad University, Alahabad 2, Uttar Pradesh, India.

CAREER: Allahabad University, Allahabad, India. lecturer, 1939-50, reader, 1950-56, professor of commerce and business administration, beginning 1956, currently head of department of commerce and business administration, and senior professor of management and director, Motilal Nehru Institute of Research and Business Administration. Saugor University, head of economics department, 1947-48; Massachusetts Institute of Technology, visiting scholar, 1960; Michigan State University, visiting professor, 1965; University of Michigan, visiting research professor, 1967-68. Government of India, research deputation, 1943-44, member of Cultural Delegation to China, 1955, member of Special Committee on Commerce Education, Ministry of Education, 1958-61, director of Agro-Economic Research Center, Ministry of Food and Agriculture; member of panel of economists and panel of agriculture, Indian Planning Commission. President of International Committee for Management Development in Developing Countries. Lecturer at universities in United States, Philippines, Singapore, and Japan.

MEMBER: Indian Commerce Association (founding member, 1947; secretary, 1947-51; vice-president, 1957; president, 1965). *Awards, honors:* Ford Foundation grant for research at American universities, 1960; U.S. Department of Justice exchange scholar, 1960-61.

WRITINGS—In English: *Insurance Finance, with Special Reference to India,* Kitab-Mahal, 1939; *Pessimism in Planning,* Kitab-Mahal, 1944; *A Critique of the Industrialists' Plan,* Nand Kishore & Brothers, 1944; *Reconstruction of Economic Science,* Kitab-Mahal, 1944, 2nd edition, 1957; *Social Insurance Planning in India,* Kitab-Mahal, 1944; *The U.K.C.C. and India,* Vora & Co., 1944; *Ghandhism, a Socialistic Approach,* Kitab-Mahal, 1944; (editor) *Public Corporations, An Expert Study of the Economics of Public Corporations,* S. Narayan, for Indian Research Association, 1945; *Some Economic Issues of Transition and Planning in India,* M. K. Dikshit, 1945; (with others) *Economic Planning and Agriculture,* East End Publishers, 1945; *Health Insurance in India,* East End Publishers, 1945; *Socialism without Prejudice,* Kitabistan, 1947; (editor) *Position and Prospects of India's Foreign Trade,* Probsthain (London), 1947; (editor) *Indian Labour Problems,* Kitabistan, 1947; (with M. K. Gosh) *Insurance Principles: Practice and Legislation,* Indian Press, 1948.

Specialized Accountancy, Kitab-Mahal, 1956; *The Government and Politics of China* (with one chapter by C. B. Arwala), Kitab-Mahal, c.1956; *Higher Science of Accountancy,* Kitab-Mahal, 1958; *Some Aspects of Economic Advancement of Underdeveloped Economics,* Kitab-Ma-

hal, 1958; (editor with S. P. Singh) *The Economics of Underdevelopment,* Oxford University Press, 1958; (with S. N. Agarwala) *Economics and Commercial Essays,* 5th edition, 1958; *Indian Economics: An Introduction,* Kitab-Mahal, 2nd edition, 1959.

A New Conception of Business Education, Motilal Nehru Institute of Research and Business Administration, University of Allahabad, 1960; *Insurance in India: A Study of Insurance Aspect of Social Security in India,* Allahabad Law Journal Press, 1960; *Life Insurance System of India,* [Allahabad], 1960; *Governing Factors of India's Economic Progress* (lectures), Agra University, 1962; (editor) *Planning of Business Education and Research in India,* Asia Publishing House, 1964; *Emerging Dimensions of Indian Business* (presidential address, All-India Commerce Conference), Poona University, 1965; *Economic Mobilization for National Defence,* Asia Publishing House, 1966; *Business Methods and Machinery,* Kitab-Mahal, 10th edition, 1966; *Economics of Metropolitan Development* (lectures), Agra University, 1967; *Agricultural Profile of a Metropolitan Region: A Study of Kanpur Region,* Agro-Economic Research Center (Allahabad), 1967; (editor with S. P. Singh) *Accelerating Investment in Developing Economics,* Oxford University Press, 1969; *Education for Business in a Developing Society,* Graduate School of Business, Michigan State University, 1969.

The Emerging Dimensions of Indian Management, Asia Publishing House, 1970; *The Working of Companies in India,* Kitab-Mahal, 1970. Also author of *Economic and Commercial Geography,* and *India's Leading Commercial Problems,* both published by Kitab-Mahal.

In Hindi; books on commerce, economics, and bookkeeping: *Buka-kipinga ka Paricaya,* 1949; *Arthasastra pravesika,* 1951; *Vyaparika Paddhati aura Yantra,* 1952; *Arthasastra ka Paricaya,* 1952.

Contributor: *Third Five Year Plan and India's Economic Growth,* 1962; *Planning of Business Education and Research in India,* Asia Publishing House, 1963. Contributor to *Industrial Times* (Bombay), *International Labour Review* (Montreal), *Economic Journal* (London), *Journal of World Business* (Columbia University), and other journals. *Indian Journal of Economics,* managing editor, 1943-47, member of editorial board, beginning 1963, chairman of editorial board, 1963-66.†

* * *

AGREE, Rose H. 1913-

PERSONAL: Born August 15, 1913, in Lutsk, Poland; came to United States, 1914, naturalized, 1943; daughter of Nathan and Minnie (Kagan) Plosker; married Morris J. Agree, December 18, 1938 (deceased); children: Peter Allan, Joel Loran. *Education:* Hunter College (now Hunter College of the City University of New York), B.A., 1932; Queens College (now Queens College of the City University of New York), M.S.E. and Diploma in Library Science, 1958; New York University, Ed.D., 1973. *Home:* 15 Hillpark Ave., Great Neck, N.Y. 11021. *Office:* Board of Education, U.F.S.D. 30, Forest Rd. School, Valley Stream, N.Y. 11581.

CAREER: Union Free School District 30, Board of Education, Valley Stream, N.Y., librarian, 1956—, head librarian, 1963—, head library media specialist. *Member:* American Library Association, American Association of School Librarians, National Education Association, New York State Teachers Association, New York Library Association, New York Library Club. *Awards, honors:* E. P. Dutton-John Macrae Award, American Library Association, 1969, for research in children's literature; award from Educational Press Association of America, 1973, for outstanding feature article, "Why Children Must Mourn."

WRITINGS: (Compiler) *How to Eat a Poem and Other Morsels* (anthology of poetry about food), Pantheon, 1967; *Black Children/White Images,* Citation Press, 1975. Contributor of articles to *Teacher, Instructor,* and other professional journals.

* * *

AGUILAR, Luis E. 1926-

PERSONAL: Born June 16, 1926, in Santiago de Cuba (now Oriente), Cuba; son of Fernando (a judge) and Ana (Leon) Aguilar; married Vera C. Mestre (a teacher), February 8, 1953; children: Luis E., George A., Elizabeth Anne. *Education:* University of Havana, doctorate (law and social sciences), 1949; University of Madrid, doctorate (law and social sciences), 1950; American University, Ph.D., 1967. *Home:* 6836 Tulip Hill Ter., Bethesda, Md. 20016. *Office:* Georgetown University, Washington, D.C. 20007.

CAREER: Practiced law in Cuba, 1950-60; University of Oriente, Oriente, Cuba, assistant professor of philosophy of law and history, 1951-56; Columbia University, New York, N.Y., visiting associate professor of Latin American literature, 1961-62; Georgetown University, Washington, D.C., associate professor, 1962-72, professor of Latin American History, 1972—. Visiting associate professor, Cornell University, 1969-70. *Member:* Academy of Political Science, Latin American Studies Association, American Association of University Professors. *Awards, honors:* Georgetown University summer study grant to El Salvador, 1967.

WRITINGS: Pasado y Ambiente en el Proceso Cubano, Sociedad de Filosofia, 1957; (editor) *Marxism in Latin America,* Knopf, 1968; *Cuba: Conciencia y Revolucion,* Ediciones Universal, 1972; *Cuba 1933: Prologue to Revolution,* Cornell University Press, 1973. Contributor to *New Leader, Reporter, Current,* and periodicals in Bogota, Lima, and Havana.

WORK IN PROGRESS: The Collapse of Democracy in Chile; Jose Marti: The Man and the Message.

SIDELIGHTS: A witness of the Cuban Revolution, Aguilar wrote against Batista and then against Castro (after being a member of the Revolutionary Institute of Culture). Aguilar told *CA* that he considers Latin America "the New Frontier." Aguilar travels extensively in Latin America, with special interest in Chile, Peru, and Panama.

* * *

AHLSTROM, Sydney E(ckman) 1919-

PERSONAL: Born December 16, 1919, in Cokato, Minn.; son of Joseph T. (a dentist) and Selma (Eckman) Ahlstrom; married Nancy Alexander (a Yale University publications editor), August 8, 1953; children: J. Alexander, Promise Ann, Constance Burton, Sydney E. *Education:* Gustavus Adolphus College, B.A., 1941; University of Minnesota, M.A., 1946; Harvard University, Ph.D., 1952. *Home:* 99 Armory St., New Haven, Conn. 06511. *Office:* American Studies Program, Hall of Graduate Studies 232, Yale University, New Haven, Conn. 06520.

CAREER: Salzburg Seminar in American Studies, Salzburg, Austria, member of faculty, 1952; Harvard University, Cambridge, Mass., instructor in history, 1952-54; Yale University, New Haven, Conn., assistant professor, 1954-60, associate professor, 1960-64, professor of modern religious history and American history, 1964—, chairman of American studies, 1967-71, 1972-73. Visiting professor, Princeton University, 1962; Brewer Lecturer, Beloit College, 1962; research fellow in France, 1964-65 and in Germany 1970-71; lecturer at American Studies Summer Seminar, Kyoto, Japan, 1972 and University of Sydney, summer, 1975. Trustee, Gustavus Adolphus College, 1967—. *Military service:* U.S. Army, 1942-46; became captain. *Member:* American Historical Association, American Society of Church History (president, 1975), American Studies Association. *Awards, honors:* Fulbright fellow at University of Strasbourg, 1951-52; National Book Award, 1973, and Brotherhood Award, National Conference of Christians and Jews, 1974, both for *A Religious History of the American People.*

WRITINGS: (Contributor) George H. Williams, editor, *The Harvard Divinity School,* Beacon Press, 1954; (contributor) J. W. Smity and A. L. Jamison, editors, *The Shaping of American Religion,* Princeton University Press, 1961; *The Protestant Encounter with World Religions,* Beloit College Press, 1962; (contributor) George Hunt, editor, *Calvinism and the Political Order,* Westminster Press, 1965; *Theology in America,* Bobbs-Merrill, 1967; *A Religious History of the American People,* Yale University Press, 1972. Contributor of articles to journals and books in his field. Member of editorial board of, "The Complete Works of Jonathan Edwards," Yale University Press.

WORK IN PROGRESS: Pictorial History of Religion in America; American Religious Thought: The Major Tradition (Otis-Stone Lectures); and *Romanticism and Religious Modernism.*

* * *

AIKEN, Michael Thomas 1932-

PERSONAL: Born August 20, 1932, in El Dorado, Ark.; son of William Floyd and Mary (Gibbs) Aiken; married, 1969. *Education:* University of Mississippi, B.A., 1954; University of Michigan, M.A., 1955, Ph.D., 1964. *Office:* Department of Sociology, University of Wisconsin, Madison, Wis. 53706.

CAREER: University of Wisconsin—Madison, assistant professor, 1963-67, associate professor, 1967-70, professor of sociology, 1970—. Visiting associate professor, Columbia University, 1967-68. *Military service:* U.S. Army, Military Intelligence, 1956-59; became sergeant. *Member:* American Sociological Association, Society for the Study of Social Problems, American Association of University Professors.

WRITINGS: (With Louis A. Ferman and Harold L. Shepherd) *Economic Failure, Alienation, and Extremism,* University of Michigan Press, 1968; (with Jerald Hage) *Social Change in Complex Organizations,* Random House, 1970; (editor with Paul E. Mott) *The Structure of Community Power: Readings,* Random House, 1970.

* * *

AINSWORTH, Mary D(insmore) Salter 1913-
(Mary D. Salter)

PERSONAL: Born December 1, 1913, in Glendale, Ohio; daughter of Charles Morgan (president of Aluminum

Goods Ltd.) and Mary (Hoover) Salter; married Leonard H. Ainsworth, June 10, 1950 (divorced, 1960). *Education:* University of Toronto, B.A., 1935, M.A., 1936, Ph.D., 1939. *Office:* Department of Psychology, Gilmer Hall, University of Virginia, Charlottesville, Va. 22901.

CAREER: University of Toronto, Toronto, Ontario, instructor, 1938-41, lecturer in psychology, 1941-42; Canadian Government, Department of Veterans' Affairs, Ottawa, Ontario, superintendent of women's rehabilitation, 1945-46; University of Toronto, assistant professor of psychology, 1946-50; Tavistock Clinic, London, England, senior research psychologist, 1950-54; East African Institute for Social Research, Kampala, Uganda, senior research fellow, 1954-55; Johns Hopkins University, Baltimore, Md., lecturer, 1956-59, associate professor, 1959-63, professor of psychology, 1963-75; University of Virginia, Charlottesville, professor of psychology, 1975—. Co-Director of research project evaluating security, Institute for Child Study, University of Toronoto, 1946-50; psychology assistant, Department of Veteran Affairs, Canada, 1947-50; psychologist, Sheppard and Enoch Pratt Hospital, 1956-61. *Military service:* Canadian Womens Army Corps, 1942-46; consultant to director of Personnel selection; became major.

MEMBER: American Psychological Association, British Psychological Society, Society for Research in Child Development, Association for Child Psychology and Psychiatry, American Association for the Advancement of Science, Eastern Psychological Association, Sigma Xi. *Awards, honors:* Fellow of Center for Advanced Study in the Behavorial Sciences, 1967-68, 1975-77.

WRITINGS: (Under name Mary D. Salter, with A. W. Ham) *Doctor in the Making,* Lippincott, 1943; (with B. Klopfer, W. G. Klopfer, and R. R. Holt) *Developments in the Rorschach Technique,* Volume I, World Book Co., 1954; (with Leonard H. Ainsworth) *Measuring Security in Personal Adjustment,* University of Toronto Press, 1958; (with J. Bowlby) *Child Care and the Growth of Love,* 2nd edition (Ainsworth was not associated with first edition), Penguin, 1965; *Infancy in Uganda: Infant Care and the Growth of Love,* Johns Hopkins Press, 1967.

(Contributor) J. L. Gewirtz, editor, *Attachment and Dependency,* V. H. Winston, 1972; (contributor) B. M. Caldwell and H. W. Ricciuti, editors, *Review of Child Development Research,* University of Chicago Press, 1974.

WORK IN PROGRESS: Research into the development of infant-mother attachment.

* * *

AITKEN, Jonathan (William Patrick) 1942-

PERSONAL: Born August 30, 1942, in Dublin, Ireland; son of Sir William Traven (a member of Parliament) and Penelope Jane (Maffey) Aitken; grandson of Lord Rugby; great nephew of Lord Beaverbrook. *Education:* Christ Church, Oxford, M.A., 1965. *Politics:* Conservative. *Religion:* Church of England. *Home:* 47 Phillimore Gardens, London W. 8, England. *Agent:* Graham Watson, Curtis Brown Ltd., 60 East 56th St., New York, N.Y. 10022. *Office:* Slater Walker Securities, 30 St. Paul's Churchyard, London E.C.4, England.

CAREER: Monitor Publishing Co. Ltd., Montreal, Quebec, and London, England, publisher, 1965-66; *Evening Standard,* London, journalist, 1966-70; Slater Walker Securities, Middle East division, London, managing director,

1970—. Private secretary to Selwyn Lloyd on tour of Australia and New Zealand, 1965-66, and on visit to Rhodesia, 1966; unsuccessfully contested a seat in Parliament as Conservative candidate in 1966 general election; elected to Parliament as Thanet East Conservative member, 1974. *Member:* Royal Institute of International Affairs, Saddlers' Company, Bow Group, Coningsby Club, Turf Club, Pratts.

WRITINGS: (With Michael Beloff) *A Short Walk on the Campus,* Atheneum, 1966; *Swinging London,* Atheneum, 1967 (published in England as *The Young Meteors,* Secker & Warburg, 1967); *Land of Fortune: A Study of the New Australia,* Atheneum, 1971; *Officially Secret,* Weidenfeld & Nicolson, 1971. Contributor to *Harper's Bazaar, Spectator, Listener, Evening Standard,* and other periodicals. Editor, *Oxford Tory,* 1962-63.

SIDELIGHTS: Jonathan Aitken headed Eton's political and debating societies in 1961, and later the Conservative Association at Oxford University; he represented Oxford on a three-month debating tour of U.S. and Canadian colleges, 1964-65. Aitken visited America again in the spring of 1967, en route home from a five-month tour of India, Pakistan, Vietnam, Australia, and New Zealand.

AVOCATIONAL INTERESTS: Ballooning, bobsledding, and squash.

* * *

AKE, Claude 1938-

PERSONAL: Born February 18, 1938, in Omoku, Nigeria (now in Republic of Biafra). *Education:* Attended University of Ibadan; University of London, B.Sc., 1962; Columbia University, M.A., 1963, Ph.D., 1966. *Religion:* Nil. *Office:* Department of Political Science, Carleton University, 268 First Ave., Ottawa, Ontario, Canada.

CAREER: Columbia University, New York, N.Y., assistant professor of political science, 1966-69; Carleton University, Ottawa, Ontario, associate professor of political science, 1969—. Visiting professor, University of Nairoby, 1970-72. *Awards, honors:* Rockefeller Foundation fellow, 1970-72.

WRITINGS: *A Theory of Political Integration,* Dorsey, 1967. Contributor to *Comparative Studies in Society and History, World Politics,* and other political science journals.

WORK IN PROGRESS: Editing and co-authoring *Philosophy of Political Dissent.*†

* * *

AKINJOGBIN, I(saac) A(deagbo) 1930-

PERSONAL: Born January 12, 1930, in Ipetumodu (Ife) Nigeria; son of Joel Esudoyin (a farmer) and Bernice (Falowo) Akinjogbin; married Josephine Adebisi Odeloye, May 6, 1959; children: Adeolu, Olufemi, Yewande. *Education:* Studied at Fourah Bay College; University of Durham, B.A. (honors in history), 1957; School of Oriental and African Studies, University of London, Ph.D., 1963. *Religion:* Christian. *Home:* Isale-Apata, Ipetumodu (Ife), West Nigeria.

CAREER: Yoruba Historical Research Scheme, Ibadan, West Nigeria, junior research fellow, 1957-60; University of Ife, Ife, West Nigeria, senior lecturer in history, beginning 1963. *Member:* Historical Society of Nigeria (council), International African Institute (London). *Awards, honors:* Commonwealth scholar at University of London, 1960-63.

WRITINGS: Dahomey and Its Neighbours, 1708-1818, Cambridge University Press, 1967; (editor) *The Story of Ketu,* 2nd edition, University of Ibadan Press, 1967; (editor) *Ewi Iwoyi* (modern Yoruba poetry), Collins, 1968. Translator of "Ede," a short history, for Nigerian Ministry of Education, 1961. Contributor of articles on West African history to professional journals; also has published short stories and poems in Yoruba.

WORK IN PROGRESS: The Oyo Empire in the 18th Century, a monograph running to about six chapters; and *The Growth and Organisation of the Ife Kingdom,* 1969.

SIDELIGHTS: Akinjogbin speaks Yoruba and English, and reads French.†

*   *   *

AL-AZM, Sadik J.   1934-

PERSONAL: Born November 7, 1934, in Damascus, Syria; son of Jalal S. (in civil service) and Naziha Al-Azm; married Fawz Tuqan (a university teacher of English), July 2, 1957. *Education:* American University of Beirut, B.A. (with distinction), 1957; Yale University, M.A., 1959, Ph.D., 1961. *Religion:* No affiliation.

CAREER: Hunter College of the City University of New York, New York, N.Y., instructor in department of philosophy, 1961-62; University of Damascus, Damascus, Syria, lecturer in department of philosophy, 1962-63; American University of Beirut, Beirut, Lebanon, assistant professor in department of philosophy, 1963-67, assistant professor in cultural studies program, 1967-68; University of Jordan, Amman, member of faculty of department of philosophy, 1968-69; author, lecturer, and critic.

WRITINGS: Dirasat Fi al-Falsafa al-Gharbiyya al-Haditha (title means "Studies in Modern Western Philosophy"), American University of Beirut Press, 1966; *Kant's Theory of Time,* Philosophical Library, 1967; (contributor) *Festival Book,* American University of Beirut Press, 1967; *Fi al-Hubb wa al-Hubb al-Uzri* (title means "Of Love and Arabic Courtly Love"), Kabbani Publications (Beirut), 1967; *Nagd al-Fikr al-Dini* (title means "Critique of Religious Thought"), Tali'a Publications (Beirut), 1970; *The Origins of Kant's Arguments in the Antinomies,* Oxford University Press, 1972; *Dirasa Nagdiah Lil-Muga wamah al-Filistiniah* (title means "A Critical Study of the Palestinian Resistance Movement"), Al-Awdah Publications (Beirut), 1973; *Al-Suhyuniah wa al-Sira' al Tabaki* (title means "Zionism and the Class Struggle"), Al-Awdah Publications, 1975. Contributor of articles and reviews to journals in the Middle East, Europe, and North America.

SIDELIGHTS: Dr. Al-Azm wrote to *CA* that "the Mufti of Lebanon declared *Nagd al-Fikr al-Dini* heretical, and the Lebanese authorities quickly banned the book. [Al-Azm] was imprisoned for a week on charges of 'inciting confessional strife,' and then released on bail. A long trial followed, resulting in the dismissal of all charges against author, book, and publisher, turning the book into a *cause celebre,* the author into the 'official atheist' of the Arab World, and the trial into the most 'notorious' and protracted intellectual controversy that the Arab World has seen for many years. The whole incident was reported and analyzed at great length in German in *Der Islam* in 1972."

Al-Azm says that he is interested in "furthering a critical re-examination and appraisal of Muslim and Arab thought in relation to the contemporary secular world and the forces shaping it." He speaks English and French.

ALBA, Victor   1916-
(Pedro Pages)

PERSONAL: Born Pedro Pages, January 19, 1916, in Barcelona, Spain; became Mexican citizen, 1948; son of Pedro and Elias (Elvira) Pages; married Noemi Boune, March 20, 1947; children: Christine. *Education:* University of Barcelona, law study, 1932-36. *Home:* 554 South Lincoln St., Kent, Ohio 44240. *Office:* Department of Political Science, Kent State University, Kent, Ohio 44242; and Valencia 184, Barcelona, Spain.

CAREER: Foreign affairs commentator for *Ultima Hora,* Barcelona, Spain, 1935-39, and *La Batalla,* Barcelona, 1936-37; *Excelsior,* Mexico, reporter, 1947-54; *Salenias Excelsior,* Mexico, director, 1956-57; World Health Organization, Washington, D.C., translator and precis writer, 1957-60; Pan American Union, Washington, D.C., chief of Editorial Division, 1960-62; Centro de Estudios y Documentacion Sociales, Mexico, director, 1962-65; University of Kansas, Lawrence, visiting professor of political science, 1965-66; American University, School of International Service, Washington, D.C., lecturer, 1966-68; Kent State University, Kent, Ohio, lecturer in political science, 1967—. Lecturer on Latin American affairs at Universities of Wisconsin, Florida, Texas, Puerto Rico, at other universities in America, and at seminars and institutes. *Member:* American Association of University Professors.

WRITINGS: Insomnie espagnole, preface by Jean Cassou, Societe des Editiones Franc Tireur, 1946, translation by Charles Duff published as *Sleepless Spain,* Cobbett Press, 1948; *Histoire des republique espagnoles,* Nord-Sud, 1948, revised edition published as *Historia de la segunda Republica Espanola,* Libra Mex, 1960.

El industrailismo: Su historia y sus problemas, Secretaria de Educacion Publica, 1950; *Le mouvement ouvrier en Amerique latine,* Editions Ouvrieres, 1953; *La Concepcion historiografica de Lucio Annes Flors,* [Madrid], 1953; *Historia de comunismo en America Latina,* Ediciones Occidentales, 1954, 3rd edition published as *Esquema historico del comunismo en Iberoamerica,* 1960; *Mexicanos para la historia: Doce figuras contemporaneas,* Libro Mex, 1955; *Coloquios de Coyoacan con Rufino Tamayo,* Costa Amic, 1956; *Israel y Egipto: Democracia o guerra en el Cerano Oriente,* Libro Mex, 1956; *Hungria 1956,* Costa Amic, 1957; *Esquema historico del movimiento obrero en America Latina,* Costa Amic, 1957; *El lider: Ensayo sobre el dirigente sindical,* Instituto de Investigaciones Sociales, Universidad Nacional, 1957; (editor) *Federico Garcia Lorca, Antologia,* [Mexico], 1957; (contributor) *La pasion de Pasternak,* Libro Mex, 1958; *Historia del frente popular: Analisis de una tactica politica,* Libro Mex, 1959; *El militarismo: Ensayo un fenomeno politicosocial iberoamericano,* Instituto de Investigaciones Sociales, Universidad Nacional, 1959.

Las ideas sociales contemporaneas en Mexico, Frondo de Cultura Economica, 1960; (contributor) Albert O. Hirachman, editor, *Latin American Issues,* Twentieth Century Fund, 1961; (contributor) John T. Johnson, editor, *The Role of the Military in Underdeveloped Countries,* Princeton University Press, 1962; *Mexique,* Editions Recontre, 1963; *El sindicato,* Centro de Estudios y Documentacion Sociales, 1963; *Historia del movimiento obrero en America Latina,* Libreros Mexicanos Unidos, 1964, translation and revision published as *Politics and the Labor Movement in Latin America,* Stanford University Press, 1968; *Historia general del campesinado,* Centro de Estudios y Documentacion Sociales, 1964; *Parasitos, mitos y sordomudos: Ensayo sobre la Arlinanza para el Progreso y colonialismo latinamericano,* Centro de Estudios y Documentacion Sociales, 1964, translation by John Pearson published as *Alliance without Allies: The Mythology of Progress in Latin America,* Praeger, 1965; *Los subamericanos,* Costa Amic, 1964; *Estadisticas comentadas,* Centro de Estudios y Documentacion Sociales, 1964; *Los sumerigidos,* Costa Amic, 1965; (with others) *El Papel de los militares en los paises subdesarrollados,* Circulo Militar, 1965; *The Mexicans: The Making of a Nation,* Praeger, 1967; *Los espanoles duera de su casa,* Las Americas, 1968; *Nationalists without Nations: The Oligarchy Versus the People in Latin America,* Praeger, 1968; *The Latin Americans,* Praeger, 1969.

Retorn a Catalunya, Portic, 1970; (contributor) Louis M. Colonese, editor, *Human Rights and the Liberation of Man in the Americas,* University of Notre Dame Press, 1970; *America Latina,* Plaza & Janes, 1971; *Catalunya sense cap ni peus,* Portic, 1971; (contributor) Harold E. Davis and Larman C. Wilson, editors, *Latin American Foreign Policies: An Analysis,* Latin American Studies Program, American University, 1971; *Las ideologias y los movimientos sociales,* Plaza & Janes, 1972; *The Horizon Concise History of Mexico,* American Heritage Publishing, 1973 (published in England as *A Concise History of Mexico,* Cassell, 1973); *Historia general de Campesinado,* Plaza & Janes, 1973; *U.S.A.: Centre de la revolucio mundial,* Portic, 1974; (with Louis K. Harris) *The Political Culture and Behavior of Latin America,* Kent State University Press, 1974; *Historia social de la mujer,* Plaza & Janes, 1974; *Homo sapiens catalanibus,* Portic, 1974; *El marxisme a Calalunya,* four volumes, Portic, 1974-75; *Cataluna de tamano natural,* Planeta, 1975; *Historia social de la juventud,* Plaza & Janes, 1975; *Catalonia: A Profile,* Praeger, 1975; *Los liquidadores de un imperio,* Nauta, 1975.

Editorial director for *Manualea de Educacion Civica* and the series "Estudios y Documentos," published by Centro de Estudios y Documentacion Sociales. Contributor to, or correspondent for, *New Leader* and *New Republic* (United States), *Franco-Tireur* (Paris), *Combat* (Paris), *Le Peuple* (Brussels), *Il Ponte* (Florence), and other journals in Europe, Mexico, and Dominican Republic. Editor, *Panoramas* (bimonthly journal), 1962-65.

WORK IN PROGRESS: The Popular Front: A Strategy.

SIDELIGHTS: William P. Lineberry, reviewing *The Latin Americans,* notes that Alba, "an astute and learned observer of Latin American history and society, offers a judicious, intelligent perspective from which to act." Alba is competent in Italian, French Portuguese, and Catalan. He has traveled in all of Latin America and Europe, and in Japan, India, Vietnam, Turkey, Philippines, Taiwan, and Canada.

BIOGRAPHICAL/CRITICAL SOURCES: New Leader, April 27, 1970.

* * *

ALBERT, Ethel M(ary) 1918-

PERSONAL: Born March 28, 1918, in New Britain, Conn.; daughter of Zundel and Dorothy (Eisenstadt) Sokolsky. *Education:* Brooklyn College (now Brooklyn College of the City University of New York), B.A., 1942; Columbia University, M.A., 1947; University of Wisconsin, Ph.D., 1949. *Politics:* Registered Democrat. *Home:*

612 Mulford St., Evanston, Ill. 60202. *Office:* Department of Anthropology, Northwestern University, Evanston, Ill. 60201.

CAREER: Brooklyn College (now Brooklyn College of the City University of New York), Brooklyn, N.Y., instructor in philosophy, 1946-47; Syracuse University, Syracuse, N.Y., instructor in philosophy, 1949-52; Harvard University, Cambridge, Mass., research associate, laboratory of social relations, 1953-55; Ford Foundation fellow in Overseas African Program, Burundi, 1955-57; Center for Advanced Study in the Behavioral Sciences, Stanford, Calif., fellow, 1957-58; University of California, Berkeley, professor of speech, 1958-66, chairman of committee for African studies (Institute of International Studies), 1963-65, vice-chairman of speech department, 1964-65; Northwestern University, Evanston, Ill., professor of anthropology and speech, 1966—, chairman of department, 1972-73. National Science Foundation Project on Educational Resources in Anthropology, assistant director for ethnology, 1960, 1961.

MEMBER: African Studies Association, American Anthropological Association, American Philosophical Association, Philosophy of Science Association. *Awards, honors:* Social Science Research Council faculty research fellow, 1962; National Science Foundation, senior postdoctoral fellowship, 1965-66, research grant for semantics, summer, 1966.

WRITINGS: (Editor with S. P. Peterfreund and T. C. Denise) *Great Traditions in Ethics: An Introduction,* American Book Co., 1953, revised edition, 1969; (with Clyde Kluckholm) *A Selected Bibliography on Values, Ethics and Esthetics in the Behavioral Sciences and Philosophy, 1920-1958,* Free Press of Glencoe, 1959; (editor with D. G. Mandelbaum and G. W. Lasker) *The Teaching of Anthropology,* University of California Press, 1963; (editor with Mandelbaum and Lasker) *Resources for the Teacher of Anthropology,* University of California Press, 1963; (editor with Evon Z. Vogt) *The People of Rimrock,* Harvard University Press, 1966.

Contributor: Joseph Casagrande, editor, *In the Company of Man: Twenty Portraits by Anthropologists,* Harper, 1960; Denise Paulme, editor, *Femmes d'Afrique Noire,* Mouton & Co., 1960, published as *Women of Tropical Africa,* University of California Press, 1963; Seymour M. Farber and Roger H. L. Wilson, editors, *Man and Civilization: The Potential of Women,* McGraw, 1963; Farber and Wilson, editors, *The Challenge of Women,* Basic Books, 1966. Contributor to *International Encyclopedia of the Social Sciences,* 1968; contributor of more than twenty articles and reviews to *American Anthropologist, Journal of Philosophy, Cahiers d'Etudes Africaines* (Paris), *Antioch Review,* and other journals.†

* * *

ALBERT, Walter E. 1930-

PERSONAL: Born July 31, 1930, in Little Rock, Ark.; son of Walter H. and Ruth (Irwin) Albert; married Margaret Cook (in public relations), January 24, 1959; children: Jennifer Ann, Byran W. *Education:* University of Oklahoma, B.A., 1955; Indiana University, M.A., 1957, Ph.D., 1961. *Home:* 7139 Meade, Pittsburgh, Pa. 15208. *Office:* University of Pittsburgh, Pittsburgh, Pa. 15213.

CAREER: Brandeis University, Waltham, Mass., instructor, 1960-62, assistant professor of French, 1962-67; University of Pittsburgh, Pittsburgh, Pa., associate professor of French, 1967—. *Military service:* U.S. Army, 1952-54. *Member:* American Association of Teachers of French, Modern Language Association of America, Phi Beta Kappa. *Awards, honors:* Fulbright scholar, University of Lyons, 1957-58.

WRITINGS: (Editor and translator) *Selected Writings of Blaise Cendrars,* New Directions, 1966; (contributor) *Critical Bibliography of Twentieth Century French Literature,* Syracuse University Press, 1976. Also contributor to *The Armchair Detective.* Contributor to language journals, and to *Beloit Poetry Journal, Approach,* and *Coastlines.*

WORK IN PROGRESS: The novels of Jean Giraudoux; studies on Rimbaud and other French writers.

SIDELIGHTS: Spire Pitou, in his review of *Selected Writings of Blaise Cendrars,* congratulates Albert for conveying so precisely the bewildering variety that characterizes Cendrars' work and the abundant experimentation which marks his writing.

In addition to French, Albert is competent in Spanish and Italian.

BIOGRAPHICAL/CRITICAL SOURCES: Books Abroad, winter, 1968.

*　　*　　*

ALBERTS, William W.   1925-

PERSONAL: Born January 6, 1925, in Pittsburgh, Pa.; son of Wallace E. (a carpenter) and Edna (Hill) Alberts; married Patricia Sibert, February 26, 1952; children: Mary, Susan. *Education:* University of Chicago, B.A., M.A., 1956, Ph.D., 1961. *Home:* 16034 38th Ave. N.E., Seattle, Wash. 98155. *Office:* Department of Economics, University of Washington, Seattle, Wash.

CAREER: Roosevelt University, Chicago, Ill., instructor in economics and finance, 1956-59; University of Chicago, Chicago, instructor, 1959-61, assistant professor, 1961-66, associate professor of economics and finance, 1966-67; University of Washington, Seattle, associate professor, 1967-71, professor of economics and finance, 1971—. *Military service:* U.S. Army, 1943-46. *Member:* American Economic Association, American Finance Association.

WRITINGS: (Editor with J. E. Segall, and contributor) *The Corporate Merger,* University of Chicago Press, 1966. Contributor to professional journals. *Journal of Finance,* editor, 1960-61, associate editor, 1961-63.

WORK IN PROGRESS: Capital Investment By the Firm, and *Capital Investment in Real Property,* both for ECD.

*　　*　　*

ALBINSKI, Henry Stephen   1931-

PERSONAL: Born December 31, 1931, in Chicago, Ill.; son of Stephen (a chemical engineer) and Josephine (Wieczerek) Albinski; married Barbara Van Why, January 30, 1954; married second wife, Ethel Bisbicos (a psychologist), September 2, 1967; children: (first marriage) Lawrence; (second marriage) Gillian, Allison. *Education:* University of California, Los Angeles, B.A. (summa cum laude), 1953, M.A., 1955; University of Minnesota, Ph.D., 1959. *Home:* 803 Cornwall Dr., State College, Pa. 16801. *Office:* Department of Political Science, Pennsylvania State University, University Park, Pa. 16802.

CAREER: University of Minnesota, Minneapolis, instructor in political science, 1959; Pennsylvania State University, University Park, instructor, 1959-61, assistant pro-

fessor, 1961-65, associate professor, 1965-68, professor of political science, 1968—. Visiting fellow, Australian National University, Research School of Pacific Studies, 1963-64; visiting professor, University of Western Ontario, 1969, University of Queensland, 1970, University of Sydney, and Flinders University of South Australia, both 1974-75. Consultant, Institute for Defense Analyses, 1969, Georgetown University Center for Strategic and International Studies, 1972-73. *Member:* American Political Science Association, Australasian Political Studies Association, New Zealand Political Studies Association, Association for Canadian Studies in the United States, Canadian Political Science Association, American Association of University Professors, Hansard Society. *Awards, honors:* Rockefeller Foundation grant, 1963-64; Institute of Humanistic Studies of Pennsylvania State University fellowship, 1968; senior Fulbright Scholar, 1974-75.

WRITINGS: Australia and the China Problem during the Korean War Period, Department of International Relations, Australian National University, 1964; *Australian Policies and Attitudes Toward China,* Princeton University Press, 1965; *The Australian Labor Party and the Aid to Parochial Schools Controversy,* Pennsylvania State University Press, 1966; (contributor) *Writings on Canadian-American Studies,* Committee on Canadian-American Studies, Michigan State University, 1967; (editor with L. K. Pettit) *European Political Processes: Essays and Readings,* Allyn & Bacon, 1968, 2nd edition, 1974; (contributor) Jan Prybyla, editor, *Communism at the Crossroads,* Pennsylvania State University Press, 1968; (contributor) Richard Preston, editor, *Contemporary Australia: Studies in History, Politics and Economics,* Duke University Press, 1969; (contributor) *American Studies Conference Proceedings,* New South Wales Department of Education, 1970; *Politics and Foreign Policy in Australia,* Duke University Press, 1970; *Australia in Southeast Asia: Interest, Capacity, and Acceptability,* Research Analysis Corp., 1970; (editor and contributor) *Asian Political Processes,* Allyn & Bacon, 1971; (contributor) Arthur Stahnke, editor, *China's Trade with the West,* Praeger, 1972; *Canadian and Australian Politics in Comparative Perspective,* Oxford University Press, 1973; (contributor) Jan Prybyla, editor, *The Pentagon of Power,* Pennsylvania State University Press, 1973; (contributor) Roy Forward, editor, *Public Policy in Australia,* F. W. Cheshire, 1974. Contributor of articles and reviews to professional journals in United States, Australia, and Canada.

WORK IN PROGRESS: Foreign Policy Under Labor, for F. W. Cheshire; editing and contributing to *Process and Policy in European Political Systems,* for Random House.

*　　*　　*

ALBRECHT, Robert C(harles)   1933-

PERSONAL: Born September 27, 1933, in Aurora, Ill.; son of Marcus Frederick (a businessman) and Marguerite (Crowell) Albrecht; married Llewellyn Wells; children: two. *Education:* University of Illinois, B.A., 1955; University of Michigan, M.A., 1957; University of Minnesota, Ph.D., 1962. *Office:* Department of English, University of Oregon, Eugene, Ore. 97403.

CAREER: University of Chicago, Chicago, Ill., 1962-67, began as instructor, became assistant professor of English; University of Oregon, Eugene, associate professor, 1967-74, professor of English, 1974—, College of Liberal Arts, associate dean, 1972-74, acting dean, 1974-75. Visiting scholar, Stanford University, 1975-76. Editorial consultant, Free Press (publishers). *Military service:* U.S. Army Reserve, 1956-68; active duty, 1957-58. *Member:* Modern Language Association of America, American Studies Association, National Council of Teachers of English. *Awards, honors:* U.S. Steel faculty fellowship at University of Chicago, 1966.

WRITINGS: Patterns of Style, Lippincott, 1967; *The World of Short Fiction,* Free Press, 1970; *Theodore Parker,* Twayne, 1971. Contributor to literature journals.

WORK IN PROGRESS: Education for What, a monograph on higher education; *Survival?,* an anthology.

* * *

ALEXANDER, Hubert G(riggs) 1909-

PERSONAL: Born December 8, 1909, in Lincoln, Neb.; son of Hartley Burr (a university professor) and Nelly (Griggs) Alexander; married Mildred Botts (a piano teacher), December 21, 1936; children: Robert Kirk, Hartley William, Thomas Milton, *Education:* University of Nebraska, student, 1926-27; Pomona College, B.A. (magna cum laude), 1930; University of Paris, graduate study, 1930-31; Yale University, Ph.D., 1934. *Home:* 603 Girard Blvd. N.E., Albuquerque, N.M. 87106.

CAREER: University of New Mexico, Albuquerque, instructor, 1935-38, assistant professor, 1938-44, associate professor, 1944-48, professor of philosophy, 1948-75, professor emeritus, 1975—, chairman of department, 1948-65. Visiting professor as Carnegie Intern, Yale University, 1954-55. *Member:* American Philosophical Association, American Society for Aesthetics, American Association of University Professors, Southwestern Philosophical Society, Mountain-Plains Philosophical Conference, New Mexico and West Texas Philosophical Society, Phi Beta Kappa, Phi Kappa Phi.

WRITINGS: Time as Dimension and History, University of New Mexico Press, 1945; (editor) H. B. Alexander, *The World's Rim,* University of Nebraska Press, 1953; *Language and Thinking,* Van Nostrand, 1967; *Meaning in Language,* Scott, 1969; *The Language and Logic of Philosophy,* University of New Mexico Press, 1972. Member of editorial board of *Philosophy and Rhetoric.*

* * *

ALEXANDER, J(onathan) J(ames) G(raham) 1935-

PERSONAL: Born August 20, 1935, in London, England; son of Boyd (an author) and Frederica (Graham) Alexander. *Education:* Magdalen College, Oxford, M.A., 1963, D.Phil., 1964. *Home:* 19 Macefin Ave., Manchester M21 2QQ, England.

CAREER: Bodleian Library, Oxford, England, assistant in department of Western manuscripts, 1963-71; University of Manchester, Manchester, England, lecturer, 1971-73, reader, 1973—. *Military service:* British Army, 1954-56; became second lieutenant.

WRITINGS: (With Otto Pacht) *Illuminated Manuscripts in the Bodleian Library, Oxford,* Oxford University Press, Volume I: *German, Dutch, Flemish, French and Spanish Schools,* 1966, Volume II: *Italian Schools,* 1970, Volume III: *British Schools,* 1973; (with A. C. De la Mare) *The Italian Manuscripts in the Library of Major J. R. Abbey,* Praeger, 1969; (editor and author of introduction) *The Master of Mary of Burgundy, A Book of Hours,* Braziller, 1970; *Norman Illumination at Mont St. Michel, 966-c.1100,* Oxford University Press, 1970.

WORK IN PROGRESS: Insular Manuscripts for the 6th-9th Centuries.

* * *

ALEXANDER, Lewis M(cElwain) 1921-

PERSONAL: Born June 15, 1921, in Summit, N.J.; son of Harry Louis (a physician) and Laura (Stryker) Alexander; married Jacqueline Peterson, December 30, 1950; children: Louise Anne, Lance Stryker. *Education:* Middlebury College, A.B., 1942; Clark University, M.A., 1948, Ph.D., 1949. *Politics:* Democrat. *Religion:* Protestant. *Home:* 28 Beach Hill Rd., Peach Dale, R.I. 02879. *Office:* University of Rhode Island, Kingston, R.I. 02881.

CAREER: Hunter College (now Hunter College of the City University of New York), New York, N.Y., instructor in geography, 1949-50; Harpur College (now State University of New York at Binghamton), Binghamton, N.Y., assistant professor, 1950-57, associate professor of geography, 1957-60; University of Rhode Island, Kingston, professor of geography, 1960—, Law of the Sea Institute, executive director, 1965-73, executive committee member, 1973—. Ohio State University, Mershon social science fellow, 1966-67. Deputy director, President's Commission of Marine Science, Engineering and Resources, 1967-68. Member, U.S. delegation to Third Law of the Sea Conference, 1975. Geography consultant, U.S. Department of State, 1963—; advisory committee member, Interagency Task Force on the Law of the Sea, 1973—; member of Ocean Affairs Board of National Academy of Sciences, 1973—. *Military service:* U.S. Army Air Forces, 1942-46; became master sergeant. *Member:* Association of American Geographers, American Geographical Society, Marine Technology Society, American Society of International Law.

WRITINGS: World Political Patterns, Rand McNally, 1957, 2nd edition, 1963; *Offshore Geography of Northwestern Europe,* Rand McNally, 1963; *Narragansett Bay: A Marine Use Profile,* University of Rhode Island Press, 1966; *Northeastern United States,* Van Nostrand, 1967, 2nd edition, 1975.

Editor of "Law of the Sea" series, published by University of Rhode Island, except as noted: *The Law of the Sea: Offshore Boundaries and Zones,* Ohio State University Press, 1967; *...The Future of the Sea's Resources,* 1968; *...International Rules and Organization for the Sea,* 1969; *...National Policy Recommendations,* 1970; *...The United Nations and Ocean Management,* 1971; *...A New Geneva Conference,* 1972; *...The Needs and Interests of Developing Countries,* 1973. Editor, *Proceedings* of the Law of the Sea Institute, 1967—. Also editor and co-editor of *Law of the Sea Workshop* reports. Member of editorial board, *Ocean Development and International Law,* 1972—, *Ocean Management,* 1972—.

WORK IN PROGRESS: A textbook on marine affairs; a research project on regional arrangements in the oceans.

* * *

ALEXANDER, Linda 1935-

PERSONAL: Born February 4, 1935, in Carthage, Mo.; daughter of William John (a chemical worker) and Maxine (Lewis) Alexander. *Education:* Studied magazine illustration through International Correspondence Schools, 1958-61. *Religion:* Protestant. *Home:* 3020 West 24th St., Joplin, Mo. 64801.

CAREER: Junior Chamber of Commerce, Joplin, Mo., telephone reservationist, 1961-67; full-time writer, 1967—. *Member:* Missouri Writer's Guild. *Awards, honors:* Awards for best juvenile story from the Jefferson City chapter of Missouri Writer's Guild, 1964, 1966, 1967, 1968, 1971, 1972.

WRITINGS: A Job Well Done, Lantern, 1967. Story anthologized in *Read-the-Picture Stories,* Word Making Production, 1967. Contributor of short stories and verse (some self-illustrated) to newspapers, Methodist publications, and children's magazines, including *Jack and Jill, Humpty Dumpty,* and *Wee Wisdom.*

SIDELIGHTS: Three years after her schooling was interrupted by rheumatoid arthritis when she was fifteen, Linda Alexander resumed high school studies via an intercommunications system between her home and the school and received a diploma at twenty-one. She now devotes full time to writing for children and does pen and ink drawings to illustrate her own rebus stories. She told *CA* that she "can't understand those who claim to be bored with life."

* * *

ALIBER, Robert Z. 1930-

PERSONAL: Born September 19, 1930, in Keene, N.H.; son of Norman H. and Sophie (Becker) Aliber; married Deborah Baltzly, September 9, 1955; children: Jennifer, Rachel, Michael. *Education:* Williams College, B.A., 1952; Cambridge University, B.A., 1954, M.A., 1957; Yale University, Ph.D., 1962. *Home:* 5638 South Dorchester Ave., Chicago, Ill. 60637.

CAREER: Commission on Money and Credit, New York, N.Y., staff economist, 1959-61; Committee for Economic Development, Washington, D.C., staff economist, 1961-64; Agency for International Development, Washington, D.C., senior economic adviser, 1964-65; University of Chicago, Graduate School of Business, Chicago, Ill., associate professor of economics and director of program of international studies, 1965—. *Military service:* U.S. Army, 1956-64. *Member:* American Economic Association, Royal Economic Society, American Political Science Association.

WRITINGS: The Management of the Dollar in International Finance, Princeton University Press, 1963; *The Future of the Dollar as an International Currency,* Praeger, 1966; (editor with George P. Shultz) *Guidelines, Informal Controls, and the Market Place,* University of Chicago Press, 1966; *The International Money Game,* Basic Books, 1973; (editor) *National Monetary Policies and the International Financial System,* University of Chicago Press, 1974; *World Inflation and Monetary Reform,* Sage Publications, 1974.

* * *

ALLAND, Alexander, Jr. 1931-

PERSONAL: Born September 23, 1931, in Newark, N.J.; son of Alexander and Alexandra (Mamlet) Alland; married Sonia Louise Feldman, August 26, 1956; children: David, Julie. *Education:* University of Wisconsin, B.S., 1954; University of Connecticut, M.S., 1958; Yale University, Ph.D., 1963. *Office:* Department of Anthropology, Columbia University, New York, N.Y. 10027.

CAREER: University of Connecticut, Stamford Campus, lecturer in sociology and anthropology, 1959-61; Vassar College, Poughkeepsie, N.Y., instructor in anthropology, 1962-63; Hunter College of the City University of New York, Bronx, N.Y., instructor in anthropology, 1963-64; Columbia University, New York, N.Y., assistant professor, 1964-68, associate professor, 1968-72, professor of anthropology, 1972—. Has done field work in Ivory Coast, West Africa. *Member:* American Ethnological Society (fellow), Royal Anthropological Institute (fellow), Current Anthropology (associate), American Association for the Advancement of Science, Sigma Xi.

WRITINGS: Evolution and Human Behavior, Natural History Press, 1967; *Adaptation in Cultural Evolution: An Approach to Medical Anthropology,* Columbia University Press, 1970; *Human Diversity,* Columbia University Press, 1971; *The Human Imperative,* Columbia University Press, 1972; *When the Spider Danced: Notes from an African Village,* Doubleday, 1975. Contributor to professional journals in United States and abroad.

WORK IN PROGRESS: The Roots of Creativity.

SIDELIGHTS: Alland speaks French. *Avocational interests:* Primitive art, French anthropology, structuralism.

* * *

ALLBECK, Willard Dow 1898-

PERSONAL: Born October 5, 1898, in Millville, Pa.; son of Montraville McHenry (a clergyman) and Lida Belle (Schwartz) Allbeck; married Marie Lydia Neve, June 6, 1923; children: Alton N., Martha (Mrs. R. K. Bolton), Katherine (Mrs. P. L. Winemiller). *Education:* Susquehanna University, A.B., 1919; Wittenberg University, B.D., 1925, S.T.M., 1932; University of Pittsburgh, A.M., 1928, Ph.D., 1936.

CAREER: Ordained Evangelical Lutheran minister, 1922; pastor in Pittsburgh, Pa., 1922-37; Wittenberg University, Hamma School of Theology, Springfield, Ohio, professor of historical theology, 1937-67, professor emeritus, 1967—. Lectured in Puerto Rico, 1955, and in Japan, 1967. Archivist, Ohio Synod of Lutheran Church in America, 1949-62, and Wittenberg University, 1966—. Member of board of trustees, Thiel College, 1935-37. *Military service:* Student Army Training Corps, 1918. *Member:* American Society of Church History, Lutheran Historical Conference, Society for Reformation Research. *Awards, honors:* D.D., Susquehanna University, 1941.

WRITINGS: (With J. L. Neve) *History of the Lutheran Church in America,* Lutheran Literary Board, 1934; *Theology at Wittenberg,* Wittenberg University Press, 1945; *Studies in the Lutheran Confessions,* Muhlenberg Press, 1952, revised edition, Fortress, 1968; *A Century of Lutherans in Ohio,* Antioch Press, 1966; *History of Florida Lutheran Retirement Center,* CSS Publishing, 1975. Contributor to *New Schaff-Herzog Encyclopedia, Encyclopedia of the Lutheran Church,* and to theological journals, including *Lutheran Quarterly.*

BIOGAPHICAL/CRITICAL SOURCES: H. T. Neve and B. A. Johnson, *The Maturing of American Lutheranism,* Augsburg, 1968.

* * *

ALLEN, A(rvon) Dale, Jr. 1935-

PERSONAL: Born April 10, 1935, in Greensburg, Ind.; son of A. Dale (a professor) and Dorothy (Thorne) Allen; married Anita G. Barton, August 12, 1961; children: Lori Lynn, Krista Gayle, Kirk Dale, Tanya Beth, Alysia Dawn. *Education:* Depauw University, student, 1953-54; Indiana University, B.S., 1959, M.B.A., 1960; University of Colorado, D.B.A., 1966. *Religion:* Protestant. *Home:* 7105 Rockhill Dr., Jenison, Mich. 49428. *Office:* Seidman Graduate School of Business, Grand Valley State Colleges, Allendale, Mich. 49401.

CAREER: Radio Corporation of America, Bloomington, Ind., personnel and labor relations representative, 1960-61; University of Evansville, Evansville, Ind., instructor in management and economics, 1961-63; University of Louisville, Louisville, Ky., assistant professor of management and labor relations, 1966-67; Kansas State University, Manhattan, professor of management and labor relations, 1967-74; Northern Illinois University, DeKalb, chairman of department of management, 1974-75; Grand Valley State Colleges, Seidman Graduate College of Business, Allendale, Mich., professor of management and labor relations, 1975—. Arbitrator, Federal Mediation and Conciliation Service. *Military service:* U.S. Army, 1955-57. *Member:* Academy of Management, American Management Association, National Academy of Arbitrators, American Arbitration Association, Industrial Relations Research Association, Society of Professionals in Dispute Resolution. *Awards, honors:* Several federal grants.

WRITINGS: (With Laurence Steinmetz and Robert Johnson) *Labor Law,* Media Masters, 1967. Author of numerous arbitration cases, and contributor to journals. Contributing editor, *Management Horizons.*

WORK IN PROGRESS: A book on basic management principles and theory; research on costs, procedures, attitudes, and techniques, as related to labor arbitration hearings and opinions.

AVOCATIONAL INTEREST: Ornithology, water sports, weight lifting, church work.

*   *   *

ALLEN, Richard Sanders   1917-

PERSONAL: Born January 4, 1917, in Saratoga Springs, N.Y.; son of Charles Rollin (a civil engineer) and Mabel (Calef) Allen; married Doris Bishop, February 8, 1938; children: Richard, Robert. *Education:* Cornell University, student, 1934-36; also attended Albany Business College. *Religion:* Protestant. *Home:* 13 Aspinwall Rd., Albany, N.Y. 12111.

CAREER: Munson Steamship Line, New York, N.Y., clerk, 1936-37; Shell Union Oil Co., Albany, N.Y., salesman, 1937-40; General Electric Co., Schenectady, N.Y., stock clerk, 1941-44; Round Lake, N.Y., postmaster, 1944-61; *Mobil Travel Guide,* Bloomfield, N.J., field representative, 1962-70; program director, New York State American Revolution Bicentennial Commission, 1970—. Consultant on engineering history, Smithsonian Institution, 1961—; historical consultant to Penfield Foundation, 1966—, New York State Historic Trust, 1967-68. *Military service:* U.S. Army Air Forces, 1945-46; became acting sergeant. *Member:* American Aviation Historical Society, Air Britain, Canadian Aviation Historical Society, Air Force Historical Foundation, Society for Industrial Archeology, Council on Abandoned Military Posts. *Awards, honors:* Guggenheim fellow, 1962-63.

WRITINGS—All published by Stephen Greene Press: *Covered Bridges of the Northeast,* 1957, revised edition, 1974; *Covered Bridges of the Middle Atlantic States,* 1959; *Rare Old Covered Bridges of Windsor County, Vt.,* 1961; *Revolution in the Sky,* 1964, revised edition, 1967; *Covered Bridges of the Middle West,* 1969; *Covered Bridges of the*

South, 1969. Contributor to journals. Editor, *Covered Bridge Topics,* 1942-52.

WORK IN PROGRESS: History of Iron Manufacture in America; study of American aircraft used in the Spanish Civil War, 1936-1939, and of U.S. Soviet aeronautical relations, 1919-1939.

BIOGRAPHICAL/CRITICAL SOURCES: Saturday Evening Post, November 23, 1953.

*   *   *

ALLEN, Richard V(incent)   1936-

PERSONAL: Born January 1, 1936, in Collingswood, N.J.; son of Charles Carroll (a salesman) and Magdalen (Buchman) Allen; married Patricia Ann Mason, December 28, 1957; children: Michael, Kristin, Mark, Karen, Kathryn, Kevin. *Education:* University of Notre Dame, B.A., 1957, M.A., 1958. *Politics:* Republican. *Religion:* Roman Catholic. *Home:* 2343 South Meade St., Arlington, Va. 22202. *Office:* Potomac International Corporation, 905 16th St. N.W., Washington, D.C. 20006.

CAREER: Lecturer, University of Maryland, Overseas Division, 1958-61; Georgia Institute of Technology, Atlanta, assistant professor of social sciences, 1961-62; Georgetown University, Center for Strategic Studies, Washington, D.C., research principal and chairman of study program on communism, 1962-66; Stanford University, Hoover Institution on War, Revolution and Peace, Stanford, Calif., senior staff member, 1966-68; International Resources Ltd., Denver, Colo., vice-president, 1969-71; Potomac International Corp., Washington, D.C., president, 1972—. Senior foreign policy advisor, Nixon-Agnew campaign committee, 1967-68; senior staff member, National Security Council, 1969; consultant, National Security Affairs, 1970-71; member, Presidential Commission on International Trade and Economic Policy, 1970-72; deputy executive director, Council on International Economic Policy, and deputy assistant to the President on International Economic Affairs, 1971-72. Member of board of directors, Foreign Policy Research Institute, Philadelphia, Pa., 1970—. Consultant, American Bar Association, 1963—. Trustee, Intercollegiate Studies Institute, Philadelphia, 1969—, and St. Francis Preparatory School, Spring Grove, Pa. *Member:* American Political Science Association. *Awards, honors:* H. B. Earhart fellow of Relm Foundation, University of Munich, 1958-61; Congressional fellowship of American Political Science Association, 1962; book award of Assembly of Captive European Nations, 1965, for *Peaceful Coexistence: A Communist Blueprint for Victory.*

WRITINGS: (Editor with David M. Abshire) *National Security: Political, Military, and Economic Strategies in the Decade Ahead,* Praeger, 1963; (co-author) *East-West Trade: Its Strategic Implications,* Center for Strategic Studies, Georgetown University, 1964; *Peaceful Coexistence: A Communist Blueprint for Victory,* American Bar Association, 1964; *Peace or Peaceful Coexistence?,* American Bar Association, 1966; (with Hal Bartlett and Kenneth Colegrove) *Democracy and Communism: Theory and Action,* Van Nostrand, 1967; (editor) *Yearbook on International Communist Affairs,* Hoover Institute Press, 1969.

Contributor: F. R. Barnett and others, editors, *Peace and War in the Modern Age,* Doubleday, 1965; J. E. Dougherty and J. F. Lehman, Jr., editors, *The Prospects for Arms Control,* MacFadden, 1965; Eleanor L. Dulles and R. D. Crane, editors, *Detente,* Praeger, 1965; C. J. Zablocki, editor, *Sino-Soviet Rivalry,* Praeger, 1966. Contributor to magazines and newspapers. Member of editorial advisory board, *Intercollegiate Review*.

SIDELIGHTS: Richard Allen is competent in German, French, Spanish and Portuguese. *Avocational interests:* Amateur radio.

* * *

ALLOWAY, David Nelson 1927-

PERSONAL: Born September 26, 1927, in Emmaus, Pa.; son of Rexford D. and Margery L. (Neumoyer) Alloway. *Education:* Muhlenberg College, A.B., 1950; Columbia University, M.A., 1955; New York University, Ph.D., 1965. *Home:* 1303-B Troy Towers, Bloomfield, N.J. 07003. *Office:* Montclair State College, Normal Ave., Upper Montclair, N.J. 07043.

CAREER: High school teacher and chairman of department of social studies in Fallsington, Pa., 1954-57; Montclair State College, Upper Montclair, N.J., instructor, 1957-59, assistant professor of social studies, 1960-69, associate professor, 1969-70, professor of sociology, 1970—. Special lecturer, Fairleigh Dickinson University, 1956-66; visiting professor, Western Illinois University, 1964, 1966, and Indiana University of Pennsylvania, 1965. Greater Montclair (N.J.) Urban Coalition, co-founder and executive director, 1968-70. Consultant in sociology, Project Headstart, Summer, 1966. Manuscript reader for Greenwood Press. *Military service:* U.S. Army, Army Service Forces, 1945-46, 11th Airborne Division, 1950-51; became sergeant. *Member:* National Educational Association, National Council for the Social Studies, American Historical Association, American Sociological Association, Middle States Council for the Social Studies (vice-president, 1964-66; president, 1968-70), New Jersey Educational Association, New Jersey Council for the Social Studies (vice-president, 1967-69), International Platform Association, International Biographical Association (fellow). *Awards, honors:* Founders Day award of New York University, 1965.

WRITINGS: American Economic History, Monarch Press, 1966; (with Mary A. Arny) *A Goodly Heritage*, Town of Montclair, N.J., 1966; (with Francesco Cordasco) *The Agony of the Cities: Urban Problems in Contemporary America*, Montclair State College Press, 1969; (with Cordasco) *Minorities and the American City*, McKay, 1970; *The German Community in America*, Burt Franklin, 1976. Contributor to *Encyclopaedia Britannica*. Reviewer of books for *Choice*.

WORK IN PROGRESS: Wellsprings of Power, a revision of doctoral dissertation; *Urban-Suburban Relationships: The View from the Suburbs*, an examination of the reasons why suburbs resist regionalization efforts and close fiscal and other cooperation with inner cities.

* * *

ALMON, Clopper, Jr. 1934-

PERSONAL: Born January 25, 1934, in Nashville, Tenn.; son of Clopper (a lawyer) and Louise (Howell) Almon; married Shirley Montag (an economist), June 14, 1958. *Education:* Vanderbilt University, B.A., 1956; Harvard University, M.A., 1961, Ph.D., 1962. *Office:* Department of Economics, University of Maryland, College Park, Md. 20742.

CAREER: Harvard University, Cambridge, Mass., instructor, 1961-62, assistant professor of economics, 1962-66; University of Maryland, College Park, associate profes-

sor, 1966-68, professor of economics, 1968—. *Military service:* U.S. Army, 1957-59; served as lieutenant.

WRITINGS: The American Economy to 1975: An Interindustry Forecast, Harper, 1966; *Matrix Methods in Economics*, Addison-Wesley, 1967; *1985: Interindustry Forecasts of the American Economy*, Heath, 1974.

WORK IN PROGRESS: Research on an international system of input-output forecasting models.

* * *

ALTMAN, Jack 1938-

PERSONAL: Born November 30, 1938, in London, England; son of Harry (a tailor) and Lily (Penn) Altman; married Michelle Kevin (cartoon editor of *Playboy*), October 2, 1966. *Education:* Pembroke College, Cambridge, B.A., 1960. *Address:* c/o *Playboy* Magazine, 919 North Michigan, Chicago, Ill. 60611.

CAREER: Reuters Ltd., London, England, foreign correspondent in Bonn, Geneva, Vienna, Berlin, Prague, and then Paris, 1960-65; *Time,* New York, N.Y., correspondent in Chicago, 1965-67; *Chicago Sun-Times,* Chicago, Ill., feature writer, 1967-69; radio station WIND, Chicago, broadcaster, 1968-71. *Member:* Authors Guild.

WRITINGS: (With Marvin Ziporyn) *Born to Raise Hell,* Grove, 1967; (translator with Sherrie Murphy) Sarane Alexandria, *Hans Bellmer,* Rizzoli International, 1975; (translator) Katalin De Walterskirchen, *Paul Klee,* Rizzoli International, 1975. Contributor to *Columbia Journalism Review, Playboy,* and newspapers.

WORK IN PROGRESS: A novel with the Russian Revolution as background.

SIDELIGHTS: Altman told *CA:* "[I] speak fluent French and German and, since spending two years as Reuters correspondent in East Berlin and Prague, have developed a particular interest in Eastern Europe.... In writing about the American scene for American readers, my being a European allows my enthusiasm or distaste for the society around me to be unencumbered by the claims of patriotism. In all my writing, try not to confuse being serious with being solemn, a distinction I feel, perhaps unfairly, that many Americans are not prepared to make."†

* * *

ALY, Lucile Folse 1913-

PERSONAL: Surname rhymes with "daily"; born July 31, 1913, in Kansas City, Mo.; daughter of Charles Druzin and Belle (Stewart) Folse; married Bower Aly (a professor of speech at University of Oregon), February 7, 1943; children: Stewart Folse; stepchildren: Joanna (Mrs. Frank Gray), Barbara (Mrs. Robert Miller), Bower Johnson, Martha, Charles. *Education:* Kansas City (Mo.) Junior College, A.A., 1932; Emerson College, student, 1932-33; University of Missouri, B.S., 1935, Ph.D., 1959; Columbia University, M.A., 1942. *Politics:* Democrat. *Religion:* Congregational. *Home:* 1138 22nd Ave. E., Eugene, Ore. 97403. *Office:* Department of English, University of Oregon, Eugene, Ore. 97403.

CAREER: High school teacher of English and speech in Edina, Mo., 1936-38, Parkville, Mo., 1938-41, and Columbia, Mo., 1942-43; University of Missouri, Columbia, instructor in English, 1945-56; University of Oregon, Eugene, instructor, 1960-63, assistant professor, 1963-71, associate professor of English, 1971—. Oregon Curriculum Study

Center, member of rhetoric planning and writing group, Project English, 1963—. *Member:* National Council of Teachers of English, Speech Association of America, Modern Language Association of America, American Association of University professors, Friends of the Library Association (Eugene; vice-president, 1966-67; president, 1967-68).

WRITINGS: (Editor with husband, Bower Aly) *Speeches in English*, Random House, 1968; (editor with B. Aly) *American Short Speeches*, Macmillan, 1968; (contributor) Harold Barrett, editor, *Rhetoric of the People: Is There Any Better or Equal Hope in the World?*, Editions Rodopi, 1973; (with B. Aly) *A Rhetoric of Public Speaking*, McGraw, 1973. Contributor of articles to *Quarterly Journal of Speech* and *Focus/Midwest*.

WORK IN PROGRESS: John G. Neihardt: A Critical Biography, an authorized biography of the American poet; an edition of Neihardt's letters.

* * *

AMARAL, Anthony 1930-

PERSONAL: Born August 19, 1930, in Yonkers, N.Y.; son of Antone and Mae (Vitola) Amaral. *Education:* California State Polytechnic College (now University), B.S., 1960. *Home:* 201 North Roop, Carson City, Nev. 89701.

CAREER: Trainer of show horses, working at the Arabian horse ranch of the Kellogg Ranch in Pomona, Calif., before turning to writing; now a librarian at Ormsby Public Library, Carson City, Nev. *Military service:* U.S. Army, 1952-55; aide-de-camp to General Bruce C. Clarke; became first lieutenant.

WRITINGS: Comanche: The Horse That Survived the Custer Battle, Westernlore, 1961; *Movie Horses: Their Treatment and Training*, Bobbs-Merrill, 1967; *Will James: The Gilt-Edged Cowboy* (biography), Westernlore, 1967. Contributor of about one hundred articles on horse subjects, and others on western Americana, to *Smithsonian, Western Horseman, True West, Frontier Times, Nevada*, and *Sports Afield;* contributor of short stories to *Point West*, and *Fiction Magazine*.

WORK IN PROGRESS: A scholarly study on the wild horse of Nevada, its history, legends, and lore, for University of Nevada Press; *How to Be a Better Horse Trainer*, for Wilshire.

* * *

AMLUND, Curtis Arthur 1927-

PERSONAL: Born November 29, 1927, in Fargo, N.D.; son of Arthur Nils and Corinne (Strand) Amlund. *Education:* University of Minnesota, B.A. (magna cum laude), 1952, Ph.D., 1959. *Home:* 7330 York Ave. S., Minneapolis, Minn. 55435. *Office:* North Dakota State University, Fargo, N.D. 58102.

CAREER: University of Oregon, Eugene, instructor, 1959-60; University of Wisconsin at Milwaukee, visiting lecturer, 1961; North Dakota State University, Fargo, assistant professor, 1961-65, associate professor, 1965-71, professor of politics, 1971—. *Military service:* U.S. Army Reserve, 1946-47, 1952-54; became captain. *Member:* American Political Science Association, American Academy of Political and Social Science, Academy of Political Science, American Association of University Professors, Midwestern Conference of Political Scientists, Southwestern Social Science Association, Rocky Mountain Social Science Association, Phi Beta Kappa.

WRITINGS: Federalism in the Southern Confederacy, Public Affairs, 1966; *New Perspectives on the Presidency*, Philosophical Library, 1969. Contributor to political science and social science journals.

WORK IN PROGRESS: Congress: Some Diverging Theories.

* * *

AMOSS, Berthe 1925-

PERSONAL: First name is pronounced "beart" (as in "bear"); born September 26, 1925, in New Orleans, La.; daughter of Sumter Davis (a lawyer) and Berthe (Lathrop) Marks; married Walter James Amoss, Jr. (president of Lykes Bros. Steamship Co.), December 21, 1946; children: Jim, Bob, Billy, Mark, Tom, John. *Education:* Tulane University of Louisiana, B.A.; studied art for a total of five years, at University of Hawaii, at Kunstschule, Bremen, Germany, and Academie des Beaux Arts, Antwerp, Belgium. *Religion:* Roman Catholic. *Home:* 3723 Carondelet St., New Orleans, La. 70115. *Agent:* Harriet Wasserman, Russell & Volkening, Inc., 551 Fifth Ave., New York, N.Y. 10017.

CAREER: Started as illustrator; now writing for children, and illustrating her own books.

WRITINGS—Self-illustrated; juveniles, except as noted: *It's Not Your Birthday*, Harper, 1966; *Tom in the Middle*, Harper, 1968; *By the Sea*, Parents Press, 1969; *The Marvellous Catch of Old Hannibal*, Parents Press, 1970; *Old Hasdrubal and the Pirates*, Parents Press, 1971; *The Very Worst Thing*, Parents Press, 1972; *The Big Cry*, Bobbs-Merrill, 1972; *The Great Sea Monster; or, A Book by You*, Parents Press, 1975; *The Chalk Cross* (young adult novel), Seabury, in press.

WORK IN PROGRESS: Illustrating a mystery book for Harcourt.

SIDELIGHTS: Berthe Amoss speaks German and French. The Amoss family has lived in Hawaii, Belgium, and Germany.

* * *

AMSTEAD, B(illy) H(oward) 1921-

PERSONAL: Born August 18, 1921, in Austin, Tex.; son of Joe, Jr. and Barbara (Sheppard) Amstead; married Margaret Jane Bell, February 26, 1947; children: Barbara Jane, William Howard. *Education:* University of Texas, B.S., 1941, M.S., 1949, Ph.D., 1955. *Religion:* Presbyterian. *Home:* 2500 Jarratt, Austin, Tex. 78703 *Office:* University of Texas, Austin, Tex. 78712.

CAREER: Mission Manufacturing Co., Houston, Tex. production manager, 1942-43; University of Texas, Austin, researcher in defense research laboratory, 1946-49, assistant professor, 1947-55 (part-time, 1947-49), associate professor, 1955-60, professor of mechanical engineering, 1960-69, assistant dean, College of Engineering, 1959-69, acting dean, 1969-70; University of Texas of the Permian Basin, Odessa, president, 1970-74; University of Texas, Austin, professor of mechanical engineering, 1974—. Private engineering consultant, 1974—; solar energy consultant, 1974—. Director at large, United Cerebral Palsy of Texas, 1965-66; also active on Austin boards of Cerebral Palsy Association and American Red Cross. *Military service:* U.S. Navy, Ordnance, 1943-46; became lieutenant junior grade. *Member:* American Foundrymen's Society, American Society of Tool and Manufacturing Engineers, American Society for Engineering Education, American Society of Mechanical Engineers, Southwest Placement Association (president, 1958), Texas Society for Professional Engineers, National Exchange Club (president, 1968-69; past president of Austin Club and Texas State Clubs), Sigma Xi, Pi Tau Sigma, Phi Kappa Phi.

WRITINGS: (Contributor) *Production Handbook,* revised edition, Ronald, 1958; (with M. L. Begeman and P. Ostwald) *Manufacturing Processes,* 5th edition, Wiley, 1963, 7th edition, 1975; (with Wilbourn McNutt) *Engineering as a Career Today,* Dodd, 1966. Contributor of about thirty articles to engineering and industrial journals. Field editor, *Tool Engineer.*

*   *   *

AMSTUTZ, Arnold E.   1936-

PERSONAL: Born July 31, 1936, in Saginaw, Mich.; son of Forrest C. and Florence (Winkler) Amstutz; married Nancy E. Clark, 1959; married Margaret Louise Bryant. *Education:* Massachusetts Institute of Technology, S.B., 1958, Ph.D., 1965. *Home:* 1010 Memorial Dr., Cambridge, Mass. 02142. *Office:* Sloan School of Management, Massachusetts Institute of Technology, Cambridge, Mass.

CAREER: Arco Recording, Midland, Mich., owner-manager, 1951-54; Scientific Development Corp., Watertown, Mass., founder, officer, and director, 1959-62; Massachusetts Institute of Technology, Sloan School of Management, Cambridge, research associate, 1961-62, assistant professor, 1962-67, associate professor, 1967-71, senior lecturer in management, 1971—; Investment Information, Inc., Cambridge, president and chief executive officer, 1970—. Founder and director, Advanced Analysis Co., 1961-67, Decision Technology Inc., 1964—, Cambridge Management Co., 1968—, Decision Technology International, 1968—; director and officer, WTBS Foundation, Inc., 1964-71; director, Technology Student Enterprises, Inc., 1964—; limited partner, Jesup & Lamont, 1965-68. Consultant to Office of the Special Assistant Secretary of the Navy, 1967—. Lecturer at universities, including Columbia University, Harvard Business School, Purdue University, Indiana University, University of Sherbrooke, and for industrial and other groups.

MEMBER: Academy of Political Science, American Marketing Association, Institute of Management Sciences, Association for Computing Machinery. *Awards, honors:* Ford Foundation faculty research fellowship, Sperry Hutchinson Foundation research award.

WRITINGS: What Is a Digital Computer?, Scientific Development Corp., 1961; *Getting Acquainted with MINI-VAC,* Scientific Development Corp., 1961; *An Introduction to Solid State Computers,* Scientific Development Corp., 1962; *Computer Simulation of Competitive Market Response,* M.I.T. Press, 1967.

Contributor: *Marketing Keys to Profits in the 1960's,* American Marketing Association, 1960; W. F. Massey and G. B. Tallman, editors, *Marketing and the Computer,* Prentice-Hall, 1962; *The Marketing Concept in Action,* American Marketing Association, 1964; *Meeting the Challenge to New Products,* American Marketing Association, 1965; *Science, Technology, and Marketing,* American Marketing Association, 1966; David B. Hertz and Jacques Milese, editors, *Proceedings of the Fourth International Conference on Operational Research,* Wiley Interscience, 1966; Frank M. Bass, Charles W. King, and Edgar A. Pessemier, editors, *Applications of the Sciences in Mar-*

keting Management, Wiley, 1968; Steuart Henderson Britt and Harper W. Boyd, Jr., editors, *Marketing Management and Administrative Action,* 2nd edition, McGraw, 1968; Robert D. Buzzell, Donald F. Cox, and Rex V. Brown, editors, *Marketing Research and Information Systems,* McGraw, 1969.

David B. Montgomery and Glen L. Urban, editors, *Applications of Management Science in Marketing,* Prentice-Hall, 1970; Erwin Grochla and Norbert Szyperski, editors, *Management-Informations-Systeme,* Betriebswirtschaftlicher Verlag (Wiesbaden, West Germany), 1971; M. S. Moyer, editor, *Managing Marketing Information,* York University Faculty of Administrative Studies, Bureau of Research, 1971; Alfonso F. Cardenas, Leon Presser, and Miguel A. Marin, editors, *Computer Science,* Wiley Interscience, 1972; Steuart Henderson Britt, editor, *Marketing Manager's Handbook,* Dartnell Press, 1973; Robert Ferber, editor, *Handbook of Marketing Research,* McGraw, 1974. Contributor to marketing and management journals.

*   *   *

ANDERSEN, Doris   1909-

PERSONAL: Born February 6, 1909, in Tanana, Alaska; daughter of Edgar and Florence Maude (Walker) Crompton; married George C. Andersen, December 23, 1929; children: Deirdre (Mrs. W. J. McKechnie), Richard, David. *Education:* University of British Columbia, B.A., 1929; University of Washington, Seattle, B.S.L.S., 1930. *Home:* 1232 Esquimalt Ave., West Vancouver, British Columbia, Canada.

CAREER: Librarian with Seattle (Wash.) Public Library, 1929-30, and Ottawa (Ontario) Public Library, 1940-45; Vancouver (British Columbia) Public Library, branch head, 1956-74. *Awards, honors:* Runner-up for Canadian Association of Children's Librarians Best Children's Book Award in 1974, for *Slave of the Haida.*

WRITINGS: Blood Brothers (juvenile), St. Martin's, 1967; *Ways Harsh and Wild* (adult), J. J. Douglas Ltd., 1973; *Slave of the Haida* (juvenile), Macmillan, 1974. Contributor to *Canadian Library* and *British Columbia Library Quarterly.*

*   *   *

ANDERSON, Colena M(ichael)   1891-

PERSONAL: Born May 30, 1891, in Buffalo, N.Y.; daughter of Charles F. and Frances (Reppien) Michael; married Elam J. Anderson (a missionary to China and college president), July 3, 1916 (deceased); children: Frances (Mrs. Clarence S. Gulick), Victor, Elam. *Education:* Cornell University, B.A., 1914; University of Chicago, M.A., 1917; Claremont Graduate School, Ph.D., 1954. *Politics:* Republican. *Religion:* Christian. *Home:* 345 South Baker, McMinnville, Ore. 97128.

CAREER: Teacher, mainly of English, in Buffalo, N.Y., 1914-16, University of Shanghai, Shanghai, China, 1917-19, and Shanghai American School, 1928-29, 1931-32; Linfield College, McMinnville, Ore., associate professor of English and history, 1946-58, professor emeritus, 1958—, dean of women, 1952-58. *Member:* Phi Beta Kappa, Delta Kappa Gamma (president, 1952-54), Shakespeare Club (McMinnville).

WRITINGS: Handbook for Christian Writers, Zondervan, 1966; *Don't Put on Your Slippers Yet,* Zondervan, 1971; *Joy Beyond Grief,* Zondervan, 1975. Contributor of articles and stories to *Christian Herald* and denominational publications.

WORK IN PROGRESS: Frances, stories of author's mother's childhood; *Four Seasons of the House of Peace,* a family biography.

AVOCATIONAL INTERESTS: Reading, gardening, flower arrangement, and making personal greeting cards.

* * *

ANDERSON, Margaret (Vance) 1917-

PERSONAL: Born June 19, 1917, in Glasgow, Ky.; daughter of James Wood (a lawyer) and Lucie (Akers) Vance; married Raymond Anderson (a high school band director), May 22, 1943; children: Martha Wood, Carolyn Elaine. *Education:* Western Kentucky State University, A.B., 1939; University of Tennessee, M.S., 1945. *Politics:* Democrat. *Home and office:* 505 Eagle Bend Rd., Clinton, Tenn. 37716.

CAREER: Williamsburg High School, Williamsburg, Ky., teacher, 1947-51; Clinton High School, Clinton, Tenn., teacher, 1953-58, assistant principal, 1958-60, guidance director, beginning 1960. Member of advisory committee, Center for Southern Education Studies, George Peabody College for Teachers, 1971-72. *Member:* American Personnel and Guidance Association, National Education Association, National Parent-Teacher Association (honorary life member), Tennessee Personnel and Guidance Association, Tennessee Education Association, East Tennessee Education Association, Delta Kappa Gamma.

WRITINGS: The Children of the South, Farrar, Straus, 1966. Contributor to *New York Times Magazine* and to professional journals.

WORK IN PROGRESS: Research on Appalachia, the region and its people; a study of the problems of disadvantaged children in the public schools.†

* * *

ANDERSON, Rachel 1943-

PERSONAL: Born March 18, 1943, in Hampton Court, Surrey, England; daughter of Donald Clive (a writer and military historian) and Verily (a writer; maiden name, Bruce) Anderson; married David Bradby (a university lecturer in French), June 19, 1965; children: Hannah, Lawrence, Donald. *Education:* Studied at Hastings School of Art, 1959-60. *Politics:* Socialist. *Religion:* "Church of England Christian." *Home:* 18 King St., Canterbury, Kent, England.

CAREER: Chatto & Windus Ltd., London, England, publicity assistant, 1963-64; brief period in editorial department of *Women's Mirror,* London, 1964; and very brief period (three days) in news department of British Broadcasting Corp., Bristol, England, 1966; these occupations "preceded, interspersed, and followed by jobs as nursemaid, cleaning woman, van driver, gardener, etc., etc., and freelance writer, and as broadcaster for BBC 'Woman's Hour.'"

WRITINGS: Pinneapple (novel), J. Cape, 1965; *The Purple Heart Throbs* (survey of romantic fiction), Hodder & Stoughton, 1974. Also author of radio play, "Tomorrow's Tomorrow," 1970. Contributor of articles to *Observer, Good Housekeeping, Homes & Gardens, Times* (London), *Weekend Telegraph, Punch, Guardian,* and other magazines and newspapers in England.

WORK IN PROGRESS: Dream Loves, a biography, publication by Hodder & Stoughton expected in 1977; *The Expatriates,* children's fiction.

SIDELIGHTS: Rachel Anderson told *CA:* "[I was] brought up in a literary family. Am incapable of doing anything else so had to be a writer. Am [a] practicing Christian in an essentially heathen age. Speak French, Italian. Main interests are domestic bliss, travel, peace". In 1975, Ms. Anderson starred in "Fateful Eclipse," a television drama by Nigerian writer Loalu Oguniyi, broadcast on Western Nigerian Television.

* * *

ANDERSON, Robert (Woodruff) 1917-

PERSONAL: Born April 28, 1917, in New York, N.Y., son of James Hewston (a businessman) and Myra Esther (a teacher; maiden name Grigg) Anderson; married Phyllis Stohl (a teacher, producer, and literary agent), June 24, 1940 (died, 1956); married Teresa Wright (an actress), December 11, 1959; stepchildren: Terence Busch, Mary Kelly Busch. *Education:* Harvard University, A.B. (magna cum laude), 1939, M.A., 1940, courses completed for Ph.D.; studied at Dramatic Workshop, New School for Social Research. *Agent:* Audrey Wood, International Creative Management, 40 West 57th St., New York, N.Y. 10019.

CAREER: Made stage debut as a troll in a seventh-grade school production; acted with South Shore Players, Cohasset, Mass., summers, 1937-38; Harvard University, Cambridge, Mass., assistant in English, 1939-42; Erskine School, Boston, Mass., teacher, 1941; teacher of playwriting at American Theatre Wing, New York City, 1946-50, and at Actors' Studio, New York City, 1955; playwright, 1946—; television and radio writer, 1948-53; Playwrights Co., New York City, producer, partner, and member, 1953-60; screenwriter, 1955—. President, New Dramatist Committee, 1959-60; member of faculty, Salzberg Seminar in American Studies, 1968; writer-in-residence, University of North Carolina, Chapel Hill, 1969; member of board of governors, American Playwrights Theatre; chairman, Harvard Board of Overseers' Committee to Visit the Performing Arts. *Military service:* U.S. Naval Reserve, active duty, 1942-46; became lieutenant senior grade; received Bronze Star.

MEMBER: Dramatists Guild (member of council; president, 1970-73), Dramatists Guild Fund (member of board of directors), Authors League of America (member of council), Authors League Fund (member of board of directors), Century Association, Harvard Club, Coffee House Club. *Awards, honors:* First prize, Army-Navy Playwriting Contest for Servicemen Overseas, 1945, for "Come Marching Home"; National Theatre Conference Fellowship, 1945, for "Come Marching Home," "Boy Grown Tall," and "The Tailored Heart"; Rockefeller fellowship, 1946; *Variety*—New York Drama Critics Poll Award, 1954, for "Tea and Sympathy"; Writers Guild of America award for best screenplay, 1970, for "I Never Sang for My Father"; Writers Guild Laurel Award for Achievement for drama adapted from another medium, 1971, for screenplay "I Never Sang for My Father"; Academy of Motion Picture Arts and Sciences Award nominations for "The Nun's Story" and "I Never Sang for My Father."

WRITINGS: After (novel), Random House, 1973. Also author of prefaces to plays in *Best Plays . . .,* edited by Otis Guernsey, Dodd, 1954, 1967, 1968, and in *Best American Plays . . .,* edited by John Gassner, Crown, 1958, 1964, 1968.

Plays: *Tea and Sympathy* (three-act; produced on Broadway at Ethel Barrymore Theatre, September 30, 1953), Random House, 1954; *All Summer Long* (two-act; adapted from the novel *A Wreath and a Curse,* by Donald Wetzel; first produced at Arena State, Washington, D.C., January 13, 1953; produced on Broadway at Coronet Theatre, September 23, 1954), Samuel French, 1955; *Silent Night, Lonely Night* (two-act; produced on Broadway at Morosco Theatre, December 4, 1959), Random House, 1960; *The Days Between* (two-act; first produced in Dallas, Tex., 1965; produced by American Playwrights Theatre across the country, 1965-66), Random House, 1965, revised edition, Samuel French, 1969; *You Know I Can't Hear You When the Water's Running* (four one-acts; produced on Broadway at Ambassador Theatre, March 13, 1967), Random House, 1967; *I Never Sang for My Father* (two-act; produced on Broadway at Longacre Theatre, January 25, 1968), Random House, 1968, screenplay edition, New American Library, 1970; *Solitaire/Double Solitaire* (two one-acts; first produced at Long Wharf Theatre, New Haven, Conn., February 11, 1971; produced at Twenty-fifth Edinburgh International Festival, Edinburgh, Scotland, July 29, 1971; produced on Broadway at John Golden Theatre, September 30, 1971), Random House, 1972.

Unpublished plays: "Hour Town" (musical comedy), produced at Harvard University, December, 1938; "Come Marching Home," first produced at State University of Iowa, 1945, produced in New York City at Blackfriars Guild, May 18, 1946; "The Eden Rose," first produced by Theatre Workshop, Ridgefield, Conn., July 27, 1949; "Dance Me a Song," produced on Broadway at Royale Theatre, January 20, 1950; "Love Revisited," produced at Westport Country Playhouse, June 25, 1951.

Plays as yet neither published nor produced: "Boy Grown Tall," 1945; "The Tailored Heart," 1945.

Film adaptions: "Tea and Sympathy" (from own play) M-G-M, 1956; "Until They Sail" (from the novel, *Return to Paradise,* by James A. Michener), M-G-M, 1956; "The Nun's Story" (from the novel by the same title, by Kathryn Hulme), Warner Brothers, 1959; "The Sand Pebbles" (from the novel by the same title, by Richard McKenna), Twentieth Century-Fox, 1965; "I Never Sang for My Father" (from own play), Columbia, 1970.

Television scripts; adaptations: "The Old Lady Shows Her Medals" (from the story by J. M. Barrie), produced for U.S. Steel Hour, December 19, 1956; "Rise Up and Walk," produced for Robert Montgomery Presents; "Still Life," produced for Schlitz Playhouse; "Biography," produced for Prudential Playhouse; "At Midnight on the Thirty-first of March," produced for Studio One.

Radio play adaptations include Maxwell Anderson's "Valley Forge," Robert Sherwood's "The Petrified Forest," and Elmer Rice's "Dream Girl." Other adaptations for Theatre Guild radio programs include "David Copperfield," "The Glass Menagerie," "A Farewell to Arms," "The Scarlet Pimpernel," "Arrowsmith," "Trilby," "Summer and Smoke," "Goodbye, Mr. Chips," "Oliver Twist," "Vanity Fair," and others.

WORK IN PROGRESS: A film adaptation of *The Days Between.*

SIDELIGHTS: "Of our playwrights, Robert Anderson is the master engraver," wrote Richard Coe. In discussing *All Summer Long,* John Gassner said: "It would have been difficult to find a more intelligent and sensitive playwright for the assignment of adapting [Wetzel's book]. Praise should be given to some excellent details of characterizations and feeling; blame to laboriousness in underscoring the lesson and for a general mildness of action and characterization.... Anderson's talent made it possible for us to take some interest in the play's character."

Tea and Sympathy is a different kind of play. Gassner noted that it had "an ascending movement. It also had a sensational conclusion and a dramatic pressure that propelled the action forward in spurts of intrigue, conflict, discoveries, and reversals." He also felt that it is a play of greater sensitivity than *All Summer Long.* Jeremy Kingston called *Tea and Sympathy* "a slick solution of what one might call the dramatic problem of the 1950's: how not to examine homosexuality while seeming to do so."

Gassner observed that *Silent Night, Lonely Night* "was an exercise in restraint. Not many reviewers appreciated the discipline he imposed on himself.... He rested his case ... solely on the shy rapprochement of two people and took the calculated risk of exhibiting nothing else.... It was worth taking for those of us, apparently a minority, who were held by the author's finely spun web of feeling and insight." Gassner felt, however, that the play might better have been a "long one-act play in two or three scenes."

You Know I Can't Hear You When the Water's Running, an evening of one-acts, was unevenly received by the critics. Harold Clurman commented: "One feels oneself in the presence of something still unborn, certainly juvenile and consequently somewhat annoying, perhaps even boring, which one still hesitates utterly to reject (much less to condemn) since it does exist on a far wider scale than one assumes. The unbalance in the construction of the four playlets ... reflects a tussle in the playwright's spirit." Mel Gussow contended that Anderson deliberately set out to suppress his insight and write something brightly commercial. Paul Velde called the play "a curious blend of middle class expose and reassurance." He said: "Life is lived and only illusions are worked at, and illusion is what Anderson's characters are up to, much as at a job. Their job, in fact, is to preserve the illusion of middle-class values and comforts." Haskel Frankel viewed the play as "whipped cream pretending to be steak, but that's no crime."

Time commented on *I Never Sang for My Father:* "Sometimes poignant, sometimes sentimental, always earnest, it essentially presents a static emotional impasse." This is because he was working with the Oedipus complex, which *Time* saw as reducing "conflict to impasse." *Newsweek* found that the "language is flat, often burdened with the cadences of soap opera." Richard Coe did not agree. He wrote of Anderson: "Meticulous in memory, emotion, and conception, he achieves a peerless refinement.... *I Never Sang for My Father* is a matter of style fitting play, an evocation of emotions lost but permanently, indelibly, finely etched."

According to Clive Barnes on *Solitaire/Double Solitaire,* "this simple double bill seems to me to be his [Anderson's] finest achievement to date. Mr. Anderson is a fluent advocate of that maligned form, the well-made play, and his advocacy is based upon the fact that he can well-make them." A *Variety* reviewer acknowledged that "in this work, Anderson again displays his insight into human emotion and expressing his ideas in terms of general identification."

A Universal made-for-television film adaptation of "Silent Night, Lonely Night," by John Vlahos, was broadcast on NBC-TV, December 16, 1969.

AVOCATIONAL INTERESTS: Swimming, tennis, reading, and playing the guitar.

BIOGRAPHICAL/CRITICAL SOURCES: John Gassner, *Theatre at the Crossroads,* Holt, 1960; *National Observer,* March 20, 1967, February 5, 1968; *Newsweek,* March 27, 1967, February 5, 1968; *Nation,* April 3, 1967; *Commonweal,* April 28, 1967; *Time,* February 2, 1968; *New Yorker,* February 3, 1968; *Washington Post,* February 7, 1968; *Hudson Review,* summer, 1968; *Punch,* July 3, 1968; *Variety,* December 18, 1968; *New York Times,* November 23, 1969; *Writer,* September, 1970.

* * *

ANDERSON, Stanley V(ictor) 1928-

PERSONAL: Born February 18, 1928, in Alameda, Calif.; son of Victor Thomas (a barber) and Stella (Hansen) Anderson; married Mary Black, June 24, 1967. *Education:* University of California, Berkeley, B.A., 1949, LL.B., 1953, Ph.D., 1961; University of Copenhagen, graduate study, 1950-51, 1959-60. *Residence:* Santa Barbara, Calif. *Office:* Department of Political Science, University of California, Santa Barbara, Calif. 93106.

CAREER: Fallon & Hargreaves, attorneys, San Francisco, Calif., lawyer, 1954; Alameda County, Calif., assistant public defender, 1957; University of California, Santa Barbara, assistant professor, 1961-66, associate professor, 1966-67, professor of political science, 1967—. *Military service:* U.S. Navy, 1946-48. *Member:* American Bar Association, American Society of International Law, American Political Science Association, State Bar of California, Bar Association of Santa Barbara, Pi Sigma Alpha. *Awards, honors:* Woodrow Wilson traveling fellow and American-Scandinavian Foundation fellow in Denmark, 1959-60; National Endowment for the Humanities fellowship, 1975-76.

WRITINGS: Canadian Ombudsman Proposals, Institute of Governmental Studies, University of California, 1966; *The Nordic Council,* University of Washington Press, 1967; (editor) *Ombudsmen for American Government?,* Prentice-Hall, 1968; *Ombudsman Papers: American Experience and Proposals,* Institute of Governmental Studies, University of California, 1969; (editor with John E. Moore) *Establishing Ombudsman Offices: Recent Experience in the United States,* Institute of Government Studies, University of California, 1972. Also author of *Abandoned Property—State Acquisition and Recovery by Rightful Owner,* 1954. Contributor to journals, including *American Journal of Comparative Law.*

WORK IN PROGRESS: A book, *Prison Ombudsman,* completion expected in 1976.

SIDELIGHTS: Stanley Anderson speaks Danish, French, and Spanish.

* * *

ANDERSON, Virginia (R. Cronin) 1920-
(Hyacinthe Hill)

PERSONAL: Born May 24, 1920, in New York, N.Y.; daughter of Joseph Thomas (veterinarian, metallurgist, and blacksmith) and Angela (a writer; maiden name, Bradley-Bruen) Cronin; married John L. Anderson (a coppersmith), July 15, 1940; children: John Luke, Matthew Mark (died, 1971). *Education:* Brooklyn College (now Brooklyn College of the City University of New York), A.B. (cum laude), 1961; Hunter College (now Hunter College of the City University of New York), M.A., 1965; Fordham University, graduate study, 1965—. *Religion:* Quaker. *Home:* 166 Hawthorne Ave., Yonkers, N.Y. 10705.

CAREER: Paul Hoffman Junior High School, Bronx, N.Y., English teacher, 1963-69; James Monroe High School, Bronx, N.Y., English teacher, 1969—. New York and American delegate to First and Second World Congress of Poets, Manila, 1971, Taiwan, 1973. New York State associate in humanities and performing arts. Judge at sixth annual awards contest, New York Poetry Forum. *Member:* Modern Language Association of America, Poetry Society of America, Academy of American Poets, National League of American Pen Women, National Association of Media Women, National Society of Literature and the Arts, National Council of Teachers of English, American Association of University Women, American Federation of Astrologers, Astrologers' Guild of America, New York City Association of English Teachers.

AWARDS, HONORS: Poetry Society of America awards, 1961, twice in 1962, 1964, and 1967; Effa Stark Sanders National Lyric Contest award, 1962; two *Mentor* poetry awards, 1966; International Poet Laureate and Poet-Leader Merittisimus Award, Manila, 1969; International Poet Laureate, golden laurel wreath and diploma of award, First and Second World Congress of Poets, Manila, 1971, Taiwan, 1973; Gold Commemoratine Medal from the Shah of Iran, 1972; distinguished service citation, World Poetry Society, 1973; York Award, 1974; Keats Poetry Prize, 1975, for poem, "The Riveter"; named an International Woman of 1975, with laureate honors, International Hall of Fame of Women of Distinction, 1975. Honorary degrees include: Ph.D. from Northern Pontifical Academy, 1969, and St. Olav's College, Sweden, 1969; Doctor of Arts and Letters, Great China Arts College, Hong Kong, 1969; D.H., International Academy of Alfred the Great, Hull, England, 1970; L.H.D. from L'Universite Libre d'Asie, 1974; H.L.D., Free University, 1974.

WRITINGS—Poetry under pseudonym Hyacinthe Hill: *Shoots of a Vagrant Vine,* New Athenaeum Press, 1950; *Promethea,* Cameo Press (Glasgow, Scotland), 1957; (editor with Charles Angoff, Gustav Davidson, and A. M. Sullivan) *The Diamond Year,* A. S. Barnes, 1970; *Squaw, No More,* Old Nokomis Publications, 1975. Also author of *Breasts and the Woman* (poetry), and editor of *Great American Poets North Atlantic Issue,* 1973.

Poetry included in numerous anthologies including: *World Bahai Anthology,* 1951; *Adventures in American Poetry,* 1954; *New Age Anthology of Poetry,* 1955; *Exile,* 1957; *Golden Year* (Poetry Society of America, 1910-1960); *Sing Loud for Loveliness,* 1962; *The Writing on the Wall,* Doubleday, 1969; *International Who's Who in Poetry Anthology,* 1972; *New Orlando Anthologies,* Volumes I, II, and III, 1973, and other collections. Poems have been published in periodicals and newspapers here and abroad.

* * *

ANDONOV-POLJANSKI, Hristo 1927-

PERSONAL: Born September 21, 1927, in Dojran, Yugoslavia; son of George Andon and Jordana (Bakalova) Andonov; married Jelica Mihailova (a museum keeper), February 16, 1958; children: Emil, Terezina. *Education:* University of Skopje, B.A., 1951, Ph.D., 1958. *Home:* Albert Ajnstein No. 1, Skopje, Yugoslavia. *Office:* Faculty of Philosophy, University of Skopje, Skopje, Yugoslavia.

CAREER: University of Skopje, Faculty of Philosophy, Skopje, Yugoslavia, assistant, 1953-59, lecturer, 1959-66, associate professor, 1966-70, professor, 1970—. Researcher for long periods at British Museum and in the Public Record Office. *Member:* Yugoslav Historical Association, Institute for History (Skopje). *Awards, honors:* Award of Republic of Macedonia, 1972, for *Gotze Delchev.*

WRITINGS: (Contributor) *Prilog kon Bibliografijata po Arheologijata na Makedonija,* Institut za Nacionalna Istorija (Skopje), 1953; *Stranskiot pecat za Ilindenskoto vostanie,* [Skopje], 1953; (editor and author of preface) *Goce Delcev vo Spomenite na Sovremenicite,* Kultura (Skopje), 1963; *Makedonija vo Karti,* Institut za Nacionalna Istorija (Glasnik), 1965; (editor and author of preface) Karl Hron, *Narodnosta na Makedonskite Sloveni,* Arhiva na Makedonija (Skopje), 1966; *Britanska Bibliografija za Makedonija,* Arhiva na Makedonija (Skopje), 1966; (editor) *Krste Misirkov,* Institut za Makedonski Jazik, 1966; *Dramata vo Cer: Niz Zivotot i Deloto na Hristo Uzunov,* Kultura, 1968; (editor) *Britanski Dokumenti za Istorijata na Makedonskiot Narod* (title means "British Documents on the History of the Macedonian People"), Arhiva na Makedonija, Volume I: *1797-1839,* 1968, Volume II: *1840-1847,* in press; *Goce Delcev: ideolog i organizator na makedonskoto nacional-noosloboditelno dvizenje,* Kultura, 1968; *Oddzivot na ilindenskoto vostanie vo svetot,* [Skopje], 1968; *San-Stefanska Bulgarija: Nenaucnoto tolkuvanje na makedonskata istorija,* Kultura, 1968; (editor) *Za Makedoncite* (poetry), Nakedonska Kniga, 1969; (member of editorial board) *Istorija na makedonskiot narod,* three volumes, Institut za Nacionalna Istorija, 1969; *Goce Delchev,* six volumes, Kultura, 1972; *Gotze Delchev: His Life and Time,* Misla (Skopje), 1973; *Velika Britanija i makedonskoto prasanje na Pariskata mirovna konferencija, 1919,* Arhiva na Makedonija, 1973. Contributor of article, in English, to *Macedonian Review.*

SIDELIGHTS: Andonov-Poljanski is competent in English, Russian, Bulgarian, Macedonian, Serbo-Croat, Slovenian, and has "literary" competency in French, German, and Italian.

*   *   *

ANDREW, Warren   1910-

PERSONAL: Born July 19, 1910, in Portland, Ore.; son of John and Alice (Lucke) Andrew; married Nancy Valerie Miellmier, August 18, 1936; children: Linda Nancy. *Education:* Carleton College, B.A. (summa cum laude), 1932; Brown University, M.S., 1933; Yale University, graduate study, 1933-34; University of Illinois, Ph.D., 1936; Baylor University, M.D., 1943; Butler University, M.A. (church history), 1974. *Home:* 5275 North Capitol Ave., Indianapolis, Ind. *Office:* Indiana University Medical Center, 1100 West Michigan St., Indianapolis, Ind. 46207.

CAREER: University of Georgia School of Medicine, Athens, instructor and fellow in anatomy, 1937-39; Baylor University School of Medicine, Dallas, Tex., instructor, 1939-41, assistant professor of anatomy, 1941-43; Southwestern Medical College, Dallas, Tex., associate professor, 1943-45, professor of histology, 1946-47; George Washington University School of Medicine, Washington, D.C., professor of anatomy and chairman of department, 1947-52; Wake Forest College, Bowman Gray School of Medicine, Winston-Salem, N.C., professor of anatomy and director of department, 1952-58; Indiana University School of Medicine, Indianapolis, professor of anatomy and chairman of department, 1958—. Visiting professor at University of Montevideo, Uruguay, 1945-46, and Washington Univer-

sity, St. Louis, 1948-49; lecturer at Tokyo University and Kyoto University, Japan, summer, 1960, and in Pakistan and India, summer, 1962; fellow at Yale University, 1974-75. U.S. representative for biology, International Research Committee on Gerontology, 1954—; chairman of biology session, 7th International Congress of Gerontology, Vienna, 1966; presented papers at other international medical congresses in England, Scotland, Netherlands, Mexico, Denmark, Portugal, and Germany. Secretary of Indiana State Anatomical Board, 1961—; chairman of research committee, Indiana State Commission on Aging and the Aged, 1966.

MEMBER: American Association of Anatomists, American Society of Zoologists, Society for Experimental Biology and Medicine, Tissue Culture Association, Gerontological Society (member of council and corporation, 1950-53, 1957—), Electron Microscope Society of America (and Midwest and New York branches), American Geriatrics Society, American Association for the Advancement of Science, Pan American Medical Association, New York Academy of Sciences, Washington Academy of Medicine, Washington Society of Pathologists, Texas State Medical Association, as well as other medical groups in Montevideo and Vienna; Philosophical Society of Washington, Phi Beta Kappa, Sigma Xi, Phi Chi, Cosmos Club (Washington, D.C.). *Awards, honors:* Distinguished service award, U.S. Junior Chamber of Commerce, 1946; national award for research, Gerontological Research Foundation, St. Louis, 1959.

WRITINGS: (Translator) E.D.P. de Robertis, Nowinski, and Saez, *General Cytology,* Saunders, 1949; *Comparative Histology* (text), Oxford University Press, 1959; *Comparative Hematology* (text), Grune, 1965; *Microfabric of Man* (histology text), Year Book, 1966; *One World of Science,* C. C Thomas, 1966; *Anatomy of Aging in Man and Animals,* Grune, 1971; (with Cleveland Pendleton Hickman) *Histology of the Vertebrates: A Comparative Text,* Mosby, 1974. Contributor to *Encyclopaedia Britannica,* 1975, and to medical journals. Member of editorial board, *Gerontologia,* 1957—, and *Gerontological Newsletter,* 1959—.

WORK IN PROGRESS: A book of verse, *Remember the War;* research on aging of human skin; studies on structure and function of lymphocytes.

AVOCATIONAL INTERESTS: Languages, biography.

*   *   *

ANDREWS, George (Clinton)   1926-

PERSONAL: Born April 7, 1926, in New York, N.Y.; son of George Clinton (a physician) and Emma (Donner) Andrews; married Tatiana Znamensky, March 5, 1949; children: Calina, Tatiana, George, Maya, Diana. *Education:* "Expelled from Hotchkiss, graduated from [preparatory school] cum laude, quit Cornell during first semester of sophomore year at age of eighteen, and have been going my own way ever since." *Politics:* "Don't believe in labels, but Che Guevara was one of the few contemporary leaders I respected." *Religion:* "Believe them all but God is one." *Agent:* Jonathan Clowes Ltd., 19 Jeffrey's Place, London NW1 9PP, England.

CAREER: Andrews disclaims any business connections since he left school, says he took LSD on British television ("had such a good trip they were afraid to show it"), and smoked hashish for German television; after publication of *The Book of Grass* the British Home Office refused to extend his visa, and he moved on to France, where he was arrested for possession of marijuana. *Member:* Society of Authors.

WRITINGS: (Editor with Simon Vinkenoog) *The Book of Grass* (anthology of writings about the uses of marijuana and hemp, or writings produced under their influence), Grove, 1967; *Burning Joy* (poems), Trigram Press (London), 1967; (with David Solomon) *Drugs and Sexuality,* Panther, 1973; (editor with Solomon) *Coca Leaf and Cocaine Papers,* Harcourt, 1975. Contributor to *Psychedelic Review, City Lights, Plus* (Brussels), and other similar journals in Europe.

WORK IN PROGRESS: Exploration of the dimensions revealed by psychedelics.†

* * *

ANGELOCCI, Angelo 1926-

PERSONAL: Surname is pronounced An-ja-*lo*-see; born October 16, 1926, in Trenton, Mich.; son of Angelo A. (a laborer) and Agatha (Cima) Angelocci; married Joyce G. Hartung (a teacher), February 9, 1951; children: Keith, Mark, Bradley, Lisa. *Education:* Eastern Michigan University, B.S., 1950; University of Michigan, M.A., 1951; Wayne State University, Ph.D., 1962. *Religion:* Episcopalian. *Home:* 963 Sherman, Ypsilanti, Mich. 48197. *Office:* Eastern Michigan University, Ypsilanti, Mich. 48197.

CAREER: Teacher of speech and art at high school in Birmingham, Mich., 1951-58; Rehabilitation Institute of Metropolitan Detroit, Detroit, Mich., speech therapist, 1958-59; Wayne State University, Detroit, Mich., research associate, 1959-62; Western Washington State College, Bellingham, assistant professor of speech pathology, 1962-65; Eastern Michigan University, Ypsilanti, professor of speech pathology, 1965—. *Military service:* U.S. Army, 1945-46; became staff sergeant. *Member:* American Association of University Professors, American Speech and Hearing Association, Alexander Graham Bell Association for the Deaf, Council for Exceptional Children, Michigan Speech and Hearing Association.

WRITINGS: (With George A. and Harriet G. Kopp) *Visible Speech Manual,* Wayne State University Press, 1967. Contributor to professional journals.

WORK IN PROGRESS: Production of color videotape of Piaget and Montessori, *Early Childhood Education.*

AVOCATIONAL INTERESTS: Skiing, bridge, bowling, reading.

* * *

ANGUS, Margaret 1908-

PERSONAL: Born May 23, 1908, in Chinook, Mont.; daughter of Ulysses S. Grant (a merchant) and Cora (Krauss) Sharp; married William Angus, August 28, 1929; children: Barbara (Mrs. Owen Morgan), James. *Education:* University of Montana, B.A., 1930. *Home:* 20 Beverley, Kingston, Ontario, Canada.

CAREER: Queen's University at Kingston, Kingston, Ontario, director of radio, 1947-63, museum curator, 1963—. Chairman, Kingston Centennial Committee, 1966-67, Kingston Committee of Architectural Review, 1970-72; director, Ontario Historical Studies Series, 1972—; president, Frontenac Historic Foundation, 1973—; governor, Heritage Canada, 1974—; director, Ontario Heritage Foundation, 1975—. Member of board of governors, Kingston General Hospital, 1972—. Consultant, Canadian Historic

Sites Division. *Member:* Ontario Historical Society (president, 1969-71), Architectural Conservancy of Ontario, Kingston Historical Society (president, 1972-74). *Awards, honors:* Named "citizen of the year" by Kingston Jaycees, 1968; Queen's University alumni award, 1968; LL.D., Queen's University, 1973; Cruikshank gold medal, 1974; travel award from Heritage Canada, 1975; Queen's University alumni medal, 1975.

WRITINGS: The Old Stones of Kingston, University of Toronto Press, 1966; *The Story of Bellevue House,* Queen's Printer, 1967; *History of Kingston General Hospital,* McGill-Queen's Press, 1972; (contributor) D. Swainson, editor, *Oliver Mowat's Ontario,* Macmillan, 1972; (contributor) I. Wilson, editor, *Kingston 300,* [Kingston], 1973. Writer of more than thirty short stories on historical subjects for Canadian Broadcasting Corp., and four documentaries, radio plays, and historical studies.

WORK IN PROGRESS: An architectural survey of Ontario.

* * *

ANTON, John P(eter) 1920-

PERSONAL: Born November 2, 1920, in Canton, Ohio; son of Peter C. and Christine (Giannopoulos) Anton; married Helen Vezos, November 26, 1955; children: James, Christopher, Peter. *Education:* College of Pedagogy, Tripolis, Greece, B.A., 1942; University of Athens, Certificate, 1945; Columbia University, B.S., 1949, M.A., 1950, Ph.D., 1954. *Politics:* Democrat. *Home:* 2582 Sugar Plum Ct. N.E., Atlanta, Ga. 30345. *Office:* Department of Philosophy, Emory University, Atlanta, Ga. 30322.

CAREER: Pace College, New York, N.Y., instructor in history and philosophy, 1953-54; University of New Mexico, Albuquerque, visiting lecturer in philosophy, 1954-55; University of Nebraska, Lincoln, assistant professor of philosophy, 1955-58; Ohio Wesleyan University, Delaware, associate professor of philosophy, 1958-62; State University of New York at Buffalo, professor of philosophy, 1962-69, associate dean of graduate school, 1967-69; Emory University, Atlanta, Ga., Fuller Callaway Professor of Philosophy and chairman of department, 1969—. Visiting summer professor at Ohio State University, 1960, and Columbia University, 1966; research associate, University of California, Berkeley, 1971-72. *Military service:* U.S. Army, Quartermaster Corps, 1946-47.

MEMBER: American Philosophical Association, American Philosophical Society (fellow), American Philological Association, Society for the History of Philosophy, International Society for Metaphysics, American Comparative Literature Association, Society for the Advancement of American Philosophy, American Classical League, American Society for Aesthetics, American Humanist Association, Society for Ancient Greek Philosophy, Modern Greek Studies Association, Society for Macedonian Studies (honorary member), Hellenic Society for Philosophical Studies (honorary member), American Council of Learned Societies, American Association of University Professors, Phi Beta Kappa (honorary member), Phi Sigma Tau, Eta Sigma Phi. *Awards, honors:* Wurlitzer Foundation fellow, 1955-56; faculty research fellow, State University of New York at Buffalo; American Philosophical Society fellow, 1967; Outstanding Educator of America, 1970; Emory University Research Award, 1971, 1975.

WRITINGS: Meaning in Religious Poetry, New York Hellenic Society, 1954; *Aristotle's Theory of Contrariety,*

Humanities, 1957; (editor, contributor, and compiler of bibliography) *Naturalism and Historical Understanding: Essays on the Philosophy of John Herman Randall, Jr.,* State University of New York Press, 1967; (translator from the Greek and editor) E. P. Papanoutsos, *Foundations of Knowledge,* State University of New York Press, 1968; *Philosophical Essays* (in Greek), Makrides & Co., 1969; (editor with G. L. Kustas) *Essays in Ancient Greek Philosophy,* State University of New York Press, 1971; (editor with Craig Walton) *Philosophy and the Civilizing Arts: Essays Presented to Herbert W. Schneider on His Eightieth Birthday,* Ohio University Press, 1975; (editor with N. P. Diamantouros, John A. Petropulos, and Peter Topping) *Hellenism and the First Greek War of Liberation (1821-1830),* Institute for Balkan Studies, 1975; *Constantine Cavafy: His Poetry and Poetics,* Twayne, in press. Contributor of more than seventy articles and reviews to journals, including *Athene, Journal of Philosophy, Western Humanities, Humanist,* and *Classical Journal.*

Member of editorial board: *Arethusa,* 1968-72, *Journal for Critical Analysis,* 1970—, *Neo-Hellenika,* 1970—; editorial consultant, *Journal of the History of Philosophy,* 1968—; co-editor, *Diotima,* 1972—; advisory editor, *Southern Journal of Philosophy,* 1974—.

SIDELIGHTS: Anton is competent in classical Greek, modern Greek, and French. He also reads German.

BIOGRAPHICAL/CRITICAL SOURCES: Nea Estia (Athens), October 15, 1966.

*   *   *

APOSTLE, Chris(tos) N(icholas) 1935-

PERSONAL: Born November 14, 1935, in Astoria, Long Island, N.Y.; son of Nicholas Christos (a funeral director) and Maria (Katsaros) Apostle. *Education:* University of Colorado, B.S., 1958; graduate study at New School for Social Research, 1959-60, and City College (now City College of the City University of New York), 1960-61, 1962; University of Maryland, M.A., 1963; New York University, Ph.D. candidate, 1963—. *Home:* 6 Pine St., Albany, N.Y. 12207.

CAREER: Commercial Analysts Corp., New York City, project director, 1963; Department of Correction, New York City, research analyst, Division of Research and Planning, 1963; Adelphi University, Oakdale Campus, Oakdale, N.Y., instructor in sociology, 1964-65; State University of New York at Albany, assistant professor of sociology, 1965-67. Co-founder and adviser, Getting Through College Clinic, Albany; founder and director of Research Institute for Student Problems, New York City, and Institute for Temporal and Durational Studies, Yorktown Heights. *Military service:* U.S. Air Force Reserve, 1958-64. *Member:* American Statistical Association, American Sociological Association, Society for the Scientific Study of Religion, American Anthropological Association, World Association for Public Opinion Research, Philosophy of Science Association.

WRITINGS: (Senior editor and contributor) *Getting Through College Using Sociological Principles,* Knowledgeable Press, 1966. Contributor to professional journals. Assistant editor, *Indian Sociological Bulletin.*

WORK IN PROGRESS: Social research directed to understanding the role time plays in social phenomena and scientific investigation.

ARCONE, Sonya 1925-

PERSONAL: Born June 27, 1925, in Boston, Mass.; daughter of Mischa (an actor) and Nina (Progulnia) Balanoff; married Anthony Arcone, September 27, 1942; married Lee Goodman (a free-lance producer and director), October 14, 1957; children: (first marriage) Steven Arcone. *Education:* Studied at New School for Social Research. *Home:* 67 Perry St., New York, N.Y. 10014. *Agent:* Elizabeth McKee, Harold Matson Co., Inc., 22 East 40th St., New York, N.Y. 10016.

CAREER: Fashion buyer in New York, N.Y., for O'Shaughnessy, Dewes & Klein, 1950-54, and Felix Lilienthal, 1954-59; writer.

WRITINGS—Novels: *The Golden Hammer,* Atheneum, 1963; *Cage of Light,* Harcourt, 1967; *The Werewolf of Hanover,* Barrie & Jenkins, in press. Contributor of short story to *Mademoiselle,* 1961.

WORK IN PROGRESS: A novel with working title, *For Fanny,* based on the life of Mary Wollstonecraft.

AVOCATIONAL INTERESTS: The theater, pre-Columbian artifacts, travel in Mexico.

*   *   *

AREEDA, Phillip E. 1930-

PERSONAL: Born January 28, 1930, in Detroit, Mich.; son of Elias Herbert and Selma (Cope) Areeda. *Education:* Harvard University, A.B. (summa cum laude), 1951, LL.B. (summa cum laude), 1954. *Politics:* Republican. *Office:* Langdell Hall, Harvard Law School, Cambridge, Mass. 02138.

CAREER: Admitted to Michigan Bar, 1954; Harvard traveling fellow, 1954-55; Office of the President, Washington, D.C., assistant special counsel, 1956-61; Harvard University, Law School, Cambridge, Mass., associate professor, 1961-63, professor of law, 1963—. Executive director, U.S. Cabinet Task Force on Oil Import Control, 1969; counsel to the President, 1974-75. *Military service:* U.S. Air Force, 1955-57; became first lieutenant. *Member:* American Law Institute.

WRITINGS: Antitrust Analysis, Little, Brown, 1967, 2nd edition, 1974. Contributor to legal journals.

AVOCATIONAL INTERESTS: Politics, skiing, tennis, and squash racquets.

*   *   *

ARGOW, Waldemar 1916-

PERSONAL: Born March 10, 1916, in Lorain, Ohio; son of W. Waldemar W. (a clergyman) and Elsie (Baker) Argow; married Isabel Catching (owner of a hi-fi and stereo business); children: Nancy Katherine. *Education:* Antioch College, A.B., 1938; Harvard Divinity School, S.T.B., 1941. *Politics:* Independent. *Address:* 224 Country Club Dr., Tequesta, Fla. 33458; Cushing, Me. 04563 (summer). *Agent:* (Lectures) Redpath Bureau, 343 South Dearborn, Chicago, Ill.

CAREER: Clergyman of Unitarian Universalist Association. Peoples Church, Cedar Rapids, Iowa, minister, 1944-57; First Unitarian Church, Toledo, Ohio, minister, 1957-74, minister emeritus, 1974—; First Unitarian Church of Palm Beach County, Fla., winter season minister, 1974—. Lectures throughout the United States on mental health, art of living, and travel subjects. Former member of board of directors, National Association for Mental Health, Antioch

College, and School of Religion at State University of Iowa; past president of Toledo Council on World Affairs; has served as president or on boards of more than twenty local, state, and national social and cultural organizations. Conducted popular Sunday radio program, "Religion for the Modern Mind," for fifteen years. *Member:* International Platform Association. *Awards, honors:* L.H.D., University of Toledo, 1973.

WRITINGS: What Do Religious Liberals Believe?, Antioch Press, 1949; *The Case for Liberal Religion,* Antioch Press, 1954. Also author of *Sermons for the Modern Mind.* Writer of pamphlets, articles, and book reviews.

WORK IN PROGRESS: The Courage to Live: Religion for the Modern Mind.

* * *

ARGYLE, Michael 1925-

PERSONAL: Born August 11, 1925, in Nottingham, England; son of George Edgar (a school teacher) and Phyllis (Hawkins-Ambler) Argyle; married Sonia Kemp (a lexicographer), June 24, 1949; children: Miranda, Nicholas, Rosalind, Ophelia. *Education:* Emmanuel College, Cambridge, M.A., 1952. *Religion:* Church of England. *Home:* 309 Woodstock Rd., Oxford, England. *Office:* Department of Experimental Psychology, South Parks Rd., Oxford, England.

CAREER: Oxford University, Oxford, England, university lecturer, 1952-69, reader in social psychology, 1969—, fellow of Wolfson College, 1965—. Center for Advanced Study in the Behavioral Sciences, Stanford, Calif., fellow, 1958-59. Visiting professor at University of Michigan, University of British Columbia, University of Delaware, University of Ghana, University of Buffalo, University of Leuven, Hebrew University (Jerusalem), and University of Adelaide; lecturer in universities in Italy, Greece, New Zealand, and Finland. *Military service:* Royal Air Force, navigator, World War II, with rank of Flying Officer. *Member:* British Psychological Society, (fellow; chairman of social psychology section, 1964-67, 1972-74), European Association for Social Psychology.

WRITINGS: The Scientific Study of Social Behaviour, Methuen, 1957; *Religious Behaviour,* Free Press of Glencoe, 1959; (with George Humphrey) *Social Psychology Through Experiment,* Methuen, 1962; (with A. T. Welford and others) *Society: Problems and Methods of Study,* Routledge & Kegan Paul, 1962; (with M. Kirton and T. Smith) *Training Managers,* Action Society Trust, 1962; *Psychology and Social Problems,* Methuen, 1964; *The Psychology of Interpersonal Behaviour,* Penguin, 1967; *Social Interaction,* Methuen, 1969, Aldine, 1970; *The Social Psychology of Work,* Taplinger, 1972; (editor) *Social Encounters: Readings in Social Interaction,* Aldine, 1973; *Bodily Communication,* Methuen, 1975; (with Benjamin Beit-Hallahmi) *The Social Psychology of Religion,* Routledge & Kegan Paul, 1975; (with M. Cook) *Gaze and Mutual Gaze,* Cambridge University Press, 1975. Editor of "Social Psychology Monographs" series, Penguin, 1967-74. Contributor to professional journals in Great Britain, Europe, and United States. Editor of *British Social and Clinical Psychology,* 1960-67.

SIDELIGHTS: Michael Argyle travels extensively, partly to observe varied cultural settings, partly to meet other workers in his field.

ARIETI, Silvano 1914-

PERSONAL: Born June 28, 1914, in Pisa, Italy; son of Elio (a physician) and Ines (Bemporad) Arieti; married second wife, Marianne Thompson, October 24, 1965; children: (first marriage) David, James. *Education:* Lycee Galileo, Pisa, Italy, B.A., 1932; University of Pisa, M.D., 1938; William A. White Institute, New York, N.Y., psychoanalytic training, 1946-52. *Office:* 125 East 84th St., New York, N.Y. 10028.

CAREER: Left Italy because of Fascist persecution, 1939; fellow in neuropathology, New York State Psychiatric Institute, 1939-41; resident in psychiatry, Pilgrim State Hospital, 1941-43; private practice as psychiatrist and psychoanalyst, New York City, 1952—. State University of New York Downstate Medical Center, Brooklyn, associate professor of clinical psychiatry, 1953-61; New York Medical College, New York City, professor of clinical psychiatry, 1961—; W. A. White Institute, New York City, member of faculty and training analyst, 1962—. Visiting fellow in primate biology laboratories, Yale University, 1940. Diplomate, American Board of Psychiatry and Neurology, 1944.

MEMBER: American Medical Association, American Psychiatric Association, Academy of Psychoanalysis, American Association of Neuropathologists, American Academy of Neurology, American Association for the Advancement of Science, William A. White Psychoanalytic Association (president, 1964-65). *Awards, honors:* Gold Medal Award of Milan Group for the Advancement of Psychotherapy, 1964; Frieda Fromm-Reichmann Award, American Academy of Psychoanalysis, 1968; National Book Award in the field of the sciences, 1975, for *Interpretation of Schizophrenia.*

WRITINGS: Interpretation of Schizophrenia, Brunner, 1955, 2nd edition, Basic Books, 1974; (editor) *American Handbook of Psychiatry,* Basic Books, Volumes I-VI, 1959-75, revised edition, Volumes I-III, 1974; *Intrapsychic Self: Feeling, Cognition and Creativity in Health and Mental Illness,* Basic Books, 1967; (editor) *The World Biennial of Psychiatry and Psychotherapy,* Basic Books, Volume I, 1970, Volume II, 1973; *The Will to Live,* Quadrangle, 1972; (editor with Gerard Chrzanowski) *New Dimensions in Psychiatry: A World View,* Wiley, 1975; *Creativity: The Magic Synthesis,* Basic Books, 1976. Contributor to *Encyclopaedia Britannica,* and of more than ninety articles to professional journals.

WORK IN PROGRESS: Research on the cognitive and conceptual aspect of psychiatry.

SIDELIGHTS: Interpretation of Schizophrenia has been translated into Japanese, Italian, and Spanish.

* * *

ARKIN, David 1906-

PERSONAL: Born December 19, 1906, in New York, N.Y.; son of Arthur (an insurance man) and Fanny (Krinsky) Arkin; married Beatrice Wortis (an educational therapist), August 6, 1929; children: Alan, Robert, Bonnie. *Education:* New York University, B.A., 1939; further study at New York University School of Architecture, National Academy of Design, and in France and Italy. *Home:* 2563 Lake View Ave., Los Angeles, Calif. 90039.

CAREER: Albert C. Martin Co., Los Angeles, Calif., architectural draftsman, 1956-57; National Technical Schools, Los Angeles, instructor in engineering and drawing, 1965-68; professional painter, exhibiting in museums and galleries, and songwriter. *Member:* American Society of Composers, Authors and Publishers, American Institute for Design and Drafting, Songmakers of Los Angeles (member of board of directors, 1967-68). *Awards, honors:* Western Book Award, 1966, for *Black and White.*

WRITINGS: Black and White (music by Earl Robinson), Ward Ritchie, 1966; *The Twenty Children of Johann Sebastian Bach,* Ward Ritchie, 1968.

(Designer and illustrator) Joseph Wortis, *Tricky Dick and His Pals,* Quadrangle, 1974. Librettist, "The Little Piano that Liked to Play" (a musical fantasy; music by Paul Schoop), performed by Los Angeles Youth Orchestra, 1968; writer of lyrics for recordings by Sammy Davis, Pete Seeger, Womenfold, Harry Simeone Chorale, Three Dog Night, and other singing groups.

SIDELIGHTS: David Arkin's song, "Black and White," sung by Three Dog Night, was No. 1 on the rock music charts in 1973. Arkin speaks French and knows some Italian.

*   *   *

ARMENS, Sven   1921-

PERSONAL: Born August 11, 1921, in Cambridge, Mass.; son of Magnus (a bus operator) and Ruth (Nyden) Armens; married Kathleen Danahy, May 31, 1942; children: Karl, Sharon. *Education:* Tufts College (now Tufts University), A.B. (summa cum laude), 1943; Harvard University, M.A., 1947, Ph.D., 1951. *Home:* 617 South Dodge St., Iowa City, Iowa 52240.

CAREER: University of Iowa, Iowa City, instructor, 1950-54, assistant professor, 1954-61, associate professor, 1961-66, professor of English, 1966—. *Military service:* U.S. Coast Guard, cadet, 1943. U.S. Army, 1944-45. *Member:* Modern Language Association of America, Renaissance Society of America, American Association of University Professors, Phi Beta Kappa.

WRITINGS: John Gay: Social Critic, Columbia University Press, 1954, 2nd edition, Octagon, 1966; *Archetypes of the Family in Literature,* University of Washington Press, 1966.

WORK IN PROGRESS: Archetypes of the Family, further considerations in poetry; *The Lechmere Trolley Coach,* a collection of poems.

SIDELIGHTS: Sven Armens is competent in Swedish, French, and German.

*   *   *

ARMERDING, Hudson Taylor   1918-

PERSONAL: Born June 21, 1918, in Albuquerque, N.M.; son of Carl and Eva May (Taylor) Armerding; married Miriam Lucille Bailey, December 26, 1944; children: Carreen A., Hudson Taylor II, Paul Timothy, Miriam Ruth, Jonathan Edwards. *Education:* Wheaton College, Wheaton, Ill., A.B., 1941; Clark University, A.M., 1942; University of Chicago, Ph.D., 1948; Harvard University, postdoctoral study, 1949-50. *Politics:* Republican. *Home:* 326 North Washington, Wheaton, Ill. 60187. *Office:* Wheaton College, Wheaton, Ill. 60187.

CAREER: Ordained to Baptist ministry, 1951; Wheaton College, Wheaton, Ill., visiting instructor in social science, 1946-48; Gordon College, Wenham, Mass., professor of history, 1950-61, dean, 1951-61; Wheaton College, professor of history, 1961—, provost, 1963-65, president of

college, 1965—. Minister in Brockton, Mass., 1951-54. *Military service:* U.S. Naval Reserve, 1942-66; active duty, 1942-46; now commander (retired). *Member:* U.S. Naval Institute.

WRITINGS: Christian Patriotism, United Evangelical Action, 1966; *Academic Freedom in the Christian College,* United Evangelical Action, 1966; (editor) *Christianity and the World of Thought,* Moody, 1968. Contributor of articles on aspects of the Christian church to periodicals.

WORK IN PROGRESS: A book, *One Christian's Perspective.*

*   *   *

ARNDT, H(einz) W(olfgang)   1915-

PERSONAL: Born February 26, 1915, in Breslau, Germany; son of Fritz Georg and Julia (Heinmann) Arndt; married Ruth Strohsahl (a research officer, Australian Department of External Affairs), July 12, 1941; children: Christopher, Nicholas, Bettina. *Education:* Lincoln College, Oxford, B.A., 1936, B.Litt., 1938, M.A., 1940. *Home:* 14 Hopetoun Circuit, Deakin, Canberra, Australian Capital Territory 2600, Australia. *Office:* Australian National University, Canberra, Australian Capital Territory 2600, Australia.

CAREER: University of London, London School of Economics and Political Science, London, England, Leverhulme research fellow, 1938-41; Royal Institute of International Affairs, London, research assistant, 1941-43; University of Manchester, Manchester, England, assistant lecturer, 1943-46; University of Sydney, Sydney, Australia, senior lecturer, 1946-50; Australian National University, Canberra, professor of economics, School of General Studies, 1950-63, professor of economics and head of department, Research School of Pacific Studies, 1963—. Visiting professor at University of South Carolina, 1953-54, and at Indian Statistical Institute, Calcutta, and Indian Planning Commission, New Delhi, 1958-59. Deputy director of Australian Studies Division, Organization for Economic Cooperation and Development, Paris, 1972. Member of Australian Capital Territory Advisory Council, 1959-63; consultant to United Nations Economics Commission for Europe, 1960-61, and to United Nations Conference on Trade and Development, 1966-67; member of governing council, United Nations Asian Institute, Bangkok. *Member:* Society for International Development (Australian vice-president), Social Science Research Council of Australia (secretary, 1957-59), Economic Society of Australia and New Zealand (president, 1958-60); Academy of Social Sciences in Australia (fellow).

WRITINGS: The Economic Lessons of the Nineteen-Thirties, Oxford University Press, 1944; *The Australian Trading Banks,* F. W. Cheshire, 1957, 4th edition (with D. W. Stammer), 1973; (editor with W. M. Corden) *The Australian Economy: A Volume of Readings,* F. W. Cheshire, 1963, 2nd edition published as *The Australian Economy: A First Volume of Readings,* 1972; (with R. I. Downing and others) *Taxation in Australia: Agenda for Reform,* Melbourne University Press, 1964; (with J. Panglaykim) *The Indonesian Economy: Facing a New Era?,* Rotterdam University Press, 1966; *A Small Rich Industrial Country: Studies in Australian Development, Aid and Trade,* F. W. Cheshire, 1968; *Australia and Asia: Economic Essays,* Australian National University Press, 1972; (editor with A. H. Boxer) *The Australian Economy: A Second Volume of Readings,* F. W. Cheshire, 1972; *Per-*

bankan di Indonesia (title means "Banking in Indonesia"), Obor (Djakarta), 1972.

Contributor: A. Davies and G. Serle, editors, *Policies for Progress,* F. W. Cheshire, 1954; *Economic Survey of Europe in 1960,* United Nations, 1961; J. Wilkes, editor, *Economic Growth in Australia,* Angus & Robertson for Australian Institute of Political Science, 1962; *Canberra: The Next Decade,* Federal Capital Press, 1963; *Economic Survey of Europe in 1962,* United Nations, 1964; *SEANZA Lectures,* Volume I, State Bank of Pakistan, 1964; *Anatomy of Australia,* Sun Books, 1968; J.D.B. Miller, editor, *India, Japan, Australia: Partners in Asia?,* Australian National University Press, 1968; *The Australian Role in Joint Ventures and Investment in Developing Countries of Asia and the Pacific: A Seminar Report,* Australian Council for Overseas Aid, 1969; B. Glassburner, editor, *The Economy of Indonesia: Selected Readings,* Cornell University Press, 1971; J.A.A. Stockwin, editor, *Japan and Australia in the Seventies,* Angus & Robertson, 1972; J. N. Bhagwati and R. S. Eckaus, editors, *Development and Planning: Essays in Honor of Paul Rosenstein-Rodan,* Allen & Unwin, 1972; G. Greenwood and N. Harper, editors, *Australia in World Affairs 1966-1970,* F. W. Cheshire, 1974; H. Bull, editor, *Asia and the Western Pacific: Towards a New International Order,* Nelson, 1975.

Author of official papers for the United Nations, India, and Australia. Contributor of more than one hundred articles to economic, banking, and other journals. Member of editorial board, *Economic Record,* 1956-74; editor, *Bulletin of Indonesian Economic Studies.*

WORK IN PROGRESS: Research on developments in the Indonesian economy; economic growth as a policy objective in the West.

* * *

ARNETT, Carroll 1927-
(Gogisgi)

PERSONAL: Born November 9, 1927, in Oklahoma City, Okla.; son of Herschel Warren (an accountant) and Ethel Mildred (Duckett) Arnett; married Claudia Wilson, August 19, 1964; children: Randall, Cassanda, Carlen. *Education:* Beloit College, B.A. (magna cum laude), 1951; University of Oklahoma, graduate study, 1953-55; University of Texas, M.A., 1958, and fifty hours graduate study beyond M.A. *Home:* Route 1, Mecosta, Mich. 49332. *Office:* English Department, Central Michigan University, Mt. Pleasant, Mich. 48859.

CAREER: Instructor in English at Knox College, Galesberg, Ill., 1958-60, Stephens College, Columbia, Mo., 1960-64, Wittenberg University, Springfield, Ohio, 1964-68; Nasson College, Springvale, Me., assistant professor of English, 1968-70; Central Michigan University, Mt. Pleasant, professor of English, 1970—. Associate editor, Elizabeth Press, 1967—. Has given readings at numerous colleges, including Bucknell University, Bowling Green State University, Ohio State University, and State University of New York at Albany. Deer Clan Chief of Overhill Band, Cherokee Nation. *Military service:* U.S. Marine Corps, 1946-47. *Member:* Phi Beta Kappa. *Awards, honors:* National Endowment for the Arts fellowship in creative writing, 1974.

WRITINGS—Poetry; all published by Elizabeth Press, except as indicated: *Then,* 1965; *The Intentions,* Ringading Editions, 1966; *Not Only That,* 1967; *Like a Wall,* 1969;

Through the Woods, 1971; *Earlier,* 1972; *Come,* 1973; *Tsalagi,* 1976.

Poetry represented in many anthologies, including: *Of Poem,* Elizabeth Press, 1966; *Best Poems of 1966,* Pacific Books, 1967; *Poems for People,* Macmillan, 1968; *Poems of the Sixties,* J. Murray, 1970; *Another Eye,* Scott, Foresman, 1971; *. . . And Be Merry!,* Grossman, 1972; *My Music Bent,* Elizabeth Press, 1973; *Voices of the Rainbow: Contemporary Poems by American Indians,* Viking, 1975. Contributor of more than one hundred fifty poems and stories, sometimes under Cherokee name Gogisgi, to more than thirty magazines, including *Antioch Review, Beloit Poetry Journal, Cosmopolitan, Poetry,* and *Saturday Review.*

WORK IN PROGRESS: La Dene, a short novel; a verse sequence on American Indian affairs.

SIDELIGHTS: On poetry Carroll Arnett told *CA:* "I write poems, when I can, because it seems sensible to do so and wasteful not to. A poem has a use insofar as it shows what it feels like to be alive or what a person does to himself or others by being alive. . . . No one writes well unless he's in love—with another person, an idea, language, himself. . . . When he writes in love, sometimes, with luck, what comes out is a poem."

On prose Carroll Arnett explained to *CA:* "I write prose because it is the hardest thing I know, and I like to do hard things. I try to please people, a few of them, when I can, but pleasing is seldom an end in itself. More often it is a means of living—with or without people—and living is the most important thing."

BIOGRAPHICAL/CRITICAL SOURCES: Trace, 1966-67; *Poetry,* February, 1967.

* * *

ARNETT, Harold E(dward) 1931-

PERSONAL: Born January 20, 1931, in Hegeler, Ill.; son of Dumous Clay (a watchman) and Amie (Netherton) Arnett; married Betty JoAnne Carter, August 30, 1952; children: John, Carl, Melia. *Education:* University of Illinois, B.S., 1955, M.S., 1957, Ph.D., 1962. *Politics:* Conservative Republican. *Religion:* Presbyterian. *Home:* 2113 Delaware Dr., Ann Arbor, Mich. 48103. *Office:* Accounting Department, University of Michigan, Ann Arbor, Mich. 48104.

CAREER: Certified public accountant, state of Illinois, 1960; University of Illinois, Urbana, instructor in accounting, 1955-60; American Institute of Certified Public Accountants, New York, N.Y., research associate, 1960-62; University of Michigan, Ann Arbor, assistant professor, 1962-66, associate professor, 1966-70, professor of accounting, 1970—, head of department, 1970-72. Faculty consultant, Federal Taxation Committee of American Institute of Certified Public Accountants, 1966-67. *Military service:* U.S. Navy, 1948-52. *Member:* American Accounting Association, Financial Executives Institute, American Institute of Certified Public Accountants, National Association of Accountants, Michigan Association of Certified Public Accountants, Phi Eta Sigma, Beta Gamma Sigma, Beta Alpha Psi, Sigma Iota Epsilon.

WRITINGS: (With others) *Reporting the Financial Effects of Price-Level Changes,* American Institute of Certified Public Accountants, 1963; (with R. Lee Brummet) *Business and Economic Evaluation of the Metal Finishing Industry* (monograph), Bureau of Business Research, University of Michigan, 1967; (contributor) *The Dental Clinics of North America* (readings), Saunders, 1967; (contributor)

R. L. Dixon, editor, *The Executive's Accounting Primer*, McGraw, 1971; (with Donald Smith) *Financial and Economic Evaluation of the Tool and Die Industry*, Bureau of Business Research, University of Michigan, 1975. Contributor to accounting and other business journals.

*   *   *

ARNOLD, Emmy (von Hollander) 1884-

PERSONAL: Born December 25, 1884, in Riga, Latvia; daughter of Heinrich (a professor of law at University of Halle) and Monika (Otto) von Hollander; married Eberhard Arnold, December 20, 1909 (died November 22, 1935); children: Emi-Margret (Mrs. Hans Zumpe), Eberhard, Johann Heinrich, Hans-Hermann (died, 1972), Monika E. (Mrs. Balthasar Truempi). *Education:* Studied nursing in Halle/Saale, Germany, 1905-07. *Address:* Society of Brothers, Woodcrest, Rifton, N.Y. 12471.

CAREER: Has served as housemother for the Society of Brothers (Bruderhof) communities, Rifton, N.Y., since 1920. Writer and editor. *Member:* Society of Brothers.

WRITINGS: (Editor) *Sonnenlieder: Songs of Joy in Nature, Peace Among Men, and Communion with God* (German language), Eberhard Arnold Verlag, 1924; (editor) Count Ludwig von Zinzendorf, *Zinzendorf: Glaube und Leben* (songs and poems; subtitle means "Faith and Life"), Hochweg Verlag (Berlin), 1925; (editor and contributor) *Eberhard Arnold: A Testimony of Church Community from His Life and Writings*, Plough Publishing, 1953; (compiler) *Inner Words for Every Day of the Year*, Plough Publishing, 1963; *Torches Together: The Beginning and Early Years of the Bruderhof Communities*, Plough Publishing, 1964; (contributor) Eberhard Arnold, *When the Time Was Fulfilled*, Plough Publishing, 1965; *The Early Christians after the Death of the Apostles*, Plough Publishing, 1972. Also author of religious poetry.

SIDELIGHTS: With her husband, Mrs. Arnold helped to found Bruderhof, a community which derives its inspiration from the early Christians. The Community, established in 1920 in Sannerz, near Frankfurt-am-Main, Germany, was conceived as an act of "reununciation of normal middle class life in its totality, with its private property, its ambitions and injustices." Mrs. Arnold has recalled that "Eberhard and I had the idea of buying ourselves a gyp·· trailer, or even several, and traveling from village to village this way, from town to town, with our family and those who wanted to join us. We would make music, bring joy and help to people, and teach our children as we went along. We would travel without destination, staying in a particular place only as long as our help was needed and accepted there by the widows, the children and the sick, whose destroyed homes we would rebuild. This idea found a good deal of response in many people." When Hitler came to power, the group moved first to Paraguay, and then to America.

Mrs. Arnold continues to assist with the work of the self-sufficient community, now located in Rifton, N.Y., and to consult with the editors of Plough Publishing, a Bruderhof establishment, concerning the posthumous publication of some of her husband's writings.

BIOGRAPHICAL/CRITICAL SOURCES: Chelsea, October, 1968.

ARNOLD, June (Davis) 1926-
(Carpenter)

PERSONAL: Born October 27, 1926, in Greenville, S.C.; daughter of Robert Cowan and Cad (Wortham) Davis; children: Kate, Roberta, Fairfax, Gus. *Education:* Vassar College, student, 1943-44; Rice University, B.A., 1948, M.A., 1958. *Politics:* "Feminist." *Religion:* "Women." *Home:* 54 Seventh Ave. South, New York, N.Y. 10014.

WRITINGS—All novels: *Applesauce*, McGraw, 1967; (under pseudonym Carpenter) *The Cook and the Carpenter*, Daughter's, Inc., 1973; *Sister Gin*, Daughter's, Inc., 1975.

WORK IN PROGRESS: A new novel.

BIOGRAPHICAL/CRITICAL SOURCES: Time, March 10, 1967; *Prairie Schooner*, spring, 1967; *Village Voice*, April 4, 1974; *Viva*, August, 1974.

*   *   *

ARNOLD, Rollo (Davis) 1926-

PERSONAL: Born January 24, 1926, in Richmond, Nelson, New Zealand; son of Richard Reeves (a farmer) and Linda (Russ) Arnold; married Elizabeth Burrows, May 11, 1955; children: Elizabeth Ann, Margaret Nell, Helen Linda, John David. *Education:* University of New Zealand, M.A., 1949; University of Melbourne, M.A., 1952; Victoria University of Wellington, Dip.Ed., 1962, Ph.D., 1972. *Religion:* Presbyterian. *Home:* 2 Maurice Ter., Wellington 1, New Zealand. *Office:* Victoria University of Wellington, Private Bag, Wellington 1, New Zealand.

CAREER: Teacher in country primary schools, Nelson Province, New Zealand, 1945-46; high school teacher of English and social studies, Napier, New Zealand, 1949-50, and Stratford, New Zealand, 1952-58; Teacher's College, Palmerston North, New Zealand, lecturer, 1959-65, head of English department, 1962-65; Victoria University of Wellington, Wellington, New Zealand, senior lecturer, 1966-75, reader in education, 1975—. *Member:* Australian and New Zealand History of Education Society (New Zealand representative), Wellington Institute for Educational Research.

WRITINGS: Bracken Block, Angus & Robertson, 1966; *The Freedom of Ariki*, Angus & Robertson, 1967. Contributor to *Australian Literary Studies, New Zealand Journal of History, New Zealand Journal of Educational Studies*, and *Past and Present*.

WORK IN PROGRESS: The Farthest Promised Land; English Villagers, New Zealand Immigrants of the 1870's, a social history; additional research on nineteenth-century English rural emigration to New Zealand; research on nineteenth-century New Zealand social and educational history; revision of doctoral thesis, a social history of the North Island bush settlements, 1869-1881.

SIDELIGHTS: Rollo Arnold told *CA:* "Childhood was spent in a rather isolated back country valley, not far removed from the pioneering stage. Primary education at a one-teacher school, secondary education by correspondence."

*   *   *

ASHBY, LaVerne 1922-

PERSONAL: Born January 25, 1922, in Lynnville, Ind.; daughter of Earl Cyrus (a barber) and Lennis (Cabage) Ashby. *Education:* Teachers College of Kansas City, Kansas City, Mo., B.S., 1942; Southwestern Baptist Theological Seminary, M.R.E., 1946; Columbia University, graduate study, 1958-59; George Peabody College for Teachers, currently candidate for doctorate in education. *Politics:* Republican. *Religion:* Baptist. *Office:* Sunday School Board of Southern Baptist Convention, 127 Ninth Ave. N., Nashville, Tenn. 37203.

CAREER: Kansas City (Mo.) public schools, elementary teacher, 1942-43; Southwestern Baptist Theological Seminary, Fort Worth, Tex., assistant librarian, 1945-46; Baptist Convention of Arkansas, Little Rock, director of youth work for Woman's Missionary Union, 1946-48; Inskip Baptist Church, Knoxville, Tenn., minister of Christian education, 1950-52; Southern Baptist Convention, Sunday School Board, Nashville, Tenn., consultant in primary religious education, beginning 1952. Gheens Lecturer, Southern Baptist Theological Seminary, 1965. *Member:* Association for Childhood Education International, National Federation of Republican Women, Southeastern Baptist Religious Education Association, Business and Professional Women's Club.

WRITINGS: (With Doris Monroe) *The Primary Leadership Manual,* Convention Press, 1959; *The Bible Is a Special Book,* Broadman, 1966. Contributor of articles to Baptist publications. Section editor, *Baptist Training Union Magazine,* beginning 1952.

WORK IN PROGRESS: Doctoral dissertation, "The Effect of Self Concept on Children's Learning in Religious Education."††

* * *

ASHER, John (A(lexander) 1921-

PERSONAL: Born January 30, 1921, in Auckland, New Zealand; son of John Alexander (a teacher) and Innes (Hargreaves) Asher; married Monica Coates (a teacher), January 12, 1942; children: Raynor John, Monica Innes, Gavin Alexander. *Education:* University of Auckland, M.A. (first class honors), 1942; University of Basle, Dr.Phil., 1948. *Politics:* None. *Religion:* Protestant. *Home:* 27 New Windsor Rd., Avondale, Auckland, New Zealand. *Office:* University of Auckland, Auckland, New Zealand.

CAREER: University of Auckland, Auckland, New Zealand, lecturer, 1948-61, professor of German and head of department of Germanic languages and literature, 1962—. Guest lecturer at various German, Austrian, Swiss, and English universities, 1955-56, 1963-64, 1968. *Member:* Australasian Universities Language and Literature Association (deputy convenor, later convenor of Germanic section, 1961—), Auckland Goethe Society (president). *Awards, honors:* Medal of Goethe-Institut (Munich).

WRITINGS: "*Der gute Gerhard*": *Rudolfs von Ems in seinem Verhaeltnis zu Hartman von Aue,* Max Glaser, 1948; *The Framework of German,* Whitcombe & Tombs, 1951, 11th edition, 1973; *Des Erdballs Letztes Inselriff,* Max Hueber Verlag, 1956; (editor) Rudolf von Ems, *Der guote Gerhart* (a critical edition), Max Niemeyer Verlag, 1962, 2nd revised edition, 1971; *A Short Descriptive Grammar of Middle High German: With Texts and Vocabulary,* Oxford University Press for University of Auckland, 1967, 3rd edition, 1975. Contributor to *Encyclopaedia Britannica;* contributor of thirty articles and reviews to journals in United States, Europe, and New Zealand. Co-editor, *Australisch-Neuseelandische Studien.*

WORK IN PROGRESS: Further work in the field of Middle High German.

ASHLEY, Paul P(ritchard) 1896-

PERSONAL: Born July 2, 1895, in Fostoria, Ohio; son of John P. (a minister and college president) and Della (Gust) Ashley; married Katherine Macrae Smith, August 20, 1932; children: Mary Macrae (Mrs. David Lee Williams), Katherine Cooper (Mrs. Robert Lee Calhoun). *Education:* University of California, student, 1916-17; University of Washington, Seattle, LL.B., 1925, J.D., 1926. *Politics:* Independent. *Religion:* Protestant. *Home:* 2009 Broadmoor Dr. E., Seattle, Wash. 98102. *Office:* 4400 Sea First Bldg., Seattle, Wash. 98154.

CAREER: Admitted to Washington State bar, 1926; in private practice of law in Seattle, Wash., 1926—. University of Washington, Seattle, associate professor of business administration, 1929-32; Pacific Coast School of Banking, lecturer, 1939-66. President of Seattle Foundation, 1952-54, Municipal League of Seattle and King County, 1958-60, and Seattle Symphony Orchestra Association, 1963-66; co-chairman of Washington chapter, National Conference of Christians and Jews; trustee of World Affairs Council, China Club, and Seattle Opera Association. *Member:* American Judicature Society, National Conference of Bar Presidents (executive committee member, 1962; vice-chairman, 1966-67; president, 1967-68), American Bar Foundation (fellow), Washington State Bar Association (member of board of governors, 1949-52; president, 1961), Seattle-King County Bar Association (president, 1941), English-Speaking Union (Seattle; president, 1942-43), Phi Beta Kappa, Order of the Coif, Phi Delta Phi, College Club (Seattle; president, 1938). *Awards, honors:* Distinguished Service award from Western Washington Chapter of Society of Professional Journalists, April 26, 1975.

WRITINGS: (With Leslie J. Ayer) *Cases on Business Law, Selected, with Notes and Problems,* Prentice-Hall, 1929; *Essentials of Libel,* University of Washington Press, 1948; *Say It Safely,* University of Washington Press, 1956, 4th edition, 1969; *You and Your Will: The Planning and Management of Your Estate,* McGraw, 1975. Contributor to legal publications. First editor, *Washington Law Review.*

WORK IN PROGRESS: A fifth edition of *Say It Safely; The Twelve Questions.*

AVOCATIONAL INTERESTS: Sailing, woodworking, and gardening.

* * *

ATKINSON, John W(illiam) 1923-

PERSONAL: Born December 31, 1923, in Jersey City, N.J.; son of Frank Gray (a business executive) and Wilhelmina (Meyer) Atkinson; married Mary Jane Wanta, April 15, 1944; children: Ann Mina (Mrs. James R. Sawusch), David John, William Frank. *Education:* Wesleyan University, B.A. (with high distinction), 1947; University of Michigan, M.A., 1948, Ph.D., 1950. *Home:* 2363 Belgrade Notch, Ann Arbor, Mich. 48103. *Office:* Psychology Department, University of Michigan, Ann Arbor, Mich. 48106.

CAREER: University of Michigan, Ann Arbor, instructor in psychology, 1948-49; Wesleyan University, Middletown, Conn., assistant professor of psychology, 1949-50; University of Michigan, assistant professor, 1950-55, associate professor, 1955-60, professor of psychology, 1960—, research associate, Survey Research Center, 1964-69. *Military service:* U.S. Army Air Forces, 1943-45; became second lieutenant. *Member:* American Psychological Association, American Association for the Advancement of Science, American Educational Research Association, American Association of University Professors. *Awards, honors:* Social Science Research Council faculty research fellow, 1952-55; Center for Advanced Study in the Behavioral Sciences fellow, 1955-56; Guggenheim fellow, 1960-61; U.S. Public Health Service special research fellow, 1969-70; American Academy of Arts and Sciences fellow, 1975.

WRITINGS: (With D. C. McClelland, R. A. Clark, and E. L. Lowell) *The Achievement Motive,* Appleton, 1953; (editor and contributor) *Motives in Fantasy, Action, and Society,* Van Nostrand, 1958; *An Introduction to Motivation,* Van Nostrand, 1964; (editor with N. T. Feather, and contributor) *A Theory of Achievement Motivation,* Wiley, 1966; (with David Birch) *The Dynamics of Action,* Wiley, 1970; (editor with J. O. Raynor, and contributor) *Motivation and Achievement,* V. W. Winston, 1974.

WORK IN PROGRESS: A book, *An Introduction to Psychology,* with David Birch.

*   *   *

ATTWOOD, William   1919-

PERSONAL: Born July 14, 1919, in Paris, France; son of Frederic (an engineer) and Gladys (Hollingsworth) Attwood; married Simone Cadgene, June 22, 1950; children: Peter, Janet, Susan. *Education:* Princeton University, B.A., 1941. *Home:* 423 Carter St., New Canaan, Conn. 06840. *Office: Newsday,* Garden City, N.Y.

CAREER: New York Herald-Tribune, New York, N.Y., foreign correspondent, 1946-49; *Collier's,* New York, N.Y., European correspondent, 1949-51; *Look,* New York, N.Y., European editor, 1951-54, national editor, 1955-57, foreign editor, 1957-61; U.S. Ambassador to Guinea, 1961-63; U.S. Delegation to United Nations, special advisor, 1963-64; U.S. Ambassador to Kenya, 1964-66; Cowles Communications, Inc., New York, N.Y., editor-in-chief, 1966-70, also vice-president and director; *Newsday,* Garden City, N.Y., president and publisher, 1971—. Member of John F. Kennedy presidential campaign staff, 1960. Member of board of directors, Planned Parenthood-World Population; alumni trustee of Princeton University, 1967-71. *Military service:* U.S. Army, 1941-45; became captain.

MEMBER: Council on Foreign Relations, and Century Association. *Awards, honors:* National Headliners Award, 1955, 1957; George Polk Memorial Award, 1956; Page One Award of New York Newspaper Guild, 1960; distinguished achievement award from University of Southern California, School of Journalism, 1966.

WRITINGS: The Man Who Could Grow Hair, Knopf, 1949; *Still the Most Exciting Country,* Knopf, 1955; (with George B. Leonard, Jr. and J. Robert Moskin) *The Decline of the American Male,* Random House, 1959; *The Reds and the Blacks,* Harper, 1967; *The Fairly Scary Adventure Book,* Harper, 1969. Contributor to about twenty-five national magazines.

SIDELIGHTS: William Attwood speaks French, some German and Spanish; he has traveled in eighty-one countries. *Avocational interests:* Sports, reading.

*   *   *

AUBEY, Robert T(haddeus)   1930-

PERSONAL: Born June 19, 1930, in Beaumont, Tex.; son of Victor Dale and Lou Etta (Holt) Aubey; married Graciela Wood, June 24, 1961; children: Robert, Jr., George William. *Education:* Lamar State College of Technology (now Lamar University), B.B.A., 1958; University of the Americas, M.A., 1960; University of California, Los Angeles, Ph.D., 1965. *Home:* 2714 Oak Bluff, San Antonio, Tex. 78230. *Office:* University of Texas, San Antonio, Tex.

CAREER: University of Wisconsin, Madison, associate professor of finance and international business, 1966-75; University of Texas, San Antonio, professor of finance, 1975—. *Military service:* U.S. Navy, Airman, 1948-49, 1950-52.

WRITINGS: Nacional Financiera and Mexican Industry, Latin American Center, University of California, Los Angeles, 1966; *Cases in Managerial Finance,* Holt, 1970; *Decisions in Financial Management,* Holt, 1972.

WORK IN PROGRESS: Research on the role of commercial banking in the process of regional development in developing countries, and on investment group formation as a factor in economic development in Latin America.

*   *   *

AUERBACH, Jerold S(tephen)   1936-

PERSONAL: Born May 7, 1936, in Philadelphia, Pa.; son of Morry and Sophie (Soloff) Auerbach; married Judith Aaron, June 29, 1961; children: Jeffrey Aaron, Pamela Jane. *Education:* Oberlin College, B.A., 1957; Columbia University, M.A., 1959, Ph.D., 1965. *Home:* 30 Hillside Terrace, Belmont, Mass. 02178. *Office:* Department of History, Wellesley College, Wellesley, Mass. 02181.

CAREER: Queens College, of the City University of New York, Flushing, N.Y., lecturer in history, 1964-65; Brandeis University, Waltham, Mass., assistant professor of history, 1965-71; Wellesley College, Wellesley, Mass., associate professor of history, 1971—. Fulbright lecturer, Tel Aviv University, 1974-75. *Member:* Organization of American Historians, American Society for Legal History.

AWARDS, HONORS: Lasker fellow, Brandeis University, 1963; Erb fellow, Columbia University, 1963-64; Pelzer Award, Organization of American Historians, 1964; American Council of Learned Societies grant, 1966; American Philosophical Society grant, 1969; Social Science Research Council grant, 1969; National Endowment for the Humanities grant, 1969; Liberal Arts fellow, Harvard University Law School, 1969-70; Guggenheim fellow, 1974-75.

WRITINGS: Labor and Liberty: The LaFollette Committee and the New Deal, Bobbs-Merrill, 1966; (editor) *American Labor: The Twentieth Century,* Bobbs-Merrill, 1969; *Unequal Justice: Lawyers and Social Change in Modern America,* Oxford University Press, 1975. Contributor of articles to *Nation, Harvard Law Review,* and other historical and legal journals.

*   *   *

AUGSBURGER, A(aron) Don(ald)   1925-

PERSONAL: Born December 21, 1925, in Elida, Ohio; son of Clarence A. (a painter) and Estella R. (Shenk) Augsburger; married Martha Kling, June 5, 1948; children: Phyllis Anne, Patricia Louise, Don Richard. *Education:* Eastern Mennonite College, A.B., 1949; Eastern Baptist Seminary, M.R.E., 1956; Temple University, D.Ed., 1963. *Home:* 1601 Hillcrest Dr., Harrisonburg, Va. 22801. *Office:* Eastern Mennonite Seminary, Harrisonburg, Va. 22801.

CAREER: Eastern Mennonite College, Harrisonburg, Va., teacher of Christian education, 1958-64, director of counselling services, 1970—, also professor of work of the Church, Eastern Mennonite Seminary. Pastor and bishop of Mennonite Church, Goshen, Ind., 1964-69; assistant dean, Goshen Biblical Seminary, 1964-65; teacher in psychology, Goshen College, 1965-67; high school guidance counsellor, 1966-68, superintendent, 1968-70. Moderator of General Assembly of the Mennonite Church, 1971-73.

WRITINGS: Creating Christian Personality, Herald, 1966.

* * *

AUSTGEN, Robert Joseph 1932-

PERSONAL: Born September 19, 1932, in Hammond, Ind.; son of Robert Joseph (a buyer) and Christine (Frichtl) Austgen. *Education:* University of Notre Dame, A.B., 1955; Gregorian University, Rome, Italy, S.T.L., 1959; University of Fribourg, S.T.D., 1963. *Home and office:* University of Notre Dame, Notre Dame, Ind. 46556.

CAREER: Roman Catholic priest of Congregation of Holy Cross (C.S.C.). University of Notre Dame, Notre Dame, Ind., assistant professor of theology, 1964—, director of summer session, 1970—, director of graduate admissions, 1971. *Member:* Catholic Theological Society of America, Indiana Academy of Religion, Council of Graduate Schools, National Association of Summer Sessions, North Central Conference of Summer Schools. *Awards, honors:* Notre Dame Man of the Year Award, 1971; distinguished service award, Air Force Institute of Technology, 1974.

WRITINGS: Natural Motivation in the Pauline Epistles, University of Notre Dame Press, 1966.

WORK IN PROGRESS: Research for a book on modern man.

AVOCATIONAL INTERESTS: Sports, art, flower gardening, antiques.

* * *

AUSTIN, William W(eaver) 1920-

PERSONAL: Born January 18, 1920, in Lawton, Okla.; son of William M. (an auto dealer) and Leone Elizabeth (Weaver) Austin; married Elizabeth J. Hallstrom, June 20, 1942; children: Ann Elizabeth, Margery Jane. *Education:* Harvard University, A.B., 1939, A.M., 1940, Ph.D., 1951. *Office:* Department of Music, Cornell University, Ithaca, N.Y. 14853.

CAREER: University of Virginia, Charlottesville, assistant professor of music, 1946-47; Cornell University, Ithaca, N.Y., assistant professor, 1947-50, associate professor, 1950-60, professor, 1960-69, Goldwin Smith Professor of Musicology, 1969—, chairman of department, 1958-63. Princeton University, visiting associate professor, 1957-58. *Military service:* U.S. Naval Reserve, active duty, 1942-46; became lieutenant senior grade. *Member:* American Musicological Society, International Musicological Society, Gesellschaft fur Musikforschung, American Academy of Arts and Sciences for Ethnomusicology, College Music Society (president, 1960-62). *Awards, honors:* Guggenheim fellow, 1961-62; E. J. Dent Prize of Royal Musical Association, and Otto Kinkeldey Award of American Musicological Society, both 1967, for *Music in the Twentieth Century.*

WRITINGS: Music in the Twentieth Century, Norton, 1966; (editor) *New Looks at Italian Opera,* Cornell University Press, 1968; (editor) Debussy, *Prelude a l'apres-midi d'un faune* (critical edition), Norton, 1970; *Everywhere I Roam: The Songs of Stephen Foster,* Macmillan, 1975. Contributor to music publications.

WORK IN PROGRESS: Studies of Stravinsky, Tchaikovsky, Andrei Eshpai, Steve Reich, and others.

SIDELIGHTS: Austin writes: "Poetry and dance are inseparable from music, for me. Science and religion are closely allied. The chance to continue performing and occasionally composing music, as well as teaching its history and appreciation, distracts me from scholarship; I hope in the long run my writing is enriched by my diverse activities." Austin has participated in national and international scholarly efforts, including reading a paper at the Moscow Congress of the International Music Council.

* * *

AVERILL, Lloyd J(ames) 1923-

PERSONAL: Born April 5, 1923, in Warrenville, Ill.; son of Lloyd James and Dorothy (Rogers) Averill; married Shirley Karr, February 9, 1944 (divorced June, 1968); married Carol Ann White, July 13, 1968; children: (first marriage) Shelly Ann, Leslie Jean, Scott Alan. *Education:* University of Wisconsin, B.A. (with honors), 1947; Colgate Rochester Divinity School, B.D., 1950, M.Th., 1966; University of Rochester, M.A., 1952; additional study in England at Westminister College and Fitzwilliam House, Cambridge, 1965-66. *Politics:* Democrat. *Office:* 4343 Oak St., Kansas City, Mo. 64111.

CAREER: Colgate Rochester Divinity School, Rochester, N.Y., instructor in practical theology and associate director of field work, 1951-54; Kalamazoo College, Kalamazoo, Mich., assistant professor, 1954-57, associate professor, 1957-62, professor of religion, 1962-67, assistant to the president, 1957-63, vice-president of college, 1963-67; Council of Protestant Colleges and Universities, Washington, D.C., president, 1967-68; Ottawa and Baker Universities and Park College, Ottawa, Kan., distinguished visiting professor, 1968-70; Davis and Elkins College, Elkins, W. Va., professor of religion and sociology, vice-president, dean of faculty, 1970-72; Kansas City Regional Council for Higher Education, Kansas City, Mo., president, 1972—. Adjunct professor, San Francisco Theological Seminary, 1965-71, Southern Methodist University, Baker University; special professor of religion, Graceland College, 1972—. Distinguished lecturer at universities, including Wilson lecturer at Southwestern University, 1967, Austin College, 1968, and Trinity University, 1968; has given occasional lectures or preached at more than 100 American colleges and universities. Member of advisory board, Danforth Foundation; member of Missouri Committee on the Humanities. Consultant to Association of American Colleges and to American Council on Education, 1967-68. *Military service:* U.S. Army Air Forces, 1943-46.

MEMBER: American Academy of Religion, American Association for Higher Education, Pi Kappa Delta. *Awards, honors:* Danforth Foundation campus ministry grant, 1958-59; L.H.D., Lewis and Clark College, 1962, College of Idaho; LL.D., Carroll College and William Jewell College, 1967; Litt.D., Augustana College, Rock Island, Ill., 1968; D.D., Tusculum College, 1968.

WRITINGS: A Strategy for the Protestant College, Westminister, 1966; *American Theology in the Liberal Tradition,* Westminister, 1967; (contributor) Donovan Smucker, editor, *Rockefeller Chapel Sermons,* University of Chicago Press, 1967; *Between Faith and Unfaith,* John Knox, 1968; *Agenda for the Protestant College* (monograph), Council of Protestant Colleges and Universities, 1968; *The Church College and the Public Good* (monograph), Council of Protestant Colleges and Universities, 1968; (contributor) G. Kerry Smith, editor, *Twenty-Five Years,* Jossey-Bass, 1970; (contributor) DeWitte Holland, editor, *Sermons in American History,* Abingdon, 1971; (editor with William W. Jellema) *Colleges and Commitments,* Westminister, 1971; *The Problem of Being Human,* Judson, 1974; (contributor) Thomas Diener and Lewis Patterson, editors, *Trends and Issues in Cooperation,* American Association for Higher Education, 1974. Contributor to *Current Issues in Higher Education,* Association for Higher Education, 1963, 1964, and to religious and educational journals. Consulting editor, *Journal of Higher Education.*

WORK IN PROGRESS: A book, *Enhancing the Human: A Mission for Colleges,* completion expected in 1976.

AVOCATIONAL INTERESTS: Plastic and graphic arts, music (playing the piano and organ), drama, and politics.

* * *

AVERITT, Robert T(abor) 1931-

PERSONAL: Born July 12, 1931, in Kaufman, Tex.; son of James Ted (a realtor) and Tina Ruth (Young) Averitt; married Brett Thomas (a teacher), September 16, 1957; children: Mark Harrison, Angela Lee. *Education:* North Texas State University, B.A., 1951; University of Texas, M.A., 1957, Ph.D., 1961. *Office:* Department of Economics, Smith College, Northampton, Mass. 01060.

CAREER: Smith College, Northampton, Mass., assistant professor, 1961-66, associate professor, 1966-69, professor of economics, 1969—. Consultant, U.S. Small Business Administration, 1964. *Military service:* U.S. Navy, 1953-55. *Member:* American Economic Association, Association for Evolutionary Economics, American Association for the Advancement of Science.

WRITINGS: The Dual Economy: The Dynamics of American Industrial Structure, Norton, 1968; (with others) *Perspectives on Business,* Arts & Sciences, 1969. Contributor to journals in his field.

WORK IN PROGRESS: A book, tentatively entitled *The Economics of American Welfare.*†

* * *

AXELSON, Eric 1913-

PERSONAL: Born July 11, 1913, in London, England; son of Charles Edmund and M.E.L. (Beddow) Axelson; married Hilda Mason (an artist, and associate of Royal College of Art), February 11, 1949; children: Ann Frances, Rafe Antony. *Education:* Natal University College (now University of Natal), B.A., 1932, M.A., 1934; graduate study at University of the Witwatersrand and King's College, University of London, 1935-37; D.Litt. (Rand), 1938. *Home:* 20 Ou Wingerd Rd., High Constantia, 7800, Cape Town, South Africa. *Office:* University of Cape Town, Rondebosch, South Africa.

CAREER: Union War Histories section of the Prime Minister's Office, Pretoria, South Africa, assistant editor, 1946-49; Central African Archives, Salisbury, Southern Rhodesia, editor, 1949-51; chief narrator, Union War Histories, 1952-54; Oppenheimer Institute of Portuguese Studies, Johannesburg, South Africa, research officer, 1955-62;

University of Cape Town, Rondebosch, South Africa, professor of history and head of department, 1962-74, dean of the faculty of Arts, 1967-69, assistant principal, 1972—. *Military service:* South African Land Forces, 1941-45; served in North Africa and Italy; became major.

MEMBER: Royal Historical Society (fellow), Royal Geographical Society (fellow), South African Historical Society (chairman, 1967-68), South African Association for the Advancement of Science (president, Section F, 1968), Academia Portuguesa da Historia, Centro de Estudos Historicos Ultramarinos of Lisbon, Historical Society of Cape Town (chairman, 1967), Owl Club (president, 1968). *Awards, honors:* Grant from Calouste Gulbenkian Foundation, 1960; travel grant from Carnegie Corp. of New York to study the teaching of African history at various American universities, 1966.

WRITINGS: South-East Africa, 1488-1530, Longmans, Green, 1940; (editor) *South African Explorers,* Oxford University Press, 1954; *Portuguese in South-East Africa 1600-1700,* Witwatersrand University Press, 1960; *Portugal and the Scramble for Africa 1875-91,* Witwatersrand University Press, 1967; *Portuguese in South-East Africa 1488-1600,* Witwatersrand University Press, 1973; *Congo to Cape: Early Portuguese Explorers,* Faber, 1973.

WORK IN PROGRESS: Portuguese in South-East Africa, 1700-1800; editing "The Brenthurst" series.

SIDELIGHTS: Eric Axelson has done research in the history of Portuguese exploration and colonization in Africa in archives and libraries in Portugal and Spain, Paris and Rome, Goa and Lourenco Marques. His archaeological discoveries include finding fragments of stone pillars erected by Dias in 1488 at Kwaaihoek and Luderitz, and Axelson has searched for crosses erected by Vasco de Gama on the Mocambique coast, and identified as Portuguese limestone the cross at Malindi. He is interested in African history generally, and started a course in the subject at the University of Cape Town in 1964. In addition to visiting U.S. universities in 1966, Axelson has traveled in Brazil, Chile, and Peru.

* * *

AXTON, W(illiam) F(itch) 1926-

PERSONAL: Born September 24, 1926, in Louisville, Ky.; son of Edwin Dymond (a manufacturer) and Blanche T. (Miller) Axton; married Joanne Virginia Lewis, June 23, 1951 (deceased); married Anne Elizabeth Millard (a teacher), August 5, 1967; children: (first marriage) Blanche Miller, Lucy Riggs, Belle Sherlock; (second marriage) Samantha Elizabeth. *Education:* Yale University, B.A., 1948; University of Louisville, M.A., 1951; Princeton University, Ph.D., 1961. *Politics:* Republican. *Religion:* Protestant. *Address:* 2421 Cherokee Pkwy., Louisville, Ky. 40204. *Office:* English Department, University of Louisville, Louisville, Ky. 40208.

CAREER: Kentucky State Department of Health, Louisville, director of field education, 1951-52; Miami University, Oxford, Ohio, instructor in English, 1952-53; Brown University, Providence, R.I., instructor in English, 1957-61; University of Kentucky, Lexington, 1961-67, began as assistant professor, became associate professor of English; University of Louisville, Louisville, Ky., associate professor, 1967-69, professor of English, 1969—, chairman of department, 1971-74. Consultant to Canada Council. *Military service:* U.S. Naval Reserve, 1944-46, 1950-53; became lieutenant junior grade. *Member:* Modern Language

Association of America, Victorian Society, Kentucky Historical Society, Dickens Society (president, 1972), Victorian Society in America, Tennyson Society, Browning Society, Browning Institute, Byron Society, Filson Club.

WRITINGS: (Editor) C. R. Maturin, *Melmoth the Wanderer,* University of Nebraska Press, 1961; *Circle of Fire: Dickens' Vision and Style,* University Press of Kentucky, 1967; *Tobacco and Kentucky,* University Press of Kentucky, 1975; *F. M. Brown, "King Lear," and the "Historical Machine,"* University Press, 1975; *The Charles Dickens Drink Book,* Tradehouse, in press; *A Thirties Childhood,* Tradehouse, in press. Contributor of scholarly and critical articles to journals. Managing editor, *Dickens Newsletter;* associate editor, *Dickens Annal;* consultant, Ohio University Press, Princeton University Press, University Press of Kentucky.

* * *

AYANDELE, E(mmanuel) A(yankanmi) 1936-

PERSONAL: Born October 12, 1936, in Ogbomosho, Nigeria; son of John and Oyeniwe Ayandele; married Margaret Oyebimpe Adeshima, August 25, 1960; children: Aderemi. *Education:* Nigerian College of Arts, Science and Technology, G.C.E. (with distinction), 1956; University College of Ibadan, B.A. (honors), 1960; King's College, University of London, Ph.D., 1964. *Religion:* Nigerian Baptist. *Office:* Office of the Principal, University of Ibadan, Jos Campus, P.M.B. 2084, Jos, Nigeria.

CAREER: Baptist Day School, Jos, Northern Nigeria, teacher, 1954; Baptist Boys' High School, Oyo, Western Nigeria, teacher, 1960; University of Ibadan, Ibadan, Nigeria, lecturer, 1963-67, senior lecturer, 1967-69, professor of history, 1969—, Jos Campus, foundation head and acting principal, 1971-74, principal, 1974—. Member of Nigerian National Archives Committee, and Emergency Committee for World Government. *Member:* International Association for Mysiological Studies, Historical Society of Nigeria (member of council), Society for African Church History (executive member), Club of Rome.

WRITINGS: The Missionary Impact on Modern Nigeria, 1842-1914: A Political and Social Analysis, Longmans, 1966, Humanities, 1967; (contributor) J. C. Anene and G. N. Brown, editors, *Africa in the Nineteenth and Twentieth Centuries,* Thomas Nelson, 1966; (author of introduction) T. J. Bowen, *Central African Adventures and Missionary Labors in Several Countries in the Interior of Africa from 1849 to 1956,* 2nd edition, Cass & Co., 1967; (editor with J. D. Omer-Cooper, R. J. Gavin, and A. E. Afigbo, and contributor) *The Making of Modern Africa,* Volume I: *The Nineteenth Century to the Partition: The Growth of African Civilisation,* Humanities, 1968, Volume II: *The Late Nineteenth Century to the Present Day,* Longman, 1971; (contributor) *The Church Crossing Frontiers: Essays on the Nature of Mission in Honour of Bengt Sunkler,* Gleerup Bokforlag (Lund), 1969.

Holy Johnson 1836-1917: Pioneer of African Nationalism, Cass & Co., 1970; (author of introduction) J.A.B. Horton, *Letters on the Political Condition of the Gold Coast,* 2nd edition, Cass & Co., 1970; (contributor) Michael Crowder and Obaro Ikeme, editors, *West African Chiefs: Their Changing Status Under Colonial Rule and Independence,* Holmes & Meier, 1970; (contributor) John E. Flint and Glyndwr Williams, editors, *Perspectives of Empire,* Longman, 1973; (contributor) *The University of Ibadan 1948-1973,* Ibadan University Press, 1973; *The Educated Elite in the Nigerian Society,* Ibadan University Press, 1974. Contributor of articles to professional journals, including *African Historical Studies, West African Journal of Education,* and *Journal of African Studies.*

SIDELIGHTS: Ayandele believes "African historiography faces a big challenge. . . . Non-Africans should learn to see African history as an entity in its own right, rather than as a mere projection of European history; on the other hand, Africans should not write nationalist history but exhume the past dispassionately and faithfully."

* * *

AYCKBOURN, Alan 1939-

PERSONAL: Surname is pronounced, Ache-born; born April 12, 1939, in Hampstead, London, England; son of Horace (a musician) and Irene (Worley) Ayckbourn; married Christine Roland, May 9, 1959; children: Steven Paul, Philip Nicholas. *Education:* Attended Haileybury and Imperial Service College, Hertfordshire, England, 1952-57. *Politics:* None. *Religion:* None. *Agent:* Margaret Ramsay Ltd., 14 A, Goodwin's Ct., St. Martin's Lane, London WC2N 4LL, England. *Office:* Theatre in the Round Co., c/o 32 Manor Rd., Scarborough, North Yorkshire, England.

CAREER: Former actor and stage manager for repertory and other companies in England; now director of productions, Theatre in the Round Co., Scarborough, England. Drama producer for North region, British Broadcasting Corp., Leeds, Yorkshire, England, 1965-70. *Awards, honors:* London Evening Standard, Best Comedy award, 1973, Best Play award, 1974; *Plays and Players* Best Play award, 1974; Playwright of the Year, from Variety Club of Great Britain, 1974.

WRITINGS—Plays: *Relatively Speaking* (produced on West End at Duke of York's Theatre, 1967), Evans Brothers, 1969; *Countdown* (one-act; produced on West End at Comedy Theatre, April 9, 1969), published in *Mixed Doubles: An Entertainment on Marriage,* Methuen, 1970; *Time and Time Again* (two-act; produced on West End at Comedy Theatre, August 16, 1972), Samuel French, 1972; *How the Other Half Loves* (produced on West End at Lyric Theatre, 1969), Evans Brothers, 1973; *Absurd Person Singular* (produced on West End at Criterion Theatre, 1973), Samuel French, 1974; *The Norman Conquests* (trilogy; includes "Table Manners," "Living Together," and "Round and Round the Garden"; produced on West End at Globe Theatre, 1974), Chatto & Windus, 1975.

Unpublished plays: "Mr. Whatnot," produced in London at Arts Theatre, 1965; "The Story So Far," produced in Scarborough at Library Theatre, August 20, 1970; "Slipper," produced in Paris at Theatre Daunou, September, 1970; "Me Times Me Times Me," produced on West End in Phoenix Theatre, August 25, 1971; "Ernie's Incredible Illucinations," produced in London at Arts Theatre, September 18, 1971; "Absent Friends," produced on West End at Garrick Theatre, July, 1975; "Jeeves" (musical; score by Andrew Lloyd Weber), produced on West End at Her Majesty's Theatre, 1975; "Bedroom Farce," produced in Scarborough, 1976; "Confusions," produced in Scarborough, 1976. Other plays produced: "The Square Cat," "Love After All," "Dad's Tale," "The Sparrow," and "Standing Room Only."

SIDELIGHTS: "All my plays are written under tremendous pressure," writes Alan Ayckbourn, " which is why I still use Scarborough. I reckon that with a bit of luck I've got one play in me a year. That's all! I never write anything else. Even then I only do it under extreme protest. In February I make out a playlist for Scarborough and announce a play by me so I make up a title which usually has nothing to do with the play. [One] year we had literally started rehearsals before I wrote *Absurd Person Singular*. I met the cast on a Sunday night in my house and mine was the second play that was going to be rehearsed in a fortnight. I suddenly got nervous, all these actors in the room saying 'I'm dying to read *yours*' and they're asking me what sort of clothes are they going to need, and I'm saying 'Well, sort of a suit, but it could be a pair of jeans.'"

Ayckbourn feels that "the interesting thing about *Time And Time Again* is that I have upset the balance. The central character should be the driving force. I wanted to write a total vacuum, a central character who took no decisions, did nothing, everything was done for him and by simply taking no decisions he affects the whole course of the play. Doing nothing, he upsets five lives. He comes through it in the most extraordinary way; everybody else ends up miserable. Like certain characters in life, he attracts people who have an irresistible impulse to push him in one direction, but he slides out of the push. Some people get angered by this type, others get concerned. . . . I have never made any decisions, they have always been made for me. I started out as an actor, and I was incredibly lucky, never out of work. Not that I was that *good,* but somehow I never wrote a letter or did an audition in my life, it just went from the end of one season to the beginning of another, *bonk, bonk, bonk*. Entirely due to circumstances and possibly because I never did take any action. I could look back on my life and say I planned it that way, but I didn't plan to be an actor, nor a director, nor a writer."

Critic Stanley Kauffmann contends that Ayckbourn is "much more than Mack Sennett of England—50 percent of Sennett, anyway. [He] calls [*Absurd Person Singular*] a comedy, but it is farce; and essentially it is not theater farce, it is film slapstick. The great farces of Feydeau and Courteline and Pinero are complicated machines of egocentric desire in monochromatic characters, people who desperately want something or other and bump violently into or frantically evade or breathlessly deceive others. Ayckbourn makes no such machine. His characters are monochrome, all right, but few of them *want* anything very much: they just behave in certain ways that are sharply and quickly defined. One wife is a compulsive housecleaner who has an addiction to cleaning, no matter whose house she's in. Another wife is a compulsive, socially pretending drinker. And so on. The result is a series of situations that lead to physical complications that lead to more physical complications. The play is so much like a series of Sennett set-ups that it could very easily be played completely silent with fifteen or twenty subtitles."

Kauffmann maintains that "Ayckbourn understands the secret of this kind of laugh-building. Each of his nests of structures begins with an action that is perfectly credible for its doer and then proceeds perfectly logically: the comedy comes from the fact that this logic has nothing to do with the logic of the other people . . . [Most] of the dialogue itself is quite unfunny. Ayckbourn almost seems to flirt with the idea of an Ionesco-like barrage of banalities, which may be the source of the 'absurd' in his title, but the dialogue never quite gets to that level of self-knowledge. If this play were not well *done,* it would be worse than unfunny, it would be embarrassing."

"From the time of *Relatively Speaking* onwards," writes J. W. Lambert, "I have been signalling . . . the merits of this alarmingly perceptive dramatist as very much more than those of an expert purveyor of light comedy. Some are still reluctant to accept this fact; others evade the issue by arguing the totally unimportant question whether he is a true writer of comedy or 'merely' an inspired farceur. (I suppose they would have wittered on in much the same way about Moliere.) But for the most part, with a paradoxical absurdity typical of cultural establishments down the ages, the opinion-formers have finally caught up with Ayckbourn's real quality (and with the general public) in welcoming *The Norman Conquests* . . . sharply perceptive and almost unbearably funny . . . Each play is virtually . . . the off-stage of the others, taking place respectively in the dining-room and the garden . . . Mr. Ayckbourn's ingenuity in thus constructing the plays positively makes the head spin if dwelt upon; but of course it should not be dwelt upon, for however valuable the challenge may have been to his inventive powers, it is to us only an incidental pleasure. The value of the work lies elsewhere—in its knife-sharp insights into the long littleness of life and in its unflagging comic exhilaration. . . .

"However inhibited or hesitant they may appear, Mr. Ayckbourn's women in these plays . . . are pillars of certainty compared to the men . . . It is the pregnant pause which more than anything else [provides] the unnerving element in Mr. Ayckbourn's plays which gives him so much in common with Harold Pinter."

BIOGRAPHICAL/CRITICAL SOURCES: Plays and Players, September, 1972; Carolyn Riley, editor, *Contemporary Literary Criticism,* Volume V, Gale, 1976.

*   *   *

AYMES, Sister Maria de la Cruz

PERSONAL: Born in Mexico. *Education:* Attended Sacred Heart College (Mexico), Catholic University of America, Notre Dame University, and University of San Francisco. *Home:* 214 Haight St., San Francisco, Calif. 94102.

CAREER: Roman Catholic religious. Entered Society of Helpers (H.H.S.) in New York, N.Y., 1939; subsequently taught and worked with young children in Paris, Spanish Harlem in New York, Hunter's Point in San Francisco, and three Indian villages in Mexico; Confraternity of Christian Doctrine Office, Archdiocese of San Francisco, San Francisco, Calif., archdiocesan supervisor; University of San Francisco, San Francisco, teacher in religious education department. Lecturer at Catholic University of America, University of Notre Dame, Fordham University, and other universities; lecturer and conductor of courses in religious education in Ireland, England, Scotland, France, Belgium, Japan, Canada, Manila, and Hong Kong. Member of International Catechetical Commission of Sacred Congregation of the Clergy, Rome, 1975-80. *Awards, honors:* S.T.D., University of San Francisco, 1973.

WRITINGS: Original "On Our Way" series, texts and teacher's guides for grades 1-6, Sadlier, 1957-62, revised Vatican II edition (with F. J. Buckley, S.J.), 1966-70; (with Buckley) "New Life" series, texts and guides for grades 1-6, Sadlier, 1970-74; *Jesus Non Dice* (Spanish-English religion text), Volume I, with guide, Sadlier, 1974. Contributor of articles on modern catechetics to *Teaching All Nations, Living Light,* and *Good Tidings.*

WORK IN PROGRESS: Volumes II and III of *Jesus Non Dice,* completion expected in 1976; a complete revision of "New Life" series.

BABIN, David E. 1925-

PERSONAL: Born May 1, 1925, in Memphis, Tenn.; son of Walter F. (a lumber broker) and Virginia (Haste) Babin; married Frances Sherrill, March 29, 1947; children: Sheryl, Patricia, Mark. *Education:* Northwestern University, B.S., 1946; Church Divinity School of the Pacific, B.D. (with honors), 1960; Chicago Theological Seminary, D.Re. *Home:* 629 Garrett Pl., Evanston, Ill. 60201. *Office:* Seabury-Western Theological Seminary, 2122 Sheridan Rd., Evanston, Ill. 60201.

CAREER: Radio Station WTAR, Norfolk, Va., public service director, 1946-48; Babin Lumber Sales Co., Memphis, Tenn., partner, 1948-57. Ordained priest of Protestant Episcopal Church, 1960; curate in Knoxville, Tenn., 1960-62; rector in Germantown, Tenn., 1962-65; Seabury-Western Theological Seminary, Evanston, Ill., professor of homiletics and liturgics, 1965—. Theologian-in-residence, Windward Coalition of Churches, Kailua, Hawaii, 1974-75. Conductor of workshops in effective preaching, using video tape-recording equipment. *Member:* Associated Parishes for Liturgy and Mission, American Academy of Homiletics Professors, Christian Preaching Conference (member of editorial board), Associated Parishes Council (member of executive committee).

WRITINGS: Introduction to the Liturgy of the Lord's Supper, Morehouse, 1968; *The Celebration of Life,* Morehouse, 1969; *Doing the Eucharist,* Morehouse, 1971; *The Supreme Festival of Life and Death,* Forward Movement Books, 1972; (contributor) *The Romance of the Prayer Book,* Forward Movement Books, 1975; *Introduction to the Prayer Book—1979,* Forward Movement Books, in press. Contributor of monographs and articles to theology journals and church periodicals. Editor, "Bookmarks," in *Tennessee Churchman,* 1963-65.

WORK IN PROGRESS: Week-In; Week-Out: A New Look at Liturgical Preaching.

*   *   *

BABLADELIS, Georgia 1931-

PERSONAL: Surname is pronounced *Bab*-le-delis; born January 30, 1931, in Manistique, Mich.; daughter of Alex N. and Bertha (Prokas) Babladelis. *Education:* University of Michigan, B.A. (honors in psychology), 1953; University of California, Berkeley, M.A., 1955; University of Colorado, Ph.D., 1959. *Office:* California State University, Hayward, Calif. 94542.

CAREER: Alameda County Probation Department, Oakland, Calif., clinical psychologist, 1959-60, senior clinical psychologist and training supervisor, 1960-63; California State University, Hayward, assistant professor, 1965-67, associate professor, 1967-1972, professor of psychology, 1972—. Manuscript reader for publishers.

WRITINGS: (With Suzanne Adams) *The Shaping of Personality,* Prentice-Hall, 1967. Contributor to *Journal of Abnormal and Social Psychology, Psychological Reports, Perceptual and Motor Skills,* and *Psychological Record.* Editor, *Journal of the Psychology of Women.*

SIDELIGHTS: Babladelis is competent in Greek, and reads French. *Avocational interests:* Travel, reading.

*   *   *

BABRIS, Peter J. 1917-

PERSONAL: Born January 31, 1917, in Atasiene, Latvia; son of Dominiks A. (a farmer) and Katrine (Pastors) Babris; married Janina Skraustins (a teacher), December 31, 1961. *Education:* University of Latvia, B.A., 1944; University of South Dakota, M.A., 1952; Northern Illinois University, graduate study, 1962-65; Walden University, Ph.D., 1973. *Religion:* Roman Catholic. *Home:* 108 South Patton, Arlington Heights, Ill. 60005. *Office:* Arlington High School, Arlington Heights, Ill. 60004.

CAREER: Elementary teacher in Latvia, 1941-44; teacher of languages in Oldenburg, Germany, 1945-50; high school teacher of foreign languages in various American schools, 1952-58; Arlington High School, Arlington Heights, Ill., teacher of foreign languages, 1958—. *Military service:* Latvian Army, 1938-40; became sergeant. *Member:* National Education Association, American Association of Teachers of Slavic and East European Languages, Illinois Education Association.

WRITINGS: Baltic Youth Under Communism, Research Publishers, 1967.

WORK IN PROGRESS: A book on religion behind the Iron Curtain; *Genocide in the Soviet Empire; Siberia: Land of Punishment.*

SIDELIGHTS: Babris is competent in German, Latin, Greek, Latvian, Russian, and other Slavic languages.

BIOGRAPHICAL SOURCES: Arlington Heights Herald, August 18, 1967.

*   *   *

BACH, Bert C(oates) 1936-

PERSONAL: Born December 14, 1936, in Jenkins, Ky.; son of Bert Clarence (a physician) and Rowena (Coates) Bach; married Diana Miller, August 25, 1957; children: Bert Coates, Jr., Nancy Elizabeth. *Education:* Eastern Kentucky University, A.B., 1958; George Peabody College for Teachers, M.A., 1959; New York University, Ph.D., 1966. *Politics:* Democrat. *Religion:* Presbyterian. *Home:* 3885 Delmar, Decatur, Ill. 62522. *Office:* Millikin University, Decatur, Ill. 62522.

CAREER: Assistant professor of English at West Georgia College, Carrollton, 1959-61, and Manhattan College, Bronx, N.Y., 1961-66; Eastern Kentucky University, Richmond, associate professor of English, 1966-67, professor, 1967-70; Millikin University, Decatur, Ill., faculty member of English department, 1970—, chairman of department, 1970-73, assistant vice-provost for academic affairs, 1974—. *Member:* Modern Language Association of America, National Council of Teachers of English, Conference on College Composition and Communication, American Association for Higher Education, South Atlantic Modern Language Association. *Awards, honors:* American Council of Education fellow, 1972-73.

WRITINGS: (With Gordon Browning) *Fiction for Composition,* Scott, Foresman, 1968; *The Liberating Form,* Dodd, 1972; (with Browning) *Drama for Composition,* Scott, Foresman, 1973.

AVOCATIONAL INTERESTS: The theater, art, music, and all sports, especially baseball.

*   *   *

BACKHOUSE, Sally 1927-

PERSONAL: Born January 21, 1927, in Wakefield, England; daughter of Harry Milton (a clerk) and Lena (Hughes) Backhouse; married Dick Wilson (a journalist and writer), September 8, 1962; children: Benjamin Garratt, Emma Maria. *Education:* St. Hugh's College, Oxford, B.A. (honors), 1948, M.A., 1955. *Politics:* Labour. *Religion:* Agnostic. *Home:* White Lodge, 67 Grove Lane, London S.E.5, England. *Agent:* H. Rubinstein, A. P. Watt & Son, Hastings House, 10 Norfolk St., Strand, London, W.C. 2, England.

CAREER: Teacher of English at High Storrs Grammar School, Sheffield, England, 1948-51, and Lady Margaret Church of England School, London, England, 1951-59; Aylwin Girls' Grammar School, London, England, head of English department, 1959-62; Lutheran World Organization, teacher in rooftop schools for refugees, Hong Kong, 1962-64; Independent Adoption Agency, volunteer case committee worker, 1974—. Teacher of modern literature, University of Sheffield, Extension, 1948-50; has also worked as shop assistant, governess, clerk, and farm hand. Camberwell Credit Union, president.

WRITINGS: Nine Dragons: An Encounter with the Far East, Hamish Hamilton, 1967; *Singapore,* Stackpole, 1972. Contributor to *Guardian, Orientations,* and *Times Literary Supplement.*

WORK IN PROGRESS: A thriller with a Far East background.

SIDELIGHTS: Ms. Backhouse has traveled in South Korea, Japan, India, Nepal, Thailand, Indonesia, East Africa, Europe, Communist China, and the United States, and lived in Singapore from 1969 to 1972. She is competent in French and Italian. *Avocational interests:* The theatre and grand opera.

* * *

BACKMAN, Melvin (Abraham)   1919-

PERSONAL: Born February 12, 1919, in Lynn, Mass.; son of David A. and Sophie (Berman) Backman; married Dorothy Weisman, December 23, 1946 (deceased); married Lisbeth-Anne Coverdale, July 27, 1971; children: (first marriage) Sherril, Maren (deceased). *Education:* Massachusetts State College at Bridgewater, B.S., 1941; Columbia University, M.A., 1947, Ph.D., 1960. *Home:* 11 Northfield Rd., Glen Cove, N.Y. 11542. *Office:* Department of English, C. W. Post Center, Long Island University, Greenvale, N.Y. 11548.

CAREER: Richmond Professional Institute, Richmond, Va., instructor in English, 1948-51; Clarkson College of Technology, Potsdam, N.Y., instructor, 1953-56, assistant professor, 1956-60, associate professor, 1960-62, professor of English and humanities, 1962-67; Long Island University, C. W. Post Center, Greenvale, N.Y., professor of English, 1967—, chairman of English department, 1973—. Professor of English, Columbia University, summers, 1967, 1968. *Military service:* U.S. Army Air Forces, 1943-46; served in China-Burma-India theater; became staff sergeant. *Member:* Modern Language Association of America, National Council of Teachers of English, American Association of University Professors, English Graduate Union (Columbia University). *Awards, honors:* Excellent teaching award, Clarkson College, 1963.

WRITINGS: Faulkner, The Major Years: A Critical Approach, Indiana University Press, 1966; (contributor) Carlos Baker, editor, *Hemingway and His Critics: An International Anthology,* Hill & Wang, 1961; (contributor) Roy B. Browne and Martin Light, editors, *Critical Approaches to American Literature,* Crowell, 1965; (contrib-

utor) T. D. Young and R. E. Fine, editors, *American Literature: A Critic's Survey,* American Book Co., 1968. Contributor to professional journals; regular reviewer for *Choice;* reader for *Papers on Language and Literature.*

WORK IN PROGRESS: Articles on Hemingway and Faulkner.

SIDELIGHTS: A French edition of *Faulkner, The Major Years* has been published by Minard (Paris); earlier critical pieces on Faulkner and Hemingway were translated and reprinted in *La Revue des Lettres Modernes* (Paris).

* * *

BAER, George Webster   1935-

PERSONAL: Born September 12, 1935, in Palo Alto, Calif.; son of George Albert and V. A. (Thornhill) Baer; married Martha Nagle, June 16, 1962 (divorced, 1975); children: Susan, Charles, Carolyn. *Education:* Stanford University, A.B., 1957; Oxford University, B.A. and M.A., 1959; Harvard University, Ph.D., 1965. *Office:* Stevenson College, University of California, Santa Cruz, Calif. 95060.

CAREER: Dartmouth College, Hanover, N.H., 1964-67, began as instructor, became assistant professor of history; Stevenson College, University of California, Santa Cruz, assistant professor, 1967-72, currently professor of history.

WRITINGS: The Coming of the Italian-Ethiopian War, Harvard University Press, 1967.

* * *

BAEZ, Joan   1941-

PERSONAL: Born January 9, 1941, in Staten Island, N.Y.; daughter of Albert V. (a physicist) and Joan (an English-Scottish drama teacher; maiden name, Bridge) Baez; married David Victor Harris, March, 1968 (divorced, 1973); children: Gabriel Earl. *Education:* Studied drama briefly at Boston University Fine Arts School, 1958. *Residence:* Carmel Valley, Calif. *Office:* c/o Chandos Productions, 934 Santa Cruz Ave., Menlo Park, Calif. 94025.

CAREER: Learned to play the guitar at age fourteen and sang in a high school choir, Palo Alto, Calif.; first performed in public, playing the guitar and singing folk ballads with other amateurs, at Club 47, a coffee house in Cambridge, Mass., 1958-60; performed regularly in coffee houses around Harvard Square, in Cambridge and Boston, Mass., 1958-60; appeared at The Gate of Horn, a folknightclub in Chicago, Ill., 1958, where she was noticed by Bob Gibson and invited to play at the Newport (R.I.) Folk Festival in the summer of 1959; performed again at the Newport Folk Festival in 1960; recorded first Vanguard Records album of folk music, "Joan Baez" ("highest selling individual female folk album in the history of long playing records"), in 1960; recordings for Vanguard Records, 1960-72; has toured colleges and concert halls around the country (first Carnegie Hall Concert, 1962), 1961—; began refusing payment of war taxes, 1964; concert tours, Europe, 1965, 1966, 1970, 1972, 1973, Japan, 1966, United States and Europe, 1967, 1968; extensive television appearances and speaking tours for anti-militarism, United States and Canada, 1967-68; arrested for civil disobedience opposing draft, October and December, 1967; recordings for A & M Records, 1972—. Founded the Institute for the Study of Nonviolence, Palo Alto, Calif., 1965, vice-president, 1965—.

WRITINGS: Daybreak (an autobiographical memoir), Dial, 1968; (with David V. Harris) *Coming Out,* Pocket Books, 1971.

SIDELIGHTS: "A folksinger of great renown, a pacifist of great conviction, and a dazzling celebrity," is Joan Baez. Chosen for *Time* magazine's cover as the indisputable "queen of the folksingers," unlike more conventional covergirl "superstars," she has also been in jail, and "lived on bread and milk for three days."

A "compelling rather than pretty" girl, she became in the early 1960's a prime mover and heroine of the folk movement that popularized old English love ballads and contemporary protest songs. Although she has been criticized by "purists" for her disregard of the origins of her songs, her concern for "how it sounds and the feeling in it" was enough for most people. She hypnotizes with a pure soprano voice (ranging over three octaves) and an unaffected style as well as the "understated passion" of her performance. Although she "hardly considers herself a singer at all," a *Time* magazine writer describes her singing voice as "a clear flow of sound. It is haunted and plaintive, a mother's voice, and it has in it distant reminders of black women wailing in the night, of detached madrigal singers performing calmly at court, and of saddened gypsies trying to charm death into leaving their Spanish caves." Jazz-writer Ralph Gleason attributes her sudden and tremendous appeal not so much to a lovely voice, as to the "utter reality, . . . the glowing humanity of her personality and remarkable gift for vocal communication."

Indeed, the impact of her individual style as a non-conformist who is dissatisfied with the way things are is as important as her singing talent. "What Joan was doing on stage was giving an extension of her own personality," according to Gleason, and this personality included letting her hair "hang long," wearing the simplest burlap shifts, and going barefoot on stage as the mood hit her. All of this was original and a new kind of honest directness for an on-stage singer, particularly in the early 60's. "At once innocent yet startlingly sophisticated, somewhat shy yet ready to do just what she damn well pleases," Simon Lazarus III, writes in *Cambridge 38,* she is appealing because she appears to scorn mere "show-business" success and its glamorous fringe benefits. With a Jaguar XKE as her only luxury, she at one time lived a simple life in remote Big Sur.

Almost without effort she became a famous and powerful image-maker for a huge student following (and became notoriously publicized as the "alienated and anti-establishment generation") who appreciated the idealism of her passions and the simple sincerity of her manner. She was the embodiment of their restlessness during the beginning of the decade. They idolized Joan Baez and made her rebellion their own.

Since then, the long hair, guitar, and supercasual dress have become a trite uniform for the young rebel. For the student activists of the end of the 60's who are increasingly relying on violence for their protests, she has no sympathy, and Margot Hentoff described her as "a nice girl whose songs and sensibilities are perhaps . . . irrelevant to the new turn of attitudes and events. . . ."

She has not stopped protesting, however; only her methods are unlike those of many youthful demonstrators, because, since her early protest days as a ban-the-bomb girl, she has always been opposed to violence. It has been said that "non-violence is the moving force in her life." She founded the Institute for the Study of Non-violence, with her good friend Ira Sandperl, because, she explains in *Daybreak,* "man organizes, buys, sells, pushes violence. The non-violenter wants to organize the opposite side. That's all

non-violence is—organized love." She admits, though, that "the only thing that's been a worse flop than the organization of non-violence has been the organization of violence," but she continues her "building . . . from the ground up, . . . experimenting with every possible alternative to violence on every level."

Her personal alternatives have included going to jail and refusing to pay "war" taxes to the U.S. Government. She served her jail term, as a disturber of the peace, after sitting-in for the cause of draft resistance at the Oakland (Calif.) Induction Center. After her refusal to pay her taxes, she was kicked off the stage at Constitution Hall by the Daughters of the American Revolution in Washington, D.C. (she sang instead in an open-air concert to an audience of thousands). Because of her vehement criticism of the war in Vietnam, her records have been banned in Army PX's all over the world. In a criticism of *Daybreak,* Robert Coles says Joan is "an example of how liberal pieties and banalities can exist side by side with obvious talent in a given person"; he calls *Daybreak* "a ridiculous failure of a book," and adds: "Joan Baez speaks in great earnest, and we have no reason to believe that her way of thinking is unusual in this nation."

In answer to her many critics H. S. Resnik says: "Super patriots will continue to see her as a threat, but *Daybreak* is a jewel of American folklore—it captures the America of our dreams."

Ms. Baez's mother told *CA:* "Her desire for human brotherhood in one world far surpasses her enjoyment of folk singing, and for that reason she felt progress for herself was made when she was dubbed lately a 'folksinging pacifist' rather than a 'pacifist folksinger'."

Recordings—All released by Vanguard Records, except as indicated: "Round Harvard Square," Veritas Recordings, 1959; "Joan Baez," 1960; "Joan Baez, Volume 2," 1961; "In Concert," 1962; "In Concert, Part 2," 1964; "5," 1964; "Farewell Angelina," 1965; "Noel," 1966; "Joan," 1967; "Baptism," 1968; "Any Day Now" (songs by Bob Dylan), 1969; (with Mimi and Richard Farina) "Memories," 1969; "David's Album," 1969; "Carry It On," 1970; "Best of Joan Baez," released by Squire; "One Day at a Time"; "Blessed Are . . ."; "The First Ten Years"; "The Ballad Book"; "Greatest Hits."

All released by A & M Records: "Come From the Shadows," 1972; "Where Are You Now, My Son?," 1973; "Gracias a La Vida," 1974; "Diamonds and Rust," 1975.

Other recordings include: "Sacco and Vanzetti" (film score); "Silent Running" (film score); "Celebration at Big Sur" (ODE Records). Contributor to "Folk Festival at Newport, 1959," Volume 2, Folk, 1961, "Newport Broadside," 1964, "Evening Concerts at Newport, 1963," Volume 1, 1964, "Newport, 1964," Volume 2, 1965.

Joan Baez and David Harris starred in the film "Carry It On," title song sung by Ms. Baez, New Film Company Production, 1970.

BIOGRAPHICAL/CRITICAL SOURCES: Cambridge 38, April, 1961; *Newsweek,* November 27, 1961, September 2, 1968, March 29, 1971, November 3, 1975; *Reporter,* January 4, 1962; *Show Business Illustrated,* January 23, 1962; *Time,* June 1, 1962, November 23, 1962, April 5, 1968, July 25, 1969, June 15, 1970; *Village Voice,* February 22, 1968, July 24, 1969, August 28, 1969; *Washington Post,* June 5, 1968; *Christian Century,* September 4, 1968; *Saturday Review,* September 7, 1968; *Book World,* September 8, 1968;

Joan Didion, *Slouching Toward Bethlehem,* Dell, 1968; *New York Times Book Review,* September 8, 1968; *New York Times,* September 18, 1968, January 26, 1969, June 18, 1972; *Nation,* September 23, 1968; *Christian Science Monitor,* October 3, 1968, September 9, 1969; *Atlantic,* October, 1968; *New York Review of Books,* November 7, 1968; *Detroit Free Press,* April 14, 1969; *New Yorker,* August 23, 1969.

* * *

BAHL, Roy W. (Jr.) 1939-

PERSONAL: Born June 28, 1939, in Miami, Fla.; son of Roy W. (a heavy equipment operator) and Vista (Becks) Bahl; married Marilyn Seifried, December 22, 1962. *Education:* Greenville College, A.B. (with honors), 1961; University of Kentucky, M.A., 1963, Ph.D., 1965. *Office:* The Maxwell School, Syracuse University, Syracuse, N.Y.

CAREER: University of Kentucky, Lexington, research associate. Bureau of Business Research, 1964-65; West Virginia University, Morgantown, assistant profssor of economics, 1965-67; Syracuse University, Syracuse, N.Y., postdoctoral fellow in urban economics, 1967-68; International Monetary Fund, Washington, D.C., economist in Fiscal Affairs Department, 1968-71; Syracuse University, professor of economics, 1971—. Member of senior staff, Committee for Economic Development intergovernmental fiscal relations project, 1965, 1967; consultant, World Bank, 1971—. *Member:* American Economic Association, National Tax Association, Regional Science Association, Southern Economic Association. *Awards, honors:* Resources for the Future postdoctoral fellowship, 1967-68.

WRITINGS: (With James W. Martin and Don M. Soule) *Budgetary Support for Kentucky Highways by System,* Bureau of Business Research, University of Kentucky, 1963; *A Bluegrass Leapfrog,* Bureau of Business Research, University of Kentucky, 1964; *A Primer on State and Local Government Finances in West Virginia,* Institute for Labor Studies, West Virginia University, 1967; (with Robert J. Saunders) *Intercounty Differences in West Virginia Government Expenditures,* Bureau of Business Research, West Virginia University, 1967; *West Virginia Local Government: Revenue Structure and Potential Reforms,* Office of Research and Development, West Virginia University Appalachian Center, 1968; *Metropolitan City Expenditures,* University Press of Kentucky, 1969; (with Alan Campbell and David Greytok) *Taxes, Expenditures and the Economic Base,* Praeger, 1975; (with Campbell) *Government Reform in the Seventies,* Free Press, 1975. Contributor to economics and finance journals.

* * *

BAHN, Eugene 1906-

PERSONAL: Born November 23, 1906, in Cape Girardeau, Mo.; son of William C. (a businessman) and Catherine (Kelly) Bahn; married Margaret E. Linton, September 12, 1939. *Education:* University of Wisconsin, B.A. (cum laude), 1929, M.A., 1930, Ph.D., 1935; postdoctoral study, Salzburg Mozarteum, 1935, Mansfield College, Oxford, 1971, St. Andrews University, 1975. *Religion:* Presbyterian. *Home:* 1386 Grayton, Grosse Pointe Park, Mich. 48230. *Office:* Wayne State University, Detroit, Mich. 48202.

CAREER: Instructor in speech at University of Iowa, Iowa City, 1932-34, and Colgate University, Hamilton, N.Y., 1934-37; Ohio State University, Columbus, assistant

professor of speech, 1937-43; American National Red Cross, official historian for Great Britain and western Europe, 1943-46; U.S. High Commission for Germany, Berlin, chief theater officer for U.S. zone and higher education adviser, 1946-52; Wayne State University, Detroit, Mich., professor of speech, 1952—. Dean, Anatolia College, Thessaloniki, Greece, 1959-60. Guest lecturer, University of Marburg; guest professor, Tohoku Gakuin University, Japan, 1973-74. *Member:* Speech Association of America, National Collegiate Players (national vice-president).

WRITINGS: (With Frances Ross) *Near-By Tales,* American Educational Press, 1939; (with Ross) *Faraway Tales,* American Educational Press, 1939; (editor) *Yanks in Britain* (anthology of American soldier verse), London Daily Mail, 1945; (with Keith Brooks and L. LaMont Okey) *The Communicative Act of Oral Interpretation,* Allyn & Bacon, 1967, 2nd edition, 1975; (contributor) Keith Brooks, editor, *The Communicative Arts and Sciences of Speech,* C. E. Merrill, 1967; (editor with Brooks and Okey) *Literature for Listening,* Allyn & Bacon, 1968; (with wife, Margaret Linton Bahn) *History of the Oral Interpretation of Literature,* Burgess, 1970; (contributor with John Cambus) Fred Casmir, editor, *International Speech Education,* Speech Association of America, 1970. Contributor to *Players, Die Buehne, Journal of the English Institute,* and other speech and theater journals.

SIDELIGHTS: Bahn is competent in German, Spanish, and French.

* * *

BAILEY, Harry A(ugustine), Jr. 1932-

PERSONAL: Born December 19, 1932, in Fort Pierce, Fla.; son of Harry Augustine (a salesman) and Ruth (Finlayson) Bailey; married Mary L. Howard, August 8, 1952; children: Harry III, Larry Berisford. *Education:* Florida Agricultural and Mechanical University, B.A., 1954; University of Kansas, M.A., 1960, Ph.D., 1964. *Politics:* Democrat. *Religion:* Episcopalian. *Home:* 11960 Dumont Rd., Philadelphia, Pa. 19116. *Office:* Department of Political Science, Temple University, Philadelphia, Pa. 19122.

CAREER: University of Kansas, Lawrence, assistant instructor in political science and western civilization, 1960-64, instructor in sociology, summer, 1964; Temple University, Philadelphia, Pa., assistant professor, 1964-68, associate professor, 1968-70, professor of political science, 1970—, chairman of department, 1968-73. Consultant-lecturer, Philadelphia Antipoverty Action Committee, 1965-66. *Military service:* U.S. Army, 1954-57; became first lieutenant. U.S. Army Reserve, 1957-65; became captain. *Member:* American Political Science Association, American Society for Public Administration, American Association of University Professors, Pi Sigma Alpha.

WRITINGS: (Editor) *Negro Politics in America,* C. E. Merrill, 1967; (editor with Ellis Katz) *Ethnic Group Politics,* C. E. Merrill, 1969. Contributor to *Public Utilities Fortnightly, Urban Affairs Quarterly, Your Government, Administrative Law Review, Publius, Illinois Quarterly,* and *Temple Alumni Review.*

AVOCATIONAL INTERESTS: Poverty problems.

* * *

BAILEY, Joan H(auser) 1922-

PERSONAL: Born December 4, 1922, in Bicknell, Ind.; daughter of Glen Norman (in insurance) and Bess (Berry)

Hauser; married E. Aubrey Bailey, Jr. (a research physical chemist), August 15, 1953. *Education:* Lake Forest College, student, 1939-40; Indiana University Extension, student, 1944-46; University of California, Los Angeles, B.A., 1956, M.A., 1959, Ph.D., 1970. *Politics:* Independent. *Home:* 10296 Kenny Lane, San Jose, Calif. 95127. *Office:* Psychology Department, San Jose State University, San Jose, Calif. 95192.

CAREER: Held clerical, accounting, and secretarial positions, 1941-55; Long Beach State College (now California State University, Long Beach), assistant professor of psychology, 1962-63; San Jose State University, San Jose, Calif., assistant professor, 1963-70, associate professor of psychology, 1971—. *Member:* American Psychological Association, Psychometric Society, American Statistical Association, National Council on Measurement in Education, Institute of Electrical and Electronics Engineers, American Association for the Advancement of Science, Western Psychological Association, California Educational Research Association, Psi Chi, Sigma Xi.

WRITINGS: (With John Jung) *Contemporary Psychology Experiments: Adaptations for Laboratory,* Wiley, 1966, 2nd edition, 1976. Contributor to professional journals.

WORK IN PROGRESS: Transitivity in young children.

AVOCATIONAL INTERESTS: History, especially history of science; cultural anthropology, philosophy of science, logic; rock-collecting and lapidary work; fishing, hiking, camping, back-packing, natural science observation.

*   *   *

BAILEY, Kenneth K(yle)   1923-

PERSONAL: Born December 3, 1923, in Coldwater, Miss.; married Mary Lou Crain, August 11, 1961. *Education:* Vanderbilt University, B.A., 1947, M.A., 1948, Ph.D., 1953. *Politics:* Democrat. *Religion:* Presbyterian. *Office:* Department of History, University of Texas at El Paso, El Paso, Tex. 79968.

CAREER: Cumberland College, Williamsburg, Ky., instructor in social science, 1949-50; New Mexico Military Institute, Roswell, instructor, 1952-53, assistant professor of history, 1953-55; Indiana University, Bloomington, instructor in history, 1955-56; assistant professor of history at Texas Western College (now University of Texas at El Paso), 1956-57, North Texas State University, Denton, 1957-58, and Louisiana State University, Baton Route, 1958-60; University of Texas at El Paso, 1960—, began as associate professor, became professor of history. *Military service:* U.S. Army, 1942-45; became sergeant. *Member:* American Historical Association, Organization of American Historians, Southern Historical Association. *Awards, honors:* Grants-in-aid from Social Science Research Council, 1955, and Louisiana State University Council for Research, 1959; Guggenheim fellowship, 1966-67.

WRITINGS: Southern White Protestantism in the Twentieth Century, Harper, 1964. Contributor to *American Historical Review* and *Journal of Southern History.*

WORK IN PROGRESS: Southern White Protestantism in the Nineteenth Century.

*   *   *

BAILEY, Norman A(lishan)   1931-

PERSONAL: Born May 22, 1931, in Chicago, Ill.; son of Percival (a surgeon) and Yevnige (Bashian) Bailey; married

Lorraine Baillargeon, September 9, 1961; married second wife, Suzin Robbins, July 8, 1966. *Education:* Oberlin College, A.B., 1953; Columbia University, M.I.A., 1955, Ph.D., 1962. *Politics:* Republican. *Religion:* Bahai. *Home:* 149 Wellington Rd., Garden City, N.Y. 11530. *Office:* Queens College of the City University of New York, Flushing, N.Y. 11367.

CAREER: With Queens College of the City University of New York, Flushing, N.Y., 1962—. Associated with Bailey, Tondu, Warwick & Co., Inc., New York, 1967—. *Military service:* U.S. Army, 1956-58. *Member:* Public Choice Society.

WRITINGS: (Editor) *Latin America,* Praeger, 1965; *Latin America in World Politics,* Walker & Co., 1967. Also co-author of *Portuguese Africa,* 1969, and *Operational Conflict Analysis,* 1973. Author of plays; contributor of articles and short stories to periodicals.

WORK IN PROGRESS: Text on politics.

SIDELIGHTS: Bailey speaks Spanish, French, Portuguese, and Italian. *Avocational interests:* Tennis, travel.

*   *   *

BAILEY, Paul   1937-

PERSONAL: Born February 16, 1937, in Battersea, London, England; son of Arthur Oswald and Helen (Burgess) Bailey. *Education:* Studied at Central School of Speech and Drama, London, 1953-56. *Politics:* Socialist. *Religion:* Agnostic. *Home:* 32 St. Stephen's Garden, London W. 2, England. *Agent:* David Machin, A. P. Watt & Son, 26-28 Bedford Row, London, WC1R 4HL, England.

CAREER: Has been an actor on television and in the theatre (repertory at Stratford and Royal Court); left a job "selling at a large Knightsbridge store" to become a full-time writer. *Awards, honors:* Arts Council of Great Britain Award, for the best novel published between 1965-67, and Somerset Maugham Travel Award, both 1968, for *At the Jerusalem.*

WRITINGS: At the Jerusalem (novel), Atheneum, 1967; *Trespasses* (novel), Harper, 1970; *A Distant Likeness,* J. Cape, 1973. Also author of four plays. Contributor to *New Statesman, Listener, Observer, London Magazine, Sunday Times, Daily Telegraph.*

WORK IN PROGRESS: A play; a filmscript for *At the Jerusalem.*

SIDELIGHTS: "Probably the most original, and certainly the most accomplished, first novel of the year," says Alan Ross in a 1967 review of *At the Jerusalem.* The "Jerusalem" is the old peoples' home to which "Mrs. Gadny" is forced to retire. Her struggle and eventual failure to adjust to the loneliness of institutional life is the subject of Bailey's cool examination. His study of the misery of growing old is convincing, as Ross said, in "giving alienation a fresh context." According to Peter Buckman, he "brings on a glut of guilt for the generation gap, without any catharsis." Miles Burrows said: "Everything in this book rings true. . . . Mr. Bailey's social comment is precise and made with an enviably light touch while never failing to be serious." Indeed, he is comic and compassionate at the same time. Writing almost entirely in dialogue, he achieves, said Ross, "a series of portraits remarkable for their insight and tenderness." His novel builds in dramatic intensity through "his economic and elliptical use of conve·sation to suggest non-communication. . . . Bailey achieves a natural, individual style without, as yet, any of the disfigurements of a mannerism." He has written a "pitilessly good novel," concludes Buckman.

Times Literary Supplement reviewer writes that in *Trespasses* "the principal strength lies in the way [Bailey] causes a small world to radiate wider and graver implications: *Trespasses,* again, is brief and self-denyingly economical; yet it manages to encompass, in a hauntingly perceptive and compassionate way, a large range of attitudes and situations. Its theme is estrangement: the subtly inevitable processes by which parents and children, men and women, draw tragically and uncomprehendingly apart from one another ... Mr. Bailey's avoidance of gimmickry or pretentiousness in his very original experimental technique, his fine, trenchant way with an old friend, the sensitive young hero, his mature skill with dialogue, and his unerring social sense, enable him to write a novel that both moves and excites."

Paul Bailey told *CA:* "I admire Chekhov, Svevo, and Henry Green inordinately. I get more inspiration to work from paintings than from books: from Rembrandt, Masaccio, Piero della Francesca, Giotto, etc." He also says, "I'm fond of my anonymity."

AVOCATIONAL INTERESTS: Music, literature, and tennis.

BIOGRAPHICAL/CRITICAL SOURCES: New York Times Book Review, May 21, 1967; *New Statesman,* June 2, 1967; *Times Literary Supplement,* June 8, 1967, April 16, 1970; *Punch,* July 5, 1967; *Listener,* July 6, 1967; *Books and Bookmen,* August, 1967; *London Magazine,* October, 1967.†

*   *   *

BAINBRIDGE, Beryl 1933-

PERSONAL: Born November 21, 1933, in Liverpool, England; daughter of Richard (a salesman) and Winifred (Baines) Bainbridge; married Austin Davies (an artist), April 24, 1954 (divorced); children: Aaron Paul, Johanna Harriet, Ruth Emmanuella. *Education:* Attended Merchant Taylor's School, Great Crosby, England. *Politics:* Socialist. *Religion:* "Lapsed Catholic." *Home:* 42 Albert St., Camden Town, London, England.

CAREER: Actress in England before marriage, appearing at Liverpool Playhouse, West End theaters, and with repertory companies in Salisbury and Windsor; also did some television work, and wrote and read stories for a children's radio program in Manchester.

WRITINGS: A Weekend with Claud (novel), Hutchinson, 1967; *Another Part of the World* (novel), Hutchinson, 1968; *Harriet Said,* Duckworth, 1972, Braziller, 1973; *The Dressmaker,* Duckworth, 1973, published as *The Secret Glass,* Braziller, 1973; *The Bottle Factory Outing,* Braziller, 1974; *Sweet William,* Braziller, 1975. Author of radio play, and articles in general magazines and children's periodicals.

SIDELIGHTS: Beryl Bainbridge told *CA:* "[I] write to work out [my] own personal obsessions. [I] believe writing, like old photographs, gives a record by which past experiences can be remembered."

AVOCATIONAL INTERESTS: Painting (the primitives she has done include fictional characters of her books).

BIOGRAPHICAL/CRITICAL SOURCES: Carolyn Riley, editor, *Contemporary Literary Criticism,* Gale, Volume IV, 1975, Volume V, 1976.

BAKAL, Carl 1918-

PERSONAL: Born January 11, 1918, in New York, N.Y.; son of William (a salesman) and Esther (Tutelman) Bakal; married Shirley Sesser (a concert pianist), December 4, 1956; children: Stephanie, Emily, Amy and Wendy (twins). *Education:* City College (now City College of the City University of New York), B.S., 1939; Columbia University, graduate study, 1949. *Home and office:* 225 West 86th St., New York, N.Y., 10024. *Agent:* Julian Bach, Jr., 3 East 48th St., New York, N.Y. 10017.

CAREER: Fotoshop, New York City, advertising manager and editor of *Fotoshop Almanac,* 1939-41; *U.S. Camera,* New York City, associate and contributing editor, 1939-43; Universal Camera Corporation, New York City, sales promotion manager, 1941-43; editorial chief of information control division with military government in Germany, 1947-48; *New York Mirror,* New York City, promotion writer, 1948-50; *Coronet* (magazine), New York City, associate editor, 1950-55; free-lance writer and photo-journalist, 1955-57, 1958—; *Real* and *See* (magazines), New York City, editor, 1957-58; U.S. Department of Commerce, public affairs consultant, 1961-62; Howard Chase Associates, New York City, senior associate, 1962-65; Carl Byoir & Associates, New York City, management department director, 1966-68; Anna M. Rosenberg & Associates, New York City, accountant supervisor, 1968—. Photojournalism columnist for *Writer's Digest.* Guest lecturer in photo-journalism, University of Wisconsin, 1953. *Military service:* U.S. Army, Signal Corps, 1943-46, 1951-52; became first lieutenant. *Member:* Society of Magazine Writers (vice-president, 1968), P.E.N., Violincello Society. *Awards, honors:* Society of Magazine Writers research grant; first prize ($25,000) in *Popular Photography* International Picture Contest, 1956.

WRITINGS: Filter Manual, Camera Craft, 1951; *How to Shoot for Glamour,* A. S. Barnes, 1955; *The Right to Bear Arms,* McGraw, 1966, revised paperback edition published as *No Right to Bear Arms,* Warner Paperback, 1968. Contributor to *Encyclopedia Photography,* 1942, and *Treasury of Tips for Writers,* 1965. Contributor of articles and photographs to *Harper's, McCall's, Esquire, Reader's Digest, Saturday Review,* and many other national magazines.

WORK IN PROGRESS: A book on charities for McKay.

*   *   *

BAKAN, Paul 1928-

PERSONAL: Born November 1, 1928, in Brooklyn, N.Y.; son of Max and Rose (Rosenstrauch) Bakan; married Rita Feierstein (a psychologist), September 3, 1950; children: Laura N., Joel C., Michael B. *Education:* New York University, B.A., 1949, M.A., 1950, Ph.D., 1954. *Office:* Psychology Department, Simon Fraser University, Burnaby, British Columbia, Canada.

CAREER: University of Illinois, Urbana, research associate, 1952-53; Michigan State University, East Lansing, instructor, 1953-55, assistant professor, 1955-59, associate professor, 1959-63, professor of psychology, 1963-70; Simon Frazer University, Burnaby, British Columbia, professor of psychology, 1969—. Visiting scientist, Cambridge University, 1961-62. *Member:* American Psychological Association, American Association for the Advancement of Science, Psychonomic Society, Experimental Psychology Society (England), Western Psychological Association. *Awards, honors:* National Science Foundation fellow, 1956-57; Thomas Welton Stanford fellowship, 1968-69.

WRITINGS: (Editor) *Attention,* Van Nostrand, 1966.

* * *

BAKER, Donald N(oel) 1936-

PERSONAL: Born December 24, 1936, in Vancouver, British Columbia, Canada; son of Jack Sidney (a plumber) and Joyce (Heap) Baker; married Marlene Joan Fletcher, July 5, 1958 (divorced, 1975); married Heather Dianne McLeod, July 12, 1975; children: (first marriage) Janet, Noel, Carol. *Education:* University of British Columbia, B.A. (honors in history), 1958; Stanford University, A.M., 1960, Ph.D., 1965. *Office:* Department of History, University of Waterloo, Waterloo, Ontario, Canada N2L 3G1.

CAREER: Stanford University, Stanford, Calif., instructor in history, 1962-65; Michigan State University, East Lansing, assistant professor, 1965-69, associate professor of history, 1969-70; University of Waterloo, Waterloo, Ontario, associate professor of history, 1970—, chairman of department, 1972-73. Trustee, Waterloo County Board of Education, 1973-74. *Member:* American Historical Association, Canadian Historical Association, Societe d'Histoire Moderne et Contemporaine, Society for French Historical Studies. *Awards, honors:* National Foundation for the Endowment of Humanities fellowship for research in France, 1967-68.

WRITINGS: (Editor with George W. Fasel) *Landmarks in Western Culture: Commentaries and Controversies,* Prentice-Hall, 1968. Contributor to *Journal of Modern History* and *Historical Reflections.*

WORK IN PROGRESS: Further research in modern French socialist and labor history.

SIDELIGHTS: Baker speaks and reads French; reads German.

* * *

BAKER, Gary G. 1939-

PERSONAL: Born February 18, 1939, in Keene, N.H.; son of Gordon Ellsworth (a salesman) and Hazel (Blair) Baker; married Barbara Herrick, September 16, 1961; children: Karen Sorine, Amy Suzanne. *Education:* University of New Hampshire, B.A., 1961; Harvard University, M.A.T., 1962. *Religion:* Protestant.

CAREER: High school teacher of history, Hamilton, Mass., 1962-66; Committee on the Study of History, Chicago, Ill., and Amherst, Mass., associate director, beginning 1966. Consultant on Experienced Teacher Fellowship Program, U.S. Office of Education. *Member:* American Historical Association, National Education Association, National Council for the Social Studies, New England History Teachers Association, Massachusetts Teachers Association, Chicago Council for the Social Studies (member of board of directors).

WRITINGS: Andrew Johnson and the Struggle for Presidential Reconstruction, 1865-1868, Heath, 1965; *Communism in America: Liberty and Security in Conflict,* with teacher's manual, Addison-Wesley, 1970. Contributor to *Independent Schools Journal.*

WORK IN PROGRESS: Minorities and Prejudice in America, in collaboration with Frank Kane.†

* * *

BAKER, George W(alter) 1915-

PERSONAL: Born June 15, 1915, in Seaford, Del.; son of E. Walter (a farmer) and Mary (Hill) Baker; married Louise Krock, May 29, 1958; children: Mary Louise. *Education:* University of Delaware, A.B., 1939; University of North Carolina, M.A., 1947, Ph.D., 1952. *Politics:* Democrat. *Religion:* Unitarian Universalist. *Home:* 7502 Nevis Rd., Bethesda, Md. 20034. *Office:* National Science Foundation, 1800 G St., Washington, D.C. 20550.

CAREER: High school teacher in Delaware, 1939-42, 1946; Human Resources Research Institute, Maxwell Air Force Base, Ala., project officer, Human Relations Division, 1951-53, program officer, 1953-54; Air Force Personnel and Training Research Center, Lackland Air Force Base, Tex., senior task scientist, Office for Social Science Programs, 1954-57; Special Operations Research Office, American University, Washington, D.C., team chairman, 1957-59; National Academy of Sciences-National Research Council, technical director of Disaster Research Group, 1959-63; National Science Foundation, Washington, D.C., staff associate, 1963—, program director for behavioral sciences in science facilities evaluation group, Division of Institutional Programs, 1964—, associate in university science development, 1965—, program manager of Research Applied to National Needs program, 1971—. *Military service:* U.S. Army, 1942-46; military government officer during Okinawa campaign; became first lieutenant.

MEMBER: American Academy of Political and Social Science, American Anthropological Association (fellow), American Association for the Advancement of Science (fellow), American Sociological Association (fellow), Society for Applied Anthropology (fellow), District of Columbia Sociological Society, Alpha Kappa Delta, Phi Kappa Phi, Cosmos Club (Washington, D.C.). *Awards, honors:* Army commendations for military research, 1953, 1955.

WRITINGS: (Editor with John H. Rohrer) *Symposium on Human Problems in the Utilization of Fallout Shelters,* National Academy of Sciences-National Research Council, 1960; (with Raymond W. Mack) *The Occasion Instant: The Structure of Social Responses to Unanticipated Air Raid Warnings,* National Academy of Sciences-National Research Council, 1961; (editor with Leonard S. Cottrell, Jr.) *Behavioral Science and Civil Defense,* National Academy of Sciences-National Research Council, 1962; (editor with Dwight W. Chapman) *Man and Society in Disaster,* Basic Books, 1962; (contributor) George H. Grosser, Henry Wechsler, and Milton Greenblatt, editors, *The Threat of Impending Disaster: Contributions to the Psychology of Stress,* M.I.T. Press, 1964; (contributor) M. H. Appley and Richard Trumbull, editors, *Psychological Stress,* Appleton, 1967. Author of prefaces to several other National Academy of Sciences-National Research Council publications on disaster studies, and of various reports on military research. Contributor of articles and reviews to journals.

* * *

BAKER, Leonard 1931-

PERSONAL: Born January 24, 1931, in Pittsburgh, Pa.; married Liva Baker (a writer), August 1, 1958; children: David, Sara. *Education:* University of Pittsburgh, B.A., 1952; Columbia University, M.S., 1955. *Home:* 606 Fourth Pl. S.W., Washington, D.C. 20024.

CAREER: Globe-Democrat, St. Louis, Mo., reporter, 1955-56; *Newsday,* Long Island, N.Y., reporter and Washington correspondent, 1956-65; free-lance writer, 1965—.

WRITINGS—All published by Macmillan, except as

noted: *The Johnson Eclipse: A President's Vice Presidency,* 1966; *Back to Back: The Duel Between FDR and the Supreme Court,* 1967; *The Guaranteed Society,* 1968; *Roosevelt and Pearl Harbor,* 1970; *Brahmin In Revolt: A Biography of Herbert C. Pell,* Doubleday, 1972; *John Marshall: A Life in Law,* 1974. Contributor to national magazines.

* * *

BAKER, Peter (Gorton)   1928-

PERSONAL: Born March 28, 1928, in Eastbourne, Sussex, England. *Education:* Educated at Roborough College. *Politics:* Apolitical. *Religion:* Agnostic. *Agent:* Hilary Rubenstein, A. P. Watt and Son, 26/28 Bedford Row, London WC1R 4HL, England.

CAREER: Sometime reporter and feature writer for *Kinematograph Weekly,* and for several years a free-lance journalist and broadcaster, specializing in serious cinema; Hansom Books Ltd., London, England, editor of *Films and Filming* (monthly magazine), 1955-68. British representative on a number of international film festival juries, including Venice Film Festival. *Member:* British Screenwriters Guild, National Union of Journalists, Arts Theatre Club (London).

WRITINGS—Novels: *To Win a Prize on Sunday,* Souvenir Press, 1966; *Cruise,* Souvenir Press, 1967, Putnam, 1968; *Casino,* Souvenir Press, 1968; *The Antibodies,* Putnam, 1969; *Minnie Swan,* Hodder & Stoughton, 1969, published as *A Killing Affair,* Houghton, 1971; *The Bedroom Sailors,* Cassell, 1971; *Babel Beach,* Cassell, 1972.

Television plays: "The Offence"; "No Feet for Friday"; "Little Girl Blue"; "Tripp's Last Balance."

SIDELIGHTS: While editor of *Films and Filming,* Baker "travelled to film production centers in the Soviet Union, Czechoslovakia, Scandinavia, France, Spain, Italy, Argentina, and Brazil"; he has also travelled to the United States, Israel, Lebanon, Greece, and Mexico. *Avocational interests:* Music, Wagner in particular.†

* * *

BAKER, Wesley C.

PERSONAL: Born in Seattle, Wash.; son of William C. (an accountant) and Evelyn (Cooney) Baker; married Delma Allgood, February 25, 1945; children: Rebecca, Ernest, Timothy. *Education:* Arizona State University, B.A., 1943; San Francisco Theological Seminary, B.D., 1946. *Politics:* Democrat ("active"). *Home:* 302 Radnor St. Rd., Wayne, Pa. 19087. *Agent:* Roland Tapp, 125 East Lancaster Ave., Wayne, Pa. 19087. *Office:* 125 East Lancaster Ave., Wayne, Pa. 19087.

CAREER: Clergyman of United Presbyterian Church, 1946—. Pastor in Redmond, Ore., 1946-50, Norwalk, Calif., 1950-55, Sunland, Calif., 1955-60, and San Rafael, Calif., 1960-67; United Presbyterian Church, Commission on Ecumenical Mission and Relations, New York, N.Y., consultant secretary for ecumenical relations, 1967-72; Wayne Presbyterian Church, Wayne, Pa., pastor, 1972—. Visiting lecturer, San Francisco Theological Seminary, 1961-67. Presbytery of Los Angeles, director of refugee resettlement, 1956-60.

WRITINGS—All published by Westminster: *The Split-Level Fellowship,* 1965; *More Than A Man Can Take,* 1966; *The Open End of Christian Morals,* 1967; *Believer in Hell,* 1968.

WORK IN PROGRESS: A novel, *Minister in Reverse.*

* * *

BAKER, William E(dwin)   1935-

PERSONAL: Born May 10, 1935, in Council, Idaho; son of E. Waldo and Bessie (Savage) Baker; married Patricia Cooper (a zoologist), December 21, 1961; children: Willa Blythe. *Education:* University of Washington, Seattle, B.A., 1956; Sorbonne, University of Paris, Certificat de la Langue, 1958; University of Hawaii, M.A., 1960; University of California, Berkeley, Ph.D., 1964. *Office:* Department of English, University of California, Davis, Calif. 95616.

CAREER: Reed College, Portland, Ore., assistant professor of English literature, 1964-68; currently English department faculty member, University of California, Davis.

WRITINGS: Jacques Prevert, Twayne, 1967; *Syntax in English Poetry, 1870-1930,* University of California Press, 1967; (editor) *Critics on George Eliot,* Allen & Unwin, 1973.

WORK IN PROGRESS: "The Milkman," a puppet play for adults; a book on literature and war; a play for puppets or mime-style actors.

SIDELIGHTS: William Baker is competent in French, German, Spanish, and Persian. *Avocational interests:* "Mexico, poker, carpentry."†

* * *

BALCOMB, Raymond E.   1923-

PERSONAL: Born February 8, 1923, in San Bernardino, Calif.; son of J. B. (an engineer) and Rose Balcomb; married Hazel Schlosser (a teacher), June 18, 1944; children: Bernice, Rosemary, Gene, Scott. *Education:* San Jose State College (now San Jose State University), A.B. (with distinction), 1944; Boston University, S.T.B. (magna cum laude), 1947, Ph.D., 1951. *Politics:* Independent. *Home:* 124 Northwest Hermosa Blvd., Portland, Ore. 97210.

CAREER: Methodist minister in Holbrook, Mass., 1945-49, Ashland, Mass., 1949-51, Portland, Ore., 1951-54, Medford, Ore., 1954-57, Corvallis, Ore., 1957-63; First Methodist Church, Portland, Ore., minister, 1963—. Conducted preaching missions in Alaska, 1954, 1961, and Hawaii, 1956. Chairman of Board of Ministerial Training and Qualifications, Oregon Conference, The Methodist Church. *Member:* American Civil Liberties Union (chairman of Oregon executive board, 1964-66), City Club (Portland). *Awards, honors:* Distinguished alumnus award, Boston University School of Theology, 1966.

WRITINGS: Stir What You've Got!, Abingdon, 1968; *Try Reading the Bible This Way,* Westminster, 1971. Contributor to other books and religious magazines.

* * *

BALIGH, Helmy H.   1931-

PERSONAL: Born October 17, 1931, in Cairo, Egypt; son of Hamdollah and Aziza (Tewfik) Baligh; married Sara Jane Walker, September, 1959; children: Aziza Leslie, Magda Giffen, Laila Anne. *Education:* Oxford University, B.A. (honors), 1954; University of California, Berkeley, Ph.D., 1963. *Home:* 1909 Rolling Rd., Chapel Hill, N.C.

CAREER: University of Illinois, Urbana, began as assistant professor, became associate professor of business administration, 1962-67; Duke University, Durham, N.C., associate professor, 1967-71, professor of business administration, 1971—.

WRITINGS: (With L. E. Richartz) *Vertical Market Structures*, Allyn & Bacon, 1967; (contributor) Bruce E. Mallen, *The Marketing Channel*, Wiley, 1967. Contributor to *Management Science, Journal of Marketing Research, Transportation Science*, and *Health Services Research*.

* * *

BALINKY, Alexander 1919-

PERSONAL: Born October 24, 1919, in Russia; son of Jacob and Esther (Schwartz) Balinky; married Jean Lahn (a school psychologist), March 29, 1951. *Education:* University of California, Los Angeles, B.A., 1940; Harvard University, M.A., 1947, Ph.D., 1953. *Politics:* Democrat. *Religion:* Jewish. *Address:* Box 777, Martinsville, N.J. *Office:* Department of Economics, Rutgers University, New Brunswick, N.J. 08903.

CAREER: Rutgers University, New Brunswick, N.J., 1947—, started as assistant professor, professor of economics, 1961—, director of Soviet and East European Program, 1967. *Member:* Association for the Study of Soviet-Type Economics, Comparative Economic Systems Association.

WRITINGS: *Albert Gallatin: Fiscal Theories and Policies*, Rutgers University Press, 1953; (with Abram Bergson, John Hazard, and Peter Wiles) *Planning and the Market in the USSR: The 1960's*, Rutgers University Press, 1967; *Marx's Economics: Origin and Development*, Heath, 1970. Contributor to *William and Mary Quarterly*, and to economics journals.

WORK IN PROGRESS: *Transition to Communism.*

* * *

BAN, Joseph D(aniel) 1926-

PERSONAL: Born April 12, 1926, in Homestead, Pa.; son of Joseph (a building contractor) and Suzannah (Petrusan) Ban; married Arline June Chapman (a writer for children), March 31, 1951. *Education:* University of Pittsburgh, B.S. in C.E., 1950; Colgate Rochester Divinity School, B.D., 1953; graduate study at University of Rochester, 1951, and Union Theological Seminary, New York, N.Y., 1956-58; University of Oregon, Ph.D., 1974. *Office:* Linfield College, McMinnville, Ore. 97129.

CAREER: Baptist clergyman. Associate pastor in Rochester, N.Y., 1950-53, and Dayton, Ohio, 1953-56; pastor in New Brunswick, N.J., 1956-58; American Baptist Home Mission Societies, New York, N.Y., and Valley Forge, Pa., program associate in Division of Evangelism, 1958-64; Pennsylvania State University, University Park, executive director of University Christian Association, 1964-66, campus minister, 1967; Linfield College, McMinnville, Ore., chaplain, 1967-73, associate professor of religious studies and history, 1967—. *Member:* American Academy of Religion, American Baptist Historical Society, American Association of University Professors. *Awards, honors: Education for Change* named American Baptist "Best Book of the Year," 1968.

WRITINGS: (Contributor) *The Church's Educational Ministry: A Curriculum Plan*, Bethany Press, 1965; *Education for Change*, Judson, 1968; (contributor) Charles L. Wallis, editor, *The Minister's Manual for 1970*, Harper, 1969; *Facing Today's Demands*, Judson, 1970; (contributor and consulting editor) "Makers of Modern Thought" series, Judson, 1972; *Jesus Confronts Life's Issues*, Judson, 1972.

With wife, Arline J. Ban: *Jesus Makes the Difference*, Judson, 1966; *God's Gift of Life*, Christian Board of Publication, 1969; *As Wide as the World*, Judson, 1971; *The New Disciple*, Judson, 1975.

Author of Baptist manuals and booklets, one in Spanish; contributor of more than one hundred articles, book reviews, and sermons to religious periodicals.

WORK IN PROGRESS: *Prophets or Priests?* (tentative title) for Judson; rewriting Ph.D. dissertation for possible publication entitled "Holocaust: The Response of the Religious Press in the Pacific Northwest to the Anti-Semitic Policies of the Third Reich."

* * *

BAN, Thomas A. 1929-

PERSONAL: Born November 16, 1929, in Budapest, Hungary; became Canadian citizen, March 1, 1962; son of Geza and Elisabeth (Rona) Ban; married Joan Evelyn Valley, November 21, 1963; children: Christopher Valley. *Education:* University of Budapest, M.D., 1954; McGill University, Diploma in Psychiatry (with distinction), 1960; Royal College of Physicians and Surgeons of Canada, fellow, 1972. *Religion:* Lutheran. *Home:* 17 Stratford Rd., Montreal, Quebec, Canada.

CAREER: Licensed to practice medicine, Canadian Medical Council, 1959; certification in psychiatry by Royal College of Physicians and Surgeons of Canada and Royal College of Physicians and Surgeons of the Province of Quebec, 1962. McGill University, Montreal, Quebec, demonstrator, 1960-63, lecturer, 1964-65, assistant professor, 1965-70, associate professor of psychiatry, 1970—, Division of Psychopharmacology of department of psychiatry, director, 1970—, and director of World Health Organization Training Program in Biological Psychiatry, 1972—. Douglas Hospital, Verdun, Quebec, senior research psychiatrist, 1961-66, associate director of research, 1966-70, chief of research services, 1970-72. Head of National Reference Center, World Health Organization International Reference Center Network for the Study of Psychotropic Drugs, 1969—. Psychiatric research consultant, Hospital des Laurentides, 1963-72, Lakeshore General Hospital, Pointe Claire, Montreal, Quebec, 1967—; consulting member of department of psychiatry at St. Mary's Hospital, Montreal, 1971—, and at Reddy Memorial Hospital, Montreal, 1972—; consulting staff member in psychiatry, Queen Elizabeth Hospital of Montreal, Montreal, 1973—.

MEMBER: Collegium Internationale Neuro-Psychopharmacologicum (vice-president), Collegium Internationale Activitatis Nervosae Superiorae (secretary-treasurer), International Brain Research Organization, International College of Psychosomatic Medicine (founding member), Societe Royale de Medecine Mentale de Belgique (honorary member), American College of Neuro-Psychopharmacology (fellow; chairman, Constitution and Rules Committee), American Society for the Advancement of Science, American Psychopathological Association, American Psychiatric Association (fellow; Task Force member on Megavitamin Therapy, 1970-73; member of Quebec chapter), American Pharmaceutical Association (scientific review panel member), Association for the Advancement of Behavior Therapies, Canadian Psychiatric Association, Canadian Medical Association, Canadian Society of Chemotherapy (charter member), Pavlovian Society of America, Psychophamacological Society of Argentina (foreign correspondent), Argentine Association of Biological Psychiatry (honorary member), Quebec Psychophamacological Research Association (executive secretary). *Awards, honors:* Honorable mention, Quebec Literary and Scientific Competition, 1965, for *Conditioning and Psychiatry;* McNeil Award, Canadian Psychiatric Association, 1969, for "Study of Psychopathological Mechanisms and Psychopharmacological Effects," 1970, for *Nicotinic Acid in the Treatment of Schizophrenias* (first report), and 1973, for *Nicotinic Acid in the Treatment of Schizophrenias* (second report); Clarke Institute of Psychiatry Annual Research Fund Award, 1970, for *Psychopharmacology;* Young Scientist Award, Semmelweis Scientific Society, 1975.

WRITINGS: Conditioning and Psychiatry, Aldine, 1964; *Psychopharmacology,* Williams & Wilkins, 1969; (with H. E. Lehmann) *Nicotinic Acid in the Treatment of Schizophrenias* (three reports), Canadian Mental Health Association, 1970-71; (with Lehmann) *Pharmacotherapy of Tension and Anxiety,* C. C Thomas, 1970; (with Lehmann) *Experimental Approaches to Psychiatric Diagnosis,* C. C Thomas, 1971; *Schizophrenia: A Psychopharmacological Approach,* C. C Thomas, 1972; *Recent Advances in the Biology of Schizophrenia,* C. C Thomas, 1973; *Depression and the Tricyclic Antidepressants,* Ronalds (Montreal), 1974.

Editor with Lehmann, except as indicated: *The Butyrophenones in Psychiatry,* Quebec Psychopharmacological Research Association, 1964; *Trimipramine: A New Anti-Depressant,* Quebec Psychopharmacological Research Association, 1965; *Toxicity and Adverse Reaction Studies with Neuroleptics and Antidepressants,* Quebec Psychopharmacological Research Association, 1968; *The Thioxanthenes,* S. Karger, 1969; (with B. Silvestrini) *Trazodone,* S. Karger, 1974.

Contributor of 295 articles to professional journals. Co-editor, *Journal of International Pharmacopsychiatry;* editorial consultant, Medcom Faculty of Medicine, and International Editorial Committee of MINERVA Psiquiatrica, Argentina; editorial reviewer, *Canadian Psychiatric Association Journal;* editorial board member, *Conditional Reflex Journal, Journal of Behavior Therapy and Experimental Therapy, Journal of Behavioral Neuro-Psychiatry, International Journal of Psychobiology, Investigacion Psicomatica, Neuropsychobiology,* and *Psychopharmacology Communications.*

*   *   *

BANDMAN, Bertram   1930-

PERSONAL: Born March 6, 1930, in Shanghia, China; son of Albert (a businessman) and Edith (Magnus) Bandman; married Elsie Lucier (a doctoral candidate in psychiatric nursing), August 8, 1951; children: Nancy. *Education:* Columbia University, B.S., 1954, M.A., 1955, Ph.D., 1962. *Home:* 3345 Reservoir Oval, Bronx, N.Y. 10467. *Office:* Long Island University Center, Brooklyn, N.Y. 11201.

CAREER: Yeshiva University, New York, N.Y., lecturer in philosophy of education, 1957-58; New York (N.Y.) public schools, teacher, 1958-62; Long Island University, Merriweather Campus (now C. W. Post Center), Brookville, N.Y., assistant professor of philosophy, 1962-65, Brooklyn Center, Brooklyn, N.Y., assistant professor, 1965-67, associate professor, 1967-72, professor of philosophy of education, 1972—. Secretary-treasurer, Conference on Methods in Philosophy and the Sciences, 1966—; visiting associate professor at New York University, summers, 1966, 1968, and Hofstra University, summer, 1967.

Member: American Philosophical Association (fellow), Philosophy of Education Society (fellow), American Society for Legal and Political Philosophy.

WRITINGS: The Place of Reason in Education, Ohio State University Press, 1967; (editor with Robert Guttchen) *Philosophical Essays on Teaching,* Lippincott, 1969; (contributor) Marvin Kohl, editor, *Beneficent Euthanasia,* Prometheus Books, 1975. Also author of *Philosophical Essays on Curriculum,* 1969, and with wife, Elsie Bandman, *Rights, Justice and Euthanasia,* 1975. Contributor to philosophy and education journals.

WORK IN PROGRESS: A Theory of Rights and Claims.

*   *   *

BANNISTER, Robert C(orwin), Jr.   1935-

PERSONAL: Born June 4, 1935, in Brooklyn, N.Y.; son of Robert Corwin and Ruth (Allen) Bannister; married Joan C. Turner (an editorial assistant), June 8, 1958; children: Robert, Emily, Paul, James. *Education:* Yale University, B.A., 1955, Ph.D., 1961; Pembroke College, Oxford, B.A., 1957, M.A., 1961. *Home:* 606 Elm Ave., Swarthmore, Pa. 19081.

CAREER: Yale University, New Haven, Conn., instructor in history, 1960-62; Swarthmore College, Swarthmore, Pa., assistant professor, 1962-68, associate professor, 1968-75, professor of American history, 1975—.

WRITINGS: Ray Stannard Baker: The Mind and Thought of a Progressive, Yale University Press, 1966; (editor) *American Values in Transition,* Harcourt, 1972; (contributor) John M. Harrison and Harry Stein, editors, *Muckraking: Past, Present, and Future,* Harcourt, 1973.

WORK IN PROGRESS: American Sociology, 1885-1920: An Intellectual History.

*   *   *

BARBOUR, Hugh (Stewart)   1921-

PERSONAL: Born August 7, 1921, in Peking, China; son of George Brown (emeritus professor and dean) and Dorothy (Dickinson) Barbour; married Sirkka Talikka (an instructor in German), September 6, 1959; children: Elisa Sirkka, Celia Margaret, Dorothy Maida. *Education:* Harvard University, A.B. (magna cum laude), 1942; Yale University, student in Divinity School, 1942-44; Ph.D. (department of religion), 1952; Union Theological Seminary, New York, N.Y., B.D. (magna cum laude), 1945. *Home:* 1840 Southwest E St., Richmond, Ind. 47374. *Office:* Earlham College, Richmond, Ind. 47375.

CAREER: Member of Society of Friends (Quakers), but pastor of Congregational church in Coventry, Conn., 1945-47; Syracuse University, Syracuse, N.Y., instructor in religion, 1947-49; Wellesley College, Wellesley, Mass., instructor in Biblical literature, 1950-53; Earlham College, Richmond, Ind., 1953—, began as assistant professor, professor of religion, 1964—. *Member:* Biblical Theologians, American Society of Church History, Quaker Theological Discussion Group, Association for Asian Studies.

WRITINGS: The Quakers in Puritan England, Yale University Press, 1964; *Reading and Understanding the Old Testament,* Association Press, 1965; (with Arthur O. Roberts) *Early Quaker Writings,* Eerdmans, 1973. Contributor to *Church History* and Quaker periodicals.

WORK IN PROGRESS: Editing an edition of William Penn's religious and ethical writings.

BARBOUR, Ian G(raeme) 1923-

PERSONAL: Born October 5, 1923, in Peking, China; son of George Brown (a dean) and Dorothy (Dickinson) Barbour; married Deane Kern, November 29, 1947; children: John Dickinson, Blair Winn, David Freeland, Heather Deane. Education: Swarthmore College, B.A., 1943; Duke University, M.A., 1946; University of Chicago, Ph.D., 1950; Yale University, B.D., 1956. Home: 106 Winona St., Northfield, Minn. Office: Carleton College, Northfield, Minn. 55057.

CAREER: Kalamazoo College, Kalamazoo, Mich., assistant professor, 1949-51, associate professor and chairman of department of physics, 1951-53; Carleton College, Northfield, Minn., assistant professor of religion, 1955-57, associate professor, 1957-65, professor of religion and physics, 1965—, chairman of department of religion, 1956. Lilly Visiting Professor of Science, Theology, and Human Values, Purdue University, 1973-74. Member: American Academy of Religion, Phi Beta Kappa, Sigma Xi. Awards, honors: Ford faculty fellow, 1953; Harbison award of Danforth Foundation, 1953; American Council of Learned Societies fellowship, 1963-64; Guggenheim and Fulbright fellowships, 1967-68.

WRITINGS: Christianity and the Scientist, Association Press, 1960; Issues in Science and Religion, Prentice-Hall, 1966; (editor) Science and Religion: New Perspectives on the Dialogue, Harper, 1968; Science and Secularity: The Ethics of Technology, Harper, 1970; (editor) Earth Might Be Fair, Prentice-Hall, 1971; (editor) Western Man and Environmental Ethics, Addison-Wesley, 1972; Myths, Models, and Paradigms, Harper, 1974. Contributor to scientific and religious journals. Member of editorial boards of Process Studies, Zygon, and Journal of Science and Religion.

* * *

BARCK, Oscar Theodore, Jr. 1902-

PERSONAL: Born October 11, 1902, in Brooklyn, N.Y.; son of Oscar Theodore (a businessman) and Viola (Silence) Barck; married Olive Marie Aschenbach, January 31, 1929; children: Barbara Jean (Mrs. Robert E. Snavely), William Brewster. Education: Hamilton College, A.B., 1923; Cornell University, graduate study, 1925; Columbia University, Ph.D., 1931. Politics: Republican. Religion: Presbyterian. Home: 2450 Canadian Way, Apt. 46, Clearwater, Fla. 33515.

CAREER: Syracuse University, Syracuse, N.Y., 1928-63, began as instructor, became professor of history; Sacramento State College (now California State University), Sacramento, professor of history, 1963-65; Syracuse University, professor of history, 1965-68, professor emeritus, 1968—, university historian, 1966-68. Visiting professor, Cornell University, Ithaca, N.Y., 1950. Member: American Historical Association, Organization of American Historians, Sons of the Revolution, New York Historical Association, Phi Beta Kappa.

WRITINGS: New York City During the War for Independence, Columbia University Press, 1931; (with Nelson M. Blake) Since 1900: A History of the United States in Our Times, Macmillan, 1947, 5th edition, 1974; (with others) The United States: A Survey of National Development, Ronald, 1950; (with Hugh T. Lefler) Colonial America, Macmillan, 1958, revised edition, 1968; (with Blake) The United States in Its World Relations, McGraw, 1960; (editor) America in the World: Twentieth-Century History in

Documents, Meridan, 1961; A History of the United States Since 1945, Dell, 1965; (with Lefler) A History of the United States, two volumes, Ronald, 1968. Also author of The United States in the World, 1961, and contributor to The History of New York State, A. C. Flick, editor, 1933.

WORK IN PROGRESS: Loyalists of the American Revolution and a non-military history of the American Revolution.

* * *

BARCUS, James E(dgar) 1938-

PERSONAL: Born October 29, 1938, in Alliance, Ohio; son of James Edgar (a minister) and Mary Emma (Weiznecker) Barcus; married Nancy Bidwell, 1961; children: Heidi Anne. Education: Houghton College, B.A., 1959; University of Kentucky, M.A., 1961; University of Pennsylvania, Ph.D., 1968. Politics: Independent. Religion: Society of Friends. Home: 23 Park Dr., Houghton, N.Y. 14744. Office: Department of English, Houghton College, Houghton, N.Y. 14744.

CAREER: Nyack College, Nyack, N.Y., visiting professor, 1963-64; Houghton College, Houghton, N.Y., associate professor, 1964-68, professor of English, 1968—, chairman of division of English and speech, 1969—. Visiting professor, University of Kentucky, summer, 1966. Partner in antique shop, Houghton, 1966-68. Evaluator for Middle States Accrediting Association; national treasurer, Conference on Christianity and Literature, 1970-71. Associate of Danforth Foundation. Member: Modern Language Association of America, National Council of Teachers of English.

WRITINGS: (Editor) The Literary Correspondence of Bernard Barton, University of Pennsylvania Press, 1966; Shelley: The Critical Heritage, Routledge & Kegan Paul, 1975. Contributor of articles and reviews to literary journals. Christian Scholar's Review, associate editor, 1970-71, member of editorial board.

WORK IN PROGRESS: Structure and Idea in Coleridge's Prose; other studies on E. G. Fitzgerald and art, Newman, and Tennyson.

AVOCATIONAL INTERESTS: Eighteenth-century American antiques, modern painting, and Renaissance music.

* * *

BARD, Patti 1935-

PERSONAL: Born May 3, 1935, in Binghamton, N.Y.; daughter of Oliver Wilbur (a production control specialist) and Jane (Purple) Haire; married Roger H. Bard (a painter and art instructor), November 21, 1959; children: Amy Carol, Jane Lynnette. Education: Keuka College, B.A., 1957; graduate study at University of Laval, summers, 1969-70, New School for Social Research, 1969-71, and Instituto Allende, 1973. Religion: "Evangelical Christian." Address: P.O. Box 736, East Quoque, N.Y. 11942.

CAREER: Worked during college field periods with New York State Historical Association at Cooperstown, for House and Garden, New York City, and with a social service mission in Oneonta, N.Y.; field director of Mid-Fairfield Council, Camp Fire Girls, Danbury, Conn., 1957-59; leader, and member of executive committee of Tioga Council Girl Scouts, 1959-62; participant in Rural Social-Help Projects, Tioga Center, N.Y., 1959-62; neighborhood worker, Full Circle, Inc., Inner-City Neighborhood Projects, New York City, 1969-70; participant in experimental school community, 1970—; volunteer teacher of creative writing, Bay Community School, Brookhaven, N.Y., 1970-72; public relations worker, Family Cooperative, Riverhead, N.Y., 1970-72; free-lance writer. *Member:* Pi Delta Epsilon, Pi Gamma Mu, Alpha Psi Omega, Chi Beta Phi. *Awards, honors:* Award for valued service, East Quoque School, 1972.

WRITINGS: (With Judi Culbertson) *Games Christians Play,* Harper, 1967, revised edition published as *Games Christians Play: An Irreverent Guide to Religion without Tears,* 1973; *The Fragmented, the Empty, the Love,* Zondervan, 1969; (with Culbertson) *The Little White Book on Race,* illustrations by Susan Perl, Lippincott, 1970; (with Maryanna Johnson; self-illustrated) *At the Risk of Being a Wife: A Dialogue between Two Wives,* Zondervan, 1971. Contributor of articles to magazines and newspapers including *Eternity, Guideposts, Newsday.*

WORK IN PROGRESS: A book with Judi Culbertson, tentatively entitled *Notes from the Christian Underground.*

AVOCATIONAL INTERESTS: Seashore exploring, art, theater, gardening, camping.†

* * *

BARISH, Jonas A. 1922-

PERSONAL: Born March 22, 1922, in New York, N.Y.; son of Philip H. (a merchant) and Mollie (Schaffer) Barish; married Mildred Seaquist, July 24, 1964; children: Judith Rose, Rachel Alexandra. *Education:* Harvard University, A.B., 1942, M.A., 1947, Ph.D., 1952. *Home:* 107 Tamalpais Rd., Berkeley, Calif. 94708. *Office:* Department of English, University of California, Berkeley, Calif. 94720.

CAREER: Yale University, New Haven, Conn., instructor in English, 1953-54; University of California, Berkeley, assistant professor, 1954-60, associate professor, 1960-66, professor of English, 1966—. *Military service:* U.S. Army, Signal Corps, 1943-46. *Member:* Modern Language Association of America, Renaissance Society of America, Malone Society. *Awards, honors:* Fulbright fellow in Paris, 1952-53, 1961-62; American Council of Learned Societies fellow, 1961-62; National Endowment for the Humanities senior fellow, 1973-74; American Academy of Arts and Sciences, fellow, 1973.

WRITINGS: (Editor) Ben Jonson, *Volpone,* Crofts, 1958; *Ben Jonson and the Language of Prose Comedy,* Harvard University Press, 1960; (editor) Shakespeare, *All's Well that Ends Well,* Pelican, 1964; (editor) Ben Jonson, *Sejanus,* Yale University Press, 1965.

WORK IN PROGRESS: A monograph, *The Antitheatrical Prejudice.*

SIDELIGHTS: Jonas Barish is competent in French, Italian, German.

* * *

BARKAN, Elliott Robert 1940-

PERSONAL: Born December 15, 1940, in Brooklyn, N.Y.; son of Carl (a printer) and Tessie (Leder) Barkan; married Margaret Lindenauer, June 7, 1964; married Esther Werblud, November 28, 1968. *Education:* Queens College of the City University of New York, A.B., 1962; Harvard University, A.M., 1963, Ph.D., 1968. *Office:* California State College, San Bernardino, Calif. 92407.

CAREER: Instructor at Pace College, New York, N.Y.,

and lecturer at Queens College of the City University of New York, Flushing, N.Y., 1964-68; California State College, San Bernardino, assistant professor, 1968-71, associate professor of history, 1971—. *Member:* American Historical Association, Organization of American Historians, American Sociological Association, Phi Beta Kappa, Phi Alpha Theta. *Awards, honors:* Pinson & Megauro Award, Queens College of the City University of New York; Woodrow Wilson fellowship.

WRITINGS: (Editor) *Edmund Burke on the American Revolution,* Harper, 1966, 2nd edition, Peter Smith 1972; *History of England,* Monarch Press, 1966; *A Diplomatic History of the United States,* Monarch Press, 1967. Contributor of book reviews to *American Historical Review, American Studies,* and *New York Historical Society Quarterly.* Also contributor to the Proceedings of the Conference on the Future of General Education in the California State Universities and Colleges, 1972.

WORK IN PROGRESS: The Price of Equality: A Comparative Analysis of the American Ethnic Experience, for Prentice-Hall.

* * *

BARKER, Thomas M. 1929-

PERSONAL: Born August 26, 1929, in Minneapolis, Minn.; son of Albert Francis (a druggist) and Ruth (Mack) Barker; married Renate Heppe-Verner, April 24, 1971; children: Brigid, Julia. *Education:* Carleton College, B.A., 1951; Harvard University, A.M., 1952; University of Vienna, further graduate study, 1952-53; University of Minnesota, Ph.D., 1957. *Home:* 177 South Manning Blvd., Albany, N.Y.

CAREER: Glassboro State College, Glassboro, N.J., assistant professor of history, 1958-62; Western Illinois University, Macomb, assistant professor of history, 1962-63; State University of New York at Albany, 1963—, began as associate professor, now professor of history. Member of U.S. Commission on Military History. *Member:* Conference Group for Central European History, New York Conference of European Historians, Phi Beta Kappa, Pi Gamma Mu. *Awards, honors:* Woodrow Wilson fellow, 1952; Fulbright scholar in Austria, 1952-53; State University of New York faculty fellow, American Philosophical Society grantee; International Research and Exchange Board fellowship.

WRITINGS: The Slovenes of Carinthia: A Natural Minority Problem, Studia Slovenica, 1961; *European History* (pocket crammer), Doubleday, 1964; *Double Eagle and Crescent: Vienna's Second Turkish Siege and Its Historical Setting,* State University of New York Press, 1967; *The Military Intellectual and Battle: Raimondo Montecuccoli and the Thirty Years War,* State University of New York Press, 1975.

SIDELIGHTS: Thomas Barker is competent in German, French, and Italian.

* * *

BARLOW, Genevieve 1910-

PERSONAL: Born June 10, 1910, in Gardena, Calif.; daughter of Charles Henry (a realtor) and Nellie (Bacon) Barlow. *Education:* University of Southern California, A.B. and teaching credential; University of Puerto Rico, M.A.; additional study at Stanford University, University of San Marcos, and University of Mexico. *Politics:* Republican. *Religion:* Protestant. *Home:* 1203 West 164th St., Gardena, Calif. 90247.

CAREER: Teacher of Spanish in Gardena, Calif., 1943-61; secretary to Consul General of Ecuador in Los Angeles, Calif., 1963-64; teacher of Spanish at American Institute, Gardena, Calif., 1964-65. Part-time teacher of English to the foreign-born in Los Angeles evening schools, storyteller in English and Spanish at Los Angeles County libraries, and translator for the Red Cross in Puerto Rico. Also speaker at international education conventions.

WRITINGS: Escenitas de Mexico, Banks Upshaw, 1946; *Latin American Tales: From the Pampas to the Pyramids of Mexico,* Rand McNally, 1966; *Leyendas Latinoamericas,* National Textbook, 1970; (contributor) Ruth Carlson, editor, *Folklore and Folktales Around the World,* International Reading Association, 1972; *Leyendas Mexicanas,* National Textbook, 1974; *Cuentos Misteriosos,* National Textbook, 1976.

WORK IN PROGRESS: Scary Stories Around the World.

SIDELIGHTS: Genevieve Barlow has visited most countries of the world, and is a tour leader for students visiting Mexico.

* * *

BARLOW, John A(lfred) 1924-

PERSONAL: Born January 22, 1924, in Gallipolis, Ohio; son of Alfred Marion (an attorney) and Marian (Sullivan) Barlow; married Dulcie Dimmette (a harpist), June 29, 1948; children: Aaron John, Joel John, Michael John. *Education:* Oberlin College, A.B., 1949; Duke University, Ph.D., 1952. *Politics:* Independent. *Religion:* Religious Society of Friends. *Office:* Kingsborough Community College of the City University of New York, Manhattan Beach, Brooklyn, N.Y. 11235.

CAREER: Georgia Institute of Technology, Atlanta, instructor, 1952-53; Denison University, Granville, Ohio, assistant professor, 1953-57; Earlham College, Richmond, Ind., associate professor and head of department of psychology, 1957-61; Emory University, Atlanta, Ga., associate professor of psychology, 1961-64; Thammasat University, Faculty of Liberal Arts, Bangkok, Thailand, Fulbright lecturer, 1964-65; Indiana University, Fort Wayne Campus, associate professor of psychology, 1965-66; Hope College, Holland, Mich., professor of psychology, 1966-68; Hamilton College, Clinton, N.Y., professor of psychology, 1968-70; Kingsborough Community College of the City University of New York, Manhattan Beach, Brooklyn, N.Y., professor of psychology, 1970—, chairman of department of behavioral sciences, 1970-72, psychology area coordinator, 1972-75. Member of advisory committee on programmed instruction, John Wiley and Sons, Inc. (publishers), 1961-64; member of executive board, Institute for Behavioral Research and Programmed Instruction, 1961-62; consultant, U.S. Public Health Service Communicable Disease Center, Atlanta, Ga., 1962-64; member of board of trustees, Friends World College, 1972—. *Military service:* U.S. Army Air Forces, 1943-46.

MEMBER: American Psychological Association (fellow), Psychonomic Society, Society for Social Responsibility in Science, American Association of University Professors, American Civil Liberties Union (member of board of directors, Brooklyn chapter), Sigma Xi. *Awards, honors:* National Science Foundation grant, 1957-60; U.S. Office of Education grant, 1959-61; Fund for the Advancement of Education grant, 1963-64.

WRITINGS: (Contributor) R. Filep, editor, *Programed Instruction in Perspective,* Macmillan, 1963; *Programed Book in General Psychology,* Thammasat University Press, 1965; *Stimulus and Response,* Harper, 1968; *Samples, Populations, and Science,* Media Masters, 1971. Contributor of more than thirty articles to professional journals. Member of editorial board, *Journal of Programed Instruction,* 1961-64; editorial adviser, *Journal of Mathematics,* 1961-62.

WORK IN PROGRESS: Studies in the psychology of learning and instruction, emotional factors in memory, contemporary Chinese education and thought reform, temporal variable in classical conditioning.

* * *

BARNARD, Ellsworth 1907-

PERSONAL: Born April 11, 1907, in Shelburne Falls, Mass.; son of David Thompson and Kate (Barnard) Barnard; married Mary Taylor, December 31, 1936. *Education:* University of Massachusetts, B.S., 1928; University of Minnesota, M.A., 1929, Ph.D., 1935. *Politics:* Independent Liberal. *Home:* 86 Leverett Rd., Amherst, Mass. 01002.

CAREER: University of Massachusetts, Amherst, instructor in English, 1930-33; University of Tampa, Tampa, Fla., assistant professor of English, 1936-37; Williams College, Williamstown, Mass., instructor in English, 1937-40; University of Wisconsin, Madison, lecturer in English, 1940-41; Alfred University, Alfred, N.Y., professor of English and head of department, 1941-50; University of Chicago, Chicago, Ill., lecturer in liberal arts, 1952-55; Bowdoin College, Brunswick, Me., visiting lecturer in English, 1955-57; Northern Michigan University, Marquette, associate professor, 1957-62, professor of English, 1962-68; University of Massachusetts, Amherst, visiting professor, 1968-69, professor of English, 1969-73, professor emeritus, 1973—. *Member:* Modern Language Association of America (member emeritus), American Association of University Professors (member emeritus), College English Association, National Council of Teachers of English.

WRITINGS: Shelley's Religion, University of Minnesota Press, 1937; (editor) *Shelley: Selected Poems, Essays, and Letters,* Odyssey, 1944; *Edwin Arlington Robinson: A Critical Study,* Macmillan, 1952; *Wendell Willkie: Fighter for Freedom,* Northern Michigan University Press, 1966; (contributor) J. R. Bryer, editor, *Fifteen Modern American Authors,* Duke University Press, 1969; (editor and contributor) *Edwin Arlington Robinson: Centenary Essays,* University of Georgia Press, 1969. Contributor to *Harper's, New York Times Magazine, Massachusetts Review,* and several other publications.

WORK IN PROGRESS: Generally Speaking: Of Usage, Grammar, and Style.

AVOCATIONAL INTERESTS: Nature study, conservation, civil liberties.

* * *

BARNES, Robert J(ay) 1925-

PERSONAL: Born July 7, 1925, in Hutchinson, Kan.; son of Everette John (a railroad dispatcher) and Mary Ellen (Bundy) Barnes; married Evelyn Josephine Kerschen, October 23, 1948; children: Allison, Madeline. *Education:* University of Kansas, B.A., 1947, M.A., 1950; University of Texas, Ph.D., 1955. *Office:* Lamar University, Beaumont, Tex. 77710.

CAREER: University of Texas, Austin, instructor in English, 1953-55; University of Southern Mississippi, Hattiesburg, assistant professor, 1955-57, associate professor of English, 1957-60; Lamar University, Beaumont, Tex., associate professor, 1960-61, professor of English, 1961—, Regents Professor, 1972—, head of department, 1966-69. *Military service:* U.S. Naval Reserve, active duty, 1943-46; served in western Pacific. *Member:* National Council of Teachers of English, Conference on College Composition and Communication, American Association of University Professors, South-Central Modern Language Association. *Awards, honors:* State of Texas research grants, 1960-62, 1970, 1975; Phi Kappa Phi Teaching Award, 1972.

WRITINGS: (With C. W. Moorman and R. G. Lowrey) *Mechanics of English,* Appleton, 1960; (with C. W. Hagelman, Jr.) *A Concordance to Byron's "Don Juan,"* Cornell University Press, 1967; *Conrad Richter,* Steck, 1968. Contributor to *Modern Drama, Explicator, Renascence,* and *Southwestern American Literature.*

WORK IN PROGRESS: A book about oil industry fiction.

* * *

BARNES, Samuel H(enry)   1931-

PERSONAL: Born January 20, 1931, in Mississippi. *Education:* Tulane University of Louisiana, B.A., 1952, M.A., 1954; graduate study, Institut d'Etudes Politiques, Paris, France, 1956-57; Duke University, Ph.D., 1957. *Office:* Department of Political Science, University of Michigan, Ann Arbor, Mich. 48104.

CAREER: University of Michigan, Ann Arbor, instructor, 1957-60, assistant professor, 1960-64, associate professor, 1964-68, professor of political science, 1968—. *Military service:* U.S. Navy, 1949-50. *Member:* American Political Science Association (secretary, 1972-74). *Awards, honors:* Fulbright fellow, 1956-57; Fulbright lecturer, University of Florence, 1962-63, University of Rome, 1967-68.

WRITINGS: Party Democracy, Yale University Press, 1967.

* * *

BARR, Pat(ricia Miriam)   1934-

PERSONAL: Born April 25, 1934, in Norwich, Norfolk, England; daughter of Spencer and Miriam Copping; married John Marshall Barr (a journalist), June 22, 1956 (deceased). *Education:* University of Birmingham, B.A. (honors), 1956; University College, London, M.A. (honors in English), 1964. *Politics:* Liberal. *Religion:* None. *Home:* 25 Montpelier Row, Blackheath, London S.E.3, England. *Agent:* Richard Scott Simon Ltd., 32 College Cross, London N.1, England.

CAREER: Teacher of English at Yokohama International School, Yokohama, Japan, 1959-61, and with University of Maryland Overseas Program in Japan, 1961-62; assistant secretary of National Old People's Welfare Council, London, England, 1965-66; full-time writer, 1966—. *Awards, honors:* Winston Churchill fellowship, 1971, for nonfiction writing.

WRITINGS: The Coming of the Barbarians, Dutton, 1967; *The Deer Cry Pavillion: A Story of Westerners in Japan, 1868-1905,* Macmillan, 1968; *A Curious Life for a Lady,* Doubleday, 1970; *To China with Love,* Doubleday, 1972. Occasional contributor to *Quarterly Review, Times Educational Supplement, Guardian,* and other journals and newspapers.

WORK IN PROGRESS: A study of Victorian women in India; an account of the residency system in nineteenth-century Malaya.

SIDELIGHTS: Pat Barr told *CA:* "Have travelled in the Far East and South America and these are my main areas of interests. Also, of course, have a general enthusiasm for the 19th [century]. . . . I aim to be, in a sense, a good and trustworthy historical journalist."

The extent to which Pat Barr accomplishes this goal in *The Deer Cry Pavillion* is apparent in Sylvia Townsend Warner's review: "Her narrative is substantial, vivid, without sentiment, without partially. It is as though she wrote with the detachment of someone observing a process of history through a telescope of impartial magnification."

* * *

BARRETT, C(harles) Kingsley   1917-

PERSONAL: Born May 4, 1917, in Salford, Lancashire, England; son of Fred (a Methodist minister) and Clara (Seed) Barrett; married Margaret Heap, August 16, 1944; children: Anne Penelope, Charles Martin Richard. *Education:* Cambridge University, B.A., 1938, M.A., 1942, B.D., 1948, D.D., 1956. *Home:* 8 Princes St., Durham, England.

CAREER: Methodist minister. Minister in Darlington, England, 1943; University of Durham, Durham, England, lecturer in theology, 1945-58, professor of divinity, 1958—. Hewett lecturer in the United States, 1961; Shaffer lecturer in the United States, 1965; Delitzsch lecturer in Germany, 1967; Cato lecturer in Australia, 1969; Tate-Wilson lecturer in the United States, 1975. *Member:* British Academy (fellow), British and Foreign Bible Society (vice-president, 1963—), Society for Old Testament Study, Studiorum Novi Testamenti Societas (president, 1973-74).

WRITINGS: The Holy Spirit and the Gospel Tradition, Macmillan, 1947; *The Gospel According to St. John,* Macmillan, 1955; (editor and reviser) Wilbert Francis Howard, *Fourth Gospel in Recent Criticism and Interpretation,* 4th edition, Epworth, 1955; (editor) *The New Testament Background: Selected Documents,* S.P.C.K., 1956, Macmillan, 1957; *Biblical Preaching and Biblical Scholarship,* Epworth, 1957; *A Commentary on the Epistle to the Romans,* Black, 1957, Harper, 1958; *Westcott as Commentator,* Cambridge University Press, 1959; *Yesterday, Today, and Forever: The New Testament Problem,* University of Durham Press, 1959; *Luke, the Historian, in Recent Study,* Epworth, 1961; *From First Adam to Last,* Scribner, 1962; *The Pastoral Epistles in the New English Bible,* Clarendon Press, 1963; *Biblical Problems and Biblical Preaching,* Fortress, 1964; *History and Faith: The Story of the Passion,* B.B.C. Publications, 1967; *Jesus and the Gospel Tradition,* S.P.C.K., 1967, Fortress, 1968; *The First Epistle to the Corinthians,* Fortress, 1968; *The Signs of an Apostle,* Epworth, 1970; *Das Johannes-evangelicum und das Judentum,* Kohlhammer, 1970; *New Testament Essays,* S.P.C.K., 1972; *The Second Epistle to the Corinthians,* Black, 1973; *The Gospel of John and Judaism,* S.P.C.K., 1975.

WORK IN PROGRESS: Research in the Acts of the Apostles and early Christian history.

SIDELIGHTS: Barrett speaks German and French, and reads several other European languages.

* * *

BARRITT, Denis P(hillips)   1914-

PERSONAL: Born December 24, 1914, in Belfast,

Northern Ireland; son of Ronald (president of a linen firm) and Sybil (Heelas) Barritt; married Monica Clipstone; children: Christopher Clipstone, Jonathan Heelas, Ronald Paul. *Education:* University of Manchester, B.A., 1935. *Politics:* Liberal. *Religion:* Society of Friends. *Home:* Hill Cottage, Ballycairn, Lisburn, Northern Ireland. *Office:* Belfast Voluntary Welfare Society, 28 Bedford St., Belfast, Northern Ireland.

CAREER: John Henning & Son Ltd. (linen firm), secretary, 1935-51; Irish Association for Cultural, Economic and Social Relations, Belfast, Northern Ireland, research assistant to science and industry committee, and later honorary member of committee, 1955-59; Society of Friends in Ireland, clerk, 1959-65; Belfast Voluntary Welfare Society, Belfast, Northern Ireland, secretary, 1964—. Member of Quaker team at United Nations, 1959, 1967. Voluntary chairman of War on Want, Northern Ireland, and organizer of Freedom from Hunger campaign for Northern Ireland. Chairman of Protestant and Catholic Encounter (PACE). *Member:* Fellowship of Reconciliation (chairman for Northern Ireland).

WRITINGS: (With Charles F. Carter) *Northern Ireland Problem,* Oxford University Press, 1962, revised edition, 1972; (with Arthur Booth) *Orange and Green,* Northern Friends Peace Board, 1967, revised edition, 1972. Contributor to *Journal of Industrial Economics, Friend, Peace News,* and local journals and newspapers.

WORK IN PROGRESS: Numerous sociological studies for Belfast Voluntary Welfare Society regarding the aged and deprived; study of violence, causes and effects for Irish Council of Churches.

* * *

BARROW, Thomas C(hurchill) 1929-

PERSONAL: Born April 30, 1929, in Ansonia, Conn.; son of George A. (a clergyman) and Helen (Choate) Barrow; married Julia Paxton, August 1, 1953; children: Catherine, Stephen. *Education:* Harvard University, A.B., 1952, M.A., 1954, Ph.D., 1961. *Home:* 6 Forest St., Worcester, Mass. 01609. *Office:* History Department, Clark University, Worcester, Mass. 01610.

CAREER: University of Missouri, Columbia, assistant professor, 1961-64, associate professor of history, 1964-67; Clark University, Worcester, Mass., associate professor of history, 1967—. Research associate at Charles Warren Center, 1970. *Military service:* U.S. Army, 1954-56. *Member:* American Historical Association, Organization of American Historians, Conference on British Studies, Colonial Society of Massachusetts. *Awards, honors:* Research grant, American Philosophical Society, summer, 1963.

WRITINGS: Trade and Empire: The British Customs Service in Colonial America, 1660-1775, Harvard University Press, 1967; *Connecticut Joins the Revolution,* Pequot Press, 1973. Contributor to historical journals.

WORK IN PROGRESS: The Expansion of Europe, completion expected in 1977; *Massachusetts Politics on the Eve of Revolution,* 1978; *Politics in Transition,* 1980.

* * *

BARTHELME, Donald 1931-

PERSONAL: Born April 7, 1931, in Philadelphia, Pa.; son of Donald (an architect) and Helen (Bechtold) Barthelme; married wife Birgit; children: Anne. *Home:* 113 West 11th St., New York, N.Y. *Agent:* Lynn Nesbit, International

Creative Management, 40 West 57th St., New York, N.Y. 10019.

CAREER: Worked as a newspaper reporter and a museum director; was managing editor, *Location,* an art and literature review. Distinguished visiting professor of English, City College of the City University of New York, 1974-75. Full-time writer. *Military service:* U.S. Army, served in Korea and Japan. *Member:* Authors Guild, P.E.N. *Awards, honors:* Guggenheim fellowship, 1966; *Time* magazine's Best Books of the Year list, 1971, for *City Life;* National Book Award for children's literature, 1972, for *The Slightly Irregular Fire Engine or the Hithering Thithering Djinn;* Morton Dauwen Zabel Award from the National Institute of Arts and Letters, 1972.

WRITINGS—All published by Farrar, Straus, except as noted: *Come Back, Dr. Caligari* (stories), Little, Brown, 1964; *Snow White* (novel; first published in *New Yorker,* February 18, 1967), Atheneum, 1967; *Unspeakable Practices, Unnatural Acts* (stories), 1968; *City Life* (stories), 1970; *The Slightly Irregular Fire Engine or the Hithering Thithering Djinn* (children's book), 1971; *Sadness* (stories), 1972; *Guilty Pleasures* (parodies and satire), 1974; *The Dead Father* (novel), 1975. Regular contributor to *New Yorker.*

SIDELIGHTS: Barthelme has been called "probably the most perversely gifted writer in the U.S." and "one of the best, most significant and carefully developing young American writers." He is, writes Richard Gilman, "one of a handful of American writers who are working to replenish and extend the art of fiction instead of trying to add to the stock of entertainments, visions and humanist documents that fiction keeps piling up."

According to Gilman, Barthelme is saying that fiction "has lost its power to transform and convince and substitute, just as reality has lost . . . its need and capacity to sustain fictions of this kind." *Snow White,* Gilman continues, "may be read . . . as the work of a highly idiosyncratic imagination, a *new* imagination, popping up like a wild-crested tropical bird in our parlors. . . . Its truest accomplishment is to be representative, to adhere with consciousness, craft and potency to a new reality. In the most summary way this new reality can be described as being open-ended, provisional, characterized by suspended judgments, by disbelief in hierarchies, by mistrust of solutions, denouments and completions, by self-consciousness issuing in tremendous earnestness but also in far-ranging mockery, by emphasis on the flesh to the anachronization of the spirit, by a wealth of possibility whose individual possibilities tend to cancel one another out, by unfreedom felt as freedom and the reverse, by cults of youth, sex, change, noise and chemically induced 'truth.' It is also a reality harboring a radical mistrust of language, writing, fiction, the imagination." Gilman further maintains that, if *Snow White* did not refuse to be a novel, it would be *The Catcher in the Rye* of this generation, for "its 'content' includes the substance of our age's newest awarenesses, . . . its behavior and bemusements, its vocabularies, costumes and stances. . . ." *Snow White* is not merely "clever" as some critics have suggested. It has several purposes. Anatole Broyard calls it "a re-statement of romance, taking off from the *locus classicus* of romance, the fairy tale." It deplores tired language: Snow White no longer wishes to hear the words she always hears. "Beneath the gags and the tricks and the puns," says Don Crinklaw, "a quiet, strangulated sobbing can be heard, and there emerges a touching picture of our unlovely world's reaction to pure loveliness. . . . The author achieves his effect by blending the rhythms and vocabulary of our own day with those of a more poetic time." And Barthelme suggests, according to Shaun O'Connell, "that the things we really treasure—which thus are worth evoking and debunking—are those great tawdry, lyrical, chintzy fantasies which exploited us when we were young. . . . Sometimes always funny, the allusions really serve [an] important function; after the reader's long trips through odd syntax and weird doings they periodically refer him to a recognizable world only, of course, to show that what he thought was inviolable is now turvy-topsy."

His novel and many of his stories question "the discursive ability of language even to express [the denial of] the possibility of providing fictional equivalents of reality," writes Stanley Trachtenberg. "Freakishness is the new idiom. . . . Accordingly, the narrative line is frustrated by the random quality of subjects introduced by alternating narrators. In addition, Barthelme employs language parodies of several cultural poses, typographical oddities, narrative fragmentation into generally page-long observations, explanatory boldface footnotes, . . . and questionnaires that review the progress of [*Snow White*]." As Jack Kroll observes, "the great thing Barthelme does is to compose a crystalline comedy of human peril: no longer the old comfortable tarnished perils—physical, social, psychological—but the new, shiny peril, the total, integrated peril of the human organism. . . . [Yet] Barthelme has some of Cummings' quality of ironic gallantry in the face of the enemy—and the enemy is what philosophers used to call the world. . . . [Barthelme is a] splendid writer who knows how to turn spiritual dilemmas into logic, and how to turn that logic into comedy which is the true wised-up story of our time." Broyard adds: "The age demanded an image of its accelerated grimace: Barthelme obliges."

"Kafka might well be not turning over but grinning in his grave at Donald Barthelme," says Broyard, "for here at last is a worthy successor. Not an imitator—a successor. . . . Where Kafka erected a castle to house his anxieties, Barthelme has opened a boutique. The reduction in scale is not Barthelme's fault. Nobody builds castles anymore." Barthelme has, in effect, shaped, controlled, and colored hysteria, "better than any current writer," says Kroll. "The world is hysteria but Barthelme doesn't get hysterical about it. He knows it's also funny." In fact, Broyard notes, "Barthelme is so funny that most readers will never know how serious he is. It figures. Punch lines are our epitaphs and most of our truths occur in jests. Black humor is nothing but the congested face of a literature choking on the truth." It is true that Barthelme's stories are at times black and gruesome, but as Robert Martin Adams notes, "his macabre is applied in touches. [And], when you have caught his rhythm, the style starts to feel mechanical to the point of predictability." Thus he sometimes fails imaginatively "precisely by succeeding so regularly—and with such unrelenting control stylistically."

His style is as diverse and dizzying as our society. Hilary Corke says of *Come Back, Dr. Caligari:* "That one cannot make a thumbnail precis of any of the 14 stories here, is an indication of the sort of stories they are, as well as a measure of the success they achieve. They defy easy boiling-down and serving-up. . . . [Even his near-misses] are vastly more interesting than the tame successes of almost anybody I can think of." Conrad Knickerbocker called these stories "a testament to the non-sequiturs of the contemporary event. The stories become prose pop art, spilling past the

hitherto agreed-on limits of fiction into realms as mysterious as daily life. Ideally, one should read them while drinking beer, reading *Time,* watching television, and listening to Dizzy Gillespie. More than stories, they are literary 'happenings.'" *Snow White,* too, is composed "in a variety of styles," says Gilman, "although if there is a predominant one it is a flat, arch, professorial tone, elevated and full of pseudo-precision, exactly suited to his mock-learned treatment of the fairy story. . . . [Barthelme] is also a minor Joyce, with a mastery over a great diversity of vocabularies—hip talk, academic cliche, pure or communal chiche, advertising jargon, novelistic 'eloquence'—and he employs them for ironic purposes, releasing through their juxtapositions and their fish-out-of-water helplessness as literary instruments a comic sense of reality's lugubrious, perpetually renewed struggle to express itself. But at the same time he incorporates them into the substance of his new literary act." As Thomas Lask notes, Barthelme's "writing is always meticulously precise and carefully structured. The sentences make up a kind of game. They reverberate with echoes—of other writings, of bits of information, of parallel sentences used in other contexts. It is what makes the prose so alive." According to Crinklaw, Barthelme manages, moreover, "to avoid most of the vices common to this sort of apparently free-swinging composition. . . . Barthelme has rather a classic sense of form—what his grouping of short chapters, with their subtle cadences and measured tag-lines reminds me of is, oddly enough, a sonnet sequence—and an honorable regard for the dignity of the language. And happily absent is that chronium-plated, heartless efficiency. . . . Wherever Barthelme's head may be, his heart is always visible."

His writing often elicits the adjective surreal (an evaluation Barthelme agrees with), and he is sometimes criticized for including the merely bizarre. But his "fantasticated grab bag of effects," which range from "advertising slogans to screenplays of Scandinavian avant-garde films," says Lask, is "as carefully calibrated as a bomb sight. Reading one of [these stories] is like listening to bits and pieces of five simultaneous conversations going on at a dinner party for 20 people. . . . Barthelme shows the logic in them. . . . In his best stories, as also in *Snow White,* the point is not lost in the witty invention or in the flow of words. He writes, to use Robert Scholes' fine phrase, 'ethically controlled fantasy.'. . . He has allied himself with those writers who are breaking down the lines between character and setting, fixed time and points of view, interior or exterior psychological states. It is a kind of writing that depends on exaggeration, wit, elaborate hoax, playfulness." His voice [in *Unspeakable Practices, Unnatural Acts*], says Kroll, "has a mannerliness that plangs like a Debussy chord and gently hints of a gallant decorousness that is both a strategy in the face of madness and an echo of the lost days when manners were an appropriate matrix for the business of civilization. . . . By now he has created a voice so clear and characteristic that the reader's ear, brain, nerves, react to it like an oscilloscope. It is the voice of the unspecialized mind of our time that sees nothing in the world but a duplicity so extensive that it has become the environment of human consciousness."

To Alan M. Kriegsman, *City Life* seems "at first blush, like so much of Barthelme, the whole thing seems totally deranged, nonsensical. At the same time, again, as with most of the author's work, it reads like a roller-coaster. Once you're on you can't get off; it pulls you along in a dizzying, veriginous spin that takes your breath away. . . .

There's more here than verbal trickery, a lot more. Barthelme's insights cut as deeply into the maze of contemporary experience as they do into the coils of discourse. I think of his writing as a kind of acupuncture—it sticks thin, pointy needles into our fears and fantasies, letting the noxious humors within escape to the outside air.'' Barthelme's devices aim at the reader's achieving insight, for ''Barthelme is a genius at self-consciousness. . . .'' writes a *Time* reviewer, ''He uses cliches to make the reader think; he uses parodies to stir emotion. Like a billiard shark trying carom shots, he plays worn emotional impacts and responses against one another. The meaning behind the meaning in his stories is that the old main lines of communication are down. The simple, the forthright, the straightforward can no longer be confidently said. For the time being at least, messages must be sent by mirrors. And at that game, Donald Barthelme knows no peer.''

The writing in *Sadness* ''is more affecting,'' claims Earl Shorris, ''the pose of the *enfant terrible* that undermined some of the earlier stories is gone, *Sadness* is the work of a writer in the bloom of maturity—the flower is dark and made of cutting angles, streaked with laughter, a strangely natural collage of unforgettable surfaces.'' Jerome Klinkowitz comments that ''from the start of his career Barthelme has shown the ability to seize our mundane moments and make them lucid, usually by an apt metaphor or deft refocusing of language and idea. Nobody ever faulted Barthelme for his perceptions, but by themselves they could be called subjective, lyrical, poetic, or any of the other terms used to disqualify fiction as fiction. *Sadness*, however, gives his visions a clarifying run through our very familiar and objective lives. . . .''

As for one of his latest books, a *Time* reviewer contends that ''by now Barthelme's fictional landscape is familiar: a plot of undifferentiated clutter, hedged about with manicured non sequiturs. Though [*Guilty Pleasures* is] billed as nonfiction, this collage of pieces reads suspiciously like his past story collections—fragmented, humming with vaguely malevolent absurdities. This book's innocent pleasures stem from seeing how far the author can jump.''

His former editor has said that Barthelme ''spends a lot of time in despair, broods a lot; he's not alienated; he knows what's going on; he makes experimental writing important; and he writes just as *he* sees things.'' Barthelme himself says: ''I try to avoid saying anything directly and just hope that something emerges from what has been [written].'' Among the writers he most admires are Beckett, Kenneth Koch, John Ashbery, Gass, Percy, and Marquez.

BIOGRAPHICAL/CRITICAL SOURCES—Books: Carolyn Riley, editor, *Contemporary Literary Criticism*, Gale, Volume I, 1973, Volume II, 1974, Volume III, 1975, Volume V, 1976, Volume VI, 1976; Joe David Bellamy, editor, *The New Fiction: Interviews with Innovative American Writers*, University of Illinois Press, 1974.

Periodicals: *New York Review of Books*, April 30, 1964, August 24, 1967, April 25, 1968; *New Republic*, May 2, 1964, June 3, 1967; *New York Times Book Review*, September 27, 1964, May 21, 1967, May 12, 1968, November 7, 1971, September 3, 1972, December 23, 1973; *Books*, April, 1967; *Book Week*, May 21, 1967; *Newsweek*, May 22, 1967, May 6, 1968; *Time*, May 26, 1967; *Life*, May 26, 1967; *Kenyon Review*, spring, 1967; *Christian Science Monitor*, June 1, 1967; *Nation*, June 19, 1967; *Hudson Review*, autumn, 1967; *Commonweal*, December 29, 1967, June 21, 1968; *Publishers' Weekly*, March 18, 1968; *New York Times*, April 24, 1968; *New York Times Magazine*, August 16, 1970; *Minnesota Review*, Fall, 1971; *Horn Book*, October, 1972.

* * *

BARTIER, Pierre 1945-
(Peter Pan)

PERSONAL: Born October 7, 1945; son of John (a professor) and Suzanne (a history professor) Bartier. *Education:* Studied humanities at Robert Catteau, a public secondary school in Brussels; attended college for one year. *Politics:* ''The Communists call me 'the remains of the provotariat [i.e., associated with the mouvement provo] and liberalism.''' *Religion:* None. *Home:* 2, rue Keyenveld, Brussels, Belgium.

CAREER: Comic strip scenario writer in Brussels and publicity writer; former movie critic for the newspaper *Special* in Paris. Spent much time creating ideas for ''un peu fou'' (a little crazy) night club, The Smog, in Brussels, and later for a discotheque and restaurant, L'Ogenblik. He previously held jobs as car washer, office worker, and ''faineant'' (loafer). *Military service:* L'Armee Belge Troupes de Transmission, 1966-67 (discharged because of tuberculosis).

WRITINGS: Les Aventures de Jodelle (illustrated by Guy Peellaert, preface by Jacques Sternberg), Le Terrain Vague, 1966, translation published as *Adventures of Jodelle*, Grove, 1968. Also author of *Bruxelles: Guide Tendancieux*, 1974, and *How to Beat Boredom in Brussells*, 1975.

Film scenarios: ''Flap, Flap, Flap'' (animated short-subject), Valisa Films, 1973; (with Boris Szulzinger) ''Lonely Killers,'' Valisa Films, 1973; (with Picha) ''Tarzoon: The Shame of the Jungle,'' Valisa Films, 1974. Bartier was also a movie critic for the satirical journal *Pan* in which he used the pseudonym Peter Pan. He also does small cartoons and articles for reviews in Belgium.

WORK IN PROGRESS: A scenario of a short footage film about an old Japanese Karate champion; a satirical book on the linguistic rivalry between a Dutchman and a Frenchman, *Comment du bon francais de parler;* a collection of interviews, *Les Belges de New York.*

SIDELIGHTS: Bartier has traveled in the United States, France, Holland, Germany, and Italy. He lists as one of his ambitions, ''To prohibit professionalism in all forms.''

* * *

BARTLETT, Gerald (Robert) 1935-

PERSONAL: Born November 16, 1935, in England; son of Ernest Richard (a shopkeeper) and Elsie (Voyce) Bartlett; married Kathleen Kirby Speller, November 26, 1955 (divorced, 1969); married Dena Stuart, June 22, 1970; children: (first marriage) Christopher Robert, Jonathan Warren. *Education:* Attended schools in London, England. *Politics:* Left-wing conservative. *Religion:* None. *Home:* 63 Wood Vale, London S.E. 23, England. *Office:* The Economists' Bookshop Ltd., 43 Gloucester Crescent, London N.W. 1, England.

CAREER: The Economists' Bookshop Ltd., London, England, general manager, 1955—. Member of Economic Research Council. *Member:* Booksellers Association (treasurer, 1968-74; president, 1974—), Society of Bookmen, Society of Young Publishers.

WRITINGS: Stock Control in Bookselling, Hutchinson, 1965; *Bookselling by Mail,* Hutchinson, 1966. Editor of five other titles in Hutchinson's "Better Bookselling" series, 1965-68.

AVOCATIONAL INTERESTS: Hi-fi, croquet.

*   *   *

BARTLETT, Irving H(enry) 1923-

PERSONAL: Born February 2, 1923, in Springfield, Mass.; son of Lewis Irving and Carrie E. (Jones) Bartlett; married Virginia Kostulski (a television producer), November 30, 1944. *Education:* Ohio Wesleyan University, B.A., 1948; Brown University, M.A., 1949, Ph.D., 1952. *Home:* 5816 Howe St., Pittsburgh, Pa. 15232. *Office:* Carnegie-Mellon University, Pittsburgh, Pa.

CAREER: Assistant professor of history at Rhode Island College, Providence, 1953-54, and Massachusetts Institute of Technology, Cambridge, 1954-60; Cape Cod Community College, Hyannis, Mass., president, 1960-64; Carnegie-Mellon University (formerly Carnegie Institute of Technology), Pittsburgh, Pa., professor of history, 1964—, chairman of department, 1964-71. John Dorrance Visiting Professor, Trinity College, 1971. Vice-chairman of board of trustees, Allegheny County Community College, 1964-71. *Military service:* U.S. Army Corps of Engineers, 1943-46; became captain. *Member:* American Historical Association, American Studies Association, American Academy of Political and Social Sciences, American Arbitration Association, Phi Beta Kappa. *Awards, honors:* Guggenheim fellowship, 1966-67.

WRITINGS: From Slave to Citizen: The Story of the Negro in Rhode Island, Providence Urban League, 1953; (editor and author of introduction) *William Ellery Channing: Unitarian Christianity and Other Essays,* Liberal Arts Press, 1957; *Wendell Phillips, Brahmin Radical,* Beacon, 1961, 2nd edition, Greenwood, 1974; (contributor) Martin Dubermar, editor, *The Antislavery Vanguard,* Princeton University Press, 1965; *The American Mind at the Mid-Nineteenth Century,* Crowell, 1967; (with Edwin Fenton, David Fowler, and Seymour Mandelbaum) *A New History of the United States,* Holt, 1974. Contributor to *Journal of Religion, Boston Public Library Quarterly,* and other journals.

WORK IN PROGRESS: A biography of Daniel Webster.

*   *   *

BARTLETT, Marie (Swan) 1918-
(Marie Swan; pseudonyms: Rowena Lee, Sara Linden, Valerie Rift)

PERSONAL: Born June 30, 1918, in Colombo, Ceylon; daughter of Victor Lesley Sheldon and Primrose (Wright) Swan; married William Harry Bartlett (a civil engineer), October 2, 1946; children: William Ralph, Anne Marie. *Education:* Educated at Catholic convents in Ceylon, Spain, and England. *Politics:* Conservative. *Religion:* Roman Catholic. *Home:* 17 Moss Close, Wickersley, Rotherham, Yorkshire, England. *Agent:* A. M. Heath & Co., 40-42 William IV St., London, England.

CAREER: Press liaison officer, later war correspondent in New Delhi, India, 1941-43; free-lance journalist, 1945-47; *East African Standard,* Nairobi, Kenya, editor of magazine section, 1947-51; free-lance writer for British Broadcasting Corp. radio news, and journalist and novelist in England, 1952—. *Military service:* Women's Royal Naval Service

(WRENS), 1943-45. *Member:* Society of Authors, Romantic Novelists' Association, P.E.N. (all England). *Awards, honors:* Historical award of Romantic Novelists' Association, 1965, for *A Diadem for Philippa.*

WRITINGS—All novels: *The Rino Stayed for Breakfast,* Jarrolds, 1958.

Under pseudonym Rowena Lee; all published by Collins: *Woman with a Secret,* 1960; *Sweet Pledge of Love,* 1960; *The Madness of Love,* 1961; *No Escape from Love,* 1962; *The Spanish Garden,* 1962; *The Barrier Between,* 1963; *A Diadem for Philippa,* 1964; *A Diadem in Jeopardy,* 1966; *Corinna's Diadem,* 1966. Also author of *A Stillness in the Sun* and *Diadems of a Duchess.*

Under pseudonym Sara Linden: *Tread Softly My Love,* Gresham, 1963.

Under pseudonym Valerie Rift; all published by Wright & Brown, except as noted: *Dim Venue,* 1955; *Tides of Zhimoni,* 1955; *So Low the Stars,* 1956; *Wake of a Moonbeam,* 1956; *No Day But This,* Jenkins, 1957; *Secret Splendour,* Jenkins, 1957; *Singing Volcanoes,* 1958; *Joyous Bondage,* Jenkins, 1958; *Dear Enchantment,* 1959; *Dangerous Delight,* 1960; *If This Be Love,* R. Hale, 1960; *Light and Flame,* R. Hale, 1960; *Reckless Love,* R. Hale, 1961; *Pitiless Rapture,* R. Hale, 1962; *Paradise Way,* 1965; *Poison Ivy,* 1966.

Writer of two television plays, "The Two Widows" and "The Other Rut," and short stories.

*   *   *

BARTOCCI, Gianni 1925-

PERSONAL: Born September 2, 1925, in Fiuminata, Italy; son of Furio (an architect) and Maria (Rubini) Bartocci; married second wife, Judith Ann Berendsen, September 9, 1966; children: (previous marriage) Kelmen David; (second marriage) Alexandra. *Education:* St. Apollinare, Rome, Italy, Licenza Liceale Classica, 1942; University of Rome, Ph.D., 1950. *Home:* 97-Z95 Water St., Guelph, Ontario, Canada. *Office:* University of Guelph, Guelph, Ontario, Canada.

CAREER: University of Dublin, Trinity College, Dublin, Ireland, lecturer in Italian, 1951-57; University of Auckland, Auckland, New Zealand, professor of Italian literature, 1958-67; University of Guelph, Guelph, Ontario, professor of Italian literature, 1967—. Professor of Italian civilization, Italian Institute, Dublin, 1954-57. *Military service:* Italian Army, noncommissioned officer, 1943-45. *Awards, honors:* Cavaliere, Ordine al Merito della Repubblica Italiana, conferred by President of Italy, 1967, for fostering cultural relations between Italy and New Zealand.

WRITINGS: Agenda per Educatori, Societa Editrice Tipografica Italiana (Rome), 1954; *Per le Vie di Dublino,* (essays) Intelisano (Parma), 1956; *Addio, Vecchia Strada* (short novel) Intelisano, 1959; *Waiting for You/La Tua Attesa* (poetry; bilingual edition), Officina Tipografica Laziale (Rome), 1966; *Viaggio Agli Antipodi* (narrative poem), Kursaal (Florence), 1967; *I Volsci a Dublino* (novel), Intelisano, 1968; *Equinozio ad Armanderiz* (novel), Kursaal, 1968; *Vento a Guelph* (poetry), Intelisano, 1969; *Stars and Solitude* (poems), Dorrance, 1969; *In margine a Gauguin* (poems), [Padua], 1971; (editor) *On Italy and the Italians,* University of Guelph, 1974. Contributor of poetry to *Crucible* (Auckland), *Poetry Review* (London), *La Carovana* (Rome), *Selva* (Turin), *Fenarete* (Milan), and *Question* (London), and of articles to Italian and English newspapers and magazines.

WORK IN PROGRESS: Stefano Guazzo: 1530-1593; Il Paese degli Aironi, a novel; Angel Ganivet, a monograph; also writing on the "idea of man" in the works of J. Ortega y Gasset.

SIDELIGHTS: Bartocci speaks Spanish and French, in addition to his native Italian and English.

* * *

BARTON, Weldon V. 1938-

PERSONAL: Born August 14, 1938, in Bastrop County, Tex.; son of William and Ella (Wilhelm) Barton; married Joan Ann Corey, August 27, 1965. Education: Southwest Texas State College (now Southwest Texas State University), B.A., 1962; Florida State University, M.A., 1963, Ph.D., 1965. Home: 9105 Wire Ave., Silver Spring, Md. 20901.

CAREER: Southwest Texas State College (now Southwest Texas State University), San Marcos, assistant professor of political science, 1965-67; Texas Technological College (now Texas Tech University), Lubbock, assistant professor of political science, 1967-69; National Farmers Union, assistant director of Legislative Services, 1970-75; U.S. House of Representatives, staff consultant on Committee on Agriculture, 1975—. Southwest Educational Development Laboratory, member of Central Texas Advisory Council. Member: American Political Science Association (Congressional fellow, 1969-70), American Society for Public Administration, Southern Political Science Association, Southwestern Social Science Association, Phi Kappa Phi, Alpha Chi, Pi Sigma Alpha, Phi Alpha Theta, Pi Gamma Mu.

WRITINGS: Interstate Compacts in the Political Process, University of North Carolina Press, 1967. Contributor to law and political science journals.

WORK IN PROGRESS: Editing symposium issue of Public Administration Review, on "Food and Agricultural Policy and Administration."

* * *

BARTZ, Albert E(dward) 1933-

PERSONAL: Born December 11, 1933, in Fergus Falls, Minn.; son of Albert F. (a teacher) and Elsie (Meyer) Bartz; married Solveig A. Moe, August 18, 1957. Education: Concordia College, Moorhead, Minn., B.A., 1955; University of North Dakota, M.A., 1957; University of Arizona, Ph.D., 1961. Home: 517 Fifth St. S., Moorhead, Minn. 56560. Office: Department of Psychology, Concordia College, Moorhead, Minn. 56560.

CAREER: Concordia College, Moorhead, Minn., instructor, 1957-59, assistant professor, 1961-64, associate professor, 1964-70, professor of psychology, 1970—. Member: American Psychological Association, American Association for the Advancement of Science, Midwestern Psychological Association, Sigma Xi, Psi Chi.

WRITINGS: Elementary Statistical Methods for Educational Measurement, Burgess, 1958, 4th edition, 1971; (with Ralph H. Kolstoe) Workbook for Introduction to Statistics for the Behavioral Sciences, Dorsey, 1968, 2nd edition, 1973. Contributor to Science, Highway Research Bulletin, and psychology journals.

WORK IN PROGRESS: A study of information processing in peripheral vision.

BAR-ZOHAR, Michael 1938-

PERSONAL: Born January 30, 1938, in Sofia, Bulgaria; son of Jacques M. and Ines (Anavi) Bar-Zohar; married Galila Schlosberg (a teacher), October 8, 1958; children: Gilles. Education: Hebrew University of Jerusalem, B.A., 1959; Institut d'Etudes Politiques, University of Paris, M.A., 1959; Foundation Nationale de Sciences Politiques, Ph.D., 1963. Politics: Labour Party (Israel). Religion: Jewish. Home and office: 109 Rotschild Blvd., Tel-Aviv, Israel.

CAREER: Lamerhav, Tel-Aviv, Israel, foreign correspondent in Paris, France, 1960-64; professional writer, 1964—. Press and public relations attache to General Moshe Dayan, Israeli Minister of Defense, 1967. Military service: Israeli Army, 1956-58; became sergeant. Awards, honors: Sokolov Prize (Israeli Pulitzer), and Foch Award of French Academy, both 1965, for Suez: Ultra-secret.

WRITINGS: Suez: Ultra-Secret, Fayard (Paris), 1964; La Chasse aux savants allemands (1944-1960), Fayard, 1964, translation by Len Ortzen published as The Hunt for German Scientists, Hawthorn, 1967; Ben Gurion, le prophete arme, Fayard, 1966, translation by Ortzen published as The Armed Prophet: A Biography of Ben Gurion, Arthur Barker, 1967, published as Ben Gurion: The Armed Prophet, Prentice-Hall, 1968; Les Vengeurs, Fayard, 1968, translation by Ortzen published as The Avengers, Arthur Barker, 1968, Hawthorn, 1969; Historie secrete de la guerre d'Israel, Fayard, 1968; Embassies in Crisis: Diplomats and Demogogues behind the Six-Day War, Prentice-Hall, 1970; Spies in the Promised Land: Iser Harel and the Israeli Secret Service, translation by M. Stearns, Poynter, 1972; The Third Truth, translation by J. Wilson, Houghton, 1973; The Spy Who Died Twice, Houghton, 1975. Also author of several series of syndicated articles.

SIDELIGHTS: Michael Bar-Zohar traveled widely to interview the fugitive or transplanted people who are the subjects of The Hunt for German Scientists. He reminds us, Edwin Tetlow points out, that "war is not only a matter of the firing of shot and shell but has secret facets which, even if less physically ghastly, are more dishonorable and sinister, and continue long after the guns have fallen silent." Willy Ley believes that Bar-Zohar "has produced a book that is interesting and often exciting reading and that is also factually correct almost all the time." Leonard C. Schneider writes that "the full value of [The Avengers] is not just to be found in its descriptive passages. It is rightly called history and it joins the front lines of those comparatively few works which look beyond atrocity to retribution. Although partisan, being written by a Jew about Jews, it is strongly objective."

The Hunt for German Scientists has been published in nine countries, and Ben Gurion: The Armed Prophet, in eight. Bar-Zohar is competent in English, Russian, and Spanish, besides his native Bulgarian. Avocational interests: Scuba diving.

BIOGRAPHICAL/CRITICAL SOURCES: New York Times Book Review, September 17, 1967; Christian Science Monitor, September 18, 1967; Jewish Quarterly, winter, 1967-68; Best Sellers, March 1, 1969, December 1, 1970.†

* * *

BASSETT, T(homas) D(ay) Seymour 1913-

PERSONAL: Born December 21, 1913, in Burlington, Vt.;

son of Samuel Eliot (a professor of Greek) and Bertha (Raymond) Bassett; married Patricia Reynolds, December 26, 1942 (died November 23, 1959); married Mary Jane Gray (a physician specializing in obstetrics and gynecology), June 15, 1963; children: (first marriage) John Eliot, Elizabeth, Miriam (Mrs. Douglas Clark French), Margot. *Education:* Yale University, A.B., 1935, graduate study, 1935-36; University of California, Berkeley, graduate study, 1936-37; Harvard University, graduate study, 1937-39, Ph.D., 1952. *Religion:* Society of Friends. *Home:* 179 North Prospect St., Burlington, Vt. 05401. *Office address:* Box 19, Waterman Building, University of Vermont, Burlington, Vt. 05401.

CAREER: National Archives, Washington, D.C., various posts, 1942-43; Princeton University, Princeton, N.J., research associate in American civilization program, 1946-48; Earlham College, Richmond, Ind., assistant professor, 1948-56, associate professor of history, 1956-57, college archivist, 1956-57; University of California, Riverside, lecturer, 1957-58; University of Vermont, Burlington, associate professor of history, 1958-65, Wilbur librarian, 1958, and university archivist, 1962—. United Nations, acting chief of archives, summers, 1957, 1959; University of California, Berkeley, lecturer, summer, 1958. Trustee of Moses Brown School, Providence, R.I., 1961-71, and Lincoln School, Providence, 1967-71. *Member:* American Historical Association, Society of American Archivists, Organization of American Historians, Friends Historical Association (Philadelphia), Friends Historical Society (London), Vermont Historical Society (trustee, 1961-66). *Awards, honors:* Social Science Research Council faculty grant, 1952-53.

WRITINGS: (Co-author, Volume I, and bibliographer, Volume II) Stow Persons and Donald D. Egbert, editors, *Socialism and American Life,* Princeton University Press, 1952; (editor) *Outsiders Inside Vermont,* Greene, 1967. Contributor to *Vermont History, New England Quarterly,* and *Quaker History.*

WORK IN PROGRESS: Vermont Geological Survey, 1844-1974.

*   *   *

BASTIN, J(ohn) S(turgus)   1927-

PERSONAL: Born January 30, 1927, in Melbourne, Australia; son of William Henry and Dora (Wentman) Bastin; married Jane Margaret Andrews, June 22, 1949; married second wife, Rita Violet Elliott, July 7, 1966; children: (first marriage) Christopher, Jennifer; (second marriage) Mark, Marianne. *Education:* University of Melbourne, B.A. and M.A., 1950; Oxford University, 1951-52, D.Phil., 1955; University of Leiden, D.Litt., 1954. *Politics:* Conservative. *Religion:* Methodist. *Home:* Denstone, Berry Lane, Chorleywood, Hertfordshire, England. *Office:* School of Oriental and African Studies, University of London, London W.C. 1, England.

CAREER: University of Queensland, Brisbane, Australia, lecturer in history, 1955-56; Australian National University, Canberra, fellow in Pacific history, 1956-59; University of Malaya, Pantai Valley, Kuala Lumpur, professor of history, 1959-63; School of Oriental and African Studies, University of London, London, England, reader in the modern history of Southeast Asia, 1963—. *Member:* Royal Asiatic Society (London; fellow), Royal Asiatic Society (Malaysian branch).

WRITINGS: Raffles' Ideas on the Land Rent System in

Java, Nijhoff, 1954; *Raffles in Java and Sumatra,* Clarendon Press, 1957; *Essays on Indonesian and Malayan History,* Eastern Universities Press (Singapore), 1961; *The British in West Sumatra 1685-1825,* University of Malaya Press, 1965; (editor with Robin Winks) *Malaysia: Selected Historical Readings,* Oxford University Press (Kuala Lumpur), 1966; *The Emergence of Modern Southeast Asia,* Prentice-Hall, 1967; (with T. E. Smith) *Malaysia,* Oxford University Press, 1967; (with Harry J. Benda) *A History of Modern Southeast Asia,* Prentice-Hall, 1968 (with Mildred Archer) *The Raffles Drawings,* Oxford University Press, 1976. General editor, "Oxford in Asia Historical Reprints." Contributor to historical journals in Netherlands, Singapore, Australia, and elsewhere.

WORK IN PROGRESS: Nineteenth-century prints of Indonesia.

*   *   *

BASTLUND, Knud   1925-

PERSONAL: Born March 12, 1925, in Denmark; son of Aage Christian and Jenny (Pedersen) Bastlund; married Carina Bell, August 16, 1952; children: Christian, Carina. *Education:* Royal Danish Academy of Fine Arts, Master of Architecture, 1950. *Home:* Uplandsgade 12, Copenhagen, Denmark 2300.

CAREER: Practicing architect in Denmark, 1950—, with exception of two periods, 1952-56, and 1960-63, when he worked as an architect in the United States. Royal Danish Academy of Fine Arts, Copenhagen, School of Architecture, professor, 1963—.

WRITINGS: Jose Luis Sert: Architecture, City Planning, Urban Design (trilingual edition), Praeger, 1967.

*   *   *

BATCHELDER, Alan Bruce   1931-

PERSONAL: Born December 30, 1931, in Medina, Ohio; son of William George (a toolmaker) and Mary (Hutchins) Batchelder; married Joan Anderson (a teacher), March 28, 1953; children: Alan Bruce, John David, Michael Edward, Elizabeth Ann. *Education:* Ohio Wesleyan University, B.A., 1953; Harvard University, M.A., 1955, Ph.D., 1961. *Politics:* Democratic. *Office:* Kenyon College, Gambier, Ohio 43022.

CAREER: Ohio Wesleyan University, Delaware, instructor in economics, 1957-60; Ohio State University, Columbus, assistant professor of economics, 1960-64; Kenyon College, Gambier, Ohio, associate professor, 1964-69, professor of economics, 1969—. General economist, Harvard Advisory Service, in Monrovia, Liberia, 1968-69. Consultant, Ohio Civil Rights Commission, 1967; consultant, Ford Foundation, 1973-74. *Military service:* U.S. Air Force, 1955-57; became captain. *Member:* American Economic Association, American Association of University Professors, American Civil Liberties Union, National Association for the Advancement of Colored People, Phi Beta Kappa.

WRITINGS: The Economics of Poverty, Wiley, 1966, 2nd edition, 1971; *Essentials of International Economics,* Grid Publishing, 1973. Contributor to industrial relations and economics journals.

WORK IN PROGRESS: Research on the burden of a college education and bureaucratic obstacles to economic growth.

AVOCATIONAL INTERESTS: Distance running.

BATTCOCK, Gregory 1938-

PERSONAL: Born July 2, 1938, in New York, N.Y.; son of Gregory and Elizabeth Battcock. *Education:* Michigan State University, A.B.; Hunter College (now Hunter College of the City University of New York), M.A.; Academia de Belli Arti, Rome, certificate. *Home:* 317 West 99th St., New York, N.Y. 10025.

CAREER: Fairleigh Dickenson University, Teaneck Campus, Teaneck, N.J., assistant professor of art; William Paterson College, Wayne, N.J., associate professor of art history. Member of board of trustees, Bronx Museum of the Arts. *Member:* International Air Transport Association.

WRITINGS—All published by Dutton: (Editor) *The New Art,* 1965, revised edition, 1972; (editor) *The New American Cinema,* 1967; (editor) *Minimal Art: A Critical Anthology,* 1968; *Idea Art,* 1973; *New Ideas in Art Education,* 1973; *Super Realism,* 1975. Editor, *Arts* (magazine); New York correspondent, *Art and Artists;* correspondent, *Domus.* Also regular contributor to *Film Culture, Soho News, Art in America, Projekt,* and art education journals.

WORK IN PROGRESS: A book on art theory, a book on artists' experiments in video, and a book on narrative art, all for Dutton.

* * *

BAUMANN, Amy (Brown) Beeching 1922-
(James Barbary, Alexis Brown)

PERSONAL: Born May 14, 1922, in Shropshire, England; daughter of George Alexis and Lily (Cartwright) Brown; married Jack Beeching (a poet and novelist), 1950 (divorced, 1970); married Heinrich Baumann, 1971; children: (first marriage) John Rutland, Laura Caroline. *Education:* Exhall College, teaching certificate, 1946. *Home:* 5, Falcon Sq., Castle Hedingham, Essex, England. *Agent:* Hope Leresche & Steele, 11 Jubilee Pl., Chelsea, London S.W. 3, England.

CAREER: Teacher, writer, and translator; lived abroad for seven years in the Balearics, Morocco, and Canary Islands; currently involved in remedial work among children with reading difficulties.

WRITINGS—Juveniles; with Jack Beeching, under pseudonym James Barbary: *The Fort in the Forest,* Parrish, 1962, published as *The Fort in the Wilderness,* Norton, 1965; *The Engine and the Gun,* Meredith Press, 1963; *Ten Thousand Heroes,* Parrish, 1963, Roy, 1964; *The Student Buccaneer,* Roy, 1963; *The Pike and the Sword,* Parrish, 1963; *The Young Cicero,* Roy, 1964; *Lawrence and His Desert Raiders,* Parrish, 1965, Meredith Press, 1968; *The Young Lord Byron,* Roy, 1965; *The Young Mutineer,* Parrish, 1966; *1066,* Parrish, 1966.

Under pseudonym Alexis Brown: *Treasure in Devil's Bay,* Blackie & Son, 1961, McGraw, 1965; *Schooner on the Rocks,* Dobson, 1966.

Translator from the Dutch, except as noted; under pseudonym Alexis Brown: W. Sevensma, *Tapestries,* Merlin Press, 1965; *Enamelling,* Merlin Press, 1965; *Playing Cards,* Merlin Press, 1966; Ben Minoti, "Little King, Big King" (children's play), produced in London at Arts Theatre, by Unicorn Theatre Co., February, 1967; *The Buccaneers of the West Indies,* Penguin, 1968, revised edition, Folio Society, 1972; Carel J. du Ry, *Art of the Ancient Near and Middle East,* Abrams, 1970; Ry, *Art of Islam,* Abrams, 1971; (from the Spanish) Jose Ortega y Grasset, *Velasquez, Goya and the Dehumanization of Art,* Norton, 1972; (from the German, with husband, Heinrich Baumann) Werner Haftmann, *Marc Chagall,* Abrams, 1973.

WORK IN PROGRESS: Three Long Years, A Valley Wide, an autobiographical account of life in the Balearic Islands; *The House from Inner Space.*

* * *

BAXT, George 1923

PERSONAL: Born June 11, 1923, in Brooklyn, N.Y.; son of Samuel and Lena (Steinhaus) Baxt. *Education:* Attended City College (now City College of the City University of New York), 1940, and Brooklyn College (now Brooklyn College of the City University of New York), 1941. *Residence:* New York, N.Y.

CAREER: Writer; motion picture and theater historian. *Awards, honors:* Mystery writers of America's Best Mystery Novel award nomination, 1967, for *A Parade of Cockeyed Creatures.*

WRITINGS: A Queer Kind of Death, Simon & Schuster, 1966; *Swing Low, Sweet Harriet,* Simon & Schuster, 1967; *A Parade of Cockeyed Creatures; or, Did Someone Murder Our Wandering Boy?,* Random House, 1967; *Topsy and Evil,* Simon & Schuster, 1968; *"I!" Said the Demon,* Random House, 1969; *The Affair at Royalties,* Macmillan (London), 1971, Scribner, 1972.

Films: "The Possessors"; "Swing Low, Sweet Harriet"; "Circus of Horrors"; "Payroll"; "Shadow of a Cat"; (with Charles Beaumont and Richard Matteson) "Burn Witch, Burn"; and others. Also author of television plays for "The Defenders," and for Philco, Kraft, and other network programs.

SIDELIGHTS: Certainly one of the best mystery novelists to appear in recent years, Baxt exhibits a talent which is being applauded by many. One reviewer called Baxt's work "New Humor infused with human-kindness, plus dazzling narrative technique." He is called "witty, clever, and knowing" by one, "horribly fashionable" by another. Baxt is all of that in each brilliantly plotted, "Baldwin-vocabularied" novel. In 1967 Anthony Boucher wrote: "It is hard to realize that only a year and a half ago fanciers of crime fiction never heard of George Baxt. In that brief time he has published three novels, and become the very paradigm by which one measures the far-out reach of other novelists of the grotesque, the macabre, the absurd in crime. *A Queer Kind of Death* is now in paperback . . . and you should not miss it. As I predicted, a few readers were offended by its campy immorality; others find it dazzling, in a nasty kind of way. His second novel, *Swing Low, Sweet Harriet,* dealt with the same set of fascinatingly unpleasant people [Baxt's first, second, and fourth novels form his "Pharoah Love" trilogy]; but here's a surprising switch in his third, *A Parade of Cockeyed Creatures.* . . . It turns out that Mr. Baxt also loves people. One cannot fault him for inconsistency. I do not see how one can contemplate oneself and one's brothers without feeling both Swiftian rage and Saroyanesque affection. . . . Certainly those who were revolted by early Baxt should try [*A Parade*]. They will find the same unpredictably absurd invention, the same brilliant techniques in dialogue and narrative (plus one virtuoso cross-cutting), this time devoted to a warm and loving portrayal of people in all their improbable variety. . . . If you have never suspected that the crime novel of the absurd could have charm, try this one."

Baxt lived in London from 1957 to 1962. He speaks French and Spanish.

BIOGRAPHICAL/CRITICAL SOURCES: New York Times Book Review, May 14, 1967, September 24, 1967, December 3, 1967, February 25, 1968, April 21, 1968; *Times Literary Supplement,* June 1, 1967.†

*   *   *

BAXTER, Ian F. G.

OFFICE: Faculty of Law, University of Toronto, Toronto, Ontario, Canada.

CAREER: Osgoode Hall Law School, Toronto, Ontario, director of commercial law program, 1963-66; University of Toronto, Toronto, Ontario, currently professor of law. Visiting professor at University of Louvain, North Atlantic Treaty Organization (NATO), 1967, and at University of Bristol, 1975-76. Director of family law project, Ontario Law Reform Commission.

WRITINGS: (Editor with Ivan R. Feltham) *Export Practice,* Carswell, 1964; *Essays on Private Law: Foreign Law and Foreign Judgments,* University of Toronto Press, 1966; *Law of Banking and the Canadian Bank Act,* Carswell, 2nd edition, 1968. Contributor to *Encyclopaedia Britannica, American Family, Law Library,* and other periodicals.

*   *   *

BAYNES, John (Christopher Malcolm)   1928-

PERSONAL: Born April 24, 1928, in Bath, Somersetshire, England; son of Rory M. S. (an Army officer, serving with the Cameronians) and Audrey (Giles) Baynes; married Shirley Dodds, June 2, 1955; children: Christopher, Timothy, Simon, William. *Education:* Attended Sedbergh School, Sedbergh, Yorkshire, England, 1941-46. *Religion:* Church of England. *Home:* The Cottage, Lake Vyrnwy Hotel, Via Oswestry, Shropshire SY10 0LY, England. *Agent:* Anthony Sheil Associates Ltd., 47 Dean St., London W.1, England.

CAREER: British Army, officer in the Cameronians (Scottish Rifles) until disbandment, 1968, Queen's Own Highlanders, beginning 1946, retired, 1972, as Lieutenant-Colonel; now hotel proprietor.

WRITINGS: Morale: A Study of Men and Courage, Praeger, 1967; *The Jacobite Rising of 1715,* Cassell, 1970; *The History of the Cameronians (Scottish Rifles), Volume IV: The Close of Empire, 1948-1968,* Cassell, 1971; *The Soldier in Modern Society,* Eyre Methuen, 1972. Occasional contributor to periodicals.

*   *   *

BEADLE, Muriel (McClure Barnett)   1915-

PERSONAL: Born September 14, 1915, in Alhambra, Calif.; daughter of Richard M. and Eunice (Bothwell) McClure; married Joseph Y. Barnett, 1942 (died, 1951); married George Wells Beadle (president emeritus of University of Chicago), August 12, 1953; children: Redmond James Barnett. *Education:* Pomona College, B.A., 1936. *Home:* 5533 Dorchester Ave., Chicago, Ill. 60637.

CAREER: Carson Pirie Scott & Co., Chicago, Ill., advertising copywriter, 1936-40; Butler Brothers, Chicago, catalogue production, 1940-42; Bullock's Pasadena, Pasadena, Calif., advertising copywriter, 1946-48; *Los Angeles Mirror-News,* Los Angeles, Calif., variously fashion editor, feature writer, and women's editor, 1948-58; free-lance writer, 1958—. Lecturer on education and social welfare.

President, Harper Court Foundation, 1962-72. *Member:* Phi Delta Kappa, Delta Kappa Gamma, Friday Club (Chicago), Fortnightly Club (Chicago). *Awards, honors:* Friends of Literature Award, 1963, for *These Ruins Are Inhabited;* D.H.L., Mundelein College, 1965; Thomas Alva Edison Foundation award, with husband 1967, for best science book for youth, *The Language of Life;* Delta Kappa Gamma award, 1971, for *A Child's Mind;* LL.D., Pomona College, 1973.

WRITINGS: These Ruins Are Inhabited, Doubleday, 1961; (with husband, George W. Beadle) *The Language of Life,* Doubleday, 1966; *A Child's Mind,* Doubleday, 1970; *Where Has All the Ivy Gone?,* Doubleday, 1972; *The Fortnightly of Chicago,* Regnery, 1973; *A Nice Neat Operation,* Doubleday, 1975.

WORK IN PROGRESS: A book about cats.

*   *   *

BEAL, George M(elvin)   1917-

PERSONAL: Born May 21, 1917, in Parkdale, Ore.; son of Isaac Thomas (a farmer) and Anna (Peters) Beal; married Evelyn Miller, June 6, 1946; children: Carolee, Linda, Dirk, David. *Education:* Iowa State University of Science and Technology, B.S., 1943, M.S., 1947, Ph.D., 1953. *Home:* 2022 McCarthy Rd., Ames, Iowa 50010. *Office:* Iowa State University, Ames, Iowa 50010.

CAREER: Iowa State University, Ames, research associate, 1948-50, assistant professor, 1950-53, associate professor, 1953-57, professor of sociology, 1957-69, Charles F. Curtiss Distinguished Professor of Agriculture, and chairman of department of sociology and anthropology, 1969—. Member of Ford Foundation's agriculture production team in India, 1959; member of Surgeon General's task force on smoking and health, 1967-68. Has served as consultant abroad for UNESCO, and been consultant or conductor of training courses for more than two hundred U.S. firms, agencies, professional groups, and voluntary associations. *Military service:* U.S. Army, Field Artillery, 1943-46; became captain; received Purple Heart. *Member:* Rural Sociological Society (president, 1968), American Sociological Association, Midwest Sociological Society.

WRITINGS: (With Joe M. Bohlen and Neil Raudabaugh) *Leadership and Dynamic Group Action,* Iowa State University Press, 1962; (with Ross C. Blount, Ronald C. Powers, and W. John Johnson) *Social Action and Interaction in Program Planning,* Iowa State University Press, 1966; (with Powers and E. Walter Coward) *Sociological Perspective of Domestic Development,* Iowa State University Press, 1971; (with Leslie D. Wilcox, Ralph M. Brooks, and Gerald E. Klonglan) *Social Indicatos and Societal Monitering,* Elsevier Nederland, 1972; (with John Middleton) *Organizational Communication and Coordination in Family Planning,* East-West Communication Institute (Honolulu), 1975.

Contributor: James H. S. Bossard, William A. Lunden, Lloyd V. Ballard, and Laurence Foster, editors, *Introduction to Sociology,* Stackpole, 1952; *Problems and Policies of American Agriculture,* Iowa State University Center for Agricultural Adjustment, 1959; E. L. Baum, Howard G. Diesslin, and Earl O. Heady, editors, *Capital and Credit Needs in a Changing Agriculture,* Iowa State University Press, 1961; James H. Copp, editor, *Our Changing Rural Society,* Iowa University Press, 1964; *Family Mobility in Our Dynamic Society,* Iowa University Center for Agricultural and Economic Development, 1965. Regular columnist, "Our Changing Rural Scene," in *Agricultural Banking and Finance;* author or co-author of more than two hundred professional papers, monographs, journal articles and popular articles.

SIDELIGHTS: Beal has conducted research in India, Guatemala, and Mexico.

* * *

BEALS, Ralph L(eon) 1901-

PERSONAL: Born July 19, 1901, in Pasadena, Calif.; son of Leon Eli and Elvina (Blickensderfer) Beals; married Dorothy Manchester, June 13, 1923; children: Ralph Carleton, Alan R., Genevieve (deceased), Mariana (Mrs. David Beatty). *Education:* University of California, Berkeley, A.B., 1926, Ph.D., 1930. *Home:* 16016 Anoka Dr., Pacific Palisades, Calif. 90272. *Office address:* HH 360, University of California, Los Angeles, Calif. 90024.

CAREER: National Park Service, Field Educational Division, museum technician, 1933-35; University of California, Berkeley, lecturer in department of anthropology, 1935; University of California, Los Angeles, instructor, 1936-38, assistant professor, 1937-41, associate professor, 1941-47, professor of anthropology, 1947-69, professor emeritus, 1969—, chairman of department of anthropology and sociology, 1941-43, 1944-48, 1964-65. Smithsonian Institution, director of Latin American ethnic studies, 1942-43, collaborator, Institute of Social Anthropology, 1944-51. Visiting professor, University of Buenos Aires, 1962. Principal field work has been done in Mexico, Ecuador, South America, and Europe. Consultant to various educational institutions, government, and professional organizations.

MEMBER: National Research Council, American Association for the Advancement of Science (member of council, 1963—), American Anthropological Association (fellow; member of executive board, 1947-49; president, 1950), Society for American Archaeology (member of executive committee, 1954-57), American Sociological Association, American Folklore Society, Society for Applied Anthropology, Latin American Studies Association, Sociedad Mexicana de Antropologia, American Ethnological Society, Archaeological Institute of America, Social Science Research Council, Academy of Human Rights, Southwest Anthropological Association (president, 1958), Phi Beta Kappa, Sigma Xi, Pi Gamma Mu. *Awards, honors:* National Research Council fellow, 1930-32; Southwest Society fellow, 1932-33; Center for Advanced Study in the Behavioral Sciences fellow, 1955-56; Guggenheim Foundation fellow, 1958-59; LL.D., University of California, Los Angeles, 1969; National Science Foundation research grants, 1964-72.

WRITINGS: Comparative Ethnology of Northern Mexico before 1750, University of California Press, 1932; *Ethnology of the Nisenan,* University of California Press, 1933; *The Aboriginal Culture of the Cahita Indians,* University of California Press, 1943; (with Thomas McCorkle and Pedros Carrasco) *Houses and House Use of the Sierra Tarascans,* Smithsonian Institution, Institute of Social Anthropology, 1944; *Ethnology of the Western Mixe Indians,* University of California Publications in American Archaeology and Ethnology, 1945; *The Contemporary Culture of the Cahita Indians,* Bureau of American Ethnology, 1945; (with George W. Brainerd and Watsons Smith) *Archaeological Studies in Northeastern Arizona,* University of California Publications in American Archaeology and Ethnology, 1945; *Cheran: A Sierra Tarascan Village,*

Smithsonian Institution, Institute of Social Anthropology, 1946; (with Harry Hoijer) *An Introduction to Anthropology,* Macmillan, 1953, 4th edition, 1971; (with Norman D. Humphrey) *No Frontier to Learning: The Mexican Student in the United States,* University of Minnesota Press, 1957; *Community in Transition: Navon, Ecuador,* Latin American Center, University of California, Los Angeles, 1966; *Politics of Social Research: An Inquiry into the Ethics and Responsibilities of Social Scientists,* Aldine, 1969; (editor) *California Indians,* Volumes I, II, III, and IV, Garland Publishing, 1974; *The Peasant Marketing System of Oaxaca, Mexico,* University of California Press, 1975.

Contributor: *Indians of the Park Region,* Rocky Mountain Nature Association, 1934; R. H. Lowie, editor, *Essays in Anthropology in Honor of A. L. Kroeber,* University of California Press, 1936; *The Civilization of the Americas,* University of California Press, 1938; *Heritage of Conquest: Ethnology of Middle America,* Free Press of Glencoe, 1952; *Human Attitudes: How They Develop and Change,* Committee on Civil Rights, United Steel Workers of America, 1954; *Race Relations in Spanish America,* University of Hawaii Press, 1955; *Estudios Antropologicos publicados en Homenaje al doctor Manuel Camio,* [Mexico], 1958; *Alfred L. Kroeber: A Memorial,* Kroeber Anthropological Society, 1961; *Anthropology Today: Selections,* University of Chicago Press, 1962; *Resources for the Teaching of Anthropology,* American Anthropological Association, 1963; Robert A. Manners, editor, *Process and Pattern in Culture,* Aldine, 1963; *Mexico: Past and Present,* Latin American Center, University of California, Los Angeles, 1967; *Handbook of Middle American Indians,* Volume VI, University of Texas Press, 1967.

Contributor to symposia and proceedings, and to *Handbook of Latin American Studies* and *New Catholic Encyclopedia;* about fifty articles have been published in *American Indigena, Scientific Monthly, Journal of American Folklore, American Antiquity, Human Organization,* and other anthropology and sociology journals in United States and Mexico. Editor, *Notes on Latin American Studies,* 1942-43, *Acta Americana,* 1943-48; *Handbook of Latin American Studies,* contributing editor, 1942-47, chairman of advisory board, 1943; associate editor, *Journal of American Folklore,* 1947-51; *American Anthropologist,* advisory editor, 1952-55, associate editor, 1955-60.

WORK IN PROGRESS: The History of Indian Mexico.

SIDELIGHTS: Ralph Beals is fluent in Spanish and reads Portuguese, French, Italian, and German.

* * *

BEAR, James A(dam), Jr. 1919-

PERSONAL: Born November 13, 1919, in Roanoke, Va.; son of James Adam and Elise (Sheppard) Bear; married Mary Caperton Braxton Armistead, May 8, 1953; children: Mary Caperton Armistead, James Adam III, Elise Sheppard. *Education:* University of Virginia, B.A., 1943, M.A., 1952; Simmons College, M.S. in Library Science, 1951. *Politics:* Democrat. *Religion:* Episcopalian. *Home address:* Box 108, Ivy, Va. 22945. *Office address:* Thomas Jefferson Memorial Foundation, Box 31b, Charlottesville, Va. 22902.

CAREER: University of Virginia, Charlottesville, assistant curator of manuscripts, 1948-54; Thomas Jefferson Memorial Foundation, Charlottesville, Va., curator, 1955—. *Military service:* U.S. Marine Corps; served in World War II and Korea. U.S. Marine Corps Reserve, now lieutenant colonel. *Member:* Albemarle County Historical Society (president, 1964-66), Grolier Club.

WRITINGS: Old Pictures of Monticello, University of Virginia Press, 1957; *Thomas Jefferson's Book Marks,* 1958; (with wife, Mary Caperton Bear) *A Checklist of Virginia Almanacs, 1732-1850,* Bibliographical Society of University of Virginia, 1962; (editor with Edwin M. Betts) *The Family Letters of Thomas Jefferson,* University of Missouri Press, 1966; (with Frederick D. Nichols) *Monticello,* Thomas Jefferson Memorial Foundation, 1967; (editor) *Jefferson at Monticello,* University Press of Virginia, 1967.

WORK IN PROGRESS: Editing Thomas Jefferson's account books; *Monticello Since 1926.*

* * *

BEAR, Roberta Meyer   1942-

PERSONAL: Born February 6, 1942, in Ukiah, Calif.; daughter of Lawrence F. and Martha (Eggers) Meyer; married Walter T. Bear, January 29, 1966; children: Jacob, Elana, Nathan. *Education:* Mills College, B.A., 1963; University of Chicago, Ph.D., 1967. *Religion:* Reform Judaism. *Office:* College of Human Learning and Development, Governors State University, Park Forest South, Ill. 60466.

CAREER: University of Chicago, Chicago, Ill., research assistant and U.S. Public Health Service trainee in research methods, Committee on Human Development, 1963-67, assistant professor and research associate, Committee on Human Development, 1967-68, lecturer on human development in infancy and childhood, Extension Divison, 1967; Roosevelt University, Chicago, lecturer in education, summer, 1975; currently at Governors State University, Park Forest South, Ill., as university professor of early childhood education. *Member:* Society for Research in Child Development, Phi Beta Kappa, Sigma Xi. *Awards, honors:* Woodrow Wilson fellowship, 1963.

WRITINGS: (Editor with Robert D. Hess) *Early Education: Current Theory, Research and Practice,* Aldine, 1968; (with R. Hess, V. Shipman, and J. Brophy) *Cognitive Environments of Urban Pre-Schoolers,* Pergamon, 1975.

* * *

BEARDEN, James Hudson   1933-

PERSONAL: Born September 25, 1933, in Marion, Ala.; son of Joseph N. and Lula W. Bearden; married Pauline Larkins, March 30, 1961; children: James Hudson, Jr., Pauline Larkins. *Education:* Marion Institute, Marion, Ala., A.A., 1953; Centenary College, Shreveport, La., B.A., 1956; East Carolina University, M.A., 1959; University of Alabama, Ph.D., 1966. *Religion:* Baptist. *Home:* 106 Crown Point Rd., Greenville, N.C. 27834. *Office:* School of Business, East Carolina University, Greenville, N.C. 27834.

CAREER: Marion Institute, Marion, Ala., business manager, 1959; East Carolina University, Greenville, N.C., instructor, 1959-60, assistant professor, 1961-63, associate professor, 1963-64, professor of business, 1964—, director of Bureau of Business Research, 1964—, assistant dean, 1967-68, dean, 1968—. Member of population and growth policy project advisory committee, North Carolina Energy; member of Board of Education, Greenville City Schools. Member of board of directors, American Cancer Society (North Carolina division), Pitt County United Fund, Tar River Basin Development Association, and Hackney & Sons, Inc. Member of Coastal Plain Planning and Development Commission, State Emergency Industrial Production

Task Group, and North Carolina World Trade Association. *Military service:* U.S. Army, Artillery, 1955-58; became second lieutenant. *Member:* American Marketing Association, American Society for Training and Development (Eastern North Carolina chapter), Newcomen Society in North America, American Association of University Professors, Southern Business Administration Association, Southern Economic Association, North Carolina Council on Economic Education, North Carolina Association of Colleges and Universities (committee member on services to institutions), Rotary Club.

WRITINGS: Personal Selling: Behavioral Science Readings and Cases, Wiley, 1967; *The Environment of Business: Perspectives and Viewpoints,* Holt, 1969. Editor of four reports published by Bureau of Business Research, East Carolina University. Contributor of numerous articles, monographs, and papers to purchasing journals.

* * *

BEAURLINE, L(ester) A(lbert)   1927-

PERSONAL: Born April 25, 1927, in St. Paul, Minn.; son of Albert E. (a businessman) and Olga W. (Faust) Beaurline; married Mary Elizabeth Jones, September 1, 1950; children: Philip, Erica. *Education:* University of Missouri, A.B. (with distinction), 1950; University of Chicago, M.A., 1951, Ph.D., 1960; King's College, London, graduate study, 1956-57. *Politics:* Democrat. *Home address:* Route 8, Box 317, Charlottesville, Va. 22901. *Office:* Department of English, University of Virginia, Charlottesville, Va. 22903.

CAREER: Augustana College, Rock Island, Ill., instructor in English, 1951-53; North Central College, Naperville, Ill., assistant professor of English, 1955-60; University of Virginia, Charlottesville, assistant professor, 1960-63, associate professor, 1963-68, professor of English, 1969—. Fellow in Co-operative Program in the Humanities, University of North Carolina-Duke University, 1968-69; Huntington Library fellow, 1973-74. *Military service:* U.S. Naval Reserve, 1945-46. *Member:* Modern Language Association of America, Renaissance Society of America, Malone Society, Phi Beta Kappa. *Awards, honors:* Fulbright fellow, University of London, 1956-57.

WRITINGS: (Editor) Ben Jonson, *Epicoene,* University of Nebraska Press, 1966; (editor) *A Mirror for Modern Scholars: Essays in Methods of Research in English and American Literature* (anthology), Odyssey, 1966; (author of introduction and commentary; text by Fredson Bowers) *Eight Plays by Dryden,* two volumes, University of Chicago Press, 1968; (editor) Sir John Suckling, *The Works of Sir John Suckling: The Plays,* Clarendon Press, 1971. *Studies in Bibliography,* assistant editor, 1964-65, associate editor, 1966-73; also editor of *The Captain, Love's Pilgrimage,* and *The Noble Gentleman* in *The Dramatic Works in the Beaumont and Fletcher Canon,* Cambridge University Press, 1966—. Contributor to *Studies in Philology, Criticism, Modern Drama,* and other professional journals.

WORK IN PROGRESS: Jonson and Elizabethan Comedy; Essays in Dramatic Rhetoric.

AVOCATIONAL INTERESTS: Printing and camping.

* * *

BEAUSAY, Florence E(dith)   1911-

PERSONAL: Born September 30, 1911, in Upper Sandusky, Ohio; daughter of J. David and Hazel F. (Smith)

Frey; married Lanne Beausay (a minister), July 27, 1930; children: William J., Phyllis (Mrs. John E. Ryerse). *Education:* Attended public schools in Upper Sandusky, Ohio. *Religion:* Independent. *Home:* 228 North Sandusky Ave., Upper Sandusky, Ohio 43351.

CAREER: Writer of religious books for children. Teacher of Sunday school classes, 1948—; instructor for children's Bible club, 1948—, and woman's Bible club, 1958—. *Awards, honors:* First prize in Zondervan's Christian Fiction Contest, 1958.

WRITINGS: Bold White Stranger, Zondervan, 1958; *Moccasin Steps,* Zondervan, 1960; *The Clouded Sky,* Zondervan, 1962. Contributor of articles to religious periodicals.

WORK IN PROGRESS: Mirth in Marble; writing *Advanced Student's Bible Course* for Mail Box Bible Club.

* * *

BEAVER, Harold (Lothar) 1929-

PERSONAL: Born June 27, 1929, in Dessau, Germany; emigrated to England with his parents, 1936; son of Joseph Curt (a lawyer) and Elsie (Hope) Beaver; married Tessa Theobald (a painter and print-maker), October 12, 1957; children: Jacob Courtenay, Abigail Hope. *Education:* St. John's College, Oxford, B.A. (honors in classics), 1951; Harvard University, M.A., 1955. *Home:* 10 Eastfield Rd., Leamington Spa, Warwickshire CV32 4EX, England.

CAREER: Oxford University Press, London, England, editor, 1955-62; Friends' School, Kamusinga, Kenya, English master, 1963-65; University of Leeds, Leeds, England, lecturer in School of English, 1966; University of Warwick, Warwickshire, England, reader in School of Literature, 1968—. Fellow of the American Council of Learned Societies, Amherst College, Amherst, Mass., 1973-74. *Member:* British Association for American Studies, Signet Society (Harvard University).

WRITINGS: (Compiler and author of introduction) *American Critical Essay: Twentieth Century,* Oxford University Press, 1959; (author of introduction) Mark Twain, *Life on the Mississippi,* Oxford University Press, 1962; (contributor) *Essays and Studies,* J. Murray, 1962; *The Confessions of Jotham Simiyu* (novel), Chatto & Windus, 1965, published as *Rogue of the African Night,* Dodd, 1966; *Pardoner's Tale* (novel), Chatto & Windus, 1966; (editor, and author of introduction and commentary) Melville, *Billy Budd, Sailor, and Other Stories,* Penguin, 1968; (editor, and author of introduction and commentary) Melville, *Moby Dick,* Penguin, 1972; (editor, and author of introduction and commentary) Poe, *The Narrative of Arthur Gordon Pym,* Penguin, 1975; (editor, and author of introduction and commentary) Melville, *Redurn,* Penguin, 1976; (editor, and author of introduction and commentary) Poe, *The Science Fiction of Edgar Allan Poe,* Penguin, 1976; (contributor) *Lewis Carroll Observed,* C. N. Potter, 1976. Regular contributor to the *Times Literary Supplement.*

WORK IN PROGRESS: Black, Red and Tattooed: Myths of Race and Colour in Classic American Literature.

* * *

BECK, Aaron T(emkin) 1921-

PERSONAL: Born July 18, 1921, in Providence, R.I.; son of Harry S. and Elizabeth (Temkin) Beck; married Phyllis Harriet Whitman (a lawyer), June 4, 1950; children: Roy, Judith, Daniel, Alice. *Education:* Brown University, A.B.

(magna cum laude), 1942; Yale University, M.D., 1946. *Home:* 406 Wynmere Rd., Wynnewood, Pa. 19096. *Office:* 204 Piersol Building, Hospital of the University of Pennsylvania, Philadelphia, Pa. 19104.

CAREER: Rhode Island Hospital, Providence, intern, 1946, resident in pathology, 1947; Cushing Veterans Administration Hospital, Framingham, Mass., resident in neurology, 1948, resident in psychiatry, 1949-50; Austen Riggs Center, Stockbridge, Mass., fellow, 1950-52; University of Pennsylvania, Philadelphia, faculty member, 1954—, assistant professor, 1956-67, associate professor, 1967-70, professor of psychiatry, 1970—. Institute of the Pennsylvania Hospital, member of visiting staff, 1956—; Philadelphia General Hospital, chief of section, department of psychiatry, 1958—; Veterans Administration Hospital, Philadelphia, consultant, 1967—. *Military service:* U.S. Army, 1943-46, 1952-54; became captain. *Member:* American Psychiatric Association, American Academy of Psychoanalysis, Philadelphia County Medical Society, Philadelphia Psychiatric Society, Phi Beta Kappa.

WRITINGS: Depression: Clinical, Experimental, and Theoretical Aspects, Harper, 1967; *Diagnosis and Management of Depression,* University of Pennsylvania, 1973; *Prediction of Suicide,* Charles Press, 1974; *Twisted Thinking,* International Universities Press, 1975. Contributor of more than eighty articles to professional journals.

WORK IN PROGRESS: Writing on psychotherapy.

* * *

BEECHING, Jack 1922-
(James Barbary)

PERSONAL: Born 1922, in Sussex, England; married Amy Brown (an author and translator), 1950 (divorced, 1970); married Charlotte Mensforth (a painter), 1971; children: (first marriage) John Rutland, Laura Caroline. *Agent:* Georges Borchardt, Inc., 145 East 52nd St., New York, N.Y. 10022; and, Hope Leresche & Steele, 11 Jubilee Pl., Chelsea, London S.W. 3, England.

CAREER: Professional writer ("poetry is my avocation; the other forms of writing are a means of livelihood"); since mid-fifties has lived outside of England and traveled widely; formerly poet-in-residence at North Dakota State University, Fargo. *Military service:* Navy service during World War II. *Awards, honors:* Arts Council of Great Britain award, 1967.

WRITINGS: Aspects of Love (poetry), A. Swallow, 1950; *Paper Doll* (novel), Heinemann, 1950; *Truth Is a Naked Lady* (poetry), Myriad, 1957; *Let Me See Your Face* (novel), Heinemann, 1959; *The Dakota Project,* Delacorte, 1968; *The Polytheme Maidenhead* (poetry), Penguin, 1970; (contributor) *Jack Beeching, Harry Guest, Matthew Mead* (poetry), Penguin, 1970; (editor and author of introduction) *Voyages and Discoveries: The Principal Navigations, Voyages, Traffiques and Discoveries of the English Nation,* Penguin, 1972; *The Chinese Opium Wars,* Harcourt, 1976. Also author of *Personal and Partisan* (poetry), 1940.

Juveniles; with Amy Baumann, under pseudonym James Barbary: *The Fort in the Forest,* Parrish, 1962, published as *The Fort in the Wilderness,* Norton, 1965; *The Engine and the Gun,* Meredith Press, 1963; *Ten Thousand Heroes,* Parrish, 1963, Roy, 1964; *The Student Buccaneer,* Roy, 1963; *The Pike and the Sword,* Parrish, 1963; *The Young Cicero,* Roy, 1964; *Lawrence and His Desert Raiders,* Parrish, 1965, Meredith Press, 1968; *The Young Lord*

Byron, Roy, 1965; *The Young Mutineer,* Parrish, 1966; *1066,* Parrish, 1966.

Sole author under pseudonym James Barbary: *The Boer War,* Hawthorn, 1968; *Captive of the Corsairs,* Macdonald & Co., 1969; *The Crimean War,* Hawthorn, 1970; *Puritan and Cavalier: The Stories of the English Civil War,* Thomas Nelson, 1976. Also translator from French and Spanish of poetry and of several plays for the London stage.

*   *   *

BEHA, Sister Helen Marie 1926-

PERSONAL: Born August 9, 1926, in Columbus, Ohio; daughter of Henry F. (a banker) and Helen (Callahan) Beha. *Education:* College of St. Francis, Joliet, Ill., B.A., 1947; St. Bonaventure University, M.A., 1958, Ph.D., 1960. *Home:* 1916 North Pleasantburg, Greenville, S.C. 29609.

CAREER: Roman Catholic nun of Order of St. Francis. St. Francis Academy, Joliet, Ill., teacher of English, 1947-57; College of St. Francis, Joliet, Ill., instructor, 1957-58, assistant professor of philosophy, 1960-66, chairman of department, 1966—. *Member:* American Catholic Philosophical Association, Metaphysical Society of America, Delta Epsilon Sigma.

WRITINGS: Mathew of Aquasparta's Theory of Cognition, Franciscan Institute, 1962; *Living Community,* Bruce, 1967; *Dynamics of Community,* Corpus Books, 1970.

WORK IN PROGRESS: Contemplative Journal, for John Knox.

SIDELIGHTS: Sister Helen Marie Beha is competent in French and German.

*   *   *

BEIER, Ernst G(unter) 1916-

PERSONAL: Born June 26, 1916, in Breslau, Germany; naturalized U.S. citizen; son of Paul (a manufacturer and businessman) and Hanna (Moses) Beier; married Frances (a pediatrician), September 7, 1949; children: Paul, Elizabeth. *Education:* Amherst College, B.A., 1940; Columbia University, M.A., 1947, Ph.D., 1949. *Home:* 1600 Michigan Ave., Salt Lake City, Utah 84105.

CAREER: Diplomate, American Board of Examiners in Professional Psychology. Syracuse University, Syracuse, N.Y., assistant professor of clinical psychology and head of mental hygiene clinic, 1948-53; University of Utah, Salt Lake City, professor of psychology and director of clinical training, 1953—. Consultant to U.S. Veterans Administration and state hospitals. *Military service:* U.S. Army, 1943-45. *Member:* Inter-American Society of Psychology, American Psychological Association (fellow; council representative), Family Service Society (president, 1971), Western Psychological Association, Rocky Mountain Psychological Association (president, 1968), Utah State Psychological Association (president, 1957), Sigma Xi.

WRITINGS: The Silent Language of Psychotherapy, Aldine, 1966; (with Valens) *People-reading,* Stein & Day, 1975. Contributor to clinical and social psychology journals.

WORK IN PROGRESS: Research in communication.

SIDELIGHTS: Beier made world lecture trip, 1966, and Israel and Africa lecture trip, 1967 and 1971, consulting at various universities and hospitals.

AVOCATIONAL INTERESTS: Sports, skiing, sailing, flying, chess.

*   *   *

BEIRNE, Brother Kilian 1896-

PERSONAL: Surname rhymes with "fern"; born September 2, 1896, in Drumshanbo, County Leitrim, Ireland, son of Patrick (a farmer) and Ellen (Beirne) Beirne. *Education:* Received early education in Ireland; University of Notre Dame, B.Sc., 1929. *Home:* St. Joseph Novitiate, Valatie, N.Y. 12184.

CAREER: Roman Catholic religious, member of Congregation of Holy Cross. Teacher of mathematics, English, and chemistry in high schools conducted by Brothers of Holy Cross, 1920-55; St. Joseph Juniorate, Valatie, N.Y., superior, 1950-56.

WRITINGS: From Sea to Shining Sea (a history of the Holy Cross Brothers in the United States), Holy Cross, 1966; *Me Grandfather,* Novitiate Press, 1969; *White Birch Abbey* (novel), Novitiate Press, 1973.

*   *   *

BELL, Marvin 1937-

PERSONAL: Born August 3, 1937, in New York, N.Y.; son of Saul and Belle (Spector) Bell; married Dorothy Murphy; children: Nathan Saul, Jason Aaron. *Education:* Alfred University, B.A., 1958; attended Syracuse University, 1958; University of Chicago, M.A., 1961; University of Iowa, M.F.A., 1963. *Office:* Writers Workshop, University of Iowa, Iowa City, Iowa 52242.

CAREER: University of Iowa, Writers' Workshop, Iowa City, visiting lecturer, 1965, assistant professor, 1967-69, associate professor, 1969-75, professor of English, 1975—. Visiting lecturer, Goddard College, 1972; member of faculty, Bread Loaf Writers' Conference, 1973-75. *Military service:* U.S. Army, 1964-65; first lieutenant. *Awards, honors:* Lamont Award from The Academy of American Poets, 1969, for *A Probably Volume of Dreams;* Bess Hopkin Award from *Poetry* (magazine), 1969; Emily Clark Balch Prize from *Virginia Quarterly Review,* 1970; Guggenheim fellowship, 1975-76.

WRITINGS—Poetry: Poems for Nathan and Saul (pamphlet), Hillside Press, 1966; *Things We Dreamt We Died For,* Stone Wall Press, 1966; *A Probable Volume of Dreams,* Atheneum, 1969; *Woo Havoc* (pamphlet), Barn Dream Press, 1971; *Escape into You,* Atheneum, 1971; *Residue of Song,* Atheneum, 1974. Work represented in many anthologies, including: *Major Young Poets,* edited by Al Lee, World Publishing, 1971; *New Voices in American Poetry,* edited by David Allan Evans, Winthrop Publishing, 1973; *Preferences,* edited by Richard Howard, Viking, 1974; *American Poetry Anthology,* edited by Daniel Halpern, Avon, 1975. Writer of column, "Homage to the Runner," for *American Poetry Review.*

Editor and publisher, *Statements,* 1959-64; poetry editor, *North American Review,* 1964-69, and *Iowa Review,* 1969-71.

BIOGRAPHICAL/CRITICAL SOURCES: Nation, February 2, 1970; *Shenandoah,* summer, 1971; *Parnassus,* fall/winter, 1972; *Stand,* Volume XIII, number 4, 1972; Karl Malkoff, *Crowell's Handbook of Contemporary American Poetry,* Crowell, 1973; *New Republic,* March 29, 1975.

BELLAH, Robert N(eelly) 1927-

PERSONAL: Born February 23, 1927, in Altus, Okla.; son of Luther Hutton and Lillian Lucille (Neely) Bellah; married Melanie Claire Hyman, August 17, 1929; children: Jennifer, Abigail, Harriet. Education: Harvard University, A.B., 1950, Ph.D., 1955. Home: 10 Mosswood Rd., Berkeley, Calif. 94704. Office: Department of Sociology, University of California, Berkeley, Calif. 94720.

CAREER: McGill University, Montreal, Quebec, research fellow at Islamic Institute, 1955-57; Harvard University, Cambridge, Mass., research associate, Center for Middle Eastern Studies, 1957-58, lecturer on social relations and world religions, 1958-61, associate professor of sociology and regional studies, 1961-66, professor of sociology, 1966-67; University of California, Berkeley, Ford Professor of Sociology and Comparative Studies, 1967—. Military service: U.S. Army, 1945-46. Member: American Sociological Association, Association for Asian Studies, Society for the Study of Religion. Awards, honors: Fulbright research grant, Japan, 1960-61; fellow, Center for Advanced Study in the Behavioral Sciences, 1964-65; Harbison Award for Gifted Teaching, 1972.

WRITINGS: Tokugawa Religion, Free Press of Glencoe, 1957; (editor) Religion and Progress in Modern Asia, Free Press of Glencoe, 1965; (editor with William G. McLoughlin) Religion in America, Houghton, 1968; Beyond Belief: Essays on Religion in a Post-Traditional World, Harper, 1970; The Broken Covenant, Seabury, 1975. Contributor to professional journals.

* * *

BELLAIRS, John 1938-

PERSONAL: Born January 17, 1938, in Marshall, Mich.; son of Frank Edward and Virginia (Monk) Bellairs; married Priscilla Braids, June 24, 1968; children: Frank. Education: University of Notre Dame, A.B., 1959; University of Chicago, M.A., 1960. Politics: Democrat. Religion: Episcopal. Home: 28 Hamilton Ave., Haverhill, Mass. 01830. Agent: Richard Curtis, 1215 Fifth Ave., New York, N.Y. 10029.

CAREER: College of St. Teresa, Winona, Minn., instructor in English, 1963-65; Shimer College, Mount Carroll, Ill., member of humanities faculty, 1966-67; Emmanuel College, Boston, Mass., instructor in English, 1968-69; Merrimack College, North Andover, Mass., member of English faculty, 1969-71; currently full-time writer. Member: Authors League, Authors Guild. Awards, honors: Woodrow Wilson fellowship.

WRITINGS: St. Fidgeta, and Other Parodies, Macmillan, 1966; The Pedant and the Shuffly, Macmillan, 1968; The Face in the Frost, Macmillan, 1969; The House With a Clock in Its Walls, Dial, 1973; The Figure in the Shadows, Dial, 1975.

WORK IN PROGRESS: A second sequel to The House With a Clock in Its Walls.

AVOCATIONAL INTERESTS: Archaeology, history, Dickens, wine-tasting, cheese, and Latin.

* * *

BELOFF, Michael 1942-

PERSONAL: Born April 18, 1942, in Adlington, Cheshire, England; son of Max (a professor) and Helen (Dobrin) Beloff. Education: Attended Eton College, 1954-60; Magdalen College, Oxford, B.A. (history; first class honors), 1963, B.A. (law), 1965, M.A., 1967. Politics: Labour. Religion: Jewish. Home: 352a Woodstock Rd., Oxford, England. Agent: G. Watson, Curtis Brown Ltd., 1 Craven Hill, London, W2 3EW, England.

CAREER: Trinity College, Oxford University, Oxford, England, lecturer in law, 1965-66; barrister-at-law, 1967—. Legal correspondent for New Society, 1969—.

WRITINGS: (With J. Aitken) A Short Walk on the Campus, Atheneum, 1966; The Plateglass Universities, Secker & Warburg, 1968. Contributor to Harper's Bazaar, Rhodesia Herald, Irish Jurist, Encounter, Minerva, and other periodicals and legal journals. Former editor, Eton College Chronicle.

WORK IN PROGRESS: The Law Relating to Sex Discrimination.

SIDELIGHTS: Michael Beloff has traveled widely in Europe, including Russia, and has visited United States on Speech Association debate tour, 1964. He speaks French and some Russian.

* * *

BELOOF, Robert 1923-

PERSONAL: Born December 30, 1923, in Wichita, Kan.; son of P. A. and Ida Anna (Dungan) Beloof; married Ruth Madeleine LaBarre, June 14, 1946 (divorced, 1971); children: Marshall H. and Laird D. (twins), Douglas E., Grant L. Education: Attended Haverford College and Swarthmore College; Friends University, B.A., 1946; Middlebury College, M.A., 1948; Northwestern University, M.A., 1948, Ph.D., 1954. Religion: Society of Friends (Quaker). Home: 1557 Beverly Pl., Berkeley, Calif. 94706. Office: Department of Rhetoric, University of California, Berkeley, Calif. 94720.

CAREER: University of California, Berkeley, lecturer, 1948-54, assistant professor, 1954-58, currently professor of interpretation of literature. Fulbright professor of American literature, Oriental Institute, Naples, 1959-60. Member: Modern Language Association of America, Speech Association of America, Speech Communication Association, California Association of Teachers of English.

WRITINGS: The One-Eyed Gunner (poems), Villiers Publications, 1956; The Performing Voice in Literature, Little, Brown, 1966; Good Poems, Sampler Press, 1973; The Children of Venus, Sampler Press, 1974. Contributor of articles and poems to literary magazines in the United States and abroad. Editor and reader, "An Historical Anthology of American Poetry," long-playing record album, Argo Records (London), 1964.

WORK IN PROGRESS: Poetry; critical and scholarly writing on poetics, and on modern American literature.

* * *

BELSHAW, Michael (Horace) 1928-

PERSONAL: Born June 23, 1928, in Auckland, New Zealand; naturalized U.S. citizen; son of Horace (an economist) and Marion (McHardie) Belshaw. Education: Columbia University, A.B., 1951, Ph.D., 1956. Politics: "Nineteenth-century liberal." Home: Quinta el Santuario, Camp Wood Route, Prescott, Ariz. 86301.

CAREER: Barnard College, New York, N.Y., instructor in economics, 1954-57; Rutgers University, Douglass College, New Brunswick, N.J., assistant professor of economics, 1957-60; Hunter College (now Hunter College of the

City University of New York), New York, N.Y., assistant professor, 1960-65, associate professor of economics, 1966-69; Prescott College, Prescott, Ariz., professor of economics, 1969-74. Owner of quarterhorse ranch near Prescott. *Member:* American Economic Association. *Awards, honors:* Social Science Research Council fellowship, 1962, for field work in Mexico.

WRITINGS: A Village Economy: Land and People of Huecorio, Columbia University Press, 1967. Contributor to *Economic Development and Cultural Change, Inter-American Affairs,* and *Engineering Economist.*

WORK IN PROGRESS: A study of modern homesteaders on the Arizona Strip; study in the theory of community.

* * *

BELVEAL, L(orenzo) Dee   1918-

PERSONAL: Born August 15, 1918, in Hailey, Idaho; son of James D. (a farmer) and Helen C. (Folsom) Belveal; married Ione L. Pflug, August 14, 1960; children: William Dee, Donald Wesley, Robert Edwin. *Education:* American University, A.B., 1938, M.A., 1945. *Home:* 3100 Country Lane, Wilmette, Ill. 60091. *Agent:* Harry E. Walton, Box 125, Wilmette, Ill. 60091.

CAREER: National Foundation for Infantile Paralysis, New York City, staff member, 1947-52; National Association of Manufacturers, New York City, executive, 1952-57; professional speculator in commodities, and consulting economist, 1957—. *Military service:* U.S. Naval Reserve, active duty, 1942-45.

WRITINGS—All published by Commodities Press: *Commodity Trading Manual,* 1966; *Commodity Speculation—With Profits in Mind,* 1967; *Charting Commodity Market Price Behavior,* 1969. Contributor to magazines.

WORK IN PROGRESS: Find Me a Man, a novel; *History of American Markets.*

AVOCATIONAL INTERESTS: Photography, music, travel.†

* * *

BENASUTTI, Marion   1908-

PERSONAL: Born August 2, 1908, in Philadelphia, Pa.; daughter of Joseph E. (a builder) and Elvira (Serafini) Gosette; married Frank I. Benasutti (a consulting engineer), August 2, 1930; children: Noel (deceased), Frank J. *Education:* Temple University, special courses. *Politics:* Democrat. *Religion:* Roman Catholic. *Home:* Mt. Vernon, Apt. 6A3, 885 Easton Rd., Glenside, Pa. 19038. *Agent:* Curtis Brown Ltd., 60 East 56th St., New York, N.Y. 10022.

CAREER: Italian-American Herald (weekly), Philadelphia, Pa., women's editor, 1960-62; National League of American Pen Women, Washington, D.C. editor of *Pen Woman,* 1964-68; free-lance writer for newspapers and magazines; lecturer at Georgetown University, Holy Angels College, Holy Family College, and in public and private schools. *Member:* National League of American Pen Women, Philadelphia Art Alliance, Professional Writers' Club of Philadelphia.

WRITINGS: No Steady Job for Papa (novel), Vanguard, 1966. Also author of a cookbook, *With Love Everything Tastes Better,* and *Rosemary for Remembrance.* Articles published in magazines, including *McCall's, Mademoiselle, Redbook, American Home,* and *Reader's Digest,* and short stories in *Seventeen, Marriage, Family Weekly* (Great Brit-

ain), *Literary Review,* and Catholic magazines; contributor of features to Philadelphia daily and Sunday newspapers and *Camden Courier-Post.* Columnist, "The Feminine View," and "Woman Talk" in *Catholic Star Herald,* Camden, and "Books and Authors," in *Delaware Valley Calendar.*

BIOGRAPHICAL/CRITICAL SOURCES: Pen Woman, April, 1964; *Horn Book,* February, 1965; Rose Basile Green, *Italian-American Novel,* Fairleigh Dickinson University Press, 1974.

* * *

BENDER, Marylin   1925-

PERSONAL: Born April 25, 1925, in New York, N.Y.; daughter of Michael (a merchant) and Janet (Sloane) Bender; married Selig Altschul (an aviation consultant), 1959; children: James. *Education:* Smith College, A.B., 1944; Columbia University, LL.B., 1947. *Agent:* Ann Elmo Agency, Inc., 52 Vanderbilt Ave., New York, N.Y. 10017. *Office: New York Times,* 229 West 43rd St., New York, N.Y. 10036.

CAREER: New York Journal American, New York City, reporter, 1951-58; *Parade,* New York City, writer, 1958-59; *New York Times,* New York City, reporter, 1959—.

WRITINGS—Nonfiction: *The Beautiful People,* Coward, 1967; *At the Top,* Doubleday, 1975. Contributor to magazines.

BIOGRAPHICAL/CRITICAL SOURCES: Christian Science Monitor, October 5, 1967; *New York Times Book Review,* October 15, 1967; *Reporter,* November 30, 1967.

* * *

BENDER, Todd K.   1936-

PERSONAL: Born January 8, 1936, in Stark County, Ohio; son of Kenneth W. and Minnie (Hill) Bender; married Patricia Ann Minor, September 6, 1958; children: Kirsten Ann, Claire Elaine. *Education:* Kenyon College, B.A., 1958; University of Sheffield, graduate study, 1958-59; Stanford University, Ph.D., 1962; postdoctoral study at Campion Hall, Oxford, 1963. *Office:* Department of English, University of Wisconsin, Madison, Wis. 53706.

CAREER: Instructor in English at Stanford University, Stanford, Calif., 1961-62, and Dartmouth College, Hanover, N.H., 1962-63; University of Virginia, Charlottesville, assistant professor of English, 1963-66; University of Wisconsin, Madison, associate professor, 1966-73, professor of English, 1973—. *Awards, honors:* Fulbright scholar at University of Sheffield, 1958-59; American Council of Learned Societies grant-in-aid for work at Oxford University, 1963, and fellowship at Bibliotheque Nationale, Paris, France, 1965-66.

WRITINGS: Gerard Manley Hopkins: The Classical Background and Critical Reception of His Work, Johns Hopkins Press, 1966; *A Concordance to Hopkins,* University of Wisconsin Press, 1970; *A Concordance to Heart of Darkness,* Southern Illinois University Press, 1973; *A Concordance to Lord Jim,* Garland Press, 1975; *Modernism in Literature,* Holt, 1976. Contributor to *Times Literary Supplement, Criticism,* and other publications.

* * *

BENFIELD, Derek   1926-

PERSONAL: Born March 11, 1926, in Bradford, Yorkshire, England; son of William Thomas (a journalist) and Pansy (Raymond) Benfield; married Susan Lyall Grant (an actress), July 17, 1953; children: Kate, Jamie. *Education:* Attended Royal Academy of Dramatic Art, 1947-49. *Politics:* Moderate socialist. *Religion:* Church of England. *Home:* 4 Berkeley Rd., Barnes, London, S.W. 13, England.

CAREER: Began professional acting career in repertory theaters of England, and first played in London in "The Young Elizabeth"; playwright, 1951—, with first play produced by Reginald Salberg at Preston, England, 1951, and first farce premiered in London, 1954; television actor, currently starring in British Broadcasting Corp.. series, "The Brothers." *Military service:* British Army, Infantry, 1943-47; served in Germany, Egypt, and Palestine; became sergeant. *Member:* League of Dramatists, British Actors' Equity, Green Room Club.

WRITINGS—Three-act plays: *The Young in Heart,* H. F. W. Deane, 1953; *Champagne for Breakfast,* H. F. W. Deane, 1954; *The Way the Wind Blows,* H. F. W. Deane, 1954; *Wild Goose Chase* (farce), Evans Brothers, 1956; *Running Riot* (farce), Evans Brothers, 1958; *Out of Thin Air* (comedy), H. F. W. Deane, 1961; *Fish Out of Water* (comedy), Evans Brothers, 1963; *Down to Brass Tacks* (comedy), H. F. W. Deane, 1964; *Post Horn Gallop* (sequel to *Wild Goose Chase*), Evans Brothers, 1965; *Murder for the Asking* (thriller), Evans Brothers, 1967; *Off the Hook* (farce), Evans Brothers, 1969; *A Bird in the Hand* (comedy), Evans Brothers, 1973; *Panic Stations* (farce), Evans Brothers, 1975; *Caught on the Hop* (comedy), Evans Brothers, 1976; *Joking Apart* (comedy), Evans Brothers, 1976.

One-act plays: *Third Party Risk,* Evans Brothers, 1964; *The Party,* Evans Brothers, 1964.

Occasional contributor to two television series, "Z Cars" and "Dixon of Dock Green."

SIDELIGHTS: Benfield's first farce, *Wild Goose Chase,* has been performed in many parts of the world and is still popular fare. *Post Horn Gallop* was presented in Turkish at the Municipal Theatre, Istanbul, in 1966.

*   *   *

BENNETT, John Jerome Nelson 1939-
(Jeremy Bennett)

PERSONAL: Born December 1, 1939, in Worthing, England; son of Denis P. (a headmaster) and Jill (Nelson) Bennett; married Tine Langkilde, August 3, 1963. *Education:* Clare College, Cambridge, B.A., 1962, M.A., 1966. *Home:* 30 Grove Lane, Camberwell, London S.E. 5, England.

CAREER: British Broadcasting Corp., London, England, producer and sometime radio broadcaster, 1966—. Has also broadcast for Danish Radio. *Member:* Hurlingham Club (London). *Awards, honors:* Churchill fellow, University of Copenhagen, 1962-63.

WRITINGS—Under name Jeremy Bennett: *British Broadcasting and the Danish Resistance Movement, 1940-45,* Cambridge University Press, 1966; (contributor) *The Strategy of Civilian Defence,* Faber, 1967. Book reviewer, *Birmingham Post.*

WORK IN PROGRESS: Britain and Norway, 1940-1945.

BIOGRAPHICAL/CRITICAL SOURCES: Birmingham Post, December 15, 1966.†

BENSMAN, Joseph 1922-
(Jay Bentham, Ian Lewis)

PERSONAL: Born January 29, 1922, in Two Rivers, Wis.; son of Louis (a shoemaker) and Mary (Zussman) Bensman; married Marilyn Dlugacz (a sociologist), June 15, 1944; children: David, Rhea, Miriam. *Education:* University of Wisconsin, B.A., 1945, M.A., 1946, Columbia University, Ph.D., 1958. *Politics:* Independent. *Home:* 6 Wilwade Rd., Great Neck, N.Y.

CAREER: Syracuse University, Syracuse, N.Y., instructor in sociology, 1948-50; U.S. Information Agency, New York City, research analyst, 1951-54; William Esty, Inc., New York City, director of market research, 1954-64; City College of the City University of New York, New York City, associate professor, 1964-68, professor of sociology, 1968—. Lecturer at Brooklyn College (now Brooklyn College of the City University of New York), 1957, and Hunter College (now Hunter College of the City University of New York), 1958; adjunct associate professor, New School for Social Research, 1958-68; visiting associate professor, University of California, Berkeley, 1966; visiting professor, University of Leicester, 1967-68; holder of Hardy Chair in Sociology, Hartwick College, 1974-75. Research director for Bedford Stuyvesant Youth in Action, 1964, and New York University Study of Unemployed Youth, 1965-67. *Military service:* U.S. Army Air Forces, 1943-46. Member of Democratic Socialist Organizing Committee. *Member:* American Sociological Association, American Academy of Political and Social Science, Eastern Sociological Society.

WRITINGS: (With Arthur Vidich) *Small Town in Mass Society,* Princeton University Press, 1958; (with Bernard Rosenberg) *Mass, Class, and Bureaucracy: The Evolution of Contemporary Society,* Prentice-Hall, 1963; (editor with Vidich and others) *Reflections on Community Studies,* Wiley, 1965; *Dollars and Sense,* Macmillan, 1967, revised edition published as *Dollars and Sense: Ideology, Ethics, and the Meaning of Work in Profit and Nonprofit Organizations,* 1974; (with Vidich) *The New American Society: The Revolution of the Middle Class,* Quadrangle, 1971; (with Robert Lilienfeld) *Craft and Consciousness: Occupation Technique and the Development of World Images,* Wiley-Interscience, 1973; (editor with Vidich) *Metropolitan Communities,* F. Watts, 1975; (editor with Rosenberg) *Sociology: Introductory Readings in Mass, Class, and Bureaucracy,* Praeger, 1975. Contributor to *Nation, Human Organization,* and other journals, and under pseudonyms to *Dissent* and various anthologies.

WORK IN PROGRESS: The Evolution of Public and Private Roles, with Robert Lilienfeld.

AVOCATIONAL INTERESTS: Music, the arts, fiction, drinking, and talking.

*   *   *

BENT, Charles N. 1935-

PERSONAL: Born October 22, 1935, in Roxbury, Mass.; son of Charles (a carpenter) and Dorothy (Burns) Bent. *Education:* Boston College, A.B, 1959, M.A., 1960; Weston College of Theology, Ph.L. (magna cum laude), 1960, S.T.L. (magna cum laude), 1967; Yale University, graduate study, 1968. *Home:* 297 Commonwealth Ave., Boston, Mass. 02115. *Office:* Department of Theology, College of the Holy Cross, Worcester, Mass. 01610.

CAREER: Roman Catholic priest, member of Society of

Jesus (Jesuits). Teacher of physics and mathematics at Cheverus High School in Portland, Me., 1960-63; Northeastern University, Boston, Mass., chaplain to Catholic students, 1964-67; College of the Holy Cross, Worcester, Mass., instructor in theology, 1967—.

WRITINGS: The Death of God Movement, Paulist Press, 1967; *Interpreting the Doctrine of God*, Paulist Press, 1969.††

*   *   *

BENY, Wilfred Roy   1924-
(Roloff Beny)

PERSONAL: Born January 7, 1924, in Medicine Hat, Alberta, Canada; son of Charles John Francis and Rosalie N. (Roloff) Beny; unmarried. *Education:* Banff School of Fine Arts, student, 1939; Trinity College, University of Toronto, B.A. and B.F.A., 1945; University of Iowa, M.A. and M.F.A., 1947; further study at Columbia University and New York University, 1947-48, and in Europe, 1948-49, 1951-52. *Religion:* Anglican. *Home and studio:* Lungotevere Ripa 3-B, Rome, Italy; and 432 13th St. S., Lethbridge, Alberta, Canada.

CAREER: Artist and photographer. His first public showing was a watercolor accepted for exhibition by Manitoba Society of Artists when he was fifteen, and two years later the first of his twenty-five one-man shows was staged in Toronto; also has prepared ten major public photographic exhibits since 1962, among them "Image Canada," a collection of thirty-eight murals commissioned for the Federal Pavilion at Expo '67. One-man shows have been held in New York, Paris, and London, as well as in the principal cities of Canada and Italy; paintings and graphic art are in the permanent collections of National Gallery of Canada, Fogg Museum of Boston, Brooklyn Museum, New York Museum of Modern Art, and in galleries and museums in Italy, London, and Jerusalem, as well as in private collections· work has been hung in numerous national exhibitions, including shows at Art Institute of Chicago, Library of Congress, Dallas Museum of Fine Arts, and Canadian National Exhibition, Toronto. In addition to Expo '67's "Image Canada," Beny has prepared other photographic exhibits, including "A Time of Gods," shown in Rome and Toronto, 1962, "Metaphysical Monuments," in Rome and Toronto, "Pleasure of Photography," in London, England, and throughout Canada, 1966, "Sculpture of the Renaissance," by National Film Board of Canada, 1967, and "The Renaissance," 1968. "A Visual Odyssey, 1958-68," a ten-year retrospective, was exhibited at the Gallery of Modern Art, New York and in 1973 was acquired for the permanent art collection of the University of Calgary. A special exhibition of Roloff Beny's books was held at Canada House, New Delhi, India, 1971, to commemorate Canada's Flag Day. *Member:* Royal Canadian Academy (life member).

AWARDS, HONORS: Guggenheim fellowship for print-making and painting, 1953; International Prize for Design at Leipzig Book Fair, 1959, for *The Thrones of Earth and Heaven; Terre des Dieux* (French edition of *A Time of Gods*) was selected as one of the fifty great books of 1965 by Comite des Arts Graphiques Francais; Centennial Medal from Government of Canada, 1967; *To Every Thing There Is a Season* was one of the books chosen by the Canadian Government for presentation to heads of state invited to Canada's Centennial celebration, 1967; Canada Council Visual Arts Award, 1968; International Book Fair at Leipzig gold medal, 1968, for *Japan in Color;* LL.D., University of Lethbridge, 1972; Officer of the Order of Canada, 1972.

WRITINGS—All self-designed photographic books, except as noted: *An Aegean Note Book* (collection of lithographs), Thames & Hudson, 1950; (text by Bernard Berenson; commentaries by Jean Cocteau and others) *The Thrones of Earth and Heaven*, Abrams, 1958; *A Time of Gods*, Viking, 1962; (text by Rose Macaulay) *Pleasure of Ruins*, Time-Life Books, 1964; *To Every Thing There Is a Season*, Thames & Hudson, 1967; (text by Anthony Thwaite) *Japan in Color*, McGraw, 1967; (with Aubrey Menen) *India*, McGraw, 1969; (text by John Lindsay Opie) *Island-Ceylon*, Thames & Hudson, 1971; (text by Anthony Thwaite and Peter Porter; epilogue by Gore Vidal) *Roloff Beny in Italy* (Book-of-the-Month Club selection), Thames & Hudson, 1974. Articles and photographs have appeared in Canadian, American, English, and continental publications, including *Catelaine, Harper's Bazaar, Canadian Art, Mayfair, Sunday Times* (London), *Vogue, Queen,* a special Italian edition of *La Revue des Voyages,* and many others.

WORK IN PROGRESS: A book of 100 poems by Desmond O'Grady inspired by 100 photographs by Beny; *Persia, Bridge of Turquoise,* a major work on Iran.

SIDELIGHTS: A *New York Times* reviewer said of "A Visual Odyssey, 1958-68": "No individual photographer has ever had this kind of space to work with in any gallery or museum in this city, if not the country." There have been foreign editions of Beny's first three photographic books; *A Time of Gods* and *Pleasure of Ruins* have been published in eight languages. *To Every Thing There Is a Season,* a Centennial book about Canada, hit the top spot on that nation's list of best sellers. Beny says that his study of etching and graphic art (largely at the University of Iowa) provided the link between his painting, photography, and book design.

BIOGRAPHICAL/CRITICAL SOURCES: New York Times, September 29, 1968.

*   *   *

BERBUSSE, Edward J(oseph)   1912-

PERSONAL: Born November 30, 1912, in Port Chester, N.Y.; son of William A., Jr. (a general contractor) and Lauretta (Lyons) Berbusse. *Education:* Loyola University, Chicago, Ill., B.A., 1938; Fordham University, M.A., 1948; Georgetown University, Ph.D., 1952. *Religion:* Roman Catholic. *Home and office:* Department of History, Fordham University, Bronx, N.Y. 10458.

CAREER: Roman Catholic priest of Jesuit order (S.J.); high school teacher in New York, 1939-42; assistant professor of history at Canisius College, Buffalo, N.Y., 1952-54, and Fordham University, Bronx, N.Y., 1954-59; Colegio San Ignacio, Rio Piedras, Puerto Rico, rector, 1959-62; University of Puerto Rico, Rio Piedras, director of Catholic Center and lecturer in U.S. history, 1962-66; historical research in National Archives and Library of Congress, Washington, D.C., 1966-67; Fordham University, assistant professor, 1967-71, associate professor of history, 1971—. *Member:* Conference on Latin American History, Conference on Latin American Studies.

WRITINGS: The Origins of the McLane-Ocampo Treaty of 1859, Academy of American Franciscan History, 1958; *The United States in Puerto Rico, 1898-1900*, University of North Carolina Press, 1966. Contributor to journals.

WORK IN PROGRESS: A Century of United States-Mexican Relations, 1823-1933.

SIDELIGHTS: Edward Berbusse speaks Spanish; he has done extensive travel, and research and teaching in Mexico.

*   *   *

BERG, David 1920-
(Dave Berg)

PERSONAL: Born June 12, 1920, in Brooklyn, N.Y.; son of Morris and Bessie (Friedman) Berg; married Vivian Lipman (a comic-book artist), March 3, 1949; children: Mitchel Ian, Nancy Ann Iva. *Education:* Studied at Pratt Institute, New School for Social Research, Cooper Union, and Art Students League. *Politics:* Registered Democrat. *Religion:* Jewish. *Home:* 40 Davenport Ave., New Rochelle, N.Y. 10805.

CAREER: Cartoonist, illustrator, lecturer, writer, and editor with Marvel Comics (comic books), Fawcett Publications, and Will Eisner Productions, New York, N.Y., working on "Captain Marvel," "Archie," and other series, 1947-55; *Mad* (magazine), New York, N.Y., artist and writer, 1955—. Boy Scouts of America, field commissioner. *Military service:* U.S. Army Air Forces, Chemical Warfare, 1942-46; war correspondent on Iwo Jima, Guam, Saipan, and in Japan; became sergeant. *Awards, honors:* Th.D., Reconstructionist Rabbinical College.

WRITINGS—Under name Dave Berg: *Mad's Dave Berg Looks at the U.S.A.*, New American Library, 1964; *Mad's Dave Berg Looks at People*, New American Library, 1966; *Mad's Dave Berg Looks at Things*, New American Library, 1967; *Mad's Dave Berg Looks at Modern Thinking*, New American Library, 1969.

Mad's Dave Berg Looks at Our Sick World, New American Library, 1971; *My Friend GOD*, New American Library, 1972; *Mad's Dave Berg Looks at Living*, Warner Paperback, 1973; *Roger Kaputnik and GOD*, Warner Paperback, 1974; *Mad's Dave Berg Looks Around*, Warner Paperbacks, 1976. Was ghost writer of several newspaper cartoon features.

WORK IN PROGRESS: The Bible According to Roger Kaputnik, for New American Library; *Mad's Dave Berg Looks with Love,* for Warner Paperbacks.

SIDELIGHTS: David Berg told *CA:* "I am motivated by the ethics of religion. I am yelling 'Hey, world, cut it out, and that goes for me too.' My vehicle is satire, and my gimmick is humor." Berg's books have been translated into Swedish, German, Danish, and Finnish.

*   *   *

BERG, Ivar E(lis), Jr. 1929-

PERSONAL: Born January 3, 1929, in Brooklyn, N.Y.; son of Ivar Elis (a carpenter) and Hjordis (Holmgren) Berg; married Winifred Welling (a research assistant), August 29, 1950; children: Geoffrey S. *Education:* Colgate University, A.B., 1954; University of Oslo, graduate study, 1954-55; Harvard University, Ph.D., 1959. *Politics:* Independent. *Office:* Graduate School of Business, Columbia University, New York, N.Y. 10027.

CAREER: Columbia University, New York, N.Y., 1959—, began as instructor, professor of sociology and business, 1968-72, George E. Warren Professor of Sociology and Business, 1972—, member of administrative

board of Bureau of Applied Social Research. Visiting lecturer, University of Toronto, 1972. Member of review panel, Center for Metropolitan Studies, National Institute of Mental Health, 1971—. Consultant to Russell Sage Foundation, 1966-68, National Commission on Crime and Administrative Justice, 1967-68, U.S. Department of Labor, 1970—, U.S. Department of Health, Education and Welfare, 1970—, American Telephone and Telegraph Co., 1971—, Ford Foundation, National Commission on Employment of Youth, and others. Member of board of governors, Center for Research and Education in American Liberties; chairman, Citizens Study Groups for Education, Hastings-on-Hudson. *Military service:* U.S. Marine Corps and U.S. Marine Corps Reserve, 1946-65; on active duty, 1946-48, 1950-52; became major. *Member:* American Sociological Association (fellow), American Association for the Advancement of Science, Society for Applied Anthropology, American Civil Liberties Union, New York Academy of Science, Phi Beta Kappa, Beta Gamma Sigma. *Awards, honors:* Fulbright scholar in Norway, 1954-55; grants from center for Urban Education, Columbia University, 1966-70, U.S. Department of Labor, 1970-72, and Ford Foundation, 1972-75.

WRITINGS: (With Eli Ginzberg) *Democratic Values and the Rights of Management,* Columbia University Press, 1964; (with Ginzberg and others) *Talent and Performance,* Columbia University Press, 1965; (with James Kuhn) *Values in a Business Society,* Harcourt, 1968; (editor and contributor) *The Business of America,* Harcourt, 1968; *Education and Jobs: The Great Training Robbery,* introduction by Ginzberg, Praeger, 1970; (editor) *Human Resources and Economic Welfare,* Columbia University Press, 1972.

Contributor: Leonard Sayles, *Individualism and Big Business,* McGraw, 1963; *Manpower Report of the President of the United States,* U.S. Government Printing Office, 1966; Ginzberg, *The Development of Human Resources,* McGraw, 1966; *Report on Juvenile Delinquency,* President's Commission on Law Enforcement and Administration of Justice, U.S. Government Printing Office, 1967; Ginzberg, *Manpower Agenda for America,* McGraw, 1968; Ginzberg, editor, *Manpower Strategy for the Metropolis,* Columbia University Press, 1968. Contributor to *Labor Law, Human Organization,* and other journals.

SIDELIGHTS: Ivar Berg is fluent in Norwegian and can "negotiate" Swedish and Danish. *Avocational interests:* Stamp collecting, travel in Norway.†

*   *   *

BERGMANN, Peter G(abriel) 1915-

PERSONAL: Born March 24, 1915, in Berlin, Germany; became U.S. citizen, 1942; son of Max (a biochemist) and Emmy (a physician; maiden name, Grunwald) Bergmann; married Margot Eisenhardt (a researcher in x-ray crystallography), May 23, 1936; children: Ernest E., John E. *Education:* Studied at Universities of Dresden, Freiburg, and Prague; University of Prague, Dr.rer.nat. (D.Sc. equivalent), 1936. *Office:* Department of Physics, Syracuse University, Syracuse, N.Y. 13210.

CAREER: Institute for Advanced Study, Princeton, N.J., member of Institute and assistant to Albert Einstein, 1936-41; assistant professor of physics at Black Mountain College, Black Mountain, N.C., 1941-42, and Lehigh University, Bethlehem, Pa., 1942-44; staff member and assistant director of sonar analysis group, Division of War Research,

Columbia University, New York, N.Y., and Woods Hole Oceanographic Institution, 1944-47; Syracuse University, Syracuse, N.Y., associate professor, 1947-50, professor of physics, 1950—. Adjunct professor, Polytechnic Institute of Brooklyn, 1947-57; Yeshiva University, visiting professor, 1959-63, 1970—, professor and chairman, department of physics, 1963-64; lecturer at King's College, University of London, at University of Stockholm, and in Italy, 1958. Member of International Committee on Relativity and Gravitation, 1959—. *Member:* American Physical Society, American Mathematical Society, Federation of American Scientists (chairman, 1963-64), European Physical Society, German Physical Society, American Association for the Advancement of Science, Sigma Xi.

WRITINGS: Introduction to the Theory of Relativity, Prentice-Hall, 1942, revised edition, Dover, 1976; *Basic Theories of Physics,* two volumes, Prentice-Hall, 1949; *The Riddle of Gravitation,* Scribner, 1968. Contributor of articles on relativity to *Encyclopedia of Physics* and *Encyclopaedia Britannica.* Associate editor of several physics journals.

WORK IN PROGRESS: Theoretical physics research, primarily in field of general relativity.

*   *   *

BERKOWITZ, Pearl H(enriette)   1921-

PERSONAL: Born September 9, 1921, in New York, N.Y.; daughter of Henry and Fannie (Hauptman) Schwartz; married Sol Berkowitz (a composer), June 27, 1945. *Education:* Queens College (now Queens College of the City University of New York), Flushing, N.Y., B.A., 1942; Columbia University, M.A., 1944; New York University, Ph.D., 1957. *Home:* 46-36 Hanford St., Douglaston, N.Y. 11362. *Office:* Edenwald School, 1250 East 229th St., Bronx, N.Y. 10466.

CAREER: Bellevue Psychiatric Hospital, New York, N.Y., teacher in hospital school, 1947-56, acting assistant principal, 1956-60; New York (N.Y.) Board of Education, principal of Edenwald School (for disturbed children), Bronx, N.Y., 1960—. Queens College of the City University of New York, Flushing, N.Y., lecturer in child and abnormal psychology, 1958—. *Member:* American Psychological Association, American Orthopsychiatric Association, Eastern Psychological Association, New York Academy of Sciences, New York State Psychological Association.

WRITINGS: (With Esther Rothman) *The Disturbed Child,* New York University Press, 1960; *Some Psychophysical Aspects of Mental Illness in Children,* Genetic Psychology Monographs, 1961; (editor with Rothman) *Public Education for Disturbed Children in New York City,* C. C Thomas, 1967; (contributor) Clayton D. Lewis and James M. Kauffman, editors, *Teaching Children with Behavior Disorders: Personal Perspectives,* C. E. Merrill, 1974. Publications include a psychological test, *Buttons: Differential Diagnosis in Childhood and Adolescence,* Western Psychological Service, 1964, and *Let's Sing a Little Action* (original songs for children), Lawson-Gould, 1955, both in collaboration with Rothman. Contributor to child psychology journals.

*   *   *

BERKSON, Bill   1939-

PERSONAL: Born August 30, 1939, in New York, N.Y.;

son of Seymour (a journalist) and Eleanor (Lambert) Berkson. *Education:* Attended Brown University, 1957-59, Columbia University, 1959-60. *Residence:* Bolinas, Calif.

CAREER: Art News, New York, N.Y., editorial associate, 1960-63; free-lance art critic, New York, N.Y., 1962-66; WNDT-TV, New York, N.Y., associate producer, "Art-New York" series, 1964-65; New School for Social Research, New York, N.Y., instructor in literature, 1964-69; Yale University, New Haven, Conn., visiting fellow, 1969-70; Big Sky (publishers), Bolinas, Calif., editor, 1971—. Part-time writer, editor, and researcher, Museum of Modern Art, New York, 1965-69; editor, Best & Co., 1969. *Awards, honors:* Dylan Thomas Memorial Award for Poetry, New School for Social Research, 1959; grant from Poets Foundation, 1968; resident at Yaddo, 1968.

WRITINGS: Saturday Night: Poems 1960-61, Tibor de Nagy, 1961; (editor) Frank O'Hara, *In Memory of My Feelings,* illustrated by 30 American artists, Museum of Modern Art, 1967; *Shining Leaves,* Angel Hair, 1969; *Recent Visitors,* Angel Hair, 1974; *Ants,* Arif, 1975; *100 Women,* Simon & Schuster, 1975; *Enigma Variations,* Big Sky, 1975. Contributor to various anthologies. Poems published in *Poetry, Big Table, Paris Review, Locus Solus,* and other publications, articles in *Mercure de France, Art and Literature, Art News, Arts,* among others.

WORK IN PROGRESS: Blue is the Hero: Poems 1960-74.

BIOGRAPHICAL/CRITICAL SOURCES: Poetry, August, 1962; *The World,* Number 29, 1974.

*   *   *

BERLIN, Irving N.   1917-

PERSONAL: Born May 31, 1917, in Chicago, Ill.; son of Solomon (a chef) and Lena (Izrealov) Berlin; married Roxie Wittenberg (a social worker), December 3, 1942; children: Walter and Gregory (twins), Suzanne. *Education:* University of California, Los Angeles, A.B., 1939; University of California, San Francisco, M.D., 1943. *Home:* 1619 Northeast 52nd St., Seattle, Wash. 98105. *Office:* Division of Child Psychiatry, University of Washington School of Medicine, Seattle, Wash. 98105.

CAREER: Los Angeles General Hospital, Los Angeles, Calif., intern, 1943; University of California Medical School, San Francisco, resident at Langley Porter Neuropsychiatric Institute, 1948, 1950, clinical instructor in child psychiatry, 1952-56, assistant clinical professor and director of training, 1956-60, associate clinical professor of child psychiatry and director of training and research, 1960-65; University of Washington School of Medicine, Seattle, professor of psychiatry and pediatrics and head of Division of Child Psychiatry, 1965—. Consultant to McAuley Neuropsychiatric Institute and to Center for training in Community Psychiatry and Administration, Berkeley, Calif. *Military service:* U.S. Army Medical Corps, 1944-46; served in Germany.

MEMBER: American Orthopsychiatric Association (fellow; board member, 1962—; vice-president, 1965-66), American Psychiatric Association (fellow), American Academy of Child Psychiatry (fellow; president, 1973-75), American College of Psychiatry (fellow), King County Medical Society.

WRITINGS: Bibliography of Child Psychiatry, Number 1, American Psychiatric Association, 1963; *Advocacy for Child Mental Health,* Brunner, 1975; *Bibliography of Child*

Psychiatry and Selected Films, Behavioral Publications, 1975.

Editor—All with S. A. Szurek; all published by Science and Behavior Press, except as noted: *Learning and its Disorders,* 1966; *Training in Therapeutic Work with Children,* 1967; *Psychosomatic Disorders and Mental Retardation in Children,* 1968; *The Antisocial Child: His Family and His Community,* 1969; (and with M. J. Boatman) *Inpatient Care for the Psychotic Child,* 1971; *Clinical Studies in Childhood Psychoses,* Brunner, 1973.

Contributor: H. I. Kaplan and A. M. Friedman, editors, *Comprehensive Textbook of Psychiatry,* Williams & Wilkins, 1967; I. Philips, editor, *Prevention and Treatment of Mental Retardation,* Basic Books, 1966. Contributor of more than ninety articles to psychiatric and related journals. Member of editorial board, *Journal of Community Mental Health, Journal of the American Academy of Child Psychiatry, American Journal of Orthopsychiatry, Archives of General Psychiatry, Journal of Autism and Childhood Schizophrenia.*

WORK IN PROGRESS: Editing a volume on *Prevention,* for Basic Books.

AVOCATIONAL INTERESTS: Photography.

* * *

BERMAN, Louise M(arguerite)   1928-

PERSONAL: Born July 6, 1928, in Hartford, Conn.; daughter of Jacob (a lawyer) and Anna (Woike) Berman. *Education:* Wheaton College, Wheaton, Ill., A.B., 1950; Columbia University, M.A., 1953, Ed.D., 1960. *Residence:* Hyattsville, Md. *Office:* College of Education, University of Maryland, College Park, Md. 20742.

CAREER: Teacher in New Jersey, 1950-51, and Connecticut, 1951-54; instructor at Central Connecticut State College, New Britain, 1954-58, and Teachers College, Columbia University, New York, N.Y., 1958-60; University of Wisconsin-Milwaukee, assistant professor, 1960-63, associate professor, 1963-65; Association for Supervision and Curriculum Development, Washington, D.C., associate secretary, 1965-67; University of Maryland, College of Education, College Park, professor of education, 1967—. *Member:* Association for Supervision and Curriculum Development, American Educational Research Association, National Council of Teachers of English, Professors of Curriculum, World Future Society, Pi Lambda Theta, Kappa Delta Pi.

WRITINGS: (With Mary Lou Usery) *Personalized Supervision: Sources and Insights,* Association for Supervision and Curriculum Development, 1966; (editor) *The Humanities and the Curriculum,* Association for Supervision and Curriculum Development, 1967; *From Thinking to Behaving,* Teachers College, Columbia University, 1967; *New Priorities in the Curriculum,* C. E. Merrill, 1968; *Supervision, Staff Development, and Leadership,* C. E. Merrill, 1971; (with Jessie Roderick) *Teaching the What, How, and Why of Living,* Charles A. Jones Publishing, in press. Contributor to education journals.

* * *

BERNARD, Hugh Y(ancey), Jr.   1919-

PERSONAL: Born July 17, 1919, in Athens, Ga.; son of Hugh Yancey (a merchant) and Marguerite (Von der Au) Bernard. *Education:* Piedmont College, student, 1937-38; University of Georgia, A.B., 1941; Columbia University,

B.S.L.S., 1947; George Washington University, J.D., 1961. *Religion:* Baptist. *Home:* 1911 Paul Spring Pkwy., Alexandria, Va. 22308.

CAREER: High school teacher of general science, Moultrie, Ga., 1941; U.S. Veterans Administration, Atlanta, Ga., clerk-supervisor, 1946; Library of Congress, Washington, D.C., cataloger, later reviser in copyright office, 1947-59, cataloger in Descriptive Catalogue Division, 1959-60; George Washington University Law School, Washington, D.C., law librarian, 1960—, member of law faculty, 1962—, professor of law, 1970—. Director, trustee, Luther Rice College, Alexandria, Va., 1972—. Law library consultant, U.S. State Department, Agency for International Development, Kabul, Afghanistan, 1974. *Military service:* U.S. Army Air Forces, 1942-46; served in the Philippines; became staff sergeant. *Member:* American Association of Law Libraries, Special Libraries Association, American Bar Association, District of Columbia Bar Association, Law Librarians' Society of Washington, D.C. (vice-president, 1964-66; president, 1966), National Lawyers' Club, Phi Beta Kappa, Phi Alpha Delta, Order of the Coif (honorary member), Masons, Knights Templar, Shriners.

WRITINGS: (Contributor) Werner Ellinger, editor, *Subject Headings for the Literature of Law and International Law,* Fred B. Rothman, 1963, revised edition, 1969; *The Law of Death and Disposal of the Dead,* Oceana, 1966; *Public Officials: Elected and Appointed,* Oceana, 1968; (contributor) Parnell J. T. Callahan, editor, *Your Complete Guide to Estate Planning,* Oceana, 1971. Contributor of notes, book appraisals, and short articles to *George Washington Law Review* and law library journals. Consultant/reviewer, *Law Books in Review* and *Reprint Bulletin Book Reviews,* 1972—.

WORK IN PROGRESS: Studies on the law governing private clubs and societies, and on alcoholism and other addictive diseases; and on law governing organ transplants and other advances in medical science.

AVOCATIONAL INTERESTS: American history, "particularly the sidelights and lightly-traveled roads of historical research from the Civil War's end until World War I."

* * *

BERNARD, Jack F.   1930-

PERSONAL: Born September 9, 1930, in Lafayette, La.; son of Fernand C. and Aline M. (Blanchet) Bernard. *Education:* University of Montreal, B.A., 1951; University of Rome, M.A., 1953; University of Paris, Ph.D., 1958; Institute of Medieval Studies, M.A., 1959.

CAREER: Doubleday & Co., Inc., New York, N.Y., editor, beginning 1962. Member of board of directors, Fire Island Pines. *Military service:* U.S. Army, 1953-56. *Member:* American Historical Association, Mediaeval Academy of America.

WRITINGS: (With John Delaney) *A Guide to Catholic Reading,* Doubleday, 1966; *Up from Caesar: A Survey of the History of Italy from the Fall of the Roman Empire to the Collapse of Fascism,* Doubleday, 1970 (published in England as *Italy: An Historical Survey,* David & Charles, 1971); (translator) Marc Oraison, *Morality for Moderns,* Doubleday, 1972; *Talleyrand: A Biography,* Putnam, 1973.

SIDELIGHTS: Bernard is fluent in French and Italian and reads Spanish, German, Latin, Attic Greek. He is particularly interested in European history, from the fall of Rome to the end of the Napoleonic Age.†

BERNARD, Jacqueline (de Sieyes) 1921-

PERSONAL: Born May 5, 1921, in Le Bourget du Lac, Savoie, France; daughter of Jacques Edouard (a diplomat) and Louise (Paine) de Sieyes; married Allen Bernard (a public relations writer), August 31, 1943 (divorced); children: Joel. *Education:* Attended Vassar College, 1939-41, and University of Chicago, 1941-42; has also attended evening classes at City College of the City University of New York, intermittently, 1960—. *Religion:* None. *Home:* 552 Riverside Dr., New York, N.Y. 10027. *Agent:* Marie Rodell, 141 East 55th St., New York, N.Y. 10022.

CAREER: ABC News Service, Jamaica, N.Y., reporter, 1946-48; all New York, N.Y.: Pare Lorentz Associates, picture researcher, 1949-51; *Pageant* (magazine), editorial assistant, 1951-53; Filmstrip House, writer, 1953-57; advertising copywriter with B. L. Mazel, Inc., 1957-59, and Young & Rubicam, 1959-61; Jewish Board of Guardians, public relations associate, 1963-68; currently working as a free-lance reporter. Co-founder and vice-president, Parents Without Partners (nation-wide organization for single parents and their children), 1957-58, currently an honorary member. *Member:* Authors Guild, Community Agencies Public Relations Association.

WRITINGS: Journey Toward Freedom: The Story of Sojourner Truth, Norton, 1967; *Voices from the Southwest,* Scholastic Book Service, 1972; *The Children You Gave Us,* Jewish Child Care Association, 1973. Also author of a book, *Daughter of the Muses,* as yet unpublished.

SIDELIGHTS: Richard Elman, in his reivew of *Journey Toward Freedom,* wrote that "the literal facts" of the career of the Black woman evangelist who called herself Sojourner Truth "would be sufficiently challenging to any ambitious biographer. To the writer for children the problems further proliferate.... Jacqueline Bernard has succeeded on nearly every count." Robert Coles calls Mrs. Bernard "a careful and lively writer, a historian as well as a storyteller." He says that to read her book is to gain "a thorough knowledge of the 19th-century America that struggled so hard over 'the race problem.'" Elman said in conclusion: "I learned from the author's quiet narrative ease and lucid prose, as well as from her careful unostentatious scholarship, her intelligent use of common speech, her choice of credible scenes and snatches of reconstructed dialogue."

Mrs. Bernard has lived in Mexico. *Avocational interests:* People, music (jazz, folk-rock, folk, blues, and classical), history, anthropology, science, art.

BIOGRAPHICAL/CRITICAL SOURCES: New York Times Book Review, November 26, 1967; *Book World,* January 21, 1968.

*   *   *

BERNHEIM, Evelyne 1935-

PERSONAL: Born January 26, 1935, in Austria; daughter of Richard and Erika (Bettelheim) Hirsch; married Marc Bernheim (a photographer). *Education:* Barnard College, B.A., 1955; Columbia University, M.A., 1956; further graduate study at Adelphi University. *Home:* 330 Ridgeway, White Plains, N.Y. 10605.

CAREER: With her husband, free-lance magazine and industrial photographer, working part of the year in Africa and part in America. *Member:* American Society of Magazine Photographers.

WRITINGS—With husband, Marc Bernheim, illustrated with their own photographs: *From Bush to City: A Look at New Africa,* Harcourt, 1966, revised edition, 1968; *A Week in Aya's World: The Ivory Coast,* Macmillan, 1969; *African Success Story: The Ivory Coast,* Harcourt, 1970; *Growing Up in Old New England,* Macmillan, 1971; *Growing Up in Old Sturbridge Village,* Macmillan, 1971; *The Drums Speak: The Story of Kofi, A Boy of West Africa,* Harcourt, 1972; *In Africa,* Atheneum, 1973.

*   *   *

BERNHEIM, Marc 1924-

PERSONAL: Born December 16, 1924, in France; son of Rene and Madeleine (Cerf) Bernheim; married Evelyne Lang (a photographer and author). *Education:* Zurich Polytechnicum, B.S., 1947; Columbia University, graduate study, 1949. *Home:* 330 Ridgeway, White Plains, N.Y. 10605. *Agent:* (Photographs) Woodfin Camp, 50 Rockefeller Plaza, Room 832, New York, N.Y. 10020.

CAREER: Formerly chemical engineer and perfume chemist, heading Evergreen Chemical Co., and Darome Products Corp., New Rochelle, N.Y., 1956-62; with his wife, free-lance magazine and industrial photographer, working part of the year in Africa and part in America. *Military service:* Swiss Army, 1943. *Member:* American Society of Magazine Photographers.

WRITINGS—With wife, Evelyne Bernheim, illustrated with their own photographs: *From Bush to City: A New Look at Africa,* Harcourt, 1966, revised edition, 1968; *A Week in Aya's World: The Ivory Coast,* Macmillan, 1969; *African Success Story: The Ivory Coast,* Harcourt, 1970; *Growing Up in Old New England,* Macmillan, 1971; *Growing Up in Old Sturbridge Village,* Macmillan, 1971; *The Drums Speak: The Story of Kofi, A Boy of West Africa,* Harcourt, 1972; *In Africa,* Atheneum, 1973.

*   *   *

BERNSTEIN, Marilyn 1929-

PERSONAL: Born April 6, 1929, in New York, N.Y.; daughter of Harry and Leona (Kandel) Gabe; married Norman Ralph Bernstein (a physician), August 30, 1953; children: Michael, Genya. *Education:* Cornell University, B.A., 1950; Columbia University, M.S., 1952. *Home:* 87 Garden St., Cambridge, Mass. 02138. *Office:* 606 Larsen Hall, Harvard Graduate School of Education, Appian Way, Cambridge, Mass.

CAREER: Jewish Board of Guardians, Bronx, N.Y., psychiatric social worker, 1952-53; Massachusetts Mental Health Center, Boston, psychiatric social worker, 1953-54; Hillcrest Remedial Reading School, Boston, Mass., teacher, 1954-56; Remedial Scholastic Services, Cambridge, Mass., co-director and teacher, 1956-62; Carroll Hall School, Cambridge, psychiatric social worker, 1963-64; Lesley-Dearborn School, Cambridge, teacher, 1964-65; Harvard University, Graduate School of Education, Cambridge, research associate in sociology of education, beginning 1965.

WRITINGS: (With Robert B. Heinemann) *The Fourth R: A Return to Learning for Sidetracked Adolescents,* Beacon Press, 1967; (with Neal C. Gross) *Implementing Organizational Innovations,* Basic Books, 1971.†

*   *   *

BERNSTEIN, Morey 1919-

PERSONAL: Born June 21, 1919, in Pueblo, Colo.; son of

Samuel and Celia (Wagner) Bernstein; married Hazel Doris Higgins, August 1, 1948. *Education:* University of Pennsylvania, graduate of Wharton School of Finance, 1941; Columbia University, graduate study, 1953. *Religion:* Jewish. *Home:* 1819 Elizabeth, Pueblo, Colo. 81003. *Office:* 134 North Mechanic St., Pueblo, Colo.

CAREER: Partner, Bernstein Brothers Investment Co. and Bernstein Brothers Equipment Co., both Pueblo, Colo., 1941—; Bernstein Brothers Machinery Co., Pueblo, president, 1946-52. Director, Minnequa Bank, 1951-55; chairman of board of Bernstein Realty and Investment Co., Double B, Inc., 1970—, and Wholesales, Inc., 1970—. Chairman, Bernstein Brothers Parapsychology Fund, 1969—.

WRITINGS: The Search for Bridey Murphy, Doubleday, 1965.

SIDELIGHTS: Morey Bernstein holds the patents for Instant Fence and Pronto Panels.

* * *

BERQUIST, Goodwin F(auntleroy)   1930-

PERSONAL: Born June 29, 1930, Rockville Center, N.Y.; son of Goodwin F. and Millicent (Gorham) Berquist; married Nancy Farquharson, June 13, 1953. *Education:* Ohio Wesleyan University, B.A., 1952; Pennsylvania State University, M.A., 1954, Ph.D., 1958. *Politics:* Independent/ Democrat. *Religion:* Unitarian Universalist. *Home:* 970 High St., Worthington, Ohio 43085. *Office:* 205 Derby, 154 North Oval Dr., Ohio State University, Columbus, Ohio 43210.

CAREER: Ohio State University, Columbus, instructor in speech, 1957-60; University of Wisconsin, Milwaukee, assistant professor, 1960-64, associate professor, 1964-68, professor of communication, 1968-69, chairman of department, 1967-68; Ohio State University, professor of communication, 1969—. Visiting professor, University of Hawaii, 1965. *Member:* Speech Communication Association, American Association of University Professors, Central States Speech Association, Speech Communication Association of Ohio. *Awards, honors:* Named outstanding young speech teacher of Ohio by Central States Speech Association, 1957; Kiekhofer award for excellence in teaching from University of Wisconsin, 1964; named outstanding college teacher of the year by Speech Communication Association of Ohio, 1975.

WRITINGS: (Editor) *Speeches for Illustration and Example,* Scott, Foresman, 1965; (with James Golden and William Coleman) *Rhetoric of Western Thought: A Survey of Major Rhetorical Theories,* Kendall/Hunt, 1976.

Editor; all published under auspices of Wisconsin Academy of Sciences, Arts, and Letters: *The Wisconsin Academy Looks at Urbanism,* 1963; *The Natural Resources of Northern Wisconsin,* 1964; *Sciences, Arts, and Letters in Wisconsin History,* 1965. Contributor to speech and history journals. Editor of inter-disciplinary research annual of Wisconsin Academy of Sciences, Arts, and Letters, 1963-66; editorial critic, *Today's Speech, Central States Speech Journal, Western Speech, Pacific Historical Review,* and *Speech Monographs.*

WORK IN PROGRESS: A Bicentennial monograph on the use of revolutionary rhetoric by Black Americans; civil war diary of Brigadier General M. Jeff Thompson, *Frontier Worthington: Civil Liberties, Social Value and the American Dream.*

SIDELIGHTS: Goodwin Berquist enjoys spending his summers reading, thinking, and writing at his summer cabin on Washington Island, Wis.

* * *

BERRY, (Julia) Elizabeth   1920-

PERSONAL: Born November 18, 1920, in Jones, Ala.; daughter of Charles Picton (in lumber manufacturing and farming) and Sarah Annie (Ousley) Berry. *Education:* Central Missouri State College (now University), B.S., 1941; University of Michigan, A.M., 1948; Columbia University, Ph.D., 1955. *Home:* 35 East 68th St., New York, N.Y., 10021. *Office:* Brooklyn College of the City University of New York, Brooklyn, N.Y. 11210.

CAREER: Social science teacher in Independence, Mo., 1941-46; Albuquerque (N.M.) public schools, English teacher and counselor, 1946-56; guidance director in Fort Lauderdale, Fla., 1956-57; Metropolitan Junior College, Kansas City, Mo., counselor, 1957-68; Brooklyn College of the City University of New York, Brooklyn, N.Y., instructor, 1970—. Also maintains a small private practice in counseling under-achieving teen-agers. *Member:* American Personnel and Guidance Association, American College Personnel Association, National Council of Teachers of English (chairman of committee on careers of English majors; member of board of directors, 1960-64), National Association for Foreign Student Affairs, North Central Association of Colleges and Secondary Schools, Greater Kansas City Psychological Association, Phi Lambda Theta, Kappa Delta Pi.

WRITINGS: Guiding Students in the English Class, Appleton, 1957; (contributor) Jerry Weiss, editor, *An English Teacher's Reader,* Odyssey, 1962; *The Careers of English Majors,* National Council of Teachers of English, 1966. Contributor of articles and poetry to education journals.

AVOCATIONAL INTERESTS: Travel, collecting sea shells, water-color painting, studying and observing people.†

* * *

BERRY, James   1932-
(Jim Berry)

PERSONAL: Born January 16, 1932, in Oak Park, Ill.; married, wife's name Heather; children: Duncan, Alex. *Education:* Attended Dartmouth College; graduated from Ohio Wesleyan University.

CAREER: Cartoonist; did animated films for television commercials and conducted training programs for a management consulting firm. Was vice-president of an automobile agency. Associated with Comic Art Department of Newspaper Enterprise Association, Cleveland, Ohio, and creator of "Berry's World," syndicated to more than 800 newspapers. Member of board of governors, and regional chairman, National Cartoonists Society. Served as deacon in the Presbyterian Church; member of Men's Advisory Board of the local League of Women Voters. *Military service:* U.S. Navy. *Member:* Sigma Delta Chi. *Awards, honors:* Best Syndicated Panel Cartoonist Award of the National Cartoonists Society, 1966 and 1967; award for consistently outstanding editorial cartoons, National Headliners Club, 1967.

WRITINGS: (Under name Jim Berry) *Berry's World* (cartoon collection), Four Winds, 1967.

SIDELIGHTS: "Berry's World," the satirical cartoon,

gives editorial comment on the news. Prominent people—from Everett Dirksen to Carol Channing—have requested his cartoon originals, and Bill Mauldin believes that "Berry has come along with the sophisticated touch that used to be found exclusively in the *New Yorker*." Berry believes that "the most important factor in cartooning is the IDEA. This is a matter of creativity and originality. . . . [However] the first impression you make is by the looks of your art work." He admits that "it's fun to be able to comment on what's happening in this 'super age.'"

AVOCATIONAL INTERESTS: Golfing, oil painting, boating, fishing, surfing, traveling, and collecting early cartoon art and rare editions containing the work of great comic artists of the past.††

*   *   *

BERRY, Thomas 1914-

PERSONAL: Born November 9, 1914, in Greensboro, N.C.; son of William Nathan and Elizabeth (Vize) Berry. *Education:* St. Michael's Monastery, Union City, N.J.; Catholic University of America, Ph.D., 1949. *Office:* Theology Department, Fordham University, Bronx, N.Y. 10458.

CAREER: Ordained Roman Catholic priest of the Passionist Congregation, 1942. Fordham University, Bronx, N.Y., associate professor of history of religions, 1966—. Founder and director of Riverdale Center for Religious Research, 1970—. *Military service:* U.S. Army, 1951-54; became first lieutenant. *Member:* American Teilhard Association for the Future of Man (president, 1975—). Association for Asian Studies, American Academy of Religion.

WRITINGS: The Historical Theory of Giambattista Vico, Catholic University of America Press, 1959; *Buddhism,* Hawthorn, 1967; *Religions of India: Hinduism, Yoga, Buddhism,* Macmillan, 1971.

WORK IN PROGRESS: Contemporary Spirituality in America, a study intended especially for college level students.

SIDELIGHTS: Father Berry can work in Classical Chinese, Sanskrit, French, German, Italian, and Latin.

*   *   *

BERTELSON, David (Earl) 1934-

PERSONAL: Born November 26, 1934, in Salt Lake City, Utah; son of Arthur Earl and Gladys (Nelson) Bertelson. *Education:* Harvard University, A.B., 1957, Ph.D., 1965. *Home:* 4942-3 Kilauea Ave., Honolulu, Hawaii 96816. *Office:* Department of American Studies, University of Hawaii, Honolulu, Hawaii 96822.

CAREER: University of California, Berkeley, assistant professor of U.S. intellectual history, 1965-71; University of Hawaii, Honolulu, associate professor of American studies, 1971—. *Military service:* U.S. Army, 1958-60; became first lieutenant. *Member:* American Studies Association, American Association of University Professors, Gay Academic Union.

WRITINGS: The Lazy South, Oxford University Press, 1967.

WORK IN PROGRESS: California and American Individualism.

*   *   *

BERTHELOT, Joseph A. 1927-

PERSONAL: Born January 3, 1927, in Detroit, Mich.; son

of Joseph Alfred and Eva M. (Atchinson) Berthelot. *Education:* Assumption College, University of Western Ontario, B.A., 1949; University of Texas, El Paso, M.A., 1955; University of Denver, Ph.D., 1962. *Home:* 2115 West Chalet, Anaheim, Calif. 92804.

CAREER: University of St. Thomas, Houston, Tex., assistant librarian, 1951-52; U.S. Air Force, active duty, 1951-72, became lieutenant colonel (retired); U.S. Air Force Academy, Colorado Springs, Colo., instructor, 1958-62, assistant professor, 1962-64, associate professor, 1964-72, professor of English, 1972. Visiting professor for U.S. Navy PACE program at Chapman College, 1974-75. *Member:* Modern Humanities Research Association, Phi Alpha Theta. *Awards, honors*—Military: Received Distinguished Flying Cross, Bronze Star, Air Medal and four Oak Leaf Clusters, and Air Force Commendation Medal.

WRITINGS: Michael Drayton, Twayne, 1967. Contributing editor, *Annual Bibliography of English Language and Literature,* 1964-71.

*   *   *

BERWANGER, Eugene H.

PERSONAL: Born in Calumet City, Ill.; son of Henry Nicholas and Cornelia (Benshop) Berwanger; married Elizabeth A. Kohl, June 10, 1967. *Education:* Illinois State University, B.A., 1951, M.A., 1952; University of Illinois, Ph.D., 1964. *Residence:* Fort Collins, Colo. *Office:* Department of History, Colorado State University, Fort Collins, Colo. 80521.

CAREER: High school teacher, Park Ridge, Ill., 1954-60; Illinois College, Jacksonville, assistant professor of history, 1964-67; Colorado State University, Fort Collins, associate professor, 1967-72, professor of history, 1972—. *Military service:* U.S. Army, 1952-54. *Member:* Organization of American Historians, American Historical Association, American Association of University Professors, Southern Historical Association, Pi Gamma Mu, Phi Alpha Theta, Theta Alpha Phi.

WRITINGS: The Frontier Against Slavery: Western Anti-Negro Prejudice and the Slavery Extension Controversy, University of Illinois Press, 1967; *As They Saw Slavery,* Holt, 1973. Contributor to historical journals.

*   *   *

BIGLER, Vernon 1922-

PERSONAL: Born March 30, 1922, in East Falmouth, Mass.; son of C. V. (a Methodist clergyman) and Jessie (Seaver) Bigler; married Patricia A. McKinney, June 30, 1945; children: Paul Vernon. *Education:* DePauw University, A.B., 1944; Boston University, S.T.B., 1947.

CAREER: Methodist clergyman. Missionary to Puerto Rico, 1947-48; pastor in Bainbridge and Union Chapel, Ind., 1948-50, Zionsville, Ind., 1950-56, West Lafayette, Ind., 1956-59, and Terre Haute, Ind., 1959-62; Syracuse University, Syracuse, N.Y., chaplain, 1962-67; First Methodist Church, Syracuse, pastor, beginning 1967. Methodist Church, member of General Board of Education, 1944-47, and General Conference, 1960. Vice-president, United Fund of Terre Haute, 1960-62. *Member:* National Association of Campus and University Ministers, American Civil Liberties Union (chairman of Upstate New York chapter, 1964-65), Rotary International.

WRITINGS: Keywords in Christian Thinking, Association Press, 1966.

WORK IN PROGRESS: The Pastor as Prophet.††

*   *   *

BILLETDOUX, Francois (Paul) 1927-

PERSONAL: Born September 7, 1927, in Paris France; son of Paul and Adrienne (Vidal) Billetdoux; married Eve-lyne Colin, August 2, 1947; children: Virginie, Rafaele. *Education:* Attended Lycee Condorcet, Sorbonne, University of Paris (Faculte de Droit and Faculte des Lettres), Ecole d'Art Dramatique Charles Dullin, and Institut des Hautes Etudes Cinematographiques. *Religion:* Catholic. *Home:* 31, square Montsouris, 75014 Paris, France.

CAREER: Radiodiffusion Francaise, producer, director, writer, 1946—, serving as director of radio and television in Fort-de-France, Martinique, 1949-50, and in General Overseas Service, 1957-58; journalist for *Combat, Arts,* and *Opera,* 1951; nightclub performer and producer of recordings, 1951-53; has worked as a producer, actor, and writer for theatre, radio, television, and records, 1959—. Novelist and filmscript writer. Member of Conseil de Developpement Culturel, beginning 1972, and Haut-Conseil de l'Audiovisuel, beginning 1973. *Awards, honors:* Grand Prix du Disque, 1957, for the production of *Une Rose pour Charles Cros;* Prix Georges Colin; Prix Triomphe (radio), Prix "U," 1959, and Prix Lugne-Poe, both for "Tchin-Tchin"; Prix Ibsen, Prix du Cercle Internationale de le Jeune Critique, and Prix Interclubs du Theatre, 1964, for "Comment va le monde, mossieu? ..."; Prix de L'Unanimite, 1965; Chevalier de la Legion d'Honneur, 1975.

WRITINGS—Plays: "Treize pieces a louer," first produced in Paris at Theatre du Quartier-Latin, 1951; "A la nuit la nuit" (one-act comedy), first produced in Paris at Theatre de l'Oeuvre, 1955; "Hi-Fi," (variety show), first produced in Paris at Theatre des Trois-Baudets, 1957; *Une Rose pour Charles Cros,* Editions du Chant du Monde, 1957; "Tchin-Tchin," first produced in Paris at Theatre de Poche-Montparnasse, 1959, translation by Mark Rudkin first produced on Broadway, with title "Tchin-Tchin," at Plymouth Theatre, October 25, 1962, published as *Chin-Chin,* Secker & Warburg, 1963.

"Le Comportement des epoux Bredburry," first produced in Paris at Theatre des Mathurins, 1960; "Va donc chez Torpe," first produced in Paris at Studio des Champs Elysees, 1961, translation by Mark Rudkin published at *Chez Torpe,* Secker & Warburg, 1963; "Pour Finalie" (one-act comedy), first produced in Paris at Studio des Champs Elysees, 1962; "Comment va le monde, mossieu? Il tourne, mossieu!" first produced in Paris at Theatre de L'Ambigu, 1964; "Il faut passer par les nuages," first produced in Paris by Jean-Louis Barrault at Theatre de France, 1964; "Silence! L'Arbre remue encore!" produced at Festival d'Avignon, 1967; "7 + Quoi?" produced at Festival de Spoleto, 1968, and at Theatre du Gymnase, 1969; "Je n'etais pas chez moi," first produced at Festival de Spolete, 1968; "Quelqu'un devrait faire quelque chose," first produced at Festival de Vaison-la-Romaine, 1969.

"Femmes Paralleles," first produced in Paris at Comedie Francaise, 1970; "Ne m'attendiz pas ce soir," first produced in Paris at Petit Odeon, 1971; "Rintru pa trou tar hin!" first produced at Theatre de la Ville, 1971; "Le nostalgie, comarade," first produced at Theatre de l'Odeon, 1974. Also author, with Eugene Ionesco and Jean Vauthier, of "Chemises de nuit." Wrote the material for the recording "Monologues pour rire," Editions Phonographiques Philips, 1961.

Novels: *L'Animal,* La Table Ronde, 1955; *Royal Garden Blues,* Laffont, 1957; *Brouillon d'un bourgeois,* La Table Ronde, 1961, translation by Ralph Manheim published as *A Man and His Master,* Secker & Warburg, 1963, Hill & Wang, 1964.

Television scripts: "Pitchi Poi ou la parole donne," 1967; "Musique pour une ville," 1969; "Famine chez les rats," 1970; (with Federic Rossif) "Cantique des creatures," 1970; (with Rossif) "L'apocalypse des animaux" (series), 1973.

Radio scripts: "Ai-je dit que je suis bossu?" 1971; "Ocean du theatre," 1972.

Omnibus volumes: *Theatre I* (contains "A la nuit la nuit," "Le Comportement des epoux Bredbury," "Va donc chez Torpe," and "Tchin-Tchin"), La Table Ronde, 1961; *Two Plays* (contains Mark Rudkin's translations of "Tchin-Tchin" and "Chez Torpe"), Hill & Wang, 1964; *Theatre II* (contains "Pour Finalie," "Comment va le monde, mossieu? Il tourne, mossieu!," and "Il faut passer par les nuages"), La Table Ronde, 1964.

SIDELIGHTS: "Few playwrights of any importance have appeared in France in recent years," Frederick Lumley said a few years ago; "it is almost as if the death of the small Left-bank theatres of the Fifties has been catastrophic for playwrights. ... Francois Billetdoux is the only playwright of any stature to appear." Paul A. Mankin assigned Billetdoux to "our school of abstract playwrights" and predicted that "we will hear (or see) more of him, I am sure." Lumley agreed that Billetdoux was a "writer to watch," and added that it was the production of "Va donc chez Torpe" that established his potential importance for contemporary theatre. Unfortunately, little has been translated; Americans can evaluate Billetdoux's playwriting ability only in terms of Mark Rudkin's translations of "Tchin-Tchin" and "Chez Torpe." Billetdoux is known to many as a television writer; his "Pitchi Poi ou la parole donne," scheduled for broadcasting in seventeen countries, was seen by Mankin as an event which would be "bound to make [him] world-famous even if the quality of [the play] will vary considerably from one country to another."

Billetdoux is also a novelist of some significance. Cade Ware, in his review of *A Man and His Master,* wrote: "It's a favorite amusement of modern French novelists to demonstrate that a totally unimaginable approach to the world is humanly possible. When this kind of novel fails, it seems no more than an affection; when it succeeds, it becomes a cold moral lesson. Francois Billetdoux ... has succeeded in this short, difficult and fearsome study: he has portrayed either a hitherto unknown kind of neurosis or a previously undiscovered form of sainthood. ... M. Billetdoux has distilled in his short book an awesome body of thought. It isn't casual reading, and at the end I don't know whether I *understand* it as much as I have been carried pell-mell to its stone-wall conclusion."

BIOGRAPHICAL/CRITICAL SOURCES: New Yorker, April 11, 1964; *Book Week,* April 19, 1964; Frederick Lumley, *New Trends in Twentieth-Century Drama,* Oxford University Press, 1967; *Books Abroad,* autumn, 1967; *L'Express,* March 8-14, 1971.

*   *   *

BILLINGTON, Monroe Lee 1928-

PERSONAL: Born March 4, 1928, in Duncan, Okla.; son of Marion Lester (an oil refiner) and Ossie (Hunt) Billington; married Mary E. Salter (a juvenile probation officer), June 2, 1951; children: Marion Lewis, Martha Reaves, Melinda Lee. *Education:* Oklahoma Baptist University, B.A. (cum laude), 1950; University of Oklahoma, M.A., 1951; University of Kentucky, Ph.D., 1955. *Politics:* Democrat. *Religion:* Disciples of Christ. *Home:* 1733 Imperial Ridge, Las Cruces, N.M. 88001. *Office:* Department of History, New Mexico State University, Las Cruces, N.M. 88003.

CAREER: East Kentucky State College (now Eastern Kentucky University), Richmond, instructor in history, 1955; University of South Dakota, Vermillion, 1955-66, began as instructor, became professor of American history; University of Toledo, Toledo, Ohio, professor of American history, 1966-68; New Mexico State University, Las Cruces, professor of history and head of department, 1968—. Visiting Fulbright professor, University of Vienna, 1962-63; visiting professor, University of Missouri, 1964. *Member:* American Historical Association, Organization of American Historians, Southern Historical Association, South Dakota Historical Society, Phi Beta Kappa, Phi Alpha Theta.

WRITINGS: Thomas P. Gore: The Blind Senator from Oklahoma, University of Kansas Press, 1967; (editor with Duane M. Leach) *Forging of a Nation,* McCutchan, 1968; (editor with Leach) *American Democracy on Trial,* McCutchan, 1968; (editor) *The South: A Central Theme?,* Holt, 1969; *The American South: A Brief History,* Scribner, 1971; *The Political South in the Twentieth Century,* Scribner, 1975. Contributor to *Dictionary of American History, Encyclopedia of Southern History,* and *Dictionary of American Biography;* contributor of forty articles and reviews to historical journals.

WORK IN PROGRESS: Research on black civil rights in the twentieth century.

*   *   *

BINGHAM, John (Michael Ward)   1908-

PERSONAL: Born November 3, 1908, son of Arthur Robert Maurice (Lord Clanmorris) and Leila (Cloete) Bingham; married Madeleine Ebel (a writer), July 28, 1934; children: Simon, Charlotte (also a writer). *Education:* Educated at Cheltenham College, Gloucestershire, England, and in France and Germany. *Religion:* Church of England. *Home:* 4 Abingdon Villas, London W8, England. *Agent:* Ursula Winant, Winant Towers Ltd., 14 Clifford's Inn, London EC4A 1DA, England.

CAREER: Seventh Baron Clanmorris, succeeding father to title, 1960. *Hull Daily Mail,* Hull, England, reporter, beginning in 1931; later joined *Sunday Dispatch,* London, England, as reporter, picture-editor, then feature-writer; served with Control Commission in Germany during the 1940's; Ministry of Defence, London, civil servant, 1950—. Author. *Military service:* British Army, Royal Engineers, 1939-40.

WRITINGS: My Name is Michael Sibley, Dodd, 1952; *The Tender Poisoner,* Dodd, 1953 (published in England as *Five Roundabouts to Heaven,* Gollancz, 1953); *The Third Skin: A Story of Crime,* Dodd, 1954; *The Paton Street Case,* Gollancz, 1955, published as *Inspector Morgan's Dilemma,* Dodd, 1956; *Murder Off the Record,* Dodd, 1957 (published in England as *Marion,* Gollancz, 1957); *Murder Plan Six,* Dodd, 1958; *Night's Black Agent,* Dodd, 1961; *A Case of Libel,* Gollancz, 1963; *Fragment of Fear,* Gollancz, 1965, Dutton, 1966; *The Double Agent,* Gollancz,

1966, Dutton, 1967; *I Love, I Kill,* Gollancz, 1968; *Good Old Charlie,* Simon & Schuster, 1968; *Vulture in the Sun,* Gollancz, 1971; *The Hunting Down of Peter Manuel: Glasgow Multiple Murderer,* Macmillan, 1973.

SIDELIGHTS: Although Baron Clanmorris inherited a castle in Northern Ireland, he was not interested in "a feudal way of life" and hence disposed of the property; the castle became Bangor's Town Hall. *Fragment of Fear* was adapted for film and released by Columbia Pictures, 1970, under the same title.

AVOCATIONAL INTERESTS: Travel and gardening.

BIOGRAPHICAL/CRITICAL SOURCES: Books and Bookmen, March, 1968.†

*   *   *

BINGHAM, Robert C(harles)   1927-

PERSONAL: Born April 12, 1927, in Kenosha, Wis.; son of Vernon Arnt and Myrtle (Kinkead) Bingham; married Patricia Ann Nixon, June 22, 1957; children: Charles William, Anne Elizabeth, Roberta Lynn Elise. *Education:* DePauw University, B.A., 1950; Northwestern University, M.A., 1954, Ph.D., 1962. *Home:* 489 Harvey St., Kent, Ohio 44240. *Office:* Department of Economics, Kent State University, Kent, Ohio 44242.

CAREER: University of Nebraska, Lincoln, instructor, 1954-57, assistant professor of economics, 1957-62; Kent State University, Kent, Ohio, assistant professor, 1962-64, associate professor, 1964-67, professor of economics, 1967—. Visiting professor, Royal University of Malta, 1968-69. *Military service:* U.S. Army, 1945-47. *Member:* American Economic Association, Midwest Economic Association, Ohio Association of Economists and Political Scientists.

WRITINGS: (Editor with Campbell R. McDonnell) *Economics Issues: Readings and Cases,* McGraw, 1963; *Economic Concepts: A Programmed Approach,* McGraw, 1966, 3rd edition, 1972; *Economics: Mathematically Speaking,* McGraw, 1972. Author of study guide to accompany Campbell R. McConnell's *Economics,* McGraw, 1960.

WORK IN PROGRESS: A textbook in intermediate price theory, for McGraw.

AVOCATIONAL INTERESTS: Military history, duplicate bridge, golf.

*   *   *

BIRKENMAYER, Sigmund Stanley   1923-

PERSONAL: Surname originally Birkenmajer; born June 5, 1923, in Warsaw, Poland; son of Joseph Anthony (a university professor of Polish language and literature in Poland and America) and Mary (Jetkiewicz) Birkenmajer; married Amina Maria Martinez, December 22, 1951. *Education:* Jagellonian University, Cracow, Poland, student, 1945-46; University of Wisconsin, B.A. and M.A. (English), 1948, M.A. (Russian), 1957, Ph.D., 1961. *Office:* N-483 Burrowes Building, Pennsylvania State University, University Park, Pa. 16802.

CAREER: University of Puerto Rico, Rio Piedras, instructor in English and German, 1951-55; Lycoming College, Williamsport, Pa., assistant professor of Russian and Spanish, 1959-60; Pennsylvania State University, University Park, assistant professor, 1960-66, associate professor, 1966-73, professor of Slavic languages, 1973—. Member of Russian Achievement Test Committee, College Entrance

Examination Board, 1967-70. *Member:* Modern Language Association of America (head of East European literature section, international bibliography committee, 1963-75), American Association of Teachers of Slavic and East European Languages (president of Pennsylvania chapter, 1965-66), Polish Institute of Arts and Sciences in America, Kosciuszko Foundation, Pennsylvania State Modern Language Association, Association for Advancement of Polish Studies (president, 1973-75).

WRITINGS: A Study of the Preparation of High-School-Trained Students of Russian for College Russian Courses, Department of Slavic Languages, Pennsylvania State University, 1963; (with Zbigniew Folejewski) *Introduction to the Polish Language,* and *Workbook,* Parts I and II, Kosciuszko Foundation, 1965, 3rd edition, 1975; (compiler) *An Accented Dictionary of Place Names in the Soviet Union,* Department of Slavic Languages, Pennsylvania State University, 1967, *Supplement,* 1970; *An Annotated Bibliography on the Teaching of Slavic Languages and Literatures in the United States and Canada Since 1942,* Pennsylvania State University Press, 1968; *Nikolaj Nekrasov: His Life and Art,* Mouton & Co., 1969; *A Modern Polish Reader,* Department of Slavic Languages, Pennsylvania State University, 1970. Contributor of articles and reviews to Slavic journals.

SIDELIGHTS: Birkenmayer speaks Russian and Spanish, and reads French, German, and Ukrainian. He notes that his interest in languages was first instilled in him by his father, who spoke seven, and who translated most of Kipling's works into Polish.

*   *   *

BISHOP, Ferman 1922-

PERSONAL: Born May 4, 1922, in Landrum, S.C.; son of Ferman (a businessman) and Sue (Sligh) Bishop; married Audrey Wierske (a speech correctionist), November 25, 1948; children: Katherine, William John. *Education:* Wofford College, A.B., 1942; University of Wisconsin, M.A., 1948, Ph.D., 1955. *Home:* R.R. #2, Bloomington, Ill. 61701. *Office:* Department of English, Illinois State University, Normal, Ill. 61761.

CAREER: University of Wisconsin-Milwaukee, instructor in English, 1946-47; University of Colorado, Boulder, instructor in English, 1951-55; University of Wichita, Wichita, Kan., assistant professor, 1955-58, associate professor of English, 1958-60; Illinois State University, Normal, associate professor, 1960-64, professor of English, 1964—. *Military service:* U.S. Naval Reserve, active duty, 1942-46; became lieutenant. *Member:* Modern Language Association of America, Midwest Modern Language Association (secretary-treasurer, 1959-66).

WRITINGS: Allen Tate, Twayne, 1967; *Henry Adams,* Twayne, 1975. Contributor to literature journals.

SIDELIGHTS: Bishop has "moderate" competence in French and German.

*   *   *

BISHOP, W(illiam) Arthur 1923-

PERSONAL: Born June 13, 1923, in London, England; son of William Avery (Air Marshal, Royal Canadian Air Force) and Margaret (Burded) Bishop; married Priscilla Aylen (a public relations executive), November 3, 1945; children: Diana, William. *Education:* Educated at Selwyn House, Montreal, Quebec, and Bishop's College School. *Religion:* Church of England. *Home:* 185 Montclair Ave., Toronto, Ontario, Canada. *Agent:* Collins-Knowlton-Wing, Inc., 60 East 56th St., New York, N.Y. 10022. *Office:* PPS Publicity Ltd., 69 Yonge St., Toronto, Ontario, Canada.

CAREER: Engaged in public relations work in Toronto, Ontario; president of Creative Services, 1960—, and PPS Publicity Ltd., Toronto, Ontario, 1963—. Member of board of directors, Canadian National Ballet Guild. *Military service:* Royal Canadian Air Force, 1939-45; became flight lieutenant. *Member:* Badminton and Racquet Club (Toronto).

WRITINGS: The Courage of the Early Morning, McKay, 1966; *Winged Warfare,* Ace Books, 1968.

*   *   *

BISKIN, Miriam 1920-

PERSONAL: Born March 17, 1920; in Cohoes, N.Y.; daughter of Eli (a merchant) and Bessie (Fishman) Newell; married Irving Biskin (a merchant), March 17, 1946; children: Anne, Deborah. *Education:* State University of New York at Albany, B.A., 1941, M.A., 1949. *Religion:* Jewish. *Home:* 2507 16th St., Troy, N.Y.

CAREER: Cohoes (N.Y.) Board of Education, 1941—, began as teacher of history and English, became teacher of high school English, now chairman of English department at Cohoes High School. *Member:* New York State Teachers Association, Cohoes Teachers Association (president, 1957-58, 1967-68), Writers' Alliance, Hadassah. *Awards, honors:* First prize ($1,200) in Roxbury short story competition, 1960; Freedoms Foundation Award, 1964.

WRITINGS: Pattern for a Heroine, Union of American Hebrew Congregations, 1967; *My Life Among the Gentiles,* A. S. Barnes, 1968. Contributor of articles, stories, and plays to more than thirty periodicals, including *Jack and Jill, Negro Digest, Jewish Heritage, Catholic Home, The Instructor, Messenger,* 'Teen, *Read, Home Life,* and *Highlights for Children.*

WORK IN PROGRESS: One a Night, an anthology of Hanukkah stories; *Yearning to Breathe Free,* an anthology of Jewish biographies; *Sour Apples,* an essay collection.

BIOGRAPHICAL/CRITICAL SOURCES: Albany Times Union, June 2, 1964.

*   *   *

BIVEN, W(illiam) Carl 1925-

PERSONAL: Born January 11, 1925, in Louisville, Ky.; son of George Monroe (a railroad yardmaster) and Mary Agnes (Vetter) Biven; married Dora Jane Duncan, June 17, 1959; children: Jane Elizabeth, Louis Duncan, Russell Monroe. *Education:* St. Mary's College of Kentucky, B.A., 1945; St. Louis University, M.A., 1953, Ph.D., 1956. *Office:* Department of Industrial Management, Georgia Institute of Technology, Atlanta, Ga. 30332.

CAREER: Emory University, Atlanta, Ga., research associate, 1957; Georgia Institute of Technology, Atlanta, 1958—, began as assistant professor, became professor of economics, 1966. *Member:* American Economic Association, Southern Economic Association.

WRITINGS: Economics and Public Policy, C. E. Merrill, 1966. Contributor to *Mercer Law Review; An Introduction to Economics,* C. E. Merrill, 1970; (editor) *Readings in Economics,* C. E. Merrill, 1970.

WORK IN PROGRESS: A textbook on advanced macroeconomics.

BLACK, Mary Childs   1922-

PERSONAL: Born April 7, 1922, in Pittsfield, Mass.; daughter of George and Isabelle (Merrill) Childs; was married; children: Merrill Elizabeth. *Education:* University of North Carolina, B.A., 1943; Catholic University of America, graduate study, 1950; George Washington University, M.A., 1951. *Home:* 149 West 94th St., New York, N.Y. 10025. *Office:* New York Historical Society, 170 Central Park W., New York, N.Y. 10024.

CAREER: Colonial Williamsburg, Williamsburg, Va., research assistant, 1956-57; Abby Aldrich Rockefeller Folk Art Collection, Williamsburg, registrar, 1957-58, curator, 1958-60, director and curator, 1960-64; Museum of American Folk Art, New York City, director, 1964-69; New York Historical Society, New York City, curator of painting, sculpture, and decorative arts, 1969—. Member of advisory board, Esther Stevens Brazer Guild; member of education and restorative advisory boards, South Street Seaport. Trustee, Westbeth Artist's Housing, New York Foundation for the Arts. Consultant, Smithsonian Institution. *Military service:* U.S. Navy Women's Reserve (WAVES), 1943-46; became lieutenant junior grade.

WRITINGS: (With Jean Lipman) *American Folk Painting,* C. N. Potter, 1967; (with Barbara Holdridge and Lawrence Holdridge) *Ammi Phillips,* C. N. Potter, 1969; *What Is American in American Art* (catalogue), C. N. Potter, 1971; (editor) *Old New York in Early Photographs,* Dover, 1973. Contributor to *Antiques, Art in America, Arts in Virginia,* and *Curator.*

WORK IN PROGRESS: Nineteenth-Century Advertising from the Bella C. Landauer Collection.

*   *   *

BLACKHAM, H(arold) J(ohn)   1903-

PERSONAL: Born March 31, 1903, in Birmingham, England; son of Walter Roland (a bookseller) and Harriet Mary (Pallot) Blackham; married Olga Florence Rock, August, 1934; children: Paul. *Education:* University of Birmingham, B.A., 1924, Secondary Teachers' Diploma, 1925. *Politics:* Radical. *Religion:* Humanist. *Home:* 22 The Avenue, Twickenham, Middlesex, England.

CAREER: Former philosophy lecturer and tutor in adult education programs of Workers' Educational Association and London County Council; Ethical Union, London, England, chairman, 1934-45, secretary, 1945-63; International Humanist and Ethical Union, secretary, 1952-66; Rationalist Press Association, London, director, 1955—; British Humanist Association, London, director, 1963-68; full-time writer and editor, 1968—. Chairman, Anglo-Austrian Society's Childrens Committee, 1950-65; chairman, Social Morality Council, 1971—. International Help for Children, founder member, vice-chairman, 1972—. *Wartime service:* National Fire Service, 1941-45. *Member:* Royal Institute of Philosophy, National Book League, Society of Authors. *Awards, honors:* International Humanist Award, 1974.

WRITINGS: (With others) *Living as a Humanist* (essays), Chaterson, 1950; *Six Existentialist Thinkers,* Macmillan (New York), 1952; *The Human Tradition,* Routledge & Kegan Paul, 1952; *Political Discipline in a Free Society,* Allen & Unwin, 1961; *Religion in a Modern Society,* Ungar, 1966; *Humanism,* Penguin, 1968, new edition, Harvester, 1975.

Editor: J. B. Bury, *A History of Freedom of Thought,* 2nd edition, Oxford University Press, 1952; (and contributor) *Objections to Humanism,* Constable, 1963; (and author of introduction) *Reality, Man and Existence* (anthology of existentialist writings), Bantam, 1965; *Moral and Religious Education in County Schools,* Social Morality Council, 1970; *Ethical Standards in Counselling,* Bedford Square Press, 1974; *Education and Drug Dependence,* Methuen Educational, 1975.

Contributor: Guy Metraux and Francois Crouzet, editors, *Religion and the Promise of the Twentieth Century,* Mentor, 1965; Julian Huxley, editor, *The Growth of Ideas,* Macdonald, 1965; Monica Taylor, editor, *Progress and Problems in Moral Education,* National Foundation for Educational Research, 1975.

Editor of series of studies in the history of ideas, for Constable in England and University of Chicago Press in United States, launched in 1969 with the publication of two volumes by Charles Trinkaus. Founder and editor, *Plain View* (quarterly), 1944-65.

WORK IN PROGRESS: Self and Society in a Welfare State.

AVOCATIONAL INTERESTS: Wildlife and the natural world ("early years spent in farming, with a passion for horses").

BIOGRAPHICAL/CRITICAL SOURCES: Observer, July 21, 1963.

*   *   *

BLACKLEDGE, Ethel H.   1920-
  (Allison Hale)

PERSONAL: Born March 2, 1920, in Mount Vernon, Ky.; daughter of Wilburn and Allie (Allen) Hale; married Walter L. Blackledge (a professor), February 25, 1960; children: Walter L. Jr., Lawrence Allen. *Education:* Ohio State University, B.S., 1949; University of Oklahoma, professional writing courses, 1949-51; University of Texas, M.Ed., 1959. *Religion:* Presbyterian. *Home:* 3620 Gary Ave., Alton, Ill. 62002.

CAREER: Former high school teacher in Ohio, and secretary for one year in Wiesbaden, Germany; University of Texas, Austin, lecturer, 1957-59; Southern Illinois University, Edwardsville Campus, Alton, lecturer, 1959-61.

WRITINGS: (With husband, Walter L. Blackledge) *Supervising Women Employees,* Dartnell, 1966; (with W. L. Blackledge and Helen J. Keily) *You and Your Job: Finding It, Getting It, and Keeping It,* South-Western, 1967; (with W. L. Blackledge and Keily) *The Job You Want: How to Get It,* South-Western, 1975; (under pseudonym Allison Hale) *23 Ways to Get A Proposal* (booklet), Personal Success Publishers, 1965. Contributor to *Reader's Digest, Family Weekly,* and business education journals.

WORK IN PROGRESS: When You Feel Discouraged, Try This!, a book of stories and anecdotes.

*   *   *

BLACKWELL, William L.   1929-

PERSONAL: Born April 7, 1929, in Jersey City, N.J.; son of William Leslie and Pearl (Lindberg) Blackwell; married Constance Taylor, July 23, 1960; children: Anne W., Leslie T., Theodore W. *Education:* Columbia University, A.B., 1952, graduate study at Russian Institute, 1957-58; New York University, M.A., 1954, Princeton University, Ph.D., 1959. *Office:* History Department, New York University, New York, N.Y. 10003.

CAREER: Instructor in history at Princeton University, Princeton, N.J., 1958-59, and American University, Cairo, Egypt, 1959-60; College of William and Mary, Williamsburg, Va., assistant professor of history, 1961-62; New York University, New York, N.Y., assistant professor, 1962-65, associate professor, 1965-71, professor of history, 1971—. *Military service:* U.S. Army, 1946-48. *Member:* American Association for the Advancement of Slavic Studies.

WRITINGS: The Beginnings of Russian Industrialization: 1800-1860, Princeton University Press, 1968; *The Industrialization of Russia,* Crowell, 1970; (editor) *Russian Economic Development from Peter the Great to Stalin,* F. Watts, 1974.

WORK IN PROGRESS: Several works dealing with Russian and European economic and social history.

* * *

BLACKWOOD, James R. 1918-

PERSONAL: Born April 30, 1918, in Columbia, S.C.; son of Andrew W. (a professor of homiletics) and Carolyn (Philips) Blackwood; married Louise Ritter, June 30, 1949; children: Paul J., Philip D., Carolyn L. *Education:* College of Wooster, B.A., 1941; Princeton Theological Seminary, B.D., 1945, Th.M., 1946. *Office:* 317 Givens St., Sarasota, Fla. 33581.

CAREER: Presbyterian clergyman, with first pastorage in St. Charles, Mo., 1947-52; College of Wooster, Wooster, Ohio, campus pastor, 1952-61; First Presbyterian Church, Winter Haven, Fla., pastor, 1962-70; Siesta Key Chapel, Sarasota, Fla., organizing pastor, 1970—. Member of American team, British-American Preachers' Exchange, 1965. *Awards, honors:* D.D., College of Wooster, 1965.

WRITINGS: The Soul of Frederick W. Robertson, Harper, 1947; *The House on College Avenue: The Comptons at Wooster, 1891-1913,* M.I.T. Press, 1968; (editor) Howard F. Lowry, *College Talks,* Oxford University Press, 1969. Contributor to *Christian Century, Pulpit Digest, Religion in Life,* and other journals.

* * *

BLAHER, Damian J(oseph) 1913-

PERSONAL: Surname is pronounced Blair; born March 16, 1913, in Boston, Mass.; son of William Joseph (a bookbinder) and Vincetta (Harrod) Blaher. *Education:* Studied at St. Joseph's Seminary, Callicoon, N.Y., 1928-32, St. Stephen's Philosophy House, Croghan, N.Y., 1933-34, and St. Anthony's Philosophy House, Butler, N.J., 1934-36; St. Bonaventure University, B.A., 1936; Holy Name College, graduate study, 1936-40; Catholic University of America, J.C.D., 1949. *Home:* 100 Arch St., Boston, Mass. 02107.

CAREER: Entered Roman Catholic order of Friars Minor (Franciscans), 1932, ordained priest, 1939; Siena College, Loudonville, N.Y., instructor in English and German, 1940-42; Military Ordinariate, New York, N.Y., assistant chancellor, 1944-54; Christ the King Seminary, St. Bonaventure, N.Y., professor of moral theology, 1954-55; Holy Name College, Franciscan House of Studies, Washington, D.C., professor of theology, 1955-70, guardian and rector, 1955-58. Professor of canon law, DeLaSalle College, Washington, D.C., 1957; professor of moral theology, Whitefriars Hall, Washington, D.C., 1966-67; lecturer in moral theology in England, Brazil, Bolivia, Peru, New Zealand, Australia, New Guinea, Singapore, Hong Kong, and Japan.

MEMBER: Catholic Theological Society of America, Canon Law Society of America (secretary, 1957-58), American Society of Christian Ethics, Society for the Scientific Study of Religion.

WRITINGS: The Ordinary Processes in Causes of Beatification and Canonization, Catholic University of America Press, 1949; *Thirty-Two Answers to Timely Questions in Moral Theology and Church Law,* Friar Press, 1963. Regular monthly contributor, *Friar Magazine,* 1954—, contributor to *Encyclopaedia Britannica, Encyclopedia Americana, Catholic Encyclopedia for Home and School,* and *Proceedings* of Franciscan Education Conference.

* * *

BLAIR, Ruth Van Ness 1912-

PERSONAL: Born June 91, 1912, in St. Michael, Alaska; daughter of Elmer Eugene (an educator and Presbyterian minister) and Eula (McIntosh) Van Ness; married Glenn Myers Blair (a professor of educational psychology), June 27, 1934; children: Glenn Myers, Jr., Sally Virginia (Mrs. Donald L. Leach). *Education:* Seattle Pacific College, graduate in elementary education, 1932; studied voice privately in Seattle and New York. *Home:* 51 Island Way, Clearwater, Fla. 33515.

CAREER: Public school teacher in Everett, Wash., 1932-34; kindergarten teacher in Champaign, Ill., 1953-62. Soprano soloist in local churches, 1938-65; pianist for adult education classes, 1961-75. Education chairman for Champaign-Urbana Symphony Guild, 1970-74. *Member:* Chicago Children's Reading Round Table. *Awards, honors:* Writer's Digest short story contest winner, 1963, and essay contest winner, 1965.

WRITINGS: Puddle Duck, Steck, 1966; *A Bear Can Hibernate—Why Can't I?,* Denison, 1972; *Willa-Willa—The Wishful Witch,* Denison, 1972; *Mary's Monster* (Junior Literary Guild Selection), Coward, 1975. Also author of stories and poems for Encyclopaedia Brittanica Education Corp., 1974. Contributor of poems to *Music Journal, Athene, Christian Living, Gourmet.* Editor of Champaign-Urbana Symphony Guild *Teacher's Guide,* 1970-74.

WORK IN PROGRESS: Ottie the Otter, for Oddo, and other children's books.

SIDELIGHTS: Ruth Blair has traveled in the Mid-east and Europe. Her book, *Mary's Monster,* is the result of journeys to Southern England. *Avocational interests:* Archaeology, music, travel.

* * *

BLAIS, Marie-Claire 1939-

PERSONAL: Born October 5, 1939, in Quebec, Quebec, Canada; daughter of Fernando and Veronique (Nolin) Blais. *Education:* Attended Pensionnat St. Roch in Quebec; studied literature and philosophy at Laval University in Quebec. *Religion:* Catholic. *Home:* 3467 Ontario Ave., Apt. 204, Montreal, Quebec, Canada. *Agent:* Georges Borchardt, 145 East 52nd St., New York, N.Y. 10022.

CAREER: Full-time writer. *Member:* P.E.N. *Awards, honors:* Prix de la Langue Francaise from L'Academie Francaise, 1961, for *La Belle bete;* Guggenheim fellowships, 1963, 1964; Le Prix France-Quebec, 1966, and Prix Medicis (Paris), 1966, both for *Une Saison dans la vie d'Emmanuel.*

WRITINGS—All novels, except as noted: *La Belle bete,* Institut Litteraire du Quebec, 1959, translation by Merloyd Lawrence published as *Mad Shadows,* Little, Brown, 1961; *Tete Blanche,* Institut Litteraire du Quebec, 1960, translation by Charles Fullman under same title, Little, Brown, 1961; *Le Jour est noir* (novella), Editions du Jour (Montreal), 1962, translation by Derek Coltman published as *The Day is Dark* (see below); *Pays voiles* (poems), Garneau (Quebec), 1963; *Existences* (poems), Garneau, 1964; *Une Saison dans la vie d'Emmanuel,* Editions du Jour, 1965, translation by Coltman published as *A Season in the Life of Emmanuel,* introduction by Edmund Wilson, Farrar, Straus, 1966; *L'Insoumise,* Editions du Jour, 1966; *The Day Is Dark* [*and*] *Three Travelers* (two novellas, translated by Coltman; the latter originally titled "Les Voyageurs sacres"), Farrar, Straus, 1967; *David Sterne,* Editions du Jour, 1967, translation by David Lobdell under same title, McClelland & Stewart, 1973; *Manuscrit de Pauline Archange,* Editions du Jour, 1968, translation by Coltman published with translation of *Vivre! Vivre!: La Suite des Manuscrits de Pauline Archange* (see below) as *The Manuscripts of Pauline Archange,* Farrar, Straus, 1970; *Vivre! Vivre!: La Suite des Manuscrits de Pauline Archange,* Editions du Jour, 1969; *Les Apparences,* Editions du Jour, 1970; *The Wolf,* McClelland & Stewart, 1971; *Un Joualonais sa Joualonie,* Editions du Jour, 1973, translation by Ralph Manheim published as *St. Lawrence Blues,* Farrar, Straus, 1974.

Plays: *L'Execution* (two-act; produced in Montreal at Theatre du Rideau Vert, 1967), Editions du Jour, 1968; *Fievre,* Editions du Jour, 1974. Also author of "La Roulotte aux Poupees" and "Eleanor," both produced in Quebec at Theatre de L'Estoc.

WORK IN PROGRESS: A novel, *Testament de J. L. Maigre.*

SIDELIGHTS: Mlle. Blais, according to Edmund Wilson, is "a writer in a class by herself." Although each of her novels is written in a different style and mood, "we know immediately," writes Raymond Rosenthal, "that we are entering a fully imagined world when we start reading any of her books." Wilson believes that Mlle. Blais is a "true 'phenomenon'; she may possibly be a genius. At the age of twenty-four, she has produced four remarkable books of a passionate and poetic force that, as far as my reading goes, is not otherwise to be found in French Canadian fiction." That was in 1964; when Wilson read *A Season in the Life of Emmanuel* in 1965, he compared the novel to works by Synge and Faulkner.

"*A Season in the Life of Emmanuel* is a particularly Canadian work of art," writes David Stouck, "for the sense of winter and of life's limitations (especially defined by poverty) are nowhere felt more strongly. Yet . . . these physical limitations serve to define the emotional deprivation that is being dramatized. That eroding sense of poverty is never externalized as a social issue, nor is the harshness of the Quebec landscape seen as an existentialist 'condition.' Rather, in the oblique and relentless manner of her writing Miss Blais remains faithful stylistically to the painful vision of her imagination and in so doing has created both a fully dramatic and genuinely Canadian work of art."

Robertson Davies believes that *The Day is Dark* and *Three Travelers* are "less substantial than *A Season in the Life of Emmanuel,*" but, he adds, "all the writing of this extraordinary young woman is so individual, so unlike anything else

being written on this continent, that admirers of her poetic vision of life may find them even more to their taste." Laurent LeSage says of the two novellas: "Although the basic structures of fiction are still recognizable, they have been weakened and distorted to prevent any illusion of realistic dimension or true-to-life anecdote from distracting us from the author's intention. Without warning the narrative shifts from one character to another, chronology is jumbled, events are sometimes contradictory, and the fancied is never clearly separated from the real. By a series of interior monologues Mlle. Blais works along the lower levels of consciousness, and only rarely does she come to the surface. The world of her revery is the somber, shadowy one of primitive urges and responses. . . . Each [character] obeys a force that resembles a tragic predestination, leading [him] in a lonely quest through life to [his] final destruction." The novellas are actually prose poems, similar in some respects to works by Walter de la Mare. Rosenthal defines the genre as "a piece of prose that should be read more than once, preferably several times. . . . If after reading it in the prescribed fashion," says Rosenthal, "the work assumes depth and color and value it did not have at the first reading, then the author has written a successful prose poem. . . . In a prose poem each word counts and Mlle. Blais generally doesn't waste a syllable."

In his study of Canadian literature, Wilson comments that "these novels of Marie-Claire Blais are the most unrelievedly painful that I remember ever to have read, and one questions . . . the inevitability of so much pain." But Irving Wardle, although he admits that "harshness and squalor are there," sees that, at least in *A Season in the Life of Emmanuel,* these elements "are transformed in the writing into the material of adolescent fantasy. [Mlle. Blais] has the myth-making faculty, and it is an exciting thing to watch." LeSage writes: "Marie-Claire Blais lets her words pour forth in a rhapsodic torrent. In *Three Travelers* they often form into verses, but everywhere they have the poetic qualities of image and cadence as they create laments and paeans, cries of love, lust, and hate for the wretched characters whose affliction is the sickness of life. The power of her writing is terrific." Wilson explains that "Mlle. Blais has grown up in this cult, and the idea that man is born to sorrow, the agony of expiation, is at the base of her tragic consciousness. . . . [Her work] is the refinement to a purer kind of poetry than that of the protesting patriots of the desperate cry that arises from the poverty, intellectual and material, the passionate self-punishing piety and the fierce defeated pride of Quebec."

Daniel M. Murtaugh observes that *A Season in the Life of Emmanuel* "has at its center an autobiographical sketch by a consumptive child whose writing is a cry of defiance against the misery of his life and the approach of his death. The manuscripts of a suffering child, a structural detail of that novel, are the sum and substance of its successor. *The Manuscripts of Pauline Archange* takes us through memories of almost unmitigated horror rendered bearable, redeemed even, for us as for the novel's heroine, by the fluid, re-creative medium of her prose. . . . What Pauline remembers does not fall into a conventional plot or lend itself easily to summary. Her life is lived out in the mental and physical squalor of a French Canadian slum, under the tyranny of repressed, frustrated adults who visit their failures in blows upon their consumptive, lamed offspring. To survive is to escape, to rebel, above all, to avoid pity. Pity 'stinks of death,' and only leads to torture and rape of the victims it cannot help. Pauline writes her manuscripts because, as her family tells her, she 'has no heart.' Only at such a cost does she live and speak to us.''

Rosenthal emphasizes that Mlle. Blais has done much to "put Canada on the literary map." He says of her work: "Mlle. Blais leaves out a great deal, almost all the familiar furniture of fiction, and yet her characters have a tenacious life and her themes, though often convoluted and as evanescent as the mist that dominates so much of her imagination, strike home with surprising force." "With *David Sterne*," writes Brian Vintcent, "Mlle. Blais has placed herself firmly and uncompromisingly in the literary tradition of the French moralists leading back through Camus, Genet and Gide to Baudelaire. The book deals in one way or another with many of the themes explored by these writers, and this makes it somewhat derivative. It owes most, perhaps, to the more abstract and less sensational works of Jean Genet, in which the passionate existential wranglings, the rebellion, the life of crime and sensation are so prominent. The confessional and didactic style of the book will also strike echoes in the reader's mind. . . . But *David Sterne* survives and transcends these comparisons. What allows it to do so is the immense compassion and tenderness Mlle. Blais displays for her characters in their whirlwind of struggle and suffering. The hard cold eye she casts on the cruel world of *Mad Shadows* has grown into one full of pity and profound sadness for the fate of men condemned to do battle with themselves.''

The *Virginia Quarterly Review* writer concludes: "These are novels to be read slowly and carefully for the unusual insights they present in often difficult but provocative images and sometimes demanding but intriguing technical innovations. This is a serious, talented and deeply effective writer.''

BIOGRAPHICAL/CRITICAL SOURCES: Edmund Wilson, *O Canada*, Farrar, Straus, 1964; *Times Literary Supplement*, March 30, 1967; *New Statesman*, March 31, 1967; *New York Times Books Review*, April, 1967; *Observer*, April 2, 1967; *Saturday Review*, April 29, 1967; *Book Week*, June 18, 1967; *Virginia Quarterly Review*, autumn, 1967; *Books Abroad*, winter, 1968; Carolyn Riley, editor, *Contemporary Literary Criticism*, Gale, Volume II, 1974, Volume IV, 1975, Volume VI, 1976.

* * *

BLAKE, I(srael) George 1902-

PERSONAL: Born August 14, 1902, in East Orange, N.J.; son of William H. (a carpenter) and Emma (Earhart) Blake; married Frances Joyce Klyver (a high school teacher), August 24, 1927; children: Martha Jane (Mrs. John Bohencamp). *Education:* Hillsdale College, A.B., 1927; Northwestern University, M.A., 1931; Indiana University, Ph.D., 1941. *Politics:* Republican. *Religion:* Baptist. *Home:* 201 East Methodist Dr., Franklin, Ind. 46131. *Office:* Franklin College, Franklin, Ind. 46131.

CAREER: High school teacher and principal in Flushing, Mich., 1927-30; Franklin College, Franklin, Ind., assistant professor, 1931-35, associate professor, 1935-41, professor of history and chairman of department of history and political science, 1941-72, professor emeritus and resident historian, 1972—. Director, Hoosier Historical Tours, 1950-70, Indiana Historical Sites Survey, 1967-70; member of Indiana Sesquicentennial Commission, 1966. Member, Franklin City Council, 1948-56; president, Franklin School Board, 1959-61. *Member:* American Historical Association,

Organization of American Historians, Indiana Historical Society, Indiana Academy of Social Sciences (past president), Society of Indiana Pioneers (honorary member), Indiana Academy, Phi Alpha Theta. *Awards, honors:* D.C.L., Hillsdale College, 1952.

WRITINGS: The Holmans of Veraestau, Mississippi Valley Press, 1943; *Paul V. McNutt: Portrait of a Hossier Statesman*, Central Publishing, 1966. Also editor of *Pioneers of Johnson County, Indiana*, 1973.

WORK IN PROGRESS: History of Indiana Baptist Convention, 1798-1983, completion expected in 1983.

* * *

BLAKE, Robert R(ogers) 1918-

PERSONAL: Born January 21, 1918, in Providence, R.I.; son of Rogers Charles and Margaret (Rogers) Blake; married Mercer Blain, September 4, 1941; children: Brooks, Carrie. *Education:* Berea College, B.A., 1940; University of Virginia, M.A., 1941; University of Texas, Ph.D., 1947. *Office address:* Scientific Methods, Inc., P.O. Box 195, Austin, Tex. 78767.

CAREER: Assistant professor, then associate professor of psychology at University of Texas, Austin; now president of Scientific Methods, Inc. (development service to industry and other groups), Austin, Tex. *Military service:* U.S. Army Air Forces, 1942-45. Diplomate of American Psychological Association. *Member:* National Training Laboratories, Psychonomic Society, American Association for the Advancement of Science, New York Academy of Sciences.

WRITINGS—All with Jane Srygley Mouton and others where noted; all published by Gulf Publishing except as noted: *Group Dynamics—Key to Decision Making*, 1962; (and Herbert Shepard) *Managing Intergroup Conflict in Industry*, 1964; *The Managerial Grid*, 1964; (and Warren Avis) *Corporate Darwinism*, 1967; *Corporate Excellence Through Grid Organization Development: A Systems Approach*, 1968; *Building a Dynamic Corporation through Grid Organization Development*, Addison-Wesley, 1969.

The Grid for Sales Excellence, McGraw, 1970; *The Marriage Grid*, McGraw, 1971; *How to Assess the Strengths and Weaknesses of a Business Enterprise*, Scientific Methods, Inc., 1972; *The Grid for Supervisory Effectiveness*, Scientific Methods, Inc., 1975; *Instrumented Team Learning*, Scientific Methods, Inc., 1975; *Consultation*, Addison-Wesley, 1976. Contributor to business periodicals. Member of editorial board, *Group Psychotherapy*, *International Journal of Sociometry*, *International Journal of Social Psychiatry*, and *Psychological Review*.

WORK IN PROGRESS: Research and development of material for use in management training, especially in applying Grid theories to the nuclear family.

* * *

BLANCH, Robert J. 1938-

PERSONAL: Born February 17, 1938, in Brooklyn, N.Y.; son of Cyril A. (a purchasing agent) and Sarah (Coogan) Blanch; married Marjorie A. Yokell, December 29, 1961; children: Robert, Jr., Sandra, Randall, Kevin, David. *Education:* College of the Holy Cross, A.B., 1959; Northeastern University, M.A., 1961; State University of New York at Buffalo, Ph.D., 1967. *Politics:* Independent. *Religion:* Roman Catholic. *Home:* 56 Walker St., Newtonville, Mass. 02160. *Office:* Department of English, Northeastern University, Boston, Mass. 02115.

CAREER: Instructor in English at Northeastern University, Boston, Mass., 1961-62, Newman Preparatory School, Boston, 1962-63, and State University of New York College at Buffalo, 1963-66; Canisius College, Buffalo, N.Y., assistant professor of English, 1966-67; Bentley College, Boston, assistant professor of English, 1967-68; Northeastern University, associate professor of English, 1968—. *Member:* Modern Language Association of America.

WRITINGS: (Editor) *Sir Gawain and Pearl: Critical Essays,* Indiana University Press, 1966; (editor) *Style and Symbolism in Piers Plowman: A Modern Critical Anthology,* University of Tennessee Press, 1969; (editor) Chaucer, *Merchant's Tale* (casebook), C. E. Merrill, 1970. Contributor to literary journals.

WORK IN PROGRESS: Editing with Thomas Bestul, *Parlement of the Thre Ages,* and *Wynnere and Wastoure,* completion expected in 1977.

*   *   *

BLANCHARD, William H(enry) 1922-

PERSONAL: Born March 25, 1922, in St. Paul, Minn.; son of Charles Edgar (a jeweler) and Ethel R. (Gurney) Blanchard; married Martha I. Lang, August 22, 1947; children: Greg, Mary. *Education:* Iowa State University of Science and Technology, B.S., 1944; University of Southern California, Ph.D., 1954. *Politics:* Democrat. *Religion:* None. *Home:* 4307 Rosario Rd., Woodland Hills, Calif. 91364. *Office:* Department of Psychology, University of Southern California, Los Angeles, Calif.

CAREER: Chemist, Goodrich Chemical Co., 1946-47; University of Southern California Medical School, Los Angeles, research chemist, 1947; U.S. Veterans Administration Hospital, Los Angeles, Calif., clinical psychology trainee, 1950-54; Los Angeles County General Hospital, Los Angeles, court psychologist, 1954; California Youth Authority, Norwalk, clinical psychologist, 1954-57; social scientist, RAND Corp., 1958-60; System Development Corp., Santa Monica, Calif., social scientist, 1960-70; University of Southern California, Los Angeles, consulting psychologist and lecturer, 1970—. Clinical associate, University of Southern California, 1955-56. President, Parents and Friends of Mentally Ill Children (nonprofit foundation), 1966-68. *Military service:* U.S. Marine Corps, 1944-45. *Member:* American Psychological Association, American Academy of Political and Social Science, American Political Science Association, American Association for the Advancement of Science, Society for the Psychological Study of Social Issues, Research Society of America, Western Psychological Association, Los Angeles County Psychological Association.

WRITINGS: Rousseau and the Spirit of Revolt, University of Michigan Press, 1967. Contributor to professional journals and newspapers.

WORK IN PROGRESS: Studying the relationship between national character and national policy, the role of national character in the search for peace, and national manpower and world resources.

SIDELIGHTS: Blanchard wrote to *CA:* "Admire Freud, Sartre, Camus, Darwin, Marx, Kafka. . . . Would like to do something to improve the quality of American life which I consider lacking in emotional range and in intellectual depth."†

BLANDINO, Giovanni 1923-

PERSONAL: Surname is pronounced Blan-*dee*-no; born April 14, 1923, in Italy; son of Domenico (a professor) and Maria (Benso) Blandino. *Education:* Pontifical Gregorian University, Rome, Italy, Ph.L., 1948, Th.L., 1955; State University of Rome, Doctorate in Biological Sciences, 1956. *Home:* Via degli Astalli 16, Rome, Italy.

CAREER: Entered Roman Catholic Society of Jesus (Jesuits), 1943, ordained priest, 1954. Full-time writer, 1956-68; Aloisianum, Pontifical Faculty of Philosophy, Gallarate (Varese), Italy, professor of biology, beginning in 1968; now professor of philosophy and biology, Pontifical Gregorian University, Rome, Italy, and Pontifical University of Lateran, Rome.

WRITINGS: Problemi e Dottrine di Biologia teorica, Minerva Medica (Torino), 1960, translation published as *Theories on the Nature of Life,* Philosophical Library, 1969; *Vita, Ordine, Caso,* Editore Morcelliana (Brescia), 1967; *Peccato originale e Poligenismo,* Ethica Centro Dehoniano (Bologna), 1967; *Una discussione sull'Etica della felicita,* Ethica Centro Dehoniano, 1968; *Il Problema della conoscenza. Filosofia della conoscenza e fondamenti di filosofia della scienza,* Abete (Rome), 1972.

*   *   *

BLASIER, (Stewart) Cole 1925-

PERSONAL: Born March 16, 1925, in Jackson, Mich.; son of Stewart P. (a business executive) and Helen (Cole) Blasier; married Martha Hiett, September 20, 1947; children: Peter Cole, Martha Hamilton. *Education:* University of Illinois, B.A., 1947; Columbia University, M.A., 1950, Ph.D., 1955. *Home:* 5306 Westminster Pl., Pittsburgh, Pa. 15232. *Office:* Mervis Hall, University of Pittsburgh, Pittsburgh, Pa. 15213.

CAREER: U.S. Department of State, Foreign Service officer in Belgrade, Bonn, and then Moscow, 1951-60; Colgate University, Hamilton, N.Y., executive assistant to president and secretary of board of trustees, 1960-63; University of Valle, Cali, Colombia, visiting professor, 1963-64; University of Pittsburgh, Pittsburgh, Pa., professor of political science and director of Center for Latin American studies, 1964-74, research professor of Latin American studies, 1974—. Visiting professor in Warsaw, Poland, 1975. *Military service:* U.S. Naval Reserve, active duty, 1943-46; became lieutenant junior grade. *Member:* American Political Science Association, Latin American Studies Association, Phi Beta Kappa.

WRITINGS: (Editor) *Constructive Change in Latin America,* University of Pittsburgh Press, 1968; *The Hovering Giant,* University of Pittsburgh Press, 1975. Contributor to political science and Latin American studies journals. Associate editor, *Latin American Research Review.*

WORK IN PROGRESS: Studies of U.S. policy toward Latin America.

SIDELIGHTS: Blasier is competent in Spanish, Russian, German, and Serbo-Croatian.

*   *   *

BLECHMAN, Burt 1932-

PERSONAL: Born March 2, 1932. *Education:* University of Vermont, B.A.; Columbia University, M.S. *Home:* 200 Waverly Pl., New York, N.Y. 10014.

CAREER: Full-time professional writer. Assistant professor, New York University Medical School, New York, N.Y. *Member:* Phi Beta Kappa. *Awards, honors:* Merrill Foundation Award.

WRITINGS: How Much?, Obolensky, 1961; *The War of Camp Omongo,* Random House, 1963; *Stations,* Random House, 1964; *The Octopus Papers,* Horizon, 1965; *Maybe,* Prentice-Hall, 1967.

WORK IN PROGRESS: School Days.

SIDELIGHTS: The *New Leader* reviewer who noted that Blechman's *Maybe* is "a *tour de force* of comic skill," recalled that Blechman "rocketed into prominence with his first novel, *How Much?,* which discerning critics all the way from W. H. Auden to Saul Bellow—a vast area of culture if you think of it—praised for its satiric sharpness and its dazzling use of idiom.... *Maybe,*" he added, "is a return to the satire of *How Much?,* but with a difference. The difference lies in the brilliantly unsparing yet sympathetic portrait of the protagonist of *Maybe,* the chirpy, restless, time-eating widow, Myra, whose inner life is really a delightful voyage through the city's despairing amusements." Bellow advises: "For the sake of your souls, read Blechman."

BIOGRAPHICAL/CRITICAL SOURCES: Observer Review, May 14, 1967; *New Leader,* July 3, 1967.

* * *

BLEND, Charles D(aniels) 1918-

PERSONAL: Born July 18, 1918, in Marion, Ind.; son of Gordon B. (an attorney) and Huldah (Daniels) Blend; married Rhoda Cook, January 2, 1953; children: Jonathan C., Patricia. *Education:* Ohio State University, B.A., 1949, M.A., 1952, Ph.D., 1955; University of Aix-Marseille, graduate study, 1949-50. *Office:* Department of Romance Languages, Michigan State University, East Lansing, Mich. 48823.

CAREER: Ohio State University, Columbus, instructor, 1954-56; assistant professor of French, 1956-61; University of North Carolina at Greensboro, professor of Romance languages and chairman of department, 1962-66; Michigan State University, East Lansing, professor of Romance languages and chairman of department, beginning 1966. *Military service:* U.S. Army, Infantry, 1943-46; served in Europe. *Member:* Modern Language Association of America, American Association of Teachers of French, American Association of University Professors, Phi Beta Kappa, Phi Eta Sigma. *Awards, honors:* Fulbright fellow in France, 1949-50; American Philosophical Society grant for France, 1956; American Council of Learned Societies grant for France, 1960.

WRITINGS: Andre Malraux, Tragic Humanist, Ohio State University Press, 1963. Contributor of translations, articles, and reviews to language journals.

WORK IN PROGRESS: Quixotism in the literature of the Spanish Civil War.

AVOCATIONAL INTERESTS: Music, photography.††

* * *

BLEZNICK, Donald W(illiam) 1924-

PERSONAL: Born December 24, 1924, in New York, N.Y.; son of Louis and Gertrude (Kleinman) Bleznick; married Rozlyn Burakoff, June 15, 1952; children: Jordan Lewis, Susan Gale. *Education:* City College (now City College of the City University of New York), B.A., 1946;

National University of Mexico, M.A., 1948; Columbia University, Ph.D., 1954. *Home:* 7870 Elbrook Ave., Cincinnati, Ohio 45237. *Office:* 352 McMicken Hall, University of Cincinnati, Cincinnati, Ohio 45237.

CAREER: Ohio State University, Columbus, instructor in Romance languages, 1949-55; Pennsylvania State University, University Park, assistant professor, 1955-60, associate professor, 1960-64, professor of Spanish literature, 1964-67; University of Cincinnati, Cincinnati, Ohio, professor of Romance languages, 1967—, head of department, 1967-72. *Military service:* U.S. Army, Counterintelligence Corps, 1946-47.

MEMBER: Modern Language Association of America, Renaissance Society of America, American Association of Teachers of Spanish and Portuguese, American Association of University Professors, Midwest Modern Language Association, Comediantes, Phi Beta Kappa (chapter president, 1971-72), Sigma Delta Pi (state director, 1968—; national executive council, 1973—), Phi Sigma Iota, Kappa Delta Pi. *Awards, honors:* American Philosophical Society grant, 1964, Charles Phelps Taft research grant, 1972.

WRITINGS: El Ensayo Espanol del Siglo XVI al XX, Studium (Mexico City), 1964; (editor) *El Ensayo Espanol del Siglo veinte,* Ronald, 1964; (editor) Juan Goytisolo, *Duelo en el Paraiso,* Blaisdell, 1967; (editor) Buero Vallejo, *Madrugada,* Blaisdell, 1969; (editor with Walter T. Pattison) *Representative Spanish Authors,* 3rd edition, Oxford University Press, 1971; *Quevedo,* Twayne, 1972; *Directions of Literary Criticism in the Seventies,* Department of Romance Languages and Literatures, University of Cincinnati, 1972; *A Sourcebook for Hispanic Literature,* Temple University Press, 1973. Contributor to *Encyclopedia Americana;* bibliographer for Modern Languages Association *International Bibliography,* 1966—. *Hispania,* associate editor and review editor, 1965-73, editor in chief, 1974—.

WORK IN PROGRESS: Research in the Spanish golden age of literature.

* * *

BLOSSOM, Thomas 1912-

PERSONAL: Born February 15, 1912, in Dedham, Mass.; son of Harold Hill (a landscape architect) and Minnie Motley (Dawson) Blossom; married Mildred Marguerite Underwood (a high school English teacher), October 11, 1940; children: Frances (Mrs. John L. Caughey III), Katherine, Mary (Mrs. Terry Springle), Martha (Mrs. James Medeiros). *Education:* Amherst College, A.B., 1934; Columbia University, M.A., 1935; Duke University, Ph.D., 1956. *Politics:* Democrat. *Religion:* Unitarian Universalist. *Home:* 1417 Rust Dr., Virginia Beach, Va. 23455. *Office:* Old Dominion University, Hampton Blvd., Norfolk, Va. 23508.

CAREER: Secondary school teacher, 1935-40; served with U.S. Department of the Interior, Indian Service, 1941, 1943-44; Western Carolina University, Cullowhee, N.C., supervisor of teacher training in mathematics and physical education, 1941-43; The Citadel, Charleston, S.C., 1946-56, began as assistant professor, became associate professor of history; Southern State College, Magnolia, Ark., chairman of social studies department, 1956-58; University of Florida, Gainesville, assistant professor of humanities, 1958-64; Old Dominion University, Norfolk, Va., associate professor, 1964-68, professor of Latin American history, 1968—. *Military service:* U.S. Navy, 1944-46; on convoy duty in Atlantic and Mediterranean. U.S. Naval Reserve, 1946-64;

now lieutenant commander (retired). *Member:* American Historical Association, Southern Historical Association, Phi Alpha Theta. *Awards, honors:* Pan American Union grant for research in Colombia, 1962; Duke Hispanic Foundation fellow in Spain, 1964, Southeast Institute of Medieval and Renaissance Studies fellow, Duke University, 1968.

WRITINGS: (With Jack Allen and others) *The Americas,* Prentice-Hall, 1964; *Narino, Hero of Colombian Independence,* University of Arizona Press, 1967; *Santander: Colombia's Man of Laws,* Twayne, in press. Contributor to *McGraw Hill Encyclopedia of World Biography,* 1972. Associate editor, *ALAS* (publication of now-defunct Association for Latin American Studies), 1960-61.

WORK IN PROGRESS: Doctors for Freedom, a book on Espejo, Vargas, Rieux, Mutis, and Caldas, and their work with Antonio Narino for Colombian independence; research in the comunero movement of 1781 and Colombian independence.

*   *   *

BLUMBERG, Myrna 1932-

PERSONAL: Born November 29, 1932, in Johannesburg, South Africa; daughter of Sidney (an insurance agent) and Edith (Joffe) Blumberg; married Kenneth Theodore Mackenzie (a writer and journalist), January 15, 1954; children: Ruth. *Education:* Attended Jeppe High School, Johannesburg, South Africa. *Home:* 2 Hamilton Ter., London N.W.8, England. *Agent:* David Higham Associates, Ltd., 5 Lower John St., London W.1., England.

CAREER: Reporter and foreign correspondent, for various newspapers, 1950-60, including South African *Sunday Times,* London *Daily Herald,* and *Guardian,* and *New York Post.*

WRITINGS: White Madam (non-fiction), Gollancz, 1962; *Two Minutes from the Sea* (novel), MacGibbon & Kee, 1965; *Ted's Here* (novel), Deutsch, 1967; *Jump for Love and Money, Or Is It Sex Again?* (novel), Quartet, 1975.

WORK IN PROGRESS: A new novel; research for a biography of George Henry Lewes.

*   *   *

BLUMENFELD, Gerry 1906-

PERSONAL: Born September 15, 1906, in New York, N.Y., daughter of William (a manufacturer) and Sadie (Odze) Krasner; married Harold Blumenfeld (an executive editor, United Press International), September 21, 1932; children: Judith Dolgins. *Education:* Attended City College of the City University of New York. *Politics:* Democrat. *Religion:* Jewish. *Home:* 137 Golden Isles Dr., Hallandale, Fla. 33009. *Agent:* Toni Mendez, Inc., 140 East 56th St., New York, N.Y. 10022.

CAREER: Raconteur of Yiddish stories at fund-raising and charitable functions. *Member:* American Jewish Congress, Anti-Defamation League of B'nai B'rith, Hadassah, Council of Jewish Women.

WRITINGS: Some of My Best Jokes are Jewish, Kanrom, 1965; *Cracks in the Steeple* (Catholic humor), World Publishing, 1967; *Tales from the Bagel Lancers* (Jewish humor), World Publishing, 1967; *Doctor's Orders: Laugh* (medical humor), Popular Library, 1970.

WORK IN PROGRESS: An interfaith humor book.

AVOCATIONAL INTERESTS: Upholstering and refin-ishing furniture, the theater, collecting autographed photos of notable people, sewing.

*   *   *

BLUNDEN, Margaret (Anne) 1939-

PERSONAL: Born May 14, 1939, in Ongar, Sussex, England; daughter of Wilfred Leon (a farmer) and Olive (Mitson) Haigh; married John Russell Blunden (a senior lecturer, Open University), August 21, 1965. *Education:* University of Exeter, B.A., 1960; Cambridge University, M.A., 1966. *Politics:* Labour/Liberal. *Religion:* Agnostic.

CAREER: North Western Polytechnic, London, England, assistant lecturer in history, 1963-66; Lewes Technical College, Lewes, Sussex, England, lecturer, beginning 1966. *Awards, honors:* English Speaking Union scholarship to United States, 1960.

WRITINGS: The Countess of Warwick, Cassell, 1967. Regular contributor to *Times Educational Supplement* and *New Education.*

WORK IN PROGRESS: Research on late Victorian ambassadors; a book on Colonial and Commonwealth history.††

*   *   *

BLYTH, Henry 1910-

PERSONAL: Born June 8, 1910, in London, England; son of Henry Montague (a sugar importer) and Mary (Calvert) Blyth. *Education:* Wadham College, Oxford, M.A. (honors in modern history), 1932. *Politics:* "Impartial." *Home:* Southerndown, Rottingdean, Sussex, England. *Agent:* Christopher Mann, 140 Park Lane, London W.1, England.

CAREER: Times, London, England, correspondent, chiefly as film critic, 1932—; author of original film stories and scripts, including fourteen feature films, 1955-67, mostly for Rank Organization, Pinewood Studios, England; author, concentrating on historical biography, 1966—. *Military service:* Royal Air Force, 1940-45; became squadron leader. *Member:* National Liberal Club and R.A.F. Club (both London).

WRITINGS: The Pocket Venus (biography of 4th Marquis of Hastings, 1842-1868), Weidenfeld & Nicolson, 1966, 2nd edition, 1967, Walker & Co., 1967; *Old Q: The Rake of Piccadilly* (biography of 4th Duke of Queensberry, 1725-1810), Weidenfeld & Nicolson, 1968; *Hell and Hazard* (biography of William Crockford, 1775-1844), Weidenfeld & Nicolson, 1969; *The High Tide of Pleasure,* Weidenfeld & Nicolson, 1970; published as *The Rakes,* Dial, 1971; *Skittles* (the life of Catherine Walters), Hart-Davis, 1970; *Caro: The Fatal Passion* (biography of Caroline Lamb), Coward, 1972; *Madeleine* (biography of Madeleine Smith), Duckworth, 1975. Has written for television as well as films.

WORK IN PROGRESS: The Age of the Peacock, a history of the Dandies.

SIDELIGHTS: Blyth became interested in historical biography more than thirty years after taking an honors degree in history at Oxford, focusing on historical figures of the eighteenth and nineteenth century in England—favoring the aristocracy and those who led a dramatic rather than a political life. Particularly interested in the Victorian era because of the paradox of its extremes of puritanism and of dissipation and immorality.

The Pocket Venus was adapted as a musical, 1968.

BOARINO, Gerald L(ouis) 1931-

PERSONAL: Born June 28, 1931, in Los Angeles, Calif.; son of Ottavio and Giuseppina (Spalla) Boarino. *Education:* University of California, Berkeley, B.A., 1955, M.A., 1957, Ph.D., 1963. *Religion:* Roman Catholic. *Home:* 31221 Ceanothus Dr., South Laguna, Calif.

CAREER: California State University, Fullerton, currently professor, department of foreign languages. *Military service:* U.S. Army, 1955-57. *Member:* American Association of Teachers of Spanish and Portuguese, American Association of Teachers of Italian, Modern Language Association of Southern California. *Awards, honors:* Fulbright fellowship to Spain, 1960-61.

WRITINGS: (Editor with D. M. Feldman) *Lecturas Contemporanas,* Blaisdell, 1968; *La actualidad espanola,* Playor (Madrid), 1972. Contributor of reviews to academic journals.

*   *   *

BOATENG, E(rnest) A(mano) 1920-

PERSONAL: Born November 30, 1920, in Aburi, Ghana; son of Christian Robert (a clergyman) and Adelaide (Asare) Boateng; married Evelyn K. Danso (a librarian), March 26, 1955; children: Akosua, Akua, Amanobea, Oduraa. *Education:* St. Peter's College, Oxford, M.A., 1953, B.Litt., 1954. *Religion:* Presbyterian. *Home:* 13, Roman Ridge, Accra, Ghana.

CAREER: University of Ghana, Legon, Accra, professor of geography, 1961-73, dean of Faculty of Social Studies, 1961-69; University of Cape Coast, Cape Coast, Ghana, principal of University College, 1969-71, vice-chancellor of university, 1971-73; currently executive chairman, Environmental Protection Council, Accra. Ghana representative, Scientific Council for Africa. *Member:* Royal Geographical Society (London), Ghana Geographical Association (president, 1959-69), Ghana Academy of Sciences (president, 1972—), Royal Society of Arts (fellow).

WRITINGS: A Geography of Ghana, Cambridge University Press, 1959, 2nd edition, 1966; (editor) *Ghana Junior Atlas,* Thomas Nelson, 1965, revised edition, International Publications Service, 1969; *West African Secondary School Atlas,* Thomas Nelson, 1968; *Independence and Nation Building in Africa,* Ghana Publishing Corp., 1973. Contributor to *Encyclopaedia Britannica,* 1961—, and to geographical journals.

WORK IN PROGRESS: A political geography of Africa.

SIDELIGHTS: Boateng has a reading knowledge of French. He has traveled in United States, most of Europe, Soviet Union, Australia, India, and a number of tropical African countries.

AVOCATIONAL INTERESTS: Photography, gardening, English literature.

*   *   *

BOATNER, Mark Mayo III 1921-

PERSONAL: Born June 28, 1921, in Alexandria, Va.; son of Mark Mayo, Jr. (an army colonel) and Amenie Nelson (Gunnell) Boatner; married Patricia Dilworth, June 15, 1957; children: Stirling (daughter), Bruce, Andrew, Nelson, Spencer, Carter. *Education:* University of Kansas, student, 1938-39; U.S. Military Academy, B.S., 1943; U.S. Army War College and George Washington University, M.S., 1966. *Politics:* "None, being second-generation regular

army officer." *Religion:* Episcopalian. *Home:* Penrith Plantation, Jackson, La. 70748. *Agent:* Oliver G. Swan, Julian Bach Literary Agency, Inc., 18 East 48th St., N.Y. 10017.

CAREER: U.S. Army, regular officer, 1943—, currently with rank of colonel. Combat service in Italy, 1944-45, and Korea, 1953-54; served at Supreme Headquarters Allied Powers Europe, Paris, France, 1959-63; current duty at the Pentagon, Arlington, Va. *Awards, honors*—Military: Bronze Star with three oak leaf clusters, Combat Infantryman's Badge with star, and Croix de Guerre. Civilian: American Revolutionary Round Table award, 1967, for *Encyclopedia of the American Revolution.*

WRITINGS: Company Duties, Combat Forces Press, 1950; *Military Customs and Traditions,* McKay, 1956; *Civil War Dictionary,* McKay, 1959; *Encyclopedia of the American Revolution,* McKay, 1966; *Landmarks of the American Revolution,* Stackpole, 1973. Contributor to *Encyclopaedia Britannica* and other encyclopedias, and to military journals.

WORK IN PROGRESS: Research in American history, principally the periods of the Revolution, the Civil War and World War II, with a view to biographical studies and, perhaps, historical novels; writing on military history and theory; assembling material for a long-range project, a study of "the military mind."

SIDELIGHTS: Boatner speaks French fluently.

*   *   *

BOBER, Stanley 1932-

PERSONAL: Born January 13, 1932, in New York, N.Y.; son of Morris and Sylvia (Buckser) Bober; children: Sharon Leslie, Mitchell Stuart. *Education:* New York University, Ph.D., 1962. *Religion:* Jewish. *Home:* 1037 Firewood Dr., Pittsburgh, Pa. 15243. *Office:* Department of Economics, Duquesne University, Pittsburgh, Pa. 15219.

CAREER: Colby College, Waterville, Me., assistant professor of economics, 1960-64; Duquesne University, Pittsburgh, Pa., associate professor of economics, 1964—.

WRITINGS: The Economics of Cycles and Growth, Wiley, 1968.

*   *   *

BOBROW, Edwin E. 1928-

PERSONAL: Born April 8, 1928; son of Abraham David (a sales manager) and Emma (Goldstein) Bobrow; married Gloria Lefkowitz, May 3, 1954; children: Mark David. *Education:* Long Island University, B.Sc., 1947; New York University, advanced study at Graduate School of Business Administration. *Home:* 4465 Douglas Ave., Riverside, N.Y. 10471. *Office:* Bobrow Sales Associates, Inc., 175 Fifth Ave., New York, N.Y. 10010.

CAREER: Decro Wall Corp., Elmsford, N.Y., former director of marketing; Bobrow Sales, Inc., New York, N.Y., chairman of the board, 1955—. President of Marketing In Depth, Inc.; vice-president of Bobrow Realty Co.; founding member of Parmar, Inc.; member of board of directors of Business Games Group, Graduate School of Business Administration, Long Island University; member of advisory board of Institute for Mass Marketing. United Jewish Appeal of Greater New York, member of Leadership Council, and past chairman of Hardware, Housewares Division; active in Bonds for Israel. *Military Service:* U.S. Army, 1945-47.

MEMBER: American Marketing Association, Authors League of America, Authors Guild, International Platform Association, Manufacturers' Agents National Association, National Council of Salesmen's Organization (past vice-president), Housewares-Hardware Representatives of Metropolitan New York (founding member; past vice-president), Hardware Boosters, Hardware Affiliated Representatives (charter member), Mass Merchandising Distributors' Association (co-founder), The Sales Executives Club of New York. *Awards, honors:* State of Israel Leadership Award; United Jewish Appeal Scroll of Honor and Leadership Citation; Manufacturers' Agents Associations Special Award; numerous citations from the Institute for Mass Marketing.

WRITINGS: How to Make Big Money as an Independent Sales Agent, Parker Publishing, 1967; *Selling the Volume Retailer: Anatomy of a Sale,* Chain Store Publishing, 1975. Author of a booklet, *Is the Independent Sales Agent for You?,* for the U.S. Government Small Business Administration; co-author of two booklets, *Checklist for Marketing Hardlines through Mass Merchandisers* and *Checklist for Successfully Marketing New Products.* Columnist, *Housewares Review,* two years, and *Income Opportunities.* Contributor to trade journals. Contributing editor, *Income Opportunities.*

*   *   *

BOEHLKE, Frederick J(ohn), Jr. 1926-

PERSONAL: Born March 6, 1926, in Philadelphia, Pa.; son of Frederick J. (a mechanic) and Freda M. (Reiss) Boehlke. *Education:* University of Pennsylvania, B.A., 1948, A.M., 1951, Ph.D., 1958; Eastern Baptist Theological Seminary, B.D., 1952. *Politics:* Republican. *Office:* Eastern Baptist College, St. Davids, Pa.

CAREER: Ordained Baptist clergyman. Judson College, Marion, Ala., assistant professor, 1955-58, associate professor, 1958-63, professor of history, 1963-67, acting dean, 1964-65, 1967; Eastern Baptist College, St. Davids, Pa., professor of history, 1967—. *Member:* American Historical Association, Southern Historical Association, Phi Beta Kappa.

WRITINGS: Pierre de Thomas, Scholar, Diplomat, and Crusader, University of Pennsylvania Press, 1966.

*   *   *

BOELL, Heinrich (Theodor) 1917-

PERSONAL: Born December 21, 1917, in Cologne, Germany; son of Viktor (a sculptor) and Maria (Hermanns) Boell; married Annemarie Cech (a translator), 1942; children: Raimund, Rene, Vincent. *Education:* University education in German philosophy. *Religion:* Roman Catholic. *Home:* 35 Belvederestrasse, Koeln-Muengersdorf, Germany.

CAREER: Worked as a joiner, at the same time receiving training in the publishing trade; full-time writer, 1947—. Founder, Word Producers Union, 1970. *Military service:* German Army, 1939-45; was an American prisoner of war, 1945. *Member:* Gruppe 47, International PEN (president, 1970-74). *Awards, honors:* Grant from Bundesverband der Deutschen Industrie; Rene Schickele Prize; Gruppe 47 prize, 1951; Kritikerpreis, 1953; *Tribune de Paris* prize, 1953; Prix du Meilleur Livre Etranger, 1955; Heydt cultural prize, 1958; award of honor, Bayerische Akademie der Schoenen Kuenste Litaratur, 1958; Nordhein-Westfalen

Grand Art Prize, 1959; Veillon Prize (Switzerland; international), 1959, for *Billard um Halbzehn;* Siehe-Heydt Preis; Cologne literature prize, 1961; Pris d'Elba, 1965; Georg Buechner prize, German Academy for Language and Poetry, 1967; Nobel Prize for Literature, 1972, for contributions to "a renewal of German Literature in the postwar era."

WRITINGS—Stories: Der Zug war puenktlich (also see below), Middelhauve, 1949, translation by Richard Graves published as *The Train Was on Time,* Criterion Books, 1956, translation by Leila Vennewitz published as *The Train Was on Time* (also see below), Seeker & Warburg, 1973; *Wanderer, kommst du nach Spa* (also see below), Middelhauve, 1950, translation by Mervyn Saville published as *Traveller, If You Come to the Spa,* Arco, 1956, bilingual edition, edited and translated by Savill and John Bednall, M. Hueber, 1956; *Die Schwarzen schafe,* Middelhauve, 1951, reprinted, 1972; *Nicht nur zur Weihnachtszeit* (also see below), Kiepenheuer & Witsch, 1955, reprinted, Deutscher Taschenbuch Verlag, 1973; *Das Brot der fruehen Jahre,* Kiepenheuer & Witsch, 1955, revised edition, edited by James Alldridge, Heinemann, 1965, translation by Savill published as *The Bread of Our Early Years,* Arco, 1957; *So ward Abend und Morgen* (also see below), Verlag der Arche, 1955; *Unberechenbare Gaeste: Heitere Erzaehlungen,* Verlag der Arche, 1956; *Im Tal der donnernden Hufe,* Insel-Verlag, 1957, revised edition, edited by Alldridge, Heinemann, 1970; *Abenteuer eines Brotbeutels, und andere Geschichten* (also see below), selected and edited by Richard Plant, Norton, 1957; *Erzaehlungen* (contains *Der Zug war puenktlich* and *Wanderer kommst du nach Spa*), Middelhauve, 1958; *Doktor Murkes Gesammeltes Schweigen, und andere Satiren,* Kiepenheuer & Witsch, 1958, revised edition published as *Doktor Murkes Gesammeltes Schweigen, and Other Stories,* edited by Gertrud Seidmann, Harrap, 1963; *Der Mann mit den Messern* (also see below), Reclam-Verlag, 1958; *Nicht nur zur Weinachtszeit* [und] *Der Mann mit den Messern,* edited by Dorthea Curger, American Book Co., 1959; *Der Bahnhof von Zimpren,* P. List, 1959: *Die Waage der Baleks, und andere Erzaehlungen* (also see below), Union-Verlag, 1959.

(Contributor) *Modern German Stories,* edited by H. M. Waidson, Faber, 1961; *1947-1951 Erzaehlungen,* Middelhauve, 1963; *18 Stories,* translated by Leila Vennewitz, McGraw, 1966; *Children Are Civilians Too,* translated by Vennewitz, McGraw, 1970; *Fuenferzaelungen* (contains *Das Abenteuer, Die Waage der Baleks,* "Die Postkarte," "Der Tod der Elsa Baskoleit," and *So war Abend und Morgen*), Hyperion-Verlag, 1971; *Erzaelungen, 1950-1970,* Kiepenheuer & Witsch, 1972.

Novels: *Wo warst du, Adam?,* Middelhauve, 1951, reprinted, Deutscher Taschenbuch Verlag, 1972, translation by Savill published as *Adam, Where Art Thou?,* Criterion Books, 1955, translation by Vennewitz published as *And Where Were You Adam?* (also see below), Seeker & Warburg, 1974; *Und sagte kein einziges Wort,* Kiepenheuer & Witsch, 1953, translation by Richard Graves published as *Acquainted with the Night,* Holt, 1954; *Haus ohne Hueter,* Kiepenheuer & Witsch, 1954, translation published as *Tomorrow and Yesterday,* Criterion Books, 1957 (translation by Savill published in England as *The Unguarded House,* Arco, 1957); *Billard um Zalbzehn,* Kiepenheuer & Witsch, 1959, translation by Patrick Bowles published as *Billards at Half Past Nine,* Weidenfeld & Nicolson, 1961, McGraw, 1963; *Als der Krieg ausbrach* [und] *Als der Krieg zer Ende war* (two novellas), Insel-Verlag, 1962, translation by Vennewitz published as *Absent without Leave* (also see below), McGraw, 1965; *Ansichten eines Clowns*, Kiepenheuer & Witsch, 1963, translation by Vennewitz published as *The Clown*, McGraw, 1965; *Entfernung von der Truppe* (novella; also see below), Kiepenheuer & Witsch, 1964; *Ende einer Dienstfahrt*, Kiepenheuer & Witsch, 1966, translation by Vennewitz published as *End of a Mission*, McGraw, 1967; *Gruppenbild mit Dame*, Kiepenheuer & Witsch, 1971, translation by Vennewitz published as *Group Portrait with a Lady*, McGraw, 1973.

Nonfiction: *Irisches Tagebuck*, Deutscher Taschenbuch Verlag, 1957, translation by Vennewitz published as *Irish Journal*, McGraw, 1967; *Brief an einen jungen Katholiken*, Kiepenheuer & Witsch, 1961; *Assissi*, Knorr & Hirth, 1962; *Hierzulande* (essays), Deutscher Taschenbuch Verlag, 1963; *Frankfuter Vorlesungen*, Kiepenheuer & Witsch, 1966; *Leiben im Zustand des Frevels*, Berliner Handpresse, 1969; *Neue politische und literarische Schriften*, Kiepenheuer & Witsch, 1973.

Plays; all radio plays, except as noted: *Zum Tee bei Dr. Borsig* (produced, 1955), Deutscher Taschenbuch Verlag, 1964; *Die Spurlosen*, Hans Bredow-Institut, 1957; *Bilanz* (first produced, 1957; published with *Klopfzeichen*, also see below), Reclam, 1961; *Klopfzeichen* (produced, 1960, translation by Anthony Reid produced as "The Knocking," British Broadcasting Corp., September, 1967), Reclam, 1961; *Ein Schucke Erde* (stage play), Kiepenheuer & Witsch, 1962; (contributor) *Hoespiele*, afterword by Ernst Schnobel, Fischer Buecherei, 1965; *Vier Hoerspiele*, edited by G. P. Sonnex, Methuen, 1966; *Hausfriedsbruch* (contains "Hausfriedsbruch" and "Aussatz"; also see below), Kiepenheuer & Witsch, 1969; "Aussatz," first produced at Aachen's City Theatre, October 17, 1970; (contributor) *Politische Meditationen zer Gleuck u[nd] Vergeblichkeit* (television scripts), Luchterlund, 1973. Also author of "Die Bruecke von Berczaba," 1952, "Ein Tag wie sonst," 1953, "Eine Stunde Aufenthalt," 1957, "Die Stunde der Wahrheit," 1958, "Ich habe nichts genen Tiere," 1958, "Die ungezehlte Geliebte," 1958, and "Der Heilige und der Raeuber."

Author of text for photography books by Karl Hargesheimer (Chargesheimer): *Im Ruhrgebiet*, Kiepenheuer & Witsch, 1958; *Unter Krahnenbaeumen*, Greven Verlag (Koeln), 1958; *Menschen am Rhein*, Kiepenheuer & Witsch, 1960.

Translator; with wife, Annemarie Boell, except as noted: Kay Cicellis, *Kein Name bei den leuten*, Keipenheur & Witsch, 1953; (with Goyert and Baechler) *Ein unordentlicher Mensch*, Biederstein, 1955; *Tod einer Stadt* (stories), Kiepenheuer & Witsch, 1956; Paul Horgan, *Weihnachtsabend in San Cristobal*, Walter, 1956; Patrick White, *Zur Ruhe kam der Baum des Menschen nie*, Kiepenheuer & Witsch, 1957; Paul Horgan, *Der Teufel in der Wueste*, Walter, 1958; Paul Horgan, *Eine Rose zur Weihnacht*, Walter, 1960; Bernard Malamud, *Der Gehilfe (The Assistant)*, Kiepenheuer & Witsch, 1960; Tomas O'Crohan, *Die Boote fahren nicht mehr aus: Bericht einer irischen Fischers*, Walter, 1960; Patrick White, *Zur Ruhe kam der Baum des Menschen nie*, Ex Buchslub Libris (Zuerich), 1960; J. D. Salinger, *Kurz vor dem Krieg gegen die Eskimos, und andere Kurzgeschichten* (stories), Kiepenheuer & Witsch, 1961; Brendan Behan, *Stuecke fuers Theater*, Luchterhand, 1962; (with Irene Muehlon) Salinger, *Der Faenger im Roggen*, Kiepenheuer & Witsch, 1962. Also translator of Salinger's *Franny und Zooey*, Shaw's *Caesar und Cleopatra*, and Flann O'Brien's *Das harte Leben*.

Omnibus volumes: *Aus unseren Tage*, edited by Gisela Stein, Holt, 1960; *Erzaehlungen, Hoerspiele, Aufsaetze*, Kiepenheuer & Witsch, 1962; *Absent without Leave, and Other Stories*, translated by Vennewitz, Weidenfeld & Nicolson, 1967; *Aufsaetze, Kritiken, Reden*, Kiepenheuer & Witsch, 1967; *Mein trauriges Gesicht*, Verlag Progress, 1968; *Hausfriedensbruch: Hoerspiel, Aussatz, Schauspiel*, Kiepenheuer & Witsch, 1969; *Adam, and The Train: Two Novels* (contains *And Where Were You, Adam*, and *The Train Was on Time*), translated by Vennewitz, McGraw, 1970.

Other: *Geschichten aus zwoelf Jahren*, Suhrkamp, 1969; *Gedichte*, Literarisches Colloquium, 1972.

SIDELIGHTS: "Conscience and craft are the two poles that delimit [Boell's] scope as a writer," writes Theodore Ziolkowski, "and neither consideration is given short shrift in his works. Small wonder, then, that perspicacious critics rate [Boell] above most of his contemporaries. Greater wonder, perhaps, that his books have been greeted not only with critical acclaim but with an enthusiastic reception by the German reading public! Two factors account, at least in part, for his popular success. In the first place, [Boell] is a master of the art of storytelling. He does not regard his books merely as vehicles to bear ponderous philosophical speculations. . . . In the second place, his main theme is one to elicit the sympathy—or, more often perhaps, to arouse the antagonism—of his countrymen: at any rate, it does not leave them bored or indifferent." Boell, as *Time* magazine has noted, "for years has turned out thoughtful novels about Germany, most of them more notable for civilized intentions than sustained artistic power."

His "civilized intentions" are largely concerned with changing the societal and moral structure of post-war Germany. The protagonist in *The Clown* is a paradigmatic character, "giving witness against all Germany," writes Bruce Cook. "But he is hardest of all on the Catholics, it is they, he feels, who are the most pretentious and hypocritical . . . [because] they lack the fundamental virtue of charity." Edwin Kennebeck notes that, "probably as much as any German novelist since World War II, Heinrich [Boell], writing of the people of his country and of the great wounds and wrenchings in their lives, has consistently kept his stories under the discipline of his craft." Kennebeck adds, "by the paradox of art, [they make] the best testimonial." They show by implication "the face of [Germany's] slightly surrealist post-war landscape," writes Richard Plant. They probe, according to Helga E. Dohse, "the schizophrenic contradictions between the law and human reactions based on conscience." Edward M. Potoker observes that in Boell's vivisection of modern Germany he uncovers "the quirks that lay, like noxious organisms, beneath Germany's values and social institutions, and [uncovers] as well the dangerous illusions which Germans cherished about these quirks." According to Victor Lange, "to [the] more independent younger readers [Boell] has sometimes seemed provincial in attitude and old-fashioned in his technique; they have not, of course, been indifferent to the integrity and seriousness of [Boell's] moral position, but they have been troubled by his reluctance—or perhaps his inability—to bring the radical resources of modern fiction to bear upon intellectual and emotional issues that cannot be fully explored in the conventional designs of his novels."

Kennebeck has said that Boell, "though writing of a milieu

that is predominantly stultifying, dreary, cynical—a defeated nation after a war of unspeakable horror, a generation of people whose lives at their very centers have been irrevocably contorted—nevertheless has extraordinary depth of feeling. . . . *Tomorrow and Yesterday,* [for example], has many strong and eloquent passages, celebrating human love and human pleasure." Even a comparatively stark novel, such as *The Clown,* "is filled with gentleness, high comic spirits, and human sympathy," writes Robert Kiely. Lange notes that what Boell calls forth in many of his stories "is not so much our compassion for the victims of a system, nor our dismay at the prevalence of evil; . . . [instead] he attacks greed, stupidity, pretentiousness and arrogance—the traditional targets of satire—and insofar as they are curable, reminds us of the rational resources that might, with varying degrees of success, be marshalled against them. . . . The gap between moral pretensions and the pursuit of a pointless existence is hauntingly explored with the fervor of a born storyteller who may at times seem in danger of being swayed by his own compassion into melodrama and sentimentality." Lange adds that Boell and Camus "have a moving emotional integrity in common, and a profound awareness of the need of individual moral commitment in a society of increasingly abstract relationships. Camus is altogether the more impressive analyst of the private dilemma, [Boell] perhaps the more specific (and satirical) recorder of public attitudes and of a collective experience desperately determined by an inheritance that is probably easier for the younger Germans totally to disavow than for their parents to transcend."

Boell has been called an existentialist writer. Hugh McGovern believes that this philosophical point of view is succinctly depicted in a statement made by one of Boell's characters: "I am a clown, and I collect moments." The clown is an individual, a victim of his society, and one who objects to "the party line, the party men, the people who begin sentences with the words, 'We Catholics . . .', just as he is against those who begin their sentences, 'We Protestants . . .', 'We Atheists . . .', 'We Socialists . . .', 'We Germans . . .' and so forth," writes D. J. Enright. Boell's novel, *Tomorrow and Yesterday,* has been called "a cry of giant despair." In "Enter and Exit" Boell writes that "the words man and stupid had become almost identical to me." Michael Wilding believes that, in *Absent without Leave,* "explicit misanthropy has been replaced by a refusal—or inability—to connect with the world," a theme that recurs in *The Clown.* As Ziolkowski notes, Boell's early story, "The Train Was On Time," is "the story of one man's destiny and his rendezvous with death," while *Adam, Where Art Thou?* "is a diatribe against the utter senselessness of war—a motif that obviously could not be developed if individual destiny were the central theme." According to Koch, Boell "has inlaid the standard German romantic theme of the poet's pathos, futility, need for love, emasculation, into the texture of the sociological-critical search for identity we have come to expect from American fiction." His characters "are depressed innocents trying hard to live decently in an indecent world," writes Paul Bailey. "Enemies loom everywhere: men and women who have surrendered their humanity become things." A *Times Literary Supplement* writer adds: "For all his distancing devices of urbane irony, Herr [Boell] is essentially a guardian of innocence against the contagion of the world; the sensitized plate of his imagination registers—as does the childish mind—nuances of deceit and turpitude beyond the range of normal vision."

One of Boell's themes, writes Ziolkowski, is the Christian ideal. "The basic trouble with contemporary society, as [Boell] sees it, is anxiety caused by the disparity between this ideal and the actual state of affairs. Now the awareness of such a glaring discrepancy between the real and the ideal, as Schiller pointed out, is the source of satire, elegy, and the idyll: the three dominant moods in [Boell's] writing." His stories are often little more than "logical elaborations of an absurd situation, . . ." according to Ziolkowski. Potoker notes that Boell's "work is never as depressing as Kafka's. There is a dash of Fielding in him that always mitigates the effects of his paranoia, a gusto and vigor that enable him to envision, eccentrically but firmly, human order as well as ordure." "At his best," writes J. P. Bauke, Boell "creates satiric close-ups of unsurpassed power," but unlike Brecht, "his assault is directed against the indolence of the heart, not the social order." His elegies are based on his childhood and on a lost society lacking in values. In Ireland he found an idyllic second home. Ziolkowski explains: "It was inevitable that [Boell] should visit, love, and write a book about Ireland. . . . Literary sympathies, in the first place, paved the way before he ever landed in Dublin; an old admirer of Yeats and Joyce, [Boell's] first act was to visit the grave of Swift, his godfather in satire. Then, Ireland is a Catholic country, but one in which Catholicism is not bruited about noisily or academically. . . . And finally, Ireland has not been afflicted by the mixed blessings of the *Wirtshaftswunder:* the people may be impoverished, but they are honest and warmhearted, displaying themselves as they are and not as they believe they ought to be."

In 1965 Potoker wrote that Boell "continues his stern and sometimes merciless probing of the conscience, values, and imperfections of his countrymen. However, [Boell's] style, which in his previous work had been relatively simple and direct, has now become an instrument of striking subtlety, maintained intricately on several levels, artfully moving back and forth in time and making use of symbols and parables both poignant and absurd. . . . *Absent Without Leave* is not only a brilliant novella, but one that indicates a major turning point in [Boell's] artistic career. If existential malaise is to propel him toward inner exile, he is bound to make his journey with dignity, sincerity, and characteristic robustness." Lange adds that, in this novella, Boell "offers the story in the bare outlines of a coloring book, which the reader himself may complete or vary." Says Boell: "Like a miserly uncle or a thrifty aunt, I take for granted the possession of a paintbox or a set of crayons. Those who have nothing but a pencil, a ballpoint, or the remains of some ink, are free to try it in monochrome." Ziolkowski notes that "much has been said about [Boell's] indebtedness to the recent American short story and to Hemingway in particular. To a certain extent this is true. His use of idiomatic speech and his skill with dialogue, the economy of style that is emphasized by occasional exaggeration and repetition, the technique of expressing complex problems by strictly external means, and the absence of traditional beginning and ending in most of his works—these, at any rate, are characteristics more typical of American than German fiction." At times his plots become exceedingly intricate as Boell weaves "a close texture that gives us an almost sensuous impression of the narrated time," writes Ziolkowski. His characters are clearly drawn and unstereotyped. Richard Plant calls him "essentially an impressionist, conveying the sensations of the world in the most concrete details," but he adds that Boell "also possesses a quiet intensity, a muted strength which equips each episode with an extraordinary impact." In his descriptive passages, writes Matthew Hodgart, "he is a worthy successor to Thomas Mann."

Enright praises Boell for his ability to be humorous and salutary, as well as sad. Ziolkowski writes: "*Billard um halbzehn* is representative, structurally, stylistically, and thematically, of [Boell's] entire work: it is an impassioned indictment of a hypocritical society, of a generation without values, of a people without Christianity. At no point, however, does the narrative suffer, for he relates, with an epic love for plot and detail, the fascinating story of a family of men and women during one of the most turbulent periods of history, establishing their way of life as a possible ideal within a world of debased values.... [Boell] is a writer of whom Germany is justly proud. Few of his contemporaries have had the courage to speak out as clearly and trenchantly as he against what he considers false in his society. Moreover, there is always implicit in his criticism the suggestion of a solution: a society based upon true Christian principles. Unlike some authors, he does not cloak his moral in history or myth, but writes about people of Germany today—people ... whose behaviour he has described in German prose that is second to none in clarity, precision, euphony, and flexibility.... [And] he is unwilling to compromise himself and his convictions at any cost." Lange writes that Boell is "concerned with the impact of war, ... but more specifically than most of his contemporaries, he defines the oppressive effects of every sort of institutional power.... All institutions of his world seem to Boell vacuous and inhuman, all political or social alternatives questionable, right and left, Catholic and Protestant, wealthy and destitute are merely the instruments of group prejudices that paralyze the individual judgment." Lane concludes that Boell "is above all a moralist whose critical intelligence and whose profound religious commitment have produced, beyond all ideological perspectives and beyond any faith in abstract principles or order, novels and stories that may in some respects seem conservative but that are bound to move us by their rare compassion and their integrity of vision and purpose."

AVOCATIONAL INTERESTS: Travel and hiking.

BIOGRAPHICAL/CRITICAL SOURCES: Saturday Review, June 2, 1956, October 19, 1957, September 11, 1965, December 10, 1966; *Commonweal,* June 29, 1956, November 1, 1957, February 12, 1965; *Time,* October 21, 1957, January 4, 1963; *Books Abroad,* summer, 1960, spring, 1967; *Manchester Guardian,* June 2, 1961; *New Statesman,* June 2, 1961, March 3, 1967; Uwe Schultz, editor, *Das Tagebuch und der moderne Autor,* C. Hanser, 1965; *America,* February 6, 1965; *Christian Science Monitor,* February 11, 1965; *New Republic,* March 20, 1965, November 27, 1965; *Nation,* May 3, 1965; *Times Literary Supplement,* November 10, 1966, March 9, 1967; *Observer Review,* March 5, 1967; *Punch,* March 15, 1967; *London Magazine,* May, 1967; Marcel Reich-Ranicki, editor, *In Sachen Boell,* Kiepenheuer & Witsch, 1968; Gunter Wirth, *Heinrich Boell,* Union Verlag, 1968; Wilhelm Johannes Schwartz, *Heinrich Boell, Teller of Tales: A Study of his Works and Characters,* Ungar, 1969; *New York Times,* October 20, 1972; Carolyn Riley, editor, *Contemporary Literary Criticism,* Gale, Volume II, 1974, Volume III, 1975, Volume VI, 1976.†

BOESCH, Mark J(oseph) 1917-

PERSONAL: Born October 31, 1917, son of Anthony Joseph and Anna (Supancheck) Boesch; married Frances Blackburn, April 2, 1951; children: Mark, David, Anna Marie. *Education:* "High school graduate and that's all any author needs." *Home:* 311 Geneva, Hamilton, Mont. 59840.

CAREER: U.S. Forest Service, fire dispatcher in Hamilton, Mont., 1946-65, press officer in Milwaukee, Wis., 1965-71; now full-time writer. Member, Environmental Resources Group. *Military service:* U.S. Marine Corps, 1942-46; became sergeant; received Purple Heart and Bronze Star. *Member:* Authors Guild.

WRITINGS: The Lawless Land, Winston, 1953; *Beyond the Muskingum,* Winston, 1953; *Fire Fighter,* Morrow, 1954; *The Cross in the West,* Farrar, 1956; *Kit Carson of the Old West,* Farrar, 1959; *John Colter,* Putnam, 1959; *The Long Search for the Truth About Cancer,* Putnam, 1960; *The World of Rice,* Dutton, 1967; *Careers in the Outdoors,* Dutton, 1975. Author of brochures; contributor of articles and short stories to magazines and newspapers.

WORK IN PROGRESS: Research for several books.

SIDELIGHTS: Boesch told CA: "[I] have a strong urge to expose the evils in our society, to champion the underdog, the so-called misnamed 'common man.' Expect this to reflect in my future writing."

* * *

BOEVE, Edgar G. 1929-

PERSONAL: Born September 27, 1929, in Marshalltown, Iowa; son of Edward (a clergyman) and Grace (Jansen) Boeve; married Ervina Van Dyke (a director of drama at Calvin College), August 13, 1955. *Education:* J. Franklin School of Professional Arts, New York, certificate, 1950; Calvin College, A.B., 1953; University of Michigan, M.S.D., 1954. *Religion:* Protestant. *Home:* 2228 Thornapple River Dr. S.E., Grand Rapids, Mich. 49506.

CAREER: Calvin College, Grand Rapids, Mich., professor of art and chairman of department, 1958—. Painter, sculptor, and illustrator, with work exhibited at several one-man shows.

WRITINGS: Childrens' Art and the Christian Teacher, Concordia, 1966; (illustrator of Christian symbols, and author of related text) *Youth Hymnal,* Eerdmans, 1966; *Revelation-Response,* seven books, National Union of Christian Schools, 1974-75.

WORK IN PROGRESS: Processions: Religious Affirmation and Celebration.

* * *

BOHLE, Bruce 1918-

PERSONAL: Born July 21, 1918, in St. Louis, Mo.; son of Edward F. (a postal employee) and Emma W. (Fricke) Bohle. *Education:* Washington University, St. Louis, Mo., B.A., 1939. *Politics:* "Normally Democratic." *Religion:* Protestant. *Home:* 260 Audubon Ave., New York, N.Y. 10033. *Office:* American Heritage Publishing Co., 1221 Avenue of the Americas, New York, N.Y. 10020.

CAREER: St. Louis Star-Times, St. Louis, Mo., film critic, 1946-51, drama and music critic, 1950-51; St. Louis Symphony Orchestra, St. Louis, Mo., assistant manager, 1951-53; *Theatre Arts,* New York, N.Y., editor, 1953-61; Grolier, Inc., New York, N.Y., encyclopedia editor, 1960-

64; American Heritage Publishing Co., New York, N.Y., usage editor, *American Heritage Dictionary*, 1964—. *Military service:* U.S. Army Air Forces, 1942-46. *Member:* Phi Beta Kappa.

WRITINGS: (Compiler) *The Home Book of American Quotations*, Dodd, 1967, published as *Apollo Book of American Quotations*, Apollo Editions, 1970; (editor with American Heritage editors) *Great Historic Places*, American Heritage Press, 1973; (editor with American Heritage editors) *Great Historic Places of Europe*, American Heritage Press, 1974; (editor) *International Cyclopedia of Music and Musicians*, 10th edition, Dodd, 1974.

*   *   *

BOHROD, Aaron   1907-

PERSONAL: Born November 21, 1907, in Chicago, Ill.; son of George (a Russian immigrant in the grocery business in Chicago) and Fanny (Feingold) Bohrod; married Ruth Bush, December 29, 1929; children: Mark, Georgi (Mrs. Stephen S. Rothe), Neil. *Education:* Studied at Crane Junior College, 1925-26, Art Institute of Chicago, 1927-29, and Art Students' League of New York, 1930-32. *Home:* 4811 Tonyawatha Trail, Madison, Wis. 53716.

CAREER: Artist. Began to draw when very young, and worked as broker's messenger, commercial artist, and at other jobs to finance his art studies in Chicago and New York; first won recognition with his paintings of the Chicago scene; awarded the landscape prize at Art Institute of Chicago, 1933; had first one-man exhibition in New York, 1937, and was commissioned that year to do murals for post offices in Vandalia, Galesburg, and Clinton, Ill.; artist-in-residence at Southern Illinois University, Carbondale, 1941-42. *Wartime service:* Covered war fronts in the South Pacific, Germany, and France as member of War Art Unit, The Engineers, U.S. Army, 1942, and for *Life*, 1943-45. Artist-in-residence at University of Wisconsin, Madison, 1948-73. Instructor in art at Art Institute of Chicago, 1940; summer instructor at Ohio University, 1949, 1954, Ball State University, 1952, and Northern Michigan University, 1953. Represented in most major American museums, including Corcoran Gallery of Art, Metropolitan Museum of Art, Whitney Museum of American Art, Art Institute of Chicago, Detroit Institute of Arts, and Swope Art Gallery. In addition to one-man shows, paintings have been exhibited in U.S. Treasury Department collection, "War Against Japan," in New York, 1945, and a number of other group showings from coast to coast. Designer of ceramics (decorated more than five hundred pieces in collaboration with F. Carlton Ball) and fabrics.

MEMBER: National Academy of Design (academician). *Awards, honors:* Guggenheim fellowship to travel in and study America, 1936-37, 1937-38; honorary D.F.A., Ripon College, 1960. Awards for paintings include: Eight awards from Art Institute of Chicago, including Logan Art Medal and $500, 1937, 1945; $1,000 Prize in "Artists for Victory" exhibition at Metropolitan Museum of Art, 1942; Clark Prize of $1,500 and Silver Medal, Corcoran Gallery of Art, 1943; Saltus Gold Medal of National Academy of Design, 1961; Child Hassam Purchase Prize of American Academy of Arts and Letters, 1962; Kirk Memorial Prize of National Academy of Design, 1965.

WRITINGS: A Pottery Sketch Book, University of Wisconsin Press, 1959, revised edition, 1968; *A Decade of Still Life* (autobiographical), University of Wisconsin Press, 1966 (with Robert Gard) *Wisconsin Sketches*, Wisconsin House, 1973.

Illustrator: James Gray, *The Illinois*, Farrar & Rinehart, 1940; Albert Halper, *The Golden Watch*, Holt, 1953; Hartzell Spence, *The Story of America's Religions*, Holt, 1960.

BIOGRAPHICAL/CRITICAL SOURCES: Esquire, March, 1940; *Time*, December 6, 1954, September 28, 1966; *New Republic*, December 2, 1957; *Design*, March, 1960; Aaron Bohrod, *A Decade of Still Life*, University of Wisconsin Press, 1966.

*   *   *

BOLL, David   1931-

PERSONAL: Surname rhymes with "roll"; born March 29, 1931, in Newcastle, England; son of William Henry (a schoolteacher) and Anne (Watson) Boll; married Antonia Sandford (a publisher's reader and editor), May 27, 1962; children: Marcus William Henry, Miranda. *Education:* Balliol College, Oxford, B.A. (honors), 1954. *Politics:* Labour Party. *Religion:* None. *Home:* 59 Coniger Rd., London S.W. 6, England. *Agent:* Curtis Brown Ltd., 1 Craven Hill, London W2 3EW, England.

CAREER: Employed in marketing and advertising positions, 1954-65; Birds Eye Frozen Foods Ltd., London, England, marketing manager, beginning 1965. *Military service:* British Army, Royal Artillery, 1949-51; became second lieutenant.

WRITINGS: The Thicket (novel), Hodder & Stoughton, 1967. Contributor of reviews to *Books and Bookmen*, 1962-63.

WORK IN PROGRESS: Under Saturn's Sign, a novel.

SIDELIGHTS: Boll told *CA:* "Determined in adolescence to be novelist. Have travelled extensively in Africa, North America, India, and virtually all countries of Europe." *Avocational interests:* Art, history.††

*   *   *

BOLLES, Robert C(harles)   1928-

PERSONAL: Born April 24, 1928, in Sacramento, Calif.; son of Walter Ehmann and Claris (Hillary) Bolles; married Ann Sonkin, March 24, 1951; children: Hilary, Richard, Elizabeth, Ronald. *Education:* Stanford University, A.B., 1948, M.S., 1949; University of California, Berkeley, Ph.D., 1956. *Religion:* Atheist. *Office:* Department of Psychology, University of Washington, Seattle, Wash. 98105.

CAREER: Princeton University, Princeton, N.J., instructor in psychology, 1956-58; University of Pennsylvania, Philadelphia, visiting assistant professor, 1958-59; Hollins College, Roanoke, Va., assistant professor of psychology, 1959-66; University of Washington, Seattle, professor of psychology, 1966—. *Member:* American Psychological Association, Psychonomic Society.

WRITINGS: Theory of Motivation, Harper, 1967, 2nd edition, 1975; *Learning Theory*, Holt, 1975.

WORK IN PROGRESS: Animal behavior; applications of psychology to the law.†

*   *   *

BOMAN, Thorleif Gustav   1894-

PERSONAL: Born June 29, 1894, in Oslo, Norway; son of Victor Julius and Bertha (Hakkerud) Boman; married Ester Sjoholm, 1927; children: Leif Gunnar, Bjarne, Ingrid, Helge. *Education:* University of Oslo, Cand.Theol., 1923, Dr.Theol., 1952. *Home:* Eckersbergs gaten 21, Oslo, Norway.

CAREER: Clergyman of Church of Norway. Seamen's pastor, Hamburg, 1924-30; Norwegian Seamen's Mission, Bergen, Norway, pastor, 1930-34; Norwegian Missionary Society, Stavanger, Norway, principal of school, 1934-37; pastor, 1937-61. University of Oslo, Oslo, Norway, lecturer in Old Testament and systematic theology. Member: Norwegian Academy of Science.

WRITINGS: Das hebraische Denken im Vergleich mit dem griechischen, Vandenhoeck & Ruprecht, 1952, 5th edition, 1968, English translation by Jules L. Moreau published as Hebrew Thought Compared with Greek, Westminster, 1960; Troslaere for fritenkere, Fabritius, 1963; Jesus, jodenes konge, Aschehoug, 1967; Die Jesueberlieferung im Lichte der neueren Volkskunde, Vandenhoeck & Ruprecht, 1967; Europas kultar og den joediske arv, Gyldendal, 1972; Hvem var Jesus?, Aschehoug, 1975. Also author of Religioese problemer, 1972, and Personlig kristendom i en irreligioes stat, 1972. Contributor to journals and newspapers.

* * *

BOMBECK, Erma 1927-

PERSONAL: Born February 21, 1927, in Dayton, Ohio; daughter of Cassius Edwin (a laborer) and Erma (Haines) Fiste; married William Bombeck (employed by Board of Education, Phoenix, Ariz.), August 13, 1949; children: Betsy, Andrew, Matthew. Education: University of Dayton, B.A., 1949. Religion: Roman Catholic. Home: Paradise Valley, Ariz. 85253.

CAREER: Dayton Journal Herald, writer, 1949-53; author of column, "At Wit's End," for Field Newspaper Sydicate, Chicago, Ill., syndicated to 541 newspapers, 1965—; lecturer. Member: Women in Communication, Sigma Delta Xi.

WRITINGS: At Wit's End (collection of columns), Doubleday, 1967; Just Wait Till You Have Children of Your Own, Doubleday, 1971; I Lost Everything in the Post-Natal Depression, Doubleday, 1973.

BIOGRAPHICAL/CRITICAL SOURCES: Life, October 1, 1971.

* * *

BOMELI, Edwin C(larence) 1920-

PERSONAL: Born September 16, 1920, in Peoria, Ohio; son of Edward J. (a teacher) and Alma (Hoffman) Bomeli; married Doreen Swaim, May 6, 1945; children: David, Daniel, Paul, Deborah, Timothy. Education: Ohio State University, B.S., 1942; Butler University, M.A., 1949; Michigan State University, Ph.D., 1963. Politics: Republican. Home: 258 South Church St., Bowling Green, Ohio 43402. Office: Bowling Green State University, Bowling Green, Ohio.

CAREER: Certified public accountant, Ohio and Indiana. Keller, Kirschner, Martin & Clinger, Columbus, Ohio, staff accountant, 1942-45; Butler University, Indianapolis, Ind., associate professor of accounting, 1946-51, 1954-56; Muskingum College, New Concord, Ohio, associate professor of economics and business administration, 1952-54; Bowling Green State University, Bowling Green, Ohio, professor of accounting, 1956—, chairman of accounting department, 1960-72, director of graduate studies in business, 1972—. Minister of Disciples of Christ, ordained 1949. Director of Mid-American National Bank, Cain's Potato Chips, and Deck-Hanneman Funeral Homes, Inc.;

financial consultant, Glidden Co. Member: American Accounting Association, American Institute of Certified Public Accountants, Financial Executives Institute, Ohio Society of Certified Public Accountants.

WRITINGS: (With Gilbert Cooke) Business Financial Management, Houghton, 1967. Contributor to professional journals.

SIDELIGHTS: Bomeli speaks some Italian; he lived in Italy for a year.

* * *

BOND, Mary Fanning Wickham 1898-
(Mrs. James Bond, Mary F. W. Lewis, Mary F. Wickham Porcher, Mary Fanning Wickham)

PERSONAL: Born June 8, 1898, in Philadelphia, Pa.; daughter of Samuel (a vice-president of Pennsylvania Railroad) and Maria Porter (Landis) Porcher; married Shippen Lewis (an attorney), November 19, 1934 (deceased); married James Bond (a biologist and author of bird guides to the West Indies), August 20, 1953. Education: Dana Hall, diploma, 1916; took extension courses in English at Columbia University, 1938, and University of Pennsylvania, 1940. Politics: Democrat. Religion: Episcopalian. Home: 721 Davidson Rd., Philadelphia, Pa. 19118. Agent: Mary Squire Abbot, McIntosh & Otis, Inc., 18 East 41st St., New York, N.Y. 10017.

CAREER: Writer. Chestnut Hill Local (weekly newspaper), Chestnut Hill, Pa., founder, and honorary editor. Chairman, Philadelphia Democratic Women's Campaign for Roosevelt, 1940, 1944; co-chairman, Volunteers for Stevenson, Philadelphia, 1953. Trustee, Free Library of Philadelphia, 1953—. Awards, honors: Browning Society of Philadelphia poetry medal, 1924.

WRITINGS—Under name Mary Fanning Wickham, except as indicated: The Tilted Cup (poetry), Dorrance, 1926; Cherique (girls' adventure), Appleton, 1928; Gloom Creek (girls' adventure), Appleton, 1929; Device and Desire (adult novel), Lippincott, 1950; The Petrified Gesture (adult novel), Lippincott, 1951; (under name Mrs. James Bond) How 007 Got His Name (nonfiction), Collins, 1966; Far Afield in the Caribbean, Livingston, 1971. Also author of verse, published under name Mary F. Wickham Porcher; contributor to Audubon under name Mary F. W. Lewis; also contributor of poetry, short stories, and nature and sports articles to other magazines, including McClure's, St. Nicholas, Ladies' Home Journal, American, Town and Country, American Lawn Tennis, Reader's Digest, Poetry of To-day (London), New York Times "Travel and Resorts," and Forum. Editor, On Leave (United Service Organizations weekly newssheet for servicemen), 1941-45.

WORK IN PROGRESS: Ants in the Sugar, a West Indian odyssey.

SIDELIGHTS: Mrs. Bond told CA: "Ian Fleming 'stole' my husband's name from title pages of one of the latter's books; inscribed a book of his 'to the real James Bond, from the thief of his identity, Ian Fleming.'"

Mrs. Bond accompanied her ornithologist-husband on an expedition to Turneffe Islands, British Honduras, in 1954, and has spent more than a dozen winters in the Caribbean; was also a member of the Phelps expedition to Venezuelan islands, 1961. In earlier years, she was a member of field hockey, tennis, and golf teams.

BONEY, William Jerry   1930-

PERSONAL: Born November 20, 1930, in New York, N.Y.; son of Cecil DeWitt (a teacher) and Myrtle E. (Cox) Boney; married Nancy J. Dyck (an artist), August 23, 1958; children: Elizabeth Jane, William Thomas, Paul DeWitt. *Education:* Princeton University, A.B., 1952; Union Theological Seminary, New York, N.Y., B.D., 1955; University of Tuebingen, graduate study, 1961-62; Drew University, Ph.D., 1963. *Politics:* Democrat. *Religion:* Presbyterian. *Home:* 2904 Noble Ave., Richmond, Va. 23222. *Office:* School of Theology, Virginia Union University, 1205 Palmyra Ave., Richmond, Va. 23227.

CAREER: Presbyterian Church in the U.S., ordained minister, 1955; Virginia Polytechnic Institute, Blacksburg, Presbyterian minister to students, 1955-58; Rutgers University, Douglas College, New Brunswick, N.J., lecturer in religion, 1962-63; Virginia Union University, School of Religion, Richmond, assistant professor, 1963-67, associate professor 1967-70, professor of theology, 1970—. Protestant consultor to Ecumenical Affairs Commission, Catholic Diocese of Richmond; member of Delegation of Presbyterian Church, U.S. to the Consultation on Church Union. *Member:* American Academy of Religion, North American Academy of Ecumenists (secretary/treasurer, 1972—), Quadrangle Club (Princeton University). *Awards, honors:* Faculty fellowship, American Association of Theological Schools, 1968-69; Institute for Ecumenical and Cultural Research, Collegeville, Minn., fellow, 1968-69.

WRITINGS: (Editor with Lawrence E. Molumby, and contributor) *The New Day: Catholic Theologians of the Renewal,* John Knox, 1968; (editor with Paul A. Crow, and contributor) *Church Union at Midpoint,* Association Press, 1972; (contributor) Richard N. Soulen, editor, *Care for the Dying,* John Knox, 1975. Contributor of articles to *Worship, Priest,* and *Ecumenical Studies.*

WORK IN PROGRESS: Studies in ecumenics.

*   *   *

BONNEVILLE, Douglas A(lan)   1931-

PERSONAL: Born April 30, 1931, in Greenfield, Mass.; son of Joseph Ernest (with Northeast Telephone Co.) and Dorothy Louise (Wait) Bonneville; married Ellen Ann Bracken, June 10, 1961; children: Anne Louise, Loretta Marie, Raymond Griffith. *Education:* Wesleyan University, Middletown, Conn., B.A., 1955; University of Bordeaux, graduate study, 1955-56; Ohio State University, M.A., 1958, Ph.D., 1961. *Home:* 600 Northeast Ninth Ave., Gainesville, Fla. 32601. *Office:* Department of Romance Languages, University of Florida, Gainesville, Fla. 32611.

CAREER: Kenyon College, Gambier, Ohio, instructor in French, 1958-59; Dartmouth College, Hanover, N.H., instructor in French, 1961-63; University of Florida, Gainesville, assistant professor of French, 1963—. *Member:* Modern Language Association of America, American Association of University Professors. *Awards, honors:* Fulbright scholarship in France, 1955-56; National Endowment for the Humanities summer stipend, 1971.

WRITINGS: Diderot's Vie de Seneque: A Swan-Song Revised, University of Florida Press, 1966; (contributor) C. G. S. Williams, editor, *Literature and History in the Age of Ideas,* Ohio State University Press, 1975.

WORK IN PROGRESS: Voltaire and the Form of the Novel.

AVOCATIONAL INTERESTS: Art, music.

BOODMAN, David M(orris)   1923-

PERSONAL: Born July 4, 1923, in Pittsburgh, Pa.; son of Abraham and Elizabeth (Small) Boodman; married Helen Citron (an artist), September 5, 1948; children: Sandra Gail, Lisa Jean. *Education:* University of Pittsburgh, B.S., 1944, Ph.D., 1950. *Home:* 4 Linmoor Ter., Lexington, Mass. 02173. *Office:* Arthur D. Little, Inc., Cambridge, Mass. 02140.

CAREER: Massachusetts Institute of Technology, Cambridge, research staff, 1950-60; Arthur D. Little, Inc. (consultants), Cambridge, Mass., member of senior staff, 1960—, vice-president and head of operations research section, 1968—. *Military service:* U.S. Navy, 1944-46. *Member:* American Association for the Advancement of Science (fellow), Operations Research Society of America, Institute of Management Sciences, Sigma Xi. *Awards, honors:* National Safety Council traffic safety award, 1967.

WRITINGS: (With J. F. Magee) *Production Planning and Inventory Control,* McGraw, 1967. Contributor to *Handbook of Manufacturing Management,* edited by H. B. Maynard, McGraw.

*   *   *

BORCHARDT, Dietrich Hans   1916-

PERSONAL: Born April 14, 1916, in Hanover, Germany; son of Max Noah (a physician) and Mina (Lewinski) Borchardt; married Janet Duff Sinclair, 1944; children: Sandra Helen, Ann Sinclair (deceased), Max William. *Education:* Received early education in Germany and Italy; Victoria University of Wellington, M.A. (honors), 1946; New Zealand Library School, Diploma, 1947; Library Association of Australia, associate, 1953. *Home:* 57 Aylmer St., North Balwyn, Victoria 3104, Australia. *Office:* La Trobe University, Bundoora, Victoria 3083, Australia.

CAREER: Farm worker in Germany, Italy, and Spain, 1934-36; second-hand book dealer in Florence, Italy, 1936-39; farm worker and general laborer in New Zealand, 1939-43; book dealer in Wellington, New Zealand, 1943-46; University of Otago, Dunedin, New Zealand, acquisitions librarian, 1947-50; University of Tasmania, Hobart, deputy librarian, 1950-53, librarian, 1953-64; La Trobe University, Bundoora, Victoria, Australia, chief librarian, 1965—. UNESCO library expert in Turkey, 1964-65; lecturer in bibliography at Graduate Library School, George Peabody College for Teachers, Nashville, Tenn., summers, 1968 and 1973. Member of Australian Advisory Council on Bibliographic Service, and chairman of Working Party on Bibliography; representative of La Trobe University on Council of Victoria Institute of Colleges; member of council, Victorian College of the Arts; consultant in subject bibliography, National Library of Australia. Director of Blackwell Scientific Publications Ltd. (Australia).

MEMBER: Library Association of Australia (fellow; past president of university and college libraries section; member of board of examiners, 1962-64, 1966-69), New Zealand Library Associaton, Library Association (United Kingdom), Bibliographical Society of Australia and New Zealand (executive member). *Awards, honors:* Carnegie grant to visit Europe and United States, 1958.

WRITINGS: (Compiler with B. Tilley and author of introduction) *The Roy Bridges Collection in the University of Tasmania,* Cremorne, Stone, 1956; *Checklist of Royal Commissions, Select Committees of Parliament and Boards of Inquiry,* Part I: *Commonwealth of Australia,*

1900-1950, Cremorne, Stone, 1958, Part II: *Tasmania, 1956-1959*, Cremorne, Stone, 1960, Part III: *Victoria, 1856-1960*, Wentworth Books, 1970, Part IV: *New South Wales, 1856-1960*, La Trobe University Library, 1975; *Australian Bibliography: A Guide to Printed Sources of Information*, F. W. Cheshire, 1963, 3rd edition, Academic Press, 1975. *Senescence and Fertility* (La Trobe University inaugural lectures), F. W. Cheshire, 1967; *How to Find Out in Philosophy and Psychology*, Pergamon, 1968; *The Spread of Printing: Australia*, Hertzberger, 1968; (with J. I. Horacek) *Librarianship in Australia, New Zealand, and Oceania*, Pergamon, 1975. Contributor of more than sixty articles and reviews to library journals. Editor, *Australia Academic and Research Libraries*, 1970—.

WORK IN PROGRESS: Checklist of Royal Commissions, Part V: Queensland 1859-1960.

AVOCATIONAL INTERESTS: Gardening.

*   *   *

BORDIN, Ruth B(irgitta) 1917-

PERSONAL: Born November 11, 1917, in Litchfield, Minn.; daughter of Emil William (a merchant) and Martha (Linner) Anderson; married Edward Bordin (a psychologist), June 20, 1941; children: Martha (Mrs. Steven A. Hillyard), Charlotte (Mrs. Sung Piau Lin). *Education:* University of Minnesota, B.S., 1938, M.A., 1940. *Politics:* Democrat. *Religion:* Unitarian Universalist. *Home:* 1000 Aberdeen, Ann Arbor, Mich. 48104. *Office:* Department of History, Eastern Michigan University, Ypsilanti, Mich. 48197.

CAREER: University of Minnesota, Minneapolis, research assistant, 1945-46; Washington State University, Pullman, research associate, 1946-48; University of Michigan, Ann Arbor, research associate, 1956-57, assistant curator of Michigan Historical Collections, 1957-60, curator, 1960-65, research associate, 1965-67; Eastern Michigan University, Ypsilanti, lecturer in history, 1967—. Dutch American Historical Society, consultant, 1966. *Member:* American Historical Association, Organization of American Historians, Phi Beta Kappa, Mortar Board.

WRITINGS: (Editor) L. V. McWhorter, *Hear Ye My Chiefs*, Claxton, 1952; (with Robert M. Warner) *The Manuscript Library*, Scarecrow, 1966; *The University of Michigan: A Pictorial History*, University of Michigan Press, 1967. Contributor to *Notable American Women*. Writer of radio scripts for "Footnote to History" program, 1963-64. Editor, "Occasional Publications of Michigan Historical Society," 1965-67.

*   *   *

BORG, Dorothy 1902-

PERSONAL: Born September 4, 1902, in Elberone, N.J.; daughter of Sidney C. (a banker) and Madeleine (Beer) Borg. *Education:* Wellesley College, B.A., 1923; Columbia University, M.A., 1931, Ph.D., 1946. *Politics:* Democrat. *Home:* 22 Riverside Dr., New York, N.Y. 10023.

CAREER: Institute of Pacific Relations, New York, N.Y., research associate, 1938-59; Harvard University, East Asian Research Center, Cambridge, Mass., research associate, 1959-61; Columbia University, New York, N.Y., lecturer in department of public law and government, 1962-68, senior research associate, East Asian Institute, 1962—. Member of political science department, Peking National University, 1947-48. *Member:* American Political Science

Association, Association for Asian Studies, American Historical Association. *Awards, honors:* Bancroft Prize of Columbia University, 1965, for *United States and the Far Eastern Crisis of 1933-1938*.

WRITINGS: American Policy and the Chinese Revolution, 1925-1928, Macmillan, 1947; *United States and the Far Eastern Crisis of 1933-1938*, Harvard University Press, 1964; (compiler) *Historians and American Far Eastern Policy*, East Asian Institute, Columbia University, 1966; (co-editor) *Pearl Harbor as History: Japanese-American Relations, 1931-1941*, Columbia University Press, 1973. Contributor to *Political Science Quarterly, Far Eastern Survey*, and other professional journals.

*   *   *

BORGES, Jorge Luis 1899-
(H[onorio] Bustos Domecq and B. Suarez Lynch, both joint pseudonyms with Adolfo Bioy Casares)

PERSONAL: Born August 24, 1899, in Buenos Aires, Argentina; son of (Dr.) Jorge (a writer) and Leonor (Acevedo) Borges; married. *Education:* Educated at College de Geneve, Switzerland. *Religion:* Says he has no personal religion, "but I hope to have one. Of course, I can believe in God, in the sense that Matthew Arnold gave to that word, something not ourselves that makes for righteousness. . . . I don't like to think of God as a person. . . . I would rather like to think of God as being a kind of adventurer . . . or perhaps as something within us making for some unknown purpose." *Home:* Mexico 564, Buenos Aires, Argentina.

CAREER: After completing his formal education he traveled in Europe, returning to Buenos Aires in 1921. There he became a leader in "ultraismo," a new literary movement based on Surrealism and Imagism; left the movement in the 1930's when he began writing essays and stories; was literary adviser to Emece Editores (publishers), Buenos Aires; professor of English literature at the University of Buenos Aires (has conducted a graduate school class in Anglo-Saxon). Municipal librarian of Buenos Aires, 1939-43; director of the Biblioteca Nacional, 1955-73, except during a period when Peron demoted him to the rank of chicken inspector; has lectured and taught in the United States; in 1967-68 he was the Elliot Norton Professor of Poetry at Harvard University, and again visited the U.S. in 1968; visiting lecturer, University of Oklahoma, 1969. *Member:* Argentinian Academy of Letters, Argentine Writer's Society (president, 1950-53), Amigos de la Literatura Inglesa (vice-president, 1950—), Goetheana Academy, Modern Language Association of America (honorary fellow, 1961—). *Awards, honors:* Municipal Literary Prize of Buenos Aires, 1928, for *El Idioma de los Argentinos*; Premio de Honor, Argentine Writers Society, 1945, for *Ficciones*; Legion d'Honneur (France); Gran Premio Nacional de Literatura, 1957, for *El Aleph*; International Publishers Prize (shared with Samuel Beckett), 1961; Ingram Merrill Foundation Award, 1966; Inter-American Literary Prize ($25,000), Bienal Foundation, 1970; D.Litt., Oxford University, 1970; Ph.D., University of Jerusalem, 1971; Alfonso Reyes Prize, 1973.

WRITINGS—Poetry: Fevor de Buenos Aires (also see below), [Buenos Aires], 1923, reprinted, Emece Editores, 1969; *Luna de enfrente* (also see below), Editorial Proa, 1925; *Cauderno San Martin* (also see below), Editorial Proa, 1929; *Poemas (1922-1943)* (includes *Fevor de Buenos Aires, Luna de enfrente, Cauderno San Martin, Muertes de*

Buenos Aires, and other poems), Editorial Losada, 1943; *Poemas, 1923-1959,* Emece Editores, 1958; *Obra poetica, 1923-1964,* Emece Editores, 1964; *Para las seis cuerdas* (songs), Emece Editores, 1965; *Obra poetica, 1923-1966,* Emece Editores, 1966; *Obra poetica, 1923-1967,* Emece Editores, 1967, translation by Norman Thomas di Giovanni published as *Selected Poems, 1923-1967,* Delacorte, 1972; *Luna de enfrente* [y] *Cauderno San Martin,* Emece Editores, 1969; *Obra poetica de Borges,* Emece Editores, Volume I: *El otro, el mismo* (also see below), Volume II: *Luna de enfrente* [and] *Cauderno de San Martin,* Volume III: *Fevor de Buenos Aires,* all 1969; *El otro, el mismo,* Emece Editores, 1969; *Obra poetica,* Alianza Editorial, 1972; *Elogio de la sombra,* Emece Editores, 1969, translation by di Giovanni published as *In Praise of Darkness,* Dutton, 1974.

Essays: *El Idioma de los Argentinos,* M. Gleizer (Buenos Aires), 1928; *Evaristo Carriego,* M. Gleizer, 1930; *Discusion,* M. Gleizer, 1932, reprinted, Emece Editores, 1964; *Historia de la Eternidad,* [Buenos Aires], 1936, revised edition, Alianza Editorial, 1971; *Aspectos de la Literatura Gauchesca,* Numero (Montevideo), 1950; (with Delia Ingenieros) *Antiguas Literaturas Germanicas,* 1951, 2nd edition, Fondo de Cultura Economica (Mexico), 1965; *Otras Inquisiciones (1937-1952),* Sur, 1952, translation by Ruth L. C. Simms published as *Other Inquisitions, 1937-1952,* University of Texas Press, 1964; (with Margarita Guerrero) *El "Martin Fierro",* Editorial Columba, 1953; (with Jose Edmundo Clemente) *El Idioma de los Argentinos* (not the same as above title), Del Giudice (Buenos Aires), 1953, new edition published as *El Lenguaje de Buenos Aires,* Emece Editores, 1963; (with Betina Edelberg) *Leopoldo Lugones,* Editorial Troquel (Buenos Aires), 1955; (with Margarita Guerrero) *Manual de Zoologia Fantastica,* Fondo de Cultura Economica (Mexico), 1957, translation published as *The Imaginary Zoo,* University of California Press, 1969, revised Spanish edition with Guerrero published as *El libro de los seres imaginarios,* Editorial Kier, 1967, translation and revision by Borges and Norman Thomas di Giovanni published as *The Book of Imaginary Beings,* Dutton, 1969; *The Spanish Language in South America: A Literary Problem* [and] *El Gaucho Martin Fierro* (two lectures), Hispanic and Luso-Brazillian Councils (London), 1964; (with Maria Esther Vazquez) *Introduccion a la Literatura Inglesa,* Editorial Columba, 1965, translation by L. Clark Keating and Robert O. Evans published as *An Introduction to English Literature,* University Press of Kentucky, 1974; (with M. E. Vazquez) *Literaturas Germanicas Medievales,* Falbo, 1966; (with Esther Zemborain de Torres) *Introduccion a la literature Northamericana,* Editorial Columba, 1967, translation by Keating and Evans published as *An Introduction to American Literature,* University Press of Kentucky, 1971. Also author of *Inquisiciones,* 1925, *El tamano de mi esperanza,* 1926, *La Kennigar,* 1933, and *Nueva refutacion del tiempo,* 1947.

Fiction: *Historia Universal de la Infamia,* Editorial Tor, 1935, reprinted, Alianza Editorial, 1971, translation by di Giovanni published as *A Universal History of Infamy,* Dutton, 1971; *El jardin de senderos que se bifurcan,* Sur, 1942; *Ficciones (1935-1944),* Sur, 1944, translation by several persons published as *Ficciones,* edited by Anthony Kerrigan, Grove, 1962 (published in England as *Fictions,* J. Calder, 1965); *El Aleph,* Editorial Losada, 1949, 3rd edition, Emece Editores, 1962, translation and revision by Borges and di Giovanni published as *The Aleph and Other Stories, 1933-1969,* Dutton, 1970; *La Muerta y la Brujula,*

Emece Editores, 1951; (with L. M. Levinson) *La Hermana de Eloisa,* Ene Editorial (Buenos Aires), 1955; *Cuentos,* Monticello College Press (Godfrey, Ill.), 1958; *El informe de Brodie,* Emece Editores, 1970, translation and revision by Borges and di Giovanni published as *Dr. Brodie's Report,* Dutton, 1972; *El matrero,* Edicom, 1970; *El Congreso,* El Archibraza Editor, 1970, translation and revision by Borges and di Giovanni published as *The Congress,* Enitharmon, 1974.

Omnibus volumes: *Obras completas,* edited by Jose Edmundo Clemente, ten volumes, Emece Editores, 1953-67; *El hacedor* (prose and poetry), Emece Editores, 1960, translation by Mildred Boyer and Harold Morland published as *Dreamtigers,* University of Texas Press, 1964; *Antologia personal* (prose and poetry), Sur, 1961, translation published as *A Personal Anthology,* edited by Anthony Kerrigan, Grove, 1967; *Labyrinths: Selected Stories and Other Writings,* edited by Donald A. Yates and James E. Irby, New Directions, 1962, augmented edition, 1964; *Nueva antologia personal,* Emece Editores, 1968.

With Adolfo Bioy Casares: (Under pseudonym H. Bustos Domecq) *Seis problemas para don Isidro Parodi,* Sur, 1942; (under pseudonym B. Suarez Lynch) *Un modelo para la muerte,* 1946; *Los Orilleros,* Editorial Losada, 1955; (under pseudonym H. Bustos Domecq) *Cronicas de Bustos Domecq,* Editorial Losada, 1967.

Editor or compiler: (With Silvina Ocampo and Adolfo Bioy Casares) *Antologia de la literatura fantastica,* Editorial Sudamericana, 1940, reprinted, 1971; (with Ocampo and Bioy Casares) *Antologia Poetica Argentina,* Editorial Sudamericana, 1941; (and translator with Bioy Casares) *Los mejores cuentos policiales,* 3rd edition, Emece, 1947, reprinted, Alianza Editorial, 1972; (with Bioy Casares) *Poesia Gauchesca,* Fondo de Cultura Economica, 1955; (with Bioy Casares) *Cuentos breves y extraordinarios,* Editorial Raigal (Buenos Aires), 1955, translation by Anthony Kerrigan published as *Extraordinary Tales,* Herder, 1971; (with Bioy Casares) *Libro del Cielo y del Infierno,* Sur, 1960; *Macedonio Fernandez,* Ediciones Culturales Argentinas, 1961; Evaristo Carriego, *Versos,* Editorial Universitaria de Buenos Aires, 1963; Carlos Mastronardi, *Cuentos: Seleccion de Carlos Mastronardi,* Centro Editor de America Latina, 1968.

Translator: Henri Michaux, *Un barbaro en Asia,* Sur, 1941; William Faulkner, *Las Palmeras Salvajes,* Editorial Sudamericana, 1956. Also translator of works by Gide, Kafka, Joyce, and Virginia Woolf.

Was a producer and scenario writer for Alfar Empresa Productora de Beliculas. Co-founder of several literary magazines, including *Proa* (with Ricardo Guiraldes), and co-editor, 1924-26, and *Sur,* 1931. Was associated with *Prisma,* a "muralist" magazine that was published on walls and billboards.

SIDELIGHTS: In the attempt to describe Borges' work critics have resorted to the word Borgesian, a word we have always needed, writes Ronald Christ, adding, "and that of course is the measure of Borges' genius." Mr. Christ describes Borges' special province as "a literature about literature. All his writings are about reading; each one contains a dual revelation. Typically, they tell of makers, authors, or wizards who invent artificial creatures only to discover the sadness of a being who is unreal yet unaware of the fact; typically they conclude with the humiliating revelation that the maker is himself the creation of still another imagination.'' What Borges essentially does, according to Anthony Kerrigan, involves restating, ''in a few allegorical pages, the circular, ceremonial direction of our curious, groping, thrilling, and atrocious ignorance.''

His characters, notes Victor Lange, ''are the ghostly seekers who are . . . in pursuit of the unequivocal formula, the image, the absolute book, the word, that would contain the universe. . . . His conviction [is] that we must accept and articulate in art the inescapable ambiguity of our world.'' Barth notes that Borges believes that ''the world is our dream, our idea, in which 'tenuous and eternal crevices of unreason' can be found to remind us that our creation is false, or at least fictive.'' Lange relates how, in ''Everything and Nothing,'' Borges ''reflects on the fate of the archpoet: 'there was no one in him; behind his face and behind his words there was nothing but a bit of cold, a dream not dreamed by anyone'; he is haunted by 'the habit of pretending that he was someone, so that it should not be discovered that he was no one'; . . . [When] he faced God and . . . demanded to be himself, the voice in the whirlwind replied, *'I am not, either. I dreamed the world the way you dreamed your work, my Shakespeare: one of the forms of my dream was you, who, like me, are many and no one.'* . . . The poet, like God, is a creator of hallucinations, uncertain and in deluded search of 'that moment, when man should know forever who he is.''' Only ''forever'' probably does not exist. ''Time is the substance of which I am made,'' writes Borges. ''Time is a river which sweeps me along, but I am the river; it is a tiger which mangles me, but I am the tiger; it is a fire which consumes me, but I am the fire. The world, unfortunately, is real; I, unfortunately, am Borges. . . . Through the years, a man peoples a space with images of provinces, kingdoms, mountains, bays, ships, islands, fishes, rooms, tools, stars, horses, and people. Shortly before his death, he discovers that the patient labyrinth of lines traces the image of his own face.''

Borges is concerned with identity in time. He once wrote: ''Any destiny at all, however long and complicated, . . . actually consists of *a single moment,* the moment in which a man once and for all knows who he is.'' Yet ''always the essential thing gets lost. . . . Music, states of happiness, mythology, faces scored by time, certain twilights, certain places, all want to tell us something, or told us something we should not have missed, or are about to tell us something. This imminence of a revelation that does not take place is, perhaps, the esthetic fact.'' Borges believes, says Ronald Christ, that ''we make characters real by reading them, and our own existence is equally tentative and dubious, resting entirely on the mind who is reading us, writing us now. Life is a literary dream.'' And man may be nothing more than ''the phantasm of another intellect,'' adds Christ; ''and the reader, like the uncomfortable spectator at *Hamlet,* is left to feel that he too, perhaps, is a pawn playing a part.'' Thus illusion and reality fuse in a Borges story so that Borges becomes ''a realist about an unreal country, time, and reality,'' writes Keith Botsford. As Mr. Christ notes, it is not ''the willing suspension of disbelief that Borges works for. On the contrary it is the unwilling suspension of belief in a literary reality that he achieves.''

Borges believes that ''there is no exercise of the intellect which is not in the final analysis useless.'' He once said: ''Many people have thought of me—of course, I can only be grateful to them—as a thinker, as a philosopher, or even as a mystic. Well the truth is that though I have found reality perplexing enough—in fact, I find it gets more perplexing all the time—I never think of myself as a thinker.'' Moreover, he would like all writers to be judged, not on the basis of their ideas, but for the enjoyment and emotional reaction that the reader finds. He told the *Paris Review,* in perfect English with no trace of an accent, that he never *intended* to write parables. ''I don't intend to show anything. I have no intentions. I describe. I write.'' As Botsford says, Borges ''imagines his profession to be to make notes on unwritten books. Notes. That is, *reductions* of some larger work. The scale is very important. Borges writes very brief works—no single work of his exceeds some twenty pages. This might lead to an almost unbearable intensity within a small area; but in fact, the first thing one notices on reading Borges is that he is not difficult to read. . . . Nothing is superfluous; all is limpid. The overall effect is as though one were reading in a science or philosophy, where exact meaning is all.'' And his meaning, his recurring ''message,'' according to John Ashbery, is that ''everything has value—an equal value, but a value nevertheless. This is implied by the colossal scale and also the intricacy which have gone into the staging of the fraudulent tableau of eternity. And though it is true, as Borges wrote in 'The Immortal,' that we know nothing of the gods 'except that they do not resemble man,' someone evidently cares enough to clothe the dream with an air of truth.''

Simon says: ''Stylistically, Borges' tales tend to be palinodes within palinodes. Two recurrent images are prototypical of Borges' art. . . . There is, first, the labyrinth. . . . Our dreams are labyrinths that reveal things we forget upon waking. . . . The maze is unreality in search of the real. . . . The second master image [is] fictions. . . . In a poem, Borges writes that he 'creates a fiction, not a living creature'; not, as he says elsewhere, 'a mirror of the world, but simply one more thing added to the universe.''' Borges does not want to express but to allude. He once said: ''Croce held that art is expression; to this exigency, or to a deformation of this exigency, we owe the worst literature of our time. . . . Sometimes I, too, sought expression. I know now that my gods grant me no more than allusion or mention.''

Both his friends and critics agree that Borges' poetry is as close as Borges can get to personal statement. He himself believes *Dreamtigers* is his most personal book. In the twenties his friends noted, ''along with his timidity, his brilliance, his intoxication, the way he is dazzled, and then dazzles, by what he sees or reads, by words, by sounds, by images,'' says Botsford. ''The largely free verse patterns of his poetry at that time gave him free play with concrete realities. . . . The later poems are among the most skillful and immaculate in Spanish. Strict in their rules and sober in their imagery, gentle in tone, recollected in tranquility, they are elegiac, formal, symmetrical: as one critic pointed out, they are in every sense of the word conventional. The true Borges is now elsewhere.''

He began writing fiction after a severe fall which left him with the feeling that his ability to write was gone. So he rationalized to himself, ''If I try fiction, that will be something new, and readers will not be able to compare my old self with the new and hold the new against me.'' Partly to compensate for his timidity about writing fiction he tried to hybridize the short story and the essay. Maloff writes: ''Typically, a Borges ficcion combines elements of fiction, the personal essay, arcane scholarship and recondite learning, the meditation, the prose poem, metaphysics, the gnostic utterance. There is either no narrative line or only a fragmentary one; little or no plot; little or no characterization. Often there are no characters. Borges' concerns lie elsewhere, [namely] in creating a mythology of an uncreated race living by the laws of a strange mathematics on a planet without atmosphere.''

A *Time* reviewer notes that Borges' ficciones are his ''most characteristic creations.... They can be unmistakably identified by their brevity, clear, laconic style, humor, and dependency on such devices as mazes, mirrors, odd beasts, and men who are really other men. In short, they deal in one way or another with the conundrums of art and identity, the treacherous nature of reality, and the silvered labyrinths of myth and imagination.'' By 1970, Borges' approach to his ficciones is observed as changing. George Steiner quotes Borges: '''I've grown weary of labyrinths and mirrors and tigers and of all that sort of thing. Especially when others are using them.... That's the advantage of imitators. They cure one of one's literary ills. Because one thinks: there are so many people doing that sort of thing now, there's no need for one to do it any more. Now let the others do it, and good riddance.'''

Borges' changing attitude is apparent in Anatole Broyard's review of *Dr. Brodie's Report:* ''But now Borges has undergone a change as odd as any of his characters': He has begun to write 'realistic' or 'straightforward' stories ... 'woven around a plot,' and often little else. In some cases, Borges has descended from the metaphysical to the supernatural.... He seems to be doubting the value of the very qualities that earned him his reputation.'' Edward G. Warner agrees: Borges' best previous stories were strange, dreamlike fables that cast an oblique, ironic light on the doings of this world. In this latest group, the world is all too much with the author. These are mostly plain, unadorned tales—some harsh, some tender—of love, hate and the inevitability of death. In his preface, Borges admits giving up the 'surprises inherent in a baroque style. Now, having passed 70, I believe I have found my own voice.' Or is it, he asks himself, only the 'fruit of weariness'?'' Warner suggests that Borges may now be seeking a ''plainer reality.''

His hereditary blindness ''is no handicap for a writer of fantasy,'' Borges says. ''It leaves the mind free and unhampered to explore the depths and heights of human imagination.'' Botsford reports that Borges walks miles ''through his mythical Buenos Aires, fancying most what is poorest there, but most rose-colored and revealing; ... he knows his city better than most men their own lives; [he] thinks animals are magic, especially cats, but that all animals of the same breed are one and the same animal; ... he is vain about trifles, baubles like [his] Legion d'Honneur, ... but infinitely humble about what matters; [he] doesn't like music or painting; and is at the same time both learned and ignorant.''

Borges' erudition, choice of forms, and style are all efficient vehicles for his world view,'' says Simon. ''His learning seems to know no boundaries.... From Old Norse to Anglo-Saxon, from Near to Far Eastern lore, from the cabala to contemporary philosophy, from the songs of the gauchos to the prose and poetry of the symbolists and even to the 'influence of Cecil B. DeMille,' everything is grist for his thorough, unostentatious, meaningful imagination. But this imagination is more than a mill, it is also a volcano, albeit an exquisite one.'' Maloff concludes that ''Borges is tough meat. Swallowed whole, he will either stick in the craw or nourish as few writers of our time do. He does not seek to please. He will not compromise

with his readers any more than he would with Juan Peron, whose regime he despised. He insists that the reader go all the way to meet him. He will never achieve mass popularity, but it is likely that he is one of the few living writers whose permanence is assured.''

Borges is currently revising and translating his works with Norman Thomas di Giovanni. Their goal, according to di Giovanni is ''to see that the piece reads as though it were written in English.''

''Invasion,'' a story written with Adolfo Bioy Casares, has been made into an Argentinian film, 1969. An Italian film, ''The Spider's Strategy,'' was based on one of Borges' stories, 1970.

BIOGRAPHICAL/CRITICAL SOURCES—Periodicals: *Atlantic,* January, 1967, August, 1967; *Paris Review* (interview), winter-spring, 1967; *New York Times Book Review,* April, 1967; *New Yorker,* April 1, 1967, October 28, 1967, June 20, 1970; *Newsweek,* April 3, 1967; *Christian Science Monitor,* April 6, 1967; *Book Week,* April 23, 1967; *Wisconsin Studies in Contemporary Literature,* spring, 1967; *New Republic,* May 20, 1967; *Commonweal,* September 29, 1967, December 1, 1967, October 25, 1968; *New York Times,* December 1, 1967, April 10, 1968, January 4, 1972; *Encounter,* April, 1969; *Time,* January 5, 1970, January 31, 1972; *Antioch Review,* fall-winter, 1970-71.

Books: Anthony Kerrigan, introduction to *Ficciones,* Grove, 1965; Ana Marie Barrenchea, *Borges the Labyrinth Maker,* edited and translated by R. Lima, New York University Press, 1965; Ronald J. Christ, *The Narrow Act: Borges' Art of Illusion,* New York University Press, 1969; Richard Burgin, *Conversations with Jorge Luis Borges,* Holt, 1969; Martin S. Stabb, *Jorge Luis Borges,* Twayne, 1970; Jorge Luis Borges, *Borges on Writing,* edited by Norman Thomas di Giovanni, Daniel Halpren, and Frank MacShane, Dutton, 1973; Carolyn Riley, editor, *Contemporary Literary Criticism,* Gale, Volume I, 1973, Volume II, 1974, Volume III, 1975, Volume IV, 1975, Volume VI, 1976; Sheldon Rodman, *Tongues of Fallen Angels: Conversations with Jorges Luis Borges and Others,* New Directions, 1974.†

*   *   *

BORKLUND, C(arl) W(ilbur) 1930-

PERSONAL: Born September 16, 1930; son of Carl Ernest (a printer) and Marian (Bon) Borklund; married Dorothy Bea Avey; children: John Edward, Debra Lu, Julie Elizabeth, Thomas Craig, Jean Marie. *Education:* University of Illinois, B.S. in Journalism, 1952. *Home:* 11605 Hitching Post Lane, Rockville, Md.

CAREER: American Aviation Publications, Washington, D.C., publisher, beginning 1957, publishing *Armed Forces Management* and *Military Export Reporter. Member:* Aviation/Space Writers Association, National Security Industrial Association, Navy League, Authors Guild, National Aviation Club. *Awards, honors:* Patriotic Civilian Service Award of U.S. Department of Army, 1965, for editorial writing in *Armed Forces Management;* Book Award (nonfiction), Aviation/Space Writers Association, 1966, for *Men of the Pentagon.*

WRITINGS: Men of the Pentagon, Praeger, 1966; *The Department of Defense,* Praeger, 1968.††

BOROSON, Warren 1935-
(Warner Brown)

PERSONAL: Born January 22, 1935, in New York, N.Y.; son of Henry (a teacher) and Cecelia (Wersan) Boroson; married F. Rebecca Kaplan, June 19, 1965; children: Bram Seth. *Education:* Columbia University, B.A. (summa cum laude), 1957; graduate courses in editing and writing at Columbia University, New School for Social Research, and New York University.

CAREER: The Record, Hackensack, N.J., reporter, 1957-59, regional and music editor, 1959, assistant magazine editor, 1960-61; *Precis,* New York City, editor, 1961; *Pageant,* New York City, associate editor, 1961-62; *Eros,* New York City, associate editor, 1962-63; *Fact,* New York City, editor, 1963-67; *Medical Economics,* Oradell, N.J., associate editor, 1967; Washington University, St. Louis, Mo., editor of *Trans-action* (social sciences magazine), 1967-68. *Member:* Phi Beta Kappa.

WRITINGS: (Editor with Ralph Ginsburg) *The Best of "Fact,"* Trident, 1967. Contributor to *Trans-action, Scholastic Roto, Word Study, Cavalier,* and other periodicals. Contributor under pseudonym Warner Brown to *Coronet* and other periodicals.††

* * *

BOSHINSKI, Blanche 1922-

PERSONAL: Born November 28, 1922, in Fort Morgan, Colo.; daughter of Joseph B. (a farmer) and Gertrude (Stroebel) Tarr; married Edward J. Boshinski, March 16, 1945; children: Laura (Mrs. Luther A. Shipley, Jr.), Sharon. *Education:* University of Denver, A.B., 1944, Teacher's Certification, 1966. *Home:* 2174 South Clarkson St., Denver, Colo. 80210.

CAREER: Rocky Mountain News, Denver, Colo., club editor, 1944-45; held office jobs in Tacoma, Wash., 1945; teacher of adult basic education in Denver (Colo.) public schools, 1966-72. *Member:* Colorado Author's League, Denver Women's Press Club. *Awards, honors:* Top Hand Award for children's literature, Colorado Author's League.

WRITINGS—All children's literature: *The Luck of the Blue Stallion,* Meredith, 1967; *Aha and the Jewel of Mystery,* Parent's Magazine Press, 1968. Contributor of short stories to children's magazines, including *Humpty Dumpty, Calling All Girls, Jack and Jill, Summer Weekly Reader,* and *Child Life.*

* * *

BOTTIGLIA, William F(ilbert) 1912-

PERSONAL: Born November 23, 1912, in Bernardsville, N.J.; son of Vincent Richard and Quintilia (Mastrobattista) Bottiglia; married Mildred MacDonald, December 21, 1943 (deceased); stepchildren: Martha (Mrs. Milton H. Morris), Janet M. *Education:* Princeton University, A.B., 1934, A.M., 1935, Ph.D., 1948. *Politics:* Independent. *Religion:* Protestant. *Home:* 50 Windsor Rd., Needham, Mass. 02192. *Office:* E52-553 Massachusetts Institute of Technology, Cambridge, Mass. 02139

CAREER: Princeton University, Princeton, N.J., instructor in French and Italian, 1937-42; J & S Tool Co., Inc., East Orange, N.J., production coordinator, became general manager, 1942-47; St. Lawrence University, Canton, N.Y., assistant professor of English, 1948; Ripon College, Ripon, Wis., professor of Romance languages and literatures and chairman of department, 1948-56; Massachu-

setts Institute of Technology, Cambridge, associate professor, 1956-60, professor of foreign literatures and humanities, 1960-73, professor of management and humanities, 1973—, head of department of foreign literatures and linguistics, 1964-73. *Member:* Modern Language Association of America, American Economic Association, American Historical Association, American Political Science Association, Dante Society of America, Ordre des Palmes Academiques, Phi Beta Kappa.

WRITINGS: Voltaire's Candide: Analysis of a Classic, Institut et Musee Voltair (Geneva), 1959, revised edition, 1964; (editor and contributor) *Voltaire: A Collection of Critical Essays,* Prentice-Hall, 1968. Editor, reports of the working committees, Northeast Conference on the Teaching of Foreign Languages, 1957, 1962, 1963.

WORK IN PROGRESS: A book dealing with the crises of our age, titled *Heroic Symphony.*

* * *

BOULDING, Elise (Biorn-Hansen) 1920-

PERSONAL: Born July 6, 1920, in Oslo, Norway; daughter of Joseph (an engineer) and Birgit (Johnsen) Biorn-Hansen; married Kenneth Boulding (a professor at University of Colorado), August 30, 1941; children: John Russell, Mark David, Christine Ann, Philip Daniel, William Frederick. *Education:* Douglass College, B.A., 1940; Iowa State University, M.S., 1949; University of Michigan, Ph.D., 1969. *Religion:* Society of Friends. *Home:* 890 Willowbrook Rd., Boulder, Colo. 80302. *Office:* Institute of Behavioral Science, University of Colorado, Boulder, Colo. 80302.

CAREER: University of Michigan, Ann Arbor, research associate at Survey Research Center, 1957-58, and secretary for seminar on research development, Center for Research on Conflict Resolution, 1960-63; editor, *International Peace Research Newsletter,* 1963-67; University of Colorado, Boulder, lecturer, 1967-68, assistant professor, 1968-69, associate professor, 1969-73, professor of sociology, 1973—. Member of advisory committee, Society for a World Services Federation; international chairperson, Women's International League for Peace and Freedom, 1968-70; member of board of directors, Institute for World Order, 1972—. Member of regional executive board, American Friends Service Committee, 1961-67; member of board, People's Clinic.

MEMBER: International Peace Research Association, International Sociological Association (co-chairman, research committee on sex roles in society, 1973—), International Studies Association, American Association for the Advancement of Science (member of executive committee, 1970-72), American Association of University Professors, American Sociological Association (chairman of committee on status of women in the profession, 1970-72, and committee on sociology of world conflicts, 1972-74; member of council, 1976—), National Council of Family Relations, Rocky Mountain Social Science Association, Society for the Scientific Study of Religion, World Future Society. *Awards, honors:* Danforth fellow, 1965-67; distinguished alumni award, Douglass College; University of Colorado faculty grant, 1974.

WRITINGS: (Translator) Fred Polak, *Image of the Future,* two volumes, Oceana, 1961, abridged edition, edited by Boulding, Jossey-Bass, 1972; (editor with Robert Kahn) *Power and Conflict in Organizations,* Basic Books, 1964; (author of introduction) Eric Graham Howe, *War Dance: A*

Study of the Psychology of War, Garland Publishing, 1972; (author of introduction) Mark May, *A Social Psychology of War and Peace,* Garland Publishing, 1972; *The Underside of History: A View of Women through Time,* Westview Press, 1976; (with Shirley Nuss and Dorothy Carson) *International Indicators on the Position of Women,* Sage Publications, 1976; *Women in the Twentieth-Century World Community,* Sage Publications, 1976.

Contributor: Reuben Hill, *Families under Stress,* Macmillan, 1949; M. Schwebel, editor, *Behavioral Science and Human Survival,* Science & Behavior Books, 1965; Magoroh Maruyama and James A. Dator, editors, *Human Futuristics,* Social Science Research Institute, University of Hawaii, 1971; Marvin Sussman and Betty Cogswell, editors, *Cross-National Family Research,* E. J. Brill, 1972; Nobuo Shimahara, editor, *Educational Reconstruction: Promise and Challenge,* C. E. Merrill, 1973; Sylvan Kaplan and Evelyn Kivy-Rosenberg, editors, *Ecology and the Quality of Life,* C. C Thomas, 1973; Christoph Wulf, editor, *Handbook on Peace Education,* International Peace Association, 1974; Robert Bundy, editor, *Images of the Future,* Prometheus Books, 1975; Shimahara and Adam Scrupski, editors, *Social Forces and Schooling,* McKay, 1975.

Author of four booklets published by Society of Friends. Contributor to annals and proceedings. Contributor of articles and reviews to *Marriage and Family Living, Human Relations, War/Peace Report, Japan Christian Quarterly, New Era* (London), *Journal of World Education, Contemporary Sociology,* and other journals. Associate editor of *American Sociologist,* 1970-73, and *International Interactions,* 1973—; member of board of editors, *Peace and Change: A Journal of Peace Research,* 1971—; *International Peace Research Newsletter,* editor, 1963-68, North American editor, 1968-73; guest editor of *Journal of Social Issues,* January, 1967, and *Journal of Conflict Resolution,* December, 1972.

WORK IN PROGRESS: Theory of Things to Come, Essays on the Future; foreword to *Recent Advances in Peace and Conflict Research: A Critical Survey* by Juergen Dedring.

*   *   *

BOURNE, Miriam Anne   1931-

PERSONAL: Born March 4, 1931, in Buffalo, N.Y.; daughter of Herbert M. (an insurance man) and Caroline (Walker) Young; married Russell Bourne (an editor), August 22, 1953; children: Sarah Perkins, Jonathan, Louise Taber, Andrew Russell. *Education:* Wheelock College, graduate, 1953. *Home:* 5705 Ogden Rd., Washington, D.C. 20016.

MEMBER: Washington Children's Book Guild.

WRITINGS: Emilio's Summer Day, Harper, 1966; *Raccoons Are for Loving,* Random House, 1968; *Tigers in the Woods,* Coward, 1971; *Second Car in Town,* Coward, 1972; *Four-Ring Three,* Coward, 1973; *Nelly Custis' Diary,* Coward, 1974; *Nabby Adams' Diary,* Coward, 1975; *Bright Lights to See By,* Coward, 1975; *Patsy Jefferson's Diary,* Coward, in press.

*   *   *

BOW, Russell   1925-

PERSONAL: Born January 23, 1925, in Bow, Ky.; son of Steven Tyler (a farmer) and Lula (King) Bow; married

Roxie Minton (a teacher), September 15, 1945; children: Micheal, Beverly. *Education:* Lindsey Wilson College, A.A., 1945; Union College, Barbourville, Ky., student, 1945-46; Kentucky Wesleyan College, A.B., 1949; Emory University, B.D., 1952. *Home:* 304 Hospital Dr., Princeton, Ky. 42445.

CAREER: Methodist minister, with pastoral assignments in Owensboro, Ky., 1952-61, and Louisville, Ky., 1961-67; Methodist Temple Methodist Church, Russellville, Ky., pastor, 1967-71; Ogden Memorial United Methodist Church, Princeton, Ky., pastor, 1971—. *Member:* Masons, Rotary Club.

WRITINGS: The Integrity of Church Membership, Word Books, 1968. Writer of curriculum materials for Methodist Publishing House, and articles for religious journals.

AVOCATIONAL INTERESTS: Conducting tours to the Bible lands.

*   *   *

BOWE, Gabriel P(aul)   1923-

PERSONAL: Surname rhymes with "crow"; born October 25, 1923, in Waterford, Ireland; son of Paul and Johanna (Morgan) Bowe. *Education:* Pontifical University Angelicum, Rome, Italy, S.T.L., 1952; National University of Ireland, Dublin, M.A., 1954. *Politics:* Democratic. *Agent:* Michael Glazier, 1401 North Bancroft Pkwy., Wilmington, Del. *Home and office:* Aquinas Institute of Philosophy, River Forest, Ill. 60305.

CAREER: Roman Catholic Priest of Dominican Order. National University of Ireland, University College, Dublin, lecturer in politics and economics, 1954-61; St. Francis de Sales College, Nagpur, India, principal, 1962; National University of Ireland, University College, Galway, visiting lecturer in sociology, 1966; Aquinas Institute of Philosophy, River Forest, Ill., visiting professor of economics and political science, 1966—. *Member:* Association of Chicago Priests.

WRITINGS: The Origin of Political Authority, Clonmore & Reynolds, 1955; *The Third Horseman,* preface by Sargent Shriver, Pflaum, 1967. Contributor of more than fifty articles on economic, political and sociological topics to journals.

WORK IN PROGRESS: The Social Church, a book on the social implications of the church's mission to the modern world.

SIDELIGHTS: Bowe conducted field studies on underdevelopment problems in southern Italy, and on the refugee problem in Berlin. He is fluent in French and Italian and has working knowledge of German and Spanish.

*   *   *

BOWEN, Howard R(othmann)   1908-

PERSONAL: Born October 27, 1908, in Spokane, Wash.; son of Henry G. (a musician) and Josephine (Menig) Bowen; married Lois B. Schilling, August 24, 1935; children: Peter Geoffrey, Thomas Gerard. *Education:* State College of Washington (now Washington State University), B.A., 1929, M.A., 1933; University of Iowa, Ph.D., 1935; postdoctoral study at Cambridge University and London School of Economics and Political Science, 1937-38. *Home:* 723 Alamosa Drive, Claremont, Calif. 91711. *Office:* Claremont Graduate School, Claremont, Calif. 91711.

CAREER: University of Iowa, Iowa City, instructor, 1935-

38, assistant professor, 1938-40, associate professor of economics, 1940-42; U.S. Government, Washington, D.C., chief of the Business Structure Unit, Department of Commerce, 1942-44, chief economist, Joint Congressional Committee on Internal Revenue Taxation, 1944-45; Irving Trust Co., New York, N.Y., economist, 1945-47; University of Illinois, Urbana, professor of economics and dean of School of Commerce and Business Administration, 1947-52; Williams College, Williamstown, Mass., professor of economics, 1952-55; Grinnell College, Grinnell, Iowa, president, 1955-64; University of Iowa, Iowa City, president, 1964-69; Claremont Schools, Claremont, Calif., professor of economics in Claremont University Center, 1969-70, president and chancellor, 1970-74; Claremont Graduate School, R. Stanton Avery Professor of Economics and Education, 1974—. Resident scholar, Bellagio Study Center, Rockefeller Foundation, 1973. Member of government missions to Japan, 1949, Thailand, 1961, and Yugoslavia, 1962; member of Committee for Economic Development, 1955-59, National Committee on Government Finance of the Brookings Institution, 1960-65, Federal Advisory Commission on Intergovernmental Relations, 1961-64, National Commission on Non-Traditional Study, 1970-72, National Board of Graduate Education, 1973-74, and National Council of Independent Colleges and Universities, 1973-74; chairman of National Commission on Technology, Automation and Economic Progress, 1966-67; chairman of Governor's Commission on Economic and Social Trends in Iowa, 1958 and National Citizen's Committee for Tax Revision and Reduction, 1963. Consultant to National Council of Churches, 1949-53, and to a number of federal and state agencies.

MEMBER: American Economic Association, American Finance Association, Royal Economic Society (London), Phi Beta Kappa, Phi Kappa Phi, Beta Gamma Sigma, University Club (Chicago), Des Moines Club. *Awards, honors:* Social Science Research Council fellowship in England, 1937-38; LL.D. from Cornell College, Mount Vernon, Iowa, 1956, Knox College, Galesburg, Ill., 1964, Drake University, 1968, and Carnegie-Mellon University, 1973; L.H.D. from Loras College, 1963, Coe College, 1965, and Marycrest College, 1968; D.Litt., Grinnell College, 1964; also received honorary degrees from University of Illinois, University of the Pacific, Union College, and Williams College; Distinguished Alumnus Award from Washington State University and University of Iowa; award of National Council of Independent Colleges and Universities, 1975, for "outstanding leadership in American higher education and unique contribution to independent colleges and universities."

WRITINGS: English Grants-in-Aid, University of Iowa Press, 1939; *Toward Social Economy,* Rinehart, 1948; *Social Responsibilities of the Businessman,* Harper, 1953; *Graduate Education in Economics,* American Economic Association, 1953; *Christian Values and Economic Life,* Harper, 1954; (editor with Garth L. Mangum) *Automation and Economic Progress,* Prentice-Hall, 1967; (with Gordon Douglass) *Efficiency in Liberal Education: A Study of Comparative Instructional Costs for Different Ways of Organizing Teaching-Learning in a Liberal Arts College,* McGraw, 1971; (editor and contributor) *Evaluating Performance for Accountability,* Jossey-Bass, 1974. Also author of *The Finance of Higher Education,* 1969. Contributor of more than 100 monographs and articles relating to economics, finance, and education to economics journals.

BOWEN, Richard M. 1928-

PERSONAL: Born October 9, 1928, in Boston, Mass.; son of George and Mary (Donigan) Bowen; married M. Patricia McGillicuddy (a teacher), January 28, 1956; children: Richard, Kathleen, Carol, Paul, Mark. *Education:* Attended New York Central Railroad's four-year training school. *Politics:* Democrat. *Religion:* Roman Catholic. *Home:* 65 Gannett Rd., North Scituate, Mass. 02060.

CAREER: Penn Central Railroad, Framingham, Mass., 1949—, began as a machinist, now an inspector. *Military service:* U.S. Marine Corps, 1945-48.

WRITINGS: Nails: A Boy at Bunker Hill and Valley Forge, Barre, 1967.

WORK IN PROGRESS: Decision on the Bristol Star, a historical novel for children.

AVOCATIONAL INTERESTS: Painting seascapes and ships; singing.

* * *

BOWERING, George 1935-

PERSONAL: Born December 1, 1935, in Keremeos, British Columbia, Canada; son of Ewart Harry (a teacher) and Pearl (Brinson) Bowering; married Angela Luoma, December 14, 1962; children: Thea Claire. *Education:* University of British Columbia, B.A., 1960, M.A., 1963; further study at University of Western Ontario. *Politics:* "Armchair revolutionary; Fidelist." *Religion:* "Resembles that of Amer-Indians." *Home:* 2499 West 37th Ave., Vancouver, British Columbia, Canada V6M 1PA. *Office:* Department of English, Simon Fraser University, Burnaby 2, British Columbia, Canada.

CAREER: University of Calgary, Calgary, Alberta, instructor, 1963-66, then assistant professor; Sir George Williams University, Montreal, Quebec, instructor in poetry and writer in residence, 1967-68, assistant professor of English, 1968-72; Simon Fraser University, Burnaby, British Columbia, associate professor of English, 1972—. Former editor of *Imago,* Montreal, a magazine devoted to long poems. *Military service:* Royal Canadian Air Force, aerial photographer, 1954-57. *Awards, honors:* Canada Council pre-doctoral grant, 1966-67, renewed, 1967-68, but not taken, senior award, 1971; Ontario Government postgraduate fellowship, 1967-68, not taken; Governor-General's Award for poetry, 1969.

WRITINGS—Poetry: Sticks and Stones, Tishbooks, 1963; *Points on the Grid,* Contact Press, 1964; *The Man in Yellow Boots,* El Corno Emplumado (Mexico), 1965; *The Silver Wire,* Quarry Press, 1966; *Baseball: A Poem in the Magic Number 9,* Coach House Press, 1967; *Rocky Mountain Foot: A Lyric, A Memoir,* McClelland & Stewart, 1968; *Two Police Poems,* Talon Books, 1968; *The Gangs of Kosmos,* House of Anansi, 1969; *Touch: Selected Poems 1961-1970,* McClelland & Stewart, 1969; *Sitting in Mexico,* Beaven Kosmos, 1970; *George, Vancouver: A Discovery Poem,* Weed/Flower Press (Toronto), 1970; *Geneve,* Coach House Press, 1971; *The Sensible,* Massasauga Editions (Toronto), 1972; *Layers,* Weed/Flower Press, 1973; *Curious,* Coach House Press, 1973; *In the Flesh,* McClelland & Stewart, 1974; *At War with the U.S.,* Talon Books, 1975; *Allophanes,* Coach House Press, 1976; *The Catch,* McClelland & Stewart, 1976.

Other: *Mirror on the Floor* (novel), McClelland & Stewart, 1967; *How I Hear "Howl"* (essay), Sir George Williams University, 1968; *Al Purdy* (monograph), Copp Clarke,

1970; (contributor) *How Do I Love Thee: Sixty Poets of Canada (and Quebec) Select and Introduce Their Favorite Poems from Their Work,* edited by John Robert Colombo, M. G. Hurtig (Edmonton), 1970; (editor) *Vibrations: Poems of Youth* (poetry), Gage, 1970; (editor) *The Story So Far* (stories), Coach House Press, 1971; *Autobiology* (novel), New Star Books, 1972; *Flycatcher* (short stories), Oberon Press, 1974.

Also author of a play, "A Home for Heroes," which appeared in *Prism International* (University of British Columbia literary journal, Vancouver), 1962, and John Stevens, editor, *Ten Canadian Short Plays,* Dell, 1975, and a television play, "What Does Eddie Williams Want?," CBC-TV, 1965.

Contributor of poems and stories in literary magazines, including *Poetry, Atlantic Monthly, Tamarack Review, London Magazine, Poetry Australia, Queen's Quarterly,* plus a number of anthologies including the Penguin and Oxford anthologies of Canadian verse. Reviews appear regularly in *Canadian Literature* and *Open Letter.* Critical articles in such magazines as *Canadian Literature, Walt Whitman Review, Aylesford Review, Kulchur,* and *Minnesota Review.*

SIDELIGHTS: Bowering tells *CA:* "I love Mexico City, Oaxaca, Vienna, Istanbul, Kavalla, London, Langres, San Francisco, Tucson, Yugoslavia. I dislike Greece in general, Geneva, Nevada, Texas. I speak Spanish and translate a good deal of Spanish American poetry, the poets being young and revolutionary. My favorite poets are Olson, Duncan, Creeley, Levertov, Jonson, Shelley, Blake, Whitman, Neruda, Vallejo. My favorite novelists are Kerouac, Dorn, Eastlake, Burroughs, Douglas Woolf."

In his first novel, *Mirror on the Floor,* Bowering so importantly captures "the intonation, the mood, and even the pretentious self-consciousness of youth," states Phyllis Grosskurth. The story of a teen-age beatnik girl, Andrea, and her brief love affair with a college student is "extraordinarily believeable," continues Grosskurth. Bowering speaks about children in a new way, he "gives his reader a poet's eye view of what is going on 'underground,'" Carol Spray finds. The "finest portions of the novel: deftest, fullest, most carefully selective," according to W. D. Godfrey, occur when Bowering depicts Andrea's mind directly. The concerned tone extends throughout his poetry. In *The Silver Wire* Bowering is without humor, he "takes every mood with equal solemnity," Martin Dodsworth notes. Dodsworth perceives that Bowering is a poet, "in love with words and with his use of them."

BIOGRAPHICAL/CRITICAL SOURCES: London Magazine, April, 1967; *Canadian Forum,* May, 1967; *Saturday Night,* May, 1967; *Fiddlehead,* summer, 1967; *Quill & Quire,* January, 1976.

*   *   *

BOYER, Richard Edwin 1932-

PERSONAL: Born May 8, 1932, in Saginaw, Mich.; son of Jonas W. (a minister) and Evelyn (Hornback) Boyer; married Shirley Darnell; children: Richard E., Jr., Elizabeth Darnell, Peter Graem, Victoria Jane. *Education:* Northeast Missouri State Teachers College (now Northeast Missouri State University), B.S., 1954, M.A., 1957; University of Missouri, Ph.D., 1960. *Politics:* Democrat. *Religion:* Presbyterian. *Home:* 2281 Country Squire, Toledo, Ohio.

CAREER: University of Missouri, Columbia, instructor in

history, 1957-60; Westminster College, Fulton, Mo., assistant professor of history, 1960-61; Eastern Illinois University, Charleston, assistant professor of history, 1961-64; University of Toledo, Toledo, Ohio, associate professor of history, 1964—. *Military service:* U.S. Army, 1954-56; became sergeant. *Member:* American Historical Association, American Catholic Historical Association, Historical Association (England), Archaeological Institute of America, American Association of University Professors, American Federation of Teachers, Midwest British History Association, Ohio Academy of History, Phi Alpha Theta.

WRITINGS: (Editor) *Oliver Cromwell and the Puritan Revolt: Failure of a Man or a Faith?,* Heath, 1966, 2nd edition, Forum Press, 1975; *English Declarations of Indulgence, 1687 and 1688,* Mouton & Co., 1968.

WORK IN PROGRESS: Father Edward Petre, Privy Councillor; research on relaxation of censorship laws in the 1960's.

AVOCATIONAL INTERESTS: Collecting stamps, rare pamphlets, and military artifacts; travel.

*   *   *

BOYLE, Ted Eugene 1933-

PERSONAL: Born November 26, 1933, in Strang, Neb.; son of John Morris (a teacher) and Zona (Beutler) Boyle; married Mary Thompson (a teacher), May 31, 1958; married Charlotte Barthona, 1971; children: (first marriage) Michael, Stephen. *Education:* University of Nebraska, B.A., 1955, M.A., 1959, Ph.D., 1962. *Home:* 1002 Emerald Lane, Carbondale, Ill. 62901.

CAREER: Kansas State University, Manhattan, instructor in English, 1962-63; Southern Illinois University, Carbondale, assistant professor, 1963-66, associate professor, 1966-71, professor of English, 1971—. *Military service:* U.S. Army, 1955-57. U.S. Army Reserve, 1957-62; became sergeant. *Member:* Modern Language Association of America, National Council of Teachers of English, American Association of University Professors.

WRITINGS: Symbol and Meaning in the Fiction of Joseph Conrad, Humanities, 1965; *Brendan Behan,* Twayne, 1969. Contributor of critical articles on Conrad, Mansfield, Forster, Golding, and Amis to professional journals.

WORK IN PROGRESS: A book on Thomas Hardy; *Sex in Western Literature.*

*   *   *

BRACKBILL, Yvonne 1928-

PERSONAL: Born October 11, 1928, in Modesto, Calif.; married Kenneth E. Little (a professor of psychology and department head), 1959. *Education:* University of California, Berkeley, B.A., 1950; University of Colorado, M.A., 1953; Stanford University, Ph.D., 1956. *Office:* Department of Psychology, University of Florida, Gainesville, Fla. 32611.

CAREER: San Jose State College (now San Jose State University), San Jose, Calif., instructor in psychology, 1956-57; National Institute of Mental Health, Bethesda, Md., research associate, Laboratory of Psychology, 1957-58; Bio-Sciences Information Exchange, Washington, D.C., professional associate, 1958-59; Johns Hopkins University, Baltimore, Md., research fellow and instructor, 1959-61; University of Colorado Medical School, Denver, 1961-70, began as assistant professor, became associate professor of clinical psychology; University of Denver, Denver, associate professor, 1961-65, research professor of psychology, 1965-70; Georgetown University, Washington, D.C., School of Medicine, professor of obstetrics, gynecology, and pediatrics (for psychology), 1970-75; University of Florida, Gainesville, graduate research professor of psychology, 1975—.

MEMBER: American Psychological Association (member of council), American Association for the Advancement of Science, Society for Obstetrical Anesthesia and Perinatology, Society for Psychophysiological Research, Conference on Research in Infancy, Society for Research in Child Development, International Union of Scientific Psychology, Eastern Psychological Association, Midwestern Psychological Association, Sigma Xi. *Awards, honors:* Research fellowship, U.S. Public Health Service, 1959; research award, National Institute of Mental Health, 1964; fellowship, Churchill College, Cambridge University, 1973-74.

WRITINGS: (Editor) *Research in Infant Behavior: A Cross-Indexed Bibliography,* Williams & Wilkins, 1964; (editor and contributor) *Infancy and Early Childhood: A Handbook and Guide to Human Development,* Free Press, 1967; (editor with G. G. Thompson, and contributor) *Behavior in Infancy and Early Childhood: A Book of Readings,* Free Press, 1967; *A Developmental Study of Classical Conditioning,* University of Chicago Press, 1968.

Contributor: R. Bauer, editor, *Some Views on Soviet Psychology,* American Psychological Association, 1962; R. J. C. Harper, editor, *The Cognitive Processes,* Prentice-Hall, 1963; M. T. Mednick and S. A. Mednick, editors, *Readings in Personality,* Holt, 1963; D. S. Palermo and L. P. Lipsitt, editors, *Research Readings in Child Psychology,* Holt, 1963; J. M. Seidman, editor, *Educating for Mental Health,* Crowell, 1963; N. S. Ender, L. R. Boulter, and H. Osser, editors, *Contemporary Issues in Developmental Psychology,* Holt, 1967; D. M. Gelfand, editor, *Social Learning in Childhood,* Brooks/Cole, 1969; Lipsitt and H. Reese, editors, *Advances in Child Development,* Volume IV, Academic Press, 1969; R. D. Parke, editor, *Readings in Social Development,* Holt, 1969.

H. E. Fitzgerald and J. P. McKinney, editors, *Developmental Psychology: Studies in Human Development,* Dorsey, 1970; Stella Chess and Alexander Thomas, editors, *Annual Progress in Child Psychiatry and Child Development,* Brunner/Mazel, Volume V, 1972, Volume VI, in press; L. J. Stone, H. T. Smith, and L. B. Murphy, editors, *The Competent Infant: A Handbook of Readings,* Basic Books, 1972; James T. Fawcett, editor, *Psychological Perspectives on Population,* Basic Books, 1973; E. Donelson, editor, *The Scientific Study of Personality,* Appleton-Century-Crofts, in press; W. J. Meyer, editor, *Readings in Child and Adolescent Psychology,* Ginn, in press; P. L. Morselli, S. Garattini, and F. Sereni, editors, *Basic and Therapeutic Aspects of Perinatal Pharmacology,* Raven Press, in press; C. B. Nelson and V. S. Sexton, editors, *Women in Psychology,* Brooks/Cole, in press. Contributor of articles and reviews to journals in her field, including *Journal of Abnormal and Social Psychology, Child Development, Journal of Experimental Child Psychology,* and *Journal of Developmental Psychology.*

WORK IN PROGRESS: Accountability and the Future of Biomedical Research; a book with A. M. Sostek, *Stability of Heart Rate and Motor Or, Habituation Rates in Infancy.*

BRACKEN, Dorothy K(endall)

PERSONAL: Born in Dallas, Tex.; daughter of J. R. (a realtor) and Robbie (Goodwin) Kendall; married Clifford F. Bracken (a salesman), June 3, 1938; children: Brenda (Mrs. James T. Whorton). *Education:* Daniel Baker College, A.B., 1929; Southern Methodist University, M.A., 1932; further graduate study at University of Chicago, 1933, and Columbia University, 1935, 1945. *Religion:* Methodist. *Home:* 3230 Daniel Ave., Dallas, Tex. 75205.

CAREER: Teacher in public schools of Dallas, Tex., 1932-38, and Highland Park, Tex., 1938-40; Southern Methodist University, Dallas, Tex., assistant professor and director of reading clinic, 1947—. Summer lecturer at University of Texas, 1946, Columbia University, 1954-56, University of Chicago, 1958, University of Alberta, 1962, and University of Alaska, 1967. Organizer for first World Congress on Reading in Paris, 1966, and co-chairman of program, second World Congress in Copenhagen, 1968; leader of reading workshops in some twenty-five states in United States, and in Canada, Australia, New Zealand, Argentina, and South Africa. Texas Education Agency, member of Language Arts Commission; chairman, Doubleday Young Readers Advisory Committee, 1964—; director of ERIC/CRIER Reading Resources Network Center, 1970. Member of advisory board, Educational Development Corp. *Member:* International Reading Association (member of board of directors, 1962-64; president, 1965-66; coordinator of study tours, 1967—), National Reading Conference (member, board of directors, 1969—), National Council of Teachers of English, College Professors of Reading (vice-president, 1972; president, 1973), Texas Association for the Improvement of Reading, Texas State Teachers Association. *Awards, honors:* Award from International Reading Association, 1970.

WRITINGS: Rodeo, Steck, 1949; *Doak Walker,* Steck, 1950; *People at Home,* Laidlaw, 1968; *Family and Social Needs,* Laidlaw, 1968; *Community and Social Needs,* Laidlaw, 1968; *Regions and Social Needs,* Laidlaw, 1968; *Many Texans* (seventh grade reader), with manual, Hendrick-Long, 1969; *Living Texans* (eighth grade reader), with manual, Hendrick Long, 1969; *Listening Skills Program,* Grades 1-6, Science Research Association, 1969, revised edition, Education Progress Corp., 1975; *Listening Progress Laboratory,* grades 7-13, Educational Progress Corp., 1970; *Specific Reading Skills,* pre-pre-primer through grade 6, with diagnostic tests, Jones-Kenilworth, 1972-75.

Co-author: *Improvement of Reading in Secondary Schools,* Texas Education Agency, 1953; *Early Texas Homes,* Southern Methodist University Press, 1956; *Marks of Lincoln on Our Land,* Hastings, 1957; *Bucky's Friends,* Lippincott, 1957; *Making Better Readers,* Heath, 1957; *Tactics in Reading,* Scott, Book I, 1961, Book II, 1963; *The New Building Better English,* Books 3-6, Row, Peterson & Co., 1961; *English Skills and Drills,* Books 3-6, Row, Peterson & Co., 1962; *Happy Ranch,* Lippincott, 1963. Also contributor to *Casebook on Reading Disabilities,* and *The Right to Read Newsbook in Reading Instruction.* Contributor to education journals. Editor, children's literature section of *Reading Teacher,* 1966-68; co-editor, *Proceedings of Third World Congress on Reading,* 1970; editor, *Newsletter* of Texas Association for the Improvement of Reading.

SIDELIGHTS: Mrs. Bracken has conducted research for a children's literature project during travel through eighty-one countries; she has toured around the world, and has spoken to groups of educators in many countries, including Egypt, Israel, Greece, Spain, and England.

* * *

BRADEN, William 1930-

PERSONAL: Born April 13, 1930, in Evanston, Ill.; son of William Kenneth (a businessman) and Albertine (Johnson) Braden; married Beatrice Brittain, September 8, 1956; children: Anne Elizabeth, Jennifer Alice. *Education:* University of Illinois, M.S.J., 1953; Northwestern University, B.S.J., 1953. *Politics:* Independent. *Residence:* West Dundee, Ill. *Office: Chicago Sun-Times,* 401 North Wabash Ave., Chicago, Ill. 60611.

CAREER: Northwestern University, Evanston, Ill., public relations writer, 1953-56; *Chicago Sun-Times,* Chicago, Ill., reporter, beginning 1956. *Awards, honors:* Marshall Field Award; Jacob Scher-Theta Sigma Phi Award; Page One Award, Chicago Newspaper Guild (three times).

WRITINGS: The Private Sea: LSD and the Search for God, Quadrangle, 1967; *The Age of Aquarius: Technology and the Cultural Revolution,* Quadrangle, 1970; *The Family Game: Identities for Young and Old,* Quadrangle, 1972. Contributor to Science Research Associates textbooks, and to readers; contributor of articles and fiction to magazines.

WORK IN PROGRESS: A textbook.

SIDELIGHTS: "Now it was bound to happen," writes Howard Moody, "that someone would write a book connecting 'radical theology' and hallucenogenic drugs." The *Chicago Sun Times* sent Braden out to find out "who killed God" and, as a result of his findings, he produced that inevitable book. Thoreau once wrote: "It is easier to sail many thousand miles through cold and storm and cannibals . . . than it is to explore the private sea [the source of Braden's title], the Atlantic and Pacific Ocean of one's being alone." Braden saw his task as the clarification of the relationship between "the LSD cults and what he calls radical theology." He interviewed several prominent atheist-pantheist theologians, then he took a trip himself. (Braden used mescaline because LSD had, by that time, been declared illegal.) He decided, according to Malcolm Boyd, that "'orthodoxy' and 'the psychedelic experience' have indeed arrived at their collision point," and proceeded to analyze theology (via Tillich, Teilhard de Chardin, Robinson, Altizer, and Hamilton), interpret his own drug experience, and set down some rather provocative conclusions.

William A. Richards writes: "Braden attempts to portray the LSD movement as one aspect of the swing of the 'psychic pendulum' from the 'rational and the conscious' to the 'intuitive and the unconscious.'" Richards applauds Braden's "creative effort to reconcile so-called 'Eastern' and 'Western' world views" and cites Braden's argument that we may be experiencing "not so much a leap to the East as the emergence at last of a possible East-West synthesis: a historic blending, as it were, of the waters of the Jordan and the Ganges." The *Virginia Quarterly Review* writer notes that Braden "discusses how the antipodal temperaments of East and West are in our times finding common grounds. Modern man's search is for an immanent God, even for pantheism, not for a transcendent God." Moody somewhat petulantly remarks that "to trade one set of illusions for another might not be progress," and, he concludes, "the analogy of the drug experience to the mystic and the poetic quality of [one's] experiences of God make little difference. It is difficult enough in these times to talk about God, but at least we can raise a serious question about whether the communion of which psychedelic religion speaks has anything to do with [the] God that comes to us through the Judeo-Christian heritage." But, Richards concludes: "It is clear that [Braden] is asking whether, having experienced mystical consciousness, a person should choose to drop out of society and join the ranks of those committed to 'psychedelic quietism,' or choose to involve himself ever more deeply in the historical process. Braden argues for the latter choice and depicts this process in the evolutionary manner envisioned by Teilhard."

Boyd writes: "The great contribution Braden makes is to bring together under the single roof of this book some hitherto unrelated questions of first-rate importance. He does not discount psychedelic insight but criticizes any claim that it might make to possess total truth. His relating of 'the radical West and the demythologized East,' in a discussion of East-West synthesis, is particularly important. . . . [Braden] has written an excellent book; it is original, interesting, exploratory, incisive, obviously a work marked by his own involvement." And Ross thinks that "what Mr. Braden lacks in depth . . . he more than makes up for in the range of his inquiry. . . . There is a good deal to think about in this swift-paced, highly readable, and honest book, and it is well worth the time to anyone who takes even the most cursory interest in today's intense religious searches."

Braden's second book, *The Age of Aquarius,* is, according to William Hamilton, a "fascinating, sometimes carelessly constructed assemblage from his wide reading and his even wider interviewing of students and seers in the general area of the youth scene, technology, and politics. . . . Braden is able to see and to feel into the world the kids see: a terrible futureless landscape, with nobody in charge." A *Time* reviewer notes that to Braden "Americans have been done in by technology. They have become producers and consumers first, people second." John Leonard concludes: "Mr. Braden can only hope: a little more eros, a little less logos; more biology (growth), less physics (manipulation); but always a mixture. Technology must be humanized, not abandoned. History must be willed, not succumbed to. . . . 'We must try harder.' Not exactly a revelation, but on his way to this sobering conclusion Mr. Braden has written an extraordinary novel of ideas—that is, a history of ideas that reads like a novel in which we all happen to be characters."

AVOCATIONAL INTERESTS: Flying (Braden holds a private pilot's license).

BIOGRAPHICAL/CRITICAL SOURCES: New York Times Book Review, April, 1967; *Christian Century,* April 5, 1967, May 10, 1967; *Saturday Review,* April 22, 1967; *Book Week,* May 7, 1967; *Virginia Quarterly Review,* winter, 1967; *Village Voice,* January 4, 1968; *New York Times,* May 13, 1970; *Time,* June 1, 1970; *Christian Century,* September 30, 1970.†

* * *

BRADLEE, Frederic 1920-

PERSONAL: Born February 6, 1920, in New York, N.Y.; son of Frederick J. and Josephine (de Gersdorff) Bradlee. *Education:* Attended Harvard University, 1938, and Columbia University, 1939. *Politics:* Democrat. *Religion:* Episcopalian. *Home:* 161 East 75th St., New York, N.Y. 10021. *Agent:* Monica McCall, International Creative Management, 40 West 57th St., New York, N.Y. 10019.

CAREER: Actor and author. Has appeared on Broadway, Off-Broadway, and with touring companies in such plays as "Theatre," "A Winter's Tale," "The Browning Version," "The Man Who Came to Dinner," "Arms and the Man," and "Second Threshold"; appeared in solo performance of "The Glory of Language," 1975. *Military service:* U.S. Army, 1942-45. *Member:* Coffee House Club (New York).

WRITINGS: (Editor with Cleveland Amory) *Vanity Fair* (anthology), Viking, 1961; *Esperie* (novel), Houghton, 1967; *A Lady in My Life* (memoir), Tashmoo Press, 1974. Contributor of articles and verse to magazines.

WORK IN PROGRESS: A novel, *Five Sittings for a Portrait.*

* * *

BRADLEY, Joseph F(rancis) 1917-

PERSONAL: Born July 22, 1917, in Locust Gap, Pa.; son of Dennis Charles and Isabel Jane (Donaghy) Bradley; married Ethel Marjorie Quigg, August 22, 1940; children: Isabelle Jane (Mrs. S. Allan Stone), Charles Torrence. *Education:* Pennsylvania State University, B.A., 1939, M.A., 1940; University of Pittsburgh, Ph.D., 1948. *Home:* 200 Highland Ave., Apt. 201, State College, Pa. 16801. *Office:* Pennsylvania State University, University Park, Pa. 16802.

CAREER: West Liberty State College, West Liberty, W. Va., professor, 1942-43; University of Pittsburgh, Pittsburgh, Pa., instructor in finance, 1946-47; Pennsylvania State University, College of Business Administration, University Park, 1947—, associate professor, 1950-59, professor of finance, 1959—. *Member:* Delta Sigma Pi, Phi Delta Kappa, Beta Gamma Sigma.

WRITINGS: Fundamentals of Corporation Finance, Holt, 1961; *Administrative Financial Management,* Holt, 1964, 3rd edition, Dryden, 1974; *The Role of Trade Associations and Professional Business Associations in America,* Pennsylvania State University Press, 1965.

* * *

BRADLEY, Robert A(ustin) 1917-

PERSONAL: Born December 11, 1917, in Atchison, Kan.; married Dorothy Bomar, June 16, 1939; married Martha W. Lindemann (a museum curator), August 5, 1972; children: Philip Bomar, Pelham Courtland, Parris Madison; (stepchildren) Martha, Marianne, Susan. *Education:* St. Benedict's College, Atchison, Kan., student, 1936-37; University of Kansas, A.B., 1940; Baylor University, M.D., 1947; University of Minnesota, post-graduate training in obstetrics and gynecology, 1947-59, 1952-53. *Home:* 4100 South University, Englewood, Colo. 80210. *Office:* 2465 South Downing, Denver, Colo. 80210.

CAREER: University of Colorado Medical School, Denver, clinical assistant in department of obstetrics and gynecology, 1953; private practice as a specialist in obstetrics and gynecology, Denver, Colo., 1953—. Pioneered in the introduction of natural childbirth in America, and in psychosomatic medicine and hypnosis; lecturer and investigator of psychic phenomena and extrasensory perception; annual guest lecturer on preparation for parenthood at universities in Colorado and Wyoming. President of American Academy of Husband-coached Childbirth. *Member:* Academy of Parapsychology and Medicine (co-founder and first president). *Military service:* U.S. Navy, medical officer, 1950-52; became lieutenant. *Member:* American Medical Association, Academy of Psychosomatic Medicine, American Society of Clinical Hypnosis (charter member), American Society of Psychical Research, American Association for the Advancement of Science, Colorado Gynecological and Obstetrical Society, Colorado Medical Society, Rocky Mountain Optimist Club (Denver; past president); honorary member of other medical and childbirth education groups.

WRITINGS: Husband-Coached Childbirth, Harper, 1965; (with wife, Dorothy Bomar Bradley) *Psychic Phenomena: Revelations and Experiences,* Parker Publishing, 1967. Contributor to *Psychosomatics, Medical Opinion & Review,* and several other periodicals. Member of advisory board, *Child and Family Magazine.*

WORK IN PROGRESS: God Knows, We Tried and *The Medical Committeeman.*

SIDELIGHTS: Psychic Phenomena was written as the result of the Bradleys' experiences in their thirty-room home on the outskirts of Denver, locally known as a haunted house.

BIOGRAPHICAL/CRITICAL SOURCES: True, August, 1963; *Parade,* December 29, 1963; *Good Housekeeping,* June, 1964; *Farm Journal,* May, 1966; *RN Magazine,* December, 1966.

* * *

BRADLEY, Sam(uel McKee) 1917-

PERSONAL: Born February 6, 1917, in Huntington, W. Va. son of Samuel McKee (a lumberman and financeer) and Clara Anita (Dyer) Bradley. *Education:* Morehead State University, A.B., 1936; University of Washington, Seattle, M.A., 1941; University of Pennsylvania, graduate study, 1956-58. *Religion:* Religious Society of Friends. *Home:* R.D. 1, Box 183, Honeybrook, Pa. 19344. *Office:* Department of English, Kutztown State College, Kutztown, Pa. 19530.

CAREER: Worked for Sharp & Bedbury (industrial advertising), Seattle, Wash., 1939-41; teacher of English at Duke University, Durham, N.C., 1945-46, Florence State College (now University), Florence, Ala., 1947-48, Lincoln University, Lincoln University, Pa., 1950-54 (and coordinator of English program for African Center, 1959-65), and at Lebanon Valley College, Annville, Pa., 1955-58; St. Augustine's College, Raleigh, N.C., associate professor of English and writer in residence, 1966-69; Kutztown State College Kutztown, Pa., associate professor of English and of African literature, 1969—. *Military service:* U.S. Navy, 1941-45.

WRITINGS: Men—In Good Measure (poetry), Golden Quill, 1966; *Alexander and One World* (poem and essay), South & West Press, 1966; (translator from the Russian, with Marianne Bogojavlensky) *Three Modern Soviet Poets: Evtushenko, Martynov, and Vinokurov,* Eastgate Press, 1967; *manspell/godspell,* Routledge & Kegan Paul, 1975. Contributor to *Poetry, Southwest Review, Beloit Poetry Journal, Prairie Schooner, Perspective, Virginia Quarterly Review, Nation, Saturday Review,* and others. Editor, *Approach,* and *Compass.*

WORK IN PROGRESS: Poetry and translations of poetry; working on a collection of African materials.

SIDELIGHTS: Etta Blum writes: "Intellectual strength, wide range of content, and richness of language distinguish the poetry of Sam Bradley.... The language is dazzling, often suggestive of the colors and shapes of tapestries...

One has the sense here of super-human landscape and the drama of beginnings. Often the poet is drunk with words as a painter with colors. . . . His passionate manner can best be described by 'Words leap like dolphins; their play/ wakes leviathan to primal day.' There are wit and large laughter in some of these poems as weapon against man's stupidity, hence inhumanity.''

BIOGRAPHICAL/CRITICAL SOURCES: Poetry, February, 1967.

* * *

BRADLEY, William L(ee) 1918-

PERSONAL: Born September 6, 1918, in Oakland, Calif.; son of Dwight Jaques (a clergyman) and Kathryn (Culver) Bradley; married Paul Anne Elliott, August 4, 1947; children: James Richard, Dwight Culver, Paul William. *Education:* Oberlin College, B.A., 1941; University of Edinburgh, Ph.D., 1949; Andover Newton Theological School, B.D., 1950. *Politics:* Democrat. *Office:* Hazen Foundation, 400 Prospect St., New Haven, Conn. 06511.

CAREER: United Church of Christ clergyman. Hartford Seminary Foundation, Hartford, Conn., professor of philosophy of religion, 1950-64; Rockefeller Foundation, New York, N.Y., temporary field staff member in Thailand, 1964-66, assistant director, 1966-68, associate director for humanities and social science, 1968-70; Edward W. Hazen Foundation, New Haven, Conn., president, 1970—. Visiting professor, Thammasat University, Thailand, 1964-66. Executive secretary of Committee for Christian Social Action, Congregational Churches of Connecticut, 1956-63. Member of Connecticut Governor's Committee on Human Services, 1962-64, and Governor's Special Committee on Libraries, 1963-64. *Military service:* U.S. Army Air Forces, 1942-45; served in South Pacific; became technical sergeant. *Member:* American Association for the Advancement of Science, American Anthropological Association, American Theological Society, Council on Foreign Relations, Society of Religion in Higher Education, International Phenomenological Society, American Society of Christian Ethics.

WRITINGS: P. T. Forsyth: The Man and His Work, Independent Press, 1952; *The Meaning of Christian Values Today,* Westminster, 1964; *Introduction to Comparative Religion,* Thammasat University Press, 1965; (contributor) Bunnag and Smithier, editors, *In Memoriam: Phya Anuman Rajudhon,* Siam Society, 1970. Contributor to *Journal of Religion and Journal of Siam Society.*

WORK IN PROGRESS: Saints and Scoundrels, a study of the American colony in Siam in the nineteenth century.

AVOCATIONAL INTERESTS: Contemporary theater, civil rights.

* * *

BRAENNE, Berit 1918-

PERSONAL: Born September 18, 1918, in Oslo, Norway; daughter of Sigmund (an architect) and Bodil (Winge) Braenne; married Hugo Frank Wathne (a sculptor; divorced); children: Tuva Braenne Wathne (daughter). *Education:* Studied ballet, 1922-34; attended housekeeping school, 1934, and Art School of the Norwegian State, 1935-37. *Politics:* Conservative. *Religion:* Protestant. *Home:* "Tuvastova," Roterud L.P., Lillehammer, Norway.

CAREER: Actress, 1938-50, appearing at Nationale Stage in Bergen, New Theater and Central Theater in Oslo, Rog-land Theater in Stavanger, and in two films; professional writer. *Member:* Norwegian Writers Guild. *Awards, honors:* Norwegian Literary Authors Union scholarship.

WRITINGS: Historien om Tamar og Trine, Aschehoug, 1958, translation by Evelyn Ramsden published as *Trina Finds a Brother,* Harcourt, 1962; *Tai-Mi, Tamars og Trines Soster,* Aschehoug, 1959, translation by Ramsden published as *Little Sister Tai-Mi,* Harcourt, 1964; *Tom Tangloppe,* Aschehoug, 1960; *Dukkemannen Tulleruskomsnusk* (title means "The Doll Tulleruskomsnusk"), Aschehoug, 1961; *Torris, gutten fra Storlidalen,* Aschehoug, 1967, translation by Lise Somme McKinnon published as *Torris, the Boy from Broad Valley,* Harcourt, 1970; *Torris og Fjellvind* (title means "Torris and Mountainwind"), Aschehoug, 1968; *Torris gror til,* Aschehoug, 1969. Author of play, "The Sunflower," produced in Stavanger, Norway, at Rogaland Theater, 1948. Writer of radio and television scripts for children's programs, and articles for newspapers.

WORK IN PROGRESS: A study of rural life in the mountains during the middle nineteenth century.

SIDELIGHTS: Braenne told *CA:* "Very fond of and interested in animals, especially the wild, after intimate studies in the mountains of 'Trollheimen,' where I lived with my daughter, 1962-67. Made there a series of films with my little dog, Snowwhite (poodle) and other animals. It was five eventful years, full of peace near the silent mountains. But the wintertime was long and dark, and those months, when I formerly wrote my books, I was just sitting there. Therefore I had to move to the little town of Lillehammer. Will always be longing back to the mountain—to the clean nature, the small foxes in the moonlight, and the big eagle on the blue sky. It was truly the real, hard, and wonderful life." The first two of Braenne's children's books were also published in London, and several have been translated into German for publication in Zurich.†

* * *

BRAND, Charles M(acy) 1932-

PERSONAL: Born April 7, 1932, in Stanford, Calif.; son of Carl Fremont (a college professor) and Nan (Surface) Brand; married Mary Shorrock, August 7, 1954; children: Catharine, Stephen. *Education:* Stanford University, A.B., 1953; Harvard University, A.M., 1954, Ph.D., 1961. *Home:* 229 North Roberts Rd., Bryn Mawr, Pa. 19010. *Office:* Bryn Mawr College, Bryn Mawr, Pa. 19010.

CAREER: Dumbarton Oaks Research Library, Washington, D.C., visiting fellow, 1961-62; San Francisco State College (now University), San Francisco, Calif., assistant professor of history, 1962-64; Bryn Mawr College, Bryn Mawr, Pa., assistant professor, 1964-69, associate professor, 1969-75, professor of history, 1975—. *Military service:* U.S. Army, 1955-57. *Member:* American Historical Association, Mediaeval Academy of America, American Association of University Professors, United States National Committee for Byzantine Studies, Phi Beta Kappa. *Awards, honors:* Fellow in post-classical studies, Gennadius Library, Athens, Greece, 1968-69; Fulbright Research Scholar, Greece, 1968-69; Guggenheim fellowship, Greece, 1972-73.

WRITINGS: Byzantium Confronts the West, 1180-1204, Harvard University Press, 1968; *Icon and Minaret: Sources of Byzantine and Islamic Civilization,* Prentice-Hall, 1969. Contributor to *Speculum* and other academic journals.

WORK IN PROGRESS: Research on Byzantine government and society in the twelfth century.

SIDELIGHTS: Charles Brand reads Latin, Greek (ancient and modern), French, German, and some Russian and Bulgarian.

* * *

BRAND, Millen 1906-

PERSONAL: Born January 19, 1906, in Jersey City, N.J.; son of Elmer (an electrician, carpenter, and farmer) and Carrie (a nurse; maiden name, Myers) Brand; married Pauline Leader (an author), 1932 (divorced); married Helen Mendelsohn, 1943; children: Elinor (Mrs. Paul Marion), Jonathan, Daniel, Carol. *Education:* Columbia University, B.A., 1929, B.Litt. (journalism), 1929. *Home:* 242 East 77th St., New York, N.Y. 10021. *Agent:* Mrs. Ad Schulberg, 300 East 57th St., New York, N.Y. 10022.

CAREER: New York Telephone Co., copywriter, 1929-37; Writing Center, New York University, New York, N.Y. instructor, c. 1940-50; Office of Civilian Defense, Washington, D.C., copywriter, 1942-43; Magazine Institute, New York, N.Y. instructor, c. 1958; Crown Publishers, New York, N.Y., editor, 1953-74. Worked for one and one-half years as a psychiatric aide in treatment centers and with private physicians. *Member:* Authors League, P.E.N., Society of American Historians. *Awards, honors:* Co-recipient of Robert Meltzer plaque and Screenwriters Guild award, both for the screenplay, "The Snake Pit."

WRITINGS: The Outward Room (novel; Book-of-the-Month Club selection), Simon & Schuster, 1937; *The Heroes* (novel), Simon & Schuster, 1939; *Albert Sears* (novel), Simon & Schuster, 1947; *Some Love, Some Hunger* (novel), Crown, 1955; *Dry Summer in Provence* (poems), C. N. Potter, 1966; *This Little Pig Named Curly* (juvenile), Crown, 1968; *Savage Sleep* (novel), Crown, 1968; (author of text; photographs by George Tice) *Fields of Rice*, Doubleday, 1970; *Local Lives* (poems), C. N. Potter, 1975. With Frank Partos, wrote screenplay for "The Snake Pit," 20th Century-Fox, 1948. Contributor to literary magazines and anthologies.

WORK IN PROGRESS: A three-act play, *The Hallway.*

SIDELIGHTS: Until the publication of *Savage Sleep*, Brand was principally known as the author of *The Outward Room*, his other major success. Both novels deal with the care of mental patients without their ever becoming case histories. Theodore Dreiser considered the first novel to be "unsparing and honest and at the same time refreshing and lovely," and Harold Brighouse noted that "there is nothing to be done about *The Outward Room* except to surrender to a narrative gripping enough to persuade one that chalk is cheese." "A brave novel," Sinclair Lewis said, "a story as devoid of sentimentality as a blizzard and yet a great love story—a real love story." The novels in between created little interest, even though Brand continued to be considered a novelist of stature. Many critics believed that *The Heroes* was an excellent piece of writing. Alfred Kazin said of this novel: "It is not often that one is moved by a novel as a whole, in which one is excited by the very sense of life caught at sudden pitch, so that one knows that what has been said is good, and that what will be said is true."

In *Savage Sleep* Brand returned to the subject he knows best, and again received much critical acclaim. Modeled on the work of the psychotherapist Dr. John N. Rosen, with whom Brand worked in Bucks County, Pa., "the book reads like an exciting detective thriller," wrote Paul D. Zimmerman. Thomas Lask viewed the book, begun when Brand was doing "The Snake Pit," as "a strong, controversial work that, despite its disclaimers as to the coincidence of fact and fiction, will be read as a serious account of the development of one method of curing the mentally ill. . . . In a sense the boundaries of *Savage Sleep* are narrow. They are confined to the doctor and his patients and the hospital world. Even the family scenes somehow always lead to the problem of therapy. But Mr. Brand . . . has made a cosmos out of these materials."

Brand began writing when he was six years old. He told *CA:* "*Dry Summer in Provence* resulted from a nine-month stay in the South of France. I'm reasonably competent in French, speak it fairly well, read it fluently. I lived in Monaco and Le Rouret. I wrote *Dry Summer* in six weeks, revised it for six years. My main interest is poetry. *Local Lives* is a portrait of a Pennsylvania German community in which I lived for ten years (I'm of Pennsylvania German descent on my mother's side). It took thirty-four years to write along with other work, and records the final flowering of a way of life."

The Outward Room, The Heroes, and *Savage Sleep* have been published in foreign editions.

BIOGRAPHICAL/CRITICAL SOURCES: Manchester Guardian, June 8, 1937; *Times Literary Supplement,* June 12, 1937; *New York Herald Tribune,* April 16, 1939; *New York Times Book Review,* April 16, 1939, May 18, 1975; *New York Times,* October 31, 1968, November 5, 1968; *Newsweek,* November 25, 1968; *Publishers Weekly,* May 12, 1975.

* * *

BRANDT, Floyd S(tanley) 1930-

PERSONAL: Born February 12, 1930, in Detroit, Mich.; son of Stanley W. (a salesman) and Pauline (Montgomery) Brandt; married Norma Anne Pirtle, December 5, 1953; children: Mary Lynn, William Stanley. *Education:* Visalia College, A.A., 1949; Texas Technological College (now Texas Tech University), B.B.A., 1951; University of Michigan, M.B.A., 1952; Harvard University, D.B.A., 1960. *Politics:* Democrat. *Religion:* Presbyterian. *Home:* 1100 Red Bud Trail, Austin, Tex. 78746. *Office:* University of Texas, BEB 502, Austin, Tex. 78712.

CAREER: West Texas State College (now University), Canyon, instructor, 1955-56; Harvard University, Boston, Mass., instructor and research associate, 1957-59; Northwestern University, Evanston, Ill., assistant professor, 1960-63; University of Texas, Austin, 1963—, currently professor of management and industrial relations, and assistant to president of university, 1975—. Lecturer, Stanford University, 1968; visiting professor, University Aix-Marseille, France, 1971. Consultant, Armstrong Cork Co.; partner, Management Analysis Center. *Military service:* U.S. Army, Field Artillery, 1952-55; became first lieutenant. *Member:* Industrial Relations Research Association, Southwest Management Association, Southwestern Social Sciences Association, Sigma Iota Epsilon. *Awards, honors:* Jack G. Taylor award for teaching excellence, College of Business, University of Texas.

WRITINGS: Collective Bargaining: Cases and Problems, Bureau of Business Research, University of Texas, 1965; (with Carroll R. Daugherty) *Conflict and Cooperation: Cases in Union-Management Behavior,* and *Instructor's*

Manual, Irwin, 1967; *Labor Relations Policy,* University of Texas, 1968; (with E. D. Bennett and C. K. Klassen) *Administrative Policy,* C. E. Merrill, 1969; *The Negotiation Process,* Incomtec, 1971; *Manpower Planning and Organizational Development,* Incomtec, 1972. Contributor of articles and reviews to journals.

*   *   *

BRANDT, Leslie F. 1919-

PERSONAL: Born February 12, 1919, in Morris, Minn.; son of Elmer F. and Clara (Johnson) Brandt; married Edith Tokle (a junior high school teacher), August 30, 1942; children: Sonia Marie, Daniel Leslie, Donald Mark. *Education:* Augsburg College, B.A., 1941; further study at Lutheran Bible Institute, Minneapolis, Minn., 1941-42, Augsburg Theological Seminary, 1942-45, College of Chinese Studies, Peking, China, 1947-48, and American Institute of Family Relations, 1959-61. *Address:* P.O. Box 4002, Blue Jay, Calif. 92317.

CAREER: Ordained to ministry of American Lutheran Church, 1945; pastor in Pukwana, S.D., 1945-46; missionary in Peking and Shanghai, China, 1946-48; evacuated from Shangai in Communist take-over, 1948; pastor in Minneapolis, Minn., 1949-51; service pastor (as civilian) in Taiwan and Japan, 1951-54, establishing service centers and acting as auxiliary chaplain on Navy ships in port; pastor in Williston, N.D., 1954-58, Westminster, Calif., 1958-63, and Los Angeles, Calif., 1963-67; Valley Lutheran Church, North Hollywood, Calif., pastor, 1967-73; Trinity Lutheran Church, Victorville, Calif., pastor, 1973—.

WRITINGS: Good Lord, Where Are You?, Concordia, 1967; *Great God, Here I Am,* Concordia, 1969; *God Is Here, Let's Celebrate,* Concordia, 1969; *Contemporary Introits and Collects for the Twentieth Century,* C.S.S. Publishing, 1970; *Can I Forgive God?,* Concordia, 1970; *The Lord Rules-Let Us Serve Him,* Concordia, 1971; *Meditations of a Radical Christian,* C.S.S. Publishing, 1973; *Psalms/Now,* Concordia, 1973; *Living Through Loving,* Concordia, 1974; *Book of Christian Prayer,* Augsburg, 1974; (with wife Edith Brandt) *Growing Together,* Augsburg, 1975; *Epistles/Now,* Concordia, 1976; *Praise the Lord,* Concordia, 1976. Contributor to religious publications; former weekly newspaper columnist in Williston, N.D., and Westminster, Calif.

*   *   *

BRANDWEIN, Chaim N(aftali) 1920-
(Ch. Naftali)

PERSONAL: Born June 22, 1920, in Jerusalem, Israel; son of Zusia (a rabbi) and Menucha (Adler) Brandwein; married Miriam Kosovsky (a teacher), October 1, 1952; children: Eran, Lilach. *Education:* Mizrachi Teachers Training College, diploma, 1941; Rabbinical College-Universal Yeshivah of Jerusalem, certificate, 1947; Hebrew University of Jerusalem, graduate study, 1950-52; Jewish Theological Seminary of America, New York, N.Y., D.H.L., 1962. *Home:* 32 Nonantum St., Newton, Mass. 02158. *Office:* Brandeis University, Waltham, Mass. 02154.

CAREER: Educational director and teacher in high schools in Tel-Aviv, Israel, 1947-50, in Jerusalem, Israel, 1950-53, and in Montreal, Quebec, 1953-56; Hebrew Cultural Foundation, Montreal, superintendent of Hebrew Schools of Canada, 1956-57; United Hebrew Teachers College, Montreal, dean, 1957-60; Jewish Theological Seminary of America, New York, N.Y., instructor, 1960-63, assistant pro-

fessor of modern Hebrew literature, 1963-66; Brandeis University, Waltham, Mass., associate professor of modern Hebrew literature, 1966-68, B. Rose Cohen Professor, 1968—, chairman of School of Humanities, 1967-70. Lecturer in Judaic studies, Sir George Williams University, 1957-59; visiting professor at University of California, San Diego, 1974-75, and University of Tel-Aviv, 1975-76. Member of academic advisory council of Jewish University without Walls; member of College Entrance Examination Board. Consultant to Examiner Corps of North Central Association of Colleges, Cornell University Press, and Indiana University Press. *Member:* Hebrew P.E.N. (secretary, 1964—), American Association of University Professors, Society of Biblical Literature, Society for Foreign Languages, Middle East Studies Association of North America, Jewish Historical Society. *Awards, honors:* Louis Lamed Prize for Hebrew Literature, 1960, for *Behazrot Yerushalayim;* Goodman Foundation grant, 1965, for book on Asher Barash.

WRITINGS: Behazrot Yerushalayim (short stories in Hebrew), Reuben Mass (Jerusalem), 1958, English translation by Hillel Halkin published as *In the Courtyards of Jerusalem,* Jewish Publication Society, 1967; *Betzel Ha'argaman* (poetry in Hebrew), Reuben Mass, 1964; *Meshorer Hashkiah* (study of the stream of consciousness in modern Hebrew literature; in Hebrew), Reuben Mass, 1964; *Asher Barash: Selection and Critical Analysis,* Goodman Foundation, 1968; (editor with Alan Mandelbaum) S. Y. Agnon, *Guest for a Night,* translation by Misha Louvish, Schocken, 1968; (contributor) George Devine, editor, *Dimensions in Religious Experience,* Alba House, 1971; (contributor) *Modern Near East: Literature and Society,* Center for International Studies, New York University, 1971. Contributor to *The Catholic Encyclopedia for School and Home.* About twenty short stories, twenty poems, and fifteen essays have been published in Jewish periodicals in Israel, Canada, and United States; regular contributor to *Gazit* (monthly journal published in Tel Aviv), for seven years; special correspondent in Europe for several Israeli newspapers, using the pen name Ch. Naftali, summer, 1952; editor of weekly column appearing in Der Adler, Montreal, 1958-59. Member of advisory board, *Hadoar Hebrew Weekly.*

WORK IN PROGRESS: Writing *The Self Anointed,* a psychological novel based on the life and death of a poet and rebel of the Israeli underground; a literary analysis of Biblical texts.

SIDELIGHTS: Brandwein published his first short story in the literary supplement of a Hebrew newspaper, *Davar,* when he was seventeen years old. His book, *Meshorer Hashkiah,* is now required reading in Israeli Universities.

BIOGRAPHICAL/CRITICAL SOURCES: J. K. Mikliszanski, *Toldot Ha'sifrut Ha'ivrit Ba'amerka,* Ogen, 1967; David Tidhar, editor, *Encyclopedia La'chalutzei Ha'yishuv Uvonav,* Volume II; G. Kressel, editor, *Encyclopedia of Modern Hebrew Literature;* A. Shaanan, editor, *Ha'sifrut Ha'ivrit Ha'chadasha,* Massada, 1967.

*   *   *

BRANNAN, Robert Louis 1927-

PERSONAL: Born May 10, 1927, in Mineral Wells, Tex.; son of Robert H. (a teacher) and Anna (Rossen) Brannan; married Lucille E. Petrick, January 1, 1952; children: Martha, Nathaniel, Robert, Jr., Diana, Mary, Paul, Tommy. *Education:* University of Texas, B.A., 1948, M.A., 1952;

Cornell University, Ph.D., 1965. *Politics:* Independent. *Religion:* Catholic.

CAREER: Cornell University, Ithaca, N.Y., teaching assistant, 1954-56, instructor, 1956-58; University of Notre Dame, Notre Dame, Ind., instructor, 1958-61, assistant professor, 1961-66; Hiram College, Hiram, Ohio, associate professor, 1966-67; Benedictine College, Atchison, Kan., associate professor of English, beginning 1967. *Military service:* U.S. Army, 1946-47. *Member:* Modern Language Association of America, National Council of Teachers of English, American Association of University Professors.

WRITINGS: Under the Management of Mr. Charles Dickens: His Production of "The Frozen Deep," Cornell University Press, 1966.†

* * *

BRASCH, Rudolph 1912-

PERSONAL: Born November 6, 1912, in Berlin, Germany; son of British nationals, Gustav and Hedwig (Mathias) Brasch; married Liselotte Buchbinder, February 16, 1952. *Education:* Studied at University of Berlin, 1931-35; University of Wurzburg, Ph.D. (summa cum laude), 1936; Jewish Theological Seminary, Berlin, Rabbi (with highest honors), 1938. *Home:* 14 Derby St., Vaucluse, Sydney, New South Wales, Australia. *Office:* Temple Emanuel, 7 Ocean St., Woollahra, New South Wales, Australia.

CAREER: Rabbi of Progressive synagogues in London, England, 1938-48, and Dublin, Ireland, 1946-47; Johannesburg Reform Congregations, Johannesburg, South Africa, rabbi and director of public relations, 1948-49; Temple Emanuel, Woollahra (Sydney), New South Wales, Australia, chief minister, 1949—. Guest professor, University of Sydney, 1952-53. Life vice-president and chairman of ecclesiastical board, Australian and New Zealand Union for Progressive Judaism; member of governing body, World Union for Progressive Judaism; director of education, Liberal Education Board of New South Wales; justice of the peace, New South Wales. *Military service:* Padre to Civil Defence during London blitz; received Coronation Medal (Queen Elizabeth II), for his work. *Member:* Royal Australian Historical Society, Society of Religious History (founding member), Rotary Club (Sydney). *Awards, honors:* D.D., Hebrew Union College-Jewish Institute of Religion, Los Angeles, 1959; made Officer of the British Empire, 1967.

WRITINGS: The Star of David, Angus & Robertson, 1955; *The Eternal Flame,* Angus & Robertson, 1958; *General Sir John Monash* (biography), Royal Australian Historical Society, 1959; *How Did It Begin?,* Longmans, Green, 1965, McKay, 1966; *Mexico: A Country of Contrasts,* McKay, 1966; *Judaic Heritage,* McKay, 1969; *The Unknown Sanctuary: The Story of Judaism, Its Teachings, Philosophy, and Symbols,* Angus & Robertson, 1969; *How Did Sports Begin? A Look at the Origins of Man at Play,* McKay, 1970; *How Did Sex Begin? The Sense and Nonsense of the Customs and Traditions that Have Separated Men and Women Since Adam and Eve,* McKay, 1973. Also author of *The Midrash Shir Ha-shirim Zuta,* 1936; *The Jewish Question Mark,* 1945; (with Lily M. Montagu) *A Little Book of Comfort for Jewish People in Times of Sorrow,* [London], 1948; *The Symbolism of King Solomon's Temple,* 1954.

Scriptwriter for Australian Broadcasting Commission. Contributor to *Mankind* and *Commentary* (both United States), and other magazines and newspapers in Australia, Europe,

and Africa; regular columnist, "Religion and Life" in Australia's *Sun-Herald.* Editor, *Progressive Jew,* Johannesburg, 1948-49.

WORK IN PROGRESS: Research in the history of religion in Australia, and in the occult.

SIDELIGHTS: Rabbi Brasch is a master of twelve languages, among them Babylonic-Assyrian (Cuneiform), Syriac, Arabic, and Persian. From his early days, has been active in interfaith relations: in Ireland stayed at a Franciscan monastery; in London conducted Hindu-Jewish service; in South Africa addressed Bantus and held Dutch Reformed-Jewish service; in Australia has spoken in the Unitarian and Catholic churches of Sydney, and at the Inland Mission Church at Alice Springs in the heart of the interior.

* * *

BRAUER, Kinley J(ules) 1935-

PERSONAL: Born April 16, 1935, in Jersey City, N.J.; son of Sigmund I. and Dora (Zack) Brauer; married Barbara Stein, August 20, 1961; children: Emily, Peter. *Education:* University of Rochester, B.A., 1957; University of California, Berkeley, M.A., 1958, Ph.D., 1963. *Office:* History Department, University of Minnesota, Minneapolis, Minn. 55455.

CAREER: Stanford University, Stanford, Calif., instructor in history, 1960-63; University of Nevada, Reno, assistant professor of history, 1963-65; University of Minnesota, Minneapolis, assistant professor, 1965-67, associate professor, 1967-75, professor of history, 1975—. *Member:* American Historical Association, American Association of University Professors, Organization of American Historians, Society for Historians of American Foreign Relations. *Awards, honors:* McKnight Foundation Humanities Prize in American History, 1965, for *Cotton Verses Conscience.*

WRITINGS: Cotton versus Conscience: Massachusetts Whig Politics and Southwestern Expansion, 1843-1848, University of Kentucky Press, 1967. Contributor to *Encyclopedia of World Biography, Encyclopedia Americana,* and historical journals.

WORK IN PROGRESS: Foreign Policy during the American Civil War; and *America in the Age of Revolutions, 1848-1871.*

* * *

BREDSDORFF, Jan 1942-

PERSONAL: Born January 19, 1942, in Denmark; son of Elias Lunn and Marlie (Brande) Bredsdorff; married Pernille Grumme (an actress). *Education:* Educated at schools in England and Denmark. *Politics:* Communist. *Religion:* None. *Home:* Baadsmandsstraede 12, Copenhagen, Denmark. *Agent:* Curtis Brown Ltd., 1 Craven Hill, London W2 3EW, England.

CAREER: Teacher of English in Canton, People's Republic of China, 1965-67; writer. *Member:* Danish Union of Writers.

WRITINGS: Et Kys Pa Vaeggen, Thaning & Appel, 1964; *Ash* (novel), Anthony Blond, 1967; *Mao Tse-tungs Taenkning,* Erichsen, 1967; *Udsigt fra de hvide skyers bjerg,* Thaning & Appel, 1968; (with wife, Pernille Grumme) *Kina billedbog,* Erichsen, 1968. Also has written for Danish State Radio, and *Politiken* and *Ekstra Bladet* (both Copenhagen).†

BRELIS, Nancy (Burns) 1929-

PERSONAL: Born April 11, 1929, in South Africa; daughter of William (a mining engineer) and Elinor (Prudden) Burns; married Dean Brelis (a journalist and writer), December 10, 1949; married second husband, Robert R. Jay (an anthropologist), December, 1967; children: (first marriage) Doron, Jane, Tia, Matthew. Education: Attended Radcliffe College, 1946-47, 1965-67; Harvard University, B.A., 1967. Residence: Cornwall, Conn. Agent: Harold Ober Associates, Inc., 40 East 49th St., New York, N.Y. 10017.

WRITINGS: The Mummy Market, Harper, 1966.

*   *   *

BREMAN, Paul 1931-

PERSONAL: Born July 19, 1931, in Bussum, Netherlands; son of Gerrit and Adriana Petronella (Pre) Breman; married Maria A. de Waard, 1952; married second wife, Willemien Marie Vroom, 1957 (divorced); children: Remco, Marc, Sacha. Education: Attended University of Amsterdam, 1949-52. Politics: "Vaguely leftish." Religion: None. Home and office: 1 Rosslyn Hill, London N.W.3, England.

CAREER: Galerie Le Canard, Amsterdam, Netherlands, public relations officer, 1952-54; Antiquariaat Erasmus (antiquarian booksellers), Amsterdam, salesman and cataloger, 1954-58; E. P. Goldschmidt & Co. Ltd. (antiquarian booksellers), London, England, cataloger of rare books, 1959-62; B. Weinreb Ltd. (antiquarian bookseller), London, director and cataloger, 1963-66; Weinreb & Breman Ltd. (antiquarian booksellers), London, owner and sales director, 1967-68; Paul Breman Ltd. (publisher and antiquarian bookseller), London, owner, 1961—. Awards, honors: First book published under his own imprint, Robert Hayden's A Ballad of Remembrance, won Grand Prix de la Poesie at Dakar World Festival of Negro Arts, 1966.

WRITINGS: (Contributor) C.W.E. Bigsby, editor, The Black American Writer, Everett/Edwards, 1969.

Editor: (And annotator with Rosey E. Pool) Ik Zag Hoe Zwart Ik Was (bilingual edition of poetry by North American Negroes), Daamen, 1958; (and author of introductory essay) 6 Over Jazz, Heijnis, 1958.

Waring Cuney, Puzzles, limited edition with woodcuts by Ru van Rossem, De Roos, 1960; (and author of historic notes; annotator of thirty-five songs) Spirituals, Servire, 3rd edition, 1961; (and compiler of bibliography; annotator of thirty-five songs) Blues, Servire, 1961; Sixes and Sevens (anthology of poetry by American Negroes), Paul Breman, 1962; (and author of historical notes) Vitruvius Britannicus (pictorial book of English Country houses, 1660-1800), Benjamin Blom, 1967-72; (and author of commentary with Denise Addis) Architectural Views (from Brockhaus Pictorial Encyclopaedia), Benjamin Blom, 1969; (and compiler) The Weinreb Catalogues: An Annotated Index, Paul Breman, 1969.

(With Jillian Norman) Dutch Phrase Book, Penguin, 1972, 2nd edition, 1973; (and compiler) You Better Believe It: Black Verse in English, from Africa, the West Indies and the United States, Penguin, 1973. Contributor to Deutsches Architektenblatt. Compiler of twenty-five catalogues, plus an index volume, of books on specialized architectural subjects for Weinreb & Breman, 1963-68. Editor of "Heritage Series" (poetry books by Black authors), twenty seven books, Paul Breman, 1962-75. Editor of a jazz magazine published in the Netherlands, 1951-53.

WORK IN PROGRESS: An annotated bibliography of Vitruvius editions.

SIDELIGHTS: Paul Breman said: "I like work (almost any kind of), and relax with different work, or in cooking, photography, and the pursuit of active love-making. I speak Dutch and English (it is hard to decide which of these two to list as foreign), German, French, and Spanish, and decipher most other European languages when professionally necessary.

"Have collected poetry by U.S. Negro authors since 1946 (this grew out of interest in blues texts) and eventually established my own publishing house in order to present each year two or three poets whose work I like but who, for various reasons, do not rate with the commercial houses in the States. On the whole I am an editor rather than an author."

*   *   *

BREMNER, Robert H(amlett) 1917-

PERSONAL: Born May 26, 1917, in Brunswick, Ohio; son of George L. (a lawyer) and Sue E. (Hamlett) Bremner; married Catherine Marting, March 18, 1950; children: Sue L., Ann R. Education: Baldwin-Wallace College, B.A., 1938; Ohio State University, M.A., 1939, Ph.D., 1943. Home: 33 Orchard Dr., Worthington, Ohio 43805. Office: Ohio State University, 230 West 17th Ave., Columbus, Ohio 43210.

CAREER: Ohio State University, Columbus, instructor, 1946-51, assistant professor, 1951-55, associate professor, 1956-60, professor of history, 1960—. Research associate at University of Wisconsin, 1958-59, and Harvard University, 1966-69. Visiting summer professor at University of Cincinnati, 1965, and University of Michigan, 1966. Member: American Historical Association, Organization of American Historians, American Studies Association, Social Welfare History Group (chairman, 1966-68), Ohio Academy of History (president, 1965-66).

WRITINGS: From the Depths: The Discovery of Poverty in the United States, New York University Press, 1956; American Philanthropy, University of Chicago Press, 1960; (editor) Essays on History and Literature, Ohio State University Press, 1966; (editor) Anthony Comstock, Traps for the Young, Harvard University Press, 1967; (editor) Children and Youth in America: A Documentary History, Harvard University Press, 1970-74.

WORK IN PROGRESS: Philanthropy and Social Welfare in the Civil War Era, for Knopf.

*   *   *

BRENNEMAN, Helen Good 1925-

PERSONAL: Born November 26, 1925, in Harrisonburg, Va.; daughter of Lewis (a minister and businessman) and Lois (Eby) Good; married Virgil John Brenneman (a campus pastor), November 27, 1921; children: Don, Lois, John Michael, Rebecca; foster children: Loretta (Mrs. Jack Birky). Education: Attended Eastern Mennonite College, 1944-45, and Goshen College, 1948-50. Religion: Mennonite. Home: 516 East Waverly, Goshen, Ind. 46526.

CAREER: U.S. Department of Agriculture, Washington, D.C., clerk, 1942-44, 1945-47; Mennonite Central Committee, relief worker (with husband) in Gronau, Germany, 1947-48; Goshen College, Goshen, Ind., secretary to dean of Biblical Seminary, 1948-50.

WRITINGS—All published by Herald Press: *Meditations for the New Mother*, 1953; *But Not Forsaken* (novel), 1954; (contributor) Elaine Sommers Rich, editor, *Breaking Bread Together*, 1958; *My Comforters*, 1966; *Meditations for the Expectant Mother*, 1968; *The House by the Side of the Road*, 1971; *Ring a Dozen Doorbells*, 1973; *Marriage: Agony and Ecstasy*, 1975; *Cope: Handibook for the Handicapped*, 1975. Writer of curriculum materials for *Family Worship*, for three years; frequent contributor to *Christian Living;* occasional contributor to other church periodicals.

SIDELIGHTS: Mrs. Brenneman wrote *My Comforters*, a book of daily inspiration for those who are ill, as a result of her own experience with multiple sclerosis, which she developed in 1963.

* * *

BRENNER, Yehojachin Simon 1926-

PERSONAL: Born December 24, 1926, in Berlin, Germany; son of Abraham (a headmaster) and Rosel (Hilb) Brenner; married Nancy Golomb (a mathematician and statistician), March 27, 1955; children: Eli (son), Yael (daughter). *Education:* University of Basel, Phil.I., 1951; Hebrew University of Jerusalem, M.A. (history), 1956; University of London, M.A. (price history), 1962. *Politics:* "Liberal—not member of any party." *Religion:* Jewish. *Home:* Bilthoven, Netherlands. *Office:* Department of Social Sciences, State University of Utrecht, Utrecht, Netherlands.

CAREER: University of Maryland, European Extension, lecturer in economics, 1960-62; University College of Cape Coast, Ghana, West Africa, head of economics department and senior lecturer in economic development, 1962-67; Institute of Social Studies, The Hague, Netherlands, professor and deputy chairman of economic planning, 1967-69; Middle East Technical University, Ankara, Turkey, professor of economics, 1969-72; State University of Utrecht, Utrecht, Netherlands, professor of economics, 1972—. Consultant to the Organization for Economic Co-operation and Development, 1969-72. *Military service:* Israeli Armed Forces, 1948.

WRITINGS: *Theories of Economic Development and Growth*, Praeger, 1966; *A Short History of Economic Progress*, Augustus M. Kelley, 1969; (with H.T.M. Wagenbuur) *Lime Farmers: A Case Study of a Cashcrop in a Subsistence Economy*, University College of Cape Coast, 1969; *Agriculture and the Economic Development of Low Income Countries*, Mouton & Co., 1971; *An Introduction to Economics*, Middle East Technical University Press, 1972. Contributor to University College of Cape Coast Social Studies series. Contributor to *Bulletin of the Institute of Historical Research* (University of London), *Economic History Review, Middle Eastern Studies,* and *Africa Quarterly.*

WORK IN PROGRESS: A book, *Looking into the Seeds of Time.*

* * *

BRENTANO, Robert 1926-

PERSONAL: Born May 19, 1926, in Evansville, Ind.; son of S. August (a civil engineer) and Kathryn (Doyle) Brentano; married Carroll Winslow (a professor of art history), September 20, 1956; children: James August Burke, Margaret Winslow, Robert Gabriel. *Education:* Swarthmore College, B.A., 1949; Oxford University, D.Phil., 1952.

Politics: Democrat. *Religion:* Roman Catholic. *Home:* 35 Robel Court, Berkeley, Calif. 94705, also maintains residence in Rome, Italy, and Newburgh, Ind. *Office:* Department of History, University of California, Berkeley, Calif. 94720.

CAREER: University of California, Berkeley, instructor, 1952-54, assistant professor, 1954-59, associate professor, 1959-65, professor of medieval history, 1965—. *Military service:* U.S. Army, 1944-46. *Member:* Mediaeval Academy of America (fellow), Society for Italian Historical Studies, Royal Historical Society. *Awards, honors:* Rhodes scholar at Oxford University, 1949-52; Fulbright fellow in Italy, 1956-57; American Council of Learned Societies fellow, 1960-61; Guggenheim fellow, 1965-66; National Endowment for the Humanities fellow, 1972-73.

WRITINGS: *York Metropolitan Jurisdiction*, University of California Press, 1959; *Early Middle Ages*, Free Press of Glencoe, 1964; *Two Churches: England and Italy in the Thirteenth Century*, Princeton University Press, 1968; *Rome before Avignon*, Basic Books, 1974. Contributor to *Mediaeval Studies, Speculum,* and other journals.

WORK IN PROGRESS: Studies on nineteenth-century historians; a history of thirteenth-century Rieti.

* * *

BRETT-SMITH, Richard 1923-

PERSONAL: Born January 1, 1923, in Oxford, England; son of Herbert Francis (a university professor) and Helena (Yates) Brett-Smith; married Patricia Karen Shields, January 31, 1953 (divorced, 1958); children: Anna, Francesca, Adam. *Education:* Oxford University, M.A., 1949. *Home:* c/o Cavalry Club, 127 Piccadilly, London W. 1, England.

CAREER: *Oxford Mail,* Oxford, England, reporter and sub-editor, 1947-48; *Daily Telegraph,* London, England, foreign correspondent and defense correspondent, 1950-64, with more than eight years as correspondent in United States; British Aircraft Corp., Weybridge, Surrey, England, head of editorial services, 1966; Westminster Press provincial newspapers, London, editorial writer, 1967; freelance journalist, writer and teacher, 1968-73; Central Office of Information, London, information officer, 1974; freelance journalist, 1975—. *Military service:* British Army, 1941-47; became captain in Eleventh Hussars; fought in Italy, France, Belgium, Netherlands, and Germany; mentioned in dispatches. *Member:* Institute of Journalists, Royal United Services, Institute for Defence Studies.

WRITINGS: *Berlin '45: The Grey City*, Macmillan, 1966, St. Martins, 1967; *The Eleventh Hussars*, Cooper, 1969; *Hitler's Generals*, Osprey, 1976. Contributor to *Purnell's History of the Second World War*, and to *Spectator, Time and Tide, Army Quarterly,* and other periodicals.

WORK IN PROGRESS: *The Retreat to Dunkirk, 1940.*

SIDELIGHTS: Brett-Smith told *CA:* "Tend to be most interested in people, places, and atmosphere." He traveled in thirty-eight states during period as foreign correspondent in America. *Avocational interests:* Aviation and aerospace activities, English literature (especially eighteenth century), English, American, and European fiction of all periods, ancient Greek and Roman literature.

* * *

BREWER, Jack A. 1933-

PERSONAL: Born April 13, 1933, in Elmore City, Okla.;

son of Jess E. (a businessman) and Opal May (Moore) Brewer; married Carolyn Wright, March 12, 1953; children: Lee Alan, Lisa Ann, Carol Lynn. *Education:* East Central State College, Ada, Okla., B.A., 1958; Southwestern Baptist Theological Seminary, M.R.E., 1960. *Politics:* Democrat. *Home:* 10659 Hazelhurst, Houston, Tex. 77043. *Office:* Boys Country, Box 94, Houston, Tex. 77001.

CAREER: Ordained minister of the Baptist Church, 1970. Minister of youth or minister of education at Baptist churches in Tulia, Tex., 1960-62, Springfield, Mo., 1962-64, Kansas City, Mo., 1964-65, and Texarkana, Tex., 1965-67; Tallowood Baptist Church, Houston, Tex., minister of youth education and church rector, 1967-70; Boys Country, Houston, executive director, 1971—. President of Youth Employment Campaign, 1966; founder of Youth Ecological Society, 1971. *Military service:* U.S. Air Force, 1951-55. *Member:* Southwestern Religious Education Association.

WRITINGS: Fellowships from A—Z, Broadman, 1968.

WORK IN PROGRESS: A Funny Thing Happened on the Way to Heaven; Devotions from A—Z.

* * *

BREWER, Thomas B.   1932-

PERSONAL: Born July 22, 1932, in Fort Worth, Tex.; son of Earl Johnson and Maurine (Bowman) Brewer; married Betty Walling, August 4, 1951; children: Lillian Diane, Linda Susan, Thomas B. Jr. *Education:* University of Texas, B.A., 1954, M.A., 1957; University of Pennsylvania, Ph.D., 1962. *Politics:* Democrat. *Religion:* Disciples of Christ. *Home:* 4301 Lanark, Ft. Worth, Tex. 76109. *Office:* Sedlea 302, Texas Christian University, Ft. Worth Tex. 76129.

CAREER: Instructor at St. Stephens Episcopal School, Austin, Tex., 1955-56, and Southwest Texas State College (now Southwest Texas State University, San Marcos, 1956-57; North Texas State University, Denton, 1959-66, began as instructor, became associate professor of history; University of Kentucky, Lexington, assistant professor of history, 1966-67; Iowa State University of Science and Technology, Ames, associate professor of history, 1967-68; University of Toledo, Toledo, Ohio, professor of history and chairman of department, 1968-71; Texas Christian University, Ft. Worth, dean of College of Arts and Sciences, 1971-72, vice-chancellor and university dean, 1972—. *Member:* Business History Association, Economic History Association, Southern Historical Association, Business History Conference, Organization of American Historians.

WRITINGS: (Editor with Thomas C. Cochran) *Views of American Economic Growth,* two volumes, McGraw, 1966; (editor) *The Robber Barons,* Holt, 1970. Contributor of articles and reviews to journals. General editor, Macmillan's "Railroads of America Series."

WORK IN PROGRESS: History of the Missouri Pacific Railway Company, for Macmillan.

* * *

BRICE, Douglas   1916-

PERSONAL: Born June 21, 1916, in London, England. *Education:* Attended St. Ignatius College, Stamford Hill, London, England; studied music under Mary Barber in Birmingham, England. *Home:* North Lease Hall, Hathersage, Derbyshire, England.

CAREER: Roman Catholic priest; curate for various parishes for five years until health deteriorated; writer. Chaplain to U.S. Army Air Forces, Stanstead and Takeley, England, during World War II. Has trained male choirs for church performance in junior and senior seminaries.

WRITINGS: The Folk-Carol of England, Jenkins, 1967. Contributor of articles and poems to *Downside Review, Month, Clergy Review, Wiseman Review,* and *Catholic Herald;* contributor of poems to *English Folk Dance and Song.*

WORK IN PROGRESS: Research for future editions of *The Folk-Carol of England,* an antiquarian work written for non-Catholics.

SIDELIGHTS: Brice told *CA* that he founded the first grammar school on the Libyan Desert where he was a private tutor to a surgeon and his six children. Covering 12 subjects, he taught as many as 13 classes a day, sometimes in temperatures reaching 120 degrees.

* * *

BRILHART, John K.   1929-

PERSONAL: Born February 23, 1929, in Johnstown, Pa.; son of John Bryan and Elizabeth (Kinter) Brilhart; married Lillian C. Cross; married Barbara Lieb; married Sue E. Simmons, April 28, 1973; children: (first marriage) Susan, Beverly Ann, John G., Keith D. *Education:* David Lipscomb College, B.A. (magna cum laude), 1952; Pennsylvania State University, M.A., 1957, Ph.D., 1962. *Religion:* None. *Home:* 3623 Giles Rd., Omaha, Neb. 68147. *Office:* Department of Speech, University of Nebraska, Omaha, Neb. 68101.

CAREER: High school teacher of speech and science, LeCenter, Ky., 1952-55; Pennsylvania State University, University Park, instructor, 1957-62, assistant professor of speech, 1962-65; University of Nebraska at Omaha, associate professor, 1965-68, professor of speech, 1968—. *Member:* Speech Communication Association, Institute of General Semantics, Central States Speech Association, Nebraska Speech Association, Pi Gamma Mu, Delta Sigma Rho.

WRITINGS: Leading Study Discussion Programs, Center for Continuing Liberal Education, Pennsylvania State University, 1959; *Effective Group Discussion,* W. C. Brown, 1967, 2nd edition, 1974. Contributor of articles to *Journal of Abnormal and Social Psychology, Journal of Perceptual and Motor Skills,* and speech journals; contributor of stories to *Beagle Journal, American Archery,* and *Hounds and Hunting.*

WORK IN PROGRESS: A book, tentatively titled, *Communicating as a Nurse.*

AVOCATIONAL INTERESTS: Hunting, fishing, beagling, woodworking.

* * *

BRINKLEY, William (Clark)   1917-

PERSONAL: Born September 10, 1917, in Custer, Okla.; son of Daniel Squire (a minister) and Ruth (Clark) Brinkley. *Education:* Attended William Jewell College, 1936-37; University of Oklahoma, B.A., 1940; Yale School of Drama, special student, 1961-1962. *Home:* 1200 Nolana Ave., Apt. 2, McAllen, Tex. 78501. *Agent:* Harold Matson Co., Inc., 22 East 40th St., New York, N.Y. 10016.

CAREER: Reporter for *Daily Oklahoman,* Oklahoma City,

Okla., 1940-41, and *Washington Post*, Washington, D.C., 1941-42, 1949-51; *Life*, New York, N.Y., staff member, 1951-58, as Washington correspondent, assistant editor, and staff writer; free-lance writer, 1958—. *Military service:* U.S. Navy, 1942-46; served chiefly in Mediterranean and Pacific; became lieutenant. *Member:* National Press Club (Washington), Overseas Press Club (New York), Phi Beta Kappa.

WRITINGS: Quicksand (novel), Dutton, 1948; *Don't Go Near the Water* (novel), Random House, 1956; *The Fun House* (novel), Random House, 1961; *The Two Susans* (novel), Random House, 1962; *The Ninety and Nine* (novel), Doubleday, 1966. Also author of *The Deliverance of Sister Cecilia*, with Sister Cecilia.

SIDELIGHTS: Don't Go Near the Water was made into the highly successful Metro-Goldwyn-Mayer film in 1957; the movie grossed $4,500,000 and ranked among the ten best pictures of the year in *Film Daily*'s poll.

* * *

BRINSMEAD, H(esba) F(ay) 1922-
(Pixie Hungerford)

PERSONAL: Born March 15, 1922, in Blue Mountains, New South Wales, Australia; daughter of Edward K. G. (missionary to Indonesia and saw-mill operator) and May (Lambert) Hungerford; married Reginald Brinsmead (owner of spray contracting company), February 11, 1943; children: Bernard Hungerford, Ken Hungerford. *Education:* Lived in isolated area as a child and received early schooling through a correspondence school; attended high school at Wahroonga, near Sydney, Australia, and then Avondale College, one year. *Politics:* Country Party ("anti-war; humanitarian"). *Religion:* Seventh-day Adventist. *Home:* Weathsotopi Shamera Rd., Terranora, New South Wales, Australia 2W8S. *Agent:* Dorothy Blewett Associates, View Hill Crescent, Melbourne, Victoria, Australia.

CAREER: Governess for two years in Tasmania, where she continued her study of speech therapy; teacher of speech therapy in western Victoria, Australia, 1945-48; later was kindergarten supervisor in Melbourne, Australia, for two years; did amateur acting with Box Hill City Drama Group, Melbourne, 1950-60; began writing after a trip to Indonesia, 1957, and has been writing more or less full time, 1960—. *Awards, honors:* Mary Gilmore Award, 1963 and Australian Children's Book Council book of the year award, 1965, both for *Pastures of the Blue Crane;* Elizabethan Medal (London), for *Isle of the Sea Horse;* Australian Children's Book Council book of the year award, 1972, for *Longtime Passing*.

WRITINGS—All published by Oxford University press, except as noted: *Pastures of the Blue Crane*, 1964, Coward, 1966; *Season of the Briar*, 1965, Coward, 1966; *Beat of the City*, 1966, Coward, 1967; *A Sapphire for September*, 1967; *Isle of the Sea Horse*, 1969; *Who Calls from Afar?*, 1971; *Longtime Passing*, Angus & Robertson, 1972; *Echo in the Wildness*, 1972; *Under the Silkwood*, Cassell, 1975. Also author of *The Ballad of Benny Perhaps* and *Once there was a Swagman*. Author of two children's serials, "The Honey Forest," 1960, and "The Apple Ship," 1962; has written short stories for Australian Broadcasting Commission; and articles and stories, some under name Pixie Hungerford, for *People, Country, Women's Weekly, Australian Letters,* and other periodicals

SIDELIGHTS: Hesba Brinsmead is particularly engrossed in young people ("are they *really* a unique generation?"), and world peace. Since her trip to Indonesia ("it jolted me into action—the plight of humanity at large"), she has been to Fiji twice, and has traveled in Europe, Canada, and other countries. Two of her books, *Pastures of the Blue Crane* and *Beat of the City,* were made into television series by the Australian Broadcasting Commission.

* * *

BRION, John M. 1922-

PERSONAL: Born December 27, 1922, in New York, N.Y.; son of Lester E. (a business executive) and Lucille (Demarest) Brion; children: John M., Jr., William R. *Education:* Yale University, B.S., 1942. *Home:* 228 W. 71st Street, New York, N.Y. 10023.

CAREER: Peter A. Frasse & Co., Inc. (metals distributors), New York City, 1947-58, vice-president of operations; Eastern Rolling Mills, Inc. (metals), New York City, general sales manager, 1959-60; Coordinated Marketing-Management Corp. (consultants), New York City, director of industrial marketing, 1961; Crane Co., Engineered Products Group, Philadelphia, Pa., manager of sales and administration, 1962-65; Day & Zimmerman Consulting Services, New York City, vice-president of corporate planning and marketing services, 1967—. *Military service:* U.S. Army Air Forces, aircraft engineering officer, 1942-45.

WRITINGS: Decisions, Organization Planning and the Marketing Concept, American Management Association, 1965; *Marketing Through the Wholesaler/Distribution Channel*, American Marketing Association, 1966; *Corporate Marketing Planning*, Wiley, 1967.

* * *

BRISSENDEN, R(obert) F(rancis) 1928-

PERSONAL: Born March 13, 1928, in Wentworthville, New South Wales, Australia; son of Arthur Piercy and Nellie (Rogers) Brissenden; married Rosemary Groves, August 1, 1959; children: Michael, Venetia, Benedick. *Education:* University of Sydney, M.A., 1954; University of Leeds, Ph.D., 1957. *Home:* 1 Solander Ct., Yarralumla, Australian Capital Territory 2600, Australia.

CAREER: University of Melbourne, Melbourne, Victoria, Australia, senior tutor in English, 1951-52; Canberra University College (now Australian National University), Canberra, Australia, lecturer in English, 1953-54, 1957-59; Australian National University, senior lecturer in English, 1960-65, senior research fellow in the history of ideas, 1966-68, reader in English, 1969—. *Member:* Modern Humanities Research Association, Australian Universities Language and Literature Association, Australian and New Zealand American Studies Association (treasurer, 1964-66), Australian and Pacific Society for Eighteenth-Century Studies (president, 1970—), Australian Society of Authors.

WRITINGS: Samuel Richardson, Longmans, Green, 1958; (editor) *Southern Harvest: An Anthology of Australian Short Stories*, Macmillan, 1964; *Patrick White*, Longmans, Green, 1966; (editor) *Studies in the Eighteenth Century*, three volumes, Australian National University Press, 1968-76; *Winter Matins* (poems), Angus & Robertson, 1971; (editor) *Australian Poetry*, Angus & Robertson, 1972; *Elegies* (poems), Brindabella Press, 1974; *Virtue in Distress: Studies in the Novel of Sentiment from Richardson to Sade*, Macmillan, 1974; *Building a Terrace* (poems), Australian National University Press, 1975.

Contributor: Grahame Johnston, editor, *Australian Literary Criticism*, Oxford University Press, 1962; John Butt, editor, *Of Books and Humankind: Essays and Poems Presented to Bonamy Dobree*, Routledge & Kegan Paul, 1964; Arthur H. Cash and John M. Stedmond, editors, *The Winged Skull*, Kent State University Press, 1971; Harold E. Pagliaro, editor, *Studies in Eighteenth-Century Culture II*, Press of Case Western Reserve University, 1972; W. S. Ramson, editor, *The Australian Experience*, Australian National University Press, 1974; John Halperin, editor, *Jane Austen: Bicentenary Essays*, Cambridge University Press, 1975.

WORK IN PROGRESS: Editing Henry Fielding's *Joseph Andrews*, for Penguin; a monograph on A. D. Hope for Twayne.

* * *

BRISTOW, Allen P.   1929-

PERSONAL: Born July 11, 1929, in Kearney, Neb.; son of George P. and Mary (Nye) Bristow; married Patricia Ann DeWeber; children: Bradley, Scott, Teresa. *Education:* Los Angeles Valley College, A.A., 1952; Los Angeles State College (now California State University at Los Angeles), B.S., 1952; University of Southern California, M.S., 1957. *Home:* 1908 Dalton Rd., Palos Verdes Estates, Calif. 90274.

CAREER: San Fernando Police Department, San Fernando, Calif., policeman, 1952-53; Los Angeles County Sheriff's Department, Los Angeles, Calif., 1953-59, began as deputy, became sergeant; California State University at Los Angeles, 1959—, began as assistant professor, became professor of police science, 1967. Part-time or visiting professor at University of Hawaii, University of Southern California, Los Angeles Harbor College, and Orange Coast College. Developer and director of police training institutes, 1960—; consultant to President's Commission on Law Enforcement and Administration of Justice, 1966. *Military service:* U.S. Army, Corps of Military Police, 1950-51. *Member:* International Association of Polygraph Examiners (vice-president, 1962), Southern California Police Training Officers Association, California State Peace Officers Association.

WRITINGS: Police Decision Making, Donner Foundation, University of Southern California, 1957; *Field Interrogation*, C. C Thomas, 1958, 2nd edition, 1964; *Analysis of Chart and Graph Tests*, Davis Publishing (San Francisco), 1959.

(With E. Carol Gabard) *Decision Making in Police Administration*, C. C Thomas, 1961; (with G. Douglas Gourley) *Patrol Administration*, C. C Thomas, 1961; *Police Film Guide*, Police Research Associates, 1962, 2nd edition, 1968; (editor) *Readings in Police Supervision*, Los Angeles State College Foundation, 1963; (with John B. Williams) *Criminal Procedure and the Administration of Justice*, Police Research Associates, 1964, 2nd edition, Glencoe Press, 1966; *Effective Police Manpower Utilization*, C. C Thomas, 1969; (with Willis Roberts) *Introduction to Modern Police Firearms*, Glencoe Press, C. C Thomas, 1969.

Police Supervision, C. C Thomas, 1971; *Police Disaster Operations*, C. C Thomas, 1972; *Search for an Effective Police Handgun*, C. C Thomas, 1973. Contributor of more than thirty articles to law enforcement publications. Member of board of editors, *Police*, 1961-72.

WORK IN PROGRESS: The development of visual aids for police science curriculum; *Famous Western Manhunts*, completion expected in 1977.

AVOCATIONAL INTERESTS: Big game bow hunting and fishing.

* * *

BRITTEN AUSTIN, Paul   1922-

PERSONAL: Born April 5, 1922, in Dawlish, England; son of Frederick Britten (an author) and Mildred (King) Austin; married Margareta Bergman; children: Derek, Veronica, Thomas, Rose, Cecelia. *Education:* Attended University of Stockholm, 1955-56. *Religion:* Church of England. *Home:* Guestling, High St., Lindfield, Sussex, England. *Agent:* Mark Paterson, 42 Canonbury Sq., London N.1, England.

CAREER: Radio Sweden, Stockholm, director of English language broadcasts, 1948-57; Swedish National Travel Association, Stockholm, director, 1957-67; translator from Swedish into English, and author. Adviser on public relations, Swedish Tourist Traffic Association, Stockholm and London. *Wartime service:* British Merchant Navy, 1941-45.

WRITINGS: The Wonderful Life and Adventures of Tom Thumb: An English Fairy Tale, two volumes, Radiojanst Stockholm, 1952-53; *The Hen-Pecked Husband, and Other Punch-and-Judy Shows*, two volumes, Folkuniversitetets Forlag, 1956; (with Lorna Downman and Anthony Baird) *The Charm of Sweden*, Bokforlaget Fabel, 1956; (with Downman and Baird) *'Round the Swedish Year*, Bokforlaget Fabel, 1960; *Famous Swedes*, Bokforlaget Fabel, 1962; *The Life and Songs of Carl Michael Bellman, Genius of the Swedish Rococo*, Bokforlaget Allhems, 1967; *On Being Swedish: Reflections toward a Better Understanding of the Swedish Character*, Secker & Warburg, 1968, University of Miami Press, 1969; *Sweden* (travel guide), Collins, 1969; *The Swedes: How They Live and Work*, Praeger, 1970; *The Organ-Maker's Wife* (novel), Robruis Forlag, 1975.

Translator: Hjalmar Soederberg, *Doctor Glas*, Atlantic-Little, Brown, 1963; Carl Michael Bellman, *17 Songs*, Reuter & Reuter, 1965; Evert Taube, *I Come from a Raging Sea*, P. Owen and Council of Europe, 1967; Ingmar Bergman, *A Film Trilogy*, Calder & Boyars, 1967, Orion Press, 1968; Erik Asklund, *Stockholm: The City on the Water*, Norstedt, 1968; Maria Gripe, *Hugo and Josephine*, Delacorte, 1969; Gripe, *Hugo*, Delacorte, 1970; Gripe, *Josephine*, Delacorte, 1970; Jan Myrdal and Gun Kessle, *Gates to Asia*, Random House, 1971; Vilhelm Moberg, *A History of the Swedish People*, Volumes I and II, Pantheon, 1972; Stig Bjoerkman, Torsten Manns, and Jonas Sima, *Bergman on Bergman: Interviews with Ingmar Bergman*, Simon & Schuster, 1973; Uno Asplund, *Chaplin's Films*, David & Charles, 1973; *Modern Nordic Plays*, Universitetsforlaget, 1973; Gardar Sahlberg, *Murder at the Masked Ball: The Assassination of Gustaf III of Sweden*, Macdonalds, 1974; Sven Lindquist, *Land and Power in South America*, Penguin, in press.

SIDELIGHTS: Britten Austin is the brother-in-law of Ingmar Bergman, some of whose work he has translated. *Avocational interests:* History, psychology, literature, music.

* * *

BROADDUS, J(ohn) Morgan, Jr.   1929-

PERSONAL: Born August 4, 1929, in El Paso, Tex.; son

of John Morgan (a realtor) and Laura (Mishell) Broaddus; married Martha Lou Florence, January 27, 1962; children: Russell Ray, Randall Cole, Morgan III, Marla Diane. *Education:* Texas Western College (now University of Texas, El Paso), B.A., 1951, M.A., 1955; University of Texas, graduate courses, 1956-63. *Religion:* Episcopalian. *Home:* 6747 Fiesta, El Paso, Tex. 79912. *Office:* University of Texas, El Paso, Tex.

CAREER: University of Texas, El Paso, member of history faculty, 1954—. *Military service:* U.S. Army, 1951-53; became lieutenant. *Member:* Organization of American Historians, Organization of Western Historians, Texas State Historical Association, El Paso Historical Society.

WRITINGS: The Legal Heritage of El Paso, Texas Western Press, 1963.

* * *

BROCK, W(illiam) H(odson) 1936-

PERSONAL: Born December 15, 1936, in Brighton, England; son of William Heron (a publisher) and Phyllis (Hodson) Brock; married Elvina Hill, September 17, 1960; children: Gareth, Susannah, Benjamin. *Education:* University College, London, B.Sc., 1959; University of Leicester, M.Sc., 1961, Ph.D., 1966. *Religion:* Agnostic. *Office:* Victorian Studies Centre, University of Leicester, Leicester, England.

CAREER: University of Leicester, Leicester, England, reader in history of science, 1960—. *Member:* Chemical Society, British Society for the History of Science, Society for the History of Alchemy and Chemistry (council member, 1967—).

WRITINGS: (Editor and contributor) *The Atomic Debates,* Leicester University Press, 1967; (editor) *H. E. Armstrong and the Teaching of Science, 1880-1930,* Cambridge University Press, 1973. Editor of *Ambix,* 1969—. Contributor of historical papers to *Medical History, Isis, History of Science, Notes and Records of the Royal Society,* and other journals.

WORK IN PROGRESS: An edition of the journals of T. A. Hirst (1830-92), for publication by Mansell.

AVOCATIONAL INTERESTS: Walking, the theater.

* * *

BROCKBANK, Reed 1923-

PERSONAL: Born May 14, 1923, in Spanish Fork, Utah; son of Wallace W. (an educator) and Estella (Manwaring) Brockbank; married Elaine Stanford, January 2, 1946; children: Carolyn, Gregory, Douglas, Bradley. *Education:* Attended University of Dubuque, 1943-44; Brigham Young University, B.S., 1946; George Washington University, M.D., 1948; also studied at Washington School of Psychiatry, Washington, D.C., 1949-50, and Institute for Psychoanalysis, Chicago, Ill., 1957-63. *Home:* 109 Crown Rd., Kentfield, Calif. 94904.

CAREER: St. Elizabeth's Hospital, Washington, D.C., intern, later resident, 1948-50; U.S. Veterans Administration, resident at Downey Hospital, Downey, Ill., and regional office, Chicago, Ill., 1950-51; University of Chicago Clinics, Chicago, member of staff, 1951-52; private practice, Chicago, 1952-63, San Francisco, beginning 1963. Consultant to Illinois State Psychiatric Institute, Park Ridge School for Girls, 1957-63, and to Peace Corps and Bureau of Indian Affairs; adjunct in psychiatry, Michael

Reese Hospital, 1960-63. University of California, School of Medicine, San Francisco, clinical instructor in psychiatry, 1963, assistant clinical professor, 1966. Chairman of professional advisory committee, San Francisco Association for Mental Health. Diplomat, American Board of Psychiatry and Neurology. *Military service:* U.S. Navy, medical officer, 1954-56; became lieutenant. *Member:* American Psychiatric Association (fellow), San Francisco Psychoanalytic Society.

WRITINGS: (Editor with Dorothy Wesby Gibson, and contributor) *Mental Health in a Changing Community,* Grune & Stratton, 1966; (contributor) Jules Masserman, editor, *Current Psychiatric Therapies,* Grune & Stratton, 1966. Also contributor to *Archives of General Psychiatry,* 1968.††

* * *

BROCKWAY, Allan R(eitz) 1932-

PERSONAL: Born March 22, 1932, in Hutchinson, Kan.; son of H. Austin (associated with mutual funds) and Esther (Reitz) Brockway; married Martha Lou King, 1956; children: Paul Crane, Scot David, Dan Eliot, Benjamin Frost. *Education:* Hendrix College, B.A., 1954; Southern Methodist University, Perkins School of Theology, B.D., 1957; University of Chicago, M.A., 1963. *Politics:* Democrat. *Home:* 3 Park Valley Rd., Silver Spring, Md. 20910. *Office:* 100 Maryland Ave. N.E., Washington, D.C. 20002.

CAREER: Clergyman of the United Methodist Church. Pastor or educational assistant at churches in Morrilton, Ark., 1953-54, Dallas, Tex., 1954-56, and Bryan, Tex., 1956-57; West Texas State University, Canyon, director of Wesley Foundation, 1957-59; Christian Faith-and-Life Community, Austin, Tex., faculty member and editor, 1959-61; *Kiwanis Magazine,* Chicago, Ill., editorial assistant, 1962, assistant editor, 1963; *Concern* (periodical), published by United Methodist Board of Church and Society, Washington, D.C., managing editor, 1963-64, editor, 1965-68; *engage* (periodical), editor, 1968-72; *engage/social action* (periodical), editor, 1973—. Director, Faith and Culture Institute (an informal faculty of clergymen teaching contemporary theology courses to laymen and youth), 1964-69.

WRITINGS: The Secular Saint, Doubleday, 1968; *Uncertain Men and Certain Change,* Graded Press, 1970. Contributor to *Christian Century, Intercollegian,* and other periodicals.

WORK IN PROGRESS: Two books, tentatively titled *Creating the Will of God,* and *The Vintouts and their Faith;* editing a book, *Evangelism and Social Justice,* to be published by Tidings.

* * *

BRODERICK, Robert C(arlton) 1913-

PERSONAL: Born June 4, 1913, in North Fond du Lac, Wis.; son of Francis Martin (a railroad conductor) and Martha Agnes (Wheir) Broderick; married Virginia Joanne Gaertner (an artist), July 3, 1941. *Education:* St. Francis Seminary (now St. Francis Seminary School of Pastoral Ministry), Milwaukee, Wis., B.A., 1934, M.A., 1936. *Politics:* "Generally Republican." *Religion:* Roman Catholic. *Home and office:* 660 Parkmoor Dr., Brookfield, Wis. 53005.

CAREER: Bruce Publishing Co., Milwaukee, Wis., fiction editor, 1936-44; *Church Property Administration* (magazine), managing editor, 1945; free-lance writer, 1945—. Currently editorial director, Catholic Publishers, Nashville, Tenn.; adviser-consultant to Postal Church Service, Inc., Youngstown, Ohio. Member of lecture bureau, National Council of Catholic Men, 1936—; president of board of directors, Catholic Interracial Council, 1963-65.

WRITINGS: (With W. Campbell) *Knight of the North,* Bruce, 1943; *Catholic Concise Dictionary,* Bruce, 1944, 2nd revised edition, Franciscan Herald and Catholic Publishers, 1967; *Paul of St. Peter's* (juvenile), Bruce, 1947; *Wreath of Song* (fictional biography of Francis Thompson), Bruce, 1948; *Inside the Bible,* Catechetical Guild Press, 1955; *Catholic Concise Encyclopedia,* Catechetical Guild Press and Golden Books, 1957; *Catholic Layman's Book of Etiquette,* Catechetical Guild Press, 1957; *Historic Churches of the United States,* Funk, 1958; *Liturgical Renewal and Catholic Devotion,* Franciscan Herald and Catholic Publishers, 1966; *The Parish Council Handbook,* Franciscan Herald, 1968; *Encyclopedia Subject Index of the Bible,* Catholic Publishers, 1968; *Your Parish Comes Alive,* Franciscan Herald, 1970; *Your Parish: Where the Action Is,* Franciscan Herald, 1974. General editor, *Catholic Family Liturgical Bible,* Catholic Publishers, 1966—. Contributor to numerous church and general magazines.

WORK IN PROGRESS: Modern Catholic Encyclopedia and Religious Reference Book, and *Religious Landmarks and Art of the United States,* both for Thomas Nelson, Inc.

*   *   *

BROOKE-LITTLE, John   1927-

PERSONAL: Born April 6, 1927, in London, England; son of Raymond and Constance (Egan) Brooke-Little; married Mary Pierce, April 30, 1960; children: Philip James Raymond, Clare Julitta Mary, Leo John Vincent, Merlin Laurence Lee. *Education:* New College, Oxford, B.A., 1952, M.A. (honors in history), 1956. *Religion:* Roman Catholic. *Home:* Heyford House, Lower Heyford, Oxford, England. *Agent:* Curtis Brown Ltd., 1 Craven Hill, London W2 3EW, England. *Office:* College of Arms, Queen Victoria St., London E.C. 4, England.

CAREER: Duke of Norfolk's Coronation Staff, gold staff officer, 1952-54; *Dod's Peerage and Parliamentary Companion,* editor, 1955-58; Bluemantle pursuivant of arms, 1956-67; Tabard Publications Ltd., London, England, chairman of board, 1960; Richmond herald of arms, 1967—. Registrar of the College of Arms, 1974—; lecturer on heraldry, genealogy, and ceremonials in Britain and United States. Vice-president for Oxfordshire, St. John's Ambulance Brigade; chairman, Council of Clayesmore School, 1971. *Member:* Society of Antiquaries of London (fellow), Institute of Heraldic and Genealogical Studies (fellow), Heraldry Society (London; fellow; founding chairman, 1947—), British Association of Knights of Malta (chancellor, 1973—), Scriveners' Company of London (freeman and liveryman). *Awards, honors:* Knight of Malta, 1956; Commander, Order of S. Raimundo de Penafort (Spain), 1957; Julian Bickersteth Medal of Institute of Heraldic and Genealogical Studies, 1967; Grand Cross of Grace and Devotion, Knights of Malta, 1973; Knight, Order of St. John of Jerusalem, 1975.

WRITINGS: Royal London, Pitkin, 1953; *Oxford* (a guide), Pitkin, 1954; (editor and reviser with C. W. Scott-Giles) Charles Boutell, *Heraldry,* Warne, 1964, 2nd revised edition, 1973; *Knights of the Middle Ages,* Hugh Evelyn, 1966; (editor and reviser) Arthur C. Fox-Davis, *A Com-*

plete Guide to Heraldry, Nelson, 1969; *The Prince of Wales,* Giniger & Harrap, 1969; (with A. Taute and D. Pottinger) *The Kings and Queens of Great Britain,* Crown, 1970; *An Heraldic Alphabet,* Macdonald, 1973; *Heraldry,* Blackwell, 1975. Occasional contributor to journals and newspapers. Honorary editor, *Coat of Arms,* 1950—.

WORK IN PROGRESS: A book on royal arms, beasts and badges for Pilgrim Press, and one on kings and queens of Britain, for Blandford.

*   *   *

BROPHY, Donald F(rancis)   1934-

PERSONAL: Born April 13, 1934, in New York, N.Y.; son of Peter F. (an engineer) and Grace (Horgan) Brophy; married Patricia McNamara, July 20, 1968; children: Christopher, Kenneth. *Education:* University of Notre Dame, A.B. (English), 1956; St. Paul's College, Washington, D.C., A.B. (philosophy), 1964. *Office:* Paulist-Newman Press, 1865 Broadway, New York, N.Y. 10023.

CAREER: Reporter for *New Haven Journal-Courier,* New Haven, Conn., 1958-60, and National Catholic Welfare Conference, Washington, D.C., 1964-66; Paulist-Newman Press, New York, N.Y., associate editor, 1966—. Member of editorial board, *New Catholic World* (periodical), 1974—. *Military service:* U.S. Army, 1956-58.

WRITINGS: (Editor) *Science and Faith in the 21st Century,* Paulist Press, 1968; *American Bread,* Paulist Press, 1975.

*   *   *

BROTHERS, Joyce (Diane Bauer)   1929-

PERSONAL: Born October 20, 1929, in New York, N.Y.; daughter of Morris K. (an attorney) and Estelle (Rapaport) Bauer; married Milton Brothers (a physician), July 4, 1949; children: Lisa. *Education:* Cornell University, B.S., 1947; Columbia University, M.A., 1950, Ph.D., 1953. *Home:* 305 East 86th St., New York, N.Y. 10028. *Office:* National Broadcasting Co., 30 Rockefeller Plaza, New York, N.Y.

CAREER: Psychologist. Hunter College (now Hunter College of the City University of New York), New York City, teaching fellow, 1948-50, instructor, 1950-52; American Association of University Women research fellow, 1952-53; conducted own television programs, "Dr. Joyce Brothers," National Broadcasting Co., 1958-63, "Consult Dr. Joyce Brothers," American Broadcasting Co., 1961-66, "Tell Me Dr. Brothers," syndicated by Triangle Films, 1964-70, and other syndicated programs, 1972—; broadcaster of own radio programs on NBC and ABC, 1966-69. UNESCO researcher, 1949. Consultant to Armstrong Cork Co., 1974—. Member of People to People Program; member of fundraising committee for Olympic Fund; co-chairman of sports committee for Lighthouse for the Blind; member of Jewish Federation of Philantropies. *Member:* Sigma Xi.

AWARDS, HONORS: Mennen Baby Foundation award, 1959; Newhouse Newspaper award, 1959; American Academy of Achievement award; Justice Lodge citation, 1963, for unselfish devotion and inspired leadership and service to community; named Woman of Achievement by Federation of Jewish Women's Organizations, 1964; Merit Award from Bar-Ilan University, 1968; L.H.D., Franklin Pierce College, 1969; award from Parkinson Disease Foundation, 1971; Sigma Delta Chi award, 1971, for excellence in broadcasting radio news; Touchdown Club award for general accomplishments for women.

WRITINGS: Ten Days to a Successful Memory, Prentice-Hall, 1959; *Woman,* Doubleday, 1961; *The Brothers System for Liberated Love and Marriage,* Peter H. Wyden, 1974. Columnist for North American Newspaper Alliance, 1961-72, Bell-McClure Syndicate, 1963-71, *Good Housekeeping,* 1963—, and King Features Syndicate, 1972—.

WORK IN PROGRESS: Better than Ever, for Simon & Schuster.

SIDELIGHTS: Mrs. Brothers, who holds a doctorate in psychology, first came to the attention of the public in 1955 because of her knowledge of boxing. To raise money to help her husband start his medical practice, she amassed $134,000 on the "$64,000 Question" and "Challenge" television programs. Three years later she had her own television show and became, she said, "a kind of middle-man between the viewer and psychological literature."

* * *

BROUGHTON, Bradford B. 1926-

PERSONAL: Born February 6, 1926, in Allentown, Pa.; son of Harold Earle (a chemical engineer) and Margaret (Browne) Broughton; married June Barnum, October 7, 1950; children: Megan, Thaddeus. *Education:* Allegheny College, B.A., 1947; University of Pennsylvania, M.A., 1949, Ph.D., 1961. *Home:* 4 Leroy St., Potsdam, N.Y. 13676. *Office:* Clarkson College of Technology, Potsdam, N.Y. 13676.

CAREER: Syracuse University, Utica College, Utica, N.Y., instructor in English, 1949-50; Clarkson College of Technology, Potsdam, N.Y., instructor, 1955-57, assistant professor, 1957-61, associate professor of liberal studies, 1961-66, professor of humanities, 1966—, chairman of department, 1973—. *Military service:* U.S. Navy, 1944-46, 1950-52; became lieutenant. *Member:* Modern Language Association of America; International Arthurian Society; Societe Rencesvals. `

WRITINGS: (Editor and translator) *Richard the Lion Hearted and Other Medieval English Romances,* Dutton, 1966; *The Legends of King Richard I, Coeur de Lion* (a study), Mouton & Co., 1966; (editor) *Twenty-seven to One: Festschrift for D. G. Stillman,* Clarkson College of Technology Press, 1970.

WORK IN PROGRESS: Charlemagne as Figure in Medieval Poetry; Handbook of Medieval Knighthood.

* * *

BROW, Robert 1924-

PERSONAL: Born August 30, 1924; son of David Barrington (an engineer) and Ann (Franchomme) Brow; married Mollie Tarrant (a nurse), December 22, 1953; children: Rachel, Peter, Timothy, Susanne. *Education:* Cambridge University, B.A. (Trinity College), 1950, M.A., 1955; University of London, B.D., 1952; Princeton Theological Seminary, M.Th., 1958; further graduate study at University of Toronto. *Home:* 57 Fairfield Rd., Toronto, Ontario, Canada.

CAREER: Anglican missionary in India, 1952-63; currently associate rector of Little Trinity Church, Toronto, Ontario. *Military service:* Indian Army, 1942-47; became captain.

WRITINGS: Religion: Origins and Ideas, Inter-Varsity, 1966; *The Church: An Organic Picture of Its Life and Mission,* Eerdmans, 1968. Also author of *Indiscriminate Baptism,* 1975.

SIDELIGHTS: Robert Brow is competent in French and Hindi; reads Latin, Greek, and classical Hebrew. Brow originally intended to specialize in economics (at Cambridge), then moved on to theology, comparative religion, and philosophy.

* * *

BROWN, Bob Burton 1925-

PERSONAL: Born February 19, 1925, in Nemaha, Neb.; son of George V. (a storekeeper and farmer) and Iva Brown; married Evelyn L. Rodgers, July 5, 1944; children: Tandel, Michel, Deborah, Scott. *Education:* Attended Peru State College, 1946-48; Kearney State College, B.A., 1952; Northwestern University, M.A., 1957; University of Wisconsin, Ph.D., 1962. *Office:* University of Florida, Gainesville, Fla. 32601.

CAREER: Elementary teacher in Nebraska and Illinois, 1948-55; elementary principal in Palatine, Ill., and later Glenview, Ill., 1955-59; University of Wisconsin, Madison, assistant to the dean, 1959-62, assistant professor of education and assistant dean of the School of Education, 1962-65; University of Florida, Gainesville, associate professor, 1965-68, professor of education, 1968—, dean of University College, 1972—. *Member:* National Education Association, American Educational Research Association, Association for Supervision and Curriculum Development, National Society of Professors of Education, John Dewey Society.

WRITINGS: The Experimental Mind in Education, Harper, 1968; (contributor) Anita Simon and E. Gil Boyer, editors, *Mirrors for Behavior: An Anthology of Observation Instruments,* Volume VIII, Research for Better Schools, Inc., 1970. Contributor of more than thirty articles to education journals.

WORK IN PROGRESS: A book, with Jeaninne N. Webb, *Teacher Watching: The Analysis of Teaching,* for Harper.

* * *

BROWN, Charles H. 1910-

PERSONAL: Born February 20, 1910, in Ochelata, Okla., son of Herman S. and Jennie (Jackenheimer) Brown. *Education:* Student at University of Missouri, 1929-30, and University of Tulsa, 1930-31; University of Oklahoma, B.A., 1932, M.A., 1933. *Residence:* Norman, Okla.

CAREER: Member of editorial staff of newspapers in Pawhuska, Okla., 1927-28, Perry, Okla., 1934, and Oklahoma City, Okla., 1935; University of Oklahoma, Norman, assistant professor of journalism, 1935-46; Pennsylvania State University, University Park, professor of journalism, 1947-72; professor emeritus, 1972—. *Military service:* U.S. Naval Reserve, 1943-46. *Member:* Association for Education in Journalism, Kappa Delta Tau. *Awards, honors: William Cullen Bryant* was listed as a Notable Book by the American Library Association and received the Frank Luther Mott—Kappa Tau Alpha Research Award for best research book in the field of journalism, both in 1971.

WRITINGS: (With J. J. Rubin) *Walt Whitman of the New York Aurora,* Bald Eagle, 1950; *News Editing and Display,* Harper, 1952; *Informing the People,* Holt, 1958; (editor with others) *The Mass Media,* Center for Continuing Education, Pennsylvania State University, 1961; *The Correspondents' War: Journalists in the Spanish-American War,* Scribner, 1967; *William Cullen Bryant: A Biography* (History Book Club alternate selection), Scribner, 1971. Contributor to journalism periodicals.

WORK IN PROGRESS: Agents of Manifest Destiny: Filibusterism in the 1850's, and a biography of Charles Anderson Dana.

*   *   *

BROWN, Evelyn M.   1911-

PERSONAL: Born March 15, 1911, in Vancouver, British Columbia, Canada; daughter of Henry Frederick (a professional engineer) and Martha (Gowan) Brown. *Education:* Attended University of British Columbia, 1927-28, Vancouver Normal School, 1928-29, Alliance Francaise, Paris, France, 1932, and Wheaton College, Wheaton, Ill., 1933-34. *Home:* 1260 Place Merici, Quebec City, Quebec, Canada.

CAREER: Teacher in private schools in British Columbia, Vancouver, 1929-31, New Westminster, 1934-35, and Victoria, 1942-45; grade school teacher, specializing in French, in British government school, Nairobi, Kenya, 1935-40; Quebec Department of Education, Quebec City, secretary and translator, 1946-65; writer and translator.

WRITINGS: Educating Eve, Palm Publishers, 1957; *Kateri Tekakwitha, Mohawk Maid,* Farrar, Straus, 1958; (translator) Alain Grandhois, *Ne a Quebec,* Palm Publishers, 1964; *Edel Quinn, Beneath the Southern Cross,* Farrar, Straus, 1967; (translator from the French) Gabrielle Bossis, *He and I,* Editions Paulines, Volume I, 1969, Volume II, 1970. Contributor to *Chambers's Journal, Catholic Digest, Ave Maria, Field,* and other publications.

*   *   *

BROWN, George Mackay   1921-

PERSONAL: Born October 17, 1921, in Stromness, Orkney Islands, Scotland; son of John and Mary Jane (Mackay) Brown, *Education:* Attended Newbattle Abbey College, 1951-53 and 1956; University of Edinburgh, M.A., 1960, graduate work on the poetry of Gerard Manley Hopkins, 1962-64. *Home:* 3, Mayburn Court, Stromness, Orkney Islands, Scotland.

CAREER: Poet and author. *Awards, honors:* Arts Council of Great Britain award for poetry, 1965; Society of Authors Travel Award, 1967; Scottish Arts Council award and Katherine Mansfield Menton short story prize, both 1969, for *A Time to Keep;* officer, Order of the British Empire, 1974.

WRITINGS: The Storm, and Other Poems, Orkney Press, 1954; *Loaves and Fishes* (poetry), Hogarth, 1959; *The Year of the Whale* (poetry), Hogarth, 1965.

The Five Voyages of Arnor (poetry), K. D. Duval, 1966; *A Spell For Green Corn* (play; broadcast, 1967; adaptation produced at Perth Theatre, March, 1972), Hogarth, 1970; *A Calendar of Love* (stories), Hogarth, 1967, Harcourt, 1968; *A Time to Keep and Other Stories,* Hogarth, 1969, Harcourt, 1970; *An Orkney Tapestry* (essays), Gollancz, 1969.

Poems New and Selected, Hogarth, 1971, Harcourt, 1973; *Fishermen with Ploughs* (poems), Hogarth, 1971; *Greenvoe* (novel), Harcourt, 1972; *Magnus* (novel), Hogarth, 1973; *The Two Fiddlers* (stories), Hogarth, 1974; *Hawkfall* (stories), Hogarth, 1974; *Letters from Hamnavoe* (selected journalism), Reprographia Press, in press; *Winterfold* (poems), Hogarth, in press; *Pictures in the Cave* (children's stories), Hogarth, in press; *A Winter Tale* (stories), Hogarth, in press. Also writer of television poem, "The Winter Islands," broadcast 1966.

SIDELIGHTS: The *Times Literary Supplement* reviewer wrote that, in *A Calendar of Love,* Brown, "at his best, . . . can produce pleasant light character sketches, or acceptable Quiller-Couch-ish fables. At his worst," says this reviewer, "he crosses [something like] *Riders to the Sea* with *Our Town;* . . . Some of his literary echoes . . . are unhappy. But his bold, clean narrative line is a strength and there are enjoyable incidentals." Hilary Corke was much more impressed, calling the book "one of the few really solid achievements of the year, . . . poem-narratives in prose. . . . But not poetical prose in the commonly accepted mode of awash-with-rich-lush. These tales, or evocations, all set in the Orkneys, make their points with a spare beautiful accuracy that echoes the emotive landscape of these islands, linear not fuzzy, exact forms of cliff, hill-heave, peat-bog skyline, sudden surprising golden sands, the halcyon or leaden or orphic sea, and never a tree except for rare hull-down outbursts in sheltering clefts; and a strange boreal light overall. Subjects of all times, all sorts. . . . To enter [this] world is like finding oneself at last on a moorland after months in cities or home counties; one is almost deafened by the wonderful silence." Brown writes to *CA:* "Since it seems to me that our civilization will possibly destroy itself before too long, I am interested in the labour and lives of the most primitive people of our civilization, the food-getters (crofters and fishermen) since it is those people living close to the sources of life who are most likely to survive and continue the human story; and since even their lives would be meaningless otherwise, I see religion as the great illuminating and stabilising force in the life of a community. Out of these things I make my poems, stories, and plays."

BIOGRAPHICAL/CRITICAL SOURCES: Times Literary Supplement, February 16, 1967; *Listener,* April 17, 1967; Carolyn Riley, editor, *Contemporary Literary Criticism,* Volume 5, Gale, 1976.

*   *   *

BROWN, John Russell   1923-

PERSONAL: Born September 15, 1923, in Bristol, England; son of Russell Alan (a butcher) and Olive Helen (Golding) Brown; married Hilary Sue Baker (a potter), April, 1961; children: Alice Amelia, Sophia Clemence, Jasper James Mallord. *Education:* Keble College, Oxford, B.A., 1949, B.Litt., 1952; University of Birmingham, Ph.D., 1960. *Office:* Arts Building, University of Sussex, Falmer, Brighton, Sussex, England; and National Theatre, South Bank, London SE1, England.

CAREER: University of Birmingham, Birmingham, England, lecturer, then senior lecturer in English literature, 1955-63; professor of drama and theater arts and head of department, 1963-71; University of Sussex, Falmer, Brighton, Sussex, England, professor of English, 1971—. Reynolds Lecturer, University of Colorado, 1957; fellow, Folger Library, Washington, D.C., 1957, 1963; Mellon Professor of Drama, Carnegie Institute (now Carnegie-Mellon University), 1964; visiting professor, University of Zurich, Switzerland, 1970-71; University Lecturer, University of Toronto, 1971. Director, Orbit Theatre Company, 1971—; associate director, National Theatre, 1973—. *Military service:* Royal Navy, 1942-46; became sub-lieutenant.

WRITINGS: (Editor) Shakespeare, *The Merchant of Venice,* Methuen, 1955; *Shakespeare and His Comedies,* Methuen, 1957, 2nd edition, Barnes & Noble, 1962; (editor) John Webster, *The White Devil,* Methuen, 1960; *Shakespeare:*

The Tragedy of Macbeth, Edward Arnold, 1963; (editor) John Webster, *The Duchess of Malfi,* Methuen, 1965; (editor) Shakespeare, *Henry V,* New American Library, 1965; *Shakespeare's Plays in Performance,* Edward Arnold, 1966, St. Martin's, 1967; *Effective Theatre,* Heinemann, 1969; *Shakespeare's Romantic Style,* Heinemann, 1970; *Theatre Language,* Allen Lane, 1972; *Free Shakespeare,* Heinemann, 1974; *Shakespeare in Performance: An Introduction through Six Major Plays,* Harcourt, 1976. General editor, "Stratford-upon-Avon Studies" and "Stratford-upon-Avon Library."

WORK IN PROGRESS: A Short History of British Drama.

*   *   *

BROWN, Marshall L. 1924-

PERSONAL: Born February 8, 1924, in Farmington, N.H.; son of Ira Sumner (a factory foreman) and Mildred (Knox) Brown; married Winifred Morrison, June 2, 1946; children: Marshall L., Jr., Richard A., Catherine L. *Education:* University of New Hampshire, B.A., 1949; Harvard University, M.A., 1951. *Home:* 450 Liberty St., Culver, Ind. 46511.

CAREER: Culver Academies, Culver, Ind., instructor in English, 1954—, chairman of department, 1975—, holder of Carter Chair in English, 1975—. Researcher on textbook materials, Indiana University, English Curriculum Study Center, 1966-67. *Military service:* U.S. Army Air Forces, bombardier-navigator, 1943-46; became first lieutenant.

WRITINGS: (With Elmer White and Edward Jenkinson) *Two Approaches to Teaching Syntax,* Indiana University Press, 1967; (with White) *A Grammar for English Sentences,* Books I-II, C. E. Merrill, 1968; *Language: The Origins of English,* C. E. Merrill, 1971.

WORK IN PROGRESS: A series of language study-composition books based on professional writings.

*   *   *

BROWN, Norman O(liver) 1913-

PERSONAL: Born September 25, 1913, in El Oro, Mexico; son of Norman C. (a mining engineer) and Marcarita Brown; married Elizabeth Potter, October 1, 1938; children: Stephen R., Thomas N., Rebecca M., Susan E. *Education:* Balliol College, Oxford, B.A., 1936; attended University of Chicago; University of Wisconsin, Ph.D., 1942. *Office:* Department of Humanities, Cowell College, University of California, Santa Cruz, Calif. 95060.

CAREER: Nebraska Wesleyan University, Lincoln, professor of languages, 1942-43; Wesleyan University, Middletown, Conn., 1946-68, began as assistant professor of classics, became J. A. Seney Professor of Greek; former Wilson Professor of Classics and Comparative Literature, University of Rochester, Rochester, N.Y.; University of California, Santa Cruz, 1971—, member of humanities faculty. *Military service:* Office of Strategic Services, 1943-46. *Member:* American Philological Association. *Awards, honors:* Commonwealth Fund fellow, 1936-38; Ford Foundation teaching fellow, 1953-54; Guggenheim fellow, 1958-59.

WRITINGS: Hermes the Thief: The Evolution of a Myth, University of Wisconsin Press, 1947; (translator and author of introduction) Hesiod, *Theogony,* Liberal Arts Press, 1953; *Life Against Death: The Psychoanalytical Meaning of History,* Wesleyan University Press, 1959; *Love's Body,* Random House, 1966; *Closing Time,* Random House, 1973.

SIDELIGHTS: Brown (like Ayn Rand and Marshall McLuhan) appeals especially to students. Though each has a different point of view on varying topics, it is particularly understandable why this appeal exists, especially in the case of Brown. Each in his own way represents a reaction against traditional patterns and values of life, Phyllis Grosskurth points out; in particular, as Brown states clearly in his introduction to *Life Against Death:* "This book is addressed to all who are ready to call into question old assumptions and to entertain new possibilities." In both *Life Against Death* and *Love's Body,* Brown achieves exactly what he has said he wants to do, "open up a new point of view."

Brown strongly believes that with the repression of sexuality comes death and destruction, individual and collective. He attempts to understand history through psychoanalysis, namely, that just as Freud saw it, mankind must be viewed as largely unaware of its own desires, hostile to life, and unconsciously bent on self-destruction. Essentially, it appears that Brown is connecting ideas that have never been connected before, and, therefore, may seem "mad," especially to his fellow scholars. Christopher Hill claims that, although at times Brown has no very clear counsel to give us, his diagnosis is "provocative and disturbing. His refusal to accept defeat is exhilarating. . . ." *Life Against Death* is an analysis of the disease called man. Brown has concluded, states Grosskurth, that society is suffering from a general neurosis. Brown "defines man as the 'animal which represses himself.' Because man has preferred death to life, repression rather than liberation, the society he has created for himself is one of insatiable discontent, in which all his instincts have been perverted into a greedy, acquisitive money system. . . . Man has convinced himself that sublimation has been a conquest of the lower instincts whereas in reality, progressively greater sublimation has meant that the death-instinct has gained."

In a sense, too, Brown is a symbolist poet. Analogies, correspondences, metaphors, these reinforce his vision of the universe whose basic substance is sexuality. He quotes frequently from Blake (one reviewer remarked, "It is a considerable accomplishment to make Freud into a romantic"). In *Love's Body,* there is a beautiful section on "Fire." Here, according to J. M. Cameron, "he takes themes out of the whole range of world literature and is able to bring them to a point where the title of James Baldwin's book *The Fire Next Time* can be associated without incongruity with a variety of references to fire. . . ." In *Love's Body* Brown expresses the belief that systematic thought condemns us to death, and he again carries the Freudian theme through his analysis.

Critics don't quite know how to approach Brown, for as E. Z. Friedenberg puts it, "it is difficult to argue with Brown . . . even when one feels strongly that he is wrong." If we listen to Brown we hear him advocating the complete abolition of 20th-century civilization, *Time* perceives, though Brown is actually giving us more possibilities for our future than at first appears. He believes that if all trappings of civilization were put aside all repressions would go with them. He wants us to attain uninhibited, innocent sexuality rather than playing everything for the "money game." The great virtue of *Love's Body,* Cameron declares, is the way in which "it brings home to us the ambiguities and self-deceptions that may underlie our fits of moralism and righteous indignation." Both "strange" books may be better understood in the light of Brown's phrase in *Love's Body:* "Wisdom is in wit, in fooling, most excellent fooling; in play, and not in heavy puritanical seriousness."

BIOGRAPHICAL/CRITICAL SOURCES: *Spectator,* December 4, 1959; *Book Week,* July 10, 1966; *Time,* July 15, 1966; *New York Review of Books,* May 4, 1967; *Shenandoah,* summer, 1967; *Saturday Night,* July, 1967; *TriQuarterly,* No. 12, spring, 1968.†

* * *

BROWN, Peter (Robert Lamont)   1935-

PERSONAL: Born July 26, 1935, in Dublin, Ireland; son of James Lamont (an engineer) and Sheila (Warren) Brown. *Education:* Attended New College, Oxford, 1953-56. *Home:* Hillslope, Pullens Lane, Headington, Oxford, England.

CAREER: Oxford University, All Souls College, Oxford, England, fellow, 1956, lecturer and tutor, faculties of ancient and modern history, beginning in 1956; currently professor of history, Royal Holloway College, Egham, Surrey, England. *Member:* Historical Association, Society for the Promotion of Roman Studies, Etudes augustiniennes (Paris), Royal Historical Society, British Academy (fellow).

WRITINGS: (Contributor) Beryl Smalley, editor, *Trends in Medieval Political Thought,* Barnes & Noble, 1965; *Augustine of Hippo: A Biography,* University of California Press, 1967; (translator with Friedl Brown) Frederic van der Meer, *Early Christian Art,* Faber, 1967, University of Chicago Press, 1968; *The World of Late Antiquity,* Harcourt, 1971; *Religion and Society in the Age of St. Augustine,* Harper, 1972. Contributor to *Concise Encyclopedia of World History* and to journals.

WORK IN PROGRESS: Work on the social and religious consequences of the rise of Christianity in the Roman Empire.

SIDELIGHTS: J. M. Cameron has remarked that *Augustine of Hippo* "is a great work, likely to be esteemed a classic, and very remarkable as coming from so young a scholar. It is an intellectual biography, a portrait in depth of the man, and a brilliant study of the period." Robert L. Wilken finds remarkable "[Brown's] incredible familiarity with the declining Roman world and his uncanny accuracy in the smallest details." He also admires him for showing Augustine as a human being, because this enables us to "place ourselves in Augustine's age."

Philip Toynbee, in reviewing *The World of Late Antiquity,* describes Brown as "an exuberant historian, who brings to his period the benefits of a rich imagination," but who also has moments of writing "too flamboyantly."

Brown is fluent in French, Italian, and German, and competent in classical and modern Greek, Latin, Hebrew, Syrian, Persian, Serbo-Croat, Czech, Russian, and Spanish.

AVOCATIONAL INTERESTS: Travel, gardens, fairy tales, the education of children.

BIOGRAPHICAL/CRITICAL SOURCES: *Christian Century,* July 17, 1968; *The New York Review of Books,* August 1, 1968.

* * *

BROWN, Robert L.   1921-

PERSONAL: Born October 12, 1921, in Belfast, Me.; son of Seth C. (a sea captain) and Ardria (Sanborn) Brown; married Evelyn McCall, August 18, 1945; children: Diana Jean, Marshall Alan. *Education:* University of Denver, B.A., 1948, M.A., 1951. *Politics:* Republican. *Religion:* Protestant. *Home:* 3100 South Lowell Blvd., Denver, Colo. 80236.

CAREER: University of Denver, Denver, Colo., instructor in education, 1948-51; School District I, Denver, Colo., teacher of western history, 1953—. Part-time teacher of history, Regis College, Denver, Colo., 1955-65; teacher of history at Denver Center of the University of Colorado evening school. *Military service:* U.S. Army Air Forces, aerial photographer, World War II; served with 15th Air Force in Europe. *Member:* Westerners (deputy sheriff, Denver Posse, 1969), State Historical Society of Colorado, Colorado Mountain Club, Colorado Authors League, Western Writers of America, Ghost Town Club of Colorado.

WRITINGS: *Jeep Trails to Colorado Ghost Towns,* Caxton, 1963; *An Empire of Silver,* Caxton, 1965; *Ghost Towns of the Colorado Rockies,* Caxton, 1968; *Holy Cross: The Mountain and the City,* Caxton, 1970; *Colorado Ghost Towns: Past and Present,* Caxton, 1972.

WORK IN PROGRESS: A book on mountain climbing.

AVOCATIONAL INTERESTS: Mountain climbing, wood carving, photography, collecting "short beer" checks.

* * *

BROWN, Stuart Gerry   1912-

PERSONAL: Born April 13, 1912, in Buffalo, N.Y.; son of Charles H., Jr. and Edith (Warner) Brown; married Katharine DuB. Franchet, September 15, 1934 (divorced, 1940); married Mildred Geneva Kraus, August 22, 1941; children: (first marriage) Antoinette; (second marriage) Thomas Stuart, Stuart Gerry, Jr. *Education:* Amherst College, A.B., 1934; Princeton University, Ph.D., 1937. *Politics:* Democrat. *Home:* 4706 Kahala Ave., Honolulu, Hawaii 96816.

CAREER: University of Wisconsin, Madison, instructor in English, 1937-40; Grinnell College, Grinnell, Iowa, associate professor of English, 1940-43, professor of English and philosophy, 1943-47; Syracuse University, Syracuse, N.Y., professor of citizenship and American culture, 1947-58, Maxwell Professor of American Civilization, 1958-65; University of Hawaii, Honolulu, visiting professor, 1961-62, 1964-65, professor of American studies, 1965—. Visiting professor, Australian National University, Royal Military College, 1971. *Member:* American Studies Association (member of executive council, 1950-54). *Awards, honors:* Grants from Rockefeller Foundation, American Philosophical Society, Alfred P. Sloan Foundation, and Chinn Ho Foundation.

WRITINGS: *The First Republicans,* Syracuse University Press, 1954; (with C. Peltier) *Government in Our Republic,* Macmillan, 1960, 4th edition, 1971; *Memo for Overseas Americans,* Syracuse University Press, 1960; *Conscience in Politics,* Syracuse University Press, 1961; *Jefferson,* Washington Square Press, 1964; *Adlai E. Stevenson,* Woodbury Press, 1965; *The American Presidency,* Macmillan, 1966; *Hamilton,* Washington Square Press, 1967; (with W. Fiser and J. Gibson) *Government in the United States,* Ronald, 1967; *The Presidency on Trial,* University Press of Hawaii, 1972; (with R. Farmer) *Government: The American System,* Macmillan, 1973.

Editor: (With Wallace Stegner and Claude Simpson) *An Exposition Workshop*, Little, Brown, 1939; (with Wright Thomas) *Reading Poems*, Oxford University Press, 1941; *We Hold These Truths*, Harper, 1941, 2nd edition, 1948; *Great Issues*, Harper, 1948; *The Social Philosophy of Josiah Royce*, Syracuse University Press, 1950; (with Thomas) *Reading Prose*, Oxford University Press, 1952; *The Religious Philosophy of Josiah Royce*, Syracuse University Press, 1952; *The Autobiography of James Monroe*, Syracuse University Press, 1959; (with H. Bragdon and S. McCutchen) *Frame of Government*, Macmillan, 1962; *Process of Government*, Macmillan, 1963; *Revolution, Confederation, and Constitution*, Appleton, 1971. Contributor of articles and reviews to professional journals. Politics editor, *Encyclopedia International*, 1962-64.

WORK IN PROGRESS: Oral History of Hawaii, 1945-1975.

SIDELIGHTS: Brown has traveled extensively in the Pacific and Southeast Asia in connection with the Peace Corps and Agency for International Development training programs.

* * *

BROWNE, Courtney 1915-

PERSONAL: Born February 3, 1915, in London, England; son of David Stanley and Elizabeth (Pethers) Browne; married Sakaye Tamoto, June 29, 1952; children: Sandra. *Education:* Attended schools in England, 1920-31. *Residence:* Vancouver, British Columbia, Canada. *Agent:* Laurence Pollinger Ltd., 18 Maddox St., London W.1, England.

CAREER: Free-lance writer, 1931-39; worked during occasional leaner periods as a musician and innkeeper; after service with British Commonwealth Occupation Force in Japan, remained in Japan as a civilian, 1949-58, working as a journalist and foreign correspondent; worked as script writer, researcher, producer, and as an executive for major television documentaries for Rediffusion Television (now Thames Television Ltd.), London, England, 1958-74; currently living in Canada. *Military service:* British and Indian Armies, 1939-49, served in India, China, and Burma; became major. *Member:* Royal Institute for International Affairs, Japan Society of London, Society of Authors. *Awards, honors:* Emmy Award for Outstanding Documentary Program Achievements, 1974, for "World at War."

WRITINGS: The Taipan and the Pillow Book, Tuttle, 1956; *The Ancient Pond*, Harper, 1967; *Tojo: The Last Banzai*, Holt, 1967; *The Tomorrow Jade*, R. Hale, 1968; *The Sadist Hunters*, New English Library, 1969; *The Photographer*, New English Library, 1970. Author of television and radio scripts including, with Carol Doncaster, the television documentary "The Unwanted," produced for World Refuge Year, and (co-writer) "World at War" documentary series. Contributor to periodicals.

WORK IN PROGRESS: A novel and a nonfiction book, both with Far East backgrounds.

SIDELIGHTS: Brown has visited twenty-one countries in the course of television and writing work. He speaks French as well as Japanese.

* * *

BROWNE, G(erald) P(eter) 1930-

PERSONAL: Born October 12, 1930, in Vancouver, British Columbia, Canada; son of Charles Gerald and Naomi (Hodson) Browne. *Education:* University of British Columbia, B.A., 1951, M.A., 1953. Oxford University, B.A., 1958, M.A., 1961, D.Phil., 1963. *Office:* Department of History, Carleton University, Ottawa, Ontario, Canada.

CAREER: Oxford University, Oxford, England, tutor in modern history, 1959-63; University of Wisconsin, Madison, assistant professor of history, 1963-66; Carleton University, Ottawa, Ontario, assistant professor, 1966-67, associate professor, 1967-75, professor of history, 1975—. *Military service:* Lieutenant in Supplementary Reserve. *Member:* Royal Commonwealth Society, United Oxford and Cambridge University Club. *Awards, honors:* Social Science Research Council publication subsidy, 1966; Canada Council post-doctoral fellowship, 1968, research grant, 1970, and leave fellowship, 1972.

WRITINGS: The Judicial Committee and the British North America Act, Volume I, University of Toronto Press, 1967; *Documents on the Confederation of British North America*, McClelland & Stewart, 1969. Contributor to *Dictionary of Canadian Biography*, Volume II.

WORK IN PROGRESS: Contributions to *Dictionary of Canadian Biography*, Volumes IV and V.

* * *

BROWNELL, John Arnold 1924-

PERSONAL: Born September 26, 1924, in Whittier, Calif.; son of Benjamin Edward (a banker) and Anna (Arnold) Brownell; married Rena Topping, February 28, 1946; children: Ann Elizabeth, William Allan, Robert Benjamin. *Education:* Whittier College, B.A., 1947, M.A., 1948; Stanford University, Ed.D., 1952. *Religion:* Protestant. *Home:* 5243 Poola St., Honolulu, Hawaii 96821.

CAREER: Teacher in Honolulu, Hawaii, 1948-50, Whittier, Calif., 1951-54; California State College (now University) at Long Beach, instructor, 1954-55, assistant professor of education, 1955-58; Claremont Graduate School, Claremont, Calif., assistant professor, 1958-59, associate professor, 1959-64, professor of education, 1965-66; University of Hawaii, Honolulu, professor of education, researcher at Education Research and Development Center, and director of Hawaii Curriculum Center, 1966-68; East West Center, Honolulu, deputy chancellor for academic affairs, 1968-75, vice-president for academic affairs, 1975—. Visiting professor, International Christian University, Graduate School of Education, Tokyo, Japan, 1964-65; visiting lecturer, Keisatsu Daigaku, Tokyo.

MEMBER: American Educational Research Association, National Council of Teachers of English (board member, 1960-64), National Conference on Research in English, American Association of University Professors, Phi Delta Kappa. *Awards, honors:* Harold Benjamin fellowship in international education (in Japan), granted by Kappa Delta Pi, 1964-65; Phi Delta Kappa International Education Research grant, 1967-68.

WRITINGS: Claremont Teaching Team Program, Claremont Graduate School, 1961; (editor) *A Sequential Course of Study in English: Grades 7-12*, Palm Springs (Calif.) Unified School District, 1962; (with Arthur R. King, Jr.) *The Curriculum and the Disciplines of Knowledge*, Wiley, 1966; *Feasibility Study for a Pacific Region Educational Laboratory*, U.S. Office of Education, 1966; *Japan's Second Language: A Critical Analysis of the English Language Program in the Japanese Secondary Schools in the 1960's*, National Council of Teachers of English, 1967; *Directory of Selected Resources for the Study of English in*

Japan, University Press of Hawaii, in press. Co-author of various study reports for California school districts.

Contributor to *Times Educational Supplement* (London), and educational journals in Japan and United States. Editor of publications, Claremont Teaching Team Program (Ford Foundation project), 1958-64.

* * *

BRUBAKER, Sterling 1924-

PERSONAL: Born September 26, 1924, in Conway Springs, Kan.; son of Jacob Otis and Grace (Foote) Brubaker; married Jutta Bothe, August 5, 1950; children: Nils C., Tina K., Wendy A., Joel M., Philip L., Seth J., Kate L. *Education:* University of California, Berkeley, A.B., 1947, Ph.D., 1959; Sorbonne, University of Paris, graduate study, 1947-48. *Home:* 11408 Rokeby Ave., Garrett Park, Md. 20766. *Office:* Resources for the Future, Inc., 1755 Massachusetts Ave. N.W., Washington, D.C. 20036.

CAREER: Bank of America, San Francisco, Calif., research analyst, later director of economic research, 1952-62; Resources for the Future, Inc. (economic research), Washington, D.C., senior research associate, 1962—. *Military service:* U.S. Army Air Forces, 1942-45; became first lieutenant; received Air Medal. *Member:* American Economic Association, Phi Beta Kappa.

WRITINGS: Trends in the World Aluminum Industry, Johns Hopkins Press, 1967; *To Live on Earth: Man and His Environment in Perspective,* Johns Hopkins Press, 1972; *In Command of Tomorrow: Resource and Environmental Strategies for Americans,* Johns Hopkins Press, 1975.

WORK IN PROGRESS: Research on land use policies in the United States.

* * *

BRUCE, Harry J. 1931-

PERSONAL: Born July 2, 1931, in Short Hills, N.J.; son of John William (a chemist) and Anna (Ackerman) Bruce; married Vivienne Jennings, September 10, 1955; children: Robert, Harry, Jr., Stacy, Beth Ann. *Education:* Kent State University, B.S., 1957; University of Tennessee, M.S., 1958. *Politics:* Republican. *Religion:* Presbyterian. *Home:* 88 Woodley Rd., Winnetka, Ill. 60093. *Office:* Illinois Central Gulf Railroad, 233 North Michigan Ave., Chicago, Ill. 60601.

CAREER: Dwight Austin Manufacturing Co., Kent, Ohio, cost accountant, 1955-57; U.S. Steel Corp., Pittsburgh, Pa., transportation research assistant, 1959-64; Spector Freight System, Inc., Chicago, Ill., vice-president of marketing, 1964-69; assistant vice-president, Jos. Schlitz Brewing Co., 1969-72; vice-president, marketing, Western Pacific Railroad Co., 1972-75; senior vice-president, Illinois Central Gulf Railroad, Chicago, 1975—. *Military service:* U.S. Army, 1952-55. *Member:* National Council of Physical Distribution Management (treasurer), American Society of Traffic and Transportation, American Economic Association, Transportation Research Forum (council member at large).

WRITINGS: How to Apply Statistics to Physical Distribution, Chilton, for *Distribution Age* magazine, 1967; (contributor) *Modern Transportation: Selected Readings,* Houghton, 1967; (co-author) *Physical Distribution,* Dartnell, 1967; *Distribution and Transportation Handbook,* Cahners, 1971. Contributor to business journals.

BRUMMET, R. Lee 1921-

PERSONAL: Born March 16, 1921, in Ewing, Ill.; son of George (a teacher) and Iva (Smith) Brummet; married Eldora R. Riddle, August 6, 1942; children: Carmen, John. *Education:* Illinois State University, B.Ed., 1942; University of Illinois, M.Sc., 1947; University of Michigan, Ph.D., 1956. *Home:* 810 Kenmore, Chapel Hill, N.C. *Office:* School of Business Administration, University of North Carolina, Chapel Hill, N.C. 27514.

CAREER: Instructor in accounting at University of Illinois, Urbana, 1947-48, Washburn University of Topeka, Topeka, Kan., 1948-49, and University of Michigan, Ann Arbor, 1949-53; Icerman, Johnson, and Hoffman (certified public accountants), Ann Arbor, Mich., accountant, 1953-54; Cornell University, Ithaca, N.Y., assistant professor of accounting, 1954-55; University of Michigan, Ann Arbor, lecturer, 1955-57, associate professor, 1957-60, professor of accounting, 1960-69, director of management education, 1966-68; University of North Carolina, Chapel Hill, Willard J. Graham Professor of Business Administration, 1970—. Visiting professor at Stichting Bedrijfkunde, Rotterdam, 1969, and University of South Africa, 1974; Ford Foundation consultant, National Institute for Management Development, Cairo, 1963-64. Member of Michigan Governor's Task Force on Expenditure Management, 1965, 1966.

MEMBER: American Institute of Certified Public Accountants (member of council, 1975-77), National Association of Accountants (member of board of directors, 1964—; member of executive committee, 1967; chairman of committee on research planning, 1967-70), American Accounting Association (secretary-treasurer and member of executive committee, 1967-68, 1973—; president, 1974-75).

WRITINGS: (With David A. Thomas) *Record Keeping for the Small Home Builder,* Housing and Home Finance Agency, 1952; *Cost Accounting for the Small Manufacturer,* U.S. Small Business Administration, 1953; *Overhead Costing,* Bureau of Business Research, University of Michigan, 1957; (contributor) *Accountant's Cost Handbook,* Ronald, 1960; (with others) *Statement of Basic Accounting Theory,* American Accounting Association, 1966; (with Harold E. Arnett) *Business and Economic Evaluation of the Metal Finishing Industry,* Bureau of Business Research, University of Michigan, 1967; (contributor) Meinholf Dierkes and Raymond A. Bauer, editors, *Corporate Social Accounting,* Praeger, 1973; (contributor) *Researching the Accounting Curriculum: Strategies for Change,* American Accounting Association, 1975. Contributor to *House and Home* and to accounting and business journals.

* * *

BRUSH, Craig B(alcombe) 1930-

PERSONAL: Born May 28, 1930, in New York, N.Y.; son of John Mitchell (a pediatrician) and Josephine (Marple) Brush. *Education:* Princeton University, B.A., 1951; Columbia University, M.A., 1955, Ph.D., 1963. *Home:* 411 West 115th St., New York, N.Y. 10025.

CAREER: Choate School, Wallingford, Conn., teacher of French, 1951-54; Columbia University, New York, N.Y., instructor, 1955-57, 1959-63, assistant professor of French, 1963-67; City College of the City University of New York, New York City, assistant professor of French, 1967-70; Fordham University, Bronx, New York, associate professor, 1970-74, professor of French, 1975—, chairman of Modern Languages Department, 1973—.

WRITINGS: (Assisted Richard H. Popkin) *Selections from Pierre Bayle's Historical and Critical Dictionary,* Bobbs-Merrill, 1965; *Montaigne and Bayle: Variations on the Theme of Skepticism,* Nijhoff, 1966; (translator and editor) *Selected Works of Pierre Gassendi,* Johnson Reprint, 1970.

WORK IN PROGRESS: Montaigne's Self-Portrait.

* * *

BRUSHWOOD, John S(tubbs) 1920-

PERSONAL: Born January 23, 1920, in Glenns, Va.; son of John Benson (a retail merchant) and Evelyn (Stubbs) Brushwood; married Carolyn Norton, May 19, 1945; children: David Benson, Paul Darrach. *Education:* Randolph-Macon College, B.A., 1940; University of Virginia, M.A., 1942; National University of Mexico, summer study, 1943; Columbia University, Ph.D., 1950. *Religion:* Episcopalian. *Home:* 2813 Maine Ct., Lawrence, Kan. 66044. *Office:* University of Kansas, Lawrence, Kan. 66044.

CAREER: Virginia Polytechnic Institute (now Virginia Polytechnic Institute and State University), Blacksburg, instructor in Spanish, 1942-44; University of Missouri, Columbia, instructor, 1946-50, assistant professor, 1950-52, associate professor, 1952-57, professor of Spanish, 1957-67, chairman of department of Romance languages, 1953-57, 1958-59; University of Kansas, Lawrence, Roy A. Roberts Professor of Latin American Literature, 1967—.

MEMBER: Modern Language Association of America (chairman of contemporary Spanish American literature, 1966; chairman of 19th century Spanish American literature, 1972), American Association of Teachers of Spanish and Portuguese (president of state chapter, 1958), Instituto Internacional de Literatura Iberoamericana, American Association of University Professors, Midwest Modern Language Association (president, 1962-63; member of executive council, 1962-64), Phi Sigma Iota, Sigma Delta Pi. *Awards, honors:* Grants from Fund for the Advancement of Education, 1951-52, American Philosophical Society, 1957, American Council of Learned Societies, 1961, and Social Science Research Council, 1971; Fulbright lectureship in Colombia, 1974.

WRITINGS: The Romantic Novel in Mexico, University of Missouri Studies, 1954; (contributor) M. E. Johnson, editor *Swan, Cygnets, and Owl,* University of Missouri Studies, 1956; (with Jose Rojas Garciduenas) *Breve historia de la novela mexicana,* Ediciones de Andrea, 1959; *Mexico in Its Novel: A Nation's Search for Identity,* University of Texas Press, 1966, revised edition published as *Mexico en su novela,* Fondo de Cultura Economica, 1973; (translator with wife, Carolyn Brushwood) Sergio Galindo, *The Precipice,* University of Texas Press, 1969; *Enrique Gonzales Martinez,* Twayne, 1969; *Los ricos en la prosa mexicana,* Editorial Diogenes, 1970; (with Manuel Zapata Olivella) *Semanario: Literatura comparada,* Centro Colombo Americano, 1975.

Contributor: *III Congreso Latinoamericano de Escritores,* Ediciones del Congreso de la Republica, 1971; *Investigaciones contemporaneos sobre historia de Mexico,* published by Universidad Nacional Autonoma Mexicana and University of Texas, 1971; Andrew P. Dedicki and Enrique Pupo-Walker, editors, *Estudios de literatura hispanoamericana en honor a Jose J. Arrom,* International Book Service, 1974. Contributor to *Collier's Encyclopedia Yearbook;* contributor of articles, poems, and reviews to journals of Hispanic studies, *Kansas City Star,* and other publications.

WORK IN PROGRESS: The Spanish American Novel: A Twentieth Century Survey, for University of Texas Press; translations of Sergio Galindo's *La Comparsa* and Demetrio Aguilera Malta's *Don Goyo,* both with Carolyn Brushwood, and Roberta Sosa's *Twenty Poems.*

BIOGRAPHICAL/CRITICAL SOURCES: El Gallo Illustrado, April 26, 1964; *La Cultura en Mexico,* May 27, 1964.

* * *

BRUTON, Henry J(ackson) 1921-

PERSONAL: Born August 30, 1921, in Dallas, Tex.; son of Guss and Mary (Clark) Bruton; married Mary Frances Barnes, April 19, 1959. *Education:* University of Texas, B.A., 1943; Indiana University, M.A., 1948; Harvard University, Ph.D., 1952. *Office:* Williams College, Williamstown, Mass. 01267.

CAREER: Yale University, New Haven, Conn., assistant professor of economics, 1952-58; International Cooperation Administration, financial adviser in Tehran, Iran, 1958-60; University of Bombay, Bombay, India, professor of economics, 1960-61; Institute of Development Economics, Karachi, Pakistan, joint director, 1961-62; Williams College, Williamstown, Mass., associate professor, 1962-65, professor of economics, 1965—. Visiting professor, University of Chile, 1965-66; consultant to governments of Indonesia, Malaysia, and Egypt. *Military service:* U.S. Army, 1943-46. *Member:* American Economic Association, Royal Economic Society.

WRITINGS: Inflation in a Growing Economy, University of Bombay Press, 1961; (with S. R. Bose) *The Pakistan Export Bonus Scheme,* Institute of Development Economics (Karachi), 1963; *Principles of Development Economics,* Prentice-Hall, 1965.

WORK IN PROGRESS: Study of rates of growth of productivity in developing countries.

* * *

BRYANT, Robert H(arry) 1925-

PERSONAL: Born September 1, 1925, in Nokesville, Va.; son of Harry Tucker and Frances (McAllister) Bryant; married Emily Christine Rentsch (a social worker), August 11, 1951; children: John Robert, Miriam Joan, Mark Phillip. *Education:* College of William and Mary, B.A., 1946; Yale University, B.D. (magna cum laude), 1949, Ph.D., 1956; additional graduate study at University of Heidelberg, 1954-55, and University of Strasbourg, 1966-67. *Politics:* Democrat. *Home:* 504 Driftwood Rd., New Brighton, Minn. 55112. *Office:* United Theological Seminary of the Twin Cities, 3000 Fifth St. N.W., New Brighton, Minn. 55112.

CAREER: Clergyman of United Church of Christ. Assistant pastor in Waterbury, Conn., 1946-47, and Westfield, Mass., 1951-52; Hamden Hall Country Day School, Hamden, Conn., teacher, 1947-48; William Jewell College, Liberty, Mo., associate professor of philosophy, 1952-53; Vanderbilt University, Divinity School, Nashville, Tenn., visiting professor of theology, 1953-54; Mount Holyoke College, South Hadley, Mass., assistant professor of religion, 1956-58; Centre College of Kentucky, Danville, associate professor and chairman of department of philosophy and religion, 1958-61; United Theological Seminary of the Twin Cities, New Brighton, Minn., professor of constructive theology, 1961—. Visiting professor at St. John's University, 1972, and Federal Theological Seminary, South Africa, 1973-74.

MEMBER: American Academy of Religion, Society for the Scientific Study of Religion, American Theological Society, American Academy of Political and Social Science, American Association of University Professors, Phi Beta Kappa. *Awards, honors:* Fulbright grant for study at University of Heidelberg, 1954-55; Danforth Foundation grant for study at University of Chicago, 1959; Eli Lilly research grant, 1960.

WRITINGS: The Bible's Authority Today, Augsburg, 1968; (contributor) F. W. Katzenbach and Vilmos Vajta, editors, *Oecumenica: Yearbook for Ecumenical Research, 1968,* Augsburg, 1968. Contributor of short stories to *Whole Earth Newsletter* and *Theological Markings;* contributor of articles and reviews to theological journals.

WORK IN PROGRESS: Research on the church's social responsibility today, the theology of culture, the struggle between churches and government in South Africa, and traditional African religions.

AVOCATIONAL INTERESTS: Photography, music, hiking, swimming.

*   *   *

BUBE, Richard H.   1927-

PERSONAL: Born August 10, 1927, in Providence, R.I.; son of Edward Neser and Ella (Baltteim) Bube; married Betty Jane Meeker, October 9, 1948; children: Mark Timothy, Kenneth Paul, Sharon Elizabeth, Meryl Lee. *Education:* Brown University, Sc.B., 1946; Princeton University, M.A., 1948, Ph.D., 1950. *Politics:* Independent. *Religion:* Evangelical Christian. *Home:* 753 Mayfield Ave., Stanford, Calif. 94305.

CAREER: Radio Corporation of American Laboratories, Princeton, N.J., member of research staff, 1948-62; Stanford University, Stanford, Calif., associate professor, 1962-64, professor of materials science and electrical engineering, 1964—, chairman of materials science and engineering 1975—. Consultant to many industrial and government electronic laboratories. *Member:* American Physical Society (fellow), American Association for the Advancement of Science (fellow), American Society for Engineering Education, American Scientific Affiliation (fellow; executive council, 1964-68; vice-president, 1967; president, 1968), Sigma Xi. *Awards, honors:* Achievement awards for research at Radio Corporation of America Laboratories, 1952, 1957.

WRITINGS: A Textbook of Christian Doctrine, Moody, 1955; *Photoconductivity of Solids,* Wiley, 1960; (editor) *The Encounter Between Christianity and Science,* Eerdmans, 1968; *The Human Quest: A New Look at Science and Christian Faith,* Word Books, 1971; *Electronic Properties of Crystalline Solids: An Introduction to Fundamentals,* Academic Press, 1974. Contributor of more than one hundred articles, chiefly in fields of photoconductivity, luminescence, and photoelectronic properties of materials, to professional journals. Editor, *Journal* of American Scientific Affiliation, 1969—; associate editor, *Annual Review of Materials Sciences.*

WORK IN PROGRESS: Science and the Whole Person, for Inter-Varsity Press.

SIDELIGHTS: Bube writes: "My chief concerns are to show that the scientific method does not provide the means for answering all the significant questions of life, but that the scientific method is a valid and reliable procedure for interpreting the revelation of God in the natural world."

*   *   *

BUCHAN, Perdita   1940-

PERSONAL: Born December 16, 1940, in Oxford, England; daughter of William (a writer) and Nesta (Crozier) Buchan; married, 1968; children: one daughter. *Education:* Radcliffe College, B.A., 1962; studied art in Florence, Italy, one year. *Residence:* Concord, Mass.

CAREER: Worked for Bantam Books, New York City, 1962-63, Corgi Books, London, England, 1963-64, and Paramount Pictures Corp., London, England, 1965; Lenox School, New York City, English teacher, 1965-66; worked for Holiday House, Inc. (publishers), New York City, 1966-67; Concord Academy, Concord, Mass., dormitory director and tutor, 1974-76. *Awards, honors:* Radcliffe Institute grant for creative writing, 1972-74.

WRITINGS: Girl with a Zebra, Scribner, 1966. Short stories have appeared in *New Yorker, Ladies Home Journal,* and *O. Henry Prize Stories for 1970.*

WORK IN PROGRESS: A novel.

AVOCATIONAL INTERESTS: Painting, theater, mythology.

*   *   *

BUCHANAN, Keith   1919-

PERSONAL: Born February 14, 1919, in Dudley, England; son of Frederick Stuart McPherson (a farmer) and Marjorie Eleanor (Dickinson) Buchanan; children: Donald Iain, Elspeth Maureen Jane, Jean Maurya Bride (Buchanan) Coe. *Education:* University of Birmingham, B.A. (first class honors in geography), 1940. *Politics:* "Scottish Nationalist; Welsh Nationalist." *Religion:* Methodist. *Address:* c/o Wing-commander Donald Buchanan, Ashley Bank, Newbiggin-on-Lune, Kirkby Stephen, Cumbria, England.

CAREER: University of Birmingham, Birmingham, England, lecturer, 1941-46; University of Natal, Durban, Natal, South Africa, lecturer in geography, 1946-48; University College, Ibadan, Nigeria, 1948-51; London School of Economics and Political Science, London, England, lecturer in geography, 1951-53; Victoria University of Wellington, Wellington, New Zealand, professor of geography, 1953-75; Victoria University of Manchester, Manchester, England, Commonwealth visiting professor, 1975-76. Visiting professor, University of Minnesota, 1962; British Council Distinguished Academic Visitor at University of London, University of Birmingham, and University of Liverpool, 1965. *Awards, honors:* Murchison grant from Royal Geographic Society; Order of Sahametrei (Cambodia).

WRITINGS: (With J. C. Pugh) *Land and People in Nigeria,* University of London Press, 1955; *The Chinese People and the Chinese Earth,* G. Bell, 1966; *The Southeast Asian World: An Introductory Essay,* G. Bell, 1967, Doubleday, 1968; *Out of Asia: Essays on Asian Themes,* University of Sydney Press, 1968; *The Transformation of Chinese Earth,* Praeger, 1970; *The Map of Love,* Pergamon, 1970; *The Geography of Empire,* Spokesman Books, 1972. Contributor of some 250 papers and reviews to journals in past twenty-five years, most with particular reference to Africa, East Asia, and the underdeveloped world. Editor, *Pacific Viewpoint* (Wellington), 1960-67; member of editorial board, *Journal of Contemporary Asia,* 1970-73.

WORK IN PROGRESS: Volumes on China, the geography of underdevelopment, and the political problems of urbanization.

SIDELIGHTS: Buchanan has visited China four times, and Southeast Asia eight times. He also has traveled widely in Africa, western and Mediterranean Europe, the American Midwest, Caribbean, and Australasia. Buchanan speaks French and German, some Italian and Spanish. He lists among his current preoccupations the widening gap between the rich and the poor nations, the de-humanization of Western society, and the increasing relevance in the contemporary world of the small society and of intermediate style technology.

* * *

BUCKLEY, Fergus Reid 1930-
(Peter Crumpet)

PERSONAL: Born July 14, 1930, in Paris, France; son of William Francis (an oilman) and Aloise (Steiner) Buckley; married Elizabeth Huntting Howell, June 9, 1951 (divorced December 17, 1971); married Rosaria Leguina, February 14, 1972; children: William Huntting, Fergus Reid, Elizabeth Hanna, Claude Langford, John Alois; stepchildren: Patricia, Borja, Santiago, Javier, Francisco. *Education:* Yale University, B.A., 1952. *Politics:* "Catholic." *Religion:* "Catholic." *Agent:* Curtis Brown Ltd., 60 East 56th St., New York, N.Y. 10022.

CAREER: Bique, S.A. (export, retail), Madrid, Spain, cofounder and president, 1961-63; Cafranga, S.A. (travel agency), Madrid, Spain, co-buyer and director, 1963-64; Pozuelo, S.A. (real estate), Madrid, Spain, founder and president, 1963-66. *Military service:* U.S. Air Force, 1952-54; became first lieutenant.

WRITINGS: Eye of the Hurricane (novel), Doubleday, 1967; *Servants and their Masters* (novel), Doubleday, 1973.

WORK IN PROGRESS: A novel, *Revelations.*

* * *

BUDD, Edward C(arhart) 1920-

PERSONAL: Born February 20, 1920, in Summit, N.J.; son of Percy H. (a civil engineer) and Mabel (Carhart) Budd; married Margaret Louise Ellsworth, February 9, 1943; children: Dennis E., Howard S., Martin E., Paul A. *Education:* Attended Santa Ana College, 1938-40; University of California, Berkeley, A.B., 1942, Ph.D., 1954. *Politics:* Democrat. *Religion:* Unitarian Universalist. *Home:* 608 West Fairmount Ave., State College, Pa. 16801. *Office:* Department of Economics, Kern Graduate Building, Pennsylvania State University, University Park, Pa. 16802.

CAREER: U.S. Office of Price Administration, economist, 1944-46; University of Illinois, Urbana, assistant professor of economics. 1949-51; University of Oregon, Eugene, instructor in economics, 1951-52; Yale University, New Haven, Conn., instructor, 1952-54, assistant professor of economics, 1954-61; Pennsylvania State University, University Park, professor of economics, 1961—. Consultant, Bureau of Economics Analysis, U.S. Department of Commerce, 1966—. *Member:* American Economic Association, Conference on Research in Income and Wealth.

WRITINGS: (Editor) *Inequality and Poverty,* Norton, 1967; (with D. B. Radner and J. C. Hinrichs) *Size Distribution of Family Personal Income Methodology and Estimates for 1964,* U.S. Department of Commerce, 1973. Contributor to *Studies in Income and Wealth,* National Bureau of Economic Research, Volume XXII, 1958, Volume XXIV, 1960, Volume XXVII, 1964, Volume XLIV, 1975, to *Grolier Encyclopedia,* and to business and economic journals.

WORK IN PROGRESS: Research into the effect of macroeconomic fluctuations on size distribution; effect of changes in the recipient unit on size distributions.

* * *

BUDD, Richard W. 1934-

PERSONAL: Born August 24, 1934, in Henderson, Md.; son of Bryan W. and Dorothea (Fouvy) Budd; married Beverly Knight (an elementary teacher), August 28, 1955; children: Kimberly, Richard, Jr., Janna. *Education:* Bowling Green State University, B.S., 1956; University of Iowa, M.A., 1962, Ph.D., 1964. *Politics:* Independent. *Regligion:* Episcopalian. *Home:* 3 Pilgrim Run, East Brunswick, N.J. 08816. *Office:* Department of Human Communication, Rutgers University, New Brunswick, N.J. 08903.

CAREER: University of Iowa, Iowa City, instructor, 1962-64, director of mass communications research bureau, 1964-71; associate director of School of Journalism, 1967-71; Rutgers University, New Brunswick, N.J., professor of human communication and chairman of department, 1971—. *Military service:* U.S. Naval Reserve, active duty, 1957-60; assigned to Operation Deepfreeze in Antarctica, 1959-60; became lieutenant. *Member:* International Communication Association (president), American Association for Public Opinion Research, Association for Education in Journalism, Kappa Tau Alpha. *Awards, honors:* Named one of outstanding young men in America by U.S. Junior Chamber of Commerce, 1967.

WRITINGS: (With Robert Thorp) *Introduction to Content Analysis,* University of Iowa Press, 1962; *Content Analysis of Communications,* Macmillan, 1967; (with Brent Ruben) *Approaches to Human Communication,* Spartan Press, 1972; *Human Communication Handbook: Simulations and Games,* Hayden, Volume I, 1975, Volume II, 1976; *Approaches to Mass Communication,* Hayden, 1976. Contributor to *Public Opinion Quarterly, Journalism Quarterly,* and other journals.

WORK IN PROGRESS: Communication and Social Change.

* * *

BUECHNER, John C(harles) 1934-

PERSONAL: Surname is pronounced Beak-ner; born July 30, 1934, in Cleveland, Ohio; son of Frank Robert and Mary (Richardson) Buechner; married Katherine Cohan, August 11, 1956; children: Mary Katherine, John Allan, Barbara Lee. *Education:* College of Wooster, B.A., 1956; University of Michigan, M.P.A., 1958, Ph.D., 1963. *Religion:* Presbyterian. *Home:* 365 Mohawk Dr., Boulder, Colo. 80302. *Office:* Department of Political Science, University of Colorado, Boulder, Colo. 80302.

CAREER: Florida State University, Tallahassee, instructor in government, 1957-60; University of Colorado, Boulder, assistant professor, 1963-65, associate professor, 1965-69, professor of political science, 1969—, director of Bureau of Government Research, 1965-69, associate dean of arts and sciences, 1969-71, director of community relations, 1972—. City of Boulder, member of planning board, 1965-67, city councilman, 1967-69, 1971-75, deputy mayor,

1969-70, mayor, 1970; member of State House of Representatives, 1972-74. *Member:* American Society for Public Administration, American Political Science Association, International City Managers' Association, National Municipal League, Council on University Bureaus of Government (member of executive council).

WRITINGS: (With Elizabeth F. Goodwin) *Federal Aids Available for County Planning in Colorado,* University of Colorado Bureau of Government Research and Planning, 1966; *State Government in the Twentieth Century,* Houghton, 1967; (editor with George Beam) *Readings in American Government,* Wadsworth, 1968; *Public Administration,* Dickenson Publishing, 1968, revised edition, in press.

WORK IN PROGRESS: City Councilmen and their Behavior.

AVOCATIONAL INTERESTS: Skiing, fishing.

*   *   *

BUELL, Victor P(aul) 1914-

PERSONAL: Born October 18, 1914, in McAlester, Okla.; son of Victor Paul (in insurance) and Genevieve (Keller) Buell; married Virginia Stevens, May 16, 1942; children: Elizabeth, Nancy, Victor III. *Education:* Pennsylvania State University, A.B., 1938. *Home:* 235 Heatherstone Rd., Amherst, Mass. 01002. *Office:* School of Business Administration, University of Massachusetts, Amherst, Mass. 01002.

CAREER: Real Silk Hosiery Mills, Indianapolis, Ind., 1938-51, became regional sales manager, marketing research manager, and operations manager; McKinsey & Co., New York, N.Y., marketing consultant, 1951-55; Hoover Co., North Canton, Ohio, manager of Marketing Division, 1955-59; Archer Daniels Midland, Minneapolis, Minn., vice-president, marketing, 1960-64; American Standard, Inc., New York, N.Y., vice-president, marketing, 1964-70; University of Massachusetts, Amherst, professor of marketing, 1970—. Lecturer on marketing and marketing management. Member of board of trustees, Graduate School of Sales Management and Marketing, Syracuse University, 1963-67; director, L. R. Nelson Corp., Peoria, Ill., 1972—; member of board of governors, Parlin Foundation, 1973—. Consultant to several corporations including Continental Can, Gulf & Western, and American Standard. *Military service:* U.S. Army, 1941-46; became major.

MEMBER: American Marketing Association (director, 1957-59; vice-president, 1960-61; president, 1968-69), Association of National Advertisers (director), American Management Association (member of planning council, 1970—), Sales and Marketing Executives International, Beta Gamma Sigma, Advertising Club of New York, Union League Club of New York.

WRITINGS: (Contributor) *Effective Marketing Action,* Harper, 1958; (contributor) *The Marketing Job,* American Management Association, 1961; *Marketing Management in Action,* McGraw, 1966; (contributor) *Handbook of Business Administration,* McGraw, 1967; (editor-in-chief) *Handbook of Modern Marketing,* McGraw, 1970; (contributor) Robert Ferber, editor, *Readings in Marketing Research,* Herrero Hermanos Sucesores, 1970; *Changing Practices in Advertising Decision-Making and Control,* Association of National Advertisers, 1973. Contributor to journals. Editorial adviser, *Journal of Marketing,* 1958—, and *Industrial Marketing,* 1969—.

BUELOW, George J. 1929-

PERSONAL: Born March 31, 1929, in Chicago, Ill.; son of George John and Florence A. (Cook) Buelow. *Education:* Chicago Musical College, B.Music, 1950, M.Music, 1951; University of Hamburg, further graduate study, 1954-55; New York University, Ph.D., 1961. *Politics:* Independent. *Office:* Department of Music, Rutgers University, New Brunswick, N.J. 08903.

CAREER: Music Educators Jounal, Washington, D.C., assistant editor, 1956-57; *Instrumentalist Music* (magazine), Evanston, Ill., associate editor, 1957-61; University of California, Riverside, associate professor of music, 1961-68; University of Kentucky, Lexington, professor of music and chairman of department, 1968-69; Rutgers University, New Brunswick, N.J., professor of music and director of graduate program, 1969—. *Member:* American Musicological Society, International Musicological Society, International Richard Strauss Gesellschaft, Society of the Friends of Bayreuth. *Awards, honors:* Fulbright fellowship in Germany, 1954-55; Guggenheim fellowship, 1967; Rutgers University Research Council Fellowship, 1974-75.

WRITINGS: Thorough-bass Accompaniment According to Johann David Heinichen, University of California Press, 1966; (with David Daviau) *The Ariadne auf Nayos of Hofmannsthal and Richard Strauss,* University of North Carolina Press, 1975. Contributor to music and musicological journals. American editor, *Acta Musicologica,* 1967—.

WORK IN PROGRESS: The Rationale of the Musical Baroque: The Distinguishing Theoretical Concepts of the Baroque; edition of opera, "Dre schoene und getreue Ariadne"; *Performance in Music History; The Baroque Era;* articles for *Grove's Dictionary of Music and Musicians,* 6th edition.

*   *   *

BUFFINGTON, Robert (Ray) 1933-

PERSONAL: Born February 11, 1933, in Belleville, Ill.; son of Ray Ferdinand (an accountant) and Emily (Welch) Buffington; married, 1958, 1971; children: Stephanie Gudrun, Anna Claire, Christopher Ray Boettcher. *Education:* Rollins College, B.A., 1954; Vanderbilt University, M.A., 1958, Ph.D., 1967; University of Iowa, M.F.A., 1962. *Politics:* Conservative. *Religion:* Episcopal. *Office:* University of Georgia Press, Athens, Ga. 30602.

CAREER: Orlando Sentinel-Star, Orlando, Fla., sports writer, 1950-54; instructor in English at Vanderbilt University, Nashville, Tenn., 1960-62, Rollins College, Winter Park, Fla., 1962-64, and Louisiana State University, Baton Rouge, 1964-66; Western Illinois University, Macomb, assistant professor of English, 1966-68; Florida State University, Tallahassee, assistant professor of English, 1968-72; Louisiana Tech University, Ruston, associate professor of English 1972-73; University of Georgia Press, Athens, associate editor, 1973—. *Military service:* U.S. Army, 1954-56.

WRITINGS: The Equilibrist: A Study of John Crowe Ransom's Poems, 1916-1963, Vanderbilt University Press, 1967.

*   *   *

BUGENTAL, James F(rederick) T(homas) 1915-

PERSONAL: Born December 25, 1915, in Fort Wayne, Ind.; son of Richard (a contractor) and Hazel (Veness) Bugental; married Mary Edith Smith, February 11, 1939 (divorced); married Elizabeth C. Keber, May 23, 1969; children: James O., Jane P., Karen M. *Education:* West Texas State University, B.S., 1940; George Peabody College for Teachers, M.A., 1941; Ohio State University, Ph.D., 1948. *Office:* The Querencia, 818 Cherry St., Santa Rosa, Calif. 95404.

CAREER: Diplomate in clinical psychology, American Board in Professional Psychology, 1953; licensed psychologist, State of California, 1958. U.S. Civil Service and Tennessee State Civil Service employee in personnel administration, 1941-44; Georgia Institute of Technology, Atlanta, assistant professor of psychology and assistant director of Veterans Guidance Center, 1944-46; University of California, Los Angeles, assistant professor of psychology, 1948-54; Psychological Service Associates, Los Angeles, Calif., partner, 1953-68; Stanford Research Institute, Educational Policy Research Center, Menlo Park, Calif., research consultant, 1968-71; Stanford University, Medical School, Stanford, Calif., associate clinical professor of psychiatry, 1971—. Private practice of psychotherapy, 1970—.

MEMBER: American Psychological Association (fellow), Association for Humanistic Psychology (president, 1962-63), American Academy of Psychotherapists, National Training Laboratories (fellow), American Ontoanalytic Association, California State Psychological Association (president, 1960-61), Southern California Psychological Association (president, 1955-56), Sigma Xi, Psi Chi, Pi Gamma Mu, Phi Delta Kappa.

WRITINGS: (With G. E. Mount, J. S. Helmick, and I. Maltzman) *Workbook,* to accompany Brown and Gilhousen's *College Psychology,* Prentice-Hall, 1951; *Psychological Interviewing,* privately printed, 1957, 3rd edition, 1966; *Processes of Communication,* privately printed, 1962, 2nd edition, 1963; *The Existential Orientation in Intensive Psychotherapy,* privately printed, 1963; *The Search for Authenticity: An Existential-Analytic Approach to Psychotherapy,* Holt, 1965; (editor and contributor) *Challenges of Humanistic Psychology,* McGraw, 1967; *The Human Possibility,* Stanford Research Institute, 1971.

Contributor: W. B. Webb, editor, *The Profession of Psychology,* Holt, 1962; L. E. Abt and B. F. Riess, editors, *Progress in Clinical Psychology,* Volume VII, Grune, 1966; R. J. Magee, editor, *Call to Adventure,* Abingdon, 1967; R. MacLeod, editor, *The Unfinished Business of William James,* American Psychological Association, 1969; C. Buhler and F. Messarik, editors. *The Human Course of Life,* Springer Publishing, 1968; C. S. Wallia, editor, *Toward Century 21,* Basic Books, 1970; W. H. Schmidt, editor, *Organizational Frontiers and Human Values,* Wadsworth, 1970; T. C. Greening, editor, *Existential Humanistic Psychology,* Brooks/Cole, 1971; K. R. S. Iyengur, editor, *Sri Aurobindo: A Centenary Tribute,* Sri Aurobindo Press (Pondicherry, India), 1974.

Contributor to *Journal of Personality, Credit Union Executive, Psychiatry, Psychology Today, Voices,* and psychology journals. Associate editor, *Psychological Reports,* 1958-65; assistant editor, *Journal of Humanistic Psychology,* 1963-66; member of editorial board, *Psychotherapy: Research, Theory and Practice,* 1963-70, *Journal of Humanistic Psychology,* 1963—, *Existential Psychiatry,* 1965—, *Journal of Transpersonal Psychology,* 1969—.

*　　　*　　　*

BULL, Angela (Mary)   1936-

PERSONAL: Born September 28, 1936, in Halifax, York-

shire, England; daughter of Eric Alexander (a company director) and Joyce (Benson) Leach; married Martin Wells Bull (a Church of England clergyman), September 15, 1962; children: Timothy Martin, Priscilla Emily. *Education:* University of Edinburgh, M.A. (honors), 1959; St. Hugh's College, Oxford, graduate study, 1959-61. *Religion:* Church of England, *Home:* St. John's Vicarage, Ingrow, Keighley, Yorkshire, England.

CAREER: Casterton School, Kirkby Lonsdale, Westmorland, England, teacher of English, 1961-62; Bodleian Library, Oxford University, Oxford, England, assistant to keeper of western manuscripts, 1963.

WRITINGS: The Friend with a Secret, Collins, 1965, Holt, 1966; (with Gillian Avery) *Nineteenth Century Children,* Hodder & Stoughton, 1965; *Wayland's Keep,* Collins, 1966, Holt, 1967; *Child of Ebenezer,* Collins, 1974; *Treasure in the Fog,* Collins, 1976.

*　　　*　　　*

BUNI, Andrew   1931-

PERSONAL: Surname is pronounced Bunny; born June 21, 1931, in Manchester, N.H.; son of Nicholas (a laborer) and Cecilia (Makar) Buni; married Joyce Kelly, July 23, 1960; children: John Frank, Catherine, James Christopher, Nicholas. *Education:* University of New Hampshire, B.A., 1958, M.A., 1959; University of Virginia, Ph.D., 1965. *Home:* 52 Newell Ave., Needham, Mass.

CAREER: University of Virginia, Mary Washington College, Fredericksburg, assistant professor, 1964-67, associate professor of American history, 1967-68; Boston College, Chestnut Hill, Mass., associate professor, 1968-75, professor of history, 1975—. *Military service:* U.S. Army, 1952-54. *Member:* American Historical Association, Organization of American Historians, Association for the Study of Negro Life and History, Southern Historical Association.

WRITINGS: The Negro in Virginia Politics, 1902-1965, University Press of Virginia, 1967; *Robert L. Vann of Pittsburgh: Politics and Black Journalism,* University of Pittsburgh Press, 1974.

WORK IN PROGRESS: Biography of Paul Robeson.

*　　　*　　　*

BUNN, Ronald F(reeze)   1929-

PERSONAL: Born August 11, 1929, in Jonesboro, Ark.; son of Neal and Velma (Freeze) Bunn; married Rita Elaine Hess (a piano and violin teacher), March 29, 1955; children: Robin Gail, Katharine Sue, Lisabeth Joanne. *Education:* Southwestern at Memphis, B.A., 1951; Duke University, M.A., 1953, Ph.D., 1956; University of Cologne, graduate study, 1954-55. *Politics:* Liberal Democrat. *Religion:* Protestant. *Home:* 12603 West Shadow Lane, Cypress, Tex. 77429.

CAREER: University of Texas, Austin, instructor, 1956-59, assistant professor of political science, 1959-64, assistant director of International Office, 1957-59; Louisiana State University, Baton Rouge, associate professor of political science, 1964-67; University of Houston, Houston, Tex., associate professor, 1967-69, professor of political science, 1969—, dean of graduate school, 1969-74, interim dean of college of arts and sciences, 1972-74, associate dean of faculties, 1974—. Visiting professor, Indiana University, 1962; chairman of board of directors, Southwest Center for Urban Research, 1975-76. *Military service:* Arkansas National Guard, 1947-48; Tennessee National Guard, 1949. *Member:* American Political Science Association, American Association of University Professors, Southern Political Science Association, Phi Beta Kappa, Omicron Delta Kappa. *Awards, honors:* Fulbright grant for study in Germany, 1954-55, and research award, 1963; NATO Senior Science fellowship, 1973; LL.D., Southwestern at Memphis, 1973.

WRITINGS: (Editor with William G. Andrews and contributor) *Politics and Civil Liberties in Europe: Four Case Studies,* Van Nostrand, 1967; *German Politics and the Spiegel Affair: A Case Study of the Bonn System,* Louisiana State University Press, 1968. Contributor to professional journals.

* * *

BURACK, Sylvia 1916-
(Sylvia E. Kamerman)

PERSONAL: Born December 16, 1916, in Hartford, Conn.; daughter of Abraham and Augusta (Chermak) Kamerman; married Abraham S. Burack (editor and publisher of *Writer*), November 28, 1940; children: Janet (Mrs. Alan D. Biller), Susan (Mrs. Chad A. Finer), Ellen (Mrs. Franklin Toker). *Education:* Smith College, B.A., 1938. *Home:* 72 Penniman Rd., Brookline, Mass. 02146. *Office:* Writer, Inc. and Plays, Inc., 8 Arlington St., Boston, Mass. 02116.

CAREER: Writer, Inc. and Plays, Inc. (publishers), Boston, Mass., associate editor, 1941—. Trustee of Massachusetts State College System, 1971—, chairman of board, 1974—; trustee of Max C. Rosenfeld Fund; member of Brookline School Committee, 1949-69, and Massachusetts Board of Higher Education, 1973-75. *Member:* National Book Critics Circle, League of Women Voters, Phi Beta Kappa, Bostonian Society, and other social, philanthropic, and civic associations.

WRITINGS—Editor, under name Sylvia E. Kamerman; all published by Plays, except as shown: *Writing the Short Short Story,* Writer, 1942; *Little Plays for Little Players,* 1952; *Blue Ribbon Plays for Girls,* 1955; *Blue Ribbon Plays for Graduation,* 1957; *A Treasury of Christmas Plays,* 1958; *Children's Plays from Favorite Stories,* 1959; *Fifty Plays for Junior Actors,* 1966; *Fifty Plays for Holidays,* 1969; *Children's Plays from Favorite Stories,* 1970; *Dramatized Folk Tales of the World,* 1971; *A Treasury of Christmas Plays,* 1972.

AVOCATIONAL INTERESTS: The theater; local politics; travel.

* * *

BURCHARD, Max N(orman) 1925-

PERSONAL: Born May 27, 1925, near Liberal, Kan.; son of Charlie and Grace (Swink) Burchard; married June Larsen, September 11, 1948; children: Denise, Clyde, Marti, Norman, Melissa, Brett, Tracey. *Education:* San Jose State College (now University), A.B., 1949; University of Nebraska, M.A., 1951, Ph.D., 1955. *Home:* 307 Poplar, Mount Pleasant, Iowa 52641.

CAREER: University of Omaha, Omaha, Neb., instructor in sociology, 1952-54; Chico State College (now California State University, Chico), instructor in sociology, 1954-55; Marietta College, Marietta, Ohio, assistant professor of sociology and acting head of department, 1955-60; University of North Dakota, Grand Forks, assistant professor,

later associate professor of sociology, 1960-64, chairman of department, 1962-64; Moorhead State College, Moorhead, Minn., associate professor of sociology and chairman of department of behavioral sciences, 1964-68; Iowa Wesleyan College, Mount Pleasant, professor of sociology and chairman of department of behavioral sciences, 1968—. *Military service:* U.S. Navy, airman, 1943-46. U.S. Air Force Reserve, 1948-53; became second lieutenant. *Member:* American Sociological Association (fellow), Society for the Study of Social Problems, American Association of University Professors, Midwest Sociological Society (board member, 1963-64).

WRITINGS: Sociology, Sernoll, 1967.

WORK IN PROGRESS: Study in Human Ecology.

* * *

BURCHARDT, Nellie 1921-

PERSONAL: Born May 13, 1921, in Philadelphia, Pa.; daughter of Donald Lewis (a mechanical engineer) and Marian Stewart (Harper) Kellogg; married Botho Burchardt (a market researcher), May 23, 1948; children: Carol Joy, Wendy Ellen; Laurens (stepson). *Education:* Queens College (now Queens College of the City University of New York), B.A., 1944; Yale University, M.A., 1946; Columbia University, graduate study in library science, 1954-55. *Politics:* Liberal. *Religion:* Unitarian Universalist. *Home:* 773 Manor Rd., Staten Island, New York, N.Y. 10314.

CAREER: New York Public Library, New York, N.Y., trainee, 1954-55.

WRITING—Juveniles: *Project Cat,* F. Watts, 1966; *Reggie's No-Good Bird,* F. Watts, 1967; *A Surprise For Carlotta,* F. Watts, 1972; *What Are We Going to Do, Michael?* F. Watts, 1973.

WORK IN PROGRESS: Another children's book.

* * *

BURGESS, C(hester) F(rancis) 1922-

PERSONAL: Born October 30, 1922, in Brockton, Mass.; son of Chester Francis (a postal clerk) and Mary (Cronin) Burgess; married Betty L. Reigan, September 1, 1945; children: Chester F. III, Deborah Ann. *Education:* Yale University, B.A., 1945; University of Colorado, graduate study, one and a half years; University of Notre Dame, M.A., 1961, Ph.D., 1962. *Politics:* Democrat. *Religion:* Roman Catholic. *Home:* 305 Letcher Ave., Lexington, Va. 24450. *Office:* Department of English, Virginia Military Institute, Lexington, Va. 24450.

CAREER: Yale University, New Haven, Conn., instructor in English, 1946-48; in business, 1949-59; University of Notre Dame, Notre Dame, Ind., instructor in English, 1960-62; Virginia Military Institute, Lexington, assistant professor, 1962-63, associate professor, 1963-67, professor of English, 1967—. *Military service:* U.S. Marine Corps, 1943-46, 1951-52; became captain. *Member:* Modern Language Association of America, American Council of Learned Societies (senior fellow), South Atlantic Modern Language Association, Shakespeare Association of America, Phi Beta Kappa. *Awards, honors:* Ford Foundation research fellowship; three research grants, American Philosophical Society; Folger Library fellowship.

WRITINGS: (Editor) *The Letters of John Gay,* Clarendon Press, 1966; (editor) *Gay's Beggar's Opera and Companion Pieces,* Appleton, 1966; *The Fellowship of the Craft,* Kennikat, 1976. Contributor to literary journals.

WORK IN PROGRESS: A biography of Thomas Davies, eighteenth-century actor, biographer, editor, and publisher; a book on Shakespearean criticism in the eighteenth century.

SIDELIGHTS: Burgess has some competence in French, German, and Japanese.

* * *

BURGETT, Donald R(obert) 1925-

PERSONAL: Born April 5, 1925, in Detroit, Mich.; son of Elmer Wilson (a policeman) and Lillian Mae (Bruce) Burgett; married Twyla Moneen Austin, June 29, 1953; children: Kenneth R., Rene L., Mark W., Gary T., Jeffrey A. *Education:* Attended public schools in Detroit, Mich. *Politics:* "Conservative (very)." *Religion:* Atheist. *Residence:* Howell, Mich. *Agent:* Frieda Fishbein, 353 West 57th St., New York, N.Y. 10019.

CAREER: Self-employed roofer, 1941—, in Detroit, Mich., and Livingston County, Mich. Has worked at numerous other jobs in off season, including heavy equipment operator, press operator and foreman in a paper-box factory, carpenter, truck driver, and foreman of a wrecking crew. *Military service:* U.S. Army, paratrooper with 101st Airborne Division, 1943-45; became sergeant; received Purple Heart with cluster, Bronze Star, two arrowheads, and four campaign stars. *Member:* 101st Airborn Division Association, Veterans of Foreign Wars, Loyal Order of Moose.

WRITINGS: Currahee, Houghton, 1967.

WORK IN PROGRESS: Three sequels to *Currahee,* covering Holland, Bastogne, and Germany and Austria; actions of the 101st Airborne Division in the Pacific; stories on the 11th Airborne Division, and on hunting and fishing.

AVOCATIONAL INTERESTS: Hunting, fishing, flying, skin diving, sketching.

* * *

BURKE, Arvid J. 1906-

PERSONAL: Born December 15, 1906, in Staatsburg, N.Y.; son of James D. and Anna M. (Persson) Burke; married Mary A. Gallagher, July 2, 1934. *Education:* State University of New York at Albany, B.A., 1928, M.A., 1930; Columbia University, Ed.D., 1936. *Politics:* Republican. *Religion:* Episcopalian. *Home:* 314 Osborne Rd., Loudonville, N.Y. 12211.

CAREER: New York State Teachers Association, Albany, director of studies, 1935-67; State University of New York at Albany, lecturer, 1960-66, professor of education, 1966-71, professor emeritus, 1971—. Visiting professor, Harvard University, 1946-47; visiting lecturer, Columbia University, 1961-63. Consultant to various New York State committees and commissions on education. *Military service:* U.S. Army, 1943-45. *Member:* National Education Association.

WRITINGS: (With A. B. Caldwell) *Study of Financial Support and Educational Opportunity in the One-Teacher School Districts of New York State 1928-29 to 1934-35,* New York State Teachers Association, 1936; (with F. W. Cyr and P. R. Mort) *Paying for Our Public Schools,* International Textbook, 1938; *Teacher Salary Policies in Public Schools,* New York State Teachers Association, 1941; *Economics of Public School Spending,* New York State Teachers Association, 1941; *Defensible Spending for Public Schools,* Columbia University Press, 1943; *Postwar*

Program of State Aid for Schools, Based Upon Four Studies of the Financing of Public Schools in New York State, New York State Teachers Association, 1946.

(With Carter Alexander) *How to Locate Educational Information and Data,* 3rd edition, Teachers College, Columbia University, 1950, 4th edition, 1958; *Financing Public Schools in the United States,* Harper, 1951, 2nd edition, 1957; (contributor) *National Policies for Education, Health and Social Welfare,* Doubleday, 1955; (contributor) *School Business Administration,* Ronald, 1956; *Staff Report on School District Government,* Special Legislative Committee on Revision and Simplification of the Constitution, State of New York, 1958; (with Wallace H. Strevell) *Administration of the School Building Program,* McGraw, 1959.

(With Alexander) *Metodos de Investigacion,* Pan American Union, 1962; *Education and the 1967 Constitutional Convention,* State University of New York, 1966; (with wife, Mary A. Burke) *Documentation in Education,* Teachers College, Columbia University, 1967; (contributor) *The Theory and Practice of School Finance,* Rand McNally, 1967; (contributor) *Dimensions of Educational Need,* Volume I, National Educational Finance Project, 1969.

(Contributor) *Educational Programs for the Culturally Deprived—Need and Cost Differentials* (special study, number 3), National Educational Finance Project, 1970; (contributor) *Planning to Finance Education,* Volume III, National Educational Finance Project, 1971; (contributor) *The Fleischmann Report on the Quality, Cost, and Financing of Elementary and Secondary Education in New York State,* Volume I, Viking, 1973.

Also contributor to *Encyclopedia of Educational Research,* 1960, *Rand McNally Handbook of Education,* 1963, *Education in the States: Nationwide Development Since 1900,* 1969, and *Preconstruction Planning for Educational Facilities,* 1972.

* * *

BURKE, Robert E(ugene) 1921-

PERSONAL: Born July 22, 1921, in Chico, Calif.; son of Ralph Ambrose (a businessman) and Frieda (Rupp) Burke; married Helen Elizabeth Blom, October 31, 1952; children: Elizabeth Anne. *Education:* Chico State College (now California State University, Chico), A.B., 1946; University of California, Berkeley, M.A., 1947, Ph.D., 1950. *Politics:* Independent. *Religion:* Presbyterian. *Home:* 7336 19th Ave. N.E., Seattle, Wash. 98115. *Office:* History Department, University of Washington, Seattle, Wash. 98105.

CAREER: University of California, Berkeley, director of Bancroft Library research project in London, England, 1950-51, head of Manuscripts Division, Bancroft Library, 1951-56; University of Hawaii, Honolulu, assistant professor of history, 1956-57; University of Washington, Seattle, assistant professor, 1957-60, associate professor, 1960-65, professor of history, 1965—, chairman of department, 1962-67. *Military service:* U.S. Army, 1942-45; served in Pacific theater; became staff sergeant. *Member:* Organization of American Historians (executive board member, 1967-70), Agricultural History Society (executive board member, 1966-69), Forest History Society, American Historical Association, Southern Historical Association, Idaho Historical Society, Washington State Historical Society (member of board of curators, 1967—).

WRITINGS: Olson's New Deal for California, University

of California Press, 1953; (with John D. Hicks and George Mowry) *The American Nation,* Houghton, 5th edition, 1971; (with J. D. Hicks and G. Mowry) *The Federal Union,* 5th edition, Houghton, 1970; (with J. D. Hicks and G. Mowry) *A History of American Democracy,* 4th edition, Houghton, 1970. General editor, "Americana Library," a reprint series, University of Washington Press, 1967—; managing editor, *Pacific Northwest Quarterly* (publication of University of Washington).

WORK IN PROGRESS: Editing bibliography on U.S. history, 1920-40; a full-length study of Franklin D. Roosevelt and the party system; a study of sources of twentieth century American history; a biography of Hiram W. Johnson.

SIDELIGHTS: Burke traveled in Europe, 1950-51, 1965, 1967, 1970, 1971, 1972, and 1974, with chief interest in Britain. He has some competence in French and German. *Avocational interests:* Music, drama, collecting records and books, fishing.

*   *   *

BURNE, Glenn S. 1921-

PERSONAL: Born April 2, 1921, in Los Angeles, Calif.; son of Stanley (an engineer) and Merle (Snyder) Burne; married Joanne Myers, April 16, 1957; children: Karin, Peter, Stephen, Alan. *Education:* University of California, Berkeley, B.A., 1947; Sorbonne, University of Paris, Diplome d'Etudes, 1950; University of Washington, Seattle, M.A., 1952, Ph.D., 1956. *Office:* Department of English, University of North Carolina, Charlotte, N.C. 28223.

CAREER: Idaho State College (now University), Pocatello, assistant professor of English, 1956-59; Kent State University, Kent, Ohio, assistant professor, 1959-62, associate professor of English, 1962-63; State University of New York at Binghamton, associate professor of English and comparative literature, 1963-68; Kent State University, professor of English and comparative literature, 1968-71, acting chairman of English department, 1969-71; University of North Carolina at Charlotte, professor of English and chairman of department, 1971—. *Military service:* U.S. Naval Reserve, active duty, 1942-46; became lieutenant junior grade. *Member:* Modern Language Association of America, American Comparative Literature Association, American Committee for Irish Studies, American Association of University Professors.

WRITINGS: Remy de Gourmont: His Ideas and Influence in England and America, Southern Illinois University Press, 1963; (editor and translator) Remy de Gourmont, *Selected Writings,* University of Michigan Press, 1966; *Julian Green,* Twayne, 1972. Contributor to literary journals.

SIDELIGHTS: Glenn Burne is competent in French and Spanish. He lived in France and traveled throughout Europe, 1949-50, 1954-55, and lived in Mexico, 1966-67.

*   *   *

BURNEY, Elizabeth (Mary) 1934-

PERSONAL: Born November 21, 1934, in Alderley Edge, Cheshire, England; daughter of Edward (a civil servant) and Mary Constance (Allan) Burney; married Colin Alan Parker (a journalist), 1968. *Education:* Lady Margaret Hall, Oxford, M.A., 1956, B.Litt., 1958. *Politics:* Left. *Religion:* Christian. *Home:* 52 Bullingham Mansions, London W.8, England. *Office: Economist,* 25 St. James's St., London S.W.1, England.

CAREER: British Broadcasting Corp., London, England, assistant on television news staff, 1958-59; *Economist,* London, editorial assistant in intelligence unit, 1959-61, staff writer, 1962—. Studied city planning in major U.S. cities, 1964; member of committee of planning forum, Town and Country Planning Association, 1966-68; member of advisory committee, Runnymede Trust, 1968—; member of advisory committee to Minister of Housing on public housing allocation policy, 1968-69.

WRITINGS: Housing on Trial: A Study of Immigrants and Local Government, Oxford University Press, 1967. Writer of articles on race relations. Contributor to McGraw's *Directors Handbook.* Regular contributor to *Director* (magazine), and to British Broadcasting Corp. radio and television.

WORK IN PROGRESS: Research in housing, local government, race relations, and town planning.

AVOCATIONAL INTERESTS: Travel, looking at buildings and pictures, cooking, collecting antiques.†

*   *   *

BURRIS, B. C(ullen) 1924-

PERSONAL: Born June 17, 1924, in Smithdale, Miss.; son of William Culley and Leonora (Gilleylen) Burris; married Shirley Beattie; children: Scott, Ann. *Education:* Mississippi College, student, 1941-43; University of Tennessee, M.D., 1946; Northwestern University, postdoctoral study in psychiatry, 1950. *Religion:* Episcopalian. *Home:* 1247 Ridge Ave., Evanston, Ill. *Office:* 707 North Fairbanks Ct., Chicago, Ill. 60611.

CAREER: Psychiatrist; licensed to practice medicine in Tennessee, 1946, Illinois, 1947, Wisconsin, 1958. Wesley Memorial Hospital, Chicago, Ill., intern, 1946-47, resident in internal medicine, 1949, resident in neuropsychiatry, 1949-50, member of staff, 1953-58; Johns Hopkins Hospital, Baltimore, Md., resident, 1950; medical director of private psychiatric hospital, Milwaukee, Wis., 1958-67; psychiatrist in private practice, Chicago, Ill., 1967—; currently member of attending staff, Northwestern Memorial Hospital, Passavant, Chicago, Ill. Albany Medical College, Albany, N.Y., former associate professor of psychiatry; Northwestern University Medical School, Evanston, Ill., psychiatry fellow, 1952-53, clinical instructor in psychiatry, 1953-58; Marquette University Medical School, Milwaukee, Wis., associate professor of psychiatry, 1958-67; Northwestern University Medical School, associate professor of psychiatry, 1967—. Member of consulting staff at Evanston Hospital, 1958-62, West Allis Memorial Hospital, Milwaukee, 1961-64, St. Josephs Hospital, Milwaukee, 1964-67; medical director, Milwaukee Sanitarium Foundation, Wauwatosa, Wis., 1961-67; chief-of-staff of psychiatry and mental services, Veterans Administration Hospital, Albany, N.Y. Psychiatric consultant to church bodies, rehabilitation centers, and Young Women's Christian Association, Chicago; site consultant to Peace Corps, University of Wisconsin, Milwaukee, 1964-67. *Military service:* U.S. Navy, Medical Corps, 1950-52; became lieutenant. *Member:* American Psychiatric Association (fellow), National Association of Private Psychiatric Hospitals, American Medical Association, Central Neuropsychiatric Association (president, 1965-66; secretary-treasurer, 1966-67).

WRITINGS: (Editor with L. Bernstein) *Contribution of the Social Sciences to Psychotherapy,* C. C Thomas, 1967; (editor and contributor with others) *Pharmacological Activity, Metabolism and Pharmacolinetics of Glycinexylidid,* Clinical Pharmacology and Therapeutics, 1975.

BURROUGHS, Margaret Taylor 1917-
(Margaret Taylor)

PERSONAL: Born November 1, 1917, in St. Rose, La.; daughter of Alex (a laborer) and Octavia (Pierre) Taylor; married Bernard Goss, 1939 (divorced, 1947); married Charles Gordon Burroughs (a museum curator), December 23, 1949; children: (first marriage) Gayle Goss Toller; (second marriage; adopted) Paul. *Education:* Chicago Teachers College (now Chicago State University), graduate, 1937; Art Institute of Chicago, B.F.A., 1944, M.F.A., 1948; Teachers College, Columbia University, graduate study, summers, 1958, 1959, 1960; Esmerelda Art School, Mexico City, 1952-53; Field Museum of Chicago, 1967-68; American Forum for African Study, fellow, 1968. *Home:* 3806 South Michigan Ave., Chicago, Ill. 60653.

CAREER: Du Sable High School, Chicago, Ill., teacher of art, 1946-69; Kennedy-King Community College, Chicago, professor of humanities, 1969—. Officer and member of board of directors, South Side Art Community Center, Chicago, 1940—; director, Du Sable Museum of African-American History, Chicago, 1961—; member of board of directors, American Forum for International Studies, 1969-72. *Member:* National Conference of Negro Artists (founder, 1959), Phi Delta Kappa. *Awards, honors:* Art prizes at Atlanta University, 1947-55; Hallmark Prize, best in show, Lincoln University, Mo., 1962; National Endowment for the Humanities grant, 1968; Field Museum of Natural History grant to study museology, 1968; American Forum for International Study, African travel grant, 1968; L.H.D., Lewis College, Lockport, Ill., 1972; Y.W.C.A. leadership award for excellence in art, 1973.

*WRITINGS—*Under name Margaret Taylor, except as noted: *Jasper, the Drummin' Boy* (self-illustrated), Viking, 1947, revised edition under name Margaret Taylor Burroughs, illustrated by T. Lewin, Follett, 1970; *Did You Feed My Cow?* (self-illustrated), Crowell, 1955, revised edition under name Margaret Taylor Burroughs, Follet, 1969; *Whip Me Whop Me Pudding,* privately printed, 1966; (with Dudley Randall) *Malcolm X,* Broadside Press, 1966; (under name Margaret Taylor Burroughs) *What Shall I Tell My Children Who Are Black?,* privately printed, 1968; *Africa, My Africa* (poems), privately printed, 1970. Contributor to educational journals.

WORK IN PROGRESS: Negro history materials for children; stories; poems.

* * *

BURROW, John W(yon) 1935-

PERSONAL: Born June 4, 1935, in Southsea, England; son of Charles Wyon (a salesman) and Alice (Vosper) Burrow; married Diane Dunnington, October 27, 1958; children: Laurence, Francesca. *Education:* Christ's College, Cambridge, B.A., 1957, M.A., 1960, Ph.D., 1961. *Office:* Arts Building, University of Sussex, Brighton, England.

CAREER: Cambridge University, Downing College, Cambridge, England, fellow, 1962-65; University of East Anglia, School of European Studies, Norwich, England, lecturer in history, 1965-69; University of Sussex, Brighton, England, reader in history, 1969—.

WRITINGS: Evolution and Society: A Study in Victorian Social Theory, Cambridge University Press, 1966; (editor and author of introduction) Charles R. Darwin, *The Origin of Species by Means of Natural Selection,* Penguin, 1968; (editor and author of introduction) Wihelm Humboldt, *The Limits of State Action: History and Theory of Political Science,* Cambridge, University Press, 1969.

WORK IN PROGRESS: A study of the sense of the past in Victorian England.

* * *

BURROWAY, Janet (Gay) 1936-

PERSONAL: Born September 21, 1936, in Tucson, Ariz.; daughter of Paul M. (a tool and die worker) and Alma (Milner) Burroway; married Walter Eysselinck, March 18, 1961 (divorced, 1973); children: Timothy Alan, Tobyn Alexander. *Education:* Attended University of Arizona, 1954-55; Barnard College, B.A., 1958; Cambridge University, B.A., 1960, M.A., 1965; additional study at Yale School of Drama, 1960-61. *Politics:* Liberal. *Home:* 1514 Mabry St., Tallahassee, Fla. 32304.

CAREER: During her school years, worked for Young Men's Hebrew Association, *New Yorker,* and for UNICEF in Paris, France; supply teacher in Binghamton, N.Y., 1961-63; director of classical music program for schools in upstate New York, 1963; University of Sussex, Brighton, England, School of English and American Studies, 1965-70, began as assistant lecturer, became lecturer; Univeristy of Illinois at Champaign-Urbana, Urbana, special assistant to the writing laboratory, 1971; Florida State University, Tallahassee, associate professor of English literature and creative writing, 1971—. *Awards, honors:* The Buzzards received a Pulitzer Prize nomination, 1970.

WRITINGS: Descend Again (novel), Faber, 1960; *But to the Season* (poems), Keele University Press, 1961; *The Dancer from the Dance* (novel), Faber, 1965, Little, Brown, 1967; *Eyes* (novel), Little, Brown, 1966; *The Buzzards* (novel), Little, Brown, 1969; *The Truck on the Track* (juvenile), J. Cape, 1970, Bobbs-Merrill, 1971; (with John V. Lord) *The Giant Jam Sandwich* (juvenile), J. Cape, 1972, Houghton, 1973.

Plays: "The Fantasy Level" and "The Beauty Operators," produced in Brighton, England, 1968, and by Thames Television Ltd. in London, 1970; "Hoddinott Veiling," produced by ATV Network Ltd., London, 1970.

WORK IN PROGRESS: A fifth novel, *Dry Goods,* about the "sin of submission."

SIDELIGHTS: According to C.D.B. Bryan, *"The Dancer from the Dance* is the sort of novel every flower-hatted member of ladies' book clubs thinks she has in her to do. . . . It is a tribute to this young author's courage that she would attempt such a book, and a tribute to her talent that she was able to do it so well. . . . Her style has the precision of John Updike's and the charm of Sir Arthur Conan Doyle. . . . Janet Burroway is a writer."

Discussing *The Buzzards,* Roger Baker asserts "what she manages to convey about America, campaign mechanics and the cruel Arizona desert . . . tells us far more than a thousand lectures by more sociologically-minded writers."

"Hoddinott Veiling" was Britain's independent television entry at the Monte Carlo festival in 1970.

* * *

BURROWS, Miles 1936-

PERSONAL: Born February 18, 1936, in Leicestershire, England; son of James David and Brenda (Lee) Burrows; married Elspeth Jones (a research assistant), April, 1962; children: Max, Tom. *Education:* Wadham College, Oxford,

M.A., B.M., B.Ch., 1966. *Home:* 79 Broadway, Grantchester, Cambridgeshire, England.

CAREER: Fulbourn Hospital, Fulbourn, Cambridgeshire, England, registrar in psychiatry, 1967-70; Cambridgeshire College of Arts and Technology, Cambridgeshire, England, lecturer in English and general studies, 1970—. *Military service:* Royal Navy, 1954-56; became lieutenant.

WRITINGS: A Vulture's Egg (poems), J. Cape, 1966; *"Extra Verse" No. 18: A Special Number for Miles Burrows,* J. Cape, 1966. Poetry anthologized in *British Poetry Since 1945,* edited by Edward Lucie-Smith, Penguin, 1970. Contributor to *Ambit, Meridian,* and a British Broadcasting Company program entitled "Poetry Now." Regular reviewer for *New Statesman.*

SIDELIGHTS: Burrows reads Latin, Greek, and Russian.

BIOGRAPHICAL/CRITICAL SOURCES: Listener, January 26, 1967.

* * *

BURT, Samuel M(athew) 1915-

PERSONAL: Born December 11, 1915, in Philadelphia, Pa.; son of Louis (a retailer) and Anna (Neuman) Burt; married Esther Amsterdam (a guidance counselor), April 27, 1937; children: Robert, Jeffrey, Carolyn. *Education:* Temple University, B.S.E., 1936; University of Pennsylvania, M.B.A., 1943. *Home:* 9704 Saxony Rd., Silver Spring, Md. 20910.

CAREER: Printing Institute, Philadelphia, Pa., director, 1949-52; Educational Testing Service, Princeton, N.J., purchasing agent, 1952-53; National Scholarship Trust Fund, Washington, D.C., executive secretary, 1953-64; Upjohn Institute for Employment Research, Washington, D.C., project director, 1964-66; U.S. Department of Labor, Employment Service, Washington, D.C., special assistant to director, 1966-68; Upjohn Institute for Employment Research, project director, 1968—. Consultant, U.S. Office of Education. *Member:* International Benjamin Franklin Society (director), American Vocational Association (chairman of industrial cooperation committee), National Association for Industrial Education Cooperation, American Industrial Arts Association, Gamma Epsilon Tau.

WRITINGS: Industry and Vocational Technical Education, McGraw, 1967; *Toward Greater Government and Industry Involvement in Manpower Programs,* Upjohn Institute, 1968; (with Leon M. Lessinger) *Volunteer Industry Involvement in Public Education,* Heath Lexington, 1970; (with Herbert E. Striner) *A Design Concept for a Total Manpower Planning System for the State of Illinois,* Advisory Council on Vocational Education (Springfield, Ill.), 1973. Contributor to professional journals.†

* * *

BURTON, Arthur 1914-

PERSONAL: Born March 10, 1914; son of Hyman and Martha (Flam) Burton; married Edith Hamilton, April 27, 1944; children: Vicki Ann. *Education:* University of California, Los Angeles, A.B., 1936, M.A., 1938; University of Southern California, graduate study, 1938; University of California, Berkeley, Ph.D., 1940. *Politics:* Democrat. *Religion:* Jewish. *Home:* 8330 La Riviera Dr., Sacramento, Calif. 95826. *Office:* 1 Scripps Dr., Sacramento, Calif. 95825.

CAREER: Associate personnel examiner, California State

Personnel Board, 1942-45; clinical psychologist, California Youth Authority, 1945-46; Idaho State University, Pocatello, associate professor, 1946-47; Willamette University, Salem, Ore., associate professor, 1947-48; chief clinical psychologist, Agnews State Hospital, 1948-56; University of California, Los Angeles, chief clinical psychologist, 1957-58; California State University, Sacramento, professor of psychology, 1965-72. Private practice as consulting psychologist, Sacramento, 1965—. *Member:* American Psychological Association (fellow), Sigma Xi.

WRITINGS: (Editor with R. E. Harris, and contributor) *Case Histories in Clinical and Abnormal Psychology,* Harper, 1947; (editor with Harris, and contributor) *Clinical Studies of Personality,* Harper, 1955, revised two-volume edition, Torchbooks, 1966; (editor and contributor) *Case Studies in Counseling and Psychotherapy,* Prentice-Hall, 1959; (editor and contributor) *Psychotherapy of the Psychoses,* Basic Books, 1961; (contributor) H. M. Ruitenbeek, editor, *Psychoanalysis and Contemporary American Culture,* Dell, 1964; (contributor) L. Pearson, editor, *The Use of Written Communications in Psychotherapy,* C. C Thomas, 1965; (editor and contributor) *Modern Psychotherapeutic Practice: Innovations in Technique,* Science and Behavior, 1965; (with K. F. Reinhardt and L. P. Ruotolo) *A Source Book of Existentialism in Psychopathology, Philosophy, Theology and Literature,* Science and Behavior, 1967; *Modern Humanistic Psychotherapy,* Jossey-Bass, 1967; *Encounter,* Jossey-Bass, 1969; *Interpersonal Psychotherapy,* Prentice-Hall, 1972; (with others) *Twelve Therapists,* Jossey-Bass, 1972; (editor) *Operational Theories of Personality,* Brunner, 1974; (with Juan J. Lopez-Ibor and Werner M. Mendel) *Schizophrenia as a Life Style,* Springer Publishing, 1974.

Author of television script, "Crisis of Marriage." Contributor of numerous articles to psychology, psychiatry, and counseling journals. Consulting editor of *Journal of Existentialism* and *Psychotherapy, Theory, Research, Practice.*

SIDELIGHTS: Arthur Burton commented, "Interested in the decline of personal and social power in the twentieth century." He speaks German and French "on a utilitarian basis."

* * *

BURTON, Edward J. 1917-
(Michael Carey)

PERSONAL: Born May 20, 1917, in New York, N.Y.; son of Edward and Mary (Ennis) Burton; married Elizabeth Bylandt, February 3, 1940; children: Geoffrey E. *Education:* Studied fiction writing at New York University; studied at Columbia University, 1945-50.

CAREER: New York City Police Department, began as patrolman, became sergeant, 1946-67. *Military service:* U.S. Coast Guard, 1941-45; chief combat correspondent in the Mediterranean theater. *Member:* Authors Guild, Mystery Writers of America, Crime Writers Association of England.

WRITINGS—Under pseudonym Michael Carey: *Vice Squad Cop,* Avon, 1957; *The Vice Net,* Avon, 1958; *The Frightened Killers,* Gallimard, 1964; *House of Evil,* Gallimard, 1965; *Doomed,* Gallimard, 1966.

WORK IN PROGRESS: The Limpet.

SIDELIGHTS: Burton writes: "Due to the fact that I had four sisters who were great talkers, as most women are, I took to writing as an expression in my own defense." He has continued to express himself in writing by inventing stories, during his off-duty hours, derived from experiences on duty as a New York City police officer. "There isn't a bit of autobiography in it, but I do know the subject so it must ring true," he says of a typical story about a vice-squad cop and a prostitute. He has written for years using the name Michael Carey in order to avoid the need for police clearance of his writing, which he would consider "an invasion of [his] privacy" as a writer of fiction. His wife carefully edits each book: "She makes a blue-eyed character brown-eyed if she thinks that's better," he says, "and she makes some of the heroines a little less voluptuous."

AVOCATIONAL INTERESTS: Reading, rock hunting, and traveling.

BIOGRAPHICAL/CRITICAL SOURCES: New York Times, January 14, 1967; *World Journal Tribune,* March 28, 1967, March 31, 1967, April 16, 1967.††

* * *

BURTON, William L(ester) 1928-

PERSONAL: Born September 20, 1928, in Moundsville, W.Va.; son of W. Lester (a civil engineer) and Harriet (Hicks) Burton; married Odelle Lee Stewart, July 2, 1950; married second wife, Ruth Ann Buzzard, August 24, 1958; children: (first marriage) James S., Carol L. *Education:* Bethany College, Bethany, W.Va., A.B., 1949; University of Wisconsin, M.S., 1952, Ph.D., 1958. *Religion:* Presbyterian. *Home:* 817 Orchard Dr., Macomb, Ill. 61455.

CAREER: High school teacher of history in Virginia, 1949-50; Western Illinois University, Macomb, assistant professor, 1957-62, associate professor, 1962-68, professor of history, 1968, chairman of history department, 1969—. *Member:* American Historical Association, Organization of American Historians, American Association of University Professors.

WRITINGS: (Co-author) *Exploring Regions Near and Far* (text), Follett, 1965; (co-author) *Exploring Regions of the Western Hemisphere* (text), Follett, 1966; *The Trembling Land: Illinois in the Age of Exploration,* Western Illinois University Press, 1966; *A Descriptive Bibliography of Civil War Manuscripts in Illinios,* Northwestern University Press, 1966; (editor) *A Manual for History Teachers,* Williamson, 1967; *Illinois: A Student's History of the Prairie State,* Panoramic, 1969; (co-author) *Studying Civilization: A Guide to World History,* Scott, Foresman, Volume I, 1969, Volume II, 1970. Contributor to historical and educational journals.

* * *

BUSCH, Briton Cooper 1936-

PERSONAL: Born September 5, 1936, in Los Angeles, Calif.; son of Niven (an author) and Phyllis (Cooper) Busch; married Deborah Stone, 1958; children: Philip, Leslie. *Education:* Stanford University, A.B., 1958; University of California, Berkeley, M.A., 1960, Ph.D., 1965. *Home:* West Lake Rd., Hamilton, N.Y. 13346. *Office:* Department of History, Colgate University, Hamilton, N.Y. 13346.

CAREER: Colgate University, Hamilton, N.Y., instructor and then assistant professor, 1963-68, associate professor, 1968-73, professor of history, 1973—. *Member:* American Historical Association, Historical Association (Great Britain), Middle East Institute, Royal Central Asian Society,

Middle East Studies Association (fellow), American Association of University Professors, Phi Alpha Thetha. *Awards, honors:* Woodrow Wilson fellow, 1962-63; National Humanities Research Foundation fellow, 1968; Social Science Research Council fellow, 1969.

WRITINGS: Britain and the Persian Gulf, 1894-1914, University of California Press, 1967; *Britain, India, and the Arabs, 1914-1921,* University of California Press, 1971; *Mudros to Lausanne: Britain's Frontier in West Asia, 1918-1924,* State University of New York Press, in press. Contributor of articles and reviews to historical journals.

WORK IN PROGRESS: A biography of Lord Hardinge of Penhurst.

* * *

BUSHMAN, Richard L(yman) 1931-

PERSONAL: Born June 20, 1931, in Salt Lake City, Utah; son of Ted (a department store executive) and Dorothy (Lyman) Bushman; married Claudia Lauper, August 19, 1955; children: Clarissa, Richard L., Jr., Karl Edward, Margaret Elizabeth, Serge James, Martin Benjamin. *Education:* Harvard University, A.B., 1955, A.M., 1960, Ph.D., 1961. *Religion:* Church of Jesus Christ of Latter-day Saints (Mormon). *Home:* 28 Oak St., Belmont, Mass. 02178. *Office:* Department of History, Boston University, Boston, Mass. 02178.

CAREER: Mormon missionary in New England, 1951-53; Brigham Young University, Provo, Utah, assistant professor of history, 1960-63; Brown University, Providence, R.I., interdisciplinary fellow in history and psychology, 1963-65; Brigham Young University, assistant professor, 1965-66, associate professor of history, 1966-68, associate director of honors program, 1965-68; Boston University, Boston, Mass., professor of history, 1968—. Visiting professor, Harvard University, spring, 1973. *Member:* National Society for Religion in Higher Education, Phi Beta Kappa. *Awards, honors:* Frederick Sheldon fellowship in England, Harvard University, 1958-59; Bancroft Prize, 1968, for *From Puritan to Yankee;* Charles Warren Center fellow, Harvard University, 1968-69; Guggenheim fellowship, 1975-76.

WRITINGS: (Editor) *Religion at Harvard,* Harvard University Student Council, 1957; *From Puritan to Yankee: Character and the Social Order in Connecticut, 1690-1765,* Harvard University Press, 1967; (editor) *The Great Awakening: Documents on the Revival of Religion, 1740-1745,* Atheneum, 1970. Contributor to journals.

* * *

BUTCHER, H(arold) J(ohn) 1920-

PERSONAL: Born September 6, 1920, in Southampton, England; son of Thomas H. and Lily R. (Hand) Butcher. *Education:* Cambridge University, B.A., 1941; University of Manchester, Diploma in Education, 1956, Ph.D., 1959. *Office:* University of Sussex, Arts Building, Falmer, Brighton BN1 9RH, England.

CAREER: University of Manchester, Manchester, England, lecturer in education, 1956-63; University of Edinburgh, Edinburgh, Scotland, lecturer in psychology, 1963-67; University of Manchester, professor of higher education, 1967-70; University of Sussex, Sussex, England, professor of educational psychology, 1970—. *Military service:* British Army, Royal Artillery, 1945; became captain. *Member:* British Psychological Society.

WRITINGS: (With R. B. Cattell) *The Prediction of Achievement and Creativity,* Bobbs-Merrill, 1967; (editor with H. B. Pont) *Educational Research in Britain,* University of London Press, 1968; *Human Intelligence: Its Nature and Assessment,* Barnes & Noble, 1968, published as *Human Intelligence: Its Natural Assessment,* Harper, 1973; (with James Freeman) *Creativity: A Selective Review of Research,* Society for Research into Higher Education, 1968, 2nd edition, 1971; (editor with Pont) *Educational Research in Britain Two,* University of London Press, 1970, Crane, Russak, 1971; (editor with Donald E. Lomax) *Readings in Human Intelligence,* Harper, 1972; (editor with Ernest Rudd) *Contemporary Problems in Higher Education: An Account of Research,* McGraw, 1972; *Educational Research in Britain Three,* University of London Press, 1974. Contributor to professional journals.†

*   *   *

BUTERA, Mary C.   1925-

PERSONAL: First syllable of surname is accented, rhymes with "view"; born September 23, 1925, in Pittston, Pa.; daughter of Ignatius (a laborer) and Margaret (Aquilina) Butera; married George E. Wine (an administrative manager), August 20, 1966. *Education:* College Misericordia, B.S., 1947. *Religion:* Roman Catholic. *Home:* 2400 41st St., N.W., Washington, D.C. 20007. *Office:* Association of Independent Colleges and Schools, 1730 M St. N.W., Washington, D.C. 20036.

CAREER: High school teacher in Delaware City, Del., 1947-49; Goldey Beacom Junior College, Wilmington, Del., chairman of secretarial department, 1949-66; Strayer Junior College, Washington, D.C., director of guidance, 1966-73; Association of Independent Colleges and Schools, executive associate, 1973—. *Member:* National Office Management Association (secretary, 1963-66), Eastern Business Teachers Association (member of board of directors, 1970-72), Delaware Business Association (secretary-treasurer, 1957-60).

WRITINGS: (With Ruthetta Krause and William A. Sabin) *College English: Grammar and Style,* McGraw, 1967. Contributor to business education journals.

*   *   *

BUTLAND, Gilbert J(ames)   1910-

PERSONAL: Born November 12, 1910, in Dartmouth, England; son of Frank and Elizabeth (Emmett) Butland; married Elsie Leeuwin Peniston, June 30, 1938; children: Jan Peniston, Lucinda Leeuwin. *Education:* University of Birmingham, B.A. (honors) and Diploma in Education, 1931, Ph.D., 1951. *Home:* 98 Mossman St., Armidale, New South Wales, Australia. *Office:* University of New England, Armidale, New South Wales, Australia.

CAREER: Whitney Institute School, Bermuda, geography master, 1932-36, headmaster, 1937-41; Mackay School, Valparaiso, Chile, geography master, 1942-43; British School, Punta Arenas, Chile, headmaster, 1943-47; University of Birmingham, Birmingham, England, lecturer, 1948-57, senior lecturer in geography, 1957-59; University of New England, Armidale, New South Wales, Australia, Foundation Professor of Geography, 1959-72, dean of faculty of arts, 1960-62, chairman of professorial board, 1964-66, pro vice-chancellor, 1972-75. Honorary consul of Chile in Birmingham, England, 1950-59. *Member:* Royal Geographical Society (fellow), Geographical Association, Institute of British Geographers, Institute of Australian Geographers.

WRITINGS: Chile: An Outline of Its Geography, Economics, and Politics, Oxford University Press, for Royal Institute of International Affairs, 1951, 3rd edition, 1956; *The Human Geography of Southern Chile,* George Philip, for Institute of British Geographers, 1957; *Latin America: Regional Geography,* Longmans, Green, 1960, 3rd edition, Longman, 1972; *Letters from Grenfell,* Sydney University Press, 1971; *The Other Side of the Pacific: Problems of Latin America,* Angus & Robertson for Australian Institute of International Affairs, 1972. Contributor to *The Annual Register,* Longmans, Green, 1949-60. Editor, *This Changing World* (publication of Geographical Association), 1956-59.

WORK IN PROGRESS: Settlement Problems in Latin America; Bermuda: Island Series, for David & Charles.

SIDELIGHTS: Butland is competent in French and Spanish. *Avocational interests:* Travel, photography, gardening.

*   *   *

BUTLER, Iris   1905-

PERSONAL: Born June 15, 1905, in Simla, India; daughter of Montagu (in Indian civil service) and Anne (Smith) Butler; married Gervas Portal (an officer in Indian Cavalry), January 6, 1927 (died December 1, 1961); children: Jane Portal (Mrs. Charles Williams), Susan (Mrs. James Batten). *Education:* Attended private boarding school at Folkstone, England, for seven years. *Politics:* Variable. *Religion:* Christian. *Home:* Marshbanks Cottage, Morston Rd., Blakeney, Norfolk, England.

CAREER: Spent part of her life as a soldier's wife in India and Pakistan, and more than twenty years in England; did some free-lance journalism through the years; writer. Broadcaster on social aspects of British India. Volunteer youth leader on a county basis for two decades. *Wartime service:* Nurse and member of St. John Ambulance Brigade, World War II; decorated Officer of the Order of St. John of Jerusalem.

WRITINGS: Rule of Three: Sarah, Duchess of Marlborough and Her Companions in Power, Hodder & Stoughton, 1967, published as *The Great Duchess: The Life of Sarah Churchill,* Funk, 1968; (editor and author of notes) *The Viceroy's Wife: Letters of Alice, Countess of Reading, from India,* Hodder & Stroughton, 1969; *The Eldest Brother: The Marquess Wellesley, The Duke of Wellington's Eldest Brother,* Hodder & Stroughton, 1974. Author of scripts for British Broadcasting Corp. Schools Programme, and articles for *Norfolk News.*

WORK IN PROGRESS: Song at Seventy, personal reminiscences; a romantic biography of William Gardner, Irish military adventurer in Hindustan during the eighteenth and nineteenth centuries.

SIDELIGHTS: Iris Butler speaks and reads French, and reads Italian. She has made a particular study of the evolution of Parliamentary democracy in seventeenth-century England. She is also interested in women's problems, history, and position in society, and in Indian history.

BIOGRAPHICAL/CRITICAL SOURCES: Books & Bookmen, April, 1967.

*   *   *

BUTTINGER, Joseph   1906-

PERSONAL: Born April 30, 1906, in Reichersbeuern,

Germany, of Austrian parents; came to United States in 1939, naturalized in 1943; son of Anton (a miner) and Maria (Birkenhauer) Buttinger; married Muriel Morris (a psychiatrist), August 1, 1939. *Education:* "Have no formal education, except six years of elementary school in a small village of Austria. I must call myself in every respect self-educated." *Home address:* R.R.1, Box 264, Pennington, N.J. 08534.

CAREER: Social-Democratic Party of Austria, secretary for Province of Carinthia, 1930-34, chairman of central committee of Social-Democratic underground movement, 1934-38; active in work for refugees from fascism, 1939—, and refugees from Iron Curtain countries, 1945—; International Rescue Committee (American private refugee and relief organization), European director, 1945-47, and again following the Hungarian revolt, member of board, 1940—; American Friends of Vietnam, executive committee chairman, 1955-65, working in Vietnam, 1954, 1958. *Member:* Authors Guild of the Authors League of America. *Awards, honors:* Great Golden Order of Merit of the Republic of Austria.

WRITINGS: In the Twilight of Socialism, Praeger, 1953; *The Smaller Dragon: A Political History of Vietnam,* Praeger, 1958; (contributor) Richard W. Lindholm, editor, *Viet-Nam: The First Five Years* (international symposium), Michigan State University Press, 1959; (contributor) Wesley Fishel, editor, *Problems of Freedom* (symposium), Free Press of Glencoe, 1961; *Vietnam: A Dragon Embattled,* two volumes, Praeger, 1967; *Vietnam: A Political History,* Praeger, 1969: *A Dragon Defiant* (a short history of Vietnam), Praeger, 1972. Wrote a number of brochures and newspaper articles published in Austria, and a brochure, "Fact and Fiction on Foreign Aid" (a critique of "Ugly American"), published by the magazine *Dissent,* summer, 1959.

WORK IN PROGRESS: A study of "the literature of anticipation"; an autobiography.

SIDELIGHTS: Buttinger speaks French, and reads Italian and Spanish.

* * *

BUTZER, Karl W(ilhelm)   1934-

PERSONAL: Born August 19, 1934, in Mulheim-Ruhr, Germany; became Canadian citizen; son of Paul A. and Wilhelmine (Hansen) Butzer; married Elisabeth Schloesser, May 12, 1959. *Education:* McGill University, B.Sc. (honors), 1954, M.Sc., 1955; University of Bonn, Dr. rer. nat. (D.Sc. equivalent), 1957. *Residence:* Flossmoor, Ill. *Office:* Department of Geography, University of Chicago, Chicago, Ill. 60637.

CAREER: Academy of Science and Literature, Germany, research associate in geography, 1957-59; University of Wisconsin, Madison, assistant professor, 1959-62, associate professor of geography, 1962-66; University of Chicago, Chicago, Ill., professor of anthropology and geography, 1966—. Director, Alexanders Fontein Project, Kimberley, South Africa, 1974-75. *Member:* Association of American Geographers, American Geographical Society, South African Archaeological Association, Deutsche Quartarvereinigung, Canadian Association of Geographers. *Awards, honors:* Citation, Association of American Geographers, 1968, for *Environment and Archaeology.*

WRITINGS: Environment and Archeology, Aldine, 1964; (with Carl L. Hansen) *Desert and River in Nubia,* Univer-

sity of Wisconsin Press, 1969; *Recent History of an Ethiopian Delta,* University of Chicago Press, 1971; *Geomorphology from the Earth,* Harper, in press; *Floodplain Ecology, Irrigation and Demography in Ancient Egypt,* University of Chicago Press, in press. Author of three monographs, published in German publications. Contributor of more than one hundred articles to scientific journals in North America, Europe, and South Africa. Editor, *Prehistoric Archaeology and Ecology;* co-editor, *Journal of Archaeological Science, Paleorient,* and *Catena.*

WORK IN PROGRESS: A study of man-environmental interactions in prehistoric times, focused on site selection, resource orientation, and patterns of territoriality.

SIDELIGHTS: Butzer has done field research or been a member of expeditions in Egypt, 1956—, Spain, 1957—, East Africa, 1967—, and South Africa, 1969—.

* * *

BYRNE, Frank L(oyola)   1928-

PERSONAL: Born May 12, 1928, in Hackensack, N.J.; son of Francis Loyola (a bank officer) and Bertha (Widman) Byrne; married Marilyn L. Sobraske, June 9, 1962; children: Anne Louise, Frank Joseph. *Education:* Trenton State College, B.S., 1950; University of Wisconsin, M.S., 1951, Ph.D., 1957. *Religion:* Roman Catholic. *Home:* 5800 Horning Rd., Kent, Ohio 44240. *Office:* Department of History, Kent State University, Kent, Ohio 44240.

CAREER: Louisiana State University, Baton Rouge, instructor in history, 1957-58; Creighton University, Omaha, Neb., assistant professor, 1958-63, associate professor of history, 1963-66; Kent State University, Kent, Ohio, associate professor, 1966-68, professor of American history, 1968—. Member, Nebraska Civil War Centennial Commission, 1960-65. *Military service:* U.S. Army, 1954-56. *Member:* American Historical Association, Organization of American Historians, Southern Historical Association, the state historical societies of Nebraska, Louisiana, Ohio, and Wisconsin. *Awards, honors:* Research grants from Wisconsin Civil War Centennial Commission, 1962-63, American Philosophical Society, 1965, and Kent State University, 1967, 1969, 1972.

WRITINGS: Prophet of Prohibition: Neal Dow and His Crusade, State Historical Society of Wisconsin, 1961; (editor) *The View from Headquarters: Civil War Letters of Harvey Reid,* State Historical Society of Wisconsin, 1965; (contributor) Allan Nevins, James I. Robertson, Jr., and Bell D. Wiley, editors, *Civil War Books: A Critical Bibliography,* Volume I, Louisiana State University Press, 1967; (editor with Andrew T. Weaver) *Haskell of Gettysburg: His Life and Civil War Papers,* State Historical Society of Wisconsin, 1970; (contributor) Edward T. James, Janet W. James, and Paul S. Boyer, editors, *Notable American Women, 1607-1905: A Biographical Dictionary,* three volumes, Harvard University Press, 1971. Contributor to *Civil War History* and regional history journals.

WORK IN PROGRESS: A general history of Civil War military and political prisons, completion expected in 1979.

* * *

BYRNE, Richard Hill   1915-

PERSONAL: Born August 3, 1915, in Lancaster, Pa.; son of Jacob Hill (a lawyer) and Mary Deborah (Allwein) Byrne; married Antoinette M. Wardell, June 12, 1954; children: Christopher, Mary, Matthew, Peter. *Education:* Franklin and Marshall College, A.B., 1938; Columbia University, M.A., 1947, Ed.D., 1952. *Home:* 15232 Red Clover Dr., Rockville, Md. 20853. *Office:* University of Maryland, College Park, Md. 20740.

CAREER: Lancaster County (Pa.) schools, high school teacher, 1940-41, 1946; Allegany County (Md.) schools, counselor, 1948-49; New Hampshire State Department of Education, director of guidance, 1950-51; University of Maryland, College Park, associate professor, 1951-57, professor of counselor education, 1957—, chairman of department, 1961-65, director of Eastern Regional Research and Demonstration Center, 1963-68. President of American Board on Counseling Services, 1960-63; consultant to U.S. Department of Labor, 1964-67. *Military service:* U.S. Army, 1941-46; became captain.

MEMBER: American Personnel and Guidance Association, Association for Counselor Education and Supervision (past chairman of membership committee), National Vocational Guidance Association, American Psychological Association, National Society for the Study of Education, Maryland Personnel and Guidance Association (first president), Maryland Psychological Association (council member, 1964-66), Pi Gamma Mu.

WRITINGS: Guidance Handbook for New Hampshire, New Hampshire State Department of Education, 1951; (with Ruth Barry and others) *Case Studies in Human Relations in Secondary Schools,* Teachers College, Columbia University, 1956; (editor) *Directory of Vocational Counseling Services,* American Board on Professional Standards in Vocational Counseling, 1958, 2nd edition, 1960; *The School Counselor,* Houghton, 1963; (contributor) Margaret Ruth Smith, editor, *Guidance-Personnel Work: Future Tense,* Teachers College, Columbia University, 1966; *Systematic Guidance,* Prentice-Hall, in press. Contributor to *International Yearbook of Education,* 1955; contributor of articles and reviews to journals. Editor, *Circuit Rider* (predecessor of *Counselor Education and Supervision*), 1957-58.

*   *   *

CACCIA-DOMINIONI, Paolo   1896-

PERSONAL: First part of surname is pronounced "Katcha"; born May 14, 1896, in Nerviano, Milan, Italy; son of Carlo (seventeenth count of Sillavengo; a diplomat) and Bianca (a marquise; maiden name, Cusani-Confalonieri) Caccia-Dominioni; married Helen Sciolette (an amateur archaeologist), May 7, 1958; children: Bianca Ottavia, Anna Francesca. *Education:* Royal High Polytechnical School of Milan, enrolled 1913, absent on military duty, 1915-19, Doctor of Civil Engineering, 1923. *Religion:* Roman Catholic. *Home and office:* 20014 Nerviano, Milan, Italy.

CAREER: Inherited title as eighteenth count of Sillavengo; civil engineer, architect, and planner with Walter Stross (builder and contractor), Cairo, Egypt, 1924-27; independent engineer and architect, 1927—, with nearly four hundred works, including several official buildings (such as embassies, monuments, and war memorials), in North Africa, Middle East, Australia, and Italy. Expert engineer and architect on Mixed Courts of Egypt, 1926-49; delegate for Egypt and Libya on Italian War Graves Commission, with residence in Alamein, 1948-59. Designer, water colorist, and engraver, with work exhibited at one-man shows in Milan, Rome, Tunis, Cairo, Alexandria, Paris, and Dues-

seldorf, 1922-64; illustrator of his own books and the books of others. Editor of all Italian-language books published by Longanesi, Milan. *Military service:* Italian Army, 1915-19, 1935-36, 1941-43; served in Libya, 1919, and Abyssinia, 1935-36; became colonel in Alpine Troops (engineers) before being disabled by wounds; received four decorations for gallantry and German Iron Cross (presented by Field Marshal Rommel). Also served with Italian Resistance, 1943-45. *Member:* Several Italian professional and military clubs. *Awards, honors:* First Prize Bancarella, 1963, for *Alamein 1933-62;* Second Prize Bagutta, 1966, for *1915-19;* Knight of Malta; commander of several orders.

WRITINGS: Amhara, Plon (Paris), 1937; *Takfir* (first Italian document on Battle of Alamein), Alfieri, 1947, 3rd edition, Longanesi, 1967; *Alamein 1933-62,* Longanesi, 1962, English translation by Dennis Chamberlin, Allen & Unwin, 1966; *1915-19,* Longanesi, 1965; *Ascari K7 1935-36,* Longanesi, 1967; *Le trecento ore a Nord di Qattara* (anthology on Battle of Alamein), Longanesi, 1972. Correspondent for *Corriere della Sera,* 1931-61, and contributor to other Italian and French newspapers.

WORK IN PROGRESS: A book about Italian explorers and warriors in Africa; editing a collection of writings from 1752 to 1975, *The Honorary Ghost;* a journal of the Italian Resistance; planning and building a residential village at Riva dei Tessali on the Apulian Jonian Coast.

SIDELIGHTS: Sales of *Alamein 1933-62* exceed 500,000 copies, with eleven printings of the Italian edition. Caccia-Dominioni is fluent in spoken and written French, German, and English, and speaks Arabic.

*   *   *

CAHILL, Audrey Fawcett   1929-

PERSONAL: Born November 21, 1929, in Port Shepstone, Natal, South Africa; daughter of Walter Clive (a station master) and Margaret (Fawcett) Cahill. *Education:* University of Natal, B.A., 1953, B.A. (honors), 1958, M.A., 1965, Ph.D., 1974; attended University of Cincinnati for a year. *Politics:* Liberal. *Religion:* Anglican. *Home:* 43 Dorchester, Cato Rd., Durban, Natal, South Africa. *Agent:* Lawrence Verry, Inc., Mystic, Conn. 06355. *Office:* University of Natal, King George V Ave., Durban, Natal, South Africa.

CAREER: Teacher of English at Durban Girls' High School, Durban, Natal, South Africa, 1953-56, and Pietermaritzburg Girls' High School, Pietermaritzburg, Natal, 1957-62; St. Anne's Diocesan College, Hilton, Natal, senior English teacher, 1963-65; University of Natal, Durban, Natal, lecturer in English, 1967-70, senior lecturer, 1971—. Taught in England two years. *Member:* South African Institute of Race Relations, Christian Institute of South Africa, English Academy of Southern Africa.

WRITINGS: T. S. Eliot and the Human Predicament, University of Natal Press, 1967; (contributor) Sheila Sullivan, editor, *Critics on T. S. Eliot,* Allen & Unwin, 1973. Contribugor to *Crux.*

WORK IN PROGRESS: A revised and supplemented version of *Studies in Structure* (doctoral dissertation) for Allen & Unwin.

SIDELIGHTS: Miss Cahill told *CA:* "Interest in literature is second only to interest in people. Have taught everything from Afrikaans to football.... Enjoy bridge-building at the personal level between races, nationalities, churches."

CAHN, Steven M. 1942-

PERSONAL: Born August 6, 1942, in Springfield, Mass.; son of Judah (an educator) and Evelyn (an educator; maiden name, Baum) Cahn; married Marilyn Ross (a physician). *Education:* Columbia University, A.B., 1963, Ph.D., 1966. *Religion:* Jewish. *Home:* Manor Woods, No. 71, South Burlington, Vt. 05401. *Office:* Department of Philosophy, University of Vermont, Burlington, Vt. 05401.

CAREER: Vassar College, Poughkeepsie, N.Y., assistant professor of philosophy, 1966-68; New York University, New York, N.Y., assistant professor, 1968-71, associate professor of philosophy, 1971-73; University of Vermont, Burlington, professor of philosophy, and chairman of department, 1973—. Consultant-panelist, Division of Fellowships and Stipends of National Endowment for the Humanities. Concert pianist and organist. *Member:* American Philosophical Association, American Association of University Professors, Phi Beta Kappa.

WRITINGS: Fate, Logic and Time, Yale University Press, 1967; (editor with Frank A. Tillman) *Philosophy of Art and Aesthetics,* Harper, 1969; (editor) *The Philosophical Foundations of Education,* Harper, 1970; (editor) *Philosophy of Religion,* Harper, 1970; *A New Introduction to Philosophy,* Harper, 1971; *The Eclipse of Excellence,* Public Affairs Press, 1973. Contributor to *Encyclopedia of Philosophy, Journal of Philosophy, Analysis, American Philosophical Quarterly, American Journal of Medicine, New York Times,* and other journals.

WORK IN PROGRESS: A book on the philosophy of education.

AVOCATIONAL INTERESTS: Chess.

* * *

CAHN, William 1912-

PERSONAL: Born May 12, 1912, in New York, N.Y.; married Rhoda Lipofsky, 1943; children: Susan, Kathe, Daniel. *Education:* Dartmouth College, B.A., 1934. *Home:* 488 Norton Pkwy., New Haven, Conn.

CAREER: Has worked as a newspaperman, and in public relations and advertising; free-lance writer. *Military service:* U.S. Army, 1943-44. *Awards, honors:* Copy Writers Association of New York, Silver Key, 1964, merit citation 1966; National Conference of Christians and Jews, certificate of recognition, 1964; American Institute of Graphic Arts, certificate of excellence, 1966; Andy Award, Advertising Club of New York, 1967; associate fellow, Calhoun College, Yale University, 1975.

WRITINGS: Guide to Political Action, United Electrical Workers, 1944; (with Herbert Montfort Morais) *Gene Debs: The Story of a Fighting American,* International Publishers, 1948; *Mill Town,* Cameron & Kahn, 1954; *Einstein: A Pictorial Biography,* Citadel, 1955; *Laugh Makers: A Pictorial History of American Comedians,* introduction by Harold Lloyd, Putnam, 1957; *The Union Democracy Built,* Retail Drug Employees Union, 1957; *The Amazing Story of a New American Hero: Van Cliburn,* Ridge Press, 1959; (with Marvin Barrett) *The Jazz Age,* Putnam, 1959; *The Story of Pitney-Bowes,* Harper, 1961; *Good Night, Mrs. Calabash: The Secret of Jimmy Durante,* Duell, Sloan & Pearce, 1963; (with wife, Rhoda Cahn) *The Story of Writing: From Cave Art to Computer,* Harvey House, 1963; *Harold Lloyd's World of Comedy,* Duell, Sloan & Pearce, 1964; *Signature of 450,000,* Ladies Garment Workers' Union, 1965; *Out of the Cracker Barrel: The Nabisco*

Story, From Animal Crackers to Zuzus, Simon & Schuster, 1969; *A Matter of Life and Death: The Connecticut Mutual Story,* Random House, 1970; *A Pictorial History of the Great Comedians,* Grosset, 1970; (with Rhoda Cahn) *No Time for School, No Time for Play: The Story of Child Labor in America,* Messner, 1972; *A Pictorial History of American Labor,* Crown, 1972.

* * *

CAIN, Glen G. 1933-

PERSONAL: Born November 24, 1933, in Chicago, Ill.; son of John Mead (a house painter) and Anna (Stevens) Cain; married Ria H. Castellanet, February 22, 1958; children: Steven M., Paula D. *Education:* Lake Forest College, B.A., 1955; University of California, Berkeley, M.A., 1957; University of Chicago, Ph.D., 1964. *Home:* 3905 Regent St., Madison, Wis. 53705. *Office:* Department of Economics, University of Wisconsin, Madison, Wis. 53706.

CAREER: Federal Reserve Bank, Chicago, Ill., associate economist, 1958-60; University of Wisconsin-Madison, 1963—, began as assistant professor, professor of economics, 1969—. Economist, U.S. Office of Economic Opportunity, 1966-67. Visiting professor at Universidad Nacional de Cuyo, Mendoza, Argentina, summer, 1964, and Princeton University, 1970-71; consulting economist, National Opinion Research Corp., 1965-66. *Member:* American Economic Association, Industrial Relations Research Association (vice-president, Wisconsin chapter, 1965-66).

WRITINGS: Married Women in the Labor Force, University of Chicago Press, 1966; (contributor) Gerald Somers, editor, *Retraining the Unemployed,* University of Wisconsin Press, 1968; (with Richard B. Freeman and W. Lee Hansen) *Labor Market Analysis and Technical Workers,* Johns Hopkins Press, 1973; (editor with Harold W. Watts) *Income Maintenance and Labor Supply,* Academic Press, 1973. Also author of discussion papers for the Institute for Research on Poverty, University of Wisconsin-Madison. Contributor of articles and reviews to professional journals.

WORK IN PROGRESS: Research projects include an economic analysis of the employment and earnings of engineers, a study of the methodology of evaluating social welfare programs.†

* * *

CAIRNS, Thomas W(illiam) 1931-

PERSONAL: Born November 13, 1931, in Hutchinson, Kan.; son of Edmund Alexander (a teacher) and Gladys (Upstone) Cairns; married Sharon Kellet, 1959; children: Janet L., M. Scot. *Education:* Oklahoma State University, B.S., 1953, M.S., 1954, Ph.D., 1959. *Home:* 1357 South 101 East Ave., Tulsa, Okla. 74128. *Office:* Department of Mathematical Sciences, University of Tulsa, 600 South College, Tulsa, Okla. 74104.

CAREER: University of Tulsa, Tulsa, Okla., assistant professor, 1959-66, associate professor, 1966-69, professor of mathematics, and head of department, 1969—. *Military service:* U.S. Army, 1954-56; became first lieutenant. *Member:* Mathematical Association of America (member of board of governors, 1972-75), Society for Industrial and Applied Mathematics, Sigma Xi, Phi Kappa Phi, Omicron Delta Kappa.

WRITINGS: (With William A. Rutledge) *Mathematics for Business Analysis,* Holt, 1964, 2nd edition, 1969; (with I. R. Taylor) *Cost and Management Accounting with Programmed Instruction,* Juta, 1970.

WORK IN PROGRESS: Biomathematics, time series analysis, and mathematical geophysics.

* * *

CALDER, Nigel (David Ritchie) 1931-

PERSONAL: Born December 2, 1931, in London, England; son of (Peter) Ritchie (Lord Ritchie-Calder, the author) and Mabel (McKail) Calder; married Elisabeth Palmer (a research assistant), May 22, 1954; children: Sarah, Penelope, Simon, Jonathan, Katharine. Education: Attended Merchant Taylors' School; Sidney Sussex College, CambridgE, B.A., 1954, M.A., 1957. Home and office: 8 The Chase, Furnace Green, Crawley, Sussex, England. Agent: Rena Feld, 16 Florence Rd., Brighton, England.

CAREER: Mullard Research Laboratories, Redhill, Surrey, England, research physicist, 1954-56; New Scientist, London, England, staff writer, 1956-60, science editor, 1960-62, editor, 1962-66. Military service: British Army, 1950-51; became lieutenant. Member: Association of British Science Writers (chairman, 1962-64). Awards, honors: UNESCO Kalinga Prize for the popularization of science, 1972.

WRITINGS: Electricity Grows Up, Phoenix House, 1958; Robots, Roy, 1958; Radio Astronomy, Roy, 1959, revised edition, Phoenix House, 1964; (editor) The World in 1984, Penguin, 1965; The Environment Game, Secker & Warburg, 1967, published as Eden Was No Garden: An Inquiry into the Environment of Man, Holt, 1967; (editor) Unless Peace Comes: A Scientific Forecast of New Weapons, Viking, 1968; Technopolis: Social Control of the Uses of Science, MacGibbon & Kee, 1969, Simon & Schuster, 1970; Violent Universe: An Eyewitness Account of the New Astronomy, BBC Publications, 1969, Viking, 1970; Living Tomorrow, Penguin, 1970; The Mind of Man, Viking, 1970; Restless Earth, Viking, 1972; The Life Game, BBC Publications, 1973, Viking, 1974; (editor) Nature in the Round, Weidenfeld & Nicolson, 1973, Viking, 1974; The Weather Machine, BBC Publications, 1974, Viking, 1975; The Human Conspiracy, Viking, 1976.

Television documentaries; produced by British Broadcasting Corp., sometimes in conjunction with National Educational Television: "Russia: Beneath the Sputniks," 1967; "The World in a Box," 1968; "The Violent Universe," 1969; "The Mind of Man," 1970; "The Restless Earth," 1972; "The Life Game," 1973; "The Weather Machine," 1974; "The Human Conspiracy," 1975.

Contributor to science journals in England and United States. Science correspondent, New Statesman, 1959-62, 1966-71.

WORK IN PROGRESS: Television scripts for the British Broadcasting Corp.; books, for Viking.

SIDELIGHTS: Nigel Calder told CA that his investigations into the great scientific discoveries of our era have taken him around the world six times. Avocational interests: Sailing.

* * *

CALDERWOOD, James L(ee) 1930-

PERSONAL: Born April 7, 1930, in Corvallis, Ore.; son of George D. (a teacher) and Ruby (Williamson) Calderwood; married Cleo Xeniades, August 14, 1955; children: Stuart Peter, Ian George. Education: University of Oregon, B.S., 1952; University of Washington, Seattle, Ph.D., 1963. Poli-

tics: Democrat. Religion: None. Home: 1323 Terrace Way, Laguna Beach, Calif. 92651. Office: University of California, Irvine, Calif. 92664.

CAREER: Michigan State University, East Lansing, instructor in English, 1961-63; University of California, Los Angeles, assistant professor of English, 1963-66; University of California, Irvine, 1966—, began as associate professor, became professor of English. Military service: U.S. Army, 1952-54; became first lieutenant.

WRITINGS: Shakespearean Metadrama: The Argument of the Play, University of Minnesota Press, 1971.

Editor with Harold E. Toliver, except as noted: Forms of Poetry, Hall, 1968; Perspectives on Drama, Oxford University Press, 1968; Perspectives on Poetry, Oxford University Press, 1968; Perspectives on Fiction, Oxford University Press, 1968; Forms of Drama, Prentice-Hall, 1969; Essays in Shakespearean Criticism, Prentice-Hall, 1970; (editor with J. Leeds Barroll, Jr.) William Shakespeare, Love's Labour's Lost, W. C. Brown, 1970; Forms of Tragedy, Prentice-Hall, 1972; Forms of Prose Fiction, Prentice-Hall, 1972. Contributor of critical articles to professional journals.

WORK IN PROGRESS: Metadrama in Shakespear's Histories: Richard II to Henry V.

* * *

CALDWELL, John C(ope) 1913-

PERSONAL: Born November 27, 1913, in Futsing, China; son of Harry Russell (a Methodist missionary) and Mary Belle (Cope) Caldwell; married Elsie I. Fletcher (a writer and importer), May 27, 1949; children: John, Jr., Kendall Eidson, David F., William O., Karen Elizabeth. Educ tion: Attended Earlham College, 1931-32; Vanderbilt University, A.B., 1935; summer study at Cornell University, 1934, and University of Tennessee, 1939-41. Religion: Methodist. Home and office: 4526 Shy's Hill Rd., Nashville, Tenn. 37215.

CAREER: Tennessee Department of Conservation, Nashville, educational director, 1935-43; U.S. Office of War Information, writer in Washington, D.C., and China, 1943-45; U.S. Department of State, U.S. Information Service, assignments in China and Korea, 1945-50; free-lance writer and lecturer, 1950—, with periods on special assignment with U.S. Department of the Army, Christian Children's Fund of Richmond, Va., and Cordell Hull Foundation, Nashville, Tenn. For several years he conducted two tours each year to the Orient; formerly owned a travel agency, now consultant for a major travel agency. Member of board of directors, American Afro-Asian Educational Exchange, Inc. Member: Society of American Travel Writers, Authors Guild of the Authors League of America, Outdoor Writers Association of America, Tennessee Ornithological Society, Nashville China Club.

WRITINGS: (With Harry R. Caldwell) South China Birds, H. M. Vanderburgh, 1931; (with J. L. Bailey and R. W. Watkins) Our Land and Our Living, Singer, 1941; (with Mark Gayn) American Agent, Holt, 1947; (with Lesley Frost) The Korea Story, Regnery, 1952; China Coast Family, Regnery, 1953 (published in England as Our Friends the Tigers, Hutchinson, 1954); Still the Rice Grows Green: Asia in the Aftermath of Geneva and Panmunjom, Regnery, 1955; Communism in Our World, Day, 1956, revised edition, 1968; Children of Calamity, Day, 1957; South of Tokyo, Regnery, 1957; Far East Travel

Guide, Day, 1959, revised edition, 1961; *South Asia Travel Guide*, Day, 1966; *Far Pacific Travel Guide*, Day, 1966; (with others) *Thailand: Social and Economic Studies in Development*, Duke University Press, 1968; (editor with C. Okonjo) *Population of Tropical Africa*, Columbia University Press, 1968; *Massage Girl, and Other Sketches of Thailand*, Day, 1968; *John C. Caldwell's Orient Travel Guide*, Day, 1970, revised edition, 1971.

"Let's Visit" series (for ages nine to eleven); all published by Day except as noted: *Let's Visit Formosa, Island Home of Free China*, 1956; *... Southeast Asia, Hong Kong to Malaya*, 1957, revised edition, 1970; *... the Middle East*, 1958, revised edition, 1972; *... Middle Africa: East Africa, Central Africa*, 1958, revised edition, 1962; *... Americans Overseas: The Story of Foreign Aid, the Voice of America, Military Assistance, Overseas Bases*, 1958; (with wife, Elsie F. Caldwell) *... Korea*, 1959; *... West Africa*, 1959, revised edition, 1969; *... China*, 1959, revised edition published as *... China Today*, 1973; *... Japan*, 1959, revised edition, 1966; *... the West Indies*, 1960, revised edition, 1963; *... India*, 1960, revised edition, 1970; *... Indonesia*, 1960; *... Ceylon*, 1960; *... Pakistan*, 1960, revised edition, 1970; *... the Philippines*, 1961; *... Argentina*, 1961, revised edition, Burke Publishing, 1968; *... Brazil*, 1961, revised edition, 1973; *... Venezuela*, 1962; *... Colombia*, 1962; *... Peru*, 1962; *... Chile*, 1963, revised edition, 1970; *... the South Pacific: Fiji, Tonga, Tahiti*, 1963, revised edition, 1969; *... Australia*, 1963; *... New Zealand*, 1963; *... Canada*, 1964, revised edition, 1970; *... Central America*, 1964, revised edition, 1973; *... Mexico*, 1965, revised edition, 1972; (with Bernard Newman) *... France*, Burke Publishing, 1965, Day, 1966, revised edition, 1969; *... Vietnam*, 1966; (with Julian Popeseu) *... U.S.S.R.*, 1967, revised edition published as *... Russia*, 1968; *... Thailand*, 1967; (with Angus MacVicar) *... Scotland*, 1967; *... Afghanistan*, 1968; *... Italy*, 1968; *... Turkey*, 1969; *... Micronesia, Guam, U.S.A.*, 1969; (with Popeseu) *... Yugoslavia*, 1969; (with Nicholas Freville) *... Nigeria*, 1970; (with Garry Lyle) *... Greece*, 1972.

"World Neighbors" series, with wife, Elsie F. Caldwell (for ages six to nine); all published by Day: *Our Neighbors in India*, 1960; *... in Japan*, 1960; *... in the Philippines*, 1961; *... in Korea*, 1961; *... in Africa*, 1961, revised edition, 1968; *... in Peru*, 1962; *... in Brazil*, 1962; *... in Central America*, 1967; *... in Australia and New Zealand*, 1967; *... in Thailand*, 1968.

Contributor to national magazines; has written syndicated newspaper column on travel.

SIDELIGHTS: Caldwell travels constantly, gathering material for new books and for updating the old. He has crossed the Pacific more than seventy times. A number of the books in the "Let's Visit" series have also been published in England.

AVOCATIONAL INTERESTS: Trout fishing, wild flower gardening.†

* * *

CALDWELL, Joseph H(erman) 1934-

PERSONAL: Born January 19, 1934, in Jacksonville, Fla.; son of Newton Frank (a corporation president) and Josephine (Zapf) Caldwell. *Education:* Florida State University, B.S., 1955, M.S., 1962; University of Florida, Ed.S., 1969. *Religion:* Roman Catholic. *Home:* 344 Ninth St., Atlantic Beach, Fla. 32233.

CAREER: Elementary teacher in Ponte Vedra, Fla., 1959-64; Mill Creek School, St. Augustine, Fla., principal, 1965-66; Florida Junior College at Jacksonville, counselor, 1966-67, counselor coordinator of Southside Campus, 1967-68, director of student personnel services, Southside Campus, 1968-69, assistant dean of student services, 1969-72, dean of student development, 1972—. Director and treasurer, Duval County Teacher's Credit Union, 1975; chairman of Florida State Community College Health Services Commission, 1973—. Member of advisory board, Jacksonville Children's Museum. *Military service:* U.S. Naval Reserve, 1956-73; active duty, 1956-59; became lieutenant commander. *Member:* American Personnel and Guidance Association, Association for Measurement and Evaluation in Guidance, American College Personnel Association, American Littoral Society, Florida Association of Community Colleges, Florida Personnel and Guidance Association (treasurer, 1974), Florida Association of Science Teachers. *Awards, honors:* Florida State Competence Award, 1962, 1963; National Science Foundation fellowship, 1964-65, 1972, 1974.

WRITINGS: (With Myra B. Cook and Lina Christiansen) *The Come-Alive Classroom*, Parker Publishing, 1967; (with Cook and Christiansen) *Dynamic Teaching in the Elementary School*, Prentice-Hall, 1970. Contributor to *Community and Junior College Journal*.

WORK IN PROGRESS: A revision of *The Come-Alive Classroom*.

AVOCATIONAL INTERESTS: Photography, cycling, boating, amateur radio (operates under call number W4TON).

* * *

CALIN, William (Compaine) 1936-

PERSONAL: Surname is pronounced *Kale*-in; born April 4, 1936, in Newington, Conn.; son of Jack and Nettie (Compaine) Calin; married Francoise Geffroy, January 5, 1971. *Education:* Yale University, B.A., 1957, Ph.D., 1960; additional study in France, 1955-56. *Home:* 2988 Powell St., Eugene, Ore. 97405. *Office:* Department of Romance Languages, University of Oregon, Eugene, Ore.

CAREER: Dartmouth College, Hanover, N.H., instructor, 1960-62, assistant professor of French, 1962-63; Stanford University, Stanford, Calif., assistant professor, 1964-65, associate professor, 1965-70, professor of French, 1970-73; University of Oregon, Eugene, professor of French, 1973—. *Member:* Modern Language Association of America, Societe Rencesvals. *Awards, honors:* Guggenheim fellowship and American Council of Learned Societies grant, both 1963-64.

WRITINGS: The Old French Epic of Revolt, Droz (Geneva), 1962; (editor with Michel Benamou) *Aux Portes du Poeme*, Macmillan, 1964; *The Epic Quest: Studies in Four Old French Chansons de Geste*, Johns Hopkins Press, 1966; (editor) *La Chanson de Roland*, Appleton 1968; (editor) *A Poet at the Fountain: Essays on the Narrative Verse of Guillaume de Machaut*, University Press of Kentucky, 1974. Contributor to journals.

WORK IN PROGRESS: A book on the epic poem in France, from the Middle Ages to the twentieth-century.

* * *

CALLAHAN, Daniel 1930-

PERSONAL: Born July 19, 1930, in Washington, D.C.;

son of Vincent F. (an editor) and Florence Anita (Hawkins) Callahan; married Sidney Cornelia deShazo (a part-time writer), June 5, 1954; children: Mark, Stephen, John, Peter, Sarah, David. *Education:* Yale University, B.A., 1948; Georgetown University, M.A., 1957; Harvard University, Ph.D., 1965. *Politics:* Democrat. *Office:* Institute of Society, Ethics and the Life Sciences, 623 Warburton Ave., Hastings-on-Hudson, N.Y. 10706.

CAREER: Harvard Divinity School, Cambridge, Mass., teaching fellow in Roman Catholic studies, 1959-61; *Commonweal,* New York, N.Y., 1961-68, became executive editor, 1967; Institute of Society, Ethics and the Life Sciences, Hastings-on-Hudson, N.Y., director, 1969—. Visiting assistant professor at Temple University, 1963, and at Brown University, 1965. Staff associate of The Population Council, 1969-70. *Military service:* U.S. Army, Counterintelligence Corps. 1952-55; became sergeant. *Member:* National Academy of Sciences, Institute of Medicine, New York Council for the Humanities. *Awards, honors:* National Catholic Book Award, 1964, for *The Mind of the Catholic Layman;* Thomas More Medal, 1970, for *Abortion: Law, Choice, and Morality.*

WRITINGS: (Editor with D. O'Hanlon and H. Oberman) *Christianity Divided,* Sheed, 1961; *The Mind of the Catholic Layman,* Scribner, 1963; (editor) *Federal Aid and Catholic Schools,* Helicon, 1964; (editor) *Generation of the Third Eye,* Sheed, 1965; *Honesty in the Church,* Scribner, 1965; *The New Church,* Scribner, 1966; (editor) *The Secular City Debate,* Macmillan, 1966; *Abortion: Law, Choice, and Morality,* Macmillan, 1970; *Ethics and Population Limitation,* Associated Booksellers, 1971; *The American Population Debate,* Doubleday, 1972; *The Tyranny of Survival: And Other Pathologies of Civilized Life,* Macmillan, 1973. Contributor to *Harper's, Atlantic, Center Magazine,* and *New York Times Magazine.*

WORK IN PROGRESS: A book on medical ethics.

BIOGRAPHICAL/CRITICAL SOURCES: Newsweek, June 8, 1970; *Washington Post,* January 19, 1974.

* * *

CALLAHAN, Sterling G. 1916-

PERSONAL: Born June 23, 1916, in Loa, Utah; son of William Henry and Frances (Grundy) Callahan; married Rebecca Morrow, September 5, 1943; children: Scott M., Jane Ann. *Education:* Brigham Young University, A.B., 1937; George Washington University, M.A., 1947; University of Virginia, E.D., 1953. *Religion:* Church of Jesus Christ of Latter-day Saints. *Home:* 1080 East 2680 North, Provo, Utah. 84601.

CAREER: Mormon missionary in Germany, 1938-39; teacher in public schools of Arlington, Va., 1946-50; University of Virginia, School of Education, Charlottesville, instructor, 1950-53; Brigham Young University, Provo, Utah, assistant professor, 1953-56, associate professor, 1956-59, professor of secondary education, 1959—. Visiting professor, University of Southern California, 1959. *Military service:* U.S. Army, Intelligence, 1941-45. *Member:* National Education Association, Utah Education Association, Phi Delta Kappa.

WRITINGS: Reference Materials for Use in Secondary School Planning and Teaching, Brigham Young University Press, 1960; *Successful Teaching in Secondary Schools,* Scott, Foresman, 1966, revised edition, 1971. Contributor to education journals.

CALLEN, William B. 1930-

PERSONAL: Born October 6, 1930, in Milwaukee, Wis.; son of Carroll Francis (an industrial engineer) and Magdalene (Behr) Callen. *Education:* Rensselaer Polytechnic Institute, B. Mech. Engrg., 1952; St. Louis University, M.A., 1960, S.T.B., 1967. *Politics:* Democrat. *Address:* Sogang College, P.O. Box 1142, Seoul, Korea.

CAREER: A C Electronics Corp., Milwaukee, Wis., junior engineer, 1953-54; entered Society of Jesus (Jesuits), 1954, ordained priest, 1967; Marquette University, Milwaukee, visiting lecturer in theology, 1968; went to Korea, 1968, to study Korean language preparatory to teaching in a Jesuit college there.

WRITINGS: (Editor with D. McCarthy) *Modern Biblical Studies,* Bruce Publishing, 1967.

WORK IN PROGRESS: Research in New Testament.††

* * *

CALLOW, Alexander B., Jr. 1925-

PERSONAL: Born November 15, 1925, in Denver, Colo.; son of Alexander B. (an engineer) and Pearl (Meadows) Callow; married Marie Eleanor Carrubba, 1953; children: Scott Alexander, Sean Michael. *Education:* University of California, Santa Barbara, B.A., 1950; University of California, Berkeley, M.A., 1955, Ph.D., 1961. *Politics:* Democrat. *Home:* 4651 La Espada Dr., Santa Barbara, Calif. 93105. *Agent:* Collins-Knowlton-Wing, Inc., 60 East 56th St., New York, N.Y. 10022.

CAREER: Purdue University, Lafayette, Ind., assistant professor, 1961-65, associate professor of history, 1965-66; University of California, Santa Barbara, associate professor of history, 1966—. *Military service:* U.S. Merchant Marine, 1943-46. U.S. Air Force, 1951-53; became staff sergeant. *Member:* American Historical Association, Organization of American Historians. *Awards, honors:* California Historical Society Prize, 1957; Woodrow Wilson Fellowship, 1960; Purdue Research Foundation grants, 1962, 1963.

WRITINGS: The Tweed Ring, Oxford University Press, 1966; *American Urban History: An Interpretive Reader with Commentaries,* Oxford University Press, 1969, 2nd edition, 1973; *The City Boss in America,* Oxford University Press, 1975. Contributor to *American Heritage, New York Times Magazine, Smithsonian, True,* and to learned journals.

WORK IN PROGRESS: Behind Those Swinging Doors: A History of the American Saloon; and a history of organized crime in America.

AVOCATIONAL INTERESTS: Sleight-of-hand, fishing, reading, travel.

* * *

CALLOWAY, Doris Howes 1923-

PERSONAL: Born February 14, 1923, in Canton, Ohio; daughter of Earl John (a lawyer and detective) and Lillian (Roberts) Howes; married Nathaniel O. Calloway, February 14, 1946 (divorced, 1956); children: David K., Candace M. *Education:* Ohio State University, B.S., 1943; University of Chicago, Ph.D., 1947. *Residence:* Berkeley, Calif. *Office:* Department of Nutritional Sciences, University of California, Berkeley, Calif. 94720.

CAREER: Johns Hopkins Hospital, Baltimore, Md., intern in dietetics, 1944; University of Illinois, College of Medicine, Chicago, research dietitian, 1945; Medical Associates, Chicago, consultant, 1948-50; Armed Forces Food and Container Institute, Chicago, nutritionist, 1951-56, head of metabolism laboratory, 1956-59, chief of nutrition branch, 1959-61; Stanford Research Institute, Menlo Park, Calif., chairman of department of food science and nutrition, 1961-64; University of California, Berkeley, lecturer in nutritional science, 1962-63, professor of nutrition, 1963—. Consultant to Food and Agricultural Organization of the United Nations, 1971 and 1975; member of Food and Nutrition Board, National Research Council, 1969-72; member of advisory panel on nutrition, World Health Organization, 1972—, and advisory council of National Institute of Arthritis, Metabolism, and Digestive Diseases, 1973-77.

MEMBER: American Dietetic Association, American Institute of Nutrition (secretary, 1969-72), Sigma Xi, Omicron Nu, Sigma Delta Epsilon, Iota Sigma Pi. *Awards, honors:* Meritorious Civilian Service Award, U.S. Department of the Army, 1959, and Certificates of Achievement, 1959, 1961.

WRITINGS: (With B. H. Ingel) *Nutrition,* Behavorial Research Laboratories, Palo Alto, 1964; (with L. J. Bogert and G. M. Briggs) *Nutrition and Physical Fitness,* 8th edition (Calloway was not associated with earlier editions), Saunders, 1966, 9th edition, 1973; (editor) *Human Ecology in Space Flight,* New York Academy of Sciences, Volume I, 1966, Volume II, 1967, Volume III, 1968; (contributor) *Handbook of Physiology,* Williams & Wilkins, 1968. Contributor of more than 100 articles to medical and nutritional journals. Associate editor, *Nutrition Reviews,* 1962-69; member of editorial boards of *Journal of Nutrition,* 1967-72, *Environmental Biology and Medicine,* 1971—, *American Dietetic Association Journal,* 1974—, *Interdisiplinary Science Review,* 1975—. Editor of and contributor to numerous reports published by Food and Agriculture Organization, and National Research Council.

WORK IN PROGRESS: An advanced human nutrition text, to be published by Saunders.

*   *   *

CALMANN, John 1935-

PERSONAL: Born December 6, 1935, in Hamburg, Germany, son of Hans M. (an art dealer) and Gerta (Hertz) Calmann. *Education:* Christ Church, Oxford, B.A. (honors in history), 1957, graduate study, 1957-59. *Politics:* Liberal Party. *Religion:* None. *Home:* 6/7 Cleveland Sq., London W2 6DA, England.

CAREER: Wall Street Journal, New York, N.Y., news assistant, 1960; European Community, Luxembourg, spokesman, 1962-63; *Times,* London, England, editor of News Service, 1964-65; Institute for Strategic Studies, London, research associate, 1966; Elek Books Ltd., London, senior editor, 1967-69; Phaidon Press Ltd., London, senior editor, 1969-73, editorial director, 1973-75.

WRITINGS: (Editor) *Western Europe: A Handbook,* Praeger, 1967; (editor) *The Rome Treaty: The Common Market Explained,* Anthony Blond, 1967; *Defense and Technology in West Europe,* Institute for Strategic Studies, 1967.

WORK IN PROGRESS: A novel, a play, and various political writings.

*   *   *

CALVERT, Monte A(lan) 1938-

PERSONAL: Born April 16, 1938, in Los Angeles, Calif.;

son of Bill Franklin and Evelyn (McDougall) Calvert; married Gertrude Baker, December 29, 1962; children: Ann Elizabeth, Laura Ellen. *Education:* Occidental College, A.B., 1960; University of Delaware, M.A., 1962; University of Pittsburgh, Ph.D., 1965. *Home:* 9 Lawrence Ave., Potsdam, N.Y. 13676. *Office:* Department of History, Clarkson College, Potsdam, N.Y. 13676.

CAREER: Archives of Industrial Society, Pittsburgh, Pa., curator, 1963-65; Smithsonian Institution, Washington, D.C., curator of tools, 1965-67; University of Pennsylvania, Philadelphia, visiting professor of history of technology, 1967, visiting lecturer in history, 1967-68, assistant professor of American civilization, 1968-69; Iowa State University of Science and Technology, Ames, associate professor of history, 1969-70; Clarkson College, Potsdam, N.Y., associate professor, 1970-73, professor of history, 1973—. *Member:* Organization of American Historians (life member).

WRITINGS: The Mechanical Engineer in America, 1830-1910: Professional Cultures in Conflict, John Hopkins Press, 1967.

WORK IN PROGRESS: The Engineer and the City (tentative title), exploring the relationships between technics and politics in American cities of the late nineteenth- and early twentieth-centuries.

*   *   *

CAMERON, Donald (Allan) 1937-
(D. A. Cameron, Silver Donald Cameron)

PERSONAL: Born June 21, 1937, in Toronto, Ontario, Canada; son of Maxwell A. (a professor of education) and Hazel (Robertson) Cameron; married Catherine Ann Cahoon (divorced, 1973); children: Maxwell, Ian, Leslie (daughter), Steven. *Education:* University of British Columbia, B.A., 1960; University of California, Berkeley, M.A., 1962; University of London, Ph.D., 1967. *Politics:* New Democratic Party. *Residence:* D'Escousse, Nova Scotia.

CAREER: High school teacher in British Columbia public schools, 1957-58, principal, 1958-59; University of British Columbia, Vancouver, lecturer in English, 1962-64; Dalhousie University, Halifax, Nova Scotia, postdoctoral fellow, 1967-68; University of New Brunswick, Fredericton, associate professor of English, 1968-71; freelance writer, broadcaster, and photographer in D'Escousse, Nova Scotia, 1971—. *Member:* Writers Union of Canada, Canadian Civil Liberties Association. *Awards, honors:* Woodrow Wilson fellowship, 1960-61; British Council Scholar, 1965-66; Canadian Centennial Commission Author's Award, 1966-67; Killam fellowship, Dalhousie University, 1967-68.

WRITINGS: Faces of Leacock, Ryerson, 1967; *Conversations with Canadian Novelists,* Macmillan, 1973. Contributor of plays, talks, interviews, and other material to Canadian radio and television. Contributor of articles under the names D. A. Cameron and Silver Donald Cameron, to journals in Canada, the United States, India, and Britain. Founding editor, *The Mysterious East* ("radical magazine").

AVOCATIONAL INTERESTS: Talk, music, woodworking, sailing his 33-foot schooner *Hirondelle.*

*   *   *

CAMERON, James 1911-

PERSONAL: Born June 17, 1911, in London, England; son

of William Ernest (a barrister at law and author) and Douglas Margaret (Robertson) Cameron; married Elma Murray, June, 1938 (died in childbirth, 1939); married Elizabeth O'Conor (an artist), November 25, 1944 (divorced); married Moneesha Sarkar, January, 1971; children: Desmond Roderic, Elma (Mrs. Gavin Roberts), Fergus Doone. *Education:* Educated in France and England. *Politics:* Socialist. *Religion:* None. *Home:* 16 Binden Rd., London, England. *Agent:* Nicholas Thompson, Queen's Gate, London, England.

CAREER: Journalist and foreign correspondent, 1930—; began writing for the *Sunday Post* in Scotland, became foreign correspondent for the *Daily Express*, London, England, 1944-50, chief foreign correspondent for the *News Chronicle*, London, 1952-60, and wrote for other British newspapers. Consultant to British Broadcasting Corporation and initiator of their "One Pair of Eyes"; appeared many times on British television; producer of "Cameron Country," a collection of international programs. Founder-member of the Campaign for Nuclear Disarmament, 1958. Governor of Mermaid Theatre. *Wartime activity:* War correspondent in World War II, Korea, and Vietnam; first western journalist in North Vietnam, 1964. *Member:* National Union of Journalists, Society of Authors, Savile Club. *Awards, honors:* Granada award as foreign correspondent of the year, 1966, and as foreign correspondent of the decade, 1957-67; Hannen Swaffer Award, 1967; Prix Italia, 1973.

WRITINGS: Touch of the Sun, Witherby, 1950; *Mandarin Red*, Rinehart, 1955; *1914*, Rinehart, 1959; *The African Revolution*, Random House, 1961; *1916*, Oldbourne, 1962; *Here Is Your Enemy*, Holt, 1965 (published in England as *Witness in Vietnam*, Gollancz, 1965); *Vicky: A Memorial*, Allen Lane, 1967; *Point of Departure: An Attempt at Autobiography*, Arthur Barker, 1967, McGraw, 1968; *What a Way to Run the Tribe*, McGraw, 1968; *An Indian Summer*, McGraw, 1974.

SIDELIGHTS: In his review of Cameron's autobiography, John Mecklin describes Cameron as "a worthy but unenviable Quixote battling the giants of the Establishment by hammering at them with his typewriter." According to Anthony Howard, "for the past 20 years [Cameron has been] the owner of perhaps one of the half-dozen best-known by-lines in the business." Not only is he one of the best-known, Cameron is also one of the most controversial of journalists. With his characteristic lack of objectivity, he does not merely describe an event, but often defines it in the terms of his personal reaction to it. "He has consistently broken all the rules about the twin journalistic duties of detachment and objectivity," says Howard. "Even as a foreign correspondent the distinguishing hallmark of his writing has always been a sense of personal involvement in whatever he is describing—whether it happened to be the first atom bomb test exploded at Bikini, the Vietnam war as lived through in the North, or . . . the plight of Arab Refugees in the Middle East." A reviewer in the *Times Literary Supplement* says that Cameron has learned that "the only way a reporter can work and still save his soul alive is to be true to his own subjective vision, whether in absolute terms it prove right or wrong." Although Cameron says without illusions that "nothing one writes makes much difference. . . . One has never altered anything," he keeps trying, with his compassionate empathy, to express his point of view. Typically, he says: "I had no professional justification left if I did not at least try to make the point that North

Vietnam, despite all official Washington arguments to the contrary, was inhabited by human beings."

So outspoken is his reportage sometimes, that Mecklin calls his book about his visit to North Vietnam, *Here is Your Enemy*, "one of the most scathing blasts at [the United States] . . . from a non-Communist writer." According to Michael Wharton, Cameron "epitomizes, on an unsophisticated level, and in a remarkably pure form, [the] orthodox liberal attitude to the world," and, he adds, "it is part of this attitude that the world ought to make sense according to liberal ideas. It is a perpetual wonderment to him that it doesn't." Indeed, Cameron may be conforming to type when he passionately states: "Nothing in the world, however base nor however good, nor however theoretically admirable can justify murder as an act of policy." David Watt says, Cameron is one of "very few journalists writing today who [is] capable of [a] precise combination of topicality, experience and controlled indignation." Howard, attempting to explain "what exactly it is that James Cameron has always had over even his most accomplished professional rivals," writes: "For them curiosity has been everything—for him, compassion has always meant more."

BIOGRAPHICAL/CRITICAL SOURCES: James Cameron, *Point of Departure*, Arthur Barker, 1967, McGraw, 1968; *Punch*, July 5, 1967, July 3, 1968; *Observer Review*, July 9, 1967, July 7, 1968; *Times Literary Supplement*, July 27, 1967; *Newsweek*, January 29, 1968; *New Yorker*, February 24, 1968; *New York Times Book Review*, April 21, 1968; *Newsman*, August, 1968; *New Republic*, December 14, 1968.

* * *

CAMERON, Kenneth Walter 1908-

PERSONAL: Born October 12, 1908, in Martins Ferry, Ohio; son of Albert Ernest (an executive) and Zoe Shockley (Barker) Cameron. *Education:* West Virginia University, A.B., 1930, A.M., 1931; General Theological Seminary, S.T.B., 1935; Yale University, Ph.D., 1940. *Politics:* Republican. *Home:* 23 Wolcott St., Hartford, Conn. 06106. *Office:* Trinity College, Zion St., Hartford, Conn. 06106.

CAREER: Ordained Episcopal priest, 1935. University of North Carolina, Raleigh, instructor in English, 1938-43; Temple University, Philadelphia, assistant professor of English, 1945-46; Trinity College, Hartford, Conn., assistant professor, 1946-58, associate professor of English, 1958—. Diocese of Connecticut, archivist and historiographer. *Member:* Modern Language Association of America, Modern Humanities Research Association, Melville Society, Thoreau Society, Emerson Society (executive secretary, 1955—).

WRITINGS—All published by Transcendental Books, except as noted: *Authorship and Sources of "Gentleness and Nobility,"* Thistle Press, 1941; *Background of John Heywood's "Witty and Wittless,"* Thistle Press, 1941; *John Heywood's "Play of the Wether,"* Thistle Press, 1941; *Ralph Waldo Emerson's Reading*, Thistle Press, 1941, reprinted, Haskell, 1973, revised edition, Transcendental Books, 1962; *Emerson the Essayist: An Outline of His Philosophical Development Through 1836*, Thistle Press, 1945.

The Presbury Family of Maryland and the Ohio Valley, 1950; *Genesis of Hawthorne's "The Ambitious Guest,"* Thistle Press, 1955; *The Genesis of Christ Church, Stratford, Connecticut*, Christ Church, 1957; *The Transcen-*

dental Workbook, 1957; An Emerson Index; or, Names, Exempla, Sententiae, Symbols, Words, and Motifs in Selected Notebooks of Ralph Waldo Emerson, 1958; The Transcendentalists and Minerva, 1958; Emerson and Thoreau as Readers (selected chapters from The Transcendentalists and Minerva), 1958, 2nd edition, 1972; Index of the Pamphlet Collection of the Diocese of Connecticut, The Historiographer, 1958.

A Commentary on Emerson's Early Lectures, 1833-1836, with Index-Concordance, 1961; Centennial History of Trinity Episcopal Church, Bridgeport, Connecticut, Trinity Episcopal Church, 1963; The Catholic Revival in Episcopal Connecticut, 1850-1925, Trinity Episcopal Church, 1963; Companion to Thoreau's Correspondence, 1964; Emerson's Workshop: An Analysis of His Reading in Periodicals Through 1836, 1964; The Pardoner and His Pardons: Indulgences Circulating in England on the Eve of Reformation, 1965; Transcendental Epilogue, 1965; Thoreau's Harvard Years, 1966; Transcendental Climate, 1967; Hawthorne Index, 1968.

Transcendental Reading Patterns: Library Charging Lists, 1970; Young Emerson's Transcendental Vision: An Exposition of His World View with an Analysis of the Structure, Backgrounds, and Meaning of Nature, 1971; Emerson the Essayist: An Outline of His Philosophical Development through 1836 with Special Emphasis on the Sources and Interpretation of Nature, also Bibliographical Appendices, 1972; Letter-book of the Reverend Henry Caner, S.P.G. Missionary in Colonial Connecticut and Massachusetts until the Revolution, 1972; Longfellow's Reading in Libraries: The Charging Records of a Learned Poet Interpreted, 1973; Response to Transcendental Concord, 1974; Young Thoreau and the Classics, 1975.

Compiler: Early Anglicanism in Connecticut, 1962; Index-Concordance to Emerson's Sermons, 1963; (and author of notes, and editor) Over Thoreau's Desk: New Correspondence 1838-1861, 1965; Emerson Among His Contemporaries: A Harvest of Estimates, Insights, and Anecdotes from the Victorian Literary World and an Index, 1967; Research Keys to the American Renaissance: Scarce Indexes of "The Christian Examiner," "The North American Review," and "The New Jerusalem Magazine," for Students of American Literature, Culture, History, and New England Transcendentalism, 1967; Connecticut Churchmanship: Records and Historical Papers Concerning the Anglican Church in Connecticut in the Eighteenth and Early Nineteenth Centuries, 1969; The Massachusetts Lyceum During the American Renaissance: Materials for the Study of the Oral Tradition in American Letters, 1969; Concord Harvest: Publications of the Concord School of Philosophy and Literature, 1970; Contemporary Dimension: An American Renaissance Literary Notebook of Newspaper Clippings, [and] Victorian Notebook: Literary Clippings from Nineteenth-Century American Newspapers, 1970; The Anglican Episcopate in Connecticut: A Sheaf of Biographical and Institutional Studies for Churchmen and Historians (1784-1899), 1970; American Episcopal Clergy: Registers of Ordinations in the Episcopal Church in the United States, 1970; Transcendental Log, 1973; Anglican Climate in Connecticut: Historical Perspectives from Imprints of the Late Colonial and Early National Years, 1974; Ammi Rogers and the Episcopal Church in Connecticut, 1790-1832: His Memoirs and Documents Illuminating Historical, Religious, and Personal Backgrounds, 1974.

Editor: (And author of introduction) Ralph Waldo Emerson, Nature (1836 edition), Scholars' Facsimiles Reprints, 1940; John Heywood, Gentleness and Nobility, Thistle Press, 1941; Emerson, Indian Superstition, Friends of the Dartmouth Library, 1954, 2nd edition 1963; Emerson, Thoreau, and Concord in Early Newspapers, 1957; Thoreau's Literary Notebook in the Library of Congress, 1964; Thoreau and His Harvard Classmates with Henry William's Memorials of the Class of 1837, 1965; Poems of Jones Very, 1965; Thoreau's Fact Book in the Harry Elkins Widener Collection in the Harvard College Library, 1966; The Works of Samuel Peters of Hebron, Connecticut, New England Historian, Satirist, Folklorist, Anti-patriot, and Anglican Clergyman, 1735-1826, with Historical Indexes, 1967; Facsimiles of Early Episcopal Church Documents (1759-1789), 1970. Editor, Emerson Society Quarterly, Historiographer of the Episcopal Diocese of Connecticut, and American Transcendental Quarterly.

AVOCATIONAL INTERESTS: American literary autographs.

*   *   *

CAMPBELL, Ann R. 1925-

PERSONAL: Born January 30, 1925, in Boston, Mass.; daughter of Jonathan Stone (a banker) and Pauline (Pollard) Raymond; married Gordon P. Baird; married second husband, Peter A. Campbell; married third husband, Peter Paul Luce (a management consultant), October 28, 1967; children: (first marriage) Jonathan Raymond Baird, Jordan Prentiss Baird. Education: Vassar College, A.B., 1946; graduate study at American University, 1954. Religion: Presbyterian.

CAREER: Miss Fine's School, Princeton, N.J., teacher, 1955-57; Brooklyn Friends School, Brooklyn, N.Y., teacher, 1957-59; H. M. Snyder & Co., New York City, promotion manager, 1960-63; Franklin Watts, Inc., New York City, advertising and promotion manager, 1963-67; free-lance editor, writer, and book illustrator, beginning 1967. Member: Publisher's Advertising Club (New York; past vice-president), Artists Equity Association.

WRITINGS: Let's Find Out about Color, F. Watts, 1966, revised edition, 1975; Let's Find Out about Boats, F. Watts, 1967; Let's Find Out about Farms, F. Watts, 1968; Start to Draw, F. Watts, 1968; Let's Find Out about a Ball, F. Watts, 1969; The Picture Life of Richard Milhous Nixon, F. Watts, 1969; Paintings: How to Look at Great Art, F. Watts, 1970.†

*   *   *

CAMPBELL, Bernard G(rant) 1930-

PERSONAL: Born April 29, 1930, in Weybridge, England; son of Donald Fraser (an engineer) and Caroline (Henry) Campbell; married Margaret Elton-Mills, May 10, 1962; children: James Sebastian, Sophia Georgina. Education: Cambridge University, M.A., 1952, Ph.D., 1957. Home: Sedgeford Hall, Hunstanton, Norfolk, England.

CAREER: Farmer, 1957—; Cambridge University, Cambridge, England, visiting lecturer in anthropology, 1967-69; University of California, Los Angeles, professor of anthropology, 1971—.

WRITINGS: The Nomenclature of the Hominidae, Royal Anthropological Institute, 1965; Human Evolution: An Introduction to Man's Adaptations, Aldine, 1966, 2nd edition, 1974; (with K. P. Oakley) Catalogue of Fossil Hominids, three volumes, British Museum, 1967-75; (editor)

Sexual Selection and the Descent of Man, 1871-1971, Aldine, 1972; (editor) *Mankind Emerging,* Little, Brown, 1976.

WORK IN PROGRESS: Research in human evolution.

* * *

CAMPBELL, David P. 1934-

PERSONAL: Born January 14, 1934, in Bridgewater, Iowa; son of Gerald L. (a grocer) and Shirley (Sullivan) Campbell; married Phyllis Jensen (a musician), August 28, 1955; children: James, Charles, Andrew. *Education:* Iowa State University, B.S., 1955, M.S., 1958; University of Minnesota, Ph.D., 1960. *Politics:* "Occasionally." *Religion:* "In crises." *Home:* 908 Dover Rd., Greensboro, N.C. 27408. *Office address:* Center for Creative Leadership, P.O. Box P-1, Greensboro, N.C. 27402.

CAREER: University of Minnesota, Minneapolis, assistant professor, 1960-63, associate professor, 1963-68, professor of psychology, 1968-74; Center for Creative Leadership, Greensboro, N.C., vice-president, 1974—. Consultant, National Computer Systems; lecturer, International Roundtable of Educational Counseling, Salzburg, Austria, 1967. *Military service:* U.S. Army Reserve, 1955-68; became captain. *Member:* American Psychological Association (fellow), American Association for the Advancement of Science (fellow), American Personnel and Guidance Association, American Association of University Professors.

WRITINGS: The Results of Counseling, Saunders, 1965; *Handbook for the Strong Vocational Interest Blank,* Stanford University Press, 1971; *If You Don't Know Where You're Going, You'll Probably Wind Up Somewhere Else,* Argus, 1974.

WORK IN PROGRESS: Research on vocational interests and leadership.

* * *

CAMPBELL, Eugene Edward 1915-

PERSONAL: Born April 26, 1915, in Tooele, Utah; son of Edward (a locomotive engineer) and Betsy Ann (Bowen) Campbell; married Beth Larsen, August 11, 1939; children: Bruce L., Mary Ann (Mrs. William Dennison Payne), Jean (Mrs. John M. Fenn), Sharon (Mrs. Tristan R. Pico), Edward L. *Education:* Snow Junior College (now Snow College), A.A., 1935; University of Utah, B.A., 1939, M.A., 1940; University of Southern California, Ph.D., 1952. *Politics:* Independent. *Home:* 1305 Briar, Provo, Utah 84601. *Office:* Brigham Young University, Provo, Utah 84601.

CAREER: High priest, Church of Jesus Christ of Latter-day Saints (Mormon). Teacher and principal in Mormon Educational System, 1940-44; Idaho State University, Pocatello, director of Latter-day Saints Institute of Religion, 1946-49; Utah State University, Logan, associate director of Latter-day Saints Institute of Religion, 1950-56; Brigham Young University, Provo, Utah, associate professor, 1956-57, professor of history, 1957—, chairman of department, 1960-67. *Military service:* U.S. Army, chaplain, 1944-46; became captain; received two battle stars for European campaigns. *Member:* Mormon History Association (national president, 1966-67), Utah History Association, Phi Kappa Alpha. *Awards, honors:* Danforth associate; Morman History Association award and Dale Morgan award, both 1973, for scholarly article.

WRITINGS: (Contributor) *The History of a Valley: Cache Valley, Utah and Idaho,* Cache Valley Centennial Commission, 1956; (with Kent Fielding) *The United States: An Interpretative History,* Harper, 1964; (with Fred K. Gowans) *Fort Bridger: Island in the Wilderness,* Brigham Young University Press, 1975; *Life and Thought of Hugh B. Brown,* Bookcraft, 1975. Contributor of articles on Mormon and Utah history to journals.

WORK IN PROGRESS: Volume six of the *Comprehensive History of The Latter-day Saints; The Early Pioneer Period, 1847-1869,* for Deseret.

* * *

CAMPBELL, Jack K(enagy) 1927-

PERSONAL: Born January 17, 1927, in Chicago, Ill.; son of Donald John (a personnel manager) and Helen (Myers) Campbell; married Susan Decker Eschenlauer, August 20, 1960; children: Martha Decker, Jonathan Myers, Arthur Olin. *Education:* Cornell College, Mount Vernon, Iowa, A.B., 1949; University of Illinois, M.A., 1956; Columbia University, Ed.D., 1965. *Home:* 1805 Shadow Wood, College Station, Tex. 77840.

CAREER: Teacher of history at high schools in Manhasset, N.Y., 1956-58, and Cranford, N.J., 1959-64; Brooklyn College of the City University of New York, Brooklyn, N.Y., assistant professor of education, 1964-67; Lycoming College, Williamsport, Pa., associate professor of education and chairman of department, 1967-70; Texas A&M University, College Station, associate professor of education, 1970—. *Military service:* U.S. Navy, 1951-55. *Member:* History of Education Society, American Historical Association, National Education Association, American Association of University Professors, American Education Research Association.

WRITINGS: Colonel Francis W. Parker, the Children's Crusader, Teachers College, Columbia University, 1967. Contributor to *Progressive Education, Teachers College Record, Kappa Delta Pi Record, Intellect,* and *Education Digest.*

* * *

CAMPBELL, Paul N. 1923-

PERSONAL: Born February 27, 1923, in Washington, D.C.; son of John Clinton (a government auditor) and Stella (Reynolds) Campbell; married Mildred Seibald, July, 1946 (divorced); married Karlyn Kohrs, September, 1967. *Education:* Grove City College, B.Mus., 1943; University of Southern California, Ph.D., 1959. *Home:* 1348 Engel Rd., Lawrence, Kan. 66044. *Office:* University of Kansas, Lawrence, Kan. 66045.

CAREER: Singer and actor, working in Hollywood, Rome, Paris, and other capitals of Europe, 1943-56; California State College (now University), Los Angeles, assistant professor, 1959-65, associate professor of speech, 1965-71; Queens College of the City University of New York, Flushing, N.Y., associate professor, 1971-72, professor of communication arts and sciences, 1972-74; University of Kansas, Lawrence, visiting professor and actor-in-residence, 1974-75, professor of theatre and drama, 1975—. Private practice of psychotherapy. Consulting editor to Macmillan Co. and Dickenson Publishing Co. *Member:* American Theatre Association, Speech Communication Association.

WRITINGS: Oral Interpretation, Macmillan, 1966; *The Speaking and the "Speakers" of Literature,* Dickenson,

1967; *Rhetoric-Ritual: A Study of the Communicative and Aesthetic Dimensions of Language*, Dickenson, 1972.

*　*　*

CAMPBELL, Peter Anthony 1935-

PERSONAL: Born January 21, 1935, in San Francisco, Calif.; son of Rupert W. and Audrie (Ford) Campbell. *Education:* Gonzaga University, B.A. (cum laude), 1957, Ph.L. and M.A., 1959; University of Santa Clara, S.T.M. and S.T.L., 1966; University of Ottawa, Ph.D., 1972. *Address:* (Current) Greeley Route, Box 3-A, Coulterville, Calif. 95311; (permanent) Department of Religious Studies, University of Ottawa, Ottawa, Ontario, Canada.

CAREER: Roman Catholic priest, ordained 1964. St. Ignatius High School, San Francisco, Calif., instructor, 1959-62; University of Santa Clara, Alma College, Los Gatos, Calif., faculty member of Sisters' Theology Program, 1964-66; experimental work developing group programs in religious renewal, in Canada, 1966-67; University of Ottawa, Ottawa, Ontario, department of religious studies, member of faculty, 1970—.

WRITINGS: (With Edwin M. McMahon) *Becoming a Person in the Whole Christ*, Sheed, 1967; *The In-Between: Evolution in Christian Faith*, Sheed, 1969; *Please Touch*, Sheed, 1969.

WORK IN PROGRESS: Research and studies to synthesize the areas of humanistic psychology, parapsychology, and religion.

SIDELIGHTS: Father Campbell has professional competence in photography which he has used in experimental group programs with religious communities and parish groups. *Avocational interests:* Bookkeeping.

*　*　*

CAMPBELL, Thomas F. 1924-
(Crosscountry)

PERSONAL: Born September 13, 1924, in Enniskillen, Northern Ireland; son of Thomas F. (a hairdresser) and Brigid (McGuire) Campbell; married Marguerite Brown, June 16, 1956; children: Thomas F., Ellen Healy. *Education:* Temple University High School, diploma, 1955; Western Reserve University (now Case Western Reserve University), B.A., 1958, M.A., 1960, Ph.D., 1965. *Politics:* Democratic. *Home:* 13713 Drexmore Rd., Cleveland Heights, Ohio 44106. *Office:* Department of History, Cleveland State University, Cleveland, Ohio.

CAREER: Baker in Ireland, 1939-50, 1952-53; volunteer with British Friends Ambulance Unit in England and Germany, 1950-52, and with American Friends Service Committee in Washington, D.C., and Mexico, 1953-54; aide in a mental hospital and baker in Philadelphia, Pa., before entering college at age thirty-two; Western Reserve University (now Case Western Reserve University), Cleveland, Ohio, lecturer in history, 1961-63; Ohio State University, Columbus, instructor at Columbus campus, 1963-64, and Lakewood branch, 1964-65, assistant professor of history at Lakewood branch, 1965-66; Cleveland State University, Cleveland, Ohio, assistant professor, 1966-67, associate professor, 1967-75, professor of history, 1975—, director of Institute of Urban Studies, 1969-75. Producer or co-producer of television series "We Who Built Cleveland," and "Urban Politics," 1973. Lecturer, City of Cleveland Police Academy, 1969-74. Trustee of Heights Council of Human Relations, 1967—, Karamu House, 1970-72, and Nationali-

ties Service, 1973. Chairman of the board, AIM Jobs, 1974—. Member of Cuyahoga County Democratic Central Committee, 1966-68. Chairman of Cleveland Irish-American Bicentennial committee, 1975. Member of Manpower Planning Council of Western Reserve Manpower Consortium; chairman of Mass Transit Sub-committee of Northeast Ohio Areawide Coordinating Agency. *Military service:* Irish National Security Force, 1939-40.

MEMBER: American Historical Association, Organization of American Historians, American Association of University Professors, Social Welfare History Group (secretary-treasurer, 1966—), Ohio Historical Society, Western Reserve Historical Society, Americans for Democratic Action (board of directors, Cleveland chapter, 1966—; vice-chairman, 1968-69), City Club of Cleveland (member board of directors, 1965-70; president, 1970), Friends of Cleveland Public Library (trustee), Rowfant Club.

WRITINGS: Freedom's Forum: The City Club 1912-1962, World Publishing and City Club of Cleveland, 1963; *Daniel E. Morgan, 1877-1949: The Good Citizen in Politics*, Western Reserve University Press, 1966; *SASS: Fifty Years of Social Work Education*, Western Reserve University Press, 1967. Sports columnist of *Ulster Post*, writing under pseudonym Crosscountry, 1950-51. Editor, *Newsletter* of Social Welfare History Group, 1966—.

WORK IN PROGRESS: Cleveland: From Tom Johnson to Carl Stokes; The History and Development of Public Housing in Metropolitan Cleveland.

AVOCATIONAL INTERESTS: Sports (runner-up for Northern Ireland marathon championship, 1949).

*　*　*

CAMPBELL-PURDIE, Wendy 1925-

PERSONAL: Born June 8, 1925, in Auckland, New Zealand; daughter of Edmund Hamilton (a mining engineer) and Janie Theodora (Williams) Campbell-Purdie. *Education:* Attended Woodford House, New Zealand. *Politics:* Socialist ("disappointed"). *Religion:* Church of England. *Home:* 84 St. Paul's Rd., London N.1, England. *Agent:* David Higham Associates Ltd., 5-8 Lower John St., London W1R 4HA, England.

CAREER: Member of Red Cross Transport Corps, Auckland, New Zealand, 1943-46; lived in England, and traveled in Europe, 1947-53; taught English in France and, later, in Corsica, 1954-57; was employed by a timber firm in Corsica, 1957-58; initiated her Sahara reclamation project, 1959, and has worked in Morocco, Tunisia, and Algeria, beginning 1959; director of Sahara Reaffrestion (now Desert Reafforestation Trust), beginning 1965.

WRITINGS: (With Fenner Brockway; forewords by Iris Murdoch and Lord Boyd Orr) *Woman Against the Desert*, Gollancz, 1967.

WORK IN PROGRESS: Studies in Arab folklore; a novel.

*　*　*

CANETTI, Elias 1905-

PERSONAL: Born July 25, 1905, in Russe, Bulgaria; son of Jacques (a businessman) and Mathilde (Arditti) Canetti; married Venetia Toubner-Calderon, February 26, 1934 (died May 1, 1963). *Education:* Attended schools in England, Austria, Switzerland, and Germany; University of Vienna, Dr. Philosophy, 1929. *Religion:* Jewish. *Residence:* London, England. *Address:* c/o Public Relations

Director, Victor Gollanz Ltd., 14 Henrietta St., Covent Garden, London W.C. 2, England.

CAREER: Full-time writer; lecturer in England and Europe. *Military service:* None. *Awards, honors:* Prix International (Paris), 1949, for *Die Blendung;* Dichterpreis der Stadt (Vienna), 1966; Deutscher Kritikerpreis (Berlin), 1967; Grosser Oesterreichischer Staatspreis (Vienna), 1968; Buchner-Preis (Munich), 1972; Franz Nabl-Preis der Stadt Graz, 1975.

WRITINGS: Hochzeit (play; first produced in Braunschweig, Germany, February 6, 1965), [Berlin], 1932, published in *Dramen,* Hanser Verlag, 1964; *Die Blendung* (novel; title means "The Deception"), H. Reichner, 1935, translation by C. V. Wedgwood published as *Auto-da-fe,* J. Cape, 1946, Stein & Day, 1964, published as *The Tower of Babel,* Knopf, 1947; *Fritz Wotruba* (criticism), Brueder Rosenbaum, 1955; *Masse und Macht* (psycho-sociological study), Claassen Verlag, 1960, translation by Carol Stewart published as *Crowds and Power,* Viking, 1962; *Welt im Kopf,* edited and introduction by Erich Fried, Stiasny Verlag, 1962; "Komoedie der Eitelkeit" (three-part play, written 1933-34; first produced in Braunschweig, Germany, November 3, 1965), published in *Dramen,* Hanser Verlag, 1964; "The Numbered" (play; first produced at Oxford Playhouse, Oxford, England, November 5, 1956), published as "Die Befristeten" in *Dramen,* Hanser Verlag, 1964; *Dramen* (contains *Hochzeit,* "Komoedie der Eitelkeit," "Die Befristeten"), Hanser Verlag, 1964; *Aufzeichnungen, 1942-1948* (notebooks), Hanser Verlag, 1965; *Die Stimmen von Marrakesch* (travelog), Hanser Verlag, 1968; *Die Andere Prozess,* Hanser Verlag, 1969, translation by Christopher Middleton published as *Kafka's Other Trial: The Letters to Felice,* Schocken, 1974; *Die Gespaltene Kukunft: Aufsaetze und Gespraeche,* Hanser Verlag, 1972; *Macht und Ueberleben: Drei Essays,* Literarisches Colloquim, 1972; *Die Provinz des Men schen: Aufzeichnungen 1942-1972,* Hanser Verlag, 1973; (contributor) Alfred Hrdlicka, *Graphik/Alfred Hrdlicka,* Propylaeen, 1973; *Der Ohrenzeuge: 50 Charaktere,* Hanser Verlag, 1974; *Das Gewissen der Worte: Essays,* Hanser Verlag, 1975.

WORK IN PROGRESS: A sequel to *Crowds and Power;* an autobiography.

SIDELIGHTS: Reviewing *Auto-da-fe,* Maurice Captianchik writes: "With the great power of his intelligence, his profound comic irony, and because, ahead of the psychologists, he implies that either all are mad or there is no such thing as madness, Canetti has created a modern masterpiece. Of those novels which tell of the despoiled life of the men of contemporary cities, this surely is the best, and will probably last the longest.... Canetti's achievement, still incomplete, is already immense. He has laid bare the most sinister secrets of the paradox we call history—that illusion-theatre in which the greatest criminals can appear as the greatest heroes. He has analysed to its roots the most tormenting problem of our time, our estrangement from each other, giving hope that we can solve it. He has, with a single novel, propagated an entire school of literature,...." Canetti speaks and reads German, French, Spanish, Italian, and English.

AVOCATIONAL INTERESTS: Canetti gave *CA* the following list: Anthropology, history, psychiatry, history of religions, philosophy, sociology, psychology, and the civilisations of Egypt, Sumer, Greece, Rome, Persia, India, China, Japan, Mexico, Maya, Inca. He added: "It is ridiculous to have so many; but they are all equally important to me and have cost me years and decades of study."

BIOGRAPHICAL/CRITICAL SOURCES: Manchester Guardian, May 10, 1946; *Spectator,* May 24, 1946; *New York Herald Tribune Book Review,* February 23, 1947; *Saturday Review of Literature,* March 8, 1947; *San Francisco Chronicle,* March 9, 1947; *Canadian Forum,* April, 1947; Uwe Schultz, editor, *Das Tagebuch und der Moderne Autor,* Hanser Verlag, 1965; *Times Literary Supplement,* July 8, 1965, January 22, 1971; *Books Abroad,* autumn, 1965, spring, 1970; *Book Week,* May 29, 1966; *Chicago Review,* Volume XX, number 4, 1969; *Books and Bookmen,* April, 1971; *New York Times,* November 17, 1972.

* * *

CANGEMI, Sister Marie Lucita   1920-

PERSONAL: Born October 11, 1920, in Summit, N.J.; daughter of Frank (owner of a shoe store) and Flora (Landolfi) Cangemi. *Education:* Catholic University of Puerto Rico, B.A., 1960; Fordham University, M.S.W., 1962.

CAREER: Roman Catholic religious, member of Missionary Servants of the Most Blessed Trinity. Has done social work in New York, Ohio, Pennsylvania, Connecticut, and Puerto Rico (where she was coordinator of the Spanish program for the Sisters Institute for Intercultural Communications), 1940-60; Catholic Charities, New York, N.Y., social worker, beginning 1960.

WRITINGS: Manhattan Mission, Doubleday, 1967.††

* * *

CAPALDI, Nicholas   1939-

PERSONAL: Born May 5, 1939, in Philadelphia, Pa.; son of Edward and Mildred (Izzi) Capaldi; married Marilyn Miller (a librarian), June 25, 1960; children: Diana Robin. *Education:* University of Pennsylvania, B.A., 1960; Columbia University, Ph.D., 1965. *Home:* 245 West 107th St., New York, N.Y. 10025. *Office:* Department of Philosophy, Queens College of the City University of New York, Flushing, N.Y. 11367.

CAREER: State University of New York College at Potsdam, professor of philosophy and chairman of department, 1965-67; Queens College of the City University of New York, Flushing, N.Y., 1967—, began as associate professor, currently professor of philosophy. *Member:* American Philosophical Association. *Awards, honors:* National Endowment for the Humanities fellowship, 1967.

WRITINGS: (Editor) *The Enlightenment: The Proper Study of Mankind,* Putnam, 1967; (editor with Boruch A. Brody) *Science: Men, Methods, Goals,* W. A. Benjamin, 1968; *Human Knowledge: A Philosophical Analysis of Its Meaning and Scope,* Pegasus, 1969; (editor and author of introduction) *Clear and Present Danger: The Free Speech Controversy,* Pegasus, 1970; *The Art of Deception,* Donald W. Brown, 1971; *David Hume: The Newtonian Philosopher,* Twayne, 1975. General editor, "Traditions of Philosophy" series, Pegasus, 1968—. Contributor to *Ethics, Journal of Philosophy,* and *Philosophical Journal.*

* * *

CAPLES, John   1900-

PERSONAL: Surname rhymes with Naples; born May 1, 1900, in New York, N.Y.; son of Byron H. (a physician) and Edith Jessie (Richards) Caples; married Mabel Veronica Watson, June 12, 1931 (died, 1956). *Education:* Columbia University, student, 1918-19; U.S. Naval Academy, B.S., 1924. *Religion:* Episcopalian. *Home:* 35 Park Ave., New York, N.Y. 10016. *Office:* Batten, Barton, Durstine & Osborn, Inc., 383 Madison Ave., New York, N.Y. 10017.

CAREER: New York Telephone Co., New York, N.Y., employed in engineering department, 1924-25; Ruthrauff and Ryan, Inc., New York, N.Y., advertising writer, 1925-27; Batten, Barton, Durstine & Osborn, Inc., New York, N.Y., began in 1927 as a writer, became vice-president, 1941. Instructor, Columbia University, 1952-53. Member of advisory board, Famous Writers School, 1958—, and Episcopal Church Foundation; member of jury, Advertising Hall of Fame. *Military service:* U.S. Navy, seaman, 1918, officer, 1942-45; became commander; received Letter of Commendation from Secretary of the Navy, 1944. *Member:* University Club (New York). *Awards, honors:* Writer of two advertisements included in book, *100 Greatest Advertisements;* elected to Advertising Copywriters Hall of Fame, 1973.

WRITINGS: Tested Advertising Methods, Harper, 1932, 4th edition, revised and enlarged, Prentice-Hall, 1974; *Advertising for Immediate Sales,* Harper, 1936; *Advertising Ideas,* McGraw, 1938; (co-author) *Copy Testing,* Ronald, 1939; *Making Ads Pay,* Harper, 1957. Writer of column for *Direct Marking Magazine,* 1972—. Contributor to *Advertising Handbook,* 1950.

WORK IN PROGRESS: Autobiographical book about his life in advertising; a book on advertising for direct response.

* * *

CAPPS, Jack Lee 1926-

PERSONAL: Born July 16, 1926, in Liberty, Mo.; son of Ernest Lee and Georgia Deane (Hall) Capps; married Marie Theodora Pappas, July 29, 1953; children: Steve George, Caroline Kate. *Education:* William Jewell College, student, 1943-44; U.S. Military Academy, B.S., 1948; University of Pennsylvania, M.A., 1960, Ph.D., 1963. *Office:* Department of English, U.S. Military Academy, West Point, N.Y. 10996.

CAREER: U.S. Army, 1944—; commissioned second lieutenant in Field Artillery, 1948; present rank, lieutenant-colonel. Imperial Ethiopian Military Academy, Addis Ababa, adviser, 1956-58; U.S. Military Academy, West Point, N.Y., instructor, 1959-61, assistant professor, 1961, associate professor, 1961-67, professor of English and deputy head of department, 1967—. Consultant and panelist, Conference on College Composition and Communication, 1966. Visiting professor at University of Massachusetts, summer, 1967, and American University of Beirut, 1971-72. Reader for College Boards and Advance Placement, Educational Testing Service. *Member:* American Association of University Professors, National Council of Teachers of English, Modern Language Association of America. *Awards, honors—Military:* Commendation Medal.

WRITINGS: Emily Dickinson's Reading 1836-1886, Harvard University Press, 1966; (editor and annotator with C. Robert Kemble) Stephen Vincent Benet, *John Brown's Body,* Holt, 1968. Contributor of articles and reviews to military and literary publications.

WORK IN PROGRESS: A concordance to the works of William Faulkner.

* * *

CAPRETTA, Patrick J(ohn) 1929-

PERSONAL: Born November 2, 1929, in Cleveland, Ohio; son of Carmen (a factory worker) and Phyllis (Sapparcerqua) Capretta; married Suzanne E. Gloor (a dietician), July 20, 1958; children: Eve, Nicholas, Christopher. *Education:* Kent State University, B.A., 1952; University of Colorado, M.A., 1954, Ph.D., 1958. *Politics:* Independent. *Home:* 6061 Joseph Dr., Oxford, Ohio 45056.

CAREER: Human Resources Research Office, Monterey, Calif., research associate in psychology, 1957-59; Washington State University, Pullman, instructor, 1959-60, assistant professor of psychology, 1960-61; Miami University, Oxford, Ohio, associate professor, 1961-64, professor of psychology, 1964—. *Member:* American Psychological Association, Sigma Xi. *Awards, honors:* National Institute of Mental Health special postdoctoral fellowship, 1966-67; National Science Foundation Research Grants, 1969—.

WRITINGS: A History of Psychology in Outline, Dell, 1967. Contributor of some twenty articles to psychological journals.

WORK IN PROGRESS: Research on the establishment and modification of food preferences in animals.

* * *

CAPRON, Jean F. 1924-

PERSONAL: Surname rhymes with "apron"; born February 16, 1924, in Englewood, N.J.; daughter of Wallace Sinclair (a railroadman) and Lucy (Schultheiser) Flint; married Harry Erlo Capron (a farmer), September 22, 1945; children: John, William, David, Susan, Bruce, Marjorie, Andrew. *Education:* Studied at Hackensack Hospital, two years; Palmer Institute of Authorship, correspondence diploma, 1962. *Politics:* Republican. *Religion:* Protestant. *Home:* Jackson Hill Rd., R.D. 2, Boonville, N.Y. 13309.

CAREER: Curtiss-Wright Aeronautics Co., Passaic. N.J., clerk-typist, 1942-43; Faxton Hospital, Utica, N.Y., nurse's assistant, 1965-66.

WRITINGS: The Trouble with Lucy, Dodd, 1967. Also author of *And Then I Hear a Voice,* and *The Horror of It All.* Contributor of short stories to confession, juvenile, and teen magazines.

WORK IN PROGRESS: A teen novel, tentatively entitled *Willis and Me.*

* * *

CAREY, Omer L. 1929-

PERSONAL: Born January 24, 1929, in Ellsworth, Ill.; son of George Franklin (a railroad telegrapher) and Nola (Thompson) Carey; married Carol Grant, June 20, 1954; children: Gayle, Craig, Dale, Bryan, Grant. *Education:* Illinois Wesleyan University, B.A., 1954; graduate study at Illinois State University, 1955-56, Southern Illinois University, 1957-59, and University of Illinois, 1957; Indiana University, M.B.A., 1960, D.B.A., 1962. *Politics:* Republican. *Religion:* Methodist. *Home:* 7625 Island Dr., Anchorage, Alaska 99504. *Office:* Department of Business Administration, Anchorage Senior College, University of Alaska, Anchorage, Alaska 99504.

CAREER: State Farm Mutual Automobile Insurance Co.,

Bloomington, Ill., 1947-49, 1952-55, began as trainee, became chief tab operator; Illinois Power Co., Havana, accountant, 1949-52, 1955; high school teacher in Bethalto, Ill., 1956-59; Indiana University, Bloomington, instructor in business, 1959-62; Idaho State University, Pocatello, assistant professor of business administration and assistant director, Bureau of Business Research, 1962-64; Washington State University, College of Economics and Business, Pullman, 1964-73, began as assistant professor, became professor of business administration, chairman of department, 1968-73; University of Alaska, Anchorage Senior College, Anchorage, professor of business administration, 1973—. Visiting assistant professor of finance, University of Washington, Seattle, summer, 1966. *Member:* American Finance Association, Western Finance Association (secretary-treasurer, 1965-70), Western Economic Association, Phi Kappa Phi, Beta Gamma Sigma, Blue Key.

WRITINGS: (With Frank Seelye, Harold White, and Donald Carrell) *Personnel Policies of Small Business,* Small Business Administration and Idaho State University, 1964; (contributor) *Trends in Distribution, Services and Transportation,* Bureau of Economic and Business Research, Washington State University, 1966; (editor) *Military-Industrial Complex and United States Foreign Policy,* Washington State University, 1969. Contributor to professional journals.

*   *   *

CAREY-JONES, N(orman) S(tewart)   1911-

PERSONAL: Born December 11, 1911, in Swansea, Wales; son of Samuel Carey (a civil engineer) and Jessie (Stewart) Jones; married Stella Myles, August 2, 1946; children: Thomas David, Owen Myles. *Education:* Merton College, Oxford, B.A., 1933. *Religion:* Christian. *Home:* Sandown, Rawdon, Leeds, England. *Office:* University of Leeds, Leeds 2, England.

CAREER: In British Colonial Service, 1935-65, serving in Gold Coast, Northern Rhodesia, British Honduras, and with final assignment as permanent secretary to the Ministry of Lands and Settlement, Kenya; University of Leeds, Leeds, England, director in development administration, 1965—. President, Kenya European Civil Servants' Association, 1951-54; fellow, Economic Development Institute, Washington, D.C., 1960—. Previously member of European Civil Service Advisory Board (Kenya), Maize Marketing Board, and Export Promotion Council. *Military service:* British Army, 1931-36, Supplementary Reserve, then lieutenant in Regular Army Reserve of Officers. *Member:* Royal Geographical Society, Royal Commonwealth Society, Political Studies Association. *Awards, honors:* Companion of St. Michael and St. George.

WRITINGS: The Pattern of a Dependent Economy, Cambridge University Press, 1952; *The Anatomy of Uhuru: Dynamics and Problems of African Independence in an Age of Conflict,* Manchester University Press, 1966, Praeger, 1967; (with S. V. Patankar and M. J. Boodhoo) *Politics, Public Enterprise, and the Industrial Development Agency: Industrialisation Policies and Practices,* Croom-Holm, 1974, Holmes & Meier, 1975. Contributor to journals. Chairman of editorial board, *East African Economics Review,* 1955-60.

WORK IN PROGRESS: Research on third world politics; agricultural development.

CARLETON, Barbee Oliver   1917-

PERSONAL: Born August 17, 1917, in Thomaston, Me.; daughter of Charles F. and Mildred (Thurlow) Oliver; married Granville E. Carleton (an engineer), September 19, 1942; children: Courtney (Mrs. T. W. MacLachlan), David. *Education:* Wellesley College, B.A., 1940. *Religion:* Unitarian Universalist. *Home:* 41 Oak St., Beverly Farms, Mass. 01915.

CAREER: Teacher at secondary schools in Maine and Massachusetts, 1940-43; Houghton Mifflin Co., Boston, Mass., assistant editor, summer, 1942; Brookwood School (independent school), Manchester, Mass., elementary teacher, beginning 1960. Member, Wellesley Publication Committee.

WRITINGS: The Wonderful Cat of Cobbie Bean, Winston, 1957; *Benny and the Bear,* Follett, 1960; *More Bedtime Stories to Read Aloud,* Grosset, 1961; *Secret of Saturday Cove* (Junior Literary Guild selection), Holt, 1961; *Chester Jones,* Holt, 1963; (with others) *Tale of Napoleon Mouse, and Other Stories,* Highlights, 1965; *The Witches' Bridge,* Holt, 1967.

WORK IN PROGRESS: Mrs. Carleton told *CA:* "As a very amateur archeologist, am digging into both old histories and early settlements, principally on the Maine coast."

BIOGRAPHICAL/CRITICAL SOURCES: Book World, January 28, 1968.††

*   *   *

CARLINSKY, Dan   1944-

PERSONAL: Born March 9, 1944, in Holyoke, Mass.; son of Louis H. and Ethel (Mag) Carlinsky; married Nancy Cooperstein, August 25, 1972. *Education:* Columbia University, B.A., 1965, M.S., 1966. *Home and office:* 301 East 78th St., New York, N.Y. 10021.

CAREER: Freelance writer.

WRITINGS: (With Edwin Goodgold) *Trivia,* Dell, 1966; (with Goodgold) *More Trivial Trivia,* Dell, 1966; *Rock 'n' Roll Trivia,* Popular Library, 1970; (compiler) *A Century of College Humor,* Random House, 1971; (with David Heim) *Bicycle Tours in and around New York,* Hagstrom, 1975; (with Goodgold) *The Compleat Beatles Quiz Book,* Warner Books, 1975; (with Goodgold) *The World's Greatest Monster Quiz,* Berkley Publishing, 1975. Author of syndicated newspaper column, "It's On the Tip of My Tongue," for Newspaper Enterprise Association. Contributor to periodicals including *New York Times, Travel and Leisure, Esquire, Sports Illustrated,* and *T.V. Guide.*

*   *   *

CARLSON, Marvin   1935-

PERSONAL: Born September 15, 1935, in Wichita, Kan.; son of Roy Edward (an accountant) and Gladys (Nelson) Carlson; married Patricia McElroy, August 20, 1961; children: Geoffrey Albert, Richard James. *Education:* University of Kansas, B.S.Ed., 1957; Cornell University, Ph.D., 1961. *Religion:* Presbyterian. *Home:* 407 North Aurora St., Ithaca, N.Y. 14850. *Office:* Department of Theatre Arts, Cornell University, Ithaca, N.Y. 14850.

CAREER: Cornell University, Ithaca, N.Y., instructor, 1961-62, assistant professor, 1962-66, associate professor, 1966-72, professor of theatre arts, 1972—, chairman of department, 1966-68, 1974—. *Member:* American Educational Theatre Association, American Society for Theatre Research, National Collegiate Players (second vice-president, 1963-67), American Association of University Professors, Phi Kappa Phi. *Awards, honors:* Guggenheim fellowship, 1969.

WRITINGS: (Translator) *Andre Antoine's Memories of the Theatre-Libre,* University of Miami Press, 1964; *The Theatre of the French Revolution,* Cornell University Press, 1966; *The French Stage in the Nineteenth Century,* Scarecrow, 1972; *The German Stage in the Nineteeth Century,* Scarecrow, 1972. Contributor to *Comparative Literature, Modern Drama, Educational Theatre Journal, Scandinavian Studies, The Drama Review, Theatre Survey, Revue d'histoire du Theatre* and *Players.*

WORK IN PROGRESS: Goethe and the Weimar Stage.

* * *

CARLSON, Vada F. 1897-
(Florella Rose)

PERSONAL: Born February 27, 1897, in Cody, Neb.; daughter of Fred Lorenzo (employed in building trades) and Hattie F. (Ditson) Rose; married Albert B. Carlson, July 22, 1917 (divorced, 1937); married Jose C. Rodriguez (an artist) January 29, 1972; children: Lois Rose (Mrs. Earl A. Toburen), Wayne B. *Education:* Attended public schools in Cody and Gordon, Neb.; took correspondence courses; attended Mexico City writing school. *Politics:* Republican. *Religion:* Methodist. *Home:* 123 West Fourth St., Winslow, Ariz. 86047. *Agent:* Mrs. T. Carter Harrison, Route 4, Box 23, Chatham, Va. 24531.

CAREER: Began working at age sixteen as telephone operator in Cody, Wyo.; writer and woman's page editor on papers in Riverton, Wyo., at various intervals, 1915-32, Concord, Calif., 1932-37, and Pittsburg, Calif., 1938-41; Columbia Steel, Pittsburg, Calif., secretary to foundry superintendent, 1942-45; news editor on paper in Concord, Calif., 1946-48; publisher of own paper in Oakley, Calif., 1948-49; woman's page editor of *Winslow Mail,* Winslow, Ariz., 1955-56, and *Flagstaff Daily Sun,* Flagstaff, Ariz., 1956-57, 1963-64; *Winslow Mail,* editor, 1965-66; A.R.E. Press, Virginia Beach, Va., editor, 1968-70. *Riverton Ranger,* special writer for golden anniverary edition, 1956, and author of anniversary pageant, *And Still the River.*

MEMBER: National Federation of Press Women (regional director, 1965-67), Arizona Press Women (president, 1957-58), Winslow Arts Association (founder; president, 1962-64), Business and Professional Woman's Club, Order of Eastern Star, Soroptimist Club. *Awards, honors:* Named Woman of Achievement by National Federation of Press Women, Winslow Woman of the Year, by Winslow Chamber of Commerce, Woman of the Year by Arizona Press Women, and Business Woman of the Year by Business and Professional Woman's Club, 1965; holder of more than sixty awards for writing.

WRITINGS: We Saw the Sundance, Graphic Press, 1948; *The Desert Speaks* (poetry), Ranger Press, 1956; *This Is Our Valley* (history of Santa Maria Valley), Westernlore, 1959; (with Elizabeth W. White [Indian name, Polingaysi Qoyawayma]), *No Turning Back,* University of New Mexico Press, 1964; (ghost writer for Clara Edge) *Tahirih,* Eerdmans, 1963; *Fluffy and the Flyaway Fly* (juvenile), Whitman Publishing, 1966; (with Gary Witherspoon) *Black Mountain Boy* (juvenile), Navaho Curriculum Center (Rough Rock, Ariz.), 1968; *Coyote Legends,* Navaho Curriculum Center, 1968; *The Vision and the Promise* (juve-

nile), A.R.E. Press, 1969; *The Sacred Summer,* A.R.E. Press, 1969.

The Great Migration, A.R.E. Press, 1970; *High Country Canvas,* Northland Press, 1972; *East of the Sun* (anthology), A.R.E. Press, 1972; *Cochise: Chief of the Chiricahuas,* Harvey House, 1973; *John Charles Fremont: Adventurer in the Wilderness* (biography), Harvey House, 1973; *John Wesley Powell: Conquest of the Canyon* (juvenile), Harvey House, 1974. Also author of introduction, *Arizona History,* 1975.

Juveniles; under pseudonym Florella Rose; all published by Whitman Publishing: *Peter Picket Pin,* 1953; *Yipee Kiyi,* 1954; *Yipee Kiyi and Whoa Boy,* 1955.

Contributor of articles and poetry to magazines.

WORK IN PROGRESS: Broken Pattern, a novel with a Hopi Indian background; *The Big Swap,* a novel about a boy's adventure in the steamboat era; *White Horses Running,* a novel concerning the sinking of the Posidea, the last island of Atlantis.

SIDELIGHTS: Vada Carlson wrote: "[I] was born near the Rosebud Reservation and have lived near Indians most of my life.... Aside from travel, which I love, [I] relax by doing oil paintings and by reading."

* * *

CARMEN, Sister (M.) Joann 1941-

PERSONAL: Born March 25, 1941, in Chicago, Ill.; daughter of Joseph (a tool and die maker) and Ann (Speciale) Fina. *Education:* Attended Mundelein College; Alverno College, B.S. in Ed.; Loyola University, Chicago, Ill., M.A. *Office:* Alvernia High School, 3900 North Lawndale Ave., Chicago, Ill. 60618.

CAREER: Roman Catholic religious of Franciscan order (O.S.F.); elementary teacher of social studies in Glenview, Ill., 1964-65; Alvernia High School, Chicago, Ill., sociology teacher, beginning 1965.

WRITINGS: Lessons in Race Relations, Pflaum, 1966.

WORK IN PROGRESS: Units on the American Indian and the Puerto Rican migrant, including teacher's manuals.††

* * *

CARNEGIE, Raymond Alexander 1920-
(Sacha Carnegie)

PERSONAL: Born July 9, 1920, in Edinburgh, Scotland; married Patricia Dawson, April 17, 1943; married second wife, the Countess of Erroll, November 27, 1964; children: (first marriage) Alexandra, Susan; (second marriage) Jocelyn. *Education:* Attended Eton College, 1933-37. *Religion:* Church of England. *Home:* Crimonmogate, Lonmay, Aberdeenshire, Scotland. *Agent:* John Johnson, 3 Albemarle St., London W1X 3HF, England.

CAREER: British Army, Scots Guards, regular officer, 1940-52, rising to major; served in Italy and Malaya; mentioned in dispatches during World War II. Author. *Member:* P.E.N. (London).

*WRITINGS—*All under name Sacha Carnegie: *Noble Purpose,* P. Davies, 1954; *Sunset in the East,* P. Davies, 1955; *Holiday from Life: A Scandinavian Interlude,* P. Davies, 1957; *The Devil and the Deep,* Appleton, 1957; *Pigs I Have Known,* P. Davies, 1958; *The Lion and Francis Conway,* P. Davies, 1958; *Red Dust of Africa,* P.

Davies, 1959; *The Dark Night,* P. Davies, 1960; *The Deer-slayers,* P. Davies, 1961; *The Golden Years,* P. Davies, 1962; *A Dash of Russia,* P. Davies, 1966, International Publications Service, 1967; *The Guardian,* Dodd, 1966; *The Banners of Love,* P. Davies, 1968, published as *Scarlet Banners of Love,* Dodd, 1968; *Banners of War,* Dodd, 1970; *Banners of Power,* P. Davies, 1972, published as *Kasia and the Empress,* Dodd, 1973. Contributor to *Scotsman, Field, Country Life, Sunday Times,* and other publications.

WORK IN PROGRESS: A series of novels with background in eastern Europe and Russia in the eighteenth century.

SIDELIGHTS: Carnegie traveled in Africa, 1957, Hungary, Poland, and Bulgaria, 1958, and four thousand miles by car in Soviet Russia, 1965.

* * *

CARNEY, James (Patrick) 1914-
(Seumas O Ceithearnaigh)

PERSONAL: Born May 17, 1914, in Ireland; son of Partick (a state official) and Constance (Grace) Carney; married Maura Morrissey (a lexicographer), June 1, 1939 (died May 1, 1975); children: Paul. *Education:* University College, Dublin, B.A., 1936; also studied at University of Bonn, 1936-37. *Religion:* Roman Catholic. *Home:* 78 Highfield Rd., Rathgar, Dublin, Ireland. *Office:* Dublin Institute for Advanced Studies, 10 Burlington Rd., Dublin, Ireland.

CAREER: Dublin Institute for Advanced Studies, Dublin, Ireland, professor of Celtic studies, 1941—. Visiting professor in Sweden, 1950-52, and at University of California, Los Angeles, 1965-66. *Member:* Royal Irish Academy. *Awards, honors:* Doctor of Philosophy, University of Uppsala, 1975.

WRITINGS: Topographical Poems, Dublin Institute for Advanced Studies, 1943; *Poems on the Butlers of Ormond, Cahir, and Dunboyne (A.D. 1400-1650),* Dublin Institute for Advanced Studies, 1945; *Poems on the O'Reillys,* Dublin Institute for Advanced Studies, 1950; *Studies in Early Irish Literature and History,* Dublin Institute for Advanced Studies, 1956; *A Genealogical History of the O'Reillys,* An Cumann Sheanchais Bhreifne (Cavan), 1959; *The Problem of St. Patrick,* Dublin Institute for Advanced Studies, 1961; *The Poems of Blathmac,* Educational Company of Ireland for the Irish Texts Society, 1964; *Early Irish Poetry,* Mercier Press, 1965; (editor and translator) *Medieval Irish Lyrics,* University of California Press, 1966; *The Irish Bardic Poet,* Dolmen Press, 1966; (editor with D. Greene) *Celtic Studies: Essays in Memory of Angus Matheson, 1912-1962,* Barnes & Noble, 1968. Also writer of articles.

Under Gaelic name Seumas O Ceithearnaigh: *Regimen na Slainte,* three volumes, Government Publications (Dublin), 1942-44; *Sgealta romansuiochta,* Government Publications, 1952; *Siabhradh Mhic na Miochomhairle,* Government Publications, 1955.

WORK IN PROGRESS: Research on medieval Irish literature.

SIDELIGHTS: James Carney is competent in German and Swedish.

* * *

CARP, Frances Merchant 1918-
PERSONAL: Born May 28, 1918, in San Diego, Calif.;

daughter of William Bluford and Pauline (Mallot) Merchant; married Abraham Carp (a psychologist), June 19, 1942; children: Bertram William, Richard Merchant. *Education:* Stanford University, A.B. (with greatest distinction), 1940, M.A., 1942, Ph.D., 1950. *Politics:* Democrat. *Religion:* Episcopalian. *Home:* 5240 Cribari Hills, San Jose, Calif. 95135. *Office:* Wright Institute, 2728 Durante Ave., Berkeley, Calif. 94074.

CAREER: Western Michigan University, Kalamazoo, assistant professor of psychology, 1950-52; U.S. Air Force, Randolph Air Force Base, Tex., technical aid to director of research, 1953; Trinity University, San Antonio, Tex., associate professor, later professor of psychology and chairman of department, 1954-65; National Institutes of Health, Bethesda, Md., scientist and administrator, 1965-67; American Institutes for Research, Palo Alto, Calif., director of human development research program, 1967-69; University of California, research specialist V at San Francisco Campus, 1969-71, at Berkeley Campus, 1971-73; Wright Institute, Berkeley, research project director, 1973—. Diplomate in clinical psychology, American Board of Examiners in Professional Psychology. *Member:* American Psychological Association, Interamerican Society of Psychology, Gerontological Society, Society for Projective Techniques, Phi Beta Kappa, Sigma Xi.

WRITINGS: A Future for the Aged: Victoria Plaza and Its Residents, University of Texas Press, 1966; (editor) *Patterns of Living and Housing,* U.S. Government Printing Office, 1967; (editor) *The Retirement Process,* U.S. Government Printing Office, 1968; (editor) *Retirement,* Behavioral Publications, 1972. Also author of environmental studies and monographs on psychology and gerontology. Contributor to psychology and gerontology journals.

WORK IN PROGRESS: The Person-Environment Transaction in Aging.

* * *

CARR, (Bettye) Jo (Crisler) 1926-
PERSONAL: Born September 29, 1926, in Greenville, Miss.; daughter of Joseph Neal (an entomologist) and Esther (Gilley) Crisler; married Galen M. Carr (an engineer), December 20, 1947 (divorced, November 9, 1967); children: Catherine Ann, Michael Joseph, Glenna Faye, Rebecca Jo, Douglas Galen. *Education:* Texas Tech University, B.S. (cum laude), 1947, M.A., 1973; University of California, Berkeley, graduate study, 1949-50. *Politics:* Independent. *Religion:* Methodist. *Home:* 4705 40th St., Lubbock, Tex. 79414.

CAREER: Girl Scouts of America, Lubbock, Tex., acting area field director, 1947-49; Methodist Board of Missions, New York, N.Y., missionary in Southern Rhodesia, 1952-57; free-lance writer, 1959—; Texas Tech University, Lubbock, instructor in English, 1975—. *Member:* Phi Upsilon Omicron.

WRITINGS: Living on Tiptoe: Devotions for Families with Children, Upper Room, 1970; *Trouble with Tikki,* Lantern Press, 1970; *Touch the Wind,* Upper Room, 1975.

With Imogene Sorley; all published by Abingdon: *Too Busy Not to Pray: A Homemaker Talks with God,* 1966; *Bless This Mess, and Other Prayers,* 1969; *The Intentional Family,* 1971; *Plum Jelly and Stained Glass, and Other Poems,* 1973; *Mockingbird and Angel Song,* 1975.

Author of teachers' guides, published by Friendship, for Alice Geer Kelsey, *Land of the Morning,* Louis Horton

Young, *No Biscuits at All!*, Lulu Hathaway, *The Boy Who Couldn't Talk,* and Audrey McKim, *Aiko and Her Cousin Kenichi;* also author of monthly column on family fun in *Christian Home,* 1973—, and bimonthly column in *Today,* 1974-75. Contributor of short stories to *Jack and Jill, Boy's Life, Golden Magazine, Humpty Dumpty,* and other magazines; also contributor of devotional material and articles to Methodist publications.

WORK IN PROGRESS: Juvenile fiction on bicycling in Europe.

AVOCATIONAL INTERESTS: Camping, ecology, crafts, reading.

* * *

CARROLL, Faye 1937-

PERSONAL: Born March 1, 1937, in Louisville, Ky.; daughter of Wilburn Owen (a farmer) and Nova (Wilson) Carroll. *Education:* Campbellsville Junior College, student, 1955-57; Western Kentucky University, A.B., 1959; University of Kentucky, Ph.D., 1963. *Home:* 1608 Hogle Dr., Bowling Green, Ky. 42101. *Office:* Department of Government, Western Kentucky University, Bowling Green, Ky. 42101.

CAREER: East Carolina University, Greenville, N.C., associate professor of political science, 1963-67; Western Kentucky University, Bowling Green, professor of international relations, 1967—, head of department of government, 1973—. *Member:* American Association of University Professors, Southern Political Science Association, Pi Sigma Alpha.

WRITINGS: Southwest Africa and the United Nations, University of Kentucky Press, 1967.

* * *

CARROLL, Sister Mary Gerald 1913-

PERSONAL: Secular name, Catherine C. Carroll; born July 8, 1913, in New York, N.Y.; daughter of James Joseph and Catherine (Roche) Carroll. *Education:* Manhattanville College of the Sacred Heart, B.Mus., 1941; Catholic University of America, M.A., 1949; also studied liturgy at University of Notre Dame, 1954. *Politics:* Democrat. *Home and office:* St. Catherine's Hall, College of New Rochelle, New Rochelle, N.Y. 10801.

CAREER: Roman Catholic religious, member of Ursuline Order, 1933—. Lay teacher of music in New York (N.Y.) schools and at Pius X School of Liturgical Music, New York N.Y., 1931-33; Ursuline Novitiate, Beacon, N.Y., teacher of music and liturgy, 1933-36; College of New Rochelle, New Rochelle, N.Y., instructor in music department, 1936-58, head of department, 1955-58; Ursuline School Grand Concourse, New York, N.Y., teacher of general music and choral, 1958-59; Ursuline School, New Rochelle, N.Y., teacher of general music and choral, 1943-55, 1959-71; Cathedral Preparatory Seminary, New York, N.Y., teacher of music, 1973—; College of New Rochelle, adjunct teacher of music, 1973—. Member of Schola Musicae Liturgicae faculty, St. John the Divine, New York, N.Y. Instructor in musicology and humanities with Foreign Study League in Europe, summers, 1969-71; lecturer on music and liturgy throughout United States. *Member:* National Catholic Music Educators Association, National Catholic Liturgical Conference, Church Music Association of America, American Guild of Organists, National Association for Humanities Education, Music Commission of

the New York Archdiocese, Music Teachers' Council of New Rochelle. *Awards, honors:* $5,000 award from Cardinal Spellman for musical composition, 1957.

WRITINGS—Texts in "Our Life With God" series: (With Mother Marie Venard Pfeiffer) *Love the Lord, Alive in Christ,* and *Christ With Us,* books for grades four-six, Sadlier, 1966-67; (with Sisters Edward Mary Magill, Mary Celene Lhota, and Mary Andrew Wank) *The Living Church,* book for grade eight, Sadlier, 1968.

SIDELIGHTS: Sister Mary Gerald Carroll has a reading knowledge of French, German, and Latin.

* * *

CARSE, James P(earce) 1932-

PERSONAL: Born December 24, 1932, in Manfield, Ohio; son of James B. (a businessman) and Constance (Keene) Carse; married Alice Fetzer, June 8, 1957; children: Alisa, Nelson, James. *Education:* Ohio Wesleyan University, A.B., 1954; Yale University, B.D., 1957, S.T.M., 1962; Drew University, Ph.D., 1966. *Office:* New York University, Washington Sq., New York, N.Y. 10003.

CAREER: Clergyman. University of North Carolina, Chapel Hill, University pastor, 1957-60; University of Connecticut, Storrs, University pastor, 1960-62; New York University, New York N.Y., assistant professor, 1966-68, associate professor of the history and literature of religion, 1968—.

WRITINGS: Jonathan Edwards and the Visibility of God, Scribner, 1967; *The Meanings of Death,* Wiley, in press. Contributor of articles and reviews to professional journals.

WORK IN PROGRESS: A book, *Death and Society,* for Harcourt.

* * *

CARSON, Robert 1909-

PERSONAL: Born October 6, 1909, in Clayton, Wash.; son of Franklin Pierce and Blanche Ethel (McClaren) Carson; married Mary Jane Irving, February 11, 1938. *Education:* Studied at American Institute of Banking, Los Angeles, Calif. *Home:* 10565 Fontenelle Way, Los Angeles, Calif. 90024. *Agent:* Brandt & Brandt, 101 Park Ave., New York, N.Y. 10017.

CAREER: Held various positions, 1928-35; worked as a scenarist, novelist, and magazine writer, 1935-42; writer, 1945—; Columbia Broadcasting System, Inc., television producer, 1954-55. *Military service:* U.S. Army Air Forces, 1942-45; became lieutenant colonel. *Member:* Writers Guild of America (council member), Screen Writers' Guild (member of executive board, 1951-53). *Awards, honors:* Academy Award for best original story, 1937, for "A Star is Born."

WRITINGS—Screen plays: "A Star is Born," United Artists, 1937; "Men With Wings," Paramount, 1938, "The Light That Failed," Paramount, 1939; "Beau Geste," Paramount, 1939; "Western Union," Twentieth Century-Fox, 1941; "The Tuttles of Tahiti," RKO, 1942; "The Desperadoes," Columbia, 1943; "Bedside Manner," United Artists, 1945; "Perilous Holiday," Columbia, 1946; "You Gotta Stay Happy," Universal, 1948; "The Reformer and the Redhead," Metro-Goldwyn-Mayer, 1950; "The Groom Wore Spurs," Universal, 1951; "Just for You," Paramount, 1952; "Bundle of Joy," RKO, 1956; "Action of the Tiger," Metro-Goldwyn-Mayer, 1957.

Novels: *Revels Are Ended,* Doubleday, 1936; *The Bride Saw Red,* Putnam, 1943; *Stranger in Our Midst,* Putnam, 1947; *Triangle With Curves,* R. Hale, 1948; *You've Gotta Stay Happy,* R. Hale, 1951; *Magic Lantern* (Book-of-the-Month Club selection), Holt, 1952; *Quality of Mercy,* Holt, 1954; *Father Came Home!,* R. Hale, 1954; *Legal Bride,* R. Hale, 1955; *Love Affair,* Holt, 1958; *My Hero,* McGraw, 1961; *An End to Comedy,* Bobbs-Merrill, 1963; *The Outsiders,* Little, Brown, 1966; *The December Syndrome,* Little, Brown, 1969; *The Golden Years Caper,* Little, Brown, 1970; *Jellybean,* Little, Brown, 1974. Contributor to *Saturday Evening Post, Holiday,* and other periodicals.

SIDELIGHTS: Carson's work has been translated into Danish, Italian, German, Dutch, Norwegian and Swedish.

BIOGRAPHICAL/CRITICAL SOURCES: New York Herald Tribune Book Review, September 21, 1958; *New York Times,* September 28, 1958; *New Yorker,* October 25, 1958, November 2, 1963; *Springfield Republican,* December 14, 1958; *New York Times Book Review,* November 3, 1963.†

*   *   *

CARTER, Byron L.   1924-

PERSONAL: Born April 18, 1924; son of John T. (a newspaper editor) and Annie Ruth (Mays) Carter; married Ella Lee McKinnis, September 26, 1945; children: Debbie, Sharon. *Education:* St. Mary's University of San Antonio, Certified Public Accountant, 1962. *Residence:* Westerville, Ohio. *Office:* 1651 North West Professional Plaza, Columbus, Ohio 43220.

CAREER: National Cash Register Co., Dayton, Ohio, various posts in Ohio, Texas, and elsewhere, 1946—, assistant vice-president, 1966. Now vice-chairman, Management Horizons, Columbus, Ohio. *Military service:* U.S. Marine Corps, 1942-45; became sergeant. U.S. Army Reserve, 1950-55; became first lieutenant. *Member:* American Institute of Certified Public Accountants.

WRITINGS: Data Processing for the Small Business, Macfadden, 1966.

WORK IN PROGRESS: Research in advanced electronic data processing systems for retailers.

AVOCATIONAL INTERESTS: Flying (holds private pilot's license with instrument and multi-engine ratings), golf, tennis.

*   *   *

CARTER, Charles W(ebb)   1905-

PERSONAL: Born May 14, 1905, in Southport, Ind.; son of Alonzo Elsworth and Anna (White) Carter; married Elizabeth Hutchinson, 1928; children: Donald Webster, Norman Lee. *Education:* Marion College, Marion, Ind., Th.B., 1933, A.B., 1947; Winona Lake School of Theology, M.A. in Th., 1933; Asbury Theological Seminary, B.D., 1949; Butler University, M.A., 1950, Th.M., 1951; also studied at Ohio State University and Chicago Lutheran Theological Seminary. *Politics:* Republican. *Home:* 4308 South Wigger St., Marion, Ind. 46952.

CAREER: Clergyman of Wesleyan Church of America. Missionary to Sierra Leone, Africa, 1928-45, as general superintendent of Wesleyan Methodist Mission, 1937-38, 1943-45; Marion College, Marion, Ind., professor of philosophy and missions, 1946-57; Higley Publishing Co., Butler, Ind., editor, 1958-59; Taylor University, Upland, Ind., professor of philosophy and religion and head of department of philosophy, 1959-71; China Evangelical Seminary, Taipei, Taiwan, professor of theology and ethics, 1971-74; Marion College, Marion, Ind., scholar-in-residence, 1974—. Pastor of churches in Michigan, Ohio, and Indiana, at various periods. Lecturer on Africa and missions, and preacher in America and abroad. *Member:* Metaphysical Society of America, Evangelical Theological Society, Wesleyan Theological Society, American Association of University Professors, Phi Kappa Phi, Theta Phi. *Awards, honors:* D.D. from Asbury Theological Seminary, 1968.

WRITINGS: Transformed Africans, Wesley Press, 1938; *Half-Century of American Wesleyan Missions in West Africa,* Wesley Press, 1940; (co-author) *Akafa Ka Maling Ma Temne* (hymnbook in Temne), 1948; *The Bible Gift of Tongues,* Wesley Press, 1952; *Road to Revival,* Higley Press, 1959; (with Ralph Earle) *The Acts of the Apostles,* Zondervan, 1959, new edition, 1973; *Higley Sunday School Lesson Commentary,* four books, Higley Press, 1960, 1961; (general editor) *Wesleyan Bible Commentary,* Eerdmans, Volume IV: *Gospels and Acts,* 1964, Volume V: *Romans through Philemon,* 1965, Volume VI: *Hebrews through Revelation,* 1966, Volume I: *Genesis through Esther,* 1967, Volume II: *Job through Song of Solomon,* 1968, Volume III: *Isaiah through Malachi,* 1969; *The Person and Ministry of the Holy Spirit: A Wesleyan Perspective,* Baker Book, 1974. Also author of *The Holy Spirit in the Early Church* for Beacon Hill.

WORK IN PROGRESS: Faith, Reason and Action, a textbook in philosophy and Christian thought.

*   *   *

CARTER, Harvey L(ewis)   1904-

PERSONAL: Born December 2, 1904, in Forest, Ind.; son of Harry Holmes (a farmer) and Martha Frances (Wyatt) Carter; married Ruth Thornton (a sociologist), June 20, 1929; children: Harvey Thornton, Cherry (Mrs. John J. Kinney). *Education:* Wabash College, A.B. (with honors), 1927; University of Wisconsin, A.M., 1928, Ph.D., 1938. *Politics:* Democrat. *Home:* 4 Cragmor Village, Colorado Springs, Colo. 80907.

CAREER: Ursinus College, Collegeville, Pa., instructor in history and public speaking, 1928-30, assistant professor, 1930-31, associate professor, 1931-41, professor of history, 1941-45; Colorado College, Colorado Springs, professor, 1945-56, John and Harriet Parker Campbell Professor of History, 1956-73, emeritus professor, 1973—, chairman of department, 1955-60, curator of Hulbert Memorial Collection of Western Americana, 1960-73. Visiting summer professor at University of Denver, 1945, and Western State College of Colorado, 1954, 1962. *Member:* American Historical Association, Organization of American Historians, American Association of University Professors (member of national council, 1956-59), Western History Association (honorary life member, 1975), Indiana Historical Society, Colorado Historical Society, American Civil Liberties Union, Winter Night Club.

WRITINGS: Zebulon Montgomery Pike: Pathfinder and Patriot, Dentan Printing Co., 1956; (editor) *The Pike's Peak Region: A Sesquicentennial History,* Dentan Printing Co., 1956; *The Far West in American History,* American Historical Association, 1960, 3rd edition published as *Far Western Frontiers,* 1972; (contributor) *Mountain Men and the Fur Trade of the Far West,* six volumes, Arthur Clark, 1965-68; (editor with Norma L. Peterson) *The Letters of*

William S. Stewart, 1861-62, Kelley Press (Columbia, Mo.), 1967; *Dear Old Kit: The Historical Christopher Carson* (with a new edition of his memoirs), University of Oklahoma Press, 1968. Contributor to *Encyclopaedia Britannica, Dictionary of American History,* and centennial calendar for Colorado Springs, Colo.; limericks and other humorous verse have been published in magazines, including *Sports Illustrated.* Contributor to professional journals.

SIDELIGHTS: "I don't bowl or fish anymore so [I have] lots of time for limericks," Carter told *CA.* "I spent some time defending Kit Carson against ignorant and unwarranted attacks" in the *Denver Westerners Brand Book* (1974).

* * *

CARY, Richard 1909-

PERSONAL: Born November 18, 1909, in New York, N.Y.; married Frances Perkins, July 17, 1954. *Education:* New York University, A.B. (magna cum laude), 1948, M.A., 1949; Cornell University, Ph.D., 1952. *Home:* 31 Highland Ave., Waterville, Me. 04901.

CAREER: Cornell University, Ithaca, N.Y., instructor in English, 1949-52; Colby College, Waterville, Me., instructor, 1952-54, assistant professor, 1954-57, associate professor, 1957-62, professor of English, 1962-75, curator of rare books and manuscripts, editor of *Colby Library Quarterly,* and director of Colby College Press. Conductor of fifteen-week television course, "Great English Novels," on Maine Network, 1959-60; member of advisory board of *American Literature Abstracts. Military service:* U.S. Army, 1943-46. *Member:* Modern Language Association of America, Phi Beta Kappa, Phi Kappa Phi, Sigma Delta Omicron. *Awards, honors:* M.A., Colby College, 1963.

WRITINGS: The Genteel Circle: Bayard Taylor and His New York Friends, Cornell University Press, 1952; *Sarah Orne Jewett* (critical biography), Twayne, 1962; *Mary N. Murfree* (critical biography), Twayne, 1967; (contributor) J. B. Pickard, editor, *Memorabilia of John Greenleaf Whittier,* Transcendental, 1968; *Early Reception of Edwin Arlington Robinson: The First Twenty Years,* Colby College Press, 1974.

Editor: *Sarah Orne Jewett Letters,* Colby College Press, 1956, enlarged and revised edition, 1967; *Deephaven and Other Stories by Sarah Orne Jewett,* College & University Press, 1966; *Edwin Arlington Robinson's Letters to Edith Brower,* Harvard University Press, 1968; Thomas Hardy, *The Return of the Native,* Cambridge Book Co., 1968; Thomas Hardy, *The Mayor of Casterbridge,* Cambridge Book Co., 1969; *Appreciation of Edwin Arlington Robinson,* Colby College Press, 1969; *The Uncollected Short Stories of Sarah Orne Jewett,* Colby College Press, 1971; *Appreciation of Sarah Orne Jewett,* Colby College Press, 1973. Contributor to *Encyclopaedia Britannica, World Encyclopedia of Twentieth Century Authors,* and *Penguin Companion to Juvenile Literature;* contributor of articles, mainly on New England authors, and poetry to scholarly and special journals.

WORK IN PROGRESS: Uncollected Poems and Prose of Edwin Arlington Robinson; two bibliographies of Walt Whitman; *The Literary Tastes of Sarah Orne Jewett.*

CARYL, Warren 1920-
(Moss Tadrack)

PERSONAL: Born October 15, 1920, in Sudbury, Vt.; son of William C. (a farmer) and Myrtle (Burt) Caryl. *Education:* University of Vermont, B.A., 1949; University of Wisconsin, M.A., 1950; Columbia University, graduate study, 1952-54, currently doctoral candidate; also studied at Sorbonne, University of Paris, 1951-52, and University of Goettingen, 1958-59. *Politics:* Democrat.

CAREER: Lawrence College (now University), Appleton, Wis., instructor in French and German, 1954-60; Emporium, San Francisco, Calif., sales supervisor, 1960-62; Victoria University, Victoria, British Columbia, eighteenth-century French specialist, 1962-63; Chico State College (now University of California, Chico), assistant professor of French, 1963-68. *Military service:* U.S. Army, 1942-45. *Awards, honors:* Fulbright fellow, 1958-59.

WRITINGS—All under pseudonym Moss Tadrack, except as noted: (Under name Warren Caryl) *Whirlpool of Thunder,* Newsstand Library, 1961; *Four for Seduction,* Novel Books, 1961; *Shocking Nymphs,* Novel Books, 1962; *Carnal College,* Novel Books, 1963; *No Green on This Mountain,* Novel Books, 1964; *Georgette,* Pike Publications, 1963; (under name Warren Caryl) *Riot Night in Cedarville,* Monarch Books, 1965; *Mistress of Evil,* Brandon House, 1966; *Halo of Sin,* Brandon House, 1967. About forty short stories have been published in magazines ranging from *Sir* to *Ingenue.*††

* * *

CASEY, Michael T. 1922-
(Mart Casey)

PERSONAL: Born November 22, 1922, in Brooklyn, N.Y.; son of Michael and Anna (Curley) Casey; married Rosemary Alice Christmann (a children's book editor), January 22, 1944; children: Brigid, Maura. *Education:* Fordham College, A.B., 1944; Columbia University, M.A., 1948, Ed.D., 1971. *Religion:* Roman Catholic. *Home:* 226 Clinton St., Brooklyn, N.Y. 11201. *Office:* St. Francis College, 180 Remsen St., Brooklyn, N.Y.

CAREER: Fordham University, Bronx, N.Y., assistant professor of economics and finance at Schools of Business and Education, 1948-62; St. Francis College, Brooklyn, N.Y., professor of economics, 1962—. *Member:* American Economic Association, American Historical Association, American Finance Association, American Association of University Professors, Academy of Political Science, Association of American Geographers, Metropolitan Economic Society, Beta Gamma Sigma, Omicron Delta Epsilon.

WRITINGS: (Under name Mart Casey; with wife, Rosemary A. Casey, and Sigmund A. Lavine) *Water Since the World Began,* Dodd, 1965. Author of "Productivity" series for International Telephone and Telegraph, 1959.

* * *

CASH, Grace (Savannah) 1915-
(Grady Cash)

PERSONAL: Born April 13, 1915, in Hall County, Ga.; daughter of Rufus Spencer (a farmer) and Lou Ella (Deaton) Cash. *Education:* Attended Perry Business School, Morehead College, Oklahoma University and Temple College; Brenau College, B.A. *Politics:* "Have voted alternately Democratic and Republican." *Religion:*

Baptist. *Home address:* Route 2, c/o Mrs. Rufus S. Cash, Flowery Branch, Ga. 30542.

CAREER: Employed in hosiery, silk, and textile mills, Gainesville, Ga., 1937-43; stenographer with American Leprosy Missions, Atlanta, Ga., 1944-46, and American Red Cross, Atlanta, 1946-49; stenographer with various Georgia State departments, Atlanta, 1949-68; currently English teacher for Marietta Tabernacle Christian Schools, Marietta, Ga. Free-lance writer for church publications.

WRITINGS—Novels: *Highway's Edge,* Moody, 1965; *Promise Unto Death,* Herald Press, 1967. Poems have been included in *Yearbook of Modern Poetry,* 1971, *Melody of the Muse,* 1972, *Lyrics of Love,* 1972.

Contributor of more than four hundred stories and numerous poems to Baptist, Church of God, Mennonite, Presbyterian, Nazarene, and other church publications; *The American Girl* and other non-denominational publications; some boys' stories in *Young Life* have appeared under pseudonym Grady Cash.

WORK IN PROGRESS: A Christian novel on migrants in the United States.

*　　*　　*

CASHIN, Edward L.   1927-

PERSONAL: Born July 22, 1927, in Augusta, Ga.; son of Edward J. (a cotton broker) and Margaret (O'Leary) Cashin. *Education:* Marist College, B.A., 1952; Fordham University, M.A., 1956, Ph.D., 1962. *Politics:* Independent. *Religion:* Roman Catholic. *Home:* 2980 Fox Spring Circle, Augusta, Ga. 30904. *Office:* Augusta College, Augusta, Ga. 30904.

CAREER: Teacher of history at Mount St. Michael Academy, Bronx, N.Y., and Christopher Columbus High School, Miami, Fla.; Marist College, Poughkeepsie, N.Y., assistant professor of history and academic vice-president, 1963-68; New York State Education Department, Office of Planning in Higher Education, consultant, 1969; Augusta College, Augusta, Ga., professor of history, 1970—. Vice-president of board of directors, Dutchess County Committee for Economic Opportunity, 1966-67. *Member:* Georgia Historical Society, Georgia Association of Historians (vice-president, 1974—), Richmond County Historical Society (president, 1974—). *Awards, honors:* Freedoms Foundation Award, 1959; E. Merton Coulter Award of Georgia Historical Society, 1975.

WRITINGS: Your Calling as a Brother, Rosen, 1966; *Higher Education in the Mid-Hudson Region,* New York State Education Department, 1969; (with Heard Robertson) *Augusta in the Decade of the Revolution 1773-1783,* Ashantilly Press, 1975; *A History of Augusta College 1783-1975,* Augusta College, 1976. Contributor to *Catholic Youth Encyclopedia for School and Home, Collier's Encyclopedia Yearbook, Georgia Historical Quarterly, Georgia Review,* and *Richmond County History.*

*　　*　　*

CASSELL, Richard A(llan)   1921-

PERSONAL: Born October 20, 1921, in Chicago, Ill.; son of John Allan (a salesman) and Naomi (Sherwood) Cassell; married Harriet Carrithers, September 8, 1950; children: John Wallace Sherwood, Edith Camilla, Robert Ludlow Baker, Judith Bessesen. *Education:* University of Chicago, B.A., 1946, M.A., 1947, Ph.D., 1959. *Home:* 502 West Hampton Dr., Indianapolis, Ind. 46208. *Office:* Butler University, Indianapolis, Ind. 46208.

CAREER: Illinois Institute of Technology, Chicago, instructor in English, 1947-50; Dakota Wesleyan University, Mitchell, S.D., associate professor of English and head of department, 1950-58; Butler University, Indianapolis, Ind., 1959—, began as associate professor, now professor of English. *Military service:* U.S. Army, 1943-46. *Member:* Modern Language Association of America, National Council of Teachers of English, American Association of University Professors, Indiana Council of Teachers of English, Phi Kappa Phi.

WRITINGS: (Contributor) Mark Schorer, editor, *Modern British Fiction,* Oxford University Press, 1961; *Ford Madox Ford: A Study of His Novels,* Johns Hopkins Press, 1961; (editor with Henry Knepler) *What Is the Play?,* Scott, Foresman, 1967; (editor) *Ford Madox Ford: Modern Judgements,* Macmillan, 1972.

WORK IN PROGRESS: A short story text; a book on impressionism in the novel.

*　　*　　*

CASSIDY, Vincent H.   1923-

PERSONAL: Born September 10, 1923, in Manchester, N.H.; son of Vincent Harold (a butcher) and Ruth (Shackett) Cassidy; married Geraldyne Woodall, June 24, 1945; married Amy Kostant Page, November 3, 1970; children: (first marriage) John Micajah, Karen Nina. *Education:* Student at University of New Hampshire, 1941, and University of Southwestern Louisiana, 1944; University of North Carolina, B.A., 1947, M.A., 1953, Ph.D., 1957. *Religion:* Unitarian Universalist. *Home:* 569 Weber Ave., Akron, Ohio 44303. *Office:* Department of History, University of Akron, Akron, Ohio.

CAREER: University of North Carolina, Chapel Hill., instructor, 1953-56, member of library staff, 1954-56; University of Southwestern Louisiana, Lafayette, assistant professor, 1956-60, associate professor, 1960-65, professor of ancient and medieval history, 1965-69; University of Akron, Akron, Ohio, professor of history, 1969—. One of founders of Lafayette Civic Theatre, Inc.; actor, director, and producer of plays and musicals; also gives readings of his own poetry. *Military service:* U.S. Marine Corps, 1942-46; received Silver Star for action with First Marine Raider Battalion, 1942.

MEMBER: Mediaeval Academy of America, Society for the History of Discoveries, American Association of University Professors, Southern Historical Association, New England Antiquities Research Association, Ohio Historical Society, Ohio Academy of History, Phi Alpha Theta. *Awards, honors:* Louisiana Library Association Literary Award, 1965; fellow, Southeastern Institute of Medieval and Renaissance Studies, 1967.

WRITINGS: (With John V. D. Southworth) *Long Ago in the Old World,* with *Teacher's Manual,* C. E. Merrill, 1964, revised edition, 1968; (with A. E. Simpson) *Henry Watkins Allen,* Louisiana State University Press, 1964; (with Simpson) *The Traveling Man,* Claitors, 1967; *Saints and Sinners at Sea,* University of Minnesota Press, 1968; *The Sea Around Them,* Louisiana State University Press, 1968. Plays include "Uncle Al," a two-act musical presented in the Municipal Auditorium of Lafayette, 1966, and "The Puppet Tree," performed in local schools by Service League of Lafayette, 1966. Poems have been published in a number of little literary magazines.

WORK IN PROGRESS: With wife, Amy Page Cassidy, a

biography of Sarah Dorsey; with Mathe Allain, annotating and translating *De Imagine Mundi,* for University of Minnesota Press, completion expected in 1977; *The Saint and Saul,* a reappraisal of the Biblical account of St. Paul; *Roman History,* a text for college freshman; *New Worlds and Every Man: The Pre-Columbian Discovery of America.*

* * *

CASTEL, J(ean) G(abriel)   1928-

PERSONAL: Born September 17, 1928, in Nice, France; son of Charles (a businessman) and Simone (Ricour) Castel; married Jane Jewett (a music and art history teacher), September 5, 1953; children: Christopher, Maria, Marc. *Education:* University of Aix-Marseille, B.Sc. and Phil., 1947; University of Paris, LL.B. and LL.M., 1950; University of Michigan, LL.B., 1953; Harvard University, S.J.D., 1958. *Religion:* Roman Catholic. *Home:* R.R.1, Schomberg, Ontario, Canada. *Office:* Osgoode Hall Law School, York University, Toronto, Ontario, Canada.

CAREER: United Nations, Department of Economic Affairs, New York City, legal research assistant, 1952; worked for Dewey, Ballantine, Busby, Palmer, & Wood (law firm), New York City, 1953; McGill University, Montreal, Quebec, assistant professor, 1954-55, associate professor of law, 1955-59; York University, Osgoode Hall Law School, Toronto, Ontario, professor of law, 1959—; barrister and solicitor, Toronto, Ontario, 1960—. Visiting professor at Laval University, and University of Montreal, both 1959-68, University of Mexico, 1963, University of Lisbon, 1964, University of Nice, 1968, and University of Puerto Rico, 1973. Consultant to Department of External Affairs, Canadian Government. *Military service:* Served with French resistance, 1944-45. *Member:* Canadian Bar Association (council, 1957—), Canadian Institute of International Affairs, Association of Canadian Law Teachers, International Law Association, International Faculty of Comparative Law. *Awards, honors:* Fulbright scholar, 1950; British Commonwealth fellow, 1962.

WRITINGS: Foreign Judgments: A Comparative Study, McGill University Press, 1956; *Private International Law,* Canada Law Book, 1960; *Cases, Notes and Materials on the Conflict of Laws,* Butterworth, 1960, 3rd edition published as *Conflict of Laws,* 1974; *Civil Law System of Quebec,* Butterworth, 1962; *International Law, Chiefly As Interpreted and Applied in Canada,* University of Toronto Press, 1965; *Canadian Conflict of Laws,* Butterworth, 1975; (with S. A. Williams), *International Criminal Law,* York University, 1975. Contributor to periodicals. Editor, *Canadian Bar Review,* 1957—.

WORK IN PROGRESS: A textbook on fine arts and the law.

AVOCATIONAL INTERESTS: Travel, riding and swimming.

* * *

CASTELNUOVO-TEDESCO, P(ietro)   1925-

PERSONAL: Born January 5, 1925, in Florence, Italy; came to United States, 1939; naturalized U.S. citizen, 1947; son of Mario (a musician and composer) and Clara (Forti) Castelnuovo-Tedesco; married Lisbeth M. Stone, October 20, 1957; children: Diana, Costanza. *Education:* University of California, Los Angeles, B.A., 1945; University of California, Berkeley, M.S., 1947; Boston University School of

Medicine, M.D., 1952. *Office:* Department of Psychiatry, Vanderbilt University, Nashville, Tenn. 37232.

CAREER: Boston City Hospital, Boston, Mass., Psychiatric Service, physician-in-charge of inpatient unit, 1958-59; University of California School of Medicine, Los Angeles, assistant professor, 1959-66, associate professor, 1966-72, professor of psychiatry, 1972-75; Vanderbilt University, Nashville, Tenn., James G. Blackmore Professor of Psychiatry, 1975—. Assistant in psychiatry, Harvard Medical School, Boston, 1958-59; chief of department of psychiatry, Harbor General Hospital, Torrance, Calif., 1959-75. *Military service:* U.S. Air Force, Medical Corps, 1955-57; became captain. *Member:* International Psychoanalytic Association, American Psychoanalytic Association, American College of Psychiatrists (fellow), American Psychiatric Association (fellow), American Psychosomatic Society, Southern California Psychiatric Society (councillor, 1966-69), South Bay Psychiatric Society (president, 1966-67), Los Angeles Psychoanalytic Society/Institute.

WRITINGS: The Twenty Minute Hour: A Guide to Brief Psychotherapy for the Physician, Little, Brown, 1965; *Psychiatric Aspects of Organ Transplantation,* Grune, 1971. Contributor to medical journals.

WORK IN PROGRESS: Research in the areas of psychosomatic medicine, psychotherapy, and psychoanalysis.

* * *

CAVALLARI, Alberto   1927-

PERSONAL: Born September 1, 1927, in Piacenza, Italy; son of Enrico (a tradesman) and Dirce (Bongiorni) Cavallari; married Marisa Astorri, June 10, 1953; children: Paolo, Andrea. *Education:* Studied philosophy and law at University of Milan. *Religion:* "Baptized Catholic." *Home:* Copernico 57, Milan, Italy. *Agent:* Agenzia Letteraria Internazionale, Milan, Italy. *Office: La Stampa,* 5 rue des Italicus, Paris 9, France.

CAREER: Journalist in Italy with *Italia Libera,* 1945-47, and *EPOCA,* 1950-53; *Corriere della Sera,* Milan, Italy, special correspondent, 1954-69; *Gazzettino,* Venice, Italy, editor, 1969; free-lance journalist, 1970-73; *La Stampa,* Turin, Italy, correspondent from Paris, 1973—. Judge, Premio Bagutta (literary prize), 1959—. *Member:* Ordine Nazionale dei Giornalist (Rome), Associazione Giornalisti Lombardi (Milan). *Awards, honors:* Palazzi Prize for reporting, 1962; Marzotta Prize for international reporting, 1963; Estense Prize for *La Russia contro Kruscev,* 1963.

WRITINGS: L'Europa intelligente, Rizzoli, 1963; *L'Europa su misura,* Vallecchi, 1963; *La Russia contro Kruscev,* Vallecchi, 1965; (with Montanelli) *Italia sotto inchiesta,* Sansoni, 1965; *Il Vaticano che cambia,* Mondadori, 1966, translation published as *The Changing Vatican,* Doubleday, 1967; *Il Potere in Italia,* Mondadori, 1967; *Una lettera da Pechino,* Garzanti, 1974; *La Cita dell' ultima Mao,* Garzanti, 1975. Adviser for American literature, Mondadori Co., 1950-54.

* * *

CAWELTI, John G(eorge)   1929-

PERSONAL: Born December 31, 1929, in Evanston, Ill.; son of Donald George (a teacher) and Florence (Mason) Cawelti; married Elizabeth Offringa, June 4, 1955; children: John Anthony, Brent Alwyn, Andrea Natalia Suellen. *Education:* Oberlin College, B.A., 1951; University of Iowa, M.A., 1956, Ph.D., 1960. *Home:* 5817 Blackstone,

Chicago, Ill. 60637. *Office:* University of Chicago, Chicago, Ill. 60637.

CAREER: University of Chicago, Chicago, Ill., instructor, 1957-59, assistant professor, 1959-63, associate professor, 1963-69, professor of English and humanities, 1969—. *Military service:* U.S. Army, 1952-54; became first lieutenant. *Member:* American Studies Association.

WRITINGS: (With Marvin Meyers and Alexander Kern) *Sources of the American Republic,* two volumes, Scott, 1960, revised edition, 1967-68; (contributor) Germaine Bree, editor, *Literature and Society,* University of Nebraska Press, 1964; *Apostles of the Self-Made Man,* University of Chicago Press, 1965; (contributor) Frederic Cople Jaher, editor, *America and the Age of Industrialism,* Free Press, 1968; *The Six-Gun Mystique,* Bowling Green University, 1971; (editor) *Focus on Bonnie and Clyde,* Prentice-Hall, 1973; *Why Pop?,* Chandler & Sharp, 1973; *Adventure, Mystery, and Romance: A Theory of Popular Story Formulas,* University of Chicago Press, 1976. Contributor of reviews, articles, and essays to professional journals.

WORK IN PROGRESS: The Secret Agent Syndrome: Spies in Literature; Images of the American West.

*   *   *

CAYCE, Edgar E(vans) 1918-

PERSONAL: Surname is pronounced Casey; born February 9, 1918, in Selma, Ala.; son of Edgar (the psychic) and Gertrude (Evans) Cayce; married Kathryn Bane (an office manager), June 13, 1942; children: Edgar Evans, Jr., Janet Gail. *Education:* Duke University, B.S. in E.E., 1939. *Religion:* Presbyterian. *Home:* 1565 Michigan Ave., Virginia Beach, Va. 23454.

CAREER: Registered professional engineer in Virginia. Virginia Electric & Power Co., Norfolk, electrical engineer in planning department, 1940-41, 1945-75, planning engineer of Eastern division, 1975—. Chairman of board, Association for Research and Enlightenment, Inc.; member of board of directors, Edgar Cayce Foundation. Trustee, Atlantic University. *Military service:* U.S. Army and U.S. Army Air Forces, 1941-45; became captain.

WRITINGS: Edgar Cayce on Atlantis, Hawthorn, 1968; (with Hugh Lynn Casey) *The Outer Limits of Edgar Cayce's Power,* Harper, 1971. Also editor of *Atlantis Fact or Fiction,* Association for Research and Enlightenment. Contributor of articles and reviews to *ARE Journal* and *Searchlight.*

AVOCATIONAL INTERESTS: Golf, bridge.

BIOGRAPHICAL/CRITICAL SOURCES: Virginian Pilot, May 5, 1968.

*   *   *

CECIL, Lamar (John Ryan, Jr.) 1932-

PERSONAL: Born March 11, 1932, in Beaumont, Tex.; son of Lamar John Ryan (a federal judge) and Mary (Reed) Cecil. *Education:* Rice University, B.A., 1954; Johns Hopkins University, Ph.D., 1962. *Office:* History Department, University of North Carolina, Chapel Hill, N.C. 27514.

CAREER: Johns Hopkins University, Baltimore, Md., instructor, 1962-63; Princeton University, Princeton, N.J., instructor, 1963-65, assistant professor of modern European history, 1965-68; University of North Carolina at Chapel

Hill, associate professor, 1968-73, professor of history, 1973—. *Military service:* U.S. Army, 1954-56. *Member:* American Historical Association.

WRITINGS: Albert Ballin: Business and Politics in Imperial Germany, 1888-1918, Princeton University Press, 1967; *The German Diplomatic Service, 1871-1914,* Princeton University Press, 1976.

WORK IN PROGRESS: A biography of Kaiser Wilhelm II, last German kaiser, 1888-1918.

*   *   *

CELA, Camilo Jose 1916-
(Don Camilo, Matilde Verdu)

PERSONAL: Surname pronounced *Sel-*lah; born May 11, 1916, in Iria Flavia, La Coruna, Spain; son of Camilo (a customs official and part-time writer) and Camila Enmanuela (Trulock Bertorini) Cela; married Maria del Rosario Conde Picavea, March 12, 1944; children: Camilo Jose. *Education:* Attended University of Madrid, 1933-36 (left without taking a degree in order to join Franco's forces), returned to study, 1939-43. *Home:* La Bonanova, Palma de Mallorca, Spain; also maintains a home in Madrid, Spain.

CAREER: Writer. Founded *Papeles de Son Armadans,* 1956, a scholarly journal of art and literature, which he continues to direct. Has traveled and lectured in England, France, Belgium, Sweden, Italy, and the United States. *Military service:* Served in Spanish Rebel Army under Franco during Spanish Civil War, 1936-39; became corporal. *Member:* Real Academia Espanola (elected in 1957), Real Academia Gallega, Hispanic Society of America, American Association of Teachers of Spanish and Portuguese. *Awards, honors:* Doctorate from Syracuse University.

WRITINGS—Novels; *La Familia de Pascual Duarte,* Aldecoa, 1942, 16th edition, Destino, 1967, translation by Anthony Kerrigan published as *The Family of Pascual Duarte,* Eyre & Spottiswoode, 1946, Altantic-Little, 1964, Spanish version edited by Harold L. Boudreau and John W. Kronik, Appleton, 1961, translation by Herma Briffault published as *Pascual Duarte and His Family,* bi-lingual edition, Las Americas Publishing (New York), 1965; *Pabellon de reposo* (first published serially in *El Espanol,* March 13 to August 21, 1943), Afrodisio Aguado, 1943, 5th edition, Destino, 1971, translation by Briffault published as *Rest Home,* bi-lingual edition, Las Americas Publishing, 1961; *Nuevas andanzas y desventuras de Lazarillo de Tormes* (derived from the 16th-century picaresque legend; first published serially in *Juventud,* July 4 to October 18, 1944), La Nave, 1944, 9th edition, Noguer, 1970; *Caminos inciertos: La Colmena,* Emece, 1951, 2nd and subsequent reprintings published as *La Colmena,* 11th edition, Noguer, 1971, translation by J. M. Cohen and Arturo Barea published as *The Hive,* Farrar, Straus, 1953; *Santa Balbina 37, gas en cada piso* (novella), Melilla Mirto y Laurel, 1952; *Timoteo, el incomprendido* (novella), Rollan, 1952; *Cafe de artistas* (novella), Tecnos, 1953; *Mrs. Caldwell habla con su hijo,* Destino, 1953, 3rd edition, 1969, translation by Jerome S. Berstein published as *Mrs. Caldwell Speaks to Her Son,* Cornell University Press, 1968; *Historias de Venezuela: La Catira* (written at the request of the Venezuelan Government; although billed as the first in the "Historias de Venezuela" series, *La Catira* remains without sequel), Noguer, 1955; *Tobogan de hambrientos,* Noguer, 1962, 2nd edition, 1964; *San Camilo, 1936: Visperas, festividad y octava de San Camilo del ano 1936 en Madrid,*

Alfaguara, 1969; *Oficio de tinieblas 5; o, Novela de tesis escrita para ser cantada por un coro de enfermos*, Noguer, 1973.

Stories: *Esas Nubes que pasan*, Afrodisio Aguado, 1945; *El Bomito crimen del carabinero, y otras invenciones*, Janes, 1947; *Baraja de invenciones*, Castalia, 1953; *Nuevo retablo de don Cristobita: Invenciones, figuraciones y alucinaciones*, Destino, 1957; *Historias de Espana: Los ciegos, los tontos*, privately printed by Papeles de Son Armadans, 1957, Arion, 1958, published as *A la pata de palo*, Alfaguara, Volume I: *Historias de Espana*, 1965, Volume II: *La familia del heroe; o, Discurso historico de los ultimos restos*, 1965, Volume III: *El cuidadano Iscariote Reclus*, 1965, Volume IV: *Viaje a U.S.A.; o, El que la sigue la mata*, 1967, single volume edition published as *El tacata oxidado: Florilegio de carpetovetonismos y otras lindezas*, Noguer, 1973; *Cajon de sastre*, Cid, 1957, 3rd edition, Alfaguara, 1970; *Los Viejos amigos*, Noguer, 1960, 2nd edition, 1973; *Gavilla de fabulas sin amor* (illustrated by Picasso), Ediciones de los Papeles de Son Armadans, 1962; *Once cuentos de futbol*, Nacional, 1963, 2nd edition, 1972; *Las Companias convenientes, y otros fingimientos y cegueras*, Destino, 1963, 2nd edition, 1969; *El Solitario* [y] *Los Suenos de Quesada*, Ediciones de los Papeles de Son Armadans, 1963; *Garito de Hospicianos; o, Guirigay de imposturas y bambollas*, Noguer, 1963, 2nd edition, 1971; *Toreo de Salon*, Lumen, 1963; *Izas, rabizas y colipoterras*, Lumen, 1964; *Nuevas escenas matritenses*, seven volumes, Alfaguara, 1965-66, single volume edition published as *Fotografias al minuto*, Sala, 1972; *Cuentos para leer despues del bano*, La Gaya Ciencia, 1974.

Poetry: *Poemas de una adolescencia cruel*, Zodiaco, 1945, published as *Pisando la dudosa luz del dia: Poemas de una adolescencia cruel*, Seix Barral, 1960; *Dos romances de ciego*, Libreria Anticuaria El Guadalhorce, 1966; *Maria Sabina* (dramatic poem), Ediciones de los Papeles de Son Armadans, 1967, 2nd edition, published with *El Carro de heno; o, El inventor de la guillotina*, Alfaguara, 1970.

Travel: *Las Botas de siete leguas: Viaje a la Alcarria, con los versos de su cancionero, cada uno en su debido lugar*, Revista de Occidente, 1948, 14th edition, Destino, 1971, Spanish version edited by Philip Polack published as *Viaje a la Alcarria*, Harrap, 1961, Health, 1962, translation by Frances M. Lopez-Morillos published as *Journey to the Alcarria*, University of Wisconsin Press, 1964; *Avila*, Noguer, 195[?], 6th revised edition, 1968, translation by John Forrester published under same title, 1956; *Del Mino al Bidasoa: Notas de un vagabundaje*, Noguer, 1952, 4th edition, 1966; *Judios, moros y cristianos: Notas de un vagabundaje por Avila, Segovia y sus tierras*, Destino, 1956, 4th edition, 1970; *Primer viaje andaluz: Notas de un vagabundaje por Jaen, Cordoba, Sevilla, Huelva y sus tierras*, Noguer, 1959; *Cuaderno del Guadarrama*, Arion, 1959; *Paginas de geografia errabunda*, Alfaguara, 1965; *Viaje al Pirineo de Lerida: Notas de un paseo a pie por el Pallars Sobira, el Valle de Aran y el Condado de Ribagorza*, Alfaguara, 1965; *Madrid*, Alfaguara, 1966; *Calidoscopio callejero, maritimo y campestre*, Alfaguara, 1966; *Barcelona*, Alfaguara, 1970; *La Mancha en el corazon y en los ojos*, EDIVSEN, 1971; *Balada del vagobundo sin suerte y otios papeles volanderos*, Espasa Calpe, 1973.

Other nonfiction: *Mesa revuelta*, Sagitario, 1945, 2nd edition, published with *Ensuenos y figuraciones* (also see below), Taurus, 1957, 4th edition, Alfaguara, 1972; (under pseudonym Matilde Verdu) *San Juan de la Cruz*, Madrid, 1948; *El Gallego y su cuadrilla, y otros apuntes carpetovetonicos*, Aguilera, 1949, published with the addition of "En el lomo de la cubierta dice," 1951, 3rd edition, corrected and augmented, Destino, 1967; *Ensuenos y figuraciones*, Ediciones G.P., 1954, published as part of 2nd edition of *Mesa revuelta*, Taurus, 1957; *Mis paginas preferidas*, Gredos, 1956; *La Rueda de los ocios*, Mateu, 1957, 3rd edition, Alfaguara, 1972; *La Obra literaria del pintor Solana*, Ediciones de los Papeles de Son Armadans, 1957, 3rd edition, Sala, 1972; *Recuerdo de don Pio Baroja*, De Andrea, 1958; *La Cucana* (memoirs), Destino, 1959; (editor) *Homenaje y recuerdo a Gregorio Maranon (1887-1960)*, Ediciones de los Papeles de Son Armadans, 1961; *Cuatro figuras del 98: Unamuno, Valle Inclan, Baroja, Azorin, y otros retratos y ensayos espanoles*, Aedos, 1961; *Poesia y cancioneros*, [Madrid], 1968; *Diccionario Secreto*, Alfaguara, Volume I, 1968, Volume II, 1972; *Al servicio de algo*, Alfaguaro, 1969; *La bola del mundo: Escenas cotidianas*, Sala, 1972; *El bonito crimen del carabineros*, Ediciones Picazo, 1972; *A vueltas con Espana*, Seminarios y Ediciones, 1973. Author of articles on bullfighting under pseudonym Don Camilo.

Plays: *Homenaje al Bosco, I: El carro de heno; o, el inventor de la guillotina*, Papelas de Son Armadans, 1969.

Omnibus volumes: *Nuevas andanzas y desventuras de Lazarillo de Tormes, y siete apuntes carpetovetonicos*, [Madrid], 1952; *El Molino de viento, y otras novelas cortas* (includes *El molino de viento, Timoteo, el incomprendido, Cafe de Artistas*, and *Santa Balbina 37: Gas en cada piso*), Noguer, 1956, 2nd edition, 1971; *Obra completa*, Destino, 1962; *Cauteloso tiento por lo pudiera tronar* (prologue to complete works which follows), Destino, 1962; *Los Tres primeras novelas* (includes *La Familia de Pascual Duarte, Pabellon de reposo*, and *Nuevas andanzas y desventuras de Lazarillo de Tormes*), Destino, 1962; *Cuentos (1941-1953)* [y] *Nuevo retablo de don Cristobita* (collected stories), Destino, 1964; *Apuntes carpetovetonicos: Novelas cortas 1949-1956*, Destino, 1965; *Viajes por Espana I (1948-1952)*, Destino, 1965; *Viajes por Espana II (1952-1958)*, Destino, 1966; *Memorias de mi: Novela*, Biblioteca ca Nueva, 1966; *Viajes por Espana III (1959-1964)*, Destino, 1968; *Antologia*, Coculsa, 1968; *Tres novelas mas (1951-55)*, Destino, 1969; *Cafe de artistas y otros Cuentos*, Salvat Editores, 1969; *Cela*, edited by Mariano Tudela, E.P.E.S.A., 1970; *Timoteo el incomprendido y otros papeles ibericos*, Editorial Magisterio Espanol, 1970; *Los amigos y otra novela (1960-62)*, Destino, 1971; *Obras selectas*, Alfaguara, 1971.

SIDELIGHTS: "Of all the young novelists of the present generation in Spain," contend Jacob Ornstein and James Causey "it is definitely Camilo Jose Cela . . . whose star shines most brilliantly in the literary firmament today." Anthony Kerrigan, Cela's translator, carries Ornstein's and Causey's claim further: "Cela is undoubtedly the finest writer of fiction in post-Civil War Spain," he writes. "Cela is certainly the writer of the most redolent Spanish today: redolent of sounding, breathing spoken Spanish."

Cela came to prominence in Spain almost immediately after the publication of his first novel. Now, according to Ornstein and Causey, "he is virtually the only recent novelist to have gained the admiration and approbation even of the Spanish exile group in the Americas." It is often noted that Cela not only writes excellent fiction, but that he has changed the entire course of the development of the novel in Spain. With *La Familia de Pascual Duarte*, Cela established himself as a master of *tremendismo* and became the most successful practitioner of the technique. In this novel, as in his later fiction, Cela "has little to say in favor of mankind." Ornstein and Causey note that "the history of the Spanish novel records few cases of such stern and merciless realism as Cela's.... Few if any rays of sunshine penetrate his pages, in which ugliness, brutality, selfishness and the principle of 'homo homini lupus' predominate.... From the very beginning of his career, Don Camilo has exhibited a predilection and a genius for portraying life, man and society at their worst." Pascual Duarte has frequently been compared with certain of Dostoevsky's psychopathic characters. Ornstein and Causey believe that "it is difficult to find in Spanish literature a novel which approaches *La Familia de Pascual Duarte* in its sustained atmosphere of impending catastrophe, its powerful portrayal of human malevolence, and in nightmarish effects."

La Familia de Pascual Duarte is the self-narrated story of a murderer awaiting execution. Pascual Duarte, writes Anthony Kerrigan, "is the most murderous *picaro* in all of the picaresque in Spain" and "the picaro's everlasting war [is] more potent and deadly than the class war, for an individual can be more venomous than an army and more tireless." But, as David W. Foster contends, "Cela's novels have attracted more attention to their forms than to their themes [as Foster points out elsewhere, "it becomes increasingly difficult, as Cela's career unfolds, to speak of plot in his novels"] and the author has stated his interest in trying out various modes of the novel." Accordingly, Foster demonstrates that each of Cela's novels can be studied as an example of an established form. (Strictly, the novels must be called free-form; but one can show that each adheres to a technique characteristic of an existing form.) Foster calls *La Familia de Pascual Duarte* an example of the traditional novel; *Pabellon de reposo* is a "novel of psychological introspection"; *Nuevas andanzas y desventuras de Lazarillo de Tormes* demonstrates the "revitalization of prototype"; *La Colmena* exemplifies the "readaptation of the novel as a vision of society"; *Mrs. Caldwell habla con su hijo* may be evaluated as a "new novel"; *La Catira* is an "experiment with the ethic archetype"; and Cela's recent fiction, says Foster, demonstrates his increasing commitment to the new novel.

Basically, however, Cela's concept of the novel is utilitarian in that he regards it as "a vehicle for information, albeit an artistic and stylistic vehicle." Further, according to Ornstein and Causey, the novel for Cela must be a "malleable and flexible instrument for the mirroring of life's realities. The novelist is to him 'the keeper of the conscience of his times and his world' whose duty it is to lash out against deceit, dishonesty and sham. His pessimism is stubborn and unrelieved.... Last year [Cela] commented: 'Life is not good; neither is man.... Upon occasion it appears that man is kind and intelligent. But let us not be deceived. He is only hiding behind his mask.'" One of the frequently recurring themes in Cela's fiction, in fact, is that man is "cursed by an original sin," a notion which does much to explain the "moral and ethical bankruptcy" of Cela's characters. His primary interest being the examination of man "as a set of human foibles," he has depicted him both in situations which have virtually no external points of reference, as in *Pabellon de reposo* and *Mrs. Caldwell,* and in the "complex web of of human society," as in most of the other novels. Regardless of the aspect from which Cela chooses to analyze human nature, it seems that it is always the individual, without respect to his back-

ground or environment, that fascinates Cela. Although Robert Kirsner says that the predominant theme of Cela's fiction has been his "search for Spain," for the "essence of Spanish existence," and that Cela's novels capture "the agony of a people who are destined to live among the ruins of their own devastation," it must be argued that Cela's indictment is not of *Spanish* society, but of all the societies of men. One realizes, then, that Cela's search for a form which will enable him to express his beliefs concerning the fundamental nature of man is primarily a personal endeavor and that his role as a novelist is, for him, of only secondary significance. Foster maintains that it is Cela's obsession with finding a "suitable form of narrative prose fiction" that has driven him to experimentation with so many novelistic forms. If the novel is indeed a personal document for Cela, and if he has only indirectly sought to improve his novelistic technique (and to consequently serve as bellwether for contemporary Spanish novelists), one must admire his achievements all the more.

In his recent work, Cela has rejected, as Foster writes, "every single device reminiscent of the novel, including the word itself" (the term *novela* does not appear in Cela's prologue to *Garito de hospicianos*), in an attempt to create an imitation of life, rather than a work of fiction. One of Cela's latest novels, *Visperas, festividad y octava de San Camilo del ano 1936 en Madrid,* David William Foster observes, "is Cela's first major novel in seven years.... Never ranging far afield from the social strata of Madrid (which he is fond of bringing together in the brothel), Cela has, in numerous works over the years, sought to give expression to his depressing vision of man's Fall, a Fall which he may attempt to hide behind the facade of his 'civilized institutions,' but which is nevertheless all the more definitive for our collective indifference and acceptance of spiritual prostitution: 'It may be that my writings are novels, but I'm just given over to writing to God to make him aware of what's going on on on Earth, it's not enough, probably it's not enough and something else is needed....'"

Foster continues: "The novel is set within the framework of an unidentified consciousness which indulges in a diatribe against itself in front of a mirror. There are several possible guiding implications for the novel here, such as the juxtaposition of the 'material' consciousness and its superficial representation in the mirror (literature, of course). But above all, this extrinsic device allows Cela to string together the most disparate (and many would say meaningless) contents of a stream of consciousness, as through the assembly of misanthropic Freudian jottings on three-by-five cards.... the novel can only be understood, not as the pseudo-objective spectacle of mankind found in Cela's previous works, but as a minute and scathing self-denunciation of Cela the man and Cela the artist for their joint impotence in the face of mankind's inevitable history."

Cela has said, according to Foster, that "reflection upon mankind's plight and any sadness thereupon are forms of atavism." But, in his role as novelist, he himself is "forced to come to grips with the plight of mankind, to ponder it, and to shape his novelistic world accordingly. In so doing," Foster continues, "Cela is practicing the very atavism against which he has spoken." Foster believes, however, that Cela's statement is simply his way of saying that the artist must remain outside the mainstream of life. Kerrigan found this note in a prologue by Cela: "We writers live a bit like the snail, sticking out our neck from time to time, only to draw it back in almost at once. We writers need a mere half dozen clear ideas . . . to keep us on the margin of institutions, which are all of them bad, without exception, all of them rotten and shopworn." Furthermore, Cela's nihilism seems to admit no possibility of future indemnification. There is still some dignity in the world, and some love; "life," as Kirsner says, "may be reduced to absurdity but never to nothingness." Cela himself claims that "this is even clearer in [my] latest novel *Oficio de tinieblas 5.*"

Foster notes that some critics have accused Cela of being "glib and slick rather than profound," and, he says, "to a certain extent, this is true. His attitude derives from a sense of superiority natural to an artist from whom we demand insights not accorded to us—which is turn produces an ironical vision of mankind's attempts at living." Foster's own principal condemnation of Cela as a novelist is his disapproval of Cela's "departure from the romantic-realist pattern in which the novelist is responsible for the creation of individuals who, although they may reflect the broader outlines of their society, must also exist as well-defined and unique individuals. It is the latter that Cela refuses to have his characters do. The characters of Cela's novels gather any importance they may possess as individuals solely from their identity with the larger human society to which they belong. Since Cela seems to feel that it is unnecessary to create individuals—perhaps even impossible—he can with little trouble reject the form, devices, and ends of the realist novel." Foster concludes that, perhaps as a result, "Cela's vision of mankind has failed to make any significant advances" in recent years. Kirsner, however, supplies this summary of Cela's work: "Blended with the specter of horror that pervades the works of Cela is a note of poetic imagery that evokes musical exaltation. Songs are shaped from the most trivial aspects of human existence. Cela, the master of horror, is also the master of delicate sensations. He perceives pathos with the same intensity that he dramatizes cruelty. Even in an atmosphere of human depravity, amidst virtual destruction, there are inextinguishable glimmers of man's love. The art of Cela seems to erupt in unexpected disproportion in form as in content. His composition is deliberately grotesque. As an artist, Cela finds no symmetry in life and he strives to express that image of his experience."

Kirsner points out that, sadly, "Cela's artistic integrity has been his personal tragedy" in that Spain has always been an oppressive censor of his work. *La Colmena,* his greatest novel, was not fully authorized for sale in Spain until 1962; *La Familia de Pascual Duarte* was seized by censors in 1943 and was not authorized until 1945. Kirsner also maintains that, in addition to censoring Cela's books, the Spanish "did not wish to understand his work." Cela left the Peninsula as an act of vengeance. Kirsner writes: "He might forgive the innocent audience, but not that body of readers who appoint themselves as judges of art by virtue of academic training."

Although Cela answered questions posed by *CA's* personal information form clearly and completely, Kirsner states that "as a child Cela understood English; today the language . . . seems to frighten him."

AVOCATIONAL INTERESTS: According to Kirsner, Cela's "passionate hobby" is collecting empty wine bottles. Because he shared the wine with a friend, each bottle represents a pleasant encounter. He also collects stamps and literary myths.

BIOGRAPHICAL/CRITICAL SOURCES: Books

Abroad, summer, 1950, spring, 1953, winter, 1971; Olga Prjevalinsky, *El Sistema estetico de Camilo Jose Cela, expresividad y estructura,* Castalia (Valencia), 1960; Alonso Zamora Vicente, *Camilo Jose Cela (acercamiento a un escritor),* Gredos (Madrid), 1962; *Revista Hispanica Moderna,* number 28, April-October, 1962; Robert Kirsner, *The Novels and Travels of Camilo Jose Cela,* University of North Carolina Press, 1963; Pau Ilie, *La Novelistica de Camilo Jose Cela,* Gredos, 1963; David W. Foster, *Forms of the Novel in the Work of Camilo Jose Cela,* University of Missouri Press, 1967; *New York Times Book Review,* May 26, 1968; Sara Suarez Solis, *El lexico de Camilo Jose Cela,* Alfaguara, 1969; D. W. McPheeters, *Camilo Jose Cela,* Twayne, 1969; Mariano Tudela, *Cela,* E.P.E.S.A., 1970; Jorge A. Maraban, *Camus y Cela: El Drama del antiheroe tragico,* Picazo, 1973.

* * *

CELL, Edward (Charles) 1928-

PERSONAL: Born October 5, 1928, in Elizabeth, N.J.; son of Samuel Wesley and Clara (Magnuson) Cell; married Mary Cashman, November 10, 1955; children: Kathryn, Robin, Terryn, Kristin. *Education:* Boston University, A.B., 1956; Andover Newton Theological School, B.D., 1956; Princeton University, M.A., 1959, Ph.D., 1964. *Politics:* Democrat. *Religion:* Quaker. *Home:* 1316 Outer Park Dr., No. 10, Springfield, Ill. 62704. *Office:* Department of Philosophy, Sangamon State University, Springfield, Ill. 62708.

CAREER: Pastor of Congregational church in Dracut, Mass., 1953-55; Danvers State Hospital, Danvers, Mass., occupational therapist, 1954-55; Simpson College, Indianola, Iowa, assistant professor, 1959-64, associate professor of philosophy and religion, 1964-66; Albion College, Albion, Mich., associate professor of philosophy, 1966-72; United States International University, San Diego, Calif., professor of philosophy, 1972-74; Sangamon State University, Springfield, Ill., professor of philosophy, 1974—. Program officer, National Endowment for the Humanities, Washington, D.C., 1971-72. *Member:* American Philosophical Association, American Academy of Religion, American Association of University Professors.

WRITINGS: (Editor) *Religion and Contemporary Western Culture,* Abingdon, 1967; *Language, Existence and God,* Abingdon, 1971.

WORK IN PROGRESS: A book, *Knowledge and Control of Persons.*

* * *

CERNEY, James Vincent 1914-

PERSONAL: Surname is pronounced Sir-nee; born January 27, 1914, in Detroit, Mich.; son of James (a toolmaker) and Anna (Hein) Cerney; married Martha Elizabeth French (an interior design coordinator), November 2, 1940; children: James F., Lee Carol, Patricia Kay (Mrs. Douglas Henry), Jeffrey Lynn, Kimberley Layne. *Education:* Attended Hiram College, 1935; Miami University, Oxford, Ohio, A.B., 1939; Ohio College of Podiatric Medicine, D.P.M., 1943; Central States College of Physiatrics, Eaton, Ohio, D.M., 1948, D.C., 1953. *Office:* 5225 North Main St., Dayton, Ohio 45415.

CAREER: While attending Miami University, wrote the radio series "Northwest School of the Air" for Station WLW, Cincinnati; Radio Station WING, Dayton, Ohio, merchandising and publicity manager, 1940-42; in private practice as a podiatrist, 1943—. Professional Research (human engineering), Dayton, Ohio, founder and president, 1944—. President, team doctor, and trainer, Dayton Triangle Professional Football Team, 1957-59; president, Central States College, Eaton, Ohio, 1961-62. President of Dayton Purple Mask Theatre and Dayton Ballet Guild, 1958. *Member:* National Athletic Trainers Association, American College of Sports Medicine, Academy of Chinese Medicine, Writers Guild, Ohio Mechanotherapists Association (president, 1960-61), Montgomery County Podiatry Society (president, 1962).

WRITINGS—All published by Parker Publishing, except as indicated: (Self-illustrated) *Encyclopedia of the Care of Athletic Injuries,* C. C Thomas, 1963; *How to Develop a Million Dollar Personality,* 1964; *Confidence and Power for Successful Living,* 1966; *Dynamic Laws of Thinking Rich,* 1967; *Stay Younger—Live Longer Through the Magic of Mental Self-Conditioning,* 1968; *Talk Your Way to Success,* 1968; *Thirteen Steps to New Personal Power,* 1969.

(Self-illustrated) *Complete Book of Athletic Taping Techniques: The Defensive Offensive Weapon in the Care and Prevention of Athletic Injuries,* 1972; *Acupuncture without Needles,* 1974; *Modern Magic of Natural Healing with Water Therapy,* 1975; *Handbook of Unusual and Unorthodox Healing Methods,* 1975; *Prevent System for Football Injuries,* Prentice-Hall, 1975; *Sports Clinic Care,* Prentice-Hall, 1975. Writer of stage play, "Blues in the Night," produced locally, 1948, and radio shows, including "Skip Holiday," a Civil Defense series, 1955. Contributor of how-to-do-it series to *Sports Trail;* columnist, *Current Podiatry,* 1965-66; contributor of stories to periodicals, including *McCall's, Coach and Athlete,* and *Police.* Editor, *Ohio Chiropody Journal,* 1944.

WORK IN PROGRESS: You Can Be Charming, for women; *Raw Juices for Health; Reach for the Sun,* the biography of a Dayton Negro poet; *Flame Durrell* and *The Dead Don't Cry,* both novels.

*   *   *

CHACONAS, D(oris) J.   1938-

PERSONAL: Born March 11, 1938; daughter of Paul (a factory employee) and Kathryn (Baratka) Kozak; married Nick Chaconas (a salesman), October 12, 1957; children: Stacy Jean and Stephanie Anne (twins). *Education:* Attended parochial schools in Milwaukee, Wis. *Religion:* Roman Catholic. *Home:* 8720 West Dallas St., Milwaukee, Wis. 53224.

CAREER: Writer for young people.

WRITINGS: A Hat for Lilly, Steck, 1967; *In a Window on Greenwater Street,* Steck, 1970; *The Way the Tiger Walked,* Simon & Schuster, 1970; *Danger in the Swamp,* Lantern Press, 1971. About twenty stories and articles have appeared in *Jack and Jill, Trailblazer, Child Life, Highlights, Family Herald,* and other periodicals.

WORK IN PROGRESS: Several books of fiction for young people.†

*   *   *

CHADBOURNE, Richard M(cClain)   1922-

PERSONAL: Born September 19, 1922, in Providence, R.I.; son of Alexander McClain and Ruth (Wilbur) Chadbourne; married Anna Gisela Golm, July 13, 1947; children: Lawrence McClain, Eric Francis, Eugene Alexander.

Education: Brown University, B.A., 1943; Yale University, M.A., 1947, Ph.D., 1950. *Home:* 3732 Underhill Dr., Calgary, Alberta, Canada T2N 4G1. *Office:* University of Calgary, Calgary, Alberta, Canada T2N 1N4.

CAREER: Fordham University, Bronx, N.Y., instructor, 1950-53, assistant professor of French, 1953-57; University of Colorado, Boulder, associate professor, 1957-61, professor of French and chairman of department, 1961-71; University of Calgary, Calgary, Alberta, professor of French and chairman of department, 1971—. Visiting professor, University of California, Los Angeles, 1967-68. *Military service:* U.S. Army, Signal Corps. 1943-45; became staff sergeant. *Member:* Modern Language Association of America, American Association of Teachers of French, American Council of Teachers of Foreign Languages, Canadian Association of University Teachers. *Awards, honors:* Modern Language Association of America, Crofts-Cornell Award, 1957, for *Ernest Renan as an Essayist;* American Council of Learned Societies fellowship for travel in France, 1962-63; Chevalier, Ordre des Palmes Academiques (France), 1967.

WRITINGS: Ernest Renan as an Essayist, Cornell University Press, 1967; *Ernest Renan,* Twayne, 1968; (contributor) *Chateaubriand,* University of Wisconsin Press, 1970. Contributor to *Essays in French Literature* (publication of University of Western Australia) and scholarly journals in the United States, Canada, and France.

WORK IN PROGRESS: Sainte-Beuve, for Twayne; a book on the great French essayists, from Montaigne to Sartre.

*   *   *

CHADWICK, Henry   1920-

PERSONAL: Born June 23, 1920, in Bromley, Kent, England; son of John (a barrister) and Edith (Horrocks) Chadwick; married Margaret Elizabeth Brownrigg, 1945; children: Priscilla, Hilary, Juliet. *Education:* Magdalene College, Cambridge, B.A. and Mus.B., 1941. *Home:* Christ Church, Oxford, England.

CAREER: Ordained priest, Church of England, 1943; Wellington College, Berkshire, England, assistant master, 1945; Cambridge University, Queen's College, Cambridge, England, fellow and chaplain, 1946-58, dean, 1950-55; Oxford University, Christ Church, Oxford, England, Regius Professor of Divinity and canon, 1959-69, dean, 1969—. Visiting professor, University of Chicago, 1957; Forwood Lecturer, University of Liverpool, 1961; Hewett Lecturer, Union Theological Seminary, 1962; Gifford Lecturer, University of St. Andrews, 1962-64; Burns Lecturer, University of Otago, 1971. Delegate, Oxford University Press, 1960—. *Member:* British Academy (fellow), American Academy of Arts and Sciences. *Awards, honors:* D.D., University of Glasgow, 1957, Yale University, 1970; D.Teol., University of Uppsala, 1967.

WRITINGS: (Editor and translator) Origen, *Contra Celsum,* Cambridge University Press, 1953, revised edition, 1965; (editor with John E. L. Oulton) *Alexandrian Christianity,* Westminster, 1954; (editor and translator) *Lessing's Theological Writings,* A. & C. Black, 1956, Stanford University Press, 1957; (editor) Wilfred Lawrence Knox, *Sources of the Synoptic Gospels,* Volume II, Cambridge University Press, 1957; (editor) *The Sentences of Sextus: A Contribution to the History of Early Christian Ethics,* Cambridge University Press, 1959.

(Editor) *St. Ambrose on the Sacraments*, Loyola University Press, 1960; *The Vindication of Christianity in Westcott's Thought*, Cambridge University Press, 1961; (contributor) M. Black and H. H. Rowley, editors, *Peake's Commentary on the Bible*, Nelson, 1962; *Early Christian Thought and the Classical Tradition*, Oxford University Press, 1966; *The Early Church*, Hodder & Stoughton, 1968, published as *The Early Christian Church*, Eerdmans, 1969. General editor of Harper's "New Testament Commentaries," 1958—. Contributor to professional journals. Editor with H. F. D. Sparks, *Journal of Theological Studies*, Clarendon Press, 1954—.

AVOCATIONAL INTERESTS: Music.

* * *

CHAFFIN, Yule M. 1914-

PERSONAL: Born December 25, 1914, in Waubeka, Wis.; daughter of Frank Benjamin (later a cattle rancher in Montana) and Minnie (Hansmann) Safford; married Darrel Fenton Chaffin (area manager of Federal Aviation Agency communications stations at Kodiak, Alaska), January 16, 1944; children: Jerry Francis, Patricia Mary. *Education:* Northern Montana College, graduate of normal training course, 1936; additional study at Great Falls College of Education (now College of Great Falls), 1941, University of Wisconsin, 1943, and Civil Aeronautics Administration Aeronautical Training Center, Seattle, Wash., 1944. *Home address:* Box 805, Kodiak, Alaska 99615.

CAREER: Elementary teacher in Montana and Wisconsin, 1936-43; ground school instructor for air cadets at Northern Montana College, Havre, and Baker School of Flying, Baker, Ore., 1943-44; airways communications specialist for Federal Aviation Agency, Kodiak, Alaska, 1945-52; elementary teacher in Kodiak, Alaska, 1955-57; now freelance writer. Public information officer, Civil Air Patrol, Kodiak, 1960. *Member:* Alaska Press Women (secretary-treasurer, 1963-64). *Awards, honors:* Three awards from Alaska Press Club, including outstanding free-lance writer in Alaska, 1962; three awards from National Federation of Press Women, including outstanding photo layout, 1966; five awards from Alaska Press Women, including outstanding series of historical articles, 1966; one award from League of Alaskan Writers.

WRITINGS: (With George C. Ameigh) *Alaska's Kodiak Island*, Deseret News Press, 1962; *Alaska's Southwest: Koniag to King Crab*, Deseret News Press, 1967. Contributor to *Alaska Travel Guide;* contributor of some fifty articles to *Alaska Call, Twelve/Fifteen, Catholic Miss, Seattle Times, Westways, Alaska Sportsman, Catholic Boy, Impact*, and other publications.

WORK IN PROGRESS: Benny Benson, a children's book on the life of Alaska's flag designer; *I Remember the Bear Paws*, about her youth on a cattle ranch in Montana; *Sammy, the Saucy Sea Otter*, for ages seven to ten; booklets on Alaska's southwest.

SIDELIGHTS: In 1963 Mrs. Chaffin made a 250-mile float trip with her husband down the Alatna, a wilderness river, through an uninhabited region of Alaska north of the Arctic circle.

BIOGRAPHICAL/CRITICAL SOURCES: Kodiak Daily Mirror, July 12, 1967; *Anchorage Daily Times*, July 28, 1967; *St. Petersburg Times*, St. Petersburg, Fla., January 25, 1968.

CHAI, Chen kang 1916-

PERSONAL: Born February 14, 1916, in Hopeh, China; son of Y. C. and M. C. (Wang) Chai; married February 3, 1954, wife's name Ling C.; children: Leon C., Jean J. *Education:* Army Veterinary College, Nanking, China, D.V.M. (equivalent), 1937; Michigan State University, M.S., 1949, Ph.D., 1951. *Home:* 19 School St., Bar Harbor, Me. 04609. *Office:* Jackson Laboratory, Bar Harbor, Me. 04609.

CAREER: Jackson Laboratory, Bar Harbor, Me., U.S. Department of State fellow, 1951-52, research associate, 1952-53, staff scientist, 1957-67, senior staff scientist, 1967—. Visiting fellow, Massachusetts Institute of Technology, 1952-53. *Military service:* Chinese Army, veterinarian, 1937-46; became major. *Member:* Genetics Society of America, American Association of Physical Anthropologists, Biometric Society, American Genetic Association, American Association for the Advancement of Science. *Awards, honors:* Guggenheim fellow at University of Taiwan and University of California, 1962-63.

WRITINGS: Taiwan Aborigines: A Genetic Study of Tribal Variations, Harvard University Press, 1967; *Genetic Evolution*, University of Chicago Press, 1976.

* * *

CHAI, Hon-chan 1931-

PERSONAL: Born March 23, 1931, in Malaya; son of Ahnam and Choo-moi (Loh) Chai. *Education:* Attended Malayan Teachers' Training College, Kirkby, Lancashire, England, 1952-53; University of Adelaide, B.A. (honors), 1959, M.A., 1961; Harvard University, Ed.D., 1968. *Politics:* Liberal. *Religion:* Agnostic. *Office:* Faculty of Education, University of Malaya, Kuala Lumpur, Federation of Malaysia.

CAREER: High school teacher in Ipoh, Malaya, 1953-56, 1960-63; University of Malaya, Kuala Lumpur, Malaysia, lecturer in education, 1963-64; Harvard University, Cambridge, Mass., teaching fellow, 1965; University of Guyana, Georgetown, visiting lecturer, 1966-67; Ministry of Education, Georgetown, Guyana, assistant in educational planning, 1967; University of Malaya, lecturer, 1968-70, associate professor, 1970-71, professor of sociological studies in education, 1971—, dean of faculty of education, 1971-74. Harvard University, research associate, Center for Studies in Education and Development, 1968-70, visiting fellow, Institute for International Development, 1975-76. Consultant to Federal Examinations Syndicate, Malaysia Ministry of Education, and external examiner for teachers' training colleges. *Member:* Phi Delta Kappa. *Awards, honors:* D.H.L., Sioux Empire College (Iowa), 1966.

WRITINGS: The Development of British Malaya, 1896-1909, Oxford University Press, 1964, 2nd edition, 1967; *Planning Education for a Plural Society*, International Institute for Educational Planning (Paris), 1971.

Contributor: Bernhard Grossmann, editor, *Studien zur Entwicklung in Sud und Ostasien*, Institut fur Asienkunde (Hamburg), 1966; *Curriculum Evaluation in Teacher Education in Southeast Asia*, Faculty of Education, University of Malaya, 1970; Bernhard Grossmann, editor, *South-East Asia in the Modern World*, Institut fur Asienkunde, 1972; K. S. Nijhar, editor, *The Role of Asian Universities in a Changing World*, University of Malaya Academic Staff Association, 1972; David Lim, editor, *Leading Issues in*

Malaysian Economic Development, Oxford University Press, 1975. Contributor to reports, *Education and Manpower Development in Asia,* 1972, and *Education of Workers' Representatives and of Management Towards Improved Labour Relations,* 1973; contributor of articles to journals, including *Journal of Research and Development in Education,* and *Jurnal Pendidikan.*

WORK IN PROGRESS: Education and Nation-Building in Malaysia, for Longman; research in problems of race relations, education and development.

*   *   *

CHAIJ, Fernando   1909-
   (E. L. Alcalde)

PERSONAL: Born February 23, 1909, in San Fernando, Argentina; son of Gabriel (a carpenter) and Agustina (Saman) Chaij; married Sara Ramos (an editor), February 19, 1942. *Education:* Attended Colegio Adventista del Plata, 1931; National University of Buenos Aires, Ph.D. (honors), 1942. *Politics:* "No affiliation." *Religion:* Seventh Day Adventist. *Home:* 1711 Cherrytree Lane, Mountain View, Calif. 94040. *Office:* 1350 Villa St., Mountain View, Calif. 94040.

CAREER: Colegio Adventista del Plata, Villa Libertador S. Martin, E. Rios, Argentina, teacher and president of the college, 1942-47; Casa Editora Sudamericana, Buenos Aires, Argentina, head of editorial department, 1948-60; Pacific Press Publishing Association, Mountain View, Calif., editor-in-chief and book editor of Spanish department, 1961—. Chairman of editorial council, *El Centinela.* *Member:* American Academy of Political and Social Science.

WRITINGS: El Desenlace del Drama Mundial, Casa Editora Sudamericana, 1950, Pacific Press Publishing Association, 1956; *Hacia una Vida Mejor,* Casa Editora Sudamericana, 1951; *Paz en la Angustia,* Casa Editora Sudamericana, 1956, Pacific Press Publishing Association, 1959; *Potencias Supranormales que Actuan en la Vida Humana,* Pacific Press Publishing Association, 1963; (with Braulio Perez Marcio and Hector Pereyra) *Libertad del Temor,* Pacific Press Publishing Association, 1964; *Preparation for the Final Crisis,* Pacific Press Publishing Association, 1966; *Glossolalia: A New Pentecost?,* Pacific Press Publishing Association, 1970; *El Dilema del Hombre,* Pacific Press Publishing Association, 1972; *Un Solo Camino,* Pacific Press Publishing Association, 1975. Contributor to *El Centinela* and *Vida Feliz,* some articles written under pseudonym.

*   *   *

CHAMPION, Larry S(tephen)   1932-

PERSONAL: Born April 27, 1932, in Shelby, N.C.; son of Flay Oren (an oil distributor) and Mary (Helms) Champion; married Nancy Ann Blanchard, December 22, 1956; children: Mary Katherine, Rebecca Jane, Larry Stephen, Jr. *Education:* Davidson College, B.A. (cum laude), 1954; University of Virginia, M.A., 1955; University of North Carolina, Ph.D., 1961. *Politics:* Democrat. *Religion:* Presbyterian. *Home:* 2010 Myron Dr., Raleigh, N.C. 27607.

CAREER: Instructor in English, Davidson College, Davidson, N.C., 1955-56, and University of North Carolina, Chapel Hill, 1959-60; North Carolina State University, Raleigh, instructor, 1960-61, assistant professor, 1961-65, associate professor, 1965-68, professor of English, 1968—,

associate head, 1968-71, head of department, 1971—. *Military service:* U.S. Army, 79th Army Band, 1956-58; served in Canal Zone, Panama. *Member:* Modern Language Association of America, Shakespeare Association of America, Renaissance Society of America, National Council of Teachers of English, South Atlantic Modern Language Association, Southeastern Renaissance Conference, North Carolina English Teachers Association, Phi Beta Kappa, Phi Kappa Phi. *Awards, honors:* Academy of Outstanding Teachers award, 1966; selected as academic administration intern by American Council on Education, 1967-68.

WRITINGS: Ben Jonson's "Dotages": A Reconsideration of the Late Plays, University of Kentucky Press, 1967; *The Evolution of Shakespeare's Comedy,* Harvard University Press, 1970; (editor) *Quick Springs of Sense: Studies in the Eighteenth Century,* University of Georgia Press, 1974; *Shakespeare's Tragic Perspective: The Development of His Dramatic Technique,* University of Georgia Press, 1975. Contributor to literary and scholarly journals. Editorial consultant, *Papers on Language and Literature,* *PMLA,* Canada Council, and Prentice-Hall.

WORK IN PROGRESS: Tragic Patterns in Jacobean and Caroline Drama: A Study in Perspective.

*   *   *

CHAMPLIN, James R(aymond)   1928-

PERSONAL: Born June 14, 1928, in Coventry, R.I.; son of Henry W. and Ida E. (Congdon) Champlin; children: Deborah Jean, Diana Kaye, Duane Jeffrey, Donna Marie. *Education:* Earlham College, A.B., 1953; Indiana University, M.S. and Re. Dir., 1956. *Religion:* Society of Friends. *Home:* 170 Keneway Dr., Bogart, Ga. 30622. *Office:* Department of Recreation and Park Administration, University of Georgia, Athens, Ga. 30602.

CAREER: Superintendent of parks and recreation, Winchester, Ind., 1952-55; Indiana State Board of Health, Indianapolis, recreation consultant, 1956-62; University of Maryland, College Park, instructor in recreation, 1962-64; University of Georgia, Institute of Community and Area Development, Athens, park and recreation consultant, 1964—, associate professor of recreation, 1968—, chairman of department of recreation and park administration, 1970—. Member, Georgia State Commission on Aging, 1966—. *Military service:* U.S. Air Force, 1946-49; became sergeant. *Member:* National Recreation and Park Association (member, Council on Accreditation, 1976-79), American Recreation Society (president, state and federal services section, 1961-62), American Association for Leisure and Recreation (president, 1974-75; member of National Council on Accreditation, 1976-79), Georgia Recreation and Parks Society (president, 1971-72). *Awards, honors:* Distinguished Service Award, American Institute of Park Executives, 1966; Professional of the Year Award, Georgia Recreation and Parks Society, 1973.

WRITINGS: (With Stone) *Recreation in Indiana,* Indiana State Board of Health, 1963; (with Keeling and Hill) *A Preliminary Development Plan for Andersonville,* Institute of Community and Area Development, University of Georgia, 1965; (with Hill) *Optimist Park—A Ten Year Development Study,* Institute of Community and Area Development, University of Georgia, 1965; *A Syllabus on Outdoor Recreation,* Department of Park and Recreation Administration, University of Georgia, 1965; (with Smith and Partain) *Rural Recreation for Profit,* Interstate, 1966; *A Syllabus on Park and Recreation Administration,* Department of Park and Recreation Administration, University of Georgia, 1966; *A Prospectus for Parks and Recreation*, Institute of Community and World Development, University of Georgia, 1967. Contributor to recreation and health periodicals. Editor of monographs on recreation published by Indiana Department of Public Instruction and Board of Health, 1958. Editor of newsletter, Indiana Park and Recreation Association, 1956-61, and Georgia Recreation Society, 1965-66; associate editor, *American Recreation Journal*, 1963-65; member of editorial board, *Leisure Today*, 1973-77.

WORK IN PROGRESS: A book, *Recreation Planning;* chapters for a book, *Leisure Today*.

*   *   *

CHANDLER, A. Bertram 1912-
(Andrew Dunstan, George Whitley)

PERSONAL: Born March 28, 1912, in Aldershot, England; son of Arthur Robert (a soldier) and Ida Florence Chandler; married Susan Schlenker (a secretary), December 23, 1962. *Education:* "Patchy." *Politics:* "Liberal—with a small 'l'." *Religion:* "Agnostic, with Judaistic hankerings." *Home:* Cell 7, Tara St., Woollahra, New South Wales, Australia. *Agent:* Scott Meredith Literary Agency, Inc., 845 Third Ave., New York, N.Y. 10022; E. J. Carnell Literary Agency, 1F Burwash Rd., London SE18 FQY, England. *Office:* 23/19 Tusculum St., Potts Point, N.S.W. 2011, Australia.

CAREER: Shipmaster, holding certificate of competency as master of foreign-going steamship; Sun Shipping Co., London, England, served apprenticeship at sea in tramp steamer, became third officer, 1928-37; Shaw Savill Line, London, sailed on cargo and passenger liners operating from United Kingdom to Australasia, and rose from fourth officer to chief officer, 1937-56; Union Steam Ship Co., Wellington, New Zealand, third officer, 1956-66, master of cargo ships in coastal and Pacific Islands service, 1966-75. Writer of science fiction. *Wartime service:* British Merchant Navy during World War II; became 2nd officer. *Member:* Science Fiction Writer of America, Australian Merchant Service Guild, Australian Society of Authors, British Interplanetary Society (fellow). *Awards, honors:* Ditmar award for best Australian science fiction, 1969, for *False Fatherland*, 1971, for short story, "The Bitter Pill," and 1974, for novel, *The Bitter Pill*.

WRITINGS—All published by Ace Books, except as noted: *The Rim of Space*, 1961; *Bring Back Yesterday*, 1961; *Rendezvous on a Lost World*, 1961; *The Ship from Outside*, 1963; *Beyond the Galactic Rim*, 1963; *The Hamelin Plague*, Monarch Books, 1963; *Glory Planet*, Avalon, 1964; *The Far Reaches of Space*, Jenkins, 1964; *The Coils of Time*, 1964; *Into the Alternate Universe*, 1964; *Empress of Outer Space*, 1965; *The Alternate Martians*, 1965; *Space Mercenaries*, 1965; *Contraband from Other Space*, 1967; *Nebula Alert*, 1967; *The Road to the Rim*, 1967; *False Fatherland*, Horwitz, 1968; *Rim Gods*, 1969; *Catch the Star Winds*, Lancer, 1969; *Spartan Planet*, Dell, 1969. *The Sea Beasts*, Curtis, 1971; *To Prime the Pump*, Curtis, 1971; *Alternate Orbits* [and] *The Dark Dimensions*, 1971; (with Robert Lory) *The Hard Way Up* [and] *The Veiled World* (the former by Chandler, the latter by Lory), 1972; *The Gateway to Never* [and] *The Inheritors*, 1972; *The Bitter Pill*, Wren, 1974; *The Broken Cycle*, Hale & Co., 1975; *The Way Back*, Hale & Co., in press. Short stories for magazines, some under the pseudonyms of An-

drew Dunstan and George Whitley, have been widely anthologized and translated.

WORK IN PROGRESS: Another novel, *Kelly Country*.

SIDELIGHTS: A. Bertram Chandler told *CA:* "[I] write science fiction because I like it. More than one unkind editor has commented that my stories are 'costume sea stories.' Admit that the personnel of my respectable interstellar liners are very Shaw Savill, whereas the officers of the Rim Runners' fleet are more than somewhat Union Steam Ship Company. Hope one day to write a *real* novel." He adds: *"The Bitter Pill* was an attempt to break out of the Rim Worlds ghetto. *Kelly Country* will be another one."

Chandler told *CA* that his novels are "widely translated into all languages from Japanese to Russian, the long way around the world."

AVOCATIONAL INTERESTS: Cookery, navigation, and harbour pilotage.

*   *   *

CHANDLER, S(tanley) Bernard 1921-

PERSONAL: Born May 31, 1921, in Canterbury, England; son of Albert Edward (in insurance) and Emma (Brown) Chandler; married Pearl Morrison (a teacher), July 22, 1954; children: Melanie Linda, Gregory Stephen. *Education:* University of London, B.A., 1947, Ph.D., 1953. *Home:* 9 Heathbridge Park, Toronto, Ontario, Canada M4G 2Y6. *Office:* University of Toronto, Toronto, Ontario, Canada.

CAREER: University of London, London, England, assistant lecturer in Italian, 1948-50; University of Aberdeen, Aberdeen, Scotland, lecturer in Italian, 1950-57; University of Toronto, Toronto, Ontario, associate professor, 1957-63, professor of Italian, 1963—, chairman of department, 1973—. *Military service:* British Army, 1941-45; became lieutenant. *Member:* Modern Language Association of America, Dante Society of America, American Association of Teachers of Italian, Dante Society of Toronto (president, 1959-60, 1964-65).

WRITINGS: (Editor with J. A. Molinaro) *The World of Dante: Six Studies in Language and Thought* (papers read at Toronto, 1964-65, in celebration of 700th anniversary of the birth of Dante), University of Toronto Press, 1966; (contributor) J. A. Molinaro, editor, *Petrarch to Pirandello*, University of Toronto Press, 1973; *Alessandro Manzoni*, University of Edinburgh Press, 1974. Contributor to professional journals in North America and Italy.

WORK IN PROGRESS: Research on Alessandro Manzoni, literature and society in Italy, 1860-1900, and Giovanni Verga.

*   *   *

CHANG, Isabelle C(hin) 1924-

PERSONAL: Born February 20, 1924, in Boston, Mass.; daughter of Que Wah (a merchant) and June (Hall) Chin; married Min-Chueh Chang (a research scientist), May 28, 1948; children: Francis Hugh, Claudia, Pamela. *Education:* Simmons College, B.S.L.S., 1946; graduate study at Yale University, 1946-47; Clark University, M.A., 1967. *Politics:* Independent. *Religion:* Society of Friends. *Home:* 15 Fiske St., Shrewsbury, Mass. 01545. *Office:* Shrewsbury Junior-Senior High School Libraries, Shrewsbury, Mass. 01545.

CAREER: Library assistant in Boston, Mass., 1943, New Haven, Conn., 1945; Harvard-Yenching Library, Cambridge, Mass., apprentice librarian, 1946; Yale Sterling Library, New Haven, Conn., cataloguer, 1946-48; Shrewsbury Public Library, Shrewsbury, Mass., library director, 1959-64; Shrewsbury (Mass.) school system, librarian, 1964—, media specialist, 1974—. Leader, Great Books Discussion Group, 1950-60. Trustee, Shrewsbury Public Library, 1958-59, 1965—. *Member:* American Library Association, New England Library Association, Round Table of Young Adult Librarians (secretary-treasurer, 1963-64), Massachusetts Library Association, Worchester Art Museum, Worchester Foundation for Experimental Biology (women's auxiliary; chairman, fund-raising committee, 1957-58), Bay Path Library Club; Women's Club, Historical Society, Congregational Professional Circle (all Shrewsbury, Mass.). *Awards, honors:* John Greene Chandler Medal for excellence in juvenile writing, 1965, for *Chinese Fairy Tale.*

WRITINGS: What's Cooking at Changs, Liveright, 1959, revised enlarged edition, 1971; *Chinese Cooking Made Easy,* Paperback Library, 1962; *Chinese Fairy Tales,* Barre, 1965; *Tales of the Far East,* Random House, 1968; *Tales from Old China,* Random House, 1969; *Gourmet on the Go,* Tuttle, 1971. Monthly contributor to *Worchester Evening Gazette, Worchester Telegram.*

WORK IN PROGRESS: Paper Folding Fun; The Living School Library; Chinese Interlude; Windows.

SIDELIGHTS: Isabelle Chang travelled around the world, lived for one year in Europe, and visited the People's Republic of China in 1972. She speaks Chinese fluently, and reads French, Italian, Spanish, and Latin.

*   *   *

CHANSKY, Norman M(orton) 1929-

PERSONAL: Born August 26, 1929, in Boston, Mass.; son of Israel (a tailor) and Sadie (Waldman) Chansky; married Elissa Ellsas, March 23, 1957; children: Linda, James, Karen, Tamar, Matthew. *Education:* Boston University, B.S., 1951, M.Ed., 1952; Columbia University, Ph.D., 1958. *Home:* 15 Benjamin West Ave., Swarthmore, Pa. 19081. *Office:* Temple University, Philadelphia, Pa. 19122.

CAREER: Manter Hall School, Cambridge, Mass., teacher of remedial reading, 1952-53; Adelphi University, Garden City, N.Y., instructor in psychology, 1954-57; State University of New York at Oswego, assistant professor of psychology, 1957-59; Ulster County Board of Education, New Paltz, N.Y., school psychologist, 1959-62; North Carolina State University at Raleigh, associate professor of psychology, 1962-66; Temple University, Philadelphia, Pa., professor of educational psychology, 1966—. Visiting associate professor, State University of New York at Albany, 1959; visiting faculty member, State University of New York at New Paltz, 1960-61; visiting professor, Tel Aviv University, 1973-74. *Member:* American Psychological Association, American Educational Research Association, National Council on Measurement in Education.

WRITINGS: Untapped Good: Rehabilitation of School Dropouts, C. C Thomas, 1966; (contributor) J. Margary, editor, *School Psychology in Theory and Practice,* Prentice-Hall, 1967. Contributor of articles to professional journals.

WORK IN PROGRESS: Reporting and Marketing Practices in American School; School Tenure Laws: Public Attitudes.

CHAPMAN, J. Dudley 1928-
(Jay Dudley)

PERSONAL: Born April 29, 1928, in Moline, Ill.; son of Joseph Dudley (a salesman) and Illlian Caroline (Pruder) Chapman; married Mary Kay Sartini, June 15, 1948; married second wife, Virginia Helene Milius (a laboratory technician), June 17, 1958; children: (first marriage) Mary Jo, Nancy Jo. *Education:* Attended University of Illinois, 1946-48; Roosevelt University, B.S., 1949; College of Osteopathic Medicine and Surgery, D.O., 1953, D.S., 1968; University of California, Irvine, M.D., 1962. *Politics:* "Ambivalent." *Religion:* Lutheran. *Home:* 6374 Lake Rd., North Madison, Ohio 44057. *Office address:* P.O. Box 253, North Madison, Ohio 44057.

CAREER: Diplomate of American Osteopathic Board of Obstetrics and Gynecology. College of Osteopathic Medicine and Surgery, Still Osteopathic Hospital, Des Moines, Iowa, associate professor of obstetrics and gynecology, 1956-58, chairman of department, 1957-58. Private practice of obstetrics and gynecology in Ohio, 1958—; Brentwood Hospital, Cleveland, Ohio, chief of obstetrics and gynecology, 1958-61; Bayview Hospital, Bay Village, Ohio, senior obstetrician and gynecologist, 1961-63, consultant, 1963—; Northeastern Ohio General Hospital, Madison, chief of staff, 1967—. Aviation medical examiner, Federal Aviation Agency. Lecturer at professional meetings, seminars, and conferences.

MEMBER: International Society of Comprehensive Medicine (charter member; member of national scientific advisory council), American College of Osteopathic Obstetricians and Gynecologists (president, 1966-67; fellow), American Osteopathic Association, Society of Psychosomatic Medicine (executive secretary), Academy of Psychosomatic Medicine (fellow), American Medical Writers' Association, Aerospace Medical Association, Ohio Society of Osteopathic Obstetricians and Gynecologists (past president), Ohio Osteopathic Association of Physicians and Surgeons.

WRITINGS: The Feminine Mind and Body, Philosophical Library, 1967. Contributor of articles and reviews to osteopathic and other journals of medicine and health. Editor-in-chief, *Osteopathic Physician,* 1968; member of editorial board, *Geriatrics,* and International Society of Comprehensive Medicine.

WORK IN PROGRESS: The Feminine Existant; My Devil Fear; Sexual Equation. Research in process thought as it affects feminine behavior and function, psychosexual problems relative to rapid management, and psychedelic agents and their relationship to hypnoidal phenomena.

AVOCATIONAL INTERESTS: Aviation (Chapman holds commercial pilot's license with instrument rating); swimming and diving.

*   *   *

CHAPMAN, Roger E(ddington) 1916-

PERSONAL: Born June 3, 1916, in Los Angeles, Calif.; son of Wayland Ayer and Dora (Sutherland) Chapman; married Cornelia Kessler, April 7, 1945; children: George Andrew, Devon, Mark Roger, Jonathan. *Education:* University of California, Los Angeles, A.B., 1937, M.A., 1951, Ph.D., 1954. *Home:* 4000 Cuervo Ave., Santa Barbara, Calif. 93110. *Office:* University of California, Santa Barbara, Calif. 93106.

CAREER: University of California, Los Angeles, lecturer,

1951-54; University of California, Santa Barbara, 1954-71, began as instructor, professor of music, 1967-71, professor emeritus, 1971—. Composer. Chairman of board of directors, Santa Barbara Symphony Association, 1958-61; conductor, Santa Barbara Choral Society, 1966-67. *Military service:* U.S. Army Air Forces, 1941-45; became first lieutenant; received Air Medal and Presidential Unit Citation. *Member:* American Musicological Society, College Music Society. *Awards, honors:* Huntington Hartford Foundation fellowship.

WRITINGS: (Translator) Marin Mersenne, *Harmonie Universelle: The Books on Instruments,* Nijhoff, 1957; *Essentials of Music,* Doubleday, 1967; *Hearing Music,* four volumes, Appleton, 1970. Composer of instrumental music published by C. F. Peters, 1961-62, and choral music published by Harold Flammer. Contributor to *Music Review.*

* * *

CHAPMAN, Stanley D(avid) 1935-

PERSONAL: Born January 31, 1935, in Nottingham, England; son of Horace (a tool-room engineer) and Dulcie (Woodward) Chapman; married Audrey Palmer (a teacher), July, 1960; children: Julian Robert, Timothy David. *Education:* London School of Economics and Political Science, B.Sc. (honors), 1956; University of Nottingham, M.A., 1960; University of London, part-time external student, 1963-65, Ph.D., 1966. *Politics:* "Floating voter." *Religion:* Methodist. *Home:* 35 Park Lane, Sutton, Bonington, Loughborough, Leichestershire, England.

CAREER: Schoolmaster in Nottingham, England, 1957-60, and Wigan, Lancashire, England, 1960-62; Dudley College of Education, Dudley, England, lecturer in history, 1962-66; University of Aston, Birmingham, England, lecturer in economic history, 1966; University of Nottingham, Nottingham, England, Pasold Lecturer in Textile History, 1968-73, reader, 1973—.

WRITINGS: (With C. Aspin) *James Hargreaves and the Spinning Jenny,* Helmshore Historical Society, 1964; *The Early Factory Masters,* David & Charles, 1967; (author of introduction) William Felkin, *History of the Hosiery and Lace Manufacturers,* centenary edition, David & Charles, 1967; (with J. D. Chambers) *The Beginnings of Industrial Britain,* University Tutorial Press, 1968; (editor) *The History of Working Class Housing: A Symposium,* David & Charles, 1971; *The Cotton Industry in the Industrial Revolution,* Macmillan, 1972; *Jesse Boot of Boots the Chemists,* Hodder & Stoughton, 1974. Contributor to journals in Britain and the United States. Co-editor, *Textile History,* 1971—.

WORK IN PROGRESS: European Calico Printers: A Comparative Study of Peel, Schuele and Oberkampf.

* * *

CHAPPLE, J(ohn) A(lfred) V(ictor) 1928-

PERSONAL: Born April 25, 1928, in Barnstaple, Devonshire, England; son of Alfred and Frances Lilian (Taylor) Chapple; married Kathleen Bolton, August 6, 1955; children: Andrew, John, Clare, James, Christopher. *Education:* University College, London, B.A. (honors in English), 1953, M.A., 1955. *Politics:* Liberal. *Home:* 173 Newland Park, Hull, England. *Office:* Department of English, University of Hull, Hull HU6 7RX, England.

CAREER: Yale University, New Haven, Conn., research assistant, 1955-58; University of Aberdeen, Aberdeen, Scotland, assistant lecturer in English, 1958-59; University of Manchester, Manchester, England, 1959-71, began as assistant lecturer, senior lecturer in English, 1967-71; University of Hull, Hull, England, professor of English, 1971—. *Military service:* British Army, Royal Artillery, 1946-49; became lieutenant. *Member:* Manchester Bibliographical Society (secreaty, 1965-71).

WRITINGS: (Editor) *Samuel Johnson's "Proposals for Printing the History of the Council of Trent,"* John Rylands Library (Manchester), 1963; (editor with Arthur Pollard) *The Letters of Mrs. Gaskell,* Manchester University Press, 1966, Harvard University Press, 1967; *Documentary and Imaginative Literature 1880-1920,* Blandford Press, 1970; *Dryden's Earl of Shaftesbury,* University of Hull, 1973. Contributor to *Critical Survey, Essays in Criticism, Yale University Library Gazette,* and other journals.

WORK IN PROGRESS: An edition of Elizabeth Gaskell's *Life of Charlotte Bronte;* editing *Early Letters to Elizabeth Gaskell.*

AVOCATIONAL INTERESTS: Calligraphy, playing piano, growing plants, art.

* * *

CHARLWOOD, D(onald) E(rnest) 1915-

PERSONAL: Born September 6, 1915, in Melbourne, Victoria, Australia; son of Ernest Joseph (a clerk) and Emily F. (Cameron) Charlwood; married Nell East (a teacher and librarian), June 8, 1944; children: Jan, Susan, Doreen, James. *Education:* Attended Frankston High School, 1927-32. *Politics:* "No affiliations—independent views." *Religion:* Church of England. *Home:* Qualicum, Mount View Rd., Templestowe, Victoria 3106, Australia. *Agent:* A. M. Heath & Co. Ltd., 40-42 William IV St., London WC2N 4DD, England.

CAREER: Australian Department of Civil Aviation, Melbourne, employed in Air Traffic Control, 1945-75, in charge of selecting and training controllers throughout Australia, 1953-75. *Military service:* Royal Australian Air Force, 1941-45; trained as navigator in Canada; served in Royal Air Force Bomber Command and Pacific Ferry Group; became flight lieutenant. *Member:* P.E.N., Fellowship of Australian Writers, Society of Australian Authors (regional vice-president).

WRITINGS—All published by Angus & Robertson: *No Moon Tonight* (memoirs), 1956; *All the Green Year* (novel), 1965; *An Afternoon of Time* (story collection), 1967; *Take-Off to Touchdown,* 1967; *The Wreck of the "Lock Ard"* (regional history), 1971. Work represented in several anthologies including *Classic Australian Short Stories,* edited by Judah Waten and Stephen Murray-Smith, Wren Publishing, 1974, and *Festival and Other Stories,* edited by Brian Buckley and Jim Hamilton, Wren Publishing, 1974. Contributor to *Blackwood's Magazine.*

WORK IN PROGRESS: Research into the life of Captain James Nicol Forbes of the Black Ball Line, 1821-72.

* * *

CHEN, Nai-Ruenn 1927-

PERSONAL: Born March 1, 1927, in Foochow, China; married Catherine Tien-pai Yang, July 1, 1961; children: Jerome, Tina. *Education:* National Taiwan University, B.A., 1950; University of Illinois, M.S., 1955, Ph.D., 1960. *Home:* 9615 Byeforde Rd., Kensington, Md. 20795. *Office:*

Bureau of East-West Trade, U.S. Department of Commerce, Washington D.C. 20230.

CAREER: University of Chicago, Chicago, Ill., economist in Laboratories for Applied Science, 1960-62; lecturer in economics at University of California, Berkeley, and research economist, Social Science Research Council Committee on the Economy of China, Berkeley, 1962-66; Cornell University, Ithaca, N.Y., assistant professor, 1966-69, associate professor of economics, 1969-73; U.S. Department of Commerce, Washington D.C., international economist, 1973—.

WRITINGS: The Economy of Mainland China, 1949-1963: A Bibliography of Materials in English, Committee on the Economy of China, Social Science Research Council, 1963; *Chinese Economic Statistics,* Aldine, 1967; (with Walter Galenson) *The Chinese Economy Under Communism,* Aldine, 1969; (contributor) John P. Hardt, editor, *China: A Reassessment of the Economy,* Government Printing Office, 1975.

WORK IN PROGRESS: China's international balance of payments.

* * *

CHERMAYEFF, Serge 1900-

PERSONAL: Surname is pronounced Sher-*may*-eff; born October 8, 1900, in Caucasia; came to United States in 1940, naturalized in 1946; son of Ivan and Rosalie (Sunshin) Chermayeff; married Barbara Maitland May, March 28, 1928; children: Ivan, Peter. *Education:* Educated in London, England, 1910-14, and at Harrow School, England, 1914-18. *Politics:* Liberal. *Religion:* Agnostic. *Residence:* Wellfleet, Mass.

CAREER: Architect in England, 1928-40; Brooklyn College (now Brooklyn College of the City University of New York), Brooklyn, N.Y., professor and chairman of department of designs, 1942-46; Institute of Design, Chicago, Ill., president, 1947-51; Harvard University, Cambridge, Mass., professor of architecture, 1953-62; Yale University, New Haven, Conn., professor of architecture, 1962-69, professor emeritus, 1969—. Abstract painter, with work exhibited at Metropolitan Museum of Art, Art Institute of Chicago, and other museums; lecturer and writer. Sometime consultant to National Resources Planning Board; consultant on architectural and art education to universities. *Member:* Royal Institute of Architects (England; fellow), Royal Society of Arts (England; fellow), Association of Architects of Columbia (South America; honorary fellow). *Awards, honors:* D.A., MacMurray College and Washington University; Royal Canadian Institute of Architects gold medal award, 1973.

WRITINGS: (With Christopher Alexander) *Community and Privacy,* Doubleday, 1962 (with Alexander Tzonis) *Shape of Community,* Penguin, 1971. Contributor of critical and other essays to the architectural and art press in America and abroad.

* * *

CHERRY, C. Conrad 1937-

PERSONAL: Born March 31, 1937, in Kerens, Tex.; son of Charles C. and Laura (Owens) Cherry; married Mary Ella Bigony, August 22, 1959; children: Kevin, Diane. *Education:* McMurry College, B.A., 1958; Drew University, B.D., 1961, Ph.D., 1965. *Home:* 630 Wayland Pl, State College, Pa. 16801. *Office:* Pennsylvania State University, University Park, Pa. 16802.

CAREER: Pennsylvania State University, University Park, 1964—, began as assistant professor, now professor of religious studies. *Member:* American Society of Church History, American Academy of Religion, Society for Religion in Higher Education. *Awards, honors: American Quarterly* Award, 1969; Society for Religion in Higher Education, post-doctoral fellow, 1970-71.

WRITINGS: The Theology of Jonathan Edwards: A Reappraisal, Anchor Books, 1966; (editor with John Fenton) *Religion in the Public Domain,* Pennsylvania State University Center for Continuing Liberal Education, 1966; *God's New Israel,* Prentice-Hall, 1971.

WORK IN PROGRESS: A book on "nature and imagination in American theology."

SIDELIGHTS: C. Conrad Cherry reads German, French, and Greek.

* * *

CHESNUT, J(ames) Stanley 1926-

PERSONAL: Born Decmeber 22, 1926, in Bokchito, Okla.; son of Atwood Wesley and Lillian (Phipps) Chesnut; married Rowena Haymond, August 15, 1948 (died, 1954); married Vlasta J. Marek, January 28, 1956; children: James Stephen, David Jon, Daniel Atwood, Teresa Leigh. *Education:* University of Tulsa, B.A., 1948; McCormick Theological Seminary, B.D., 1951; Yale University, M.A., 1957, Ph.D., 1959. *Politics:* Democrat. *Home:* 6335 30th St. S., St. Petersburg, Fla. 33712. *Office address:* Eckerd College, P.O. Box 12560, St. Petersburg, Fla. 33733.

CAREER: Clergyman of United Presbyterian Church of the U.S.A. Trinity University, San Antonio, Tex., instructor in religion, 1951-52; pastor in Milford, Conn., 1953-56; University of Tulsa, Tulsa, Okla., assistant professor of religion, 1956-63; Eckerd College, St. Petersburg, associate professor, 1963-68, professor of religion, 1968—, director of continuing education, 1967—, chairman of humanities division, 1970-73, interim provost, 1975. Staff member of Drew-McCormick Archaeological Expedition to Schechem, Jordan, summers, 1960, 1962. Hoxie Thompson Lecturer, Austin Presbyterian Theological Seminary, 1962. *Member:* American Academy of Religion, Society of Biblical Literature, American Schools of Oriental Research, American Association of University Professors. *Awards, honors:* University of Tulsa research grants, 1960 and 1962; Ford Foundation faculty fellowship, 1964; Danforth Foundation grant, 1966-67.

WRITINGS: The Old Testament Understanding of God, Westminster, 1968. Contributor to theological journals.

WORK IN PROGRESS: A Western View of Eastern Religions; Sayings: Religious Thoughts from Around the World.

* * *

CHESTER, Edward W(illiam) 1935-

PERSONAL: Born November 9, 1935, in Richmond, Va.; son of Edward W. (a fire insurance agent) and Elizabeth (Lewis) Chester. *Education:* Morris Harvey College, A.B. (summa cum laude), 1956; University of Pittsburgh, M.A., 1958, Ph.D., 1961. *Politics:* Independent. *Religion:* Protestant. *Home:* 3915 Staunton Ave., Charleston, W.Va. 25304.

CAREER: Lambuth College, Jackson, Tenn., assistant professor of history, 1961-62; University of Kentucky, Lexington, instructor in history, 1962-64; Inter-American University of Puerto Rico, San German, assistant professor of history, 1964-65; University of Texas at Arlington, assistant professor, 1965-68, associate professor of history, 1968—. *Member:* American Historical Association, Organization of American Historians, Southern Historical Association, American Association for State and Local History, American Association of University Professors.

WRITINGS: Europe Views America, Public Affairs, 1961; *Issues and Responses in State Political Experience,* Littlefield, 1968; *Radio, Television and American Politics,* Sheed, 1969; *Clash of Titans: Africa and U.S. Foreign Policy,* Orbis, 1974; *Sectionalism, Politics, and American Diplomacy,* Scarecrow, 1975. Contributor to journals.

WORK IN PROGRESS: Studies of political platforms; World War II Atlantic military bases; diplomacy of oil.

AVOCATIONAL INTERESTS: Listening to records.

*　　*　　*

CHEYNEY, Arnold B. 1926-

PERSONAL: Born February 23, 1926, in Massillon, Ohio; son of Ray A. and Viola May (Zurcher) Cheyney; married Jeanne Smith, September 3, 1948; children: Steven, Timothy. *Education:* Kent State University, B.S., 1944, M.Ed., 1951; Ohio State University, Ph.D., 1964. *Religion:* Baptist. *Home:* 5861 Southwest 51st Ter., Miami, Fla. 33155. *Office:* School of Education, University of Miami, Coral Gables, Fla. 33124.

CAREER: Elementary teacher in public schools of Suffield, Ohio, 1949-50, Canton, Ohio, 1950-55; elementary principal in Canton, 1955-58, supervisor of elementary education, 1958-61; Ohio State University, Columbus, instructor in education, 1961-64; University of Miami, Coral Gables, Fla., 1964—, began as associate professor, now professor of elementary education. *Military service:* U.S. Marine Corps, 1944-46; served in South Pacific, Okinawa, and China; received Purple Heart. *Member:* International Reading Association, Association for Childhood Education International, National Council of Teachers of English, National Education Association (life), National Committee on the Education of Migrant Children. *Awards, honors:* American Library Association Outstanding Academic Book award, 1973, for *The Ripe Harvest.*

WRITINGS: Teaching Culturally Disadvantaged in the Elementary School, C. E. Merrill, 1967; *Teaching Reading Skills Through the Newspaper,* International Reading Association, 1971; (editor) *The Ripe Harvest: Educating Migrant Children,* University of Miami Press, 1972; *Puppet Enrichment Program,* Ideal School Supply Company, 1973; *Curriculum for Grades Two and Three,* Baptist Publications, 1973. Contributor of about 150 articles and short stories to educational, denominational, children's periodicals, and newspapers.

WORK IN PROGRESS: Teaching Multicultured Children in the Classroom, for C. E. Merrill.

*　　*　　*

CHICK, Edson M(arland) 1924-

PERSONAL: Born May 29, 1924, in Boston, Mass.; son of Louis S. (a business executive) and Carolyn (Rowse) Chick; married Barbara Waldo, June 13, 1953; children: Edson, Peter, Susan, Amy. *Education:* Brown University, A.B., 1944; Princeton University, Ph.D., 1953. *Politics:* Democrat. *Religion:* Protestant. *Home:* 9 Gale Rd., Wil-

liamstown, Mass. 01267. *Office:* Department of German, Williams College, Williamstown, Mass. 01267.

CAREER: Wesleyan University, Middletown, Conn., assistant professor of German, 1952-57; University of California, Riverside, assistant professor of German, 1957-60; Harpur College (now State University of New York at Binghamton), associate professor of German, 1961-64; Dartmouth College, Hanover, N.H., associate professor of German, 1964-72; Williams College, Williamstown, Mass., member of faculty, department of German, 1972—. *Military service:* U.S. Naval Reserve, active duty, 1943-46; became lieutenant junior grade. *Member:* Modern Language Association of America, American Association of Teachers of German, Modern Humanities Research Association. *Awards, honors:* Fullbright research grant for work in Germany, 1960-61.

WRITINGS: Ernst Barlach, Twayne, 1967. Contributor of articles on Ernst Barlach, Ernst Wiechert, Droste-Huelshoff, and Sternheim to journals.

WORK IN PROGRESS: A monograph on modern German dramatic satire.

*　　*　　*

CHILCOTE, Ronald H. 1935-

PERSONAL: Born February 20, 1935, in Cleveland, Ohio; son of Lee A. (a businessman) and Katherine (Hodell) Chilcote; married Frances Tubby, January 6, 1961; children: Stephen, Edward. *Education:* Dartmouth College, B.A., 1957; Stanford University, M.B.A., 1959, M.A., 1963, Ph.D., 1965; University of Lisbon, Diploma Superior, 1960; University of Madrid, Diploma Estudios Hispanicos, 1961. *Home:* 1940 San Remo Dr., Laguna Beach, Calif. 92651. *Office:* Department of Political Science, University of California, Riverside, Calif. 92502.

CAREER: Stanford University, Stanford, Calif., assistant director to Institute of Hispanic American and Luso-Brazilian Studies, 1961-63; University of California, Riverside, 1963—, began as assistant professor, now professor of political science, coordinator of Latin American research program, 1964-70. *Member:* Latin American Studies Association, African Studies Association, American Political Science Association. *Award, honors:* University of California faculty fellowship, 1965; Haynes Foundation fellowship, 1966; Organization of American States grant, 1971; Social Science Research Council grants, 1971 and 1974-75.

WRITINGS: The Press in Spain, Portugal, and Latin America: A Summary of Recent Developments, Institute Of Hispanic American and Luso-Brazilian Studies, Stanford University, 1963; *Portuguese Africa,* Prentice-Hall, 1967; *Spain's Iron and Steel Industry* (monograph), Bureau of Business Research, University of Texas, 1968; *Emerging Nationalism in Portuguese Africa: A Bibliography of Documentary Ephemera Through 1965,* Hoover Institution on War, Revolution, and Peace, 1969; *Revolution and Structural Change in Latin America: A Bibliography on Ideology, Development, and the Radical Left (1930-1965),* two volumes, Hoover Institution on War, Revolution, and Peace, 1970; (compiler) *Protest and Resistance in Angola and Brazil,* University of California Press, 1972; (compiler) *Emerging Nationalism in Portuguese Africa* (documents), Hoover Institution on War, Revolution, and Peace, 1972; *The Brazilian Communist Party: Conflict and Integration, 1922-1972,* Oxford University Press, 1974; (editor with Joel C. Edelstein) *Latin America: The Struggle with Dependency and Beyond,* Schenkman, 1974.

Contributor to encyclopedias and yearbooks; contributor of about sixty articles and reviews to journals and newspapers, including *Nation, New Republic, Contemporary Review, Cuadernos* (Paris), *Africa Studies Bulletin, Journal of Modern African Studies, Africana Journal, Africa Today, Latin American Perspectives, International Journal of Comparative Sociology,* and *Los Angeles Times.* Assistant editor, *Hispanic American Report,* 1961-63, and volume on "The Americas," *Worldmark Encyclopedia of Nations,* 1963; managing editor, *Latin American Perspectives,* 1974—.

WORK IN PROGRESS: Ruling Classes and Dependency in Two Communities of Backlands Brazil.

* * *

CHILDS, Barney 1926-

PERSONAL: Born February 13, 1926, in Spokane, Wash.; son of Robert Barney (an electrical engineer) and Alice (Sanford) Childs; married Charlotte Brown, April 16, 1949 (divorced); married Mary Hinson, December 24, 1961 (divorced); children: Dirje Andrea, Margaret Alice. *Education:* Deep Springs College, student, 1943-45; University of Nevada, B.A., 1949; Oxford University, B.A., 1951, M.A., 1955; Stanford University, Ph.D., 1959. *Politics:* "Determinedly a-political." *Religion:* "None." *Home:* 864 Hartzell, Redlands, Calif. 92373.

CAREER: Composer. Tucson New Art Wind Ensemble, Tucson, Ariz., director, 1962-65; Deep Springs College, Deep Springs, Nev., dean, 1964-69; Wisconsin College Conservatory, Milwaukee, composer in residence, 1969-71; University of Redlands, Redlands, Calif., professor of composition, 1971—. *Military service:* U.S. Army, 1945-46. *Member:* American Composers Alliance, American Music Center (New York), American Music Society, American Society of University Composers (member of executive committee, 1971-74, of national council, 194—). *Awards, honors:* Rhodes scholar at Oxford University; MacDowell Colony fellowships, 1963, 1968, 1970, and 1974.

WRITINGS: (Editor with Elliott Schwartz) *Contemporary Composers on Contemporary Music,* Holt, 1967. Composer of music published by BMI Canada, Tritone Press, McGinnis & Marx, Theodore Presser, Ensemble Publications, Composer/Performer Editions, and others. Contributor of articles to *Bandwagon, Source, The Composer, Perspectives of New Music,* and other journals.

SIDELIGHTS: Barney Childs has recorded for CRI, Advance, Gregorian, and Ars Nova labels. *Avocational interests:* Hiking.

* * *

CHRIST, Carl F(inley) 1923-

PERSONAL: Born September 19, 1923, in Chicago, Ill.; son of Jay Finley (a professor) and Maud (Trego) Christ; married Phyllis Tatsch, March 16, 1951; children: Alice, John, Lucy. *Education:* Colorado College, student, 1940-42; University of Chicago, B.S., 1943, Ph.D., 1950. *Office:* Johns Hopkins University, Baltimore, Md. 21218.

CAREER: Manhattan Project, junior physicist, 1943-45; Princeton University, Princeton, N.J., instructor in physics, 1945-46; Cowles Commission for Research in Economics, research associate, 1949-50; Johns Hopkins University, Baltimore, Md., assistant professor, 1950-53, associate professor of political economy, 1953-55; University of Chicago, Chicago, Ill., associate professor of economics, 1955-

61; Johns Hopkins University, professor of political economy, 1961—, chairman of department, 1961-66, 1969-70. Senior Fulbright research scholar, University of Cambridge, 1954-55; fellow, Center for Advanced Study in the Behavioral Sciences, 1960-61; chairman of committee for economic research, Universities-National Bureau, 1967-74. Visiting professor of economics, University of Tokyo, 1959; Keynes Visiting Professor of Economics, University of Essex, 1966-67. Member of the Maryland Governor's Council of Economic Advisers, 1969—.

MEMBER: American Economic Association, Econometric Society (fellow), Royal Economic Society, American Statistical Association (fellow), American Finance Association, Phi Beta Kappa. *Awards, honors:* Social Science Research Council fellow, 1948-50.

WRITINGS: Econometric Models and Methods, Wiley, 1966; (contributor) *International Encyclopedia of the Social Sciences,* Volume IV, Macmillan, 1968. Contributor of papers and articles to professional publications in his field. Member of board of editors, *American Economic Review,* 1969-73.

WORK IN PROGRESS: Research in monetary and fiscal policy in relation to inflation and unemployment.

* * *

CHRISTIAN, C(urtis) W(allace) 1927-

PERSONAL: Born February 11, 1927, in Dallas, Tex.; son of J. B. (a choral director and musician) and Ella (Vause) Christian; married Betty Purvis (a secretary), August 9, 1952; children: Anne, Robert, Sue, David. *Education:* Baylor University, B.A., 1948, M.A., 1957; Southwestern Baptist Theological Seminary, B.D., 1951; Vanderbilt University, Ph.D., 1964. *Politics:* "More or less Democrat." *Home:* 717 Bellaire, Waco, Tex. 76710. *Office:* Baylor University, Waco, Tex. 76703.

CAREER: Baptist clergyman; Baylor University, Waco, Tex., instructor, 1954-58, assistant professor, 1958-63, associate professor, 1964-75, professor of religion, 1975—. Has held several church-related positions, including pastor. *Member:* American Academy of Religion, Association of Baptist Teachers of Religion.

WRITINGS: (With Glenn R. Wittig) *Radical Theology: Phase II,* Lippincott, 1967; *Shaping Your Faith: A Guide to a Personal Theology,* Word Books, 1973.

WORK IN PROGRESS: Research and writing on radical theology and process theology; work on Paul Tillich; an introduction to the theology of Friederich Schleiermacher.

* * *

CHRISTIANSON, John Robert 1934-

PERSONAL: Born January 21, 1934, in Mankato, Minn.; son of K. O. (in business) and Marian Christine (Peterson) Christianson; married Birgitte Povelsen, June 20, 1964; children: Erik Kenneth Gyde, Paul Frederik Gyde. *Education:* Mankato State College, B.A. (honors), 1956; University of Copenhagen, graduate study, 1956-57, 1962-63; University of Minnesota, M.A., 1959, Ph.D., 1964. *Religion:* Lutheran. *Home:* 110 Pleasant Hill, Decorah, Iowa 52101. *Office:* Luther College, Decorah, Iowa 52101.

CAREER: University of South Dakota, Vermillion, assistant professor of history, 1964-66; University of Minnesota, Minneapolis, visiting assistant professor, 1966-67; Luther College, Decorah, Iowa, associate professor, 1967-72, professor of history, 1972—, chairman of department, 1967—. Assistant director, Norwegian-American Museum, 1969—. *Military service:* U.S. Army, 1958-60. *Member:* American Historical Association, Den Danske Historiske Forening, Society for the Advancement of Scandinavian Study, American-Scandinavian Foundation, Norwegian-American Historical Association (executive committee member, 1972—).

WRITINGS: (Contributor) Louise B. Young, editor, *Exploring the Universe,* McGraw, 1963; (contributor) J. D. Holmquist and A. H. Wheeler, editors, *Diving Into the Past,* Minnesota Historical Society, 1964; (with E. S. Ress, G. Liebow, I.I. Olicker) *Man Builds Tomorrow,* Creative Educational Society, 1966. Contributor to *American Scandinavian Review, Scientific American, Centaurus, Isis, Sixteenth Century Journal,* and other journals.

WORK IN PROGRESS: A biography of Tycho Brahe, sixteenth-century astronomer.

* * *

CHURCHILL, Linda R. 1938-

PERSONAL: Born September 26, 1938, in Evanston, Ill.; daughter of Orville Vinton (a realtor) and Ruth Jane (Markham) Ruler; married E. Richard Churchill (a teacher), August 18, 1961; children: Eric Richard and Robert Sean. *Education:* Attended Colorado State University, 1956-58; Colorado State College (now University of Northern Colorado), A.B., 1961, M.A., 1962. *Religion:* Episcopalian. *Home address:* Route 1, Box 329B, Kersey, Colo. 80644.

CAREER: Greeley (Colo.) Public Library, assistant, 1958-61; Greeley (Colo.) public schools, history teacher, 1961—.

*WRITINGS—*With husband, E. Richard Churchill: (And with Edward H. Blair) *Fun with American History,* Abingdon, 1966; (and with Blair, and Kay Reynolds) *Fun with American Literature,* Abingdon, 1968; *Puzzle It Out,* Scholastic Book Services, 1971. *Short Lessons in World History,* J. Weston Walch, 1971; *How Our Nation Became Great,* J. Weston Walch, 1971; *Community Civics Case Book,* J. Weston Walch, 1973; *Enriched Social Studies Teaching,* Fearon, 1973; *Puzzles and Quizzes,* Scholastic Book Services, 1973; *American History Activity Reader,* J. Weston Walch, 1974; *World History Activity Reader,* J. Weston Walch, 1975; *Casebook on Marriage and the Family,* J. Weston Walch, 1975.

* * *

CHURCHMAN, C(harles) West 1913-

PERSONAL: Born August 29, 1913, in Philadelphia, Pa.; son of Clarke Wharton and Norah (Fassitt) Churchman; married Gloria King, September 27, 1950; children: Daniel. *Education:* University of Pennsylvania, A.B., 1935, M.A., 1936, Ph.D., 1938. *Home:* 657 Lovell Ave., Mill Valley, Calif. 94941.

CAREER: University of Pennsylvania, Philadelphia, instructor in philosophy, 1937-42; U.S. Ordnance Laboratory, Frankfort Arsenal, head of mathematics section, 1942-45; University of Pennsylvania, assistant professor of philosophy and head of department, 1945-48; Wayne State University, Detroit, Mich., associate professor of philosophy, 1948-51; Case Institute of Technology (now Case Western Reserve University), Cleveland, Ohio, professor of engineering administration, 1951-58; University of California, Berkeley, visiting professor, 1957-58, professor of

business administration, 1958—. Co-founder, Institute for Experimental Method, Philadelphia, Pa., 1945-48; director of research, System Development Corp., 1962-63. *Member:* American Association for the Advancement of Science (fellow), Philosophy of Science Association (member of board), American Philosophical Association, Institute of Management Sciences (president, 1962), American Statistical Association (fellow). *Awards, honors:* Dr. Sci., Washington University, 1974.

WRITINGS: Elements of Logic and Formal Science, Lippincott, 1940; (editor with R. L. Ackoff and M. Wax) *Measurement of Consumer Interest,* University of Pennsylvania Press, 1947; *Theory of Experimental Inference,* Macmillan, 1948; (with Ackoff) *Methods of Inquiry: An Introduction to Philosophy and Scientific Theory,* Educational Publishers, 1950; (with Ackoff and E. L. Arnoff) *Introduction to Operations Research,* Wiley, 1957; (editor with P. Ratoosh) *Measurement: Definitions and Theories,* Wiley, 1959; *Prediction and Optimal Decision,* Prentice-Hall, 1961; *Challenge to Reason,* McGraw, 1968; *The Systems Approach,* Delacorte, 1968; *Design of Inquiring Systems,* Basic Books, 1972; (with L. Auerbach and S. Sadan) *Thinking for Decisions,* Scientific Research Associates, 1975. Contributor to *Management Science, Operations Research.* Editor, *Philosophy of Science,* 1948-57, *Management Science,* 1954-60.

WORK IN PROGRESS: The Systems Approach and Its Enemies, an evaluation of large scale systems thinking.

* * *

CIPES, Robert M. 1930-

PERSONAL: Surname rhymes with "types"; born February 9, 1930, in Mount Vernon, N.Y.; son of Bernard J. (a dental surgeon) and Ida (Solow) Cipes; married Amy Rabkin, September 5, 1954; children: Peter, Judith, Eric. *Education:* Harvard University, A.B., 1950; Yale University, LL.B., 1957. *Religion:* Jewish.

CAREER: Family Weekly (magazine), New York City, associate editor, 1953-54; New York Court of Appeals, Albany, confidential law assistant, 1957-59; Rabkin & Johnson, Esqs., New York City, attorney, 1959-62; U.S. Department of Justice, attorney and sometime special assistant U.S. Attorney, New York City, and Washington, D.C., 1962-64; Georgetown University, Institute of Criminal Law and Procedure, Washington, D.C., senior research attorney, 1966-67; University of California, Santa Barbara, lecturer in sociology, beginning 1968.

WRITINGS: Rules of Criminial Procedure, Matthew Bender, 1965; *The Crime War,* New American Library, 1968; (editor) *Criminal Defense Techniques,* Matthew Bender, 1969. Contributor to *Playboy, Look, Atlantic Monthly,* and *New Republic.†*

* * *

CLAFFEY, William J. 1925-

PERSONAL: Born March 1, 1925, in Boston, Mass.; son of William J. and Grace (Hanson) Claffey; married Nancy R. Brown, January 4, 1952; married Patricia R. Hutchings, May 6, 1972; children: (first marriage) Leslie Anne, Brent Steven, Scott Wentworth, Devin Merrill. *Education:* Boston University, B.S., 1950, graduate study, 1951; California State College (now University), Long Beach, graduate study, 1957, 1958; University of Southern California, M.S. in Ed., 1964. *Home:* 2157 Loma Alta Dr., Fullerton,

Calif. 92633. *Agent:* John Crain, 464 Maylin St., Pasadena, Calif.

CAREER: Reno Business College, Reno, Nev., teacher, 1951-52; Occidental Life Insurance Co., manager in Los Angeles, Calif., 1952-56; employed by General Dynamics (Convair), Pomona, Calif., 1957; Buena Park High School, Buena Park, Calif., teacher, 1957-61; employed by Hughes Aircraft Ground Systems, Fullerton, Calif., 1961-62; Fullerton Junior College, Fullerton, Calif., data processing coordinator, beginning in 1962; currently chairman of Business Division, Cypress Junior College, Cypress, Calif. *Military service:* U.S. Navy, aviation radioman, 1942-46. *Member:* Society for Automation in Business Education, California Teachers Association, California Business Education Association, California Junior College Faculty Association.

WRITINGS: Principles of Data Processing, Dickenson, 1967; *Principles of Programming the IBM 1620 Computer,* Dickenson, 1968; *Keypunch Operation,* Dickenson, 1969, alternate edition, 1972; *Flowcharting, Logic, Programming in BASIC,* Wiley, 1976. Contributor to California Bureau of Business Education handbook on data processing, 1963.

* * *

CLARENS, Carlos (Figueredo y) 1936-

PERSONAL: Born July 7, 1936, in Havana, Cuba; son of Pedro (a financier) and Maria (Clarens) Figueredo. *Education:* Studied at Sorbonne, University of Paris, and Institut d'Urbanisme, Paris, 1955-57; University of Havana, Master of Arts and Architecture, 1958. *Residence:* Paris, France. *Agent:* Maxine Groffsky, 104 Greenwich Ave., New York, N.Y. 10011.

CAREER: Clarens told *CA:* "Began writing film criticism around 1954, for Latin American periodicals. Worked as designer, barman, film researcher, film editor, finally in production. Lived in France for many years."

WRITINGS: An Illustrated History of the Horror Film, Putnam, 1967; (with John Kobal) *Spectacular!,* Derbibooks, 1974; *George Cukar,* Secker & Warburg, in press.

* * *

CLARIDGE, Gordon S. 1932-

PERSONAL: Born January 23, 1932, in Walsall, Staffordshire, England; son of Albert Sidney and Bertha (Bayliss) Claridge. *Education:* University College, London, B.A. (honors), 1953; Institute of Psychiatry, London, England, Ph.D., 1956. *Home:* 30 Davenant Rd., Oxford, England OX2 8B7. *Office:* Department of Experimental Psychology, Oxford University, South Parks Rd., Oxford, England.

CAREER: Leavesden Hospital, Watford, England, clinical psychologist, 1956-57; Institute of Psychiatry, London, England, research psychologist, 1957-61; University of Bristol, Bristol, England, lecturer in psychology, 1961-64; Barrow Hospital, Bristol, clinical psychologist, 1961-64; University of Glasgow, Glasgow, Scotland, lecturer, 1964-67, senior lecturer, 1967-72, reader in psychology, 1972-74; Oxford University, Oxford, England, lecturer in abnormal psychology, 1975—, fellow of Magdalen College. *Member:* British Psychological Society, American Psychological Association, Royal Medico-Psychological Association. *Awards, honors:* D.Sc., University of Glasgow, 1971.

WRITINGS: (Contributor) H. J. Eysenck, editor, *Experiments in Personality,* Routledge & Kegan Paul, 1960; (contributor) Eysenck, editor, *Experiments with Drugs,* Pergamon, 1963; *Personality and Arousal,* Pergamon, 1967; *Drugs and Human Behavior,* Penguin, 1970, new edition, 1972; (with W. I. Hume, and Sandra Canter) *Personality Differences and Biological Variations: A Study of Twins,* Pergamon, 1973. Regular contributor to scientific journals, with more than twenty papers published on drugs, personality, and the psychophysiology of mental illness.

WORK IN PROGRESS: Psychosomatics, for Penguin; research on psychophysiology of personality, especially schizophrenia.

* * *

CLARK, Donald E. 1933-

PERSONAL: Born April 25, 1933, in Silverton, Ore.; son of Harold Edward and Vera (Lang) Clark; married Barbara June Bollen (a dental hygienist), September 27, 1952; married second wife, Shirley Paulus, May 5, 1971; children: (first marriage) Donald E. II, Donna Kim. *Education:* Vanport College, student, 1951-53; San Francisco State College (now San Francisco State University), A.B., 1956; Portland State College (now University), graduate courses, 1958-60, master's program, beginning 1966. *Politics:* Democrat. *Home:* 4327 Southwest Tunnelwood Dr., Portland, Ore. 97221. *Office:* Law Enforcement Programs, Urban Studies Center, Portland State University, P.O. Box 751, Portland, Ore. 97207.

CAREER: Elementary teacher in Portland, Ore., 1959-62; Multnomah County (Ore.) Sheriff's Office, deputy, 1956-62, sheriff (elected), 1963-66; Portland State University, Portland, Ore., assistant professor of law enforcement and associate director of Law Enforcement Programs, 1967—. County commissioner, Multnomah County, 1969—. Police Design Associates, director and consultant; special consultant to Public Administration Service, Chicago, Ill., and National Council on Crime and Delinquency, New York, N.Y.; member of Oregon Criminal Law Revision Commission. Member of board of directors, Boys' Club of Portland, Boys and Girls Aid Society, and local chapters of National Association for the Advancement of Colored People, Urban League.

MEMBER: American Correctional Association, International Association of Chiefs of Police, International Association of Police Professors, National Sheriffs' Association (life member), American Society of Criminology, American Association of University Professors, Navy League (member of board of directors), Oregon Historical Society, City Club (Portland).

WRITINGS: (With Samuel G. Chapmen) *A Forward Step:* Educational journals.†

* * *

CLARK, Frederick Stephen 1908-
(Clive Dalton)

PERSONAL: Born May 21, 1908, in Gravesend, Kent, England; son of Frederick George (an army officer) and Mabel (Dalton) Clark; married Agnes Staples, September 25, 1937; children: Anne (Mrs. John Sheppard), Richard. *Education:* Attended army-operated schools in various parts of the world. *Religion:* Church of England. *Home:* Green Bushes, Harewood Rd., Canstock, Cornwall, England. *Agent:* Winant, Towers Ltd., 14 Clifford's Inn, London, E.C.4A, England.

CAREER: Malay Mail, correspondent in London, England, 1936-39; *British Malaya,* London, sub-editor, 1936-39; writer. *Military service:* Royal Artillery, 1939-45; became sergeant.

WRITINGS—All under pseudonym Clive Dalton; all published by Brockhampton Press, except where noted: *Malay Canoe,* Coward, 1960; *Malay Boy,* 1961; *Malay Island,* 1962; *Malay Cruise,* 1964; *Malay Schooner,* 1965, Chilton, 1966; (contributor) *The Decorative Arts of the Mariner,* Cassell, 1966; *Malay Treasures,* 1967; *Malay Pirate,* 1972.

SIDELIGHTS: Frederick Clark stated, "All my writing stems from a childhood spent in the Malay islands, in close association with Malay children." His books have been translated into German and Polish; *Malay Cruise* has been issued as a school reader in Australia. *Avocational interests:* Swimming, boating, music.†

*   *   *

CLARK, James M(ilford) 1930-

PERSONAL: Born April 11, 1930, in Wayne, Mich.; son of Roy Wesley (a farmer) and Florence (Grice) Clark; married Patricia Ann Haynes, March 11, 1960; children: Pamela Flannery, Matthew Scott, Timothy James. *Education:* University of Michigan, B.A., 1952, Ph.D., 1962; University of the Philippines, M.A., 1955. *Home:* 15 Mayo St., Orono, Me. 04473. *Office:* Alumni Hall, University of Maine, Orono, Me. 04473.

CAREER: University of Maine, Orono, assistant professor, 1960-64, associate professor of political science, 1964—, assistant to the president, 1966-68, vice-president for academic affairs, 1968—. Fulbright professor, Institut d'Etudes Politiques, University of Toulouse, 1965-66. *Military service:* U.S. Army, 1952-55. *Member:* American Political Science Association, American Association of University Professors, Phi Beta Kappa, Phi Kappa Phi, Phi Eta Signa, Pi Sigma Alpha.

WRITINGS: Teachers and Politics in France, Syracuse University Press, 1967.

*   *   *

CLARK, Jere Walton 1922-

PERSONAL: Born January 31, 1922, in Rex, Ga.; son of Grover Cleveland and Jessie (Butler) Clark; married Juanita Stone, June 13, 1947; children: Merrilyn, Melissa. *Education:* Attended Berry College; University of Georgia, B.B.A., 1947, M.A., 1949; University of Virginia, Ph.D., 1953. *Politics:* Independent. *Religion:* Methodist. *Home:* 179 Bradford Dr., Cheshire, Conn. 06410. *Office:* Department of Economics, Southern Connecticut State College, 501 Crescent St., New Haven, Conn. 06515.

CAREER: West Virginia University, Morgantown, assistant professor of economics, 1952-55; University of Chattanooga, Chattanooga, Tenn., assistant professor, 1955-57, associate professor of economics, 1957-62; Southern Connecticut State College, New Haven, professor of economics, chairman of department, and director of Center for Interdisciplinary Creativity, 1962—. Coordinator and moderator of fifty-program series on nursing education for radio and television, 1959-60; faculty member of twelve annual creative problem-solving institutes at State University of New York at Buffalo; chairman and director of annual national workshop on systems education, New Haven, 1967-70. Member of board, Wesley Foundation, New Haven, 1966—. *Military service:* U.S. Army, Infantry, 1943-45; served in Europe.

MEMBER: American Economic Association, Society for General Systems Research (national chairman of Task Force on General Systems Education, 1967—), Electronic Industries Association, International Cooperation Council (member of advisory council, 1974—). *Awards, honors:* Southern Fellowship Foundation grant, 1958; Volker Fund fellowship, 1959; Ford Foundation fellowship, 1961; first place in national awards program of Kazanjian Economics Foundation for best college course in economics, 1962-63; U.S. Office of Education grant, 1974-75.

WRITINGS—Editor and contributor: *Economic Education Experiences of Enterprising Teachers,* three volumes, Joint Council on Economic Education, 1963, 1965, 1966; *Systems Education Patterns on the Drawing Boards of the Future,* Kazanjian Economics Foundation, 1969; *Practical Action Programs in Education,* Kazanjian Economics Foundation, 1969; *Launching Operation Man to Mankind,* Kazanjian Economics Foundation, 1971.

Contributor: Milton Rubin, editor, *Man in Systems,* Gordon & Breach, 1971; Ervin Laszlo, editor, *The Relevance of General Systems Theory,* Gordon & Breach, 1972; Laszlo, editor, *Introduction to Systems Philosophy,* Gordon & Breach, 1972; Edward Haskell, editor, *Full Circle: The Moral Force of Unified Diversity,* Gordon & Breach, 1973; D. Smith and D. Washburn, editors, *Unity in Diversity,* Gordon & Breach, 1973. Also contributor to *Death and Creativity,* edited by F. Hetzler, 1976.

Author of two booklets, *Synergistic Tools for Designing Global Democracy,* and *The Market Structure of West Virginia Industry.* Contributor to education, economic, scientific, and psychic journals. Consulting editor, *Journal of Creative Behavior,* 1968—; associate editor, *General Systems Bulletin,* 1969-72; systems creativity editor, *International Associations* (Brussels), 1970.

WORK IN PROGRESS: Writing on the quest for economic democracy and on the general systems approach to synthesizing knowledge.

*   *   *

CLARK, Miles (Morton) 1920-

PERSONAL: Born May 9, 1920, in St. Paul, Minn.; son of Glenn (a professor of English and author) and Louise (Miles) Clark; married Virginia Sanford, April 2, 1949; children: Louise Sieglinde, Miles Robert, Kristen Elizabeth, Edgar Lewis. *Education:* Macalester College, A.B., 1943; George Washington University, M.A., 1962. *Politics:* Democrat. *Religion:* Episcopalian. *Home:* 1686 Homewood Dr., Altadena, Calif.

CAREER: Macalester Park Publishing Co., St. Paul, Minn., co-editor, 1947-50; *Rural Electrification* (magazine), Washington, D.C., associate editor, 1950-53; *Coachella Valley Sun* (weekly), Coachella, Calif., editor, 1953-54; *Northridger,* Northridge, Calif., editor-publisher, 1954-59; *Pasadena Independent Star News,* Pasadena, Calif., business editor, 1959-62; KABC-TV, Los Angeles, Calif., editorial director, 1962-63; *Los Angeles Daily Journal* (legal newspaper), Los Angeles, editor, 1963-68; Parker & Sons Publications, Los Angeles, editorial director, 1968—. Lecturer at University of Southern California, California State University, and Ambassador College. *Military service:* U.S. Army Air Forces, 1943-46; radar officer in India and China; became captain in Reserve; received Presidential Unit Citation. *Awards, honors:* California Newspaper Publishers Association Award for financial writing, 1961; California Bar Association Press Award, 1966.

WRITINGS: The Original Desert Almanac, Northridge Press, 1958; Glenn Clark: The Man Who Tapped the Secret of Creative Power, Macalester College Press, 1962; Every Day I Have a Journey, Harper, 1967; Glenn Clark: His Life and Writings, Abingdon, 1975. Contributor to professional journals.

WORK IN PROGRESS: Several books on public affairs.

SIDELIGHTS: Clark told CA: "[I] feel we need constant probing of our times from every direction. We non-attached writers have freedom to dig in but not as much time as the academic, foundation-sponsored writers. Yet we can do the wild things that shock and stir the creative firmament." Avocational interests: Reading "in great spurts."

*   *   *

CLARKE, Mary Stetson   1911-

PERSONAL: Born December 27, 1911, in Melrose, Mass.; daughter of Horace (a manufacturers' representative) and Mabel Pitts (Russell) Stetson; married Edwin L. Clarke (an electrical engineer), June 8, 1937; children: Edwin Stetson, Susan E. (Mrs. Spence W. Perry), Joyce Russell (Mrs. David M. Hockman). Education: Boston University, A.B., 1933; Columbia University, graduate study, 1937-38. Religion: Protestant. Home: 333 West Emerson St., Melrose, Mass. 02176.

CAREER: Christian Science Monitor, Boston, Mass., advertising copywriter, 1933-37; Boston Center for Adult Education, Boston, teacher of creative writing, 1959-60; author of historical fiction and nonfiction for young people. Has served as member of Melrose Conservation Commission, member of executive board of Experiment in International Living, and director of Community Council, currently trustee of Melrose Public Library. Member: Boston Authors Club (director, 1966-67), Society for the Preservation of New England Antiquities, Middlesex Canal Association.

WRITINGS: Petticoat Rebel, Viking, 1964; The Iron Peacock, Viking, 1966; The Limner's Daughter, Viking, 1967; Pioneer Iron Works, Chilton, 1968; The Glass Phoenix, Viking, 1969; Piper to the Clan, Viking, 1970; Bloomers and Ballots: Elizabeth Cady Stanton and Women's Rights, Viking, 1972; Immigration in Colonial Times, Grossman, 1974; The Old Middlesex Canal, Hilltop Press, 1974; A Visit to the Ironworks, U.S. National Park Service, 1975. Contributor to magazines and newspapers.

*   *   *

CLARKE, Ronald Francis   1933-

PERSONAL: Born May 29, 1933, in Poole, England; son of Harold Bertram (a chartered surveyor) and Doris (Basquerville) Clarke; married Dorothy Elizabeth Milligan (a teacher), 1958; children: Catharine Sarah, Julian Francis. Education: Cambridge University, B.A. (honors), 1957, M.A., 1962; University of London, P.G.C.E., 1958. Politics: Liberal ("radical tendencies"). Religion: Anglican.

CAREER: Makerere University, Kampala, Uganda, East Africa, tutor, 1961-67, senior tutor, 1967-68, deputy director of Center for Continuing Education, 1968, professor of adult education, beginning 1968. Military service: Royal Air Force, interpreter, 1952-54.

WRITINGS: The Growth and Nature of Drama, Cambridge University Press, 1965; (editor with R. C. Presser) A Guidebook for Adult Teachers, East Africa Publishing House, 1968; (editor) Continuing Literacy, Proceedings of the Third Conference of the African Adult Education Association, 1968.

WORK IN PROGRESS: Understanding in a Second Language; research in the assessment of mental ability in adult students.††

*   *   *

CLASTER, Daniel S(tuart)   1932-

PERSONAL: Born December 8, 1932, in Harrisburg, Pa.; son of Harold (a communications executive) and Mildred (Lintz) Claster; married Jill Nadell (a history professor), June 17, 1960 (divorced, 1969); married Flavia Agnello, October 4, 1969; children: (first marriage) Elizabeth (deceased); (second marriage) Rebecca, Andrew. Education: Yale University, A.B., 1954; Columbia University, Ph.D., 1961. Politics: Democrat. Religion: Jewish. Home: 1176 Beach Ninth St., Far Rockaway, N.Y. 11691. Office: Department of Sociology, Brooklyn College of the City University of New York, Brooklyn, N.Y. 11210.

CAREER: University of Kentucky, Lexington, instructor in sociology, 1958-62; Hawthorne Cedar Knolls School, Hawthorne, N.Y., research associate, 1962-67; Brooklyn College of the City University of New York, Brooklyn, N.Y., assistant professor, 1967-73, associate professor of sociology, 1973—. Member: American Sociological Association, American Psychological Association, Law and Society Association.

WRITINGS: (With Howard Polsky) The Dynamics of Residential Treatment: A Social System Analysis, University of North Carolina Press, 1968; (editor with Polsky and Carl Goldberg) Social System Perspectives in Residential Institutions, Michigan State University Press, 1970. Occasional contributor to sociology journals.

*   *   *

CLAYTON, Keith (M.)   1928-

PERSONAL: Born September 25, 1928, in London, England; son of Edgar Francis and Constance (Clark) Clayton; married Jean Mary Wilkinson, August 4, 1952; children: Richard, Jill, Michael, Ian. Education: University of Sheffield, B.Sc., 1949, M.Sc., 1951; University of London, Ph.D., 1958. Home: 100 Pottergate, Norwich NR2 1EQ, England. Office: University of East Anglia, Norwich NR4 7TJ, England.

CAREER: State University of New York at Binghamton, professor of geography, 1960-62; University of London, London School of Economics and Political Science, London, England, reader in geography, 1962-67; University of East Anglia, Norwich, England, dean of environmental sciences, 1967-71, professor of environmental sciences, 1972—.

WRITINGS: The Earth's Crust, Aldus Books, 1966, published as The Crust of the Earth, Natural History Press, 1967; (editor with I. B. Kormoss) Oxford Regional Economic Atlas: Western Europe, Clarendon Press, Cartographic Department, 1971; (editor) Pollution Abatement, David & Charles, 1973. Editor, Oliver & Boyd's "Geomorphology Series," including Cliff Ollier's Weathering, 1969; editor and publisher, Geo Abstracts A & G.

WORK IN PROGRESS: Introduction to Geomorphology; co-editing Physique of Britain, to be published by Methuen.

CLEAVER, (Leroy) Eldridge 1935-

PERSONAL: Born August 31, 1935, in Wabbaseka, Ark.; son of Leroy (a dining car waiter) and Thelma (a janitress) Cleaver; married Kathleen Neal, December, 1967; children: two. *Education:* Attended junior college; also educated in the California state prisons of San Quentin, Folsom, and Soledad.

CAREER: First job was shining shoes in Phoenix, Ariz.; hustled marijuana which led to reform school and then, on June 18, 1954, he began his first term in Soledad Prison. Was paroled in two and a half years, but eleven months later was again arrested and convicted of assault with intent to commit murder and assault with a deadly weapon. Was sentenced from one to fourteen years in Folsom Prison, where he began introspective process which brought about *Soul on Ice.* His correspondence with white attorney Beverly Axelrod blossomed into a love affair which, in addition to the publicity he received from *Ramparts,* as well as public pressure, resulted in his parole in December, 1966. He had been guaranteed a job on the staff of *Ramparts,* and became senior editor and contributing writer. Shortly after his release from prison he became involved with the Black Panther Party for Self-Defense in Oakland, California, and in the fall of 1967 became their minister of information. In April, 1968, was arrested as a parole violator as the result of a gun battle with the Oakland Police in which he was involved and was shot in the foot. Was freed after two months by a California superior-court judge who ruled that he was a political prisoner. This ruling was overturned by the higher apellate court which decided he had violated his parole and must return to prison. The date for his surrender was set at November 27, 1968. He disappeared two days before that date. He lived in Havana, Cuba until July, 1969 then moved to Algiers. In 1971, split with the Black Panther Party in an ideological dispute. Returned to the United States, November 18, 1975, and was immediately arrested by Federal authorities. In August, 1976, he was released on $100,000 bond, and is awaiting trial for charges relating to the Oakland gun battle.

Was presidential candidate of the Peace and Freedom Party, 1968. Guest lecturer at the University of California at Berkeley, October, 1968, and speaker at numerous other universities throughout the United States. Was once a Black Muslim, but while in exile, he experienced a conversion to Christianity.

WRITINGS: Soul on Ice, introduction by Maxwell Geismar, McGraw, 1968; *Eldridge Cleaver: Post-Prison Writings and Speeches,* edited by Robert Scheer, Random House, 1969; *Eldridge Cleaver's Black Papers,* McGraw, 1969; (author of introduction) Jerry Rubin, *Do It!,* Simon & Schuster, 1970. Also author, with others, of *War Within: Violence or Nonviolence in Black Revolution,* 1971, and of pamphlets for the Black Panther Party and People's Communications Network. Contributor to *Ramparts, Commonweal,* and other periodicals.

SIDELIGHTS: "The devil now wears a black beret, a leather jacket, sunglasses and a .50-calibre shell slung around his neck on a thong. He regards Martin Luther King, Roy Wilkins and Whitney Young as Uncle Toms, and Adam Clayton Powell as a sellout to the black bourgeoisie. He advocates a programme which, to most Americans, is simply unthinkable, involving as it does the total exemption of black citizens from military service and the establishment of all-black juries to try negroes. He preaches armed insurrection as a political technique. His

name is Eldridge Cleaver, and he has spent eight of his thirty-four years in various state prisons in the U.S.A., where he wrote a collection of essays entitled *Soul on Ice.*" "*Soul on Ice* is not a book about the prison life of a black man, although a very good picture of prison life does emerge secondarily. The book is about the imprisonment of men's souls by society," writes Charlayne Hunter. Jervis Anderson says that Cleaver expresses "the profound alienation from America which black nationalists feel and the extreme political and cultural view of its future which they take." Cleaver is, however, as Steven V. Roberts points out, "one of the few black militants who advocates a form of interracial tolerance." In Cleaver's words: "Black power to black people; white power to white people."

While in prison, Cleaver read and was influenced by many writers: Tom Paine, Rousseau, Voltaire, Marx, Lenin, Bakunin, Nechayev, Baldwin, Mailer, Ellison, Wright, Malcolm X. He became a Black Muslim for a while, and followed Malcolm X when he broke away from Elijah Muhammed. Cleaver says: "I have, so to speak, washed my hands in the blood of the martyr, Malcolm X, whose retreat from the precipice of madness created new room for others to turn about in, and I am now caught up in that tiny space, attempting a maneuver of my own." The "maneuver" he attempts to carry out is called by Richard Gilman "an effort at grace, complexity and faithfulness. It is to *be* Negro, with no concessions, no adaptations to white expectations, but at the same time to hold back from excess." *Playboy* says Cleaver "has been called the first black leader since Malcolm X with the potential to organize a militant mass movement of 'black liberation.' Whether he will succeed in forging it, whether he will remain free—or even alive—to lead it, and whether, if he does, it will be a force for racial reconciliation or division remains to be seen. But there is no denying that Cleaver, like Malcolm X, has great impact on the young in the ghettos." Cleaver has many enemies as well. *Playboy* continues: "They have charged him with intensifying racial hostilities to the detriment of black equality; and with providing racists—in and out of uniform—with precisely the provocation that can lend legal legitimacy to suppression."

Cleaver's position as a leader not only of the Black Panthers but of the whole black and even the whole liberal community can be seen in the support for him in the face of the revoking of his parole as a result of the gun battle between the Panthers and the Oakland police in which he was involved. The protest was not limited only to the Oakland area but was widespread throughout the country and world. In New York the *Times* reported a demonstration in which actor Gary Merrill and writer Susan Sontag took part. *The Washington Post* reported that, in London, French film director Jean Luc Godard protested some changes in his latest film and suggested that the people in the audience should ask for their money back and should send it to Eldridge Cleaver for his parole fund. The Peace and Freedom Party chose him as their nominee for president in 1968 in the midst of the hassle over the possibility or probability of his return to jail. Cleaver told Nat Hentoff in the *Playboy* interview: "I never exactly dreamed of waking up in the White House after the November election, but I took part in that campaign because I think it's necessary to pull a lot of people together, black and white."

Cleaver has gained a widespread hearing through *Soul on Ice.* It has even gotten him out of prison. Cleaver told Hentoff: "If I had been just another black man, I wouldn't have had a chance in the world of getting out before my maximum sentence was served—especially not me, because I was involved in a lot of prison politics. . . . It wasn't until I smuggled the manuscript of *Soul on Ice* out of prison and got it into the hands of people who had the book published that the attitude of the prison officials toward me started changing. And even then it took a whole mobilization of prominent literary figures writing letters to get me out." Beverly Axelrod, a white attorney, was the first to try to get Cleaver out of prison. His correspondence with her forms a part of the book, and Robert Coles says of Cleaver: "He loves his lawyer, a white woman, and pours out his love to her in three beautiful, incredibly subtle and blunt and unsparing and unforgettable letters."

Comments on *Soul on Ice* vary widely. "Not strictly satire or autobiography," Michael Cook writes, "*Soul on Ice* strikes one as a *satura* tentatively placed on an autobiographical stand, a mixed dish of letters, dramatic vignettes, politics, history or historiography, journal, character sketch, psychology, reportage, and sacred address. What sustains it, along the way, is its clear sense that formal circumstances differ from substantive conditions, a sense of freedom and candor that continually promises, and delivers, the 'creative moment.'" Thomas Lask says: "Mr. Cleaver's thoughts on the Negro in America, on black power, on white and black sexuality, on people such as the Rev. Dr. Martin Luther King, James Baldwin, Muhammed Ali and others will stimulate all those remotely concerned with the position of black and white people in the United States today. The response will certainly not be unanimous. What will be agreed is that it is an exceptional volume both in what it says and how the author came to say it." *Time* says: "It is Cleaver's thesis—as it is James Baldwin's, among others—that the root cause of racial prejudice in America is sexual. He argues that as a result of the Negro's years of servity the black male has been systematically robbed of his masculinity. Thus 'castrated,' the Negro also has been denied his development as a positive intellectual and social force." True, Cleaver does agree with Baldwin on this, but he also has some harsh things to say about him. "Cleaver," says Jervis Anderson, launches "a brilliant but mean and unfair attack upon Baldwin. . . . It is an essay of such sustained nastiness that one suspects it was really Cleaver's way of demolishing Baldwin in order the more sensationally to announce his own arrival upon the scene." David Llorens writes: "Cleaver on Baldwin is penetrating, consuming and not without the ambiguity one comes upon in the best of art, but it leaves you feeling that he saved his most vicious screams for the man he *really* loves, as indeed he should, which says something else about Eldridge Cleaver. Something beautiful."

Robert Coles comments: "I don't like the way he talks about Baldwin's life and his personality." He continues: "I don't like the way he lumps white men, all of them, indiscriminately together, and I'm sick and tired of a rhetoric that takes three hundred years of complicated, tortured American history and throws it in the face of every single white man alive today. Mr. Cleaver rightly wants to be seen for the particular man *he* is, and I don't see why he should by the same token confuse the twentieth-century traveling salesman with the seventeenth-century slave trader. If he wants us to understand American history, and in fact see its economic and political continuities, all well and good; but it is really stupid to tell today's white people that they caused what in fact gradually and terribly happened. What can anyone do with that kind of historical

burden . . .?" Coles is not completely down on Cleaver, however. He feels that he is "a promising and powerful writer, an intelligent and turbulent and passionate and eloquent man." David Evanier comments on Cleaver's style: "The style throughout the book is pop-Leftism, a mixture of sex and revolution characteristic of the New Left around the world." "Cleaver," writes Lita Eliscu, "is still searching and digging. He uses a lush, prosey prose which often becomes a frenzied, intellectualized echolalia of superabundant sound, as though he just discovered cinematic, polyphonic multi-syllabic speech. But often enough, more than enough, the symphonic effect becomes complete and the voice speaks so truly, if heavily, all is forgiven by the intent. Eldridge Cleaver replaces cool, throwaway witticism with an earnest passion to reveal all he can about his human condition."

About Cleaver as a writer Evanier says: "Cleaver restricts his own potential, confining his writing to a series of machine-gun blasts that capture the mood of the black militants. He reveals an innate gift for language at every turn, but he makes it the servant of the fashions of a political movement. . . . Hopefully Cleaver will find that his stylish Leftism was a small achievement measured against the talent he could develop if he tries." *Playboy* comments: "The fact that he is a self-generating writer, re-creating in print his own passionately felt experience and trying as much to educate himself as to educate others, gives his voyage of self-discovery as a black man an appealing freshness, even though he finally arrives at a familiar port of call." Anderson concludes his comments by saying: "He is an immensely talented essayist, one of the best in America at the present moment, who at the same time is lacking in certain fundamental moral qualities. His urgent concern for the humanity of black people . . . does not translate into a concern for the humanity of all people. His vision is so narrow and racially determined that it is incapable of accomodating the tragic sense of displaying any interest in what we are used to calling the sadness and ambiguity of the human condition. . . . He has a mind which is neither broad, complex, nor compassionate enough to be really interesting. His passion takes him to the peripheries of hate, a tendency or a temptation that succeeds only in reducing the beauty which passion, anger, and outrage can take on in writing that is controlled by the moral imagination." Robert Hughes writes: "*Soul on Ice,* as a cumulative statement about the Afro-American and the world he inhabits, is worth a thousand white papers prepared on 'the problem' by Washington sociologists. It is a deeply invigorating, challenging book: what is more, it is, I believe, one of the rare books without which our history—let alone our future—cannot be understood." Coles concludes his comments by saying: "Above all we must notice what he has done: begun (and only begun) to master the writer's craft. For that achievement Eldridge Cleaver deserves our unashamed awe, our admiration, and our insistence that like every other writer he work harder, rid himself of unnecessary baggage, and put to word the startling ironies that he knows from real life but sees and comprehends out of his mind's life."

Reading *Post Prison Writings*, according to Stuart Hood, is not a comfortable experience; nor does he intend it to be. He is a revolutionary and polemicist whose aim is to shock and disturb his audience, to force it to consider the world as seen by a man who grew up in the black ghettoes." Lindsay Patterson writes that the book is "up to a point, brilliant and revealing. Beyond that point, lurked some empty although eloquent abstractions, patently incorrect in their assumptions, judgments and conclusions." Patterson adds, however, that in reading this "urgently important book, no one should fail to realize how accurately Cleaver pinpoints the American malaise and its relationship to current world affairs—or just how remarkable a man he is, or how valuable."

Jack Newfield believes that the book "does perform two valuable and necessary functions. It gives evidence that Cleaver is *not* anti-white. And it provides the more plausible Panther version of the now mythicized shoot-out in Oakland that killed Bobby Hutton." "To the accusation that the Black Panthers advocate violence," Hood notes that "Cleaver's reply is that the violence was there already and that the coloured people of America are now beyond the points where they put any trust in passive resistence." Patterson comments: "Unlike some militants who have no play or design other than to level society and kill off whites, . . . Cleaver realizes that a coalition of responsible persons is needed."

On his return to the United States in 1975, Cleaver noted that "with all its faults the American system is the freest . . . in the world."

In 1969, Cleaver traveled to North Korea, China, and the U.S.S.R. A speech, "Dig," was recorded by the More Record Co. Documentary films on Cleaver were produced in 1969 and 1970.

BIOGRAPHICAL/CRITICAL SOURCES: Soul on Ice, McGraw, 1968; *Saturday Review,* March 9, 1968; *New Republic,* March 9, 1968, March 13, 1968, November 30, 1968; *New York Times,* March 13, 1968, November 27, 1968, December 1, 1968, October 7, 1969, November 1, 1970, September 9, 1972; *New York Times Book Review,* March 24, 1968, April 27, 1969; *New Leader,* March 25, 1968; *Time,* April 5, 1968, September 20, 1968; *Village Voice,* April 11, 1968, March 6, 1969; *Ramparts,* May, 1968, June, 1968, December, 1968, September, 1969; *Playboy,* May, 1968, December, 1968; *Atlantic,* June, 1968; *Negro Digest,* June, 1968; *Yale Review,* autumn, 1968; *Antioch Review,* fall, 1968; *Evergreen Review,* October, 1968; *Saturday Evening Post,* November 16, 1968; *Commentary,* December, 1968; *Washington Post,* December 1, 1968; *Newsweek,* December 9, 1968, December 1, 1975; *Spectator,* February 2, 1969, September 13, 1969; *National Review,* December 5, 1975; *Nation,* December 6, 1975; *Detroit Free Press,* August 30, 1976.†

*   *   *

CLEVELAND, Harold van B(uren)   1916-

PERSONAL: Born May 12, 1916, in Cincinnati, Ohio; son of Stanley Matthews and Marian (van Buren) Cleveland; married Joan Borkow, April 19, 1963; children: Helen, Marian, Mark, Hollis, Alice. *Education:* Harvard University, A.B., 1938, LL.B., 1942. *Home:* 49 East 96th St., New York, N.Y. 10028. *Office:* First National City Bank, 399 Park Ave., New York, N.Y. 10022.

CAREER: Admitted to practice of law in Massachusetts, Maryland, and District of Columbia. U.S. Government, Washington, D.C., industrial specialist with War Production Board, 1942-44, assistant chief of Middle East Division, Foreign Economic Administration, 1944, assistant chief of Division of Investment and Economic Development, U.S. Department of State, 1945-48, deputy director and special economic adviser, European Program Division, Economic Cooperation Administration, 1948-51; Com-

mittee for Economic Development, Washington, D.C., international economist and assistant director of research, 1951-56; John Hancock Mutual Life Insurance Co., Boston, Mass., counsel, 1956-63; Council on Foreign Relations, New York, N.Y., director of Atlantic policy studies, 1963-65; First National City Bank, New York City, vice-president for international economics, 1965—. *Military service:* U.S. Army, Office of Strategic Services, 1944-45. *Member:* American Bar Association, Council on Foreign Relations.

WRITINGS: (With Theodore Geiger) *Making Western Europe Defensible,* National Planning Association, 1951; (with others) *The Political Economy of American Foreign Policy,* Holt, 1955; *The Trade Expansion Program and Its Meaning for New England,* New England Council, 1962; *The Atlantic Idea and Its European Rivals,* Council on Foreign Relations, 1966. Contributor of articles on international, economic, and legal subjects to journals.

*   *   *

CLEVELAND, Ray L(eRoy)   1929-

PERSONAL: Born April 29, 1929, in Scottsbluff, Neb.; son of Harold Ziba (a carpenter) and Florence (Allison) Cleveland. *Education:* Westmont College, A.B., 1951; Johns Hopkins University, M.A., 1956, Ph.D., 1958. *Home:* West Route 2, Bayard, Neb. 69334. *Office:* University of Regina, Regina, Saskatchewan, Canada S4S 0A2.

CAREER: American Schools of Oriental Research, Jerusalem, fellow, 1955-56; Johns Hopkins University, Baltimore, Md., research associate in Arabian archaeology, 1956-64; American Foundation for the Study of Man, Honolulu, Hawaii, research fellow in Jordan, 1964-66; University of Saskatchewan, Regina, visiting associate professor of history, 1966-67, associate professor, 1967-71, professor of history, 1971-74; University of Regina, Regina, Saskatchewan, professor of history, 1974—. *Member:* American Oriental Society, American Research Center in Egypt, Middle East Institute, British School of Archaeology in Jerusalem, Royal Canadian Geographical Society, Royal Central Asian Society, Middle East Studies Association of North America, Royal Asiatic Society, Royal Geographical Society, International Linguistic Association, Hakluyt Society.

WRITINGS: The Excavation of the Conway High Place (Petra) and Soundings at Khirbet Ader, American Schools of Oriental Research, 1960; *An Ancient South Arabian Necropolis,* Johns Hopkins Press, 1965; (editor) *The Middle East and South Asia,* Stryker-Post Publications, 1968, 9th edition, 1975. Associate editor, *Bulletin of the American Schools of Oriental Research,* 1960-64; assistant editor of publications, American Foundation for the Study of Man, 1956—.

*   *   *

CLIFFORD, Nicholas R(owland)   1930-

PERSONAL: Born October 12, 1930, in Radnor, Pa.; son of Henry (a curator) and Esther (Rowland) Clifford; married Deborah Pickman, June 22, 1957; children: Mary, Sarah, Susannah, Rebecca. *Education:* Princeton University, B.A., 1952; Harvard University, M.A., 1957, Ph.D., 1961. *Politics:* Democrat. *Religion:* Roman Catholic. *Home:* R.D. 2, Cornwall, Middlebury, Vt. 05753. *Office:* Department of History, Middlebury College, Middlebury, Vt. 05753.

CAREER: Massachusetts Institute of Technology, Cambridge, instructor in humanities, 1961-62; Princeton University, Princeton, N.J., instructor in history, 1962-66; Middlebury College, Middlebury, Vt., assistant professor, 1966-68, associate professor, 1968-75, William R. Kenan Professor of History, 1975—, chairman of department, 1971-73, dean of East Asian Summer Language School, 1972—. *Military service:* U.S. Navy, 1952-56; became lieutenant. *Member:* American Historical Association for Asian Studies, Conference on British Studies.

WRITINGS: Retreat from China: British Policy in the Far East, 1937-41, University of Washington Press, 1967. Contributor to *Journal of Modern History, Journal of British Studies,* and *Commonweal.*

WORK IN PROGRESS: The May 30th Movement (1925) in China.

* * *

CLIVE, Mary   1907-

PERSONAL: Born August 23, 1907, in London, England; daughter of Thomas and Mary (Child-Villiers) Longford; married M.G.D. Clive, December 30, 1939 (killed in action, 1943); children: George, Alice. *Education:* Educated privately. *Religion:* Protestant. *Address:* c/o Macmillan & Co. Ltd., Little Essex St., London, England.

CAREER: Journalist on *Evening Standard,* London, England, before her marriage; for some years has been living quietly in the English countryside, writing "entirely to please myself."

WRITINGS: Caroline Clive, Bodley Head, 1949; *Christmas with the Savages,* Macmillan, 1955; *The Day of Reckoning,* Macmillan, 1964; *Jack and the Doctor* (biography of John Donne), Macmillan, 1966; *The Sun of York: A Biography of Edward IV,* Macmillan, 1973.

* * *

CLUTTERBUCK, Richard   1917-
(Richard Jocelyn)

PERSONAL: Born November 22, 1917, in London, England; son of Lewis St. John Rawlinson (a colonel, British Army) and Isabella (Jocelyn) Clutterbuck; married Angela Barford, May 1, 1948; children: Peter, Robin, Julian. *Education:* Cambridge University, M.A. (mechanical sciences), 1939; University of Singapore, graduate study, 1966-68; University of London, Ph.D. (politics), 1971. Military schooling has included British Army Staff College, 1948, and Imperial Defence College, 1965. *Office:* Department of Politics, University of Exeter, Exeter, England.

CAREER: British Army, officer, 1937-72, became Engineer-in-Chief of the Army, with rank of major general; served in more than fifteen countries around the world, including France, Belgium, Ethiopia, Egypt, Algeria, Palestine, Malaya, and the United States; University of Exeter, Exeter, England, lecturer in politics, 1972—. Member of General Advisory Council of the British Broadcasting Corp. *Member:* Institute of Civil Engineers (London; fellow), Institute for the Study of Conflict (council member). *Awards, honors*—Military: Officer of Order of the British Empire, 1958, for services in Malaya; Companion of the Order of the Bath, 1972, for services as Engineer-in-Chief of the Army. Literary: George Knight Clowes Prize of *Army Quarterly,* 1954; Bertrand Stewart Prize of Ministry of Defence, 1960; Toulmin Medal of Society of American Military Engineers, 1963.

WRITINGS: (Under pseudonym Richard Jocelyn) *Across the River,* Constable, 1957; *The Long Long War,* Praeger, 1966; *Riot and Revolution in Singapore and Malaya, 1942-63,* Faber, 1973; *Protest and the Urban Guerrilla,* Cassell, 1973, Abelard, 1974; *Living with Terrorism,* Faber, 1975; (contributor) Anthony Deane-Drummond, editor, *Riot Control,* Royal United Services Institute of Defence Studies, 1975. Author of play, "A Means to an End," broadcast by Radio Malaya, 1958. Contributor of more than forty articles to British and American periodicals.

WORK IN PROGRESS: Research project on "Political Violence in Great Britain," funded by the Social Science Research Council.

AVOCATIONAL INTERESTS: Canoeing at sea (led a canoe party of twenty-four soldiers across the English Channel to France in 1960).

* * *

COATS, George W.   1936-

PERSONAL: Born August 13, 1936, in Knox City, Tex.; son of George Wesley (a banker) and Bonnie (McClellan) Coates; married Sandra Sue Colley, June 25, 1939; children: George Andrew, Charissa Suzanne. *Education:* McMurry College, B.A., 1958; Southern Methodist University, B.D., 1961; Yale University, M.A., 1963, Ph.D., 1966; graduate study at University of Goettingen, 1964-66, and University of Heidelberg, 1970-71. *Religion:* Methodist. *Home:* 1316 Tanforan Dr., Lexington, Ky. 40502. *Agent:* Pierce Ellis, 201 Eighth Ave. S., Nashville, Tenn. 37202. *Office:* 631 South Limestone, Lexington, Ky. 40508.

CAREER: McMurry College, Abilene, Tex., assistant professor of religion, 1965-68; Lexington Theological Seminary, Lexington, Ky., associate professor, 1968-71, professor of Old Testament, 1971—. *Member:* Society of Biblical Literature, Catholic Biblical Association, American Philosophical Society (fellow), Institute for Antiquity and Christianity (corresponding member), British Society of Old Testament Studies, American Association of University Professors. *Awards, honors:* Fulbright fellowship in Germany, 1964-65; Hebrew Union College fellowship in Israel, 1968-69; Humboldt Fellow, 1970-71, 1976-77.

WRITINGS: (Contributor) *Vetus Testamentum,* E. J. Brill, Volume XVII, 1967, Volume XVIII, 1968; *Rebellion in the Wilderness: The Murmuring Motif in the Wilderness Traditions of the Old Testament,* Abingdon, 1968; *From Canaan to Egypt: Structural and Theological Context for the Joseph Story,* Catholic Biblical Association, 1975. Contributor to *Catholic Biblical Quarterly* and *Lexington Theological Quarterly.*

WORK IN PROGRESS: Heroic Man and Man of God: Theological Exposition of the Moses Tradition, for John Knox.

SIDELIGHTS: Coats is competent in German, French, Hebrew, Greek, and Aramaic.

* * *

COBB, Carl W(esley)   1926-

PERSONAL: Born August 11, 1926, in Yazoo City, Miss.; son of Clifford C. and Mable (Jones) Cobb; married Jane Kimbrough, December, 1958; children: Kimbrough, Karen, Carolyn. *Education:* George Peabody College for Teachers, B.A., 1950, M.A., 1952; Mexico City College, summer study, 1949; graduate study at Harvard University, 1953, and National University of Columbia, 1957-58; Tulane

University of Louisiana, Ph.D., 1961. *Religion:* Protestant. *Home:* 9501 Mobile Dr., Knoxville, Tenn. 37919. *Office:* Department of Romance Languages, University of Tennessee, Knoxville, Tenn. 37916.

CAREER: Virginia Intermont College, Bristol, member of faculty, 1952-58; Middle Tennessee State University, Murfreesboro, assistant professor of Spanish, 1961-62; Furman University, Greenville, S.C., associate professor of Spanish, 1962-66; University of Tennessee, Knoxville, 1966—, began as associate professor, currently professor of modern Spanish literature. *Military service:* U.S. Naval Reserve, 1944-46. *Member:* American Association of Teachers of Spanish and Portuguese, American Association of University Professors, South Atlantic Modern Language Association, Phi Sigma Iota. *Awards, honors:* Buenos Aires Convention fellowship to Colombia, 1956-57; Ford Foundation fellowship to write book on Federico Garcia Lorca, 1965-66.

WRITINGS: Federico Garcia Lorca, Twayne, 1967; *Antonio Machado,* Twayne, 1971. Also author of *Spanish Poetry of the 20th Century,* 1975. Contributor of articles and reviews to learned journals, including *Hispania, Philological Quarterly,* and *Romance Notes.*

* * *

COBBS, Price M(ashaw) 1928-

PERSONAL: Born November 2, 1928, in Los Angeles, Calif.; son of Peter Price (a physician) and Rosa Cobbs; married Evadne Priester (a teacher), May 30, 1957 (deceased); children: Price Priester, Marion Renata. *Education:* University of California, Berkeley, B.A., 1954; Meharry Medical College, M.D., 1958. *Office:* Pacific Management Systems, 3528 Sacramento St., San Francisco, Calif. 94118.

CAREER: Practicing psychiatrist. University of California, San Francisco, assistant clinical professor of psychiatry, 1963—; Pacific Training Associates, San Francisco, Calif., co-director, 1967—; also senior partner of Pacific Management Systems. *Military service:* U.S. Army, 1951-52. *Member:* American Psychiatric Association, American Medical Association, Black Behavioral Scientists, University of California Black Caucus.

WRITINGS: (With William H. Grier) *Black Rage,* Basic Books, 1968; (with Grier) *The Jesus Bag,* McGraw, 1971.

SIDELIGHTS: Thomas Frazier writes of *Black Rage:* "No book I have read so convincingly portrays the condition of black America. Even the intensely personal disclosures of Richard Wright, James Baldwin, John A. Williams and other novelists do not have its impact." One of the book's greatest values, according to Henrietta Buckmaster, is "its hard reminder that slavery has left shocking residual effects on both black and white." Charles Valentine calls *Black Rage* "a brilliant book which combines highly passionate eloquence with thoroughly intellectual seriousness."

BIOGRAPHICAL/CRITICAL SOURCES: Time, July 26, 1968; *Washington Post,* August 6, 1968; *New Republic,* August 17, 1968; *New York Times Book Review,* August 17, 1968, September 22, 1968; *Book World,* September 8, 1968; *New Yorker,* September 28, 1968; *Christian Science Monitor,* November 14, 1968; *Nation,* January 6, 1969.

* * *

COCHRANE, Willard W(esley) 1914-

PERSONAL: Born May 15, 1914, in Fresno, Calif.; son of Willard W. (a rancher) and Clare A. (Chambers) Cochrane; married Mary Herget, August 23, 1942; children: W. Wesley, Stephen A., James M., Timothy S. *Education:* University of California, B.S., 1937; Montana State University, M.S., 1938; Harvard University, M.P.A., 1942, Ph.D., 1945. *Politics:* Democrat. *Religion:* Protestant. *Home:* 12490 Norell Ave. N., Stillwater, Minn. 55082. *Office:* 332 G Classroom—Office Bldg., University of Minnesota, St. Paul, Minn.

CAREER: U.S. Government, Washington, D.C., economist for Farm Credit Administration, 1939-41, War Food Administration, 1943, and Bureau of Agricultural Economics, U.S. Department of Agriculture, 1943-47; United Nations Food and Agricultural Organization, Washington, D.C., economist, 1947-48, member of U.S. Mission to Siam, 1948; Pennsylvania State University, University Park, associate professor, 1948-49, professor of agricultural economics, 1950-51; University of Minnesota, Minneapolis, professor of agricultural economics, 1951-61; U.S. Department of Agriculture, Washington, D.C., director of agricultural economics and economic adviser to Secretary of Agriculture, 1961-64; University of Minnesota, St. Paul, professor of agricultural economics, 1964—, dean of international programs, 1965-70. Visiting professor at University of Wisconsin, summer, 1951, and University of Chicago, 1958-59. Consultant to Commodity Credit Corp., 1964-68, to Agency for International Development on food problems of India, 1964-65, to United Nations Food and Agriculture Organization, 1965-68, to Ministry of Agriculture, Saudi Arabia, 1973-74; Ford Foundation consultant to India's Ministry of Food and Agriculture, 1967, 1970, Thailand, 1970, and the Philippines, 1973. *Military service:* U.S. Naval Reserve, active duty as ensign 1942-43.

MEMBER: American Economic Association, American Farm Economic Association (vice-president, 1954-55; president, 1959-60; fellow), American Academy of Political and Social Science. *Awards, honors:* Distinguished Service Award, U.S. Department of Agriculture, 1964; LL.D., Montana State University, 1967.

WRITINGS: (With Walter W. Wilcox) *Economics of American Agriculture,* Prentice-Hall, 1951, 3rd edition, 1974; (with Carolyn Shaw) *Economics of Consumption,* McGraw, 1956; *Farm Prices—Myth and Reality,* University of Minnesota Press, 1958; *The City Man's Guide to the Farm Problem,* University of Minnesota Press, 1965; *The World Food Problem,* Crowell, 1969; *Agricultural Development Planning: Economic Concepts, Procedures, and Political Process,* Praeger, 1974. Writer of more than one hundred articles, reviews, and bulletins, including the prize-winning article, "Farm Price Gyrations—An Aggregative Hypothesis" in *Journal of Farm Economics,* 1947.

SIDELIGHTS: Cochrane has made many trips to India on technical assistance projects, and traveled extensively in Latin America and South and Southeast Asia. *Avocational interests:* History of the exploration of the Rocky Mountains; camping and fishing in the Rocky Mountains and High Sierras; raising, driving, and riding Morgan horses.

* * *

COENS, Sister Mary Xavier 1918-

PERSONAL: Born January 16, 1918, in Chicago, Ill.; daughter of Henry H. (vice-president of a coal company) and Daisy M. (Rothgeb) Coens. *Education:* Mundelein College, B.A., 1939; Catholic University of America, M.A., 1947; graduate study in theater at University of

Iowa, 1945, University of Minnesota, 1950, and University of Kansas, 1965. *Office:* Department of Drama, Clarke College, Dubuque, Iowa 52001.

CAREER: Roman Catholic nun, member of Sisters of Charity of the Blessed Virgin Mary (B.V.M.). Teacher in Chicago (Ill.) public schools, 1939-40, and at Mount Carmel Academy, Wichita, Kan., 1943-47; Clarke College, Dubuque, Iowa, associate professor of speech and drama, and chairman of drama department, 1948—. Was first nun to travel overseas for United Service Organizations (U.S.O.), touring the European Command, 1963, and Northeastern Command, 1967; pioneered Children's Theatre Arena and Coffee House Theatre in Midwest. Director of drama for National Endowment of Arts and Iowa Arts Council, 1974-76; member of board of chiropractic examiners, 1975-77. Panelist and frequent guest on national television. *Member:* Speech Association of America, American Educational Theatre Association, Catholic Theatre Conference, Children's Theatre Conference, American Association of University Women. *Awards, honors:* Honorary colonel in U.S. Army.

WRITINGS: G I Nun, Kenedy, 1967. Contributor to *Reader's Digest, Critique,* and *Catholic Theatre.*

* * *

COFFEY, (Helen) Dairine 1933-

PERSONAL: Given name pronounced Darina; born December 28, 1933, in Dublin, Ireland; daughter of Diarmid and Sheela (Trench) Coffey. *Education:* University of Dublin, B.A., 1956; has studied art in recent years at Byam-Shaw School of Drawing and Painting, London, England. *Home:* Glendarragh, Newtown Mount Kennedy, County Wicklow, Ireland.

CAREER: Cambridge University, Trinity Hall, Cambridge, England, secretary, 1958-59; *Observer* (newspaper), London, England, secretary to "Pendennis," 1959-61; Studio-Vista (publishers), London, editor, 1962-64; Atheneum Publishers, New York, N.Y., editor of children's books, 1965-66.

WRITINGS: (Compiler) *The Dark Tower* (anthology of nineteenth-century narrative poems), Atheneum, 1967.

WORK IN PROGRESS: Illustrating and compiling books for children.††

* * *

COFFIN, Tristram 1912-

PERSONAL: Born July 25, 1912, in Hood River, Ore.; son of Clarence Eugene and Lenora (Smith) Coffin; married Margaret Avery, June 26, 1933; children: Stephen A., Lynne A. Coffin Cronyn. *Education:* DePauw University, A.B., 1933. *Home:* 5601 Warwick Pl., Chevy Chase, Md. 20015.

CAREER: Reporter for *Indianapolis Times,* 1933-37; assistant to governor of Indiana, 1937-41; assistant to director, Office of War Information, 1941-44; commentator for Columbia Broadcasting System, 1944-47, and American Broadcasting Companies, 1947-51; free-lance writer, 1951—; currently editor of *The Washington Spectator* (newsletter).

WRITINGS: Missouri Compromise, Little, Brown, 1947; *Your Washington,* Duell, Sloan & Pearce, 1954; *Not to the Swift,* Norton, 1961; *The Passion of the Hawks: Militarism in Modern America,* Macmillan, 1964; *Mine Eyes Have Seen the Glory,* Macmillan, 1964; *The Sex Kick: Eroticism in Modern America,* Macmillan, 1966; *Senator Fulbright: Portrait of a Public Philosopher,* Dutton, 1966.

WORK IN PROGRESS: A novel, *Dominique;* a nonfiction book, *The Foreign Policy Apparatus.*

SIDELIGHTS: William Chapman writes of *Not to the Swift:* "One can scarcely quarrel with the moral of this novel of the Presidency—that peril awaits the nation entrusted to a manufactured idol lacking the courage or ability to face the hard facts of power. But *Not to the Swift* has the effect of transforming this uncomfortably familiar truth into unconvincing fiction." Several critics compare this novel to Allen Drury's *Advise and Consent.* Margaret Parton says that, while "Mr. Drury seemed to accept his world, . . . Mr. Coffin is angry about the cynicism, the chicanery, the callous attitude of 'insiders' toward the loathsome risk of war."

The Passion of the Hawks: Militarism in Modern America was both praised and criticized. L. E. Fichtelburg writes that the work is "done with sparkling, sharp wit and occasional oversimplification, [and is] impressionistic, popular, almost slick." He notes, however, that it "is colorful writing, delightful reading." G. M. Lyons, on the other hand, thinks that "Tristram Coffin has written about an important subject, but unfortunately he has written a terrible book. *The Passion of the Hawks* is a potpourri of quotations and anecdotes, strung together with simple journalistic logic, and ending with a hawk-like shriek at the perversity of man."

George Adelman calls *The Sex Kick* "a wide-ranging journalistic review . . . a provocative, occasionally sensational (how could it not be with this topic!) but withal, interesting and valuable book."

BIOGRAPHICAL/CRITICAL SOURCES: New York Herald Tribune Lively Arts, April 2, 1961; *New York Times Book Review,* April 2, 1961; *Booklist,* May 1, 1961; *New Republic,* May 15, 1961, December 3, 1966; *American Political Science Review,* September, 1964; *Saturday Review,* November 26, 1966; *Harper's,* December, 1966.

* * *

COGER, Leslie Irene 1912-

PERSONAL: Born January 18, 1912, in Huntsville, Ark.; daughter of Ira M. (a pharmacist) and Minna Lee (Presley) Coger. *Education:* Crescent Junior College, A.A., 1931; Curry School of Expression, Boston, Mass., Diploma, 1932; College of the Ozarks, B.A. (magna cum laude), 1933; University of Arkansas, M.A., 1939, Northwestern University, Ph.D., 1952. *Home:* 941 South Weller St., Springfield, Mo. 65802. *Office:* Southwest Missouri State University, Springfield, Mo. 65802.

CAREER: Arkansas State Vocational School, Huntsville, instructor in English and speech, 1933-38; Central College, North Little Rock, Ark., instructor in speech and physical education, 1938-43; Southwest Missouri State University, Springfield, instructor, 1943-46, assistant professor, 1946-48, associate professor, 1948-52, professor of speech and theater, 1952—, director of Tent Theatre, 1963—. Visiting summer professor, Queens College of the City University of New York, 1966. Director of shows for American Education Theatre Association on United Service Organizations (U.S.O.) tours abroad, 1961, 1965, 1968, and 1972. *Member:* Speech Association of America (chairman of legislative assembly, 1972), American Educational Theatre Association.

WRITINGS: (With Melvin White) *Studies in Readers' Theatre*, S and F Press, 1963; (with Melvin White) *Readers' Theatre Handbook*, Scott, Foresman, 1967, revised edition, 1973; (contributor) Erika Munk, editor, *Stanislavski and America*, Fawcett, 1967; (contributor) *Studies in Interpretation*, Rodopi NV (Amsterdam), 1972. Contributor to handbook, "From the Printed Page," 1964; also contributor to magazines and professional journals. Editor, *Newsletter* of Interpretation Interest Group, Speech Association of America, 1963-65.

WORK IN PROGRESS: Adapting scripts for Readers' Theatre; the study of kinesics as applied to the oral performer.

*   *   *

COHEN, Edward M(artin) 1936-

PERSONAL: Born April 15, 1936, in New York, N.Y.; son of Harry M. (an attorney) and Betty (Mendell) Cohen; married Sheila H. Miller, 1955 (divorced, 1958); married Susan Simon, June 22, 1969; children: (first marriage) Noel Aram, Joy Alison. *Education:* Queens College (now of the City University of New York), student, 1952-55. *Home:* 949 West End Ave., New York, N.Y. 10025. *Agent:* Candida Donadio & Associates, Inc., 111 West 57th St., New York, N.Y. 10019. *Office address:* c/o KLR Agency, 853 7th Ave., New York, N.Y. 10022.

CAREER: Westminster Records, New York City, production manager, 1955-58; Everest Records, New York City, operations manager, 1958-59; Interdisca, Inc., New York City, general manager, 1959-63; Dubbins Electronics, Inc., New York City, director of artists and repertoire, 1963—. *Member:* Actor's Studio, O'Neill Playwrights Group. *Awards, honors:* National Playwright Conference, Eugene O'Neill Memorial Theatre Foundation, playwright fellow, 1971.

WRITINGS: Two Hundred and Fifty Thousand Dollars (novel), Putnam, 1967; "The Complaint Department Closes at Five" (play), first produced in Waterford, Conn., at Eugene O'Neill Memorial Theatre, 1971. Also author of two plays "Cakes with the Wine," 1970, and "Breeding Ground," 1970. Short stories have been published in *Carleton Miscellany* and *Evergreen Review.*

WORK IN PROGRESS: A Little Scare, a novel.

SIDELIGHTS: According to Leo Harris, *Two Hundred and Fifty Thousand Dollars* tells a tale of a New York Jewish family, and "a nastier, meaner, dirtier, *horribler* family . . . would be difficult . . . to imagine." He concludes that "there is no let-up in the sordity, but somehow an underlying reality emerges through the brutally parodied stereotypes."

BIOGRAPHICAL/CRITICAL SOURCES: Books and Bookmen, March, 1968.†

*   *   *

COHEN, Leonard (Norman) 1934-

PERSONAL: Born September 21, 1934, in Montreal, Quebec, Canada; son of Nathan B. and Marsha (Klinitsky) Cohen. *Education:* McGill University, B.A., 1955; did graduate work at Columbia University. *Residence:* Montreal, Quebec, Canada. *Office:* Stranger Music, Inc., 1501 Broadway, New York, N.Y. 10036.

CAREER: Poet, novelist, singer, and composer; currently associated with Stranger Music, Inc., New York City.

Worked in Montreal before going to Europe in 1959; has lived in London, Greece, and New York City. *Awards, honors:* McGill Literary Award, 1956; Canada Council grant, 1960-61; Quebec Literary Award, 1964; LL.B., Dalhousie University, 1971.

WRITINGS—Poetry: *Let Us Compare Mythologies,* Contact Press (Toronto), 1956; *The Spice Box of Earth,* McClelland & Stewart, 1961, Viking, 1965; *Flowers for Hitler,* McClelland & Stewart, 1964; *Parasites of Heaven,* McClelland & Stewart, 1966; *Selected Poems, 1956-1968,* Viking, 1968; *The Energy of Slaves,* McClelland & Stewart, 1972, Viking, 1973.

Novels: *The Favorite Game,* Viking, 1963; *Beautiful Losers,* Viking, 1966.

Work represented in many anthologies, including *The Penguin Book of Canadian Verse,* edited by Ralph Gastafson, Penguin, 1967, and *How Do I Love Thee: Sixty Poets of Canada (and Quebec) Select and Introduce Their Favourite Poems from Their Own Work,* edited by John Robert Colombo, M. G. Hurtig (Edmonton), 1970. Contributor of poetry to magazines.

Recordings include "Songs of Leonard Cohen," Columbia, 1968, "Songs of Love and Hate," Columbia, 1971, and "Leonard Cohen: Live Songs," Columbia, 1973. His songs have been recorded by many other singers. *Leonard Cohen's Song Book* was published by Collier, 1969.

SIDELIGHTS: Leonard Cohen once wrote: "Without song, the language is dead. A good song does something to the language. It gives people a house they can live in forever. A great singer creates hospitals, institutions, healers—with his words."

A *National Observer* critic, reviewing *Selected Poems: 1956-68,* wrote ". . . without voice and music, these poems stand naked in their triteness." A reviewer from *Beloit Poetry Journal* also pointed out that Cohen ". . . writes vague romantic verse or weak protest poetry neither as enchanting nor compelling as some of his better recordings. When forced to stand on their words alone his songs are not successful."

BIOGRAPHICAL/CRITICAL SOURCES: Canadian Literature, winter, 1965; Guy Sylvestre and others, editors, *Canadian Writers,* revised edition, Ryerson, 1966; *New York Times,* April 27, 1966; *New York Review of Books,* April 28, 1966; *New York Times Book Review,* May 8, 1966; *New Leader,* May 23, 1966; *Canadian Forum,* July, 1967; September, 1970; *Books,* January, 1968, June, 1970; *Saturday Night,* February, 1968; *Life,* June 28, 1968; *Time,* September 13, 1968; *McCall's,* January, 1969; *National Observer,* September 9, 1968; *Beloit Poetry Journal,* Volume XIX, number 2, winter 1968-69.

*   *   *

COHEN, Warren I. 1934-

PERSONAL: Born June 20, 1934, in Brooklyn, N.Y.; son of Murray and Fay (Phillips) Cohen; married Janice Prichard, June 22, 1957; children: Geoffrey Scott, Anne Leslie. *Education:* Columbia University, A.B., 1955; Fletcher School of Law and Diplomacy, A.M., 1956; University of Washington, Seattle, Ph.D., 1962. *Home:* 1233 Tanager Lane, East Lansing, Mich. 48823.

CAREER: University of California, Riverside, lecturer in history, 1962-63; Michigan State University, East Lansing, assistant professor, 1963-67, associate professor, 1967-71, professor of history, 1971—. Visiting professor, National

Taiwan University, Taipei, 1964-66; Fulbright lecturer, Tokyo, 1969-70. Foreign policy consultant. *Military service:* U.S. Navy, 1956-59; became lieutenant.

WRITINGS: (Editor) *Intervention, 1917: Why America Fought,* Heath, 1966; *The American Revisionists,* University of Chicago Press, 1967; *America's Response to China,* Wiley, 1971. Contributor of articles and reviews to *Journal of Asian Studies, Orbis, Journal of American History,* and other historical journals.

WORK IN PROGRESS: Three Who Found China; a study of Dean Rusk for "American Secretaries of State" series.

*   *   *

COLE, Wayne S. 1922-

PERSONAL: Born November 11, 1922, in Manning, Iowa; son of Roy E. and Gladys (Granseth) Cole; married Virginia Miller, December 24, 1950; children: Thomas Roy. *Education:* Iowa State Teachers College (now University of Northern Iowa), B.A., 1946; University of Wisconsin, M.S., 1948, Ph.D., 1951. *Religion:* Protestant. *Home:* 10203 McGovern Dr., Silver Spring, Md. 20903. *Office:* Department of History, University of Maryland, College Park, Md. 20742.

CAREER: University of Arkansas, Fayetteville, instructor, 1950-52, assistant professor of history, 1952-54; Iowa State University, Ames, assistant professor, 1954-56, associate professor, 1956-60, professor of history, 1960-65; University of Maryland, College Park, professor of history, 1965—. Fulbright lecturer, University of Keele, Keele, Staffordshire, England, 1962-63. *Military service:* U.S. Army Air Forces, 1943-45; became first lieutenant. *Member:* Organization of American Historians, Society for Historians of American Foreign Relations (president, 1973). *Awards, honors:* Summer research grants, American Philosophical Society, 1958-1960, and Social Science Research Council, 1959; fellow, Woodrow Wilson International Center for Scholars, 1973.

WRITINGS: America First: The Battle Against Intervention, 1940-1941, University of Wisconsin Press, 1953; *Senator Gerald P. Nye and American Foreign Relations,* University of Minnesota Press, 1962; *An Interpretive History of American Foreign Relations,* Dorsey, 1968, revised edition, 1974; *Charles A. Lindbergh and the Battle Against American Intervention in World War II,* Harcourt, 1974. Contributor to professional journals.

WORK IN PROGRESS: President Roosevelt and the Isolationists, 1932-1945.

SIDELIGHTS: Cole told *CA:* "My avocation is flying. I am a commercial airplane pilot with an instrument rating and a flight instructor certificate."

*   *   *

COLE, Wendell 1914-

PERSONAL: Born May 15, 1914, in Chicago, Ill.; son of Herbert F. (an accountant) and Susan (a teacher; maiden name, Richards) Cole; married Charlotte Klein (a librarian), December 14, 1948. *Education:* Albion College, A.B., 1936; University of Michigan, A.M., 1937; Stanford University, Ph.D., 1951. *Home:* 853 Esplanada Way, Stanford, Calif. 94305. *Office:* Memorial Hall, Stanford University, Stanford, Calif. 94305.

CAREER: Alma College, Alma, Mich., assistant professor

of history and English, 1943-45; Stanford University, Stanford, Calif., instructor, 1945-51, assistant professor, 1951-54, associate professor, 1954-63, professor of speech and drama, 1963—, acting executive head of department of speech and drama at various periods between 1956-63, and 1963—. *Member:* American Educational Theatre Association, Society of Architectural Historians, U.S. Institute for Theatre Technology.

WRITINGS: (Editor) *The Story of the Meininger,* University of Miami Press, 1963; *Kyoto in the Momoyama Period,* University of Oklahoma Press, 1967.

AVOCATIONAL INTERESTS: Architecture.

*   *   *

COLEMAN, Kenneth 1916-

PERSONAL: Born April 28, 1916, in Devereux, Ga.; son of John Amoss (a merchant) and Nolia (Lee) Coleman. *Education:* University of Georgia, A.B., 1938, M.A., 1940; University of Wisconsin, Ph.D., 1952. *Politics:* Democrat. *Religion:* Episcopalian. *Home:* 220 Dearing St., Athens, Ga. 30601. *Office:* University of Georgia, Athens, Ga. 30602.

CAREER: University of Georgia, instructor, later assistant professor of history at Atlanta Campus, 1949-55, associate professor of history at Athens Campus, 1955-68, professor, 1968—. Member of board of directors, Athens-Clarke Heritage Foundation; member, Georgia Bicentennial Commission. *Military service:* U.S. Army Reserve, 1941-56; active duty, 1941-46, with service in European theater; became lieutenant colonel. *Member:* American Historical Association, Southern Historical Association, Georgia Historical Society, Athens Historical Society (past president).

WRITINGS: Georgia History in Outline, Georgia State College of Business Administration, 1955, 2nd edition, University of Georgia Press, 1960; *The American Revolution in Georgia,* University of Georgia Press, 1958; (contributor) Horace Montgomery, editor, *Georgians in Profile. Historical Essays in Honor of Ellis Merton Coulter,* University of Georgia Press, 1958; (with Sarah B. Gover Temple) *Georgia Journeys. Being an Account of the Lives of Georgia's Original Settlers and Many Other Early Settlers from the Founding of the Colony in 1732 until the Institution of Royal Government in 1754,* University of Georgia Press, 1961; *Confederate Athens,* University of Georgia Press, 1968; *Athens, 1861-1865: As Seen Through Letters in the University of Georgia Libraries,* University of Georgia Press, 1969. Contributor to *Agricultural History* and regional history journals.

WORK IN PROGRESS: A History of Colonial Georgia, to be published by Scribner; editor with Milton Ready, *The Colonial Records of the State of Georgia,* for University of Georgia Press.

AVOCATIONAL INTERESTS: Architecture and how it reflects life of the period in which the house was built.

*   *   *

COLLIER, David S(wanson) 1923-

PERSONAL: Born September 28, 1923, in Baltimore, Md.; son of John P. (a business executive) and Anna (Swanson) Collier. *Education:* Attended Oberlin College, 1941-42; Northwestern University, B.S., 1947, M.A., 1949, Ph.D., 1952. *Home and office:* 743 North Wabash Ave., Chicago, Ill. 60611.

CAREER: Northwestern University, Evanston, Ill., instructor, 1948-50; American University of Beirut, Beirut, Lebanon, Smith-Mundt Visiting Professor of International Relations, 1952-53; University of Tokyo, Tokyo, Japan, Fulbright research professor, 1953-54; American Friends of the Middle East, Washington, D.C., executive director, midwest region, 1954-57; Foundation for Foreign Affairs, Chicago, Ill., executive director, 1957-69, president, 1970—. *Military service:* U.S. Army, military intelligence and military government, 1943-46, 1950-51; became captain. *Member:* Institute for Philosophical and Historical Studies (member of board of directors), Japan-America Society (member of board of directors), American Political Science Association, American Economic Association, Association for Asian Studies, Council for Basic Education, American Society for Public Administration, Middle East Institute, Asia Society of New York, Japan Society of New York, Executives Club of Chicago. *Awards, honors:* Order of the Golden Emblem, Republic of South Africa, 1974.

WRITINGS: (With William M. McGovern) *Radicals and Conservatives*, Regnery, 1958; (editor with Kurt Glaser) *Berlin and the Future of Eastern Europe*, Regnery, 1963; (editor with Glaser) *Western Integration and the Future of Eastern Europe*, Regnery, 1964; (editor with Glaser) *Western Policy and Eastern Europe*, Regnery, 1966; (editor with Glaser) *The Conditions for Peace in Europe*, Public Affairs Press, 1968; (editor with John Barratt, Simon Brand, and Glaser) *Accelerated Development in Southern Africa*, St. Martin's, 1974; (editor with Barratt, Brand, and Glaser) *Strategy for Development in Southern Africa*, St. Martin's, 1976. Editor, "Foreign Policy" Series, Foundation for Foreign Affairs. Publisher and associate editor, *Modern Age: A Quarterly Review*, 1957-69, publisher and editor, 1970—.

WORK IN PROGRESS: The United States and Japan, 1945-1952: An Analysis of the Occupation.

SIDELIGHTS: Collier has good command of Japanese and French, reads and speaks some German and Spanish and knows a little Italian and Arabic.

*   *   *

COLLIER, Simon   1938-

PERSONAL: Born June 6, 1938, in England; son of D. H. and M. K. (Winter) Collier. *Education:* Trinity Hall, Cambridge, B.A. (honors), 1961, M.A. and Ph.D., 1965. *Politics:* "Europeanist."

CAREER: University of Essex, Essex, England, 1965—, senior lecturer in Latin American history, and director of Latin American Centre, 1968-70, dean, School of Comparative Studies, 1971-74, chairman of history department, 1972-74. *Military service:* Royal Air Force, 1956-58; became pilot officer. *Member:* Society for Latin American Studies (United Kingdom), Conference on Latin American History (United States), Association of University Teachers.

WRITINGS: Latin America, Anthony Blond, 1967; *Ideas and Politics of Chilean Independence 1808-1833*, Cambridge University Press, 1967; *From Cortes to Castro: An Introduction to the History of Latin America 1492-1973*, Macmillan, 1974.

WORK IN PROGRESS: A monograph on the political history of Chile between 1830 and 1862.

SIDELIGHTS: Collier is fluent in Spanish and French. He has traveled in nine countries of South America, and in Mexico, United States, Canada, Europe, and the South Pacific. *Avocational interests:* Music, literature, astronomy.

*   *   *

COLLINS, David A(lmon)   1931-

PERSONAL: Born January 9, 1931, in Caribou, Me.; son of Samuel W. (a banker) and Elizabeth (Black) Collins; married Vera Edfors, June 23, 1951; children: Sheryl, David, Mark, Peter, Amy. *Education:* University of Maine, B.A., 1952; Yale University, M.A.T., 1953; Brown University, Ph.D., 1962. *Politics:* Independent Democrat. *Religion:* Unitarian Universalist. *Home:* 1616 Grand Ave., Kalamazoo, Mich. 49007.

CAREER: Denver Country Day School, Denver, Colo., French master, 1953-56; instructor in French at Brown University, Providence, R.I., 1959-60, and University of New Hampshire, Durham, 1960-63; Kalamazoo College, Kalamazoo, Mich., assistant professor 1963-68, associate professor of French, 1968—, chairman of department, 1966—. Director, W. K. Kellogg Latin American Orientation Program, 1968. Member of Fulbright national screening committee, 1975-76. *Member:* Modern Language Association of America, American Association of Teachers of French, Alliance Francaise of Kalamazoo (president and board member, 1966-68), Old Music Society, Phi Beta Kappa, Phi Kappa Phi. *Awards, honors:* Fulbright grant, 1956; Kalamazoo College faculty grant for travel and study in France, 1967.

WRITINGS: Thomas Corneille: Protean Dramatist, Mouton & Co., 1966.

*   *   *

COLLIS, Louise   1925-

PERSONAL: Born January 29, 1925, in Arakan, Burma; daughter of Maurice (an author) and Eleanor (Bourke) Collis. *Education:* University of Reading, honors degree in history, 1945. *Politics:* "Vague." *Religion:* "Unbeliever." *Home:* 65, Cornwall Gardens, London S.W.7, England.

CAREER: Writer.

WRITINGS: Without a Voice (novel), Faber, 1951; *A Year Passed* (novel), Faber, 1952; *After the Holiday* (novel), Faber, 1954; *The Angel's Name* (novel), Faber, 1955; *Seven in the Tower* (historical essay), Faber, 1958; *The Apprentice Saint* (biography), M. Joseph, 1964, published as *Memoirs of a Medieval Woman*, Crowell, 1964; *Soldier in Paradise* (biography), M. Joseph, 1965, Harcourt, 1966; *The Great Flood* (novel), Macmillan (London), 1966; *A Private View of Stanley Spencer* (biography), Heinemann, 1972; (editor) Maurice Collis, *Diaries 1949-1969*, Heinemann, 1976.

WORK IN PROGRESS: Radio plays.

SIDELIGHTS: Louise Collis lived in the Far East as a child, and has traveled in most European countries. She speaks French and Italian. *Avocational interests:* Reading books.

*   *   *

COLMAN, John E.   1923-

PERSONAL: Born March 8, 1923, in Philadelphia, Pa.; son of Joseph Aloysius (a dentist) and Loretta (Murphy) Colman. *Education:* St. Joseph's College, Philadelphia, Pa., B.A., 1943; Johns Hoskins University, M.A., 1956,

Ph.D., 1958. *Home and office:* St. John's University, Jamaica, N.Y. 11432.

CAREER: Roman Catholic priest, member of Congregation of the Mission. Immaculata College, Immaculata, Pa., instructor in mathematics, 1946-47; Niagara University, Niagara, N.Y., professor of education, 1958-61, dean of Graduate School and School of Education, 1959-61; St. John's University, Jamaica, N.Y., professor of education, 1961-63, assistant dean of School of Education, 1963-66, director of government and research grants, 1966—. Member of advisory board, State University of New York Board of Regents. *Military service:* U.S. Navy, 1942-45; received Presidential Unit Citation for service in invasion of Normandy; became lieutenant. *Member:* American Association of School Administrators, Association for Higher Education, American Educational Research Association, National Catholic Educational Association, National Education Association, National Council of University Research Administrators, American Academy of Political and Social Science, Phi Delta Kappa, Kappa Delta Pi, Delta Epsilon Sigma.

WRITINGS: The History of the Administration at St. John's, Johns Hopkins Press, 1956; *The Effect of Certain Factors on College Policy Regarding Enrollment,* Johns Hopkins Press, 1958; (editor) *Teachers and Teaching Today,* St. John's University Press, 1963; *The Master Teachers and the Art of Teaching,* Pitman, 1967. Contributor of articles on various aspects of education to journals.

WORK IN PROGRESS: Research concerning government and foundation grants; *Professionalism among Research Administrators.*

* * *

COLONIUS, Lillian   1911-

PERSONAL: Born March 19, 1911, in Irvine, Calif.; daughter of John S. (a farmer) and Annie (Brady) McDonald; married Allen B. Colonius, August 1, 1942. *Education:* Attended Santa Ana College, 1928-30; Occidental College, A.B., 1932. *Politics:* Republican. *Religion:* Protestant. *Home:* 905 East Buffalo Ave., Santa Ana, Calif. 92706.

CAREER: Elementary teacher in Santa Ana, Calif., 1934-67.

WRITINGS—Juvenile; all published by Melmont, except as indicated: *At the Harbor,* 1953, revised edition, 1954; *At the Bakery,* 1953, revised edition, 1967; *At the Airport,* 1953, revised edition, 1967; *At the Zoo,* 1953, revised edition, 1967; *At the Post Office,* 1953, revised edition, 1967; *At the Library,* 1954, revised edition, 1967; *Here Comes the Fireboat,* Elk Grove Press, 1967.

* * *

COMFORT, Richard A(llen)   1933-

PERSONAL: Born October 16, 1933, in Los Angeles, Calif.; son of Charles B. and Anne (Jaehne) Comfort; married Louise Kloos (an assistant professor of political science), August 24, 1958; children: Nathaniel Charles, Honor Louise. *Education:* University of California, Berkeley, A.B. (with honors), 1958; Princeton University, M.A., 1960, Ph.D., 1962. *Home:* 5248 Golden Gate Ave., Oakland, Calif. 94618. *Office:* History Department, Mills College, Oakland, Calif. 94613.

CAREER: Stanford University, Stanford, Calif., instructor, 1962-64, lecturer in history, 1964-65, research asso-

ciate, Institute of Political Studies, 1964; Mills College, Oakland, Calif., assistant professor, 1965-68, associate professor of European history, 1968—. *Military service:* U.S. Air Force, 1951-55; served in Korea, 1953; became staff sergeant; received Air Medal with cluster. *Member:* American Historical Association, Phi Beta Kappa. *Awards, honors:* Woodrow Wilson fellowship, 1960; Penfield travel fellowship, 1960-61; Hoover Institution research grant, 1963.

WRITINGS: Revolutionary Hamburg: Politics and Labor in the Early Years of the Weimar Republic, Stanford University Press, 1966; *Twentieth Century Europe,* Rand McNally, 1968. Contributor to *Studies on the Left, International Review of Social History, Journal of Modern History, Canadian Journal of History,* and other journals.

WORK IN PROGRESS: Research focused on the history of U.S.-German relations since World War II.

SIDELIGHTS: Comfort is competent in French, German, and Russian. *Avocational interests:* Sailing, medieval music and musical instruments.††

* * *

COMMAGER, Henry Steele   1902-

PERSONAL: Born October 25, 1902, in Pittsburgh, Pa.; son of James Williams and Anna Elizabeth (Dan) Commager; married Evan Carroll, July 3, 1928; children: Henry Steele, Nellie Thomas McColl, Elisabeth Carroll. *Education:* University of Chicago, Ph.B., 1923, M.A., 1924, Ph.D., 1928; attended University of Copenhagen, Cambridge University, M.A.; Oxford University, M.A. *Politics:* Independent Democrat. *Home:* 405 South Pleasant St., Amherst, Mass.

CAREER: New York University, New York, N.Y., instructor in history, 1926-29, assistant professor, 1929-30, associate professor, 1930-31, professor, 1931-38; Columbia University, New York, N.Y., professor of American history, 1939-56, adjunct professor, 1956-59, Speranza Lecturer, 1960; Amherst College, Amherst, Mass., Smith Professor of History, 1956-72, Simpson Lecturer, 1972—. Pitt Professor of American History, Cambridge University, 1941, 1947-48; Bacon Lecturer, Boston University, 1943; Richards Lecturer, University of Virginia, 1944; Harmsworth Professor of American History, Oxford University, 1952-53; Gottesman Lecturer, Uppsala University, 1953; Ziskind Professor, Brandeis University, 1955; Commonwealth Lecturer, University of London, 1963; Harris Lecturer, Northwestern University, 1964. Visiting professor or lecturer at Duke University, Harvard University, University of Chicago, and University of California, 1926-38, University of Copenhagen, 1956, University of Jerusalem, 1958, University of Mexico, 1965, New York University, and Massachusetts Institute of Technology, 1975; lecturer for the Department of State at universities in Germany, 1954, Israel and Italy, 1955, Trinidad, 1959, Italy, spring, 1960, Chile, 1963, Mexico, 1964, and Japan, 1975. Member of War Department Commission on History of the War; travelled to Britain for War Department, Office of War Information, summer, 1943, and to France and Belgium, 1945. *Military service:* Served with U.S. Army Information and Education Division, 1945.

MEMBER: American Academy of Arts and Letters, American Scandinavian Society (fellow), American Antiquarian Society, Massachusetts Historical Society, Phi Beta Kappa, Century Association, St. Botolph's (Boston), Athenaeum Club (London). *Awards, honors:* Herbert B.

Adams Award of the American Historical Association, 1929; Guggenheim fellowship, 1960-61; decorated Knight, Order of Dannebrog. Honorary degrees from colleges and universities include: Litt.D., Washington College (Maryland), 1958, Ohio Wesleyan University, 1958, Monmouth College, 1959, Cambridge University, 1962; D.C.L., Alfred University; Ed.D., Rhode Island College; LL.D., Brandeis University, 1960, Michigan State University, 1960, Franklin and Marshall College, 1962; L.H.D., University of Hartford, 1962, University of Puget Sound, 1963.

WRITINGS: The Literature of the Pioneer West, [Saint Paul], 1927; (with Samuel Eliot Morison) *The Growth of the American Republic,* Oxford University Press, 1931, 5th edition, 1962; *Our Nation's Development,* Harper, 1934; *Theodore Parker,* Little, Brown, 1936, reissued with a new introduction, Beacon Press, 1960; (with Eugene Campbell Barker) *Our Nation,* Row, Peterson, 1941; (with Allan Nevins) *America: The Story of a Free People,* Little, Brown, 1942, reissued in paperback as *The Pocket History of the United States,* Pocket Books, 1943, revised edition, 1956; *Majority Rule and Minority Rights,* Oxford University Press, 1943; (with Nevins) *A Short History of the United States,* Modern Library, 1945, 5th edition, 1966; *The American Mind: An Interpretation of American Thought and Character Since the 1880's,* Yale University Press, 1950; *America's Robert E. Lee* (juvenile), Houghton, 1951; (with others) *Civil Liberties Under Attack,* University of Pennsylvania Press, 1951; *Chestnut Squirrel* (juvenile), Houghton, 1952; (contributor) Courtlandt Canby, editor, *The World of History,* New American Library, 1954; (with Geoffrey Brunn) *Europe and America Since 1492,* Houghton, 1954; *Freedom, Loyalty, Dissent,* Oxford University Press, 1954; *Federal Centralization and the Press,* University of Minnesota, 1956; *The First Book of American History* (juvenile), F. Watts, 1957; *The Great Declaration* (juvenile), Bobbs-Merrill, 1958; *A Picture History of the United States of America* (juvenile), F. Watts, 1958; (contributor) *Conference on the American High School,* University of Chicago Press, 1958

The Great Proclamation (juvenile), Bobbs-Merrill, 1960; (with Robert W. McEwen and Brand Blanshard) *Education in a Free Society,* University of Pittsburgh Press, 1961; *The Great Constitution* (juvenile), Bobbs-Merrill, 1961; *Crusaders for Freedom* (juvenile), Doubleday, 1962; *The Nature and the Study of History,* C. E. Merrill, 1965; *The Role of Scholarship in an Age of Science,* Laramie, 1965; *Freedom and Order: A Commentary on the American Political Scene,* Braziller, 1966; *The Study of History,* C. E. Merrill, 1966; (with Elmo Giordonetti) *Was America a Mistake?: An Eighteenth Century Controversy,* Harper, 1967; *The Search for a Usable Past, and Other Essays in Historiography,* Knopf, 1967; (with Richard B. Morris) *Colonies in Transition,* Harper, 1968; *The Commonwealth of Learning,* Harper, 1968; *The Defeat of America,* Simon & Schuster, 1974; *Britain Through American Eyes,* McGraw, 1974; *Jefferson, Nationalism, and the Enlightment,* Braziller, 1974.

Editor: *Documents of American History* (Volume I, to 1898; Volume II, from 1865), F. S. Crofts, 1934, 8th edition, 1969; (with Allan Nevins) *The Heritage of America,* Little, Brown, 1939, revised and enlarged edition, 1949; (and author of historical narrative) *The Story of the Second World War,* Little, Brown, 1945; (and author of introduction and notes) *America in Perspective: The United States Through Foreign Eyes,* Random House, 1947, abridged edition, New American Library, 1959; Alexis de Tocque-ville, *Democracy in America,* translated by Henry Reeve, Oxford University Press, 1947; *St. Nicholas Anthology,* Random House, 1948; *Selections from "The Federalist,"* Appleton, 1949; (with others) *Years of the Modern: An American Appraisal,* Longmans, Green, 1949; *Second St. Nicholas Anthology,* Random House, 1950; *The Blue and the Gray: The Story of the Civil War as Told by Participants,* two volumes, Bobbs-Merrill, 1950; *William Dean Howells, Selected Writings,* Random House, 1950; *Living Ideas in America,* Harper, 1951; (with Richard B. Morris) *The Spirit of 'Seventy-Six: The Story of the American Revolution as Told by the Participants,* two volumes, Bobbs-Merrill, 1958; *Official Atlas of the Civil War,* Yoseloff, 1958.

Living Documents of American History, [Washington], 1960; *The Era of Reform, 1830-1860,* Van Nostrand, 1960; *Theodore Parker: An Anthology,* Beacon Press, 1960; James Bryce, *Reflections on American Institutions: Selections from "The American Commonwealth,"* Fawcett, 1961; *Immigration and American History: Essays in Honor of Theodore C. Blegen,* University of Minnesota Press, 1961; Chester Bowles, *The Conscience of a Liberal,* Harper, 1962; Winston Churchill, *History of the English-Speaking Peoples* (one volume of a four volume series), Bantam, 1963; *Noah Webster's American Spelling Book,* Teachers College Press, 1963; *The Defeat of the Confederacy: A Documentary Survey,* Van Nostrand, 1964; *Fifty Basic Civil War Documents,* Van Nostrand, 1965; (consulting editor) *Encyclopedia of American History,* Harper, 1965; *Lester Ward and the Welfare State,* Bobbs-Merrill, 1966; *The Struggle for Racial Equality: A Documentary Record,* Harper, 1967; Winston Churchill, *Marlborough: His Life and Times,* Scribner, 1968. With Richard B. Morris, editor of "New American Nation" series, forty-one volumes, published by Harper. Contributor to *Book Week, New York Times Book Review, New Republic, Saturday Review, New York Review of Books, American Scholar,* and other publications.

WORK IN PROGRESS: Editing "The Rise of the American Nation," a projected fifty-volume series.

SIDELIGHTS: Commager's first book length work, *The Growth of the American Republic,* written in collaboration with Samuel Eliot Morison, was said by Allan Nevins to be "the most entertaining, stimulating and instructive single-volume history of the United States as yet written on the plane that meets a demand for all principal facts." In 1961, *The Christian Century* found that the fifth edition of *The Growth of the American Republic* "constitutes the standard by which other inclusive American histories are to be judged." The two-volume fifth edition was extended through the Presidential election of 1960, and a final chapter was devoted to world power in the nuclear age. In 1934 Commager completed what he has suggested to be his most valuable work, *Documents of American History.* It contains over six hundred documents illustrating the course of American history from the age of discovery to the present.

BIOGRAPHICAL/CRITICAL SOURCES: Christian Science Monitor, April 6, 1936; *Saturday Review (of Literature),* April 1, 1944, January 5, 1946, January 28, 1967; *New York Herald Tribune Book Review,* May 30, 1954; *Christian Century,* October 24, 1962; *New York Times Book Review,* October 23, 1966, June 25, 1967; *New Republic,* May, 1967; *New Statesman,* June 2, 1967; Harold Hyman and Leonard Levy, editors, *Freedom and Reform: Essays in Honor of H. S. Commager* (includes a bibliography), Harper, 1967.

*   *   *

CONDON, John C(arl)   1938-

PERSONAL: Born September 5, 1938; son of John Carl (a businessman) and Esther (Simpson) Condon; married Emily Carroll Harland, December 23, 1965; children: Christina Bahati, Michael Franklyn. *Education:* Attended Mexico City College (now University of the Americas), 1956-57; Northwestern University, B.S., 1959, Ph.D., 1964, study of Swahili, 1965-66; San Francisco State College (now University), M.A., 1960. *Home:* 4-15-3 Kyonan-cho, Musashino-shi, Tokyo 180, Japan. *Office:* Communication Department, International Christian University, Mitaka, Tokyo 181, Japan.

CAREER: Northwestern University, School of Speech, Evanston, Ill., associate professor of public address and group communication, 1968-69; International Christian University, Mitaka, Tokyo, Japan, associate professor of communication, 1969—.

WRITINGS: Semantics and Communication, Macmillan, 1966, 2nd edition, 1975; *Kotoba no Sekai*, Simul Press, 1971; (editor with M. Saito) *Intercultural Encounters with Japan*, Simul Press, 1974; (with K. Kurata) *In Search of What's Japanese about Japan*, Shufunotomo Co., 1974; (with F. Yousef) *An Introduction to Intercultural Communication*, Bobbs-Merrill, 1975; *Simple Pleasures*, Shufunotomo Co., 1975. Contributor to *Journal of Modern African Studies, Today's Speech, ETC.: A Quarterly Journal of General Semantics*, and many other journals.

WORK IN PROGRESS: A textbook on interpersonal communication for Macmillan; research on cultural patterns of communication and intercultural communication; a survey of Japanese patterns of communication.

*   *   *

CONFER, Vincent   1913-

PERSONAL: Born June 12, 1913, in Greencastle, Ind.; son of Carl Vincent and Louise (Kiefer) Confer; married Elizabeth Davis, June 17, 1939. *Education:* DePauw University, A.B., 1934; University of Pennsylvania, A.M., 1935, Ph.D., 1939. *Religion:* Presbyterian. *Home:* 15 Centennial Dr., Syracuse, N.Y. 13207. *Office:* Department of History, Syracuse University, Syracuse, N.Y. 13210.

CAREER: Assistant professor of history at Hartwick College, Oneonta, N.Y., 1940-41, Moravian College, Bethlehem, Pa., 1941-43, and University of Delaware, Newark, 1943-44; Salem College, Winston-Salem, N.C., associate professor of history, 1944-46; Syracuse University, Syracuse, N.Y., assistant professor, 1946-52, associate professor, 1952-66, professor of history, 1966—. *Member:* American Historical Association, Society for French Historical Studies, French Colonial Historical Society, International Institute of Differing Civilizations (Brussels), Societe d'Histoire Moderne et Contemporaine (Paris), New York State Association of European Historians (president, 1957-58); member of executive committee, 1966-67), Phi Beta Kappa, Sigma Delta Chi, Phi Sigma Iota. *Awards, honors:* Guggenheim fellow, 1949-50.

WRITINGS: (Contributor) Daniel H. Thomas and Lynn M. Case, editors, *Guide to the Diplomatic Archives of Western Europe*, University of Pennsylvania Press, 1959; *France and Algeria: The Problem of Civil and Political Reform, 1870-1920*, Syracuse University Press, 1966. Contributor to history journals.

WORK IN PROGRESS: Studies of French colonial policies, 1870-1920.

AVOCATIONAL INTERESTS: Travel, photography.

*   *   *

CONN, Charles William   1920-

PERSONAL: Born January 20, 1920, in Atlanta, Ga.; son of Albert C. and Rosa Bell (Brimer) Conn; married Edna Louise Minor, April 7, 1941; children: Philip, Sarah (Mrs. R. Stephen Wesson), Stephen, Paul, Sharon (Mrs. Dale Cannon), Raymond, Camilla, Mark, Catherine, Bruce, Jeffrey, Melody. *Home:* 2408 Peerless Rd., Cleveland, Tenn. 37311. *Office:* Office of the President, Lee College, Cleveland, Tenn. 37311.

CAREER: Church of God, Cleveland, Tenn., Sunday school and youth director for state of Louisiana, 1940-41, ordained minister, 1946, director of Sunday school and youth literature, 1948-52, member of executive council, 1952—, editor-in-chief of church publications, 1952-62, assistant general overseer, 1962-66, general overseer, 1966-70; Lee College, Cleveland, Tenn., president, 1970—. *Awards, honors:* D.Litt., Lee College, 1962.

WRITINGS—All published by Pathway Press: *Like a Mighty Army*, 1955; *Pillars of Pentecost*, 1956; *The Evangel Reader*, 1958; *Where the Saints Have Trod*, 1959; *The Rudder and the Rock*, 1960; *The Bible: Book of Books*, 1961; *A Guide to the Pentateuch*, 1963; *Christ and the Gospels*, 1964; *Acts of the Gospels*, 1965; *A Certain Journey*, 1965; *Why Men Go Back*, 1967; *A Survey of the Epistles*, 1969; *The Pointed Pen*, 1973; *Highlights of Hebrew History*, 1975; *A Balanced Church*, 1975. Former editor, *Church of God Evangel* and *Lighted Pathway*.

SIDELIGHTS: Conn has traveled in more than seventy countries, lecturing and doing research for his writings.

*   *   *

CONNIFF, James C(lifford) G(regory)   1920-
(John Coolwater, Anthropophagus Minor)

PERSONAL: Born August 27, 1920, in New York, N.Y.; son of John Aloysius and Julia (Badaracco) Conniff; married Dorothy Eulalia Donnelly, July 3, 1943; children: Gregory, Sue, Dorothy Deborah, Cynthia, Richard, Mark, Robert Pierre. *Education:* St. Peter's College, A.B. (honors), 1942; Fordham University, graduate study, 1942-43. *Religion:* Roman Catholic. *Address:* Box 736, Upper Montclair, N.J. 07043.

CAREER: Republic Pictures, New York, N.Y., and Hollywood, Calif., public relations director (for magazines), 1943-45; St. Peter's College, Jersey City, N.J., director of prose control program, 1947—. President of MEGADOT (public relations firm); executive secretary and trustee, Cerebrovascular Disease Foundation, 1960—. Public relations consultant to Hoffmann-La Roche Pharmaceutical Co., 1960-66, and Marsalin Institute for Psychiatric Research, 1966-67. *Member:* Society of Magazine Writers, Authors Guild. *Awards, honors:* Howard W. Blakeslee Award of American Heart Foundation, 1961, for national magazine reporting on progress in stroke diagnosis and therapy; grant from World Law Fund for research in psychiatry and war.

WRITINGS: Rocky Mountain Empire, Doubleday, 1949;

Story of the Mass, Ace Books, 1953; *Bishop Sheen Story*, Fawcett, 1954; *Holy Life of Eugenio Pacelli, Pope Pius XII*, Fawcett, 1955; *Story of Easter*, Ace Books, 1955; *Good Shepherd Story*, Garrison, 1957; (with James A. Farley) *Governor Al Smith*, Farrar, Straus, 1958. Contributor of more than nine hundred articles to magazines in English-speaking countries and in about eighty foreign countries.

WORK IN PROGRESS: Man Tomorrow, molecular biological research; *The Great Gray Knout*, brain physiology; *Blueprint for an End to Madness*, psychiatry and war; *Writing for Readers*, prose control techniques for colleges.

SIDELIGHTS: Conniff considers the "ultimate wedding of Medicine (mainly psychiatry) and Religion (grown-up version, not current spookery) to be man's best hope of survival. Believe in far more intelligent life as likely occupant of extraterrestrial worlds; could hardly be less intelligent than life too often is on this one."

* * *

CONRAD, Sybil 1921-

PERSONAL: Born June 16, 1921, in New York, N.Y.; daughter of Louis and Libbie (Feldman) Winsten; married Milton Conrad (an orthodontist), May 30, 1944 (divorced, 1975); children: Jeffrey Bruce, Ronald Scott. *Education:* Attended Antioch College, 1939-40, and Columbia University, 1940-41; University of Michigan, B.A., 1943. *Politics:* Democrat. *Home:* 30 Edgewood Rd., Scarsdale, N.Y. 10583. *Agent:* Curtis Brown Ltd., 60 East 56th St., New York, N.Y. 10022.

CAREER: National Broadcasting Co., New York City, public relations writer, 1943-44; Erwin Wasy Advertising Agency, New York City, writer in radio department, 1944-45; Meyer Both Syndicate, fashion copywriter in New York City, 1945-49; producer and moderator for public affairs program, "Youth on the Watch," Radio WFAS, 1969-70; actress and lecturer. Adjunct lecturer, Pace University, 1974; conductor of communications seminar, School of New Resources, College of New Rochelle, 1975; conductor of workshops for women and corporation groups on "The Art of Communicating." Communications consultant, Associated Colleges of Mid-Hudson Area, 1973, IBM, 1974, and Ladycliff College, 1975. *Member:* Authors League of America, America Federation of Radio and Television Artists, Y.W.C.A.

WRITINGS: The Golden Summer, Holt, 1955; *Enchanted Sixteen*, Holt, 1957; *Sorority Rebel*, Holt, 1958; *Believe in Spring*, Vanguard, 1968. Writer of book and lyrics for musical comedy, "The Dream Stops Here." Contributor of articles to *Westchester* and *Nassau*.

WORK IN PROGRESS: A nonfiction book, *The Art of Communicating: Acquiring Facility in Writing and Speaking*, based on her workshops.

AVOCATIONAL INTERESTS: Travel, water sports, photography, psychology, theatre, and related media.

* * *

CONSTANTELOS, Demetrios J. 1927-
(Dimitris Stachys)

PERSONAL: Born July 27, 1927, in Spilia, Messenia, Greece; became U.S. citizen in 1958; son of John B. (a farmer) and Christine (Psilopoulos) Constantelos; married Stella Croussouloudis, August 15, 1954; children: Christine, John, Helen, Maria. *Education:* Holy Cross Greek

Orthodox Theological School, Diploma in Theology, 1951, B.A. in Th., 1958; Princeton Theological Seminary, Th.M., 1959; Rutgers University, M.A., 1963, Ph.D., 1965. *Home:* 304 Forest Dr., Linwood, N.J. 08221. *Office:* Arts and Humanities, Stockton State College, Pomona, N.J. 08240.

CAREER: St. Demetrios Greek Orthodox Church, Perth Amboy, N.J., pastor, 1955-64; Dumbarton Oaks Research Library, Washington, D.C., junior fellow, 1964-65; Holy Cross Greek Orthodox Theological School, Brookline, Mass., assistant professor, 1965-67, associate professor of history, 1967-71; Stockton State College, Pomona, N.J., professor of history and religious studies, 1971—. Visiting lecturer in history, Boston College, 1967-68. Representative of Greek Orthodox Archdiocese of North and South America at national and international congresses. *Member:* American Historical Association, American Society of Church History, Mediaeval Academy of America, American Academy of Religion, Orthodox Theological Society of America (president, 1968-71), U.S. National Committee for Byzantine Studies.

WRITINGS: An Old Faith for Modern Man, Greek Orthodox Archdiocese (New York), 1964; *The Greek Orthodox Church: History, Faith and Practice*, Seabury, 1967; *Byzantine Philanthropy and Social Welfare*, Rutgers University Press, 1968; *Marriage, Sexuality, and Celibacy: A Greek Orthodox Perspective*, Light & Life Press, 1975; (editor) *Encyclicals and Documents of the Greek Orthodox Archdiocese*, Institute for Patristic Studies, 1975. Contributor of more than thirty studies, essays, articles, and reviews to theological and historical journals, and about fifty articles and reviews of a more popular nature to *Orthodox Observer, Detroit Greek Tribune, National Herald, Christian Herald*, and Greek publications, some under pseudonym Dimitris Stachys.

WORK IN PROGRESS: Poverty and Philanthropy in the Late Medieval Greek World.

* * *

CONWAY, Thomas D(aniel) 1934-

PERSONAL: Born June 15, 1934, in Medford, Mass.; son of John M. (director of a vocational high school) and Helen F. (Hurley) Conway. *Education:* Attended Boston College, 1952-53, and Cardinal O'Connell Seminary, Boston, Mass., 1953-54; St. John's Seminary, Brighton, Mass., B.A., 1956, M.A. in Ed., 1960, M.Div., 1973; Emmanuel College, M.A.R.E., 1970. *Home:* 67 Atlantic Rd., Gloucester, Mass. 01930.

CAREER: Roman Catholic priest. Assistant pastor in Marlboro, Mass., 1960-69; St. John Parish, Haverhill, Mass., assistant pastor, 1969-73; Archdiocese of Boston, Office of Religious Education, assistant director, 1973—. Conductor of teacher training workshops and institutes on religious education.

WRITINGS: (With Eileen E. Anderson) *Forming Catechists*, Sadlier, 1966; (with Frank Martino) *Handbook of Creative Activities*, Sadlier, 1972; *Journey into the Spirit*, Sadlier, 1975.

* * *

COOGAN, Daniel 1915-

PERSONAL: Born July 14, 1915, in Philadelphia, Pa.; son of Daniel Francis (a stockbroker) and Harriet Elizabeth (Reeve) Coogan; married Inge Bruns (a librarian), June 7, 1941; children: Michael, Mrs. Michael F. Horan, Margaret

McCarthy, Mrs. H. Mark Lueke, James, Anne. *Education:* Haverford College, A.B., 1936; University of Wisconsin, M.A., 1937, Ph.D., 1941. *Politics:* Democrat. *Religion:* Catholic. *Residence:* Shelter Island Heights, N.Y. 11965. *Office:* Southampton College, Southampton, N.Y.

CAREER: Haverford School, Haverford, Pa., teacher of German, 1937-38; Ripon College, Ripon, Wis., instructor, 1941-43, associate professor of German, 1943-46; Brooklyn College of the City University of New York, Brooklyn, N.Y., assistant professor, 1947-57, associate professor, 1957-66, professor of German and classics, 1966-67, deputy chairman of department of modern languages, 1960-67; York College of the City University of New York, Jamaica, N.Y., professor of languages, 1967-74, dean of humanities, 1967-70; Southampton College, Southampton, N.Y., adjunct professor of humanities, 1975—. Visiting associate professor, Haverford College, 1946-47. Secretary, Lynbrook Citizens Advisory Committee on Public Schools, 1966; member of executive board, Long Island Association of Laymen. *Member:* Modern Language Association of America, Catholic Interracial Council of New York, Phi Beta Kappa. *Awards, honors:* Award for excellence in teaching, Brooklyn College of the City University of New York, 1964, York College of the City University of New York, 1973.

WRITINGS—Textbooks: (With M. E. Valk) *Nachkriegserzaehlungen,* Whittier Books, 1952; (with W. R. Gaede) *Stimmen der Zeit,* Holt, 1957, 2nd edition, 1963; (with E. P. Kurz) *Auswahl Deutscher Essays,* Appleton, 1966.

Translator from the German: F. W. Foerster, *Christ and the Human Life,* Philosophical Library, 1953; Parsch, *The Church's Year of Grace,* Liturgical Press, 1953; Pieper, *Temperance and Fortitude,* Pantheon, 1954, Dirks, *The Monk and the World,* McKay, 1954; Hermann, *Experience of Faith,* Kenedy, 1966; Goethe, *Hermann and Dorothea* (in English hexameters), Ungar, 1966. Contributor of over ninety articles and reviews to periodicals, including *Catholic World, America, Monatshefte,* and *Long Island Catholic.* Consulting editor and contributor, *Lyrica Germanica.*

*   *   *

COOK, George Allan   1916-

PERSONAL: Born June 14, 1916, in Unionville, Mo.; son of Ed Robert (a blacksmith) and Adda (Burnhardt) Cook. *Education:* University of Missouri, A.B. and B.S. in Ed., 1938, M.A., 1939; Columbia University, Ph.D., 1951. *Politics:* Republican. *Religion:* Episcopalian. *Home:* 1201 South 11th St., Kingsville, Tex. 78363. *Office:* Box 2228, Texas A & I University, Kingsville, Tex. 78363.

CAREER: Wentworth Military Academy, Lexington, Mo., instructor in English, 1939-41; lecturer at Polytechnic Institute of Brooklyn, Brooklyn, N.Y., 1947, and Columbia University, New York, N.Y., 1947-48; Wagner Lutheran College, Staten Island, N.Y., assistant professor of English and American literature, 1950-56; East Carolina University, Greenville, N.C., 1956-64, started as assistant professor, professor of English and American literature, 1961-64; American University, Cairo Egypt, associate professor of English and American literature, 1964-66; Texas A & I University, Kingsville, professor of American literature, 1966—. Fulbright senior lecturer and professor of American literature, University of the Saar, Saarbrucken, West Germany, 1958-60. *Military service:* U.S. Army, Infantry, 1941-46; became captain; received Purple Heart and Bronze Star with two oak-leaf clusters, for Leyte and Oki-

nawa campaigns. *Member:* Modern Language Association of America, National Council of Teachers of English, South Central Modern Language Association, Phi Beta Kappa.

WRITINGS: John Wise, Early American Democrat, King's Crown Press, 1952; (author of introduction) John Wise, *The Churches Quarrel Espoused,* Scholars' Facsimiles, 1966. Contributor of articles, reviews, and poems to professional journals.

AVOCATIONAL INTERESTS: Bird-watching, gardening, duplicate bridge, choir work.

*   *   *

COOK, Melva Janice   1919-

PERSONAL: Born August 1, 1919, in Texas; daughter of Ancel and Irene (Frazier) Cook. *Education:* North Texas State University, B.S., 1940; additional study at Southwestern Baptist Theological Seminary. *Home:* 2308 Woodmont Blvd., Nashville, Tenn. 37215. *Office:* 127 Ninth Ave. N., Nashville, Tenn. 37203.

CAREER: Baptist Convention of Texas, director of children's work, 1950-54; First Baptist Church, Muskogee, Okla., director of children's work, 1954-56; Baptist Sunday School Board, Nashville, Tenn., editorial coordinator.

WRITINGS: I Know God Loves Me, Broadman, 1960; *Christmas at Kyle's House,* Broadman, 1964; *The Thinking Book,* Broadman, 1966; (with A. V. Washburn) *Administering the Bible Teaching Program of a Church,* Convention Press, 1969. Also author of *Bible Teaching for Fours and Fives,* published by Convention Press. Editor, "Beginner Lesson Courses," Baptist Sunday School Board, 1957-64.

*   *   *

COOK, Myra B.   1933-

PERSONAL: Born September 12, 1933, in Atlanta, Ga.; daughter of James Randolph (a manufacturers representative) and Myra (Boynton) Brown; married Donald M. Cook (an officer, U.S. Army), September 3, 1961; children: Elizabeth Jean, Donald Michael, Daniel Lewis, Roger Randolph. *Education:* Attended Rollins College, 1951-53; University of Florida, B.A., 1955; Cornell University, M.Ed., 1957. *Politics:* Democrat. *Religion:* Episcopalian. *Address:* P.O. Box 346, Ponte Vedra Beach, Fla. 32082.

CAREER: Elementary teacher in Ponte Vedra, Fla., 1957-59, Hohenfels, Germany, 1959-61, Fort Sill, Okla., 1962, and Fort Chaffee, Ark., 1963; Dixie Precision Manufacturing Co., Jacksonville Beach, Fla., vice-president and advertising manager, 1961—. Resource consultant and teacher aide, Mt. Clemens (Mich.) Schools, 1972-76.

WRITINGS: (With Joseph H. Caldwell and Lina J. Christiansen) *The Come-Alive Classroom,* Parker Publishing, 1967; *Chalk Dust* (poems), Dorrance, 1969; *Dynamic Teaching in the Elementary School,* Parker Publishing, 1970; (with Ann B. Piechowiak) *Complete Guide to the Elementary Learning Center,* Parker Publishing, in press.

WORK IN PROGRESS: Innovative Techniques in the Audio-Visual Learning Center, with Michael Pattison; *Career Education Learning Centers,* with Ann Piechowiak.

SIDELIGHTS: Myra Cook traveled through Europe every summer, 1958-61. Each December for more than a decade she has issued a book, running around ninety pages, of cartoons that she creates and reproduces for distribution to friends.

COOK, Richard I(rving) 1927-

PERSONAL: Born August 3, 1927, in St. Louis, Mo.; son of Marcus (a chemical engineer) and Rachel (Atlas) Cook; married Margaret Scruggs, November 25, 1955; children: Helen Rachel. *Education:* Washington University, St. Louis, Mo., B.A., 1950, M.A., 1953; graduate study at Sorbonne, University of Paris, 1954-55; University of California, Berkeley, Ph.D., 1960. *Home:* 218 Rellim Dr., Kent, Ohio 44240. *Office:* English Department, Kent State University, Kent, Ohio 44240.

CAREER: Rutgers University, New Brunswick, N.J., instructor in English, 1960-62; University of Washington, Seattle, assistant professor, 1962-65, associate professor of English, 1965-67; Kent State University, Kent, Ohio, professor of English, 1967—. *Military service:* U.S. Navy, 1945-46. *Member:* Modern Language Association of America, Philological Association of the Pacific Coast.

WRITINGS: Jonathan Swift as a Tory Pamphleteer, University of Washington Press, 1967; *Bernard Mandeville,* Twayne, 1974. Contributor of about fifteen articles and reviews to journals.

WORK IN PROGRESS: Sir Samuel Garth: A Critical Biography.

SIDELIGHTS: In his review of *Johathan Swift as a Tory Pamphleteer,* James J. Stathis writes: "This study—throughout—is objective and judicious. Professor Cook deserves more than a little credit for his urbane and lucid style, for his unpedantic treatment of the subject, and particularly for ignoring any temptation to white-wash, excuse, or tame Swift." Stathis states that "of particular interest to some will be the chapter concerning Swift's polemical characters. To my knowledge, it constitutes the first attempt to discuss, in a systematic and detailed fashion, the various devices Swift uses in the portrayal of character."

BIOGRAPHICAL/CRITICAL SOURCES: Georgia Review, Spring, 1969.

* * *

COOLEY, Richard A(llen) 1925-

PERSONAL: Born June 15, 1925, in Raton, N.M.; son of Harlie E. and Imogene (Dorman) Cooley; married Alice Sigismund, September 6, 1952; children: Brigham John, Matthew Sigismund. *Education:* Texas Technological College (now Texas Tech University), student, 1947-49; University of New Mexico, A.B., 1951; University of Chicago, M.A., 1955; University of Michigan, Ph.D., 1962. *Religion:* None. *Home:* 1335 Branciforte Ave., Santa Cruz, Calif. *Office:* Board of Environmental Studies, University of California, Santa Cruz, Calif.

CAREER: Alaska Resource Development Board, Juneau, research economist, 1952-55; Conservation Foundation, New York, N.Y., assistant director of research, 1958-59; Alaska Natural Resources Research Center, Juneau, director, 1959-65; University of Washington, Seattle, associate professor of geography, 1965-70; University of California, Santa Cruz, professor of environmental studies and chairman of department, 1970—. Part-time research professor of economics, University of Alaska, 1962-65. Consultant to State of Alaska and to Federal resource agencies in Alaska; member of Joint Federal-State Land Use Planning Commission for Alaska, 1972—; member of Marine MAMMAC Commission (presidential appointment), 1974—. *Military service:* U.S. Navy, 1943-46. *Member:* Various technical societies in political science, economics,

and geography; Phi Kappa Phi, Pi Sigma Alpha. *Awards, honors:* Research grants from Conservation Foundation, 1959—; Western Political Science Association Award for *Politics and Conservation,* 1963.

WRITINGS: An Economic Study of Haines, Alaska, Alaska Resource Development Board, 1953; *Fairbanks, Alaska: A Study of Progress,* Alaska Resource Development Board, 1954; (with George W. Rogers) *Alaska's Population and Economy: Regional Growth, Development and Future Outlook,* two volumes, University of Alaska Press, 1962; *Population and Economy of the Haines Region, Alaska,* Alaska Housing Authority, 1963; *Politics and Conservation,* Harper, 1963; *Land Policy and the Future of Alaska,* Conservation Foundation, 1964; *Alaska: A Challenge in Conservation,* University of Wisconsin Press, 1966, revised edition, 1967; (editor with Geoffrey Wandesforde-Smith) *Congress and the Environment,* University of Washington Press, 1970.

WORK IN PROGRESS: Conservation in the Arctic: A Case Study in Problems of International Cooperation.

* * *

COOPER, John C(harles) 1933-

PERSONAL: Born April 3, 1933, in Charleston, S.C.; son of Chauncey Miller (in U.S. Navy) and Margarete Anna (Gerard) Cooper; married Ann Johnston, June 6, 1954; children: Martin Christopher, Catherine Marie, Cynthia Ann, Paul Conrad. *Education:* University of South Carolina, B.A. (cum laude), 1955; Lutheran Theological Southern Seminary, B.D. (cum laude), 1958; Lutheran School of Foreign Mission, certificate, 1959; Chicago Lutheran Theological Seminary, S.T.M., 1960; University of Chicago, M.A., 1964, Ph.D., 1966. *Home:* 3337 Ridgeview Dr., Findlay, Ohio 45840. *Office:* Winebrenner Theological Seminary, Findlay, Ohio.

CAREER: Ordained minister of The Lutheran Church in America, 1958; Thiel College, Greenville, Pa., lecturer in English and Bible, 1959-60; pastor in Tampa, Fla., 1960-61; Newberry College, Newberry, S.C., assistant professor of Bible and philosophy, 1961-63, associate professor, 1965-66, professor of philosophy, 1968, head of department, 1966-68; Eastern Kentucky University, Richmond, professor of philosophy and chairman of department, 1968-71; Winebrenner Theological Seminary, Findlay, Ohio, professor of systematic theology and dean of academic affairs, 1971—. Member of Commission on Youth Activities, The Lutheran Church in America, 1967-72. Supply pastor, St. John's Lutheran Church, McComb, Ohio. *Military service:* U.S. Marine Corps, 1950-52; served in Korea and Japan; became sergeant; received Presidential Unit Citation. *Member:* American Academy of Religion, American Philosophical Association, Phi Beta Kappa.

WRITINGS: The Roots of the Radical Theology, Westminster Press, 1967; (editor with Charles Sauer) *Wine in Separate Cups,* Commission on Youth Activities, Lutheran Church, 1967; *The Christian and Politics,* pupil's books and teacher's book, Lutheran Church Press, 1968; *Radical Christianity and Its Sources,* Westminster Press, 1968; *The New Mentality,* Westminster Press, 1969; *The Turn Right,* Westminster Press, 1970; (with Carl Skrade) *Celluloid and Symbols,* Fortress, 1970; *Religion in the Age of Aquarius,* Westminster Press, 1971; *Paul for Today,* Lutheran Church Press, 1971; *A New Kind of Man,* Westminster Press, 1972; *Getting It Together,* Lutheran Church Press, 1972; *The Recovery of America,* Westminster Press, 1973; *Reli-*

gion After Forty, Pilgrim Press, 1973; *Finding A Simpler Life,* Pilgrim Press, 1974; *Fantasy and the Humane Spirit,* Seabury, 1975; *Faith, Fear and Hope in Middle Life,* Word, Inc., 1976. Contributor of poetry, reviews, and more than two hundred articles to religious and secular journals and newspapers.

SIDELIGHTS: John Cooper reads French, German, Spanish, and Italian; he has knowledge of classical Greek and biblical languages.

*   *   *

COOPER, John L.   1936-

PERSONAL: Born March 19, 1936, in Philadelphia, Pa.; son of Allen Albertus (a laborer) and Mabel (Scriven) Cooper; married Estelle Boockoff, October 26, 1966; children: Melanie Joyce, Armin Ari. *Education:* Temple University, B.S., 1964; New School for Social Research, M.A., 1970, Ph.D., 1974. *Home:* 788 Columbus Ave., Apt. 6E, New York, N.Y. 10025.

CAREER: Free Library of Philadelphia, Philadelphia, Pa., library assistant, 1961-65; New York University, New York City, researcher, 1965-67; City of New York, human resources administration specialist, beginning 1967; John Jay College of Criminal Justice of the City University of New York, New York City, assistant professor of Black studies and sociology, 1974—, chairman of Black studies department, 1975—. *Military service:* U.S. Army, 1956-59.

WRITINGS: Opus One, Maelstrom Press, 1966; *Unreality of This Reality,* R. Rajeshwari Publications (India), 1972. Contributor of essays to *Sarika, Avesh, Alochna, Tathastha* (all India), and *Buenos Aires Herald;* contributor of a short story to *Kahankar.*

WORK IN PROGRESS: Fantasy Vs. Reality, a study of the illusion that is the modern social reality and the importance of dreams; *Hospitals: The Modern Medieval Estates,* a study of the medieval character of the modern hospital system.

SIDELIGHTS: Cooper credits his brother, composer Allen King Cooper, with being the inspirational force behind his writing. *Avocational interests:* Travel.

*   *   *

COOPER, John M(iller)   1912-

PERSONAL: Born February 6, 1912, in Smith Mills, Ky.; married Charlianna Wilson, August 30, 1940; children: Carolyn M., John M., Jr., Joanna. *Education:* University of Missouri, A.B., 1934, M.A., 1937, Ed.D., 1946; Columbia University, graduate study. *Home:* 2431 Barbara Ave., Bloomington, Ind. 47401. *Office:* School of Health, Physical Education, and Recreation, Indiana University, Bloomington, Ind. 47401.

CAREER: University of Missouri, Columbia, instructor in physical education, 1940-42; University of Southern California, Los Angeles, member of physical education staff, 1945-66; Indiana University, School of Health, Physical Education, and Recreation, Bloomington, associate dean and director of graduate studies, 1966—. Producer of more than two hundred films on human motion. *Military service:* U.S. Army Air Forces, 1942-45; became captain. *Member:* American Association for Health, Physical Education and Recreation (president of research council, 1961-62), American Academy of Physical Education, College of Sports Medicine, National Education Association, Indiana Association for Health, Physical Education and Recreation,

Sigma Xi, Phi Delta Kappa, Phi Epsilon Kappa, Kiwanis Club. *Awards, honors:* National Honor Award for work in kinesiology, American Association for Health, Physical Education and Recreation.

WRITINGS: (Editor) *The Physical Education Curriculum,* 6th edition, College Book Co. (Los Angeles), 1955, 8th edition, 1975; (with Mortensen) *Track and Field for the Coach and Athlete* (textbook), Prentice-Hall, 1959, 2nd edition, 1970; (with Ruth Glassow) *Kinesiology* (textbook), Mosby, 1963, revised edition, 1976; (with Wakefield and Harkins) *Track and Field Fundamentals for Girls and Women,* Mosby, 1966, revised edition, 1976; *Beginning Track and Field,* Wadsworth, 1969; (with D. Siedentop) *Theory and Science of Basketball,* Lee & Febiger, 1969; (editor) *Biomechanics,* Athletic Institute, 1972. Author of pamphlets and articles.

WORK IN PROGRESS: Cinematographic research, such as light tracing.

*   *   *

COOPER, Mario   1905-

PERSONAL: Born November 26, 1905, in Mexico City, Mexico; son of U.S. citizens, Luis Rodrigo and Maria (a physician; maiden name, Garfias) Cooper; married Aileen Whetstine, February 26, 1927 (divorced April, 1964); married G. Dale Meyers (an artist), October 10, 1964; children: (first marriage) Vincent, Patricia. *Education:* Attended schools in Mexico until parents returned to United States when he was ten; studied art at Otis Art Institute, Los Angeles, 1924, Chouinard Art Institute, Los Angeles, 1925, and Grand Central School of Art, New York, 1927-37; also studied at Columbia University. *Home and studio:* 1 West 67th St., New York, N.Y. 10023.

CAREER: Illustrator, painter, sculptor, and teacher of art. Staff artist with advertising agencies in Dallas, Tex., 1925, San Francisco, Calif., 1926, and Batten, Barton, Durstine & Osborn, New York City, 1927-28; art director at Lord & Thomas, New York City, 1929-31; instructor in illustration and advertising art in New York City, at Columbia University, 1937-41, Grand Central School of Art, 1941-44, veterans class in illustration, Society of Illustrators, 1945-50, Art Students' League of New York, 1945—, Pratt Institute, 1950-55, National Academy of Design, 1959—, and City College of the City University of New York, 1961—. Freelance Illustrator for Shell Oil Co., U.S. Steel, General Electric Co., and other industrial clients; also illustrator for magazines, including *Woman's Home Companion, Cosmopolitan, Good Housekeeping, True,* and *American.* Watercolors are in the collection of the Metropolitan Museum of Art, New York, and other museums, and both watercolors and sculpture have been exhibited by Pennsylvania Academy of Fine Art, Metropolitan Museum, Brooklyn Museum, California Watercolor Society, and in other shows in United States, Tokyo, Kyoto, Mexico City, and London; has had numerous one-man shows; worked on commissions for U.S. Air Force in Far East, 1954, Korea, Formosa, and Alaska, 1956, and Europe, 1960.

MEMBER: National Academy of Design (academician), Society of Illustrators (life member; secretary, 1949), American Watercolor Society (president 1959—), Allied Artists of America, National Sculpture Society (fellow), Audubon Artists (honorary member; president, 1954-58), Royal Society of Arts (London), National Society of Painters in Casein (director), Texas Watercolor Society, Salmagundi Club (honorary member). *Awards, honors:*

Friedrichs Prize for watercolor, Allied Artists of America, 1956; first prize for watercolor, National Academy of Design, 1956; Samuel B. Morse Medal, National Academy of Design, 1967; numerous other awards for watercolors, including nine awards in the American Watercolor Society annuals, and several awards for sculpture.

WRITINGS: Flower Painting in Watercolor, Van Nostrand, 1962; *Drawing and Painting the City,* Van Nostrand, 1967; *Painting with Watercolor,* Van Nostrand, 1971.

Illustrator: Henry C. Pitz, *The Brandywine Tradition,* Houghton, 1969; Walt Reed, *Harold von Schmidt Draws and Paints the Old West,* Northland Press, 1972. Also illustrator of stories by Eric Maria Remarque, Conrad Bercovici, Agatha Christie, Quentin Reynolds, Clarence Budington Kelland, and other writers.

* * *

COOPERSMITH, Stanley 1926-

PERSONAL: Born July 15, 1926, in New York, N.Y.; son of David and Clara (Felix) Coopersmith; married Alice Mae Levine, February 6, 1955; children: Mark, Erik, Karen. *Education:* Yeshiva University, B.A., 1946; Brandeis University, M.A., 1955; Cornell University, Ph.D., 1957. *Politics:* Democrat. *Religion:* Jewish. *Home:* 1311 Brewster Ct., El Cerrito, Calif. 94530. *Office:* University of California, Davis, Calif. 95616.

CAREER: Wesleyan University, Middletown, Conn., assistant professor of psychology, 1957-63; University of California, Davis, associate professor of psychology, 1963—, chairman of department, 1963-66. Director of Self Esteem Institute, 1975. Member of Board of Education, Cromwell, Conn., 1960-62. *Member:* American Psychological Association, Society for Research in Child Development, Western Psychological Association, Sigma Xi. *Awards, honors:* Social Science Research Council fellow, 1961-62; National Science Foundation fellow, 1965-66.

WRITINGS: (Editor) *Personality Research,* Munksgaard, 1962; (editor) *Frontiers of Psychological Research,* W. H. Freeman, 1966; *Antecedents of Self-Esteem,* W. H. Freeman, 1967; (editor) *The Formative Years,* Albion, 1974; *The Myth of the Generation Gap,* Albion, 1975; *Developing Motivation in Children,* Albion, 1975.

WORK IN PROGRESS: A general introduction to psychology; research in procedures for changing self-esteem and developing personality.

AVOCATIONAL INTERESTS: Art, politics.

* * *

COPEL, Sidney L(eroy) 1930-

PERSONAL: Born August 29, 1930, in Philadelphia, Pa.; son of Manuel and Anna (Snyder) Copel; married Joan Danzig, December 28, 1954; children: Valerie, Kenneth. *Education:* Temple University, B.A., 1951, M.Ed., 1953, Ed.D., 1958. *Religion:* Jewish. *Home:* 615 East Manoa Rd., Havertown, Pa. 19083. *Office:* Youth Psychotherapy Center, Bryn Mawr Hospital, Bryn Mawr, Pa.

CAREER: Camden (N.J.) public schools, psychologist, 1953-56; Devereux Foundation, Devon, Pa., 1956-58, began as assistant director of clinical psychology, administrator of psychological clinic, 1966-68, consulting psychologist, 1968—; Jefferson Medical College, Hospital School of Nursing, Philadelphia, Pa., instructor in psychology and sociology, 1964—; Bryn Mawr Hospital, Youth Psycho-

therapy Center, Bryn Mawr, Pa., chief psychologist, 1968—. Consulting psychologist, Chester (Pa.) public schools, 1967—. *Member:* American Psychological Association, Society for Projective Techniques and Rorschach Institute (fellow), American Association for the Advancement of Science, Eastern Psychological Association, Pennsylvania Psychological Association (fellow), Philadelphia Society of Clinical Psychologists.

WRITINGS: Psychodiagnostic Study of Children and Adolescents, C. C Thomas, 1967; (editor) *Behavior Pathology of Children and Adolescents,* Basic Books, 1973.

AVOCATIONAL INTERESTS: Do-it-yourself home projects and target shooting.

* * *

COPLIN, William D(avid) 1939-

PERSONAL: Surname rhymes with "*rope*-in"; born September 22, 1939, in Baltimore, Md.; son of Isidor (a salesman) and Dubbie (Lebowitz) Coplin; married Merry Roseman, September 2, 1963; children: Deborah, Laura. *Education:* Johns Hopkins University, B.A., 1960; American University, M.A., 1962, Ph.D., 1964; University of Michigan, post-doctoral study, 1968-69. *Office:* Syracuse University, Syracuse, N.Y. 13210.

CAREER: Instructor in political science at Howard University and American University, both Washington, D.C., 1962-64; Wayne State University, Detroit, Mich., assistant professor, 1964-67, associate professor of political science, 1967-69; Syracuse University, Syracuse, N.Y., associate professor, 1969-72, professor of political science, 1972—, director of International Relations Program, 1970-75, director of Public Affairs Program, 1975—. Consultant to Industrial College of the Armed Forces, 1967-69, National War College and Consolidated Analysis Centers, Inc., both 1971, Department of State, External Research Bureau, 1972, *New York Times* Educational Division for College Utilization, 1975—, and Presidential Commission to Study the Organization of the Government for the Conduct of Foreign Policy, 1975-76; lecturer, Foreign Service Institute, 1973-75. Member of executive committee of Consortium for International Studies Education, 1972—.

MEMBER: American Political Science Association (chairman of International Relations Panels, 1974), American Society of International Law (member of executive council, 1975-77), International Studies Association (chairman of Education Commission, 1971-75), Social Science Education Consortium. *Awards, honors:* National Science Foundation faculty fellowship, 1968-69.

WRITINGS: The Functions of International Law, Rand McNally, 1966; (editor) *Simulation in the Study of Politics,* Markham, 1968; (editor with Charles W. Kegley, Jr.) *A Multi-Method Introduction to International Politics: Readings in Observation, Explanation, and Prescription,* Markham, 1971; *Introduction to International Politics: A Theoretical Overview,* Markham, 1971, 2nd edition, 1974; (with Michael K. O'Leary) *Everyman's PRINCE: A Guide to Understanding Political Problems,* Duxbury, 1972, 2nd edition, 1976; (with others) *A Description of the PRINCE Model,* Learning Resources in International Relations, 1974; (with others) *American Foreign Policy,* Duxbury, 1974; (with O'Leary, and Stephen L. Mills) *Participant's Guide to PRINCE: Concepts, Environments, Procedures,* Learning Resources in International Relations, 1974; (with O'Leary) *Quantitative Techniques in Foreign Policy Forecasting and Analysis,* Praeger, 1975; (with O'Leary, and

Robert F. Rich) *Towards an Improvement of Foreign Service Reporting*, U.S. Government Printing Office, 1975; (with Kegley) *The Analysis of International Politics: A Multi-Method Introduction*, Praeger, 1975; *An Introduction to the Analysis of Public Policy Issues from a Problem-Solving Perspective*, Learning Resources in International Studies, 1975; (with Mills and O'Leary) *PRINCE-DOWN Student Manual: A Gaming Approach to the Study of Policy Issues*, Learning Resources in International Studies, 1975.

Contributor: Richard A. Falk, and Wolfram F. Hanrieder, editors, *International Law and Organization*, Lippincott, 1968; Michael Barkun, and Robert W. Gregg, editors, *The United Nations System*, Van Nostrand, 1968; Abdul A. Said, editor, *Theory of International Relations: The Crisis of Relevance*, Prentice-Hall, 1968; James N. Rosenau, editor, *International Politics and Foreign Policy: A Reader in Research and Theory*, revised edition, Free Press, 1969; Gregg and Charles W. Kegley, editors, *After Vietnam: The Future of American Foreign Policy*, Doubleday, 1971.

Writer of exercises for "American Government Simulation Series," and teaching materials for *Learning Packages in International Relations*. Author of *Student Manual*, and editor of *Test Item Catalogue* of Mentorex for American Politics, a testing-tutorial system, for Cognitive Systems, Inc. Contributor to *Political Science Annual*, Volume II, and *Proceedings of the National Gaming Council*, both 1969, and *Sage International Yearbook of Foreign Policy Studies*, 1974; articles and reviews have appeared in political science journals. Member of editorial board, *Simulation and Games*, 1971—, and *Teaching Political Science*, 1973—.

WORK IN PROGRESS: Designing all-computer simulations to study foreign policy at the comparative level.

* * *

CORCORAN, Barbara 1911-
(Paige Dixon, Gail Hamilton)

PERSONAL: Born April 12, 1911, in Hamilton, Mass.; daughter of John Gilbert (a physician) and Anna (Tuck) Corcoran. *Education:* Wellesley College, B.A., 1933; University of Montana, M.A., 1955. *Politics:* Democrat. *Religion:* Episcopalian. *Home:* 1875 Kalanianaole, Hilo, Hawaii 96720. *Agent:* McIntosh & Otis, Inc., 18 East 41st St., New York, N.Y. 10017.

CAREER: Celebrity Service, Hollywood, Calif., researcher, 1945-53; Station KGVO, Missoula, Mont., copywriter, 1953-54; University of Kentucky, Covington, instructor in English, 1956-57; Columbia Broadcasting System, Hollywood, Calif., researcher, 1957-59; Marlboro School, Los Angeles, Calif., teacher of English, 1959-60; University of Colorado, Boulder, instructor in English, 1960-65; Palomar College, San Marcos, Calif., instructor in English, 1965-69. *Member:* Authors League of America, California Teachers Association. *Awards, honors:* Samuel French Award for original play, 1955; *The Long Journey* was named a Child Study Association children's book of the year, 1970; William Allen White Children's Book Award, 1972, for *Sasha, My Friend;* Pacific Northwest Book Sellers' Award, and National Science Teachers' Award, both 1975.

WRITINGS—For young people; all published by Atheneum, except as noted: *Sam*, 1967; (with Jeanne Dixon and Bradford Angier) *The Ghost of Spirit River*, 1968; *Sasha, My Friend*, 1969; *A Row of Tigers*, 1969; *The Long Jour-*

ney, 1970; (with Angier) *A Star to the North* (Junior Literary Guild Selection), Thomas Nelson, 1970; *The Lifestyle of Robie Tuckerman*, Thomas Nelson, 1971; *This is a Recording*, 1971; *A Trick of Light* (Junior Literary Guild Selection), 1972; *Don't Slam the Door when You Go*, 1972; *All the Summer Voices*, 1973; *The Winds of Time*, 1974; *A Dance to Still Music*, 1974; *Meet Me at Tamerlane's Tomb*, 1975; *The Clown*, 1975; *Axe-Time, Sword-Time*, 1976.

Under pseudonym Paige Dixon: *Lion on the Mountain*, 1972; *Silver Wolf*, 1973; *The Young Grizzly*, 1974; *Promises to Keep*, 1974; *May I Cross Your Golden River*, 1975; *Cabin in the Sky*, 1976; *Summer of the White Goat*, 1976; *The Search for Charlie*, 1976; *Pimm's Cup for Everybody*, 1976.

Under pseudonym Gail Hamilton: *Titania's Lodestone*, 1975; *A Candle to the Devil*, 1975.

Contributor of short stories to *Woman's Day*, short stories and a novel to *Redbook*, and a novel to *American Girl*.

WORK IN PROGRESS: Other books for young people.

BIOGRAPHICAL/CRITICAL SOURCES: Book World, October 22, 1967; *Young Reader's Review*, November, 1967.

* * *

CORCOS, Lucille 1908-

PERSONAL: Born September 21, 1908, in New York, N.Y.; daughter of Joseph and Amelia (Abrams) Corcos; married Edgar Levy (an artist, writer, and teacher), May 7, 1928; children: David C., Joel C. *Education:* Art Students League, New York, N.Y., student, 1927-31. *Home:* 167 South Mountain Rd., New City, N.Y. 10956. *Agent:* McIntosh & Otis, Inc., 475 Fifth Ave., New York, N.Y. 10017.

CAREER: Artist and illustrator, with work including paintings, murals, full-page color reproductions for *Life, Vogue, Fortune*, and other national magazines, and book illustrations. Has had one-woman shows in New York; paintings exhibited at museums throughout United States, in Europe, and South America; represented in permanent collections of Whitney Museum of American Art, Museum of Tel Aviv, and in corporate and private collections; murals include "Kaleidoscope" for Waldorf Astoria Hotel, 1945. *Member:* Artists Equity Association (director, New York chapter, 1964-66), Audubon Artists. *Awards, honors:* Honorable mention award, first Portrait of America Show, 1944; Grumbacher purchase award, Audubon Artists, 1956.

WRITINGS—All self-illustrated: *Joel Gets a Haircut*, Abelard, 1952; *Joel Spends His Money*, Abelard, 1954; *Joel Gets A Dog*, Abelard, 1958; *From Ungskah to Oyaylee: A Counting Book for all Little Indians*, Pantheon, 1965; *The City Book*, Golden Press, 1972.

Illustrator: *Treasury of Gilbert and Sullivan* (Book-of-the-Month Club selection), Simon & Schuster, 1941; *Chicikov's Journey*, Limited Editions Club, 1944; *A Treasury of Laughter*, 1946; *The Adventures of a Brownie*, Grosset, 1948; *Follow the Sunset*, Doubleday, 1952; *Women Today*, 1953; *The Picture of Dorian Gray*, Limited Editions Club, 1958; *Songs of the Gilded Age* (Book-of-the-Month Club selection), 1960; *Grimm's Fairy Tales*, four-volume edition, Limited Editions Club, 1962.

BIOGRAPHICAL/CRITICAL SOURCES: Life, July 12, 1954.†

CORD, Steven Benson 1928-

PERSONAL: Born July 22, 1928, in New York, N.Y.; son of Mandel E. and Bertha Cord; married Edith Mayer (a professor of French and German), February 21, 1954; children: Emily, Louise. *Education:* City College (now City College of the City University of New York), B.A., 1948; Columbia University, M.A., 1955, Ed.D., 1962. *Home:* 580 North Sixth St., Indiana, Pa. 15701.

CAREER: High school teacher of history in Yonkers, N.Y., 1956-62; Indiana University of Pennsylvania, Indiana, associate professor, 1962-64, professor of history, 1964—. *Military service:* National Guard, 1948-51. *Awards, honors:* Two foundation grants for research in urban renewal, 1967.

WRITINGS: Henry George: Dreamer or Realist?, University of Pennsylvania Press, 1965. Currently editor, *Incentive Taxation.*

WORK IN PROGRESS: Research on the moral basis of history and the social sciences.

SIDELIGHTS: Cord told *CA:* "I regard ethical relativism as being a basic error in current approaches to history and the social sciences, as well as the chief underminer of both our individual and national life. Consequently, I am currently attempting to find an absolute ethical standard as susceptible to proof as any facts or laws are. I am attempting to reconcile the reigning logical positivism with an absolute ethical standard, a difficult but not impossible and certainly necessary task."

*   *   *

CORMIER, Frank 1927-

PERSONAL: Born August 21, 1927, in Worcester, Mass.; son of E. Edmund (an auto dealer) and Catherine (Markley) Cormier; married Margot Anne Bumiller, October 11, 1952; children: Elizabeth, Anne (deceased), John, William, Michael. *Education:* Northwestern University, B.S., 1950, M.S., 1952. *Residence:* Fairfax, Va. *Agent:* Michael S. Hamilburg, 292 South LaCienega Blvd., Beverly Hills, Calif. 90211. *Office:* Associated Press, 2021 K St. N.W., Washington, D.C. 20006.

CAREER: Associated Press, reporter in Chicago, Ill., 1951-54, and Washington, D.C., 1954-62, White House correspondent, 1962—. *Military service:* U.S. Army, 1946-47. *Member:* White House Correspondents Association (president, 1967-68), Sigma Delta Chi, Gridiron Club of Washington. *Awards, honors:* Page One Award in college division, Chicago Newspaper Guild, 1949; Northwestern University Alumni Award of Merit, 1975.

WRITINGS: Wall Street's Shady Side, Public Affairs Press, 1962; *Presidents Are People Too,* Public Affairs Press, 1966; (with William J. Eaton) *Reuther,* Prentice-Hall, 1970; (contributor) Charles A. Grumich, editor, *Reporting/Writing from Front Row Seats,* Simon & Schuster, 1971; (contributor) Richard Wilson, editor, *The President's Trip to China,* Bantam, 1972.

WORK IN PROGRESS: A personal memoir of Lyndon B. Johnson for Doubleday.

SIDELIGHTS: According to Frank Porter, the Cormier and Eaton biography, *Reuther,* "may well stand as the authoritative text on Reuther for labor students as well as a worthwhile experience for laymen with only an incidental interest in the labor movement."

CORNER, Philip 1933-

PERSONAL: Born April 10, 1933, in Bronx, N.Y. *Education:* City College (now City College of the City University of New York), New York, N.Y., B.A., 1955; Paris Conservatory, music studies, 1955-57; Columbia University, M.A., 1959. *Residence:* New York, N.Y.

CAREER: Composer. Works include: "Frozen Motion," "Evolving Extremities," "Concert," and "Flairs," all for ensembles; "Oracle, a War Cantata," an electronic composition; and other instrumental pieces. Active in Fluxus movement, 1962-63, and peace and civil rights movements, especially in Mississippi, 1963—. *Military service:* U.S. Army, 1959-61; served in Korea.

WRITINGS: The Four Suits (musical compositions), Something Else, 1965; *Popular Entertainments,* Something Else, 1967.

WORK IN PROGRESS: Starting from the Keyboard and Not Necessarily Stopping There, a book on piano technique and musical philosophy.†

*   *   *

CORRADI, Gemma 1939-

PERSONAL: Born January 15, 1939, in Rome, Italy; daughter of Cosimo (a geologist) and Maria (Pizzo) Corradi. *Education:* Barnard College, B.A., 1960; University of Rome, Ph.D., 1963. *Home:* Via Fratelli Bandiera, 24-26, Rome, Italy 00152.

CAREER: University of Rome, Rome, Italy, lecturer in philosophy, 1963—.

WRITINGS: Philosophy and Coexistence, Sijthoff, 1966. Free-lance writer for television.

WORK IN PROGRESS: A book on ideologies.††

*   *   *

CORTAZAR, Julio 1914-
(Julio Denis)

PERSONAL: Born August 26, 1914, in Brussels, Belgium; son of Julio Jose and Maria Herminia (Descotte) Cortazar; married Aurora Bernardez, August 23, 1953. *Education:* Received literature degree from the teachers college, Buenos Aires, 1935. *Home:* Saignon par Apt, Vaucluse, France.

CAREER: Grew up in Argentina; taught in secondary schools in several small towns and in Mendoza, Argentina, 1935-45; translator for editorial houses, 1945-51; left in 1951 because he was opposed to the dictatorship of Juan Peron; returns to Argentina periodically, but has lived in Paris since 1951, where he works four months out of each year for UNESCO as a free-lance translator of French and English into Spanish. Has been an amateur jazz trumpeter. Member of jury, Casa de las Americas Award.

WRITINGS: (Under pseudonym Julio Denis) *Presencia* (poems), [Buenos Aires], 1938; *Los reyes* (play), Gulab y Aldabahor (Buenos Aires), 1949; *Bestiario* (stories), Editorial Sudamericana, 1951; *Final del juego* (stories), Los Presentes (Mexico), 1956, translation by Paul Blackburn published as *End of the Game, and Other Stories* (includes selections from *Bestiario* and *Las armas secretas*), Pantheon, 1967, published as *Blow-Up, and Other Stories,* Collier, 1968; *Las armas secretas* (stories), Editorial Sudamericana, 1959.

Los premios (novel), Editorial Sudamericana, 1960, translation by Elaine Kerrigan published as *The Winners*, Pantheon, 1965; *Historias de cronopios y de famas*, Ediciones Minotauro (Buenos Aires), 1962, translation by Blackburn published as *Cronopios and Famas*, Pantheon, 1969; *Rayuela* (novel), Editorial Sudamericana, 1963, translation by Gregory Rabassa published as *Hopscotch*, Pantheon, 1966; *Cuentos* (stories), Casa de las Americas (Havana), 1964; *Todos los fuegos el fuego* (stories), Editorial Sudamericana, 1966, translation by Suzanne Jill Levine published as *All Fires the Fire, and Other Stories*, Pantheon, 1973; *La vuelta al dia en ochenta mundos*, Siglo Veintiuno Editores (Mexico), 1967; *El perseguidor, y otros cuentos*, Centro Editor de America Latina (Buenos Aires), 1967; *62: Modelo para armar* (novel), Editorial Sudamericana, 1968, translation by Rabassa published as *62: A Model Kit*, Pantheon, 1972; *Ceremonias* (includes selections from *Final del juego*, and *Las armas secretas*), Seix Barral (Barcelona), 1968; (with others) *Cuba por argentinos*, Editorial Merlin (Buenos Aires), 1968; *Buenos Aires, Buenos Aires* (edition includes French and English translations), Editorial Sudamericana, 1968; *Ultimo round*, Siglo Veintiuno Editores, 1969.

Relatos (includes *Bestiario, Las armas secretas*, and *Todos los fuegos el fuego*), Editorial Sudamericana, 1970; *Viaje alrededor de una mesa*, Editorial Rayuela (Buenos Aires), 1970; (with Oscar Collazos and Mario Vargas Llosa) *Literatura en la revolucion y recolucion en la literature*, Siglo Vientiuno Editores, 1970; *La isla a mediodia y otros relatos*, Salvat, 1971; *Pameos y meopas*, Editorial Llibres de Sinera (Barcelona), 1971; (with Antonio Galvez) *Prosa del observatorio*, Lumen (Barcelona), 1972; *Libro de Manual*, Editorial Sudamericana, 1973; (contributor) Julio Ortega, compiler, *Convergencias, divergencias, incidencias* (anthology), Tusquets (Barcelona), 1973; *La casilla de los Morelli*, edited by Julio Ortega, Tusquets, 1973; *Octaedro*, Editorial Sudamericana, 1974.

Translator: Edgar Allan Poe, *Obras en prosa*, Ediciones de la Universidad de Puerto Rico (Madrid), 1956; Poe, *Cuentos*, Alianza Editorial, 1970. Has also translated the works of Andre Gide, Walter de la Mare, G. K. Chesterton, Daniel Defoe, and Jean Giono, published in Argentina between 1948 and 1951.

SIDELIGHTS: Cortazar, who has been called Latin America's first great novelist, and whose novel, *Hopscotch*, has been called the continent's first great novel, has received even greater praise as a writer of short stories; there is, at least, less display of critical irritation when his stories are reviewed. Both as novelist and short story writer, however, Cortazar is an experimenter, playing with language, form, and place, with the absurd, with correspondences between reality and illusion, with contradictions within the imaginary world itself, and with existential situations. Daniel Stern asserts that, "at this point in the development of a freer form for prose writing, Cortazar is indispensable.... If one reads [as Stern does] 'straight books' with suspicion, and is still unconvinced by the self-indulgent extravagances of many of the 'advanced writers,' ... one turns, it seems, to ... Julio Cortazar. When Cortazar's most successful novel, *Hopscotch*, was published here ..., I read it with great pleasure ... and boredom ... and irritation! Here was a man whose writing flashed with wit, superb imagery, and who obviously was possessed of—and by—a fantastic imagination. But what of the endless self-indulgences? The tricks and games played not with or for—but on the reader."

"In [*The End of the Game*]," Stern continues, "the shorter form allows no time for the merely tricky. Yet what magnificent tricks Cortazar *does* play. A woman dreams about a beggar woman on a bridge in Budapest (a city foreign to her). Then she arrives in Budapest and finds the beggar woman on the same bridge. They embrace—and in horror the woman stands rooted while watching herself leave.... This playing with time ... is characteristic. But it is only one of Cortazar's techniques for breaking down reality, mixing it with various illusions, and scrambling them to make a brand new reality—or is it a brand new illusion?" But, as a *Times Literary Supplement* reviewer notes, Cortazar manipulates the absurd and the mysterious "with sufficient skill to make the contrived seem impressively natural."

"In reading such experimental work," says Stern, "there is the temptation to overdo the concentration on influences. In the case of Cortazar it is interesting and valid to consider them. While a number of European influences are clearly indicated, it is two compatriot authors who strike this reader as most important to Cortazar's growth: the classic Machado de Assis and, most significantly, the great modernist Jorge Luis Borges.... Like Borges, [Cortazar] often combines elements of the essay with the fictional elements of his stories.... He shares with Borges, also, a pervading sense of the mysteriousness of natural objects and banal daily life. Cortazar writes with all the ambiguity, irony and attention to objects common to [certain other current novelists].... The difference is that Cortazar, in [his] stories, knows precisely when to stop. Brevity, in the land of advanced writing, attains to a kind of morality." There is present "the compelling sense that what has been left out is playing an important part in the final work of art."

This sense of significant brevity is, of course, most prevalent in the short stories. Many are masterful representations of the surreal, metaphysical, horror-filled world which prevail upon Cortazar's imagination. The *Times Literary Supplement* reports that Cortazar "started as a writer of slightly Kafkaesque, slightly Borgesian short stories, most of them, on his own admission, the description of dreams in which an ordinary situation slipped almost imperceptibly into fantasy." He has admitted that a great deal of his writing originates in his dreams, "real dreams, dreams in sleep. When I don't know where my writing is going, I stop. Then I dream and the ending comes." Perhaps this explains why, in Cortazar's stories, narrative switches and suspensions of time, space, and identity, "just happen," as Robert Sale says. In one story for example, "a man has an embarrassing habit of vomiting rabbits; in another a man becomes the murder victim in the detective story he is reading; in a third a man meets a transmogrified self." Guy Davenport adds that Cortazar's stories "are strangely asymmetrical, lacking a beginning or an end. As with ... Borges, the conundrum is the essence, and the writer is not the explainer but the discoverer of the conundrum.... If Cortazar were not a poet, [his] puzzles would seem gratuitous and a bit cheap; but he is a poet and can manage the weather, the odd slant of light, the unfamiliar pace that make these stories so readable." Of his *Presencia*, Marta Morello-Frosch wrote: "The earlier volume of poems is a collection of sonnets... which anticipate many of his constant and recurrent themes: The preoccupation with the unreal in the presence of the real, the longing for the ultimate harmony of the self with the universe, a determined search for the absolute to be achieved against the demands of logic or reason and glimpses of such an absolute in special moments: in children, in ritualistic games, in music.''

His stories ''pivot on children's games, the camera's eye, labyrinths, mirrors,'' says Alexander Colemen. It is the world ''of what Cortazar calls 'the figures.' In an interview he said 'apart from our individual lots, we all inadvertently form part of larger figures. For instance, we at this moment may be a part of a structure that prolongs itself at a distance of perhaps 200 meters from here. I'm constantly sensing the possibility of certain links, of circuits that close around us.' Cortazar's short stories are full of juxtapositions and flukes: *deja vu* is everywhere.'' Morello-Frosch perceives these ''links'' in *Las armas secretas* where ''Cortazar reveals a marked predilection for what could be called participatory experience, in which the self, at times reluctantly, participates with, or in, other selves' experiences.'' The *Times Literary Supplement* adds that, like Borges, Cortazar ''is often concerned with the point at which an ordinary situation slips without explanation into mystery, falling into the grip of elusive metaphysical forces....'' He plays games continually, but at the same time he ''displays throughout his stories the ability to elevate them above the condition of those gimmicky tales which depend for effect solely on a twist ending,'' writes Donald A. Yates. ''His genius here lies in the knack for constructing striking, artistically 'right' subordinate circumstances out of which his fantastic and metaphysical whimsies appear normally to spring.'' *Cronopios and Famas*, Melvin Maddocks has noted, is a ''miscellaneous collection of fables, fantasia, and general whimsy [which] spells out Cortazar's credo of absurdity, his theology of the metaphysical joke.'' Neil Millar suggests that ''the very young accept the world's mystery.... To us older children the world is no less mysterious, and if we forget that fact our mornings come stale and too easy upon us ... our perceptions drowse behind their dusty windows. Cortazar stings them alert again ... he engulfs us in his dreams of Earth.''

The stories ''work'' as *Hopscotch* does not, says Stern. This ''anti-novel'' begins with a preface by Cortazar which gives the reader a choice between two possible ways of reading the book. The first 56 chapters are to be read in order, then the reader is to begin, this time leaping about (according to Cortazar's instructions) on a course that would involve, said one reviewer, ''reading 56 chapters twice and one chapter four times—all told, 900 pages.'' (Or, the reader may simply read the first 56 chapters in order and stop.) Cortazar explained this back-and-forth construction thus: ''I was trying to break the habits of readers—not just for the sake of breaking them, but to make the reader free. The characters were searching for a new road in life—a new reason for the world. There is something wrong in Western civilization today: it has missed its route. But the way to find a new route is not to go back into history. The new route is to be found in the soul—in the heart—in the depths of each man. We should abandon much of our culture, our judgments, our civilization in seeking the new route. I wrote *Hopscotch* as I did to enable the reader to grow very angry and independent and to hurl my book out the window if he chose.'' Martin Shuttleworth calls this novel ''a baggy monster,'' but adds: ''the beauty of the book is in the hymns to the baby who dies; in the hymns to places, to moments, to life. The strength of the book is in all that, baggy and tortuous though the narrative 'line' is....'' Yates considers *Hopscotch* ''a long, difficult but undeniably masterful work, the product of a writer whose intellectual grasp of the essence of the novelistic genre is so thorough that he is compelled to play (in the creative sense)

with its elements and to elaborate on its traditional form.'' As the *Times Literary Supplement* reviewer notes, Cortazar here ''sees human beings not as characters in a conventional sequence (his characterization is deliberately superficial) but as constellations in a vast structure outside time. His characters are involved in a sort of ritual dance, the more meaningless the dance, the more pleasing the patterns.... Unfortunately Senor Cortazar is not content merely to present some sort of abstracted aesthetic pattern, but is constantly straining for meanings which this pattern [cannot adequately] embody. The game of hopscotch not only symbolizes the abstract dance of human beings. The hopper's arrival at the last square or 'heaven' is called upon to symbolize some sort of mystical truth, an ultimate meaning beyond the false superstructure of society. The game of hopscotch is in fact a highly unsatisfactory mandala.'' The same reviewer concludes that if the novel had been left at its ''rather dotty, basically humorous level, it would be far better than it is,'' or at least less pretentious.

The Argentinian critics, according to Cortazar, searched for allegory in *The Winners*. Cortazar, however, ''intended the novel primarily as an exercise in style. I wanted to prove to myself that I could handle 18 characters at the same time. Of course, its various conflicts do have a universal appeal, and that is why the book was so well received in France in 1961. You see, I'm not a modest person.'' This novel bears an epigraph from Dostoevsky which tells of the difficulty of dealing with ordinary people in fiction. Capouya notes that, fortunately, Cortazar ''understands that ordinary people partake of the miraculous.'' Capouya adds: ''Cortazar's talent as revealed in *The Winners,* is chiefly comic and lyrical, and if the lyricism is widely exuberant, the comedy is in the solid tradition of Latin social realism. All in all, [it is] an absorbing novel that sometimes stumbles into portentousness—what with rape, near-rape, murder, and, above all, metaphysics—but a pleasure or a pleasurable irritant throughout.'' Orville Prescott, who called the novel merely tiresome, was unable to see through, as William Goyen did, to the beauty of the monologues. ''It is in these passages of the novel,'' says Goyen, ''brooding and beautiful and passionate, that Mr. Cortazar shows himself to be a dazzling writer. He creates a language and rhythm and sensuality as mysterious and terrible as Melville's but all in his own voice.'' Morello-Frosch believes *The Winners* ''is a novel without climax or denouement in the real sense, except for what the characters reveal or learn about themselves ... an eventful interior voyage in the psychological realms.'' *The Winners,* R. D. Spector believes, ''might well have come from a Parisian pen. Its allusions to jazz and American fiction strike a curiously Gallic note. Its ridicule of bourgeois comforts and values echoes the tones of Sartre and Simone de Beauvoir. But particularly in its central concern—the problem of existentialist anguish—[the] novel most closely resembles contemporary French literature.... Cortazar's own strength derives from his ability to create a Kafka-like suspense, fraught with the frustrations of his interestingly juxtaposed characters.... Cortazar has weaknesses. He protests too much the microcosmic significance of his ship and its passengers. He [sometimes] strikes too didactic a posture.... Nevertheless, he possesses a good narrative sense that finally gives fictional realism to this sometimes too philosophical meandering.''

Aside from the influences of Borges, Kafka, and the existentialists, critics have found parallels in Huxley and Italo Svevo. Cortazar's predilections, however, are for Fielding,

Smollett, Sterne, and Stendhal. *Time* notes that, "however much Cortazar may remind readers of Poe, Maupassant, and Camus, his . . . style and gothic viewpoint make him a unique storyteller. He can induce the kind of chilling unease that strikes like a sound in the night. What is it—a burglar, beast or spectral thing? If it occurs in a Cortazar story, it is likely to be something nameless and decidedly lethal." This spirit, and the language used to convey it, Cortazar believes, are very Argentinian, contrary to what others may speculate. "They forget," he says, "that we are Europeans too—descendants of the Spanish, the Italians, the French. . . . Of all the Latin-American countries, the Argentine is the one most influenced by Europe."

Cortazar told one interviewer: "Good writing, I think, must tap the subconscious. Writing is imagination, culture, metier, but, above all it is something you cannot explain. When I write a short story, even I do not know when I begin what the ending will be. My stories are often fantastic . . . ." He contrasted novels and stories: "A novel," he said, "is like a chain of mountains. It can go on and on. A short story must be neat, complete, closed. Everything in it must be perfect, and that is why it is the more difficult of the two to write. Novel writing, as far as I am concerned, is a craft. It is something one can learn to do, but one must be born a short-story writer." A short story is also a more spontaneous form, he asserts. It is "like a poem; it falls upon you. Both the writer and the reader must be plunged into it from the fifth line if it is any good." Cortazar's stories, for the most part, fulfill this requirement. As the *New Yorker* notes, Cortazar "takes full advantage of the power of the short story for immediate and violent effects." When Cortazar is not writing of traveling he says he is "unwriting—a dreary trade because one hurts the Narcissus inside."

Antonioni's film, "Blow-Up," was loosely based on Cortazar's story with the same title.

BIOGRAPHICAL/CRITICAL SOURCES: New York Times Book Review, March 21, 1965, July 9, 1967; *New York Times,* March 22, 1965; *Saturday Review,* March 27, 1965, April 29, 1966, July 22, 1967; *Book Week,* April 4, 1965; *New Yorker,* May 8, 1965, February 17, 1968; *New Republic,* April 23, 1966, July 15, 1967; *Time,* April 29, 1966, August 11, 1967; *Times Literary Supplement,* February 9, 1967, March 9, 1967; *Punch,* March, 1967; *Observer Review,* March 5, 1967; *Best Sellers,* July 15, 1967; *National Review,* July 25, 1967; *Christian Science Monitor,* August 15, 1967; *Nation,* September 18, 1967; *Hudson Review,* winter, 1967-68; *Books Abroad,* winter. 1968; Carolyn Riley, editor, *Contemporary Literary Criticism,* Gale, Volume II, 1974, Volume III, 1975, Volume V, 1976.

*   *   *

COSTA, Richard Hauer   1921-

PERSONAL: Born July 5, 1921, in Philadelphia, Pa.; son of Leonard A. (an insurance agent) and Marie (Hauer) Costa; married Marie Jo Basilio (a news correspondent), June 10, 1950; children: Philip. *Education:* West Chester State College, B.S., 1943; Syracuse University, M.A., 1950; Purdue University, Ph.D., 1968. *Politics:* Independent. *Religion:* Protestant. *Home:* 1119 Neal Pickett Dr., College Station, Tex. 77840. *Office:* South Central Modern Language Association Headquarters, Texas A&M University, College Station, Tex. 77843.

CAREER: Syracuse Post-Standard, Syracuse, N.Y., reporter, 1947-49; *Utica Observer-Dispatch,* Inc., Utica,

N.Y., editor, columnist, and reporter, 1951-61; Syracuse University, Utica College, Utica, N.Y., assoiate professor of English, 1961-70; Texas A&M University, College Station, Tex., professor of English, 1970—. Executive secretary, South Central Modern Language Association, 1975—. *Military service:* U.S. Army, Infantry, 1942-46; served in European theater; became sergeant; received Bronze Star. U.S. Army Reserves; now captain (retired). *Member:* Modern Language Association of America, American Association of University Professors, College English Association, South Central Modern Language Association, Sigma Delta Chi.

WRITINGS: H. G. Wells, Twayne, 1967. *Malcolm Lowry,* Twayne, 1972. Contributor to *Nation, University of Toronto Quarterly, Journal of Modern Literature,* and *Modern Language Quarterly.* Book reviewer for *Modern Fiction Studies, Western Humanities Review.* Editor and publisher, *Quartet Magazine,* 1968—.

WORK IN PROGRESS: The Seignorial Stance: Conversations with Edmund Wilson, 1962-72, completion expected in 1976.

*   *   *

COUGHLAN, John W.   1927-

PERSONAL: Born 1927, in Canada; married Betty J. Boyd, November 12, 1954; children: Victoria Ruth, Brian Walker, John Anthony. *Education:* University of Alberta, B.A., 1948, B.Com., 1949; University of Western Ontario, M.A., 1951; Johns Hopkins University, Ph.D., 1955. *Office:* 1601 Connecticut Ave., N.W., Washington, D.C. 20009.

CAREER: Worked for Interprovincial Pipeline Corp., 1949-50, the Canadian Army at various times, Brown University, 1951-52, and Olin Mathieson Chemical Corp., 1952-54; certified public accountant in Maryland and District of Columbia, and practicing public accountant in District of Columbia, 1955—; George Washington University, Washington, D.C., professor of accounting, 1963-67, chairman of department, 1963-66; Loyola College, Baltimore, Md., professor of accounting, 1968—. *Member:* American Institute of Certified Public Accountants, National Association of Accountants, American Association of University Professors (national treasurer, 1967-71), Toastmasters 888, Junior Chamber of Commerce of Washington, D.C., Alpha Kappa Psi.

WRITINGS: What the Businessman Should Know about Public Utilities, Public Affairs Press, 1958; *Return on Capital,* National Association of Accountants, 1959; *Techniques in Inventory Management,* National Association of Accountants, 1964; *Guide to Contemporary Theory of Accounts,* Prentice-Hall, 1965; *Accounting Manual for Radio Stations,* National Association of Broadcasters, 1975. Contributor to *Reinhold Encyclopedia of Management;* contributor of articles, reviews, and fiction to periodicals.

*   *   *

COUGHRAN, Larry C.   1925-
(Larry Craig)

PERSONAL: Surname is pronounced *Ko-ran;* born October 19, 1925, in Berkeley, Calif.; son of Lyle (an industrial engineer) and Lois (Springmeyer) Coughran; married Rose Hittner, 1952; children: Annette, Loretta, Sharon. *Education:* Woodbury College, B.A., 1952; San

Fernando Valley State College, law courses, beginning 1963.

CAREER: Private investigator. *Military service:* U.S. Army, Paratroops, 1944-46.

WRITINGS—With Gene LeBell: *Your Handbook of Judo,* Thomas Nelson, 1962; *Your Personal Handbook of Self Defense,* Thomas Nelson, 1964. Writer of television scripts.††

* * *

COULSON, Robert S. 1928-
(Thomas Stratton, Roberta Black, joint pseudonyms)

PERSONAL: Surname is pronounced *Col*-son; born May 12, 1928, in Sullivan, Ind.; son of Springer (a house painter) and Mary (Stratton) Coulson; married Juanita Wellons (a writer and artist), August, 1954; children: Bruce. *Education:* International Correspondence Schools, completed course in electrical engineering, 1960. *Politics:* "Political liberal, economic conservative." *Religion:* Agnostic. *Home:* Route 3, Hartford City, Ind. 47348.

CAREER: Heckman Bindery (bookbinding), North Manchester, Ind., factory hand, 1947-57; Honeywell, Inc., Wabash, Ind., draftsman, 1957-59, technical writer, 1959-65; Overhead Door Co., Hartford City, Ind., lead draftsman, 1965. *Member:* Science Fiction Writers of America (secretary, 1972-74). *Awards, honors:* Joint winner, with wife, Juanita Wellon Coulson, of Hugo Award at 1965 World Science Fiction Convention, for editing and publishing best amateur science fiction magazine, *Yandro.*

WRITINGS—With Gene DeWeese: *Gates of the Universe,* Laser Books, 1975; *Now You See Him/It/Them . . . ,* Doubleday, 1975. Author, with DeWeese, of short stories published in *Amazing Stories* and *Fantasy and Science Fiction.*

With DeWeese under joint pseudonym Thomas Stratton: *The Invisibility Affair,* Ace Books, 1967; *The Mind-Twisters Affair,* Ace Books, 1967; (contributor) L. Sprague DeCamp and George Scithers, *The Conan Grimoire: Essays in Swordplay and Sorcery,* Mirage Press, 1972.

Editor and publisher with wife, Juanita W. Coulson, of monthly magazine, *Yandro,* 1953—; editor of *SFWA Forum,* 1971-72.

WORK IN PROGRESS: "Soy la Libertad," a short story to be included in anthology *Beyond Time,* edited by Sandra Ley, for Pocket Books; two novels, *To Renew the Ages,* for Harlequin Books and *The Art of Terror,* with Sandra Miesel under pseudonym Roberta Black.

* * *

COVEY, Cyclone 1922-

PERSONAL: First syllable of surname rhymes with "dove"; born May 21, 1922, in Guthrie, Okla; son of Cyclone Davis (an oil fields wildcatter) and Lola (a teacher; maiden name, Best) Covey; married Bonnie Hansen, June 12, 1949; children: Christopher, Nicholas, Julie Kristiana, Jonathan, Timothy. *Education:* Stanford University, B.A., 1944, Ph.D., 1949; also studied at University of Chicago, 1944-45, University of Oklahoma, 1945-46, and Harvard University, 1953-54. *Politics:* Democrat. *Religion:* "Biblical ecumenical Christian." *Residence:* Winston-Salem, N.C. *Office:* Department of History, Wake Forest University, Winston-Salem, N.C.

CAREER: Reed College, Portland, Ore., instructor in history and humanities, 1947-50; Oklahoma Agricultural and Mechanical College (now Oklahoma State University), Stillwater, instructor, 1950-51, assistant professor, 1957-65, professor of music and humanities, 1965-68, part-time research in history, 1958-68; McKendree College, Lebanon, Ill., professor of history, government, and foreign languages, 1951-56; Amherst College, Amherst, Mass., Carnegie visiting assistant professor of American studies, 1956-57; conducted research in United Kingdom and Ireland, 1967; Wake Forest University, Winston-Salem, N.C., professor of history, 1968—, director of Wake Forest in Venice, 1972. Conducted research and taught in Turkey, Greece, Crete, and Egypt, 1972-73, 1975-76. *Awards, honors:* Fund for the Advancement of Education (Ford Foundation), postdoctoral fellowship to Harvard University, 1953-54; Oklahoma State University Research Foundation grants for Colonial research, 1958-68; Danforth Foundation associate, 1962—.

WRITINGS: The Wow Boys: The Story of Stanford's Historic 1940 Football Season Game by Game, Exposition Press, 1957; *The American Pilgrimage,* Oklahoma State University, 1960, published as *The American Pilgrimage: The Roots of American History, Religion and Culture,* Collier. 1962; (translator and editor) Cabeza de Vaca *Adventures in the Unknown Interior of America,* Collier, 1961; *A Cyclical Return to the Timeless Three-Clock Revolution,* Oklahoma State University, 1966; *The Gentle Radical: A Biography of Roger Williams,* Macmillan, 1966; *Calalus: A Roman Jewish Colony in America from the Time of Charlemagne through Alfred the Great,* Vantage, 1975.

Contributor of chapters on music: Max Savelle, *Seeds of Liberty,* Knopf, 1948; Anatole Mazour, *Russia Past and Present,* Van Nostrand, 1951; Anatole Mazour, *Russia: Tsarist and Communist,* Van Nostrand, 1962. Contributor to *Encyclopedia of Morals,* Philosophical Library, 1956, and to journals.

WORK IN PROGRESS: Elizabeth and America, books on 14th and 15th century music, and on the preclassic Aegean and Near East.

SIDELIGHTS: Covey told *CA:* "Vocations and avocations are indistinguishable. . . . [I] worry over teaching an understanding of tradition and of creative self-maturation." In addition to teaching he is interested in wide-angle photography of ruins, classical music composition, criticism, and study.

* * *

COWAN, Michael H(eath) 1937-

PERSONAL: Born July 26, 1937, in Kansas City, Mo.; son of Heath Hal (a land agent) and Lewellyn (Bolen) Cowan; married Ann Curtis Ewbank, August 10, 1963; children: David Andrew, Susanna Martin. *Education:* Yale University, B.A., 1959; Ph.D., 1964; St. Catharine's College, Cambridge, graduate study, 1962-63. *Home:* 1040 Western Dr., Santa Cruz, Calif. 95060. *Office:* 119 Merrill College, University of California, Santa Cruz, Calif. 95064.

CAREER: Yale University, New Haven, Conn., instructor in English, 1963-66, dean of Branford College, 1964-66, assistant professor of English and American studies, 1966-69; University of California, Santa Cruz, associate professor of community studies and literature, 1969-73, professor of literature, 1973—. *Member:* Modern Language Association of America, American Studies Association, Phi Beta Kappa.

WRITINGS: City of the West: Emerson, America, and Urban Metaphor, Yale University Press, 1967; (editor) *The Sound and the Fury: A Collection of Critical Essays,* Prentice-Hall, 1968.

WORK IN PROGRESS: Research on environmental metaphors in American literature; and research on the city in literature and on the history of attitudes toward urban civilization.

BIOGRAPHICAL/CRITICAL SOURCES: Yale Review, spring, 1968; *Virginia Quarterly Review,* spring, 1968.

*   *   *

COWAN, Peter (Walkinshaw) 1914-

PERSONAL: Born November 4, 1914, in Perth, Western Australia; son of Norman Walkinshaw and Marie (Johnson) Cowan; married Edith Howard, June 18, 1941; children: Julian Walkinshaw. *Education:* University of Western Australia, B.A., 1941, Diploma in Education, 1946. *Home:* 149 Alfred Rd., Mount Claremont, Western Australia. *Office:* English Department, University of Western Australia, Nedlands, Western Australia.

CAREER: Clerk, farm laborer, and casual worker in Australia, 1930-39, and teacher, 1941-42; University of Western Australia, Nedlands, part-time teacher, 1946-50; Scotch College, Swanbourne, Western Australia, senior English master, 1950-62; University of Western Australia, senior tutor in English, 1964—. *Military service:* Royal Australian Air Force, 1943-45. *Member:* Australian Society of Authors. *Awards, honors:* Commonwealth literary fellowship, 1963, to write *Seed;* Australian Council for the Arts fellowship, 1975.

WRITINGS: Drift (short stories), Reed & Harris, 1944; *The Unploughed Land* (short stories), Angus & Robertson, 1958; *Summer* (novel), Angus & Robertson, 1964; (editor) *Short Story Landscape* (anthology), Longmans, Green, 1964; *The Empty Street* (short stories), Angus & Robertson, 1965; *Seed* (novel), Angus & Robertson, 1966.

(Editor with Bruce Bennett) *Spectrum One: Narrative Short Stories,* Longman, 1970; (editor with Bennett) *Spectrum Two: Modern Short Stories,* Longman, 1970; (editor) *Today* (short stories), Longman, 1971; (contributor) *This is Australia,* Hamlyn, 1975. Short stories anthologized in various collections including *The Tins and Other Stories,* University of Queensland Press, 1973. Contributor to *Meanjin Quarterly.*

WORK IN PROGRESS: Short stories and a biography; articles on the environment.

AVOCATIONAL INTERESTS: Nature and wild life conservation, particularly in Australia.

BIOGRAPHICAL/CRITICAL SOURCES: Meanjin Quarterly, number 2, 1960, number 2, 1966; Evan Jones, editor, *Commonwealth Literary Fund Lectures,* Australian National University Press, 1961; Dorothy Hewett, editor, *Sandgropers,* University of Western Australia Press, 1973; *Westerly,* number 3, 1973; John Barnes, *An Australian Selection,* Angus & Robertson, 1974.

*   *   *

COWLES, S(amuel) Macon, Jr. 1916-

PERSONAL: Born December 27, 1916, in Memphis, Tenn.; son of Samuel Macon (a Young Men's Christian Association secretary) and Rebecca (Kendall) Cowles; married Virginia Ballard (an administrative secretary); chil-

dren: Douglas, Cheryl, Macon III, Marcia. *Education:* Oberlin College, B.A., 1938; Union Theological Seminary, New York, N.Y., B.D., 1944, S.T.M., 1953; graduate study at New School for Social Research, 1960-61, and Boston University, 1961. *Politics:* Democrat. *Home:* 6845 Downing Circle E., Littleton, Colo. 80120. *Office:* Center for Pastoral Counseling and Human Development, 1100 East Evans Ave., Denver, Colo.

CAREER: Clergyman of United Church of Christ. City College (now City College of the City University of New York), New York City, executive secretary of Student Christian Association, 1939-44; minister at Presbyterian church in New York City, 1946, at Congregational churches in Wellsville, N.Y., 1946-50, and Spring Valley, N.Y., 1951-53, and at community church in Salt Lake City, Utah, 1953-59; program secretary for Congregational Churches Missions Council, New York City, 1959-61, and United Church of Christ Stewardship Council, Philadelphia, Pa., 1961-62; United Church in Cherry Knolls, Littleton, Colo., minister, 1962-67; University of Colorado, Denver Center, community development consultant, 1968-70; Center for Pastoral Counseling and Human Development, Denver, director, 1970—. Chairman of Littleton (Colo.) Council for Human Relations; director of United Housing Development Board in Denver. *Military service:* U.S. Navy, chaplain, 1944-46; served in Pacific theater. *Member:* American Association of Pastoral Counselors. National Association for the Advancement of Colored People. *Awards, honors:* D.D. from Westminster College, Salt Lake City, Utah, 1959.

WRITINGS: Ministers All, United Church, 1967; *Living the Incarnation,* United Church, 1967. Contributor to church periodicals.

*   *   *

COX, Constance 1915-

PERSONAL: Born October 25, 1915, in Sutton, Surrey, England; daughter of J. Frederick (an educator) and Anne E. (Vince) Shaw; married Norman C. Cox (a Royal Air Force pilot), June 7, 1933 (deceased). *Education:* Attended schools in England. *Home:* 2 Princes Ave., Hove, Sussex, England. *Agent:* Eric Glass Ltd., 28 Berkeley Sq., London W. 1, England.

CAREER: Playwright and adapter of classics for stage, 1942—; writer and adapter for television, 1955—. Former racing and competition driver; amateur actress and producer at Brighton Little Theatre Co. and New Venture Theatre, both Brighton, England. *Member:* Sussex Playwrights' Club (honorary treasurer), West Sussex Writer's Club. *Awards, honors: News Chronicles* Award for best television play of the year, 1956; Television and Screenwriters' Guild Special Award for adaptations of the classics, 1964; Prix Jeunesse International (second place) for thirteen-part television serial, "The Old Curiosity Shop," 1964; Television and Screenwriters' Guild Award, 1967, for television serial "The Forsythe Saga."

WRITINGS—Published plays: *Vanity Fair* (adapted from the novel by Thackeray), Samuel French, 1947; *The Picture of Dorian Gray* (adapted from the novel by Wilde), Fortune Press, 1948; *Madame Bovary* (adapted from the novel by Gustave Flaubert), Fortune Press, 1948; *Northanger Abbey* (adapted from the novel by Jane Austen), Fortune Press, 1950; *Mansfield Park* (adapted from the novel by Jane Austen), Evans Brothers, 1950; *The Count of Monte Cristo* (adapted from the novel by Dumas), Fortune Press, 1950; *Spring at Marino,* Samuel French, 1951; *The Desert Air,* English Theatre Guild, 1951; *Because of the Lockwoods,* Evans Brothers, 1953; *Three Knaves of Normandy,* Evans Brothers, 1958; *Jane Eyre* (adapted from the novel by Charlotte Bronte), J. Garnet Miller, 1959.

The Caliph's Minstrel, Evans Brothers, 1961; *Lord Arthur Saville's Crime,* Samuel French, 1963; *A Miniature 'Beggar's Opera'* (adapted from the work by John Gay), Evans Brothers, 1964; *The Three-Cornered Hat* (adapted from the work by Alarcon), Evans Brothers, 1966; *Trilby* (adapted from the novel by George duMaurier), Evans Brothers, 1967; *The Woman in White* (adapted from the novel by Wilkie Collins), Evans Brothers, 1967; *Everyman* (adapted from the anonymous morality play, c1500), Samuel French, 1967; *Miss Letitia,* Samuel French, 1970; *Wuthering Heights* (adapted from the novel by Emily Bronte), English Threatre Guild, 1974.

Other stage plays produced: "The Romance of David Garrick," 1942; "The Nine Days' Wonder," 1944; "Remember Dick Sheridan," 1944; "The Hunchback of Notre Dame," 1944; "Elizabeth and Darcy," 1945; "Sleeping Dogs," 1947; "Georgia Story," 1949; "The Enemy in the House," 1951; "The Woman in White," 1953; "Trilby," 1954; "Heathcliff," 1959; "Nightmare," 1963; "Pride and Prejudice," 1970.

Television plays: "The Trial of Admiral Byng"; "Trilby"; "Heathcliff"; "Lord Arthur Saville's Crime"; "Georgia Story"; "The Nine Days' Wonder"; "Spring at Marino"; "Miss Letitia."

Television serials: "Jane Eyre"; "Vanity Fair"; "Precious Bane"; "The History of Mr. Polly"; "The Lost King"; "Champion Road"; "Thunder in the West"; "The Golden Spur"; "Pride and Prejudice"; "Little Women"; "Good Wives"; "Jo's Boys"; "Bleak House"; "Angel Pavement"; "Oliver Twist"; "The Old Curiosity Shop"; "Lorna Doone"; "Martin Chuzzlewit"; "Rogue Herries"; "Silas Marner"; "Judith Paris"; "A Tale of Two Cities"; "John Halifax, Gentleman"; "Jane Eyre" (new version); "The Master of Ballantrae"; "The Franchise Affair"; "The House Under the Water"; "Katy, and What Katy Did at School"; "The Forsythe Saga," parts four, five, and seven.

Radio serials: "The Herries Chronicle," 1969; "War and Peace," 1971; "The Barchester Chronicles," 1974.

AVOCATIONAL INTERESTS: Music, motoring, and croquet.

*   *   *

COX, Eugene L. 1931-

PERSONAL: Born April 12, 1931, in Teaneck, N.J.; son of John H. (a mechanical engineer) and Maritta (Hunt) Cox. *Education:* College of Wooster, B.A., 1953; Johns Hopkins University, Ph.D., 1958; University of Dijon, graduate study, 1955-57. *Home:* 72 Denton Rd., Wellesley, Mass. 02181. *Office:* Wellesley College, Wellesley, Mass. 02181.

CAREER: Maryland Institute of Art, Baltimore, Md., director of history program, 1958-59; Wellesley College, Wellesley, Mass., instructor, 1959-61, assistant professor, 1961-67, associate professor, 1967-73, professor of history, 1973—. *Member:* American Historical Association, Mediaeval Academy of America, American Association of University Professors, Phi Beta Kappa. *Awards, honors:* Fulbright scholarship to France, 1955-57; Huber Founda-

tion awards, 1962, 1963; American Philosophical Society Award, 1971.

WRITINGS: The Green Count of Savoy, Princeton University Press, 1967; *The Eagles of Savoy,* Princeton University Press, 1974. Contributor of reviews to history journals.

WORK IN PROGRESS: A translation of Rigord's *Vie de Philippe Auguste.*

SIDELIGHTS: Cox told *CA:* "European travel is my avocation. [I] have lived in France (two years), Italy, and Switzerland. Spend almost every summer in Europe, partly working in archives and libraries, but also traveling in search of the curious, the beautiful, the forgotten. 'Lifestyles' of the present world interest me almost as much as do the different 'life-styles' of ages past." Cox is competent in French, Italian, Latin, and German.

*   *   *

COX, Richard 1931-

PERSONAL: Born March 8, 1931, in Winchester, England; son of Hubert Eustace (an engineer) and Joan (Thornton) Cox; married Caroline Jennings, October, 1963; children: Lorna Katherine, Ralph Pelham, Jeremy Philip. *Education:* St. Catherine's College, Oxford (second class honors in English language and literature, 1955). *Politics:* Conservative. *Religion:* Church of England. *Agent:* Curtis Brown, Ltd., 1 Craven Hill, London W.2, England. *Office:* 15 Carendish Square, London W.1, England.

CAREER: Colman, Prentis & Varley (advertising agency), London, England, advertising executive, 1957-59; *Sunday Times,* London, staff foreign correspondent, 1961-64; with foreign office, 1964-66; *Daily Telegraph,* London, correspondent, 1966-73; Thomas Cox Ltd., and Brassey's Publishers, London, managing director, 1974—. Radio and television commentator on African and British Commonwealth affairs, British Broadcasting Corp.; temporary African correspondent, Westinghouse Broadcasting Corp. Private Pilot. Chelsea borough councillor, 1962-65. *Military service:* British Army, Royal Artillery, 1949-51; became reserve major. Royal Air Force Volunteer Reserve, 1951-56. *Member:* Army and Navy Club.

WRITINGS: Pan-Africanism in Practice, Oxford University Press, 1964; *Kenyatta's Country,* Hutchinson, 1965, Praeger, 1966; (editor) *Institute of Directors Guide to Europe,* Thornton Cox, 1968, 2nd edition, 1970; (editor) *Traveller's Guide to Majorca, Minorca, Ibiza, and Formentera,* Hastings House, 1973; *Operation Sea Lion,* Thornton Cox, 1975.

AVOCATIONAL INTERESTS: Flying, studying art and architecture, and traveling.

*   *   *

CRABB, Richard 1914-

PERSONAL: Born January 20, 1914, in Wabash, Ind.; son of Carle Ray (a newspaper publisher) and Lida (an editor and writer; maiden name, Milne) Crabb; married Rachel Lemon (a home economist), December 24, 1936; children: Owen L., Sarah Ann. *Education:* Western Illinois University, B.A., 1934; attended University of Illinois, 1938-45. *Politics:* Independent. *Religion:* Methodist. *Home address:* P.O. Box 306, Wheaton, Ill. 60187.

CAREER: Regional correspondent for newspapers in Quincy and Peoria, Ill., during college days; *Moline Dis-*

patch, Moline, Ill., farm editor; western Illinois correspondent for *Chicago Daily News*, 1937-45, and *Chicago Tribune*, 1939-42; did public relations and promotion for business organizations serving the agricultural industry, 1945-62; Day Publications (subsidiary of Field Enterprises), Arlington Heights, Ill., political editor, 1967-70; editorial writer, Capley Newspapers, 1970—. *McDonough Times* (weekly newspaper), Macomb, Ill., founder, 1934, and contributor, beginning 1934. Professional lecturer on topics connected with the winning of the West and the origin of the motor car in the United States.

WRITINGS: The Hybrid Corn-Makers, Rutgers University Press, 1947; *Empire on the Platte*, World Publishing, 1967; *Birth of a Giant: The Men and Incidents that Gave America the Motorcar*, Chilton, 1969. Contributor to *Farm Journal, Progressive Farmer*, and other agricultural magazines, for twenty years.

* * *

CRABTREE, T(homas) T(avron)   1924-

PERSONAL: Born August 2, 1924, in Bells, Tenn.; son of Tom T. (a farmer) and Fay Laverne (Taylor) Crabtree; married Bennie Elizabeth Cole, April 21, 1946; children: Thomas Taylor, Robert Cody, Anna Beth. *Education:* Union University, Jackson, Tenn., A.B., 1946; Southern Baptist Theological Seminary, B.D., 1949, Th.D., 1953. *Politics:* Republican. *Home:* 2915 East Crestview, Springfield, Mo. 65804. *Office:* 525 South Ave., Springfield, Mo. 65806.

CAREER: Baptist clergyman. Pastor of Putnam City Baptist Church, Oklahoma City, Okla., beginning 1963; currently pastor of First Baptist Church, Springfield, Mo. Director of Ozark Christian Counseling Center. Member of board of directors of Springfield Chapter of American Red Cross, and Lester E. Cox Medical Center; trustee of Southwest Baptist College, and Southern Baptist Theological Seminary. *Member:* Rotary International.

WRITINGS: The Zondervan Pastor's Annual, Zondervan, 1968, 1969, (author and editor) 1970-76.

WORK IN PROGRESS: Editing *The Life and Work Annual*.

* * *

CRAIN, Robert L(ee)   1934-

PERSONAL: Born January 28, 1934, in Louisville, Ky.; son of John Lewis (a construction foreman) and Elizabeth (Duncan) Crain; married Barbara Fourmont, September 3, 1959; children: Alex Sandor, Colin Andrew. *Education:* University of Louisville, B.A., 1955; University of Chicago, Ph.D., 1963. *Politics:* Independent Democrat. *Religion:* None. *Office:* Department of Social Relations, Johns Hopkins University, Baltimore, Md. 21218.

CAREER: University of Chicago, Chicago, Ill., assistant professor of sociology, 1962-68, senior study director, National Opinion Research Center, 1964-68; Johns Hopkins University, Baltimore, Md., associate professor of social relations, 1968—. *Member:* American Sociological Association. *Awards, honors:* Ford Foundation research grant, 1967; Carnegie Corp. research grant, 1967.

WRITINGS: (With Morton Inger) *School Desegregation in New Orleans: A Comparative Study of the Failure of Social Control*, National Opinion Research Center, University of Chicago, 1966; (with Elihu Katz and Donald Rosenthal) *The Politics of Community Conflict*, Bobbs-Merrill, 1967; *The Politics of School Desegregation*, Aldine, 1967; (with Carol Sachs Weisman) *Discrimination, Personality, and Achievement: A Survey of Northern Blacks*, Seminar Press, 1972; (with David J. Kirby) *Political Strategies in Northern School Desegregation*, Lexington Books, 1973. Contributor to *Saturday Review, Journal of Politics, Social Forces, Urban Affairs Quarterly*. Associate editor, *American Journal of Sociology*.

WORK IN PROGRESS: Further studies of school desegregation, city politics, and American Negroes.

AVOCATIONAL INTERESTS: Amateur politics and photography.†

* * *

CRAMER, George H.   1913-

PERSONAL: Born June 9, 1913, in Conestoga, Pa.; son of Ralph E. (a carpenter) and Barbara (Warfel) Cramer; married Elva Glick, September 16, 1939; children: James and John (twins), George II. *Education:* Lancaster School of the Bible, student, 1936-39; Wheaton College, B.A., 1948, M.A., 1951; Brown University, further graduate courses, 1955-60. *Politics:* Republican. *Religion:* Conservative Baptist. *Home:* 424 South Chase St., Wheaton, Ill. 60187. *Office:* Director of Admissions, Wheaton College, Wheaton, Ill. 60187.

CAREER: Barrington College, Barrington, R.I., registrar and director of admissions, 1951-66, professor of biblical studies, registrar, and director of institutional research, 1966-69; Wheaton College, Wheaton, Ill., registrar and director of admissions, 1969—. College representative, Higher Education Facilities Commission for Rhode Island; member, Barrington Town Planning Board. *Member:* American Association of Collegiate Registrars and Admissions Officers, National Association of Foreign Student Advisers, Association for Institutional Research.

WRITINGS: First and Second Peter (volume in "Everyman's Bible Commentary"), Moody, 1967. Contributor to *Bibliotheca Sacra*.

* * *

CRAMER, James   1915-

PERSONAL: Born July 1, 1915, in Portsmouth, Hampshire, England; son of James Isaac (an inspector, British Admiralty) and Margaret (Power) Cramer; married Patricia Barbara Bailey; children: Ian James, James Anthony, Christopher Ranville, Judith Patricia, Ruth Theresa. *Education:* Portsmouth College of Education, Teacher's Certificate, 1967; Open University, England, B.A., 1973. *Politics:* "English Republican." *Religion:* Roman Catholic. *Home:* 7 Invergordon Ave., Cosham, Hampshire, England.

CAREER: Member of city police force, Portsmouth, England, 1933-39, 1947-65, retiring with rank of inspector; teacher at junior school in Portsmouth, 1967-73; teacher in adolescent tutorial units (for disruptive teen-aged pupils), Portsmouth, 1973—. *Military service:* British Army, 1939-47; served five years with 6th Airborne Division; became sergeant major.

WRITINGS: The World's Police, Cassell, 1964; *History of the Police of Portsmouth*, Portsmouth City Council, 1967; *Uniforms of the World's Police*, C. C Thomas, 1968; *Police Animals of the World*, Cassell, 1968. Contributor of articles on police history and foreign police administrations to *Police Review* and *Hampshire Telegraph*.

CRAMPTON, C(harles) Gregory 1911-

PERSONAL: Born March 22, 1911, in Kankakee, Ill.; married Helen Mickelsen (a professor of sociology); children: Patricia, Juanita. Education: University of California, Berkeley, A.B., 1935, M.A., 1936, Ph.D., 1941. Home: 327 South 12th St., Salt Lake City, Utah 84102. Office: American West Center, 1038 Annex, University of Utah, Salt Lake City, Utah 84112.

CAREER: U.S. Department of Justice, Washington, D.C., member of staff, 1943-44; U.S. War Department, Washington, D.C., historian, 1944-45; University of Utah, Salt Lake City, 1945—, began as assistant professor, professor of history, 1951—, director of Western History Center, 1966-68. U.S. Department of State exchange professor at University of Panama, 1955. Member of board, American West Publishing Co. Member: American Historical Association, Organization of American Historians, Phi Alpha Theta (vice-president, 1941-48; president, 1949-50). Awards, honors: Rockefeller Foundation fellowships, 1941-42, 1948-49; Rockefeller Foundation gold medal from University of Panama, 1965, for Standing Up Country.

WRITINGS—All published by University of Utah Press, except as indicated: (Co-editor) Greater America, Essays in Honor of Herbert E. Bolton, University of California Press, 1945; (editor) The Mariposa Indian War, 1850-1851: Diaries of Robert Eccleston, the California Gold Rush, Yosemite and the High Sierra, 1957; Outline History of the Glen Canyon Region, 1776-1922, 1959; Historical Sites in Glen Canyon: Mouth of San Juan River to Lee's Ferry, 1960; (editor with Dwight L. Smight) Robert B. Stanton, The Hoskaninni Papers: Mining in Glen Canyon, 1897-1902, 1961; Historical Sites in Glen Canyon: Mouth of Hansen Creek to Mouth of San Juan River, 1962; The San Juan Canyon Historical Sites, 1964; Historical Sites in Cataract and Narrow Canyons, and in Glen Canyon to California Bar, 1964; Standing Up Country: The Canyonlands of Utah and Arizona, Knopf, 1964; Land of Living Rock: The Grand Canyon and the High Plateaus, Knopf, 1972; (editor with W. L. Rusho) Desert River Crossing: Historic Lee's Ferry on the Colorado River, Peregrine Smith, 1975; (editor) Sharlot Hall on the Arizona Strip: A Diary of a Journey Through Northern Arizona in 1911, Northland Press, 1975. Writer of historical articles. Editor, American West, 1964-66.

* * *

CRASSWELLER, Robert D. 1915-

PERSONAL: Born September 17, 1915, in Duluth, Minn.; son of Arthur H. (a lawyer) and Mary (Doell) Crassweller; married Mildred Clarke, March 21, 1942; children: Peter, Karen, Pamela. Education: Attended University of Minnesota, 1935-36; Carleton College, B.A., 1937; Harvard University, LL.B., 1941. Religion: Universalist. Home: East Lane, Revonah Woods, Stamford, Conn. 06905. Agent: McIntosh & Otis, Inc., 475 Fifth Ave., New York, N.Y. 10017.

CAREER: Partner in law firms, Duluth, Minn., 1941-43, 1945-51; U.S. Department of State, Washington, D.C., assistant division assistant, 1943-45; West Indies Mining Corp., San Juan, Puerto Rico, officer and director, 1951-53; Pan American World Airways, New York, N.Y., staff lawyer, 1954-67; Council on Foreign Relations, visiting council fellow, 1967-69; International Telephone & Telegraph Corp., New York, N.Y., staff counsel, senior counsel for multinational corporate affairs, and general

counsel for Latin America, 1970—. Director, Minnesota United Nations Committee, 1947-51. Visiting professor, Brooklyn College of the City University of New York and Sarah Lawrence College, 1968-69. Member of state central committee, Minnesota Republican Party, 1948-49. Member: Minnesota Bar Association (founding director of tax law section, 1948), Council on Foreign Relations, Center for Inter-American Relations.

WRITINGS: Trujillo: The Life and Times of a Caribbean Dictator, Macmillan, 1966; The Caribbean Community: Changing Societies and U.S. Policy, Praeger, 1972. Occasional contributor to Reporter.

* * *

CRAVERI, Marcello 1914-

PERSONAL: Born March 23, 1914, in Turin, Italy; son of John (a bank manager) and Lina (Clivio) Craveri; married Carla Moretti (a primary teacher), October 10, 1952. Education: University of Turin, Doctorate in Arts and Philosophy, 1940. Politics: Socialist.

CAREER: Civilta Proletaria (weekly newspaper), Bari, Italy, editor, 1944-45; teacher of Italian and Latin literature in High Scientific School, Turin, Italy, beginning 1946. Military service: Italian Army, Infantry, 1941-43; became sergeant; punished for refusing to cooperate with German detachment at time of American landing in Sicily, and for giving aid to American troops.

WRITINGS: Il Tema Letterario (studies on Italian literature), Paravia (Turin), 1955, 13th edition, 1967; Syntaxis Ornata (Latin stylistic art), La Nuova Italia (Florence), 1961, 6th edition, 1967; Sermo Facilis (a Latin grammar), La Nuova Italia, 1966, 2nd edition, 1967, Volume II, 1968; La Vita di Gesu, Feltrinelli (Milan), 1966, translation by Charles Lam Markham published as The Life of Jesus, Grove, 1967; (compiler) I Vangeli Apocrifi, G. Einaudi, 1969. Contributor to La Nuova Rivista Storica (Milan).

WORK IN PROGRESS: A novel and a book of tales for publication by Feltrinelli; doing an Italian translation from Greek and Latin of all the Apocryphal Gospels, for Einaudi.

SIDELIGHTS: "When [The Life of Jesus] was published in Italy . . . the dust jacket informs us, there was 'a storm both of protest and approval in newspapers, magazines, even special pamphlets.' It has been called 'libelous,' 'blasphemous,' 'profound,' 'solid,' 'objective,'" writes M. I. Finley. "Although he [Craveri] writes in a respectful tone most of the time, there is a deep current of passionate humanitarianism and conviction. He takes his risks knowingly (as during the war when he refused to cooperate with a German detachment). 'If we intend to conduct a serious historical investigation,' he writes, 'we must necessarily examine in what circumstances and on what bases the tradition of each of the miracles recounted in the New Testament might have arisen, and we must study their meanings, notwithstanding the penalty of anathema with which the Church threatens all who do not believe in the reality of the miracles.'"

Craveri says in his introduction: "I have undertaken the life of Jesus, . . . the history of his life, of his teachings, of the development of Christianity—with full consideration for all current and recent theories, but with the intention of remaining as impartial as possible toward the often contradictory approaches of the various schools. . . . Never losing sight of Jesus as an individual born into a clearly defined society as a clearly defined point in history, and hence of striving to understand his life, his ideas, his behavior as the product of a particular culture and unique historical circumstances." Henrietta Buckmaster feels that this is too great a task, and that it cannot fail to have problems that Craveri is unable to avoid. She feels that he fails in "that area of scriptural interpretation known as the exegesis." This is an area almost impossible for one to explore and remain objective. "One would not object," she continues, "if exegesis were labeled speculative, but it always carries with it the assumptions of authority. The explanations are catagoric . . . and this seems to me *bad* scholarship, no matter how one looks at it."

Hugh J. Schonfield believes, along with others, that the book in many ways is closer to the nineteenth century than the twentieth. It has been pointed out that he does not make use of the information found in the Dead Sea Scrolls, but relies on earlier works for much of his information. Schonfield feels that this is probably inevitable, however, because he was writing for "Italians with a Roman Catholic background, to whom much that has been familiar to others is still extremely novel and perturbing." He feels the book "is well written, extremely readable, and follows an orderly plan; but curiously it blends a progressive narration of the story of Jesus, and an exposition of his teaching founded upon the Gospels, with the frequent denial that their information is dependable." George MacRae writes that Craveri "just does not seem to understand what the Gospels are, nor is it clear that he wants to." Schonfield and others felt that there was a lack of focus in the work, since he included many of his own feelings and digressions, and this takes away from the effect he was trying to achieve. Miss Buckmaster states: "In spite of these criticisms, however, Dr. Craveri has written a book which can be of value to the Bible student who, knowing that ignorance is not bliss, wishes to explore a vast and fascinating area with an inquiring mind." Schonfield concludes: "We must treat this book . . . not as the production of a New Testament scholar . . . but as the thinking on paper of a man independently eager to discover for himself the Jesus behind the myths and marvels of an adoring Church. His findings should at least help to clear away some of the cobwebs which still cling to the traditionalists, and if he succeeds at all in this, the years he has devoted to his task will not have been spent in vain."

Craveri knows English, French, German, and Spanish, in addition to ancient Latin, Greek, and Hebrew. His greatest interest is the "fight against all forms of superstition and fanaticism in religious, social, racial opinions."

BIOGRAPHICAL/CRITICAL SOURCES: Book Week, June 25, 1967; *Commonweal,* September 8, 1967; *Nation,* October 9, 1967; *Observer Review,* November 12, 1967; *Christian Science Monitor,* January 31, 1968.†

* * *

CRAWFORD, Ann Fears 1932-

PERSONAL: Born August 26, 1932, in Beaumont, Tex.; daughter of Thaddeus Alvin (a physician) and Dorothy (Huey) Fears; married Frank B. Crawford, Jr., September 19, 1953 (divorced, 1957); children: Kevin Brooks. *Education:* University of Texas, B.F.A., 1953, doctoral candidate, 1975—; Los Angeles State College (now California State University, Los Angeles), M.A., 1956. *Politics:* Democratic. *Religion:* Episcopalian. *Home:* 2104 Indian Trail, Austin, Tex. 78703. *Agent:* Bertha Klausner, 71 Park Ave., New York, N.Y. 10016.

CAREER: Steck-Vaughn Co. (publishers), Austin, Tex., editor, 1958-62; Texas Butane Dealers Association, Austin, magazine editor, 1965; Eugene Wukasch, Austin, public relations writer, 1965—; Institute of Texan Cultures, Austin, research associate, 1966-68; *Austin People Today,* Austin, editor, 1973-74. Freelance writer and editor. *Member:* Texas State Historical Society, Austin Heritage Society, Women in Communications, Texas Women's Political Caucus, National Organization for Women, Phi Kappa Phi.

WRITINGS: (With Norman Schacter) *Experience,* Books 1-3, Steck, 1965-66; *A Boy Like You,* Pemberton, 1966; (editor with William D. Wittliff) *The Eagle: The Autobiography of Santa Anna,* Pemberton, 1967; *Experience* (high school text), Steck, 1968; (editor) June Rayfield Welch, *Texas: New Perspectives* (high school text), Steck, 1973; (with Jack Keener) *John Connally: Portrait in Power,* Jenkins Publishing, 1973; *Viva: The Story of Mexican Americans,* Steck, 1976.

WORK IN PROGRESS: A biography of Governors Jim and Mirian Ferguson of Texas, for Pemberton; a history of O'Connor ranch.

* * *

CREAMER, Robert W. 1922-

PERSONAL: Born July 14, 1922, in Tuckahoe, N.Y.; son of Joseph J. (in real estate) and Marie (Watts) Creamer; married Margaret Schelz, August 23, 1947; children: James, Thomas, John, Ellen, Robert. *Education:* Studied at Syracuse University, 1940-41, Fordham University, 1941-43, 1945-46, City College (now City College of the City University of New York), 1943-44. *Residence:* Tuckahoe, N.Y. 10707. *Agent:* Sterling Lord, 660 Madison Ave., New York, N.Y. 10021. *Office: Sports Illustrated,* Time & Life Building, New York, N.Y. 10020.

CAREER: Grey Advertising, New York City, junior copywriter, 1946-48; *Bronxville Review-Press,* Bronxville, N.Y., advertising manager, 1948-49; *Westchester Herald,* White Plains, N.Y., advertising manager, 1949; William Weintraub (now Norman, Craig, & Kummel; advertising), New York City, junior account executive, 1949-50; P. F. Collier & Co., New York City, assistant editor of *Collier's Encyclopedia,* 1950-54; *Sports Illustrated,* New York City, senior editor, 1954—. *Military service:* U.S. Army, 1942-45. *Member:* Magazine Sports Writers Association, Authors Guild.

WRITINGS: (With Mickey Mantle) *The Quality of Courage,* Doubleday, 1964; (with Jocko Conlan) *Jocko,* Lippincott, 1967; (with Red Barber) *Rhubarb in the Catbird Seat,* Doubleday, 1968; *Babe: The Legend Comes to Life,* Simon & Schuster, 1974. Contributor to *Sports Illustrated, Collier's Encyclopedia, Collier's Yearbook,* and other publications.

WORK IN PROGRESS: A biography.

SIDELIGHTS: Creamer told *CA,* "Writing is something you do because you know how to do it and because it gives economic and emotional satisfaction when you do it competently."

* * *

CRITCHLEY, Edmund M(ichael) R(hys) 1931-

PERSONAL: Born December 25, 1931, in Bury St. Edmunds, England; son of A. Michael (a physician and professor of public health) and Doris (Rees) Critchley; married Mair Bowen (a physician), October 8, 1963; children: Giles

Roderic, Hugo Dyfrig. *Education:* Studied at Lincoln College, Oxford, 1950-54, and King's College Hospital Medical School, London, 1954-57. *Politics:* Liberal. *Office:* Preston Royal Infirmary, Lancashire, England.

CAREER: University College Hospital, London, England, senior register in neurology, 1964-65; University of Kentucky Medical Center, Lexington, instructor in neurology, 1967-68; Preston Royal Infirmary, Lancashire, England, consultant neurologist, beginning 1968. *Military service:* Royal Army Medical Corps, 1959-60; served in Malaya; became captain. *Member:* Royal College of Physicians (London), Royal College of Physicians (Edinburgh), Royal Society of Medicine (London; fellow). *Awards, honors:* Donald Patterson Prize in pediatrics, London, England, 1966.

WRITINGS: Speech Origins and Development, C. C Thomas, 1967.

WORK IN PROGRESS: Research in pediatric neurology; and analysis of typing errors.

SIDELIGHTS: Critchley lived in Iraq at one period; he has traveled in the Far and Middle East and western Europe.††

* * *

CROOK, J(ohn) A(nthony) 1921-

PERSONAL: Born November 5, 1921, in London, England; son of Herbert (a musician) and Hilda (Flower) Crook. *Education:* St. John's College, Cambridge, M.A., 1949. *Home and office:* St. John's College, Cambridge University, Cambridge, England.

CAREER: University of Reading, Reading, England, lecturer in classics, 1948-51; Cambridge University, St. John's College, Cambridge, England, research fellow, 1951-53, university assistant lecturer, 1953-55, lecturer in classics, 1955-71, reader in Roman history and law, 1971—, president of St. John's College, 1971—. *Military service:* British Army, 1941-45; became sergeant.

WRITINGS: Consilium Principis, Cambridge University Press, 1955; *Law and Life of Rome,* Thames & Hudson, 1967.

WORK IN PROGRESS: Further research in the field of Roman law and social institutions.

SIDELIGHTS: A reviewer in the *Times Literary Supplement* comments that Crook's *Law and Life of Rome* "fulfills a need because, in dealing with the relations between law and society, he is aiming at the student not of law but of history." He adds that Crook "handles the theme, subject by subject, with impressive mastery."

BIOGRAPHICAL/CRITICAL SOURCES: Times Literary Supplement, September 28, 1967.†

* * *

CROSS, Claire 1932-
(M. Claire Cross)

PERSONAL: Born October 25, 1932, in Lincoln, England; daughter of Frederick Leonard (a bank cashier) and Rebecca (Newton) Cross. *Education:* Girton College, Cambridge, B.A., 1955, Ph.D., 1959. *Religion:* Church of England. *Office:* Department of History, University of York, Heslington, Yorkshire, England.

CAREER: County archivist, Cambridgeshire, England, 1958-61; University of Reading, Reading, England, re-

search fellow, 1962-65; University of York, Heslington, Yorkshire, England, lecturer in history, 1965—. *Member:* Royal Historical Association (fellow). *Awards, honors:* American Association of University Women fellowship for research at Huntington Library, 1961-62.

WRITINGS: (Under name M. Claire Cross) *Free Grammar School of Leicester,* Leicester University Press, 1953; *The Puritan Earl: Henry Hastings, Third Earl of Huntingdon, 1536-1595,* Macmillan, 1966; *The Royal Supremacy in the Elizabethan Church,* Barnes & Noble, 1969; (editor) *The Letters of Sir Francis Hastings, 1574-1609,* Somerset Record Society, 1969; (contributor) Gerald Edward Aylmer, editor, *The Interregnum: The Quest for Settlement,* Macmillan, 1972; *Church and People: The Triumph of the Laity in the English Church,* Fontana, 1976. Contributor to learned periodicals.

WORK IN PROGRESS: Research in sixteenth- and seventeenth-century English history, especially church history.

SIDELIGHTS: Claire Cross knows a "smattering" of French, German, Italian, Latin, and Greek. *Avocational interests:* Gardening, travel in Europe and America.

* * *

CROTTY, William J(oseph) 1936-

PERSONAL: Born April 14, 1936, in West Somerville, Mass.; children: three. *Education:* University of Massachusetts, A.B. (cum laude), 1958; University of North Carolina, Ph.D., 1963. *Office:* Department of Political Science, Northwestern University, Evanston, Ill. 60201.

CAREER: University of North Carolina, Chapel Hill, part-time instructor, 1959-62; University of Georgia, Athens, assistant professor, department of political science, 1963-65; University of Oregon, Eugene, research associate of Center for Advanced Study of Educational Administration, 1965-66; Northwestern University, Evanston, Ill., assistant professor, 1966-70, associate professor, 1970-74, professor of political science, 1974—. Co-director of task force on political assassinations, National Commission on the Causes and Prevention of Violence, 1969-70; executive director of American political parties project, National Municipal League, 1972-75. Consultant, Democratic Party Reform, 1968-72. *Member:* American Political Science Association, Midwest Political Science Association, Western Political Science Association, Southern Political Science Association, Southwestern Social Science Association, Pi Sigma Alpha. *Awards, honors:* Research grants from Falk Foundation, 1963, Stern Foundation, 1964-65, National Center for Education in Politics, 1964, Northwestern University, 1966-67, and Russell Sage Foundation and Twentieth Century Fund, 1972-74; American Political Science Association fellowship, 1970-71.

WRITINGS: (Editor with Donald M. Freeman and Douglas S. Gatlin) *Political Parties and Political Behavior,* Allyn & Bacon, 1966; (editor and contributor) *Approaches to the Study of Party Organization,* Allyn & Bacon, 1967; (contributor) Henry Kariel and Michael Haas, *Approaches to Political Science,* Chandler Publishing, 1968; (with Robert T. Golembiewski and others) *A Methodological Primer for Political Scientists,* Rand McNally, 1968; (compiler) *Public Opinion and Politics: A Reader,* Holt, 1970; (with James F. Kirkham) *Assassination and Political Violence,* Praeger, 1970; (editor with others) *Political Parties and Political Behavior,* Allyn & Bacon, 1971; (editor and contributor) *Assassinations and the Political Order,* Harper, 1972; *Presidential Nominating Practices,* National Municipal League, 1974; *Political Reform,* Crowell, 1975. Contributor of articles and reviews to professional journals.

*   *   *

CROWCROFT, Andrew 1923-

PERSONAL: Born November 25, 1923, in Watford, England; son of Heber Ewart (an engineer) and Zenaida (Katchorovskia) Crowcroft; married Kyla Greenbaum (a professor of music), February 29, 1956; children: Jonathan, Natasha. *Education:* University of London, B.Sc., 1950, M.B. and B.S., 1956; also received L.R.C.P. and M.R.C.S., 1956, and D.P.M., 1960. *Politics:* "Nil." *Religion:* "Nil."

CAREER: Physician holding a number of hospital and teaching posts in psychiatry, London, England, 1958-61; consultant psychiatrist to Queen Elizabeth Hospital for Children, London, England, beginning 1961. Consultant to School for Autistic Children and several voluntary and statutory community organizations. Speaker on British Broadcasting Corp. radio and television. *Military service:* British Army, commando with Combined Operations, 1942-46; received Burma Star and France-Germany Star. *Member:* British Medical Association, Association of Child Psychologists and Psychiatrists, Royal Medico-Psychological Association.

WRITINGS: The Psychotic—Understanding Madness, Penguin, 1967; (contributor) *Trends in the Service for Youth,* Pergamon, 1967; (contributor) John G. Howells, editor, *Modern Perspectives in International Child Psychiatry,* Oliver & Boyd, 1969, Brunner, 1971. Contributor to scientific and some popular journals.

WORK IN PROGRESS: The Evolution of Identity; research in family dynamics, adolescence, and pathological mourning.

AVOCATIONAL INTERESTS: Travel, general literature, "the adventure of ideas of science," talking, listening ("this less than talking").†

*   *   *

CROWLEY, Daniel J(ohn) 1921-

PERSONAL: Born November 27, 1921, in Peoria, Ill.; son of Michael Bartholomew (a plumbing contractor) and Elsie (Schnebelin) Crowley; married Pearl Ramcharan (a teacher), February 4, 1958; children: Peter Mahendranath Njoya, Eve Lakshmi Lueji, Magdalene Lilawati Balchis. *Education:* Northwestern University, A.B., 1943, Ph.D., 1956; Bradley University, M.A., 1948. *Politics:* Democrat. *Religion:* Roman Catholic. *Home:* 726 Peach Lane, Davis, Calif. 95616. *Office:* 224 Young Hall, University of California, Davis, Calif. 95616.

CAREER: Bradley University, Peoria, Ill., instructor in art history, 1948-50; University of the West Indies, Port-of-Spain, Trinidad, tutor in anthropology, 1953-56; Northwestern University, Evanston, Ill., instructor in anthropology, 1956-57; University of Notre Dame, Notre Dame, Ind., assistant professor of sociology, 1958-59; University of California, Davis, assistant professor, 1961-62, associate professor, 1962-67, professor of anthropology and art, 1967—. Field research in Bahama Islands, 1952, 1953, Trinidad, Tobago, and Santa Lucia, 1953-56, 1958, 1966, 1972, 1973-74, Congo, Angola, Zambia, and Tanzania, 1960, Mexico, 1962, Ghana, Logo, and Dahomey, 1969-71. Member of executive board, Davis Art Center, 1966-68.

Military service: U.S. Naval Reserve, active duty, 1942-47; became lieutenant junior grade.

MEMBER: American Anthropological Association (fellow), Society for Ethnomusicology (councillor, 1961-65, 1967—), American Folklore Society (executive board member, 1963-65; president, 1969-71), American Society for Aesthetics (president of California division, 1964-65), African Studies Association, Royal Anthropological Institute (fellow), Southwestern Anthropological Association (fellow), Trinidad Ethnographic Society, California Folklore Society (Northern regional vice-president, 1971-73), Sigma Xi. *Awards, honors:* Jo Stafford Prize in American Folklore, 1952; Ford Foundation fellow, 1959-61.

WRITINGS: I Could Talk Old-Story Good: Creativity in Bahamian Folklore, University of California Press, 1966.

Contributor: Richard M. Dorson, editor, *Folklore Research Around the World,* Indiana University Press, 1961; D. K. Wilgus, editor, *Folklore International: Essays in Traditional Literature, Belief, and Custom in Honor of Wayland Hand,* Folklore Association, 1967; Gwendolyn M. Carter and Ann Paden, editors, *Expanding Horizons in African Studies,* Northwestern University Press, 1969; John F. Szwed, editor, *Black Americans,* Basic Books, 1970; Carol F. Jopling, editor, *Art and Aesthetics in Primitive Societies,* Dutton, 1971; Douglas Fraser and Herbert M. Cole, editors, *African Art and Leadership,* University of Wisconsin Press, 1972; Warren L. d'Azevedo, editor, *The Traditional Artist in African Societies,* Indiana University Press, 1973.

Also contributor to *Encyclopaedia Britannica, Encyclopedia International, International Encyclopedia of the Social Sciences, Catholic Encyclopaedia,* and also to journals. Book review editor, *Journal of American Folklore,* 1961-64; contributing editor, *African Arts,* 1971—.

WORK IN PROGRESS: With wife, a translation of *Plastiek van Kongo* (title means "Congolese Sculpture") by Frans M. Olbrechts; writing a monograph on African art, based on Zaire and Ghana field research; with wife, a study on diffusion of African folktales; preparing a collection of Caribbean folktales; monograph on Trinidad Creole culture.

SIDELIGHTS: Crowley speaks French, Spanish, some Portuguese; reads German, and Antillean Creole.

*   *   *

CROWLEY, James B. 1929-

PERSONAL: Born July 11, 1929, in Hartford, Conn.; son of William George and Edith (Buckley) Crowley; married Joan Sullivan, December 9, 1950; children: Barbara, Jonathan, Sheila. *Education:* University of Connecticut, B.A., 1950, M.A., 1951; University of Michigan, M.A., 1956, Ph.D., 1960. *Office:* History Department, Yale University, New Haven, Conn. 06520.

CAREER: University of Michigan, Ann Arbor, instructor in history, 1959-60; Amherst College, Amherst, Mass., assistant professor of history, 1960-63; Yale University, New Haven, Conn., assistant professor, 1963-67, associate professor, 1967-72, professor of history, 1972—. Research associate, Columbia University, 1961; research fellow, Hoover Institute, 1964; Fulbright research professor, Tokyo University, 1965-66. *Member:* Association for Asian Studies, American Historical Association. *Awards, honors:* American Council of Learned Societies grant, 1969; National Defense Education Act grant, 1969-70.

WRITINGS: Japan's Quest for Autonomy, Princeton University Press, 1966; (editor) *Modern East Asia: Essays in Interpretation*, Harcourt, 1970. Contributor to historical and political science journals. Advisory editor, *Journal of Asian Studies.*†

* * *

CRUICKSHANK, C(harles) G(reig) 1914-

PERSONAL: Born June 10, 1914, in Fyvie, Aberdeenshire, Scotland; son of George Leslie and Annie (Duncan) Cruickshank; married Maire Kissane, June 16, 1943; children: Christopher, Charles, Matthew. *Education:* University of Aberdeen, M.A., 1936; Hertford College, Oxford, D.Phil., 1940; University of Edinburgh, postdoctoral study, 1940-41. *Home:* 15 McKay Rd., Wimbledon Common, London SW20 OHT, England.

CAREER: British Civil Service, London, England, Ministry of Supply, a principal, 1941-45, Board of Trade, a principal, 1945-51, British trade commissioner in Colombo, Ceylon, 1951-55, and Ottawa, Ontario, 1955-58, British senior trade commissioner in Wellington, New Zealand, 1958-62, Commonwealth Secretariat, London, director of Commodities Division, 1965-68, Board of Trade, regional export director, 1969-71, Foreign and Commonwealth office, inspector, 1971-72, Civil Aviation Authority, 1972-73, Department of Trade and Industry, assistant secretary, 1973—. *Member:* Royal Wimbledon Golf Club.

WRITINGS: Elizabeth's Army, Oxford University Press, 1946, revised and enlarged edition, Clarendon Press, 1966; *Army Royal: Henry VIII's Invasion of France, 1513*, Clarendon Press, 1969; *The English Occupation of Tournai*, Clarendon Press, 1971; (co-editor) *A Guide to the Sources of British Military History*, University of California Press, 1971; *The German Occupation of the Channel Islands*, Oxford University Press, 1975; *Greece 1940-41*, Davis-Poynter, 1975; *The V-Mann Papers* (spy novel), R. Hale, 1976. Contributor to *English Historical Review, Army Quarterly, Punch, Men Only, History Today*, and other periodicals.

WORK IN PROGRESS: The Tang Murders, for R. Hale.

* * *

CRUMP, Kenneth G(ordon), Jr. 1931-

PERSONAL: Born January 25, 1931, in Pittsburgh, Pa.; son of Kenneth Gordon (an educator) and Evangeline (Fisher) Crump; married Marcia Louise Freeland, August 29, 1954; children: David Wesley, Thomas Edward. *Education:* San Jose State College (now San Jose State University), B.A., 1956, M.A., 1958; graduate study at University of California, Berkeley, 1965, and American University, 1967. *Religion:* Protestant. *Home:* 20602 Carniel Ave., Saratoga, Calif. 95070.

CAREER: Teacher of world geography at El Dorado High School in Placerville, Calif., 1957-60, and of world history at Fremont High School in Sunnyvale, Calif., 1960-63; Homestead High School, Cupertino, Calif., curriculum associate and chairman of department of social sciences, 1963—; Stanford University, Stanford, Calif., social science intern supervisor, 1964-70. Instructor in European history, Zwettl, Austria, in cooperation with the Austro-American Institute of Education and Fremont Union High School District, 1974-75. *Military service:* U.S. Air Force, 1948-52; combat photographer in Korean War; became sergeant. *Member:* California Council for the Social Studies,

California Teachers Association, California Council of Geographers.

WRITINGS: Napoleon Bonaparte, Scholastic Book Services, 1966; (with Nicholas Ferentinos) *The Islands*, Evergreen Press, 1975.

* * *

CRUMP, Spencer (M., Jr.) 1923-

PERSONAL: Born November 25, 1923, in San Jose, Calif.; son of Spencer M. (a dentist) and Jessie (Person) Crump; married Mary Dalgarno, January 12, 1963 (divorced, 1975); children: John Spencer, Victoria Elizabeth Margaret. *Education:* University of Southern California, B.A., 1960, M.Sc. (education), 1962, M.A. (journalism), 1969, doctoral studies, 1974—. *Politics:* Democrat. *Religion:* Unitarian Universalist. *Office address:* P.O. Box 38, Corona del Mar, Calif. 92625.

CAREER: Long Beach Independent, Long Beach, Calif., picture editor, 1952-56; *Los Angeles Times*, Los Angeles, Calif., editor of suburban sections (South Bay and Orange County), 1959-62; Trans-Anglo Books, Los Angeles, editorial director, 1962—; Orange Coast College, Costa Mesa, Calif., chairman of communications department, 1966—. Managing director, Person Properties Co., Lubbock, Tex., 1951—. Elected member, Los Angeles Democratic Central Committee, 1960-61. *Member:* Railway and Locomotive Historical Society, Society of Professional Journalists, American Civil Liberties Union, Fellowship of Reconciliation, California Historical Society, Book Publishers Association of Southern California, Orange County Press Club, Masons.

WRITINGS—All published by Trans-Anglo, except as noted: *Ride the Big Red Cars*, 1962; *Redwoods, Iron Horses, and the Pacific*, 1963; *Western Pacific: The Railroad That Was Built Too Late*, 1963; *California's Spanish Missions Yesterday and Today*, 1964; *252 Historic Places You Can See in California*, 1964; *Black Riot in Los Angeles*, 1966; *Henry Huntington and the Pacific Electric*, 1970; *Fundamentals of Journalism*, McGraw, 1974; *California's Spanish Missions: An Album of Their Yesterdays and Todays*, 1975.

AVOCATIONAL INTERESTS: Collector of western books.

* * *

CSICSERY-RONAY, Istvan 1917-

PERSONAL: Name is pronounced *Eesht-vahn Chee-cherry Ro-noy*; born December 13, 1917, in Budapest, Hungary; son of Stephen A. (member of Parliament) and Maria Alexandra (Flesch) Csicsery-Ronay; married Elizabeth Tariska (a librarian), July 27, 1945; children: Elizabeth M., Istvan, Jr. *Education:* Konsularakademie (now Diplomatische Akademie), Vienna, diploma, 1939; Royal Hungarian University, Budapest, Ph.D., 1940; Technical University, Budapest, certificate, 1943; University of Geneva, summer student, 1943; School of Diplomacy, Budapest, certificate, 1944; Catholic University of America, M.S.L.S., 1957, further graduate study, 1956-59, 1974-75. *Religion:* Protestant. *Home address:* P.O. Box 1005, Washington, D.C. 20013. *Office:* McKeldin Library, University of Maryland, College Park, Md. 20742.

CAREER: Served in Anti-Nazi Resistance Movement, 1944-45; Foreign Ministry of Hungary, ministerial secretary, 1944-47; School of Foreign Affairs, Budapest, Hungary, director, 1945-46; Smallholder Party (majority party in Hungary at that time), chief of Foreign Affairs Division, 1945-47; arrested by Communist political police in 1947 and sentenced to two years' imprisonment; released pending appeal after eight months in jail; escaped to Austria late in 1947, then lived in Paris, France, before coming to United States; Free Europe Committee, Inc., New York, N.Y., political analyst, 1949-56; University of Maryland, McKeldin Library, College Park, associate librarian II, 1956—. Acting vice-president, Teleki Pal Munkakozosseg, 1943-47. Lecturer, University of Montreal, University of Maryland. *Military service:* Hungarian Army, Artillery, 1936-37, 1942-43; awarded rank of first lieutenant for work in Anti-Nazi Resistance Movement. *Member:* American Academy of Political and Social Science, Academy of Political Science, Klub der Absolveuten und Freunde der Diplomatischen Akademie, International P.E.N., U.S. Chess Federation, Federal Aviation Club, Phi Kappa Phi. *Awards, honors:* American Council of Learned Societies grants, 1961, 1962, for producing Hungarian literary records.

WRITINGS: Russian Cultural Penetration in Hungary, Free Europe Committee (New York), 1950, 4th edition, Occidental Press, 1976; *Szamuzottek naptara* (title means "Calendar of Exiles"), Occidental Press, 1954; (editor) *Koltok forradalma* (title means "Poets' Revolution"), Occidental Press, 1957; (contributor) Alexander S. Preminger and others, editors, *Encyclopedia of Poetry and Poetics,* Princeton University Press, 1965; *The First Book of Hungary,* F. Watts, 1967, 2nd edition, 1976; (contributor) Paul S. Horecky, editor, *East Central Europe: A Guide to Basic Publications,* University of Chicago Press, 1969; (contributor) *Lands and Peoples,* seven volumes, Grolier, 1972. Author of television script "Stephen I: His Life and His Reign," 1969, and of radio scripts for Voice of America and Radio Free Europe. Contributor to *Collier's Encyclopedia;* contributor of more than one hundred articles and reviews to American, Swiss, Yugoslav, and Hungarian language newspapers and journals.

Editor and producer of six literary records and a recording of Hungarian folk songs on the Ady label. Editor of *Eb Ura Fako* (an underground weekly), 1944, *Hirunk a Vilagban,* 1951-64, and *Bibliografia,* 1957-64 (the last two are quarterlies published in Washington, D.C.).

SIDELIGHTS: Csicsery-Ronay speaks and writes French, German, and Russian and reads Latin and Greek. *Avocational interests:* Playing the piano, photography, sailing, tennis, aviation, chess, and riding horses.

*   *   *

CULLINAN, Gerald 1916-

PERSONAL: Born January 6, 1916, in San Francisco, Calif.; son of Eustace and Katherine (Lawler) Cullinan; married Barbara Lynch, January 2, 1943; children: Mary Patricia, Thomas Anthony. *Education:* Oxford University, B.A., 1937, M.A., 1938. *Religion:* Roman Catholic. *Home:* 6205 Nebraska Ave. N.W., Washington, D.C. 20015. *Office:* 100 Indiana Ave. N.W., Washington, D.C. 20001.

CAREER: San Francisco Call-Bulletin, San Francisco, Calif., reporter and department editor, 1938-43; Mooney & Cullinan (public relations), Dallas, Tex., partner, 1946-53; U.S. Post Office Department, Washington, D.C., assistant to Postmaster General, 1953-58; Edward K. Moss International (public relations), Washington, D.C., consultant, 1958-60; National Association of Letter Carriers, Washing-

ton, D.C., assistant to president, 1960—. Adviser to an international commission to translate Roman Catholic liturgy into English. *Military service:* U.S. Army Air Forces, 1943-46; became master sergeant. *Member:* National Press Club (Washington, D.C.), Newcomen Society in North America, Serra International, Kenwood Country Club (Washington, D.C.).

WRITINGS: Four Thousand Years in San Antonio, Naylor, 1948; *The Mail Man,* Merkle Press, 1967; *The Post Office Department,* Praeger, 1968; *The United States Postal Service,* Praeger, 1973. Ghostwriter of twelve books on a variety of subjects. Writer of television and radio scripts and articles.

WORK IN PROGRESS: A history of the U.S. Senate.

AVOCATIONAL INTERESTS: Latin, literary and art criticism.

*   *   *

CULSHAW, John (Royds) 1924-

PERSONAL: Born May 28, 1924, in Southport, Lancashire, England; son of Percy Ellis and Doris (Crowther) Culshaw. *Education:* Educated at King George V School, Southport, England. *Home:* 16 Arlington Ave., London N. 1, England.

CAREER: Decca Record Co. Ltd., London, England, chief producer of classical recordings, 1956-67; British Broadcasting Corp., London, England, director of television music, 1967-75; free-lance author and television producer, 1975—. Frequent broadcasting commentator for the Metropolitan Opera performances. Broadcaster on musical topics for British Broadcasting Corp. prior to joining the staff; occasional lecturer for extramural departments of University of London and Oxford University. *Military service:* Royal Navy, Fleet Air Arm, 1942-46; became lieutenant. *Awards, honors:* Co-recipient of Nicolai Medal presented by Vienna Philharmonic Orchestra, 1959, and Schalk Medal, 1967; Order of the British Empire, 1966, for services to music.

WRITINGS: Sergei Rachmaninov, Oxford University Press, 1948; *The Sons of Brutus* (novel), Secker & Warburg, 1950; *A Century of Music,* Dobson, 1951; *The Concerto,* Parrish, 1951; *A Place of Stone* (novel), Secker & Warburg, 1952; *Ring Resounding: The Stirring Account of How Wagner's "Der Ring des Nibelungen" Was Recorded for the First Time,* Viking, 1967; *Reflections on Wagner's "Ring,"* Viking, in press. Contributor to *Encyclopaedia Britannica Book of the Year,* 1948-53, and to *High Fidelity, Saturday Review, Gramophone,* and other periodicals.

SIDELIGHTS: Culshaw and his team of engineers began recording Wagner's monumental "Ring" in Vienna in 1958, a project that took seven years to complete. He says he speaks "bad French and worse German." *Avocational interests:* Flying (licensed pilot).

*   *   *

CUMMINGS, Paul 1933-

PERSONAL: Born January 24, 1933, in Detroit Lakes, Minn. *Education:* Attended University of Minnesota and Goldsmiths' College, London. *Office:* 41 East 65th St., New York, N.Y. 10021.

CAREER: Louis Alexander Gallery, New York City, director, 1962-63; *New York Arts Calendar,* New York

City, editor, 1963-65; *Gallery Guide,* New York City, editor and publisher, 1965-67; Smithsonian Institution, Archives of American Art, New York City, interviewer, 1968-70, director of oral history program, 1970—. Founder and publisher, *Print Collector's Newsletter.* Organizer, installer, and curator of exhibitions for art galleries, museums, and corporations. Consultant on cultural programs to institutions and corporations, including Ruder & Finn, Inc., New York City, 1963-67; also consultant to departments of fine arts at State University of New York at Stony Brook, 1963-67. *Member:* Drawing Society (member of executive committee). *Awards, honors: Fine Arts Market Place* named book of the year, American Library Association, 1973.

WRITINGS: A Dictionary of Contemporary American Artists, St. Martin's, 1966, 3rd edition, 1976; (editor) *Fine Arts Market Place,* Bowker, 1973, 2nd edition, 1975; *American Drawings: Twentieth Century,* Viking, 1976. Editor of "Documentary Monographs in Modern Art" series, seven books, Praeger. Editor, *Archives of American Art Journal,* 1974—.

* * *

CUNLIFFE, Marcus 1922-

PERSONAL: Born July 5, 1922; son of Keith Harold and Kathleen (Falkner) Cunliffe; married Mitzi Solomon, July 3, 1949 (divorced, 1971); married Lesley Hume, November 18, 1971; children: (first marriage) Antonia, Sharon, Jason. *Education:* Oriel College, Oxford, B.A., 1944, M.A., 1946, B.Litt., 1947. *Home:* 19 Clifton Terrace, Brighton, Sussex BN1 3HA, England. *Office:* University of Sussex, Falmer, Brighton, Sussex, England.

CAREER: Yale University, New Haven, Conn., Commonwealth Fund fellow, 1947-49; University of Manchester, Manchester, England, lecturer in American studies, 1949-56, senior lecturer, 1956-60, professor of American history and institutions, 1960-64; University of Sussex, Sussex, England, professor of American studies, 1965—. Fellow, Center for Advanced Study in the Behavioral Sciences, Stanford, Calif., 1957-58; visiting professor at Harvard University, 1959-60, City College of the City University of New York, 1970, and at University of Michigan, 1973. *Military service:* British Army, 1942-46; became lieutenant. *Member:* American Historical Association, Massachusetts Historical Society.

WRITINGS: The Royal Irish Fusiliers, 1793-1950, Oxford University Press, 1953; *The Literature of the United States,* Penguin, 1954, 3rd revised edition, 1967; *History of the Royal Warwickshire Regiment, 1919-1953,* Clowes, 1957; *George Washington: Man and Monument,* New American Library, 1958; *The Nation Takes Shape, 1789-1837,* University of Chicago Press, 1959; (editor) M. L. Weems, *Life of Washington,* Harvard University Press, 1962; (with R. B. Morris) *George Washington and the Making of a Nation* (juvenile literature), American Heritage Press, 1966; *The Presidency,* American Heritage Press, 1968; *Soldiers and Civilians,* Little, Brown, 1968; (with the editors of American Heritage) *The American Heritage History of the Presidency,* American Heritage Press, 1968; (with others) *The Making of America,* BBC Publications, 1968; *Soldiers and Civilians: The Martial Spirit in America, 1775-1865,* Little, Brown, 1968; *American Presidents and the Presidency,* Eyre & Spottiswoode, 1969, American Heritage Press, 1972; (editor with Robin Winks) *Pastmasters: Some Essays on American Historians,* Har-

per, 1969; (editor) *The London Times History of Our Times,* Norton, 1971 (published in England as *The Times History of Our Times,* Weidenfeld & Nicolson, 1971); *The Ages of Man: From Sav-age to Sew-age,* American Heritage Press, 1971; *The Age of Expansion, 1848-1917,* Weidenfeld & Nicolson, 1974; (editor) *Sphere History of Literature,* Volume VIII and Volume IX: *American Literature,* Sphere Books, 1975.

WORK IN PROGRESS: A history of the idea of private property in the United States, completion expected in 1977; a book on comparative approaches to American history, completion expected in 1977.

AVOCATIONAL INTERESTS: Cinema, theatre, imaginative literature, walking.

* * *

CURLEY, Arthur 1938-

PERSONAL: Born January 22, 1938, in Boston, Mass.; son of Alphonsus M. and Lillian (Norton) Curley. *Education:* Harvard University, B.A., 1959; Simmons College, M.S. in L.S., 1962. *Residence:* Lakewood, Ohio. *Office:* Cuyahoga County Library, 4510 Memphis Ave., Cleveland, Ohio 44144.

CAREER: Boston Public Library, Boston, Mass., adults' librarian, 1959-61; library director, Avon Public Library, Avon, Mass., 1961-64, Palatine Public Library, Palatine, Ill., 1964-68, Montclair Public Library, Montclair, N.J., 1968-75, Cuyahoga County Library, Cleveland, Ohio, 1975—. Executive director, National Library Week in Massachusetts, 1963-64. Lecturer on management, Rutgers University, 1973-75. *Member:* American Library Association (councillor-at-large, 1970-74), Public Library Association (legislation chairman, 1971-74), Ohio Library Association. *Awards, honors:* Avon Public Library received the American Library Association Book-of-the-Month Club Library Award for 1964; writings included in *Library Journal* citation of outstanding reference books of 1967.

WRITINGS: (With Dorothy Curley) *Modern Romance Literatures,* Ungar, 1967; (contributor) Melvin Voigt, editor, *Advances in Librarianship,* Volume IV, Academic Press, 1974; (contributor) Bill Katz, editor, *The Best of Library Literature: 1974,* Scarecrow, 1975; (contributor) John Wakeman, editor, *World Authors,* H. W. Wilson, 1975. Contributor to *Encyclopedia of Library and Information Sciences,* 1968—, and to *Library Journal.* Editor, *New Jersey Libraries,* 1971-74.

WORK IN PROGRESS: Continued research in modern American and Romance literatures, and in librarianship.

* * *

CURRAN, Charles E. 1934-

PERSONAL: Born March 30, 1934, in Rochester, N.Y. *Education:* St. Bernard's Seminary and College, Rochester, N.Y., B.A.; Gregorian University, Rome, Italy, S.T.B., 1957, S.T.L., 1959, S.T.D., 1961; Academia Alfonsiana, Rome, Italy, S.T.D., 1961. *Office:* Department of Theology, Catholic University of America, Washington, D.C. 20017.

CAREER: Ordained Roman Catholic priest, 1958. St. Bernard's Seminary, Rochester, N.Y., professor of moral theology, 1961-65; Catholic University of America, Washington, D.C., assistant professor, 1965-67, associate professor, 1967-71, professor of moral theology, 1971—. *Member:* American Society of Christian Ethics (president, 1971-72),

American Theological Society, Catholic Theological Society of America (vice-president, 1968-69; president, 1969-70), College Theology Society.

WRITINGS: Christian Morality Today: The Renewal of Moral Theology, Fides, 1966; *A New Look at Christian Morality,* Fides, 1968; (editor) *Absolutes in Moral Theology?,* Corpus Books, 1968; (with others) *The Responsibility of Dissent: The Church and Academic Freedom,* Sheed, 1969; (editor) *Contraception: Authority and Dissent,* Herder & Herder, 1969; (with Robert E. Hunt and others) *Dissent in and for the Church,* Sheed, 1970; *Contemporary Problems in Moral Theology,* Fides, 1970; (editor with George J. Dyer) *Shared Responsibility in the Local Church,* Catholic Theological Society of America, 1970; *Catholic Moral Theology in Dialogue,* Fides, 1972; *The Crisis in Priestly Ministry,* Fides, 1972; *Politics, Medicine and Christian Ethics: A Dialogue with Paul Ramsey,* Fortress, 1973; *New Perspectives in Moral Theology,* Fides, 1974.

Contributor: S. H. Miller and G. E. Wright, editors, *Ecumenical Dialogue at Harvard,* Harvard University Press, 1964; James E. Biechler, editor, *Law for Liberty,* Helicon, 1967; Harvey Cox, editor, *The Situation Ethics Debate,* Westminster, 1968; William Jerry Boney and Lawrence E. Molumby, editors, *The New Day,* John Knox, 1968; Gene H. Outka and Paul Ramsey, editors, *Norm and Context in Christian Ethics,* Scribner, 1968. Contributor to *Jurist, Commonweal, Homiletic,* and other journals in his field.

WORK IN PROGRESS: Articles and monographs on medical ethics, Roman Catholic social ethics in the United States, and questions of fundamental moral theology.

SIDELIGHTS: In April 1967, Curran became a *cause celebre* for priestly academic freedom when he was fired by Catholic University of America, supposedly (although the university gave no reasons for the dismissal) for his liberal views on birth control. The popular teacher choose to fight the ouster, and CU's faculty voted 400 to 18 not to hold classes until he was reinstated. The boycott closed the university for three days before Curran was rehired with the announcement that he would be promoted to associate professor the following semester.

In the summer of 1968, Curran was, as he told *CA,* "the organizer and chief spokesman of a group of American Catholic theologians ultimately totalling about 600 who dissented from the papal encyclical *Humanae Vitae.* The day after the encyclical was issued in Rome I spoke for 89 Roman Catholic theologians . . . indicating that one could be a loyal Roman Catholic and still disagree with this particular teaching. This dissent was widely carried in the newspaper and television accounts of those days. . . . These events are recorded in . . . *Dissent in and for the Church.*"

BIOGRAPHICAL/CRITICAL SOURCES: National Observer, April 24, 1967, May 1, 1967; *Christian Century,* August 27, 1969.

*   *   *

CURRIER, Alvin C. 1932-

PERSONAL: Born March 13, 1932, in Minneapolis, Minn.; married Patricia Dredge, June, 1952; children: Cathryn, Christopher, Matthew, Richard. *Education:* Macalester College, B.A., 1953; Union Theological Seminary, New York, N.Y., B.D., 1956; St. Mary's College, University of St. Andrews, further theological study. *Politics:* Democratic. *Office:* Macalester College, St. Paul, Minn. 55101.

CAREER: Ordained to Presbyterian ministry, 1956; pastor of parish embracing Mountain Lake, Butterfield, and Alpha, Minn., 1956-59, 1960-61; exchange pastor in Haslach im Kinzigtal, Germany, 1959-60; Free University of Berlin, Berlin, Germany, researcher on communism and the churches in eastern Europe at Eastern European Institute, 1961-63; Macalester College, St. Paul, Minn., assistant chaplain, beginning 1964. Co-founder of Minnesota Clergy and Laymen Concerned About Vietnam and of Dissenting Democrats (now Minnesota Conference of Concerned Democrats); member of American Civil Liberties Union and active in civil rights movement.

WRITINGS: No Easter for East Germany, Augsburg, 1968.††

*   *   *

CURTIS, Charles J(ohn) 1921-

PERSONAL: Born September 7, 1921, in Isanti, Minn.; married Norma Nason (a high school teacher), July 21, 1946; children: Beth (deceased), Linell, Susan. *Education:* Gustavus Adolphus College, B.A., 1943; Augustana Theological Seminary, Rock Island, Ill., B.D., 1946; University of Chicago, M.A., 1950, Ph.D., 1965; additional study at Princeton Theological Seminary. *Politics:* Democrat. *Office:* Department of Theology, DePaul University, Chicago, Ill. 60614.

CAREER: Clergyman of Lutheran Church in America. Pastor in San Lorenzo, Calif., 1950-53, and Chicago, Ill., 1953—, with pastorate at Immanuel Lutheran Church, 1959—; DePaul University, Chicago, associate professor of theology, 1967—. Special lecturer at Loyola University, Chicago, and Lutheran institutions. Dean of North Chicagoland district, Illinois Synod, Lutheran Church in America. Member of board of directors of Augustana Hospital. *Member:* American Academy of Religion, American Theological Society, Lutheran Academy for Scholarship, Society for the Scientific Study of Religion, Swedish Pioneer Historical Society, Swedish Club of Chicago. *Awards, honors:* D.D., Carthage College, 1966; James M. Yard Brotherhood Award, National Conference of Christians and Jews.

WRITINGS: Nathan Soederblom: Theologian of Revelation, Covenant Press, 1966; *Facets of Ecumenicity* (Loyola University Ecumenical Forum lectures), Academy Library Guild, 1966; *Soederblom: Ecumenical Pioneer,* Augsburg, 1967; *The Task of Philosophical Theology,* Philosophical Library, 1967. Contributor of more than fifty articles to Protestant and Catholic journals in United States and Europe.

WORK IN PROGRESS: Eight Trialogue books; *Nathan Soederblom: Evangelical Catholic; Evangelical Catholicity; Systematic Process Theology; Soederblom Anthology; Soederblom Studies; Contemporary Religious Thought; The Mystery of the Church.*

*   *   *

CURTIS, David 1942-

PERSONAL: Born June 24, 1942; son of Charles and Rebecca (Lillenstein) Curtis; married Janice Van Raay (an artist), March 24, 1968; children: Cassidy Jonathan. *Education:* Cornell University, B.A., 1964; Stanford University, M.A., 1965; New York University, further graduate study, 1965-67. *Home:* 135 Eastern Pkwy., Brooklyn, N.Y. 11238. *Office:* 919 Third Ave., New York, N.Y. 10022.

CAREER: Bill Adler Books, New York City, managing editor, 1966-68; Ketchum MacLeod & Grove Advertising, New York City, copywriter, 1969-71; Spitzer/Bogan Advertising, New York City, copy supervisor, beginning 1972.

WRITINGS: (With Stephen Crane) *Dayan*, Citadel, 1967; *Experimental Cinema*, Universe Books, 1971.†

* * *

CUTLER, Donald R. 1930-

PERSONAL: Born November 20, 1930, in Sharon, Pa.; son of John B. (an educator) and Elmo (Carnes) Cutler; married Virginia Barone, June 20, 1958; children: Julia, Anne, Gavin. *Education:* Pennsylvania State University, A.B., 1953; Protestant Episcopal Theological Seminary in Virginia, B.D., 1957; Harvard University, Ph.D., 1965. *Office:* Beacon Press, 25 Beacon St., Boston, Mass. 02138.

CAREER: Episcopal clergyman. Pennsylvania State University, University Park, Episcopal chaplain, 1957-59; Harvard University, Cambridge, Mass., associate Episcopal chaplain, 1959-62; Church Society for College Work, Cambridge, director of research, 1963-66; Beacon Press, Boston, Mass., an editor, beginning 1966. *Member:* Harvard Club (Boston).

WRITINGS: (Editor) *The Religious Situation: 1968*, Beacon Press, 1968 (published in England as *World Year Book of Religion: The Religious Situation*, Volume I, Evans Brothers, 1969); (editor) *The Religious Situation: 1969*, Beacon Press, 1969 (published in England as *World Year Book of Religion: The Religious Situation*, Volume II, Evans Brothers, 1970); (editor) *Updating Life and Death: Essays in the Ethics of Religion*, Beacon Press, 1969; (editor with Herbert W. Richardson) *Transcendence*, Beacon Press, 1969.

BIOGRAPHICAL/CRITICAL SOURCES: Christian Century, May 29, 1968; *Commonweal*, October 17, 1969.†

* * *

CUTLER, Irving H. 1923-

PERSONAL: Born April 11, 1923, in Chicago, Ill.; son of Zelig (a newsman) and Frieda (Wopner) Cutler; married Marian Horovitz, August 31, 1951; children: Daniel, Susan. *Education:* Herzl Junior College, Chicago, Ill., A.A., 1942; University of Chicago, M.A., 1948; Northwestern University, Ph.D., 1964. *Home:* 3217 Hill Lane, Wilmette, Ill. *Office:* Department of Geography, Chicago State University, 95th St. and King Dr., Chicago, Ill. 60628.

CAREER: U.S. Department of Labor, Chicago, Ill., regional labor and housing investigator, 1946-47; Crane Junior College, Chicago, instructor in social science, 1954-59; U.S. Army, Corps of Engineers, Chicago, transportation geographer, 1957; Chicago State University, Chicago, professor of geography, 1961—, chairman of department, 1974—. Consultant to Ginn & Co., 1964-65, U.S. Office of Economic Opportunity, 1965-66, and Journal Films, 1967-68. Member of Wilmette Human Relations Committee, 1967-70. *Military service:* U.S. Navy, 1943-46; became lieutenant junior grade. *Member:* International Geographical Union, Association of American Geographers, National Council for Geographic Education, Illinois Geographical Society, Geographic Society of Chicago, Sigma Xi. *Awards, honors:* Haas research grant.

WRITINGS: The Chicago-Milwaukee Corridor: A Geographic Study of Intermetropolitan Coalescence, Northwestern University Studies in Geography, 1965; (with John Beck and John Hobgood) *Pembroke Township: A Research Report on Problems and Possibilities*, U.S. Office of Economic Opportunity, 1966; (editor) *The Chicago Metropolitan Area: Selected Geographic Readings*, Simon & Schuster, 1970; *Chicago: Metropolis of the Mid-Continent*, Geographic Society of Chicago, 1973.

Contributor: Harold Mayer, editor, *1967 Conference on Mass Transportation*, Brotherhood of Railroad Trainmen, 1968; Herbert Gross, editor, *A Modern City: Its Geography*, National Council for Geographic Education, 1970; Ronald E. Nelson, editor, *Geography of Illinois*, Kendall/Hunt, 1976; Brian J. L. Berry, editor, *Chicago: Transformation of an Urban System*, Association of American Geographers, 1976. Contributor to geography and transportation journals.

WORK IN PROGRESS: Contributing to a book tentatively entitled *The City*, for C. E. Merrill.

* * *

CUTTINO, G(eorge) P(eddy) 1914-

PERSONAL: Surname is accented on first syllable; born March 9, 1914, in Newnan, Ga.; son of David Smith II and Katie May (Peddy) Cuttino. *Education:* Swarthmore College, B.A., 1935; University of Iowa, M.A., 1936; Oxford University, D.Phil., 1938; University of London, postdoctoral study, 1938-39. *Politics:* Independent Democrat. *Religion:* Protestant. *Home:* 1270 University Dr. N.E., Atlanta, Ga. 30306. *Office:* Department of History, Emory University, Atlanta, Ga. 30322.

CAREER: University of Iowa, Iowa City, instructor, 1939-42, assistant professor of history, 1946; assistant professor at Swarthmore College, Swarthmore, Pa., and Bryn Mawr College, Bryn Mawr, Pa., 1946-49, associate professor of history at both colleges, 1949-52; Emory University, Atlanta, Ga., associate professor, 1952-55, professor of history, 1955—. Visiting honors examiner, Swarthmore College, 1940-41, 1958, 1961, University of Virginia, 1966; academic consultant, Bishop College, 1963-65. *Military service:* U.S. Army, Intelligence, 1942-46, 1951-52; became major; received Bronze Star.

MEMBER: Royal Historical Society (fellow), Mediaeval Academy of America, American Historical Association, Association of American Rhodes Scholars, American Association of University Professors, Historical Association (England), British Records Society, Huguenot Society of America, Huguenot Society of Georgia, Huguenot Society of South Carolina, Phi Beta Kappa. *Awards, honors:* Rhodes scholar, 1936-39; Guggenheim fellowships, 1947-48, 1953-54.

WRITINGS: English Diplomatic Administration, 1259-1339, Oxford University Press, 1940, 2nd edition, 1971; *The Gascon Calendar of 1322*, Royal Historical Society, 1949; *I Laugh Through Tears: The Ballades of Francois Villon*, Philosophical Library, 1955; *Le Livre d'Agenais*, Association Marc Bloch, 1956; (with J. R. Major and R. L. Scranton) *Civilization in the Western World*, Lippincott, 1967; *Gascon Register A (Series of 1318-1319)*, three volumes, Oxford University Press, 1975. Contributor to historical journals.

SIDELIGHTS: Cuttino is competent in Medieval Latin, French, Old French, Gascon, Italian, and Spanish.

CUYLER, Louise E. 1908-

PERSONAL: Born March 14, 1908, in Omaha, Neb.; daughter of A. Rust (a dentist) and Stella (Slade) Cuyler. *Education:* University of Rochester, B.M., 1929, Ph.D., 1948; University of Michigan, A.M., 1931. *Office:* Department of Music, University of Michigan, Ann Arbor, Mich. 48105.

CAREER: University of Michigan, Ann Arbor, assistant professor of music theory, 1935-42, associate professor, 1945-53, professor of musicology, 1953-75, professor emeritus, 1975—, chairman of department, 1955-70. Visiting professor, Stanford University, 1965, Indiana University, 1975; William Allen Neilson Research Professor, Smith College, 1975; visiting lecturer, University of California, Santa Barbara, 1976. *Member:* American Musicological Society (national secretary, 1955-70), Renaissance Society of America, Music Library Association. *Awards, honors:* Rackham research and publication grants, 1948, 1951; Fulbright research grant for work in Belgium, 1953-54; American Council of Learned Societies grant, 1960.

WRITINGS: Choralis Constantinus, Book III, University of Michigan Press, 1950; *Five Polyphonic Masses of H. Isaac,* University of Michigan Press, 1956; (contributor) G. Reese and R. Brandel, editors, *A Commonwealth of Music,* Free Press of Glencoe, 1964; (contributor) J. LaRue, editor with others, *Aspects of Medieval and Renaissance Music,* Norton, 1966; *The Emperor Maximilian I and Music,* Oxford University Press, 1973; *The Symphony,* Harcourt, 1973.

WORK IN PROGRESS: The Contrafactum in Sixteenth-Century Anthologies of Polyphonic Music.

* * *

DAANE, James 1914-

PERSONAL: Born May 31, 1914, in Grand Haven, Mich.; son of James and Martina (Ringelberg) Daane; married Jean Temple, June 19, 1940; children: Marilyn Jean, Bruce James. *Education:* Calvin College, B.A., 1937; Calvin Seminary, Th.B., 1940; Princeton Theological Seminary, Th.D., 1947; post-doctoral study at Free Reformed University, Amsterdam, Netherlands, 1952-53. *Home and office:* 1771 East Mendocino St., Altadena, Calif. 91001.

CAREER: Clergyman of Christian Reformed Church; minister in New Jersey, 1943-45, and Lafayette, Ind., 1945-49; First Christian Reformed Church Los Angeles, Calif., minister, 1949-61; *Christianity Today,* Washington, D.C., associate editor, 1961-66; Fuller Theological Seminary, Pasadena, Calif., professor of practical theology and director of professional doctorate program, 1966-74, professor of theology and ministry, 1974—.

WRITINGS: The Theology of Grace: An Inquiry into and Evaluation of Cornelius Van Til's Doctrine of Common Grace, Eerdmans, 1954; *The Anatomy of Anti-Semitism, and Other Essays on Religion and Race,* Eerdmans, 1965; *The Freedom of God: Study of Election and Pulpit,* Eerdmans, 1973. Contributor to religious journals. Member of editorial staff, *Reformed Journal,* 1951—.

WORK IN PROGRESS: A book on preaching.

BIOGRAPHICAL/CRITICAL SOURCES: Cornelius Van Til, *The Theology of James Daane,* Presbyterian & Reformed, 1959.

DABNEY, Ross H. 1934-

PERSONAL: Born June 10, 1934, in Dallas, Tex.; son of Lewis Meriwether (a lawyer) and Crystal (Ross) Dabney; married Charlotte Gmelin, August 1, 1959; children: Susan, Barbara. *Education:* Princeton University, A.B., 1955; Harvard University, Ph.D., 1964. *Office:* Department of English, Sweet Briar College, Sweet Briar, Va. 24595.

CAREER: Smith College, Northampton, Mass., instructor in English, 1960-65; University of Virginia, Charlottesville, visiting assistant professor of English, 1965-66; currently member of faculty, department of English, Sweet Briar College, Sweet Briar, Va. *Military service:* U.S. Army Reserve, 1955-64; active duty, 1956; became lieutenant. *Member:* Modern Language Association of America.

WRITINGS: Love and Property in the Novels of Dickens, University of California Press, 1967.

WORK IN PROGRESS: A book on the English novel.†

* * *

DAHLBERG, Jane S. 1923-

PERSONAL: Born February 7, 1923, in New York, N.Y.; daughter of Sidney and Aimee (Rothschild) Silsdorf; married Charles Clay Dahlberg (a psychoanalyst), June 28, 1959; children: John, James, Charles, Robert. *Education:* Hunter College (now Hunter College of the City University of New York), B.A., 1944; Syracuse University, M.P.A., 1945; New York University, Ph.D., 1964. *Home:* 516 East 87th St., New York, N.Y. 10028. *Office:* Empire State College of the State University of New York, 300 Park Ave. S., New York, N.Y. 10010.

CAREER: New York University, University College, Bronx, N.Y., assistant professor of politics and assistant dean, 1965-68; Sarah Lawrence College, Bronxville, N.Y., associate dean, 1968-69, member of political science faculty, 1969-70; Empire State College of the State University of New York, New York, N.Y., professor of political science, 1971—, dean, 1972—. *Member:* American Political Science Association, American Society for Public Administration, Phi Beta Kappa.

WRITINGS: The New York Bureau of Municipal Research: Pioneer in Public Administration, New York University Press, 1966; *Introduction to American Government,* Empire State College, 1974; *The Interpersonal Theory of Harvey Stack Sullivan,* Empire State College, 1975.

* * *

DAHMUS, Joseph Henry 1909-

PERSONAL: Born March 11, 1909, in St. Maurice, Ind.; son of Henry Herman and Rosa (Rahe) Dahmus; married Mildred M. Kling; children: John, Rosemary, Helen, Claire, Edward, Mary, Robert, Margaret, James, Elizabeth. *Education:* Pontifical College Josephinum, A.B., 1930; St. Louis University, M.A., 1933; University of Illinois, Ph.D., 1938. *Office:* Department of History, Pennsylvania State University, University Park, Pa.

CAREER: Instructor in history at College of Mount St. Vincent, New York, N.Y., 1939-43, Aquinas College, Grand Rapids, Mich., 1944-46, and St. John's University, Brooklyn, N.Y., 1946-47; Pennsylvania State University, University Park, 1947—, began as assistant professor, professor of medieval history, 1955—. *Member:* Mediaeval Academy of America, American Historical Association.

WRITINGS: The Metropolitan Visitations of William

Courtenay, University of Illinois Press, 1950; *The Prosecution of John Wyclyf*, Yale University Press, 1952; *A History of Medieval Civilization*, Odyssey, 1964; *William Courtenay, Archbishop of Canterbury 1381-1396*, Pennsylvania State University Press, 1966; *Seven Medieval Kings*, Doubleday, 1967; *The Middle Ages: A Popular History*, Doubleday, 1968; *Seven Medieval Queens*, Doubleday, 1972. Contributor to *Speculum* and *Catholic Historical Review*.

* * *

DALAND, Robert T(heodore) 1919-

PERSONAL: Born October 3, 1919, in Milton, Wis.; son of John Norton (a dean) and Nellie (Furrow) Daland; married Dorothy Shaw (a sculptor), June 6, 1942; children: David Norton, William Christopher. *Education:* Milton College, B.A., 1942; University of Wisconsin, M.A., 1947, Ph.D., 1952. *Religion:* Unitarian Universalist. *Home:* Pine Bluff Trail, Chapel Hill, N.C. 27514. *Office:* Department of Political Science, University of North Carolina, Chapel Hill, N.C. 27514.

CAREER: University of Alabama, University, 1949-56, began as instructor, became assistant professor; University of Connecticut, Storrs, assistant professor of political science, 1956-58; University of North Carolina, Chapel Hill, associate professor of political science, 1959-61; University of Southern California, member of Brazil faculty, 1961-63; University of North Carolina, professor of political science, 1963—, director of public administration program, 1963-70. *Military service:* U.S. Army, 1942-45. *Member:* American Political Science Association, American Society for Public Administration, International Political Science Association, National Municipal League, Southern Political Science Association, Pi Sigma Alpha. *Awards, honors:* Ford faculty fellow at University of California, 1954-55; Metropolitan Region Program fellow at Columbia University, 1958-59.

WRITINGS: Government and Health, University of Alabama Press, 1955; (editor) *Perspectives of Brazilian Public Administration*, University of Southern California Press, 1963; *Brazilian Planning: Development Politics and Administration*, University of North Carolina Press, 1967. Contributor to journals. Member of editorial board, *Public Administration Review*.

WORK IN PROGRESS: A study of certain aspects of the Brazilian national bureaucracy.†

* * *

DALE, D(ion) M(urray) C(rosbie) 1930-

PERSONAL: Born August 28, 1930, in Wanganui, New Zealand; son of Daniel Sutor (a teacher) and Ida Victoria (also a teacher; maiden name, Gillions) Dale; married Elizabeth M. Slade (a teacher), 1967. *Education:* University of Auckland, B.A. and Diploma in Education, 1954; University of Manchester, Ph.D., 1958. *Office:* Institute of Education, University of London, Malet St., London W.C.1, England.

CAREER: School for Deaf Children, Auckland, New Zealand, principal, 1962-65; University of London, London, England, senior lecturer in education of deaf and partially hearing children, 1965—.

WRITINGS: Applied Audiology for Children, C. C Thomas, 1962, 2nd edition, 1967; *Deaf Children at Home and at School*, University of London Press, 1967; *Language Development in Deaf and Partially Hearing Children*, C. C Thomas, 1974.

* * *

DALE, Reginald R. 1907-

PERSONAL: Born April 11, 1907, in Widnes, Lancashire, England; son of Rowland Blease and Florence Emma (Harrison) Dale; married Margaret Watson Pollard, August, 1933; children: F. Rowland, Rosemary, Jonathan, Jeremy Watson. *Education:* University of Liverpool, B.A. (honors in history), 1928, M.A., 1931; University of Leeds, M.Ed., 1936. *Politics:* Socialist. *Religion:* Society of Friends. *Home:* 81 West Cross Lane, Swansea, Wales.

CAREER: Teacher of music, and later, history in British grammar schools, 1929-46; University College of Swansea, Swansea, Wales, 1946-72, began as assistant, senior lecturer, 1962-69, reader in education, 1969-72. Summer lecturer, University of British Columbia. *Member:* British Psychological Society (fellow; past chairman, education section). *Awards, honors:* Leverhulme research award, 1967.

WRITINGS: From School to University, Routledge & Kegan Paul, 1954; (with S. Griffith) *Downstream: A Study of Academic Deterioration*, Routledge & Kegan Paul, 1965; (contributor) H. J. Butcher, editor, *Educational Research in Britain*, University of London Press, 1968; *Mixed or Single-Sex School?*, Routledge & Kegan Paul, Volume I, 1969, Volume II, 1971, Volume III, 1974. Contributor of articles to educational journals.

AVOCATIONAL INTERESTS: Walking, chess, collecting rare books, music.

* * *

DALRYMPLE, Willard 1921-

PERSONAL: Born June 21, 1921, in Newton, Mass.; son of Sidney Collingwood (a physician) and Dorothy (Chester) Dalrymple; married Margaret Lothrop, November 18, 1950; children: Frederick Lothrop, Thomas Starbuck. *Education:* Harvard University, A.B. (cum laude), 1943, M.D., 1946. *Religion:* Presbyterian. *Home:* 24 Vernon Circle, Princeton, N.J. 08540. *Office:* McCosh Infirmary, Princeton University, Princeton, N.J. 08540.

CAREER: Massachusetts General Hospital, Boston, intern, 1946-47, fellow, 1949-50; U.S. Veterans Administration Hospital, West Roxbury, Mass., resident, 1949-50, 1951-52; Massachusetts Institute of Technology, Cambridge, assistant physician in medical department, 1952-56; Harvard University, Cambridge, Mass., instructor in medicine at medical school, 1952-61, physician with university health services, 1956-60; Princeton University, Princeton, N.J., director of university health services, 1961—. Columbia University, instructor in medicine, 1964-66, assistant physician at Vanderbilt Clinic. Assistant clinical professor of medicine, Rutgers University Medical School, 1970—. Trustee, Princeton Day School and Westminster Choir College. *Military service:* U.S. Air Force, 1947-49. *Member:* American College Health Association (president, 1972-73), Massachusetts Medical Association, New Jersey Medical Association, Mercer County Medical Association.

WRITINGS: The Foundations of Health, Allyn & Bacon, 1959; (contributor) G. B. Blaine, Jr. and C. C. McArthur, editors, *Emotional Problems of the Student*, Appleton, 1961; (editor with Lawrence A. Pervin and Louis E. Reik) *The College Dropout and the Utilization of Talent*,

Princeton University Press, 1966; (with Harold S. Diehl) *Healthful Living,* 8th edition, McGraw, 1968, 9th edition, 1973; *Sex Is for Real: Human Sexuality and Sexual Responsibility,* McGraw, 1969; (with Diehl) *Elements of Healthful Living,* 4th edition, McGraw, 1969. Contributor of about twenty articles to medical journals, a number of them on infectious mononucleosis and its management. Editor, *Journal of the American College Health Association,* 1973—.

* * *

DALTON, Dorothy 1915-
(Dorothy Dalton Kuehn)

PERSONAL: Born September 25, 1915, in New York, N.Y.; daughter of John Aloysius (a printer) and Mary Agnes (Ferris) Dalton; married John Raymond Birmingham, November 14, 1936 (divorced, 1945); married LeRoy Edward Kuehn (a sign artist, Kuehn Signs), January 12, 1946; children: (second marriage) Christine, Stephanie. *Education:* B.A., University of Wisconsin. *Politics:* Republican. *Religion:* "No church affiliation." *Home:* 1125 Valley Rd., Menasha, Wis. 54952.

CAREER: Worked for electrical specialties company, 1933-36; receptionist-assistant to doctors, 1937-42; New York (N.Y.) public library, assistant librarian, 1942-44. *Military service:* Women's Army Corps (WACS), Medics, 1944-46. *Member:* Poetry Society of America, Oregon State Poetry Association, American Legion Post 38. *Awards, honors:* Hatshaker's Prize for poetry of Olivant Press, 1966; *Writer's Digest* poetry contest winner, 1970, 1972; Touchstone Poetry award of Viterbo College, 1974.

WRITINGS:—Poems: *Poems,* Olivant, 1967; *Midnight and Counting,* Charas Press, 1973. Poetry anthologized in *New Orlando Anthology II, New Poets* from James Decker Press, and *Poetry Ventured.* Contributor of poetry to *New York Quarterly, Red Cedar Review, Southern Poetry Review, Christian Science Monitor, Outposts* (England), *Poet* (India), *Wisconsin Review,* and others. Contributor of short stories and humorous essays, some under name Dorothy Dalton Kuehn, to periodicals and newspapers, including *St. Anthony Messenger, Sacred Heart Messenger, Exclusively Yours,* and *Spokesman-Review.* Editor, *Poetry View,* 1970—.

WORK IN PROGRESS: A fourth book of poetry, and a gothic novel laid in Ireland, tentatively entitled *Carriga Castle.*

AVOCATIONAL INTERESTS: Painting in oils. Guitar.

* * *

D'AMBROSIO, Charles A. 1932-
(Dollar Investor)

PERSONAL: Born August 31, 1932, in Chicago, Ill.; son of Anthony Joseph and Della (Melpede) D'Ambrosio; married Marilyn Ann Hilgert, June 8, 1957; children: Charles A., Jr., Mary Margaret, Mary Catherine, Mary Christine, Mary Patricia, Michael Charles, John Charles Daniel. *Education:* John Carroll University, student, 1950-52; Loyola University, Chicago, Ill., B.S.C., 1955; University of Illinois, M.S., 1958, Ph.D., 1962. *Religion:* Roman Catholic. *Home:* 3604 42nd Ave., Northeast, Seattle, Wash. 98105. *Office:* University of Washington, Seattle, Wash. 98195.

CAREER: University of Washington, Seattle, assistant professor, 1960-63, associate professor, 1963-70, professor

of finance, 1970—. Member of faculty, Pacific Coast Banking School and American Savings and Loan Institute; consultant to Pacific Northwest Bell Telephone Co. and investment firms. *Member:* American Economic Association, American Finance Association, Association for Social Economics, Financial Management Association, Western Finance Association, Western Economic Association, Seattle Society of Investment Analysts.

WRITINGS: (With Stephen H. Archer) *Business Finance: Theory and Management,* and *Instructor's Manual,* Macmillan, 1966, 2nd edition, 1972; (editor with Archer) *Theory of Business Finance: A Book of Readings,* Macmillan, 1967; (contributor) Bayard O. Wheeler, *Business: An Introductory Analysis,* and *Workbook,* Harper, 1967; *Bulls, Bears, and Bucks: An Elementary Guide to Successful Investing,* Prentice-Hall, 1969; *Mister Dollar Investor,* Prentice-Hall, 1969; (under pseudonym, Dollar Investor) *My Stockbroker is a Bum: Or, Where Are All the Customers' Yachts,* Exposition Press, 1972. Writer of telecourse, "Bulls, Bears, and Bucks," carried by University of Washington educational television station, 1967. Contributor to economic and finance journals. Consulting editor, McGraw's "Finance Series"; co-founder, and presently managing editor, *Journal of Financial and Quantitative Analysis.*

WORK IN PROGRESS: Analysis of risk rate-of-return.

* * *

DANIELS, Guy 1919-

PERSONAL: Born May 11, 1919, in Gilmore City, Iowa; son of Guy Emmett (a gentleman farmer) and Gretchen (Van Alstine) Daniels; married Margaret Holbrook (a teacher), November 14, 1943; married second wife, Anne McCrea, January 13, 1963; married third wife, Vernell Groom, December 2, 1967; children: (first marriage) Brooke (Mrs. Donald Hinrichsen); (second marriage) Matthew. *Education:* University of Iowa, B.A., 1941, graduate study, 1941-42. *Home and office:* 416 East 65th St., New York, N.Y. 10021. *Agent:* Gunther Stuhlmann, 65 Irving Pl., New York, N.Y. 10003.

CAREER: Trans-World Airlines, International Division, chief language instructor at Training School, Reading, Pa., and Newark, Del., 1946-47; U.S. Government, Washington, D.C., "petty bureaucrat," 1947-52; full-time writer and translator, 1952—. *Military service:* U.S. Navy, 1942-45; became lieutenant junior grade; received combat star. *Member:* P.E.N., Phi Beta Kappa. *Awards, honors:* Fellow, Chapelbrook Foundation, 1967.

WRITINGS: Poems and Translations, Inferno Press, 1959; *Progress, U.S.A.* (novel), Macmillan, 1968. Work represented in many anthologies, including *Poetry Los Angeles I,* Villiers Publications, 1958, and *A Treasury of American Political Humor,* edited by Leonard C. Lewin, Delacorte, 1964.

Translations: Erich Auerbach, *An Introduction to Romance Languages and Literature,* Putnam, 1961; Stendhal, *Racine and Shakespeare,* Crowell-Collier Press, 1962; *A Lermontov Reader,* Macmillan, 1965; *Fifteen Fables of Krylov* (juvenile), Macmillan, 1965; *Ivan the Fool, and Other Tales of Leo Tolstoy* (juvenile), Macmillan, 1966; *The Tsar's Riddles* (juvenile), McGraw, 1967; Nikolai Leskov, *The Wild Beast* (juvenile), Funk, 1968; *The Complete Plays of Vladimir Mayakovsky,* Washington Square Press, 1968; *The Falcon Under the Hat: Favorite Russian Merry Tales and Fairy Tales* (juvenile), Funk, 1969; *Rus-*

sian Comic Fiction, New American Library, 1970; Ivan Bunin, *Velga* (juvenile), S. G. Phillips, 1970; Vladimir Mayakovsky, *Timothy's Horse* (juvenile), Pantheon, 1970; *Foma the Terrible* (juvenile), Delacorte, 1970; Andre Castelot, *Napoleon,* Harper, 1971; Yevgeny Riabchikov, *Russians in Space,* Doubleday, 1971; Anton Chekhov, *The Wolf and the Mutt* (juvenile), McGraw, 1971; Colette Portal, *The Beauty of Birth* (juvenile), Pantheon, 1971; *The Peasant's Pea Patch* (juvenile), Delacorte, 1971; Pierre Louys, *Mimes des Courtisanes,* Cercle des Editions Privees, 1973; Honore de Balzac, *The Unknown Masterpiece,* Cercle des Editions Privees, 1973; Henry de Montherlant, *Pasiphae,* Cercle des Editions Privees, 1973; Valery Chalidze, *To Defend These Rights,* Random House, 1974; Andrei Sakharov, *My Country and the World,* Knopf, 1975; Roy Medvedev, *A History of the Civil War in the Don,* Knopf, in press; *The Autobiography of Sergei Prokofiev,* Doubleday, in press; Andre Bazin, *The Cinema of Cruelty,* Third Press, in press.

Contributor of original poetry, fiction, and articles to periodicals, including *New Republic, Nation, New Directions, Kenyon Review,* and *Beloit Poetry Journal.* Associate editor, *Trace* (magazine), 1956-58; member of advisory board, *Soviet Studies in Literature.*

WORK IN PROGRESS: Translations of *The Russian Ballet: Past and Present* by A. Demidov, and *The Soviet General Staff at War* by S. M. Shtemenko, both for Doubleday.

SIDELIGHTS: Guy Daniels told *CA:* "Rather deeply involved in 'classical' (i.e., largely nineteenth-century) Russian authors, especially the poets. Am getting mired down in this vast bog to the detriment of my poetry (abandoned) and fiction (lately resumed with a vengeance)." In addition to translating ability in Russian and French, he has some competence in Spanish and Italian.

*   *   *

DARLING, Richard L(ewis) 1925-

PERSONAL: Born January 19, 1925, in Great Falls, Mont.; son of Harry (a farmer) and Faye (Willey) Darling; married Persis Ann Williams (a librarian), December 11, 1947 (divorced, 1973); married Pamela Ann Wood (a librarian), May 5, 1973; children: Richard Lewis, Jere Andrew, Katherine Elizabeth. *Education:* University of Montana, B.A. (honors), 1948, M.A., 1950; University of Michigan, A.M.L.S., 1954, Ph.D., 1960. *Politics:* Democrat. *Religion:* Episcopalian. *Home:* 560 Riverside Dr., New York, N.Y. 10027. *Office:* School of Library Service, Columbia University, New York, N.Y. 10027.

CAREER: University of Michigan, University High School, Ann Arbor, librarian, 1951-56; University of Montana, Missoula, assistant professor of library science, 1956-59; Livonia (Mich.) public schools, coordinator of libraries, 1959-62; U.S. Office of Education, Library Service Bureau, Washington, D.C., school library specialist, 1962-64; Montgomery County Public Schools, Rockville, Md., supervisor of libraries, 1964-65, assistant director of department of instructional materials, 1965-66, director of department of educational media and technology, 1966-70; Columbia University, New York, N.Y., dean of School of Library Service, 1970—. Visiting summer instructor, University of Montana, 1954, 1955, 1960, and 1963; visiting summer lecturer, University of Michigan, 1961, and Columbia University, 1969. Consultant, National Library Statistics Coordinating Project, 1964. *Military service:* U.S. Army, 1943-46; became technical sergeant.

MEMBER: American Library Association (second vice-president, 1970-71), American Association of School Librarians (president, 1966-67), Association of American Library Schools, New York Library Association, Freedom to Read Foundation (trustee; president, 1974—). *Awards, honors:* E. P. Dutton-John McRae Award of American Library Association, 1959; Broome Award, Montgomery County Education Association, 1969, for *The Rise of Children's Book Reviewing in America.*

WRITINGS: Public School Library Statistics, 1962-63, U.S. Office of Education, 1964; *Survey of School Library Standards,* U.S. Office of Education, 1964; (with James T. Taylor and Mary Helen Mahar) *Library Facilities for Elementary and Secondary Schools,* U.S. Office of Education, 1965; (with Henry T. Drennan) *Library Manpower,* U.S. Office of Education, 1966; *The Rise of Children's Book Reviewing in America, 1865-1881,* Bowker, 1968. Contributor to journals. Children's book review editor, *Childhood Education,* 1965-68.

*   *   *

DARROW, Richard W(illiam) 1915-

PERSONAL: Born September 23, 1915, in Champaign County, Ohio; son of Benjamin H. and Mary Frances (Carter) Darrow; married Nelda Darling, September 17, 1938; children: William R., John H. *Education:* Ohio Wesleyan University, B.A. (cum laude), 1936. *Home:* 16 Sutton Place, New York, N.Y. 10022. *Office:* Hill & Knowlton, Inc., 633 Third Ave., New York, N.Y. 10017.

CAREER: Daily Citizen, Urbana, Ohio, reporter, circulation promotion, 1933-34; International News Service, Washington, D.C., reporter, 1935; *Columbus Citizen,* Columbus, Ohio, reporter, aviation editor, then assistant city editor, 1936-41; Curtiss-Wright Corp., manager of public relations, Columbus, Ohio, 1941-43, assistant director of public relations for airplane division, Buffalo, N.Y., 1943-44, and New York, N.Y., 1944-45; American Meat Institute, Chicago, Ill., assistant to president, 1945-46; Glenn L. Martin Co., Baltimore, Md., director of public relations, 1946-52; Hill & Knowlton, Inc. (public relations), New York, N.Y., vice-president, 1952-55, executive vice-president, 1955-66, president, 1966-71, chairman of board and chief executive officer, 1971—. Ohio Wesleyan University, trustee, 1957—, chairman of board of trustees, 1968-72; Scarsdale Village, member of board of trustees, 1967-71, mayor, 1971-73. Chairman of civilian public relations advisory committee, U.S. Military Academy; member of national executive board, Boy Scouts of America, 1962—. Also member of numerous other civic, public, and community organizations.

MEMBER: Public Relations Society of America, Ohio Wesleyan University Alumni Association (national president, 1952-54; New York area president, 1957-58), Aviation/Space Writers Association, Association of Petroleum Writers, Overseas Press Club, National Press Club, Phi Beta Kappa, Phi Gamma Delta, Omicron Delta Kappa, Pi Delta Epsilon, Pi Sigma Alpha. *Award, honors:* Awards from Trans World Airlines for aviation writing, 1940, 1941, and from American Public Relations Association for fostering Latin American public relations, 1947; *Public Relations News* Public Relations Professional of the Year, 1971; U.S. Army Outstanding Civilian Service Medal, 1972; Scarsdale Town Club Medal, 1973; Scarsdale Bowl (for civic service), 1974; Boy Scouts of America Silver Beaver, Silver Buffalo and Distinguished Eagle awards; Boy Scouts of the Philippines, Bronze Tamaray.

WRITINGS: (With Dan J. Forrestal and Aubrey O. Cookman) *Dartnell Public Relations Handbook,* Dartnell, 1967, revised edition, 1968. Contributor to magazines, newspapers, and company publications.

AVOCATIONAL INTERESTS: Golf, photography, travel, youth recreation projects.

* * *

DAVIDSON, Roger H(arry) 1936-

PERSONAL: Born July 31, 1936, in Washington, D.C.; son of Ross Wallace (a botanist) and Mildred (Younger) Davidson; married Nancy Dixon (an editorial assistant), September 29, 1961; children: Douglas Ross, Christopher Reed. *Education:* University of Colorado, B.A. (magna cum laude), 1958; Columbia University, Ph.D., 1963. *Office:* Department of Political Science, University of California, Santa Barbara, Calif. 93106.

CAREER: Fort Collins Coloradoan, Fort Collins, Colo., municipal reporter, summers, 1957-59; Brookings Institution, Washington, D.C., research assistant, 1960; Dartmouth College, Hanover, N.H., assistant professor of government, 1962-68; University of California, Santa Barbara, associate professor, 1968-71, professor of political science, 1971—. Staff associate, W. E. Upjohn Institute for Employment Research, Washington, D.C., 1965-66; chairman, Upper Valley Human Rights Council, Hanover, N.H., 1967-68; scholar-in-residence, National Manpower Policy Task Force, 1970-71; professional staff member, Select Committee on Committees, U.S. House of Representatives, 1973-74. Member of Gioleta Valley Citizens Planning Group, Santa Barbara, Calif., 1974-75. *Member:* American Political Science Association, American Association of University Professors, Western Political Science Association, Phi Beta Kappa, Delta Sigma Rho. *Awards, honors:* Faculty fellowship, Dartmouth College, 1965-66.

WRITINGS: (With D. M. Kovenock and M. K. O'Leary) *Congress in Crisis: Politics and Congressional Reform,* Wadsworth, 1966; (with J. F. Bibby) *On Capitol Hill: Studies in Legislative Politics,* Holt, 1967, 2nd edition, 1972; *The Role of the Congressman,* Bobbs-Merrill, 1969; *The Politics of Comprehensive Manpower Legislation,* Johns Hopkins Press, 1972. Contributor to *American Behavioral Scientist, American Journal of Politics, Western Political Quarterly,* and other journals.

WORK IN PROGRESS: Continuing research into public opinion and attitudes of the public toward legislative bodies.

* * *

DAVIES, (David) Ioan 1936-

PERSONAL: Given name is pronounced Yow-an; born August 28, 1936, in Stanleyville, Congo; son of Ivor (a missionary) and Rosalie (Sore) Davies; married Virginia Antoinette Keiner (a mental health officer), April 5, 1960; children: Miranda, Erich Mervyn Gareth. *Education:* Attended The Polytechnic, London, England, 1956-57; London School of Economics and Political Science, B.Sc. (honors), 1959. *Politics:* Anarchist. *Religion:* None. *Office:* Department of Sociology, University of Essex, Colchester, Essex, England.

CAREER: Worked as a journalist in London, 1957-58; University of London, London School of Economics and Political Science, London, England, research fellow in sociology, 1961-62; Cambridge University, Cambridge, England, tutor in sociology, 1962-65; University of Essex, Colchester, England, lecturer in sociology, beginning 1965. Consultant editor for sociology texts for Faber & Faber Ltd. *Military service:* British Army, National Service education office, 1956-58; became lieutenant. *Member:* British Sociological Association, Society for Latin American Studies, Society for Study of Labour History, Political Science Association, African Studies Association, Fabian Society, British Film Institute.

WRITINGS: African Trade Unions, Penguin, 1966; *Social Mobility and Political Change,* Praeger, 1970; (editor with Kathleen Herman) *Social Space: Canadian Perspectives,* New Press (Toronto), 1971. Contributor to *Presence Africaine, New Left Review, Political Quarterly,* and other journals.

WORK IN PROGRESS: Introduction to Comparative Sociology, for Basic Books; *Transitional Man; Labour Mobility and Politics in Latin America;* a survey, "Student in the Market-Place," for British Department of Education and Science; periodic work on two novels and a play.

SIDELIGHTS: Davies reads Spanish, French, Swahili, and a little Portuguese and Welsh. *Avocational interests:* Folk art, sectarian religion, and folk songs.†

* * *

DAVIES, L(eslie) P(urnell) 1914-
(Leo Berne, Robert Blake, Richard Bridgeman, Morgan Evans, Ian Jefferson, Lawrence Peters, Thomas Philips, G. K. Thomas, Leslie Vardre, Rowland Welch)

PERSONAL: Born October 20, 1914, in Cheshire, England; son of Arthur (a gardener) and Annie (Sutton) Davies; married Wynne Tench, November 13, 1940. *Education:* Manchester College of Science and Technology, University of Manchester, qualified as optometrist (F.B.O.A.), 1939. *Home:* EL Botanico, Puerto de la Cruz, Tenerife, Canary Islands. *Agent:* Howard Moorepark, 444 East 82nd St., New York, N.Y. 10024; and Carl Routledge, Charles Lavell Ltd., Mowbray House, Norfolk St., London W.C.2, England.

CAREER: Assistant dispensing pharmacist in Crewe, England, 1930-39; optometrist in private practice, 1939—; freelance writer. Professional artist in Rome, Italy, 1945-46; postmaster in Birmingham, England, 1947-57. *Military service:* British Army, Royal Army Medical Corps, World War II; served in France, and with 8th Army in North Africa and Italy; became staff sergeant.

WRITINGS: The Paper Dolls, Jenkins, 1964, Doubleday, 1966; *Man Out of Nowhere,* Jenkins, 1965, published as *Who Is Lewis Pinder?,* Doubleday, 1966; *The Artificial Man,* Jenkins, 1965, Doubleday, 1967; *Psychogeist,* Jenkins, 1966, Doubleday, 1967; *The Lampton Dreamers,* Jenkins, 1966, Doubleday, 1967; (under pseudonym Leslie Vardre) *Tell It to the Dead,* Long, 1966, published as *The Reluctant Medium,* Doubleday, 1967; *Twilight Journey,* Jenkins, 1967, Doubleday, 1968; (under pseudonym Leslie Vardre) *The Nameless Ones,* Jenkins, 1967, published as *A Grave Matter,* Doubleday, 1968; *The Alien,* Jenkins, 1968; *Dimension A,* Doubleday, 1969; *Stranger to Town,* Doubleday, 1969; *Adventure Holidays, Ltd.,* Doubleday, 1970; *Genesis Two,* Doubleday, 1970; *The White Room,* Barrie & Rockliff, 1970; *The Shadow Before,* Doubleday, 1970; *Give Me Back Myself,* Doubleday, 1971; *What Did I Do Tomorrow,* Barrie & Jenkins, 1971, Doubleday, 1973; *As-*

signment Abacus, Doubleday, 1975; *Macumba,* Doubleday, 1976. Author of more than 250 short stories published under various pseudonyms in United Kingdom and abroad.

SIDELIGHTS: The Artificial Man was filmed with title "Project X," Paramount, 1968, and *The Alien* was filmed as "The Groundstar Conspiracy," Universal, 1970. The film rights to *Psychogeist* have been sold. *Avocational interests:* Reading about the unusual; painting.

* * *

DAVIS, Allen F(reeman) 1931-

PERSONAL: Born January 9, 1931, in Hardwick, Vt.; son of Harold Freeman (owner of a store) and Bernice (Allen) Davis; married Roberta Green (a secretary), June 16, 1956; children: Gregory, Paul. *Education:* Dartmouth College, A.B., 1953; University of Rochester, M.A., 1954; University of Wisconsin, Ph.D., 1959. *Home:* 107 Columbia Ave., Swarthmore, Pa. 19081. *Office:* Department of History, Temple University, Philadelphia, Pa. 19122.

CAREER: Wayne State University, Detroit, Mich., instructor in history, 1959-60; University of Missouri, Columbia, assistant professor, 1960-63, associate professor of history, 1963-68; Temple University, Philadelphia, Pa., professor of history, 1968—. *Military service:* U.S. Army, 1954-56. *Member:* American Historical Association, Organization of American Historians, American Association of University Professors, American Civil Liberties Union, American Studies Association (executive secretary, 1972-76). *Awards, honors:* Christopher Award, 1974, for *American Heroine.*

WRITINGS: (With Jacob Cooke and Robert Daly) *March of American Democracy,* Volume V, Scribner, 1965; (editor with Harold Woodman) *Conflict or Consensus in American History,* Heath, 1966, 2nd edition published as two volumes, Volume I: *Conflict or Consensus in Early America,* Volume II: *Conflict or Consensus in Modern America,* 1967, 4th edition published as, Volume I: *Conflict and Consensus in Early American History,* Volume II: *Conflict and Consensus in Modern American History,* 1976; *Spearheads for Reform: The Social Settlements and the Progressive Movement, 1890-1914,* Oxford University Press, 1967; (editor with Mary Lynn McCree) *Eighty Years at Hull House,* Quadrangle, 1969; (author of introduction) Jane Addams, *Spirit of Youth and the City Streets,* University of Illinois Press, 1972; *American Heroine: The Life and Legend of Jane Addams,* Oxford University Press, 1973; (editor with Mark Haller) *The Peoples of Philadelphia: A History of Ethnic Groups and Lower-Class Life, 1790-1940,* Temple University Press, 1973; (with Jim Watts) *Generations: Your Family in Modern American History,* Knopf, 1974. Contributor to *American Quarterly, Mid-America, Labor History, Journal of Politics, American Historical Review,* and other history and social studies journals.

WORK IN PROGRESS: A Reinterpretation of American Culture from 1876-1920: The Story of a Nineteenth-Century Family.

* * *

DAVIS, Horace B(ancroft) 1898-

PERSONAL: Born August 10, 1898, in Newport, R.I.; son of Horace A. and Anna N. (Hallowell) Davis; married Marian Rubins, June 22, 1925 (died October, 1960); children: Chandler, Barbara (Mrs. Robert D. Crowley), Wil-

helmina (Mrs. Thomas H. Caulfield), Terry (Mrs. Robert Koth), Cynthia Quentin (Mrs. John Bassett). *Politics:* Independent. *Religion:* Atheist. *Education:* Harvard University, A.B., 1921; Columbia University, Ph.D., 1934. *Home:* Shawm Hill, Sandwich, Mass. 02563.

CAREER: Southwestern at Memphis, Memphis, Tenn., instructor, 1929-30; writer in New York, N.Y., 1930-33; Escola Livre de Sociol e Polit, Sao Paulo, Brazil, contracted professor, 1933-34; Simmons College, Boston, Mass., instructor, later assistant professor of economics, 1936-41; University of Kansas City (now University of Missouri at Kansas City), associate professor of economics, 1947-53; Benedict College, Columbia, S.C., professor of economics, 1955-57; University of Guyana, Georgetown, professor of economics, 1963-66, and former dean. Hofstra University, Hempstead, N.Y., special professor of economics, 1967, 1968. *Awards, honors:* Two grants from Rabinowitz Foundation.

WRITINGS: Labor and Steel, International Publishers, 1934; *Shoes: The Workers and the Industry,* International Publishers, 1940; *Nationalism and Socialism: Marxist and Labor Theories of Nationalism to 1917,* Monthly Review, 1967; (editor and translator) Rosa Luxemburg, *The National Question: Selected Writings,* Monthly Review, in press; *Towards a Marxist Theory of Nationalism,* Monthly Review, in press. Also author of *NRA: Fascismo e Communismo,* 1934. Contributor of more than thirty articles to professional journals; former contributor to labor press and editor of labor papers.

SIDELIGHTS: Davis is fluent in French and Portuguese; he can read all the western European languages, including German and Dutch, and has studied Russian.

* * *

DAVIS, Lew A(rter) 1930-

PERSONAL: Born January 3, 1930, in Marietta, Okla.; son of Louie Albert and Marie (Petree) Davis; married Dorothy Armstrong, July 12, 1950; children: John, Bruce, Carolyn, Glenn. *Education:* Phillips University, B.A., 1951; Texas Christian University, B.D., 1954, M.Th., 1968; additional study at Oklahoma State University and Hartford Seminary Foundation. *Office:* First Christian Church, 306 East Coolidge, Blackwell, Okla. 74631.

CAREER: Clergyman of Christian Churches (Disciples of Christ); United Christian Missionary Society, Indianapolis, Ind., missionary to India, 1954-71; First Christian Church, Blackwell, Okla., pastor, 1971—.

WRITINGS: The Layman Views World Missions, Bethany, 1964. Contributor to religious journals.

* * *

DAVIS, Terence 1924-

PERSONAL: Born March 29, 1924, in England; son of Leonard and Evelyn (Hunt) Davis. *Education:* Educated in England. *Religion:* Church of England.

CAREER: House Beautiful, assistant editor of British edition, 1956-57; *House and Garden,* executive editor of British edition, 1957-59; *Decorative Art,* editor of British edition, 1959-61. Lecturer to Victorian Society, National Trust, American Museum in Britain, and to other societies.

WRITINGS: The Architecture of John Nash, Studio Books, 1961; *John Nash: The Prince Regent's Architect,* Country Life, 1966, new edition, David & Charles, 1973;

(contributor) *Great Interiors,* Weidenfeld & Nicolson, 1967; *Rococo: A Style of Fantasy,* Orbis, 1973; *The Gothick Taste,* David & Charles, 1974, Fairleigh Dickinson University Press, 1975. Contributor of articles on architecture and allied subjects to newspapers and magazines, including *Sunday Times* and *Connoisseur.*

WORK IN PROGRESS: Research on neo-Gothicism.

SIDELIGHTS: Davis has made many visits to ancient architectural sites in the Middle East; he has made other study visits to Baroque buildings in Austria, Portugal, and Spain, and to the Pallavian villas in Italy.

BIOGRAPHICAL/CRITICAL SOURCES: Times Literary Supplement, January 12, 1967.†

*   *   *

DAWSON, Mary   1919-

PERSONAL: Born September 13, 1919, in Beckenham, Kent, England; daughter of William Harbutt (an author) and Else (Munsterberg) Dawson; married John Blackett Jeffries (a psychiatrist), August 22, 1944 (died February 25, 1963); children: Pamela, Timothy, Douglas, Rosalind. *Education:* Trained as state registered nurse, 1940-44. *Religion:* Church of England. *Home:* 1 Woodshears Dr., Malvern, Worchestershire, England. *Agent:* Anthony Sheil Associates Ltd., 52 Floral St., Covent Garden, London WC2E 9DA, England.

CAREER: Writer, mainly for children. Justice of the Peace, serving on both juvenile and adult benches, 1971—. *Member:* Malvern Writers Circle (chairman, 1965-66), Poetry Society, Malvern Music Society.

WRITINGS: Tecwyn, the Last of the Welsh Dragons, Parents Magazine Press, 1967; *How Do You Do,* Schoenigh (West Germany), 1972; *Tinker Tales,* Parents Magazine Press, 1973. Also writer of published songs and carols. Contributor of stories and poems to British Broadcasting Corp. programs, and to *Punch, Christian Science Monitor, Humpty Dumpty, Mother,* and *Lady.*

WORK IN PROGRESS: A sequel to *Tecwyn, the Last of the Welsh Dragons;* a collection of poems for children.

*   *   *

DAWSON, (John) Philip   1928-

PERSONAL: Born November 28, 1928, in Ann Arbor, Mich.; son of John P. (a professor of law) and Emma (McDonald) Dawson; married Ellen Greene, February 6, 1954; children: John, Elizabeth. *Education:* University of Michigan, A.B., 1950, A.M., 1951; Harvard University, Ph.D., 1961. *Home:* 115 Willow St., Brooklyn, N.Y. 11201. *Office:* Department of History, Brooklyn College of the City University of New York, Brooklyn, N.Y. 11201.

CAREER: Washington Post, Washington, D.C., reporter, 1952-55; Harvard University, Cambridge, Mass., instructor in history, 1961-64; Stanford University, Stanford, Calif., assistant professor, 1964-70, associate professor of history, 1970-73; Brooklyn College of the City University of New York, Brooklyn, N.Y., professor of history, 1973—. *Member:* American Historical Association, Society for French Historical Studies, Societe d'Histoire Moderne. *Awards, honors:* Summer research grant, American Philosophical Society, 1962.

WRITINGS: (Editor and translator) *The French Revolution,* Prentice-Hall, 1967; *Provincial Magistrates and Revolutionary Politics in France, 1789-1795,* Harvard University

Press, 1972; (contributor) W. O. Aydelotte, A. G. Boque, and R. W. Fogel, editors, *The Dimensions of Quantitative Research in History,* Princeton University Press, 1972. Contributor to *French Historical Studies, Annales Historiques de la Revolution Francaise,* and other historical journals.

*   *   *

DAWSON, Robert (Merril)   1941-

PERSONAL: Born November 10, 1941, in Wells, Minn; son of Robert (an auto-mechanic) and Jane (Giese) Dawson; married former wife, Joan Goguen (a painter), June 20, 1964. *Education:* Harvard University, B.A. (cum laude), 1964; San Francisco State University, M.A., 1975. *Politics:* "Red." *Religion:* "Disinterested." *Home:* 127 Downey St., San Francisco, Calif. 94117.

CAREER: Has worked as a worm salesman, truck driver, photo-lab technician, lithographer's apprentice, fruit picker, cannery worker, delivery boy, elementary school teacher, machine operator in a wool-reprocessing plant, usher, and fair-exhibit builder; he is currently occupied as a union organizer and secretary for American Federation of Teachers, and as a musician. *Military service:* None; conscientious objector.

WRITINGS: Six Mile Corner (poems), Houghton, 1966; *Sculpture,* Lane Book Co., 1966; (contributor) Jonathan D. Culler, editor, *Harvard Advocate Centennial Anthology,* Schenkman, 1966; (contributor) R. S. Barker, P. L. Van Osdol, editors, *The World on Wheels: Reading/Thinking/ Writing About the Automobile in America,* Allyn & Bacon, 1972.

WORK IN PROGRESS: The Whore of the High Sierra and Other Poems, completion expected in 1976; *Revolutionary Lives: Psychohistorical Essays on the Autobiographers of the Revolution,* 1977.

SIDELIGHTS: Virginia Quarterly Review wrote: "A brilliant imagist who has got inventive hold of the American colloquial idiom and not boxed himself in with pretentiousness is Robert Dawson, a . . . migrant and itinerant who has crisscrossed America in the Fords, Buicks, Nashes, and Chevys of his Whitman-Yevtushenko lyrics and also edited the *Harvard Advocate.*" Dawson isn't an enemy of rhyme and form nor their victim, *Virginia Quarterly Review* continued, and in his first short collection, *Six Mile Corner,* he "perceives and vividly evokes an overlooked America, the Nebraska and Michigan and Dakotas that will seem to some readers as exotic and alien and yet as inexorably real as Yevtushenko's Zima Junction. . . . He is neither a nostalgic Twain nor a grimacing Garland, but simply a new and large poet worth keeping an eye on."

BIOGRAPHICAL/CRITICAL SOURCES: New York Times Book Review, January 8, 1967; *Virginia Quarterly Review,* summer, 1967; *Poetry,* December, 1967.

*   *   *

DAY, A(rthur) Grove   1904-

PERSONAL: Born April 29, 1904, in Philadelphia, Pa.; son of Arthur Sinclair (a salesman) and Clara Tomlinson (Hogeland) Day; married Virginia T. Molina (a college instructor), July 2, 1928. *Education:* Stanford University, A.B., 1926, M.A., 1942, Ph.D., 1944. *Home:* 1434 Punahou St., Apt. 1223, Honolulu, Hawaii 96822. *Agent:* Paul R. Reynolds, Inc., 12 East 41st St., New York, N.Y. 10017. *Office:* c/o University Press of Hawaii, 535 Ward Ave., Honolulu, Hawaii 96814.

CAREER: Columbia University, New York, N.Y., research assistant, Institute of Educational Research, 1926-27; free-lance writer, 1927-30; Stanford University, Stanford, Calif., research assistant, 1932-36, assistant director of engineering, science, and management war training, 1943-44; University of Hawaii, Honolulu, assistant professor, 1944-46, associate professor, 1946-50, professor, 1950-61, senior professor of English, 1961-69, professor emeritus, 1969—, chairman of department, 1948-53. Proprietor, White Knight Press, Honolulu, Hawaii, 1948—. Fulbright senior research fellow in Australia, 1955; Smith-Mundt Visiting Professor of American Studies, University of Barcelona, 1957-58; Fulbright visiting professor of American studies, University of Madrid, 1961-62. *Member:* Modern Language Association of America, Modern Humanities Research Association, Honolulu Academy of Arts, Bernice P. Bishop Museum, Phi Beta Kappa, Phi Kappa Phi, Elks, Adventurers' Club of Honolulu.

WRITINGS: (With Fred J. Buenzle) *Bluejacket,* Norton, 1939; *Coronado's Quest: The Discovery of the Southwestern States,* University of California Press, 1940, new edition, 1964; (with Ralph S. Kuykendall) *Hawaii: A History,* Prentice-Hall, 1948, revised edition, 1961; *The Sky Clears: Poetry of the American Indians,* Macmillan, 1951, new edition, 1964; *Hawaii and Its People,* Duell, Sloan & Pearce, 1955, revised edition, 1968; (with James A. Michener) *Rascals in Paradise,* Random House, 1957; *Hawaii, Fiftieth Star,* Duell, Sloan & Pearce, 1960, 2nd edition, Meredith, 1969; *The Story of Australia,* Random House, 1960; *James A. Michener,* Twayne, 1964; *They Peopled the Pacific,* Duell, Sloan & Pearce, 1964; *Louis Becke,* Twayne, 1966; *Explorers of the Pacific,* Duell, Sloan & Pearce, 1966; *Coronado and the Discovery of the Southwest,* Meredith, 1967; *Pirates of the Pacific,* Meredith, 1968; *Adventurers of the Pacific,* with foreword by James A. Michener, Meredith, 1969.

Jack London in the South Seas, Four Winds Press, 1971; *Pacific Islands Literature: One Hundred Basic Books,* University Press of Hawaii, 1971; (with Edgar C. Knowlton, Jr.) *V. Blasco Ibanez,* Twayne, 1972; *What Did I Do Right?* (auto-bibliography), privately printed, 1974; *Robert D. Fitzgerald,* Twayne, 1974; *Kamehameha, First King of Hawaii,* edited by Dorothy Hazama, Hogarth Press, 1974; *All the Missionaries,* edited by Hazama, Hogarth Press, 1975.

Editor: (In Spanish) *Fernando Cortes: Despatches from Mexico,* American Book Co., 1935; (with Carl Stroven) *The Spell of the Pacific: An Anthology of Its Literature,* Macmillan, 1949; (with William F. Bauer) *The Greatest American Short Stories,* McGraw, 1953, published as *The Greatest American Short Stories: Twenty Classics of Our Heritage,* 1970; (with Stroven) *A Hawaiian Reader,* with introduction by James A. Michener, Appleton, 1959; (with Stroven) *Best South Sea Stories,* Appleton, 1964; Jack London, *Stories of Hawaii,* Appleton, 1965; *Mark Twain's Letters from Hawaii,* Appleton, 1966; (with Stroven) *True Tales of the South Seas,* Appleton, 1966; Louis Becke, *South Sea Supercargo,* University Press of Hawaii, 1967; (with Stroven) *The Spell of Hawaii,* Meredith, 1968; (and author of introduction) *Melville's South Seas: An Anthology,* Hawthorn, 1970; *The Art of Narration: The Novella,* McGraw, 1971; *The Art of Narration: The Short Story,* McGraw, 1971; (and author of introduction) Robert L. Stevenson, *Travels in Hawaii,* University Press of Hawaii, 1973.

Contributor to *Encyclopedia of Poetry and Poetics,* 1965, and *Encyclopaedia Britannica,* 1968; also contributor of short stories and articles to national magazines. Editor-in-chief, *Pacific Science,* 1947-48.

SIDELIGHTS: Several of Day's books have had foreign editions.

BIOGRAPHICAL/CRITICAL SOURCES: New Statesman, June 23, 1967.†

* * *

DAY, LeRoy Judson 1917-

PERSONAL: Born December 12, 1917, in Clinton Falls, Minn.; son of Judson LeRoy (a dentist) and Blanche Leona (Finch) Day; married Bette Mae Keith (a librarian), December 27, 1942; children: Judson, Nancy, Marilyn, Sara, Dorothea. *Education:* University of Minnesota, B.A., 1939; Colgate Rochester Divinity School, B.D., 1942; University of Wisconsin, M.A., 1944, Ph.D., 1951. *Politics:* Democrat. *Home:* 1113 South Lake, Sioux Falls, S.D. 57105. *Office:* Sioux Falls College, 1501 South Prairie, Sioux Falls, S.D. 57101.

CAREER: Pastor of Baptist churches in Ohio and Wisconsin, 1944-55; Ottawa University, Ottawa, Kan., assistant professor of sociology, 1948-51; Alderson-Broaddus College, Philippi, W.Va., professor of sociology and chairman of department, 1955-65; Sioux Falls College, Sioux Falls, S.D., professor of sociology and chairman of department, 1965—. Rural Church Center, Green Lake, Wis., instructor, 1946, 1951-55. *Member:* American Sociological Association, Rural Sociological Society, American Association of University Professors, Gerontological Society, Christian Rural Fellowship, Alpha Kappa Delta, Lions Club.

WRITINGS: (With John H. Kolb) *Interdependence in Town and Country Relations in Rural Society: A Study of Trends in Walworth County, Wisconsin, 1911-13 to 1947-48,* Wisconsin Agriculture Experiment Station, 1950; *Dynamic Christian Fellowship,* Judson, 1960, revised edition, 1968; *Toward a Christian Style Life,* Judson, 1970. Editor of *Baptist Town and Country Fellowship Bulletin,* 1954-56.

* * *

DAYAN, Moshe 1915-

PERSONAL: Born May 20, 1915, in Deganya (first Jewish kibbutz established in the Jordan Valley); son of Russian immigrants, Shmuel (a farmer) and Devora Dayan; married Ruth Schwartz, 1935 (divorced, 1972); married Rachel Corem, 1973; children: (first marriage) Yael (wife of Colonel Dovsion; a novelist and correspondent under name Yael Dayan, and also a colonel in the Israeli Army), Ehud, Assaf. *Education:* Graduated from Nahalal Agriculture School; later attended British Staff College at Camberly; resumed formal schooling in his forties and received LL.B. from Faculty of Law, University of Tel Aviv, 1959. *Home:* 11 Yoav, Zahala, Tel Aviv, Israel.

CAREER: Grew up in the village of Nahalal, where he trained for farming; joined the Hagana in 1929, taking part in skirmishes against the Arabs; in 1937 met Orde Wingate, the British officer who organized Israel's commandos in Palestine, and eventually became Wingate's second in command; sentenced to five year's imprisonment by the British when the Hagana was declared illegal in 1939; after two years in Acre Prison was released in 1941 to do intelligence work with Allied troops fighting the Vichy French in Syria (black patch covering his one eye dates from the Syrian campaign when binoculars he was using were hit by a bullet, shattering the eye); sent to Jordan Valley front in 1948 as commander of 8th Brigade of the Israeli Army, swiftly rising to lieutenant commander, then to commanding general of Southern Region, 1950, commanding general of Northern Region, 1951, head of General Staff Branch at General Headquarters, 1952, and chief of General Staff, 1953-58; left the Army in 1958 and entered Israeli politics and Parliament; appointed Minister of Agriculture, 1959, holding that post until 1964 when he resigned from the government; joined Ben Gurion's splinter Rafi party, and was elected to the Knesseth, 1965; went back into uniform as Minister of Defence on the eve of the "Six-Day War" in June, 1967, directing the Israeli blitz that defeated the Arabs on every front, resigned from the government, May, 1974.

WRITINGS: Diary of the Sinai Campaign, Harper, 1966. Also author of *Mapa Kadasha, Yadassim Aherim* (title means "New Map, Other Relations"), 1969. Publications include a series of articles on the Vietnam War, written after his trip to the Vietnam front in 1966.

SIDELIGHTS: Diary of the Sinai Campaign, a blueprint of the type of attack followed again by Israeli forces in their sweep of June, 1967, attracted little general notice when it was published; shortly after Dayan's 1967 victory, paperback rights to the book reportedly sold for $40,000. In "Father and Hero" (*Look,* August 22, 1967), Yael Dayan characterized her father as "a lone man . . . out of choice, consciously, deliberately. He holds the key to his own jail, and he controls the traffic in and out of it." She mentioned his legendary courage, the reaction of warmth and admiration that young soldiers extract from him, and his passion for archaeological digging and reconstructing his finds. In March, 1968, Dayan was buried by an earth slide while engaged in archaeological exploration on the Mediterranean coast near Tel Aviv; he was unconscious when freed, and hospitalized with rib and spine injuries.

BIOGRAPHICAL/CRITICAL SOURCES: Time, June 16, 1967, November 30, 1970; *Newsweek,* June 19, 1967, December 21, 1970; *U.S. News & World Report,* June 19, 1967; *New York Times Magazine,* July 9, 1967; Yael Dayan in *Look,* August 22, 1967; *Life,* September 29, 1967; N. Lau-Lavie, *Moshe Dayan,* Prayer Book Press, 1969; I. I. Taslitt, *Soldier of Israel,* Funk, 1969; P. Jurman, editor, *Moshe Dayan: A Portrait,* Dodd, 1969; Shabtai Teveth, *Moshe Dayan: The Soldier, the Man, the Legend,* Weidenfeld & Nicolson, 1972, Houghton, 1973.

*   *   *

DEAKIN, James   1929-

PERSONAL: Born December 3, 1929, in St. Louis, Mo.; son of Rogers (a surgeon) and Dorothy (Jeffrey) Deakin; married Doris Kanter (a free-lance writer), April 14, 1956; children: David Andrew. *Education:* Washington University, St. Louis, Mo., B.A., 1951, graduate study, 1951-52. *Politics:* Independent. *Religion:* Jewish. *Home:* 6406 Whittier Ct., Bethesda, Md. 20034. *Office:* 1701 Pennsylvania Ave. N.W., Washington, D.C. 20006.

CAREER: With *St. Louis Post-Dispatch,* 1951—, Washington Bureau, Washington, D.C., 1954—, White House correspondent, 1965—. *Member:* White House Correspondents' Association (president, 1974-75). *Awards, honors:* Distinguished Alumnus Citation, Washington University, 1973.

WRITINGS: The Lobbyist, Public Affairs Press, 1966; *Lyndon Johnson's Credibility Gap,* Public Affairs Press,

1968. Contributor to *New Republic, Esquire, Washingtonian,* and other magazines.

*   *   *

DEAN, Nell Marr   1910-
(Virginia Roberts)

PERSONAL: Born September 28, 1910, in Tulsa, Okla.; daughter of Ren Dow (a banker) and Nell (Wilson) Marr; married George Douglas Dean (a newspaper editor; deceased), January 22, 1939; children: Robert Marr, George Rex. *Education:* Attended University of Oklahoma, 1933-34. *Politics:* Democrat. *Religion:* Presbyterian. *Home:* 4800 American River Dr., Carmichael, Calif. 95608.

CAREER: Member of editorial department of *Tulsa Tribune,* Tulsa, Okla., 1929-32, and *Oklahoma News,* Oklahoma City, Okla., 1934-35; editorial librarian for *Great Falls Tribune,* Great Falls, Mont., 1935-36, *Sacramento Bee,* Sacramento, Calif., 1936-39; *San Francisco Chronicle,* San Francisco, Calif., war research librarian, 1939-41; full-time free-lance writer, 1941—. Real estate agent, 1970-75. *Member:* California Writers' Club (president, 1972).

WRITINGS—All published by Bouregy, except as indicated: *Thief of Hearts,* Arcadia House, 1950; *Honeymoon in the Sky,* Arcadia House, 1951; *Deep in Her Heart,* Arcadia House, 1952; *Front Page Girl,* Arcadia House, 1953; *Circus Girl,* Arcadia House, 1954; *A Business in Pets,* Messner, 1956; *Nurse Howard's Assignment,* 1957; *Fashions for Carol,* 1958; *Desert Doctor,* 1959.

Nurse on Skis, 1960; *Society Doctor,* 1961; *Jacklyn Lane—Fashion Model,* 1962; *Allison Day—Weather Girl,* Messner, 1962; *Flight Nurse,* Messner, 1963; *Sandy and the Lavender Tub,* 1963; *The Vet is a Girl,* Messner, 1963; *The Girl at the Teller's Window,* 1963; *The Nurse on Paradise Isle,* 1964; *Circus Nurse,* 1965; *Trials of Doctor Carol,* Belmont Publishing, 1965; *Strength in Her Hands,* Belmont Publishing, 1966; *A Nurse in Vietnam,* Messner, 1969; *Nurse Kelly's Crusade,* 1969; *Reach for the Moon,* 1969.

Assignment to Danger, 1971; *Nurse at Mission Canyon,* 1971; *Nurse at Golden Gate,* 1971; *Courage to Suffer,* 1972; *Romance on Capri,* 1973; *Terror Over Bluehaven,* 1975.

Under pseudonym Virginia Roberts; all published by Bouregy: *Photo by Nicky,* 1957; *Nurse on Location,* 1958; *Lady and the Ranger,* 1959; *Wish on a Star,* 1959; *The Right Man,* 1960; *Studio Nurse,* 1961; *The Desert Angel,* 1962; *Beauty by Diane,* 1965; *False Haven,* 1970.

WORK IN PROGRESS: A historical novel, *Sweeter Than Wine,* and a juvenile mystery.

*   *   *

DEATS, Richard L(ouis)   1932-

PERSONAL: Born February 8, 1932, in Big Spring, Tex.; son of Charles Wesley (a dentist) and Helen (Mueller) Deats; married Janice Baggett (a pianist), June 2, 1956; children: Mark Richard, Stephen Michael, Elizabeth Helen, Katherine Anne. *Education:* McMurry College, B.A. (magna cum laude), 1953; Southern Methodist University, B.D. (with honors), 1956; Boston University, Ph.D., 1964. *Politics:* Liberal Democrat.

CAREER: United Methodist clergyman. Associate pastor in Big Spring, Tex., 1956-57, and pastor in Manila, Philippines, 1959-60; Union Theological Seminary, Manila, Philippines, associate professor, 1960-72, professor of social ethics, 1972—. Trustee, Philippine Wesleyan College; chairman of board of directors, Methodist Social Center, Manila. Chairman, United Nations-Washington Christian Citizenship Seminar, 1955. *Member:* Philippine Theological Society (secretary-treasurer, 1964-66), National Association for the Advancement of Colored People, American Civil Liberties Union, United World Federalists, International Fellowship of Reconciliation (member of executive committee; director of inter-faith activities), American Association for the United Nations, National Wildlife Federation, Alpha Chi, Sigma Tau Delta. *Awards, honors:* Cokesbury Award for academic achievement, 1957.

WRITINGS: The Story of Methodism in the Philippines, National Council of Churches in the Philippines, 1964; *Nationalism and Christianity in the Philippines,* Southern Methodist University Press, 1967; (contributor) Gerald H. Anderson, editor, *Studies in Philippine Church History,* Cornell University Press, 1968; (contributor) Vitaliano Gorospe and S. J. Manila, editors, *Responsible Parentnood in the Philippines,* Ateneo Publications, 1970; (contributor) Stephen Neill, John Goodwin, and Anderson, editors, *Concise Dictionary of the Christian World Mission,* Lutterworth Press, 1970; (editor with Gorospe and Manila) *The Filipino in the Seventies: An Ecumenical Perspective,* New Day Publishers, 1973. Contributor of articles to secular and religious periodicals, including *Christian Century, National Catholic Reporter,* and *Progressive.*

WORK IN PROGRESS: A study of the religious roots of peacemaking.

SIDELIGHTS: Deats has participated in work camps in Germany, Mexico, and the Philippines.

*   *   *

DeBOLD, Richard C.   1927-

PERSONAL: Born July 20, 1927, in New York, N.Y.; son of William John (a railroad inspector) and Emma (Herzog) DeBold; married Marjorie Cope Warren (a teacher), September 26, 1957. *Education:* New York Maritime Academy, student, 1945-47; University of California, Berkley, B.A. (with highest honors), 1957, Ph.D., 1963; Yale University, M.S., 1959. *Office:* Department of Psychology, Brooklyn Center, Long Island University, Brooklyn, N.Y. 11201.

CAREER: Gulf Oil Co., marine engineer, 1947-50; Air Reduction Co., field engineer, 1953-55; Wesleyan University, Middletown, Conn., assistant professor of psychology, 1963-66, associate professor, 1966-67; Hobart College, Geneva, N.Y., associate professor of psychology and dean of the college, 1967-71; Long Island University, Brooklyn Center, Brooklyn, N.Y., professor of psychology, 1971—. Visiting associate professor of social relations, Harvard University, summer, 1966. *Military service:* U.S. Navy, instructor in nucleonics and radiological safety, 1951-53; served in Korea; received two battle stars. U.S. Naval Reserve; currently lieutenant. *Member:* American Association for the Advancement of Science, American Psychological Association. *Awards, honors:* Grants from U.S. Public Health Service, 1963-66, 1967—, and National Science Foundation, 1967-68.

WRITINGS: (Editor with Russel C. Leaf) *LSD, Man and Society,* Wesleyan University Press, 1967; *A Manual of Current Experiments in Psychology,* Prentice-Hall, 1968; (editor with Leaf) Bernard Palmer, *Danny Orlis and Trouble on the Circle R Ranch,* Moody, 1968; (with W. R. Thompson) *Psychology: A Systematic Introduction,* Mc-

Graw, 1971. Contributor of about twenty articles to psychology and other journals.†

*   *   *

de BONO, Edward   1933-

PERSONAL: Born May 19, 1933, in Malta; son of Joseph Edward (a physician) and Josephine (Burns) de Bono. *Education:* Royal University of Malta, B.Sc., 1953, M.D., 1955; Oxford University, M.A., 1957, D.Phil., 1961; Cambridge University, Ph.D., 1963. *Home:* 11 Warkworth St., Cambridge, England. *Agent:* Michael Horniman, A. P. Watt, 26/28 Bedford Row, London W.C.1, England. *Office:* Cambridge University, Cambridge, England.

CAREER: Oxford University, Oxford, England, research assistant, 1957-60, lecturer, 1960-61; University of London, London, England, lecturer, 1961-63; Cambridge University, Cambridge, England, assistant director of research, 1963—. Research associate, Harvard University, Cambridge, Mass., 1965-66. Lecturer to industry and education on research cognitive processes. Inventor; designer of the L-game. Honorary director and founding member of Cognitive Research Trust. *Member:* Medical Research Society. *Awards, honors:* Rhodes scholar.

WRITINGS: The Use of Lateral Thinking, J. Cape, 1967, published as *New Think: The Use of Lateral Thinking in The Generation of Ideas,* Basic Books, 1968; *The Five-Day Course in Thinking,* Basic Books, 1967; *The Mechanism of Mind,* Simon & Schuster, 1969.

Lateral Thinking: Creativity Step by Step, Harper, 1970 (published in England as *Lateral Thinking: A Textbook of Creativity,* Ward, Lock, 1970); *The Dog Exercising Machine,* J. Cape, 1970, Simon & Schuster, 1971; (editor) *Technology Today,* Routledge & Kegan Paul, 1971; *Lateral Thinking for Management: A Handbook of Creativity,* American Management Association, 1971; *Practical Thinking: Four Ways to be Right, Five Ways to be Wrong, Five Ways to Understand,* J. Cape, 1971; *Children Solve Problems,* Penguin, 1972, Harper, 1974; *About Think,* J. Cape, 1972; *PO: A Device for Successful Thinking,* Simon & Schuster, 1972 (published in England as *PO: Beyond Yes and No,* Penguin, 1973); (editor) *Eureka: A History of Inventions,* Holt, 1974.

Writer of television items, and of feature stories for *Sunday Mirror, Telegraph Magazine, Nova, Oz, Mind Alive, Science Journal, Sunday Times, Fashion, Honey;* contributor of articles to professional journals.

AVOCATIONAL INTERESTS: Polo, canoeing (paddled 112 miles from Oxford to London non-stop while at Oxford University), and games design.

BIOGRAPHICAL/CRITICAL SOURCES: Realites (France), August, 1967; *Realites* (United States), November, 1967.

*   *   *

DEBRAY, (Jules) Regis   1942-

PERSONAL: Born in 1942, in Paris, France; son of a lawyer and a city councilwoman; married Elizabeth Bugos, February 12, 1968; (it is rumored that he was previously married). *Education:* Ecole Normale Superieure, Agrege de Philosophie; former student of Fidel Castro.

CAREER: Writer specializing in French Marxism. University of Havana, Havana, Cuba, lecturer, 1966; journalist, formerly with the Mexican magazine, *Sucesos;* went to Bolivia as a journalist to interview Che Guevara, 1967, where he was arrested and later convicted for taking part in the guerrilla movement, began serving a 30-year prison sentence in Casino Militar, Bolivia, November 17, 1967; released from prison, 1970.

WRITINGS: Revolution das la Revolution?: Lutte Armee et Lutte Politique en Amerique Latine, F. Maspero, 1967, translation by Bobbye Ortis published as *Revolution in the Revolution?: Armed Struggle and Political Struggle in Latin America,* Monthly Review Press, 1967; *La Frontiere* [et] *Un jeune homme a la page,* Editions du Seuil, 1967, translation by Helen R. Lane published as *The Border* [and] *Young Man in the Know,* Grove, 1968, translation by Louis Allen published as *The Frontier* [and] *A With-It Young Man,* Sheed & Ward, 1968; *Essais sur l'Amerique latine,* F. Maspero, 1967; (with Fidel Castro) *On Trial,* translation by Marianne Alexander, Lorrimer, 1968; *Defensa en Camiri,* Siglo Ilustrado, 1968; *Strategy for Revolution: Essays on Latin America,* edited by Robin Blackburn, J. Cape, 1970; *Entretiens avec Allende sur la situation au Chili,* F. Maspero, 1971, translation by Ben Brewster and others published as *The Chilean Revolution: Conversations with Allende,* postscript by Salvador Allende, Random House, 1971, translation by Peter Beglan published as *Conversations with Allende: Socialism in Chile,* New Left Books, 1971; *Prison Writings of Regis Debray,* translation by Rosemary Sheed, Random House, 1973; *La Critique des armes,* Editions du Seuil, 1974; *La guerilla du Che,* Editions du Seuil, 1974, translation published as *Che's Guerrilla War,* Penguin, 1976. Also author of *L'Anniversaire* (two long essays on the continental strategy of revolution plus a third essay), 1967. Contributor to *Evergreen Review, New Left Review,* and *Marcha.*

SIDELIGHTS: Debray's book, *Revolution in the Revolution?,* must be considered as one chapter among many important chapters in the long-range thinking of Fidel Castro. In another sense, the book is essentially part of a larger scheme, too. A European intellectual, Debray was curious to see first hand the things he had dealt with abstractly in his book. He went to Bolivia as a correspondent for a Mexican magazine, fell into the hands of troops searching for Bolivian guerrillas, and had the fabulous luck of not being killed. Although Sartre (who has deeply influenced Debray) has said that Debray was jailed for having written *Revolution in the Revolution?,* he could well be alive today *because* he wrote the book. "It gave him worldwide notoriety, and by the time the Bolivian military leaders realized whom they held prisoner, the scandal produced in Europe and America was such that it would have been dangerous to eliminate the young writer," writes Juan Bosch. At the moment that the English translation of his book appeared, Debray was undergoing a typical Latin American feudal ordeal. He faced a trial for crimes which it would have been an honor to be guilty of, and was sentenced for 30 years although he may have never committed the crimes.

The series of essays which constitute *Revolution in the Revolution?* have already made Debray something of a legend. The book was written after a stay in Havana where Debray had extensive conversations with leaders of the revolutionary and communist movements from every Latin American country. Robin Blackburn notes that "the passion and revolutionary romanticism which infuse Debray's writing remind one more of the young Malraux. Debray is concerned not so much with predicting how revolution might occur in Latin America as with how the instrument that will make possible that revolution will be forged."

Blackburn continues: "His essay does not explore conceivable scenarios of revolution in the manner now fashionable among Pentagon academics nor does he provide a learned 'Marxist' account of the relationship of class forces and the continent's economic future. He addresses himself to the predicament of the lonely, hunted guerrilla, the embattled miners of Bolivia, the desperate inhabitants of the Caracas slums and the bitter peasantry of the under-developed, over-exploited interior—in these he sees the truth and the future of the South American continent." Debray admits in the book that three characteristic mistakes stem from an over-estimation of the revolutionary movement's own strength—namely the strategies of "armed self-defence," "armed propaganda" and the guerrilla base. Debray argues that "the armed self-defence of the miners in Bolivia or of the Colombian peasant republics placed them in an overexposed position leading to a premature armed confrontation with the government forces." He recommends that the guerrillas should be a roving force with, initially, quite modest social objectives, and adds that few Latin American guerrilla movements have been as independent of outside political direction as Fidel Castro's was. In Debray's defense it must be recognized that the Left's most urgent task in Latin America is to acquire striking power so that they may intervene effectively in their continent's history, rather than speculate about its passing future.

Debray's compatriot, Che Guevara, is a prime example of the kind of activist who helped change the course of Latin American history. (Guevara, however, was missing for two years and although he is now dead, his disappearance has never really been explained.) One must note that if it weren't for Debray's important associations, this book would probably have attracted little serious attention as a theoretical work, according to Eqbal Ahmad. Debray and his fellow revolutionaries are basically against Latin American parties (Communists, Trotskyists, Reformists) who claim to be revolutionary but are actually selling out to and begging to be "co-opted by the capitalist establishment," writes Ahmad.

Debray also describes Latin America's thirst for freedom from United States domination and the need for the Latin American countries to adopt tactics suited to their unique conditions. (Debray believes that the study of the Russian, Chinese, and Vietnamese revolutions would be misleading for other South American countries because each revolution must be effected in accord with its regional and national peculiarities. Debray believes that "one may consider it a stroke of good luck that Fidel had not read the military writings of Mao Tse-tung before disembarking on the coast to Oriente....") Debray stresses the military *foco* (a Spanish word used to describe the unitary focus of guerrilla operation) in the formative stages of an armed revolution. For Debray, T. Richard Snyder points out, revolution, and not reconciliation, is the key to the creation of a genuinely new and human future, and "violence is an essential ingredient of revolution...." Debray's thorough study of the Cuban revolution convinced him that no revolution can succeed by peaceful means. The lesson of the Cuban revolution is that violence must determine the form of politics, not vice versa.

Debray claims, in a letter from his Bolivian cell entitled "A Message to My Friends," that *he* was not being accused, but that actually Cuba, through him, was being indicted. He states: "Over the two month period [before my trial], I was not once accused of being a guerrilla.... The Bolivian government left me in the hands of the CIA in the hope of obtaining, through its intermediary, some sensational confession proving that I was 'Fidel's envoy,' 'an international spy in the service of Cuba,' or some such nonsense.... The case against Cuba came to naught, given their failure to unearth any convincing evidence or obtain the hoped-for confession; thus they had to settle for a case against Debray." He feels that his predicament is now the responsibility of the French Government (he is a French citizen and requested protection from the French Embassy), but Debray knows that President Barrientos of Bolivia wants people to believe that Cuba and Bolivia are at war, and that he (Debray) was an envoy to Cuba. In fact, on January 4, 1968, Barrientos offered to trade Debray for Major Huber Matos, a Cuban who fought beside Castro as a revolutionary but who was sentenced in 1959 to 20 years imprisonment as a counter-revolutionary. Barrientos said that he would make the exchange as a "gesture." Since Bolivia was unable to prove that Debray was an "agent," they had to prove he was a "guerrilla"—in fact a leader, and one of the heads of the guerrilla movement. Debray had to admit, unhappily, that he was not a guerrilla, though he says that for a long time he had "planned and intended to join the guerrillas.... Che decided that the time was not yet ripe for that ... and that for the moment it was better I served by keeping the outside world informed." Debray adds, that, though *Revolution in the Revolution?* "does express many of Che's ideas, it did not play any part in the organization of the guerrilla movement in Bolivia."

Writers, professors, and academicians of all political shades from Sartre to Mauriac emerged in Debray's defense. (Debray has often been pictured by the French, however, as a victim of his own idealism.) In Britain and the United States Herbert Marcuse, Noam Chomsky, Graham Greene, Bertrand Russell, and others protested his incarceration. "Debray, Bustos and Roth, [captured together in Bolivia], are all convinced that only the international publicity saved them from being silently eliminated," Blackburn and Perry Anderson conclude. Yet, in "A Message to My Friends," Debray condemns the "vile publicity which the bourgeois press and the mass-circulation magazines gave to my situation, deforming and dissimulating its real meaning, which would be to describe a historical rather than a personal situation." He was appalled by "The circus they were staging with me in the role of the clown," while he remained in solitary confinement. He detested the "sentiment" displayed and especially the active support of his family as indicated by their query, "My son isn't a bandit; who do you take him for? He's a decent young man, [etc.]" Debray, therefore, makes this plea: "I ... ask my friends to right the helm. Instead of the Debray affair serving as a mirror to the indignation of rightious souls or as a source of revenue for the weekly emotion-merchants, it should be utilized to arouse public opinion to some degree concerning the overall problems of America [and] the revolutionary struggle.... Let people talk less about Debray ... and talk more about the Bolivian guerrillas and others, about those who have died in battle and those who are still alive and fighting in a terrain that is unbelievably difficult. Let them tell the story of the miners, of their silicosis and their massacre. The application of Fidel's and Che's ideas—several Vietnams to save Vietnam and bring down once and for all those responsible for Vietnam—does not require supermen but a great deal of sacrifice from all of us: a renunciation of everything, and perhaps of life itself; it requires endurance, stubbornness, and a stomach that can stand being empty for weeks on end."

Stanley Reynolds, reviewing *The Frontier* [*and*] *A With-It Young Man,* states that "Debray is a writer of power, already accomplished with the short story, and holding great promise as a novelist.... Debray has an objectivity that would be impressive in any writer so politically committed.... One hopes that he will turn his hand in prison back to literature." John L. Hess notes that Debray, prior to his release from prison, commented that his "'greatest joy' would be 'to recover the anonymity from which I emerged for reasons independent of my will.'" Hess continues, however, that "for the author of 'Revolution in the Revolution?' the wish seems rather optimistic." Since his release from prison in 1970, Debray has traveled to Cuba and Chile.

BIOGRAPHICAL/CRITICAL SOURCES: News Statesman, April 28, 1967, August 9, 1968; *New York Times,* July 21, 1967, July 3, 1968, December 12, 1969, December 25, 1970, February 17, 1971; *Observer,* August 27, 1967; *Ramparts,* September, 1967, August, 1968; *New York Review of Books,* October 26, 1967; *Christian Century,* January 17, 1968; *Nation,* January 29, 1968; *Evergreen Review,* February, 1968; *Time,* September 12, 1968; *Washington Post,* May 4, 1969; Leo Huberman and Paul M. Sweezy, editors, *Regis Debray and the Latin American Revolution,* Monthly Review Press, 1968; Carlos Maria Gutierrez, *Note sulla situazione politica boliviana,* Edizioni della Liberia, 1970.†

* * *

de CAMP, Catherine C(rook) 1907-

PERSONAL: Born November 6, 1907, in New York, N.Y.; daughter of Samuel (a lawyer) and Mary E. (Beekman) Crook; married Lyon Sprague de Camp (an author under name of L. Sprague de Camp), August 12, 1939; children: Lyman Sprague, Gerard Beekman. *Education:* Barnard College, B.A. (magna cum laude), 1933; graduate study at Western Reserve (now Case Western Reserve) University, Columbia University, and Temple University, between 1934-38. *Politics:* "Uncommitted." *Religion:* Episcopalian. *Home:* 278 Hothrope Lane, Villanova, Pa. 19085.

CAREER: Oxford School, Hartford, Conn., teacher of English, 1934-35; teacher of English and history at Laurel School, Shaker Heights, Ohio, 1935-37, and Calhoun School, New York, N.Y., 1937-39; Temple University, Philadelphia, Pa., instructor in child development, 1949; editor of books and radio scripts for husband, L. Sprague de Camp, 1949-62; writer in collaboration with husband, 1962—. At times, social worker with the handicapped, tutor, and substitute teacher. *Member:* Academy of Natural Sciences (Philadelphia), University Museum of University of Pennsylvania, Historical Society of Pennsylvania, Fellows in American Studies (fellow), Phi Beta Kappa, Cum Laude Society, Barnard Club of Philadelphia (president, 1956-59).

WRITINGS: The Money Tree, New American Library, 1972; *Teach Your Child to Manage Money,* U.S. News & World Report, 1975.

With husband, L. Sprague de Camp: *Ancient Ruins and Archaeology,* Doubleday, 1964, published as *Citadels of Mystery,* Ballantine, 1973; *Spirits, Stars and Spells,* Canaveral, 1967; *The Story of Science in America,* Scribner, 1967; *The Day of the Dinosaur,* Doubleday, 1968; *Darwin and His Great Discovery,* Macmillan, 1972; *Three Thousand Years of Fantasy and Science Fiction,* Lothrop, 1972; *Tales Beyond Time.* Lothrop, 1973; *Science Fiction Hand-*

book, revised edition, Owlswick, 1975. Writer of scripts on developments in science for Voice of America, 1949-50.

Contributor of an article to *Time,* and *South.*

AVOCATIONAL INTERESTS: Modern dance, genealogical and historical research, travel, lecturing, gardening, interior decoration, and antique hunting.

BIOGRAPHICAL/CRITICAL SOURCES: Philadelphia Sunday Bulletin, December 6, 1964; *Main Line Times,* March 3, 1966.

*   *   *

de CERVERA, Alejo 1919-

PERSONAL: Born July 17, 1919, in Santander, Spain; son of Jesus-Ricardo de Cervera Zubieta and Maria-Teresa (Gabilondo) de Cervera; married Marianne Almryd, November 12, 1949. *Education:* College of San Jose, Santander, Spain, B.A., 1935; University of Oviedo, Licence in Law, 1941; Columbia University, M.C.L., 1955, LL.M., 1956, J.S.D., 1966. *Religion:* Catholic. *Home:* Darlington, Rio Piedras 00925, Puerto Rico. *Office:* Faculty of Law, University of Puerto Rico, Rio Piedras 00931, Puerto Rico.

CAREER: Appointed judge, 1948, and held first judgeship in Guia, Canary Islands, 1948-50; University of Stockholm, Stockholm, Sweden, scientific guest, 1950-51; judge in Valls, Tarragona, Spain, 1952-55; Columbia University, Parker School, New York, N.Y., associate in comparative law, 1955-56; University of Puerto Rico, Rio Piedras, professor of law, beginning 1957. *Member:* International Association for Philosophy of Law and Social Philosophy (member of American Section).

WRITINGS: The Statute of Limitations in American Conflict of Laws, Oceana and University of Puerto Rico, 1966. Contributor to legal periodicals.

WORK IN PROGRESS: Research in civil law, jurisprudence, and theory of law.

SIDELIGHTS: In addition to his native language and English, de Cervera is competent in French, German, and Swedish. *Avocational interests:* Travel ("for relaxation and adequate contact with the world; my intellectual commitment leaves no room for other things").††

*   *   *

DECHERT, Charles R(ichard) 1927-

PERSONAL: Born March 16, 1927, in Philadelphia, Pa.; son of Alfred Charles and Kathryn (Schubert) Dechert; married Anna Leone, May 26, 1957; children: Michel. *Education:* Catholic University of America, A.B., 1949, M.A., 1950, Ph.D., 1952. *Office:* Department of Politics, Catholic University of America, Washington, D.C. 20017.

CAREER: U.S. Government, Office of Secretary of Defense, Washington, D.C., analyst, 1955-56; Johns Hopkins University, School of Advanced International Studies, Bologna Center, Bologna, Italy, Mazzini fellow and assistant to director, 1956-57; International University of Social Studies "Pro Deo," Rome, Italy, visiting professor of comparative economic and social policy, and director of North American Institute, 1957-59; Purdue University, Lafayette, Ind., associate professor of government, 1959-65, professor of political science, 1965-67; Catholic University of America, Washington, D.C., professor of politics, 1967—. Consultant to Joint Economic Committee of U.S. Congress, Columbia University Graduate School of Business, Italian Ministry of Justice, and other public and pri-

vate agencies. *Military service:* U.S. Air Force Reserve, 1950-52. U.S. Air Force, 1952-55; became first lieutenant.

MEMBER: American Political Science Association, American Association of University Professors, American Society for Cybernetics (charter member), American Catholic Philosophical Association, Society for General Systems Research, Istituto Luigi Sturzo (corresponding member), Phi Beta Kappa, Pi Sigma Alpha. *Awards, honors:* Knights of Columbus fellow, 1949-52; Harman Prize in philosophical anthropology, 1964; Fulbright-Hays research fellow in Italy, 1965-66.

WRITINGS: Ente Nazionale Idrocarburi: Profile of a State Corporation, E. J. Brill, 1963; (co-author) *Congress: The First Branch of Government,* American Enterprise Institute for Public Policy Research, 1966; (editor and contributor) *The Social Impact of Cybernetics,* University of Notre Dame Press, 1966; (co-author) *Positive Feedback,* Pergamon, 1967. Author of numerous monographs on the theory of management, published by Edizioni Sociali Internazionali (Rome), 1958-59. Contributor of articles to professional journals in the United States and Europe.††

*   *   *

de GRAFT-JOHNSON, John Coleman 1919-

PERSONAL: Born March 21, 1919, in Accra, Gold Coast (now Ghana); son of John Coleman and Hannah (Hammond) de Graft-Johnson; married second wife, Nancy Opoku-Afari (a teacher), August 20, 1960; children: (first marriage) John Coleman, Hannah Hammond: (second marriage) Elizabeth Hagan, Josephine. *Education:* Early education in Ghana; University of Edinburgh, medical student, 1937-39, B.Com., 1942, M.A., 1944, Ph.D., 1946. *Religion:* Protestant. *Home:* 2 Ayido Circle, Legon, Accra, Ghana. *Office:* Department of Economics, University of Ghana, Legon, Accra, Ghana.

CAREER: British Colonial Office, London, England, administrative assistant in Economic Department, 1946-48; Gold Coast Department of Commerce and Industry, Accra, assistant controller of commerce and industry, 1950; University College of the Gold Coast (now University of Ghana), Legon, Accra, resident tutor, Institute of Extra-Mural Studies, 1950-56; Delhi University, Delhi, India, professor of economics, department of African studies, 1956-58; University College of Ghana (now University of Ghana), senior resident tutor, Institute of Extra-Mural Studies, 1958-61; University of Ghana, associate professor, 1962, director of Institute of Public Education (now Institute of Adult Education), 1962-65, associate research professor, department of economics, 1965-67, master of Commonwealth Hall, 1961-65; ambassador to the Netherlands and Belgium, 1967-70; University of Ghana, professor of economics, 1970—, chairman of department, 1974—.

Member of board of directors, Ghana Commerical Bank, 1966-67; chairman of board of directors, State Insurance Corp., 1966-67, and Ghana National Manganese Corp., 1973—; chairman of Ghana Government's Committee of Ghana and the European Economic Community, 1972-74. Deputy chairman of Retail Trade Workers Wages Board, 1952-56, 1958-61; member of First National Committee on the Volta River Project, 1953; chairman of Committee on the Local Purchasing of Cocoa, 1966.

MEMBER: Ghana Academy of Arts and Sciences (honorary secretary, 1971-72; chairman of Prizes and Awards Committee, 1970, 1973—, and Committee on Documents, Oral Tradition and Cultural Heritage, 1971—), Council for

Scientific and Industrial Research (chairman of Finance and Development Committee, 1971-72), Economic Society of Ghana (fellow), Institute of Bankers (London), British Institute of Management (London), Royal Economic Society (fellow), Scottish Economic Society, Historical Society of Ghana (president, 1961-67). *Awards, honors:* Grand Cross of Order of Merit, Luxembourg, 1970.

WRITINGS: African Glory: The Story of Vanished Negro Civilisations, C. A. Watts, 1954, Praeger, 1955; *Background to the Volta River Project*, Abura Press (Kumasi), 1955; *The Gold Coast in Perspective* (monograph), Indian Council for World Affairs, 1956; *African Experiment: Cooperative Agriculture and Banking in British West Africa*, C. A. Watts, 1958; *An Introduction to the African Economy*, Delhi University School of Economics, 1959, Asia Publishing House, 1961; *Sons and Daughters* (play), Oxford University Press, 1964; (contributor) R. A. Kotey, C. Okali, and B. G. Rourke, editors, *Cooperative Marketing of Cocoa in Ghana, 1929-72*, Institute of Statistical, Social and Economic Research, 1974. Joint author of report on the local purchasing of cocoa, 1966.

Contributor to *Proceedings of the Ghana Academy of Arts and Sciences*, Volume VII, 1970, *Encyclopaedia Britannica*, 1974, and *World Encyclopedia of Black Peoples*, 1975. Contributor of articles to *Economic Bulletin of Ghana*, and *Social Science Journal* (Ghana). Editor, *Economic Bulletin of Ghana*, 1970-75, and *Christian Sentinel*, 1974—.

WORK IN PROGRESS: Writing on the economic history of Ghana, problems of agricultural development in Ghana, aspects of African history, and banking in West Africa; an industrial survey of Accra, Kumasi, and other cities in Ghana.

*   *   *

De HAAN, Richard W. 1923-

PERSONAL: Born February 21, 1923, in Holland, Mich.; son of Martin R. (a physician and minister) and Lena Priscilla (Venhuizen) De Haan; married Margaret Blohm, August 24, 1945; children: Martin R., Richard W., Kurt Edward, Stephen Jon. *Education:* Attended Calvin College, 1940-42, Wheaton College, Wheaton, Ill., 1942-44, and Northern Baptist Seminary, 1944-48. *Religion:* Protestant. *Home address:* P.O. Box 22, Grand Rapids, Mich. 49501. *Office:* 2303 Kalamazoo Ave. S.E., Grand Rapids, Mich. 49507.

CAREER: Radio Bible Class, Grand Rapids, Mich., associate teacher, 1950-65, president-teacher, 1965—; voice of "Radio Bible Class" radio program; speaker for "Day of Discovery" television program, 1969—.

WRITINGS: The Living God, Zondervan, 1967; *Israel and the Nations in Prophecy*, Zondervan, 1968; *The World on Trial: Studies in Romans*, Zondervan, 1970; *Happiness is Not an Accident*, Zondervan, 1971; *The World's Last Hope*, Victor, 1971; (editor with Henry G. Bosch) *Our Daily Bread Favorites*, Zondervan, 1971; (with Herbert Vander Lugt) *Satan, Satanism, and Witchcraft*, Zondervan, 1972; (with Vander Lugt) *The Wonderful Difficult Years*, Victor, 1973; (with Vander Lugt) *The Art of Staying Off Dead End Streets*, Victor, 1974; *Good News for Bad Times*, Scripture Press, 1975. Author of seven pamphlets for Scripture Press including *How to Talk to God*, and *The Middle East Prophecy*, both 1975.

DELANEY, Jack J(ames) 1921-
(Richard Stone)

PERSONAL: Born March 2, 1921, in Great Falls, Mont.; son of James R. (a salesman) and Frances (Schneider) Delaney. *Education:* College of Great Falls, B.A., 1946; Our Lady of the Lake College M.S. in L.S., 1953; further study at Columbia University, 1960, and Harvard University, 1962. *Home:* Stony Brook Lodge, Stony Brook, N.Y. 11790.

CAREER: Social worker for Montana Department of Public Welfare, 1949-50, and at Fort Riley, Kan., 1950-52; Texas Technological College (now Texas Tech University), Lubbock, order librarian, 1954-56; school librarian in Houston, Tex., 1956-57, and Galveston, Tex., 1957-58; Middle Country School District 11, Centereach, N.Y., librarian, 1958—. *Military service:* U.S. Army, 1943-46, 10th Infantry Division, 1950-51. *Member:* American Academy of Political and Social Science, American Association of School Librarians. *Awards, honors: The New School Librarian* appeared on the *Collier's Encyclopedia* list of best books on education.

WRITINGS: The School Librarian, Shoe String, 1961; *The New School Librarian*, Shoe String, 1968; *The Library Club*, Shoe String, 1970; (under pseudonym Richard Stone) *The Good Teacher*, Philosophical Library, 1970; *The Media Program in the Elementary School: Administration*, Shoe String, 1976. Contributor to educational and library journals.

WORK IN PROGRESS: Where the Good Books Are, an annotated bibliography.

*   *   *

DeLAURA, David J(oseph) 1930-

PERSONAL: Born November 19, 1930, in Worcester, Mass.; son of Louis and Helen A. (Austin) DeLaura; married Ann Beloate, August 19, 1961; children: Michael, Catherine, William. *Education:* Boston College, A.B., 1955, A.M., 1958; University of Wisconsin, Ph.D., 1960. *Home:* 305 Bryn Mawr Ave., Bryn Mawr, Pa. 19010. *Office:* Department of English, University of Pennsylvania, Philadelphia, Pa.

CAREER: University of Texas, Austin, instructor, 1960-62, assistant professor, 1962-64, associate professor, 1964-68, professor of English, 1968-74; University of Pennsylvania, Philadelphia, Avalon Foundation Professor in the Humanities and professor of English, 1974—. *Member:* Modern Language Association of America, American Association of University Professors. *Awards, honors:* Award for outstanding article in *PMLA*, Modern Language Association of America, 1964; Guggenheim fellow, 1967-68.

WRITINGS: (Editor) John Henry Newman, *Apologia pro Vita Sua*, Norton, 1968; *Hebrew and Hellene in Victorian England: Religion and Humanism in Newman, Arnold, and Pater*, University of Texas Press, 1969; (editor) *Matthew Arnold: A Collection of Essays*, Prentice-Hall, 1973; (editor) *Victorian Prose: A Guide to Research*, Modern Language Association of America, 1973. Author of numerous monographs, chapters, articles, and reviews; has contributed to *Dublin Review, Victorian Poetry, French Review*, and other journals.

WORK IN PROGRESS: Matthew Arnold's Literary Theory; a book-length study of the main problems of Victorian literary theory.

DELEAR, Frank J. 1914-

PERSONAL: Surname is pronounced *Dee-leer;* born January 21, 1914, in Boston, Mass.; son of Joseph F. (an architectural sculptor) and Adelaide (von der Luft) Delear; married Marion Robertsen, September 3, 1940; children: Susan (Mrs. Richard Noel), David, Betsy, James, Janet. *Education:* Boston College, B.A., 1936. *Religion:* Episcopalian. *Home:* 100 Brenair Ter., Stratford, Conn. 06497. *Office:* Sikorsky Aircraft, Stratford, Conn. 06602.

CAREER: Quincy Patriot Ledger, Quincy, Mass., assistant sports editor, 1936-37; *Bridgeport Post Telegram,* Bridgeport, Conn., reporter, aviation editor, 1937-42; Chance Vought Aircraft, Stratford, Conn., publicity representative, 1942-47; United Aircraft Corp., East Hartford, Conn., assistant to public relations director, 1947-48; Socony-Vacuum Oil Co., New York, N.Y., writer in public relations department, 1948-52; Hamilton Standard (division of United Aircraft Corp.), Windsor Locks, Conn., assistant public relations director, 1952-57; Sikorsky Aircraft (division of United Aircraft Corp.), Stratford, Conn., public relations manager, 1957—. *Member:* Aviation/Space Writers Association (chairman of National Writing Awards Committee), American Helicopter Society, Helicopter Association of America. OX-5 Club of America, Brownson Country Club. *Awards, honors:* Aviation/Space Writers Association writing award citation, 1970, for *Igor Sikorsky.*

WRITINGS: Wings for the Navy, Chance Vought Aircraft, 1944; *Miracle of the Helicopter,* Sikorsky Aircraft, 1961; *The New World of Helicopters,* Dodd, 1967; *Igor Sikorsky: His Three Careers in Aviation,* Dodd, 1969. Writer of scripts for company-produced movies. Contributor to *Yankee,* to newspapers and aviation magazines.

SIDELIGHTS: As a boy Delear built model planes and worked at an airport; he later learned to fly, but poor eyesight prevented a pilot's career. He has followed at first hand the development of the helicopter since its beginnings in 1939. Delear stated: "The twentieth century is the most dangerous and barbaric yet known to man and if man's intellect does not soon prevail over his emotions and prejudices the twenty-first century will be the quietest ever known."

*   *   *

DELESSERT, Etienne 1941-

PERSONAL: Born January 4, 1941, in Lausanne, Switzerland; son of Ferdinand (a minister) and Berengere (de Mestral) Delessert. *Education:* Attended College Classique, Lausanne, 1951-56, and Gymnase Classique, Lausanne, 1957-58. *Religion:* Protestant.

CAREER: Free-lance graphic designer and illustrator in Paris, France, 1962-65; author and illustrator of children's books, 1965—. *Military service:* Swiss Army, 1961.

WRITINGS: (With Eleonore Schmid) *The Tree,* Quist, 1966; (with Schmid, and illustrator) *The Endless Party,* Quist, 1967; (and illustrator) *How the Mouse Was Hit on the Head by a Stone and So Discovered the World,* with foreword by Jean Piaget, Good Book, 1971. Also author and illustrator of *The Boy with Whiskers,* published by Doubleday.

Illustrator: Eugene Ionesco, *Story Number 1 for Children under Three Years of Age,* Quist, 1968; Betty Jean Lifton, *The Secret Seller,* Norton, 1968; Ionesco, *Story Number 2 for Children under Three Years of Age,* Quist, 1969; Rudyard Kipling, *Just So Stories,* anniversary edition, Double-

day, 1972; Gordon Lightfoot, *The Pony Man,* Harper Magazine Press, 1972; Joseph G. Rapaso, *Being Green,* Western Publishing, 1973. Contributor of editorial illustrations to *Fortune, Playboy, Punch, Fact, Elle,* and other magazines.

AVOCATIONAL INTERESTS: Motion picture directing.

BIOGRAPHICAL/CRITICAL SOURCES: Idea (Japan), number 66, 1964, number 71, 1965; *Graphis,* number 128, 1967; Jacques Chessex, *Les dessins d'Etienne Delessert,* Bertil Galland, 1974.†

*   *   *

DeLEY, Herbert (Clemone, Jr.) 1936-

PERSONAL: Born November 24, 1936, in Altadena, Calif.; son of Herbert Clemone and Lilian L. (Stone) DeLey; married Margo Ynes Corona (a teacher), February 3, 1962. *Education:* University of California, Los Angeles, B.A., 1958, graduate study, 1958-59; University of Paris, Diplome d'etudes francaises, 1957; Yale University, Ph.D., 1963. *Office:* Department of French, University of Illinois, Urbana, Ill. 61801.

CAREER: Wilson College, Chambersburg, Pa., instructor in French, 1961-62; University of Illinios, Urbana, instructor, 1962-63, assistant professor, 1963-66, associate professor of French, 1966—. Visiting associate professor, University of California, Riverside, 1967-68, and University of Chicago, 1969. *Member:* Modern Language Association of America, American Association of Teachers of French, Societe des Amis de Marcel Proust, Association Internationale d'Etudes Francaises, American Association of University Professors. *Awards, honors:* American Philosophical Society grant.

WRITINGS: Marcel Proust et le duc de Saint-Simon, University of Illinois Press, 1966; *Saint-Simon Memorialist,* University of Illinois Press, 1975. Contributor to professional journals.

WORK IN PROGRESS: Research in French classicism; baroque eroticism.

*   *   *

DELFGAAUW, Bernard(us Maria Ignatius) 1912-

PERSONAL: Born November 24, 1912, in Amsterdam, Netherlands; son of Henri (a teacher) and Mathilde (de Jong) Delfgaauw; married Christina Niesten, April 13, 1944; children: Thomas, Maria. *Education:* University of Amsterdam, Ph.D., 1947. *Politics:* Socialist. *Religion:* Roman Catholic. *Home:* 23 Botanicuslaan, Haren, Groningen, Netherlands. *Office:* Philosophical Institute, Kraneweg 74, Groningen, Netherlands.

CAREER: Teacher in Catholic high school, Haarlem, Netherlands, 1939-61; University of Amsterdam, Amsterdam, Netherlands, lecturer in philosophy, 1947-61; University of Groningen, Groningen, Netherlands, professor of philosophy, 1961—, director of Philosophical Institute, 1961-73, chairman of philosophical faculty, 1965-73. Lecturer and conferee in Belgium, Germany, Italy, Spain, Denmark, and Sweden. *Member:* Soeren Kierkegaard Society (Copenhagen), Instituto Antonio Rosmini (Italy), Societas Ethica (Basel), Societe Philosophique (Louvain).

WRITINGS: Louis Lavelle, Het Wereldvenster, 1947; *Wat is Existentialisme?,* Het Wereldvenster, 1948; *Beknopte geschiedenis der wijsbegeerte,* Het Wereldvenster, 1950, translation by N. D. Smith published as *The Student His-*

tory of Philosophy, Magi Books, 1968, same translation also published as *A Concise History of Philosophy*, Sidney, Gill & Son, 1968; *Wijsbegeerte van de 20e eeuw*, Het Wereldvenster, 1951, translation by Smith published as *Twentieth-Century Philosophy*, Macmillan and M. H. Gill & Son, 1969; *Teilhard de Chardin*, Het Wereldvenster 1961, translation published as *Teilhard de Chardin and the Problem of Evolution*, Harper, 1968, also published as *Evolution: The Theory of Teilhard de Chardin*, Harper, 1969; *De jonge Marx*, Het Wereldvenster, 1962, translation published as *The Young Marx*, Newman, 1967; *Geschiedenis en Vooruitgang*, three volumes, Het Wereldvenster, 1962-65; *Over de Schreef*, Het Wereldvenster, 1965; (with others) *Evolutie en de filosofie, de biologie, de kosmos*, Het Spectrum, 1967; *Vietnam: Verdragen als vodjes papier*, Het Wereldvenster, 1975. Studies on philosophical themes have been published in *Man and World* (United States), *Tijdschrift voor Philosophie* (Belgium), *Zeitschrift fur philosophische Forschung* (Germany), *Etudes Philosophiques* (France), *Giornale di Metafisica* (Italy), and *Eranos-Jahrbuch* (Switzerland).

WORK IN PROGRESS: Philosophy of history and politics.

SIDELIGHTS: James Heisig believes *Evolution: The Theory of Teilhard de Chardin* "allows the neophyte to break into the stream" of Teilhard's evolutionary theory since "it is concentrated enough to merit careful reading, and yet does not demand a scholar's knowledge of science and philosophy."

All but one of Delfgaauw's books have been translated into Spanish for publication in Buenos Aires; five have been published in German, and two in Italian. He speaks English, French, and German and has a passive command of Latin, Greek, Hebrew, Italian, Spanish, Portuguese, Danish, Swedish, Norwegian, and Frisian.

* * *

DeLUCA, A(ngelo) Michael 1912-

PERSONAL: Born October 1, 1912, in Brooklyn, N.Y.; son of Nicola (a businessman) and Francesca (Staiano) DeLuca; married Rose Pully (an elementary teacher), September 20, 1936; children: Vincent Arthur. *Education:* Brooklyn College (now Brooklyn College of the City University of New York), B.A., 1934; Columbia University, M.A., 1936, Ph.D., 1951; additional study at University of Florence, 1936-37. *Politics:* Independent. *Religion:* Roman Catholic. *Home:* 58 Strathmore Gate Dr., Stony Brook, N.Y. 11790.

CAREER: Brooklyn College (now Brooklyn College of the City University of New York), Brooklyn, N.Y., instructor in Romance languages, 1937-42, 1945-46; Hofstra University, Hempstead, N.Y., 1946-60, began as instructor, became associate professor of Romance languages; Suffolk Community College, Selden, N.Y., professor of foreign languages and chairman of Humanities Division, 1960-64; Long Island University, C. W. Post College, Greenvale, N.Y., professor of foreign languages and chairman of department, 1964-72. Member of board, Uniondale Public Library, 1955-60.

MEMBER: Modern Language Association of America, American Association of Teachers of Spanish, American Association of Teachers of Italian (vice-president), American Council on Teaching Foreign Languages, Dante Society of America, Italian Culture Council, New York State Federation of Foreign Language Teachers (director), Sigma Delta Pi, Touring Club Italiano. *Awards, honors:* Italian Government travel award; Eleanora Duse fellowship to University of Florence; distinguished educator award of Suffolk County Community College.

WRITINGS: (Editor with Vincenzo Cioffari) *Corrierino delle Famiglie*, Heath, 1962; (editor and translator with William Giuliano) *Selections from Italian Poetry* (bilingual book), Harvey House, 1966; *The Fourth Estate* (poetry), Great Society Press, 1971; *Doves Fly Homeward: Medley of Moods for Balladry* (poetry), Great Society Press, 1972; *Legacy of Life: Ariel and Frankenstein Come to Grips* (poetry), Great Society Press, 1973. Contributor to journals.

WORK IN PROGRESS: Contemporary Italian Prose and Poetry, a textbook for intermediate Italian.

SIDELIGHTS: A. Michael DeLuca has traveled repeatedly and extensively in Italy, Greece, and Spain, and visited elsewhere in Europe, Mexico, the Caribbean, Algiers, and Turkey.

* * *

deMARE, George 1912-

PERSONAL: Born November 11, 1912, in Denver, Colo.; son of Joseph S. and Marie (Healy) deMare; married Mercedes Moore, May 16, 1936; children: Gregory Moore, Malcolm Moore, Gilbert Healy, Adrienne. *Education:* Yale University, B.A., 1936. *Politics:* Independent. *Home:* 7230 Woodstock Rd., Saugerties, N.Y. *Office:* 687 Leaington Ave., New York, N.Y. 10022.

CAREER: Collier's, New York City, associate editor, 1936-41; Western Electric Co., New York City, publications work, 1943-56; Price Waterhouse & Co., New York City, director of communications, 1956-72. Instructor in creative writing, New York University, 1946-50. *Member:* International Society for the Communicating Arts (president, 1967-68), Industrial Communications Council (director, 1966-69), New York Association of Industrial Communicators (president, 1963-65), Authors League of America, Graduates Club.

WRITINGS: The Empire (novel), Putnam, 1956; *The Ruling Passion* (novel), Putnam, 1958; *Communicating for Leadership* (a guide for opinion leaders), Ronald, 1968. Contributor to *Reporting* and other professional journals. Editor, *Price Waterhouse Review*.

WORK IN PROGRESS: Corporate Lives, an exploration of the quality of life in the corporation, part of a series on American life styles.

* * *

De MENTE, Boye 1928-

PERSONAL: Born November 12, 1928, in Redford, Mo.; son of Elza Lafayette and Ruby (Bounds) De Mente; married Margaret Warren, September 29, 1958; children: Dawn Rubi, Demetra (both daughters). *Education:* Studied at American Institute of Foreign Trade (now Thunderbird Graduate School of International Management), BFT, 1953; Jochi University, Tokyo, Japan, B.S., 1956. *Residence:* Phoenix, Ariz.

CAREER: In military service with U.S. Navy, 1946-48, and U.S. Army Security Agency, 1948-52, leaving service as sergeant; did public relations for Japan Travel Bureau, Tokyo, 1953-54; editor in Tokyo, Japan, of *Kembun* (weekly newspaper), 1954-55, *Today's Japan* (cultural magazine), 1955-57, and *Importer* (trade journal), 1958-62; free-lance writer, 1962—.

WRITINGS: Japanese Manners and Ethics in Business, East Asia Publishing, 1961, 2nd revised edition, Simpson-Doyle & Co., 1975; *The Tourist and the Real Japan,* Tuttle, 1961, revised edition, 1966; *Bachelor's Japan,* Tuttle, 1962, revised edition, 1966; *How Business Is Done in Japan,* Simpson-Doyle & Co., 1963, revised edition published as *How to Do Business in Japan: A Guide for International Businessmen,* Center for International Business, 1972; *Oriental Secrets of Graceful Living,* Wilshire, 1963; *Once a Fool—From Tokyo to Alaska by Amphibious Jeep,* Simpson-Doyle & Co., 1964; *Bachelor's Hawaii,* Tuttle, 1964, revised edition, 1966; *Mizu Shobai: The Pleasure Girls and Fleshpots of Japan,* Medco Books, 1966; *Some Prefer Geisha—The Lively Art of Mistress-Keeping in Japan,* Wayward Press, 1966; *Faces of Japan—Twenty-Three Critical Essays,* Simpson-Doyle & Co., 1966; *Bachelor's Mexico,* Tuttle, 1967; (with Fred Thomas Perry) *The Japanese as Consumers—A General Description of Asia's First Mass Market,* Weatherhill/Walker, 1968; *Face-Reading for Fun and Profit,* Bachelor Books, 1968; *International Businessman's After-hours Guide to Japan,* East Asia Publishing, 1968, revised edition, Phoenix Books, 1975; *Girl-Watcher's Guide to the Far East,* Bachelor Books, 1969; *Aphrodisiac Recipes for Swingers,* Bachelor Books, 1969, revised edition published as *Cookbook for Lovers,* Phoenix Books, 1975.

Insiders' Guide to Phoenix, Scottsdale and Tucson, Phoenix Books, 1972, revised edition, 1975; *Retiring in Arizona: Senior Citizen's Shangri La,* Phoenix Books, 1973, revised edition, 1975; (with Mario De La Guente) *I Like You, Gringo—But!,* Phoenix Books, 1973; *Fifteen Ways to Kick the Smoking Habit,* Phoenix Books, 1974; *P's and Cues for Travelers in Japan,* Japan Publications, 1974; *Insiders' Guide to Rocky Point, Guaymas, Mazatalan and La Paz,* Phoenix Books, 1975; *Exotic Japan: The Land, the People, the Places, the Pleasures,* Phoenix Books, 1975.

WORK IN PROGRESS: How to Make Retirement the Best Years of Your Life; Visitor's Guide to Arizona's Indian Reservations; a collection of short stories, *Hai-ior no Sekai* (title means "The Grew World"); a novel, *The Mixed-Blood.*

*   *   *

DEMETRIUS, James Kleon   1924-

PERSONAL: Born August 23, 1924, in Chicopee Falls, Mass.; son of James (a professor, poet, and dramatist) and Bess (Stephens) Demetrius. *Education:* Brooklyn College (now Brooklyn College of the City University of New York), B.A., 1948; Columbia University, M.A., 1949. *Politics:* Democrat, "but preferably independent voter." *Religion:* Eastern Orthodox. *Home and office:* 507 Fifth Ave., New York, N.Y. 10017.

CAREER: Teacher of foreign languages at Iona College, New Rochelle, N.Y., 1955-59, Pennsylvania Military College (now Wildener College), Chester, 1961-63, and Washington College, Chestertown, Md., 1963-64; Bloomfield College, Bloomfield, N.J., professor of Spanish and Greek studies, 1964-69; St. Francis College, Loretto, Pa., visiting professor of ancient and modern languages, 1971-72; Touro College, New York, N.Y., professor of ancient and modern languages, 1972—. Visiting professor at Abbe Institute, and Interboro College. *Military service:* U.S. Army Air Forces, 1942-45. *Member:* American Association of

Teachers of Spanish and Portuguese, Classical League of America, Mediaeval Academy of America, Center for Neo-Hellenic Studies, International Hispanists, Philosophical Society (England), Classical Association (England), Classical Society of Spain-Byzantine Studies, Hellenic Society of London, Alpha Sigma Phi.

WRITINGS: A Bibliography of Greek Studies in Spain (monograph), privately printed, 1962; *Los Griegos en Espana* (monograph), privately printed, 1962; *An Essay on Greek Influence in Spanish Literature,* privately printed, 1962; (contributor) I. A. Langnas and B. Sholod, editors, *Studies in Honor of M. J. Benardete,* Las Americas, 1966; *Greek Scholarship in Spain and Latin America,* Volume I, Argonaut, 1966; (with Luis Leon) *Spanish Grammar Explained,* privately printed, 1972; (contributor) *Studies in Honor of Dr. Quintino Cautadella,* University of Catania, 1972. Also author of *Pandelis Prevelakis: The Muse of Prevelakis,* 1973.

Contributor to *Modern Greek Literature, Modern Greek Poetry,* both 1974, and *The Marvels of Modern Greek,* 1975. Contributor to *New York Times, Hispania, Athene, Greek Herald, Atlantis, Books Abroad, Slavic Review,* and other publications (Demetrius states: "661 book reviews, 221 articles"). Regular columnist, *Chicago Greek Press,* 1962-74; member of editorial board and regular columnist, *New York Hellenic Times,* 1974—.

WORK IN PROGRESS: A novel, *Only the Stars are Neutral; Stratis Myrivilis: The Man and His Work,* for Twayne; *Spanish Spoken Language;* a monograph on Nikos Kazantzakis; *Dictionary of Greek Thought in Spain.*

SIDELIGHTS: Demetrius spent 1970 and 1971 doing research for volumes two and three of *Greek Scholarship in Spain and Latin America.* He speaks Greek, Spanish, Italian, and French.

BIOGRAPHICAL/CRITICAL SOURCES: New York Times, May 2, 1955; *Baltimore News-Post,* October 1, 1963.

*   *   *

de MILLE, Richard   1922-
(B. Grayer Dimrecken)

PERSONAL: Born February 12, 1922, in Monrovia, Calif.; son of Cecil Blount (a motion picture director) and Constance (Adams) de Mille; married Margaret Belgrano, August 7, 1955; children: Anthony B. van Fossen, Cecil Belgrano. *Education:* Attended Columbia University, 1940-42, and University of California, Los Angeles, 1942-43; Pepperdine College, B.A., 1955; University of Southern California, Ph.D., 1961. *Home:* 960 Lilac Dr., Santa Barbara, Calif. 93108.

CAREER: KTLA-TV, Hollywood, Calif., director, 1946-50; free-lance writer, 1952—; University of Southern California, Los Angeles, research associate, 1961-62; University of California, Santa Barbara, lecturer in psychology, 1962-65; General Research Corp., Santa Barbara, Calif., scientist, 1967-70, consulting research psychologist, 1970—. *Military service:* U.S. Army Air Forces, 1943-46. *Member:* American Psychological Association, Authors Guild.

WRITINGS: Introduction to Scientology: An Introductory Survey and Evaluation to Thirty Years' Work in the Field of Human Thought by L. Ron Hubbard, Scientology Council, 1953; *Put Your Mother on the Ceiling: Children's Imagination Games,* Walker & Co., 1967, revised edition, Viking, 1973; (with R. P. Barthol) *Project ECHO,* Management Information Services, 1969; *Two Qualms and a Quirk* (stories), Capra, 1973; (under pseudonym B. Grayer Dimrecken) *A Skeleton Key to "The Transuxors,"* Capra, 1973. Co-author of *The Measurement of Social Intelligence,* for the University of Southern California, and of three publications for Sheridan Supply, *Missing Cartoons, Missing Pictures,* and *Picture Exchange,* all 1965. Contributor to scientific journals and popular periodicals, including *Astounding Science Fiction, This Week, National Review,* and *Reason.* Consulting editor, Capra Press, 1972—.

WORK IN PROGRESS: A philosophical book, *Boundaries of Understanding;* a book of reminiscences, *Glimpses of Henry,* for Capra.

*   *   *

DEMING, Robert H.   1937-

PERSONAL: Born October 12, 1937, in Hartford, Conn.; son of David F. and Augusta M. (Sanford) Deming; married Anne L. Bruggy, March 3, 1962; children: Michael S., Maura K., Sean F. *Education:* Union College, Schenectady, N.Y., A.B., 1959; University of Kansas, M.A., 1961; University of Wisconsin, Ph.D., 1965. *Home:* 189 Temple St., Fredonia, N.Y. 14063. *Office:* State University of New York College, Fredonia, N.Y. 14063.

CAREER: Miami University, Oxford, Ohio, assistant professor of English, 1965-70; State University of New York College at Fredonia, associate professor of English, 1970—. *Member:* Modern Language Association of America, Renaissance Society of America.

WRITINGS: A Bibliography of James Joyce Studies, University of Kansas Libraries, 1964; (editor and author of introduction) *James Joyce: The Critical Heritage,* Volume I: *1902-1927,* Volume II: *1928-1941,* Barnes & Noble, 1970; *Ceremony and Art: Robert Herrick's Poetry,* Mouton & Co., 1974.

WORK IN PROGRESS: Some Uses of the Past: Classicism and the Native Traditions in Renaissance Poetry.

*   *   *

Den BOER, James (Drew)   1937-

PERSONAL: Born August 21, 1937, in Sheboygan, Wis.; son of Jacob (a welding engineer) and Jeanette (Verhulst) Den Boer; married Daphne R. Kingma, June 6, 1961 (divorced, 1969); married Emily Cady Williams, 1970; children: (first marriage) Megali Stuart (daughter); (second marriage) Joshua Reeve. *Education:* Calvin College, A.B., 1960; University of California, Santa Barbara, M.A., 1969. *Politics:* Independent. *Religion:* None. *Home:* 228 Ortega Ridge Rd., Santa Barbara, Calif. 93108.

CAREER: New Jersey State Department of Health, Trenton, epidemiologist, 1961-62; U.S. Public Health Service, Washington, D.C., writer and editor, 1963-67; Unicorn Press, Santa Barbara, Calif., assistant director, 1968-69; Office of Special Events, White House Conference on Children and Youth, Washington, D.C., deputy director, 1970-71; free-lance writer and consultant, 1972-73; University of California, Santa Barbara, research information officer, 1973—. *Military service:* U.S. Naval Reserve, 1955-63. *Awards, honors:* U.S. Award of International Poetry Forum ($2,000), 1967, for *Learning the Way;* National Council of the Arts Selection ($500), 1971, for *Trying to Come Apart;* grants from National Institute of Arts and Letters, Carnegie Fund for Authors, and Authors League of America, 1971-73.

WRITINGS: Learning the Way (poems), University of Pittsburgh Press, 1968; *Trying to Come Apart* (poems), University of Pittsburgh Press, 1971; *Nine Poems,* Christopher Books, 1972; (with Charles Olson) *A Letter: Charles Olson—James Den Boer,* Christopher Books, 1975; *Firewood,* University of Pittsburgh Press, 1976. Assistant editor, *Voyages;* editor-at-large, *Black Box.*

WORK IN PROGRESS: A book of poetry; a novel; a biography of Jimmy Angel, pioneer aviator and explorer; an anthology of essays on the morphologies of natural, artifactual, and artistic forms.

*   *   *

DENHAM, Alice   1933-

PERSONAL: Born January 21, 1933, in Jacksonville, Fla.; daughter of T. B. Simkins (a Federal Housing Administration official) and Leila (Meggs) Denham; married S. Lee Kutz, 1953 (divorced, 1954). *Education:* University of North Carolina, B.A., 1953; University of Rochester, M.A., 1954. *Religion:* "Peace." *Home and office:* 96 Grove St., New York, N.Y. 10014. *Agent:* Elaine Markson, 44 Greenwich Ave., New York, N.Y. 10011.

CAREER: Professional model (*Playboy*'s Playmate of the Month, 1956), and actress in films and television commercials, 1955-64; free-lance writer and author, 1964—. Teacher of fiction at summer writers' conferences at Georgetown University, 1966, Ryerson Institute, Toronto, 1968-69, York University, 1970-73, and University of Toronto, 1974-75; John Jay College of Criminal Justice of the City University of New York, adjunct lecturer, 1970-71, adjunct assistant professor, 1971-74, adjunct associate professor of creative writing, speech, and English, 1974—. Lecturer on radio and at universities including Yale University, and Smith College. Member of board of sponsors, Westbeth Feminists Playwrights Cooperative. *Member:* P.E.N., National Organization for Women, MacDowell Colonists, Phi Beta Kappa. *Awards, honors:* MacDowell Colony fellowships, 1969, 1970, 1971.

WRITINGS: My Darling from the Lions (novel), Bobbs-Merrill, 1967, published as *Coming Together,* Lancer, 1969; *The Ghost and Mrs. Muir* (based on television series of same name), Popular Library, 1968; *Adios, Sabata* (based on a movie), Popular Library, 1971; *AMO* (novel), Coward, 1974.

Adaptations: Ruth Montgomery, *Mrs. L.B.J.,* Avon, for U.S. Information Agency, 1967; William Inge, *Picnic* (play), Washington Square Press, for U.S. Information Agency, 1969; Henry James, *The Bostonians,* Washington Square Press, for U.S. Information Agency, 1971.

Work represented in anthologies including *Discovery 5,* Pocket Books, 1955, and *Great Tales of City Dwellers,* Lion Library, 1955. Writer of educational filmstrip, "New Dimensions in Public Housing," for Housing and Urban Development Agency. Contributor of feature stories to *Cosmopolitan, Topic,* and *Washingtonian;* contributor of essays and reviews to *Village Voice, New York Times Book Review,* and *Nation's Cities,* and of a short story to *Playboy, Man,* and *Dialog.*

WORK IN PROGRESS: "Currently working on yet another picaresque novel."

SIDELIGHTS: Alice Denham describes her novel, *My Darling from the Lions,* as "a feminist novel ahead of its time." She told *CA:* "Have appeared on 25-30 radio and TV shows to promote my novels ... and to discuss the

Woman's Movement. I was interviewed on the Walter Cronkite CBS-TV News in March 1970 in the first national TV news interview with individual feminists. I read the Media Women's demands over ABC-TV during the *Ladies' Home Journal* takeover in February 1970. (Such fun).''

BIOGRAPHICAL/CRITICAL SOURCES: New York Times Book Review, January 7, 1968; *Village Voice,* January 18, 1968.

*   *   *

DENIS, Paul   1909-

PERSONAL: Surname originally Dejerenis: born July 1, 1909, in New York, N.Y.; son of Nicholas and Amelia (Rozakis) Dejerenis; married Helen Martin (an editorial researcher), May 17, 1942; children: Michael, Christopher. *Education:* New York University, student, 1926-30. *Politics:* Independent Democrat. *Religion:* Greek Orthodox. *Home:* 518 Tulfan Ter., New York, N.Y. 10463.

CAREER: Writer, editor, and columnist specializing in show business, New York, N.Y., 1926—. Began as reporter for *Vaudeville News* and *Star,* 1926-30; associate editor of *New York Star,* 1930-31; managing editor, *Billboard,* 1931-43; drama reporter, radio-television editor, and vaudeville columnist for *New York Post,* 1943-45, radio and television writer, 1946-49; columnist for *New York Daily Compass,* 1949-51; associate editor of *Why* (magazine), 1951, and *Academy* (magazine), 1952-53; daytime television editorial director for Sterling's Magazines Inc., 1969—. Columnist for *TV World, TV People, Modern Screen,* and other periodicals. Lecturer on radio, television, and show business. Founder and chairman of Radio Critics Circle, 1947-49. *Member:* Writers Guild of America (East), American Academy of Television Arts and Sciences, Silurians Society, New York Newspaper Guild. *Awards, honors:* Award for fighting bigotry, Radio Station WNYC, 1948; Comedy Writers Institute award, 1949.

WRITINGS: Your Career in Show Business, Dutton, 1948; (compiler) *Paul Denis' Celebrity Cook Book,* Rockport Press, 1951; *Jackie Gleason's Life Story,* Goodman Publications, 1955; *Opportunities in Dancing,* Vocational Guidance Manuals, 1957, 2nd edition, Universal Publishing & Distributing Corp., 1966; *Unexpected Answers on Radio and TV,* Lyle Stuart, 1958; (with sons, Michael and Christopher Denis) *Singer Super Sound,* Rutledge Books, 1969. Contributor to national magazines.

WORK IN PROGRESS: A book on Greek-American creative artists; a book on the impact of television on American life; and a third book on daytime television dramatic serials.

SIDELIGHTS: Paul Denis speaks and reads Greek. He is interested in teen-age behavior and rock and roll music.

*   *   *

DENISON, Edward F(ulton)   1915-

PERSONAL: Born December 18, 1915, in Omaha, Neb.; son of Edward Fulton (member of national council, Young Men's Christian Association) and Edith (Brown) Denison; married Elsie Lightbown (an economist), June 14, 1941; children: Janet (Mrs. Alfred Hunt Howell, Jr.), Edward Brown. *Education:* Attended Central Young Men's Christian Association College, Chicago, Ill., 1933-34, and Loyola University, Chicago, 1935; Oberlin College, B.A., 1936; Brown University, M.A., 1938, Ph.D., 1941; National War College, graduate, 1951. *Politics:* Democrat. *Religion:* Presbyterian. *Home:* 560 N St. S.W., Apt. N-902, Washington, D.C. 20024. *Office:* Brookings Institution, 1775 Massachusetts Ave. N.W., Washington D.C. 20036.

CAREER: Brown University, Providence, R.I., instructor in economics, 1940-41; U.S. Department of Commerce, Washington, D.C., economist, 1941-47, assistant director of Office of Business Economics, 1947-56; Committee for Economic Development, Washington, D.C., member of research staff, 1956-60, associate director of research, 1961-62; Brookings Institution, Washington, D.C., senior fellow in economics, 1962—. Lecturer, American University, 1946; Ford Rotating Research Professor of Economics, University of California, Berkeley, 1967-68.

MEMBER: American Economic Association, American Statistical Association (fellow), International Association for Research in Income and Wealth, Conference on Research in Income and Wealth (former chairman of executive committee), National Economists Club, Massachusetts Society of Mayflower Descendants, Sherwood Forest Club. *Awards, honors:* Woytinsky Award of University of Michigan, 1967, for *Why Growth Rates Differ.*

WRITINGS: The Sources of Economic Growth in the United States and the Alternatives Before Us, Committee for Economic Development, 1962; (with Jean-Pierre Poullier) *Why Growth Rates Differ: Postwar Experience in Nine Western Countries,* Brookings Institution, 1967; *Accounting for United States Economic Growth, 1929-1969,* Brookings Institution, 1974.

Contributor: *The Residual Factor and Economic Growth,* [Paris], 1964; Marshall D. Ketchum and Leon D. Kendall, editors, *Readings in Financial Institutions,* Houghton, 1965; Seymour E. Harris and Alan Levensohn, editors, *Education and Public Policy,* McCutchan, 1965; E.A.G. Robinson and J. E. Vaisey, editors, *The Economics of Education,* St. Martin's, 1966; Heinz Kohler, editor, *Readings in Economics: An Introduction to Economics,* Holt, 1968; *Readings in the Economics of Education,* UNESCO, 1968; *Britain's Economic Prospects,* Brookings Institution, 1968; William E. Mitchell and Ingo Walter, editors, *Readings in Macroeconomics,* McGraw, 1974. Also translator of economic articles into numerous languages including Italian, German, and Hungarian. Contributor to economic journals and to publications of National Bureau of Economic Research.

WORK IN PROGRESS: With William K. Chung, *How Japan's Economy Grew So Fast.*

BIOGRAPHICAL/CRITICAL SOURCES: Jean-Jacques Servan-Schreiber, *The American Challenge,* Atheneum, 1968; *Forbes,* July 1, 1969.

*   *   *

DePAUW, Linda Grant   1940-

PERSONAL: Born January 19, 1940, in New York, N.Y.; daughter of Phillip and Ruth (Marks) Grant; married John W. DePauw (a social science analyst), October 23, 1960 (divorced January, 1973); children: Jolie Diane, Benjamin Grant. *Education:* Swarthmore College, B.A., 1961; Johns Hopkins University, Ph.D., 1964. *Home:* 210 East Fairfax St., Apt. 603, Falls Church, Va. 22046. *Office:* George Washington University, Washington, D.C. 20052.

CAREER: University of Virginia, Fairfax, assistant professor of history, 1964-65; National Historical Publications

Commission, Washington, D.C., assistant editor of First Federal Congress project, 1965-66; George Washington University, Washington, D.C., assistant professor, 1966-69, associate professor of history, 1969—. Member of Columbia University Seminar on Early American History and Culture; lectured to women's rights groups including Women's Equity Action League and National Organization for Women; member of board of Women's Coalition for the Third Century; former chairperson of Columbia University seminar on early American history and culture. Consultant to many civic and historical groups including National Archives, National Park Service, Stanton Project, National Public Radio, and others. *Member:* American Historical Association, American Studies Association, American Society for Legal History, Women's Equity Action League, American Association of University Professors, Southern Historical Association. *Awards, honors:* American Historical Association Albert J. Beveridge Award, 1964, for *The Eleventh Pillar: New York State and the Federal Constitution.*

WRITINGS: The Eleventh Pillar: New York State and the Federal Constitution, Cornell University Press, 1966; (editor) *Documentary History of the First Federal Congress, 1789-1791,* four volumes, Johns Hopkins Press, 1972-76; *Founding Mothers: Women of America in the Revolutionary Era,* Houghton, 1975. Contributor to *New York History, Prologue, Maryland Historical Magazine,* and *Ms.*

WORK IN PROGRESS: Editing last fourteen volumes of *Documentary History of the First Federal Congress, 1789-1791,* to be completed by 1989; a biography of Abigail Adams.

SIDELIGHTS: Linda DePauw has spoken on radio and television and made tape presentations for Voice of America and British Broadcasting Corporation.

* * *

DERIC, Arthur J. 1926-

PERSONAL: Born July 20, 1926, in Philadelphia, Pa.; married Claire Brandt; children: Mark, Alexa D., Beverly J. *Education:* Temple University, A.B., 1950, J.D., 1952; University of Pennsylvania, M.B.A., 1959. *Home:* 8 Upton Lane, Yardley, Pa. 19067. *Office:* Fred S. James & Co. of New York Inc., 55 Water St., New York, N.Y. 10041.

CAREER: Admitted to Pennsylvania and Federal Bars, 1953; law clerk to judges in several courts, Philadelphia, Pa., 1952-54; United States Fidelity and Guaranty Co., Philadelphia, engaged in multiple-lines claims, 1954-61; chartered property and casualty writer, 1959; American Management Association, Inc., New York City, division manager, insurance, 1961-69; Bucks County Community College, Newtown, Pa., associate professor of law, marketing, and management, 1969-70; Fred S. James & Co. of New York Inc., New York City, president and account executive, 1970—. Adjunct lecturer, University of Pennsylvania, Wharton School, 1959. *Military service:* U.S. Army, 1944-46; became captain. *Member:* American Bar Association, Society of Chartered Property and Casualty Underwriters, American Society of Insurance Management (New York chapter), Insurance Company Education Directors Society, American Pension Conference.

WRITINGS: The Total Approach to Employee Benefits, American Management Association, 1967.

WORK IN PROGRESS: Several books on insurance, risk management and employee benefits.

DeROSA, Peter 1932-

PERSONAL: Born November 12, 1932, son of Louis Leopold and Ruby (Read) DeRosa. *Education:* Studied at St. Ignatius College, London, England, at St. Edmund's College of Divinity, 1950-56, and Gregorian University, Rome, Italy, 1956-59. *Home:* 182 Mildmay Rd., Martins Wood, Stevenage, Hertfordshire, England.

CAREER: Corpus Christi College, London, England, lecturer in philosophy, 1960-65, vice-principal, 1965-71. BBC producer. Assistant director, National Catechetical Center, London.

WRITINGS: (With H. J. Richards) *Christ in Our World,* Bruce, 1966; *Christ and Original Sin,* Bruce, 1967; *God Our Saviour,* Bruce, 1967; *Jesus Who Became Christ,* Dimension, 1974; *The Bee and the Rose,* Argus, 1975; *Not I, Not I, But the Wind that Blows Through Me,* Argus, 1975; *Cloud Cuckoo Land,* Argus, 1975. Contributor to theological journals in United Kingdom and United States.

AVOCATIONAL INTERESTS: Literature, especially the great French and Russian novelists.

* * *

DERTOUZOS, Michael L. 1936-

PERSONAL: Surname is pronounced Der-*two*-zos; born November 5, 1936, in Athens, Greece; son of Leonidas M. (an admiral in the Greek Navy) and Rozana (Maris) Dertouzos; married Hadwig Gofferje (a chemist), November 21, 1961; children: Alexandra, Leonidas. *Education:* Athens College, Athens, Greece, Diploma, 1954; University of Arkansas, B.S.E.E., 1957, M.S.E.E., 1959; Massachusetts Institute of Technology, Ph.D., 1964. *Religion:* Greek Orthodox. *Home:* 15 Bernard Lane, Waban, Mass. 02168. *Office:* Massachusetts Institute of Technology, Cambridge, Mass. 02139.

CAREER: D. H. Baldwin, Cincinnati, Ohio, and Baldwin Electronics, Inc., Little Rock, Ark., head of advance development, 1958-60; Massachusetts Institute of Technology, Cambridge, instructor, 1963-64, assistant professor, 1964-68, associate professor of electrical engineering, 1968-73, professor of computer science and electrical engineering, 1973—, director of Project MAC, 1974—. *Member:* Institute of Electrical and Electronics Engineers, Sigma Xi, Pi Mu Epsilon, Tau Beta Pi. *Awards, honors:* Browder Thomson Award of Institute of Electrical and Electronics Engineers for best paper by a writer under thirty, 1968; Terman Award for best young educator, American Society of Engineering Education, 1975.

WRITINGS: Threshold Logic, M.I.T. Press, 1965; (with others) *Systems, Networks, and Computation: Basic Concepts,* two volumes, McGraw, 1972, 2nd edition, 1975. Contributor of more than forty papers to technical journals.

WORK IN PROGRESS: A book, *Structure and Interpretation of Programming Languages;* research in computer science.

AVOCATIONAL INTERESTS: Sailing, skiing, cabinet-making.

* * *

DESCHNER, Donald (Anthony) 1933-

PERSONAL: Born December 16, 1933, in Portland, Ore.; son of Frank Henry and Carolyn (Schetem) Deschner. *Education:* St. Mary's College of California, B.A., 1956; University of Southern California, graduate study, 1957.

Office: 1809½ North Las Palmas Ave. No. 5, Hollywood, Calif. 90028.

MEMBER: India-America Society, Cinemists (executive secretary, 1963), Filmex, Shaw Society of Southern California, Westerners.

WRITINGS: The Films of W. C. Fields, Citadel, 1966; *The Films of Spencer Tracy,* Citadel, 1968; *The Films of Cary Grant,* Citadel, 1973. Author of two plays, "Earth" and "Creation of Women," both produced in 1964.

WORK IN PROGRESS: A book on American opera; a play with a religious theme, set in eighteenth-century England; articles on Alaskan history and western Americana.

* * *

DeSEYN, Donna E. 1933-

PERSONAL: Surname is pronounced "design"; born November 7, 1933, in Canandaigua, N.Y.; daughter of Lewis J. and Mercie (Peer) DeSeyn. *Education:* State University Teachers College (now State University of New York College at Geneseo), B.S., 1955; Syracuse University, M.S., 1960. *Religion:* Presbyterian. *Home:* 66 Chapel St., Canandaigua, N.Y. 14424.

CAREER: Fairport Central School, Fairport, N.Y., science consultant, 1960-72, director, earth-space science education center, 1968-71, chairman, science department, 1974—. Member of board, Friends of Sonnenberg Gardens, 1973—. *Member:* National Science Teachers Association, National Education Association, Science Teachers Association of New York State (member of board of directors; fellow), New York State Teachers Association, Central Western Zone Science Teachers (president, 1965; member of board of directors), Rochester Council of Scientific Societies (delegate). *Awards, honors:* Phi Delta Kappa Outstanding Service Award, 1974; Science Teachers Association of New York Distinguished Service Award, 1974.

WRITINGS: Termite Works for His Colony, Holiday, 1967; *Teaching Earth Science with Behavioral Objectives and Investigations,* Parker & Son, 1973. Contributor to science and education journals.

AVOCATIONAL INTERESTS: Watercolor painting, music, and photography.

* * *

DETHLOFF, Henry C(lay) 1934-

PERSONAL: Born August 10, 1934, in New Orleans, La.; son of Carl Curt and Camelia (Jordan) Dethloff; married Myrtle Anne Elliott, August 27, 1961; children: Clay, Carl. *Education:* University of Texas, B.A., 1956; Northwestern State College (now University) of Louisiana, M.A., 1960; University of Missouri, Ph.D., 1964. *Religion:* Methodist. *Home:* 1202 Westover St., College Station, Tex. *Office:* Department of History, Texas A&M University, College Station, Tex. 77840.

CAREER: University of Southwestern Louisiana, Lafayette, instructor, 1962-64, assistant professor, 1964-66, associate professor of history, 1966-69, director of Southwestern Archives, 1965-69; Texas A&M University, College Station, associate professor, 1969-75, professor of history, 1975—. *Military service:* U.S. Naval Reserve, active duty, 1956-58; became lieutenant. *Member:* Agricultural History Society, Southern Historical Association, Louisiana History Society, Louisiana Studies Institute, Texas Historical Association, Phi Alpha Theta, Phi Kappa Phi.

WRITINGS: (Editor and author of introduction) *Huey P. Long: Southern Demagogue or American Democrat?,* Heath, 1967; (with Allen E. Begnaud) *Our Louisiana Legacy* (text), Steck, 1968; (editor) *Thomas Jefferson and American Democracy,* Heath, 1971; (with Begnaud) *The American People,* two volumes, Steck, 1972; *The Centennial History of Texas A&M University, 1876-1976,* Texas A&M University Press, 1976.

WORK IN PROGRESS: A History of the American Rice Industry.

* * *

DEUTSCH, Harold C(harles) 1904-

PERSONAL: Born June 7, 1904, in Milwaukee, Wis.; son of Herman Carl (a grain jobber) and Julia (Wettendorf) Deutsch; married Marie Margaret Frey, August 25, 1923; children: Harold Charles, Jr., Janet (Mrs. Robert E. Leaf), Dorothy (Mrs. Richard Thews). *Education:* University of Wisconsin, A.B., 1924, M.A., 1925; Harvard University, M.A., 1927, Ph.D., 1929; also studied at University of Paris, 1928-29, University of Vienna, 1929, and University of Berlin, 1935-36. *Home address:* Star Route, Garrison, Minn. 56450. *Office:* Department of History, University of Minnesota, Minneapolis, Minn. 55455.

CAREER: University of Minnesota, Minneapolis, member of faculty, 1929—, began as assistant professor, professor of history, 1945—, chairman of department, 1960-66. Visiting summer professor at University of Missouri, 1932, and University of Southern California, 1954, 1956, 1965; visiting professor at Free University of Berlin, 1963. Government posts include war service with Board of Economic Warfare, 1942-43, Office of Strategic Services (OSS), in France and Germany, 1944-45, and State Department Special Interrogation Mission, 1945; member of faculty, National War College, 1948, 1950, 1972-74, and Army War College, 1974—. News analyst, Station WCCO, Minneapolis, 1940-42, 1955-57, and Station WTCN-TV, Minneapolis, 1961-62.

MEMBER: American Historical Association, American Military History Foundation, Foreign Policy Association, International Institute for Strategic Studies, Inter-University Seminar on Armed Forces and Society, Oral History Association, Phi Alpha Theta (national president, 1941-46), Savage Club (London; honorary member), Informal Club (St. Paul). *Awards, honors:* Medal of Freedom for war services; Fulbright fellowship for research in Germany, 1957-58, 1969-70.

WRITINGS: The Genesis of Napoleonic Imperialism, Harvard University Press, 1938; *Present and Future United States Policy Toward Germany,* North Central Association, 1956; *Our Changing German Problems,* North Central Association, 1956; *Problems of Western Europe,* North Central Association, 1958; *America's Stake in Western Europe,* North Central Association, 1959, revised edition, 1962; *The Conspiracy Against Hitler in the Twilight War,* University of Minnesota Press, 1968; (with others) *The Changing Structure of Europe,* University of Minnesota Press, 1970; (editor with Helmut Krausnick) Helmuth Groscurth, *Die Tagebuecher eines Abwehroffiziers 1938-40* (title means "Diaries of an Abwehr Officer"), Deutsches Verlags-Anstalt, 1970; *Hitler and His Generals: The Hidden Crisis, January-June, 1938,* University of Minnesota Press, 1974; (contributor) Gerhard L. Weinberg, editor, *The Transformation of a Continent: Problems and Issues of Twentieth-Century Europe,* Burgess, 1975. Also author of *The New Europe, the Common Market and the*

United States, 1964. Contributor to *Journal of Modern History, Annals of the Academy of Political Science, The Historian, Social Science Review, Minnesota Review,* and other periodicals. Member of board of editors, *Journal of Modern History,* 1948-52.

WORK IN PROGRESS: Editing *The Diaries of Sir Henry Howard;* writing *The First Round of Conspiracy Against Hitler, 1938-39.*

SIDELIGHTS: Deutsch has spent a total of eleven years in Europe since 1928, traveling extensively in all west and central European countries, in most of eastern Europe, and in much of the Middle East, Far East, and Africa. He is fluent in German and French; less so in Italian and Spanish.

*   *   *

DEVINS, Joseph H(erbert), Jr.   1930-

PERSONAL: Born September 25, 1930, in New York, N.Y.; son of Joseph Herbert (an advertising public relations executive) and Florence (Barber) Devins; married Elizabeth Short, 1972; children: Dorian D. (daughter); stepchildren: six. *Education:* U.S. Military Academy, B.S., 1952; U.S. Army Command and General Staff College, graduate, 1968. *Address:* (Permanent) 2612 Alteza Place, Colorado Springs, Colorado 80917. *Agent:* Bill Berger Associates, Inc., 444 East 58th St., New York, N.Y. 10022.

CAREER: U.S. Army, Infantry officer, 1952-75, retired from active duty with rank of lieutenant colonel; overseas assignments in Korea, Italy, Panama, and Vietnam.

WRITINGS: The Vaagso Raid, R. Hale, 1967, Chilton, 1968. Occasional contributor to military journals.

WORK IN PROGRESS: A book on military history.

SIDELIGHTS: Devins told *CA:* "The *Vaagso Raid* started as an article for a professional journal but it 'just growed.' I claim to speak Brazilian Portuguese, rusty Italian and some Spanish, but natives of those countries might not agree."

*   *   *

DEVORE, Irven   1934-

PERSONAL: Born October 7, 1934, in Joy. Tex.; son of Boyd Irven (a minister) and Clara (Hurt) Devore; married Nancy Skiles, April 20, 1956; children: Gregory Irven, Marie Claire. *Education:* University of Texas, B.A., 1956; University of Chicago, M.A., 1959, Ph.D., 1962. *Home:* 33 Hurlbut St., Cambridge, Mass., 02138. *Office:* Department of Social Relations, Harvard University, Cambridge, Mass. 02138.

CAREER: University of California, Berkeley, assistant professor of anthropology, 1960-61, Miller fellow in basic research, 1961-62; Center for Advanced Study in the Behavioral Sciences, Palo Alto, Calif., fellow, 1962-63; Harvard University, Cambridge, Mass., lecturer, 1963-66, associate professor, 1966-69, professor of anthropology, 1969—. Consultant to Education Development Center, Cambridge, Mass., Committee on Primate Research Centers, National Institutes of Health, and Danforth Foundation. Field work on baboons, orangutans, and African bushmen has been done in Kenya, 1959, the Kalahari Desert, 1964, 1967-69, and Borneo, 1968. *Member:* American Anthropological Association (member of executive board), American Academy of Arts and Sciences, American Association for the Advancement of Science. *Awards,*

honors: M.A. from Harvard University, 1966; Walker Prize for Meritorious Scientific Investigation and Discovery, Museum of Science (Boston), 1970.

WRITINGS: (Editor) *Primate Behavior: Field Studies of Monkeys and Apes,* Holt, 1965; (with S. Eimerl) *The Primates,* Time/Life, 1965, young readers' edition, 1968; (editor with Richard B. Lee) *Man the Hunter,* Aldine, 1968. Editor of three films on baboon behavior and ecology for University of California, Berkeley, and seven films on baboons for Education Development Center.

WORK IN PROGRESS: Continuing research on primates and on the Kung bushmen of the Kalahari.†

*   *   *

De VORSEY, Louis, Jr.   1929-

PERSONAL: Born April 6, 1929, in Newark, N.J.; son of Louis Joseph and Eleena (Carpenter) De Vorsey; married Rosalyn W. Dennis, March 25, 1960; children: Megan Caroline, Kirsteen Anne, Kevin Louis. *Education:* Montclair State College, B.A., 1952; Indiana University, M.A., 1954; University of Stockholm, graduate study, 1958-59; University of London, Ph.D., 1965. *Home:* 355 Kings Rd., Kingswood, Athens, Ga. 30601. *Office:* Department of Geography, University of Georgia, Athens, Ga. 30601.

CAREER: East Carolina College (now University), Greenville, N.C., assistant professor of geography, 1961-64; University of North Carolina, Chapel Hill, assistant professor of geography, 1964-67; University of Georgia, Athens, 1967—, began as associate professor, now professor of geography. *Military service:* U.S. Naval Reserve, 1954—; active duty, 1954-58; now commander. *Member:* American Geographical Society, Association of American Geographers, Society for History of Discoveries, Georgia Historical Society, Sigma Xi. *Awards, honors:* Association of American Geographers Citation, 1975, for meritorious service in the field of geography.

WRITINGS: The Indian Boundary in the Southern Colonies, 1763-1775, University of North Carolina Press, 1966; *West Europe-East Europe,* Sadlier, 1968; *Europe and Asia,* Sadlier, 1968; *Neighbors in Eurasia,* Sadlier, 1968; (editor) *De Brahm's Report of the General Survey in the Southern District of North America,* University of South Carolina Press, 1971; *The Peoples of Western Europe,* Sadlier, 1972; *The Atlantic Pilot,* University Presses of Florida, 1974. Contributor to geography and history journals.

SIDELIGHTS: Louis De Vorsey, Jr. is active as an expert witness in boundary and land litigations.

*   *   *

DeVOS, George A(lphonse)   1922-

PERSONAL: Born July 25, 1922, in Detroit, Mich.; married Winifred Olsen (a psychiatric social worker), May 4, 1944; children: Laurie, Eric, Susan, Michael. *Education:* University of Chicago, B.A., 1946, M.A., 1948, Ph.D., 1951. *Office:* Department of Anthropology, University of California, Berkeley, Calif. 94720.

CAREER: Michael Reese Hospital, Chicago, Ill., research associate in psychology, 1950-51; Elgin State Hospital, Elgin, Ill., chief psychologist, 1951-53; Nagoya National University, Nagoya, Japan, Fulbright research fellow, 1953-55; University of Michigan, Ann Arbor, assistant professor of psychology and director of Ford Foundation's Japanese Personality and Culture Research Project, 1955-57; University of California, Berkeley, associate professor of social welfare, 1957-65, professor of anthropology, 1965—, chairman of Center for Japanese and Korean Studies, 1965-68, associate research psychologist and director of comparative research on delinquency, Institute of Human Development, 1960-68, research associate, Institute of Personality Assessment and Research, 1969-70. Research fellow of National Institute for Training Research on Delinquency, French Ministry of Justice, Vaucresson, France, 1963-64; visiting professor of anthropology and research psychologist, University of Hawaii, 1966-67; consultant on family planning research, Korean Institute of the Behavioral Sciences, Seoul, Korea, 1970-71; principal investigator, National Science Foundation Project, The Korean Minority in Japan, 1974-75. *Military service:* U.S. Army, 1943-46. *Member:* American Psychological Association, American Anthropological Association. *Awards, honors:* Fulbright, Ford Foundation, and National Institute for Mental Health research grants.

WRITINGS: (With Hiroshi Wagatsuma) *Japan's Invisible Race: Caste in Culture and Personality,* University of California Press, 1966; *American Japanese InterCultural Marriages,* Chinese Association for Folklore (Taipei), 1973; *Socialization for Achievement: Essays on the Cultural Psychology of the Japanese,* University of California Press, 1973; (with William Wetherall) *Japan's Minorities,* Minority Rights Group (London), 1974; (editor with Lola Romanucci-Ross) *Ethnic Identity: Cultural Continuities and Change,* Mayfield, 1975; (editor) *Responses to Change,* Van Nostrand, 1975.

Contributor: Yehudi A. Cohen, editor, *Social Structure and Personality,* Holt, 1961; Francis L. K. Hsu, editor, *Psychological Anthropology,* Dorsey, 1961; Robert J. Smith and Richard K. Beardsley, editors, *Japanese Culture: Its Development and Characteristics,* Aldine, 1962; Mildred B. Kantor, editor, *Mobility and Mental Health,* C. C Thomas, 1965; Bernard E. Segal, editor, *Racial and Ethnic Relations,* Crowell, 1966; Staten W. Webster, editor, *The Disadvantaged Learner,* Chandler Publishing, 1966; R. P. Dore, editor, *Aspects of Social Change in Modern Japan,* Princeton University Press, 1967; H.L.P. Resnick, editor, *Suicidal Behaviors: Diagnosis and Management,* Little, Brown, 1968; Edward Norbeck, Douglass Price-Williams, and William M. McCord, editors, *Personality: An Interdisciplinary Appraisal,* Holt, 1968; Joseph C. Finney, editor, *Culture Change, Mental Health, and Poverty,* University of Kentucky Press, 1969.

Georgene H. Seward and Robert C. Williams, editor, *Sex Roles in Changing Society,* Random House, 1970; Minako Kurokawa, editor, *Minority Responses,* Random House, 1970; Nevitt Sanford and Craig Comstock, editors, *Sanctions for Evil,* Jossey-Bass, 1971; Norman R. Yetman and C. Hoy Steele, editors, *Majority and Minority,* Allyn & Bacon, 1971; William P. Lebra, editor, *Transcultural Research in Mental Health,* University of Hawaii Press, 1972; Ben Whitaker, editor, *The Fourth World Victims of Group Oppression,* Sidgwick & Jackson, 1972; Takie Sugiyama Lebra and William Lebra, editors, *Japanese Culture and Behavior,* University Press of Hawaii, 1974; William P. Lebra, editor, *Youth, Socialization and Mental Health,* University Press of Hawaii, 1974; Irwin Scheiner, editor, *Modern Japan: An Interpretive Anthology,* Macmillan, 1974; *Modern Japanese Organization and Decision Making,* University of California Press, 1975. Contributor of articles and reviews to psychology and anthropology journals.

DEW, Charles B(urgess)   1937-

PERSONAL: Born January 5, 1937, in St. Petersburg, Fla.; son of Jack Carlos and Amy (Meek) Dew; married Robb R. Forman, January 26, 1968. *Education:* Williams College, A.B., 1958; Johns Hopkins University, Ph.D., 1964. *Office:* Department of History, University of Missouri, Columbia, Mo. 65201.

CAREER: Wayne State University, Detroit, Mich., instructor, 1963-64, assistant professor of history, 1964-65; Louisiana State University, Baton Rouge, assistant professor of history, 1965-68; University of Missouri, Columbia, associate professor, 1968-72, professor of history, 1972—. Visiting associate professor, University of Virginia, 1970-71. *Member:* American Historical Association, Organization of American Historians, Southern Historical Association (member of executive council, 1975-78), Virginia Historical Society. *Awards, honors:* Fletcher Pratt Award, 1967, for *Ironmaker to the Confederacy;* American Association for State and Local History, Award of Merit, 1966.

WRITINGS: Ironmaker to the Confederacy: Joseph R. Anderson and the Tredegar Ironworks, Yale University Press, 1966. Contributor to *South Atlantic Quarterly, Louisiana History, Civil War History, American Historical Review, Journal of Southern History,* and *William and Mary Quarterly.*

*   *   *

DIAS, Earl Joseph   1916-

PERSONAL: Born March 23, 1916, in New Bedford, Mass.; son of John Felisberto (an insurance agent) and Virginia (Alexander) Dias; married Edith G. Kenny (a teacher), August 18, 1951. *Education:* Bates College, A.B. (magna cum laude), 1937; Boston University, M.A. 1938; also studied summers at Shakespeare Institute, Stratford on Avon, England, 1957, 1960, and University of London, 1960. *Home:* 52 Walnut St., Fairhaven, Mass. 02719. *Office:* Southeastern Massachusetts University, North Dartmouth, Mass. 02747.

CAREER: High school teacher of English, Fairhaven, Mass., 1939-57; New Bedford Institute of Technology, New Bedford, Mass., associate professor of English, 1958-63; Southeastern Massachusetts University, North Dartmouth, professor of English, 1963—, chairman of department, 1971—. *New Bedford Standard-Times,* drama and music critic, 1947—, regular Sunday columnist, "A Look at the Arts," 1948—. Reader in English composition, College Entrance Examination Board. Corporator, Fairhaven Institution for Savings; member, Fairhaven Town Meeting; chairman of board of trustees, Millicent Library, Fairhaven; member of board of directors, New Bedford Symphony Orchestra and New Bedford Concert Series. *Member:* College English Association, Shakespeare Association of America, American Association of University Professors, Thoreau Society, Phi Beta Kappa.

WRITINGS: Melodramas and Farces for Young Actors, Plays, 1956; *One-Act Plays for Teen-Agers: A Collection of Royalty-Free Comedies,* Plays, 1961, revised edition, 1971; *New Comedies for Teen-Agers: A Collection of One-Act, Royalty-Free Comedies, Farces, and Melodramas,* Plays, 1967; *Henry Huttleson Rogers: Portrait of a 'Capitalist,'* Millicent Library, 1974. Also author of *Mark Twain's Letters to the Rogers Family,* 1970. Plays anthologized in *A Treasury of Christmas Plays,* Plays, 1956, *A Treasury of Holiday Plays,* Plays, 1963, *Basic Reading,* Book 7, Lippincott, 1965, and *Favorite Plays for Classroom Reading*, Plays, 1965. Contributor to *Coronet, Drama Critique, New England Quarterly,* and other journals.

WORK IN PROGRESS: More Plays for Young Actors; Brains to Brawn: A History of Detective Fiction.

SIDELIGHTS: Earl Dias speaks French and Portuguese; he has made twelve trips to Europe.

* * *

Di CERTO, J(oseph) J(ohn) 1933-

PERSONAL: Born February 27, 1933, in New York, N.Y.; son of Rocco (a barber) and Severina (Basile) Di Certo; married Josephine Valle, September 5, 1964; children: Lisa Ann, David, Jennifer Ann. *Education:* Hunter College of the City University of New York, B.A., 1968. *Politics:* Independent. *Religion:* Roman Catholic. *Residence:* New York, N.Y. *Office:* Sperry Rand Corp., 1290 Avenue of the Americas, New York, N.Y. 10019.

CAREER: Curtiss Wright Corp., Woodridge, N.J., senior technical writer, 1956-59; American Machine & Foundry, Greenwich, Conn., technical writer and editor, 1959-62; Sperry Gyroscope, Great Neck, N.Y., publication engineer, 1962-66; Sylvania Electric Products, New York City, advertising supervisor, 1966-72; worked at Al Paul Lefton Co., Inc. (advertising agency), 1972-73, Marstella Advertising Agency, 1973-74; Sperry Rand Corp., New York City, manager of special projects, 1974—. *Military service:* U.S. Air Force, 1952-56.

WRITINGS: Planning and Preparing Data Flow Diagrams, Hayden, 1963; *Missile Base Beneath the Sea,* St. Martin's, 1967; *The Electric Wishing Well,* Macmillan, in press. Also author of six audiovisual training programs published by Educational Activities. Contributor to *Electronic Design.*

WORK IN PROGRESS: A science fiction novel based on computers.

* * *

DICK, Bernard F(rancis) 1935-

PERSONAL: Born November 25, 1935, in Scranton, Pa.; son of Jacob Nelson and Anita (Sarambo) Dick; married Katherine M. Restaino (a college administrator), July 31, 1965. *Education:* University of Scranton, B.A. (summa cum laude), 1957; Fordham University, M.A., 1960, Ph.D., 1962. *Religion:* Roman Catholic. *Home:* 989 Wilson Ave., Teaneck, N.J. 07666. *Office:* Department of English, Fairleigh Dickinson University, Teaneck, N.J. 07666.

CAREER: Iona College, New Rochelle, N.Y., instructor, 1960-64, assistant professor, 1964-67, associate professor of classics, 1967-70, chairman of department, 1967-70; Fairleigh Dickinson University, Teaneck, N.J., associate professor, 1970-73, professor of English, and chairman of department, 1973—. Adjunct lecturer in Latin, College of New Rochelle, 1962-63. *Member:* Modern Language Association of America, American Association of University Professors, American Comparative Literature Association.

WRITINGS: William Golding, Twayne, 1967; *The Hellenism of Mary Renault,* Southern Illinois University Press, 1972; *The Apostate Angel: A Critical Study of Gore Vidal,* Random House, 1974.

WORK IN PROGRESS: Two books, *The Anatomy of Film* and *The Modern Mythic Novel.*

AVOCATIONAL INTERESTS: Music, theater, and film.

DICKEY, Franklin M(iller) 1921-

PERSONAL: Born April 19, 1921, in Milwaukee, Wis.; son of Cromwell Bartlett and Edna (Miller) Dickey; married former wife, Rita M. Durkee, 1947; married Claude-Marie Senninger, 1972; children: (first marriage) Sarah Coulter. *Education:* University of Wisconsin, B.A., 1942; University of California, Los Angeles, Ph.D., 1954. *Home:* 5949 Guadalupe Trail, N.W., Albuquerque, N.M. 87107. *Office:* Department of English, University of New Mexico, Albuquerque, N.M. 87106.

CAREER: University of Michigan, Ann Arbor, instructor in English, 1950-55; University of Oregon, Eugene, assistant professor of English, 1955-58; University of New Mexico, Albuquerque, assistant professor, 1958-59, associate professor, 1959-64, professor of English, 1964—. *Military service:* U.S. Army, 1942-43. *Member:* Modern Language Association of America, Malone Society, Bibliographical Society (London), Renaissance Society of America, Renaissance English Text Society, American Association of University Professors. *Awards, honors:* Fellowships from Guggenheim Memorial Foundation, 1957, Folger Shakespeare Library, summer, 1957, 1959, Huntington Library, summer, 1960, and Newberry Library, summer, 1963.

WRITINGS: Not Wisely but Too Well: Shakespeare's Love Tragedies, Huntington Library, 1957; (editor of translation) *Amyntas* [and] *The Lamentations of Amyntas* (the former edited by Walter F. Station, Jr.) University of Chicago Press, 1968. Contributor to professional journals.

WORK IN PROGRESS: Studies in intellectual history, including Renaissance aesthetics, contemporary drama, film, and psychology and literature.

SIDELIGHTS: Franklin Dickey traveled and studied in England, France, and Italy for three years.

* * *

DICKIE-CLARK, H(amish) F(indlay) 1922-

PERSONAL: Born May 20, 1922, in Bloemfontein, Orange Free State, South Africa; son of William (a secretary) and Margaret (Findlay) Dickie-Clark; married Elaine Kirkness (a psychologist), March 15, 1947; children: Anthony, Katherine, Margaret, Findlay. *Education:* Rhodes University, B.A., 1947, B.A. (with honors), 1954; University of Cape Town, Teacher's Certificate, 1948; University of Natal, Ph.D., 1965. *Politics:* Liberal. *Religion:* None.

CAREER: High school teacher of history and English at Healdtown, South Africa, 1949-53; Grahamstown Coloured Secondary School, Grahamstown, Cape Province, South Africa, headmaster, 1955; University of Natal, Durban, South Africa, research assistant, 1955-57, lecturer, 1957-65, professor of sociology and dean of Faculty of Social Science, beginning 1966. *Military service:* South African Army, 1940-45.

WRITINGS: The Marginal Situation: A Sociological Study of a Coloured Group, Department of Sociology, University of Natal, 1964, Humanities, 1966.

WORK IN PROGRESS: Studies in German sociology and education in South African plural societies; a translation of Max Weber's *Der Socialismus.*†

* * *

DICKINSON, Donald C. 1927-

PERSONAL: Born June 9, 1927, in Schenectady, N.Y.; son of Charles William (a teacher) and Stella (Sheldon)

Dickinson; married Colleen Schindler, August 11, 1954; children: Ann, Jean, Ellen, Mary, Kathleen, Sheila. *Education:* New York College for Teachers (now State University of New York at Albany), A.B., 1949; University of Illinois, M.S. in L.S., 1951; University of Michigan, Ph.D., 1964. *Politics:* Democrat. *Religion:* Methodist. *Home:* 8451 Malvern, Tucson, Ariz. 85710.

CAREER: Central Missouri State College (now University), Warrensburg, reference librarian, 1951-53; Eastern Michigan University, Ypsilanti, assistant reference librarian, 1953-56; University of Kansas Library, Lawrence, assistant acquisition librarian, 1956-58; Bemidji State College, Bemidji, Minn., head librarian, 1958-66; University of Missouri Library, Columbia, associate librarian, 1966-69; University of Arizona, Tucson, director of Graduate Library School, 1969—. *Member:* American Library Association, Bibliographical Society of America, American Association of Library Schools, Arizona Library Association. *Awards, honors:* College and Research Library Association travel grant, 1960.

WRITINGS: A Bio-Bibliography of Langston Hughes, 1920-1967, preface by Arna Bontemps, Archon Books, 1967; (compiler) *Checklist of Writings of Helmut Lehmann-Haupt,* Bibliophile Society, 1975.

WORK IN PROGRESS: Bibliography of James Weldon Johnson.

AVOCATIONAL INTERESTS: Negro-American literature, jazz, tennis, chess.

*   *   *

DICKSON, Robert J(ames)   1919-

PERSONAL: Born December 29, 1919, in Belfast, Northern Ireland; son of John and Sarah J. (Cassells) Dickson; married Annette Getty, June 4, 1944; children: Jennifer, Moore. *Education:* Queen's University of Belfast, B.A., 1941, M.A., 1943, Ph.D., 1949. *Religion:* Church of Ireland. *Home:* 119 Castlehill Rd., Belmont, Belfast 4, Northern Ireland. *Office:* County Hall, Ballymena, County of Antrim, Northern Ireland.

CAREER: Teacher of history at Methodist College, Belfast, Northern Ireland, and Rainey Endowed School, County Londonderry, Northern Ireland, 1943-50; Tyrone County Education Committee, Omagh, Northern Ireland, deputy director of education, 1950-67; Antrim County Education Committee, Belfast, Northern Ireland, director of education, 1967-73; Northeastern Education and Library Board, Ballymena, Northern Ireland, chief officer, 1973—.

WRITINGS: Ulster Emigration to Colonial America, 1718-1775, Routledge & Kegan Paul, 1966.

AVOCATIONAL INTERESTS: Books, articles, and music concerning the American Civil War.

*   *   *

DIETRICH, R(ichard) F(arr)   1936-

PERSONAL: Born January 16, 1936, in Sandusky, Ohio; son of Richard Franklin (a hospital accountant) and Marion (Farr) Dietrich; married Linnea S. Stonesifer (an assistant professor of visual arts); children: Richard Fredrick. *Education:* Miami University, Oxford, Ohio, A.B., 1958; Bowling Green State University, M.A., 1960; Florida State University, Ph.D., 1963. *Politics:* "Creeping Socialist (when not an anarchist)." *Home:* 905 Bellemeade Ave., Temple Terrace, Fla. 33617.

CAREER: University of Delaware, Newark, assistant professor of English, 1963-68; University of South Florida, Tampa, assistant professor, 1968-70, associate professor of English, 1970—. *Member:* Modern Language Association of America, Shaw Society of America, Shaw Society of England, American Association of University Professors. *Awards, honors:* Summer faculty fellowship, University of Delaware, 1966; University of Florida research grants, 1969, 1973, and 1975.

WRITINGS: (With Roger H. Sundell) *The Art of Fiction,* Holt, 1967, 2nd edition, 1974; (compiler with William E. Carpenter and Kevin Kerrane) *The Art of Drama,* Holt, 1969, 2nd edition, 1976; (compiler with Carpenter and Kerrane) *The Art of Modern Drama,* Holt, 1969; (with Carpenter and Kerrane) *Instructor's Manual for The Art of Drama and The Art of Modern Drama,* Holt, 1969; *Portrait of the Artist as a Young Superman: A Study of Shaw's Novels,* University of Florida Press, 1969; (compiler) *The Realities of Literature,* with teacher's manual, Xerox College Publishing, 1971; (editor and author of introduction) Bernard Shaw, *An Unsocial Socialist,* W. W. Norton, 1972. Also author of *Earth Angel* (novel) and a play "Alphabetical Order," both as yet unpublished.

WORK IN PROGRESS: The Romance of the Real: A Study of Modernism.

AVOCATIONAL INTERESTS: Sports, carpentry, and architecture.

*   *   *

DIETZ, Norman D.   1930-

PERSONAL: Born June 24, 1930, in Buffalo, N.Y.; son of Donald J. (a contractor) and Irene (Kientzler) Dietz; married Sandra Rae Spotts (an actress), September 24, 1960. *Education:* Attended Concordia Preparatory School and Concordia Junior College, Bronxville, N.Y., 1944-50, and Washington University, St. Louis, Mo., 1950, 1954; Concordia Seminary, St. Louis, Mo., B.A., 1955. *Address:* Box 218, Orient, N.Y. 11957.

CAREER: KFUO Radio, St. Louis, Mo., announcer, 1953-55; KTBS-TV, Shreveport, La., cameraman and floor manager, 1955; WGAL-TV, Lancaster, Pa., assistant news editor, 1958-60; Lutheran Foundation for Religious Drama, New York City, executive director, 1960-61; with his wife Sandra, Dietz formed Theatre of Concern, a touring repertory company of five plays, 1962; tours with Sandra, giving two-character performances of his plays, 1963—. Artistic director, Barn Playhouse, Stony Point, N.Y., 1962, 1968; with Sandra, opened Theatre-at-Noon, New York City, 1968; producer and director, Noonshow, New York City, 1969. *Military service:* U.S. Navy, detached service with NATO, 1955-57.

WRITINGS: Fables & Vaudevilles & Plays: Theatre More-or-Less at Random (six plays), John Knox, 1968; *The Life Guard and the Mermaid and Other Plays* (four plays), Judson Press, 1976.

Plays: "Le Drugstore"; "Deus Ex Machinist"; "Tilly Tutweiler's Silly Trip to the Moon"; "I Used to See My Sister"; "Old Ymir"; "The Apple Bit"; "Harry and the Angel"; "The Well-Spoken Acrobat"; "Millenimum"; "Robinson Crusoe Eats It"; "The Firemen's Picnic"; "Jesustory"; "Son of the Beach"; "Noah Webster's Electrick Arktype"; "Scenario for an Unmovie"; "The Phonebooth Fable"; "The Doll Factory."

SIDELIGHTS: Dietz has said, according to Jerome Nilssen, that he "understands his work, both as writer and actor, in terms of celebration. And this means, he says, 'making holy whoopee about what it means, as we see it, to be human, to be alive in a world full of strangers impossible to understand.'" Nilssen wrote: "All six plays [in *Fables & Vaudevilles & Plays*] are highly satisfying as entertainment. They read well, they play better. On occasion they are reminiscent of some of the better television sketches of Sid Caesar and Ernie Kovacs; and there are hints of Woody Allen, too, in the delight in word play and the building of absurd yet disconcertingly plausible situations. In other words, when Dietz says vaudeville, he means it. . . . His is a thoughtful but not a cerebral theatre. . . ." Dan Sullivan called Dietz's work "a kind of theologically tinged humor" and said the plays "skip happily down a line separating secular skepticism and churchy gush." Many of Dietz's plays are for two players; "Sandra and I are kind of the mad Hansel and Gretel of the underground theatre," noted Dietz. And David Grambs saw them as "sort of like Dylan Thomas and Mike Nichols and Elaine May all at once."

BIOGRAPHICAL/CRITICAL SOURCES: New York Times, January 9, 1968; *Religious Theatre,* summer, 1968.

* * *

DIETZE, Gottfried 1922-

PERSONAL: Born November 11, 1922, in Kemberg, Germany; son of Paul (a mayor) and Susanne (Pechstein) Dietze. *Education:* University of Heidelberg, J.U.D., 1949; Princeton University, Ph.D., 1952; postdoctoral study at University of California, Los Angeles, 1950-51, and Harvard University, 1951-52; University of Virginia, S.J.D., 1961. *Religion:* Lutheran. *Office:* Department of Political Science, Johns Hopkins University, Baltimore, Md. 21218.

CAREER: Dickinson College, Carlisle, Pa., instructor in political science, 1952-54; Johns Hopkins University, Baltimore, Md., assistant professor, 1954-58, associate professor, 1958-62, professor of political science, 1962—. Visiting professor, University of Heidelberg, 1956, 1958, 1959, 1960, Brookings Institution, 1960-61, 1967. *Member:* American Political Science Association, American Society for Political and Legal Philosophy, Mont Pelerin Society, Academy of Human Rights.

WRITINGS: Ueber Formulierung der Menschenrechte, Duncker & Humbolt, 1956; *The Federalist,* Johns Hopkins Press, 1960; *In Defense of Property,* Regnery, 1963; (editor) *Essays on the American Constitution,* Prentice-Hall, 1964; *Magna Carta and Property,* University Press of Virginia, 1965; *America's Political Dilemma: From Limited to Unlimited Democracy,* Johns Hopkins Press, 1968; *Youth, University and Democracy,* Johns Hopkins Press, 1970; *Bedeutungswandel der Menschenrechte,* C. F. Mueller, 1972; *Two Concepts of the Rule of Law,* Liberty Fund, 1973.

SIDELIGHTS: Gottfried Dietze speaks French, Spanish, Portuguese, and Italian (listed in order of fluency).

* * *

DIETZEL, Paul (Franklin) 1924-

PERSONAL: Born September 5, 1924, in Fremont, Ohio; son of Clarence Harland and Catherine (Bihmer) Dietzel; married Anne Wilson, September 25, 1944; children: Stephen Paul, Kathie Anne. *Education:* Duke University, student, 1942-43; Miami University, Oxford, Ohio, B.S. in

Ed., 1948. *Religion:* Baptist. *Home:* The Oaks, No. 20, 395 Redding Rd., Lexington, Ky. 40502.

CAREER: Assistant football coach at U.S. Military Academy, West Point, N.Y., 1948, University of Cincinnati, Cincinnati, Ohio, 1949-50, University of Kentucky, Lexington, 1951-52, U.S. Military Academy, 1953-54; head football coach at Louisiana State University, Baton Rouge, 1955-62, U.S. Military Academy, 1962-66; University of South Carolina, Columbia, director of athletics and head football coach, 1966-75; Ohio Valley Conference (athletic), commissioner, 1975—. Radio and television broadcaster during football season. Trustee and past president of American Football Coaches Association; trustee and past national president of Fellowship of Christian Athletes. *Military service:* U.S. Army Air Forces, 1943-45; pilot; became lieutenant; received Air Medal with clusters, Presidential Citation. *Member:* Rotary, Junior Chamber of Commerce, Omicron Delta Kappa (president), Kappa Delta Pi (president). *Awards, honors:* National Football Coach of the year, 1958; Atlantic Coast Conference Coach of the Year, 1969.

WRITINGS: Wing T and the Chinese Bandits, privately printed, 1959; (with Ev Houghton) *Go Shorty Go,* Bobbs-Merrill, 1965; *Coaching Football,* Ronald, 1971. Writer of poems, and contributor to periodicals.

SIDELIGHTS: Paul Dietzel has coached seven all-star teams during his twenty seven years as a collegiate football coach.

* * *

DIGGORY, James C(lark) 1920-

PERSONAL: Born November 4, 1920, in Philadelphia, Pa.; son of Benjamin James (a real estate appraiser) and Alice Adeline (Clark) Diggory; married Daisy Elliot (a teacher), September 3, 1944; married second wife, Sylvia Farnham (a psychologist), June 6, 1961; children: (first marriage) Terence, Edith; stepchildren: Matthew, Jonathan. *Education:* King's College, New Castle, Del., B.A., 1942; University of Pennsylvania, M.A., 1943, Ph.D., 1948. *Politics:* "Mixed, usually Democratic." *Religion:* None. *Home:* 5976 Adler St., Pittsburgh, Pa. 15232. *Office:* Department of Psychology, Chatham College, Pittsburgh, Pa. 15232.

CAREER: University of Pennsylvania, Philadelphia, assistant professor, 1948-56, associate professor of psychology, 1956-66; Chatham College, Pittsburgh, Pa., professor of psychology and chairman of department 1966—. *Member:* American Psychological Association, American Association for the Advancement of Science, American Association of University Professors, New York Academy of Sciences, Sigma Xi.

WRITINGS: Self-Evaluation: Concepts and Studies, Wiley, 1966. Contributor to professional journals.

WORK IN PROGRESS: A book on existentialism in psychology, tentatively entitled *The Cult of Existence;* a textbook on personality; continuing research on self-evaluation; studies of suicidal behavior.

SIDELIGHTS: James Diggory reads German, French, Spanish, and has some speaking ability in those languages; he can decipher Italian and a little Dutch and studied Arabic, Hebrew, classical Greek, and Russian ("cannot read them now for any practical use"). *Avocational interests:* Singing, baroque music, playing the guitar, painting, sculpturing in wood and clay, designing and making furniture, and the study of history.

Di LELLA, Alexander A. 1929-

PERSONAL: Born August 14, 1929, in Paterson, N.J.; son of Alexander (a textile worker) and Adelaide (Grimaldi) Di Lella. *Education:* St. Bonaventure University, B.A., 1952; Catholic University of America, S.T.L., 1959, Ph.D., 1962; Pontifical Biblical Institute, Rome, Italy, S.S.L., 1964. *Politics:* Democrat. *Home:* Holy Name College, 14th and Shepherd Sts. N.E., Washington, D.C. 20017.

CAREER: Roman Catholic priest of Order of Friars Minor (Franciscan), member of Province of the Holy Name. Holy Name College, Washington, D.C., lecturer in Old Testament, 1964-67; Catholic University of America, Washington, D.C., assistant professor, 1966-68, associate professor of Semitic languages, 1968—. Adjunct professor, Washington Theological Coalition, 1969-72. *Member:* Catholic Biblical Association of America (president, 1975-76), Society of Biblical Literature. *Awards, honors:* Fellowship to American School of Oriental Research, Jerusalem, 1962-63; Guggenheim fellow, 1972-73.

WRITINGS: The Hebrew Text of Sirach: A Text—Critical and Historical Study, Mouton & Co., 1966. Contributor to *New Catholic Encyclopedia* and *Interpreter's Dictionary of the Bible, Supplement;* also contributor to biblical and religious journals. Associate editor, *Cithara.*

WORK IN PROGRESS: Co-author of the *Anchor Bible* volume on the Prophet Daniel, for Doubleday; a critical edition of the "Book of Proverbs" in Syriac, for E. J. Brill.

SIDELIGHTS: DiLella reads French, German, Italian, Latin, Greek, Hebrew, Aramaic, Syriac, Ugaritic, and modern Israeli Hebrew.

*   *   *

DILLARD, R(ichard) H(enry) W(ilde)   1937-

PERSONAL: Born October 11, 1937, in Roanoke, Va.; son of Benton O. (a lawyer) and Mattie (Mullins) Dillard. *Education:* Roanoke College, B.A., 1958; University of Virginia, M.A., 1959, Ph.D., 1965. *Politics:* Democrat. *Religion:* Baptist. *Home:* 6910 Ardmore Dr. N.W., Roanoke, Va. 24019. *Agent:* Blanche C. Gregory, Inc., 2 Tudor City Pl., New York, N.Y. 10017.

CAREER: University of Virginia, Charlottesville, Va., instructor, 1961-64; Hollins College, Hollins College, Va., assistant professor, 1964-68, associate professor, 1968-74, professor of English, 1974—. Member of Novel Award Committee, William Faulkner Foundation, 1963-66. *Member:* Authors Guild of the Authors League of America, American P.E.N., Poe Studies Association, Emerson Society, Melville Society, Society for the Study of Southern Literature, Count Dracula Society. *Awards, honors:* American Academy of Poets Prize, 1961.

WRITINGS: The Day I Stopped Dreaming About Barbara Steele, and Other Poems, University of North Carolina Press, 1966; (editor with Louis D. Rubin, Jr.) *The Experience of America,* Macmillan, 1969; *News of the Nile,* University of North Carolina Press, 1971; (editor with George Garrett and John R. Moore) *The Sounder Few,* University of Georgia Press, 1971; *After Borges,* Louisiana State University Press, 1972; *The Book of Charges,* Doubleday, 1974; *Horror Films,* Simon & Schuster, 1976.

Poems represented in anthologies including: *Southern Writing in the Sixties/Poetry,* Louisiana State University Press, 1967; *The Young American Writers,* edited by Richard Kostelanetz, Funk, 1967; *Nabokov,* edited by Charles Newman and Alfred Appel, Northwestern University Press, 1970; *Contemporary Poetry in America,* edited by Miller Williams, Random House, 1972; *Poetry: Points of Departure,* edited by Henry Taylor, Winthrop, 1974. Stories included in *The Girl in the Black Raincoat,* Duell, Sloan & Pearce, 1966; *Southern Writing in the Sixties/Fiction,* Louisiana State University Press, 1967. Author with Garrett and John Rodenbeck of film script, "Frankenstein Meets the Space Monster." Contributor to literary journals. Member of editorial board, *Hollins Critic,* 1966—.

WORK IN PROGRESS: Mysteries, a collection of three novellas, completion expected in 1976; *High Water,* a book-length poem, 1976; *The First Man on the Sun,* a novel, 1977.

SIDELIGHTS: Dillard's originality, according to a *Virginia Quarterly Review* writer, "is rooted in a long literary tradition. His ancestors are in the musical tradition of Southern poetry, especially the world of Poe. His immediate literary cousins are those modern poets of prose: Borges, Nabokov, Robbe-Grillet. And the burden of his theme . . . is Christian joy, the marvelous transforming power whereby man and his history are redeemed. . . . For those accustomed to the cliches and conventions of much contemporary poetry, this book will come as a delightful surprise. For all who weary of the habitual gesture and the mechanical response, Dillard's poetry offers a bright promise for the future."

AVOCATIONAL INTERESTS: Movies, baseball, and book collecting.

BIOGRAPHICAL/CRITICAL SOURCES: New York Times Book Review, April, 1967; *Virginia Quarterly Review,* summer, 1967; Carolyn Riley, editor, *Contemporary Literary Criticism,* Volume V, Gale, 1976.

*   *   *

DILLEHAY, Ronald C(lifford)   1935-

PERSONAL: Born November 2, 1935, in Malvern, Iowa; son of Clifford M. (a certified public accountant and comptroller) and Lela (Raines) Dillehay; married Valerie R. Sherbourne, December 22, 1954; children: Pamela Ann, Ronald, Jr., Darin. *Education:* Fresno State College (now California State University, Fresno), student, 1953-55; University of California, Berkeley, A.B., 1957, Ph.D., 1962. *Politics:* Democrat. *Religion:* Protestant. *Home:* 1848 McDonald Rd., Lexington, Ky. 40503. *Office:* University of Kentucky, Lexington, Ky. 40506.

CAREER: University of California, School of Public Health, Berkeley, assistant research behavioral scientist and lecturer in public health, 1962-64; University of Kentucky, Lexington, 1964-66, began as assistant professor, became associate professor of behavioral science and psychology; Texas Christian University, Fort Worth, associate professor of psychology, 1966-69; University of Kentucky, 1969—, began as associate professor, became professor of psychology and behavioral science, chairperson of department, 1973—. Consultant, California State Department of Public Health, 1963—; research psychologist, U.S. Public Health Service Clinical Research Center, Fort Worth, 1968. *Member:* American Psychological Association, Society for the Psychological Study of Social Issues, American Association of University Professors, Southeastern Psychological Association, Midwestern Psychological Association, Sigma Xi.

WRITINGS: (Contributor) A. L. Knutson, *The Individ-*

ual, Society, and Health Behavior, Russell Sage, 1965; (with J. P. Kirscht) Dimensions of Authoritarianism: A Critical Review of Research and Theory, University of Kentucky Press, 1967. Contributor to Dimensions of Personality, edited by Harvey London and John Exner; also contributor to public health and psychology journals.

WORK IN PROGRESS: A monograph on the behavior patterns of normal children; current research projects include psychological aspects of law and criminal justice, and moral evaluation.

*   *   *

DILLIARD, Irving (Lee) 1904-

PERSONAL: Born November 27, 1904, in Collinsville, Ill.; son of James Irving (a businessman) and Mary Beedle (Look) Dilliard; married Dorothy Alice Dorris, June 20, 1931; children: Doris Lee (Mrs. James V. Sprong), Mary Sue (Mrs. Ernest L. Schusky). Education: University of Illinois, B.A., 1927; Harvard University, graduate study, 1928-29, Nieman fellow, 1938-39 (in first class). Politics: "Independent, but elected to state office as Democrat." Religion: Methodist. Home and office: 407 Crestwood Dr., Collinsville, Ill. 62234.

CAREER: St. Louis Post-Dispatch, St. Louis, Mo., local correspondent, 1923-27, reporter, 1927-30, editorial writer, 1930-60, editor of editorial page, 1949-57; writer and lecturer, 1960-62; Chicago's American, Chicago, Ill., editorial columnist, 1962-65; Princeton University, Princeton, N.J., Ferris Professor of Journalism, 1963-73, professor emeritus, 1973—. Christian Science Monitor, Harvard reporter, 1928-29, St. Louis correspondent, 1929-38; articles also have appeared in other newspapers. U.S. Department of State, public member of Selection Board, 1965, overseas specialist in Netherlands and Yugoslavia, 1960, and India, Hong Kong, and Japan, 1966. Lecturer at Salzburg Seminar in American Studies, 1960, 1966, and in other European countries; Edmund Janes James lecturer at University of Illinois, 1949, and holder since of distinguished lectureships at a dozen American universities and colleges, including Universities of Michigan, California, Colorado, Kansas, Oregon, Nevada, and New Mexico; also has spoken at numerous other universities across the country. National committeeman, American Civil Liberties Union, 1964—. Illinois State Historical Society, director, 1941-48, president, 1947-48. Director, Illinois State Department on Aging, 1974-75. Member of advisory council, Illinois Fair Employment Practices Committee, 1961-70; citizen member, Illinois State Library Advisory Committee, 1947-53; member, Illinois Arts Council, 1965-73, National News Council, 1973—. Trustee and secretary, Illinois State Historical Library Board, 1938-48; state-wide elected trustee, University of Illinois, 1961-67; trustee, Missouri Historical Society, 1962-65. Collinsville Memorial Public Library, trustee, 1936—, president of board, 1957—. Military service: U.S. Army, 1943-46; served in Psychological Warfare Division, Supreme Headquarters, Allied Expeditionary Forces (Europe), 1944-45, later as commanding officer of Information Control Division, Office of Military Government, Bavaria; became lieutenant colonel; received Bronze Star, Army Commendation Medal, Order of the British Empire (military), Chevalier de la Legion d'Honneur, Medaille Argent de la Reconnaissance Francaise.

MEMBER: American Association of University Professors, Phi Beta Kappa (senator-at-large, 1958-70; national historian, 1970—), Sigma Delta Chi (national president, 1940-41), Alpha Kappa Lambda (national president, 1936-38), Kappa Tau Alpha, Phi Kappa Epsilon. Awards, honors: Litt.D., MacMurray College, 1951; L.L.D., Colby College, 1953, Washington University, St. Louis, 1961; L.H.D., New School for Social Research, 1954, Southern Illinois University, 1958; C.L.D., Brandeis University, 1961. Newberry fellow, 1940; Sigma Delta Chi fellow, 1951; Elijah P. Lovejoy fellow, 1953; Florina Lasker Award, New York Civil Liberties Union, 1958; Silver Gavel Award, American Bar Association, 1959, for series of articles on U.S. Supreme Court; Newsman's Newsman Award, Mound City Press Club, St. Louis, 1959, and other awards for journalism, public service, and work in fostering inter-group relations.

WRITINGS: Building the Constitution, Pulitzer Publishing Co., 1937; (editor) Mr. Justice Brandeis: Great American, Modern View Press, 1941; The Development of a Free Press in Germany, University of Illinois Press, 1949; I'm from Missouri, Hastings, 1951; (editor) Learned Hand, The Spirit of Liberty: Papers and Addresses of Learned Hand, Knopf, 1952, 2nd edition, 1953; (editor) Hugo Black, One Man's Stand for Freedom: Mr. Justice Black and the Bill of Rights, Knopf, 1964.

Contributor: Missouri: A Guide to the Show-Me State, Duell, Sloan & Pearce, 1941; Old Cahokia, St. Louis Historical Documents Foundation, 1949; Lincoln for the Ages, Doubleday, 1960; Quarrels That Have Shaped the Constitution, Harper, 1964; The Missouri Reader, University of Missouri Press, 1964; Reporting the News, Harvard University Press, 1965; The Responsibility of the Press, Fleet, 1966; Hugo Black and the Supreme Court, Bobbs-Merrill, 1967; Legends and Lore of Southern Illinois, Southern Illinois University, 1963; It Happened in Southern Illinois, Southern Illinois University, 1968; Modern American Democracy: Readings, Holt, 1969; Politics and the Press, Acropolis Books, 1970; The Challenges of Change, Public Affairs Press, 1971; Muckraking: Past, Present and Future, Pennsylvania State University Press, 1973.

Contributor to Dictionary of American Biography, Dictionary of American History, Encyclopedia of the Social Sciences, Dictionary of Political Science, Encyclopaedia Britannica, World Book Encyclopedia, Notable American Women, Collier's Encyclopedia, and Home Encyclopedia. Contributor of articles and occasional reviews to Atlantic Monthly, Harper's, Journal of Negro History, Nation, Public Opinion Quarterly, Saturday Review, Yale Law Journal, New Republic, American Scholar, and other magazines and journals. Member of Dictionary of American Biography committee, American Council of Learned Societies, 1953—.

WORK IN PROGRESS: Research and writing on aspects of the history of American journalism, the Lincoln administration, and the U.S. Supreme Court.

SIDELIGHTS: Irving Dilliard told CA: "Enjoy my own vine and fig tree (only they are hackberry and pawpaw) but also like to travel. Have been in 50 states and around the world twice (1957 and 1966), going west once and east once, and it works either way.... My chief concern as a writer and editor has been the preservation and practice of the civil liberties and rights of the citizen...."

BIOGRAPHICAL/CRITICAL SOURCES: Nieman Reports, June, 1963.

DINGWALL, W(illiam) Orr   1934-

PERSONAL: Born March 9, 1934, in Washington, D.C.; son of James Davidson and Marion (Orr) Dingwall. *Education:* University of Heidelberg, student, 1952-53; Georgetown University, B.S. in Foreign Service (summa cum laude), 1957, Ph.D., 1964. *Home:* 6511 Wilson Lane, Bethesda, Md. 20034. *Office:* Department of Linguistics, University of Maryland, College Park, Md. 20742.

CAREER: Georgetown University, Institute of Languages and Linguistics, Washington, D.C., formerly instructor in theoretical linguistics; currently chairman of linguistics program at University of Maryland. *Member:* Linguistic Society of America, British Philological Society, Linguistic Circle of New York, Gold Key Society. *Awards, honors:* Notz Medal for economics; Walsh Medal for International Law.

WRITINGS: Transformational Generative Grammar: A Bibliography, Center for Applied Linguistics (Washington, D.C.), 1965; *Survey of Linguistic Science,* University of Maryland Press, 1971; (contributor) B. Kachru and others, editors, *Issues in Linguistics: Papers in Honor of Henry and Renee Kahane,* University of Illinois Press, 1973; *The Species: Specificity of Speech,* Georgetown University Press, 1975. Contributor of articles to learned journals including *Annual Review of Anthropology.*

WORK IN PROGRESS: Editing *Readings in Language and the Brain,* for Plenum.

SIDELIGHTS: Dingwall is competent in German, Russian, Spanish, French, and Japanese.

*   *   *

DINNERSTEIN, Leonard   1934-

PERSONAL: Born May 5, 1934, in New York, N.Y.; son of Abraham and Lillian (Kubrik) Dinnerstein; married Myra Rosenberg, August 20, 1961; children: Andrew, Julie. *Education:* City College (now City College of the City University of New York), B.A., 1955; Columbia University, M.A., 1960, Ph.D., 1966. *Politics:* Democratic. *Religion:* Jewish. *Home:* 5821 East 7th St., Tucson, Ariz. 85711. *Office:* Department of History, University of Arizona, Tucson, Ariz. 85721.

CAREER: New York Institute of Technology, New York City, instructor in American history, 1960-65; City College (now City College of the City University of New York), New York City, lecturer in American history, 1966-67; Fairleigh Dickinson University, Teaneck, N.J., assistant professor of American history, 1967-70; University of Arizona, Tucson, professor of history, 1970—. Adjunct assistant professor at Columbia University, summers, 1969, 1972, 1974, and at New York University, 1969-70. *Member:* American Historical Association, Organization of American Historians. *Awards, honors: Saturday Review* Anisfield-Wolf Award, 1969, for *The Leo Frank Case;* National Endowment for the Humanities summer fellowship, 1970; University of Arizona faculty research fellowships, 1971 and 1972.

WRITINGS: The Leo Frank Case, Columbia University Press, 1968; (with David M. Reimers) *Ethnic Americans: A History of Immigration and Assimilation,* Dodd, 1975.

Editor: (With Fred Jaher) *The Aliens: A History of Ethnic Minorities in America,* Appleton, 1970; (with Kenneth T. Jackson) *American Vistas,* Oxford University Press, 1971, 2nd edition, 1975; *Antisemitism in the United States,* Holt, 1971; (with Mary Dale Palsson) *Jews in the South,* Louisiana State University Press, 1973; (with Jean Christie) *Decisions and Revisions: Interpretations of Twentieth-Century American History,* Praeger, 1975; (with Christie) *Since 1945,* Praeger, 1976.

Contributor: Jaher, editor, *The Age of Industrialism in America,* Free Press, 1968; Leon Friedman and Fred L. Israel, editors, *The Justices of the United States Supreme Court, 1789-1969: Their Lives and Major Decisions,* four volumes, Bowker, 1969; A. M. Schlesinger, editor, *History of American Presidential Elections,* four volumes, McGraw, 1971; Schlesinger, editor, *History of United States Political Parties,* four volumes, Chelsea House, 1973; (with George Lankevich) *The Study of American History,* two volumes, Dushkin, 1974.

Also author of papers presented at historical association conferences across the country. Contributor of articles to *American Jewish Historical Quarterly, Jewish Social Studies, American Jewish Archives, Alabama Review, Virginia Magazine of History and Biography,* and *New York History.* Contributor of book reviews to *American Jewish Historical Quarterly, Arizona and the West, American Journal of Sociology, International Migration Review, Jewish Social Studies, Journal of American History, New Jersey History,* and *New York History.*

WORK IN PROGRESS: An ethnic history of the United States, for Oxford University Press.

BIOGRAPHICAL/CRITICAL SOURCES: Spectator, July 5, 1968.

*   *   *

DIRRIM, Allen Wendell   1929-

PERSONAL: Born June 11, 1929, in DeKalb County, Ind.; son of Clarence Franklin and Madge (DeLong) Dirrim; married Loretta Binns (a registered nurse), November 25, 1953; children: Mark, Peter, Lisa. *Education:* DePauw University, B.A., 1950; University of Cincinnati, M.A., 1951; Indiana University, Ph.D., 1959. *Politics:* Democratic. *Home:* 10204 Lasine Ave., Northridge, Calif. 91324. *Office:* Department of History, California State University, Northridge, Calif. 91324.

CAREER: Indiana University, Bloomington, lecturer in history, 1958-59; California State University, Northridge, assistant professor, 1959-64, associate professor, 1964-68, professor of history, 1968—; visiting associate professor of history, Ohio University, 1968-69. Foundation for Reformation Research, St. Louis, Mo., senior fellow, 1963, research director, summer, 1968. Member of California State Democratic Central Committee, 1974-75. *Military service:* U.S. Naval Reserve, active dutiy 1952-55; became lieutenant. *Member:* American Historical Association, Renaissance Society of America, American Association for Reformation Research, Phi Beta Kappa, Phi Eta Sigma, Phi Alpha Theta.

WRITINGS: (With John Stipp and Warren Hollister) *The Rise and Development of Western Civilization,* two volumes, Wiley, 1967, 2nd edition, 1972, published as three volumes, 1968, 2nd edition, 1972, published as one volume, 1969.

WORK IN PROGRESS: A history of the German Peasants Revolt, 1524-1526.

*   *   *

DIRSCHERL, Denis   1934-

PERSONAL: Born May 10, 1934, in Troy, Ohio; son of

Albert Nicholas (an insurance man) and Margaret (Schief) Dirscherl. *Education:* Studied at University of Dayton, 1956-57, later at West Baden College and other Jesuit institutions; Loyola University, Chicago, Ill., B.A., 1961; summer Russian studies at Fordham University, 1961, 1962, 1964, and Middlebury College, 1965, 1966, M.A., 1968; Bellarmine School of Theology, student, 1967; Georgetown University, Ph.D., 1971; George Washington University, post-doctoral study, 1975. *Home:* Georgetown Preparatory School, Rockville, Md. 20852.

CAREER: Entered Society of Jesus (Jesuits), 1957; ordained Roman Catholic priest in Aurora, Ill., 1967. St. Ignatius High School, Chicago, Ill., teacher of Latin and speech, and coach of debate and baseball, 1963-64; freelance writer. Teacher, Loyola Academy, Wilmette, Ill., summer, 1963. *Military service:* U.S. Air Force, Intelligence, 1952-56; studied Russian at Army Language School; served in Alaska. U.S. Air Force Reserve, chaplain. *Member:* American Association for the Advancement of Slavic Studies, Knights of Columbus, United States Lawn Tennis Association (honorary life member), Washington Area Tennis Officials Association, Rockville Tennis Association.

WRITINGS: (Editor and contributor) *Speaking of God* (essays on belief and unbelief), Bruce, 1967; (editor) *The New Russia,* Pflaum, 1968. Contributor of more than one hundred articles and seventy-five reviews in the area of Russian studies to scholarly journals, Catholic periodicals, and newspapers.

* * *

DISCH, Thomas M. 1940-
(Thom Demijohn, a joint pseudonym)

PERSONAL: Born February 2, 1940, in Des Moines, Iowa; son of Felix Henry and Helen (Gilbertson) Disch. *Education:* Attended New York University, 1959-62. *Agent:* Marie Rodell-Frances Collin Agency, 141 East 55th St., New York, N.Y. 10022.

CAREER: Checkroom attendant at Majestic Theater, New York, N.Y., sporadically from 1957-62; copywriter for Doyle Dane Bernbach, Inc., New York, N.Y., 1963-64; free-lance writer, 1964—. Visiting lecturer at University of Minnesota, Michigan State University, and Wesleyan University. *Awards, honors:* O. Henry Prize, 1975, for short story, "Getting into Death."

WRITINGS: The Genocides, Berkley Publishing, 1965; *Mankind Under the Leash,* Ace, 1966; *102 H-Bombs, and Other Stories,* Compact Books, 1966, American edition with somewhat different stories, Berkley Publishing, 1969; *Echo 'Round His Bones,* Berkley Publishing, 1967; (with John Sladek, under joint pseudonym Thom Demijohn) *Black Alice,* Doubleday, 1968; *Camp Concentration,* Hart-Davis, 1968, Doubleday, 1969; *Under Compulsion* (short stories), Hart-Davis, 1968, published as *Fun with Your New Head,* Doubleday, 1969; (editor) *The Ruins of Earth: An Anthology of Stories of the Immediate Future,* Putnam, 1971; *The Right Way to Figure Plumbing* (poetry), Basilisk, 1972; (editor) *Bad Moon Rising: An Anthology of Political Foreboding,* Harper, 1973; *Getting into Death* (short stories), Hart-Davis, 1973, Knopf, in press; *Three Thirty-Four,* Avon, 1974; (editor) *The New Improved Sun,* Harper, 1975; (editor) *New Constellations,* Harper, in press. Contributor to *Harper's, Playboy, American Review,* and other periodicals.

WORK IN PROGRESS: Two novels, *The Pressure of Time,* and *Acts of the Apostles;* a libretto for full-length opera *Kierkegaard.*

SIDELIGHTS: Disch has been living in New York and abroad since 1964.

BIOGRAPHICAL/CRITICAL SOURCES: Punch, September 7, 1968.

* * *

DIX, Robert H. 1930-

PERSONAL: Born August 18, 1930, in Elizabeth, N.J.; son of Allen Gilbert (an engineer) and Sara (Heller) Dix; married Mary Seaton (an editor), May 5, 1956. *Education:* Harvard University, B.A., 1951, M.A., 1953, Ph.D., 1962. *Office:* Department of Political Science, Rice University, Houston, Tex. 77001.

CAREER: U.S. Department of State, Foreign Service officer in Bogota, Colombia, 1957-60; Yale University, New Haven, Conn., assistant professor of political science, 1962-67; Harvard University, Center for International Affairs, Cambridge, Mass., research associate in political development, 1967-68; Rice University, Houston, Tex., associate professor, 1968-70, professor of political science, 1970—, chairman of department, 1972-75. Academic researcher in Chile, 1966-67. *Military service:* U.S. Army, 1953-55. *Member:* American Political Science Association, Latin American Studies Association. *Awards, honors:* Social Science Research Council fellowship, 1966-67.

WRITINGS: Colombia: The Political Dimensions of Change, Yale University Press, 1967; (contributor) Robert Dahl, editor, *Regimes and Oppositions,* Yale University Press, 1974.

WORK IN PROGRESS: Studies in mass-based authoritarianism in Latin America.

* * *

DMYTRYSHYN, Basil 1925-

PERSONAL: Born January 14, 1925, in Poland; naturalized U.S. citizen; married Virginia Roehl, July 16, 1949; children: Sonia, Tania. *Education:* University of Arkansas, B.A., 1950, M.A., 1951; University of California, Berkeley, Ph.D., 1955. *Politics:* Democrat. *Home:* 11300 Southwest 92nd Ave., Portland, Ore. 97223. *Office:* Department of History, Portland State University, Portland, Ore. 97207.

CAREER: University of California, Berkeley, research associate, 1955-56; Portland State University, Portland, Ore., assistant professor, 1956-59, associate professor, 1959-64, professor of history, 1964—. Visiting professor at University of Illinois, 1964-65, and Harvard University, summer, 1971. Conductor of college credit course in history on both Oregon educational television and commercial television. *Member:* American Historical Association, American Association for the Advancement of Slavic Studies, Canadian Association of Slavicists. *Awards, honors:* Fulbright fellowship for research in Germany, 1967-68.

WRITINGS: Moscow and the Ukraine, 1918-53, Bookman Associates, 1956; (translator with John M. Letiche and Richard Pierce) *A History of Russian Economic Thought,* University of California Press, 1964; *USSR: A Concise History,* Scribner, 1965, 2nd edition, 1971; (editor) *Medieval Russia: A Source Book, 900-1700,* Holt, 1967, 2nd edition, Dryden, 1973; (editor) *Imperial Russia: A Source Book, 1700-1917,* Holt, 1967, 2nd edition, Dryden, 1974;

(editor) *Modernization of Russia under Peter I and Catherine II,* Wiley, 1974; *A History of Russia,* Scribner, 1975. Contributor to professional journals in United States, Canada, and Germany.

WORK IN PROGRESS: Research in Russian expansion to the Pacific, mercantilist thought, and the impact of Adam Smith on Russia.

SIDELIGHTS: Dmytryshyn speaks German, Russian, Czechoslovak, and Ukrainian. He also reads French and church Slavonic.

* * *

DOEBLER, Charles H. 1925-

PERSONAL: Born May 25, 1925, in Huntington, W.Va.; son of Charles H. (an engineer) and Phyllis (Leavitt) Doebler; married Marilyn Janet Hill (a teacher), March 28, 1953; children: Christine von Schuler, Charles Hay. *Education:* Brown University, A.B., 1948. *Politics:* Liberal Republican. *Religion:* Episcopalian. *Home:* 86 Brown St., Providence, R.I. 02906. *Agent:* Donald MacCampbell, Inc., 12 East 41st St., New York, N.Y. 10017. *Office:* 86 Brown St., Providence, R.I.

CAREER: Brown University, Providence, R.I., director of admission, 1951-69; self-employed as educational counselor and consultant in Providence, 1969—. Director of Society for Crippled Children and Adults of Rhode Island, and of Providence Athenaeum. Member of board of overseers, Lincoln School. *Military service:* U.S. Naval Reserve, active duty, 1943-45; served on minesweepers, became ensign. *Member:* Providence Art Club.

WRITINGS: Who Gets into College and Why: Planning Your Child's Education, Macfadden, 1964, hardcover edition, Putnam, 1966, new edition, Prentice-Hall, 1971.

WORK IN PROGRESS: A possible book on the perils of educating fourteen-year-olds, or one on alternates to college.

* * *

DOHERTY, Robert W. 1935-

PERSONAL: Born November 9, 1935, in Detroit, Mich.; son of J. Kenneth (a professor) and Lucile (Mason) Doherty; married Marilyn Green; children: Robert, Kathryn. *Education:* Denison University, B.A., 1957; University of Pennsylvania, M.A., 1958, Ph.D., 1962. *Office:* History Department, University of Pittsburgh, Pittsburgh, Pa.

CAREER: Pennsylvania Military College, Chester, instructor, 1959-62; Rutgers University, Douglass College, New Brunswick, N.J., assistant professor, 1962-65; University of Massachusetts, Amherst, assistant professor, 1965-68; University of Pittsburgh, Pittsburth, Pa., associate professor of history, beginning 1968. *Awards, honors:* Junior fellowship, National Endowment for the Humanities, 1967-68.

WRITINGS: The Hicksite Separation: A Sociological Analysis of Religious Schism in Early Nineteenth-Century America, Rutgers University Press, 1967.

WORK IN PROGRESS: A study of the social impact of industrialization on American society from 1800 to 1850.††

* * *

DOLMETSCH, Carl R(ichard, Jr.) 1924-

PERSONAL: Surname is pronounced *Doll*-metch; born July 5, 1924, in Kingston, Pa.; son of Carl Richard (a chemist) and Margaret (Hollister) Dolmetsch; married Joan Downing (a curator in graphic arts), February 7, 1948; children: Carl Richard III, Christopher Lee. *Education:* Drake University, B.A., 1948, M.A., 1949; Columbia University, graduate study, 1954-55; University of Chicago, Ph.D., 1957. *Home:* 108 Hermitage Rd., Williamsburg, Va. 23185. *Office:* College of William and Mary, Williamsburg, Va. 23185.

CAREER: Drury College, Springfield, Mo., instructor in English, 1949-51; high school teacher in Illinois, 1951-56; Drake University, Des Moines, Iowa, assistant professor of English, 1956-59; College of William and Mary, Williamsburg, Va., assistant professor, 1959-63, associate professor, 1963-67, professor of English, 1967—, chairman of department, 1970-76. Fulbright visiting professor, Free University of Berlin, 1964-66. *Military service:* U.S. Army Air Forces, 1943-45; became sergeant. *Member:* Modern Language Association of America, American Studies Association, American Association of University Professors, Tau Kappa Epsilon, Alpha Phi Omega. *Awards, honors:* John Hay Whitney fellow, 1954; Willett research award, College of William and Mary, 1963; American Philosophical Society research grants, 1963, 1964, 1967.

WRITINGS: (Editor with J. A. Servies) *The Poems of Charles Hansford,* University of North Carolina Press, 1961; *The Smart Set: A History and Anthology,* introduction by S. N. Behrman, Dial, 1966. Contributor to *Menckeniana, Dickensian* (London), *Jahrbuch fuer Amerikastudien* (Heidelberg), *Early American Literature,* and other journals.

WORK IN PROGRESS: William Byrd II, a critical biography, for publication by Twayne; an edition of the unpublished essays of St. George Tucker.

* * *

DONALD, Aida DiPace 1930-

PERSONAL: Born April 9, 1930, in Brooklyn, N.Y.; daughter of Victor E. and Bessie (Catania) DiPace; married David Donald (a university professor and author), October 31, 1955; children: Bruce Randall. *Education:* Barnard College, A.B., 1952, Columbia University, M.A., 1953; University of Rochester, graduate study, 1953-55, Ph.D., 1961; Oxford University, graduate study, 1959-60. *Home:* Lincoln Rd., Lincoln, Mass. 01773.

CAREER: Columbia University, New York City, instructor in history, 1955-56; Hill & Wang, Inc. (publishers), New York City, consulting editor, 1959—, general editor of "American Profiles" series, 1967—, and "World Profiles" series, 1970—. History and humanities editor, Johns Hopkins University, 1972-73; social sciences editor, Harvard University Press, 1973—. *Member:* American Historical Association, American Association of University Women, League of Women Voters. *Awards, honors:* American Association of University Women fellowship, 1957-58; Fulbright fellowship to Oxford University, 1959-60.

WRITINGS: (Editor with husband, David Donald) *Diary of Charles Francis Adams,* two volumes, Harvard University Press, 1964; *John F. Kennedy and the New Frontier,* Hill & Wang, 1966. Contributor of articles and book reviews to scholarly journals.

* * *

DONEY, Willis (Frederick, Jr.) 1925-

PERSONAL: Born August 19, 1925, in Pittsburgh, Pa.;

son of Willis Frederick (a banker) and Ora (Powell) Doney. *Education:* Princeton University, B.A., 1946, M.A. and Ph.D., 1949. *Address:* Box 298, Norwich, Vt. 05055. *Office:* Philosophy Department, Dartmouth College, Hanover, N.H. 03755.

CAREER: Cornell University, Ithaca, N.Y., instructor in philosophy, 1949-52; Ohio State University, Columbus, assistant professor of philosophy, 1953-58; Dartmouth College, Hanover, N.H., associate professor, 1958-66, professor of philosophy, 1966—. Visiting lecturer at University of Michigan, 1953, and Harvard University, 1963. Member of Institute for Advanced Study, 1972-73. *Member:* American Philosophical Association, Aristotelian Society. *Awards, honors:* George Santayana fellowship to Harvard University, 1956-57; M.A. from Dartmouth College, 1967.

WRITINGS: (Editor) *Descartes: A Collection of Critical Essays,* Doubleday, 1967. Contributor to *Encyclopedia of Philosophy* and philosophical journals.

WORK IN PROGRESS: Studies in the philosophy of Descartes.

* * *

DONNELLY, Alton S(tewart) 1920-

PERSONAL: Born November 30, 1920, in Springville, Utah; son of Alton Chance and Ruby (Stewart) Donnelly; married Kathleen Riley (a high school teacher), July 11, 1958. *Education:* University of California, Berkeley, B.S., 1948, M.A., 1955, Ph.D., 1960; Leningrad State University, graduate study, 1958-59. *Religion:* Church of Jesus Christ of Latter-day Saints (Mormon). *Home:* 125 Southwood Dr., Vestal, N.Y. 13850. *Office:* State University of New York, Binghamton, N.Y. 13901.

CAREER: University of Wisconsin—Madison, lecturer in Russian history, 1957; Northern Illinois University, DeKalb, assistant professor of history, 1960-63; Parsons College, Fairfield, Iowa, associate professor of history, 1963-64; Northern Illinois University, assistant professor of history, 1964-66; State University of New York at Binghamton, associate professor of history, 1966—. *Military service:* U.S. Naval Reserve, 1942—; active duty, 1942-46, 1950-52; current rank, captain. *Member:* American Historical Association, American Association for the Advancement of Slavic Studies.

WRITINGS: The Russian Conquest of Bashkiria, 1552-1740, Yale University Press, 1968. Contributor to *Cities of Central Asia* (guide book), Central Asian Research Centre, 1961.

WORK IN PROGRESS: A monograph on Peter the Great's Asian policies and activities.

SIDELIGHTS: During Donnelly's year as an exchange student in the Soviet Union, he worked one summer as a guide at the American National Exhibition in Moscow.

* * *

DONOVAN, James A., Jr. 1917-

PERSONAL: Born May 23, 1917, in Chicago, Ill.; son of James A. (a banker) and Nellie B. Donovan; married May 16, 1950; wife's name, Kay Virginia; children: Kathryn B., Deborah V. *Education:* Dartmouth College, A.B., 1939; also studied at Industrial College of the Armed Forces, 1957-58, and various Marine Corps schools. *Home:* 7365 Hunters Branch Dr., Atlanta, Ga. 30328. *Office:* Engineering Experiment Station, Georgia Institute of Technology, Atlanta, Ga. 30309.

CAREER: J. Walter Thompson Co. (advertising), Chicago, Ill., production staff, 1939-40; U.S. Marine Corps, regular officer, 1940-63, rising from second lieutenant to colonel; *Journal of the Armed Forces,* Washington, D.C., publisher and president, 1963-67; Georgia Institute of Technology, Atlanta, research scientist with Industrial Development Division, 1967-72, with Engineering Experiment Station, 1972—. Member of board of advisors, Center for Defense Information. Editorial cartoonist and painter. *Member:* Marine Corps Association, Inter-University Seminar on Armed Forces and Society, SANE (member of national board). *Awards, honors*—Military: Silver Star; Bronze Star; Presidential Unit Citation (for action on Tarawa).

WRITINGS: The United States Marine Corps, Praeger, 1967; *Militarism, U.S.A.,* Scribner, 1970. Editor-publisher, *Leatherneck* (magazine), 1948-51; columnist and writer for *Marine Corps Gazette* and *Leatherneck,* 1951-66.

WORK IN PROGRESS: A book, *Arms. Power. Peace.*

* * *

DONSON, Cyril 1919-
(Via Hartford, Russ Kidd)

PERSONAL: Born May 26, 1919, in Mexborough, Yorkshire, England; son of Ernest (a miner) and Ada (Wagstaffe) Donson; married Dorothy Denham (a teacher), May 23, 1942; children: Valeria Norma (Mrs. Reginald MacKinnon). *Education:* Educated at Bristol College, Loughborough College, and University of Nottingham; received Teacher's Certificates in psychology and education, and Diploma of Loughborough College. *Politics:* Liberal. *Religion:* Nonconformist. *Home and office:* 24 Eaton Close, Hartford, Huntingdonshire, England.

CAREER: Newspaper journalist in England, 1941-43; schoolmaster, 1944-62, intermittently deputy headmaster and head of handicraft department in a bilateral school; public relations officer for a short period in 1964; writer. *Military service:* Royal Air Force, 1936-40. *Member:* Royal Society of Arts, Crime Writers' Association, United Writers.

WRITINGS: (With Armand Georges) *Lonelyland* [and] *Bedsitterland,* Bala Press, 1967; *Born in Space,* R. Hale, 1968; *The Perspective Process,* R. Hale, 1969. Author of three crossword puzzle books; also author of *Draco the Dragon* (horror novel), *Guide to Authors,* and *Planet of the Gargantua.*

Under pseudonym Russ Kidd; all published by Ward, Lock: *Brannan of Bar B,* 1964; *Thunder at Bushwhack,* 1965; *Jinx Ranch,* 1966; *Gun Law at Concho Creek,* 1966; *Throw a Tall Shadow,* 1967; *Fight for Circle C,* 1967; *Dead Man's Colts,* 1968. Writer of romantic short stories for women under pseudonym Via Hartford.

* * *

DORMON, James H(unter), Jr. 1936-

PERSONAL: Born September 26, 1936, in Monroe, La.; son of James Hunter (an attorney) and Ethel C. (Shaw) Dormon; divorced; children: James Mahlon. *Education:* University of Southwestern Louisiana, B.A., 1957; University of North Carolina, M.A., 1959, Ph.D., 1966. *Politics:* Liberal Democrat. *Home:* 226 River Dr., Lafayette, La. 70501. *Office:* Box 454, University of Southwestern Louisiana, Lafayette, La. 70501.

CAREER: University of Southwestern Louisiana, Lafayette, assistant professor, 1962-63, 1966-67, associate professor of history, 1967—. *Military service:* U.S. Naval Reserve, 1956-64. *Member:* Organization of American Historians, American Studies Association, American Association of University Professors, Southern Historical Association, Louisiana Historical Association.

WRITINGS: Theater in the Ante-Bellum South, 1815-1861, University of North Carolina Press, 1966; (with Robert R. Jones) *The Afro-American Experience: A Cultural History through Emancipation,* Wiley, 1974. Contributor of articles and reviews to journals in his field.

WORK IN PROGRESS: Several projects in early American history and culture; a novel.

*   *   *

DORN, Jacob H(enry)   1939-

PERSONAL: Born September 21, 1939, in Chicago, Ill.; son of Francis Jacob Henry and Mary (Young) Dorn; married Carole R. Johnson (a teacher), August 15, 1964; children: Jonathan Andrew, Elizabeth Ann. *Education:* Wheaton College, Wheaton, Ill., B.A., 1960; University of Oregon, M.A., 1962, Ph.D., 1965. *Religion:* Baptist. *Home:* 6 Forrer Blvd., Dayton, Ohio 45419. *Office:* Department of History, Wright State University, Dayton, Ohio.

CAREER: Wright State University, Dayton, Ohio, assistant professor, 1965-68, associate professor, 1968-74, professor of history, 1974—, director of university honors program, 1972—. Member, Dayton Area Campus Ministry Board. *Member:* American Historical Association, American Society of Church History, Organization of American Historians, Ohio Academy of History, Ohio Historical Society. *Awards, honors:* Ohioana Library Association Annual Book Award, 1969.

WRITINGS: Washington Gladden: Prophet of the Social Gospel, Ohio State University Press, 1967; (editor with Carl Becker and Paul Merriam) *A Bibliography of Sources for Dayton, Ohio, 1850-1950,* Wright State University, 1972.

*   *   *

DORO, Edward   1910-

PERSONAL: Born February 3, 1910, in Dickinson, N.D. *Education:* University of Southern California, B.A., 1930; University of Pennsylvania, M.A., 1931; University of Paris, language study, 1932-33; University of California, Berkeley, M.L.S., 1957. *Address:* P.O. Box 235, Seaside, Calif. 93955.

CAREER: Yale University Library, New Haven, Conn., senior assistant in rare books, 1958-59; Northwestern University Library, Evanston, Ill., curator of rare books, 1959-62; New School for Social Research, New York, N.Y., teacher of literature, 1962-63; Museum of Fine Arts, Houston, Tex., lecturer and librarian, 1963-65; Franconia College, Franconia, N.H., instructor in creative writing and college librarian, 1965-67; John F. Kennedy University, Martinez, Calif., professor of humanities and university librarian, 1967-69; Monterey Institute of Foreign Studies, Monterey, Calif., professor of humanities, 1969-73. Poet-reader for Library of Congress Archives of American Poets, 1962. *Member:* American Library Association (life member). *Awards, honors:* Russell Loines Memorial Award ($1,000) of National Institute of Arts and Letters, 1933, for *The Boar & Shibboleth;* Guggenheim fellowship in poetry, 1936; L.H.D., Sussex Institute of Technology, 1971.

WRITINGS—Poetry: *Alms for Oblivion,* Casa Editorial Hispano-Americana (Paris), 1931; *The Boar & Shibboleth,* Knopf, 1932; *Shiloh,* Putnam, 1936; *Mr. Zenith,* Bookman Associates, 1942; *Parisian Interlude,* Doan, 1960; *The Furtherance,* Franconia College Press, 1966, 2nd edition, 1966. Poetry anthologized in *Great Poems of the English Language, Twentieth-Century American Poetry, Bartlett's Quotations,* and other collections.

Plays: "The Prophet from Izmir," 1972; "The Spanish Locket," 1974.

WORK IN PROGRESS: Adapting "The Prophet from Izmir," with C. P. van Lidth de Jeude, and "The Spanish Locket," with C. P. Burkholder, for operatic theatre; a poetic satire, *The Rise and Fall of Academia,* with Gordon Curtis.

SIDELIGHTS: As a creative artist Edward Doro is concerned "with the relationship of *esthesis,* reality, *gnosis,* human knowledge, and *sophia,* divine wisdom."

*   *   *

DORONZO, Emmanuel   1903-

PERSONAL: Born February 3, 1903, in Barletta, Italy; son of Pasquale and Concetta (Vannella) Doronzo. *Education:* Apostolic School of Oblates of Mary Immaculate, Naples, Italy, seminarian, 1913-18; Gregorian University, Rome, J.C.B. and Ph.D., 1925; St. Thomas Aquinas University, Rome, S.T.D., 1927. *Office:* Notre Dame Institute for Advanced Studies in Religious Education, Middleburg, Va. 22117.

CAREER: Roman Catholic priest of Oblate Fathers of Mary Immaculate, ordained in Rome, Italy, 1925; professor of theology at Oblate Major Seminary, Turin, Italy, 1927-36, and Oblate College of the Southwest, San Antonio, Tex., 1936-46; Catholic University of America, Washington, D.C., professor of theology, 1947-51, Ordinary Professor of Theology, 1952-68; Notre Dame Institute for Advanced Studies in Religious Education, Middleburg, Va., consultant in sacred theology, 1970—. Member of Preparatory Commission for Vatican Council II. *Member:* Catholic Theological Society of America, Roman Pontifical Academy of St. Thomas Aquinas. *Awards, honors:* Cardinal Spellman Theology Award, 1947, 1952.

WRITINGS: (Translator from the Italian) Pietro Parante, *Dictionary of Dogmatic Theology,* Bruce, 1951; *Introduction to Theology* (pamphlet), Notre Dame Institute Press, 1974; *The Channels of Revelation* (pamphlet), Notre Dame Institute Press, 1974; *Revelation,* Notre Dame Institute Press, 1974.

All published in Latin: *Tractatus dogmaticus de Sacramentis in genere,* Bruce, 1946; *De Baptismo et Confirmatione,* Bruce, 1947; *Tractatus dogmaticus de Eucharistia,* two volumes, Bruce, 1947; *De Paenitentia,* four volumes, Bruce, 1949-53; *De Extrema Unctione,* two volumes, Bruce, 1954-55; *De Ordine,* three volumes, Bruce, 1957; *De Matrimonio,* Bruce, 1964; *Theologia Dogmatica,* Montepio Diocesano (Vitoria, Spain), Volume I, 1966, Volume II, 1968.

WORK IN PROGRESS: The Church, God, the Trinity.

BIOGRAPHICAL/CRITICAL SOURCES: American Ecclesiastical Review, Number 153, 1965.

*   *   *

DORSETT, Lyle W(esley)   1938-

PERSONAL: Born April 17, 1938, in Kansas City, Mo.;

son of Albert Wesley (a sales executive) and Eda Rose (Hilderbrand) Dorsett; married Mary Ann Hayes, July 9, 1970. *Education:* Junior College of Kansas City, A.A., 1958; University of Missouri, B.A., 1960, M.A., 1962, Ph.D., 1965. *Home:* 2185 Goddard Pl., Boulder, Colo. 80303. *Office:* Department of History, University of Denver, Denver, Colo. 80210.

CAREER: University of Missouri at St. Louis, assistant professor of history, 1965-66; University of Southern California, Los Angeles, assistant professor of history, 1966-68; University of Missouri at St. Louis, associate professor of history, 1968-71; University of Colorado, Boulder, associate professor of history, 1971-72; University of Denver, Denver, Colo., professor of history, 1972—. *Member:* American Historical Association, Organization of American Historians, Southern Historical Association. *Awards, honors:* American Philosophical Society grant; National Endowment for the Humanities summer fellowship.

WRITINGS: The Pendergast Machine, Oxford University Press, 1968; (editor) *The Challenge of the City, 1860-1910,* Heath, 1968; *The Early American City,* Forum Press, 1973. Contributor to *Arizona and the West, New England Quarterly, Journal of Southern History, Pacific Northwest Quarterly, Colorado Magazine,* and other history journals.

WORK IN PROGRESS: Franklin Roosevelt and the City Bosses; a history of Denver.

* * *

DOUGLAS, Louis H(artwell) 1907-

PERSONAL: Born September 5, 1907, in Bloomington, Neb.; son of Ralph S. and Mary (Hamilton) Douglas; married Mary Burton, 1933; children: Kathryn Marie (Mrs. John E. Hodge), Stephen A., Merrie Lou. *Education:* Hastings College, Hastings, Neb., A.B., 1931; University of Nebraska, M.A., 1937, Ph.D., 1950; Yale University, graduate study, 1947-48. *Politics:* Democrat. *Religion:* Congregational. *Home:* 415 Oakdale, Manhattan, Kan. 66504. *Office:* Kansas State University, Manhattan, Kan. 66502.

CAREER: McCook College, McCook, Neb., instructor, 1942-43; Hastings College, Hastings, Neb., 1943-46, began as instructor, became acting dean; Miami University, Oxford, Ohio, assistant professor of government, 1946-49; Kansas State University, Manhattan, professor of political science, 1949—. Visiting professor, Tottori National University, Japan, 1951-52; Fulbright professor, University of the Philippines, 1960-61; visiting professor, University of Illinois, summer, 1963. *Member:* American Political Science Association, Midwest Political Science Association.

WRITINGS: (With V. Sweedlun, Golda Crawford, and J. Kenyon) *Men in Society,* American Book Co., 1956; (editor with J. Hajda) *Readings and Exercises in American Government,* Burgess, 1958; (editor with Hajda and L. Lambert) *Readings and Projects in American Government,* American Book Co., 1960; (contributor) R. Stauber, editor, *Approaches to Study of Urbanization,* University of Kansas Press, 1964; (with Wayne C. Rohrer) *Dualism and Change: The Agrarian Transition in America,* Bobbs-Merrill, 1969; (editor) *Agrarianism in American History,* Heath, 1969. Contributor to professional journals.

WORK IN PROGRESS: Poverty and Powerlessness: Studies in Rural Political Culture, completion expected in 1977.

DOUGLAS, Mack R. 1922-

PERSONAL: Born November 27, 1922, in Fort Worth, Tex.; son of Edgar Lamar (a college professor) and Lona (Rushing) Douglas; married Aline Goodwin, December 27, 1946. *Education:* Mississippi College, B.A., 1948; Millsaps College, student, 1943-44; Southwestern Baptist Theological Seminary, Master of Religious Education, 1951. *Politics:* Republican.

CAREER: Baptist minister; First Baptist Church, Pompano Beach, Fla., pastor, beginning 1962; Baptist Village, Inc. (retirement center), Pompano Beach, president, beginning 1963. Speaker on trips to Europe, Middle East, Orient, and South America; professional speaker in United States, and instructor in Dale Carnegie leadership and sales courses. Chairman of Pompano Beach Community Relations Committee. *Military service:* U.S. Marine Corps, Intelligence, 1943-46. *Member:* Sales and Marketing Executives (speakers bureau), Kiwanis Club, Masons, Shriners (Miami chaplain).

WRITINGS: How to Build an Evangelistic Church, Zondervan, 1963; *How to Make a Habit of Succeeding,* Zondervan, 1966; *How to Cultivate the Habit of Succeeding,* Zondervan, 1968; *How to Succeed in Your Life's Work,* Droke, 1971; *Success Can Be Yours,* Zondervan, 1972.†

* * *

DOWSE, Robert E. 1933-

PERSONAL: Born April 17, 1933, in London, England; son of Robert Edward and Elizabeth Ivy Dowse; married Patricia Anne Thoday; children: Robert Edward, Simon Geoffrey. *Education:* London School of Economics and Political Science, Ph.D., 1960. *Politics:* Socialist. *Religion:* None. *Home:* 148 Heavitree Rd., Exeter, England. *Office:* University of Exeter, Exeter, England.

CAREER: University of Edinburgh, Edinburgh, Scotland, lecturer in political science, 1960-61; University of Hull, Hull, England, lecturer in political science, 1961-64; University of Exeter, Exeter, England, lecturer in political science, 1964—. *Military service:* National Service, 1954-56.

WRITINGS: Left in the Centre, Longmans, Green, 1966; (editor with Robert Benewick) *Readings on British Politics and Government,* University of London Press, 1968; *Ghana and USSR: A Comparative Study,* Routledge & Kegan Paul, 1969; *Political Sociology,* Wiley, 1972; *The Labour Ideal,* Harvester Press, 1975. Contributor to journals in his field.

* * *

DRAKE, William D(onovan) 1922-

PERSONAL: Born August 22, 1922, in Russell, Iowa; son of George C. (a meat inspector, U.S. Department of Agriculture) and Elsie (Boyd) Drake; married Elizabeth D'Arbantes Ward. *Education:* University of Iowa, B.A., 1945, M.A., 1948; University of Arizona, Ph.D., 1967. *Home:* 166 West Third St., Oswego, N.Y. 13126. *Office:* Department of English, State University of New York, Oswego, N.Y. 13126.

CAREER: Instructor in English at University of Iowa, Iowa City, 1946-48, and University of Wyoming, Laramie, 1948-49; Contra Costa County Library, Pleasant Hill, Calif., consultant, 1953-56; Nature Conservancy, western regional director, Berkeley, Calif., 1956-61; University of Arizona, Tucson, instructor in English, 1961-67; State University of New York College at Oswego, associate professor, 1967-71, professor of English and chairman of department, 1971—. Director of summer studies program, University of London, 1973; chairman of American literature division, State University of New York Awards Committee, 1973-76. *Member:* Modern Language Association of America, National Council of Teachers of English, Thoreau Society. *Awards, honors:* Merit award in conservation education from California Conservation Council, 1957; faculty fellowship from State University of New York, summers, 1968 and 1974.

WRITINGS: (Contributor) Sherman Paul, editor, *Thoreau,* Prentice-Hall, 1962; *The Way to Spell,* Chandler Publishing, 1967; *The Way to Punctuate,* Chandler Publishing, 1970; (contributor) Richard Benton, editor, *Eureka,* Transcendental, 1975.

WORK IN PROGRESS: Love, Death, and Beauty: The Feminine Tragedy of Sara Teasdale.

BIOGRAPHICAL/CRITICAL SOURCES: Walter Harding, *The Thoreau Handbook,* New York University Press, 1959.

*   *   *

DREYER, Edward C.   1937-

PERSONAL: Born May 28, 1937, in Long Beach, Calif.; son of J. Henry (a grocer) and Flonnie E. (Callahan) Dreyer; married Norma L. Steeples, August 21, 1960; children: Eric Christopher, Mark Edward. *Education:* University of Redlands, B.A. (cum laude), 1959; University of North Carolina, graduate study, 1960-63, Ph.D., 1968. *Religion:* Lutheran. *Home:* 221 East 24th Place, Tulsa, Okla. 74114. *Office:* Department of Political Science, University of Tulsa, 600 South College Ave., Tulsa, Okla. 74104.

CAREER: University of North Carolina, Chapel Hill, instructor, 1962; San Diego State College (now San Diego State University), San Diego, Calif., assistant professor of political science, 1963-68; University of Missouri, St. Louis, assistant professor of political science, 1968-71; University of Tulsa, Tulsa, Okla., professor of political science and chairman of department, 1971—. Consultant to various government agencies and political groups. *Member:* American Political Science Association, Southern Political Science Association.

WRITINGS: (With Walter A. Rosenbaum) *Political Opinion and Electoral Behavior: Essays and Studies,* Wadsworth, 1966, 3rd edition, Durbury, 1975; (contributor) Norman R. Luttbeg, editor, *Public Opinion and Public Policy: Models of Political Linkage,* revised edition, Dorsey Press, 1974. Contributor to *Journal of Politics* and other periodicals.

WORK IN PROGRESS: The American Electorate, for Prentice-Hall.

*   *   *

DROR, Yehezkel   1928-

PERSONAL: Surname originally Freeman; born August 12, 1928, in Vienna, Austria; emigrated to Palestine, 1938; son of Isidor (a business executive) and Stephania (Altman) Freeman; married Rachel Elboim (a university lecturer), January 19, 1954; children: Asrael E., Otniel I. E., Itiel E. *Education:* Hebrew University of Jerusalem, Mag.Jur. and B.A., 1953; Harvard University, LL.M., 1955, S.J.D., 1957. *Religion:* Jewish. *Home:* 48 Shimoni St., Jerusalem, Israel. *Office:* Hebrew University, Jerusalem, Israel.

CAREER: Hebrew University of Jerusalem, Jerusalem, Israel, faculty member, 1957—, senior lecturer in political science and public administration, 1963—, associate professor, 1966-73, professor, 1973—. Visiting professor, Institute of Social Studies, The Hague, Netherlands, annually, 1960—; guest professor at universities in Puerto Rico, United States, the Netherlands, Turkey, England, Belgium, Yugoslavia, Sweden, Germany, Brazil, Venezuela, Denmark, and other countries. Consultant on policy and administration to government departments, international agencies, and public agencies in Israel and abroad. Senior staff member, RAND Corp., 1968-69. *Military service:* Haggana and Israeli Defence Army, 1946-49; became staff officer.

MEMBER: International Institute of Differing Civilizations, International Political Science Association, International Futures Research Association (member of executive committee and research council). *Awards, honors:* Eliashiv Prize of Israeli General Federation of Labour for distinguished essay in social science, 1957; United Nations fellowship to study planning practices in Europe, 1958; fellow, Center for Advanced Study in the Behavioral Sciences, Stanford, Calif., 1962-63; Rosolio Award of Israeli National Public Administration Conference, 1965; Levi Eshkol Prize, for best study of Israeli public administration, 1972.

WRITINGS: Minhal tsiburi, [Jerusalem], 1957; (editor) *Hoveret mekorot,* [Jerusalem], 1957; *Ha-Mishpat mibehinat ha-minhal ha-tsiburi,* [Jerusalem], 1958; *Komunikatsiyah ve-minhal,* [Jerusalem], 1958; (editor) *Law from the Point of View of Administration,* Hebrew University, Eliezer Kaplan School of Economics and Social Sciences, 1958; *Ekronot le-hitnahagutam shel 'ovde tsibur,* [Jerusalem], 1958; *Some Recent Developments of the Doctrine of Precedent in Israel,* Hebrew University, 1958; *Re 'organizatsiyah,* [Jerusalem], 1959; *A General Model of Planning,* Institute of Social Studies, The Hague, 1960(?); (editor with Edwin Emanuel Gutmann) *Mishtar medinat Yisrael,* [Jerusalem], 1961; *Organizational Functions of a Domestic Tribunal,* [London], 1963(?); *The Government of Israel,* Hebrew University, Eliezer Kaplan School of Economics and Social Sciences, 1964; (with Benjamin Akzin) *Israel: High Pressure Planning* (published in Hebrew language in Israel, 1964), Syracuse University Press, 1966; *Tikhnun le'umi be-Holand,* [Israel], 1965, published as *National Planning in the Netherlands,* Syracuse University Press, 1967; *Public Policymaking Reexamined* (published in Hebrew language in Israel, 1966), Chandler, 1967; *Design for Policy Sciences,* Elsevier, 1971; *Ventures in Policy Sciences,* Elsevier, 1971; *Crazy States: A Counterconventional Strategic Problem,* Heath, 1971, revised edition published in German. Also author of *Senior Civil Service Policy for Israel* (in Hebrew), 1972.

Contributor of about fifty articles to professional journals in Israel, India, the Philippines, the United States, and European countries. Member of editorial board, *Policy Sciences, Policy and Politics, Futures, Technological Forecasting and Social Change, Journal of the American Institute of Planners, Computers and Urban Society, Social Indicators Research, Policy Studies Journal, International Journal of General Systems, Sage Yearbooks in Politics and Public Policy,* and *Jerusalem Journal of International Relations.*

WORK IN PROGRESS: The Compleat Policy Analyst; Top Decision Making; Policymaking for British Futures.

DRUKS, Herbert 1937-

PERSONAL: Born April 1, 1937, in Vienna, Austria; son of Charles Druks (a businessman). *Education:* City University of New York (now City College of the City University of New York), B.A., 1958; Rutgers University, M.A., 1959; New York University, Ph.D., 1964. *Address:* P.O. Box 164, Jackson Heights, N.Y. 11372.

CAREER: Works as college professor of history and international relations.

WRITINGS: Harry S Truman and the Russians, Robert Speller, 1967; *From Truman through Johnson,* two volumes, Robert Speller, 1971; *Cities in Civilization,* Volume I, Robert Speller, 1971.

WORK IN PROGRESS: Cities in Our Time.

* * *

DUBLIN, Jack 1915-

PERSONAL: Born February 24, 1915, in Denver, Colo.; son of Max (a tailor) and Goldie (Aaron) Dublin; married Selma Morris, March 28, 1943; children: Mark David, Kirk Andrew, Lance Edward, Hollis Tobe. *Education:* University of Denver, student, 1932-33; George Washington University, A.B., 1941. *Politics:* Independent. *Religion:* Jewish. *Home and office:* 6303 Crathie Lane, Washington, D.C. 20016.

CAREER: Bureau of Federal Credit Unions, employee, 1937-55, as regional representative in Chicago, Ill., and various posts in Philadelphia, Pa., and Washington, D.C.; Michigan Credit Union League, Detroit, Mich., director of member services, 1955-62; Credit Union National Association and CUNA International, Inc., special representative for East Africa, Moshi, Tanzania, 1963-64, regional director of East Africa Project, Moshi, 1965-67, assistant global project director, Washington, D.C., 1967-68; Agency for International Development, Washington, D.C., chief of cooperatives development services, 1968-75; International Technical Services, Washington, D.C., president, 1975—. *Military service:* U.S. Army, 1944-46. *Member:* International Research Center on Rural Cooperative Communities.

WRITINGS: Credit Unions: Theory and Practice, Wayne State University Press, 1966, revised edition, 1967. Contributor to *Contact, Credit Union Way, Credit Union Bridge* (now *Credit Union Magazine*), *Journal of Rural Cooperation, Journal of Law and Economic Development,* and *Co-op News.*

AVOCATIONAL INTERESTS: Trailering and fishing.

BIOGRAPHICAL/CRITICAL SOURCES: Detroit News Pictorial Magazine, December 9, 1962; *Detroit Free Press,* August 15, 1965.

* * *

DuBOSE, LaRocque (Russ) 1926-

PERSONAL: Born April 24, 1926, in San Antonio, Tex.; son of Milton Lafayette (owner and operator of a motion picture theater) and Ethel (Gardner) DuBose; married Estelle Griner (a college teacher of French), January 29, 1951; children: Dennis Devereaux, Adam Campbell. *Education:* Trinity University, San Antonio, Tex., B.A., 1949; University of Texas, M.A., 1955; University of London, graduate study, summer, 1968. *Religion:* Episcopalian. *Agent:* Maurice Crain, Inc., 18 East 41st St., New York, N.Y. 10017. *Office:* Department of English, Western State College of Colorado, Gunnison, Colo. 81230.

CAREER: University of Texas Press, Austin, assistant editor, 1954-56; Indiana University Press, Bloomington, advertising and promotion manager, 1956-58; manager of motion picture theaters in Cotulla, Tex., 1958-63; Montana State University, Bozeman, instructor in English, 1963-66; Western State College of Colorado, Gunnison, assistant professor of English, 1966—. Member, Webster Players Ltd. (little theater group), Gunnison. *Military service:* U.S. Marine Corps, 1944-45, 1948; antiaircraft gunner aboard U.S.S. *Franklin* in World War II; became sergeant. *Member:* Modern Language Association of America, National Council of Teachers of English, American Association of University Professors.

WRITINGS: Aye, Aye, Sir! (juvenile novel), Lothrop, 1958; *Wild Horse, Wild Rider* (juvenile novel), Steck, 1967. Writer of study guides to *For Whom the Bell Tolls,* Cliff's Notes, 1965, *Of Human Bondage,* Barron's, 1968, and *Cyrano De Bergerac,* Cliff's Notes, 1969.

WORK IN PROGRESS: A study guide for *Barchester Towers,* for Cliff's Notes; *Shorty,* an adult novel; *The Great Adventure: A History of the Exploration of the Pacific* (junior or senior high school level).

AVOCATIONAL INTERESTS: "Range from skiing in the winter to amateur archaeology/anthropology in the summer—and there are dozens of things between."††

* * *

Du BROFF, Sidney 1929-

PERSONAL: Born July 18, 1929, in Chicago, Ill.; son of Harry (a proofreader) and Anna (Rubin) Du Broff; married Nedra Geiser (a psychologist), October 30, 1954. *Education:* Attended Los Angeles City College, one year. *Politics:* Socialist. *Religion:* "None. Culture: Jewish." *Home:* 7 The Corner, Grange Rd., London W.5, England.

CAREER: Author, journalist. *Member:* British Society of Authors. *Awards, honors:* One of winners of Golden Hedgehog international literary contest for story, "After All," and again for story, "The Happy Birthday."

WRITINGS: Woe to the Rebellious Children (novel), Geiser Productions, 1967; *Black Fuse* (novel), Everest, 1975; *Shooting, Fishing, and Gun Book I,* Spur Publications, 1976. Writer of radio and television scripts, and of short stories, articles, and reviews published in seventeen countries; correspondent for several German publications.

WORK IN PROGRESS: Shooting, Fishing, and Gun Book II.

SIDELIGHTS: Du Broff told *CA:* "My wife and I have lived abroad since 1960, having visited every country in Europe, except Albania, which continues to exclude U.S. citizens."

* * *

DUBUS, Andre 1936-

PERSONAL: Surname is pronounced De-*buse;* born August 11, 1936, in Lake Charles, La.; son of Andre Jules and Katherine (Burke) Dubus; married Patricia Lowe, February 22, 1958 (divorced, 1970); married Tommie Gail Cotter, June, 1975; children: (first marriage) Suzanne, Andre Jeb, Nicole. *Education:* McNeese State College, B.A., 1958; University of Iowa, M.F.A., 1966. *Politics:* "Vague." *Religion:* Roman Catholic. *Agent:* Philip G. Spitzer, 111-25 76th Ave., Forest Hills, N.Y. 11375. *Office:* Bradford College, Bradford, Mass. 01830.

CAREER: U.S. Marine Corps, commissioned lieutenant, 1958, left service as captain, 1964; Bradford College, Bradford, Mass., teacher of modern fiction and creative writing, 1966—.

WRITINGS: The Lieutenant (novel), Dial, 1967; *Separate Flights* (novella and seven stories), David R. Godine, 1975. Stories published in *Sewanee Review, Midwestern University Quarterly, Sage, New Yorker, Carlton Miscellany, Northwest Review, North American Review, Viva, Southern Writing in the Sixties,* and *Ploughshares.*

*   *   *

DUFF, Raymond S(tanley)   1923-

PERSONAL: Born November 2, 1923, in Hodgdon, Me.; son of Maurice C. (a farmer) and Ruth (Barton) Duff; married G. Joyce London (an elementary school teacher), November 28, 1945; children: Jane, Carole, Lori. *Education:* University of Maine, B.A., 1948; Yale University, M.D., 1952, M.P.H., 1959. *Home:* Newton Rd., Woodbridge, Conn. 06525. *Office:* School of Medicine, Yale University, New Haven, Conn. 06520.

CAREER: Yale-New Haven Hospital, New Haven, Conn., intern, then resident in pediatrics, 1952-55; New Haven Health Department, New Haven, Conn., director of Bureau of Medical Services, 1955-56; Yale-New Haven Hospital, director of ambulatory services, 1956-59; Yale University, New Haven, Conn., instructor in pediatrics and public health, 1956-59, instructor in pediatrics and sociology, 1959-62, assistant professor, 1962-67, associate professor of pediatrics, 1967—. *Military service:* U.S. Army, 1943-46; became second lieutenant. *Member:* American Association for the Advancement of Science, American Public Health Association (fellow), Academy of Pediatrics (fellow).

WRITINGS: (With A. B. Hollingshead) *Sickness and Society,* Harper, 1968; (contributor) John Kosa and Irving Fola, editors, *Poverty and Health,* Harvard University Press, 1974. Contributor to medical journals.

WORK IN PROGRESS: Several articles on research in pediatrics.

*   *   *

DUGGER, Ronnie   1930-

PERSONAL: Born April 16, 1930, in Chicago, Ill.; son of William Leroy and Mary (King) Dugger; married Jean Williams (a teacher), June 13, 1950; children: Gary McGregor, Celia Williams. *Education:* University of Texas, B.A., 1950; graduate study at University of Texas and Oxford University. *Home:* 1017 West 31st St., Austin, Tex. 78705. *Office: The Texas Observer,* 600 W. Seventh St., Austin, Tex. 78701. *Agent:* Mrs. Anton Myrer, McIntosh & Otis Inc., 18 East 41st St., New York, N.Y. 10017.

CAREER: Worked as newscaster, sports announcer, sports writer for *San Antonio Express,* San Antonio, Tex., political reporter for International News Service, British correspondent for Texas newspapers, assistant to the executive director for writing and research of National Security Training Commission, Washington, D.C.; *Texas Observer,* Austin, editor, 1954-61, 1963-66, editor-at-large and publisher, 1966—. Special correspondent to newspapers and magazines. Member of national advisory council of American Civil Liberties Union. *Member:* Authors Guild, Texas Institute of Letters, Texas Philosophical Society, Texas Folklore Society, Town and Gown (Austin).

WRITINGS: Dark Star: Hiroshima Reconsidered in the Life of Claude Eatherly of Lincoln Park, Texas, World, 1967; (editor) *Three Men in Texas; Bedichek, Webb, and Dobie: Essays by Their Friends in the "Texas Observer,"* University of Texas, 1967; *Our Invaded Universities: Form, Reform, and New Starts,* Norton, 1974. Contributor of articles to periodicals.

*   *   *

DUKES, Paul   1934-

PERSONAL: Born April 5, 1934, in Wallington, England; son of James Albert (an electrical contractor) and Margaret (Newman) Dukes; married Sara Dodd, March 28, 1966 (divorced December 6, 1972); married Rosemary Ann Mackay, May 6, 1974. *Education:* Peterhouse, Cambridge, B.A. (honors), 1954; University of Washington, Seattle, M.A., 1956; University of London, Ph.D., 1964. *Politics:* Socialist (Labour Party). *Religion:* Atheist. *Home:* 4 South Square, Aberdeenshire, Scotland. *Office:* History Department, Taylor Building, King's College, Aberdeen, Scotland.

CAREER: University of Maryland, Overseas Program, lecturer, 1959-64; University of Aberdeen, Aberdeen, Scotland, King's College, lecturer, 1964-71, senior lecturer in history, 1972—, reader, 1975—. *Military service:* British Army, 1956-58. *Member:* Historical Association, British Universities Association of Slavists, British Association for American Studies.

WRITINGS: Catherine the Great and the Russian Nobility, Cambridge University Press, 1967; *The Emergence of the Super-Powers,* Harper, 1970; *A History of Russia,* McGraw, 1974.

WORK IN PROGRESS: Pugachev Revolt; and a book on global impact of the Russian Revolution.

SIDELIGHTS: Paul Dukes is competent in French, Russian, and German.

*   *   *

DUNBAR, John Greenwell   1930-

PERSONAL: Born March 1, 1930, in London, England; son of John (a marine engineer) and Marie (Alton) Dunbar; married Elizabeth Mill Blyth, 1974. *Education:* Balliol College, Oxford, B.A., 1952, M.A., 1954. *Home:* Patie's Mill, Carlops, by Penicuik, Midlothian, Scotland. *Office:* Royal Commission on Ancient Monuments, 52-4 Melville St., Edinburgh, Scotland.

CAREER: Royal Commission on Ancient Monuments, Edinburgh, Scotland, staff member, 1953—. *Member:* Society of Antiquaries of London, Society of Antiquaries of Scotland (member of council, 1965-68, 1971-74), National Trust for Scotland (member of council, 1967-74), New Club (Edinburgh).

WRITINGS: The Historic Architecture of Scotland, Batsford, 1966; (contributor) Howard Colvin and John Harris, editors, *The Country Seat: Studies in the History of the British Country House,* Penguin, 1970; (contributor) John G. Hurst and M. W. Beresford, editors, *Deserted Medieval Villages: Studies,* Lutterworth Press, 1971, St. Martin's, 1972. Contributor to publications of Royal Commission on Ancient Monuments and to learned journals.

*   *   *

DUNDES, Alan   1934-

PERSONAL: Surname is pronounced *Dun*-deez; born September 8, 1934, in New York, N.Y.; son of Maurice (an attorney) and Helen (Rothschild) Dundes; married Carolyn Browne, September 8, 1958; children: Alison, Lauren, David. *Education:* Yale University, B.A., 1955, M.A.T., 1958; Indiana University, Ph.D., 1962. *Home:* 1590 La Vereda, Berkeley, Calif. 94708. *Office:* Department of Anthropology, University of California, Berkeley, Calif. 94720.

CAREER: University of Kansas, Lawrence, instructor in English, 1962-63; University of California, Berkeley, assistant professor of anthropology, 1963-65, associate professor, 1965-68, professor of anthropology and folklore, 1968—. *Military service:* U.S. Navy, 1955-57; became lieutenant. *Member:* American Folklore Society, American Anthropological Association, California Folklore Society. *Awards, honors:* Second place in Chicago Folklore Prize competition for *The Morphology of North American Indian Folktales;* Guggenheim fellowship, 1966-67; senior fellowship, National Endowment for the Humanities, 1972-73.

WRITINGS: The Morphology of North American Indian Folktales, Academic Scientarium Fennica, 1964; (editor) *The Study of Folklore,* Prentice-Hall, 1965; (editor) *Every Man His Way: Readings in Cultural Anthropology,* Prentice-Hall, 1968; (editor) *Mother Wit from the Laughing Barrel: Readings in the Interpretation of Afro-American Folklore,* Prentice-Hall, 1973; (with Alessandro Falassi) *La Terra in Piazza: An Interpretation of the Palic of Siena,* University of California Press, 1975; (with Carl R. Pagter) *Urban Folklore from the Paperwork Empire,* American Folklore Society, 1975; *Analytic Essays in Folklore,* Mouton, 1975. Contributor to journals in his field.

BIOGRAPHICAL/CRITICAL SOURCES: California Monthly, Volume LXXVI, number 1, October, 1965.

* * *

DUNN, Ethel (Deikman) 1932-

PERSONAL: Born March 30, 1932, in Pueblo, Calif.; daughter of Herman (an auto-parts dealer) and Eva (Lader) Deikman; married Stephen Porter Dunn (an anthropologist), October 6, 1956. *Education:* Rollins College, B.A. (with distinction), 1954; Columbia University, M.A. and Certificate of Russian Institute, 1956. *Home and office:* Highgate Road Social Science Research Station, 32 Highgate Rd., Berkeley, Calif. 94707.

CAREER: Fordham University, Bronx, N.Y., research associate, Institute of Contemporary Russian Studies, 1959-63; University of California, Berkeley, research anthropologist, Center for Slavic Studies, 1964-68; Highgate Road Social Science Research Station, Berkeley, Calif., executive secretary, 1969—.

WRITINGS: (With husband, Stephen P. Dunn) *The Peasants of Central Russia,* Holt, 1967; (editor with S. P. Dunn) *Introduction to Soviet Ethnography,* two volumes, Highgate Road Social Science Research Station, 1974. Collaborator with husband on articles, translations, and critical reviews in the field of Soviet anthropology and sociology.

WORK IN PROGRESS: A book on the history of religious sectarianism in the Soviet Union; a history of Molokans in America.

* * *

DUNN, Jerry G. 1916-

PERSONAL: Born June 30, 1916, in Dayton, Ohio. *Education:* Attended Ohio Wesleyan University, Northwestern University, and Newspaper Institute of America. *Office:* People's City Mission, Lincoln, Neb.

CAREER: A former advertising and public relations executive, Dunn says he "hit the alcoholic skids and came to his senses at the end of a two-year drunk when he picked up a Bible in a Texas prison cell"; following his release from prison, worked for newspapers until entering the ministry; he was ordained a Baptist minister, and served a church in Union, Neb.; staff member of Open Door Mission, Omaha, Neb., as director of public relations and rehabilitation, 1955-68; People's City Mission, Lincoln, Neb., executive director, 1968—. Lecturer at University of Nebraska School of Medicine, and for religious, civic, and other groups; conducts weekly half-hour television programs, "Plain Talk with Pastor Jerry," on Station KMTV, and "Slices from the Bread of Life," on Station KFAB, both Omaha. Member of board of directors and executive committee of Lincoln Council on Alcoholism and Drugs; chairman of Comprehensive Alcoholic Planning Committee for Lancaster County, Neb.; vice-president of Better Lincoln Committee; member of Region IV Mental Health Planning Committee; vice-president in charge of education for Nebraska Council on Alcohol Education Inc.

MEMBER: Agency Executives Association of Lincoln Community Services, Lincoln Evangelical Minister's Fellowship (president), Omaha Press Club (honorary member), Rotary International. *Awards, honors:* Service to Mankind award of Sertoma Club, 1959; Good Neighbor Award of National Conference of Christians and Jews, 1962; Omaha Lion's Club public service award, 1965; Citizen of Year award from Concord Club, 1965; Doulos (servant to community) award of Lincoln Fellowship of Churches, 1975.

WRITINGS: God Is for the Alcoholic, Moody, 1965; *Alcoholic Victorious,* Moody, 1969; *Yeah, Why Not Try God,* Light and Life Evangel, 1971; *The Christian in a Drinking Society,* Good News Broadcasting Association, 1974. Contributor to periodicals.

* * *

DUNNER, Joseph 1908-
(Germanicus, Alexander Roth)

PERSONAL: Born May 10, 1908, in Fuerth, Germany; son of Samuel (a government official) and Ella (Laske) Dunner; married Ada Bier, December 24, 1935; married Ruth Bevan (a political scientist), January 29, 1971. *Education:* Attended University of Berlin, 1927-30; University of Frankfurt am Main, M.A., 1932; University of Basel, Ph.D., 1934. *Politics:* Republican. *Religion:* Jewish. *Home:* 630 Shore Rd., Long Beach, N.Y. 11561. *Office:* Yeshiva Uniersity, Amsterdam Ave. and 186th St., New York, N.Y. 10033.

CAREER: Research fellow at International Institute of Social Research, 1930-35, and Brookings Institution, Washington, D.C., 1936-37; United Jewish Appeal, American Joint Distribution Committee, New York City, consultant on refugee problems and lecturer, 1937-42; Harvard University, Cambridge, Mass., lecturer, 1943-44; U.S. Office of War Information, chief of Intelligence Section, London, England, 1944-45, and of Press Control Section, Munich, Germany, 1945-46; Grinnell College, Grinnell, Iowa, professor of government, 1946-63, chairman of department of political science and director of Institute of International Affairs, 1946-58; Yeshiva University, New York City, David Petegorsky Professor of Political Science and International Relations, 1964—. Research fellow, New York University, 1942-43; visiting professor, Hebrew University of Jerusalem, 1950; Fulbright professor, University of Freiburg, 1963-64. Trustee, Institute for Mediterranean Affairs; director, American Friends of the Hebrew University.

MEMBER: International Political Science Association, American Political Science Association, American Society of International Law, American Academy of Political and Social Science. *Awards, honors:* Decorated by Government of France; Americanism Medal of Jewish War Veterans; Order of Ouissam Alaouite Cherifien by Sultan of Morocco, 1954.

WRITINGS: Die Gewerkschaften im Arbeitskampf, Philographischer Verlag, 1934; *If I Forget Thee . . .,* Dulane Press, 1937; (contributor) C. J. Fredrich, editor, *American Experiences in Military Government in World War II,* Rinehart, 1948; (contributor) Stuart G. Brown, editor, *Internationalism and Democracy,* Syracuse University Press, 1949; *The Republic of Israel: Its History and Its Promise,* McGraw, 1950; (contributor) Arnold J. Zurcher, editor, *Constitutions and Constitutional Trends Since World War II,* New York University Press, 1951; *Democratic Bulwark in the Middle East,* Grinnell College Press, 1952; *Baruch Spinoza and Western Democracy,* Philosophical Library, 1955; *Links-und Rechtsradikalismus in der Amerikanischen Politik,* Athenaum Verlag, 1964; *Zu Protokoll Gegeben* (autobiography), Desch Verlag, 1971.

Editor: *Major Aspects of International Politics,* Grinnell College Press, 1948; *Dictionary of Political Science,* Philosophical Library, 1964; *Hand Book of World History,* Philosophical Library, 1967.

Also co-author of *The Palestine Refugee Problem,* 1959, and editor of *Leftist and Rightest Radicalism in American Politics,* 1964. Contributor, under pseudonyms Germanicus and Alexander Roth, to the Swiss press and *Deutsche Freiheit,* 1933-35; also contributor to newspapers and magazines, including *Des Moines Register, Nation,* and *University Bookman.*

SIDELIGHTS: Dunner is fluent in French, and has some competence in Spanish and modern Hebrew.

BIOGRAPHICAL/CRITICAL SOURCES: Leo Schwartz, *The Redeemers,* Farrar, Straus, 1953; Joseph Dunner, *Zu Protokoll Gegeben,* Desch Verlag, 1971.

*   *   *

DUNNINGTON, Hazel Brain   1912-

PERSONAL: Born October 31, 1912, in Thorp, Wash.; daughter of George and Alice Pearl (Ellison) Brain; married Robert J. Dunnington, December 28, 1949 (deceased); children: Robert James, David Arthur. *Education:* Central Washington State College, B.A. in Ed., 1935; Northwestern University, M.A., 1940; also studied at Moholy Nagy School of Design, Chicago, Ill., 1942, and University of Washington, Seattle, at various periods between 1946-62. *Religion:* Protestant. *Home:* 111 East 10th, Ellensburg, Wash. 98926. *Office:* Edison Hall, Central Washington State College, Ellensburg, Wash. 98926.

CAREER: Elementary school teacher, Washington, 1932-38; Stanford University, Stanford, Calif., instructor in theatre arts, 1940-43; American Red Cross, recreation club director in India and China, 1943-46; Central Washington State College, Ellensburg, assistant professor of English and children's drama, 1946-50, assistant professor of children's drama, 1956-68, associate professor of children's

drama, 1968—. Creative dramatics workshop director, San Jose State College (now University), 1964, University of Toledo, 1965. Director of National Defense Education Act Institute in Poetry (for elementary school children), 1966. *Member:* Children's Theatre Conference, American Educational Theatre Association, American Association of University Professors, National Education Association, Washington Education Association, Northwest Drama Conference, Zeta Phi Eta, Delta Kappa Gamma.

WRITINGS: (Contributor) Geraldine Brain Siks, editor, *Creative Dramatics: An Art for Children,* Harper, 1958; (editor with sister, Geraldine Brain Siks) *Children's Theatre and Creative Dramatics,* University of Washington Press, 1961; (contributor of adaptations of works of Tolstoy and Ruskin) Siks, editor, *Children's Literature for Dramatization,* Harper, 1964; (contributor) Siks, editor, *Drama with Children,* Harper, 1976.

WORK IN PROGRESS: Drama curriculum for the elementary school; research in language development through oral interpretation of children's literature; research in work of James Barrie.

*   *   *

DUNSTAN, Reginald (Ernest)   1914-

PERSONAL: Born April 10, 1914, in Sunderland, Durham, England; son of Ernest Greenough (a proofreader) and Beatrice Alice (Hughes) Dunstan; first wife died in 1949, and second wife in 1964. *Education:* Educated at schools in Manchester and Salford, England; took economics subjects at North-West Polytechnic, London, England, 1951-54. *Politics:* Apolitical. *Religion:* None. *Home:* 7 Rosecroft Ave., London N.W.3, England. *Office:* Aims for Freedom and Enterprise, 5 Plough Pl., Fetter Lane, London E.C. 4, England.

CAREER: Journalist in Manchester, England, 1928-30; *Newcastle Journal,* Newcastle-upon-Tyne, England, variously reporter, radio editor, flying correspondent, and subeditor, 1930-39; Kemsley Newspapers Ltd., London, England, reporter and radio and light flying correspondent, 1946-47; Aims for Freedom and Enterprise (advocacy of free enterprise), London, England, 1947—, writer, editor of *Voice of Industry,* 1947-63, managing editor, 1963, and editorial director, 1965—. Managing director, Property Newspapers and Periodicals Ltd.; director, Tomorrow's Business Ltd. *Military service:* British Army, 1939-45; became warrant officer second class. *Member:* Institute of Public Relations, National Union of Journalists, Royal Automobile Club.

WRITINGS: (Editor with Michael Ivens) *The Case for Capitalism,* M. Joseph, 1967. Writer of pamphlets on government ownership and nationalization published by Aims of Industry Ltd. (now Aims for Freedom and Enterprise). Contributor to magazines and newspapers, including *Sunday Times, Headlight, Sunday Graphic.* Former editor, *Property.*

SIDELIGHTS: Dunstan has traveled widely in Europe and the United States, often on business. He has some proficiency in French, German, and Spanish, and knows a smattering of Italian, modern Greek, Serbo-Croat, Norwegian, and Dutch. *Avocational interests:* Jazz, the arts, fashion, changing mores, continental food and wine, and "everything except sports and politics."

DURBIN, Mary Lou 1927-

PERSONAL: Born April 3, 1927, in LaFayette, Ohio; daughter of Charles Frederick (a contractor) and Eunice Mildred (Parr) Durbin. Education: Eastern Michigan University, B.S., 1952, M.A., 1960, Specialist in Arts, 1966; University of Michigan, doctoral candidate, 1976—. Home: 11341 Parkview Dr., Plymouth Township, Mich.

CAREER: Custer Consolidated Schools, Munro, Mich., elementary teacher, 1947-55; Garden City (Mich.) public schools, primary teacher, 1958-60, teacher of trainable mentally retarded, 1960-66, teacher-consultant, 1966—, supervisor of special education, 1967-68, director of special services, 1973—. Evaluator of instructional materials for Instructional Materials Center for Handicapped Children and Youth, Michigan State University. Member: Michigan Teachers of the Mentally Handicapped (vice-president, 1966-67), Garden City Education Association, Phi Delta Kappa.

WRITINGS: Teaching Techniques: For Retarded and Pre-Reading Students, C.C Thomas, 1967. Contributor to education journals.

WORK IN PROGRESS: A book, tentatively entitled Learner Difficulties: Techniques for Their Correction.

* * *

DURNBAUGH, Donald F. 1927-

PERSONAL: Born November 16, 1927, in Detroit, Mich.; son of Floyd D. (an office worker) and Ruth E. (Tombaugh) Durnbaugh; married Hedwig T. Raschka (an instructor in German), July 10, 1952; children: Paul, Christopher, Renate. Education: Manchester College, B.A., 1949; University of Michigan, M.A., 1953; University of Pennsylvania, Ph.D., 1960. Politics: Independent. Religion: Church of the Brethren. Home: 18W647 22nd St., Lombard, Ill. 60148. Office: Bethany Theological Seminary, Oak Brook, Ill. 60521.

CAREER: Brethren Voluntary Service, relief worker in Austria and Germany, 1949-51; Brethren Service Commission, director of program in Austria, 1953-56; Juniata College, Huntingdon, Pa., instructor, 1958-60, assistant professor of church history, 1960-62; Bethany Theological Seminary, Oak Brook, Ill., associate professor, 1962-69, professor of church history, 1969—. European director in Marburg and Strasbourg, Brethren Colleges Abroad, 1964-65; Menno Simons lecturer, Bethel College, 1974. Member: American Historical Association, American Society of Church History, Organization of American Historians, North American Academy of Ecumenists, Brethren Journal Association. Awards, honors: Colonial Society of Pennsylvania Award, 1957, for best essay on colonial heritage by graduate student at University of Pennsylvania; Association of Theological Schools fellowship, 1971-72.

WRITINGS: (Compiler and translator) European Origins of the Brethren, Brethren Press, 1958; (with Lawrence W. Schultz), A Brethren Bibliography, 1713-1963, Brethren Press, 1964; The Brethren in Colonial America, Brethren Press, 1967; The Believers Church: The History and Character of Radical Protestantism, Macmillan, 1968; The Church of the Brethren: Past and Present, Brethren Press, 1971; (editor) Every Need Supplied: Mutual Aid and Christian Community in the Free Churches, 1525-1675, Temple University Press, 1974; (editor) To Serve the Present Age: The Brethren Service Story, Brethren Press, 1975. Contributor to church and historical journals.

WORK IN PROGRESS: Research on German-American religious communities in the United States, American Civil religion, and peace churches in the American revolution.

SIDELIGHTS: Durnbaugh's extensive travel in western Europe has provided him opportunities to study European-founded church groups such as the peace churches and Moravians, and to trace interrelationships back and forth across the Atlantic.

* * *

DURRANT, Digby 1926-

PERSONAL: Born March 18, 1926, in Rochester, Kent, England; son of Frank Baston (a company director) and Irene Maud (Drury) Durrant; married Cecily Katherine Barnes, June 18, 1959; children: Charlotte Fable. Education: University of Edinburgh, M.A. (honours), 1952. Politics: "It all depends." Religion: Church of England. Home: 11 Selwood Ter., London S.W. 7, England. Agent: Jonathan Clowes Ltd., 19 Jeffrey's Place, London NW1 9PP, England. Office: J. Walter Thompson, 40 Berkeley Sq., London W. 1, England.

CAREER: Former journalist and drama critic, including a period on the Daily Mail, Scotland; J. Walter Thompson (advertising), London, England, currently a director. Member: Savile Club (London).

WRITINGS: A Dragon World (novel), Hodder & Stoughton, 1967.

WORK IN PROGRESS: Daylight, a novel; "Strip Down an Onion and You've Nothing But Tears in Your Eyes," a television play.

SIDELIGHTS: Digby Durrant told CA, "Started to write to fulfill a long-standing need and found it 'seemed' to come naturally and satisfyingly, though clearly I have a lot to learn."

BIOGRAPHICAL/CRITICAL SOURCES: Books & Bookmen, July, 1967.††

* * *

DURRELL, Jacqueline Sonia Rasen 1929-
(Jacquie Durrell)

PERSONAL: Born November 17, 1929, in Manchester, England; daughter of John Thomas and Helen (Miles) Wolfenden; married Gerald Malcolm Durrell (a zoologist and author), February 26, 1951. Education: Attended state schools in England, 1933-48; music student in Manchester, England, 1948-51. Home and office: Les Augres Manor, Trinity, Jersey, Channel Islands. Agent: John Cushman Associates, Inc., 25 West 43rd St., New York, N.Y. 10036.

CAREER: Personal assistant to husband, founder of Jersey Zoological Park, Jersey, Channel Islands, 1951—; has accompanied him on major zoological expeditions, 1954—, including trips to Africa, South and Central America, Far East, and Australasia.

WRITINGS—Under name Jacquie Durrell: Beasts in My Bed (autobiographical), Atheneum, 1967. Contributor of articles to magazines in England and abroad.

WORK IN PROGRESS: Intimate Relations.

AVOCATIONAL INTERSTS: Music of all kinds, still photography, tennis, cricket, all types of internal combustion engines.

DURRENBERGER, Robert Warren 1918-

PERSONAL: Born October 2, 1918, in Perham, Minn.; son of John George (in real estate) and Angela (Weibeler) Durrenberger; married Bernadine Ann Steigel, July 15, 1946; children: Daniel Joseph, Mary Ann. *Education:* Moorhead State College, B.S., 1940; California Institute of Technology, B.S., 1941; University of Wisconsin, M.S., 1949; University of California, Los Angeles, Ph.D., 1955. *Home:* 3406 N. Valencia Lane, Phoenix, Ariz. 85018. *Office:* Laboratory of Climatology, Arizona State University, Tempe, Ariz. 85281.

CAREER: Junior high school teacher in Minnesota, 1940; R. S. Bacon Veneer Corp., Chicago, Ill., office manager, 1945-46; Western Auto Store, Gibbon, Wis., manager, 1946-47; University of Kentucky, Lexington, instructor, 1948-49; Los Angeles State College (now California State University), Los Angeles, assistant professor of geography and chairman of department, 1949-56; San Fernando Valley State College (now California State University), Northridge, associate professor, 1956-59, professor of geography, 1959-70, chairman of department, 1956-60, dean of graduate studies, 1960-63; California State College System, associate dean of academic planning, 1963-64; Arizona State University, Tempe, professor of geography, 1971—, director of laboratory of climatology and state climatologist for Arizona, 1970—. Project meteorologist for U.S. Air Force, summer, 1958. Visiting professor, University of California, Los Angeles, 1965-66, Adams State College, summer, 1967, University of Illinois, summer, 1968, Northern Arizona University, 1970. Instructor, University of California, Berkeley, extension services, 1968—. Member of California State Department of Education textbook review committee, 1956-60, and social studies curriculum committee, 1958; member of State Coordinating Council for Higher Education committee on faculty need and supply, 1961-63. *Military service:* U.S. Army Air Forces; served as meteorologist in South Pacific, 1940-45.

MEMBER: International Solar Energy Society, Association of American Geographers, American Meteorological Society (professional member), American Water Resources Association, Association of Pacific Coast Geographers, Sigma Xi. *Awards, honors:* National Science Foundation visiting scientist of Association of American Geographers, 1969-70.

WRITINGS: (Editor) *Patterns on the Land: Geographical, Historical and Political Maps of California,* Brewster Map, 1957, 3rd edition, Aegeus Publishing, 1965; (editor) *Readings in the Geography of California,* Brewster Map, 1959.

Sources of Information About California, Roberts Publishing (Northridge), 1961, 2nd edition published as *Sources of Information about California and the West,* Pacific Books, 1969; *Selected List of Social Science Publications,* Conservation Foundation (Northridge), 1961; *California and the Western States,* Roberts Publishing, 1963; (compiler with Leonard Pitt and Richard Preston), *The San Fernando Valley: A Selected Bibliography,* Urban Studies Institute, San Fernando Valley State College, 1966; (contributor) *Investigating the Earth,* Houghton, 1967; *Elements of California Geography,* National Press Books, 1968; *Aids to Geographical Research,* San Fernando Valley State College, 1968; *California: The Last Frontier,* Van Nostrand, 1969.

Environment and Man: A Bibliography, National Press Books, 1970; (editor), *California: Its People, Its Problems,*

Its Prospects, National Press Books, 1971; *Geographical Research and Writing,* Crowell, 1971; (editor and compiler) *Dictionary of the Environmental Sciences,* National Press Books, 1973; (contributor) *Regions of the United States,* Harper, 1972. Editor of Educational Outline Map Series for Brewster Map, 1957. Author of motion picture script, "California's Natural Regions," Arthur Barr Productions, 1963. Contributor of about twenty-five articles and reviews to journals. *California Geographer,* editor, 1969-70, member of editorial advisory board, 1971—; editor, *California* (wall map), 1976—.

WORK IN PROGRESS: The Climate of Arizona: An Atlas.

* * *

DURST, Paul 1921-
(Peter Bannon, John Chelton, Jeff Cochran, John Shane)

PERSONAL: Born April 23, 1921, in Archbald, Pa.; married W. Z. June Radcliffe, June 16, 1942 (died, 1972); married Doris L. Lamb, May 5, 1973; children: (first marriage) Donald P., Robin (Mrs. Bruno Koraca). *Education:* Attended Colorado State College (now Colorado State University), 1938-40, and Northwest Missouri State College (now Northwest Missouri State University), 1940-41. *Religion:* Catholic. *Home:* Robin's Roost, Thruxton, Andover, Hampshire, England. *Agent:* (Literary) Tony Masters, Whitewood Cottage, Swyffe Lane, Broad Oak, Heathfield, Sussex, England; (films) Gordon Harbord, Flat 9, Parkside, Knightsbridge, London SW1, England.

CAREER: St. Joseph News-Press, St. Joseph, Mo., reporter and editorial writer, 1946-48; Southwest Bell Telephone Co., Kansas City and St. Louis, Mo., advertising copywriter, 1948-50; advertising manager of Crofts Ltd. (engineers), Bradford, Yorkshire, England, 1959-60, and J. G. Graves Ltd. (mail order firm), Sheffield, England, 1960-62; free-lance writer. *Military service:* U.S. Naval Reserve, aviator, 1941-46; became lieutenant commander.

WRITINGS: Die Damn You!, Lion, 1952; *Bloody River,* World's Work, 1955; *Kid From Canadian,* World's Work, 1956; *Prairie Reckoning,* Fawcett, 1956; *John Law, Keep Out,* Ace, 1957; *Ambush at North Platte,* John Long, 1957; *River Flows West,* John Long, 1958; *Kansas Guns,* Avalon, 1958; *Dead Man's Range,* R. Hale, 1958; *Gun Doctor,* Bouregy, 1959; *Johnny Nation,* Mills & Boon, 1960; *Backlash,* Cassell, 1967; *Badge of Infamy,* Cassell, 1968; *Intended Treason: What Really Happened in the Gunpowder Plot,* W. H. Allen, 1970, A. S. Barnes, 1971; *A Roomful of Shadows* (autobiography), Dobson, 1975. Author with Alun Falconer of script for "The Informer"; researcher for film "Those Magnificent Men and Their Flying Machines"; author of "George Sand," a film script for Warner Bros.-Seven Arts Ltd., and "The Two Faces of Evil," a television mystery film for Moving Picture Co., London.

Under pseudonym Peter Bannon: *They Want Me Dead,* Jenkins, 1958; *If I Should Die,* Jenkins, 1959; *Whisper Murder Softly,* Jenkins, 1963.

Under pseudonym John Chelton: *My Deadly Angel,* Fawcett, 1955.

Under pseudonym Jeff Cochran: *Guns of Circle 8,* Mills & Boon, 1955.

Under pseudonym John Shane: *Along the Yermo Rim,* Mills & Boon, 1955; *Sundown in Sundance,* Mills & Boon, 1956; *Six-Gun Thursday,* Mills & Boon, 1956; *Gunsmoke Dawn,* Mills & Boon, 1957.

WORK IN PROGRESS: A historical novel, *Not a Stone upon a Stone*, built around the fulfillment of Christ's prophecy of the destruction of Jerusalem, 70 A.D.; *A Pocketful of Dreams*, second volume of autobiography.

SIDELIGHTS: Durst told *CA:* "For over two decades have financed globe-trotting by writing potboiling Westerns and suspense books . . . intend to concentrate on autobiography in future. Live quietly in modest little XVth century thatched cottage in small village in rural England, occasionally besieged by some of nine grandchildren. Love collecting antiques, especially clocks and guns, when we can find a bargain at an auction-sale."

* * *

DWORKIN, Rita 1928-

PERSONAL: Born December 28, 1928, in Brooklyn, N.Y.; daughter of Louis (a builder) and Helen (Rosenfeld) Sokolov; married Paul Dworkin (a production manager in construction), October 30, 1949; children: Steven Allen, Betsy Ruth. *Education:* University of California, Los Angeles, student, 1946-47; Brooklyn College (now Brooklyn College of the City University of New York), B.A., 1949; Long Island University, M.S., 1964. *Politics:* Democrat. *Religion:* Jewish. *Home:* 12 McLane Dr., Dix Hills, N.Y. 11746.

CAREER: Clerical employee at Pace College (now Pace University), New York, N.Y., 1949-50, and Associated Hospital Service of New York, 1950-51; East Meadow (N.Y.) Public Library, trainee, 1963-64, assistant reference librarian, 1964-67, head of adult services, 1967—. *Member:* Nassau County Library Association.

WRITINGS: (With Irving Adelman) *Modern Drama: A Checklist of Critical Literature on Twentieth-Century Plays,* Scarecrow, 1967; (editor with Adelman) *The Contemporary Novel: A Checklist of Critical Literature on the British and American Novel Since 1945,* Scarecrow, 1972.

WORK IN PROGRESS: With Irving Adelman, *Poetry Criticism: A Checklist of Critical Literature on British and American Poetry,* publication by Scarecrow expected in 1978.

* * *

DYAL, William M., Jr. 1928-

PERSONAL: Born May 13, 1928, in Austin, Tex.; son of William M. (an electrician) and Mildred (Taylor) Dyal; married Edith Colvin, May 6, 1950. *Education:* Baylor University, A.B., 1949; Southern Baptist Theological Seminary, B.D., 1953. *Office:* Inter-American Foundation, 1515 Wilson Blvd., Rosslyn, Va. 22209.

CAREER: Southern Baptist Foreign Mission Board, missionary in Guatemala and Costa Rica, 1953-59, field secretary in Buenos Aires, Argentina, 1960-61, associate personnel secretary in Richmond, Va., 1962-63; Southern Baptist Convention, Christian Life Commission, Nashville, Tenn., director of organization, 1963-67; Peace Corps of Colombia, Bogota, director, 1967-69, regional director for North Africa, Near East, and South Asia, 1969-71; Inter-American Foundation, Rosslyn, Va., president, 1971—. *Awards, honors:* Association Press Award ($2,000) for best manuscript on youth and contemporary issues, 1966, for *It's Worth Your Life;* Gold Medal of Santander for outstanding service to country, presented by President Lleras Restrepo of Columbia, 1969.

WRITINGS: *It's Worth Your Life: A Christian Challenge to Youth Today,* Association Press, 1967; *Un Desefio al Discipulado,* Mundo Hispano (Buenos Aires), 1970.

WORK IN PROGRESS: *The Responsible Funder: A New Look at Foundations.*

* * *

DYE, David L. 1925-

PERSONAL: Born August 5, 1925, in Seattle, Wash.; son of Ira W. (an engineer) and Helen (Stonecypher) Dye; married Bernice Born, June 25, 1952; children: Daniel, Rebecca, Stephanie. *Education:* University of Washington, Seattle, B.S.E.E., 1945, Ph.D., 1952. *Religion:* Protestant. *Home:* 12825 Southeast 45th Place, Bellevue, Wash. 98006.

CAREER: University of California Medical Center, San Francisco, research associate in radiological laboratory, 1954-55, 1958-59; Gordon College, Rawalpindi, West Pakistan, head of physics department, 1955-58; Boeing Co., Seattle, Wash., research specialist, Aerospace Division, 1959-62, chief of radiation effects laboratory, 1962-64, chief of radiation effects unit, 1964-68; U.S. Air Force Special Weapons Center, Kirtland Air Force Base, N.M., senior scientist (TREES), 1968-70; Boeing Co., nuclear and space physics scientist, 1970—. *Military service:* U.S. Naval Reserve, active duty, 1942-46, 1952-53; became lieutenant. *Member:* American Physical Society, American Association for the Advancement of Science, American Scientific Affiliation, Institute of Electrical and Electronics Engineers.

WRITINGS: (Contributor) E. G. Stanford, editor, *Progress in Applied Materials Research,* Volume V, Heywood & Co., 1964; *Faith and the Physical World,* Eerdmans, 1966.

WORK IN PROGRESS: A book on limitations that people place on their ideas of God; research on radiation environment correlation; a science fiction novel.

* * *

DYE, James W(ayne) 1934-

PERSONAL: Born December 22, 1934, in Appalachia, Va.; son of Earnest Pierce (a railroad carman) and Zella Mae (McCloud) Dye; married Loreata Phipps (a purchasing assistant), July 25, 1955; children: Melissa Diane. *Education:* Carson-Newman College, A.B., 1955; New Orleans Baptist Theological Seminary, B.D., 1958; Tulane University of Louisiana, Ph.D., 1960. *Home:* 405 Fairmont Dr., De Kalb, Ill. 60115. *Office:* Northern Illinois University, De Kalb, Ill. 60115.

CAREER: New Orleans Baptist Theological Seminary, New Orleans, La., fellow, 1958-60; Washington University, St. Louis, Mo., instructor, 1960-63, assistant professor of philosophy, 1963-66; Northern Illinois University, De Kalb, associate professor of philosophy and director of Philosophy Institute, 1966—. *Member:* American Philosophical Association, Metaphysical Society of America, Society for Phenomenology and Existential Philosophy, Society for Ancient Greek Philosophy, Society for the Study of Process Philosophy, American Association of University Professors, Charles S. Peirce Society, American Civil Liberties Union, Southern Society for Philosophy and Psychology, Southern Society for the Philosophy of Religion, Illinois Philosophy Conference, Northern Illinois Philosophical Association.

WRITINGS: (Editor with William H. Forthman) *Religions of the World,* Appleton, 1967. Contributor to *Encyclopedia of Philosophy;* also contributor to professional journals. Associate editor, *Philosophy Forum.*

WORK IN PROGRESS: A book on Plato's concept of causation; research in the philosophy of culture and the history of philosophy.

SIDELIGHTS: James Dye reads Latin, Greek, Spanish, French, German. *Avocational interests:* Electronics, music, psychology, photography.

* * *

DYER, Charles (Raymond) 1928-
(C. Raymond Dyer, Raymond Dyer, R. Kraselchik, Charles Stretton, Renshaw Stretton)

PERSONAL: Born July 5, 1928, in Shrewsbury, Shropshire, England; son of James Sidney (an actor) and Florence (Renshaw) Dyer; married Fiona Susan Thomson (an actress), July 7, 1959; children: John, Peter, Timothy. *Education:* Attended Queen Elizabeth's School, Hertfordshire, England. *Home:* Old Wob, Austenwood Common, Gerrards Cross, Buckinghamshire, England.

CAREER: Playwright, novelist, actor, director. Worked as a call-boy at Hippodrome Theatre, Manchester, England, 1938. Actor in stage plays in as many as 250 roles, including: Made his debut as Lord Harpenden in "While the Sun Shines," New Theatre, Crewe, Cheshire, 1947; Duke, "Worm's Eye View," Whitehall Theatre, London, March 5, 1947, tour, 1948-50; Digger, "The Hasty Heart," tour, 1950; Wilkie, "No Trees in the Street," tour, 1951; Turtle, "Turtle in the Soup," London, 1953; Launcelot Gobbo, "The Merchant of Venice," London, 1954; Flash Harry, "Dry Rot," Whitehall Theatre, London, August 31, 1954, tour, 1954; Maitre d'Hotel, "Room for Two," Prince of Wales' Theatre, London, March 7, 1955; Syd Fish, "Painted Sparrow," Opera House Theatre, Cork, Ireland, summer, 1956; Shylock, "The Merchant of Venice," Bromley, Kent, 1959; Viktor, "Red Cabbages and Kings," Portsmouth, Hampshire, and tour, 1960; Percy, "Rattle of a Simple Man," London, 1963; Mickleby, "Wanted—One Body!," Guildford, Surrey, 1966. Actor in screenplays include: "Cuptie Honeymoon," 1947; "Britannia Mews," 1949; "Road Sense," 1950; "Off the Record," 1952; "Pickwick Papers," 1952; "Dockland Case," 1953; "Strange Case of Blondie," 1953; "Naval Patrol," 1959; "Loneliness of a Long Distance Runner," Continental, 1962; "Mouse on the Moon," 1962; Chalky in "Rattle of a Simple Man," Reade-Sterling, 1964; "Knack," United Artists, 1965; "How I Won the War," 1967; "Staircase," 1968. Also acted in television series, "Hugh and I," BBC-TV, 1965. Director of many plays for stage, screen, and television, including his television adaptation of "Wanted—One Body!," BBC-TV, 1958. *Military service:* Royal Air Force, 1943-46; served as navigator; became flying officer.

WRITINGS—Plays: (Under name C. Raymond Dyer) "Clubs Are Sometimes Trumps," first produced in Staffordshire at Hippodrome Theatre, April 12, 1948; (under name C. Raymond Dyer) "Who On Earth," first produced in London at Q Theatre, July 24, 1951; (under name C. Raymond Dyer) "Turtle in the Soup," first produced in London at Intimate Theatre, December 14, 1953; "The Jovial Parasite," first produced in London at Intimate Theatre, December 6, 1954; "Single Ticket Mars," first produced in stock at New Theatre, Kent, December 12, 1955; *Time, Murderer, Please* (first produced in Portsmouth at King's Theatre, October 15, 1956; subsequently

toured British Isles, 1957-58, with "Poison in Jest," 1956), English Theatre Guild, 1962; *Wanted—One Body!* (toured British Isles, 1956-58), English Theatre Guild, 1961; (author and actor) "Poison in Jest," staged by Dyer for tour of British Isles, 1958-59; (and composer of theme music under name Stretton) "Prelude to Fury," first produced in London at Intimate Theatre, November 23, 1959; (playwright under pseudonym Kraselchik; composer of theme music under name Stretton) "Red Cabbages and Kings," first produced in stock at Southsea at King's Theatre, summer, 1960; *Rattle of a Simple Man* (first produced in London at Garrick Theatre, September 19, 1962; opened on Broadway at Booth Theatre, April 17, 1963), Samuel French, 1963; "Gorillas Drink Milk" (adaption of a play by John Murphy), first produced in Coventry, 1964; *Staircase* (first produced by Royal Shakespeare Company, at Aldwych Theatre, November 2, 1966; opened on Broadway at Biltmore Theatre, January 10, 1968), Penguin, 1966, Grove, 1969; *Mother Adam* (directed by the author; two-act; first produced in London's West End at Arts Theatre, November 30, 1971), Davis-Poynter, 1972; *A Hot Godly Wind* (one-act; first produced by British Youth Theatre at Manchester Festival, March 9, 1975), Hutchinson, 1972.

Others: *Rattle of a Simple Man* (novelization of his original play), Elek, 1964; *Rattle of a Simple Man* (screenplay), Elstree, 1964; "Insurance Italian Style" (screenplay), Twentieth Century-Fox, 1967; "Staircase" (screenplay), Twentieth Century-Fox, 1969; *Staircase* (novelization), Doubleday, 1969 (published in England as *Staircase; or, Charlie Always Told Harry Almost Everything,* W. H. Allen, 1969); "Brother Sun and Sister Moon" (screenplay), Paramount, 1969.

WORK IN PROGRESS: A play, "The Ducking Stool."

SIDELIGHTS: Dyer specialises in commenting upon human loneliness, as in "Staircase" and "Rattle"; and, to bring home its potency, he uses few actors. A French critic recently called Dyer "England's master of the duologue—one might almost say 'dyerlogue.'" Walter Lucas wrote: "Dyer, who is a considerable craftsman, in both of his works 'Staircase' and 'Rattle' makes no concessions to shrillness but instead gives us pictures of human beings who are not particularly good or bad but are alive."

When *Staircase* opened on Broadway, Brendan Gill wrote: "You must see *Staircase* as nearly as possible without pre-possession; let your instruction and astonished pleasure start with the rising of the curtain." Gill, certainly, did not anticipate his own favorable response to the play. "If some sort of prize had been offered for the play that, before it reached Broadway, sounded most likely to render any theatre as dark as the grave," he wrote, "I think my candidate this season would have been the English import *Staircase,* by a playwright named Charles Dyer." But Gill came away predicting that "the Biltmore will be bright and ungrave-like for many a month to come, thanks to the admirable dovetailing of the talents of Mr. Dyer."

Jack Kroll, on the other hand, found *Staircase* "just much whoopdedo about nothing." Kroll called the play "soggy" and "sticky," and he added: "Dyer takes advantage of the new permissiveness to write a tinny little oratorio full of as many swishes and giggles as he can muster.... Dyer's view of human relationships, sexual, emotional and tonsorial, is simply so much cornball shaving-soap opera." Gill agreed that Dyer "has taken terrible chances in the course of his play, beginning with the calculated skimpiness of its plot and the moral and intellectual poverty of his protagonists. They are miserable creatures in thought, word, and deed, and in real life we would not consent to endure their whining talkativeness for five minutes." But, Gill concludes, "Mr. Dyer finds in them—and encourages us to find in them—genuine humor, genuine pathos."

Walter Kerr feels that Dyer's *Staircase* is "the simplest and most honest treatment of homosexuality I have come across in the theatre.... Outlines are indicated, though, and the play can be seen for what it is: small, special, surprisingly understanding."

Director Stanley Donen says of the film "Staircase," that "This is a story that says attention must be paid. It's aimed at people who feel that those who may be different have no right to any feelings. You know, the ones who say, 'He's a freak and has no feelings.' And it says to those critical stone-throwers, 'Are *you* human beings? Now that you've seen the Charlies and Harrys, do you tell them you don't care for them?' I wanted to do this as an extremely personal human document." Co-star of the film, Rex Harrison, concurs that "... there is pathos and deep humanity in this work. The story is really about loneliness and human failure. These two subjects are so much a part of everyone's life that most people will not, or do not, recognize their presence. I would like to hope that in 'Staircase' I can shed a little more light on these universal frailties. If so, we shall have accomplished our artistic purpose."

Rattle of a Simple Man, Staircase, and *Mother Adam* form a trilogy on loneliness. Of the most recent, *Mother Adam,* a reviewer for *Variety* states that "In this new work, Dyer again analyzes and dissects the agony of loneliness, this time centering on an arthritic, bed-ridden mother, who lives with and dominates her grown son. While she teases and browbeats her way through each demanding day, he tries to maintain his sanity by acting out a number of fantasies for her, but the wind up of the virtually plotless play finds the two still tragically linked."

Dyer writes *CA* that he "still concentrates on one play every four-or-so years, first writing a novel to establish his facts." He states that he is "trying to bring a more elaborate language into live drama, more poetry and extravagance, which had occasionally piqued critics."

Staircase and *Rattle of a Simple Man* have been translated into about twenty languages and, as most of his other plays, have been performed all over the world.

BIOGRAPHICAL/CRITICAL SOURCES: Sunday Times, April 24, 1966, December 5, 1971, April 29, 1973; *Drama,* winter, 1967; *New Yorker,* January 20, 1968; *Newsweek,* January 22, 1968; *Irish Tatler and Sketch,* December, 1969.

* * *

DYSON, Anne Jane 1912-

PERSONAL: Born March 5, 1912, in Amite, La.; daughter of Andrew Jackson and Estelle (Vernon) Holton; married Harold F. Dyson (an accountant), June 18, 1937; children: Deanna Barnard (Mrs. Marshall Lyne Posey, Jr.). *Education:* Louisiana State University, A.B., 1934, B.S. in L.S., 1935. *Politics:* Democratic. *Religion:* Baptist. *Home:* 7575 Jefferson Hwy., Baton Rouge, La. 70806. *Office:* Louisiana State University Library, Baton Rouge, La. 70803.

CAREER: Louisiana State University Library, Baton Rouge, general assistant, 1935-37, reference librarian, 1937-62, assistant librarian, Humanities Division, 1962—. Active in Baton Rouge Little Theatre and Community Concert Association. *Member:* American Library Association, American Association of University Women, Louisiana Library Association, Baton Rouge Library Club (president, 1958-59), Campus Club (Louisiana State University).

WRITINGS—All compiled with Helen H. Palmer; all published by Shoe String: *American Drama Criticism; Interpretations, 1890-1965 inclusive, of American Drama since the First Play Produced in America,* 1967; *European Drama Criticism,* 1968; *American Drama Criticism: Supplement 1,* 1970; *European Drama Criticism: Supplement 1,* 1970, *Supplement 2,* 1974; *English Novel Explication Criticisms to 1972,* 1973.

* * *

EAGLE, Dorothy 1912-

PERSONAL: Born March 10, 1912, in Newcastle upon Tyne, England; daughter of Edwin (keeper of National Gallery, London) and Eva (Postance) Glasgow; married Charles Henry Eagle, April 29, 1941; children: Roger Charles, Martin Swinburne, John Richard. *Education:* Bedford College, University of London, B.A., 1934. *Home:* 25 Linkside Ave., Oxford, England. *Office:* Clarendon Press, Oxford, England.

CAREER: London County Council, London, England, children's care (medical) organizer, 1936-38; city almoner (social worker), Oxford, England, 1938-42; Clarendon Press, Oxford, England, member of editorial staff, 1953—. Director, Mary Glasgow Publications Ltd. (language magazines for schools). *Member:* National Council of Women (Oxford committee, 1966-69).

WRITINGS—All published by Oxford University Press: (Editor with J. Coulson, C. T. Carr, and L. M. Hutchinson) *The Oxford Illustrated Dictionary,* 1962, 2nd edition (sole editor), 1975; (editor with Paul Harvey) *The Oxford Companion to English Literature,* 4th edition, 1967; (editor) *The Concise Dictionary of English Literature,* 2nd edition (Eagle was not associated with first edition), 1970; (assistant to editor) *The Oxford Companion to Art,* 1970; (assistant to editor) *The Oxford English-Arabic Dictionary,* 1972. Assistant to editor, *Review of English Studies.*

WORK IN PROGRESS: A literary guide to the British Isles.

* * *

EARLE, Olive L(ydia) 1888-

PERSONAL: Born 1888, in London, England; daughter of E. J. Vavasour (an importer) and Elizabeth (Bedbrook) Earle; married Sydney Hannon, January 16, 1920 (deceased); married Harry R. Daugherty (an artist), September 12, 1934 (deceased). *Education:* Attended a private school in England and National Academy of Design, New York, N.Y. *Politics:* Liberal. *Religion:* Unitarian Universalist. *Home:* 154 Highview Ave., Staten Island, N.Y. 10301.

CAREER: Writer and illustrator of nature books for children; illustrator on nature subjects for encyclopedias. Work has been exhibited in group shows at American Museum of Natural History, Brooklyn Museum, Los Angeles Museum, and elsewhere.

WRITINGS—Self-illustrated; all published by Morrow: *State Birds and Flowers,* 1951; *Thunder Wings,* 1951; *Birds and Their Nests,* 1952; *Robins in the Garden,* 1953; *Paws, Hoofs, and Flippers,* 1954; *The Octopus,* 1955; *Swans of*

Willow Pond, 1955; *Mice at Home and Afield,* 1957; *Crickets,* 1956; *White Patch: A City Sparrow,* 1958; *Pigs: Tame and Wild,* 1959; *State Trees,* 1960, revised edition, 1973; *Camels and Llamas,* 1961; *Birds of the Crow Family,* 1962; *Squirrels in the Garden,* 1963; *Strange Lizards,* 1964; *Birds and Their Beaks,* 1965; *Strange Companions in Nature,* 1965; *The Strangler Fig and Other Strange Plants,* 1967; *Strange Fishes of the Sea,* 1968; *Praying Mantis,* 1969; *The Rose Family,* 1970; *Peas, Beans, and Licorice,* 1971; *Pond and Marsh Plants,* 1972; *Scavengers,* 1973; (with Michael Kantor) *Animals and Their Ears,* 1974; (with Kantor) *Nuts,* 1975. Contributor of illustrations and articles to nature magazines.

WORK IN PROGRESS: Another nature book.

SIDELIGHTS: Olive Earle told *CA:* "I garden like crazy. The other aspects of my life I do not consider of public interest."

*   *   *

EAST, John Marlborough 1936-

PERSONAL: Born September 10, 1936, in London, England. *Home and office:* 22, Gibson's Hill, Norbury, London S.W. 16 3JP, England.

CAREER: Actor in England since his teens, playing on tour, in vaudeville and pantomime, and in more than 450 television productions; stage roles include Polyte le Mou in "Irma la Douce" at Lyric Theatre, London; has appeared with most of the leading British television comedians, and presented entertainment and current affairs programs on both radio and television. Has made over one thousand radio broadcasts. Runs own publicity and public relations company.

WRITINGS: '*Neath the Mask: The Story of the East Family,* Allen & Unwin, 1967. Contributor to *The Oxford Companion to the Theatre* and *Film Review.* Author of radio and television scripts. Contributor of articles and drama criticism to periodicals.

WORK IN PROGRESS: Two books, *The Cheeky Chappie* and *The Other Side of Show Business.*

SIDELIGHTS: East is the grandson and namesake of John M. East, and a member of a family identified for generations with the music halls and working class theatres of London.

*   *   *

EASTMAN, Arthur M(orse) 1918-

PERSONAL: Born September 8, 1918, in Roslyn, N.Y.; son of Fred (a teacher and writer) and Lilla Frances (Morse) Eastman; married Berenice Miller, June 1, 1941; married Ann Heibreder, November 10, 1973; children: (first marriage) Barbara, Richard W., John M., Martha. *Education:* Oberlin College, B.A., 1940; Yale University, M.A., 1942, Ph.D., 1947. *Office:* Carnegie-Mellon University, Schenley Park, Pittsburgh, Pa. 15213.

CAREER: University of New Hampshire, Durham, instructor in English, 1946-47; University of Michigan, Ann Arbor, instructor, 1947-51, assistant professor, 1951-57, associate professor, 1957-63, professor of English, 1963-68; Carnegie-Mellon University, Pittsburgh, Pa., professor of English and head of department, 1968—. Writer and teacher of taped American literature course, "Franklin to Frost," for Midwest Program of Television Instruction, 1961-62; Ann Arbor chairman of Democratic Party, 1950-52. *Military service:* U.S. Army, 1943-46; became sergeant. *Member:* Modern Language Association of America, National Council of Teachers of English (member of commission on curriculum), Shakespeare Association of America. *Awards, honors:* University of Michigan Class of 1923 Award for excellence in teaching, 1956; Guggenheim fellowship, 1957-58; National Endowment for the Humanities senior fellow, 1973-74.

WRITINGS: (Editor with A. W. Allison and A. J. Carr) *Masterpieces of the Drama,* Macmillan, 1957, 3rd edition, 1974; (editor with G. B. Harrison) *Shakespeare's Critics,* University of Michigan Press, 1964; (general editor with others) *The Norton Reader,* Norton, 1965, 3rd edition, 1973; *A Short History of Shakespearean Criticism,* Random House, 1968; (editor with others) *The Norton Anthology of Poetry,* Norton, 1970.

WORK IN PROGRESS: Editing the manuscript autobiography of John Wrenshall, 1761-1821.

*   *   *

EASTON, Loyd D(avid) 1915-

PERSONAL: Born July 29, 1915, Rockford, Ill.; son of Boyd John (a securities dealer) and Elda (Holden) Easton; married Millison Shedd, June 14, 1942 (died December 21, 1962); married Martha Hutchison, November 28, 1963; children: (first marriage) David Shedd, Carol Beth, Judith Ann; (stepchildren) Martha C. (Mrs. David Anderson), Anne S. (Mrs. G. Edward Lundin). *Education:* De Pauw University, B.A., 1937; Boston University, M.A., 1939, Ph.D., 1942; additional graduate study at Harvard University, 1941-42, and University of Glasgow, 1946. *Politics:* Social Democrat. *Religion:* Methodist. *Home:* 998 Braumiller Rd., Delaware, Ohio 43015. *Office:* Department of Philosophy, Ohio Wesleyan University, Delaware, Ohio 43015.

CAREER: Ohio Wesleyan University, Delaware, instructor, 1946-47, assistant professor, 1947-50, associate professor, 1950-55, professor of philosophy, 1955—, chairman of department, 1952—. Visiting professor at Ohio State University, 1957, and Methodist Theological School in Ohio, 1960-61, 1963-64. *Military service:* U.S. Army, 1942-46; served in Europe; received Commendation Ribbon.

MEMBER: American Philosophical Association, Society for Religion in Higher Education (fellow), American Association of University Professors (president of Ohio Conference, 1950-52; member of national council, 1960-63), League for Industrial Democracy, American Civil Liberties Union, Ohio Philosophical Association (president, 1964-67), Phi Beta Kappa, Omicron Delta Chi. *Awards, honors:* Grants from American Council of Learned Societies, 1961-62, and American Association for State and Local History, 1963.

WRITINGS: (Co-author) *Values and Policy in American Society,* William C. Brown, 1954; (co-editor) *Readings in Social Policy,* William C. Brown, 1954; *Ethics, Policy and Social Ends,* William C. Brown, 1955; (contributor) J. Sherwood Weber, editor, *Good Reading,* revised edition, New American Library, 1964; *Hegel's First American Followers: The Ohio Hegelians,* Ohio University Press, 1966; (editor and translator with Kurt Guddat) *Writings of the Young Marx on Philosophy and Society,* Doubleday, 1967; (editor and author of introduction) D. S. Miller, *Philosophical Analysis and Human Welfare: Essays and Chapters from Six Decades,* D. Reidel, 1975. Contributor of articles and reviews to professional journals.

WORK IN PROGRESS: Writing on Owenite and Fourierist Socialist colonies in Ohio, 1825-1850; a study of Marx's view of individual liberty.

SIDELIGHTS: Easton reads German and French. Avocational interests: Gardening and lawn care, sailing, stamp collecting.

* * *

EATON, Leonard K. 1922-

PERSONAL: Born February 3, 1922, in Minneapolis, Minn.; son of Leo Kimball (a lawyer) and Elizabeth (Barber) Eaton; married Carrol Faith Kuehn, August 15, 1947; children: Mark R., Elisabeth K. Education: Williams College, B.A., 1943; Harvard University, M.A., 1948, Ph.D., 1951. Politics: Democrat. Religion: Episcopalian. Home: 2601 Heather Way, Ann Arbor, Mich. 48104. Office: School of Architecture and Design, University of Michigan, Ann Arbor, Mich. 48104.

CAREER: University of Michigan, Ann Arbor, instructor, 1950-56, assistant professor, 1956-60, associate professor, 1960-63, professor of architecture, 1963—. Visiting professor of history, Wayne State University, Detroit, Mich., summers, 1959-60. Military service: U.S. Army, 10th Mountain Division, World War II. Member: Society of Architectural Historians, American Institute of Architects (associate member), Research Club (University of Michigan). Awards, honors: Ford Foundation fellow, 1954-55; Rehmann fellowship of the American Institute of Architects, 1956; Fulbright Foundation fellow, 1962-63.

WRITINGS: New England Hospitals 1790-1833, University of Michigan Press, 1956; Landscape Artist in America, University of Chicago Press, 1964; Two Chicago Architects and Their Clients: Frank Lloyd Wright and Howard Van Doran Show, M.I.T. Press, 1969; American Architecture Comes of Age, M.I.T. Press, 1972. Contributor of articles to learned journals.

WORK IN PROGRESS: Warehouses and Warehouse Districts in Midwestern Cities.

* * *

EATON, Trevor 1934-

PERSONAL: Born March 26, 1934, in London, England; son of William (a postmaster) and Cecilia (Davies) Eaton; married Beryl Conley (a teacher), September 29, 1958; children: Michael, Rachel, Ruth, William. Education: New College, Oxford, M.A. (honors), 1958. Religion: Church of England. Home: 18 Highfield Rd., Willesborough, Ashford, Kent, England.

CAREER: University of Erlangen, Erlangen, West Germany, lecturer in English, 1958-60; University of New South Wales, Newcastle, Australia, lecturer in Old and Middle English and English language, 1961-64; Norton Knatchbull School, Ashford, Kent, England, teacher, 1965—, head of philosophy department, 1974—. Member of Examination Panel in Logic, University of London, 1972—. Military service: Royal Air Force, National Service, 1953-55. Member: Linguistics Association of Great Britain (section convener, Linguistics and Literature Section, 1972—).

WRITINGS: The Semantics of Literature, Mouton & Co., 1966; Theoretical Semics, Mouton & Co., 1972; (editor) Poetries, Their Media and Ends: A Collection of Essays by I. A. Richards Published to Celebrate his 80th Birthday, Mouton & Co., 1974; (contributor) A. P. Foulks, editor, The Uses of Criticism, Herbert Lang Verlag, 1975. Editor, Journal of Literary Semantics, 1970—.

AVOCATIONAL INTERESTS: Natural history, astronomy, music.

* * *

EBON, Martin 1917-

PERSONAL: Born May 27, 1917, in Hamburg, Germany; son of Julius (a manufacturer) and Martha (Ludwig) Ebon; married Chariklia S. Baltazzi, April 25, 1949; children: Andrew Richard. Education: University of Hamburg, M.A., 1934. Home: 5616 Netherland Ave., New York, N.Y. 10471. Office: Lombard Associates, Inc., 355 Lexington Ave., New York, N.Y. 10017.

CAREER: Settled in the United States in 1938; held various positions in book and magazine retailing, and was managing editor of Foreign Language Division, Overseas News Agency; during World War II was on the staff of U.S. Office of War Information, and served briefly as an information officer with the U.S. Department of State; U.S. Information Agency, New York City, information officer on Far Eastern desks, 1950-52; Hill & Knowlton, Inc. (public relations), New York City, account executive, 1952-53; Parapsychology Foundation, Inc., New York City, administrative secretary and editor, 1953-65; Lombard Associates, Inc. (public relations and publications consultants), New York City, president, 1962—. Consulting editor, New American Library (publishers), 1966—; executive editor of hardcover book division, Playboy Press, 1971-72. Lecturer in Division of Social Sciences, New School for Social Research, 1949-50, 1955-56, 1967. Consultant, Foundation for Research on the Nature of Man, 1966-67.

MEMBER: American Association for the Advancement of Science, American Sociological Association, American Academy of Political and Social Science, American Society for Psychical Research. Awards, honors: Freedoms Foundation Award for editorials in Saturday Evening Post, 1948-62.

WRITINGS: World Communism Today, McGraw, 1948; Malenkov: Stalin's Successor, McGraw, 1953; Svetlana: The Story of Stalin's Daughter, New American Library, 1967; Prophecy in Our Time, New American Library, 1968; Che: The Making of a Legend, Universe Books, 1969; (translator) The Last Days of Luther, Doubleday, 1970; Lin Piao: The Life and Writings of China's New Ruler, Stein & Day, 1970; Every Woman's Guide to Abortion, Universe Books, 1971; They Knew the Unknown, World Publishing, 1971; The Truth about Vitamin E, Bantam, 1972; The Devil's Bride: Exorcism, Past and Present, Harper, 1974; The Essential Vitamin Counter, Bantam, 1974; Which Vitamins Do You Need?, Bantam, 1974; (translator) Johannes Lehmann, The Jesus Establishment, Doubleday, 1974; (translator) Demosthenes Savramis, Satanizing of Woman: Religion versus Sexuality, Doubleday, 1974; Saint Nicholas: Life and Legend, Harper, 1975; (translator) Adolf Rodewyk, Possessed by Satan: The Church's Teaching of the Devil, Possession and Exorcism, Doubleday, 1975; The Satan Trap: Dangers of the Occult, Doubleday, 1976; The Relaxation Controversy, New American Library, 1976.

Compiler or editor; all published by New American Library, except as indicated: True Experiences in Prophecy (also see below), 1967; True Experiences in Telepathy (also see below), 1967; Beyond Space and Time: An ESP Casebook (contains True Experiences in Prophecy and True Experiences in Telepathy), 1967; Communicating with the Dead, 1968; Maharishi, the Guru: An International Sympo-

sium, 1968, published as *Maharishi: The Founder of Transcendental Meditation*, 1976; *True Experiences with Ghosts*, 1968; *True Experiences in Exotic ESP*, 1968; *The Psychic Reader*, World Publishing, 1969; *Reincarnation in the Twentieth Century*, 1969; (and author of introduction) Danton M. Walker, *I Believe in Ghosts: True Stories of Some Haunted Celebrities and Their Celebrated Haunts*, Taplinger, 1969; *Test Your ESP*, World Publishing, 1970; *Psychic Discoveries by the Russians*, 1971; *Witchcraft Today*, 1971; (and author of introduction) *The Psychic Scene*, 1974; *Exorcism: Fact Not Fiction*, 1974; *The Amazing Uri Geller*, 1975; *The Riddle of the Bermuda Triangle*, 1975; *Five Chinese Communist Plays*, John Day, 1975; *TM: How to Find Peace of Mind through Meditation*, 1976.

Managing editor, *Tomorrow*, 1953-62; executive editor, *International Journal of Parapsychology*, 1959-62, *Spiritual Frontiers* (quarterly), 1969-71, 1976—; member of editorial board, *International Reports* (foreign currencies and finance), 1960-67.

WORK IN PROGRESS: Biographical research; psychology of economics and public affairs; contemporary events.

* * *

ECHLIN, Edward P.   1930-

PERSONAL: Born January 15, 1930, in Detroit, Mich.; son of Edward Patrick (an attorney) and Helen (Kelly) Echlin. *Education:* Loyola University, Chicago, Ill., A.M., 1959; University of Ottawa, Ph.D., 1967; Universite Saint Paul, S.T.D., 1968. *Home and office:* John Carroll University, Cleveland, Ohio 44118.

CAREER: Roman Catholic priest of Society of Jesus (Jesuits). Union Theological Seminary, New York, N.Y., visiting scholar, 1966-67; Gregorian University, Rome, Italy, visiting scholar, 1967; John Carroll University, Cleveland, Ohio, assistant professor of theology, beginning 1968; University of Durham, Durham, England, lecturer in ecclesiology, 1972-73. *Member:* Catholic Theological Society of America.

WRITINGS: The Anglican Eucharist in Ecumenical Perspective, Seabury, 1968; *The Deacon in the Church: Past Time and Future*, Alba, 1971; *The Priest as Preacher: Past and Future*, Fides, 1973; *The Story of the Anglican Ministry*, St. Paul Publications, 1974. Contributor to *America, Emmanuel, Homilitic and Pastoral Review*, and other journals.

WORK IN PROGRESS: Research and writing on Christianity in the secular age, the problem of God, the problem of the ministry.†

* * *

EDDY, Elizabeth M.   1926-

PERSONAL: Born January 8, 1926, in Albany, N.Y.; daughter of George Roberts and Marie (Betts) Eddy. *Education:* Wellesley College, B.A., 1947; Columbia University, M.A., 1958, Ph.D., 1961. *Religion:* Episcopalian. *Home:* 1642 Northwest 14th Ave., Gainesville, Fla. 32605. *Office:* Department of Anthropology, University of Florida, Gainesville, Fla. 32601.

CAREER: Director of religious education at Episcopal churches in Wellesley, Mass., 1947-50, Winnetka, Ill., 1950-54, and Lynchburg, Va., 1954-57; Columbia University, School of Social Work, New York, N.Y., assistant

project director, Research Center, 1960-63; Hunter College (now Hunter College of the City University of New York), New York, N.Y., lecturer in sociology, 1963, project director, Teacher Resources for Urban Education (TRUE), 1963-67; University of Florida, Gainesville, associate professor of sociology and director of Urban Studies Bureau, 1967-72, associate professor of anthropology, 1971-74, professor of anthropology, 1974—, project director of Dissemination and Diffusion Study in Selected Florida Schools, College of Education, 1972-73. Columbia University, secretary of Seminar on Content and Methods in the Social Sciences, 1960-66, and corresponding member of the Seminar, 1967—, lecturer at Teachers College, 1965; visiting lecturer, State University of New York at Stony Brook, 1967. Consultant, Culture of Schools Project, 1965-67, National Assessment of Educational Progress Project, Education Commission of the States, 1972, Project Ruroe, ABT Associates, 1975—.

MEMBER: American Anthropological Association (fellow), American Sociological Association (fellow), Society for Applied Anthropology (fellow), American Association for the Advancement of Science, Council on Anthropology and Education (second vice-president, 1972-73; president, 1973-74; first vice-president, 1974-75), Southern Anthropological Society, Phi Beta Kappa.

WRITINGS: (Contributor) Thomas J. Hennessey, editor, *The Interdisciplinary Roots of Guidance*, Fordham University Press, 1966; (with Julius A. Roth) *Rehabilitation for the Unwanted*, Atherton, 1967; *Walk the White Line: A Profile of Urban Education*, Doubleday Anchor (original paperback), and Praeger, 1967; *Becoming a Teacher*, New York Teachers College Press, 1969; (editor) *Urban Anthropology: Research Perspectives and Strategies*, University of Georgia Press, 1969. Contributor to sociology and anthropology journals.

WORK IN PROGRESS: Crossing Classroom Boundaries: Educational Innovation and Desegregation.

* * *

EDWARDS, Ward   1927-

PERSONAL: Born April 5, 1927, in Morristown, N.J.; son of Corwin D. (an economist) and Janet (Ward) Edwards; married Sylvia Callegari, December 12, 1970; children: Tara Anne, Page Corwin. *Education:* Swarthmore College, B.A. (honors), 1947; Harvard University, M.A., 1950, Ph.D., 1952. *Home:* 11466 Laurelcrest Rd., Studio City, Calif. *Office:* Social Science Research Institute, University of Southern California, Los Angeles, Calif.

CAREER: Instructor in psychology at Brooklyn College (now of the City University of New York), Brooklyn, N.Y., 1947-48, and Johns Hopkins University, Baltimore, Md., 1951-54; U.S. Air Force Personnel and Training Research Center, research psychologist at Lackland Air Force Base, San Antonio, Tex., 1954-56, and chief of intellectual functions section in the Operator Laboratory at Lowry Air Force Base, Denver, Colo., 1956-58; University of Michigan, Ann Arbor, lecturer, 1958-60, associate professor, 1960-63, professor of psychology, 1963-73, research psychologist in engineering psychology laboratory, Institute of Science and Technology, 1958-63, and head of laboratory, 1963-73; University of Southern California, Los Angeles, professor of psychology and industrial and systems engineering and director of Social Science Research Institute, 1973—. Consultant to North American Aviation Co., 1961—, Army Personnel Research Office, 1963-64, and

RAND Corp., 1964—. *Military service:* U.S. Navy, 1945-46. *Member:* American Psychological Association (fellow), Association of Aviation Psychologists (president, 1967), Psychonomic Society, Midwestern Psychological Association, Sigma Xi.

WRITINGS: (Editor with Amos Tversky) *Decision Making: Selected Readings,* Penguin, 1967.

Contributor: C. T. Morgan, editor, *Introduction to Psychology,* McGraw, 1956; M. J. Bowman, editor, *Expectations, Uncertainty, and Business Behavior,* Social Science Research Council, 1958; H. Gulliksen and S. Messick, editors, *Psychological Scaling: Theory and Applications,* Wiley, 1960; Albert H. Rubenstein and Chadwick J. Haberstroh, editors, *Some Theories of Organization,* Irwin, 1960; R. M. Gagne, editor, *Psychological Principles in System Development,* Holt, 1962; G. L. Bryan and M. W. Shelly, editors, *Human Judgments and Optimality,* Wiley, 1964; *New Directions in Psychology II,* Holt, 1965. Author of Air Force research reports. Contributor to *International Encyclopedia of the Social Sciences,* and of about seventy articles to professional journals.

WORK IN PROGRESS: Research on human information processing and decision making, and on the design of man-machine systems for information processing and decision making.

* * *

EELLS, George 1922-

PERSONAL: Born January 20, 1922, in Winslow, Ill.; son of Clark V. (a teacher) and Martha (Hardle) Eells. *Education:* Attended Northwestern University, 1940-43. *Politics:* Democrat. *Home:* 41 West Eighth St., New York, N.Y. 10011. *Agent:* Scott Meredith Literary Agency, Inc., 845 Third Ave., New York, N.Y. 10022.

CAREER: Look, New York City, entertainment editor, 1944-60; *Theatre Arts,* New York City, editor, 1962; *Signature* (Diners Club magazine), New York City, editor, 1963-67. *Member:* Writers Guild of America. *Awards, honors:* National Theater Conference fellowship, 1947; *New York Times'* outstanding non-fiction list, 1967, for *The Life That Late He Led; Reader's Digest's* most unforgettable characters anthology includes *The Life That Late He Led,* 1968; first annual Deems Taylor Award of American Society of Composers, Authors, and Publishers ($300), 1968.

WRITINGS: The Life That Late He Led: A Biography of Cole Porter, Putnam, 1967; *Hedda and Louella* (biographies of Hedda Hopper and Louella Parsons), Putnam, 1972; *Six Women,* Putnam, 1976. Contributor to magazines.

WORK IN PROGRESS: Entertainment Americana, about circuses, carnivals, marathon dances, and medicine shows; also writing about tent repertoire shows, 1890's to the present.

SIDELIGHTS: Robert Wise Productions has purchased *The Life That Late He Led* for filming; the working title is "The Incredible Cole Porter Machine."

* * *

EFEMEY, Raymond (Frederick) 1928-

PERSONAL: Born July 2, 1928, in Romsey, Hampshire, England; son of Frederick Elijah (a clergyman) and Gladys (De Ste. Croix) Efemey; married Anne Sylvia Pratley (a part-time writer and public relations officer), September 13, 1958; children: Simon Paul, Rachel Jane. *Education:* Oxford University, B.A., 1951, M.A., 1963.

CAREER: Clergyman, Church of England, 1953—. Assistant curate in Croydon, Surrey, 1953-57, and Yeovil, Somersetshire, 1957-60; vicar of Arley, Worcestershire, and industrial chaplain in Kidderminster, 1960-66; vicar of Dudley, Worcestershire, beginning 1966. *Wartime service:* Friends Ambulance Unit, worked with displaced children in Northern France, 1946-48. *Member:* Society of Authors.

WRITINGS: Devils Are for Yesterday: Considerations of Morality and Tolerance, Hodder & Stoughton, 1966, Abingdon, 1967; (reviser) Arthur Pearce Shepherd, *The Story of the Parish Church of St. Thomas,* 3rd edition (Efemey was not associated with earlier editions), British Publishing Co., 1967, 5th edition, 1972. Regular columnist, *National Christian News;* contributor to *Church Times.*

WORK IN PROGRESS: The Passion and the Love, a study of the Redemption of the human situation.

SIDELIGHTS: Efemey writes: "[My] writing arose out of work in industrial mission.... Wanted to say something about how the church was not really adapting to change. Believe orthodox Christianity was perverted by the Middle Ages.... Have been described as 'an orthodox radical.'" He is bilingual in French and English, and is competent in Italian. *Avocational interests:* All forms of artistic activity; science fiction.

BIOGRAPHICAL/CRITICAL SOURCES: Church Times, July 23, 1965; *Birmingham Post,* November 10, 1967.†

* * *

EFROS, Israel (Isaac) 1891-
(Efrot)

PERSONAL: Born May 28, 1891, in Ostrog, Poland; son of David (a teacher) and Gittel-Leah (Krusman) Efros; married Mildred Blaustein, December 20, 1925; children: Ghela (Mrs. Ben-Ami Scharfstein). *Education:* New York University, B.A., 1913; Columbia University, M.A., 1914, Ph.D., 1915. *Religion:* Jewish. *Home and office:* 11 Mapu St., Tel Aviv, Israel.

CAREER: Professor of Hebrew at Hunter College (now Hunter College of the City University of New York), and of philosophy and literature at Dropsie College for Hebrew and Cognate Learning (now Dropsie University), Philadelphia, Pa., 1941-55; Tel Aviv University, Tel Aviv, Israel, professor of philosophy and literature, and rector, 1955-62; Dropsie University, visiting professor of philosophy and literature, 1962—. *Member:* American Academy for Jewish Research (vice-president, 1954-55), Hebrew Writers Association of State of Israel (chairman, 1966—). *Awards, honors:* L.H.D., Jewish Theological Seminary of America, 1937; honorary Doctor of Philosophy, University of Tel Aviv, 1974. Bialik Award (Israel), for four books of poetry; Jewish Book Council of America Award for *Ancient Jewish Philosophy;* Tchernichovsky Prize for translations of Shakespeare's *Hamlet, Coriolanus,* and *Timon of Athens;* La Med Prize for poem, *Gold;* Henrietta Szold Medal for advancement of higher education in Israel; Wallenrod Prize, 1970, for Hebrew poetry.

WRITINGS: The Problem of Space in Jewish Mediaeval Philosophy, Columbia University Press, 1917; *The Bloody Jest* (a drama in four acts), R. G. Badger, 1922; *Philosophical Terms in the Moreh Nubukim,* Columbia University Press, 1924; (with Judah Ibn-Shmuel Kaufman and Benjamin Silk) *Milon Angli-'ivri,* edited by Kaufman, [Tel Aviv], 1929, translation published as *English-Hebrew Dic-*

tionary, Dvir (Tel Aviv), 1956; *Shirim,* [Tel Aviv], 1932; *Vigvamim Shotkim,* [Tel Aviv], 1933; *Palquera's Reshit Hokmah and Alfarabi's Ihsa Al'ulum,* Dropsie College for Hebrew and Cognate Learning, 1935; *Maimonides Treatise on Logic,* American Academy of Jewish Research, 1938; *Hayyim Nahman Bialik,* Hebrew P.E.N. Club of U.S.A., 1940; *Judah Halevi as Poet and Thinker,* Histadruth Ivrith of America, 1941; *Zahav,* Posy-Shoulson Press, 1942; *Saadia's Theory of Knowledge,* Dropsie College for Hebrew and Cognate Learning, 1942; *Anahnu Ha-dor* (title means "We are the Generation"), [New York], 1944; *Heimlose Yidn,* [Buenos Aires], 1947; (editor) Hayyim Nahman Bialik, *Complete Poetic Works,* Histadruth Ivrith of America, 1948; (editor) *Selected Poems of Bialik,* Bloch, 1948, revised edition, 1965; *Zakharti Iakh,* [New York], 1950; *Ha-mahashavah Ha-genuzah: The Philosophy of the Apocrypha,* [New York], 1953; (translator) *Timon ish Atunah,* [Tel Aviv], 1953; *Goral U-pit'om: Destiny and Studdenly* (poems), [Jerusalem], 1954; *Ha-filosofyah Ha-yehudit Ha-'atikah,* [Jerusalem], 1959; *Ben Hofim Nistarim,* [Tel Aviv], 1960; *Ancient Jewish Philosophy,* Wayne State University Press, 1964; *Studies in Medieval Jewish Philosophy,* Columbia University Press, 1974.

Other works: *Ha-filosofyah Ha-vrit Ha'atikah: Ancient Hebrew Philosophy—A Study in Metaphysics and Ethics,* 1964; *Ha-filosofyah Ha-yehudit Bi-yeme Ha-benayim: Mediaeval Jewish Philosophy Systems and Problems,* 1964; (translator) *Hamlet* [*and*] *Coriolanus,* Am-ha-sefer (Tel Aviv), 1964. Also author of verse in Hebrew published in Tel Aviv, 1966.

WORK IN PROGRESS: A book of essays in Hebrew on poetry and philosophy; original Hebrew verse.

*   *   *

EGAN, E(dward) W(elstead)   1922-
(Eamon MacAedhagan)

PERSONAL: Born March 26, 1922, in New York, N.Y.; son of Edward Bulger (a railroad executive) and Irene (Welstead) Egan. *Education:* Hamilton College, B.A., 1947; University of Paris, graduate study, 1948-49. *Politics:* "Enrolled Republican but vote as I please." *Religion:* "Catholic by background but non-religious." *Home:* 105 East 15th St., New York, N.Y. 10003. *Office:* Sterling Publishing Co., Inc., 419 Park Ave. S., New York, N.Y. 10016.

CAREER: U.S. Department of State, Washington, D.C., technical assistance project analyst for Economic Cooperation Administration, Mutual Security Agency, and then Foreign Operations Administration in Paris, France, 1949-56; free-lance writer, 1956-67; Sterling Publishing Co., Inc., New York, N.Y., reference book editor, 1967—. Theatre in Education, Inc., consultant, 1956—, member of board, 1964—, vice-president, 1965—. *Military service:* U.S. Army Air Forces, 1942-46.

WRITINGS: France in Pictures, Sterling, 1965, 2nd revised edition, 1972; *Italy in Pictures,* Sterling, 1966, revised edition, 1972; *Belgium and Luxembourg in Pictures,* Sterling, 1966; *Ceylon in Pictures,* Sterling, 1967; *Brazil in Pictures,* Sterling, 1967; (editor with Leonard F. Wise) *Kings, Rulers, and Statesmen,* Sterling, 1967; *Argentina in Pictures,* Sterling, 1967; (adapter) Stenuit, *The Dolphin: Cousin to Man,* translation by Catherine Osborne, Sterling, 1968; (translator) Robert Girard, *Learn Art in One Year,* Sterling, 1968; (translator) J. M. Guilcher and R. H. Noailles, *The Hidden Life of Flowers,* Sterling, 1971;

(adapter) Guilcher and Noailles, *A Fern is Born,* translation by Rhea Rollin, Sterling, 1971; (translator with Rollin) Guilcher and Noailles, *A Tree Grows Up,* Sterling, 1972; (translator and adapter) J. P. Vanden Eeckhoudt, *The Secret Life of Small Animals,* Sterling, 1972; (translator and adapter) E. Bosiger and P. Faucher, *Birds That Fly in the Night,* Sterling, 1973; (translator) Edourd Cauvin, *Tiny Living Things,* Sterling, 1973; (translator) Marie-Claude Rivier, *Pin Pictures,* Sterling, 1975. Uses pseudonym Eamon MacAedhagan for "unpublished and/or rejected verse."

SIDELIGHTS: Egan says that he does not "disbelieve in saints, angels, and flying saucers, but suspend belief in them pending actual confrontation. However if such beliefs help others to refrain from killing one another (or me) I am all for them. Man's problem is to do his work and keep his identity without destroying his fellows." He is competent in French, reads Latin, and knows a smattering of Italian, German, Bengali, Russian, and Greek. Egan has traveled in Europe, Australia, India, and Middle East.

AVOCATIONAL INTERESTS: Language, literature, arts, history, natural sciences, reading, television, cycling, gardening, walking, and swimming.

*   *   *

EGGERT, Gerald G(ordon)   1926-

PERSONAL: Born April 12, 1926, in Berrien County, Mich.; son of Gordon D. (a farmer) and E. Marguerite (Inman) Eggert; married Jean Higgins, June 20, 1953; children: Michael, Susan, Christine. *Education:* Western Michigan University, B.A., 1949; University of Michigan, M.A., 1951, Ph.D., 1960. *Religion:* Episcopalian. *Home:* 517 Nimitz Ave., State College, Pa. 16801. *Office:* Department of History, Pennsylvania State University, University Park, Pa. 16802.

CAREER: Battle Creek (Mich.) public schools, teacher of social studies, 1949-54; University of Maryland, College Park, instructor in history, 1957-60; Bowling Green State University, Bowling Green, Ohio, assistant professor of history, 1960-65; Pennsylvania State University, University Park, assistant professor, 1965-67, associate professor of history, 1967-72, professor of American history, 1972—. Visiting lecturer in history, University of Michigan, 1963. *Military service:* U.S. Army, Quartermaster Corps, 1946-48. *Member:* American Historical Association, Organization of American Historians, American Association of University Professors, Pennsylvania Historical Association.

WRITINGS: Railroad Labor Disputes: The Beginnings of Federal Strike Policy, University of Michigan Press, 1967; *Richard Olney: Evolution of a Statesman,* Pennsylvania State University Press, 1974. Contributor to historical journals.

WORK IN PROGRESS: William Brown Dickson: A Case Study of Welfare; Capitalism in the Steel Industry; editing the diary of Thomas M. Cooley.

*   *   *

EGGLESTON, Wilfrid   1901-

PERSONAL: Born March 25, 1901, in Lincoln, England; son of Samuel (a farmer) and Ellen (Cowham) Eggleston; married Magdalena Raskevich, June 28, 1928; children: Anne Elisabeth. *Education:* Queen's University at Kingston, B.A., 1926. *Home:* 234 Clemow Ave., Ottawa, Ontario, Canada.

CAREER: Left home at fifteen; *Toronto Star* and *Star Weekly,* Toronto, Ontario, reporter, then head of Ottawa bureau, 1926-33; Reuter's, correspondent, 1934-36; Royal Commission on Federalism, press secretary, 1937-39; Press Censor for Canada, 1940-43, Director of Censorship, 1944; Carleton University, Ottawa, Ontario, founder of Canada's first school of journalism, professor of journalism and director of School of Journalism, 1947-66, professor emeritus, 1966—. *Awards, honors:* Order of the British Empire, 1943, for war services in censorship; LL.D., Carleton University, 1966; D.Litt., University of Western Ontario, 1967; National Press Club Award, 1968; Alex Award, Media '75, 1975.

WRITINGS: The High Plains (fiction), Macmillan, 1938; *The Road to Nationhood,* Oxford University Press, 1946; *Scientists at War,* Oxford University Press, 1950; *The Frontier and Canadian Letters,* Ryerson, 1957; (editor) *The Green Gables Letters,* Ryerson, 1960; *The Queen's Choice: A Story of Canada's Capital,* Queen's Printer, 1961; *Canada's Nuclear Story,* Clarke, Irwin, 1965; *While I Still Remember* (autobiography), Ryerson, 1968; *Newfoundland: The Road to Confederation,* Queen's Printer, 1974.

WORK IN PROGRESS: A history of the first fifty years of the National Research Council of Canada, 1916-1966; *Homestead on the Range,* a documentary on the semi-arid plains of Alberta.

* * *

EHRLICH, Robert S. 1935-

PERSONAL: Born March 18, 1935, in Boston, Mass.; son of Simon (a physician) and Lillian (Sherman) Ehrlich; married Margery Cohen (a teacher), July 30, 1961. *Education:* Boston University, A.B., 1957, M.A., 1959; Brandeis University, M.A., 1961, Ph.D., 1968. *Politics:* Democrat. *Religion:* Jewish. *Home:* 797 Washington St., Brookline, Mass. 02146. *Office:* Department of History, Boston State College, 625 Huntington Ave., Boston, Mass. 02115.

CAREER: Mohawk Valley Community College, Utica, N.Y., instructor in humanities, 1961-63; Fitchburg State College, Fitchburg, Mass., associate professor of history and humanities, 1963-68; Boston University, Boston, Mass., assistant professor of social science, 1968-70; Boston State College, Boston, Mass., professor of history, 1970—. Consultant to President's Crime Commission, 1966. *Military service:* U.S. Army, 1958; became lieutenant. *Member:* American Historical Association, American Philosophical Association, American Association of University Professors.

WRITINGS: Twentieth-Century Philosophy, Monarch, 1965; *Spinoza,* Monarch, 1965; *Bertrand Russell,* Monarch, 1966; *History of Man,* Simon & Schuster, 1973. Contributor to academic journals.

* * *

EICKHOFF, Andrew R(obert) 1924-

PERSONAL: Born October 3, 1924, in New York, N.Y.; son of Andrew B. (a Disciples of Christ minister) and Ruth Lois (Wolfe) Eickhoff; married Joan Jordan Dietz, December 22, 1946; children: Andrew Robert, Jr., Joan Jordan. *Education:* Loyola College, Baltimore, Md., B.S., 1944; Boston University, S.T.B., 1949, Ph.D., 1953; University of Geneva, Certificate in Ecumenics, 1956. *Home:* 333 East College Ave., Jacksonville, Ill. 62650. *Office:* MacMurray College, Jacksonville, Ill. 62650.

CAREER: Pastor of Methodist churches in Clinton, Mass., 1948-50, and West Fitchburg, Mass., 1950-53; Columbia College, Columbia, S.C., professor of religion and acting head of department, 1953-55; Bradley University, Peoria, Ill., professor of religion and chairman of department, 1956-67; Union College, Barbourville, Ky., dean of faculty, 1967-74; MacMurray College, Jacksonville, Ill., dean, 1974—. Marriage and psychological counselor. Delegate to World Methodist Conference, Oslo, and member of World Congress for Mental Health, Paris, both 1961. *Military service:* U.S. Navy, 1943-46; line officer with Pacific Fleet; became lieutenant junior grade.

MEMBER: World Federation for Mental Health, American Academy of Religion (president of Midwestern section, 1966-67), Academy of Religion and Mental Health (president of Peoria chapter, 1960), American Psychological Association, American Association for the United Nations (member of board of directors, Illinois State Division, 1965-67), American Conference of Academic Deans.

WRITINGS: A Christian View of Sex and Marriage, Free Press, 1966. Contributor to *Pastoral Psychology, Christian Home, Journal of Bible and Religion,* and other journals.

WORK IN PROGRESS: A book concerning Christian sexual ethics; the relationship of psychology and religion; a book on academic administration.

* * *

EIDELBERG, Paul 1928-

PERSONAL: Born June 21, 1928, in Brooklyn, N.Y.; son of Harry and Sarah (Leimseider) Eidelberg; married Phyllis Lief, December 27, 1947; children: Steven, Sharen, Sarah Elizabeth. *Education:* University of Chicago, Ph.D., 1966. *Religion:* Hebrew. *Office:* Claremont Men's College, Claremont, Calif. 91711.

CAREER: U.S. Air Force, 1946-52, leaving service as first lieutenant; Sweet Briar College, Sweet Briar, Va., visiting professor of government, 1966-67; North Carolina State University at Raleigh, assistant professor of politics, 1967-68; Kenyon College, Gambier, Ohio, associate professor of political science, 1968-70; University of Dallas, Irving, Tex., associate professor of political science, 1970-74; Claremont Men's College, Claremont, Calif., visiting professor of political science, 1974—. *Member:* American Political Science Association.

WRITINGS: The Philosophy of the American Constitution, Free Press, 1968; *A Discourse on Statesmanship,* University of Illinois Press, 1974. Contributor to journals in .his field.

WORK IN PROGRESS: A three-volume work on the foundations of Soviet foreign policy, the first two entitled *On the Silence of the Declaration of Independence* and *Beyond Detente.*

* * *

EIGNER, Edwin M(oss) 1931-

PERSONAL: Born April 3, 1931, in Boston, Mass.; son of Harry (a lawyer) and Gladys (Lowett) Eigner; married Ruth Aglaya Hanka, September 21, 1956; children: Nancy Carol, Barton Lowett. *Education:* Cornell University, B.A., 1953; University of Iowa, M.F.A., 1955, Ph.D., 1963. *Home:* 2255 Quantz Pl., Riverside, Calif. 92507. *Office:* Department of English, University of California, Riverside, Calif. 92502.

CAREER: Instructor in English, University of Maryland Overseas Program in Germany, 1956-57, and Northwestern University, Evanston, Ill., 1960-63; University of Kansas, Lawrence, assistant professor, 1963-66, associate professor of English, 1966-70; University of California, Riverside, professor of English, 1970—, chairman of department, 1972-75, director of University of California Study Center for the United Kingdom and Ireland, 1975-77. Fulbright lecturer in American studies, University of Erlangen-Nuernberg, 1967-68; senior visiting fellow, Westfield College, University of London, 1975-77. Member: Modern Language Association of America. Awards, honors: Elizabeth M. Watkins research scholarship of University of Kansas Endowment Association, 1966; Younger Scholar Fellowship from National Foundation on the Arts and Humanities, 1969; honorable mention in The Explicator contest for Robert Louis Stevenson and Romantic Tradition.

WRITINGS: Robert Louis Stevenson and Romantic Tradition, Princeton University Press, 1966. Contributor to literary journals.

WORK IN PROGRESS: A book on Romantic fiction in England and America.

*   *   *

EIMERL, Sarel (Henry) 1925-

PERSONAL: Born February 28, 1925, in Chester, England. Education: Exeter College, Oxford, B.A., 1948; Rice University, M.A., 1950.

CAREER: Middlebury College, Middlebury, Vt., instructor in political science, 1949-50; information officer for British government, New York City, 1950-52; Scholastic Magazine, New York City, editor, 1952-56; full-time writer, 1956—. Military service: Royal Navy, 1943-46.

WRITINGS: The Cautious Bachelor, Crown, 1958; Title Deeds, Elek, 1960; (adapter) The Wonders of Life on Earth, Golden Press, 1961; (adapter) The History of Flight, Golden Press, 1964; The Primates, Time-Life, 1965, young readers edition, 1968; (with Russel V. Lee) The Physician, Time-Life, 1967; Revolution!: France, 1789-1794, Little, Brown, 1967; The World of Giotto, Time-Life, 1967; Baboons, Simon & Schuster, 1968; Gulls, Simon & Schuster, 1969; Hitler over Europe: The Road to World War II, Little, Brown, 1972.†

*   *   *

EISENSTEIN, Ira 1906-

PERSONAL: Born November 26, 1906, in New York, N.Y.; son of Isaac and Sadie (Luxenberg) Eisenstein; married Judith Kaplan (a teacher), June 10, 1934; children: Miriam R., Ann. N. Education: Columbia University, B.A., 1927, Ph.D., 1941; Jewish Theological Seminary of America, Rabbi, 1931. Home: Rittenhouse Claridge Apts., Rittenhouse Square, Philadelphia, Pa. 19103. Office: Jewish Reconstructionist Foundation, 15 West 86th St., New York, N.Y. 10024; Reconstructionist Rabbinical College, 2308 North Broad St., Philadelphia, Pa. 19132.

CAREER: Society for the Advancement of Judaism, New York City, executive director, 1930-31, assistant leader, 1931-33, associate leader, 1933-45, leader, 1945-54; rabbi of congregation in Chicago, Ill., 1954-59; Jewish Reconstructionist Foundation, New York City, president and editor of Reconstructionist, 1959—. Visiting professor of homiletics, Jewish Theological Seminary of America, 1951. Member of

board of directors, Cejwin Camps, 1966—. Member: Rabbinical Assembly of America (president, 1952-54). Awards, honors: D.D. from Jewish Theological Seminary of America, 1958.

WRITINGS: Creative Judaism, Reconstructionist Press, 1936, revised edition, 1953; What We Mean by Religion, Reconstructionist Press, 1938, revised and enlarged edition, 1958; The Ethics of Tolerance, King's Crown Press, 1941; (editor with E. Kohn) Mordecai M. Kaplan: An Evaluation, Reconstructionist Press, 1952; Judaism Under Freedom, Reconstructionist Press, 1956; (editor) Varieties of Jewish Belief, Reconstructionist Press, 1966; (contributor) Alfred Jospe, editor, Tradition and Contemporary Experience: Essays on Jewish Thought and Life, Schocken, 1970. Also translator of Z. Feierberg's Whither (from Hebrew), Abelard.

Co-editor of New Haggadah Prayer Book, Sabbath Prayer Book, High Holiday Prayer Book, Festival Prayer Book and Daily Prayer Book, Reconstructionist Press, 1963. Writer of five cantatas with wife, Judith K. Eisenstein. Contributor to periodicals.

AVOCATIONAL INTERESTS: Music, photography.

*   *   *

EISINGER, Chester E(manuel) 1915-

PERSONAL: Born May 11, 1915, in Chicago, Ill.; son of Harry (a manufacturer) and Clara (Brownstein) Eisinger; married Marjorie Kendall, July 31, 1937; children: Peter, Steven, Joel. Education: University of California, Los Angeles, B.A., 1937; University of Michigan, M.A., 1938, Ph.D., 1945. Politics: Democrat. Religion: "None." Home: 1729 Sheridan Rd., West Lafayette, Ind. 47906. Office: Department of English, Purdue University, Lafayette, Ind. 47907.

CAREER: University of Michigan, Ann Arbor, assistant editor of Dictionary of Proverbs in English, 1940-45; Purdue University, Lafayette, Ind., 1945—, associate professor, 1953-57, professor of English and chairman of committee on American studies, 1957—. Fulbright lecturer at Fuad University, Cairo, Egypt, 1951-52, University of Innsbruck, Innsbruck, Austria, 1960-61, and Toritsu Daieaku and Aoyama Eakuin Universities, Tokyo, Japan, 1971. Member: Modern Language Association of America, American Studies Association (president of Ohio-Indiana branch, 1959-60), American Association of University Professors. Awards, honors: Fulbright grants, 1951-52, 1960-61; Purdue Research Foundation grant, 1956; senior fellow, National Endowment for the Humanities.

WRITINGS: Fiction of the Forties, University of Chicago Press, 1963; (author of introduction) Norman Mailer, The Naked and the Dead, Rinehart, 1968; (contributor) D. Madden, editor, Proletarian Writers of the Thirties, Southern Illinois University Press, 1968; (editor and author of introduction) The 1940's: Profile of a Nation in Crisis, Anchor Books, 1969. Contributor of essays and articles to literary journals in United States and Austria; also contributor of reviews to Saturday Review.

WORK IN PROGRESS: Traditionalism and Modernism in American Fiction, 1950-1970, for University of Chicago Press.

*   *   *

ELAZAR, Daniel J(udah) 1934-

PERSONAL: Born August 25, 1934, in Minneapolis,

Minn.; son of Albert (an educator) and Nettie (Barzon) Elazar; married Harriet Fienberg, January 22, 1961; children: Naomi, Jonathan. *Education:* Attended Wayne State University, 1951-54; University of Chicago, M.A., 1957, Ph.D., 1959. *Politics:* "Democratic—Farmer—Labor." *Religion:* Jewish. *Home:* 2334 North 50th St., Wynnefield, Philadelphia, Pa. 19131. *Office:* Center for the Study of Federalism, Temple University, Philadelphia, Pa. 19122.

CAREER: United Hebrew Schools, Detroit, Mich., librarian, 1951-54, consultant, 1954-59; University of Illinois, Institute of Government and Public Affairs, Urbana, Ill., assistant professor, 1959-63; University of Minnesota, Minneapolis, visiting assistant professor of political science, 1963-64; Temple University, Philadelphia, Pa., associate professor, 1964-67, professor of political science, 1967—, director, Center for the Study of Federalism, 1967—. Hebrew University of Jerusalem, Fulbright senior lecturer and visiting professor of political science and American studies, 1968-69, visiting professor of contemporary Jewry, 1970-71; Bar Ilan University, Ramat Gan, Israel, professor of political science and head of Institute of Local Government, 1973—. Associate member, Center for Advanced Study in the Behavioral Sciences, 1959; chairman of City-County Library Committee, Citizens League of Minneapolis and Hennepin County, 1964-65; lecturer of executive training program, U.S. Civil Service Commission, 1966—; chairman, State Political Cultures Committee, 1966—, Allocations Committee of Jewish Federation, Champaign and Urbana, Ill.; consultant, Minneapolis Attorney General, 1967-68, Advanced Commission of Education Commission of the States, 1967—; chairman and member of chief executive office, Center of Jewish Community Studies, Jerusalem and Philadelphia, 1970—; chairman of executive council, Joint Center for Federal and Regional Studies, Basil, Switzerland, 1975—.

MEMBER: American Political Science Association, American Society for Public Administration, World Congress of Jewish Studies, American Jewish Historical Society, American Jewish Committee, Association for Jewish Studies, Israel Political Science Association (member of executive council), Conference for Federal Studies (chairman), Northwestern Political Science Association, Western History Association, Minnesota Academy of Science, Minnesota Historical Society, Colorado Historical Society, Illinois Historical Society, Montana Historical Society, Pennsylvania Political Science and Public Administration Association, Phi Beta Kappa. *Awards, honors:* Leonard D. White award, American Political Science Association, 1960; Huntington Library fellow, 1963, 1964; Guggenheim fellow, 1964-65, Fulbright fellow, 1968-69; Woodrow Wilson Award, honorable mention, 1971.

WRITINGS: The American Partnership: Federal State Relations in the Nineteenth Century, University of Chicago Press, 1962; *American Federalism: A View from the States,* Crowell, 1966, revised edition, 1972; (editor) Morton Grodzins, *The American System: A New View of Government in the United States,* Rand McNally, 1966; (editor) *The Politics of Federalism,* Heath, 1968; (co-author) *A Classification System for Libraries of Judaica,* Kresge Science Library, Wayne State University, 1968; (co-editor) *Cooperation and Conflict: Readings in American Federalism,* F. E. Peacock, 1968; (editor and author of introduction) *The Politics of American Federalism,* Heath, 1969; *Land Space and Civil Society in America,* Center for the Study of Federalism, Temple University, 1970; *Cities of the Prairie: The Metropolitan Frontier of American Poli-*

tics, Basic Books, 1970: *The Politics of Belleville,* Temple University Press, 1971.

Contributor: *Illinois Local Government,* University of Illinois Institute of Government and Public Affairs, 1961, revised edition, 1965; *The Office of Governor in Illinois,* University of Illinois, 1963; *Regional Development and the Wabash Basin,* University of Illinois Press, 1964; *Economic Change in the Civil War Era,* Eleutherian Mills—Hagley Foundation, 1965; Jacob and Vines, *Politics in the American States: A Comparative Analysis,* Little, Brown, 1965; Robert A. Goldwin, editor, *A Nation of Cities,* Rand McNally, 1968. Contributor to *Britannica Book of the Year,* 1964, 1965, 1966, 1967, and to *International Encyclopedia of the Social Sciences;* contributor to society yearbooks, annals, and proceedings, of articles and reviews to *Huntington Library Quarterly,* and other learned journals. Editor, *Publius, The Journal of Federalism,* 1971—.

WORK IN PROGRESS: Federal Democracy, a basic text in American government; books on political planning in Minneapolis, St. Paul, and Jerusalem; a book on the Jewish communities of the world.

*   *   *

ELBING, Alvar O(liver), Jr.   1928-

PERSONAL: Born September 24, 1928, in Minneapolis, Minn.; son of Alvar Oliver and Martha (Malmquist) Elbing; married Carol Jeppson (a writer and researcher), October, 1950; children: Kristofer Erik, John Rolf. *Education:* University of Minnesota, B.A., 1950; University of California, Berkeley, B.S., 1956; Sacramento State College (now California State University, Sacramento), M.S., 1959; University of Washington, Seattle, D.B.A., 1962. *Office:* Department of Management, School of Business, State University of New York, Albany, N.Y. 12203.

CAREER: Procter & Gamble Distributing Co., sales representative, 1954-55; State Personnel Board, Sacramento, Calif., personnel analyst, 1956-58; Sacramento State College (now California State University, Sacramento), lecturer in business administration, 1958-59; University of Washington, Seattle, associate in human relations, 1959-62; Dartmouth College, Amos Tuck School of Business Administration, Hanover, N.H., assistant professor, 1962-66, associate professor of organizational behavior, 1966-67; State University of New York at Albany, professor of management, 1967—. *Military service:* U.S. Air Force, 1951-53; became first lieutenant. U.S. Air Force Reserve, 1953-62. *Member:* Academy of Management, American Economic Association, American Association for the Advancement of Science, Beta Gamma Sigma. *Awards, honors:* Ford Foundation fellow, 1961.

WRITINGS: (With wife, Carol Elbing) *The Value Issue of Business,* McGraw, 1967; *Behavioral Decisions in Organizations,* Scott, Foresman, 1970. Contributor to *American Economic Review, Personnel Journal,* and *Personnel Psychology.*

WORK IN PROGRESS: With Carol Elbing, a book on values in business; a long-term study of values and attitudes of businessmen and students.

SIDELIGHTS: Alvar Elbing traveled in Sweden as guest of the Swedish Government, 1966, visiting industry, education, and government. He is competent in Swedish.†

ELBING, Carol J(eppson) 1930-

PERSONAL: Born March 15, 1930, in West Ellis, Wis.; daughter of Ralph Victor (an upholsterer) and Claire (Fredell) Jeppson; married Alvar O. Elbing, Jr. (a university professor), October, 1950; children: Kristofer Erik, John Rolf. *Education:* University of Minnesota, B.A., 1951; Sacramento State College (now California State University, Sacramento), M.A., 1958; University of Washington, Seattle, graduate study, 1958-62.

CAREER: California Department of Social Welfare, social worker in Eureka, Oakland, and Richmond; Dartmouth College, Hanover, N.H., instructor in speech and oral interpretation. *Member:* Phi Beta Kappa.

WRITINGS: (With husband, Alvar O. Elbing, Jr.) *The Value Issue of Business,* McGraw, 1967.

WORK IN PROGRESS: A book on values in business, in collaboration with Alvar Elbing.††

* * *

ELDEFONSO, Edward 1933-

PERSONAL: Born April 20, 1933, in Honolulu, Hawaii; son of Bartold (a laborer) and Cecelia (Jardine) Eldefonso; married Mildred Ann Prastalo, December 1, 1956; children: Jaime Christine, Mitchell Edward. *Education:* San Jose State College (now San Jose State University), B.A., 1959, M.S., 1962, junior college teaching credential, 1963. *Politics:* "None." *Home:* 5070 Northlawn Dr., San Jose, Calif. 95130. *Office:* 840 Guadalupe Pkwy., San Jose, Calif. 95110.

CAREER: Santa Clara County Juvenile Probation Department, San Jose, Calif., staff member, 1957—, supervisor, 1965—. Teaching instructor at DeAnza College, Cupertino, and West Valley College, Campbell, 1963—. *Military service:* U.S. Marine Corps Reserve, 1953-57.

WRITINGS: Law Enforcement and the Youthful Offender, Wiley, 1967, 2nd edition, 1973; (with Alan R. Coffey and Richard C. Grace) *Principles of Law Enforcement,* Wiley, 1968, 2nd edition, 1974; (with Coffey) *Human Relations: Law Enforcement in a Changing Community,* Prentice-Hall, 1971; (with Coffey) *Police-Community Relations,* Prentice-Hall, 1971; (with Coffey and James Sullivan) *Police and the Criminal Law,* Goodyear Publishing, 1972; *Youth Problems and Law Enforcement,* Prentice-Hall, 1972; (compiler) *Readings in Criminal Justice,* Glencoe Press, 1973; (with Walter Hartinger) *Corrections,* Goodyear Publishing, 1973; (compiler) *Issues in Corrections: A Book of Readings,* Glencoe Press, 1974; (with Coffey) *An Introduction to the Criminal Justice System and Process,* Prentice-Hall, 1974; (with Coffey) *Process and Impact of Justice,* Glencoe Press, 1975; (with Hartinger) *Treatment and Rehabilitation of Juvenile Offenders,* Glencoe Press, in press.

WORK IN PROGRESS: Probation and Parole, a text.†

* * *

ELFORD, Homer J. R. 1912-

PERSONAL: Born June 15, 1912, in Rochester, Minn.; son of Jonathan Rodney (a mail carrier and farmer) and Mida E. (Dean) Elford; married Margaret Mann, June 15, 1937; children: Cary Mann, Mary Margaret Elford Price. *Education:* Attended Rochester State Junior College, 1930-32; Hamline University, A.B., 1934; Boston University, S.T.B., 1937. *Politics:* Republican. *Home:* 532 Tod Lane, Youngstown, Ohio 44504.

CAREER: Methodist clergyman, serving churches in Stillwater, Minn., 1937-40, Grand Forks, N.D., 1940-45, Minneapolis, Minn., 1945-47, and St. Paul, Minn., 1947-52; Trinity United Methodist, Youngstown, Ohio, senior minister, 1952—. Trustee, Methodist Theological School in Ohio, Methodist Community Center, Youngstown, Copeland Oaks Methodist Retirement Home, Sebring, Ohio; chairman of board Penn-Ohio College, Youngstown; member of executive committee, Youngstown Council of Churches. *Member:* Youngstown Chamber of Commerce, Masons. *Awards, honors:* D.D. from Hamline University, 1951, and Mount Union College, 1960.

WRITINGS: I Will Uphold the Church, Tidings, 1949, 2nd edition, 1968; *A Guide to Church Ushering,* Abingdon, 1961; *A Layman's Guide to Worship,* Abingdon, 1963. Sermons published in *Pulpit Preaching, The New Pulpit Digest,* and included in booklets.

* * *

ELKHOLY, Abdo A. 1925-

PERSONAL: Born July 16, 1925, in Elmansoura, Egypt (now a region of United Arab Republic); son of Abdel-Rahman A. (a merchant) and Kawkab (Qandeel) Elkholy; married August 11, 1956; wife's name, Margaret Jesse; children: Atif Fred, Deena Elizabith, Nadia Marie. *Education:* Al-Azhar University, B.A., 1952, M.A., 1954; Ein Shams University, Diploma in Education and Psychology, 1953; Princeton University, M.A., 1957, Ph.D., 1960, postdoctoral study, 1964-65. *Religion:* Moslem. *Home:* 921 West Taylor St., De Kalb, Ill. 60115. *Office:* Northern Illinois University, De Kalb, Ill. 60115.

CAREER: Assistant professor of sociology at Al-Azhar University and American University in Cairo, both Cairo, Egypt, 1960-63, and concurrently director of Congress for Cultural Freedom in Cairo; State University of New York College at New Paltz, associate professor of sociology, 1963-65; Northern Illinois University, De Kalb, associate professor of sociology, 1965—. *Member:* American Sociological Association, Middle East Institute, Midwest Sociological Society. *Awards, honors:* State University of New York research grant, 1964, and faculty scholarship in Oriental studies, 1964-65.

WRITINGS: (Co-author) *Principles of Sociology* (published in Arabic), Al-Bayan Al-Arabi Press, 1961; *The Arab Moslems in the United States: Religion and Assimilation,* College and University Press, 1966. Contributor to Arabic journals and newspapers.

WORK IN PROGRESS: Personal and National Aspiration in Modern Egypt; further research on traditional Moslems in North America and their conditions.

AVOCATIONAL INTERESTS: Travel, classical music, swimming.

* * *

ELLER, Vernard (Marion) 1927-

PERSONAL: Born July 11, 1927, in Everett, Wash.; son of Jay Vernard (a professor) and Geraldine (Crill) Eller; married Phyllis Kulp, July 9, 1955; children: Sander Mack, Enten, Rosanna. *Education:* La Verne College, B.A., 1949; Bethany Theological Seminary, Oak Brook, Ill., B.D., 1955; Northwestern University, M.A., 1958; Pacific School of Religion, Th.D., 1964. *Politics:* Democratic. *Home:* 2448 Third St., La Verne, Calif. 91750. *Office:* La Verne College, La Verne, Calif. 91750.

CAREER: Clergyman, Church of the Brethren. Church of the Brethren, Elgin, Ill., editor of youth publications, 1950-56; La Verne College, La Verne, Calif., assistant professor, 1958-63, associate professor, 1963-68, professor of religion, 1968—. Member: American Academy of Religion, American Society of Christian Ethics, American Society of Church History, Brethren Journal Association, Swenson-Kierkegaard Foundation.

WRITINGS: Kierkegaard and Radical Discipleship: A New Perspective, Princeton University Press, 1968; His End Up, Abingdon, 1969; The Promise: Ethics in the Kingdom of God, Doubleday, 1970; The MAD Morality or the Ten Commandments Revisited, Abingdon, 1970; The Sex Manual for Puritans, Abingdon, 1971; In Place of Sacraments: A Study of Baptism and the Lord's Supper, Eerdmans, 1972; King Jesus' Manual of Arms for the 'Armless: War and Peace from Genesis to Revelation, Abingdon, 1973; The Simple Life: The Christian Stance toward Possessions, Eerdmans, 1973; The Most Revealing Book of the Bible: Making Sense out of Revelation, Eerdmans, 1974.

Contributor: Donald Durnbaugh, editor, The Church of the Brethren Past and Present, Brethren Press, 1971; Paul M. Robinson, editor, Call the Witnesses, Brethren Press, 1974; A. J. Klassen, editor, Bonhoeffer and the Believers Church, Harper, in press. Regular contributor to Christian Century and periodicals of Church of the Brethren; occasional contributor to other religious journals.

WORK IN PROGRESS: The Eccentricity of the Gospel, theological comments upon the graphic works of the Dutch artist, M. C. Escher; Cleaning Up the Christian Vocabulary, a study of the communications gap that arises when Christians try to categorize one another, for Brethren Press; Pieces Falling Into Place, a collection of his periodical pieces tracing the growth of a theological stance.

BIOGRAPHICAL/CRITICAL SOURCES: Church of the Brethren Messenger, January, 1968.

*   *   *

ELLETT, Marcella H.   1931-

PERSONAL: Born November 20, 1931, in Bloomington, Ind.; daughter of Myron (a stonesawyer) and Geneva (Franklin) Howard; children: John Franklin, Jean Marie, Anthony D. Education: Indiana University, B.S., 1952; Cornell University, M.S., 1955. Religion: American Baptist. Home: 6821 Woodcrest Dr., Fort Wayne, Ind. 46805.

CAREER: Teacher of home economics in Curlew, Wash., 1952-54, Huntertown, Ind., 1956-58, New Haven, Ind., 1962-67, and Fort Wayne, Ind., 1967—. Consultant to Fort Wayne Community Schools. Member: National Education Association, Omicron Nu, Phi Kappa Phi, Phi Lamba Theta.

WRITINGS: Textiles for Teens, Burgess, 1956; The World of Children, Burgess, 1966.

WORK IN PROGRESS: Research in nutrition for the teen-age population; revisions of Textiles for Teens and The World of Children.

*   *   *

ELLINGSWORTH, Huber W.   1928-

PERSONAL: Born August 13, 1928, in Corydon, Iowa; son of Arthur J. (a farmer) and Helen (Kirk) Ellingsworth; married June G. Davis (a teacher of speech and English), August 14, 1952; children: Claudia, Denise, Louise. Education: Simpson College, student, 1945-48; Pacific University, Forest Grove, Ore., B.A., 1949; Washington State University, M.A., 1950; Florida State University, Ph.D., 1955. Politics: Democrat. Religion: Protestant. Home: 202 Hawaii Loa St., Honolulu, Hawaii 96821. Office: University of Hawaii, Honolulu, Hawaii 96822.

CAREER: Michigan State University, East Lansing, assistant professor of communication, 1956-63; Frostburg State College, Frostburg, Md., professor of speech and head of department, 1963-66; University of Hawaii, Honolulu, professor of speech-communication, 1966—. Member of training and program staff, Resources Development Corp., East Lansing, Mich., 1961—; consultant to Agency for International Development, U.S. Weather Bureau, National Project in Agricultural Communication, Pacific and Asian Affairs Council, and Hawaii Department of Education. Member: Speech Association of America, National Society for the Study of Communication, American Association of University Professors, Pacific Speech Association. Awards, honors: Ford Foundation grant, 1961-63; curriculum development grant, University of Hawaii Foundation, 1967; East-West Communication Institute, senior fellow, 1971-72.

WRITINGS: (With Theodore Clevenger) Speech and Social Action, Prentice-Hall, 1967; (with Paul Deutschmann and John McNelly) Communication and Technological Change in Latin America, Praeger, 1967; (with Sarah Sanderson) Weather Communication: A Programmed Introduction, Program Associates, 1967. Contributor to communication and speech journals. Editor, Journal of the Alleganies, 1965; associate editor, Pacific Speech, 1967.

WORK IN PROGRESS: A field study on the communication behavior of population communication administrators in the Philippines and Malaysia.

*   *   *

ELLIOT, Edith M(arie Farmer)   1912-

PERSONAL: Born May 23, 1912, in Seattle, Wash.; daughter of Ernest Melvin (a lawyer) and Cora Lillian (Van Ornum) Farmer; married Wilmar Alexander Laing Elliot (a railway clerk), November 30, 1939; children: Ernest Alexander, Wesley Scott, Wilmar Bruce, Mary Edith. Education: University of Washington, Seattle, B.S., 1935. Politics: "Middle of the road Republican." Religion: United Church of Christ. Home: 7636 Northeast 33rd Dr., Portland, Ore. 97211.

CAREER: San Francisco Chronicle, San Francisco, Calif., writer in home service department, 1935-36; Los Angeles Examiner, Los Angeles, Calif., writer and assistant to Prudence Penny, 1936-37; home service director and radio and news columnist for two public utilities in Hilo, Hawaii, 1937-41; later public health nutritionist in Hawaii, and then writer in home economics departments of Oregon Journal and Oregonian, Portland, Ore.; free-lance writer. Member: National League of American Pen Women, Willamette Writers Club, Alpha Delta Pi Alumnae.

WRITINGS: Christopher's Hoppy Day, Whitman Publishing, 1967. Contributor of nonfiction to periodicals.

WORK IN PROGRESS: Two biographies completed, but as yet unpublished, entitled Look Back In Love and Murder on Molokai.

*   *   *

ELLIS, Mary Leith   1921-

PERSONAL: Born October 5, 1921, in Hodges, S.C.;

daughter of William Hartnette (a farmer) and Lucy (Haddon) Leith; married Richard Bourne Ellis (a structural engineer), July 3, 1948; children: Lucy Marie, Carol Louise. *Education:* Erskine College, A.B., 1941; Yale University, M.P.H., 1945; Georgia State University, Ed.S., 1975. *Politics:* Democrat. *Religion:* Presbyterian. *Home:* 2381 Eastway Rd., Decatur, Ga. 30033.

CAREER: Teacher of English and science at high school in Simpsonville, S.C., 1941-43, and of science in Piedmont, S.C., 1943-44; South Carolina State Board of Health, health educator in Charleston, 1945-48, and Columbia, 1948-51; Dekalb County McLendon Elementary School, Decatur, Ga., teacher, 1968—.

WRITINGS: Jesus Christ, Son of God (adaptation of *The Sun of God*), with teacher's guide, John Knox, 1967; *Growing in Faith and Knowledge,* with teacher's guide, Covenant Life Curriculum Press, 1968. Also author of teacher's guide to *Story of the Church,* 1966.

*   *   *

ELMSLIE, Kenward 1929-

PERSONAL: Born April 27, 1929, in New York, N.Y.; son of William Gray (a speculator) and Constance (Pulitzer) Elmslie. *Education:* Harvard University, B.A., 1950. *Home:* The Eyrie, Calais, Vt.

CAREER: Writer. Composer/librettist panel member, National Endowment of the Arts, 1973-76. Publisher of Z Press; editor of *Z Magazine. Member:* Dramatists Guild, American Society of Composers, Authors and Publishers (ASCAP), American Guild of Authors and Composers. *Awards, honors:* National Endowment for the Arts award, 1967, for poem, "The Power Plant Sestina"; Frank O'Hara Award for poetry, 1971.

WRITINGS: Pavilions (poems), Tibor de Nagy Editions, 1961; *The Baby Book,* Boke Press, 1965; *Power Plant Poems,* C Press, 1967; *The Champ,* Black Sparrow Press, 1968; *Album* (poems), Kulchur Press, 1970; *Circus Nerves* (poems), Black Sparrow Press, 1971; *Motor Disturbance* (poems), Columbia University Press, 1971; *The Grass Harp* (musical adaptation of the novel by Truman Capote; music by Claibe Richardson; first produced on Broadway at Martin Beck Theatre, November 2, 1971), Samuel French, 1972; *The Orchid Stories* (novel), Doubleday, 1972; *Tropicalism* (poems), Z Press, 1975.

Opera libretti: *Miss Julie* (music by Ned Rorem; produced by New York City Opera, 1965), Boosey & Hawkes, 1965; *Lizzie Borden* (music by Jack Beeson; produced by New York City Opera, 1965), Boosey & Hawkes, 1965; *The Sweet Bye and Bye* (music by Jack Beeson; produced by Julliard Opera Co., 1956), Boosey & Hawkes, 1966; *The Seagull* (music by Thomas Pasatieri; produced by Houston Grand Opera, 1973), Belwin-Mills, 1973. Has done translations from the French, German, and Italian, in collaboration with Ruth Yorck. Art critic, *Art News,* 1966-67.

WORK IN PROGRESS: Washington Square, an opera libretto, music by Thomas Pasatieri, based on the novel by Henry James.

AVOCATIONAL INTERESTS: Attending rehearsals of something he has written, cooking, weeding, walking, tennis, movies, reading newspapers, seeing friends.

*   *   *

ELSNER, Henry, Jr. 1930-

PERSONAL: Born December 13, 1930, in Detroit, Mich.; son of Henry (a watchmaker) and Augusta (Heise) Elsner; married Charlotte M. Schwimmer, January 13, 1968. *Education:* University of Michigan, B.A., 1952, M.A., 1953, Ph.D., 1963. *Home:* 319 South 44th St., Philadelphia, Pa. 19104.

CAREER: University of Pennsylvania, Philadelphia, instructor in sociology, 1961-63; Temple University, Philadelphia, Pa., instructor in sociology, 1963-65; Villanova University, Villanova, Pa., associate professor of sociology, 1965—. *Military service:* U.S. Army, 1953-55. *Member:* American Sociological Association.

WRITINGS: The Technocrats: Prophets of Automation, Syracuse University Press, 1967; (editor and author of introduction) Robert E. Park, *The Crowd and the Public and Other Essays,* University of Chicago Press, 1972.

WORK IN PROGRESS: Research in the field of social movements, social-political change, and collective behavior.

*   *   *

EMERSON, Donald (Conger) 1913-

PERSONAL: Born September 17, 1913, in Toronto, Ontario, Canada; son of Henry Conger and Isabel (Rife) Emerson; married Glenys Truax, 1943; children: Margaret, John. *Education:* University of Wisconsin, B.A., 1937, M.A., 1946, Ph.D., 1950. *Home:* 3233 North Hackett Ave., Milwaukee, Wis. 53211. *Agent:* Larry Sternig, 2407 North 44th St., Milwaukee, Wis. 53210. *Office:* University of Wisconsin, Milwaukee, Wis. 53201.

CAREER: University of Wisconsin-Milwaukee, instructor, 1948-54, associate professor, 1955-59, professor of English, 1960—, assistant dean of College of Letters and Science, 1958-62. *Military service:* U.S. Army, Infantry, 1942-45; became master sergeant; received Bronze Star Medal. *Member:* Modern Language Association of America, National Council of Teachers of English, American Studies Association, American Association of University Professors, Authors Guild, Midwest Modern Language Association (vice-president, 1962-63), Wisconsin Council of Teachers of English, Wisconsin Regional Writers Association, Council for Wisconsin Writers (president, 1965).

WRITINGS: Span across a River, McKay, 1966; *Court Decision,* McKay, 1967. Contributor of articles and reviews to scholarly periodicals.

WORK IN PROGRESS: Adult and juvenile novels.

*   *   *

EMERSON, Thomas I(rwin) 1907-

PERSONAL: Born July 12, 1907, in Passaic, N.J.; son of Luther Lee (an engineer) and Wilhelmina (Runft) Emerson; married Bertha Paret, October 9, 1934 (died, 1958); married Ruth Calvin (a tutor), May 27, 1960; children: (first marriage) Joan Paret, Robert Madden, Luther Lee. *Education:* Yale University, B.A., 1928, LL.B., 1931, M.A., 1946. *Politics:* Independent. *Religion:* None. *Home:* 2271 Ridge Rd., North Haven, Conn. 06473. *Office:* Yale Law School, New Haven, Conn. 06520.

CAREER: Admitted to New York Bar, 1932, and practiced law with a New York City firm, 1932-33; U.S. Government, Washington, D.C., attorney with National Labor Relations Board, and Social Security Board, 1933-37, assistant general counsel, later associate general counsel for National Labor Relations Board, 1937-40, special assistant to U.S. Attorney General, Department of Justice, 1940-41, associate general counsel, later deputy administrator for enforcement, Office of Price Administration, 1941-45, general counsel for Office of Economic Stabilization, 1945, and Office of War Mobilization and Reconversion, 1945-46; Yale University Law School, New Haven, Conn., Lines Professor of Public Law, 1946—. *Member:* National Lawyers Guild (president, 1951-52). *Awards, honors:* Guggenheim fellow, 1953-54; Ford Foundation faculty fellow, 1960-61; Fulbright fellowship to Japan, 1974-75.

WRITINGS: (With David Haber) *Political and Civil Rights in the United States,* foreword by Robert M. Hutchins, Dennis, 1952, 3rd edition (with Haber and Norman Dorsen), Little, Brown, 1967; *Toward a General Theory of the First Amendment,* Random House, 1966; *The System of Freedom of Expression.,* Random House, 1970. Contributor to *Nation, Saturday Review,* and legal journals.

SIDELIGHTS: A view of the importance of Emerson's work was expressed by C. Herman Pritchett when he wrote: "Thomas I. Emerson is not the father of the Bill of Rights but surely he must rank at least as a son-in-law. For no other member of the legal profession has so tirelessly and so effectively combined scholarly exposition with public defense of the constitutional principles of an open society. Many constitutional scholars can ably dissect Supreme Court opinions, but few would have been able to bring into relationship the various components of the system of free expression as skillfully as he has done in this monumental work."

BIOGRAPHICAL/CRITICAL SOURCES: Virginia Quarterly Review, Autumn, 1970.

* * *

ENDLER, Norman S(olomon) 1931-

PERSONAL: Born May 2, 1931, in Montreal, Quebec, Canada; son of Elie (a cutter of men's clothing) and Pearl (Segal) Endler; married Beatrice Kerdman, June 26, 1955; children: Mark, Marla. *Education:* Bet Berl College, Kfar Saba, Israel, student, 1950-51; McGill University, B.Sc., 1953, M.Sc., 1954; University of Illinois, Ph.D., 1958. *Religion:* Jewish. *Home:* 52 Sawley Dr., Willowdale, Ontario, Canada. *Office:* York University, Toronto, Ontario, Canada M3J 1P3.

CAREER: University of Illinois, Urbana, clinical intern in Student Counseling Service and Psychological Clinic, 1957-58; Pennsylvania State University, University Park, psychologist, Division of Counseling, 1958-60; York University, Toronto, Ontario, research associate and lecturer, 1960-62, assistant professor, 1962-65, associate professor, 1965-68, professor of psychology, 1968—, chairman of department, 1974—. University of Illinois, research assistant professor, summer, 1964, research associate professor, summers, 1965-67; visiting professor, University of Stockholm, 1974.

MEMBER: American Psychological Association (fellow), Canadian Psychological Association (fellow), Society for the Psychological Study of Social Issues, Canadian Association of University Teachers, Society for Research in Child Development, Ontario Psychological Association (member of board of directors, 1968-70), Sigma Xi. *Awards, honors:* Research grants from National Research Council of Canada, 1964-65, 1966-67, U.S. Public Health Service, 1964-67, Joseph E. Atkinson Foundation, 1965, Laidlaw Foundation, 1966, Ontario Mental Health Foundation, 1968-69; Canada Council senior fellowship, 1967-68; John B. C. Watkins Leave Fellowship, 1973-74.

WRITINGS: (Editor with L. R. Boulter and H. Osser) *Contemporary Issues in Developmental Psychology,* Holt, 1968, 2nd edition, 1975; (editor with David Magnusson) *Interactional Psychology and Personality,* Hemisphere, 1975; (with E. J. Shipton and F. D. Kemper) *Maturing in a Changing World,* Prentice-Hall, 1971; (editor with Magnusson) *Interactional Psychology: Current Issues in Theory and Research,* Halsted, 1976. Contributor of more than twenty articles on anxiety, social conformity, and hostility to journals, a number of them reprinted in books.

WORK IN PROGRESS: Research in anxiety and conformity.

* * *

ENGBERG, Edward 1928-

PERSONAL: Born March 5, 1928; son of Molts Ivan and Corrine (Olson) Engberg; married Catherine Lilek, February 19, 1949; children: Anton, Karen, Kristin, Elizabeth. *Education:* University of Chicago, A.B., 1952. *Home:* 221 East Constance, Santa Barbara, Calif. 93105.

CAREER: Fund for the Republic, New York City, managing editor of *Business International,* 1951-59; *Fortune,* New York City, associate editor, 1952-54; Cowles Communications, New York City, senior editor, 1959-65; Center for the Study of Democratic Institutions, Santa Barbara, Calif., senior fellow, 1967—; Forum for Contemporary History, editorial chairman, 1971-75; Committee Against Government Secrecy, national chairman, 1972-75; Christopher, Edwards & Henry, partner, 1975—. Consultant to Dreyfus Corp. *Military service:* U.S. Army, 1945-47. *Member:* Overseas Press Club, National Press Club, University of Chicago Club of New York (president, 1966).

WRITINGS: (With others) *Blacklisting in the Entertainment Industry,* Fund for the Republic, 1956; *The Spy in the Corporate Structure and the Right to Privacy,* World Publishing, 1967. Contributor to magazines, including *Fortune, New Republic, Commonweal, New Leader, Chicago Tribune Magazine, Center Magazine,* and *Skeptic.*

WORK IN PROGRESS: A biography of Thorstein Veblen.

* * *

ENGEL, James F. 1934-

PERSONAL: Born March 3, 1934, in Des Moines, Iowa; son of Frederick E. and Lucille (Anderson) Engel; married Sharon Kay Callies, August 18, 1957; children: Janet, Joanne, Susan. *Education:* Drake University, B.S., 1956; University of Illinois, M.S., 1957, Ph.D., 1960. *Religion:* Methodist. *Home:* 707 Howard, Wheaton, Ill. 60187. *Office:* Graduate School Communications Department, Wheaton College, Wheaton, Ill. 60187.

CAREER: University of Illinois, Champaign, instructor in marketing, 1959-60; University of Michigan, Ann Arbor, assistant professor of marketing, 1960-63; Ohio State University, Columbus, associate professor, 1963-66, professor of marketing, 1967-72; Wheaton College, Wheaton, Ill., professor and director of the Billy Graham Graduate Program in Communications, 1972—. Visiting professor at University of New South Wales; national faculty coordinator, Campus Crusade for Christ International. *Member:* American Marketing Association, Association for Consumer Research (founder and first president), American Economic Association, Academy of Advertising, Alpha Kappa Psi, Columbus Advertising Club.

WRITINGS: (With Hugh G. Wales and Martin R. Warshaw) *Promotional Strategy,* Irwin, 1967, 3rd edition, 1975; (with Theodore N. Beckman and William R. Davidson) *Marketing,* 8th edition, Ronald, 1967; (with Roger D. Blackwell and David T. Kollat) *Consumer Behavior,* Holt, 1968, 2nd edition, 1973; *Consumer Behavior: Selected Readings,* Irwin, 1968; (with Blackwell and Kollat) *Cases in Consumer Behavior,* Holt, 1969; (with Blackwell and Kollat) *Research in Consumer Behavior,* Holt, 1970; (with W. Wayne Talarzyk and Carl M. Larson) *Cases in Promotional Strategy,* Irwin, 1971; (with M. A. Cayley and Henry Riorillo) *Market Segmentation: Concept and Applications,* Holt, 1972; (with H. Wilbert Norton) *What's Gone Wrong with the Harvest? A Communication Strategy for the Church and World Evangelization,* Zondervan, 1975. Contributor of articles to marketing and religion journals. Member of editorial board, *Journal of Marketing.*

* * *

ENGEL, Louis (Henry, Jr.)   1909-

PERSONAL: Born November 27, 1909, in Jacksonville, Ill.; son of Louis Henry (an auditor) and Maude (Salyers) Engel; married Viola De Berrienne, July 29, 1932 (divorced); married Mary June Montgomery, June 19, 1943 (divorced); married Nina Phillips Washburn, August 8, 1954; children: (second marriage) James Montgomery, Thomas Edward, Jonathan Clark. *Education:* University of Chicago, Ph.B., 1930. *Home:* Revolutionary Rd., Scarborough, N.Y. 10510.

CAREER: University of Chicago Press, Chicago, Ill., staff member, 1930-32; *Advertising and Selling,* New York City, staff member, 1932, managing editor, 1933-34; *Business Week,* New York City, news editor, 1934-35, marketing editor, 1935-36, managing editor, 1937-46; Merrill Lynch, Pierce, Fenner & Smith, Inc. (investments), New York City, advertising manager, 1946-69, vice-president, 1954-69. Elected trustee, Village of Ossining, N.Y., 1970-74. *Member:* Phi Beta Kappa, Wall Street Club.

WRITINGS: How to Buy Stocks, Little, Brown, 1953, 6th edition, 1976. Work included in Watkins' *100 Greatest Advertisements* and *100 Great Copywriters.*

* * *

ENGELMANN, Siegfried E.   1931-

PERSONAL: Born November 26, 1931, in Chicago, Ill.; son of Victor E. (a physician) and Rose (Onixt) Engelmann; married Therese Piorkowski (a lawyer), June 28, 1953; children: Eric, Kurt and Owen (twins), Joyce. *Education:* University of Illinois, B.A., 1955. *Politics:* "Slightly liberal." *Religion:* Atheist. *Home:* 1910 Fairmont, Eugene, Ore. 97401. *Office:* Department of Education, University of Oregon, Eugene, Ore. 97403.

CAREER: Self-employed investment counselor, 1955-60; creative director, vice-president, and holder of various other positions in advertising agencies, 1960-64; University of Illinois, Institute for Research on Exceptional Children, Urbana, research associate, 1964-66, senior educational specialist, 1966-70; University of Oregon, Eugene, professor of special education, 1970—. Visiting professor at Ontario Institute for Studies in Education, summer, 1966, and Colorado State University, summer, 1971; visiting research associate, Oregon Research Institute, 1972—. Researcher and administrator of government-funded projects on the education of disadvantaged children, and on the effectiveness of various methods of instruction. Consultant

to the Office of Education, Office of Economic Opportunity, and numerous school districts, libraries, and other education centers. Visiting speaker at educational conferences and workshops, and at numerous colleges and universities, including University of California, Michigan State University, Stanford University, University of the Pacific, and Pennsylvania State University.

WRITINGS: (With wife, Therese Engelmann) *Give Your Child a Superior Mind,* Simon & Schuster, 1966; (with Carl Bereiter) *Teaching Disadvantaged Children in the Preschool,* Prentice-Hall, 1966; (with Bereiter) *Language Learning Activities for the Disadvantaged Child,* Anti-Defamation League of B'nai B'rith, 1966; (with S. Osborn and B. Lundeen) *Learning Language: Part-Whole Relationships,* University of Illinois Press, 1967; (with Osborn and Lundeen) *Learning Language: Concept and Action Stories,* University of Illinois Press, 1968; *Conceptual Learning,* Dimensions Publishing Co., 1969; *Preventing Failure in the Primary Grades,* Science Research Associates, 1969; (with Wesley C. Becker and Don R. Thomas) *Teaching: A Course in Applied Psychology,* Science Research Associates, 1971, 2nd edition published as *Teaching 1: Classroom Management,* and *Teaching 1: Cognitive Learning and Instruction,* both 1975; *Your Child Can Succeed: How to Get the Most Out of School for Your Child,* Simon & Schuster, 1975.

Contributor: F. M. Hechinger, editor, *Preschool Education Today,* Doubleday, 1966; F. W. McDowell, editor, *Education and Training of the Mentally Retarded,* Council for Exceptional Children, National Education Association, 1967; D. W. Brison and E. Sullivan, editors, *Psychology and Early Childhood Education,* Ontario Institute for Studies in Education, 1967; K. E. Berry and B. Bateman, editors, *Dimensions in Early Learning Series,* Dimensions Publishing Co., 1969; F. Williams, editor, *Language and Poverty: Perspectives on a Theme,* Markham, 1970; J. G. Morrey, editor, *Failure Prevention: A Programming Necessity,* Idaho State University, 1971; *Socio-Linguistics Cross-Disciplinary Perspective,* Center for Applied Linguistics, 1971; D. R. Green, M. P. Ford, and G. B. Flamer, *Measurement and Piaget,* California Test Bureau, 1971; *New Books in Reading Instruction, Series I,* Multimedia Publishing, 1971; M. Csapo and B. Poutt, *Education for All Children,* Federation of the Council for Exceptional Children (Vancouver, B.C.), 1974.

Co-author of more than thirty instructional programs, including texts, tests and teacher's manuals, for Science Research Associates. Contributor of articles to education journals.

* * *

ENGLISH, James W(ilson)   1915-

PERSONAL: Born January 13, 1915, in Phoenix, Ariz.; son of James Henderson (a farmer) and Fannie (Briedlove) English; married Dolores V. Hoffelder, December 18, 1948; children: Jamee Dolores, James W., Jr., Diane Marie, Richard Gregory, Stevan Michael, Jeffrey Douglas. *Education:* Phoenix Junior College, A.A., 1935; Vanderbilt University, B.A., 1937. *Politics:* Liberal Republican. *Religion:* Methodist. *Home:* 1046 Beau Brummel Dr., Route 1, Dundee, Ill. 60118. *Office:* D. C. Cook Publishing Co., Elgin, Ill. 60120.

CAREER: Worked at variety of writing assignments with United Press, *Arizona Highways,* U.S. Social Security Board, and others, 1937-40; *Boys' Life,* New York, N.Y., writer, and later executive editor, 1940-41, 1945-51; D. C. Cook Publishing Co. (religious publisher), Elgin, Ill., 1952—, began as editorial director, then director of marketing, became director of denominational sales. Private consultant on marketing, public relations, the religious market, and selling the Negro market. *Military service:* U.S. Army, Counterintelligence Corps, 1941-45, 1951-52; served in Southwest Pacific; became first lieutenant (field commission). *Member:* Authors Guild, Rotary International.

WRITINGS: The Rin Tin Tin Story, Dodd, 1949; *Border Adventure,* Abelard, 1952; *Tailbone Patrol,* Holiday House, 1955; *Tops in Troop 10,* Macmillan, 1966; *Handyman of the Lord* (biography of William Holmes Borders, a Negro minister), Meredith, 1967; (with Rose Butler Browne) *Love My Children* (Mrs. Browne's autobiography), Meredith, 1969; *The Prophet of Wheat Street,* David C. Cook, 1973.

WORK IN PROGRESS: The Camera Bug Spy, a teen-age mystery, for Putnam; a novel.

SIDELIGHTS: James English camped out with Boy Scouts in all fifty states while on assignments for *Boys' Life,* shot the Colorado River rapids, and hunted wild pigs in Hawaii.

BIOGRAPHICAL/CRITICAL SOURCES: Boys' Life, February, 1967.

*   *   *

ENGLIZIAN, H. Crosby   1923-

PERSONAL: Surname is pronounced En-*glee*-zian; born August 12, 1923, in Chelsea, Mass.; son of S. (a shoemaker) and Virginia (Noradunkian) Englizian; married Eleanor F. Harvey (a secretary), June 4, 1949; children: Mark, Gail, Lois. *Education:* Grace Theological Seminary and Grace College, Winona Lake, Ind., B.A. and B.D., 1956; Western Baptist Seminary (now Western Conservative Baptist Seminary), Portland, Ore., Th.M., 1962; Dallas Theological Seminary and Graduate School of Theology, Th.D., 1966. *Politics:* Independent. *Office:* 5511 Southeast Hawthorne Blvd., Portland, Ore. 97215.

CAREER: Baptist clergyman in South Dakota and Idaho, 1956-61; Western Baptist Seminary (now Western Conservative Baptist Seminary), Portland, Ore., professor of church history and director of postgraduate studies, 1966—. *Military service:* U.S. Army, 1943-45; became sergeant. *Awards, honors:* George Washington Honor Medal of Freedoms Foundation in sermon category, 1961.

WRITINGS: Brimstone Corner: History of Park Street Church, Boston, Moody, 1968; (contributor) *The New International Dictionary of the Christian Church,* Zondervan, 1974. Occasional contributor to Baptist and other religious periodicals.

*   *   *

ENOMIYA-LASSALLE, Hugo M(akibi)   1898-

PERSONAL: Original name, Hugo Lassalle; born November 11, 1898, in Nieheim, Germany; son of Georg (a judge) and Elisabeth (Feltmann) Lassalle. *Education:* Educated in Germany, 1905-16, in the Netherlands at St. Ignatius College, Valkenburg, 1921-23, and in England at Stonyhurst, St. Mary's Hall, 1923-24, and Heythrop College, 1926-28. *Home:* Zen-Retreathouse, 8.702 Hinohara-mura, Nisitamagun, Tokyo 190-02, Japan. *Office:* Sophia University, Kioicho 7, Chiyoda-Ku, Tokyo, Japan; Elisabeth University of Musik, Hiroshima, Japan.

CAREER: Roman Catholic priest of Jesuit order (S.J.). Sophia University, Tokyo, Japan, professor of German, 1929-38; superior of Jesuit mission in Japan, 1935-49; Hiroshima University, Hiroshima, Japan, faculty member, 1943-45, 1947-49; Elisabeth University of Musik, Hiroshima, Japan, professor of religious science, 1948—. *Military service:* German Army, 1916-19.

WRITINGS: "Hiroshima," los Talleres Graficus de la Compania Impressora Argintina, [Buenos Aires], 1948; *Shinri to Onkei,* Enderle (Tokyo), 1959; *Zen—Weg zur Erleuchtung,* Herder (Vienna), 1960, translation published as *Zen—Way to Enlightenment,* Burns & Oates, 1967; *Zen-Buddhismus,* Bachem (Cologne), 1966; *Meditation als weg zur Gotteserfahrung,* Bachem, 1972; *Zen unter Christen,* Styria, 1973; *Zen-Meditation fur Christen,* 3rd edition, O. W. Barth, 1973, translation published as *Zen Meditation for Christians,* Open Court, 1974; *Zazen und die Exerzitien des heiligen Ignatius,* Bachem, 1975; *Zen-Meditation,* Benziger, 1975.

SIDELIGHTS: Father Enomiya-Lassalle has studied Zen, as it is practiced in Japan, for about thirty years. Of German birth, educated in the Netherlands and England, and now a Japanese national, he finds no conflicts of faith between being a follower of the teachings of Ignatius and systematically taking part in Zen meditation.

BIOGRAPHICAL/CRITICAL SOURCES: Times Literary Supplement (London), March 23, 1967, June 7, 1967.

*   *   *

ENTINE, Alan D(avid)   1936-

PERSONAL: Second syllable of surname rhymes with "dine"; born June 30, 1936, in New York, N.Y.; son of Ben and Jeanne (Schimmel) Entine; married Jean Marks (a social worker), July 22, 1967. *Education:* Middlebury College, B.A., 1956; University of Melbourne, graduate study, 1958; Columbia University, M.A., 1960, Ph.D., 1963. *Office:* Undergraduate studies, State University of New York, Stony Brook, N.Y. 11790.

CAREER: Procter & Gamble Co., Cincinnati, Ohio, public relations staff, 1956-57; Columbia University, New York, N.Y., assistant professor of economics, 1963-70, School of General Studies, assistant dean, 1965-67, associate dean, 1967-70; State University of New York at Stony Brook, adjunct associate professor of economics and assistant vice-president of undergraduate studies, 1970—. Consultant to New York Moreland Commission, 1963, and to New York Temporary Commission on City Finances, 1964. *Military service:* U.S. Army, 1961-62; Army Reserves, 1962-66. *Member:* American Economic Association, American Finance Association, American Association for the Advancement of Science, American College Public Relations Association, American Association of University Professors, American Alumni Council, Phi Beta Kappa.

WRITINGS: (Editor) *Monetary Economics: Readings,* Wadsworth, 1968; (with Peter Kenen and Albert Hart) *Money, Debt and Economic Activity,* 4th edition, Prentice-Hall, 1969; (editor) *Americans in Middle Years: Career Options and Educational Opportunities,* University of Southern California Press, 1974; (editor with Ann Zambrano) *Job Seekers Guide for Academics,* Change Magazine, 1976. Contributor to professional journals.†

EPSTEIN, Howard M(ichael) 1927-

PERSONAL: Born April 27, 1927, in New York, N.Y.; son of Samuel and Florence (Gilbert) Epstein; married Cynthia Fuchs (a sociologist), July 4, 1954; children: Alexander Maxim. *Education:* Queens College (now Queens College of the City University of New York), Flushing, N.Y., B.A.; Institut d'Etudes Politiques, University of Paris, Certificate. *Politics:* Democrat. *Home:* 425 Riverside Dr., New York, N.Y. 10025. *Office:* Facts on File, Inc., 119 West 57th St., New York, N.Y. 10019.

CAREER: Xenia Gazette, Xenia, Ohio, news editor, 1952-55; Facts on File, Inc. (news reference publishers), New York, N.Y., managing editor and vice-president of company, 1958—. Free-lance book editor. *Military service:* U.S. Navy, 1945-46.

WRITINGS: Revolt in the Congo, Facts on File, 1965; (editor) *News Dictionary,* Facts on File, annually, 1965—.

* * *

ERDMAN, Howard Loyd 1935-

PERSONAL: Born August 29, 1935, in Boston, Mass.; son of Simon (a teacher) and Eva (Friedman) Erdman; married Joan Barbara Landy, March 7, 1940 (divorced, 1973); children: Karen, Deborah. *Education:* Harvard University, B.A., 1958, M.A., 1960, Ph.D., 1964. *Religion:* Jewish. *Home:* 28 East Wheelock, Hanover, N.H. 03755. *Office:* 217 Silsby, Dartmouth College, Hanover, N.H. 03755.

CAREER: Dartmouth College, Hanover, N.H., assistant professor, 1964-69, associate professor, 1969-75, professor of government, 1975—. *Member:* American Council of Learned Societies, American Philosophical Society, Association for Asian Studies, Phi Beta Kappa. *Awards, honors:* Sheldon traveling fellowship, Harvard University, 1962-63; Fulbright grant, 1962-63, and American Institute of Indian Studies grant, 1966-67, for work in India; Social Science Research Council grant, 1956; Dartmouth faculty fellowship, 1966-67; Fulbright grant, 1971-72, for research in London and India.

WRITINGS: The Swatantra Party and Indian Conservatism, Cambridge University Press, 1967; *Political Attitudes of Indian Industry,* Institute of Commonwealth Studies (London), 1971; *Politics and Economic Development in India,* D. K. Publishing House (Delhi), 1973. Contributor to *Asian Survey, Pacific Affairs,* and *Journal of Developing Areas.*

WORK IN PROGRESS: Public Policy Making for Fertilizer Production in India.

* * *

ERNST, Margot Klebe 1939-

PERSONAL: Born November 1, 1939, in Philadelphia, Pa.; daughter of Charles Eugene (an artist) and Mary (Klaer) Klebe; married Robert Clark Ernst (a restaurant owner), August 11, 1962; children: Andrew Robert, Laura Jane. *Education:* Tufts University, B.A. (cum laude), 1962. *Home:* 259 Main St., West Harwich, Mass. 02671.

CAREER: Elementary teacher in Ithaca, N.Y., 1962-63; substitute teacher in Cape Cod, Mass., 1966-67.

WRITINGS: (With father, Gene Klebe) *Penguin Family,* Putnam, 1968.

WORK IN PROGRESS: Articles or book based on two years in Germany and a three-month camping trip throughout Europe.††

ERNST, Robert 1915-

PERSONAL: Born March 1, 1915, in New York, N.Y.; son of Arthur O. (a lawyer) and Florence (Pakas) Ernst; married Esther Boyden, July 29, 1950; children: David Arthur, Thomas Boyden. *Education:* Columbia University, A.B., 1936, Ph.D., 1947; Brown University, A.M., 1937. *Office:* Department of History, Adelphi University, Garden City, N.Y. 11530.

CAREER: University of North Carolina, Chapel Hill, instructor in social science, 1940-41; Briarcliff College, Briarcliff Manor, N.Y., instructor in history and economics, 1944-45; Adelphi University, Garden City, N.Y., instructor, 1946-47, assistant professor, 1947-54, associate professor, 1954-58, professor of history, 1958—. Member, Lay Advisory Committee on Adult Education, Great Neck, N.Y., 1953-54; director, Westbury (N.Y.) Education Association, 1963-68. *Military service:* U.S. Army, 1942-44; became second lieutenant. *Member:* American Historical Association, Organization of American Historians, American Association of University Professors, American Civil Liberties Union, New York Historical Society. *Awards, honors:* Grants-in-aid from American Philosophical Society, 1958, and Huntington Library, 1960.

WRITINGS: Immigrant Life in New York City, 1825-1863, King's Crown Press, 1949; *Rufus King, American Federalist,* University of North Carolina Press, 1968. Contributor of articles and reviews to professional journals.

* * *

ESCARRAZ, Donald Ray 1932-

PERSONAL: Born November 24, 1932, in Chicago, Ill.; son of Enrique and Edith May (Porter) Escarraz; married Barbara Fay Swartz, May 24, 1952; children: Pamela Kay, Paul Edward, Peter James, Patricia Marie, Phyllis Ann, Philip Lee. *Education:* University of Tampa, B.S., 1960; University of Wisconsin, M.B.A., 1961; Oklahoma State University, Ph.D., 1964. *Religion:* Presbyterian. *Home:* 5001 Meadow Lane, Dickinson, Tex. 77539. *Office:* University of Houston at Clear Lake City, Houston, Tex. 77058.

CAREER: N. Shure Co., Chicago, Ill., assistant buyer and later buyer for stationery department, 1950-53; O. J. Swartz Co. (wholesale bleach firm), Melrose Park, Ill., business manager, 1955-57; University of Florida, Gainesville, assistant professor of economics, 1964-66; University of Georgia, Athens, associate professor of finance, 1966-74; University of Houston at Clear Lake City, Houston, Tex., associate professor of finance, 1974—. *Military service:* U.S. Army, Signal Corps, 1953-54. *Member:* Academy of Political Science, American Economic Association, National Tax Association, Southern Economic Association, Public Choice Society.

WRITINGS: (With Robert L. Sandmeyer) *A Study of Expenditures and Sources of Revenue for Mental Health and Retardation Services in the State of Oklahoma: 1963,* Research Institute, Oklahoma State University, 1963; *The Price Theory of Value in Public Finance,* University of Florida Press, 1967; (contributor) *Planning, Programming, Budgeting Systems for Government* (readings), University of Georgia Press, 1968; *State Government Revenue Sources: Georgia,* Institute of Government, University of Georgia, 1969; (contributor) Horst Claus Recktenwald, editor, *Nutzen-Kosten-Analyse und Programmbudget,* J.C.B. Mohr (Tubingen), 1970; *A History of State Debt Georgia,* Institute of Government, University of Georgia, 1975.

WORK IN PROGRESS: The Economics of Higher Education.

* * *

ESLER, Anthony (James) 1934-

PERSONAL: Born February 20, 1934, in New London, Conn.; son of James Arthur (an artist, sheetmetal worker, and shipfitter) and Helen (Kreamer) Esler; married Carol Clemeau (a college professor), 1961; children: Kenneth Campbell, David Douglas. *Education:* University of Arizona, B.A., 1956; Duke University, M.A., 1958, Ph.D., 1961; University of London, postdoctoral study, 1961-62. *Office:* College of William and Mary, Williamsburg, Va. 23185.

CAREER: College of William and Mary, Williamsburg, Va., assistant professor, 1962-67, associate professor, 1967-72, professor of history, 1972—. Visiting associate professor, Northwestern University, 1968-69. *Member:* American Association of University Professors, American Historical Association, National Association for the Advancement of Colored People, Williamsburg Human Relations Council. *Awards, honors:* Fulbright scholar in London, 1961-62; American Council of Learned Societies research fellow, Chicago, 1969-70; College of William and Mary research fellow, 1975-76.

WRITINGS: The Aspiring Mind of the Elizabethan Younger Generation, Duke University Press, 1966; *Bombs, Beards and Barricades,* Stein & Day, 1971; (contributor) Robert Bezucha, editor, *Modern European Social History,* Heath, 1972; *The Youth Revolution,* Heath, 1974; *The Blade of Castlemayne,* Morrow, 1974; *Hellbane,* Morrow, 1975; *Generations in History,* Exposition Press, 1975; *Lord Libertine,* Morrow, 1976.

WORK IN PROGRESS: Dreamers in the Streets, a study of rebellious youth in France, c. 1830, completion expected in 1976.

AVOCATIONAL INTERESTS: Drawing, travel, islands (Barbados, Lamu, Molokai), and beaches ("any good ocean beach, for as much of the summer as possible").

* * *

EVANS, George W(illiam) II 1920-

PERSONAL: Born June 8, 1920, in Houston, Tex.; son of Griffith Conrad (a professor) and Isabel (John) Evans; married Marjorie Woodard (a director of Poulter Laboratory, Stanford Research Institute), January 30, 1943; children: George W. III, Anne Garvin. *Education:* University of Colorado, student, 1938-39; University of California, Berkeley, A.B., 1942, M.A., 1943; New York University, Ph.D., 1951. *Home:* 14511 DeBell Dr., Los Altos Hills, Calif. 94022. *Office:* Department of Mathematics, University of Santa Clara, Santa Clara, Calif. 95053.

CAREER: New York University, New York, instructor in mathematics, 1946-49; Argonne National Laboratory, Lemont, Ill., research mathematician, 1949-53; University of California Radiation Laboratory, Livermore, research mathematician, 1953-54; Stanford Research Institute, Menlo Park, Calif., research mathematician, 1954-62, senior research mathematician, 1966-68, manager of mathematics and science departments, 1962-66; University of Santa Clara, Santa Clara, Calif., associate professor of mathematics, 1966—. *Military service:* U.S. Naval Reserve, active duty, 1943-45; became lieutenant; Submarine Reserve, 1946-51; Naval Research Reserve, 1951-55. *Member:* American Mathematical Society.

WRITINGS: (With C. L. Perry) *Programming and Coding for Automatic Digital Computers,* McGraw, 1961; (with G. F. Wallace and G. L. Sutherland) *Simulation Using Digital Computers,* Prentice-Hall, 1967. Contributor to professional journals.†

* * *

EVANS, Joseph W(illiam) 1921-

PERSONAL: Born December 10, 1921, in Dublin, Ontario, Canada; son of Peter Joseph and Catherine (Murray) Evans. *Education:* University of Western Ontario, B.A., 1942; Assumption College (now University of Windsor), Windsor, Ontario, M.A., 1947; University of Notre Dame, Ph.D., 1951. *Religion:* Roman Catholic. *Home:* 501 West Washington, South Bend, Ind.

CAREER: Assumption College (now University of Windsor), Windsor, Ontario, librarian, 1943-47; University of Notre Dame, Notre Dame, Ind., assistant professor, 1951-58, associate professor of philosophy and director of Jacques Maritain Center, 1958—. *Awards, honors:* Ford faculty fellowship to Yale University, 1953-54.

WRITINGS—Editor: (With Leo R. Ward) *The Social and Political Philosophy of Jacques Maritain: Selected Readings,* Scribner, 1955; Jacques Maritain, *On the Philosophy of History,* Scribner, 1957; (and author of introduction and contributor) *Jacques Maritain: The Man and His Achievements,* Sheed, 1963; (and author of comments with Ward) Maritain, *Challenges and Renewals: Selected Readings,* University of Notre Dame Press, 1966.

Translator: (And reviser with Peter O'Reilly) Maritain, *St. Thomas Aquinas,* Meridian, 1958; Jacques Maritain and Raissa Maritain, *Liturgy and Contemplation,* Kenedy, 1960; Maritain, *Art and Scholasticism and the Frontiers of Poetry,* Scribner, 1962; Maritain, *God and the Permission of Evil,* Bruce, 1966; Maritain, *Integral Humanism,* new edition, Scribner, 1968; Maritain, *On the Church of Christ: The Person of the Church and Her Personnel,* University of Notre Dame Press, 1973; Maritain, *Approaches without Shackles,* University of Notre Dame Press, in press. Contributor to *Encyclopaedia Britannica, Encyclopedia of Philosophy, New Catholic Encyclopedia,* and to learned journals.

SIDELIGHTS: Evans is competent in German and Latin, in addition to French.

* * *

EVANS, N(orman) Dean 1925-

PERSONAL: Born March 22, 1925, in Springfield, Pa.; son of Norman H. and Mae (Dean) Evans; married Jacqueline Lentz, June 23, 1951; children: Alan, Jennifer. *Education:* Ursinus College, A.B., 1948; University of Pennsylvania, M.S., 1951; Temple University, Ed.D., 1958; Princeton Theological Seminary, M.A., 1975. *Home:* 31 Hiawatha Trail, Medford Lakes, N.J. 08055. *Office:* Burlington County College, Pemberton, N.J. 08068.

CAREER: Lansdowne-Aldan Joint School System, Lansdowne, Pa., elementary principal, 1955-59; Delaware County Schools, Media, Pa., assistant county superintendent, 1959-65; West Chester State College, West Chester, Pa., area curriculum coordinator, 1965-67; Burlington County College, Pemberton, N.J., president, 1967—. Visiting professor at Temple University, University of Delaware, and University of New Hampshire. Formerly assistant minister, Church of the Redeemer, Springfield, Pa.;

currently assistant minister, St. Peter's Episcopal Church, Medford, N.J., and director of Christian education, Diocese of New Jersey. *Military service:* U.S. Army, 1943-46; served in Pacific Theater; became first sergeant. *Member:* National Education Association (life member), American Association of School Administrators (life member), Phi Delta Kappa.

WRITINGS: (With Ross L. Neagley) *Handbook for Effective Supervision of Instruction,* Prentice-Hall, 1964, revised edition, 1970; (with Neagley) *Handbook for Effective Curriculum Development,* Prentice-Hall, 1967; (with Neagley) *Planning and Developing Innovative Community Colleges,* Prentice-Hall, 1973. Contributor to educational journals.

AVOCATIONAL INTERESTS: Travel, color motion picture photography, music.

* * *

EVANS, Robert Henry 1937-

PERSONAL: Born April 1, 1937, in Bristol, England; son of Henry H. (an engineer) and Marguerita Evans; married Maria Antonietta Cappellini, August 5, 1961; children: Philippe, Francesca. *Education:* Institute of Political Studies, Paris, France, Diploma, 1959; Johns Hopkins University, Bologna (Italy) Center, Diploma, 1960; University of Denver, M.A., 1961, Ph.D., 1966. *Office:* Department of Government, University of Virginia, Charlottesville, Va. 22903.

CAREER: University of Notre Dame, Notre Dame, Ind., assistant professor of government, 1966-71; University of Virginia, Charlottesville, associate professor of government, 1971—. Visiting assistant professor, University of Denver, 1968. *Awards, honors:* Gold medal, First International Biennial of Scientific Publications, Italy, 1969.

WRITINGS: Coexistence, Communism and Its Practice in Bologna, 1946-1965, University of Notre Dame Press, 1967; (contributor) E. A. Goerner, editor, *Democracy in Crisis: New Challenges to Constitutional Democracy in the Atlantic Area,* University of Notre Dame Press, 1971; (with Enzo Bandelloni) *Arqua Petrarca: Profilo di una comunita Euganea,* Marsilio (Padua, Italy), 1971; (contributor) Leo Moulin, editor, *Les Eglises comme Institutions Politiques,* Institut Belge de Science Politique (Bruxelles), 1972; (contributor) Franco Cazzola and Zerzy Wiatr, editors, *Partecipazione e Sviluppo nella Politica Locale,* Officina Edizioni (Roma), 1974; (contributor) Donald C. Rowat, editor, *Recent Reorganizations of Local Governments Throughout the World,* University of Toronto Press, 1975.

WORK IN PROGRESS: Study of the Bank of Italy; The Life and Politics of a Venetian Community.

* * *

EVANS, Rowland, Jr. 1921-

PERSONAL: Born April 28, 1921, in White Marsh, Pa.; son of Rowland and Elizabeth Wharton (Downs) Evans; married Katherine Winton, June 18, 1949; children: Rowland Winton, Sarah Warren. *Education:* Attended Yale University, 1940-41, and George Washington University, 1950. *Religion:* Episcopalian. *Home:* 3125 0 St. N.W., Washington, D.C. 20007. *Office:* 1750 Pennsylvania Ave. N.W., Washington, D.C. 20006.

CAREER: Associated Press, reporter, 1945-55; *New York Herald Tribune,* New York, N.Y., editorial staff, 1955-63; syndicated columnist, "Inside Report," Washington, D.C., 1963—. News commentator and television panelist. *Military service:* U.S. Marine Corps Reserve, active duty, 1942-44.

WRITINGS: (With Robert D. Novak) *Lyndon B. Johnson: The Exercise of Power,* New American Library, 1966; (with Novak) *Nixon in the White House: The Frustration of Power,* Random House, 1971, revised edition, Vintage Books, 1972. Articles on the political scene and other topics have been published in *Reporter, Harper's, Saturday Evening Post, New Republic, Esquire, Atlantic Monthly,* and other national magazines.

BIOGRAPHICAL/CRITICAL SOURCES: Time, December 2, 1966.

* * *

EVANS, W(illiam) McKee 1923-

PERSONAL: Born September 17, 1923, in St. Pauls, N.C.; son of John Browne (in real estate business) and Alfreda (Pittard) Evans; married Ruth Van Camp (a college teacher), November 27, 1955 (divorced December, 1970); children: Owen Thomas, Katherine Ann, Daniel George, Laura Ellen. *Education:* Attended Davidson College, 1941-43, and American University at Biarritz, 1945; University of North Carolina, A.B., 1948, M.A., 1950, Ph.D., 1965. *Office:* Department of History, California State Polytechnic University, Pomona, Calif. 91766.

CAREER: Westminster College, Salt Lake City, Utah, lecturer in history, 1952-64; California Lutheran College, Thousand Oaks, assistant professor of history, 1964-68; California State Polytechnic University, Pomona, assistant professor of history, 1968—. *Military service:* U.S. Army, 1943-46; served in Europe. *Member:* Organization of American Historians, American Historical Association, Southern Historical Association. *Awards, honors:* American Association for State and Local History Prize, 1966, for *Ballots and Fence Rails.*

WRITINGS: Ballots and Fence Rails: Reconstruction on the Lower Cape Fear, University of North Carolina Press, 1967; *To Die Game: The Story of the Lowry Band, Indian Guerrillas of Reconstruction,* Louisiana State University Press, 1971.

SIDELIGHTS: Evans is competent in French, Spanish, and German.

* * *

EVANS, William Howard 1924-

PERSONAL: Born April 28, 1924, in Spring Lake, N.J.; son of Howard J. and Frances (Haselden) Evans; married Frances Marie Fox, June 11, 1949; children: Jenifer Marie, Stephen Michael (deceased), William Howard, Jr. *Education:* Florida Southern College, student, 1946-48; University of Colorado, B.A., 1950; Syracuse University, M.A., 1951; University of Florida, certified for teaching English in secondary schools and junior colleges, 1952; Florida State University, Ed.D., 1961. *Office:* Department of English, Southern Illinois University, Carbondale, Ill. 62901.

CAREER: Teacher of English in St. Petersburg, Fla., 1953-56; Pinellas County (Fla.) Board of Public Instruction, English supervisor, 1957-58; Florida State University, Tallahassee, instructor in English education, 1958-61; University of Illinois, Urbana, associate professor of English education, 1961-66; Southern Illinois University, Carbondale, professor of English, 1966—. Consultant to test department, Harcourt, Brace & World, Inc.; Chairman of English consultants, American Education Publications; associate director, Illinois State-Wide Curriculum Study Center, Preparation for Secondary School English Teachers, 1964-

66. Fund drive chairman, Tri-C United Fund, Williamson County, Ill., 1967. *Military service:* U.S. Navy, 1942-46.

MEMBER: National Council of Teachers of English, Conference on English Education (member of executive committee, 1963-68; program co-chairman, 1965; national chairman, 1968-70), Association for Higher Education, American Association of Colleges for Teacher Education, Illinois Association of Teachers of English, Phi Delta Kappa.

WRITINGS: Introduction to the Novel, Bantam, 1963; (contributor) *Research in Written Composition,* National Council of Teachers of English, 1963; (with Michael J. Cardone) *Specialized Courses in Methods of Teaching English,* National Council of Teachers of English, 1964; (with J. N. Hook) *Individualized English,* Follett, Set J, 1964, Set H, 1965; (compiler with Arno Jewett and Mary Ellen Chase) *Values in Literature* (anthology) Houghton, 1965, 2nd edition, 1968; (with Jerry L. Walker) *New Trends in the Teaching of English in Secondary Schools,* Rand McNally, 1966; (with Paul H. Jacobs) *Illinois Tests in the Teaching of English,* Southern Illinois University Press, 1969; (editor) *The Creative Teacher,* Bantam, 1971. Writer of other teaching materials for Science Research Associates, tests for Educational Testing Service, and guides for American Education Publications. Contributor to yearbooks and journals; compiler and editor of "Testing in English," special issue of *Illinois English Bulletin,* February, 1965.†

* * *

EVERITT, Alan (Milner) 1926-

PERSONAL: Born August 17, 1926, in Sevenoaks, Kent, England; son of Robert Arthur and Grace (Milner) Everitt. *Education:* Attended Sevenoaks School, 1938-43; University of St. Andrews, M.A., 1951; University of London, Ph.D., 1957. *Home:* Fieldedge, Kimcote, Lutterworth, England. *Office:* University of Leicester, Leicester, England.

CAREER: University of Leicester, Leicester, England, research assistant in agrarian history, 1957-59, research fellow in urban history, 1960-65, lecturer in English local history, 1965-68, Hatton Professor and head of English local history department, 1968—. Member, Northampton-shire Archives Committee; trustee, Marc Fitch Fund. *Member:* Historical Association, Economic History Society, Past and Present Society, British Agricultural History Society (executive committee member, 1964—), Kent Archaeological Society, Standing Conference for Local History (member of executive committee, 1968—), Leicestershire Archaeological Society (executive committee member, 1968—), Leicestershire Local History Council (vice-president, 1970—).

WRITINGS: The County Committee of Kent in the Civil War, Leicester University Press, 1957; *Suffolk and the Great Rebellion, 1640-1660,* Suffolk Records Society, 1960; *The Community of Kent and the Great Rebellion, 1640-1660,* Leicester University Press, 1966; *Change in the Provinces: The Seventeenth Century,* Leicester University Press, 1969; *The Local Community and the Great Rebellion,* Historical Association, 1969; *New Avenues in English Local History* (lecture), Leicester University Press, 1970; *Ways and Means in Local History,* National Council of Social Service for the Standing Conference for Local History, 1971; *The Pattern of Rural Dissent: The Nineteenth Century,* Leicester University Press, 1972; (editor) *Perspectives in English Urban History,* Macmillan, 1973.

Contributor: Joan Thirsk, editor, *The Agrarian History of England, 1500-1640,* Cambridge University Press, 1967; T. G. Cook, editor, *Local Studies and the History of Education,* Methuen, 1972; H. T. Dyos, editor, *Urban History Yearbook,* Leicester University Press, 1974; C. E. Chalkin and M. A. Harinden, editors, *Rural Change and Urban Growth, 1500-1800,* Longman, 1974.

WORK IN PROGRESS: Studies in Northampton evangelicalism, 1700-1850, the market town in English history, and early English settlement; three books, *The Making of the Kentish Landscape,* for Hodder & Stoughton, *The Grass Roots of History,* for Penguin, and *The History of Northampton, 1500-1760.*

SIDELIGHTS: Everitt states his historical studies are concentrated on the period between 1530 and 1880, when the "cast of thought of English people was more conditioned by local/environment than by national events and politics." He adds: "[I] believe deeply that history is an art as well as a science. . . . Exploring the past is like exploring another country." *Avocational interests:* Walking, music.

* * *

EVERTTS, Eldonna L(ouise) 1917-

PERSONAL: Born May 19, 1917, in South Bend, Ind.; daughter of Clay H. and Bertha A. (Weiss) Becker; married Lyston C. Evertts, July 19, 1941 (deceased); children: Irene Mary (Mrs. David Anthony LePage), James Lyston. *Education:* Manchester College, B.S., 1953; Indiana University, M.A., 1956, Ed.D., 1961. *Home:* 2506 Stanford Dr., Champaign, Ill. 61820. *Office:* College of Education, University of Illinois, Urbana, Ill. 61801.

CAREER: Elementary teacher in Indiana, 1937-41, 1948-58; Indiana University, Bloomington, lecturer and then instructor in language arts, and assistant director of research in children's use of oral language, 1959-62; University of Wisconsin, Milwaukee, assistant professor of elementary education, 1962-63; University of Nebraska, Lincoln, associate professor of elementary education, 1963-65; University of Illinois, Urbana, associate professor of elementary education, 1965—. Assistant executive secretary of National Council of Teachers of English, 1965-69.

MEMBER: International Reading Association, Association for Childhood Education International, National Council of Teachers of English, National Conference on Research in English, Conference on English Education, National Education Association, Association for Supervision and Curriculum Development, American Educational Research Association, American Association of University Professors, Illinois Association of Teachers of English, Pi Lambda Theta, Delta Kappa Gamma.

WRITINGS—All with Bryon H. Van Roekel, except as noted: *Traveling Trade Winds,* Harper, 1966; *Coming to Cross Roads,* Harper, 1966; *Spanning the Seven Seas,* Harper, 1966, 2nd edition, 1972. Author with Bernard Weiss and Lyman Hunt of "The Holt Basic Reading System" series, Holt, 1973.

Editor; all published by National Council of Teachers of English: *Dimensions of Dialect,* 1967; *Aspects of Reading,* 1970; *Explorations in Children's Writing,* 1970; *English and Reading in a Changing World,* 1972. Contributor to professional journals.

* * *

EVSLIN, Bernard 1922-

PERSONAL: Born April 9, 1922, in Philadelphia, Pa.; son

of Leo (an inventor) and Tillie (Stalberg) Evslin; married Dorothy Shapiro (a teacher), April 18, 1942; children: Thomas, Lee, Pamela, Janet. *Education:* Studied at Rutgers University. *Home:* 158 Sutton Manor, New Rochelle, N.Y. 10805.

CAREER: Full-time professional writer and producer of documentary films shot in United States and various parts of Europe and Asia. *Military service:* U.S. Army, 1942-45. *Member:* Dramatists Guild. *Awards, honors:* "Face of the Land" was named best television film of 1959 in *Variety* poll; National Education Association Award for best television documentary on an educational theme, 1961.

WRITINGS: Merchants of Venus, Fawcett, 1964; *Heroes, Gods and Monsters of the Greek Myths* (juvenile), Four Winds, 1967; *Adventures of Ulysses,* Scholastic Book Services, 1969; *The Trojan War,* Scholastic Book Services, 1971; *Gods, Demigods and Heroes,* Scholastic Book Services, 1975; *The Green Hero,* Four Winds, 1975. Author of two plays, "Step on a Crack," produced on Broadway, and "Geranium Hat," and scripts for many documentaries and shorts.

WORK IN PROGRESS: Roaring Girls and Talking Beasts, under contract with Four Winds; a novel, *Raskalnikov in Oz.*

*   *   *

EYRE, S(amuel) R(obert)   1922-

PERSONAL: Born April 14, 1922, in Cheadle, Cheshire, England; son of Robert Henry and Ada (Spittlehouse) Eyre; married Blanche Mary Hickes (a primary teacher), August, 1948; children: Jonathan Robert, Nicholas James. *Education:* University of Nottingham, B.Sc., 1949; University of Sheffield, Ph.D., 1952. *Home:* 51 Gledhow Lane, Leeds 8, England. *Office:* Department of Geography, University of Leeds, Leeds, England.

CAREER: University of Sheffield, Sheffield, England, research demonstrator in geography, 1949-52; University of Leeds, Leeds, England, senior lecturer in geography, 1952—. *Military service:* Royal Navy, Fleet Air Arm, 1942-46; served as meteorologist in the North Atlantic and Australia. *Member:* Royal Meteorological Society (fellow; member of council), British Association for the Advancement of Science (recorder of geography section; member of council), Institute of British Geographers, British Agricultural History Society, British Ecological Society.

WRITINGS: Vegetation and Soils—A World Picture, Edward Arnold, 1963, 2nd edition, Aldine, 1968; (editor with G.R.J. Jones) *Geography as Human Ecology—Methodology by Example,* St. Martin's, 1966; (editor) *World Vegetation Types,* Macmillan, 1971. Contributor to journals of history and geography.

WORK IN PROGRESS: The study of organic and mineral productivity of the earth and its allocation between different political units.

*   *   *

FABIAN, Donald L(eroy)   1919-

PERSONAL: Born July 5, 1919, in Chicago, Ill.; son of William Leroy and Edith (Born) Fabian. *Education:* University of Chicago, B.A. and M.A., 1941, Ph.D., 1950. *Home:* 4753 Zenith Ave. S., Minneapolis, Minn. 55410. *Office:* Department of Spanish, Macalester College, 1600 Grand Ave., St. Paul, Minn. 55101.

CAREER: Tulane University of Louisiana, New Orleans, instructor in Spanish, 1946-49; University of Chicago, Chicago, Ill., instructor, 1949-51, assistant professor of Spanish, 1951-58; Southern Methodist University, Dallas, Tex., assistant professor, 1958-59, associate professor, 1959-62, professor of Spanish, 1962-65; Macalester College, St. Paul, Minn., professor of Spanish, 1965—. Visiting assistant professor, University of Puerto Rico, 1952-53. *Member:* American Association of Teachers of Spanish and Portuguese, American Association of University Professors.

WRITINGS: Essentials of Spanish, Houghton, 1957; *Tres ficciones breves,* Houghton, 1968. Contributor to journals in his field.

WORK IN PROGRESS: An anthology of nineteenth-century Spanish literature; research in twentieth-century Spanish literature.

*   *   *

FABRYCKY, Wolter Joseph   1932-

PERSONAL: Born December 6, 1932, in Springfield, N.Y.; son of Louis Ludwig (a businessman) and Stephanie (Wadis) Fabrycky; married Luba Swerbilow, September 4, 1954; children: David Jon, Kathryn Marie. *Education:* Wichita State University, B.S.I.E., 1957; University of Arkansas, M.S.I.E., 1958; Oklahoma State University, Ph.D., 1962. *Politics:* Varies. *Religion:* Protestant. *Home:* 1200 Lakewood Dr., Blacksburg, Va. 24061. *Office:* Virginia Polytechnic Institute and State University, Blacksburg, Va. 24061.

CAREER: Cessna Aircraft Co., Wichita, Kan., junior design engineer, 1954-57; University of Arkansas, Fayetteville, instructor in industrial engineering, 1957-60; Oklahoma State University, Stillwater, associate professor of industrial engineering, 1962-65; Virginia Polytechnic Institute and State University, Blacksburg, associate professor, 1965-66, professor of industrial engineering, 1966—, associate dean of engineering, 1970—. Consultant to Brown Engineering, Huntsville, Ala., 1962-64, Prentice-Hall, Englewood Cliffs, N.J., 1964—, and Inland Motors Corp., Radford, Va., 1965-67. *Member:* American Society for Engineering Education, American Institute of Industrial Engineers (vice-president, 1974—), Operations Research Society of America, Sigma Xi, Alpha Pi Mu, Sigma Tau. *Awards, honors:* American Institute of Industrial Engineers Book of the Year Award, 1974, for *Industrial Operations Research.*

WRITINGS: (With H. G. Thuesen) *Engineering Economy,* 3rd edition (Fabrycky was not associated with earlier editions), Prentice-Hall, 1964, 4th edition (with H. G. Thuesen and G. J. Thuesen), 1972; (with P. E. Torgersen) *Operations Economy: Industrial Applications of Operations Research,* Prentice-Hall, 1966, revised edition (with Torgersen and P. M. Ghare) published as *Industrial Operations Research,* 1971; (with J. Banks) *Procurement and Inventory Systems: Theory and Analysis,* Reinhold, 1967; (contributor) W. G. Ireson and E. L. Grant, editors, *Handbook of Industrial Engineering and Management,* Prentice-Hall, 1971; (with G. J. Thuesen) *Economic Decision Analysis,* Prentice-Hall, 1974. Co-editor, "International Series in Industrial and Systems Engineering," for Prentice-Hall. Contributor to *Industrial Engineering and Operations Research.*

SIDELIGHTS: Engineering Economy has been published in New Delhi, and in Spanish and Italian, and has been marketed in thirteen countries of Southeast Asia.

FACKENHEIM, Emil L(udwig) 1916-

PERSONAL: Born June 22, 1916, in Halle, Germany; son of Julius F. and Meta (Schlesinger) Fackenheim; married Rose Komlodi, December 28, 1957; children: Michael, Susan, David. *Education:* Attended University of Halle, 1937-38; Hochschule fuer die Wissenchaft des Judentums, Berlin, Germany, Rabbi, 1939; studied at University of Aberdeen, 1939-40; University of Toronto, Ph.D., 1945. *Home:* 563 Briar Hill Ave., Toronto, Ontario, Canada. *Agent:* Georges Borchardt, Inc., 145 East 52nd St., New York, N.Y. 10022. *Office:* Department of Philosophy, University of Toronto, Toronto, Ontario, Canada.

CAREER: Rabbi in Hamilton, Ontario, 1943-48; University of Toronto, Toronto, Ontario, lecturer, 1948-53, assistant professor, 1953-56, associate professor, 1956-61, professor of philosophy, 1961—. *Member:* Canadian Philosophical Association, Royal Society of Canada (fellow). *Awards, honors:* President's Medal of University of Western Ontario for best scholarly article published in Canada, 1954; Guggenheim fellowship, 1957-58; LL.D from Laurentian University, 1969, and Sir George Williams University, 1971; D.D. from St. Andrews College, 1972; D.Hu.L., Hebrew Union College, 1974.

WRITINGS: Paths to Jewish Belief, Behrman, 1960; *Metaphysics and Historicity,* Marquette University Press, 1961; *The Religious Dimension in Hegel's Thought,* Indiana University Press, 1968; *Quest for Past and Future: Essays in Jewish Theology,* Indiana University Press, 1968; *God's Presence In History: Jewish Affirmations and Philosophical Reflections,* New York University Press, 1970; (contributor) Herbert W. Richardson and Donald Culter, editors, *Transcendence,* Beacon Press, 1970; (contributor) Arthur A. Cohen, editor, *Arguments and Doctrines: A Reader of Jewish Thinking in the Aftermath of the Holocaust,* Harper, 1970; *Encounters between Judaism and Modern Philosophy: A Preface to Future Jewish Thought,* Basic Books, 1973. Contributor of essays and papers to learned journals in United States, Canada, Israel, and Germany, and to *Proceedings* of Inter-American Congress of Philosophy.

WORK IN PROGRESS: Philosophy of religion in German idealism; Jewish theology.

* * *

FAGER, Charles E(ugene) 1942-

PERSONAL: Born December 11, 1942, in St. Paul, Kan.; son of Callistus Eugene (a U.S. Air Force officer) and Alice Clare (O'Brien) Fager; married Letitia Hastings, August 6, 1964; children: Annika, Molly. *Education:* Colorado State University, B.A., 1967; attended Harvard Divinity School, 1968-72. *Politics:* "Worried independent, pacifist." *Religion:* "Convinced Quaker." *Home:* c/o Fager, 101 Greentree Dr., Vacaville, Calif. 95688.

CAREER: Friends World Institute, Westbury, N.Y., faculty member, 1966-68; editor, Harvard University Press, 1969-70; *Newton Times,* Newton, Mass., editor, 1971; *Real Paper,* Cambridge, Mass., president and staff writer, 1972-74. Free-lance writer, 1970—. *Military service:* None; conscientious objector. *Member:* Sigma Tau Delta, Phi Kappa Theta, Farmhouse Fraternity. *Awards, honors:* Award as editor of best college magazine in Rocky Mountain region, 1964.

WRITINGS: White Reflections on Black Power, Eerdmans, 1967; *Uncertain Resurrection: The Poor People's Washington Campaign,* Eerdmans, 1969; *Selma, 1965: The March That Changed the South,* Scribner, 1974; (editor) *Taking Charge,* Bantam, 1976. Contributor to *Boston Globe, Boston Phoenix, National Catholic Reporter, WIN Magazine, San Francisco Bay Guardian, Harper's,* and others. Weekly columnist, *CSU Collegian,* 1963-64; member of staff of *WIN Magazine,* 1974-75.

WORK IN PROGRESS: A historical novel about the Quakers of Nantucket Island during the American Revolution; a narrative history of the 1971 Mayday demonstrations in Washington.

SIDELIGHTS: Fager told *CA:* "After six years of apprenticeship, it appears I have finally attained journeyman status as a working writer. I would like to be able to concentrate on book projects and do less week to week journalistic stuff. Such a shift in emphasis would also enable me to spend more time raising my daughters, a task which is, now that the Indochina War is finally over, among the highest of my personal priorities."

* * *

FALK, Irving A. 1921-

PERSONAL: Born August 11, 1921, in Paterson, N.J.; son of Hyman A. (a contractor) and Yetta (Golden) Falk; reared by Minnie Hoffman. *Education:* New York University, A.B., 1942, Ph.D., 1970; Yale University, M.F.A., 1948; Columbia University, special studies, 1951-53. *Home:* 5-26 Sixth St., Fair Lawn, N.J. 17410. *Office:* Film-TV Institute, School of the Arts, New York University, Washington Sq., New York, N.Y. 10003.

CAREER: WNEW, New York City, continuity and publicity writer, 1943; U.S. Information Agency, editor-writer in Washington, D.C., and Petersburg, Va., 1943-45; United Illuminating Co., New Haven, Conn., writer of industrial films, 1946; Bacharach-Gardner Agency, New York City, writer and researcher, 1948-50; New York University, School of the Arts, New York City, instructor, 1948-55, assistant professor, 1955-60, associate professor in Film and Television Institute, 1960—. Writer and producer for radio and television; conductor of summer writing and communications workshops at New School for Social Research, 1954-55, and Fairleigh Dickinson University, 1956-58; spent 1965 at Universal Films in North Hollywood, representing Music Corp. of America in study of studio methods and current shows. *Military service:* U.S. Army, 1942-43.

MEMBER: International Radio and Television Society, American Association of University Professors. *Awards, honors:* Samuel French Award for excellence in teaching playwriting, 1952; Association for Education by Radio and Television Award, 1953; Ohio State University Radio-Television Award, 1955; Urban League Award for public service as producer of "The Urban League Presents," on occasion of 1000th broadcast, 1963.

WRITINGS: (Editor) *Radio and Television Continuity Writing,* Pitman, 1962; *The Idea Invaders,* Hastings, 1963; (with George N. Gordon) *Your Career in TV and Radio,* Messner, 1966; (with Gordon) *On-the-Spot Reporting: Radio Records History,* Messner, 1967; (with Gordon) *TV Covers the Action,* foreword by Walter Cronkite, Simon & Schuster, 1968; (with Gordon) *Your Career in Film Making,* Messner, 1969; (editor) *Prophecy for the Year 2000,* Messner, 1970; (with Gordon) *The War of Ideas: America's International Identity Crisis,* Hastings House, 1973. Author of several plays produced by Yale University

Theatre. Writer of nationally syndicated review and feature column on television distributed by Bell Syndicate, 1951-52.

* * *

FALK, Ze'ev W(ilhelm) 1923-

PERSONAL: Born May 11, 1923, in Breslau, Silesia; immigrated to Israel, 1939; son of Meyer (a physician) and Frieda (David) Falk; married Miriam Strauss, October 29, 1952; children: Hayim, Orah. Education: Hebron Rabbinical College, student, 1940-45; Israeli Government Law Classes, Advocate, 1951; Hebrew University of Jerusalem, M.A., 1952, Ph.D., 1959. Religion: Jewish. Home: 10 Harav Berlin, Jerusalem, Israel. Office: Faculty of Law, Hebrew University of Jerusalem, Mount Scopus, Israel.

CAREER: Private law practice, 1952-55; Hebrew University of Jerusalem, Jerusalem, Israel, external teacher and fellow, 1959-67; Tel-Aviv University, Tel-Aviv, Israel, senior lecturer in Jewish law, 1965-70; Hebrew University of Jerusalem, associate professor of family and succession law, 1970—. Legal adviser to Israeli Ministry of Social Welfare, 1955-60, Israeli Ministry of Interior, 1960-67; judge, Advocates' Chamber Superior Tribunal, 1962-66. Member of board of directors, Government Legal Service Union, 1960-67. Visiting lecturer at University of London, Oxford University, University of Murcia, University of Navarra, 1966. Awards, honors: Israeli Fighters' Decoration.

WRITINGS: Nisu'in Ve-gerushin, Hebrew University Faculty of Law, 1961, enlarged English edition published as Jewish Matrimonial Law in the Middle Ages, Oxford University Press, 1966; Hebrew Law in Biblical Times, Wahrmann Books, 1964; Halakhah u-ma'aseh bi-medinat Yisrael (title means "Halakhah and Reality in the State of Israel"), Wahrmann Books, 1967; Mavo le-dine Yisrael, [Tel Aviv], 2 volumes, 1969-71, translation published as Introduction to Jewish Law of the Second Commonwealth, Volume I, E. J. Brill, 1972. Also author of Mekorot ba-mishpat ha-'ivri, 1968; Tevi'at gerushin mi-tsad ha-ishah be-dine Yisrael, 1973. Author of booklets on Jewish law.

Contributor to encyclopedias and learned journals. Coeditor of Dine Israel: Annual on Jewish and Israeli Family Law; member of secretariat, Rivista Internazionale di Diritto Romano e Antico.

WORK IN PROGRESS: Three books: Values of Jewish Law: Towards a Philosophy of Law, The Family and Succession Law of Israel, and Illegitimacy in Jewish Law.

SIDELIGHTS: Ze'ev Falk speaks Hebrew, English, German, and French. Avocational interests: Writing Hebrew poetry; travel; books.

* * *

FALKNER, Leonard 1900-

PERSONAL: Born July 7, 1900, in Cleveland, Ohio; son of John (a farmer) and Emma (Piersdorf) Falkner; married Irene Steiner, December 18, 1922; children: Doris Irene (Mrs. James W. Hart). Education: Attended public schools in Cleveland, Ohio. Politics: Independent. Religion: Methodist. Home: Candlewood Isle, Conn. Agent: Lurton Blassingame, 60 East 42nd St., New York, N.Y. 10017. Office: 90 Morningside Dr., New York, N.Y. 10027.

CAREER: American Magazine, New York City, staff writer, 1930-32; New York World-Telegram and Sun, New York City, news editor, 1937-48, features editor, 1948-65.

WRITINGS: Forge of Liberty, Dutton, 1959; Painted Lady Eliza Jamel: Her Life and Times, Dutton, 1962; The President Who Wouldn't Retire, Coward, 1967; John Adams: Reluctant Patriot of the Revolution, Prentice-Hall, 1969; For Jefferson and Liberty, Knopf, 1972. Contributor of articles and short stories to American Heritage, Reader's Digest, Redbook, and Liberty.

* * *

FALK-ROENNE, Arne 1920-

PERSONAL: Born May 12, 1920, in Copenhagen, Denmark; son of Svend and Inge (Andersen) Falk-Roenne; married Katia Bryn, March 7, 1944; children: Adele, Christel, Synnoeve, Arne. Education: Attended Frederiksberg Gymnasium, Copenhagen, Denmark; University of Copenhagen, B.A., 1941. Religion: Lutheran. Home: 64 Rymarksvej, Hellerup, Copenhagen, Denmark.

CAREER: Journalist, beginning 1943, covering much of the world as traveling correspondent for Allers Familie Journal (magazine published in Danish, Norwegian, and Swedish). Member: Danish Writers Association, Danish Journalists Association, Adventurers Club of Denmark. Awards, honors: Norwegian-Danish Anker Prize for Vejen til Betlehem (title means "The Road to Bethlehem"), 1965.

WRITINGS: Det Bedste for Min Rejsevaluta, [Denmark], 1953; Eventyrfaerden til Greven af Montechristo's Oe, [Denmark], 1953; Eventyrfaerden til Robinson Crusoe's Oe, Branner & Korch, 1954; I Udlandet paa Knallert, [Denmark], 1955; Se Neapel og Spis Sovs til, Hirschsprungs Forlag, 1956; Det var pa Capri, Hirschsprungs Forlag, 1957; For Graensen Lukkes, Hirschsprungs Forlag, 1958; Hyklere og Myklere pa Mallorca, Hirschsprungs Forlag, 1958; Skaebnens Flod, [Denmark], 1959.

Tafiya, Lohses Forlag, 1960; Djaevlens Diamanter, Gyldendals Forlag, 1961; Tilbage til Tristan, Lohses Forlag, 1963, translation published as Back to Tristan, Allen & Unwin, 1967; Vejen til Betlehem, Lohses Forlag, 1963; I Morges ved Amazonfloden, Lohses Forlag, 1964; Paradis om Bagbord, Steen Hasselbalchs Forlag, 1965; Mine venner Kannibalerne, Steen Hasselbalchs Forlag, 1965; Vejen Paulus Gik, Lohses Forlag, 1967; Sydhavets syv boelger, Lohses Forlag, 1969; Doede Indianere sladrer ikke, Steen Hasselbalchs Forlag, 1969; I Stanleys fodspor gennem Afrika, Lohses Forlag, 1972; (with Farbbildern and Kt.-Skizze) Wo Salome tanzie, Stocker, 1973; Kannibalernes Ny Guinea, Fremed, 1974. Author of television scripts, and articles for magazines and newspapers.

SIDELIGHTS: Readers of Allers Familie Journal (more than a million circulation) have adventured vicariously in such remote spots as Alexander Selkirk's Island, Masatierra, where Falk-Foenne spent a month in Selkirk's (the real Robinson Crusoe) cave. In 1962 Falk-Roenne joined an advance party of Tristaners returning to Tristan de Cunha, where eruption of a dormant volcano the previous year forced evacuation of all the inhabitants to England. He also has visited Pitcairn Island, made four expeditions to remote Amazon tributaries, written about the original German Mennonite sect in Paraguay, searched for descendants of the Incas in Ecuador, and traveled in the New Hebrides, New Guinea, India, Soviet Union, and Africa. Most of Falk-Roenne's books have been published in other Scandinavian countries, and a number in Germany, Netherlands, Czechoslovakia, and Austria.†

FALUDY, George 1913-
(Gyoergy Faludy)

PERSONAL: Born September 22, 1913, in Budapest, Hungary; son of Eugene Faludy (a professor); wife deceased; children: Andrew. *Education:* Attended University of Vienna, University of Paris, University of Berlin, and University of Bologna, 1930-35. *Religion:* Catholic. *Home:* 2601 Bathurst, Apt. 206, Toronto, Ontario, Canada. *Agent:* Gemini, 9 Abbey House, Abbey Rd., London N.W.8, England.

CAREER: Professional writer in Hungary, 1936-38; lived in Paris, France, 1938, Africa, 1940, the United States, and England; Free Hungary Movement, New York, N.Y., secretary and editor of *Fight* (weekly), 1941-42; *Nepszava* (Hungarian daily), literary editor, 1946-50; political prisoner in Hungary, 1950-54; unemployed in Hungary, 1954-57; *Hungarian Literary Gazette,* London, England, editor in chief, 1957-61; full-time writer, 1961—. Visiting lecturer at Columbia University, 1968-71. *Military service:* U.S. Army, 1942-45. *Member:* International P.E.N. (honorary secretary, Center for Writers in Exile).

WRITINGS: Villon Balladai (poems after Villon; title means "The Ballads of Villon"), [Budapest], 1937 (burned by the Nazis, 1944), new edition, 1947 (confiscated by the Communists, 1949), new edition, Big Ben Publishing (London), 1958, Pannonia Press (Denville, N.J.), 1968; *Heine Nemetorszaga* (title means "Heine's Germany"), [Rumania], 1937, 2nd edition, [Budapest], 1947 (confiscated, 1950); *Laudetur* (poems), [Budapest], 1938 (confiscated, 1948); *A Pompeji Strazsan* (poems; title means "At the Gates of Pompeii"), [Budapest], 1938 (burned by Hungarian Nazis, 1944), 2nd edition, 1945 (pulped by the Communists, 1950); (editor) *Anthology of European Poets,* [Budapest], 1938 (burned, 1944), 2nd edition, 1946 (confiscated, 1950); (translator) *Dicsertessek* (poems after the Church Fathers and the Catholic poetry of the Middle Ages and Renaissance; title means "The Commendable Ones"), [Budapest], 1938; *Spanyolorszag* (poems; title means "Spain"), [Budapest], 1946; *Oszi Harmat Utan* (title means "After the Dew of Autumn"), [Budapest], 1947.

(With Maria Tatar and Gyorgy Paloczi-Horvath) *Tragoedie eines Volkes* (German language), [Vienna], 1957; *Emlekkonyv a Rot Bizancrol* (poems; title means "A Keepsake Book of the Red Byzantium"), [London], 1961; *My Happy Days in Hell* (autobiography), translated from the Hungarian by Kathleen Szasz, Deutsch, 1962, Morrow, 1963; *City of Splintered Gods,* translated from the Hungarian by Flora Papastavrou, Morrow, 1966 (published in England as *Karoton,* Eyre & Spottiswoode, 1966); *Erasmus,* Stein & Day, 1970 (published in England as *Erasmus of Rotterdam,* Eyre & Spottiswoode, 1970); *Levelek as utokorhos* (poems; title means "Letters to Posterity"), [Toronto], 1975. Translator into Hungarian of works of Villon, Rabelais, Shakespeare, Milton, Garcia Lorca, and others.

WORK IN PROGRESS: A novel about Giovanni Pico della Mirandola; a novel about the Cordovan Caliphate; *A History of Humanism,* for Stein & Day.

SIDELIGHTS: My Happy Days in Hell has been published in France, Germany, Denmark, England, the United States, and other countries. Faludy speaks French, German, Italian, Greek, and English, as well as his native Hungarian.

FAN, Kuang Huan 1932-

PERSONAL: Born September 1, 1932, in Taiwan, China; son of Chao Teng (a statesman) and Twei Mei (Chen) Fan; married Sophie S. M. Chen, September 10, 1966; children: Alice C. *Education:* Bethel College, B.A., 1956; Brooklyn College (now Brooklyn College of the City University of New York), M.A., 1958; New York University, Ph.D., 1964. *Home:* 4017 Kinney Gulf Rd., Cortland, N.Y. 13045. *Office:* Department of Political Science, State University of New York College, Cortland, N.Y. 13045.

CAREER: University of Idaho, Moscow, visiting assistant professor of political science, 1963-64; College of Great Falls, Great Falls, Mont., assistant professor of political science, 1964-65; University of Idaho, assistant professor of political science, 1965-68; State University of New York College at Cortland, associate professor, 1968-73, professor of political science, 1974—, chairman of department, 1973-75. Member of senior associate faculty, St. Anthony's College, Oxford University, 1975. *Member:* American Political Science Association, International Studies Association. *Awards, honors:* Fulbright scholar, University of Singapore, 1968; American Heritage Award, 1974.

WRITINGS: (Editor) *The Chinese Cultural Revolution: Selected Documents,* Monthly Review Press, 1968; (compiler with Donald E. Leon) *Politics in a Changing World,* McCutchan, 1971; (editor) *Mao Tse-tung and Lin Piao: Post-Revolutionary Writings,* Anchor-Doubleday, 1973; *From the Other Side of the River: A Self Portrait of China Today,* Anchor-Doubleday, 1975.

SIDELIGHTS: Fan is fluent in Japanese as well as his native tongue and English.

* * *

FARBER, Bernard 1922-

PERSONAL: Born February 11, 1922, in Chicago, Ill.; son of Benjamin and Esther (Axelrod) Farber; married Annette Shugan, December 21, 1947 (divorced, 1970); married Rosanna Bodanis Gaines, 1970; children: (first marriage) Daniel, Michael, Lisa, Jacqueline; (second marriage) Tanya. *Education:* Central YMCA College (now Roosevelt University), A.B., 1943; University of Chicago, A.M., 1949, Ph.D., 1953. *Religion:* Jewish. *Home:* 739 East Loyola, Tempe, Ariz. 85282. *Office:* Department of Sociology, Arizona State University, Tempe, Ariz. 85281.

CAREER: University of Chicago, Chicago, Ill., research associate in sociology, 1951-53; Henderson State Teachers College (now Henderson State College), Arkadelphia, Ark., assistant professor of social sciences, 1953-54; University of Illinois, Urbana, instructor, 1954-57, assistant professor, 1957-60, associate professor, 1960-64, professor of sociology, 1964-71, member of Institute for Research on Exceptional Children, 1954-69, and associate director of institute, 1967-68; Arizona State University, Tempe, professor of sociology, 1971—, chairman of department, 1971-74. Consultant to California Study Committee on Mental Retardation, 1964, and Vanderbilt University Medical School Project on deviant development, 1967-71. Member of board of directors, Illinois Council on Family Relations, 1958-59; member of mental retardation research committee, National Institute of Child Health and Human Development, 1971-75.

MEMBER: American Sociological Association (fellow; family section council member, 1966-69), American Anthropological Association, Pacific Sociological Society, Illinois Sociological Association (first president, 1965-66). *Awards, honors:* E. W. Burgess Award, 1975, for contributions to family sociology; research grants for studies on exceptional children from Illinois Departments of Public Welfare and Mental Health, National Institute of Mental Health, and U.S. Office of Education.

WRITINGS: Predicting Marital Success, Russell Sage, 1953; *The Prevalence of Exceptional Children in Illinois in 1958,* Illinois Department of Public Instruction, 1959; (editor) *Directions of Future Sociological Research in Mental Retardation,* National Association for Retarded Children, 1961; (editor with B. V. Sheets) *The Handicapped Child in the Family,* United Cerebral Palsy Research and Educational Foundation, 1962; (contributor) W. J. Goode, editor, *Readings on the Family and Society,* Prentice-Hall, 1964; *Family: Organization and Interaction,* Chandler Publishing, 1964; (editor) *Kinship and Family Organization,* Wiley, 1966; *Comparative Kinship Systems,* Wiley, 1968; *Mental Retardation: Its Social Context and Social Consequences,* Houghton, 1968.

Kinship and Class: A Midwestern Study, Basic Books, 1971; *Guardians of Virtue: Salem Families in 1800,* Basic Books, 1972; *Family and Kinship in Modern Society,* Scott, Foresman, 1973. Also author of four monographs published by Society for Research in Child Development and Council for Exceptional Children; contributor to journals. Consulting or advisory editor for various sociological journals.

WORK IN PROGRESS: Kinship and Family Organization.

* * *

FARGIS, Paul (McKenna) 1939-

PERSONAL: Surname pronounced with soft "g"; born March 19, 1939, in New York, N.Y.; son of George Bertrand (an attorney) and Elizabeth (McKenna) Fargis; married Elizabeth Hackett, August 22, 1965; children: John Hackett. *Education:* Catholic University of America, student, 1957; Fairfield University, B.A., 1961; New York University, M.A. in Ed., 1962. *Religion:* Roman Catholic.

CAREER: Hawthorn Books, Inc., New York, N.Y., vice-president and editorial editor, 1962—. *Military service:* U.S. Army Reserve, 1962-68; became sergeant. *Member:* National Association of Book Editors, American Book Publishers Council.

WRITINGS: (Editor) *The Consumer's Handbook,* Hawthorn, 1967, revised edition, 1974.

WORK IN PROGRESS: An inspirational anthology; a consumer's guide to finances.

AVOCATIONAL INTERESTS: Swimming, carpentry, antiques, travel.†

* * *

FARLEY, Jean 1928-

PERSONAL: Born October 17, 1928, in Philadelphia, Pa.; daughter of David Labauve (a physician) and Jean (Clark) Farley; married Ellington White (a writer), June 19, 1954; children: David, Nancy, Susan. *Education:* University of North Carolina at Greensboro, B.A., 1950; Johns Hopkins University, M.A., 1953, graduate study in Romance languages, 1953-54. *Politics:* Democrat.

CAREER: Instructor in English at Richmond Professional Institute, Richmond, Va., 1954-56, and Hollins College,

Roanoke, Va., 1966-67; *Kenyon Review,* Gambier, Ohio, associate poetry editor, beginning 1968. *Member:* Phi Beta Kappa.

WRITINGS: (Contributor) Louis Rubin, editor, *The Hollins Poets,* University Press of Virginia, 1967; (contributor) J. W. Corrington and M. Williams, editors, *Southern Writing in the Sixties: Poetry,* Louisiana State University Press, 1967; (contributor) R. W. Watson and G. Ruark, editors, *The Greensboro Reader,* University of North Carolina Press, 1968; *Figure and Field* (poems), University of North Carolina Press, 1970. Contributor to *Poetry, New Yorker, Kenyon Review, Sewanee Review, Reporter,* and to other literary periodicals. Associate editor, *Hopkins Review,* 1952-54.†

* * *

FARMER, Albert J. 1894-

PERSONAL: Born May 2, 1894, in Manchester, England; became a French citizen, 1924; son of Alexander Hay Farmer; married Renee Lorin, November 13, 1924. *Education:* Victoria University, Manchester, England, B.A. (honors), 1913, M.A., 1919; University of Toulouse, docteur, 1920, agregation, 1921; University of Paris, D.Litt., 1931. *Politics:* None. *Religion:* None. *Home:* Residence Voltaire, Chatenay, Malabroy, Hauts de Seine, France.

CAREER: Teacher of English at a lycee in Toulouse, France, 1919-24; University of Grenoble, Grenoble, France, assistant professor of English, 1924-31; University of Bordeaux, Bordeaux, France, professor of English, 1931-45; Sorbonne, University of Paris, Paris, France, professor of English, 1945-64. Visiting professor at Brown University, 1931-33, Harvard University, 1936-37, Wayne State University, 1963, University of Natal, 1964, and University of Cape Town, 1967. *Military service:* British Army, Royal Fusiliers, 1914-19; became sergeant; received Meritorious Service Medal. *Awards, honors:* French Legion of Honor, 1949; commander, Ordre des Palmes Academiques, 1961.

WRITINGS: Scevole de Sainte-Marthe (1536-1623), Privat, 1920; *Le Mouvement Esthetique et Decadent en Angleterre,* Champion, 1931; *Walter Pater as a Critic of English Literature,* Didier, 1931; *Les Ecrivains Anglais d'Aujourd'hui,* Presses Universitaires de France, 1966; *George Farquhar,* Longmans, Green, for British Council, 1966; (editor with G. A. Marks) J. Marks, *French-English Dictionary of Slang and Colloquialisms,* Harrap, 1970. Contributor of articles and reviews to *Etudes Anglaises* (France), *Erasmus* (Germany), and other journals.

WORK IN PROGRESS: A book on the contemporary theater in England.

* * *

FARMER, Martha L(ouise) 1912-

PERSONAL: Born December 17, 1912, in Cincinnati, Ohio; daughter of William Silas (a manufacturer) and Genevieve (Fye) Farmer. *Education:* Wheaton College, Norton, Mass., B.A., 1935; Wellesley College, graduate study, 1936; Columbia University, M.A., 1937, Professional Diploma, 1948, Ed.D., 1956. *Politics:* Republican. *Religion:* Episcopalian. *Home:* 348 Lake St., Upper Saddle River, N.J. 07458. *Office:* City College of the City University of New York, 137th St. and Convent Ave., New York, N.Y. 10031.

CAREER: Manhattanville College of the Sacred Heart,

New York City, associate professor of physical education, 1936-43, 1946-48; City College of the City University of New York, New York City, professor of student personnel services, 1948-75, professor emeritus, 1975—. Visiting associate professor, New York University, 1967-68. Member of resident and management committees, Emma Ransom Residence of Young Women's Christian Association, 1958-60. *Military service:* U.S. Navy Women's Reserve (WAVES), 1943-46; became lieutenant.

MEMBER: American Association of University Professors, American College Personnel Association (chairman of commission on student personnel programs for adults in higher education, 1964-67), American Personnel and Guidance Association (delegate to senate, 1968), Adult Student Personnel Association (founder and first president; honorary trustee, 1975), Association of University Evening Colleges (chairman of legislative committee, 1965-66; vice-chairman, 1967-68), International Association of Evening Student Councils (trustee, 1964-70; honorary trustee, 1975), U.S. Commission on Civil Rights (member of New Jersey advisory committee, 1971—). *Awards, honors:* Bernard Webster Reed Memorial Award of Adult Student Personnel Association; medal of Instituto de las Espanas-Sangre de Hispania Fecunda.

WRITINGS: (Editor) *Student Personnel Services for Adults in Higher Education,* Scarecrow, 1967; (editor) *Counseling Services for Adults in Higher Education,* Scarecrow, 1971. Contributor to journals.

WORK IN PROGRESS: Research in leisure time as it will affect adults in the twenty-first century.

AVOCATIONAL INTERESTS: Training three-and five-gaited horses; learning dressage from Captain Fritz Bader, former riding master at the Spanish School of Riding, Vienna, Austria.

* * *

FARMER, Robert Allen 1938-

PERSONAL: Born September 20, 1938, in Cleveland, Ohio; son of Sterling (a business executive) and Eleanor (Sandberg) Farmer. *Education:* Dartmouth College, B.A., 1960; Harvard University, LL.B., 1963, graduate study at School of Business Administration, 1966. *Religion:* Protestant. *Home:* 1501 Beacon St., Brookline, Mass.

CAREER: Robert A. Farmer & Associates, Inc. (educational consulting and publishing firm), Boston, Mass., president, 1964—. President of Health Funds Institute, Inc., 1965—, and Education for Management, Inc., 1968—.

WRITINGS—All published by Arco: *How to Adopt a Child,* 1967; *The Rights of the Mentally Ill,* 1967; *Crime, the Law, and You,* 1967; *How to Collect on Personal Injuries,* 1967; *One Thousand Ideas for English Term Papers,* 1967; (with R. W. Sawyer) *New Ideas for Science Fair Projects,* 1967; *How to Avoid Problems with Your Will,* 1968; *The Truth about Inheritance,* 1968; *The Last Will and Testament,* 1968; *One Thousand Ideas for Term Papers in Sociology,* 1969; *One Thousand Ideas for Term Papers in American History,* 1969; *One Thousand Ideas for Term Papers in Social Science,* 1969; *One Thousand Ideas for Term Papers in World Literature,* 1969; *What You Should Know about Contracts,* 1969.

* * *

FARRANT, Leda 1927-

PERSONAL: Born June 15, 1927, in Rome, Italy; daughter of Nello and Wanda (Nuccorini) Ventani; married Juan Farrant (managing director of a Kenya firm), June 10, 1945; children: Robert, Gary. *Education:* Studied at Instituto Paolina de Malinkraud, Rome, Italy, and at a school in Addis Ababa, Ethiopia. *Religion:* Roman Catholic. *Address:* P.O. Box 10.002, Nairobi, Kenya.

WRITINGS: Eleven-and-a-Half (novel), Deutsch, 1967; *The Daughter of the Sun* (children's stories), Oxford University Press, 1969; *Fables from Kenya,* Macmillan, 1971; *Tippu Tip and the East African Slave Trade,* St. Martin's, 1975.

SIDELIGHTS: In addition to her native Italian, Leda Farrant speaks English, French, Spanish, and Swahili.

* * *

FARRIS, Martin T(heodore) 1925-

PERSONAL: Born November 5, 1925, in Spokane, Wash.; son of Jacob B. (an editor, publisher, and insurance agent) and Edith (Gunderson) Farris; married Rhoda F. Harrington, August 20, 1948; children: Christine Ann, Lynn Farris Harned, Elizabeth Louise, Martin Theodore II. *Education:* Attended Montana State University, 1943; University of Montana, B.A. (with honors), 1949, M.A., 1950; Ohio State University, Ph.D., 1957. *Religion:* Episcopalian. *Home:* 5010 East Calle Tuberia, Phoenix, Ariz. 85018. *Office:* College of Business Administration, Arizona State University, Tempe, Ariz. 85281.

CAREER: Ohio State University, Columbus, instructor in economics, 1955-57; Arizona State University, Tempe, assistant professor, 1957-59, associate professor, 1959-62, professor of economics, 1962-73, chairman of department, 1967-69, professor of transportation, 1973—, assistant director of bureau of business and economic research, 1964-66. Visiting professor, University of Hawaii, 1969-70. Consultant to business and government agencies. *Military service:* U.S. Army, Signal Corps, 1944-46; received two battle stars and Philippine Liberation Medal with Bronze Star. *Member:* American Economic Association, American Society of Traffic and Transportation (member of board of examiners, 1962-74), Association of Interstate Commerce Commission Practitioners, Transportation Research Forum, Western Economic Association (member of executive committee, 1966-69), Phoenix Traffic Club (president, 1960), Delta Nu Alpha (president, 1967-68), Phi Kappa Phi, Beta Gamma Sigma, Omicron Delta Epsilon, Delta Sigma Pi, Sigma Phi Epsilon.

WRITINGS: (Contributor) P. A. Kolb and Otis Lipstreu, editors, *New Concepts and Current Issues in Public Utility Regulation,* Peerless Publishing, 1963; (with Roy J. Sampson) *Domestic Transportation: Practice, Theory, and Policy,* Houghton, 1966, 3rd edition, 1975; (editor with Paul T. McElhiney) *Modern Transportation: Selected Readings,* Houghton, 1967, 2nd edition, 1973; (with Sampson) *Public Utilities: Regulation, Management, and Ownership,* Houghton, 1973; (with Grant M. Davis and Jack V. Holder, Jr.) *Management of Transportation Carriers,* Praeger, 1975; (with Forrest E. Harding) *Passenger Transportation,* Prentice-Hall, 1976. Contributor of about eighty articles and reviews to journals.

* * *

FARWELL, George Michell 1911-

PERSONAL: Born October 3, 1911, in Bath, England; son of George Douglas (a civil engineer) and Eleanor Grace

(Jones) Farwell; married Patricia Minty, February 15, 1938 (divorced, 1953); married Noni Irene Rowland (a journalist), September 6, 1958; children: (first marriage) Anne Michele (Mrs. Angelo Mathos), Miles Christopher. *Education:* Educated in England. *Address:* c/o Bank of New South Wales, 138 Castereagh St., Sydney, Australia. *Agent:* Bertha Klausner International Literary Agency, Inc., 71 Park Ave., New York, N.Y. 10016.

CAREER: Worked in early years as seaman, gold-miner, actor, and in cattle country of Australia, and lived "on the beach" in Tahiti; editor for *Australian Books News,* 1946-48, *London Sphere,* London, England, 1949-51, and for *Air Travel, New York Times, London Financial Times,* and Australian journals; former literary critic for Australian Broadcasting Commission and *Sydney Morning Herald;* currently a full-time free-lance writer. Public relations officer for Adelaide Festival of Arts, South Australia, 1959-64, and for Australian Government Pavilion at EXPO 67 (exposition), Montreal, Quebec, Canada. *Member:* Australian Society of Authors, Australian Journalists Association. *Awards, honors:* Australian Broadcasting Commission prize, 1941, for radio play; Commonwealth Jubilee Stage Play Prize, Australia, 1951; First Prize for documentary script, New York Film Festival, 1966; Commonwealth Literary Fund fellow, 1971.

WRITINGS: Down Argent Street, F. H. Johnson, 1948; *Surf Music, and Other Stories,* Australian Publishing Co., 1949; *Land of Mirage,* Cassell, 1950; *Traveller's Tracks,* Melbourne University Press, 1950; *The Outside Track,* Melbourne University Press, 1951; *Australian Setting,* Evans Brothers, 1952; *Vanishing Australians,* Rigby, 1961; *Cape York to Kimberley,* Rigby, 1962; *Riders to an Unknown Sea,* St. Martin's, 1963; *Last Days in Paradise,* Gollancz, 1964; *Ghost Towns of Australia,* Rigby, 1965; *Mask of Asia: The Philippines,* Praeger, 1966; *Around Australia on Highway One,* Thomas Nelson, 1967; *The Seven Thousand Isles* (juvenile), Landsdowne, 1968; *Australian Landscapes,* Thomas Nelson, 1968.

Ned Kelly: The Life and Adventures of Australia's Notorious Bushranger, Cheshire, 1970; *Requiem for Woolloomooloo,* Hodder & Stoughton, 1972; *Squatter's Castle, the Store of a Pastoral Dynasty: Life and Times of Edward David Stewart Ogilvie, 1814-96,* Lansdowne, 1973. Also author of *Sun Country,* 1970, and *The House that Jack Built,* 1971. Short stories, poetry, and non-fiction represented in Australian anthologies.

SIDELIGHTS: Farwell has lived in the Philippine Islands, New Guinea, Tahiti, Fiji, and various parts of Australia.†

* * *

FASEL, George W(illiam) 1938-

PERSONAL: Surname rhymes with "hazel"; born May 28, 1938, in Elgin, Ill.; son of George W. and Louise (Bumgarner) Fasel; children: Kimberley, Marion, Mason. *Education:* University of the Pacific, A.B., 1959; Stanford University, M.A., 1960, Ph.D., 1965. *Home:* 1001 University Ave., Apt. 408, Columbia, Mo. 65201. *Office:* Department of History, University of Missouri, Columbia, Mo. 65201.

CAREER: Reed College, Portland, Ore., instructor, 1963-65, assistant professor, 1965-67, associate professor of French history, 1967-70; University of Missouri, Columbia, associate professor, 1970-76, professor of history, 1976—. *Member:* American Historical Association, Society for French Historical Studies. *Awards, honors:* Woodrow

Wilson fellowship, 1959; Arnold L. and Lois P. Graves Award, 1968; National Endowment for the Humanities summer stipend, 1975.

WRITINGS: (Editor with Donald N. Baker) *Landmarks in Western Culture,* two volumes, Prentice-Hall, 1968; *Europe in Upheaval: The Revolutions of 1848,* Rand McNally, 1970; *Modern Europe in the Making,* Dodd, 1974; *Edmund Burke,* Twayne, in press. Contributor to professional journals.

* * *

FATOUT, Paul 1897-

PERSONAL: Surname is pronounced Fa-too; born March 4, 1897, in Indianapolis, Ind.; son of Daniel Hosbrook and Margaret (Traub) Fatout; married Roberta Smith, October 23, 1933. *Education:* Purdue University, B.S., 1920; Pennsylvania State College (now Pennsylvania State University), M.S., 1925; Columbia University, M.A., 1926. *Politics:* "Usually Democratic, but play the field." *Religion:* Protestant. *Home:* 808 Rose St., West Lafayette, Ind. 47906.

CAREER: Pennsylvania State College (now University), assistant professor of agriculture, 1920-25; Washington State College (now Washington State University), Pullman, assistant professor of English, 1925-26; Purdue University, Lafayette, Ind., 1927-65, began as instructor, became professor of English, professor emeritus, 1965—. *Military service:* U.S. Navy, 1918-19. *Member:* American Association of University Professors, Phi Beta Kappa (honorary). *Awards, honors:* American Association for State and Local History Award of Merit, 1964, for *Mark Twain in Virginia City.*

WRITINGS: Ambrose Bierce, the Devil's Lexicographer, University of Oklahoma Press, 1951; *Ambrose Bierce and the Black Hills,* University of Oklahoma Press, 1956; *Mark Twain on the Lecture Circuit,* Indiana University Press, 1960; (editor) *Letters of a Civil War Surgeon,* Purdue University Studies, 1961; *Mark Twain in Virginia City,* Indiana University Press, 1964; *Meadow Lake: Gold Town,* Indiana University Press, 1969; *Indiana Canals,* Purdue University Press, 1972; (editor) *Mark Twain Speaking,* University of Iowa Press, in press.

Contributor: *Models for Writing Prose,* Richard R. Smith, 1931; *Exposition of Ideas,* Heath, 1948; *Mark Twain: A Profile,* Hill & Wang, 1967. Contributor to *Encyclopaedia Britannica,* 1959, and *Collier's Encyclopedia,* 1960; contributor to *Harper's, Musical Quarterly, Pacific Historical Review, American Literature,* and other periodicals.

SIDELIGHTS: Fatout told *CA* that he is "not a hobbyist" and that he does not "play golf, tinker with things, or collect ancient waffle irons, swizzle sticks or rare old brandies. At threescore and ten, I should have sage views on all sorts of vital subjects, but I'm blessed if I know what they are...."

* * *

FAUSOLD, Martin L. 1921-

PERSONAL: Born November 11, 1921, in Irwin, Pa.; son of Samuel and Edna Fausold; married Daryl Ethel Clement; children: Sharon Ann, Cynthia Lynn, Marti Clement, Martin Samuel. *Education:* Gettysburg College, A.B., 1944; California State College, California, Pa., Secondary Teaching Certificate, 1946; Syracuse University, D.S.Sc., 1953. *Office:* State University of New York College, Geneseo, N.Y. 14454.

CAREER: Fausold Dairy Co., Blairsville, Pa., partner, 1946-49; State University of New York College at Cortland, assistant professor of social studies, 1952-54, associate professor of history and government, 1955-57, professor, 1957-58; State University of New York College at Geneseo, professor of history, 1958—, chairman of social studies department, 1958-65, chairman of Division of Social Sciences, 1965-69, chairman of university awards committee, 1971-77, member of joint awards council, 1971—. Member of Cortland County Civil Service Commission, 1957; chairman of Cortland Board of Public Works, 1957-58. Military service: U.S. Naval Reserve, active duty, 1944-46; served in European and Asiatic theaters; became lieutenant junior grade.

WRITINGS: (Co-author) A Guide to the American Story (workbook), McGraw, 1957; Gifford Pinchot: Bull Moose Progressive, Syracuse University Press, 1961; Annotated Bibliography of American History, National Council for the Social Studies, 1968; James W. Wadsworth, Jr.: The Gentleman from New York, Syracuse University Press, 1975. Contributor of occasional articles and numerous reviews to education journals.

WORK IN PROGRESS: The American Presidency Series: The Presidency of Herbert Hoover.

* * *

FEDDER, Norman J(oseph) 1934-

PERSONAL: Born January 26, 1934, in New York, N.Y.; son of Abraham Herbert (a rabbi) and Harriet (Solomon) Fedder; married Deborah Pincus, November 24, 1955; children: Jordan Michael, Tamar Beth. Education: Attended Johns Hopkins University, 1950-52; Brooklyn College (now Brooklyn College of the City University of New York), B.A., 1955; Columbia University, M.A., 1956; New York University, Ph.D., 1962. Religion: Jewish. Home: 1309 Nichols St., Manhattan, Kan. 66502.

CAREER: Trenton State College, Trenton, N.J., assistant professor of English, 1960-61; associate professor of English at Indiana State College (now Indiana University of Pennsylvania), Indiana, Pa., 1961-64, and Florida Atlantic University, Boca Raton, 1964-67; University of Arizona, Tucson, associate professor of drama, 1967-70; Kansas State University, Manhattan, associate professor of speech-theatre program, 1970—. Judge at American College Theatre Festival; theatre consultant to B'nai B'rith, Hillel Foundation, and American Baptist Church; director of religious theatre project for American Theatre Association. Member: American Theatre Association, American Association of University Professors, Kansas Association of the Religious Communities, the Arts, and the American Revolution (president), Association of Kansas Theatre (chairman of religious theatre division). Awards, honors: Honorable mention in Charles H. Sergel Drama Competition, University of Chicago; winner of Sacramento State College National Drama Competition.

WRITINGS: The Influence of D. H. Lawrence on Tennessee Williams, Mouton & Co., 1966.

Plays: "The Eternal Kick," produced at Indiana State College, 1963; "My Old Room," produced at University of Arizona, 1968; "The Planter May Weep," first produced at University of Arizona, 1968; "A Thousand at the Branches," produced at University of Arizona, fall, 1969; "Some Events Connected with the Early History of Arizona," first produced by Arizona Pioneers Historical Society, 1970; "Earp!" (musical), produced in Abilene at Kansas State

Historical Theatre, 1971; "Monks" (musical), produced at Kansas State University, 1972; "PUBA," produced at University of North Carolina, 1973; "The Betrayal," produced in Baptist churches throughout Kansas, 1974; "The Decision," produced in Colby at Kansas Baptist Conference, 1974. Also author of Readers Theatre scripts: "Proud to be a Baptist," "Tevye in the Golden Land," and "The Matter with Kansas," produced on tour throughout Kansas, 1975. Television scripts: "We Can Make Our Lives Sublime," produced by Columbia Broadcasting System, Inc., 1970.

WORK IN PROGRESS: A full length play, "A Light to the Nations"; a bibliography of Jewish theatre, and a critical study of Jewish plays.

SIDELIGHTS: Fedder writes that his play "The Matter with Kansas" was designated an official bicentennial project.

* * *

FEGAN, Camilla 1939-

PERSONAL: Born August 14, 1939, in Belfast, Northern Ireland; daughter of B.T.O. (a colonel, British Army) and Merrill C. (Gotto) Fegan; married, 1972; children: one son; two stepchildren. Education: Studied at various schools in England, Ireland, and Germany. Politics: Conservative. Home: Caberfeidh, Clachan, Locheport, Isle of North Uist, Outer Hebrides, Scotland.

MEMBER: Museums Association of Great Britain, Surrey Archaeological Society.

WRITINGS: Late for Hallowe'en, Methuen, 1966, Criterion, 1967.

WORK IN PROGRESS: Children's books.

SIDELIGHTS: Camilla Fegan is fairly fluent in German; lived eight years in Germany, and eighteen months in Malta. Avocational interests: Archaeology (spends several weeks each summer on archaeological excavations), reading, browsing in second-hand book shops.

* * *

FEHREN, Henry 1920-

PERSONAL: Surname originally Foehrenbacher; born August 19, 1920, in St. Cloud, Minn.; son of Henry and Martha (Engel) Foehrenbacher. Education: St. John's University, Collegeville, Minn., B.A., 1944; St. John's Seminary, Collegeville, Minn., seminarian, 1944-48; Moorhead State College, M.S.Ed., 1964. Politics: Democrat. Address: Box 22, Kent, Minn. 56553.

CAREER: Roman Catholic priest, ordained 1948. St. Donatus Church, Brooten, Minn., pastor, 1953-60; St. Joseph Church, Foxhome, Minn., pastor, 1960-69; St. Thomas Church, Kent, Minn., pastor, 1969—. Conductor of retreats.

WRITINGS: Christ Now, Kenedy, 1966; God Spoke One Word, Kenedy, 1967; (contributor) G. S. Sloyan, editor, Secular Priest in the New Church, Herder & Herder, 1967; Never Quite Ready for Heaven, Claretian, 1972; That's the Spirit, Claretian, 1974. Author of booklets; columnist, U.S. Catholic, 1965—; contributor of articles and reviews to Encyclopedia Americana, Encyclopedia International, Worship, Ave Maria, My Sunday Visitor, Continuum, Liturgical Arts, Preaching, My Daily Visitor, Today's Family, Pastoral Life, National Catholic Reporter, and to other magazines and thirty diocesan weekly papers. Editor, Benziger's Sunday Bulletin.

WORK IN PROGRESS: Art and Architecture for the New Liturgy.

AVOCATIONAL INTERESTS: Travel, hiking, swimming, collecting Bach records.

* * *

FEJES, Claire 1920-

PERSONAL: Born December 14, 1920, in New York, N.Y.; daughter of Samuel and Deborah Specht; married Joseph Fejes (owner of an art shop), December 21, 1947; children: Mark, Yolanda. Education: Attended University of Alaska, 1950-58. Home: 1003 Cushman St., Fairbanks, Alaska. Agent: Russell & Volkening, Inc., 551 Fifth Ave., New York, N.Y. 10017.

CAREER: Teaches intermittently in public schools in Fairbanks, Alaska, and at University of Alaska, College; professional artist, and owner with husband of Alaska House and Alaska Art Gallery, Fairbanks, 1967—. Has had one-woman shows in New York, N.Y. at Roko Gallery, 1959, 1962, Larcada Gallery, 1974, Coe Kerr Gallery, 1975; work exhibited at Norfolk Museum, State Capitol Museum of Olympia, Washington Frye Art Museum, Seattle, 1967 and 1974, and Charles Bowers Memorial Museum, Santa Ana, Calif., 1968; also represented in "American Painters in the Artic." Awards, honors: First prize for poetry, Alaska division of League of Western Writers, 1959-60.

WRITINGS—Self-illustrated: People of the Noatak, Knopf, 1966; Enuk, My Son (juvenile), Pantheon, 1969. Issued a handmade edition of her own poems about Alaska, 1959. Contributor of articles to Alaska Sportsman and Beaver.

WORK IN PROGRESS: A self-illustrated book about the Athapaskan Indians along the Yukon.

SIDELIGHTS: The illustrations for People of the Noatak, were done by Claire Fejes in the Artic.

* * *

FELD, Werner (Joachim) 1910-

PERSONAL: Born April 10, 1910, in Dusseldorf, Germany; son of Bruno and Irma (Loebl) Feld; married Betty Tandy, October 1, 1957. Education: University of Berlin, LL.B., 1933; Tulane University of Louisiana, Ph.D., 1962. Religion: Episcopalian. Home: 2362 Killdeer St., New Orleans, La. 70122.

CAREER: Dixie Specialty Co., Inc., Mobile, Ala., president, 1947-61; North Georgia College, Dahlonega, assistant professor of political science, 1961-62; Moorhead State College, Moorhead, Minn., 1962-65, began as assistant professor, became professor of political science; University of New Orleans, New Orleans, La., professor of political science, 1965—. Civil Defense director, Mobile, Ala., 1956-57; consultant to U.S. Department of State, 1965-70. Military service: U.S. Army Reserve, 1943-63, with active duty in World War II and Korean War; became lieutenant colonel. Member: American Political Science Association, International Studies Association (executive committee, 1966-67), Southern Political Science Association (secretary, 1966-67).

WRITINGS: Reunification and West German-Soviet Relations, Nijhoff, 1963; The Court of the European Communities: New Dimension in International Adjudication, Nijhoff, 1964; The European Common Market and the World, Prentice-Hall, 1967; (editor with others) The En-

during Questions of Politics, Prentice-Hall, 1969, revised edition, 1974; Transnational Business Collaboration Among Common Market Countries, Praeger, 1970; Nongovernmental Forces and World Politics, Praeger, 1972. Contributor to political science, law, and other journals.

WORK IN PROGRESS: The European Community in World Politics: Economic Power and Political Influence; and Domestic Politics and Political Integration in the European Community.

* * *

FELDMAN, Gerald D(onald) 1937-

PERSONAL: Born April 24, 1937, in New York, N.Y.; son of Isadore and Lillian (Cohen) Feldman; married Philippa Blume, June 22, 1958; children: Deborah Eve, Aaron. Education: Columbia University, B.A. (magna cum laude), 1958; Harvard University, M.A., 1959, Ph.D., 1964. Politics: Democrat. Religion: Jewish. Residence: Berkeley, Calif. Office: Department of History, University of California, Berkeley, Calif. 94720.

CAREER: University of California, Berkeley, assistant professor, 1963-68, associate professor, 1968-70, professor of history, 1970—, Institute of International Studies, member of advisory and program committees, 1969-70, acting chairman of committee on Advanced Industrial Societies and West European Studies, 1971-72. Delegate to Council for European Studies, 1971-72; member of Curatorium for State and the Economy in the Weimer Republic conference, 1973; co-chairman of conference on Twentieth Century Capitalism, 1974. Member: American Historical Association, Phi Beta Kappa. Awards, honors: American Council of Learned Societies fellowships, 1966-67, 1970-71; Social Science Research Council grant, 1966-67; Conference Group on Central European History honorary mention for best article, 1970; Guggenheim fellowship, 1973-74.

WRITINGS: Army, Industry and Labor in Germany, 1914-1918, Princeton University Press, 1966; (editor) German Imperialism, 1914-1918: The Development of a Historical Debate, Wiley, 1972; (editor with Thomas G. Barnes) A Documentary History of Modern Europe, Little, Brown, 1972, Volume I: Renaissance, Reformation, and Absolutism, 1400-1660, Volume II: Rationalism and Revolution, 1660-1815, Volume III: Nationalism, Industrialization, and Democracy, 1814-1914, Volume IV: Breakdown and Rebirth, 1914 to the Present.

Contributor: Gerhard A. Ritter, editor, Entsehung und Wandel der modernen Gesellschaft: Festschrift fur Hans Rosenberg zum 65. Geburtstag, De Gruyter, 1970; I. Geiss and B. Wendt, editors, Deutschland in der Weltpolitik des 19. und 20 Jahrhunderts: Fritz Fischer zum 65. Geburtstag, Bertelsmann Universitasverlag, 1973; Hans-Ulrich Wehler, editor, Sozialgeschichte heute: Festschrift fur Hans Rosenberg zum 70. Geburtstag, Vandenhoeck & Ruprecht, 1974; Henrich Winkler, editor, Organisierter Kapitalismus: Voraussetzunger und Anfange, Vandenhoeck & Ruprecht, 1974. Contributor to proceedings, and historical journals in the United States and Germany. Member of editorial board, Journal of Social History, Central European History, and Journal of Modern History.

WORK IN PROGRESS: Iron and Steel in the German Inflation, 1916-1923, for Princeton University Press.

* * *

FELKER, Jere L. 1934-

PERSONAL: Born February 11, 1934, in Monroe, Ga.;

son of Paul McDaniel (an attorney) and Anne Graham (Reeves) Felker; married Martha Douglass, December 22, 1961; children: Alexandria Anne. *Education:* Vanderbilt University, B.A., 1956; New York University, M.B.A., 1961; Center of Industrial Studies, Geneva, Switzerland, M.Sc., 1962; Graduate Institute of International Studies, Geneva, Switzerland, Ph.D., 1966. *Politics:* Independent. *Religion:* Methodist.

CAREER: F. W. Dodge Corp., New York, N.Y., marketing consultant, 1956-61; Center of Industrial Studies, Geneva, Switzerland, professor of marketing, 1962-63; Unilever Ltd., London, England, senior economist, 1965-68; McKinsey & Co., London, management consultant, beginning 1968. *Member:* American Marketing Association, American Economic Association, Society for Long-Range Planners, Reform Club (London). *Awards, honors:* Rockefeller and Ford Foundation grants for study in Switzerland.

WRITINGS: Soviet Economic Controversies: The Emerging Marketing Concept and Changes in Planning, 1960-65, M.I.T. Press, 1967.

SIDELIGHTS: Felker has traveled extensively in Europe, and has done research in the Soviet Union. He is fluent in French and Russian.††

* * *

FELKNOR, Bruce L(ester) 1921-

PERSONAL: Born August 18, 1921, in Oak Park, Ill.; son of Audley Rhea and Harriet (Lester) Felknor; married Joanne Sweeney, February 8, 1942 (divorced January, 1952); married Edith Johnson, March 1, 1952; children: (first marriage) Susan Harriet; (second marriage) Sarah A. D., Bruce Lester, Jr. *Education:* University of Wisconsin, student, 1939-41. *Politics:* Democrat. *Religion:* Presbyterian. *Home:* 620 Smith Ave., Lake Bluff, Ill. 60044. *Office: Encyclopaedia Britannica,* 425 North Michigan Ave., Chicago, Ill. 60611.

CAREER: Worked as newspaper reporter in Menomonie, Wis., 1937-39, brakeman, then assistant yardmaster with Pennsylvania Railroad, 1941-42, production coordinator for a trailer company, 1943, radio officer in U.S. Maritime Service, 1944-45, and as public relations writer for American Airlines, 1945, and International Telephone and Telegraph, 1946; regional public relations director, Ford Motor Co., Chester, Pa., 1946-48; public relations executive in New York City, with Geyer, Newell & Ganger, 1948-49, and Foote, Cone & Belding, Inc., 1950-53; Market Relations Network (public relations), New York City, vicepresident, 1954-55; Fair Campaign Practices Committee, Inc., New York City, executive director, 1956-66; *Encyclopaedia Britannica,* Chicago, Ill., assistant to the publisher and chairman, 1966-70, director of marketing information (international), 1970-73, director of public information and corporate advertising, and editor of quarterly magazine *Know,* 1973—. Visiting lecturer, Hamilton College, 1966 and 1975. Consultant to Office of Economic Opportunity and American Arbitration Association, 1965-66. Member of counsel on church and society, United Presbyterian Church in the U.S.A., 1966-74. *Member:* American Political Science Association, Authors Guild, National Capital Democratic Club, Dutch Treat Club, Arts Club of Chicago, Chicago Press Club.

WRITINGS: Fair Play in Politics, Fair Campaign Practices Committee, 1960; (with Charles P. Taft) *Prejudice and Politics,* Anti-Defamation League, 1960; *Dirty Politics,* Norton, 1966; (editor with Frank Jonas and others) *Polit-*

ical Dynamiting, University of Utah Press, 1970. Author of series, "State by State Study of Smear," published by Fair Campaign Practices Committee, 1957, 1959, 1961, 1963. Also author of occasional syndicated newspaper features on political and campaign ethics. Contributor to encyclopedia yearbooks and periodicals.

WORK IN PROGRESS: A small book of outdoor essays tentatively entitled *In Praise of Woodcraft;* a popular analysis of contemporary problems in American electoral politics and executive-congressional relations.

AVOCATIONAL INTERESTS: Trout fishing, deer hunting, camping, self-directed study of the written Japanese language.

* * *

FELT, Jeremy P(ollard) 1930-

PERSONAL: Born December 26, 1930, in Miami, Fla.; son of Henry William and Georgia (Tallent) Felt; married Kaye W. Williams, March 26, 1955; children: Dana, Katharine, Timothy. *Education:* Duke University, A.B., 1951, M.A., 1956; Syracuse University, Ph.D., 1959. *Home:* 81 Dunder Rd., Burlington, Vt. 05401. *Office:* History Department, University of Vermont, Burlington, Vt. 05401.

CAREER: University of Vermont, Burlington, instructor, 1957-60, assistant professor, 1960-65, associate professor, 1965-69, professor of history, 1969—, acting chairman of department, 1966-67, chairman, 1969-74, director of area and international studies, 1973—. Fulbright professor of history, Helsinki University, 1969. *Military service:* U.S. Air Force, 1951-53; became second lieutenant. *Member:* American Historical Association, Organization of American Historians, Phi Beta Kappa.

WRITINGS: Hostages of Fortune: Child Labor Reform in New York State, Syracuse University Press, 1965; (contributor) H. J. Steffens and H. N. Muller, editors, *Science, Technology and Culture,* AMS Press, 1974. Also author of several scholarly articles.

WORK IN PROGRESS: The Progressive Era: A New Interpretation for publication by Praeger.

* * *

FEMIANO, Samuel D. 1932-

PERSONAL: Born October 6, 1932, in Rochester, N.Y.; son of Dominic (buyer for a chain store) and Florence (Ciccariello) Femiano. *Education:* University of Toronto, B.A., 1956, M.A., 1962; University of Rochester, M.Ed., 1958; Institute Catholique de Paris, Ph.D., 1966. *Office:* Department of Religious Studies, Seton Hall University, South Orange, N.J. 07079.

CAREER: Roman Catholic priest. University of St. Thomas, Houston, Tex., associate professor of theology, beginning 1966; currently faculty member in religious studies, Seton Hall University, South Orange, N.J. *Member:* College Theology Society.

WRITINGS: Infallibility of the Laity, Herder & Herder, 1967.†

* * *

FENANDER, Elliot W(atkins) 1938-

PERSONAL: Born November 14, 1938, in New York, N.Y.; son of Edmund Albert (a patent lawyer) and Genevieve (Watkins) Fenander; married Margaret Flaccus, June

23, 1962; children: Sara, Amy, Jennifer, Rebecca. *Education:* Haverford College, B.A., 1961; Harvard University, M.A.T., 1962; Middlebury College, M.A., 1967. *Politics:* Independent. *Religion:* Society of Friends. *Home:* Hancock Rd., Williamstown, Mass. 01267.

CAREER: William Penn Charter School, Philadelphia, Pa., teacher of English, 1962-65; Mount Greylock Regional High School, Williamstown, Mass., teacher of English, 1965—. *Member:* National Education Association, National Council of Teachers of English, Massachusetts Teachers Association, George Eastman House Associates, Circus Fans Association of America, Circus Historical Society, Northeastern Beekeeper's Association, Franklin County Beekeeper's Association.

WRITINGS: (Editor with Peter H. Reinke and Edward O. Shakespeare) *Understanding the Essay,* Odyssey, 1966. Contributor to *Atlantic.*

WORK IN PROGRESS: A text of essays; a book of photographs with related material for teaching composition; a manual on woodburning stoves.

SIDELIGHTS: Elliot Fenander has some competence in reading French, German, and Latin. *Avocational interests:* Photographing circus life.

*   *   *

FERDINAND, Theodore N(ichols)   1929-

PERSONAL: Born June 8, 1929, in South Bend, Ind.; married Jane Phyllis Fisher, August 26, 1960; children: two sons. *Education:* University of Notre Dame, B.S. (cum laude), 1951; Purdue University, M.A., 1953; University of Michigan, Ph.D., 1961. *Politics:* Democratic. *Office:* Department of Sociology, Northern Illinois University, DeKalb, Ill. 60115.

CAREER: Michigan Department of Corrections, vocational training program evaluator and organizer at Camp Pugsley, 1957-59; Central Michigan University, Mount Pleasant, assistant professor of sociology, 1959-61; Northeastern University, Boston, Mass., assistant professor, 1961-65, associate professor of sociology, 1965-70; Northern Illinois University, DeKalb, professor of sociology, 1970—. Senior research analyst, Community Progress, Inc., and research associate at Yale University, 1966-67. Consultant to ABCD (anti-poverty agency in Boston). *Member:* American Sociological Association, American Society of Criminology, Society for the Study of Social Problems, American Association for the Advancement of Science, Midwestern Sociological Society, Sigma Xi.

WRITINGS: Typologies of Delinquency: A Critical Analysis, Random House, 1966; (with Ruth Cavan) *Juvenile Delinquency,* 3rd edition (Ferdinand was not associated with earlier editions), Lippincott, 1975. Contributor of articles and reviews to professional journals.

WORK IN PROGRESS: Studies of the police and courts, both contemporary and historical.

*   *   *

FERDON, Edwin N(elson), Jr.   1913-

PERSONAL: Born June 14, 1913, in St. Paul, Minn.; son of Edwin Nelson and Julie B. (Omeyer) Ferdon; married Constance Etz, October 14, 1939 (died January 20, 1969); married Lola V. Galbraith, June 18, 1972; children: (first marriage) Richard, Derre, Julie. *Education:* Marietta College, student, 1931-33; University of New Mexico, B.A.,

1937; University of Southern California, M.A., 1942; University of Michigan, graduate study, 1952-54. *Religion:* Unitarian Universalist. *Home:* 2141 East Juanita St., Tucson, Ariz. 85719.

CAREER: Museum of New Mexico, Santa Fe, curator, 1937-40, research associate in Hispanic studies, 1940-57, associate director in charge, Museum of International Folk Art, 1958-60, coordinator of interpretation, 1960-61; Arizona State Museum, Tucson, associate director, 1961—. Field work since 1935 includes archaeological and geographic expeditions in Bolivia, Peru, Ecuador, Guatemala, Mexico, and eastern Polynesia; during World War II worked as procurement specialist with U.S. Cinchona Mission in Ecuador harvesting wild cinchona bark (from which quinine is derived) in the Andes Mountains. *Member:* American Association for the Advancement of Science, Sigma Xi, International Students' Club of University of Arizona (honorary member).

WRITINGS: Studies in Ecuadorian Geography, School of American Research, 1950; *Tonala, Mexico: An Archaeological Survey,* School of American Research, 1953; (editor with Thor Heyerdahl, and contributor) *Reports of the Norwegian Archaeological Expedition to Easter Island and the East Pacific,* School of American Research, Part I, 1961, Part II, 1965; *One Man's Log,* Rand McNally, 1966. Contributor to professional journals.

WORK IN PROGRESS: Research on Polynesian peoples and cultures as they were regarded by the early European voyagers, with an ethnographic report and popular book projected.

AVOCATIONAL INTERESTS: Photography and travel.

*   *   *

FERGUSON, James M(ilton)   1936-

PERSONAL: Born May 19, 1936, in Evanston, Ill.; son of Milton and Dorothy (Cooper) Ferguson; married Frances Moore, August 26, 1961; children: Diane, Douglas. *Education:* Stanford University, A.B., 1958; University of Chicago, Ph.D., 1962. *Office:* University of Rochester, Rochester, N.Y. 14627.

CAREER: University of Virginia, Charlottesville, assistant professor, later associate professor of economics, 1961-65; University of Chicago, Chicago, Ill., faculty research fellow, 1965-66; University of Rochester, Rochester, N.Y., associate professor of economics, 1965—. *Member:* American Economic Association. *Awards, honors:* Thesis was one of five winners in fourth annual Ford Foundation doctoral dissertation competition, 1962.

WRITINGS: The Advertising Rate Structure in the Daily Newspaper Industry, Prentice-Hall, 1963; (editor) *Public Debt and Future Generations,* University of North Carolina Press, 1964; *Advertising and Competition: Theory, Measurement, Fact,* Ballinger, 1974.

WORK IN PROGRESS: Writing on the economic effects of liquor regulation, on a general theory of tie-in sales, and on restrictions on the distribution of golf equipment.

*   *   *

FERKISS, Victor C(hristopher)   1925-

PERSONAL: Born August 2, 1925, in New York, N.Y.; son of Joseph (a salesman) and Pauline (Kiss) Ferkiss; married Barbara Jouvenal, October 16, 1948; children: Michael, Deborah, Ethan. *Education:* University of California, Berkeley, A.B., 1948, A.M., 1949; Yale University, M.A., 1950; University of Chicago, Ph.D., 1954. *Politics:* Democrat. *Religion:* Roman Catholic. *Office:* Department of Government, Georgetown University, Washington, D.C. 20007.

CAREER: State of California Compensation Insurance Fund, field service representative, 1948-49; Montana State University (now University of Montana), Missoula, assistant professor of political science, 1954-55; St. Mary's College, St. Mary's, Calif., assistant professor, 1955-60, associate professor of political science, 1960-62; Georgetown University, Washington, D.C., 1962—, visiting associate professor of government, professor of government, 1966—. Visiting summer professor at University of California, Berkeley, 1958, 1972, and at Simon Fraser University (British Columbia), 1973; visiting professor, Johns Hopkins University, 1966; visiting Fulbright Professor, University of West Indies, 1968-69; Eli Lilly Visiting Professor of Science, Theology and Human Values, Purdue University, 1976. Director of International Cooperation Association Personnel Training for Africa, Boston University, 1959-60. Consultant on Africa to Peace Corps, 1961. Member of National Board, Americans for Democratic Action, 1962-66, of board of directors, Catholic Association for International Peace, 1962-64. *Military service:* U.S. Army, 1943-46, 1951-52; became first lieutenant; received Bronze Star. U.S. Army Intelligence Reserve, 1954-68; became major.

MEMBER: American Political Science Association, American Association for the Advancement of Science, American Society for Public Administration, World Future Society. *Awards, honors:* Rockefeller Foundation fellow in political philosophy, 1959-60; National Book Award special commendation, 1971, for *Technological Man.*

WRITINGS: Communism Today: Belief and Practice, Paulist Press, 1962; *Foreign Aid: Moral and Political Aspects,* Council on Religion and International Affairs, 1965; *Africa's Search for Identity,* Braziller, 1966; *Technological Man: The Myth and the Reality,* Braziller, 1969; *The Future of Technological Civilization,* Braziller, 1974.

Contributor: Ferral Heady and S. L. Stokes, editors, *Papers in Comparative Public Administration,* Institute of Public Administration, University of Michigan, 1962; James Baker and John A. Davis, editors, *Southern Africa in Transition,* Praeger, 1964; William Lewis, editor, *French Speaking Africa: The Search for Identity,* Walker & Co., 1965; Jeffrey E. Butler and A. A. Castagno, editors, *Boston University Papers on Africa: Transition in African Politics,* Praeger, 1967; Daniel McCracken, editor, *Public Policy and the Expert,* Council on Religion in International Affairs, 1971. Contributor to *Commonweal, Nation, Ramparts,* and other magazines and professional journals.

WORK IN PROGRESS: A book on the relationship between politics and culture in technological society, for Braziller.

* * *

FERM, Betty 1926-

PERSONAL: Born December 4, 1926, in New York, N.Y.; daughter of Jack and Libby (Wetsky) Chefetz; married Max A. Ferm (senior vice-president of an advertising agency), July 3, 1957; children: Matthew Lewis, Stephanie Ellen. *Education:* Educated in public schools of New York, N.Y.; has taken special courses at New York University. *Home:* 86-21 Avon St., Jamaica Estates, N.Y. 11432. *Agent:* Betty Anne Clarke, International Creative Management, 40 West 57th St., New York, N.Y. 10019.

CAREER: House of Alexander (interior decoration), Brooklyn, N.Y., owner, 1951-55; worked in advertising posts in New York, N.Y., with Revlon, 1955, and Swirl, Inc., 1955-57. *Member:* Women's National Book Association, Authors League of America, Authors Guild.

WRITINGS: Flair for Fashion (teen novel), Simon & Schuster, 1967; *The Vengeance of Valdone,* Dell, 1973; *Eventide,* Dell, 1974; *Edge of Beauty,* Dell, 1974; *False Idols,* Putnam, 1974. Short stories published in *American Girl* and *Golden Magazine,* and one anthologized in *Everygirl's Companion,* Lantern, 1968.

WORK IN PROGRESS: Original fiction for Fawcett; a book on the publishing industry.

AVOCATIONAL INTERESTS: Gardening, interior decorating, traveling.

* * *

FESLER, James W(illiam) 1911-

PERSONAL: Born March 14, 1911, in Duluth, Minn.; son of Bert (a judge) and Vinnie (King) Fesler; married Frances Martin, March 15, 1940; children: Janet Martin, James Martin. *Education:* University of California, Berkeley, student, 1928-30; University of Minnesota, A.B. (cum laude), 1932; Harvard University, M.A., 1933, Ph.D., 1935. *Politics:* Democratic. *Office:* Department of Political Science, Yale University, New Haven, Conn. 06520.

CAREER: Brookings Institution, Washington, D.C., research fellow, 1934-35; University of North Carolina, Chapel Hill, assistant professor, 1935-37, associate professor, 1937-45, professor of political science, 1945-51, research professor, Institute for Research in Social Science, 1946-51; Yale University, New Haven, Conn., Alfred Cowles Professor of Government, 1951—, chairman of department of political science, 1951-55, 1962-64, Ford research professor, 1961-62. Visiting professor, University of California, Berkeley, 1949-50. U.S. War Production Board, Washington, D.C., assistant to executive secretary, 1941-43, chief of Policy Analysis and Records Branch, 1943-45, historian, 1945-46. Member of advisory board to committee for improvement of management in government, Committee for Economic Development, 1965-72; consultant at various times to United Nations, and U.S. Government departments. Member of New Haven Redevelopment Agency, 1962-64.

MEMBER: American Political Science Association (vice-president, 1968-69), American Society for Public Administration, American Association for the Advancement of Science (fellow), American Association of University Professors, National Academy of Public Administration. *Awards, honors:* Rockefeller Foundation research fellow, 1937-38; M.A. from Yale University, 1951; Carnegie Corp. grant, 1952, for work in East and Central Africa, and, 1957-60, for comparative field administration project at Yale University; Social Science Research Council faculty fellow, 1964-65.

WRITINGS: The Independence of State Regulatory Agencies, Public Administration Service, 1942; *Area and Administration,* University of Alabama Press, 1949; (editor and contributor) *Industrial Mobilization for War: History of the War Production Board and Predecessor Agencies, 1940-1945,* U.S. Government Printing Office, 1947; (editor with Clifford C. Nelson and contributor) *The Forty-Eight States: Their Tasks as Policy Makers and Administrators,* American Assembly, Columbia University, 1955; (editor and contributor) *The 50 States and Their Local Governments,* Knopf, 1967.

Contributor: *Regional Factors in National Planning and Development,* U.S. Government Printing Office, for National Resources Committee, 1935; *Report with Special Studies,* U.S. Government Printing Office, for President's Committee on Administrative Management, 1937; *Washington-Field Relationships in the Federal Service,* U.S. Department of Agriculture Graduate School, 1942; *The University Bureaus of Public Administration,* University of Alabama Press, 1946; Fritz Morstein Marx, editor, *Elements of Public Administration,* Prentice-Hall, 1946, revised edition, 1959; Edwin A. Bock, editor, *Essays on the Case Method in Public Administration,* International Institute of Administrative Sciences (Brussels), 1962; Ferrel Heady and Sybil L. Stokes, editors, *Papers on Comparative Public Administration,* Institute of Public Administration, University of Michigan, 1962; *Management Concepts and Practice,* Industrial College of the Armed Forces, 1963; Leigh E. Grosenick, editor, *The Administration of the New Federalism,* American Society for Public Administration, 1973; Frederick C. Mosher, editor, *American Public Administration: Past, Present, Future,* University of Alabama Press, 1975. Contributor to *International Encyclopedia of the Social Sciences,* 1968, and *Encyclopaedia Britannica;* contributor of articles, editorials, and reviews to political and social science journals. Associate editor, *American Political Science Review,* 1949-51; editor-in-chief, *Public Administration Review,* 1958-60.

*   *   *

FESSEL, Murray 1927-

PERSONAL: Born May 28, 1927, in Long Island, N.Y.; son of Sam and Molly (Gerlich) Fessel; married Marilyn Goldman (a teacher), January 30, 1949; children: Keith, Jerry. *Education:* Long Island University, B.A., 1949; Queens College (now Queens College of the City University of New York), M.A., 1952. *Religion:* None. *Home:* 9 Candy Lane, Huntington Station, N.Y. 11746.

CAREER: Teacher in New York, N.Y., 1950-58, Plainview, N.Y., 1958-59; Central School District Number 4, Plainview, assistant principal, 1959-61, principal, 1961—. *Military service:* U.S. Navy, 1945-46. *Member:* National Education Association, New York State Teachers Association.

WRITINGS: (With Lillian Glogau) *The Nongraded Primary School: A Case Study,* Parker Publishing, 1967.†

*   *   *

FEUERWERKER, Albert 1927-

PERSONAL: Born November 6, 1927, in Cleveland, Ohio; son of Martin and Gizella (Feuerwerker) Feuerwerker; married Yi-tsi Mei (a lecturer in literature, University of Michigan), June 11, 1955; children: Alison, Paul M. *Education:* Harvard University, A.B., 1950, Ph.D., 1957. *Home:* 1224 Ardmoor Ave., Ann Arbor, Mich. 48103. *Office:* Department of History, University of Michigan, Ann Arbor, Mich. 48104.

CAREER: University of Toronto, Toronto, Ontario, lecturer in history, 1955-58; Harvard University, Cambridge, Mass., research fellow, Center for East Asian Studies, 1958-60; University of Michigan, Ann Arbor, associate professor, 1960-63, professor of history, 1963—, director of Center for Chinese Studies, 1961-67, 1972—. Social Science Research Council-American Council of Learned Societies Joint Committee on Contemporary China, member, 1966—, chairman, 1970-75; member of National Academy of Sci-

ence committee on Scholarly Communication with the People's Republic of China, 1971—, vice-chairman, 1975—. *Military service:* U.S. Army, 1945-46. *Member:* American Historical Association, Association for Asian Studies, American Association of University Professors. *Awards, honors:* Research grants from Social Science Research Council, 1962, and Social Science Research Council-American Council of Learned Societies, 1962-63; National Endowment for the Humanities senior fellowship, 1971-72.

WRITINGS: China's Early Industrialization, Harvard University Press, 1958; (with S. Cheng) *Chinese Communist Studies of Modern Chinese History,* Harvard University Press, 1961; (editor and contributor) *Modern China,* Prentice-Hall, 1964; (editor with R. Murphey and M. C. Wright, and contributor) *Approaches to Modern Chinese History,* University of California Press, 1967; (editor and contributor) *History in Communist China,* M.I.T. Press, 1968; *The Chinese Economy, 1912-1949,* University of Michigan Center for Chinese Studies, 1968; *The Chinese Economy, ca. 1870-1911,* University of Michigan Center for Chinese Studies, 1969; *Rebellion in Nineteenth-Century China,* University of Michigan Center for Chinese Studies, 1974. Contributor to history journals. Associate editor, *Journal of Asian Studies,* 1958-62; member of editorial board, *American Historical Review,* 1970-75.

WORK IN PROGRESS: Modern Chinese history.

*   *   *

FICKETT, Lewis P., Jr. 1926-

PERSONAL: Born May 28, 1926, in Winthrop, Mass.; son of Lewis P. (a lumberman) and Phyllis (Macpherson) Fickett; married Constance Marsh (a teacher), May 29, 1964; children: Karin, Sybil. *Education:* Bowdoin College, A.B. (summa cum laude), 1948; Harvard University, LL.B., 1952, Ph.D., 1956. *Politics:* Democrat. *Religion:* Unitarian Universalist. *Office:* Department of Political Science, Mary Washington College, Fredericksburg, Va. 22401.

CAREER: Northeastern University, Boston, Mass., instructor, 1954-55; U.S. Department of State, Foreign Service officer, 1958-63, with posts in Bonn, Germany, Algiers, and Washington, D.C.; Mary Washington College, Fredericksburg, Va., assistant professor, 1963-64, associate professor, 1964-68, professor of political science, 1968—, chairman of department, 1969—. Exchange professor, Women's College Exchange Program, Delhi, India, 1967-68. *Military service:* U.S. Naval Reserve, 1944-46; became commander. *Member:* American Political Science Association, Association for Asian Studies, American Association of University Professors, Unitarian Fellowship of Fredericksburg (chairman), Phi Beta Kappa.

WRITINGS: Problems of the Developing Nations: Readings and Case Studies, Crowell, 1966.

WORK IN PROGRESS: The Praja-Socialist Party of India.†

*   *   *

FIEDLER, Fred E(dward) 1922-

PERSONAL: Born July 13, 1922, in Vienna, Austria; son of Victor (a businessman) and Hilda (Schallinger) Fiedler; married Judith Joseph (assistant director of University of Washington Educational Assessment Center), April 14, 1946; children: Phyllis, Ellen Victoria, Robert J., Carol Ann. *Education:* University of Chicago, A.M., 1947,

Ph.D., 1949. *Home:* 1250 Northwest 126th Street, Seattle, Wash. 98177. *Office:* Department of Psychology, University of Washington, Seattle, Wash. 98195.

CAREER: University of Chicago, Chicago, Ill., research associate and instructor, 1950-51; University of Illinois, Urbana, assistant professor, 1951-55, associate professor, 1955-59, professor of psychology, 1960-69, director of Group Effectiveness Research Laboratory, 1953-69; University of Washington, Seattle, professor of psychology and of management and organization, 1969—. Consultant to various government agencies, corporations, and industries. *Military service:* U.S. Army, 1942-45; served in Germany.

MEMBER: International Association of Applied Psychology, American Psychological Association (fellow), Society for Experimental Social Psychology, Midwestern Psychological Association. *Awards, honors:* Award for outstanding research, American Personnel and Guidance Association, 1953, honorable mention, 1960; Fulbright research scholarship to University of Amsterdam, 1957-58; Ford Foundation faculty research fellowship to University of Louvain, 1963-64; letter of commendation from U.S. Chief of Naval Operations for work with Belgian Navy, 1963-64; American Psychological Association, Division of Consulting Psychology research award, 1971.

WRITINGS: Leader Attitudes and Group Effectiveness, University of Illinois Press, 1958; (with E. P. Godfrey and D. M. Hall) *Boards, Management, and Company Success,* Interstate, 1959; *A Theory of Leadership Effectiveness,* McGraw, 1967; (with M. M. Chemers) *Leadership and Effective Management,* Scott, Foresman, 1974.

Contributor: O. H. Mowrer, editor, *Psychotherapy: Theory and Research,* Ronald, 1953; R. Tagiuri and L. Petrullo, editors, *Person Perception and Interpersonal Behavior,* Stanford University Press, 1958; D. Cartwright and A. Zander, editors, *Group Dynamics,* 2nd edition, Harper, 1960, 3rd edition, 1968; Leonard Berkowitz, editor, *Advances in Experimental Social Psychology,* Academic Press, 1964; H. M. Proshansky and B. Seidenberg, editors, *Basic Studies in Social Psychology,* Holt, 1965; C. W. Backman and P. F. Secord, editors, *Problems in Social Psychology,* McGraw, 1966; *Kleingruppenforschung und Gruppe im Sport,* Westdeutches Verlag (Cologne), 1966; E. A. Fleishman, editor, *Studies in Personnel and Industrial Psychology,* Dorsey, 1967; Joseph McGuire, editor, *Contemporary Management: Issues and Viewpoints,* Prentice-Hall, 1974. Contributor of over one hundred articles and reviews to journals in the fields of social psychology, psychotherapy, and organizational theory.

* * *

FIELD, Frank 1936-

PERSONAL: Born October 31, 1936, in Wakefield, Yorkshire, England; son of Arthur and Daisy (Smith) Field; married Barbara Hawkins (a university lecturer), July 22, 1965; children: two daughters. *Education:* Studied at Balliol College, Oxford, 1957-60, and Nuffield College, Oxford, 1960-62; Oxford University, D.Phil., 1965. *Home:* Greenacres, Highway Lane, Keele, Staffordshire, England. *Office:* Department of History, University of Keele, Keele, Staffordshire, England.

CAREER: University of Keele, Keele, England, lecturer, 1962-70, senior lecturer in history, 1970—.

WRITINGS: The Last Days of Mankind: Karl Kraus and His Vienna, Macmillan, 1967; *Three French Writers and the Great War: Studies in the Rise of Communism and Fascism,* Cambridge University Press, 1975.

WORK IN PROGRESS: Research on literature and politics in modern France for a book on Jean Jaures and Charles Peguy.

SIDELIGHTS: Frank Field is competent in French, German, and Russian.

* * *

FIELD, Stanley 1911-

PERSONAL: Born May 20, 1911, in the Ukraine; son of Henry (a merchant) and Nina (Zibulski) Field; married Joyce S. Stillman (an artist and editor), December 7, 1935; children: Jeffrey Michael, Constance Elyse. *Education:* Brooklyn College (now Brooklyn College of the City University of New York), B.A., 1934. *Home:* 3520 Duff Dr., Falls Church, Va. 22041.

CAREER: Radio announcer for WLTH, WNYC, and WMCA, New York, N.Y., 1934-36; Emil Mogul Advertising Agency, New York, N.Y., copywriter, 1936-38; National Broadcasting Co., New York, N.Y., contract writer, 1938-40; U.S. Department of Defense, Washington, D.C., radio-television information specialist, 1942—; American University, Washington, D.C., adjunct professor of broadcasting, 1952-68. Instructor, Adult Education Program, Arlington County, Va. *Member:* Author's Guild, Broadcast Education Association, Associated Writing Programs. *Awards, honors:* Special award for script writing, YMCA International.

WRITINGS: Television and Radio Writing, Houghton, 1959; *Guide to Scholarships, Fellowships and Grants,* Public Affairs Press, 1967; *Bible Stories for Adults Only,* David, 1967; *Professional Broadcast Writer's Handbook,* TAB Books, 1974; *The Making of the Mini-Documentary,* TAB Books, 1975.

Television scripts include: "Life in Washington" (series of documentaries), broadcast by WRC, "Womanpower" (hour-long documentary starring Helen Hayes) and "Fond Recollections" (hour-long musical), both broadcast by National Broadcasting Co. Also author of special material for Tallulah Bankhead and Ray Milland.

Radio scripts include: "Shakespeare's England" (series of weekly dramas) and "Words at War," National Broadcasting Co.; "Your Rights and Mine," "Together We Live," "Legend of the Great Hope," "This Small World," and other dramas; transcribed series for Veterans of Foreign Wars and American National Red Cross.

Film scripts; all produced by Stuart Finley Productions, include: "Cash for Trash," "Recycling," "Garbage Is a Dirty Word," and "Realities of Recycling." Contributor of short stories and articles to *Green's Magazine, Woman's Life, Home Life, Pollution Control Journal,* and *Journal of Broadcasting.*

WORK IN PROGRESS: The Television Documentary, for TAB Books; *Cathy,* a novel.

* * *

FIELDING, Temple (Hornaday) 1913-

PERSONAL: Born October 8, 1913, in New York, N.Y.; son of George T. Fielding II (an executive) and Helen Ross (Hornaday) Fielding; married Nancy Parker (a literary agent and writer), October 17, 1942; children: Dodge Temple. *Education:* Princeton University, B.A. (cum laude), 1939. *Politics:* "Professionally 100 percent a-political." *Religion:* Unitarian Universalist. *Home and European office:* Villa Fielding, Formentor, Mallorca, Balearic Isles, Spain. *Headquarters:* Fielding Publications, 105 Madison Ave., New York, N.Y. 10016.

CAREER: Professional writer, 1940—, primarily identified with travel guides to Europe. Wrote for a number of national magazines, 1940-47, doing special correspondence abroad at various times for *Town and Country, Reader's Digest, Saturday Evening Post,* and other magazines; author of *Fielding's Travel Guide to Europe,* 1948—; producer of National Broadcasting Co. travel program, "The Fieldings in Europe," 1954; columnist, Hall Syndicate, 1956-57; founder and president, Temple Fielding's Epicure Club of Europe, 1958—; chairman and president, Fielding Publications, New York, N.Y., 1965—. *Military service:* U.S. Army, 1940-45; on detached service with Office of Strategic Services for two years, at one point as member of the first American military mission to Tito in Yugoslavia; became major; received Bronze Star and Army Commendation Medal with palm.

MEMBER: American Society of Authors and Journalists (past president), Society of American Travel Writers, Arctic Institute, Overseas Press Club of America (past governor), Adventurers' Club of New York (past governor), Travelers' Century Club (Los Angeles), Ski Club of Great Britain, Arabian Knights (Cairo), Banshees (New York), Het Jagertje (The Hague), King Christian IV Guild (Denmark), Century Club (New York); honorary member of other clubs and societies in Europe. *Awards, honors:* Commander of Order of Merito Civil and Knight's Cross of the Order of Isabel la Catolica (Spain); Commander of Merito della Repubblica Italiana (Italy); Gold Cross of Honor (Austria); Knight of the Royal Order of Vasa (Sweden); Knight of the Royal Order of Dannebrog, Knight's Cross of the Order of Haederstegn, and Danish Information Foundation Award (all Denmark); Officer of the Commanderie de Cotteaux (France); and other awards from cities in Europe; Red Badge of Courage from U.S. Marine Corps, 1963; Non Sibi, Sed Patriae Award from Marine Corps Reserve Association, 1964.

WRITINGS: Fielding's Travel Guide to Europe, Sloane, annually, 1948-52, Morrow, annually, 1953-64, Fielding Publications, annually, 1965—; (with wife, Nancy Fielding) *Fieldings' Currency Guide to Europe,* annually, 1950-65, Fielding Publications, annually, 1965—; (with Nancy Fielding) *The Temple Fieldings' Shopping Guide to Europe,* Morrow, annually, 1957-65, Fielding Publications, annually, 1965—; (with Nancy Fielding) *The Fieldings' Low Cost Guide to Europe,* Fielding Publications, 1967—; *Fieldings' Currency Guide for the Far, Near, and Middle East,* Fielding Publications, 1967—; *Fieldings' Word Time Converter,* Fielding Publications, 1967—.

SIDELIGHTS: Fielding, his wife, and three members of their staff fan out (usually separately, but occasionally in pairs) for six months every year, covering twenty-three European countries. Then from early summer to fall they incorporate their findings into new editions—rating hotels, restaurants, airlines, motoring conditions, and other categories encountered on a scale which runs from "superb" to "dreadful."

"Our primary obsession wherever we move is to be accepted as Mr. and Mrs. John Smith, routine American tourists," Fielding writes. "We never voluntarily introduce ourselves. We always insist, as our most basic policy rule,

upon paying *all* bills in full. . . . This total independence and candor have activated forty-six libel actions to date by disgruntled agencies or institutions—only one of which we have lost (1952). . . . We merely tell the truth, as we see it. . . . Although we speak from four to six languages (all of them badly), our roles as typical American tourists require that we stick to English always when we are in public."
Sales of the guides now total more than six million copies.

BIOGRAPHICAL/CRITICAL SOURCES: New Yorker, January 6, 1968; *Life,* May 3, 1968; *Time,* June 6, 1969; *Publishers Weekly,* December 8, 1975.

* * *

FIENNES, Richard N(athaniel Twisleton-Wykeham) 1909-

PERSONAL: Surname is pronounced Fines; born November 26, 1909, in London, England; son of Gerard Yorke and Gwendolen (Gisborne) Twisleton-Wykeham-Fiennes; married Alice Isobel Cowie, 1946; children: Frances Elizabeth, Richard George. *Education:* Cambridge University, B.A., 1935; Royal (Dick) Veterinary College, Edinburgh, Scotland, M.R.C.V.S., 1934. *Politics:* "Agin the Government!" *Religion:* Church of England. *Address:* c/o Zoological Society, Regents Park, London N.W.1, England.

CAREER: British Colonial Veterinary Service, 1935-53, serving successively as veterinary officer, veterinary research officer, and dean of Veterinary School in Uganda, and senior veterinary research officer in Kabete, Kenya; University of Ghana, Legon, Accra, senior lecturer in veterinary science, 1953-56; London Zoo, London, England, resident veterinary pathologist, 1956—; Nuffield Institute of Comparative Medicine, London, England, head of pathology department, 1964—. Member of chemotherapy panel and of tsetse and trypanosomiasis committee, British Ministry of Overseas Development. Councillor, Richmond Borough Council, 1961-64. *Military service:* Uganda Defence Force, World War II. *Member:* Royal Society of Medicine (secretary of comparative medicine section), and other scientific societies.

WRITINGS: Man, Nature, and Disease, Weidenfeld & Nicolson, 1964, New American Library, 1965; (editor) *Some Recent Developments in Comparative Medicine,* Academic Press, 1966; *Zoonoses of Primates: The Epidemiology and Ecology of Simian Diseases in Relation to Man,* Cornell University Press, 1967; (with wife, Alice Fiennes) *Natural History of the Dog,* Weidenfeld & Nicolson, 1968, published as *The Natural History of Dogs,* Natural History Press, 1970; (editor) *Biology of Nutrition: The Evolution and Nature of Living Systems,* Pergamon, 1972; (editor) *Pathology of Simian Primates,* Karger, Volume I: *General Pathology,* 1972, Volume II: *Infectious and Parasitic Diseases,* 1972.

WORK IN PROGRESS: A Handbook of Zoo Pathology, for Edward Arnold; editing *Handbook of Primate Pathology,* for Tulane University's Delta Regional Primate Center.

SIDELIGHTS: Fiennes intends to "retire to a beautiful sea-front site in the Bahamas, where my wife and I will build our house. I shall then bathe, boat, fish, and write—and I hope be visited by my friends." *Avocational interests:* Photography, travel.†

* * *

FILENE, Peter G. 1940-

PERSONAL: Born January 28, 1940, in New York, N.Y.;

son of Herman and Ursula (Spiero) Filene; married Jeanette Strasser, June 6, 1960 (divorced, 1972); children: Benjamin, Rebecca. *Education:* Swarthmore College, B.A., 1960; Harvard University, M.A., 1961, Ph.D., 1965. *Office:* University of North Carolina, Chapel Hill, N.C. 27514.

CAREER: Harvard University, Graduate School of Education, Cambridge, Mass., research associate, 1964-65; Lincoln University, Jefferson City, Mo., assistant professor of history and Woodrow Wilson teaching intern, 1965-67; University of North Carolina, Chapel Hill, assistant professor, 1967-69, associate professor of history, 1969—. *Member:* American Historical Association, Organization of American Historians, Phi Beta Kappa.

WRITINGS: Americans and the Soviet Experiment 1917-1933, Harvard University Press, 1967; (editor) *American Views of Soviet Russia, 1917-1965,* Dorsey, 1968; *Him/Her/Self: Sex Roles in Modern America,* Harcourt, 1975.

*   *   *

FILLMER, Henry Thompson   1932-

PERSONAL: Born April 13, 1932, in Martins Ferry, Ohio; son of Henry Zimmer (a city clerk) and Vera (Thompson) Fillmer; married Dorothy Clutter, June 12, 1954; children: Susan Jane, Constance Ann, Thompson Donald. *Education:* Ohio University, B.S., 1954, M.Ed., 1959, Ph.D., 1962. *Home:* 900 Northwest 51st Ter., Gainesville, Fla. 32601. *Office:* University of Florida, Gainesville, Fla. 32601.

CAREER: Starr Commonwealth for Boys, Albion, Mich., teacher of high school English, 1956-57; teacher at public schools in Chauncey, Ohio, 1957-58, and in Athens, Ohio, 1958-59; Hiram College, Hiram, Ohio, assistant professor of education, 1962-64; Emory University, Agnes Scott College, Decatur, Ga., assistant professor of education, 1964-67; University of Florida, Gainesville, 1967—, began as associate professor, currently professor of education. Visiting summer professor at University of Alaska, 1963, and Ohio University, 1964. Consultant to U.S. Office of Economic Opportunity for Job Corps project. *Military service:* U.S. Army, 1954-56. *Member:* International Reading Association, National Council of Teachers of English, National Society for Programmed Instruction, National Society for the Study of Education, Florida Reading Association, Phi Delta Kappa.

WRITINGS: (With others) *Our Language Today* (texts), Books III-VI, with workbooks, American Book Co., 1967, revised edition, 1971; (with others) *Composition Through Literature,* Books A-C, American Book Co., 1967, revised edition, 1971; (with others) *Patterns of Language,* Books III-VI, with workbooks, American Book Co., 1974. Contributor to education journals.

*   *   *

FINE, Warren   1943-

PERSONAL: Born January 24, 1943, in Fort Smith, Ark.; son of Jack Eugene and Dortha (Amerine) Fine. *Education:* Attended University of Kansas, 1961-66 (took no degrees); Johns Hopkins University, M.A., 1970. *Agent:* Lynn Nesbit, International Creative Management, 1301 Avenue of the Americas, New York, N.Y. 10019.

CAREER: Mill Creek Valley Intelligencer, St. Louis, Mo., contributing editor, 1966-68; University of Kansas, Lawrence, project director, writer, and editor at extension cen-

ter, 1969; University of Wisconsin, Milwaukee, assistant professor of English, 1970-74. Writer. *Awards, honors:* Grants from Ariadne Foundation, 1969-70, University of Wisconsin, 1970-71, National Endowment for the Arts, 1972-73.

WRITINGS: The Artificial Traveler (novel), Coward, 1968; *The Mousechildren and the Famous Collector* (fiction), Harper, 1970; *In the Animal Kingdom* (novel), Knopf, 1971; *Their Family* (novel), Knopf, 1972. Contributor of poems, short stories, and articles to *Beloit Poetry Journal, New American Review, Triquarterly,* and *Playboy.*

WORK IN PROGRESS: A novel, *American Confession;* a play about Christopher Columbus; a collection of poetry; radio and film scripts.

AVOCATIONAL INTERESTS: "Baseball, I love, and other modern or ancient rituals."

BIOGRAPHICAL/CRITICAL SOURCES: Kansas City Star, January 14, 1968; *Book World,* February 11, 1968; *New Yorker,* March 9, 1968.

*   *   *

FINKEL, Donald   1929-

PERSONAL: Born October 21, 1929, in New York, N.Y.; son of Saul Aaron (an attorney) and Meta (Rosenthal) Finkel; married Constance Urdang (a writer), August 14, 1956; children: Liza, Thomas Noah, Amy Maria. *Education:* Columbia University, B.S., 1952, M.A., 1953. *Office:* Washington University, St. Louis, Mo. 63130.

CAREER: State University of Iowa (now University of Iowa), Iowa City, instructor, 1957-58; Bard College, Annandale-on-Hudson, N.Y., instructor, 1958-60; Washington University, St. Louis, Mo., poet in residence, 1960—. Visiting professor, Bennington College, 1966-67. *Member:* Antarctican Society, Author's Guild, Phi Beta Kappa. *Awards, honors:* Helen Bullis Prize, *Poetry Northwest,* for *Simeon;* Guggenheim fellow, 1967-68; Ingram Merrill Foundation grant, 1973; Theodore Roethke Memorial Award for *Adequate Earth.*

WRITINGS—Poetry; all published by Atheneum: *Simeon,* 1964; *A Joyful Noise,* 1966; *Answer Back,* 1968; *The Garbage Wars,* 1970; *Adequate Earth,* 1972; *A Mote in Heaven's Eye,* 1975. Work included in anthology, *Poets of Today VI,* edited by S. J. R. Saunders, Scribner, 1959. Contributor to *Poetry, New Yorker,* and other publications.

SIDELIGHTS: Simeon, according to De Witt Bell, is "a book of great *elan,* robust in world view and vigorous in style," and only occasionally prosaic. Chad Walsh adds: "Finkel reveals an impressive sense of poetic architecture, ... while an unsolemn but not frivolous vitality charges through much of his verse." The vitality continues in the second book. R. J. Mills writes that Finkel is "a creator of comic extravagance, of an imagination which responds to the seemingly chance, grotesque and unreal nature of present-day life in its own terms." His poems are grimly and outrageously funny, bawdy, satirical, and dreamlike. His characters comprise, according to Mills, "a Jewish-French-Irish stew whose chefs might be Isaac Singer, Andre Breton, and Samuel Beckett." Joseph Bennett adds, however, that Finkel "is so gifted he does not need subjects for his poems.... He has, above all, the gift of wonderment." When he succeeds, it is not "with constructions but with clusters. His successful effects are purely linguistic; his organizations do not function."

Walsh writes: "*Answer Back* . . . is T. S. Eliot reborn, so far as much of the technique is concerned." The book is actually one long poem, which, says Walsh, "zigzagging between the neolithic past and the napalm present, creates a sense of the human condition in which all times are blended into a dimension of eternal experience. This poet is worthy grist for the scholarly commentators, but meanwhile I pause to celebrate his extraordinary sense of language and acuteness of observation." Bennett concludes that in the end, Finkel makes a joyful noise indeed.

Louis Coxe says: "[*Adequate Earth*] is a splendid piece of work, I think: rich, complex, resonant and simple, in the best sense. You can READ it. . . . Finkel writes: he weaves syntactical patterns in accordance with the integrity and the dynamics of the lines—each line as a unit, each unit of several lines as part of a whole."

BIOGRAPHICAL/CRITICAL SOURCES: New York Times Book Review, December 20, 1964, September 4, 1966; *Saturday Review,* January 2, 1965; *Poetry,* November, 1966, February, 1969; *Book World,* July 28, 1968; *New Republic,* February 3, 1973.

*   *   *

FINKELSTEIN, Leonid Vladimirovitch 1924-
(Leonid Vladimirov)

PERSONAL: Born May 22, 1924, in Tsherkassy, Ukraine; son of Vladimir E. (a mathematician) and Rebecca M. (Shwartsbraim) Finkelstein; married Julia I. Bogouslavskaya, November 3, 1958; married Kira Y. Szuchman (a translator), March 27, 1968; children: Anatoly, Dmitry, Andrew. *Education:* Moscow Automotive Engineering Institute, graduated, 1955. *Religion:* Jewish. *Address:* Box 355, G.P.O. London E.C.1, England. *Agent:* Robert Harben Literary Agency, 3 Church Vale, London N2 9DD, England.

CAREER: Magazine editor, journalist, and writer, Moscow, U.S.S.R., 1958-66; free-lance journalist and writer, London, England, 1966—. Also free-lance lecturer on Russian topics at Oxford University, University of Glasgow, Harvard University, Massachusetts Institute of Technology, and other universities. *Military service:* Soviet Army Reserves, lieutenant.

WRITINGS—Under name Leonid Vladimirov: *Dorogi k Nezrimomu Kladu* (title means "The Ways to the Invisible Treasure"), Moloydaya Guardia (Moscow), 1962; *Putj K Nulju* (title means "To the Zero"), Moloydaya Guardia, 1963; *Prikosnovenie Maga* (title means "The Touch of a Magician"), Znanije (Moscow), 1965; *The Russians,* Praeger, 1968; *The Russian Space Bluff: The Inside Story of the Soviet Drive to the Moon,* translated from the Russian manuscript by David Floyd, Tom Stacey, Ltd., 1971, Dial, 1973. Also author of a novella, "Do Pensii Sorok Let," published as "Forty Years to Pension Time," in *Soviet Literature,* November, 1965. Contributor to *Daily Telegraph* (London), and other newspapers.

WORK IN PROGRESS: Research on current events in the Soviet Union.

SIDELIGHTS: It has been reported that Finkelstein was visiting in London, as a journalist permitted to travel from the Soviet Union, when he decided to request political asylum and was granted it. In Russia, he had been a foreman in an automobile factory and a tractor driver on a collective farm, before turning to journalism, and spent some eight years in Stalinist prison camps as a result of talking about the growth of anti-Semitism.

FINKLE, Jason L(eonard) 1926-

PERSONAL: Born August 11, 1926, in Winthrop, Mass.; son of John and Sarah (Zimble) Finkle; married Patricia Brodsky, 1959; children: Lisa, Nina, Clea, Moira. *Education:* University of Miami, A.B., 1949; University of Michigan, M.A., 1951, Ph.D., 1959. *Home:* 2645 Bedford Rd., Ann Arbor, Mich. 48104. *Office:* Center for Population Planning, School of Public Health, University of Michigan, Ann Arbor, Mich. 48109.

CAREER: University of Florida, Gainesville, instructor in political science, 1953-59; Michigan State University, East Lansing, assistant professor of political science, 1959-62; University of Southern California, Los Angeles, associate professor of public administration, 1962-65; University of Michigan, Ann Arbor, visiting associate professor of political science, 1964, associate professor, 1965-72, professor of population planning, 1972—. Academic adviser and director of case-research program, National Institute of Administration, Saigon, 1959-61. Consultant to Ford Foundation and Government of India on national population planning program, 1965-67; member of Southeast Asia Development Advisory Group of Asia Society, 1967—. *Military service:* U.S. Army, Infantry, 1944-46; served with U.S. Military Government in Berlin District, 1945-46.

MEMBER: American Political Science Association, American Society for Public Administration, Association for Asian Studies, International Union for the Scientific Study of Population, Population Association of America. *Awards, honors:* Michigan State University International Programs research grant, 1961-62; Ford Foundation research grant, 1963-64; Rockefeller Foundation research grant, 1972-76.

WRITINGS: The President Makes a Decision: A Study of Dixon-Yates, Institute of Public Administration, University of Michigan, 1960; (contributor) Frank Persons Sherwood and William B. Storm, editors, *Teaching and Research in Public Administration,* University of Southern California Press, 1960; *Vietnam's Emerging Bureaucracy: A Profile of Nia Students* (monograph), Michigan State University Press, 1961; *Provincial Government in Vietnam* (monograph), Michigan State University Press, 1961; (contributor) *Area Handbook for Vietnam,* Foreign Areas Studies Division of Special Operations Research Office, 1962; (contributor) John M. Swarthout and Ernest R. Bartley, editors, *Materials on National American Government,* 2nd edition, Oxford University Press, 1962; (with William B. Storm) *American Professionals in Technical Assistance* (monograph), University of Southern California Press, 1965; (editor with Richard W. Gable) *Political Development and Social Change,* Wiley, 1966. Contributor to *Anthology of Counter-Insurgency,* U.S. Air Force, 1963, and to professional journals.

WORK IN PROGRESS: The Response of the United Nations System to the Population Problem.

*   *   *

FIRCHOW, Evelyn Scherabon 1932-
(Evelyn Scherabon Coleman)

PERSONAL: Born November 29, 1932, in Vienna, Austria; naturalized U.S. citizen; daughter of Raimund (a government official) and Hildegard (Nickl) Scherabon; married Peter E. Firchow; children: (previous marriage) Filicitas Giselle. *Education:* University of Texas, B.A., 1956; University of Manitoba, M.A., 1957; Harvard University, Ph.D., 1963. Also attended University of Vienna, 1950-51, and University of Munich, 1960-61. *Office:* German Department, University of Minnesota, Minneapolis, Minn. 55455.

CAREER: Balmoral Hall School, Winnipeg, Manitoba, teacher of mathematics, 1953-55; University of Maryland Overseas Branch, Munich, Germany, lecturer, 1961; University of Wisconsin, Madison, 1962-65, began as instructor, became assistant professor of German; University of Minnesota, Minneapolis, associate professor, 1965-69, professor of German philology, 1969—. Guest professor, University of Florida, 1973.

MEMBER: Modern Language Association of America (member of executive committee of German I, 1970-73; member of Delegate Assembly, 1970-72), American Association of Teachers of German, American Association of University Professors, Mediaeval Academy of America, Internationale Vereinigung der Germanisten, International Comparative Literature Association, Modern Humanities Research Association, Association for Literary and Linguistic Computing, Society for the Advancement of Scandinavian Study, Midwest Modern Language Association, Lambda Alpha Psi.

AWARDS, HONORS: Fulbright scholar, University of Texas at Austin, 1951-52; Fulbright-Hays fellow at University of Iceland, 1967-68; MacMillan Travel grant for research in Iceland, 1969; Institute for Advanced Studies (Edinburgh) grant for research in Scotland, 1973-74; Alexander Von Humboldt-Stiftung fellow in Germany, 1974; numerous grants from the University of Wisconsin and University of Minnesota for research.

WRITINGS—Under the name E. S. Coleman: (Editor with Werner Betz and Kenneth Northcott, and contributor) *Taylor Starck—Festschrift,* Mouton & Co., 1964, Humanities, 1965; (contributor) F. A. Raven, W. K. Legner, and J. C. King, editors, *Germanic Studies in Honor of Edward Henry Sehrt,* University of Miami Press, 1968; *Stimmen aus dem Studenglas: Deutsche Gedichte und Lieder,* Prentice-Hall, 1968; (translator and author of introduction) *Einhard: Vita Karoli Magni, Das Leben Karls des Grossen,* [Stuttgart], 1968, new edition (under name E. S. Firchow, with E. H. Zeydel) published as *Einhard: The Life of Charlemagne (Vita Karoli magni): The Latin Text with a New English Translation, Introduction, Notes and Illustrations,* University of Miami Press, 1972.

Under the name E. S. Firchow: (Author of introduction and notes) W. L. van Helten, *Die altostniederfrankischen Psalmenfragmente: Die Lipsius'schen Glossen und die altsudmittelfrankischen Psalmenfragmente,* Johnson Reprint, 1969; (editor with others) *Studies by Einar Haugen,* Mouton & Co., 1972; (editor with others) *Studies for Einar Haugen,* Mouton & Co., 1972; (author of introduction) Eduard Sievers, *Die Murbacher Hymnen,* Johnson Reprint, 1972; (editor with Karl Van D'Elden) *Was Deutsche lesen: Modern German Short Stories,* McGraw, 1973; (editor with others) *Deutung und Bedeutung: Studies in German and Comparative Literature,* Mouton & Co., 1973; (editor and translator) *Icelandic Short Stories,* Twayne, 1974. Contributor to *Dictionnaire international des termes litteraires.* Contributor of articles and about fifty-six reviews to professional journals.

WORK IN PROGRESS: Johannes von Telp: Der Ackermann aus Bohmen, for Metzler Verlag; a critical text edition of the old Icelandic *Elucidarius,* with Kaaren E. Grimstad, for MS Institute, University of Iceland; with husband, Peter E. Firchow, an anthology of East German

short stories in English translation for Twayne; an analysis of the language of Notker III's translation of Aristotle's *De interpretatione* with the help of a computer.

SIDELIGHTS: Evelyn Firchow is competent in French, Spanish, Latin, and Modern Icelandic.

*   *   *

FISCHER, Gerald C(harles) 1928-

PERSONAL: Born April 11, 1928, in Buffalo, N.Y.; son of Charles Arthur and Ivalo Fischer; married Janice Everingham, August 29, 1953; children: Alyson Beth. *Education:* University of Buffalo, B.S., 1952; Columbia University, M.S., 1953, Ph.D., 1960. *Politics:* Republican. *Religion:* Episcopalian. *Home:* 7616 Huron St., Philadelphia, Pa. 19118. *Office:* 1432 Philadelphia National Bank Building, Philadelphia, Pa. 19107.

CAREER: Marine Midland Corp., Buffalo, N.Y., portfolio analyst, 1954-56; Jamestown Community College, Jamestown, N.Y., instructor in economics and banking, 1956-57; Canisius College, Buffalo, assistant professor of banking and finance, 1957-58, 1960-62; Indiana University, Graduate School of Business, Bloomington, 1962-67, began as assistant professor, became associate professor of finance; Temple University, Philadelphia, Pa., research professor of business administration, 1967—. Consultant to American Bankers Association, 1964-65, Robert Morris Associates, 1967—, and other corporations. *Military service:* U.S. Army, 1945-48; became staff sergeant. *Member:* American Finance Association. *Awards, honors:* Ford Foundation faculty research grant, 1964-65.

WRITINGS: Bank Holding Companies, Columbia University Press, 1961; *American Banking Structure,* Columbia University Press, 1968; (editor) *Commercial Banking 1975 and 1980: A First Step in Long-Range Planning,* Robert Morris Associates, 1970; (co-author) *Economic Power of Commercial Banks,* American Bankers Association, 1971; *The Future of the Registered Bank Holding Company,* Association of Registered Bank Holding Companies, 1972. Contributor to financial journals.

WORK IN PROGRESS: Loan quality control in bank holding companies, commercial banking, lending, and manpower in the next decade.

*   *   *

FISHEL, Leslie H(enry), Jr. 1921-

PERSONAL: Born November 14, 1921, in New York, N.Y.; son of Leslie Henry and Thelma R. (Minzie) Fishel; married Barbara G. Richards (a teacher), June 30, 1943; children: R. Lynne (Mrs. John R. Barry), Timothy R., Lesley G. (Mrs. Gregg R. Hanson), Andrew M., John Jefferson. *Education:* Oberlin College, A.B., 1943; Harvard University, A.M., 1947, Ph.D., 1954. *Religion:* Congregational. *Office:* Heidelberg College, Tiffin, Ohio 44883.

CAREER: Massachusetts Institute of Technology, Cambridge, instructor, 1948-52, assistant professor of history, 1952-55; Oberlin College, Oberlin, Ohio, executive director of Alumni Association, 1955-59, lecturer in history, 1956-59; State Historical Society of Wisconsin, Madison, director, 1959-69; Heidelberg College, Tiffin, Ohio, president, 1969—. National Science Foundation Project, research associate, 1953-55; Library of Congress, member of advisory committee, National Union Catalogue of Manuscripts Collections, 1965—; University of California, Berkeley, consultant to Bancroft Library, 1967; Cooperative Educational Research Laboratory, Inc., member of regional council, 1968-70; National Council for the Humanities, member, 1970-75. Wisconsin Civil War Centennial Commission, secretary, 1959-66; Historic Sites Foundation, executive vice-president, 1961-69; Wisconsin Governor's Committee on the Portage Canal, chairman, 1965-66; Wisconsin Executive Residence and State Capitol Committee, chairman, 1967-69. Ohio College Association, chairman, 1975-76. *Military service:* U.S. Naval Reserve, active duty, 1943-46; served at sea with antisubmarine forces; became lieutenant junior grade.

MEMBER: Organization of American Historians, American Association for State and Local History (council member, 1963—), Wisconsin Academy of Sciences, Arts and Letters (vice-president for letters, 1965-66), Alumni Association of Oberlin College (board member, 1968-71), Madison Friends of the National Urban League (president, 1962-65; first vice-president, 1965-68). *Awards, honors:* Litt.D., Lakeland College, 1969.

WRITINGS: (Editor with Benjamin Quarles) *The Negro American: A Documentary History,* text edition, Scott, 1967, trade edition, Morrow, 1968, revised edition published as *The Black American: A Documentary History,* Scott, Foresman, 1970; (contributor) Melvin Kranzberg and Carroll Pursell, editors, *Technology in Western Civilization,* Oxford University Press, 1967. Contributor to *Journal of Negro History, Journal of Negro Education, Midwest Journal, Civil War History,* and other journals.

*   *   *

FISHER, John H(urt)   1919-

PERSONAL: Born October 26, 1919, in Lexington, Ky.; son of C. Bascom (a teacher) and Franke (Sheddan) Fisher; married Jane Elizabeth Law, February 21, 1942; children: Janice Carol, John Craig, Judith Law. *Education:* Maryville College, B.A., 1940; University of Pennsylvania, M.A., 1942, Ph.D., 1945. *Home:* 505 Scenic Dr., Knoxville, Tenn. 37919. *Office:* McClung Tower, University of Tennessee, Knoxville, Tenn. 37916.

CAREER: University of Pennsylvania, Philadelphia, instructor in English, 1942-45; New York University, New York City, instructor, 1945-48, assistant professor of English, 1948-55; Duke University, Durham, N.C., associate professor, 1955-58, professor of English, 1958-60; Indiana University, Bloomington, professor of English, 1960-62; New York University, professor of English, 1962-72; University of Tennessee, Knoxville, John C. Hodges Professor of English, 1972—, head of department, 1976—. Executive secretary, Modern Language Association of America, New York City, 1963-71. Summer instructor at Yale University, 1944; lecturer at University of Southern California, 1955, and University of Michigan, 1956. Consultant to U.S. Office of Education, 1962-64; member of U.S. Commission to UNESCO, 1962-68. *Member:* Modern Language Association of America (treasurer, 1952-55; president, 1974), National Council of Teachers of English, Linguistic Society of America, Mediaeval Academy of America, Century Association (New York). *Awards, honors:* L.H.D., Loyola University of Chicago, 1970; Litt.D., Middlebury College, 1970; National Endowment for the Humanities senior fellowship, 1975-76.

WRITINGS: (Editor) *Tretyse of Love,* Oxford University Press, 1951; (co-author) *The College Teaching of English,* Appleton, 1965; *John Gower, Moral Philosopher and*

Friend of Chaucer, New York University Press, 1965; (editor) *The Medieval Literature of Western Europe: A Review of Research,* New York University Press, 1966; (with D. Bornstein) *In Forme of Speche is Chaunge,* Prentice-Hall, 1974. Editor, *PMLA,* 1963-71.

WORK IN PROGRESS: Medieval studies; study of English linguistics.

*   *   *

FISHER, Marvin   1927-

PERSONAL: Born November 20, 1927, in Detroit, Mich.; son of Julius and Helen (Goldman) Fisher; married Jill Ann Jones, January 6, 1956; children: Ann, Sarah, Laura. *Education:* University of Michigan, student, 1945-46; Wayne State University, A.B., 1950, A.M., 1952; University of Minnesota, Ph.D., 1958. *Home:* 2425 South Newberry Rd., Tempe, Ariz. 85282.

CAREER: Instructor in English at Wayne State University, Detroit, Mich., 1951-52, General Motors Institute, Flint, Mich., 1952-53, and University of Minnesota, 1953-58; Arizona State University, Tempe, assistant professor, 1958-60, associate professor, 1960-66, professor of English, 1966—. Visiting professor of American civilization at Aristotelian University, Thessaloniki, Greece, 1961-63, and University of Oslo, 1966-67; visiting professor of American studies and acting chairman of department, University of California, Davis, 1969-70. *Military service:* U.S. Army, 1946-47. *Member:* Modern Language Association of America, American Studies Association, National Council of Teachers of English, American Association of University Professors. *Awards, honors:* Huntington Library Research fellowship, 1960; Fulbright-Hays lectureships, 1961, 1966.

WRITINGS: Workshops in the Wilderness: The European Response to American Industrialization, 1830-1960, Oxford University Press, 1967; (contributor) Hennig Cohen, editor, *The American Culture,* Houghton, 1968; (contributor) Sigmund Skard, editor, *Americana Norvegica,* University of Pennsylvania Press, 1968; (contributor) David Madden, editor, *American Dreams, American Nightmares,* Southern Illinois University Press, 1970; *The Fallen World: Melville's Short Fiction and the American 1850's,* Oxford University Press, in press. Contributor to learned journals, including *New England Quarterly, Journal of Aesthetics and Art Criticism, Journal of the History of Ideas,* and *Southern Review.*

WORK IN PROGRESS: A study of the surrealistic novel in America.

SIDELIGHTS: Marvin Fisher is competent in German and modern Greek.

*   *   *

FISHER, Morris   1922-

PERSONAL: Born March 13, 1922, in Baltimore, Md.; son of Harry and Lillian (Hill) Fisher; married Ruth Jeff (a market researcher), October 29, 1941; children: Gary, Bruce. *Education:* Studied at Baltimore City College, Johns Hopkins University, and University of Maryland. *Politics:* Democrat. *Office:* Leon Levi, Inc., 316 West Lexington, Baltimore, Md. 21209.

CAREER: Leon Levi, Inc. (jewelry and appliance retailer), Baltimore, Md., buyer and merchandiser, beginning 1949. *Military service:* U.S. Maritime Service; became lieutenant junior grade.

WRITINGS: Provinces and Provincial Capitals of the World, Scarecrow, 1967.

WORK IN PROGRESS: Research in occupational and career references.††

*   *   *

FISHER, Wallace E. 1918-

PERSONAL: Born March 29, 1918, in Greensburg, Pa.; son of Daniel Rhoads (a realtor) and Rose Elizabeth (Brantner) Fisher; married Margaret Elizabeth Stauffer, September 2, 1942; children: Paul Mark. Education: Gettysburg College, A.B., 1940; Lutheran Theological Seminary, Philadelphia, Pa., B.D., 1943; University of Pittsburgh, M.A., 1945; University of Pennsylvania, graduate study, 1949-51. Politics: Republican. Home: Doe Run Hills, Route 6, Lancaster, Pa. 17603. Office: Holy Trinity Church, 31 South Duke St., Lancaster, Pa. 17602.

CAREER: Lutheran clergyman. Gettysburg College, Gettysburg, Pa., professor of history, pastor of college church, and counselor, 1947-52; Holy Trinity Lutheran Church, Lancaster, Pa., senior minister, beginning 1952. Lecturer in homiletics at Lancaster Theological Seminary of the United Church of Christ, 1962, 1964, 1965, and Gettysburg Seminary, 1963-64. Pastor at Tabernacle, Ocean City, N.J.; pastor elsewhere in United States, and in Canada and Europe. Member of board of directors of Mental Health Organization, Community Chest, Planned Parenthood, Human Relations Committee, all Lancaster. Member: Lancaster Historical Society, Phi Beta Kappa, Phi Alpha Theta. Awards, honors: Freedoms Foundation Award, 1954; Sertoma Freedom Award, 1955; honorary D.D. from Gettysburg College, 1958; B'nai B'rith Citizenship Award, 1963.

WRITINGS: (Contributor) Preaching the Passion, Fortress, 1963; (contributor) A Man Named John Kennedy, Paulist Press, 1964; From Tradition to Mission, Abingdon, 1965; Preaching and Parish Renewal, Abingdon, 1966; (contributor) Renewing the Congregation, Augsburg, 1967; A Preface to Parish Renewal, Abingdon, 1968.

Affable Enemy: Letters to a Christian Dropout, Abingdon, 1970; Can Man Hope to be Human?, Abingdon, 1971; Politics, Poker, and Piety: A Perspective on Cultural Religion in America, Abingdon, 1972; Because We Have Good News: A Layman's Guide for Person-to-Person Evangelism in the Community, Abingdon, 1974. Contributor to reviews to church periodicals, including Christian Century, Religion and Life, Lutheran.†

*   *   *

FITCH, Robert Beck 1938-
(Bob Fitch)

PERSONAL: Born December 27, 1938, in Chicago, Ill.; stepson of Marvin Fitch (an architect) and son of Josephine (Beck) Fitch. Education: Oberlin College, student, 1956-58; University of Illinois, B.A., 1960; University of California, Berkeley, M.A., 1966, further study, beginning 1966. Politics: "Revolutionary Socialist." Religion: Atheist. Home: 361 Osage St., Park Forest, Ill.

MILITARY SERVICE: U.S. Army, 1961-64.

WRITINGS—All under name Bob Fitch: (With Mary Oppenheimer) Ghana: End of an Illusion, Monthly Review Press, 1966; (with Lynne Fitch) Say Chicano: I Am Mexican-American, Creative Educational Society, 1970; My Eyes have Seen, introduction by Daniel Berrigan,

Glide Publications, 1971; (with L. Fitch) Mark Witt Ward: A Black Family in the City, edited by Paul J. Deegan, Creative Educational Society, 1972. Contributor to Free Student and Marcha (Uruguay).†

*   *   *

FITTS, William Howard 1918-

PERSONAL: Born October 24, 1918, in Martin, Tenn.; son of Paul Morris (a jeweler) and Lucile (Dodd) Fitts; married Gladys Moerner (a statistician), February 11, 1943; children: Robert William, Patricia Alann. Education: University of Tennessee, B.S., 1941; Vanderbilt University, Ph.D., 1954. Politics: Independent. Religion: Methodist. Home: 4209 Sneed Ave., Nashville, Tenn. 37215. Office: Dede Wallace Center, 700 Craighead Ave., Nashville, Tenn. 37204.

CAREER: U.S. Veterans Administration, Nashville, Tenn., counseling psychologist, 1946-52; U.S. Veterans Administration Hospital, Nashville, psychology intern, 1954-55; Dede Wallace Center (formerly Nashville Mental Health Center), Nashville, chief clinical psychologist and assistant director, 1955-66, director of research, 1966-73, scientist-in-residence, 1973—. Psychologist in private practice. Member, Tennessee Board of Examiners in Psychology. Consultant to Vanderbilt Counseling Center, Tennessee Department of Mental Health, U.S. Veterans Administration, Peabody College, University of Tennessee, Meharty Medical College. Military service: U.S. Army Air Forces, 1942-46; became technical sergeant. Member: American Psychological Association, Southeastern Psychological Association, Tennessee Psychological Association (president, 1961-62), Sigma Xi.

WRITINGS: The Experience of Psychotherapy: What It's Like for Client and Therapist, Van Nostrand, 1965; (contributor) H. N. Maloney, editor, The Psychologist-Christian, Baker Book, 1973; (compiler) Tennessee Self-Concept Scale Bibliography of Research Studies, Dede Wallace Center, 1973; (with Randolph W. Parks and Glen L. Larsen) The Dede Wallace Center Maze, Dede Wallace Center, 1974. Author of monographs on psychological topics. Compiler of a self-concept scale (test) published in 1965; author of a filmscript, "Counseling for Church Vocations," for the Television, Radio and Film Commission of The Methodist Church, 1954. Contributor of numerous articles to professional journals.

WORK IN PROGRESS: Research projects concerning the self concept and human behavior; research into group therapy; development of a new behavioral test, the Parks Maze.

AVOCATIONAL INTERESTS: Performing and composing music; tennis and golf.

*   *   *

FITZGERALD, Arlene J.
(Monica Heath)

PERSONAL: Born in Orleans, Neb.; daughter of William Franklin and Laura Mae (Sell) Daily; married Ralph L. Fitzgerald (a safety engineer); children: Ralph A., Fawn J. (Mrs. David M. Machado), Dawn A. (Mrs. Michael L. McGuire). Education: Attended Southern Oregon College. Home: 4520 Foots Creek Rd., Gold Hill, Ore. 97525. Agent: Donald MacCampbell, Inc., 12 East 41st St., New York, N.Y. 10017.

CAREER: Professional writer and artist.

WRITINGS: Northwest Nurse, Ace Books, 1964; *Young Nurse Rayburn,* Pyramid Books, 1964; *Harbor Nurse,* Avon, 1964; *Daredevil Nurse,* Pyramid Books, 1964; *Log Camp Nurse,* Avon, 1966; *Volunteer Nurse,* Avon, 1967; *Double Duty Nurse,* Belmont, 1968; *Pamela's Palace,* Manor Books, 1971, 2nd edition, 1975; *Everything You Always Wanted to Know about Sorcery (But Were Afraid),* Manor Books, 1973; *Satanic Sex,* Manor Books, 1973; *House of Tragedy,* Manor Books, 1973; *Numbers for Lovers,* Manor Books, 1974; *The Devil's Gate,* Popular Library, 1975. Contributor of historical articles to western magazines.

Under pseudonym Monica Heath; all published by Signet Books: *Falconlough,* 1966; *Dunleary,* 1967; *Secrets Can Be Fatal,* 1967; *The Secret of the Vineyard,* 1968; *Clerycastle,* 1969; *Return to Clerycastle,* 1970; *Mistress of Ravenstone,* 1973; *Chateau of Shadows,* 1973; *Duncraig,* 1974; *The Legend of Crownpoint,* 1974; *Woman in Black,* 1974; *The Secret Citadel,* 1975; *Calderwood,* 1975; *The Legend of Blackhurst,* in press; *Raneslough,* in press.

WORK IN PROGRESS: Several books.

SIDELIGHTS: Many of Arlene Fitzgerald's books have had foreign editions.

*   *   *

FLEISHER, Frederic   1933-

PERSONAL: Born January 31, 1933, in Tokyo, Japan; son of Wilfred (an author and journalist) and Greta (Sundberg) Fleisher; divorced; children: Linn Marie. *Education:* Attended University of Lund, 1951-52; University of Stockholm, B.A., 1954, Ph.D., 1967; Salzburg Seminar in American Studies, student, 1959. *Home:* Malungsvagen 151, 191 71 Sollentuna, Sweden. *Office:* TRU, Stocksund, Sweden.

CAREER: Variety, New York City, correspondent in Sweden, 1958-70, in Finland, 1962-70; *Christian Science Monitor,* Boston, Mass., regular contributor from Scandinavia, 1960-68; *San Francisco Chronicle,* San Francisco, Calif., correspondent in Sweden, 1961-71, in Finland, 1962-71; *New York Herald Tribune,* New York City, Scandinavian correspondent, 1964-66; TRU, Storksund, Sweden, producer/director of television programs, 1968—. *Member:* Publicistklubben (Stockholm). *Awards, honors:* Award for translating Swedish literature, 1964.

WRITINGS: (Editor and annotator with Johannes Hedberg) *Views of America: An Anthology of American Prose and Poetry,* Almqvist & Wiksell, 1960; (translator and editor) *Seven Swedish Poets,* Cavefors, 1963, enlarged and revised edition published as *Eight Swedish Poets,* 1969; (with Finn Havnevik) *Introducing the U.S.A.,* Gleerups, 1964, enlarged 3rd edition, 1972; (with W. G. Simpson and Brita af Ekenstam) *American Words, with British and Swedish Equivalents,* Svenska Bokforlaget, 1966; *The New Sweden: The Challenge of a Disciplined Democracy,* McKay, 1967; *Folk High Schools in Sweden,* Swedish Institute for Cultural Relations with Foreign Countries, 1968; *Voices from Black American,* Liber/Gleerups, 1975. Also co-editor of *Prose of the Other Culture,* 1970. Author of documentary film, "The Quiet Revolution," and writer of television scripts.

SIDELIGHTS: Fleisher's books have been published in the Netherlands and Canada as well as the United States and Sweden.

FLEISHMAN, Avrom (Hirsch)   1933-

PERSONAL: Born July 27, 1933, in New York, N.Y.; son of Louis (a shopkeeper) and Sarah (Kaminetzky) Fleishman; married Sophia Abraham (a pianist), August 9, 1960; children: Franz Derek, Ilya Ian. *Education:* Columbia University, B.A. (with honors), 1954; Johns Hopkins University, M.A., 1956, Ph.D., 1963. *Politics:* Socialist. *Religion:* None. *Office:* Department of English, John Hopkins University, Baltimore, Md. 21218.

CAREER: Associate editor of *Industrial Design,* 1956-58, and *Printers' Ink,* 1958; instructor in English at Columbia University, New York, N.Y., 1958-59, and Hofstra University, Hempstead, N.Y., 1960-63; assistant professor of English at University of Minnesota, Minneapolis, 1963-66, and Michigan State University, East Lansing, 1966-67; Johns Hopkins University, Baltimore, Md., associate professor, 1968-70, professor of English, 1970—. *Member:* Modern Language Association of America. *Awards, honors:* Guggenheim fellowship in England, 1967-68; American Council of Learned Societies grant, 1970; research grants from University of Minnesota and Johns Hopkins University.

WRITINGS: A Reading of "Mansfield Park": An Essay in Critical Synthesis, University of Minnesota Press, 1967; *Conrad's Politics: Community and Anarchy in the Fiction of Joseph Conrad,* Johns Hopkins Press, 1967; *The English Historical Novel: Walter Scott to Virginia Woolf,* Johns Hopkins Press, 1971; *Virginia Woolf: A Critical Reading,* Johns Hopkins Press, 1975. Contributor to *Victorian Studies* and other professional journals. Editor, *E.L.H.: A Journal of English Literary History,* 1969—.

*   *   *

FLEISHMAN, Edwin A(lan)   1927-

PERSONAL: Born March 10, 1927, in New York, N.Y.; son of Harry E. and Sera (Weinblatt) Fleishman; married Pauline S. Utman, February 6, 1949; children: Jeffrey B., Alan R. *Education:* Loyola College, Baltimore, Md., B.S., 1945; University of Maryland, M.A., 1949; Ohio State University, Ph.D., 1951. *Home:* 8201 Woodhaven Blvd., Bethesda, Md. 20134.

CAREER: U.S. Air Force, Skill Components Research Laboratory, San Antonio, Tex., director, 1951-56; Yale University, New Haven, Conn., professor of industrial administration and psychology, 1957-63; American Institutes for Research, Washington, D.C., senior vice-president and director of Washington office, 1963—. Visiting professor, Israel Institute of Technology, 1962-63, University of California, Irvine, 1975-76. Consultant to Army Surgeon General's Office and Office of Naval Research; member of advisory panel on social science, Office of Secretary of Defense. *Military service:* U.S. Navy, 1945-46. *Member:* American Psychological Association (president, Division of Industrial and Organizational Psychology, 1973-74), American Association for the Advancement of Science, International Association of Applied Psychology (president, 1974-82), Psychometric Society, Sigma Xi, Cosmos Club (Washington, D.C.). *Awards, honors:* Guggenheim fellow, 1962-63; Franklin V. Taylor award of Society of Engineering Psychologists for distinguished contributions.

WRITINGS: (With E. F. Harris and H. E. Burtt) *Leadership and Supervision in Industry,* Ohio State University, 1955; (with R. M. Gagne) *Psychology and Human Performance: An Introduction to Psychology,* Holt, 1959; *Manual* for Administering the Leadership Opinion Questionnaire, Science Research Associates, 1960, supplement, 1963; (editor) Studies in Personnel and Industrial Psychology, Dorsey, 1961, 2nd revised edition, 1974; The Structure and Measurement of Physical Fitness, with Examiner's Manual and Performance Record, Prentice-Hall, 1964; (with J. C. Hunt) Current Developments in the Study of Leadership, Southern Illinois University Press, 1973.

Contributor: Readings in Experimental Industrial Psychology, edited by M. L. Blum, Prentice-Hall, 1952; Aspects of Leadership Organization, edited by R. M. Stogdill, Personnel Research Board, Ohio State University, 1953; Leader Behavior: Its Description and Measurement, edited by Stogdill and A. E. Coons, Bureau of Business Research, Ohio State University, 1957; The Study of Leadership, edited by C. G. Browne and T. S. Cohn, Interstate, 1958; Drugs and Behavior, edited by J. G. Miller and L. Uhr, Wiley, 1960; Some Views on Soviet Psychology, American Psychological Association, 1962; Training Research and Education, edited by R. Glaser, University of Pittsburgh Press, 1962; People and Productivity, edited by R. A. Sutermeister, McGraw, 1963; The Acquisition of Skill, edited by E. A. Bilodeau, Academic Press, 1966; Learning and Individual Differences, edited by R. M. Gagne, C. E. Merrill, 1966.

Author of technical and research reports for U.S. Air Force and Navy. Contributor to International Encyclopedia of the Social Sciences, 1967, Encyclopedia of Educational Research, 4th edition, 1968, and International Encyclopedia of Neurology, Psychiatry, Psychoanalysis, and Psychology, 1976. Contributor of more than 100 articles to professional publications. Editor in chief, Journal of Applied Psychology, 1971-76; associate editor of Personnel Psychology, Organizational Behavior and Human Performance, and Journal of Motor Behavior.

*   *   *

FLETCHER, Joseph (Francis III) 1905-

PERSONAL: Born April 10, 1905, in Newark, N.J.; son of Joseph Francis II (a businessman) and Julia (Davis) Fletcher; married Forrest Hatfield, September 5, 1928; children: Joseph Francis IV, Jane Elizabeth (Mrs. Robert J. Geniesse). Education: West Virginia University, A.B., 1925; Yale University, graduate study, 1928-30; Berkeley Divinity School, B.D., 1929; University of London, S.T.D., 1932. Politics: Independent. Home: 52 Van Ness Rd., Belmont, Mass. 02178. Office: Box 325, Medical School, University of Virginia, Charlottesville, Va. 22903.

CAREER: Ordained minister of Protestant Episcopal Church, 1929; St. Peter's Church, London, England, curate, 1930-32; St. Mary's Junior College, Raleigh, N.C., lecturer and chaplain, 1932-35; Graduate School of Applied Religion, Cincinnati, Ohio, dean, 1936-44; St. Paul's Cathedral, Cincinnati, Ohio, dean, 1936-40; University of Cincinnati, Cincinnati, Ohio, lecturer in labor history and Bible literature, 1939-43; Episcopal Theological School, Cambridge, Mass., professor of pastoral theology and Christian ethics, 1944-70; University of Virginia, Charlottesville, visiting professor of medical ethics, 1970—. Supervisor, Episcopal Summer Training Program, West Indies, 1955; Lilly Visiting Professor, International Christian University, Tokyo, Japan, 1963-64; visiting professor, University of Texas at Houston, 1973—; lecturer, Harvard Divinity School, 1964-65, and at University of St. Andrews, summer, 1966; visiting fellow, Cambridge University, 1967-68.

Director of National Religion and Labor Foundation, Musser Seminar of Harvard Business School, and Institute of Pastoral Care.

MEMBER: Association for the Study of Abortion (vice-president), Association for Voluntary Sterilization, American Society of Christian Ethics, Institute of Society, Ethics and Life Sciences (fellow), Soviet-American Friendship Society, Planned Parenthood Federation, Episcopal League for Social Action.

WRITINGS: The Church and Industry, Longmans, Green, 1930; Christianity and Property, Westminster, 1948; Morals and Medicine, Princeton University Press, 1954; William Temple: 20th Century Christian, Seabury, 1963; Situation Ethics, Westminster, 1966; Moral Responsibility, Westminster, 1967; (with T. A. Wassmer) Hello Lovers! An Introduction to Situation Ethics, Corpus Books, 1970; The Ethics of Genetic Control, Doubleday, 1974. Contributor to Encyclopedia of Religious Knowledge, 1955, and to Die Religion in Geschichte und Gegenwart, 1956. Associate editor, Anglican Theological Review, 1936-48, Journal of Pastoral Care, 1947-57, Christendom, 1935-47, Witness, 1935-71, Churchman, 1963—, International Journal, and Science, Medicine, and Man.

WORK IN PROGRESS: Conscience on the Medical Frontiers; Re-Thinking Right and Wrong.

AVOCATIONAL INTERESTS: Reading; bass and lake trout fishing and photography.

*   *   *

FLETCHER, William C(atherwood) 1932-

PERSONAL: Born October 13, 1932, in Oakland, Calif.; son of Edwin Teed (an American Baptist missionary) and Virginia (Barrett) Fletcher; married Diane Chase, June 17, 1956; children: Stephen Mark, Laurie Ann, Linda Susan. Education: University of Redlands, student, 1950; University of California, Los Angeles, B.A. (cum laude), 1958; California Baptist Theological Seminary, B.D., 1964; University of Southern California, Ph.D., 1964. Office: Department of Slavic and Soviet Area Studies, University of Kansas, Lawrence, Kan. 66045.

CAREER: University of Southern California, School of International Affairs, Los Angeles, research associate in religion, Research Institute, 1964-65; Center for Research and Studies of Religion Institute, Geneva, Switzerland, director of religion of East Europe and the Soviet Union, 1965-70; University of Kansas, Lawrence, professor of Slavic and Soviet area studies and director of department, 1970—. Member of board, College du Leman, beginning 1967; lecturer and trustee, Kansas School of Religion, 1970—. Military service: U.S. Navy, 1951-55. Member: Phi Beta Kappa, Phi Eta Sigma, Lambda Mu Gamma.

WRITINGS: Unlikely Saints of the Bible, Zondervan, 1961; The Moderns: Molders of Contemporary Theology, Zondervan, 1962; Christianity in the Soviet Union: An Annotated Bibliography, University of Southern California Press, 1963; A Study in Survival: The Church in Russia, 1927-43, Macmillan, 1965; (editor with Anthony J. Stover) Religion and the Search for New Ideals in the USSR, Praeger, 1966; Nikolai: Portrait of a Dilemma, Macmillan, 1968; (editor with Max Hayward) Religion and the Soviet State: A Dilemma of Power, Praeger, 1969; The Russian Orthodox Church Underground, 1917-1970, Oxford University Press, 1971; Religion and Soviet Foreign Policy, 1945-1970, Oxford University Press, 1973. Contributor to magazines and journals, including *Frontiers, Communist Affairs, Studies on the Soviet Union, Crusader.*

WORK IN PROGRESS: Editing *Laws on Religion in Eastern Europe,* a collection of documents; research on the history of underground religion in Russia.†

*   *   *

FLIESS, Peter J(oachim) 1915-

PERSONAL: Surname is pronounced Fleece; born May 8, 1915, in Stargard, Germany; son of Julius (a lawyer) and Stephanie M. (Gottheil) Fliess; married Helen Horowitz, July 5, 1941; children: Linda. *Education:* Columbia University, student, 1939-43; Stanford University, B.A., 1944; Harvard University, M.A., 1947, Ph.D., 1951. *Home:* 6 Winston Ct., Amherst, Mass. 01002. *Office:* Department of Political Science, University of Massachusetts, Amherst, Mass. 01002.

CAREER: Former bank employee in Germany and United States; Louisiana State University, Baton Rouge, assistant professor, 1948-54, associate professor, 1954-59, professor of government, 1959-67; University of Massachusetts, Amherst, professor of political science, 1967—. Consultant to Puerto Rican Constitutional Project, and summer lecturer, University of Puerto Rico, 1951; Maurice Falk lecturer, Carnegie Institute of Technology, 1962; visiting summer professor, University of Massachusetts, 1965; guest professor, University of Freiburg, 1971-72; visiting professor, Mt. Holyoke College, 1973-74. *Military service:* U.S. Army, Intelligence, 1943-46; became captain. *Member:* American Political Science Association, American Society of International Law, American Association of University Professors, International Association for Philosophy of Law and Social Philosophy, Southern Political Science Association (member of executive council, 1957-60), Phi Beta Kappa, Phi Kappa Phi, Pi Sigma Alpha. *Awards, honors:* Ford Foundation fellow, 1951-52; Fulbright professor at University of Frankfurt, 1955-56; Earhart Foundation travel and research grant, 1975.

WRITINGS: Freedom of the Press in the German Republic, 1918-1933, Louisiana State University Press, 1955; *Thucydides and the Politics of Bipolarity,* Louisiana State University Press, 1966; *International Relations in the Bipolar World,* Random House, 1968; (contributing editor) *Dictionary of Political Science,* Philosophical Library, 1964. Contributor to political science and law journals in United States and abroad. Editor, *Polity,* 1975—.

WORK IN PROGRESS: Profile of Imperialism, a long-range project.

SIDELIGHTS: Besides his native German, Fliess speaks French and Spanish and reads Greek, Latin, Italian, Portuguese, and Russian. *Avocational interests:* Music, walking.

*   *   *

FLINDERS, Neil J. 1934-

PERSONAL: Born July 11, 1934, in Ogden, Utah; son of Percy James (a contractor) and Reta (Herrick) Flinders; married Joan D. Robertson, June 3, 1960; children: Leisa, Erin, Karalee, Tracy, Scott, David, Shelley. *Education:* Weber State College, student, 1952-54; Brigham Young University, B.S., 1960, M.R.E., 1962, Ed.D., 1968. *Religion:* Church of Jesus Christ of Latter-day Saints. *Home address:* R.F.D. 2, Box 400-F, Pleasant Grove, Utah.

CAREER: Church of Jesus Christ of Latter-day Saints, missionary, 1954-56, teacher of theology and supervisor of

seminary teacher training, Department of Education, Utah, 1960—, director of research and evaluation, Department of Seminaries and Institutes of Religion, 1969-75. Consultant and trainer in human relations at Weber State College and Brigham Young University, 1963—. *Military service:* U.S. Army, Medical Corps, 1957-59; served in the Far East.

WRITINGS: Personal Communication: How to Understand and Be Understood, Deseret, 1966; *Leadership and Human Relations: A Handbook for Parents, Teachers and Executives,* Deseret, 1970; *Continue in Prayer,* Publishers, 1975. Author of curriculum course outlines, and articles for Mormon and non-Mormon publications.

WORK IN PROGRESS: Moral and Religious Education: Teaching Right from Wrong, completion expected in 1978.

AVOCATIONAL INTERESTS: Sports, especially hunting and fishing.

*   *   *

FLINT, Betty M. 1920-

PERSONAL: Born August 20, 1920, in Toronto, Ontario, Canada; daughter of Frederick Cecil and Margaret (Arthurs) Talbot; married Lyman G. B. Flint (a trust officer), January 5, 1951; children: Margaret Elizabeth, George F. B. *Education:* University of Toronto, Diploma in Child Study, 1944, M.A., 1948. *Religion:* Protestant. *Home:* 18 Apsley Rd., Toronto , Ontario, Canada M5M 2X8.

CAREER: Registered psychologist, Province of Ontario. University of Toronto, Toronto, Ontario, research associate, Institute of Child Study, 1948—, assistant professor, 1962-71, associate professor of psychology, 1971—. Clinical psychologist and consultant, Children's Aid, Toronto, and lecturer at Ryerson Institute of Technology, Toronto. Chairman, Blatz Memorial Committee. *Member:* Canadian Psychological Association, Nursery Association of Ontario (past president; honorary member).

WRITINGS: The Security of Infants, University of Toronto Press, 1959; *The Child and the Institution: A Study of Deprivation and Recovery,* University of Toronto Press, 1967. Contributor to *Child Study: Manual and Scale-The Flint Infant Security Scale.*

WORK IN PROGRESS: Reporting the results of a seventeen- year longitudinal study of a group of children reared in a severely depriving environment during infancy and early childhood and later reared in families.

*   *   *

FLOWER, Dean S. 1938-

PERSONAL: Born August 17, 1938, in Milwaukee, Wis.; son of Forrest Wayne (a painter) and Margo (Miller) Flower; married Judith Pickard, June 20, 1959; children: Benjamin, Ann, Sarah, Jonah. *Education:* Attended Oberlin College, 1956-58; University of Michigan, A.B. (with honors), 1960; Stanford University, Ph.D., 1966. *Home:* 25 Henshaw Ave., Northampton, Mass. 01060. *Office:* Neilson Library, Smith College, Northampton, Mass. 01060.

CAREER: University of Southern California, Los Angeles, assistant professor of English, 1964-69; Smith College, Northampton, Mass., assistant professor, 1969-72, associate professor of English, 1972—.

WRITINGS—Editor: Great Short Works of Henry James, Harper, 1966; *Eight Short Novels,* Fawcett, 1967; *Counterparts: Classic and Contemporary American Stories,* Fawcett, 1971; *Henry David Thoreau: Essays, Journals, and Poems*, Fawcett, 1975. Also author of *Henry James in Northampton*, Smith College Library, 1971.

WORK IN PROGRESS: A book-length study of Vladimir Nabokov.

* * *

FLYNN, James Joseph 1911-

PERSONAL: Born September 1, 1911, in Brooklyn, N.Y.; son of Francis Xavier (a policeman) and Helen (McKay) Flynn; married Mary C. Quinn, January 31, 1945. *Education:* Fordham University, B.S. (with honors), 1935, M.A., 1937, Ph.D., 1953. *Politics:* Democrat. *Religion:* Roman Catholic. *Home:* 1825 Norman St., Brooklyn, N.Y. 11227. *Office:* St. Francis College, 180 Remsen St., Brooklyn, N.Y. 11201.

CAREER: High school teacher, 1938-40; Fordham University, Bronx, N.Y., 1940-61, started as instructor, associate professor of history, 1954-61; St. Francis College, Brooklyn, N.Y., professor of history, 1961—, chairman of Social Studies Division, beginning 1961, dean of Continuing Education, 1975—. Provost of Alphonsus College; member of Queens School Board Number 24. *Military service:* U.S. Navy, Seabees, 1943-46; became chief specialist, Office of Naval History. *Member:* American Historical Association, American Academy of Political and Social Science, Southern Historical Association, Pacific Historical Association. *Awards, honors:* Foundation for Economic Education fellow and Voelker Foundation fellow, summer, 1962.

WRITINGS: (With Ross Hoffman) *Medieval History*, Littlefield, 1953; *Comparative Government*, Monarch Books, 1966; *Political Science*, Monarch Books, 1967; *Famous Justices of the Supreme Court*, Dodd, 1968; *Negroes of Achievement in Modern America*, Dodd, 1969; *Winning the Presidency: The Difficulty of Elections*, Gaus, 1975. Editor, Bruce "Social Studies" series.

* * *

FLYNN, James R. 1934-

PERSONAL: Born April 28, 1934, in Washington, D.C.; son of Joseph R. (a journalist and civil servant) and Mae (Scott) Flynn; married Emily F. Malkin, August 27, 1961; children: Eugene Victor, Natalie Claire. *Education:* University of Chicago, B.A., 1952, M.A., 1955, Ph.D., 1958. *Politics:* Democratic Socialist. *Religion:* None. *Home:* 50 Queen St., Dunedin, New Zealand. *Office:* Department of Political Studies, University of Otago, Dunedin, New Zealand.

CAREER: Assistant professor of political science at Eastern Kentucky University, Richmond, 1957-61, Wisconsin State University (now University of Wisconsin), Whitewater, 1961-62, and Lake Forest College, Lake Forest, Ill., 1962-63; University of Canterbury, Christchurch, New Zealand, began as lecturer, became senior lecturer in political science, 1963-67; University of Otago, Dunedin, New Zealand, professor of political studies and head of department, 1967—. Chairman of Madison County (Ky.) Congress of Racial Equality, 1960-61; member of Wisconsin State Executive Committee of the Socialist Party, 1962; member of local New Zealand executive committee on Vietnam, 1965—. *Member:* Australasian Political Studies Association, New Zealand Political Studies Association.

WRITINGS: American Politics: A Radical View, Black-

wood & Janet Paul (Auckland), 1967; *Humanism and Ideology: An Aristotelian View*, Routledge & Kegan Paul, 1973. Regular contributor on American themes to *New Zealand Listener* and New Zealand Broadcasting Corp.; also contributor of articles to journals in the United States, Australasia, Britain and Norway.

WORK IN PROGRESS: A book, tentatively titled *The Justification of Humanism: Four Approaches.*

* * *

FODOR, Eugene 1905-

PERSONAL: Born October 14, 1905, in Leva, Hungary; came to United States in 1938, naturalized in 1942; son of Matthew Gyula (a businessman) and Malvine (Kurti) Fodor; married Vlasta Maria Zobel, December 4, 1948; children: Eugene, Jr. *Education:* Sorbonne, University of Paris, student, 1924-25; University of Grenoble, licencie es economie politique, 1927. *Residence:* Litchfield, Conn. *Office:* Fodor's Modern Guides, Inc., Box 784, Litchfield, Conn. 06759.

CAREER: Travel correspondent, *Prague Hungarian Journal*, 1930-33; editor of travel guides, London, England, 1934-38, of *Query* (foreign affairs magazine), London, 1938, and at Hyperion Press (publishers of art books), New York, N.Y., 1939-42; Fodor's Modern Guides, Inc., Litchfield, Conn., president, 1949—; Fodor's Modern Guides Ltd., London, vice-chairman, 1966—. *Military service:* U.S. Army, 1942-47; became captain; received six battle stars and other decorations. *Member:* International Federation of Travel Journalists and Writers, International Union of Official Travel Organizations, Society of American Travel Writers, Pacific Area Travel Association, South American Travel Association, Caribbean Travel Association. *Awards, honors:* Grand Prix de Litterature de Tourisme (Paris), 1959; awards from Caribbean Travel Association, 1960, Pacific Area Travel Association, 1960, 1962, National Association of Travel Organizations, 1966, International Travel Book Contest, 1969, British Tourist Authority, 1972, Discover America Travel Organizations, 1975; Vienna Travel Book Exposition honor list, 1963; Silver Medal, Austrian government, 1970.

WRITINGS—Editor; all published by McKay, except as indicated: *1936 ... On the Continent*, Aldor, 1936, 2nd edition published as *1937 ... In Europe*, Houghton, 1937, 3rd edition published as *1938 in Europe*, Houghton, 1938 (published in England as *Aldor's Entertaining Annual*, two volumes, Aldor, 1938).

Britain in 1951, 1951, 3rd edition, 1955; *France in 1951*, 1951, latest edition, 1976; *Italy in 1951*, 1951, latest edition, 1976; *Switzerland in 1951*, 1951, latest edition, 1976; *Benelux: Belgium, the Netherlands, Luxembourg*, 1952, 3rd edition, 1958, published as *Belgium and Luxembourg*, 1959, latest edition, 1976, and *Holland*, 1959, latest edition, 1976; *Scandinavia in 1952*, 1952, latest edition, 1976; *Spain and Portugal in 1952*, 1952, 7th edition, 1966, published (with William Curtis) as *Spain, 1967*, 1967, latest edition, 1976, and *Portugal, 1967*, latest edition, 1976; *Woman's Guide to Europe*, 1952, 4th edition, 1956; *Austria, 1953*, 1953, latest edition, 1976; *Germany, 1953*, 1953, latest edition, 1976; *The Men's Guide to Europe*, 1955, 2nd edition (with Frederick Rockwell), 1957; *Britain and Ireland, 1956*, 1956, 8th edition, 1967, published (with Robert C. Fisher) as *Great Britain*, 1968, latest edition, 1976, and *Ireland*, 1968, latest edition, 1976; *Yugoslavia, 1958*, 1958, latest edition, 1976; *Fodor's Jet Age Guide to Europe*, 1959, also published as

Fodor's Guide to Europe, 1959, 3rd edition, 1967, also published as *Guide to Europe, 1964*, 1964, latest edition, 1976.

Fodor's Guide to the Caribbean, Bahamas, and Bermuda, 1960, latest edition, 1976; *Greece, 1960*, 1960, latest edition (with Curtis), 1976; *Hawaii, 1961*, latest edition, 1976; (with Fisher) *Fodor's Guide to Japan and East Asia*, 1962, latest edition, 1974; (with Curtis) *Fodor's Guide to India*, 1963, latest edition, 1976; (with Curtis) *Morocco, 1965-66*, 1965, latest edition, 1976; (with Fisher) *Fodor's Guide to South America, 1966*, 1966, latest edition, 1976; (with Fisher and Barnett D. Laschever) *Fodor Shell Travel Guides U.S.A.*, Fodor's, Volume I: *New England*, Volume II: *New York-New Jersey*, Volume III: *Mid-Atlantic*, Volume IV: *Southeast*, Volume V: *South Central*, Volume VI: *Midwest*, Volume VII: *Rockies and Plains*, Volume VIII: *Pacific States*, all 1966, 2nd editions, 1967; (with Curtis) *Israel, 1967-68*, 1967, latest edition, 1976; (with Curtis) *Turkey, 1969*, 1969, latest edition, 1976.

Czechoslovakia, 1970-71, 1970, latest edition, 1975; *Hungary, 1970-71*, 1970, latest edition, 1976; *London*, 1971, latest edition, 1975; Georgina Masson, *Fodor's Rome*, revised edition, 1971; Hugh Honour, *Fodor's Venice*, revised edition, 1971; Odile Cail, *Peking*, 1972, revised edition, 1973; (with Marjorie Lockett) *Mexico*, 1972, latest edition, 1976; *Europe under 25*, 1972, latest edition, 1974; *Europe on a Budget*, 1972, latest edition, 1974; (with Curtis) *Islamic Asia*, 1973; (with Curtis) *Tunisia*, 1973, latest edition, 1976; *Paris*, 1974; *Vienna*, 1974; *Guide to the Soviet Union, 1974-75*, 1974, latest edition, 1976; (with Jamake Highwater) *Indian America*, 1975; *Japan and Korea*, 1975; *Southeast Asia*, 1975; (with Robert V. Daniels) *Europe Talking*, 1975; *Guide to the U.S.A.*, 1976, one volume, 1976.

WORK IN PROGRESS: Books on Canada, the South Pacific, and the Middle East.

SIDELIGHTS: Fodor told *CA:* "Passionately believe that travel is the most effective shortcut to tolerance, understanding and recognition of the others' rights to their own values." Most of his books have been published in French, German, Italian, Spanish, Dutch, Hungarian, and Japanese. In addition to his native Hungarian, Fodor speaks French, German, Italian, Czech, and Slovak.

*   *   *

FOGARTY, Michael P(atrick)   1916-

PERSONAL: Born October 3, 1916, in Maymyo, Burma; son of Philip Christopher and Mabel (Pye) Fogarty; married Phyllis Clark, September 11, 1939; children: Sally Margaret, Priscilla Mary, Bernard Michael Charles, Kiernan Patrick. *Education:* Christ Church, Oxford, B.A. (first class honors), 1938, M.A., 1941. *Politics:* Labour, 1934-59; Liberal, 1959—. *Religion:* Roman Catholic. *Home:* Red Copse, Foxcombe Rd., Boars Hill, Oxford, England. *Office:* Centre for Studies in Social Policy, 62 Doughty St., London WC1N 2LS, England.

CAREER: Oxford University, Nuffield College, Oxford, England, research staff, 1941-44, fellow, 1944-51; University of Wales, University College, Cardiff, Montague Burton Professor of Industrial Relations and head of department, 1951-66; Political and Economic Planning (independent social research institute), London, England, consultant, 1966-68; Economic and Social Research Institute, Dublin, Ireland, professor and director, 1968-72; Centre for Studies in Social Policy, London, senior fellow, 1973—.

Research officer, Ministry of Town and Country Planning, London, 1944-45; research associate, National Institute of Economic and Social Research, London, 1950-51; visiting professor, University of Notre Dame, 1956; professor associate, Brunel University, and Administrative Staff College, 1973—. Former chairman of Oxford City Labour Party, and municipal and parliamentary candidate. Liberal party, vice-president, 1964-66, parliamentary candidate, 1964, 1966, 1974, and member of council and standing committee, 1973—. *Military service:* British Army, Royal Artillery, 1939-41; discharged as lieutenant after being wounded at Dunkirk.

MEMBER: British Institute of Management, British Sociological Association, Royal Economic Society, Association of University Teachers (vice-president, 1964-66), Newman Association (president, 1957-59; honorary president, 1966—), Catholic Social Guild (chairman, 1959-63). *Awards, honors:* Doctor of Political and Social Science, University of Louvain, 1964.

WRITINGS: Prospects of the Industrial Areas of Great Britain, Methuen, 1944; (editor) *Further Studies in Economic Organisation*, Methuen, 1947; *Plan Your Own Industries* (regional planning), Basil Blackwell, 1947; *Town and Country Planning*, Hutchinson, 1948; *Economic Control*, Routledge & Kegan Paul, 1955; *Personality and Group Relations in Industry*, Longmans, Green, 1956; *Christian Democracy in Western Europe, 1820-1953*, University of Notre Dame Press, 1957.

The Just Wage, Geoffrey Chapman, 1961; *Under-Governed and Over-Governed*, Geoffrey Chapman, 1962; *The Rules of Work*, Geoffrey Chapman, 1964; *Company and Corporation—One Law?*, Geoffrey Chapman, 1965; *Wider Business Objectives: American Thinking and Experience*, Political and Economic Planning, 1966; *A Companies Act 1970?*, Political and Economic Planning, 1967; (with Rhona Rapoport and Robert Rapoport) *Women and Top Jobs: The Next Move*, Political and Economic Planning, 1967; (with others) *Women in Top Jobs: Four Studies in Achievement*, Allen & Unwin, 1971; (with Rhona Rapoport and Robert Rapoport) *Sex, Career and Family*, Sage Publications, 1971; *Irish Entrepreneurs Speak for Themselves*, Economic and Social Research Institute (Dublin), 1973; *Company Responsibilities and Participation*, Political and Economic Planning, 1975; *Forty to Sixty: How We Waste the Middle-Aged*, Bedford Square Press, 1975; *Work and Industrial Relations in the European Community*, Political and Economic Planning, 1975.

Author of monographs on industrial and social topics; also author of scripts for British Broadcasting Corp. and Independent Television. Contributor to professional journals in England, western Europe, and the United States. Former British correspondent for *Commonweal;* deputy editor, *Economist, 1946-47.*

WORK IN PROGRESS: Research on the social role of the churches in northwestern Europe, and on the problem of the older worker and retirement.

SIDELIGHTS: Michael Fogarty speaks French and German, reads Spanish, Italian, Dutch, and Latin, and is learning Russian. *Avocational interests:* Swimming, walking.

*   *   *

FOLLETT, Robert J. R.   1928-

PERSONAL: Born July 4, 1928, in Oak Park, Ill.; son of

Dwight W. (an executive) and Mildred (Johnson) Follett; married Nancy L. Crouthamel, December 30, 1950; children: Brian L., Kathryn R., Jean A., Lisa W. *Education:* Brown University, A.B., 1950; Columbia University, graduate study, 1950-51. *Religion:* Presbyterian. *Home:* 508 North Oak Park Ave., Oak Park, Ill. 60302. *Office:* 1010 West Washington Blvd., Chicago, Ill. 60607.

CAREER: Follett Publishing Co., Chicago, Ill., publisher, 1951—. Director of Follett Corp.; director of Educational Systems Corp., 1967—; president of Alpine Research Institute, 1973—. *Military service:* U.S. Army, Psychological Warfare School, 1951-53. *Member:* American Educational Research Association, Chicago Publishers Association, Chicago Book Clinic, Cliff Dwellers, River Forest Tennis Club, Caxton Club.

WRITINGS: Your Wonderful Body, Follett, 1962. Contributor to professional journals.

WORK IN PROGRESS: Research in computer-assisted educational systems.

AVOCATIONAL INTERESTS: Wood sculpture, painting, outdoor sports, photography, poetry, and reading.

* * *

FOLLEY, Terence T. 1931-

PERSONAL: Born September 5, 1931, in Birmingham, England; married; children: four. *Education:* National University of Ireland, B.A., 1951, M.A., 1956, Ph.D., 1969; additional study at universities in Spain, France, and Germany. *Religion:* Roman Catholic. *Home:* Kerry Pike, Carrigrohane, County of Cork, Ireland. *Office:* Spanish Department, University College, Cork, Ireland.

CAREER: During his early career taught English in Spain for three years, and taught general subjects in London for two years; U.S. Air Force Central High School, Teddington, England, teacher of Spanish and German, 1957-60; College of Advanced and Commercial Studies, London, England, head of modern languages department, 1960-63; University College, National University of Ireland, Cork, lecturer in Spanish department, 1963—. Co-examiner, Irish Civil Service Appointments Commission, 1965; chief examiner in Spanish, Irish Government intermediate and leaving school certificate examinations, chief examiner in Spanish, 1967 and 1970—. *Member:* Association of Hispanists of Great Britain and Ireland, Irish Federation of University Teachers.

WRITINGS: A Dictionary of Spanish Idioms and Colloquialisms, Blackie & Son, 1965; *Spanish Aide-Memoire* (also published as *Spanish Vocabulary*), G. Bell, 1966; *Contemporary Spanish Passages for Advanced Study,* Harrap, 1967; *Spanish Parallel Passages,* Harrap, 1968; *Spanish Comprehension Passages,* Gill & Macmillan, 1972; *Los españoles viven su historia,* Harrap, in press. Contributor to *Bulletin of Hispanic Studies;* also contributor of articles in English and Spanish to professional journals in Ireland, England, and Spain.

WORK IN PROGRESS: Aspects of linguistic usage in the works of several modern and contemporary Spanish writers.

SIDELIGHTS: Folley is fluent in French and Gaelic; speaks Portuguese, Italian, and Polish; reads Russian and Rumanian.

FOLSOM, Kenneth E(verett) 1921-

PERSONAL: Born January 17, 1921, in Reno, Nev.; son of Ernest Gilman and Eileen (Everett) Folsom; married Elizabeth Wales, August 24, 1945; married second wife, Gwen Harmsen (a contract administrator), August 21, 1955. *Education:* Princeton University, A.B., 1943; University of California, Berkeley, A.B. (with honors), 1955, M.A., 1957, Ph.D., 1964. *Home:* 4216 Woodberry St., University Park, Md. 20782. *Office:* Department of History, University of Maryland, College Park, Md. 20742.

CAREER: KLM Royal Dutch Airlines, New York, N.Y., assistant airport manager, 1946-47; Indemnity Insurance Co. of North America, Newark, N.J., special agent, 1947-49; Colgate Palmolive Peet Co., Jersey City, N.J., advertising staff, 1949-52; Purex Corp. Ltd., South Gate, Calif., associate advertising manager, 1953-54; University of Maryland, College Park, assistant professor, 1964-67, associate professor of history, 1967—. *Military service:* U.S. Naval Reserve, active duty, 1943-46; became lieutenant junior grade. *Member:* Association for Asian Studies.

WRITINGS: Friends, Guests, and Colleagues: The Mu-fu System in the Late Ch'ing Period, University of California Press, 1968; (contributor) David I. Eggenberger, editor, *Encyclopedia of World Biography,* McGraw, 1973.

WORK IN PROGRESS: Chinese Communist Political Indoctrination and Education, 1921-1927.

* * *

FORCE, William M. 1916-

PERSONAL: Born August 15, 1916, in Newark, N.J.; son of George M. (a civil engineer) and Ethel T. (Binzen) Force; married Patricia E. Laverty, August 14, 1949; children: William M., Jr., Elizabeth, Barbara. *Education:* Colgate University, B.A., 1940, M.A., 1948; Northwestern University, additional graduate studies, 1949-50. *Address:* 106 Shady Dr., Indiana, Pa. 15701. *Office:* Indiana University of Pennsylvania, Indiana, Pa. 15701.

CAREER: Missouri Valley College, Marshall, Mo., associate professor of English and drama, 1951-58; Clarion State College, Clarion, Pa., member of speech department, 1959-60; Indiana University of Pennsylvania, Indiana, Pa., associate professor of English, 1961—. *Military service:* U.S. Army Air Forces, 1941-46; became first lieutenant.

WRITINGS: (Editor) Euripides, *Orestes & Electra* (anthology), Houghton, 1968.†

* * *

FORD, Amasa B. 1922-

PERSONAL: Born July 13, 1922, in Cleveland, Ohio; son of David Knight and Elizabeth Kingsley (Brooks) Ford; married Mary Elizabeth Simmons, 1951; children: Edward Clark, Charles Keith, Donald Brooks. *Education:* Yale University, B.A., 1944; Harvard University, M.D. (cum laude), 1950. *Home:* Mather Lane, Chagrin Falls, Ohio 44022. *Office:* School of Medicine, Case Western Reserve University, Cleveland, Ohio 44106.

CAREER: Took internship and residency at Massachusetts General Hospital, Boston, 1950-52, and University Hospitals of Cleveland, Cleveland, Ohio, 1952-54; private practice of internal medicine, Cleveland, 1954—; University Hospitals of Cleveland, assistant physician, 1954-71, associate physician, 1971—; Case Western Reserve University, School of Medicine, Cleveland, teaching fellow, 1954-56, instructor, 1956-58, senior instructor, 1958-60, assistant professor, 1960-72, associate professor of medicine, 1972—, assistant professor, 1969-71, associate professor, 1971-75, professor of community health, 1975—, acting director of department of community health, 1973-75, on sabbatical leave, 1968-69, to study at London School of Hygiene and Tropical Medicine. Benjamin Rose Hospital, assistant physician, 1954-68, medical director, 1960-68. Geauga East Suburban Drug Center, medical director, 1971—, member of board of trustees, 1972—. Cleveland Neighborhood Health Services, Inc., member of board of trustees, 1972—, president, 1975—. Member of board of trustees, Metropolitan Health Planning Corp., 1972—. Member of nursing research study, National Institutes of Health, 1961-65; member, Ohio Health Planning Council, 1973—. Diplomate, American Board of Internal Medicine, 1957. *Military service:* U.S. Army, Infantry, 1943-46; became second lieutenant.

MEMBER: American Medical Association, American Public Health Association (fellow), Association of American Medical Colleges, American Federation for Clinical Research, American Heart Association, National League for Nursing (board of directors, 1966-68), Association of Teachers of Preventative Medicine, Society of Teachers of Family Medicine, Royal Society of Medicine, Academy of Medicine of Cleveland and Cuyahoga County Medical Society, Phi Beta Kappa, Sigma Xi, Alpha Omega Alpha.

WRITINGS: (With R. E. Liske, R. S. Ort, and J. C. Denton) *The Doctor's Perspective: Physicians View Their Patients and Practice,* Press of Case Western Reserve University, 1967; (with others) *The Effects of Continued Care: A Study of Chronic Illness in the Home,* U.S. Department of Health, Education, and Welfare, 1972; *Urban Health in America,* Oxford University Press, 1975. Contributor to monographs published by American Heart Association, and to proceedings of medical conferences; also contributor of more than thirty articles and reviews to professional journals.

*   *   *

FORD, Gordon B(uell), Jr. 1937-

PERSONAL: Born September 22, 1937, in Louisville, Ky.; son of Gordon Buell (a certified public accountant) and Rubye (Allen) Ford. *Education:* Princeton University, A.B., 1959; Harvard University, A.M., 1962, Ph.D., 1965; graduate study at University of Sofia and University of Madrid, 1963, at University of Oslo, University of Uppsala, and University of Stockholm, 1963-64. *Home:* 1939 College St., Cedar Falls, Iowa 50613. *Office:* Department of English Language and Literature, University of Northern Iowa, Cedar Falls, Iowa 50613.

CAREER: Northwestern University, Evanston, Ill., assistant professor of Indo-European and Baltic linguistics and Medieval Latin, 1965-72, assistant professor of anthropology, 1971-72; University of Northern Iowa, Cedar Falls, associate professor, 1972-74; professor of English and linguistics, 1974—. Visiting assistant professor and lecturer, University of Chicago, 1966-67, 1970-72. *Member:* International Linguistic Association, Linguistic Society of America, American Philological Association, Modern Language Association of America, American Association of Teachers of Slavic and East European Languages, Mediaeval Academy of America, Societas Linguistica Europaea, Association for the Advancement of Baltic Studies, Institute of Lithuanian Studies, Phi Beta Kappa, Sons of the American Revolution, Princeton Club (New York).

WRITINGS: The Ruodlieb: The First Medieval Epic of Chivalry from Eleventh-Century Germany, E. J. Brill, 1965; *The Old Lithuanian Catechism of Baltramiejus Vilentas (1579): A Phonological, Morphological, and Syntactical Investigation,* Mouton & Co., 1969.

Editor: *The Lithuanian Catechism of Baltramiejus Vilentas (1579),* Pyramid Press, 1964, 3rd revised edition, 1966; *The Ruodlieb: The Facsimile Edition,* Pyramid Press, 1965, 2nd revised edition, 1967; *The Wolfenbuttel Lithuanian Postile Manuscript of the Year 1573,* three volumes, Pyramid Press, 1965-66; *The Ruodlieb: Linguistic Introduction, Latin Text, and Glossary,* E. J. Brill, 1966; *Baltramiejus Vilentas' Lithuanian Translation of the Gospels and Epistles (1579),* Pyramid Press, 1966; (and compiler) *Old Lithuanian Texts of the Sixteenth and Seventeenth Centuries with a Glossary,* Mouton & Co., 1969; *The Old Lithuanian Catechism of Martynas Mazvydas (1547),* Van Gorcum, 1971.

Translator: Jan Gonda, *A Concise Elementary Grammar of the Sanskrit Language,* University of Alabama Press, 1966; (with Guido Donini) *Isidore of Seville's History of the Kings of the Goths, Vandals, and Suevi,* E. J. Brill, 1966, 2nd revised edition published as *Isidore of Seville's History of the Goths, Vandals, and Suevi,* 1970; Antoine Meillet, *The Comparative Method in Historical Linguistics,* Libraire Honore Champion (Paris), 1967; Manfred Mayrhofer, *A Sanskrit Grammar,* University of Alabama Press, 1972.

WORK IN PROGRESS: Isidore of Seville: On Grammar, for Adolf M. Hakkert; *Readings in Historical Linguistic Methodology,* for University of Miami Press; a translation of Antoine Meillet's *Introduction to the Comparative Study of the Indo-European Languages,* for University of Alabama Press.

SIDELIGHTS: Ford is competent in French, German, Spanish, Norwegian, Swedish, Danish, Bulgarian, Lithuanian, Latvian, Greek, Latin, and Sanskrit.

*   *   *

FORD, Norman Dennis 1921-

PERSONAL: Born January 8, 1921, in United Kingdom; son of Frederick William (an accountant) and Jessie (Shortland) Ford; married Angela Lawrence, September 17, 1964; children: Eric, Kirk. *Education:* Educated in Wales. *Politics:* Liberalism. *Religion:* Agnostic. *Home:* 1428 North L St., Lake Worth, Fla. 33460; and 3055 North 6th St., Boulder, Colo. 80302.

CAREER: Free-lance writer on travel and retirement. *Military service:* Royal Navy, World War II. *Member:* Society of American Travel Writers, Sierra Club, American Natural Hygiene Society, International Bicycle Touring Society, Cyclists Touring Club, Sivananda Yoga Vidanta Centre, Globetrotters Club.

WRITINGS—All published by Harian: *How to Entertain Yourself on a Ship,* 1949; *Ship Lore: An Introduction to Life at Sea for Landlubber Passengers and Young Seamen,* 1949; *Retire Young, and Start Living,* 1950; *Lands in the Sun,* 1950; *How to Earn an Income While Retired,* 1950, 5th revised edition published as *Increasing Your Retirement and Other Income,* 1968, 6th revised edition, 1969; *Harian's French Recommendations* (booklet), 1950; *Harian's English Recommendations* (booklet), 1950; *Where to Retire on a Small Income,* 1950, 19th edition, 1975; *Your Ship,* 1951; (with William J. Redgrave) *Bargain Paradises of the World*, 1952, 13th revised edition (sole author), 1967, 15th revised edition, 1971; *Where to Find Opportunity Today*, 1952, published as *Today's Lands of Opportunity*, 1955; *Where to Vacation on a Shoestring*, 1952, 8th revised edition, 1959; *Where to Stay, Eat, and Shop in Western Europe, and What to See*, 1953, 5th edition, 1960; *Why Not Write?*, 1953; *The Fiesta Lands*, 1953, 7th edition, 1959; *Florida: A Complete Guide to Finding What You Seek in Florida*, 1953, 17th edition, 1975; *All of Europe at Low Cost*, 1953, 6th edition, 1971.

(With Fredric Ewald Tyarks [pseudonym for Fred Tyler]) *Europe on a Shoestring*, new edition, 1954 (Ford was not associated with earlier editions), 18th revised edition, 1973; *How to Travel without Being Rich*, 1954, 17th edition, 1976; *How to Get a Job that Takes You Traveling*, 1954, 8th revised edition published as *How to Travel and Get Paid for It*, 1963, 12th revised edition, 1971; *Air Routes of the World*, 1955, 2nd edition, 1956; *America's 50 Best Cities in Which to Live, Work, and Retire*, 1957, 3rd edition, 1960; *Off the Beaten Path*, 1957, 15th edition, 1976; *America by Car*, 1957, 15th edition, 1975; *Today's Best Buys in Freighter Travel*, 1959, 14th edition, 1972; *Today's Best Buys in American Vacations*, 1959.

(With Tyarks) *Today's Best Buys in Travel*, 1960, 5th revised edition, 1971; *Freighter Days*, 1960, 7th revised edition, 1973; *Fabulous Mexico: Where Everything Costs Less*, 1960, published as *Mexico: Where Everything Costs Less!*, 1960, 12th edition, 1974; *All the World*, 1960, 3rd revised edition (with Richard Leavitt) published as *All the World at Low Cost*, 1969; *It's Cheaper to Travel*, 1961, 2nd edition published as *It's Cheaper to Travel—When You Travel on Your Own*, 1966; *Mexico and Guatemala by Car*, 1962; *Utopia Is an Island*, 1963, 4th edition, 1971; *What to See in All America*, 1964, 4th revised edition, 1971; *Around the World for $1500: Norman Ford's Guide to All the World*, 1964; *How to Travel by Freighter*, 1964, 5th revised edition, 1969; *All of Mexico and Guatemala at Low Cost*, 1967, 3rd revised edition published as *All of Mexico at Low Cost*, 1970, 4th revised edition, 1972; *Investing for a Sound 6% and More*, 1969, 9th edition, 1974; *Norman Ford's Favorite Travel Bargains*, 1969; *Travel without Your Car*, 1975. Travel editor, *Retirement Living* (formerly *Harvest Years*).

SIDELIGHTS: Norman Ford described himself to *CA* as a founder of positive evolution, "a scientific way of living based on the premise that through accelerated evolution one may develop his body, mind and spirit to the highest levels attainable . . . to become simultaneously an athlete, a student, and a self-realized individual."

*   *   *

FORD, Patrick 1914-

PERSONAL: Born August 7, 1914, in Cobram, Victoria, Australia; son of Peter Leo and Maude (Squires) Ford. Studied in Australia at St. Columba's College, 1931-32, and St. Patrick's College, 1933-36; University of Melbourne, B.A., 1940. *Home:* Old South Head Rd., Watson's Bay, New South Wales, Australia.

CAREER: Roman Catholic priest. Lecturer in ethics at St. Patrick's College, Manly, New South Wales, Australia, 1943-59, and St. Columba's College, Springwood, New South Wales, 1961; parish priest in Watson's Bay, New South Wales, 1962—. *Military service:* Royal Australian Air Force, chaplain, 1941-42.

WRITINGS: Cardinal Moran and the A.L.P., Melbourne

University Press, 1966, Cambridge University Press, 1967. Also author of a pamphlet, *The Right to Freedom in Health and Medicine*, ACTD Publications (Melbourne), 1973.

*   *   *

FORD, Thomas W(ellborn) 1924-

PERSONAL: Born December 23, 1924, in Houston, Tex.; son of Henry Harrison (an independent oil operator) and Natalia (Wellborn) Ford; married Cora Lewis, August 29, 1953; children: Tommy, Emily. *Education:* Rice University, B.A., 1950; University of Texas, M.A., 1951, Ph.D., 1959. *Politics:* "No party affiliation—independent voter." *Religion:* Episcopalian. *Home:* 6126 Sugar Hill, Houston, Tex. 77027. *Office:* Department of English, University of Houston, Houston, Tex. 77004.

CAREER: Instructor in English at Kinkaid Preparatory School, Houston, Tex., 1953-55, and University of Texas, Austin, 1958-59; University of South Carolina, Columbia, instructor, 1959-61, assistant professor of English, 1961-66; University of Houston, Houston, Tex., associate professor, 1966-71, professor of English, 1971—. *Military service:* U.S. Army Air Forces, 1943-46; served as aerial gunner on B-24; became sergeant; received Asiatic-Pacific Campaign Medal, Philippine Liberation Ribbon. *Member:* Modern Language Association of America, College Conference of Teachers of English, South Central Modern Language Association, Western American Literature Association, Southwestern American Literature Association, Phi Kappa Phi.

WRITINGS: Heaven Beguiles the Tired: Death in the Poetry of Emily Dickinson, University of Alabama Press, 1966. Also author of *A. B. Guthrie, Jr.* (booklet), Steck, 1968. Contributor of poetry to magazines, and articles to learned journals, including *Southern Folklore Quarterly, University Review, Midwest Quarterly, Texas Studies in Literature and Language, Mark Twain Journal, Walt Whitman Review, Western American Literature*, and *New England Quarterly*.

WORK IN PROGRESS: A book on A. B. Guthrie, Jr., for Twayne, completion expected in 1977.

AVOCATIONAL INTERESTS: Travel in Mexico, tennis.

BIOGRAPHICAL/CRITICAL SOURCES: Midwest Quarterly, autumn, 1962.

*   *   *

FOREMAN, Michael 1938-

PERSONAL: Born March 21, 1938, in Lowestoft, England; son of Walter Thomas (a crane operator) and Gladys (Goddard) Foreman; married Janet Charters, September 26, 1959 (divorced); children: Mark. *Education:* Lowestoft School of Art, National Diploma in Design (painting), 1958; Royal College of Art, A.R.C.A. (first honors), 1963. *Home:* 353 Liverpool Rd., London, England.

CAREER: Graphic artist. Lecturer in graphics at St. Martins School of Art, London, England, 1963-66, London College of Printing, London, 1966-68, and Royal College of Art, London, 1968-69. Art director of *Ambit* and *Playboy*, 1965, and *King*, 1966-67. *Awards, honors:* Schweppes traveling scholarship to United States, 1961-63; Gimpel Fils Prize for a young painter, 1962.

WRITINGS—All self-illustrated: (With Janet Charters) *The General*, Dutton, 1961; *The Perfect Present*, Coward,

1967; *The Two Giants,* Pantheon, 1967; *The Great Sleigh Robbery,* Hamish Hamilton, 1968, Pantheon, 1969; *Horatio,* Hamish Hamilton, 1970, published as *The Travels of Horatio,* Pantheon, 1970; *Moose,* Hamish Hamilton, 1971, Pantheon, 1972; *The Living Arts of Nigeria,* Studio Vista, 1972; *Dinosaurs and All That Rubbish,* Hamish Hamilton, 1972; *War and Peas,* Crowell, 1974; (with Georgess McHargue) *Private Zoo,* Viking, 1975.

Illustrator: Sergei Vladimirovich Mikhalkov, *Let's Fight, and Other Russian Fables,* Pantheon, 1968; William Ivan Martin, *Adam's Balm,* Bowmar, 1970; Barbara Adachi, *The Living Treasures of Japan,* Wildwood House, 1973; Janice Elliott, *Alexander in the Mog,* Brockhampton Press, 1973; Janice Elliott, *The Birthday Unicorn,* Penguin, 1973; Jane H. Yolen, *Rainbow Rider,* Crowell, 1974; Barbara K. Walker, *Teeny-Tiny and the Witch-Woman,* Pantheon, 1975.

WORK IN PROGRESS: The Rain, Snow, and Fog Men, for Pantheon; *The Rainbow,* for Hamish Hamilton; six animated color children's films for British Broadcasting Corp. and Danish and Swedish television.

BIOGRAPHICAL/CRITICAL SOURCES: Isis, November, 1966.†

* * *

FORRESTER, (William) Ray 1911-

PERSONAL: Born January 14, 1911, in Little Rock, Ark.; son of William Thomas and Mary Louise (Lucas) Forrester; married Celine Mortee Penn, October 31, 1942; children: William Ray, Jr., Catherine Lucas, David, Stephen. *Education:* University of Arkansas, A.B., 1933; University of Chicago, J.D., 1935. *Office:* Cornell University, Ithaca, N.Y. 14850.

CAREER: Admitted to Illinois Bar, 1935; Defrees, Buckingham, Jones & Hoffman, Chicago, Ill., attorney, 1935-41; Tulane University of Louisiana, New Orleans, assistant professor, 1941-43, professor of law, 1943-49; Vanderbilt University, Nashville, Tenn., professor of law and dean of Law School, 1949-52; Tulane University of Louisiana, professor of law and dean of Law School, 1952-63; Cornell University, Ithaca, N.Y., professor of law and dean of Law School, 1963-73, Stevens Professor, 1973—. Interim chairman of Board of Conciliation and Arbitration, U.S. Steel and United Steel Workers of America, 1950-52; permanent arbitrator, International Harvester Co. and United Automobile Workers, 1951-52; member of board of governors, National Academy of Arbitrators. Commissioner on Uniform State Laws, 1956-63. *Awards, honors:* LL.D., University of Arkansas, 1963.

WRITINGS: (Editor with A. M. Dobie) *Cases and Material on Federal Jurisdiction and Procedure,* 2nd edition, West Publishing, 1950; *Constitutional Law: Cases and Materials,* West Publishing, 1959, supplement, 1966; (editor with T. S. Currier) *Cases on Federal Jurisdiction and Procedure,* West Publishing, 1962, 2nd edition (with Currier and J. Moye), 1970, supplement (with Moye), 1973. Contributor to legal journals. Member of board of editors, *University of Chicago Law Review,* 1934; faculty editor, *Tulane Law Review,* 1942-46.

WORK IN PROGRESS: Third edition of *Cases on Federal Jurisdiction and Procedure.*

* * *

FORSBERG, Malcolm I. 1908-

PERSONAL: Born December 14, 1908, in Tacoma, Wash.; son of John Victor (a machinist and lay preacher) and Hannah (Bjur) Forsberg; married Enid Hattersely Miller, March 14, 1935; children: Leigh, James R., Malcolm I., Jr., Dorothy June. *Education:* Wheaton College, Wheaton, Ill., Ph.B., 1932. *Politics:* Independent Republican. *Religion:* Presbyterian. *Home:* 1017 East Jefferson Ave., Wheaton, Ill. 60187. *Agent:* Muriel Fuller, Box 193, Grand Central Station, New York, N.Y. 10017. *Office:* Sudan Interior Mission, 164 West 74th St., New York, N.Y. 10023.

CAREER: Ordained missionary. Sudan Interior Mission, New York, N.Y., missionary to Ethiopia, 1933-37, missionary to Sudan, 1938-64, candidate secretary for personnel, 1964-74. *Awards, honors:* Litt.D., Wheaton College, 1960.

WRITINGS: Land Beyond the Nile (autobiographical), Harper, 1958; *Last Days on the Nile* (autobiographical), Lippincott, 1966. Also author with wife, Enid Forsberg, of *In Famine He Shall Redeem Thee,* 1974.

* * *

FORSTER, Kent 1916-

PERSONAL: Born December 4, 1916, in New York, N.Y.; son of Theodore (a merchant) and Elise (Strobel) Forster; married Jean Elizabeth Brown, November 27, 1943; children: Kristine Forster Brecht, Ann Forster Lyon, Jon Secor, Peter Kent, Elise Jane. *Education:* Johns Hopkins University, student, 1936; Washington and Lee University, A.B., 1937; University of Pennsylvania, M.A., 1939, Ph.D., 1941. *Religion:* Christian. *Office:* Department of History, Pennsylvania State University, University Park, Pa. 16802.

CAREER: Pennsylvania State University, University Park, instructor, 1941-42, 1944-45, assistant professor, 1945-48, associate professor, 1948-54, professor of history, 1954—. Fulbright lecturer at University of Helsinki, 1956-57, and University of Vienna, 1962-63; visiting professor at Bowling Green State University, 1964, University of Alaska, 1965, and American University of Beirut, 1967-68. *Military service:* U.S. Army Air Forces, 1942-44; became captain. *Member:* American Historical Association, Phi Beta Kappa, Omicron Delta Kappa.

WRITINGS: Failures of Peace, American Council on Public Affairs, 1941; (with Elton Atwater and others) *World Affairs,* Appleton, 1958; *Recent Europe: A Twentieth Century History,* Ronald, 1965; (with Robert Forster and Donald Worcester) *Man and Civilization,* Lyons & Carnahan Books, 1965; (with Elton Atwater and Jan Prybyla) *World Tensions: Conflict and Accommodation,* Appleton, 1967. Contributor to professional journals.

WORK IN PROGRESS: A history of Finnish foreign policy.

SIDELIGHTS: Kent Forster has lived for extended periods in Europe and the Middle East and is competent in French and German.

* * *

FORTMAN, Edmund J. 1901-

PERSONAL: Born July 21, 1901, in Chicago, Ill.; son of Fred and Louise (Smith) Fortman. *Education:* Loyola University, Chicago, Ill., A.B., 1922; St. Louis University, M.A., 1927; Gregorian University, S.T.D., 1937. *Politics:* Democrat. *Home and office:* Bellarmine School of Theology, North Aurora, Ill. 60542.

CAREER: Roman Catholic priest, member of Society of Jesus; Bellarmine School of Theology (formerly West Baden College, located in West Baden Springs, Ind.), North Aurora, Ill., professor of dogmatic theology, beginning 1939.

WRITINGS: (Editor) The Theology of Man and Grace, Bruce, 1966; The Triune God: A Historical Study of the Doctrine of the Trinity, Westminster, 1971.†

* * *

FOSTER, David William (Anthony) 1940-

PERSONAL: Born September 11, 1940, in Seattle, Wash.; son of William Henry (a mechanic) and Rosamond (Pepin) Foster; married Virginia Maria Ramos (a professor), May 31, 1966. Education: University of Washington, Seattle, B.A. (magna cum laude), 1961, M.A., 1963, Ph.D., 1964. Politics: Democrat. Religion: Roman Catholic. Home: 928 West Palm Lane, Phoenix, Ariz. 85007. Office: Department of Foreign Languages, Arizona State University, Tempe, Ariz. 85281.

CAREER: University of Missouri, Columbia, assistant professor of Spanish, 1964-66; Arizona State University, Tempe, assistant professor, 1966-68, associate professor, 1968-71, professor of Spanish, 1971—. Fulbright lecturer in linguistics, Universidad de la Plata and Instituto Nacional de Lenguas Vivas, Argentina, 1967, 1973; Inter-American Development Bank Visiting Professor, Universidad Catolica de Chile, 1975. Member: American Association of Teachers of Spanish and Portuguese, Modern Language Association of America, Hispanic Institute, Linguistic Society of America, Instituto Internacional de Literatura Iberoamericana, American Association of University Professors, Dante Society of America, Philological Association of the Pacific Coast, Rocky Mountain Council for Latin American Studies, Missouri Academy of Science, Phi Sigma Iota.

WRITINGS: (Co-author) Research on Language Teaching: An Annotated International Bibliography for 1945-1961, University of Washington Press, 1962, revised edition, 1965; Forms of the Novel in the Work of Camilo Jose Cela, University of Missouri Press, 1967; The Myth of Paraguay in the Fiction of Augusto Roa Bastos, University of North Carolina Press, 1969.

(Compiler with wife, Virginia Ramos Foster) Manual of Hispanic Bibliography: An Annotated Handbook of Basic Sources, University of Washington Press, 1970; (with Virginia Ramos Foster) Research Guide to Argentine Literature, Scarecrow, 1970; Christian Allegory in Early Hispanic Poetry, University Press of Kentucky, 1971; The Early Spanish Ballad, Twayne, 1971; The Marques de Santillana, Twayne, 1971; (with Virginia Ramos Foster) Luis de Gongora, Twayne, 1973; Unamumo and the Novel as Expressionistic Conceit, Inter American University Press, 1973; (with Gary L. Brower) An Annotated Bibliography of Haiku in Western Languages, American Haiku Press, 1974; Currents in the Contemporary Argentine Novel, University of Missouri Press, 1975; (compiler) A Dictionary of Contemporary Latin American Authors, Center for Latin American Studies, Arizona State University, 1975; (compiler) Latin American Government Leaders, 2nd edition, Center for Latin American Studies, Arizona State University, 1975; (editor with Virginia Ramos Foster) Modern Latin American Literature, two volumes, Ungar, 1975; The Twentieth Century Spanish-American Novel: A Bibliographic Guide, Scarecrow, 1975. Contributor of about seventy articles to professional journals.

WORK IN PROGRESS: Contemporary Argentine Literary Criticism: An Analytical Study; Narrative Structures in the Contemporary Latin American Short Story.

* * *

FOSTER, Paul 1931-

PERSONAL: Born October 15, 1931, in Salem, N.J.; son of Eldridge M. and Mary (Manning) Foster. Education: Rutgers University, B.A., 1954; attended St. John's University Law School, 1955, 1957-58. Religion: Protestant. Home: 236 East Fifth St., New York, N.Y. 10003.

CAREER: Playwright. La Mama Experimental Theatre Club, New York, N.Y., president and co-founder, 1962—. Military service: U.S. Naval Reserve, Judge's Advocate General Corps, 1955-57. Member: P.E.N., Dramatist's Guild, Societe des Auteurs et Compositeurs (Paris), Eugene O'Neill Theatre Foundation. Awards, honors: Rockefeller Foundation fellowship for playwriting, 1967, 1968; New York Drama Critics Award, 1968, for Tom Paine; Creative Artists Public Service grants, 1972, 1974; National Endowment for the Arts fellowship, 1973, 1975; British Arts Council award, 1973, for Elizabeth I; Guggenheim literature fellowship, 1974.

WRITINGS: Minnie the Whore, The Birthday, and Other Stories, Ediciones Zodiaco (Caracas), 1962.

Plays: Hurrah for the Bridge (one-act; first produced Off-Off Broadway at Caffe Cino, 1963), Canal Ramirez, 1963; Balls and Other Plays (contains "Balls," first produced Off-Off Broadway at Cafe La Mama, 1965; "The Recluse," first produced Off-Off Broadway at Cafe La Mama, 1964; "Hurrah for the Bridge," [see above]; "The Hessian Corporal," first produced Off-Off Broadway at Cafe La Mama, 1966), Calder & Boyars, 1967, Samuel French, 1968; Tom Paine (full-length; first produced Off-Off Broadway at Cafe La Mama, May 15, 1967; produced on the West End at the Vaudeville Theatre, 1967; produced Off-Broadway at Stage 73, 1968), Calder & Boyars, 1967, Grove Press, 1968; "The Madonna in the Orchard" (full-length; first produced Off-Off Broadway at Cafe La Mama, 1965), published in Germany as Die Madonna im Apfelhag, S. Fischer Verlag, 1968, published as The Madonna in the Orchard, Breakthrough Press, 1971; Heimskringla; or The Stoned Angels (written for television in order to utilize the videospace electronic technique; first produced by National Education Television for "Theatre America" series, 1969), Samuel French, 1970; Satyricon (first produced Off-Broadway at La Mama Theatre, 1972), published in The Off-Off Broadway Book, edited by Bruce Mailman and Albert Poland, Bobbs-Merrill, 1972; Elizabeth I (first produced on Broadway at the Lyceum Theatre, 1972), Samuel French, 1972; Silver Queen Saloon (first produced Off-Broadway at La Mama Theatre, 1973), Samuel French, 1975; Marcus Brutus (first produced at Stage West, Springfield, Mass., 1975), Calder & Boyars, 1975.

WORK IN PROGRESS: A new drama.

SIDELIGHTS: Foster considers himself "prodigiously energetic." Leonard Harris of CBS Television said, "Foster's thinking is original. Here is a man born to write for the theater." William Raidy of the Newhouse National News Service said, "It [Elizabeth I] has a vitality and a zest and it is truly an inventive and inspired piece of theater."

In a review of Marcus Brutus, Clive Barnes of the New York Times said, "Foster is an important playwright. He wants to push theater beyond its conventionally realistic bounds and to use it as an arena for philosophic and historic thought.'' Raidy said of *Marcus Brutus* ''A compelling, fascinating, unusual drama . . . his characters are divinely human.'' Charles Smith of the *Boston Advocate* said, ''[*Marcus Brutus* is a] play that will leave your mind gasping for air. It is an excellent work. . . .''

Foster speaks French and German.

BIOGRAPHICAL/CRITICAL SOURCES: New Statesman, October 27, 1967; *Listener,* November 2, 1967; *Village Voice,* March, 1968; *New Yorker,* April 6, 1968; *Newsweek,* April 8, 1968; *Hudson Review,* summer, 1968; *Los Angeles Free Press,* November 22, 1968; *Long Island Press,* April 6, 1972; *Boston Advocate,* January 12, 1975; *New York Times,* January 20, 1975.

*   *   *

FOUNTAIN, Leatrice   1924-

PERSONAL: First name is pronounced *Lee*-ah-tris; born September 6, 1924, in Los Angeles, Calif.; daughter of film stars, John Gilbert and Leatrice Joy (maiden surname, Zeidler); married first husband, Henry Clay Hart, Jr. (an advertising executive); married John Fountain, 1950; children: (first marriage) Lorin (daughter); (second marriage) John, Christopher, Anthony, Gideon. *Politics:* Democrat. *Religion:* Society of Friends (Quaker). *Residence:* Riverside, Conn. *Agent:* Fifi Oscard Associates, Inc., 19 West 44th St., New York, N.Y. 10036.

WRITINGS: Love to the Irish (novel), Doubleday, 1967. Contributor to *Redbook, McCalls,* and *Woman's Day.*

WORK IN PROGRESS: A biography of John Gilbert.

BIOGRAPHICAL/CRITICAL SOURCES: New York Post, July 22, 1967.

*   *   *

FOWLER, Austin   1928-

PERSONAL: Born January 26, 1928, in New York, N.Y.; son of Jeremiah S. (a writer and civil servant) and Julia Anne (Byrne) Fowler; married Joan C. Hafemann (a teacher), September 11, 1955; children: Justin, Christopher, Jonathan, Benjamin. *Education:* Iona College, B.A., 1949; Fordham University, M.A., 1959; Columbia University, graduate study, 1958—. *Home:* 170 Ave. C, New York, N.Y. 10009. *Office:* Department of Speech, John Jay College of Criminal Justice of the City University of New York, 315 Park Ave. S., New York, N.Y. 10010.

CAREER: City University of New York, New York City, City College, instructor in English, 1958-64, John Jay College of Criminal Justice, assistant professor of English and speech, 1964-72, lecturer in speech, 1972—. Adjunct associate professor of speech and English, Pace College, New York City, 1962—; lecturer in communications, Roosevelt Hospital School of Nursing, 1962—. President, Alpha Five Publications, Inc.; contributing editor, Simon & Shuster, Inc. President, Manhattan Community Planning Board Number 6. *Military service:* U.S. Army, 1950-52. *Member:* Modern Language Association of America, American Association of University Professors, Andiron Club, Anawanda Club.

WRITINGS: (Editor) *Longfellow's Evangeline,* Monarch, 1965; (editor) *Stevenson's Treasure Island,* Monarch, 1955; *Tolstoy's War and Peace,* Monarch, 1965; *The Poetry of Wallace Stevens,* Monarch, 1965, revised edition, 1966; *Albert Camus,* Monarch 1965; *Hemingway's Short Stories,*

Monarch, 1966; *Franklin's Autobiography,* Monarch, 1966; *Stevenson's Kidnapped,* Monarch, 1966; *Fitzgerald's The Great Gatsby,* Simon & Schuster, 1967; *Henry James' The Turn of the Screw,* Simon & Schuster, 1967; *Stephen Crane's The Red Badge of Courage,* Simon & Schuster, 1967. Contributor to *Spirit, Sign, Phoenix,* and other journals. Associate editor of *Journal of Communication Disorders* and *Express;* co-editor of ''Black Man in America'' reprint series, AMS Press.

WORK IN PROGRESS: Greek Minded (poems), for Elsinore Press; *Tennyson's Historical Plays; Wallace Stevens: Poet's Poet; Linguistics for Freshmen; Rhetoric: The Compleat Kit;* in collaboration with R. W. Rieber, *The Psychology of Communication;* in collaboration with Russell Gillis, *The Act of Poetry;* three novels.†

*   *   *

FOX, G(eoffrey) P.   1938-

PERSONAL: Born April 20, 1938, in Manchester, England; son of Frederick Platts (a furnishing consultant) and Marjorie (Percival) Fox; married Sara Hughes (a clinical nursing tutor), September 2, 1961; children: Jane, Alison. *Education:* Oxford University, M.A.; Associate of the Drama Board (Education), 1974. *Politics:* Liberal. *Home:* 4A, Thornton Hill, Exeter, Devonshire, England.

CAREER: Manchester Grammar School, Manchester, England, teacher, 1961-69; University of Manchester, Manchester, tutor in extramural department; University of Exeter, Exeter, England, faculty member of School of Education. Exchange teacher, Newton High School, Newton, Mass., 1966-67; master teacher, Harvard-Newton Summer School, 1967-72; lecturer at universities in the United States and England; teacher of drama courses and director of dramatic works; external examiner for Oxford and Cambridge Universities Examination Board, St. Luke's College, and University of Southampton. *Military service:* Royal Air Force, 1956-58; became senior aircraftsman.

WRITINGS: (With Brian A. Phythian) *Starting Points,* English Universities Press, 1967; *Shakespeare's ''Winter's Tale,''* Basil Blackwell, 1967; (contributor) Phythian, editor, *Considering Poetry: An Approach to Criticism,* English Universities Press, 1970; *Writers, Critics and Children* (collection of articles), APS Publications, 1976. Contributor of articles and reviews to journals in his field. Co-editor, *Children's Literature in Education.*

AVOCATIONAL INTERESTS: Playing hockey, walking, camping, acting.

*   *   *

FOX, Jack C(urtis)   1925-

PERSONAL: Born July 25, 1925, in Los Angeles, Calif.; son of William Oldham and Grace (Curtis) Fox. *Education:* University of Southern California, B.Arch., 1950. *Politics:* Republican. *Home:* 1688 Guadalupe Ave., San Jose, Calif. 95125.

CAREER: Automobile Club of Southern California, Los Angeles, cartographer and architectural consultant, 1949-61; H. M. Gousha Co., San Jose, Calif., research cartographer and assistant copy editor in charge of auto racing publications, 1961-69. Official photographer for auto racing associations, 1948—. *Military service:* U.S. Army Air Forces, 1943-45; became staff sergeant; received Air Medal with three oak leaf clusters. *Member:* British-American

Club, Indianapolis 500 Old Timers Club, Bay Cities Racing Association (official photographer), Gilbert and Sullivan Society of San Jose (vice-president).

WRITINGS: The Indianapolis 500, World Publishing, 1967. Compiler and publisher, *Bay Cities Racing Association Midget Racing Yearbook,* 1964, 1970—, and *California Midget Racing Annual,* 1965. Historic editor, *Indianapolis 500 Yearbook,* 1973, 1974. Columnist, *Illustrated Speedway News,* 1949—, and *Motor Sports World,* 1953. West Coast editor, *Desert Dust,* 1954-55.

WORK IN PROGRESS: An illustrated history of midget auto racing, *The Mighty Midgets,* and a six-volume history of the Indianapolis 500, both for Carl Hungness and Associates.

SIDELIGHTS: Jack Fox told *CA:* "Have been attending auto races since 1934 and collecting data and photos since 1936 (except for stock and sports cars, for which I have a strong dislike). Photographer and writer at Indianapolis 500 since 1951; own one of the largest collections of '500' photos in existence."

* * *

FOX, Willard 1919-

PERSONAL: Born May 22, 1919, in Springfield, Mass.; son of Willard and Bessie (Prouty) Fox; married Dorothy Earline Grote, March 20, 1944; children: Willard III, Nancy Lee, Judith Ann. *Education:* Springfield Young Men's Christian Association College, student, 1938-40; Southeast Missouri State College, B.S., 1947; University of Wyoming, M.A., 1953; Stanford University, graduate study, 1954; Wayne State University, Ed.D., 1959. *Office:* Department of Educational Administration and Supervision, Bowling Green, Ohio. 43403.

CAREER: High school teacher in Cape Girardeau, Mo., 1946-47, in LeMay, Mo., 1947-48; superintendent of schools in Chugwater, Wyo., 1948-51, LaGrange, Wyo., 1951-53, and Wheatland, Wyo., 1953-55; Bowling Green State University, Bowling Green, Ohio, assistant professor, 1959-62, associate professor of education and chairman of department, 1962-65, professor of school administration, 1965—. Visiting summer professor at universities including Ohio University, 1960, Wayne State University, 1963, University of Toledo, 1964, Drake University, 1965, University of Arkansas, 1966, and University of Cincinnati, 1968-69. Vice-president, School Management Institute, 1970. Executive director, Ohio School Boards Association, 1970-72. Chairman of County Welfare Board, 1953. Member of Governor's Commission to Study Education, 1954; member of Bowling Green School Board, 1968-70, 1974—. Consultant to Ohio School Management Institutes, 1962—, and to more than fifty boards of education in Michigan and Ohio. *Military service:* U.S. Army Air Forces, 1941-46.

MEMBER: American Association of School Administrators (life member), National Conference of Professors of Educational Administration, Association of Higher Education, National Education Association (life member), Ohio Education Association (life member), Ohio Association of School Administrators (president, 1968-69), Northwest Ohio Education Association, Northwest Ohio Association of School Administrators, Northwest Ohio County Superintendents Association, Buckeye Association of School Administrators (president, 1969), Phi Delta Kappa, Phi Kappa Phi, Alpha Phi Omega.

WRITINGS: (With Alfred Schwartz) *Managerial Guide for School Principals,* C. E. Merrill, 1965; (contributor) Robert J. Simpson, editor, *Education and the Law in Ohio,* W. H. Anderson, 1968. Author of education booklets. Contributor of reviews and more than fifty articles to bulletins and journals.

* * *

FRANCE, Malcolm 1928-

PERSONAL: Born August 13, 1928, in Wood Norton, Norfolk, England; son of Walter Frederick (an Anglican priest) and Marjorie (Norris) France; married Elisabeth Stonehouse, June 15, 1956; children: Richard Michael, Caroline Sarah, Miranda Louise. *Education:* Oxford University, B.A., 1953, M.A., 1957; Westcott House, Cambridge, England, passed general ordination examination, 1955; University of Essex, Ph.D., 1975. *Home:* Wood Hall, Little Waldingfield, Sudbury, Suffolk, England.

CAREER: Church of England, clergyman, 1955—, serving as assistant curate in Ipswich, Suffolk, England, 1955-58, and vicar in Bradford, Yorkshire, England, 1958-64; Institute for Advanced Pastoral Studies, Bloomfield Hills, Mich., graduate fellow, 1964; University of Essex, Colchester, Essex, England, Anglican chaplain, 1964-73. Director of Bradford branch, Telephone Samaritans (international organization offering help to thwart suicides), 1961-64. *Military service:* Royal Air Force, 1947-49. *Member:* Clinical Theology Association (Nottingham; member of council, 1962-69; vice-chairman, 1967).

WRITINGS: The Paradox of Guilt, United Church Press, 1967.

WORK IN PROGRESS: The origins of personal identity in personal communications.

* * *

FRANCIS, (Alan) David 1900-

PERSONAL: Born December 2, 1900, in Copythorne, Hampshire, England; son of Alan Ogilvie (an army officer) and Helen Constance (Wyllie) Francis; married Norah Turpin, January 26, 1932; children: M. J. O. Francis, Charles S. D. Drace-Francis. *Education:* Attended Winchester College, 1914-19; Magdalen College, Oxford, B.A., 1922, M.A., 1927; Corpus Christi College, Cambridge, B.A., 1923. *Religion:* Church of England. *Home:* 21 Cadogan St., London S.W.3, England.

CAREER: British Consular Service, 1923-58, with posts in Antwerp, Rotterdam, Panama, Bagota, 1925-37; consul at Brussels, 1937-40, Lisbon, 1941-42, Barcelona, 1942-44, Caracas, 1944-46; consul-general at Danzig, 1949-51, New Orleans, La., 1951-55, Oporto, 1955-58. Member, Lord Chancellor's Advisory Council on Public Records, 1962-67. *Member:* Royal Geographical Society (fellow), Royal Historical Society (fellow), Society of Geneologists. *Awards, honors:* Member of Royal Victorian Order, 1957; Commander of Order of the British Empire, 1959.

WRITINGS: The Methuens and Portugal, Cambridge University Press, 1966; *The Wine Trade,* A & C Black, 1972; *The First Peninsular War, 1702-1713,* St. Martin's, 1975. Contributor to historical journals.

WORK IN PROGRESS: Research on Anglo-Portuguese history, 1690-1750; a study of Anglo-Dutch relations in the Iberian Peninsula, 1702-1713; research on the movement of trade out of the Common Market, 1715.

SIDELIGHTS: David Francis speaks French, German, Spanish, and Portuguese.

*   *   *

FRANCIS, Dorothy Brenner 1926-

PERSONAL: Born November 30, 1926, in Lawrence, Kan.; daughter of Clayton (a district judge) and Cecile (Goforth) Brenner; married Richard M. Francis (a professional musician), August 30, 1950; children: Lynn Ann, Patricia Louise. Education: University of Kansas, Mus.B., 1948. Politics: Republican. Religion: Methodist. Home: 1505 Brentwood Ter., Marshalltown, Iowa 50158.

CAREER: Band and vocal instructor in Orange, Calif., 1948-50, Pleasant Hill, Mo., 1950-51, Cache, Okla., 1951-52, and Gilman, Iowa, 1961-62; now teaches piano and trumpet privately. Board member of community Chamber Orchestra, Marshalltown, 1967. Member: P.E.O. Sisterhood, Marshalltown Tuesday Music Club (former president), Mu Phi Epsilon.

WRITINGS: Adventure at Riverton Zoo, Abingdon, 1966; Mystery of the Forgotten Map, Follett, 1968; Laugh at the Evil Eye, Messner, 1970; Another Kind of Beauty, Criterion, 1970; Hawaiian Interlude, Avalon, 1970; Studio Affair, Avalon, 1972; Nurse on Assignment, Avalon, 1972; A Blue Ribbon for Marni, Avalon, 1973; Nurse Under Fire, Avalon, 1973; Nurse in the Caribbean, Avalon, 1973; Murder in Hawaii, Scholastic, 1973; Nurse in the Keys, Avalon, 1974; Golden Girl, Scholastic, 1974; Nurse at Spirit Lake, Avalon, 1975; Allamanda House, Avalon, 1975; The Flint Hills Foal, Abingdon, 1976. Short stories included in Augsburg publications. Contributor of light verse to magazines.

WORK IN PROGRESS: Two Against the Arctic, an adaptation of a Walt Disney Productions television script, "Tundra Summer," for Pyramid.

*   *   *

FRANCO, Jean 1924-

PERSONAL: Born March 31, 1924, in England; daughter of William (a shopkeeper) and Ella (Newton) Swindells; formerly married to Juan Antonio Franco; children: Alexis Parke. Education: University of Manchester, B.A. (first class honors), 1944, M.A., 1946; King's College, London, first class honors degree in Spanish, 1960, Ph.D., 1964. Home: 60 Pearce Mitchell Pl., Stanford, Calif. 94305. Office: Department of Spanish and Portuguese, Stanford University, Stanford, Calif. 94305.

CAREER: University of London, London, England, lecturer at Queen Mary College, 1960-64, reader at King's College, 1964-68; University of Essex, Colchester, England, professor of Latin American literature, 1968-72; Stanford University, Stanford, Calif., professor of Spanish, 1972—. Member: Society for Latin American Studies (founder-member; treasurer, 1965-67; vice-chairman, 1967-68).

WRITINGS: (Editor) Cuentos Americanos de Nuestros Dias, Harrap, 1965; (editor) Short Stories in Spanish, Penguin, 1966; The Modern Culture of Latin America: Society and the Artist, Praeger, 1967, revised edition, Penguin, 1970; (editor) Horacio Quiroga, Cuentos Escogidos, Pergamon, 1968; An Introduction to Spanish-American Literature, Cambridge University Press, 1969; A Literary History of Spain, Volume VII: Spanish-American Literature since Independence, Harper, 1973. Editor of Latin American

section, Penguin Companion to Literature, Volume III: United States and Latin America. Contributor to Times Literary Supplement and Spectator.

WORK IN PROGRESS: Literature and the Ideology of Colonialism; a book on Caesar Vallejo, Poetry and Silence.

SIDELIGHTS: Jean Franco lived in Latin America, 1953-57, mostly in Guatemala and Mexico. Besides Spanish, she speaks some Portuguese, French, and Italian.

*   *   *

FRANDA, Marcus F. 1937-

PERSONAL: Born August 16, 1937, in Nassawaupee Township, Wis.; son of Simon John and Esther Mary (Schallie) Franda; married Vonetta Jane Pedlow, August 9, 1959; children: Charles Arthur, Stephanie Jane. Education: Beloit College, B.A., 1959; University of Chicago, A.M., 1960, Ph.D., 1966. Home: 51 University Ave., Hamilton, N.Y. 13346. Office: Department of Political Science, Colgate University, Hamilton, N.Y. 13346.

CAREER: Colgate University, Hamilton, N.Y., assistant professor, 1965-71, associate professor of political science, 1971—. Associate, American Universities Field Staff. Member: Association for Asian Studies, American Political Science Association, American Academy of Political and Social Science. Awards, honors: Shell Oil Co. award for excellence in teaching, 1967-68.

WRITINGS: West Bengal and the Federalizing Process in India, Princeton University Press, 1968; (co-author) State Politics in India, Princeton University Press, 1968; (translator from the Bengali with S. K. Chatterjee) Narendranath Mitra, Mahanagar, InterCulture Associates, 1968; Political Development and Political Decay in Bengal, Firma K. L. Mukhopadhyay (Calcutta), 1971; Radical Politics in West Bengal, M.I.T. Press, 1971; (translator with Chatterjee) Tarasankar Banerjee, Panchagram, South Asia Books, 1973; (with Paul R. Brass) Radical Politics in South Asia, M.I.T. Press, 1973; (editor) Responses to Population Growth in India: Changes in Social, Political and Economic Behavior, Praeger, 1975. Also author of numerous monographs on Indian social and environmental subjects.

*   *   *

FRANK, Andre Gunder 1929-

PERSONAL: Born February 24, 1929, in Berlin, Germany; son of Leonhard and Elena (Pevsner) Frank; married Marta Guentes Enberg (a librarian), December 21, 1962; children: Paulo Rene, Miguel Leonardo. Education: Swarthmore College, B.A. (with honors), 1950; University of Michigan, graduate study, 1951; University of Chicago, M.A., 1952, Ph.D., 1957. Politics: "Revolutionary socialist."

CAREER: Michigan State University, East Lansing, assistant professor, 1957-61; University of Brasilia, Brasilia, Brazil, visiting professor, 1963; National University of Mexico, Mexico City, visiting professor, 1965; Sir George Williams University, Montreal, Quebec, visiting professor in department of economics and history, beginning 1966. Consultant, United Nations Economic Commission for Latin America, 1965. Awards, honors: Louis M. Rabinowitz Foundation research grant.

WRITINGS: Capitalism and Underdevelopment in Latin America: Historical Essays of Chile and Brazil, Monthly Review Press, 1967, revised edition, 1969; Development of Underdevelopment: Essays on Imperialism Society and Politics in Latin America, Monthly Review Press, 1968;

Latin America: Underdevelopment or Revolution, Monthly Review Press, 1970; (translator) Marion D. Berdicio, *Lumpenbourgeoisie: Lumpendevelopment, Dependence, Class and Politics in Latin America,* Monthly Review Press, 1973; *Raices del desarrollo y el subdesarrollo en el Nuevo Mundo: Smith y Marx contra los weberianos,* Universidad Central de Venezuela, Facultad de Ciencias Economicas y Sociales, 1975. Contributor to magazines and professional journals.

WORK IN PROGRESS: Editing with Said Shah, *Underdevelopment: History, Theory, Policy, Politics,* a reader in two volumes; study of the growth of latifundium in Mexico and Latin America.

SIDELIGHTS: Frank told *CA:* "My interests are political, not vocational; the latter are means for a political end, which is revolution and socialist transformation of society." He is competent in French, Spanish, and Portuguese, in addition to his native German. His first two books have been translated into four languages.†

* * *

FRANK, Charles E(dward) 1911-

PERSONAL: Born May 5, 1911, in Philadelphia, Pa.; son of Harry Jacob (a wagon builder) and Carrie (Miller) Frank; married Dorothy Almira Berry (an art teacher), June 7, 1941; children: Charles W., Geoffrey, Constance (Mrs. John Ronald), Barbara and David (twins). *Education:* Haverford College, A.B., 1933; Princeton University, M.A., 1938, Ph.D., 1939. *Politics:* Republican. *Religion:* Episcopalian. *Home:* 236 Park St., Jacksonville, Ill. 62650; (summer) White Birch Point, Antrim, N.H. 03440. *Office:* Illinois College, Jacksonville, Ill. 62560.

CAREER: Haverford College, Haverford, Pa., instructor in English, 1935-37; Illinois College, Jacksonville, assistant professor, 1939-42, professor of English, 1945-55; University of Nevada, Reno, associate professor of English, 1955-57; Illinois College, professor of English and co-chairman of department, 1957—, Dunbaugh Distinguished Professor, 1973. Research consultant, Illinois Legislative Council, 1959-61; elected alderman, sixth ward, Jacksonville. Representative, Woodrow Wilson Foundation, 1962—. *Military service:* U.S. Naval Reserve, 1942-55; on active duty, 1942-45, 1950; became lieutenant commander. *Member:* Modern Language Association of America, American Association of University Professors, Charles Lamb Society, Literary Union, Phi Beta Kappa. *Awards, honors:* Ford Foundation faculty fellowship, 1953-54.

WRITINGS: Six Franks Abroad: One Man's Sabbatical, World Publishing, 1967. Contributor to educational journals.

WORK IN PROGRESS: An edition of *Love of Fame,* the satires of Edward Young; a study of Henry James' obituary writings; *Abroad at Home: The American Field Service Story; An Oral History of Illinois College,* completion expected in 1979.

BIOGRAPHICAL/CRITICAL SOURCES: Peterborough Transcript, July 27, 1967.

* * *

FRANK, Jeffrey 1942-

PERSONAL: Born April 10, 1942, in Baltimore, Md.; son of Adam and Rachel (Brody) Frank; married Diana Crone, March 17, 1967. *Education:* Attended Knox College. *Home address:* R.D. 1, Box 128, Alpine, N.Y. 14805. *Agent:* Cyrilly Abels, 119 West 57th St., New York, N.Y. 10019.

CAREER: Free-lance writer.

WRITINGS: The Creep (novel), Farrar, Straus, 1968.

WORK IN PROGRESS: Working on new novels.

SIDELIGHTS: The *Virginia Quarterly Review* writer says that "with an unheroic hero, bumbling, ineffectual, and evidently repulsive on sight, Mr. Frank has adroitly created for his character sketch the very portrait of a lonely man, introspective, adrift, and friendless in a large and unresponsive city. His tragi-comic study is a pointed one, wringing with pathos one moment and slyly inducing derisive laughter the next."

AVOCATIONAL INTERESTS: Reading, music, hiking, and Oriental art. He has a special interest in nineteenth-century Scandinavian literature, and is fluent in Danish.

BIOGRAPHICAL/CRITICAL SOURCES: Saturday Review, January 6, 1968; *Book World,* February 11, 1968; *Virginia Quarterly Review,* spring, 1968; *Harper's,* May, 1968.

* * *

FRANKE, C(arl) W(ilfred) 1928-

PERSONAL: Born November 30, 1928; son of Centennial Grant (a farmer) and Bonnie (Hopkins) Franke; married Letty Jane Adelmann (a public school teacher), July 24, 1951; children: David, Dwight, Daniel, Carolyn, Carmen. *Education:* Westmar College, A.B., 1953; Evangelical Theological Seminary, Naperville, Ill., B.D., 1956. *Home:* 3203 Huffman Blvd., Rockford, Ill. 61103.

CAREER: Beth Eden United Methodist Church, Rockford, Ill., pastor, 1959—. Rockford Area Council of Churches, member of board of directors, 1966—, president, 1968-70; member of board, Protestant Welfare Council, Rockford, 1967—; member of board of trustees, Wesley Willow Home, 1969—. *Member:* Rockford Ministerial Association (president, 1967-68).

WRITINGS: How to Stay Alive All Your Life, Zondervan, 1967; *Defrost Your Frozen Assets,* Word, 1969; *Christian Be a Real Person,* Thomas Nelson, 1974. Contributor to denominational magazines.

WORK IN PROGRESS: Two books, one on humor and one on greatness.

AVOCATIONAL INTERESTS: Aircraft, airlines, and aerospace developments; photography.

* * *

FRANKLIN, R(alph) W(illiam) 1937-

PERSONAL: Born August 20, 1937, in Ojus, Fla.; son of John Bryan and Lillie May (Perry) Franklin. *Education:* University of Puget Sound, B.A., 1959; Northwestern University, M.A., 1960, Ph.D., 1965; University of Chicago, M.A., 1968. *Office:* Washington State Library, Olympia, Wash. 98504.

CAREER: University of Wisconsin—Madison, lecturer, 1964-65, assistant professor of English, 1965-66; Tacoma (Wash.) public schools, instructor, 1966-67; Middlebury College Library, Middlebury, Vt., curator of special collections, 1968-70; Washington State Library, Olympia, assistant chief of technical services and development, 1970-71, consultant, 1971-74, bibliographic systems consultant, 1974—. Assistant professor and dean of students, Graduate Library School, University of Chicago, 1971-74. *Member:* Bibliographical Society of America, American Library Association.

WRITINGS: The Editing of Emily Dickinson: A Reconsideration, University of Wisconsin Press, 1967. Contributor to literature and library journals.

AVOCATIONAL INTERESTS: Mountain climbing, hiking, camping, skiing, water sports, music.

* * *

FRANKLIN, Richard 1918-

PERSONAL: Born May 11, 1918, in Jamestown, Ohio; son of C. B. (a farmer) and Alta V. (Earley) Franklin; married Grace Kelly (deceased); married Paula A. Fowler; children: (first marriage) Jan; (second marriage) Tim; (adopted) Edward. *Education:* Ohio Wesleyan University, B.S., 1939; Ohio State University, M.A., 1948; Columbia University, Ed.D., 1955. *Home:* 3946 Cloverhill Rd., Baltimore, Md. 21218. *Office:* Johns Hopkins University, Baltimore, Md. 21218.

CAREER: Newspaperman in Marion and Toledo, Ohio, prior to 1943; following World War II, taught journalism at New Mexico State University, University Park, supervised educational broadcasting in El Paso, Tex., and was news editor for Church World Service, New York City; National Conference of Christians and Jews, New York City, research associate, 1952-54; Kansas State University Extension, Manhatten, assistant professor of adult education and consultant, 1954-56; Southern Illinois University, Carbondale, assistant professor of community development and consultant, 1956-57, assistant director of Community Development Institute, 1957-59, director of Community Development Institute and associate professor of sociology, 1959-66; West Virginia University, Morgantown, professor of sociology and education, and training coordinator for Appalachian Center, 1966-71; Johns Hopkins University, Baltimore, Md., director of Division of Arts and Sciences, Evening College, 1971-74, adjunct faculty member, 1974—. Fulbright lecturer at University of New England, Australia. Delegate to UNESCO Regional Seminar on Adult Education, Sydney, Australia, 1964. Associate of National Training Laboratories Institute for Applied Behavioral Sciences; consultant to Job Opportunities Through Better Skills (JOBS), and other development programs. *Military service:* U.S. Army Air Forces, bomber pilot, World War II.

MEMBER: International Association of Applied Social Scientists (charter member), Adult Education Association of the U.S.A., Society for the Psychological Study of Social Issues, American Sociological Association, American Association of University Professors, Phi Delta Kappa. *Awards, honors:* Carnegie Corp. postdoctoral fellowship, 1963-64.

WRITINGS: (Contributor) Dorothy Mial and H. Curtis Mial, editors, *Forces in Community Development,* National Training Laboratory in Group Development, 1961; (editor) *Patterns of Community Development,* Public Affairs Press, 1966; (with wife, Paula Franklin) *Urban Decision Making,* National Training Laboratory in Group Development, 1967; *Toward the Style of the Community Change Educator,* National Training Laboratories Institute for Applied Behavioral Sciences, 1969; (with P. Franklin) *Tomorrow's Track: Experiments with Learning to Change,* New Community Press, 1976.

* * *

FRANZWA, Gregory M. 1926-

PERSONAL: Born February 27, 1926, in Glidden, Iowa; son of Frederick W. (a postmaster) and Mabel (Henderson) Franzwa; married second wife, Laura Brockmeyer Goehri, November 22, 1966; children: (first marriage) Theodore, Christian, Patrice; Scott (stepchild). *Education:* University of Iowa, B.A., 1950. *Politics:* Republican. *Religion:* None. *Home:* 9528 Old Bonhomme Rd., St. Louis, Mo. 63132.

CAREER: Self-employed as owner of Gregory M. Franzwa Public Relations, St. Louis, Mo., 1955—, and Patrice Press, St. Louis, 1966—. *Military service:* U.S. Naval Reserve, 1943-46; became lieutenant junior grade.

WRITINGS: The Old Cathedral, Archdiocese of St. Louis, 1965; *The Story of Old Ste. Genevieve,* Patrice Press, 1967; *The Oregon Train Revisited,* Patrice Press, 1972; *A History of St. Louis,* Patrice Press, in press.

WORK IN PROGRESS: The California Trail Revisited, completion expected in 1977.

AVOCATIONAL INTERESTS: Jazz musician.

BIOGRAPHICAL/CRITICAL SOURCES: St. Louis Magazine, June, 1967.

* * *

FRASER, Colin 1935-

PERSONAL: Born September 29, 1935, in Reading, England; son of Angus Alexander (an army officer) and Dorothy Jane (Sullivan) Fraser; married Elizabeth Johnson, February 14, 1959; children: Stuart Austin, Iain Sullivan. *Education:* Seal-Hayne Agricultural College, 1954-56, diploma of the College and national diploma in agriculture, 1956. *Religion:* Anglican. *Address:* Azienda Agricola Collefiorito, Rocca Sinibalda, Rieti, Italy.

CAREER: Massey-Ferguson, Coventry, England, lecturer in farm mechanization, 1957-61; self-employed as plant hire-contractor in Coventry, England, 1961-63; free-lance writer and journalist, Italy, 1963—; United Nations Food and Agriculture Organization, Rome, Italy, information officer, 1967-69, development support communication branch, chief, 1969—. *Member:* Society for International Development, Ski Club of Great Britain, Club Alpino Italiano, Eagle Ski Club, Alpine Ski Club, Kandahar Ski Club.

WRITINGS: The Avalanche Enigma, Rand McNally, 1966; *Harry Ferguson: Tractor Pioneer,* Ohio State University Press, 1973. Writer of script for hour-long documentary film, "Avalanche," and a script of the same title for British Broadcasting Corp. educational radio. Contributor to *Autocar, New Scientist, Times, Guardian, Financial Times, International Science and Technology,* and other journals and newspapers.

WORK IN PROGRESS: A novel based on development assistance projects.

AVOCATIONAL INTERESTS: Traveling, skiing, sailing, fishing, and farming.

* * *

FREND, W(illiam) H(ugh) C(lifford) 1916-

PERSONAL: Born January 11, 1916, in Shottermill, Surrey, England; son of Edwin George (a clerk in holy orders) and Edith (Bacon) Frend; married Mary Crook, June 2, 1951; children: Sarah Anne, Simon William Clifford. *Education:* Keble College, Oxford, B.A. (first class honors in history), 1937, D.Phil., 1940. *Politics:* Unionist. *Religion:* Church of England. *Home:* Marbrae, Balmaha, Glasgow, Scotland. *Office:* University of Glasgow, Glasgow, Scotland.

CAREER: Civil servant in British War Office and then in Cabinet Office, 1940-42; Allied German War Documents Project, member of editorial board, 1947-51; University of Nottingham, Nottingham, England, research fellow, 1951-52; Cambridge University, Cambridge, England, S. A. Cook bye-fellow at Gonville and Caius College, 1952-56, fellow of Gonville and Caius College and University Lecturer in divinity, 1956-69, university proctor, 1957-59, Birkbeck lecturer in ecclesiastical history, 1967-68; University of Glasgow, Glasgow, Scotland, professor of ecclesiastical history, 1969—, dean of divinity, 1972-75. Visiting professor at Rhodes University, 1964; associate director of excavations of Egypt Exploration Society at Qasribrim, Nubia, 1964. Chairman, of Cambridge City Liberal Party, 1968-69. *Military service:* British Army, Political Intelligence Service, 1942-46; received Gold Cross of Merit with Swords (Poland). Commissioned in the Territorial Army, Brigade Intelligence Officer (retired 1967). *Member:* European Commission for Comparative Study of Ecclesiastical History (vice-president, 1964), Society of Antiquaries (fellow), Royal Historical Society (fellow), Society for Promotion of Roman Studies (member of council, 1966). *Awards, honors:* B.D., Cambridge University, 1964; D.D. from Oxford University in recognition of contribution to historical theology, 1966, and University of Edinburgh, 1974.

WRITINGS: The Donatist Church, Oxford University Press, 1952; *Martyrdom and Persecution in the Early Church,* Basil Blackwell, 1965, Doubleday, 1967; *The Early Church,* Lippincott, 1965; (contributor) Arthur J. Arberry, editor, *Religion in the Middle East,* two volumes, Cambridge University Press, 1969; *The Rise of the Monophysite Movement,* Cambridge University Press, 1972. Contributor to *Journal of Theological Studies, Journal of Ecclesiastical History,* and other journals. Editor, *Modern Churchman,* 1963—.

WORK IN PROGRESS: The Early Christians; Jesus in His Time; reports on archaeological work done at Qasribrim, Nubia, 1972-74.

SIDELIGHTS: Frend wrote to *CA:* "I'm basically a bridge subject man with an interest in archaeology, history, and theology. Am against narrow specialization, believe that the proper study of man is man. Am interested in politics from a national rather than a party point of view. Believe in seeing things on the spot and have a deep dislike of any policy which places creative workers in the hand of administrators."

BIOGRAPHICAL/CRITICAL SOURCES: Journal of Roman Studies, Volume LVI, 1966.

* * *

FRENKEL, Richard E(ugene) 1924-

PERSONAL: Born July 28, 1924, in New York, N.Y.; son of Herman (a businessman) and Renee (Roth) Frenkel; married Barbara Gamm, December 20, 1971; children: Robert Harold, Joseph Lawrence. *Education:* New York University, B.A., 1949; University of Lausanne Medical School, Lausanne, Switzerland, M.D., 1957; New York Medical College, certified psychoanalyst, 1972. *Home and office:* 17 Kingston Rd., Scarsdale, N.Y. 10583.

CAREER: Cornell University Medical College, Department of Medicine, New York City, research assistant, 1948-51; Kings County Hospital, Brooklyn, N.Y., rotating intern, 1957-58; Bellevue Psychiatric Hospital, New York City, U.S. Public Health Service fellow, 1958-59; Hillside Hospital, Queens, N.Y., resident psychiatrist, 1959-60;

Manhattan State Hospital, New York City, senior psychiatrist, 1961-62; New York State Department of Mental Hygiene, Upper Manhattan After-Care Clinic, New York City, supervising psychiatrist, 1962-72; Telecommunications Research Associates, New York City, director for psychiatry and social sciences, 1963—; Arista Center for Psychotherapy, Queens, medical director, 1971-75; Mount Vernon Mental Health Clinic, Mt. Vernon, N.Y., psychiatrist, 1972-73. *Military service:* U.S. Army, Medical Corps, 1943-46; served in Pacific Theater. *Member:* American Psychiatric Association, American Medical Association, Society of Medical Psychoanalysts, American Academy of Psychiatry and Neurology (fellow), American Academy of Psychoanalysis (fellow). *Awards, honors:* D.Sc., Pilathea College, 1969.

WRITINGS: Fundamentals of the Frenkel Minor Image Projective Technique (monograph), Psychological Library, 1963; (with Herbert M. Frenkel) *World Peace via Satellite Communications: A Psychoanalytic Examination of Its Aspects and Prospects,* Telecommunications Research Associates, 1965. Contributor to *Journal of Existential Psychiatry, Journal of the American Academy of Psychiatry and Neurology,* and other professional journals. Editorial consultant, Psychological Library Publishers, 1963-71; executive editor, *Satellite Communications Research News,* 1965—; editor, *Journal of the American Academy of Psychiatry and Neurology,* 1975—.

WORK IN PROGRESS: Psychiatry, for Riverwood; *Theory and Technique of the Minor Image Projective Technique.*

SIDELIGHTS: Frenkel has patented a multicolor light-reflecting and sound-recording psychiatric observation apparatus. Other patents include a cooking utensil for the blind and adjustable grips for medical instruments, tennis rackets, and other tools. He is competent in French, German, and Hungarian.

* * *

FRERE, Sheppard (Sunderland) 1916-

PERSONAL: Born August 23, 1916, in Graffham, Sussex, England; son of Noel Gray (a civil servant) and Agnes Barbara (Sunderland) Frere; married Janet Cecily Hoare, July 3, 1961; children: Sarah, Bartle. *Education:* Magdalene College, Cambridge, B.A., 1938, M.A., 1944. *Religion:* Church of England. *Home:* Netherfield House, Marcham, Abingdon, Berkshire, England. *Office:* All Souls College, Oxford University, Oxford, England.

CAREER: Epsom College, Surrey, England, master, 1938-40; served with National Fire Service, 1940-45; Lancing College, Sussex, England, master, 1945-54; University of Manchester, Manchester, England, lecturer in archaeology, 1954-55; Institute of Archaeology, University of London, London, England, reader, 1955-62, professor of archaeology of the Roman provinces, 1963-66; Oxford University, Oxford, England, professor of the archaeology of the Roman Empire, 1966—. Director of Canterbury excavations, 1946-60, and Verulamium excavations, 1955-61. Member of Royal Commission on Historical Monuments and Ancient Monuments Board for England, 1966. *Member:* Society of Antiquaries (fellow; vice-president, 1962-66), Society for the Promotion of Roman Studies (vice-president, 1967), German Archaeological Institute (fellow).

WRITINGS: (Editor) *Problems of the Iron Age in Southern Britain,* Institute of Archaeology, University of

London, 1961; *Britannia: A History of Roman Britain,* Harvard University Press, 1967, 2nd edition, 1974; *Verulamium Excavations,* Volume I, Society of Antiquaries, 1972. Contributor to learned journals.

AVOCATIONAL INTERESTS: Gardening.

* * *

FRIED, Morton H(erbert) 1923-

PERSONAL: Born March 21, 1923, in New York, N.Y.; son of Norton and Sally (Solomon) Fried; married Martha Nemes (a cookbook compiler), June 22, 1945; children: Nancy, Elman Steven. *Education:* City College (now City College of the City University of New York), B.S., 1942; Columbia University, Ph.D., 1951. *Politics:* "Middle-age left." *Religion:* None. *Residence:* Leonia, N.J. *Office:* Department of Anthropology, Columbia University, New York, N.Y. 10027.

CAREER: City College (now City College of the City University of New York), New York City, lecturer in anthropology, 1949-50; Columbia University, New York City, instructor, 1950-52, assistant professor, 1952-55, associate professor, 1955-61, professor of anthropology, 1961—, chairman of department, 1966-69, staff member of East Asian Institute, 1956—. Visiting professor at University of Michigan, 1961-62, and National Taiwan University, 1963-64, Yale University, 1965-66, Florida Atlantic University, 1971, University of British Columbia, 1972, and University of Colorado, 1973. Chairman of Asia Committee, Division of Psychology and Anthropology of National Academy of Sciences-National Research Council, 1957-62; member of board of directors of Social Science Research Council; member of Sino-American Committee for Cooperation in Humanities and Social Sciences; consultant to National Science Foundation, 1969-72, National Institute of Mental Health, 1973—, and National Endowment for the Humanities, 1974—. *Military service:* U.S. Army, 1943-45; became sergeant.

MEMBER: American Anthropological Association (fellow), American Ethnological Society, Association for Asian Studies. *Awards, honors:* Social Science Research Council fellow in China, 1947-49; National Science Foundation grants, 1963, 1964; Guggenheim fellow, 1963.

WRITINGS: Fabric of Chinese Society, Praeger, 1953; (editor) *Readings in Anthropology,* Crowell, Volume I: *Physical Anthropology, Linguistics, and Archeology,* 1959, Volume II: *Cultural Anthropology,* 1959, 2nd edition, 1968; *The Evolution of Political Society,* Random House, 1967; (editor with Marvin Harris and Robert Murphy) *War: The Anthropology of Armed Aggression,* American Museum of Natural History Press, 1968; (with Chen Shao-hsing) *The Distribution of Family Names in Taiwan,* two volumes, Department of Sociology, Columbia University, 1968-70; *The Study of Anthropology,* Crowell, 1972; (editor) *Explorations in Anthropology,* Crowell, 1973; *The Notion of Tribe,* Cummings, 1975. Editor with Marvin Harris, "Random House Studies in Anthropology." Contributor to journals.

WORK IN PROGRESS: The Halls of the Ancestors: A Study of Clans in Taiwan (tentative title), a book based on research underway since 1963 under a National Science Foundation grant, completion expected about 1977.

SIDELIGHTS: Fried has carried out research in Mainland China, Taiwan, and in the Caribbean, particularly in Guyana (where the subject was Huach'iao, or Overseas Chinese).

FRIEDBERG, Gertrude (Tonkonogy)

PERSONAL: Born in New York, N.Y.; daughter of George and Sylvia Tonkonogy; married Charles K. Friedberg (a cardiologist); children: Richard, Barbara. *Education:* Barnard College, B.A. *Home:* 1185 Park Ave., New York, N.Y. 10028.

CAREER: Substitute teacher of mathematics in New York City public schools, 1964—. Free-lance writer.

WRITINGS: Three Cornered Moon (play), Samuel French, 1933; (contributor of five stories) *Short Story Two,* Scribner, 1959; *The Revolving Boy* (science fiction novel), Doubleday, 1966. Contributor of short stories to *Atlantic, Harper's, Esquire,* and other magazines.

* * *

FRIEDHEIM, Robert L(yle) 1934-

PERSONAL: Born August 1, 1934, in New York, N.Y.; son of Joseph N. and Blanche (Vogel) Friedheim; married Robin Rudolph (an editor), June 17, 1956; children: Amy, Jessica. *Education:* Columbia University, B.A., 1955, M.A., 1957; University of Washington, Seattle, Ph.D., 1962. *Politics:* Democrat. *Office:* Center for Naval Analyses, 1401 Wilson Blvd., Arlington, Va. 22209.

CAREER: Purdue University, Lafayette, Ind., assistant professor, 1961-66, associate professor of political science, 1966; Center for Naval Analyses, Arlington, Va., 1966—, began as researcher, director of Law of the Sea Project, 1972—. *Military service:* U.S. Army, Intelligence, 1957-58. *Member:* International Studies Association, American Political Science Association, American Society of International Laws. *Awards, honors:* American Council of Learned Societies grant, 1962; Purdue University research grants, 1963, 1964; Center for Naval Analyses fellowship, 1971-72; National Science Foundation grant, 1974-75.

WRITINGS: The Seattle General Strike, University of Washington Press, 1964; (contributor) L. Alexander, editor, *The Law of the Sea,* Ohio State University Press, 1967; *Offshore Boundaries and Zones,* Ohio State University Press, 1967; (contributor) *Pacem in Maribus,* Royal University Press of Malta, 1971; (contributor) George H. Quester, editor, *Readings on International Politics,* Little, Brown, 1971; (contributor) Robert Jordan, editor, *Multinational Cooperation: Economic, Social and Scientific Development,* Oxford University Press, 1972; (co-author) *The Navy and the Common Sea,* U.S. Government Printing Office, 1972; (contributor) John Lawrence Hargrove, editor, *Who Protects the Ocean?,* West Publishing, 1975; (contributor) Michael MacGuire, Ken Booth, and John McDonnell, editors, *Soviet Naval Policy, Objectives, and Constraints,* Praeger, 1975. Contributor to *Monograph Series in World Affairs,* University of Denver Press, 1968-69, and to proceedings. Contributor of reviews and articles on labor and international diplomacy to *Pacific Northwest Quarterly, World Politics,* and other periodicals; author of numerous studies for Center for Naval Analyses.

* * *

FRIEDLANDER, Albert H(oschander) 1927-

PERSONAL: Born May 10, 1927, in Berlin, Germany; came to United States in 1940; son of Alex (a textile broker) and Sali (Hoschander) Friedlander; married Evelyn Philipp (a pianist), July 9, 1961; children: Ariel Judith, Michal Sali, Noam Ilana. *Education:* University of Chicago, Ph.B., 1946; Hebrew Union College—Jewish Institute of Religion, Cincinnati, Ohio, B.H.L., 1950, Rabbi, 1952; Columbia University, Ph.D., 1966. *Politics:* Democrat. *Home:* Kent House, Rutland Gardens, London S.W. 7, England. *Agent:* David H. Scott, 225 East 57th St., New York, N.Y. 10022. *Office:* Leo Baeck College, 33 Seymour Pl., London, England.

CAREER: Rabbi in Fort Smith, Ark., 1952-57, Wilkes-Barre, Pa., 1957-61, and Easthampton, Long Island, N.Y., 1961-65; Columbia University, New York, N.Y., religious counselor, 1961-66; Wembley Liberal Synagogue, Harrow, Middlesex, England, rabbi, 1966-71; Westminster Synagogue, London, England, rabbi, 1971—; Leo Baeck College, London, lecturer, 1966-71, director, 1971—. Visiting professor at Emory University, 1975. *Member:* Central Conference of American Rabbis (chairman of committee on art and literature, 1961-66), World Union for Progressive Judaism (member of American board, 1964-66; member of European board, 1967—), B'nai B'rith.

WRITINGS: Early Reform Judaism in Germany: An Introduction, published in two parts, Union of American Hebrew Congregations, 1954-55; (editor) *The Words They Spoke: Statements from the Speeches and Writings of Early Leaders of Reform Judaism,* Union of American Hebrew Congregations, 1954; *Isaac M. Wise: The World of My Books,* American Jewish Archives, 1954; (translator) Leo Baeck, *This People Israel* (original title, *Dieses Volk*), Holt, 1965; (editor) *Never Trust a God Over 30: New Styles in Campus Ministry,* with an introduction by Paul Goodman, McGraw, 1967; (editor) *Out of the Whirlwind: A Reader of Holocaust Literature,* Doubleday, 1968; *Leo Baeck: Teacher of Theresienstadt,* Holt, 1968; *Leo Baeck: Leben und Lehre,* Deutsche Verlags-Anstalt, 1973.

Librettoes: "The Two Brothers," 1971; "The Harp and the Lovers," 1974; "The Burning City," 1975; "The Five Scrolls," 1975.

Also author of monographs including *Jews and God,* 1972, *Jewish View of Suffering,* 1974, and *Leo Baeck's Theology of Suffering,* 1974. Contributing editor, *Jews from Germany in the United States,* 1955. Contributor of reviews, articles, and notes to *Saturday Review, Dimensions, American Judaism, Encounter, Reconstructionist,* and other journals in the United States and Germany. Member of editorial board, *European Judaism.*

WORK IN PROGRESS: Section on Leo Baeck for *Three Thinkers: Baeck, Heschel, Kaplan,* edited by Alfred Jospe for publication by Schocken; editing *Jewish Emancipation Reader,* commissioned by B'nai B'rith; *Contemporary Theology; Anthology of Holocaust Poetry.*

SIDELIGHTS: "It is to Albert Friedlander's credit that, despite his profound love for his late teacher, he does not permit emotion to interfere with objective scholarly appraisal," according to Alan W. Miller reviewing *Leo Baeck: Teacher of Theresienstadt.* He further describes Friedlander's work as a "sensitive and thoughtful exploration of the tension between the mind and the man. . . ."

Friedlander told *CA* his motivation encompasses "the need to communicate, to preserve and to transmit the past, to enlarge the role of the rabbi in contemporary life."

BIOGRAPHICAL/CRITICAL SOURCES: New Republic, March 15, 1969; *Christian Century,* September 3, 1969.

*   *   *

FRIEDMAN, Melvin J(ack) 1928-
PERSONAL: Born March 7, 1928, in Brooklyn, N.Y.; son

of Julian (a lawyer) and Edith (Block) Friedman; married Judith Zervitz, October 12, 1958; children: Jennifer Ann, James Alan. *Education:* Bard College, A.B., 1949; Columbia University, M.A., 1951; Yale University, Ph.D., 1954. *Religion:* Jewish. *Home:* 1211 East Courtland Pl., Milwaukee, Wis. 53211. *Office:* Department of Comparative Literature, University of Wisconsin, Milwaukee, Wis. 53201.

CAREER: University of Maryland, College Park, instructor in English, 1956-59; University of Wisconsin, Madison, instructor, 1959-60, assistant professor of English, 1960-62; University of Maryland, associate professor of English and comparative literature, 1962-66; University of Wisconsin, Milwaukee, professor of comparative literature, 1966—. Visited India under U.S. Department of State auspices, 1960, to investigate teaching possibilities in American literature and history. *Military service:* U.S. Army, 1954-56. *Member:* International Comparative Literature Association, Modern Language Association of America, American Comparative Literature Association, American Committee for Irish Studies, Popular Culture Association, Wisconsin Academy of Sciences, Arts and Letters.

WRITINGS: Stream of Consciousness: A Study in Literary Method, Yale University Press, 1955.

(Editor and author of introduction) *Configuration critique de Samuel Beckett,* Lettres Modernes, 1964; (editor with Lewis A. Lawson, and author of introduction) *The Added Dimension: The Art and Mind of Flannery O'Connor,* Fordham University Press, 1966; (editor with August J. Nigro, and author of introduction) *Configuration critique de William Styron,* Lettres Modernes, 1967.

(Editor with John B. Vickery, and author of introduction) *The Shaken Realist: Essays in Modern Literature in Honor of Frederick J. Hoffman,* Louisiana State University Press, 1970; (editor and author of introduction) *Samuel Beckett Now,* University of Chicago Press, 1970; 2nd revised edition, 1975; (editor with Irving Malin, and author of preface) *William Styron's "The Confessions of Nat Turner": A Critical Handbook,* Wadsworth, 1970; (editor and author of introduction) *The Vision Obscured: Perceptions of Some Twentieth-Century Catholic Novelists,* Fordham University Press, 1970; (with J. R. Bryer, Peter Hoy, and R. J. Davis) *Calepins de bibliographie Samuel Beckett,* Lettres Modernes, 1971; *William Styron,* Bowling Green University/Popular Press, 1974.

Contributor: *Configuration critique de William Faulkner,* Lettres Modernes, 1959; Joseph J. Waldmeir, editor, *Recent American Fiction: Some Critical Views,* Houghton, 1963; Frederic Will, editor, *Hereditas,* University of Texas Press, 1964; J. H. Matthews, editor, *Un Nouveau Roman,* Lettres Modernes, 1964. Contributor to yearly bibliography published in *The Yearbook of Comparative and General Literature,* 1958-60; contributor of articles on F. Scott Fitzgerald, Henry James, James Starkey and Irish literature to *Lexikon der Weltliteratur im 20. Jahrhundert,* Volume I, 1960, Volume II, 1961. Contributor of articles, review essays, and about seventy-five short reviews to professional journals. Associate editor, *Yale French Studies,* 1952-54; editor, *Wisconsin Studies in Contemporary Literature,* 1961-62, and *Comparative Literature Studies,* 1962-66; review editor for comparative literature, *Modern Language Journal,* 1963-70; member of editorial boards, *Renascence, Journal of Popular Culture,* and *Studies in the Novel.*

WORK IN PROGRESS: Two books, one on the American Jewish novel, and one on the Southern novel; preparing, as guest editor, a double issue of *TriQuarterly* on American "little magazines."

* * *

FRIEL, Brian 1929-

PERSONAL: Born January 9, 1929, in Ireland; son of Patrick (a teacher) and Christina (MacLoone) Friel; married Anne Morrison, December, 1955; children: Paddy (daughter), Mary, Judy. *Education:* St. Patrick's College, Maynooth, Ireland, B.A., 1948; St. Joseph's Teachers Training College, graduate study, 1949-50. *Home:* Ardmore, Muff, Lifford, County Donegal, Ireland. *Agent:* Curtis Brown Ltd., 60 East 56th St., New York, N.Y. 10022.

CAREER: Teacher at primary and post-primary schools in and around Derry City, Northern Ireland, 1950-60; professional writer, 1960—. *Awards, honors:* McAuley fellowship from Irish Arts Council; D.Litt., Rosary College (Chicago), 1974.

WRITINGS: A Saucer of Larks (stories), Doubleday, 1963; *The Gold in the Sea* (stories), Doubleday, 1966. Also has written for British and Irish radio and television. Contributor of stories to periodicals.

Plays: *Philadelphia, Here I Come!* (first produced in Dublin at Gaiety Theatre, September 28, 1964; first produced on Broadway at Helen Hayes Theatre, February 16, 1966), Farrar, Straus, 1967; *The Loves of Cass McGuire* (first produced on Broadway at Helen Hayes Theatre, October 6, 1966), Farrar, Straus, 1967; *Lovers* (two one-acts, "Winners" and "Losers"; first produced in Dublin at Gate Theatre, summer, 1967; produced on Broadway at Vivian Beaumont Theatre, June 25, 1968; moved on Broadway to Music Box Theatre, November, 1968), Farrar, Straus, 1968; *Crystal and Fox* [and] *The Mundy Scheme* (*Crystal and Fox* first produced in Dublin; produced in Los Angeles at Mark Taper Forum, February, 1969; produced in New York, March, 1972; *The Mundy Scheme,* first produced in Dublin at Olympia Theatre, June 11, 1969; produced on Broadway at Royale Theatre, December 11, 1969), Farrar, Straus, 1970; "The Gentle Island" (two-act), first produced in Dublin at Olympia Theatre, 1971; "The Freedom of the City," first produced in Dublin at Abbey Theatre, 1972, produced in Chicago at Goodman Theatre, 1974, produced on Broadway, 1974; "Volunteers," first produced in Dublin at Abbey Theatre, 1975.

SIDELIGHTS: The Loves of Cass McGuire was produced on television in Dublin.

BIOGRAPHICAL/CRITICAL SOURCES: Carolyn Riley, editor, *Contemporary Literary Criticism,* Volume V, Gale, 1976.

* * *

FRIELINK, A(braham) Barend 1917-

PERSONAL: Born November 17, 1917, in Amsterdam, Netherlands; married Jenny J. de Vries, April 26, 1952; children: Barend, Maarten, Albertine. *Education:* Netherlands Institute of Accountants, Amsterdam, accountant's certification, 1948. *Home:* Linnaeusparkweg 45, Amsterdam, Netherlands. *Office:* Van Dien & Co., Fizeaustroat 2, Amsterdam, Netherlands.

CAREER: De Haan, Stol & Co. (accountants), Amsterdam, Netherlands, partner, 1955-69; Van Dien & Co. (accountants), Amsterdam, partner, 1970—. University of Amsterdam, part-time lecturer, 1957-65, part-time professor of accounting, auditing, and methodology of automatic in-

formation processing, 1965—; Netherlands Information Processing Research Centre, Amsterdam, managing director, 1958-64, member of Scientific Bureau, 1964-73. Member of Netherlands Institute of Registeraccountants, 1953—, vice-president, 1974-75, president, 1975—.

WRITINGS: De Accountantscontrole bij huishoudingen met geautomatiseerde administratie, Studiecentrum Administratieve Automatisering, 1959 published as *Auditing Automatic Data Processing,* Elsevier, 1961; (editor) *Economics of Automatic Data Processing,* North Holland Publishing, 1965; *Inleiding tot het Organisatieonderzoek,* Samsom, 1966; *Inleiding tot de automatische informatieverwerking,* Agon Elsevier, 1968; *De GBR Verklaard,* Kosmos Uitg-Mij, 1974; (editor) *Economics of Informatics,* American Elsevier, 1975. Contributor to proceedings and journals. Member of editorial board, *Maandblad voor Accountancy en Bedrijfshuishoudkune.*

WORK IN PROGRESS: A textbook on auditing; research in man-machine communication.

SIDELIGHTS: Auditing Automatic Data Processing has also been published in German and Danish. Frielink is competent in English, French, and German.

* * *

FRIENDLY, Fred W. 1915-

PERSONAL: Surname originally Wachenheimer, but adopted mother's maiden name early in career; born October 30, 1915, in New York, N.Y.; son of Samuel and Therese (Friendly) Wachenheimer; married Dorothy Greene (a magazine researcher); married second wife, Ruth W. Mark (an educator), June, 1968; children: Andrew, Lisa, David, Jon, Michael, Richard. *Education:* Nichols Junior College (now Nichols College), Dudley, Mass. *Office:* Ford Foundation, 320 East 43rd St., New York, N.Y. 10017; and Columbia University, New York, N.Y. 10027.

CAREER: Began career in radio in 1938 as writer, producer, and narrator of "Footprints in the Sands of Time," a local series aired in Providence, R.I. (received $8 a broadcast from the sponsor); met Edward R. Murrow in 1948 and collaborated with him on an oral history of the period from 1932 to 1945, which resulted in the best-selling Columbia Records album, "I Can Hear It Now," issued in 1948, and two subsequent albums covering the 1920's and the post-World War II period; became associated with Columbia Broadcasting System in 1951 as joint producer with Murrow of radio network series, "Hear It Now," and eventually, the television series, "See It Now" and "Small World"; executive producer of "CBS Reports," 1959-64, arranging, among other specials, Walter Lippmann's series of conversations on the program; as president of CBS News, 1964-66, was responsible for the "Town Meeting of the World," "Vietnam Perspective," "National Drivers Test," and other landmark broadcasts; resigned from Columbia Broadcasting System in a celebrated conflict with Network opinions regarding ratings, February, 1966; two months later became Edward R. Murrow Professor of Journalism at Columbia University and adviser on television to the Ford Foundation, New York, N.Y., teaching and directing the Graduate School's Television Workshop at Columbia. *Military service:* U.S. Army, Information and Education Section, 1941-45; served in the Pacific and Europe; received Legion of Merit, four battle stars, and Soldier's Medal (the last was bestowed for heroism in rescue work following a dock explosion in Bombay, India; Friendly had been discharged from the Army, and was in India for Columbia Broadcasting System at the time).

AWARDS, HONORS: "See It Now" series received thirty-five major awards, garnering in one year (1954) the Overseas Press Club Award, Page One Award of New York Newspaper Guild, National Headliners Club Award, *Saturday Review* Award, *Look* TV Award, and *TV Guide* Gold Medal; "CBS Reports" earned forty major awards, becoming the most decorated series on network television; Friendly personally received ten George Foster Peabody Awards; D.H.L., University of Rhode Island, 1966, and Grinnell University, 1967.

WRITINGS: (With Edward R. Murrow) *See It Now,* Simon & Schuster, 1955; *Due to Circumstances Beyond Our Control,* Random House, 1967; *The Good Guys, the Bad Guys and the First Amendment: Free Speech Vs. Fairness in Broadcasting,* Random House, 1976.

BIOGRAPHICAL/CRITICAL SOURCES: Time, April 7, 1967; *New Leader,* May 22, 1967; *Kenyon Review,* June, 1967; *Esquire,* August, 1967; *Listener,* November 2, 1967.

* * *

FROMM, Harold 1933-

PERSONAL: Born July 19, 1933, in New York, N.Y. *Education:* Brooklyn College (now Brooklyn College of the City University of New York), B.A., 1954; Columbia University, M.A., 1956; University of Wisconsin, Ph.D., 1962. *Office:* Department of English, Indiana University Northwest, Gary, Ind. 46408.

CAREER: Oakland University, Rochester, Mich., instructor in English, 1960-62; Wayne State University, Detroit, Mich., 1962-67, began as instructor, became assistant professor of English; Brooklyn College of the City University of New York, Brooklyn, N.Y., assistant professor of English, 1968-70; Indiana University Northwest, Gary, Ind., associate professor of English, 1970—. *Awards, honors:* Faculty research grant ($2,500), Wayne State University, 1966.

WRITINGS: Bernard Shaw and the Theater in the Nineties: A Study of Shaw's Dramatic Criticism, University of Kansas Press, 1967. Contributor of essays on Spenser, Virginia Woolf, Emerson, and Kierkegaard to *Massachusetts Review* and *English Miscellany,* and an article on rock music to *New Republic.*

WORK IN PROGRESS: Virginia Woolf's Triumphs.

AVOCATIONAL INTERESTS: Music and philosophy.

BIOGRAPHICAL/CRITICAL SOURCES: Times Literary Supplement, July 25, 1968.

* * *

FROOMKIN, Joseph 1927-

PERSONAL: Born February 7, 1927, in Harbin, China; son of Nathan A. and Rachel (Sineikin) Froomkin; married Maya Pines (a writer), December 12, 1959; children: Michael, Daniel. *Education:* St. John's University, Shanghai, China, B.A., 1946; University of Chicago, Ph.D., 1950. *Home:* 4724 32nd St. N.W., Washington, D.C. 20008. *Office:* Joseph Froomkin Inc., 1015 18th St. N.W., Washington, D.C. 20036.

CAREER: United Nations, Fiscal Division, economist, 1950; New York City Mayor's Commission on Management Survey, member, 1950-51; research associate, Columbia University, Bureau of Applied Social Research, New York, N.Y., 1951, and Harvard University, Law School, Cambridge, Mass., 1954-55; Aeronautical Research

Foundation, senior economist, 1955-57; International Business Machines Corp., White Plains, N.Y., planner, 1959-66; U.S. Office of Education, Washington, D.C., assistant commissioner, 1966-68; Joseph Froomkin Inc., Washington, D.C., president, 1969—. Consultant to Agency for International Development, 1960, 1965; director of Educational Policy Center for Higher Education and Society, 1975—. *Military service:* U.S. Army, 1952-53.

WRITINGS: (With A. J. Jaffe) *Technology and Jobs,* Praeger, 1968; *Aspirations, Enrollments and Resources,* U.S. Government Printing Office, 1970. Contributor to a number of anthologies on management and taxation, and to journals.

* * *

FROST, Lesley 1899-

PERSONAL: Born April 28, 1899, in Boston, Mass.; daughter of Robert (the poet) and Elinor M. (White) Frost; married Joseph W. Ballantine (a professor), 1952 (died, 1973); children: (first marriage) Elinor (Mrs. Malcolm Wilber), Lesley Lee (Mrs. Stanislav Zimic). *Education:* Attended Wesley College, one year; attended Barnard College after World War I; attended University of Michigan; attended University of Mexico, one year. *Home:* 127 East 10th St., New York, N.Y. 10003.

CAREER: After World War I, worked as a journalist in New York, N.Y.; apprenticed to Marion Dodd in the Hampshire Book Shop, Northampton, Mass.; owned and operated, with her sister, Marjorie, The Open Book, Pittsfield, Mass., 1923-34, and, from this shop, operated a bookshop-on-wheels throughout New England and then around the world on the S.S. Franconia, 1928-29; Rockford College, Rockford, Ill., assistant professor and director of Maddox House Cultural Center, 1935-37; King-Smith Studio School, Washington, D.C., director, three years; owner and director of Frost Studio School for adult education. Was associated with Office of War Information in Madrid, Spain as cultural officer and director of U.S. Information Library, 1945-47, then with the State Department as a lecturer on American literature in Latin America, 1949-50. Regular lecturer, formerly for Columbia Lecture Bureau, and Wide World Lecture Bureau in New York, currently for Eastman Boomer Bureau of New York. *Wartime activity:* During World War I, worked in the Curtis airplane factory in Gloucester, Mass.; during World War II, served as an electrical mechanic in the Washington airport of the Air Transport Command.

MEMBER: Women's Press Club of New York City (chairman of literature), Women's National Republican Club, International P.E.N., Daughters of the American Revolution (New York City chapter), New York Browning Society.

WRITINGS: (Editor) *Come Christmas* (anthology), Coward, 1929; *Murder at Large* (fiction), Coward, 1932; *Not Really!* (stories for children), introduction by Louis Untermeyer, Coward, 1939; (with John Caldwell) *The Korea Story,* Regnery, 1952; *Really Not Really* (juvenile), Channel, 1962; *Digging Down to China* (juvenile), Devin-Adair, 1966; *Derry Journals of Lesley Frost,* State University of New York Press, 1969; *Going on Two* (poems), Devin-Adair, 1973.

SIDELIGHTS: In 1964 Miss Frost purchased an estate in La Granja, Spain, where she opened La Escuela de la Tahona, a two-month summer language school (Spanish and French), for 15- to 17-year-olds. The school is still in operation.

Every year since 1964, Miss Frost has presented a segment of her father's library to New York University's Division of Special Collections. When the presentation is completed, the collection will be installed in the Robert Frost Room of the new library building on Washington Square.

Miss Frost has recorded a collection of her father's poems, entitled "Derry Down Derry," for Folkways Records.

*   *   *

FRUMKIN, Robert M. 1928-

PERSONAL: Born March 20, 1928, in Newark, N.J.; son of Solomon and Anna (Gruber) Frumkin; married Miriam Zisenwine, 1950 (divorced, 1964); married Beverly Crouch Babcock, 1964 (divorced, 1966); married Grace Butcher, 1970 (divorced, 1973); children: (first marriage) Judith. *Education:* Upsala College, B.A., 1948; New School for Social Research, graduate student, 1948-49; Ohio State University, M.A., 1951, Ph.D., 1961; postdoctoral study at Syracuse University, 1963-64, and Case Western Reserve University, 1967-68. *Home:* 952 South Lincoln St., Kent, Ohio 44240. *Agent:* Vickie Stoller, 1228 Easton Ave., Somerset, N.J. 08873. *Office:* 311 Education Building, Kent State University, Kent, Ohio 44242.

CAREER: Ohio State Department of Mental Hygiene and Correction, Columbus, social research analyst, 1952-54; State University of New York College for Teachers at Buffalo (now State University of New York at Buffalo), instructor in sociology and psychology, 1954-57; State University of New York at Oswego, 1957-63, began as assistant professor, became associate professor of sociology and anthropology; Benjamin Rose Institute, Cleveland, Ohio, research associate in gerontology, 1964-65; director of research for Community Action for Youth, Cleveland, Ohio, 1965-66, and Cleveland Society for the Blind, Cleveland, 1966-67; Kent State University, Kent, Ohio, associate professor of rehabilitation counseling, 1967—. Lecturer, Cuyahoga Community College, 1965; research consultant, Cleveland Psychiatric Institute, 1966—. Licensed psychologist, State of Ohio, 1974—; certified rehabilitation counselor, 1974—. *Military service:* U.S. Navy, Hospital Corps, 1946-47.

MEMBER: American Humanist Association, American Art Therapy Association, Middle East Friendship League (founder), Society for the Scientific Study of Sex (fellow), American Sociological Association (fellow), American Psychological Association, American Association of University Professors, American Civil Liberties Union, Mensa, National Rehabilitation Association. *Awards, honors:* Fellowships from Ericsson Society of New York, in science, 1945-46, and State University of New York Research Foundation, summer, 1963; research grants from National Institutes of Mental Health, 1965-66, and Cleveland Foundation, 1966; first prize for nonfiction writing, Sigma Tau Delta literary competition, 1965.

WRITINGS: The Measurement of Marriage Adjustment, Public Affairs, 1954; *The Meaning of Sociology,* University of Buffalo, 1956; *The Patient as a Human Being,* University of Buffalo, 1956; *Freedom to Love,* Paine Press, 1956; *Hospital Nursing: A Sociological Interpretation,* University of Buffalo, 1956; *The Nurse as a Human Being,* University of Buffalo, 1956; *Social Problems, Pathology and Philosophy: Selected Essays and Studies,* Frontiers Press, 1962. Also author of "Kangaroo Court" (play), 1974.

Contributor: *Mental Health and Mental Disorder: A Socio-logical Approach,* edited by A. M. Rose, Norton, 1955; *Contemporary Sociology,* edited by J. S. Roucek, Philosophical Library, 1961; *Encyclopedia of Sexual Behavior,* edited by A. Ellis and A. Abarbanel, Hawthorn, 1961; *The Heritage of American Education,* edited by R. E. Gross, Allyn & Bacon, 1962; *The Unusual Child,* edited by J. S. Roucek, Philosophical Library, 1965; *Life in Families,* edited by H. M. Hughes, Allyn & Bacon, 1970; *New Developments in Modern World Sociology,* edited by D. Martindale and R. Mohan, Greenwood Press, 1975.

Contributor of more than 180 articles and reviews to sociology, psychology, education, religious, literary, medical, nursing, and other journals. Abstractor, *Psychological Abstracts,* 1954-63; editor, *Heritage* (literary magazine), 1949-51, and *Ethos* (literary magazine), 1955-58; research editor, *Journal of Human Relations,* 1958-70.

WORK IN PROGRESS: The Ivy Conspiracy; The Sexual Potential of the Handicapped; Social Psychological Aspects of Disability; Open Relationships; "The Measure of Love," a play; *Thunder in the Snow,* a novel.

AVOCATIONAL INTERESTS: Drawing, painting, sculpture, wood carving, piano, tennis, table tennis, track and field, hiking, rowing, ice skating, and other forms of outdoor recreation.

*   *   *

FRYE, (Charles) Alton 1936-

PERSONAL: Born November 3, 1936, in Nashville, Tenn.; son of Edgar Alton (a businessman) and Virginia Kathleen (Hannah) Frye; married Patricia Ann Davis, September 29, 1953; children: Wesley, Andrew, Felicia Emily. *Education:* St. Louis University, B.S. (summa cum laude), 1958; Yale University, Ph.D., 1961. *Politics:* Independent. *Religion:* Congregationalist. *Home:* 1242 Titania Lane, McLean, Va. *Office:* Suite 900, 11 Dupont Circle, N.W., Washington, D.C. 20036.

CAREER: Announcer-reporter for WNAH and WMAK, Nashville, Tenn., 1953-54, and WTMV, KXLW, and WEW, St. Louis, Mo., 1954-56; Division of Parks and Recreation, St. Louis, director of public relations and personnel supervisor, 1956-58; WELI, New Haven, Conn., news director, 1959-61; RAND Corp., staff member in Santa Monica, Calif., and Washington, D.C., 1962-68; legislative and administrative assistant to U.S. Senator Edward W. Brooke, 1968-71; fellow, Woodrow Wilson International Center for Scholars, 1971-73; director of Institute for Congress Project, Carnegie Endowment for International Peace, 1974—. Visiting assistant professor, University of California, Los Angeles, 1964; research associate and lecturer in government, Centre for International Affairs, Harvard University, 1965-66; consultant to Senator Brooke, 1971—, and to Subcommittee on National Security Decision-Making, Committee on Economic Development, 1972—. *Member:* American Political Science Association, American Historical Association, American Academy of Political and Social Science, Council on Foreign Relations (fellow; director of special projects, 1973—), Institute for Strategic Studies (London), Pangloss Society. *Awards, honors:* Congressional fellow, American Political Science Association, 1961-62.

WRITINGS: The Hazards of Atomic Wastes: Perspectives and Proposals on Oceanic Disposal, Public Affairs Press, 1962; *Nazi Germany and the American Hemisphere, 1933-1941,* Yale University Press, 1967; *A Responsible Congress: The Politics of National Security,* McGraw, 1975.

Contributor: *Reflections on Space,* U.S. Air Force Academy, 1964; *Outer Space: Prospects for Man and Society,* 2nd edition (Frye was not associated with first edition), Prentice-Hall, 1968; *The Role of Analysis in Defense Planning,* RAND Corp., 1968; Mason Willrich & John B. Rhinelander, editors, *SALT: The Moscow Agreement and Beyond,* Free Press, 1974. Contributor of articles to numerous journals and newspapers, including *Ripon Forum, Foreign Policy, Journal of Conflict Resolution,* and *Christian Science Monitor.*

WORK IN PROGRESS: Continuing research on foreign policy issues, arms control, and legislative-executive relations.

AVOCATIONAL INTERESTS: Photography.

* * *

FUCHS, Jacob 1939-

PERSONAL: Born December 2, 1939; son of Daniel and Susan (Chessen) Fuchs; married Freya Cummings, June 15, 1963; children: three. *Education:* University of California, Berkeley, B.A., 1961, M.A., 1964, Ph.D., 1972. *Home:* 695 Ensenada Ave., Berkeley, Calif. 94707. *Office:* English Department, California State University, Hayward, Calif.

CAREER: Orange Coast College, Costa Mesa, Calif., teacher of English, 1964-68; California State College (now California State University), Los Angeles, instructor in English, beginning 1968; presently professor at California State University at Hayward.

WRITINGS: (Editor with Roslyn Snow) *Man: Alternatives of Experience,* Wadsworth, 1967. Contributor to journals.

WORK IN PROGRESS: A translation of Horace's *Satires and Epistles,* for Norton.

* * *

FUCHS, Josef 1912-

PERSONAL: Born July 5, 1912, in Bergisch Gladbach, Germany. *Education:* Attended Pontifical Gregorian 'University, Rome, and Universities of Bonn and Freiburg; University of Muenster, Dr.theol., 1946. *Home:* 4 Piazza della Pilotta, Rome, Italy.

CAREER: Roman Catholic priest of Society of Jesus (Jesuits); Pontifical Gregorian University, Rome, Italy, professor of moral theology, 1954—.

WRITINGS: Magisterium, Ministerium, Regimen—Zum Entstehen: Einer ekklesiologischen Trilogie, Kollen, 1941; *Die Sexualethik des Hl. Thomas v. Aquin,* Bachem, 1949; *Situation und Entscheidung,* Knecht, 1952; *Lex Naturae: Zur Theologie des Naturrechts,* Patmos, 1955, translation by Helmut Reckter and John A. Dowling published as *Natural Law: A Theological Investigation,* Sheed, 1965; *Moral und Moraltheologie nach dem Konzil,* Herder, 1967; *Human Values and Christian Morality,* translated from the original German by M. H. Heelan, Gill & Macmillan, 1970; *Existe-t-il une morale chretienn?,* Duculot, 1973. Author of several textbooks on moral theology published in Latin by Gregorian University Press.

* * *

FUGATE, Joe K. 1931-

PERSONAL: Born October 31, 1931, in East St. Louis, Ill.; son of Ott B. (a railroad man) and Elizabeth (Kemp) Fugate; married Louise Reid, February 21, 1953; children: John Eric, Karl Richard, Erika Leah. *Education:* Southern Illinois University, A.B., 1954; Princeton University, M.A., 1959, Ph.D., 1962. *Politics:* Independent. *Religion:* Baptist. *Home:* 1301 Grand, Kalamazoo, Mich. 49007. *Office:* Kalamazoo College, Kalamazoo, Mich. 49001.

CAREER: Ohio University, Athens, instructor in German, 1959-61; Kalamazoo College, Kalamazoo, Mich., assistant professor, 1961-66, associate professor, 1966-71, professor of German, 1971—, chairman of German department, 1965-74, assistant director of foreign study, 1965-74, director, 1974—, director of neglected languages program, 1965—. *Military service:* U.S. Army, 1955-57. *Member:* American Association of Teachers of German, Modern Language Association of America, Association of Departments of Foreign Languages (member of executive committee), American Council on Foreign Language Teaching.

WRITINGS: The Psychological Basis of Herder's Aesthetic, Mouton & Co., 1966. Contributor of reviews to *Choice, Library Journal,* and language journals.

WORK IN PROGRESS: A German cultural-historical reader for intermediate students; a revision of the English translation of Herder's *Ideen.*

SIDELIGHTS: Fugate has made numerous trips to universities in Europe, the Middle East, and Africa. *Avocational interests:* Old books, manuscripts, and antiques.

* * *

FULD, James J. 1916-

PERSONAL: Born February 16, 1916, in New York, N.Y.; son of Gus and Blanche (Weill) Fuld; married Elaine Gerstley, September 12, 1942; children: Joan, James, Jr., Nancy. *Education:* Harvard University, A.B., 1937, LL.B., 1940. *Office:* Room 2100, 300 Park Ave., New York, N.Y. 10022.

CAREER: Admitted to New York Bar, 1940; Proskauer, Rose, Goetz & Mendelsohn (law firm), New York, N.Y., attorney, 1940—, partner, 1952—. Director of various corporations. Trustee, Federation of Jewish Philanthropies of New York; member of executive committee, New York chapter of American Jewish Committee. *Military service:* U.S. Army, 1942-46; became major; received Commendation Ribbon. *Member:* American Bar Association, and state, county, and city bar associations; International Musicological Society, American Musicological Society, Phi Beta Kappa, Sunningdale Country Club.

WRITINGS: American Popular Music, 1875-1950, Musical Americana, 1955; *A Pictorial Bibliography of First Editions of Stephen C. Foster,* Musical Americana, 1957; *The Book of World-Famous Music: Classical, Popular and Folk,* Crown, 1966. Contributor to legal periodicals. Editor, *Harvard Law Review,* 1939-40.

AVOCATIONAL INTERESTS: Collecting first editions of well-known classical, popular, and folk music of all countries, from 1600 to the present time.

* * *

FULLER, John (Leopold) 1937-

PERSONAL: Born January 1, 1937, in Ashford, Kent, England; son of Roy Broadbent (a poet and lawyer) and Kathleen (Smith) Fuller; married Cicely Prudence Martin, July 20, 1960; children: Sophie Claire, Louisa Charlotte, Emily Renira Alice. *Education:* New College, Oxford,

B.A., 1960, M.A., 1964, B.Litt., 1965. *Home:* 4 Benson Place, Oxford, England. *Office:* Magdalen College, Oxford University, Oxford, England.

CAREER: State University of New York at Buffalo, visiting lecturer in English, 1962-63; University of Manchester, Manchester, England, assistant lecturer, 1963-66; Oxford University, Magdalen College, Oxford, England, fellow and tutor in English, 1966—. *Awards, honors:* Newdigate Prize, 1960; Richard Hillary Award, 1961; E. C. Gregory Award, 1965; Faber Memorial Prize, 1974.

WRITINGS—Poetry: *Fairground Music,* Chatto & Windus, with Hogarth Press, 1961; *The Tree That Walked,* Chatto & Windus, with Hogarth Press, 1967; *The Art of Love,* The Review (Oxford, England), 1968; *The Labours of Hercules: A Sonnet Sequence,* Manchester Institute of Contemporary Arts, 1970; *The Wreck,* limited edition, Turret Books, 1970; *Cannibals and Missionaries,* Secker & Warburg, 1972; *Boys in a Pie,* Steam Press (London), 1972; *Hut Groups,* limited edition, Cellar Press (Hertfordshire, England), 1973; (with Adrian Mitchell and Peter Levi) *Penguin Modern Poets 22,* Penguin, 1973; *Epistles to Several Persons,* Secker & Warburg, 1973; *Poems and Epistles,* David R. Godine, 1974; *Squeaking Crust,* Chatto & Windus, 1974; *A Bestiary,* Sycamore Press, 1974; *The Mountain in the Sea,* Secker & Warburg, 1975.

Plays: *Herod Do Your Worst: A Nativity Opera* (produced in Thame, Oxfordshire, England, 1967; music by Bryan Kelly), Novello (London), 1968; *Three London Songs,* music by Kelly, Novello, 1969; *Half a Fortnight* (produced in Leicestershire, England, 1970; music by Kelly), Novello, 1973; *The Spider Monkey Uncle King* (produced in Cookham, Berkshire, England, 1971; music by Kelly), Novello, 1974.

Unpublished plays: "Fox-Trot" (music by Kelly), produced in Leicestershire, 1972; "The Queen in the Golden Tree" (music by Kelly), produced in Edinburgh, 1974.

Editor: (With J. Mitchell and others) *Light Blue Dark Blue,* Macdonald & Co., 1960; *Oxford Poetry 1960,* Fantasy Press (Oxford), 1960; *Poetry Supplement,* Poetry Book Society (London), 1962; (with Harold Pinter and Peter Redgrove) *New Poems 1967: A P.E.N. Anthology of Contemporary Poetry,* Hutchinson, 1968; *Poetry Supplement,* Poetry Book Society, 1970; *Nemo's Almanac,* three volumes, Sycamore Press, 1971-73.

Criticism: *A Reader's Guide to W. H. Auden,* Farrar, 1970.

Novels: *The Last Bid,* Deutsch, 1975.

Other: *The Sonnet,* Methuen, 1972.

Contributor of poetry to *Oxymoran* (Oxford University's Magdalen College magazine).

SIDELIGHTS: David Harsent of *Spectator* commented: "John Fuller is a poet of formidable intelligence and skill; he is also rewardingly susceptible to the oddities of experience: the strange lesions in our lives around which lines of poetry accrete. His two . . . collections, *Fairground Music* and *The Tree That Walked,* are books one goes back to repeatedly for their wit, their depth and their sheer entertainment value. *Cannibals and Missionaries* displays all those qualities. . . ." Peter Porter of the *Observer* noted in reference to *Epistles to Several Persons:* "These enormously resourceful poems are a pleasure to read—only one doubt remains with me: is this stanza a little light for what are often serious matters? Burns, writing in dialect, made it surprisingly tough. Fuller is sometimes too bland. His

rhyming is prodigious but not cumbrous, his marshalling of proper names always apt, and his syntax gives the necessary lift to the metre. One is always being delighted by the touch of a master . . ."

BIOGRAPHICAL/CRITICAL SOURCES: Observer, November 12, 1961; *Poetry Review,* summer, 1967; Ian Hamilton, *A Poetry Chronicle: Essays and Reviews,* Harper, 1973.

* * *

FUNK, Arthur Layton 1914-

PERSONAL: Born May 10, 1914, in Brooklyn, N.Y.; son of Merton Layton (a physician) and Marion (Thompson) Funk; married Genevieve Standard, June 10, 1944; children: Laurence L., James T. *Education:* Dartmouth College, B.A., 1936; University of Chicago, Ph.D., 1940. *Home:* 1717 Northwest 23rd Blvd., Gainesville, Fla. 32601. *Office:* 108 Peabody Hall, University of Florida, Gainesville, Fla. 32601.

CAREER: St. Petersburg Junior College, St. Petersburg, Fla., instructor in history, 1940-42; Drake University, Des Moines, Iowa, assistant professor of history, 1946; University of Florida, Gainesville, associate professor of humanities, 1946-56; U.S. Information Agency, cultural attache and public affairs officer, 1956-62, serving in Damascus, Syria, Madras, India, and Tananarive, Madagascar; University of Florida, professor of humanities and history, 1962—, chairman of history department, 1973—. *Military service:* U.S. Naval Reserve, active duty, 1942-46; highest rank in Reserve, commander. *Member:* American Historical Association, American Committee on the Second World War (secretary), Southern Historical Association. *Awards, honors:* Guggenheim fellow, 1954-55.

WRITINGS: Charles de Gaulle: The Crucial Years, 1943-1944, University of Oklahoma Press, 1959; (compiler) *Europe in the Twentieth Century,* Dorsey, 1968; *The Politics of TORCH: The Allied Landings and the Algiers Putsch, 1942,* University Press of Kansas, 1974.

WORK IN PROGRESS: Resistance movements in World War II.

SIDELIGHTS: Funk lived in france, 1950-51, 1954-55.

* * *

FUNK, Peter V(an) K(euren) 1921-

PERSONAL: Born May 11, 1921, in Montclair, N.J.; son of Wilfred John (president of publishing firms bearing the family name for many years; editor and author) and Eleanor MacNeal (Hawkins) Funk; married Mary Estelle Pettit, November 25, 1942; children: Peter, Jr., Wilfred John II, Celine, Mary, Mark, Paul, Eleanor. *Education:* Princeton University, A.B., 1943. *Politics:* Independent Republican. *Religion:* Episcopalian. *Home address:* Box 128, Lambertville, N.J. 08530. *Agent:* Monica McCall, Inc., 667 Madison Ave., New York, N.Y. 10021.

CAREER: With Hearst Publications, 1946; *Newsweek,* editorial work, 1947-49; Wilfred Funk, editorial work, 1949, 1951-53; Harper & Row, editorial work, 1952; *Reader's Digest,* Pleasantville, N.Y., author of monthly feature, "It Pays to Increase Your Word Power," 1965; Van Keuren Funk, Inc., president, 1952-58, Knickerbocker Shares Inc., New York, N.Y., vice-president, 1958-65, director, 1965—. Chairman of finance committee, Formall Corp., New Hope, Pa. *Military service:* U.S. Marine Corps Reserve, 1941-45; active duty, 1942; became first lieutenant; received Unit Citation.

WRITINGS: My Six Loves, Popular Library, 1963; *Love and Consequences,* Chilton, 1966; *It Pays to Increase Your Word Power,* Funk, 1968; (with Ernest Gordon) *Guidebook for the New Christian,* Harper, 1972.

BIOGRAPHICAL/CRITICAL SOURCES: New York Times, January 21, 1968.†

* * *

FURBANK, P(hilip) N(icholas) 1920-

PERSONAL: Born May 23, 1920, in Cranleigh, Surrey, England; son of William Percival and Grace (Turner) Furbank. *Education:* Emmanuel College, Cambridge, M.A., 1947. *Politics:* Socialist. *Home:* 2 Regent's Park Ter., London N.W.1, England. *Agent:* Curtis Brown Ltd., 1 Craven Hill, London, W2 3EW, England.

CAREER: Cambridge University, Emmanuel College, Cambridge, England, fellow, 1947-53; Macmillan & Co. Ltd., London, England, editor, 1964-70; Cambridge University, King's College, fellow, 1970-72; Open University, Milton Keynes, England, lecturer, 1972—.

WRITINGS: Samuel Butler: 1835-1902, Cambridge University Press, 1948; *Italo Svevo: The Man and the Writer,* Secker & Warburg, 1966, University of California Press, 1967; *Reflections on the Word "Image,"* Secker & Warburg, 1970. Regular contributor to *Listener;* contributor to *Guardian, Observer, Encounter,* and other publications.

WORK IN PROGRESS: A biography of E. M. Forster.

SIDELIGHTS: Furbank is competent in French and Italian. *Avocational interests:* Painting, architecture.

* * *

FURNISH, Victor Paul 1931-

PERSONAL: Born November 17, 1931, in Chicago, Ill.; son of Reuben McKinley (a clergyman) and Mildred (Feller) Furnish; married Jody Carmichael (a teacher), May 25, 1963; children: Brianna Ruth, Rebecca Joann. *Education:* Cornell College, Mount Vernon, Iowa, A.B., 1952; Garrett Theological Seminary, B.D. (with highest distinction), 1955; Yale University, M.A., 1958, Ph.D., 1960. *Politics:* Democrat. *Home:* 6806 Robin Rd., Dallas, Tex. 75209. *Office:* Perkins School of Theology, Southern Methodist University, Dallas, Tex. 75275.

CAREER: Ordained elder, The Methodist Church, 1955. Southern Methodist University, Perkins School of Theology, Dallas, Tex., instructor, 1959-60, assistant professor, 1960-65, associate professor, 1965-71, professor of New Testament, 1971—. *Member:* Society of Biblical Literature, American Academy of Religion, Studiorum Novi Testamenti Societas, New Testament Colloquium, Archaelogical Institute of America, Phi Beta Kappa, Tau Kappa Alpha. *Awards, honors:* Faculty fellow, American Association of Theological Schools, 1964; Alexander von Humboldt Foundation, research fellow, 1965-66, 1972-73.

WRITINGS: Theology and Ethics in Paul, Abingdon, 1968; (contributor) C. M. Layman, editor, *The Interpreter's One-Volume Commentary on the Bible,* Abingdon, 1971; (contributor) H. D. Betz, editor, *Christology and a Modern Pilgrimage,* Scholars' Press, 1971, revised edition, 1974; *The Love Command in the New Testament,* Abingdon, 1972; (with J. H. Snow) *Easter: Series A,* Fortress, 1975; (co-editor and contributor) *The Interpreter's Dictionary of the Bible: Supplementary Volume,* Abingdon, 1976. Contributor to theology journals and Methodist periodicals.

WORK IN PROGRESS: A commentary on Corinthians II for *The Anchor Bible.*

SIDELIGHTS: Furnish traveled in Mediterranean countries and the Middle East, 1964. He did research and writing at University of Bonn, 1965-66, and University of Munich, 1972-73. *Avocational interests:* Music and art.

* * *

FUSS, Peter 1932-

PERSONAL: Surname rhymes with "goose"; born February 11, 1932, in Berlin, Germany; naturalized U.S. citizen; son of Ernest Martin and Ruth (Sonnemann) Fuss; married Carol Ann Wimsatt, November 25, 1961; children: Tobin, Jenna. *Education:* Fordham University, B.S., 1954; Harvard University, M.A., 1956, Ph.D., 1962. *Home:* 6326 McPherson, St. Louis, Mo. 63130. *Office:* Department of Philosophy, University of Missouri, St. Louis, Mo. 63121.

CAREER: University of Michigan, Ann Arbor, lecturer in philosophy, 1960-61; University of California, Riverside, lecturer, 1961-62, assistant professor, 1962-68, associate professor of philosophy, 1968-69; University of Missouri, St. Louis, associate professor, 1969-75, professor of philosophy, 1975—. Visiting associate professor, University of Washington, Seattle, 1966-67. *Member:* American Society for Political and Legal Philosophy, Society for Phenomenology and Existential Philosophy, Hegel Society of America, American Association of University Professors. *Awards, honors:* Humanities Institute fellowship, University of California, 1968-69; summer faculty fellowship, University of Missouri, 1973.

WRITINGS: (Editor and translator with Philip Wheelwright) *Five Philosophers,* Odyssey, 1963; *The Moral Philosophy of Josiah Royce,* Harvard University Press, 1965; (editor and translator with Henry L. Shapiro) *Friedrich Nietzsche: A Self-Portrait from His Letters,* Harvard University Press, 1971; (contributor) Peter A. French, *Conscientious Actions: Revelation of the Pentagon Papers,* General Learning Corp., 1974. Contributor of essays and reviews to professional journals. Editorial consultant, *Journal of History of Philosophy.*

WORK IN PROGRESS: With John Dobbins, a translation and critical commentary of Hegel's *Phenomenology of Spirit.*

* * *

GABLEHOUSE, Charles 1928-

PERSONAL: Born April 16, 1928, in New York, N.Y.; married Marge Holman (an educator), June 21, 1964. *Education:* Attended College of William and Mary, Fordham University, New York University, Academy of Aeronautics at LaGuardia Airport, and Sig Ulydert Flying School, Amityville, N.Y. *Home:* 299 Howard Ave., Passaic, N.J. 07055.

CAREER: DeLackner Helicopters, Inc., Mount Vernon, N.Y., field service engineer, 1956-58; Grumman Aircraft Engineering Corp., Bethpage, N.Y., technical editor and project director, 1958-61; *Business/Commercial Aviation* (magazine), New York City, technical editor, 1961-62; Port Authority of New York and New Jersey, New York City, aviation writer and editor, and aviation department public services representative, 1962—. Holds commercial pilot's license for landplanes and seaplanes, and teacher's license for aviation (New York City high schools); has owned and operated two airplanes for charter work, aerial photography, and personal use. *Military service:* U.S. Army, Aviation Section of 955th Field Artillery Battalion, 1950-52; became staff sergeant; received Bronze Star. *Member:* American Helicopter Society, American Institute of Aeronautics and Astronautics, Experimental Aircraft Association, Society of Technical Writers and Publishers, Convertible Aircraft Pioneers, American Society of Civil Engineers. *Awards, honors:* Annual award of New York chapter of Society of Technical Writers and Publishers, 1963, for article on maintenance of jet aircraft; National Publications Society of Technical Writers and Publishers Award, 1969, for *Helicopters and Autogiros;* National Public Relations Award, Aviation/Space Writers Association, 1974, for promoting aviation activities.

WRITINGS: Helicopters and Autogiros: A Chronicle of Rotating-Wing Aircraft (historical narrative), Lippincott, 1967, revised edition, 1969. Author of aircraft maintenance and inspection manuals; co-author of film script "Flight of the Vin Fiz," 1972. Contributor of more than seventy articles on aviation to journals.

WORK IN PROGRESS: A book on the Battle of Britain; a book about cats.

*   *   *

GAGLIARDO, John G(arver)   1933-

PERSONAL: Born August 13, 1933, in Chicago, Ill., son of Domenico (a professor) and Ruth (Garver) Gagliardo. *Education:* University of Kansas, A.B., 1954, M.A., 1957; University of Marburg, graduate study, 1954-55; Yale University, M.A., 1958, Ph.D., 1962. *Politics:* Republican. *Religion:* Protestant. *Office:* Department of History, Boston University, Boston, Mass. 02215.

CAREER: Amherst College, Amherst, Mass., instructor, 1960-63, assistant professor of history, 1963-65; University of Illinois at Chicago Circle, assistant professor, 1965-67, associate professor of history, 1967-68; Boston University, Boston, Mass., associate professor, 1968-70, professor of history, 1970—. *Member:* American Historical Association, Conference Group on Central European History, American Association of University Professors, New England Historical Association (president, 1974-75).

WRITINGS: Enlightened Despotism, Crowell, 1967; *From Pariah to Patriot: The Changing Image of the German Peasant, 1770-1840,* University Press of Kentucky, 1969. Contributor of articles and reviews to historical journals.

*   *   *

GAGNON, Jean-Louis   1913-

PERSONAL: Born February 21, 1913, in Quebec City, Quebec, Canada; son of Adhemar and Marie-Elise (Nadeau) Gagnon; married Helene Jobidon (a journalist and writer), September 12, 1936. *Education:* Educated at College St. Marie in Montreal, University of Ottawa, and University of Laval. *Politics:* Liberal. *Religion:* Roman Catholic. *Office:* 171 rue Slater, Ottawa, Ontario, Canada.

CAREER: Founded *Vivre* (political and literary magazine), 1933; *Voix de l'est,* Granby, Quebec, editor-in-chief, 1935-40; *Evenement-Journal,* Quebec City, Quebec, editor-in-chief, 1940-41; *Soleil,* war correspondent in London, England, 1941-42; West African Broadcasting Unit, Accra, Gold Coast (now Ghana), director, 1942-43; Agence France-Afrique, Canadian director, Montreal, Quebec, 1943-44; Agence France-Presse, chief of Washington

(D.C.) Bureau, 1944-46; Brazilian Traction, Light and Power Co. Ltd., Rio de Janeiro, director of information services and public relations, 1946-49; CKAC, Montreal, news commentator, 1949-53; *Ecrits du Canada Francais* (literary quarterly), Montreal, editor, 1953-55; *Reforme,* Montreal, editor and general manager, 1955-58; *Presse,* Montreal, editor, 1958-61; *Nouveau Journal,* Montreal, vice-president and editor, 1961-62; CKLM, Montreal, news editor and commentator, 1962-70; Information Canada, Ottawa, Ontario, director-general, 1970—. Member Royal Commission on Bilingualism and Biculturalism.

MEMBER: Academie Canadienne-Francaise, Conseil des Arts du Quebec, Royal Society of Canada (fellow). *Awards, honors:* Lafleche trophy for most significant contribution to Canadian radio, 1957; Grand Prix of Journalism of Canadian Union of French-Speaking Journalists, 1962; Commentary Trophy for program, "Choc," 1963.

WRITINGS: Vent du Large, Parizeau, 1944; *Le Fin des Haricots* (novel), Ecrits du Canada Francais, 1955; *La Mort d'un Negre* (novel), Editions du Jour, 1961; (editor of French selections) *A Century of Reporting–Un Siecle de Reportage,* National Press Club (Ottawa), 1967. Wrote prefaces to an album of Robert Lapalme's caricatures published by Le Cercle du Livre de France, 1950, and an album of Berthio's caricatures, published by Editions du Jour, 1960.†

*   *   *

GALBRAITH, John Kenneth   1908-
(Mark Epernay, Herschel McLandress)

PERSONAL: Born October 15, 1908, in Iona Station, Ontario, Canada; son of William Archibald (a politician and farmer) and Catherine (Kendall) Galbraith; married Catherine Atwater, September 17, 1937; children: John Alan, Peter, James. *Education:* University of Toronto, B.S. in agriculture, 1931; University of California, M.S., 1933, Ph.D., 1934; attended Cambridge University, 1937-38. *Politics:* Democrat. *Home:* 30 Francis Ave., Cambridge, Mass.; (summer) Newfane, Vt. *Office:* Harvard University, Cambridge, Mass. 02138.

CAREER: Harvard University, Cambridge, Mass., instructor and tutor, 1934-39; Princeton University, Princeton, N.J., assistant professor of economics, 1939-42; U.S. Office of Price Administration, Washington, D.C., administrator in charge of price division, 1941-42, department administrator, 1942-43; member of board of editors of *Fortune,* 1943-48; Harvard University, lecturer, 1948-49, professor of economics, 1949—, Paul M. Warburg Professor of Economics, 1959-60, 1963—. Visiting fellow, Trinity College, Cambridge, 1969-70. Director of U.S. Strategic Bombing Survey, 1945, and Office of Economic Security Policy, U.S. Department of State, 1946. American Ambassador Extraordinary and Plenipotentiary in India, 1961-63; presidential advisor to John F. Kennedy and Lyndon B. Johnson. National chairman, Americans for Democratic Action, beginning 1967.

MEMBER: National Institute of Arts and Letters, American Academy of Arts and Sciences (fellow), Twentieth Century Fund (trustee), American Economic Association, American Farm Economists Association, Century Club, Harvard Club (New York). *Awards, honors:* University of California, research fellow, 1931-34; Social Science Research Council, fellow, 1937-38; Medal of Freedom, 1946; L.L.D. from Bard College, 1958, Miami University, Ohio, 1959, University of Toronto, 1963, University of Guelph,

1965, and University of Saskatchewan, 1965; Sarah Josepha Hale Award of Friends of the Richards Free Library, 1967.

WRITINGS: California County Expenditures, University of California Press, 1934; *Branch Banking and Its Bearing upon Agricultural Credit,* [Lancaster, Pa.], 1934; (with Henry Sturgis Dennison) *Modern Competition and Business Policy,* Oxford University Press, 1938; (editor with Carl J. Friedrich) *Public Policy, 1953-1955,* Littauer Center (Cambridge, Mass.), 1940; *Beyond the Marshall Plan,* National Planning Association (Washington), 1949.

America and Western Europe, Public Affairs Committee (New York), 1950; *A Theory of Price Control,* Harvard University Press, 1952; *American Capitalism: The Concept of Countervailing Power,* Houghton, 1952, revised edition, 1956; *The Great Crash, 1929,* Houghton, 1955, 3rd edition, 1972; (with Richard H. Houlton and others) *Marketing Efficiency in Puerto Rico,* Harvard University Press, 1955; *Inequality in Agriculture: Problem and Program,* Ontario Agricultural College, 1956; *Economic Planning in India,* Indian Statistical Institute, 1956; (contributor) Henry Jarrett, editor, *Perspectives on Conservation,* Johns Hopkins Press, 1958; *Latin American Journal, July-September, 1958,* Cambridge University Press, 1958; *Journey to Poland and Yugoslavia,* Harvard University Press, 1958; *Farm Policy: The Problem and the Choices,* Cambridge University Press, 1958; *The Affluent Society,* Houghton, 1958, 2nd edition, 1969.

Some Thoughts on Public Policy and the Dollar Problem, [Cambridge, Mass.], 1960; *The Liberal Hour,* Houghton, 1960; *El Desarollo Economico y la Politica Agraria,* [Montevideo], 1960; *The Causes of Poverty,* Gujarat University (Ahmedabud, India), 1962; *Economic Development in Perspective,* Harvard University Press, 1962, revised edition published as *Economic Development,* Houghton, 1964; *The Economics of Banking Operations,* McGill University Press, 1963; (under pseudonym Mark Epernay) *The McLandress Dimension* (a satire), Houghton, 1963, revised edition, 1968; *The Scotch* (a memoir), Houghton, 1964 (published in England as *The Non-potable Scotch: A Memoir on the Clansman in Canada,* Penguin, 1964; also published as *Made to Last,* Hamish Hamilton, 1964); (with others) *Economic Strategy and the Third Plan,* Taplinger, 1964; *Perspectiva del Desarollo Economico,* Agencia Para el Desarollo Internacional, 1965; *Underdevelopment: An Approach to Classification,* Rehovoth, 1965; *The Underdeveloped Country* (text of radio broadcasts presented in fall of 1965), Canadian Broadcasting Corp., 1965.

Economic Discipline, Houghton, 1967; (with Mohinder Singh Randhawa) *The New Industrial State,* Houghton, 1967, 2nd edition, 1971; (with Randhawa) *Indian Painting,* Houghton, 1967; *How to Get Out of Vietnam: A Workable Solution to the Worst Problem of Our Time,* New American Library, 1967; *The Triumph* (novel; Book-of-the-Month Club selection), Houghton, 1968; *How to Control the Military* (originally published in *Harper's*), Doubleday, 1969; *Ambassador's Journal: A Personal Account of the Kennedy Years,* Houghton, 1969.

Who Needs the Democrats, and What It Takes to Be Needed, Doubleday, 1970; (author of introduction) David Levine, *No Known Survivors: David Levine's Political Prank,* Gambit, 1970; *A Contemporary Guide to Economics, Peace, and Laughter,* Houghton, 1971; *Economics and the Public Purpose,* Houghton, 1973; *A China Passage,* Houghton, 1973; (with Edward Howe) *John Kenneth Galbraith Introduces India,* Deutsch, 1974.

Editor, "Harvard Economic Studies" series, Harvard University Press. Contributor to many economic and scientific journals. Has composed numerous drafts for major speeches for such luminaries as Adlai Stevenson, Lyndon Johnson, and John, Robert, and Edward Kennedy. Galbraith reviewed the pseudonymous *Report from Iron Mountain* under the pseudonym Herschel McLandress.

SIDELIGHTS: Paul A. Samuelson, himself a widely recognized economist and former Kennedy advisor, called Galbraith the "non-economist's economist." Arthur Selwyn Miller said Galbraith "posed some of the basic questions" in *The New Industrial State,* but one might say it is just typically "Galbraithian" to never stop questioning economic policy in the United States, in the rest of the world, and in the United States in relation to the rest of the world. From a close look at his major writings, at his role as lecturer, diplomat, and as *Time* dubs him, "current cynosure of the Eastern intellectual set," Galbraith, says Samuelson, "is the philosopher of the younger generation.... Sage of the Mixed Economy, he is part of our affluence." But Michael Laurence says simply that Galbraith really "defies categorization."

The Affluent Society, Galbraith's major assessment of America's economic situation, has become a key reference (and key phrase along with such terms as "countervailing power" and "conventional wisdom") among economists and laymen alike. It has appeared on the reading lists of more than 100 American colleges, and has been published in a dozen foreign languages, including Gujarate, Hindu, and Tamil. In *The Affluent Society,* Galbraith raises the question of priorities and how wealth is to be divided; he poses the same question again in *The New Industrial State.* "Galbraith is an antenna and a synthesizer," says Samuelson. "He senses what is in the air and puts it together and packages it." Although his opinions are topics of much debate among economists, Galbraith has ready answers for all his critics (a group which includes University of Chicago economist Milton Friedman, Barry Goldwater's former economic advisor, and his personal friend but philosophical foe, William F. Buckley). According to Galbraith, economists are "trapped by assumptions and preconceptions which belong to an economic order that has passed into history," writes Harry Magdoff. Galbraith believes that "economics, as it is conventionally taught, is in part a system of belief designed less to reveal truth than to reassure its communicants about established social arrangements." Probably the best known economist of all time (with the possible exceptions of Adam Smith and John Maynard Keynes), Galbraith is also an outspoken critic of governmental policy, and a continual "purveyor of predictions," according to *Time.* Ken (he dislikes the name John, which honors an uncle with whom he never got along) Galbraith credits Keynes with influencing his own conversion to economics and Henry Luce for teaching him to write. Paul Booth writes "The bulk of Galbraith's proposals are for intellectuals," because Galbraith "calls for using the power he believes they have to solve the problems he outlines." And it is the work of intellectuals—their strategies for change—that give body and substance to Galbraith's theories. Galbraith's book, *The Great Crash, 1929,* is one of his first major statements on the importance of change in our economic system, although he had carefully defined his principles of economics in *A Theory of Price Control* and again in *American Capitalism: The Concept of Countervailing Power.*

Before *American Capitalism,* Galbraith had written *A Theory of Price Control,* which, although he claims "maybe fifty people read it and it had absolutely zero influence," was to him "the best book I ever wrote in many ways." He decided at that time to "engage a larger audience . . . [because then,] other economists would have to react to me. My work would not be ignored." Arthur Schlesinger, Jr., a close friend, encouraged him to write about the year 1929 (Schlesinger would say to Galbraith: "Why is it that economists have never explained the crash?"). In many ways, too, *The Great Crash, 1929* explains Galbraith's feelings about the need for our present society to be open to criticism and, thus, to want to change for what may be a better way of life. D. F. Dowd recommends *1929* to "those who have grown complacent about the present." Galbraith admits that "many things in the stock market today grow from the factors that were at work in 1929. . . . We have a new generation of innocents . . . who believe there is something about computers that's certain to make them rich."

Galbraith, who describes himself as a writer, has assigned himself the task of explaining to the public the most vital issues: the poor and big business. (Galbraith claims his height, 6 feet 8 inches, has much to do with the responsibilities he has assumed. He observed in *The Scotch:* "The superior confidence which people repose in the tall man is well merited. Being tall, he is more visible than other men and being more visible, he is much more closely watched. In consequence, his behavior is far better than that of smaller man." He's lived with the comforting belief that everyone around him is abnormally short.) He explained his method of presenting these issues to Victor Navasky: "Galbraith told me that his system is four drafts, and then on the fifth, he put in that note of spontaneity everybody likes. It is very important to develop your basic system of defense. Many people have a good case but affirm it by overstating it." Undoubtedly, Galbraith's dry wit is one of the reasons for the tremendous success of *The Affluent Society.* Gerald Carson thinks Galbraith has never been in better form "as discussant and epigrammatist. . . . [He demonstrates that] we are fighting our modern economic battles with antique weapons: muskets in the missile age. Galbraith can hit a vested interest at any range and shoot folly as it flies, in business thinking, in Washington circles, even in the professorate." The question Galbraith asks, according to the *New Republic,* is "haven't things got twisted when we produce in order to provide jobs, instead of get jobs in order to produce?" E. L. Dale points out that Galbraith finds the urgency of production "a myth." A treatise on the difficulty of avoiding depressions and inflation in our present society, *The Affluent Society* raises, in particular, three issues. Robert L. Heilbroner (who claims he has referred to *The Affluent Society* more than to any other book in the past 10 years) explains: "One of these [three issues] is the moral problem of how an Affluent Society may be prevented from becoming merely a Rich one. A second is the efficacy of Mr. Galbraith's reforms to offset the inertia and the vested interests of a powerful social structure. A third is what form of social cohesion can replace our troublesome but useful absorption in Production." According to Galbraith, "private wants could [have been] satisfied by the pluralistic economy but 'public squalor' was the outcome, for no force represented the general interest of the society in the pluralistic give-and-take of the economy," writes Booth. Finally, in his lucid and pleasantly mordant style, Galbraith offers a re-adapta-

tion of economic ideas and attitudes to the society of affluence.

As exemplified by reactions to *The Affluent Society,* misunderstanding is sometimes generated by Galbraith's work. "His book may be assailed by rightists and leftists and perhaps by middle-roaders," Nate White concludes. D. M. Potter, referring to *The Liberal Hour,* perceives that "insofar as Galbraith represents liberalism today it is a vastly different thing from the liberalism of the Thirties." Basically, Galbraith (as in *Economic Development in Perspective*) believes that money is far less important than the way society is organized and run, and that new nations should imitate each other, learning from the mistakes made by the more advanced. He has very definite beliefs on the future status of the United States; at 33 he was, in effect, personally responsible for fixing the price of virtually every item sold in the United States. Though he labels himself "Democrat" he would in any case vote for the better man. In 1969, he was quite critical of the administration, and specifically of its obsolete foreign policy. He discussed, in an interview with Michael Laurence, the major errors in our foreign policy over the past 20 years. "First," he said, "[U.S. foreign policy] relied excessively on the mystique of military power. Second, it had the vision of a unified, international Communist conspiracy, just at the time the Communist world was breaking up and giving way to the stronger force of nationalism. Third, it was rigidly and narrowly anti-Communist. Far too many issues were decided in accordance with whether they seemed to advance or impede the Cold War with what was called the Sino-Soviet bloc. And fourth, it terribly exaggerated the possible American role in bringing about desirable social change in other countries." These problems are discussed in detail in *How to Get Out of Vietnam* which deals with a war in which he believes our objectives were never really defined. Personally, Galbraith opposes all censorship and has an unabashed commitment to reform. He felt compelled for example, to expose the State Department in *The Triumph;* he believes that too many people are assuming too much responsibility for too many things. Likewise, he admits that the Chinese must be deriving a certain pleasure out of the ill will the United States is generating throughout Europe. Galbraith, who claims he has never devoted himself to any subject as much as he has to the war, told Laurence that "one major consequence of our enterprise in Vietnam was that not since the Russian Revolution has Soviet policy in Europe looked so good in comparison with that of the Western powers." He is sure that the economic consequences of peace would be most favorable.

"The test of writing about political economy is its ability to explain individual phenomena with a more fundamental analysis," and, according to Booth, "*The New Industrial State* meets that test." S. S. Smith finds that "Galbraith is a political economist like Adam Smith, Marx and Keynes. He is also, like Veblen, a social satirist, but possessed of a deadpan Scots Canadian irony and humor. . . ." This description seems to accurately characterize Galbraith as author of *The New Industrial State.* Scores of reviewers have concerned themselves with the corporate and government issues Galbraith presents therein. Probably the economic publishing event of the year, *The New Industrial State* was the stuff of a thousand debates. Galbraith believes, contrary to established liberal doctrine, that "it is no longer possible to accept the view that individual free choice is the guiding force in the economic system." He demonstrates that modern business "uses its political influence to persuade the Government to maintain full employment and total demand for all output of all firms. Moreover, by advertising, it attempts to persuade the consumer to buy what it has to sell," writes Alan Day. Galbraith "addresses himself to the social class which has been gaining in power—'the educational and scientific estate responsible for producing the educated talent and new technological knowledge on which the industrial system increasingly depends'—urging them to understand their society and to use their power to correct its deficiencies," the *Spectator* reviewer writes. *Spectator* points out that, in contrast to Marx, "Galbraith has a unique personal knowledge of the mainsprings of power in modern society and he writes extremely readably...." *Spectator* adds that *The New Industrial State* is "the crowning piece of a life-time effort to understand modern capitalism." In it, Galbraith exposes the myths. Naomi Bliven writes: "He thinks the industrial system and state are bad because they offer no higher human purpose than consumption to use up the products of industry—a lifetime of eating to guarantee the cook's job." He challenges big business. Saville R. Davis writes: "Since the men who hold the power in these big corporations do not make profits for themselves like the Rockefellers and Fords of old (the profits are paid out to countless stockholders), they are motivated by something other than profit. What is it? The exhilaration of power? The goal of constant growth measured in sales? Autonomy for their business empires? A big role in society and even in shaping society? Probably all of these.... But profits—no." Galbraith detests blind faith. He continually argues that change is built into the social structure. For Galbraith the "educational and scientific estate" offers the only possible challenge to the technostructure. In other words, the reality of the industrial system, Galbraith shows us, is the opposite of everything highlighted in the text books.

As a consequence of these economic, social, and political issues, "Galbraith finds the quality of American life defective," writes Saul Maloff; "he raises questions of the most urgent importance. In an industrial system with its 'peculiar association with weapons of unimaginable ferocity and destructiveness,' he asks: 'How are we to be saved from these?' Where the system requires, 'both in production and consumption, that individuality be suppressed,' by what means, he asks, 'if at all, is human personality to be saved?'" Galbraith has no easy answers, "but it [is] his vision, of the good in a humane society, that 'esthetic goals will have pride of place' and the 'subordinate' industrial system will become an 'essentially technical arrangement for providing convenient goods and services in adequate volume.' He calls upon those who agree with his analysis to reject the system's 'monopoly of social purpose.' Therein 'the chance for salvation lies.'"

BIOGRAPHICAL/CRITICAL SOURCES: Nation, July 20, 1955; *Christian Science Monitor,* May 29, 1958, June 17, 1967; *Chicago Sunday Tribune,* June 1, 1958; *New York Herald Tribune Book Review,* June 1, 1958; *New Republic,* June 9, 1958, July 8, 1967; *Saturday Review,* August 13, 1960; *Observer Review,* June 3, 1967; *New York Times Book Review,* June 25, 1967; *Newsweek,* June 26, 1967, July 3, 1967; *Spectator,* November 10, 1967; *New Yorker,* January 6, 1968; *Time,* February 16, 1968; *Motive,* March, 1968; *Playboy* (interview), June, 1968; *Look,* March 27, 1970; M. D. Hancock and G. Sjoberg, editors, *Politics in the Post-Welfare State,* Columbia University Press, 1972.

GALLOWAY, David D(arryl)   1937-

PERSONAL: Born May 5, 1937, in Memphis, Tenn.; son of James Henry (an attorney) and Kathlyn (Snipes) Galloway; married Sally Lee Gantt, August 22, 1959; children: Gantt Perkins. *Education:* Harvard University, B.A. (with honors), 1959; State University of New York, Ph.D., 1962. *Home:* 4 Duesseldorf-Urdenbach, Dorfstrasse 19, West Germany. *Office:* English Seminar, Ruhr University, Bochum, West Germany.

CAREER: Calasanctius Preparatory School for Gifted Boys, Buffalo, N.Y., chairman of department of English, 1961-64; State University of New York at Buffalo, lecturer in English and American studies, 1962-64; University of Sussex, Sussex, England, lecturer in English and American studies, 1964-67; University of Hamburg, Hamburg, Germany, professor of American literature, 1967-68; Case Western Reserve University, Cleveland, Ohio, associate professor of modern literature, 1968-72; Ruhr University, Bochum, Germany, chairman of American studies, 1972—. Editor, Albright-Knox Art Gallery, Buffalo, 1962-64. Lecturer on tours throughout Europe, Africa, and the Middle East; guest professor in Egypt, Kuwait, England, Scotland, and Ireland; guest curator of museum exhibitions in Europe and the Middle East. *Member:* Modern Language Association of America, American Studies Association, British Association for American Studies. *Awards, honors:* Ford Foundation grant.

WRITINGS: The Absurd Hero in American Fiction: Updike, Styron, Bellow, Salinger, University of Texas Press, 1966, revised edition, 1970; *Henry James: "The Portrait of a Lady,"* Edward Arnold, 1967; (editor, and author of introduction) Edgar Allen Poe, *Selected Writings,* Penguin, 1967; (editor with John Whitley) *Ten Modern American Short Stories,* Methuen, 1968; *Melody Jones* (novel), Calder & Boyars, 1976. Also editor and author of introduction of conference papers, *The Elizabethan Theatre,* 1969-73. Editor, *Audit Magazine,* 1960-63.

WORK IN PROGRESS: A critical biography of Edward Lewis Wallant, for Twayne; a third novel; and *The Ceremony of Innocence,* a collection of essays on the American novel.

SIDELIGHTS: Galloway speaks French, German, and Spanish. *Avocational interests:* Fine arts—a collector, dealer, and editor.

*   *   *

GALVIN, John R(ogers)   1929-

PERSONAL: Born May 13, 1929, in Melrose, Mass.; son of John James (a contractor) and Mary Josephine (Logan) Galvin; married Virginia Lee Brennan, June 5, 1961; children: Mary Jo, Elizabeth Ann. *Education:* U.S. Military Academy, B.S., 1954; Columbia University, M.A., 1962; University of Pennsylvania, further graduate study, 1963-64. *Residence:* Springfield, Va.

CAREER: U.S. Army, cadet, 1950-54, regular Infantry officer, beginning 1954, with current rank of lieutenant colonel. U.S. Army adviser to Colombian Army Rangers on counter-guerrilla operations, 1956-58; commander of rifle companies in 101st Airborne Division, 1958-60; instructor at U.S. Military Academy, West Point, N.Y., 1962-65; plans officer of 1st Calvary Division in Vietnam, 1967; military assistant to the Secretary of the Army, beginning 1968. *Member:* Thoreau Society. *Awards, honors—*Military: Bronze Star Medal, Air Medal with oak-leaf cluster, Vietnamese Honor Medal (first class). *Literary:* Revolutionary Round Table Annual Award for the year's most significant contribution to the history of the American Revolution, 1968, for *The Minute Men.*

WRITINGS: (Editor) *Western America in 1846-1847: The Original Travel Diary of Lieutenant J. W. Abert,* John Howell, 1967; *The Minute Men,* Hawthorn, 1967; *Air Assault: The Development of Airmobile Warfare,* Hawthorn, 1969; *Three Men of Boston,* Crowell, 1976. Contributor of about twenty articles to military journals.†

* * *

GANNETT, Ruth Stiles 1923-

PERSONAL: Born August 12, 1923, in New York, N.Y.; daughter of Lewis Stiles (a book reviewer) and Mary (Ross) Gannett; married H. Peter Kahn (a professor and artist), March 21, 1947; children: Charlotte, Margaret, Sarah, Hannah, Louise, Catherine, Elizabeth. *Education:* Vassar College, B.A., 1944. *Home:* 309 Mitchell St., Ithaca, N.Y. 14850.

CAREER: Author of children's books. *Awards, honors:* First prize in medium-age children's category, *New York Herald Tribune* Children's Spring Book Festival, 1948, for *My Father's Dragon.*

WRITINGS—All published by Random House: *My Father's Dragon* (Junior Literary Guild selection), 1948; *The Wonderful House-Boat Train,* 1949; *Elmer and the Dragon* (Junior Literary Guild Selection), 1950; *The Dragons of Blueland* (Junior Literary Guild selection), 1951; *Katie and the Sad Noise,* 1961.

SIDELIGHTS: Ruth Gannett told *CA:* "I do not write for children so much as for my own pleasure. Of course, I am happy if children like the stories."

* * *

GARBINI, Giovanni 1931-

PERSONAL: Born October 8, 1931, in Rome, Italy; son of Vittorio and Margherita (Virgili) Garbini; married Maria Enrica Mognaschi (a teacher), August 23, 1956; children: Paolo, Enrica. *Education:* Studied at University of Rome, 1950-54. *Religion:* Roman Catholic. *Home:* Via Piave 41, Rome, Italy 00187.

CAREER: University of Rome, Rome, Italy, associate professor of Semitic epigraphy, 1957-68; Oriental Institute, Naples, Italy, professor of Semitic philology, 1964—. Has taken part in archaeological expeditions at Ramat Rahel (Jerusalem), Tas Silg (Malta), Motya (Sicily), Monte Sirai (Sardinia), and in northern Yemen. *Military service:* Italian Army, officer, 1955-56.

WRITINGS: Il Semitico di Nord-Ovest, Oriental Institute (Naples), 1960; *Le Origini della Statuaria Sumerica,* University of Rome Press, 1962; *The Ancient World,* McGraw, 1966; *Le lingue semitiche: Studi di storia linguistica,* Oriental Institute, 1972.

WORK IN PROGRESS: Studies in Semitic historical linguistics; studies in ancient history of Yemen.

* * *

GARDINER, Judy 1922-

PERSONAL: Born May 18, 1922, in London, England; daughter of Godfrey (a major, British Army) and Millicent (onetime chorus girl) Collier; married George Gardiner (an engineer), April 6, 1946; children: David Mills, Angela Sarah-Louisa. *Education:* Educated in England. *Politics:* "Have none." *Religion:* "Have none." *Home:* Poplar Cottage, High Easter, Chelmsford, Essex, England. *Agent:* Rupert Crew Ltd., King's Mews, Gray's Inn Rd., London WC1N 2JA, England.

CAREER: Writer of fiction. *Military service:* Women's Auxiliary Air Force, 1940-43.

WRITINGS: The Power of Sergeant Mettleship (three novellas), M. Joseph, 1967; *The Dimbug* (novel), M. Joseph, 1969. Also author of television plays including "Anniversary" and "You and Your Old German." Short stories have been published in *Argosy, Housewife, Good Housekeeping, Woman's Journal, She, Woman's Realm,* and other popular magazines in Britain.

WORK IN PROGRESS: A full-length novel, *Living Doll.*

SIDELIGHTS: Judy Gardiner told *CA:* "Love France and speak French reasonably. Other great interests are music, gardens and cats. Live very harmoniously with all three in a house that is 400 years old."

* * *

GARDINER, Robert K. A. 1914-

PERSONAL: Born September 29, 1914, in Kumasi, Ghana; son of Philip H. D. and Nancy (Ferguson) Gardiner; married Linda Charlotte Edwards, July 24, 1943; children: Charlotte, George, Roberta. *Education:* University of London, extension studies, 1939-40; Cambridge University, B.A. (honors), 1941; Oxford University, graduate study, 1941-42. *Religion:* Church of England. *Office:* Commonwealth Foundation, Marlborough House Pall Mall, London S.W.1, England.

CAREER: Fourah Bay College, Freetown, Sierra Leone, lecturer, 1943-46; United Nations, New York, N.Y., member of Trusteeship Department, 1947-49; University College of Ibadan (now University of Ibadan), Ibadan, Nigeria, director of extramural studies, 1949-53; Gold Coast (now Ghana) Government, director of social welfare and community development, 1953-55; Ghana Government, permanent secretary, Ministry of Housing, 1955-57, head of Civil Service, 1957-59; United Nations, deputy executive secretary, Economic Commission for Africa, Addis Ababa, Ethiopia, 1959-60, member of U.N. Mission to the Congo, 1961, director of U.N. Division of Public Administration, 1961-62, officer in charge, U.N. Operations in the Congo, 1962-63, executive secretary, Economic Commission for Africa, Addis Ababa, Ethiopia, 1962—. Reith Lecturer, British Broadcasting Corp., 1965; Gilbert Murray Memorial Lecturer, Oxford University, 1969; J. B. Danquah Memorial Lecturer, Ghana, 1970; David Livingstone Visiting Professor, Strathclyde University, 1970—. Chairman of Commonwealth Foundation, London, England, 1970—.

MEMBER: Society for International Development. *Awards, honors:* D.C.L. from University of East Anglia, 1966, University of Sierra Leone and Tuskegee Institute, 1969, and University of Liberia, 1972; LL.D. from University of Bristol, 1966, University of Ibadan, 1967, University of East Africa, 1968, and Haile Sellassie I University, 1972; Ph.D., University of Uppsala, 1966; D.Sc. from Kumasi University, 1968, and Bradford University, 1969.

WRITINGS: (With H. O. Judd) *The Development of Social Administration,* Oxford University Press, 1955, 2nd edition, 1959; *A World of Peoples,* Longmans, Green, 1965; (editor with others) *Africa and the World,* Oxford University Press, 1970.†

GARDNER, Alan (Harold) 1925-

PERSONAL: Born August 25, 1925, in Ilford, Essex, England; son of Alfred (a toy wholesaler and retailer) and Gladys (May) Gardner; married August 23, 1951, wife's name Joan Rosemary; children: Sally Anne, Simon Alan. *Education:* Attended Newton College, Devonshire, England, and Downing College, Cambridge. *Politics:* Rightwing Conservative. *Home:* 82 Riverside Dr., Solihull, West Midlands, England. *Office:* Lucas Industries, Great King St., Birmingham, England.

CAREER: Formerly on staff of *Daily Mail,* London, England, and foreign correspondent in New York, Washington, D.C., and Rome; Ford Motor Co., Warley, Essex, England, press and information manager, 1962-67; public affairs director, Cameras/Rothmans (tobacco company), 1967-71; affiliated with Lucas Industries, Birmingham, England, 1971—. *Military service:* Royal Air Force, 1939-45; served in Far East; became sergeant; received Burma Star and Air Medal.

WRITINGS: The Escalator, Muller, 1962; *Assignment Tahiti,* Muller, 1964; *Six-Day Week,* Coward, 1966; *The Man Who Was Too Much,* Muller, 1967; *The Hibernation of Ginger Scrubb,* Muller, 1968. Contributor to *Saturday Review.*

SIDELIGHTS: Gardner's manuscripts and papers are held by Chenery Library, Boston University. He speaks Italian and French, plays golf for recreation, and has a waterfront apartment in Santa Ponsa, Mallorca where he spends all of his spare time.

* * *

GARDNER, David P(ierpont) 1933-

PERSONAL: Born March 24, 1933, in Berkeley, Calif.; son of Reed Snow (a banker) and Margaret (Pierpont) Gardner; married Elizabeth Fuhriman (a dental hygienist), June 27, 1958; children: four daughters. *Education:* Brigham Young University, B.S., 1955; University of California, Berkeley, M.A., 1959, Ph.D., 1966. *Religion:* Church of Jesus Christ of Latter-day Saints. *Home:* 2951 Sherwood Dr., Salt Lake City, Utah 84108. *Office:* Office of the President, 202 Park Building, University of Utah, Salt Lake City, Utah 84112.

CAREER: California Farm Bureau Federation, Berkeley, administrative assistant, 1958-60; University of California Alumni Association, Berkeley, field and scholarship director, 1960-62, director of California Alumni Foundation, 1962-64; University of California, Santa Barbara, assistant to the chancellor, 1964-67, assistant chancellor, 1967-69, vice chancellor, 1969-70, assistant professor, 1966-69, associate professor, 1969-70, professor of higher education, 1970-73; University of California, Berkeley, vice-president of public service programs and university dean of University Extension, all campuses, 1971-72, vice-president of extended academic and public service programs, all campuses, 1972-73; University of Utah, Salt Lake City, professor of higher education, 1973—, president, 1973—. University of California, member and chairman of numerous committees and boards, 1968-73, representative on Title I Advisory Committee at State of California Coordinating Council for Higher Education, 1971-73; chairman of national board for courses by newspaper, National Endowment for the Humanities; member of presidents council, National Association of State Universities and Land-Grant Colleges, and Western Athletic Conference. Member of board of directors of Utah Symphony, Utah Power and Light Co., and Salt Lake City Branch of Federal Reserve Bank of San Francisco; member of Greater Salt Lake Council of Boy Scouts of America. *Military service:* U.S. Army, 1955-57; served with Army Intelligence in Japan and Korea. *Member:* American Association for Higher Education, American Association of University Professors, Phi Kappa Phi.

WRITINGS: The California Oath Controversy, University of California Press, 1967; (contributor) Verne A. Stadtman, editor, *The Centennial Record of the University of California,* University of California Press, 1967; (contributor) Dale L. Brubaker, editor, *Social Studies in a Mass Society,* International Textbook, 1969; (contributor) *A Convocation Anthology: Problems, Goals and Research in Higher Education,* Campus Convocation Committee, University of California, 1969; (contributor) Douglas Knight, editor, *Cybernetics Simulation and Conflict Resolution,* Spartan Books, 1970; (contributor) Ann M. Heiss, Joseph R. Mixer, and James G. Paltridge, editors, *Participants and Patterns in Higher Education: Research and Reflections—A Festschrift for T. R. McConnell,* School of Education, University of California, 1973; (contributor) Sterling M. McMurrin, editor, *On the Meaning of the University,* University of Utah Press, in press. Contributor to *Los Angeles Times,* and professional journals.

* * *

GARDNER, Mary A(delaide) 1920-

PERSONAL: Born July 19, 1920, in Kingston, Ohio; daughter of J. P. (a veterinarian) and Wyland (Davis) Gardner. *Education:* Stephens College, A.A., 1940; Ohio State University, B.A., 1942, M.A., 1953; University of Minnesota, Ph.D., 1960; also studied creative writing at Evansville College (now University of Evansville), 1942-43, and Spanish at Mexico City College, 1952, and University of San Marcos, 1954-55. *Office:* School of Journalism, Michigan State University, East Lansing, Mich. 48824.

CAREER: Mead Johnson & Co., Evansville, Ind., bacteriologist, 1942-43; U.S. Army, Special Services, club director (as civilian), in Austria, 1948-51; *Minneapolis Star,* Minneapolis, Minn., assistant for World Affairs Program, 1957-59, copy editor, 1960-61; University of Texas, Austin, assistant professor of journalism, 1961-66; Michigan State University, East Lansing, assistant professor, 1966-70, associate professor, 1970-75, professor of journalism, 1975—. Guest lecturer, University of Minnesota, 1960-61. Consultant, El Norte, Mexico, summers, 1970, 1972, 1974, and 1975. *Military service:* U.S. Marine Corps Reserve, 1943—; active duty, 1943-46; now colonel, and liaison officer at Michigan State University. *Member:* Association for Education in Journalism, Latin American Studies Association, Women in Communications, Delta Sigma, Chi Delta Pi. *Awards, honors:* Stephens College Alumna Recognition Award, 1965; Teaching Excellence Award, University of Texas, 1966.

WRITINGS: The Inter-American Press Association: Its Fight for Freedom of the Press, 1926-60, Institute of Latin American Studies, University of Texas, 1967; *The Press of Latin America: A Tentative and Selected Bibliography in Spanish and Portuguese,* Institute of Latin American Studies, University of Texas, 1973. Also author of *Press of Guatemala* (monograph), 1971. Contributor to newspapers and magazines.

WORK IN PROGRESS: Research on the right of reply as a journalistic concept; the professionalization of journalists in Chile and Costa Rica through colegiacion (formation of a collegiate group).

*   *   *

GARDNER, Richard 1931-
(Dic Gardner; pseudonyms, John Carver, Richard Cummings, Richard Orth; Clifford Anderson, a joint pseudonym)

PERSONAL: Surname originally Orth; born August 26, 1931, in Bremerton, Wash.; son of Maurice (an attorney) and Alice (Cummine) Orth; married Lois Schriner, June 21, 1952 (divorced); children: Diana, Adam. Education: Washington State College (now Washington State University), B.A., 1953. Residence: New York, N.Y. Agent: Don Congdon, Harold Matson Co., Inc., 22 East 40th St., New York, N.Y. 10016.

CAREER: Station KMO-TV, Tacoma, Wash., floor manager, 1953; Station KOMO-TV, Seattle, Wash., writer, performer, puppeteer, producer, director, 1954-55, 1959-61; Macfadden Publications, New York, N.Y., junior editor, 1956; full-time professional writer, 1961—.

WRITINGS: The Impossible (nonfiction), Ballantine, 1962; Scandalous John (adult novel), Doubleday, 1963; Grito! Reies Tijerina and the New Mexico Land Grant War of 1967 (nonfiction), Bobbs-Merrill, 1970; The Adventures of Don Juan (novel), Viking, 1974; Mandrill (novel), Pocket Books, 1975; The Dragon Breath Papers (novel), Viking, 1976.

Juveniles under name Dic Gardner; all published by John Day, except as noted: (Self-illustrated) Your Backyard Circus (nonfiction), 1959; (self-illustrated) Be on TV (nonfiction), 1960; Danny and the Ape, Komba, 1962; (self-illustrated) Is My Job for You? (nonfiction), 1962; The Bridge (Junior Literary Guild selection), 1963; The Baboon (nonfiction), Macmillan, 1972.

Paperback novels under pseudonym John Carver; all published by Universal Publishing: The Sex Twist, 1962; The Shame of Jenny, 1963; The Scuba Set, 1964; Campus Nymphs, 1964; Undress Rehearsal, 1965; The Fair Young Wives, 1966; Weekend Partners, 1966; That Motorcycle Boy, 1966; Suburban Hotbed, 1967; Wolverine, 1967.

Paperback novels under name Richard Orth: The Pad Upstairs, Universal Publishing, 1966; Girl in a Go-Go Cage, Universal Publishing, 1967.

Juvenile nonfiction under pseudonym Richard Cummings; all published by McKay: (Self-illustrated) 101 Hand Puppets, 1962; The Alchemists, 1966; 101 Masks, 1967; 101 Costumes for All Ages, All Occasions, 1972; Make Your Own Comics for Fun and Profit, 1976.

With Clifford Irving and Robert Anderson, under joint pseudonym Clifford Anderson: The Hollow Hero (novel), Ace Books, 1959.

Author of one-act play, "Family Shelter," produced by Overplayers, San Francisco, 1962.

WORK IN PROGRESS: Freud and Jung at Niagara Falls, a novel for Viking; a musical comedy, "Bernarr"; a three-act play, "The Death of Errol Flynn."

SIDELIGHTS: Gardner told CA: "Primary interest in writing comic and satirical novels. . . . Write because I do not believe we live in the best of all possible worlds."

*   *   *

GARMON, William S. 1926-
PERSONAL: Born May 17, 1926, in Centre, Ala.; son of John Russell and Jewel (Harris) Garmon; married Virginia Miller (a secretary), December 21, 1947 (divorced); children: William S. II, Clayton T. M. Education: Auburn University, student, 1942-44; Samford University, B.A., 1948; George Peabody College for Teachers, M.A., 1949; New Orleans Baptist Theological Seminary, B.D. and Th.D., 1956. Politics: Democrat. Home address: Box 508A, Route 5, Danville, Va. 24541.

CAREER: Baptist clergyman; served small rural churches as pastor, 1948-56; New Orleans Baptist Theological Seminary, New Orleans, La., associate professor of social ethics, 1956-68; Averett College, Danville, Va., professor of sociology and co-ordinator of department of sociology and social work, 1968—. Military service: U.S. Army Air Forces, 1944-46; special agent, Counterintelligence Corps, 1946; became sergeant. Member: Religious Research Association, National Council on Crime and Delinquency, Southern Sociological Association.

WRITINGS: The Many Faces of Ethyl, Broadman, 1966; (contributor) Ross Coggins, editor, The Gambling Menace, Broadman, 1966; Mission Action Group Guide: Prisoner Rehabilitation, Brotherhood Commission of the Southern Baptist Convention, 1968; Who Are the Criminals?, Broadman, 1968; (with Phil D. Strickland) How to Fight the Drug Menace, Broadman, 1970. Contributor to religious journals.

AVOCATIONAL INTERESTS: Gardening and reading.

*   *   *

GARNER, William R(obin) 1936-
PERSONAL: Born May 4, 1936, in Dallas, Tex.; son of William Calvin (a contractor) and Lora V. (Robinson) Garner; married Mary Louise Blietz. Education: Baylor University, B.A., 1957; Southern Methodist University, M.A., 1959; Tulane University, Ph.D., 1963. Politics: Democratic. Religion: Roman Catholic. Home: 904 Glenview Dr., Carbondale, Ill. 62901. Office: Department of Political Science, Southern Illinois University, Carbondale, Ill. 62901.

CAREER: University of Southwestern Louisiana, Lafayette, instructor, 1960-63, assistant professor of political science, 1963; North Texas State University, Denton, assistant professor of government, 1963-66; Southern Illinois University, Carbondale, associate professor of government, 1966—. Visiting professor, Midwestern University, 1968, and Tulane University, 1971. U.S. Episcopal delegate to World Council of Churches Latin American Conference on the Life and Mission of the Church, Mexico City, 1962. Member: International Studies Association, American Political Science Association, American Academy of Political and Social Science, American Association of University Professors, Latin American Studies Association, Midwest Conference of Political Scientists, Midwest Association for Latin American Studies, Southwestern Political Science Association, Southwestern Social Science Association, Southwest Conference of Latin American Studies, Southern Political Science Association. Awards, honors: Graham Distinguished Teaching Award, North Texas State University, 1966.

WRITINGS: The Chaco Dispute: A Study of Prestige Diplomacy, Public Affairs Press, 1966; (contributor) Stephen L. Wasby, editor, Political Science, The Discipline and Its Dimensions: An Introduction, Scribner, 1970.

WORK IN PROGRESS: A text, Latin American Government and Political Processes: A Psychological Interpretation.

* * *

GARRIGAN, Owen (Walter) 1928-

PERSONAL: Born September 20, 1928, in Newark, N.J.; son of Walter Clark and Helen Salmi (Chase) Garrigan. Education: Seton Hall University, A.B., 1950; Catholic University of America, S.T.L., 1954; Columbia University, Ph.D., 1960. Home and office: Seton Hall University, South Orange, N.J. 07079.

CAREER: Roman Catholic priest, ordained 1954; Seton Hall Preparatory School, South Orange, N.J., teacher, 1954-56; Seton Hall University, South Orange, N.J., instructor, 1960-61, assistant professor, 1961-64, associate professor of chemistry, 1964—. Member: American Chemical Society (national councilor, 1964-69), American Association for the Advancement of Science, Catholic Theological Society of America, Chemical Society (London), New York Lipid Club, Sigma Xi, Phi Lambda Upsilon. Awards, honors: U.S. Public Health Service research grant, 1961-67.

WRITINGS: Man's Intervention in Nature, Hawthorn, 1967. Contributor to New Catholic Encyclopedia, Catholic World, and to scientific and theological journals.

* * *

GATENBY, Rosemary 1918-

PERSONAL: First syllable of surname rhymes with "late"; born October 8, 1918, in Muncie, Ind.; daughter of Samuel Orr (an automotive engineer) and Edna (Cooper) White; married William Hal Gatenby (an executive), September 14, 1945; children: Halley, Jane. Education: Wellesley College, B.A., 1940; additional study at Columbia University, 1940-41, and University of Toledo, 1948. Politics: Republican. Religion: Presbyterian. Residence: Weston, Conn.

CAREER: Sperry Gyroscope Co., Long Island, N.Y., secretary, 1942-45; free-lance writer.

WRITINGS—All mystery novels, except as noted: Evil Is as Evil Does, Mill, 1967; Aim to Kill, Mill, 1968; Deadly Relations, Morrow, 1970; Hanged for a Sheep, Dodd, 1973; (contributor) A. S. Burack, editor, Techniques of Novel Writing (text), Writer, Inc., 1973; The Season of Danger, Dodd, 1974.

* * *

GATES, Natalie

PERSONAL: Born in Indianapolis, Ind.; daughter of John Tomlinson and Elsie (Lombard) Brush; married Bennett Gates, April 6, 1926 (divorced); married Rene DeGendron, July 20, 1965 (divorced); stepchildren: three. Education: Studied at Baldwin School, Columbia University, New School for Social Research, and City University of New York. Politics: Republican. Religion: Agnostic. Address: 1056 Fifth Ave., New York, N.Y. 10028. Agent: Blanche C. Gregory, Inc., 2 Tudor City Pl., New York, N.Y. 10017.

CAREER: Ran a motion picture theater (as a public service) for more than two decades. Nantucket Cottage Hospital, director and chairman of accreditation committee. Member: Association of the Junior Leagues of America (past vice-president).

WRITINGS: Hush Hush Johnson (novel), Holt, 1967; Decoy in Diamonds (novel), Putnam, 1971.

SIDELIGHTS: Natalie Gates told CA: "[I] have flown around the world and traveled up and down it and sailed on most of the seas."

* * *

GATLIN, Douglas S. 1928-

PERSONAL: Born May 2, 1928, in Jacksonville, Fla.; son of William Arthur (an insurance executive) and Claire (Denby) Gatlin. Education: University of Florida, B.A., 1955, M.A., 1956; University of North Carolina, Ph.D., 1963. Office: Florida Atlantic University, Boca Raton, Fla. 33432.

CAREER: Wake Forest College (now University), Winston-Salem, N.C., assistant professor of political science, 1960-64; Florida Atlantic University, Boca Raton, associate professor, 1964-70, professor of political science, 1970—, chairman of department, 1975—. Military service: U.S. Army, 1951-53. Member: American Political Science Association, Southwestern Political Science Association, Southern Political Science Association.

WRITINGS: (Editor with William J. Crotty and Donald M. Freeman) Political Parties and Political Behavior, Allyn & Bacon, 1966; (contributor) William C. Crotty, editor, New Approaches to the Study of Party Organizations, Allyn & Bacon, 1968; (contributor) James A. Robinson, editor, State Legislative Innovations, Praeger, 1973. Contributor of articles and book reviews to Social Science Quarterly, Public Opinion Quarterly, Journal of Politics, and American Political Science Review.

* * *

GAY, Kathlyn 1930-

PERSONAL: Born March 4, 1930, in Zion, Ill.; daughter of Kenneth Charles and Beatrice (Anderson) McGarrahan; married Arthur L. Gay (an elementary principal), August 28, 1948; children: Martin, Douglas, Karen. Education: Attended Northern Illinois University, two years. Politics: Registered Democrat. Religion: "No affiliation." Home and office: 1711 East Beardsley Ave., Elkhart, Ind. 46514. Agent: Hoffman-Sheedy Literary Agency, 145 West 86th St., New York, N.Y. 10024.

CAREER: Church World Service, Christian Rural Overseas Program (CROP), editor and public relations writer in Elkhart, Ind., and New York, N.Y., 1962-65; Juhl Advertising Agency, Elkhart, publicity and public relations writer, 1966; free-lance writer, 1966—; partner in promotional services business, 1971—. Writing consultant to Lyons & Carnahan, 1969-70, Ginn & Co., 1971, and Science Research Association, 1972-73; instructor in creative writing, Elkhart Area Career Center. Staff writer, Mayor Richard J. Daley's political campaign in Chicago, 1967. Member: Authors Guild. Awards, honors: Honorable mention in Writer's Digest short story contest, 1962; first prize in literary section, Northern Indiana Arts Festival, 1965, for one-act play.

WRITINGS: Girl Pilot, Messner, 1966; Money Isn't Everything: The Story of Economics, Delacorte, 1967; Meet the Mayor of Your City, Hawthorn, 1967; Beth Speaks Out, Messner, 1968; Meet the Governor of Your State, Hawthorn, 1968; Careers in Social Service, Messner, 1969; Where the People Are: Cities and Their Future, Delacorte, 1969.

The Germans Helped Build America, Messner, 1971; *Core English: English for Speakers of Other Languages,* Ginn, 1972; *A Family is for Living,* Delacorte, 1972; *Body Talk,* Scribner, 1974; *Be a Smart Shopper,* Messner, 1974. Also prepared teachers manuals including activities and stories for Ginn & Co., Science Research Associates, and Lynons & Carnahan. Contributor of articles to *American Home, Ebony, Women's World, Women in Business, Popular Medicine, Family Digest,* and other periodicals; contributor of short stories to *Highlights for Children, Child Life, Instructor,* and other magazines.

WORK IN PROGRESS: An adult novel based on the history of a theocratic community in Illinois at the turn of the century; a young adult novel about an interracial family; *Care and Share,* for Messner; a documentary about black-white marriages/unions.

*   *   *

GAYLIN, Willard M.   1925-

PERSONAL: Born February 23, 1925, in Cleveland, Ohio; son of Harry C. and Fay (Baumgard) Gaylin; married Betty Schafer, June 15, 1947; children: Joan Deborah, Ellen Andrea. *Education:* Harvard University, A.B., 1947; Western Reserve (now Case Western Reserve) University, M.D., 1951; Columbia University, Certificate in Psychoanalytic Medicine, 1956. *Office:* Psychoanalytic School, Columbia University, New York, N.Y. 10027.

CAREER: Cleveland City Hospital, Cleveland, Ohio, intern, 1951-52; Veterans Administration Hospital, Bronx, N.Y., resident in psychiatry, 1952-54; Columbia University, Psychoanalytic School, faculty member, 1956—, training and supervising psychoanalyst, 1961, clinical professor of psychiatry, 1972—. President of Institute of Society, Ethics and the Life Sciences, 1970—; adjunct professor of psychiatry, Union Theological Seminary (N.Y.); adjunct professor of psychiatry and law at Columbia University, School of Law. Visiting professor at Emory University, Medical School; Elizabeth Cutter Morrow Lecturer at Smith College, 1970; visiting lecturer at colleges and universities throughout the United States, and at University of Paris, Sorbonne. Consultant to American Medical Association Judicial Council, and to Institute de la Vie at University of Paris; member of Commission on Psychoanalytic Education and Research. Member of board of directors, Field Foundation, and Penal Reform Institute. American Civil Liberties Union, named to Prisoner's Rights Study, member of advisory committee on amnesty; member, Committee for Public Justice, and Goodell Commission for Studies of Incarceration. *Military service:* U.S. Navy, 1943-45. *Member:* American Psychoanalytic Association, American Psychiatric Association (fellow), New York Psychiatric Society. *Awards, honors:* George E. Daniels Medal of Merit for contributions to psychoanalytic medicine; *In the Service of Their Country* named one of fifteen notable books of the year by American Library Association; Yale University Chubb Fellow, 1972.

WRITINGS: (With H. Hendrin and A. Carr) *Psychoanalysis and Social Research,* Doubleday, 1965; (compiler) *The Meaning of Despair,* Science House, 1968; *In the Service of Their Country: War Resisters in Prison,* Viking, 1970; (contributor) Harry M. Clor, editor, *Censorship and Freedom of Expression: Essays on Obscenity and the Law,* Rand, 1971; (contributor) Murray Polner, editor, *When Can I Come Home: A Debate on Amnesty for Exiles, Antiwar Prisoners, and Others,* Anchor Press, 1972; (with R.

Veatch and C. Morgan) *The Teaching of Medical Ethics,* Hastings Center Publications, 1973; *At the Heart of Judgement: A Study of Bias in Judges,* Knopf, 1974; (editor with others) *Operating on the Mind,* Basic Books, 1974; *Partial Justice: A Study of Bias in Sentencing,* Knopf, 1974. Contributor to newspapers and journals.

WORK IN PROGRESS: A study on judicial bias under a grant from Field Foundation; a two year study on ethics of behavior control.

*   *   *

GEARHEART, B(ill) R.   1928-

PERSONAL: Born September 5, 1928, in Wichita, Kan.; son of H. Floyd (a decorator) and Lucille (Hooker) Gearheart; married Jean Wood, June 4, 1950 (divorced); children: Mark, Leslie Jean, Susan. *Education:* Friends University, Wichita, Kan., B.A., 1949; Wichita State University, M.Ed., 1955; Colorado State College (now University of Northern Colorado), Ed.D., 1963. *Religion:* Methodist. *Home:* 2209 20th Street Rd., Greeley, Colo. 80631.

CAREER: Wichita (Kan.) public schools, teacher of mathematics and science, 1949-51, principal, 1953-59; Cedar Rapids (Iowa) public schools, director of special services and assistant superintendent, 1960-66; University of Northern Colorado, Greeley, 1966—, began as associate professor, now professor of special education. *Military service:* U.S. Naval Reserve, 1951-53; served in the Atlantic and with Sixth Fleet; became lieutenant junior grade.

WRITINGS: Administration of Special Education, C. C Thomas, 1967; (with E. Willenberg) *Application of Pupil Assessment Information: For the Special Education Teacher,* Love Publishing, 1970, revised edition, 1974; (editor and contributor) *Education of the Exceptional Child: History, Present Practices and Trends,* International Textbook, 1972; *Learning Disabilities: Educational Strategies,* Mosby, 1973; *Organization and Administration of Programs for the Exceptional Child,* C. C Thomas, 1974; (with F. Litton) *The Trainable Retarded: A Foundations Approach,* Mosby, 1975; (with M. Weishahn) *The Handicapped Child in the Regular Classroom,* Mosby, 1976; *Teaching the Learning Disabled: A Combined Task/Process Approach,* Mosby, 1976.

*   *   *

GEIER, Woodrow A.   1914-

PERSONAL: Born October 3, 1914, in Anniston, Ala.; son of Louis Charles (an iron worker) and Minnie (Parsons) Geier; married Rosemary Parkman (a social worker), December 9, 1939; children: Janet Lynn (Mrs. French W. Jernigan), Gail Ellen (Mrs. Richard C. Wilkerson), Carl David. *Education:* University of Alabama, B.A., 1938; Vanderbilt University, B.D., 1943, Ph.D., 1959. *Politics:* Independent Democrat. *Home:* 4036 Overbrook Ct., Nashville, Tenn. 37204.

CAREER: Ordained Methodist clergyman. Reporter, and later editor of a newspaper in Anniston, Ala., 1937-40; Methodist Publishing House, Nashville, Tenn., assistant editor, 1940-41, editor of *Pastor* (magazine), 1941-47, associate editor of adult publications, 1947-53; The Methodist Church, Board of Education, Nashville, Tenn., associate director of public relations and finance, 1953-57, director of information and publications, 1957-75; free-lance writer. Visiting professor of drama, Scarritt College, 1960—; sometime teacher of journalism at Vanderbilt University and University of Tennessee at Nashville, Consultant to church editorial projects.

WRITINGS: (Editor) *Studies in Christian Higher Education,* fourteen volumes, Board of Education, The Methodist Church, 1956-74; *The Campus Ministry of the Methodist Church,* Board of Education, The Methodist Church, 1967; *A Mayfarer's Book of Devotion,* Abingdon, 1973; *Sanctuary for Lust,* Abingdon, 1974. Also author of *The Corinthian Correspondence,* a curriculum resource, 1976. Contributor of articles and reviews to *Christian Century, Religion in Life, School and Society,* and other periodicals.

WORK IN PROGRESS: A book on language, drama, and the devotional life; a book on the Christian view of economics; monographs on contemporary dramatists as interpreters of religion.

AVOCATIONAL INTERESTS: Community theater, music, gardening, travel.

* * *

GELERNT, Jules 1928-

PERSONAL: Surname is pronounced Gel-*urnt;* born July 13, 1928, in Berlin, Germany; son of Henoch and Anya (Kaminska) Gelernt; married Rosalie Sacks, August 3, 1958; children: Mark David, Karen Beth. *Education:* City College (now City College of the City University of New York), B.A., 1949; Columbia University, M.A., 1950, Ph.D., 1963. *Office:* Department of English, Brooklyn College of the City University of New York, Brooklyn, N.Y. 11210.

CAREER: Hofstra University, Hempstead, N.Y., instructor in English, 1956-63; Brooklyn College of the City University of New York, Brooklyn, N.Y., 1963—, began as assistant professor, became professor of English, chairman of department, 1975—. *Military service:* U.S. Army, 1951-53. *Member:* Modern Language Association of America, Renaissance Society of America, Dante Society of America, Phi Beta Kappa.

WRITINGS: World of Many Loves: The Heptameron of Marguerite de Navarre, University of North Carolina Press, 1966. Writer of review notes for Dante's *Divine Comedy,* Monarch Books, 1963.

WORK IN PROGRESS: Literary Theory in Dante; a comparative study of Italian, French, and English Renaissance lyrics.

* * *

GELLINEK, Christian 1930-

PERSONAL: Surname is accented on first syllable, and pronounced with hard "g"; born May 5, 1930, in Potsdam, Germany; son of Christian (a professor) and Margaretha (Lorenzen) Gellinek; married Jose E. Schellekens, June 26, 1975. *Education:* University of Goettingen, student, 1953-57; University of Toronto, B.A., 1959; Yale University, M.A., 1963, Ph.D., 1964. *Religion:* "Calvinist-reformed." *Home:* 6510 Lakeshore Dr., Gainesville, Fla. 32611. *Office:* German Department, University of Florida, Gainesville, Fla. 32601.

CAREER: Pickering College, Newmarket, Ontario, head of German and Latin department, 1959-61; Yale University, New Haven, Conn., instructor, 1964-66, assistant professor, 1966-68, associate professor of German, 1968-71; University of Florida, Gainesville, professor of German,

1971—. *Member:* Modern Language Association of America, Mediaeval Academy of America, American Association of Teachers of German, Anglo-Norman Text Society, American Association of University Professors. *Awards, honors:* Morse fellow, 1965-66.

WRITINGS: Koenig Rother: Studie zur literarischen Deutung, Francke (Berne), 1968; *Programmed German Dictionary,* Prentice-Hall, 1968; *Kaiserchronik,* Athenaeum-Verlag (Frankfurt), 1971. Contributor to *Studia Gratiana* and other journals.

WORK IN PROGRESS: Prolegomena to Twelfth-Century Poetics; studies on the language learning process and the epistemological analysis of German.

* * *

GEMME, Francis Robert 1934-

PERSONAL: Surname is pronounced Gem; born May 3, 1934, in Hartford, Conn.; son of Emmet Richard (a rigger) and Mary (Hannon) Gemme; married Leila Frances Boyle (a teacher), August 20, 1964; children: Michael Antisdale. *Education:* University of Hartford, B.A., 1957; Trinity College, Hartford, Conn., graduate courses, 1957-63; University of Connecticut, M.A., 1966; University of Massachusetts, graduate study, 1966-68. *Agent:* Leon Balukas Associates, Hartford, Conn.

CAREER: Part-time jobs, 1950-57, included over the road van driver and psychiatric aide; English teacher in Hoosick, N.Y., 1957-58; *Hartford Courant,* Hartford, Conn., proofreader, 1958-59; Milford Academy, Milford, Conn., instructor in English, 1959-66, chairman of department, 1961-66, alumni director, 1964-66; American Education Publications (a Xerox company), Middletown, Conn., manager of elementary paperback programs, 1968-70; Young Readers Press, New York, N.Y., publisher and president, 1970—. Lecturer in American literature and language, Middlesex College, Middletown, 1968-70; faculty consultant, Institute for Children's Literature, 1970—. *Member:* Modern Language Association of America, College English Association, National Council of Teachers of English, Connecticut Historical Society, Milford Historical Society, Northampton Historical Society, Conference of Early American Literature.

WRITINGS: (Author of critical commentary) John Hersey, *A Bell for Adano and Hiroshima,* Monarch Press, 1966; (contributor) Robert F. Beauchamp, editor, *Creative Approaches to Reading Fiction,* Xerox Education Division, 1968; (contributor) Robert M. Bleiweiss, editor, *Marching to Freedom: The Life of Martin Luther King,* Xerox Education Division, 1968; (contributor) Mary Lou Kennedy, editor, *Paperbacks in the Elementary School,* Xerox Education Division, 1969. Publications include "Monarch Review Notes" to works of Thornton Wilder, Sinclair Lewis, Washington Irving, Esther Forces, and Owen Wister, Monarch Books, 1965-66, and introductions to about twenty paperback classics, Airmont, 1964-68. Contributor of articles and reviews to education journals.

WORK IN PROGRESS: Jonathan Edwards: The Northampton Years, a book-length biography; *Robert Wooster Stallman: A Bibliography; Stephen Vincent Benet: A Bibliography; Witchcraft in the Connecticut Valley.*

SIDELIGHTS: Gemme has reading knowledge of Latin, French, and German. *Avocational interests:* The Connecticut River Valley, its antiquities and folklore.†

GENDZIER, Irene Lefel 1936-

PERSONAL: Surname is pronounced Gen-zir; born March 24, 1936, in Paris, France; children: Alexander Amos. Education: Barnard College, B.A. (with honors in history), 1957; Columbia University, M.A., 1959, Ph.D., 1964. Office: History Department, Boston University, 226 Bay State Rd., Boston, Mass. 02215.

CAREER: Barnard College, New York, N.Y., lecturer in history, 1958-60; Boston University, Boston, Mass., instructor, 1961-64, assistant professor, 1965-69, associate professor, 1969-74, professor of history, 1974—. Harvard University, Center for Middle Eastern Studies, Cambridge, Mass., research fellow, 1964-65, honorary research associate, 1966—, member of Extension School faculty, 1967-69, 1972. Lecturer at various educational institutions including: University of Chicago, University of London, University of Texas at Austin, Hiatt Institute (Israel), Harvard University, and others. Member: American Historical Association, Middle East Institute, Middle East Studies Association (fellow), Society of Radcliffe Institute, Phi Beta Kappa. Awards, honors: Woodrow Wilson fellowship, 1957; Ford Foundation grant for studies in the Middle East, 1957-58; National Endowment for the Humanities fellowship, 1969-70; Radcliffe Institute fellow, 1972-73.

WRITINGS: The Practical Visions of Yaqub Sanu', Harvard University Press, 1966; (editor) Middle East Reader, Pegasus, 1970; (contributor) H. Mason, editor, Reflections on the Middle East, Mouton, 1970; Frantz Fanon: A Critical Study, Pantheon, 1973; (contributor) Noam Chomsky, editor, Peace in the Middle East? Reflections on Justice and Nationhood, Pantheon, 1974; (contributor) Emmanuel Hansen, editor, Frantz Fanon: Social and Political Thought, Ohio State University, in press. Contributor to Die Welt des Islams, Partisan Review, Etudes Mediterraneennes (Paris), The Middle East Journal, American Anthropologist, and others.

WORK IN PROGRESS: A Critique of Modernization Theory: Selected Problems, for Pantheon.

*   *   *

GEORGESCU-ROEGEN, Nicholas 1906-

PERSONAL: Born February 4, 1906, in Constanza, Rumania; son of Stavru (an army officer) and Maria (Niculescu) Georgescu; married Otilia Busuioc, September 2, 1934. Education: University of Bucharest, M.A., 1926; Sorbonne, University of Paris, D.Stat., 1930; University College, University of London, postdoctoral research, 1930-31. Religion: Orthodox. Home: 2614 Hemingway Dr., Nashville, Tenn. 37215. Office: Vanderbilt University, Nashville, Tenn. 37235.

CAREER: University of Bucharest, Bucharest, Rumania, professor of statistics, 1932-46; Harvard University, Cambridge, Mass., lecturer and research associate in econometrics, 1948-49; Vanderbilt University, Nashville, Tenn., professor of economics and statistics, 1949-69, Distinguished Professor of Economics, 1969—. Posts in Rumania included assistant director of Central Statistical Institute, Bucharest, 1932-39, economic adviser to Treasury Department, 1938-39, delegate to Committee on Peaceful Change, League of Nations, 1938, and secretary-general of the Rumanian Armistice Commission, 1944-45. Rockefeller visiting professor in Japan, 1962-63; Ford Foundation visiting lecturer and consultant in Brazil, 1964; visiting professor at University of Sao Paulo, 1966, adviser, 1966-67. Member of National Research Council, 1973—.

MEMBER: Econometric Society (fellow), International Institute of Sociology (fellow), International Institute of Statistics, American Economic Association (distinguished fellow), American Academy of Arts and Sciences (fellow), American Association for the Advancement of Science, Southern Economic Association, Societe de Statistique de Paris. Awards, honors: Rockefeller fellowship in United States, 1934-36; Guggenheim fellow and Fulbright scholar in Italy, 1958-59; Harvie Branscomb Distinguished Professor Award, 1967.

WRITINGS: Methoda Statistica, Institului Central de Statistica (Bucharest), 1933; Un quantum-index pentru comertul exterior al Romaniei, Institutului Central de Statistica, 1938; (associate editor and contributor of three chapters) Activity Analysis of Production and Allocation, edited by T. C. Koopmans, Wiley, 1951; Analytical Economics: Issues and Problems, Harvard University Press, 1966; La Science eonomique: Ses Problemes et ses difficultes, Dunod, 1970; The Entropy Law and the Economic Problem, University of Alabama Press, 1971; The Entropy Law and the Economic Process, Harvard University Press, 1971; Analisi economica e processo economico, Sansoni (Italy), 1973; Economic Essays, Ottawa University Press, 1976.

Contributor: Jean Mary Bowman, editor, Expectations, Uncertainty, and Business Behavior, Social Science Research Council, 1958; Essays on Econometrics and Planning, Presented to Professor P. C. Mahalanobis, Pergamon, 1964; C. Eicher and L. Witt, editors, Agriculture in Economic Development, McGraw, 1964; R. E. Kuenne, editor, Monopolistic Competition: Studies in Impact, Wiley, 1967; U. Papi, editor, Economic Problems of Agriculture in Industrial Societies, Macmillan, 1969; C. R. Wharton, Jr., editor, Subsistence Agriculture and Economic Development, Aldine, 1969; G. M. Meier, editor, Leading Issues in Economic Development, Oxford University Press, 1970; Paul M. Sweezy and others, editors, La Teoria dello sviluppo capitalistico, Boringheri, 1970; H. Daly, editor, Toward a Steady-State Economy, W. H. Freeman, 1973; R. E. Neel, Readings in Price Theory, Southwestern Co., 1973.

Editor and contributor, Enciclopedia Romaniei, four volumes, [Bucharest], 1938-43. Contributor to International Encyclopedia of Social Sciences, Dictionary of the History of Ideas, and to economic journals in England, France, Italy, Rumania, Brazil, and the United States. Associate editor, Econometrica, 1951-68.

SIDELIGHTS: Georgescu-Roegen told CA, "My singular tendency of clarifying in every detail even the most obvious must be imputed to the able mathematical school of Rumania." In addition to his native language Georgescu-Roegen speaks French, Italian, and German.

*   *   *

GERBER, Helmut E. 1920-

PERSONAL: Born July 7, 1920, in Germany; naturalized U.S. citizen; son of W. Emil (a businessman) and Hedwig (Tanz) Gerber; married Helga Schrank (a teacher), June 29, 1947; children: Ellen, Donald. Education: Rutgers University, B.S. in Ed., 1942; New York University, M.A., 1946; University of Pennsylvania, Ph.D., 1952. Office: Department of English, Arizona State University, Tempe, Ariz. 85281.

CAREER: Lafayette College, Easton, Pa., instructor, 1946-52, assistant professor of English, 1952-57; Purdue

University, West Lafayette, Ind., assistant professor, 1957-62, associate professor of English, 1962-68; Northern Illinois University, De Kalb, professor of English, 1968-71; Arizona State University, Tempe, professor of English, 1971—. *Military service:* U.S. Army, Intelligence, 1942-46; served in European theater; became captain. *Member:* National Council of Teachers of English, International Society for Anglo-Irish Literature, Modern Language Association of America, English Institute, Rocky Mountain Modern Language Association, Kipling Society, H. G. Wells Society. *Awards, honors:* Ford Foundation fellowship, 1955-56; Purdue Research Foundation grants, 1959, 1961, 1962; Northern Illinois University Council of Academic Deans grant, 1970; Arizona State University faculty research grants, 1971, 1972; American Philosophical Society grant, 1974; Arizona Commission on the Arts, and Humanities grant, 1975.

WRITINGS: (Editor) *The English Short Story in Transition, 1880-1920,* Pegasus, 1967; *George Moore in Transition,* Wayne State University Press, 1968; (with Bruce Teets) *Joseph Conrad: An Annotated Secondary Bibliography,* Northern Illinois University Press, 1971; (with W. Eugene Davis) *Thomas Hardy: An Annotated Secondary Bibliography,* Northern Illinois University Press, 1973. Contributor to scholarly journals. Editor, *English Literature in Transition* (journal), 1957—; general editor, *Annotated Secondary Bibliography Series on English Literature in Transition,* 1970—, published by Northern Illinois University Press; member of advisory or editorial boards, *Modern Fiction Studies, Literature and Psychology, American Literary Realism, Conradiana, Hartford Studies in Literature,* and *Virginia Woolf Quarterly.*

WORK IN PROGRESS: Studies of late nineteenth-century English criticism; a critical history of English literature, 1880-1920, completion expected in 1979; bibliographical works on George Moore and others; *George Moore on Parnassus: 1910-1933,* completion expected in 1976.

* * *

GERMAR, William H(erbert) 1911-
(Herb Germar)

PERSONAL: Born October 20, 1911, in Des Moines, Iowa; son of William Edward (a pharmacist) and Caroline (Zimbelman) Germar; married Monica Healy, September 10, 1938; children: William H., Jr., Annette Marie. *Education:* Drake University, B.A., 1934. *Home:* 6810 37th Ave. N., Minneapolis, Minn. 55427.

CAREER: Associated Press, wirephoto technician in Des Moines, Iowa, 1934-37; *Des Moines Register and Tribune,* Des Moines, Iowa, picture editor, 1937-42; U.S. Army Signal Corps, civilian instructor, 1942-46; *Minneapolis Star and Tribune,* Minneapolis, Minn., picture editor, 1947—. Instructor at University of Minnesota, 1960 and Augsburg College, 1961-62. Audiovisual consultant. *Member:* Sigma Delta Chi, Omicron Delta Phi. *Awards, honors:* Photo layout award of National Press Photographers Association, 1963.

WRITINGS—Under name Herb Germar: *The Student Journalist and Photojournalism,* Rosen, 1967. Writer-producer of industrial motion picture and sound slide films.

* * *

GERSTL, Joel E. 1932-
PERSONAL: Born August 20, 1932, in Prague, Czechoslo-vakia; son of Max (an architect) and Clarie (Ehrman) Gerstl; married Judith Jelinek, December 18, 1966; children: Jonathan, Javis. *Education:* Columbia University, B.A., 1954, M.A., 1955; University of Minnesota, Ph.D., 1959. *Home:* 7103 McCallum St., Philadelphia, Pa. 19119. *Office:* Sociology Department, Temple University, Philadelphia, Pa. 19122.

CAREER: Lecturer at University of Michigan, Ann Arbor, 1958-60, University of South Wales and Monmouthshire, Cardiff, 1960-62, and Cambridge University, Cambridge, England, 1962-63; Purdue University, Lafayette, Ind., assistant professor of sociology, 1963-65; Temple University, Philadelphia, Pa., associate professor of sociology, 1965—. *Member:* American Sociological Association, Eastern Sociological Association.

WRITINGS: (With S. P. Hutton) *Engineers: The Anatomy of a Profession,* Tavistock Publications, 1966; (editor with Donald A. Hansen) *On Education—Sociological Perspectives,* Wiley, 1967; (editor with Robert Perrucci) *Profession Without Community,* Random House, 1969; (editor with Perrucci) *The Engineers and the Social System,* Wiley, 1969; (with Glen Jacobs) *Professions for the People: Politics of Skill,* Schenkman, 1975. Contributor to sociology journals in America and England.

WORK IN PROGRESS: Further research and writing in the sociology of occupations and professions.

* * *

GERTEINY, Alfred G(eorges) 1930-
PERSONAL: Second syllable of surname rhymes with "rain"; born October 13, 1930, in Heliopolis, Egypt; son of Georges J. (an Egyptologist) and Nabiha (Negm) Gerteiny; married Elizabeth Folsom Leppert (a free-lance writer and poet), April 16, 1955; children: Cynthia, Celia, Frederick. *Education:* College Sainte Famille, Cairo, B. es lettres, 1950; University of Paris, D.E.S., 1956; specialized work at Hague Academy of International Law, Columbia University and St. John's University, Jamaica, N.Y., 1957-62; St. John's University, Ph.D., 1963. *Home:* 31 Tamarac Rd., Westport, Conn. 06880. *Office:* University of Bridgeport, Bridgeport, Conn. 06602.

CAREER: La Semaine Financiere et Politique, Paris, France, foreign correspondent, 1952-53; North Atlantic Treaty Organization, Paris, France, administrative assistant, 1953-55; Lebanese delegation to UNESCO, Paris, France, research assistant, 1955; Grolier Society, Inc., New York, N.Y., managing editor of French department, 1957-59; St. John's University, Jamaica, N.Y., assistant editor, university press, 1959-60, instructor, 1959-63, assistant professor of Mid-Eastern and African studies, 1963-66; University of Bridgeport, Bridgeport, Conn., associate professor, 1966-70, professor of Mid-Eastern and African history, and chairman of department, 1970—. Consultant, Associated Universities for Research in Astronomy, 1973; consultant, Peace Corps.

MEMBER: American Political Science Association, American Historical Association, Middle East Institute, African Studies Association (fellow), Middle East Studies Association (fellow), American Association of University Professors, University of Bridgeport Scholar's Group. *Awards, honors:* Grant from Africa Service Institute of New York, 1963-64; fellow in Islamic studies, State University of New York, 1966; senior Fulbright research fellow, 1970-71; National Endowment for the Humanities fellow in diplomacy, 1975.

WRITINGS: (Contributor) Michael Martin, *The Language of Love,* Bantam, 1961; *Mauritania: A Survey of a New African Nation,* Praeger, 1967; (contributor) James Kritezek, editor, *Islam in Africa,* Van Nostrand, 1968. Also contributor to *Aspects of West African Islam,* edited by D. McCall. Contributor to *Encyclopedia Americana,* and to *American Political Science Review, Africa Today, RACE,* and other periodicals.

WORK IN PROGRESS: A study of revolutionary Egypt's foreign policy.

SIDELIGHTS: Gerteiny has travelled extensively in Europe, Africa, and the Middle East. He is fluent in French and Arabic.

*   *   *

GESCH, Roy G(eorge)   1920-

PERSONAL: Born December 30, 1920, in Milwaukee, Wis.; son of Walter Frederick and Stella (Scholz) Gesch; married Dorothy Katherine Gesch, April 8, 1945; children: Gary Richard. *Education:* Concordia Junior College, Milwaukee, Wis., graduate, 1939; Concordia Seminary, St. Louis, Mo., B.A., 1941, Diploma, 1944. *Home:* 1572 Skyline Dr., Laguna Beach, Calif. 92651. *Office address:* Lutheran Bible Translators, P.O. Box 5566, Orange, Calif. 92667.

CAREER: Lutheran clergyman, 1944—. Pastor in Buffalo, N.Y., 1944-46, Brawley, Calif., 1946-50, Oceanside, Calif., 1950-61, Wahiawa, Oahu, Hawaii, 1961-62, and Whittier, Calif., 1962-70; St. Paul's Lutheran Church, Laguna Beach, Calif., pastor, 1970-75; currently director of development, Lutheran Bible Translators, Orange, Calif. Armed Services Commission of Lutheran Church, contact pastor and counselor at Camp Pendleton, Calif., 1950-61, and Schofield Barracks, Wheeler Air Force Base, and Pearl Harbor, Hawaii, 1961-62; area counselor for Lutheran Churches in California, 1949-50, 1953-60, 1964-68.

WRITINGS—All published by Concordia: (Contributor) *Of Such Is the Kingdom,* 1964; (contributor) *Adventuring with God,* 1965; *On Active Duty* (meditations for servicemen), 1967; *A Husband Prays,* 1968; *A Wife Prays,* 1968; *Parents Pray,* 1968; *God's World Through Young Eyes* (juvenile), 1969; *Help! I'm in College,* 1969; *Man at Prayer,* 1970; *Lord of the Young Crowd,* 1971; (with wife, Dorothy Gesch) *Discover Europe: A Guide to the Unique and Exceptional,* 1973; *And Yet the Church Goes On!,* 1974. Regular contributor to *My Devotions;* contributor to other religious periodicals.

WORK IN PROGRESS: More of God's World; Discover Hong Kong.

AVOCATIONAL INTERESTS: Travel, photography, skin diving, sailing, and philately.

*   *   *

GEWECKE, Clifford George, Jr.   1932-

PERSONAL: Surname is pronounced Gay-wicky; born June 8, 1932, in Evanston, Wyo.; son of Clifford George and Edna Marie (Smith) Gewecke. *Education:* University of Southern California, B.A., 1954, M.A., 1955. *Religion:* Protestant. *Home:* 1707 Micheltorena, Apt. 204, Los Angeles, Calif. 90026. *Agent:* Lurton Blassingame, 60 East 42nd St., New York, N.Y. 10017. *Office: Daily Signal,* 6414 Rugby Ave., Huntington Park, Calif. 90255.

CAREER: Daily Signal, Huntington Park, Calif., sports editor, 1958—; southern California sports correspondent for *Christian Science Monitor,* 1964-74. *Military service:* U.S. Army, 1955-57. *Member:* Sigma Delta Chi.

WRITINGS: Advantage Ashe (as told by Arthur Ashe, Jr.), Coward, 1967. Contributor to *Sport* and *West.*

SIDELIGHTS: Gewecke's coverage of sports events includes Olympic Games in Rome, Tokyo, and Mexico City. *Avocational interests:* Reading, movies, plays, dancing, and participating in sports.

*   *   *

GHAI, Dharam P.   1936-

PERSONAL: Born June 29, 1936, in Nairobi, Kenya; son of Basti Ram (a businessman) and Vidya (Vati) Ghai; married Neela Korde (a barrister), March 29, 1963; children: Kamini (daughter), Aniket (son). *Education:* Queen's College, Oxford, B.A., 1958, B.Phil., 1959; Yale University, M.A., 1961, Ph.D., 1965. *Address:* Case Postale 500, CH 1211 Geneva 22, Switzerland.

CAREER: Makerere University College, Kampala, Uganda, lecturer in economics, 1961-65; Institute for Development Studies, Nairobi, Kenya, 1966-74, began as deputy director, became director; United Nations, International Labor Organization, Geneva, Switzerland, chief of research branch of World Employment Programme, 1974—. Consultant to Government of Kenya Salaries Review Commission, 1966-67; member of Pearson Commission Secretariat, 1968-69.

WRITINGS: (Editor) *Portrait of a Minority: Asians in East Africa,* Oxford University Press, 1965; *Taxation for Development: A Case Study of Uganda,* East African Publishing House, 1966; (editor) *Economic Independence in Africa,* East African Literature Bureau, 1973; (editor with D. Court) *Education, Society and Development: New Perspectives from Kenya,* Oxford University Press, 1974.

SIDELIGHTS: Ghai speaks Swahili, Hindi, and Punjabi, and reads French. *Avocational interests:* Travel, photography, reading.

*   *   *

GHOSH, Arun Kumar   1930-

PERSONAL: First "h" of surname is pronounced; born February 1, 1930, in Burdwan, West Bengal, India; son of Ashutosh (a lawyer in District Judge's Court, Burdwan) and Induprova (Roy Mitter) Ghosh. *Education:* Vidyasagar College, B.A. (honors in economics), 1948; University of Calcutta, M.A., 1950. *Politics:* Former radical humanist; "at present, a leftist and a democrat, and believer in wider democratic movement." *Religion:* "Hindu by birth, but accept some of its cultural aspects only; accept the role of religion in life, in some form or other." *Home:* Late Ashutosh Ghosh's House, Nawab Dust Kayum Lane, Burdwan, West Bengal, India. *Office:* Institute of Cost and Works Accountants of India, 12, Sudder St., Calcutta, India.

CAREER: Burdwan Town School, Burdwan, West Bengal, India, assistant teacher of civics and English, 1950-51; University of Calcutta, Calcutta, India, postgraduate research fellow in economics, 1952-55; Seth Anandaram Jaipuria College, Calcutta, lecturer in economics and commerce, 1955-56; University of Calcutta, examiner and scrutineer of intermediate and bachelor examinations, 1955—, research assistant in industrial finance, department of economics, 1956-66; Institute of Cost and Works Accountants of India, Calcutta, part-time tutor, 1965-70, assistant director of research, 1970—, part-time lecturer, 1971-72. Visiting professor, Indian Institute of Management, 1973. *Member:* Indian Economic Association, Bardhaman Sahitya Sabha (literary society of Burdwan; member of executive committee, 1956—), Mukta Meda (cultural society). *Awards, honors:* University of Calcutta, Banco Behari Banerjee Gold Medal, 1950, Beereshwar Mitter Gold Medal, 1966.

WRITINGS: Fiscal Problem of Growth with Stability (monograph), Calcutta University Press, 1959; *Fiscal Policy and Economic Growth: A Cross-Section Study* (monograph), Calcutta University Press, Part I, 1962, Part II, 1963; (contributor) *Monetary Policy of the Reserve Bank of India,* Popular Prakasan (Bombay), 1963; *Cost Accounting in Commercial Banking Industry,* Institute of Cost and Works Accountants of India, in press. Also author of *Fiscal Policy, Stability and Growth: The Experience and Problems of the Underdeveloped Economy, Capital Market in a Developing Economy, with Special Reference to India, Cost and Output in Banking,* and *Inflation and Price Control.* Frequent contributor to *Radical Humanist,* 1954-57, to *Calcutta Review, Indian Economic Journal,* and other professional journals in India.

WORK IN PROGRESS: Investigating fiscal problems of the underdeveloped economies of Latin America, Middle East and Africa, and Asia and the Far East, 1929-39, 1945-65; collecting material for an industrial economics textbook; *Fiscal Policy of India, 1945/46-1965/66.*

SIDELIGHTS: Ghosh is competent in Sanskrit and Hindi. *Avocational interests:* Debate, sports (was a chief scorer of University of Calcutta's Post-Graduate Athletic Club), architecture, sculpture, painting, and music.

*   *   *

GIANNONE, Richard 1934-

PERSONAL: Born October 9, 1934, in Newark, N.J.; son of Salvatore and Nellie (Cordileone) Giannone. *Education:* Catholic University of America, A.B. (with honors), 1956; University of Michigan, M.A., 1957; University of Notre Dame, Ph.D., 1964. *Home:* 330 East 19th St., New York, N.Y. 10003. *Office:* Department of English, Fordham University, Rose Hill Campus, Bronx, N.Y. 10458.

CAREER: University of Notre Dame, Notre Dame, Ind., assistant professor of English, 1964-67; Fordham University, Rose Hill Campus, Bronx, N.Y., associate professor, 1967-74, professor of English, 1974—. *Awards, honors:* Fulbright scholar in Italy, 1960-61; postdoctoral grant, American Philosophical Society.

WRITINGS: Music in Willa Cather's Fiction, University of Nebraska Press, 1968; *The Shapes of Fiction,* Holt, 1971; *John Keats: A Thematic Reader,* Scott, Foresman, 1971; (contributor) John J. Murphy, editor, *Five Essays on Willa Cather: The Merrimack Symposium,* Cather Book, 1974.

WORK IN PROGRESS: A critical study of Kurt Vonnegut, Jr.

*   *   *

GIBSON, Charles 1920-

PERSONAL: Born August 12, 1920, in Buffalo, N.Y.; son of William W. and Helen (Jones) Gibson; married Alice Klauss. *Education:* Yale University, B.A., 1941, Ph.D., 1950; University of Texas, M.A., 1947. *Home:* 2872 Glacier Way, Ann Arbor, Mich. 48105.

CAREER: University of Iowa, Iowa City, assistant professor, 1949-52, associate professor, 1952-59, professor of history, 1959-65; University of Michigan, Ann Arbor, professor of history, 1965—. Visiting lecturer at Harvard University, 1956-57. *Military service:* U.S. Army, 1942-45; became staff sergeant. *Member:* American Historical Association. *Awards, honors:* Guggenheim fellow, 1952; Rockefeller Foundation fellow, 1960-61.

WRITINGS: The Inca Concept of Sovereignty and the Spanish Administration in Peru, University of Texas Press, 1948, reprinted, Greenwood Press, 1969; *Tlaxcala in the Sixteenth Century,* Yale University Press, 1952; (editor) *Guide to the Hispanic American Historical Review, 1946-1955,* Duke University Press, 1958; *The Aztecs under Spanish Rule,* Stanford University Press, 1964; *Spain in America,* Harper, 1966; (compiler) *The Spanish Tradition in America,* University of South Carolina Press, 1968; (editor with Howard Peckham) *Attitudes of the Colonial Powers toward the American Indians,* University of Utah Press, 1969; (compiler) *The Black Legend: Anti-Spanish Attitudes in the Old World and the New,* Knopf, 1971. Contributing editor, *Handbook of Latin American Studies,* 1953—; associate managing editor, *Hispanic American Historical Review,* 1955-69.

WORK IN PROGRESS: Further research in Spanish and Spanish-American history.

*   *   *

GIBSON, Derlyne 1936-

PERSONAL: Born November 27, 1936, in St. Louis, Okla.; daughter of Wayne Derl and Cora (McKown) Simpson; married John Lanier Gibson, August 22, 1959; children: John Baudelaire. *Education:* University of Arkansas, B.A., 1963. *Religion:* Episcopalian. *Home:* Route 4, Berryville, Ark. 72616.

CAREER: Harrison Regional Arts & Crafts Center, Harrison, Ark., art instructor, 1967-69; Berryville High School, Berryville, Ark., art instructor, 1974—. *Member:* American Association of University Women, Arkansas Educational Association.

WRITINGS—Juvenile; all published by Reilly & Lee: How Fast Can It Go?, 1967; *How Far Can It Go?,* 1970; *How Big Can It Grow?,* 1971; *How Old Can It Get?,* 1972.

*   *   *

GIBSON, Raymond E(ugene) 1924-

PERSONAL: Born March 10, 1924, in Shelbyville, Ky.; son of Wallace and Laura (Lee) Gibson; married Susan Cochran, June 29, 1945; children: Cyrus Noel, Mark Scott, Christopher Watt, Laurence Kristen, Jonathan Geoffrey. *Education:* Berea College, A.B., 1944; Union Theological Seminary, New York, N.Y., B.D., 1947; Columbia University, Ph.D., 1962. *Politics:* Independent. *Religion:* Protestant. *Home:* 283 Wayland Ave., Providence, R.I. 02906.

CAREER: Ordained minister of Congregational Church, 1947; Institute for Religious and Social Studies, New York, N.Y., administrative assistant, 1947-48; pastor in New Lebanon, N.Y., 1948-49, and Pittsfield, Mass., 1950-61; Central Congregational Church, Providence, R.I., pastor, 1961—; Providence College, Providence, professor of religious studies, 1971—. Chairman of Rhode Island Advisory Committee to U.S. Commission on Civil Rights, 1962—; member of board of directors of Rhode Island Congregational Conference, 1965—. Trustee of Berea College. *Mili-*

tary service: U.S. Navy, 1943-46. *Member:* Academy of Religion and Mental Health. *Awards, honors:* Named one of the four outstanding young men of the state by Massachusetts Junior Chamber of Commerce, 1959.

WRITINGS: (Editor and author of introduction) Myrtle L. Elmer, *Conversations with God: The Devotional Journals of Myrtle L. Elmer,* Eerdmans, 1962; (editor) *Pastoral Prayers of William C. Wilson,* privately printed, 1964; *God, Man, and Time,* United Church Press, 1966. Contributor to *Christian Century, Religion in Life,* and other journals. Associate editor, *Minister's Quarterly,* 1958-66.

*   *   *

GIDDINGS, Robert (Lindsay) 1935-

PERSONAL: Born June 29, 1935, in Worcester, England; son of Arthur Wesley (a cabinetmaker) and Stella Mary (McCallum) Giddings; married Marie Ethel Matthews, December 8, 1963; children: James Nield (adopted son), Giles. *Education:* Studied at College of Commerce, Bristol, England, 1954-55; University of Bristol, B.A., 1958, M.A., 1960, Dip.Ed., 1961, M.Litt., 1967; University of Keele, Ph.D., 1974. *Politics:* Labour. *Religion:* None. *Home:* Somerset House, Swineford-Bitton, Bristol, England. *Agent:* A. M. Heath & Co. Ltd., 40-42 King William IV St., London WC2N 4DD, England. *Office:* City of Bath Technical College, Bath, Somersetshire, England.

CAREER: Master at schools in Bristol, England, 1961-63, and Yeovil, England, 1963; Yeovil Technical College, Yeovil, assistant lecturer in English, 1963-64; City of Bath Technical College, Bath, England, 1964—, began as assistant lecturer in English and history, now lecturer in literature; Open University, Milton Keynes, Buckinghamshire, England, tutor and lecturer in literature, beginning 1973; University of Bath, Bath, associate tutor in English, 1971—. Visiting lecturer at Florissant Valley Community College (St. Louis, Mo.), 1975-76. Regular radio correspondent and reporter for British Broadcasting Corp, in Bristol, England. *Member:* Society of Authors, Association for Programmed Learning, Association of Teachers in Technical Institutions, Conservation Society.

WRITINGS: The Tradition of Smollett, Methuen, 1967; *British Trade Unions,* Bristol Tutor Group, 1968. Also author of six-volume programmed course, "British History 1660-1763," Bristol Tutor Group, 1967. Television scripts include autobiographical documentary. "Sitting Target," produced by British Broadcasting Corp., June, 1967. Contributor to *New Society, Music & Letters, Dickens Studies,* and other professional journals; regular contributor to *Western Daily Press,* 1960-64.

WORK IN PROGRESS: An autobiography, *Sitting Target; Dickens and the Changing World,* a study of Dickens' early political and social ideas; a melodrama for radio, "The Last Illusion"; a radio reading, "Mincepiety," for British Broadcasting Corp.; a novel, *Heads I Win; How Green Was My Belt: A Study of the Politics of Ecology,* a personal account of environmental campaigning in England.

SIDELIGHTS: Giddings contracted polio in 1946 when he was eleven, and came out of the hospital in 1953. For a time he was completely paralyzed, but now he can move his head, left arm, and has partial use of his right arm. Giddings teaches from a wheelchair, hates patronage, but "burns with anger at the usual attitude toward the disabled." At the University of Bristol he edited the university newspaper and magazine, and produced plays, revues, and films; the films included Chaucer's "Pardoner's Tale,"

shown at Edinburgh Festival, 1959. He has an enduring interest in Wagner, and is a conservationist and environmentalist. Giddings has traveled widely in Europe and the United States.

*   *   *

GIERTZ, Bo H(arald) 1905-

PERSONAL: Born August 31, 1905, in Rapplinge, Sweden; son of Knut Harald (a professor) and Anna (Ericsson) Giertz; married Ingrid Andren, September 24, 1932 (died July 2, 1942); married Elisabeth af Heurlin, September 17, 1945 (died July 3, 1968); children: (first marriage) Lars, Birgitta Hemstrom, Ingrid Giertz Martenson, Martin. *Education:* University of Uppsala, B.A. (classic linguistics), 1928, B.A. (theology), 1931. *Home:* Tandasgatan 15, 41266 Gothenburg, Sweden.

CAREER: Evangelical-Lutheran clergyman. Diocese of Linkoping, Sweden, pastor in different congregations, 1934-38, vicar of Torpa, 1938-49; Bishop of Gothenburg, 1949-70. Lutheran World Federation, vice-president, 1957-63, member of executive committee, 1957-70, chairman of National Committee in Sweden, 1963-72; member of board of Church of Sweden Mission, 1964-70. *Awards, honors:* D.Div., University of Lund, Sweden, 1974.

WRITINGS: Kristi Kyrka (title means "The Church of Christ"), Verbum, 1939; *Kyrkofromhet* (title means "Living in the Church"), Verbum, 1939; *Stengrunden,* Verbum, 1941, translation by Clifford Anagar Nelson published as *The Hammer of God: A Novel About the Cure of Souls,* Augustana Press, 1960; *Grunden* (title means "The Foundation"), Verbum, 1942; *Tron allena* (title means "By Faith Alone"), Verbum, 1943; *Den stora lognen och den stora sanningen* (title means "The Big Lie and the Great Truth"), Verbum, 1945; *Kampen om manniskan* (title means "Struggle for Man"), Verbum, 1947; *Med egna ogon,* Verbum, 1948, translation by Maurice Michael published as *With My Own Eyes: A Life of Jesus,* Macmillan, 1960; *Herdabrev* (title means "Pastoral Letter"), Verbum, 1949; *The Message of the Church in a Time of Crisis and Other Essays,* translated from the Swedish by Clifford Ansgar Nelson, Augustana Book Concern, 1958; *Brytningstider* (title means "Times of Change"), Pro Caritate, 1957; *Vad sager Guds Ord?,* Verbum, 1957, translation by Nelson published as *Preaching from the Whole Bible: Background Studies in the Preaching Texts for the Church Year,* Augsburg, 1967; *23 teser om skriften kvinnan och praesteambetet,* Diakonistyrelsens Bokfoerlag, 1958.

Ratt och oratt i sexuallivet, Verbum, 1960; *Afrikanska overrasknigar* (title means "African Surprises"), Verbum, 1961; *Folkvandring* (title means "Migration"), Pro Caritate, 1962; *I smaeltdegeln* (title means "In the Melting Pot"), Pro Caritate, 1967; *Trons ABC* (title means "ABC of Faith"), Verbum, 1971; *Riddarna pa Rhodos* (title means "The Knights of Rhodes"; novel), Askild & Karnekull, 1972; *Att kunna laesa sin Bibel* (title means "How to read the Bible"), Verbum, 1973; *Att tro pa Kristus* (title means "Faith in Christ"), Verbum, 1973; *Att leva med Kristus* (title means "Life with Christ"), Verbum, 1974.

WORK IN PROGRESS: Five Letters of St. Paul, translated and explained for non-professionals, for Verbum.

SIDELIGHTS: For a number of years Bishop Giertz served a small parish, giving him the opportunity, he says, "to do a lot of writing—novels and essays on Christian items. I suppose these books were the reason why I was elected bishop of Gothenburg." His writings have been translated into German, Norwegian, Danish, Finnish, Icelandic, Hungarian, Tamil, and Zulu. He speaks German and English fluently, and can read six other languages. In addition to five trips to the United States, he has made several visits in Africa and Asia, and one trip in South America. His friends honored him on his sixtieth birthday, 1965, with a festschrift in Swedish, *Till Bo Giertz.*

* * *

GIH, Andrew 1901-

PERSONAL: Born January 10, 1901, in Shanghai, China; son of You-Run (a Confucian scholar) and Tsai-Liem (Loh) Gih; married Dorcas Tsai-yin Chang (secretary of Evangelize China Fellowship, Inc.). *Education:* Attended Bethel Seminary, Shanghai, China, 1925-27. *Home and office address:* P.O. Box 550, Los Angeles, Calif. 90053.

CAREER: Bethel missionary evangelist, 1925-46; founder, 1947, and president of Evangelize China Fellowship, Inc., an organization supporting schools and orphanages in China, and two Bible colleges, forty churches, and a publication department; publisher of *Life* (in Chinese) and *His Faithfulness* (in English). *Member:* Royal Geographical Society (fellow). *Awards, honors:* Award from Chinese National Government for relief services during Japanese war in China; Litt.D. from Cascade College, Portland, Ore.

WRITINGS: Twice Born—and Then? The Autobiography and Messages of Andrew Gih, Marshall, Morgan & Scott, 1936, Zondervan, 1937, 2nd edition, Marshall, Morgan & Scott, 1954; *Into God's Family,* Marshall, Morgan & Scott, 1937, revised edition, 1955; *Launch Out Into the Deep!,* Marshall, Morgan & Scott, 1938; *Bands of Soldiers for War!,* Marshall, Morgan & Scott, 1939; *Power of the Gospel in War-Torn China,* Zondervan, 1940; *The Church Behind the Bamboo Curtain,* Attic Press, 1961; *When War Comes,* Marshall, Morgan & Scott, 1964, Attic Press, 1969; *What Saved Chinese Churches in Indonesia?,* Marshall Morgan & Scott, 1968; *Revival Follows Revolution in Indonesia,* Marshall, Morgan & Scott, 1975.

SIDELIGHTS: Andrew Gih traveled all over China, in other parts of Asia, and in Europe, Australia, and New Zealand.

* * *

GILBERT, (Agnes) Joan (Sewell) 1931-
(Jill Baer)

PERSONAL: Given name is pronounced Jo-ann; born November 7, 1931, in Dixon, Mo.; daughter of Daniel Boone and Blanche Evelyn (Gilbert) Sewell; married Dewey Franklin Lipscomb, January 24, 1953; married second husband, Ira Joseph Gilbert, October 9, 1961. *Education:* Southwest Missouri State College (now University), B.S. in Ed., 1954. *Home:* Box 326, Dixon, Mo. 65459.

CAREER: Columbia Daily Tribune, Columbia, Mo., women's editor, 1955-58; also wrote continuity for Radio Station KGBX, Springfield, Mo., worked in society department of newspaper in Springfield, and did public relations work for Gascosage Electric Cooperative; free-lance writer. Book chairman of Dixon library board. *Member:* Missouri Writer's Guild.

WRITINGS: Summerhill Summer (teen-age mystery), Bethany Press, 1967; (under pseudonym Jill Baer) *House of Whispers,* Paperback Library, 1971. Contributor of about

three hundred articles to newspapers, religious weeklies for teenagers, and magazines including *Writer's Digest, Health, Calling All Girls, Ebony, American Girl,* and *Today's Farmer.* Contributing editor, *Management Quarterly.*

WORK IN PROGRESS: Teen novels and gothics.

AVOCATIONAL INTERESTS: Photography, animals, outdoors, books, music.

* * *

GILCHRIST, Alan W. 1913-
(Alan Cowan)

PERSONAL: Born July 3, 1913, in Hove, Sussex, England; son of Adam Cowan (a clerk) and Kate Hannah (Bettesworth) Gilchrist; married Joan Clare Purser, December 16, 1939; children: James Adam, Patric Alan. *Education:* University of London, B.A., 1934. *Politics:* "None—except for pacifism." *Agent:* A. D. Peters, 10 Buckingham St., Adelphi, London WC2N 6BU, England.

CAREER: Schoolmaster, teaching English literature, Worcestershire, England, 1946-66. *Military service:* Fought with International Brigades, Spanish Civil War, 1937-38; British Army, Royal Artillery, 1940-46; became major; received Order of the British Empire (M.B.E.).

WRITINGS: Modern English Readings, Longman, 1973, 2nd edition, 1974; *A New Secondary English Course,* Longman, Book 1, 1973, Book 2, 1974; *Language for Living: A Caribbean English Course,* 'O' Level, Longman, 1974.

All under pseudonym Alan Cowan: *A Kind of Truth,* Hutchinson, 1961; *Nowhere to Go,* Hutchinson, 1964; *A Backward Glance,* Hutchinson, 1966; *Fortunately in England,* Hutchinson, 1968; *Two or Three Questions,* Hutchinson, 1969; *Here Be Dragons,* Hutchinson, 1972. Author of three radio plays broadcast by British Broadcasting Corp., and in Australia and New Zealand.†

* * *

GILFOND, Henry

PERSONAL: Son of Louis and Vera Gilfond; wife, Edythe, is a costume designer; children: Michael, Pamela. *Home and office:* 455 Franklin D. Roosevelt Dr., New York, N.Y. 10002.

CAREER: Teacher in New York (N.Y.) schools for a number of years; author and ghost-writer. *Member:* American National Theatre and Academy, Dramatists Guild of the Authors League of America.

WRITINGS: Journey Without End, Philosophical Library, 1958; *How to Run for School Office,* Hawthorn, 1969; *Heroines of America,* Fleet Press, 1971; *The Reichitag Fire, February, 1933: Hitler Utilizes Arson to Extend His Dictatorship,* F. Watts, 1973; *Black Hand at Sarajevo,* Bobbs-Merrill, 1975.

With Gene Schoor; juvenile biographies; all published by Messner: *The Jim Thorpe Story,* 1952; *The Story of Ty Cobb,* 1952; *Red Grange,* 1952; *Christy Mathewson,* 1953; *Casey Stengel,* 1953; *The Jack Dempsey Story,* 1954; *The Ted Williams Story,* 1954; *The Stan Musial Story,* 1955.

Editor; all published by Walker & Co.: *Plays for Reading,* 1966; *American Plays for Reading,* 1966; *Holiday Plays for Reading,* 1967; *Plays for Today,* 1967; *Mythology Plays,* 1967; *African Plays for Reading,* 1967; *Latin-American Plays for Reading,* 1967; *Favorite Short Stories,* 1967; *Asian Plays for Reading,* 1968.

Ghost-writer on subjects ranging from pediatrics to politics. Author of radio and television scripts, and a full-length play, "The Wick and the Tallow," recorded by Folkways, 1967. Contributor to *New York Times Book Review.* Former editor, *New World Monthly* (literary magazine), and *Dance Observer.*

WORK IN PROGRESS: *Voodoo,* for F. Watts.

*   *   *

GILL, (Ronald) Crispin   1916-

PERSONAL: Born March 10, 1916, in England; son of Joseph Henry (a builder) and Margaret Jane (Crispin) Gill; married Mary Beatrice Grills Foot, August 4, 1939 (died February 19, 1971); married Betty Theed, August 26, 1972; children: (first marriage) Jane Elford (Mrs. F. N. Dowling), Crispin Owen, Sarah Margaret Foot. *Education:* Attended grammar school in Plymouth England, 1926-34. *Religion:* Church of England. *Home:* Greyhounds, Sheep St., Burford, Oxfordshire, England.

CAREER: *Western Morning News,* Plymouth, England, assistant editor, 1950-71; *Countryman* (magazine), Burford, Oxfordshire, England, editor, 1971—. Member, Friends of Buckland Abbey Committee, 1951-71, Dartmoor National Park Committee, 1954-66; chairman of Plymouth Lifeboat Committee, 1967-71. West Devon scout commissioner, 1951-62. *Military service:* Royal Army, Service Corps, 1940-46; became captain. *Member:* Society for Nautical Research, Hakluyt Society, Royal Institution of Cornwall, Devon and Cornwall Record Society, Devonshire Association, Royal Western Yacht Club of England.

WRITINGS: *The Westcountry,* Oliver & Boyd, 1962; *Plymouth, a New History: Ice Age to the Elizabethans,* Volume I, David & Charles, 1966, Taplinger, 1967; (with Frank Booker and Tony Soper) *The Wreck of the Torrey Canyon,* David & Charles, 1967; *Plymouth in Pictures,* David & Charles, 1968; *Sutton Harbour,* Sutton Harbour Improvement Co., 1970; (editor) *Dartmoor: A New Study,* David & Charles, 1970; *Mayflower Remembered: A History of the Plymouth Pilgrims,* Taplinger, 1970; *The Isles of Scilly,* David & Charles, 1975.

WORK IN PROGRESS: Editing Volume II of *Plymouth, a New History.*

AVOCATIONAL INTERESTS: The sea, travel, and maritime history.

*   *   *

GILL, Richard T(homas)   1927-

PERSONAL: Born November 30, 1927, in Long Branch, N.J.; son of Thomas Grant (a commercial artist) and Myrtle (Sickles) Gill; married Elizabeth Bjornson, January 6, 1950; children: Thomas Grandon, Peter Severin, Geoffrey Karl. *Education:* Harvard University, A.B., 1948, Ph.D., 1956; Jesus College, Oxford, graduate study, 1948-49. *Home and office:* 22 Possum Trail, Upper Saddle River, N.J. 07458.

CAREER: Harvard University, Cambridge, Mass., assistant dean, 1949-52, instructor in economics, 1952-55, Allston Burr Senior Tutor, 1955-63, assistant professor of economics, 1958-63, lecturer in economics and master of Leverett House, 1963-71; New York City Opera Co., New York City, principal bass, 1971—; Metropolitan Opera Co., New York City, principal bass, 1973—. Has presented fifteen-part television series, "Economics and the Public Interest," on New England Educational Television.

Member of board of governors of American Guild of Musical Artists. *Military service:* U.S. Army, 1946-47. *Member:* Harvard Signet Society (president, 1965-66). *Awards, honors:* Atlantic Monthly "First" Award, 1954, for short story, "The Secret."

WRITINGS: *Economic Development: Past and Present,* Prentice-Hall, 1963, 3rd edition, 1972; *Evolution of Modern Economics,* Prentice-Hall, 1967; *Economics and the Public Interest,* Goodyear Publishing, 1968, 2nd edition, 1972; (contributor) Maurice Sheehy, editor, *Michael/Frank: Studies on Frank O'Connor,* Knopf, 1969; *Economics and the Private Interest,* Goodyear Publishing, 1973, 2nd edition, 1975. Contributor of short stories to *New Yorker* and *Atlantic Monthly,* 1954-57.

*   *   *

GILLHAM, D. G.   1921-

PERSONAL: Born May 6, 1921, in Benoni, South Africa; son of Frederick and Blanche (Tovey) Gillham; married Sheila Hammett (a university lecturer), January 1, 1955. *Education:* University of the Witwatersrand, B.A., 1949; University of South Africa, M.A., 1960; University of Bristol, Ph.D., 1964. *Home:* 1 Highways, Derwent Rd., Gardens, Cape Province, South Africa. *Office:* Department of English, University of Cape Town, Private Bag Rondebosch, 7700 Cape Province, South Africa.

CAREER: University of Stellenbosch, Stellenbosch, South Africa, 1956-67, became senior lecturer; University of Natal, Pietermaritzburg, Natal, South Africa, professor, 1968-71; University of Cape Town, Cape Town, Cape Province, South Africa, professor of English, 1972—. *Military service:* South African Air Force, 1940-45; became lieutenant.

WRITINGS: *Blake's Contrary States,* Cambridge University Press, 1966; *William Blake,* Cambridge University Press, 1972.

WORK IN PROGRESS: A study on Blake.

*   *   *

GILLMORE, David   1934-

PERSONAL: Born August 16, 1934, in Swindon, England; son of Alan David (an officer in Royal Air Force) and Kathleen (Morris) Gillmore; married Lucile Morin, December 16, 1964; children: Julian. *Education:* Attended King's College, Cambridge, 1955-58. *Home:* 19 Ashlone Rd., London S.W. 15, England.

CAREER: Reuters (news service), London, England, subeditor, 1958-60; Polypapier S.A., Paris, France, assistant to director, 1960-64; Inner London Education Authority, London, England, teacher, 1965—. *Military service:* Royal Air Force, 1953-55.

WRITINGS: *A Way from Exile* (novel), Macdonald & Co., 1967. Assistant editor, *Gemini,* 1957-58.

WORK IN PROGRESS: A novel, as yet untitled.

SIDELIGHTS: Gillmore is fluent in French; he also speaks Russian, Spanish, and Italian.††

*   *   *

GILPATRICK, Eleanor G(ottesfocht)   1930-

PERSONAL: Born October 29, 1930, in Brooklyn, N.Y.; daughter of Murry and Essie (Hirsch) Gottesfocht; married Jerome Gilpatrick, September 8, 1956 (divorced August, 1959). *Education:* Brooklyn College (now Brooklyn College of the City University of New York), B.A., 1951; New

School for Social Research, M.A., 1959; Cornell University, Ph.D., 1964. *Home:* 302 West 12th St., New York, N.Y. 10014.

CAREER: Boni Watkins Jason & Co., New York City, junior research analyst, 1959-60; United Furniture Workers of America, New York City, assistant research director and secretary to president, 1960-61; University of Illinois, Urbana, assistant research professor, Bureau of Economic and Business Research, 1964-66; Skill Advancement, Inc., New York City, senior research associate, 1966-67; City University of New York, New York City, director of Research Foundation's health services mobility study, 1967—. *Member:* American Economic Association, Industrial Relations Research Association, American Association of University Professors, Metropolitan Economic Association, Phi Beta Kappa.

WRITINGS: Structural Unemployment and Aggregate Demand, Johns Hopkins Press, 1966; *Use of Job Vacancies to Select Promising Industries for Training Programs,* Skill Advancement, Inc., 1967; *Aspects of Manpower Supply in Illinois Regions, 1940, 1950 and 1960,* Department of Business and Economic Development, State of Illinois, 1967; *Train Practical Nurses to Become Registered Nurses: A Survey of the PN Point of View,* Research Foundation, City University of New York, 1968; (with Paul K. Corliss) *The Occupational Structure of New York City Municipal Hospitals,* Praeger, 1970; (with Christina Gullion) *The Design Guidelines for Educational Ladders Using Task Data,* Research Foundation, City University of New York, 1973. Contributor to *The Annals* of the American Academy of Political and Social Science, 1975.

WORK IN PROGRESS: Reports on health services mobility study, concerned with career ladders, education and evaluation, funded by U.S. Department of Labor Manpower Administration.

* * *

GINSBURG, Seymour 1927-

PERSONAL: Born December 12, 1927, in Brooklyn, N.Y.; son of William (a grocer) and Bessie (Setomer) Ginsburg; married Eleanor Shore, June 13, 1954; children: Diane, David. *Education:* City College (now City College of the City University of New York), B.S., 1948; University of Michigan, M.S., 1949, Ph.D., 1952. *Home:* 14031 Margate St., Van Nuys, Calif.

CAREER: University of Miami, Coral Gables, Fla., assistant professor of mathematics, 1951-55; Northrop Corp., Los Angeles, Calif., computer engineer, 1955-56; National Cash Register Co., Electronics Division, Los Angeles, senior research engineer, 1956-59; Hughes Aircraft Co., Information Processing Research Department, Los Angeles, head of systems, synthesis, and organization section, 1959-60; System Development Corp. (programming), Santa Monica, Calif., senior research mathematician, 1960—. Teacher of mathematics, University of California, Los Angeles, 1956-65; professor of computer science, University of Southern California, 1966—. Referee for mathematical and computer journals. *Military service:* U.S. Army, Infantry, 1946-47; served in Korea and the Philippines.

MEMBER: American Mathematical Society, Association for Computing Machinery, Society for Industrial and Applied Mathematics, Mathematical Association of America, Institute of Electrical and Electronic Engineers, Phi Beta Kappa, Sigma Xi, Phi Kappa Phi.

WRITINGS: An Introduction to Mathematical Machine Theory, Addison-Wesley, 1962; (contributor) R. D. Luce, R. R. Bush, and E. Galanter, editors, *Readings in Mathematical Psychology,* Volume II, Wiley, 1965; *The Mathematical Theory of Context Free Languages,* McGraw, 1966; *Algebraic and Automata Theoretic Properties of Formal Languages,* North-Holland Publishing, 1975. Also author of monographs for System Development Corp. Contributor of more than eighty research articles to journals; reviewer for *Mathematical Reviews, Computing Reviews,* and *IEEE Transactions on Electric Computers.* Associate editor, *Journal of Computer and Systems Sciences;* editor, *Journal of the Association for Computing Machinery.*

* * *

GINZBURG, Ralph 1929-

PERSONAL: Born October 28, 1929, in Brooklyn, N.Y.; son of Raymond (a housepainter) and Rachel Guta (Lipkin) Ginzburg; married Shoshana Brown (a poet and the promotion director of *Avant Garde*), December 16, 1958; children: Bonnie, Shepherd, Lark. *Education:* Received Diploma from Henry George School of Economics, 1945; City College (now City College of the City University of New York), B.B.A., 1949. *Politics:* Independent. *Religion:* None. *Office: Moneysworth,* 251 West 57th St., New York, N.Y. 10019.

CAREER: New York Daily Compass, New York City, reporter, 1949-50; *Washington Times-Herald,* Washington, D.C., rewrite man, 1950-51; writer for National Broadcasting Co., 1952; *Look* Magazine, New York City, director of circulation and promotion, 1953-55; *Esquire* Magazine, New York City, articles editor, 1956-58; *Eros* (quarterly magazine), New York City, editor and publisher, 1962-63 (four issues published); at the same time he was publisher of Documentary Books, Inc. and "Liaison Newsletter"; began *Fact* Magazine, New York City, 1963-67, was editor and publisher until publication was suspended; *Avant Garde* (bimonthly magazine), New York City, editor and publisher, 1967—; *Moneysworth* (consumer newspaper), New York City, editor and publisher, 1971—. *Military service:* U.S. Army, 1950-51 (concurrently working for the *Times-Herald* at night); became corporal. *Member:* American Civil Liberties Union, Sierra Club (New York); Trails Conference, Friends of the Earth, Friends of Animals (all New Jersey). *Awards, honors:* Best Article of the Year Award from *Playboy.*

WRITINGS: (Contributor) *Best Sports Stories,* edited by I. T. Marsh and E. Ehre, Dutton, 1951; *An Unhurried View of Erotica,* introduction by Theodor Reik and George Jean Nathan, privately printed by Helmsman Press, 1958; (editor) *100 Years of Lynchings,* Olive Branch Press, 1961, Lancer, 1962; *"Eros" on Trial,* Book Division of *Fact* Magazine, 1966; (editor with Warren Boronson) *The Best of "Fact,"* Trident, 1967; *Castrated: My Eight Months in Prison,* Avant Garde Books, 1973. Contributor to *Reader's Digest, Harper's, Coronet, Parade, This Week, Look, Esquire, Collier's,* and other publications.

WORK IN PROGRESS: A biography of Anthony Comstock.

SIDELIGHTS: In 1963 Ginzburg was indicted, tried, and convicted in a Federal Court in Philadelphia for "pandering" through the allegedly "salacious" promotional methods he used to sell his hard-cover erotic art magazine, *Eros.* On March 21, 1966, the U.S. Supreme Court, with a five to four vote, upheld the lower court's decision and sentenced Ginzburg to five years in prison and attached a $42,000 fine. He petitioned for a rehearing. After the Supreme Court handed down its decision, Ginzburg called a press conference before a statue of Benjamin Franklin, "the founder of our post office and America's first postmaster general, [who] said that nothing should be banned from the mails except inflammables and perishables and that no form of censorship should be tolerated by the American people," said Ginzburg. While the Court did not rule that Ginzburg's publications as such (*Eros, The Housewife's Handbook on Selective Promiscuity,* and "Liaison") were necessarily obscene, it decided instead that Ginzburg's promotional mailing, postmarked Middlesex, N.J., was "shoddy" and pervaded by "the leer of the sensualist." The Court thus added a new dimension to the establishment of what may or may not be obscene, basing its judgment on something entirely extraneous to the material being judged. In his press conference Ginzburg added: "I am confident that future Americans will look back at today's decision with shame and remorse and will regard it not only as the triumph of censorship over free speech but of psychopathy over mental health. Today's decision was worthy of a Russian court, not of the United States Supreme Court. I am confident that history will vindicate me, and that eventually America will stop branding its artists, writers, and publishers as criminal."

Ginzburg maintained that, "although we did mail from Middlesex, N.J., we had no intention of exploiting the sexual connotation of the name." He told *Playboy:* "We mailed from Middlesex simply because one of the largest mail-order facilities in the Eastern United States was located there. Anyone who thinks otherwise is really doing my sense of humor an injustice." Furthermore, he did not believe his promotional matter was in any way tasteless: "It was elegantly written and handsomely printed. We used beautiful old engravings for art, and we reproduced them on expensive antiqued paper.... Personally, I think most cigarette ads are vulgar. I think photographs showing B-52s dropping napalm on Vietnamese civilians are vulgar. No, let me make that stronger. They're grotesque, they're obscene. But I wouldn't put a man in jail for publishing such pictures. Good taste is absolutely indefinable in any legal sense." Obscenity, too, is indefinable, no more definable than witchery, said Ginzburg, adding: "I think the comparison is valid and our descendants in future generations will look back with profound shame that publishers like myself who dealt honestly with sex had been hounded into prison as criminals in the middle of the twentieth century."

A U.S. District Court later lowered Ginzburg's jail term to three years. In February, 1971, the U.S. Appeals Court rejected Ginzburg's appeal and later that year the U.S. Supreme Court denied a hearing on the sentence. Ginzburg began serving his prison sentence in February, 1972; he was paroled from the Federal prison in Allenwood, Penn., October 10, 1972, after serving eight months.

Ginzburg thought of *Eros* as "an *antidote* to the average conception of obscenity. With very few exceptions, sex has traditionally been relegated to slimy, tawdry, mean, crude, and inartistic publications by our society. *Eros* was the direct opposite of all these things.... *Eros* contained reproductions of many masterpieces of art, as well as original contributions by some of the most gifted contemporary writers, artists, and photographers." The magazine won more awards for artistic excellence than any other American publication. The U.S. State Department supposedly planned to send portions of *Eros* to the U.S.S.R. as examples of excellence in American design.

Ginzburg told *Playboy* that it was only because of previous Supreme Court rulings that he believed it possible to publish *Eros* and advertise as he did. "I was stunned when they came out of left field and ... hit me with the advertising bit. I had no idea I would be accused of intending to 'pander,' and, accordingly, I had no opportunity to make an adequate defense." He said, however, that he would not continue to publish *Eros* "until the Supreme Court clearly establishes that erotica can be dealt with honestly.... I'm a law-abiding crusader. You know, I could have pleaded guilty at the trial and received a suspended sentence.... But I chose to fight. I lost, and now I'll respect the decision."

Ginzburg admitted that he is "a vigorous, energetic promoter and hustler, but that doesn't preclude my being a serious publisher, too. Under all the razzle-dazzle, flash, noise, and promotion I come up with, there is a very real, beautiful, important, and worthwhile philosophy. It is a philosophy that will endure, and I express it in my publications.... It boils down to two words: *simple honesty.*" This philosophy was perhaps best expressed in *Fact,* a publication which the *New Statesman* called "the sawn-off shotgun of American critical writing" and the magazine which Barry Goldwater brought suit against, and won.

Ginzburg told *CA:* "I believe that within my lifetime I shall see the eradication of the anti-'obscenity' statutes which have done so much to hinder the dissemination of so many great works of art and literature dealing with sex."

Ginzburg speaks and writes Spanish and Yiddish.

BIOGRAPHICAL/CRITICAL SOURCES: New York Times, March 22, 1966, May 26, 1968, April 30, 1972, May 21, 1972, December 3, 1972; *Playboy,* July, 1966; *Publishers Weekly,* February 21, 1972.

*   *   *

GIRSON, Rochelle

PERSONAL: Born in Spokane, Wash.; daughter of David and Minnie (Parson) Girson. *Education:* Attended Montana State University. *Home:* 60 Sutton Place S., New York, N.Y. 10022. *Agent:* James Brown Associates, Inc., 22 East 60th St., New York, N.Y. 10022.

CAREER: Saturday Review, New York, N.Y., writer of syndicated columns, "Among Books and Authors" and "This Week's Personality," for Saturday Review Book Service for newspapers prior to 1958, book review editor, 1958-73. *Member:* P.E.N.

WRITINGS: Maiden Voyages: A Lively Guide for the Woman Traveler, Harcourt, 1967.

WORK IN PROGRESS: Study of self-fulfillment in leisure time.

SIDELIGHTS: Miss Girson has visited more than sixty countries in Europe, Near East, Africa, Asia, and Central and South America.

BIOGRAPHICAL/CRITICAL SOURCES: Emily Kimbrough, "One With the World," *Saturday Review,* April 29, 1967.

*   *   *

GIST, Ronald R. 1932-

PERSONAL: Born May 15, 1932, in St. Louis, Mo.; son of Noel P. and Mabel (Wilkes) Gist; married Shirley Turner,

March 14, 1953; children: Tony, Johnalea, Robin, Marty. *Education:* University of Missouri, B.S., 1958, M.S., 1959; University of Illinois, Ph.D., 1964. *Home:* 7102 South Platte Canyon Dr., Littleton, Colo. 80123. *Office:* Department of Marketing Management, University of Denver, Denver, Colo. 10210.

CAREER: University of Missouri, Columbia, instructor, 1959-60, assistant professor, 1963-64; University of Southern California, Los Angeles, assistant professor, 1964-66; Oregon State University, Corvallis, associate professor, 1966-67; University of Nebraska, Lincoln, associate professor of marketing, 1967-69; University of Denver, Denver, Colo., Beaumont professor of business administration, 1969—. Consultant to Auto Club of Southern California, Lockheed, Modern Market Research Associates, and other business firms. *Military service:* U.S. Army, 1954-55. *Member:* American Marketing Association (director, Omaha-Lincoln chapter), Beta Gamma Sigma.

WRITINGS: (Editor) *Management Perspectives in Retailing,* Wiley, 1967, 2nd edition, 1971; *Retailing: Concepts and Decisions,* Wiley, 1968; *Marketing and Society: A Conceptual Introduction,* Holt, 1971; (editor) *Readings: Marketing and Society,* Holt, 1971; *Basic Retailing: Text and Cases,* Wiley, 1971; *Cases in Marketing Management,* Holt, 1972.

*   *   *

GITTELL, Marilyn   1931-

PERSONAL: Born April 3, 1931, in New York, N.Y.; daughter of Julius and Rose (Meyerson) Jacobs; married Irwin Gittell (a certified public accountant), August 20, 1950; children: Amy, Ross. *Education:* Brooklyn College (now Brooklyn College of the City University of New York), B.A., 1952; New York University, M.P.A., 1953, Ph.D., 1960. *Home:* 110-21 73rd Ave., Forest Hills, N.Y. 11375. *Office:* Brooklyn College of the City University of New York, Brooklyn, N.Y. 11210.

CAREER: Tax Foundation, New York, N.Y., research assistant, 1952-55; Government Affairs Foundation, Albany, N.Y., research associate, 1955-60; Queens College of the City University of New York, Flushing, Long Island, N.Y., instructor, 1960-62, assistant professor, 1962-65, associate professor, 1965-67, professor of political science, 1967-71, professor of urban studies and chairman of department, 1971-73, director of Institute for Community Studies, 1967-73; Brooklyn College of the City University of New York, Brooklyn, N.Y., professor of political science, 1973—, assistant vice-president and associate provost, 1973—. Consultant to numerous organizations including New York State Constitutional Revision Commission, 1958-59, United Nations, 1966, and Ford Foundation, 1967; member of Associate Task Force on Manpower, U.S. Department of Labor, 1970-74, of advisory board, Puerto Rican Research Center, 1971—, New York State Task Force on Post Secondary Education, 1971—, National Study Commission on undergraduate and teacher education, 1972—, and New York State Regents Committee on Examinations, 1974—. Conductor of series of forty radio programs, "Megalopolis: U.S.A.," for WNYC, 1960. Member of community committee, New York Metropolitan Museum of Art, 1971—.

MEMBER: American Political Science Association, American Society for Public Administration, Northeastern Regional Political Science Association (member of executive committee, 1972), New York State Political Science Association (member of executive board, 1966-67), Phi Beta Kappa. *Awards, honors:* Grants from Ford Foundation, 1967-70, 1975-76, City University of New York, 1970-71, New York Foundation, 1971, New World Foundation, 1971-72, and Carnegie Foundation, 1972-74.

WRITINGS: (Co-author) *Metropolitan Communities: A Bibliography,* Public Administration Service, 1956; (co-author) *Metropolitan Surveys: A Digest,* Public Administration Service, 1958; (editor) *Educating an Urban Population,* Sage Publications, 1967; *Participants and Participation: A Study of School Policy in New York City,* Praeger, 1967; (with T. E. Hollander) *Six Urban School Systems: A Comparative Study of Institutional Response,* Praeger, 1968; (editor with Alan Hevesi) *The Politics of Urban Education,* Praeger, 1969; (editor with Maurice Berube) *Confrontation at Ocean Hill-Brownsville,* Praeger, 1969; (with Mario Fantini and Richard Magat) *Community Control and the Urban School,* Praeger, 1970; *Local Control in Education,* Praeger, 1972; (with Fantini) *Dencentralization: Achieving Reform,* Praeger, 1973; *School Boards and School Policy,* Praeger, 1973; (editor with Ann Cook and Herb Mack) *City Life: A Documentary History of the American City,* Praeger, 1973; (editor with Cook and Mack) *What Was It Like: When Your Grandparents Were Your Age,* Knopf, 1976.

Monographs: *Megalopolis, U.S.A.: A Radio Course,* Queens College Press, 1960; (with William Fredericks) *State Technical Assistance to Local Government,* Council of State Governments, 1962; *Governing the Public Schools,* Temporary Commission on City Finances (New York), 1966; (with T. E. Hollander and William Vincent) *Investigation of Fiscally Independent City School Districts,* U.S. Office of Education, 1967; *The Community School in the Nation,* Institute for Community Studies, Queens College of the City University of New York, 1970; *School Decentralization and School Policy in New York City,* Institute for Community Studies, Queens College of the City University of New York, 1971; *An Evaluation of the Impact of the Emergency Employment Act in New York City,* National Manpower Task Force, 1972.

Contributor: Louis Masotti and Dan Bowen, editors, *Civil Violence in the Urban Community,* Sage Publications, 1968; Alan Rosenthal, editor, *Governing Education: A Reader on Politics, Power and Public School Policy,* Doubleday, 1969; H. R. Mahodd and Edward L. Angus, editors, *Urban Politics and Problems,* Scribner, 1969; *Needs of Elementary and Secondary Education for the Seventies,* U.S. Government Printing Office, 1970; Henry M. Levin, editor, *Community Control of Schools,* Brookings Institution, 1970; Annette Rubinstein, editor, *Schools against Children: The Case for Community Control,* Monthly Review Press, 1970; Jewel Bellush and Stephen David, editors, *Race and Politics in New York City: Six Case Studies in Decentralization,* Praeger, 1971; *Freedom, Bureaucracy and Schooling,* National Education Association, 1971; Susan Fainstein and Norman Fainstein, editors, *The View from Below: Urban Politics and Social Policy,* Little, Brown, 1972; Allan Gartner, Colin Greer, and Frank Riessman, editors, *What Nixon is Doing to Us,* Harrow Books, 1974; Sar A. Levitan and Robert Taggart, editors, *Emergency Employment Act,* Olympus, 1974; Antonia Pantoja, Barbara Blourock, and James Bowman, editors, *Badges and Indicia of Slavery: Cultural Pluralism Redefined,* Study Commission on Undergraduate Education and the Education of Teachers, 1975; Maynard C. Reynolds, editor, *Special Education in School System Decentrali-*

zation, Leadership Training Institute, University of Minnesota, 1975; Frederick B. Rough, editor, *Milliken vs. Bradley: Implication for Metropolitan Desegregation*, U.S. Government Printing Office, 1975; Carl A. Grant, editor, *Community Participation in Education: What Is/What Should Be*, Pendell, 1976.

Contributor to *Encyclopedia Americanna*, 1964, *Proceedings of the Academy of Political Science*, 1968, and *Encyclopedia of Education*, 1971. Contributor of articles to professional journals, including *Change, Social Policy, Public Administration Review, New Generations, Journal of Negro Education*, and *American Behavioral Scientist*. Editor, *Urban Affairs Quarterly*, 1965-70; member of editorial advisory board, *Urban Affairs Annual Review*, 1966-74; member of editorial board, *Social Policy*, 1969—.

* * *

GITTINGS, John 1938-

PERSONAL: Born September 24, 1938, in London, England; son of Robert William Victor and Katherine (Campbell) Gittings; married Aelfthryth Georgina Buzzard (a social worker); children: Daniel John, Thomas Fidel. *Education:* School of Oriental and African Studies, London, Civil Service Diploma (Chinese), 1958; Corpus Christi College, Oxford, Oriental studies, 1958-61 (first honors). *Politics:* Socialist. *Religion:* Atheist. *Home:* Dodds, East Dean, near Chichester, West Sussex, England. *Office:* Instituto de Estudios Internacionales, Casilla 14187-Correo 15, Santiago, Chile.

CAREER: Royal Institute of International Affairs, London, England, Chinese specialist, 1963-66; Instituto de Estudios Internacionales, Santiago, Chile, specialist in Asian studies, 1966—. Consultant, International Confederation for Disarmament and Peace. *Awards, honors:* Harkness fellowship of Commonwealth Fund, 1961-62.

WRITINGS: *The Role of the Chinese Army*, Oxford University Press, 1967; *Survey of the Sino-Soviet Dispute: A Commentary and Extracts from the Recent Polemics, 1963-67*, Oxford University Press, 1968; *A Chinese View of China*, Pantheon, 1973; *The World and China, 1922-1972*, Harper, 1974.

SIDELIGHTS: Gittings is competent in written and spoken Chinese, French, Italian, and Spanish.†

* * *

GITTLEMAN, Edwin 1929-

PERSONAL: Born January 20, 1929, in Brooklyn, N.Y.; son of Joseph (a physician) and Esther (Cohen) Gittleman; married Rosalyn Leinwand (a music teacher), June 29, 1952; children: Neal Jay. *Education:* Columbia University, A.B., 1950, M.A. (with highest honors), 1957, Ph.D., 1965. *Politics:* Democrat. *Religion:* Jewish. *Home:* 5 Great Rock Rd., Lexington, Mass. 02173. *Office:* English Department, University of Massachusetts, Boston, Mass. 02125.

CAREER: Stevens Institute of Technology, Hoboken, N.J., assistant professor of humanities, 1959-65; Dartmouth College, Hanover, N.H., assistant professor of English, 1965-69; University of Massachusetts, Boston, associate professor, 1969-75, professor of English, 1975—, associate dean of faculty, 1973-75. Norwich delegate, Windsor County, Vermont Democratic Organization, 1966-67. *Military service:* U.S. Naval Reserve, 1954-57; served in Panama; became lieutenant. *Member:* Modern Language Association of America, College English Association,

American Association of University Professors, English Graduate Union (Columbia University), Archaeological Society of Panama, Emerson Society, Thoreau Society.

WRITINGS: *Naval Communications Procedures in the Fifteenth Naval District*, U.S. Navy, 1956; *Jones Very: The Effective Years, 1833-1840*, Columbia University Press, 1967; (contributor) Irving Malin, editor, *Critical Views of Isaac Bashevis Singer*, New York University Press, 1969. Author of scholarly articles on American literature. Guest editor, *Emerson Society Quarterly*.

WORK IN PROGRESS: *Emerson's Women: Love and Friendship in the Nineteenth Century; Emerson the Poet*, a critical study of major and important minor poems; essays on the Black presence in American literature; Crevecoeur's place in American literature.

SIDELIGHTS: Gittleman stated "[I] remain convinced that Ralph Waldo Emerson is the crucial figure in American literary history, and that the Transcendental Movement is at the center of a vital American tradition which reaches back to Puritan times and is now reflected in contemporary American writing from Hemingway to Ginsberg." Gittleman is competent in Latin, French, and German; he reads Middle English. *Avocational interests:* Pre-Colombian archaeology (collected pottery and stone artifacts in Panama), and collecting nineteenth-century primitive New England handicrafts and furniture.

* * *

GLAD, Betty 1929-

PERSONAL: Born September 27, 1929, in Salt Lake City, Utah; daughter of Harluf A. (a businessman) and Edna (Geertsen) Glad. *Eduation:* University of Utah, B.S. (magna cum laude), 1949; University of Chicago, Ph.D., 1962. *Office:* 382 Lincoln Hall, University of Illinois, Urbana, Ill. 61820.

CAREER: United Airlines, Chicago, Ill., staff member, 1949-53; University of Chicago, Center for Study of American Foreign Policy, Chicago, Ill., researcher, 1955-56; instructor in political science at Wilson Junior College, Chicago, Ill., 1957-58, and Mount Holyoke College, South Hadley, Mass., 1958-59; Brooklyn College of the City University of New York, Brooklyn, N.Y., lecturer, 1959-64; University of Illinois, Urbana, associate professor, 1964-74, professor of political science, 1974—. *Member:* American Political Science Association, Authors Guild, Phi Beta Kappa, University of Utah Beehive Society.

WRITINGS: *World Affairs Programs in Illinois*, University of Illinois, 1965; *Charles Evans Hughes and the Illusions of Innocence: A Study in American Diplomacy*, University of Illinois Press, 1966; (contributor) Jeanne N. Knutson, editor, *Handbook of Political Psychology*, Jossey-Bass, 1974.

WORK IN PROGRESS: *Personality and Role Performance; Sex Roles and Society; Psychology of the Tyrant*.

* * *

GLADDEN, E(dgar) Norman 1897-
(Norman Mansfield)

PERSONAL: Born August 4, 1897, in Reading, England; son of Edgar Mansfield (a builder) and Evelyn (Ladyman) Gladden; married Alice Ryan, 1944. *Education:* University of London, B.Sc., M.Sc., Ph.D. *Home:* 79 Bulwer Rd., New Barnet, Hertfordshire, England.

CAREER: Executive in British Civil Service, 1913-58, with posts in General Post Office, 1913-41, Ministry of Labour and National Service, 1942-47, and Ministry of Pensions and National Insurance, 1948-58. Since his retirement, has traveled to Liberia, Tanzania, and Ethiopia on short missions for United Nations and UNESCO. *Military service:* British Army, 1916-19. *Member:* Royal Institute of Public Administrators (member of London executive council, 1958—).

WRITINGS: Civil Service Staff Relationships, foreword by Sir Horace Wilson, Hodge & Co., 1943; *The Civil Service: Its Problems and Future,* Staples, 1948; *An Introduction to Public Administration,* Staples, 1952; *The Essentials of Public Administration,* Staples, 1953; *Civil Service or Bureaucracy,* Staples, 1956; *British Public Service Administration,* Staples, 1961; *Approach to Public Administration,* Staples, 1966; *Civil Services of the United Kingdom, 1855-1970,* Augustus Kelley, 1967; *Ypres 1917,* Kimber & Co., 1967; (editor) *Across the Piave: Personal Account of the British Forces in Italy, 1917-19,* H.M.S.O., 1971; *A Student's Guide to Public Administration,* two volumes, Beekman, 1972; *A History of Public Administration,* two volumes, Cass & Co., 1972; *Local Corporational and International Administration,* Staples, 1972; *Central Government Administration,* Staples, 1972; *The Somme 1916,* Kimber & Co., 1974.

Under pseudonym Norman Mansfield: *The Failure of the Left,* Staples, 1947.

WORK IN PROGRESS: Autobiography of a Civil Servant.

AVOCATIONAL INTERESTS: Music appreciation, history, travel, philately.

* * *

GLADSTONE, Josephine 1938-
(Josephine Marquand)

PERSONAL: Born January 5, 1938, in London, England; daughter of Sir Frederick Elwyn (Lord Chancellor of Great Britain) and Pearl (an author and illustrator; maiden name, Binder) Jones; married Richard Marquand (a documentary film producer), July 23, 1960, (annulled, 1972); married J. Francis Gladstone (a documentary film director and television writer); children: two daughters and two sons. *Education:* Attended Newnham College, Cambridge, M.A., 1960; Harvard University, graduate study, 1975—. *Politics:* Social Democrat. *Religion:* Quaker Attender. *Home:* 193 Fuller St., Brookline, Mass. 02146. *Agent:* Betty Ann Clark, International Creative Management, 40 West 57th St., New York, N.Y. 10019. *Office:* History of Science Department, Harvard University, Cambridge, Mass. 02135.

CAREER: Diocesan Girls School, Kowloon, Hongkong, biology teacher, 1960-62; free-lance reader, editor, and illustrator, 1962-67; Anthony Blond Ltd. (publishers), London, England, editor of juvenile and educational books, beginning 1967; British Broadcasting Corp., London, science program researcher for series "Horizon," beginning 1967; chief researcher, art editor, and script assistant to Jacob Bronowski, for series "The Ascent of Man," for British Broadcasting Corp., 1969-73.

WRITINGS—Under name Josephine Marquand: *Chi Ming and Tiger Kitten* (juvenile), F. Watts, 1965; *Life, Its Nature, Origins and Distribution,* Oliver & Boyd, 1968; (illustrator) H. F. King, *Life Around Us,* Heinemann Educational Books, 1968; *Ching Ming and the Writing Lesson* (juvenile), Dobson, 1969; *Ching Ming and the Lion Dance* (juvenile), illustrations by mother, Pearl Binder, Dobson, 1969. Also author of *Stories from Ladder Street,* Dobson, 1975; *Zadig* (juvenile), British Broadcasting Publications, 1975.

WORK IN PROGRESS: Aspects of the history of birth control in China.

* * *

GLAETTLI, Walter E(ric) 1920-

PERSONAL: Born August 23, 1920, in Winterthur, Switzerland; son of Rodolphe and Frieda (Muller) Glaettli; married Beatrice Hoer, 1960. *Education:* Attended University of Lausanne, University of Geneva, and University of Edinburgh; University of Zurich, Ph.D. (magna cum laude), 1949. *Home:* Budd Lake Rd., Hackettstown, N.J. 07840. *Office:* Centenary College for Women, Hackettstown, N.J. 07840.

CAREER: James Gillespie's High School for Girls, Edinburgh, Scotland, teacher, 1946-47; Hohere Tochterschule, Zurich, Switzerland, teacher, 1949-50; Northwestern University, Evanston, Ill., instructor in German, 1950-53; Centenary College for Women, Hackettstown, N.J., professor of French and German, 1953—. *Military service:* Swiss Army, 1942-46. *Member:* Modern Language Association of America, Swiss American Historical Society (board of directors).

WRITINGS—College-level German textbooks, with C. R. Goedsche, except as indicated; all published by American Book Co., except as noted: *Sutter,* 1953; *Steuben,* 1953; *Carl Schurz,* 1953; *Einstein,* 1954; *Schweitzer,* 1956; *Thomas Mann,* 1957; *Heine,* 1958; *Beethoven,* 1959; *Steinmetz,* 1961; (sole author) *Die Vierte Kurve,* 1962; (with E. R. Backenstoss) *Conversational German Review Grammar,* 1966, revised edition, Van Nostrand, 1971. Contributor to journals.

SIDELIGHTS: Glaettli is also fluent in French; has good working knowledge of Italian and Spanish. *Avocational interests:* Travel; symphonic music and seriously-written contemporary music.

* * *

GLASER, E(ric) M(ichael) 1913-

PERSONAL: Born June 20, 1913, in Bratislava, Czechoslovakia; son of Charles (a lawyer) and Mila Maria Glaser; married Dorothy Isabella Hunter, March 10, 1948; children: Rosalind Ann, Mary Elizabeth, Caroline Mila. *Education:* University of Komensky, M.D., 1938; Cambridge University, Ph.D., 1949. *Politics:* Conservative. *Religion:* Church of England. *Home:* Bratach Bhan, Ballachulish, Argyll PA 39 4JX, Scotland.

CAREER: Appointed to a teaching hospital in Czechoslovakia, 1939, but left for England when the Nazis marched in; Postgraduate Medical School, London, England, research assistant, 1939-40; Cambridge University, Cambridge, England, research assistant in department of experimental medicine, 1947-51; University of Malaya, Singapore, professor of physiology, 1952-56, dean of Faculty of Medicine, 1954; University of London, London, professor of physiology, 1956-61, head of department, 1960-61; Evans Medical Laboratories (Glaxo Group), director of research, 1961-65; Riker Laboratories, Welwyn Garden City, Hertfordshire, England, director of research and development, 1965-69; Mid-West Medical Research, Columbus, Ohio, president, 1970-76. Royal Naval Survival at Sea Subcommittee, member, 1948-52, 1957-61; Medical Research Council Climatic Physiology Committee, member, 1956-61; Association of the British Pharmaceutical Industry, member of Code of Practice Committee. Broadcaster on scientific subjects on British television and radio. *Military service:* Czechoslovakian Army, volunteer sapper in France, 1940, medical orderly under English command, 1940-41. Royal Army Medical Corps, 1941-47; became captain; received Military Cross in Italian Campaign.

MEMBER: Royal College of Physicians of England, British Pharmacological Society, International Society for Biometeorology, Medical Research Society, Physiological Society, Institute of Biology (fellow), Royal Society of Medicine (fellow), Athenaeum Club (London).

WRITINGS: (Contributor) R. A. McCance, editor, *Studies of Undernutrition, Wuppertal 1946-49,* H.M.S.O., 1951; (contributor) L. J. Witts, editor, *Medical Surveys and Clinical Trials,* Oxford University Press, 1959, 2nd edition, 1964; (contributor) W. D. M. Paton, editor, *Pharmacological Analysis of Central Nervous Action,* Pergamon, 1962; *The Physiological Basis of Habituation,* Oxford University Press, 1966; (contributor) Edmund L. Harris and J. D. Fitzgerald, editors, *The Principles and Practice of Clinical Trials,* E. & S. Livingstone, 1970. About eighty-five articles and research reports have been published, a number of them on survival trials at sea, motion sickness, adaptation, means of slowing the growth of tumors by drugs, and effects of cold and heat on the body.

WORK IN PROGRESS: A revision of earlier monographs on habituation.

SIDELIGHTS: Glaser was the only civilian member of a Royal Navy team that conducted ten full-scale survival exercises in waters ranging from the Arctic to tropical seas off Singapore. He also was a member of a survival party put down in the mid-Atlantic in a gale in 1960; the team was supposed to remain adrift on the raft for five days, but had to shoot distress flares for rescue after one hour. *Avocational interests:* Walking, skiing and riding in Scotland.

*   *   *

GLASER, Lynn 1943-

PERSONAL: Born June 25, 1943, in Bryn Mawr, Pa.; son of Charles John (a chemist) and Martha (Fuhs) Glaser; married Nosta Boll, October 1, 1966. *Education:* Philadelphia College of Art, B.F.A., 1966. *Politics:* None. *Religion:* Quaker. *Home:* 4710 Chester Ave., Philadelphia, Pa. 19143.

WRITINGS: Counterfeiting in America, C. N. Potter, 1968; *Engraved America: American Iconography to 1800,* Roy Boswell, 1970; (author of introduction) Manasseh Ben Israel, *Hope of Israel,* Roy Boswell, 1973. Columnist, "Numismatically Speaking," in *Numismatic News;* contributor of more than one hundred articles to numismatic magazines.

WORK IN PROGRESS: Further research in studies relating to American life; work in urban re-development efforts.

*   *   *

GLASS, Stanley T(homas) 1932-

PERSONAL: Born September 7, 1932, in Liverpool, England; son of Charles (a railway clerk) and Mary (Forbes) Glass; married Maureen Simpson, July 26, 1958; children: David Charles Maurice, Michael Vincent. *Education:* University of Durham, B.A. (honors), 1958; St. Catherine's College, Oxford, B.Litt., 1963. *Religion:* Church of England. *Home:* 159 Sandbach Rd., North Alsager, Stoke-on-Trent, England. *Office:* Department of Politics, University of Keele, Keele, Staffordshire, England.

CAREER: City Passenger Transport Department, Liverpool, England, local government officer, 1948-50, 1954; Queen's University of Belfast, Belfast, Northern Ireland, assistant lecturer in politics, 1960-63; University of Keele, Keele, Staffordshire, England, assistant lecturer, 1963-64, lecturer in politics, 1964—. *Military service:* Royal Air Force, 1951-53; served in Egypt two years; became senior aircraftsman. *Member:* Political Studies Association of the United Kingdom, Protofour Society, Historical Model Railway Society, St. Catherine's Association (Oxford).

WRITINGS: The Responsible Society: The Ideas of the English Guild Socialists, Barnes & Noble, 1966.

WORK IN PROGRESS: Political ideologies.

AVOCATIONAL INTERESTS: Reading, walking, railway history, and historical railway modeling.

*   *   *

GLAUS, Marlene 1933-

PERSONAL: Born November 24, 1933, in Mantorville, Minn.; daughter of Vernon and Ardis (Mott) Glaus. *Education:* Winona State College, B.S., 1954; University of Minnesota, graduate study. *Religion:* Congregationalist. *Home:* 6601 Fifth Ave. S., Richfield, Minn. 55423.

CAREER: Elementary teacher in Minnesota, 1954—, currently at Centennial Elementary School, Richfield. Teacher of adult evening classes for Betty Crocker Creative Learning Center. *Member:* National Education Association, Minnesota Education Association, Richfield Education Association.

WRITINGS: From Thoughts to Words, National Council of Teachers of English, 1965; *Good and Right and Beautiful,* Giant Photos, 1971. Contributor of poems to *My Weekly Reader* (children's newspaper), *Instructor,* and other education journals.

SIDELIGHTS: Marlene Glaus has traveled in Europe, around the world, and in the United States and Canada.

*   *   *

GLEN, Duncan (Munro) 1933-

PERSONAL: Born January 11, 1933, in Cambuslang, Lanarkshire, Scotland; son of John Kennedy and Margaret (Tennent) Glen; married Margaret Eadie, January 4, 1957; children: Ian Kenneth, Alison Rosemary. *Education:* Educated at Rutherglen Academy, and then Edinburgh College of Art, 1953-56. *Home:* 14 Parklands Ave., Penwortham, Preston, Lancashire, England. *Office:* Preston Polytechnic, Corporation St., Preston, Lancashire, England.

CAREER: H.M. Stationery Office, London, England, typographer, 1958-60; Watford College of Technology, Watford, Hertfordshire, England, lecturer in typographic design, 1960-63; Robert Gibson & Sons Ltd. (publishers), Glasgow, Scotland, editor, 1963-65; Preston Polytechnic, Preston, Lancashire, England, lecturer, 1965-69, senior lecturer in graphic design, 1969-74, head of graphic design division, 1974—. Founder and owner of Akros Publications, 1965—. *Military service:* Royal Air Force, national service, 1956-58.

WRITINGS—All published by Akros Publications, except as noted: *Hugh MacDiarmid: Rebel Poet and Prophet,* Drumalban Press, 1962; *Hugh MacDiarmid and the Scottish Renaissance,* W. & R. Chambers, 1964; *The Literary Masks of Hugh MacDiarmid,* Drumalban Press, 1964; *Scottish Poetry Now,* 1966; *Idols: When Alexander Our King Was Dead: Poem,* 1967; (editor) *Poems Addressed to Hugh MacDiarmid,* 1967; *Kythings and Other Poems,* Caithness Books, 1969; *Sunny Summer Sunday Afternoon in the Park?,* 1969; (editor) *Selected Essays of Hugh MacDiarmid,* J. Cape, 1969, University of California Press, 1970.

Unnerneath the Bed: Poem, 1970; (editor) *The Akros Anthology of Scottish Poetry, 1965-70,* 1970; *A Small Press and Hugh MacDiarmid,* 1970; (with Hugh MacDiarmid) *The MacDiarmids: A Conversation,* 1970; *In Appearances: A Sequence of Poems,* 1971; *Clydesdale: A Sequence of Poems,* 1971; (editor) *Whither Scotland?,* Verry, 1971; *The Individual and the Twentieth-Century Scottish Literary Tradition,* 1971; *Feres: Poems,* 1971; (editor) *Hugh MacDiarmid: A Critical Survey,* Scottish Academic Press, 1972, University of California Press, 1973; *A Journey Past: A Poem,* privately printed, 1972; *A Cled Score: Poems,* 1974; (compiler) *A Bibliography of Scottish Poets from Stevenson to 1974,* 1974; *Mr. & Mrs. J. L. Stoddart at Home: A Poem,* 1975; (with John Brook) *The New Buildings of Preston,* Harris Press, 1975; (editor with Nat Scammacca) *Scottish Poetry for Sicily,* Celebes, 1975. Editor, *Akros,* 1965—, *Graphic Lines,* 1975—.

SIDELIGHTS: Glen told *CA,* "Scottish literary renaissance has given me the sense of belonging to a Scottish culture ... rather than a subsidiary of English literature with only parochial interests."

* * *

GLENDINNING, Richard 1917-

PERSONAL: Surname is pronounced Glen-*din*-ing; born October 10, 1917, in Elizabeth, N.J.; son of Richard Edwin and Alice May (Summers) Glendinning; married Sara Helena Wilson (a journalist), December 27, 1941; children: Elizabeth Ann. *Education:* Dartmouth College, A.B., 1940. *Home:* 1638 South Dr., Sarasota, Fla. 33579.

CAREER: Vogue, New York City, member of advertising staff, 1940; *Country Life,* New York City, associate editor, 1940-41; Museum of Art, Baltimore, Md., public relations work, 1941; full-time free-lance writer, 1945—. Chairman of Sarasota County Historical Commission; director of Historical and Natural Sciences Center. *Military service:* U.S. Naval Reserve, 1942-45; became lieutenant commander. *Member:* Society of American Historians, Mystery Writers of America, Authors Guild, Forest Lakes Country Club.

WRITINGS: Terror in the Sun, Gold Medal Books, 1952; *Who Evil Thinks,* Gold Medal Books, 1952; *Mission to Murder,* Gold Medal Books, 1954; *Retreat into Night,* Gold Medal Books, 1954; *Too Fast We Live,* Popular Library, 1954; *Passion Road,* Popular Library, 1955; *Carnival Girl,* Popular Library, 1956; (with Wyatt Blassingame) *The Mountain Men,* F. Watts, 1962; (with Blassingame) *The Frontier Doctors,* F. Watts, 1963; (with Blassingame) *Man Who Opened the West,* Putnam, 1966; *When Mountain Men Trapped Beaver,* Garrard, 1967; *Circus Days Under the Big Top,* Garrard, 1969; (with Sally Glendinning) *The Ringling Brothers: Circus Family,* Garrard, 1972; (with S. Glendinning) *Gargantua: The Mighty Gorilla,* Garrard, 1974. Author of radio plays. Contributor of short stories and articles to newspapers and magazines.

WORK IN PROGRESS: Continuing research on the early West and Florida history.

* * *

GLICK, Edward Bernard 1929-

PERSONAL: Born February 12, 1929, in Brooklyn, N.Y.; son of Louis (a butcher) and Ray (Schwartz) Glick; married Florence Joy Wolfson (a public school teacher), June 18, 1950; children: Reuven (son), Marnina (daughter). *Education:* Attended New York University, 1946-48; Brooklyn College (now Brooklyn College of the City University of New York), B.A. (cum laude), 1950; University of Florida, M.A., 1952, Ph.D., 1955. *Politics:* Democrat. *Religion:* Jewish. *Home:* 302 Fox Lane, Broomall, Pa. 19008. *Office:* Department of Political Science, Temple University, Philadelphia, Pa. 19122.

CAREER: University of Florida, Gainesville, instructor in political science, 1955-56; American Jewish Congress, New York, N.Y., director of Commission on International Affairs, 1956-59; System Development Corp., human factors scientist in Paramus, N.J., and Falls Church, Va., 1959-64; Bendix Corp., Office of National Security Studies, Washington, D.C., senior political scientist, 1964-65; Temple University, Philadelphia, Pa., associate professor, 1965-68, professor of political science, 1968—. Consultant to U.S. Office of Naval Research, 1964-67, and Bendix Corp., 1965-70. *Member:* American Political Science Association, International Studies Association, American Association of University Professors, Inter-University Seminar on Armed Forces and Society (fellow), Association of Canadian Studies in the United States. *Awards, honors:* Stackpole Award for "the most significant contribution to military thinking," 1967, for *Peaceful Conflict: The Non-Military Use of the Military.*

WRITINGS: Latin America and the Palestine Problem, Herzl Press, 1958; *Straddling the Isthmus of Tehuantepec,* University of Florida Press, 1959; *Peaceful Conflict: The Non-Military Use of the Military,* Stackpole, 1967; *Soldiers, Scholars, and Society: The Social Impact of the American Military,* Goodyear Publishing, 1971; *Between Israel and Death,* Stackpole, 1974. Contributor to *Commonweal, Congress Weekly, Midstream, Military Review, Jewish Frontier, Americas,* and other journals.

WORK IN PROGRESS: Soldier and State in Israeli Society, a monograph for the Labor Zionist Alliance.

SIDELIGHTS: Glick has traveled in Israel and Latin America; he speaks Spanish, French, modern Hebrew, Yiddish, and German.

BIOGRAPHICAL/CRITICAL SOURCES: Washington Post, April 28, 1964; *Philadelphia Inquirer* (Northwest edition), October 1, 1967; *Philadelphia Jewish Exponent,* June 7, 1974.

* * *

GLOCK, Marvin D(avid) 1912-

PERSONAL: Born November 19, 1912, in San Jose, Ill.; son of David W. (a farmer) and Lydia (Gruensfelder) Glock; married Ruth Snell, April 13, 1941; children: Carol Sue, Sandra Kay. *Education:* Blackburn College, student, 1930-32; University of Nebraska, A.B., 1934; University of Illinois, M.S., 1938; University of Iowa, Ph.D., 1946. *Religion:* Presbyterian. *Home:* 101 Homestead Ter., Ithaca, N.Y. 14850. *Office:* 217 Stone Hall, Cornell University, Ithaca, N.Y. 14850.

CAREER: High school teacher in Nebraska, 1934-36, and in Illinois, 1936-37; high school principal in Mason City, Ill., 1937-43; Michigan State University, East Lansing, assistant professor of education, 1947-49; Cornell University, Ithaca, N.Y., professor of educational psychology, 1949—. Visiting professor at University of Chicago, summer, 1954. Licensed psychologist, New York State. *Military service:* U.S. Navy, 1943-45; became lieutenant. *Member:* American Psychological Association (fellow), American Educational Research Association, International Reading Association, National Council on Measurement in Education, National Society for the Study of Education, Sigma Xi, Phi Delta Kappa, Phi Kappa Phi. *Awards, honors:* Fulbright scholar at University of Ceylon, 1962-63.

WRITINGS: (With J. Stanley Ahmann and Helen Wardeberg) *Evaluating Elementary School Pupils,* Allyn & Bacon, 1960; *The Improvement of College Reading,* Houghton, 1954, 2nd edition, 1967; (with Ahmann) *Evaluating Pupil Growth,* Allyn & Bacon, 1958, 5th edition, 1975; (with Ahmann) *Test Manual on Evaluating Pupil Growth,* Allyn & Bacon, 1964, 4th edition, 1975; (with Richard E. Ripple and Jason Millman) *Learner Characteristics and Instructional Mode: The Relationship of Anxiety, Compulsivity, Creativity, and Exhibitionism to Success in Learning from Programed and Conventional Instruction,* Cornell University Press, 1967; (editor) *Guiding Learning: Readings in Educational Psychology,* Wiley, 1971; (with Ahmann) *Measuring and Evaluating Educational Achievement,* Allyn & Bacon, 1971, 2nd abridged edition, 1975; (with David Bender and Ann Dennis) *Probe,* C. E. Merrill, 1975.

WORK IN PROGRESS: Research in imagery as it relates to comprehension.

* * *

GLOS, Raymond E(ugene) 1903-

PERSONAL: Born February 5, 1903, in Wayne, Ill.; son of Frederick A. (an accountant) and Flora (Mapes) Glos; married Dorothy Styan, July 9, 1927; children: Carol (Mrs. David E. Hinshaw), Alan S. *Education:* University of Illinois, B.S., 1925, M.S., 1926; Ohio State University, Ph.D., 1939. *Politics:* Republican. *Religion:* Congregational. *Home:* 110 East Spring St., Oxford, Ohio 45056.

CAREER: Certified public accountant, state of Illinois, 1926, Ohio, 1938. University of Illinois, Urbana, assistant to dean of men, 1926-27; Miami University, Oxford, Ohio, assistant professor, 1927-30, associate professor, 1930-37, professor of accounting, 1937-47, professor of business, 1947-69, dean of School of Business Administration, 1937-63, chairman of department of business, 1963-69, dean emeritus, 1969—. Member of board of directors, Citizens Bank, Hamilton, Ohio. *Member:* American Institute of Certified Public Accountants, American Accounting Association (vice-president, 1947), American Association of Collegiate Schools of Business (president, 1952), Alpha Sigma Phi (national president, 1966-68), Beta Gamma Sigma (national vice-president, 1954-58), Phi Eta Sigma (national treasurer, 1937—), Delta Sigma Pi. *Awards, honors:* LL.D., Miami University, 1972.

WRITINGS: (With Harold A. Baker) *Introduction to Business,* South-Western Publishing, 1947, 8th edition (with Richard D. Steade and James R. Lowry) published as *Business: Its Nature and Environment, An Introduction,* 1976.

AVOCATIONAL INTERESTS: Golf, numismatics.

GLUCK, Jay 1927-

PERSONAL: Born January 11, 1927, in Detroit, Mich.; son of Harry J. (a musician) and Lillian Mary Veronica Friar (Campbell-Phillips) Gluck; married Sumiye Hiramoto (a writer), May 9, 1955; children: Cellin Phillip, Garet Arthur. *Education:* Attended City College (now of the City University of New York), 1943-44, and George Washington University, 1946-47; University of California, Berkeley, B.A. in anthropology, 1949; Asia Institute School for Asian Studies, New York, N.Y., graduate study, 1950-51. *Politics:* Democrat by Oriental resignation. *Religion:* "Jew by temper; Buddhist inclination." *Agent:* Ruth Aley, Maxwell Aley Associates, 145 East 35th St., New York, N.Y. 10016. *Office:* Asia Institute Books, Tehran, Iran; and Asia Institute Books, 149 Nishiyama-cho, Ashiya 659, Japan.

CAREER: Asian Publications, Tokyo, Japan, editor, 1952-53; *Orient Asia Grafix,* Tokyo, owner, publisher, and editor of *Orient Digests,* 1953-57; Wakayama National University, Wakayama, Japan, professor of English, 1957-63; Asia Institute Books, Shiraz, Iran, and Ashiya, Japan, owner and publisher, 1963—; Pahlavi University, Shiraz, assistant director of Asia Institute, 1966-70. Commutes quarterly between Iran and Japan. Museum consultant on Near Eastern art; art collector. *Military service:* U.S. Navy, 1943-45.

WRITINGS: Ah So (cartoon misadventures of a foreigner in Japan), Orient Asia Grafix (Tokyo), 1953, new edition, 1964; *Zen Combat* (martial arts of Japan), Ballantine, 1964, new edition, 1974; (translator with Grace Sizuki and others, and editor) *Ukiyo: Stories of the "Floating" World of Postwar Japan,* Universal Library, 1964; (with wife, Sumiye Gluck) *Japan Inside Out* (guidebook), five volumes, Asia Institute Books, 1964-65, new edition, 1976; (editor) *Survey of Persian Art,* Volume XII: *A Bibliography of Pre-Islamic Persian Art,* Asia Institute Books, 1975. Translator with wife, S. Gluck, and editor-publisher of series on agriculture and anthropology of Southeast Asia, Asia Institute Books for Kyoto National University Center for Southeast Asian Studies, 1966-67.

Author of two documentary films for Iranian National Television. Contributor to *Encyclopedia of Sexual Behaviour,* and of more than four hundred articles to various Asian publications. Former columnist, *Japan Times,* Tokyo. Roving editor, *France-Asie/Asia,* 1960-66; contributing editor, *Arts of Asia,* 1975—.

WORK IN PROGRESS: Editing and contributing to Volume XV, Volume XVI and Volume XVII of *Survey of Persian Art;* editing series, and writing with wife, S. Gluck, two books in series "Introduction to Persian Art"; editing and publishing special project on handicrafts and folk art of Persia for the Empress of Iran; a novel on the Mongol empire, *Kamikaze;* editing and contributing to special issue of *Arts of Asia;* directing own documentary films for Iranian National Television.

SIDELIGHTS: Gluck describes himself as a "dilettante of the type one laughingly refers to today as an Asian expert," antisocial, and a non-joiner. His motivation is "to clarify Asia to America, America to Asia, as a contribution to Yugen and to enjoy myself doing the absurd."

* * *

GLUSTROM, Simon W. 1924-

PERSONAL: Born March 4, 1924, in Atlanta, Ga.; son of Solomon and Ida (Okun) Glustrom; married Helen Stein,

June 9, 1948; children: Jan, Beth, Aliza. *Education:* Yeshiva University, B.A., 1944; Jewish Theological Seminary of America, Rabbi, 1948. *Office:* Fair Lawn Jewish Center, Fair Lawn, N.J.

CAREER: Beth El Congregation, Durham, N.C., rabbi, 1948-50; Fair Lawn Jewish Center, Fair Lawn, N.J., rabbi, 1950—. *Member:* Rabbinical Assembly of America (president of New Jersey region, 1961), Associated Clergy of Fair Lawn (past president), Rotary (past president).

WRITINGS: When Your Child Asks: A Handbook for Jewish People, Bloch Publishing, 1956; *Living With Your Teenager,* Bloch Publishing, 1961; *The Language of Judaism,* Jonathan David, 1966, 2nd revised edition, Ktav, 1973.

* * *

GODDARD, Burton L(eslie) 1910-

PERSONAL: Born July 4, 1910, in Dodge Center, Minn.; son of William Bliss and Myra (Beckwith) Goddard; married Esther Anna Hempel (a teacher), July 16, 1940. *Education:* University of Minnesota, student, 1928-30; University of California, Los Angeles, A.B. (with highest honors), 1933; Westminster Theological Seminary, Th.B., 1937; Harvard Divinity School, S.T.M., 1938, Th.D., 1943; Simmons College, S.M. (library science), 1957. *Politics:* Republican. *Home and office:* Gordon-Conwell Theological Seminary, South Hamilton, Mass. 01982.

CAREER: Clergyman of the Orthodox Presbyterian Church. Pastor of Congregational church in Carlisle, Mass., 1937-41; Gordon College of Theology and Missions (now Gordon College), Wenham, Mass., instructor in Bible and Christian education, 1941-44, professor of Old Testament, 1944-51; Gordon-Conwell Theological Seminary, South Hamilton, Mass., instructor in Bible and Christian education, 1941-44, professor of Old Testament, 1944-51, professor of biblical languages and exergisis, 1951—, dean, 1944-61, director of library, 1961-73, library consultant, 1973—. Committee on Bible Translation, executive secretary, 1966-68, editorial coordinator, 1968-69, vice-chairman, 1969-73. Deerwander Bible Conference Association, member of board of directors, 1938—, and former president; member of board of directors, Chinese Evangelical Literature Committee, 1963—; member, Committee to Assist Missionary Education Overseas, 1964-70. Trustee, Boston Theological Institute, 1971-74. *Member:* Society of Biblical Literature, Evangelical Theological Society (president, 1964), American Theological Library Association, Phi Beta Kappa, Pi Gamma Mu, Phi Alpha Chi, Alpha Gamma Omega.

WRITINGS: Animals of the Bible, National Foundation for Christian Education, 1963; (editor with others) *The Encyclopedia of Modern Christian Missions: The Agencies,* Thomas Nelson, 1967. Joint editor of *New International Version of New Testament,* Zondervan, 1973.

Contributor to *Baker's Dictionary of Theology, Zondervan Pictorial Bible Dictionary,* and *Encyclopedia of Christianity;* also contributor of articles and reviews to theological and church journals.

WORK IN PROGRESS: Editing a new version of the Old Testament.

SIDELIGHTS: Burton Goddard is competent in biblical Hebrew and Greek, and has studied biblical Aramaic, Arabic, Assyrian, Syriac, Latin, French, and German. *Avocational interests:* Photography.

GOELLER, Carl 1930-

PERSONAL: Born May 20, 1930, in Wichita, Kan.; son of Carl G. and Sarah (Nothstine) Goeller; married Kay Branson (a stained glass designer), June 9, 1951; children: Sheila Kay Engelhardt, Ben Dee. *Education:* University of Wichita (now Wichita State University), A.B., 1951; University of Kansas City (now University of Missouri—Kansas City), graduate study, 1959-61. *Politics:* Independent. *Religion:* Lutheran. *Home:* 30200 Ashton Lane, Bay Village, Ohio 44140.

CAREER: Wichita Beacon, Wichita, Kan., advertising representative, 1951; Hallmark Cards, Inc., Kansas City, Mo., managing editor, 1953-61; Rust Craft, Inc., Dedham, Mass., editor, research director, and then director of advertising and sales, 1961-68; American Greetings Corp., Cleveland, Ohio, 1968—, began as editorial director and consultant, currently research director, and director of public relations. President, SPV&P, Inc. (writing service), Westwood, Mass. *Military service:* U.S. Army, 1951-53; became first lieutenant. *Member:* American Marketing Association, Armed Forces Writing League.

WRITINGS: Selling Poetry, Verse and Prose, Doubleday, 1962, revised edition, Writer, Inc., 1967; (with W. Uraneck) *Thirteen Steps to a More Dynamic Personality,* Prentice-Hall, 1971; *Writing to Communicate,* Doubleday, 1974. Also author of *How to Get Your Ideas Across,* 1972. Writer of television commercials and radio scripts; contributor of articles to newspapers and magazines and of cartoons to trade publications. Advisory editor, *Author & Journalist,* 1962—.

WORK IN PROGRESS: A book on public speaking, and one on greeting card history.

AVOCATIONAL INTERESTS: History, religion, philosophy, and mixtures of the three; stained glass designing.

* * *

GOETZMANN, William H. 1930-

PERSONAL: Born July 20, 1930, in Washington, D.C.; son of Harry William (an executive) and Viola M. (Nelson) Goetzmann; married Mewes M. Mueller (a games designer), August 26, 1953; children: William Nelson, Anne Stimson, Stephen Russell. *Education:* Yale University, B.A., 1952, Ph.D., 1957. *Politics:* Independent. *Home:* 4802 Timberline Dr., Austin, Tex. *Office:* University of Texas, Austin, Tex. 78712.

CAREER: Yale University, New Haven, Conn., instructor, 1957-59, assistant professor, 1959-63, associate professor of history and American studies, 1963-64; University of Texas, Austin, associate professor, 1964-66, professor of history and American studies, 1966-67, Stiles Professor of American Studies and History, 1967—, director of American studies program. Vice-president, Wilgo Games, Inc.; chief historical consultant, U.S. National Atlas Project.

MEMBER: American Studies Association, American Historical Association, Society of American Historians, Organization of American Historians, Western History Association, Texas State History Association, Texas Academy of Arts and Letters, Phi Beta Kappa. *Awards, honors:* Buffalo Award of New York Posse of The Westerners, 1960, for *Army Exploration in the American West;* Pulitzer Prize in history, Francis Parkman Award, and Friends of the Dallas Public Library Award, all 1967, for *Exploration and Empire;* LL.D., St. Edward's University, Austin, Tex., 1967; Golden Plate Award, American Academy of Achievement, 1968.

WRITINGS: Army Exploration in the American West, Yale University Press, 1959; (editor with Wallace E. Davies) *The New Deal and Business Recovery*, Holt, 1960; (editor with David M. Potter) *The New Deal and Employment*, Holt, 1960; *When the Eagle Screamed*, Wiley, 1966; *Exploration and Empire*, Knopf, 1966; (editor) *Colonial Horizon: America in the Sixteenth and Seventeenth Centuries*, Addison-Wesley, 1969; (editor with Dixon Pratt) *The American Hegelians*, Knopf, 1973. Editor: "Western American Series," Lippincott; "Transitions in American Thought Series," Prentice-Hall; and "American History in Focus Series," Addison-Wesley. Consulting editor, "Western Americana Series," Yale University Press. Contributor to *American Heritage* and professional journals.

WORK IN PROGRESS: An intellectual history of the United States; a biography of William H. Holmes.

SIDELIGHTS: "Regard good writing as one form of teaching," Goetzmann wrote. "Also interested in cartography, the development of various kinds of games as teaching devices and in the use of television and other modern media." His prize-winning *Exploration and Empire* is described by John Higham as an "imposing narrative of the expeditions and travels during the nineteenth century that opened up the land beyond the great bend of the Missouri River." Higham observes that it is "the first account that is both panoramic and detailed," and says that "it will stand for a long time as a valuable work of reference."

BIOGRAPHICAL/CRITICAL SOURCES: Kenyon Review, November, 1966; *New York Review of Books*, April 25, 1968.

*   *   *

GOFFMAN, Erving   1922-

PERSONAL: Born June 11, 1922, in Canada; son of Max and Anne Goffman; widower; children: one son. *Education:* University of Toronto, B.A., 1945; University of Chicago, M.A., 1949, Ph.D., 1953. *Office:* University of Pennsylvania, Philadelphia, Pa. 19174.

CAREER: University of Chicago, Chicago, Ill., assistant in the Division of Social Sciences, 1952-53, resident associate, 1953-54; National Institute of Mental Health, Bethesda, Md., visiting scientist, 1954-57; University of California, Berkeley, assistant professor, 1958-59, associate professor, 1959-62, professor of sociology, 1962-68; University of Pennsylvania, Philadelphia, Benjamin Franklin Professor of Anthropology and Sociology, 1968—.

WRITINGS: The Presentation of Self in Everyday Life (monograph), University of Edinburgh Social Sciences Research Centre, 1956, revised and expanded edition, Anchor Books, 1959; *Encounters: Two Studies in the Sociology of Interaction*, Bobbs-Merrill, 1961; *Asylums: Essays on the Social Situation of Mental Patients and Other Inmates*, Anchor Books, 1961; *Stigma: Notes on the Management of Spoiled Identity*, Prentice-Hall, 1963; *Behavior in Public Places: Notes on the Social Organization of Gatherings*, Free Press of Glencoe, 1963; *Interaction Ritual: Essays on Face-to-Face Behavior*, Doubleday, 1967; *Strategic Interaction*, University of Pennsylvania Press, 1969; *Relations in Public: Micro-Studies of the Public Order*, Basic Books, 1971; *Frame Analysis: Essays on the Organization of Experience*, Harper, 1974. Contributor to such periodicals as *Psychiatry* and the *American Journal of Sociology*.

BIOGRAPHICAL/CRITICAL SOURCES: Annals of American Academy of Political and Social Science, November, 1962, September, 1964; *American Journal of Sociology*, November, 1962; *American Anthropologist*, December, 1962; *American Sociological Review*, June, 1964.

*   *   *

GOFFSTEIN, M(arilyn) B(rooke)   1940-

PERSONAL: Born December 20, 1940, in St. Paul, Minn.; daughter of Albert A. (an electrical engineer) and Esther (Rose) Goffstein; married Peter Schaaf (a photographer and concert pianist), August 15, 1965. *Education:* Bennington College, B.A., 1962. *Religion:* Jewish. *Home:* 697 West End Ave., New York, N.Y. 10025.

CAREER: Author and illustrator; has had several one-woman exhibitions of pen and ink and watercolor drawings in New York, N.Y., and St. Paul, Minn. *Awards, honors: Sleepy People* was selected for the American Institute of Graphic Arts' Children's Book Show of 1965-66; *The Gats!* was an honor book in *Book Week's* Children's Spring Book Festival, 1966.

WRITINGS—All self-illustrated; all published by Farrar, Straus, except as noted: *The Gats!*, Pantheon, 1966; *Sleepy People*, 1966; *Brookie and Her Lamb*, 1967; *Across the Sea*, 1968; *Goldie the Dollmaker*, 1969; *The Two Piano Tuners*, 1970; *The Underside of the Leaf* (novel), 1972; *A Little Schubert*, Harper, 1972; *Me and My Captain*, 1974; *Daisy Summerfield's Style* (novel), Delacorte, 1975; *Fish for Supper*, Dial, 1976; *My Crazy Sister*, Dial, 1976.

*   *   *

GOLBURGH, Stephen J.   1935-

PERSONAL: Born September 21, 1935, in Boston, Mass.; son of M. Harry (a lawyer) and Mary (Cohen) Golburgh; married Linda Glaser (a speech pathologist), April 15, 1962; children: Vicki, Lawrence. *Education:* Boston University, A.B., 1957, Ed.D., 1960; Harvard University, Ed.M., 1958. *Religion:* Jewish. *Home:* 277 St. Paul St., Brookline, Mass. *Office:* 150 Freeman St., Brookline, Mass.

CAREER: Certified psychologist, Massachusetts Board of Certification in Psychology. Spencer Associates, Cambridge, Mass., clinical psychologist, 1958; Massachusetts Mental Health Center, Boston, Mass., rehabilitation psychologist, 1958-60; Boston University, Boston, 1960-63, began as instructor, became assistant professor of psychology and guidance; Northeastern University, Boston, lecturer in psychology, 1961-63, assistant professor of psychology in education, beginning 1963. Consultant, Jewish Big Brother Association, 1967—; consultant psychologist for Massachusetts Rehabilitation Commission, 1958-59, Solomon Schechter School, beginning 1960, and Jewish Family and Children's Service, 1964-65. Private practice, beginning 1960. Psychologist and lecturer in psychology at Camp Young Judea, 1959-60. Assessment officer for Volunteers in Service to America, 1965. Staff clinical psychologist, Boston V.A. Hospital, Boston, 1966—; clinical consultant in research, McLean Hospital, Harvard Medical School, 1966-67.

MEMBER: American Personnel and Guidance Association, American Psychological Association, American Society of Clinical Hypnosis, Psychologists Interested in the Advancement of Psychotherapy, American Association of University Professors, New England Psychological Association, Massachusetts Psychological Association (fellow), Phi Delta Kappa, Everett C. Benton Lodge.

WRITINGS: (Contributor) E. C. Glanz, *Groups in Guidance*, Allyn & Bacon, 1962; *The Experience of Adolescence*, Schenkman, 1965; (contributor) M. Kornrich, *Underachievement*, C. C Thomas, 1965; (contributor) J. C. Gowan and G. D. Demos, *The Guidance of Exceptional Children*, McKay, 1965. Contributor of articles and reviews to professional journals.

WORK IN PROGRESS: Research on attitudes of college students towards personal death, and on drug addiction among adolescents, hypnosis in the treatment of intractable pain, hypnotherapy in the treatment of drug addiction.††

* * *

GOLD, Doris B. 1919-

PERSONAL: Born November 21, 1919, in New York, N.Y.; daughter of Saul and Gertrude (Reiss) Bauman; married Wilson Branch, February, 1947; married second husband, Bernard George Gold (a bakery foreman), August, 1953; children: (second marriage) Albert, Michael. *Education:* Brooklyn College (now Brooklyn College of the City University of New York), B.A., 1946; Washington University, St. Louis, Mo., M.A., 1955; attended Pratt Institute and University of Kansas. *Religion:* Jewish. *Home:* 89-25 187th St., Hollis, Queens, N.Y. 11423. *Office:* Pete McGuinness Senior Center, 715 Leonard St., Brooklyn, N.Y. 11222.

CAREER: University of Kansas, Lawrence, instructor in English, 1946-47; evening instructor in English at State University of New York at Farmingdale, and for Levittown (N.Y.) adult education program, 1958-60; substitute teacher of English and art in secondary schools of New York City, 1953, 1960-64, and in Levittown, N.Y., 1956-60; *Young Judaean* (magazine), New York City, editor, 1964-72. Teacher of English to new Americans for Young Men's Hebrew Association and Young Women's Hebrew Association, St. Louis, Mo., 1950, and for New York Association for New Americans, 1962. East coast coordinator of Volunteerism Task Force, National Organization for Women, 1972-75. *Member:* American Jewish Historical Society. *Awards, honors:* American Scene Poetry Award, Poetry Society of Colorado, 1945; Carruth Poetry Award, University of Kansas, 1947; Allan Tate poetry scholarship at Indiana University, 1949; New York State Council on the Arts grant, 1970-73, for work on juvenile education program.

WRITINGS: (Editor, and adapter of twenty stories) *Stories for Jewish Juniors*, Jonathan David, 1967; (contributor) Vivian Gornick and B. K. Moran, editors, *Woman in Sexist Society: Studies in Power and Powerlessness*, Basic Books, 1971. Plays include "Golden Land," "Lincoln and Liberty Too," and several others produced by synagogue and church groups, and "Time Out of Joint," a Shakespearean burlesque; also dramatized sections of Mary Antin's *The Promised Land*. Contributor of poetry to *Tiger's Eye, Experiment,* and *Writer,* feature stories to *Levittown Tribune* and *Newsday,* book reviews to *New York Times,* and *Kansas City Star,* and feature articles to *Jerusalem Post, Jewish Weekly,* and *Woman's Day.*

WORK IN PROGRESS: A collection of poems dating from 1946, *Street Cry and Other Poems;* a book on the debate concerning volunteer work in America.

* * *

GOLD, Joseph 1933-

PERSONAL: Born June 30, 1933, in London, England; son of Maurice and Kitty (Goldberg) Gold; married Sandra Abramson, December 23, 1955; children: Deborah, Anna Michelle, Joel Martin Kit. *Education:* University of Birmingham, B.A., (honors), 1955; University of Wisconsin, Ph.D., 1959. *Politics:* Socialist. *Religion:* Jewish. *Residence:* Baden, Ontario, Canada. *Office:* Department of English, University of Waterloo, Waterloo, Ontario, Canada.

CAREER: University of Manitoba, Winnipeg, 1960-70, associate professor, then professor of English; University of Waterloo, Waterloo, Ontario, professor of English, 1970—, chairman of English department, 1970-73. Broadcaster of talks, and drama, film, and play criticism for Canadian Broadcasting Corp.

WRITINGS: *William Faulkner: A Study in Humanism,* University of Oklahoma Press, 1966; (editor) Charles G. D. Roberts, *King of Beasts, and Other Stories,* Ryerson, 1967; (compiler) *The Stature of Dickens: A Centenary Bibliography,* University of Toronto Press, 1971; *Charles Dickens: Radical Moralist,* Copp, 1972; (editor) Charles G. D. Roberts, *The Heart of the Ancient Wood,* McClelland & Stewart, 1973; (editor) *In the Name of English,* Macmillan, 1975. Contributor to *Canadian Literature, Dalhousie Review, Mississippi Quarterly,* and other journals.

* * *

GOLDBERG, Barney 1918-

PERSONAL: Born March 11, 1918, in Philadelphia, Pa.; son of Sam (a merchant) and Anna (Schwartz) Goldberg; married Erondina Valladares, May 20, 1939; children: Elisa Victoria, Paul Victor. *Education:* Temple University, B.S. in Ed., 1939. *Politics:* Socialist ("unaffiliated"). *Religion:* None. *Home:* 7145 Lincoln Dr., Philadelphia, Pa. 19119. *Agent:* Maximilian Becker, 115 East 82nd St., New York, N.Y. 10028.

CAREER: Worked as secondary school teacher, photographer, welder, and commodity trader; Grace Line, New York, N.Y., chief radio officer on S.S. *Santa Rosa,* 1949-66. Young People's Socialist League, organizer of Philadelphia branch, 1937-40.

WRITINGS: *Channel Fever* (novel), Jonah, 1967.

WORK IN PROGRESS: *Forgetful Let Me Dream,* a psychological novel; an untitled novel dealing with life aboard a luxury cruise ship.††

* * *

GOLDEN, L(ouis) L(awrence) L(ionel)

PERSONAL: Born in Toronto, Ontario, Canada; son of Samuel B. and Bluma Golden; married Mary Macmillan, April 8, 1960. *Education:* University of Toronto, B.A.; Osgoode Hall Law School, member of Ontario Bar. *Home:* 320 East 57th St., New York, N.Y. 10002. *Office:* 680 Fifth Ave., New York, N.Y. 10019.

CAREER: Ottawa correspondent, *Saturday Night,* 1938-42; *Globe And Mail,* Toronto, Ontario, editorial writer, 1942-50; public affairs consultant, New York, N.Y., 1951—. *Member:* Overseas Press Club, Canadian Society.

WRITINGS: *Only by Public Consent,* Hawthorn, 1968. Columnist, *Saturday Review,* 1960-72.

* * *

GOLDFARB, Ronald L. 1933-

PERSONAL: Born October 13, 1933, in Jersey City, N.J.;

son of Robert S. and Aida Goldfarb; married June 9, 1957; children: Judy Anne, Nicholas, Maximilian. *Education:* Syracuse University, A.B., 1954, LL.B., 1956; Yale University, LL.M., 1960, J.S.D., 1962. *Home:* 7312 Rippon Rd., Alexandria, Va. *Office:* 1616 H St. N.W., Washington, D.C.

CAREER: Admitted to practice before District of Columbia, New York, and California Bars, and Bar of U.S. Supreme Court. Commission on Law and Social Action, New York, N.Y., staff counsel, 1960-61; U.S. Department of Justice, Washington, D.C., special prosecutor, Organized Crime and Racketeering Section, 1961-64; Twentieth Century Fund, New York, N.Y., research director, 1964-65; Kurzman and Goldfarb (law firm), Washington, D.C., partner, 1965-70; Goldfarb and Singer (law firm), Washington, D.C., partner, 1970—. Member, President's Task Force for the War Against Poverty, 1964; special counsel, U.S. House of Representatives Select Committee (Adam Clayton Powell investigation), 1967. Consultant to President's Advisory Commission on Civil Disorders, Brookings Institution, California Legislature, George Washington University Law School, and Westinghouse Broadcasting Co.; member of board of directors, Common Cause. *Military service:* U.S. Air Force, staff judge advocate, 1957-60. U.S. Air Force Reserve, 1960-64; became captain.

MEMBER: American Bar Association, American Trial Lawyers Association (faculty), Federal Bar Association, New York State Bar Association, California State Bar Association, Cosmos Club (Washington, D.C.). *Awards, honors:* Federal Bar Association prize for best work in field of constitutional law, 1965-66, for *Ransom: A Critique of the American Bail System.*

WRITINGS: The Contempt Power, Columbia University Press, 1963; *Ransom: A Critique of the American Bail System,* Harper, 1965; (with Alfred Friendly) *Crime and Publicity: The Impact of News on the Administration of Justice,* Twentieth Century Fund, 1967; (contributor) *How to Try a Criminal Case,* American Trial Lawyers Association, 1967; (with Linda Singer) *After Conviction: A Review of the American Correction System,* Simon & Schuster, 1973; *Jails: The Ultimate Ghetto of the Criminal Justice System,* Doubleday, 1975. Contributor to legal journals, newspapers, and general periodicals.

*   *   *

GOLDING, Morton J(ay)   1925-
(Stephanie Lloyd, Jay Martin, M. M. Michaeles, Patricia Morton)

PERSONAL: Born July 24, 1925, in New York, N.Y.; son of Samuel H. and Sue Golding; married Patricia Gibbons, April 2, 1949; children: Geoffrey E., Gower Edward. *Education:* University of Denver, B.A., 1949, M.A., 1950; New York University, graduate study. *Politics:* Democrat. *Religion:* Jewish. *Residence:* New Canaan, Conn. *Agent:* Henry Morrison, Inc., 58 West 10th St., New York, N.Y. 10011.

CAREER: Barkas & Shalit (publicity), New York City, copywriter, 1953-54; Enterprise Magazine Management, New York City, associate editor, 1954-56; J. B. Publications, New York City, features editor, 1956-57; full-time free-lance writer, 1957—. Lecturer in creative writing, Hunter College of the City University of New York, 1966-67. *Military service:* U.S. Army, 1943-46; became sergeant. *Member:* Authors Guild.

WRITINGS—Fiction, except as noted: *Bridges* (juvenile nonfiction), Putnam, 1967; *Night Mare* (Science Fiction), Dell, 1970; *The Mystery of the Vikings in America* (juvenile nonfiction), Lippincott, 1973; *A Short History of Puerto Rico* (nonfiction), 1973.

Under pseudonym Stephanie Lloyd: *Graveswood,* Paperback Library, 1966.

Under pseudonym Jay Martin: *Make Love, Not Waves,* Lancer Books, 1967; *Ban the Bra,* Lancer, 1968; *Erotica Caper,* Lancer Books, 1968; *Fondle With Care,* Lancer Books, 1968; *Sexy Egg Love-In,* Lancer Books, 1969; *Another Piece of Candy,* Berkley Publishing, 1969; *Laying the Ghost,* Berkley Publishing, 1970; *Digging the Love Goddess,* Berkley Publishing, 1971; *Plugged In,* Berkley Publishing, 1972.

Under pseudonym M. M. Michaeles: *Suicide Command,* Lancer, 1967.

Under pseudonym Patricia Morton: *A Gathering of Moondust,* Lancer Books, 1965; *Child of Value,* Lancer Books, 1966; *In the Province of Darkness,* Banner Books, 1967; *Destiny's Child,* Belmont, 1967; *Caves of Fear,* Lancer Books, 1968; *Daughter of Evil,* Lancer Books, 1973.

Author of four plays for American Broadcasting Co.'s "Radio Theatre Five." Contributor of articles and fiction to *Redbook, Popular Mechanics, Family Circle, Pageant,* and other magazines.

WORK IN PROGRESS: Under pseudonym Jay Martin, *Happy Bottom,* for Dell; two mysteries and two other novels.

AVOCATIONAL INTERESTS: Reading ("admire fine fiction of all sorts, poetry, and nonfiction, especially in the areas of politics and anthropology/archaeology"), opera and other music.

*   *   *

GOLDMAN, Peter L(ouis)   1933-

PERSONAL: Born February 8, 1933, in Philadelphia, Pa.; son of Walter (a sales representative) and Dorothy (Semple) Goldman; married Helen Dudar (a writer), July 16, 1961. *Education:* Williams College, A.B., 1954; Columbia University, M.S., 1955. *Religion:* Jewish. *Home:* 36 Gramercy Pk., New York, N.Y. 10003. *Office:* Newsweek, 444 Madison Ave., New York, N.Y.

CAREER: St. Louis Globe-Democrat, St. Louis, Mo., reporter, 1955-62; *Newsweek,* New York, N.Y., senior editor, 1962—. *Member:* American Civil Liberties Union. *Awards, honors:* Nieman fellow, Harvard University, 1960-61; Sigma Delta Chi award for magazine reporting, 1963; National Headliners award, 1963, for coverage of riot at University of Mississippi, 1962; Robert F. Kennedy Journalism Award, 1972; American Bar Association Silver Gavel Award, 1972, for a report on criminal justice in America.

WRITINGS: Civil Rights: The Challenge of the Fourteenth Amendment, Coward, 1965; *Report from Black America,* Simon & Schuster, 1970; *The Death and Life of Malcolm X,* Harper, 1973.

*   *   *

GOLDMAN, Ronald

PERSONAL: Born in Manchester, England. *Education:* University of Manchester, B.A., 1946, B.D., 1947; University of Chicago, M.A., 1948; University of Birmingham,

M.A., 1958, Ph.D., 1962. *Home:* 8 Robert Court, Viewbank, Victoria, Australia.

CAREER: Teacher at state schools in England, 1948-51; University of Birmingham, Birmingham, England, lecturer in psychology and head of department, 1951-58; University of Reading, Reading, England, senior lecturer in educational psychology and head of department, 1958-66; Didsbery College of Education, Manchester, England, principal, 1966-69; La Trobe University, Bundoora, Victoria, Australia, professor and dean of School of Education, 1969—. *Member:* British Psychological Society (fellow).

WRITINGS: "The Readiness for Religion Series" (curriculum series for children seven to thirteen), Hart-Davis, 1966-68; *Readiness for Religion,* Seabury, 1968; *Religious Thinking from Childhood to Adolescence,* Seabury, 1968; *Breakthrough* (autobiographies of poverty children), Routledge & Kegan Paul, 1968; *Angry Adolescents: Case Studies,* Sage Publications, 1969. Contributor to educational journals.

*   *   *

GOLDMAN, Sheldon 1939-

PERSONAL: Born September 18, 1939, in New York, N.Y.; son of Yehuda (a businessman) and Anne (Slochower) Goldman; married Marcia Liebeskind, June 16, 1963; children: Ellen, Jeremy, Sara. *Education:* New York University, B.A., 1961; Harvard University, M.A., 1964, Ph.D., 1965. *Politics:* Democrat. *Office:* Department of Political Science, University of Massachusetts, Amherst, Mass. 01002.

CAREER: University of Massachusetts, Amherst, assistant professor, 1965-69, associate professor of government, 1970-73, professor of political science, 1974—. *Member:* International Political Science Association, American Political Science Association, Law and Society Association, American Association of University Professors, American Civil Liberties Union, Northeastern Political Science Association, Midwest Political Science Association, Western Political Science Association, Phi Beta Kappa. *Awards, honors:* Woodrow Wilson fellowship; Social Science Research Council grant.

WRITINGS: (Editor with Thomas P. Jahnige) *The Federal Judicial System: Readings in Process and Behavior,* Holt, 1968; *Roll Call Behavior in the Massachusetts House of Representatives,* Bureau of Government Research, University of Massachusetts, 1968; (with Jahnige) *The Federal Courts as a Political System,* Harper, 1971, 2nd edition, 1975; *The Policies and Politics of the United States Court of Appeals,* Sage Publications, in press. Contributor to professional journals.

WORK IN PROGRESS: With Austin Sarat, *The Massachusetts Judicial System.*

AVOCATIONAL INTERESTS: Travel, cinema, the arts.

BIOGRAPHICAL/CRITICAL SOURCES: Harvard Law Review, June, 1966; *Journal of Politics,* May, 1967.

*   *   *

GOLDSTEIN, Sidney 1927-

PERSONAL: Born August 4, 1927, in New London, Conn.; son of Max (a dairy manager) and Bella (Hoffman) Goldstein; married Alice Dreifuss (a part-time statistical researcher), June 21, 1953; children: Beth Leah, David Louis, Brenda Ruth. *Education:* University of Connecticut, B.A., 1949, M.A., 1951; University of Pennsylvania, Ph.D., 1953. *Religion:* Jewish. *Home:* 95 Kiwanee Rd., Warwick, R.I. 02888. *Office:* Brown University, Providence, R.I. 02912.

CAREER: University of Pennsylvania, Philadelphia, instructor in sociology, 1953-55, research associate, Wharton School of Finance and Commerce, 1955-58; Brown University, Providence, R.I., assistant professor, 1955-57, associate professor, 1957-60, professor of sociology, 1960—, chairman of department of sociology and anthropology, 1963-70, director of population studies and training center, 1966—. Member of ad hoc committee of experts on demographic aspects of urbanization, United Nations; member of advisory committee on 1970 Census, U.S. Bureau of the Census. Consultant to Institute for Neurological Diseases and Blindness, 1960-71, National Institutes of Health, 1960—, Ford Foundation and Rockefeller Foundation, 1971—, Urban Institute, and the RAND Corp., 1974—. Member of board of directors, Bureau of Jewish Education.

MEMBER: American Sociological Association (fellow), Population Association of America (president, 1975-76), American Statistical Association, International Union for the Scientific Study of Population, Gerontological Society (fellow), Association for Jewish Demography and Statistics (member of board of directors, 1965—), Eastern Sociological Association, Sociological Research Association, Institute of Contemporary Jewry (Jerusalem), Rhode Island Jewish Historical Society (member of board of directors), Phi Beta Kappa. *Awards, honors:* Social Science Research Council grant, 1956-57, and fellowship, 1961-62; Guggenheim fellowship, 1961-62; Fulbright research scholarship to Denmark, 1961-62; Alexander Dushkin fellowship from Hadassah, 1965-66; Chulalongkorn University (Bangkok) medal for distinguished service, 1968.

WRITINGS: Patterns of Mobility, 1910-1950: A Method for Measuring Migration and Occupational Mobility in the Community, University of Pennsylvania Press, 1958; *Consumption Patterns of the Aged,* University of Pennsylvania Press, 1960; *The Norristown Study: An Experiment in Interdisciplinary Research Training,* University of Pennsylvania Press, 1961; *The Greater Providence Jewish Community: A Population Survey,* General Jewish Committee of Greater Providence, 1964; (contributor) William Gomberg and Arthur B. Shostak, editors, *Blue Collar World,* Prentice-Hall, 1964; (with Calvin Goldscheider) *Jewish-Americans: Three Generations in a Jewish Community,* Prentice-Hall, 1968; (contributor) Charles B. Nam, editor, *Population and Society,* Houghton, 1968; *A Population Survey of the Greater Springfield Jewish Community,* Springfield Jewish Community Council, 1968.

(With Alden Speare, Jr. and William H. Frey) *Residential Mobility, Migration, and Metropolitan Change,* Ballinger, 1975; (editor with David F. Sly) *Working Paper I: Basic Data Needed for the Study of Urbanization,* International Union for the Scientific Study of Population, 1975; (editor with Sly) *Working Paper II: The Measurement of Urbanization and the Projection of Urban Population,* International Union for the Scientific Study of Population, 1975.

All with Kurt B. Mayer: *Migration and Economic Development in Rhode Island,* Brown University Press, 1958; *The First Two Years: Problems of Small Business Growth and Survival,* U.S. Small Business Administration, 1961; *Metropolitanization and Population Change in Rhode Island,* Rhode Island Development Council, 1962; *Residential Mobility, Migration, and Commuting in Rhode Island,*

Rhode Island Development Council, 1963; *The People of Rhode Island, 1960,* Rhode Island Development Council, 1963. Contributor of about seventy articles to *Gerontology, Sales Management, Vanderbilt Law Review,* and sociology, demography, and history journals.

WORK IN PROGRESS: Writing on problems of urbanization, fertility, and population redistribution in developing countries in conjunction with earlier work with the Population Division of the United Nations and recent research in Thailand; also writing on differential fertility by religious identification; further research in social and demographic aspects of the Rhode Island population.

SIDELIGHTS: Goldstein has traveled extensively in Europe, and made several trips to Australia and the Far East, including a sabbatical year at Chulalongkorn University in Bangkok, Thailand, 1968-69. He speaks and reads French and German, and reads Danish.

*   *   *

GOLLINGS, Franklin O. A.   1919-

PERSONAL: Born June 12, 1919, in Llandudno, Wales; son of John Henry and Mary Ann (Martin) Gollings; married Mary McKechnie Munro, October 31, 1945; children: Christine Miranda, Alison Claire. *Education:* Attended British Institute of Engineering Technology. *Politics:* Conservative. *Religion:* Baptist. *Office:* (In United States) Four Cities International Corp., Suite 407, 224 West 49th St., New York, N.Y. 10019.

CAREER: British Board of Admiralty, London, England, film production adviser, 1945-48; Rayant Pictures, London, writer, director, and producer of shorts and documentaries, 1948-52; assistant director and production manager in London, for Metro-Goldwyn-Mayer, 1952-55, and Ealing Studios, 1955-56; Associated-Rediffusion (television), London, executive producer, 1956-57; writer, producer, and director of motion pictures, including "Yangtse Incident," 1957-66; currently director, Four Cities International Corp., New York, N.Y. *Military service:* Royal Naval Volunteer Reserve; became sub-lieutenant. Royal Marines; became captain. *Member:* Association of Cinema and Television Technicians (London; treasurer, 1948-52), Screenwriters Guild of Great Britain.

WRITINGS: (Co-compiler) *Dictionary of 1,001 Famous People,* Lion Press, 1966; (with Samuel Nisenson) *Great Moments in American History,* Lion Press, 1968. Motion picture scripts include "The Stirling Moss Story," "Tempt Not the Stars," "Woman of Destiny," and "Overkill"; also writer of filmscripts for television and documentary productions. Contributor to film and other periodicals.

WORK IN PROGRESS: Biographies of Aaron Burr and Simon Bolivar; research on the Tang Dynasty.

SIDELIGHTS: Gollings has traveled extensively throughout India, Africa, Europe, and United States.††

*   *   *

GOMORI, George   1934-

PERSONAL: Born April 3, 1934, in Budapest, Hungary; son of Lajos and Rosalie (Fein) Gomori; married Gudrun Linhart, September 16, 1961; children: Beata Csilla, Anna Serena.. *Education:* Attended University of Eotvos Lorand, 1953-56; University of London, B.A. (honors), 1958; Oxford University, B.Litt., 1962. *Home:* 55 Eltisley Ave., Cambridge, England. *Office:* Department of Slavonic Studies, Cambridge University, Cambridge, England.

CAREER: Left Hungary in 1956, and studied at English universities, 1956-59, 1961-62, spending the academic year, 1960-61, at Jogjakarta, Indonesia; University of California, Berkeley, lecturer in Polish and Hungarian, 1963-64; Harvard University, Cambridge, Mass., research fellow in Polish studies at Russian Research Center, 1964-65; University of Birmingham, Birmingham, England, research associate at Centre for Russian and East European Studies, 1965-67, senior research associate and librarian of Centre, 1967-69; Cambridge University, Cambridge, England, assistant lecturer, 1969-73, lecturer in Slavonic studies, 1973—. Fellow, Darwin College, 1970—. *Member:* British University Association of Slavists, P.E.N., Hungarian Writers Association in Exile (executive committee, 1958-60). *Awards, honors:* Paderewski scholarship for study in Indonesia 1960-61; Jurzykowski Award for Translation, 1972.

WRITINGS: Virag-bizonysag (poems), Otthon Ktado (London), 1958; *Hajnali uton* (poems), Poets' and Painters' Press, 1963; (translations from the poetry of Boris Pasternak, with Vince Sulyok), *Karacsonyi csillag,* Occidental, 1965; *Hungarian and Polish Poetry, 1945-1956,* Clarendon Press, 1966; (editor with C. H. Newman) *New Writing of East Europe,* Quadrangle, 1968; *Atvaltozasok* (poetry), Szepsi Csombor Kor (London), 1969; *Cyprian Norwid,* Twayne, 1974; (editor with James Atlas) Attila Jozsef, *Selected Poems and Texts,* Carcanet Press, 1974; (editor) Laszlo Nagy, *Love of the Scorching Wind,* translation by T. Connor and K. McRobbie, Oxford University Press, 1974.

Work anthologized in *Norwid zywy,* edited by W. Gunther, Swiderski (London), 1962 and *Histoire du soulevement hongrois 1956,* edited by G. Gosztony, Editions Horvath, 1966. Author of articles in Hungarian, Polish, and English; many of those written between 1961-65 were focused on Indonesia. Edited special eastern European literature edition of *Tri-Quarterly* (published in Evanston, Ill.), spring, 1967.

WORK IN PROGRESS: A study of Polish-Hungarian literary connections at the end of the sixteenth century; a history of modern Hungarian literature.

SIDELIGHTS: Gomori is fluent in English and Polish. He also speaks Russian, French, German, and Indonesian.

*   *   *

GOODGOLD, Edwin   1944-

PERSONAL: Born June 12, 1944, in Tel Aviv, Israel; son of Eugene (a factory foreman) and Ahuva Goodgold. *Education:* Columbia University, B.A., 1965; New York University, graduate studies. *Religion:* Jewish. *Home:* 1902 Ave. L, Brooklyn, N.Y.

CAREER: Writer-researcher for metropolitan Sunday newspapers, New York, N.Y., 1964—.

WRITINGS: (With Dan Carlinsky) *Trivia,* Dell, 1966; (with Carlinsky) *More Trivial Trivia,* Dell, 1966; *I Spy: Robert Culp and Bill Cosby, the Swift and Swinging Story of TV's Favorite Spies,* Grosset, 1967; (with Carlinsky) *Rock 'n' Roll Trivia,* Popular Library, 1970; (editor with Ken Weiss) *To Be Continued: A Complete Guide to Over 220 Motion Picture Serials with Sound Tracks,* Crown, 1972; (with Carlinsky) *The Compleat Beatles Quiz Book,* Warner Books, 1975; (with Carlinsky) *World's Greatest Monster Quiz,* Berkeley Publishing, 1975. Contributor to *Playboy, Playbill, Show,* and other magazines.

WORK IN PROGRESS: A television series on the academic world; a farce based on fictional heroes.†

* * *

GOODING, John (Ervine) 1940-

PERSONAL: Born July 16, 1940, in Bristol, England; son of William George (an engineer) and Kathleen (Tinney) Gooding. *Education:* Merton College, Oxford, B.A., 1962; University of Moscow, research student, 1962-63; St. Anthony's College, Oxford, graduate study, 1964-67. *Religion:* Agnostic. *Home:* Hollyside, Brockweir, Chepstow, Monmouthshire, England.

CAREER: University of Edinburgh, Edinburgh, Scotland, lecturer in department of history, 1967—.

WRITINGS: The Catkin and the Icicle: Aspects of Russia, Constable, 1965; *People of Providence Street* (novel), Viking, 1967.

WORK IN PROGRESS: A second novel.†

* * *

GOODMAN, George J(erome) W(aldo) 1930- ("Adam Smith")

PERSONAL: Born August 10, 1930, in St. Louis, Mo.; son of Alexander Mark and Viona (Cremer) Goodman; married Sallie Cullen Brophy, October 6, 1961; children: Alexander Mark, Susannah Blake. *Education:* Harvard University, B.A. (magna cum laude), 1952; further study as Rhodes Scholar at Oxford University, 1952-54. *Office: New York* Magazine, 207 East 32nd St., New York, N.Y. 10016.

CAREER: Reporter in New York City, for *Collier's,* 1956; and *Barron's,* 1957; *Time* and *Fortune,* New York City, associate editor, 1958-60; Lincoln Fund, New York City, vice-president, 1960-62; screenwriter in Los Angeles, Calif., 1962-65; *Institutional Investor,* New York City, editor, 1967-72; *New York* Magazine, New York City, cofounder, 1967, contributing editor, and vice-president, 1967—. Glassboro (N.J.) State College, trustee, 1967-71, co-chairman, presidential selection committee, 1968; executive vice-president and director, Institutional Investor Systems, 1969-72; member of advisory council, economics department, Princeton University, 1970—; occasional columnist, *Newsweek,* 1973; occasional lecturer, Harvard University. *Military service:* U.S. Army, 1954-56. *Member:* Writers Guild of America (West), Authors Guild. *Awards, honors:* G. M. Loeb Award for Distinguished Achievement in Writing about Business and Finance, University of Connecticut, 1969.

WRITINGS—Novels: *The Bubble Makers,* Viking, 1955; *A Time for Paris,* Doubleday, 1957; (with Winthrop Knowlton) *A Killing in the Market,* Doubleday, 1958; *Bascombe, the Fastest Hound Alive* (juvenile), Morrow, 1958; *The Wheeler Dealers,* Doubleday, 1959.

Nonfiction; under pseudonym "Adam Smith": *The Money Game,* Random House, 1968; *Supermoney,* Random House, 1972; *Powers of Mind,* Random House, 1975.

Screenplays include "The Wheeler Dealers," Metro-Goldwyn-Mayer, 1963, and "The Americanization of Emily," Metro-Goldwyn-Mayer, 1964. Contributor of articles to periodicals.

SIDELIGHTS: The Money Game has been published in five languages including Japanese and Portuguese. Charles J. Rolo calls it ". . . one of the best and most original books written about the stock market, and certainly the most en-

tertaining." He goes on to state that ". . . for all its fun and frolics, it is a serious and searching book, full of good sense and permeated with an awareness that the game is a rough one in which the players stand to lose not only their money but their very identity." Melvin Maddocks writes: "The charm of 'Adam Smith' is that he treats money as if he were writing about love, or art, or religion but heavens! not business. The stodgy old market becomes a sort of feminine principle; one does not graph it, one seduces her. Nor will the investor finally be satisfied with anything so crude as a conquest: 'the end object of investment is serenity.'"

BIOGRAPHICAL/CRITICAL SOURCES: New York Times Book Review, May 26, 1968, July 14, 1968; *Book World,* June 2, 1968; *National Observer,* June 10, 1968; *Newsweek,* June 17, 1968; *Commonweal,* November 29, 1968; *Life,* December 20, 1968; *New York,* April 7, 1969, August 18, 1969; *Virginia Quarterly Review,* winter, 1969; *Saturday Review,* September 9, 1972, October 21, 1972; *Time,* November 27, 1972.†

* * *

GOODMAN, Roger B. 1919-

PERSONAL: Born May 18, 1919, in New York, N.Y.; son of Henry (a teacher) and Mollie (Bernstein) Goodman; married Laura S. Rosenblum (a teacher of library science), November 14, 1942; children: Peter W., David W. *Education:* City College (now City College of the City University of New York), B.S.S., 1940; Columbia University, M.A., 1946. *Religion:* Jewish. *Home:* 2005 Pearson St., Brooklyn, N.Y. 11234.

CAREER: New York (N.Y.) Board of Education, teacher of English, 1948-75, chairman of department of English at Grover Cleveland High school, 1960-63, chairman of department of English at Stuyvesant High School, 1963-75. Assistant to New York Board of Examiners. Actor and reader with semi-professional companies for more than ten years, including New York's Roundabout Theatre and Brooklyn Public Library Reading Ensemble. *Military service:* U.S. Army, 1940-46, 1948-51; became first lieutenant. *Member:* Council of Supervisory Associations, Association of Chairman of English of New York.

WRITINGS: (Editor) *Just for Laughs,* Oxford Book Co., 1955; (with David Lewin) *New Ways to Greater Word Power,* Dell, 1955; (editor) *Short Masterpieces of the World's Greatest Literature,* Bantam, 1957; *A Concise Handbook of Better English,* Bantam, 1960; (editor) *The World's Best Short Short Stories,* Bantam, 1965; (editor) *World Wide Short Stories,* Globe Book, 1966; (with Charles Spiegler) *Modern Mythology,* AMSCO School Publications, in press. Conductor of "Sharpen Your Word Sense" in *Coronet,* 1955-58.

WORK IN PROGRESS: Compiling two anthologies, *Morality for Today,* with Spiegler, and *Cast of Characters;* a book of colloquial philosophy, *Instant Happiness.*

AVOCATIONAL INTERESTS: Reading modern poetry and writing poetry.

* * *

GOODRICH, Frances C. 1933-

PERSONAL: Born September 25, 1933, in Solon, Me.; daughter of Alfred Barney (a woodsman) and Delima (Berube) Worster; married Charles R. Minyard, July 5, 1952; married second husband, Charles E. Goodrich (an ironworker), April 17, 1962; children: (first marriage) Donna

Lee, Vanessa Gail; (second marriage) Janell Lynn. *Education:* Attended Indiana University.

CAREER: Secretary or clerical worker for contractors, construction, and supply companies in Louisiana, Indiana, and California, 1956-61; full-time evangelistic work as ordained minister of Faith Missionary Ministerial Association, traveling throughout United States, 1961-63; writer on metaphysics. *Military service:* U.S. Air Force, Women in the Air Force (WAF), 1952-53.

WRITINGS: The Third Adam, Philosophical Library, 1967.

WORK IN PROGRESS: Research for a book, *Golden Nuggets;* research on Calvin's works and similar materials to be applied to modern spiritual thinking.††

* * *

GOODWYN, Lawrence 1928-

PERSONAL: Born July 16, 1928, at Fort Huachuca, Ariz.; son of Carey Edwin (an officer, U.S. Army) and Helen (Corbett) Goodwyn; married Nell De Reese, April 12, 1958; children: Wade, Laurie. *Education:* Texas A&M University, B.A., 1949; Trinity University, M.A., 1956; University of Texas at Austin, Ph.D., 1971. *Politics:* Liberal.

CAREER: Texas Observer, Austin, associate editor, 1958-60; free-lance writer, beginning 1960. *Military service:* U.S. Army, 1950-52; became captain. *Awards, honors: South Central States* was one of five books nominated for Texas Institute of Letters award for best nonfiction by a Texan, 1967.

WRITINGS: South Central States, Time-Life Books, 1967. Contributor of fiction and articles, both popular and scholarly, in fields of history and contemporary issues, to magazines.

WORK IN PROGRESS: A book on New Orleans, for Time-Life Books; a work on the Populist movement.†

* * *

GORDENKER, Leon 1923-

PERSONAL: Born October 7, 1923, in Detroit, Mich.; son of Samuel (a merchant) and Anna (Posalsky) Gordenker; married Belia Emilie Strootman, 1956; children: Robert J. M., Hendrik W. P., Emilie E. S. *Education:* University of Michigan, A.B., 1943; studied at Wayne State University, 1944-45, New York University, 1948-50, and Institut d'-Etudes Politiques, Paris, France, 1951-52; Columbia University, M.A., 1954, Ph.D., 1958. *Home:* 492 Riverside Dr., Princeton, N.J. *Office:* Corwin Hall, Princeton University, Princeton, N.J. 08540.

CAREER: Newspaperman in Detroit, Mich., with *Detroit Times,* 1943, Associated Press, 1943-44, *Detroit Free Press,* 1944-45; National War Labor Board, editor-writer, 1945; United Nations, New York, N.Y., information officer, 1945-53, consultant to Office of Public Information, 1954-56, 1961; Dartmouth College, Hanover, N.H., instructor, 1956-58; Princeton University, Princeton, N.J., lecturer, 1958-59, assistant professor, 1959-63, associate professor, 1963-66, professor of politics, 1966—, faculty associate, Center of International Studies. Visiting professor at Makerere University, 1970-71. Director, Carnegie Corp. Experimental European Summer Research Program, 1962; consultant, United Nations Institute for Training and Research, 1966. *Awards, honors:* Fulbright grant for study

in Paris, France, 1951-52; Netherlands Institute for Advanced Study, fellow, 1972-73.

WRITINGS: The United Nations and the Peaceful Unification of Korea, Nijhoff, 1959; *The UN Secretary-General and the Maintenance of Peace,* Columbia University Press, 1967; (with E. Miles) *Basic Course in International Law and Organization,* Sage, 1969; *The United Nations in International Politics,* Princeton University Press, 1971; *International Aid and National Decisions,* Princeton University Press, 1976. Contributor to *World Politics, International Organization, American Political Science Review,* and other journals.

WORK IN PROGRESS: International Executives, leadership in global organization.

* * *

GORDON, Patricia 1909-

PERSONAL: Born March 20, 1909, in London, England; daughter of Louis and Rebecca Nina (Shapira) Meyer; married Alban Godwin Gordon (a lawyer), January 23, 1937 (died, 1947). *Education:* Attended Cheltenham Ladies' College. *Home:* The Studio, Mynthurst, Leigh, Surrey, England.

CAREER: Professional artist, and dramatist. Justice of the peace in Dorking, Surrey, England, beginning 1961. Civil Defence worker during World War II. *Member:* Magistrates Association, Sussex Artists' Association, Dorking Artist Association, North Weald Group of Artists.

WRITINGS—Plays: *Begger My Neighbour,* Evan Brothers, 1957; *Thought for the Morrow,* Kenyon House Press, 1957; *Three's Company,* Evan Brothers, 1958; *Sauce for the Gander,* Evan Brothers, 1959; *Mid-Autumn Madness,* Evan Brothers, 1959; *Snow Cakes,* Kenyon Press, 1959; *Brief Suspicion,* Evan Brothers, 1960; *The Wonderful Day,* Evan Brothers, 1961; *Magic Carpet,* Evan Brothers, 1966; *Tangled Web,* H.W.F. Deane, 1966; (with Ned Hoopes) *Great Television Plays 2,* Dell, 1975.

WORK IN PROGRESS: A novel, *Pattern in the Sand;* another novel.

SIDELIGHTS: Patricia Gordon has traveled widely, mostly for painting purposes. She does not care for pop art, action paintings, and certain trends in modern literature.†

* * *

GORELICK, Molly C. 1920-

PERSONAL: Born September 19, 1920, in New York, N.Y.; daughter of Morris and Jean Chernow; married Leon Gorelick, April 12, 1941; children: Walter, Peter. *Education:* University of California, Los Angeles, B.A., 1948, M.A., 1955, Ed.D., 1962; University of Southern California, graduate study, 1950. *Home:* 600 North June St., Los Angeles, Calif. 90004.

CAREER: Licensed psychologist, and marriage, family, and child counselor. Los Angeles (Calif.) city schools, teacher, 1948-62, counselor, 1957-58; University of California, Los Angeles, instructor in psychology and education departments, 1957-63, research assistant, 1961-62, supervisor in psychology clinic, 1962-63; University of Southern California, School of Education, Los Angeles, assistant professor, 1964-66; Exceptional Childrens Foundation, Los Angeles, chief of guidance services, 1963-70; California State University, Northridge, professor of psychology, 1970—. Visiting associate professor, University of Hawaii, summers, 1967, 1969, 1971, 1973. *Member:* American Association on Mental Deficiency (member, regional executive board), Council for Exceptional Children (member, executive board, mental retardation division), National Rehabilitation Association (member, regional executive board), American Psychological Association, and Western and California State branches; Phi Beta Kappa, Pi Gamma Mu, Pi Lambda Theta.

WRITINGS—With Jean Boreman; all published by Ward Ritchie: *Fire on Sun Mountain*, 1967; *Flood at Dry Creek*, 1967; *Storm at Sand Point*, 1967; *Fog Over Sun City*, 1968; *Snow Storm at Green Valley*, 1968. Also author of *Careers in Integrated Early Childhood Settings*, 1975, *A Teacher in the Making*, 1975, *Recipes for Teaching*, 1975. Contributor to *Children Limited, American Journal of Mental Deficiency,* and other educational and guidance journals.

* * *

GOSHEN, Charles E(rnest) 1916-

PERSONAL: Born September 2, 1916, in Altoona, Pa.; son of Charles W. (a merchant) and Pearl (Rice) Goshen; married Patricia McGuire (a registered nurse), September 22, 1940; children: Charles Robert, Anne Elizabeth. *Education:* Columbia University, A.B., 1938, M.D., 1942; New York Medical College, Certificate in Psychoanalysis, 1952. *Politics:* Independent. *Religion:* None. *Home:* 6029 Ashland Dr., Nashville, Tenn. *Office:* School of Engineering, Vanderbilt University, Nashville, Tenn. 37203.

CAREER: Boston City Hospital, Boston, Mass., intern, 1942-43; U.S. Veterans Administration Hospital, Bronx, N.Y., resident, 1946-48; diplomate, American Board of Psychiatry, 1948; Nassau Neuropsychiatric Clinic, Hempstead, N.Y., director, 1948-57; Robbins Institute, New York, N.Y., executive director, 1954-57; American Psychiatric Association, Washington, D.C., research director, 1957-59; National Research Council, Washington, D.C., professional associate, Division of Medical Sciences, 1959-60; Operations Research, Inc., Silver Spring, Md., research physician, 1960; West Virginia University, School of Medicine, Morgantown, associate professor of psychiatry, 1960-67; Vanderbilt University, School of Engineering and School of Medicine, Nashville, Tenn., associate professor of engineering management, 1967—. *Military service:* U.S. Army, Medical Corps, 1942-46; became captain; received two battle stars.

MEMBER: American Psychiatric Association (fellow), American Association for the Advancement of Science, American Medical Writers Association, Association of American Medical Colleges, American Association of University Professors, Human Factors Society, American Society of Engineering Education, Institute of Management Science.

WRITINGS: Psychiatric Architecture, American Psychiatric Association, 1959; (co-author) *Human Factors in Accident Prevention,* U.S. Public Health Service, 1960; *Documentary History of Psychiatry,* Philosophical Library, 1967. Contributor of seventy articles to medical journals.

WORK IN PROGRESS: A textbook, *Systems Analysis Applied to Human Behaviour;* a transcultural study of Appalachian people; a transcultural study of the youth offender population.

AVOCATIONAL INTERESTS: Collecting antique tools, old classics in psychology, psychiatry, and early American technology; inventing (holder of two U.S. patents on navigational devices).

GOTTFRIED, Martin 1933-

PERSONAL: Born October 9, 1933, in New York, N.Y.; son of Isidore (a book dealer) and Rachel (Weitz) Gottfried; married Jane Lahr (an artist), April 15, 1968; children: Maya (daughter). *Education:* Columbia University, B.A., 1955, law student, 1955-57. *Politics:* Independent. *Religion:* None. *Home:* 17 East 96th St., New York, N.Y. 10028. *Agent:* William Morris Agency, 1350 Avenue of the Americas, New York, N.Y. 10019. *Office: New York Post,* 110 South St., New York, N.Y. 10022.

CAREER: Village Voice, New York City, music critic, 1960-62; Fairchild Publications, New York City, editor, 1962-63; drama critic for *Women's Wear Daily,* 1963-72; drama critic for *New York Post,* 1973—. Also drama critic for WPAT radio. *Military service:* U.S. Army, Military Intelligence, 1957-59. *Member:* New York Drama Critics Circle. *Awards, honors:* Rockefeller Foundation grant, 1966-67, 1967-68; George Jean Nathan Award for Dramatic Criticism, 1968, for *A Theatre Divided.*

WRITINGS: A Theater Divided, Little, Brown, 1968; *Opening Nights,* Putnam, 1969. Contributor to national magazines.

WORK IN PROGRESS: A book on American musical theater, for Little, Brown; several plays.

BIOGRAPHICAL/CRITICAL SOURCES: Time, Press Section, November 5, 1967.

* * *

GOULD, Cecil (Hilton Monk) 1918-

PERSONAL: Born May 24, 1918, in England; son of R. T. (a lieutenant commander, Royal Navy) and Muriel Hilda (Estall) Gould. *Education:* Attended Westminster School, England, 1931-36; educated privately in Germany, 1936-37, and at Courtauld Institute of Art, University of London, 1937-39. *Home:* 6 Palace Gate, London W.8, England. *Office:* National Gallery, London W.C.2, England.

CAREER: National Gallery, London, England, assistant keeper, 1946-62, deputy keeper, 1962-73, keeper, 1973—. *Military service:* Royal Air Force, 1940-46; served in France, Middle East, Italy, Belgium, and Germany. *Member:* Royal Society of Arts (fellow).

WRITINGS: An Introduction to Italian Renaissance Painting, Phaidon, 1957; *The Sixteenth-Century Italian Schools Excluding the Venetian,* National Gallery, 1962; *Italian Painting: The High Renaissance,* McGraw, 1963; *Trophy of Conquest: The Musee Napoleon and the Creation of the Louvre,* Faber, 1965.

Compiler of National Gallery catalogs, including: *Early Renaissance: Fifteenth-Century Italian Painting,* 1965; (and author of introduction and notes) *Corot,* 1965; *Michelangelo: Battle of Cascina* (Charlton Lecture), 1966; (with Sebastiano del Piombo) *The Raising of Lazarus, By Sebastiano del Piombo,* 1967; *The Studio of Alfonso d'Este and Titian's Bacchus and Ariadne: A Re-examination of the Chronology of the Bacchanals and of the Evolution of One of Them,* 1969; *Titian,* 1969; *Raphael's Portrait of Pope Julius II: The Re-emergence of the Original,* 1970; "The School of Love" and Correggio's Mythologies, 1970; (with Kenneth Clark) *The Leonardo Cartoon,* 1962; *The Draped Figure,* 1972; *Failure & Success: 150 Years of the National Gallery, 1824-1974,* 1974; *Space in Landscape,* 1974.

Contributor to *Encyclopaedia Britannica, Chamber's Encyclopaedia,* and *Dizionario Biografico degli Italiani;* also contributor to *Burlington Magazine, Art Quarterly, Art Bulletin*, and other journals in America and Europe.

SIDELIGHTS: Cecil Gould speaks French, German, and Italian. *Avocational interests:* Travel, music, skiing.

*   *   *

GOVEIA, Elsa V(esta)   1925-

PERSONAL: Born April 12, 1925, in British Guiana; daughter of Alfred (a salesman) and Florence (Hood) Goveia. *Education:* University of London, B.A., 1948, Ph.D., 1952. *Home:* 25 Hope Mews, Kingston 6, Jamaica. *Office:* Department of History, University of the West Indies, Kingston 7, Jamaica.

CAREER: University of the West Indies, Kingston, Jamaica, teacher of history, 1950—. *Member:* West Indies Group of University Teachers.

WRITINGS: Historiography of the British West Indies, Instituto Panamericano de Geografia e Historia, 1956; *Slave Society in the British Leeward Islands at the End of the Eighteenth Century,* Yale University Press, 1965; *West Indian Slave Laws of the Eighteenth Century* [and] *A New Balance of Power: The Nineteenth Century* (the latter by C. J. Bartlett), Ginn, 1970.

WORK IN PROGRESS: Research on West Indian history, chiefly in the eighteenth and early nineteenth centuries; co-editing and contributing to a history of the West Indies.

*   *   *

GOVINDA, (Lama) Anagarika   1898-

PERSONAL: Born May 17, 1898, in Waldheim, Germany; now a citizen of India. *Education:* Studied at University of Freiburg, University of Naples, University of Cagliari, and at Buddhist monasteries in Ceylon. *Home and office:* Kasar Devi Ashram, P.O. Dinapani, District Almora, Kumaon Himalaya, India.

CAREER: Helped to organize Buddhist movements in Europe, Ceylon, Burma, and India; former general secretary, International Buddhist University Association; lecturer at Visva-Bharati University, Santiniketan, West Bengal, India, for several years; Readership lecturer at Patna University, Patna, India, 1936-37; became a personal pupil of Tomo Geshe Rimpoche; spent several years in Tibet, eventually joining the bKah-rgyud-pa order; now lama and acharya (head) of Buddhist order of Arya Maitreya Mandala, Kasar Devi Ashram, Kumaon Himalaya, India.

WRITINGS: The Fundamental Ideas of Buddhism, Altmann (Leipzig), 1920; *Gedanken und Gesichte* (title means "Thoughts and Visions"), Pandora (Dresden), 1926; *Rhythmische Aphorismen* (title means "Rhythmic Aphorisms"), Pandora, 1927; *Abhidhammattha-Sangaha: A Compendium of Buddhist Philosophy,* Benares Verlag (Munich), 1930; *Art and Meditation,* Roerich Centre of Art and Culture (Allahabad), 1936; *Stupa Symbolism,* [London], 1940; (author of introductory essay and commentaries) *The Tibetan Book of the Dead,* Oxford University Press, 1947, revised and enlarged edition, 1965; *Solar and Lunar Symbolism in the Development of Stupa Architecture,* MARG (Bombay), 1950; *Foundations of Tibetan Mysticism,* Rascher (Zurich), 1957, Dutton, 1959.

Mandala, Origo (Zurich), 1960, 2nd enlarged edition, 1961; *The Psychological Attitude of Early Buddhist Philosophy* (Readership lectures at Patna University, 1936-37), Dutton,

1961; Buddhist section in *Die Antwort der Religionen* (title means "The Answer of Religions"), Szczesny Verlag (Munich), 1964; *The Way of the White Clouds: Experiences of a Buddhist Pilgrim in Tibet,* Hutchinson, 1965; *The Psycho-Cosmic Symbolism of the Buddhist Stupa,* Nyingma Institute (Berkeley, Calif.), 1975; *Creative Meditation and Multidimensional Consciousness,* Quest Books, 1976. Contributor to other works dealing with Buddhist thought, art, and tradition, and to journals in United States, Europe, India.

SIDELIGHTS: Govinda's books have been issued in translation in Switzerland, Japan, France, Italy, and other countries.

*   *   *

GRAEFF, Grace M.   1918-

PERSONAL: Surname rhymes with "safe"; born October 22, 1918, in Mayville, N.Y.; original name, Julia Martha Lirie Henninger; adopted by Karl H. (a men's clothier) and Lucile M. (Crowther) Shearer; married Myron Jay Graeff, March 29, 1941 (deceased); children: Christopher, Ronald, Geoffrey, Valerie. *Education:* Studied at Oberlin Conservatory, 1936-39, Cleveland Institute of Music, 1939-41, Western Reserve University (now Case Western Reserve University), 1965-66; Empire State College of State University of New York, B.A., 1974. *Religion:* Methodist. *Residence:* Chautauqua County, N.Y.

CAREER: Welch Grape Juice Co., Westfield, N.Y., receptionist, 1959-61; Carnahan Shearer Co., Westfield, N.Y., partner-manager, 1961-65; Western Reserve University (now Case Western Reserve University), Cleveland, Ohio, house director, 1965-67; Chautauqua County, N.Y., assistant special deputy to commissioner jurors and court clerk, 1967. Vice-president, Westfield Chamber of Commerce, 1963.

WRITINGS: House Not Made with Hands, Philosophical Library, 1967.

*   *   *

GRAHAM, Hugh Davis   1936-

PERSONAL: Born September 2, 1936, in Little Rock, Ark.; son of Otis Livingstone (a Presbyterian minister) and Lois (Patterson) Graham; married Ann Clary (a lawyer), June 11, 1966. *Education:* Yale University, B.A. (magna cum laude), 1958; Stanford University, M.A., 1961; Ph.D., 1964. *Home:* 213 Southway, Baltimore, Md. 21218.

CAREER: Tennessean, Nashville, Tenn., reporter, 1960; Foothill Junior College, Los Altos Hills, Calif., instructor in history, 1962-63; San Jose State College (now University), San Jose, Calif., assistant professor of history, 1963-66; Stanford University, Stanford, Calif., visiting assistant professor of history, 1967; Johns Hopkins University, Baltimore, Md., associate professor of history, 1967-71, assistant director of Institute of Southern History, 1967-71; University of Maryland, Baltimore County, professor of history and dean of social sciences, 1971—. Peace Corps, Office of Public Affairs, training officer, later director of Western Region, 1965-66. *Military service:* U.S. Marine Corps, Artillery, 1958-60; served on Okinawa; became captain. *Member:* American Historical Association, Organization of American Historians, American Association of University Professors, Southern Historical Association (chairman of membership committee). *Awards, honors:* Woodrow Wilson fellow, 1960; Woodrow Wilson dissertation fellow, 1963; Award of Merit, American Association for State and Local History, for *Crisis in Print*.

WRITINGS: Crisis in Print: Desegregation and the Press in Tennessee, Vanderbilt University Press, 1967; (editor with Ted Robert Gurr) *The History of Violence in America*, Bantam, 1969; (editor) *Huey Long*, Prentice-Hall, 1970; (editor) *Violence: The Crisis of American Confidence*, Johns Hopkins Press, 1971; *Desegregation: The U.S. Supreme Court and the Schools*, Harper, 1972; (with Numan V. Bartley) *Southern Politics and the Second Reconstruction*, Johns Hopkins Press, 1975. Contributor to newspapers and professional journals, including *Tennessee Historical Quarterly*, *Baltimore Sunday Sun*, *Southern Education Reports*, and *Virginia Quarterly Review*.

WORK IN PROGRESS: Preparing a data book on southern (United States) primaries and elections, 1948-72, for Johns Hopkins Press.

* * *

GRAHAM, Loren R. 1933-

PERSONAL: Born June 29, 1933, in Hymera, Ind.; son of Ross R. (a teacher) and Hazel (McClanahan) Graham; married Patricia Albjerg (a college professor), September 6, 1955; children: Marguerite. *Education:* Purdue University, B.S., 1955; Columbia University, M.A., 1960, Ph.D., 1964; University of Moscow, graduate study, 1960-61. *Home:* 15 Claremont Ave., New York, N.Y. 10027. *Office:* Department of History, Columbia University, New York, N.Y. 10027.

CAREER: Dow Chemical Co., Midland, Mich., research engineer, 1955; Indiana University, Bloomington, assistant professor of history, 1963-66; Columbia University, New York, N.Y., assistant professor, 1966-67, associate professor, 1967-72, professor of history, 1972—. *Military service:* U.S. Naval Reserve, 1955-63; on active duty, 1955-58. *Member:* American Historical Association, History of Science Society, American Association for the Advancement of Science, American Association for the Advancement of Slavic Studies. *Awards, honors:* Woodrow Wilson fellowship; Guggenheim fellow, 1969-70.

WRITINGS: The Soviet Academy of Sciences and the Communist Party, 1927-32, Princeton University Press, 1967; *Science and Philosophy in the Soviet Union*, Knopf, 1972.

WORK IN PROGRESS: History of science in Russia; a general history of science.

* * *

GRAHAM, Otis L., Jr. 1935-

PERSONAL: Born June 24, 1935, in Little Rock, Ark.; son of Otis L. (a clergyman) and Lois (Patterson) Graham; married Ann Zemke; children: Ann, Wade. *Education:* Yale University, B.A., 1957; Columbia University, M.A., 1961, Ph.D., 1966. *Office:* University of California, Santa Barbara, Calif. 93106.

CAREER: University of California, Santa Barbara, associate professor of history, 1966—. *Military service:* U.S. Marine Corps, 1957-60; served in Hawaii; became captain. *Member:* American Historical Association, Organization of American Historians.

WRITINGS: An Encore for Reform: The Old Progressives and the New Deal, Oxford University Press, 1967; *The Great Campaigns: Reform and War in America*, Prentice-

Hall, 1971; (editor) *From Roosevelt to Roosevelt*, Appleton, 1971; (editor) *The New Deal: The Critical Issues*, Little, Brown, 1971.

WORK IN PROGRESS: A history of planning in America, 1932-1975.

* * *

GRAHAM, Sean 1920-

PERSONAL: Born June 26, 1920, in Berlin, Germany; married Catherine Darquier, October 26, 1958; children: Valerie, Dominique. *Education:* Attended Bryanston School, Blandford, England, and Peterhouse, Cambridge. *Home:* 36 Westbourne Park Rd., London W.2, England.

CAREER: Between 1949 and 1958, wrote, produced and directed more than fifty films in West Africa. *Military service:* British Army, Intelligence Corps, 1939-45. *Member:* Writers Guild, Association of Cine and Television Technicians. *Awards, honors:* Various awards for documentaries at film festivals in Europe.

WRITINGS: Surfeit of Sun (novel), Weidenfeld & Nicolson, 1965, Doubleday, 1966; *Hippo's Coup* (novel), Weidenfeld & Nicolson, 1968.

Screenplays: "Two Weeks in September," produced, 1967; "The High Commissioner," produced, 1967; "The Shells," for production by Warner Bros. Also author of "Moon in an Empty Sky," "A Sudden Rage," "Coup," "Clea," "Turquoise Garden," and "Games"; author of a stage play, "Lola," and of programs for British television.

WORK IN PROGRESS: A play about 18th-century Turkey.

SIDELIGHTS: Graham has spent a total of ten years in Africa in the course of his career.

* * *

GRAHAM, Thomas F(rancis) 1923-

PERSONAL: Born December 8, 1923, in Niles, Ohio. *Education:* Kent State University, B.S., 1946, M.A., 1947; University of Ottawa, Ph.D., 1952. *Office:* Walsh College, Canton, Ohio 44720.

CAREER: Certified as psychologist by Ohio Psychological Association. University of Akron, Akron, Ohio, instructor in psychology, 1947-48; Massillon State Hospital, Massillon, Ohio, chief psychologist and director of psychology research and training, 1948-67; Walsh College, Canton, Ohio, professor of psychology and philosophy, 1967—. Adjunct professor of psychology, University of Youngstown, 1956-59. Consultant and group therapist, Canton Aultman Hospital. *Member:* Ohio Psychological Association (fellow).

WRITINGS: Dynamic Psychopathology: Introduction to Abnormal Psychology, Christopher, 1957; *Mental Status Manual*, Sandoz, 1965; *Parallel Profiles: Pioneers in Mental Health*, Franciscan Herald, 1966; *Medieval Minds: Mental Health in the Middle Ages*, Allen & Unwin, 1967, Beacon-Bell Books, 1969; *Stars and Shadows: Mental Health in Ancient Times*, Beacon-Bell Books, 1967; *Anatomy of Aggression: Bases of War*, Beacon-Bell Books, 1967; *Anatomy of Avarice: Bases of Greed*, Beacon-Bell Books, 1967; *Principles of Psychology: Management Manual*, Beacon-Bell Books, 1967; *Profiles in Protest: Rebels in the Renaissance*, Beacon-Bell Books, 1968.

Abnormal Psychology, Lansford, 1973; *Human Development*, Littlefield, 1973; *Basic Statistics*, Kendall/Hunt,

1975; *Anatomy of an Asylum,* Human Services House, 1975; *Recovery Revisited,* Human Services House, 1975. Contributor to *The International Handbook of Group Psychotherapy,* Philosophical Library, 1966, and to professional journals.

WORK IN PROGRESS: Personality Theories; Readings in Behavior; Sexuality in Society.

*   *   *

GRANOWSKY, Alvin 1936-

PERSONAL: Born June 27, 1936, in Brooklyn, N.Y.; son of Samuel (a laundry plant operator) and Helen (Golden) Granowsky; married Seena Abramsky, June 18, 1961; children: Eric, Sedra, Richard. *Education:* Colgate University, B.A., 1958; Harvard University, M.A. in Teaching, 1959. *Religion:* Jewish.

CAREER: High school teacher of English in Central Valley, N.Y., 1959-60; assistant editor, Miller-Freeman Publications, New York, N.Y., 1960-62; teacher of English in Poughkeepsie, N.Y., 1962—, at Spackenkill Junior High School, 1965—. Marist College, Poughkeepsie, communications arts instructor in Upward Bound (program for deprived high school students), 1966—, and member of Upward Bound advisory board. *Member:* National Education Association, New York State Teachers Association, Dutchess County Council of English Teachers.

WRITINGS: The Schoolteachers, Fell, 1967.

SIDELIGHTS: Alvin Granowsky writes: "To support myself by writing, especially of novels, has been a longstanding hope."††

*   *   *

GRANT, Judith 1929-

PERSONAL: Born October 2, 1929, in New York, N.Y.; daughter of Havens (a corporation lawyer) and Carolyn (Hall) Grant; married Chris Sakellariadis (an engineer in Greece), March 26, 1949; children: Spyro Steven. *Education:* Swarthmore College, student, 1946-47; Stanford University, B.A. (with highest honors), 1951. *Politics:* Liberal. *Religion:* Episcopalian. *Address:* c/o Dr. James M. Grant, 19 Joann Circle, Westport, Conn. *Agent:* David Higham Associates Ltd., 5-8 Lower John St., London W1R 4HA, England.

CAREER: Harvard University, Cambridge, Mass., music librarian, 1951-52. *Member:* Phi Beta Kappa.

WRITINGS: A Pillage of Art, R. Hale, 1966, Roy, 1968. Contributor to *Gourmet* and *Your New Baby.*

WORK IN PROGRESS: Parsons Prejudice, a study of unusual English parsons; *Worms in the Bidet,* personal reminiscence of life in Portugal.

SIDELIGHTS: Judith Grant has lived in Europe since 1952, principally in Greece, Turkey, and Portugal, but also at times in Italy, France, and England. She is competent in French and modern Greek, and knows some Italian, Turkish, and Portuguese.††

*   *   *

GRANT, Kay
(Jan Hilliard)

PERSONAL: Born in Yarmouth, Nova Scotia, Canada; married Joseph Howe Grant, June 20, 1945 (deceased). *Agent:* Paul R. Reynolds, Inc., 12 East 41 St., New York, N.Y. 10017.

CAREER: Writer. *Awards, honors:* Leacock Medal for best humorous book by a Canadian author, 1951, for *The Salt Box.*

WRITINGS—Light adult novels under pseudonym Jan Hilliard: *The Salt Box,* Norton, 1951; *A View of the Town,* Abelard, 1954; *The Jameson Girls,* Abelard, 1956; *Dove Cottage,* Abelard, 1958; *Miranda,* Abelard, 1960; *Morgan's Castle,* Abelard, 1964.

Under own name: *Samuel Cunard, Pioneer of the Atlantic Steamship* (juvenile), Abelard, 1967; (with William S. Brett) *Small City Gardens,* Abelard, 1967; *Robert Stevenson: Engineer and Sea Builder* (juvenile), Meredith, 1969. Contributor to *Story* and other magazines.

*   *   *

GRAY, Nicholas Stuart 1922-

PERSONAL: Born October 23, 1922, in Scotland; son of William Stuart and Lenore May (Johnston) Gray. *Education:* Educated at "various private grammar schools, names forgotten. No degrees, as never tried for any, and probably wouldn't have got them if had done so." *Politics:* None. *Religion:* None. *Home:* Timewells, Bradford-on-Tone, Taunton, Somerset, England; and Langamull, Calgary, Isle of Mull, Scotland. *Agent:* Samuel French, Inc., 25 West 45th St., New York, N.Y. 10036; and Lawrence Fitch, 113 Wardour St., London, England.

CAREER: Playwright, novelist, actor and stage director, and illustrator. Had his first play produced professionally when he was seventeen; actor and director in repertory in London theaters and throughout England; has directed many of his plays, and appeared in some, including "New Clothes for the Emperor," "The Imperial Nightingale," "The Tinder-Box," "The Marvellous Story of Puss in Boots," "The Wrong Side of the Moon," and "The Princess and the Swineherd"; has also played Hamlet, Richard II, and Iago in "Othello," at the Malvern Festival Theatre. *Member:* P.E.N., Societe des Auteurs (Paris).

WRITINGS—Novels: *Over the Hills to Fabylon,* Oxford University Press, 1954; *Down in the Cellar,* Dobson, 1961; *The Seventh Swan,* Dobson, 1962; *The Stone Cage,* Dobson, 1963; *Grimbold's Other World,* Faber, 1963; *The Apple Stone,* Dobson, 1965; *Mainly in Moonlight,* Faber, 1965, Meridith, 1966; *Boys,* Meridith, 1969; *The Edge of Evening,* Faber, 1976; *Killer's Cookbook,* Dobson, 1976.

Plays; all published by Oxford University Press, except as indicated: *Beauty and the Beast,* 1951; *The Princess and the Swineherd,* 1952; *The Tinder-Box,* 1952; *The Hunters and the Henwife,* 1953; *The Marvellous Story of Puss in Boots,* 1955; *The Imperial Nightingale,* 1956; *New Clothes for the Emperor,* 1957; *The Other Cinderella,* 1958; *The Seventh Swan,* Dobson, 1962; *The Stone Cage* (now titled *The Wrong Side of the Moon*), Dobson, 1963; *Gawain and the Green Knight,* Dobson, 1967; *New Lamps for Old,* Dobson, 1967. Also writer of television plays.

WORK IN PROGRESS: A novel based on the life story of Sir Gawain, involving research in early Celtic legends, Welsh legends, medieval writings and poems of England and France, and later works; full-length adaptation of "Tinder-Box" with music; a folk-musical, "The Singing Shell."

SIDELIGHTS: Gray told *CA:* "Think it most important that people have a world of imagination into which they can escape from the turmoils of life. Myths used to provide this escape route. Now it is usual to hear people say they are not interested in 'fairytales,' and then proceed to weave themselves a fairytale based on what they would do if they suddenly became rich or famous. Materialism is no proper substitute, and I have been trying, in writing modern fantasies, to give children and adults some sort of temporary passport to a dream-world. It is interesting to find with what relief most of them take it. Speak French adequately (cannot spell)." *Avocational interests:* Archaeology, history, art, literature, animals, mythology, gardening.

* * *

GRAY, Ralph D(ale) 1933-

PERSONAL: Born October 13, 1933, in Otwell, Ind.; son of Lee M. (a grocer) and Voris R. (Gray) Gray; married Janice R. Everett, September 2, 1956; children: Karen, David, Sarah. *Education:* Hanover College, B.A., 1955; University of Durham, graduate student, 1955-56; University of Delaware, M.A., 1958; University of Illinois, Ph.D., 1962; *Home:* 1724 West 73rd Pl., Indianapolis, Ind. 46260.

CAREER: Ohio State University, Columbus, instructor in history, 1961-64; Indiana University, Kokomo Regional Campus, assistant professor, 1964-67, associate professor of history, 1967-68; Indiana University, Indianapolis, associate professor, 1968-72, professor of history, 1972—. Special consultant to Monon Railroad, 1966 and Cabot Corp., 1971. *Member:* American Historical Association, Organization of American Historians, Economic History Association, Business History Conference, American Association of University Professors, Delaware Historical Society, Indiana Historical Society, Indiana Oral History Roundtable (president, 1975-76), Howard County (Indiana) Historical Society (director, 1965-68). *Awards, honors:* Fulbright scholar in England, 1955-56; Dickerson Award, University of Illinois, 1966, for *The National Waterway.*

WRITINGS: The National Waterway: A History of the Chesapeake and Delaware Canal, 1769-1965, University of Illinois Press, 1967; (contributor) David I. Eggenberger, editor, *Encyclopedia of World Biography,* McGraw, 1973. Also author of *Stellite: A History of the Stellite Company, 1912-1972,* 1974. Contributor of articles and reviews to business history and regional history journals.

WORK IN PROGRESS: Editing *Gentlemen from Indiana: National Party Candidates, 1840-1940;* a biographical study of Elwood Haynes, a Hoosier automobile and metallurgical pioneer; research on Indiana waterways.

AVOCATIONAL INTERESTS: All sports, woodworking, photography.

* * *

GRAY, Simon 1936-
(James Holliday, Hamish Reade)

PERSONAL: Born October 21, 1936, in Hayling Island, Hampshire, England; son of James Davidson (a pathologist) and Barbara Celia Mary (Holliday) Gray; married Beryl Mary Kevern (a picture researcher), August 20, 1964; children: Benjamin. *Education:* Dalhousie University, B.A. (honors in English), 1958; Cambridge University, B.A. (honors in English), 1962. *Politics:* None. *Religion:* None. *Residence:* London, England. *Agent:* Clive Goodwin, 79 Cromwell Rd., London S.W.7, England. *Office:* Queen Mary College, Mile End Rd., London E.1, England.

CAREER: Author and playwright, residing in France, 1960-61, and Spain, 1962-63; University of London, Queen Mary College, London, England, lecturer in English, 1965—. *Awards, honors: Evening Standard* award for best play of the year, 1972, for "Butley."

WRITINGS: Colmain (novel), Faber, 1962; *Simple People* (novel), Faber, 1964; *Little Portia* (novel), Faber, 1966; (compiler) *Anthology of British Prose,* Faber, 1967; (under pseudonym Hamish Reade) *A Comeback for Stark,* Putnam, 1968.

Plays: *Wise Child* (produced on the West End at Wyndham's Theatre, 1967; produced on Broadway at Helen Hayes Theatre, January 27, 1972) Faber, 1968; *Dutch Uncle* (produced on the West End at Aldwych Theatre, March 26, 1969), Faber, 1969; *The Idiot* (adaptation from the novel by Dostoevsky; produced in London at National Theatre, July 15, 1970) Methuen, 1971; *Spoiled* (also see below; produced on the West End at Haymarket Theatre, February 24, 1971), Methuen, 1971; *Butley* (produced on the West End at Criterion Theatre, June 14, 1971; produced on Broadway at Morosco Theatre, 1972; screen adaptation by Gray for American Film Theatre, 1974) Methuen, 1971, Viking, 1972; *Otherwise Employed* (produced on the West End at Queen's Theatre, 1975), Methuen, 1975.

Television plays: "The Caramel Crises," 1966; "Death of a Teddy Bear," 1967; "A Way with the Ladies," 1967; *Sleeping Dog,* 1967, Faber, 1968; "Spoiled," 1968; "Pig in a Poke," 1969; "The Dirt on Lucy Lane," 1969; "Style of a Countess," 1970; "The Princess," 1970; "The Man in the Sidecar," 1971; *Plaintiffs and Defendants,* Methuen, 1975; *Two Sundays,* Methuen, 1975.

SIDELIGHTS: Film rights to "Death of a Teddy Bear" have been purchased by Avco Embassy.

BIOGRAPHICAL/CRITICAL SOURCES: Observer, April 23, 1967; *Listener,* August 31, 1967; *Punch,* May 1, 1968; *Prompt,* Number 12, 1968; *Variety,* January 29, 1969, April 2, 1969.

* * *

GREBANIER, Bernard 1903-

PERSONAL: Surname is pronounced Greb-an-yer; born March 8, 1903, in New York, N.Y.; son of Benjamin (an accountant) and Ottillie (von Sternberg) Grebanier; formerly married to Frances Winwar (a writer). *Education:* City College (now City College of the City University of New York), B.A., 1926; New York University, M.A., 1930, Ph.D., 1935. *Home:* 215 West 88th St., New York, N.Y. 10024. *Agent:* Cyrilly Abels, 119 West 57th St., New York, N.Y. 10019.

CAREER: Brooklyn College (now Brooklyn College of the City University of New York), Brooklyn, N.Y. instructor, 1930-35, assistant professor, 1936-47, associate professor, 1948-54, professor of English, 1954-64, professor emeritus, 1964—. *Member:* P.E.N., Authors Guild, Poetry Society of America, American Guild of Authors and Composers (vice-president, 1975—), Players Club. *Awards, honors:* Samuel French Award for the best teaching of playwriting in the United States, 1957, 1958.

WRITINGS: (With S. Thompson) *English Literature and Its Backgrounds,* Holt, 1939, revised edition, 1950; *Fauns, Satyrs and a Few Sages,* Mosher Press, 1945; *Mirrors of the Fire,* Mosher Press, 1946; *Essentials of English Literature,* Barron's, 1951; (with V. Hopper) *Essentials of European Literature,* Barron's, 1952; (with V. Hopper) *Bibliography of European Literature in English,* Barron's, 1953; *The Other Love,* Bookman Associates, 1957; *Racine's*

"Phaedra" in *English Verse* (acting version), Barron's, 1958; *Moliere's "The Misanthrope" in English* (acting version), Barron's, 1959.

The Heart of Hamlet, Crowell, 1960; (with S. Reiter) *Introduction to Imaginative Literature,* Crowell, 1960; *Playwriting,* Crowell, 1961; *The Truth About Shylock,* Random House, 1962; *Thornton Wilder,* University of Minnesota Press, 1963; *The Great Shakespeare Forgery,* Norton, 1965; *Armenian Miniatures,* Mechitarist Press (Venice), 1967; *Barron's Simplified Approach to Chaucer,* Barron's, 1964; *Barron's Simplified Approach to Moliere,* Barron's, 1965; *Barron's Simplified Approach to Rousseau: Emile and Other Works,* Barron's, 1965; *Barron's Simplified Approach to Shakespeare's Henry IV, Part I,* Barron's, 1965; *Barron's Simplified Approach to Milton: Paradise Lost and Other Works,* Barron's, 1966; *Barron's Simplified Approach to Shakespeare's Richard II,* Barron's, 1967; *The Uninhibited Byron: An Account of His Sexual Confusion,* Crown, 1970; *The Enjoyment of Literature,* Crown, 1975; *Then Came Each Actor: Shakespearen Actors, Great and Otherwise, including Players and Princes, Rogues, Vagabonds and Actors Motley,* McKay, 1975; *Players Hide,* McKay 1975.

WORK IN PROGRESS: A biography of Byron.

SIDELIGHTS: Grebanier told *CA:* "[I] started out in life to be a concert pianist; music still major avocational interest. Have collected fine paintings, sculptures (all periods), tanagras, intaglios and vases (all ancient). Spend much time in Europe, particularly in Italy."

*   *   *

GREEN, Elizabeth A(dine) H(erkimer) 1906-

PERSONAL: Born August 21, 1906, in Mobile, Ala.; daughter of Albert Wingate (a musician) and Mary (Timmerman) Green. *Education:* Wheaton College, Wheaton, Ill., B.S. and Mus.B., 1928; Northwestern University, M.Mus., 1939; studied violin under father, Albert Wingate Green, and Jacques Gordon and Ivan Galamian; studied viola under Clarence Evans. *Politics:* Republican. *Religion:* Presbyterian. *Home:* 1225 Ferdon Rd., Ann Arbor, Mich. 48104.

CAREER: High school teacher of stringed instruments and conductor of orchestras in Waterloo, Iowa, 1928-42; teacher in public schools of Ann Arbor, Mich., 1942-48; University of Michigan, Ann Arbor, assistant professor, 1948-49, associate professor in music education, 1957-63, professor of music, 1963-75. Concertmaster of Ann Arbor Civic Orchestra, 1942-56, 1965-68; formerly concertmaster of other community orchestras and staff viola player for two years on WMT, Waterloo, Iowa. Lecturer and music clinician throughout the country. *Member:* Music Educators National Conference, American String Teachers Association, National School Orchestra Association, American Association of University Professors, Pi Kappa Lambda, Delta Omicron (national honorary member).

WRITINGS—Texts: Orchestral Bowings, Edwards Letter Shop, 1949, revised edition published as *Orchestral Bowings and Routines,* Ann Arbor Publishers, 1953; *The Modern Conductor,* Prentice-Hall, 1962, 2nd edition, 1969; *Teaching Stringed Instruments in Classes,* Prentice-Hall, 1966; (with N. Malko) *The Conductor and His Score,* Prentice-Hall, 1975.

Music: "Theme and Variations for Orchestral Bowings," Carl Fischer, 1950; "Musicianship and Repertoire for the High School Orchestra," Book I, Theodore Presser, 1962; "Twelve Modern Etudes for the Advanced Violinist," Elkan-Vogel, 1967. Adapter, "Hohmann for the String Class," Carl Fischer, 1959. Former columnist on strings, *School Musician;* contributor to other music journals.

SIDELIGHTS: Elizabeth Green spent the summer of 1958 in the Soviet Union, visiting classes and conferring with musicians at Moscow Conservatory and Stoliarsky School in Odessa; lived in Paris, 1964-65; returned to Europe in 1968 to be guest speaker at second Nicolai Malko International Competition for Young Conductors at Danish Royal Conservatory of Music, Copenhagen. She is proficient in French; speaks some German, and less Danish and Russian.

*   *   *

GREEN, Julien (Hartridge) 1900-
(Theophile Delaporte, David Irland)

PERSONAL: Born September 6, 1900, in Paris, France; christened Julian, but has chosen to use the French spelling, Julien, since the late 1920's; kept U.S. citizenship from birth, though France remained his adopted country; son of Edward Moon (a business agent) and Mary Adelaide (Hartridge) Green (both U.S. citizens); brother of novelist Anne Green. *Education:* Attended Lycee Janson-de-Sailly (Paris); University of Virginia, Charlottesville, student, 1919-22; studied drawing at La Grande Chaumiere (Paris), 1922-23. *Religion:* Roman Catholic convert, 1916. *Address:* c/o Editions Plon, 8 rue Garanciere, Paris 6e France.

CAREER: Went to America for the first time, 1919; University of Virginia, Charlottesville, assistant professor of French, 1921-22; returned to France, summer, 1922; in 1924, embarked on full-time literary career; stayed several times in the United States, including a second visit to Virginia, 1933-34; went to America in 1940 after France fell to Germany; lectured on French writers at Princeton University, Goucher College, Mills College, and a number of Jesuit colleges, October, 1940-September, 1942; returned to Paris, 1945. *Wartime service*—World War I: Volunteered for the American Field Service, 1917; served on the French front at Verdun; later worked for six months with the Norton-Harjes Service (as the Red Cross was then called) in Italy until May, 1918; then joined the French Army, training at the artillery school, Fontainebleau; served in the region of Strasbourg, and, after the armistice, went with his regiment to the Rhineland on occupation duty; demobilized, 1919. World War II: Joined U.S. Army, 1942; later held post in the U.S. Office of War Information; made radio broadcasts to France, 1943.

MEMBER: Academie de Baviere, L'Academie Royale de Belgique, Academie Francaise, Academy of Arts and Letters, Academie of Mainz, Conseil litteraire de Monaco. *Awards, honors:* Prix Paul Flat, of the Academie Francaise, and Femina-Bookman Prize, for *Adrienne Mesurat;* Harper Prize, 1929-30, for *Leviathan;* Harper 125th Anniversary Award, 1942, for *Memory of Happy Days;* Officier de la Legion d'Honneur; Grand Prix Litteraire de Monaco, 1951, for the whole of his work; Grand Prix National des Lettres, 1966; Prix Ibico Reggino, 1968; Grand Prix, Academie Francaise, 1970; Prix des Universites Alemaniques; Grand Prix Arts, Sciences et Lettres de Paris.

WRITINGS—Nonfiction: (Under pseudonym Theophile Delaporte) *Pamphlet contre les Catholiques de France* (essay), Editions de la Revue des Pamphletaires (Paris), 1924, reprinted in *Deux pamphlets contre les bien pensants,* with an introduction by Albert Beguin, Editions de la Baconniere (Neuchatel, Switzerland), 1944, new separate edition, with a preface by Jacques Maritain, Plon, 1963; *Suite anglaise* (essays on Samuel Johnson, William Blake, Charles Lamb, and Charlotte Bronte), Cahiers de Paris, 1927, reprinted, Plon, 1972; *Un Puritain homme de lettres: Nathaniel Hawthorne*, Editions des Cahiers Libres, 1928; *Liberte* (essay), Plon, 1974.

Fiction: *Mont-Cinere* (novel), Plon, 1926, translation by Marshall A. Best (containing fifty pages not included in the original French edition) published as *Avarice House*, Harper, 1927, complete French edition (containing the additional fifty pages), Plon, 1928, new English edition published as *Monte-Cinere*, edited by C. T. Stewart, Harper, 1937; *Adrienne Mesurat* (novel), Plon, 1927, translation by Henry Longan Stuart published as *The Closed Garden* (Book-of-the-Month Club selection), with an introduction by Andre Maurois, Harper, 1928, new French edition (containing some pages of the author's manuscript), Club des Libraries de France, 1957, reprinted, Plon, 1973; *Le Voyageur sur la terre* (tale; illustrated with a portrait of the author by Jean Cocteau), Gallimard, 1927, translation by Courtney Bruerton published as *The Pilgrim on the Earth*, Harper, 1929; "Christine" (tale), printed by Paillart in the collection, *Les Amis d'Edouard*, [Abbeville], 1927; *La Traversee inutile* (tale), Plon, 1927, published as "Leviathan," in *Christine, suivi de Leviathan*, Editions des Cahiers Libres, 1928; *Les Clefs de la Mort* (tale), J. Schiffrin (Paris), 1928; all four preceding tales published in a single French edition under the title *Le Voyageur sur la terre*, Plon, 1930, translation published as *Christine, and Other Stories*, with an introduction by Courtney Bruerton (containing "Leviathan," "Christine," "The Keys of Death," and "The Pilgrim on the Earth"), Harper, 1930; *Leviathan* (novel; not the same work as the tale, "Leviathan"), Plon, 1929, revised edition, with a preface by J. C. Brisville, Editions Recontre (Lausanne), 1962, translation by Vyvyan Holland published as *The Dark Journey*, Harper, 1929, reprinted, Greenwood Press, 1972.

L'Autre Sommeil (novel), Gallimard, 1931, reprinted, Plon, 1971; *Epaves* (novel), Plon, 1932, translation by Holland published as *The Strange River*, Harper, 1932; *Le Visionnaire* (novel), Plon, 1934, reprinted, 1962, translation by Holland published as *The Dreamer*, Harper, 1934; *Minuit* (novel), Plon, 1936, reprinted, 1963, translation by Holland published as *Midnight*, Harper, 1936; *Varouna* (novel), Plon, 1940, translation by James Whitall published as *Then Shall the Dust Return*, Harper, 1941; *Si j'etais vous* (novel), Plon, 1947, revised edition, 1970, translation by J.H.F. McEwen published as *If I Were You*, Harper, 1949; *Moira* (novel), Plon, 1950, translation by Denise Folliot published as *Moira*, Macmillan, 1951; *Le Malfaiteur* (novel; in *Oeuvres Completes*, Volume V), Plon, 1955, general edition, 1956, augmented edition, 1974, translation by Anne Green published as *The Transgressor*, Pantheon, 1957; *Chaque homme dans sa nuit* (novel), Plon, 1960, translation by Anne Green published as *Each in His Darkness*, Pantheon, 1961; *L'Autre* (novel), Plon, 1971, translation by Bernard Wall published as *The Other One*, Harcourt, 1973.

Drama: *Sud* (three-act play; produced in Paris at Athenee Theatre, 1953), Plon, 1953, reprinted, 1972, translation published as "South" in *Plays of the Year*, Volume XII, Elek, 1955 (produced by Peter Hall in London at Arts Theatre Club, 1955; opera, with music by Kenton Coe, produced at Opera de Paris, 1973); *L'Ennemi* (three-act play; produced

at Theatre des Bouffes Parisiens, March, 1954), Plon, 1954; *L'Ombre* (three-act play; produced at Theatre Antoine, September, 1956), Plon, 1956.

Autobiographical works: *Memories of Happy Days* (originally written in English), Harper, 1942, reprinted, Greenwood Press, 1969; "Quand nous hibitions tous ensemble" (reminiscences), in *Les Oeuvres nouvelles*, Editions de la Maison Francaise (New York), 1943; *Partir avant le jour*, Grasset, 1963, translation by Anne Green published as *To Leave Before Dawn*, Harcourt, 1967; *Mille chemins ouverts*, Grasset, 1964; *Terre Lointaine*, Grasset, 1966; *Jeunesse*, Grasset, 1974.

Journal, nine volumes, all published by Plon, except as noted: Volume I: *Les Annees faciles, 1928-34*, 1938, revised edition published as *Les Annees faciles, 1926-34*, 1970, Volume II: *Derniers beaux jours, 1935-39*, 1939, translation of Volumes I-II by Jocelyn Godefroi published in one volume as *Personal Record, 1928-39*, Harper, 1939, Volume III: *Devant la porte sombre, 1940-43*, 1946, Volume IV: *L'Oeil de l'ouragan, 1943-46*, 1949, Volume V: *Le Revenant, 1946-50*, 1951, Volume VI: *Le Miroir interieur, 1950-54*, 1955, Volume VII: *Le Bel aujourd'hui, 1955-58*, 1958, omnibus edition (contains Volumes I-VII) published as *Journal: 1928-1958*, 1961, translation by Anne Green published in an abridged edition as *Diary, 1928-57*, edited by Kurt Wolff, Harcourt, 1964, Volume VIII: *Vers l'invisible, 1959-66*, 1967, new omnibus edition (contains Volumes I-VIII) published in two volumes as *Journal, 1928-66*, 1969, Volume IX: *Ce qui reste de jour, 1966-72*, 1972.

Omnibus volumes: *Oeuvres Completes*, ten volumes, Plon, 1954-65; *Bibliotheque de la Pleiade*, five volumes, Gallimard, 1971-75.

Translator: (With Anne Green) Charles Peguy, *Basic Verities: Prose and Poetry*, Pantheon, 1943; (with Anne Green) Peguy, *Men and Saints*, Pantheon, 1944; Peguy, *God Speaks: Religious Poetry*, Pantheon, 1945; Peguy, *The Mystery of the Charity of Joan of Arc*, Pantheon, 1949.

Filmscripts: "Leviathan," 1962; (with Eric Jourdan) "La Dame de pique," 1965. Also, with Eric Jourdan, author of television and radio scripts, "Je est un autre," 1954, and "La Mort de Ivan Ilytch," 1955.

Contributor: *Etapes d'une pensee: Rencontres avec Albert Beguin*, Editions de la Baconniere, 1957. Has also contributed to *Revue Hebdomadaire*, *Revue Europeenne*, *Nouvelle Revue Francaise*, *Revue Universelle*, *La Parisienne*, *Revue des Deux Mondes*, *University of Virginia Magazine*, *American Scholar*, and other periodicals.

WORK IN PROGRESS: A new volume of the *Journal*, for Plon; a translation of *Memories of Happy Days* into French; a play; a tale for children.

SIDELIGHTS: In 1930 Courtney Bruerton wrote: "As Julien Green is the first American novelist to choose French as his medium of expression, so he is the first American to be ranked by competent critics as a great French writer." L. Clark Keating comments on the "irresistible appeal" which Green's work has held for critics, "many of whom have tried to find American sources and models for his characters and situations." Among his works which have American settings is *Avarice House;* this story, notes Keating, "is laid in a Virginia farmhouse, modeled on an uncle's manor house near Warrenton [where] Green spent several weeks during his first American sojourn." Discussing the similarities between Green and Hawthorne, the same writer suggests that "Green's sombre and fantastic imagination, and his preoccupation with violence and death, are often reminiscent of the nineteenth-century New Englander." He concludes that Hawthorne, "if not a model, has been an inspiration."

Andre Maurois, on the other hand, does not recognize a predominant English or American influence on Green's work: "For my part," writes Maurois, "I see very well wherein Green resembles the Brontes, but I see also wherein he resembles Balzac." According to I. W. Brock, Green is "unmistakably French" and "may be called American only because of his parentage. His ideas, language and philosophy are primarily French."

However, the unusual nature of his background tends to elude classification. Marilyn Gaddis points out: "By temperament and training Green was perhaps as much as ten years behind most boys of his generation. To begin with, he was the most confirmed French-speaking member of a household that was a miniature bilingual community.... Teased about his Confederate sympathies and Protestantism by his French schoolmates, Green withdrew into his own creative fantasy world." Samuel Stokes writes that Green's parents "brought to Europe all sorts of furniture which caused considerable consternation among their French friends, but," he continues, "its appearance created an atmosphere." James Lord affirms: "The emotional stress of this formative duality had a decisive effect upon the young author" which is "starkly reflected" in his works. For instance, Peter Hall, the London producer of *South,* has said that it is a play about "extremes: North versus South, white man against coloured man, the old world of Europe in contrast with the new world of America, the difficulty that the sexually normal have in understanding the sexually abnormal."

For I. W. Brock, the main strength of Green's work lies in its "psychological naturalism." Robert Kanters, emphasizing a different aspect, feels that the use of dreams in Green's work "is a natural way less between reality and the fantastic than between two different levels of reality."

L. Clark Keating says of Green as a man, that he is "solitary and takes pains to avoid a crowd. Although a traveler he has few of the earmarks of the tourist. Even in his diary he does not choose to write of the issues of the day." Defending his position, Marilyn Gaddis states: "It would be incorrect—and basically unfair—to call either his solitude or his lack of social commitment an escape. On the contrary he has faced and transcended the alienation which most of his readers bury or ignore. After a period of doubt and religious crisis, Green became "reconverted" to the Roman Catholic faith in 1939, and James Lord writes: "His personal, intellectual and moral adherence to the tenets of Roman Catholicism appears to be complete."

Although he is bilingual in English and French, Green found that when he tried to write in English, it was like "wearing clothes that were not made for me." His only imaginative story in English is "The Apprentice Psychiatrist," published in the *University of Virginia Magazine,* May-June, 1920. He has mastered a number of other languages; Robert de Saint-Jean reports: "During a voyage in Italy, I had the surprise of hearing Julien Green express himself easily in Italian; I knew he was reading Dante in the original text, but thought that he understood the language without being able to speak it, and especially to make himself understood. In Germany, the same experi-

ence...." The same writer also reports that Green has studied Greek and Latin assiduously. In 1935, he took lessons in Hebrew from a rabbi in Paris "after much time spent in floundering among contradictory versions of the Bible."

In 1971, Green became the first foreign member of the Academie Francaise.

Extracts from his work, including a reading by Green himself, have been recorded in the series "Auteurs du 20e Siecle," Philips.

BIOGRAPHICAL/CRITICAL SOURCES—Books: Anne Green, *With Much Love,* Harper, 1948; Samuel Stokes, *Julian Green and the Thorn of Puritanism,* King's Crown Press, Columbia University, 1955; Marilyn Gaddis, *The Critical Reaction to Julien Green (1926-56),* unpublished thesis, University of Missouri, 1958; M. G. Cooke, *Hallucination and Death as Motifs of Escape in the Novels of Julien Green,* Catholic University of America Press, 1960; Jean-Claude Joyce, *Julien Green et le monde de la fatalite,* Arnaud Druck (Berne), 1964; Robert de Saint Jean, *Julien Green,* Editions du Seuil, 1967; Jacques Petit, *Julien Green: L'Homme qui orient d'ailleurs,* Desclee, 1969; Peter C. Hoy, *Julien Green: Essai de bibliographie des etudes en langue francaise consarcees a Julien Green (1923-1967),* Lettre Modernes, 1970; Antonio Mor, *Julien Green: Memoir de l'invisible,* Plon, 1972; Carolyn Riley, editor, *Contemporary Literary Criticism,* Volume III, Gale, 1975.

All by Julien Green: *Journal* (also see above), nine volumes, Plon, 1938-72, translation of Volumes I-VII by Anne Green published in an abridged edition as *Diary, 1928-57,* edited by Kurt Wolff, Harcourt, 1964; *Memories of Happy Days,* Harper, 1942, reprinted, Greenwood Press, 1969; *Partir avant le jour,* Grasset, 1963, translation by Anne Green published as *To Leave Before Dawn,* Harcourt, 1967; *Mille chemins ouverts,* Grasset, 1964; *Terre Lointaine,* Grasset, 1966; *Jeunesse,* Grasset, 1974.

Articles: *Sewanee Review,* April, 1932; *Bookman,* August, 1932; *PMLA,* June, 1939; *Saturday Review of Literature,* November, 1939; *New York Times Book Review,* May 11, 1941, October 1, 1967; *Emory University Quarterly,* March, December, 1945; *Biblio,* December, 1949; *French Review,* March, 1950, May, 1955; *New Yorker,* September 1, 1951; *London Magazine,* January, 1967; *Livres de France,* February, 1967; *L'Express,* February 15-21, 1971.

*   *   *

GREENBAUM, Leonard 1930-

PERSONAL: Born September 30, 1930, in Boston, Mass.; son of Noah and Sarah (Hookness) Greenbaum; married Judith Levine (a research administrator), June 22, 1952; children: Daniel, Joshua, Sara, Susannah. *Education:* University of Michigan, B.A., 1952, M.A., 1953, Ph.D., 1963; University of California, Berkeley, graduate study, 1952-53. *Office:* Michigan-Memorial Phoenix Project, University of Michigan, Ann Arbor, Mich. 48105.

CAREER: University of Michigan, Ann Arbor, fellow, 1957-58, producer and writer for university TV office, 1958-60, Michigan-Memorial Phoenix Project, staff member, 1961-64, assistant to director, 1962-64, assistant director, 1964—, assistant professor of English, College of Engineering, 1963-68. Danforth Foundation associate, 1969—; consultant to KMS Industries, 1971—, and Manpower Science Service, 1972—.

WRITINGS: The Hound and Horn, Mouton & Co., 1966; *Out of Shape,* Harper, 1969; (with Rudolf B. Schmerl) *Course X: A Left Field Guide to Freshman English,* Lippincott, 1970; *A Special Interest: The Atomic Energy Commission, Argonne National Laboratory, and the Midwestern Universities,* University of Michigan Press, 1971. Writer of educational television scripts.

WORK IN PROGRESS: Fiction.†

*   *   *

GREENBLUM, Joseph   1925-

PERSONAL: Born December 1925, in New York, N.Y.; son of Harry (a grocer) and Bella (Fogel) Greenblum; married Erika Gerner (a high school teacher), June 18, 1950; children: Eli, Judith, Miriam. *Education:* City College (now City College of the City University of New York), B.S.S., 1949; University of Wisconsin, M.S., 1951; Columbia University, M.P.H., 1959. *Religion:* Jewish. *Office:* Office of Research and Statistics, Social Security, Baltimore, Md.

CAREER: Columbia University, School of Public Health, New York City, assistant in social epidemiology, 1959-61; American Jewish Committee, New York City, study director, Division of Scientific Research, 1962-67; Yeshiva University, New York City, instructor in department of sociology, 1967-74; Social Security Administration, Office of Research and Statistics, Baltimore, Md., social science research analyst, 1974—. Lecturer, Hunter College of the City University of New York, 1965-68; research associate in department of psychiatry, Columbia University, 1970-74. *Member:* American Sociological Association, American Association for Public Opinion Research, Association for the Sociological Study of Jewry, Phi Beta Kappa.

WRITINGS: (Contributor) Reinhard Bendix and Seymour M. Lipset, editors, *Class, Status, and Power,* Free Press of Glencoe, 1953; (contributor) Marshall Sklare, editor, *The Jews: Social Patterns of an American Group,* Free Press of Glencoe, 1957; (with Sklare) *Jewish Identity on the Suburban Frontier: A Study of Group Survival in the Open Society,* Basic Books, 1967. Contributor to sociology journals.

WORK IN PROGRESS: Research on national vocational rehabilitation programs; contributing to monographs on sociomedical health indicators.

*   *   *

GREENE, David H.   1913-

PERSONAL: Born November 4, 1913, in Boston, Mass.; son of Herbert Alva (an engineer) and Ann (Roche) Greene; married Catherine J. Healy, June 24, 1939; children: Mrs. Bruce Fields, Catherine J., Gail E., David G., Helen C. *Education:* Harvard University, A.B., 1936, M.A., 1938, Ph.D., 1943. *Politics:* Democrat. *Religion:* Roman Catholic. *Home:* 47 Oakwood Ave., Upper Montclair, N.J. *Office:* Department of English, New York University, New York, N.Y. 10003.

CAREER: Instructor in English at Boston College (now University), Boston, Mass., 1939, and College of New Rochelle, New Rochelle, N.Y., 1939-41; U.S. Naval Academy, Annapolis, Md., professor of English, 1941-43, 1945-46; New York University, New York, N.Y., member of faculty, 1946—, professor of English, 1959—, head of all-university department of English, 1963—. *Military service:* U.S. Naval Reserve, active duty, 1943-45; became lieutenant junior grade. *Member:* Modern Language Association of America, International Association of University Professors of English, Royal Society of Antiquaries of Ireland, American Committee for Irish Studies.

WRITINGS: (Editor with Vivian Mercier) *One Thousand Years of Irish Prose,* Devin-Adair, 1952; (editor and author of introduction) *An Anthology of Irish Literature,* Modern Library, 1954, published in two volumes, New York University Press, 1971; (with E. M. Stephens) *J. M. Synge, 1871-1909,* Macmillan, 1959; (editor with D. H. Laurence) *G. B. Shaw: The Matter with Ireland,* Hart-Davis, 1962; (editor) *Great Stories by Chekhov,* Dell, 1962; (editor with James Carney) *Celtic Studies: Essays in Memory of Angus Matheson,* Barnes & Noble, 1968. Also author of *The Irish Language,* 1966, and *Writing in Irish Today,* 1972.

*   *   *

GREENE, Maxine   1917-

PERSONAL: Born December 23, 1917, in New York, N.Y.; daughter of Max C. and Lillian (Greenfield) Meyer; married Joseph M. Krimsley, March 19, 1938 (deceased); married Orville N. Greene (a patent attorney), August 7, 1947; children: (first marriage) Linda; (second marriage) Timothy F. *Education:* Barnard College, B.A., 1938; New York University, M.A., 1949, Ph.D., 1955. *Politics:* Liberal Democrat. *Home:* 1080 Fifth Ave., New York, N.Y. 10028. *Office:* Teachers College, Columbia University, 525 West 120th St., New York, N.Y. 10027.

CAREER: New York University, New York City, instructor, 1949-56; Montclair State College, Upper Montclair, N.J., assistant professor of English, 1956-57; New York University, assistant professor, 1957-59, associate professor, 1959-62; Brooklyn College of the City University of New York, Brooklyn, N.Y., associate professor of education, 1962-65; Columbia University, Teachers College, New York City, associate professor, 1965-67, professor of English and philosophy of education, 1967—. *Member:* Philosophy of Education Society (president, 1966-67), National Council of Teachers of English, American Association of University Professors, John Dewey Society (lecturer; chairman, 1970—), Middle Atlantic States Philosophy of Education Society (president, 1965-67), Kappa Delta Pi, Phi Beta Kappa.

WRITINGS: The Public School and the Private Vision, Random House, 1965; *Existential Encounters for Teachers,* Random House, 1967; (author of introduction, preface, and notes) Nathaniel Hawthorne, *The Birthmark and Other Stories,* Scholastic Book Services, 1968; *Teacher as Stranger: Educational Philosophy for the Modern Age,* Wadsworth, 1973. Author of prefaces to Collier Books editions of Conrad and Eliot novels, 1963. Contributor to *Saturday Review* and to education journals. Editor, *Record* (publication of Teachers College, Columbia University), 1965-70.

WORK IN PROGRESS: Literature as Human Quest.†

*   *   *

GREENE, Wilda   1911-

PERSONAL: Born January 25, 1911, in Falkville, Ala.; daughter of Frank T. and Ida Dixie (Lovelady) Witt; married Wallace S. Greene, Jr., March 2, 1936; children: Donna (Mrs. William T. Miller). *Education:* Attended public schools. *Religion:* Baptist. *Home and office:* 155 Boxwood Dr., Franklin, Tenn. 37064.

MEMBER: National League of American Pen Women,

National Federation of Press Women, Authors Guild, Tennessee Woman's Press and Authors Club, Nashville Woman's Press and Authors Club.

WRITINGS: Visitation Evangelism, Moody, 1955; *The Disturbing Christ* (devotional study of Hebrews), Broadman, 1968. Contributor to *Broadman Devotional Annual,* 1973. Writer of articles, biblical background material, and curriculum materials for religious publications.

WORK IN PROGRESS: What the Bible Says about the Right to Live and Die.

*   *   *

GREENFIELD, Patricia Marks   1940-

PERSONAL: Born July 18, 1940, in Newark, N.J.; daughter of David Marks, Jr. (a life insurance salesman) and Doris (Pollard) Marks; married Sheldon Greenfield (a physician), March 13, 1965; children: Lauren. *Education:* Radcliffe College, A.B. (summa cum laude), 1962; University of Dakar, additional study, 1963-64; Harvard University, Ph.D., 1966. *Office:* Department of Psychology, University of California, Los Angeles, Calif. 90024.

CAREER: Syracuse University, Syracuse, N.Y., investigator at Research and Development Center in Early Childhood Education, 1967, research associate, 1967-68; Harvard University, Cambridge, Mass., research fellow in psychology, Center for Cognitive Studies, 1968-72, lecturer on social relations, 1970; Stanford University, Stanford, Calif., acting assistant professor of psychology, 1972-73; University of California, assistant professor, Santa Cruz Campus, 1973-74, associate professor of psychology, Los Angeles Campus, 1974—. Visiting lecturer, Clark University, 1971. Program advisor, Bromley-Health Infant Daycare Center, 1969-70. Consultant on child development to Urban Systems Research and Engineering, 1972. *Member:* Phi Beta Kappa. *Awards, honors:* First Award of Sixth Annual Creative Talent Awards Program of American Institute for Research, 1967, for dissertation, "Culture, Concepts, and Conservation: A Comparative Study of Cognitive Development in Senegal."

WRITINGS: (With Jerome S. Bruner, R. R. Olver, and others) *Studies in Cognitive Growth,* Wiley, 1966; (with E. Tronick) *Infant Curriculum: The Bromley-Health Guide to the Care of Infants in Groups,* Media Projects, 1973; (with J. Smith) *The Structure of Communication in Early Language Development,* Academic Press, in press.

Contributor: D. Price-Williams, editor, *Cross-Cultural Studies: Selected Readings,* Penguin, 1969; R. Cancro, editor, *Intelligence: Genetic and Environmental Influences,* Grune, 1971; P. Adams, editor, *Language in Thinking,* Penguin, 1972; V. P. Clark, P. A. Escholz, and A. F. Rosa, editors, *Language: Introductory Readings,* St. Martin's, 1972; H. C. Lindgren, editor, *Child Behavior,* National Press Books, 1975; D. Walter, editor, *Human Brain Function,* Brain Research Institute, in press; G. Steiner, editor, *Piaget and Beyond: The Psychology of the Twentieth Century,* Volume VII, Kindler, in press; P. Dasen, editor, *Cross-Cultural Piagetian Psychology,* Gardner Press, in press. Also author, with Allegra M. May and Jerome S. Bruner, of filmscript, "Early Words: Language and Action in the Life of a Child," Wiley, 1972. Contributor of articles and reviews to professional journals. Member of editorial board, *Child Development,* 1969-71.

WORK IN PROGRESS: Contributing to *The Developing Individual in a Changing World,* Volume I, edited by K. F.

Riegel and J. A. Meacham, for Mouton, and to *Culture, Child and School: Socio-Cultural Influences in Learning,* edited by M. Maehr, for Brooks/Cole; research on psychological relations between language and action structure, children's construction activity, physical environment and child behavior, and on response to interruption in a narrative structure.

SIDELIGHTS: Patricia Greenfield is competent in French and Wolof, a major Sengalese language. *Avocational interests:* Travel, sailing, and "social action."

*   *   *

GREENFIELD, Sidney M(artin)   1932-

PERSONAL: Born April 30, 1932, in New York, N.Y.; son of Solomon and Edith Greenfield; married Eleanor Stolz, August 21, 1954; children: Beth, David, Suzanne. *Education:* Brooklyn College (now Brooklyn College of the City University of New York), A.B., 1954; Columbia University, Ph.D., 1959. *Home:* 2605 East Beverly Rd., Milwaukee, Wis. 53211. *Office:* Department of Sociology, University of Wisconsin, Milwaukee, Wis. 53201.

CAREER: Hunter College (now Hunter College of the City University of New York), New York, N.Y., instructor in anthropology, 1958; Connecticut College, New London, instructor in anthropology and sociology, 1958-59; Purdue University, Lafayette, Ind., assistant professor of anthropology and sociology, 1959-63; University of Wisconsin—Milwaukee, associate professor of sociology, 1963—. *Member:* American Anthropological Association, American Ethnological Society, Society for Applied Anthropology. *Awards, honors:* Fulbright-Hays and Social Science Research Council grants for research in Brazil and the Caribbean; National Science Foundation grant for research in Portugal.

WRITINGS: English Rustics in Black Skin, College & University, 1966; (editor with Arnold Strickon) *Structure and Process in Latin America: Patronage, Clientage, and Power Studies,* University of New Mexico Press, 1972. Contributor to journals and books in his field.

*   *   *

GREENHAW, H(arold) Wayne   1940-

PERSONAL: Born February 17, 1940, in Colbert County, Ala.; son of Harold Reed (a salesman) and Lee (Able) Greenhaw; married Faye Berry, September, 1965 (divorced August, 1967); married Sarah Virginia Maddox, August, 1972. *Education:* Attended Instituto Allende, San Miguel, Mexico, summer, 1959; University of Alabama, B.S. in Ed., 1966. *Residence:* Montgomery, Ala. *Agent:* Writers House, 303 West 42nd St., New York, N.Y. 10036. *Office: Alabama Journal,* Washington St., Montgomery, Ala. 36102.

CAREER: Tuscaloosa News, Tuscaloosa, Ala., part-time sports reporter, 1958-62; Tuscaloosa Country Club, Tuscaloosa, assistant manager, 1960-63; *Graphic Weekly,* Tuscaloosa, sports columnist, 1963-64; Draper Correctional Center, Elmore, Ala., writer for experimental educational project, 1964-65; *Alabama Journal,* Montgomery, general assignment reporter, 1965—. *Awards, honors:* First place in investigative reporting and second place in feature writing, Alabama Associated Press Awards, 1966; Nieman fellow, Harvard University, 1972-73.

WRITINGS: The Golfer, Lippincott, 1967. Writer of two six-part series for Alabama Educational Television. Entertainment editor, *Montgomery Advertiser.* Contributor of more than 100 articles to magazines.

WORK IN PROGRESS: Nonfiction book about modern politics in Alabama.

SIDELIGHTS: Greenshaw has traveled, mostly by hitchhiking or motorcycle, in every state in the United States and Mexico.

* * *

GREENWOOD, Duncan 1919-

PERSONAL: Born August 30, 1919, in Bradford, Yorkshire, England; son of Angus (a cloth manufacturer) and Edith (Jackson) Greenwood; married Joyce Black, February 24, 1949; children: David, John, Robin. *Education:* Bradford Technical College (now Bradford University), B.Sc., 1941. *Home:* 58 High View, Pinner, Middlesex, England. *Agent:* Curtis Brown Ltd., 1 Craven Hill, London, W2 3EW, England.

CAREER: British Ministry of Transport, civil engineer on design of highway and transportation systems, 1946—, currently as assistant chief engineer in charge of division dealing with urban transport problems. *Military service:* British Army, Royal Engineers, 1941-46; became lieutenant. *Member:* Institution of Civil Engineers (associate member).

WRITINGS—Plays; all published by Samuel French: *Cat Among the Pigeons,* 1957; *Strike Happy,* 1960; *Murder Delayed,* 1961; (with Robert King) *No Time for Fig Leaves,* 1966.

Plays produced: "Bid for Fame" (television), Associated British Cinemas Television Ltd., 1956; (with Robert King) "In at the Death," premiered at Phoenix Theatre, London, 1967. Radio version of *Murder Delayed* has been broadcast in Australia, South Africa, West Germany, and Switzerland.

AVOCATIONAL INTERESTS: Sketching and painting, caravan vacations with his family in western Europe, gardening, and poultry keeping.

* * *

GREENWOOD, Gordon 1913-

PERSONAL: Born September 17, 1913, in Terowie, South Australia; son of R. O. and L. A. (Hales) Greenwood; married Thora J. Smeal, February 16, 1939; children: Helen (Mrs. Geoffrey Derrick), David, Stephen, Andrew. *Education:* University of Sidney, B.A. (first class honors), 1935, M.A. (first class honors), 1937; University of London, Ph.D., 1939. *Home:* 164 Victoria St., Chelmer, Brisbane, Queensland, Australia. *Office:* University of Queensland, St. Lucia, Brisbane, Queensland, Australia.

CAREER: New England University College, Armidale, Australia, lecturer in history, 1939-41; University of Sydney, Sydney, Australia, lecturer, 1942-43, senior lecturer, 1944-46, acting professor of history, 1947-49; University of Queensland, Brisbane, Australia, professor of history, 1949—, dean of Faculty of Arts, 1951-55, member of senate, 1953—. Member of Commonwealth Advisory Committee on Advanced Education. *Member:* Australian Institute of International Affairs (Commonwealth president, 1961-65), Social Science Research Council of Australia, Australian Humanities Research Council, University of Queensland Football Club (president). *Awards, honors:* Carnegie and Commonwealth fellow, 1956; United States Leader Award, 1964.

WRITINGS: Early American-Australian Relations, Melbourne University Press, 1944; *The Future of Australian Federalism,* Melbourne University Press, 1946; (contributor) C. Hartley Grattan, editor, *Australia,* University of California, 1947; (contributor) *Federalism in Australia,* Wadley & Ginn, 1949; (editor and contributor) *Australia: A Social and Political History,* Angus & Robertson, 1955, Praeger, 1956; (editor with Norman Harper, and contributor) *Australia in World Affairs,* F. W. Cheshire, Volume I, 1957, Volume II, 1963, Volume III, 1968; (editor and co-author) *Brisbane 1859-1959,* Oswald Ziegler, 1959; *The Modern World,* Volume I, Angus & Robertson, 1964. Contributor to professional journals. Editor, *Australian Journal of Politics and History.*

SIDELIGHTS: Gordon Greenwood has traveled in Europe, Asia, and United States. *Avocational interests:* Literature, drama, and sports.†

* * *

GREER, Thomas H(oag) 1914-

PERSONAL: Born April 18, 1914, in New York, N.Y.; son of Thomas H. (a builder) and Lillian (Marmion) Greer; married Margarette Cheney, December 17, 1939; children: Thomas M., Margarette E. *Education:* San Diego State College (now University), student, 1931-34; University of California, Berkeley, A.B., 1935, M.A., 1936, Ph.D., 1938. *Home:* 427 Collingwood Dr., East Lansing, Mich. 48823. *Office:* Department of Humanities, Michigan State University, East Lansing, Mich. 48823.

CAREER: San Diego State College (now University), San Diego, Calif., instructor in history, 1938-42; U.S. Department of the Air Force, Washington, D.C., chief of Historical Studies Section, 1946-47; Michigan State University, East Lansing, assistant professor of history, 1947-51, associate professor, 1951-56, professor of humanities, 1956—, chairman of department of humanities, 1963-68. *Military service:* U.S. Army Air Forces, 1942-46; became captain; received Commendation Medal. *Member:* American Historical Association, Organization of American Historians, American Association of University Professors, Phi Beta Kappa. *Awards, honors:* American Council of Learned Societies faculty fellowship, 1952; Distinguished Faculty Award of Michigan State University, 1960.

WRITINGS: American Social Reform Movements, Prentice-Hall, 1949; *The Army Air Forces in World War II,* Volume VI, University of Chicago Press, 1954; *Development of Air Doctrine in Army Air Arm,* Air University, 1955; *What Roosevelt Thought,* Michigan State University Press, 1958; (contributor) *Curriculum Building in General Education,* W. C. Brown, 1960; *A Brief History of Western Man,* Harcourt, 1967, 2nd edition, 1972. General editor of "Classics of Western Thought," three volumes, Harcourt, 1964-68.

WORK IN PROGRESS: Research in problems of world peace and international order.

* * *

GREGG, James E(rwin) 1927-

PERSONAL: Born May 3, 1927, in Harrisburg, Pa.; son of Clarence Richard (a barber) and Mabel (Elicker) Gregg; married Lyla Korb, June 11, 1955; children: William, Richard, Joan, Michael, Robert. *Education:* Lebanon Valley College, B.A., 1950; University of California, Berkeley, M.A., 1954, Santa Barbara, Ph.D., 1964. *Politics:* Democrat. *Home:* 1655 Filbert Ave., Chico, Calif. 95926. *Office:* Graduate School, California State University, Chico, Calif. 95926.

CAREER: Teacher of social science and journalism in Redding, Calif., 1952-59; California State University, Chico, assistant professor of journalism and political science, 1959-64, associate professor, 1964-66, professor of political science and chairman of department, 1966-70, dean of graduate school, 1970—. Summer teaching at University of California at Santa Barbara, Western State College, and University of Oregon. Member of Democratic County Central Committee, 1956-72; staff secretary for education, to governor of California, 1965-66. *Military service:* U.S. Navy, 1945-46. *Member:* American Political Science Association, Western Political Science Association, Northern California Political Science Association, California Association for Public Administration Education.

WRITINGS: (With John Egan and Clyde Parker) *Journalism Advisor's Guide,* R. Wallace Pischel, 1966; *Newspaper Editorial Endorsements and Local Elections in California* (monograph), University of California, Davis, 1966; (contributor) Royce Dehnatier, Earl Waters and Clarence McIntosh, editors, *The Rumble of California Politics,* Wiley, 1970; *Newspaper Editorial Endorsements: Their Influence on California Ballot Measure Elections, 1964-68* (monograph), University of California, Davis, 1970. Contributor to *Journalism Quarterly* and newspapers.

AVOCATIONAL INTERESTS: Skiing, soaring, photography, and outdoor life in northern California.

*   *   *

GREGG, James R.   1914-

PERSONAL: Born October 26, 1914, in Napoleon, Ohio; son of Edgar M. and Minnie (Lauerman) Gregg; married Bernice Klopf, 1938; children: Janell, Ronald. *Education:* Ohio State University, B.S., 1942; Los Angeles College of Optometry (now College of Optometry), D.O., 1948, D.Ocular Sci., 1953. *Politics:* Republican. *Religion:* Presbyterian. *Home:* 412 Rolling Hills Pl., Anaheim, Calif. 92807.

CAREER: Optometrist in private practice, 1947—; College of Optometry, Fullerton, Calif., associate professor, 1948-60, professor of optometry, 1960—. *Member:* American Optometric Association, American Academy of Optometry (fellow), California Optometric Association (president, 1957), Los Angeles County Optometric Society (president), Beta Gamma Sigma, South Los Angeles Optimist Club. *Awards, honors:* Named Optometrist of the Year, California Optometric Association, 1956; Doctor of Optometric Letters, Los Angeles College of Optometry, 1965; Distinguished Service Award, American Optometric Association, 1970.

WRITINGS: Your Future in Optometry, Richard Rosen, 1960; (with Gordon Heath) *The Eye and Sight,* Heath, 1963; *The Story of Optometry,* Ronald, 1965; *Experiments in Visual Science for Home and School,* Ronald, 1966; *How to Communicate in Optometric Practice,* Chilton, 1969; *The Sportsman's Eye,* Winchester Press, 1971; *The Business of Optometric Practice,* Advisory Enterprises (New York), 1975. Editor of *Guide to Occupational and Other Visual Needs,* 1958; writer of column "Your Vision," *Los Angeles Herald Examiner,* 1958—. Contributor of about fifty articles to optometric journals, including *Popular Science, Instructor, U.S. Camera, Library Journal,* and *Better Homes and Gardens.*

AVOCATIONAL INTERESTS: Outdoor activities.

*   *   *

GREWER, Eira M(ary)   1931-

PERSONAL: Born November 26, 1931, in Bristol, England; daughter of Robert Hughes (a physician) and E. Joan (a physician; maiden name, Williams) Parry; married Robin Spencer Grewer (a bank official), September 10, 1960; children: David A. J., Ruth S. *Education:* University of Bristol, B.A. (honors in history), 1953; University of London, Diploma in Health Education, 1956. *Home:* 5, The Nook, Newton, Chester, England.

CAREER: Former teacher; worked for McGraw-Hill Book Co. in Toronto, Ontario, and London, England, 1954-55; education officer in Nigeria, West Africa, 1957-62.

WRITINGS: Everyday Health, Pergamon, 1966; *Caring for Your Health,* Pergamon, 1968.††

*   *   *

GRIFFIN, A(rthur) H(arold)   1911-

PERSONAL: Born January 15, 1911, in Liverpool, England; son of James Arthur (a decorator) and Annie Elizabeth (Jackson) Griffin; married Mollie Barker, October 23, 1937; children: Robin M. M., Sandra E. *Education:* Attended Barrow Grammar School. *Home:* Cunswick End, Plumgarths, Kendal, Cumbria, England.

CAREER: Journalist in England on weekly newspapers, 1928-32, *Lancashire Evening Post,* 1932-37, *Daily Mail,* Manchester, and other papers, 1937-46, and *Lancashire Evening Post,* Kendal, 1946-76. Free-lance journalist and writer for radio and television; authority on English Lake District. *Military service:* British Army, 1940-46; became lieutenant colonel. *Member:* Rotary Club of Kendal (past president), various climbing and skiing clubs.

WRITINGS: Inside the Real Lakeland, Guardian Press, 1961; *In Mountain Lakeland,* Guardian Press, 1963; *Pageant of Lakeland,* R. Hale, 1966; *The Roof of England,* R. Hale, 1968; *Still the Real Lakeland,* R. Hale, 1970; *Long Days in the Hills,* R. Hale, 1974; *A Lakeland Notebook,* R. Hale, 1975; *A Lakeland Year,* R. Hale, in press. Contributor to "Country Diary" in *Guardian* for more than twenty-five years (*Pageant of Lakeland* is based on these contributions); also contributor to other newspapers, and climbing, skiing, and other outdoor magazines.

AVOCATIONAL INTERESTS: Travel and exploration, particularly in mountain areas; mountaineering, skiing, music.

*   *   *

GRIFFIN, William Lloyd   1938-

PERSONAL: Born May 7, 1938, in Meadow Bridge, W.Va.; son of William Daniel (a farmer and railroader) and Ina (Ballenger) Griffin; married Toby Ann Bragg (a beautician), January 2, 1958. *Education:* Marshall University, A.B., 1961, M.A., 1964. *Agent:* Philip T. Berkley Associates, 132 West Broadway, San Diego, Calif. 92101.

CAREER: Professional boxer in Cleveland, Ohio, and Baltimore, Md., 1957; high school teacher of English and Spanish, Russell, Ky., 1962-64; West Liberty State College, West Liberty, W.Va., instructor in English, 1964-66; Penn Metal Co., Parkersburg, W.Va., member of sales office staff, 1966-67; Star Book Store, Huntington, W.Va., owner and operator, 1968—. *Military service:* U.S. Army

Reserve, 1955-1964; active duty, 1956. *Member:* Committee of Small Magazines and Publishers.

WRITINGS—All published by Valley Publications, except as noted: *Brahma's Drum* (poetry), Royal, 1965; *Beneath the Varnish* (novel), 1967; *Quality American Poetry,* Volume I, 1973, Volume II, 1974, Volume III, in press; *Moment of Vision* (short stories), 1975; *Cross Fire* (novel), 1975. Editor and publisher, *El Viento* (literary magazine).

WORK IN PROGRESS: Wormwood, a novel.

SIDELIGHTS: Griffin's interest in publishing first emerged when as a child he published a neighborhood newspaper which sold for three cents per copy.

* * *

GRIFFITH, Paul 1921-

PERSONAL: Born December 11, 1921, in Huntington, Pa.; son of George Cupp (a cardiologist) and Stella (McQuain) Griffith; married Ethel Moore (a painter; divorced). *Education:* Yale University, B.A., 1943. *Religion:* Quaker. *Home:* 34 Witherspoon St., Princeton, N.J. 08540.

CAREER: Life, New York City, researcher, 1943-46; University of Iowa, Writers' Workshop, Iowa City, instructor, 1947-49; *Presbyterian Life,* Philadelphia, Pa., art editor, 1950-63; Religious News Service, New York City, photo editor, 1964—. *Member:* Franklin Inn Club (Philadelphia). *Awards, honors:* Yaddo fellowships in creative writing, 1949, 1963, 1964.

WRITINGS: (Contributor) Martha Foley, editor, *The Best American Short Stories of 1947,* Houghton, 1948; *The Mare's Nest,* Macmillan, 1950; *Square,* Manhattan East, 1966; *My Stillness,* Vanguard, 1972. Contributor of short stories to magazines.

WORK IN PROGRESS: Green Memories.

AVOCATIONAL INTERESTS: Opera, making needlepoint rugs.

* * *

GRIFFITH, Thomas 1915-

PERSONAL: Born December 30, 1915, in Tacoma, Wash.; son of Thomas and Anne (O'Reilly) Griffith; married Caroline Coffman, September 26, 1937. *Education:* University of Washington, Seattle, A.B., 1936; Harvard University, 1942-43. *Home:* 25 East End Ave., New York, N.Y. 10028.

CAREER: Seattle Times, Seattle, Wash., reporter, later assistant city editor, 1936-42; *Time,* New York City, contributing editor, 1943-49, national affairs editor, 1949-51, foreign news editor, 1951-60, assistant managing editor, 1960-63; Time, Inc., New York City, senior staff editor of publications, 1963-67; *Life,* New York City, editor, 1968-72; columnist, *Atlantic,* 1973—. *Member:* Coffee House, Century Association, and University Club (all New York).

WRITINGS: The Waist-High Culture, Harper, 1959; *How True,* Little, Brown, 1974. Contributor to *Time* and *Fortune.*

* * *

GRITSCH, Eric W. 1931-

PERSONAL: Born April 19, 1931, in Neuhaus, Austria; son of Matthew and Irene (Mattes) Gritsch; married Ruth Sandman, June 5, 1955. *Education:* Oberschuetzen Gymnasium, Austria, Matura (B.A. equivalent), 1950; Yale University, S.T.M., 1955, M.A., 1958, Ph.D., 1960; University of Vienna, Cand.Theol. (B.D. equivalent), 1956; other study at University of Zurich, University of Basel, and University of Heidelberg. *Politics:* Democrat. *Home and office:* Lutheran Theological Seminary, Gettysburg, Pa. 17325.

CAREER: Vicar (pastor) in Bruck an der Mur, Austria, 1955-57; Wellesley College, Wellesley, Mass., instructor in department of Bible literature, 1959-61; Lutheran Theological Seminary, Gettysburg, Pa., professor of church history, 1961—. Director of Institute for Luther Studies; member of International Luther Research Congress. *Member:* Society for Reformation Research, American Society of Church History, American Association of University Professors. *Awards, honors:* Fulbright-Smith-Mundt fellowship, 1955-56; American Association of Theological Schools fellowship to University of Heidelberg, 1967-68.

WRITINGS: Reformer Without a Church: The Life and Thought of Thomas Muentzer, 1468-1525, Fortress, 1967; (editor) *Luther's Works,* Fortress, Volume XLI, 1967, Volume XIL, 1970; *The Continuing Reformation,* Lutheran Church Press, 1971; (with Roland H. Bainton) *Bibliography of the Continental Reformation,* Archon Books, 1972. Contributor of articles and reviews to *Church History, Lutheran Quarterly, Dialog, Erasmus, Journal of Ecumenical Studies,* and other journals.

WORK IN PROGRESS: With Robert W. Jenson, *The Lutheran Confessions,* for Fortress.

* * *

GROLLMAN, Earl A. 1925-

PERSONAL: Born July 4, 1925, in Baltimore, Md.; son of Gerson S. (a bookseller) and Dora (Steinbach) Grollman; married Netta Levinson, August 14, 1949; children: David, Sharon, Jonathan. *Education:* University of Cincinnati, B.A., 1947; Hebrew Union College–Jewish Institute of Religion, Cincinnati, Ohio, M.H.L., 1950; Boston University, graduate study at School of Theology and School of Legal Medicine. *Home:* 79 Country Club Lane, Belmont, Mass. 02178. *Office:* Beth El Temple Center, 2 Concord Ave., Belmont, Mass. 02178.

CAREER: Temple Israel, Boston, Mass., assistant rabbi, 1950-51; Beth El Temple Center, Belmont, Mass., rabbi, 1951—. Chairman of United Rabbinical Chaplaincy Commission; past president of Massachusetts Board of Rabbis. Chairman of Massachusetts Ecumenical Council on Health and Morality; member of Governor's Council on Action for Mental Health and Massachusetts Committee for the Aged; social action chairman of Belmont Religious Council. *Awards, honors:* D.D. from Portia Law School, 1964, and Hebrew Union College–Jewish Institute of Religion, 1975.

WRITINGS: Judaism in Sigmund Freud's World, Appleton, 1965; (editor and contributor) *Rabbinical Counseling,* Bloch Publishing, 1966; (editor and contributor) *Explaining Death to Children,* Beacon Press, 1967; (editor and contributor) *Explaining Divorce to Children,* Beacon Press, 1969; *Suicide: Prevention, Intervention, Postvention,* edited by Clyde and Barbara Dodder, Beacon Press, 1971; *Concerning Death: A Practical Guide for the Living,* Beacon Press, 1974; *Talking about Divorce: A Dialogue Between Parent and Child,* Beacon Press, 1975. Contributor to *Psychiatric Opinion, American Imago, Pastoral Psychology,* and other periodicals.

GROMAN, George L. 1928-

PERSONAL: Born September 8, 1928, in New York, N.Y.; son of Benno (a musician) and Hella (Weil) Groman; married C. Diane Walsh, September 16, 1961; children: Paul B. *Education:* New York University, B.A., 1949, Ph.D., 1963; Columbia University, M.A., 1951. *Home:* 150 West 87th St., New York, N.Y. 10024. *Office:* La Guardia Community College, City University of New York, 31-10 Thomson Ave., Long Island City, N.Y. 11101.

CAREER: Columbia University Press, New York City, editorial assistant, 1951-53; Macmillan Co., New York City, production editor, 1954-57; New York University, New York City, instructor in English, 1957-62; Rutgers University, Newark Campus, Newark, N.J., assistant professor of English, 1963-70; La Guardia Community College of the City University of New York, Long Island City, N.Y., associate professor, 1970-72, professor of language and culture, 1972—, chairman of division, 1970—. Consultant to National Endowment for the Humanities, 1974—. *Member:* Modern Language Association of America, American Studies Association, College English Association. *Awards, honors:* Woodrow Wilson fellowship for dissertation research, 1962-63.

WRITINGS: (Editor, and author of introduction and notes) *Political Literature of the Progressive Era,* Michigan State University Press, 1967; (editor and contributor) *The City in the Seventies,* Harper, 1976.

* * *

GROSS, Shelley 1938-

PERSONAL: Born September 3, 1938, in New York, N.Y.; daughter of Julius and Gertrude (Davidson) Gross. *Education:* Studied at Hunter College of the City University of New York, 1959-61, New School for Social Research, 1960-61, and Emerson College, Monterey, Calif., 1962-63. *Religion:* Jewish and Vedanta ("essence of Hinduism"). *Residence:* Hollywood, Calif.

CAREER: Has worked since 1957 as editorial assistant, editor, copywriter, and book reviewer, in New York City, and San Francisco and Los Angeles, Calif.; editor of *Emerson Review* (literary magazine) 1963; *The Executive Woman* (national monthly newsletter), New York City, co-founder and editor-in-chief, 1973-74. Public speaker to professional women's and co-ed groups, and on radio and television.

WRITINGS: (Compiler) *The Mystic in Love* (anthology of world mystical poetry), Citadel, 1966. Poems published in a small poetry magazine, and reviews in *San Francisco Examiner.*

WORK IN PROGRESS: How to Awaken Spiritual Power through Singing.

AVOCATIONAL INTERESTS: Gregorian chants, classical and Indian music; abstract pen drawings, painting; comparative religions; women's rights.

* * *

GROSS, Walter 1923-

PERSONAL: Born August 17, 1923, in New York, N.Y.; son of Albert and Sophie (Reichner) Gross; married Florence Geld, June 10, 1950; children: Linda, Arleene, Marshall. *Education:* Brooklyn College (now Brooklyn College of the City University of New York), B.A., 1944; New York University, M.B.A., 1948, Ph.D., 1963. *Home:* 330 University Circle, Athens, Ga. 30601.

CAREER: Arizona State University, Tempe, assistant professor of economics and marketing research, 1950-53; owned and operated a retail store in Phoenix, Ariz., 1953-58; Texas College of Arts and Industries (now Texas A&I University), Kingsville, assistant professor, 1958-60, associate professor, 1961-63; University of Georgia, Athens, associate professor, 1964-65, professor of marketing, 1966—. *Member:* American Marketing Association, American Economic Association, American Association of University Professors, Southern Marketing Association, Southwestern Social Science Association. *Awards, honors:* Fulbright lecturer, Linz University, Austria, 1974-75.

WRITINGS: (With others) *Marketing Handbook,* Ronald, 1965; (with Alfred Gross) *Business Policy,* Ronald, 1967. Contributor to business and marketing journals. Senior editor, *Journal of Marketing,* 1975—.

* * *

GROSSMAN, Ronald P(hilip) 1934-

PERSONAL: Born November 18, 1934, in Chicago, Ill.; son of Arthur M. (a salesman) and Ethel (Weinberg) Grossman; married Tina Tomberlin, February 19, 1972; children: Julie Ellen, Lev, Jenifer Elizabeth. *Education:* University of Illinois, student, 1952-55; Illinois Institute of Technology, student, 1955; University of Chicago, B.A., Ph.D., 1965. *Politics:* Independent. *Religion:* None. *Home:* 554 Roscoe, Chicago, Ill. 60614. *Office:* Department of History, Lake Forest College, Lake Forest, Ill. 60045.

CAREER: University of Nebraska, Lincoln, instructor in history, 1963-64; St. Olaf College, Northfield, Minn., assistant professor of history, 1964-65; Michigan State University, East Lansing, assistant professor of the humanities, 1965-67; Lake Forest College, Lake Forest, Ill., associate professor of history, 1967—. *Member:* American Historical Association, American Association of University Professors.

WRITINGS: The Italians in America, Lerner, 1966. Research assistant and contributor of reviews, *Playboy,* 1964—. Regular contributor to newspapers and magazines on various social issues.

WORK IN PROGRESS: A monograph, *The Financing of the Crusades; A History of the Western Tradition,* a study of the contours of Western society and culture, for Holt.

SIDELIGHTS: Grossman has knowledge of Latin, Greek, French, German, and Italian. *Avocational interests:* Photography (exhibitor in several shows).

* * *

GROSSMAN, Sebastian P. 1934-

PERSONAL: Born January 21, 1934, in Coburg, Bavaria, Germany; came to United States in 1954, naturalized in 1955; son of Otto (a professor) and Arnet (Peipers) Grossman; married Lore Bensel (a research associate), June 30, 1955. *Education:* University of Maryland, B.A., 1958; Yale University, M.S., 1959, Ph.D., 1961. *Religion:* Protestant. *Home:* 1159 East 56th St., Chicago, Ill. 60637. *Office:* University of Chicago, 5848 South University, Chicago, Ill. 60637.

CAREER: University of Iowa, Iowa City, assistant professor of psychology, 1961-64; University of Chicago, Chicago, Ill., associate professor, 1964-67, professor of biopsychology, 1967—, chairman of section, 1967-73. Participant in International Congress of Physiological Sciences at Leiden, 1962, Tokyo, 1965, Washington, 1968, and New Delhi, 1975, and in International Congress of Pharmacology, Prague, 1963. *Military service:* U.S. Army, 1954-56; served in Germany. *Member:* American Psychological Association (fellow), American Association for the Advancement of Science (fellow), American Physiological Society, Psi Chi.

WRITINGS: A Textbook of Physiological Psychology, Wiley, 1967; *Essentials of Physiological Psychology,* Wiley, 1973. Contributor of more than 100 articles to professional journals. Regional editor, *Physiology and Behavior,* 1965—; consulting editor, *Psychopharmacologia,* 1968—, *Psychobiology,* 1969—, and *Pharmacology.* Member of editorial board of *Biochemistry and Behavior,* 1970—.

* * *

GUANDOLO, John 1919-

PERSONAL: Born September 11, 1919, in Beaver County, Pa.; son of Vincent and T. (Meta) Guandolo; married Betty Wade, February 13, 1942; children: Joseph Wade. *Education:* University of Illinois, A.B., 1940; University of Maryland, LL.B. and J.D., 1943. *Home:* 10905 Rosemont Dr., Rockville, Md. 20852.

CAREER: Attorney, in private practice of law specializing in transportation and antitrust law, Washington, D.C., 1957—; admitted to practice before the Supreme Court; member of the District of Columbia Bar, and the state bars of Illinois, Maryland, and Missouri. Lecturer in regulation of transportation, American University. *Member:* American Bar Association, Federal Bar Association, Association of Interstate Commerce Commission Practitioners (president elect), Motor Carrier Lawyers Association, American Society of Traffic and Transportation, District of Columbia Bar Association.

WRITINGS: Federal Procedure Forms, Dennis, 1949, annual supplements, 1951-57, cumulative supplement, 1950-58, three volume edition, Dennis, 1961; (author of revision with Marvin L. Fair) Joseph H. Tedrow, *Regulation of Transportation: Practice and Procedure before the Interstate Commerce Commission,* 6th edition, W. C. Brown, 1964, 7th edition published as *Transportation Regulation: Practice and Procedure before the Interstate Commerce Commission,* 1972; *Transportation Law,* W. C. Brown, 1965, 2nd edition, 1973. Writer of articles on transportation and administrative law. Editor-in-chief, *I.C.C. Practitioners' Journal.*

WORK IN PROGRESS: Revised editions of *Transportation Law, Transportation Regulation,* and *Federal Procedure Forms.*

* * *

GUERRANT, Edward Owings 1911-

PERSONAL: Surname is pronounced Gair-*rant;* born February 2, 1911, in Danville, Va.; son of Peter Dutois and Grace (Guerrant) Guerrant; married Helen Louise Daggett, February 14, 1936 (died, 1939); married Charlotte Edwina Tompkins, August 12, 1944; children: (first marriage) Helen Louise (Mrs. Stewart A. Toy); (second marriage) Lucy Allison, Edward Owings, Jr. *Education:* Davidson College, A.B., 1933; University of Southern California, M.A., 1939, Ph.D., 1942. *Politics:* Democrat. *Religion:* Presbyterian. *Home:* 1431 North Coolidge Ave., Pasadena, Calif. 91104. *Office:* Department of History,

California State University, 5151 State University Dr., Los Angeles, CA 90032.

CAREER: California Institute of Technology, Pasadena, instructor in history, 1942-44; U.S. Government, Washington, D.C., political analyst with Office of Coordinator of Inter-American Affairs, 1944-45, and Department of State, 1945-46; Davidson College, Davidson, N.C., 1946-54, began as associate professor, became professor of history; California State University, Los Angeles, assistant professor, 1954-57, associate professor, 1957-60, professor of history, 1960—, chairman of department, 1957-64. Visiting professor at University of Southern California, summers, 1947-54, University of Hawaii, 1963. *Awards, honors:* Ford Foundation fellowship, 1952-53.

WRITINGS: Roosevelt's Good Neighbor Policy, University of New Mexico Press, 1950; *Modern American Diplomacy,* University of New Mexico Press, 1954; *Comparisons and Contrasts—Franklin D. Roosevelt and Herbert Hoover,* Howard Allen, 1960; (with K. A. Martyn) *Toward a More Perfect Union,* Heath, 1967.

WORK IN PROGRESS: A book, *Race and the Supreme Court.*

* * *

GULLASON, Thomas A(rthur) 1924-

PERSONAL: Born July 1, 1924, in Watertown, Mass.; son of Sarkis (a businessman) and Rebecca (Sahagian) Gullason; married Elizabeth Bakalian, June 26, 1955; children: Edward. *Education:* Suffolk University, B.A., 1948; University of Wisconsin, M.A., 1949, Ph.D., 1953. *Politics:* Independent. *Religion:* Protestant. *Office:* Department of English, University of Rhode Island, Kingston, R.I. 02881.

CAREER: Instructor in English at Heidelberg College, Tiffin, Ohio, 1952-53, and Wisconsin State College (now University of Wisconsin—Eau Claire), 1953-54; University of Rhode Island, Kingston, instructor, 1954-57, assistant professor, 1957-60, associate professor, 1960-64, professor of English, 1964—. Vice-president of board of trustees, Kingston Free Library, 1965-67. *Military service:* U.S. Army, Signal Corps, 1943-46. *Member:* Modern Language Association of America, American Association of University Professors.

WRITINGS: (Editor with Leonard Casper) *The World of Short Fiction: An International Collection,* Harper, 1962, 2nd edition, 1971; (editor, and author of introduction) *The Complete Short Stories and Sketches of Stephen Crane,* Doubleday, 1963; (editor, and author of introduction) *The Complete Novels of Stephen Crane,* Doubleday, 1967; *Stephen Crane: Perspectives and Evaluations of His Art,* New York University Press, 1972; (contributor) *American Literary Naturalism: A Reassessment,* Carl Winter University, Press, 1975. Contributor of more than thirty articles to professional journals; book reviewer for *American Literature, Studies in Short Fiction,* and *Boston Sunday Herald.* Member of editorial committee, *Studies in Short Fiction.*

WORK IN PROGRESS: Stephen Crane: A Critical Biography, for New York University Press.

SIDELIGHTS: Thomas Gullason told *CA:* "Dedicated admirer of Anton Chekhov. Motivated or inspired by good poems and good short stories, classical music, and fishing at the ocean's edge (especially for mackerel)." Other hobbies: Gardening, tennis, and stamp collecting. He has studied Armenian, Spanish, French.

GUPTA, Ram Chandra 1927-
(Rama)

PERSONAL: Born January 20, 1927, in Palwal, Punjab, India; son of Omkar Prasad and Vidyavati (Bindal) Agrawal; married Saraswati Mangla, December 14, 1945; children: Roop Rekha (daughter), Himanshu Kumar (son), Reita (daughter). *Education:* Attended Punjab University, 1946; Agra University, M.A. (political science), 1950, M.A. (philosophy), 1954; Maharaja Sayajirao University of Baroda, Ph.D., 1961. *Politics:* "Believe in a free and independent society where there is no exploitation of any kind." *Religion:* Humanism. *Home:* Street Number 2, Bungalow 7, South Tukoganj, Indore 1, Madhya Pradesh, India. *Office:* I.K. College, Indore University, Sanyogitaganj, Indore, Madhya Pradesh, India.

CAREER: M.N. College, Visnagar, Gujrat, India, lecturer in political science, 1951-54; Government Arts and Commerce College, Indore, Madhya Pradesh, India, lecturer in political science, 1958-63; I.K. College, Indore University, Indore, Madhya Pradesh, assistant professor and head of department of political science, 1965—, principal, 1968—. *Member:* Society of State Politics (Varanasi).

WRITINGS: Ghandhian Philosophy, Gupta Publishing House, 1958; *Great Political Thinkers: East and West,* Lakshmi Narain Agrawal, 1963; *Political Philosophies of Eminent Americans,* University Publishers (Delhi), 1964; *Socialism, Democracy, and India,* Ram Prasad & Sons, 1965; *Harold J. Laski,* Ram Prasad & Sons, 1966; *Lal Bahadur Shastri: The Man and His Ideas,* Sterling Publishers (Delhi), 1966; (editor) *Youth in Ferment,* Sterling Publishers, 1968, Verry, 1969. Also author of *Who Rules a Country?,* 1968.

Books in Hindi: *Mahadevi Varma* (literary criticism), Saraswati Sadan, 1955; *Sumitra Nandan Pant* (literary criticism), Saraswati Sadan, 1956; (co-editor) *Biyani Mitron Ki Nazar Men,* Sahitya Sadan, 1965; *Brajlal Biyani,* N. R. Printers (Indore), 1966.

Contributor of more than fifty articles to *American Rationalist, Calcutta Review, Triveni, Modern Review,* and other journals in India and abroad. Writes also under pseudonym Rama.

WORK IN PROGRESS: A work on Jawaharlal Nehru, for Litt.D. degree; monograph on Lord Sri Krishna.

*   *   *

GUSS, Leonard M.   1926-

PERSONAL: Born December 8, 1926, in Philadelphia, Pa.; son of David (in manufacturing) and Fay (Rosner) Guss; married Marianne Gailey, February 17, 1950; children: Matthew, Stuart, Peter, Jonathan, Gavin. *Education:* University of Pennsylvania, B.A., 1949; Drexel Institute of Technology, M.B.A., 1955; Ohio State University, Ph.D., 1965. *Home:* 619 North Yakima, Tacoma, Wash. *Office:* Leonard Guss Associates, Inc., 4041 Ruston Way, Tacoma, Wash. 98402.

CAREER: E. F. Houghton Co. (chemicals), Philadelphia, Pa., 1950-55, started as researcher, became production superintendent; Battelle Institute (research), Columbus, Ohio, economist, 1955-60; Weyerhaeuser Co. (forest products), Tacoma, Wash., manager of marketing, director of economic and marketing research, 1960-69; Leonard Guss Associates, Inc., Tacoma, Wash., president, 1969—. Vice-president, Pierce County Mental Health and Retardation Association, 1965—; board member, Tacoma Art Museum.

Military service: U.S. Navy, 1945-46. *Member:* American Marketing Association (president of Puget Sound chapter, 1967-68), National Association of Business Economists, American Economic Association, National Industrial Conference Board—West Coast Council, United Nations Association of Tacoma.

WRITINGS: Packaging IS Marketing, American Management Association, 1967; (contributor) Victor P. Buell, editor, *Handbook of Modern Marketing,* McGraw, 1970; (contributor) Steuart Henderson Britt, editor, *The Dartnell Marketing Manager's Handbook,* Dartnell, 1973.

*   *   *

GUSTAFSON, Ralph (Barker)   1909-

PERSONAL: Surname is pronounced Gus-*taf*-son; born August 16, 1909, in Lime Ridge, Quebec, Canada; son of Carl Otto (a photographer) and Gertrude (Barker) Gustafson; married Elisabeth Renninger, October 4, 1958. *Education:* Bishop's University, B.A. (first class honors), 1929, M.A., 1930; Oxford University, B.A. (honors), 1933, M.A., 1963. *Address:* P.O. Box 172, North Hatley, Quebec, Canada. *Office:* Department of English, Bishop's University, Lennoxville, Quebec, Canada.

CAREER: Bishop's College School, Lennoxville, Quebec, music master, 1930; St. Alban's School, Brockville, Ontario, master, 1934; lived in London, England, 1934-38; when he returned to Canada, worked for the British Information Service, 1942-46; lived and wrote in New York, N.Y., 1946-63; Bishop's University, Lennoxville, lecturer, 1963-64, assistant professor, 1965-66, associate professor, 1967-71, professor of English, 1971—, poet in residence, 1965—. Music critic, frequently broadcasting for Canadian Broadcasting Corp. *Member:* Canadian Association of University Teachers, Association of Canadian University Teachers of English, Humanities Association, Keble Association, League of Canadian Poets. *Awards, honors:* Prix David, awarded by the Quebec Government, 1935, for *The Golden Chalice;* senior fellowship of Canada Council, 1959-60, 1971-72; D.Litt., Mount Allison University, 1973; Governor General's Award for Poetry, 1974, and A.J.M. Smith Award, Michigan State University, 1974, both for *Fire on Stone.*

WRITINGS—Poetry: *The Golden Chalice,* Nicholson & Watson, 1935; *Alfred the Great* (a poetic drama), M. Joseph, 1937; *Epithalamium in Time of War,* privately printed, 1941; *Lyrics Unromantic,* privately printed, 1942; *Flight into Darkness,* Pantheon, 1944; *Rocky Mountain Poems,* Klanak Press, 1960; *Rivers Among Rocks,* McClelland & Stewart, 1960; *Sift in an Hourglass,* McClelland & Stewart, 1966; *Ixion's Wheel,* McClelland & Stewart, 1969; *Theme and Variations for Sounding Brass,* privately printed, 1972; *Selected Poems,* McClelland & Stewart, 1972; *Fire on Stone,* McClelland & Stewart, 1974.

Editor: *Anthology of Canadian Poetry* (English), Penguin, 1942; *A Little Anthology of Canadian Poets,* New Directions, 1943; *Canadian Accent* (a collection of stories and poems by contemporary writers from Canada), Penguin, 1944; *The Penguin Book of Canadian Verse,* Penguin, 1958, 2nd revised edition, 1975.

Other writings: *Poetry and Canada,* Canadian Legion Educational Services, 1945; *The Brazen Tower* (short stories), Roger Ascham Press, 1975. Short stories included in *The Best American Short Stories,* 1948, 1950, *Canadian Short Stories,* 1960, and *A Book of Canadian Stories,* 1962; poetry included in *The Best Poems of 1961, Oxford Modern*

Canadian Verse, 1967, and *Canadian Poetry,* 1974. Edited the Canadian poetry issue of *Voices,* 1943. Contributor of poetry, short stories, and critical articles to literary periodicals and journals in Canada, the United States, and abroad.

WORK IN PROGRESS: Poetry.

AVOCATIONAL INTERESTS: Music ("have a collection of piano records since the inception of the gramophone"), and travel.

BIOGRAPHICAL/CRITICAL SOURCES: C. Klinck, editor, *Literary History of Canada,* University of Toronto Press, 1965.

*   *   *

GUTHEIM, Frederick   1908-

PERSONAL: Born March 3, 1908, in Cambridge, Mass.; son of August George and Augusta (Meiser) Gutheim; married Mary Purdon, June 8, 1935; children: Nicholas. *Education:* University of Wisconsin, B.A., 1931; University of Chicago, graduate student, 1933-36; additional study at Ecole des Hautes Etudes Urbaines, London School of Economics and Political Science, and University of Heidelberg.

CAREER: Brookings Institution, Washington, D.C., junior staff member of Institute for Government Research, 1931-33; Illinois Housing Association, Chicago, executive secretary, 1933-34; directed U.S. Government exhibit programs at New York and San Francisco World's Fairs, 1936-37; U.S. Housing Authority, Division of Research and Information, Washington, D.C., assistant director, 1938-40; U.S. Federal Works Agency, Washington, D.C., consultant, 1940-41; National Housing Agency, Hampton Roads, Va., area representative, 1941-43; French Mission for Urbanism and Reconstruction, Washington, D.C., assistant chief, 1945-46; National Housing Agency, Land and Public Services Division, Washington, D.C., principal urban development specialist, 1946-47; *New York Herald Tribune,* New York, N.Y., staff and editorial writer, 1947-50; American Institute of Architects, Washington, D.C., assistant executive director, 1950-52; Galaxy, Inc., Washington, D.C., in private practice as consultant in city and regional planning, 1953-59; U.S. Congress, Washington, D.C., staff director of Joint Committee on Metropolitan Problems, 1959-60; Washington Center for Metropolitan Studies, Washington, D.C., president, 1960-65; in independent practice as consultant on urban affairs, Washington, D.C., 1965—. Williams College, Williamstown, Mass., assistant professor, 1968-69; Central Washington State College, Ellensburg, distinguished visiting professor, 1970; George Washington University, Washington, D.C., professor of history, 1971-74, professor of American studies, 1974—. Washington Regional Planning Council, chairman, 1950-52; Upper Montgomery County Planning Commission, commissioner, 1950-57; National Capital Regional Planning Council, member, 1952-57; National Capital Transportation Agency, member of advisory board, 1961—, chairman, 1961-63; President's Council on Pennsylvania Avenue, member, 1962-65; Joint Committee on the National Capital, chairman, 1963—; Interior Department Task Force on the Potomac, member, 1965—. Washington Arts Council, chairman, 1962—; Neighborhood Commons, Inc., chairman, 1963-65. Member of visitors committee of schools of architecture at Princeton University, 1950-53, Harvard University, 1950-55, and Carnegie-Mellon University, 1964—. Consultant to colleges and universities including Williams College, Central Washington State College, and

George Washington University. *Military service:* U.S. Army, 1943-45.

WRITINGS: (Editor, and author of introduction) *Frank Lloyd Wright, Selected Writings, 1894-1940,* Duell, Sloan & Pearce, 1941, published later that year as *Frank Lloyd Wright on Architecture; Houses for Family Living,* Women's Foundation, 1948; *The Potomac,* Rinehart, 1949, revised edition, Grosset, 1969; (with Coleman Woodbury) *Rethinking Urban Redevelopment,* Public Administration Service (Chicago), 1949; *Planning for the Future in the Potomac River Basin,* Interstate Commission on the Potomac River Basin, 1950; *One Hundred Years of Architecture in America, 1857-1957, Celebrating the Centennial of the American Institute of Architects,* Reinhold, 1957; *Alvar Aalto,* Braziller, 1960; *Urban Space and Urban Design,* Washington Center for Metropolitan Studies, 1962; (contributor) Lowden Wingo, editor, *Cities and Space,* Johns Hopkins Press, 1963; (contributor) Roger Revelle and Hans H. Landsberg, editors, *America's Changing Environment,* Houghton, 1970; (author of introduction) Alexander Papageorgiou, *Continuity and Change: Preservation in City Planning,* Pall Mall, 1971; (editor, and author of introduction) *In the Cause of Architecture: Frank Lloyd Wright,* McGraw, 1975. Also author of *Housing as Environment,* 1953. Architectural critic, *Washington Post,* 1960-62. Advisory editor, *Magazine of Art,* 1935-40; corresponding editor, *Urbanistica,* 1950-58, and *Progressive Architecture,* 1954-59.

*   *   *

GUTMAN, Judith Mara   1928-

PERSONAL: Born May 22, 1928, in New York, N.Y.; daughter of Victor (shirtmaker and retail merchant) and Anna (Zimmerman) Markowitz; married Herbert George Gutman (a historian), June 18, 1950; children: Marta, Nell. *Education:* Queens College (now of the City University of New York), Flushing, N.Y., B.A., 1949; Bank Street College of Education, M.A., 1950; graduate study at New York University. *Politics:* Independent. *Religion:* None. *Home:* 97 Six Ave., Nyack, N.Y.

CAREER: University of Wisconsin—Madison, instructor in psychology, 1952-54; Montefiore (Hospital) Nursery School, Bronx, N.Y., director, 1954-58; Hunter College (now of the City University of New York), New York, N.Y., lecturer in education, 1959-60; now a full-time writer. *Member:* Authors Guild, Authors League of America.

WRITINGS: The Colonial Venture: An Autobiography of the American Colonies from Their Beginnings to 1763, Basic Books, 1966; *Lewis W. Hine and the American Social Conscience,* Walker & Co., 1967; (contributor of visual material) Edwin C. Rozwenc, *The Making of American Society,* Allyn & Bacon, 1972; *Is America Used Up?,* Grossman, 1973; *Lewis W. Hine: Two Perspectives,* Viking, 1974; *Buying,* Bantam, 1975. Also film strip writer and visual editor of "Our Ethnic Heritage," a six strip film strip series on immigration, migration, and urbanization. Contributor to *Nation* and *Dictionary of American Biography.*

*   *   *

GUTSCHE, Thelma   1915-

PERSONAL: Born January 7, 1915, in Cape Province, South Africa; daughter of Jesse (a synthetic chemist) and Agnes Patricia Anne (Mackintosh) Gutsche. *Education:* University of Cape Town, B.A., 1933, M.A., 1935, Ph.D.,

1947. *Politics:* None. *Religion:* Agnostic. *Home:* 314 Gleneagles, Killarney, Johannesburg, South Africa.

CAREER: Forum, Johannesburg, South Africa, cinema/theatre critic and literary reviewer, 1939-43; film adviser, Government of South Africa, 1940-47; African Consolidated Films Ltd., Johannesburg, South Africa, head of educational films department, 1947-58; consultant on film and historical matters to various enterprises, 1958—; writer of historical books, 1963—. Member of executive committee, National War Fund; member of advisory committee, Africana Museum and National Film Institute. *Member:* Institute for the Study of Man in Africa, Africana Society (founding member), Simon van der Stel Foundation (founding member), Historical Society of Port Elizabeth and Walmer, Johannesburg Country Club. *Awards, honors:* C.N.A. Literary Prize, 1966, for *No Ordinary Woman.*

WRITINGS—All published by Howard Timmons, except as noted: (With Patricia Knox) *Do You Know Johannesburg?,* Unie Volkspers, 1947; *No Ordinary Woman,* 1966; *Old Gold,* 1966; *The Microcosm,* 1968; *A Very Smart Medal,* 1970; *The Bishop's Lady,* 1970; *The History and Social Significance of the Cinema in South Africa 1895-1940,* 1972. Contributor of articles to newspapers.

WORK IN PROGRESS: A biography of Sir Arnold Theiler (a veterinary scientist).

* * *

HAAR, James 1929-

PERSONAL: Born July 4, 1929, in St. Louis, Mo.; son of George B. (in advertising) and Marie (Zukoski) Haar. *Education:* Harvard University, A.B., 1950, Ph.D., 1961; University of North Carolina, M.A., 1954. *Home:* 129 Pacific St., Brooklyn, N.Y. 11201. *Office:* Department of Music, New York University, New York, N.Y. 10003.

CAREER: Harvard University, Cambridge, Mass., instructor, 1960-63, assistant professor, 1963-67; University of Pennsylvania, Philadelphia, associate professor of music, 1967-69; New York University, New York, N.Y., professor of music, 1969—. *Military service:* U.S. Army, 1952-54. *Member:* American Musicological Society (council member, 1966—), Renaissance Society of America, Italian Musicological Society, Phi Beta Kappa.

WRITINGS: (Editor) *Chanson and Madrigal, 1480-1530,* Harvard University Press, 1964; *The Tugendsterne of Harsdorffer and Staden: An Exercise in Musical Humanism,* American Institute of Musicology (Rome), 1965; (editor) *The Duos of Jhan Gero,* Broude, 1975. Contributor to music journals. Editor-in-chief, *Journal of the American Musicological Society,* 1966—.

WORK IN PROGRESS: Studies of aspects of the sixteenth-century madrigal; musical settings of Ariosto, *Orlando Furioso.*

* * *

HAAS, Albert E. 1917-

PERSONAL: Born September 14, 1917, in Rifton, N.Y.; married Mary Yealy, June 21, 1941; children: Judith (Mrs. Frederic Ornellas), Mary Carol. *Education:* Rider College, B.Ed., 1937; University of Pennsylvania, M.S. in Ed., 1942; Columbia University, professional diploma in supervision of business education, 1966. *Home:* 93 Hemlock Dr., Farmingdale, N.Y. 11735.

CAREER: Southampton High School, Southampton, Pa.,

teacher, 1937-43; Pittston Stevedoring Corp., New York, N.Y., payroll clerk, 1946-47; Butler High School, Butler, N.J., teacher, 1947; Mercantile Stores Co., secretary to the president and assistant buyer, 1947-50; School Thrift, Inc., office work, 1950-51; State University of New York Agricultural and Technical College at Farmingdale, 1951—, began as instructor, associate professor, 1958-61, professor of business, 1961—, chairman of Business Division, 1968—. *Military service:* U.S. Maritime Service, 1943-46; became lieutenant junior grade. *Member:* Sales and Marketing Executives.

WRITINGS: (Contributor) *College Typewriting,* Pitman, 1960; (with Herman B. Henderson) *Industrial Organization and Management Fundamentals,* Industrial, 1961.

* * *

HABERMAN, Donald (Charles) 1933-

PERSONAL: Born July 12, 1933, in Passaic, N.J.; son of Charles Alfred (a manufacturer of medical instruments) and Elsa (Spellman) Haberman; married Lidia Wachsler (a professor of classics), August 10, 1957; children: Sofia Margaret, Alice Helene. *Education:* Rutgers University, B.A., 1955; Yale University, Ph.D., 1962. *Office:* Department of English, Arizona State University, Tempe, Ariz. 85281.

CAREER: Lafayette College, Easton, Pa., instructor, 1959-62, assistant professor of English, 1962-65; University of Montana, Missoula, associate professor of English, 1965-67; Arizona State University, Tempe, associate professor of English, 1967—. *Member:* Phi Beta Kappa, Delta Upsilon.

WRITINGS: The Plays of Thornton Wilder, Wesleyan University Press, 1967. Contributor to *Four Quarters.*

WORK IN PROGRESS: G.B.S.: A Bibliography of Writings about Him, 1951-1975.

* * *

HACKNEY, Vivian 1914-

PERSONAL: Born November 1, 1914, in Robertson County, Tenn.; daughter of Jordan (a farmer) and Minnie Melissa (Castelow) Hackney. *Education:* Attended public schools in Nashville, Tenn. *Religion:* Southern Baptist. *Home:* 1304 Stainback Ave., Nashville, Tenn. 37207.

CAREER: Southern Baptist Convention, Sunday School Board, Nashville, Tenn., stenographer, 1951-60, editorial assistant, 1960-66, assistant editor, 1966—. *Member:* National League of American Pen Women, Nashville Woman's Press and Authors Club, Nashville Federation of Baptist Business Women.

WRITINGS: Invitation to Prayer, Broadman, 1965; (with Jimmy R. Key) *Hymns to Know and Sing,* Convention Press, 1973. Author of song texts included in children's religious albums; contributor of articles, poems, devotional materials, and curriculum materials to religious journals. Assistant literary editor, *Music Makers, Young Musicians,* and *The Music Leader.*

* * *

HADAWI, Sami 1904-

PERSONAL: Born March 6, 1904, in Jerusalem; came to United States in 1952; son of Elias and Sarah (Jacob) Hadawi; married Nora Badr, June 25, 1931 (deceased); children: Nabil (son), Aida (Mrs. Roy Karaoglan). *Education:* Privately educated. *Religion:* Christian. *Home:* 191 Classen Dr., Dallas, Tex. 75218.

CAREER: Secretarial work with Governor of Jerusalem, 1920-26; chief clerk, Palestine Land Settlement Department, 1927-35; land valuer in Palestine, 1935-48; head of Jordanian land tax department, 1949-52; United Nations, New York, N.Y., land specialist, 1952-55, adviser to Iraq Mission to United Nations, 1955-59, director of public relations, Arab States Delegations Office, and adviser to Yemen Mission to United Nations, 1959-60; Arab Information Center, Dallas, Tex., director, 1960-64; Institute for Palestine Studies, Beirut, Lebanon, director, 1965-67; writer and lecturer. *Awards, honors:* Member, Order of the British Empire, 1943.

WRITINGS: Palestine: Loss of a Heritage, Naylor, 1963; (editor) *Palestine before the United Nations,* Institute for Palestine Studies, 1965; *Bitter Harvest: Palestine between 1941 and 1967,* New World Press, 1967; *Palestine in Focus,* edited by Yusif A. Sayigh, Palestine Research Center, 1968; *Village Statistics, 1945: A Classification of Land and Area Ownership in Palestine,* Palestine Liberation Organization Research Center, 1970; (with Robert John) *The Palestine Diary,* 2 volumes, New World Press, 1970. Author of monographs published by Arab Information Center (New York), the Jordan Government, the Institute for Palestine Studies, and the Palestine Research Center (Beirut).†

* * *

HADWIGER, Don F. 1930-

PERSONAL: Born April 3, 1930, in San Bernardino, Calif., son of Claude L. (a farmer) and Edith (Hamann) Hadwiger; married Ellen B. Van Laanen, July 4, 1953; children: Mary, Stephen, David, Edith, Arlis. *Education:* University of Santa Clara, student, 1947-49; University of Oklahoma, B.A., 1953; University of Nebraska, M.A., 1954; University of Iowa, Ph.D., 1956. *Politics:* Democrat. *Religion:* Roman Catholic. *Home:* 311 South Riverside, Ames, Iowa.

CAREER: Southwest Missouri State University, Springfield, associate professor, 1956—. *Military service:* U.S. Army, 1950-52. *Awards, honors:* Congressional fellow, American Political Science Association, 1959-60.

WRITINGS: (With Ross B. Talbot) *Pressures and Protests,* Chandler Publishing, 1965; (with Talbot) *Policy Process in American Agriculture,* Chandler Publishing, 1968; *Federal Wheat Commodity Legislation,* Iowa State University Press, 1969; *Low-Income Housing Programs in Iowa: A Manual for Community Leaders,* Iowa State University Press, 1974.

WORK IN PROGRESS: Leave The City; Future Oriented Community Leaders; Agricultural Research Policy.

* * *

HAGELMAN, Charles W(illiam), Jr. 1920-

PERSONAL: Born November 9, 1920, in Houston, Tex.; son of Charles William and Anna Marie (Griffin) Hagelman; married Elizabeth Drisler Sloan, September 7, 1946; children: Lucy Ann, Charles William III, John F. *Education:* University of Texas, B.A., 1942, Ph.D., 1956; Columbia University, M.A., 1947. *Religion:* Episcopalian. *Residence:* Dixon, Ill. *Office:* Department of English, Northern Illinois University, De Kalb, Ill. 60115.

CAREER: Muhlenberg College, Allentown, Pa., instructor in English, 1947-51; University of Texas, Austin, instructor in English, 1953-55; University of Houston, Houston, Tex.,

instructor, 1955-56, assistant professor, 1956-58, associate professor of English, 1958-59; Lamar State College of Technology (now Lamar University), Beaumont, Tex., professor of English and head of department, 1959-66; University of Toledo, Toledo, Ohio, professor of English and associate dean, 1966-68; Northern Illinois University, De Kalb, professor of English, 1968—. *Military service:* U.S. Army, 1942-46.

MEMBER: Modern Language Association of America, Keats-Shelley Association of America, Conference of College Teachers of English (president, 1964-65), American Association of University Professors, South Central Modern Language Association (chairman of contemporary literature section, 1957-58), Midwest Modern Language Association (member of executive council, 1972-74). *Awards, honors:* Award for excellence of teaching, United States Steel Co., 1958; State of Texas research grants, 1960-64.

WRITINGS: (Editor with Robert J. Barnes) *A Concordance to Byron's "Don Juan,"* Cornell University Press, 1967; (editor) Mary Wollstonecraft, *A Vindication of the Rights of Woman,* Norton, 1967. Contributor to *Keats-Shelley Journal.* Editorial consultant, *Survival Planning Project for the Houston-Harris County Area,* 1956-57, and *Business Review,* 1957-59.

WORK IN PROGRESS: A John Keats' medical notebook.

* * *

HAGSTROM, Warren Olaf 1930-

PERSONAL: Born May 27, 1930, in Minneapolis, Minn.; son of Andrew (a postal supervisor) and Borghild (Aune) Hagstrom; married Lois Mendum (an artist), July 30, 1956; children: Eric, Susan. *Education:* University of Minnesota, B.A., 1952, M.A., 1954; University of California, Ph.D., 1963. *Religion:* Unitarian Universalist. *Office:* Department of Sociology, University of Wisconsin, Madison, Wis. 53706.

CAREER: University of Wisconsin–Madison, assistant professor, 1962-65, associate professor, 1965-68, professor of sociology, 1968—, chairman of department, 1973-76. *Military service:* U.S. Army, 1954. *Member:* American Sociological Association, American Association for the Advancement of Science, American Association of University Professors, Society for the Study of Social Problems.

WRITINGS: (With William Kornhauser) *Scientists in Industry,* University of California Press, 1962; *The Scientific Community,* Basic Books, 1965. Contributor to professional journals.

WORK IN PROGRESS: Surveys of physical, formal, and biological scientists; studies of the organization of American universities.

* * *

HALEY, Gail E. 1939-

PERSONAL: Born November 4, 1939, in Charlotte, N.C.; daughter of George C. (an advertising manager) and P. Louise (Bell) Einhart; married Joseph A. Haley (a mathematician), August 15, 1959; married second husband, Arnold F. Arnold (a designer, writer, and artist), February 14, 1966; children: (second marriage) Marguerite Madeline. *Education:* Student at Richmond Professional Institute, 1957-59, and University of Virginia, 1960-64. *Home:* 3 Market Pl., London N. 2, England. *Agent:* Marilyn Marlowe, Curtis Brown Ltd., 575 Madison Ave., New York, N.Y. 10022; and A. P. Watt, 26-28 Bedford Row, London WC1R 4HL, England.

CAREER: Manuscript Press, New York, N.Y., vice-president, beginning 1965. Artist, illustrator of children's books and educational material, and designer of toys and fashion items; graphics and illustrations exhibited at libraries and museums in southern states and New York. Work included in permanent collections at the University of Minnesota, and Jacksonville (Fla.) Children's Museum. *Awards, honors:* Caldecott Medal, American Library Association, 1971, for *A Story, A Story;* Czechoslovak Children's Film Festival Award for best animated children's film of the year, 1974.

WRITINGS—All self-illustrated: *My Kingdom for a Dragon,* Crozet Print Shop, 1962; *The Wonderful Magical World of Marguerite,* McGraw, 1964; *Round Stories About Things That Live on Land,* Follett, 1966; *Round Stories About Things That Live in Water,* Follett, 1966; *Round Stories About Things That Grow,* Follett, 1966; *Round Stories About Our World,* Follett, 1966; *A Story, A Story,* Atheneum, 1970; *Noah's Ark,* Atheneum, 1973; *Jack Jouett's Ride,* Viking, 1973; *The Abominable Swampman,* Viking, 1975; *The Post Office Cat,* Scribner, 1976; *Costumes for Plays and Playing,* Methuen, in press; *Go Away, Stay Away!,* Scribner, in press.

Illustrator: *The Skip Rope Book,* Dial, 1962; *One, Two Buckle My Shoe,* Doubleday, 1964; *The Three Wishes of Hu,* Putnam, 1964; *Koalas,* Prentice-Hall, 1965; *Which Is Which?,* Prentice-Hall, 1966; *P.S. Happy Anniversary,* World Publishing, 1966; *Peek-A-Boo Book of Puppies and Kittens,* Nelson, 1966; *All Together, One at a Time,* Atheneum, 1971. Also illustrator of syndicated column, "Parents and Children," written by husband, Arnold F. Arnold. Contributor of children's stories to magazines.

SIDELIGHTS: Gail Haley writes: "More than a personal catharsis, my work is an effort designed to stimulate verbal and visual responses and a preparation for literacy. My books are for children. They are also frames of reference for the story reader who needs to dramatize, explain, and discuss the ideas I express, the pictures I draw and the words I use. My object is to involve both adult and child." She also explained that "a child brings his own understanding and experience to the book and is enriched by what the book gives him back. He must supply movement, image, sound and sequence of time. This is a far greater challenge to his brain than sitting passively before a TV set and having these things fed to him without any effort on his part."

A Story, A Story was made into a filmstrip, 1972, and an animated film, 1973, both produced by Weston Woods Studios. *Jack Jouett's Ride* was made into a filmstrip, Weston Woods Studios, 1975. An animated film with the same title is planned. Gail Haley appeared in a documentary film, *Animating Picture Books.*

BIOGRAPHICAL/CRITICAL SOURCES: New York Times Book Review, April 12, 1970, November 8, 1970; *Publishers' Weekly,* September 6, 1971; *Charlotte (N.C.) Observer,* July 29, 1973.

* * *

HALEY, Jay 1923-

PERSONAL: Born July 19, 1923, in Midwest, Wyo.; son of Andrew J. and Mary (Sneddon) Haley; married Eliza-

beth Kuehn (a musician), December 25, 1950 (divorced, 1971); children: Kathleen, Andrew, Gregory. *Education:* University of California, Los Angeles, B.A., 1948; University of California, Berkeley, B.L.S., 1951; Stanford University, M.A., 1953. *Home:* 520 Woodland Ter., Philadelphia, Pa. 19104. *Office:* Philadelphia Child Guidance Clinic, 34th St. and Civic Center Blvd., Philadelphia, Pa. 19104.

CAREER: Project for Study of Communication (Veterans Administration and Stanford University), Palo Alto, Calif., research associate, 1953-62; Mental Research Institute, Palo Alto, Calif., director of family experimentation, 1962-67; Philadelphia Child Guidance Clinic, Philadelphia, Pa., director of family research, 1967—.

WRITINGS: Strategies of Psychotherapy, Grune, 1963; (editor) *Advanced Techniques of Hypnosis and Therapy,* Grune, 1967; (with Lynn Hoffman) *Techniques of Family Therapy,* Basic Books, 1967; *The Power Tactics of Jesus Christ: And Other Essays,* Grossman, 1969; (editor) *Changing Families,* Grune, 1971; *Uncommon Therapy,* Norton, 1972.

* * *

HALL, Andrew 1935-

PERSONAL: Born September 15, 1935, in London, England; son of James Henry (a physician) and Monica (Macdonald) Hall. *Education:* Attended Uppingham School, Rutland, England, 1949-54. *Politics:* "Vacillating." *Religion:* Church of England. *Home:* 58 Washington Rd., Maldon, Essex, England. *Agent:* A. M. Heath & Co. Ltd., 35 Dover St., London W1X 4EB, England; and Brandt & Brandt, 101 Park Ave., New York, N.Y. 10017.

CAREER: Tatler, London, England, photographic editor, 1957-58; free-lance film researcher, 1958-60; Central Office of Information, London, England, member of film production unit, 1960-64; full-time writer, 1964—. *Military service:* British Army, 1955-57; became lieutenant. *Member:* Writer's Guild of Great Britain, Malta Union Club.

WRITINGS—Novels: *Man in Aspic,* Cassell, 1965; *Frost,* Cassell, 1966, Putnam, 1967; *Safe Behind Bars,* Cassell, 1968. Author of several television series, and a film script for Twentieth Century-Fox. Contributor of short stories to Putnam's *Pick of Today's Short Stories,* and to *Tatler* and *Young Elizabethan.*

WORK IN PROGRESS: A fourth novel, as yet untitled; two television plays for British Broadcasting Corp.; an original film script.

SIDELIGHTS: Hall's first short story was published when he was sixteen. He told *CA* that his later writing was influenced by Graham Greene and F. Scott Fitzgerald. Hall owns a large collection of children's books dating from 1600 to 1935, many signed first editions. He noted that his ambition is to direct the film of one of his novels. He likes France and the French (he also speaks French), and cinema, walking, children of any nationality, and acting; he dislikes curry, women who wear slacks, tobacco, snobs, and hypocrites.

AVOCATIONAL INTERESTS: Tennis, fives, swimming, rugby football.††

* * *

HALL, Angus 1932-

PERSONAL: Born March 24, 1932, in Newcastle on Tyne, Northumberland, England; son of Angus Henry (a timber merchant) and Anne (Calvert) Hall; married Theresa Geraldine Garcia (an artist), July 12, 1963; children: Andrew Henry. *Education:* Attended Skerries Commercial College, Newcastle on Tyne, England, 1954-55. *Politics:* "Apolitical. A believer in world peace and brotherhood." *Religion:* Agnostic. *Home:* Little House, West St., Old Town, Hastings, Sussex, England.

CAREER: Newcastle Evening Chronicle, Newcastle on Tyne, England, news reporter and feature writer, 1955-56; *Daily Mirror,* London, England, feature writer, 1956-57; *Daily Sketch,* London, England, theater and film critic and show business columnist, 1957-61; novelist, 1961—. Speech and script writer. *Member:* P.E.N., London Press Club.

WRITINGS—Novels: *Love in Smoky Regions,* Constable, 1962, Dell, 1967; *The High-Bouncing Lover* (consists of one section from each of two unpublished novels—"Wild About Harry" and "Gigolo"), Hammond, Hammond, 1966, Dell, 1968; *Live Like a Hero,* Hammond, Hammond, 1967, Dell, 1968; *The Come-Uppance of Arthur Hearne,* Hammond, Hammond, 1967, Dell, 1968; *Qualtrough,* Jenkins, 1968; *The Late Boy Wonder,* Jenkins, 1969; *Devilday,* Sphere, 1969.

A Long Way to Fall, W. H. Allen, 1971; *The Scars of Dracula,* Sphere, 1971; *To Play the Devil,* Sphere, 1971; *The Gentle Sex,* Sphere, 1972; *On the Run,* Harrap, 1974; *Madhouse,* Universal Publishing & Distributing, 1974; *Signs of Things to Come,* Doubleday, 1975; *Monsters and Mythic Beasts,* Doubleday, 1976. Adapted *Love in Smoky Regions* for the screen. Book reviewer for *Look & Learn* (London educational periodical), and for *Books and Bookmen.*

WORK IN PROGRESS: A novel, as yet untitled, based on the case of Philip Yale Drew, an American actor tried for murder in England in 1929.

SIDELIGHTS: According to several critics, Hall is a funny, ingenious, and very good novelist. According to Hall, his first novel was published "to a welcome of muted trumpets and qualified cheers." His second and third novels were rejected. When Hall presented his second novel, "Wild About Harry," his publisher said: "The trouble with your novel is something quite elementary. It is no good." When a similar lack of enthusiasm greeted his third, "Gigolo," Hall recounts: "I showed low literary cunning. . . . By cutting out one half of 'Gigolo,' and grafting it to another half of 'Harry' I had a new and hybrid novel which I decided to call *The High-Bouncing Lover.* It was a piece of skilful creative surgery, which combined one man's career with another man's marriage, and which was published . . . with a gratifying amount of success."

When Hall published *The Come-Uppance of Arthur Hearne,* John Foss wrote: "This is Angus Hall's fourth novel and there is no doubt that he is developing his own unique style. He specializes in the picaresque, and his heroes, with one exception, are all gay rogues, shiftless deceivers with few cares and no responsibilities. In many ways they reflect modern society, and sooner or later this author is bound to come up with a character immediately recognisable as the man all men want to be."

Qualtrough is based on a 1931 murder case in which a Liverpudlian named William Herbert Wallace was indicted for the murder of his wife. Richard Whittington-Egan explains: "The arraigned widower apart, the sole suspect was the insubstantial Mr. R. M. Qualtrough—a mysterious voice calling from a public telephone box, and heard by five witnesses. Qualtrough! An old Manx name which Wallace swore pseudonymously masked the ugly persona of his wife's killer." Wallace was subsequently exonerated. (Whittington-Egan most provocatively adds, however, that he has "the soundest reasons for believing that [he has] actually met the so-elusive Qualtrough in the flesh"!) At any rate, Whittington-Egan continues, "the enigmatic Wallace case is . . . merely the inspirational touchstone of Mr. Hall's remarkable novel. . . . For, the eponymous reality of its title notwithstanding, this is no mere fictionalised revivification of an old crime upon which the blood has long since dried and crusted. It is an imaginative artefact that lives and breathes in its own right, and demands consideration on its own creative terms. Mr. Hall's writing is extremely good, his variations on his seminal theme alarmingly ingenious, and the appalling lack of effect that characterises his psychopathic—query schizophrenic—killer chills by its verisimilitude. Mr. Hall carries us most convincingly into terrifyingly cerebral territory at a compulsive pace."

Ronald Pearsall in his review of Hall's *The Late Boy Wonder,* wrote: "There is a thoroughly professional use of research and background material, and Angus Hall handles the bizarre convolutions of the plot with expert glee. . . . Mr. Hall has a good ear for dialogue and his character-drawing has a perky precision that can only come from the clinical observation of a born novelist."

Hall told *CA* that he has "no 'literary views' on writing," that he "regards it as a nine-to-five job," and that he writes because he believes, justifiably so, that he can. He notes that he's an avid newspaper reader, "as they provide much valuable information and data." Hall lived in Spain, mainly on the island of Ibiza, for three years. (He told *Books and Bookmen* that, while trying to write his second novel, he "remembered Thomas Wolfe, and what he called 'the naked desperation' of attempting to complete *his* second novel. . . . Wolfe had solved his problem by working abroad. *He* went to Paris and London; so *I* went to the Baliaric [sic] island of Ibiza.)"

American International Pictures purchased *The Late Boy Wonder* for filming.

AVOCATIONAL INTERESTS: Watching English Association football.

BIOGRAPHICAL/CRITICAL SOURCES: Times Literary Supplement, July 7, 1966; *Books and Bookmen,* January, February, and June, 1968, July and September, 1969.†

* * *

HALL, Lynn 1937-

PERSONAL: Born November 9, 1937, in Lombard, Ill.; daughter of Raymond Edwin (a city official) and Alice (a high school teacher; maiden name, Seeds) Hall; married Dean W. Green, May 1, 1960 (divorced September, 1961). *Education:* Attended schools in Iowa. *Religion:* Protestant. *Home:* Touchwood, Volga, Iowa 52077.

CAREER: Author, 1968—. Member of Garnavillo Library Board. *Member:* Collie Club of America, Cedar Valley Collie Club, Dubuque Kennel Club. *Awards, honors:* Charles W. Follett award, 1971, for *A Horse Called Dragon.*

WRITINGS—Juveniles; all published by Follett, except as noted: *The Shy Ones,* 1967; *The Secret of Stonehouse,* 1968; *Ride a Wild Dream,* 1969; *Too Near the Sun* (Junior Literary Guild selection), 1970; *Gently Touch the Milkweed* (Junior Literary Guild selection), 1970; *A Horse Called Dragon,* 1971; *The Famous Battle of Bravery*

Creek, Garrard, 1972; *The Seige of Silent Henry*, 1972; *Sticks and Stones*, 1972; *Lynn Hall's Dog Stories*, 1972; *Flash, Dog of Old Egypt*, Garrard, 1973; *Barry, the Bravest St. Bernard*, Garrard, 1973; *Riff, Remember*, 1973; *To Catch a Tartar*, 1973; *Stray*, 1974; *Bob, Watchdog of the River*, Garrard, 1974; *Troublemaker*, 1975; *Kids and Dog Shows*, 1975; *New Day for Dragon*, 1975; *Captain: Canada's Flying Pony*, Garrard, 1976.

WORK IN PROGRESS: Flowers of Anger, for Follett; an untitled sequel to *New Day for Dragon*, for Follett.

SIDELIGHTS: Lynn Hall told *CA*: "My primary interest, aside from writing, is the breeding and exhibiting of show dogs—collies. This hobby dovetails nicely with my ambition to specialize in the area of dog stories of high literary quality."

* * *

HALL, Mary Bowen 1932-
(Mary Bowen)

PERSONAL: Born June 13, 1932, in Oakland, Calif.; daughter of Donald A. (a public health administrator) and Margaret (Maack) Cordray; married Robert W. Bowen (an insurance broker), April 9, 1953; married Thomas F. Hall, June 13, 1970; children: Steven, Donald, Paul. *Education:* Attended Santa Rosa Junior College and San Jose State College (now University); Sacramento State College (now California State University, Sacramento), A.B., 1961, M.A., 1970. *Home:* 1350 42nd St., Sacramento, Calif. 95819.

CAREER: Educational communicator, division of agricultural sciences, University of California. *Member:* American Association of Agricultural College Editors, Mensa, California Writers Club, Sierra Club.

WRITINGS: (Under name Mary Bowen, with Walter Petty) *Slithery Snakes and Other Aids to Children's Writing*, Appleton, for Sacramento County Schools and Folsom-Cordova School District, 1968. Contributor to *Parents' Magazine, National Parks, True West*, and to local newspapers.

WORK IN PROGRESS: Writings on agricultural economics.

* * *

HALL, Patrick 1932-

PERSONAL: Born May 16, 1932, in Birmingham, England; son of Frederick Charles (a bricklayer) and Mary (Pearks) Hall; married Kathleen Blackman, August 27, 1955; children: Brendan, Sally, Louise. *Education:* Attended schools in Birmingham, England, until sixteen. *Home:* 25 Regal Close, London W.5, England. *Agent:* A. D. Peters, Ltd., 10 Buckingham St., London WC2N 6BU, England. *Office:* Ofrex House, Stephen St., London W1A 1EA, England.

CAREER: Kalamazoo Ltd., (business systems manufacturers), Birmingham, England, employed in various positions in marketing, 1953-63; C.S. International Ltd. (telecommunications equipment manufacturers), London, England, overseas marketing manager, 1963-65; Ofrex Group Ltd. (international business equipment manufacturers), London, England, international director of exports, 1965-74, managing director, 1974—. Vice-chairman, Fordigraph Consolidated, Australia, 1971—. *Military service:* British Army, Infantry, 1950-52; served with Twenty-ninth Brigade in Korea; became sergeant.

WRITINGS—Novels: *The Harp That Once*, Heinemann, 1967; *The India Man*, Chatto & Windus, 1968; *The Power Sellers*, Putnam, 1969; *Sun and Grey Shadow*, W. H. Allen, 1974.

WORK IN PROGRESS: A novel, *The Directorate*, for W. H. Allen.

SIDELIGHTS: In the past ten years Patrick Hall has visited every country in Europe, spent lengthy periods in Africa, and also traveled in Asia, Europe and the United States. Much of his time is currently spent in Australia, where his novel, *Sun and Grey Shadow*, is set.

John McGrath's screenplay, "The Reckoning," Columbia Pictures, 1969, was based on *The Harp That Once*.

BIOGRAPHICAL/CRITICAL SOURCES: Birmingham Mail, January 4, 1967; *Books and Bookmen*, April, 1967; *Best Sellers*, February 15, 1969.

* * *

HALL, Walter (Earl, Jr.) 1940-

PERSONAL: Born October 15, 1940, in Detroit, Mich.; son of Walter Earl (a mechanic) and Mary (Applegate) Hall. *Education:* Attended Wayne State University, 1960-67. *Politics:* Democrat. *Religion:* None. *Home:* 609½ Bloomington, Iowa City, Iowa 52240.

CAREER: MacManus, John & Adams, Inc. (advertising firm), Bloomfield Hills, Mich., copywriter, 1966; Wayne State University, Detroit, Mich., director of literary programs for WDET-FM Radio and part-time instructor in creative writing, 1966-69; Richard Abel & Co., Portland, Ore., assistant buyer and literary advisor, 1969-70; Colorado Mountain College, Aspen, Colo., instructor in creative writing, 1971-72; visiting poet, California Poetry-in-the-Schools, 1972-73, and North Creede Poetry Center, Creede, Colo., 1973-75; Custer County, Colo., zoning officer and geologic hazards observer, 1975-76; Iowa City/Johnson County Arts Council, Iowa City, Iowa, community poet, 1976—. Master poet-in-residence, State of Oregon, 1970-71; poet-in-residence, Aspen Community Schools, Aspen, Colo., 1971-72. *Military service:* U.S. Army, 1959, 1961-62. *Awards, honors:* Miles fellowships, 1964, 1966; Keith Waldrop Memorial Award, 1964; Tompkins Award, 1965; National Endowment for the Arts discovery grant, 1970.

WRITINGS: The Spider Poems, Perishable Press, 1967; *The Music Threat*, Trask House Books, 1971; *Glowing in the Dark*, Burning Deck Press, 1972; *Vestiges*, Diana's Bimonthly, 1975. Poetry represented in anthologies, including *Under Thirty*, Indiana University Press, 1970, and *The Yes! Press Anthology*, Christopher Books, 1972. Contributor of poetry to *Approach, Tri-Quarterly, Open Places*, and other journals.

WORK IN PROGRESS: Miners Getting off the Graveyard; A Guide to the Wilderness Off-the-Trail; a sequence of poems; a novel.

* * *

HALLAM, H(erbert) E(noch) 1923-

PERSONAL: Born September 28, 1923, in Pembridge, Herefordshire, England; son of Thomas Enoch (a coal miner) and Edith (Neighbours) Hallam; married Sylvia Joy Maycock (a university lecturer), June 11, 1948; children: John Richard, David Leslie, Thomas William, Elizabeth Ann. *Education:* Jesus College, Cambridge, B.A., 1948,

M.A., 1952; University of Nottingham, Ph.D., 1957. *Home:* 13 Walter St., Claremont, Western Australia 6010.

CAREER: Spalding Grammar School, Spalding, Lincolnshire, England, assistant history master, 1950-55; Loughborough Training College, Loughborough, Leicestershire, England, lecturer, 1955-60, senior lecturer in charge of history 1960-61; University of Western Australia, Nedlands, senior lecturer, 1961-64, reader, 1965, professor of medieval history, 1966—, head of department, 1966-67, 1970-71, 1973-75, dean of faculty of arts, 1969-71. *Military service:* Royal Air Force, ground staff, 1942-45. *Member:* Royal Historical Society (fellow), Australian Academy of the Humanities (fellow), Economic History Society, British Agricultural History Society, Society for Mediaeval Archeology. *Awards, honors:* Ellen McArthur Prize, Cambridge University, 1959, for study later published as *Settlement and Society.*

WRITINGS: The New Lands of Elloe, Leicester University Press, 1954; *Settlement and Society: Study of Early Agrarian History of South Lincolnshire,* Cambridge University Press, 1965. Contributor to learned periodicals.

WORK IN PROGRESS: Editing Volume II of *Agrarian History of England and Wales, 1042-1350;* a book on medieval England to 1350.

SIDELIGHTS: Hallam is fluent in French; knows Latin, Italian, Dutch, Spanish, Portugese, Danish, Norwegian, Swedish, and German. *Avocational interests:* Wine, music, and walking.

* * *

HALLECK, Seymour L(eon) 1929-

PERSONAL: Born April 16, 1929, in Chicago, Ill.; son of Irving and Eva Halleck; married Helen L. Goldberg, August 27, 1950; children: Nancy, Judith, Elizabeth. *Education:* University of Chicago, Ph.B., 1948, B.S., 1950, M.D., 1952. *Home:* 500 Laurel Hill Rd., Chapel Hill, N.C. 27514. *Office:* North Carolina Memorial Hospital, University of North Carolina, Chapel Hill, N.C. 27514.

CAREER: U.S. Public Health Service intern, San Francisco, Calif., 1952-53; Menninger Foundation, Topeka, Kan., resident, 1955-58; University of Wisconsin—Madison, associate professor, 1963-66, professor of psychiatry, 1966-72, director of student health psychiatry, 1963-72, lecturer in department of sociology, 1963-64; University of North Carolina, North Carolina Memorial Hospital, Chapel Hill, professor of psychiatry and director of psychiatry residency training program, 1972—. State of Wisconsin, Division of Corrections, chief of psychiatric services, 1961-63, chief psychiatric consultant, beginning 1963; member of advisory committee (parole board), Central State Hospital, beginning 1960. *Member:* American Psychiatric Association, North Carolina Neuropsychiatric Association, Wisconsin Psychiatric Association, Durham-Orange County Medical Society, Dane County Medical Society, Isaac Ray Society. *Awards, honors:* Sc.D., Rockford University, 1969; Arthur Marshall Distinguished Alumnus Award, Menninger School of Psychiatry, 1974.

WRITINGS: (Editor with L. Roberts and M. Loeb) *Community Psychiatry,* University of Wisconsin Press, 1966; *Psychiatry and the Dilemmas of Crime,* Harper, 1967; (with Walter Bromberg) *Psychiatric Aspects of Criminology,* C. C Thomas, 1968; *The Politics of Therapy,* Science House, 1971; (editor with others) *1974 Aldine Annual of Crime and Justice,* Aldine, 1975. Contributor to newspapers and journals in his field.

HALM, George N(ikolaus) 1901-

PERSONAL: Born September 10, 1901, in Munich, Germany; son of Peter (a professor) and Katherina (Muller) Halm; married Lore Friedlander (a lecturer) March 18, 1927; children: Klaus, Ruth (Mrs. Wallace F. Caldwell). *Education:* University of Munich, doctorate, 1924. *Home:* 134 Valley Lakes Dr., Santa Rosa, Calif. 95405.

CAREER: University of Munich, Munich, Germany, assistant in economics, 1927-28; University of Wuerzburg, Wuerzburg, Germany, professor of economics, 1928-36; Tufts University, Medford, Mass., professor of economics, 1937-44, professor of international economic relations at Fletcher School of Law and Diplomacy, 1944-71. *Member:* American Academy of Arts and Sciences.

WRITINGS: Die Konkurrenz, Duncker & Humblot, 1929; *Ist der Sozialismus wirtschaftlich moglich?,* Junker & Dunnhaupt, 1929; *Der Wirtschaftliche Kreislauf und seine Gesetze,* Reclam, 1934; *Geld, Banken, Borsen,* Duncker & Humblot, 1935; *Monetary Theory,* Blakiston Co., 1942, 2nd edition, 1946; *International Monetary Cooperation,* University of North Carolina Press, 1945; *Economic Systems,* Holt, 1951, 3rd edition, 1968; *Economics of Money and Banking,* Irwin, 1956, 2nd edition, 1963; *The "Band" Proposal,* Princeton University Press, 1965; *A Guide to International Monetary Reform,* Lexington Books, 1975. Contributor to *Encyclopaedia Britannica* and *Handworterbuch der Sozialwissenschaften.* Also contributor to yearbooks and professional journals in both English and German.

SIDELIGHTS: Halm's books have been translated into German, Japanese, Spanish, Portuguese, French, Chinese, and Hindi.

* * *

HALPERT, Inge D. 1926-

PERSONAL: Born August 5, 1926, in Berlin, Germany; daughter of Paul (a businessman) and Irma (Pollak) David; married Henry Halpert (an electronics engineer), February 8, 1948; children: Stephen C., Karen D. *Education:* Hunter College (now of the City University of New York), B.A., 1948; Columbia University, M.A., 1950, Ph.D., 1957. *Home:* 445 Riverside Dr., New York, N.Y. 10027. *Office:* 607 Lewisohn Hall, Columbia University, 116th and Broadway, New York, N.Y. 10027.

CAREER: Columbia University, New York, N.Y., instructor, 1950-57, assistant professor, 1957-61, associate professor, 1961-73, professor of German language and literature, 1973—, chairman of department of German, School of General Studies, 1965—. *Member:* Modern Language Association of America, American Association of Teachers of German, American Association of University Professors, American Council of Teachers of Foreign Languages, Phi Beta Kappa, Delta Phi Alpha. *Awards, honors:* Hunter College Achievement Award, 1958; American Philosophical Society grant, 1964.

WRITINGS: "Playway to German" (children's language course), Foreign Language Studies, 1959; (editor of textbook edition) Rilke, *Ewald Tragy,* Appleton, 1961; (with Margarita Madrigal) *See It and Say It in German,* New American Library, 1962; (contributor) John Gearey and Willy Schumann, editors, *Einfuehrung in die deutche Literatur,* Holt, 1964; *Auditory and Reading Comprehension Exercises in German,* Latin American Institute Press, 1966; (with Ellen V. Nardroff) *In Wort und Schrift* (advanced German conversation and composition), Appleton, 1971; (contributor) *Columbia Dictionary of Modern European Literature,* Columbia University Press, in press. Contributor to journals.

*   *   *

HALSELL, Grace   1923-

PERSONAL: Born May 7, 1923, in Lubbock, Tex.; daughter of Harry H. (a cattleman) and Ruth (Shanks) Halsell. *Education:* Attended Texas Technological College (now Texas Tech University) and Texas Christian University. *Agent:* Julian Bach Literary Agency, Inc., 3 East 48th St., New York, N.Y. 10017.

CAREER: Former newspaper columnist and correspondent in Latin American countries, Japan, and Korea; White House, Washington, D.C., staff writer during President Johnson's administration, 1965-68.

WRITINGS: Getting to Know Colombia, Coward, 1964; *Getting to Know Guatemala and the Two Honduras,* Coward, 1964; *Getting to Know Peru,* Coward, 1964; *Soul Sister,* World Publishing, 1969; *Peru,* Macmillan, 1969; (editor and author of introduction) Charles Evers, *Evers* (autobiography), World Publishing, 1971; *Black/White Sex,* Morrow, 1972; *Bessie Yellowhair,* Morrow, 1973; *Los Viejos, Secrets of Health and Long Life from the Sacred Valley,* Rodale Press, in press.

SIDELIGHTS: After leaving her White House job, Miss Halsell spent three months darkening her skin under a doctor's care and then lived as a black woman in the deep South and Harlem. *Soul Sister* is an account of her six months as a white Texan-turned black.

*   *   *

HALSMAN, Philippe   1906-

PERSONAL: Born May 2, 1906, in Riga, Latvia; came to United States in 1940, naturalized in 1949; son of Max (a dentist) and Ita (a school principal; maiden name, Grintuch) Halsman; married Yvonne Moser (a photographic assistant), April 1, 1937; children: Irene Aline, Jane Ellen. *Education:* Vidus Vacu Skola, Riga, Latvia, B.A., 1924; Technische Hochschule, Dresden, Germany, student, 1924-28; additional study for one year at Sorbonne, University of Paris. *Home and studio:* 33 West 67th St., New York, N.Y. 10023.

CAREER: Photographer with own studio in Paris, France, 1931-40, doing portraits of the fashionable and work for *Vogue, Vu, Voila,* and other magazines; free-lance photographer in New York, N.Y., 1940—, with subjects for portraits including Sir Winston Churchill, Katherine Cornell, Albert Einstein, Helen Hayes, Eleanor Roosevelt, Andre Gide, Dwight D. Eisenhower, Harold Macmillan, and others. Member of guiding faculty, Famous Photographers School, Westport, Conn., 1963—; professional lecturer, 1967—. Portraits have been exhibited at shows in Paris, New York, and Tokyo, and are in the permanent collections of Metropolitan Museum of Art and Museum of Modern Art; has shot 101 covers for *Life,* and also was commissioned by the magazine to travel around the world to find and photograph the most beautiful girls; commissioned by *Time* on another world tour to photograph the most beautiful queens and president's wives; his portraits of Adlai Stevenson and Einstein have appeared on U.S. postage stamps.

MEMBER: American Society of Magazine Photographers

(first president, 1944, re-elected, 1954), Dutch Treat Club (New York). *Awards, honors:* Named one of world's ten greatest photographers in international poll conducted by *Popular Photography,* 1958; Newhouse Citation of Syracuse University School of Journalism, 1963; Golden Plate Award, American Academy of Achievement, 1967.

WRITINGS—All illustrated with his own photographs: *The Frenchman: A Photographic Interview* (with French comedian Fernandel), Simon & Schuster, 1948; *Piccoli* (juvenile), Simon & Schuster, 1951; *Dali's Mustache,* Simon & Schuster, 1954; *Jump Book,* Simon & Schuster, 1959; *Philippe Halsman on the Creation of Photographic Ideas,* Ziff-Davis, 1961; *Halsman Sight and Insight,* Doubleday, 1972. Portraits included in "Mental Giants" series in *Saturday Evening Post;* did series for *Picture Post* (England), and also has had work published in *Look* and other national magazines in United States and in photography journals.

BIOGRAPHICAL/CRITICAL SOURCES: Photography Workshop, fall, 1950; *American,* June, 1953; *Popular Photography,* December, 1958; *Pageant,* November, 1965.

*   *   *

HAM, Wayne   1938-

PERSONAL: Born May 13, 1938, in Toronto, Ontario, Canada; son of Albert F. and Edna (Dempster) Ham; married Marliene Miller, December 24, 1959; children: Terry Russell, Brian Neal. *Education:* Graceland College, B.A., 1959; Brigham Young University, M.A., 1961; College of the Siskiyous, graduate study, 1962; St. Paul's School of Theology, M.Div., 1969; Central Missouri State College, teaching certificate, 1970; University of Florida, Ph.D. candidate. *Religion:* Reorganized Church of Jesus Christ of Latter Day Saints. *Home address:* Route 1, Box 174T, Wildwood, Fla. 32785.

CAREER: High school teacher of Spanish, German, and Latin in Dunsmuir, Calif., 1961-62; University of Valle, Cali, Colombia, assistant professor of English, 1962-63; Reorganized Church of Jesus Christ of Latter Day Saints, Independence, Mo., member of department of religious education, 1963-70; Florida School System, Sumter County, supervisor, 1970—.

WRITINGS—All published by Herald Publishing House: *Enriching Your New Testament Studies,* 1966; *Man's Living Religions,* 1967; *Call to Covenant,* 1970; *Publish Glad Tidings,* 1970; *Yesterday's Horizons,* 1975.

*   *   *

HAMILTON, Horace E(rnst)   1911-

PERSONAL: Born November 20, 1911, in Madison, Ind.; son of Guy Wheeler (a physician) and Alice Pauline (Ernst) Hamilton; married Evelyn Ahrenhold, 1941; children: Philip, Patricia (Mrs. John Chapman), Lee (daughter). *Education:* College of Wooster, B.A., 1933; Yale University, Ph.D., 1941; Columbia University, postdoctoral study, 1952-53. *Politics:* Independent ("though registered Republican"). *Religion:* Presbyterian ("but non-active"). *Home:* 312 Raritan Ave., Middlesex, N.J. 08846. *Office:* Rutgers University, New Brunswick, N.J. 08903.

CAREER: Columbian Preparatory School, Washington, D.C., master, 1934-35; instructor at Hofstra University, Long Island, N.Y., 1937-40, Rensselaer Polytechnic Institute, Troy, N.Y., 1941-43; Rutgers University, New Brunswick, N.J., assistant professor, 1946-62, professor of English, 1963—. Carnegie visiting professor at Columbia

College, Columbia University, 1956-57. *Military service:* U.S. Navy, 1943-45; served aboard destroyer-escort in Atlantic and Pacific. *Awards, honors:* Ford Foundation Fellow for the Advancement of Education, 1952-54; Borestone Mountain Poetry Award, 1955.

WRITINGS: Through the Moongate (Chinese sketches), Dorrance, 1947; *The Dry Scratch of Laurel* (poems), Twayne, 1954; *China Two Generations Ago* (memoirs), A. Swallow, 1957; (contributor) *Essays in Literary Criticism,* Rutgers University Press, 1960; *Before Dark* (poems), Rutgers University Press, 1965; *The Cage of Form: Likeness and Difference in Poetry,* Dickinson, 1972. Contributor of articles, short stories, and poems to *New Yorker, Nation, Saturday Review, Virginia Quarterly Review,* and other magazines.

WORK IN PROGRESS: A novel on China, tentatively entitled, *North China Mission; Homer and the Essential Prototype;* and a volume of poetry, *Etude for the Left Hand.*

SIDELIGHTS: Hamilton lived in China as a child. *Avocational interests:* Building, boating on Lake Champlain.

* * *

HAMILTON-EDWARDS, Gerald (Kenneth Savery) 1906-

PERSONAL: Born July 24, 1906, in Southsea, Hampshire, England; son of Frederick Charles (a lieutenant general, Royal Marines) and Nona Louisa (Stevens) Edwards. *Education:* Keble College, Oxford, B.A., 1927, M.A., 1932; University of London, Diploma in Librarianship, 1930. *Politics:* Conservative. *Home:* 32 Bowness Ave., Headington, Oxford, England.

CAREER: Plymouth Proprietary Library, Plymouth, England, assistant librarian, 1937-39; University of London, Queen Mary College, London, England, assistant librarian, 1945-47; Devon County Library, England, librarian of Pymstock branch, 1947-48, regional librarian for South West Devon, 1948-54; Society of Genealogists, London, secretary, 1955; writer, 1955—. Part-time teacher in technical and grammar schools. Member of Plymouth City Libraries and Museum Committee, 1932—, and Oxford City Council, 1967-72. Governor of Oxford Polytechnic, 1967-72, and Magdalen College School, 1970-72. *Military service:* British Army, Royal Signals, Territorial Army, 1934-55; on active service, 1939-45; became major; received Territorial Decoration, 1946, and Coronation Medal, 1953. *Member:* Library Association (fellow), Royal Overseas League (chairman of Plymouth branch, 1953-54), Society of Genealogists (fellow), Scottish Genealogy Society, English Speaking Union, Society of Authors, Radio Writers Association, Oxford Society.

WRITINGS: The Stevens Family of Plymouth, privately printed, 1947; *Twelve Men of Plymouth,* privately printed, 1951; *The Leisured Connoisseur,* privately printed, 1954; (editor) *A Cadet in the Baltic: The Letters of Frederick Edwards, 1855-1857,* privately printed, 1956; (editor) Nona Louisa Edwards, *My Memory Walks beside Me,* privately printed, 1963; *In Search of Ancestry,* M. Joseph, 1966, published as *Tracing Your British Ancestors: A Guide to Genealogical Sources,* Walker & Co., 1967, 3rd edition published as *In Search of British Ancestry,* Genealogical Publishing Co., 1974; *In Scottish Ancestry,* Genealogical Publishing Co., 1972. Author of short stories and radio scripts for British Broadcasting Corp.; contributor to *Dictionary of National Biography,* and to *Trident, Apollo,*

Weekly Scotsman, Westcountry Magazine, Times, Times Literary Supplement, Independent, and other publications.

WORK IN PROGRESS: Research on Army, Navy, and East India Company records of biographical and genealogical value.

AVOCATIONAL INTERESTS: Music, art, photography, economics.

* * *

HANCOCK, Leslie 1941-

PERSONAL: Born December 4, 1941, in Miami, Fla.; son of Frank and Helen (Schlappich) Hancock. *Education:* Duke University, student, 1959-61; University of Miami, Coral Gables, Fla., B.A., 1963, M.A., 1966; New York University, graduate study, 1966—. *Home:* 305 Lexington Ave., New York, N.Y. 10016.

WRITINGS: Word Index to James Joyce's Portrait of the Artist, Southern Illinois University Press, 1967.

BIOGRAPHICAL/CRITICAL SOURCES: Modern Language Review, January, 1970.

* * *

HANDEL, Gerald 1924-

PERSONAL: Born August 8, 1924, in Cleveland, Ohio; son of Louis and Pearl (Seidman) Handel; married Ruth Doman, February 5, 1956; children: Jonathan, Michael. *Education:* University of Chicago, A.B., 1947, A.M., 1951, Ph.D., 1962; additional graduate study at Michael Reese Hospital. *Office:* City College of the City University of New York, New York, N.Y. 10031.

CAREER: University of Chicago, Chicago, Ill., research associate and instructor, 1952-56; Social Research, Inc., Chicago, research associate, 1956-62, assistant director, 1962-65, vice-president, 1965-66; Center for Urban Education, New York City, senior research psychologist, 1966-67; City College of the City University of New York, associate professor, 1967-72, professor of sociology, 1973—. *Member:* American Sociological Association, American Psychological Association, Eastern Sociological Society.

WRITINGS: (With Robert Hess) *Family Worlds,* University of Chicago Press, 1959; (with Lee Rainwater and Richard Coleman) *Workingman's Wife: Her Personality, World and Life Style,* Oceana, 1959; (editor) *The Psychosocial Interior of the Family,* Aldine, 1967, 2nd edition, 1972; (with Frederick Elkin) *The Child and Society: The Process of Socialization,* Random House, 1972. Contributor to professional journals.

* * *

HANDLER, Julian Harris 1922-

PERSONAL: Born April 19, 1922, in New York, N.Y.; son of Irving (a realtor) and Mathilde (Fromkes) Handler; divorced; married second wife, Phyllis Gabrielle Supplice, February 5, 1967; children: (first marriage) Russell Hartmann, Frederick John. *Education:* Syracuse University, B.A., 1943. *Home and office:* 400 East 89th St., New York, N.Y. 10028.

CAREER: Fairchild Publications, Inc., New York City, editor, 1949-61; Profit Press, Inc. (publishers of business books and newsletters), New York City, publisher, 1963-66; *Grocery Manufacturer* (business periodical), New York City, editor, 1966-72; Profit Press, Inc., publisher, 1972—. *Military service:* U.S. Navy, 1942-46; became lieutenant junior grade.

WRITINGS: Fundamentals of Selling the Supermarkets, Fairchild, 1956, 2nd edition published as *How to Sell the Supermarkets,* 1959, 3rd edition, 1966; (editor) *Food Industry Yearbook,* Profit Press, 1964-66; *You and Food Marketing,* Profit Press, 1968; (editor) *The Food Industry Executive's Pleasure Reader* (anthology), Media Books, 1969.

* * *

HANNAU, Hans W(alter) 1904-

PERSONAL: Born August 5, 1904, in Vienna, Austria; son of Julius and Jeanette (Karolyi) Hannau; married Elizabeth Ann Roeder, June 23, 1934; children: George P., Michael P. *Education:* Academy of Music, Vienna, Austria, student, 1923-24; University of Vienna, doctorate in law, 1928. *Religion:* Roman Catholic. *Home:* 423 East Rivo Alto Island, Miami Beach, Fla. 33139.

CAREER: Author/photographer, producing a series of pictorial books. Hannau, Inc., Miami, Fla., president, 1961—; chairman of the board, Hannau-Robinson Color Productions, Inc., New York, N.Y., 1964-67, and Argos, Inc., Miami, Fla., 1964—. President of Caribbean Trade Council, 1967-73. *Member:* Caribbean Travel Association, Caribbean Hotel Association, Austrian-American Society (president), English Speaking Union, Rotary Club and La Gorce Country Club (both Maimi Beach).

WRITINGS—Pictorial books, self-illustrated with color photographs; all published by W. Andermann, except as noted: *Florida: A Photographic Journey,* Hastings House, 1948; *Jamaica,* 1962; *Islands of the Caribbean: A Pictorial Book of Color Photographs,* 1963; *Nassau in den Bahamas* (captions to pictures in English, French, and German), 1963; *Badgastein, the Springs of Eternal Youth,* 1964; *Austria,* 1965; *The Virgin Islands, St. Thomas, St. Croix, St. John: The Islands where Angels Pause to Rest,* 1965; *The California Missions,* 1966; *Costa del Sol,* 1966; *San Francisco,* 1966; *Trinidad and Tobago,* 1966; *Virginia,* 1966; *Curacao,* 1967; *Romantic Danube,* 1967; *Arizona,* 1967; *Colorado,* 1967; *Barbados,* 1967; *Los Angeles,* 1967; *Martinique,* 1967; *New Orleans,* 1967; *Wachau,* 1967; *Guadeloupe,* 1967; *Cape Cod,* 1967; *Yosemite,* 1967; *Puerto Rico,* 1967; *Aruba,* 1968; *New York City,* 1968; *Palm Beach,* 1968; *Hawaii,* 1968; *New Jersey,* 1968; *Georgia,* 1968; *Freeport-Lucaya: Grand Bahama Island,* 1969.

Flowers of the Caribbean, Argos, 1970; *Flowers of Florida,* Argos, 1970; *Bermuda in Full Color,* Doubleday, 1970; *Islands of the Bahamas in Full Color,* Doubleday, 1971, revised edition published as *The Bahama Islands in Full Color,* 1974; *The Caribbean Islands in Full Color,* Doubleday, 1972; *USA in Full Color,* Meriani, 1972; *Flowers of Bermuda,* Hastings House, 1972; *Flowers of the Bahamas,* Argos, 1972; *Beneath the Seas of the West Indies,* Hastings House, 1973; *Tropical Flowers,* Doubleday, 1973; *Eleuthera, Puerto Rico, Curacao, St. Maarten, Aruba,* Argos, 1973; *In the Coral Reefs of the Caribbean, Bahamas, Florida and Bermuda,* Doubleday, 1974; *Antigua, West Indies,* Argos, 1974; *The Netherlands Antilles,* Argos, 1974; *Islands of the Caribbean,* Hastings House, 1974.

* * *

HANNEMAN, Audre (Louise) 1926-

PERSONAL: Born July 27, 1926, in Council Bluffs, Iowa; daughter of Homer William (a railway clerk) and Nettie (Smith) Hanneman. *Education:* Attended evening courses at New School for Social Research and New York Univer-

sity, 1959-60. *Politics:* Democrat. *Religion:* Protestant. *Home:* 2 Horatio St., New York, N.Y. 10014. *Office:* McGraw-Hill Book Co., 1221 Avenue of the Americas, New York, N.Y. 10020.

CAREER: Heritage Press, New York City, clerical work, 1959; Corner Book Shop, New York City, assistant to owner, 1960-61; secretary and manuscript typist for an author, New York City, 1961-62; McGraw-Hill, Inc., New York City, indexer for Sweet's Industrial Catalog Services, 1963-69, index editor for Book Co., 1969—. *Member:* American Society of Indexers, Bibliographical Society of America, National Association for the Advancement of Colored People (secretary of Greenwich Village/Chelsea branch, 1959-60, 1962-63), Greenwich Village Brotherhood Congress (secretary, 1960-61).

WRITINGS: (Compiler) *Ernest Hemingway: A Comprehensive Bibliography,* Princeton University Press, 1967, *Supplement,* 1975.

WORK IN PROGRESS: Two novels.

SIDELIGHTS: Audre Hanneman's comprehensive bibliography of Hemingway includes "just about everything of the author that ever appeared in print," according to a reviewer in the *Virginia Quarterly Review.* This includes high school publications as well as later journalism. Also included are all library holdings of Hemingway manuscripts and letters, and a second section with all secondary material about the author. With an index and annotations, this is called "the major contribution to Hemingway scholarship in recent years."

BIOGRAPHICAL/CRITICAL SOURCES: Virginia Quarterly Review, summer, 1968.

* * *

HANRIEDER, Wolfram F. 1931-

PERSONAL: Born May 9, 1931, in Munich, Germany; son of Josef and Barbara (Laubmeier) Hanrieder. *Education:* University of Chicago, B.A., 1958, M.A., 1959; University of California, Berkeley, Ph.D., 1963. *Home:* 4812 Winding Way, Santa Barbara, Calif. 93111.

CAREER: Princeton University, Princeton, N.J., research associate at Center of International Studies, 1963-64, assistant professor, 1964-67; University of California, Santa Barbara, associate professor, 1967-71, professor of political science, 1971—.

WRITINGS: West German Foreign Policy, 1949-1963: International Pressure and Domestic Response, Stanford University Press, 1967; (editor with R. A. Falk) *International Law and Organization,* Lippincott, 1968; *The Stable Crisis: Two Decades of German Foreign Policy,* Harper, 1970; (editor and contributor) *Comparative Foreign Policy: Theoretical Essays,* McKay, 1971; (editor and contributor) *The United States and Western Europe: Political, Economic and Strategic Perspectives,* Winthrop Publishing, 1974.

WORK IN PROGRESS: A book on comparative foreign policy.

* * *

HANSEN, Klaus J(uergen) 1931-

PERSONAL: Born November 29, 1931, in Kiel, Germany; became U.S. citizen; son of H. G. and M. C. (Paetau) Hansen; married Joan Patricia Dunn (an instructor in English), December 28, 1959; children: Eric, Christian, Evan,

Britt. *Education:* Brigham Young University, B.A., 1957, M.A., 1959; Harvard University, Diploma of Archival and Historical Institute, 1958; Wayne State University, Ph.D., 1963. *Politics:* Democrat. *Religion:* Church of Jesus Christ of Latter-Day Saints (Mormon). *Home:* 422 Albert St., Kingston, Ontario, Canada. *Office:* Department of History, Queen's University, Kingston, Ontario, Canada.

CAREER: Eastern Michigan University, Ypsilanti, instructor in history, 1963; Ohio State University, Columbus, instructor in history, 1963-65; Utah State University, Logan, assistant professor of history, 1965-68; Queen's University, Kingston, Ontario, associate professor, 1968-76, professor of history, 1976—. Research fellow, Yale University, 1974-75. Canada Council Fellow, 1974-75. *Member:* American Historical Association, American Studies Association, Organization of American Historians, American Civil Liberties Union (member of Columbus board of directors, 1964-65), Western History Association, Utah State Historical Society. *Awards, honors:* Award of Merit, American Association For State and Local History, 1968, for *Quest For Empire;* Mormon History Association award, 1968, for *Quest For Empire.*

WRITINGS: Quest for Empire: The Political Kingdom of God in Mormon History, Michigan State University Press, 1967, revised edition, University of Nebraska Press, 1974; (editorial consultant) *The American Heritage Dictionary,* American Heritage, 1969; *Mormonism and American Culture,* University of Chicago Press, 1976. Contributor to historical journals.

WORK IN PROGRESS: Millennialism in American Thought; Romanticism in American Thought and Culture; Sex, Death and Race in Nineteenth-Century America: The Case of the Mormons.

AVOCATIONAL INTEREST: Piano, painting, sailing.

* * *

HANSON, Anne Coffin 1921-

PERSONAL: Born December 12, 1921, in Kinston, N.C.; daughter of Francis Joseph (a clergyman) and Annie (Coffin) Coffin; married Warfield Garson, June 6, 1942; married second husband, Bernard Alan Hanson (a professor), June 27, 1962; children: (first marriage) James Warfield, Robert Coffin, Ann Blaine. *Education:* University of Southern California, B.F.A., 1943; University of North Carolina, M.A.C.A., 1951; Bryn Mawr College, Ph.D., 1962. *Home:* 28 Lincoln St., New Haven, Conn. 06511. *Office:* Department of History of Art, Yale University, New Haven, Conn. 06520.

CAREER: Wagner College, Staten Island, N.Y., lecturer, 1949-50; Miss Fine's School, Princeton, N.J., art teacher, 1952-55; University of Buffalo (now State University of New York at Buffalo), Buffalo, N.Y., instructor in art, 1955-58; Swarthmore College, Swarthmore, Pa., assistant professor of art, 1963-64; Bryn Mawr College, Bryn Mawr, Pa., assistant professor of art, 1964-68; Museum of Modern Art, New York, N.Y., director of International Study Center, 1968-70; Yale University, New Haven, Conn., professor of art, 1970—, chairman, Department of History of Art, 1974—. *Member:* College Art Association of America (president, 1972-74). *Awards, honors:* American Council of Learned Societies grant, summer, 1963; National Endowment for the Humanities fellowship, 1967-68.

WRITINGS: Jacope della Quercia's Fonte Gaia, Clarendon Press, 1965; *Edouard Manet: 1832-1886,* Philadel-phia Museum of Art, 1966; *Manet and the Modern Tradition,* Yale University Press, 1976. Contributor of articles on Manet to art publications.

* * *

HANSON, Anthony Tyrrell 1916-

PERSONAL: Born November 24, 1916, in London, England; son of Philip Herbert (a civil servant) and Deena (Tyrrell) Hanson; married Miriam Joselin, September 25, 1945; children: Philip, Andrew. *Education:* Attended Cheltenham College; Trinity College, University of Dublin, B.D., 1942, D.D., 1953. *Home:* 197 Victoria Ave., Hull, Humberside, England. *Office:* Department of Theology, University of Hull, Hull, Humberside, England.

CAREER: Clergyman of Anglican Church. Curate in County Down, Ireland, 1941-43; Student Christian Movement, London, England, secretary, 1943-46; Andhra United Theological College, Dornakal, Andhra Pradesh, South India, tutor, 1947-55; United Theological College, Bangalore, South India, tutor, 1955-59; St. Anne's Cathedral, Belfast, Northern Ireland, canon theologian, 1959-62; University of Hull, Hull, England, professor of theology, 1963—. Helped to organize interdenominational theology department (Roman Catholic, Reformed, Anglican) at Lesotho, South Africa; also helped to obtain affiliation of Irish School of Ecumenics, Dublin, to the University of Hull.

WRITINGS: (With R. H. Preston) *Revelation of St. John the Divine,* S.C.M. Press, 1949; (with wife, Miriam Hanson) *The Book of Job,* S.C.M. Press, 1953, revised edition, 1970; *The Wrath of the Lamb,* S.P.C.K., 1957; *The Pioneer Ministry,* S.C.M. Press, 1961; *The Church of the Servant,* S.C.M. Press, 1962; *St. Paul's Understanding of Jesus,* University of Hull Press, 1963; *Beyond Anglicanism,* Longman & Todd, 1965; *Jesus Christ in the Old Testament,* S.P.C.K., 1965; (editor) *The Pastoral Letters,* Cambridge University Press, 1966; (editor) *Vindications,* S.C.M. Press, 1966; *Studies in the Pastoral Epistles,* S.P.C.K., 1968.

(Editor) *Teilhard Reassessed,* Longman & Todd, 1970; *Studies in Paul's Technique and Theology,* Eerdmans, 1974; *Grace and Truth,* S.P.C.K., 1975; *Church, Sacraments, and Ministry,* Mowbrays, 1975.

WORK IN PROGRESS: Further study of Paul's writing against Rabbinic background.

* * *

HANSON, Howard Gordon 1931-

PERSONAL: Born December 29, 1931, in Colorado, Tex.; daughter of Alexander Barraud (an Episcopal minister) and Howard (Gordon) Hanson. *Education:* South Georgia College, student, 1948-50; Vanderbilt University, B.A., 1952, M.A., 1953, Ph.D., 1957. *Agent:* Esther Brown, 1199 Park Ave., New York, N.Y. 10028.

CAREER: Young Harris College, Young Harris, Ga., instructor in English literature and foreign languages, 1957-62; Campbell College, Buies Creek, N.C., associate professor of English literature, German, and world literature, 1962-65; poet. Reader in poetry, Ridgecrest Writers Conference, 1963. *Member:* American Association of University Women, American Association of University Professors, South Atlantic Modern Language Association, North Carolina Poetry Society, Phi Beta Kappa, Delta Phi Alpha. *Awards, honors:* Androcles Foundation grants in writing, 1965, 1967; *Arizona Quarterly* prize for poetry, 1968, 1969, 1974, 1975.

WRITINGS: Ageless Maze: Poems, Robert Moore Allen, 1963; *Future Coin or Climber, and Other Poems,* Blair, 1967. Poetry anthologized in four North Carolina Poetry Society collections, 1965, 1966, and in *Award Winning Poems,* Rochester Festival of Religious Arts (Rochester, N.Y.), 1967. Contributor of poetry to *Vagabond, Arizona Quarterly, New Mexico Quarterly, Literary Review,* and other periodicals.

WORK IN PROGRESS: The Western Spirit, a reinterpretation of English literary history; a novel; *Against Dark Angles,* a volume of poetry; short stories; *Collision Course,* a juvenile science fiction novel.

SIDELIGHTS: Howard Hanson speaks French and Spanish in addition to German. *Avocational interests:* Music and sculpture.

BIOGRAPHICAL/CRITICAL SOURCES: A Time for Poetry: An Anthology of the North Carolina Poetry Society, Blair, 1966.

*   *   *

HANSON, R(ichard) P(atrick) C(rosland)   1916-

PERSONAL; Born November 24, 1916, in London, England; son of Sir Philip (a civil servant) and Lady (maiden name, Tyrrell) Hanson; married Mary Dorothy Powell, August 29, 1950; children: Catherine Mary, Daniel Alexander, Monica Brigid, Simon John. *Education:* Trinity College, Dublin, B.A. in classics and in ancient history (both degrees with first class honors), 1938, B.D., 1941, D.D., 1950, M.A., 1962. *Home:* 24 Styal Rd., Wilmslow, Cheshire SK9 4AG, England. *Office:* Faculty of Theology, University of Manchester, Manchester M13 9PL, England.

CAREER: Clergyman of Church of Ireland, 1941—; pastoral work as priest in Dublin and County Down, Ireland, 1941-45; Queen's College, Birmingham, England, vice-principal, 1945-50; St. John's, Shuttleworth, Bury, England, vicar, 1950-52; University of Nottingham, Nottinghamshire, England, lecturer, 1952-58; senior lecturer, 1958-61, reader in theology, 1961-62; University of Durham, Durham, England, Lightfoot Professor of Divinity, 1962-64; University of Nottingham, professor of Christian theology and head of department, 1964-70; bishop of Clogher (Ireland), 1970-73; University of Manchester, Manchester, England, professor of historical and contemporary theology, 1973—. Honorary canon of Southwell Cathedral, 1965—, and Coventry Cathedral, 1967—; assistant bishop of Manchester, 1973—. Chairman of Council of Christians and Jews (Manchester area), 1975—. *Member:* Royal Irish Academy, Society for the Study of Theology, Association of Teachers of Theology in British Universities, Association of University Teachers, Society of Authors.

WRITINGS—All published by S.C.M. Press, except as noted: (With R. H. Fuller) *The Church of Rome: A Dissuasive,* 1948; *II Corinthians,* 1954; *The Summons to Unity,* Edinburgh House Press, 1954; *Origen's Doctrine of Tradition,* S.P.C.K., 1954; *Allegory and Event,* 1959; *God: Creator, Saviour, Spirit,* 1960; *Tradition in the Early Church,* 1962; (translator and abridger) *Justin Martyr's Dialogue with Trypho,* World Christian Books, 1963; *Clarendon Commentary on Acts,* Oxford University Press, 1965, revised edition published as *The Acts: A New Clarendon Commentary,* 1967; (editor) *Difficulties for Christian Belief,* Macmillan (London), 1967; (editor with M. W. Barley) *Christianity in Britain 300-700,* Leicester University Press, 1968; *Saint Patrick: His Origins and Career,* Oxford University Press, 1968; (editor) *The Pelican Guide to Modern Theology,* two volumes, Penguin, 1969-70; *The Attractiveness of God,* S.P.C.K., 1973; *Mystery and Imagination: Reflections on Christianity,* S.P.C.K., 1976.

Contributor: Alfred Robert C. Leaney, editor, *A Guide to the Scrolls,* S.C.M. Press, 1958; N. Ehrenstrom and W. G. Muelder, editors, *Institutionalism and Church Unity,* Association Press, 1963; W. Browning, editor, *The Anglican Synthesis,* Derby, 1964; R. J. W. Bevan, *The Christian Way Explained,* Mowbray, 1964; A. T. Hanson, editor, *Vindications,* S.C.M. Press, 1966; *Lambeth Conference 1968: Preparatory Essays,* S.P.C.K., 1968; *Eucharistic Agreement,* S.P.C.K., 1975; *Theology and Change* (memorial to Alan Richardson), S.C.M. Press, 1975. Contributor to *Studia Patristica,* Volumes III, XII, and XIII, 1961, 1976, *The Cambridge History of the Bible,* 1970, 1975. and *Latin Script and Letters* (festschrift to Ludwig Bieler), 1976. Contributor to *Modern Churchman, Vigiliae Christianae, Expository Times, Times Literary Supplement, London Times, Irish Theological Quarterly, Zeitschrift fuer Kirchengeschichte,* and others theology and denominational journals.

WORK IN PROGRESS: An edition of the works of St. Patrick in the original Latin, with an introduction and commentary to be translated into French, for the series, "Sources Chretiennes."

SIDELIGHTS: Hanson reads ancient Hebrew, ancient Greek, Latin, French, German, and Italian; he speaks a little French.

*   *   *

HARBESON, Gladys Evans

PERSONAL: Born in Princeton, Ill.; daughter of Ernest (a Congregational minister) and Clara (Palmer) Evans; married Robert W. Harbeson (a university professor), August 27, 1936; children: John Willis. *Education:* Grinnell College, A.B., 1921; University of Iowa, A.M., 1926; University of Michigan, graduate study, 1931-32. *Politics:* Independent. *Religion:* Congregationalist. *Home:* 808 West William St., Champaign, Ill. 61820.

CAREER: Teacher of high school English and social sciences in Audubon, Iowa, 1921-23, in Ames, Iowa, 1923-25; State College of Iowa (now University of Northern Iowa), Cedar Falls, associate professor of teacher training, 1926-36; Rutgers University, New Brunswick, N.J., supervisor of practice teaching in College of Education, 1937-38. Freelance writer. *Member:* American Association of University Women (president, Champaign-Urbana branch, 1965-67), Delta Gamma.

WRITINGS: Choice and Challenge for the American Woman, Schenkman, 1968, 2nd edition, 1972. Contributor to *AAUW Journal* (American Association of University Women), and to *Journal of the Royal Historical Society of Victoria* (Australia).

WORK IN PROGRESS: Continuing research on subjects of women's changing life patterns and higher education programs for women.

*   *   *

HARBIN, Calvin E(dward)   1916-

PERSONAL: Born March 26, 1916, in Puxico, Mo.; son of Samuel Wesley and Ada Maria (Shelton) Harbin; married Dorothy Comoh, June 26, 1947; children: Maria Catherine, Ruth Ella, Charles Edward. *Education:* Southeast Missouri State College, B.S., 1949; George Peabody College for

Teachers, M.A., 1949; University of Missouri, Ed.D., 1952. *Politics:* Republican, *Religion:* Presbyterian. *Home:* 303 West 19th St., Hays, Kan. 67601. *Office:* Department of Education, Fort Hays Kansas State College, Hays, Kan. 67601.

CAREER: Marks, Henderson and Mahon, Bakersfield, Calif., law clerk, 1937-41; Fort Hays Kansas State College, Hays, professor of education, 1954—, chairman of Division of Education and Psychology, 1954—. *Military service:* U.S. Army, 1941-46. U.S. Army Reserve, 1946-74; retired as colonel. *Member:* National Education Association, History of Education Society, Kansas Educators Club, Kansas State Teachers Association, Kansas Association of School Administrators, Phi Kappa Phi, Pi Gamma Mu, Phi Delta Kappa, Faculty Men's Club.

WRITINGS: Teaching Power, Philosophical Library, 1967. Composer of published hymns including: "We Who Would Worship," "Open the Door, Lord," "In a Moment of Love." Contributor of articles and poetry to magazines.

* * *

HARDING, Thomas G(rayson) 1937-

PERSONAL: Born May 20, 1937, in Detroit, Mich.; son of Leonard Joseph (a business executive) and Helen (Gardner) Harding; married Patricia Ann Norman, August 16, 1958; children: Evan Grayson, Sara Ann. *Education:* University of Michigan, A.B., 1958, M.A., 1960, Ph.D., 1965; University of Bergen, postdoctoral study, 1965-66. *Home:* 2014 Garden St., Santa Barbara, Calif. *Office:* Department of Anthropology, University of California, Santa Barbara, Calif. 93106.

CAREER: University of California, Santa Barbara, instructor in anthropology, 1961-63; University of Michigan, Ann Arbor, research associate, 1963-64, visiting assistant professor, 1965; University of California, Santa Barbara, assistant professor, 1966-68, associate professor, 1968-71, professor of anthropology, 1971—, chairman of department, 1970-75. *Awards, honors:* National Science Foundation postdoctoral fellow in Norway, 1965-66.

WRITINGS: (With David Kaplan, Marshall D. Sahlins, and Elman R. Service) *Evolution and Culture,* University of Michigan Press, 1960; (contributor) D. G. Bettison, C. A. Hughes, and P. W. van der Veur, editors, *The Papua-New Guinea Elections 1964,* Australian National University Press, 1965; *Voyagers of the Vitiaz Strait,* University of Washington Press, 1967; (editor and author of introduction with Ben J. Wallace) *Cultures of the Pacific: Selected Readings,* Free Press, 1970; (contributor) A. L. Epstein, R. S. Parker, and M. Reay, editors, *The Politics of Dependence: New Guinea 1968,* Australian National University Press, 1971; (contributor) H. I. Hogbin, editor, *Anthropology in Papua and New Guinea,* Melbourne University Press, 1973. Contributor to *Encyclopaedia of Papua and New Guinea,* and to professional journals.

* * *

HARDY, Evelyn 1902-

PERSONAL: Born October, 1902, in Philadelphia, Pa.; daughter of Thornton (on *Saturday Evening Post* staff) and Beulah Ashley (a painter; maiden name, Greenough) Hardy. *Education:* Smith College, B.A., 1924; University of London, art student. *Home:* Bramshott Court, West Wing, Liphook, Hampshire, England. *Agent:* Peter Janson-Smith Ltd., 31 Newington Green, Islington, London N16 9PU, England.

CAREER: Employed at U.S. Consulate General, London, England, 1925-31; broadcaster in England on literary, artistic, and country subjects; author. Honorary adviser on Thomas Hardy manuscripts, Dorchester County Museum; discoverer of some unpublished poems by Thomas Hardy and his "Plots for Short Stories." *Awards, honors:* Leverhulme research grant, 1955-57, for work on Thomas Hardy papers; grant from Society of Authors, 1967, for work on *The Dynasts.*

WRITINGS: Donne: A Spirit in Conflict, Constable, 1942, reprinted, Folcroft, 1969; *The Conjured Spirit, Swift: A Study in the Relationship of Swift, Stella, and Vanessa,* Hogarth, 1949, reprinted, Greenwood Press, 1973; (editor, and author of introduction) *Swift: Selected Prose,* Falcon Press, 1950; *Summer in Another World,* Gollancz, 1950; *Thomas Hardy: A Critical Biography,* St. Martin's, 1954; (editor, and author of notes) Thomas Hardy, *Notebooks, and Some Letters from Julia Augusta Martin,* St. Martin's, 1955; (editor and author of notes with Robert Gittings) *Some Recollections by Emma Hardy,* Oxford University Press, 1961; *Survivors of the Armada,* Constable, 1966; *Midnight Festival* (poems), Dufour, 1968; (editor with F. B. Pinion) *One Rare Fair Woman: Thomas Hardy's Letters to Florence Henniker, 1893-1922,* University of Miami Press, 1972.

Adviser to William Emrys Williams on his Penguin edition of *Selected Poems of Thomas Hardy;* analytical indexer for Harold Williams' two-volume edition of Swift's *Journal to Stella.* Contributor of articles to *New Stories, London Magazine, History Today, Listener, Guardian, Country Life, English, Times Literary Supplement,* and other periodicals and newspapers; contributor of poems to literary journals.

WORK IN PROGRESS: An autobiographical novel; a new biography; a volume of essays on Hardy; *Tristan in Cornwall,* a serious work of archeological and literary interest.

SIDELIGHTS: Evelyn Hardy's first poems were published when she was thirteen. Both her grandfathers were writers, one an Ambassador to Spain and Greece, and the other president of University of Massachusetts. *Thomas Hardy: A Critical Biography* was commissioned by Leonard Woolf, the husband of Virginia Woolf. *Avocational interests:* Painting, sculpture, architecture, history, music, the English countryside.

* * *

HARE, John 1935-

PERSONAL: Born March 21, 1935, in Hastings, Sussex, England; son of Jack Charles (a motor mechanic) and Beatrice (Watford) Hare; married Diana Joy Staton, May 9, 1959; children: Ian Paul, Stephen Keith. *Education:* Oxford University, B.A., 1959, M.A., 1960; University of Reading, Diploma in Education, 1960. *Politics:* New Democratic Party. *Religion:* Agnostic. *Home:* 48 Slattery Rd., St. John's, Newfoundland, Canada. *Office:* Memorial University, St. John's, Newfoundland, Canada.

CAREER: Ecole Normale, Gueret, Creuse, France, assistant in English, 1957-58; Remo Secondary School, Sagamu, West Nigeria, schoolmaster, 1960-62; Memorial University of Newfoundland, St. John's, assistant professor, 1962-67; Sevenoaks School, Sevenoaks, England, schoolmaster, 1967-72; Memorial University of Newfoundland, associate professor, 1972—.

WRITINGS: The Literature of France: A Short Introduction, Macmillan (Canada), 1967. Also contributor of articles to language journals.

WORK IN PROGRESS: A literary study of Du Bellay's *Songe* sequence; translation of Delvaille's *Histoire de l'- Idee du Progres.*

* * *

HARLAN, Louis R(udolph)   1922-

PERSONAL: Born July 13, 1922, in West Point, Miss.; son of Allen Dorset (an agricultural economist) and Isabel (Knaffl) Harlan; married Sadie Morton (a research assistant), September 6, 1947; children: Louis, Benjamin W. *Education:* Emory University, B.A., 1943; Vanderbilt University, M.A., 1948; Johns Hopkins University, Ph.D., 1955. *Home:* 6924 Pureway, Hyattsville, Md. 20782.

CAREER: East Texas State University, Commerce, 1950-59, began as instructor, associate professor of history, 1955-59; University of Cincinnati, Cincinnati, Ohio, 1959-66, began as associate professor, became professor of history; University of Maryland, College Park, professor of history, 1966—. *Military service:* U.S. Navy, 1943-46; became lieutenant junior grade. *Member:* American Historical Association, Organization of American Historians, Association for the Study of Negro Life and History (member of executive council, 1968—), American Association of University Professors, American Civil Liberties Union, Southern Historical Association, Phi Beta Kappa. *Awards, honors:* American Philosophical Society grants-in-aid, summers, 1961-64; American Council of Learned Societies fellowship, 1963; Academic Freedom Award, University of Cincinnati chapter of American Association of University Professors, 1964; Bancroft Prize in American History, 1972, for *Booker T. Washington: The Making of a Black Leader;* Guggenheim fellowship, 1974.

WRITINGS: Separate and Unequal: Public School Campaigns and Racism in the Southern Seaboard States, 1901-1915, University of North Carolina Press, 1958; *Negro in American History* (pamphlet), American Historical Association, 1965; *Booker T. Washington: The Making of a Black Leader, 1856-1901,* Oxford University Press, 1972. General editor of *Booker T. Washington Papers,* four volumes, University of Illinois Press, 1972—. Articles on Black history included in various anthologies. Contributor to professional journals.

* * *

HARMON, A(llen) J(ackson)   1926-

PERSONAL: Born June 1, 1926, in Connellsville, Pa.; son of E. R. and Edith (Colborn) Harmon. *Education:* Cornell University, B.Arch., 1950. *Residence:* Southampton, N.Y.

CAREER: Employed by Twentieth Century-Fox Film Corp., 1949-54, and Loews Inc., 1954-57; Harrison & Abramovitz, Architects, New York City, architect and designer, 1958-59; Holt, Rinehart & Winston, Inc., New York City, editor and writer on architecture, 1959-64; private practice in architecture, 1964—. *Member:* American Institute of Architects.

WRITINGS: The Guide to Home Remodeling, Holt, 1967, revised edition, Grosset, 1972; *Remodeling,* Grosset, 1975; *Porches and Terraces,* Grosset, 1975; *Closets and Storage Areas,* Grosset, 1976; *Kitchens,* Grosset, 1976; *Recreation Rooms,* Grosset, 1976.

WORK IN PROGRESS: Four books.

SIDELIGHTS: Harmon has lived and worked in the Orient and South America. *Avocational interests:* Painting, sculpture, and travel.

* * *

HARMON, James Judson   1933-
(Jim Harmon)

PERSONAL: Born April 21, 1933, in Mount Carmel, Ill.; son of John Russell and Valeria Irene (Odom) Harmon. *Education:* Attended Los Angeles City College, one year. *Politics:* Democrat. *Religion:* None. *Home:* (Winter) 1255 Seward, Hollywood, Calif.; (summer) 427 East Eighth, Mount Carmel, Ill.

CAREER: Free-lance writer. Radio, television, and motion picture performer; consultant to National Broadcasting Co., Canadian Broadcasting Corp., Hollywood Museum on Broadcasting. *Member:* Science Fiction Writers of America.

WRITINGS—Under name Jim Harmon; all novels, except as noted: *Vixen Hollow,* Art Enterprises, 1961; *Celluloid Scandal,* Art Enterprises, 1961; *Twist Session,* France, 1962; *Silent Siren,* France, 1962; *Passion Strip,* France, 1963; *Sex Burns Like Fire,* P.E.C. Publications, 1964; *The Great Radio Heroes* (nonfiction), Doubleday, 1967; *The Great Radio Comedians,* Doubleday, 1970; (with D. F. Glut) *The Great Movie Serials,* Doubleday, 1972; *Jim Harmons Nostalgia Catalogue,* J. P. Tarcher, 1973; (with Glut) *The Great Television Heroes,* Doubleday, 1975.

Author with Ron Haydock of feature film, "The Lemon Grove Kids," 1967; writer-producer-narrator of radio series, "Radio Rides Again," 1964, and "Pop Art Review," 1965; writer-producer of radio drama series, "Curley Bradley." Contributor to science fiction magazines, with stories anthologized in *Fourth Galaxy Reader,* Doubleday, 1959, *Rare Science Fiction,* Belmont Books, 1963, and *Tenth Galaxy Reader,* Doubleday, 1967. Co-editor, *Fantastic Monsters of the Films* (magazine); editor, *Monsters of the Movies* (magazine), 1974-75; editor of newspapers published for Congress of Racial Equality, Los Angeles, 1964.

SIDELIGHTS: A reviewer for the *New York Times Book Review* says of Jim Harmon's *The Great Radio Heroes:* "If you owe some of the magic of your childhood to radio's halcyon era, Jim Harmon's unabashedly nostalgic scrapbook of stars and scripts, 'cereals' and 'soaps,' is a grand way to tune in and drop out for a few pleasurable hours back in the golden, simpler world of yesteryear."

BIOGRAPHICAL/CRITICAL SOURCES: New York Times Book Review, October 22, 1967.

* * *

HARMON, Lyn S.   1930-

PERSONAL: Born May 2, 1930, in New York, N.Y.; daughter of Leo and Lillian (Guenzberg) Spielberger; married Robert Benjamin Harmon (a broker on the Commodity Exchange), August 26, 1951; children: Robert, Jr., Nicholas, Alexander Lee. *Education:* New York University, B.A., 1952. *Religion:* Unitarian Universalist. *Home:* 24 Helena Ave., Larchmont, N.Y. *Agent:* McIntosh & Otis, Inc., 475 Fifth Ave., New York, N.Y. 10017.

CAREER: Town and Country, New York City, editorial assistant, 1952-53; writer. United Nations Children's Fund

(UNICEF), volunteer in Public Information Division, New York City, 1950-52. *Member:* Authors Guild, Amateur Astronomers Association.

WRITINGS: Clyde's Clam Farm, Lippincott, 1966; *Flight to Jewell Island,* Lippincott, 1967.

WORK IN PROGRESS: A novel.

SIDELIGHTS: Mrs. Harmon spent a summer in Italy under the experiment in "International Living" program, 1950, and has since traveled in Asia, North Africa, Europe, the South Pacific Islands, and most of the West Indies.

*　　*　　*

HARMON, Maurice 1930-

PERSONAL: Born June 21, 1930, in Dublin, Ireland; son of Patrick and Mary (Owens) Harmon; married Maura Lynch, October 17, 1951; children: Diarmaid, Maura. *Education:* University College, Dublin, B.A., 1951, H.D.E., 1953, M.A., 1955, Ph.D., 1961; Harvard University, A.M., 1957. *Home:* 20 Sycamore Rd., Mount Merrion, Dublin, Ireland. *Office:* University College, Dublin 2, Ireland.

CAREER: Harvard University, Cambridge, Mass., teaching fellow, 1955-57; Lewis and Clark College, Portland, Ore., assistant professor of English and Anglo-Irish literature, 1958-60; University of Notre Dame, Notre Dame, Ind., assistant professor, 1961-64; University College, National University of Ireland, Dublin, lecturer in English and Anglo-Irish literature, 1964—. University of Massachusetts, visiting professor, 1967. Swift Tercentenary Committee, executive secretary, 1967. Executive secretary, J. M. Synge Centenary Committee, 1971. *Member:* International Association for the Study of Anglo-Irish Literature, American Committee for Irish Studies (Irish representative).

WRITINGS: Sean O'Faolain: A Critical Introduction, University of Notre Dame Press, 1967; *Modern Irish Literature, 1800-1967,* Dolmen Press, 1967; (editor) *Fenians and Fenianism: Centenary Essays,* Scepter Publishers, 1968, University of Washington Press, 1970; *The Celtic Master,* Dolmen Press, 1969, Dufour, 1970; *J. M. Synge Centenary Papers, 1971,* Humanities, 1972; (editor) William Shakespeare, *Coriolanus,* Education Co. of Ireland, 1972; *The Poetry of Thomas Kinsella,* Wolfhound Press, 1974, Humanities, 1975. Also editor of Shakespeare's *King Lear, King Richard II,* and *Romeo and Juliet.* Contributor to *University of Massachusetts Review, Northwest Review,* and other journals. Editor, *Irish University Review.*

*　　*　　*

HARPER, Howard M., Jr. 1930-

PERSONAL: Born October 2, 1930, in Wikinsburg, Pa.; son of Howard M. (a teacher and engineer) and Marjorie (Campbell) Harper; married Jeanne Castner; children: David, Richard, Andrew. *Education:* State Teachers College at Slippery Rock (now Slippery Rock State College), B.S., 1952; Pennsylvania State University, M.A., 1957, Ph.D., 1964. *Home:* 718 Caswell Rd., Chapel Hill, N.C. 27514. *Office:* Department of English, University of North Carolina, Chapel Hill, N.C. 27514.

CAREER: Pennsylvania State University, University Park, instructor in English, 1958-59; HRB-Singer, Inc. (electronics research and development), State College, Pa., proposal writer, 1959-64; University of North Carolina, Chapel Hill, assistant professor, 1964-68, associate professor of English, 1968—. Consultant on proposal writing

for various companies. *Military service:* U.S. Navy, 1952-55; became lieutenant junior grade; U.S. Navy Reserves, 1955—, currently commander.

WRITINGS: Desperate Faith: A Study of Bellow, Salinger, Mailer, Baldwin and Updike, University of North Carolina Press, 1967; (editor with Charles Edge) *The Classic British Novel,* University of Georgia Press, 1972. Contributor of reviews to *Washington Star.*

WORK IN PROGRESS: Research on Faulkner and Beckett.†

*　　*　　*

HARRE, John 1931-

PERSONAL: Surname is pronounced *Hare*-ay; born December 31, 1931, in New Zealand; son of Horace Romano (a schoolteacher) and Susan (Jack) Harre; married Charmian Yock, July 6, 1957; children: Nicole, Christopher, Laila, Ivan. *Education:* University of Auckland, B.A., 1959; London School of Economics and Political Science, Ph.D., 1963. *Politics:* Liberal. *Office:* Hawke's Bay Community College, Taradale, New Zealand.

CAREER: Rangitoto College, Auckland, New Zealand, assistant master, 1956-57; University of London, London School of Economics and Political Science, London, England, assistant lecturer, 1962-63; University of Otago, Dunedin, New Zealand, senior lecturer in social anthropology, 1963-68; University of the South Pacific, Suva, Fiji, reader in sociology and professor of social anthropology, 1969-74; Hawke's Bay Community College, Taradale, New Zealand, director, 1975—. Regular broadcaster on New Zealand Broadcasting Crop. television. *Member:* Polynesian Society (council member, 1964-72), Association of Social Anthropologists of the Commonwealth, Royal Society of New Zealand.

WRITINGS: Maori and Pakeha: A Study of Mixed Marriages in New Zealand, Pall Mall, 1966; (with William K. Jackson) *New Zealand,* Walker & Co., 1969; (editor) *Living in Town: Problems and Priorities in Urban Planning in the South Pacific,* South Pacific Social Sciences Association, in cooperation with University of the South Pacific, 1973. Script writer for three documentary films produced by New Zealand Broadcasting Corp., "The Pitcairners," "Maori Urbanization," and "Maori Land." Contributor of articles to *Race, Landfall,* and *Journal of the Polynesian Society.*

*　　*　　*

HARRELL, Irene B(urk) 1927-
(Amos Amor, Mildred Waylan)

PERSONAL: Born March 10, 1927, in Montcalm County, Mich.; daughter of Howard Lofton (a builder) and Marguerite (Weatherby) Burk; married Allen Waylan Harrell (a District Court judge), June 22, 1952; children: Thomas Burk, Alice Elizabeth, James Britton, Susan Irene, Marguerite Owens, Maria Weatherby. *Education:* Ohio State University, B.A. (summa cum laude), 1948; University of North Carolina, B.S. in L.S., 1949; Famous Writers School, graduate, 1965. *Religion:* "Non-denominational." *Home:* 408 Pearson St., Wilson, N.C. 27893.

CAREER: Westerville Public Library, Westerville, Ohio, librarian, 1949-52; University of North Carolina, Chapel Hill, librarian in sociology, anthropology and city planning library, 1952-53; Halifax County Library, Halifax, N.C., director, 1953-54; Atlantic Christian College, Wilson,

N.C., staff of C. L. Hardy Library, 1958-64, began as cataloger, became assistant librarian, acting head librarian, and then librarian, before resignation in 1964; free-lance writer, 1964—. Editor and assignment writer, Logos International, 1970—. *Member:* Phi Beta Kappa.

WRITINGS—All published by Word Books, except as noted: *Prayerables: Meditations of a Homemaker*, 1967; *Good Marriages Grow*, 1968; (compiler) *God Ventures: True Accounts of God in the Lives of Men*, 1970; *Lo, I Am with You: Prayersteps to Faith*, Logos, 1970, published as *Miracles Through Prayer*, 1970; *Ordinary Days with an Extraordinary God: Prayerables II*, 1971; (with husband Allen W. Harrell) *The Opposite Sex*, 1972; (with Floyd Miles) *Black Tracks: A Junkie Turns to God and Kicks the Habit*, Logos, 1972; (with John Herbert and Lucille Walker) *God's Living Room*, Logos, 1972; *Security Blankets—Family Size*, 1973; *Muddy Sneakers and Other Family Hassles*, Abingdon, 1974; (with Harold Hill) *How to Live Like a King's Kid*, Logos, 1974; *The Windows of Heaven: Prayerables III*, 1975. Poems, articles, and stories have been published in numerous magazines including *Jack and Jill*, *Guideposts*, *Christian Life*, *Logos Journal*, and *Faith at Work*.

WORK IN PROGRESS: Three books on Bible centered meditations, *I Love You*, *Is Someone Sick?*, and *Thank You*; *Open My Eyes, Lord: Prayerables IV*; *How to Walk in the Spirit*; two books of poetry entitled, *A Sand Dollar and Other Impressions of Sea and Shore* and *NC Scene*, both for Logos.

* * *

HARRIGAN, Anthony (Hart) 1925-

PERSONAL: Born October 27, 1925, in New York, N.Y.; son of Anthony H. (a physician) and Elise (Hutson) Harrigan; married Elizabeth Ravenel, August 16, 1950; children: Anthony H. III, Elliot, Chardon, Mary. *Education:* Studied at Kenyon College, 1948, and University of Virginia, 1949-51. *Religion:* Episcopalian. *Home:* 54 Legare St., Charleston, S.C. 29401. *Office:* 918 Stahlman Building, Nashville, Tenn. 37201.

CAREER: Charleston News and Courier, Charleston, S.C., associate editor, 1955-70, covering foreign assignments at various times. Foreign Policy Research Institute of South Carolina, director, 1960-62; *Canadian Military Journal*, Ottawa, Ontario, U.S. correspondent, 1964-71; American Security Council, Chicago, Ill., secretary of national strategy committee, 1965-69; executive vice-president, U.S. Industrial Council, 1970—. Director, Center for Science and Technology, Boulder, Colo. Lecturer at National War College, and various colleges and military institutions in the United States and abroad. *Military service:* U.S. Marine Corps, 1943-45; received *Military Review* award of U.S. Army Command and General Staff College twice. *Awards, honors:* George Washington Medal of Freedoms Foundation, 1961; Relm Foundation grant for study of Canada, 1966.

WRITINGS: The Editor and the Republic, University of North Carolina Press, 1954; *Red Star Over Africa*, Nasionale Boekhandel Beperk, 1964; *Defense Against Total Attack*, Nasionale Boekhandel Beperk, 1965; *The New Republic*, J. L. Van Schaik, 1966; *One Against the Mob*, Crestwood, 1966; *A Guide to the War in Vietnam*, Panther, 1966; (co-author) *The Indian Ocean and the Threat to the West*, Stacey International, 1975. Also author of *American Perspectives*, 1972. Contributor to more than fifty U.S. and foreign periodicals. Former advisory editor, *Modern Age.*

WORK IN PROGRESS: A collection of essays.

SIDELIGHTS: Harrigan has covered overseas assignments in Vietnam, Cuba, Dominican Republic, Israel, Greece, Panama, Japan, South Africa, Rhodesia, Germany, Turkey, and other countries.

* * *

HARRIMAN, Margaret 1928-

PERSONAL: Born April 27, 1928, in Luton, Bedforshire, England; daughter of Oliver Kenneth (a hatter) and Olive (Gregg) Webb; married William Harriman, November 23, 1956 (divorced). *Education:* Monmouthshire College of Agriculture, Certificate in General Agriculture, 1946. *Home:* Claridge, Pietermaritzburg, Natal, South Africa. *Office address: Natal Witness*, P.O. Box 362, Pietermaritzburg, Natal, South Africa.

CAREER: National Health Service, London, England, medical secretary, 1952-57; Federal Government of Rhodesia and Nyasaland (now Malawi), Salisbury, civil servant, 1959-62; Rhokana Corp. (copper mine), Kitwe, Zambia, reporter, 1962-65; S. A. Philips Ltd. (electronics), Johannesburg, South Africa, editorial assistant and staff member of *Philips Focus*, 1967-68; *Natal Witness*, Pietermaritzburg, South Africa, sub-editor, 1972—.

WRITINGS: Bring Me My Bow, Gollancz, 1967.

SIDELIGHTS: Margaret Harriman has competed in Paralympics and Commonwealth Paraplegic Games in Rome, Perth, Tokyo, Tel Aviv, Heidelberg, and represented South Africa at World Archery Championships in Oslo, 1961 and Interlaken, 1975. She has traveled the Indian Ocean to the remote Chagos Archipelago and other islands by copra schooner. Paints.

* * *

HARRINGTON, Donald Szantho 1914-

PERSONAL: Born July 11, 1914, in Newton, Mass.; son of Charles Elliot Marshall (a druggist) and Leita (Hersey) Harrington; married Vilma Szantho (a minister), March 28, 1939, in Hungary; children: Ilonka Harrington Hancock, David. *Education:* Antioch College, student, 1932-35; University of Chicago, B.A., 1936; Meadville Theological School, B.D., 1938; University of Leyden, graduate study, 1938-39; Starr King School for Ministry, Berkeley, Calif., S.T.D., 1959. *Politics:* Liberal Party. *Home and office:* 10 Park Ave., New York, N.Y. 10016.

CAREER: Unitarian minister at churches in Hobart, Ind., 1936-38, Chicago and Beverly Hills, Ill., 1939-44; Community Church, New York City, junior colleague, 1944-49, senior minister, 1949—. New School for Social Research, New York City, instructor in human relations, 1966—. State chairman, Liberal Party of New York; past president, United World Federalists; co-chairman, American Committee on Africa; chairman of planning committee, American Association for the United Nations; chairman, Professional Household Workers of America. *Awards, honors:* Cruft traveling fellowship to Europe, 1938-39; D.D., Meadville Theological School, 1965.

WRITINGS: As We Remember Him, Beacon, 1965; *Religion in an Age of Science*, Beacon, 1965. Columnist, *Saturday Review.*

WORK IN PROGRESS: Several books on religion.

HARRIS, Clyde E., Jr.

PERSONAL: Born in Arkadelphia, Ark.; son of Clyde E. (a barber) and Manie P. (Honea) Harris; married Billie I. Bearden, November 13, 1952; children: Ralph P., James R., Paula S. *Education:* Ouachita Baptist College (now University), B.A., 1952; University of Arkansas, M.B.A., 1960, Ph.D., 1964. *Religion:* Methodist. *Home:* 240 Pendleton Dr., Athens, Ga. 30601. *Office:* College of Business Administration, University of Georgia, Athens, Ga. 30601.

CAREER: University of Georgia, College of Business Administration, Athens, 1962—, began as assistant professor, associate professor of marketing, 1966—. *Military service:* U.S. Army, 1952-56. U.S. Army Reserve, 1956—; current rank, major. *Member:* American Marketing Association, Ozark Economic Association, Southern Marketing Association, Sales and Marketing Executives (Atlanta), Phi Sigma Epsilon, Beta Gamma Sigma.

WRITINGS: (With Robert E. Tritt) *Sales Management Organization Game,* with player's manual and administrator's manual, Irwin, 1967, revised edition, Bureau of Business Research, University of Georgia, 1973; (with R. R. Still) *Cases in Marketing: Decisions, Policies, and Strategies,* with teacher's manual, Prentice-Hall, 1972. Contributor to *Southern Journal of Business, Journal of Marketing, Business Facts and Ideas,* and *Training and Development Journal.*

WORK IN PROGRESS: Research in salesman selection, sales coverage determination, and domestic and international marketing strategy.

* * *

HARRIS, F(rank) Brayton 1932-
(Kirkpatrick West)

PERSONAL: Born April 25, 1932, in Ann Arbor, Mich.; son of Walter Orville (a cost accountant) and E. Lucille (Atkinson) Harris; married Nancy Pendleton Shanks, September 7, 1963; children: Walter Kirkpatrick, Jennifer Shelton. *Education:* University of Illinois, B.A., 1953; graduate study at University of California, Los Angeles, 1957, and San Francisco State College (now University), 1958-60. *Religion:* Episcopalian. *Home:* 11312 Wedge Dr., Reston, Va. 22090.

CAREER: U.S. Navy, 1953-57; Troubadour Press (publishers), San Francisco, Calif., and New York, N.Y., managing partner, 1957-61; U.S. Navy, public relations specialist, 1961—, with present rank of captain, assigned as assistant chief of information, Washington, D.C. Crown & Anchor, Inc. (developers), Philadelphia, Pa., president, 1966—; Wellington Group Ltd. (public relations), New York, N.Y., associate, 1966—. *Member:* Armed Forces Writer's League (national director, Navy, 1964-66). *Awards, honors:* Silver Anvil Award, Public Relations Society of America, 1966; Blue Pencil Award for magazine layout, Federal Editors Association, 1966.

WRITINGS: The Age of the Battleship, 1890-1922, F. Watts, 1965; *Johann Gutenberg and the Invention of Printing,* F. Watts, 1972. One-act play, "Introduction," included in *Three San Francisco Playwrights,* Troubador Press, 1963. Author of 1966 official pamphlet on the future of the Negro in the U.S. Navy, and other Navy publications (some ghosted). Developed plot outlines for "Buz Sawyer" comic strip, 1965-68. Contributor of about one hundred articles to trade and military magazines. Former editor, *Law Enforcement Review, California Homeowner, Taluga News, Direction,* and *Navnews.*

WORK IN PROGRESS: Untitled history of Black Americans in maritime and naval service from colonial times to the present, for Bellwether Publishing.

SIDELIGHTS: Frank Harris intended to be a painter, but was sidetracked by father's dictum that he attend college before art school; he still paints occasionally, and has sold some of his work through galleries in New York and San Francisco. Harris speaks some Russian, Spanish, and German.

* * *

HARRIS, Robin S(utton) 1919-

PERSONAL: Born October 27, 1919, in Toronto, Canada; son of George Henry Ronalds (an engineer) and Lorna Craig (Gibbons) Harris; married Mary Patricia Gunn, June 22, 1946; children: Catherine A., David R., Mary M. *Education:* University of Toronto, B.A., 1941, M.A., 1947; University of Michigan, Ph.D., 1952. *Religion:* Anglican. *Home:* 228 Douglas Dr., Toronto, Ontario, Canada. *Office:* University of Toronto, Toronto, Ontario, Canada.

CAREER: Ridley College, St. Catharines, Ontario, schoolmaster, 1941, 1945-46; University of Western Ontario, London, Ontario, instructor in English, 1947-49; University of Toronto, Toronto, Ontario, 1952—, began as lecturer, became assistant professor, then associate professor of English, college principal, 1963-71, professor of higher education, 1964—. Member, UNESCO, Educational Planning Team, 1961. Member, Toronto Board of Education, 1959-63. *Military service:* Canadian Army, 1941-45; became captain.

WRITINGS—All published by University of Toronto Press: (With Robert L. McDougall) *The Undergraduate Essay,* 1958; (editor with Arthur Tremblay) *A Bibliography of Higher Education in Canada,* 1960, editor of *Supplement,* 1965; (editor) *Changing Patterns of Higher Education in Canada,* 1966; *Quiet Evolution: A Study of the Ontario Educational System,* 1967; (editor) *Cold Steel and Lady Godiva: Engineering Education at Toronto 1920-1972,* 1973. Also author of *A History of Higher Education in Canada,* 1976.

WORK IN PROGRESS: A History of the University of Toronto, 1900-1972, completion expected in 1977.

BIOGRAPHICAL/CRITICAL SOURCES: Canadian Forum, November, 1967.

* * *

HARRIS, William C. 1933-

PERSONAL: Born February 7, 1933, in Mount Pleasant, Ala.; son of Orrie Nelson (a civil service employee) and Ethel (Weatherford) Harris; married Betty Glenn (an assistant professor of nursing), May 29, 1960; children: Nelson Glenn, Frances Virginia, Sehoya Elizabeth. *Education:* University of Alabama, A.B., 1954, M.A., 1959, Ph.D., 1965. *Politics:* Democrat. *Religion:* Baptist. *Home:* 6516 Brookhollow Dr., Raleigh, N.C. 27609.

CAREER: Millsaps College, Jackson, Miss., assistant professor, 1963-67, associate professor of history, 1967-68; North Carolina State University, Raleigh, member of history department faculty, 1969—. *Military service:* U.S. Air Force, 1955-58; became first lieutenant. *Member:* Organization of American Historians, American Association of University Professors, Southern Historical Association, Historical Society of North Carolina.

WRITINGS: Leroy Pope Walker: Confederate Secretary of War, Confederate, 1962; *Presidential Reconstruction in Mississippi*, Louisiana State University Press, 1967; (editor, and author of introduction) John R. Lynch, *The Facts of Reconstruction*, Bobbs-Merrill, 1970.

WORK IN PROGRESS: A book on Republican reconstruction in Mississippi.

* * *

HARRISON, Saul I.   1925-

PERSONAL: Born November 4, 1925, in New York, N.Y., son of Jacob (a certified public accountant) and Flora (Weinstein) Harrison; married Susan Ormond; children: Susan Ruth, Richard Lawrence, James Woods, Lisa Woods, Rebecca Esther. *Education:* University of Michigan, M.D., 1948; additional study at Philadelphia Psychoanalytic Institute, 1957. *Home:* 3400 Andover, Ann Arbor, Mich. 48105. *Office:* Children's Psychiatric Hospital, University of Michigan Medical Center, Ann Arbor, Mich. 48109.

CAREER: Western Pennsylvania Hospital, Pittsburgh, intern, 1948-49; Temple University School of Medicine and Hospital, Philadelphia, Pa., resident in psychiatry, 1950-52, instructor, 1954-56; University of Michigan Medical School, Ann Arbor, assistant professor, 1956-61, associate professor, 1961-66, professor of psychiatry, 1966—, training director, Children's Psychiatric Hospital, 1956-75. *Military service:* U.S. Naval Reserve, 1943-45, 1948-50, 1952-54; became lieutenant. *Member:* American Psychiatric Association, American Psychoanalytic Association, American Academy of Child Psychiatry (member of council, 1966-69), American College of Psychiatrists, Group for the Advancement of Psychiatry, American Ortho-psychiatric Association (director, 1967-70), Sigma Xi. *Awards, honors:* Commonwealth Fund fellow, 1966.

WRITINGS: (With Donald Carek) *A Guide to Psychotherapy*, Little, Brown, 1966; (with John F. McDermott) *Childhood Psychopathology*, International Universities Press, 1972.

Contributor: (With M. W. Brody) S. R. Slavson, editor, *The Fields of Group Psychotherapy*, International Universities Press, 1956; Waggoner and Carek, editors, *Communication in Clinical Practice*, Little, Brown, 1964; A. M. Freedman and H. I. Kaplan, editors, *Comprehensive Textbook of Psychiatry*, Williams & Wilkins, 1967, 2nd edition, 1975; (with McDermott, J. Schrager, P. Wilson) E. Thomas, editor, *Behavioral Science for Social Workers*, Free Press, 1967; (with H. Copollilo) H. Conn, editor, *Current Diagnosis*, Saunders, 1968; (with McDermott and others) S. Chess and A. Thomas, editors, *Annual Progress in Child Psychiatry and Child Development, 1968*, Brunner, 1968; (with McDermott and others) Chess and Thomas, editors, *Annual Progress in Child Psychiatry and Child Development, 1969*, Brunner, 1969.

J. B. McDevitt and C. F. Settlage, editors, *Separation-Individuation: Essays in Honor of Margaret Mahler*, International Universities Press, 1971; (with McDermott and others) M. Levitt and A. Rubenstein, editors, *The Mental Health Field: A Critical Appraisal*, Wayne State University Press, 1971; Freedman and Kaplan, editors, *The Major Psychological Disorders and Their Treatment*, Atheneum, 1971; (with J. H. Hess and J. P. Zrull) *Health Problems of U.S. and North American Indian Populations*, Mss Information, 1972; (with C. W. Davenport and McDermott) *Effects of Early Parent Death*, Mss Information, 1973; (with

H. Burks) G. C. Morrison, editor, *Emergencies in Child Psychiatry*, C. C Thomas, 1975. Contributor to books by others, and to professional journals. Member of editorial board, *Journal of the American Academy of Child Psychiatry* and *Journal of Autism and Childhood Schizophrenia*.

* * *

HARTMANN, Ernest   1934-

PERSONAL: Born February 25, 1934, in Vienna, Austria; son of Heinz and Dora Hartmann; married Barbara Hengst, December 26, 1961; children: Jonathan. *Education:* University of Chicago, A.B., 1952; Yale University, M.D., 1958. *Home:* 20 Claremont St., Newton, Mass. *Office:* 591 Morton St., Boston, Mass. 02124.

CAREER: Massachusetts Mental Health Center, Boston, resident (psychiatry), 1960-62; Tufts University, School of Medicine, Boston, Mass., assistant professor, 1964-69, professor of psychiatry, 1969—; Boston State Hospital, Boston, Mass., director of Sleep and Dream Laboratory and consultant in psychiatry, 1964—. Director of sleep clinic, Peter Bent Brigham Hospital. *Military service:* U.S. Public Health Service, 1962-64; became major. *Member:* American Psychiatric Association, American Association for the Advancement of Science, Association for the Psychophysiological Study of Sleep, Society for Psychophysiological Research, Massachusetts Medical Society, Boston Psychoanalytic Society, Society for Neuroscience. *Awards, honors:* American Cancer Society fellowship, 1958-59; Yale University, Holt Book Prize, 1956; A. E. Bennett Award, for psychiatric research, 1966.

WRITINGS: The Biology of Dreaming, C. C Thomas, 1967; *Adolescents in a Mental Hospital*, Grune, 1968; (editor and contributor) *Sleep and Dreaming*, Little, Brown, 1970; *The Function of Sleep*, Yale University Press, 1973. Contributor of over 130 articles to scientific journals. Author of poetry and fables.

WORK IN PROGRESS: Research on sleep and dreaming.

* * *

HARTMANN, Klaus   1925-

PERSONAL: Born September 5, 1925, in Berlin, Germany. *Education:* University of Bonn, Dr.Phil., 1953; Yale University, postdoctoral study, 1953-55. *Home:* Eschenweg 15, 74 Tuebingen, West Germany. *Office:* Philosophisches Seminar, Universitaet Tuebingen, Bursagasse 1, 74 Tuebingen, West Germany.

CAREER: University of Bonn, Bonn, West Germany, teaching assistant, 1957-62, privatdozent, 1962-64, lecturer in philosophy, beginning 1964; University of Tuebingen, Tuebingen, West Germany, professor of philosophy, 1972—. Visiting professor, University of Texas, 1965-66. *Awards, honors:* Commonwealth Fund fellow at Yale University, 1953-55.

WRITINGS: (Editor with Hans Wagner) *Lebendiger Realismus*, Bouvier & Co., 1962; *Grundzuege der Ontologie Sartres in ihrem Verhaeltnis zu Hegels Logik*, W. de Gruyter & Co., 1963; *Sartre's Ontology*, Northwestern University Press, 1966; *Sartres Sozialphilosophie*, W. de Gruyter & Co., 1966; *Die Marxsche Theorie*, W. de Gruyter & Co., 1970.

WORK IN PROGRESS: Studies in modern European philosophy; studies concerning Hegel.

HART-SMITH, William 1911-

PERSONAL: Born November 23, 1911, in Tunbridge Wells, Kent, England; son of George May Coleridge (a banker) and Florence (Gomez) Hart-Smith; married Mary Wynn, October 17, 1939; married second wife, Patricia Ann McBeath (an astrologer), January 8, 1949; children: Katherine, Christopher, Julian, *Education:* Had short periods of formal schooling in Scotland and England, and one year of high school in Auckland, New Zealand. *Politics:* Democracy. *Religion:* "Sufi influences." *Office:* Charles Kidd & Co. Pty. Ltd., 128 Arthur St., North Sydney, New South Wales 2060, Australia.

CAREER: Radio mechanic in Auckland, New Zealand (where he operated one of the earliest "ham" radio stations), and Sydney and Hobart, Australia, 1927-41; Radio Station 2CH, Sydney, Australia, copywriter, 1941-45; freelance journalist, and publicity officer for Australian Broadcasting Commission, 1945-46; University of Canterbury, Christchurch, New Zealand, tutor-organizer in adult education department, 1948-55; Charles Kidd & Co. Pty. Ltd. (mail order business), North Sydney, New South Wales, Australia, advertising manager, 1959—. Lecturer on poetry and on the culture and mythology of Australian aborigines; gives public poetry readings. *Military service:* Australian Military Forces, 1941-43; became sergeant. *Member:* Poetry Society of Australia (president, 1963-64; vice-president, 1964—). *Awards, honors:* Crouch Memorial Medal for best book of poems (Australia), 1959, for *Poems of Discovery;* Grace Leven Prize for best book of poems (Australia), 1966, for *The Talking Clothes.*

WRITINGS—Poetry, except as noted: *Columbus Goes West,* Jindyworobak Club, 1943; *Harvest,* Georgian House, 1945; *The Unceasing Ground,* Angus & Robertson, 1946; *Christopher Columbus, a Sequence,* Caxton Publishing Co. (New Zealand), 1948; *On the Level,* Timaru Herald (New Zealand), 1950; *Poems of Discovery,* Angus & Robertson, 1959; *The Talking Clothes,* Angus & Robertson, 1966; (author of foreword) Leslie Horsphol, *Transubstantiation and Other Poems,* F. P. Leonard (Sydney, Australia), 1967; (with Judith Wright) *Poetry from Australia,* compiled by Howard Sergeant, Pergamon, 1969. Author of a book on graphology, privately printed. Contributor to poetry anthologies, books of verse for schools, and other publications. Reviewer, *New Zealand Listener, Sydney, Bulletin,* and others.

WORK IN PROGRESS: Poetry (as "illuminations" that "can be understood on different levels of meaning").

SIDELIGHTS: Although he had only six and a half years of formal schooling, Hart-Smith has educated himself by reading "vastly" in a wide range of subjects. He has "always had a passion for science," and he told *CA* that he "became obsessed by Time! Chiefly because of unusually frequent and vivid flashes of visual pre-cognition." His greatest enthusiasm and influence during recent years has been a book about the mystic sect of Muslims, *The Sufis,* by Idries Shah (with a foreword by Robert Graves). He says that D. H. Lawrence "first awakened poetry in me," but that American poets such as Ezra Pound and the Imagists were a greater influence on his work than English poets. He comments on his poetry, saying, "I will *not* write out of negative emotion. . . . I want my poetry to mean something to children and still be adult poetry."

AVOCATIONAL INTERESTS: Collector of New South Wales Cowrie shells (discovered a new species which was named after him, "Notadusta hartsmithi"). He told *CA*

that he "*must* spend as much time as possible outside, in the open."†

*   *   *

HARWOOD, Lee 1939-

PERSONAL: Born June 6, 1939, in Leicester, England; son of Wilfred Travers Lee (a teacher) and Grace (Ladkin) Harwood. *Education:* Attended St. George's College, Weybridge, Surrey, England, 1951-58; Queen Mary College, University of London, B.A., 1961. *Politics:* Socialist. *Religion:* None. *Home:* 21 Chatsworth Rd., Brighton, Sussex, England.

CAREER: Held various jobs including stonemason's mate, library assistant, bookshop assistant, forester, and bus conductor, 1961-69; writer in residence, Aegean School of Fine Arts, Paros, Greece, 1971-72; post office clerk, 1974—. Writer, mainly of poetry. Has given readings of his poetry in the United States, in London, and at English universities. *Awards, honors:* Poets Foundation (New York) annual award, 1967.

WRITINGS: title illegible, Writers Forum, 1965; (with William Burroughs) *Darazt,* Lovebooks, 1965; *The Man with Blue Eyes,* Angel Hair Books, 1966; *The White Room,* Fulcrum Press, 1968; *Landscapes,* Fulcrum Press, 1969; *The Beautiful Atlas,* Hand Press, 1969; (translator) Tristan Tzara, *Cosmic Realities Vanilla Tobacco Dawnings,* ARC Publications, 1969; (translator) Tristan Tzara, *Destroyed Days,* Voiceprint Editions, 1971; (with John Ashbery and Tom Raworth) *Penguin Modern Poets,* Volume 19, Penguin, 1971; *The Sinking Colony,* Fulcrum Press, 1971; *Captain Harwood's Log of Stern Statements and Stout Sayings,* Writers Forum, 1973; (compiler) *Tristan Tzara: A Bibliography,* Aloes Books, 1974; (translator) Tristan Tzara, *Selected Poems,* Trigram, 1975; *Freighters,* Pig Press, 1975.

Poems anthologized in *Children of Albion,* edited by Michael Harowitz, Penguin, 1969, *British Poetry Since 1954,* edited by Lucie-Smith, 1970, and *Twenty three Modern British Poets,* edited by John Matthias, Swallow Press, 1971. Contributor of poetry to magazines and journals including *Art and Literature, Paris Review, Angel Hair, Ole, Poetry Review* (London), *London Magazine,* and *Six Pack.* Former editor of *Tzarad.*

WORK IN PROGRESS: H.M.S. Little Fox: Poems, 1967-72, for Oasis Books.

*   *   *

HASKETT, Edythe Rance 1915-

PERSONAL: Born December 28, 1915, in Suffolk, Va.; daughter of Edgerton L. H. (a dentist) and Ivy M. (Miller) Rance; divorced; children: John Oswald. *Education:* Shaw University, A.B., 1939; New York University, M.A., 1949; graduate study at Columbia University, 1966, and University of the West Indies, 1970. *Religion:* Episcopalian. *Home:* 2741 Woodland Ave., Norfolk, Va. 23504.

CAREER: Public school teacher in North Carolina, 1934-35; elementary school supervisor in Louisa County, Va., 1945-50; art teacher in elementary school, Norfolk, Va., 1950—. Elementary and high school teacher-principal in Liberia, West Africa, 1962-64. Member of Norfolk chapter board of directors, Human Relations Council, 1967-69; member of board of directors, Fair Housing, Inc. *Member:* American Association of University Women, National Education Association, National Art Education Association, African Studies Association, Virginia Education Association, Alpha Kappa Alpha. *Awards, honors:* Distinguished Community Service Award of Alpha Kappa Alpha, 1968; received an award from St. Paul's College, 1975.

WRITINGS: Grains of Pepper (tales from Liberia), Day, 1967; *Some Gold, a Little Ivory* (tales from Ghana and the Ivory Coast), Day, 1971.

WORK IN PROGRESS: Hawa's Village in West Africa; an autobiography entitled *But You Don't Know Me.*

BIOGRAPHICAL/CRITICAL SOURCES: Norfolk Journal and Guide, Norfolk, Va., September 21, 1968.

*   *   *

HASSENGER, Robert (Leo)   1937-

PERSONAL: Born March 2, 1937, in Sioux City, Iowa; son of Leo M. (president of a savings and loan company) and Louise (Gross) Hassenger; married Teresa R. Smith, June 27, 1959 (divorced); married Nancy C. Camara, December 27, 1969; children: Raissa (daughter), Courtney, Robert. *Education:* University of Notre Dame, B.A. (cum laude), 1959; Marquette University, M.A., 1961; University of Chicago, Ph.D., 1965. *Home:* 4417 Chestnut Ridge Rd., Tonawanda, N.Y. 14222.

CAREER: Instructor in psychology at Marquette University, Milwaukee, Wis., 1961, St. Xavier College, Chicago, Ill., 1961-62, and Mundelein College, Chicago, 1962-65; University of Notre Dame, Notre Dame, Ind., assistant professor of sociology, 1965-71, assistant professor of education, 1967-71; Kalamazoo College, Kalamazoo, Mich., visiting associate professor of sociology, 1971-72; State University of New York, Empire State College, Saratoga Springs, 1972—, began as associate professor of sociology and education, currently associate dean. Member of American Council on Education, 1968-71. *Member:* American Sociological Association, Association for Higher Education, American Association of University Professors, American Civil Liberties Union.

WRITINGS: (Editor) *The Shape of Catholic Higher Education,* University of Chicago Press, 1967.

Contributor: Lois Vaccaro and James Covert, editors, *Student Freedom in American Higher Education,* Columbia University Press, 1969; William T. Kiu and Nathaniel V. Pallone, editors, *Catholics, U.S.A.: Perspectives from the Behavioral Sciences,* Wiley, 1970; Julian Foster and Durward Long, editors, *Protest! Student Activism in America,* Morrow, 1970; Joseph Boskin and Robert Rosenstone, editors, *Seasons of Rebellion: Protest and Radicalism in Recent America,* Holt, 1972. Contributor of articles and reviews to sociology, education, and other professional journals. Editor, *Sociological Analysis,* 1971-74.

*   *   *

HATCH, Raymond N(orris)   1911-

PERSONAL: Born February 6, 1911, in Plymouth, Ohio; son of Walter O. and Nora (Anderson) Hatch; married E. Grace Norris, June 5, 1939; children: David R. *Education:* Ashland College, B.S., 1939; Michigan State University, M.A., 1947; Oregon State University, Ed.D., 1950. *Politics:* Republican. *Religion:* Protestant. *Home:* 448 Tulip Tree Lane, East Lansing, Mich. *Office:* College of Education, Michigan State University, East Lansing, Mich. 48823.

CAREER: High school teacher and guidance director in

Ohio, 1934-43; East Lansing (Mich.) Board of Education, director of guidance, 1946; Michigan State University, East Lansing, College of Education, member of faculty, 1946-54, director of Bureau of Research, 1954-55, assistant dean of education, 1955-61, professor, 1961—, chairman of department of counseling, personnel services, and educational psychology, 1962-64. Chief of party, Michigan State University contract at University of Ryukyus, 1961-62, and in Thailand, 1964-68. *Military service:* U.S. Army, 1943-46; became first lieutenant. *Member:* American Personnel and Guidance Association (executive council, 1956-58), National Vocational Guidance Association (president, 1957), National Education Association, Michigan Education Association. *Awards, honors:* National Vocational Guidance Association, National Merit Award, 1975.

WRITINGS: (With Paul Dressel and James Costar) *Guidance Services in the Secondary School,* W. C. Brown, 1953, revised edition, 1963; (with Buford Stefflre) *Administration of Guidance Services: Organization, Supervision, Evaluation,* Prentice-Hall, 1958, revised edition, 1965; (with Willa Norris and Frank Zeran) *Information Service in Guidance,* Prentice-Hall, 1960, 3rd edition, Rand McNally, 1972; (with Costar) *Guidance Services in the Elementary School,* W. C. Brown, 1961; (with Morgan Parmentar and Stefflre) *Planning Your Future,* McKnight, 1962; (with Parmentar and Stefflre) *Planning Your Life's Work,* McKnight, 1962; (with Parmentar and Stefflre) *Planning Your School Life,* McKnight, 1962; (editor) *The Organization of Pupil Personnel Program,* Michigan State University Press, 1974. Also author of *Vocational Counseling in Secondary Education: Thailand.*

*   *   *

HATCH, Richard A(llen)   1940-

PERSONAL: Born August 18, 1940, in Anderson, Ind.; son of Clarence Wilbur (a clergyman) and Mildred (Sutton) Hatch; married Ann Marie Menchinger, August 27, 1960. *Education:* Anderson College, Anderson, Ind., student, 1957-59; Boston University, B.S., 1961; University of Illinois, Ph.D., 1969. *Home:* 8715 Lake Murray Blvd., San Diego, Calif. *Office:* San Diego State University, San Diego, Calif.

CAREER: Illinois State Legislature, Springfield, intern, 1966-67; University of Illinois, Urbana, assistant to director of public information, 1966, instructor in business and technical writing, 1967-69; Western Michigan University, Kalamazoo, associate professor and coordinator of communication studies in business, 1969-75; San Diego State University, San Diego, Calif., assistant professor of communications study, 1975—. *Member:* American Business Communication Association (vice-president, 1974-75).

WRITINGS: (Compiler) *Some Founding Papers of the University of Illinois,* University of Illinois Press, 1967; (editor) *An Early View of the Land-Grant Colleges,* University of Illinois Press, 1967; (with Francis W. Weeks) *Business Writing Cases and Problems,* Stipes, 1972; (with Irene S. Caldwell, Beverly Welton) *Basics for Communication in the Church,* Warner Press, 1971. Associate editor, *Bostonia* (Boston University), 1960-61.

WORK IN PROGRESS: A business writing text.

*   *   *

HATT, Harold E(rnest)   1932-

PERSONAL: Born September 6, 1932, in Vancouver,

British Columbia, Canada; naturalized American citizen, 1968; son of Fred (a Canadian customs official) and Margaret Louise (Tarling) Hatt; married Martha Ann Smith, July 14, 1957; children: Frederick Harold, Franklin Kenneth, Daniel Ernest. *Education:* University of British Columbia, B.A., 1953; Southwestern Baptist Theological Seminary, B.D., 1956; Baylor University, M.A., 1957; Vanderbilt University, Ph.D., 1963. *Home:* 1706 East Elm, Enid, Okla., 73701. *Office:* Graduate Seminary, Phillips University, Enid, Okla. 73701.

CAREER: Clergyman, Disciples of Christ. Minister in Carthage, Tenn., 1958-59; North Texas State University, Denton, Ecumenical Bible Chair Professor of Religion, 1960-62; Phillips University, Graduate Seminary, Enid, Okla., associate professor, 1962-66, professor of theology and philosophy, 1966—. *Member:* American Academy of Religion, American Philosophical Association, Association of Disciples for Theological Discussion, Oklahoma Christian Ministers Theological Discussion Group. *Awards, honors:* Grants from Association of Theological Schools and Phillips University, for research.

WRITINGS: Encountering Truth: A New Understanding of How Revelation, as Encounter, Yields Doctrine, Abingdon, 1966; *Cybernetics and the Image of Man: A Study of Freedom and Responsibility in Man and Machine,* Abingdon, 1968; (contributor) Alton M. Motter, editor, *Preaching About Death,* Fortress, 1975. Also author of church school curriculum materials. Contributor to religious journals.

WORK IN PROGRESS: Research at the School of Theology at Claremont, University of California, Los Angeles, and University of Southern California on film study in a theological context.

SIDELIGHTS: Harold Hatt reads French; has also studied German, Latin, Greek, Hebrew, and Aramaic. *Avocational interests:* Humor ("would like to write a book on the philosophy of humor"); collecting ethnic and unusual phonograph records; refereeing soccer games (registered referee with Oklahoma and U.S. Soccer Federations).

*   *   *

HAUGEN, Einar (Ingvald) 1906-

PERSONAL: Born April 19, 1906, in Sioux City, Iowa; son of John Ellingsen (a cabinetmaker) and Kristine (Gorset) Haugen; married Eva Lund, June 18, 1932; children: Anne Margaret Littlefield, Camilla Christine Conley. *Education:* Attended Morningside College, 1924-27; St. Olaf College, B.A. (summa cum laude), 1928; University of Illinois, M.A., 1929, Ph.D., 1931. *Politics:* Independent ("usually Democratic"). *Religion:* ("Mildly") Unitarian Universalist. *Office:* Widener Library, Harvard University, Cambridge, Mass. 02138.

CAREER: University of Wisconsin, Madison, assistant professor, 1931-36, associate professor, 1936-38, Thompson Professor of Scandinavian Languages, 1938-62, Vilas Research Professor of Scandinavian and Linguistics, 1962-64, director of Linguistic Institute, 1943-44; Harvard University, Cambridge, Mass., Victor S. Thomas Professor of Scandinavian and Linguistics, 1964-75, professor emeritus, 1975—. University of Oslo, visiting lecturer, 1938, Fulbright research professor, 1951-52; visiting summer lecturer at universities including University of Michigan, 1949, and Georgetown University, 1954; U.S. Department of State lecturer at University of Iceland, 1956. Cultural Officer at U.S. Embassy, Oslo, Norway, 1945-46; consultant to English Language Educational Council, Tokyo, Japan, 1958-60. President of Ninth International Linguistic Congress, 1962; Permanent International Council of Linguists, president, 1966-72, life member, 1972—.

MEMBER: American Academy of Arts and Sciences, Linguistic Society of America (president, 1950), American Dialect Society (president, 1965, 1966), Modern Language Association of America, Norwegian-American Historical Association, Society for Advancement of Scandinavian Society (president, 1938), Oslo Academy of Science (corresponding member), Icelandic Academy of Science (corresponding member). *Awards, honors:* Order of St. Olaf, first class, Norway, 1940; Guggenheim fellowship, 1942-43; Center for Advanced Study in the Behavioral Sciences fellowship, 1963-64; Litt.D., University of Michigan, 1953; Ph.D., St. Olaf College, 1958, University of Oslo, 1961, University of Wisconsin, 1969, University of Reykjavik, 1971, University of Trondheim, 1972, University of Uppsala, 1975; Commander, Order of the North Star, Sweden, 1970.

WRITINGS: Beginning Norwegian, Appleton, 1937, 3rd edition, 1975; *Norsk i Amerika,* Cappelen (Oslo), 1938; *Reading Norwegian,* Appleton, 1938; *Norwegian Word Studies,* two volumes, University of Wisconsin Press, 1941; *Voyages to Vinland,* Knopf, 1941, 2nd edition, 1942; *Spoken Norwegian,* Holt, 1945, revised edition (with K. G. Chapman), 1964.

First Grammatical Treatise, Linguistic Society of America, 1950, 2nd edition, Longman, 1972; *The Norwegian Language in America,* two volumes, University of Pennsylvania Press, 1953, 2nd edition, Indiana University Press, 1969; *Bilingualism in the Americas,* American Dialect Society, 1956; (translator and editor) *Beyer's History of Norwegian Literature,* New York University Press, 1957; (editor) *Norwegian-English Dictionary,* University of Wisconsin Press, 1965; *Language Conflict and Language Planning,* Harvard University Press, 1966; (translator and editor) *Fire and Ice: Three Icelandic Plays,* University of Wisconsin Press, 1967; *The Norwegians in America,* Columbia University Press, 1967.

(Translator) Guomundur Kamban, *We Murderers,* University of Wisconsin Press, 1970; (translator) H. Koht, *Life of Ibsen,* Benjamin Blom, 1971; *The Ecology of Language: Essays by Einar Haugen,* edited by Anwar S. Dil, Stanford University Press, 1972; (contributor) T. A. Sebeok, editor, *Current Trends in Linguistics,* Volume X, Mouton & Co., 1973; (editor) Georges Dumezil, *Gods of the Ancient Northmen,* University of California Press, 1973; *A Bibliography of Scandinavian Languages and Linguistics, 1900-1970,* Oslo University Press, 1974; (editor with Morton Bloomfield) *Languages as a Human Problem,* Norton, 1974. Contributor to professional journals in United States and abroad.

WORK IN PROGRESS: History and Structure of the Scandinavian Languages; editing Bjornson's *Letters from America; The Oppdal Dialect of Norwegian;* editing Snovri Starluson's treatise on medieval Icelandic metrics, *Hattatal* (1224).

SIDELIGHTS: Haugen has lived in Japan and the Scandinavian countries, and has traveled around the world. He is known as a pioneer and specialist in the field of bilingualism and Scandinavian.

BIOGRAPHICAL/CRITICAL SOURCES: Studies for Einar Haugen, Mouton & Co., 1972.

HAVIGHURST, Robert J(ames)   1900-

PERSONAL: Born June 5, 1900, in DePere, Wis.; son of Freeman A. and Winifred (Weter) Havighurst; married Edythe D. McNelly, June 21, 1930; children: James Parsons, Walter M., Helen (Mrs. Marvin S. Berk), Ruth (Mrs. Samuel H. Neff), Dorothy (Mrs. Thomas Kucera). *Education:* Ohio Wesleyan University, B.A., 1921; Ohio State University, M.A., 1922, Ph.D., 1924. *Religion:* Protestant. *Home:* 5844 Stony Island Ave., Chicago, Ill. 60637. *Office:* Department of Education, University of Chicago, Chicago, Ill.

CAREER: Harvard University, Cambridge, Mass., National Research Council fellow in physics, 1924-26; Miami University, Oxford, Ohio, assistant professor of chemistry, 1927-28; University of Wisconsin—Madison, assistant professor of physics, 1928-32; Ohio State University, Columbus, associate professor of science education, 1932-34; Rockefeller Foundation, General Education Board, New York, N.Y., assistant director, 1934-37, director, 1937-41; University of Chicago, Chicago, Ill., professor of education and human development, 1941—, chairman of department, 1947-50. Co-director of Government Center for Educational Research, Brazil, 1956-58. Visiting professor at University of Missouri at Kansas City, 1965-69. *Military service:* U.S. Army, 1918.

MEMBER: American Educational Research Association, National Society for the Study of Education, American Association of University Professors, Phi Beta Kappa, Sigma Xi, Phi Delta Theta. *Awards, honors:* National Research Council fellowship, 1924-26; Fulbright grants to University of New Zealand, 1953-54, and University of Buenos Aires, 1961.

WRITINGS: (Co-author) *Who Shall Be Educated?*, Harper, 1944; (with Allison Davis) *Father of the Man: How Your Child Gets His Personality*, Houghton, 1947; (with William Lloyd Warner) *Should You Go to College?*, Science Research Associates, 1948, 2nd edition (with Esther E. Diamond), 1961; (with Hilda Taba, Andrew W. Brown, and others) *Adolescent Character and Personality*, Wiley, 1949; (co-author) *Personal Adjustment in Old Age*, Science Research Associates, 1949; *Developmental Tasks and Education*, University of Chicago Press, 1949, 3rd edition, McKay, 1972.

(With others) *The American Veteran Back Home: A Study of Veteran Readjustment*, Longmans, Green, 1951; (with H. Gerthon Morgan) *The Social History of a War Boom Community*, Longmans, Green, 1951; (co-author) *Intelligence and Cultural Differences*, University of Chicago Press, 1951; (co-author) *A Community Youth Development Program*, University of Chicago Press, 1952; (with Ruth Albrecht) *Older People*, Longmans, Green, 1953; (with Eugene A. Friedmann, William H. Harlan, and others) *The Meaning of Work and Retirement*, University of Chicago Press, 1954; (with Bernice L. Neugarten) *American Indian and White Children*, University of Chicago Press, 1955; (with Eugene Stivers and Robert F. DeHaan) *A Survey of the Education of Gifted Children*, University of Chicago Press, 1955; (with Betty Orr) *Adult Education and Adult Needs*, Center for the Study of Liberal Education for Adults (Chicago), 1956; (editor with Irma Gross and others) *Potentialities of Women in the Middle Years*, Michigan State University Press, 1956; (with Neugarten) *Society and Education*, Allyn & Bacon, 1957, 4th edition, 1975; (with Robert F. DeHann) *Educating Gifted Children*, University of Chicago Press, 1957, 2nd edition, 1961.

American Higher Education in the 1960's, Ohio State University Press, 1960; (with others) *The Coming Crisis in the Selection of Students for College Entrance* (symposium), 1960; (co-author) *Psychology of Moral Character*, Wiley, 1960; *Human Development and Education* (expansion of *Developmental Tasks and Education*), Longmans, Green, 1953, McKay, 1961; (with others) *Growing Up in River City*, Wiley, 1962; (with others) *La Sociedad y la Education en America Latina*, Editorial Universitaria de Buenos Aires, 1962, 4th edition, 1971; *Psicologia Social de la Adolescencia*, Union Panamericana, 1962, 2nd edition, 1969; (with others) *Las Actitudes Personales y Sociales de Adolescentes de Buenos Aires y de Chicago*, Union Panamericana, 1963, translation published as *A Cross-National Study of Buenos Aires and Chicago Adolescence*, S. Karger, 1964; *The Public Schools of Chicago*, Board of Education, City of Chicago, 1964; *The Educational Mission of the Church*, Westminster, 1965; (with J. Robert Moreira) *Society and Education in Brazil*, University of Pittsburgh Press, 1965; *Education in Metropolitan Areas*, Allyn & Bacon, 1966, 2nd edition (with Levine), 1971; (editor with Neugarten and Jacqueline M. Falk) *Society and Education: A Book of Readings*, Allyn & Bacon, 1967, 2nd edition, 1971; (editor and author of introduction) *Comparative Perspectives on Education*, Little, Brown, 1968; (editor with others) *Adjustment to Retirement*, Van Gorcum, 1969, 2nd edition, 1970; (with Aparecida J. Gouveia) *Brazilian Secondary Education and Socio-Economic Development*, Praeger, 1969.

(With Winton M. Ahlstrom) *400 Losers: Delinquent Youth in High School*, Jossey-Bass, 1971; (editor) *Leaders in American Education*, University of Chicago Press, 1971; (compiler with Daniel U. Levine) *Farewell to Schools???*, Charles A. Jones Publishing, 1971; (with Guy J. Manaster) *Cross-National Research: Social Psychological Methods and Problems*, Houghton, 1972; (with Estelle Fuchs) *To Live on This Earth: American Indian Education*, Doubleday, 1972; *Optometry: Education for the Profession*, National Commission on Accrediting, 1973.

Editor with Philip Dreyer, *YOUTH*, 74th Yearbook of the National Society for the Study of Education, 1971. Author of reports for Rockefeller Foundation, 1947, and for International Sociological Association, 1968, and of numerous booklets on education. Contributor of articles to professional journals.

*   *   *

HAWKINS, Arthur   1903-

PERSONAL: Born April 9, 1903, in Cumberland, Md.; son of Arthur Hanson (a surgeon) and Louise (Price) Hawkins; married Patricia Laporte, 1930; married Nancy Pilson (a writer), June 28, 1940; children: Arthur III, Barbara (Mrs. Julian Palmore III), Nancy (Mrs. Richard N. Field), Gilbert Huston. *Education:* University of Virginia, B.S., 1925; studied at Art Students League of New York, 1925-27. *Politics:* Independent Democrat. *Religion:* Episcopalian. *Home and office:* 396 Allaire Ave., Leonia, N.J. 07605.

CAREER: Designer, painter, art director; currently working as consulting art director in book publishing and advertising sales promotion fields. Speaker on advertising arts and judge of exhibitions. *Member:* Society of Illustrators, Art Directors Club (New York).

WRITINGS: (Editor with Edward N. Gotshall) *Advertising Directions: Trends in Visual Advertising*, Art Directions Book Co., 1959; (editor) *The Art Director at Work:*

How Fifteen Medal-winning Exhibits Were Conceived and Executed, Hasting House, 1959; *The Steak Book*, Doubleday, 1966; *Who Needs a Cookbook: How to Make 222 Delicious International Dishes with a Minimum of Direction*, Prentice-Hall, 1968; *The Complete Seafood Cookbook*, Prentice-Hall, 1970; (with Aileen Paul) *Kids Cooking*, Doubleday, 1970; *Cook It Quick: 203 Delicious Half-Hour Recipes*, Prentice-Hall, 1971; (co-author) *Chef's Special*, Prentice-Hall, 1972; (co-author) *Chef's Magic*, Prentice-Hall, 1972; (with wife, Nancy Hawkins) *The Low Cost Meat Book: First Class Fare with Economy Meats*, Doubleday, 1974; (with Aileen Paul) *Candies, Cookies, Cakes*, Doubleday, 1974; *The Architectural Cookbook*, Architectural Record, 1975; (with Nancy Hawkins) *The American Regional Cookbook: Recipes from Yesterday & Today for the Modern Cook*, Prentice-Hall, 1976.

Illustrator: Aileen Paul, *Kids Gardening: A First Indoor Gardening Book for Children*, Doubleday, 1972.

Also author of *The Antisocial Cookbook*. Contributor of articles about art to trade journals. Editor, *Illustrators '59* (yearbook), 1959.

* * *

HAWKINS, Brett W(illiam) 1937-

PERSONAL: Born September 15, 1937, in Buffalo, N.Y.; son of Ralph Charles and Irma (Rowley) Hawkins; married Linda Knuth, November 30, 1974; children: (first marriage) Brett William, Jr. *Education:* University of Rochester, A.B., 1959; Vanderbilt University, M.A., 1962, Ph.D., 1964. *Politics:* Democrat. *Religion:* Christian Scientist. *Home:* 3909 North Murray, Milwaukee, Wis. 53211. *Office:* Department of Political Science, University of Wisconsin, 3203 North Downer, Milwaukee, Wis. 53201.

CAREER: Vanderbilt University, Nashville, Tenn., instructor in political science, 1963; Washington and Lee University, Lexington, Va., assistant professor of political science, 1963-65; University of Georgia, Athens, assistant professor, 1965-68, associate professor in department of political science and Institute of Government, 1968-70; University of Wisconsin-Milwaukee, associate professor, 1970-71, professor of political science, 1971—. *Member:* American Political Science Association, Southern Political Science Association, Phi Beta Kappa.

WRITINGS: Nashville Metro, Vanderbilt University Press, 1966; (editor with Thomas R. Dye) *Politics in the Metropolis*, C. E. Merrill, 1967, 2nd edition, 1971; (editor with Robert Lorinskas) *The Ethnic Factor in American Politics*, C. E. Merrill, 1970; *Politics and Urban Policies*, Bobbs-Merrill, 1971. Contributor of numerous chapters to books; also contributor of articles to professional journals.

* * *

HAWKINS, Robert 1923-

PERSONAL: Born April 6, 1923, in Highmore, S.D.; son of Francis Edwards (a builder) and Lunetta (Bloomenrader) Hawkins. *Education:* Trinity College, Hartford, Conn., B.A., 1945; University of Edinburgh, graduate study, 1947-48. *Politics:* Republican. *Religion:* Episcopalian. *Office:* The Hotchkiss School, Lakeville, Conn. 06039.

CAREER: The Hotchkiss School, Lakeville, Conn., master in English, beginning 1945.

WRITINGS: (Editor with Denise Restout) *Landowska on Music*, Stein & Day, 1964; *Preface to Poetry*, Basic Books, 1965; (editor) Robert Louis Stevenson, *Dr. Jekyll and Mr.*

Hyde, Dell, 1966; (editor with John G. Bowen) Shakespeare, *Macbeth*, Basic Books, 1967.

WORK IN PROGRESS: Two books in collaboration with Denise Restout, *Biography of Landowska*, and *What Is Music?;* and with John G. Bowen, editing *Julius Caesar*.

SIDELIGHTS: Robert Hawkins is competent in French and Italian. *Avocational interests:* Ornithology and cooking.

* * *

HAWKINSON, John (Samuel) 1912-

PERSONAL: Born November 8, 1912, in Chicago, Ill.; son of John S. (a contractor) and Amy (Jackson) Hawkinson; married Lucy Ozone (an author and illustrator), September 20, 1954 (died December 6, 1971); children: Anne, Julia. *Politics:* Democrat. *Home:* R.R. 2, Lawrence, Mich. 49014.

CAREER: Artist and illustrator. Scoutmaster, thirteen years. Chairman of parks and recreation committee, Hyde Park Kenwood Community Conference, one year. *Military service:* U.S. Army, 1941-45; received Bronze Star.

WRITINGS—Children's books; all published by Albert Whitman, except as indicated: (With wife, Lucy Hawkinson) *Winter Tree Birds*, 1956; (with L. Hawkinson) *City Birds*, 1957; *Robins and Rabbits*, 1960; *Collect, Print, and Paint from Nature*, 1963; *More to Collect and Paint from Nature*, 1964; (with L. Hawkinson) *Birds in the Sky*, Childrens Press, 1965; (self-illustrated) *The Old Stump*, 1965; *Our Wonderful Wayside*, 1966; (author and illustrator with L. Hawkinson) *Little Boy Who Lives Up High*, 1967; (self-illustrated) *Where the Wild Apples Grow*, 1967; (self-illustrated) *Pastels Are Great!*, 1968; (with Martha Faulhaber and illustrator) *Music and Instruments for Children to Make*, 1969; (with Faulhaber and illustrator) *Rhythms, Music, and Instruments to Make*, 1970; (self-illustrated) *Who Lives There?*, 1970; (self-illustrated) *Paint a Rainbow*, 1970; (self-illustrated) *The Mouse that Fell off the Rainbow*, 1971; (self-illustrated) *Let Me Take You on a Trail*, 1972; (self-illustrated) *A Ball of Clay*, 1974.

Illustrator; all published by Childrens Press, except as indicated: Ruth Orbach, *Ekorn the Squirrel*, Albert Whitman, 1961; Dorothy Koch, *Up the Big Mountain*, Holiday House, 1964; Janet Konkle, *Schoolroom Bunny*, 1965; Natalie Miller, *Story of the White House*, 1966; Solveig P. Russell, *How Shall We Ride Away?*, Melmont, 1966; Patricia M. Martin, *One Special Dog*, Rand McNally, 1968; Julian May, *Moving Hills of Sand*, Hawthorn, 1969; Illa Podendorf, *Things Are Alike and Different*, 1970; Margaret Friskey, *Indian Two Feet and the Wolf Cubs*, 1971; Podendorf, *Every Day Is Earth Day*, 1971; Ruth B. Gross, *What Is That Alligator Saying?*, Hastings House, 1972; Friskey, *Indian Two Feet and the Grizzly Bear*, 1974.

Illustrator with wife, Lucy Hawkinson: Carla Greene, *I Want to Be a Fisherman*, 1957; Mabel Gee and Mary Bongiorno, *How Can I Find Out*, 1963; Margaret Friskey, *Mystery of the Farmer's Three Fives*, 1963; Jane Hefflefinger and Elaine Hoffman, *At the Pet Hospital*, 1964; Natalie Miller, *Story of the Statue of Liberty*, 1965; Friskey, *Indian Two Feet and His Eagle Feather*, 1967; Helen R. Russell, *The True Book of Buds: Surprise Packages*, 1970.

* * *

HAWLEY, Jane Stouder 1936-

PERSONAL: Born December 17, 1936, in Indianapolis,

Ind.; daughter of Albert Edwin (a physician) and Ruby (Heaston) Stouder; married Searle Edward Hawley, Jr. (a journalist), December 28, 1966; children: Alison Gail, Elizabeth Ann. *Education:* Indiana University, A.B., 1958, M.A. (in journalism), 1966; University of California, Berkeley, M.A. (in English), 1960; Claremont Graduate School, secondary teaching internship, 1960-61; Northwestern University, Ph.D. (in English education), 1970. *Home:* 2332 Lawndale Ave., Evanston, Ill. 60201. *Office:* Department of Education, Northeastern Illinois University, Bryn Mawr and St. Louis Avenues, Chicago, Ill. 60625.

CAREER: High school English and journalism instructor in California, 1960-63; Lyons & Carnahan (publishers), Chicago, Ill., language arts editor, 1964-65; *Chicago Tribune,* Chicago, reporter, 1965; Indiana University, Bloomington, assistant director of English curriculum study center, 1965-66; Science Research Associates, Chicago, language arts editor, 1967-70; Northeastern Illinois University, Chicago, associate professor of secondary education, 1970—. *Member:* National Council of Teachers of English, American Association of Higher Education, Conference on English Education.

WRITINGS: (Editor with Edward B. Jenkinson, and author of introduction and basic poetry program) *Teaching Literature in Grades Seven through Nine,* Indiana University Press, 1967; (editor with Jenkinson) *On Teaching Literature: Essays for Secondary School Teachers,* Indiana University Press, 1967; (with James S. Ackerman, and editor) *On Teaching the Bible as Literature: A Guide to Selected Biblical Narratives for Secondary Schools,* Indiana University Press, 1967. Contributor to education publications.

* * *

HAY, Peter 1935-

PERSONAL: Born September 17, 1935, in Berlin, Germany; son of Euward Arthur (a lawyer) and Margot Hedwig (Tull) Hay; married Norma Gossman, January 31, 1958 (divorced, 1973); married Grazina Parokas, 1974; children: (first marriage) Cedric Peter. *Education:* University of Michigan, A.B. and J.D., 1958; graduate study at University of Goettingen, 1959, and University of Heidelberg, 1960. *Home:* 2302 Shurts Circle, Urbana, Ill. 61801. *Office:* College of Law, University of Illinois, Champaign, Ill. 61820.

CAREER: University of Michigan, Ann Arbor, instructor in law, 1960-61; University of Pittsburgh, Pittsburgh, Pa., assistant professor of law, 1961-63; University of Illinois, Champaign, assistant professor, 1963-64, associate professor, 1964-66, professor of law, 1966—, director of Office of Graduate and International Legal Studies, 1971—, associate dean, 1974—. Visiting professor at University of Michigan, 1963, Stanford University, 1966, and University of Freiburg, 1966, 1970, 1973. *Member:* American Association of University Professors, American Foreign Law Association, American Society of Comparative Law, Societe de Troit Compare, Phi Beta Kappa, Phi Kappa Phi, Order of the Coif. *Awards, honors:* American Council of Learned Societies, grant-in-aid, 1964, and travel grant, 1966; honorary professor of law, University of Freiburg, 1975—.

WRITINGS: Federalism and Supranational Organization, University of Illinois Press, 1966; (editor with W. R. LaFave) *International Trade, Investments, and Organization,* University of Illinois Press, 1967; (author and editor

with Eric Stein) *Law and Institutions in the Atlantic Area,* Bobbs-Merrill, 1967. Also author of *Introduction to U.S. Law* (originally published in German), 1976, and, with Stein and Michael Waelbroeck, *European Community Law,* 1976. Contributor of articles to law journals. Member of board of editors and contributor, *American Journal of Comparative Law.*

WORK IN PROGRESS: Problems of international unification of law, including work of the Hague Conference on Private International Law.

SIDELIGHTS: Besides German, Hay is competent in French and knows some Spanish and Italian.

* * *

HAYCRAFT, Howard 1905-

PERSONAL: Born July 24, 1905, in Madelia, Minn.; son of Julius Everett (a lawyer, legislator, and district judge) and Marie (a teacher; maiden name, Stelzer) Haycraft; married Molly Randolph Costain (daughter of author Thomas B. Costain), October 9, 1942. *Education:* University of Minnesota, A.B., 1928. *Religion:* Episcopalian. *Office:* H. W. Wilson Co., 950 University Ave., Bronx, N.Y. 10452.

CAREER: University of Minnesota Press, Minneapolis, staff member, 1928; H. W. Wilson Co. (publishers of reference works and indexes for libraries), Bronx, N.Y., promotional and editorial work, 1929-34, member of board of directors, 1934—, assistant secretary of firm, 1934-39, vice-president, 1940-52, president, 1953-67, chairman of board, 1967. Forest Press, Inc., member of board of directors, 1951-68, president, 1961-62. U.S. War Department Specialist, associated with publication of "G.I. Guides," 1942; member of President's Committee on Employment of the Handicapped, beginning, 1963. *Military service:* U.S. Army, Special Services, 1942-46; became major; received Army Commendation Medal. *Member:* Mystery Writers of America (president, 1963), Kappa Sigma. *Awards, honors:* Mystery Writers of America, Edgar Allan Poe Award ("Edgar"), 1947, for criticism, Special Award, 1975, for distinguished contribution to mystery criticism and scholarship; Outstanding Achievement Award, University of Minnesota, 1954; first recipient of Sir Francis Campbell Medal and citation, American Library Association, 1966, for outstanding contributions to library service for the blind; L.H.D., Gustavus Adolphus College, 1975.

WRITINGS: Murder for Pleasure: The Life and Times of the Detective Story, Appleton, 1941, enlarged edition, Biblo & Tannen, 1968; *Books for the Blind: A Postscript and an Appreciation,* Library of Congress, 1965, 4th edition, 1972.

Editor: (And author of introduction) Arthur Conan Doyle, *The Boys' Sherlock Holmes,* Harper, 1936, new edition, 1961; *The Boys' Book of Great Detective Stories,* Harper, 1938; *The Boys' Second Book of Great Detective Stories,* Harper, 1940; *Crime Club Encore,* Doubleday, 1942; *The Art of the Mystery Story* (critical essays), Simon & Schuster, 1946; (and author of introduction) *Fourteen Great Detective Stories,* Modern Library, 1949; (with John Beecroft) *Treasury of Great Mysteries,* two volumes, Simon & Schuster, 1957; (with Beecroft) *Ten Great Mysteries,* Doubleday, 1959; (and author of introduction) *Five Spy Novels,* Doubleday, 1962; (with Beecroft) *Three Times Three* (mystery story collection), Doubleday, 1964; (and author of introduction) Arthur Conan Doyle, *Sherlock Holmes' Greatest Cases,* F. Watts, 1967.

Editor, "Wilson Authors Series": (With Stanley Kunitz and W. C. Hadden) *Authors of Today and Yesterday*, 1933, 2nd edition, 1934; (with Kunitz, Hadden, and others) *The Junior Book of Authors*, 1934, 3rd edition, 1956; (with Kunitz) *British Authors of the Nineteenth Century*, 1936; (with Kunitz) *American Authors, 1600-1900*, 1938; (with Kunitz) *Twentieth Century Authors*, 1942; *First Supplement*, 1955; (with Kunitz) *British Authors Before 1800*, 1952.

Mystery critic for *Harper's*, 1941-42, and *Ellery Queen's Mystery Magazine*, 1946-48; contributor to other magazines. Editorial consultant, Doubleday Mystery Guild, 1948-61.

BIOGRAPHICAL/CRITICAL SOURCES: John L. Lawler, *The H. W. Wilson Company: Half a Century of Biographical Publishing*, University of Minnesota Press, 1950; *Saturday Review*, February 3, 1951; *New York Times*, February 25, 1968.

* * *

HAYES, Margaret 1925-

PERSONAL: Born April 5, 1925, in London, England; daughter of Edward James and Louise (Evans) Hayes. *Education:* Watford Isolation Hospital, R.F.N., 1946; Withington Hospital, S.R.N., 1949; Mother's Hospital, S.C.M., 1950; Institut Leopold II, Belgium, C.M.T., 1957 (degrees indicate fever nurse, gene.al nurse, midwifery, and certification in tropical medicine). *Home:* 7 Pinewood Close, Paddock Wood, Kent, England.

CAREER: Head nurse in London, England, 1950-57; Unevangelised Fields Mission, missionary nurse in Congo, 1957-65; held as prisoner of war; head nurse in London, England, 1965—, currently in Niger Republic.

WRITINGS: Captive of the Simbad (autobiographical), Hodder & Stoughton, 1966, Harper, 1967. Contributor of technical articles to nursing journals.††

* * *

HAYES, Ralph E(ugene) 1927-
(Nick Carter)

PERSONAL: Born September 3, 1927, in Columbus, Ind.; son of Ralph Emmons and Ruth (Lister) Hayes; married Donna Ford (an artist), July 21, 1951. *Education:* University of Michigan, B.A., 1951, J.D., 1954. *Home:* 826 Eaton, Key West, Fla. 33040.

CAREER: Admitted to Michigan Bar, 1954; White & Block (attorneys), Grand Rapids, Mich., attorney, 1954-55; Preferred Insurance Co., Grand Rapids, Mich., attorney, 1955-57; Travelers Insurance Co., attorney and examiner, 1957-69, first in Grand Rapids, Mich., later in Hartford, Conn; free-lance writer, 1969—. *Military service:* U.S. Army Air Forces, 1945-47. *Member:* Grand Rapids Bar Association, State Bar of Michigan.

WRITINGS: Ellen Matthews, Bouregy, 1966; *Mission to Hong Kong*, Bouregy, 1967; *Virgie Tate*, Vega Books, 1967; *One Springtime in Venice*, Bouregy, 1967; *Nurse in Hong Kong*, Bouregy, 1967; *Nurse in Istanbul*, Avalon, 1970; *The Visiting Moon*, Lenox Hill, 1971; *Hunter's Moon*, Lenox Hill, 1972; *The Name is O'Brien*, Lenox Hill, 1972; *O'Brien-Buffalo Hunter: Four Ugly Guns*, Belmont-Tower, 1973; *O'Brien-Buffalo Hunter: Gunslammer*, Belmont-Tower, 1973; *Hellhole*, Belmont-Tower, 1973; *The Treasure of Rio Verde*, Lenox Hill, 1973; *Nightmare Island*, Manor, 1975.

"Agent for Cominsec" series; all published by Belmont-Tower: *The Bloody Monday Conspiracy*, 1974; *The Doomsday Conspiracy*, 1974; *The Turkish Mafia Conspiracy*, 1974; *The Hellfire Conspiracy*, 1974; *The Nightmare Conspiracy*, 1974; *The Death Makers Conspiracy*, 1975.

"The Hunter" series; all published by Belmont-Tower: *The Scavenger Kill*, 1975; *Night of the Jackals*, 1975; *A Taste for Blood*, 1975; *Track of the Beast*, 1975; *The Deadly Prey*, 1975.

"Check Force" series; all published by Manor: *100 Megaton Kill*, 1975; *Clouds of War*, 1975; *Judgment Day*, 1975; *The Peking Plot*, 1975; *Seeds of Doom*, 1976.

Under pseudonym Nick Carter; all published by Award House, 1971-73: *Assault on England; The Cairo Mafia; The Omega Terror; The Butcher of Belgrade; Agent Counter-Agent; Strike Force Terror; Vatican Vendetta; Code Name Vulture.*

Also author of three travel guides, on Greece, Netherlands, and Russia, for Simon & Schuster, 1974. More than thirty short stories have appeared in men's, mystery, travel, and sports magazines.

WORK IN PROGRESS: A new adventure series based on treasure hunting; a suspense novel.

SIDELIGHTS: Hayes has traveled in twenty-six countries, and uses a foreign setting for about two-thirds of his fiction. His favorite places are East Africa and Italy. He thinks that more storytellers are needed, and that a writer should regard "*all* the fiction he writes as *art,* regardless of genre or degree of literary significance."

* * *

HAYS, David G(lenn) 1928-

PERSONAL: Born November 17, 1928, in Memphis, Tenn.; son of Oliver Glenn (a warehouse manager) and Adele (de Long) Hays; married Marguerite Thompson (a physician and researcher), February 4, 1950 (separated, 1974); children: Dorothy Adele, Warren Stith Thompson, Thomas Glenn. *Education:* Harvard University, B.A., 1951, M.A., 1954, Ph.D., 1956. *Politics:* Democrat. *Residence:* Twin Willows, Wanakah, N.Y. 14075. *Office:* Department of Linguistics, Spaulding Quadrangle, State University of New York, Ahmerst Campus, Buffalo, N.Y. 14261.

CAREER: Center for Advanced Study in the Behavioral Sciences, Stanford, Calif., fellow in sociology, 1954-55; RAND Corp., Santa Monica, Calif., social scientist, 1955-68; State University of New York at Buffalo, professor of linguistics, 1968—. Lecturer at University of Southern California, 1956-58, and University of California, Los Angeles, 1950. Visiting scientist in computational linguistics, Euratom Research Center, Ispra, Italy, 1962-63. Member of Mathematical Social Science Board, 1967-71. Director of Linguistic Institute, 1971; member of Social Science Advisory Committee of National Science Institute, 1970-72. *Member:* Association for Computational Linguistics (president, 1964), International Committee on Computational Linguistics (chairman, 1965-69). *Awards, honors:* Bronze Medal, University of Brno, 1971, and University of Piza, 1973; Chancellor's Award for Excellence in Teaching, 1975.

WRITINGS: (Editor) *Readings in Automatic Language Processing*, American Elsevier, 1966; (editor) *Introduction to Computational Linguistics*, American Elsevier, 1967. Series editor, Elsevier's "Mathematical Linguistics and

Automatic Language Processing." Contributor of about forty-five articles to journals. Editor, *American Journal of Computational Linguistics,* 1974—.

WORK IN PROGRESS: Cognitive structures; cross-cultural linguistics.

SIDELIGHTS: David Hays speaks French and a little of a dozen other languages.

* * *

HAYTER, William Goodenough 1906-

PERSONAL: Born August 1, 1906, in Oxford, England; son of Sir William Goodenough (an adviser to the Egyptian Government) and Alethea (Slessor) Hayter; married Iris Hoare, October 19, 1938; children: Teresa Margaret. *Education:* Attended Winchester College; New College, Oxford, M.A., 1929. *Home:* Warden's Lodgings, New College, Oxford University, Oxford, England. *Office:* New College, Oxford, England.

CAREER: Entered the British Diplomatic Service, 1930, and served abroad in Vienna, Moscow, and China prior to World War II; postwar posts included assistant Under-Secretary of State, 1948, H.M. Minister in Paris, 1949, Ambassador to Soviet Union, 1953-57, and deputy Under-Secretary of State, 1957-58; New College, Oxford, England, warden, 1958—. Trustee, British Museum. *Member:* Brooks's Club. *Awards, honors:* Companion of St. Michael and St. George, 1948; Knight Commander of St. Michael and St. George, 1953.

WRITINGS: The Diplomacy of the Great Powers, Hamish Hamilton, 1959, Macmillan, 1961; *The Kremlin and the Embassy,* Hodder & Stoughton, 1967; *Russia and the World: A Study of Soviet Foreign Policy,* Secker & Warburg, 1970. Contributor to *Observer.*

BIOGRAPHICAL/CRITICAL SOURCES: New Leader, May 22, 1967; *Times Literary Supplement,* August 24, 1967.

* * *

HAZO, Robert G. 1931-

PERSONAL: Born February 11, 1931, in Pittsburgh, Pa.; son of Sam (a merchant) and Lottie (Abdou) Hazo. *Education:* St. John's College, Annapolis, Md., B.A., 1953; further study at Princeton University, 1953-54, Sorbonne, University of Paris, 1954-55, and American University of Beirut, 1955-57. *Office:* University of Pittsburgh, Pittsburgh, Pa.

CAREER: Institute for Philosophical Research, Chicago, Ill., associate director, 1957-63; *Encyclopaedia Britannica,* Chicago, Ill., senior editor, 1964-70; University of Pittsburgh, Pittsburgh, Pa., lecturer and director of special seminars, 1971—. *Member:* Nockian Society.

WRITINGS: The Idea of Love, Praeger, 1967. Contributor to *New Republic, Nation, Commonweal, America Illustrated, Commentary, American Scholar, New York Times Book Review,* and to newspapers.

SIDELIGHTS: Hazo's *The Idea of Love* is one of the books resulting from a project of the Institute for Philosophical Research: to compile and analyze all of philosophical thought on the major subjects of freedom, justice, happiness, progress, and love. These exhaustive studies, according to Brand Blanchard, might produce the phenomenon of "philosophers agreed on their terms before advancing to do battle." Material for each subject in the

books has developed out of years of discussion among philosophers at the Institute on every aspect of thought in each area. It was Hazo's task to write up the final compilation and analysis of "love," probably "the hardest of the subjects, where analysis is almost as unmanageable as the emotion," observes Blanchard. Despite the difficulty of the task Blanchard says that Hazo "balances the arguments with judicial gravity" (these ranging from the Freudian id to the Christian love of God), and accomplishes his analysis "illuminatingly."

BIOGRAPHICAL/CRITICAL SOURCES: New York Times Book Review, February 25, 1968.

* * *

HECHT, Marie B(ergenfeld) 1918-

PERSONAL: Born October 21, 1918, in New York, N.Y.; daughter of Frank F. (a lawyer) and Marie (Trommer) Bergenfeld; divorced; children: Ann (Mrs. David Bloomfield), Margaret (Mrs. Jason Crum), Laurence, Andrew. *Education:* Goucher College, B.A. (honors in political science), 1939; Johns Hopkins University, graduate study, 1940-42; C. W. Post College (now Long Island University), Teaching Certificate, 1960; New School for Social Research, M.A., 1971. *Politics:* Democrat. *Home:* 5 Hewlett Pl., Great Neck, N.Y. 11024. *Office:* Mineola High School, Garden City Park, N.Y. 11530.

CAREER: Mineola High School, Garden City Park, N.Y., teacher of history, 1960—. *Member:* Organization of American Historians, New York Historical Society, New York State Historical Association, Goucher College Club.

WRITINGS: (With Herbert S. Parmet) *Aaron Burr: Portrait of an Ambitious Man,* Macmillan, 1967; (with Parmet) *Never Again: A President Runs for a Third Term,* Macmillan, 1968; *John Quincy Adams,* Macmillan, 1972; (editor with others) *The Women, Yes!,* Holt, 1973; *Beyond the Presidency,* Macmillan, 1976. Contributor to *New York Historical Society Quarterly.*

SIDELIGHTS: Marie Hecht is competent in French. *Avocational interests:* Stamp collecting and gardening.

* * *

HECKMAN, Hazel 1904-

PERSONAL: Born April 6, 1904, in Liberty, Kan.; daughter of William Norman and Alice (Dudgeon) Price; married Earle D. Heckman (a foundryman), September 4, 1926; children: James C. *Education:* Studied at University of Kansas, 1922-23, 1925-26, University of Puget Sound, summer, 1952, and has taken various correspondence courses at University of Kansas, University of Chicago, and University of Oklahoma. *Home:* Anderson Island, Wash. 98303.

CAREER: Teacher in rural Kansas, 1923-25; reporter for University of Kansas News Bureau and Associated Press, 1925-26; proofreader and feature writer for *Blackwell News Tribune,* Blackwell, Okla., 1926-29; free-lance writer. Teacher of creative writing in adult education classes, Auburn, Wash., 1960-61. *Member:* Tacoma Writers Club, Seattle Free Lances. *Awards, honors:* Short story prize, *Country Home;* first prize for radio script, University of Oklahoma, 1935; Pacific Northwest Booksellers nonfiction award, 1967, for *Island in the Sound;* Governor's citation, 1968; Achievement of the Year award from Allied Arts of Tacoma, 1968; Governor's citation, 1973, for *Island Year.*

WRITINGS: Island in the Sound, University of Washington Press, 1967; *Island Year,* University of Washington Press, 1972; (with Willet J. Price) *Boots and Forceps,* Iowa State University Press, 1973. Also author of several radio plays.

Work represented in anthologies, including *Best Humor Annual,* edited by Louis Untermeyer and Ralph Shikes, Holt, 1952. Short stories, articles, and verse have been published in *Saturday Evening Post, Harper's, Collier's, Woman's Day, Argosy, Family Circle, Housewife* (England), and other magazines, and feature stories in *Kansas City Star, Seattle Magazine, Farm Journal,* and *Daily Oklahoman.*

WORK IN PROGRESS: A novel, tentatively entitled *Afterthought.*

SIDELIGHTS: Some of Mrs. Heckman's short stories have been adapted for use in high school speech contests. Her other writings were adapted for Washington Archives radio programs, sponsored by Washington State University. *Avocational interests:* Natural history, conservation and preservation of wildlife and natural areas everywhere.

BIOGRAPHICAL/CRITICAL SOURCES: Harper's, January 1952, March, 1952; *Saturday Review,* June 10, 1967; *Seattle Times,* November 19, 1967.

* * *

HECKMAN, William O(scar) 1921-

PERSONAL: Born July 7, 1921, in State College, Pa.; son of William Oscar (a high school teacher) and Ruth (Rossman) Heckman; married Opal McNeill, December 27, 1944; children: William Frederic, Ann Elizabeth. *Education:* Rutgers University, B.A., 1947; Columbia University, M.A., 1949. *Religion:* Protestant. *Home:* 1218 Holly St., Anaheim, Calif. 92801. *Office:* Fullerton Junior College, 321 East Chapman Ave., Fullerton, Calif. 92634.

CAREER: Carroll College, Waukesha, Wis., assistant professor of English and director of publicity, 1949-53; Cornell College, Mount Vernon, Iowa, assistant professor of English and journalism, 1953-54; Community Chest of Des Moines, Iowa, director of public relations, 1954-56; Iowa State University of Science and Technology, Ames, instructor in English, 1956-59; Fullerton Junior College, Fullerton, Calif., instructor in English, 1959—. California State College at Fullerton, part-time instructor in English, 1966—. *Military service:* U.S. Army, 1942-46; became first lieutenant. *Member:* National Council of Teachers of English, International Reading Association, National Education Association.

WRITINGS: (With P. Joseph Canavan) *The Way to Reading Improvement,* Allyn & Bacon, 1966. Contributor of poetry to journals.

WORK IN PROGRESS: A volume of poetry; programmed instruction in reading, literature, and grammar.††

* * *

HEIBY, Walter A(lbert) 1918-

PERSONAL: Born September 19, 1918, in Washington, D.C.; son of Albert A. (a mathematics teacher) and Laura (Jarmuth) Heiby; married Eunice Strehlow (an advertising executive), April 15, 1944; children: Ronald, Pamela. *Education:* University of Chicago, B.S., 1939; University of Illinois, graduate study, 1941. *Office:* General Industrial Co., 4744 West Peterson Ave., Chicago, Ill. 60646.

CAREER: Industrial Condenser Co., Chicago, Ill., assis-

tant design engineer, 1941-42; Austin Evening High School, Chicago, instructor in mathematics, 1941-43; Precision Scientific Co., Chicago, assistant advertising manager, 1942-43; Walker-Jimieson, Inc., advertising manager, 1943-45; Precision Equipment Co., Chicago, president and chairman of board, 1945-75; General Industrial Co., Chicago, president and chairman of board, 1953—; Institute of Dynamic Synthesis, Inc., Chicago, president, 1965—. *Member:* Mail Advertising Club of Chicago (former director).

WRITINGS: Stock Market Profits through Dynamic Synthesis, Institute of Dynamic Synthesis, 1965; *Live Your Life,* Harper, 1966; *The New Dynamic Synthesis,* Institute of Dynamic Synthesis, 1967. Contributor to *Encyclopedia of Stock Market Techniques.*

WORK IN PROGRESS: A book, *Great Sex, a Long Life and the Foods You Eat.*

* * *

HEIJKE, John 1927-

PERSONAL: Born June 28, 1927, in Amsterdam, Netherlands; son of Gerard John (a tailor) and Anna (Smit) Heijke. *Education:* Jesuit Faculty of Theology at Louvain, Th.Lic., 1954; Catholic University of Nijmegen, doctoral examination in theology, 1957. *Home:* Hollestraat 30, Nederasselt, Netherlands.

CAREER: Ordained Roman Catholic Priest, July 19, 1953; Seminary of the Holy Ghost Fathers, Gemert, Netherlands, professor of fundamental theology, 1957-66; Theological Institute, Eindhoven, Netherlands, professor of fundamental theology, beginning 1966; Catholic University of Nijmegen, Nijmegen, Netherlands, reader in Missiology, 1974—. Duquesne University, visiting professor of theology, 1963-64.

WRITINGS: St. Augustine's Comment on "Imago Dei," Supplement III of "Classical Folia," College of the Holy Cross Press, 1960; *De Bijbel over geloven,* Romen en Zonen (Roermond, Netherlands), 1965, published as *The Bible on Faith,* St. Norbert Abby Press, 1966; *An Ecumenical Light on the Renewal of Religious Community Life: Taize,* Duquesne University Press, 1967; *Theology for Missionaries,* Holy Ghost Fathers (Netherlands), 1974.

* * *

HELLER, Herbert L. 1908-

PERSONAL: Born March 12, 1908, in New Castle, Ind.; son of Herbert and Mary Elizabeth (Smith) Heller; married Evelyn Crim (a teacher), May 31, 1942; children: Carol Lynn (Mrs. James A. Bruen), David Crim. *Education:* Attended James Millikin University, 1926-28, and Alaska Agricultural College and School of Mines (now University of Alaska), 1928-30; Indiana University, A.M., 1931, Ed.D., 1952; Ball State University, M.A., 1938. *Religion:* Presbyterian. *Home address:* R.R. #3 Sherwood Dr., Greencastle, Ind. 46135.

CAREER: J. C. Penney Co., New Castle, Ind., salesman, 1934-36; New Castle Senior High School, New Castle, history teacher, 1936-42; Philco Radio Corp., Philadelphia, Pa., technical writer, 1946-47; Hanover College, Hanover, Ind., registrar, 1947-48; DePauw University, Greencastle, Ind., associate professor of education, 1950-59; Alaska Methodist University, Anchorage, academic dean, 1959-62; California Western University (now United States International University), San Diego, administrative assistant to dean, 1962-65; Baldwin-Wallace College, Berea, Ohio, professor of education, 1965-1973, professor emeritus, 1973—. Assistant director, Educational Development Center (non-profit organization directed at re-educating college failures who show potential), 1966-68. Teacher in summer camps, American Youth Foundation, 1935-41; field archivist, Indiana State Library, summers, 1957-58. *Military service:* U.S. Naval Reserve, electronics officer, 1942-45; served in South Pacific; became lieutenant commander.

MEMBER: American Association of University Professors, National Education Association, Ohio Education Association, Indiana Historical Society (chairman of schools committee), Kiwanis International, Phi Delta Kappa, Phi Alpha Theta.

WRITINGS: (Editor) *Readings in the History of New Castle, Indiana,* two volumes, privately printed, 1941; (editor) *Newspaper Readings in the History of New Castle, Indiana,* five volumes, privately printed, 1942; *Servicing Television Receivers,* Philco Radio Corp., 1946; (with Ross Lockridge) *The Story of Indiana,* Harlow, 1955, revised edition, 1958; *The Indiana Conference of the Methodist Church, 1832-1956,* Historical Society of the Indiana Conference, 1956; (editor) *Sourdough Sagas: The Journals, Memoirs, Tales, and Recollections of the Earliest Alaskan Gold Miners, 1883-1923,* World Publishing, 1967; *The Schools of New Castle, Indiana, 1832-1932,* New Castle School Corp., 1970; *The Presbyterian Church (1825-1975),* Mitchell-Fleming, 1975. Writer of faculty handbooks for Alaska Methodist and California Western universities, and similar university materials. Contributor to *Indianapolis Star Magazine* and education journals. Weekly columnist, "Justice in the Good Old Days," in *Berea News* and other local newspapers, 1968-69; columnist, "Historic Henry County," in *New Castle Courier-Times,* 1974—.

WORK IN PROGRESS: An Alaskan Odyssey: Life in the Gold Camps along the Yukon 1898-1923.

AVOCATIONAL INTERESTS: Collecting books on Indiana and Alaska history.

* * *

HELLER, Walter W(olfgang) 1915-

PERSONAL: Born August 27, 1915, in Buffalo, N.Y.; son of Ernst and Gertrude (Warmburg) Heller; married Emily Karen Johnson, September 16, 1938; children: Walter Perrin, Eric Johnson, Kaaren Louise. *Education:* Oberlin College, B.A., 1935; University of Wisconsin, M.A., 1938, Ph.D., 1941. *Home:* 2203 Folwell St., St. Paul, Minn. 55108. *Office:* Department of Economics, University of Minnesota, Minneapolis, Minn. 55455.

CAREER: University of Wisconsin, Madison, instructor, 1941-42; U.S. Treasury Department, Washington, D.C., fiscal economist, 1942-46; University of Minnesota, Minneapolis, associate professor, 1946-50, professor, 1950-67, Regents' Professor of Economics, 1967—, chairman of department, 1957-60. Visiting professor at University of Wisconsin, University of Washington, Seattle, and Harvard University. Chief of internal finance, U.S. Military Government in Germany, 1947-48; member, Economic Cooperation Administration Mission on German Fiscal Problems, 1951; fiscal adviser to governor of Minnesota, 1955-60; President's Council of Economic Advisors, chairman, 1961-64, consultant, 1974—; consultant, Executive Office of the President, 1965-69; member, U.S. Treasury Committee on Internal Monetary Arrangements, 1965-69; member, Federal Energy Office Advisory Panel, 1974—. Tax adviser to King Hussein and Royal Commission of Jordan,

1960; member of Minnesota State Council on Economic Education, 1961—, and Minnesota State Planning Board, 1965-71; chairman of group of fiscal experts, Organization for Economic Cooperation and Development, 1966-68; consultant at various times to the United Nations, Minnesota Department of Taxation, Brookings Institution, and U.S. Census Bureau; currently director of International Multifoods, Inc., National City Bank of Minneapolis, Northwestern National Life Insurance Co., and Commercial Credit Co. Trustee of Oberlin College, 1966—, College Retirement Equities Fund, 1968-72, and General Growth Properties, Inc.

MEMBER: American Economic Association (president, 1974), National Bureau of Economic Research (director, 1960—, chairman, 1971-74), American Finance Association, National Tax Association, Association for Evolutionary Economics, American Philosophical Society, American Council on Germany, American Academy of Arts and Sciences, Phi Beta Kappa, Beta Gamma Sigma, Alpha Kappa Psi, Federal City Club (Washington, D.C.), Skylight Club (Minneapolis). *Awards, honors:* LL.D., Oberlin College, 1964, and Ripon College, 1967; D.Litt., Kenyon College, 1965.

WRITINGS: (Editor with Francis M. Boddy and Carl L. Nelson) *Savings in the Modern Economy,* University of Minnesota Press, 1953; (with Clara Penniman) *State Income Tax Administration,* Public Administration Service (Chicago), 1959; *New Dimensions of Political Economy,* Harvard University Press, 1966; (co-author) *Revenue-Sharing and the City,* edited by Harvey Perloff and R. P. Nathan, Resources for the Future, 1968; (editor) *Perspectives on Economic Growth,* Random House, 1968; (with Milton Friedman) *Monetary vs. Fiscal Policy: A Dialogue,* Norton, 1969; *Economic Growth and Environmental Quality: Collision or Co-Existence?,* General Learning Press, 1973.

Contributor: *Financing the War,* Tax Institute, 1941; H. J. Morgenthau, editor, *Germany and the Future of Europe,* University of Chicago Press, 1951; *Limits of Taxable Capacity,* Tax Institute, 1953; Francis Godwin and others, editors, *The Hidden Force,* Harper, 1962; B. H. Wilkins and C. B. Friday, editors, *The Economists of the New Frontier,* Random House, 1963; James MacGregor Burns, editor, *To Heal and to Build,* McGraw, 1968. Also author of *Taxes and Fiscal Policy in Underdeveloped Countries,* 1954. Contributor to *Encyclopaedia Britannica,* professional journals, and congressional compendia on taxation, government expenditures, and economic growth and stability.

WORK IN PROGRESS: What's Right with Economics and Wrong with the Economy, for Norton.

AVOCATIONAL INTERESTS: Travel, wood-chopping, clam-digging.

BIOGRAPHICAL/CRITICAL SOURCES: Time, March 3, 1961, June 8, 1962; *Business Week,* December 15, 1962, January 25, 1964 (cover story); *Look,* December 15, 1963; *New York Review of Books,* October 10, 1968.

* * *

HEMPHILL, W(illiam) Edwin 1912-

PERSONAL: Born June 28, 1912, in Wake County, N.C.; son of J. Edwin (a minister) and Nellie Stuckey (Jackson) Hemphill; married Susan Langhorne Moffett (a teacher), June 6, 1939; children: Alice Gammon (Mrs. Thomas Bennett Clark), Susan Langhorne (Mrs. James Francis Steadman). *Education:* Hampden-Sydney College, B.A. (with first honors), 1932; Emory University, M.A., 1933; University of Virginia, Ph.D., 1937. *Religion:* Presbyterian. *Home:* 846 Camellia St., Columbia, S.C. 29205. *Office address:* South Carolina Department of Archives and History, P.O. Box 11669, Columbia, S.C. 29211.

CAREER: Teacher of history at Hampden-Sydney College in Virginia, Hampden-Sydney, 1934-35, Davidson College, Davidson, N.C., 1937-38, University of Virginia, Charlottesville, 1938-39, and Emory University, Atlanta, Ga., 1940-41; Mary Washington College, Fredericksburg, Va., assistant professor of history, 1939-40, 1941-44; Virginia World War II History Commission, Charlottesville, assistant director, 1944-45, director, 1946-50; Virginia State Library, Richmond, director of history division, 1950-59; South Carolina Department of Archives and History, Columbia, editor of *The Papers of John C. Calhoun,* 1959—. Member of board of trustees, Presbyterian College, 1966-75. *Member:* American Historical Association, Society of American Archivists (fellow), Organization of American Historians, American Association for State & Local History, Southern Historical Association, Phi Beta Kappa, Omicron Delta Kappa, Chi Phi, Kiwanis Club.

WRITINGS: (Editor) *Gold Star Honor Roll of Virginians,* Virginia World War II History Commission, 1947; (editor) *Pursuits of War: The People,* Albemarle County Historical Society, 1948; (editor) *Aerial Gunner from Virginia,* Virginia State Library, 1950; (with Marvin W. Schlegel and Sadie E. Engelberg) *Cavalier Commonwealth: History and Government of Virginia,* McGraw, 1957; (editor) *Extracts from the Journals of the Provincial Congresses of South Carolina, 1775-1776,* South Carolina Archives Department, 1960; (editor with Wylma Anne Wates and R. Nicholas Olsberg) *Journals of the General Assembly and House of Representatives, 1776-1780,* University of South Carolina Press, 1970. Contributor to historical journals. Editor, *Papers of the Albemarle County Historical Society,* Volumes VI-VIII, 1946-48, and *The Papers of John C. Calhoun,* Volumes II-VIII, 1963-75. Editor of *Virginia Cavalcade* (pictorial quarterly of Virginia State Library), 1951-59.

WORK IN PROGRESS: Additional volumes of *The Papers of John C. Calhoun.*

* * *

HENDERSON, Keith M. 1934-

PERSONAL: Born May 24, 1934, in Bakersfield, Calif.; son of John Dale (a consultant) and Ethel (McGough) Henderson; married Behi Lotfi, September 1, 1966. *Education:* Reed College, student, 1952-55; University of California, Berkeley, summer student, 1955; Occidental College, B.A., 1956; University of Southern California, M.S., 1957, D.P.A., 1961; Columbia University, postdoctoral study, 1964-65. *Religion:* Presbyterian. *Home:* 105 Middlesex Rd., Buffalo, N.Y. 14216. *Office:* Department of Political Science, State University of New York College, 1300 Elmwood, Buffalo, N.Y. 14222.

CAREER: City of Los Angeles, Calif., various posts in civil service department and city administrative office, 1956-60, field deputy of city council, 1961; American University of Beirut, Beirut, Lebanon, assistant professor of public administration, 1961-64; New York University, Graduate School of Public Administration, New York, N.Y., associate professor of public administration, 1964-69; State University of New York College at Buffalo, professor of political science, 1969—. Consultant to Civil Service Commission of Jordan. *Military service:* U.S. Army, 1959-60.

MEMBER: American Society for Public Administration, American Political Science Association, International Political Science Association, International Institute of Administrative Sciences, Royal Institute of Public Administration, American Association for the Advancement of Science, American Academy of Political and Social Science, American Real Estate and Urban Economics Association, American Association of University Professors, Middle East Institute, Middle East Studies Association (fellow), Society for International Development, Comparative Administration Group, National Wildlife Federation, Psi Chi.

WRITINGS: Emerging Synthesis in American Public Administration, Asia Publishing House, 1966; (contributor) Vera Micheles Dean, editor, *The Nature of the Non-Western World,* revised edition, New American Library, 1966; (contributor) Joseph Dunner, editor, *Handbook of Historical Concepts,* Philosophical Library, 1967. Contributor of about thirty articles and reviews to journals.

WORK IN PROGRESS: Administrative Management in Government.

* * *

HENDRICKSON, James E. 1932-

PERSONAL: Born May 1, 1932, in Tofield, Alberta, Canada; son of George E. and Magda P. (Anderson) Hendrickson; married Sonja J. K. Gotaas, July 14, 1958; children: Joy, David, Mark, Mary. *Education:* University of Saskatchewan, B.A., 1955; University of Alberta, B.Ed., 1958; University of Oregon, M.A., 1961, Ph.D., 1965. *Religion:* Lutheran. *Home:* 2511 Sinclair Rd., Victoria, British Columbia, Canada V8N 1B5. *Office:* History Department, University of Victoria, Victoria, British Columbia, Canada.

CAREER: University of Victoria, Victoria, British Columbia, lecturer, 1964-65, assistant professor, 1965-67, associate professor of history, 1967—, chairman of department, 1969—. Member of board of regents, Camrose Lutheran College. Member, Historic Sites Advisory Board of British Columbia, 1972—. *Member:* American Historical Association, Organization of American Historians. *Awards, honors:* Marion F. McClain Prize, University of Oregon, 1967; Canadian Council fellow, 1971-72.

WRITINGS: Joe Lane of Oregon: Machine Politics and the Sectional Crisis, 1849-1861, Yale University Press, 1967. Contributor of articles to professional journals.

* * *

HENLEY, Arthur 1921-
(Kenneth Eric, Webb Jones)

PERSONAL: Born September 9, 1921, in New York, N.Y.; son of Nathan (a salesman) and Tessie (Hohauser) Henley; married Janet Radskin, June 3, 1950; children: Eric, Kenneth. *Education:* Pratt Institute, E.A., 1943; City College of the City University of New York, B.A., 1969. *Home:* 73-37 Austin St., Forest Hills, N.Y. 11375. *Office:* 507 Fifth Ave., New York, N.Y. 10017.

CAREER: Fairchild Instruments Co., New York City, technical writer, 1944; Arthur Henley Productions, New York City, television-radio writer and producer, 1945-61; free-lance writer, 1961—. Television consultant; lecturer in creative writing at New York University, 1970-71, and at other colleges and universities. *Member:* National Association of Science Writers, American Federation of Television and Radio Artists, Society of Magazine Writers. *Awards, honors:* Crusade for Freedom, U.S. Treasury Department, and Veterans of Foreign Wars awards, 1967, for *Make Up Your Mind;* Russell Sage Foundation award, 1973.

WRITINGS: Comedy: How to Write It, privately printed, 1948; *Demon In My View,* Trident, 1966; *Make Up Your Mind,* Pocket Books, 1967; (with Robert L. Wolk) *Yes Power,* Peter H. Wyden, 1969; (with Wolk) *The Right to Lie: A Psychological Guide to the Uses of Deceit in Everyday Life,* Peter H. Wyden, 1970; (with Adelio Montanari) *The Montanari Book: What Other Child-Care Books Won't Tell You,* Stein & Day, 1971 (published in England as *The Montanari Method: What Other Child-Care Books Won't Tell You,* W. H. Allen, 1973); *Schizophrenia: Current Approaches to a Baffling Problem,* Public Affairs Press, 1971; (with Mort Weisinger) *The Complete Alibi Handbook,* Citadel, 1972; *The Difficult Child,* Stein & Day, 1973. Columnist, *Brides,* 1969-70. Work anthologized in several books on creative writing; contributor to popular and professional periodicals.

WORK IN PROGRESS: A novel; a book on moods.

*   *   *

HENNESSY, Mary L.   1927-

PERSONAL: Born January 4, 1927, in St. Paul, Minn.; daughter of Hugh J. (a chemist) and Gertrude (Luger) Hennessy. *Education:* College of St. Catherine, B.A., 1948. *Politics:* Democrat. *Home:* 2514 K St. N.W., Washington, D.C. 20037. *Office:* Labor Relations Training Center, U.S. Civil Service Commission, Washington, D.C.

CAREER: Building Service Employees International Union, Chicago, Ill., research assistant, 1961-63; Public Personnel Association, Chicago, Ill., member of staff, 1963-69; American Federation of State, County, and Municipal Employees International Union, Washington, D.C., assistant director of research, 1969-74; Federal Mediation and Conciliation Service, Washington, D.C., labor economist, 1974-76; Labor Relations Training Center, U.S. Civil Service Commission, Washington, D.C., member of staff, 1976—.

WRITINGS: Public Management at the Bargaining Table, Public Personnel, 1967; *Contract Clauses,* Public Personnel, 1968; (contributor) Loewenberg and Moskow, editors, *Collective Bargaining in Government,* Prentice-Hall, 1971.

*   *   *

HENZE, Donald F(rank)   1928-

PERSONAL: Born August 24, 1928, in Plymouth, Wis.; son of Francis Frank (an insurance man) and Florence (Dassow) Henze; married Jean Justiliano, October 30, 1953 (divorced, 1968); children: Ingrid Kirsten, Christopher Ernest. *Education:* University of Wisconsin, B.A., 1950, M.A., 1951, Ph.D., 1954; University of California, Berkeley, graduate study, 1951-52. *Home:* 13044 Hartsook St., Sherman Oaks, Calif. 91423. *Office:* Department of Philosophy, California State University, 18111 Nordoff St., Northridge, Calif. 91324.

CAREER: Instructor in philosophy at Trinity College, Hartford, Conn., 1956-58, and University of Maryland, College Park, 1958-59; University of Northern Illinois, De

Kalb, assistant professor of philosophy, 1959-60; California State University, Northridge, assistant professor, 1960-63, associate professor, 1963-67, professor of philosophy, 1967—. *Military service:* U.S. Army, 1954-56. *Member:* Desert Protective Council, Wilderness Society. *Awards, honors:* American Council of Learned Societies grant, 1974.

WRITINGS: (With John Turk Saunders) *The Private-Language Problem: A Philosophical Dialogue,* Random House, 1967. Contributor to professional journals in United States, Britain, and Australia.

WORK IN PROGRESS: A book, *Other Minds: The History of a Problem from Descartes to Reid.*

AVOCATIONAL INTERESTS: Chamber music, mountain climbing, desert camping, raising cacti.

*   *   *

HEPPENSTALL, Margit Strom   1913-

PERSONAL: Born March 8, 1913, in Trondheim, Norway; daughter of Anton Margido (an army officer) and Magdalena (Weyergang) Strom; married Edward Heppenstall (a university professor), June 6, 1938; children: Malcolm Edward, Astrid Margaret. *Education:* Attended University of Norway, 1933-36; Andrews University, B.A. (with honors), 1938, M.A., 1963. *Politics:* Republican. *Religion:* Seventh-day Adventist. *Residence:* Riverside, Calif.

CAREER: Primary teacher in public schools of Corona, Calif., 1954-55, Langley Park, Md., 1955-58, Silver Spring, Md., 1959-60, St. Joseph, Mich., 1960-62, 1963-66, and San Bernardino, Calif. 1962-63.

WRITINGS: Treasure in the West, Pacific Press Publishing Association, 1954; *The Book and the Quest,* Review & Herald, 1961; *Deborah,* Southern Publishing, 1967; *Secret Mission,* Southern Publishing, 1972. Contributor to Seventh-day Adventist publications.

SIDELIGHTS: Margit Strom Heppenstall speaks German and French in addition to her native Norwegian; reads and "can communicate" in Danish and Swedish. *Avocational interests:* Reading, gardening, listening to classical music, needlework, and travel (United States, Canada, Europe, Africa, the Orient and the Caribbean).

*   *   *

HERBER, Bernard P.   1929-

PERSONAL: Born November 11, 1929, in Ottumwa, Iowa; son of Nicholas William (an office worker) and Anne (Sheridan) Herber; married Jean Marie Carey, January 16, 1960; children: Mary Frances, Ann Terese; stepchildren: Kathleen, Sandra, Michael. *Education:* Loyola University of Los Angeles, B.A., 1954; University of Arizona, M.A., 1955; University of Washington, Seattle, Ph.D., 1960. *Home:* 5623 East 14th St., Tucson, Ariz. 85711. *Office:* Department of Economics, University of Arizona, Tucson, Ariz. 85721.

CAREER: University of Arizona, Tucson, 1957-61, began as instructor, became assistant professor of economics; University of Texas at El Paso, associate professor of economics, 1961-62; University of Arizona, assistant professor, 1962-64, associate professor, 1964-67, professor of economics, 1967—, assistant dean of College of Business and Public Administration, 1964-67. *Member:* American Economic Association, National Tax Association, Tax Institute of America, Western Economic Association.

WRITINGS: Modern Public Finance (textbook), Irwin, 1967, 2nd edition published as Modern Public Finance: The Study of Public Sector Economics, 1971, 3rd edition, 1975; Fiscal Federalism in the USA (monograph), Australian National University, 1975. Contributor to business, tax, public utilities, and economics journals.

WORK IN PROGRESS: Public and Private Goods Trends in the American Economy; The Vertical and Horizontal Fiscal Effects of General Revenue Sharing.

* * *

HERBERT, John 1924-

PERSONAL: Born March, 1924. Education: University of London, London School of Economics and Political Science, B.Sc., 1950, Institute of Education, Diploma, 1954; Cornell University, M.Ed., 1958; Columbia University, Ed.D., 1964. Office: Center for Educational Studies, Universiti Sains Malaysia, Minden, Pulau Pinang, Malaysia.

CAREER: LMS Railway, London, England, skilled engine fitter and apprentice engineer, 1942-45; teacher at elementary, high school, and evening college level in England, 1945-55; director of youth camps in England, Holland, and Belgium, 1949-50; high school teacher in New York and Massachusetts, 1955-58; supervising principal of school in Northfield, Minn., 1958-62; Columbia University, Teachers College, New York, N.Y., research assistant, Institute of Field Studies and Horace Mann-Lincoln Institute for School Experimentation, 1962-64; Reed College, Portland, Ore., associate professor of education and director of graduate program for teachers, 1964-67; University of Toronto, Toronto, Ontario, associate professor of educational theory, School of Graduate Studies, and associate professor of curriculum and instruction, Ontario Institute for Studies in Education, 1967-74; expert in educational psychology for UNESCO, 1974-76, currently in Malaysia.

MEMBER: American Educational Research Association, Canadian Educational Research Association, Association for Supervision and Curriculum Development, National Principals Association (life member), American Psychological Association, National Education Association (life member), Canadian Association for Curriculum Studies, Canadian Society for the Study of Education.

WRITINGS: (Contributor) Wilbur Schramm, editor, Four Case Studies in Programmed Education, Fund for the Advancement of Education, 1964; Team Teaching: A Working Bibliography, Horace Mann-Lincoln Institute for School Experimentation, 1964; (with John Swayze) Wireless Observation, Teachers College, Columbia University, 1964; A System for Analyzing Lessons, Teachers College, Columbia University, 1967; (editor with David Ausubel) Psychology in Teacher Preparation, Ontario Institute for Studies in Education, 1969; (contributor) Anita Simon, editor, Mirrors for Behavior, Research for Better Schools, 1970; (contributor) Educational Objectives and the Teaching of Educational Psychology, Methuen, 1972; (editor with Geoffry Milburn) National Consciousness and the Curriculum, Ontario Institute for Studies in Education, 1974; (contributor) Phillip Taylor and Mauritz Johnson, editors, Curriculum Development: A Comparative Study, National Foundation for Educational Research, 1974; (contributor) National Consciousness and the Curriculum, Ontario Institute for Studies in Education, 1974. Contributor to education journals. Founding editor, Curriculum Theory Network, 1968-74; Journal of Curriculum Studies, member of editorial board, 1970-74, Far East editor, 1974—.

HERN, (George) Anthony 1916-
(Andrew Hope; Potiphar, a joint pseudonym)

PERSONAL: Born November 4, 1916, in Camberley, Surrey, England; son of George Frederick and Marion Margaret (Hogan) Hern; married Frances Josephine Starr, October 7, 1939; children: Nicholas, Justin. Education: Attended grammar school in Surrey, England, 1927-34. Home: Maycot, Woodland Way, Kingswood, Tadworth, Surrey, England. Office: Evening Standard, 47 Shoe Lane, London E.C.4, England.

CAREER: Daily Express, London, England, editorial staff, 1945-61; Evening Standard, London, England, literary editor, 1962—. Member: National Union of Journalists, Society of Authors, Savage Club (London; committee member, 1967—).

WRITINGS: (With J. F. Marrack, under joint pseudonym Potiphar) They Must Not Starve, Gollancz, 1945; (ghost writer) Ian Fraser, Frogman VC, Angus & Robertson, 1954; (ghost writer) Arthur Shaw, Doctors for Hire, R. Hale, 1960; The Seaside Holiday (social history), Cresset, 1967. Regular contributor to Bookman, 1963—.

WORK IN PROGRESS: A social history of invective and bad manners; a social history of etiquette; a novel set in the thirties, under pseudonym Andrew Hope.

SIDELIGHTS: Hern told CA: "Belated, possibly arrogant, conviction that academic historians tend to lack humor and knowledge of ordinary people has led me to adopt role of serious but unpompous historian. Particularly interested in social nuances affecting behaviour patterns, and have sketched ambitious plan for series of novels on this theme.... Have been intellectually influenced by the great liberators—Joyce, Eliot, Picasso—but newspaper work had disciplined my half-Irish exuberance, which is probably A Good Thing. Chief professional failing is occasional flippancy; my only virtue that I work."††

* * *

HERO, Alfred O(livier) Jr. 1924-

PERSONAL: Born February 7, 1924, in New Orleans, La.; son of Alfred Olivier (a planter and textile executive) and Effel Anita (Pearson) Hero; married Barbara Ann Ferrell (an artist), May 22, 1954 (divorced, 1971); children: Alfred O. III, Barbara Ann, Michelle Claire, David Evans. Education: Virginia Military Institute, student, 1941-42; U.S. Military Academy, B.S., 1945; Vanderbilt University, M.A. (psychology), 1949, M.A. (political science), 1950; Georgetown University, graduate study, 1950-51; George Washington University, Ph.D., 1954. Home: 67 Larch Rd., Cambridge, Mass. 02138. Office: World Peace Foundation, 40 Mount Vernon St., Boston, Mass. 02108.

CAREER: U.S. Army, regular officer, 1945-54, serving in Germany, 1945-48, in the office of Chief of Personnel, Washington, D.C., 1950-53, and as member of staff and faculty, Infantry School, Fort Benning, Ga., 1953-54; captain at time of resignation from Regulary Army, 1954; World Peace Foundation, Boston, Mass., executive secretary, 1954-71, member of board of editors and executive committee, 1972—. Secretary, Boston Committee on Foreign Relations, 1954—; member of board of directors, World Affairs Council of Boston and Boston Council for International Visitors; member of international relations committee, National Council of Churches and Massachusetts Council of Churches. Member: American Political Science Association.

WRITINGS: Studies in Citizen Participation in International Relations, World Peace Foundation, Volume I: *Americans in World Affairs,* 1959, Volume IV: *Mass Media and World Affairs,* 1960, Volume V: *Voluntary Organizations in World Affairs Communications,* 1961, Volume VI: *Opinion Leaders in American Communities,* 1961; *The Southerner and World Affairs,* Louisiana State University Press, 1965; *The Reuther-Meany Foreign Policy Dispute,* Oceana, 1971; *American Religious Groups View Foreign Policy,* Duke University Press, 1973; (co-editor and contributor) *Le Nationalisme quebecois a la croisee des chemins,* Centre Quebecois des Relations Internationales and Universite Laval, 1975; (co-editor and contributor) *Canada and the United States: Transnational and Transgovernmental Relations,* Columbia University Press, 1976. Managing editor, *International Organization,* 1954-71.

*   *   *

HERRESHOFF, David   1921-

PERSONAL: Born November 21, 1921, in New York, N.Y.; son of James Brown (a metalurgist) and Constance (Mills) Herreshoff; married Doris Kaplan (a librarian), December 21, 1943; children: Robert, Peter, Matthew. *Education:* University of Akron, B.A., 1951; University of Minnesota, M.A., 1957, Ph.D., 1959. *Politics:* Socialist. *Home:* 75 McLean, Highland Park, Mich. 48203. *Office:* Department of English, Wayne State University, Detroit, Mich. 48202.

CAREER: Industrial worker, 1938-43; United Rubber Workers, Akron, Ohio, tirebuilder, 1943-51; American Federation of Teachers, Detroit, Mich., staff member of local union paper, 1959—; Wayne State University, Detroit, instructor, 1959-64, assistant professor of English, 1964—, chairman of Program in American Studies, 1965-66. Member of executive board, American Civil Liberties Union, Detroit. *Military service:* U.S. Army, T/5 Signal Corps, 1942-43. *Member:* Modern Language Association, American Studies Association, Melville Society. *Awards, honors:* Research fellowships from Wayne State University, 1964, 1966.

WRITINGS: (Contributor) Harvey Goldberg, editor, *American Radicals,* Monthly Review Press, 1957; (contributor) Bert Cochran, editor, *American Labor in Midpassage,* Monthly Review Press, 1958; *American Disciples of Marx: From the Age of Jackson to the Progressive Era,* Wayne State University Press, 1967, published as *Origins of American Marxism: From the Transcendentalist to De Leon,* Monad Press, 1973. Contributor to *Journal of Human Relations.*

WORK IN PROGRESS: Work and character (occupation as a device for characterization) in American literature; the Bible as a source in American literature.

SIDELIGHTS: Herreshoff writes to *CA:* "I have a strong active and scholarly interest in radical politics and labor organizations." His book, *American Disciples of Marx: From the Age of Jackson to the Progressive Era,* deals with the way in which Marx's ideas were interpreted and modified in the United States during those years. It concerns both the impact of Marxism on America and the influence of America on Marxism.

BIOGRAPHICAL/CRITICAL SOURCES: Times Literary Supplement, August 24, 1967; *Choice,* January, 1968.

HERRICK, Walter R(ussell), Jr.   1918-

PERSONAL: Born January 1, 1918, in New York, N.Y.; son of Walter Russell and Helen (Aull) Herrick; married Joan Alexandre, July 19, 1941; married second wife, Catrina Norris, April 14, 1959; children: Walter R. III, Patricia A., Frederick R., Charles A., Joan A., Catrina F. *Education:* Yale University, A.B., 1940; Columbia University, A.M., 1959; University of Virginia, Ph.D., 1962. *Politics:* Republican. *Home:* 40 Mohawk Dr., West Hartford, Conn. 06117. *Office:* Department of History, Quinnipiac College, Hamden, Conn. 06517.

CAREER: Pomfret School, Pomfret, Conn., history master, 1940; Salisbury School, Salisbury, Conn., instructor in history, Latin, and French, 1946-53, assistant headmaster, 1949-53; Haley Travel Service, New York City, commercial accounts agent, 1955-56; Hornblower & Weeks, New York City, registered representative, 1956-58; University of Virginia, Charlottesville, instructor in American history, 1961-62; Rollins College, Winter Park, Fla., associate professor of modern history, 1962-67; Quinnipiac College, Hamden, Conn., associate professor, 1967-72, professor of modern history, 1972—. *Military service:* U.S. Naval Reserve, active duty, 1941-45; became lieutenant commander. *Member:* American Historical Association, U.S. Naval Institute, Naval Historical Foundation, American Military Institute, Organization of American Historians, Maritime Historical Association (Mystic, Conn.).

WRITINGS: The American Naval Revolution, Louisiana State University Press, 1966.

WORK IN PROGRESS: Five chapters for a two-volume work, *American Secretaries of the Navy,* edited by Paolo Coletta.

AVOCATIONAL INTERESTS: Boating, dramatics, tennis.†

*   *   *

HERRICK, William   1915-

PERSONAL: Born January 10, 1915, in Trenton, N.J.; son of Nathan and Mary (Saperstein) Horvitz; married Jeannette Esther Wellin, August 31, 1948; children: Jonathan, Michael, Lisa. *Education:* Educated in public schools, New York, N.Y. *Residence:* Stockbridge, Mass. *Agent:* Roberta Pryor, International Creative Management, 40 West 57th St., New York, N.Y. 10019.

CAREER: Court reporter, 1943-69; began writing in 1956.

WRITINGS: The Itinerant (novel), McGraw, 1967; *Strayhorn* (novel), McGraw, 1968; *Hermanos!* (novel), Simon & Schuster, 1969; *The Last to Die* (novel), Simon & Schuster, 1971.

WORK IN PROGRESS: A novel, *Golcz: All-Universe.*

SIDELIGHTS: Hermanos! is to be filmed by Avco Embassy, 1976, with the screenplay by Reginald Rose.

*   *   *

HERRMANN, Frank   1927-

PERSONAL: Born May 18, 1927; married Patricia Robinson, 1954; children: Camilla, Lucilla, Paul, Piers. *Education:* Attended Magdalen College, Oxford. *Office:* Marshall, Morgan & Scott, Ltd., 116 Baker St., London W.1., England.

CAREER: Associated Book Publishers Ltd., London, England, publisher, director of editorial planning, and production director, beginning 1965; currently managing director of Marshall, Morgan & Scott, Ltd., London. Director of World Distributors Ltd., and Pentos Ltd.; chairman of Ward Lock Ltd., and Hudsons Bookshops Ltd. *Member:* Society of Antiquaries (fellow), Walpole Society, English Ceramics Circle, Double Crown Club.

WRITINGS: (Translator from the German) Peter Bamm, *The Invisible Flag,* Faber, 1956; *The Giant Alexander,* McGraw, 1964; *The Giant Alexander and the Circus,* McGraw, 1966; *The Giant Alexander in America,* McGraw, 1968; *The Giant Alexander and Hannibal the Elephant,* McGraw, 1971; *The English as Collectors,* Norton, 1972; *All about the Giant Alexander,* Methuen, 1975. Contributor to magazines.

WORK IN PROGRESS: The History of Sotheby's, for Norton.

* * *

HERTZ, Richard C(ornell) 1916-

PERSONAL: Born October 7, 1916, in St. Paul, Minn.; son of Abram J. (in insurance business) and Nadine (Rosenberg) Hertz; married Mary Louise Mann, November 25, 1943; children: Nadine, Ruth Mann. *Education:* University of Cincinnati, B.A., 1938; Hebrew Union College, Cincinnati, Ohio, M.H.L. (honors), 1942; Northwestern University, Ph.D., 1948. *Office:* Temple Beth El, 7400 Telegraph Rd., Birmingham, Mich.

CAREER: Rabbi (Reform Judaism), 1942—; assistant rabbi of congregation in Glencoe, Ill., 1942-47; associate rabbi of congregation in Chicago, Ill., 1947-53; Temple Beth El, Birmingham, Mich., senior rabbi, 1953—. Adjunct professor of Jewish thought, University of Detroit, 1970—. Former chairman of board of overseers, Hebrew Union College-Jewish Institute of Religion. Former member of board of directors, Boys' Clubs of Detroit, Detroit Institute of Technology, and United Foundation, Detroit. *Military service:* U.S. Army, chaplain, 1943-46; became captain.

MEMBER: Central Conference of American Rabbis (former executive board member), Religious Education Association (member of national executive committee), World Union for Progressive Judaism, American Legion (department chaplain for Michigan, 1954), Jewish War Veterans (department chaplain, 1956), Economic Club of Detroit, Rotary Club, Wrangler's Ministerial Association (president, 1958-59). *Awards, honors:* Hebrew Union College, D.D., 1967.

WRITINGS: This I Believe (sermons), privately printed, 1952; *Education of the Jewish Child,* Union of American Hebrew Congregations, 1953; *Our Religion above All,* Temple Beth El, 1953; *Inner Peace for You,* Temple Beth El, 1954; *Positive Judaism,* Temple Beth El, 1955; *Wings of the Morning,* Temple Beth El, 1956; *Prescription for Heartache,* Pageant, 1958.

The Responsibilities of Lay Leadership in Large Congregations, Union of American Hebrew Congregations, 1960; *Faith in Jewish Survival* (sermons), Temple Beth El, 1961; *Jewish Life Today* (sermons), Bloch Publishing, 1962; *The American Jew in Search of Himself,* Bloch Publishing, 1962; *What Counts Most in Life?,* Bloch Publishing, 1963; *What Can a Man Believe?,* Bloch Publishing, 1967. Also author of *Winning the Peace,* 1956, *Impressions of Israel* (collection of articles first published in *Detroit Times*), 1956, and *Juvenile Delinquency: How to Understand It?*

What to Do about It?, 1958. Contributor to scholarly and popular Jewish and secular journals.

SIDELIGHTS: Dr. Hertz traveled to the U.S.S.R. in 1959, on a special mission for the White House to investigate the status of Jews and Judaism behind the Iron Curtain. His report to President Eisenhower and the U.S. Department of State was printed in the *Congressional Record.* In 1963, Dr. Hertz was the first American rabbi received in private audience at the Papal Palace by Pope Paul VI. He has conducted retreats for Jewish personnel in the U.S. Armed Forces stationed in Europe and in 1974 went on a mission to the Arab countries and Israel with Christian and Jewish leaders to study refugee problems and explore alternatives of peace in the Middle East.

* * *

HERZ, Martin F(lorian) 1917-

PERSONAL: Born July 9, 1917, in New York, N.Y.; son of Gustave L. and Edith (Flammerschein) Herz; married Elisabeth Kremenak (a gynecologist), April 6, 1957. *Education:* Columbia University, B.S., 1937, graduate study, 1939-41. *Office:* U.S. Department of State, Washington, D.C. 20520; and U.S. Embassy, Sofia, Bulgaria.

CAREER: Wessel, Duval & Co., New York, N.Y., junior executive, 1940-41; U.S. Department of State, Foreign Service officer, 1946—. Assigned to Vienna, 1946-48; officer in charge of Austrian cultural and information affairs, Washington, D.C., 1949-50; second secretary, U.S. Embassy, Paris, France, 1950-54; second secretary, then first secretary of U.S. Embassy, Phnom Penh, Cambodia, 1955-57; first secretary of U.S. Embassy, Tokyo, Japan, 1957-59; political-military adviser, Bureau of African Affairs, Washington, D.C., 1960-61; special assistant for planning, Bureau of African Affairs, 1961-63; counselor for political affairs, U.S. Embassy, Tehran, Iran, 1963-67; country director, Bureau of East Asian Affairs, 1967-68; minister-counselor for political affairs, Saigon, Vietnam, 1968-70; deputy assistant secretary of state, Washington, D.C., 1970-74; ambassador to the People's Republic of Bulgaria, Sofia, 1974—. *Military service:* U.S. Army, 1941-46; served in Europe; became major; received Purple Heart and Bronze Star. *Member:* American Foreign Service Association (board member, 1961-63, 1967-68; vice-chairman of board, 1963). *Awards, honors:* Commendable Service Award, U.S. Department of State, 1961.

WRITINGS: (With Zack Hanle) *The Golden Ladle,* Ziff-Davis Publishing, 1943; *A Short History of Cambodia,* Praeger, 1958; *Beginnings of the Cold War,* Indiana University Press, 1966. Contributor to *Foreign Service Journal, Army Digest, Public Opinion Quarterly,* and *Military Review.*

WORK IN PROGRESS: Two novels.

SIDELIGHTS: Herz speaks French, German, Italian, Spanish, Japanese, and Farsi (Persian).

BIOGRAPHICAL/CRITICAL SOURCES: Daniel Lerner, *Psywar,* George W. Stewart, 1949; Morris Janowitz and William E. Daugherty, editors, *Psychological Warfare Casebook,* Johns Hopkins Press, 1958.

* * *

HESS, Gary R(ay) 1937-

PERSONAL: Born March 23, 1937, in Pittsburgh, Pa.; son of John C. (an accountant) and Dorothy (Brombach) Hess; married Rose Cycler (a teacher), August 29, 1966. *Educa-*

tion: University of Pittsburgh, A.B., 1959; University of Virginia, M.A., 1962, Ph.D., 1965. *Politics:* Democrat. *Home:* 216 Baldwin Ave., Bowling Green, Ohio 43402. *Office:* Department of History, Bowling Green State University, Bowling Green, Ohio 43402.

CAREER: Bowling Green State University, Bowling Green, Ohio, instructor, 1964-65, assistant professor, 1965-68, associate professor, 1968-72, professor of history, 1972—, chairman of department, 1973—. *Member:* American Historical Association, Society of American Historians, Society of Historians of American Foreign Relations, Phi Beta Kappa. *Awards, honors:* Woodrow Wilson fellowship, 1959-60; Fulbright grant to India, 1963-64; National Humanities Foundation summer research grant, 1967; Harry S. Truman Library Institute research grant, 1974.

WRITINGS: Sam Higginbottom of Allahabad, Pioneer of Point Four to India, University Press of Virginia, 1967; *America Encounters India, 1941-47,* Johns Hopkins Press, 1971; (editor) *America and Russia: Cold War Confrontation to Coexistence,* Crowell, 1973. Contributor of articles to history and political science journals.

WORK IN PROGRESS: A book, *American Policy in Southeast Asia, 1940-54.*

* * *

HESS, John M(ilton) 1929-

PERSONAL: Born November 24, 1929, in Grand Island, Neb.; son of August Theodore (a merchant) and Amy Jane (Blofield) Hess; married Delpha Louise Balster, October 28, 1950; children: Delphia Lynn, John Steven, Amy Ann. *Education:* University of Iowa, B.S., 1951; University of Oregon, M.B.A., 1955; Stanford University, Ph.D., 1959. *Religion:* Lutheran. *Home:* Mesa Canyon Rd., Boulder, Colo. 80302. *Office:* Department of Marketing, University of Colorado, Boulder, Colo. 80302.

CAREER: University of Colorado, Boulder, assistant professor, 1957-59, associate professor, 1959-66, professor of marketing, 1966—. Visiting distinguished professor, U.S. International University, 1969-70. Managing associate, Mentor Associates; director of several corporations. *Military service:* U.S. Air Force, 1951-53; became first lieutenant. *Member:* American Marketing Association, Lutheran Academy for Scholarship.

WRITINGS: Trade-In Housing Management, Stanford University Press, 1958; (editor) *The Trouble with Marketing Today,* University of Colorado Press, 1960; (editor) *New Product Marketing,* University of Colorado Press, 1961; (editor with P. R. Cateora) *The Industrial Marketing Environment,* University of Colorado Press, 1965; (with Cateora) *International Marketing,* Irwin, 1966, 3rd edition, 1975.

WORK IN PROGRESS: A series, "Great American Salesmen."

* * *

HESS, Robert D(aniel) 1920-

PERSONAL: Born March 10, 1920, in Shambaugh, Iowa; son of John (a minister) and Alillian Hess; divorced; children: Jared, Alyssa, Devin, Bradley. *Education:* University of California, Berkeley, B.A., 1947; University of Chicago, Ph.D., 1950. *Home:* 3903D Middlefield Rd., Palo Alto, Calif. 94303. *Office:* School of Education, Stanford University, Stanford, Calif. 94305.

CAREER: University of Chicago, Chicago, Ill., instructor and secretary of Committee on Human Development, 1949-53, assistant professor, 1953-59, associate professor and chairman of Committee on Human Development, 1959-64, professor of human development and education, and director of Urban Child Center, 1964-67, director of Early Education Research Center, 1965-67; Center for Advanced Study in the Behavioral Sciences, Stanford, Calif., fellow, 1966-67; Stanford University, Stanford, Lee L. Jacks Professor of Child Education and professor of psychology, 1967—. *Military service:* U.S. Marine Corps Reserve, active duty, 1942-46; became captain.

MEMBER: American Association for the Advancement of Science, American Educational Research Association, American Psychological Association, American Sociological Association, Society for Research in Child Development.

WRITINGS: (With Gerald Handel) *Family Worlds: A Psychosocial Approach to Family Life,* University of Chicago Press, 1959; (with Benjamin Bloom and Allison Davis) *Compensatory Education for Cultural Deprivation,* Holt, 1965; (with Judith V. Torney) *The Development of Political Attitudes in Children,* Aldine, 1967; (editor with Roberta Bear, and contributor) *Early Education: Current Theory, Research, and Practice,* Aldine, 1968; (with Doreen J. Croft) *Teachers of Young Children,* Houghton, 1972, 2nd edition, 1975.

Contributor: *New Definitions of School Library Service,* edited by S. I. Fenwick, University of Chicago Press, 1960; *The Adolescent: A Book of Readings,* edited by J. M. Seidman, Holt, 1960; *Readings in Child and Adolescent Psychology,* edited by L. D. Crow and A. Crow, Longmans, Green, 1961; *Culture and Social Character: The Work of David Riesman,* edited by S. M. Lipset and L. Lowenthal, Free Press of Glencoe, 1961; *Studies in Adolescence,* edited by R. E. Grinder, Macmillan, 1963; *Mental Health and Educational Achievement,* edited by R. Strom and P. Torrance, Wiley, 1965; *The Disadvantaged Child: Issues and Innovations,* edited by J. Frost and G. Hawkes, Houghton, 1966; *Minnesota Symposia in Child Psychology,* edited by J. P. Hill, University of Minnesota Press, 1967; *The New Elementary School,* edited by A. Frazier, National Education Association, 1968; *Developing Programs for the Educationally Disadvantaged,* edited by A. H. Passow, Teachers College Press, 1968; *L. Carmichael's Manual of Child Psychology,* 2nd edition, edited by P. H. Mussen, Wiley, 1968; *Contemporary Issues in Developmental Psychology,* edited by N. S. Endler, H. Osser, and others, Holt, 1968. Contributor of about forty articles to professional journals.

SIDELIGHTS: Hess's research has been concerned with the socialization processes of children, including such areas as: the effect of social class and ethnic backgrounds upon learning, the mechanics of transferring learning, socialization of educability in lower class Negro children, and political socialization, in particular. The research involved in his book with Judith V. Torney, *The Development of Political Attitudes in Children,* produced interviews with grade-schoolers which are "pungent and entertaining," according to a *New York Times Book Review* interviewer. One of the revelations of their work was the surprise that teachers have more influence on children's political concepts than do their parents. Hess told *CA* "There is, in my view, too little attempt to involve the youth of this country in the major problems that face our society, and indeed, all societies throughout the world. In this sense, there is the need for more integrity in education, integrity in the sense that what is learned in the classroom is taught, learned and understood in terms of the connections that link individuals to families, families to communities, communities to nations, and nations to each other."

BIOGRAPHICAL/CRITICAL SOURCES: New York Times Book Review, February 11, 1968.

*   *   *

HESSLINK, George K.   1940-

PERSONAL: Born June 10, 1940, in Sheboygan, Wis.; married Joanne Mersberger, June 24, 1961; children: one son. *Education:* Northwestern University, A.B., 1961; University of Chicago, A.M., 1963, Ph.D., 1966. *Politics:* Democrat. *Office:* Department of Sociology, Pomona College, Claremont, Calif. 91711.

CAREER: Indiana University, South Bend Campus, lecturer, 1963-65, assistant professor of sociology, 1965-66; Rutgers University, New Brunswick, N.J., assistant professor of sociology, 1966-69; Pomona College, Claremont, Calif., associate professor of sociology, 1969—. *Member:* American Sociological Association, Midwest Sociological Society, Eastern Sociological Society. *Awards, honors:* Bobbs-Merrill Publishing Co. grant, 1970.

WRITINGS: Black Neighbors: Negroes in a Northern Rural Community, Bobbs-Merrill, 1967, 2nd edition, 1974.

WORK IN PROGRESS: A comparative study of negro communities; analysis of patterns of racial extremism, and analysis of "New Cities Research."

*   *   *

HETH, Meir   1932-

PERSONAL: Born September 24, 1932, in Haifa, Israel; son of Nachum (a lawyer) and Michal (Levin) Heth; married Rina Zmirin, May 27, 1958; children: Hadas, Noam. *Education:* Hebrew University of Jerusalem, B.A., 1956, M.Jur., 1958, Ph.D., 1971; Harvard University, LL.M., 1967. *Religion:* Jewish. *Home:* 23 Etzel St., Jerusalem, Israel. *Office:* Bank of Israel, P.O.B. 780, Jerusalem, Israel.

CAREER: Maurice Falk Institute for Economic Research in Israel, Jerusalem, research assistant, 1955-57, research supervisor, 1958-59; admitted to Israel Bar, 1960; attorney in private practice, Haifa, Israel, 1960-61; Bank of Israel, Jerusalem, senior economist in research department, 1962-68, examiner of banks, 1969-75, director of Open Market Operations, 1976—. Hebrew University of Jersulem, lecturer in economics, 1963-66, lecturer in law, 1968—; lecturer in economics and law, Tel Aviv University, 1967—. Deputy chairman of Securities Authority, Jerusalem, 1975—. *Military service:* Israel Defence Forces, 1950-52. *Awards, honors:* The Penetz Naphtali Prize for economic and sociological research of Tel Aviv municipality, 1964, for Hebrew edition of *Banking Institutions in Israel,* and, 1968, for *The Flow Funds in Israel.*

WRITINGS: Ha-Mosadot ha-banka'iyim be-Yisrael, published as *Banking Institutions in Israel,* Maurice Falk Institute for Economic Research in Israel, 1966; *The Legal Framework of Economic Activity in Israel,* Praeger, in cooperation with Bank of Israel, 1967; *The Flow of Funds in the Israeli Economy, 1959-66,* Praeger, in cooperation with Bank of Israel, Hebrew edition, 1968, English edition, 1970.

AVOCATIONAL INTERESTS: Sports (long distance running), photography.

HETTICH, David William   1932-

PERSONAL: Born October 9, 1932, in La Porte, Ind. *Education:* Creighton University, B.S., 1954; Marquette University, M.A., 1956; Wayne State University, Ph.D., 1961. *Home:* 1255 Plumas St., Reno, Nev. 89502. *Office:* University of Nevada, Reno, Nev. 89507.

CAREER: Wayne State University, Detroit, Mich., instructor in English, 1959-61; University of Nevada, Reno, associate professor of English, 1961—. Supervising director, Reno Little Theatre. *Member:* Modern Language Association of America, National Council of Teachers of English, Conference on College Composition and Communication.

WRITINGS: (With William C. Miller) *The Fundamentals of English,* Allyn & Bacon, 1966.

*   *   *

HEWETT, Anita   1918-

PERSONAL: Born May 23, 1918, in Wellington, Somerset, England; daughter of Harold Frank and Agnes (Welsh) Hewett; married Richard Duke, October 29, 1966. *Education:* Attended University of Exeter, three years. *Home:* 29 Esher Road, East Molesey, Surrey, England.

CAREER: Primary school teacher at various schools for seven years; principal of Shirley Hall School, Kingston Hill, Surrey, England, eight years; British Broadcasting Corp., London, England, producer in School Broadcasting Department, 1962-70.

WRITINGS—All published by Bodley Head, except as noted: *Elephant Big and Elephant Little, and Other Stories,* 1955, A. S. Barnes, 1960; *Little Yellow Jungle Frogs, and Other Stories,* 1956, A. S. Barnes, 1960; *Honey Mouse, and Other Stories,* 1957; *Think, Mr. Platypus,* Sterling, 1958; *Koala Bear's Walkabout,* Sterling, 1959; *Laughing Bird,* Sterling, 1959.

A Hat for Rhinoceros, and Other Stories, A. S. Barnes, 1960; *Piccolo,* 1960, A. S. Barnes, 1961; *The Tale of the Turnip,* McGraw, 1961; *The Little White Hen,* 1962, McGraw, 1963; *Piccolo and Maria,* 1962; *The Elworthy Children,* 1963; *Dragon from the North,* McGraw, 1965; *The Bull Beneath the Walnut Tree, and Other Stories,* 1966, McGraw, 1967; *Mrs. Mopple's Washing Line,* 1966; *Mr. Faksimily and the Tiger,* 1967, Follett, 1969; *The Anita Hewitt Animal Story Book,* 1972. Also author of *The Pebble Nest,* 1962.

SIDELIGHTS: Virginia Haviland writes: "Though prodigally inventive, [Miss Hewett] is often close to the folk-tale pattern. . . . [She] writes with fine-sounding words, with an ear for rhythm, pattern and repetition, and her tales have a smooth roundness of story structure."

BIOGRAPHICAL/CRITICAL SOURCES: Children's Book World, November 5, 1967.

*   *   *

HEWETT, William S.   1924-

PERSONAL: Born July 28, 1924, in St. Paul, Minn.; son of Maurice W. (a civil engineer) and Jesse Lee (Berry) Hewett; married Evelyn Ruth Fischer, August 14, 1948; children: Joanne, Charles, Susan, John, Thomas. *Education:* University of Minnesota, student, 1942-43; College of Wooster, B.A., 1949. *Home:* 2380 Saga Circle N.E., East Canton, Ohio 44730.

CAREER: New York Life Insurance Co., agent in Wooster, Ohio, 1949-51; Merrill Lynch, Pierce, Fenner & Smith, salesman in Canton, Ohio, 1951-58; Paine, Webber, Jackson & Curtis, salesman in Canton, 1958-62; Hayden Miller & Co. (stockbrokers), Canton, salesman, 1962-64, branch manager, 1964, vice-president, 1966-68; Stone Webster Co., Canton, salesman, 1968-73; Butcher & Singer Co. (stockbrokers), Canton, salesman, 1973—. Real estate developer. *Military service:* U.S. Navy, 1943-46. *Member:* Canton Ski Club, Keelhaulers Canoe Club, Soaring Thunderbird Gliding Club, Toastmasters Club (Canton; past president).

WRITINGS: Common Stock for the Uncommon Man, Fell, 1966.

*   *   *

HICKEN, Victor 1921-

PERSONAL: Born September 28, 1921, in Witt, Ill.; son of Thomas and Anne (Atherton) Hicken; married Mary Patricia O'Connell, December 28, 1943; children: Jeffrey, Brian, Elizabeth, Daniel. *Education:* Southern Illinois University, B.Ed., 1943; University of Illinois, M.A., 1947, Ph.D., 1953. *Politics:* Independent. *Religion:* Episcopalian. *Home:* 615 Lincoln Dr., Macomb, Ill. 61455. *Office:* Department of History, Western Illinois University, Macomb, Ill. 61455.

CAREER: Western Illinois University, Macomb, 1947—, began as instructor, became professor of history, 1956, chairman of department, 1967-70. Visiting professor, Salzburg University, 1971. *Military service:* U.S. Naval Reserve, 1943-46; became lieutenant. *Member:* American Historical Association, Illinois State Historical Society (president). *Awards, honors:* Outstanding Teacher Award, Western Illinois University, 1964; award of merit, American Association for State and Local History, 1967, for *Illinois in the Civil War.*

WRITINGS: Settlement in Western Illinois, Western Illinois University Press, 1966; *Illinois in the Civil War,* University of Illinois Press, 1966; *The American Fighting Man,* Macmillan, 1969; *The Purple and the Gold: The Story of Western Illinois University,* Western Illinois University Foundation, 1970; *The World Is Coming to an End: An Irreverent Look at Modern Doomsayers,* Arlington House, 1975. Also author of books on the history of Illinois. Contributor to *Chicago Tribune Sunday Magazine, Nashville Tennessean,* and to scholarly journals.

WORK IN PROGRESS: A bicentennial series.

*   *   *

HIEATT, A(llen) Kent 1921-

PERSONAL: Born January 21, 1921, in Indianapolis, Ind.; son of Allen Andrew (a businessman) and Violet (Kent) Hieatt; married Constance Bartlett (a college professor), October 25, 1958; children: Alice K., Katherine Marsh. *Education:* University of Louisville, B.A., 1943; Columbia University, Ph.D., 1954. *Home:* 4 Grosvenor St., London, Ontario, Canada N6A 1Y4.

CAREER: Columbia University, New York, N.Y., instructor, 1944-55, assistant professor, 1955-60, associate professor of English, 1960-67; University of Western Ontario, London, Ontario, professor of English, 1968—.

WRITINGS: Short Time's Endless Monument, Columbia University Press, 1960; (with wife Constance Hieatt) *The Canterbury Tales of Geoffrey Chaucer,* Golden Books, 1961; (contributor) William Nelson, editor, *Form and Con-*

vention in the Poetry of Edmund Spenser, Columbia University Press, 1961; (editor and translator with Constance Hieatt) Geoffrey Chaucer, *Canterbury Tales,* Bantam, 1963; (editor with William Park) *The College Anthology of British and American Verse,* Allyn & Bacon, 1964, 2nd edition, 1972; (author of introduction) Constance Hieatt, editor and translator, *Beowulf, and Other Old English Poems,* Odyssey, 1967; (editor with Constance Hieatt) Edmund Spenser, *Selected Poetry,* Appleton, 1969.

(Contributor) Judith M. Kennedy and James A. Reither, editors, *A Theatre for Spenserians,* University of Toronto Press, 1973; *Chaucer, Spenser, Milton: Mythopoeic Continuities and Transformations,* McGill-Queen's University Press, 1975; (contributor) Richard C. Frushell and Bernard J. Vondersmith, editors, *Contemporary Thought on Edmund Spenser,* Southern Illinois University Press, 1975; (translator with Maristella Lorch) Lorenzo Valla, *On Pleasure,* Abaris, 1976; (contributor) *Essays in Honor of Arthur Barker,* University of Toronto Press, in press. Senior editor, *Spenser Newsletter,* 1970-74. Contributor to *Funk and Wagnall's Standard Encyclopedia, Encyclopaedia Britannica, Encyclopedia Americana,* and professional journals.

*   *   *

HIFLER, Joyce (Sequichie) 1925-

PERSONAL: Surname is pronounced High-fler; born March 31, 1925, in Nowata, Okla.; daughter of Charles Arch and Nellie (Leab) Sequichie; married second husband, Charles J. Zofness (a menswear retailer), 1972; children: Jane Evelyn, David. *Education:* Verian Masters Chaney Studio. *Politics:* Republican. *Religion:* Protestant. *Office:* Joyce Sequichie Hifler Enterprises, P.O. Box 788, Bartlesville, Okla. 74003.

CAREER: Phillips Petroleum Co., Bartlesville, Okla., employee, 1948—, presently assigned to American Indian affairs. Weekly columnist, "Thoughts for Every Day," *Nowata Daily Star,* beginning 1956; daily columnist, "Think on These Things," *Tulsa Daily World,* beginning 1963, syndicated by Joyce Sequichie Hifler Enterprises. President, Cherokee Foundation, Inc., 1967—. Member of board of trustees, Unity School of Christianity, Bartlesville, Okla. Former vice-president, State Health Planning Advisory Council, 1970. *Awards, honors:* Honored by Cherokee Nation, 1965, for advancing Cherokee culture through her writing.

WRITINGS—All published by Doubleday: *Think on These Things* (collection of columns), 1966; *To Every Thing a Season,* 1968; *All Rivers to the Sea,* 1970; *Pathways,* 1975.

WORK IN PROGRESS: A book of Indian poetry; a book on the Cherokee wood sculptor, Willard Stone.

AVOCATIONAL INTERESTS: Collecting old and rare books, Blue Willow ware, painting, and embroidery.

BIOGRAPHICAL/CRITICAL SOURCES: Tulsa Daily World, October 6, 1966.

*   *   *

HIGH, Dallas M. 1931-

PERSONAL: Born November 14, 1931, in Van Wert, Ohio; son of Orval H. (a farmer) and Mary (Baltzell) High; married Diane Ayres, June 23, 1957; children: Kevin Craig, Scott Andrew, Bradley Stuart. *Education:* Ohio Wesleyan University, B.A. (with honors), 1956; Yale University,

B.D., 1959; Duke University, Ph.D., 1965. *Home:* 3353 Hunter Rd., Lexington, Ky. 40502.

CAREER: Hiram College, Hiram, Ohio, assistant professor, 1964-68, associate professor of philosophy, 1968-69; University of Kentucky, Lexington, associate professor, 1969-72, professor of philosophy, 1972—, chairman of department, 1969—. *Member:* American Philosophical Association, American Academy of Religion, Society for Religion in Higher Education, Mind Association, American Association of University Professors, Kentucky Philosophical Association, Phi Beta Kappa. *Awards, honors:* Summer research grants, Hiram College, 1965, 1967; Danforth fellowship; National Endowment to the Humanities research grant, 1968; Rockefeller Foundation fellowship, 1975-76.

WRITINGS: Language, Persons, and Belief, Oxford University Press, 1967; (editor) *New Essays on Religious Language,* Oxford University Press, 1969; (co-editor and contributor) *Medical Treatment of the Dying: Moral Issues,* Schenkman, 1975.

WORK IN PROGRESS: Research into philosophy of religion and philosophy of medicine.

* * *

HILDUM, Donald C(layton) 1930-

PERSONAL: Born September 20, 1930, in Plainfield, N.J.; son of Edward Barkdoll (a mechanical engineer) and Isabel (Morrison) Hildum; married Priscilla Ames, July 5, 1952; children: Edward Ames, Robert Morrison, David Waldau. *Education:* Princeton University, B.A., 1952; Harvard University, M.A., 1953, Ph.D., 1960. *Politics:* Democrat. *Religion:* Unitarian Universalist. *Home:* 424 Gunder Dr., Rochester, Mich. 48063. *Office:* Department of Speech Communication, Oakland University, Rochester, Mich. 48063.

CAREER: Case Institute of Technology (now Case Western Reserve University), Cleveland, Ohio, instructor, 1956-60, assistant professor of psychology, 1960-61; Oakland University, Rochester, Mich., assistant professor, 1961-64, associate professor, 1964-69, professor of psychology, 1969—, professor of speech communication, 1972—, chairman of department of speech communication, 1975—. Fulbright lecturer, University of Ghent, 1967-68. *Member:* International Communication Association, International Society for General Semantics, Linguistic Society of America, Speech Communication Association, Michigan Speech Association, Michigan Academy of Science, Arts, and Letters, Phi Beta Kappa.

WRITINGS: (Editor) *Language and Thought,* Van Nostrand, 1967. Contributor to *Language* and *Journal of Abnormal and Social Psychology.*

WORK IN PROGRESS: Working on semantic theory and its application to individual associative structure, especially in education and group processes; a textbook of communication theory.

SIDELIGHTS: Professor Hildum is proficient in Dutch; knows some French, Spanish, and German.

* * *

HILL, Alfred T(uxbury) 1908-

PERSONAL: Born May 17, 1908, in Montclair, N.J.; son of Charles (a businessman) and Edith (Tuxbury) Hill; married Eunice Garland, June 23, 1934; children: Geraldine

(Mrs. Alexander Jenkins III), Kate G. *Education:* Haverford College, student, 1926-28; Brown University, A.B., 1933; Harvard University, Ed.M., 1937; Columbia University, Ph.D., 1950. *Politics:* Republican ("slightly to the right of center"). *Religion:* Episcopalian. *Address:* P.O. Box 724, Falmouth, Mass. 02541. *Office:* 340 Capitol Ave., Hartford, Conn. 06115.

CAREER: Instructor in English at Cushing Academy, Ashburnham, Mass., 1933-36, and Culver Military Academy, Culver, Ind., 1937-43; U.S. War Department, Office of the Chief of Ordnance, Detroit, Mich., executive assistant and personnel counselor, 1943-44; government contract service specialist and chief of employment and placement, Western Electric Co., Radio Division, 1944-45; Herrick, Waddell and Co., securities analyst, 1945-46; Lake Erie College, Painesville, Ohio, vice-president and acting president, 1949-51; director of Dana Hall Schools and president of Pine Manor Junior College, Wellesley, Mass., 1951-56; Council for Financial Aid to Education, Washington, D.C., staff associate, 1956; Council for the Advancement of Small Colleges, Inc., Washington, D.C., executive secretary, 1956-67; vice-president, Heald, Hobson & Associates (educational consultants), 1968; Connecticut Commission for Higher Education, Hartford, associate in higher education, 1969—. Member of New England Junior College Council. Volunteer worker in Labrador with Wilfred Grenfell while in college.

MEMBER: American Association of Junior Colleges (member of executive committee), American Council on Education, American Association for Higher Education, Phi Delta Theta, Phi Delta Kappa, Harvard Club (Boston and New York). *Awards, honors:* H.H.D., Nasson College, 1957; D.C.L., New England College, 1958; Ped.D., Salem College, Salem, W.Va., 1960; LL.D., Los Angeles Pacific College, 1961; Litt.D., College of St. Joseph on the Rio Grande, 1962.

WRITINGS: Campus and Classroom, Harper, 1942; *The Small College Meets the Challenge,* McGraw, 1959; (editor) *Management for Success: A Report on the Twelfth Annual Summer Workshop of the Council for the Advancement of Small Colleges,* [Washington], 1967; (editor) Thomas Cambell, *The Poetical Works,* Books for Libraries, 1972; (editor) *Essays upon Educational Subjects Read at the Educational Conference of June 1857,* Augustus M. Kelley, 1973. Contributor of about fifty articles on educational subjects to general and professional magazines.

AVOCATIONAL INTERESTS: Travel (Europe, around the world, United States), sailing, swimming, golf, tennis, riding, reading, music.†

* * *

HILL, Claude 1911-

PERSONAL: Born July 28, 1911, in Berlin, Germany; naturalized U.S. citizen; son of Arthur and Lotte (Friebus) Hilzheimer; married Helen Leiter, November 18, 1938; children: Thomas Charles. *Education:* Studied at University of Vienna, 1931, and University of Goettingen, 1931-33; University of Jena, Ph.D., 1937. *Politics:* Independent liberal. *Home:* 245 Varsity Ave., Princeton, N.J. 08540. *Office:* Rutgers University, New Brunswick, N.J. 08901.

CAREER: Asheville College, Asheville, N.C., instructor in world literature, radio, and drama, 1940-43; U.S. Department of State, Voice of America, New York, N.Y., commentator and program director for German broadcasts, 1943-45; Rutgers University, New Brunswick, N.J., assistant professor, 1946-51, associate professor, 1951-61, professor of German and graduate director of German studies, 1961—. German consultant, Harper & Row, Publishers, Inc. *Member:* American Association of Teachers of German (vice-president, New Jersey chapter, 1961), American Association of University Professors. *Awards, honors:* Honorary fellow, Yale University, 1940; American Council of Learned Societies faculty study fellowship, 1951-52.

WRITINGS: Das Drama der deutschen Neuromantik, Akademischer Verlag, 1938; (editor) *Drei Nobelpreistrager,* Harper, 1948; (editor) *Drei zeitgenoessische Erzaehler,* American Book· Co., 1951; (with Ralph Ley) *The Drama of German Expressionism,* University of North Carolina Press, 1960; *Zwei Hundert Jahre Deutscher Kultur,* Harper, 1966; (editor) *Kaestner fuer Studenten,* Harper, 1968; (editor) *Lesen mit Gewinn,* Harper, 1972; *Bertolt Brecht,* Twayne, 1975. Author of eight full-length plays. Editor of a German series for Harper. Contributor to *Saturday Review, New York Times, Modern Drama,* and other journals.

* * *

HILL, L(eslie) A(lexander) 1918-

PERSONAL: Born January 6, 1918, in Athens, Greece; son of Arthur Edwin and Anastasia (Tsaousopoulou) Hill; married Margaret Beryl Barrett, September 26, 1946; married second wife, Jane Elizabeth Hose, January 14, 1963; children: (first marriage) Rosemary Anne, Julian Alexander, Judith Mary, Katherine Jane. *Education:* Cambridge University, B.A. (honors), 1939, M.A., 1948; University of London, B.A. (first class honors), 1953, M.A. (mark of distinction), 1956. *Home and office:* La Prairie, St. Mary, Jersey, Channel Islands.

CAREER: British Council, service in Greece, Iran, Indonesia, and then in India, 1939-41, 1946-61; University of Indonesia, Djakarta, professor of English and head of department, 1953-58; Oxford University Press, Oxford, England, adviser on the teaching of English as a second (foreign) language, 1961-71; full time writer, 1972—. English language adviser, United Nations Development Programme, 1971-72; chairman, Hill Publications Ltd. *Military service:* British Army, 1941-46; became major; received Military Cross. *Member:* International Phonetic Association, Audio-Visual Language Association, International Association of Teachers of English as a Foreign Language, Society of Authors, Mensa, Linguistic Circle of New York.

WRITINGS—All published by Oxford University Press, except as noted: Comprehension and Precis Pieces for Overseas Students, Longmans, Green, 1950; *The Teaching of English in Indonesia: Problems and Suggestions,* Wolters (Djakarta), 1955; (with others) *Indonesian Ministry of Education's English Language Syllabus,* Year I, with *Teacher's Guide* and *Drill Book,* Indonesian Ministry of Education, 1955, Years II-III, 1957; (with R. D. S. Fielden) *Further Comprehension and Precis Pieces for Overseas Students,* Longmans, Green, 1956; *A Corrective Course for Indonesian Students of English,* Ganaco (Bandung), 1957; (with Fielden) *Vocabulary Tests and Exercises for Indonesian Students of English,* Ganaco, 1958.

Picture Stories for Composition and *Teacher's Guide,* Longmans, Green, 1960; *Drills and Tests in English Sounds,* Longmans, Green, 1961; (contributor) *Recent Trends in Educational Practice,* Longmans, Green, 1961; (with Derwent J. May) *Advanced Comprehension and Appreciation Pieces,* 1962; (with J. M. Ure) *English*

Sounds and Spellings, 1962, with *Tests,* 1963, and *Dictation Pieces,* 1964; (with Fielden) *Vocabulary Tests and Exercises,* 1962; (with May) *Literary Comprehension and Appreciation Pieces,* 1963; *Letter Writing,* 1963; *Elementary Comprehension Pieces,* 1963; *Elementary Composition Pieces,* 1964; *An Elementary Refresher Course,* 1964; *An Intermediate Refresher Course,* 1964; *English Letters for All Occasions,* Diesterweg (Frankfurt), 1965; *An Advanced Refresher Course,* 1965; *A Picture Vocabulary,* with *Student's Book* and *Teacher's Book,* 1965; *A Guide to Correct English,* 1965, 2nd edition, 1968; (contributor) H. B. Allen, editor, *Teaching English as a Second Language,* McGraw, 1965; *Stress and Intonation, Step by Step,* with *Workbook* and *Companion,* 1965; *Elementary Stories for Reproduction,* 1965; *Advanced Stories for Reproduction,* 1965.

Outline Composition Book, 1966; *Free Composition Book,* 1966; *Intermediate Stories for Composition,* with *Workbook* and *Companion,* 1967; *Selected Articles on the Teaching of English as a Foreign Language,* 1967; *Note-Taking Practice,* 1968; (with Prema Popkin) *A First Crossword Puzzle Book,* 1968; *Exercises for Senior Pupils,* Verlag Moritz Diesterweg, 1968; *Easy Pieces,* Gleerups (Sweden), 1968; *Prepositions and Adverbial Particles,* 1968; *Intermediate Comprehension Pieces,* 1969; *A First Reader,* 1969, 2nd edition, two volumes, 1973; *A Prelude to English,* 1969; (with Popkin) *Second Crossword Puzzle Book,* 1969.

(With Popkin) *Third Crossword Book,* 1970; *Contextualized Vocabulary Tests,* three books, 1970-75; *Contemporary Short Stories,* 1970; (with M. Sinha) *Elementary Stories for Translation into Hindi or English,* 1970; (with Popkin) *A Fourth Crossword Puzzle Book,* 1970; (with K. Shimizu and T. Shimaoka) *Study Guide to Elementary Stories for Reproduction: Spoken English through Humorous Stories,* 1970.

(With Shimizu and Shimaoka) *Study Guide for Intermediate Stories for Reproduction,* 1971; (with others) *English Language Course for Colleges,* Book 1, 1971, Book 2, 1974; *A Second Reading Book,* 1972; *A Third Reading Book,* 1972; *A Fourth Reading Book,* 1972; *A Fifth Reading Book,* 1972; (with D. Mallet and K. Shimizu) *English through Cartoons,* Book 1, 1973, Book 2, 1975; *English Language Teaching Games for Adult Students,* Evans Brothers, 1974, Book 1: Elementary, Book 2: (with R. D. S. Fielden) Advanced; *What Would You Say?,* Evans Brothers, 1975; (with K. Ando and Shimizu) *Listen and Speak,* with 10 cassettes, 1975.

Editor: "Oxford Graded Readers," junior level, stage 1, 1971: *The Three Goats and the Dwarf; The Grasshopper and the Ant; The Lion, the Wolf, and the Fox; The Eagle, the Pig, and the Cat; The Boy in the Moon; The Old Woman and Her Pig; The Father, His Son and Their Donkey; Goldilocks and the Three Bears; The Happy Dragon; Hansel and Gretel;* (with O. Dunn) *Japanese Talking Workbook; The Ugly Duckling; The Boy and the Ice.* Junior level, stage 2, 1972: *Big Claus and Small Claus; Thumbelisa; The Tinder Box; Nasreddin; The Ruined House,* 1973.

Editor: "Oxford Graded Readers," senior level, stage 1, 1971: *Ali Baba and the Forty Thieves; The Giant's Garden; Tom Gold; The Two Dingoes.* Senior level, stage 2: *Funny Stories,* 1972.

Other series: "Programmed English Course," student and teacher books, 1-12, 1966-68; "Books Adapted for Use with the Stillitron Teaching Machine," eight books, Stillit Books, 1967-68; (with Derwent J. May) "A New Introduction to English Literature," five books, 1969-73; "Cartoons for Students of English," five books, 1972.

Educational materials include "Stress and Intonation, Step by Step" (recordings), Oxford University Press, 1965; "Drills and Tests in English Sounds" (tapes), Longmans, Green, 1966-67.

Scriptwriter for radio series, "Ear and Speech Training," British Broadcasting Corp., 1961, and television series, "English for Everyone," Center for Educational Television Overseas, 1963-65. Contributor of more than sixty articles to professional journals in England, United States, Taiwan, India, France, Japan, Ethiopia, Nigeria and Germany. Editor, *Teaching English* (Calcutta), 1959-61.

WORK IN PROGRESS: Techniques of Discussion, for Evans Brothers.

SIDELIGHTS: Hill is fluent in German, modern Greek, French, and Italian; he has some competence in Spanish, Russian, and Dutch; "rusty" in Persian and Indonesian; has studied about ten other languages. Hill's interest in linguistics extends to "human behaviour and its similarities/variations between different cultures." *Avocational interests:* Travel (especially in the Mediterranean and Southeast Asia), music (chiefly pre-1800 and classical Indian), photography.

* * *

HILTON, Earl (Raymond) 1914-

PERSONAL: Born December 22, 1914, in Beulah, Wyo.; son of David Butler and Mabel (Peterson) Hilton; married Miriam Elder, June 22, 1947; children: Ann, Susan, John, Margaret, Robert. *Education:* University of Wyoming, B.A., 1938; University of Wisconsin, M.Ph., 1939; University of Minnesota, Ph.D., 1950. *Home:* 403 East Arch St., Marquette, Mich. 49855. *Office:* Department of English, Northern Michigan University, Marquette, Mich. 49855.

CAREER: Iowa State University, Ames, instructor in English, 1946-47; Central Washington College of Education (now Central Washington State College), Ellensburg, assistant professor of English, 1949-50; Northern Michigan University, Marquette, assistant professor, 1950-55, associate professor, 1955-59, professor of English, 1959—. *Military service:* U.S. Army, 1941-46; became first lieutenant. *Member:* Modern Language Association of America, American Association of University Professors, National Association for the Advancement of Colored People, American Civil Liberties Union, Wilderness Society. *Awards, honors:* Ford Foundation fellow, 1951-52.

WRITINGS: (With Darwin Shrell) *Exposition,* Wadsworth, 1967. Contributor of literary history and criticism to journals.

AVOCATIONAL INTERESTS: Biology, conservation, anthropology, mythology.

* * *

HINSON, E(dward) Glenn 1931-

PERSONAL: Born July 27, 1931, in St. Louis, Mo.; son of Allen Lloyd and Docia F. Hinson; married Martha Ann Burks, September 1, 1956; children: Christopher Glenn, Elizabeth Leora. *Education:* Washington University, St. Louis, Mo., B.A., 1954; Southern Baptist Theological Seminary, B.D., 1957, Th.D., 1962; Oxford University, D.Phil., 1974. *Politics:* Democrat. *Home:* 120 Heady Ave., Louisville, Ky. 40207. *Office:* Southern Baptist Theological Seminary, 2825 Lexington Rd., Louisville, Ky. 40206.

CAREER: Baptist clergyman. Southern Baptist Theological Seminary, Louisville, Ky., instructor in New Testament, 1959-60, instructor in church history, 1960-62, assistant professor, 1962-66, associate professor, 1966-73, David T. Porter Professor of Church History, 1973—. *Member:* American Society of Church History, American Academy of Religion, Society for the Scientific Study of Religion. *Awards, honors:* American Association of Theological Schools fellowship to Oxford University, 1966-67; Association of Theological Schools in the United States and Canada fellowship, 1975-76.

WRITINGS: The Church: Design for Survival, Broadman, 1967; (with Frank Stagg and Wayne E. Oates) *Glossolalia: Tongue Speaking in Biblical, Historical and Theological Perspectives,* Abingdon, 1967; *Seekers After Mature Faith,* Word Books, 1968; *A Serious Call to a Contemplative Lifestyle,* Westminster, 1974; *Jesus and His Times,* Volume I, Consortium, 1976.

Contributor: George Torney, editor, *Towards Creative Urban Strategy,* Word Books, 1970; Clifton J. Allen, general editor, *Broadman Bible Commentary,* Volume XI, Broadman, 1971; Watson Mills, editor, *Tongue Speaking: Let's Talk about It,* Word Books, 1974; A. Frazier, editor, *What Faith Has Meant to Me,* Westminster, 1975. Contributor to *Religion in Life, Journal of Ecumenical Studies, Revue de Qumran, Christian Century,* and Baptist periodicals.

WORK IN PROGRESS: A comparative study of the church's teaching authority in Roman Catholic, Orthodox, and selected Protestant traditions.

SIDELIGHTS: Hinson is competent in Latin, Greek, German, French, and Biblical Hebrew.

* * *

HITCHMAN, Janet 1916-

PERSONAL: Born July 5, 1916, in Oulton Broad, England; daughter of Margaret Mayhew; orphaned in infancy; married Michael Hitchman (an actor), February 18, 1939 (deceased); children: Rachael Glennon Button. *Education:* Educated in England. *Politics:* Socialist. *Religion:* Quaker. *Home:* Putnams, Long Thurlow Rd., Badwell Ash, Bury St. Edmunds, Suffolk, England.

CAREER: Stage director for various companies in England, 1940-47; domestic servant, 1947-60; writer and broadcaster for British Broadcasting Corp. and Independent Television Network, 1960—. *Member:* British Actors Equity, Society of Authors.

WRITINGS: The King of the Barbareens (autobiography), Putnam, 1960; *They Carried the Sword,* Gollancz, 1966; *Meeting for Burial* (novel), Gollancz, 1967, Atheneum, 1968; *Such a Strange Lady: A Biography of Dorothy L. Sayers,* Harper, 1975. Author of about one hundred talks, short stories, plays, and documentaries for British Broadcasting Corp.; articles include a number on deprived children in *Observer, Times,* and *Guardian.*

WORK IN PROGRESS: A book on Victorian novelist, Quida.

BIOGRAPHICAL/CRITICAL SOURCES: New York Times Book Review, September 1, 1968.

* * *

HITTE, Kathryn 1919-

PERSONAL: Surname is pronounced Hit; born November

23, 1919, in Pana, Ill.; daughter of Dudley Clement (a musician) and Zeta (Kelligar) Hitte; married William D. Hayes (an author of children's books and illustrator), April 2, 1960. *Education:* Illinois College, A.B. (cum laude), 1942; University of Illinois, B.S. in Library Science, 1944. *Residence:* New York, N.Y. *Office:* 500 Fifth Avenue, LL 21-22, New York, N.Y. 10036.

CAREER: Children's librarian in Whiting, Ind., 1944-45; New York (N.Y.) Public Library, children's librarian, 1945-50; editorial consultant and writer for children, beginning 1950. Active in civil defense in New York City, beginning 1951; volunteer supervisor, Civil Defense Communications Division, Borough of Manhattan, 1965—. *Member:* Authors League of America, Authors Guild.

WRITINGS: Surprise for Susan, Abingdon, 1950; *Lost and Found,* Abingdon, 1951; *A Letter for Cathy,* Abingdon, 1953; *Bugs Bunny at the Easter Party,* Simon & Schuster, 1954; *The Button Book,* Golden Press, 1959; *Hurricanes, Tornadoes, and Blizzards,* Random House, 1960; *I'm an Indian Today,* Golden Press, 1961; *The Golden Shoe Book,* Golden Press, 1962; *The Other Side of the Fence,* American Book Co., 1963; *Richie and the Junk,* American Book Co., 1963; *The Brave and Free,* American Book Co., 1964; *Where Will We Go?,* American Book Co., 1965; *New in the City,* American Book Co., 1965; (with husband, William D. Hayes) *Let's Fly,* American Book Co., 1965; (contributor) George Manolakes, editor, *Reading Round Table: Goldbook,* American Book Co., 1965; (contributor) Manolakes, editor, *Reading Round Table: Silverbook,* American Book Co., 1965; *When Noodlehead Went to the Fair,* Parents' Magazine Press, 1968; *Boy Was I Mad!,* Parents' Magazine Press, 1969; (with W. D. Hayes) *Mexicali Soup,* Parents' Magazine Press, 1970; *What Can You Do Without a Place to Play?,* Parents' Magazine Press, 1971.

Contributor to reading textbooks and anthologies, including Child Study Association's *Read Me Another Story,* and *Klumpe-Dumpe Sagor,* published in Sweden. Author of audio-visual materials, including "Pathways to Phonic Skills" (three recordings). Plays for children include adaptations of "Beauty and the Beast," "Cinderella," and "Pinocchio" for The Playmart, professional children's theater in New York. Also author of original adult plays for The Actors' Quarter, San Diego, and studio workshop productions in New York. Contributor of fiction, nonfiction, and verse to *Jack and Jill, Humpty Dumpty's, Children's Digest, Vacation Fun,* and other periodicals.

WORK IN PROGRESS: A book of fiction based on certain legends of American history; an adult drama.

AVOCATIONAL INTERESTS: Reading, travel, theater, acting.

*   *   *

HIXSON, Richard F.   1932-

PERSONAL: Born February 1, 1932, in Youngstown, Ohio; son of Frederick Grant and Thelma (Young) Hixson; married Anetta Pichford, October 16, 1953 (divorced February, 1960); married second wife, Cynthia Moore, August 13, 1960; children: (second marriage) Todd Milton, Nancy Sommer. *Education:* Kent State University, student, 1950-51; Youngstown University, A.B., 1957; Western Reserve University (now Case Western Reserve University), A.M., 1960. *Politics:* Democrat. *Religion:* Protestant. *Home:* 242 Stanton Mountain Rd., R.D. 1, Lebanon, N.J. 08833. *Office:* Rutgers University, New Brunswick, N.J. 08903.

CAREER: Boardman News and Poland Press, Boardman, Ohio, reporter and editor, 1951-52; *Youngstown Vindicator,* Youngstown, Ohio, reporter, 1954-57; Firestone Tire & Rubber Co., Akron, Ohio, advertising and public relations, 1957-60; Rutgers University, New Brunswick, N.J., professor of journalism and consultant to Institute of Management and Labor, 1960—. *Military service:* U.S. Army, 1952-54. *Member:* Association for Education in Journalism, American Association of University Professors, Sigma Delta Chi.

WRITINGS: Introduction to Journalism, Monarch, 1966; *Isaac Collins: A Quaker Printer in Eighteenth-Century America,* Rutgers University Press, 1968; *Mass Media: A Casebook,* Crowell, 1973.

WORK IN PROGRESS: Writing on printing and publishing in colonial America.

*   *   *

HOBBS, Cecil (Carlton)   1907-
(Maung Hauk)

PERSONAL: Born April 22, 1907, in Martins Ferry, Ohio; son of John A. and Mary (Whitten) Hobbs; married Cecile Jackson; children: Mary Louise. *Education:* University of Illinois, B.A., 1929; Colgate Rochester Divinity School, B.D., 1933, Th.M., 1942. *Politics:* Democrat. *Home and office:* 5100 Backlick Rd., Annandale, Va. 22003.

CAREER: Methodist clergyman. American Board of Foreign Missionary Societies, missionary field administrator in Burma, 1935-40; Pierce Divinity College and Burman Theological Seminary, Insein, Burma, professor, 1940-41; Library of Congress, Washington, D.C., head of South Asia Section and specialist on Southeast Asia, 1943-72, consultant, 1972—. Consultant on Southeast Asia at the Australian National University Library, 1972-73, and National Library of Australia, 1973. *Member:* Association for Asian Studies (chairman of committee on American library resources for Southeast Asia), Bibliographical Society of the Philippines, Burma Research Society.

WRITINGS: Christian Education and the Burmese Family, Colgate Rochester Divinity School, 1942; (compiler with others) *Indochina: A Bibliography of the Land and People,* Library of Congress, 1950; (compiler) *Southeast Asia: An Annotated Bibliography of Selected Reference Sources,* Library of Congress, 1952; *An Account of an Acquisition Trip in the Countries of Southeast Asia,* Cornell University, 1952; *The Burmese Family: An Inquiry into Its History, Customs, and Traditions,* privately printed, 1952; *Account of a Trip to the Countries of Southeast Asia for the Library of Congress, 1952-1953,* Cornell University, 1953; (with Frank Trager) *Burma,* Human Relations Area Files Press, 1956.

Southeast Asia Publication Sources: An Account of a Field Trip, 1958-1959, Cornell University, 1960; *Southeast Asia: An Annotated Bibliography of Selected Reference Sources in Western Languages,* Library of Congress, 1964; *Understanding the Peoples of Southern Asia: A Bibliographical Essay,* University of Illinois, 1967; *Account of a Trip to the Countries of Southeast Asia for the Library of Congress, August-December 1965,* Department of Far Eastern Studies, Cornell University, 1967; (editor) *Conference on Access to Southeast Asian Research Materials: Proceedings,* Library of Congress, 1971; *Southeast Asia Field Trip for the Library of Congress, 1970-71,* Cornell University, 1972; (editor) *Southeast Asia Subject Catalog,* six volumes, G. K. Hall. 1972. Contributor to *Asian Student, Far*

Eastern Quarterly, and similar journals. Associate editor, *Journal of Asian Studies,* 1946-48.

WORK IN PROGRESS: Southeast Asia: A Research Guide.

AVOCATIONAL INTERESTS: Woodcraft, photography.

* * *

HOBBS, William (Beresford) 1939-

PERSONAL: Born January 29, 1939, in London, England; son of Kenneth Beresford and Joan Francis (Lindsay) Hobbs; married Janet Milner-Riley, April 1, 1961; children: Laurence Beresford, Edwin Bizley. *Education:* Attended Central School of Speech and Drama, London, 1957-59. *Religion:* Church of England. *Residence:* London, England. *Agent:* (Theatre) Neil Landor, Progressive Management, 11 Blenheim St., New Bond St., London W.1, England.

CAREER: Actor with Shakespeare Memorial Theatre Company and Old Vic Company on tour in Australia, 1956-57; actor with repertory companies in Colchester, Worthing, and Bristol, England, 1959-61; actor and fight director (stage) at Old Vic Theatre, 1961, for various stage plays and television films, 1961-63, with National Theatre, London, England, 1963-73, and with the Royal Shakespeare Company, 1974—. Owner and director, Mandala Musical Theatre Co.; part-time tutor of stage fights, Central School of Speech and Drama; director of fights for many productions in Germany and films including Lester's "Three Musketeers" and "Royal Flash," Polanski's "Macbeth," and Olivier's "Othello."

WRITINGS: Techniques of the Stage Fight, Studio Vista, 1967.

AVOCATIONAL INTERESTS: Fencing (won New South Wales state schools foil championship and was selected for New South Wales Olympic foil training squad); music and chess.

* * *

HOBERECHT, Earnest 1918-

PERSONAL: Surname is pronounced Hoe-bright; born January 1, 1918, in Watonga, Okla.; son of Earnest T. (a banker, later dealing in abstracts, land, and oil) and Grace (Woolman) Hoberecht; married Laurette Heger, May 6, 1959; married second wife Mary Ann Karns, April 26, 1970; children: Antonia Grace, Earnest III, Nathalie, Shelley. *Education:* University of Oklahoma, B.A. in Journalism, 1941. *Religion:* Presbyterian. *Home:* 1317 North Noble Ave., Watonga, Okla. *Office:* 100 West Main, Watonga, Okla.

CAREER: Began reporting for a newspaper in Watonga, Okla., 1935, and published his own magazine, *Reflector,* in Watonga, 1936; during college did free-lance and part-time work on *Oklahoma News* and *Daily Oklahoman,* Oklahoma City, Okla.; reporter for *Memphis Press Scimitar,* Memphis, Tenn., 1941-42; laborer at Pearl Harbor Navy Yard, Pearl Harbor, Hawaii, 1942-43, and editor of *Pearl Harbor Bulletin,* 1944-45; United Press International, war correspondent with Third Fleet, 1945, correspondent in Japan, 1946-48, bureau manager, Tokyo, Japan, 1948-51, general manager for Asia, 1951-66, vice-president of UPI, 1953-66; president, American Suppliers, Inc., 1966—. Owner and president of Blaine County Abstract Co., Inc., and The Watonga Abstract Co., Inc.; president of American Southeast Asia Corp. Saigon and Oklahoma Land Trust; owner, Earnest Hoberecht Insurance. *Member:* National Association of Insurance Agents, American Land Title Association, Foreign Correspondents Club of Japan (founder; charter member), Oklahoma Association of Insurance Agents, Oklahoma Land Title Association, Sigma Delta Chi. *Awards, honors:* Elected to Oklahoma Journalism Hall of Fame, 1972.

WRITINGS: Tokyo Romance (in English and Japanese), Didier, 1947; *Asia Is My Beat,* Tuttle, 1961. Author of four other books published in Japanese: *Tokyo Diary,* 1947, *Democratic Etiquette,* 1948, *Fifty Famous Americans,* 1949, and *Shears of Destiny,* 1949.

SIDELIGHTS: Hoberecht covered International War Crimes Trials, Wedemeyer Mission to China, outbreak of the Korean War, and other epic events of the past two decades in Asia; as general manager of United Press for Asia, he ran a news beat stretching from Midway Island to the border of Iran, with an Asia staff numbering about 130. His *Tokyo Romance* was a best seller in Japan.

BIOGRAPHICAL/CRITICAL SOURCES: Quill, July, 1957.

* * *

HOETINK, H(armannus) 1931-

PERSONAL: Surname is pronounced *Hoo*-tink; born January 7, 1931, in Groningen, Netherlands; son of Gradus J. G. (a public accountant) and Hendrika (Rijtema) Hoetink; married Ligia C. A. Espinal (a translator), April 25, 1957; children: Harman Antonie. *Education:* University of Amsterdam, B.A., 1950, M.A., 1953; University of Leyden, Ph.D., 1958.

CAREER: University of Puerto Rico, Rio Piedras, associate professor, 1960-64; Netherlands Economic University, Rotterdam, professor extraordinary, 1964-68; University of Amsterdam, Amsterdam, Netherlands, director of Center for Latin American Research and Documentation, 1964-68; Yale University, New Haven, Conn., visiting professor of sociology, 1968; University of Texas at Austin, visiting professor, department of anthropology, 1969. *Member:* Royal Anthropological Society of the Netherlands (member of board, 1966—).

WRITINGS: Het Patroon van de oude Curacaose samenleving: Een sociologische studie, Van Gorcum, 1958, 2nd edition, De Wit, 1966; *De Gespleten samenleving in het Caribisch Gebied,* Van Gorcum, 1962, translation by Eva M. Hooykaas published as *Caribbean Race Relations: A Study of Two Varients,* shortened edition, Oxford University Press, 1967; *Het Nieuwe Evolutionisme,* Van Gorcum, 1965; (editor-in-chief) *Encyclopedie van de Nederlandse Antillen,* Elsevier, 1969; *El Pueblo Dominicano, 1850-1900: A puntes para su sociologia historica,* UCMM (Santiago, Dominican Republic), 1971; *Slavery and Race Relations in the Americas,* Harper, 1973.

WORK IN PROGRESS: "The New Evolutionism" for reader, *Dutch Anthropology Today,* for Van Gorcum.

BIOGRAPHICAL/CRITICAL SOURCES: J.A.A. van Doorn, *Beeld en Betekenis van de Nederlandse Sociologie* (title means "Image and Significance of Dutch Sociology"), [Rotterdam], 1964.†

* * *

HOFFMAN, Abbie 1936-
(Free, Spiro Igloo, George Metesky)

PERSONAL: Born November 30, 1936, in Worcester,

Mass.; son of John and Florence (Schanberg) Hoffman; married; wife's name, Sheila (divorced); married Anita Kushner, June 10, 1967; children: (first marriage) Andrew, Amy; (second marriage) "america". *Education:* Expelled from high school at 17 for striking a teacher; Brandeis University, B.A., 1959; University of California, Berkeley, M.A. (psychology), 1960. *Politics:* Revolutionary. *Religion:* Neo-American.

CAREER: Worked briefly as a psychologist at Worcester State Hospital, Worcester, Mass., and as a pharmaceuticals salesman, 1964-65; an active civil rights worker for the Student Non-Violent Coordinating Committee (S.N.C.C.), in Mississippi, 1966; founded the Youth International Party (YIP), 1968; former vice-president of Congress of Racial Equality (CORE); founder of Pirate Editions (publisher); travel editor, *Crawdaddy* (magazine), 1976—; has also worked as camp counselor and pool hustler.

WRITINGS: F—— the System (pamphlet), privately printed, 1968; (under pseudonym Free) *Revolution for the Hell of It,* Dial, 1968; *Woodstock Nation: A Talk-Rock Album,* Vintage Books, 1969; (contributor) Bob Abel, Peter Babcox, and Deborah Babcox, editors, *The Conspiracy,* introduction by Noam Chomsky, Dell, 1969; (with Izack Haber) *Steal This Book,* Pirate Editions, 1971; (with Jerry Rubin and Ed Sanders) *Vote!,* Warner Paperback, 1972; (with wife, Anita Hoffman) *To America with Love: Letters from the Underground,* Stonehill Publishing, 1976. Contributor of articles to magazines and newspapers, including *East Village Other, Village Voice, Los Angeles Free Press, Eye, Realist, Harper's, Esquire.*

WORK IN PROGRESS: The Book-of-the-Month Selection, a sequel to *Steal This Book.*

SIDELIGHTS: Abbie Hoffman first became involved in the radical movement by participating in a demonstration in May, 1960. He subsequently became interested in such causes as the Vietnam war, nuclear disarmament, changes in the governmental system, and, Hoffman explained, "gradually, civil rights became the crux of my involvement." As *Saturday Night* related, in 1968 Hoffman and Jerry Rubin "started Yippie, the Youth International Party, to bring together the hippies who were beginning to turn political and the New Left types who were getting bored with picket lines and parades." Arrested more than thirty times for various sorts of disruptive behavior, he was one of the Chicago Seven tried for his activities at the Democratic National Convention in 1968. Of the eight people originally indicted and the seven who were tried, Hoffman, along with David Dellinger, Tom Hayden, Rennie Davis, and Jerry Rubin, was convicted for crossing state lines to foment violence in the Chicago streets. *Newsweek* reported: "The trial of the seven was a landmark in American life and law—and not just for its almost daily pyrotechnics. It had produced the most devastating use of a judge's contempt-of-court power that any lawyer could remember, raised questions about the proper limits on that power and opened up the possibility that the trial system itself might have to be modified in order to cope with defendants and lawyers who refuse to observe its fragile rules of decorum. It had offered the first court test of the controversial 'Rap Brown law' which makes it a crime simply to cross a state line with riotous intent. And it had locked Attorney General John Mitchell's Justice Department into its starkest confrontation with the radical movement, prompting charges from radicals and some liberals that the Administration was embarked on a campaign of political repression against the militant left." Hoffman's conviction

resulted in a sentence of five years in prison, a $5000 fine, and court costs. An appeal was immediately requested and granted. The sentence was postponed.

On August 28, 1973, as the *New Yorker* reported, "Hoffman was arrested and charged with selling cocaine to two undercover narcotics policemen. A defense committee sprang up immediately, like a mushroom after a storm, and raised ten thousand dollars in cash to bail him out." "The bust brought out the love of Abbie's friends," Anita Hoffman explained. "When it's an obvious case of political harassment, everybody's on your side. But when it's a drug bust, especially involving a drug like cocaine, which people are afraid of, only the people who genuinely love you come forward. I've never known anybody who had as many friends as Abbie." Mayer Vishner, a friend of Abbie and Anita Hoffman's, concurred: "A lot of people in the Movement think Abbie's politics are ideologically frivolous, or they think his attention span is too short, and maybe they're right. But everybody respects him, because he's always put himself on the line." Hoffman was released pending trial on the cocaine charges, and shortly afterwards, in October, 1973, the Chicago Court of Appeals struck down the sentence resulting from the Chicago Seven trial. A few months later, early in 1974, Hoffman disappeared to avoid standing trial on the cocaine charges, which he claimed to be a result of research for *The Book-of-the-Month Club Selection* [see WORK IN PROGRESS]. He explained his decision to go underground: "We didn't have the money to put on an adequate defense. I guess the odds are probably two to one that I could have won the case, but if I'd lost, the penalty was a mandatory life sentence. Mandatory. That means there weren't even any options. It's the same as if it were a murder case."

After over fifteen years in the revolutionary movement, Hoffman views his role as that of helping to "create a government that serves the needs of the people, not only in this country but throughout the world. I don't believe change is going to come peacefully in the United States, not without conspiring with anti-imperialist forces abroad. We need a true Communist Party in the United States—one that knows how to reach people. And because of infiltration and harassment, we have to build that party secretly.... I'm helping to build an underground network in the United States that will last a number of years and will be used in different ways, depending on the political climate. War is built into this society and as each war comes along, more and more progressive people will resist it. That's why an underground will be needed."

Abbie Hoffman's life-style and beliefs, thought by some to be unorthodox and dramatic, are reflected in his writings. Commenting on *Revolution for the Hell of It,* Daniel Greene notes: "As literature, [it] is a mess, yet if it were anything else it wouldn't be honest. For as a revolutionary, Hoffman is pretty much of a mess himself—brazen, brilliant revel-rogue dedicated to disrupting the American System, but only if he can have fun doing it." A *Variety* reviewer writing about *Woodstock Nation* says: "The anti-establishment Yippie attitude permeates the entire book. Hoffman bases his philosophy on subjective environment, a stand that works well in this accounting, since both Yippies and Woodstock were products of environment and indications of social change. The result is a collection of thoughts from the head of the new subculture about an unprecedented social event. The differences and similarities between Yippies and Woodstock give the reader a survey of the possible changes society can anticipate in the near future."

Unable to secure a publisher for *Steal This Book,* Hoffman founded Pirate Editions to publish the book himself. He describes *Steal This Book* as "a handbook for living free, stealing, and making violent revolution. . . . I traveled cross-country interviewing doctors, fugitives, dope dealers, draft dodgers, private detectives, country communalists, veterans, organizers, and shoplifters. Every time I met an interesting person I asked if he knew a good rip-off or survival scheme. People loved telling how they screwed the Establishment." D.J.C. Brundnoy, however, feels that *Steal This Book* "is a sort of *Ripping-Off Amerika on Minus $5 a Day* for citizens of Woodstock Nation, complete with diagrams on how to make Molotov cocktails, lessons in getting the right gun to do the job, and other useful tidbits for survival in 'Pig Empire,' this 'prison that is Amerika.' . . . the light stuff in this sequel to *Revolution for the Hell of It* is sandwiched between the ugliness for which Abbie is beloved by the Left: little lessons on how to kill people, kick cops in the groin—friendly, friendly. Abbie's concern for The People is touching." He wrote *Steal This Book,* Hoffman explained, because "big political trials cost hundreds of thousands of dollars. You get the money either by robbing the ruling class or conning it. The bulk of your finances does not come from comrades who march in the streets. And so, determined to effect great social change, fight injustice wherever it reared its ugly head, forge the great proletarian revolution, the be 'one of the people,' I decided to tell all."

BIOGRAPHICAL/CRITICAL SOURCES: New York (magazine), September, 1968; *Time,* December 20, 1968; *Eye* (articles by Hoffman's wife), January, 1969; *National Observer,* January 13, 1969; *Washington Post,* January 30, 1969, October 5, 1971; *Commonweal,* February 7, 1969; *Saturday Night,* July, 1969; *Variety,* November 19, 1969; *Newsweek,* March 2, 1970, July 13, 1970; *Nation,* January 11, 1971; *National Review,* June 1, 1971; *Harper's,* May, 1974; *New Yorker,* May 6, 1974; Anita Hoffman and Abbie Hoffman, *Love Letters from the Underground,* Stonehill Publisher, 1976; *Esquire,* April, 1976; *Playboy,* May, 1976.†

* * *

HOFFMAN, William 1925-

PERSONAL: Born May 16, 1925, in Charleston, W. Va.; son of Henry William and Julia (Beckley) Hoffman; married Alice Sue Richardson, April 17, 1957; children: Ruth Beckley, Margaret Kay. *Education:* Hampden-Sydney College, B.A., 1949; graduate study at Washington and Lee University, 1949-50, University of Iowa, 1951. *Religion:* Presbyterian. *Address:* P.O. Box 241, Charlotte Courthouse, Va. 23923. *Agent:* Curtis Brown Ltd., 60 East 56th St., New York, N.Y. 10022.

CAREER: Hampden-Sydney College, Hampden-Sydney, Va., assistant professor, 1952-59, author in residence, 1966-70; novelist and short story writer. Breeder of horses at farm, Wynard, in Charlotte County, Va.; director of Elk Grocery Co., Elk Storage and Warehouse Co., and Kay Co. *Military service:* U.S. Army, 1943-46. *Member:* Authors Guild.

WRITINGS—Novels; all published by Doubleday: *The Trumpet Unblown,* 1955; *Days in the Yellow Leaf,* 1958; *A Place for My Head,* 1960; *The Dark Mountains,* 1963; *Yancey's War,* 1966; *A Walk to the River,* 1970; *A Death of Dreams,* 1973. Also author of play "The Love Touch."

Contributor of short stories to *Playboy, Cosmopolitan, Virginia Quarterly Review, Carleton Miscellany, Sewanee Review, McCall's, Gentlemen's Quarterly,* and *Scholastic.*

WORK IN PROGRESS: Another novel; a play; and short stories.

SIDELIGHTS: Hoffman told *McCall's* that he had always intended to become a lawyer. "Then," he recounts, "one term, to fill out my schedule, I signed for a course in creative writing. I meant it just as a lark. Next thing I knew, I was trapped." *Yancey's War* has been sold to Judd Bernard for filming.

BIOGRAPHICAL/CRITICAL SOURCES: McCall's, July, 1969.

* * *

HOGG, Garry 1902-

PERSONAL: Born January 5, 1902, in London, England; son of Robert and Kathleen (Lester) Hogg; married second wife, Elizabeth Toothill, 1950; children: (first marriage) Peter. *Education:* Wadham College, Oxford, M.A., 1923. *Home:* Coach House, Leyswood, Groombridge, Sussex, England.

CAREER: Schoolmaster in England, 1923-33, 1939-45; university extension lecturer, 1927-45; author of books for adults and young people, 1936—. Lecturer; broadcaster on travel and books.

WRITINGS: Muddle Headed Postman, and Other Stories, Burns & Oates, 1937, new edition, Hollis & Carter, 1943; *Explorers Awheel,* Thomas Nelson, 1938; *Explorers on the Wall,* Thomas Nelson, 1939.

Explorers Afloat, Thomas Nelson, 1940; *Secret of the Shuttered Lodge,* Thomas Nelson, 1941; *Houseboat Holiday,* Thomas Nelson, 1944; *And Far Away,* Phoenix House, 1946; *Stirring Yarns of Bosun Bill,* Hollis & Carter, 1947; *The Road Before Me,* Phoenix House, 1948; *Sealed Orders,* Thomas Nelson, 1948.

Secret of Hollow Hill, Thomas Nelson, 1950; *Turf Beneath My Feet,* Museum Press, 1950; *Norwegian Journey,* Museum Press, 1951; *Norwegian Holiday,* Thomas Nelson, 1952; *Brittany Roundabout,* Museum Press, 1953; *Riddle of Dooley Castle,* Thomas Nelson, 1953; *Granite Men,* Thomas Nelson, 1954; *Portuguese Journey,* Museum Press, 1954; (with wife, Beth Hogg) *The Young Traveler in Norway,* Phoenix House, 1954, Dutton, 1955; *The Crystal Skull,* Thomas Nelson, 1956; *Swiss Spring,* Museum Press, 1956; *Dutch Treat,* R. Hale, 1957; *Bavarian Journey,* R. Hale, 1958; *Cannibalism and Human Sacrifice,* R. Hale, 1958, Citadel, 1966; *In the Nick of Time,* Roy, 1958; *Country Crafts and Craftsmen,* Hutchinson, 1959; *Dangerous Trades,* Phoenix House, 1959.

Lust for Gold, R. Hale, 1960, A. S. Barnes, 1962; *With Peter Fleming in Tartary,* Muller, 1960; *Climbers' Glory,* Bodley Head, 1961; *Ann and Peter in Norway,* Muller, 1961; *Deep Down,* Hutchinson, 1961, revised edition, Criterion, 1962; *The Far-Flung Isles: Orkney and Shetland,* R. Hale, 1961; *With Burke and Wills Across Australia,* Muller, 1961; *Safe Bind, Safe Find: The Story of Locks, Bolts, and Bars,* Phoenix House, 1961, Arco, 1968; *The Overlanders,* R. Hale, 1961; *Exploring Switzerland,* Weidenfeld & Nicolson, 1962; *Pathfinders in New Zealand,* R. Hale, 1963; *Hammer and Tongs: Blacksmithery Down the Ages,* Hutchinson, 1964; *Inns and Villages of England* (also see below), Arco, 1966; (self-illustrated) *Engineering Magic,* Criterion, 1966; *A Second Book of Inns and Vil-*

lages of England (also see below), Arco, 1967; Blind Jack of Knaresborough: Road Builder Extraordinary, Phoenix House, 1967; Union Pacific: The Birth and Life of a Great Train, Hutchinson, 1968, Walker & Co., 1969; Malta: Blue Water Island, A. S. Barnes, 1968; Orient Express, Hutchinson, 1968; Odd Aspects of England, Arco, 1969; Airship Over the Pole, Abelard, 1969; The Suez Canal, Hutchinson, 1969.

The Hovercraft Story, Abelard, 1970; A Guide to English Country Houses, Arco, 1970; Castles of England, Arco, 1970; Customs and Traditions of England, Arco, 1971; The Batsford Colour Book of London, Batsford, 1971; The Shell Book of Exploring Britain, Hastings House, 1971; London, Batsford, 1971; Inns and Villages of England (based on Inns and Villages of England [1966] and The Second Book of Inns and Villages of England [1967]), Spring Books, 1972; Priories and Abbeys of England, Drake, 1972; They Did It the Hard Way: Some Great Twentieth-Century Journeys, Abelard, 1972, published as They Did It the Hard Way: Seven Astounding Journeys, Pantheon, 1973; Corsica: The Fragrant Isle, Allen & Unwin, 1973; Facets of the English Scene, David & Charles, 1973; Museums of England, David & Charles, 1973, Arco, 1974; The Batsford Colour Book of the Colswolds, Batsford, 1973, Hastings House, 1974; The Best of England, Arco, 1974; Pagentry of Britain in Colour, Batsford, 1974; The English Country Inn, Batsford, 1974, Hastings House, 1975; Market Towns of England, David & Charles, 1974; The Shell Guide to Viewpoints of England, Osprey Publishing, 1975. Contributor to Country Life, Guardian, Countryman, Books and Bookmen, and other periodicals.

SIDELIGHTS: "Now write only when commissioned by a publisher," Hogg told CA. "And an 'on call' from several London publishers to produce books, usually requiring research in the British Museum Reading Room/Library and other sources, since some of the subjects are unusual. E.g., Cannibalism and Human Sacrifice, which is the only book on the subject in the English language." Avocational interests: Country crafts, the outdoors, geology.†

* * *

HOHNEN, David 1925-

PERSONAL: Surname is pronounced Hoe-nen; born March 3, 1925, in London, England; son of Frederick Henry (an engineer) and Arline (King) Hohnen; married Ingrid Hansen, August 20, 1947; children: Michael, Peter. Education: Educated in England. Home: Gunderod, 2970 Horsholm, Denmark.

CAREER: Held various jobs in Denmark, Switzerland, and Morocco, 1947-51; scriptwriter and dubbing director, Madrid, Spain, 1952-55; free-lance writer, translator, and film narrator, with residence in the Scandinavian countries (principally Denmark), 1956—. Military service: British Army, Royal Armoured Corps, North Irish Horse, 1942-47. Member: Society of Authors, Translators Association (both London).

WRITINGS: 3 Mal Skandinavien (written in English, translated by Hanko de Tolly), Piper Verlag (Munich), 1962; A Portrait of Denmark, Hosts Forlag (Copenhagen), 1966. Writer of approximately 100 original scripts for his talks in English on Danish affairs, broadcast on home and overseas programs of Radio Denmark; also writer of many original commentaries for documentary or short films made in Scandinavia and a few short stories published in England, Denmark, Canada, and Switzerland.

Reviser: English text of Knut Hanneborg, Anthropological Circles, Munksgaard (Copenhagen), 1962; (also editor and enlarger) Hosts' English-Danish and Danish-English Pocket Dictionary, Hosts Forlag, 1966; (also translator of various sections into English) Knut Hanneborg, The Study of Literature, University of Oslo Press, 1967.

Translator from Danish into English: Alex Secher, Greenland Revisited, Christian Erichsen Forlag (Copenhagen), 1958; Hans Christian Andersen, The Little Mermaid, Hosts Forlag (Copenhagen), 1959; Palle Lauring, A History of the Kingdom of Denmark, Hosts Forlag, 1960, 3rd edition, 1968; Erik Lassen, Knives, Forks and Spoons, Hosts Forlag, 1960; Hans Christian Andersen, First Three Tales, Hosts Forlag, 1960; Poul Hoffman, The Burning Bush (first volume of "The Moses Trilogy"), Muhlenberg Press, 1961; Poul Hoffman, The Eternal Fire (second volume of "The Moses Trilogy"), Muhlenberg Press, 1962; Ingolf Boisen, Turkey and Denmark through the Ages, Kampsax (Copenhagen), 1962; Henrik Bramsen, Danish Marine Painters, Burmeister & Wain (Copenhagen), 1962; Inge Hegeler and Sten Hegeler, An ABZ of Love, Christian Erichsen Forlag, 1962, Medical Press (New York), 1964; Theodor Moller, Old Danish Military Weapons, Hosts Forlag, 1963; Poul Hoffman, The Brazen Serpent (third volume of "The Moses Trilogy"), Muhlenberg Press, 1963; Ingolf Boisen, Denmark and Iran through the Ages, Kampsax, 1965; Facts About Denmark, edited by M. K. Bjornsen and L. E. Bramsen, 13th edition, Politikens Forlag, 1965, 16th edition, 1967; Ole Wanscher, The Art of Furniture, Reinhold, 1967; Anders Bodelsen, Think of a Number, M. Joseph, 1969; Inge Hegeler and Sten Hegeler, The XYZ of Love, MacGibbon & Kee, 1970; Inge Hegeler and Sten Hegeler, Living Is Loving, Neville Spearman, 1972; Kaj Thaning, N.F.S. Grundtvig, The Danish Institute, 1972. Also translator from Danish into English of over twenty-five other books and monographs.

Translator of screenplays and writer of English subtitles for over eighty Danish and Norwegian feature films; also translator from Danish into English of fourteen radio plays.

SIDELIGHTS: Hohnen has lived at one time or another in most European countries, and at present lives in Denmark. He speaks several European languages. Hohnen's book 3 Mal Skandinavien has been published in Spanish and French.

* * *

HOLLAND, Isabelle 1920-

PERSONAL: Born June 16, 1920, in Basel, Switzerland; daughter of Philip (a U.S. Foreign Service officer) and Corabelle (Anderson) Holland. Education: Educated at private schools in England and University of Liverpool; Tulane University of Louisiana, B.A., 1942. Politics: Independent. Religion: Christian. Home: 1199 Park Ave., New York, N.Y. 10028. Agent: Jane Wilson, John Cushman Associates, 25 West 43rd St., New York, N.Y. 10036.

CAREER: Worked for various magazines, including McCall's, prior to 1960; Crown Publishers, Inc., New York City, publicity director, 1956-60; J. B. Lippincott Co., New York City, publicity director, 1960-66; Harper's, New York City, assistant to publisher, 1967-68; G. P. Putnam's Sons, New York City, publicity director, 1968-69; freelance writer, 1969—. Member: Authors Guild, P.E.N.

WRITINGS—All juvenile except as indicated: Cecily, Lippincott, 1967; Amanda's Choice, Lippincott, 1970; The Man without a Face, Lippincott, 1972; Heads You Win,

Tails I Lose, Lippincott, 1973; *Kilgaren* (adult), Weybright, 1974; *Trelawny* (adult), Weybright, 1974; *Journey for Three,* Houghton, 1975; *Of Love and Death and Other Journeys,* Lippincott, 1975; *Moncrieff* (Gothic novel), Weybright, 1975.

SIDELIGHTS: Isabelle Holland noted that her "childhood was a study in contrasts. The challenge of adapting from sun-drenched Guatemala City with its earthquakes, fiestas and revolutions to the somber, sodden countryside near Liverpool, England, entailed great personal adjustment for a sensitive seven-year-old. My father was a Foreign Service Officer, which accounts for the family's wanderings. When I was three, we moved to Guatemala City, where we remained for four and a half years. This probably accounts for my fondness for things Spanish—music, fiestas, the sound of the language."

Alice Low wrote that Isabelle Holland "understands childrearing, psychological nuances and social problems, but she uses her characters to carry messages rather than to tell their flesh and blood stories. Isabelle Holland makes important points [in *Amanda's Choice*]: among them that emotional deprivation scars more deeply than material deprivation and that Spanish Harlem has a richer, more genuine life than Amanda's insulated island."

BIOGRAPHICAL/CRITICAL SOURCES: New York Times Book Review, May 3, 1970.

* * *

HOLLINGSHEAD, (Ronald) Kyle 1941-

PERSONAL: Born July 29, 1941, in Baird, Tex.; son of Olaf M. (a groceryman) and Pearlie (Gillit) Hollingshead. *Education:* Texas Technological College (now Texas Tech University), student, 1959-61. *Politics:* Democrat. *Religion:* Methodist. *Address:* 5437 42nd St., Lubbock, Texas 79414.

CAREER: Partner in H & H Food Market, 1961-68, and 4th St. Laundry, 1968—, both in Lubbock, Texas. *Member:* Western Writers of America.

WRITINGS—All published by Ace Books: *Echo of a Texas Rifle,* 1967; *The Franklin Raid,* 1968; *Ransome's Debt,* 1970; *Ransome's Move,* 1971; *Ransome's Army,* 1974.

WORK IN PROGRESS: Two Western novels; a science fiction novel; a suspense novel.

AVOCATIONAL INTERESTS: Collecting and reading books, golf.

* * *

HOLLISTER, Leo E. 1920-

PERSONAL: Born December 3, 1920, in Cincinnati, Ohio; son of William Burton and Ruth (Appling) Hollister; married Louise P. Palmieri, February 1, 1950 (divorced); children: Stephen, David, Cynthia, Matthew. *Education:* University of Cincinnati, B.S., 1941, M.D., 1943. *Home:* 3237 Benton St., Santa Clara, Calif. 95051. *Office:* Veterans Administration Hospital, 3804 Junipero Serra Blvd., Palo Alto, Calif. 94304.

CAREER: Veterans Administration Hospital, Palo Alto, Calif., chief of Medical Service, 1953-60, associate chief of staff, 1960-70, medical investigator, 1970—. Member of executive committee of Veterans Administration Cooperative Studies of Chemotherapy in Psychiatry, 1956—. *Military service:* U.S. Naval Reserve, active duty, 1945-46,

1950-51; became commander. *Member:* American Therapeutic Society (president), American College of Neuropsychopharmacology, Collegium Internationale Neuropsychopharmacologicum (president), American College of Physicians (president), American Society for Pharmacology and Experimental Therapeutics. *Awards, honors:* Meritorius Service Award, U.S. Veterans Administration, 1960; William S. Middleton Award for outstanding achievement in medical research, 1966.

WRITINGS: Chemical Psychoses, LSD and Related Drugs, C. C Thomas, 1968; *Clinical Use of Psychotherapeutic Drugs,* C. C Thomas, 1973. Writer of more than 200 scientific and medical papers.

WORK IN PROGRESS: A revision of *Clinical Use of Psychotherapeutic Drugs.*

* * *

HOLLO, Anselm 1934-
(Sergei Bielyi, Anton Hofman)

PERSONAL: Born April 12, 1934, in Helsinki, Finland; son of Juho A. (a translator and university professor) and Iris (Walden) Hollo; married Josephine Wirkus (a poet and translator), December 23, 1957; children: Hannes, Karina, Tamsin. *Education:* Studied science at Helsinki University and modern languages at Tuebingen University, 1952-56. *Address:* c/o English Department, University of Maryland Baltimore County, Baltimore, Md. 21228.

CAREER: Worked as a journalist doing book and film reviews and interviews for the Finnish press in Germany, Sweden, and Austria, 1950-58; British Broadcasting Corp., London, England, radio producer, 1958-66; State University of New York at Buffalo, visiting professor of English, 1967; University of Iowa, Iowa City, visiting professor in Poetry Workshop, 1968-73; Hobarte & William Smith Colleges, Geneva, N.Y., professor of English, 1973-75; University of Maryland Baltimore County, Baltimore, professor of English, 1975—. Free-lance writer, translator, and lecturer, 1966—.

WRITINGS—Poetry: *Sateiden Valilla* (title means "Rainpause"), Otava (Helsinki), 1956; *Loverman,* the dead language press (New York), 1961; *St. Texts and Finnpoems,* Migrant Press (Birmingham, England), 1961; (with David Ball) *We Just Wanted to Tell You,* Writers Forum (England), 1963; *And What Else Is New,* New Voice (Kent, England), 1963; *History,* Matrix Press (England), 1963; (with eight German poets) *Zwischenraume,* Limes Verlag (Wiesbaden), 1963; *Trobar: Loytaa,* Otava, 1964; *And It Is a Song,* Migrant Press, 1965; *Faces and Forms,* Ambit Books (London), 1965; *Here We Go,* Stranger's Press, 1965.

The Claim, Goliard Press (London), 1966; *The Going-On Poem,* Writers Forum, 1966; *Isadora, and Other Poems,* Writers Forum, 1967; *Poems/Runoja* (bi-lingual edition), Otava, 1967; *The Man in the Treetop Hat,* Turret Books (London), 1968; *The Coherences,* Trigram Press, 1968; *Maya: Works, 1959-69,* Grossman, 1971; *Sensation 27,* Institute of Further Studies (New York), 1973; *Black Book No. 1,* Bowling Green State University Writing Program, 1975; *Heavy Jars,* Toothpaste Press, 1976.

Editor and translator: Allen Ginsberg, *Kaddisch* (poems), Limes Verlag, 1962; Yevgeni Yevtushenko, Andrei Voznesensky, and Semyon Kirsanov, *Red Cats* (poems), City Lights, 1962 (German translation published as *Gegen Grenzen,* Limes Verlag, 1962); *Some Poems by Paul Klee,*

Scorpion Press, 1963; Gregory Corso, *In der Fluechtigen Hand der Zeit* (poems), Limes Verlag, 1963; Ginsberg, *Huuto ja Muita Runoja* (poems), Tajo, 1963; (co-translator) Ginsberg, *Kuolema van Goghin Korvalle* (poems), Tajo, 1963; *Idan ja Lannen Runot* (anthology of modern American poetry), Weilin & Goos, 1963; Voznesensky, *Selected Poems*, Grove, 1964; (with Matti Rossi) *Nain Ihminen Vastaa* (anthology of modern Latin American poetry), Tajo, 1964; Rolf-Gunter Dienst, *Five Feet Two* (poems), Tarasque Press, 1965; *Word from the North: New Poetry from Finland*, Screeches Press, 1965.

Translator: Vladimir Maximov, *A Man Survives* (novel), Grove, 1963; *John Lennon Panee Omiaan* (translation of *John Lennon in His Own Write*), Otava, 1964; Veijo Meri, *Das Manilaseil* (novel), Carl Hanser Verlag, 1964; Lars Gorling, *491* (novel), Grove, 1966; Matti Rossi, *The Trees of Vietnam* (poems), El Corno Emplumado, 1966; Lars Ullerstam, *The Erotic Minorities* (essays), Grove, 1966; Bertolt Brecht, *Jungle of Cities* (plays), Grove, 1966; John Lennon, *Hispanjalainen Jakovainaa* (prose), Otava, 1966; Pentti Saarikoski, *Helsinki* (poems), Rapp & Carroll, 1967; Paavo Haavikko, *Selected Poems*, Cape Goliard, 1968; Jean Genet, *Querelle* (novel), Grove, 1975; Emmanuelle Arsan, *Emmanuelle II* (novel), Grove, 1975; Franz Innerhofer, *Beautiful Days* (novel), Urizen Books, 1976.

Others: (With Gregory Corso and Tom Raworth) *The Minicab War* (satire), Matrix Press, 1961; (editor) *Jazz Poems* (anthology of modern English poetry), Vista Books, 1963; (editor) *Negro Verse* (anthology), Vista Books, 1964. Also author of numerous radio scripts for British Broadcasting Corp. and for Finnish and German broadcasts (some under pseudonym Anton Hofman).

SIDELIGHTS: Hollo told *CA* that his "major area" is "the poetry and music of the world" and that he delights in "travel, people, all sentient beings." Tom Clark says Hollo writes "cheerful, sentimental and around-the-house" poems which make one suspect that it would be "pleasant to meet the poet on the street and say hello to him." Ian Vine adds: "Hollo is a poet of great warmth, with eyes directed unflinchingly on himself and his surroundings, but with heart still in the accepting world of childhood."

Clark believes that the peculiarity of Hollo's vision, which becomes in the poems an attractive strangeness, is sometimes weakened by a "rib-nudge sort of wryness"; but he adds, "if Hollo can adhere more closely to [his unique vision] his poems will move and fascinate us even more." Vine attributes this strangeness to the influence of Apollinaire in Hollo's work. "The closeness of his links with Apollinaire is not primarily stylistic [as with Apollinaire's "bizarre, sometimes apparently random, imagery, and the easy conversational style of some of his poems"], but in his approach to the definition of experience in poetry."

Of Hollo's technique Clark writes: "His sense of phrasing is casual and musical. The poems are really songs celebrating affection.... His temperament is romantic, but in a generous, not a moody way. And he pays enough attention to the domestic things he writes about to make them unusual, interesting to me. The poetry has a talking diction that's good-natured, colorful, truthful, and accurate.... You feel that the language of his poems does the job it has to do without being especially new. Hollo manages to keep going on the strength of feeling rather than that of conscience, and that's its advantage." Adrian Mitchell says simply: "His poems storm, they weep, they are full of peace."

Edward Dorn wrote: "When I first met Anselm Hollo I noticed he laughed quite a bit, sort of all the time. I didn't know what it meant or *if* it was supposed to mean because it didn't like most laughter seem to be about something. And anyway was it laughing. More like rapid fire. Then there is poetry and the world of men who mean something by that, laughing or weeping. That *is* international, just that part of it more than the tiresome questions about whether these or those languages will cohabit.... At last I understood experiences are important—if something happens to you simple or otherwise you then have that, in some form of yourself and the transfer is that direct: this happens. Happens to be us. The language can be difficult just like what happened. Or end before anything 'recognisable' began. That's one of the discoveries Anselm has made about the language most natives never get to. And it can be immensely probable like watching the seas far below come in come on when you know the sound is there too. The sound is in everything you can see."

BIOGRAPHICAL/CRITICAL SOURCES: Nation, January 6, 1962; *Kulchur*, summer, 1962; *Resuscitator*, May, 1965; *Sunday Times*, January 2, 1966; *Track*, February, 1967; *Poetry*, May, 1967.

*   *   *

HOLLOWAY, Mark   1917-

PERSONAL: Born October 10, 1917, in London, England; adopted son of G. C. and M. E. (Thomson) Holloway; married Victoria Strachey, November 5, 1952; children: two sons, two daughters. *Education:* Trinity Hall, Cambridge, B.A. (honors in English literature), 1940, M.A., 1948. *Agent:* A. M. Heath & Co. Ltd., 40-42 William IV St., London, WC2N 4DD, England.

CAREER: Wrote book reviews and worked occasionally as a bookseller, 1947-55; writer. *Member:* Society of Authors. *Wartime service:* Conscripted into Royal Navy, 1940; became conscientious objector and worked as forester, on a farm and in hospitals, 1941-46.

WRITINGS: Heavens on Earth: Utopian Communities in America, 1680-1880, Turnstile Press, 1951, 2nd edition, Dover, 1966; *Poems,* Fantasy Press, 1956; *William Harvey, 1578-1657,* Tower, 1957; (with Sydney Carter, Derek Savage, Clifford Simmons, and Stuart Smith) *The Objectors,* Gibbs & Phillips, 1965; *Ten Poems,* Tragara Press, 1969.

WORK IN PROGRESS: A biography of Norman Douglas (1868-1952).

AVOCATIONAL INTERESTS: Eccentrics, literature, architecture, cities, history of the South Seas, the years 1780-1830, gardening, good food.

*   *   *

HOLMES, Paul Carter   1926-

PERSONAL: Born September 10, 1926, in Niagara Falls, N.Y.; son of Frederick Greenwood and Helen Louise (Carter) Holmes. *Education:* Santa Rosa Junior College, A.A., 1955; University of California, Berkeley, B.A., 1957; San Francisco State College (now University), M.A., 1964. *Politics:* Democrat. *Religion:* Episcopalian. *Home:* 47 Buena Vista Ter., San Francisco, Calif. 94117. *Office:* College of San Mateo, San Mateo, Calif. 94402.

CAREER: San Leandro (Calif.) Unified School District, teacher of English and reading, 1959-62; College of San Mateo, San Mateo, Calif., 1964—, began as instructor in

English and reading, currently instructor in English and supervisor of reading program. President, Northern California College Teachers of Reading. *Military service:* U.S. Army, 1950-52. *Member:* American Association of University Professors, International Reading Association, American Federation of Teachers, National Council of Teachers of English, Western College Reading Association, California Teachers Association.

WRITINGS: (With Anita J. Lehman) *Keys to Understanding: Receiving and Sending the Essay,* Harper, 1968, 2nd edition, 1974; (with Lehman) *Keys to Understanding: Receiving and Sending the Poem,* Harper, 1969; *Keys to Understanding: Receiving and Sending Drama,* Harper, 1970; (with Lehman) *A Parade of Lines,* Canfield Press, 1971; (with Harry Souza) *The Touch of a Poet,* Harper, 1975; (with Lehman) *The Challenge of Conflict* (short story anthology), Harper, 1976.

WORK IN PROGRESS: A Frame of Reference, with L. Hazelton; revising *Passway to Reading,* with Anita J. Lehman.

* * *

HOLSTI, Kalevi J(acque) 1935-

PERSONAL: Born April 25, 1935, in Geneva, Switzerland; became a Canadian citizen; son of Rudolf W. and Liisa (Franssila) Holsti; married Mina E. Machado, June 23, 1973; children: Liisa, Matthew, Karina. *Education:* Stanford University, B.A., 1956, M.A., 1958, Ph.D., 1961. *Home:* 1672 Roxbury Pl., North Vancouver, British Columbia, Canada. *Office:* Department of Political Science, University of British Columbia, Vancouver, British Columbia, Canada.

CAREER: University of British Columbia, Vancouver, instructor, 1961-63, assistant professor, 1963-67, associate professor, 1967-71, professor of political science, 1971—, acting director of Institute of International Relations, 1970-71. Visiting associate professor at University of Hawaii, summer, 1967. External member of the board of directors, Centre for Foreign Policy Studies, Dalhousie University, 1970—. *Member:* International Studies Association (vice-president of Western division, 1966-67); Canadian Political Science Association (member of executive committee, 1968-71). *Awards, honors:* Fulbright scholarship to Finland, 1959-60; Ford Foundation research fellowship, 1961; Canada Council senior research fellowship, Royal Institute of International Affairs, 1967-68, and McGill University, 1972-73.

WRITINGS: Suomen Ulkopolitiikka Suuntaansa Etsimmassa, Tammi Publishing (Helsinki), 1963; *International Politics: A Framework for Analysis,* Prentice-Hall, 1967, 2nd edition, 1972; (contributor) Kenneth Waltz and Steven Spiegel, editors, *Conflict in World Politics,* Winthrop Publishers, 1971; (contributor) Gavin Boyd, James Rosenau, and Kenneth Thompson, editors, *World Politics,* Free Press, 1976. Contributor to *American Political Science Review, Journal of Conflict Resolution, Western Political Quarterly,* and other journals in his field. Editor, *International Studies Quarterly,* 1970-75.

WORK IN PROGRESS: Research on sources of isolationism in Burma and Bhutan.

AVOCATIONAL INTERESTS: Fishing, water polo (member of British Columbia team playing in Canadian Championships in Edmonton, 1965, and Montreal, 1966, and captain of team in Canada Games, 1970).

HOLUB, Miroslav 1923-

PERSONAL: Born September 13, 1923, in Pilsen, Czechoslovakia; son of Josef (a railway clerk) and Frantiska (Dvorakova) Holub; married former wife, Vera Koktova (an actress), November 30, 1948; married Marta Svikruhova (editor of an encyclopedia), January 31, 1963; children: two sons, Radovan Jiri and Radovan. *Education:* Charles University, School of Medicine, M.D., 1953; Czechoslovak Academy of Sciences, Institute of Microbiology, Ph.D. (immunology), 1958. *Politics:* "Not organized." *Religion:* Czechoslovak Church (protestant). *Home:* Hrncire 107, 149 00 Prague 4, Czechoslovakia. *Office:* Institute for Clinical and Experimental Medicine, Budejovicka 800, 146 22 Prague 4, Czechoslovakia.

CAREER: Bulovka Hospital, Prague, Czechoslovakia, clinical pathologist, 1953-54; Czechoslovak Academy of Sciences, Institute of Microbiology, Prague, scientific worker, 1954-65; Public Health Research Institute of the City of New York, New York, N.Y., visiting investigator, 1965-67; Czechoslovak Academy of Sciences, Institute of Microbiology, Prague, scientific worker, 1968-71; Institute for Clinical and Experimental Medicine, Prague, scientific worker, 1972—. *Member:* Czechoslovak Writers Union (former member of central committee), Union of Czechoslovak Scientists (former member of central committee). *Awards, honors:* Publishers' awards for *Achilles a zelva, Tak zvane srdce, Andel na koleckach,* and *Die explodierende Metropole.*

*WRITINGS—*Poetry: *Denni sluzba* (title means "Day Duty"), Ceskoslovensky Spisovatel, 1958; *Achilles a zelva* (ttile means "Achilles and the Tortoise"), Mlada Fronta, 1960, 2nd edition, 1962; *Slabikar* (title means "Primer"), Ceskoslovensky Spisovatel, 1961, 2nd edition, 1964; *Jdi a otevri dvere* (title means "Go and Open the Door"), Mlada Fronta, 1962; *Zcela nesoustavna zoologie* (title means "A Completely Unsystematic Zoology"), Mlada Fronta, 1963; *Kam tece krev* (title means "Where the Blood Flows"), Ceskoslovensky Spisovatel, 1963; *Tak zvane srdce* (title means "The So-Called Heart"), Mlada Fronta, 1963; *Anamneza* (title means "Anamnesis"), Mlada Fronta, 1964; *Selected Poems,* translation by Ian Milner and George Theiner, introduction by A. Alvarez, Penguin, 1967; *Ackoli,* Ceskoslovensky Spisovatel, 1969, translation by I. Milner and J. Milner published as *Although,* J. Cape, 1971; *Beton* (title means "Concrete"), Mlada Fronta, 1970; (contributor) *Aktschluesse/Halbgedichte* (published only in German), translation by F. P. Knnzel, Hanser, 1974.

Prose: *Andel na koleckach* (reports from America; title means "Angel on Wheels"), Ceskoslovensky Spisovatel, 1963, 4th edition, 1967; *Tri kroky po zemi* (title means "Three Steps on the Earth"), Nase Vojsko (Prague), 1965; *Die explodierende Metropole* (written in Czech; title means "The Exploding City" and refers to New York), German translation published by Verlag Volk und Welt (Berlin), 1967; *Zit v New Yorku* (title means "To Live in New York"), Melantrich, 1969; *Poe cili udoli neklidu* (title means "Poe or Valley of Unrest"), Ceskoslovensky Spisovatel, 1971. Also author of monographs and sixty papers on cellular immunology. Editor, *Vesmir* (magazine devoted to the popularization of science), 1951-65; member of editorial board, *Lidove Noviny* (newspaper of the Czech Writers Union), 1963-65, 1968.

SIDELIGHTS: Holub is a scientist by vocation and considers his poetry a pastime. Holub told Stephen Stepanchev that the Czech Writers Union had offered him a stipend equivalent to his salary as a research scientist to enable him to devote two years to his poetry. "But I like science," he said. "Anyway, I'm afraid that, if I had all the time in the world to write my poems, I would write nothing at all."

Holub told Stepanchev that, for him, science and poetry enjoy an "uneasy relationship." "In scientific circles," he said, "I try to hide the fact that I write verse. Scientists tend to be suspicious of poets; they feel that poets are, somehow, irresponsible." And he admitted that his profession was similarly held suspect by his literary friends. But Holub sees no real conflict between science and poetry. As a scientist, he says, he believes in "an objective reality" and hates superstition. But, he adds, "I'm open-minded about all the phenomena of experience, including the irrational." Graham Martin, reviewing *Selected Poems,* explains how such tenets are effected in Holub's poems: "Where [others register] the savagery of our epoch indirectly, Holub's urbanity stands upon unstated but direct knowledge of everything that could swamp it. These are wonderful poems, sane, witty, courageous, inventive.... Holub is a pathologist, and so experimental, pragmatic, free of the taint of ideology. But he has his articles of faith, that the specifically human quality is the mind, its inventiveness, moral energy, its fantasies. And his art can absorb the different kinds of knowledge of the universe which science offers, not I think because he practises one but because he can grasp reality both as known and impersonal (a body of assumptions, a method of inspection) and as the experience of knowing it, even of not liking a good deal of it."

Holub often employs scientific metaphors in his poems, a technique which, although he considers it "a risk," allows him to "find poetic equivalents for the new reality of the micro-world." Holub told Stepanchev that one of the reasons he uses metaphors at all is "to avoid the aridities of rationalism." "The other reason," he adds, "is that I like the play or dance of metaphors, just as I like the play of ideas in a poem. My poems, by the way, always begin with an idea, an obsessive idea of some sort.... I try to achieve effects of suspense with my long lines and tremendous emphases with my short ones."

Julian Symons, after reading Holub's poems in translation, was impressed by the fact that "in quotation Holub may sound whimsical. In fact his effects are gay or surrealistically odd, although always informed by a social certain sharpness." A *Times Literary Supplement* reviewer writes: "These are all poems where the argument is stated with direct, even rhetorical candour and simplicity. Sometimes it is as simple as scolding ... or humorous exhortation ... or clever, lucid fable.... But there are only occasionally poems where the tone is obvious, naive, or ungenerous.... Most frequently the movement of the reasoning in these poems—always disconcerting and resourceful—is from the large, the general and the scientific back to the human," as all significant truths are to be found, ultimately, in man's own nature. "Holub's is finally a fertile and ingenious humanist imagination," the *Times Literary Supplement* writer concludes, "re-creating very simple truths with new excitement and appealing topicality."

In 1965, Holub read his poems at the Spoleto Festival, Italy, in 1967 at the YMHA Poetry Center in New York under the auspices of the Lincoln Center Festival, in 1968 at the Harrogate Festival, England, in 1974 at Poetry International, Rotterdam, Holland, and in 1975 at the Cambridge Poetry Festival, Cambridge, England. Holub speaks English, French, and German.

BIOGRAPHICAL/CRITICAL SOURCES: A. Hoffmeister, *Cas se nevraci,* Ceskoslovensky Spisovatel, 1965; *Landfall,* Number 4, 1966; *New Scientist,* January 26, 1967; *Tri-Quarterly,* spring, 1967; *New Statesman,* April 7, 1967; *Times Literary Supplement,* April 27, 1967; *Listener,* July 6, 1967; (interview) *New Leader,* September 25, 1967; B. Svozil, *Vule k intelektualni poezii* (title means "Will to Intellectual Poetry"), Ceskoslovensky Spisovatel, 1971; Carolyn Riley, editor, *Contemporary Literary Criticism,* Volume IV, Gale, 1975.

*   *   *

HOMANS, Peter   1930-

PERSONAL: Born June 24, 1930, in New York, N.Y.; married Celia Ann Edwards (a director of field work, National Opinion Research Center); children: Jennifer, Patricia, Elizabeth. *Education:* Princeton University, A.B., 1952; Protestant Episcopal Theological Seminary in Virginia, B.D., 1957; University of Chicago, M.A., 1962, Ph.D., 1964. *Office:* Divinity School, University of Chicago, Chicago, Ill. 60637.

CAREER: Institute for Juvenile Research, Chicago, Ill., supervisor of residential treatment for children, 1961-62; University of Toronto, Trinity College, Toronto, Ontario, instructor in department of religion, 1962-64; Hartford Seminary Foundation, Hartford, Conn., assistant professor of theology and psychology, 1964-65; University of Chicago, Divinity School, Chicago, Ill., associate professor of religion and psychological studies, 1965—. *Member:* American Association of University Professors, American Academy of Religion.

WRITINGS: (Editor) *The Dialogue between Theology and Psychology,* University of Chicago Press, 1968; *Theology After Freud: An Interpretive Inquiry,* Bobbs-Merrill, 1970.

WORK IN PROGRESS: Two books.

*   *   *

HONE, Ralph E(merson)   1913-

PERSONAL: Born July 27, 1913, in Toledo, Ohio; son of Henry Ralph and Ethel (Skeldon) Hone; married Harriet Crawford (an elementary school teacher), December 27, 1944; children: Beth (Mrs. Kenneth Kearse), Hannah (Mrs. James Leckman), Martha, Philip. *Education:* Ohio State University, B.A., 1943, M.A., 1945; New York University, Ph.D., 1955. *Home:* 229 Anita Ct., Redlands, Calif. 92373. *Office:* University of Redlands, Redlands, Calif. 92373.

CAREER: Associate professor of English at Gordon College, Boston, Mass., 1949-54, and Wheaton College, Wheaton, Ill., 1954-56; University of Redlands, Redlands, Calif., associate professor, 1956-59, professor of English and Latin, 1959—, director of Division of Language and Literature, 1960—, director of Redlands in Europe, Salzburg, Austria, 1961-62, dean of humanities, 1972—. Visiting professor, University of California, Los Angeles, summer, 1959; Fulbright professor at University of Helsinki, 1965-66. *Member:* Modern Language Association of America, Renaissance Society of America, Milton Society of America, California Writers Guild, Omicron Delta Kappa, Torch International, Redlands Fortnightly Club. *Awards, honors:* Mortar Board Distinguished Teacher Award, 1964.

WRITINGS: The Voice Out of the Whirlwind: The Book of Job, Chandler Publishing, 1960, revised edition, 1972;

(editor) John Milton, *Samson Agonistes: The Poem and Materials for Analysis,* Chandler Publishing, 1965. Contributor to *Huntington Library Quarterly, Studies in Philology, Notes and Queries* (London); staff reviewer, *Los Angeles Times.*

WORK IN PROGRESS: A book, *Dorothy Leigh Sayers.*

* * *

HONG, Edna H. 1913-

PERSONAL: Born January 28, 1913, in Thorpe, Wis.; daughter of Otto (a farmer) and Ida (Nordby) Hatlestad; married Howard V. Hong (a professor of philosophy at St. Olaf College), June 8, 1938; children: Irena (Mrs. Roy Elveton), Erik, Peder, Rolf, Mary (Mrs. Tom Loe), Judith, Theodore, Nathaniel. *Education:* St. Olaf College, B.A., 1938. *Politics:* Independent. *Religion:* Lutheran. *Home address:* R.F.D. 1, Northfield, Minn. 55057.

CAREER: Homemaker and writer. *Awards, honors:* With Howard V. Hong, co-recipient of National Book Award, 1968, for *Kierkegaard's Journals and Papers,* Volume I.

WRITINGS: (With husband, Howard V. Hong) *Muskego Boy,* Augsburg, 1943; *The Boy Who Fought With Kings,* Augsburg, 1946; *Paving Block Stories,* Northfield News, 1955; (with Mary Hinderlie) *Festival of Christmas,* Augsburg, 1957; (translator with H. V. Hong) Kierkegaard, *Works of Love,* Harper, 1962; (editor and translator with H. V. Hong) *Kierkegaard's Journals and Papers,* Indiana University Press, Volume I, 1967, Volume II, 1970, Volumes III-VII, 1975-76; *Clues to the Kingdom,* Augsburg, 1968; (editor and translator with H. V. Hong) Kierkegaard, *Armed Neutrality* [and] *An Open Letter,* Indiana University Press, 1968; *Turn Over Any Stone,* Augsburg, 1970; *The Gayety of Grace,* Augsburg, 1970; *From This Good Ground,* Augsburg, 1974.

SIDELIGHTS: See HONG, Howard V(incent), below.

* * *

HONG, Howard V(incent) 1912-

PERSONAL: Born October 19, 1912, in Wolford, N.D.; son of Peter B. (a businessman) and Ada J. (Cooper) Hong; married Edna Hatlestad (a writer), June 8, 1938; children: Irena (Mrs. Roy Elveton), Erik, Peder, Rolf, Mary (Mrs. Tom Loe), Judith, Theodore, Nathaniel. *Education:* St. Olaf College, B.A., 1934; State College of Washington (now Washington State University), graduate study, 1934-35; University of Minnesota, Ph.D., 1938; University of Copenhagen, postdoctoral study, 1938-39. *Politics:* Independent. *Religion:* Lutheran. *Home address:* R.F.D. 1, Northfield, Minn. 55057. *Office:* Department of Philosophy, St. Olaf College, Northfield, Minn. 55057.

CAREER: St. Olaf College, Northfield, Minn., instructor, 1938-40, assistant professor of philosophy and English, 1940-46, associate professor of philosophy and psychology, 1946-49, professor of philosophy and chairman of department, 1949—. Visiting lecturer at University of Minnesota, 1954, and Pacific Lutheran Theological Seminary, 1956. World Young Men's Christian Association, Geneva, Switzerland, field secretary for war prisoners' aid in Germany, Scandinavia, and United States, 1943-46; senior field officer in Germany, Refugee Division, World Council of Churches, 1947-48. Senior representative in Europe, Lutheran World Federation Service to Refugees, 1947-49; director of Christian Service Institute, 1957-60.

MEMBER: American Philosophical Association, Phi Beta Kappa. *Awards, honors:* American-Scandinavian Foundation fellowship, 1938-39; American Council of Learned Societies fellowship, 1951-52; J.A.O. Preus Award, 1953; Rockefeller Foundation grant, 1958-59; Fulbright grant to Denmark, 1959-50, 1968; with Edna H. Hong, co-recipient of National Book Award, 1968, for translation of *Kierkegaard's Journals and Papers,* Volume I; National Endowment for the Humanities, senior scholar, 1970-71, research scholar, 1972-73.

WRITINGS: (Translator with wife, Edna H. Hong) Kierkegaard, *For Self Examination,* Augsburg, 1940; (with E. H. Hong) *Muskego Boy,* Augsburg, 1943; *This World and the Church,* Augsburg, 1955; (editor and contributor) *Integration and the Christian Liberal Arts College,* St. Olaf College Press, 1956; (contributor) *Christian Social Responsibility,* Muhlenberg, 1957; (editor and contributor) *Christian Faith and the Liberal Arts,* Augsburg, 1960; (translator and reviser) Kierkegaard, *Philosophical Fragments,* Princeton University Press, 1962; (editor and translator with E. H. Hong) Kierkegaard, *Works of Love,* Harper, 1962; (editor and translator with E. H. Hong) *Kierkegaard's Journals and Papers,* Indiana University Press, Volume I, 1967, Volume II, 1970, Volumes III-VII, 1975-76; (editor and translator with E. H. Hong) Kierkegaard, *Armed Neutrality* [and] *An Open Letter,* Indiana University Press, 1968; (editor and translator with E. H. Hong) G. Malantschuk, *Kierkegaard's Thought,* Princeton University Press, 1971.

SIDELIGHTS: Presenting the National Book Award for translation to Howard and Edna Hong, the jury said: "In undertaking the first complete English translation [of Kierkegaard, the Hongs] have brought to the task solid scholarship, linguistic competence, and imaginative and useful arrangement of the material, and a scrupulous self-effacement before the work."

BIOGRAPHICAL/CRITICAL SOURCES: Publishers' Weekly, March 18, 1968.

* * *

HONIGMANN, E(rnest) A(nselm) J(oachim) 1927-

PERSONAL: Born November 29, 1927, in Breslau, Germany; son of H. D. (a physician) and U. M. (Heilborn) Honigmann; married Elsie M. Packman, July 1, 1958; children: Elaine, Paul, Richard. *Education:* University of Glasgow, M.A., 1948; Oxford University, B.Litt., 1950. *Religion:* Protestant. *Office:* University of Newcastle upon Tyne, Newcastle upon Tyne 2, England.

CAREER: Shakespeare Institute, Stratford on Avon, England, fellow, 1951-54; University of Glasgow, Glasgow, Scotland, lecturer, 1954-66, senior lecturer in English, 1966-67; University of Newcastle upon Tyne, Newcastle upon Tyne, England, reader, 1968-70, professor of English literature, 1970—. Visiting professor at University of Washington, summer, 1967. *Awards, honors:* D.Litt., University of Glasgow, 1966.

WRITINGS: (Editor) *King John,* Harvard University Press, 1954; *The Stability of Shakespeare's Text,* University of Nebraska Press, 1965; (editor) *Milton's Sonnets,* St. Martin's, 1966; (editor) William Shakespeare, *Richard III,* Penguin, 1968; (editor) Shakespeare, *Twelfth Night,* Macmillan, 1971.

* * *

HOOD, Robert E. 1926-

PERSONAL: Born April 15, 1926, in Mildred, Pa., son of

Charles E. (a coal miner) and Alice V. (Johnson) Hood; married Ann M. King, October 15, 1955; children: Carol Ann, Eric Charles. *Education:* Harpur College (now State University of New York at Binghamton), B.A., 1951; New York University, graduate study, 1951-53. *Politics:* Democrat. *Home:* 12 Berwick Rd., Kendall Park, N.J. 08824. *Agent:* Sterling Lord Agency, 660 Madison Ave., New York, N.Y. 10021. *Office: Boy's Life,* Boy Scouts of America, New Brunswick, N.J. 08903.

CAREER: Boy's Life, New Brunswick, N.J., editorial assistant, 1953-54, assistant editor, 1954-58, associate editor, 1958-62, executive editor, 1962-64, editor, 1964-70, editor-in-chief, 1970—. Special consultant for Community Relations Service, 1964. Volunteer speech and pamphlet writer for Senator John F. Kennedy, 1960; speech writer for Senator Harrison Williams, 1964, and Governor LeRoy Collins, 1964-66. *Military service:* U.S. Navy Reserve, 1944-46. *Member:* American Society of Magazine Editors.

WRITINGS—All published by Putnam except as indicated: *Find a Career in Photography,* 1959; *Twelve at War: Great Photographers under Fire,* 1967; *Let's Go to a Baseball Game,* 1973; *Let's Go to a Stock Car Race,* 1973; *Let's Go to a Football Game,* 1974; *Let's Go to a Basketball Game,* 1975; *The Gashouse Gang,* Morrow, 1976. Editor, Putnam's "Sports Series," 1958—, and Coward's "States of the Nation Series," 1964-66. Contributor of articles and reviews to *World Book Yearbook, New York Times, Popular Photography, American Swedish Monthly, Infinity, Famous Writers Magazine.*

WORK IN PROGRESS: The Withered Branch, a novel, completion expected in 1977.

SIDELIGHTS: Hood describes himself as "a frustrated fiction writer and an amateur sportsman.... Trained myself to be a competent photographer by shooting dozens of photo essays for publication. In 1962, I took my family to Sweden for the summer to research a novel and trace my maternal ancestors, in the process acquiring a crude competence in spoken Swedish [he also speaks Spanish].... In 1964, for the *World Book Yearbook* and *Harper's,* I went to Colombia to photograph and write about the Peace Corps.... As a writer, I am a personalist, emotional, with instincts toward Nordic gloom and pessimism. Love to golf and fish, ... dislike travel, public appearances, patronization, sentimentality.

* * *

HOOD, (Martin) Sinclair (Frankland) 1917-

PERSONAL: Born January 31, 1917, in Queenstown, Ireland; son of Martin (a lieutenant commander, Royal Navy) and Frances (Winants) Hood; married Rachel Simmons, March 5, 1957; children: Martin, Mary, Dictynna. *Education:* Magdalen College, Oxford, M.A., 1939; University of London, Diploma in Prehistoric Archaeology, 1947; studied at British School of Archaeology, Athens, 1947-48, 1951-53, and British Institute of Archaeology, Ankara, 1948-49. *Politics:* Liberal-Conservative. *Religion:* Church of England. *Home:* Old Vicarage, Great Milton, Oxford, England.

CAREER: British School of Archaeology, Athens, Greece, assistant director, 1949-51, director, 1954-62. Archaeology work has been mainly centered in Greece and Turkey; took part in excavations in England at Dorchester, Oxford, 1937, Compton, 1946-47, and Southwark, 1946, in Turkey, at Smyrna, 1948-49, Atchana, 1949-50, Sakca-Gozu, 1950, in Greece at Mycenae, 1950-52, in Palestine, at Jericho,

1952; in charge of excavations at Emporio in Chios, 1952-55, and Knossos in Crete, 1950-61. *Wartime service:* Conscientious objector, serving with British Civil Defence, 1939-46. *Member:* Society of Antiquaries, Athenaeum Club (London).

WRITINGS: (With D. Smollett and P. de Jong) *Archaeological Survey of the Knossos Area,* Oxford University Press, 1958; *The Home of the Heroes: The Aegean before the Greeks,* McGraw, 1967; (editor with Mark Cameron) Sir Arthur Evans, *Knossos Fresco Atlas,* Gregg, 1968; *The Minoans: Crete in the Bronze Age,* Thames & Hudson, 1971. Contributor to *Anatolian Studies, Annual of the British School at Athens, Antiquity, Kadmos, Journal of Hellenic Studies,* and other professional journals.

WORK IN PROGRESS: Reports on archaeological excavations at Emporio and Knossos.

SIDELIGHTS: Hood writes to *CA:* "Began to take a serious interest in history and archaeology after reading Gibbon's *Decline and Fall of the Roman Empire* and Baikie's *Sea Kings of Crete* when about sixteen.... Much interested in problems of dating prehistoric periods, and skeptical of the value of results so far obtained by scientific methods of dating...." Hood speaks modern Greek, French, and German, and formerly spoke Turkish; he can read some Italian and Spanish.

* * *

HOOGENBOOM, Olive 1927-

PERSONAL: Born September 24, 1927, in Calcutta, India; daughter of Alfred Grover (a minister) and Bertha (Oss) Youngberg; married Ari Hoogenboom (a history professor), August 28, 1949; children: Lynn, Ari, Jr., Jan. *Education:* Atlantic Union College, B.A., 1949; Columbia University, M.A., 1955. *Religion:* Unitarian Universalist. *Home:* 1451 East 21st St., Brooklyn, N.Y. 11210.

WRITINGS: (Editor with husband Ari Hoogenboom) *The Gilded Age,* Prentice-Hall, 1967; (editor with A. Hoogenboom) *An Interdisciplinary Approach to American History,* two volumes, Prentice-Hall, 1973; (with A. Hoogenboom) *A History of the ICC: From Panacea to Palliative,* Norton, 1976.

WORK IN PROGRESS: Editing *San Francisco in 1854: The California Letters of Montgomery Blair;* collaborating with Ari Hoogenboom on *Bureaucracy in America,* for McGraw, and *Fox of the Union Navy,* a biography of Lincoln's close friend and assistant Secretary of the Navy, Gustavus Vasa Fox.

* * *

HOOK, Frank S(cott) 1922-

PERSONAL: Born May 12, 1922, in Harrisonville, Mo.; son of Frank (a farmer) and Cora (Savage) Hook; married Mary Jane Chinn (a college teacher), August 9, 1948; children: Barrett Lewis, Catherine Grace, Cora Ellen. *Education:* University of Missouri, B.A., 1942, M.A., 1947; Yale University, Ph.D., 1952. *Politics:* Democrat. *Home:* 1849 Richmond Ave., Bethlehem, Pa. 18018. *Office:* Lehigh University, Bethlehem, Pa. 18015.

CAREER: University of Missouri, Columbia, instructor in English, 1947-49; Lehigh University, Bethlehem, Pa., assistant professor, 1952-57, associate professor, 1957-65, professor of English, 1965—. *Military service:* U.S. Army Air Forces, 1942-45; served in Southwest Pacific. *Member:* Modern Language Association of America, National

Council of Teachers of English, American Association of University Professors, Shakespeare Association of America, Malone Society, Pennsylvania Council of Teachers of English (past president), Phi Beta Kappa, Eta Sigma Phi, Phi Eta Sigma, Omicron Delta Kappa.

WRITINGS: (Editor) *Fenton's Bandello,* University of Missouri Studies, 1948; (editor) George Peele, *Edward I* (in Volume II of *The Works of Peele*), Yale University Press, 1961; *A Guide to an Exhibition of Rare Books Relating to Shakespeare,* Lehigh University Library, 1964; (editor) George Peele, *Old Wives Tale* (in *The Works of Peale*), Yale University Press, 1970. Editor, *Bulletin* of Pennsylvania Council of Teachers of English.

* * *

HOOKER, James Ralph 1929-

PERSONAL: Born May 13, 1929, in Auburn, N.Y.; son of Ralph James (a research engineer) and Marjorie Jean (Smith) Hooker; married Dana Sue Downing (an instructor in linguistics; died August 3, 1969); married Naomi Ware, April 11, 1970; children: (first marriage) Alison Briggs, Ralph James II; (second marriage) Antonia. *Education:* Michigan State University, B.A., 1950, Ph.D., 1957; attended University of Michigan Law School, 1950-51; University of London, graduate study, 1955-56. *Politics:* "Left-wing Democratic Party." *Religion:* None. *Home:* Oakes Farm, Route 3, Perry, Mich. 48872. *Office:* Department of History, Michigan State University, East Lansing, Mich. 48823.

CAREER: Michigan State University, East Lansing, assistant professor, 1961-63, associate professor of African history, 1963—, faculty adviser to Student Nonviolent Coordinating Committee (SNCC). Faculty associate, American Universities Field Staff. *Military service:* U.S. Army, Infantry, 1952-54; served in Korea; received Combat Infantry Badge. *Member:* American Historical Association, African Studies Association, American Civil Liberties Union.

WRITINGS: Black Revolutionary: George Padmore's Path from Communism to Pan-Africanism, Praeger, 1967; *Henry Sylvester Williams,* Rex Collings, 1975. Contributor of reviews to professional journals.

WORK IN PROGRESS: A biography of C. L. R. James, principal Negro assistant of Leon Trotsky; studies of Trinidad personalities and of calypso music.

AVOCATIONAL INTERESTS: Planting trees and raising English and Irish setters and Siamese cats on his farm; camping, hunting upland game birds, puttering with his tractor.

* * *

HOOLE, Daryl Van Dam 1934-

PERSONAL: Born March 5, 1934, in Salt Lake City, Utah; daughter of Donovan H. (a property manager) and Ada (Strong) Van Dam; married Hendricus J. M. Hoole, Jr., March 25, 1957; children: Jean, Roger, Diane, Elaine, Rebecca, Nancy, Spencer, Gregory. *Residence:* Salt Lake City, Utah.

CAREER: Served as secretary to Adam S. Bennion of the Council of the Twelve Apostles, Church of Jesus Christ of Latter-day Saints; Brigham Young University, Provo, Utah, member of extension faculty, 1960—. Lecturer on homemaking. Member of editorial staff of Family Achievement Institute, scripts of which have been recorded for family use throughout the nation.

WRITINGS: The Art of Homemaking, 5th edition, Deseret, 1963; *The Art of Teaching Children,* Deseret, 1964; *With Sugar'n Spice,* Deseret, 1966; *The Joys of Homemaking,* Deseret, 1975. Contributor to *Improvement Era* and *Ensign.*

* * *

HOOPES, Roy 1922-

PERSONAL: Born May 17, 1922, in Salt Lake City, Utah; son of Roy H. (a lawyer) and Lydia Hoopes; married; wife's name, Cora; children: Spencer, Sallie, Tommy. *Education:* George Washington University, A.B., 1946, M.A., 1949. *Politics:* Democrat. *Home:* 7708 Hackamore Dr., Potomac, Md. 20854.

CAREER: U.S. Department of State, Washington, D.C., research analyst, 1946-48; assistant world editor, *Pathfinder* (magazine), 1949-52; Time, Inc., New York, N.Y., general promotion manager of Time-Life International, 1952-53; managing editor of *High Fidelity,* 1953-56, and *Democratic Digest,* 1956-61; *National Geographic,* Washington, D.C., editor and writer, 1963-65; *Washingtonian* (magazine), Washington, D.C., associate editor, 1965-66; worked for U.S. Department of Health, Education, and Welfare, 1967-73, and *Newsday,* 1973-74; free-lance writer, 1974—. *Member:* Oral History Association, National Press Club (Washington, D.C.).

WRITINGS: (Editor) *Wit From Overseas,* Avon, 1953; (editor) *Building Your Record Library,* McGraw, 1958; (editor) *The "High Fidelity" Reader,* Hanover House, 1958; *The Complete Peace Corps Guide,* introduction by R. Sargent Shriver, Dial, 1961, 4th edition, 1968; *The Steel Crisis: 72 Hours That Shook the Nation,* John Day, 1962; *What the President Does All Day,* John Day, 1962; (editor) *State Colleges and Universities,* Luce, 1962; *A Report on Fallout in Your Food,* New American Library, 1962; (editor) *The Peace Corps Experience,* preface by Hubert H. Humphrey, C. N. Potter, 1968; *Getting with Politics: A Young Person's Guide to Political Action,* Delacorte, 1968.

All published by John Day, except as indicated: *What a United States Senator Does,* 1970; (with son, Spencer Hoopes) *What a Baseball Manager Does,* 1970; *What a United States Congressman Does,* 1972; *What a Pro Football Coach Does,* 1972; *What a State Governor Does,* 1973; *What the President of the United States Does,* Crowell, 1974; *The Presidency: A Question of Power,* edited by Erwin Hargrove, Little, Brown, 1975. Contributor to numerous magazines and newspapers; weekly newspaper columnist for several years under an undisclosed pseudonym.

WORK IN PROGRESS: An Oral History of the American Homefront during World War II.

* * *

HOOVER, Helen (Drusilla Blackburn) 1910-
(Jennifer Price)

PERSONAL: Born January 20, 1910, in Greenfield, Ohio; daughter of Thomas Franklin (a factory manager) and Hannah (Gomersall) Blackburn; married Adrian Everett Hoover (an illustrator), February 13, 1937. *Education:* Ohio University, student, 1927-29; took special and night courses in sciences at De Paul University and University of Chicago, 1943-49. *Politics:* Independent. *Agent:* Brandt & Brandt, 101 Park Ave., New York, N.Y. 10017.

CAREER: Audit Bureau of Circulations, Chicago, Ill., proofreader, 1930-43; Pittsburgh Testing Laboratory, Chicago, analytical chemist, 1943-45; Ahlberg Bearing Co., Chicago, metallurgist, 1945-48; International Harvester Co., Chicago, research metallurgist, 1948-54; free-lance writer for general, nature, and juvenile magazines, 1954-70. Patentee of agricultural implement discs.

MEMBER: Mystery Writers of America, Authors Guild, American Platform Society, International Council for Bird Preservation, International Union for Preservation of Nature, National Audubon Society, National Catholic Society for Animal Welfare, Humane Society of the United States, Sierra Club, Wilderness Society, Defenders of Wildlife, Committee for Preservation of the Tule Elk, Fauna Preservation Society, Save-the-Redwoods League, Jersey Wildlife Preservation Trust, Minnesota Ornithologists Union, Minneapolis Audubon Society. *Awards, honors:* Annual Achievement Award of Metal Treating Institute, 1959; Blue Flame Ecology Salute, 1973; ZIA award of New Mexico Presswomen, 1973, for *Years of the Forest.*

WRITINGS: The Long-Shadowed Forest, Crowell, 1963; *The Gift of the Deer,* Knopf, 1966; *Animals at My Doorstep* (juvenile), Parents Magazine Press, 1966; *Great Wolf and the Good Woodsman* (juvenile fiction), Parents Magazine Press, 1967; *Place in the Woods,* Knopf, 1969; *Animals Near and Far* (juvenile), Parents Magazine Press, 1970; *The Years of the Forest,* Knopf, 1973. Regular contributor of feature, "Nature Story," to *Humpty Dumpty,* 1959-69, and column, "Wilderness Chat," to *Defenders of Wildlife News,* 1963-73. Contributor of adult and juvenile nature articles and some juvenile fiction to magazines. Contributor of adult pieces to periodicals, including *Audubon, American Mercury, Gourmet, Organic Gardening and Farming, Saturday Review, Woman's Journal* (London), and *Living Wilderness,* and of women's fiction under pseudonym Jennifer Price.

WORK IN PROGRESS: "Considering an autobiographical book on changes in life style, with reasons for changes and ways of adaptation."

SIDELIGHTS: Mrs. Hoover once wrote to *CA:* "Most of my writing is about life—wild and human—in the north woods. My husband and I moved in 1954 to a border lake Minnesota cabin. We were forty-five miles from town on a one-way road, had no car for nine years, and spent early-year winters with no human neighbors within fifteen miles." She stated of her hobbies: "For fun *when I have time:* Read mysteries; play piano (who else has a baby grand in a two-room log cabin forty-five miles from a town?); embroider and make lace; work *big* jigsaw puzzles, study languages with perhaps more interest in linguistics than in competency—right now Swahili, Polish, and Spanish." The following quote from *The Long-Shadowed Forest* explains the attitude of the author and her husband toward their ten acres: "When Ade and I had the opportunity of receiving electric power and telephone service at the cost of felling a swath through our old trees, we decided in favor of the trees." *The Long-Shadowed Forest* has been published in England; *The Gift of the Deer* and *Place in the Woods* in numerous countries and languages on all the continents. *Year of the Forest* is following the same pattern.

BIOGRAPHICAL/CRITICAL SOURCES: Farm Implement News, March 10, 1958; *Implement and Tractor,* May 20, 1964.

*   *   *

HOPE, A(lec) D(erwent) 1907-

PERSONAL: Born July 21, 1907, in Cooma, New South Wales, Australia; son of Percival (a clergyman) and Florence Ellen (Scotford) Hope; married Penelope Robinson, May 27, 1937; children: Emily, Andrew, Geoffrey. *Education:* Sydney University, B.A., 1928; Oxford University, B.A., 1930. *Politics:* None. *Home:* 66 Arthur Circle, Forrest, Canberra, Australian Capital Territory, Australia. *Office:* Australian National University, Canberra, Australian Capital Territory, Australia.

CAREER: New South Wales Department of Education, New South Wales, Australia, teacher of English, 1933-36; New South Wales Department of Labor and Industry, administrator of vocational tests and guidance counselor for Youth Employment Bureau, two years during the period, 1933-36; Sydney Teachers' College, Sydney, New South Wales, lecturer in English and education, 1937-45; Melbourne University, Melbourne, New South Wales, senior lecturer in English, 1945-50; Canberra University College, Canberra, Australian Capital Territory, professor of English, 1950-60; Australian National University, Canberra, Australian Capital Territory, professor of English, 1960-68.

MEMBER: Australian Academy of Humanities, Australian Society of Authors (president, 1966). *Awards, honors:* Britannica Australian Award for Literature, 1966; Arts Council of Great Britain award for poetry, 1965; Levinson Prize for Poetry, 1969; Ingram Merrill Award for Literature, 1969; Officer (of the Order) of the British Empire, 1972; Litt.D., Australia National University, 1972, University of New England, 1973.

WRITINGS: The Wandering Islands (poems), Edwards & Shaw (Sydney), 1955; *Poems,* Hamish Hamilton, 1960, Viking, 1961; *Selected Poems,* Angus & Robertson (Sydney), 1963; *Australian Literature, 1950-1965,* Melbourne University Press, 1963; *The Cave and the Spring* (essays), Rigby (Adelaide), 1965, 2nd edition, Sidney University Press, 1970; *Collected Poems, 1930-1965,* Viking, 1966.

New Poems: 1965-1969, Viking, 1970; *Dunciad Minor: An Heroick Poem,* Melbourne University Press, 1970; *Midsummer Eve's Dream: Variations on a Theme by William Dunbar,* Viking, 1970; *Collected Poems: 1930-1970,* Angus & Robertson, 1972; *Judith Wright,* Oxford University Press, 1973; *Native Companions,* Angus & Robertson, 1974.

WORK IN PROGRESS: Biographical and critical studies of Christopher Brennan.

SIDELIGHTS: Hope, Australia's foremost poet, has been called "one of the two or three best poets writing in English." David Kalstone notes that "his poise and sophistication remind one often of Auden," and Samuel French Morse claims that, "of the books to own from 1966, Hope's [*Collected Poems, 1930-1965*] is certainly the one."

Jean Garrigue has said that, "in a sense, Hope is literary the way many poets have ceased to be. He is not breaking down form and inviting chaos." Morse explains: "The powerful satiric thrust, the extraordinary sense of self-possession, the sensuality of his imagination, and the all but arrogant clarity of his poems are apparent from the beginning; and these qualities and characteristics are the more surprising in a time when the significant rhetorical gesture has grown increasingly flabby." Miss Garrigue adds: "Syntax is never ambiguous [in Hope's poems]; he favors coherence and logical connections. . . . He rhymes, he works in stanzaic forms. He seems grandly at home in his orderly arrangements. The right word is usually in the right place, but since the poems move in terms of the line, not in terms of the word, the emphasis is on the large unit."

Hope himself, according to Miss Garrigue, has said that "poetry is principally concerned to 'express' its subject and in doing so to create an emotion which is the feeling of the poem and not the feeling of the poet." His success in creating such a poetry might be confirmed by Kalstone, who writes: "It is rare to find—as one does with Hope—poems that depend so successfully on a shared sense of community. His audience is fixed in position, ready to follow the action within the proscenium his poems assume."

Kalstone believes that Hope's skill is "partly one of reinterpretation. The literary scene is one we know, but the characters have been assigned new positions on stage...." Kalstone continues: "We are led through a very familiar gallery of mythological, historical and Biblical subjects, and we are asked to see the flash of energy behind the traditional pose.... To put it another way, modern settings draw forward Hope the satirist, jaunty but rather uniformly critical of mechanized, overcivilized lives. But he rises to the challenge of the fable. His real gift is for narrative—not so much telling a story, as retelling it with an air of wisdom and experience. The story is a *tableau vivant*, action halted at a moment of high feeling, nuances revealed by the measured order in which we are directed to gestures and landscapes. It is an index of the success of recent American poetry, introspective, often jagged, that declarative sentences, direct syntax, firmly rhymed stanzas should sound now a little strange. These last are precisely Hope's resources, his assured way of drawing us from detail to detail, finishing a picture which stands powerful and separate."

Marius Bewley, on the other hand, adds qualification to his praise of Hope, although he agrees that the poet is "an accomplished and attractive writer." Bewley writes: "Hope is usually, but not always, intelligent in his poetry. One of the hesitations one feels about him is that he often seems to arrive at his intelligent ideas and clever arguments first, and wraps them up in skillful metrics later." And "only very rarely does his language and thought seem organically fused, to share one bloodstream, one flesh, one life...." But, Bewley adds, "at his best—and [Hope] is often at his best—his poems achieve a sustained, assured, and musical rhetorical mode of speech."

Both Kalstone and Miss Garrigue believe that Hope's love poems are his best; "they are sensual, sumptuous, dazzling," writes Miss Garrigue. "Without bizarreries or mad touches, they are 'square,' if you will, dedicated to the myth of beauty and joy."

Hope told *CA* that he is interested in philosophy, biology, and history, and that he has no interest in hobbies or sports. He has "some knowledge" of Latin, French, German, Italian, and Spanish. He adds that he has "no very fixed convictions on anything" and adjures us to "(see Keats on negative capability)."

BIOGRAPHICAL/CRITICAL SOURCES: New Leader, March 27, 1967; *New York Review of Books,* May 18, 1967; *Village Voice,* June 15, 1967; *Partisan Review,* fall, 1967; *A. D. Hope: A Bibliography,* Libraries Board of South Australia, 1968; *Contemporary Literature,* winter, 1968; Carolyn Riley, editor, *Contemporary Literary Criticism,* Volume III, Gale, 1975.

* * *

HOPKE, William E. 1918-

PERSONAL: Surname is pronounced *Hop*-key; born September 7, 1918, in Elmira, N.Y.; son of William Ernest (a farmer and poultryman) and Hilda (Koch) Hopke; married Carvie Thomas Estes, June 14, 1975; children: (former marriage) Carol L., Andrea N. *Education:* State University of New York at Albany, B.A., 1939, M.A., 1946; Teachers College, Columbia University, Ed.D., 1950. *Politics:* Democrat. *Religion:* Episcopalian. *Home:* 204 Myers Ave., Raleigh, N.C. 27604. *Office:* School of Education, North Carolina State University, Raleigh, N.C. 27607.

CAREER: Teacher in Ravena, N.Y., 1940-42; Armstrong Junior College, Savannah, Ga., counselor, 1946-48; Stevens Institute of Technology, Hoboken, N.Y., counselor, 1948-50; Columbia University, Teachers College, New York, N.Y., executive assistant, Office of Placement, 1950-53; Montgomery County Board of Cooperative Educational Services, Canajoharie, N.Y., board director and guidance supervisor, 1953-57; Florida State University, Tallahassee, associate professor in department of guidance, and counseling, 1957-67; North Carolina State University at Raleigh, professor and head of department of guidance and personnel services, 1967—. Consultant to Bureau of Hearings and Appeals, U.S. Social Security Administration; consultant to Counselor Films, Inc. *Military service:* U.S. Army and Army Air Forces, 1942-46; became first lieutenant.

MEMBER: American Personnel and Guidance Association, Association for Counselor Education and Supervision (treasurer, 1966-67), National Vocational Guidance Association, American School Counselor Association, National Education Association, American Association of University Professors, Phi Delta Kappa. *Awards, honors:* Certificate of Merit of National Vocational Guidance Association, 1966.

WRITINGS: (With H. F. Cottingham) *Guidance in the Junior High School,* McKnight & McKnight, 1961; (editor) *Encyclopedia of Careers and Vocational Guidance,* two volumes, J. G. Ferguson Publishing, 1967, 3rd edition, Doubleday, 1975; (with B. M. Parramore) *Children's Dictionary of Occupations,* Counselor Films, Inc., 1974; (editor) *Dictionary of Guidance and Personnel Terms,* Doubleday, in press. Contributor to professional journals.

* * *

HOPKINS, Marjorie 1911-

PERSONAL: Born May 19, 1911; daughter of Newton Fisher (a civil engineer) and Emma (Lambert) Hopkins. *Education:* Chatham College, A.B., 1933; University of Iowa, M.A., 1935. *Home:* 526 South Ardmore Ave., Los Angeles, Calif. 90005.

CAREER: Junior high school teacher of English and journalism, and counselor, 1939-73, in Pittsburgh, Pa., New York State, and in San Jose, Calif. Spent one year in Baghdad, Iraq, as Fulbright exchange teacher. *Military service:* U.S. Navy Women's Reserve (WAVES), 1944-46; became ensign.

WRITINGS—All published by Parents: *The Three Visitors* (picture book), 1967; *The Glass Valentine,* 1968; *And the Jackal Played the Masinko,* 1969; *A Gift for Jolum,* 1972. Contributor of short stories to juvenile magazines.

* * *

HOPPER, David H. 1927-

PERSONAL: Born July 31, 1927, in Cranford, N.J.; son of Orion Cornelius (a minister) and Julia (Weitzel) Hopper; married Nancy Nelson (an elementary teacher), June 10, 1967. *Education:* Yale University, B.A., 1950; Princeton

Theological Seminary, B.D., 1953, Th.D., 1959; University of Bonn, graduate study, 1953-54. *Home:* 28 South Wheeler St., St. Paul, Minn. 55105. *Office:* Macalester College, St. Paul, Minn. 55105.

CAREER: Macalester College, St. Paul, Minn., assistant professor, 1959-67, associate professor of religion, 1967-73; James Wallace Professor of Religion, 1973—. Ordained minister of United Presbyterian Church in the U.S.A., 1961. *Military service:* U.S. Navy, 1945-46. *Member:* American Association of University Professors, American Academy of Religion.

WRITINGS: Tillich: A Theological Portrait, Lippincott, 1968; *A Dissent on Bonhaeffer,* Westminster, 1975.

AVOCATIONAL INTERESTS: Gardening and fishing.

*   *   *

HOPSON, Dan, Jr.   1930-

PERSONAL: Born September 23, 1930, in Phillipsburg, Kan.; son of Dan (an attorney) and Ruth (Whitaker) Hopson; married Phyllis Ann Gray, November 23, 1956; children: Daniel Gray, Christopher Paul, Bruce Edward. *Education:* University of Kansas, A.B., 1951, LL.B., 1953; Yale University, LL.M., 1954; Cambridge University, graduate study, 1954-55. *Politics:* Democrat. *Religion:* Episcopalian. *Home:* 2316 Sussex Dr., Bloomington, Ind. 47401.

CAREER: University of Kansas, Law School, Lawrence, assistant professor, 1955-59, associate professor, 1959-63, professor of law, 1963-67; Indiana University, School of Law, Bloomington, professor of law, 1967—, associate dean of faculties, 1974—. Yale University, School of Law, research associate, 1959-60. *Member:* American Bar Association, National Council of Juvenile Court Judges (associate member), American Sociological Association (associate member), Indiana Bar Association, Phi Beta Kappa, Order of the Coif, Phi Alpha Delta. *Awards, honors:* International Rotary fellowship.

WRITINGS: (With Quinton Johnstone) *Lawyers and Their Work,* Bobbs-Merrill, 1967. Contributor to law reviews.

*   *   *

HORN, Daniel   1934-

PERSONAL: Born October 23, 1934, in Vienna, Austria; son of Herman M. (a businessman) and Bertha (Goldman) Horn; married Marcia Ginsburg (a college instructor), March 18, 1958; children: Shari, Deborah, Jeremy. *Education:* Brooklyn College (now of the City University of New York), B.A., 1956; Columbia University, M.A., 1957, Ph.D., 1963. *Religion:* Jewish. *Home:* 328 Graham St., Highland Park, N.J. 08904. *Office:* History Department, Douglass College, Rutgers University, New Brunswick, N.J. 08903.

CAREER: City College of the City University of New York, New York, N.Y., lecturer in history, 1962-63; Temple University, Philadelphia, Pa., instructor in history, 1963-64; Rutgers University, Douglass College, New Brunswick, N.J., assistant professor, 1964-68, associate professor of history, 1968—, chairman of department, 1975—. Livingston Lecturer, New Brunswick Theological Seminary, 1975—. *Military service:* National Guard, 1957-60. *Member:* American Historical Association, Conference Group for Central European History, American Association of University Professors. *Awards, honors:* National Endowment for the Humanities, fellow, 1969-70.

WRITINGS: (Translator, editor, and author of introduction) *War, Mutiny and Revolution in the German Navy: The World War I Diary of Seaman Richard Stumpf,* Rutgers University Press, 1967; *The German Naval Mutinies of World War I,* Rutgers University Press, 1969 (published in England as *Mutiny on the High Seas: Imperial German Naval Mutinies of World War I,* Frewin, 1973); *Adolf Hitler and the Third Reich,* Forum Press, 1975. Contributor to *Journal of Social History.*

*   *   *

HORN, Henry Eyster   1913-

PERSONAL: Born May 30, 1913, in New York, N.Y.; son of William Melchior (a clergyman) and Marguerite (Jacobs) Horn; married Catherine Stainken, June 9, 1939; children: Jean Louise Horn Swanson, Henry Stainken, David Jacobs, Charles Michael, William Melchior, Marguerite Eyster, Richard Downing, Eleanor Ann, Michael Jacobs, Andrew Gregg. *Education:* Cornell University, A.B., 1933; Lutheran Theological Seminary, Philadelphia, Pa., B.D., 1936, S.T.M., 1939. *Home:* 338 Harvard St., Cambridge, Mass. 02139. *Office:* University Lutheran Church, Cambridge, Mass.

CAREER: Clergyman of Lutheran Church. Immanuel Lutheran Church, Philadelphia, Pa., pastor, 1938-43; Marion College, Marion, Va., president, 1943-49; Lutheran Church of the Resurrection, Augusta, Ga., pastor, 1949-53; University Lutheran Church, Cambridge, Mass., pastor, 1953—. Member of board of theological education, Lutheran Church in America, 1962-72; chairman of advisory board, Cambridge Community Service Center, 1972—. *Member:* Cambridge Mental Health Association (president, 1973—).

WRITINGS: O Sing Unto the Lord, Fortress, 1956; *Liturgy and Life,* Lutheran Church Press, 1966; *The Christian in Modern Style,* Fortress, 1968; *Lutherans in Campus Ministry,* National Lutheran Campus Ministry, 1968; *Worship in Crisis,* Fortress, 1970.

*   *   *

HORN, Walter (William)   1908-

PERSONAL: Born January 18, 1908, in Waldangelloch, Germany; came to United States in 1938, naturalized in 1943; son of Karl and Mathilde (Peters) Horn; married Ann Binkley Rand; married second wife, Alberta West Parker (a physician), April 14, 1949; children: (second marriage) Michael Peters, Peter Mathew, Rebecca Ann. *Education:* Studied at Universities of Heidelberg, Berlin, and Hamburg; University of Hamburg, Ph.D., 1934. *Religion:* Lutheran. *Home:* 339 Western Dr., Richmond, Calif. 94801. *Office:* 238 Kroeber Hall, University of California, Berkeley, Calif. 94720.

CAREER: German Institute of Art, Florence, Italy, research associate, 1934-37; University of California, Berkeley, visiting lecturer, 1938-39, assistant professor, 1939-40, associate professor, 1940-48, professor of art, 1948—, chairman of department, 1957-60, professor of arts and science, 1967-68. Member of board of directors, Patrons of Art and Music, California Palace of Legion of Honor, 1964—. *Military service:* U.S. Army, Infantry, 1943-46; member of Third Army Intelligence Center, assigned to tracing looted and illegally hidden works of art during invasion of Germany; became captain. *Member:* College Art Association of America (director, 1950-54, 1964-68), Society of Architectural Historians (director, 1964-68), Faculty Club (Berkeley). *Awards, honors:* Guggenheim fellow, 1960-61; humanities research fellow, University of California, 1964.

WRITINGS: Die Fassade von St. Gilles, Paul Evert (Hamburg), 1937; (with Ernest Born) *The Barns of the Abby of Beaulieu at its Granges of Great Coxwell and Beaulieu St. Leonard,* University of California Press, 1965; *The Plan of St. Gall: A Study of the Architecture, Economy, and Life of a Paradigmatic Carolingian Monastery,* three volumes, University of California Press, in press. Contributor to art publications and bulletins in United States and Germany. General editor, "California Studies in the History of Art."

WORK IN PROGRESS: With Rainer Berger, writing on the potentialities and limitations of radiocarbon dating for medieval archaeology, for the Isotope Laboratory at University of California, Los Angeles.†

* * *

HORNSBY, Roger A. 1926-

PERSONAL: Born August 8, 1926, in Nye, Wis.; son of Huntley Burton (an engineer) and Lucile (James) Hornsby; married Jessie Gillespie (a professor), June 8, 1960. *Education:* Western Reserve University (now Case Western Reserve University), A.B., 1949; Princeton University, A.M., 1951, Ph.D., 1952. *Religion:* Episcopalian. *Home:* 19 Woolf Ave., Iowa City, Iowa 52242. *Office:* Schaeffer Hall, University of Iowa, Iowa City, Iowa 52242.

CAREER: University of Iowa, Iowa City, instructor, 1954-56, assistant professor, 1956-61, associate professor, 1961-67, professor of classics, 1967—, chairman of department of classics, 1966—. Chief reader for Latin IV, Educational Testing Service. *Member:* American Philological Association (director, 1974-77), American Numismatic Society (member of council), Archaeological Institute of America, Vergilian Society, Renaissance Society of America, Classical Association of Middle West and South (president).

WRITINGS: Reading Latin Poetry, University of Oklahoma Press, 1967; *Patterns of Action in the Aeneid,* University of Iowa Press, 1970.

WORK IN PROGRESS: Stoicism in Latin Literature.

* * *

HORST, Samuel (Levi) 1919-

PERSONAL: Born July 18, 1919, in Lancaster, Pa.; son of Elmer K. and Katie (Buckwalter) Horst; married Elizabeth Good, June 19, 1948; children: Kenneth, Hannah, Sylvia, Barbara, Mary, Carol. *Education:* Eastern Mennonite College, student, 1946-48; Goshen College, A.B., 1949; University of Virginia, M.Ed., 1957; American University, M.A., 1965. *Religion:* Mennonite. *Office:* Eastern Mennonite College, Harrisonburg, Va. 22801.

CAREER: Eastern Mennonite College, Harrisonburg, Va., instructor, 1949-51, assistant professor of history, 1954-58, now professor of American and Latin American history and political science. *Member:* American Historical Association, Organization of American Historians, Southern Historical Association, Southern Political Science Association. *Awards, honors:* Fellow, Institute of Southern History, Johns Hopkins University, 1967-68.

WRITINGS: Mennonites in the Confederacy: A Study in Civil War Pacifism, Herald, 1967.

HORWOOD, Harold 1923-

PERSONAL: Born February 11, 1923, in St. John's, Newfoundland, Canada; son of Andrew (a businessman) and Vina (Maidment) Horwood. *Education:* Attended Prince of Wales College and took special courses at Memorial University College. *Politics:* New Democratic Party (social-democrat). *Home and office:* Beachy Cove, via Portugal Cove, Newfoundland, Canada.

CAREER: Evening Telegram, St. John's, Newfoundland, Canada, reporter, columnist, then editorial page editor, 1952-58; full-time free-lance writer, 1958—; *The Examiner,* St. John's, managing editor, 1960-61; *The Evening Telegram,* St. John's, associate editor, 1968-70. Member of Newfoundland House of Assembly (provincial parliament), for District of Labrador, 1949-51. Teacher of creative writing, Memorial University, 1969; has assisted organized labor in planning, organizing and writing briefs. *Member:* Writers' Union of Canada (vice-chairman), Association of Canadian Television and Radio Artists.

WRITINGS: Tomorrow Will Be Sunday (novel), Doubleday, 1966; *Foxes of Beachy Cove* (nonfiction), Doubleday, 1967; *Newfoundland,* St. Martin's, 1969; *White Eskimo* (novel), Doubleday, 1972; (editor) *Voices Underground* (poetry), New Press, 1972; (with Cassie Brown) *Death on the Ice,* Doubleday, 1972. Author of television and radio documentaries for Canadian Broadcasting Corp. Contributor of articles and historical sketches to magazines.

WORK IN PROGRESS: A book of short stories; two novels; a biography of Captain Robert Bartlett.

AVOCATIONAL INTERESTS: Camping, science, mathematics.

* * *

HOSTLER, Charles W(arren) 1919-

PERSONAL: Born December 12, 1919, in Chicago, Ill.; son of S. Marvin and Catherine (Marshall) Hostler; divorced; children: Charles Warren, Jr. *Education:* University of California, Los Angeles, B.A., 1942; University of Bucharest, law student, 1945-46; Georgetown University, M.A. (international affairs), 1950, Ph.D., 1955; American University of Beirut, M.A. (Middle East studies), 1954; also attended American, British, Turkish, and Lebanese military schools. *Religion:* Protestant. *Home:* 1200 North Nash St., Arlington, Va. 22209. *Office:* Director, Bureau of International Commerce, U.S. Department of Commerce, Washington, D.C. 20230.

CAREER: U.S. Army Air Forces and U.S. Air Force, regular officer for more than twenty years, retiring as colonel; director of International Operations, Douglas Aircraft Co., 1963-69; president of Hostler Investment Company, 1969—; currently deputy assistant secretary and director of Bureau of International Commerce, U.S. Department of Commerce, Washington, D.C. Foreign assignments with Air Force included: liaison officer in France, Balkans, Middle East, North Africa, Italy, Germany, Austria, and England, 1942-45; member of U.S. military representation to Allied Control Commission for Rumania, Bucharest, 1945-47; chief of Combat Information Branch, American Mission for Aid to Turkey, Ankara, 1948-50; politico-military affairs officer attached to American Embassy, Beirut, Lebanon, 1953-55; U.S. air attache diplomatically accredited to Lebanon and Jordan, 1958-61; interim posts were in Washington, D.C., with final assignment, beginning in 1962, as member of policy planning staff, Office of Secretary of Defense/International Security Affairs. Former adjunct professor, School of International Service, American University, Washington, D.C.

MEMBER: Middle East Institute (Washington, D.C.; member of board of governors), Sons of the American Revolution, Gold Key Society, Phi Kappa Sigma. *Awards, honors*—Military: U.S. Legion of Merit, Army Commendation Medal; grand commander, Order of the Phoenix, Order of Holy Sepulchre, and Order of Saints Peter and Paul (all Greece); Order of the Cedars (Lebanon); Order of Honor and Merit (Haiti).

WRITINGS: Turkism and the Soviets: The Turks of the World and Their Political Objectives, Praeger, 1957; (contributor) *The Challenge of Soviet Education,* Philosophical Library, 1959. Writer of military, commercial and government reports. Contributor to *Commerce America, Middle Eastern Journal, Middle Eastern Affairs, Airman,* and other military and economic journals.

SIDELIGHTS: Hostler is fluent in French, competent in Spanish, and has working ability in Arabic, Turkish, and Rumanian.

*   *   *

HOTCHKISS, Jeanette 1901-

PERSONAL: Born August 8, 1901, in Milwaukee, Wis.; daughter of Kossuth Kent (a lawyer) and Florence (James) Kennan; married Eugene Hotchkiss (an investment banker), August 25, 1923; children: Frank Emerson, Eugene III and James Kennan (twins). *Education:* Attended Milwaukee State Normal School, Milwaukee-Downer Seminary, and University of Wisconsin; University of Chicago, Ph.B., 1924. *Politics:* Independent. *Religion:* Protestant. *Home:* 901 Baldwin Rd., Highland Park, Ill. 60035.

MEMBER: League of Women Voters of Highland Park (past president), Friends of the Highland Park Library, The Writers (Highland Park), Society of Childrens' Book Writers, Highland Park Historical Society, Children's Reading Round Table.

WRITINGS: European Historical Fiction for Children and Young People, Scarecrow, 1967, 2nd edition, 1972; *American Historical Fiction and Biography for Children and Young People,* Scarecrow, 1973; *African-Asian Readers' Guide for Children and Young Adults,* Scarecrow, 1975. Author of a biography for Stefanssen Collection in Baker Library, Dartmouth College.

*   *   *

HOU, Chi-ming 1924-

PERSONAL: Born December 3, 1924, in Hopei, China; married Irene Liu, June 20, 1953; children: Donald, William, Victor. *Education:* Fu Jen University of Peiping, LL.B., 1945; University of Oregon, M.A. (with honors), 1949; Columbia University, Ph.D., 1954. *Home:* 39 Maple Ave., Hamilton, N.Y. 13346. *Office:* Colgate University, Hamilton, N.Y. 13346.

CAREER: Hobart and William Smith Colleges, Geneva, N.Y., assistant professor of economics, 1953-56; Colgate University, Hamilton, N.Y., assistant professor, 1956-61, associate professor, 1961-64, professor of economics, 1964-68, Charles A. Dana Professor of Economics, 1968—. *Member:* American Economic Association, Association for Asian Studies.

WRITINGS: Foreign Investment and Economic Develop-

ment in China, 1840-1937, Harvard University Press, 1965. Contributor to academic journals.

WORK IN PROGRESS: Employment and Economic Development in China.

*   *   *

HOUGH, Joseph C(arl), Jr. 1933-

PERSONAL: Surname rhymes with "rough"; born August 8, 1933, in Kingston, N.C.; son of Joseph Carl (a minister) and Edith (Wooldridge) Hough; married Heidi Nussbaumer, March 19, 1960; children: Joseph Mark, David Matthew. *Education:* Wake Forest College, B.A., 1955; studied at University of Edinburgh, 1955-56, and Southeastern Baptist Seminary, 1956-57; Yale University, B.D., 1959, M.A., 1964, Ph.D., 1965. *Politics:* Democrat. *Home:* 169 West Seventh St., Claremont, Calif. 91711. *Office:* School of Theology at Claremont, Claremont, Calif. 91711.

CAREER: Associate minister of Baptist churches in Clarksville, Tenn., 1959-60, and Danville, Va., 1960-62; School of Theology at Claremont, Claremont, Calif., professor of Christian ethics, 1965—, Willis Fisher Lecturer, 1969, dean of graduate studies, 1968-72, academic dean, 1973—. Ordained minister in United Church of Christ, 1971. Chairman, graduate faculty of religion, Claremont Graduate School, 1967-73. Visiting instructor, Claremont Men's College, 1966-67; Willson Lecturer, Southwestern University, 1969; Scott Lecturer, Texas Christian University, 1970; Robinson Lecturer, Wake Forest University, 1971. Director of Leadership Survey Project in Los Angeles, 1967; president of board of directors of Center of Metropolitan Mission In-Service Training, Los Angeles, 1966-69; project director, Project Understanding, 1969-74. *Member:* American Society of Christian Ethics, Phi Beta Kappa.

WRITINGS: Black Power and White Protestants: A Christian Response to the New Negro Pluralism, Oxford University Press, 1968; (contributor) Paul T. Jerslid and Dale A. Johnson, editors, *Moral Issues and Christian Response,* Holt, 1971; (contributor) Charles M. Olsen, editor, *The Base Church,* Forum, 1973; (contributor) Norbert Brockman and Nicholas Piediscalzi, editors, *Contemporary Religion and Social Responsibility,* Alba House, 1973. Contributor to journals in his field.

BIOGRAPHICAL/CRITICAL SOURCES: Christian Century, August 28, 1968.

*   *   *

HOUGHTON, (Charles) Norris 1909-

PERSONAL: Born December 26, 1909, in Indianapolis, Ind.; son of Charles D. M. (a lumber dealer) and Grace (Norris) Houghton. *Education:* Princeton University, A.B., 1931. *Religion:* Presbyterian. *Home:* 11 East Ninth St., New York, N.Y. 10003. *Office:* State University of New York College, Purchase, N.Y. 10577.

CAREER: Began Broadway career as set designer for "Carry Nation," 1932; stage manager or designer for "Both Your Houses," 1933, "They Shall Not Die," 1934, "Libel," 1935, "High Tor," 1937, "Whiteoaks," 1938, and a number of other New York and summer theater productions, 1933-38; set designer for eighteen musical productions at St. Louis Municipal Opera, summers, 1939-40; made London debut as a director with Michael Redgrave's "Macbeth," 1947, returning to Broadway with that production, 1948, and directing "Clutterbuck," 1949, and "Billy

Budd," 1951; founder with T. Edward Hambleton of New York's Phoenix Theatre, 1953, staging more than fifty works while managing director, 1953-62; Vassar College, Poughkeepsie, N.Y., adjunct professor, 1959-60, professor of drama and director of Experimental Theatre, 1962-67; State University of New York College at Purchase, dean of theatre arts, 1967-75, professor of theatre arts, 1975—. Princeton University, lecturer in drama and director of dramatics, 1941-42; Smith College, guest professor of drama, 1947; Columbia University, lecturer in comparative literature, 1948-54; Columbia Broadcasting System, producer and director of Television Workshop, 1951-52; Barnard College, adjunct professor of drama, 1954-58; Harvard University, visiting professor and guest director, 1963. Lecturer on educational television, New York City, 1958-59; lecturer on the American theater, in Europe, for U.S. Department of State, 1961. Vice-president of Theatre, Inc.; trustee of National Repertory Theatre Foundation. *Military service:* U.S. Naval Reserve, active duty, 1943-45; became lieutenant.

MEMBER: American Academy of Arts and Sciences (fellow), National Theatre Conference (president, 1968-69), American Educational Theatre Association, Phi Beta Kappa, Century Club and Coffee House (both New York), Bucks' Club (London). *Awards, honors:* Guggenheim fellowships, 1934, 1935, 1960-61; special citation (jointly with T. Edward Hambleton) from American National Theatre and Academy, 1954, for accomplishments of the Phoenix Theatre; D.F.A. from Denison University, 1959; *Village Voice* Off-Broadway Award (Obie), 1962, for settings in "Who'll Save the Ploughboy."

WRITINGS: Moscow Rehearsals: An Account of Methods of Production in the Soviet Theatre, Harcourt, 1936, published as *Moscow Rehearsals: The Golden Age of the Soviet Theatre,* Grove, 1962; *Advance from Broadway: 19,000 Miles of American Theatre,* Harcourt, 1941; *But Not Forgotten: The Adventure of the University Players,* Sloane, 1952; *Return Engagement: A Postscript to "Moscow Rehearsals,"* Holt, 1962; *The Exploding Stage,* Weybright & Talley, 1972, Dell, 1974.

Editor: *Great Russian Short Stories,* Dell, 1958; *Great Russian Plays,* Dell, 1960; *The Golden Age,* Dell, 1963; *The Romantic Influence,* Dell, 1963; *Seeds of Modern Drama: In Modern Translations,* Dell, 1963. Contributor to magazines and newspapers, including *Atlantic Monthly, Stage, New Yorker, New York Times Magazine,* and *Saturday Review.* Associate editor, *Theatre Arts,* 1945-48.

* * *

HOUN, Franklin W. 1920-
(Fu-Wu Hou)

PERSONAL: "N" in surname is silent; born April 10, 1920, in Pao-tow, China; son of Tien (an educator) and Yueh-ying (Chou) Houn; married Frances Lu, April 25, 1963; children: Fred Wei-han, Florence, Flora. *Education:* National Cheng-chih University, B.A., 1946; University of Denver, M.A., 1950; University of Wisconsin, Ph.D., 1953. *Home:* 222 Glendale Rd., Amherst, Mass. 01002. *Office:* Department of Government, University of Massachusetts, Amherst, Mass. 01002.

CAREER: Presidential Office, Nanking, China, administrative secretary, 1946-48; National Assembly, China, press-liaison secretary, 1947-48; Stanford University, Stanford, Calif., research associate, 1955-57; Michigan State University, East Lansing, assistant professor of political

science, 1957-59; University of Dubuque, Dubuque, Iowa, associate professor of political science, 1959-60; University of Nebraska, Lincoln, associate professor of political science, 1960-63; University of Massachusetts, Amherst, associate professor, 1963-68, professor of government, 1968—. Stanford University, research associate, 1965-66. Chinese Association of Social Sciences, executive director, 1947-48. *Member:* American Political Science Association, Association for Asian Studies, American Association of University Professors.

WRITINGS: Central Government of China, 1912-1928, University of Wisconsin Press, 1957, reprinted, Greenwood Press, 1974; *To Change a Nation: Propaganda and Indoctrination in Communist China,* Free Press of Glencoe, 1961; *Chinese Political Traditions,* Public Affairs Press, 1965; *A Short History of Chinese Communism,* Prentice-Hall, 1967, revised edition, 1973; (contributor) Yuan-li Wu, editor, *Communist China: A Handbook,* Praeger, 1969. Contributor of articles to professional journals, including *Journal of Asian Studies, Public Opinion Quarterly, Journalism Quarterly, American Political Science Review, Tsing-hua Journal of Chinese Studies,* and *Bulletin of the Atomic Scientists.*

WORK IN PROGRESS: Book length studies on Maoism and traditional Chinese political culture and Chinese foreign policy.

SIDELIGHTS: An Asian edition of *To Change A Nation* was published in India, 1965; updated and expanded translations of *Short History of Communism* have been published in Germany and Sweden, and one is planned for publication in Spanish, in Mexico.

* * *

HOUTS, Marshall (Wilson) 1919-

PERSONAL: Surname is pronounced Howts; born June 28, 1919, in Chattanooga, Tenn.; son of Thomas Jefferson (a Methodist preacher) and Mary (Alexander) Houts; married Mary Dealy, April 27, 1946; children: Virginia, Kathy, Marsha, Patty, Thomas, Cindy, Tim. *Education:* Brevard Junior College, Brevard, N.C., A.A., 1937; University of Minnesota, B.S.L., 1941 (converted to J.D.). *Politics:* Republican. *Religion:* "Eclectic." *Home:* 313 Emerald Bay, Laguna Beach, Calif. 92651. *Agent:* Collins-Knowlton-Wing, Inc., 60 East 56th St., New York, N.Y. 10022.

CAREER: Federal Bureau of Investigation, special agent in the United States, Rio de Janiero, and legal attache to the American Embassy in Havana, 1941-44; Palmer & Houts, Pipestone, Minn., attorney, 1946-51. Michigan State University, School of Police Administration, East Lansing, professor of criminal law and evidence, 1955-57. *Trauma* (medico-legal periodical for lawyers), founder and editor-in-chief, 1959—. Special municipal judge, Pipestone, Minn., 1947-51; deputy coroner, Pipestone County, Minn., 1947-61. University of California, Los Angeles, School of Law, visiting professor, 1954. Served as member and general counsel of Erle Stanley Gardner's Court of Last Resort.

WRITINGS: From Gun to Gavel, Morrow, 1954; *From Evidence to Proof,* C. C Thomas, 1956; *The Rules of Evidence,* C. C Thomas, 1956; *Courtroom Medicine,* C. C Thomas, 1958; *From Arrest to Release,* C. C Thomas, 1958; *Courtroom Medicine: Death,* Bender, 1965; *Photographic Misrepresentation,* Bender, 1965; *Lawyers' Guide to Medical Proof,* Bender, 1967; *Where Death Delights:*

The Story of Dr. Milton Helpern and Forensic Medicine,
Coward, 1967; *They Asked for Death,* Cowles, 1970;
Proving Medical Diagnosis and Prognosis, Bender, 1971;
*King's X: Common Law and the Death of Sir Harry
Oakes,* Morrow, 1972. Also author of *Cyclopedia of Sudden, Violent, and Unexplained Death,* published by International Association of Coroners and Medical Examiners.

*WORK IN PROGRESS: Transcripts of the Trials of Jesus
Christ.*

*   *   *

HOVANNISIAN, Richard G.   1932-

PERSONAL: Born November 9, 1932, in Tulare, Calif.;
son of Kaspar and Siroon (Nalbandian) Hovannisian; married Vartiter Kotcholosian (a physician), March, 1957; children: Raffi, Armen, Ani, Garo. *Education:* University of
California, Berkeley, B.A. and General Secondary
Teaching Credential, 1955, M.A., 1958; University of California, Los Angeles, Ph.D., 1966. *Religion:* Armenian
Apostolic. *Office:* Department of History, University of
California, Los Angeles, Calif. 90024.

CAREER: Teacher in Fresno, Calif. city schools, 1958-62;
University of California, Los Angeles, lecturer in Armenian studies program, 1962-69, associate professor, 1969-72,
professor of Armenian and Near Eastern history, 1972—.
Associate professor of Near Eastern and Russian studies,
Mount St. Mary's College, Los Angeles, 1966-69.
Founding member and executive board member of Armenian Assembly of America; chairman of board of directors
of Armenian Monument Council; active in educational activities of Armenian community in North America.
Member: Society for Armenian Studies (coordinator, 1973-
75), Middle East Studies Association of North America,
American Historical Association, American Association
for the Advancement of Slavic Studies, Oral History Association, National Association for Armenian Studies and
Research, Phi Alpha Theta. *Awards, honors:* Guggenheim
fellow, 1974-75.

WRITINGS: Armenia on the Road to Independence, University of California Press, 1967, 3rd edition, 1974; *The
Republic of Armenia,* Volume 1, University of California
Press, 1971, 2nd edition, 1974; (contributor) Stanley E.
Kerr, editor, *The Lions of Marash,* State University of
New York Press, 1973. Contributor to journals in his field,
published in the United States, England, and Germany.
Member of editorial board, *International Journal of Middle
East Studies, Haigazian Armenological Review,* and *Armenian Review.*

WORK IN PROGRESS: Second volume of the history of
the Republic of Armenia (1918-1921).

SIDELIGHTS: Hovannisian spent a year teaching in Beirut, Lebanon. He has since made six return trips to the
Middle East and seven trips to the Soviet Union, including
research in Soviet Armenia. In addition to Armenian he is
competent in French, German, and Russian.

*   *   *

HOWARD, Christopher   1913-

PERSONAL: Born June 10, 1913, in Folkestone, England;
son of Robert H. and Mabel Howard; married Edith Bosshard, August 17, 1957; children: Catherine, Emma, Edward, Lucy, Gregory. *Education:* Wadham College, Oxford, B.A., 1935, M.A., 1944. *Home:* 15 Sunnydale
Gardens, Mill Hill, London, NW7 3PD, England.

CAREER: University of London, King's College, London,
England, 1938—, began as assistant lecturer, reader in his-

tory, 1954—. Seconded to British Council, 1940-45.
Member: Royal Historical Society (fellow).

WRITINGS: Sir John Yorke of Nidderdale, Sheed (London), 1939; (editor) Joseph Chamberlain, *A Political Memoir,* Batchworth Press, 1953; *Splendid Isolation,* Macmillan
(London), 1967; *Britain and the Casus Belli,* Athlone
Press, 1975; (editor with P. Gordon) *The Cabinet Journal
of Dudley Ryder, Viscount Sandon,* Institute of Historical
Research, 1975. Contributor to historical journals in Britian
and Germany.

WORK IN PROGRESS: Origins of the War of 1914.

SIDELIGHTS: Howard is proficient in French, German,
and Spanish.

*   *   *

HOWARD, Ian P.   1927-

PERSONAL: Born July 20, 1927, in Rochdale, England;
son of Thomas (a trade-union organizer) and Annie (Porteous) Howard; married Antonie Eber, June 23, 1956; children: Ruth, Neil, Martin. *Education:* Attended Stockport
School, 1946-47; University of Manchester, B.Sc., 1952;
University of Durham, Ph.D., 1966. *Home:* 49 Dove Lane,
Thornhill, Toronto, Ontario, Canada.

CAREER: University of Durham, Durham, England, lecturer in psychology, 1953-65; New York University, New
York, N.Y., associate professor of psychology, 1965-66;
York University, Toronto, Ontario, associate professor,
1966-68, professor of psychology and chairman of department, 1968—. Defence Research Establishment, Toronto,
Ontario, consultant, 1966-67. *Member:* British Psychological Society (fellow), Experimental Psychology Society,
American Psychological Association, Psychonomic Society, Canadian Psychological Association.

WRITINGS: (With W. B. Templeton) *Human Spatial Orientation,* Wiley, 1966.

Contributor: J. A. Deutsch and D. Deutsch, editors, *Physiological Psychology,* Dorsey, 1966; S. J. Freedman, editor,
The Neuropsychology of Spatially Oriented Behavior,
Dorsey, 1968; K. J. Connolly, editor, *Mechanisms of
Motor Skill Development,* CIBA, 1971; E. C. Carterette
and M. Freedman, editors, *Handbook of Perception,*
Volume III, Academic Press, 1973. Contributor of thirty
articles to scientific journals.

*   *   *

HOWE, Reuel L(anphier)   1905-

PERSONAL: Born May 15, 1905, in Vashon, Wash.; son
of Lincoln Grant (U.S. Army) and Jennie Corner (Beall)
Howe; married Marjorie Stryke, August 24, 1932; children:
Reuel Lanphier, Jr., Marjorie Martin. *Education:* Whitman
College, A.B., 1927; Philadelphia Divinity School, S.T.B.,
1930, Th.M., 1931, S.T.D., 1941. *Home:* 2770 Somerset,
Troy, Mich. 48084. *Office:* Institute for Advanced Pastoral
Studies, 380 Lone Pine Rd., Bloomfield Hills, Mich. 48013.

CAREER: Ordained deacon, Protestant Episcopal Church,
1929, and priest, 1930; vicar in Elsmere, N.Y., 1931-37;
Philadelphia Divinity School, Philadelphia, Pa., professor
of pastoral theology, 1937-44; Protestant Episcopal Theological Seminary in Virginia, Alexandria, professor of pastoral theology, 1944-57; Institute for Advanced Pastoral
Studies, Bloomfield Hills, Mich., founder and director,
1957-73, associate director, 1973—. *Member:* Association
of Seminary Professors in the Practical Fields (president,

1962-64), Society for the Advancement of Continuing Education for the Ministry. *Awards, honors:* D.D. from Whitman College, 1960, Chicago Theological Seminary, 1960, and Protestant Episcopal Theological Seminary in Virginia, 1967.

WRITINGS: Man's Need and God's Action, Seabury, 1953; *The Creative Years,* Seabury, 1959; *Herein Is Love,* Judson, 1961; *Miracle of Dialogue,* Seabury, 1963; *Youth Considers Personal Moods,* Thomas Nelson, 1966; *Partners in Preaching,* Seabury, 1967; *Survival Plus,* Seabury, 1971; *How to Stay Younger While Growing Older,* Word, Inc., 1974.

Contributor: *Sex and Religion Today; The Church's Mental Health; Making the Ministry Relevant.* Contributor to professional journals and popular magazines. Member of editorial board, *Journal of Pastoral Psychology.*

* * *

HOWELL, John C(hristian) 1924-

PERSONAL: Born February 24, 1924, in Miami, Fla.; son of Heman M. and Laura (Andersen) Howell; married Doris D. Dooley, March 8, 1947; children: Michael Christian, John Mark. *Education:* Stetson University, B.A. (magna cum laude), 1949; Southwestern Baptist Theological Seminary, B.D., 1952, Th.D., 1960. *Home:* 5621 North Doniphan, Kansas City, Mo. 64118. *Office:* Midwestern Baptist Theological Seminary, Kansas City, Mo.

CAREER: Baptist minister in Crowley, Tex., 1950-56, and Bradenton, Fla., 1956-60; Midwestern Baptist Theological Seminary, Kansas City, Mo., professor of ethics, 1960—, academic dean, 1976—. Member of executive board, Christian Counseling Services, Jefferson City, Mo.; associate counselor, Midwest Christian Counseling Center. *Military service:* U.S. Army, 1943-46. *Member:* American Society of Christian Ethics, National Council on Family Relations, American Association of Pastoral Counselors, Missouri Council on Family Relations, Kansas City Society for Theological Studies, Kansas City Association for Mental Health.

WRITINGS: Teaching About Sex: A Christian Approach, Broadman, 1966; (contributor) Ross Coggins, editor, *The Gambling Menace,* Broadman, 1966; *Growing in Oneness,* Convention Press, 1972; (contributor) E. S. West, editor, *Extremism Left and Right,* Eerdmans, 1972; *Teaching Your Children about Sex,* Broadman, 1973. Contributor to publications in his field.

* * *

HOWELL, Roger (Jr.) 1936-

PERSONAL: Born July 3, 1936, in Baltimore, Md.; son of Roger (a university dean and professor of law) and Katherine (Clifford) Howell; married Marcia Lunt, June 11, 1966; children: Tracy Walker, Ian Christopher. *Education:* Bowdoin College, A.B. (summa cum laude), 1958; St. John's College, Oxford, B.A., 1960, M.A. (first class honors), 1964, D.Phil., 1964; Johns Hopkins University, graduate study, 1960-61. *Politics:* Republican. *Religion:* Episcopalian. *Home:* 85 Federal St., Brunswick, Me. 04011.

CAREER: Oxford University, St. John's College, Oxford, England, research fellow and tutor in Honour School of Modern History, 1961-64, junior dean of arts, 1962-64; Bowdoin College, Brunswick, Me., assistant professor, 1964-66, associate professor, 1966-68, professor of history, 1968—, chairman of department, 1967-68, acting dean of the

college, 1967-68, president, 1969—. Visiting professor, University of Maine, 1967-68. Member of Maine State and New England Rhodes Scholarship Selection Committees.

MEMBER: American Historical Association, Conference on British Studies, Renaissance Society of America, Economic History Society, Royal Historical Society (fellow), Historical Association (Great Britain), Royal Anthropological Institute of Great Britain and Ireland (fellow), Scottish History Society, Societe d'Etude du Dix-septieme Siecle, Past and Present Society, Society of Antiquaries (Newcastle), Stubbs Society (Oxford), New England Conference on British Studies (executive secretary, 1967-69), Anglo-American Associates (executive committee member, 1974—), Phi Beta Kappa, London Scottish Football Club. *Awards, honors:* Rhodes Scholarship, 1958-60; LL.D. from Colby College and from Nasson College, 1970; L.H.D. from University of Maine, 1971.

WRITINGS: (Editor) *Prescott: The Conquest of Mexico,* Twayne, 1966; *Newcastle upon Tyne and the Puritan Revolution,* Clarendon Press, 1967; *Sir Philip Sidney: The Shepherd Knight,* Little, Brown, 1968; *The Constitutional and Intellectual Origins of the English Revolution,* Forum Press, 1975. Contributor of articles and reviews to *History Today, Archaeologia Aeliana, Canadian Journal of History,* and numerous other periodicals in his field. Editor, *British Studies Monitor,* 1969—; co-editor, *Erasmus,* 1975—.

WORK IN PROGRESS: Oliver Cromwell for Little, Brown; an edition of papers relating to Ralph Gardiner, for Northumberland (England) Record Society; a study of urban politics in the English revolution.

SIDELIGHTS: Howell is competent in French and German. *Avocational interests:* Rugby football (former member of Oxford City Rugby Club), tennis, pre-Columbian archaeology.

BIOGRAPHICAL/CRITICAL SOURCES: Baltimore Sunday Sun Magazine, April 19, 1959.

* * *

HOWELLS, John G(wilym) 1918-

PERSONAL: Born June 24, 1918, in Amlwch, Wales; son of Richard David and Mary (Hughes) Howells; married Ola Harrison, December 11, 1943; children: David John Barry, Richard Keith, Cheryll Mary, Roger Bruce. *Education:* University of London, B.S. and M.B., 1943, M.D., 1951; L.R.C.P. (London), 1943; University of Goettingen, graduate study, 1947. *Office:* Institute of Family Psychiatry, 23 Henley Rd., Ipswich, England.

CAREER: Charing Cross Hospital, London, England, house physician and senior house surgeon, 1943; University of London, London, England, registrar, Institute of Psychiatry and Institute of Neurology, 1947-49; consulting psychiatrist, 1949—; Institute of Family Psychiatry, Ipswich, England, director, 1949—. World Health Organization, fellow in United States, 1961, and consultant; University of Nebraska, visiting professor, 1962. Originator of family psychiatry system of practice, and organizer of first hospital department of family psychiatry. Member of council, Institute of Social Research. Member of faculty board of clinical medicine, University of Cambridge; Suffolk area Health Authority. *Member:* Royal College of Surgeons, Royal College of Psychiatrists (fellow; member of board of examiners), World Psychiatric Association, Royal Society of Medicine, British Medical Association, American Psychiatric Association (fellow).

WRITINGS: Family Psychiatry, Oliver & Boyd, 1963; Theory and Practice of Family Psychiatry, Oliver & Boyd, 1968; Remember Maria, Butterworth, 1974; (editor) World History of Psychiatry, Brunner/Mazel, 1974; Contemporary Issues in Psychiatry, Butterworth, 1974; Principles of Family Psychiatry, Brunner/Mazel, 1975. Editor of "Modern Perspectives in Psychiatry" series, seven volumes, 1965-76. Deviser, with J. R. Lickorish, of psychological test, "Family Relations Indicator." Contributor of about 100 articles to medical journals.

WORK IN PROGRESS: Continued work on "Modern Perspectives in Psychiatry Series"; research in family psychiatry and in parent-child separation and problem families.

AVOCATIONAL INTERESTS: Growing roses; music, art, poetry, and "rumination."

*   *   *

HOY, Cyrus H. 1926-

PERSONAL: Born February 26, 1926, in St. Marys, W.Va.; son of Albert Pierce and Marie (West) Hoy. Education: University of Virginia, B.A., 1950, M.A., 1951, Ph.D., 1954. Office: Department of English, University of Rochester, Rochester, N.Y.

CAREER: Vanderbilt University, Nashville, Tenn., assistant professor, 1956-60, associate professor of English, 1960-64; University of Rochester, Rochester, N.Y., professor of English, 1964—. Awards, honors: Guggenheim fellow, 1962-63.

WRITINGS: (Editor) Shakespeare, Hamlet, Norton, 1963; The Hyacinth Room: An Investigation into the Nature of Comedy, Tragedy, and Tragicomedy, Knopf, 1964; (editor) Philip Massinger, The City Madam, University of Nebraska Press, 1964; (contributor) F. Bowers, editor, The Dramatic Works in the Beaumont and Fletcher Canon, Cambridge University Press, Volume I, 1966. Author of "The Shares of Fletcher and His Collaborators in the Beaumont and Fletcher Canon," run in seven parts in Studies in Bibliography, 1956-62; Part I was reprinted in The Practice of Modern Literary Scholarship, edited by Sheldon P. Zitner, Scott, 1966, and Evidence for Authorship: Essays on Problems of Attribution, edited by David V. Erdman and Ephim G. Fogel, Cornell University Press, 1966. Contributor to Shakespeare Survey, and other literature and language journals.

WORK IN PROGRESS: Renaissance and Restoration dramatic style.

*   *   *

HOY, John C. 1933-

PERSONAL: Born December 5, 1933, in Yonkers, N.Y. Education: Wesleyan University, B.A., 1955, M.A., 1960; graduate study in psychology and education at University of Chicago and University of Pennsylvania. Home: 2418 South Louise St., Santa Ana, Calif. Office: University of California, Irvine, Calif. 92664.

CAREER: St. Louis Country Day School, St. Louis, Mo., teacher of English and history, 1955-56; Wesleyan University, Middletown, Conn., assistant director of admissions, 1956-59; Morgan Park Academy, Chicago, Ill., director of development and guidance, and teacher of English, 1959-60; Lake Forest College, Lake Forest, Ill., director of admissions, 1960-62; Swarthmore College, Swarthmore, Pa., dean of admissions, 1962-64; Wesleyan University, dean of admissions and assistant to president, 1964-67, dean of admissions and freshmen, 1967-69, dean of special academic affairs, 1968-69; University of California, Irvine, vice-chancellor of university and student affairs, 1969—. National Scholarship Service and Fund for Negro Students, member of advisory board, 1964-66, trustee, 1966—; member of Commission on Tests, College Entrance Examination Board and College Scholarship Service, 1966—; African Scholarship Program of American Universities, trustee, 1966—, and member of selection committee; member of scholarship selection committees of various foundations and corporations; trustee of Independent Day School, Middletown, 1964-67. Member: National Association of College Admissions Counselors (member of executive board, 1962—), Center for the Study of the Presidency (member of board of educators), New England Association of Colleges and Secondary Schools (member of commission on higher education).

WRITINGS: Choosing a College: The Test of a Person, Delacorte, 1967; (contributor) Asa S. Knowles, editor, Handbook of College and University Administration, McGraw, 1970; The Effective President, Palisades, 1976. Author of syndicated column distributed through Newspaper Enterprise Association. Contributor of articles and reviews to professional journals and newspapers, including Christian Science Monitor, New York World Telegram and Sun; also contributor of poetry to Approach, Beloit Poetry Journal, and other periodicals. Chairman of advisory board, Association of College Admissions Counselors (now National Association of College Admissions Counselors) Journal, 1961-63.

WORK IN PROGRESS: A book on the present generation of college students; a book on university management.

*   *   *

HOYLAND, Michael 1925-

PERSONAL: Born April 1, 1925, in Nagpur, India; son of John Somervell (a lecturer) and Jessie (Marais) Hoyland; married Marette Fraser, July 21, 1948; children: Denys, Jane, Graham, Vhairi. Education: Birmingham College of Art, 1942-43, 1946-49; received Art Teacher's Diploma, 1949. Politics: "Formatist." Religion: "Formatist." Home: Foxfoot House, South Luffenham, Oakham, Leicestershire, England.

CAREER: Part-time teacher of art in England, 1949-54; full-time teacher at Whitford Hall, Bromsgrove, England, 1954-57, and Patchway School, Bristol, England, 1957-63; Kesteven College of Education, Lincolnshire, England, 1963—, began as lecturer, now senior lecturer in art. Broadcaster of programs on Romantic poets and Russian short stories. Military service: Royal Naval Volunteer Reserve, 1943-46; became sub-lieutenant. Member: National Union of Teachers, National Society for Art Education (fellow).

WRITINGS: (With Rachel Bush, Christopher Hampton, Roy Watkins, and John Wheway) Introduction 3 (stories by five new writers), Faber, 1967; Art for Children, Macmillan, 1970; (contributor) Variations, Macmillan, 1975. Contributor to London Magazine, Views, and The Scotsman.

WORK IN PROGRESS: A book of poems; a play, completion expected in 1977.

*   *   *

HOYT, Jo Wasson 1927-

PERSONAL: Born August 13, 1927, in Princeton, Ind.; daughter of James Richard (an investor) and Charlotte

(Moser) Wasson; married Michael Phelps Evans Hoyt (a U.S. Foreign Service officer); children: Reed Wasson, Phelps Wasson Clark, Scot (daughter), Evans Wasson. *Education:* Attended Stephens College, 1943-44, and University of New Mexico, 1944-49. *Religion:* Protestant. *Address:* Box 360, Boonville, Ind.

WRITINGS: (With Frank Graham, Jr.) *For the Love of Mike,* Random House, 1966.

SIDELIGHTS: As the wife of a Foreign Service officer, Jo Wasson Hoyt has lived in Pakistan, Morocco, and the Congo.††

* * *

HSU, Kai-yu 1922-

PERSONAL: Born July 5, 1922, in China; now U.S. citizen; married Jeanne M. Horbach, 1950; children: Jean-Pierre, Roland. *Education:* National Tsing Hua University, B.A., 1944; University of Oregon, M.A., 1948; Stanford University, Ph.D., 1959. *Office:* Department of Comparative Literature, San Francisco State University, San Francisco, Calif. 94132.

CAREER: Chinese World Daily, San Francisco, Calif., successively reporter, foreign news editor, and associate editor, 1948-52; Stanford Research Institute, Stanford, Calif., assistant analyst, China Project, 1952-53; U.S. Army Language School, Monterey, Calif., instructor in Chinese-Mandarin department, 1953-55; Stanford University, Stanford, Calif., research assistant, China Project, 1955-56, lecturer then instructor, 1956-59; San Francisco State University, San Francisco, Calif., associate professor, 1959-63, professor of humanities and foreign languages, 1963—, chairman of department of foreign languages, 1960-65, and department of comparative literature, 1974—. Chairman, Advisory Committee on Chinese Language Instruction in California Public Schools, 1962-67. *Military service:* Chinese Army, 1943-47; chief interpreter, Chinese Air Force Detachment in United States, 1945-46; military aide, Chinese Embassy, Washington, D.C., 1946-47.

MEMBER: Association for Asian Studies, Modern Language Association of America, Philological Association of the Pacific Coast, Foreign Language Association of Northern California. *Awards, honors:* American Council of Learned Societies award for travel to Belgium, 1960; National Endowment for the Humanities senior fellowship for travel to the People's Republic of China, 1973.

WRITINGS: (Contributor) *China Handbooks,* Human Relations Area Files, Yale University, 1956; (editor and translator) *Twentieth Century Chinese Poetry,* Doubleday, 1963; *Chinese: Mandarin,* Levels I, II, III, and IV, Altoan Press, 1965-67; (contributor) Howard L. Boorman, editor, *Biographical Dictionary of Republican China,* Columbia University Press, 1967; *Chou En-lai: China's Gray Eminence,* Doubleday, 1968; *Asian-American Authors,* Houghton, 1972; *Chinese Civilization,* Asian Language Publications, 1972; *The Chinese Literary Scene: A Writer's Visit to the People's Republic,* Random House, 1975. Contributor to *Encyclopaedia Britannica, Philosophical Reviews, Show,* and language journals. Editor of Oriental languages section, *MLA Abstracts,* and *MLA-Chinese Conference Newsletter.*

* * *

HUBBARD, D(onald) L(ee) 1929-

PERSONAL: Born May 26, 1929, in Ottawa, Kan.; son of Robert Lee and Jennie (Poteet) Hubbard; married B. Karyl Rogers, December 29, 1950; children: Michael, Kimberly, Matthew, Harla, Jennifer. *Education:* University of California, A.A., 1950.

CAREER: Brown Brothers (insurance adjusters), Oakland, Calif., assistant manager, beginning 1956. *Military service:* U.S. Army, 1950-52; became sergeant; received Air Medal. *Member:* California Writers' Club.

WRITINGS: Dragons, Dragons (juvenile), Reilly & Lee, 1967; *The Dragon Comes to Admela* (juvenile), Reilly & Lee, 1967.

WORK IN PROGRESS: A Whisper of Magic; a picture book, *A Guide to the Flat Earth;* an insurance column, "A Capitalistic Manifesto."

SIDELIGHTS: D. L. Hubbard told *CA:* "Interested in any advance in human nature that may in time elevate humanity." *Avocational interests:* Flying, sailing.††

* * *

HUBER, Jack T(ravis) 1918-

PERSONAL: Born November 21, 1918, in San Antonio, Tex.; son of Fred W. (a grain merchant) and Agnes (Gruber) Huber; divorced. *Education:* University of Texas, B.A., 1940; Columbia University, M.A., 1947, Ph.D., 1952. *Home:* 310 East 55th St., New York, N.Y. 10022. *Office:* Hunter College of the City University of New York, 695 Park Ave., New York, N.Y. 10021.

CAREER: Diplomate (clinical) of American Board of Examiners in Professional Psychology. Vocational Advisory Service, New York City, director of psychiatric clinic, 1950-53; Rohrer, Hibler & Replogle, New York City, psychological consultant, 1953-55; Adelphi University, Garden City, N.Y., professor of education, 1955-67; Hunter College of the City University of New York, New York City, professor of psychology, department of special educational services, 1967—. Consultant, Vocational Advisory Service, 1962-69. *Military service:* U.S. Army Air Forces, 1943-46. *Member:* American Psychological Association, American Personnel and Guidance Association, New York State Psychological Association, Alpha Kappa Delta, Kappa Delta Pi.

WRITINGS: Report Writing in Psychology and Psychiatry, Harper, 1961; *Psychotherapy and Meditation,* Gollancz, 1965, published as *Through an Eastern Window,* Houghton, 1967; (editor with Howard L. Millman) *Goals and Behavior in Psychotherapy and Counseling,* C. E. Merrill, 1972; (with D. R. Diggins) *The Human Personality,* Little, Brown, 1976.

* * *

HUBY, Pamela M(argaret Clark) 1922-

PERSONAL: Surname is pronounced Hew-by; born April 21, 1922, in London, England; daughter of George Herbert (a civil servant) and Agnes (Young) Clark; married Ronald Huby (a theoretical physicist), September 1, 1956; children: Adam, Bartholomew, Priscilla. *Education:* Lady Margaret Hall, Oxford, M.A., 1947. *Home:* 14 Marine Ter., Wallasey, England.

CAREER: Oxford University, St. Anne's College, Oxford, England, lecturer in philosophy, 1947-49; University of Liverpool, Liverpool, England, lecturer, 1949-71, senior lecturer in philosophy, 1971—. *Member:* Mind Association, Classical Association, Society for Psychical Research, Parapsychological Association.

WRITINGS: (Contributor) D. J. O'Connor, *Critical History of Western Philosophy,* Free Press of Glencoe, 1964; *Greek Ethics,* Macmillan, 1967, revised edition published in *New Studies in Ethics,* edited by W. D. Hudson, 1974; *Plato and Morality,* Macmillan, 1972; (contributor) S. C. Thakur, *Philosophical Foundations of Psychical Research,* Allen & Unwin, in press. Contributor to philosophical and classical journals.

WORK IN PROGRESS: A book on the dating of Aristotle's writings by style and spelling.

SIDELIGHTS: Pamela Huby is competent in French, Latin, Ancient Greek, German, Italian.

*   *   *

HUCKINS, Wesley C.   1918-

PERSONAL: Born August 12, 1918, in Sundance, Wyo.; son of Guy W. (a lumberman) and Gertrude (Schloredt) Huckins; married Fern Shreeves, September 20, 1942; children: Kathy (Mrs. Arthur Capell), Shirley (Mrs. Donald Beckwith), Trudy, Greg. *Education:* Black Hills State College, B.S. (with high honor), 1953; University of Wyoming, M.A., 1955, Ed.D., 1963. *Religion:* Methodist. *Home:* 2309 Randy Drive, Kettering, Ohio 45440.

CAREER: Teacher in Crook County, Wyo., 1939-41, and Sundance, Wyo., 1945-47; Black Hills State College, Spearfish, S.D., instructor, 1954; Sundance (Wyo.) public schools, superintendent, 1955-59; Oregon State System of Higher Education, Portland, associate professor of education, 1963-68; Wright State University, Dayton, Ohio, associate professor, 1968-70, professor of education, 1970—. Consultant, Kettering Foundation, 1967-68. *Military service:* U.S. Army Air Forces, 1941-45; became first lieutenant; received Air Medal with four oak-leaf clusters. *Member:* American Personnel and Guidance Association, American Psychological Association, National Education Association, Phi Delta Kappa, Phi Kappa Phi.

WRITINGS: (Editor with Harold Bernard) *Readings in Educational Psychology,* International Textbook, 1967; (editor with Bernard) *Readings in Human Development,* Allyn & Bacon, 1967; *Ethical and Legal Aspects of Guidance,* Houghton, 1968; (editor with Bernard) *Psycho Social Dynamics of Effective Behavior,* Holbrook, 1971; (with Bernard) *Dynamics of Personal Adjustment,* Holbrook, 1971, 2nd edition, 1975; (editor with Bernard) *Exploring Human Development,* Allyn & Bacon, 1972; (with Bernard) *Humanism in the Classroom: An Eclectic Approach to Teaching and Learning,* Allyn & Bacon, 1974.

AVOCATIONAL INTERESTS: Woodworking.

*   *   *

HUDDLESTON, Lee Eldridge   1935-

PERSONAL: Born October 19, 1935, in Seagraves, Tex.; son of Clavin O. and Anna (Crockett) Huddleston. *Education:* Texas Technological College (now Texas Tech University), B.A., 1959; University of Texas, Ph.D., 1966. *Politics:* Democrat-Liberal. *Religion:* None. *Office:* North Texas State University, Box 13707, Denton, Tex. 76203.

CAREER: University of Arkansas, Fayetteville, instructor, 1965-66, assistant professor of history, 1966-67; North Texas State University, Denton, assistant professor, 1967-71, associate professor of history, 1971—. Visiting assistant professor of history at Kansas State University, summer, 1964, Colorado State University, summer, 1966, PMC Colleges, Pa., summer, 1967. *Member:* American Historical

Association, American Association of University Professors, Texas State Historical Association, Texas Association of College Teachers. *Awards, honors:* Woodrow Wilson fellowship, 1959-60.

WRITINGS: The Origins of the American Indians: European Concepts 1492-1729, University of Texas Press, 1967.

WORK IN PROGRESS: The question of Indian origins in relation to the development of anthropology, 1680 to present.

AVOCATIONAL INTERESTS: Pre-classical vocal music and nineteenth-century travelers in Latin America.†

*   *   *

HUESSY, Hans R.   1921-

PERSONAL: Born August 15, 1921, in Frankfurt, Germany; son of Eugene Rosenstock (a professor) and Margaret Huessy; married Ellen Nora West, December 22, 1943; married second wife, Mariot Gardner, March 1, 1958; children: eleven. *Education:* Dartmouth College, A.B., 1942; summer graduate study at Harvard University, 1940, and University of New Hampshire, 1941; Yale University, M.D., 1945; University of Colorado, M.S., 1951. *Religion:* Protestant. *Home:* Jericho, Vt. 05465. *Office:* College of Medicine, University of Vermont, Burlington, Vt. 05401.

CAREER: Licensed to practice medicine in New York, Vermont, and Missouri; certified in psychiatry by American Board of Psychiatry and Neurology, 1952, and in child psychiatry, 1963. Johns Hopkins Hospital, Baltimore, Md., pediatric intern, 1945-46; U.S. Public Health Service, officer, 1946-53, resigning with rank of senior surgeon (lieutenant colonel), after assignments in Fort Worth, Tex., Springfield, Mo., and as resident and clinical instructor in psychiatry at University of Colorado Medical Center, Denver; director of tri-county mental health program in New York State, 1953-58; Albany Medical College, Albany, N.Y., associate clinical professor of psychiatry, 1956-58; private practice of psychiatry, Burlington, Vt., 1959—; University of Vermont, College of Medicine, Burlington, clinical instructor in psychiatry, 1959-64, assistant professor, 1964-66, associate professor, 1966-69, professor of psychiatry, 1969—. Psychiatric consultant, International Business Machines, Essex Junction, Vt., 1966-70. Member of Vermont Governor's Committee on Children and Youth, and Vermont State Board of Mental Health, 1963-75.

MEMBER: World Federation for Mental Health, American Academy of Child Psychiatry (fellow), American Orthopsychiatric Association (fellow), American Public Health Association (fellow), American Psychiatric Association (fellow), Vermont State Medical Society, Chittenden County Medical Society, Phi Beta Kappa.

WRITINGS: Mental Health with Limited Resources, Grune, 1966; (with Walter Twellman and Karlheinz Walter) *Lese Schwache Schuler,* August Bagel Verlag (Dusseldorf), 1967; (contributor) Harvey H. Barten and Leopold Bellak, editors, *Progress in Community Mental Health,* Volume II, Grune, 1972; (contributor) Stuart E. Golann and Carl Eisdorfer, editors, *Handbook of Community Mental Health,* Prentice-Hall, 1972; (contributor with Craig Messersmith) James E. Lieberman, editor, *Mental Health: The Public Challenge,* American Public Health Association, 1975. Contributor to professional journals; author of numerous scientific papers.

HUFTON, Olwen H. 1938-

PERSONAL: Born June 2, 1938, in Oldham, England; daughter of Joseph Hufton (a textile engineer); married Brian Murphy (a teacher), July 3, 1965. *Education:* University of London, B.A. (first class honors), 1959, Ph.D., 1962. *Home:* 40 Shinfield Rd., Reading, England.

CAREER: University of Leicester, Leicester, England, lecturer in European history, 1962-66; University of Reading, Reading, England, 1966—, began as lecturer, professor of European history, 1975—.

WRITINGS: Bayeux in the Late Eighteenth Century: A Social Study, Oxford University Press, 1967; (contributor) Alfred Cobban, editor, *The Eighteenth Century,* McGraw, 1969; *The Poor of Eighteenth-Century France,* Oxford University Press, 1974.

WORK IN PROGRESS: Women and the Family Economy in Eighteenth-Century France.

* * *

HUGHES, Colin A(nfield) 1930-

PERSONAL: Born May 4, 1930, on Harbour Island, Bahamas; son of John Anfield (a civil servant) and Byrle (Johnson) Hughes; married Gwen Glover, August 6, 1955; children: John Anfield. *Education:* George Washington University, student, 1946-48; Columbia University, B.A., 1949, M.A., 1950; London School of Economics and Political Science, Ph.D., 1952. *Home:* 2 Ambalindum St., Hawker, A.C.T. 2614, Australia. *Office:* Australian National University, Box 4, Canberra, A.C.T. 2600, Australia.

CAREER: McKinney, Bancroft & Hughes (attorneys), Nassau, Bahamas, counsel and attorney, 1954-56; University of Queensland, St. Lucia, Australia, lecturer, 1956-59; McKinney, Bancroft & Hughes, counsel and attorney, 1959-61; Australian National University, Canberra, Australian Capital Territory, fellow, 1961-65; University of Queensland, professor of political science, 1965-74; Australian National University, Canberra, professorial fellow, 1975—.

WRITINGS: (Editor with David G. Bettison and Paul W. van der Veur) *The Papua-New Guinea Elections, 1964,* Australian National University, 1965; (with John S. Western) *The Prime Minister's Policy Speech,* Australian National University Press, 1966; (editor) *Readings in Australian Government,* University of Queensland Press, 1968; (with B. D. Graham) *A Handbook of Australian Government and Politics 1890-1964,* Australian National University Press, 1968; *Issues and Images,* Australian National University Press, 1969.

(Editor with D. J. Murphy and R. B. Joyce) *Prelude to Power,* Jacaranda Press, 1970; (with John S. Western) *The Mass Media in Australia: Use and Evaluation,* University of Queensland Press, 1971; (with B. D. Graham) *Voting for the Australian House of Representatives, 1901-1964,* Australian National University Press, 1974; *Mr. Prime Minister: Australian Prime Ministers, 1901-1972,* Oxford University Press, in press. Editor, *The Australian University,* 1975—.

* * *

HUGHES, G(eorge) E(dward) 1918-

PERSONAL: Born June 8, 1918, in Waterford, Ireland; son of George James (a photographer) and Gertrude (Sparks) Hughes; married Beryl Tilsley (a university lecturer), December 27, 1943; children: Roger David, Nigel Edward, Richard William, Jonathan Mark, Catherine Beryl. *Education:* University of Glasgow, M.A., 1940; also studied at Trinity College, Cambridge. *Home:* 24 Verviers St., Wellington 5, New Zealand. *Office:* Department of Philosophy, Victoria University of Wellington, Private Bag, Wellington, New Zealand.

CAREER: University of Glasgow, Glasgow, Scotland, assistant in moral philosophy, 1942-45; University of Wales, lecturer in philosophy at University College of South Wales and Monmouthshire, Cardiff, 1946-47, and University College of North Wales, Bangor, 1948-50; Victoria University of Wellington, Wellington, New Zealand, professor of philosophy, 1951—. Anglican Church, ordained deacon, 1949, and priest, 1950; currently holds license to officiate in Diocese of Wellington. *Member:* Aristotelian Society, Mind Association, Society for Psychical Research (London), Australasian Association of Philosophy.

WRITINGS: (Contributor) Donald M. MacKinnon, editor, *Christian Faith and Communist Faith,* Macmillan, 1953; (contributor) Abraham I. Melden, editor, *Essays in Moral Philosophy,* University of Washington Press, 1958; (with D. G. Londey) *The Elements of Formal Logic,* Harper, 1965; (with M. J. Cresswell) *An Introduction to Modal Logic,* Methuen, 1968. Contributor to philosophy journals in England, Australia, the United States, Sweden, and Poland.

WORK IN PROGRESS: Investigations in modal logic.

* * *

HUGHES, Owain (Gardner Collingwood) 1943-

PERSONAL: Born November 21, 1943, in Bath, England; son of Richard (Arthur Warren; the novelist, poet, and playwright) and Frances (Bazeley) Hughes; married Elisabeth Brandon. *Education:* Keble College, Oxford, B.A., 1966. *Politics:* "Detested." *Religion:* "Don't know." *Home:* 438 Broome St., New York, N.Y. 10013. *Agent:* Sheila Watson, Bolt & Watson, Ltd., 8 Storey's Gate, London S.W.1, England.

CAREER: "Author and specialist in the mechanics of kinetic art."

WRITINGS: The Beholding Runner, Chatto & Windus, 1966, Morrow, 1967; *Hermit's Reprieve,* Chatto & Windus, 1969.

WORK IN PROGRESS: A novel on the future of New York, a social satire.

SIDELIGHTS: Hughes' first novel, *The Beholding Runner,* is the story of a young English expatriate living and traveling in Morocco. Reviewing this book Goeffrey Godsell writes, ". . . [Hughes] shows an impressive skill in evoking for us scenes and atmosphere. Only a writer who has heard and smelt these things for himself could so effectively share them with his readers."

AVOCATIONAL INTERESTS: World-travel, sailing, underwater fishing.

* * *

HUIE, William O(rr) 1911-

PERSONAL: Born September 15, 1911, in Arkadelphia, Ark.; son of Robert W. (an attorney) and Minnie Belle (Smith) Huie; married Hugh Mae Wolff, August 27, 1935 (deceased); married Grace E. Bishop, June 10, 1972; children: (first marriage) William Orr, Jr., Robert Wolff. *Education:* Henderson State College, B.A., 1932; University of Texas, LL.B., 1935. *Politics:* Democrat. *Religion:* Methodist. *Home:* 3401 Barranca Circle, Austin, Tex. 78731. *Office:* School of Law, University of Texas, Austin, Tex. 78705.

CAREER: Admitted to Texas State Bar. Attorney in private practice, Austin, Tex., 1935-36; University of Texas, School of Law, Austin, assistant professor, 1936-39, associate professor, 1939-46, professor of law, 1946—, Sylvan Lang Professor of Law, 1965—. Visiting professor at University of California, Berkeley, summer, 1956, University of California, Los Angeles, summer, 1961, and Harvard Law School, 1961-62. Senior attorney, U.S. Office of Price Administration, 1942-43. Co-drafter of Texas Probate Code, adopted 1955; consultant to committee revising marital property laws of Texas, 1967. *Military service:* U.S. Navy, 1943-46. *Member:* State Bar of Texas, Order of the Coif, Phi Delta Phi, Chancellors. *Awards, honors:* S.J.D., Harvard University, 1953.

WRITINGS: Texas Cases and Materials on the Law of Marital Rights, West Publishing, 1955; (with A. W. Walker, Jr. and Marion K. Woodward) *Cases and Materials on Oil and Gas,* West Publishing, 1960, 2nd edition (with M. K. Woodward and Ernest E. Smith, III), 1972; *The Community Property Law of Texas,* revised edition, Vernon Law Book Co., 1960; *Texas Cases and Materials on the Law of Marital Property Rights,* West Publishing, 1966. Editor-in-chief, *Texas Law Review,* 1934-35. Contributor to legal journals.

WORK IN PROGRESS: With Ernest E. Smith, III, a casebook on community property in the United States.

* * *

HUMBLE, William F(rank) 1948-

PERSONAL: Born December 22, 1948, in Carshalton, Surrey, England; son of Frank Wilkinson and Frances (Dennis) Humble. *Education:* University of Birmingham, B.A. (with honors), 1970. *Politics:* Labour. *Religion:* None. *Home:* 9 Mark Mansions, Westville Rd., London W.12 9P.S., England. *Agent:* Marc Berlin, London Management, 235 Regent St., London W.1, England.

CAREER: English and drama teacher, 1970-72; script editor, British Broadcasting Corp., 1973—.

WRITINGS: A Tale of Arthur (farcial novel), Anthony Blond, 1967; (author and director) "The Rosebed," play, first produced at University of Birmingham, July 4, 1968; "Do It Yourself," a play, first produced at Three Horseshoes Theatre, Hampstead, England, September, 1975.

SIDELIGHTS: Humble's first novel *A Tale of Arthur* was written when he was fifteen.

* * *

HUNT, John W(esley) 1927-

PERSONAL: Born January 19, 1927, in Tulsa, Okla.; son of John Wesley (a lawyer) and Alta (Johnson) Hunt; married Marjorie Louise Bowen (a publications editor), August 8, 1951; children: Stuart, Susan, Emily. *Education:* University of Oklahoma, B.A., 1949; University of Chicago, Ph.D., 1961. *Politics:* Democrat. *Religion:* United Presbyterian Church. *Residence:* Springtown, Pa. *Office:* College of Arts and Science, Maginnes Hall No. 9, Lehigh University, Bethlehem, Pa. 18015.

CAREER: Earlham College, Richmond, Ind., assistant professor, 1956-62, associate professor, 1962-66, professor of English, 1966-72, Bain-Swiggett Professor of English Language and Literature and chairman of the English department, 1968-71, associate academic dean, 1971-72; Lehigh University, Bethlehem, Pa., dean of College of Arts and Science and professor of English, 1972—. Member of board of directors, Great Lakes Colleges Association, 1971-72; council member of Lawrence Henry Gipson Institute for Eighteenth-Century Studies, 1972—. *Military service:* U.S. Naval Reserve, 1944-46, duty as ensign, 1951-53. *Member:* Modern Language Association of America, National Council of Teachers of English, Society for Religion in Higher Education (fellow). *Awards, honors:* Lilly fellowship, 1964-65, for research in England; E. Harris Harbison Award for distinguished teaching, 1965; Ira Doan Distinguished Teacher Travel Award, 1970.

WRITINGS: William Faulkner: Art in Theological Tension, Syracuse University Press, 1965; (contributor) Nathan A. Scott, Jr., editor, *Adversity and Grace in Recent American Fiction,* University of Chicago Press, 1968. Contributor of articles and reviews to *Criterion, Encounter, Critique, Lex et Scientia,* and other journals; regular reviewer, *Choice.* Associate editor, *Bulletin of the Illinois Society for Medical Research,* 1954-56; member of editorial board of *Quest,* 1952-56, and of *Earlham Review,* 1966-72.

WORK IN PROGRESS: A study of Faulkner and history.

* * *

HUNT, Robert C(ushman) 1934-

PERSONAL: Born May 30, 1934, in Binghamton, N.Y.; son of Robert Cushman (a psychiatrist) and Fanny (Cassidy) Hunt; married Eva Verbitsky (an anthropologist), September 21, 1960; children: Melissa Gabriela. *Education:* Hamilton College, B.A., 1956; University of Chicago, M.A., 1959; Northwestern University, Ph.D., 1965. *Home:* 5314 South Hyde Park, Chicago, Ill.

CAREER: Northwestern University, Evanston, Ill., instructor, 1964-65, assistant professor of anthropology, 1965-66; University of Illinois at Chicago Circle, Chicago, assistant professor of anthropology, 1966-69; Brandeis University, Waltham, Mass., associate professor of anthropology, 1969—. *Member:* American Anthropological Association (fellow), American Ethnological Society (fellow), Current Anthropology (associate), American Association for the Advancement of Science.

WRITINGS: (Editor) *Personalities and Cultures,* Natural History Press, 1967.

WORK IN PROGRESS: Irrigation and social structure.

* * *

HUNTER, J(ames) Paul 1934-

PERSONAL: Born June 29, 1934, in Jamestown, N.Y.; son of Paul Wesley (a clergyman) and Florence (Walmer) Hunter; married Kathryn Montgomery, July 1, 1971; children: Debra, Lisa, Paul III, Anne. *Education:* Indiana Central College, A.B., 1955; Miami University, Oxford, Ohio, M.A., 1957; Rice University, Ph.D., 1963. *Home:* 1251 Fairview Rd. N.E., Atlanta, Ga. 30306. *Office:* Emory University, Atlanta, Ga. 30322.

CAREER: Instructor in English at University of Florida, Gainesville, 1957-59, and Williams College, Williamstown, Mass., 1962-64; University of California, Riverside, assistant professor of English, 1964-66; Emory University, Atlanta, Ga., associate professor, 1966-68, professor of English, 1968—, department chairman, 1973—. *Member:* Modern Language Association of America, American Society of Eighteenth Century Studies.

WRITINGS: The Reluctant Pilgrim: Defoe's Emblematic Method and Quest for Form in "Robinson Crusoe," Johns Hopkins Press, 1966; (editor) Daniel Defoe, *Moll Flanders* (critical edition), Crowell, 1970; (editor) *Norton Introduction to Literature: Poetry,* Norton, 1973; *Occasional Form: Henry Fielding and the Chains of Circumstance,* Johns Hopkins Press, 1975. Contributor to *Twentieth Century Literature, Review of English Studies, Journal of English and Germanic Philology, Novel,* and *Scriblerian.*

WORK IN PROGRESS: A critical study of parody, and a book on forms of 18th Century fiction.

* * *

HUNTINGTON, Virginia 1889-

PERSONAL: Born September 15, 1889, in Freeport, Ill.; daughter of Frederick William (a clergyman) and Mae (Brubaker) Haist; married D. Trumbull Huntington (an Episcopal bishop), December 7, 1916 (deceased); children: Jane (Mrs. Manuel Weiner), Mary (Mrs. Peter Poanessa), Jonathan Trumbull, Elizabeth (Mrs. Joseph Van Horn). *Education:* Northwestern University, A.B., 1912; Church Training School, Philadelphia, Pa., additional study, 1912-14. *Politics:* Democrat. *Religion:* Episcopalian. *Home:* 8 Craigie Circle, Cambridge, Mass. 02138.

CAREER: Missionary work in China, 1914-40. *Member:* Society of Companions of the Holy Cross (president, 1954-62), Women's International League for Peace and Freedom (vice-president, 1941-43), League of Women Voters, Poetry Society of England, Saturday Morning Club (Boston).

WRITINGS: The Shining Moment, Morehouse, 1937; *Enough to Hunger,* Morehouse, 1939; *Along the Great River,* National Council of Protestant Episcopal Church, 1940; *The Singing Hour,* Exposition, 1951; *The Festive Heart,* Hathaway House, 1955; *Green Autumn,* Dorrance, 1959; *Sun on the Land,* Newell Press, 1964; *The Resonant World,* Golden Quill, 1966; *The Frolic Life,* Newell Press, 1970; *Celebrations,* Golden Quill, 1971; *The Curious Eye,* Golden Quill, 1974. Author of articles on China, economics, religion, and race relations.

WORK IN PROGRESS: A book of poetry.

SIDELIGHTS: Virginia Huntington is fluent in Spanish; has reading knowledge of Latin, Greek, Chinese, French, and German. Her poetry has been recorded and set to music.

* * *

HUNTON, Richard E(dwin) 1924-

PERSONAL: Born December 23, 1924, in Boonville, Ind.; son of Edwin Chandler (a photographer) and Nellie (Wright) Hunton; married Agnes Setser, August 22, 1953; children: Jenifer Leigh, Richard E., Jr. *Education:* George Washington University, A.A., 1947, A.B., 1949, M.D., 1952; also studied organ at Lander College, 1964-66. *Politics:* Independent. *Religion:* Baptist. *Home:* 112 Wendover Rd., Forest Hills, Greenwood, S.C. 29646. *Office address:* Scurry Clinic, P.O. Box 609, Greenwood, S.C. 29646.

CAREER: U.S. Naval Observatory, Washington, D.C., instrument-maker, 1942-44; Gallinger Municipal Hospital, Washington, D.C., intern, 1952-53; Spartanburg General Hospital, Spartanburg, S.C., resident, 1953-54; Scurry Clinic, Greenwood, S.C., physician, 1954—. Vice-president of staff, Brewer Hospital, 1955-68; president-elect of staff, Self Memorial Hospital. *Military service:* U.S. Army, Infantry, 1944-45; received Purple Heart. *Member:* American Medical Association, American Academy of General Practice, National Rehabilitation Association, Disabled Veterans of America, National Rifle Association of America, 95th Infantry Division Association, South Carolina Medical Association, Greenwood County Mental Health Association (member of board of directors), Phi Beta Kappa.

WRITINGS: Formula for Fitness, Revell, 1966.

AVOCATIONAL INTERESTS: Photography, carpentry, gardening, stamp collecting, organ, piano, and harpsicord making.

* * *

HURNE, Ralph 1932-

PERSONAL: Born June 2, 1932, in Romford, Essex, England; son of Charles Reginald and Dorothy (Unwin) Hurne; married Maryrose Stephens (a secretary), August 13, 1956. *Agent:* A. M. Heath & Co. Ltd., 35 Dover St., London W1X 4EB, England.

WRITINGS: Larks in Cages, Redman, 1963; *What Will You Do, Jim?,* M. Joseph, 1966; *The Yellow Jersey* (novel), Simon & Schuster, 1973. Contributor of articles on antique firearms to *Shooting Times.*†

* * *

HURST, Michael (Charles) 1931-

PERSONAL: Born June 23, 1931, in England; son of Charles (an engineer) and Elsie (Bell) Hurst; married Beatrice Stehlin, August 6, 1960; children: Katrina Madeleine, Elizabeth Christina. *Education:* Oxford University, B.A. (first class honors in modern history), from Magdalen College, 1955, research student at St. Antony's College, 1955-57. *Religion:* Church of England. *Home:* 10 Rawlinson Rd., Oxford, England. *Office:* St. John's College, St. Giles St., Oxford, England.

CAREER: Oxford University, St. John's College, Oxford, England, fellow and tutor in modern history, 1957—. *Member:* Royal Historical Society (fellow), Northhamptonshire Record Society (counsellor), Suffolk Record Society.

WRITINGS: Joseph Chamberlain and West Midland Politics, Oxford University Press, 1963; *Joseph Chamberlain and Liberal Reunion,* University of Toronto Press, 1967; *Parnell and Irish Nationalism,* Routledge & Kegan Paul, 1968; *Maria Edgeworth and the Public Scene: Intellect, Fine Feeling, and Landlordism in the Age of Reform,* University of Miami Press, 1969; (editor) *Key Treaties for the Great Powers, 1814-1914,* St. Martin's, Volume I: *1814-1870,* 1972, Volume II: *1871-1914,* 1972. Editor of Routledge & Kegan Paul's "Political History" series. Literary editor, *Oxford Magazine.*

WORK IN PROGRESS: Two books, *Harty-Tarty: A Crutch for the Conservatives* and *Joseph Chamberlain: The Man from Birmingham,* both for Macmillan.

AVOCATIONAL INTERESTS: Travel, reading, walking†

* * *

HUSEN, Torsten 1916-

PERSONAL: Born March 1, 1916, in Lund, Sweden; son

of Johan S. (an executive director) and Betty Maria (Prawitz) Husen; married Ingrid Joensson (a language teacher), April 10, 1940; children: Sven-Torsten, Mats O., Goerel. *Education:* University of Lund, B.A., 1937, M.A., 1938, Fil.lic., 1941, Ph.D., 1944. *Home:* Armfeltsgatan 10, S-11534 Stockholm, Sweden. *Office:* University of Stockholm, S-10405 Stockholm 50, Sweden.

CAREER: University of Stockholm, Stockholm, Sweden, reader, 1947-52, professor of educational psychology, 1953-56, professor of education and director of Institute of Educational Research, 1959-71, professor of international education, 1971—. Visiting professor, University of Chicago, 1959, University of Hawaii, 1968, Ontario Institute for Studies in Education, 1971. Chairman of governing board, International Institute for Educational Planning, 1970—. Member of panel of scientific advisers to Swedish Government, 1963-69. Adviser to Minister of Education on Swedish school reform, 1957-65. Consultant to Organization for Economic Co-operation and Development, 1968—. *Military service:* Swedish Armed Forces, senior psychologist, 1944-51. *Member:* International Association for the Evaluation of Educational Achievement (chairman), National Academy of Education (United States; foreign associate), Swedish Royal Academy of Scientists. *Awards, honors:* Prize for educational authorship, Swedish Literary Foundation, 1961; fellow, Center for Advanced Study of the Behavioral Sciences, 1965-66; medal for distinguished service, Teachers College, Columbia University, 1969; honorary degrees from University of Chicago, 1967, Brunel University, 1974, and University of Rhode Island, 1975.

WRITINGS: Psykologisk krigfoering, C.W.K. Gleerup, 1942; *Adolescensen: Undersoekningar roerande manlig svensk ungdom i aaldern 17-20 ar,* Almqvist & Wiksell, 1944; *Studier roerande de eidetiska fenomenen,* C.W.K. Gleerup, Volume I, 1946, Volume II, 1952; *Begavning och miljo: studier i begavningsutvecklingens och begavning-survalets psykologisk-pedagogiska och sociala problem,* H. Geber, 1948; *Om innerborden av psykologiska matningar: Nagra bidrag till psykometrikens metodlara,* C.W.K. Gleerup, 1949; *Anders Berg under folkskolans pionjaeraar,* Erlanders Bookstore, 1949.

Raettstavningsfoermagans psykologi: nagra experimentella bidrag, Svensk Lararetidnings Forlag, 1950; *Testresultatens prognosvarde: En Undersokning av den teoretiska skolningens inverkan pa testresultaten, intelligenstedens prognosvarde och de sociala faktorernas inverkan pa urvalet till hogre laroanstalter,* H. Geber, 1950; (with Sven-Eric Henricson) *Some Principles of Construction of Group Intelligence Tests for Adults: A Report on Construction and Standardization of the Swedish Induction Test (the I-test),* Almqvist & Wiksell, 1951; *Tvillingstudier: undersokningar rorande begavningsforhallanden, skolprestationer, intraparrelationer, antropometriska matt, handstilslikhet samt diagnosproblem m.m. inom en representativ population likkonade tvillingar,* Almqvist & Wiksell, 1953; *Psykologi,* Svenska Bokforlaget, 1954, 5th edition with Lars Larsson, 1966; (with others) *Betyg och standardprov; en orientering for foraldrar och larare,* Almqvist & Wiksell, 1956; (with others) *Standardproven; en redogoerselse foer konstruktion och standardisering,* Almqvist & Wiksell, 1956; *Militart och civilt,* Norstedt, 1956; *Ur psykologisk synvinkel,* Almqvist & Wiksell, 1957; *Pedagogisk psykologi,* Svenska Bokforlaget, 1957, 4th edition, 1968; (with Artur Olsson) *Akademiska studier: studieteknik for studenter,* Svenska Bokforlaget, 1958; *Psychological Twin Research: A Methodological Study,* Almqvist & Wiksell,

1959; *Att undervisa studenter,* Almqvist & Wiksell, 1959; (editor with Sten Henrysson) *Differentiation and Guidance in the Comprehensive School: Report on the Sigtuna Course Organized by the Swedish Government under the Auspices of the Council of Europe, August, 1958,* Almqvist & Wiksell, 1959.

(With Urban Dahllof) *Matematik och modersmaalet i skola och yrkesliv: studier av kunskapskrav, kunskapsbehallning och undervisningens upplaggning,* Studieforbundet Naringsliv och Samhalle, 1960, translation published as *Mathematics and Communication Skills in School and Society: An Empirical Approach to the Problem of Curriculum Contest,* Industrial Council for Social and Economic Studies, 1960; *Psykologi, introduktion til psykologien af i dag,* A. Busck, 1960; *Skolan i ett foranderligt samhalle,* Almqvist & Wiksell, 1961, 2nd edition, 1963; *De Farliga psykologerna,* Raben & Sjogren, 1961; *Studieteknik foer gymnasiet,* Svenska Bokforlaget, 1961; (with Elvy Johanson) *Fysik och kemi i skola och yrkesliv,* Studienfoerbundet Naaringsliv och Samhalle, 1961; *School Reform in Sweden,* U.S. Department of Health, Education and Welfare, 1961; *Tonaaringarna i utbildningssamhaelle; naagra maenniska ocho miljoe: studier i Amerikansk pedagogik,* Almqvist & Wiksell, 1962; (with Gosta Ekman) *Att studera psykologi och pedagogik,* Svenska Bokforlaget, 1962; *Problems of Differentiation in Swedish Compulsory Schooling,* Svenska Bokforlaget, 1962; (with Malcolm Shepherd Knowles) *Erwachsene lernen,* E. Klett, 1963; *Skola foer 60-talet,* Almqvist & Wiksell, 1963; (with Gunnar Boalt) *Skolans sociologi,* Almqvist & Wiksell, 1964, 3rd edition, 1967; *Det nya gymnasiet: information och debatt,* Almqvist & Wiksell, 1964; (with Karl-Erik Warneryd) *Psykologi for fackskolan,* Svenska Bokforlaget, 1966; *Skola i foervandling,* Almqvist & Wiksell, 1966; (editor with Ingvar Carlson) *Tonaringarna och skolan,* Almqvist & Wiksell, 1966; (editor) *International Study of Achievement in Mathematics: A Comparison of Twelve Countries,* Wiley, 1967; (with Boalt) *Educational Research and Educational Change: The Case of Sweden,* Wiley, 1968; *Skola foe 80,* Almqvist & Wiksell, 1968; (compiler) *Livsaaskaadning och religion,* Svenska bokforlaget, 1968; *Talent, Opportunity and Career: A Twenty-Six Year Follow-Up of 1500 Individuals,* Almqvist & Wiksell, 1969; (compiler with Sune Askaner) *Litteratur: Konst och musik,* Laromedelsforlaget, 1969.

(Compiler with Ulf Hard af Segerstad) *Samhaallsfraagor: Planering ocho miljoe,* Laromedelsforlaget, 1971; *Present Trends and Future Developments in Education: A European Perspective,* Ontario Institute for Studies in Education, 1971; *Social Background and Educational Career: Research Perspectives on Equality of Educational Opportunity,* Organization for Economic Co-operation and Development, 1972; *Skolans kris ocha andra uppsatser om utbildning,* Almqvist & Wiksell, 1972; *Svensk skola i internationell belysning: naturorienterande amnen,* Almqvist & Wiksel, 1973; *Talent, Equality and Meritocracy,* Nijhoff, 1974; *The Learning Society,* Methuen, 1974; *Social Influences on Educational Attainment,* Organization for Economic Co-operation and Development, 1975; *Universiteten och forskningen,* Natur och Kultur, 1975.

Editor, *Scandinavian Encyclopedia of Psychology and Education;* member, international board of consultants, *World Book Encyclopedia.*

WORK IN PROGRESS: The Future Role of the School as an Institution, for Methuen.

SIDELIGHTS: Torsten Husen is competent in French and German in addition to English. *Avocational interests:* Collecting old books.

* * *

HUSTVEDT, Lloyd (Merlyn) 1922-

PERSONAL: Born April 18, 1922, in Cannon Falls, Minn.; son of Lars and Mathilda (Underdahl) Hustvedt; married Ester Vegan, 1954; children: Siri, Liv, Astrid, Ingrid. *Education:* St. Olaf College, B.A., 1949; graduate study at University of Minnesota, 1949-50, and University of Oslo, 1950-51; University of Wisconsin, Ph.D., 1958. *Religion:* Lutheran. *Home:* Route 1, Northfield, Minn. 55057. *Office:* Department of Norwegian, St. Olaf College, Northfield, Minn. 55057.

CAREER: Luther College, Decorah, Iowa, assistant professor of Norwegian, 1951-54; St. Olaf College, Northfield, Minn., assistant professor, 1954-61, associate professor, 1961-67, professor of Norwegian, 1969—, chairman of department, 1963-67. Visiting summer lecturer at University of Minnesota, 1966. *Military service:* U.S. Army, 1943-46; became sergeant. *Member:* Modern Language Association of America, American-Scandinavian Foundation, Norwegian-American Historical Association (executive secretary), Society for the Advancement of Scandinavian Study, American Association of University Professors. *Awards, honors:* McKnight Prize in literature, 1967, for *Rasmus Bjorn Anderson;* Fulbright research scholar, Iceland, 1968.

WRITINGS: Rasmus Bjorn Anderson: Pioneer Scholar, Norwegian-American Historical Association, 1966.

* * *

HUTCHINS, Francis Gilman 1939-
(Frank Madison)

PERSONAL: Born October 29, 1939, in Berea, Ky.; son of Francis S. (a college president) and Louise (Gilman) Hutchins. *Education:* Harvard University, B.A., 1960, M.A., 1963, Ph.D., 1966. *Home:* 64 West Rutland Square, Boston, Mass. 02118.

CAREER: Harvard University, Cambridge, Mass., instructor in government, 1966-73; Institute for Advanced Study, Princeton, N.J., member, 1973-74. *Awards, honors:* Guggenheim Memorial fellow, 1974-75.

WRITINGS: The Illusion of Permanence: British Imperialism in India, Princeton University Press, 1967; (under pseudonym Frank Madison) *A View from the Floor: The Journal of a U.S. Senate Page Boy,* Prentice-Hall, 1967; *India's Revolution: Gandhi and the Quit India Movement,* Harvard University Press, 1973.

* * *

HUTCHISON, William Robert 1930-

PERSONAL: Born May 21, 1930, in San Francisco, Calif.; son of Ralph Cooper (a college president) and Harriet (Thompson) Hutchison; married Virginia Quay, August 16, 1952; children: Joseph Cooper, Catherine Eaton, Margaret Sidney, Elizabeth Quay. *Education:* Hamilton College, B.A., 1951; Oxford University, B.A., 1953, M.A., 1957; Yale University, Ph.D., 1956. *Politics:* Democrat. *Religion:* Society of Friends. *Home:* 966 Memorial Dr., Cambridge, Mass. 02138. *Office:* Divinity School, Harvard University, Cambridge, Mass. 02138.

CAREER: Hunter College (now of the City University of New York), New York, N.Y., instructor in history, 1956-58; American University, Washington, D.C., associate professor, 1958-64, professor of history and American studies, 1964-68; Harvard University, Cambridge, Mass., Charles Warren Professor of the History of Religion in America, 1968—, master of Winthrop House, 1974—. Visiting associate professor, University of Wisconsin, 1963-64; Danforth associate, 1968. Lecturer, U.S. Department of State Foreign Service Institute, 1960-68; editorial consultant to UNESCO, 1962-72; lecturer in Peace Corps Training Programs, 1962-66, and to business groups and foreign officials. Member of Melcher Prize Award Committee, 1970—. Trustee, Cambridge Friends School.

MEMBER: American Historical Association, Organization of American Historians, American Studies Association (president of Chesapeake chapter, 1968), American Society of Church History, Society for Religion in Higher Education (fellow), Unitarian Historical Society, American Association of University Professors, Phi Beta Kappa. *Awards, honors:* Fulbright scholarships, 1951-52, 1952-53; Brewer Prize of American Society of Church History for manuscript of *Transcendentalist Ministers,* 1957; Guggenheim fellowship, 1960; American Philosophical Society grants-in-aid, 1962, 1965; fellow, Charles Warren Center for Studies in American History, 1966-67; M.A., Harvard University, 1968.

WRITINGS: (Contributor) *The Utilization of Teaching Resources,* Studies in Higher Education, 1959; *The Transcendentalist Ministers: Church Reform in the New England Renaissance,* Yale University Press, 1959; (contributor) *Learning and the Professors,* American Council on Education, 1968; (editor) *American Protestant Thought: The Liberal Era,* Harper, 1968; *How New is the New Radicalism?,* American University, 1968; (compiler, contributor, and editorial consultant) *History of the Scientific and Cultural Development of Mankind,* Volume V, Laffont (Paris), 1969; (contributor) *American Civilization: Readings in the Cultural and Intellectual History of the United States,* Scott, Foresman, 1972; (contributor) Brian Barbour, editor, *American Transcendentalism: An Anthology of Criticism,* University of Notre Dame Press, 1973; (contributor) John K. Fairbanks, editor, *The Missionary Enterprise in China and America,* Harvard University Press, 1974; *The Modernist Impulse in American Protestantism,* Harvard University Press, 1976.

Author of biographical script, "William Ellery Channing," for television "Hall of Fame" series, 1959. Contributor to *Encyclopaedia Britannica* and *Dictionary of American Biography.* Contributor to educational, theological, and history journals, and to other periodicals, and to yearbooks and the proceedings of learned societies.

WORK IN PROGRESS: "American Religious Expansionism"; "The Ideology of American Protestant Missions."

AVOCATIONAL INTERESTS: Music, sports, camping, travel.

* * *

HUTHMACHER, J. Joseph 1929-

PERSONAL: Surname is pronounced Hut-mock-er; born November 1, 1929, in Trenton, N.J.; son of Jacob John (driver for a bakery) and Matilda (Goehrig) Huthmacher; married Marilyn Catana (an office manager), June 22, 1957; children: David James. *Education:* Rutgers University, B.A., 1951; Harvard University, M.A., 1952, Ph.D., 1957.

Politics: Democrat. *Home:* 47 The Horseshoe, Covered Bridge Farms, Newark, Del. 19711. *Office:* Department of History, University of Delaware, Newark, Del. 19711.

CAREER: Ohio State University, Columbus, instructor in history, 1956-57; Georgetown University, Washington, D.C., instructor, 1957-59, assistant professor, 1959-63, associate professor of history, 1963-66; Rutgers University, New Brunswick, N.J., professor of history, 1966-70; University of Delaware, Newark, Richards Professor of American History, 1970—. Visiting professor, Columbia University, 1968-69. *Member:* American Historical Association (chairman of Feature Films Project, 1967-72), Organization of American Historians, American Association of University Professors, Southern Historical Association, Immigrant History Group, Historians Film Committee, Fellows in American Studies, Phi Beta Kappa, Phi Alpha Theta. *Awards, honors:* American Council of Learned Societies faculty research fellowship, 1961-62; Eagleton Foundation research fellowship, 1963.

WRITINGS: Massachusetts People and Politics, 1919-1933, Harvard University Press, 1959; *Twentieth-Century America: An Interpretation with Readings,* Allyn & Bacon, 1966; *American History Transparencies,* Ginn, 1967; *A Nation of Newcomers: Ethnic Minority Groups in American History,* Dell, 1967; (with Vincent P. De Santis) *America Past and Present: An Interpretation with Readings,* Allyn & Bacon, 1968; *Senator Robert F. Wagner and the Rise of Urban Liberalism,* Atheneum, 1968.

The Truman Years: The Reconstruction of Postwar America, Dryden, 1973; *Trial by War and Depression: 1917-1941,* Allyn & Bacon, 1973; (editor with Warren Susman) *Herbert Hoover and the Crisis of American Capitalism,* Schenkman, 1973; (editor with Susman) *Wilson's Diplomacy: An International Symposium,* Schenkman, 1973. General editor, ''From Colony to Global Power: A History of the United States in Six Volumes,'' Allyn & Bacon. Contributor of articles and reviews to history journals.

WORK IN PROGRESS: Seedtime of Social Change: The Home Front during World War II; The Kennedy Assassination, for Wiley.

BIOGRAPHICAL/CRITICAL SOURCES: Arthur Mann, *The Progressive Era,* Holt, 1963; Gerald Grob and George Billias, *Interpretations of American History,* Free Press, 1971.†

*   *   *

HUTTON, J(oseph) Bernard 1911-

PERSONAL: Born July 7, 1911, in Bohemia; son of Frederick William (a businessman) and Margaret (Anton) Hutton; married Ellen Kohl, October 10, 1940 (died, 1950); married Pearl Gold (a company director), December 12, 1950; children: (first marriage) Thomas Edward, Marion Margaret; (second marriage) Harold Frederick. *Education:* University of Berlin, degree in literature. *Home:* 16 Beehive Lane, South Ferring, Worthing, West Sussex BN1Z 5NN, England.

CAREER: Press and cultural attache, Czechoslovak Embassy, London, England. Diplomatic and special correspondent, Thomson Newspapers, Free-lance writer and journalist. Broadcaster, lecturer, and psychic researcher. Guest lecturer on economics and politics, University of Moscow, 1936-37. *Member:* International Federation of Journalists, Society of Authors, National Union of Journalists, Society for Psychical Research, Paternosters, Monday

Club. *Awards, honors:* Honorary degree, University of Moscow, 1936; Military Cross, 1943; Knight of Mark Twain, 1973; Man of Achievement, Cambridge University, 1973.

WRITINGS: Frogman Spy, Obolensky, 1960 (published in England as *Frogman Extraordinary,* Neville Spearman, 1960); *Danger from Moscow,* Neville Spearman, 1960; *School for Spies: The ABC of How Russia's Secret Service Operates,* Neville Spearman, 1961, Coward, 1962; *Stalin, the Miraculous Georgian,* Neville Spearman, 1961; (with Jack Fishman) *The Private Life of Josif Stalin,* W. H. Allen, 1962; *The Traitor Trade,* Obolensky, 1963; *Out of This World,* Psychic Press, 1965, published as *On the Other Side of Reality,* Award Books, 1969; *Healing Hands,* W. H. Allen, 1966, McKay, 1967; *Commander Crabb Is Alive,* Award Books, 1968; (with Liam Nolan) *The Life of Smetana: The Pain and the Glory,* Harrap, 1968; *Struggle in the Dark: How Russian and Other Iron Curtain Spies Operate* (sequel to *School for Spies*), Harrap, 1969.

The Fake Defector, Howard Baker, 1970; *Hess: The Man and His Mission,* Bruce & Watson, 1970, Macmillan, 1971; *The Great Illusion* (autobiography), Bruce & Watson, 1970; *Women Spies,* W. H. Allen, 1971, published as *Women in Espionage,* Macmillan, 1972; *The Subverters,* Arlington House, 1972 (published in England as *The Subverters of Liberty,* W. H. Allen, 1972); *Lost Freedom,* Bruce & Watson, 1973; *The Healing Power,* Frewin, 1975; *Step into the Unknown: A Study of All Aspects of Parapsychology,* Frewin, 1976.

WORK IN PROGRESS: Take Your Pickism: A Guide to Understanding the Many and Varied 'isms, for Harrap; work on press, radio, and television series.

SIDELIGHTS: J. Bernard Hutton speaks German, Czech, Slovak, and Russian, and he understands other languages. *Avocational interests:* Classical music, travel.

*   *   *

HUXLEY, George 1932-

PERSONAL: Born September 23, 1932, in Leicester, England; son of Leonard George Holden (former vice-chancellor of Australian National University; knighted in 1964) and Ella Mary (Copeland) Huxley; married Davina Best, 1957; children: three daughters. *Education:* Magdalen College, Oxford, B.A., 1955, M.A., 1959. *Office:* Queen's University, Belfast, Northern Ireland.

CAREER: Oxford University, All Souls College, Oxford, England, fellow, 1955-61; Queen's University of Belfast, Belfast, Northern Ireland, professor of Greek, 1962—. Visiting lecturer at Harvard University, 1958-59, and 1961-62. Assistant director of British School of Archaeology at Athens, 1956-58. *Military service:* Royal Engineers, commissioned, 1951. *Member:* Royal Irish Academy, Society of Antiquaries (fellow), Athenaeum Club (London). *Awards, honors:* Cromer Greek Prize of British Academy, 1963.

WRITINGS: Achaeans and Hittites [Oxford], 1960; *Crete and the Luwians* [Oxford], 1961; *Early Sparta,* Harvard University Press, 1962; (contributor) Michael Grant, editor, *The Birth of Western Civilization,* McGraw, 1964; *The Early Ionians,* Humanities, 1966; *Greek Epic Poetry: From Eumelos to Panyassis,* Harvard University Press, 1969; (editor with J. N. Coldstream) *Kythera: Excavations and Studies Conducted by the University of Pennsylvania Museum and the British School of Athens,* Noyes Press, 1973; *Pindar's Vision of the Past,* [Belfast], 1975. Contributor of articles on Greek literature, history and archaeology to learned journals, and articles on railway subjects to other periodicals.

WORK IN PROGRESS: Articles on Byzantine history and literature.

AVOCATIONAL INTERESTS: Railway history and operation, especially in Great Britain and Ireland.

* * *

HYDE, Simeon, Jr. 1919-

PERSONAL: Born February 25, 1919, in Charleston, S.C.; son of Simeon (a lawyer) and Isabella (Cheves) Hyde; married Ann Olcott Mills, October 21, 1942; children: Elizabeth A. (Mrs. Edward H. Washburn), Simeon, III, Olcott. *Education:* Princeton University, A.B., 1941; Harvard University, A.M., 1947; graduate study, University of New Mexico, 1973-75. *Home:* 316 15th St., Northwest, Albuquerque, N.M. 87104.

CAREER: Cambridge School, Weston, Mass., teacher of English, 1947-50; Phillips Academy, Andover, Mass., teacher of English, beginning 1950, dean of the faculty, 1968-71, acting headmaster, 1971-72, associate headmaster, 1972-73. *Military service:* U.S. Naval Reserve, active duty, 1941-45; became lieutenant commander.

WRITINGS: (With William H. Brown) *Composition of the Essay,* Addison-Wesley, 1967.

WORK IN PROGRESS: Designing housing and service centers for the elderly.

* * *

HYGEN, Johan B(ernitz) 1911-

PERSONAL: Born July 16, 1911, in Oslo, Norway; son of Johannes (a clergyman) and Borghild (Dahl) Hygen; married Ragnhild Wolner, June 14, 1941; children: Hans Wolner, Elisabeth, Anne-Sophie. *Education:* University of Oslo, cand.theol., 1935, dr.theol., 1948; also studied at Universities of Berlin, Zurich, Tuebingen, and Leipzig, 1936-39. *Home:* Jacob Aallsgate 30, Oslo 3, Norway. *Office:* University of Oslo, Blindern, Oslo 3, Norway.

CAREER: Clergyman of Evangelical-Lutheran Church. University of Oslo, Oslo, Norway, assistant professor, 1939-42, associate professor, 1942-53, professor of Christian ethics and philosophy of religion, 1954—. Pastor in Oslo, Norway, 1940-45.

WRITINGS: Moralen og Guds rike, Land og Kirke, 1948; *Albert Schweitzer's tanker om kulturen,* Land og Kirke, 1954; *Elementaer etikk,* Fabritius, 1958; *Kunst, livssyn og moral,* Land og Kirke, 1958, translation by Harris E. Kaasa published as *Morality and the Muses: Christian Faith and Art Forms,* Augsburg, 1965; *Guds allmakt og det ondes problem,* Universitetsforlaget, 1973.

* * *

HYMAN, Herbert H(iram) 1918-

PERSONAL: Born March 3, 1918, in New York, N.Y.; son of David Elihu (a physician) and Gisella (Mautner) Hyman; married Helen Raphael Kandel (a writer), September 30, 1945; children: Lisa, David, Alex. *Education:* Columbia University, A.B., 1939, A.M., 1940, Ph.D., 1942. *Religion:* Jewish. *Home:* 38 Woodside Ave., Westport, Conn. 06880. *Office:* Department of Sociology, Wesleyan University, Middletown, Conn. 06457.

CAREER: U.S. Department of Agriculture, Washington, D.C., social science analyst, 1942; U.S. Office of War Information, Washington, D.C., public opinion analyst, 1942-44; U.S. Strategic Bomb Survey, Morale Division, assistant director of field surveys in Germany and Japan, 1944-45; Brooklyn College (now Brooklyn College of the City University of New York), Brooklyn, N.Y., assistant professor of psychology, 1945-47; National Opinion Research Center, Chicago, Ill., research associate, 1947-50; University of Oslo, Oslo, Norway, Fulbright professor, 1950-51; Columbia University, New York, N.Y., assistant professor, 1951-53, associate professor, 1953-56, professor of sociology, 1956-69, chairman of department, 1965-68; Wesleyan University, Middletown, Conn., professor of sociology, 1969—. Visiting professor at University of California, Berkeley, 1950, and University of Ankara, 1957-58; program director, United Nations Research Institute, Geneva, Switzerland, 1964-65.

MEMBER: American Sociological Association (chairman of methodology section, 1962-63; chairman of psychology section, 1970-71), American Association for Public Opinion Research (president, 1959-60), Society for the Psychological Study of Social Issues (fellow; executive council member), Sociological Research Association (president, 1974). *Awards, honors:* Ford Foundation special grant, 1952; Guggenheim fellow, 1957-58; Julian Woodward Memorial Award of American Association for Public Opinion Research.

WRITINGS: (Senior author) *Interviewing in Social Research,* University of Chicago Press, 1954; *Survey Design and Analysis,* Macmillan, 1955; *Political Socialization,* Macmillan, 1959; (with Charles Wright and Terence Hopkins) *Applications of Methods of Evaluation,* University of California Press, 1962; (editor with Eleanor Singer) *Readings in Reference Group Theory and Research,* Free Press, 1968; *Secondary Analysis of Sample Surveys,* Wiley, 1972; (with Wright and John Reed) *The Enduring Effects of Education,* University of Chicago Press, 1975. Member of editorial boards at various times, *Public Opinion Quarterly, Sociometry, Journal of Abnormal and Social Psychology,* and *Journal of Social Issues.*

WORK IN PROGRESS: A monograph on the social world of the totally blind, completion expected in 1976; a collection of readings and a systematic essay to revive *The Scientific Study of the Social Sentiments,* 1977.

SIDELIGHTS: Herbert Hyman has lived, taught, or done research in Norway, England, Germany, Austria, Japan, Italy, and Turkey.

* * *

HYMAN, Ronald T. 1933-

PERSONAL: Born October 16, 1933, in Chicago, Ill.; son of Maurice H. (a salesman) and Matilda (Grossman) Hyman; married Suzanne Linda Katz, February 13, 1958; children: Jonathan, Elana, Rachel. *Education:* University of Miami, Coral Gables, Fla., B.A., 1955; Vanderbilt University and George Peabody College for Teachers, M.A.T., 1956; Columbia University, Ed.D., 1965. *Politics:* Liberal. *Religion:* Jewish. *Home:* 227 Lincoln Ave., Highland Park, N.J. 08904. *Office:* Graduate School of Education, Rutgers University, New Brunswick, N.J. 08903.

CAREER: Public school teacher, 1956-62; Queens College of the City University of New York, Flushing, N.Y., assistant professor, 1964-66; Rutgers University, New Brunswick, N.J., associate professor, 1966-74, professor of education, 1974—. Visiting summer professor at Hofstra

University, 1965 and 1966. *Member:* Association for Supervision and Curriculum Development, American Educational Research Association, National Society for the Study of Education, National Council for the Social Studies, American Association of University Professors, Curriculum Theory Network, Association of Teacher Educators.

WRITINGS: The Principles of Contemporary Education, Monarch, 1966; (with A. A. Bellack, H. M. Kliebard, and F. L. Smith) *The Language of the Classroom,* Teachers College Press, 1966; (editor) *Teaching: Vantage Points for Study,* Lippincott, 1968, 2nd edition, 1974; *Ways of Teaching,* Lippincott, 1970, 2nd edition, 1974; (editor) *Contemporary Thought on Teaching,* Prentice-Hall, 1971; (editor with Maurie Hillson) *Change and Innovation in Elementary and Secondary Organization,* 2nd edition (Hyman was not associated with previous edition), Holt, 1971; (editor) *Approaches in Curriculum,* Prentice-Hall, 1973; (editor with Samuel L. Baily and contributor) *Perspectives on Latin America,* Macmillan, 1974; *Administrators Handbook of Supervision and Evaluation Methods,* Prentice-Hall, 1975. Co-general editor of "Latin America Social Studies" series for Macmillan, 1974-75. Contributor of articles and reviews to education journals.

WORK IN PROGRESS: A book, *The Prisoner's Dilemma.*

* * *

IKE, Nobutaka 1916-

PERSONAL: Born June 6, 1916, in Seattle, Wash.; son of Yasuji and Tsuya (Tanaka) Ike; married Tai Inui (a librarian), August 23, 1942; children: Linda, Brian. *Education:* University of Washington, Seattle, B.A., 1940, graduate student, 1940-42; Johns Hopkins University, Ph.D., 1949. *Politics:* Democrat. *Home:* 621 Alvarado Row, Stanford, Calif. 94305. *Office:* Department of Political Science, Stanford University, Stanford, Calif. 94305.

CAREER: Johns Hopkins University, Baltimore, Md., lecturer in Walter Hines Page School of International Relations, 1948-49; Stanford University, Stanford, Calif., curator of Japanese collections at Hoover Institution on War, Revolution, and Peace, 1949-58, associate professor, 1958-64, professor of political science, 1964—. *Member:* American Political Science Association, Association for Asian Studies. *Awards, honors:* Ford Foundation and Rockefeller Foundation fellowships.

WRITINGS: Beginnings of Political Democracy in Japan, Johns Hopkins Press, 1950; *Japanese Politics,* Knopf, 1957; (translator) *Japan's Decision for War,* Stanford University Press, 1967; *Japanese Politics: Patron-Client Democracy,* Knopf, 1972; *Japan the New Superstate,* Freeman, 1974. Associate editor, *Far Eastern Quarterly,* 1950-55.

WORK IN PROGRESS: A Theory of Japanese Democracy.

* * *

INGLIS, James 1927-

PERSONAL: Surname rhymes with "jingles"; born August 12, 1927, in Edinburgh, Scotland; son of Neil McNeill (an engineer) and Jean (Rourke) Inglis; married Lily Brandl (an architect), September 5, 1953; children: Jane, Katrin. *Education:* University of Edinburgh, M.A. (first class honors), 1952; University of London, Dip.Psychol., 1953,

Ph.D., 1958. *Home:* 23 Sydenham St., Kingston, Ontario, Canada K7L 3G8. *Office:* Department of Psychology, Queen's University, Kingston, Ontario, Canada.

CAREER: University of London, Institute of Psychiatry, London, England, assistant lecturer, 1953-54, lecturer in psychology, 1955-59; Queen's University, Kingston, Ontario, assistant professor, 1959-61, associate professor of psychology, 1961-65; Temple University Medical School, Philadelphia, Pa., professor of psychology, department of behavioral science, 1966-68; Queen's University, Kingston, professor of psychology, 1968—. *Military service:* Royal Air Force, 1945-48. *Member:* American Psychopathological Association, American Psychological Association (fellow), American Association for the Advancement of Science (fellow), British Psychological Society (fellow), Canadian Psychological Association (fellow), Experimental Psychology Society (United Kingdom), Royal College of Psychiatrists (corresponding associate), Gerontological Society (fellow), Biofeedback Research Society. *Awards, honors:* D.Sc., University of London, 1971.

WRITINGS: The Scientific Study of Abnormal Behavior, Aldine, 1966; (contributor) C. G. Costello, editor, *Symptoms of Psychopathology,* Wiley, 1970. Contributor to professional journals. Editor, *Canadian Journal of Behavioural Science,* 1970-74.

WORK IN PROGRESS: Electroconvulsive Therapy and Human Behaviour, for Pergamon.

* * *

INNES, Brian 1928-

PERSONAL: Born May 4, 1928, in London, England; son of Stanley George (a civil servant) and Laura (Thornton) Innes; married Felicity Wilson, October 4, 1956 (divorced); children: Simon Alexander. *Education:* King's College, London, B.Sc., 1949; also studied at Chelsea School of Art, Central School of Arts and Crafts, and London School of Printing. *Home:* 8 Cambridge Gate Mews, London N.W.1, England. *Agent:* Jonathan Clowes Ltd., 19 Jeffrey's Place, London NW1 9PP, England.

CAREER: Benn Brothers Ltd. (publishers), London, England, assistant editor of *Chemical Age,* 1953-55; Maclean-Hunter (publishers), London, assistant editor of *British Printer,* 1955-59, associate editor, 1959-60; Paul Hamlyn Ltd. (publishers), London, art director, 1960-62; Animated Graphic and Publicity Designers, London, director, 1963-65; Immediate Books (book production), London, proprietor, 1965—. Production consultant, Bancroft & Co. Ltd.; design consultant, BPC Publishing Ltd. *Member:* Institute of Printing (associate), Society of Authors, National Union of Journalists, Institute of Journalists.

WRITINGS: The Book of Pirates, Bancroft & Co., 1966; *The Book of Spies: 4000 Years of Cloak and Dagger,* Bancroft & Co., 1967, Grosset, 1969; *The Book of Revolutions,* Bancroft & Co., 1967; *The Book of Outlaws,* Bancroft & Co., 1968; *My Best Book of Flight,* Purnell, 1970; *The Saga of the Railways,* Purnell, 1973. Co-editor, "Facts of Print" series, Vista Books, 1958. Contributor to *Encyclopaedia Britannica,* 1964; also contributor to *Scotsman* and other periodicals.

WORK IN PROGRESS: Man and His Art, for Card Publications; art director for "Cordon Bleu Cookery Course" and *Man, Myth and Magic,* both for BPC; art director of *Pictorial Knowledge,* for International Learning Systems Corp.†

IRION, Mary Jean 1922-

PERSONAL: Surname is pronounced *Ear*-e-on; born November 6, 1922, in Newport, Ky.; daughter of V. A. (a public utilities consultant) and Mary (McNeal) McElfresh; married Paul E. Irion (a professor), August 29, 1944; children: Mark S., Lisa N. *Education:* Millersville State College, B.A. (magna cum laude), 1966, graduate study, 1966-71. *Politics:* Democrat. *Religion:* United Church of Christ. *Home:* 149 Kready Ave., Millersville, Pa. 17551.

CAREER: Teacher at Lancaster Country Day School, Lancaster, Pa., 1968-73; Franklin and Marshall College, Lancaster, teacher in "Et Cetera" Program, 1975. Teacher at retreats and conferences on religion and poetry.

WRITINGS: From the Ashes of Christianity, Lippincott, 1968; *Yes, World: A Mosaic of Meditation,* Baron, 1970. Columnist for *United Church Herald;* contributor of poetry to *Ladies' Home Journal, Literary Review, Christian Century, Trace,* and other periodicals.

WORK IN PROGRESS: Carrying Soup and Bread, a collection of poems; research on Thomas Hardy.

SIDELIGHTS: Mrs. Irion told *CA:* "[I am] particularly interested in the area of myth and symbol. Here is the meeting ground for theology and poetry, and the means for their vitality at the core of life both personal and communal."

* * *

IRION, Paul E(rnst) 1922-

PERSONAL: Surname is pronounced *Ear*-e-on; born July 15, 1922, in Akron, Ohio; son of Ernst F. (a minister) and Elsie (Schergens) Irion; married Mary Jean McElfresh (a writer), August 29, 1944; children: Mark S., Lisa N. *Education:* Elmhurst College, B.A., 1943; Eden Theological Seminary, B.D., 1945; University of Chicago, M.A., 1952, further study in theology, 1959-60. *Politics:* Democrat. *Home:* 149 Kready Ave., Millersville, Pa. 17551. *Office:* Lancaster Theological Seminary, Lancaster, Pa. 17603.

CAREER: Clergyman of United Church of Christ. Pastor in Tioga, Ill., 1945-50, in Long Grove, Ill., 1950-56; Evangelical Deaconess Hospital, St. Louis, Mo., chaplain, 1956-59; Lancaster Theological Seminary, Lancaster, Pa., professor of pastoral theology, 1959—. Housing chairman, Lancaster Human Relations Committee, 1966—; president of board of directors, Family and Children's Service of Lancaster, 1974—. *Member:* Institute of Pastoral Care, Association of Seminary Professors in the Practical Fields, Association for Clinical Pastoral Education, American Protestant Hospital Chaplains Association.

WRITINGS: The Funeral and the Mourners, Abingdon, 1954; *The Funeral: Vestige or Value?,* Abingdon, 1966; *Cremation,* Fortress, 1968; (contributor) William B. Oglesby, Jr., editor, *The New Shape of Pastoral Theology,* Abingdon, 1969; *A Manual and Guide for Those Who Conduct a Humanist Funeral,* Waverly, 1971; (contributor) Earl A. Grollman, editor, *Concerning Death,* Beacon Press, 1974. Guest editor of several special issues, *Pastoral Psychology.*

WORK IN PROGRESS: Research on the personal and interpersonal response to radical shifts in belief, conviction, philosophical understanding; the effect of secularization on the meaning of death.

AVOCATIONAL INTERESTS: Music, printing, collecting historical autograph letters and documents.

ISRAEL, John (Warren) 1935-

PERSONAL: Born June 16, 1935, in New York, N.Y.; son of Bert (a jobber) and Audrey (Schuman) Israel; married Mary Horn (a teacher), August 25, 1957; children: Melinda, Tania. *Education:* University of Wisconsin, B.S., 1955; Harvard University, A.M., 1957, Ph.D., 1963. *Residence:* Charlottesville, Va. 22901. *Office:* Department of History, University of Virginia, Charlottesville, Va. 22901.

CAREER: Did research in Taiwan, 1959-62; Claremont Men's College, Claremont, Calif., assistant professor of history, 1963-68; University of Virginia, Charlottesville, associate professor, 1968—. Visiting scholar at East Asian Research Center, Harvard University, 1966-67, 1968. *Member:* Association for Asian Studies, American Association of University Professors, Phi Beta Kappa.

WRITINGS: Student Nationalism in China, 1927-1937, Stanford University Press, 1966; (with Donald W. Klein) *Rebels and Bureaucrats: China's December 9ers,* University of California Press, 1975. Contributor to *China Quarterly, Claremont Quarterly, New Republic, Daedalus,* and *Book World.*

WORK IN PROGRESS: Researching a book on Southwest Associated University (Kunming), 1938-1946.

* * *

JABAY, Earl 1925-

PERSONAL: Born March 30, 1925, in Lansing, Ill.; son of William (a farm manager) and Jennie (Eenigenburg) Jabay. *Education:* Calvin College, A.B., 1949; Calvin Theological Seminary, Th.B., 1952. *Home:* 62 East Somerset St., Raritan, N.J. 08869.

CAREER: Clergyman of Reformed Church in America; certified as clinically trained pastor by Council for Clinical Training, Inc.; New Jersey Neuro-Psychiatric Institute, Princeton, resident Protestant chaplain, 1959—. Lecturer in pastoral counseling at New Brunswick Theological Seminary and Princeton Theological Seminary.

WRITINGS: Search for Identity, Zondervan, 1967; *The God-Players,* Zondervan, 1969; *The Kingdom of Self,* Logas International, 1974.

* * *

JACKSON, Barbara Garvey Seagrave 1929-

PERSONAL: Born September 27, 1929, in Normal, Ill.; daughter of Neil Ford (a university professor) and Eva (Burkhart) Garvey. *Education:* University of Illinois, B.M. (with highest honors), 1950; University of Rochester, M.M., 1952; Stanford University, Ph.D., 1959. *Home:* 235 Baxter Lane, Fayetteville, Ark. 72701. *Office:* Music Department, University of Arkansas, Fayetteville, Ark. 72701.

CAREER: University of Arkansas, Fayetteville, instructor in music, 1954-56; Los Angeles (Calif.) public schools, special music teacher, 1956-57; Arkansas Polytechnic College, Russellville, assistant professor, 1957-61; University of Arkansas, assistant professor, 1961-62, associate professor, 1962-69, professor of music, 1969—. Broadcaster of radio series "American Music for the Bicentennial," on KUAF-FM (Fayetteville). *Member:* American String Teachers Association, American Musicological Society, College Music Society, Music Teachers National Association, Sigma Alpha Iota. *Awards, honors:* Southern Fellowships Fund grant, 1959.

WRITINGS: (With Bruce Benward) *Practical Beginning Theory,* W. C. Brown, 1963, 3rd edition, 1976; (with Wesley Thomas) *The Songs of the Minnesingers* (including a recording), University of Illinois Press, 1966; (with Joel Berman) *Dictionary of Bowings,* American String Teachers Association, 1969; (with Thomas) *The Songs of the Minnesinger, Prince Wizlaw of Ruegen,* University of North Carolina Press, 1969.

WORK IN PROGRESS: Studies of early eighteenth-century violin music; *The Sonatas of Giovanni Antonio Piani* (1712).

* * *

JACKSON, Carlton (Luther) 1933-

PERSONAL: Born January 15, 1933, in Blount County, Ala.; son of Luther H. (a farmer) and Winnie (Forrester) Jackson; married Patricia Dow, 1954; children: Beverly, Daniel, Matthew, Hilary. *Education:* Birmingham-Southern College, B.A. and M.A., 1959; University of Georgia, Ph.D., 1963; Exeter College, Oxford, graduate study, 1966. *Religion:* Episcopalian. *Home:* 307 Leslie Dr., Bowling Green, Ky. 42101. *Office:* Western Kentucky University, Bowling Green, Ky. 42101.

CAREER: Birmingham Post Herald, Birmingham, Ala., reporter, 1956-57; teacher in Birmingham public schools, 1957-59; Western Kentucky University, Bowling Green, assistant professor, 1961-63, associate professor, 1963-67, professor of history, 1967—. Visiting summer professor at College of William and Mary, 1965, University of Maryland Overseas Program at Upper Heyford Air Force Base, England, 1966, and Tufts University, 1968, 1970; Fulbright lecturer in U.S. history, University of Bangalore, India, 1971-72; Fulbright lecturer in American studies, Islamabad University, Pakistan, 1974-75. *Military service:* U.S. Air Force, 1951-54; became staff sergeant. *Member:* American Association of University Professors, Southern Historical Society, Phi Alpha Theta.

WRITINGS: Presidential Vetoes, 1792-1945, University of Georgia Press, 1967; (co-author) *Foundations of Freedom,* Laidlaw Brothers, 1973; (co-author) *Challenge and Change,* Laidlaw Brothers, 1973; *Zane Grey,* Twayne, 1973; (co-author) *Two Centuries of Progress,* Laidlaw Brothers, 1974; *J. I. Rodale: Apostle of Nonconformity,* Pyramid Press, 1974. Contributor of articles to professional journals, and short stories to *Link* and *Southern Humanities Review.*

WORK IN PROGRESS: The Great Lili: A Footnote to World War II.

* * *

JACKSON, Gabriel 1921-

PERSONAL: Born March 10, 1921, in Mount Vernon, N.Y.; son of Walter (an engineer) and Julia (Goldberg) Jackson; married Elizabeth K. Riddle (a professor), December 23, 1948; children: Katharine, Rachel. *Education:* Harvard University, A.B. (magna cum laude), 1942; Stanford University, M.A., 1950; University of Toulouse, Ph.D., 1952. *Office:* Department of History, University of California at San Diego, La Jolla, Calif. 92037.

CAREER: Teacher of English and Spanish at Putney School, Putney, Vt., 1946-49, and history at Goddard College, Plainfield, Vt., 1952-55; Wellesley College, Wellesley, Mass., instructor, 1955-56, assistant professor of history, 1956-60; Knox College, Galesburg, Ill., assistant professor,

1962-63, associate professor of history, 1963-65; University of California at San Diego, La Jolla, professor of history, 1965—. Former teacher of flute, and flutist with Vermont State Symphony. Consultant to Hispanic Foundation and Library of Congress. *Military service:* U.S. Army, Military Intelligence, 1942-45; served in Pacific; received direct commission as second lieutenant, 1945.

MEMBER: American Historical Association, American Association of University Professors, Phi Beta Kappa. *Awards, honors:* Fulbright fellowship to University of Toulouse, 1950, and grant for research in Spain, 1960; Social Science Research Council fellowship, 1961; Herbert Baxter Adams Prize, American Historical Association, 1966, for *The Spanish Republic and the Civil War;* American Council of Learned Societies fellowship, 1967.

WRITINGS: The Spanish Republic and the Civil War, Princeton University Press, 1965; (editor) *The Spanish Civil War: Domestic Crisis or International Conspiracy,* Heath, 1967; *Historian's Quest,* Knopf, 1969; *The Making of Medieval Spain,* Thames & Hudson, 1972; *A Concise History of the Spanish Civil War,* Thames & Hudson, 1974. Contributor to historical journals, *Nation, Commonweal,* and *Estudios de Historia Moderna.*

WORK IN PROGRESS: A cultural history of Spain, c. 1840-1940, completion expected in 1978.

SIDELIGHTS: Gabriel Jackson speaks, reads, and writes French and Spanish; he reads German and Catalan. *The Spanish Republic and the Civil War* has appeared in Spanish and Italian editions.

* * *

JACKSON, Kenneth T. 1939-

PERSONAL: Born July 27, 1939, in Memphis, Tenn.; son of Kenneth Gordon (an accountant) and Elizabeth (Willins) Jackson; married Barbara Ann Bruce (a teacher), August 25, 1962; children: Kevan Parish, Kenneth Gordon II. *Education:* Memphis State University, B.A., 1961; University of Chicago, M.A., 1963, Ph.D., 1966. *Religion:* Episcopalian. *Office:* Department of History, Columbia University, New York, N.Y. 10027.

CAREER: Wittenberg University, Springfield, Ohio, lecturer in history, 1967-68; Columbia University, New York, N.Y., assistant professor, 1968-71, associate professor, 1971-76, professor of history, 1976—. Visiting professor, Princeton University, 1974. *Military service:* U.S. Air Force, research and development director at Air Force Institute of Technology, 1965-68; became captain. *Member:* American Historical Association, Organization of American Historians, Society of American Historians (fellow), American Association of University Professors. *Awards, honors:* Woodrow Wilson fellowship, 1961-62, 1964-65; National Endowment for the Humanities fellowship, 1969-70; American Council of Learned Societies fellowship, 1972-73.

WRITINGS: The Chicago Council on Foreign Relations: A Record of Forty Years, Chicago Council on Foreign Relations, 1963; *The Ku Klux Klan in the City, 1915-1930,* Oxford University Press, 1967; (editor with Leonard Dinnerstein) *American Vistas,* Oxford University Press, 1971; (editor with Stanley K. Schultz) *Cities in American History,* Knopf, 1972.

WORK IN PROGRESS: A history of annexation and suburbanization in the United States, completion expected in 1977.

JACKSON, Philip W(esley) 1928-

PERSONAL: Born December 2, 1928, in Vineland, N.J.; son of Raymond and Estelle (Sword) Jackson; married Josephine Dandrea, May 1, 1948; children: Nancy, David, Steven. Education: Glassboro State College, B.S., 1951; Temple University, M.Ed., 1952; Columbia University, Ph.D., 1954. Office: Department of Education, University of Chicago, Chicago, Ill. 60637.

CAREER: Wayne State University, Detroit, Mich., instructor, became assistant professor of educational psychology, 1954-55; University of Chicago, Chicago, Ill., assistant professor, 1955-59, associate professor, 1959-62, professor of education and human development, 1962—, chairman of department, 1973—, David Lee Shillinglaw Distinguished Service Professor, 1973—, principal of laboratory nursery school, 1966-70, director of laboratory schools, 1970-75, dean of Graduate School of Education, 1973—. Fellow, Center for Advanced Study in the Behavioral Sciences, 1962-63, Center for Policy Study, 1973; visiting summer professor at University of Victoria, 1967, 1970, and Harvard University, 1972; Simon Visiting Professor of the Social Sciences, University of Manchester, 1968-69. Member of committee on learning and development, Social Science Research Council; member of national advisory board, University of Texas Research and Development Center; member of National Panel on High Schools and Adolescent Education. Military service: U.S. Naval Reserve, 1947-48. Member: American Psychological Association, Society for Research in Child Development (member of governing council), American Association for the Advancement of Science, American Educational Research Association, American Association of University Professors, National Academy of Education. Awards, honors: Distinguished Alumnus Award, Glassboro State College, 1970.

WRITINGS: (With J. W. Getzels) Creativity and Intelligence, Wiley, 1962; Life in Classrooms, Holt, 1968; The Teacher and the Machine, University of Pittsburgh Press, 1968. Author of monographs and articles. Member of editorial board, Psychology in the Schools; member of advisory board, Instructor.

*   *   *

JACKSON, William Vernon 1926-

PERSONAL: Born May 26, 1926, in Chicago, Ill.; son of William O. and Lillian (Scharenberg) Jackson. Education: Northwestern University, B.A. (summa cum laude), 1945; University of California, Berkeley, graduate student, 1945; Harvard University, A.M., 1948, Ph.D., 1952; University of Illinois, M.S. in L.S., 1951. Politics: Republican. Office: Vanderbilt University, Nashville, Tenn. 37235.

CAREER: High school teacher in Elmhurst, Ill., 1946-47; University of Illinois, Urbana, assistant professor and librarian of undergraduate library, 1952-58, associate professor of library science, 1958-62; University of Wisconsin-Madison, associate professor of Spanish and Portuguese, 1963-65; University of Pittsburgh, Pittsburgh, Pa., professor of library science and director of International Library Information Center, 1966-70; Vanderbilt University, Nashville, Tenn., professor of Spanish and Portuguese, 1970—; George Peabody College for Teachers, Nashville, professor of library science, 1970—. Fulbright research scholar in France, 1956-57; University of Cordoba, Cordoba, Argentina, Fulbright lecturer, 1958, advisor, 1970; advisor, National University of San Marcos, Lima, 1962,

1974; University of Antioquia, Medellin, Colombia, visiting professor, 1960, 1968, adviser to international executive council of Inter-American Library School, 1961-63. Visiting summer lecturer at University of Minnesota, 1954-56, Columbia University, 1960, Syracuse University, 1962, Simmons College, 1974, 1975. Consultant to U.S. Department of State on libraries in Argentina, 1956, in Brazil and Ecuador, 1959, in Latin America, 1961, 1962, 1967, and in Europe, 1962; consultant to Agency for International Development, 1965—, and to other public and private agencies.

MEMBER: American Library Association, Modern Language Association of America, Latin American Studies Association, American Association of Teachers of Spanish and Portuguese, Association of American Library Schools, Association of College and Research Libraries, Theatre Library Association, Bibliographical Society of America, Illinois Library Association, Pittsburgh Bibliophiles.

WRITINGS: Handbook of American Library Resources, Illini Union Bookstore, 1955, 2nd edition, 1962; Basic Library Techniques, Illini Union Bookstore, 1955; Studies in Library Resources, Illini Union Bookstore, 1958; Aspects of Librarianship in Latin America, Illini Union Bookstore, 1962; Library Guide for Brazilian Studies, University of Pittsburgh Book Center, 1964; The National Textbook Program and Libraries in Brazil, University of Pittsburgh Book Center, 1967; Resources of Research Libraries: A Selected Bibliography, University of Pittsburgh Book Center, 1969.

(With Paxton P. Price and Maria Sanz) Steps Toward the Future Development of a National Plan for Library Services in Colombia, Vanderbilt University Bookstore, 1971; (compiler) Latin American Collections, Vanderbilt University Bookstore, 1974; (author of introduction) Guide to the Research Collections of the New York Public Library, American Library Association, 1975. Also writer of reports to governmental and private agencies on work in Latin America. Contributor to professional journals. Member of editorial staff, Library Trends, 1958-62, and Encyclopedia of Library and Informational Sciences, 1971—; editor, Association of College and Research Libraries "Monograph Series," 1961-66.

WORK IN PROGRESS: A study on books and libraries in Latin America; contemporary Spanish theater; and comparative librarianship.

*   *   *

JACOB, Piers A(nthony) D(illingham) 1934-
(Piers Anthony)

PERSONAL: Born August 6, 1934, in Oxford, England; son of Alfred Bennis and Norma (Sherlock) Jacob; married Carol Marble (a computer programmer), June 23, 1956; children: Penelope Carolyn. Education: Goddard College, B.A., 1956; University of South Florida, Teaching Certificate, 1964. Politics: Independent. Religion: "No preference." Home: 800 75th Street N., St. Petersburg, Fla. 33710. Agent: (For foreign markets) E. J. Carnell, 17 Burwash Rd., London SE18 7QY, England.

CAREER: Electronic Communications, Inc., St. Petersburg, Fla., technical writer, 1959-62; free-lance writer, 1962-63; Admiral Farragut Academy, St. Petersburg, Fla., English teacher, 1965-66; free-lance writer, 1966—. Military service: U.S. Army, 1957-59. Member: Science Fiction Writers of America. Awards, honors: Pyramid/Fantasy & Science Fiction Contest winner, 1967, for manuscript of SOS the Rope.

WRITINGS—Under pseudonym Piers Anthony: *Chthon*, Ballantine, 1967; *Omnivore*, Ballantine, 1968; *SOS the Rope*, Pyramid Books, 1968; (with Robert E. Margroff) *The Ring*, Ace Books, 1968; *The Macroscope*, Avon, 1969; *Phthor*, Berkeley Publishing, 1975; *Neq the Sword*, Corgi, 1975; *Var the Stick*, Corgi, 1975. Contributor of short stories to science fiction magazines and other periodicals.

WORK IN PROGRESS: *Hasan*, an Arabic fantasy: *The Pretender*, an historical novel; research in paleontology for a science fiction novel, *Paleo;* research in world history and archaeology for a work of historical fiction.

SIDELIGHTS: Jacob told *CA*, "Major motivation as a writer has been my inability to quit writing, and my dissatisfaction with all other modes of employment."†

* * *

JACOBS, Harvey (Collins) 1915-

PERSONAL: Born September 6, 1915, in Trafalgar, Ind.; son of Ralph L. (a farmer) and Ruth (Ragsdale) Jacobs; married Florence Giddings, April 5, 1942; children: Phillip, Kenneth. *Education:* Franklin College of Indiana, B.A., 1938; Indiana University, A.M., 1952; graduate study at Northwestern University, 1957, and California State College (now University), Los Angeles, 1963. *Politics:* Independent. *Religion:* Baptist. *Home:* 700 North Alabama, Indianapolis, Ind. 46204. *Agent:* Malcolm Reiss, 559 Fifth Ave., New York, N.Y. 10017. *Office:* Indianapolis News, 307 North Pennsylvania St., Indianapolis, Ind. 46206.

CAREER: Newspaper reporter and columnist in Franklin, Ind., 1937-44; Franklin College of Indiana, Franklin, director of public relations, 1941-46, head of department of journalism, 1949-55; Rotary International, Evanston, Ill., assistant editor of *Rotarian*, 1955-56, head of Program Division, 1956-60, undersecretary, 1960-64; New Mexico State University, University Park, chairman of department of mass communications, 1964-74; *Indianapolis News*, Indianapolis, Ind., editor, 1974—.

MEMBER: Association for Education in Journalism, American Society of Newspaper Editors, National Council of Editorial Writers, National Education Association, Authors Guild, Indianapolis Press Club, Indiana Historical Society, Broadcast Pioneers, Sigma Delta Chi, Rotary International (president of Franklin club, 1949-50; district governor, 1954-55), Indianapolis Chamber of Commerce, Chicago Headline Club. *Awards, honors:* Gold Key Award from Columbia University for service to the scholastic press, 1954; Distinguished Alumnus Citation, Franklin College of Indiana, 1958; National Headliner Award, University of Oklahoma, 1970; Cooney Award, 1973; D.Litt., Sussex College, 1973, Franklin College of Indiana, 1974; Golden Crown Award, Columbia University, 1975.

WRITINGS: (Contributor) *Rural Community Organization*, Wiley, 1939; (contributor) *Journalism for Today*, Judson, 1952; *Rotary: 50 Years of Service*, Rotary International, 1955; (contributor) Lew Sarett and W. T. Foster, editors, *Basic Principles of Speech*, Riverside Editions, 1958; *Seven Paths to Peace*, Rotary International, 1959; *Adventure in Service*, Rotary International, 1961; *We Came Rejoicing*, Rand McNally, 1967. Writer of column syndicated in Indiana daily newspapers, 1938-44; contributor to magazines.

WORK IN PROGRESS: A book on group dynamics and industrial communications; a novel on rural life in the 1920's and 1930's; a handbook for program chairmen.

AVOCATIONAL INTERESTS: Music.

JACOBS, Jane 1916-

PERSONAL: Born May 4, 1916, in Scranton, Pa.; daughter of John Decker (a physician) and Bess (Robison) Butzner; married Robert Hyde Jacobs, Jr. (an architect), 1944; children: James Kedzie, Edward Decker, Mary Hyde. *Education:* Completed high school. *Residence:* Toronto, Ontario, Canada. *Address:* c/o Random House, 457 Madison Ave., New York, N.Y.

CAREER: After spending a year as a reporter on the *Scranton Tribune*, went to New York where she worked as a stenographer and wrote free-lance articles about the city's working districts. Has had a number of writing and editing jobs, ranging in subject matter from metallurgy to geography of the United States for foreign readers. *Architectural Forum*, associate and senior editor, 1952-62.

WRITINGS: (Contributor) The editors of *Fortune*, *The Exploding Metropolis*, Doubleday, 1958; *The Death and Life of Great American Cities*, Random House, 1961; *The Economy of Cities*, Random House, 1969.

SIDELIGHTS: Mrs. Jacobs is among those who opposed the construction of the expressway which would displace families and businesses along the route from the Manhattan Bridge to the Holland Tunnel. She stated: "The inference seems to be . . . that anybody who criticizes a state program is going to get it in the neck." It seems that even while an editor of *Architectural Forum*, she gradually became more skeptical of conventional planning beliefs. In fact, she noticed that the city rebuilding projects she was assigned to write about seemed neither safe, interesting, alive nor economically advisable for the cities involved. As a result, she voiced her objections and proposals in *The Death and Life of Great American Cities*. Although Lloyd Rodwin believes that she is not always "scientific" in her approach to city planning, he feels Mrs. Jacobs' book will become the most influential work on cities since Lewis Mumford's classic, *The Culture of Cities*. According to Phoebe Adams, "the great merit of Mrs. Jacobs' book is that she has looked at cities not as inanimate conglomerations of buildings but as the intricate working organisms that they really are. . . ."

Mrs. Jacobs formerly resided in Greenwich Village with her family, surrounded by old "interesting buildings" which, she believes, a city neighborhood needs to survive.

BIOGRAPHICAL/CRITICAL SOURCES: *Atlantic*, November, 1961; *New York Times Book Review*, November 5, 1961; *Christian Science Monitor*, November 9, 1961; *New York Times*, April 18, 1968; *Washington Post*, May 10, 1969; *New York Review of Books*, January 1, 1970.

* * *

JACOBS, John (Kedzie) 1918-

PERSONAL: Born April 5, 1918, in New Paltz, N.Y.; son of Edward C. (a farmer) and Bertha (Deyo) Jacobs; married Katia Altschuller (a bacteriologist), June 10, 1952; children: John, Eleanor, Lucia, Katherine. *Education:* Antioch College, B.A.; Columbia University, law studies. *Politics:* Democrat. *Office:* c/o Department of State, Washington, D.C. 20421.

CAREER: American Institute of Public Opinion, Princeton, N.J., writer, 1940-43; U.S. Information Agency, Washington, D.C., editor of *America*, 1948—. *Military service:* U.S. Army Air Forces, 1943-46; became captain.

WRITINGS: *Against All Odds*, Crowell-Collier, 1967.†

JACOBS, Lou(is), Jr. 1921-

PERSONAL: Born July 24, 1921, in Dayton, Ohio; son of Louis R. (a salesman) and Clara (Beigel) Jacobs; married Barbara Mills, September 24, 1965; children: Jordan, Kevin, Barry, Ethan. *Education:* Carnegie Institute of Technology (now Carnegie-Mellon University), B.A. in Industrial Design, 1942; Art Center College of Design, further study, 1947-50. *Home:* 13058 Bloomfield St., Studio City, Calif. 91604. *Agent:* Ann Elmo Agency, Inc., 52 Vanderbilt Ave., New York, N.Y. 10017.

CAREER: Peter Muller-Munk Associates, Pittsburgh, Pa., industrial designer, 1942-43, 1946; free-lance magazine photographer, 1950—. *Military service:* U.S. Army, 1943-46; served with Army Engineers in European and Pacific theaters; became sergeant. *Member:* American Society of Magazine Photographers (president, Southern California chapter, 1956-58; member of board, 1958).

WRITINGS—Children's books with text and photographs: *Wonders of an Oceanarium,* Golden Gate, 1965; *Duncan the Dolphin,* Follett, 1966; *SST: Plane of Tomorrow,* Golden Gate, 1967; *Oil, U.S.A.,* Elk Grove Press, 1967; *Airports, U.S.A.,* Elk Grove Press, 1967; *Four Walruses: From Arctic to Oceanarium,* W. R. Scott, 1968; *Shamu: The Killer Whale,* Bobbs-Merrill, 1968; (photographs with wife, Barbara Jacobs) *Beautiful Junk,* Little, Brown, 1968; *Aircraft, U.S.A.,* Elk Grove Press, 1968; *Jumbo Jets,* Bobbs-Merrill, 1969; *Truck Cargo, Air Cargo,* Elk Grove Press, 1970; *The Shapes of Our Land,* Putnam, 1970; *You and Your Camera,* Lothrop, 1971; *Space Station '80,* Hawthorn, 1974; *By Jupiter!: The Remarkable Journey of Pioneer 10,* Hawthorn, 1975.

Photography texts: *How to Use Variable Contrast Papers,* Amphoto, 1960, 3rd edition, 1970; *The ABC's of Lighting,* Amphoto, 1961; *Electronic Flash,* Amphoto, 1962, 2nd edition, Chilton, 1971; *Free-lance Magazine Photography,* Amphoto, 1965; *Petersen's Basic Guide to Photography,* Petersen, 1973; *How to Take Great Pictures with Your SLR,* H. P. Books, 1974. Also author of *The Knoica Autoreflex Manual,* 1974.

* * *

JACOBS, Roderick A(rnold) 1934-

PERSONAL: Born May 29, 1934, in London, England; son of George (an engineer) and Lena (Flank) Jacobs; married Suzanne Eberhart (a college instructor), June 24, 1962; children: Laura Kathryn, Eric John. *Education:* King's College, London, B.A. (honors), 1956; Harvard University, Ed.M., 1962; University of California, San Diego, M.A., 1970, Ph.D., 1972; Massachusetts Institute of Technology, graduate study, 1962-64. *Home:* 426 Poipu Dr., Honolulu, Hawaii 96825. *Office:* Department of Linguistics, University of Hawaii, Honolulu, Hawaii 96822.

CAREER: Teacher of Latin, English, and French in London County Council schools, London, England, 1954-57; Saint John (New Brunswick) public schools, teacher of English and French, 1957-60; Newton (Mass.) public schools, instructor in English in secondary schools, 1960-64; Tuxedo (N.Y.) public schools, coordinator of English and reading, kindergarten to twelfth grade, 1964-66; State University of New York College at Oneonta, associate professor of English, 1966-68; University of California, San Diego, research fellow in linguistics, 1968-72; University of Hawaii, Honolulu, professor of linguistics and English language, 1973—. *Military service:* Royal Air Force Volunteer Reserve, 1954-56. *Member:* Linguistic Society of America,

Modern Language Association of America, National Council of Teachers of English (chairman of poetry study group, 1965; chairman of committee on poetry in the schools, 1967-70), Linguistic Circle of New York, Phi Delta Kappa.

WRITINGS: (Editor with S. E. Jacobs) *Vanity Fair,* Harper, 1964; (editor with Jacobs) *Wuthering Heights,* Harper, 1965; (with P. S. Rosenbaum) *Grammar,* two volumes, Ginn, 1967; (with Rosenbaum) *English Transformational Grammar,* Blaisdell, 1968; *On Transformational Grammar,* New York State English Council, 1968.

(Editor with Rosenbaum) *Readings in English Transformational Grammar,* Wiley, 1970; (editor with Rosenbaum) *Transformations, Style, and Meaning,* Wiley, 1971; *Studies in Language,* Wiley, 1973; (with S. E. Jacobs) *College Writer's Handbook,* Wiley, 1973; *Syntactic Change,* University of California Press, 1975. Contributor to Ginn's "English Language and Composition" series, Books 7-10. Contributor of articles on poetry, linguistics, and politics to *Lucifer* (London) and other journals.

WORK IN PROGRESS: With P. S. Rosenbaum, a revision of *English Transformational Grammar,* for Wiley; *A Grammar of Gilbertese,* for University of Hawaii Press.

AVOCATIONAL INTERESTS: Indo-European, American Indian, and Austronesian language groups, mythology, children's literature (eastern and western), bilingual studies and translation.

* * *

JACOBSON, Nolan Pliny 1909-

PERSONAL: Born March 27, 1909, in Hudson, Wis.; son of Jacob Albert and Lena (Engen) Jacobson; married Grace Webb (a teacher), November 24, 1939; children: Albert Page, Susan Faye. *Education:* Attended University of Wisconsin, 1930-32; Emory University, A.B., 1940, B.D., 1942; University of Chicago, Ph.D., 1946. *Home:* 1612 Clarendon Pl., Rock Hill, S.C. 29730.

CAREER: Huntingdon College, Montgomery, Ala., professor of philosophy, 1946-49; University of Oregon, Eugene, interim head of department of religion, 1949-51; University of Florida, Gainesville, associate professor of religion, 1951-54; Winthrop College, Rock Hill, S.C., professor of philosophy, 1954-74, distinguished professor, 1962-63, chairman of department, 1963-69. Summer visiting professor at Emory University, 1948, and University of Denver, 1957; lecturer at University of Florida, 1961; visiting professor, Queens College of the City University of New York, 1974-76. *Military service:* U.S. Navy, chaplain, 1943-46; participated in invasion of Okinawa.

MEMBER: Philosophy of Education Society (past president, Southeastern region), Southern Society for Philosophy of Religion (past president), South Carolina Philosophy Society (past president), South Carolina Committee for Non-Western Studies (chairman), Phi Kappa Phi, Phi Sigma Tau. *Awards, honors:* Ford Foundation grant for research at International Institute for Advanced Buddhistic Studies, Rangoon, Burma, 1961-62; Swearinger grant for study in Japan, 1972.

WRITINGS: (Contributor) John Nordskog, editor, *Social Change,* University of Southern California Press, and McGraw, 1960; *Buddhism: The Religion of Analysis,* Allen & Unwin, 1966, Southern Illinois University Press, 1970; (contributor) Nicholas Steneck, editor, *Science and Society: Past, Present and Future,* University of Michigan

Press, 1975. Contributor of essay to souvenir volume presented to President Radhakrishnan of India on his sixty-seventh birthday, 1965; also contributor to professional journals in India, France, Mexico, England, and the United States.

WORK IN PROGRESS: Buddhism and the Modern World.

* * *

JACOBY, Neil H(erman) 1909-

PERSONAL: Surname is pronounced Ja-*co*-by; born September 19, 1909, in Dundurn, Saskatchewan, Canada; became U.S. citizen, 1937; son of Herman Reynold and Christina (MacMillan) Jacoby; married Clair Gruhn, December 23, 1933; children: Neil Herman, Jr., Christina C. *Education:* University of Saskatchewan, B.A. (high honors), 1930; University of Chicago, Ph.D., 1938. *Home:* 1434 Midvale Ave., Los Angeles, Calif. 90024. *Office:* Graduate School of Management, University of California, Los Angeles, Calif. 90024.

CAREER: State of Illinois, Springfield, assistant director of finance, 1933-36; chairman of Saskatchewan Taxation Commission, 1936; Lawrence Stern and Co. (investment bankers), Chicago, Ill., manager of research department, 1937; University of Chicago, Chicago, Ill., assistant professor, 1938-40, associate professor, 1940-42, professor of finance, 1942-48, vice-president of university, 1945-48; University of California, Graduate School of Management, Los Angeles, professor of business economics and policy, 1948—, dean, 1948-68. Moscowitz Lecturer, New York University, 1966; P. S. Ross Lecturer, McMaster University, 1968. Member of research staff, National Bureau of Economic Research, 1940-47; member of research advisory board, Committee for Economic Development, 1944-48, 1958-62; member of Council of Economic Advisers to President Eisenhower, 1953-55; U.S. representative to committee of experts, Organization for European Economic Cooperation, 1954; U.S. economic adviser, Indian Planning Commission, New Delhi, 1955; member of economic panel, President's Commission on National Goals, 1959-60; head of fiscal mission to Laos, 1960, and of U.S. aid evaluation mission to Taiwan, 1965. Consultant to RAND Corp., 1951—; consultant to other governmental and industrial groups, including U.S. Treasury Department, Bank of America, and General Motors Corp. Director of Occidental Petroleum Corp., 1958—, Electronics Capital Corp., 1960-65, Electronics Investment Corp., 1960-65, and Ultra Electronics Ltd., 1962-64. International Student Center, Los Angeles, director, 1961—, president, 1962-64.

MEMBER: American Economic Association (member of executive committee, 1965-68), American Finance Association (president, 1949), Royal Economic Society, American Management Association (director, 1963-66), Council for International Progress in Management (director, 1966-69), National Tax Association, Western Economic Association, Beta Gamma Sigma, Pi Gamma Mu. *Awards, honors:* LL.D., University of Saskatchewan, 1950.

WRITINGS: Economics of Retail Sales Taxation, Commerce Clearinghouse, 1938; (with S. E. Leland and others) *Intergovernmental Fiscal Relations in Illinois,* University of Chicago Press, 1938; *Can Prosperity Be Sustained?,* Holt, 1956; (editor and contributor) *United States Monetary Policy,* American Assembly, Columbia University, 1958, 2nd edition, Praeger, 1964; (with Frank Norton) *Bank Deposits and Legal Reserve Requirements,* Graduate School of Business Administration, University of California, 1959; *An Evaluation of U.S. Economic Aid to Free China, 1961-65,* Agency for International Development, 1966; *U.S. Aid to Taiwan,* Praeger, 1966; (with James E. Howell) *European Economics: East and West,* World Book Co., 1967; *Corporate Power and Social Responsibility: A Blueprint for the Future,* Macmillan, 1973; *Multinational Oil: A Study in Industrial Design,* Macmillan, 1974; *The Business-Government Relationship: A Reassessment,* Goodyear Publishing, 1975. Author or co-author of a number of monographs published by National Bureau of Economic Research, 1942-58.

Contributor: *Essays on Canadian Economic Problems,* Royal Bank of Canada, Volume II, 1929, Volume III, 1930; *Tax Barriers to Trade,* Tax Institute (Philadelphia), 1940; *Lectures for Bankers and Business Executives,* American Economic and Business Foundation, 1940; *Fundamental Research in Administration: Horizons and Problems,* Carnegie Press, 1953; Gerhard Colm, editor, *The Employment Act: Past and Future,* National Planning Association, 1956; *Problems of U.S. Economic Development,* Volume I, Committee for Economic Development, 1958; *Economics and the Policy Maker,* Brookings Institution, 1959; *Management Sciences, Models and Techniques,* Volume II, Pergamon, 1960; J. Fred Weston, editor, *Procurement and Profit Renegotiation,* Wadsworth, 1960; J. A. Stockfisch, editor, *Planning and Forecasting in the Defense Industries,* Wadsworth, 1962; Paul R. Hanna, editor, *Education: An Instrument of National Goals,* McGraw, 1962; Harold Koontz, editor, *Management Theory for Improved Management,* McGraw, 1963; Dean Carson, editor, *Banking and Monetary Studies,* Irwin, 1963; Helen A. Cameron and William Henderson, editors, *Public Finance: Selected Readings,* Random House, 1966; Richard A. Ward, editor, *Monetary Theory and Policy,* International Textbook, 1966; *Modern Industrial Management,* Chandler Publishing, 1966; *Government Wage-Price Guideposts in American Economy,* New York University Press, 1967. Contributor of more than fifty articles to professional journals. Member of editorial board, "Petroleum Industry Studies," Yale University Press, 1950—.

* * *

JAFFE, Louis Leventhal 1905-

PERSONAL: Born December 18, 1905, in Seattle, Wash.; son of Aaron L. and Rae (Leventhal) Jaffe; married Mildred Miles, June 6, 1936; children: H. Miles, Deborah (Mrs. Frank S. Yeomans). *Education:* Attended Stanford University, 1923-25; Johns Hopkins University, A.B., 1926; Harvard University, LL.B., 1928, S.J.D., 1932. *Politics:* Democrat. *Home:* 164 Brattle St., Cambridge, Mass. *Office:* Harvard Law School, Cambridge, Mass.

CAREER: Admitted to California State Bar, 1928, New York State Bar, 1942; law clerk to Justice Brandeis, Supreme Court of the United States, 1933-34; U.S. Government, lawyer for Agricultural Adjustment Administration, 1934-35, National Labor Relations Board, 1935-36; University of Buffalo, Buffalo, N.Y., professor of law, 1936-47, dean of Law School, 1948-50; Harvard University, Law School, Cambridge, Mass., Byrne Professor of Administrative Law, 1950—. Visiting fellow, All Souls College, Oxford, 1967; Thomas Professor, University of Colorado, summer, 1968. Public member of ship-building commission, National War Labor Board, 1944-45; labor arbitrator. *Member:* American Academy of Arts and Sciences, American Arbitration Association.

443

WRITINGS: *Judicial Aspects of Foreign Relations,* Harvard University Press, 1933, reprinted, Johnson Reprint, 1968; *Administrative Law: Cases and Materials,* Prentice-Hall, 1954, 2nd edition (with N. L. Nathanson), Little, Brown, 1961, 3rd edition (with Nathanson), 1968, supplement, 1972; *Judicial Control of Administrative Action,* Little, Brown, 1965; *English and American Judges as Lawmakers,* Clarendon Press, 1969; (with Laurence H. Tribe) *Environmental Protection,* Bracton Press, 1971. Contributor of articles and reviews to law journals and magazines.†

* * *

JAFFE, (Andrew) Michael 1923-

PERSONAL: Born June 3, 1923, in London, England; son of Arthur Daniel and Marie (Strauss) Jaffe; married Patricia Anne Milne Henderson, October 16, 1964; children: Daniel Gideon, Deborah Ruth. *Education:* King's College, Cambridge, M.A., 1949. *Office:* School of Architecture, Cambridge University, Cambridge, England.

CAREER: Washington University, St. Louis, Mo., professor of Renaissance art, 1960-61; Cambridge University, Cambridge, England, lecturer, 1961-68, university reader, 1968-73, professor in the history of Western art, 1973—, head of department, 1970-73, director of Fitzwilliam Museum, 1973—. Visiting professor, Harvard University, summer, 1961, fall, 1968-69. Organizer of Jordaens Exhibition for National Gallery of Canada, 1969. *Military service:* Royal Naval Volunteer Reserve, World War II; became lieutenant commander. *Awards, honors:* Commonwealth Fund fellow at New York University and Harvard University, 1951-53.

WRITINGS: *Van Dyck's Antwerp Sketchbook,* two volumes, Macdonald & Co., 1966; *Jordaens,* National Gallery of Canada, 1968. Contributor to periodicals in United States and Europe.

* * *

JAMES, P(hyllis) D(orothy) 1920-

PERSONAL: Born August 3, 1920, in Oxford, England; daughter of Sidney Victor (a tax officer) and Dorothy May (Hone) James; married Ernest Conner Bantry White (a medical practitioner), August 8, 1941 (deceased). *Education:* Attended Cambridge High School for Girls, 1931-37. *Politics:* "I belong to no political party." *Religion:* Church of England. *Home:* 31 Dorset Sq., London N.W. 1, England. *Agent:* Elaine Greene Ltd., 31 Newington Green, London N16 9PU, England.

CAREER: North West Metropolitan Regional Hospital Board, London, England, principal administrative assistant; currently civil servant with Department of Home Affairs. *Member:* Institute of Hospital Administration (fellow).

WRITINGS: *Cover Her Face,* Faber, 1962, Scribner, 1966; *A Mind to Murder,* Faber, 1963, Scribner, 1967; *Unnatural Causes,* Scribner, 1967; *Shroud for a Nightingale,* Scribner, 1971; (with Thomas A. Critchley) *The Maul and the Pear Tree,* Constable, 1971; *An Unsuitable Job for a Woman,* Faber, 1972, Scribner, 1973; *The Black Tower,* Scribner, 1975.

WORK IN PROGRESS: A detective novel.

* * *

JAN, George P(okung) 1925-

PERSONAL: Born January 6, 1925, in Peking, China; son of Yu-nan (a businessman) and Yin-chieh (Lee) Jan; married Norma Y. Wen, September 28, 1946; children: Gregory, David, Daniel. *Education:* National Chengchi University, A.B., 1949; Southern Illinois University, A.M., 1956; New York University, Ph.D., 1960. *Home:* 2253 Goddard Rd., Toledo, Ohio 43606. *Office:* Asian Studies Program, University of Toledo, Toledo, Ohio 43606.

CAREER: University of South Dakota, Vermillion, assistant professor, 1961-64, associate professor, 1964-66, professor of government, 1966-68; University of Toledo, Toledo, Ohio, professor of political science and chairman of Asian Studies Program, 1968—. *Member:* American Political Science Association, Association for Asian Studies, International Congress of Orientalists, American Society of International Law, American Association of University Professors, Midwest Political Science Association, Phi Beta Kappa, Pi Sigma Alpha, Phi Kappa Phi.

WRITINGS: *Practical English Grammar for Junior Middle Schools,* Central Book Co., 1953; *A Study of English Words,* Central Book Co., 1955; (editor and contributor) *Government of Communist China,* Chandler Publishing, 1966; *International Politics of Asia,* Wadsworth, 1969. Also author of *The Chinese Commune Experiment,* 1964. Contributor to numerous professional journals.

WORK IN PROGRESS: *Local Government in Communist China; Politics in Communist China; Japan's Policy Toward Communist China.*

BIOGRAPHICAL/CRITICAL SOURCES: *Chinese Journal* (New York), June 8, 1960; *Young China* (San Francisco), December 7, 1962; Associated Press Wire Service, March 1, 1965.

* * *

JANSEN, John Frederick 1918-

PERSONAL: Born April 9, 1918, in Netherlands; son of Berthus (a florist) and Gerarda C. (Holscher) Jansen; married Mary Cabiness, August 7, 1947; children: John F., Tyler C., Mark B., David C., Andrew P. *Education:* Princeton University, A.B., 1939; Princeton Theological Seminary, Th.B., 1942, Th.D., 1945; graduate study at Yale Divinity School, 1943-44, Union Theological Seminary, New York, N.Y., 1958, and University of Utrecht, 1963. *Politics:* Democrat. *Home:* 2522 Tanglewood Trail, Austin, Tex. 78703. *Office:* Austin Presbyterian Theological Seminary, 100 East 27th St., Austin, Tex. 78705.

CAREER: Presbyterian clergyman. Minister in Flemington, N.J., 1946-49; Carroll College, Waukesha, Wis., associate professor of Bible and dean of men, 1949-52; Hanover College, Hanover, Ind., professor of religion, 1952-58; Austin Presbyterian Theological Seminary, Austin, Tex., professor of New Testament interpretation, 1958—. *Member:* Society of Biblical Literature.

WRITINGS: *Calvin's Doctrine of the Work of Christ,* James Clarke, 1956; *Guests of God* (Religious Book Club selection), Westminster, 1956; *The Meaning of Baptism,* Westminster, 1958; *O Povo de Deo* (studies in I Peter translated into Portuguese), Paperlaria Fernandes (Lisbon), 1964; *Let Us Worship God,* Covenant Life Curriculum, 1966; *No Idle Tale,* John Knox, 1967; *Exercises in Interpreting Scripture,* Geneva Press, 1968. Contributor to theological journals and church publications.

SIDELIGHTS: John Jansen is competent in New Testament Greek and reads French and German.

JARDINE, Jack 1931-
(Larry Maddock; Howard L. Cory, a joint pseudonym)

PERSONAL: Born October 10, 1931, in Eaton Rapids, Mich.; son of John William (a sales executive) and Blanche (a newspaperwoman; maiden name, Owen) Jardine; married Julie Shohor (a writer under pseudonym Corrie Howard), April 18, 1958 (divorced February 2, 1967); married Marilyn McBirney (a reference librarian), January 9, 1968; children: (first marriage), Sabra Yola Elgin (daughter). *Education:* Attended Hillsdale College, two years. *Religion:* Atheist. *Residence:* Mesa, Ariz. *Agent:* Henry Morrison, Inc., 58 West 10th St., New York, N.Y. 10014.

CAREER: Associated with various radio stations as writer and announcer, 1954-57; tried free-lancing, 1958; editor-in-chief of a dozen "sophisticated" magazines for men, American Art Agency, North Hollywood, Calif., 1959-61; free-lance writer, 1962, followed by assorted jobs, 1963-65; performer-writer, KALF Radio, Mesa, Ariz., 1965-68; president of Grafniks, Inc. (manufacturer of graphic novelties), Mesa, Ariz., 1967—. *Military service:* "The military and I did not take kindly to each other, producing consequences which influenced my decision to learn the writer's craft." *Member:* Science Fiction Writers of America.

WRITINGS—Under pseudonym Larry Maddock, except as noted: *Single and Pregnant* (nonfiction), Genell, 1962; (with Corrie Howard [pseudonym], under joint pseudonym Howard L. Cory) *Sword of Lankor*, Ace Books, 1966; (with Corrie Howard, under joint pseudonym Howard L. Cory) *The Mind Monsters*, Ace Books, 1966.

"Agent of T.E.R.R.A." series, published by Ace Books: *The Flying Saucer Gambit*, 1966; *The Golden Goddess Gambit*, 1967; *The Emerald Elephant Gambit*, 1967; *The Time Trap Gambit*, 1968.

Author of a dozen novels published under almost as many pseudonyms in the early 1960's, and contributor of more than a hundred short stories to small magazines; contributor of shorts, novelettes, and articles, mainly to mystery and science fiction magazines, under pseudonym Larry Maddock.

WORK IN PROGRESS: Volar the Mighty, a science fiction novel, for Belmont Books; a science fiction novel with working title of *Sleepfreeze,* for Paperback Library; updating *Single and Pregnant;* compiling data for a book on the so-called new morality, tentatively titled *Teen Sex and Reality;* five or six more "Agent of the T.E.R.R.A." novels; short stories, predominantly crime yarns; also writing pilot script for a comedy television series.

SIDELIGHTS: Jardine told *CA:* "Write because (a) playing with ideas is the second most enjoyable pursuit I know and fortunately it allows me to indulge in (b) the first most enjoyable pursuit, which gets expensive, what with alimony and child support. Along the way I take joyous potshots at sacred cows, scoring few direct hits, but relishing the sound of the popgun. Usually, writing is more fun than work, and as I have a deep-seated abhorrence for work, I'm delighted to be paid for having fun. If I have a consistent 'message' it is simply that Reason is preferable to Romanticism; I believe most of us do too little rational thinking, and suffer needlessly because of it."††

*   *   *

JASTROW, Robert 1925-

PERSONAL: Born September 7, 1925, in New York, N.Y.; son of Abraham and Marie (Greenfield) Jastrow. *Education:* Columbia University, B.A., 1944, M.A., 1945, Ph.D., 1948. *Home:* 22 Riverside Dr., New York, N.Y. 10023. *Office:* Goddard Institute for Space Studies, 2880 Broadway, New York, N.Y. 10025.

CAREER: Columbia University, New York City, lecturer in physics, 1944-47; Cooper Union, New York City, instructor in School of Engineering, 1947-48; postdoctoral fellow at University of Leiden, Leiden, Netherlands, 1948-49, Institute for Advanced Study, Princeton, N.J., 1949-50, 1953, and Radiation Laboratory, University of California, Berkeley, 1950-53; Yale University, New Haven, Conn., assistant professor of physics, 1953-54; U.S. Naval Research Laboratory, Washington, D.C., consultant in nuclear physics, 1954-58; National Aeronautics and Space Administration, chief of Theoretical Division, Washington, D.C., 1958-61, director of Goddard Institute for Space Studies, New York City, 1961—. Adjunct professor of geophysics, Columbia University, 1961—; adjunct professor of earth sciences, Dartmouth College, 1974. Wright Brothers Memorial lecturer, 1961.

MEMBER: American Institute of Aeronautics and Astronautics, American Physical Society, American Geophysical Union (fellow; vice-president of planetary science section), International Academy of Astronautics, American Association for the Advancement of Science, Royal Astronomical Society (England; fellow), Council on Foreign Relations. *Awards, honors:* Columbia University Medal for excellence, 1962; Arthur S. Flemming Award for outstanding federal service, 1964; Columbia University Graduate Faculties Alumni Award for excellence, 1967, National Aeronautics and Space Administration medal, 1968.

WRITINGS: (Editor) *Exploration of Space,* Macmillan, 1960; (editor with A. G. W. Cameron) *Origin of the Solar System,* Academic Press, 1963; *Red Giants and White Dwarfs: The Evolution of Stars, Planets and Life,* Harper, 1967, revised edition, 1971; *Atmosphere of Venus,* Gordon & Breach, 1969; (with Malcolm H. Thompson) *Astronomy: Fundamentals and Frontiers,* Wiley, 1972, 2nd edition, 1974. Editor, *Journal of the Atmospheric Sciences.*

WORK IN PROGRESS: Second layman's book on science (*Red Giants and White Dwarfs* was the first); a high school text on astronomy.

*   *   *

JAZAYERY, M(ohammad) Ali 1924-

PERSONAL: Born May 27, 1924, in Shushtar, Iran; son of S. Kazim (an accountant) and Batul (Jazayery) Jazayery. *Education:* University of Tehran, Licence, 1950; National Teachers College, Tehran, Licence, 1950; University of Texas, Ph.D., 1958. *Home:* 705 Laurel Valley Rd., Austin, Tex. 78746. *Office:* Department of Oriental and African Languages and Literature, University of Texas, Austin, Tex. 78712.

CAREER: Anglo-Iranian Oil Co., Ahwaz, Iran, employee, 1944-45; co-editor of *Jahan-e Pak* (daily newspaper), 1945-46, and *Daftarha-ye-Mahaneh* (journal), 1945-50, both published in Tehran, Iran; Iranian Ministry of Education, Ahwaz, high school teacher of English, 1950-51; American Council of Learned Societies, Washington, D.C., textbook writer (English-Persian), 1954-55; University of Texas at Austin, lecturer in English, 1955-58; University of Tehran, Tehran, associate professor of English, 1958-59, also concurrently assistant to U.S. cultural attache at American Embassy, Tehran; University of Michigan, Ann Arbor, lecturer in Persian, 1959-62; University of Texas at Austin, associate professor, 1962-68, professor of linguistics, 1968—, assistant director of Middle East Center, 1966—. Summer lecturer in Persian at Johns Hopkins University, 1957, Harvard University, 1958, and Princeton University, 1967; visiting summer professor at New York University, 1968, and Portland State University, 1972.

MEMBER: Linguistic Society of America (life member), American Oriental Society, Modern Language Association of America, National Council of Teachers of English, International Phonetic Association, American Association of University Professors, Middle East Studies Association of North America (life member).

WRITINGS: Aludegiha-ye Ejtema'e Ma (title means "The Abuses of Our Society"), Sepehr (Tehran), 1947; (translator from the English) "Practical Psychology in Plain Language" series, seven volumes, Sepehr, 1947-50; (with H. H. Paper) *English for Iranians,* American Council of Learned Societies, 1955; (with Paper) *The Writing System of Modern Persian,* American Council of Learned Societies, 1955; (editor with M. Farzan and others) *Modern Persian Reader,* three volumes, University of Michigan Press, 1963. Also author of *Elementary Lessons in Persian,* 1968. Contributor to *Rahnema-ye Ketab* (Tehran), 1959—; also contributor to *Language, Bulletin of Oriental and African Studies,* and other journals. Member of editorial board, *Literature East and West.*

WORK IN PROGRESS: Three books with working titles *The Arabic Element in Contemporary Persian, The French Element in Contemporary Persian,* and *English Loanwords in Contemporary Persian;* a book about the life and work of Ahmad Kasravi (1890-1946), Iranian historian, linguist, and social reformer; various aspects of contemporary Persian grammar.

* * *

JEAL, Tim 1945-

PERSONAL: Born January 27, 1945, in London, England; son of Clifford Freeman and Norah (Pasley) Jeal. *Education:* Christ Church, Oxford, M.A. *Home:* 2 Healey St., London N.W.1, England. *Agent:* Toby Eady Associates, 64 Lexham Gardens, London W.8, England.

CAREER: Before and during attendance at Oxford University, held temporary jobs as wine steward, radio actor, art teacher in Johannesburg, South Africa, and staff member of an advertising agency; British Broadcasting Corp., London, England, work on production of television documentaries, 1966-70; full time writer, 1970—. Arts Council Bursary, 1970. *Member:* Writers Guild.

WRITINGS: For Love or Money (novel), McGraw, 1967; *Somewhere Beyond Reproach* (novel), Macmillan (London), 1968, McGraw, 1969; *Livingstone* (biography), Putnam, 1973; *Cushing's Crusade* (novel), Heinemann, 1974. Contributor to *Observer Colour, Punch,* and other periodicals.

WORK IN PROGRESS: An historical novel tentatively entitled, *Hostages to Fortune.*

AVOCATIONAL INTERESTS: Travel, reading.

* * *

JEBB, (Hubert Miles) Gladwyn 1900-

PERSONAL: Born April 25, 1900, in Rotherham, Yorkshire, England; son of Sydney Gladwyn and Rose (Chichester) Jebb; married Cynthia Noble, January 22, 1929; children: one son, two daughters. *Education:* Magdalen College, Oxford, first in history, 1922. *Politics:* Liberal. *Religion:* Church of England. *Home:* 62 Whitehall Court, London, England; and 2 Bramfield Hall, Halesworth, Suffolk, England. *Agent:* David Higham Associates Ltd., 5-8 Lower John St., London W1R 4HA, England.

CAREER: British diplomat, 1924-60. Served in Tehran, Rome, and in Foreign Office, 1924-29; private secretary to parliamentary Under-Secretary of State, 1929-31, and to permanent Under-Secretary, 1937-40; assistant Under-Secretary in Ministry of Economic Warfare, 1940; acting counsellor in Foreign Office, 1941, and head of Reconstruction Department, 1942; counsellor, participating in conferences at Quebec, Cairo, Tehran, Dunbarton Oaks, Yalta, San Francisco, and Potsdam, 1943-45; executive secretary of Preparatory Commission of United Nations, 1945, and acting Secretary-General of United Nations, 1946; assistant Under-Secretary of State, 1946-47; representative on Brussels Treaty Permanent Commission, with rank of ambassador, 1948; deputy Under-Secretary of State, 1949-50; representative to United Nations, 1950-54; British Ambassador to France, 1954-60; president of North Atlantic Treaty Association, 1963-67; member of parly delegations to Council of Europe and Western European Union, 1966-73. Deputy leader of Liberal Party in House of Lords. Chairman of Britain in Europe. *Military service:* British Army, 1918-19.

MEMBER: Turf Club and Garrick Club (both London). *Awards, honors:* Companion of the Order of Bath, 1945; Companion of St. Michael and St. George, 1947, Knight Commander, 1949, and Knight Grand Cross of St. Michael and St. George, 1954, Knight Grand Cross of Royal Victorian Order, 1957; D.C.L. from Oxford University, 1954, and Essex University, 1974; Grand Cross of the Legion of Honor (France), 1957; created first Baron Gladwyn, 1960.

WRITINGS: The European Idea, Weidenfeld & Nicolson, 1966; *Half-Way to 1984,* Columbia University Press, 1966; *Europe after De Gaulle,* Weybright, 1968; *De Gaulle's Europe: Or, Why the General Says No,* Seeker & Warburg, 1969; *Memoirs of Lord Gladwyn,* Weybright, 1973. Also author of *Is Tension Necessary?,* 1959, and *Peaceful Co-Existence,* 1962.

AVOCATIONAL INTERESTS: Sports.

* * *

JEFFERY, Ransom 1943-

PERSONAL: Born December 31, 1943, in Aurora, Ill.; son of Robert S. (a carpenter) and Margorie (Swanson) Jeffery; married Rosemary J. High, July 7, 1963; children: Phaedra Marie, Nicole Rosa, Xanthus High (son). *Education:* North Texas State University, B.S., 1966; University of Iowa, M.F.A., 1969. *Politics:* None. *Religion:* None.

CAREER: Held various odd jobs, including work as a dishwasher and a plumber, 1959-61; speech teacher and drama coach, West High School, Iowa City, Iowa, while studying for master's degree; University of Michigan, Ann Arbor, playwright in residence, 1969-71; currently affiliated with Southwest Missouri State University, Springfield. *Awards, honors:* Award of Merit in Samuel French Playwriting contest, 1967, and scholarship for drama conference at United Nations, 1967, both for "The Refusal"; first prize ($2,000) in American National Theatre and Academy (ANTA) playwriting contest, 1969, for "The Guest"; Shubert Theatre Foundation fellowship in playwriting at University of Michigan, 1969-70; first prize, Avery Hopwood Awards, 1970, for "The Refusal," "The Union," and "The Guest"; Rackham grant, University of Michigan, 1970-71.

WRITINGS—All plays except as noted: "Tenfold Laughs and a Few Tears," produced at North Texas State University, 1964; "The Retreat," produced at North Texas State University, 1965; "The Witness," produced in Denton, Tex., 1965; "The Refusal," produced at North Texas State University, 1966, produced in New York, 1974; "The Off-Season," produced Off-Off Broadway at Dramarena, 1968; "Friends," produced at Dramarena, 1968; "Three Pieces Left," produced by Experimental Theatre Co., Springfield, Mo., and at Dramarena, 1969; "The Guest," produced by Theatre Unlimited, Dallas, Tex., and North Texas State University, 1969; "The Union," produced at University of Michigan, 1970; (with John Keeble) *Mine* (novel), Grossman, 1974.

WORK IN PROGRESS: A novel, *The Last Kid at School;* a new play.

SIDELIGHTS: Jeffery told *CA:* "Things are happening and since I can't paint, I write. Hopefully, things I see are the same things you see. I like Bob Dylan, Albert Camus, The Doors, Jesus, John Keeble, my wife, the earth, beer, health, new typewriter ribbons, etc. I don't like old photographs and the likes. I have been deeply influenced by things outside and inside my head, by friends and enemies, by injustice and justice, and mostly by the physical properties of the rubber band."

In his review of "The Off-Season," the *Village Voice* writer described the play as "the work of a playwright of considerable talent. His curious characters are strange without being grotesque, and the rituals they enact are unique but not incredible." Specifically, "the protagonists are a husband-and-wife team of carnival actors who . . . are eventually forced back into confrontation with their own lives, their own failures, and the ultimate realization that only the death of one of them will provide their act with new material."

BIOGRAPHICAL/CRITICAL SOURCES: Village Voice, August 1, 1968.

* * *

JENKINS, John Geraint   1929-

PERSONAL: Born January 4, 1929, in Cardiganshire, Wales; son of David James (a master mariner) and Mary Jane (Thomas) Jenkins; married Anne Elizabeth Jarman, January 8, 1954; children: David, Richard, Gareth. *Education:* University of Wales, B.A., 1950, M.A., 1951. *Politics:* Liberal Party (Wales). *Religion:* Congregationalist. *Home:* St. Fagans Castle, Cardiff, Wales.

CAREER: City of Leicester Museum and Art Gallery, Leicester, England, assistant, 1951-52; University of Reading, Reading, England, curator at Rural Life Museum, 1952-60; National Museum of Wales, Welsh Folk Museum, Cardiff, assistant keeper, 1960-69, keeper, 1969—. Secretary, Welsh Radical Group, 1964-69; head of research, Welsh Liberal Party, 1967-69. Secretary, British Ethnography Committee, 1956-60; chairman, Educational Textbooks Committee, Wales, 1964-67; examiner and tutor, Museums Association, 1964—. *Member:* British Association (member of anthropology committee, 1958-60; recorder, 1969-74), Royal Anthropological Institute (fellow), Society of Antiquaries (fellow), Society for Folk Life Studies (secretary, 1961-65), Society of Authors, Society

for the Interpretation of Heritage (chairman, 1975—), Group for Regional Studies (chairman, 1974—).

WRITINGS: The English Farm Wagon, University of Reading Press, 1962; *Agricultural Transport in Wales,* National Museum of Wales, 1963; *Traditional Country Craftsmen,* Routledge & Kegan Paul, 1965; *Esgair Moel Woollen Mill,* National Museum of Wales, 1965; (editor) *Traditional Tools and Equipment,* Museum Assistants Group (London), 1966; *The Welsh Woollen Industry,* National Museum of Wales, 1967; (editor) *Studies in Folk Life,* Routledge & Kegan Paul, 1968, Barnes & Noble, 1969; *Commercial Salmon Fishing in Welsh Rivers,* National Museum of Wales, 1971; *Cooper's Craft,* National Museum of Wales, 1972; (editor) *The Wool Textile Industry in Great Britain,* Routledge & Kegan Paul, 1972; *Wood Turner's Craft,* National Museum of Wales, 1973; *Nets and Coracles,* David & Charles, 1974; *Boat House and Net House,* Welsh Folk Museum, 1974. Contributor to country magazines and learned journals. Editor, *Folk Life* (publication of Society for Folk Life Studies), 1964—.

SIDELIGHTS: Jenkins notes that he is striving for the academic recognition of folk life studies in educational institutions, both in Britain and North America. He aims to write readable but academic books that can serve as textbooks, and, he adds, he has "little time for sentiment" in his writings.

* * *

JENKINSON, Edward B(ernard)   1930-

PERSONAL: Born October 23, 1930, in Muncie, Ind.; son of Joseph G. (a toolmaker) and Alma L. (Parcher) Jenkinson; married Ronna Marasco, April 10, 1954; children: Mark Edward, Andrea Marie. *Education:* Ball State University, A.B., 1951; Indiana University, M.A., 1956. *Home:* 3609 Longview Dr., Bloomington, Ind. 47401. *Office:* English Curriculum Study Center, Indiana University, 1125 Atwater Ave., Bloomington, Ind. 47401.

CAREER: High school English teacher in Tyner, Ind., 1951-53, and South Bend, Ind., 1953-56; Northern Illinois University, De Kalb, alumni executive secretary and magazine editor, 1956-58; American University of Beirut, Beirut, Lebanon, instructor in journalism, 1958-60; Indiana University, Bloomington, 1960—, began as lecturer, now coordinator for school English language arts, director of English Curriculum Study Center, and professor of education. *Member:* National Council of Teachers of English (public relations representative; vice-president, 1971), Indiana Association for Supervision and Curriculum Development, Indiana Council of Teachers of English (vice-president; 1972-74; president, 1974-76), Phi Delta Kappa. *Awards, honors:* Research grants from U.S. Office of Education, Cummins Engine Foundation, and newspaper fund of *Wall Street Journal.*

WRITINGS: (With Marshall Brown and Elmer White) *Two Approaches to Teaching Syntax,* Indiana University Press, 1967; *What is Language? And Other Teaching Units for Grades Seven through Twelve,* Indiana University Press, 1968; *A Student Guide to the Random House Dictionary of the English Language,* Random House, *College Edition,* 1968, *School Edition,* 1970; *People, Words, and Dictionaries,* Harcourt, 1972; (with Donald A. Seybold) *Points of View in Writing,* Harcourt, 1972.

Editor: *Two Units on Journalism for English Classes,* Indiana State Department of Public Instruction, 1964; *Teacher's Guide to High School Speech,* Indiana State Department of Public Instruction, 1966; (with Jane Stouder Hawley) *On Teaching Literature: Essays for Secondary School Teachers,* Indiana University Press, 1967; (with Hawley) *Teaching Literature in Grades Seven Through Nine,* Indiana University Press, 1967; (with Philip B. Daghlian) *Teaching Literature in Grades Ten Through Twelve,* Indiana University Press, 1968; (with Daghlian) *Books for Teachers of English: An Annotated Bibliography,* Indiana University Press, 1968; (with J. Jeffrey Auer) *On Teaching Speech in Elementary and Junior High Schools,* Indiana University Press, 1971; (with Auer) *Essays on Teaching Speech in the High School,* Indiana University Press, 1972; (with James S. Ackerman, Alan W. Jenks, and Jan Blough, and contributor) *Teaching the Old Testament in English Classes,* Indiana University Press, 1972; *Some Questions and Answers about Planning Phase-Elective Programs in English,* Indiana Council of Teachers of English, 1972. Editor, *Newsletter* of Indiana University Curriculum Study Center.

WORK IN PROGRESS: Editing, with Mescal Evler and Leandra Uplinger, *Basic Objectives in English for Grades One through Twelve,* for Indiana Department of Public Instruction; writing *Projecting Images: A Personal Approach to Composition,* for Indiana University Press; writing a series of language and composition texts for pupils in grades four through eight.

* * *

JENNER, Delia 1944-

PERSONAL: Born June 9, 1944, in Bath, England; daughter of Daniel Marcus (an author) and Winifred (Gonley) Davin; married W.J.F. Jenner (a university teacher), December 2, 1961. *Education:* Studied at Oxford College of Technology, 1962-63, and University of Leeds, 1965-68. *Politics:* Anti-imperialist. *Religion:* None. *Residence:* Leeds, England. *Address:* c/o Oxford University Press, 37 Dover St., London W1X 4AH, England.

CAREER: At nineteen went to China with her husband to spend the years, 1963-65; throughout their stay she taught at Peking Broadcasting Institute.

WRITINGS: Letters from Peking (selection of her letters home), Oxford University Press, 1967.

WORK IN PROGRESS: Research on modern China.

SIDELIGHTS: Delia Jenner speaks French in addition to Chinese. *Avocational interests:* The history, literature, and current history of China, and current affairs in general.††

* * *

JENSEN, Ann

PERSONAL: Born in Marfa, Tex.; daughter of Alonzo (a rancher) and Laura (Carr) Van Oden; married Andrew R. Jensen; children: Andrew O., C. Al. *Education:* Attended Southern Methodist University, Columbia University, and University of Oklahoma. *Religion:* Christian. *Home:* 1115 Sunnybrook Lane, Enid, Okla. 73701.

CAREER: Lectures on parapsychology to groups throughout the United States and Mexico, and on radio and television. Chairman of board, Texas Society for Psychical Research. *Member:* Southwest Writers, Poetry Society of Texas, Dallas Press Club. *Awards, honors:* Texas Writers Roundup Award of Theta Sigma Phi, 1967, for *The Time of Rosie.*

WRITINGS: Diary and Scrapbook of a Texas Ranger, Kaleidograph Press, 1936; *The Droniest Bee in the Hive,* Bethany Press, 1966; *The Time of Rosie,* Steck, 1967; (with Mary Lou Watkins) *Franz Anton Mesmer: Physician Extraordinaire,* Helix Press, 1967.

WORK IN PROGRESS: The Pink Stallion, a juvenile book; *Haunted Houses of Mexico and the Southwest.*

* * *

JENSEN, John H(jalmar) 1929-

PERSONAL: Born May 16, 1929, in Baltimore, Md.; son of Jacob and Mabel (Marshall) Jensen; married Frances Journey, August 25, 1951; children: Susan, Kai (son), Gwenda, Katherine, Benedikte (daughter). *Education:* Houghton College, B.A., 1951; University of Pennsylvania, M.A., 1956, Ph.D., 1959. *Home:* 1 Dawson St., Hamilton, New Zealand. *Office:* University of Waikato, Hamilton, New Zealand.

CAREER: Rutgers University, College of South Jersey, Camden, lecturer, 1955-58, assistant professor of history, 1958-64; Massey University of Manawatu, Palmerston North, New Zealand, senior lecturer, 1964-67, reader in history, 1967-70; University of Waikato, Hamilton, New Zealand, professor of history and chairman of department, 1970—. Visiting assistant professor, University of Pennsylvania, 1959-60, 1962. *Military service:* U.S. Army, 1952-54. *Member:* Royal Society of New Zealand (vice-president, Manawatu branch, 1967-69), Australian and New Zealand Association for the Advancement of Science, New Zealand History Society.

WRITINGS: (Editor with James D. Hardy, Jr., and Martin Wolfe) *The Maclure Collection of French Revolutionary Materials,* University of Pennsylvania Press, 1966; (with others) *The European Experience: Topics in Modern History,* A. H. & A. W. Reed, Volume I: *Forces of Change,* 1970, revised edition, 1975, Volume II: *In Africa and India,* 1970, Volume III: *The Balance of Power,* 1972, Volume IV: *The Bigger Battalions,* 1974, Volume V: *Society under Seige,* in press; (with others) *Perspectives in Modern History,* A. H. & A. W. Reed, Volume I: *International Relations,* 1975, Volume II: *Cultural Interaction,* 1975, Volumes III-VII, in press. Contributor of articles and reviews to *Library Chronicle, Historical News, International Archives of Ethnography,* and other professional journals; also has done book reviews and scripts for New Zealand Broadcasting Corp.

WORK IN PROGRESS: Research in twentieth-century European history, economic and social history of eastern Europe, and history of Romanian sociological thought; articles and a book on railway and river transport in eastern Europe, on Romanian engineering, and on nationalism; a child's adventure story in a medieval setting.

SIDELIGHTS: The comprehensive guide to the collection that William Maclure presented to the Philadelphia Academy of Sciences in 1821 represents ten years' work on the part of Jensen, his co-editors, and the University of Pennsylvania library staff. The University of Pennsylvania acquired the collection of French Revolutionary printed material in 1949.

Jensen's textbook series, *The European Experience* and *Perspectives in Modern History,* are widely used in secondary schools in Australia and New Zealand; several have been used as university texts.

JENSEN, Rolf (Arthur)   1912-

PERSONAL: Surname is pronounced Yensen; born April 19, 1912, in Wallasey, England; son of Harold R. (an industrial chemist) and Edith (Pritchard) Jensen; married Elfrida Snell (a writer), April 9, 1936; children: Peter Rolf, Rodney John. *Education:* University of Liverpool, B.Arch. (honors), 1933; London School of Planning, B.E., 1947. *Home:* Bledlow, Fulton Crescent, Woodley, South Australia. *Office:* Faculty of Architecture and Town Planning, University of Adelaide, Adelaide, South Australia.

CAREER: Private practice as architect in London, England, 1933-38; served with British Admiralty in United Kingdom and Singapore, 1938-41; acting city architect, Singapore, 1945-46; North Westminister, London, England, director of housing, 1947-56; University of Adelaide, Adelaide, South Australia, professor of architecture and dean of Faculty of Architecture and Town Planning, 1956—. Lecturer at universities in America, 1964, in the Far East and Great Britain, 1970-71. Designer of banks, schools, hotels, housing developments, and civic buildings on three continents. *Military service:* Royal Engineers, 1942-56, with active duty in Far East, 1942-46; became lieutenant colonel. Royal Australian Engineers Reserve of Officers, 1956—.

MEMBER: Royal Institute of British Architects (fellow), Royal Australian Institute of Architects (fellow; member of council and honorary secretary, South Australian chapter), International Congress of Modern Architecture, Modern Architectural Research Group, City and Borough Architects Society (honorary member), Royal Australian Planning Institute (fellow), Royal Town Planning Institute (London; fellow), Royal Institute of British Architects (fellow), Royal Australian Institute of Architects (fellow), Institution of Royal Engineers, Board of Architectural Education of South Australia, Royal Overseas Racing Club, Royal Engineers Yacht Club. *Awards, honors:* Rose Shipman Award, Royal Institute of British Architects, 1954.

WRITINGS: High Density Living, Praeger, 1966; *Cities of Vision,* Applied Science, 1973, Wiley, 1974; (contributor) *Changing South East Asian Cities,* University of Singapore Press, 1975. Also author of *Colonial Architecture in Southern Australia,* with wife, Elfrida Jensen, for Rigby. Contributor of about sixty articles to architectural journals in Europe and Australia.

WORK IN PROGRESS: Housing, Urban Renewal and Urban Transportation.

AVOCATIONAL INTERESTS: Linguistics, travel, archaeology, yachting, photography.

*   *   *

JIANOU, Ionel   1905-

PERSONAL: Born October 23, 1905, in Bucharest, Rumania; son of Leon and Charlotte Susan Stark; married Margaret Grosswald, March 29, 1931; children: Ion-Alexander. *Education:* University of Paris, master's degree. *Politics:* "No." *Home:* 10, Avenue Stephane Mallarme, Paris 75017, France. *Office:* Arted, Editions d'Art, 6, Avenue du Coq, Paris 75009, France.

CAREER: Gallery Caminul Artei, Bucharest, Rumania, artistic manager, 1942-47; Editura de Stat Pentru Literatura si Arta (ESPLA) and Meridiane Publishing House, Bucharest, manager of artistic section, 1951-61; Popular University, Fine Arts Institute, Bucharest, professor of history of

art, 1954-61; Arted, Editions d'Art, Paris, France, president, 1962—. *Member:* Association Internationale des Critiques d'Art, P.E.N. (Paris).

WRITINGS: P. Iorgulescu-Yor, Arta si Technica Grafica, 1938; *T. Pallady,* Caminul Artei, 1944; *N. Tonitza,* Caminul Artei, 1945; *G. Petrascu,* Editura Fundatiilo Regale, 1945; *Luchian,* Caminul Artei, 1947; *I. Negulici,* Editura de Stat Pentru Literatura si Arta (ESPLA), 1951; *I. Rosenthal,* ESPLA, 1951; *B. Iscovescu,* ESPLA, 1953; (with Ion Frunzetti) *Maestrii Picturii Romanesti in Muzeul de Arta al Republicii Populare Romane,* ESPLA, 1953; *St. Dumitrescu,* ESPLA, 1954; *N. Grigorescu,* Editions de l'Etat pour les Langues Etrangeres, 1955; (with P. Comarnescu) *Stefan Luchian,* ESPLA, 1956; (with M. Popescu) *Maestrii Picturii Romanesti,* ESPLA, 1957; (with W. Benes) *Marturii Despre N. Grigorescu,* ESPLA, 1957; (with Comarnescu) *Les Maitres de la Peinture Roumaine au XX siecle,* Editions de l'Etat pour les langues etrangeres, 1958; *A. Ciucurencu,* ESPLA, 1958.

Brancusi, Arted-Editions d'Art, 1963, translation by Anette Michelson published under same title, Tudor, 1963; *Zadkine,* Arted-Editions d'Art, 1964, translation published under same title, New York Graphic Society, 1965; (with Michel Dufet) *Bourdelle,* Arted-Editions d'Art, 1965, translation by Kathleen Muston and Bryan Richardson published under same title, Tudor, 1966; *La Sculpture et les sculpteurs, de la prehistoire a nos jours et dans le monde entier,* F. Nathan, 1966; (with Cecile Goldscheider) *Rodin,* Arted-Editions d'Art, 1967, translation by Muston and Geoffrey Skelding published under same title, Tudor, 1967; (with Mircea Eliade and Petru Comarnescu) *Temoignages sur Brancusi,* Arted-Editions d'Art, 1967; *Lardera,* Arted-Editions d'Art, 1968; (with Waldemar George) *Henri Georges Adam,* Arted-Editions d'Art, 1968; *Henry Moore,* Arted-Editions d'Art, 1968, translation by Skelding, published under same title, Tudor, 1968; *Valentine Prax,* Arted-Editions d'Art, 1968; *Couturier,* Arted-Editions d'Art, 1969; *Cinq mille ans d'architecture,* F. Nathan, 1970; (with Waldemar George) *Dimitrios Demou,* Arted-Editions d'Art, 1970; (with Helene Lassalle) *Gilioli,* Arted-Editions d'Art, 1971; *Etienne Hajdu,* Arted-Editions d'Art, 1972; *Jean Arp,* Arted-Editions d'Art, 1973; (with Annick Pely) *Marta Pan,* Arted-Editions d'Art, 1974; (with Enzo Carli) *Vittorio Tavernari,* Arted-Editions d'Art, 1975. Contributor to periodicals in Rumania and France.

WORK IN PROGRESS: An article on Froso Eftimadi.

SIDELIGHTS: Jianou's 1955 book on Grigorescu was translated into four languages.

*   *   *

JOHNPOLL, Bernard K(eith)   1918-

PERSONAL: Born June 3, 1918, in New York, N.Y.; son of I. Joseph and Rachel (Elkin) Johnpoll; married Lillian Kirtzman, 1944; children: two daughters. *Education:* Boston University, A.B. (magna cum laude), 1959; Rutgers University, A.M., 1963; State University of New York, Ph.D., 1966. *Politics:* Independent. *Religion:* None. *Home:* 19 Haddington Lane, Delmar, N.Y. *Office:* Department of Political Science, State University of New York, Albany, N.Y.

CAREER: Boston Record-American, Boston, Mass., news editor, 1950-60; Rutgers University, New Brunswick, N.J., lecturer in political science, 1962-63; Hartwick College, Oneonta, N.Y., assistant professor of political science, 1963-65; University of Saskatchewan, Regina, visiting assistant professor, 1965-66; State University of New York at Albany, associate professor, 1966-71, professor of political science, 1971—.

WRITINGS: Canadian News Index, University of Saskatchewan Press, 1966; *The Politics of Futility: The General Jewish Workers Bund of Poland, 1917-1943,* Cornell University Press, 1967; *Pacifist's Progress: Norman Thomas and the Decline of Socialism,* Quadrangle, 1970; (editor and author of introduction) Norman Thomas, *Norman Thomas on War: An Anthology,* Garland Publishing, 1974.

WORK IN PROGRESS: The Impossible Dream: The American Left, 1826-1976, for Macmillan.

SIDELIGHTS: Johnpoll has a good knowledge of Yiddish and German. He can read Russian, Swedish, Norwegian, Danish, Spanish, and Portuguese.

* * *

JOHNS, Warren L. 1929-

PERSONAL: Born June 9, 1929, in Nevada, Iowa; son of Varner J. (a clergyman) and Ruby C. (Morrison) Johns; married Elaine C. Magnuson, July 24, 1955; children: Richard Warren, Lynn Cherie. *Education:* Loma Linda University, B.A., 1950; Andrews University, M.A., 1951; University of Southern California, J.D., 1958. *Home:* 1200 Prospect Ave., Takoma Park, Md. 20012.

CAREER: Admitted to California Bar, 1959; admitted to practice before U.S. Supreme Court, 1963. Attorney in general practice, Sacramento, Calif., 1966-75, in Takoma Park, Md., 1975—. Executive vice-president and general counsel, Church State Council, 1967—; legal adviser and member of executive board, Pacific Union Conference of Seventh-day Adventists; chief counsel, General Conference of Seventh-day Adventists, 1975—; president, Freedom House (book publisher), 1972—. Member of board, Loma Linda Foods and Pacific Union College. *Member:* International Religious Liberty Association (advisory committee member), Americans United (national advisory council member), American Bar Association, American Judicature Society, National Association of College and University Attorneys, Sacramento County Bar Association.

WRITINGS: Dateline Sunday, U.S.A., Taplinger, 1967. Contributor to magazines and newspapers. Contributing editor, *Liberty.*

* * *

JOHNSON, Arthur Menzies 1921-

PERSONAL: Born July 24, 1921, in Waltham, Mass.; son of Frederick P. (a businessman) and Florence M. (Bishop) Johnson; married Emily Ann Wilford, December 28, 1946; children: Robert M., Nancy R. *Education:* Harvard University, A.B., 1944, M.A., 1948; Vanderbilt University, Ph.D., 1954. *Home:* Perkins St., Castine, Me. 04421.

CAREER: Instructor at Thayer Academy, 1946-47, and Cambridge School, 1948-50; U.S. Naval Academy, Annapolis, Md., assistant professor of government and economics, 1954-58; Harvard Business School, Boston, Mass., assistant professor, 1958-61, associate professor, 1961-65, professor of business history, 1966-70; University of Maine, Orono, A. & A. Bird Professor of History, 1970—. Member of advisory committee, Maine State Archives. Eleutheurian Mills-Hagley Foundation, member of advisory committee, 1967-69, 1971-73, trustee, 1973—. *Military*

service: U.S. Army Air Forces, 1943-46; became first lieutenant. U.S. Air Force, 1951-53; became captain.

MEMBER: American Historical Association, Economic History Association (past chairman of membership committee), Organization of American Historians, Business History Conference (president, 1972-73), New England Economic Education Council (secretary, 1967; president, 1968—). *Awards, honors:* Albert J. Beveridge Award ($1,000 and publication), American Historical Association, 1954, for *Development of American Petroleum Pipelines, 1862-1906.*

WRITINGS: Development of American Petroleum Pipelines, 1862-1906, Cornell University Press, 1956; *Government-Business Relations,* C. E. Merrill, 1965; (with Barry E. Supple) *Boston Capitalists and Western Railroads,* Harvard University Press, 1967; *Public Policy and Petroleum Pipelines, 1906-1959,* Harvard University Press, 1967; *Winthrop W. Aldrich: Lawyer, Banker, Diplomat,* Harvard University Press, 1968; *The American Economy: An Historical Introduction to the Problems of the 1970's,* Free Press, 1974. Contributor to encyclopedias and professional journals. Editor, *Business History Review,* 1963-66.

SIDELIGHTS: Johnson told *CA* that he is "particularly interested in shedding light on the changing relationships between the private and public sectors of our economy, because the progress of the country depends so heavily on their interaction."

* * *

JOHNSON, Benjamin A. 1937-

PERSONAL: Born June 29, 1937, in Melby, Minn.; son of Ben Arvid (an insurance agent) and Ruth Ulrika (Werner) Johnson; married Suzanne Wasgatt, May 13, 1960; children: Samuel Perry, Jennie Ruth, Krister Davis, Jesse Jerome. *Education:* Gustavus Adolphus College, B.A., 1959; Lutheran School of Theology, Chicago, Ill., B.D., 1961; Harvard Divinity School, Th.D., 1966; studied at Oxford University, 1971-72. *Politics:* Democrat. *Home:* 264 South Broadmoor Blvd., Springfield, Ohio 45504. *Office:* Hamma School of Theology, Wittenberg University, Springfield, Ohio 45501.

CAREER: Ordained minister of Lutheran Church in America, 1965; Wittenberg University, Hamma School of Theology, Springfield, Ohio, 1965—, began as associate professor, now professor of New Testament, and dean. *Member:* Society for Religion in Higher Education, Society of Biblical Literature.

WRITINGS: (Editor with Herbert T. Neve) *The Maturing of American Lutheranism,* Augsburg, 1968; *The Church in the New Testament,* Lutheran Church in America, 1968; (with Daniel B. Stevick) *Proclamation—Holy Week: Aids for Interpreting the Lessons of the Church Year,* Fortress, 1973; *The Mark of the Christian Community,* CSS Publishing, 1975.

SIDELIGHTS: Johnson is competent in Greek, German, and French, and has some competence in Hebrew, Aramaic, and Latin.

* * *

JOHNSON, Byron Lindberg 1917-

PERSONAL: Born October 12, 1917, in Chicago, Ill.; son of Theodore (a builder) and Ruth E. (Lindberg) Johnson; married Catherine Teter, October 22, 1938; children: Steven, Christi, Eric. *Education:* University of Wisconsin,

B.A., 1938, M.A., 1940, Ph.D., 1947. *Politics:* Democrat. *Religion:* United Church of Christ. *Home:* 2451 South Dahlia Lane, Denver, Colo. 80222. *Office:* University of Colorado, 1100 14th St., Denver, Colo. 80202.

CAREER: State of Wisconsin, Madison, statistician, 1938-42; U.S. Government, Washington, D.C., fiscal analyst for Bureau of the Budget, 1942-44, economist for Social Security Administration, 1944-47; University of Denver, Denver, Colo., assistant professor, 1947-51, associate professor of economics, 1951-57; administrative assistant to Governor of Colorado, 1957-58; member of U.S. Congress from Colorado, 1959-60; Agency for International Development, Washington, D.C., 1961-64, served as consultant and U.S. delegate to conferences in Santiago, Chile, 1961, Geneva, Switzerland, 1962, Melbourne, Australia, 1962, and others; University of Colorado, Denver, professor of economics, 1965—, regent, 1970—. Summer professor at Columbia University, 1951. Member of House of Representatives, Colorado General Assembly, 1954-56. Member of Commission of Church and Economic Life, and Department of International Affairs, both National Council of Churches, 1959-69, of Council for Christian Social Action, United Church of Christ, 1961-67. Trustee of Voice of Youth of Denver, Colo., 1951-65.

MEMBER: American Economic Association, American Political Science Association, National Tax Association, Western Social Science Association, Phi Kappa Phi, Delta Sigma Rho, Artus. *Awards, honors:* Whitehead Award, 1960.

WRITINGS: The Principle of Equalization Applied to the Allocation of Grants in Aid, Social Security Administration, 1947; (with others) *Revolution and Renewal,* Disciples of Christ, 1965; (with Barbara Ward and others) *Christianity Among Rising Men and Nations,* Association Press, 1965; *Need Is Our Neighbor,* Friendship, 1966. Contributor to religion and industry journals.

WORK IN PROGRESS: The Laws of Bureaucratic Immobility; New Approaches to Urban and Rural Environments.

AVOCATIONAL INTERESTS: Gardening and mountaineering.

*   *   *

JOHNSON, James L.   1927-

PERSONAL: Born February 26, 1927, in Dollar Bay, Mich.; son of Eric R. (a laborer) and Anna (Backman) Johnson; married Rosemary Lorts, June 7, 1952; children: Jay. *Education:* Suomi College, student, 1947-49; Moody Bible Institute, B.Th., 1959; University of Michigan, B.A. in Journalism, 1963. *Politics:* Republican. *Home:* 505 Lyon St., Wheaton, Ill. 60187.

CAREER: Baptist minister. *Africa Challenge* (magazine), Lagos, Nigeria, editor, 1956-59; minister of Bible church in Chicago, Ill., 1959-61; Evangelical Literature Overseas, Wheaton, Ill., director, beginning 1963; professor of journalism and director of department, Wheaton College, Wheaton. Christian Writers Institute, Wheaton, former staff instructor, currently consultant. *Military service:* U.S. Navy, 1944-45. *Member:* Sigma Delta Chi. *Awards, honors:* $1,000 prize for essay, "Take the Fear Out of Integration," from *Christian Herald,* 1967.

WRITINGS—All fiction, except as indicated: *Code Name Sebastian,* Lippincott, 1967; *The Nine Lives of Alphonse,* Lippincott, 1968; *A Handful of Dominoes,* Lippincott,

1970; *The Nine to Five Complex* (nonfiction), Zondervan, 1972; *The Death of Kings,* Doubleday, 1974; *A Piece of the Moon Is Missing,* A. J. Holman, 1974; (with Eugene B. McDaniel) *Before Honor* (nonfiction), A. J. Holman, 1975.

WORK IN PROGRESS: A nonfiction book, *What Every Woman Should Know about a Man,* and a novel, *Compass Zero,* both for Zondervan.

SIDELIGHTS: James L. Johnson speaks Yoruba, a West African tribal language, and German. *Avocational interests:* Reading, sports.

BIOGRAPHICAL/CRITICAL SOURCES: Decision, June, 1967.

*   *   *

JOHNSON, Jean Dye   1920-

PERSONAL: Born February 24, 1920, in Minna, Nigeria, West Africa; daughter of Guy William (a missionary) and Elizabeth (Christie) Playfair; married second husband, Robert W. Dye, May 10, 1943; married second husband, Lawrence H. Johnson (student advisor of a language school for missionary candidates), December 6, 1956; children: (second marriage) Verne, Marge Colleen. *Education:* Columbia Bible College, Columbia, S.C., B.A. *Home and office:* New Tribes Institute, Camdenton, Mo. 65020.

CAREER: Missionary in Bolivia, 1943-58; language teacher and linguistic consultant, Waukesha, Wis., beginning 1958. Bible translations consultant.

WRITINGS: Idiomatic Spanish Course for Missionaries, Nueva Vida, 1955; *God Planted Five Seeds,* Harper, 1966, reprinted, Brown Gold Publications, 1972; *Situational Spanish for Missionaries,* New Tribes Language-Orientation Institute, 1972. Prepared grammars of two tribal languages in Bolivia.

*   *   *

JOHNSON, Robert J.   1933-

PERSONAL: Born August 1, 1933, in Denver, Colo.; son of Wilton Ernest (a fireman) and Imo Pearl (Gustofson) Johnson; married Catherine Verhage, August 20, 1959; children: Mark William, Robert James II. *Education:* University of Colorado, B.S., 1965. *Religion:* Christian Reformed. *Home:* 5730 173rd Pl. S.W., Lynnwood, Wash. 98036.

CAREER: Mountain States Telephone Co., Denver, Colo., combination man, 1951-62; Boeing Co., Seattle, Wash., methods analyst, 1965-67, change board representative for industrial engineering, 1967-68, in charge of manual and automated data documentation systems for industrial engineering, 1968-69; Pacific Northwest Bell Telephone Co., Seattle, local area telephone forecaster, 1969-70, administrative revenue forecaster, 1971—. Management consultant in marketing research. *Military service:* U.S. Army, 1954-56.

WRITINGS: (With Lawrence L. Steinmetz and A. Dale Allen) *Labor Law: A Program of Instruction on Labor Law,* Media Masters, 1967.

*   *   *

JOHNSON, Rossall J(ames)   1917-

PERSONAL: Born December 31, 1917, in Evanston, Ill.; married, 1944; three children. *Education:* Northwestern University, B.S.M.E., 1942, M.B.A., 1946; Purdue University, Ph.D., 1954. *Home:* 624 Garrett Pl., Evanston, Ill.

60201. *Office:* Northwestern University, Evanston, Ill. 60201.

CAREER: Bendix Aviation Corp., South Bend, Ind., production research engineer, 1942-45; Radio Corp. of America, Indianapolis, Ind., production foreman, 1946-48; Firecraft Corp., Chicago, Ill., personnel administrator and industrial engineer, 1948-49; Mississippi State College (now University), Starkville, assistant professor of industrial management, 1949-51; Purdue University, Lafayette, Ind., member of psychology faculty, 1951-52; Northwestern University, Graduate School of Management, Evanston, Ill., assistant professor, 1953-57, associate professor, 1958-64, professor of business administration, 1964—, chairman of department, 1956-59. Ford Foundation, director of executive development program at University of Indonesia, 1959-61, senior research consultant in India, 1964-66, management education consultant in Nigeria, 1971-73, in Indonesia, 1973.

MEMBER: Academy of Management, American Association for the Advancement of Science, American Psychological Association, American Sociological Association, Industrial Relations Research Association, L'Association Internationale de Psychologie Appliquee, Society for the Psychological Study of Social Issues, Sigma Xi, Beta Gamma Sigma.

WRITINGS: Personnel and Industrial Relations, Irwin, 1960; (co-author) *Indonesian Cases in Business Administration,* Volumes I-III, University of Indonesia Press, 1961; (co-author) *Readings in Business Administration and Economics,* University of Indonesia Press, 1961; *Executive Decisions: Human Factors, Management Functions, Social Responsibility,* South-Western Publishing, 1963, 3rd edition, 1976; (co-author) *Business Environment in an Emerging Nation,* Northwestern University Press, 1966. Contributor to professional journals.

WORK IN PROGRESS: An investigation of the interaction awareness factors in decision making, with emphasis on public sector industry; research on organization structure and control mechanisms of parastatal corporations.

*   *   *

JOHNSON, Stanley Patrick 1940-

PERSONAL: Born August 18, 1940, in Penzance, Cornwall, England; son of Wilfred (a farmer) and Irene (Williams) Johnson; married Charlotte Fawcett, July 20, 1963; children: Alexander, Rachel, Leo, Joseph. *Education:* Oxford University, B.A. (honors), 1963, Diploma in Agricultural Economics, 1965. *Home:* 37 Avenue de la Sapiniere, 1180 Brussels, Belgium; 174 Regents Park Rd., London NW1, England; Nethercote Cottage, Winsford, Minehead, Somerset, England. *Agent:* John Cushman Associates, Inc., 24 East 38th St., New York, N.Y. 10016.

CAREER: World Bank, Washington, D.C., writer and economist, 1966-68; member, Conservative Research Department, 1969-70; International Planned Parenthood Federation, London, England, staff member, 1971-73; Commission of the European Communities, Brussels, Belgium, head of Prevention of Pollution and Nuisances Division, 1973—. Consultant, United Nations Fund Population Activities, 1971-73. Member, Countryside Commission, 1971-73. *Awards, honors:* Sir Roger Newdigate Prize for English verse, 1962, for "May Morning."

WRITINGS: Gold Drain (novel), Heinemann, 1967; *The Presidential Plot* (novel), Simon & Schuster, 1968 (published in England as *Panther Jones for President,* Heinemann, 1968); *Life Without Birth: A Journey through the Third World in Search of the Population Explosion,* Heinemann, 1970, published as *Life Without Birth,* Little, Brown, 1971; *The Green Revolution,* Harper, 1972; *The Politics of the Environment,* Stacey, 1973; (editor) *The Population Problem,* David & Charles, 1974; *God Bless America* (novel), Doubleday, 1975.

*   *   *

JOHNSON, Virginia E. 1925-

PERSONAL: Born February 11, 1925, in Springfield, Mo.; daughter of Harry Hershel and Edna (Evans) Eshelman; married George Johnson, June 13, 1950 (divorced September, 1956); married William H. Masters (a medical doctor and researcher), January 7, 1971; children: (first marriage) Scott Forstall, Lisa Evans. *Education:* Attended Drury College, 1940-42, University of Missouri, 1944-47, and Washington University, St. Louis, Mo. 1964. *Office:* Reproductive Biology Research Foundation, 4910 Forest Park Blvd., St. Louis, Mo. 63108.

CAREER: St. Louis Daily Record, St. Louis, Mo., administrative secretary and reporter, 1947-50; Columbia Broadcasting System (KMOX), St. Louis, staff member of advertising department, 1950-51; Washington University School of Medicine, Division of Reproductive Biology, St. Louis, member of research staff, 1957-64, research assistant, 1960-62, research instructor, 1962-64; Reproductive Biology Research Foundation, St. Louis, research associate, 1964-69, assistant director, 1969-73, co-director, 1973—. Member of board of directors, Family and Children's Services, and Sex Information and Education Council of the United States (SIECUS); member of advisory board, Homosexual Community Counseling Center.

MEMBER: Society for the Scientific Study of Sex (fellow), International Society for Research in the Biology of Reproduction, Society for the Study of Reproduction, American Association for the Advancement of Science, International Platform Association, Author's Guild, Eastern Missouri Psychiatric Society (honorary member), Women's Association of St. Louis Symphony Society, Women's Society of Washington University, Bridle Spur Hunt Club. *Awards, honors:* Society for the Scientific Study of Sex annual award, 1967; Paul H. Hoch Award of American Psychopathological Association, 1971; SIECUS citation award, 1972.

*WRITINGS—*With William H. Masters: *Human Sexual Response,* Little, Brown, 1966; *Human Sexual Inadequacy,* Little, Brown, 1970; *The Pleasure Bond,* Little, Brown, 1975.

Contributor with W. H. Masters: G. W. Winokur, editor, *Determinants of Human Sexual Behavior,* C. C Thomas, 1963; C. W. Lloyd, editor. *Human Reproduction and Sexual Behavior,* Lea & Febiger, 1964; J. Money, editor, *Sex Research: New Developments,* Holt, 1965; F. A. Beach, editor, *Sex and Behavior,* Wiley, 1965; M. Diamond, editor, *Perspectives in Reproduction and Sexual Behavior,* Indiana University Press, 1968; M. Stuart, editor, *The Emerging Woman: The Impact of Family Planning,* Little, Brown, 1970; H. S. Kaplan and C. J. Sager, editors, *Progress in Group and Family Therapy,* Brunner, 1972; J. Zubin and J. Money, editors, *Contemporary Sexual Behavior: Critical Issues in the 1970's,* Johns Hopkins Press, 1973; M. S. Calderone, editor, *Sexuality and Human Values,* Association Press, 1974.

(Author of foreword) L. C. Schaefer, *Women and Sex,* Pantheon, 1973. Contributor to journals and periodicals in her field. Member of advisory committee, *Pastoral Psychology Journal.*

SIDELIGHTS: With regard to the research work into human sexual behavior that she and Dr. Masters have done, Mrs. Johnson said: "We never defend our work. We will discuss it with those people truly interested in it. But the thing that speaks for us most is scientific productivity. We've so much more to do. We just keep plodding on." The results of their research are published in two books, *Human Sexual Response* and *Human Sexual Inadequacy.*

Reviewing *Human Sexual Response,* Marion K. Sanders writes: "Although their book is confined to stark physiological facts, they are well aware that human sexuality cannot be considered apart from its psychological and social implications. Over the years they have themselves worked closely with social agencies and with juvenile courts; they are compassionate people much more concerned with the human tragedies that result from distorted sexual concepts than with the mechanics of sex."

Alan F. Guttmacher calls *Human Sexual Inadequacy* "a powerful document in demonstrating the urgent necessity of sex education for youths as well as adults. Human sexual dysfunction has many causes, almost all psychological; most of these are preventable in an intelligent society concerned with humanizing its sex standards and practices. Masters and Johnson show that the most difficult and baneful sexual influence to be neutralized is religious dogmatism; . . ." While Martin Roth finds Masters' and Johnsons' positive approach towards sexual life in the elderly "commendable", he finds that "their judgment appears to be coloured by that wishful kind of illusion according to which if only an adequate effort were mounted there would be a remedy for all forms of disturbed and maladaptive human conduct, no matter how complex, old and baffling, not in 20 years or a century but now."

BIOGRAPHICAL/CRITICAL SOURCES: New Statesman, May 6, 1966; *New York Times Book Review,* May 29, 1966, July 12, 1970; *Book Week,* July 17, 1966; *Scientific American,* August, 1966; Ruth Brecher and Edward Brecher, editors, *An Analysis of "Human Sexual Response,"* Little, Brown, 1966; *Playboy* (interview), May, 1968; *Harpers,* May, 1968, August, 1970; *Newsweek,* June 10, 1968, May 4, 1970, August 24, 1970, February 22, 1971; *New York Times,* April 27, 1970; *Time,* May 25, 1970; *Listener,* June 18, 1970.

*   *   *

JOHNSON-MARSHALL, Percy E. A.   1915-

PERSONAL: Born January 20, 1915, in Ajmer, India; son of Felix W. Norman and K. J. Johnson-Marshall; married April Phyllis Trix; children: Mary Tara, Peter, Katherine, Caroline, Stirling, Nicholas, Ursula. *Education:* Liverpool School of Architecture, Diploma (distinction in architecture); University of Liverpool, Certificate in Civic Design. *Office:* Bella Vista 64, The Causeway, Duddingston, Edinburgh EH15 3PZ, Scotland.

CAREER: Architect in London, England, and later senior architect in charge of reconstruction of city center after bombing of Coventry, England, 1936-41; adviser on planning to Government of Burma, 1945-46; Ministry of Town and Country Planning, London, staff of Planning Technique Office, 1946-48; London County Council, London, head of reconstruction areas groups and then group plan-

ning officer for northeast London, 1948-59; University of Edinburgh, Edinburgh, Scotland, senior lecturer, 1959-63, reader, 1963-64, professor or urban design and regional planning, 1964—, director of architectural research unit and planning research unit. Planning consultant in private practice. Participant with University of Glasgow in Lothians Regional Survey Plan. Member of Board of Architectural Education and of World Housing Organization expert panel on environmental health and planning. *Military service:* British Army, Royal Engineers, 1941-46; served in India and Burma; became major. *Member:* Royal Institute of British Architects (associate; council member, 1953-70), Town Planning Institute (associate; council member). *Awards, honors:* Distinction in Town Planning Award of Royal Institute of British Architects.

WRITINGS: Rebuilding of Cities, Aldine, 1966; (with Robert Mathew and others) *Central Lancashire: Study for a City,* H.M.S.O., 1967; (with Mathew and others) *Central Lancashire New Town Proposal: Impact on North East Lancashire,* H.M.S.O., 1968; (author of introduction) Patrick Geddes, *Cities in Evolution: An Introduction to the Town Planning Movement and to the Study of Civics,* Fertig, 1969; (with Mathew and others) *New Life in Old Towns,* H.M.S.O., 1971.†

*   *   *

JOHNSTON, Arthur   1924-

PERSONAL: Born November 24, 1924, in Bradford, Yorkshire, England; son of Arthur Stephen and Lilian (Milthorpe) Johnston; married Charlotte Stephanie Ware (a lecturer in philosophy), September 15, 1951; children: Catherine, Stella, David, Stephen. *Education:* Queen's College, Oxford, M.A., 1949, D.Phil., 1956. *Religion:* Church of England. *Home:* King's Heath, St. David's Rd., Aberystwyth, Dyfed, Wales. *Office:* University College of Wales, Aberystwyth, Dyfed, Wales.

CAREER: University of London, London, England, assistant lecturer at Bedford College, 1951-54, lecturer in English at Birkbeck College, 1954-65; University College of Wales, Aberystwyth, professor of English, 1965—. *Military service:* Royal Air Force, 1943-46; became sergeant. *Member:* Bibliographical Society (London), Bibliographical Society of University of Virginia, English Association, Honorable Society of Cymmrodorion.

WRITINGS: (Editor) W. Hazlitt, *Lectures on the English Comic Writers,* Dent, 1963; *Enchanted Ground: The Study of Medieval Romance in the 18th Century,* Athlone Press, 1964; (editor) *Francis Bacon: Selections,* Batsford, 1965; (editor) *Selected Poems of Thomas Gray and William Collins,* E. J. Arnold, 1967; (editor) *Francis Bacon: Advancement of Learning New Atlantis,* Clarendon Press, 1974; *The Poetry of William Collins,* British Academy, 1976. Contributor to *National Library of Wales Journal, Review of English Studies,* and other professional journals.

WORK IN PROGRESS: Edition of Shakespeare's *Much Ado About Nothing,* for "New Arden" series.

*   *   *

JONAS, Manfred   1927-

PERSONAL: Born April 9, 1927, in Mannheim, Germany; U.S. citizen; son of Walter and Antonie (Dannheisser) Jonas; married Nancy Jane Greene, July 19, 1952; children: Andrew Miles, Kathryn Leslie, Emily Susan, Matthew Greene. *Education:* City College (now of the City University of New York), B.S., 1949; Harvard University, A.M., 1950, Ph.D., 1959. *Office:* Department of History, Union College, Schenectady, N.Y. 12308.

CAREER: U.S. Department of Defense, Salzburg, Austria, intelligence analyst, 1950-53; Free University of Berlin, Berlin, Germany, visiting assistant professor of American history, 1959-62; Pennsylvania Military College, Chester, associate professor of history, 1962-63; Union College, Schenectady, N.Y., assistant professor, 1963-64, associate professor, 1964-67, professor of history, 1967—, director of graduate program in American studies, 1964-74, chairman, department of history, 1970—. Summer lecturer at City College (now of the City University of New York), 1950, University of Maryland Extension Division, 1954, and Northeastern University, 1958; senior Fulbright-Hays lecturer, University of the Saarland, 1973. Radio commentator and lecturer on American topics in Germany, 1960-62; conductor of discussion program on public issues, WMHT, Schenectady, 1965. Member of board of directors, Freedom Forum, Inc., 1966—. *Military service:* U.S. Naval Reserve, 1945-51, active duty, 1945-46. *Member:* American Historical Association, Organization of American Historians, American Association of University Professors, German Association for American Studies, Society for Historians of American Foreign Relations.

WRITINGS: Die Unabhangigkeitserklarung der Vereinigten Staaten, Hans Pfeiffer Verlag, 1965; *Isolationism in America, 1935-1941,* Cornell University Press, 1966; (editor) *American Foreign Relations in the Twentieth Century,* Crowell, 1967; (co-editor) *Roosevelt and Churchill: Their Secret Wartime Correspondence,* Saturday Review Press, 1975.

Contributor: Richard Wernicke, editor, *Welt im Prisma,* [Hamburg], 1962; *Die U.S.A. und Deutschland: Zeitgeschichtliche Fragen,* [Brunswick], 1962; John Braeman and others, editors, *Twentieth-Century American Foreign Policy,* Ohio State University Press, 1971; Charles Chatfield, editor, *Peace Movements in America,* Schocken, 1973. Contributor to historical periodicals in United States and Germany. Member of editorial board, *Studies in American History and Literature* (Berlin).

WORK IN PROGRESS: U.S.-German Relations since 1871; articles for *Dictionary of the History of American Foreign Policy,* edited by Alexander De Conde, and *America: An Illustrated History of the United States,* edited by Henry S. Commager and Maldwyn A. Jones.

AVOCATIONAL INTERESTS: Skiing, sailing, and acting.

*   *   *

JONES, Billy M(ac) 1925-

PERSONAL: Born April 5, 1925, in Abilene, Tex.; son of William Anderson (a salesman) and Faye (Barton) Jones; married Doris Jane Hudson, March 10, 1948; children: Jeffrey Hudson, Woodrow Edward, Russell Anderson, Scott Ellis. *Education:* Vanderbilt University, B.A., 1950; George Peabody College for Teachers, M.A., 1952; Texas Technological College (now Texas Tech University), Ph.D., 1963. *Religion:* Church of Christ. *Home:* 4035 Grandview, Memphis, Tenn. 38111. *Office:* Memphis State University, Memphis, Tenn. 38111.

CAREER: High school mathematics teacher and coach in Nashville, Tenn., 1950-54; Middle Tennessee State College (now University), Murfreesboro, teacher of history and

coach, 1954-58; Texas A&M University, College Station, assistant football coach, 1958-59; San Angelo College (now Angelo State University), San Angelo, Tex., head of department of social sciences, 1959-61; Texas Technological College (now Texas Tech University), Lubbock, instructor in history, 1961-63; Angelo State College, dean of student life, 1963-69; Southwest Texas State University, San Marcos, president, 1969-73; Memphis State University, Memphis, Tenn., president, 1973—. American Council on Education intern in academic administration, University of Colorado, 1967-68. *Military service:* U.S. Navy, 1943-46.

MEMBER: National Education Association (life), American Historical Association, American Association State Colleges and Universities, Western History Association, Southwestern Historical Association, Texas State Historical Association (president, 1975), Tennessee Historical Association, West Texas Historical Association, Economic Club of Memphis, Omicron Delta Kappa, Phi Theta Kappa, Phi Kappa Phi, Phi Alpha Theta, Rotary International. *Awards, honors:* Minnie Stevens Piper Foundation Award for teaching, 1967; fellowships from Texas State Historical Association, 1967, and American Council on Education, 1967; 1974 Liberty Bowl Classic Distinguished American Award; Silver Anniversary Top Five Award, from National Collegiate Athletic Association, 1975.

WRITINGS: The Search for Maturity, 1875-1900, Steck, 1965; *Health-Seekers in the Southwest, 1817-1900,* University of Oklahoma Press, 1967; (with Billy R. Brunson) *Texans All: The People of Texas,* W. S. Benson, 1973.

Contributor: *Protest: Student Activism in America,* Morrow, 1969; *Rangers of Texas,* Texian Press, 1969; *Capitols of Texas,* Texian Press, 1970; *Indian Tribes of Texas,* Texian Press, 1971; *Women of Texas,* Texian Press, 1972; *Soldiers of Texas,* Texian Press, 1973.

*   *   *

JONES, Christopher 1937-

PERSONAL: Born June 7, 1937, in New York, N.Y.; son of William Creed (a salesman) and Genevieve (Basilotta) Jones. *Education:* Studied at seminaries in New York, Washington, D.C., and Ohio. *Home:* Transfiguration Retreat, Route 1, Pulaski, Wis. 54162.

CAREER: Father Christopher describes himself as "author, Benedictine monk, ordained Orthodox Catholic priest and bishop." Founder of the Transfiguration Retreat, Pulaski, Wis.

WRITINGS: Listen, Pilgrim (prose poem), foreword by Daniel Berrigan, Bruce, 1968; *Look Around, Pilgrim,* Bruce, 1968.

WORK IN PROGRESS: To Touch the Heart of God; Scott: Letter From the Save; Now is the Time; Cost of Becoming.

SIDELIGHTS: Father Christopher told *CA,* "at one time known as the 'hippy priest,' [I] left the activity of the late sixties and founded a tiny monastic community in Wisconsin." Commenting on his change from activity to cloister, he said, "Sometimes there is nothing to do but ache . . . and that awful aching, is prayer."

*   *   *

JONES, D(avid) Mervyn 1922-

PERSONAL: Born July 29, 1922, in Sheffield, England; son of John David (a university lecturer) and Gladys Alicia

(Coombs) Jones; married Nan Vance Dunbar (a fellow of Somerville College, Oxford University), 1972. *Education:* Trinity College, Cambridge, M.A., 1948. *Residence:* London, England.

CAREER: Cambridge University, Cambridge, England, research fellow in classics at Trinity College, 1949-51; Oxford University, Oxford, England, fellow and lecturer in classics at Exeter College, 1951-61, fellow in Hungarian at Exeter College, 1961-62, senior research fellow at St. Antony's College, 1962-63; with Foreign and Commonwealth Office, 1963—.

WRITINGS: Five Hungarian Writers, Oxford University Press, 1966; (with Nigel G. Wilson) *Scholia in Aristophanis Equites,* Wolters-Noordhoff BV (Groningen, Netherlands), 1969. Contributor to classical journals.

WORK IN PROGRESS: Six Hungarian Writers, a sequel to his first book, which dealt with Zrinyi, Mikes, Vorosmarty, Eotvos, and Petofi.

SIDELIGHTS: Jones is competent in French, German, Hungarian, Italian, Polish, and Rumanian. His writing thus far has been geared "to interest the non-specialist reader in Hungarian literature." *Avocational interests:* Music.

* * *

JONES, Douglas C. 1924-

PERSONAL: Born December 6, 1924, in Winslow, Ark.; son of Marvin Clyde (an auto mechanic) and Bethel (Stockburger) Jones; married Mary Arnold (sales clerk), January 1, 1949; children: Mary Glenn, Martha Claire, Kathryn Greer, Douglas Eben. *Education:* University of Arkansas, B.A., 1949; U.S. Army Command and General Staff College, graduate study, 1961; University of Wisconsin, M.S., 1963. *Home address:* Route #2, West Fork, Ark. 72774.

CAREER: Career officer in U.S. Army, 1949-68, commandor of infantry rifle companies in Europe and Korea, served as information officer, Philadelphia Army Air Defense Command, and in the Office of Assistant Secretary of Defense (Public Affairs), Pentagon, Washington, D.C., as chief of Armed Forces Press Branch. Artist; had one-man show of Indian studies at Washington Gallery of Art, 1967, and presently showing his paintings in Fayetteville, Ark. and Tulsa, Okla. *Awards, honors*—Military: Army Commendation Medal (three times); Legion of Merit.

WRITINGS: The Treaty of Medicine Lodge, University of Oklahoma Press, 1966. Contributor to *Journalism Quarterly.*

WORK IN PROGRESS: Two nineteenth-century based novels.

* * *

JONES, DuPre Anderson 1937-

PERSONAL: Born May 16, 1937, in Charlotte, N.C.; son of William Burns (a physician) and Elizabeth (Anderson) Jones; married Georgie Hoole, June, 1958; married second wife, Priscilla Samuel (a journalist), July, 1964; children: (first marriage) DuPre Anderson, Jr., W. Burns; (second marriage) Matthew Adam. *Education:* University of the South, student, 1954-58; George Washington University, B.A., 1960. *Politics:* None. *Religion:* Atheist. *Home:* 2800 Ontario Rd. N.W., Washington, D.C. 20009.

CAREER: New York Times, librarian, Washington bureau, beginning 1964.

WRITINGS: The Adventures of Gremlin, Lippincott, 1966.

WORK IN PROGRESS: The Last Ditch and *The Dog Who Sang like Vaughn Monroe,* both fiction.††

* * *

JONES, G(eorge) William 1931-

PERSONAL: Born February 26, 1931, in Austin, Tex.; son of George Willis (a church business administrator) and Mary (Patterson) Jones; married Frances Joanne Baggett, May 29, 1954; children: Christopher Shaw, David Whitefield. *Education:* Southern Methodist University, B.A., 1951, B.D. (Perkins School of Theology), 1956; Syracuse University, Ph.D., 1971. *Home:* 3040 Binkley, Apt. 3, Dallas, Tex. 75205. *Office:* Department of Broadcast-Film Art, Southern Methodist University, Dallas, Tex. 75275.

CAREER: Keitz & Herndon Film Co., Dallas, Tex., writer and salesman, 1952-53; Tyler Street Methodist Church, Dallas, minister to youth, 1953-56; pastor in Justin, Tex., 1956-58, and Grand Prairie, Tex., 1958-63; Casa View Methodist Church, Dallas, minister of education, 1963-65; Southern Methodist University, Dallas, assistant professor, 1965-70, professor of broadcast-film art, 1970—. Director of Southwest Film Archive, 1969—, and U.S.A. Film Festival, 1970—. Moderator of Dallas Youth Film Forum, 1966-68. Appointed by President Johnson as member of Commission on Obscenity and Pornography, 1968-70. Consultant on use of screen media in religious education to film companies, church organizations, and U.S. Navy. *Military service:* U.S. Air Force, 1951-52.

MEMBER: Methodist Association for Study and Training (chairman of board of directors, 1966), Sex Information and Education Council of U.S. (member of executive board, 1972—), Texas Commission on Arts and Humanities, Texas Film Commission, Lambda Chi Alpha.

WRITINGS: Dialogue with the World, Encyclopaedia Britannica, 1966; *Sunday Night at the Movies,* John Knox, 1967; *The Innovator, and Other Modern Parables,* Abingdon, 1969; *Relationship of Screen-Mediated Violence to Anti-Social Behavior,* Syracuse University Press, 1971; *Landing Right-Side Up in TV and Film,* Abington, 1973. Reviewer for *Southwest Review,* 1964-65. Contributor of more than forty articles to magazines and journals.

* * *

JONES, Gene 1928-

PERSONAL: Born April 4, 1928, in Wichita, Kan.; son of Horace Hill (a carpenter) and Billie Ann (Jenkins) Jones; married Laura Shadd (an advertising media director), March, 1956; children: Hugh Hill Miron. *Education:* University of Arizona, B.F.A., 1951. *Residence:* Cold Spring, N.Y. 10516.

CAREER: Smith College, Northampton, Mass., teaching fellow, 1951-53; stage manager of theatrical productions in New York, N.Y., and summer stock, 1953-64, including the New York City Ballet, 1961-63; free-lance editor for several publishers, 1964—.

WRITINGS: Where the Wind Blew Free, Norton, 1967. Contributor of stories to *Manhunt, West, Real West.*

WORK IN PROGRESS: A novel; research for another book.

SIDELIGHTS: The grandson of Texas pioneers, Jones grew up in Arizona, and has been influenced by the American West in both his writings and interests. Has a "nodding acquaintance" with Spanish, French, Italian, and

German. *Avocational interests:* Cats, theater history, gardening.††

* * *

JONES, Kenneth S. 1919-

PERSONAL: Born August 17, 1919, in Glen Rock, N.J.; son of Howard Kenneth (a photographer) and Bessie (Appelgate) Jones; married Edlea Janice Kelly (an elementary school librarian), June 5, 1948; children: Jeffrey, Bruce, Kelly. *Education:* American University, B.A., 1948; Yale University, M.Div., 1951. *Politics:* Democrat. *Home:* 12101 Old Bridge Rd., Rockville, Md. 20852.

CAREER: Ordained Methodist minister, 1951; pastor in Baltimore, Md., 1951-56, and at the American Church, Brussels, Belgium, 1956-57; missionary in the Congo before and after independence (evacuated during the Katanga-United Nations War, 1962); The Methodist Church, Washington Area Office of Information, Washington, D.C., director, 1962-67; Faith United Methodist Church, Rockville, Md., pastor, 1967—. Director of Methodist Missions Tour to Africa, 1965. Served for a short time as public attitude analyst for U.S. Economic Cooperation Administration. *Military service:* U.S. Army, World War II; became first lieutenant.

WRITINGS: Twelve Came Riding, Abingdon, 1967. Contributor to *Christian Advocate, Today, Washingtonian,* and *Lutheran.*

* * *

JONES, (Everett) LeRoi 1934-
(Imamu Amiri Baraka)

PERSONAL: Born October 7, 1934, in Newark, N.J.; son of Coyette Leroy (a postman and elevator operator) and Anna Lois (Russ) Jones; married (divorced, August, 1965); married Sylvia Robinson (Bibi Amina Baraka), 1966; children: (first marriage) Kellie Elisabeth, Lisa Victoria; (second marriage) four sons, one daughter. *Education:* Attended Rutgers University for one year; Howard University, B.A., 1954; attended Columbia University and New School for Social Research. *Residence:* Newark, N.J. *Office:* Congress of African People, 13 Belmont, Newark, N.J.

CAREER: Founded *Yugen* magazine and Totem Press, 1958; New School for Social Research, New York, N.Y., instructor, 1961-64. Visiting professor, University of Buffalo, summer, 1964, Columbia University, fall, 1964, and 1966-67, and San Francisco State University. Founder, April, 1964, and director, 1964-66, of Black Arts Repertory Theatre, which was disbanded after it was disclosed that Jones was using Harlem Youth (HARYOU) funds to finance his war on white America; founder, 1966, and currently director of Spirit House (also known as Heckalu Community Center), Newark, a black community theatre, and head of advisory group at Treat Elementary School, Newark. Arrested some years ago for sending allegedly obscene literature through the mails—one of his plays and a William Burroughs burlesque of Franklin Delano Roosevelt. Visited Cuba 1960, to demonstrate support for Fidel Castro; subsequently arrested. Accused, August, 1966, of beating and robbing Shepard Sherbell, editor of *East Side Review,* over non-payment for the publication of one of Jones's plays; charges dismissed, January 19, 1967. Arrested, July 14, 1967, in Newark, for allegedly carrying weapons in Newark during the riots; sentenced to two-and-a-half to three years in the New Jersey State Penitentiary

and fined $1,000, January 4, 1968; released, January 9, 1968, on $25,000 bail; his first appeal was rejected by the U.S. Supreme Court, March 5, 1968; decision reversed, December 24, 1968; acquitted; arrested November 26, 1968, charged with loud and abusive language, fined $100 and sentenced to 60 days. In 1968 Jones ran for a seat on a Newark community council which would oversee slum rehabilitation, but lost the election. *Military service:* U.S. Air Force, 1954-57; weather-gunner; stationed for two and a half years in Puerto Rico with intervening trips to Europe, Africa, and the Middle East. *Member:* National Black Political Assembly (secretary general), Congress of African People (chairman), United Brothers. *Awards, honors:* John Whitney Foundation fellowship for poetry and fiction, 1962; Obie Award, 1964, for *Dutchman;* Longview Foundation Award; Guggenheim fellowship, 1965-66.

*WRITINGS—*Plays: "A Good Girl Is Hard to Find," first produced in Montclair, N.J., 1958; *Dutchman [and] The Slave (Dutchman,* one-act, first produced Off-Broadway at Cherry Lane Theatre, March 24, 1964, produced in London, 1967; *The Slave,* one-act, first produced Off-Broadway at St. Mark's Playhouse, December, 1964, produced in London, 1972), Morrow, 1964, *Dutchman* was published alone by Faber & Faber, 1967; "Dante" (first produced in New York City, 1961; produced as "The 8th Ditch" in New York City, 1964), published in *The System of Dante's Hell,* Grove, 1965 (see below); *The Baptism [and] The Toilet (The Baptism,* one-act, first produced Off-Broadway, 1964, produced in London, 1971; *The Toilet,* one-act, first produced Off-Broadway, 1964), Grove, 1967; *Arm Yourself, or Harm Yourself* (one-act; first produced in Newark, N.J., by Jihad Productions, 1967), Jihad, 1967; "Home on the Range" (first produced at Spirit House, spring, 1968; produced in New York City at a Town Hall rally, March, 1968), published in *Drama Review,* summer, 1968; "Police," published in *Drama Review,* summer, 1968; *Four Black Revolutionary Plays: All Praises to the Black Man* (contains: "Experimental Death Unit # One," first produced in New York City, by Black Arts Repertory Theatre, 1965; "A Black Mass," first produced in Newark, by Black Arts Repertory Theatre, 1966; "Great Goodness of Life (A Coon Show)," first produced with three other plays by Ben Caldwell, Ronald Milner, and Ed Bullins under program title "A Black Quartet" at Tambellini's Gate Theatre, July 30, 1969; "Madheart," first produced in San Francisco, 1967), Bobbs-Merrill, 1969 (published in England as *Four Black Revolutionary Plays,* Calder & Boyars, 1971); *Slave Ship* (one-act; first produced in Newark, by Jihad Productions, 1967; first produced in New York City, November 19, 1969), Jihad, 1969; "A Recent Killing," first produced Off-Broadway, 1969; "The Death of Malcolm X," published in *New Plays from the Black Theatre,* edited by Ed Bullins, Bantam, 1969; (under pseudonym Imamu Amiri Baraka) *Jello* (first produced by Black Arts Repertory Theatre, 1965), Third World Press, 1970; "Junkies Are Full of (SHHH...), and Bloodrites" (first produced in Newark, 1970), published in *Black Drama Anthology,* edited by Woodie King and Ronald Milner, New American Library, 1971; "BA-RA-KA," published in *Spontaneous Combustion: Eight New American Plays,* edited by Rochelle Owens, Winter House, 1972.

Poetry: *April 13* (broadside), number 133, Penny Poems (New Haven), 1959; *Spring & So Forth* (broadside), number 111, Penny Poems, 1960; *Preface to a Twenty Volume Suicide Note,* Totem-Corinth, 1961; *The Dead Lecturer,* Grove, 1964; *Black Art,* Jihad, 1966; *A Poem for*

Black Hearts, Broadside Press, 1967; *Black Magic: Sabotage, Target Study, Black Art; Collected Poetry, 1961-1967,* Bobbs-Merrill, 1969; (under pseudonym Imamu Amiri Baraka) *It's Nation Time,* Third World Press, 1970; (under pseudonym Imamu Amiri Baraka) *Spirit Reach,* Jihad, 1972; (under pseudonym Imamu Amiri Baraka) *Afrikan Revolution: A Poem,* Jihad, 1973.

Essays: *Blues People: Negro Music in White America,* Morrow, 1963, published as *Negro Music in White America,* 1965; *Home: Social Essays,* Morrow, 1966; *Black Music,* Morrow, 1968; (under pseudonym Imamu Amiri Baraka) *A Black Value System,* Jihad, 1970; (under pseudonym Imamu Amiri Baraka; with Billy Abernathy, under pseudonym Fundi) *In Our Terribleness,* Bobbs-Merrill, 1970; (under pseudonym Imamu Amiri Baraka) *Raise, Race, Rays, Raze: Essays since 1965,* Random House, 1971; (under pseudonym Imamu Amiri Baraka) *Kawaida Studies: The New Nationalism,* Third World Press, 1972.

Editor, except as noted: (Compiler) *January 1st 1959: Fidel Castro,* Totem, 1959; *Four Young Lady Poets,* Corinth, 1962; *The Moderns: An Anthology of New Writing in America,* Corinth, 1963, published as *The Moderns: New Fiction in America,* 1964 (published in England under original title, MacGibbon & Kee, 1965); (and co-author) *In-Formation* (prose), Totem, 1965; Gilbert Sorrentino, *Black & White,* Corinth, 1965; Edward Dorn, *Hands Up!,* Corinth, 1965; (and contributor) *Afro-American Festival of the Arts Magazine,* Jihad, 1966, published as *Anthology of Our Black Selves,* 1969; (with Larry Neal) *Black Fire: An Anthology of Afro-American Writing,* Morrow, 1968; (with Neal and A. B. Spellman) *The Cricket: Black Music in Evolution,* Jihad, 1968, published as *Trippin': A Need for Change,* New Ark, 1969; (under pseudonym Imamu Amiri Baraka, and author of introduction) *African Congress: A Documentary of the First Modern Pan-African Congress,* Morrow, 1972.

Other: *The Disguise* (broadside), [New Haven], 1961; *Cuba Libre,* Fair Play for Cuba Committee (New York City), 1961; (contributor) Herbert Hill, editor, *Soon, One Morning,* Knopf, 1963; *The System of Dante's Hell* (novel; contains "Dante"), Grove, 1965; *Striptease,* Parallax, 1967; *Tales* (short stories), Grove, 1967; "Dutchman" (screenplay), Gene Persson Enterprises Ltd., 1967; "Black Spring" (screenplay), Black Arts Alliance (San Francisco), 1968; "Supercoon" (screenplay; animated short), Gene Persson, 1971; "A Fable" (screenplay of *The Slave*), MFR Productions, 1971.

Contributor to *The Trembling Lamb,* and to numerous anthologies. Poetry editor, Corinth Books; editor with Diane Di Prima, *The Floating Bear,* 1961-63. Contributor to *Evergreen Review, Poetry, Downbeat, Metronome, Nation, Negro Digest, Saturday Review,* and other publications.

WORK IN PROGRESS: Essays, *Toward Idealogical Clarity.*

SIDELIGHTS: As late as 1965 Jones was generally considered to be simply a talented poet and playwright, a gifted essayist, a unique militant. Once lionized by whites even while he attacked white society, he became the literary leader of Black Nationalism in America and the scourge of many white liberals. Growing blacker and blacker, he left the Village and his white wife for Harlem, and has since left Harlem for Newark. White praise has diminished considerably. As Stephen Schneck explains, "the intellectual establishment could and did take the insults, obscenities, bad

manners and name-calling. But what was unforgivable, the one thing they couldn't take, was to be deserted, stood up. LèRoi Jones left them."

Along the way Jones left behind many Negroes as well, dismissing such writers as Ralph Ellison and James Baldwin (the latter he considers too hip to be truly black). Yet he will never deny that these men are his brothers, while white liberals and "white Negroes" such as Norman Mailer are the enemy and should, ideally, be destroyed. Negro alienation, he feels, must be proudly displayed. Jazz as sublimation of frustrations will no longer suffice. Blacks cannot be assimilated into the dying white society. "We must eliminate the white man," he says, "before we will ever be able to draw a free breath on this planet." He tells his followers that the white man "owes you everything, even his life," and exhorts them to "smash their jelly-white faces" across the world, and set up an independent nation which would have the right to make treaties, set boundaries, control its currency and business, appoint ambassadors, and even devise a mathematics which would have no whiteness in it. The blacks must also reject the white God, "the dead Jew," affirm what Jones terms their genetic superiority ("we are the beautiful people with African imaginations"), and discourage peaceful negotiations because "no amount of pacifism is going to break Charlie's back." Jones wrote in 1967: "We want a post-American form. An afterwhiteness color to live and re-erect the strength of the primitive. . . . The first learnings of man. While we fly into the next epoch." William Harris, calling Jones a Utopian, believes that, "with the power of his rhetoric, Jones makes the black city-state sound almost possible."

Jones's position in America has always been paradoxical. John Tryford (one of many such observers) notes that "Jones goes further than Martin Luther King and Stokely Carmichael, further even than Malcolm X or Elijah Muhammad in his condemnation of 'Whitey.' He has even called for total extermination of the whites, his hatred is so great. Yet . . . he depends on the white world to a great extent. . . . He writes books intended for white readers and published by white publishing houses." This position doesn't worry him: "I don't have any ego hangups about my ideas," he says. In Newark, he has been cooperating with white racists, the police department, and even (indirectly) with the House Un-American Activities Committee. Why not? He is, in his own way, maintaining what Stewart Alsop calls a balance of terror. Integrity, equality, and justice are not the issues; one does not, for example, speak of justice to a man who, in 1967, received the severest punishment ever meted out for any similar offense, a punishment which the judge himself admits was based to a great extent on a racist poem which Jones published in *The Evergreen Review.* Jones, moreover, has sworn that he was not carrying guns into the riot and that he was severely attacked by several policemen. Nevertheless, "Jones is very guilty," says Schneck. "Of something. Of poetry, probably. Of speaking in persuasive tongues to that part of the heart that is better left unaroused." Jones's most pertinent comment on the affair was "Bail, hell! $25,000 isn't bail, it's a goddamned ransom." And of course Jones's white friends are still there: the American Center of P.E.N. protesting the impropriety of the sentence.

Mailer explaining Jones's purpose cryptically—"Who is this man, why are we here, will we survive?"; Schneck adding, "He is no martyr, unless we martyr him. Neither is he a black bogey-man, a Mau-Mau monster or, as several of his former white friends have described him, a bad-talking clown. He is a poet, a playwright, a conscience, a consciousness." Stanley Kauffman still believes that anyone preaching violence while at the same time working and profiting in a society he wants overthrown is a fake. But Jones merely says, "The black people will judge me. History will absolve me."

Jones is also a black artist who has attacked middle-class literature, whether it be white or black. The Negro writer, he says "is in a peculiar position, because if he is honest most of what he has seen and experienced in America will not flatter it. . . . I have always thought of writing as a moral art; that is, basically, I think of the artist as a moralist, as demanding a moral construct of the world, as asking for a cleaner vision of society. . . ." Harris notes that Jones's aesthetic theory essentially consists of "truth over beauty, complexity over simplicity, roughness over smoothness." Jones aspires, he says, "to the craziness that will make a man keep talking even after everyone else says he shouldn't." He disallows the white man's definition of reality and maintains that "the word 'art' is something the West has never understood. Art is supposed to be a part of a whole life of the community."

Such communal art is best represented by the theatre—for Jones, the revolutionary theatre which "must Accuse and Attack because it is a theatre of Victims." Larry Neal claims that the term "Black Arts" was first used in a positive sense by Jones in a poem: ". . . We are black magicians/Black arts we make/in black labs of the heart." Neal further believes that Jones's plays represent the most advanced form of this movement. Jones writes of this Theatre of the Spirit: "The Revolutionary Theatre should force change: it should be change. (All their faces turned into the lights and you work on them black nigger magic, and cleanse them at having seen the ugliness. And if the beautiful see themselves, they will love themselves.) We are preaching virtue again, but by that to mean NOW, toward what seems the most constructive use of the word. . . . Our theatre will show victims so that their brothers in the audience will be better able to understand that they are the brothers of victims, and that they themselves are blood brothers. And what we show must cause the blood to rush, so that pre-revolutionary temperaments will be bathed in this blood, and it will cause their deepest souls to move. . . . We will scream and cry, murder, run through the streets in agony, if it means some soul will be moved, moved to actual life understanding of what the world is, and what it ought to be. We are preaching virtue and feeling, and a natural sense of the self in the world." He adds: "White men will cower before this theatre because it hates them. Because they have been trained to hate. The Revolutionary Theatre must hate them for hating. For presuming with their technology to deny the supremacy of the Spirit. They will all die because of this."

Jones once said: "Basically, I want to write plays that will make good people happy and will frighten evil people. In America, it usually turns out to be white and black—through no doing of my own. That's the way it's been shaped in this country." Broadway, he notes, "is stupid, filthy, meaningless, boring, vacuous. . . . But it reflects the American mind, because the American mind is exactly that. Would I mind having a play done on Broadway? I don't care where my plays are done as long as somebody sees them." Those who do see his plays, even if they are opposed to the ideas, the savagery, the destruction of white by black, the obsession with murder, the "artless-ness," the "twisted logic," are for the most part moved by Jones's power as a dramatist. An English critic, Ronald Bryden, who saw *Dutchman* on a bill with a work by another playwright, called *Dutchman* "a posturing, inflammatory, deliberately dishonest work, destructive for the malicious excitement of destruction. . . . Yet," he added, "such is the talent of its writing that, after it, it's difficult even to remember what the first play had to say." Mailer believes it is the best one-act American play. Frederick Lumley considers this play "strong stuff: the pride and unabashed hatred of the American Negro is given the dimension of fable; it is the total repudiation of Uncle Tom." But Jones's plays are not all blood and terror; there is always wit and lyricism. Neal writes that Jones's "particular power as a playwright does not rest solely on his revolutionary vision, but is instead derived from his deep lyricism and spiritual outlook. In many ways, he is fundamentally more a poet than a playwright. And it is his lyricism that gives body to his plays." Harold Clurman believes that Jones uses his poetic inspiration in order to "make the words used and the setting chosen emblems of the inchoate savagery which possesses him, his characters, and, to a degree unsuspected by most of us, our civilization as a whole." And Allan Lewis speaks of Jones's "powerful imagery." Jones, however, insists that none of his plays is symbolic: "I don't deal in symbols. In *Dutchman* that girl isn't supposed to be Eve, just a girl I knew who walked around eating apples. Whatever associations you draw from the play are yours; I have no responsibility for them." Robert Brustein, who generally dislikes Jones's work, believes that the later plays are nothing more than sado-masochistic racial fantasies. Jones says simply: "I was dealing with victims. It is very hard for the people who do the victimizing to understand what the world looks like through their victims' eyes." Victims and Enemies. As Emile Capouya says of *The Slave*, here the "Negro revolutionary tells the 'white liberal' that he would rather talk sports or literature with him than with any of his own cohorts—but that, nevertheless, the white man is his deadly enemy. How," adds Capouya, "can one not recognize the pathos and the truth of that position?"

Ruby Cohn summarizes Jones' playwriting accomplishments in a somewhat different way: "After *The Dutchman*, Jones' plays devalue dialogue in favor of film, ritual, and incantation. The rich images and controlled rhythms of the earlier plays give way to exclamations, blows, shots, montage effects. Conceived to carry a simple message—usually of hatred against whites—to black audiences, these plays ruthlessly smother Jones' verbal gifts."

In examining Jones' politics and plays, Clive Barnes summarizes many basic points and questions in his review of *Slave Ship:* "This is a propaganda play. It is a black militant play. It is a racist play. It purports to counsel black revolution. It is a 'get whitey' play. Its attitudes are ugly and prejudiced, and its airily total condemnation of the white American is as sick as a Ku Klux Klanner at a rally. . . . Were I black, I would, I think, be militant. But I am not black, and my concerns are for justice, not revenge. Every white man, every black man, seeing this play is forced to look at himself very carefully in the mirror of his heart.

"Is black racism less reprehensible than white racism? You cannot possible see 'Slave Ship' without confronting this question, for it is a play that is as much a political statement as a work of art. What are you going to choose? If you are like me you will perhaps decide that black racism is less reprehensible because it is more understandable. To be brought to a country as a fettered slave is very different from arriving as even the poorest immigrant. Also, black racism is perhaps a token affair. It may be part of the business of establishing racial pride. The shooting that this play clearly advocates has luckily not yet started. If it ever does then we will all have decisions to make far more important than the consideration of a play.

"Mr. Jones is a clumsy, fantastically gifted playwright. I understand his political concerns, but as a drama critic rather than a man, I cannot but observe wryly that if he could spare the time and energy to the business he could be a most unusual playwright.

"'Slave Ship' is riveting. But it is riveting on two accounts for its deliberately segregated audience. The whites feel shame, compassion and that kind of pointless guilt that can have no absolution because it has no cause. The blacks—and here I am guessing—feel shame, compassion and a certain self-righteous satisfaction in the discomfiture of whitey. It is—ritually turning the other cheek—their all too civil right. . . . The play ends with the symbolic destruction of white America. Whitey is got—black panther banners are unfurled. This scared and horrified me. I am whitey. . . .

"Mr. Jones is a poet of politics. I would like to call him brother, but I am too smart to be that presumptuous. Are we all, including Mr. Jones, going to be too smart? Peace 'Slave Ship'—do your thing."

"Ambitions?" Jones asked rhetorically. "To write beautiful poems full of mystical sociology and abstract politics. To show America it is ugly and full of middle-class toads (black and white)." "I'm always aware," he explained to David Ossman, "in anything I say, of the 'sociological configuration'—what it *means* sociologically. But it doesn't have anything to do with [the poetry I'm writing] at the time." Although such a statement may no longer be valid for Jones, he still seeks "the holiness of life [in] the constant possibility of widening the consciousness. . . . What is called the imagination (from image, magi, magic, magician, etc.) is a practical vector from the soul. It stores all data, and can be called on to solve all our 'problems.' The imagination is the projection of ourselves past our sense of ourselves as 'things.' Imagination (image) is all possibility." For *The New American Poetry* he wrote: "There cannot be anything I must *fit* the poem into. Everything must be made to fit into the poem. There must not be any preconceived notion or *design* for what the poem *ought* to be. . . . I'm not interested in writing sonnets, sestinas or anything . . . only poems. . . . The only 'recognizable tradition' a poet need follow is himself . . . & with that, say, all those things out of tradition he can use, adapt, work over, into something for himself. . . . MY POETRY is whatever I think I am. . . . I CAN BE ANYTHING I CAN. . . . What I see, am touched by (CAN HEAR) . . . wives, gardens, jobs, cement yards where cats pee, . . . ALL are a poetry, & nothing moves (with any grace) pried apart from these things. There cannot be closet poetry. Unless the closet be wide as God's eye."

Robert Bone notes that, in Jones's "emphatic rejection of formal art, of tradition and of classical restraint, [he] betrays his affinity for that neo-Romantic permissiveness, that unbridled self-indulgence, which links him to the poets of the Beat generation." Jones admits the primary influence of Garcia Lorca, Pound, Olson, and Williams, and adds: "E-

liot, earlier (rhetoric can be so lovely, for a time . . .). And there are so many young wizards around . . ., Whalen, Snyder, McClure, O'Hara, Loewinsohn, Wieners, Creeley, Ginsberg &c.&c.&c." Denise Levertov called his first collection beautiful in its sensuousness and incantatory language: "His special gift is an emotive music that might have made him predominantly a lyric poet, but his deeply felt preoccupation with more than personal issues enlarges the scope of his poems beyond what the term is often taken to mean." According to Richard Howard, Jones in *The Dead Lecturer* is "much surer of his own voice, much braver with it and gayer, for in wrestling with the solipsistic violence of his feelings he appears to have discovered his identity: he is the man who says, 'wherever I go to claim my flesh, there are entrances of spirit.'" Howard continues: "these are the agonized poems of a man writing to save his skin, or at least to settle in it, and so urgent is their purpose that not one of them can trouble to be perfect. . . . As before, the energies are centrifugal, explosive, and the technical devices which convey those energies merely blur their uncertain margin of intent: single parentheses, slash marks, phonetic spellings, Poundian contractions, aberrant punctuation, broken lines, the absence of any 'formality' beyond the decorum of arrangement on the page and, perhaps, a pattern of breathing." His more recent polemic poetry is not as well received as his earlier work. Tryford believes that Jones's poetry "is most solid when he follows a 'hard' romantic line. It is weakest when he tries to put across a political or racist message. [But] poetry, one might say, is Jones's first metier, since he himself says that he started writing in college and by the age of twenty considered himself 'a kind of poet.'"

Jones is also highly regarded as a prose stylist. "He has taken the language of the ghetto," says Harris, "and has created a beautiful but somewhat poisonous black poetry [in prose]. . . . Of course, it isn't pure ghetto speech; there is the echo of Beckett, Kerouac, and Olson." A work such as *The System of Dante's Hell* is by no means ordinary narrative. "In the complete work," says Jones, "I have tried to provide some parallels, i.e., emotional analogies, between my own life and Dante's Hell. The work is modeled after the Hell, and I go into each bolgia (ditch) of each circle of the Hell and drag out some corresponding horror in my own soul."

In his fiction, according to Capouya, "Jones rejects the formal logic of exposition; he invites verbal and emotional accidents, willingly or wilfully connecting ideas and impressions that have no common focus outside his own mind. Thus, he puts into practice the essential program of contemporary art—to find esthetic value in chaos, accidental juxtapositions, happenings." Jones believes that "the most successful fiction of Negro writing is in its emotional content. The Negro protest novelist postures, and invents a protest quite amenable within the tradition of bourgeois American life. He never reaches the hard core of the America which *can* cause that protest. The intellectual traditions of the white middle class prevent such exposure of reality, and the black imitators reflect this." Jones is no imitator, but, he says, "I write now full of trepidation, because I know the death that society intends for me. I see Jimmy Baldwin almost unable to write about himself any more. I've seen Du Bois die on another continent, Chester Himes driven away, Ellison silenced and fidgeting away in some college. I think I almost feel the same forces massing against me, almost before I've begun, but let them understand that this is a fight without quarter and I'm very fast."

His voice is still strong in *Tales* which are, according to S. K. Oberbeck, "a blend of mellow fiction and shrill fantasy from the black activist's point of view, ... difficult to read comfortably if one is white.... The telling moments are always overcast with darkness; Jones's daydreams are a white man's nightmares. The frequency of his pathological fantasies, some of which have come true in Newark and Detroit, [is a] key to an understanding of his angry soul. 'Blood Everywhere,' ends one story, 'And the heroes march thru smiling.'" Oberbeck admits, however, that Jones's prose keeps improving. "There is still a familiar, childish narcissism in his prose, and an unsurprising revving-up of vindictive violence often more funny than fearsome. But several [of these] stories are rare cameos in onyx."

Jones' *Home* and *Raise, Race, Rays, Raze* contain essays in which Jones discusses his political and ideological beliefs. A *New York Times* reviewer notes the possible and numerous causes for Jones' transition from young poet/playwright to militant Black Nationalist. "The two dozen essays that constitute this book [*Home*] were written during a five year span—a turbulent and critical period for Negroes and whites. The Cuban Revolution, the Birmingham bombings, Robert Williams' Monroe Defense movement, the Harlem riots, the assassination of Malcolm X ... each changed the way LeRoi Jones looked at America. The progressive change is recorded with honesty, anger and passion in his writings. *Home* is, in effect, LeRoi Jones' ideological autobiography. Mr. Jones usually speaks as a Negro—and always as an American. He is eloquent, he is bold. He demands rights—not conditional favors." In *Raise, Race, Rays, Raze*, Jones continues to expound on his beliefs, summing up the further growth of his views. A *Time* reviewer quotes Jones in this collection of essays: "'Do not talk Marx or Lenin or Trotsky when you speak of political thinkers. Abdel Rahman, Nkrumah, Sekou Toure, Mao, DuBois, Fanon, Nyerere, Garvey, Lumemba, Malcolm, Guevara, Elijah, Abu Dekr will plot, have already plotted, our way.' Naturally, Jones fails to note that Allah and Egypt's gods were divine sanctions for slave societies, and that many of the distinguished mortals he names learned their politics from the writings of Marx, Lenin and Trotsky. But why complicate the issue and disrupt Jones' totalitarian fantasies about white evil and righteous black revenge?" Recently, however, Jones has written to *CA* stating that he has now indeed "made transition to ideology of Marxism, Leninism, Mao Tse-tung thought, [and] scientific socialism." Thus, one more transition for Jones has occurred.

Jack Newfield maintains that Jones possesses "a gift that is more controlled and complex" than that of other Negro authors. Kaufmann merely insists that Jones is "the luckiest man of our times, a writer who ... would be less than lightly held if he did not happen to be a Negro at this moment in American history." In 1965 Irving Howe characterized him as a "pop-art guerilla warrior" who proposed verbal terrorism because he had little faith in his capacity to effect social change. Jones, says *Newsweek*, "fights dirty—he is an eye-gouger and a groin-kicker. His answer to this would be (indeed tirelessly is): 'So are you. You're a worse one. You taught me how.'" Harris, the "assimilated Negro," adds that, "in short, Jones is doing what the white man has been doing to the Negro for 400 years: he is dehumanizing him. [But] the unhappy truth that most men are moral cripples is blurred [by Jones] into the lie that all white men are bad. And the Negro is romanticized; Jones

feels there is some mystical unity in color." Yet "it is Jones with whom we are entranced," writes Sally Eisenberg, "for in the spew of his venom and hatred of all that is sordid and ugly in the polluted stream of white American life, there buds the seeds of a truly prophetic vision for his own people when he exhorts them to find their own salvation, to find their own truth.... LeRoi Jones speaks the language of hatred, but he speaks truth nevertheless. He is a prophet without honor in his own time."

Jones has recorded his work for the Library of Congress.

BIOGRAPHICAL/CRITICAL SOURCES—Books: Donald M. Allen, editor, *The New American Poetry, 1945-60*, Grove, 1960; Rosey E. Pool, editor, *Beyond the Blues*, Hand & Flower Press, 1962; David Ossman, interviewer, *The Sullen Art*, Corinth, 1963; Herbert Hill, *Soon, One Morning*, Knopf, 1963; Ralph Ellsion, *Shadow and Act*, Random House, 1964; Allan Lewis, *American Plays and Playwrights*, Crown, 1965; Stephen Stepanchev, *American Poetry Since 1945*, Harper, 1965; Herbert Hill, editor, *Anger and Beyond*, Harper, 1966; Frederick Lumley, *New Trends in 20th Century Drama*, Oxford University Press, 1967; M. L. Rosenthal, *The New Poets: American and British Since World War II*, Oxford University Press, 1967; Ruby Cohn, *American Drama*, Indiana University Press, 1971; Jerome Klinkowitz, *Negro American Literature Forum*, Indiana University Press, 1973; Donald B. Gibson, editor, *Modern Black Poets*, Prentice-Hall, 1973; Carolyn Riley, editor, *Contemporary Literary Criticism*, Gale, Volume I, 1973, Volume II, 1974, Volume III, 1975, Volume V, 1976.

Periodicals: *Nation*, November 14, 1961, January 4, 1965, March 15, 1965, January 22, 1968; *Saturday Review*, April 20, 1963, January 9, 1965; *New Yorker*, April 4, 1964, December 26, 1964, March 4, 1967; *Cue*, June 6, 1964; *National Observer*, June 29, 1964; *Chronicle* (San Francisco), August 23, 1964; *Village Voice*, December 17, 1964, May 6, 1965, May 19, 1965; *Time*, December 25, 1964, November 19, 1965, January 12, 1968, June 28, 1971; *New Republic*, January 23, 1965; *Detroit Free Press*, January 31, 1965, December 1, 1965; *Dissent*, spring, 1965; *National Review*, March 23, 1965; *New York Herald Tribune*, April 12, 1964, December 13, 1964, October 27, 1965; *New York Times Book Review*, November 28, 1965, May 8, 1966, February 4, 1968, March 17, 1968; *Negro Digest*, April, 1966, April, 1967, April, 1968, January, 1969, April, 1969; *Newsweek*, May 2, 1966, March 6, 1967; *Esquire*, June, 1966; *New York Times*, August 10, 1966, September 14, 1966, October 5, 1966, October 26, 1966, January 20, 1967, February 28, 1967, July 15, 1967, January 5, 1968, January 6, 1968, January 9, 1968, January 10, 1968, February 7, 1968, August 16, 1968, November 27, 1968, August 26, 1969, November 23, 1969, February 6, 1970, June 11, 1972, November 14, 1972, November 23, 1972; *Poetry*, February, 1967; *New Leader*, March 13, 1967; *Observer Review*, May 14, 1967, February 25, 1968; *Literary Times*, May-June, 1967; *Trace*, summer, 1967; *Life*, August 4, 1967; *Antioch Review*, fall, 1967; *Evergreen Review*, December, 1967; *Book Week*, December 24, 1967; *Kenyon Review*, Issue 5, Volume XXX, 1968; *Minnesota Review*, Volume VIII, number 2, 1968; *International Times*, February 2-15, 1968; *Listener*, March 14, 1968; *American Dialog*, spring, 1968; *Commonweal*, June 28, 1968; *Drama Review*, summer, 1968, winter, 1970; *Ramparts*, June 29, 1968; *Saturday Evening Post*, July 13, 1968; *Washington Post*, August 15, 1968, September 12, 1968, November 27, 1968; *Avant Garde*, September, 1968; *Newsday,* August 20, 1969; *New York Review of Books,* July 2, 1970; *Essence,* September, 1970; *CLA Journal,* Volume XIV, number 3, March, 1971; *Black World,* April, 1971; *Best Sellers,* August 1, 1971.

* * *

JONES, Madeline Adams 1913-

PERSONAL: Born January 22, 1913, in Washington, D.C.; daughter of Leason Heberling (a scientist) and Jeannette (Blaisdell) Adams; widowed; children: Donna (Mrs. Anthony Prisendorf), Sharon (Mrs. Jeffery Casdin), Margot K. *Education:* College of William and Mary, student, 1930-32; University of Illinois, A.B., 1934. *Religion:* Episcopalian. *Home:* 21 East Tenth St., New York, N.Y. 10003. *Office:* Funk & Wagnalls, Inc., 666 Fifth Ave., New York, N.Y. 10019.

CAREER: Crown Publishers, Inc., New York City, an editor, 1963-66; Arco Publishing Co., New York City, promotion manager, 1966-69; Cowles Book Co., Chicago, Ill., senior editor, 1969-71; Funk & Wagnalls, Inc., New York City, writer and editor, 1971—. *Member:* Chi Omega.

WRITINGS: The Mysterious Flexagons, Crown, 1966; *Young Students Encyclopedia Yearbook,* Funk & Wagnalls, 1974 and 1975.

WORK IN PROGRESS: Three juveniles, *The Unicorn and the S-Shaped Cake, Down, Around, and Over,* and *I Can Write My Name.*

AVOCATIONAL INTERESTS: Reading, crossword puzzles, skiing, horseback riding.

* * *

JONES, Mary Voell 1933-

PERSONAL: Born August 1, 1933, in Fond du Lac, Wis.; daughter of John Raymond (a salesman) and Gladys (Glynn) Voell; married J. Penrod Jones (president of a printing firm), September 21, 1957; children: Margaret, Elizabeth, Katherine, Emily. *Education:* Westminster Choir College, student, 1951-53; University of Wisconsin-Milwaukee, B.A., 1956. *Home:* 2167 Mohawk Trail, Maitland, Fla. 32751.

CAREER: Whitman Publishing Co., Racine, Wis., writer and editor, 1956-59; free-lance writer, 1959—. Choir director at churches in Hannibal, Mo., 1965-66, and Cambridge, Md., 1966-71. Secretary, Community Concerts, Inc., Hannibal, Mo., 1963-66; member of Bach Festival Choir, Winter Park, Fla.

WRITINGS—All published by Whitman Publishing: *Captain Kangaroo's Picnic,* 1959; *Huckleberry Hound Helps a Pal,* 1960; *Captain Kangaroo and Tick Tock Trouble,* 1961; *Yogi Bear's Secret,* 1963; *Little Red Riding Hood Retold,* 1964; (with Norma R. Knoche) *What Do Mothers Do?,* 1966.

WORK IN PROGRESS: First Songs: The Little Child Sings, for Paulist Press.

* * *

JONES, Vane A. 1917-

PERSONAL: Born December 11, 1917, in Indianapolis, Ind.; son of Anderson Rosencrans (a carpenter) and Mary Kathern (Haines) Jones; married Virginia June Corey (a teacher), July 30, 1941; children: Corey A., Virginia Carol. *Home:* 6710 Hampton Dr. E., Indianapolis, Ind. 46226.

CAREER: Real estate broker with own firm, Indianapolis,

Ind., 1950-63; Federal Housing Administration, Indianapolis, Ind., evaluator, 1963—. Publisher of *Traction & Models* (monthly hobby magazine) and *Traction Heritage* (bi-monthly historical magazine), beginning 1965; founder of Model Traction Manufacturers Guild; builder of professional models for Smithsonian Institution, Indianapolis Water Co., Eli Lily & Co., and others. President, Indiana Museum of Transport and Communication, Inc., Noblesville. *Member:* National Model Railroad Association, Electric Railroaders Association, National Railway Historical Society, Central Electric Railfan's Association, National Radio Club, Indianapolis Northeast Exchange Club (director).

WRITINGS: Traction Fan's Directory, Vane A. Jones Co., 1948, 3rd edition, 1965; *Jones' North American AM-FM Radio-TV Station Listing,* Vane A. Jones Co., 1958, 3rd edition, 1961; *North American Radio-TV Station Guide,* Sams, 1963, 11th edition, 1975; *Rail Fan's Directory,* Vane A. Jones Co., 1964.†

* * *

JONES-EVANS, Eric 1898-

PERSONAL: Born October 2, 1898, in West Coker, Somersetshire, England; son of John Llewellyn (a clergyman, Church of England) and Caroline Theresa (Jones) Jones-Evans; married Agnes Maude Edwards (died, 1952); children: Mervyn De Vere. *Education:* University of London and St. Thomas's Hospital Medical School, M.R.C.S. and L.R.C.P., 1921. *Religion:* Church of England. *Home:* The Treshams, Fawley, near Southampton, England. *Agent:* Margery Vosper Ltd., Suite 8, 26 Charing Cross Rd., London WC2H 0DG, England.

CAREER: Managed his own theatrical company, producing and playing the leads in Shakespearean, romantic, and Dickensian plays, 1932-39; toured his one-man, quick-change "Dickens Entertainment," playing a total of seventy-three Dickensian characters, 1948-62; toured the Netherlands with his two-hour solo act, 1959; retired from the stage in 1963 to write plays and articles on the old-time theater. Writer and broadcaster of radio series "Southampton's Theatres and Music-Halls," for British Broadcasting Corp. Occasional television performer. Assisted with the exhibition "The Actor Knight-A Tribute to Sir Henry Irving," at Russell-Cotes Art Gallery, Bournemouth, England. *Military service:* Royal Naval Volunteer Reserve, 1917-18. *Member:* Dickens fellowship. *Awards, honors:* First prize in Festival of Britain playwriting competition, 1951, for "The Blue Cockade."

WRITINGS: Character Sketches from Charles Dickens, Samuel French, 1947; *In the Footsteps of Barnaby Rudge,* Samuel French, 1947.

Plays; all published by G. F. Wilson, except as noted: *John Jasper's Secret* (four-act play based on Charles Dickens' unfinished novel, "The Mystery of Edwin Drood"), Samuel French, 1951; *Suicide Isn't Murder* (one-act), Samuel French, 1951; *Death on the Line* (one-act play adapted from Dickens' story, "The Signalman"), Pitman, 1954; *The Black Bag* (one-act), Samuel French, 1957.

Lucky Venture (three-act), 1961; *Death of a Lawyer* (three-act play based on Dickens' *Bleak House*), 1962; *Scrooge the Miser* (dramatized version of Dickens' *A Christmas Carol*), 1962; *The Haunted Man* (three-act play based on Dickens' novel), 1962; *The Weaver of Raveloe* (three-act play based on George Eliot's *Silas Marner*), 1963; *The Murder of Nancy* (Dickensian sketch from *Oliver Twist*),

1963; *The Jackal* (four-act play based on Dickens' *A Tale of Two Cities*), 1964; *The Blue Cockade* (four-act play based on Dickens' *Barnaby Rudge*), 1964; *Mr. Crummles Presents* (Dickensian play in prologue and three acts), 1966; *David Copperfield* (three-act play), 1970.

Contributor to *Southern Evening Echo,* which published fifteen chapters of his autobiography, "Footlight Fever," as a serial, 1962-65, and a series of articles on acting under the title "Beginners Please," 1963; a number of articles on theatrical history and Charles Dickens have appeared in *Hampshire;* contributor to *Kent Life* of the series "Pages from an Actor's Scrapbook." Adapted "The Dream Woman," 1973, "The Body-Snatchers," 1974, and "Markheim," 1974, all for British Broadcasting Corp. Radio.

WORK IN PROGRESS: Original plays and further stage versions of novels by Charles Dickens; writing on the theater during the Victorian and Edwardian era; television scripts on pictorial posters (1870-1930), Henry Irving and contemporary actor-managers, and other subjects.

SIDELIGHTS: Several of his plays have been broadcast on radio in Australia, New Zealand, and South Africa.

BIOGRAPHICAL/CRITICAL SOURCES: F. Dubrez Fawcett, *Dickens the Dramatist,* W. H. Allen, 1952; *Bransby Williams by Himself,* Hutchinson, 1954.

*   *   *

JORDAN, Terry G(ilbert) 1938-

PERSONAL: Born August 9, 1938, in Dallas, Tex.; son of Gilbert John (a college professor) and Vera Belle (Tiller) Jordan; married Marlis Anderson, August 18, 1962; children: Tina, Sonya, Eric. *Education:* Southern Methodist University, B.A., 1960; University of Texas, M.A., 1961; University of Wisconsin, Ph.D., 1965. *Home:* 315 Ridgecrest Circle, Denton, Tex. 76201. *Office:* Department of Geography, North Texas State University, Denton, Tex. 72603.

CAREER: Arizona State University, Tempe, assistant professor of geography, 1965-69; North Texas State University, Denton, professor of geography, and chairman of department, 1969—. *Member:* Association of American Geographers, American Geographical Society, Pioneer America Society, Texas State Historical Association, Texas Folklore Society, Phi Beta Kappa. *Awards, honors:* Woodrow Wilson fellow.

WRITINGS: German Seed in Texas Soil: Immigrant Farmers in Nineteenth-Century Texas, University of Texas Press, 1966; *The European Culture Area: A Systematic Geography,* Harper, 1973; *The Human Mosaic: A Thematic Introduction to Cultural Geography,* Canfield Press, 1976; *Deep East Texas Folk,* S.M.V. Printing Dept. (Dallas, Tex.), 1976.

WORK IN PROGRESS: Work on the cultural geography of Texas.

*   *   *

JOYNER, William T. 1934-

PERSONAL: Born March 9, 1934, in Franklin, Va.; son of Ulysses P. and Gertrude Joyner; married Bouneva F. Farlow, February 14, 1958 (divorced, 1974); married Ruth A. Bew; children: (first marriage) Bryant, Clista, Eric, Sherri. *Education:* Elon College, B.A., 1959; Duke University, B.D., 1963. *Politics:* Democrat. *Home:* Boca Pinar, Second Ave., Boca Raton, Fla. *Office address:* P.O. Box 218, Hallandale, Fla. 33009.

CAREER: U.S. Navy, Seabees, chaplain's assistant, 1951-55; clergyman of United Church of Christ, 1963—; minister in Portsmouth, Va., 1963-66; United Church of Christ, Philadelphia, Pa., associate editor of *Colloquy,* 1966-68; Wilton Congregational Church, Wilton, Conn., associate minister, 1968-72; free lance, 1972-75; Union Church, Hallandale, Fla., pastor, 1975—.

WRITINGS: Wheels in the Air, United Church, 1968. Contributor to denominational and other religious journals.

WORK IN PROGRESS: Jerusalem, Virginia 1831, a free form narrative account of the Nat Turner slave revolt presented as a photo essay of the region today.

*   *   *

JUDAH, J(ay) Stillson 1911-

PERSONAL: Born July 7, 1911, in Leavenworth, Wash.; son of Stillson (a physician) and Maude Alice (Cannon) Judah; married Lucile Elaine Baker (a secretary), December 2, 1935; children: Jay Stillson, Jr., Elaine Lucile (Mrs. Phillip Keller), Diane Francis (Mrs. Paul Moore). *Education:* University of Washington, Seattle, A.B., 1935, graduate student, 1935-36; University of California, Berkeley, Certificate of School of Librarianship, 1941, further graduate work, 1946-50. *Religion:* Disciples of Christ. *Home:* 818 Oxford St., Berkeley, Calif. *Office:* Graduate Theological Union Library, Berkeley, Calif. 94709.

CAREER: Pacific School of Religion, Berkeley, Calif., librarian, 1941-69, professor of history of religions, 1955-69, adjunct professor, 1974—; Graduate Theological Union, Berkeley, director of bibliographic center, 1966-69, head librarian, and professor of history of religions, 1969—. *Military service:* U.S. Navy, Intelligence, 1944-46; became lieutenant. *Member:* American Theological Library Association (vice-president, 1962-63; president, 1963-64), International Institute of Arts and Letters (fellow), International Association of Theological Libraries (secretary-treasurer, 1955-60), Western Theological Library Association (president, 1954-55), Sigma Pi, El Cerrito Tennis Club (president, 1954-59). *Awards, honors:* Guggenheim fellowship, 1934; Litt.D., Chapman College, 1955; American Association of Theological Schools faculty fellowship, 1957-58.

WRITINGS: (Editor and compiler) *Index to Religious Periodical Literature, 1949-52,* American Theological Library Association, 1953; *The History and Philosophy of the Metaphysical Movements in America,* Westminster, 1967; *Hare Krishna and the Counterculture,* Wiley, 1974; (contributor) Irving I. Zaretsky and Mark P. Leone, editors, *Religious Movements in Contemporary America,* Princeton University Press, 1974. Contributor to library and religious journals. Book review editor, *Pacific School of Religion Bulletin,* 1960—.

WORK IN PROGRESS: Two books, *Countercultural Religions in America* and *History of World Religions.*

SIDELIGHTS: J. Stillson Judah speaks German and Japanese, and reads German, French, Sanskrit, Pali, Latin, with "descending facility."

*   *   *

JUERGENSEN, Hans 1919-

PERSONAL: Born December 17, 1919, in Myslowice, Germany; naturalized U.S. citizen; foster son of Hermann Anton and Dora (Grossmann) Juergensen; married Ilse Dina Loebenberg (a poet and teacher of poetry in elementary schools), October 27, 1945; children: Claudia Jeanne

(Mrs. James W. Noble). *Education:* Upsala College, East Orange, N.J., B.A., 1942; Johns Hopkins University, Ph.D., 1951. *Religion:* Jewish. *Home:* 7815 Pine Hill Dr., Tampa, Fla. 33610. *Office:* University of South Florida, Tampa, Fla. 33620.

CAREER: University of Kansas, Lawrence, instructor in German, 1951-53; Quinnipiac College, Hamden, Conn., 1953-61, began as assistant professor, became associate professor of English and chairman of department; University of South Florida, Tampa, assistant professor, 1961-63, associate professor, 1963-68, professor of humanities, 1968—. Silvermine College of Art, lecturer in humanities, 1948-61, acting dean and member of board, 1960-61. Coordinator, Poetry in the Schools, Hillsborough County, Florida, 1972—. Graphic artist, exhibiting at a number of one-man shows. *Military service:* U.S. Army, 1942-45; served in three campaigns; wounded at Anzio; received Purple Heart and Unit Citation. *Member:* Poetry Society of America, Poetry Society of Florida, Connecticut Academy of Arts and Science (fellow), International Poetry Society (fellow). *Awards, honors:* Florida poet of the year, 1965; Stephen Vincent Benet Award, 1970.

WRITINGS: I Feed You From My Cup (poems), Quinnipiac College Press, 1958; *In Need for Names* (poems), Linden Press, 1961; *Existential Canon, and Other Poems,* South & West, 1965; *Florida Montage* (poems), South & West, 1966; *Sermons from the Ammunition Hatch of the Ship of Fools,* Vagabond, 1968; *From the Divide* (poems), Olivant, 1970; *Hebraic Modes* (poems), Olivant, 1972.

Contributor: *Where Is Vietnam?,* Doubleday, 1967; Robin Gregory, editor, *Ipso Facto* (poetry anthology), Hud Publications, 1975; Walter Lowenfels, editor, *For Neruda, For Chile,* Beacon Press, 1975. Editor of *Children's Poetry Anthology,* 1975. Contributor of art criticism to *Tampa Times,* 1961-67. Co-editor, *Orange Street Poetry Journal,* 1958-62, and *University of South Florida Language Quarterly,* 1961-74; editor, *Gryphon* (University of South Florida), 1974—.

WORK IN PROGRESS: Journey Toward the Roots (poems and drawings).

SIDELIGHTS: In addition to English, and his native German, Juergensen is competent in French and has some knowledge of Latin and Hebrew.

*   *   *

JUPP, James 1932-

PERSONAL: Born August 23, 1932, in Croydon, England; son of James Thomas (a Merchant Navy officer) and Florence C. (McCone) Jupp. *Education:* London School of Economics and Political Science, B.Sc., 1953, M.Sc., 1956, Ph.D., 1975. *Politics:* Labour Party. *Religion:* None. *Home:* 54 Peel Close, Heslington, York, England. *Office:* Department of Politics, University of York, Heslington, York, England.

CAREER: University of Melbourne, Melbourne, Victoria, Australia, lecturer in politics, 1957-66; University of York, York, England, lecturer in politics, 1966—. *Member:* Association of University Teachers, Political Studies Association of the United Kingdom, Fabian Society.

WRITINGS: Australian Party Politics, Melbourne University Press, 1964, 2nd edition, 1968; *Arrivals and Departures,* Cheshire-Lansdowne, 1966; *Political Parties,* Humanities, 1968; *From Ceylon to Sri Lanka,* Cass & Co., 1976. Contributor to *Canberra Times* and to political science journals. Editor, *Dissent* (Melbourne), 1961-63.

WORK IN PROGRESS: The Left in Britain, 1931-1941.

*   *   *

KADAI, Heino Olavi 1931-

PERSONAL: Born August 20, 1931, in Tartu, Estonia; son of Friedrich (a businessman) and Elizabeth (Neubaum) Kadai. *Education:* Columbia University, B.A., 1953; Concordia Theological Seminary, Springfield, Ill., B.Th., 1958; Concordia Seminary, St. Louis, Mo., M.Div. and S.T.M., 1960, Th.D., 1969; graduate study, Union Theological Seminary, New York, N.Y., 1963, and Stanford University, 1971-72. *Home:* 1014 North Fifth St., Springfield, Ill. 62702. *Office:* Concordia Theological Seminary, Springfield, Ill. 62702.

CAREER: Lutheran clergyman. Concordia Theological Seminary, Springfield, Ill., assistant professor, 1960-69, associate professor of historical theology, 1969—, chairman of department, 1967—. Visiting professor at Concordia Seminary, St. Louis, 1970. Member of Hermeneutics Committee, Lutheran Church-Missouri Synod. *Member:* American Historical Association, American Society of Church History, American Society for Reformation Research, Lutheran Academy of Scholarship, Lutheran Society for Worship, Music and the Arts. *Awards, honors:* Luther faculty fellowship, 1963-64; American Association of Theological Schools fellowship, 1971-72.

WRITINGS: (Editor and contributor) *Accents in Luther's Theology,* Concordia, 1967; (with Lewis W. Spitz) *Guide to Reformation Literature,* Concordia, 1967. Acting editor, *Springfielder,* 1963. General editor, "Profiles in Lutheranism" series, Concordia, 1969—.

SIDELIGHTS: Professor Kadai is competent in Estonian, German, French, Latin, Greek, and Hebrew. *Avocational interests:* Christian art and literature.

*   *   *

KAFKA, Sherry 1937-

PERSONAL: Born September 11, 1937, in Jonesboro, Ark.; daughter of Leonard McCurry (a minister) and Norene (Wiles) Kafka; married Cyrus Wagner (an architect and professor); children: (first marriage) Kimberlea, Robyn; (second marriage) Adam. *Education:* Baylor University, student, three years; University of Iowa, B.A., 1962. *Politics:* Democrat. *Home:* 2524 Springlane, Austin, Tex. *Agent:* Warren Bayless, International Creative Management, 555 Madison Ave., New York, N.Y. 10022. *Office:* 407 Eighth St., San Antonio, Tex.

CAREER: Formerly teacher of drama at Methodist Children's Home, Waco, Tex., and director of children's program at William Edrington Scott Theater of Fort Worth Art Center, Fort Worth, Tex.; worked on exhibit development for 1968 Hemis Fair (world fair), and as consultant to "Unlimited Potential," an innovation program for public school children. Scriptwriter for Public Broadcast Service bilingual television production for children, "Carraseolendas". *Awards, honors:* Texas Writers Roundup award of Theta Sigma Phi, and Friends of American Writers award, both for *Hannah Jackson.*

WRITINGS: Hannah Jackson, Morrow, 1966; *Big Enough* (juvenile), Putnam, 1970; *I Need a Friend* (juvenile), Putnam, 1970. Work included in *Best Plays of 1968,* Chilton, 1968.

WORK IN PROGRESS: Two juvenile books, *Clangor City's Last Parade* and *The Stable Boy of Bethlehem.*

KAGAN, Benjamin 1914-

PERSONAL: Born December 5, 1914, in Dyneburg, Poland; son of Arie (a businessman) and Dora Kagan; married Sara Anikster; children: Arie, Dorit. *Education:* Graduated from Zygmunta Augusta College, Bialystok, Poland, 1933; studied at Sorbonne, University of Paris, and at National Technical School of Aeronautics, 1939. *Religion:* Jewish. *Home:* 3 Yonatan Zahala, Tel Aviv, Israel.

CAREER: British Army, commando, 1940-45; Israeli Air Force, regular officer, 1948-63, retiring as colonel; KLIL Metal Industries, Haifa, Israel, managing director, 1963—. *Member:* Commando Association (London), Tzeyet (Israeli Army association). *Awards, honors*—Military: Cross of Merit (Poland), Officer of Legion of Honor (France).

WRITINGS: They Have Taken Off at Dawn, Davar (Tel-Aviv), 1958; *Combat secret pour Israel,* Hachette (Paris), 1961, translation published as *The Secret Battle for Israel,* World Publishing, 1966.

WORK IN PROGRESS: A book of espionage, with the 1956 war as a background.

SIDELIGHTS: Benjamin Kagan is competent in Russian, Polish, French, English, and Hebrew. He has traveled in North America, Europe (excluding Russia), Africa, Central America, and Middle East.

* * *

KAGAN, Donald 1932-

PERSONAL: Born May 1, 1932, in Lithuania; naturalized U.S. citizen; son of M. and Leah (Benjamin) Kagan; married Myrna Dabrusky (a teacher), January 13, 1955; children: Robert William, Frederick Walter. *Education:* Brooklyn College (now Brooklyn College of the City University of New York), A.B., 1954; Brown University, M.A., 1955; Ohio State University, Ph.D., 1958; American School of Classical Studies in Athens, postdoctoral studies, 1958-59. *Politics:* Democrat. *Religion:* Jewish. *Home:* 10 Fairy Glen Dr., North Haven, Conn. 06473. *Office:* History Department, Yale University, New Haven, Conn. 06520.

CAREER: Instructor in history at Capital University, Columbus, Ohio, part-time, 1957-58, and at Pennsylvania State University, University Park, 1959-60; Cornell University, Ithaca, N.Y., assistant professor, 1960-63, associate professor, 1964-67, professor of ancient history, 1967-69; Yale University, New Haven, Conn., professor of history and classics, 1969—, chairman of classics department, 1972-75. *Awards, honors:* Fulbright grant to Greece, 1958-59; American Philosophical Society research grant and New York University summer seminar grant, 1960; fellowship to Center for Hellenic Studies, 1966-67; National Endowment for the Humanities senior fellowship, 1971-72.

WRITINGS: (Editor) *The Decline and Fall of the Roman Empire in the West,* Heath, 1962; *The Great Dialogue: A History of Greek Political Thought from Homer to Polybius,* Free Press, 1965; (editor) *Readings in Greek Political Thought,* Free Press, 1965; (editor) *Problems in Ancient History,* two volumes, Macmillan, 1966; (editor with L. P. Williams and Brian Tierney) *Great Issues in Western Civilization,* two volumes, Random House, 1967; *The Outbreak of the Peloponnesian War,* Cornell University Press, 1969; *The Archidamian War,* Cornell University Press, 1974. Contributor to professional journals.

KAIM-CAUDLE, Peter Robert 1916-

PERSONAL: Born December 14, 1916, in Charlottenburg, Germany; son of Otto (a company director) and Stephanie (Schweitzer) Kaim; married Patricia Mary Caudle (a British Council correspondent), May 24, 1945; children: Robert, Helen, Katherine, Stephen. *Education:* London School of Economics and Political Science, B.Sc., 1938, graduate study, 1938-39. *Home:* Beechwood, Princes St., Durham City, England. *Office:* Department of Sociology and Social Administration, University of Durham, Elvet Riverside, New Elvet, Durham City, England.

CAREER: Barrister-at-law, Lincoln's Inn. School of Economics, Dundee, Scotland, lecturer in economics, 1947-50; University of Durham, Durham, England, senior lecturer in social administration, 1950—. Fourah Bay College-The University College of Sierra Leone, head of department of economics, 1954-55, 1961; Economic and Social Research Institute (formerly Economic Research Institute), Dublin, Ireland, research associate, 1963-64, research professor, 1968-70. Visiting professor of social science at University of Calgary, 1975. Member of Durham County Social Service Committee; member of Social Administration Association.

WRITINGS: Social Security in Ireland and Western Europe, Economic Research Institute, 1964; *Housing in Ireland: Some Economic Aspects,* Economic Research Institute, 1965; *Social Policy in the Irish Republic,* Routledge & Kegan Paul, 1967; (contributor) Peter Townsend, editor, *Social Services for All,* Fabian Society, 1968; *Dental Services in Ireland,* Economic and Social Research Institute, 1969; *Pharmaceutical Services in Ireland,* Economic and Social Research Institute, 1970; *Opthalmic Services in Ireland,* Economic and Social Research Institute, 1970; (with J. G. Byrne) *Irish Pension Schemes 1969,* Economic and Social Research Institute, 1971; (contributor) Townsend, editor, *Labor and Inequality,* Fabian Society, 1972; *Comparative Social Policy and Social Security,* Dunellen, 1973; (with G. N. March) *Team Care in General Practice,* Croom Helm, 1975. Contributor to journals in England and Ireland.

WORK IN PROGRESS: Primary Health Care Services in England and Canada.

* * *

KALES, Emily Fox 1944-

PERSONAL: Surname rhymes with "sales"; born February 18, 1944, in New York, N.Y.; daughter of Gordon (a teacher) and Rose (Berson) Fox; married David Kales (a journalist), June 12, 1965. *Education:* Barnard College, B.A. (magna cum laude), 1964; City University of New York, M.A., 1967, currently Ph.D. candidate. *Politics:* Liberal Party. *Religion:* Jewish. *Office:* Department of English, Hunter College of the City University of New York, New York, N.Y. 10021.

CAREER: New York (N.Y.) Department of Welfare, social caseworker, 1964-65; Hunter College of the City University of New York, New York, N.Y., lecturer in English, 1967—. Editorial assistant at Grosset & Dunlap, Inc., Harper & Row, Inc., and Clarkson N. Potter, Inc., summers, 1963-67. *Member:* American Association of University Professors, Phi Beta Kappa.

WRITINGS—With husband, David Kales: *Masters of Art,* Grosset, 1967; *Complete Guide to the Boston Harbor Islands,* Herman Publishing, 1975.

SIDELIGHTS: Emily Kales is competent in French and Spanish. *Avocational interests:* Art history, folk music (guitar), Chinese affairs.†

* * *

KAMARCK, Andrew M(artin)   1914-

PERSONAL: Surname is pronounced *Kay*-mark; born November 10, 1914, in Newton Falls, N.Y.; son of Martin and Frances (Earl) Kamarck; married Margaret Ellen Goldenweiser, 1941; children: Ellen Mary (Mrs. David Davies), Elizabeth Anne (Mrs. Lawrence Minnich), Martin Alexander. *Education:* Harvard University, B.S. (summa cum laude), 1936, M.A., 1944, Ph.D., 1951. *Religion:* Unitarian Universalist. *Home:* 126 Third St. S.E., Washington, D.C. 20003. *Office:* World Bank, 1818 H St. N.W., Washington, D.C. 20433.

CAREER: Allied Control Council, Germany, deputy director of Finance Division, 1945; U.S. Treasury, Washington, D.C., chief of National Advisory Council Secretariat, 1946-48, representative in Italy, 1948-50; International Bank for Reconstruction and Development, Washington, D.C., chief of African Section, 1950-52, economic adviser to department of operations, Europe, Africa, and Australia, 1953-65, director of economics department, 1965-71, director of Economic Development Institute, 1972—. Lecturer on African affairs, Johns Hopkins School of Advanced International Studies, 1957—. Regents professor at University of California, Los Angeles, 1964-65. *Military service:* U.S. Army, Field Artillery, 1942-44; became major; received two battle stars. *Member:* American Economic Association, African Studies Association (fellow; director, 1962-65), Society for International Development (council member, 1967-70), Economics Institute (policy and advisory board member), Council on Foreign Relations, Phi Beta Kappa.

WRITINGS: (Co-author) *The Economic Development of Uganda,* Johns Hopkins Press, 1962; *The Economics of African Development,* Praeger, 1967, revised edition, 1972. Contributor to journals.

* * *

KAMINSKY, Jack   1922-

PERSONAL: Born March 19, 1922, in New York, N.Y.; son of Rubin and Lena Kaminsky; married Alice Richken (a college professor), October 11, 1947; children: Eric. *Education:* City College (now City College of the City University of New York), B.S.S., 1944; Yale University, student, 1943-44; New York University, M.A., 1947, Ph.D., 1950. *Office:* Department of Philosophy, State University of New York at Binghamton, Binghamton, N.Y. 13901.

CAREER: Instructor in philosophy at University of Akron, Akron, Ohio, 1950-51, and City College (now City College of the City University of New York), New York, N.Y., 1952-53; State University of New York at Binghamton, assistant professor, 1953-57, associate professor, 1957-61, professor of philosophy, 1961—, chairman of department, 1953-61. *Military service:* U.S. Army, Infantry, 1943-46; received Bronze Star. *Member:* American Philosophical Association, Mind Association, Creighton Philosophy Club (president, 1961-62). *Awards, honors:* American Council of Learned Societies fellowship, 1951-52; distinguished research fellowship of State University of New York, 1967.

WRITINGS: (With B. F. Huppe) *Logic and Language,*

Knopf, 1956; *Hegel on Art: An Interpretation of Hegel's Aesthetics,* State University of New York, 1962; *Language and Ontology,* Southern Illinois University Press, 1969; (with wife, Alice R. Kaminsky) *Logic: An Introduction,* Addison-Wesley, 1974.

WORK IN PROGRESS: With wife, Alice R. Kaminsky, *Readings in Philosophy of Logic,* for Addison-Wesley; *Essays in Linguistic Ontology.*

* * *

KAMPF, Abraham   1920-
   (Avram Kampf)

PERSONAL: Born January 1, 1920; son of Joseph and Rosa Kampf. *Education:* New York University, B.S., 1951; New School for Social Research, Ph.D., 1962; Columbia University, graduate study, 1955-62. *Home:* 372 Central Park W., New York, N.Y.

CAREER: Montclair State College, Upper Montclair, N.J., associate professor of fine arts, beginning 1957. Associate of art history department, Columbia University, 1961-65; Fulbright professor, Hebrew University of Jerusalem, 1965-67. Adviser on research and planning, Jewish Museum, New York, N.Y., 1966-67.

WRITINGS: Contemporary Synagogue Art, Jewish Publication Society, 1965. Contributor to journals.

WORK IN PROGRESS: Synagogue and Church Architecture Today.

AVOCATIONAL INTERESTS: Painting, sculpture, architecture, social sciences, travel.††

* * *

KAPLAN, Boche   1926-
   (A. K. Roche, joint pseudonym)

PERSONAL: Born December 7, 1926, in Oceanside, N.Y.; daughter of Harry and Anna (Brown) Spiegelman; married Max M. Kaplan (a salesman), January 4, 1950; children: Lisa, Howard. *Education:* Attended Cooper Union Day Art School, 1947-49. *Religion:* Hebrew. *Home and office:* 166 West Waukena Ave., Oceanside, N.Y. 11572.

CAREER: Textile designer, 1954-64; teacher of painting, sculpture, and graphic arts to children and adults, 1964—. *Member:* Authors Guild.

WRITINGS—With Roslyn Kroop Abisch, under joint pseudonym A. K. Roche; all children's literature: *I Can Be,* Prentice-Hall, 1967; *The Pumpkin Heads,* Prentice-Hall, 1968; *The Onion Maidens,* Prentice-Hall, 1968; (adaptor) *The Clever Turtle* (African folktale), Prentice-Hall, 1969; *Even the Promise of Freedom,* Prentice-Hall, 1970; *The City . . . in Haiku,* Prentice-Hall, 1970.

Illustrator under own name: Van Gelder, *Monkeys Have Tails,* McKay, 1966.

Illustrator under own name; written by Roz Abisch: *Open Your Eyes,* Parents' Magazine Press, 1964; *Anywhere in the World,* McKay, 1966; *Art Is for You,* McKay, 1967; *Do You Know What Time It Is?,* Prentice-Hall, 1969; *'Twas in the Moon of Wintertime,* Prentice-Hall, 1969; *Mai-Ling and the Mirror* (adapted from a Chinese folk tale), Prentice-Hall, 1969; *The Shoe for Your Left Foot Won't Fit on the Right,* McCall Publishing, 1970; *Sweet Betsy from Pike,* McCall Publishing, 1970; *If I Could, I Would,* F. Watts, 1971; *Silly Street,* F. Watts, 1971; *Smile If You Meet a Crocodile,* F. Watts, 1971; *Blast Off!,* F. Watts, 1971; *Out in the Woods,* F. Watts, 1971; *Under the Ocean, Under the Sea,* F. Watts, 1971; *Let's Find Out about Butterflies,* F. Watts, 1972; *Around the House that Jack Built,* Parents' Magazine Press, 1972; *Easy to Make Holiday Fun Things,* Xerox Education Publications, 1973; *Mixed Bag of Magic Tricks,* Xerox Education Publications, 1973, hard cover edition, Walker & Co., 1975; *What's the Good Word?,* Urban Media Materials, 1973; *Star Books for Learning,* New Dimensions in Education, Series I, 1973, Series II, in press; *The Make-It, Play-It Game Book,* Walker & Co., 1974; (compiler) *Textiles,* F. Watts, 1974; *The Reading Works,* New Dimensions in Education, 1975; *Word Builders,* two volumes, Urban Media Materials, 1975.

Illustrator under own name; written by Roz Abisch, under pseudonym Mr. Sniff: *Wishes, Whiffs, and Birthday Gifts,* F. Watts, 1971; *Circus Tents and Circus Scents,* F. Watts, 1971; *Scented Rhymes for Story Times,* F. Watts, 1971; *Scents and Sun and Picnic Fun,* F. Watts, 1971.

Also illustrator under own name of *Spring, Summer, Fall, Winter,* by Roz Abisch, under pseudonym Mr. McGillicuddy, 1970, and *Big, Little, Tall, Short,* by Abisch, under pseudonym Mr. Sniff, 1974.

WORK IN PROGRESS: More children's books, in collaboration with Roz Abisch.

BIOGRAPHICAL/CRITICAL SOURCES: See also **ABISCH, Roslyn Kroop.**

*   *   *

KAPLAN, Frederick I(srael)   1920-

PERSONAL: Born December 1, 1920, in New York, N.Y.; son of Harry (a manufacturer) and Sadie-Alexandra (Finkelstein) Kaplan. *Education:* University of California, Berkeley, B.A., 1942, M.A., 1947, Ph.D., 1957. *Office:* Department of Humanities, Michigan State University, East Lansing, Mich. 48823.

CAREER: Michigan State University, East Lansing, instructor, 1958-60, assistant professor, 1960-65, professor of history, 1965—. *Military service:* U.S. Army, 1942-46; became staff sergeant. *Member:* American Historical Association, American Association for the Advancement of Slavic Studies. *Awards, honors:* Traveling research fellow, Columbia University, 1956-57; research fellow at University of Moscow in United States-Soviet Russia scholarly exchange program, 1960-61.

WRITINGS: Bolshevik Ideology and the Ethics of Soviet Labor, 1917-1920: The Formative Years, Philosophical Library, 1968. Contributor of articles and reviews to journals in United States and Europe.

WORK IN PROGRESS: The Edge of the Webb, a novel.

SIDELIGHTS: Frederick Kaplan is competent in Russian, French, German, and Japanese (Japanese translator while in Army). He did research at the University of Helsinki Library, the University of Stockholm, the Institute for Social History in Amsterdam, the British Museum, the Feltrinelli Library in Milan, the Lenin Library, the Library of University of Moscow, and the Saltykov Schedrin Library in Leningrad.

*   *   *

KAPLAN, Jacob J.   1920-

PERSONAL: Born August 23, 1920, in Somerville, Mass.; son of Louis (a merchant) and Esther (Baker) Kaplan; married Roberta Rabinoff (a teacher), May 1, 1971; children:

(first marriage) Beatrice Balgley, Esther Pauline. *Education:* Harvard University, A.B., 1940, A.M., 1941, Ph.D., 1950; Iowa State University of Science and Technology, graduate study, 1941-42. *Home:* 1221 Massachusetts Ave. N.W., Washington, D.C. 20005. *Office:* 1730 Rhode Island Ave. N.W., Washington, D.C. 20036.

CAREER: U.S. Department of State, Washington, D.C., international economist, 1946-48; Yale University, New Haven, Conn., research associate, Institute of International Studies, 1948-50; Economic Cooperation Administration, Washington, D.C., assistant chief, later chief of European regional organizations staff, 1951-54; U.S. Department of State, American representative to managing board of European Payments Union, Paris, France, 1954-59, assistant coordinator for foreign assistance programs, Washington, D.C., 1959-61; Agency for International Development, Washington, D.C., director of international development organizations staff, 1961-65; consultant in international finance and economics, Washington, D.C., 1966—. Council on Foreign Relations, consultant, 1949-50. *Military service:* U.S. Army, 1942-46; became first lieutenant; received Bronze Star. *Member:* American Economic Association, American Association for the Advancement of Science, Phi Beta Kappa, International Club and Harvard Club (both Washington, D.C.). *Awards, honors:* Ford Foundation research grant, 1965-66.

WRITINGS: The Challenge of Foreign Aid, Praeger, 1967; (contributor) *Technical Assistance and Development,* Harry S Truman Research Institute, 1971; *International Aspects of a National Materials Policy,* National Commission on Materials Policy, 1973; (co-author with R. V. Hatfield) *Foreign Maritime Aids,* U.S. Department of Commerce/National Bureau of Standards, 1974; (contributor) Isaiah Frank, editor, *The Japanese Economy in International Perspective,* Johns Hopkins University Press, 1975.

BIOGRAPHICAL/CRITICAL SOURCES: New Republic, June 3, 1967; *Reporter,* June 15, 1967; *Annuals,* January, 1968; *World Politics,* January, 1968.

*   *   *

KAPLAN, Lawrence Jay   1915-

PERSONAL: Born October 28, 1915, in New York, N.Y.; son of Harris (a tailor) and Estelle (Wilner) Kaplan; married Jeanne Leon (a teacher of English in senior high school), June 9, 1946; children: Harriet, Sanford S., Marcia. *Education:* Brooklyn College (now Brooklyn College of the City University of New York), B.A., 1937; Columbia University, M.A., 1938, Ph.D., 1958. *Politics:* Democrat. *Religion:* Jewish. *Home:* 69-18 225th St., Bayside, N.Y. 11364. *Office:* John Jay College of Criminal Justice of the City University of New York, New York, N.Y. 10003.

CAREER: New York (N.Y.) high schools, teacher of economics, 1938-41; U.S. Office of the Housing Expediter, Washington, D.C., economist, 1946-47; Organization for Rehabilitation through Training, New York City, chief statistician, 1947-49; U.S. Department of Labor, Bureau of Labor Statistics, New York City, chief information officer, 1949-57; New York (N.Y.) Departments of City Planning and Relocation, director of planning and research, 1957-65; John Jay College of Criminal Justice of the City University of New York, New York City, 1965—, began as associate professor, currently professor of economics. Part-time lecturer in economics and statistics at Barnard M. Baruch College of the City University of New York, 1950-68. Research director, New York State Joint Legislative Committee on Consumer Protection, 1965-72. Oakland Jewish Center, Bayside, N.Y., president, 1959-60, member of board of trustees, 1953-75. *Military service:* U.S. Army, Military Intelligence, 1942-45; received five battle stars in European campaigns. *Member:* American Economic Association, American Statistical Association, Metropolitan Economic Association.

WRITINGS: Factors Affecting Productivity in the Home-building Industry, Faculty of Political Science, Columbia University, 1958; (with C. Morris Horowitz) *The Estimated Jewish Population of the New York Area, 1900-1975,* Federation of Jewish Philanthropies, 1959; *Elementary Statistics for Economics and Business,* Pitman, 1966, *Workbook and Problems,* 1967, *Solutions,* 1967; (with Leo C. Loughrey) *Ins and Outs of On-Track and Off-Track Betting,* Gould Publications, 1970; (with Dennis Kessler) *An Economic Analysis of Crime,* C. C Thomas, 1975. Author of about twenty-five bulletins, studies, reports, and articles in journals.

WORK IN PROGRESS: Personal Economics for Consumers, completion expected in 1976; second edition of *Elementary Statistics for Economics and Business,* 1977.

AVOCATIONAL INTERESTS: Playing piano, gardening.

* * *

KAPLAN, Samuel 1935-

PERSONAL: Born December 20, 1935, in Brooklyn, N.Y.; son of Joseph and Sadie (Matin) Kaplan; married Sharron Louise Walther, November 13, 1960. *Education:* Cornell University, B.S., 1957. *Home:* 15 Shore Rd., Port Washington, N.Y. 11050.

CAREER: New York Times, New York City, reporter, 1958-66; New Haven Redevelopment Agency, New Haven, Conn., downtown renewal director, 1966-67; New York City Educational Construction Fund, New York City, director of development, 1968—. Adjunct professor at City College of the City University of New York, 1969-76. *Military service:* U.S. Army, 1957-58.

WRITINGS: (With Gilbert Tauber) *The New York City Handbook,* Doubleday, 1966; *The Dream Deferred,* Seabury, 1976. Author of documentaries for National Broadcasting Co. and National Educational Television. Contributor of articles and reviews to newspapers and periodicals.

* * *

KAPLON, Morton F(ischel) 1921-

PERSONAL: Born February 11, 1921, in Philadelphia, Pa.; son of Myer and Ida (Abramson) Kaplon; married Anita J. Harle, June 16, 1946; children: Keith V., Bryna M., Andrea J. *Education:* Lehigh University, B.Sc., 1941, M.S., 1947; University of Rochester, Ph.D., 1951. *Home:* 11 White Birch Dr., Pomona, N.Y. 10970. *Office:* Administration Building, City College of the City University of New York, New York, N.Y. 10031.

CAREER: University of Rochester, Rochester, N.Y., research associate in physics, 1951-52, assistant professor, 1952-55, associate professor, 1955-60, professor of physics, beginning 1960, associate dean of College of Arts and Sciences, 1963-65, chairman of physics and astronomy department, 1964-69; City College of the City University of New York, New York, N.Y., provost, 1971—. *Military service:* U.S. Army Air Forces, 1941-45; became first lieutenant. *Member:* American Physical Society (fellow), American

Association for the Advancement of Science, American Geophysical Union, Italian Physical Society, Sigma Xi.

WRITINGS: (Editor) *A Homage to Galileo,* M.I.T. Press, 1965. Contributor of more than fifty articles to professional journals.

WORK IN PROGRESS: Research in cosmic ray physics, space physics, and very high energy interactions.

* * *

KARG, Elissa Jane 1951-

PERSONAL: Born January 5, 1951, in New York, N.Y.; daughter of Lester Albert (an electronic engineer) and Dorothy (Schwartz) Karg. *Education:* Attended Oberlin College. *Politics:* None. *Religion:* None.

WRITINGS: How to Be a Noncomformist, Silvermine Publishers, 1967. Contributor to *Youth* and *Seventeen.*††

* * *

KARMEL, Alex 1931-

PERSONAL: Born September 15, 1931, in New York, N.Y.; married Marjorie Low, December 15, 1953 (deceased); children: Joseph, Marianne, Philippa. *Education:* Columbia University, B.A., 1952, M.A., 1953. *Home:* 5024 Klingle St. N.W., Washington, D.C. 20016. *Agent:* Phyllis Jackson, International Creative Management, 40 West 57th St., New York, N.Y. 10019.

CAREER: Writer.

WRITINGS: Mary Ann (novel), Viking, 1958; *Last Words* (novel), McGraw, 1968; *My Revolution: Diary of Retif de la Bretonne* (novel), McGraw, 1970; *Guillotine in the Wings* (historical essay), McGraw, 1972. Author of screenplay, "Something Wild."

WORK IN PROGRESS: Master Jack, a novel.

* * *

KARNES, Thomas L(indas) 1914-

PERSONAL: Born August 21, 1914, in Kenosha, Wis.; son of James H. (a hardware dealer) and Jennie (Lindas) Karnes; married Virginia Perry, December 23, 1941; children: Stephen P., Michele S. *Education:* De Pauw University, student, 1932-34; University of Colorado, A.B., 1940; Stanford University, M.A., 1949, Ph.D., 1953. *Office:* Arizona State University, Tempe, Ariz. 85281.

CAREER: U.S. Veterans Administration, Corvallis, Ore., training officer, 1945-47; Stanford University, Stanford, Calif., instructor in history, 1951-54; Tulane University of Louisiana, New Orleans, 1954-68, began as assistant professor, became professor of history; Arizona State University, Tempe, professor of history, 1968—. Director of conferences on Latin America for students, Army Reserve forces, and the public. *Military service:* U.S. Army Air Forces, 1941-45; became lieutenant colonel. *Member:* American Historical Association, Organization of American Historians, Conference on Latin American History, Southern Historical Association, Phi Beta Kappa.

WRITINGS: (Contributor) *The Caribbean,* University of Florida Press, 1957; *Failure of Union: Central America, 1824-1960,* University of North Carolina Press, 1961; *William Gilpin: Western Nationalist,* University of Texas Press, 1969; *The Latin American Policy of the United States,* University of Arizona Press, 1972. Contributor to *Britannica Book of the Year,* 1959-63, *Lands and Peoples,* 1964, and to *Encyclopaedia Britannica;* also contributor of articles to history journals in United States and Latin America.

WORK IN PROGRESS: A book, Standard Fruit and Steamship Company in Latin America.

*   *   *

KAROLIDES, Nicholas J(ames)   1928-

PERSONAL: Third syllable of surname is accented, pronounced to rhyme with "slides"; born August 5, 1928, in Albany, N.Y.; son of James Nicholas and Katherine (Kaplanides) Karolides; married Inga Schaumann, November 24, 1962; children: Milissa and Alexis (both daughters). Education: New York University, B.S., 1950, M.A., 1951, Ph.D., 1962. Home address: Route 1, River Falls, Wis. 54022. Office: Department of English, University of Wisconsin, River Falls, Wis. 54022.

CAREER: Pierre Van Cortlandt School, Croton-on-Hudson, N.Y., teacher of English, 1954-59, guidance counselor, 1960-64; New York University, School of Education, teaching fellow, 1959-60, part-time instructor in English, 1960-64; University of Wisconsin—River Falls, assistant professor, 1964-66, associate professor, 1966-68, professor of English and English education, 1969—. Military service: U.S. Army, 1951-53. U.S. Army Reserve, 1957-64; became captain. Member: National Council of Teachers of English, Conference on English Education, Conference on College Composition and Communication, American Association of University Professors, Wisconsin Council of Teachers of English (member of executive committee), Wisconsin Conference on English Education (chairman), Phi Delta Kappa.

WRITINGS: The Pioneer in the American Novel, 1900-1950, University of Oklahoma Press, 1967. Contributor, Wisconsin Studies in Contemporary Literature. Editor, Wisconsin English Journal, English Education, Arizona English Bulletin.

AVOCATIONAL INTERESTS: Skiing.

*   *   *

KARPAT, Kemal H(asim)   1925-

PERSONAL: Born February 15, 1925, in Turda-Tulca, Rumania; son of Hasim and Zubeyde (Cavus) Omer; married, 1962 (divorced, 1967). Education: University of Istanbul, LL.B., 1948; University of Washington, Seattle, M.A., 1950; New York University, Ph.D., 1957. Office: Department of History, University of Wisconsin, Madison, Wis. 53706.

CAREER: United Nations Secretariat, New York City, staff member, 1952-53, assistant representative, U.N. Technical Assistance Board, 1955; Montana State University, Missoula, assistant professor, 1957-60, associate professor, 1960-62; New York University, New York City, associate professor of government, 1962-67; University of Wisconsin, Madison, professor of history, 1967—, and chairman of Middle East Studies Program. Acting chairman of department of public administration, Middle East Technical University, Ankara, Turkey, 1958-59. Military service: Turkish Army, 1953-55; became second lieutenant. Member: American Political Science Association, American Historical Association, International Political Science Association, Middle East Studies Association of North America, American Oriental Society, Middle East Institute, Pi Sigma Alpha. Awards, honors: Social Science Research Council grant, 1962; fellow of Center for Middle East Studies, Harvard University, 1960-61.

WRITINGS: Turkey's Politics, Princeton University Press, 1959; (contributor) R. Ward and D. A. Rustow, editors, Political Modernization in Japan and Turkey, Princeton University Press, 1964; (editor) Political and Social Thought in the Contemporary Middle East, Praeger, 1968; Social Change and Politics in Turkey, E. J. Brill, 1973; An Inquiry into the Social Foundations of Nationalism in the Ottoman State, Center of International Studies, Princeton University, 1973; (editor) The Ottoman State and Its Place in World History, E. J. Brill, 1974; The Foreign Policy of Turkey in Transition, 1950-1974, E. J. Brill, 1975; Rural Migration and Urbanization: The Gecekondu, Cambridge University Press, 1976. Contributor to journals and to the Turkish press.

WORK IN PROGRESS: Elite Formation and Populism: Modern History of Turkey.

SIDELIGHTS: Karpat speaks French, Italian, Spanish, and Bulgarian, in addition to Rumanian and Turkish.

*   *   *

KARPLUS, Walter J.   1927-

PERSONAL: Born April 23, 1927, in Vienna, Austria. Education: Cornell University, B.E.E., 1949; University of California, Berkeley, M.S.E.E., 1951, Los Angeles, Ph.D., 1954. Office: Department of Computer Science, University of California, Los Angeles, Calif. 90024.

CAREER: Sun Oil Co., Newton Square, Pa., electrical engineer, 1949-50; International Geophysics, graduate research geophysicist, 1951-52; University of California, Los Angeles, assistant professor, 1955-59, associate professor, 1959-65, professor of computer science, electrical circuits and electronics, 1965—, chairman of computer science department, 1972—. Consulting research engineer, Hughes Aircraft Co., 1955-56. Consultant to North Atlantic Treaty Organization, Organization for Economic Co-operation and Development, U.S. Information Service seminars for French university students, and U.S. Department of State Agency for International Development program in India. Military service: U.S. Navy, 1944-46. Member: Institute of Electrical and Electronic Engineers (fellow). Awards, honors: Fulbright research fellow, 1961; Guggenheim fellow, 1968; Senior Simulation Award, Society of Computer Simulation, 1972.

WRITINGS: Analog Simulation: Solution of Field Problems, McGraw, 1958; (with W. Soroka) Analog Methods: Computations and Simulation, McGraw, 1959; (editor of analog computer section, and contributor) Handbook of Automation Computation and Control, Wiley, 1959; (contributor) Computer Handbook, McGraw, 1961; (contributor) Computer Control Technology, McGraw, 1961; (with R. Tomovic) High Speed Analog Computers, Wiley, 1964; (contributor) System Engineering Handbook, McGraw, 1965; (editor) On-Line Computing, McGraw, 1966; (with G. Bekey) Hybrid Computation, Wiley, 1967. Member of editorial board, Simulation; reviewer, IEEE Transactions.

*   *   *

KASE, Francis J(oseph)   1910-

PERSONAL: Born September 21, 1910, in Most, Czechoslovakia; naturalized U.S. citizen; son of Francis (a government official) and Bertha (Retovska) Kase. Education: Charles University, Dr.jur., 1934; Academy of Political and Social Sciences, Prague, Czechoslovakia, D.S.P., 1934; George Washington University, Ph.D., 1963. Home:

5206 Little Falls Dr., Green Acres, Md. 20016. *Office:* Patent Office, U.S. Department of Commerce, Washington, D.C. 20231.

CAREER: Ministry of Foreign Commerce, Prague, Czechoslovakia, counsellor and division chief, 1945-48; International Peasant Union, Washington, D.C., treasurer and research analyst, 1950-53; U.S. Library of Congress, Copyright Office, Washington, D.C., librarian, 1956-66; U.S. Department of Commerce, Patent Office, Washington, D.C., librarian, 1966-71; Executive Office of the President, Washington, D.C., law librarian for Price Commission, 1971-72; U.S. Department of Commerce, Patent Office, librarian, 1972—. *Member:* American Political Science Association, American Academy of Political and Social Science, Patent Office Professional Organization, Copyright Office Lawyers' Association, Patent Office Society, Pi Gamma Mu, St. Alban's Tennis Club, Arlington Y Tennis and Squash Club, Washington Athletic Club.

WRITINGS: Copyright in Czechoslovakia, New York University Law Center, 1966; *Copyright Thought in Continental Europe*, Fred B. Rothman, 1967; *People's Democracy: A Contribution to the Study of the Communist Theory of State and Revolution*, A. W. Sijthoff, 1968; *Foreign Patents: A Guide to Official Patent Literature*, Oceana, 1972; *Trademarks: A Guide to Official Trademark Literature*, Oceana, 1974; *Designs: A Guide to Official Literature on Design Protection*, Oceana, 1975. Contributor to library journals.

*   *   *

KASH, Don E(ldon)   1934-

PERSONAL: Born May 29, 1934, in Macedonia, Iowa; son of Albert (a businessman) and Blanche (Smith) Kash; married Beverly Ann Brendes; children: Kelli Denise, Jeffrey Paul. *Education:* University of Iowa, B.A., 1959, M.A., 1960, Ph.D., 1963. *Office:* Science and Public Policy Program, University of Oklahoma, 432 Physical Science Bldg., Norman, Okla. 73069.

CAREER: Texas Technological College (now Texas Tech University), Lubbock, instructor, 1960-61; Arizona State University, Tempe, assistant professor of political science, 1963-65; University of Missouri at Kansas City, assistant professor of political science, 1965-66; Purdue University, Lafayette, Ind., associate professor of political science and director of program in science and public policy, 1966-70; University of Oklahoma, Norman, professor of political science and director of science and public policy program, 1970—. Consultant to council on economic growth, technology, and public policy, Committee on Institutional Cooperation and to Argonne Universities Association. *Military service:* U.S. Army, 1954-56. *Member:* American Association for the Advancement of Science, American Political Science Association, American Association of University Professors.

WRITINGS: The Politics of Space Cooperation, Purdue University Press, 1967; (with others) *Energy under the Ocean: A Technology Assessment*, University of Oklahoma Press, 1973. Contributor to *Impact of Science and Technology on Politics*, edited by Paul Dembling and Stephen E. Doyle, American Institute of Aeronautics and Astronautics. Also contributor to *Western Political Quarterly*, *Bulletin of the Atomic Scientists*, and *Science.*

WORK IN PROGRESS: Study of inter-university research organizations; a book on interaction of technology and politics.†

KASSOF, Allen   1930-

PERSONAL: Born December 17, 1930, in New York, N.Y.; son of Morris and Sophia (Baron) Kassof; married Arianne Scholz, February 14, 1953; children: Andrea, Arlen, Anita. *Education:* Rutgers University, A.B., 1952; Harvard University, A.M., 1954, Ph.D., 1960. *Home:* 949 Mercer Rd., Princeton, N.J. 08540. *Office:* 110 East 59th St., New York, N.Y.

CAREER: Smith College, Northampton, Mass., 1957-61, began as instructor, became assistant professor of sociology; Princeton University, Princeton, N.J., assistant professor, 1961-65, associate professor of sociology, 1965-73, lecturer, 1973-75, assistant dean of the college, 1965-69; International Research and Exchanges Board, New York, N.Y., executive director, 1968—. Member of Joint Committee on Slavic Studies, American Council of Learned Societies and Social Science Research Council. *Member:* American Sociological Association, American Association for the Advancement of Slavic Studies, Council on Foreign Relations.

WRITINGS: The Soviet Youth Program: Regimentation and Rebellion, Harvard University Press, 1965; (editor) *Prospects for Soviet Society*, Praeger, for Council on Foreign Relations, 1968.

*   *   *

KAST, Fremont E.   1926-

PERSONAL: Born January 27, 1926, in Modesto, Calif.; son of Fremont H. (a teacher) and Arlette E. (Bradley) Kast; married Phyllis J. Hames, June 20, 1948; children: Karen Ann, Cheryl Jean. *Education:* San Jose State College (now San Jose State University), B.A., 1946; Stanford University, M.B.A., 1949; University of Washington, Seattle, D.B.A., 1956. *Politics:* Democrat. *Religion:* Protestant. *Home:* 10749 Lakeside N.E., Seattle, Wash. 98125. *Office:* Graduate School of Business, University of Washington, Seattle, Wash. 98195.

CAREER: Syracuse University, Syracuse, N.Y., instructor, 1949-51; University of Washington, Graduate School of Business, Seattle, instructor, 1951-53, assistant professor, 1953-56, associate professor, 1956-61, professor of management, 1961—. Visiting associate professor, Columbia University, 1957-58; Fulbright professor, Netherlands School of Economics, 1963-64; visiting professor, University of California, Los Angeles, 1973. Consultant to Boeing Co., U.S. Air Force Institute of Technology, U.S. Corps of Engineers (Seattle District), and Port of New York Authority. *Military service:* U.S. Naval Reserve, 1944-46; became lieutenant. *Member:* American Sociological Association, Academy of Management, American Academy of Political and Social Science, American Association of University Professors. *Awards, honors:* James A. Hamilton Book Award of American College of Hospital Administrators, 1965, for *The Theory and Management of Systems.*

WRITINGS: (With Richard Johnson and J. E. Rosenzweig) *The Theory and Management of Systems*, McGraw, 1963, 3rd edition, 1973; (with Rosenzweig) *Science, Technology, and Management*, McGraw, 1963; (with Rosenzweig) *Organization and Management: A Systems Approach*, McGraw, 1969, 2nd edition, 1974; (with Rosenzweig) *Contingency Views of Organization and Management*, Science Research Associates, 1973; (contributor) Joseph W. McGuire, editor, *Contemporary Management: Issues and Viewpoints*, Prentice-Hall, 1974. Contributor to *Encyclopaedia Britannica* and to management journals.

KATOPE, Christopher G. 1918-

PERSONAL: Surname is accented on second syllable; born April 1, 1918, in Lowell, Mass.; son of George and Bessie (Savas) Katope; married Marjorie Spencer King (a teacher), June 6, 1942; children: Theodora (Mrs. Charles Rowland), Christopher Lawrence. *Education:* University of Louisville, student, 1938-41; University of Chicago, M.A., 1947; Vanderbilt University, Ph.D., 1954. *Politics:* Democrat. *Religion:* Unitarian Universalist. *Home:* 514 Euclid Ave., Saegertown, Pa. *Office:* Department of English, Allegheny College, Meadville, Pa.

CAREER: Westminster College, Fulton, Mo., assistant professor of English, 1947-50; Allegheny College, Meadville, Pa., associate professor of English, 1952—, chairman of department, 1976. Fulbright professor in Greece at Athens College, 1959-60, and Anatolia College, 1960-61; visiting summer professor at Columbia University, 1968. Member of Saegertown School Board. *Military service:* U.S. Navy, 1941-45; became chief petty officer. *Member:* Modern Language Association of America, American Association of University Professors, Meadville Round Table.

WRITINGS: (Editor with Paul G. Zolbrod) *Beyond Berkeley: A Sourcebook in Student Values,* World Publishing, 1966; (editor with Zolbrod) *The Rhetoric of Revolution,* Macmillan, 1970. Contributor to journals in his field.

WORK IN PROGRESS: A book, *Romanticism and the Twentieth-Century Novel;* a monograph, *F. Scott Fitzgerald's Romanticism.*

* * *

KATZ, Leonard 1926-

PERSONAL: Born September 15, 1926, in New York, N.Y.; son of Joseph (a cab driver) and Alice (Meyer) Katz; married Betty Kronfeld, January 28, 1951. *Education:* University of Colorado, B.A., 1951. *Politics:* Liberal Democrat. *Religion:* Hebrew. *Residence:* New York, N.Y.

CAREER: New York Post, New York, N.Y., general assignment reporter, beginning 1951, thoroughbred racing columnist, 1962-63. *Military service:* U.S. Navy, 1944-46. *Member:* New York Reporters Association. *Awards, honors:* Award for best coverage of a fire story, Uniformed Fireman's Association, 1958.

WRITINGS: The Coppolino Murder Trial, Bee-Line Books, 1967; *Uncle Frank: The Biography of Frank Costello,* foreword by Anthony Quinn, W. H. Allen, 1974. Contributor to *Coronet.*

AVOCATIONAL INTERESTS: Horse racing, anthropology, and all forms of gambling.†

* * *

KATZ, Martin 1929-

PERSONAL: Born April 1, 1929, in Carmel, Calif.; son of Frank Agliano and Anna Katz; married Georgia M. Henderson (a teacher), August 20, 1967. *Education:* Stanford University, A.B., 1951; University of California, Berkeley, M.A., 1953, Ph.D., 1962. *Office:* Department of History, University of Alberta, Edmonton, Alberta, Canada.

CAREER: University of Alberta, Edmonton, assistant professor, 1962-69, associate professor of history, 1969—. *Military service:* U.S. Air Force, 1953-56; became first lieutenant. *Member:* American Historical Association, American Association for the Advancement of Slavic Stud-

ies, Canadian Association of Slavists. *Awards, honors:* Inter-University Committee on Travel Grants award; Canada Council grant and fellowship, 1968-69.

WRITINGS: Mikhail N. Katkov: A Political Biography, 1818-1887, Mouton & Co., 1966. Contributor to journals in his field. Contributing editor, *Canadian Slavic Studies.*

WORK IN PROGRESS: Research on T. N. Granovskii for a monograph, and M. P. Bestuzhev-Riumin for an article.

* * *

KATZ, William Loren 1927-

PERSONAL: Born June 2, 1927, in New York, N.Y.; son of Bernard (a researcher) and Phyllis (Brownstone) Katz; married Glorida Gray, April 6, 1952 (divorced, 1969); married Jacqueline Hunt, March 6, 1970; children (first marriage): Naomi, Michael. *Education:* Syracuse University, B.A., 1950; New York University, M.A., 1952. *Religion:* Jewish. *Home:* 34 East 10th St., New York, N.Y. 10003.

CAREER: New York (N.Y.) public schools, teacher of American history, 1955-60; Greenburgh District 8 School System, Hartsdale, N.Y., high school teacher of American history, 1960-68; writer, 1968—. Scholar-in-residence and research fellow, Columbia University, 1971-73; lecturer on American Negro history at teacher institutes; teacher of black history at Toombs Prison. Producer of audio-visual materials on minorities for classrooms. Consultant to President Kennedy's Committee on Juvenile Delinquency and Youth Development, and to Smithsonian Institution. *Military service:* U.S. Navy, 1945-46. *Member:* United Federation of Teachers.

WRITINGS: Eyewitness: The Negro in American History, Pitman, 1967, 3rd edition, 1974; *Teachers' Guide to American Negro History,* Quadrangle, 1968, revised edition, 1971; (with Warren J. Halliburton) *American Minorities and Majorities: A Syllabus of United States History for Secondary Schools,* Arno, 1970; *The Black West: A Documentary and Pictorial History,* Doubleday, 1971, revised edition, 1973; (with Halliburton) *A History of Black Americans,* Harcourt, 1973; *An Album of Reconstruction,* F. Watts, 1974; *An Album of the Civil War,* F. Watts, 1974; (with Bernard Gaughran) *The Constitutional Amendments,* F. Watts, 1974; *Minorities in American History,* six volumes, F. Watts, 1974-75; (with wife, Jacqueline Hunt) *Making Our Way,* Dial, 1975.

General editor, "The American Negro: His History and Literature" series, 147 volumes, Arno, 1968-71, "Minorities in America: Picture Histories" series, 1972—, "Teaching Approaches to Black History in the Classroom," 1973; editor, "The Anti-Slavery Crusade in America" series, 70 volumes. Contributor to professional journals. Member of editorial board, *Black Studies,* 1970—.

* * *

KAUFMAN, Gerald (Bernard) 1930-

PERSONAL: Born June 21, 1930, in Leeds, England; son of Louis (a tailor) and Jane (Pantirer) Kaufman. *Education:* Queen's College, Oxford, M.A., 1953. *Politics:* Labour. *Religion:* Jewish. *Home:* 87 Charlbert Ct., Eamont St., London N.W.8, England. *Office:* House of Commons, London S.W.1, England.

CAREER: Fabian Society, London, England, assistant secretary, 1954-55; *Daily Mirror,* London, member of political staff, 1955-64; *New Statesman,* London, political correspondent, 1964-65; British Labour Party, London, parliamentary press liaison officer, 1965-70; member of parliament, representing Ardwick Division of Manchester, 1970—; under-secretary of state, Department of the Environment, 1974—. Governor, Balham and Tooting College of Commerce, 1954-55. *Member:* British Film Institute, Fabian Society.

WRITINGS: (With David Frost, Christopher Booker, and Herb Sargent) *How to Live under Labour,* Heinemann, 1964; (editor and author of introduction) *The Left,* Anthony Blond, 1966; *To Build the Promised Land,* Weidenfeld & Nicolson, 1973. Also writer of script for British Broadcasting Corp. television program, "ABC of Britain," and contributor of scripts for "That Was the Week That Was" and other television programs. Weekly columnist, *Jewish Chronicle;* former film critic, *Listener.* Contributor to other British periodicals and newspapers, including *Time and Tide, Queen, Town, Guardian,* and *Observer.*

AVOCATIONAL INTERESTS: Cinema, travel (has traveled widely in Europe, including Soviet Union, and in the Near East and United States).

*   *   *

KAUFMAN, Irving 1920-

PERSONAL: Born October 4, 1920, in New York, N.Y.; son of Herman (a clerk) and Sylvia (Leinstein) Kaufman; married Mabel Goldfarb (an instructor at Columbia University), January 15, 1943; children: Alan Brent, Marc Steven. *Education:* Art Students League, New York, student, 1940-41, 1946-49; New York University, B.A., 1951, M.A., 1952. *Home:* 34 Corell Rd., Scarsdale, N.Y. 10583.

CAREER: New Canaan (Conn.) public schools, teacher of art and art supervisor, 1952-54; University of Michigan, College of Architecture and Design, Ann Arbor, associate professor of art, 1956-64; City College of the City University of New York, professor of art, 1964—. Lecturer at New York University, Wayne State University, Ohio State University, National Gallery of Art. Member of board of directors, Dramatic Arts Center, Ann Arbor, Mich., 1958-64; president, Institute for the Study of Art in Education, 1972-74. Consultant to Central Atlantic Regional Education Laboratory, Washington, D.C., and Center for Urban Education, New York, N.Y. Paintings exhibited at U.S. museums and national shows; exhibits regularly at Rehn Gallery, New York. *Military service:* U.S. Army, Corps of Engineers, 1942-46; became captain. *Member:* College Art Association, National Art Education Association. *Awards, honors:* Horace H. Rackham awards for travel in France, 1959, in Greece, 1962; MacDowell Colony fellowship, 1964.

WRITINGS: (Editor) *Education and the Imagination,* published jointly by Museum of Modern Art and University of Michigan, 1958; *Art and Education in Contemporary Culture,* Macmillan, 1966; (contributor) *Concepts in Art and Education,* Macmillan, 1970; (contributor) *Confronting Curriculum Reform,* Little, Brown, 1970; (contributor) *New Ideas in Art Education,* Dutton, 1972. Contributor to journals.

*   *   *

KAUFMANN, Ulrich George 1920-

PERSONAL: Born June 21, 1920, in Magdeburg, Germany; came to United States in 1938, naturalized in 1942; son of Max (a judge) and Margarete Ernestine (Dietzsch)

Kaufmann; married Ruth S. Loewenstein (a social worker), August 9, 1947; children: Karen. *Education:* Syracuse University, law courses, 1945-59; studied at various advanced and technical U.S. Government schools in America and abroad between 1950-63. *Home:* 19 Melissa Lane, Old Bethpage, N.Y. 11804. *Office:* Organization Security Services, Inc., Hicksville, N.Y.

CAREER: U.S. Department of Defense, Intelligence/Counterintelligence Section, 1949-64, began as special agent, became special agent-in-charge in twenty-four countries on four continents; Ulrich Security Services (physical security consultants), Old Bethpage, N.Y., owner, 1965-71; Organization Security Services, Inc., Hicksville, N.Y., president, 1971—. Lecturer on protection, security, and electronic devices. *Military service:* U.S. Army, 1941-45; became major; received five battle stars and D-Day Invasion Arrowhead. *Member:* American Society for Industrial Security (chairman, Long Island chapter, 1969-70), Whaler's Cove Yacht Club (member of board of directors, 1967).

WRITINGS: How to Avoid Burglary, Housebreaking and Other Crimes, Crown, 1967. Contributor of articles to various magazines and newspapers.

WORK IN PROGRESS: Research for an up-to-date directory of all security devices on the market as well as devices for countermeasures.

SIDELIGHTS: During his years as a government agent, Kaufmann was engaged in tracking down not only spies but also criminals. Initial printing of his first book, intended for the average citizen, was sold out prior to publication.†

*   *   *

KAY, George 1936-

PERSONAL: Born August 19, 1936, in Wath upon Dearne, Yorkshire, England; son of John William (a mine worker) and Gertrude (Watson) Kay; married Pauline Mary Wroe, December 30, 1961; children: Jane Helen, Gillian Lesley, Linda. *Education:* University of Liverpool, B.A. (honors in geography), 1957, M.A., 1959; University of Hull, Ph.D., 1965. *Religion:* Christian. *Home:* 1 Hoober St., Wath-on-Dearne, South Yorkshire, 563 GAX, England.

CAREER: Rhodes-Livingstone Institute, Lusaka, Zambia, research officer in human geography, 1959-62; University of Hull, Hull, England, Leverhulme fellow and lecturer in department of geography, 1962-67; University of Rhodesia, Salisbury, professor of geography and head of department, 1968-74, dean, Faculty of Arts, 1969-71. *Member:* Royal Geographical Society (fellow), Institute of British Geographers, Geographical Association, Royal Scottish Geographical Society, Royal Africa Society, African Studies Association (United Kingdom).

WRITINGS: A Social and Economic Study of Fort Rosebery Township and Peri-urban Area, Rhodes-Livingstone Institute, 1960; *Chief Kalaba's Village: A Preliminary Survey of Economic Life in an Ushi Village,* Manchester University Press, 1964; *Changing Patterns of Settlement and Land Use in the Eastern Province of Northern Rhodesia,* University of Hull Press, 1965; *A Social Geography of Zambia,* University of London Press, 1967; *Rhodesia: A Human Geography,* University of London Press, 1970; (with M. A. Smout) *Salisbury: A Geographical Survey of Rhodesia's Capital,* University of London Press, 1976. Writer of other, shorter research reports on population distribution and social aspects of village regrouping in Rhodesia and Zambia.

WORK IN PROGRESS: Principles and Concepts in Human Geography, an advanced textbook.

* * *

KAZAN, Elia 1909-

PERSONAL: Born Elia Kazanjoglous, September 7, 1909, in Constantinople (now Istanbul), Turkey; son of George (a rug dealer) and Athena (Sismanoglou) Kazan; married Molly Day Thatcher (a playwright), December 2, 1932 (died December 14, 1963); married Barbara Loden (an actress), June 5, 1967; children: (first marriage) Judy, Chris, Nick, Katharine. *Education:* Williams College, A.B., 1930; Yale University School of Drama, graduate study, 1930-32; Group Theatre, apprentice to Lee Strasbourg and Harold Clurman, 1932-33. *Residence:* Connecticut. *Office:* 850 Seventh Ave., New York, N.Y. 10019.

CAREER: Actor, 1932-41: Made his Broadway debut as Louis in "Chrysalis" (also assistant stage manager), Martin Beck Theatre, November 15, 1932; Orderly, "Men in White" (also stage manager), Broadhurst Theatre, September 26, 1933; Polyzoides, "Gold-Eagle Guy" (also stage manager), Morosco Theatre, November 28, 1933; Baum, "Till the Day I Die," 1934; Agate Keller, "Waiting for Lefty," Longacre Theatre, March 26, 1935; Kewpie, "Paradise Lost," Longacre Theatre, December 9, 1935; "Case of Clyde Griffiths," 1936. Actor with Group Theatre, New York City, 1936-41, including: Private Kearns, "Johnny Johnson," Forty-Fourth Street Theatre, November 19, 1936; Eddie Fuselli, "Golden Boy," Belasco Theatre, November 4, 1937; Joe Bonaparte, "Golden Boy," tour, 1938-39; made his London debut as Eddie Fuselli in "Golden Boy," St. James' Theatre, June 21, 1938; returned to New York City as Eli Lieber in "The Gentle People," Belasco Theatre, January 5, 1939; Steve Takis, "Night Music," Broadhurst Theatre, February 22, 1940; Ficzum ("The Sparrow"), "Liliom," Forty-Fourth Street Theatre, March 25, 1940; Adam Boguris, "Five Alarm Waltz," Playhouse Theatre, March 13, 1941. Actor in screenplays, including: Googie, "City for Conquest," Warner Brothers, 1940; the clarinetist, "Blues in the Night," Warner Brothers, 1941.

Director of stage plays, 1935-64, including: (With Alfred Saxe) "The Young Go First," Park Theatre, May 28, 1935; "Casey Jones," Fulton Theatre (now Helen Hayes Theatre), February 19, 1938; "Thunder Rock," Mansfield Theatre (now Brooks Atkinson Theatre), November 14, 1939; "Cafe Crown," Cort Theatre (now television studio), January 23, 1942; "The Strings, My Lord, Are False," Royale Theatre, May 19, 1942; "The Skin of Our Teeth," Plymouth Theatre, November 18, 1942; "Harriet," Henry Miller's Theatre, March 3, 1943; "One Touch of Venus," Imperial Theatre, October 7, 1943; "It's Up to You," 1943; "Jacobowsky and the Colonel," Martin Beck Theatre, March 14, 1944; "Deep Are the Roots," Fulton Theatre (now Helen Hayes Theatre), September 26, 1945; "Dunningan's Daughter," John Golden Theatre, December 26, 1945; (and producer with Harold Clurman and Walter Fried) "All My Sons," Coronet Theatre (now Eugene O'Neill Theatre), January 29, 1947; (and producer with Harold Clurman) "Truck-line Cafe," Belasco Theatre, February 27, 1947; "A Streetcar Named Desire," Ethel Barrymore Theatre, December 3, 1947. Actors Studio, New York City, co-founder with Cheryl Crawford and Robert Lewis, 1947, co-director, 1947-62, sole director of Actors Studio productions, including: "Sundown Beach," Belasco Theatre, September 7, 1948; "Love Life," Forty-

Sixth Street Theatre, October 7, 1948; (and producer) "Death of a Salesman," Morosco Theatre, February 10, 1949, Phoenix Theatre, London, July 28, 1949; "Point of No Return," 1951; "Flight into Egypt," Music Box Theatre, March 18, 1952; "Camino Real," National Theatre (now Billy Rose Theatre), March 19, 1953; "Tea and Sympathy," Ethel Barrymore Theatre, September 30, 1953; "Cat on a Hot Tin Roof," Morosco Theatre, March 24, 1955; (and producer with Saint Subber) "The Dark at the Top of the Stairs," Music Box Theatre, December 5, 1957; "J. B.," A.N.T.A. (American National Theatre & Academy) Theatre, December 11, 1958; "Sweet Bird of Youth," Martin Beck Theatre, March 10, 1959. The Repertory Theatre of Lincoln Center for the Performing Arts, New York City, at the A.N.T.A. Washington Square Theatre, director of company with Robert Whitehead, 1963-64, sole director of productions, including: "After the Fall," January 23, 1964; "But for Whom Charlie," March 12, 1964; "The Changeling," 1964; other productions include "Marco Millions" and "Incident at Vichy," both 1964.

Director of screenplays, 1944—, including: "A Tree Grows in Brooklyn," Twentieth Century-Fox, 1945; "Sea of Grass," Metro-Goldwyn-Mayer, 1947; "Boomerang," Twentieth Century-Fox, 1947; "Gentleman's Agreement," Twentieth Century-Fox, 1947; "Pinky," Twentieth Century-Fox, 1949; "Panic in the Streets," Twentieth Century-Fox, 1950; "A Streetcar Named Desire," Warner Brothers, 1951; "Viva Zapata!," Twentieth Century-Fox, 1952; "Man on a Tightrope," Twentieth Century-Fox, 1953; "On the Waterfront," Columbia, 1954; "East of Eden," Warner Brothers, 1955; (formed film company, Newton Productions, under which Kazan was director and producer) "Baby Doll," Warner Brothers, 1956; "A Face in the Crowd," Warner Brothers, 1957; "Wild River," Twentieth Century-Fox, 1960; "Splendor in the Grass," Warner Brothers, 1961; (and author and producer) "America, America," Warner Brothers, 1964 (produced in England as "The Anatolian Smile"); (and producer) "The Arrangement" (based on Kazan's novel), Warner Brothers, 1969; "The Visitors," United Artists, 1972.

Radio performer on "The Philip Morris Hour," "The Kate Smith Hour," and "The Group Theatre Radio Program."

MEMBER: Screen Directors Guild of America, Screen Actors Guild, Actors Equity Association, Screen Writers Guild, Phi Beta Kappa. *Awards, honors:* Variety New York Drama Critic's Poll, in 1943, for his direction of "The Skin of Our Teeth," 1947, for "All My Sons," 1949, for "Death of A Salesman," and 1959, for "Sweet Bird of Youth"; Donaldson Award and Antoinette Perry (Tony) Award in 1947, for direction of "All My Sons," and 1949, for "Death of a Salesman"; Donaldson Award in 1948, for "A Streetcar Named Desire," 1954, for "Tea and Sympathy," and 1955, for "Cat on a Hot Tin Roof"; Antoinette Perry (Tony) Award, 1959, for "J. B."; Academy Award (Oscar) in 1947, for direction of "Gentleman's Agreement," and 1954, for "On the Waterfront"; National Board of Review, Venice Film Festival Award, 1951, for "A Streetcar Named Desire"; D.Litt., Wesleyan University, 1954, and Carnegie Institute of Technology, 1962; Handel Medallion, New York City's Cultural Award, 1972, for forty-year contribution to the arts.

WRITINGS: America, America (autobiography), Stein & Day, 1962; *The Arrangement* (novel), Stein & Day, 1966; *The Assassins* (novel), Stein & Day, 1972; *The Understudy* (novel), Stein & Day, 1974. Also author of the screenplay for *The Arrangement*. Contributor of articles to *Theatre Arts* and *Esquire*.

WORK IN PROGRESS: Directing a screenplay, "The Last Tycoon," from F. Scott Fitzgerald's uncompleted manuscript; directing a screenplay, "In the Streets."

SIDELIGHTS: "When I was in my [thirties] and [forties]," Kazan told Cleveland Amory, "I could psych myself into Tennessee Williams' shoes, or Miller's. I could get involved with their problems and causes. As I've become more myself, it's become increasingly difficult to be somebody else. At my age you slowly resign yourself to being yourself. You're not trying to be somebody else. You finally realize this is it." With this realization, Kazan has scrapped an extremely lucrative and artistic career in theatre and motion pictures for that of a writer. "I found simply that I wanted to be separate and alone as much as possible. I envied writers who lived within themselves. This of course is so opposite to the gregarious activity of the theatre and motion-picture making. And so . . . I retreated from the performing arts and the public life I'd led and began to work within my own self."

The result of his "retreat" was *The Arrangement,* the story of an influential and successful man who at a critical point in his life is forced to meet the hypocrisy of "arrangements" by which he and society live their lives. In spite of their frequent criticism of the crude language and preoccupation with sex, reviewers agreed that the book was not without merit. "I am not going to . . . say that the cliches of language and action—smelling of the entertainment world or sensational journalism—the ineptitudes of construction, and the calloused crudity of observation make no difference to the effect of this novel," wrote R. V. Cassill. "Of course they do. They give it a curious, garish surface of unreality that is nearly impossible to square with our experience of the texture of life. Yet . . . something unique and impressive emerges from the mass of artifice—a kind of lyric scream. Mr. Kazan knows the terror of the flimsy pinnacle on which a variety of representative Americans sit. In composing an image of the passion a man on such a pinnacle would feel for an almost featureless young female, he has rendered the pitch of that terror with compelling fidelity."

James Baldwin commented on this same effect. "Kazan's book," he said, "has a certain raw gracelessness which I have not often encountered, and which I find difficult to describe. It is a terribly naked book—not blatantly so, but uncomfortably direct. He does not seem to have invented anything, though obviously, he must have, and he seems not so much to have drawn his characters as to have yanked them, bleeding, dismembered, and still in a state of shock, from the scene of their hideous accident. . . . The tone of the book is extremely striking, for it really does not seem to depend on anything that we think of as a literary tradition, but on something older than that: the tale being told by a member of the tribe to the tribe."

Granville Hicks noted that, if Kazan "has proved to be less than a master of the form he has adopted, he has at least shown an awareness of the novel's possibilities in this age."

Kazan cannot understand the "intellectuals'" criticism of his book. "I think the sex puts them off. Maybe I put too much in at the beginning, but I think it's integral and organic to the theme." His theme is "concerned with the cracking up that's happening all over. The middle classes

are questioning themselves, their lives. In this book I've tried to touch the feeling of people who have self-propelled themselves in life and have been successful at attaining something they find they don't really want. People profess certain ideals and standards, but the way they live is another thing. The gulf is widening; personal disruption is growing in this country. I think we have much more hypocrisy now than ever before."

Kazan continued his examination of the discouraging aspects of the human condition in his third novel, *The Assassins.* R. Z. Sheppard noted that "Kazan's subject is the whole United States of America—as a terminal case. Military hardware lies slowly disintegrating in the desert, the law softens and bends, violence flourishes, youths rot their minds with chemicals. This is certainly not the country of Kazan's autobiographical novel *America, America,* the young immigrant's dream and fulfillment."

Kazan's own quest for fulfillment has led him through various aspects of the theatrical world. His fourth novel combines his literary and theatrical personae to write *The Understudy,* which Larry Swindell has called Kazan's "homage to actors. It is his commemoration of thespian ego thrust, of the monumental vanity that precludes certain actors from ever being anything else. (Finally, they cannot even be their original selves; and that's perhaps the real reason that made Kazan decide, back there at that big fork in the road, that acting wasn't his path.)"

After forty years as a director, Kazan combined his talents to produce several novels, the first three of which, as Phil Thomas commented, deal well with "the lack of understanding—the refusal to understand, in fact, that which one finds repugnant . . . The author's ideas are thought-provoking and happily, as has happened in so many other novels of ideas, do not interfere with the action." "'Writing a book is an effort to understand other people,'" Kazan told Mel Gussow. In comparing novels to films, Kazan continued: "'Books can be complex and contradictory. Contradiction in dramatic form raises problems. If I did *The Assassins* on film, it would be unilinear. I would have to lop off the side reflections. In some way it would dilute the complexity of the event.'" However, for his earlier work, Kent E. Carroll said that Kazan "feels that the film version of *The Arrangement* is better organized, more compressed and compact than the book and in that sense superior."

At age sixty, Kazan insisted that he had "left the theatre forever." However, when it comes to films, Kent E. Carroll quoted him as having said: "'I'll go on making film the rest of my life or at least as long as I can maintain the kind of complete artistic freedom I've had in the past. It wouldn't be worth leaving my house to make a picture that somebody else cut. I've had final cut since "Viva Zapata!".... I'm not the highest paid or most praised director, but when it comes to final cut, I am one of the few.' Acknowledging that 'whether I received a credit as such or not, I've effectively been my own producer for the past 15 or 16 years.' He owns a piece of all his films made during that period."

Kazan has stated that he likes the life of a writer, although he only began writing in his fifties. Swindell summarized that "late starter that he may be, Elia Kazan should be one of the most successful novelists and also one of increasing literary importance over many years to come. Writing is his elixir, and he has an incredible wealth of experience, fortified by mature perspective."

Kazan is credited with having discovered many stage and screen stars, including: Marlon Brando, Paul Newman, Lee J. Cobb, Maureen Stapleton, Karl Malden, Geraldine Page, Eli Wallach, and James Dean.

America, America was filmed by Warner Bros. in 1963; *The Arrangement* was filmed by Warner Bros., 1969.

BIOGRAPHICAL/CRITICAL SOURCES: Elia Kazan, *America, America,* Stein & Day, 1962; *Book Week,* February 26, 1967; *New York Times Book Review,* February 26, 1967; *Christian Science Monitor,* March 2, 1967; *Saturday Review,* March 4, 1967; *New Republic,* March 4, 1967; *New York Review of Books,* March 23, 1967; *Books and Bookmen,* May, 1967; *Punch,* May 3, 1967; *Illustrated London News,* May 6, 1967; *This Week,* October 1, 1967; *Variety,* November 26, 1969; *Show,* February, 1970; *New York Times,* February 7, 1972; Michel Ciment, *Kazan on Kazan,* Viking, 1974; *Philadelphia Inquirer,* February 23, 1975; Carolyn Riley, editor, *Contemporary Literary Criticism,* Volume VI, Gale, 1976.

*   *   *

KAZEMZADEH, Firuz   1924-

PERSONAL: Born October 27, 1924, in Moscow, Russia; son of Kazem (a diplomat and lawyer) and Tatiana (Yevseyev) Kazemzadeh; married Caterina Bosio, January 5, 1959; children: Tatiana, Allegra, Monireh. *Education:* Stanford University, B.A., 1946, M.A., 1947; Harvard University, Ph.D., 1950. *Religion:* Baha'i. *Office:* Yale University, 1211 Yale Station, New Haven, Conn. 06520.

CAREER: Hoover Institution on War, Revolution and Peace, Stanford, Calif., research fellow, 1949-50; U.S. Department of State, Publicity Branch, New York City, consultant and writer, 1951-52; Radio Free Europe, New York City, chief analyst, Soviet Affairs Unit, 1952-54; Harvard University, Cambridge, Mass., research fellow at Russian Research Center and Center for Middle Eastern Studies, 1954-56; Yale University, New Haven, Conn., instructor, 1956-57, assistant professor, 1957-61, associate professor, 1961-67, professor of history, 1967—, director of graduate studies program in history, 1976—. Director, American National Institute for Social Advancement. *Member:* American Historical Association, American Association for the Advancement of Slavic Studies, Phi Beta Kappa. *Awards, honors:* Morse fellow, 1957-58; Ford Foundation faculty research grant, 1962-63; D.H.L., Parsons College, 1970.

WRITINGS: The Struggle for Transcaucasia, 1917-21, Ronald, 1952; (contributor) W. Z. Laqueur, editor, *The Middle East in Transition,* Praeger, 1958; (co-author) J. Lederer, editor, *Russian Foreign Policy: Essays in Historical Perspective,* Yale University Press, 1961; *Russia and Britain in Persia, 1864-1914: A Study in Imperialism,* Yale University Press, 1968. Contributor to *Harvard Slavic Studies,* Volume IV, 1957, *Slavic and East European Review* and other professional journals. Editor, *World Order.*

AVOCATIONAL INTERESTS: Music and the arts.

*   *   *

KEATING, L(ouis) Clark   1907-

PERSONAL: Born August 20, 1907, in Philadelphia, Pa.; son of Louis A. (a publisher and bookseller) and Blanche A. (De Young) Keating; married Lucille E. Tate (a librarian), July 23, 1936; children: Richard C., Geoffrey T., Anne E. *Education:* Colgate University, A.B., 1928; Har-

vard University, A.M., 1930, Ph.D., 1934; Sorbonne, University of Paris, graduate study, 1932-33; additional summer study at University of Heidelberg, 1931, and Centro de Estudios Historicos, Madrid, Spain, 1933. *Politics:* Democrat. *Religion:* Presbyterian. *Home:* 608 Raintree Rd., Lexington, Ky.

CAREER: Instructor in Romance languages at Colgate University, Hamilton, N.Y., 1928-29, and Harvard University, Cambridge, Mass., 1933-34; assistant professor at Macalester College, St. Paul, Minn., 1934-36, and Monticello College, Godfrey, Ill., 1936-37; University of Illinois, Urbana, associate in Romance languages, 1937-39; George Washington University, Washington, D.C., 1939-57, began as assistant professor, professor of Romance languages and head of department, 1946-57; University of Cincinnati, Cincinnati, Ohio, professor of Romance languages and head of department, 1957-60; University of Kentucky, Lexington, professor of modern languages, 1962-74, head of department, 1963-66. Member of faculty of Chapman College, World Campus Afloat, spring, 1967, fall, 1974. U.S. Operations Mission, Peru, director of education, 1960-62. Arlington County (Va.) School Board, member, 1953-57, chairman, 1956-67. *Military service:* U.S. Army, Signal Corps, 1943-46; became captain.

MEMBER: Modern Language Association of America, American Association of Teachers of French, American Association of University Professors, Phi Beta Kappa. *Awards, honors:* Palmes Academiques (France).

WRITINGS: (With C. C. Gullette) *Learning a Modern Language,* F. S. Crofts, 1938; *Studies on the Literary Salon in France, 1550-1615,* Harvard University Press, 1941; (with Gullette and C. P. Viens) *Teaching a Modern Language,* F. S. Crofts, 1942; (editor with J. S. Flores) *El Gaucho y la Pampa,* American Book Co., 1943; (with H. V. Besso) *Conversational French,* Hastings, 1944; (with R. L. Grismer) *Spanish Conversation for Beginners,* Dryden, 1946; (with C. A. Choquette) *A Short Review of French Grammar,* Holt, 1948; (with C. D. Eldridge) *Souvenirs de la France,* American Book Co., 1949; (editor with James O. Swain) Francois Mauriac, *Les Chemins de la mer,* Heath, 1953; (with W. G. Clubb) *Journal Parisien,* Appleton, 1955; (with M. I. Moraud) *Cultural Graded Readers: Elementary Series,* three volumes, American Book, 1958; (with Moraud) *Audubon, Lafayette, Lafitte, Moliere,* 1958; (with Moraud) *Les du pont* (a reader), American Book Co., 1959; *Carnet de Voyage,* Appleton, 1959.

(With Moraud) *Moliere* (a reader), American Book Co., 1961; *Critique of Civilization: Georges Duhamel and His Writings,* University of Kentucky Press, 1965; *Tierra de los Incas: Primeras lecturas,* Ronald, 1966; *Andre Maurois,* Twayne, 1969; (with K. Huvos) *Impressions d'-Amerique,* St. Martin's, 1970; *Joachim du Bellay,* Twayne, 1971; *Etienne Pasquier,* Twayne, 1972; *Audubon: The Kentucky Years,* University Press of Kentucky, 1976.

Translator: P. J. Arriaga, *La Extirpacion de la idolatria en el Peru,* University of Kentucky Press, 1968; (with R. O. Evans) Jorge Luis Borges, *Introduction to American Literature,* University Press of Kentucky, 1971; (with Evans) Borges, *Introduction to English Literature,* University Press of Kentucky, 1974. Associate editor of "Romance Monograph Series" for University Press of Kentucky. Contributor of articles and reviews to journals. Associate editor, *Romance Quarterly.*

AVOCATIONAL INTERESTS: Antiques and stamps.

KEDOURIE, Elie 1926-

PERSONAL: Born January 25, 1926, in Baghdad, Iraq. Education: London School of Economics and Political Science, B.Sc., 1950; St. Antony's College, Oxford, graduate study, 1951-53. Office: London School of Economics and Political Science, University of London, Houghton St., Aldwych, London W.C. 2, England.

CAREER: University of London, London School of Economics and Political Science, London, England, professor of politics, 1965—. Member: British Academy (fellow).

WRITINGS: England and the Middle East: The Destruction of the Ottoman Empire, 1914-1921, Bowes, 1956; Nationalism, Praeger, 1960; Afghani and Abduh: An Essay on Religious Unbelief and Political Activism in Modern Islam, Cass & Co., 1966; The Chatham House Version, Weidenfeld & Nicolson, 1970; (editor and author of introduction) Nationalism in Asia and Africa, New American Library, 1971; Arabic Political Memoirs and Other Stories, Cass & Co., 1974; In the Anglo-Arab Labyrinth, Cambridge University Press, 1976. Editor, Middle Eastern Studies (quarterly journal).

WORK IN PROGRESS: A book on British conservatism.

*   *   *

KEE, Howard Clark 1920-

PERSONAL: Born July 28, 1920, in Beverly, N.J.; son of Walter Leslie and Regina (Corcoran) Kee; married Janet Burrell, December 19, 1951; children: Howard Clark III, Christopher Andrew, Sarah Leslie. Education: Temple University, student, 1937-38; Bryan College, B.A., 1940; Dallas Theological Seminary, Th.M., 1944; Yale University, Ph.D., 1951. Politics: Democrat. Religion: Protestant. Home: 129 Fishers Rd., Bryn Mawr, Pa. 19010. Office: Bryn Mawr College, Bryn Mawr, Pa. 19010.

CAREER: University of Pennsylvania, Philadelphia, instructor in religion, 1951-53; Drew University, Madison, N.J., professor of New Testament, 1953-68; Bryn Mawr College, Bryn Mawr, Pa., Rufus Jones Professor of the History of Religion, 1968—. Lecturer at German universities. Participant in archaeological expeditions to Jordan Valley, 1949-50, Mount Siani, 1950, Biblical Shechem, Jordan, 1956, 1966, Pella, 1967, and Ashdod, 1968. President, Mohawk Trail Concerts Association. Member: American Bible Society (member of board of managers, 1957—), Society of Biblical Literature, American Academy of Religion, Society for Religion in Higher Education, Studiorum Novi Testamenti Societas. Awards, honors: American Association of Theological Schools fellow, 1959-60; Guggenheim fellow in Israel, 1966-67.

WRITINGS: (With F. W. Young) Understanding the New Testament, Prentice-Hall, 1957, third edition, 1973; Making Ethical Decisions, Westminster, 1957; Jesus and God's New People, Westminster, 1959; The Renewal of Hope, Association Press, 1959; Jesus in History: An Approach to the Study of the Gospels, Harcourt, 1970; (translator from the German with S. MacLean Gilmour) Werner G. Kummel, The New Testament: The History of the Investigations of Its Problems, Abingdon, 1972; (compiler) The Origins of Christianity: Sources and Documents, Prentice-Hall, 1973; (with Gerard S. Sloyan) Proclamation: Pentecost 3, Fortress, 1974.

WORK IN PROGRESS: Socio-Cultural Setting of the Gospel of Mark.

KEEFER, T(ruman) Frederick 1930-

PERSONAL: Born February 25, 1930, in Frederick, Md.; son of Truman Franklin (a retail farm supplier) and Mary (Mehring) Keefer; married Susie Rolle, January 17, 1975. Education: Western Maryland College, A.B. (summa cum laude), 1951; Duke University, M.A., 1953, Ph.D., 1960. Politics: Independent. Religion: Lutheran. Home: 3681 Knollbrook Dr., Franklin, Ohio 45005. Office: Miami University-Middletown, 4200 University Ave., Middletown, Ohio 45042.

CAREER: West Virginia University, Morgantown, instructor in English, 1955-56; assistant professor of English at Georgia Southern College, Statesboro, 1956-58, and State University of New York College at Fredonia, 1958-60; Transylvania College, Lexington, Ky., associate professor, 1960-61; University of Cincinnati, Cincinnati, Ohio, assistant professor, 1961-66; Miami University, Middletown Campus, Middletown, Ohio, assistant professor, 1966-75, associate professor of English, 1975—, deputy chairman of department, 1966-73.

WRITINGS: Ernest Poole (critical biography), College & University, 1966.

WORK IN PROGRESS: A biographical and critical study of Philip Wylie, for Twayne.

AVOCATIONAL INTERESTS: Collecting and listening to classical music, color photography, travel.

*   *   *

KEEPING, Charles 1924-

PERSONAL: Born September 22, 1924, in London, England; son of Charles Clark (a boxer and newspaperman) and Eliza Ann (Trodd) Keeping; married Renate Meyer (an artist), September 20, 1952; children: Jonathan, Vicki, Sean, Frank. Education: The Polytechnic, London, England, art studies, 1949-52, received National Diploma in Design. Politics: Individualist. Religion: None. Home: 16 Church Rd., Shortlands, Bromley BR2 OHP, England. Agent: B. L. Kearley Ltd., 59 George St., London W.1, England. Office: Croyden College of Art, Croydon, England.

CAREER: Apprenticed to printing trade at age of fourteen; after war service, worked as engineer and rent collector before starting full-time art studies in 1949; teacher of lithography at The Polytechnic, London, England, 1956-63; visiting lecturer in drawing at Croydon College of Art, Croydon, England, 1963—. Lithographs exhibited in London, Italy, Australia, and United States, including International Exhibition of Lithography at Cincinnati, 1958; prints in many collections, including the Victoria and Albert Museum, London; book illustrator, advertiing artist, and designer of wall murals, posters, and book jackets. Military service: Royal Navy, telegraphist, 1942-46. Awards, honors: Kate Greenaway Medal, Library Association, 1968, for illustrations in Charley, Charlotte and the Golden Canary, and 1971, for illustrations in The God Beneath the Sea; Francis Williams Memorial Bequest Prize, 1972, for Tinker Tailor.

WRITINGS—Books for children, self-illustrated: Shaun and the Carthorse, F. Watts, 1966; Molly o' the Moors, World Publishing, 1966 (published in England as Black Dolly: The Story of a Junk Cart Pony, Brockhampton Press, 1966); Charley, Charlotte and the Golden Canary, Oxford University Press, 1967; Alfie and the Ferryboat, Oxford University Press, 1968; Tinker Tailor: Folk Song

Tales, Brockhampton Press, 1968; *Alfie Finds the Other Side of the World,* F. Watts, 1968; *The Christmas Story,* F. Watts, 1969; *Joseph's Yard,* F. Watts, 1969; *Through the Window,* F. Watts, 1970; *Garden Shed,* Oxford University Press, 1971; *The Spider's Web,* Oxford University Press, 1972; *The Nanny Goat and the Fierce Dog,* Abelard, 1973.

Illustrator: Rosemary Sutcliff, *Silver Branch,* Walck, 1958; Sutcliff, *Lantern Bearers,* Walck, 1959; Sutcliff, *Knight's Fee,* Walck, 1960; John Murphy, *Canals,* Oxford University Press, 1961; Paul Berna, *Flood Warning,* Pantheon, 1963; James Holding, *King's Contest and Other North African Tales,* Abelard, 1964; Henry Treece, *Last Viking,* Pantheon, 1966; Holding, *Poko and the Golden Demon,* Abelard, 1968; Nicholas Stuart Gray, *The Apple Stone,* Meredith Press, 1969; James Reeves, *The Cold Flame,* Meredith Press, 1969; Roger Lancelyn Green, *The Tale of Ancient Israel,* Dutton, 1969; Margaret J. Miller, editor, *Knights, Beasts and Wonders: Tales and Legends from Medieval Britain,* David White, 1969; Lee Cooper, *Five Fables from France,* Abelard, 1970; Gray, *Over the Hills to Babylon,* Hawthorn, 1970; Leon Garfield and Edward Blishen, *The God beneath the Sea,* Longmans, Green, 1970; Pamela L. Travers, *Friend Monkey,* Harcourt, 1971; William Cole, compiler, *The Poet's Tales: A New Book of Story Poems,* World Publishing, 1971; Mary Francis Shura, *The Valley of the Frost Giants,* Lothrop, 1971; Roger Squire, *Wizards and Wampum: Legends of the Iroquois,* Abelard, 1972; Treece, *The Invaders: Three Stories,* Crowell, 1972; Robert Newman, *The Twelve Labors of Hercules,* Crowell, 1972; Garfield and Blishen, *The Golden Shadow,* Pantheon, 1973; Ursula Synge, *Weland: Smith of the Gods,* S. G. Phillips, 1973; Helen Hokes, compiler, *Monsters, Monsters, Monsters,* F. Watts, 1974; Travers, *About the Sleeping Beauty,* McGraw, 1975; Hoke, editor, *Wierdies, Wierdies, Wierdies,* F. Watts, 1975; Robert Swindells, *When Darkness Comes,* Morrow, 1975.

SIDELIGHTS: Charles Keeping's maternal ancesters were seafarers, and his paternal, London street traders. He was born in Lambeth Walk in South London, grew up in the docks and market area, and his work is mainly concerned with the people in the work streets of London.

Jessica Jenkins views *Joseph's Yard* as "a recreation of the myth of Adonis in a bleak backyard. There is no question of finding an alternative to its impact in words and no point in considering the words on their own. With a brief text and a combination of resist-work techniques (wax and scratch, wax and watercolor, water and waterproof ink), Charles Keeping creates page after page of visual stimulus and an extraordinary range and depth of emotion.... To most children *Joseph's Yard* will probably and rightly be just one more book: one from which they will absorb as much visual and emotional experience as they are ready for."

Anne Wood writes that in *Through the Window* Charles Keeping draws "upon the background of his own childhood, he seeks to show the effect of a child's closeness to a particular environment upon his developing understanding of some of the texture of life. Here the child views everything in a frame of heavy net so that the scene is widened or narrowed or even swirled as he moves and is moved by the violence of the action.... Keeping sets out the truth about feelings in the uncompromising context of his wonderfully beautiful art, and we owe him a debt for his courage in widening the scope of the picture book in this way."

AVOCATIONAL INTERESTS: Driving ponies, good conversation over a pint of beer in a pub, modern jazz, and folk singing.

BIOGRAPHICAL/CRITICAL SOURCES: Books, March, 1970, November, 1970.†

* * *

KEHOE, Monika 1909-

PERSONAL: Born September 11, 1909, in Dayton, Ohio; daughter of Thomas Joseph and Josephine (Martin) Kehoe. *Education:* Mary Manse College, A.B., 1932; Ohio State University, Ph.D., 1935. *Home:* Dial Apts. #6, Tuinon Bay, Guam 96910. *Office:* University of Guam, Agana, Guam 96910.

CAREER: Instructor in English at Mundelein College, Chicago, Ill., 1935-36, and Mills College, Oakland, Calif., 1936-41; director of adult education (English as a second language), for National Housing Authority Mexican-American Project, San Pedro, Calif., 1941-42, and War Relocation Authority Japanese Evacuation Program, Gila River, Ariz., 1942-44; Brooklyn College (now of the City University of New York), Brooklyn, N.Y., associate dean, 1944-46; education specialist, adviser to the Ministry of Education, and director of American Language Institute, Seoul, Korea, 1946-48; United Nations, staff counselor and adviser to director of Bureau of Personnel, New York City, and later, chief of Tokyo Division, Prisoner of War Education Program, Japan, 1948-52; associate in Bureau of Adult Education, New York State Department of Education, and lecturer at Russell Sage College, Albany, N.Y., 1952-54; regional officer, Adult Education Board, Tasmania, and later education officer, Sydney, Australia, 1955-57; Russell Sage College, Albany and Troy, N.Y., visiting professor, 1957-58; Youth Education Systems, New York City, textbook editor, 1958-61; Columbia University, Teachers College, New York City, visiting scholar, 1961; associate professor of English at Haile Sellassie I University, textbook consultant to Ethiopian Ministry of Education, and adviser on English-language newspapers to Ethiopian Minister of Information, Addis Ababa, Ethiopia, 1961-64; Marianopolis College, Montreal, Quebec, professor of English and chairman of applied linguistics, 1964-71; University of Guam, Agana, professor of English, 1971—. *Member:* International Association of University Professors, Teachers of English to Speakers of Other Languages, National Organization for Women.

WRITINGS: (With Margaret Gillett) *The Laurel and the Poppy,* Vanguard, 1968; (editor and contributor) *Applied Linguistics: A Survey for Language Teachers,* Collier-Macmillan, 1968; (contributor) Frank King, editor, *Oceania and Beyond,* Greenwood Press, 1976. Contributor of more than thirty articles to professional journals. First editor, *Journal of Ethiopian Studies.*

WORK IN PROGRESS: Manual for Teachers of English in the Polyglot Classroom, for Macmillan.

SIDELIGHTS: Ms. Kehoe told *CA:* "Perhaps my residence in bilingual areas has served to intensify my appreciation of 'the two solitudes' created by a language barrier. Whatever the reason, I am convinced that better cross-cultural communication is necessary for the one world we all dream about."

* * *

KEISLAR, Evan R(ollo) 1913-

PERSONAL: Born August 8, 1913, in Mussoorie, India; son of native American parents; married Janet L. Rushworth, 1948; children: Helen J., Robert E., Kathryn. *Edu-*

cation: College of the Pacific, B.A., 1933; Pacific School of Religion, M.A., 1936; University of California, Berkeley, Ph.D., 1944. *Home:* 373 North Kenter, Los Angeles, Calif. 90049. *Office:* Department of Education, University of California, Los Angeles, Calif. 90024.

CAREER: College Entrance Examination Board, Princeton, N.J., research associate, 1945-46; Princeton University, Princeton, instructor in psychology, 1946; Tufts University, Medford, Mass., assistant professor of education, 1946-48; University of California, Los Angeles, assistant professor, 1948-54, associate professor, 1954-61, professor of education, 1961—. Member of committee on learning and the educational process, Social Science Research Council, 1962-66; fellow, Center for Advanced Study in the Behavioral Sciences, 1963-64. *Member:* American Psychological Association, American Education Research Association, Phi Delta Kappa.

WRITINGS: (With Lee S. Shulman) *Learning by Discovery,* Rand McNally, 1966.

Contributor: J. Coulson, editor, *Programmed Learning and Computer-Based Instruction,* Wiley, 1962; R. Filep, editor, *Prospectives in Programming,* Wiley, 1963; John Krumboltz, editor, *Learning and the Educational Process,* Rand McNally, 1965; *Language and Language Behavior,* Appleton, 1968. Co-author of various research reports on learning for U.S. Office of Education. Contributor of articles to journals. *American Educational Research Journal,* review editor, 1966-67, consulting editor.

WORK IN PROGRESS: Series of research studies at the kindergarten-primary level.†

*   *   *

KELLER, Werner Rudolf (August Wolfgang) 1909-

PERSONAL: Born August 13, 1909, in Nutha, Anhalt, Germany; son of August Heinrich and Elisabeth (Eggert) Keller; married Helga Maemecke, April 6, 1940; children: Christiane (Mrs. Adam Balogh-Keller), Dorothee (Mrs. Claus M. Busch), Angela Maria (Mrs. Stammerjohann). *Education:* Studied at Universities of Berlin, Rostock, Zurich, Geneva, and Jena; received Dr.jur., 1933. *Religion:* Protestant. *Home:* Casa Romantica, Ascona (Ti), Switzerland.

CAREER: Writer. *Awards, honors:* Premio Bancarella di Pontremoli (Italy), 1957; Premio Internationale "Le Muse" (Florence), 1973.

WRITINGS: Und die Bibel hat doch recht, Econ-Verlag, 1956, translation by William Neil published as *The Bible as History: A Confirmation of the Book of Books* (Book-of-the-Month Club selection), Morrow, 1956 (published in England with subtitle *Archaeology Confirms the Book of Books,* Hodder & Stoughton, 1957); *Ost minus West = Null; der Aufbau Russlands durch den Westen,* Droemer/Knaur, 1960, translation by Constantine FitzGibbon published as *East Minus West = Zero: Russia's Debt to the Western World, 862-1962* Putnam, 1962 (published in England as *Are the Russians Ten Feet Tall,* Thames & Hudson, 1962); *Und die Bibel hat doch recht: In Bildern,* Econ-Verlag, 1963, translation by William Neil published as *The Bible as History in Pictures,* Morrow, 1964; *Und wurden zerstreut unter alle Volker. Die nachbiblische Geschichte des Judischen Volkes,* Droemer/Knaur, 1966, translation by Richard Winston and Clara Winston published as *Diaspora,* Harcourt, 1969; *Denn sie entzuendeten das Licht: Geschichte der Etrusker—die Loesung eines Raetsels,*

Droemer/Knaur, 1970, translation by Alexander Henderson and Elizabeth Henderson published as *The Etruscans: A Journey into History and Archaeology in Search of a Great Lost Civilization,* Knopf, 1974; *Da aber staunte Heredot,* Droemer/Knaur, 1972; *Was gestern noch als Wunder galt—Die Entdeckung geheimnisvoller Kraefte des Menschen,* Droemer/Knaur, 1973.

SIDELIGHTS: Und die Bibel hat doch recht has been published in at least twenty-four countries.

*   *   *

KELLOW, Norman B. 1914-

PERSONAL: Born March 27, 1914, in Wind Gap, Pa.; son of Norman Auraucher (an accountant) and Edith (Bates) Kellow; married Frederica Lees, July 6, 1938; children: Joanne (Mrs. Judson Jerome Young), Dan Norman. *Education:* Gettysburg College, A.B., 1935; Gettysburg Theological Seminary, M.Div., 1938. *Politics:* Republican. *Religion:* Presbyterian. *Home:* 333 West Merion Ave., Carney's Point, N.J. 08069. *Office:* 140 Churchtown Rd., Pennsville, N.J. 08070.

CAREER: Protestant clergyman, 1938—; King's College, Braircliff Manor, N.Y., chaplain, 1948-66; currently director of department of pastoral care, Salem County Memorial Hospital, Salem, N.J. Director, Pinebrook Book Clubs, Pennsville, N.J., beginning 1942. *Awards, honors:* D.D., King's College, 1951

WRITINGS: Daily Will I Praise Thee, Revell, 1966. Editor, *Bookcast.*

WORK IN PROGRESS: A devotional commentary on the New Testament book of Romans.

*   *   *

KELLY, Faye L(ucius) 1914-

PERSONAL: Born November 22, 1914, in Ocala, Fla.; daughter of J. William and Blanche (Proctor) Lucius; married Bruce William Kelly (with Statistical Reporting Service, U.S. Department of Agriculture), October 22, 1936; children: Josephine (Mrs. John Robert Moore), Bruce William, Jr. *Education:* University of Florida, B.A., 1941, M.A., 1950, Ph.D., 1965. *Home:* 7503 Long Pine Dr., Springfield, Va. 22151. *Office:* Department of English, American University, Massachusetts and Nebraska Aves. N.W., Washington, D.C. 20016.

CAREER: High school teacher, Gainesville, Fla., 1941-53; Stetson University, De Land, Fla., assistant professor of English literature and humanities, 1956-57, 1959-61; University of Maryland, College Park, assistant professor of English and world literature, 1957-59; American University, Washington, D.C., assistant professor of English and world literature, 1962-65, associate professor of English literature, 1965—, director of graduate studies, 1968—. *Member:* Modern Language Association of America, College English Association, Shakespeare Association of America, Southern Atlantic Modern Language Association, Phi Theta Kappa.

WRITINGS: Prayer in Sixteenth-Century England: A Study in Elizabethan Popular Culture, University of Florida Press, 1966.

WORK IN PROGRESS: A monograph on prayers, oaths, and curses in Elizabethan drama.

SIDELIGHTS: Faye Kelly is competent in German, French, Italian, and Latin.†

KELLY, Lawrence C(harles) 1932-

PERSONAL: Born December 3, 1932, in Oklahoma City, Okla.; son of Charles Lawrence (an office manager) and Esther (Beavin) Kelly; married Mary Margaret Keating, August 6, 1955; children: Kathleen, Sean, Eileen, Sheila, Kevin. *Education:* Marquette University, B.S., 1954, M.A., 1959; University of New Mexico, Ph.D., 1961. *Politics:* Democrat. *Religion:* Catholic. *Home:* 2608 Emerson Dr., Denton, Tex. 76201. *Office:* Department of History, North Texas State University, Denton, Tex. 76203.

CAREER: Lewis College, Lockport, Ill., instructor, 1961-63, assistant professor of American history, 1963-64; Indiana University, Fort Wayne Regional Campus, assistant professor, 1964-66, associate professor of history, 1966-68; North Texas State University, Denton, associate professor, 1968-71, professor of American history, 1971—. *Military service:* U.S. Naval Reserve, 1955-63; active duty, 1955-58; became lieutenant junior grade. *Member:* American Historical Association, Organization of American Historians. *Awards, honors:* Association for State and Local History, certificate of merit, 1969, for *The Navajo Indians and Federal Policy,* and 1972, for *The Navajo Roundup;* National Endowment for the Humanities fellow, 1970-71.

WRITINGS: The Navajo Indians and Federal Indian Policy, University of Arizona Press, 1968. Also author of *The Navajo Roundup,* 1970.

WORK IN PROGRESS: John Collier and The Indian New Deal.

* * *

KELLY, Maurice N. 1919-

PERSONAL: Born October 10, 1919, in Sydney, New South Wales, Australia; son of Olof Nicholson (a teacher) and Hilda (Le Souef) Kelly; married Gwen Smith (a lecturer), November 5, 1945; children: Bronwyn Haddock, Jillian Herrmann. *Education:* University of Sydney, B.A., 1942, M.A., 1945, Diploma in Education, 1946; University of Laval, Ph.D., 1961. *Politics:* Labour Party. *Agent:* Colonel Sheppard, 104 Bathurst St., Sydney, New South Wales 2000, Australia. *Office:* University of New England, Armidale, New South Wales 2351, Australia.

CAREER: Department of Education, New South Wales, Australia, teacher, 1946-54; University of New England, Armidale, New South Wales, Australia, classics lecturer, 1954-63, senior lecturer, 1963-67, associate professor of Greek, 1967—.

WRITINGS: View from Olympus (history of Greece), F. W. Cheshire, 1964; (editor) *For Service to Classical Studies,* F. W. Cheshire, 1965; *View from the Forum* (history of Rome), F. W. Cheshire, 1969.

* * *

KELSEY, Morton T(rippe) 1917-

PERSONAL: Born January 12, 1917, in Depue, Ill.; son of Weston Maynard and Myra Etta (Trippe) Kelsey; married Barbara Jones, February 11, 1944; children: Myra Louise (Mrs. Stephen Allan Johnson), Morton Trippe, Jr., John Colburn. *Education:* Washington and Lee University, B.A. (summa cum laude), 1938; Episcopal Theological Seminary, B.D., 1943; additional study at Princeton University, 1939, Pomona College, 1956, and C. G. Jung Institute, Zurich, Switzerland, 1958. *Office:* Memorial Library, University of Notre Dame, Notre Dame, Ind. 46556.

CAREER: Episcopal clergyman. Emmanuel Church, East Syracuse, N.Y., priest-in-charge, 1943-46; Trinity Cathedral, Phoenix, Ariz., assistant to dean, 1946-49, canon, 1949-50; St. Luke's Episcopal Church, Monrovia, Calif., rector, 1950-70; University of Notre Dame, Notre Dame, Ind., professor, 1969—. University of California, Los Angeles, extension lecturer, 1963, 1964. Marriage, family, and child counselor.

WRITINGS: Tongue Speaking: An Experiment in Spiritual Experience, foreword by Upton Sinclair, Doubleday, 1964; *Dreams: The Dark Speech of the Spirit,* Doubleday, 1968; *Encounter with God,* Bethany Fellowship, 1972; *Healing and Christianity,* Harper, 1973; *Myth, History and Faith,* Paulist/Newman, 1974; *God, Dreams and Revelation,* Augsburg, 1974. Contributor to religious journals.

WORK IN PROGRESS: Four books: *Meditation: The Other Side of Silence, Christianity and the Supernatural, Can Christians be Educated,* and one on healing.

* * *

KELTON, Elmer 1926-
(Lee McElroy)

PERSONAL: Born April 29, 1926, in Andrews Co., Tex.; son of R. W. (a cowman) and Beatrice (Parker) Kelton: married Anna Lipp (a native of Austria), July 3, 1947; children: Gary, Stephen, Kathryn. *Education:* University of Texas, B.A. in Journalism, 1948. *Politics:* "Very independent." *Religion:* Methodist. *Home and office:* 2460 Oxford, San Angelo, Tex. 76901. *Agent:* August Lenniger, Lenniger Literary Agency, 437 Fifth Ave., New York, N.Y. 10016.

CAREER: San Angelo Standard-Times, San Angelo, Tex., farm and ranch editor, 1948-63; *Ranch* (magazine), San Angelo, Tex., editor, 1963-58; *West Texas Livestock Weekly,* associate editor, 1968—. Free-lance writer. *Military service:* U.S. Army, Infantry, 1944-46; served in Europe. *Member:* Western Writers of America (director, 1960-62, 1963-64; president, 1962-63), Sigma Delta Chi. *Awards, honors:* Western Writers of America Spur Awards, for best western novel, 1957, for *Buffalo Wagons,* 1972, for *The Day the Cowboys Quit,* and 1974, for *The Time It Never Rained;* National Cowboy Hall of Fame Western Heritage Award, 1974, for *The Time It Never Rained;* state awards from Associated Press for news stories and pictures.

WRITINGS—All published by Ballantine, except as noted: *Hot Iron,* 1956; *Buffalo Wagons,* 1957; *Barbed Wire,* 1957; *Shadow of a Star,* 1959; *The Texas Rifles,* 1960; *Donovan,* 1961; *Bitter Trail,* 1962; *Horsehead Crossing,* 1963; *Massacre at Goliad,* 1965; *Llano River,* 1966; *After the Bugles,* 1967; *Captain's Rangers,* 1969; *Hanging Judge,* 1969; *The Day the Cowboys Quit,* Doubleday, 1971; *The Time It Never Rained,* Doubleday, 1973; (under pseudonym Lee McElroy) *Joe Pepper,* Doubleday, 1975. Contributor of about fifty short stories to magazines and several hundred articles to farm periodicals.

* * *

KEMPER, Donald J. 1929-

PERSONAL: Born April 14, 1929, in St. Louis, Mo.; son of Fred B. and Anna (Hanlon) Kemper. *Education:* Cardinal Glennon College, A.B., 1950; Gregorian University, S.T.L., 1954; University of Missouri, M.A., 1960, Ph.D., 1963. *Home and office:* 107 Waugh, Columbia, Mo. 65201.

CAREER: Roman Catholic priest. Assistant pastor in Columbia, Mo., 1954-59; University of Missouri, Columbia, instructor in history, 1960-61, professor of church history, 1963—, director of Newman Center, 1963-74. Visiting professor of history, Notre Dame University, Notre Dame, Ind., 1974-75; pastor, Sacred Heart Catholic Church, Columbia, Mo., 1975—. *Member:* American Historical Association, Organization of American Historians, American Society of Church History, Missouri Historical Society, Catholic Historical Association, Phi Beta Kappa.

WRITINGS: Decade of Fear: Senator Hennings and Civil Liberties, University of Missouri Press, 1966.

WORK IN PROGRESS: History of Black Catholics.

* * *

KENDRICK, David Andrew 1937-

PERSONAL: Born November 14, 1937, in Gatesville, Tex.; son of Andrew Greene (a banker) and Nina (Murray) Kendrick; married Gail Tidd, July 4, 1964; children: Ann Murray, Colin Andrew. *Education:* University of Texas, B.A., 1960; Massachusetts Institute of Technology, Ph.D., 1965, postdoctoral study, 1965-66. *Home:* 7209 Lamplight Lane, Austin, Tex. 78731. *Office:* Department of Economics, University of Texas, Austin, Tex. 78712.

CAREER: Harvard University, Cambridge, Mass., assistant professor of economics, 1966-70; University of Texas at Austin, professor of economics, 1970—. Visiting scholar, Stanford University, 1969-70. Consultant to U.S. Bureau of the Budget. *Military service:* U.S. Army Reserve, on active duty, 1960-61; now captain. *Member:* Econometric Society, Phi Beta Kappa, Pi Tau Sigma.

WRITINGS: Programming Investment in the Process Industries, M.I.T. Press, 1967; *Notes and Problems in Economic Theory,* Markham, 1970; (editor with M. Intriligator) *Frontiers of Quantitative Economics,* North-Holland Publishing, 1975.

* * *

KENNER, (William) Hugh 1923-

PERSONAL: Born January 7, 1923, in Peterborough, Ontario, Canada; son of Henry Rowe Hocking (a high school principal) and Mary Isabel (Williams) Kenner; married Mary Josephine Waite, August 30, 1947 (died, 1964); married Mary Anne Bittner, August 13, 1965; children: (first marriage) Catherine, Julia, Margaret, John, Michael; (second marriage) Robert, Elizabeth. *Education:* University of Toronto, B.A., 1945, M.A., 1946; Yale University, Ph.D., 1950. *Religion:* Roman Catholic. *Home:* 103 Edgevale Rd., Baltimore, Md. 21210. *Agent:* Sterling Lord Agency, 660 Madison Ave., New York, N.Y. 10021. *Office:* Johns Hopkins University, Baltimore, Md. 21218.

CAREER: Assumption College (now University of Windsor), Windsor, Ontario, assistant professor, 1946-48; University of California, Santa Barbara, instructor, 1950-51, assistant professor, 1951-56, associate professor, 1956-58, professor of English, 1958-73, department chairman, 1956-62; Johns Hopkins University, Baltimore, Md., professor of English, 1973—. *Member:* Royal Society of Literature (fellow). *Awards, honors:* American Council of Learned Societies fellow, 1949; American Philosophical Society fellow, 1956; Guggenheim fellow, 1957-58, 1963; National Institute of Arts and Letters/American Academy of Arts and Letters prize, 1968; Christian Gauss Award, 1972, for *The Pound Era.*

WRITINGS: Paradox in Chesterton, introduction by Mar-

shall McLuhan, Sheed, 1947; *The Poetry of Ezra Pound,* New Directions, 1951; *Wyndham Lewis,* New Directions, 1954; *Dublin's Joyce,* Chatto & Windus, 1955, Indiana University Press, 1956; *Gnomon* (essays), McDowell, Obolensky, 1958; (editor) *The Art of Poetry,* Rinehart, 1959; *The Invisible Poet: T. S. Eliot,* McDowell, Obolensky, 1959.

Samuel Beckett, Grove, 1961, new edition with supplementary chapter published as *Samuel Beckett: A Critical Study,* University of California Press, 1968; *Flaubert, Joyce and Beckett: The Stoic Comedians,* Beacon, 1962; (editor) *T. S. Eliot: A Collection of Critical Essays,* Prentice-Hall, 1962; *Seventeenth Century Poetry: The Schools of Donne and Johnson,* Holt, 1964; (editor) *Studies in Change: A Book of the Short Story,* Prentice-Hall, 1965; *The Counterfeiters: An Historical Comedy,* Indiana University Press, 1968; (editor and author of introduction) *The Translations of Ezra Pound,* enlarged edition, Faber, 1970; *The Pound Era,* University of California Press, 1971; *Bucky: A Guided Tour of Buckminster Fuller,* Morrow, 1973; *A Reader's Guide to Samuel Beckett,* Farrar, Straus, 1973; *A Homemade World,* Knopf, 1975; *Geodesic Math and How to Use It,* University of California Press, 1975. Contributing editor, *Poetry.*

SIDELIGHTS: Kenner once told *Book World:* "I neither debar the importunate world from my courses nor manuever to get it in. Literature imposes its own relevances. So the reading lists for my fall courses . . . will continue to reflect my literary rather than my topical judgment. The satire course I teach from time to time brushes against the world of student dissent rather often, and I've never felt a need to accommodate that world more explicitly.

"As to the relationship of dissent to education: it takes up time, and absorbs passion, and the more of both it exhausts, the less of either the student has to get educated with. And it isn't just the dissenters who suffer. Like the foehn wind, the climate of dissent wearies everyone exposed to it."

BIOGRAPHICAL/CRITICAL SOURCES: Book World, August 4, 1968.

* * *

KENNETT, Lee 1931-

PERSONAL: Born August 11, 1931, in Greensboro, N.C.; son of Lee Boone (an attorney) and Dorothy (Van Nostrand) Kennett; married Julianne Smyth, June 24, 1961; children: John Calvin, Caroline Allison. *Education:* Guilford College, student, 1948-50; University of North Carolina, B.A., 1952; University of Mississippi, M.A., 1956; University of Paris, graduate study, 1960-61; University of Virginia, Ph.D., 1962. *Office:* Department of History, University of Georgia, Athens, Ga. 30602.

CAREER: Converse College, Spartanburg, S.C., assistant professor of history, 1958-60; Southern Illinois University, Carbondale, lecturer, 1961-62; University of Georgia, Athens, associate professor of history, 1962—. Visiting professor, University of Toulouse, 1966-67; Fulbright Bicentennial lecturer in France, 1974-75. *Military service:* U.S. Navy, 1952-54. *Member:* Society for French Historical Studies, American Military Institute, Societe d'Histoire Moderne.

WRITINGS: The French Armies in the Seven Years' War, Duke University Press, 1967; *The Russian Campaign, 1812,* University of Georgia Press, 1970; (with James L. Anderson) *The Gun in America,* Greenwood Press, 1975.

WORK IN PROGRESS: Research on evolution of armaments, on military history, and on Napoleonic France.

*   *   *

KENYON, Kathleen Mary   1906-

PERSONAL: Born January 5, 1906, in England; daughter of Sir Frederic George (director of the British Museum) and Amy (Hunt) Kenyon. *Education:* Somerville College, Oxford, B.A., 1928, M.A., 1932. *Religion:* Church of England. *Home:* Rose Hill, Erbistock, Wrexham, Clwyd, Wales LL13 0DE.

CAREER: Member of archaeological expeditions in Southern Rhodesia, England, and Palestine, 1929-35; Institute of Archaeology, University of London, London, England, secretary, 1935-48, acting director, 1942-46, lecturer on Palestinian archaeology, 1948-62; St. Hugh's College, Oxford University, Oxford, England, principal, 1962-73. British School of Archaeology in Jerusalem, director, 1951—. Director of excavations at six sites in England during period, 1936-51, at Sabratha, Tripolitania, 1948-49, 1951, Jericho, Jordan, 1952-58, and Jerusalem, Israel, 1961-62. Norton Lecturer, Archaeological Institute of America, 1959; Schweich Lecturer, British Academy, 1964. Treasurer, Palestine Exploration Fund, 1948-55; trustee, British Museum, 1965—.

MEMBER: British Academy (fellow; vice-president, 1964-65), Royal Archaeological Institute (vice-president, 1956-62), Society of Antiquaries (fellow; vice-president, 1957-61), British Institute of Archaeology at Ankara (secretary, 1944-48), Roman Society, Surrey Archaeological Society (president, 1961—). *Awards, honors:* Commander, Order of the British Empire, 1954; D.Lit., University of London, 1952; Oxford University, fellow, 1960, D.Litt., 1964, D.B.E., 1973; L.H.D., Kenyon College.

WRITINGS: (With others) *Samaria-Sebaste*, British School of Archaeology in Jerusalem, Volume I, 1942, Volume III, 1958; *Excavations at the Jewry Wall Site, Leicester*, Society of Antiquaries, 1948; *Beginning in Archaeology*, Praeger, 1952, 3rd enlarged edition, 1961, revised paperback edition, 1961; *Digging Up Jericho*, Praeger, 1957; *Excavations in Southwark, 1945-47*, Billing & Sons, 1959.

Excavations at Jericho, British School of Archaeology in Jerusalem, Volume I, *The Tombs Excavated in 1952-54*, 1960, Volume II, *The Tombs Excavated in 1955-58*, 1965; *Archaeology in the Holy Land*, Praeger, 1960, 2nd edition, Benn, 1965; *Amorites and Canaanites* (Schweich Lectures), Oxford University Press for British Academy, 1966; *Jerusalem*, Thames & Hudson, 1966; *Digging Up Jerusalem*, Praeger, 1974. Also author of *Verulamium Theatre Excavations*, 1935, *Excavations at Viroconium*, 1940, *Excavations on the Wrekin*, 1943, *Excavations at Breedon-on-the Hill*, 1950, and *Excavations at Sutton Walls, Herefordshire*, 1954. Contributor to archaeology journals.

WORK IN PROGRESS: Volume III of *Excavations at Jericho*.

AVOCATIONAL INTERESTS: Gardening.

*   *   *

KERBER, August Frank   1917-

PERSONAL: Born December 4, 1917, in Detroit, Mich.; son of August (a brewer) and Helen (Christians) Kerber; married Adriana Hemsing (a teacher), February 28, 1942; children: Karla (Mrs. William Sanders), Kerry, Kevin, Paul. *Education:* Wayne State University, B.S., 1941, M.A., 1950, Ph.D., 1956. *Politics:* "Ex-state chairman of Socialist Party; presently Democratic." *Religion:* "Scientific Humanist." *Home:* 150 Eastlawn, Detroit, Mich. 48215. *Office:* College of Education, Wayne State University, Detroit, Mich. 48202.

CAREER: Detroit (Mich.) public schools, teacher, 1946-56; Wayne State University, Detroit, Mich., professor, 1956—, former chairman of department of educational sociology, College of Education. *Military service:* U.S. Navy, Air Operations, 1941-46. *Member:* International Education Association (president, 1965-66, 68-69), American Sociological Association, American Civil Liberties Union.

WRITINGS: (With W. C. Smith) *Educational Issues in a Changing Society*, Wayne State University Press, 1962, 3rd edition, 1968; (editor with Barbara Bommarito) *The Schools and the Urban Crisis*, Holt, 1964; (with J. E. Hill) *Models, Methods, and Analytical Procedures in Educational Research*, Wayne State University Press, 1966; (editor) *Quotable Quotes on Education*, Wayne State University Press, 1968; (with Edith King) *Sociology of Early Childhood Education*, American Book Co., 1968; (with Smith) *A Cultural Approach to Education*, Kendall/Hunt, 1972; (with Daniel B. Kennedy) *Resocialization: An American Experiment*, Behavioral Publications, 1973. Also author of three-act play, "Mourn Not the Dead," produced by an experimental theater, 1965; compiler with Gertrude Gordon of three song books, "Sounds of Freedom and Brotherhood."

SIDELIGHTS: Kerber has served as leader of a travel-study program to 55 countries in various parts of the world.

*   *   *

KESSEL, John H(oward)   1928-

PERSONAL: Born October 13, 1928, in Dayton, Ohio; married Margaret Wagner, August, 1954; children: Robert, Thomas. *Education:* Purdue University, student, 1946-48; Ohio State University, B.A., 1950; Columbia University, Ph.D., 1958. *Politics:* Republican. *Religion:* Protestant. *Office:* Ohio State University, Columbus, Ohio 43210.

CAREER: Mount Holyoke College, South Hadley, Mass., instructor, 1957-58; Amherst College, Amherst, Mass., instructor, 1958-60, assistant professor of political science, 1960-61; University of Washington, Seattle, assistant professor of political science, 1961-65; Allegheny College, Meadville, Pa., Arthur E. Braun Professor of Political Science, 1965-70; Ohio State University, Columbus, professor of political science, 1970—. Nixon-Lodge Volunteers of Massachusetts, executive director, 1960; Republican National Committee, director of Arts and Sciences Division, 1963-64. *Military service:* U.S. Navy, 1950-53; became lieutenant junior grade. *Member:* American Political Science Association (executive council member, 1969-71), Inter-University Consortium for Political Research (council member, 1964-64, 1967-68), Midwest Political Science Association. *Awards, honors:* National Center for Education in Politics fellowship, 1963-64; Governmental Affairs Institute fellowship, 1964.

WRITINGS: The Goldwater Coalition: Republican Strategies in 1964, Bobbs-Merrill, 1968; (editor with George Cole and Robert Seddig) *Micropolitics*, Holt, 1970; *The Domestic Presidency: Decision-Making in the White House*, Duxbury, 1975.

Contributor: Paul Tillett, editor, *Inside Politics*, Oceana,

1962; Kent Jennings and Harmon Zeigler, editors, *The Electoral Process,* Prentice-Hall, 1966; Demetrious Caraley, editor, *Party Politics and National Elections,* Little-Brown, 1966; Donald R. Matthews, editor, *Perspectives on Presidential Selection,* Brookings Institution, 1973; James David Barber, editor, *Choosing the President,* Prentice-Hall, 1974. Contributor to *Political Science Annual,* 1973, and of articles and reviews to political science journals. Co-editor, *Political Science Annual,* 1970—; member of editorial board, *American Journal of Political Science,* 1971-73, editor, 1974-76.

* * *

KETCHAM, Orman W(eston) 1918-

PERSONAL: Born October 1, 1918, in Brooklyn, N.Y.; son of Walter S. (a sales manager) and Arline (Weston) Ketcham; married Anne Phelps Stokes (a teacher), December 22, 1947; children: Anne W., Helen L.P., Elizabeth M., Susan S. *Education:* Princeton University, B.A. (cum laude), 1940; Yale University, LL.B., 1947. *Religion:* Congregational. *Home:* 2 East Melrose St., Chevy Chase, Md. 20015. *Office:* Superior Court of District of Columbia, 410 E St. N.W., Washington, D.C. 20001.

CAREER: Admitted to Bar of U.S. District Court, 1948, of U.S. Court of Appeals, 1948, and of Supreme Court of the United States, 1952. Covington & Burling, Washington, D.C., associate attorney, 1947-52; Fund for the Republic, Washington, D.C., executive assistant, 1953; U.S. Foreign Operations Administration, Washington, D.C., assistant general counsel, 1953-55; U.S. Department of Justice, Washington, D.C., trial attorney in Antitrust Division, 1955-57; Juvenile Court of the District of Columbia, Washington, D.C., judge, 1957-70; Superior Court of the District of Columbia, Washington, D.C., associate judge, 1970—. Adjunct professor of law at Georgetown University, 1963-67, and University of Virginia, 1971—. National Council on Crime and Delinquency, member of council of judges, 1959—, member of board of directors, 1973—; member of Coordinating Committee for Effective Justice, 1965—; member of U.S. delegation, United Nations Congress on Prevention of Crime and Treatment of Offenders, 1965; member of the visiting committee to Brookings Institute, 1971—; chairman of advisory board, Ford Foundation's "Lawer in Juvenile Court" project, 1966-68; adviser to American Law Institute, 1970—, National Committee on Secondary Education, 1970-74, and President's Commission on Law Enforcement and Administration of Justice. *Military service:* U.S. Naval Reserve, active duty in Atlantic and Pacific theaters, 1941-46; became lieutenant commander.

MEMBER: American Bar Association, National Council of Juvenile Court Judges (president, 1965-66), International Association of Youth Magistrates (vice-president, 1966-74), District of Columbia Bar Association, Washington Metropolitan Area Council of Juvenile Court Judges (chairman, 1961-64), Phi Delta Phi, Cosmos Club, Chevy Chase Club.

WRITINGS: (Contributor) Margaret Rosenheim, editor, *Justice for the Child,* Free Press of Glencoe, 1962; (with Monrad G. Paulsen) *Cases and Materials Relating to Juvenile Courts,* Foundation Press, 1967. Contributor to *Crime and Delinquency, Northwestern University Law Review, Virginia Law Review, Cornell Law Review,* and other professional journals.

KHANNA, J(aswant) L(al) 1925-

PERSONAL: Born July 5, 1925, in Lahore, Pakistan; son of S. L. and Savitri (Devi) Khanna; married Prabha Bhagat (an associate professor of psychiatry), July 30, 1951; children: Kanwal, Mukti. *Education:* Panjab University, B.Sc., 1943, M.A., 1948; B.R. Medical College, diploma, 1945; University of Colorado, Ph.D., 1956; also did graduate work at University of Tennessee. *Office:* Department of Psychiatry, University of Tennessee, Memphis, Tenn. 38103.

CAREER: Panjab University, New Delhi, India, member of psychology faculty, 1950-53, senior lecturer in psychology, 1956-57; Larned State Hospital, Larned, Kan., senior staff psychologist, 1957-61; University of Kansas, Lawrence, member of faculty, Extension Division, 1958-61; University of Tennessee, College of Medicine, Memphis, assistant professor, 1961-65, associate professor, 1965-71, professor of psychiatry, 1971—. Adjunct professor, LeMoyne College, 1962—; lecturer, Memphis State University, 1967—. Consultant to Jackson Mental Health Center, Memphis Mental Health Center, UNESCO and Veterans Hospital. UNESCO research reviewer for all psychology research in Southeast Asia, 1951-53. *Member:* American Psychological Association, American Psychotherapy Association, British Psychological Society (associate), Kansas Psychological Association (fellow), Sigma Xi.

WRITINGS: Brain Damage and Mental Retardation, C. C Thomas, 1967; *New Treatment Approaches to Juvenile Delinquency,* C. C Thomas, 1974. Contributor to *Directory of Social and Economic Research in Health;* contributor of about twenty-five articles to professional journals.

WORK IN PROGRESS: A book on human relations training and education.

SIDELIGHTS: In addition to Hindi, Khanna speaks Urdu and Sanskrit.

* * *

KHERDIAN, David 1931-

PERSONAL: Born December 17, 1931, in Racine, Wis.; son of Melkon (a chef) and Veronica (Dumajian) Kherdian; married Kato Rozeboom, January 21, 1967 (divorced, 1970); married Nonny Hogrogian (an artist and illustrator), March 17, 1971. *Education:* University of Wisconsin, B.S. (philosophy), 1960. *Politics:* None. *Religion:* Armenian Orthodox. *Home address:* Box 162, East Chatham, N.Y. 10206.

CAREER: Was a door-to-door magazine salesman and became, at nineteen, the company's youngest field manager; worked as shoe salesman, bartender, day laborer, factory worker; The Sign of the Tiger (used book store), Racine, Wis., owner, 1961-62; The Book House (used book store), Fresno, Calif., manager, 1962-63; Northwestern University, Evanston, Ill., literary consultant, 1965; Giligia Press, East Chatham, N.Y., founder and editor, 1966-73. Instructor in poetry, Fresno State College (now California State University, Fresno), 1969-70; poet-in-the-schools, State of New Hampshire, 1971-72. Writer and designer of theatre program, Santa Fe Theatre Co., 1968. Poetry judge, Vincent Price awards in creative writing, Institute of American Indian Arts, Santa Fe, 1968. *Military service:* U.S. Army, 1952-54. *Member:* P.E.N.

WRITINGS: David Meltzer: A Sketch from Memory and Descriptive Checklist, Oyez, 1965; *A Biographical Sketch* and Descriptive Checklist of Gary Snyder, Oyez, 1965; A Bibliography of William Saroyan, 1934-1964, Roger Beacham, 1965; (compiler) William Saroyan Collection (catalog), Fresno County Free Library, 1966; Six Poets of the San Francisco Renaissance: Portraits and Checklists, introduction by William Saroyan, Giligia, 1967; (with Gerald Hausman) Eight Poems, Giligia, 1968; (author of introduction) Hausman, compiler, The Shivurrus Plant of Mopant, and Other Children's Poems, Giligia, 1968; Six San Francisco Poets, Giligia, 1969; On the Death of My Father and Other Poems, introduction by Saroyan, Giligia, 1970; (editor with James Baloin) Down at the Santa Fe Depot: Twenty Fresno Poets, Giligia, 1970; Homage to Adana, limited edition, Perishable Press, 1970; Looking over Hills, illustrations by wife, Nonny Hogrogian, Giligia, 1972; (editor) Visions of America: By the Poets of Our Time, illustrations by N. Hogrogian, 1973; A David Kherdian Sampler, COF Press, 1974; The Nonny Poems, Macmillan, 1974; (editor) Settling America: The Ethnic Expression of Fourteen Contemporary Poets, Macmillan, 1974; Any Day of Your Life, Overlook Press, 1975; (translator with Garig Basmadjian) Yeghishe Charentz, Poems, Michael Barour, 1975; (editor) Poems Here and Now, illustrations by N. Hogrogian, Morrow, 1976; (editor) The Dog Writes on the Window with His Nose and Other Poems, illustrated by N. Hogrogian, Four Winds Press, 1976.

Broadsides: Letter to Virginia in Florence from Larkspur, California, Giligia, 1966; Mother's Day, Gary Chafe and Sanford M. Dorbin, 1967; Kato's Poem, Giligia, 1967; My Mother Takes My Wife's Side, illustrations by Judi Russell, Giligia, 1969; O Kentucky, Giligia, 1969; Outside the Library, privately printed, 1969; Root River, illustrations by Bob Totten, Perishable Press, 1970; Bird in Suet, illustrations by N. Hogrogian, Giligia, 1971; Hey Nonny, illustrations by N. Hogrogian, privately printed, 1972; Poem for Nonny, illustrations by N. Hogrogian, Phineas Press, 1973; Onions from New Hampshire, illustrations by N. Hogrogian, privately printed, 1973; In the Tradition, illustrations by N. Hogrogian, University of Connecticut, 1974; 16:IV:73, illustrations by N. Hogrogian, Arts Action Press, 1975; Anniversary Song, Bellevue Press, 1975.

Work represented in many anthologies, including: Jack Antreassian, editor, Ararat: A Decade of Armenian-American Writing, Armenian General Benevolent Union of America, Inc., 1969; Gerald Hausman and David Silverstein, editors, The Berkshire Anthology, Bookstore Press, 1972; Ward Abbott, editor, Desert Review Anthology, Desert Review Press, 1974; Michael McMahon, Flowering After Frost: The Anthology of Contemporary New England Poetry, Branden Press, 1975. Contributor to magazines. Editor, Ararat, 1970-71.

WORK IN PROGRESS: Editing a contemporary American poetry anthology entitled Traveling America: With Today's Poets, for Macmillan; editing and translating with Garig Basmadjian, Six Armenian Poets of the Twentieth Century, to include twenty poems by each poet, as well as biographies, chronologies, and introductory material.

AVOCATIONAL INTERESTS: Trout fishing.

BIOGRAPHICAL/CRITICAL SOURCES: Fresno Bee, September 2, 1962, July 26, 1964, April 16, 1966; Booklover's Answer, September-October, 1963; Racine Journal Times, May 19, 1967, July 14, 1971; The New Mexican, March 5, 1968, July 28, 1968; Hoosharar, December 1, 1970; The Armenian-Mirror Spectator, February 6, 1971, July 24, 1971; Boston Herald Traveler, March 1, 1972;

Moses Yanes, The Visit, COF Press, 1974; Carolyn Riley, editor, Contemporary Literary Criticism, Volume VI, Gale, 1976.

*   *   *

KIDD, Walter E. 1917-
(Conrad Pendleton)

PERSONAL: Born May 2, 1917, in Kickinghorse Flat, Ore.; son of William B. (an engineer) and Leetta (Conger) Kidd; married Nancy O. Pendleton (a teacher), June 27, 1946. Education: University of Oregon, B.A. (with highest honors), 1934, M.A., 1935; University of Denver, Ph.D., 1954. Politics: Republican. Religion: Methodist. Home: 1325 Southeast Umatilla St., Portland, Ore. 97202.

CAREER: University of Nebraska, Lincoln, instructor in English, 1946-50; Stephen F. Austin State College (now University), Nacogdoches, Tex., assistant professor, 1950-53; Fresno State College (now California State University, Fresno), assistant professor, 1955-58; Stephen F. Austin State University, associate professor, 1959-64, professor of English and resident writer, 1965-73. Visiting professor, University of Michigan, 1958-59. Director of Pineywoods Writers Conference. Member: Southern Modern Language Association, Poetry Society of Texas, East Texas Writers Association (president), Texas Association of College Teachers, Poetry Society of Louisiana. Awards, honors: Texas Institute of Letters Poetry Award, 1962, for Time Turns West; Southwestern Poetry Prize, 1967, for West: Manhattan to Oregon.

WRITINGS: (Editor with Warren G. French) American Winners of the Nobel Literary Prize, University of Oklahoma Press, 1967; (editor) British Winners of the Nobel Literary Prize, University of Oklahoma Press, 1973.

Under pseudonym Conrad Pendleton; all poetry, except as indicated: Slow Fire of Time, A. Swallow, 1956; Time Turns West, American Weave, 1961; Adventures of the Freckled Elf (novelette), Golden Hour Press, 1963; West: Manhattan to Oregon, 1966; Oregon Odyssey of Wheels, South & West, 1973.

Editor, Twentieth Century Literature; guest editor, Voices.

WORK IN PROGRESS: On the Face of Earth, a novel; Latin American Winners of the Nobel Literary Prize; a study of symbolism in the poetry of Robert Frost and William Butler Yeats.

AVOCATIONAL INTERESTS: Ranching in the cow country of east Oregon; travel (has been in Europe, Mexico, Hawaii, and Canada).

*   *   *

KILBORNE, Virginia Wylie 1912-
(Virginia Wylie Egbert)

PERSONAL: Born February 7, 1912, in Iowa City, Iowa; daughter of Dwight W. and Alice (McGee) Wylie; married former husband, Donald D. Egbert (a university professor), August 9, 1946; married William S. Kilborne, 1974. Education: Vassar College, A.B., 1934; New York University, M.A., 1941. Politics: Independent. Religion: Presbyterian. Home: 164 Moore St., Princeton, N.J. 08540.

CAREER: Brearley School, New York, N.Y., teacher, 1936-38; Princeton University, Princeton, N.J., research staff, Index of Christian Art, 1939—. Member: Phi Beta Kappa.

WRITINGS—All under name Virginia Wylie Egbert: The

Mediaeval Artist at Work, Princeton University Press, 1967; *On the Bridges of Medieval Paris,* Princeton University Press, 1974. Contributor to *Art Bulletin.*

SIDELIGHTS: Mrs. Kilborne speaks French, reads Italian; has done research in libraries in London, Paris, and Vienna, and traveled to Russia and all the Iron Curtain countries except Albania.

* * *

KILBOURN, William (Morley) 1926-

PERSONAL: Born December 18, 1926, in Toronto, Ontario, Canada; son of Kenneth and Mary Rae (Fawcett) Kilbourn; married Mary Elizabeth Sawyer, September 10, 1949; children: Nicholas, Timothy, Michael, Philippa, Hilary. *Education:* University of Toronto, B.A., 1948; Harvard University, A.M., 1949, Ph.D., 1957; Oxford University, M.A., 1954. *Religion:* Anglican. *Office:* Humanities Division, York University, Toronto, Ontario, Canada; and Executive Office, City Hall, Toronto, Ontario, Canada.

CAREER: McMaster University, Hamilton, Ontario, 1951-53, 1955-62, began as lecturer, became associate professor of history; York University, Toronto, Ontario, professor of history and humanities, 1962—, chairman of Humanities Division, 1962-67. Alderman for city of Toronto, 1970—; member of the Metropolitan Toronto Council, 1973—. Planner, writer, and host-interviewer for films and television and radio documentaries on the politics of the Labour movement, the Common Market, town planning, the church, and other topics; drama critic on Canadian Broadcasting Corp. weekly panel, "Views on the Shows"; has done other broadcasting in Canada and on American educational network. *Awards, honors:* President's Medal for biography, University of British Columbia, 1957, for *The Firebrand.*

WRITINGS: The Firebrand: William Lyon Mackenzie and the Rebellion in Upper Canada, Clarke, Irwin, 1956; *The Elements Combined,* Clarke, Irwin, 1960; (contributor) Bissell and others, editors, *The Literary History of Canada,* University of Toronto Press, 1965; (editor) *The Restless Church* (collection of commissioned articles), Lippincott, 1966; *The Making of the Nation,* McClelland & Stewart, 1966, revised edition, 1973; (contributor) *The Canadians,* Macmillan, 1967; (author of introduction) Cornell, Trudel, and others, *Unity in Diversity,* Holt, 1967; *Religion in Canada,* McClelland & Stewart, 1968; *Pipeline: Trans-Canada and the Great Debate,* Clarke, Irwin, 1970; (editor) *Canada: A Guide to the Peaceable Kingdom* (anthology), Macmillan, 1971; (editor) *The Toronto Book* (anthology), Macmillan, 1975.

WORK IN PROGRESS: A biography of D. D. Howe.

* * *

KILDAHL, Phillip A. 1912-

PERSONAL: Born June 13, 1912, in Chicago, Ill.; son of Harold B. (a clergyman) and Carrie (Olson) Kildahl; married Helen Alice Bolstad, February 17, 1940; children: David Douglas, Stephen Wallace. *Education:* Augsburg College, B.A., 1935; Luther Theological Seminary, St. Paul, Minn., student, 1935-37; University of Minnesota, A.M., 1940, Ph.D., 1959. *Politics:* Democrat. *Religion:* Lutheran. *Home:* 1310 Fourth Ave. S.W., Waverly, Iowa 50677. *Office:* Department of English, Wartburg College, Waverly, Iowa 50677.

CAREER: Augsburg College, Minneapolis, Minn., 1940-

51, became associate professor of history, head of department, 1947-51; Concordia College, St. Paul, Minn., associate professor, 1951-53; Hastings College, Hastings, Neb., assistant professor of English, 1956-61; Wartburg College, Waverly, Iowa, associate professor, 1961-64, professor of English, and chairman of department, 1964—. *Military service:* U.S. Army, Infantry, 1943-46; served in Germany. *Member:* National Council of Teachers of English, Modern Language Association of America, American Association of University Professors, Phi Alpha Theta. *Awards, honors:* Research grant of American Lutheran Church.

WRITINGS: Caius Marius, Twayne, 1968. Contributor of articles on history and English literature to journals.

WORK IN PROGRESS: A biography of Dionysius I of Syracuse; the epigraphical evidence for a complete restudy of Roman roads in North Africa.

* * *

KILLIAN, Ray A. 1922-

PERSONAL: Born May 9, 1922, in Conover, N.C.; son of Albert O. and Cora Virginia Killian; married Betty Pharr, June 5, 1947; children: Ray A., Jr., C. Ann. *Education:* Lenoir Rhyne College, A.B., 1948; University of North Carolina, graduate study; special courses in journalism at George Washington University, and in management at Harvard University. *Religion:* Presbyterian. *Home:* 155 Canterbury Rd. S., Charlotte, N.C. 28211. *Office:* Belk Stores Services, Inc., 308 East Fifth St., Charlotte, N.C. 28234.

CAREER: U.S. Government, Committee on Scientific Research and Development, Washington, D.C., administrative assistant, 1941; North Carolina Department of Revenue, Raleigh, personnel director, 1949; Belk Brothers Co., Charlotte, N.C., personnel director, 1949-61; Belk Stores Services, Inc., Charlotte, vice-president, 1961—. Teacher of evening classes at Queens College, Charlotte, and in University of Virginia System. Professional speaker on training and management in Europe, Mexico, South America, and United States, and for Presidents Association of American Management Association. Chairman of Development Board of Lenoir Rhyne College. Member of Business Advisory Committee for Wingate College and Appalachian State University. *Military service:* U.S. Navy, fighter pilot on aircraft carrier, World War II; received Distinguished Flying Cross and Air Medal with six gold stars.

MEMBER: Society for Advancement of Management (chapter president and national director), National Retail Merchants Association (member of board of directors), Public Relations Society of America, Personnel Directors Association, Charlotte Chamber of Commerce. *Awards, honors:* Honorary doctorate from Lenoir Rhyne College, 1973; National Retail Merchants Association Silver Plaque, 1974, for outstanding service to retailing.

WRITINGS: A Practical Guide to Store Security, Dowd Press, 1961; *Job Performance Evaluation,* Belk Stores, 1963; *Employment and Interview Guide,* Belk Stores, 1964; *Managers Must Lead!,* American Management Association, 1966; *Managing by Design: For Maximum Executive Effectiveness,* American Management Association, 1968; *The Working Woman—A Male Manager's View,* American Management Association, 1970. Contributor to *American Management Association Book of Employment Forms,* 1967, and *American Management Handbook,* 1970. Also contributor to newspapers and to national periodicals.

WORK IN PROGRESS: ROI in Human Resources: For Benefit of Individual and Company.

*   *   *

KILPATRICK, F(ranklin) P(eirce)   1920-

PERSONAL: Born April 30, 1920, in Okanogan, Wash.; son of Wilbur Carlton (a veterinarian) and Alberta (Peirce) Kilpatrick; married Mary F. Reynolds, October 30, 1943; children: Dean James, Karen Mary, Joan Terese, Carol Anne. *Education:* University of Washington, Seattle, B.A. (magna cum laude), 1942, M.S., 1947; Princeton University, M.A. and Ph.D., 1950. *Office:* Behavioral Sciences Center, Nova University, 3301 College Ave., Fort Lauderdale, Fla. 33314.

CAREER: Princeton University, Princeton, N.J., instructor, 1950-52, assistant professor of psychology, 1952-55; National Analysts, Inc., Philadelphia, Pa., head of Consumer Research Division and research development, 1955-59; Brookings Institution, Washington, D.C., senior staff member, Governmental Studies Division, 1959-67; University of Delaware, Newark, Delaware, dean of College of Graduate Studies, 1967-71; Ohio State University, Columbus, dean of College of Social and Behavioral Sciences, 1971-75; Nova University, Fort Lauderdale, Fla., director of Behavioral Sciences Center, 1975—. *Military service:* U.S. Army, 1942-46, became first lieutenant; received Bronze Star and Purple Heart. *Member:* American Psychological Association (fellow), Phi Beta Kappa, Sigma Xi.

WRITINGS: Human Behavior from the Transactional Point of View, Institute for Associated Research, 1952; (editor) *Explorations in Transactional Psychology,* New York University Press, 1961; (with Milton C. Cummings and M. Kent Jennings) *The Image of the Federal Service,* Brookings, 1964; (with Cummings and Jennings) *Source Book of a Study of Occupational Values and The Image of the Federal Service,* Brookings Institution, 1964. Contributor to professional journals.

*   *   *

KIM, Young Hum   1920-

PERSONAL: Born December 19, 1920, in Korea; son of Chung H. and Sukyung (Hwang) Kim; married Marie C. W. Nols, July 9, 1958. *Education:* Bradley University, B.S., 1955; University of Southern California, M.A., 1956, Ph.D., 1960. *Home:* 3001 Conner Way, San Diego, Calif. 92117. *Office:* United States International University, San Diego, Calif. 92131.

CAREER: United States International University, San Diego, Calif., assistant professor, 1961-64, associate professor, 1964-66, professor of history and political science, 1966—. Former executive assistant to U.S. Army in Korea, U.S. Embassy, Seoul, Korea. *Member:* American Academy of Political and Social Science, American Historical Association, Association for Asian Studies, American Association of University Professors, Phi Alpha Theta, Pi Sigma Alpha.

WRITINGS: East Asia's Turbulent Century, Appleton, 1966; *Patterns of Competitive Coexistence: USA vs. USSR,* Putnam, 1966; (editor) *Central Intelligence Agency: Problems of Secrecy in a Democracy,* Heath, 1968; *Twenty Years of Crises: The Cold War Era,* Prentice-Hall, 1968; (contributor) *Struggle against History: U.S. Foreign Policy in an Age of Revolution,* Simon & Schuster, 1968.

WORK IN PROGRESS: America's Asian Frontiers: United States-Asian Relations in the Twentieth Century.

SIDELIGHTS: Young Hum Kim is competent in Japanese and Chinese.

*   *   *

KIMBALL, Solon T(oothaker)   1909-

PERSONAL: Born August 12, 1909, in Manhattan, Kan.; son of Charles A. (a lawyer) and Matie (Toothaker) Kimball; married Hannah J. Price, December 24, 1935; children: Sally (Mrs. S. J. Makielski), John Price. *Education:* Kansas State University, B.S., 1930; Harvard University, A.M., 1933, Ph.D., 1936. *Office:* Department of Anthropology, University of Florida, Gainesville, Fla. 32611.

CAREER: U.S. Government, section head with Office of Indian Affairs, Window Rock, Ariz., 1936-42, and with War Relocation Authority, Washington, D.C., 1942-45; Michigan State University, East Lansing, associate professor of anthropology, 1945-48; University of Alabama, Tuscaloosa, professor of sociology and head of department of sociology and anthropology, 1948-53; Columbia University, Teachers College, New York, N.Y., professor of anthropology and education, 1953-66; University of Florida, Gainesville, graduate research professor of anthropology, 1966—. Former visiting professor at University of Oklahoma, University of California, University of Puerto Rico, Princeton Theological Seminary, and University of Chicago. Consultant to Wellesley School of Community Affairs, 1946; UNESCO consultant to Brazilian Center for Education Research, 1958-59. Anthropological researcher in Ireland, 1932-33, with Navajo Indians, 1936-42, 1949, and in rural communities of Michigan, 1945-48, and Alabama, 1951-53. Coordinator, Teachers College—AID Educational Development in Peru, 1963-64. Member of State Department Team to Brazil, Fulbright Commission, 1966-67.

MEMBER: American Anthropological Association (fellow; president, 1953), American Ethnological Society (president, 1971), American Association for the Advancement of Science (fellow), Society for Applied Anthropology (fellow), Southern Anthropological Society, Alpha Kappa Delta, Sigma Delta Chi, Beta Theta Pi. *Awards, honors:* Social Science Research Council faculty fellowship, 1961-62; D.Sc. from Kansas State University, 1963; Guggenheim fellowship, 1966-67.

WRITINGS: (With C. M. Arensberg) *Family and Community in Ireland,* Harvard University Press, 1940, 2nd edition, 1968; (editor) *Readings in the Science of Human Relations,* University of Alabama Press, 1949; (with M. Pearsall) *The Talladega Story,* University of Alabama Press, 1954; (with J. E. McClellan) *Education and the New America,* Random House, 1962; (with Arensberg) *Culture and Community,* Harcourt, 1965; (with James B. Watson) *Crossing Cultural Boundaries,* Chandler Publishing, 1972; (editor with Jacquetta Burnett) *Learning and Culture,* University of Washington Press, 1973; *Culture and the Educative Process,* Teachers College Press, 1974. Contributor to scientific and professional journals. Associate editor, *Human Organization,* 1955-56.

WORK IN PROGRESS: Race and culture in school and community.

*   *   *

KIMBLE, Gregory A(dams)   1917-

PERSONAL: Born October 21, 1917, in Mason City, Iowa; son of Howard (an engineer) and Iola (Adams)

Kimble; married Lucille Laird, December 30, 1943; children: Jeffrey, Judith. *Education:* Carleton College, A.B., 1940; Northwestern University, M.A., 1942; University of Iowa, Ph.D., 1945. *Home:* 443 Wewoka Dr., Boulder, Colo. 80303. *Office:* Department of Psychology, University of Colorado, Boulder, Colo. 80309.

CAREER: Brown University, Providence, R.I., instructor, 1945-47, assistant professor of psychology, 1947-50; Yale University, New Haven, Conn., assistant professor of psychology, 1950-52; Duke University, Durham, N.C., associate professor, 1952-59, professor of psychology, 1959-68; University of Colorado, Boulder, professor of psychology, 1968—, chairman of department, 1968-74. *Member:* American Psychological Association, American Association for the Advancement of Science, Psychonomic Society, Society of Experimental Psychologists, Midwestern Psychological Association, Eastern Psychological Association, Phi Beta Kappa, Sigma Xi.

WRITINGS: Principles of General Psychology, Ronald, 1956, 3rd edition (with Norman Garmezy), 1968, 4th edition (with Garmezy and Edward Zigler), 1974; *Hilgard and Marquis Conditioning and Learning,* Appleton, 1961; *Foundations of Conditioning and Learning,* Appleton, 1967. Contributor of more than eighty articles to journals. Editor, *Journal of Experimental Psychology: General.*

WORK IN PROGRESS: The Uses and Misuses of Statistics.

AVOCATIONAL INTERESTS: Jazz music, photography, cooking.

*   *   *

KINDREGAN, Charles P(eter) 1935-

PERSONAL: Born June 18, 1935, in Philadelphia, Pa.; son of Charles P. (a writer) and Catherine (Delaney) Kindregan; married Patricia Patterson, August 18, 1962; children: Charles III, Helen Christina, Patricia, Brian. *Education:* LaSalle College, B.A. (cum laude), 1957, M.A., 1958; Chicago—Kent College of Law (now Illinois Institute of Technology), J.D. (honors), 1965; Northwestern University, LL.M., 1967. *Religion:* Roman Catholic. *Home:* 15 Emerson Place, Boston, Mass. 02114. *Office:* Law School, Suffolk University, 41 Temple St., Boston, Mass. 02114.

CAREER: Virginia Military Institute, Lexington, senior counselor and administrator of reading laboratory, 1960-62; St. Mary's College, Notre Dame, Ind., instructor, 1962-64; Loyola University, Chicago, Ill., assistant professor, 1964-67; Suffolk University, Law School, Boston, Mass., assistant professor, 1967-69, associate professor, 1969-72, professor of law, 1972—. Member of the Bars of Illinois and Massachusetts. *Member:* American Bar Association.

WRITINGS: A Theology of Marriage, Bruce Publishing, 1967; *The Quality of Life: Reflections on the Moral Values of American Law,* Bruce Publishing, 1969; *Abortion, the Law, and Defective Children,* Corpus, 1969; *Marriage and Sex: A Christian Perspective,* Bruce Publishing, 1970. Also author of *Family Planning Law,* 1974. Contributor to law and medical journals. Associate editor, *Family Law Quarterly.*

*   *   *

KING, Mary Louise 1911-
(Mary Louise Johnson)

PERSONAL: Born February 26, 1911, in New Canaan, Conn.; daughter of Thomas Wells (a manufacturer of printing machinery) and Rosalie (Rogers) Hall; married Arthur F. Johnson, September 19, 1936; married second husband, John King (an art director and photographer), August 2, 1952; children: John King, Jr. *Education:* Vassar College, A.B., 1932. *Politics:* Democrat. *Religion:* Congregationalist. *Home:* 37 St. John Pl., New Canaan, Conn. 06840.

CAREER: New Canaan Gazette, New Canaan, Conn., editor, 1932-34; New Canaan Historical Society, New Canaan, researcher, 1934-36; James T. White & Co., New York City, editor, 1936-45; Henry Holt & Co., New York City, associate editor in college department, 1945-52; Wilfred Funk, Inc., New York City, managing editor, 1952-53; free-lance editor, 1953—.

WRITINGS: (Under name Mary Louise Johnson, with David Klein) *They Took to the Sea,* Rutgers University Press, 1948, published as *Great Adventures in Small Boats,* Macmillan, 1963; *History of Western Architecture,* Walck, 1967; *The Making of Main Street,* photographs by husband, John King, New Canaan Historical Society, 1971.†

*   *   *

KING, Preston (Theodore) 1936-

PERSONAL: Born March 3, 1936, in Albany, Ga.; son of Clennon Washington (a businessman) and Margaret (Slater) King; married Hazel Stern (a teacher), January 8, 1963. *Education:* Fisk University, B.A. (magna cum laude), 1956; London School of Economics and Political Science, M.Sc. (with distinction), 1958, Ph.D., 1966; additional study at University of Vienna, University of Paris, and University of Strasburg.

CAREER: University of London, London School of Economics and Political Science, London, England, tutor in political philosophy and government, 1958-60; lecture tour in United States, speaking on African politics, winter, 1961; lecturer in philosophy at University of Maryland Overseas, England, summer, 1961, and at University of Keele, Keele, England, 1961-63; University of Ghana, Accra, lecturer in political philosophy, 1963-66; University of Sheffield, Sheffield, England, lecturer in political philosophy, beginning 1966. *Member:* Phi Beta Kappa.

WRITINGS: Fear of Power: An Analysis of Anti-Statism in Three French Writers, Humanities, 1967; (editor with B. C. Parekh) *Politics and Experience: Essays Presented to Professor Michael Oakeshott on the Occasion of His Retirement,* Cambridge University Press, 1968; *The Ideology of Order: A Comparative Analysis of Jean Bodin and Thomas Hobbes,* Barnes & Noble, 1974; *Toleration,* St. Martin's, 1976. Contributor to periodicals and newspapers, including *Political Quarterly, Books and Bookmen, Presence Africaine, African Review, Guardian, Observer, African Digest.*

WORK IN PROGRESS: Research on military government in Africa.

SIDELIGHTS: Preston King is fluent in French and can cope with Italian, German, and Spanish.†

*   *   *

KING, Ray A(iken) 1933-

PERSONAL: Born October 11, 1933, in Atlanta, Ga.; son of Robert Earl (a lawyer) and Elsie (Aiken) King; married Brenda Kay Taylor, December 21, 1963; children: Ray Aiken, Jr., Wayne Starr, Kay Allison. *Education:* Erskine College, A.B., 1955; Erskine Theological Seminary, B.D.,

1958; further study at New College, University of Edinburgh, 1959-61; Austin Presbyterian Theological Seminary, Th.M., 1971; Emory University, Ph.D. candidate. *Home:* North Main St., Due West, S.C. 29639. *Office:* Erskine Theological Seminary, Due West, S.C. 29639.

CAREER: Ordained a minister of Associate Reformed Presbyterian Church, 1958; pastor in Hickory Grove, S.C., 1958-59; Erskine Theological Seminary, Due West, S.C., associate professor of church history, 1962—. *Member:* American Academy of Religion, Presbyterian Historical Society, American Association of University Professors, Historical Foundation of Presbyterian and Reformed Churches.

WRITINGS: A History of the Associate Reformed Presbyterian Church, Board of Christian Education, General Synod of Associate Reformed Presbyterian Church, 1966. Contributor to church newspaper. Bicentennial editor, *Presbyterian Outlook.*

AVOCATIONAL INTERESTS: The study and collecting of antiques; woodworking.

* * *

KING, Richard A(ustin) 1929-

PERSONAL: Born March 26, 1929, in Philadelphia, Pa.; son of Richard Edwin (a salesman) and Dorothy (Bates) King; married Margaret Skeel, June 1, 1956; children: Richard Roland, Gordon Thomas. *Education:* University of Cincinnati, A.B., 1954, M.A., 1955; Duke University, Ph.D., 1959; University of Washington, Seattle, postdoctoral fellow, 1963-65. *Politics:* Democrat. *Religion:* Protestant. *Office:* Department of Psychology, University of North Carolina, Chapel Hill, N.C. 27514.

CAREER: University of North Carolina, Chapel Hill, instructor, 1958-59, assistant professor, 1959-65, associate professor, 1965-70, professor of psychology, 1970—, associate director of Neurobiology Program, 1973—. *Military service:* U.S. Army, 1951-53; became sergeant. *Member:* American Psychological Association.

WRITINGS: (With C. T. Morgan) *Introduction to Psychology,* 3rd edition, McGraw, 1966, 5th edition, 1975; (editor) *Readings for an Introduction to Psychology,* 3rd edition, McGraw, 1971. Contributor to journals.

* * *

KING, Robert G. 1929-

PERSONAL: Born October 4, 1929, in Caneyville, Ky.; son of Greenup and Hazel (Embry) King. *Education:* Georgetown College, Georgetown, Ky., A.B., 1951; Columbia University, M.A., 1958, Ph.D., 1964. *Home:* 400 West End Ave., New York, N.Y. 10024. *Office:* Bronx Community College of the City University of New York, Bronx, N.Y. 10453.

CAREER: Columbia University, Columbia College, New York, N.Y., instructor in speech, 1958-62; Queens College (now Queens College of the City University of New York), Flushing, N.Y., instructor in speech, 1962-65; Eastern Kentucky University, Richmond, professor of speech and chairman of speech and drama department, 1965-69; Bronx Community College of the City University of New York, Bronx, N.Y., associate professor of speech, 1969-74, professor of communication arts and sciences, 1974—. *Member:* Speech Communication Association, American Forensic Association, Eastern Communication Association, Southern Speech Association, Phi Delta Kappa, Delta Sigma Rho-Tau Kappa Alpha.

WRITINGS: (With Eleanor DiMichael) *Improving Articulation and Voice,* Macmillan, 1966; *Forms of Public Address,* Bobbs-Merrill, 1969; (with DiMichael) *Articulation and Voice: A Communication Approach,* Macmillan, 1976. Associate editor, *New York State Speech Journal,* 1964-65.

WORK IN PROGRESS: Fundamentals of Human Communication.

AVOCATIONAL INTERESTS: Travel, piano, photography.

* * *

KING, William R(ichard) 1938-

PERSONAL: Born December 24, 1938, in McKeesport, Pa.; son of Dewey Clark and Cambria (Jones) King; married Fay Eileen Bickerton, June 20, 1958; children: James David, Suzan Lorain. *Education:* Pennsylvania State University, B.S. (honors), 1960; Case Institute of Technology (now Case Western Reserve University), M.S., 1962, Ph.D., 1964. *Home:* 3012 Sturbridge Ct., Allison Park, Pa. 15101. *Office:* University of Pittsburgh, Pittsburgh, Pa. 15260.

CAREER: Case Institute of Technology (now Case Western Reserve University), Cleveland, Ohio, assistant professor, 1964-65; Air Force Institute of Technology, Dayton, Ohio, assistant professor, 1965-67; University of Pittsburgh, Pittsburgh, Pa., associate professor, 1967-69, professor of business administration, 1969—. Consultant to industrial firms and governmental agencies. Director and president of Western Pennsylvania Montessori School; director of Pittsburgh Commerce Institute. *Military service:* U.S. Air Force, 1965-67; became first lieutenant.

MEMBER: Operations Research Society of America, Institute of Management Sciences, American Association for the Advancement of Science, American Marketing Association, Society for Management Information Systems. *Awards, honors:* McKinsey Foundation Award, 1969, for *Systems Analysis and Project Management.*

WRITINGS: Quantitative Analysis for Marketing Management, McGraw, 1967; *Probability for Management Decisions,* Wiley, 1968; (with D. I. Cleland) *Systems Analysis and Project Management,* McGraw, 1968, 2nd edition, 1975; (editor with Cleland) *Systems, Organizations, Analysis Management: A Book of Readings,* McGraw, 1968; (with Cleland) *Management: A Systems Approach,* McGraw, 1972. Contributor to journals. Associate editor, *Management Science.*

WORK IN PROGRESS: A book with D. I. Cleland, *Strategic Planning: Systems, Organization and Information.*

* * *

KINGDON, Robert M(cCune) 1927-

PERSONAL: Born December 29, 1927, in Chicago, Ill.; son of Robert Wells (a minister) and Anna Catherine (McCune) Kingdon. *Education:* Oberlin College, A.B., 1949; Columbia University, M.A., 1950, Ph.D., 1955; University of Geneva, graduate study, 1951-52. *Residence:* Madison, Wis. *Office:* Institute for Research in the Humanities, University of Wisconsin, Madison, Wis. 53706.

CAREER: University of Massachusetts, Amherst, 1952-57, began as instructor, became assistant professor of history; University of Iowa, Iowa City, assistant professor, 1957-59, associate professor, 1959-61, professor of history, 1961-65; University of Wisconsin—Madison, professor of history, 1965—, member of Institute for Research in the Humanities, 1974—. Member of Institute for Advanced Study, Princeton, N.J., 1965-66. *Member:* American Society for Reformation Research (secretary-treasurer, 1963-69; president, 1970-71), Renaissance Society of America (council member, 1967-69; member of executive board, 1973-75), International Federation of Societies and Institutes for the Study of the Renaissance (secretary-treasurer, 1967—), American Historical Association. *Awards, honors:* American Philosophical Society grant, summer, 1957, 1968; American Council of Learned Societies fellowship, 1960-61; Folger Shakespeare Library fellowship, summer, 1963, 1973-74; Guggenheim fellowship, 1969-70.

WRITINGS: Geneva and the Coming of the Wars of Religion in France, 1555-1563, Droz, 1956; (editor with Jean-Francois Bergier) *Registres de la Compagnie des Pasteurs de Geneve au temps de Calvin.* Droz, Volume I, 1964, Volume II, 1962; (editor) William Cecil, *The Execution of Justice,* [and] William Allen, *A True, Sincere, and Modest Defense of English Catholics,* two volumes in one, Cornell University Press, 1965; *Geneva and the Consolidation of the French Protestant Movement, 1564-1572,* University of Wisconsin Press, 1967; (editor with Robert D. Linder) *Calvin and Calvinism: Sources of Democracy?,* Heath, 1970; (editor) Theodore de Beze, *Du Droit des magistrats,* Droz, 1971; (editor and contributor) *Transition and Revolution: Problems and Issues of European Renaissance and Reformation History,* Burgess, 1974. Contributor to encyclopedias and learned journals.

WORK IN PROGRESS: The international impact of the St. Bartholomew's Massacre of 1572; the political thought of Peter Martyr Vermigli.

SIDELIGHTS: Robert Kingdon lived in Europe for two years; he speaks French fluently, and knows a smattering of German, Italian, Dutch, and Latin.

*   *   *

KINGSTON, Albert J(ames) 1917-

PERSONAL: Born November 25, 1917, in Brooklyn, N.Y.; son of Albert James and Mabel M. (Brown) Kingston; married Martha Ann Heddens, June 14, 1947; children: Barbara Ann, Elizabeth Lucas, John Heddens, Martha Jean. *Education:* New York State College for Teachers (now State University of New York College at Buffalo), Buffalo, B.S., 1939; Cornell University, M.S. in Ed., 1948, Ph.D., 1950. *Politics:* Democrat. *Religion:* Episcopalian. *Home:* Plum Nelly Rd., Athens, Ga. 30601. *Office:* University of Georgia, Athens, Ga. 30601.

CAREER: U.S. Veterans Administration, training officer, 1946-47; Cornell University, Ithaca, N.Y., vocational appraiser at Guidance Center, 1948-50; Texas A&M University, College Station, associate professor of psychology, 1950-55, director of guidance, 1952-55; U.S. Operations Mission to Ethiopia, Addis Ababa, remedial education and reading improvement adviser, 1955-56; Atlanta (Ga.) public schools, remedial specialist, 1956-58; University of Georgia, Athens, professor of education, 1958—. Director of research, Reading Research Services, Inc., 1965—. *Military service:* U.S. Army Air Forces, 1943-46; became sergeant.

MEMBER: American Psychological Association, American Educational Research Association, National Reading Conference (member of board of directors, 1960-63; vice-president, 1963-64; president, 1965-66), International Reading Association, National Education Association,

Georgia Educational Association, Phi Delta Kappa, Psi Chi.

WRITINGS: (With Embree W. Johnson) *Tachistoscopic Training,* U.S. Cooperative Education Program, 1956; (with James B. Chandler) *Hints on Teaching English in Ethiopia,* U.S. Cooperative Education Program, 1956; (with Karl C. Garrison, Fred Schab, and J. A. Wash) *Exercises in Educational Psychology,* Edwards Brothers, 1962; (with Garrison and Arthur S. McDonald) *Educational Psychology,* Appleton, 1964; (with Schab, Wash, and William F. White) *A Study Guide for Educational Psychology,* Edwards Brothers, 1966; (editor) *The Use of Theoretical Models in Research in Reading,* International Reading Association, 1966; (with Garrison and Harold W. Bernard) *The Psychology of Childhood,* and *Student's Workbook* (with Garrison and Ocie T. Dekle), Scribner, 1967; (with M. J. Rice) *Language,* University of Georgia Anthropology Curriculum Project, 1968; (with White) *Human Psychology: Learning,* Harcourt, 1975; (editor) *Toward a Psychology of Reading and Language: Selected Papers of W. W. Weaver,* University of Georgia Press, 1976.

Co-editor of Southwest Reading Conference *Yearbook,* 1954, and National Reading Conference *Yearbook,* 1961. Contributor of more than seventy-five articles to yearbooks and professional journals. Member of advisory board, *Journal of Reading,* 1964-65; contributing editor, *Research for the Classroom,* 1966-67; member of advisory board, *ERIC-CRIER* (Indiana University), 1966—.

*   *   *

KINNISON, William A(ndrew) 1932-

PERSONAL: Born February 10, 1932, in Springfield, Ohio; son of Errett Lowell and Audrey M. (Smith) Kinnison; married Lenore B. Morris (a teacher), June 11, 1960; children: William E., Linda E., Amy E. *Education:* Wittenberg University, A.B., 1954, B.Sc.Ed., 1955; University of Wisconsin, M.A., 1963; Ohio State University, Ph.D., 1967. *Religion:* Lutheran. *Home:* 1820 Timberlane Dr., Springfield, Ohio 45504. *Office:* Wittenberg University, Springfield, Ohio 45501.

CAREER: Wittenberg University, Springfield, Ohio, assistant director of admissions, 1958; State Historical Society of Wisconsin, Madison, assistant, 1958-59; Wittenberg University, assistant director of admissions, 1959-63, assistant dean of admissions, 1963-65; Ohio State University, Columbus, administrative assistant to director of School of Education, 1965-67; Wittenberg University, assistant to president, 1967-69, vice-president for university affairs, 1969-72, vice-president for administration, 1972-74, acting president, 1974-75, president, 1975—. *Military service:* U.S. Army, 1956-58. *Member:* Association for Higher Education, Clark County Historical Society, Men's Literary Society of Springfield.

WRITINGS: Samuel Shellabarger: Lawyer, Jurist, Legislator, Antioch Press, 1968; (editor with Mary A. Skardon) *World War I Armistice: Fiftieth Anniversary, 1918-1968,* Clark County Historical Society, 1968; *Wittenberg in Clark County, 1845-1970,* Clark County Historical Society, 1970; *Building Sullivant's Pyramid: An Administrative History of the Ohio State University, 1870-1907,* Ohio State University Press, 1970. Contributor to education journals.

WORK IN PROGRESS: Writing on the disputed Hayes-Tilden election of 1876, and on the "parade" of Masons, Odd Fellows, Knights of Pythias, and other fraternalists through nineteenth-century America.

KINSELLA, Paul L. 1923-

PERSONAL: Born June 15, 1923, in Louisville, Ky.; son of Lawrence V. (a tobacco manufacturer) and Mary (Kelly) Kinsella. Education: University of Louisville, B.A., 1952, M.A., 1955. Religion: Roman Catholic. Home: 3511 Nanz Ave., Louisville, Ky. 40207. Office: Jefferson Community College, First and Broadway, Louisville, Ky.

CAREER: Instructor in English at University of Louisville, Louisville, Ky., 1955-59, University of Evansville, Evansville, Ind., 1960-61, Western Illinois University, Macomb, 1961-62, University of Alabama, Huntsville, 1962-64, Indiana University Center, Jeffersonville, 1964-68; teaching at Jefferson Community College, Louisville, Ky., 1968—. Military service: U.S. Navy, 1944-46.

WRITINGS: The Techniques of Writing, Harcourt, 1967, 2nd edition, 1975. Contributor of short stories to Views.

WORK IN PROGRESS: A novel with a theme related to the ecumenical movement in the Catholic Church; a group of essays relating literary works to the basic concepts of psychology and psychiatry; The Key to Spanish; Logic for Composition.

* * *

KINZER, Betty 1922-

PERSONAL: Born November 14, 1922, in Camp Lewis, Wash.; daughter of Francis Henry (an Army officer) and Marie (Johnson) Boucher; married John Marvin Kinzer (a brigadier general, U.S. Army), December 1, 1945; children: Jeanne Marie, John Francis, Daniel Marion. Education: University of Missouri, B.S., 1944. Religion: Episcopalian. Home: 4909 Northwest 16th Pl., Gainesville, Fla. 32605.

MEMBER: Daughters of the United States Army, Museum Associates, Phi Beta Phi.

WRITINGS: (With Marian Leach) What Every Army Wife Should Know, Stackpole, 1966.

* * *

KIRDAR, Uner 1933-

PERSONAL: Born January 1, 1933, in Izmir, Turkey; son of Lutfi and Hayriye Kirdar; married Berna Benson, 1966; children: Konca. Education: University of Istanbul, Licence en droit, 1954; London School of Economics and Political Science, graduate study, 1957; Jesus College, Cambridge, Ph.D., 1962. Office: 330 East 33rd St., No. 3M, New York, N.Y. 10016.

CAREER: With Turkish Ministry of Foreign Affairs, 1957-66, as director of section of International Economic Institutions, 1963-66, member of Turkish delegation to United Nations General Assembly, 1959, to the first and second United Nations Trade and Development Conference, 1964 and 1968, and to the Trade and Development Board Sessions; deputy permanent representative for economic affairs, Permanent Turkish Delegation to United Nations at Geneva, Switzerland, 1966-71; United Nations Secretariat, New York, N.Y., 1972—, secretary, United Nations Conference on Human Settlements (HABITAT), secretary, Group of Experts on the Structure of the United Nations System, 1975, currently senior officer, Inter-Agency Affairs, Office for Inter-Agency Affairs and Coordination. Military service: Turkish Army, Engineer Corps, 1958.

WRITINGS: The Structure of United Nations Economic Aid to Underdeveloped Countries, Nijhoff, 1966. Also author of The Saving Gap in the Turkish Economy and Problem of External Finance: Problems of Multinational Corporations, 1975. Contributor to British Yearbook of International Law, 1962.

* * *

KIRKLAND, Bryant M(ays) 1914-

PERSONAL: Born May 2, 1914, in Essex, Conn.; son of Henry Burnham (a clergyman) and Helen Josephine (Mays) Kirkland; married Bernice Tanis, August 19, 1937; children: Nancy Tanis (Mrs. Tom L. Thompson), Elinor Ann, Virginia Lee. Education: Wheaton College, Wheaton, Ill., B.A., 1935; Princeton Theological Seminary, B.D., 1938; Eastern Theological Seminary, Th.M., 1948. Home: 1158 Fifth Ave., New York, N.Y. 10028. Office: 7 West 55th St., New York, N.Y. 10019.

CAREER: Ordained to ministry of Presbyterian Church at Philadelphia, Pa., 1938; minister in Willow Grove, Pa., 1938-40, Narberth, Pa., 1940-46, Haddonfield, N.J., 1946-57, Tulsa, Okla., 1957-62; Fifth Avenue Presbyterian Church, New York, N.Y., minister, 1962—. Visiting lecturer, Princeton Theological Seminary, 1951-56, 1964. Member of Commission on Ecumenical Mission and Relations, United Presbyterian Church, 1948-60. Trustee of Princeton Theological Seminary; member of board of managers, American Bible Society. Broadcaster on "Protestant Hour" and television programs. Traveler on mission surveys and preaching tours to South America, 1951, India, 1955, and Europe, 1960.

MEMBER: Rotary International, University Club (New York), Tulsa Club (Tulsa, Okla.). Awards, honors: D.D., Beaver College, 1948, Lafayette College, 1962, Denison University, 1964; LL.D., University of Tulsa, 1962; named national church preacher of the year by General Assembly of the Presbyterian Church in the U.S.A., 1963.

WRITINGS: (Contributor) A. W. Blackwood, editor, Evangelical Sermons of Our Day, Harper, 1959; (contributor) G. P. Baker and E. Ferguson, editors, A Year of Evangelism in the Local Church, Tidings, 1960; Growing in the Christian Faith, Tidings, 1963; Booklet-Prayer in the Life of the Nation, Tidings, 1963; Sermons from the Protestant Hour Broadcast, National Council of Churches, 1964; Home Before Dark, Abingdon, 1965; Living in a Zigzag Age, Abingdon, 1972. Contributor to Presbyterian Life and Christianity Today.

* * *

KIRKPATRICK, Dow (Napier) 1917-

PERSONAL: Born January 3, 1917, in Sesser, Ill.; son of Hiram Singleton (a railroad station agent) and Effie (Dycus) Kirkpatrick; married Marjorie Savage, June 1, 1938; children: Dow Napier II, David Earl. Education: Illinois Wesleyan University, student, 1933-34; Asbury College, A.B., 1934; Emory University, B.D., 1940; Drew University, Ph.D., 1945; Oxford University, postdoctoral study, 1946-47. Home: 77 Sheridan Dr. N.E., Atlanta, Ga. 30305.

CAREER: Ordained to Methodist ministry, 1940; minister in Milford, Pa., 1941-45, in Young Harris, Ga., 1947-51, in Athens, Ga., 1951-57, and in Atlanta, Ga., 1957-62; First Methodist Church, Evanston, Ill., pastor, 1962-75; Board of Global Ministries, Latin America, interpreter-at-large, currently in Lima, Peru, 1975—. Member of World Methodist Council, Division of Overseas Ministries, and National Council of Churches; co-chairman of Oxford Institute on Methodist Theological Studies, 1958, 1962, 1965,

1969, and 1973. President of Church Federation of Greater Chicago, 1965-66. *Military service:* U.S. Navy, chaplain, 1945-46.

WRITINGS: The Doctrine of the Church, Abingdon, 1964, (editor) *The Finality of Christ,* Abingdon, 1966, *Six Days—and Sunday,* Abingdon, 1968; (editor) *The Living God,* Abingdon, 1971. Contributor to religious journals.

WORK IN PROGRESS: Editing *The Holy Spirit, Tidings; Future Faith Now.*

* * *

KIRSNER, Robert 1921-

PERSONAL: Born July 9, 1921, in Lithuania; naturalized U.S. citizen; son of Samuel and Anna (Levine) Kirsner; married Mildred Warshofsky, April 11, 1947; children: David, Steven, Barbara, Kenneth, Tamara. *Education:* University of Cincinnati, A.B., 1943, M.A., 1945; Princeton University, M.A., 1947, Ph.D., 1949. *Politics:* Democrat. *Religion:* Jewish. *Home:* 500 Alminar, Coral Gables, Fla. 33146. *Office:* University of Miami, Coral Gables, Fla. 33124.

CAREER: Princeton University, Princeton, N.J., instructor in Spanish, 1945-49; University of Cincinnati, Cincinnati, Ohio, assistant professor, 1949-54, associate professor, 1954-61, professor of Romance languages, 1961-64; University of Miami, Coral Gables, Fla., professor of Spanish, 1964—, chairman of department of foreign languages, 1965-73. Visiting summer professor at Johns Hopkins University, 1948, National University of Guatemala, 1951, Tulane University, 1957, NDEA Language Institute at San Francisco State College (now University), 1959, NDEA Language Institute at Michigan State University, 1961, University of Arizona, 1964, University of California at Berkeley, 1966; resident director, Rollins College Semester in Bogota, Columbia, 1963-64. *Military service:* U.S. Army, 1943-44.

MEMBER: American Association of Teachers of Spanish and Portuguese (member of executive committee, 1959-61), Modern Language Association of America (committee chairman, 1951-54, 1962), American Association of University Professors, Central States Modern Language Association, South Atlantic Modern Language Association, Ohio Modern Language Teachers Association (president, 1960-61, B'nai Brith.

WRITINGS: (Editor with Albert Brent) *Cuentos Espanoles,* Holt, 1950; (editor with T. B. Irving) *Paisajes del Sur: An Anthology of Latin American Literature and Life,* Ronald, 1954; (editor with W. A. Kinne) *A Repasar: A Spanish Review Grammar,* Crowell, 1954; (editor with Brent) *Bibliography of Americo Castro's Writings,* [Mexico City], 1956; *The Novels and Travels of Camilo Jose Cela,* University of North Carolina Press, 1964; (editor with Brent) *New Bibliography of Castro's Writings,* Ohio State University Press, 1964; *Historia de una Escalera: A Play in Search of Characters,* Editorial Castalia (Madrid), 1966; *Buero's Un Sonador para un Pueblo,* University of North Carolina Press, 1966. Contributor to *Kentucky Romance Quarterly, Revista, Papeles,* and other journals. Associate editor, *Caribe* (journal), 1975—.

* * *

KIRVAN, John J. 1932-

PERSONAL: Born February 25, 1932, in Guelph, Ontario, Canada; son of Norman Joseph (a mail carrier) and Victo-

rine (Courtney) Kirvan. *Education:* St. Charles College, Baltimore, Md., student, 1949-51; St. Paul's College, Washington, D.C., A.B., and M.A.; Catholic University of America, M.S.L.S. *Home:* 6600 Boulevard E., West New York, N.J. 07093. *Office:* Paulist Press, 1865 Broadway, New York, N.Y. 10023.

CAREER: Ordained Roman Catholic priest of Paulist order (C.S.P.), 1958. St. Peter's College, Baltimore, Md., librarian and teacher of English, 1959-63; Wayne State University, Detroit, Mich., Roman Catholic chaplain, 1963-69, director of Newman Apostolate, 1966-69; Paulist Press, New York, N.Y., associate editor, 1969—; vicepresident, Dendron Publishing, 1974—. *Awards, honors:* Ronald Knox Literary Award of National Newman Chaplains Association, 1965.

WRITINGS: Restless Believers, Paulist Press, 1967; *The Infallibility Debate,* Paulist Press, 1971. Editor, *Newman/A Review,* 1963-69; editor, *New Catholic World,* 1969—.

* * *

KISKER, George W. 1912-

PERSONAL: Born May 22, 1912, in Cincinnati, Ohio; son of George and Margerite (Orlik) Kisker; married Florence Ray, November 24, 1932. *Education:* Ohio State University, A.B., 1939, M.A., 1940, Ph.D., 1943. *Home:* 700 Elsinboro Dr., Cincinnati, Ohio 45226. *Office:* Department of Psychology, University of Cincinnati, Cincinnati, Ohio 45221.

CAREER: University of Cincinnati, Cincinnati, Ohio, professor of psychology, 1946—; chief psychologist at Longview State Hospital, 1957-60, Hamilton County Juvenile Court, 1960-75; Behavioral Science Associates (consulting psychologists), Cincinnati, Ohio, president, 1962-72. *Military service:* U.S. Army, 1942-46; became captain. *Member:* American Psychological Association, British Psychological Society, French Psychological Society.

WRITINGS: (Editor) *World Tension: The Psychopathology of International Relations,* Prentice-Hall, 1951; *The Disorganized Personality,* McGraw, 1964, 3rd edition, in press. Contributor to magazines, including *Saturday Evening Post, Reader's Digest, Coronet,* and *Pageant.*

WORK IN PROGRESS: Research in human behavior and abnormal psychology.

* * *

KISSLING, Fred R., Jr. 1930-

PERSONAL: Born February 10, 1930, in Nashville, Tenn.; son of Fred R. and Sarah Fitzgerald (Geistman) Kissling; married Jane Kirkpatrick, September 14, 1959; children: Sarah Fitzgerald, Jane Kirkpatrick. *Education:* Vanderbilt University, B.S., 1952, M.A., 1958. *Religion:* Presbyterian. *Home:* 728 Old Dobbin Circle, Lexington, Ky. 40502. *Office:* Northwestern Mutual Life Insurance Co., 98 Dennis Dr., Lexington, Ky. 40503.

CAREER: Northwestern Mutual Life Insurance Co., Lexington, Ky., general agent, 1962—. Chartered life underwriter. *Member:* National Association of Life Underwriters, Kentucky General Agents and Managers Association (past president), Lexington General Agents and Managers Association (past president), Lexington Estate Planning Council.

WRITINGS: Sell and Grow Rich, Lexington House, 1966. Publisher, *Leader's Magazine.*

KISTIAKOWSKY, Vera 1928-
(Vera Kistiakowsky Fischer)

PERSONAL: Born September 9, 1928, in Princeton, N.J.; daughter of George Bogdan (a chemist) and Hildegard (Moebius) Kistiakowsky; children: Marc Laurenz, Karen Marie. *Education:* Mount Holyoke College, A.B., 1948; University of California, Berkeley, Ph.D., 1952. *Home:* 226 Upland Rd., Cambridge, Mass. 02140. *Office:* Massachusetts Institute of Technology, Cambridge, Mass. 02139.

CAREER: U.S. Naval Radiological Defense Laboratory, San Francisco, Calif., chemist, 1952-53; University of California, Berkeley, Berliner fellow, in Lawrence Radiation Laboratory, 1953-54; Columbia University, New York, N.Y., research associate and instructor in physics, 1954-59; Brandeis University, Waltham, Mass., 1959-63, began as assistant professor, became associate professor of physics; Massachusetts Institute of Technology, Cambridge, member of scientific staff, 1963-69, senior research scientist, 1969-72, professor of physics, 1972—. *Member:* American Association of Physics Teachers, Phi Beta Kappa, Sigma Xi.

WRITINGS: (Under name Vera Kistiakowsky Fischer) *One Way is Down,* Little, Brown, 1967. Contributor to professional journals.

WORK IN PROGRESS: Research in experimental elementary particle physics and on women scientists.

*   *   *

KITSON CLARK, George Sydney Roberts 1900-

PERSONAL: Born June 14, 1900, in Leeds, England; son of Edwin (engineer and lieutenant colonel in the British Territorial Army) and Georgina (Bidder) Kitson Clark. *Education:* Trinity College, Cambridge, B.A., 1921, Litt.D., 1954. *Religion:* Church of England. *Home and office:* Trinity College, Cambridge University, Cambridge, England.

CAREER: Cambridge University, Cambridge, England, fellow in history at Trinity College, 1922—, lecturer in history at Trinity College, 1928-54, and tutor, 1933-45, university lecturer in history, 1929-54, and reader in constitutional history, 1954-67, Birkbeck lecturer, 1967. Visiting lecturer at University of Pennsylvania, 1953-54. Ford's lecturer at Oxford University, 1960; Maurice lecturer at King's College, University of London, 1960; George Scott fellow at University of Melbourne, 1965; also lecturer in United States, Canada, Switzerland, India, Australia, New Zealand, and Ireland. Founder of Cambridge University Educational Film Council, 1947; first chairman of British University Film Council, 1948-51.

MEMBER: Royal Commonwealth Society (fellow; chairman of Cambridgeshire branch, 1956-66), Royal Institute of International Affairs, Royal Historical Society (fellow), American Academy of Arts and Sciences (foreign honorary member), Athenaeum Club (London). *Awards, honors:* D.Litt., University of Durham.

WRITINGS: Peel and the Conservative Party, G. Bell, 1929, 2nd edition, Cass & Co., 1964; *Sir Robert Peel,* Duckworth, 1936; *The English Inheritance,* S.C.M. Press, 1950; *Elizabeth by the Grace of God* (William Ainslie Memorial Lecture), St. Martins-in-the-Field, 1953; (contributor) J. H. Plumb, editor, *Studies in Social History,* Longmans, Green, 1955; *The Making of Victorian England,* Harvard University Press, 1962; (author of introduction) R. T. Shannon, *Gladstone and the Bulgarian Agita-*

tion 1876, Thomas Nelson, 1963; *The Critical Historian,* Basic Books, 1967; *An Expanding Society: Britain 1830-1900,* Cambridge University Press, 1967; *Guide for Research Students Working on Historical Subjects,* Cambridge University Press, 1968, 2nd edition, 1969; *Churchmen and the Condition of England, 1832-1885,* Methuen, 1973.

Author of two guides for research students in history, first published by Cambridge University Press, 1958 and 1963, and a booklet on the art of lecturing, published by Heffer & Sons, Cambridge. Contributor of articles and reviews to *Economic History Review, Transactions of Royal Historical Society, Journal of Modern History* (Chicago), *University Review* (Ireland), and other journals.

SIDELIGHTS: Kitson Clark is mainly engaged in teaching research students at Cambridge; four of his students are now professors in the United States, and others are teaching in Canada, Australia, and Ireland, as well as in England.

BIOGRAPHICAL/CRITICAL SOURCES: Robert Robson, editor, *Ideas and Institutions of Victorian Britain: Essays in Honour of G. Kitson Clark,* G. Bell, 1967.

*   *   *

KLAASSEN, Leo H(endrik) 1920-

PERSONAL: Born June 21, 1920, in Rotterdam, Netherlands; son of Cornelis Hendrik Leonardus (an administrator) and Alida (Bakker) Klaassen; married Maria Ablinger, June 19, 1957; children: Marianne Elizabeth, Hendrik Leonardus. *Education:* Netherlands School of Economics, M.A., 1946, Ph.D., 1959. *Home:* Joost Banckertsplaats 133, Rotterdam, Netherlands. *Office:* Netherlands Economic Institute, Pieter de Hoochweg 118, Rotterdam, Netherlands.

CAREER: Economic Technological Institute, Rotterdam, Netherlands, research fellow, 1943-45; Netherlands Economic Institute, Rotterdam, research fellow, 1945-51, chief of research, 1951-59, director, 1959-68, president, 1968—; Erasmus University, Netherlands School of Economics, Rotterdam, lecturer, 1951-59, professor, 1959—. Visiting professor, University of California, Los Angeles, 1962, 1966. Adviser to Netherlands Ministries of Transport, Agriculture, and Communication, to World Bank on transport study in Zambia, 1964, to NEDECO transportation mission to Brazil, 1965-67, to Iranian Government on city planning of Tehran, 1967-68, to Portuguese Government on industrialization policies and on amenity planning, 1968—, to Spanish Government, 1973-74, to Institute of Land Reform, Wageningen, and to Ministry of Communication, The Hague.

Supervisor of studies on economic development of Curacao, 1960-68, on the economic consequences of the Euphrates Dam in Syria, 1964, on mineral development possibilities in Turkey, 1964, on economic evaluation of the Jordan Valley irrigation project in Jordan, 1967-68, on national transportation in the Netherlands, 1967—, on regional development in Algecia, Spain, on the industry in the Ruhr Area, 1969—, and on the national accounts and the administrative structure of the Netherlands Antilles, 1973—.

Director of study on the development potentials of Clyde area in Scotland, 1971-73; trustee for regional development study of Malaysia, 1967-69; member of other transportation or survey teams in Niger and Dahomey, 1961-62, Finland,

1964-65, Korea, 1965-66, Cameroon and Central African Republic, 1967-69, South Korea, 1968-70, Nigeria, 1970, and Iran, 1971. Member of Common Market Committee on Capital-coefficients and Investment Forecasts, and Government (Netherlands) Committee on the Profitability of Infrastructural Investments. *Member:* American Geographic Society (fellow), Econometric Society, Society for Statistics, Netherlands Demographic Association, Regional Science Association (vice-president of Philadelphia branch, 1972). *Awards, honors:* Medal of honor, University of Gdansk; World Academy of Art and Science fellow.

WRITINGS: (With D. H. van Dongen Torman and L. M. Koyck) *Hoofdlijnen van de Sociaal-Economische Ontwikkeling der Gemunte Amersfoort van 1900-1970* (title means "The Development of the City of Amersfoort 1900-1970"), H. E. Stenfert Kroese, 1949; (with J. Tinbergen and E. H. Mulder) *Observations on the Planned Provision of Nitrogen Fertilizers for the World,* H. E. Stenfert Kroese, 1956; (with A. de Klerk) *De Verwarming van de Volkswoning* (title means "Heating of Low Rent Houses"), H. E. Stenfert Kroese, 1959; (with W. C. Kroft, W. M. van Liefland, and D. Zuiderhoek) *Deventer, Stad van 250,000 inwoners* (title means "Deventer, City of 250,000"), A. E. Kluwer, 1959; *Richtlijnen voor het toegepast economisch onderzoek* (title means "Principles of Economic Research"), H. E. Stenfert Kroese, 1959.

(With E. H. van den Poll) *Economische Aspecten van de Wegenbouw* (title means "Economic Aspects of Road Construction"), Het Nederlandse Wegencongres, 1960; (contributor) J. L. Mey, editor, *Depreciation and Replacement Policy,* North-Holland Publishing, 1961; (with others) *Capital Formation for Housing in Latin America,* Pan American Union, 1963; (with others) *Area Redevelopment Policy in Great Britain and the Countries of the Common Market,* U.S. Department of Commerce, 1965; *Area Economic and Social Redevelopment,* Organization for Economic Co-operation and Development, 1965; (co-author) *Energie in Perspectief* (title means "Energy in Perspective"), Steenkolen Handels-Vereniging, 1966; *Kurzfristige Sozialloesungen contra langfristige Regionalpolitik* (title means "Short-term Social Solutions and Longrun Regional Policy") [Hamburg], 1966; *Methods of Selecting Industries for Depressed Areas: An Introduction to Feasibility Studies,* Organization for Economic Co-operation and Development, 1967; *Social Amenities in Area Economic Growth: An Analysis of Methods of Defining Needs for Local Social Amenities,* Organization for Economic Co-operation and Development, 1967; (with van de Poll) *Lineamenti della politica economica nei Paesi Bassi* (title means "Economic Policy in the Netherlands"), Istituto per gli Studi Sullo Sviluppo Economico e il Progresso Tecnico, [Rome], 1968; (with others) *Theory and Practice in Transport Economics,* European Conference of Ministers of Transport, 1969; (with others) *The Future of European Ports,* College of Europe, 1970; (co-author and editor) *Regionale economie* (title means "Regional Economics"), Noordhoff, 1972; (with others) *Growth Poles,* United National Research Institute for Social Development, 1972; *The Impact of Changes in Society on the Demand for Passenger and Freight Transport,* European Conference of Minister of Transport, 1973; (editor) *Economie dezer dagen* (title means "Economics of These Days"), University Press of Rotterdam, 1973; (with Paul Drewe) *Migration Policy in Europe: A Comparative Study,* Lexington Books, 1973; (with G. Rehn and A. Bernfeld) *Manpower in Germany,* Organization for Economic Co-operation and Develop-

ment, 1974; (with Jean J. P. Paelinck) *Integration of Socio-Economic and Physical Planning,* University Press Rotterdam, 1974. Also author of *The Influence of Centralization on the Future,* 1970, *Amenity and Recreation in High Density Zones,* 1971, *Energy Conservation: Ways and Means,* 1974, *The Quality of Life in European Cities,* 1974, and numerous books and pamphlets on economy, regional development, and society, in Russian, German, Dutch, French, Italian, Spanish, and Polish.

WORK IN PROGRESS: Several studies in regional economics and development programming.

*   *   *

KLAGSBRUN, Francine (Lifton)

PERSONAL: Born in Brooklyn, N.Y.; daughter of Benjamin (a businessman) and Anna (Pike) Lifton; married Samuel C. Klagsbrun (a psychiatrist), January 23, 1955; children: Sarah Devora. *Education:* Brooklyn College (now of the City University of New York), B.A. (magna cum laude), 1952; Jewish Theological Seminary of America, B.H.L., 1952; New York University, M.A., 1959. *Home and office:* 1010 Fifth Ave., New York, N.Y. 10028.

CAREER: Field Enterprises Educational Corp., Chicago, Ill., assistant editor, 1957-59, subject editor, 1959-61, senior editor, 1961-64; Grolier, Inc., New York City, executive editor of *Encyclopedia Americana,* 1964-65; Cowles Book Co., New York City, executive editor, 1965-68; editorial director, U.E.C., Inc., 1969-73. Member of board of governors, Melton Research Foundation. *Member:* Authors League of America, Authors Guild, Jewish Publication Society of America, Phi Beta Kappa.

WRITINGS—All published by F. Watts, except as noted: *Sigmund Freud,* 1967; *First Book of Spices,* 1968; *The Story of Moses,* 1968; (editor with D. C. Whitney) *Assassination: Robert F. Kennedy,* Cowles, 1968; *Psychiatry—What It Is, What It Does: A Book for Young People,* 1969; (with husband, Samuel C. Klagsbrun) *Your Health: Nutrition,* 1969; *Read About the Teacher,* 1970; *Read About the Librarian,* 1970; *Read About the Parkman,* 1971; *Read About the Sanitation Man,* 1972; *Freedom Now! The Story of the Abolitionists,* Houghton, 1972; (editor) *The First Ms. Reader,* Warner Paperback, 1973; *Free to Be . . . You and Me,* McGraw, 1974; (editor and compiler) *Words of Women,* Doubleday, 1975; *Too Young to Die: Youth and Suicide,* Houghton, 1976. Contributor to *World Book Encyclopedia,* 1964; contributor to *Ms.*

WORK IN PROGRESS: The Jewish Answers, for Pantheon Books.

*   *   *

KLASS, Sholom   1916-

PERSONAL: Born March 8, 1916, in Brooklyn, N.Y.; son of Morris (in textile business) and Ethel (Epstein) Klass; married Irene Schreiber (a writer), August 31, 1940; children: Naomi Klass Schwartz, Hindy. *Education:* Mesifta Theological Seminary, Rabbi. *Home:* 219 Amherst St., Brooklyn, N.Y. 11235. *Office:* 338 Third Ave., Brooklyn, N.Y. 11215.

CAREER: Brooklyn Daily, Brooklyn, N.Y., publisher and editor, 1950—; *Jewish Press,* Brooklyn, N.Y., publisher, editor, and regular columnist, 1960—. Surf Realty Corp., Brooklyn, N.Y., president.

WRITINGS: Responsa of Modern Judaism, Jewish Press, Volume I, 1965, Volume II, 1966; *Tales of Our Gaonim,* Jewish Press, 1967.

KLAUSLER, Alfred P(aul) 1910-

PERSONAL: Born February 22, 1910, in Hankinson, N.D.; son of Joseph Paul (a clergyman) and Amanda (Hunziker) Klausler; married Signe Fox, June 28, 1934; children: Peter, Paula, Thomas. *Education:* Concordia College, St. Paul, Minn., diploma, 1929; Concordia Seminary, St. Louis, Mo., diploma, 1932; Loyola University, Chicago, Ill., M.A., 1961; additional study at Columbia University and University of Chicago. *Politics:* Democrat. *Home:* 2520 South 60th Ct., Chicago, Ill. 60650.

CAREER: Ordained to ministry of Lutheran Church, 1934; pastor in Glendive, Mont., 1934-42; Walther League, Chicago, Ill., editor of *Messenger* and *Arena,* 1946-66; Associated Church Press, Chicago, Ill., executive secretary, 1961-74; *Christian Century,* Chicago, Ill., editor-at-large, 1974—. Instructor at Valparaiso University, 1950-52, and Concordia Teachers College, River Forest, Ill., 1954; lecturer at Wartburg Seminary, Kent State University, and Concordia Seminary. *Military service:* U.S. Army, 1942-46, 1961-62. U.S. Army Reserve, 1946-61, 1962-66; became colonel; received Army Commendation Medal with oakleaf cluster. *Member:* Chicago Headline Club, Alpha Lambda Phi, Pi Gamma Mu, Sigma Delta Chi. *Awards, honors:* Litt.D., Valparaiso University; William B. Lipphard Award for distinguished service to religious journalism, 1974.

WRITINGS: Growth in Worship, Concordia, 1956; *Christ and Your Job,* Concordia, 1956; *The Midnight Lion* (fiction), Augsburg, 1957; *Meditations for Youth,* Concordia, 1959; *Lutheran Church and New Deal,* Loyola University Press, 1962; *Censorship, Obscenity, and Sex,* Concordia, 1967; (editor with John DeMott) *The Journalist's Prayer Book,* Augsburg, 1972. Contributor to magazines. Editorial coordinator, *Christian Ministry.*

* * *

KLEIN, Martin A. 1934-

PERSONAL: Born April 9, 1934, in New York, N.Y.; son of Joseph and Etta (Marcus) Klein; married Suzanne Silk (a political scientist), February 2, 1963. *Education:* Northwestern University, B.S., 1955; University of Chicago, M.A., 1959, Ph.D., 1964. *Office:* Department of History, University of Toronto, Toronto, Ontario, Canada.

CAREER: University of Rhode Island, Providence, instructor, 1961-62; University of California, Berkeley, assistant professor of African history, 1965-70, University of Toronto, Toronto, Ontario, associate professor of history, 1970—.

WRITINGS: Islam and Imperialism in Senegal: Sine-Saloum, 1847-1914, Stanford University Press, 1968; (editor with G. W. Johnson) *Perspectives on the African Past,* Little, Brown, 1972.

* * *

KLEIN, Rose (Shweitzer) 1918-

PERSONAL: Born October 19, 1918, in New York, N.Y.; daughter of Isidore (a contractor) and Lillian (Gershkopf) Shweitzer; married Bernard Klein (a research chemist), August 8, 1942; children: David Andrew, Peter Alan. *Education:* Hunter College (now Hunter College of the City University of New York), B.A., 1941; Columbia University, M.A., 1942. *Religion:* Hebrew. *Home:* 129 Patton Blvd., New Hyde Park, N.Y. 11040.

CAREER: Jewish Hospital and Medical Center of Brooklyn, Brooklyn, N.Y., nutrition instructor, 1958—. *Member:* American Public Health Association, American Dietetic Association, Long Island Dietetic Association, Food and Nutrition Council of Greater New York, Greater New York Dietetic Association.

WRITINGS: (With Thelma Wayler) *Applied Nutrition,* Macmillan, 1965.

WORK IN PROGRESS: A revision of *Applied Nutrition; Nutrition and Brain Function; Nutrition Program for Comprehensive Child Care.*††

* * *

KLEINMANN, Jack H(enry) 1932-

PERSONAL: Born September 1, 1932, in New York, N.Y.; son of Max and Helen (Weinstein) Kleinmann; married Ellen Kalberman, June 30, 1954 (divorced, 1970); married Joi Hase, September 16, 1972; children: (first marriage) Laura Beth, Deborah Rachel; (second marriage) Jason Hase. *Education:* Brooklyn College (now Brooklyn College of the City University of New York), B.A., 1953, M.A., 1954; Columbia University, Ed.D., 1960. *Politics:* Democrat. *Religion:* Jewish. *Home:* 6315 Utah Ave. N.W., Washington, D.C. 20015. *Office:* National Education Association, 1201 16th St. N.W., Washington, D.C. 20036.

CAREER: New York (N.Y.) public schools, teacher, 1953-58; White Plains (N.Y.) public schools, administrative assistant to superintendent, 1959-61; National Education Association, Washington, D.C., salary consultant, 1962-64, assistant director of Research Division, 1964-66, director of Special Services Division, 1966-68, executive secretary, Commission on Profession Rights and Responsibilities, 1968-69, director of Planning and Organizational Development, 1969—. *Military service:* U.S. Army, 1954-56. *Member:* National Education Association, American Association of School Administrators, American Association of School Personnel Administrators, Phi Delta Kappa.

WRITINGS: (With W. S. Elsbree and others) *Principles of Staff Personnel Administration in the Public Schools,* Teachers College, Columbia University, 1959; *Fringe Benefits for Public School Personnel,* Teachers College, Columbia University, 1962; (with T. M. Stinnett and Martha Ware) *Professional Negotiation in Public Education,* Macmillan, 1966; *Profiles of Excellence,* National Education Association, 1966.

* * *

KLERER, Melvin 1926-

PERSONAL: Born February 17, 1926, in New York, N.Y.; son of Benjamin (in retail business) and Sadie (Horowitz) Klerer; married Leona Wilt, June 17, 1951; children: Burton, Robert. *Education:* New York University, B.A., 1948, M.S., 1950, Ph.D., 1954. *Home:* 1160 Midland Ave., Bronxville, N.Y. 10708. *Office:* Department of Operation Research and System Analysis, Polytechnic Institute of New York, Brooklyn, N.Y. 11201.

CAREER: Columbia University, Hudson Laboratories, Dobbs Ferry, N.Y., director of computing and data processing facility, 1957-67; New York University, New York, N.Y., professor of industrial engineering, 1967-73; Weizmann Institute of Science, Rehovot, Israel, visiting scientist, 1973-74; Polytechnic Institute of New York, Brooklyn, professor of computer science, 1974—. *Military service:* U.S. Army, 1944-45. *Member:* Institute of Electrical and Electronics Engineers Computer Society, Association for

Computing Machinery (chairman of joint users group, 1966-68; national lecturer, 1967-68), American Association for the Advancement of Science, Society for Information Display, Pattern Recognition Society.

WRITINGS: (Coeditor) *Digital Computer User's Handbook,* McGraw, 1967; (coeditor) *Interactive Systems for Experimental Applied Mathematics,* Academic Press, 1968; (coauthor) *A Table of Indefinite Integrals,* Dover, 1971.

WORK IN PROGRESS: The Laboratory, a novel.

* * *

KLIMOWICZ, Barbara 1927-

PERSONAL: Surname is pronounced Klim-o-wits; born September 11, 1927, in Mansfield, Ohio; daughter of Everett K. (a mechanical engineer) and Dorothy (Hunter) Tingley; married Charles H. Klimowicz (a petroleum engineer), October 20, 1951; children: Mark, Lynn. *Education:* Ohio State University, B.F.A., 1949, B.S. in Ed., 1951. *Religion:* Presbyterian. *Home address:* c/o Amoseas, Box 237, Killiney Rd. P.O., Singapore 9; (residence) Rumbai, Sumatra, Indonesia.

CAREER: Kindergarten teacher in Salem, Ill., 1960-65, and remedial reading teacher, 1967.

WRITINGS—All published by Abingdon: *Fred, Fred, Use Your Head,* 1966; *Strawberry Thumb,* 1968; *The Word-Birds of Davy McFifer,* 1970; *My Sister the Horse,* 1971; *When Shoes Eat Socks,* 1971; *The Great Green Apple War,* 1973; *Ha, Ha, Ha, Henrietta,* 1975.

* * *

KLINDT-JENSEN, Ole 1918-

PERSONAL: Born March 31, 1918, in Naestved, Denmark; married Tove E. Dam, May 1, 1945; children: Karsten, Henrik, Marianne. *Education:* Studied at University of Copenhagen, 1936-44. *Religion:* Danish Lutheran Church. *Home:* 87 V. Strandalle, Risskov, Denmark. *Office:* Moesgard, Hojbjerg, Denmark.

CAREER: National Museum, Copenhagen, Denmark, inspector, 1949-61; University of Aarhus, Aarhus, Denmark, professor of prehistoric archaeology, 1961—. Secretary general of Union Internationale des Sciences Prehistoriques et Protohistoriques, 1966—.

WRITINGS: Foreign Influences in Denmark's Early Iron Age, Munksgaard, 1950; *Bronzekedelen fra Braa,* Jysk Arkaeologisk Selskab (Aarhus), 1953; *Denmark before the Vikings,* Thames & Hudson, 1957; *Istidens Kunst,* Fremad, 1957; *Bornholm i Folkevandringstiden,* National Museum (Copenhagen), 1957; *Viking Art,* Allen & Unwin, 1966; *Vikingarnas Vorld,* Forum (Stockholm), 1967, translation published as *The World of the Vikings,* Luce, 1970; *A History of Scandinavian Archaeology,* Thames & Hudson, 1975.

WORK IN PROGRESS: Excavations at Bornholm.

* * *

KNACHEL, Philip A(therton) 1926-

PERSONAL: Born June 23, 1926, in Indianapolis, Ind.; son of Firman F. (an attorney) and Mary Esther (Atherton) Knachel; married Pierrette Annie Roy, July 1, 1955; children: Sylvette K., Eric C. *Education:* Northwestern University, B.S., 1948; University of Poitiers, Certificate, 1951; Johns Hopkins University, M.A., 1952, Ph.D., 1953; Syracuse University, M.S.L.S., 1959. *Home:* 5807 Phoenix

Dr., Bethesda, Md. 20034. *Office:* Folger Shakespeare Library, Washington, D.C. 20005.

CAREER: Instructor in history at Johns Hopkins University, Baltimore, Md., 1952-53, and Hunter College (now Hunter College of the City University of New York), New York, N.Y., 1953-57; U.S. Air Force, Rome Air Development Center, Rome, N.Y., center historian, 1957-59; Folger Shakespeare Library, Washington, D.C., assistant director, 1959-68, acting director, 1968-69, associate director, 1969—. Visiting lecturer, University of Maryland, 1968-70. *Military service:* U.S. Navy, active duty, 1944-46; became ensign in Naval Reserve. *Member:* American Historical Association, Conference on British Studies, Society for French Historical Studies, Renaissance Society of America, Modern Language Association of America. *Awards, honors:* Fulbright fellowship in France, 1950-51.

WRITINGS: (Editor) *Eikon Basilike,* Cornell University Press, 1966; *England and the Fronde,* Cornell University Press, 1967; (editor) Marchamont Nedham, *The Case of the Commonwealth of England, Stated!,* University Press of Virginia, 1969.

* * *

KNAPP, Lewis M(ansfield) 1894-

PERSONAL: Born March 4, 1894, in Groton, Mass.; son of George S. (a farmer) and Susan (Lewis) Knapp; married Louise Ansley, June 24, 1922 (died, 1936); married Helen June Heath (pastor of a Spanish mission in Colorado Springs, Colo.), March 26, 1938; children: (first marriage) Margaret L. (Mrs. Christopher Wright); (second marriage) Hugh H. *Education:* Amherst College, B.A., 1916; Columbia University, M.A., 1920; Yale University, Ph.D., 1928. *Religion:* Congregationalist. *Home:* 115 East Del Norte, Colorado Springs, Colo. 80907.

CAREER: Teacher at Bishops' College School, Lennoxville, Quebec, 1916-17, at Hopkins Grammar School, New Haven, Conn., 1920-22; University of Colorado, Boulder, instructor in English, 1922-25; Williams College, Williamstown, Mass., 1928-38, began as instructor, became assistant professor of English; Colorado College, Colorado Springs, 1939—, began as assistant professor, professor of English, 1947-62, chairman of department, 1947-59, professor emeritus, 1962—. Carnegie Visiting Professor, 1962-63. *Military service:* U.S. Army, 1917-19; became sergeant. *Member:* Modern Language Association of America, Phi Beta Kappa. *Awards, honors:* Litt.D., Colorado College, 1966; American Council of Learned Societies and American Philosophical Society research grants.

WRITINGS: Tobias Smollett, Doctor of Men and Manners, Princeton University Press, 1949, reprinted, Russell, 1969; (editor and author of introduction) Tobias Smollett, *The Expedition of Humphry Clinker,* Oxford University Press, 1966; (editor) Smollett, *The Letters of Tobias Smollett,* Clarendon Press, 1970. Contributor to literary journals.

AVOCATIONAL INTERESTS: Music, poetry, travel.

BIOGRAPHICAL/CRITICAL SOURCES: G. S. Rousseau and P. G. Bouce, editors, *Tobias Smollett Bicentennial Essays Presented to Lewis M. Knapp,* Oxford University Press, 1971.†

* * *

KNEPLER, Henry (William) 1922-

PERSONAL: Born May 8, 1922, in Vienna, Austria; son of

Hugo (a concert manager) and Hedwig (Moser) Knepler; married Myrna Cohn, April 23, 1961; children: Elizabeth, Elinor, Anne. *Education:* Queen's University, Kingston, Ontario, B.A., 1945, M.A., 1946; University of Chicago, Ph.D., 1950. *Home:* 1344 East Madison Park, Chicago, Ill. 60615. *Office:* Illinois Institute of Technology, Chicago, Ill. 60616.

CAREER: Queen's University, Kingston, Ontario, lecturer, 1946; Illinois Institute of Technology, Chicago, instructor, 1947-52, assistant professor, 1952-58, associate professor, 1958-61, professor of English and chairman of department of language and literature, 1961—. Visiting professor, University of Paris, Sorbonne, 1971-73. *Member:* Modern Language Association of America, National Council of Teachers of English.

WRITINGS: (Editor with S. K. Workman) *A Range of Writing,* Prentice-Hall, 1958; (editor with Richard Cassell) *What is the Play?,* Scott, Foresman, 1967; *The Gilded Stage,* Morrow, 1968; *Man About Paris,* Morrow, 1970. Contributor to *Theatre Annual, Anglo-German and German-American Crosscurrents, Modern Drama,* and *Queen's Quarterly.*

WORK IN PROGRESS: A book on modern American drama.

* * *

KNIGHT, Etheridge 1931-

PERSONAL: Born April 19, 1931, in Corinth, Miss.; son of Bushie and Belzora (Cozart) Knight; married; children: Stephanie Tandiwe, James Bambata. *Education:* Attended high school for two years; self-educated at "various prisons, jails." *Politics:* "Freedom." *Religion:* "Freedom." *Home:* 3323 West 33rd Pl., Indianapolis, Ind. 46222.

CAREER: Poet. Writer-in-residence, University of Pittsburgh, Pittsburgh, Pa., 1968-69, and University of Hartford, Hartford, Conn., 1969-70; Lincoln University, Jefferson City, Mo., poet-in-residence, 1972. Inmate at Indiana State Prison, Michigan City, 1960-68. *Military service:* U.S. Army, 1947-51. *Awards, honors:* National Endowment for the Arts grant, 1972; National Book Award and Pulitzer prize nominations, both 1973, for *Belly Song and Other Poems;* Self-Development through the Arts grant, for local workshops, 1974; Guggenheim fellowship, 1974.

WRITINGS: Poems from Prison, preface by Gwendolyn Brooks, Broadside Press, 1968; (with others) *Voce Negre dal Carcere* (anthology), [Laterza, Italy], 1968, translation published as *Black Voices from Prison,* Pathfinder Press, 1969; *Belly Song and Other Poems,* Broadside Press, 1973. Work represented in many anthologies, including: *Norton Anthology of American Poets, Black Poets, A Broadside Treasury, Broadside Poet, Dices and Black Bones, A Comprehensive Anthology of Black Poets.* Contributor of poems and articles to many magazines and journals, including *Black Digest, Essence, Motive, American Report,* and *American Poetry.* Poetry editor, *Motive,* 1969-71; contributing editor, *New Letters,* 1974.

WORK IN PROGRESS: A historical novel on the life of Dermark Vesey.

SIDELIGHTS: Knight believes that a definition of art and aesthetics assumes that "every man is the master of his own destiny and comes to grips with the society by his own efforts. The 'true' artist is supposed to examine his own experience of this process as a reflection of his self, his ego." Knight told *CA* that he feels "white society denies art, because art unifies rather than separates; it brings people together instead of alienating them." The western/ European esthetic dictates that "the artist speak only of the beautiful (himself and what *he* sees); his task is to edify the listener, to make him see *beauty* of the world." Black artists must stay away from this because "the red of this aesthetic rose got its color from the blood of black slaves, exterminated Indians, napalmed Vietnamese children." According to Knight, the black artist must "perceive and conceptualize the collective aspirations, the collective vision of black people, and through his art form give back to the people the truth that he has gotten from them. He must sing to them of their own deeds, and misdeeds."

Of *Poems from Prison,* Jewel Latimore says that "Etheridge Knight brings the strength and hardness of black existence through his poetry to his people." Latimore notes that the forms and means of the black artist "are not of necessity confined in traditional 'mainstream' garb—but are the forms and constructs created by him, or adapted, as a set form like the Japanese Haiku"; or, as Knight has written, "making jazz swing in/Seventeen syllables AIN'T/no square poet's job." Knight has forged his art from the experience he expresses. "No universal laws/Of human misery/Create a common cause/Or common history/That ease black people's pains/Nor break black people's chains." Latimore concludes: "Etheridge Knight's poetry is just that—poetry. And as such, it is art, and a living experience for the reader."

BIOGRAPHICAL/CRITICAL SOURCES: Negro Digest, January, 1968, July, 1968.

* * *

KNIGHT, Harold V(incent) 1907-

PERSONAL: Born March 16, 1907, in Cameron, Mo.; son of George Newton (a college professor) and Hope Veii (Smith) Knight; married Ruth Gallup, March 25, 1961. *Education:* Jamestown College, Jamestown, N.D., B.A., 1929; Brookwood Labor College, Katonah, N.Y., student, 1936-37. *Politics:* "Liberal Democrat, but dissenting and concerned." *Religion:* Methodist. *Home:* 1136 Emerson St., Denver, Colo. 80218.

CAREER: Stutsman County Record, Jamestown, N.D., reporter, 1930-36; North Dakota Farmers Union, Jamestown, N.D., editor, 1938-49; free-lance reporter on legislative matters, and author, 1950—. Executive director, American Civil Liberties Union of Colorado, 1954-63. *Member:* Authors Guild, American Civil Liberties Union, Americans for Democratic Action, American Friends Service Committee, United Cerebral Palsy Association, Fellowship of Reconciliation. *Awards, honors:* Cited as outstanding handicapped citizen of North Dakota by National Society for Crippled Children and Adults, 1949; Whitehead Award of American Civil Liberties Union, 1963.

WRITINGS: With Liberty and Justice for All: The Meaning of the Bill of Rights Today, Oceana, 1967; *Working in Colorado,* University of Colorado, 1971. Also author of *Handicapped Coloradoan,* 1968. Author of three book-length pamphlets published by National Farmers Union and North Dakota Farmers Union. Contributor to *Denver Post* and to magazines. Weekly columnist, "Statehouse Drama," 1952—; political columnist for labor, *Colorado Scene,* 1951-74.

WORK IN PROGRESS: An autobiography, *To Get Up, First Fall Down.*

SIDELIGHTS: Knight told *CA:* "My wife and I enjoy travel here and abroad, and all the creative arts which reveal the human spirit. As one cerebral palsied since birth, reaching maturity in a small college town during dustbowl and depression days, I suppose I naturally identify with the underdog, a rebel not without causes, but recognizing that no Utopia lies ahead—only a stumbling that somehow moves ahead."

*   *   *

KNIGHT, Oliver (Holmes) 1919-

PERSONAL: Born June 16, 1919, in Brownwood, Tex.; son of Oliver Holmes (a railroad telegrapher) and Kathleen (Egg) Knight. *Education:* University of Oklahoma, B.A. (with distinction), 1953, M.A., 1954; University of Wisconsin, Ph.D., 1959. *Politics:* Independent. *Religion:* Protestant. *Home:* 5125 Camino de la Vista, El Paso, Tex. 79932. *Office:* Department of History, University of Texas at El Paso, El Paso, Tex. 79999.

CAREER: Reporter in Longview, Tex., 1938, for Washington (D.C.) bureau of United Press, 1938-41, Washington (D.C.) bureau of *National Petroleum News,* 1941-43, and *Fort Worth Star-Telegram,* Fort Worth, Tex., 1946-51; University of Oklahoma Extension Division, Norman, news bureau writer, 1952-54; *Norman Transcript,* Norman, Okla., city editor, 1954; *Wisconsin State Journal,* Madison, Wis., copy editor, 1954; University of Wisconsin, Madison, news bureau writer, 1955-56, coordinator of public information, Extension Division, 1956-58; Indiana University, Bloomington, assistant professor of journalism, 1958-61; *Indianapolis News,* Indianapolis, Ind., copy editor, 1960; University of Wisconsin, visiting assistant professor, 1961-62, associate professor, 1962-66, professor of journalism, 1966-67; University of Texas at El Paso, professor of history, 1967—. *Military service:* U.S. Army, 1943-46; became captain.

MEMBER: American Historical Association, Organization of American Historians, Western History Association. *Awards, honors:* Frank Luther Mott Award for research in journalism, from Kappa Tau Alpha, for *I Protest: Selected Disquisitions of E. W. Scripps;* James L. Sellers Memorial Award, Nebraska State Historical Society, 1974; faculty research award, University of Texas at El Paso, 1975.

WRITINGS: Fort Worth: Outpost on the Trinity, University of Oklahoma Press, 1953; *Following the Indian Wars: The Story of the Newspaper Correspondents among the Indian Campaigners,* University of Oklahoma Press, 1960; (author of introduction) John F. Finerty, *War-Path and Bivouac,* University of Oklahoma Press, 1961; (author of foreword) James B. Gillett, *Six Years with the Texas Rangers,* Yale University Press, 1963; (editor) *I Protest: Selected Disquisitions of E. W. Scripps,* University of Wisconsin Press, 1966. Contributor to various history journals.

WORK IN PROGRESS: Aspects of the history of the American frontier.

*   *   *

KNOWLES, Joseph W(illiam) 1922-

PERSONAL: Born June 4, 1922, in Headland, Ala.; son of Orbit Earnest (a farmer) and Willie (Solomon) Knowles; married Elizabeth McNeil (a rehabilitation counselor); children: Katherine Louise. *Education:* Howard College (now Samford University), B.A., 1944; Southwestern Baptist Theological Seminary, Th.M., 1947; Southern Baptist Theological Seminary, B.D. and Th.D., 1954. *Politics:* Democrat.

CAREER: Baptist clergyman. Minister in Wellington, Ala., 1942-44, Fort Worth, Tex., 1945-57, Patriot, Ind., 1947-48; Central State Hospital, Lakeland, Ky., chaplain supervisor, 1948-54; Los Angeles City Mission Society, Los Angeles, Calif., director of department of counseling, 1954-57; Texas Medical Center, Institute of Religion, Houston, Tex., professor, 1957-62; Church of the Saviour, Washington, D.C., director of renewal center, 1962—. *Member:* American Association of Marriage Counselors, American Association of Pastoral Counselors, American Association for Clinical Pastoral Education.

WRITINGS: Group Counseling, Prentice-Hall, 1964; (contributor) John L. Casteel, editor, *The Creative Role of Interpersonal Groups in the Church Today,* Association Press, 1968.

WORK IN PROGRESS: A book on anxiety and fear to be used by ministers in counseling.††

*   *   *

KOCHEN, Manfred 1928-

PERSONAL: Born July 4, 1928, in Vienna, Austria; son of Max (a businessman) and Pepi (Figur) Kochen; married Paula Landerer, August 15, 1954; children: David J., Mark N. *Education:* Massachusetts Institute of Technology, B.S., 1950; Columbia University, M.A., 1951, Ph.D., 1955. *Politics:* Democrat. *Religion:* Jewish. *Home:* 2026 Devonshire, Ann Arbor, Mich. 48104. *Office:* University of Michigan, MHRI, Ann Arbor, Mich. 48104.

CAREER: Institute for Advanced Study, Princeton, N.J., staff, 1953-55; International Business Machines, researcher at Thomas J. Watson Research Center, Yorktown Heights, N.Y., 1956-60, manager of information retrieval, 1960-64; University of Michigan, Ann Arbor, professor of information science at Medical School, professor of urban/regional planning, and research mathematician, 1965—. Visiting expert at Euratom, Ispra, Italy. Member of survey team on automation for Library of Congress. Consultant to Radio Corporation of America and United Aircraft Systems Center, 1965—, RAND Corp., 1968—, and Smithsonian Institution. National lecturer for Association for Computing Machines, 1967.

MEMBER: American Mathematical Society, American Physical Society, Society for Industrial and Applied Mathematics, Art Students League of New York (life member). *Awards, honors:* Ford Foundation fellow, Harvard University, 1955-56; American Society for Information Sciences, distinguished lecturer, 1968, award of merit, 1974.

WRITINGS: (With G. W. King) *Automation and the Library of Congress,* United States Government Printing Office, 1963; *Some Problems in Information Science,* Scarecrow, 1965; (editor) *The Growth of Knowledge: Selected Readings on Organization and Retrieval of Information,* Wiley, 1967; *Principles of Information Retrieval,* Wiley, 1974; *Integrative Mechanisms in Literature Growth,* Greenwood Press, 1974; (editor) *Information for Action: From Knowledge to Wisdom,* Academic Press, 1975; (editor with J. Donohue) *Information for the Community,* American Library Association, 1975; (with K. W. Deutsch) *Toward a Theory of Decentralization,* Harvard University Press, 1976. Contributor to society proceedings and annuals, and to professional journals. Associate editor, *Behavioral Science,* and *International Association for Computer Machines.*

WORK IN PROGRESS: Social Contact Nets, in collaboration with I. de Sola Pool; *Cognitive Mechanisms.*

SIDELIGHTS: Manfred Kochen is fluent in German, French, and Italian, and has reading knowledge of Hebrew and Russian. *Avocational interests:* Painting, sculpture, and sports.

* * *

KOENIG, Allen Edward 1939-

PERSONAL: Born February 11, 1939, in Los Angeles, Calif.; son of Edward Francis (a civil engineer) and Eva Barnes) Koenig. *Education:* University of Southern California, A.B., 1961; Stanford University, A.M., 1962; Northwestern University, Ph.D., 1964. *Office:* Capital University, Columbus, Ohio 43209.

CAREER: Radio Station KFAC, Los Angeles, Calif., news editor, 1959-61; KPIX Television, San Francisco, Calif., editorial writer, 1962; Eastern Michigan University, Ypsilanti, assistant professor and director of broadcasting education, department of speech and dramatic arts, 1964-65; University of Wisconsin, Milwaukee, assistant professor of speech, 1965-67; Ohio State University, Columbus, assistant professor of speech, 1967-69; director of communications, American Association of University Professors, 1969-70; Capital University, Columbus, Ohio, vice-president of university relations, 1970—. Consultant, WTMJ Television, Milwaukee, Wis., 1965-67. *Member:* Association for Professional Broadcasting Education, Department of Audiovisual Instruction, National Association of Education Broadcasters, University Film Association, Alpha Epsilon Rho, Alpha Kappa Delta. *Awards, honors:* Broadcast Preceptor Award from Broadcast Industry Conference, 1969, and San Francisco State University, 1971.

WRITINGS: (Senior editor) *The Farther Vision: Educational Television Today,* University of Wisconsin Press, 1967; (editor) *Broadcasting and Bargaining: Labor Relations in Radio and Television,* University of Wisconsin Press, 1970. Contributor to broadcasting journals. Editor, *Educational Broadcasting Review,* 1967-69.†

* * *

KOENIG, C(lyde) Eldo 1919-

PERSONAL: Born October 17, 1919, in Marissa, Ill.; son of Herman C. (a farmer) and Clara (Spleth) Koenig; married Gloria J. Houting, February 4, 1950; children: Lloyd W., Evan F., Eva L., Beth E. *Education:* Washington University, St. Louis, Mo., B.S.E.E., 1943; Illinois Institute of Technology, M.S.E.E., 1949; University of Wisconsin, M.S.E., 1951, Ph.D., 1956. *Religion:* Lutheran. *Home:* 2748 Kendall Ave., Madison, Wis. 53705. *Office:* Department of Computer Science, University of Wisconsin, Madison, Wis. 53706.

CAREER: Allis-Chalmers Manufacturing Co., Milwaukee, Wis., design engineer, 1943-52, director of computing operations, 1954-62; University of Wisconsin, Madison, associate professor of numerical analysis, 1962-63, associate professor of computer science, 1963-66, associate professor of instructional research and associate director of synnoetics laboratory, 1966-71, associate professor of computer science, 1971—. *Member:* Society for Industrial and Applied Mathematics, American Institute of Electrical and Electronics Engineers, Association for Computing Machinery, American Association for the Advancement of Science, Sigma Xi, Tau Beta Pi, Eta Kappa Nu.

WRITINGS: (With Charles H. Davidson) *Computers,* Wiley, 1967.

WORK IN PROGRESS: Research on intelligence systems.

* * *

KOGINOS, Manny T. 1933-

PERSONAL: Surname is pronounced Ka-gee-nus; born March 12, 1933, in New Castle, Pa.; son of Andrew and Katherine (Keneklis) Koginos. *Education:* Bowling Green State University, B.A., 1954; American University, M.A., 1960, Ph.D., 1965. *Office:* Department of History, State University of New York College at Buffalo, 1300 Elmwood Ave., Buffalo, N.Y. 14222.

CAREER: New Castle News, New Castle, Pa., reporter, 1957-58; Library of Congress, Washington, D.C., research assistant, 1959-60; Ohio Wesleyan University, Delaware, instructor in history, 1964-65; Purdue University, Lafayette, Ind., assistant professor of history, 1965-67; State University of New York College at Buffalo, associate professor of history, 1967—. Assistant professor, University of Delaware, summer, 1966; American University, assistant professor, summer, 1967, associate professor, summer, 1968; visiting professor, University of Manchester, 1971-72. *Military service:* U.S. Army, 1955-57; became first lieutenant. *Member:* American Historical Association, Organization of American Historians, Society of American Historians of American Foreign Relations, Western Historical Association of American-Far Eastern and American-Japanese Relations, American Association of University Professors, Phi Alpha Theta. *Awards, honors:* New York State grant-in-aid, 1968.

WRITINGS: The Panay Incident: Prelude to War, Purdue University Studies, 1967.

WORK IN PROGRESS: Illusion and Reality: America in the Far East, 1919-1941.

SIDELIGHTS: Manny Koginos is competent in German, French, Greek, and Japanese. *Avocational interests:* Skiing, tennis.

* * *

KOHLER, Heinz 1934-

PERSONAL: Born August 19, 1934, in Berlin, Germany; son of Arthur Oskar (a salesman) and Gertrud Anna (Forster) Kohler; married Mary Elaine Schmiege, June 4, 1955; children: Marjorie Ann, Victoria Rose. *Education:* Free University of Berlin, B.A. equivalent, 1956; University of Michigan, M.A., 1958, Ph.D., 1961. *Home:* 278 Middle St., Amherst, Mass. 01002. *Office:* Department of Economics, Amherst College, Amherst, Mass. 01002.

CAREER: Amherst College, Amherst, Mass., assistant professor, 1961-64, associate professor, 1964-69, professor of economics, 1969—, chairman of economics department, 1963-64, 1970-71. Visiting professor at University of Massachusetts, Mount Holyoke College, and Smith College. *Member:* American Economic Association, Aircraft Owners and Pilots Association. *Awards, honors:* American Council of Learned Societies Slavic fellow, 1962; Ford Foundation Asian studies fellow, 1967; M.A., Amherst College, 1969; National Science Foundation faculty fellow, 1974-75.

WRITINGS: Economic Integration in the Soviet Bloc, with an East German Case Study, Praeger, 1965; *Welfare and Planning: An Analysis of Capitalism versus Socialism,* Wiley, 1966; *Scarcity Challenged: An Introduction to Economics,* with Study Guide and Instructor's Manual, Holt, 1968; (editor) *Readings in Economics,* Holt, 1968, revised edition, 1969; *Economics: The Science of Scarcity,* with programmed Study Guide and Instructor's Manual, Dryden, 1970; *What Economics Is All About,* Dryden, 1972; *Economics and Urban Problems,* Heath, 1973; *Scarcity and Freedom,* Heath, in press. Contributor to economics journals.

AVOCATIONAL INTERESTS: Flying airplanes.

*   *   *

KOLB, Ken(neth) 1926-

PERSONAL: Born July 14, 1926, in Portland, Ore.; son of Fred (a railroad brakeman) and Ella (Bay) Kolb; married Emma Sanford, June 7, 1952; children: Kevin, Lauren, Kimrie. *Education:* University of California, Berkeley, B.A. (cum laude), 1950; San Francisco State College (now San Francisco State University), M.A., 1953. *Politics:* Peacenik. *Religion:* Universalist. *Home address:* Box 22, Cromberg, Calif. 96103. *Agent:* Scott Meredith Literary Agency, 580 Fifth Ave., New York, N.Y. 10036; (for screen and TV) Adams, Ray and Rosenberg, 9220 Sunset Blvd., Los Angeles, Calif. 90069.

CAREER: Free-lance writer of magazine fiction, 1950-56; free-lance television writer, 1956—, with credits for more than one-hundred plays. Fire lookout with U.S. Forest Service, 1954, 1955. *Military service:* U.S. Navy, 1944-46; served at sea aboard U.S.S. "Sicily." *Member:* Writers Guild of America, Mensa, Phi Beta Kappa. *Awards, honors:* Writers Guild of America award, 1956, for best half-hour television drama.

WRITINGS: Getting Straight (novel), Chilton, 1967; *The Couch Trip* (novel), Random House, 1970; *Night Crossing* (novel), Playboy Press, 1974. Television play, "She Walks in Beauty," included in *Prize Plays of Television,* 1956, Random House, 1957, and *A Variety of Short Plays,* Scribner, 1966. Author of motion picture script, "Seventh Voyage of Sinbad," Columbia Pictures, 1958. More than thirty short stories published in magazines.

WORK IN PROGRESS: A new novel, as yet untitled.

SIDELIGHTS: Kolb's motivation to write includes "a hatred of boring, routine work, . . . a love of freedom, travel, money." Travels with his family include trips to Tahiti, New Zealand, Fiji, Hawaii, Jamaica, and Mexico. *Getting Straight* was made into a motion picture with the same title, Columbia, 1970.

*   *   *

KOLTUN, Frances (Lang)

PERSONAL: Born in New York, N.Y.; daughter of Samuel and Rebecca (Lang) Koltun. *Education:* Brooklyn College (now Brooklyn College of the City University of New York), B.A. (magna cum laude); Columbia University, M.A. *Home:* 45 East 66th St., New York, N.Y. 10021.

CAREER: Employed in New York City, by Abraham & Strauss, 1939-45, and by U.S. Government, 1945-46; *American Girl,* New York City, fashion merchandise editor, 1946-50; *Charm,* New York City, fashion merchandise editor, 1950-55, travel and vacation editor, 1955-59; *Mademoiselle,* New York City, travel editor, 1959—; broadcaster of syndicated radio program for Air Transport Association of America. Member of advisory committee, U.S. Travel Service; lecturer at New York University and Fordham University. *Member:* American Society of Travel Agents, International Union of Official Travel Organizations, Discover America Travel Organizations, Society of American Travel Writers, Travel Writers of New York (first woman president), Propylea.

WRITINGS: Frances Koltun's Complete Book for the Intelligent Woman Traveler, Simon & Schuster, 1967. Author of syndicated column, "The Woman Traveler." Contributor to *Christian Science Monitor, Reader's Digest, Ladies Home Journal, Holiday,* and other periodicals.

SIDELIGHTS: Since travel is Miss Koltun's profession, she often logs as many as 95,000 miles in one year. She has served on numerous international travel committees and has talked on travel at the White House.

*   *   *

KONADU, S(amuel) A(sare) 1932-
(Asare Konadu; pseudonyms: Bediako Asare, K. A. Bediako)

PERSONAL: Born January 18, 1932, in Asamang, Ghana; son of Kofi (a farmer) and Abena (Anowuo) Konadu; married Alice Dede, February 26, 1958; children: Samuel Asare, Jr., Cecilia, Lucy. *Education:* Attended Abuakwa State College, Kibi, Ghana, 1948-51, The Polytechnic, London, England, 1956-58, and University of Strasbourg, 1958. *Religion:* Seventh-day Adventist. *Home:* 100 Aburaso St., Asamang, Ashanti, Ghana. *Office address:* 2R McCarthy Hill, Box 3918, Accra, Ghana.

CAREER: Ghana Information Services, Accra, junior reporter, 1952-56, journalist, 1956-58; Ghana News Agency, Accra, editor, 1958-60, chief editor, 1961-63; full-time writer, 1963—. Anowuo Educational Publishers, Accra, publisher and director. *Member:* Ghana Writers Club, Ghana Journalists Association. *Awards, honors:* University of Strasbourg fellowship for research in history of the Ghanaian press, 1959.

WRITINGS—Published variously under above listed names and pseudonyms: *Wizard of Asamang,* Waterville Publishing, 1962; *Shadow of Wealth,* Anowuo Educational Publishers, 1966; *Don't Leave Me Mercy,* Anowuo Educational Publishers, 1966; *Night Watchers of Korlebu,* Anowuo Educational Publishers, 1967, Humanities Press, 1969; *A Husband for Esi Ellua,* Anowuo Educational Publishers, 1967, Humanities Press, 1969; *A Woman in Her Prime,* Heinemann, 1967, Humanities Press, 1969; *Ordained by the Oracle,* Heinemann, 1968, Humanities Press, 1969; *Come Back Dora,* Humanities Press, 1969.

WORK IN PROGRESS: Research into traditional healing and Ghanaian customs.

SIDELIGHTS: In 1961 Konadu toured the Soviet Union with Kwame Nkrumah, ex-president of Ghana, visiting all of its states. He traveled in Europe in 1958 and 1962, and in the Congo, Rwanda, and Burundi, 1963. In 1968 Konadu was the guest of the U.S. State Department and spent ninety days on a publishing tour of eleven states.

*   *   *

KONCZACKI, Zbigniew Andrzej 1917-

PERSONAL: Surname is pronounced Kon-*chat*-ski; born March 10, 1917, in Lwow, Poland; son of Andrzej Adam (a physician) and Romana (Kawecka) Konczacki; married Janina Maria Waydowicz (a historian), July 3, 1952. *Educa-*

tion: Studied at Academy of Foreign Trade, Lwow, Poland, 1935-39, and University of Rome, 1946; University of London, B.Sc., 1951, Ph.D., 1964; University of Natal, B.Econ. (honors), 1957. *Home:* 27 Briarwood Crescent, Clayton Park, Halifax, Nova Scotia, Canada. *Office:* Department of Economics, Dalhousie University, Halifax, Nova Scotia, Canada.

CAREER: University of Alberta, Edmonton, associate professor of economics, 1963-67; Dalhousie University, Halifax, Nova Scotia, senior research fellow, 1967, professor of economics, 1968—. Economic adviser to Somali Republic, 1965. *Military service:* British Army, Polish Corps, World War II; served with 8th Army in Italian Campaign. *Member:* Canadian Economics Association, Canadian Association of African Studies, Canadian Committee on African Studies (vice-president, 1965-66), Royal Economic Society (England). *Awards, honors:* I. W. Killam senior research fellowship, 1967-68.

WRITINGS: Public Finance and Economic Development of Natal, 1893-1910, Duke University Press, 1967; (contributor) S. Chandrasekhar and C. W. Hultman, editors, *Problems of Economic Development,* Heath, 1967; (contributor) G. Maasdorp and A. S. B. Humphreys, editors, *From Shantytown to Township,* Juta & Co., 1975. Contributor to learned journals.

WORK IN PROGRESS: Problems of Pastoralism in Developing African Countries; Economic History of Sub-Saharan Africa.

SIDELIGHTS: Zbigniew Konczacki is competent in French and Italian. He has traveled extensively in South Africa, Zambia, Rhodesia, Somalia, the Near East, Middle East, Europe, Mexico, and the United States.

* * *

KONIGSBERG, Conrad Isidore 1916-

PERSONAL: Born March 7, 1916, in London, England; son of Herrschl and Eva (Bederova) Konigsberg; married Hildegard Schnitzler, March 25, 1948. *Education:* University College, London, B.A. (honors), 1937; Birkbeck College, London, M.A., 1954, Ph.D., 1959. *Home:* 97 Balmoral Rd., Harrow, Middlesex, England.

CAREER: Little Ealing School, England, deputy head master, 1959-60; Samuel Pepys School, London, England, head of English department, 1960-66; Wood Green School, head of modern languages, 1966-68; Tottenham School, Tottenham, England, head of department of modern languages, 1968—. *Military service:* International Brigade, fought with Fifty-seventh British Battalion on the side of Spanish Republic during Civil War in Spain. British Army, 1939-46; served with Rifle Brigade and Intelligence Corps; wounded in Western desert (Africa), 1941. *Member:* Society of Authors. *Awards, honors:* Peter Floud Memorial Prize of William Morris Society.

WRITINGS: (With J. Klavins) *Exercises in Oral Russian,* Harrap, 1964; (with A. Servel) *Voix francaises,* Leonard Hill, 1967; *Deutsche Stimmen,* Leonard Hill, 1968; *Ferien mit Schuss,* Cambridge University Press, 1969; *Pierre en Forme,* Cambridge University Press, 1969; (with Servel) *C'est la vie,* Macmillan, 1972. Contributor to *Adam, Catholic Herald, Tablet, Jewish Chronicle, Times Educational Supplement, Modern Language Quarterly, Modern Language Review, Der Roller, Book Collector,* and other periodicals.

KONIGSBURG, E(laine) L(obl) 1930-

PERSONAL: Born February 10, 1930, in New York, N.Y.; daughter of Adolph (a businessman) and Beulah (Klein) Lobl; married David Konigsburg (a psychologist), July 6, 1952; children: Paul, Laurie, Ross. *Education:* Carnegie Institute of Technology (now Carnegie-Mellon University), B.S., 1952; University of Pittsburgh, graduate study, 1952-54. *Religion:* Jewish. *Residence:* Jacksonville, Fla. 32217.

CAREER: Shenago Valley Provision Co., Sharon, Pa., bookkeeper, 1947-48; Bartram School, Jacksonville, Fla., science teacher, 1954-55, 1960-62. *Awards, honors: Jennifer, Hecate, Macbeth, William McKinley, and Me, Elizabeth* was chosen as an honor book in *Book Week* Children's Spring Book Festival, 1967; Newbery Medal, 1968, for *From the Mixed-Up Files of Mrs. Basil E. Frankweiler;* Newbery Honor Book, 1968, for *Jennifer, Hecate, Macbeth, William McKinley, and Me, Elizabeth;* William Allen White Award, 1970, for *From the Mixed-Up Files of Mrs. Basil E. Frankweiler;* Carnegie-Mellon Merit Award, 1971; American Library Association notable book, 1974, for *A Proud Taste for Scarlet and Miniver;* National Book Award nominee, 1974, for *A Proud Taste for Scarlet and Miniver.*

WRITINGS—All juveniles; all self-illustrated, except as noted; all published by Atheneum: *Jenifer, Hecate, Macbeth, William McKinley, and Me, Elizabeth,* 1967; *From the Mixed-Up Files of Mrs. Basil E. Frankweiler,* 1967; *About the B'nai Bagels,* 1969; *(George),* 1970; *Altogether, One at a Time,* illustrated by Gail E. Haley, Mercer Meyer, Gary Parker, and Laurel Schindelman, 1971; *A Proud Taste for Scarlet and Miniver,* 1973; *The Dragon in the Ghetto Caper,* 1974; *The Second Mrs. Giaconda,* illustrated with museum plates, 1975.

BIOGRAPHICAL/CRITICAL SOURCES: Horn Book, August, 1968, December, 1970, August, 1971; *Saturday Review,* November 9, 1968; *Chicago Tribune Children's Book World,* November 8, 1970; Ann Block and Carolyn Riley, editors, *Children's Literature Review,* Volume I, Gale, 1976.

* * *

KOSCHADE, Alfred 1928-

PERSONAL: Born December 22, 1928, in Finschhafen, New Guinea; son of Victor (a lay missionary from Australia) and Ida (an American deaconess-nurse from Iowa; maiden name, Voss) Koschade; married B. Beatrice Weiland (a part-time pharmacist), December 5, 1951; children: Miriam, Marcia, Mark, Ernest, Esther. *Education:* Studied in Adelaide, South Australia, at Immanuel College, 1942-45, and Immanuel Theological Seminary, 1946-49; Luther Theological Seminary, St. Paul, Minn., M.Th., 1964; Lutheran School of Theology, Chicago, Ill., summer graduate study, 1965, 1966; Northwestern Lutheran Theological Seminary, St. Paul, Minn., S.T.M., 1973. *Home:* 201 Spruce Ave. W., Montgomery, Minn. 56069.

CAREER: Lutheran clergyman. Served in New Guinea at Hopoi Teachers Training School, 1950-52, and then in Kaiapit, Mumeng, and the Kapau River area, 1952-56; organized congregations among the native laborers in a number of New Guinea industrial centers, 1956; toured and lectured in Australia, 1957; pastor of congregations at Maple Leaf and Clinton, Iowa, 1957-62; St. John's Lutheran Church, Montgomery, Minn., pastor, 1962—

WRITINGS: New Branches on the Vine, Augsburg, 1967; *The Cost of Bread and Wine,* Graphic Publishing, 1974. Also writer of church materials in the Jabem and Neo-Melanesian languages.

WORK IN PROGRESS: New Guinea Nurse.

* * *

KOVACS, Imre 1913-

PERSONAL: Born March 10, 1913, in Hungary; son of Imre and Carola (Kek) Kovacs; married Edna Harvey Campbell; children: Andrea. *Education:* University of Economics (now Karl Marx University of Economics), Budapest, Hungary, student, 1932-37. *Religion:* Calvinist. *Home:* 99-05 63rd Dr., Rego Park, N.Y. 11374. *Agent:* Greenburger Associates, 757 Third Ave., New York, N.Y. 10017.

CAREER: Author. Hungarian National Peasant Party, Budapest, secretary-general, 1939-46; Hungarian Parliament, Budapest, member, 1945-47; International Center for Social Research, Inc., New York City, president, 1962-63; Free Europe, Inc., New York City, senior editor of publications and special projects, 1963—. *Member:* International P.E.N.

WRITINGS: A Nema Forradalom (title means "The Silent Revolution"), Cserepfalvi, 1937; *Kivandorlas* (title means "Emigration"), Cserepfalvi, 1938; *Kolonto* (novel), Cserepfalvi, 1939; *A Paraszteletforma Csodje* (about the bankruptcy of the traditional way of life of the peasantry), Bolyai Akademia, 1940; *Magyar Feudalizmus-Magyar Parasztsag* (title means "Hungarian Feudalism—Hungarian Peasantry"), Cserepfalvi, 1941; *Szovjet-Oroszorszag Agrarpolitikaja* (title means "The Agricultural Policy of the U.S.S.R."), Cserepfalvi, 1943; *Elsullyedt Orszag* (title means "The Sunken Country"), Cserepfalvi, 1945; *Agrarpolitikai Feladatok* (on Hungarian agrarian problems), Misztotfalusi, 1946; *Im Schatten der Sowjets* (title means "In the Shadow of the Soviets"), Thomas Verlag (Zurich), 1948; *D'une occupation a l'autre: La Tragedie Hongroise* (title means "From One Occupation to Another: The Tragedy of Hungary"), Calmann-Levy (Paris), 1949; *The Ninety and Nine* (novel), Funk, 1955; (editor) *Facts About Hungary,* Hungarian Committee (New York), 1958, 3rd edition, 1966. Contributing editor, *Uj Latohatar* (literary and political review published in Munich).

* * *

KRADER, Lawrence 1919-

PERSONAL: Born December 8, 1919, in New York, N.Y.; married Barbara Ann Lattimer, May 14, 1952. *Education:* City College (now City College of the City University of New York), B.A., 1941; Harvard University, graduate study, 1950-53, Ph.D., 1954. *Office:* Institute of Ethnology, Free University of Berlin, 1 Berlin 33, West Germany.

CAREER: University of Washington, Seattle, research associate, 1947-50; American University, Washington, D.C., lecturer and research associate, 1953-58, professor of anthropology, 1958-63; professor of anthropology at Ohio State University, Columbus, 1963-64, and Syracuse University, Syracuse, N.Y., 1964-67; City University of New York, New York, N.Y., professor of anthropology, beginning 1967; University of Waterloo, Waterloo, Ontario, chairman of department of sociology and anthropology, 1970-72; Free University of Berlin, Berlin, West Germany,

professor of ethnology, 1972—. Lecturer at University of Michigan, 1955, and Columbia University, 1956. Consultant to Peace Corps. Secretary-general of International Union of Anthropological and Ethnological Sciences. *Member:* American Anthropological Association (fellow), American Association for the Advancement of Science.

WRITINGS: Peoples of Central Asia, Indiana University Press, 1963, 3rd edition, 1971; *Social Organization of Mongols,* Mouton & Co., 1963; *Formation of the State,* Prentice-Hall, 1967; *Anthropology and Early Law,* Basic Books, 1967; (editor) *The Ethnological Notebooks of Karl Marx: Studies of Morgan, Phear, Maine, Lubbock,* Van Grocum, 1972. Also author of *Asiatic Mode of Production,* 1975, and *Dialectic of Civil Society,* 1976. Contributor to professional journals.

SIDELIGHTS: Lawrence Krader has traveled for research in Siberia, the Arctic, and in the deserts and arid zones of Asia. He is competent in French, German, and Russian.

* * *

KRAFT, Virginia 1932-

PERSONAL: Born February 19, 1932, in New York, N.Y.; daughter of George John and Jean (Gillis) Kraft; married Robert Dean Grimm, December 31, 1955 (divorced, 1972); children: Tana Aurland, Tara Kraft, Robert Dean, Jr., Jill Chisholm. *Education:* Barnard College, B.A., 1951; Columbia University, graduate study, 1951-52. *Politics:* Republican. *Religion:* Roman Catholic. *Home and office:* Gipsy Trail, Carmel, N.Y.

CAREER: Field and Stream, New York City, outdoors writer, 1952-54; *Sports Illustrated,* New York City, associate editor, 1954—. Trustee, Hunting Hall of Fame; director and founding trustee, International Wilderness Leadership Foundation; director, Safari Club International Conservation Fund. Sometime game hunter, has hunted on six continents with such prominent people as Franco of Spain, the Shah of Iran, and King Hussein of Jordan. *Member:* International Women's Fishing Association, Shikar-Safari Society, American Museum of Natural History, New York Zoological Society, African Safari Club of New York (vice-president), Alaska Sled-Dog Racing Association (honorary life member). *Awards, honors:* Headliner's Award, for contribution to sporting journalism; record class trophies in Alaska moose, grizzly bear, caribou, and Asian buffalo.

WRITINGS: The Compleat Book of Dog Training, Lippincott, 1960; (with Ezra Bowen) *The Book of Small Boat Sailing,* Lippincott, 1962; *The Book of Shotgun Shooting,* Lippincott, 1966; *The Book of Shotgun Sports,* Lippincott, 1966; *Tennis Instruction for Fun and Competition,* Grosset, 1976.

WORK IN PROGRESS: Hunting Around the World.

* * *

KRAMER, Aaron 1921-

PERSONAL: Born December 13, 1921, in Brooklyn, N.Y.; son of Hyman and Mary (Click) Kramer; married; two children. *Education:* Brooklyn College (now Brooklyn College of the City University of New York), B.A., 1941, M.A., 1951; New York University, Ph.D., 1966. *Politics:* Independent. *Home:* 96 Van Bomel Blvd., Oakdale, N.Y. 11769. *Agent:* John Payne, Lenniger Literary Agency, 437 5th Ave., New York, N.Y. 10016. *Office:* Department of English, Dowling College, Oakdale, N.Y. 11769.

CAREER: New York Guild for the Jewish Blind, New York, N.Y., lecturer, 1955-58, dramatics director, 1958-59; high school teacher of English, Bogota, N.J., 1959-61; Dowling College, Oakdale, N.Y., 1961—, began as instructor, associate professor, 1966-70, professor, 1970—, graduate professor of English, 1975. Lecturer in English, Queens College of the City University of New York, 1966-68; lecturer in Shakespearean studies, University of Guanajuato, 1974; guest poetry teacher at many schools and colleges. Originator and director of poetry therapy program, Hillside Hospital, Glen Oaks, N.Y., 1956-60; co-director of poetry therapy program, Cleary School for the Deaf, Ronkonkama, N.Y. and Central Islip State Hospital, 1969—. Producer of poetry programs on radio; judge of various Poetry Society of America contests, 1948-58; chairman of judges for Reynolds Lyric Award, 1956, and Arthur Davison Ficke Memorial Award, 1957; judge for Lyric (magazine) Awards, 1974.

MEMBER: Modern Language Association of America, American Society of Composers, Authors, and Publishers, American Association of University Professors, Association for Poetry Therapy. Awards, honors: Award for New York State Poetry Day prize poem, "Nocturne," 1953; Reynolds Lyric Award of Lyric (magazine), 1961, for "Forest Vapors"; Lyric (magazine) Award, 1967, for "Cadenza"; Virginia Prize of Lyric (magazine) and Hart Crane Memorial Award, 1969, for "A Hundred Planets"; annual American Society of Composers, Authors and Publishers awards, 1971-74; Outstanding Educators of America awards, 1971, 1972, 1974; All Nations Poetry Contest Awards, Triton College, 1975, for "For Three Days," "Wedding in Los Angeles," and "Grandparents in London." Musical works and a film incorporating his poetry have won several other prizes.

WRITINGS—Poetry: Another Fountain, privately printed, 1940; Till the Grass Is Ripe for Dancing, Harbinger House, 1943; Thru Our Guns, privately printed, 1945; The Glass Mountain, B. Ackerman, 1946; The Thunder of the Grass, International Publishers, 1948; The Golden Trumpet, International Publishers, 1949; Thru Every Window, William-Frederick, 1950; Denmark Vesey, privately printed, 1952; Roll the Forbidden Drums!, Cameron & Kahn, 1954; (with Saul Lishinsky) The Tune of the Calliope, Yoseloff, 1958; Moses, O'Hare Books, 1962; Rumshinsky's Hat, Yoseloff, 1964; Henry at the Grating, Folklore Center, 1968; On the Way to Palermo, A. S. Barnes, 1973.

Other books: (With others) Seven Poets in Search of an Answer, B. Ackerman, 1944; (translator with F. Ewen) The Poetry and Prose of Heinrich Heine, Citadel, 1948; (translator and editor) Morris Rosenfeld, The Teardrop Millionaire, Emma Lazarus Federation, 1955; (translator) Songs and Ballads: Goethe, Schiller, Heine, O'Hare Books, 1963; (translator with S. Mandel) Rilke, Visions of Christ, University of Colorado Press, 1967; The Prophetic Tradition in American Poetry: 1835-1900, Fairleigh Dickinson University Press, 1968; (with others) Poetry Therapy, Lippincott, 1969; (translator) Poems by Abraham Reisen, Dowling College Press, 1971; (editor) Melville's Poetry: Toward the Enlarged Heart, Fairleigh Dickinson University Press, 1972; (compiler) On Freedom's Side, Macmillan, 1972; (with others) Poetry the Healer, Lippincott, 1975.

Scripts: "When Every Tear is Turned to Stone," commissioned by United Nations Film Division, 1949; "Ballad of August Bondi," music by Serge Hovey, Brooklyn Academy of Music, 1955; "In Us Lives the Music," Carnegie Hall, 1956; "A Garland of Music," New York Town Hall, 1957; "The Tinderbox," music by Tristram Cary, British Broadcasting Corp., 1957; (with others) "An Autumn Sequence," music by Donald Swann, British Broadcasting Corp., 1970; "Chelm," music by Eugene Glickman, Garden City Cathedral, 1970; "Neglected Poems of Herman Melville," British Broadcasting Corp., 1973; (translation) "The Emperor of Atlantis," music by Viktor Ullmann, 1975.

Reader of his own and other works for "Serenade," a Folkways album and "On Freedom's Side: The Songs and Poems of Aaron Kramer," a Freneau album. Poems have been used as texts by many composers and choreographers. Work anthologized in From Goethe to Ibsen, Poems of the United Nations, The Jews in the United States, Lift Every Voice, Treasury of Jewish Poetry, and other collections. Contributor to journals and newspapers, including Carleton Miscellany, Massachusetts Review, Prairie Schooner, San Francisco Review, Midstream, Mediterranean Review, Modern Poetry Studies, Journal of Humanistic Psychology, Denver Quarterly, New York Times, and Poetry Northwest; former staff contributor to Harlem Quarterly, Sing Out, and Village Voice.

WORK IN PROGRESS: A new volume of poems, Carousel Parkway; an opera, "The Cross and the Arrow," music by Eugene Glickman; translating and editing The Poems of Ingeborg Bachmann, with S. Mandel; Poetry the Mind Mender, with others.

*   *   *

KRAMER, (Simon) Paul 1914-

PERSONAL: Born August 17, 1914, in Cincinnati, Ohio; son of Simon Pendleton (a physician) and Minnie (Halle) Kramer; married Marie Louise Belden, January 15, 1955; children: Theresa. Education: Princeton University, B.A., 1935; Trinity College, Cambridge, M.Litt., 1938. Agent: Toni Mendez, Inc., 140 East 56th St., New York, N.Y. 10022. Office: 1346 Connecticut Ave. N.W., Washington, D.C. 20036.

CAREER: U.S. Government, Washington, D.C., special assistant to Coordinator of Inter-American Affairs, 1940-43, staff of Central Intelligence Agency, 1947-51; Brookings Institution, Washington, D.C., researcher, 1952-53; Auerbach, Pollak & Richardson, New York, N.Y., member of New York Stock Exchange and partner, 1954-57; Corporacion Industrial (Panama Cooperative Fisheries), Panama, president and director, 1955-60. National Academy of Sciences, member of secretariat, U.S. National Committee, International Geophysical Year, 1956-57, consultant, 1960-62. Member of board of directors, District of Columbia Social Hygiene Society, and delegate to D.C. Health and Welfare Council. Military service: U.S. Navy, Intelligence, 1943-46; became lieutenant.

WRITINGS: (Editor) Ch'ing Hsuan-t'ung, The Last Manchu Autobiography, translation by Kuo Ying Paul Tsai, Putnam, 1967; (editor with Robert E. McNicoll, and contributor) Latin American Panorama, Putnam, 1968; (editor with F. Holborn, and contributor) The City in American Life: A Historical Anthology, Putnam, 1970. Contributor to Journal of Inter-American Studies and yearbook of National Council for Social Studies.

SIDELIGHTS: Ch'ing Hsuan-t'ung's autobiography was first published in Peking in 1964. The shortened English version edited, with introduction and epilogue, by Kramer also has been published in England, France, Spain, and Italy.

*   *   *

KRANZBERG, Melvin 1917-

PERSONAL: Born November 22, 1917, in St. Louis, Mo.; son of Samuel (a businessman) and Rose (Fitter) Kranzberg; married Nancy Lee Fox, 1943 (divorced, 1955); married second wife, Eva Mannering, 1956; married third wife, Adelaide H. Waltz, 1962; married Dolores Campen, 1972; children: (first marriage) Steven J., John F. *Education:* Amherst College, A.B., 1938; Harvard University, M.A., 1939, Ph.D., 1942; graduate study at several other universities, including University of Paris, 1945. *Home:* 4850 Kendall Ct. N.E., Atlanta, Ga. 30342. *Office:* Georgia Institute of Technology, Atlanta, Ga. 30332.

CAREER: U.S. Office of Price Administration, Washington, D.C., administrative assistant, 1942; Harvard University, Cambridge, Mass., instructor in history, 1946; Stevens Institute of Technology, Hoboken, N.J., instructor in history, 1946-47; Amherst College, Amherst, Mass., assistant professor of history, 1947-52; Case Institute of Technology (now Case Western Reserve University), Cleveland, Ohio, associate professor, 1952-59, professor of history, 1959-72; Georgia Institute of Technology, Atlanta, Callaway Professor of the History of Technology, 1972—. Sigma Xi, national lecturer, 1966-67, bicentennial lecturer, 1974-75; Harris lecturer, Northwestern University, 1970; Mellon lecturer, Lehigh University, 1975. *Military service:* U.S. Army, Military Intelligence, 1943-46; became master sergeant; received Bronze Star Medal, Combat Infantry Badge, and three battle stars.

MEMBER: Society for the History of Technology (secretary, 1959—), American Association for the Advancement of Science (vice-president, 1966), American Society for Engineering Education (chairman of humanistic-social division, 1957), Society for French Historical Studies (vice-president, 1959), Sigma Xi (member of national board of directors, 1970—). *Awards, honors:* L.H.D., Denison University, 1967; Leonardo da Vinci Medal of Society for the History of Technology, 1967; Litt.D., from Newark College of Engineering (now New Jersey Institute of Technology), 1968, and Northern Michigan University, 1972.

WRITINGS: The Siege of Paris, 1870-71, Cornell University Press, 1951; (editor) *1848: A Turning Point?,* Heath, 1959; (editor with Carroll W. Pursell, Jr.) *Technology in Western Civilization,* two volumes, Oxford University Press, 1967; (editor with William H. Davenport) *Technology and Culture: An Anthology,* Schocken, 1972; (with Joseph Geis) *By the Sweat of Thy Brow: Work in the Western World,* Putnam, 1975. Contributor to encyclopedias and professional journals. Editor, *Technology and Culture.*

WORK IN PROGRESS: Research on innovations, and technology-society relations.

*   *   *

KRASSNER, Paul 1932-

PERSONAL: Born April 9, 1932; son of Michael E. (a printer) and Ida (Garlock) Krassner; married Jeanne Johnson, June 30, 1963 (separated); children: Holly. *Education:* Attended City College of New York (now City College of the City University of New York) for four years. *Politics:* "Independent Dupe." *Religion:* Atheist.

CAREER: Was a free-lance writer for *Mad* Magazine and "The Steve Allen Show," and a nightclub comedian; *The Independent* (newspaper), New York City, managing editor, 1954-58; *The Realist* (magazine), New York City, founder, 1958, and editor, 1958—. Founder, Youth International Party (Yippie), 1967. Member of faculty, Free University, New York City. Member of Board, Lower Eastside Action Project, and Parents Aid Society. Ordained minister, Universal Life Church. *Member:* American Civil Liberties Union.

WRITINGS: Impolite Interviews, Lyle Stuart, 1961; (author of introduction) *R. Crumb's Head Comix,* Viking, 1968; *How a Satirical Editor Became a Yippie Conspirator in Ten Easy Years,* Putnam, 1971. Wrote a hippie version of the Book of Job for the film, "Seven Deadly Virtues." Society editor, *Ramparts;* film critic, *Cavalier.*

WORK IN PROGRESS: A novel.

SIDELIGHTS: There is general agreement on the statement, once made by *Books,* that Krassner, editor of the country's most popular underground newspaper, "is rapidly becoming America's best-known iconoclast and, to many, a humorist who will fill the void left by Lenny Bruce's death." Bruce, Krassner's idol, "was part of everything he indicted," says Krassner, as indeed *The Realist* is. Krassner refuses to sell *The Realist,* which he founded with about $2,000, to any corporation, discouraging interested parties by showing them his most offensive issues.

Perhaps *the* most offensive issue of this irregularly published paper carried the sections allegedly left out of William Manchester's *The Death of a President.* It was also the most popular issue, and, most incredibly, a great many readers believed *The Realist's* account. Why did Krassner publish it? "I got sort of a perverse satisfaction from getting subscription cancellations because you know you're still hitting raw nerves," he says. "And we just got a letter from someone saying, 'I didn't think the Manchester stuff was so bad, but this! Cancel my subscription!' And he circles the part about making fun of the humane slaughter of Jews." The Manchester story was simply another put-on with a purpose. These put-ons are so common with *The Realist* that a competing magazine, striving for a similar tone, once ran Krassner's obituary.

Krassner describes *The Realist* as a magazine of "free thought, criticism, and satire." It has been, he adds, "a personal chronology of the things I've been involved in: war protest, censorship, obscenity, psychedelics, and the stage it's currently at is revolution, more or less. But it's grown and changed because it's an extension of my personality which has grown and changed." He insists that he is not a crusader: "I just want to do it. . . . The theory comes after the practice."

Krassner told John Stickney: "If I had one thing to tell everybody, it would be: do it now. Take up music, read a book, proposition a girl—but do it now. We know we are all sentenced to death. People cannot become prisoners of guilts and fears. They should cling to each moment and take what enjoyment they can from it. I do not mean reckless, hedonistic pleasure. There just should not be a dichotomy between doing and being, spirit and flesh, pleasure and principles, work and play, orgasm and love."

"I read *The Realist,*" Paul's father told *Books,* "but I don't subscribe. Paul sends it to us. I don't understand it. All those big words. And I think he goes too far. Why is it necessary to use so many four-letter words? We never cursed in this house." His mother, who relates how her son the violinist, at the age of six, was the youngest soloist to ever play at Carnegie Hall, doesn't read *The Realist*, but she tolerantly admits that Paul "was always a nonconformist. Even when he was a tiny baby he would stand in the play pen on our lawn and grunt at the kids on their way to school."

BIOGRAPHICAL/CRITICAL SOURCES: *Books*, April, 1967, February, 1968; *Fifth Estate*, February 15, 1968; *Avant Garde*, May, 1968; *Life*, July, 1968; *Chicago Literary Review*, January, 1969; *Saturday Night*, July, 1969.†

* * *

KRAUS, W. Keith 1934-

PERSONAL: Born April 11, 1934, in Oscoda, Mich.; son of W. A. (an educational representative for *Reader's Digest*) and Margaret (Eby) Kraus; married Loretta Mase, September 15, 1956; children: Linda, David, Stephen. *Education:* Eastern Michigan University, B.A., 1957, M.A., 1963; Southern Illinois University, Ph.D., 1974. *Politics:* "Vaguely Democratic." *Religion:* Episcopalian. *Home:* R.D. 2, Shippensburg, Pa. 17257. *Office:* Department of English, Shippensburg State College, Shippensburg, Pa. 17257.

CAREER: Teacher of English in Michigan high schools and at State College of Iowa, Cedar Falls, between 1958-63; Shippensburg State College, Shippensburg, Pa., associate professor of English, 1964—. *Military service:* U.S. Army, 1957; became second lieutenant. *Member:* National Council of Teachers of English. *Awards, honors:* Honorable mention for short story, "And There Was Light," in *Writer's Digest* short story contest, 1962, and fourth prize in poetry contest, 1965.

WRITINGS: *Book Notes on David Copperfield*, Barnes & Noble, 1966. Contributor of poetry to *Concepts, Cyclotron, Cardinal Poetry Quarterly,* and short stories and articles to other periodicals and newspapers; regular contributor to *Teacher's Guide to Literature*, published by Xerox Education Publications.

WORK IN PROGRESS: Development of freshman English textbook, and survey of adolescent literature.

* * *

KRAUSE, Sydney J(oseph) 1925-

PERSONAL: Born July 22, 1925, in Paterson, N.J.; married Evelyn Wolff (an occupational therapist), 1952; children: Robert James, Catherine Ann. *Education:* University of Missouri, B.A. (honors), 1949; Yale University, M.A., 1951; Columbia University, Ph.D., 1956. *Home:* 512 Harvey Ave., Kent, Ohio 44240. *Office:* Department of English, Kent State University, Kent, Ohio 44240.

CAREER: University of Missouri, Columbia, instructor, 1950-52; College of William and Mary, Williamsburg, Va., assistant director of English program for foreign students, 1953; Ohio State University, Columbus, instructor in English, 1953-55; University of Akron, Akron, Ohio, assistant professor of English, 1955-62; Kent State University, Kent, Ohio, associate professor, 1962-66, professor of English, 1966—. Fulbright lecturer in American literature, University of Copenhagen, 1968-69. *Military service:* U.S. Army, 1943-46; received Purple Heart and European Theater Medal with three battle stars. *Member:* Modern Language Association of America, Midwest Modern Language Association of America, North East Ohio College English Group (officer, 1965—), Phi Beta Kappa, Phi Eta Sigma.

Awards, honors: American Philosophical Society research grants, 1959, 1960, 1962; American Council of Learned Societies grant, 1961.

WRITINGS: (Editor) *Essays on Determinism in American Literature*, Kent State University Press, 1964; *Mark Twain as Critic*, Johns Hopkins Press, 1967; (editor) *C. B. Brown, Wieland and Carwin*, Kent State University Press, 1975; (contributor) *Artful Thunder: Versions of the Romantic Tradition in American Literature*, Kent State University Press, 1975; (contributor) *Naturalism: A Re-Assessment*, Karl Winter Universitatsverlag, 1975. Contributor to *Yearbook of the American Philosophical Society;* contributor of articles, reviews, and research reports to literary journals. General editor, Modern Language Association-Kent State University definitive edition of the works of Charles Brockden Brown.

WORK IN PROGRESS: Editing Charles Brockden Brown's *Edgar Huntly;* writing on C. B. Brown, and American realism.

* * *

KREBS, Alfred H. 1920-

PERSONAL: Born September 9, 1920, in Medina, N.Y.; married Jean Erath (a counselor), December 2, 1944. *Education:* Cornell University, B.S., 1941, M.S., 1943, Ph.D., 1950. *Office:* 201 Burruss Hall, Virginia Polytechnic Institute and State University, Blacksburg, Va. 24061.

CAREER: Vocational agriculture teacher in New York State, 1941-44; training officer for U.S. Veterans Administration, 1946-47; State University of New York, College of Agriculture at Cornell University, Ithaca, extension teacher, 1948-50; University of Illinois, Urbana, 1950-66, began as instructor, became professor of agricultural education; University of Maryland, College Park, professor of agricultural education, 1966-69; Virginia Polytechnic Institute and State University, Blacksburg, professor of agricultural education and department head, 1969-72, director of summer school, 1970-72, assistant vice-president of academic affairs, 1972-74, acting vice-president of academic affairs, 1974—. *Military service:* U.S. Army, 1944-46.

MEMBER: American Association of Teacher Educators in Agriculture (president), American Vocational Association (member of executive committee, agricultural division), Adult Education Association of the U.S.A., American Educational Research Association, American Personnel and Guidance Association, Rural Education Association of National Education Association, National Society of College Teachers of Education, National Vocational Agricultural Teachers Association, National Vocational Guidance Association, American Association of University Professors, Alpha Tau Alpha (national first vice-president), Phi Kappa Phi, Gamma Sigma Delta, Phi Delta Kappa.

WRITINGS: *Agriculture in Our Lives*, Interstate, 1964, 3rd edition, 1973; (with P. E. Hemp) *A Study Guide for Placement-Employment Programs in Agricultural Business and Industry*, Interstate, 1964; *For More Effective Teaching: A Problem Solving Approach for Teachers of Vocational Agriculture*, Interstate, 1967; (contributor) *Teacher Education in Agriculture*, Interstate, 1967; (editor and contributor) *The Individual and His Education*, American Vocational Association, 1972. Author of about twenty-five monographs and journal articles. *Agricultural Education*, editor, 1957-61, consulting editor, 1961-65, and member of editing-managing board.

KREDENSER, Gail 1936-

PERSONAL: Born December 6, 1936, in Everett, Mass.; daughter of Hyman and Frances (Gershon) Kredenser; married Stanley Mack (an art director and illustrator), December 7, 1965. *Education:* Boston University, B.S. in Journalism, 1958.

CAREER: Boston Traveler, Boston, Mass., education editor, 1958-62; *New York Herald Tribune,* New York City, editor of educational supplements and staff reporter, 1962-66; *New York Times,* New York City, Book and Educational Division promotion writer, 1966-67; currently director of publications for Camp Fire Girls, Inc. *Member:* Newspaperwomen's Club of New York. *Awards, honors:* First prize in Catherine L. O'Brien National Contest (for women's interest news writing), 1959; runner-up as New England newspaperwoman of the year, 1960; citation for distinguished achievement from Boston University School of Public Communication, 1966.

WRITINGS: The ABC of Bumptious Beasts, Quist, 1966; *Express Yourself in Writing,* Sterling, 1968; (with Stanley Mack) *One Dancing Drum: A Counting Book for Children (and Parents) Who are Tired of Puppies and Chickens and Horses,* S. G. Phillips, 1971; *Write It Right,* Barnes & Noble, 1972.

WORK IN PROGRESS: Additional children's books.†

* * *

KREML, Anne Lee 1930-

PERSONAL: Born October 27, 1930, in Pontiac, Mich.; daughter of Max Richard (a minister) and Eliza Frances (Hoskins) Flickinger; married Warren Jay Kreml (dean of Unity School for Ministers), August 19, 1951; children: Christopher Lane, Marilee Anne, Deanne Lynne. *Education:* Student at Chaffey College, 1948-49; Occidental College, B.A., 1953; Chicago Theological Seminary, M.A., 1970. *Religion:* Unity. *Office:* Johnson County Union Church, 7660 West 75th St., Overland Park, Kan. 66204.

CAREER: Pasadena (Calif.) city schools, elementary teacher, 1953-54; University of Chicago, Chicago, Ill., assistant librarian at University Library, 1954-55; director of religious education, Unity Church, San Gabriel, Calif., 1956-61, Corina, Calif., 1959-61, and Ventura, Calif. 1961-64; Unity School of Christianity, Unity Village, Mo., preschool teacher, 1964-65; Westview Elementary School, Lee's Summit, Mo., teacher, 1966-67; Unity School of Christianity, School for Ministers, Unity Village, instructor in religious education, 1967-68; Association for Unity Churches, Unity Village, consultant in religious education, 1967-71; Omega Center for Human Potential, Unity Village, consultant in creative family living, 1970-72; Johnson County Union Church, Overland Park, Kan., member of team ministry, 1972—. *Member:* Religious Educational Association, National Council of Family Relations, American Civil Liberties Union, Common Cause, Southeast Jackson County Mental Health Association (member of board of directors, 1969-71).

WRITINGS: Guidelines for Parents, Unity Books, 1967.†

* * *

KRENTZ, Edgar (Martin) 1928-

PERSONAL: Born May 27, 1928, in Macomb County, Mich.; son of Arnold Fred (a clergyman) and Magdalena (Droegemueller) Krentz; married Marion Grace Becker, September 14, 1952; children: Peter, Michael, Elizabeth, Susanna, Matthew, Christopher. *Education:* Concordia Seminary, St. Louis, Mo., B.D., 1952; Washington University, St. Louis, Mo., M.A., 1953, Ph.D., 1960; University of Tuebingen, postdoctoral study, 1963-64, 1973-74. *Home:* 6306 San Bonita, St. Louis, Mo. 63105. *Office:* Concordia Seminary in Exile, 306 North Grand Blvd., St. Louis, Mo. 63103.

CAREER: Concordia Seminary, St. Louis, Mo., instructor, 1953-54, assistant professor, 1955-64, librarian, 1955-64, associate professor, 1964-69, professor of New Testament, 1969-75; Concordia Seminary in Exile, St. Louis, professor of New Testament, 1975—. Member of board of directors, Foundation for Reformation Research, 1957-59. Field supervisor and member of executive committee, joint expedition for the excavation of Caesarea Martima, Israel. *Member:* American Philological Association, Society of Biblical Literature, Archaeological Institute of America, Studiorum Novi Testamenti Societas, Society for Ancient Greek Philosophy, American Theological Library Association, Phi Beta Kappa.

WRITINGS: Biblical Studies Today, Concordia, 1966; *The Historical Critical Method,* Fortress, 1975. Contributor to theology, philology, and library journals.

WORK IN PROGRESS: Creation Theology in the New Testament.

SIDELIGHTS: Edgar Krentz is fluent in German, and reads French. *Avocational interests:* Greek and Roman art, archaeology, and literature.

* * *

KRUEGER, John R(ichard) 1927-

PERSONAL: Born March 14, 1927, in Fremont, Neb.; son of Edward Walter (a merchant) and Winifred Ada (Munger) Krueger; married Constance Orrice Peek, March 22, 1957; children: Curtis E., Catherine A. *Education:* George Washington University, B.A. (with distinction), 1948, graduate study, 1948-51; University of Copenhagen, Fulbright scholar, 1952-54; University of Washington, Seattle, Ph.D., 1960. *Religion:* Methodist. *Office address:* P.O. Box 606, Bloomington, Ind. 47401.

CAREER: U.S. Department of the Army, Arlington, Va., research analyst for Soviet and Eastern European affairs, 1948-52; University of Washington, Seattle, instructor in German, 1956-57; Reed College, Portland, Ore, instructor in German and linguistics, 1958-60; University of California, Berkeley, lecturer in Oriental languages, 1961; Indiana University, Bloomington, began as assistant professor, currently professor of Uralic-Altaic studies. *Member:* American Oriental Society, American Name Society, Mongolia Society, Tibet Society, Phi Beta Kappa. *Awards, honors:* Fulbright grants, 1952-54, 1968.

WRITINGS: (With K. Gronbech) *Introduction to Classical Mongolian,* Harrasowitz (Germany), 1955; *Poetical Passages in the Erdeni-yin Tobci,* Mouton & Co., 1961; *Chuvash Manual,* Indiana University Press, 1961; *Yakut Manual,* Indiana University Press, 1962; (editor) *Turkic Peoples,* Indiana University Press, 1963; (contributor) *Current Trends in Linguistics,* Volume I, Mouton & Co., 1963; *Mongolian Epigraphical Dictionary,* Indiana University Press, 1967; (editor) J. G. Hangin, *Basic Mongolian,* Indiana University Press, 1967; (editor) *Mongolian Folktales and Proverbs,* Mongolia Society, 1967.

American co-editor of "Central Asiatic Studies," a monograph series; editor of "Uralic and Altaic Series," Indiana

University; co-editor of "Kalmyk Monograph Series." Contributor to *Encyclopaedia Britannica* and professional journals.

WORK IN PROGRESS: Compiling a documentary dictionary of Oirat (western) Mongolian literary and historical texts from 1648 to the twentieth century; preparing a grammar and manual of Tuvinian language; translating and editing Russian works on Mongolia and Buddhism; preparing a general study of language and dialect.

SIDELIGHTS: In addition to his knowledge of European and Asian languages, Krueger lived on a Flathead Indian reservation in the summer of 1957 to study the Salishan language. *Avocational interests:* Music (violin and "amateur Gospel Pianist").

* * *

KRUEGER, Thomas A.   1936-

PERSONAL: Born March 4, 1936, in St. Louis, Mo.; son of Paul A. and Alice M. (Reed) Krueger; married Susan Newhall, August, 1965 (divorced, 1972). *Education:* Antioch College, B.A., 1959; University of Wyoming, M.A., 1960; University of Minnesota, Ph.D., 1965. *Politics:* Independent left. *Religion:* None. *Home:* 1008 West Church, Champaign, Ill. 61820. *Office:* Department of History, University of Illinois, Champaign, Ill. 61801.

CAREER: San Diego State College (now University), San Diego, Calif., assistant professor of history, 1965-66; University of Illinois, Champaign, assistant professor of history, 1966—. *Member:* Organization of American Historians, American Federation of Teachers, American Association of University Professors.

WRITINGS: And Promises to Keep: The Southern Conference for Human Welfare, 1938-1948, Vanderbilt University Press, 1967; (contributor) F. C. Jaher, editor, *The Rich, the Well-Born, and the Powerful: Elites and Upper Classes in History,* University of Illinois Press, 1973.

WORK IN PROGRESS: Working on American political and intellectual history, 1918-1941, and American radicalism since the Civil War.

* * *

KRUPP, Nate   1935-

PERSONAL: Born September 7, 1935, in Fostoria, Ohio; son of Paul Howard (in industrial advertising) and Cleo Mae (Allis) Krupp; married Joanne Sheets Brannon, September 16, 1961; children: Gerald Brannon, Elizabeth Ann. *Education:* Purdue University, B.S. in Mechanical Engineering, 1957; studied at Marion College, 1960-61. *Religion:* Protestant. *Home:* 4001 South Boots, Marion, Ind. 46952. *Office address:* Lay Evangelism, Inc., P.O. Box 3063, Marion, Ind. 46952.

CAREER: Navigators, Colorado Springs, Colo., construction superintendent, 1959-60; director of Lay Evangelism, Inc., 1963—. *Military service:* U.S. Navy, Civil Engineer Corps, 1957-59; became lieutenant junior grade.

WRITINGS: You Can Be a Soul Winner: Here's How, Lay Evangelism, 1963; *A World to Win,* Bethany Fellowship, 1966. Also author of other books and pamphlets on religious subjects.

* * *

KRUTILLA, John Vasil   1922-

PERSONAL: Born February 13, 1922, in Tacoma, Wash.; married, 1954; children: two sons, one daughter. *Education:* Reed College, B.A., 1949; Harvard University, M.A., 1951, Ph.D., 1952. *Office:* Resources for the Future, 1755 Massachusetts Ave. N.W., Washington, D.C. 20036.

CAREER: Tennessee Valley Authority, industrial economist, 1952-53, economist in Office of the General Manager, 1953-54, acting chief economist, 1954-55; Resources for the Future (foundation for research and education in conservation and development of natural resources), Washington, D.C., research associate, 1955-60, associate director of Water Resources Research Program, 1961-63, senior staff member, 1963-68, director of Natural Environments Program, 1968—. Professorial lecturer, George Washington University, 1960-61; visiting professor at University of Colorado, summer, 1959, National University of Mexico, summer, 1960, and University of Michigan, 1969. National Academy of Sciences, member of advisory committee on interrelation of agricultural land use and wildlife resources, 1967, member of Assembly of Life Sciences, 1974—. Consultant to United Nations Economic Commission for Latin America, 1959, and Economic Commission for Asia and the Far East, 1961-62, and United Nations Development Program, 1969-72; also consultant to U.S. Department of Commerce, Department of Interior, and Bureau of the Budget. *Military service:* U.S. Coast Guard, 1942-46.

WRITINGS: (With Otto Eckstein) *Multiple Purpose River Development: Studies in Applied Economic Analysis,* Johns Hopkins Press, 1958; *Sequence and Timing in River Basin Development with Special Application to Columbia River Development* (monograph), Johns Hopkins Press, for Resources for the Future, 1960; *The Columbia River Treaty: An International Evaluation* (monograph), Resources for the Future, 1963; *The Columbia River Treaty: The Economics of an International River Basin Development,* Johns Hopkins Press, 1967; *Natural Environments: Studies in Theoretical and Applied Analysis,* Johns Hopkins Press, 1972; (with A. C. Fisher) *The Economics of Natural Environments: Studies in the Valuation of Commodity and Amenity Resources,* Johns Hopkins Press, 1975. Co-author of *Unemployment, Idle Capacity, and Public Expenditure Criteria,* 1968; also co-author of government reports on water resource development, flood loss management, and cost analysis of conservation programs.

Contributor: *TVA: The First Twenty Years,* University of Alabama Press, 1956; *Land and Water: Planning for Economic Growth,* University of Colorado Press, 1961; *Economics and Public Policy in Water Resource Development,* Iowa State University Press, 1964; *Regional Development and Planning,* M.I.T. Press, 1964; *Water Research,* Johns Hopkins Press, 1966; *Economic Aspects of Anti-Trust,* Random House, 1969; *America's Changing Environment,* Houghton, 1970; *Environmental Quality Analysis: Research Studies in the Social Sciences,* Johns Hopkins Press, 1972; *Benefit-Cost and Policy Analysis,* Aldine, 1973; *Pollution, Resources and the Environment,* Norton, 1973; *The Governance of Common Property Resources,* Johns Hopkins Press, 1974. Contributor to economic and natural resource journals.

* * *

KUCERA, Henry   1925-

PERSONAL: Surname is pronounced *Koo-* chera; born February 15, 1925, in Trebarov, Czechoslovakia; became U.S. citizen; son of Jindrich (in civil service) and Marie (Kral) Kucera; married Jacqueline M. Fortin, October 6,

1951; children: Thomas H., Edward J. *Education:* Charles University, Prague, M.A., 1947; Harvard University, Ph.D., 1952. *Home:* 196 Bowen St., Providence, R.I. 02906. *Office address:* Box E, Brown University, Providence, R.I. 02912.

CAREER: Harvard University, Russian Research Center, Cambridge, Mass., research associate, 1952; University of Florida, Gainesville, assistant professor of foreign languages, 1952-55; Brown University, Providence, R.I., assistant professor, 1955-58, associate professor, 1958-63, professor of Slavic languages, and of linguistics, 1963—, chairman of department of Slavic languages, 1965-68. Research associate, Computing Laboratory, Massachusetts Institute of Technology, 1960-63; visiting professor at University of Michigan, 1967, and University of California, Berkeley, 1969. Member of board of directors, International Institute, Providence, 1963-67.

MEMBER: Linguistic Society of America, International Linguistic Association, Association for Computational Linguistics, Modern Language Association of America, American Committee of Slavists (member of executive committee, 1966-68), Czechoslovak Society of Arts and Sciences in America, American Association of Teachers of Slavic and East European Languages. *Awards, honors:* Ford Foundation fellow, 1954-55; Guggenheim and Howard Foundation fellow, 1960-61; National Endowment for the Humanities, senior fellow, 1968-69; American Council of Learned Societies fellow, 1969-70.

WRITINGS: The Phonology of Czech, Mouton & Co., 1961; (with W. N. Francis) *Computational Analysis of Present-Day American English,* Brown University Press, 1967; (with G. K. Monroe) *A Comparative Quantitative Phonology of Russian, Czech, and German,* American Elsevier, 1968; (editor) *American Contributions to the Sixth International Congress of Slavists,* Mouton & Co., 1968; *Computers in Linguistics and in Literary Studies,* Brown University Press, 1969, revised edition, 1975; (with K. Trnka) *Time in Language,* University of Michigan Press, 1975. Contributor to journals.

WORK IN PROGRESS: A study of language acquisition and of performance grammars for Brown University.

* * *

KUEHL, John 1928-

PERSONAL: Surname rhymes with "reel"; born March 19, 1928, in Davenport, Iowa; son of Hans H. and Genevieve V. (Mills) Kuehl; married Linda Kandel (a college teacher), January 31, 1974. *Education:* University of Iowa, A.B., 1952; University of California, Los Angeles, M.A., 1955; Columbia University, Ph.D., 1958. *Residence:* Jamaica Estates, N.Y. *Agent:* Roslyn Targ, 250 West 57th St., New York, N.Y. 10019. *Office:* Department of English, New York University, 19 University Pl., New York, N.Y. 10003.

CAREER: Princeton University, Princeton, N.J., instructor, 1958-62, assistant professor of English, 1962-66; New York University, New York, N.Y., associate professor of English, 1966—. *Military service:* U.S. Marine Corps, 1946-47. U.S. Marine Corps Reserve, 1947-52. *Member:* Modern Language Association of America, Phi Beta Kappa.

WRITINGS: (Editor) *The Apprentice Fiction of F. Scott Fitzgerald, 1909-1917,* Rutgers University Press, 1965; (editor) *Creative Writing and Rewriting: Contemporary American Novelists at Work,* Appleton, 1967, also published as *Write and Rewrite: A Study of the Creative Process,* Meredith, 1967; *The Fool-Spy* (novel), For Now Press, 1967; (editor with Jackson R. Bryer) *Dear Scott/Dear Max: The Fitzgerald-Perkins Correspondence,* Scribner, 1971; (editor with Bryer) F. Scott Fitzgerald, *The Basil and Josephine Stories,* Scribner, 1973; *John Hawkes and the Craft of Conflict,* Rutgers University Press, 1975. Contributor of more than twenty articles and stories to *Yale Review, Modern Fiction Studies,* and other journals.

WORK IN PROGRESS: A second novel.

* * *

KUH, Edwin 1925-

PERSONAL: Born April 13, 1925, in Chicago, Ill.; son of Edwin J., Jr. (a grain-broker) and Charlotte (Greenebaum) Kuh; married; wife's name, Barbara; children (previous marriage): Joanna M., Elizabeth N., Thomas, Sarah, Daniel. *Education:* Williams College, B.A., 1949; Harvard University, Ph.D., 1955. *Home:* 39 Foster St., Cambridge, Mass. 02138. *Office:* Sloan School of Management, Massachusetts Institute of Technology, Cambridge, Mass. 02139.

CAREER: U.S. Economic Cooperation Administration, London, England, economist, 1949-50; economist, President's Materials Policy Commission, 1951; Johns Hopkins University, Baltimore, Md., lecturer in economics, 1953-55; Massachusetts Institute of Technology, Cambridge, assistant professor of finance, 1955-58, associate professor of economics and finance, 1959-62, professor of economics and finance, 1962—. Director, National Bureau of Economic Research, 1971—. Member of advisory research committee, Brookings-Social Science Research Council Econometric Model, 1964—. Consultant, U.S. Treasury, 1959—. *Military service:* U.S. Army, 1943-46. *Member:* Econometric Society (fellow), American Economic Association, American Statistical Association, American Academy of Arts and Sciences (fellow). *Awards, honors:* Ford Foundation faculty research fellow, 1961-62.

WRITINGS: (With J. R. Meyer) *The Investment Decision: An Empirical Study,* Harvard University Press, 1957; *Capital Stock Growth: A Micro-Econometric Approach,* North Holland Publishing, 1963, 2nd edition, 1971; (editor with J. S. Dusenberry, G. Fromm, and L. R. Klein) *The Brookings Quarterly Econometric Model of the United States,* North Holland Publishing, 1965; (with Richard L. Schmalensee) *An Introduction to Applied Macroeconomics,* American Elsevier, 1973. Contributor to professional journals.

WORK IN PROGRESS: Research on the application of computers to econometrics, and construction of an econometric forecasting model.

* * *

KUH, Richard H. 1921-

PERSONAL: Born April 27, 1921, in New York, N.Y.; son of Joseph Hellmann (a salesman) and Fannie M. R. (Rees) Kuh; married Joyce Dattel (an editor), July 31, 1966; children: Michael Joseph. *Education:* Columbia University, B.A., 1941; Harvard University, LL.B., 1948. *Politics:* Enrolled Democrat. *Religion:* Jewish. *Home:* 14 Washington Pl., New York, N.Y. 10003. *Agent:* Oliver Swan, Julian Bach Literary Agency, 18 East 48th St., New York, N.Y. 10007.

CAREER: Admitted to the Bar of New York State, 1948;

associate in law firm of Cahill, Gordon, Reindel & Ohl, New York City, 1948-53; assistant district attorney, New York County, 1953-64; attorney in private practice under own name, New York City, 1964-71; district attorney, 1974; partner in law firm of Kuh, Shapiro, Goldman, Cooperman & Levitt, New York City, 1975—. Chief of Criminal Court Bureau, 1956-64; lecturer in criminal procedure at New York University, 1958-64; coordinator, New York State Combined Council of Law Enforcement Officials, 1964-66. *Military service:* U.S. Army, Infantry, 1942-45; became sergeant. *Member:* American Bar Association, National District Attorneys Association (member of board of directors, 1963-66), New York City Bar Association.

WRITINGS: Foolish Figleaves?: Pornography in, and out of, Court, Macmillan, 1967. Contributor to legal, police, and popular journals.

* * *

KUHN, Thomas S(amuel) 1922-

PERSONAL: Born July 18, 1922, in Cincinnati, Ohio; son of Samuel L. (an industrial engineer) and Minette (Stroock) Kuhn; married Kathryn Louise Muhs, November 27, 1948; children: Sarah, Elizabeth, Nathaniel Stroock. *Education:* Harvard University, S.B. (summa cum laude in physics), 1943, A.M., 1946, Ph.D., 1949. *Home:* 3 Evelyn Rd., Princeton, N.J. 08540. *Office:* 220 Palmer Hall, Princeton University, Princeton, N.J. 08450.

CAREER: U.S. Office of Scientific Research and Development, civilian employee at Harvard University, Cambridge, Mass., 1943-44, and in Europe, 1944-45; Harvard University, junior fellow, 1948-51, instructor, 1951-52, assistant professor of general education and history of science, 1952-56; University of California, Berkeley, assistant professor of history and philosophy, 1956-58, associate professor, 1958-61, professor of history of science, 1961-64; Princeton University, Princeton, N.J., professor of history of science, 1964-68, M. Taylor Pyne Professor of the History of Science, 1968—. Director of project, Sources of History for Quantum Physics, sponsored by the American Physical Society and American Philosophical Society; member, Institute for Advanced Study.

MEMBER: American Academy of Arts and Sciences, History of Science Society (president), American Philosophical Society, American Historical Association, Social Science Research Council (member of board of directors), American Association for the Advancement of Science, Academie Internationale d'Histoire des Sciences (membre effectif), Phi Beta Kappa, Sigma Xi. *Awards, honors:* Guggenheim fellowship, 1954-55; fellow, Center for Advanced Study in the Behavioral Sciences, 1958-59; LL.D., University of Notre Dame, 1973.

WRITINGS: The Copernican Revolution: Planetary Astronomy in the Development of Western Thought, Harvard University Press, 1957, 2nd edition, 1959; *The Structure of Scientific Revolutions,* University of Chicago Press, 1962, 2nd edition, 1964; (with J. L. Heilbron, P. L. Forman, and Lini Allen) *Sources for History of Quantum Physics,* American Philosophical Society, 1967. Member of board of editors, *Dictionary of Scientific Biography,* 1964—.

Contributor: I. B. Cohen, editor, *Isaac Newton's Papers and Letters on Natural Philosophy,* Harvard University Press, 1958; Marshall Clagett, editor, *Critical Problems in the History of Science,* University of Wisconsin Press, 1959; Harry Woolf, editor, *Quantification: A History of Measurement in the Natural and Social Sciences,* Bobbs-Merrill, 1961; B. Barber and W. Hirsch, editors, *The Sociology of Science,* Free Press of Glencoe, 1961; C. W. Taylor and F. Barron, editors, *Scientific Creativity: Its Recognition and Development,* Wiley, 1963; A. C. Crombie, editor, *Scientific Change,* Basic Books, 1963; I. B. Cohen and R. Taton, editors, *Melanges Alexandre Koyre,* Volume II: *L'Aventure de l'esprit,* Hermann, 1964. Contributor to *Encyclopedia of the Social Sciences,* 1968; also contributor to *Isis, Science,* and to symposium volumes.

WORK IN PROGRESS: Research in the history of quantum physics and in philosophy of scientific development.

SIDELIGHTS: Kuhn's first exposure to the history of science came as an assistant to J. B. Conant in a course designed to present science to non-scientists. He states that he was attracted to this field "by the great difference between the image of science provided by historical study, on the one hand, and by scientific training or philosophy of science, on the other."

* * *

KUHNS, William 1943-

PERSONAL: Surname rhymes with "moons"; born January 20, 1943, in Cleveland, Ohio; son of William Augustus (a manager) and June (Diekman) Kuhns. *Education:* University of Dayton, B.A., 1966. *Religion:* Roman Catholic. *Home address:* R.R. 1, Alcove Quebec, Canada.

CAREER: Teacher in field of film education at Xavier University, Cincinnati, Ohio, and Fordham University, Bronx, N.Y., 1967; assistant professor of communications, University of Texas, 1969-70, and Loyola University, New Orleans, La., 1970-73. Consultant in television production, Lutheran Church of America. Director, Institute for Environmental Response.

WRITINGS: Short Films in Religious Education, Pflaum, 1967; *In Pursuit of Dietrich Bonhoeffer,* Pflaum, 1967; *Environmental Man,* Harper, 1968; (with Robert Stanley) *Exploring the Film* (textbook), Pflaum, 1968; *The Electronic Gospel: Religion and Media,* Herder, 1969; *Why We Watch Them: Interpreting Television,* Benziger, 1969.

Movies in America, Pflaum, 1970; *Behind the Camera,* Pflaum, 1970; *Exploring Television,* Loyola University Press, 1971; *The Post-Industrial Prophets: Interpretations of Technology,* Weybright & Talley, 1971; *The Reunion* (novel), Morrow, 1973; *Themes II: Short Films for Discussion,* Pflaum, 1974; *The Moving Picture Book,* Pflaum, 1975.

* * *

KUISEL, Richard F(rancis) 1935-

PERSONAL: Born October 17, 1935, in Detroit, Mich.; son of Harold F. and Florence (Stoll) Kuisel; married Johness Watts, April 23, 1960; children: Wade, Courtney. *Education:* University of Michigan, A.B., 1957; University of California, Berkeley, M.A., 1959, Ph.D., 1963. *Office:* History Department, State University of New York, Stony Brook, N.Y. 11790.

CAREER: Stanford University, Stanford, Calif., instructor in history, 1961-63; University of Illinois, Urbana, assistant professor of history, 1963-67; University of California, Berkeley, assistant professor of history, 1967-70; State University of New York at Stony Brook, associate professor of history, 1970—. *Member:* American Historical Association, Society for French Historical Studies, Phi

Beta Kappa. *Awards, honors:* Woodrow Wilson fellow; Koren Prize, 1970, for best article on French history.

WRITINGS: Ernest Mercier: French Technocrat, University of California Press, 1967; *The Grandeur of Charles de Gaulle,* Forum Press, 1975. Contributor to history journals in Europe and the United States.

WORK IN PROGRESS: Research on the development of economic planning in France in the twentieth-century.

SIDELIGHTS: Richard Kuisel is competent in French and German. He spent 1960-61 in Europe and returned there in 1964, 1966, and 1974.

* * *

KULSKI, Julian Eugene   1929-

PERSONAL: Born March 3, 1929, in Warsaw, Poland; son of Julian S. (in public administration) and Eugenia (Solecka) Kulski; married Isabel Gagian (an editor), September 3, 1959; children: Helena, Julian. *Education:* Yale University, B.Arch., 1953, M.Arch., 1953; Warsaw Institute of Technology, Ph.D., 1966. *Home:* 6030 Woodland Ter., McLean, Va. 22101. *Office:* Howard University, Washington, D.C. 20001.

CAREER: University of Notre Dame, Notre Dame, Ind., professor of architecture and city planning, 1960-65; George Washington University, Washington, D.C., professor of city planning, 1965-67; Howard University, Washington, D.C., professor of city planning, 1967—. Consultant to U.S. Agency for International Development, World Bank, and municipal and industrial agencies. Chairman of continuing education committee, Association of Collegiate Schools of Architecture, 1964-66. *Member:* American Institute of Architects, American Institute of Planners, American Society for Public Administration, American Association of University Professors, American Society of Planning Officials, National Association of Housing and Redevelopment Officials.

WRITINGS: Land of Urban Promise, University of Notre Dame Press, 1967; *Architecture in a Revolutionary Era,* Aurora, 1971. Contributor to professional journals.

WORK IN PROGRESS: Philosophy of architecture; new communities; black power.

* * *

KULUKUNDIS, Elias   1937-

PERSONAL: Born July 23, 1937, in London, England; son of Michael Elias (in shipping business) and Nitsa (Yannaghas) Kulukundis. *Education:* Harvard University, A.B., 1959, A.M.T., 1962. *Residence:* New York, N.Y.

CAREER: Phillips Exeter Academy, Exeter, N.H., instructor in English, 1961-62, and summer, 1964.

WRITINGS: (Translator, and author of introduction) Viktor Nekrasov, *Both Sides of the Ocean,* Holt, 1964; *The Feasts of Memory: A Journey to a Greek Island,* Holt, 1967 (published in England as *Journey to a Greek Island,* Cassell, 1968).

WORK IN PROGRESS: A novel; short fiction; articles on current Greek politics.††

* * *

KUNTZ, J(ohn) Kenneth   1934-

PERSONAL: Born January 20, 1934, in St. Louis, Mo.; son of John Frederick (principal of an elementary school) and Zula (Reed) Kuntz; married Ruth Stanley, July 7, 1962; children: David Kenneth, Nancy Ruth. *Education:* Grinnell College, B.A., 1956; Yale University Divinity School, B.D., 1959; Union Theological Seminary, New York, N.Y., Ph.D., 1963. *Home:* 1517 Oakcrest Ave., Iowa City, Iowa 52240. *Office:* School of Religion, University of Iowa, Iowa City, Iowa 52242.

CAREER: The United Methodist Church, ordained minister, 1959, now member of Iowa Conference; Union Theological Seminary, New York, N.Y., tutor in Old Testament, 1961-63; Wellesley College, Wellesley, Mass., instructor, 1963-65, assistant professor of Biblical history, literature, and interpretation, 1965-67; University of Iowa, Iowa City, assistant professor, 1967-70, associate professor of religion, 1970—. *Member:* Society of Biblical Literature, American Academy of Religion, American Schools of Oriental Research, American Association of University Professors, Chicago Society of Biblical Research, Phi Beta Kappa. *Awards, honors:* Huber Award (faculty research grant), Wellesley College; Old Gold Award (faculty research grant), University of Iowa; National Endowment for the Humanities grant; Alexander von Humboldt Award for study in Germany.

WRITINGS: The Self-Revelation of God, Westminster, 1967; *The People of Ancient Israel: An Introduction to Old Testament Literature, History, and Thought,* Harper, 1974.

WORK IN PROGRESS: Research in the Psalms and wisdom literature of the Old Testament.

SIDELIGHTS: J. Kenneth Kuntz is competent in Biblical Hebrew, and can use Greek, Aramaic, Ugaritic, and Akkadian as tools in research. *Avocational interests:* Music (plays organ and occasionally serves as church organist), photography.

* * *

KUNZ, Virginia B(rainard)   1921-

PERSONAL: Surname pronounced "coons"; born October 5, 1921, in Fairmont, Minn.; daughter of Dudley Shattuck (an educator and writer) and Merl (Anderson) Brainard; married Richard Carl Kunz, April 22, 1950; children: Susan Virginia, David Brainard. *Education:* St. Cloud State College, student, 1939-40; Iowa State University, B.S., 1943. *Politics:* Republican. *Religion:* Episcopalian. *Home:* 3976 Princeton Ave. S., Minneapolis, Minn. 55416. *Office:* 2097 Larpenteur Ave. W., St. Paul, Minn. 55113.

CAREER: Minneapolis Star and Tribune, Minneapolis, Minn., work as reporter, feature writer, and section editor, 1944-51, 1953-57; Minnesota Association for Retarded Children, state public information director, 1958-62; Ramsey County Historical Society, St. Paul, Minn., executive director, 1962—, and founding editor of *Ramsey County History* (semi-annual publication). *Awards, honors:* Five National Federation of Press Women first place awards; Page One Award of Twin Cities Newspaper Guild, 1950, 1953.

WRITINGS: Muskets to Missiles: A Military History of Minnesota, Minnesota Statehood Centennial Commission, 1958; *The French in America,* Lerner, 1966; *The Germans in America,* Lerner, 1966; (editor) *Farming in Early Minnesota,* Ramsey County Historical Society, 1968; (co-author) *The Collector's Book of Railroadiana,* Hawthorn, 1976.

KUPER, Jack 1932-

PERSONAL: Surname, pronounced Cooper, was originally Kuperblum; born April 16, 1932, in Zyrardow, Poland; son of Aaron Zelig (a shoemaker) and Edzia (Chuen) Kuperblum; married Terrye Swadron, June 26, 1955; children: Ellen, Mark, Shaul, Simca. *Education:* Central Technical School, Toronto, Ontario, diploma, 1953. *Religion:* Hebrew. *Home:* 67 Elwood Blvd., Toronto, Ontario, Canada. *Office:* Kuper Productions Ltd., 179 Carlton St., Toronto, Ontario, Canada M5A 2K3.

CAREER: Canadian Broadcasting Corp., Toronto, Ontario, supervisor of graphic design, 1953-64; Kenyon & Eckhardt (advertising firm), Toronto, Ontario, creative director, 1967-70; Kuper Productions Ltd. (a motion picture company), Toronto, Ontario, founder and creative director, 1971—.

WRITINGS: Child of the Holocaust (autobiography), General Publishing, 1967, Doubleday, 1968.

Television plays: "Sun in My Eyes"; "Lost in a Crowd"; "On a Streetcar"; "Street Music." Also author of a radio script, "The Palace."

WORK IN PROGRESS: The Messenger.

*   *   *

KUPER, Leo 1908-

PERSONAL: Born November 24, 1908, in Johannesburg, South Africa; son of Morris (a merchant) and Pesha Kuper; married Hilda Beemer (a professor of anthropology), January 14, 1934; children: Jenny, Mary. *Education:* University of the Witwatersrand, B.A. (honors), 1928, LL.B., 1930; University of North Carolina, M.A., 1949; University of Birmingham, Birmingham, England, Ph.D., 1952. *Politics:* Liberal. *Religion:* Jewish. *Home:* 1282 Warner Ave., Los Angeles, Calif. 90024. *Office:* University of California, Los Angeles, Calif. 90024.

CAREER: Practiced law, 1931-40; University of Natal, Durban, South Africa, professor of sociology and social work, and dean of the Faculty of Social Science, 1952-61; University of California, Los Angeles, professor of sociology, 1961—, director of African Studies Center, 1968-72. Organizing secretary, National War Memorial Health Foundation, 1946-49; Liberal Party executive, 1954-60. *Military service:* South African Army, 1940-45; became lieutenant. *Member:* International Sociological Association, American Sociological Association, British Sociological Association, African Studies Association. *Awards, honors:* Herskovits Book Award, 1966, for *An African Bourgeoisie.*

WRITINGS: (Editor) *Living in Towns,* Cresset, 1952; *Passive Resistance in South Africa,* Yale University Press, 1957; (with Hilstan Watts and Ronald Davies) *Durban: A Study in Racial Ecology,* Columbia University Press, 1958; *College Brew* (satirical novel), privately printed, 1960; *An African Bourgeoisie,* Yale University Press, 1965; (editor with wife, Hilda Kuper) *African Law: Adaptation and Development,* University of California Press, 1966; (editor with M. G. Smith) *Pluralism in Africa,* University of California Press, 1969; *Race, Class and Power,* Duckworth, 1974.

WORK IN PROGRESS: The Pity of It All, an analysis of polarization in race and ethnic relations, completion expected in 1977.

KUPFERBERG, Naphtali 1923-
(Tuli Kupferberg)

PERSONAL: Born September 28, 1923, in New York, N.Y.; son of Lemuel and Jennie (Weledniger) Kupferberg; married Sylvia Topp; children: Joseph, Noah, Samara. *Education:* Brooklyn College (now of the City University of New York), B.A. (cum laude), 1944; graduate study at New School for Social Research, 1944-45; also attended Columbia University, Queens College of the City University of New York, and Long Island University. *Politics:* "Anarchist, pacifist." *Religion:* "Revolution." *Home:* 210 Spring St., New York, N.Y. 10012.

CAREER: Was a medical librarian, a medical research editor, and co-founder of a messenger co-op; in 1964, with Ed Sanders, founded The Fugs, a folk-rock group; publisher, Birth Press, New York City; teacher at Free University of New York. Actor; appearing in films, including "WR: Function of the Organism" and "Voukz vous Couchez avec God?" Educational director, League for Sexual Freedom, New York. Founder and director, The Revolting Theater, New York City.

WRITINGS—Under Tuli Kupferberg: *Beating,* Birth Press, 1959; (compiler with Sylvia Topp) *Children as Authors: A Big Bibliography,* Birth Press, 1959; *Selected Fruits & Nuts, From One Crazy Month in Spring Not So Long Ago* (cartoons), Birth Press, 1959; *Snow Job: Poems, 1946-1959,* Pup Press (New York), 1959.

Stimulants: An Exhibition, Birth Press, 1960; *Beatniks; or, The War Against the Beats,* Birth Press, 1961, also published as *300000000000 Beatniks; or, The War Against the Beats,* Birth Press, 1961; *The Grace and Beauty of the Human Form,* Birth Press, 1961; *1001 Ways to Live Without Working,* Birth Press, 1961, Grove, 1967; *Sex and War,* Birth Press, 1962; (translator) *The Rub-ya-out of Omore Diem,* Birth Press, 1962; *The Mississippi,* Birth Press, 1962; *The Christine Keeler Colouring Book & Cautionary Tale,* Birth Press, 1963; *Kill for Peace,* Birth Press, 1965; (with Robert Bashlow) *1001 Ways to Beat the Draft,* Oliver Layton, 1966, Grove, 1967; *Caught in the Act: A Legal Vaudeville* (play), Birth Press, 1966; *1001 Ways to Make Love,* Grove, 1969.

News poems, Birth Press, 1971; *Listen to the Mockingbird* (songs), Times Change Press, 1973; (with wife, Sylvia Topp) *As They Were,* Links Books, 1973. Also author of *Book of the Body* (aphorisms), Birth Press, and "F--k-nam," a play. Editor of *Birth, Yeah, Swing,* and *Crazy Paper.* Staff member of *East Village Other;* contributor to various alternative newspapers including *Soho Weekly News.*

Wrote words and music for "Supergirl," "Seize the Day," "Nothing," "Kill for Peace," "Morning Morning," "Life is Strange," and other Fug songs.

WORK IN PROGRESS: With wife, Sylvia Topp, *First Glance* and *The Worst of Everything;* a novel, *The F——s.*

SIDELIGHTS: Kupferberg called himself "the oldest rock 'n' roll star in America." He enriched The Fugs with his maracas, his pantomimes, and with the erectarine, a kind of vertical tambourine which he invented.

Ideologically he is a philosophical, not a traditional, anarchist. He told Martin Cohen: "I don't believe in violence. I think the traditional anarchist and Marxist theories have failed and really new things have to be developed." He remains one of the most prolific of anarchist pamphleteers. And, as the *Village Voice* noted, "virtually everything he produces is rich in humor and social comment." One of his 1001 ways to beat the draft, for example, enjoins the potential inductee to "tell them you are a wandering Jew and you have to get going." Another instructs one to "give away copies of *The Communist Manifesto* to other inductees." Or, as the ultimate cop-out goes, "marry your mother." His interest is serious, however. He told *CA* that he is "very concerned about whether there will be a country a year from now."

Allen Ginsberg in *Howl* alludes to Kupferberg simply as the man who "jumped off the Brooklyn Bridge" and survived.

Kupferberg has recorded pop poetry on "No Deposit, No Return," for ESP Records, as well as recording with The Fugs.

BIOGRAPHICAL/CRITICAL SOURCES: Village Voice, September 16, 1965; *Avant Garde,* January, 1968; *New Yorker,* October 22, 1973.

*   *   *

KURATOMI, Chizuko   1939-

PERSONAL: Born March 30, 1939, in Tokyo, Japan; daughter of Kazuma and Matsuko (Kawamura) Kuratomi; married Kei Abe (a management consultant), December 10, 1967. *Education:* Attended Aoyama Gakuin Women's College, 1957-59, 1963-64. *Home:* 17-9 2-chome, Shinmachi, Setagaya-ku, Tokyo, Japan.

CAREER: Shiko-Sha Co., Ltd. (publisher), Tokyo, Japan, editor of children's books, 1964—. *Awards, honors:* Sankei Press prize, 1968, for *Mr. Bear Goes to Sea.*

WRITINGS—All originally published by Shiko-Sha: *Okasan wa doko,* 1966, translation by R. Hyman and I. Hyman published as *Barnabas Ball at the Circus,* Evans, 1967; *Donkumasan,* 1966, translation published as *Remember Mr. Bear,* MacDonald & Co., 1968; *Boku Hanataro,* 1967, translation by R. Hyman and I. Hyman published as *Runaway James and the Night Owl,* Evans, 1968; *Donkumasan umi e iku,* 1967, translation published as *Mr. Bear Goes to Sea,* MacDonald & Co., 1968; *Ohayo,* 1968, translation by R. Hyman and I. Hyman published as *Run, Chase the Sun,* Evans, 1969; *Donkumasan sora o tobu* (title means "Mr. Bear Goes to Fly"), 1968.

Donkumasan no rappa, 1970, translation published as *Mr. Bear's Trumpet,* MacDonald & Co., 1970; *Donkumasan no otetsudai,* 1971, translation published as *Mr. Bear and the Robbers,* MacDonald & Co., 1971; *Donkumasan wa eki-cho,* 1972, translation published as *Mr. Bear, Station-Master,* MacDonald & Co., 1972; *Norainu,* 1973, translation by Nancy Chambers published as *Pim and the Fisherboy,* MacDonald & Co., 1975; *Jam-jam Donkumasan,* 1973, translation published as *Mr. Bear and Apple Jam,* MacDonald & Co., 1974; *Donkumasan no Christmas,* 1974, translation published as *Mr. Bear's Christmas,* MacDonald & Co., 1974; *E-o-kaku Donkumasan,* 1975, translation published as *Mr. Bear's Drawing,* MacDonald & Co., 1975.

Editor and contributor of poems for children to *Kodomo-no-Sekai* (a children's pictorial magazine).

*   *   *

KUTLER, Stanley I.   1934-

PERSONAL: Born August 10, 1934, in Cleveland, Ohio; son of Robert P. (a printer) and Zelda (Coffman) Kutler; married Sandra J. Sachs, June 24, 1956; children: Jeffrey,

David, Susan, Andrew. *Education:* Bowling Green State University, B.A., 1956; Ohio State University, Ph.D., 1960. *Religion:* Jewish. *Home:* 6417 Masthead, Madison, Wis. 53705. *Office:* University of Wisconsin, Madison, Wis. 53706.

CAREER: Pennsylvania State University, University Park, instructor in history, 1960-62; San Diego State College (now University), San Diego, Calif., assistant professor, 1962-64; University of Wisconsin—Madison, associate professor, 1964-71, professor of history, 1971—. *Member:* American Historical Association, Law and Society Association, Organization of American Historians. *Awards, honors:* American Philosophical Society research grants, 1961, 1963; Guggenheim fellowship, 1973.

WRITINGS: The Dred Scott Decision, Houghton, 1967; *Judicial Power and Reconstruction Politics,* University of Chicago Press, 1968; *The Supreme Court and the Constitution,* Houghton, 1969; *Power, Growth, and Law,* Lippincott, 1971; *Looking for America,* Harper, in press. Contributor of articles and reviews to history and law journals.

*   *   *

LABOR, Earle G.   1928-

PERSONAL: Born March 3, 1928, in Tuskahoma, Okla.; son of Phillips P. (an IBM operator) and Sylvia (Kirkpatrick) Steger; married Betty Garrett, September 21, 1952; children: Royce, Kirk, Kyle, Isabel. *Education:* Southern Methodist University, B.A., 1949, M.A., 1952; University of Wisconsin, Ph.D., 1961. *Politics:* Independent. *Religion:* Methodist. *Home:* 244 Forest Ave., Shreveport, La. 71104. *Office:* Department of English, Centenary College of Louisiana, Shreveport, La. 71104.

CAREER: Haggar Co., Dallas, Tex., assistant sales manager, 1954-55; Centenary College of Louisiana, Shreveport, instructor, 1955-56, assistant professor of English, 1959-62; Adrian College, Adrian, Mich., Lyman Edwyn Davis Professor of English Literature, chairman of English department and Division of Humanities, 1962-66; Centenary College of Louisiana, professor of English, 1966—. *Military service:* U.S. Navy, 1952-54, recruit instructor. *Member:* College English Association, Modern Language Association of America, National Council of Teachers of English, American Studies Association, American Association of University Professors, Phi Beta Kappa. *Awards, honors:* Weightlifting champion, Texas, 1952; Huntington Library fellow, 1972-73; American Philosophical Society grant, 1973; National Endowment for the Humanities senior fellow, 1974-75; twelve national prizes for photography.

WRITINGS: (Editor) Jack London, *Great Short Works,* Harper, 1965, 2nd edition, 1970; (with Wilford L. Guerin and others) *A Handbook of Critical Approaches to Literature,* Harper, 1966; (editor with Guerin and others) *Mandala: Literature for Critical Analysis,* Harper, 1970; (editor) *The Future of College English,* College English Association, 1972; *Jack London,* Twayne, 1974. Editor, *Newsletter of Lambda Iota Tau,* 1964-66; *CEA Critic,* managing editor, 1967-70, editor of publications, 1970-75.

WORK IN PROGRESS: A collection of Jack London's early short stories for Huntington Library, a biographical study of Jack London's farming career, *Jack London and the Valley of the Moon; Jack London and "The Game,"* a critical study of London's prize-fighting writings.

LACEY, Peter 1929-

PERSONAL: Born October 5, 1929, in Chicago, Ill.; son of Clyde M. and Jacqueline (Dooley) Lacey; married Sheila Sax, February 4, 1961 (divorced, 1975); children: Jennifer. *Education:* University of Chicago, B.A., 1953. *Home:* 29 West 76th St., New York, N.Y. 10023.

CAREER: City News Bureau, Chicago, Ill., reporter, 1957-58; Magnum Photos, New York City, assistant editor, 1958-60; Ridge Press, New York City, picture editor, 1960-65; Playboy Press, Chicago, Ill., associate editor, 1965-67; *American Sportsman,* New York City, managing editor, 1967; *Reader's Digest,* New York City, senior editor of general books, 1968—.

WRITINGS: History of the Nude in Photography, Bantam, 1964; *The Wedding,* Grosset, 1967.

* * *

LACHS, John 1934-

PERSONAL: Born July 17, 1934, in Budapest, Hungary; left Hungary after Communist take-over in 1949, and went to Canada, 1951; married Shirley Mellow, 1967. *Education:* McGill University, B.A. (first class honors), 1956, M.A., 1957; Yale University, Ph.D., 1961. *Religion:* Episcopalian. *Office:* Vanderbilt University, Nashville, Tenn. 37235.

CAREER: College of William and Mary, Williamsburg, Va., assistant professor, 1959-62, associate professor, 1962-66, professor of philosophy, 1966-67; Vanderbilt University, Nashville, Tenn., professor of philosophy, 1967—. Visiting fellow, Duke University and University of North Carolina, 1965-66; president, Society for the Advancement of American Philosophy; director, National Endowment for the Humanities, Nashville Human Rights Project; lecturer to civic and academic groups. *Member:* American Philosophical Association, Canadian Philosophical Association, Metaphysical Society of America, Aristotelian Society, Mind Association, Royal Institute of Philosophy, American Association of University Professors, Southern Society for Philosophy and Psychology (co-chairman of program committee), Virginia Philosophical Association. *Awards, honors:* Phi Beta Kappa Faculty Award, 1962; Harbison Award, Danforth Foundation, 1967, for distinguished teaching; grants from American Philosophical Society, Titmus Foundation, Vanderbilt University Research Council, Chancellor's Corp., and National Endowment for the Humanities.

WRITINGS: (Editor) *Animal Faith and Spiritual Life: Unpublished and Uncollected Works of George Santayana with Critical Essays on His Thought,* Appleton, 1967; *Marxist Philosophy: A Bibliographical Guide,* University of North Carolina Press, 1967; (contributor) Harvey Cox, editor, *The Situation Ethics Debate,* Westminster, 1968; (author of introduction) *Dialectics,* Greenwood Reprint, 1968; (translator with Peter Heath) J. G. Fichte, *The Science of Knowledge,* Appleton, 1969; (editor with wife, Shirley Lachs) George Santayana, *Physical Order and Moral Liberty* (previously unpublished essays), Vanderbilt University Press, 1969; *The Ties of Time,* Delta Canada, 1970. Contributor of about fifty articles to philosophy journals in Europe and North America; contributor of poetry to *Delta, Queen's Quarterly,* and other journals.

WORK IN PROGRESS: Intermediate Man, a study of alienation; a book on George Santayana for Twayne.

La CLAIR, Earl E. 1916-

PERSONAL: Born August 24, 1916, in Buffalo, N.Y.; son of Edward J. and Louise (Yager) La Clair; married Carol Beth Wilder, January 7, 1942. *Education:* Canisius College, B.S., 1941, M.Ed., 1950; University of Buffalo (now State University of New York at Buffalo), further graduate study, 1950-51. *Politics:* Republican. *Religion:* Roman Catholic. *Home:* 5007 West Colonial Dr., Apt. 16, Tampa, Fla. 33611.

CAREER: U.S. Army and Army Air Forces, 1941-46, became captain; served in Europe with Air Transport Command, 1945-46; U.S. Veterans Administration, Buffalo, N.Y., training officer, 1946-48; West Seneca (N.Y.) School District, high school teacher of social sciences, 1948-51; U.S. Air Force, 1951-70, served in Korea as manpower management advisor to ROK Air Force, 1956-57; assigned as Military Training Officer for African Nations, Directorate of Military Assistance, Headquarters U.S. Strike Command, 1964-68; Executive Officer to the Base Commander at Naha Air Base, Okinawa, 1968-70; retired as major; currently adjunct professor of creative writing and history, St. Leo College, St. Leo, Fla., and an adult education instructor, Tampa, Fla.

MEMBER: International Poetry Association, American Poets Fellowship Society, Academy of American Poets, National Historical Society, Retired Officers Association, Phi Delta Kappa. *Awards, honors*—Military: Joint Services Commendation Medal, Army Commendation Medal, Air Force Commendation Medal, additional citations from U.S. Army, U.S. Air Force, and Korean Air Force. Literary: Awards for poetry include first prize from *Sydell Quarterly* for year's best poem, 1965; *Poet Lore,* narrative poetry, second prize, 1966, descriptive poetry, second prize, 1972, third prize, 1973.

WRITINGS: The Wood and the Wool, Golden Quill, 1966; *Spring Moon for Naha,* Hoshi Press (Okinawa), 1969; *Time Is a Twice Told Tale,* Branden Press, 1972; *A Street Called Singil Dong,* Prairie Poet Books, 1975; *The Essence of Time,* Peacock Press, 1975. Also author of *Promise: He Who Opens a Window to the Dawn,* 1975. Poetry anthologized in *Poetry Parade, The Melody of the Muse, Flame, Modern American Lyrics,* and *Golden Quill Anthology.* Poems have been published in numerous periodicals and newspapers, including *Haiku Highlights, Whispers, Prairie Poet, Bitteroot, Trace, Dust, South and West, Goodly Company, Poet Lore, Korea Report,* and *Voices International.*

WORK IN PROGRESS: Four collections of poems, *Gathering Places, Peace: That Time of War between Battles, Sashimas,* and *Ku-rim on Chong-i.*

SIDELIGHTS: La Clair is fluent in German and has a "basic get-get" knowledge of French, Spanish, Italian, Hongul, and Japanese. He has traveled in some thirty countries, taught courses in American history and literature at universities in Korea, Japan, and at University of Southern Mississippi (in off-duty time).

* * *

LAKE, Frank 1914-

PERSONAL: Born June 6, 1914, in Lancashire, England; son of John (in stock exchange at Liverpool) and Mary (Tasker) Lake; married Sylvia Madeline Smith, April 18, 1944; children: David, Monica, Marguerite. *Education:* University of Edinburgh, M.B. and Ch.B., 1937; University of Liverpool, Diploma in Tropical Medicine, 1938; University of Leeds, D.P.M., 1954, M.R.C., 1973. *Religion:* Church of England. *Home:* 5 Weston Ave., Bramcote, Nottingham NG7 4BA, England. *Office:* Lingdale, Weston Ave., Mount Hooton Rd., Nottingham, England.

CAREER: Specialist in tropical medicine and lecturer in parasitology, 1938-50; in practice of psychiatry, 1951—. Clinical Theology Association, director, 1958—, and developer of clinical theology seminars. Member of executive council, Institute of Religion and Medicine; visiting professor of pastoral care, Luther Theological Seminary, St. Paul, Minn., 1976. *Military service:* Indian Army, Medical Corps, 1941-45; became lieutenant colonel. *Member:* British Medical Association, Royal College of Psychiatrists, Edinburgh University Theological Society (president, 1967-68).

WRITINGS: Clinical Theology, Darton, Longman & Todd, 1966; (contributor) H. Montefiore, editor, *We Must Love One Another or Die,* Hodder & Stoughton, 1966.

WORK IN PROGRESS: A book for Darton, Longman & Todd.

*   *   *

LAL, Kishori Saran 1920-

PERSONAL: Born February 26, 1920, in Jhang, Punjab, India; son of Bisheshwar Dayal; married Urmilla Srivastava, June 18, 1946; children: Meenakshi (daughter), Rajeev (son), Deepak (son), Manju (daughter). *Education:* Kayasth Pathshala Intermediate College, certificate, 1937; Allahabad University, B.A., 1939, M.A., 1941, D.Phil., 1945. *Home:* (Permanent) E-1/143 Arera Colony, Bhopal-462014, India. *Office:* Department of History, Faculty of Arts and Social Sciences, University of Jodhpur, Jodhpur-342001, India.

CAREER: Allahabad University, Allahabad, Uttar Pradesh, India, part-time lecturer, 1944-45; Madhya Pradesh Educational Service, 1945-63, began as lecturer at Morris College, Nagpur, 1945-50, assistant professor at Robertson College, Jabalpur, 1950-57, professor at Hamidia College, Bhopal, 1957-63; Delhi University, Delhi, India, reader in history, 1963-72; University of Jodhpur, Jodhpur, India, professor of history and head of department, 1973—. *Military service:* National Cadet Corps, 1949-57; became lieutenant. *Member:* Indian History Congress (president, medieval section, 1958; treasurer, 1965-67).

WRITINGS: History of the Khaljis (1290-1320), Indian Press (Allahabad), 1950; *Muslim State in India,* Vichar Prakasham (Allahabad), 1950, revised edition, Asia Publishing House, 1967; *Yurop ka Adhunik Itihas* (title means "History of Modern Europe"), Indian Press, Volume I, 1956, Volume II, 1957; *Twilight of the Sultanate (1398-1526),* Asia Publishing House, 1963; *Studies in Medieval Indian History,* Ranjit Publishers (Delhi), 1966; (editor) *Studies in Asian History,* Asia Publishing House, 1969; *Growth of Muslim Population in Medieval India,* Research Publications in Social Sciences, 1973. Contributor of more than forty articles to historical journals in India.

WORK IN PROGRESS: A book tentatively entitled *Bases of Muslim Political Power in India, 1000-1800,* completion expected in 1978.

SIDELIGHTS: Kishori Lal is competent in English, Hindi, Urdu, and Persian.

LALUMIA, Joseph 1916-

PERSONAL: Born May 24, 1916, in Robertsdale, Pa.; son of John and Josephine (Insalac) Lalumia; children: Daniel, Catherine, Claudia. *Education:* St. Bernard's Seminary and College, Rochester, N.Y., A.B., 1941; graduate study at University of Toronto, 1945, and University of Rochester, 1946-47; Cornell University, Ph.D., 1950. *Office:* Department of Philosophy, Hofstra University, Hempstead, N.Y. 11550.

CAREER: Kent State University, Kent, Ohio, associate professor of philosophy, 1950-56; Hofstra University, Hempstead, Long Island, N.Y., professor of philosophy, 1956—.

WRITINGS: The Ways of Reason, Humanities, 1966.

WORK IN PROGRESS: A book on the evolution of the concept of matter; several articles on the history of science and philosophy.

*   *   *

LAMB, Antonia 1943-

PERSONAL: Born October 3, 1943, in New York, N.Y.; daughter of Robert Gustave (an engineer) and Marion (an artist; maiden name, Heller) Blick; children: Jim, Joanna. *Education:* Attended Columbia University, 1962-63. *Politics:* "Anarchic." *Religion:* Susila Budhi Dharma. *Agent:* Seligmann & Collier, 280 Madison Ave., New York, N.Y. 10016.

CAREER: Worked as ballet dancer, off-Broadway actress, B-girl, ballet teacher, artists' and photographers' model, sales clerk, credit analyst, and in a Christmas ornament company, 1959-63; currently a practicing astrologer, writer, and musician.

WRITINGS: Greystones, Pyramid, 1966; *The Greenhouse,* Pyramid, 1966; *Lady in Shadows,* Lancer, 1968; *Remember the Summer,* Lancer, 1973. Contributor to *The Witches' Almanac,* Grosset, 1971—.

WORK IN PROGRESS: A book on sex and astrology; a gothic novel set on California's redwood coast in 1906.

SIDELIGHTS: Mrs. Lamb told *CA:* "I generally am writing for money, a sad state of affairs in that the artist, major or minor, has a built-in ambivalence toward working for direct profit. This ambivalence makes it hard to write the best book possible every time. [However] I am working to overcome my ambivalence to money by repeating 'money is okay! money is good!' at odd intervals." Her usual method of writing is "whenever I can."

*   *   *

LAMB, H(ubert) H(orace) 1913-

PERSONAL: Born September 22, 1913, in Bedford, England; son of Ernest Horace (a university professor) and Lilian Lamb; married B. Moira Milligan, February 7, 1948; children: Catherine Ann, Kirsten Mary, Norman Peter. *Education:* Trinity College, Cambridge, B.A. (honors in natural science and geography), 1935, M.A., 1947. *Residence:* Ketteringham, Norfolk, England. *Office:* Climatic Research Unit, University of East Anglia, Norwich, NR4 7TJ, England.

CAREER: Scientist for United Kingdom Meteorological Office, 1936-40; held various posts including head of main forecasting office with Republic of Ireland Meteorological Service, 1940-44; scientist with various posts at home and abroad, United Kingdom Meteorological Office, mainly doing research on long range forecasting, climatic changes, and polar meteorology, 1945-71; University of East Anglia, Norwich, England, honorary professor and director of Climatic Research Unit, 1972—. Member of British National Committee for Antarctic Research, 1959—, and World Meteorological Organization Working Group on Climatic Fluctuations, 1962-65, chairman, 1969-73; member of International Commission on Polar Meteorology, 1967-74.

MEMBER: Royal Meteorological Society (fellow; councillor, 1956-59; vice-president, 1975—), Royal Geographical Society (fellow), Glaciological Society (fellow). *Awards, honors:* L. G. Groves Prize, Meteorological Office, 1960, 1971, and Darton Prize, Royal Meteorological Society, 1964, for contributions to understanding of climatic variations.

WRITINGS: (Contributor) A. E. M. Nairn, editor, *Descriptive Palaeoclimatology*, Wiley, 1961; *The English Climate*, English Universities Press, 1964; (contributor) Nairn, editor, *Problems in Palaeoclimatology*, Wiley, 1964; (contributor) Sir Raymond Priestley and others, editors, *Antarctic Research*, Butterworth & Co., 1964; *The Changing Climate: Selected Papers*, Barnes & Noble, 1966; *Climate: Present, Past, and Future*, Volume I, Barnes & Noble, 1972. Contributor to *A New Dictionary of Birds*, 1964, *Encyclopaedia Britannica*, 1974, and to scientific journals in Britain, Germany, Sweden, and United States.

WORK IN PROGRESS: Research for books on climatic history and on the scientific basis of climatic variability.

SIDELIGHTS: Lamb made a voyage to the Antarctic, 1946-47. He lived in Germany, 1951-52, in the Mediterranean area, 1952-54, and has traveled in America (former member of American Meteorological Society), Canada, Iceland, and many European countries. *Avocational interests:* Languages, social and economic history, archaeology.

* * *

LAMBORN, LeRoy L(eslie)   1937-

PERSONAL: Born May 12, 1937, in Marion, Ohio; son of LeRoy Leslie (a right-of-way agent for a public utility) and Lola Fern (Grant) Lamborn. *Education:* Oberlin College, A.B., 1959; Western Reserve University (now Case Western Reserve University), LL.B., 1962; Yale University, LL.M., 1963; Columbia University, J.S.D., 1973. *Home:* 630 Merrick Ave., Detroit, Mich. 48202. *Office:* Wayne State University Law School, Detroit, Mich. 48202.

CAREER: University of Florida, College of Law, Gainesville, assistant professor of law, 1965-69; Wayne State University Law School, Detroit, Mich., professor of law, 1970—.

WRITINGS: Legal Ethics and Professional Responsibility, American Bar Foundation, 1963.

* * *

LAMPARSKI, Richard

PERSONAL: Parents changed their surname to Lynch, but he adopted the original family name on reaching legal age; born in Grosse Pointe, Mich.; son of Benjamin Walter and Virginia (Downey) Lynch. *Education:* Attended schools in Michigan. *Home:* 3289 Carse Canyon Dr., Hollywood, Calif. 90068. *Agent:* Arnold Stiefel, 9255 Sunset Blvd., Los Angeles, Calif. 90069.

CAREER: Prior to 1965, was associate producer of several

television pilot films and worked as press agent for motion picture actors and actresses, both in New York and Hollywood; WBAI-FM, New York, N.Y. (listener-supported station operated by Pacifica Foundation of Berkeley, Calif.), producer, 1965-73, host and producer of "Whatever Became of . . .?," a series of half-hour interviews with celebrities of the past, which was also carried over KPFA-FM, San Francisco, another station operated by Pacifica Foundation, and KPFK-FM, Los Angeles.

WRITINGS: Whatever Became Of . . .?, Crown, first series, 1967, second series, 1968, third series, 1971, fourth series, 1973, fifth series, 1975. Contributor to *New York Times* and *Nostalgia* (magazine).

* * *

LANCASTER, Richard

PERSONAL: Born in Webberville, Tex.; son of John J. (a diplomat) and Mabel (Lundgren) Lancaster. *Education:* University of Texas, B.A., 1960. *Residence:* Austin, Tex.

CAREER: Jobs have included hospital attendant, laborer, fruit picker, lumberjack, prison guard, bodyguard, assistant to a university professor, professional hunter and wrangler; currently a breeder of horses. *Military service:* U.S. Army. *Awards, honors:* Knights of Mark Twain Award, 1966; Governor's Award of the State of Washington, 1967.

WRITINGS: Piegan, Doubleday, 1966. Contributor to *And Horns on the Toads,* Texas Folklore Society annual, 1959; contributor of short stories to magazines.

WORK IN PROGRESS: Three nonfiction books on the American Indian; a contemporary novel about the American Indian; a collection of short stories.

SIDELIGHTS: Richard Lancaster is fluent in French and Spanish and less fluent in German, Italian, and Blackfoot. He lived for a time with Blackfoot Indians.

* * *

LANCOUR, (Adlore) Harold   1908-

PERSONAL: Born June 27, 1908, in Duluth, Minn.; son of Adlore Dealor and Mino (Hoffer) Lancour; married Marie McClellan (a librarian), September 30, 1936; children: Joan. *Education:* University of Washington, Seattle, A.B., 1931; Columbia University, B.S. in L.S., 1936, M.S. in L.S., 1941, Ed.D., 1948; also studied in Geneva, Switzerland, 1930-31. *Politics:* Liberal. *Religion:* Presbyterian. *Home:* Tuckernuck Knob Farm, Morgan Hill, Weston, Vt. 05161. *Office:* Graduate School of Library and Information Sciences, University of Pittsburgh, Pittsburgh, Pa. 15213.

CAREER: Windjammer Book Shop, Seattle, Wash., owner-operator, 1931-35; New York (N.Y.) Public Library, reference assistant, 1935-37; Cooper Union, New York, N.Y., museum librarian, 1937-39, librarian and professor of bibliography, 1939-47; University of Illinois, Urbana, associate director of Graduate Library School and professor of library science, 1947-61; University of Pittsburgh, Pittsburgh, Pa., dean of Graduate School of Library and Information Sciences and professor of library science, 1961-74, dean and professor emeritus, 1974—, acting director of university libraries, 1963-64. Director of U.S. Information Service libraries in France, 1952-53; member, UNESCO International Committee on Social Science Documentation, 1953-57; surveyed libraries in Ghana, Nigeria, Sierra Leone, and Gambia for Carnegie Corp., 1957; Ford Foundation consultant to Liberian Department of Public Instruction, 1960-61; Agency for International Development, consultant to Ministry of Education, Mali, 1963, and University of San Carlos, Guatemala, 1964-65, 1967, and conductor of book surveys in Chile, and Iran, 1966. Director, International Graduate Summer School in Librarianship, Aberystwyth, Wales, 1973—. *Military service:* U.S. Army, instructor at Information and Education Staff School, 1943-45; became sergeant.

MEMBER: American Library Association (member of council, 1956-60), Association of American Library Schools (president, 1954-56, 1958-60), American Antiquarian Society, Beta Phi Mu (executive secretary, 1953-73; honorary secretary, 1973—), Phi Delta Phi, Alpha Beta Alpha, Grolier Club (New York), Caxton Club (Chicago), University Club (Pittsburgh). *Awards, honors:* Senior Fulbright scholar in England, 1950-51.

WRITINGS—Compiler: *Passenger Lists of Ships Coming to North America, 1607-1825,* New York Public Library, 1937, 2nd edition, 1938; *Heraldry: A Guide to Reference Books,* New York Public Library, 1938; *American Art Auction Catalogues, 1785-1942: A Union List,* New York Public Library, 1944; *A Bibliography of Ship Passenger Lists, 1538-1825: Being a Guide to Published Lists of Early Immigrants to North America,* New York Public Library, 1963; (editor) *Encyclopedia of Library and Information Science,* Dekker, 1968.

Surveys and reports: (Editor) *Issues in Library Education,* Council of National Library Associations, 1949; (editor) *The School Library Supervisor,* American Library Association, 1956; *Libraries in British West Africa,* University of Illinois Library School, 1958; (with C. Walter Stone) *Public Library Service in Highland Park, Illinois,* University of Illinois Library School, 1959; *The University of Liberia Library,* University of Illinois Library School, 1960; (with Harold Goldstein) *A Survey of Elmhurst Public Library,* University of Illinois Library School, 1961; (with Goldstein and K. Gesterfield) *Nebraska Libraries Face the Future,* Nebraska Library Commission, 1961; (editor with J. Clement Harrison) *Education for Librarianship Abroad in Selected Countries,* University of Illinois Library School, 1963; *Educating the Librarian for 2001,* Louisiana State University, 1973. Also author of *Survey of Springfield, Vt. Town Library,* 1975. Contributor to library journals. Editor, *Library Trends,* 1952-62, and *Journal of Education for Librarianship,* 1960-63.

*   *   *

LANDEN, Robert Geran   1930-

PERSONAL: Born July 13, 1930, in Boston, Mass.; son of Harry James (an insurance executive) and Evelyn (Geran) Landen; married Patricia Kizzia, July 19, 1958; children: Michael Geran, Robert Kizzia, Jill Arnett, Amy Patricia. *Education:* College of William and Mary, A.B., 1952; University of Michigan, M.A., 1953; Princeton University, A.M., 1958, Ph.D., 1961. *Religion:* Roman Catholic. *Home:* 2810 Augusta Dr., Arlington, Tex. 76010. *Office:* Dean of Liberal Arts, University of Texas at Arlington, Arlington, Tex. 76010.

CAREER: Ball State University, Muncie, Ind., assistant professor of social science, 1959-60; University of Michigan, Ann Arbor, assistant professor of Near East studies, 1960-61; Dartmouth College, Hanover, N.H., assistant, later associate professor of history, 1961-67, assistant dean of freshmen, 1963-64; Virginia Polytechnic Institute, Blacksburg, 1967-69, associate professor, later professor of history and chairman of department; University of South

Carolina, Columbia, professor of history, 1969-75, associate provost, 1971-73, dean of College of Social and Behavioral Sciences, 1972-75; University of Texas at Arlington, professor of history and dean of College of Liberal Arts, 1975—. *Military service:* U.S. Army, 1953-55. *Member:* American Historical Association, American Oriental Society, Middle East Institute, Middle East Studies Association of North America.

WRITINGS: Oman since 1856: Disruptive Modernization in a Traditional Arab Society, Princeton University Press, 1967; *The Emergence of the Modern Middle East,* Van Nostrand, 1969; (with A. Al-Marayati) *Governments and Politics of the Middle East,* Duxbury, 1972. Contributor to professional journals.

WORK IN PROGRESS: A history of the modern Persian Gulf.

SIDELIGHTS: Landen is competent in Arabic, Spanish, French, and German. He has lived and traveled in the Middle East and Europe.

*   *   *

LANDYNSKI, Jacob W.   1930-

PERSONAL: Born May 6, 1930, in Gateshead on Tyne, England; now U.S. citizen; son of Nachman D. (a clergyman) and Estera Malka (Bezozo) Landynski; married Miriam E. Eichenstein, September 1, 1962; children: Sori, Fayga, Moshe, Shalom, Avrom, Dvora. *Education:* Brooklyn College (now Brooklyn College of the City University of New York), B.A. (summa cum laude), 1958; Johns Hopkins University, M.A., 1959, Ph.D. (honors), 1962. *Religion:* Jewish Orthodox. *Home:* 1703 President St., Brooklyn, N.Y. 11213. *Office:* New School for Social Research, New York, N.Y. 10011.

CAREER: New School for Social Research, New York, N.Y., instructor, 1962-63, assistant professor, 1963-65, associate professor, 1965-72, professor of political science, 1972—, chairman of department, 1972—. Instructor, City College (now City College of the City University of New York), summer, 1960; visiting professor, Brooklyn College of the City University of New York, 1965-67, and Rutgers University, 1969—. *Member:* American Political Science Association, Phi Beta Kappa, Pi Sigma Alpha. *Awards, honors:* Ford Foundation grant, faculty fellowship, 1968-69.

WRITINGS: Search and Seizure and the Supreme Court: A Study in Constitutional Interpretation, Johns Hopkins Press, 1966; (contributor) Stuart S. Nagel, editor, *The Rights of the Accused: In Law and Action,* Sage Publications, 1972. Contributor of monographs and articles to professional journals.

WORK IN PROGRESS: Research in right to privacy, Fourteenth Amendment due process, and fundamental rights of accused persons; a book, *The Presidency and the Constitution.*

*   *   *

LANE, Richard   1926-

PERSONAL: Born February 9, 1926, in Florida. *Education:* Attended Rollins College, 1943-44; University of Hawaii, A.B., 1948; Columbia University, A.M., 1949, Ph.D., 1958; graduate study at Tokyo University and Kyoto University, 1950-53, University of London, 1953, and Tokyo National Museum, 1956-60. *Home:* Yamashina Koyama, Gobo-No-Uchi 57, Higashiyama-Ku, Kyoto, Japan 607.

CAREER: Columbia University, New York, N.Y., lecturer in Japanese, 1953-55; Kanta College, Fatebayashi, Japan, lecturer in comparative literature, 1956-57; University of Maryland, Far East Program, Tokyo, Japan, instructor in Japanese, 1957-60; Honolulu Academy of Arts, Honolulu, Hawaii, research associate, 1959—. Writer, lecturer, and research scholar. *Military service:* U.S. Marine Corps, 1944-46. *Member:* Phi Kappa Phi. *Awards, honors:* Cutting Traveling fellow, 1950-52; overseas training and research fellow, Ford Foundation, 1952-53, 1954-55; grants-in-aid from Rockefeller Foundation, 1960-63, and Honolulu Academy of Arts, 1963—.

WRITINGS: (Contributor) Saikaku Ihara, *Five Women Who Loved Love,* translation by W. T. De Bary, Tuttle, 1956; (translator and adaptor) Naoteru Uyeno, *Japanese Arts and Crafts in the Meiji Era,* Pan Pacific Press, 1958; *Six Masterpieces of Ukiyo-e* (folio plates with text), Mitsumura, 1958; (contributor of translations from Hokusai's *Manga*) James A. Michener, *The Hokusai Sketchbooks,* Tuttle, 1958; *Kaigetsudo,* Tuttle, 1959; (with Michener) *Japanese Prints: From the Early Masters to the Modern,* Tuttle, 1959.

(Author of English notes) *Hokusai,* Kodansha, 1960; *Masters of the Japanese Print: Their World and Their Work,* Doubleday, 1962; (with Oliver Statler) *The Black Ship Scroll,* Weatherhill, 1963; (technical editor) *The Clarence Buckingham Collection of Japanese Prints,* Volume II: *Harunobu, Koryusai, Shigemasa,* Art Institute of Chicago, 1965; (contributor) Philip Rawson, editor, *Erotic Art of the East,* Weidenfeld & Nicolson, 1968; (contributor) *The Fascinating World of the Japanese Artist,* Society for Japanese Arts and Crafts, 1971; (with M. Beurdeley and others) *Chant de l'Oreiller,* Office du Livre, 1973; *Kaitai Shinsho; or, The New Anatomy,* Nakao, 1976; *Hokusai and Hiroshige,* Gabundo, 1976; *Masterworks of Japanese Erotic Painting,* Weatherhill, in press; *Images from the Floating World: The Japanese Print,* Office du Livre, in press; *Studies in Edo Literature,* Dawson, in press.

Translations of stories included in *Anthology of Japanese Literature,* Grove, 1955, and *The Wonder World of Reading,* Macaraig (Manila), 1964. Editor, "Shungo Books of the Ukiyo-e School" series, Gabundo, 1973-76. Contributor to *Encyclopaedia Britannica,* 1974; contributor of translations, articles, and reviews, both in English and Japanese, to periodicals, including *Inside Japan, Journal of the Royal Asiatic Society, Atlantic, Monumenta Nipponica, Japan Quarterly,* and *Oriental Art.* Editor, *Journal of Oriental Literature,* 1947-48, and *Ukiyo-e Art,* 1962-63; arts section editor, *Asia Scene,* 1966-69; associate editor, *Ukiyo-e,* 1968—.

WORK IN PROGRESS: Further research and publication on seventeenth- and eighteenth-century Japanese art and literature.

SIDELIGHTS: Lane is one of the few Occidentals able to read and write the classical Japanese scripts. His current goal is "to introduce scholarly methods into fields of Japanese art—in particular, ukiyo-e—hitherto left to amateurs." His *Masters of the Japanese Print* was published simultaneously in 1962 in English, French, German, Italian, Spanish, and Dutch. Lane does color photography of Japanese subjects, and, since 1963, his work has been used for the covers of several issues of *Inside Japan.*

* * *

LANGACKER, Ronald W(ayne) 1942-

PERSONAL: Surname is pronounced *Lan*-acker; born December 27, 1942, in Fond du Lac, Wis.; son of George R. (a bookkeeper) and Florence (Hinesley) Langacker; married Margaret Fullick, June 5, 1966. *Education:* University of Illinois, A.B., 1963, A.M., 1964, Ph.D., 1966. *Home:* 3286 Galloway Dr., San Diego, Calif. 92122. *Office:* Department of Linguistics, University of California, San Diego, Calif. 92037.

CAREER: University of California, San Diego, assistant professor, 1966-70, associate professor, 1970-75, professor of linguistics, 1975—. *Member:* Linguistic Society of America, American Association of University Professors, American Civil Liberties Union, Phi Beta Kappa. Phi Kappa Phi, Phi Eta Sigma, Pi Delta Phi.

WRITINGS: Language and Its Structure, Harcourt, 1968; *Fundamentals of Linguistic Analysis,* Harcourt, 1972; *Non-Distinct Arguments in Uto-Aztecan,* University of California Press, 1975. Contributor of articles and reviews to linguistics journals.

WORK IN PROGRESS: Research on the structure of English and the Uto-Aztecan languages; linguistic theory; diachronic syntax.

* * *

LANGDON, Frank C(orriston) 1919-

PERSONAL: Born June 3, 1919, in La Grange, Ill.; son of Ernest Warren (an engineer) and Julia Ida (Mondeng) Langdon; married Virginia Irene Osborne (a social worker), May 25, 1956; children: Peter John, Marc Christopher. *Education:* Harvard University, A.B., 1941, M.A., 1949; University of California, Berkeley, Ph.D., 1953. *Politics:* Democrat. *Religion:* Presbyterian. *Home:* 4736 West Fourth Ave., Vancouver, British Columbia, Canada V6T 1C2. *Office:* Department of Political Science, University of British Columbia, Vancouver, British Columbia, Canada V6T 1W5.

CAREER: U.S. War Department, Tokyo, Japan, civilian economic analyst, 1946-47; University of California Extension, university lecturer in Korea, Guam, and Japan, 1953-54; Canberra University College (now Australian National University), Canberra, senior lecturer, 1955-58; University of British Columbia, Vancouver, assistant professor, 1958-63, associate professor, 1963-67, professor of political science, 1967—. *Military service:* U.S. Naval Reserve, 1941—; active duty 1941-46; currently lieutenant commander; received eleven battle stars for service in Pacific Theater. *Member:* Canadian Political Science Association, Association for Asian Studies, Canadian Society for Asian Studies, International House of Japan. *Awards, honors:* Canada Council grant.

WRITINGS: (Contributor) F. H. Hinsley, editor, *New Cambridge Modern History,* Volume XI, Cambridge University Press, 1962; *Politics in Japan,* Little, Brown, 1967; (with Arnold J. Heidenheimer) *Business Associations and the Financing of Political Parties,* Nijhoff, 1968; (contributor) J. W. Morley, editor, *Forecast for Japan: Security in the 1970's,* Princeton University Press, 1972; *Japan's Foreign Policy,* University of British Columbia Press, 1973. Contributor to *Pacific Affairs, Asian Survey, American Political Science Review,* and other professional journals.

WORK IN PROGRESS: Research on Canadian-Japanese relations.

AVOCATIONAL INTERESTS: Figure skating, skiing.

LANGDON, George D(orland), Jr.   1933-

PERSONAL: Born May 20, 1933, in Putnam, Conn.; son of George D. (a headmaster) and Anne Claggett (Zell) Langdon; married Patricia Bull Smith, June 25, 1954; children: George D. III, Campbell Brewster. *Education:* Harvard University, A.B., 1954; Amherst College, M.A., 1957; Yale University, Ph.D., 1961. *Religion:* Episcopalian. *Office:* Office of the Provost, Yale University, New Haven, Conn. 06520.

CAREER: Yale University, New Haven, Conn., instructor in history and American studies, 1959-62; California Institute of Technology, Pasadena, assistant professor of history, 1962-64; Vassar College, Poughkeepsie, N.Y., assistant professor, 1964-67, associate professor of history, 1967-68, special assistant to the president, 1968; Yale University, New Haven, lecturer in history, 1968—, assistant provost, 1968-70, associate provost, 1970-72, deputy provost, 1972—. *Military service:* U.S. Army, 1954-56; became first lieutenant. *Member:* American Historical Association, Organization of American Historians.

WRITINGS: Pilgrim Colony: A History of New Plymouth, 1620-1691, Yale University Press, 1966. Contributor to history journals and *Encyclopedia Americana.*

WORK IN PROGRESS: A textbook on general American history; an analysis of George Washington's presidency.†

*   *   *

LANGLEY, Harold D.   1925-

PERSONAL: Born February 15, 1925, in Amsterdam, N.Y.; son of Walter Benedict and Anna Mae (McCaffrey) Langley; married Patricia A. Piccola, June 12, 1965; children: Erika, David. *Education:* Catholic University of America, A.B., 1950; University of Pennsylvania, M.A., 1951, Ph.D., 1960. *Religion:* Roman Catholic. *Home:* 2515 North Utah St., Arlington, Va. 22207.

CAREER: Library of Congress, Manuscripts Division, Washington, D.C., manuscripts assistant, 1951-52, manuscripts specialist, 1954-55; University of Pennsylvania Libraries, Philadelphia, manuscripts specialist, rare book collection, 1952-54; Marywood College, Scranton, Pa., assistant professor of history, 1955-57; U.S. Department of State, Washington, D.C., diplomatic historian, 1957-64; Catholic University of America, Washington, D.C., associate professor, 1964-68, professor, 1968-71, adjunct professor of American history, 1971—; Smithsonian Institution, Washington, D.C., associate curator of naval history, 1969—. *Military service:* U.S. Army, 1943-46; received Meritorious Service Award, Asiatic-Pacific Campaign Medal. *Member:* American Historical Association, Organization of American Historians, U.S. Naval Institute, American Military Institute, Society for Nautical Research, Society of Historians of American Foreign Relations, American Society for Legal History, Columbia Historical Society, Western History Association, Pennsylvania Historical Association.

WRITINGS: (Editor with others) *Documents on Germany, 1944-59,* U.S. Government Printing Office, 1959; (editor with others) *Documents on Disarmament, 1960,* U.S. Government Printing Office, 1961; (compiler and co-editor) *Documents on International Aspects of the Exploration and Use of Outer Space, 1954-1962,* U.S. Government Printing Office, 1963; *Social Reform in the United States Navy, 1798-1862,* University of Illinois Press, 1967; (editor) *To Utah with the Dragoons,* University of Utah Press,

1974; (editor with Francis Loewenheim) *Roosevelt and Churchill: Their Secret Wartime Correspondence,* Saturday Review Press, 1975. Also author of *St. Stephen Martyr Church and Community, 1867-1967,* for St. Stephen Martyr Centennial Committee, 1968. Contributor to *Proceedings* of U.S. Naval Institute, government publications, and historical journals.

WORK IN PROGRESS: Studies in U.S. naval and diplomatic history.

*   *   *

LANGLOIS, Walter G(ordon)   1925-

PERSONAL: Born May 27, 1925, in Springfield, Mass.; son of Walter E. (a businessman) and Ann Mae (Doyle) Langlois; married Sheila Wood, May 30, 1959; children: Walter Rawson, Rebecca Ann. *Education:* Yale University, B.A., 1950, M.A., 1952, Ph.D., 1955; University of Paris, Certificat (honors), 1949; additional study at University of Florence, 1952-53, and Harvard University, 1960-61. *Office:* Modern and Classical Languages, University of Wyoming, Laramie, Wyo. 82071.

CAREER: University of Wisconsin, Madison, instructor in French and Italian, 1954-56; Lycee Sisowath, Pnom-Penh, Cambodia, Smith-Mundt Professor, 1956-57; Boston College, Boston, Mass., assistant professor of French and Asian studies, 1957-64; University of Kentucky, Lexington, associate professor, 1964-67, professor of French literature, 1967-74; University of Wyoming, Laramie, professor of modern languages and head of Department of Modern and Classical Languages, 1974—. *Military service:* U.S. Army, 1943-46; received Bronze Star and Croix de Guerre. *Member:* Modern Language Association of America, American Association of Teachers of French, Manuscript Society (member of board of directors, 1968—), Phi Beta Kappa. *Awards, honors:* Fulbright scholar in Italy, 1952-53; Harvard University postdoctoral fellow, 1960-61; Guggenheim fellow in France, 1967-68; American Council of Learned Societies fellow, 1971-72.

WRITINGS: Andre Malraux: The Indochina Adventure, Praeger, 1966, augmented edition published in French as *Andre Malraux: L'Aventure indochinoise,* Mercure de France, 1967; (editor) *The Persistent Voice: Hellenism in French Literature since the Eighteenth Century,* New York University Press, 1971; (editor) *Andre Malraux: Du 'farfelu' aux Antimemoires,* Lettres Modernes, 1972; *Essai di bibliographie des etudes en langue anglaise consacrees a Andre Malraux, 1924-1970,* Lettres Modernes, 1972; (editor) *Andre Malraux: Visages du romancier,* Lettres Modernes, 1973. Contributor to literary journals. Editor, *Melanges Malraux Miscellany.*

WORK IN PROGRESS: Malraux et la croixade espagnole (1936-37), for Mercure de France.

AVOCATIONAL INTERESTS: Collecting books and manuscripts.

*   *   *

LAPIDE, Pinchas E.   1922-
(Phinn E. Lapide)

PERSONAL: Born November 28, 1922, in Fort St. John, British Columbia, Canada; son of Alexander and Bertha (Pinchas) Lapide; married Ruth Rosenblatt, April 26, 1960; children: Yuval. *Education:* University of Vienna, B.A., 1947; Hebrew University of Jerusalem, M.A., 1967; also studied Italian and Latin literature for two years in Milan,

Italy. *Home:* 24 Radak, Jerusalem, Israel. *Office:* Government Press Office, Jerusalem, Israel.

CAREER: Israeli Foreign Service, diplomat with Posts in Milan, Rio de Janeiro, Rome, 1951-62; Government Press Office, Jerusalem, Israel, director of publications, 1964—. *Military service:* British Army, liaison officer between Allied and Russian Armies, 1945-46. Israeli Defense Forces, officer in three wars, 1948-49, 1956, 1967. *Member:* Israeli Authors Association. *Awards, honors:* Literary award of Jewish Book Guild (New York), 1954, for *The Prophet of San Nicandro.*

*WRITINGS—*All under name Phinn E. Lapide: *The Prophet of San Nicandro,* Beechhurst Press, 1953; *Shalom, Shalom!,* Longanesi (Milan), 1958; *Kubah—lehavah be-lev Amerikah* (title means "Cuba—Between Eagle and Bear"), Karni (Tel Aviv), 1963; *A Century of U.S. Aliyah,* Jerusalem, 1963; *Pilgrim's Guide to Israel,* Harrap, 1963; *The Last Three Popes and the Jews,* Hawthorn, 1967; *Border Village,* Kiefel (West Germany), 1967; *Israel Kaleidoscope,* de Haan (Amsterdam), 1967; *Roma e gei Ebrei,* Mondadori (Milan), 1967; *Das Grenzdorf,* Kiefel, 1967; *Die Verwendung des Hebraeischen in den christlichen Religionsgemeinschaften mit besonderer Beruecksichtigung des Landes Israel,* Koeln, 1971; *Oekumene aus Christen und Juden,* Neukirchener Verlag, 1972; *Der Rabbi von Nazaret,* Spec-Verlag, 1974. Editor, *Israel Digest.*

SIDELIGHTS: Lapide speaks Russian, Hebrew, German, English, French, Italian, Spanish, Portuguese, and Arabic. *Shalom, Shalom!* was translated into seven languages, *The Prophet of San Nicandro* into nine languages, and *Three Popes and The Jews* into eight languages.†

*   *   *

LAPIDUS, Elaine   1939-
(Lee Coleman, Lane Peters)

PERSONAL: Born December 11, 1939, in New York, N.Y.; daughter of Sam and Dora (Oshins) Lapidus. *Education:* Brooklyn College (now Brooklyn College of the City University of New York), B.A., 1959; Columbia University, M.L.S., 1961. *Home:* 201 East 17th St., New York, N.Y. 10003. *Office:* William Douglas McAdams, 110 East 59th St., New York, N.Y.

CAREER: William Douglas McAdams, New York, N.Y., medical copywriter, 1961—. *Member:* Writer's Guild of America.

*WRITINGS—*Under pseudonym Lane Peters: *Promise Him Anything,* Ace Books, 1966; *Mystery at the Moscow Fair,* Criterion, 1967; *Here Comes Charlie,* Scholastic Book Services, 1970.

Television scripts, under pseudonym Lee Coleman, have been written for "Bonanza," "Marcus Welby, M.D.," "Room 222," and "Cannon."

*   *   *

LARSEN, Lawrence H.   1931-

PERSONAL: Born January 18, 1931, in Racine, Wis.; son of Elmer A. and Eileen Larson; married Barbara Cottrell, October 12, 1963. *Education:* Lawrence College (now Lawrence University), B.A., 1953; University of Wisconsin, M.A., 1955, Ph.D., 1962. *Home:* 1250 West Gregory Blvd., Kansas City, Mo. *Office:* University of Missouri—Kansas City, 5100 Rockhill Rd., Kansas City, Mo. 64110

CAREER: State Historical Society of Wisconsin, Madison, assistant state archivist, 1959-61; Carroll College, Wankesha, Wis., lecturer, 1961-62; Wisconsin State University, Oshkosh, assistant professor of history, 1962-63; State Historical Society of Wisconsin, director of Urban History Project, 1963-64; University of Missouri—Kansas City, professor of United States history, 1964—. *Member:* Organization of American Historians, State Historical Society of Wisconsin.

WRITINGS: The President Wore Spats: A Biography of Glenn Frank, State Historical Society of Wisconsin, 1965; (with Charles N. Glaab) *Factories in the Valley: Neenah-Menosha, 1870-1915,* State Historical Society of Wisconsin, 1968; (with Robert L. Branyon) *Aspects in American History, 1776-1970,* two volumes, Kendall/Hunt, 1970-71; (with Branyon) *Crisis in Urban America,* Heath, 1971; (with Branyon) *The Eisenhower Administration, 1953-1961: A Documentary History,* two volumes, Random House, 1971. Also author, with Glaab, of *Neenah-Menosha, Wisconsin: A Study of Urbanization and Industrialization, 1870-1915,* State Historical Society of Wisconsin. Contributor of articles and reviews to historical journals.

WORK IN PROGRESS: A history of urban sanitation; a four-volume history, by sections, of the American city in 1880.

AVOCATIONAL INTERESTS: Sports.

*   *   *

LARSON, Jean Russell   1930-

PERSONAL: Born July 25, 1930, in Marshalltown, Iowa; daughter of Charles Reed and Myrtle (Koester) Russell; married Richard O. Larson, September 25, 1954; married second husband, Harold Parks, June 3, 1971; children: Kathleen, Richard O., Jr., David, Rosemarie, William John, Michael, Harold, Daniel. *Education:* Attended Winthrop College, University of Iowa, University of Chicago, and University of Northern Iowa. *Religion:* Roman Catholic. *Home:* 509 South Fifth St., Marshalltown, Iowa. *Agent:* Ruch Candor, 156 Fifth Ave., New York, N.Y. 10010.

CAREER: Writer. Active in American-Arab relations as an "Arabist." *Awards, honors:* Lewis Carroll Shelf Award, 1973, for *Jack Tar.*

WRITINGS: Palace in Bagdad: Seven Tales from Arabia, Scribner, 1966; *The Silkspinners* (juvenile), Scribner, 1967; *Jack Tar* (juvenile), Macrae, 1969; *The Glass Mountain and Other Arabian Tales,* Macrae, 1972. Also author of *Muggins' Mules,* for Dillon. Contributor of nonfiction to *Mid East, Early American Life,* and other periodicals; contributor of poetry to magazines including *Michigan Quarterly Review.*

WORK IN PROGRESS: An anthology of Arab literature; a children's book, *The Marvelous Adventures of Ali the Peddler.*

SIDELIGHTS: Jean Larson told *CA:* "Interested in Arab literature, the military architecture of the Crusades, ... Arab-American relations, ... [and] love poetry. Read some of Malory's *Le Morte d'Arthur* almost daily. Consider T. E. Lawrence, Charles Gordon, Richard I, and Saladin the greatest men who ever lived (not necessarily in that order)." Her manuscripts and personal papers were accepted by the late King Faisal on behalf of the children of Saudi Arabia.

AVOCATIONAL INTERESTS: Formula 1 car racing, skiing, archaeology.

LARSON, Muriel 1924-

PERSONAL: Born February 9, 1924, in Orange, N.J.; daughter of Eugene Louis and Helen (Fretz) Koller; married Alfred J. Larson, November 3, 1942; children: Gay (Mrs. James Verhey), Lori. Education: South River Bible Institute, diploma, 1957; Bob Jones University, part-time student, 1967-69. Politics: Independent. Religion: Baptist. Home: 10 Vanderbilt Circle, Greenville, S.C. 29609.

CAREER: Stenographer with printing company in Dunellen, N.J., 1955-57, and with Tennessee Valley Authority, Chattanooga, S.C., 1962-63; Bob Jones University, Greenville, S.C., public relations writer, 1967-69; full-time writer, 1969—. Has also served as a piano teacher, choir director, substitute teacher, and home missionary.

WRITINGS: Devotions for Women's Groups, Baker Book, 1967; How to Give a Devotion, with Suggested Outlines, Baker Book, 1967; (contributor) James R. Adair, editor, God's Power to Triumph, Moody, 1968; Devotionals for Children's Groups, Baker Book, 1969; (contributor) Adair, editor, Unhooked, Baker Book, 1971; Living Miracles, Warner Press, 1973; It Took a Miracle, Warner Press, 1974; You Are What You Think, Bible Voice, 1974; God's Fantastic Creation, Moody, 1975; The Bible Says Quiz Book, Moody, in press. Contributor of numerous articles and five hymns to periodicals, mainly religious; also prepares crossword puzzles for several publishers. Editor, Reinhearter (monthly church paper), Dallas, Tex., 1966-67.

WORK IN PROGRESS: I Give Up, God.

AVOCATIONAL INTERESTS: Music (plays piano, organ, accordian, clarinet, and sings), gardening, camping.

BIOGRAPHICAL/CRITICAL SOURCES: Greenville News, Greenville, S.C., November 20, 1967.

*   *   *

LARSON, William H. 1938-

PERSONAL: Born June 3, 1938, in La Crosse, Wis.; son of George H. and Mabel (Carlsson) Larson; married Karen Nelsestuen, July 30, 1960; children: Christopher William, Andrew Joseph, Daniel James. Education: Wisconsin State College (now University of Wisconsin—La Crosse), B.S., 1960. Home: 2321 James Blvd., Racine, Wis. 53403. Office: Western Publishing Co., Inc., 1220 Mound Ave., Racine, Wis. 53404.

CAREER: High school English teacher in Racine, Wis., 1960-64; Western Publishing Co., Inc., Racine, editorial assistant, 1964-67, director of publishing services, 1967-68, editor, 1968-73, senior editor, 1973—.

WRITINGS: (Editor) Stand By for Adventure, Whitman Publishing, 1967; (editor) Seven Great Detective Stories, Whitman Publishing, 1968; (editor with N. Gretchen Greiner) Adventure Calling, Whitman Publishing, 1969; Let's Go to Animal Town, Golden Press, 1975.

*   *   *

LARUE, Gerald A(lexander) 1916-

PERSONAL: Born June 20, 1916, in Calgary, Alberta, Canada; son of Thomas Henry (a salesman) and Christena (Weber) Larue; married Lois Knight, September 18, 1944; children: Gerald Alexander, Jr., David Knight. Education: University of Alberta, B.A., 1943, B.D., 1947; St. Stephen's College, Edmonton, Alberta, Testamur, 1945; Pacific School of Religion, Th.D., 1953; Hebrew Union College, Jerusalem, Israel, postdoctoral fellow, 1967. Home:

3136 Barkentine Rd., Palos Verdes Peninsula, Calif. 90274. Office: School of Religion, University of Southern California, Los Angeles, Calif. 90007.

CAREER: Ordained clergyman of the United Church of Canada, 1945. Held pastorates at Notikewin, Alberta, 1945-46, Edmonton, Alberta, 1946-49, Lincoln, Calif. (Methodist), 1949-50, and Suisun, Calif. (Congregational), 1950-53; Church Divinity School of the Pacific, Berkeley, Calif., lecturer in Old Testament, 1951-52; Pacific School of Religion, Berkeley, lecturer in Bible, 1953-54; National Council of Churches, New York, N.Y., member of executive staff, 1954-58; University of Southern California, Los Angeles, associate professor, 1958-66, professor of Biblical history and archaeology, 1966—, director of research center in archaeology. Visiting professor of Bible history, Hebrew Union College, Los Angeles, 1961-62; visiting scholar, University of California, Santa Barbara, summer, 1974. Associate director of American excavations in Hebron, 1966; excavated at El Kom, 1967; leader of University of Southern California expedition to excavate at Khirbet Mazra'a, 1968.

MEMBER: Society of Biblical Literature, American Schools of Oriental Research, American Oriental Society, Archaeological Institute of America, American Academy of Religion (president of Pacific Coast section, 1963).

WRITINGS: (Author of introduction) Nelson Glueck, editor, Hesed in the Bible, Hebrew Union College Press, 1967; Old Testament Life and Literature, Allyn & Bacon, 1968; Babylon and the Bible, Baker Book, 1969; Your Future in Archaeology, Richards Rosen Press, 1970; Ancient Myth and Modern Man, Prentice-Hall, 1975. Contributor to religious journals. Editor, Bulletin of American Academy of Religion, 1964-70.

WORK IN PROGRESS: A book on death and dying; a book on ancient myths and modern woman.

*   *   *

LASSITER, Roy L(eland), Jr. 1927-

PERSONAL: Born March 27, 1927, in Clermont, Fla.; son of Roy Leland (a citrus grower) and Lelia (Boring) Lassiter; married Dorothy Seaver, January 26, 1947; children: Linda Lee, William Leonard, Glenn Robert. Education: University of Florida, B.S.A. (with honors), 1953, Ph.D., 1957. Politics: Republican. Religion: Baptist. Home address: Route 15, Box 226A, Maxville, Fla. 32265. Office: University of North Florida, Jacksonville, Fla. 32216.

CAREER: Central and Southern Florida Flood Control District, West Palm Beach, analyst and economic consultant, 1954-56; University of Florida, Gainesville, instructor, 1955-57, assistant professor, 1957-59, associate professor, 1959-64, professor of economics, 1964-69, assistant dean, 1966-68, associate dean of academic affairs, 1968-69, dean of faculties, 1969-70; University of North Florida, Jacksonville, professor of economics, dean of faculties, and vice-president of the university, 1970—. Consultant to Florida East Coast Railway Co., and to legal firms. Member of State Mission Board, Florida Baptist Convention, 1963-65. Military service: U.S. Coast Guard, 1945-46. U.S. Army, 1950-52; became first lieutenant. U.S. Army Reserve, beginning 1952, retired as lieutenant colonel. Member: American Economic Association, Southern Economic Association, Alpha Kappa Psi, Phi Kappa Phi, Omicron Delta Epsilon.

WRITINGS: (With W. K. McPherson) Agricultural Land

Prices in Palm Beach County, 1940-1965, Agricultural Experimentation Station, University of Florida, 1959; *Utilization of U.S. Otter-Trawl Shrimp Vessels in the Gulf Area, 1959-1961*, Bureau of Economic and Business Research, University of Florida, 1964; (with R. J. Garrett) *The Burden of Ad Valorem Real Property Taxes Under Varying Assessment Rates*, Public Administration Clearing Service, University of Florida, 1965; (contributor) Sol Schreibner, editor, *Damages in Personal Injury and Wrongful Death Cases*, Practising Law Institute, 1965; *The Association of Income and Educational Achievement*, University of Florida Press, 1966; *Instructional Productivity and the Utilization of Faculty Resources in the State University System of Florida*, Institute of Higher Education, University of Florida, 1976.

WORK IN PROGRESS: Further research on faculty productivity and resource utilization.

* * *

LAUFER, Leopold 1925-

PERSONAL: Born December 27, 1925, in Czechoslovakia; came to United States in 1941, naturalized in 1944; son of Robert (a businessman) and Anna (Vrba) Laufer; married Rita S. Freeman (a public health nurse), November 16, 1952; children: David, Michael, Miriam, Daniel. *Education:* Queens College (now Queens College of the City University of New York), B.A., 1949; Columbia University, M.A. and Certificate of Russian Institute, 1951, Ph.D., 1968. *Home:* 306 Hillsboro Dr., Silver Spring, Md. 20902.

CAREER: Policy adviser and writer in Washington, D.C., and overseas, for U.S. Information Agency, 1952-62; U.S. Department of State, Agency for International Development, Washington, D.C., development officer, 1962—. Project director, Twentieth Century Fund, 1964-66; part-time teacher. *Military service:* U.S. Army, 1944-46; served in European and Pacific Theaters; became staff sergeant. *Member:* Society for International Development, Academy of Political Science.

WRITINGS: Israel and the Developing Countries: New Approaches to Cooperation, Twentieth Century Fund, 1967. Writer of pamphlet, "World Without War," and contributor to *Reconstructionist, Problems of Communism, International Development Review, Development Digest*, and *Span* (New Delhi).

WORK IN PROGRESS: Projects in modernization and political development.

SIDELIGHTS: Laufer has traveled widely in all continents except Australia. He is competent in seven languages.

* * *

LAUGHLIN, James 1914-

PERSONAL: Born October 30, 1914, in Pittsburgh, Pa.; son of Henry Hughart and Marjory (Rea) Laughlin; married Margaret Keyser, 1942 (divorced, 1952); married Ann Clark Resor, May 19, 1957; children: (first marriage) Paul, Leila; (second marriage) Robert, Henry. *Education:* Harvard University, A.B., 1939. *Politics:* Republican. *Religion:* Presbyterian. *Home:* Mountain Rd., Norfolk, Conn. 06058. *Office:* New Directions Publishing Corp., 333 Sixth Ave., New York, N.Y. 10014.

CAREER: New Directions Publishing Corp., New York City, founder, 1937, editor and president, 1937—; Intercultural Publications, Inc., New York City, president, 1952-

69. Alta Lodge Co., Alta, Utah, vice-president, 1948-58, president, 1958-59; vice-president, Alta Ski Lifts Co., 1950—. Consultant, Indian Southern Languages Book Trust, Madras, 1956-58; member of U.S. National Commission for UNESCO, 1962-63, and National Commission for International Cooperation Year, 1966. Member of visiting committees to German departments at Princeton and Harvard Universities. *Member:* American Academy of Arts and Sciences, Authors League of America. P.E.N.; Century Association, and Harvard Club (both New York). *Awards, honors:* Chevalier, Legion of Honor, for cultural service in publishing translations of French literature; D.Litt., Hamilton College, 1970.

*WRITINGS—*Poetry: *Some Natural Things*, New Directions, 1945; *A Small Book of Poems*, New Directions, 1948; *The Wild Anemone, and Other Poems*, New Directions, 1957; *Selected Poems*, New Directions, 1960. Translator of other books of poetry for publication abroad. Editor of *New Directions in Prose and Poetry*, New Directions, 1937—(Number 30 published in 1975), and various numbers of *Perspectives USA* and "Perspectives" supplements to *Atlantic Monthly*, 1952-58. Contributor of articles on skiing to *Town and Country, Harper's Bazaar, Ski, Sports Illustrated, Ski Annual*, and other publications.

* * *

LAVINE, Richard A. 1917-

PERSONAL: Surname is accented on second syllable, which rhymes with "pine"; born January 7, 1917, in Los Angeles, Calif.; son of Isaac (a merchant and manufacturer) and Edith (Glazer) Lavine; married Ruth Jacobson (an attorney), April 12, 1944; children: Catherine J., Raymond A. *Education:* Attended California Institute of Technology, 1935-36; University of California, Los Angeles, A.B., 1939; University of Southern California, LL.B., 1942, LL.M., 1955. *Politics:* Democrat. *Religion:* Jewish. *Office:* 121 South Beverly Dr., Beverly Hills, Calif. 90212.

CAREER: Assistant attorney and chief of Civil Division, U.S. Attorney's Office, Southern District of California, 1957-60; attorney in private practice, Beverly Hills, Calif., 1961-74; deputy assistant attorney general, U.S. Department of Justice, 1974—. *Military service:* U.S. Army Air Forces, 1943-46; became captain. U.S. Air Force Reserve, on active duty, 1951-53; became major. *Member:* Federal Bar Association (Los Angeles chapter president, 1960-61).

*WRITINGS—*Co-author: *Radio and the Law*, Parker & Son, 1948; *Federal Civil Practice*, California Continuing Education of the Bar, 1961; *Manual of Federal Practice*, McGraw, 1967.

WORK IN PROGRESS: A supplement to *Manual of Federal Practice*.

* * *

LAW, Howard W(illiam) 1919-

PERSONAL: Born June 22, 1919, in Long Beach, Calif.; son of Raymond Andrew (a salesman) and Martha (Waring) Law; married Joan Lambourne (a university instructor), December 15, 1944; children: Gloria May (Mrs. William Perkins, Jr.), Susan Joan. *Education:* Attended University of California, Los Angeles, 1937-38; Bible Institute of Los Angeles, Th.B., 1943; Seattle Pacific College, B.A., 1951; University of Texas, M.A., 1960, Ph.D., 1962. *Politics:* Republican. *Religion:* Baptist. *Office:* Simpson College, 801 Silver Ave., San Francisco, Calif. 94134.

CAREER: Missionary, translator, linguist, and teacher among the Aztecs of southern Veracruz, Mexico, 1943-62, as member of Wycliffe Bible Translators, Inc., and Summer Institute of Linguistics, Inc., both Huntington Beach, Calif.; University of Texas at Austin, research associate, 1962-63, lecturer in anthropology, 1963; University of California, Los Angeles, visiting lecturer in anthropology and linguistics, 1963-65; Hartford Seminary Foundation, Hartford, Conn., assistant professor of linguistics, 1965-67; University of Minnesota, Minneapolis, associate professor of linguistics, 1967-72; Simpson College, San Francisco, Calif., professor of anthropology and missions, and academic dean, 1972—. University of Oklahoma, Summer Institute of Linguistics, teacher, 1946-65, head of grammar department, 1964-65. Visiting lecturer at Fuller Theological Seminary, 1964, and University of Toronto, 1966-67. *Member:* American Anthropological Association (fellow), Linguistic Society of America.

WRITINGS: Obligatory Constructions of Isthmus Nahuat Grammar, Mouton & Co., 1966; *Winning a Hearing: An Introduction to Missionary Anthropology and Linguistics,* Eerdmans, 1967; (contributor) Americo Paredes, editor, *Folktales of Mexico,* University of Chicago Press, 1970. Compiler of *Concordance of Sahagun's Works in Nahuatl,* and, with wife, Joan Law, of an Aztec primer, 1946, 2nd revision, 1956. Translator of the Gospel of Mark and six of the General Epistles of the New Testament into Isthmus Nahuat. Contributor of articles and reviews to anthropological and linguistic journals.

WORK IN PROGRESS: An article, "Culture Shock/Suffering: Either or Both?"

AVOCATIONAL INTERESTS: Woodworking, stamps, sports (especially football).

* * *

LAWRENCE, Merle 1915-

PERSONAL: Born December 26, 1915, in Remsen, N.Y.; son of George William (a clergyman) and Alice (Bowne) Lawrence; married Roberta Harper, August 8, 1942; children: Linda Alice (Mrs. E. Robert Nolt, Jr.), Roberta Harper (Mrs. James E. Henderson), James Bowne. *Education:* Princeton University, A.B., 1938, M.A., 1940, Ph.D., 1941. *Religion:* Protestant. *Residence:* Ann Arbor, Mich. 48104. *Office:* Kresge Hearing Research Institute, Ann St., Ann Arbor, Mich. 48104.

CAREER: Princeton University, Princeton, N.J., assistant professor, 1946-50, associate professor, 1950-52; University of Michigan, Ann Arbor, professor of otorhinolaryngology and professor of physiology, Medical School, professor of psychology, College of Literature, Science and Arts, and research associate, Institute of Industrial Health, 1952—, director of Kresge Hearing Research Institute, 1961—. *Military service:* U.S. Navy, 1941-46, 1950-51; received Purple Heart and Secretary of the Navy's Commendation.

MEMBER: Acoustical Society of America, American Physiological Society, American Association for the Advancement of Science, Otosclerosis Study Group, American Academy of Ophthalmology and Otolaryngology, American Triological Society, American Otological Society, Collegium Oto-Rhino-Laryngologicum Amicitiae Scarum, Association for Research in Otolaryngology, Sigma Xi. *Awards, honors:* Awards of merit, American Academy of Ophthalmology and Otolaryngology, 1965, and American Otological Society, 1967; Princeton University class of 1938 distinguished service award, 1973.

WRITINGS: Studies in Human Behavior, Princeton University Press, 1949; (with E. G. Wever) *Physiological Acoustics,* Princeton University Press, 1954; (with M. Alpern and D. Wolsk) *Sensory Processes,* Brooks/Cole Publishing, 1967; (with J. E. Hawkins and W. P. Work) *Otophysiology,* S. Karger, 1973.

* * *

LAWRENCE, Samuel A. 1928-

PERSONAL: Born September 20, 1928, in Providence, R.I.; son of W. Appleton (a clergyman) and Hannah (Cobb) Lawrence; married Mary Miller, June 30, 1956; children: Susan W., Samuel A., Jr., Mary W. *Education:* Harvard University, A.B., 1950; American University, M.P.A., Ph.D., 1965. *Office:* Vice-President for Administration, Cornell University, Ithaca, N.Y. 14850.

CAREER: U.S. Bureau of the Budget, Washington, D.C., staff, 1954-67; U.S. Commission on Marine Science, Engineering and Resources, Washington, D.C., executive director, 1967-69; affiliated with Aluminum of Canada, 1969-70; Cornell University, Ithaca, N.Y., vice-president for administration, 1970—. *Military service:* U.S. Army, 1951-53.

WRITINGS: Battery Additive ADX2: A Case Study, University of Alabama Press, 1965; *United States Merchant Shipping Policies and Politics,* Brookings Institution, 1966; *International Sea Transport: The Years Ahead,* Heath Lexington, 1972.

* * *

LAWSON, Lewis A. 1931-

PERSONAL: Born November 13, 1931, in Bristol, Tenn.; son of James Calvin (a clerk) and Nannie Belle (Mays) Lawson; married Barbara Anna Hahn, April 6, 1957; children: Rachel, John. *Education:* East Tennessee State University, B.S., 1957, M.A., 1959; University of Wisconsin, Ph.D., 1963. *Home:* 6706 44th Avenue, Hyattsville, Md. *Office:* Department of English, University of Maryland, College Park, Md. 20742.

CAREER: East Tennessee State University, Johnson City, instructor in English, 1959-60; University of Maryland, College Park, instructor, 1963-65, assistant professor, 1965-67, associate professor, 1967-71, professor of English, 1972—. *Military service:* U.S. Navy, airman, 1951-54. *Member:* Society for the Study of Southern Literature, American Association of University Professors, South Atlantic Modern Language Association.

WRITINGS: (Editor with Melvin J. Friedman) *The Added Dimension: The Art and Mind of Flannery O'Connor,* Fordham University Press, 1966. Essays included in several collections. Contributor to professional journals, including *Texas Quarterly, American Imago, Renascence, Literature and Psychology, Southern Literary Journal,* and *Journal of the American Academy of Religion.*

WORK IN PROGRESS: Studies of modern Southern literature.

* * *

LAYTON, Robert 1930-

PERSONAL: Born May 2, 1930, in London, England; married Ingrid Nina Thompson. *Education:* Worcester College, Oxford, M.A., 1953; further study at University of Uppsala and University of Stockholm, 1953-55. *Home:* 112 Goldhurst Ter., London N.W. 6, England.

CAREER: Pianist and composer; British Broadcasting Corp., London, England, producer of music talks for Third Programme. Compositions include a symphony and works for piano. *Awards, honors:* Swedish Government scholarship, 1953-55.

WRITINGS: Franz Berwald, Bonniers, 1956, translation published as *Franz Berwald, Swedish Symphonist,* Anthony Blond, 1959; (contributor) Rollo Myers, editor, *Twentieth-Century Music,* J. Calder, 1960; *Sibelius,* Dent, 1965, Octagon, 1966; (contributor) Robert Simpson, editor, *The Symphony,* Penguin, 1967; *Sibelius and His World,* Viking, 1970 (published in England as *The World of Sibelius,* Thames & Hudson, 1970); (with Humphrey Searle) *Twentieth-Century Composers: Britain, Scandinavia and the Netherlands,* Weidenfeld & Nicolson, 1972, Holt, 1973; *Dvorak: Symphonies and Concertos,* University of Washington Press, 1975; (translator) Erik Tawaststjerna, *Sibelius,* Volume I, University of California Press, 1976; *Prokofiev: Symphonies and Concertos,* University of Washington Press, in press. Also author of *Penguin Stereo Guide,* 1975, and with Edward Greenfield and Ivan March, *Stereo Record Guide,* Volumes V-X. Editor, "BBC Music Guides," University of Washington Press, 1975—. Contributor of reviews and a quarterly retrospect feature to *Gramophone.*

WORK IN PROGRESS: A translation of Erik Tawaststjerna's *Sibelius,* Volume II; a book on Sibelius.

* * *

LAZARUS, Harold 1927-

PERSONAL: Born January 16, 1927, in New York, N.Y.; son of Louis (a retailer) and Anna (Fritz) Lazarus; married Carol Nunes, June 22, 1952; children: Mark Leander, Eric Lewis. *Education:* New York University, B.A., 1949; Columbia University, M.S., 1952, Ph.D., 1963. *Politics:* Democrat. *Religion:* Jewish. *Home:* 225 Wellington Rd., Garden City, N.Y. 11530. *Office:* School of Business, Hofstra University, Hempstead, N.Y. 11550.

CAREER: Hofstra University, Hempstead, N.Y., assistant professor of management, 1951-63; New York University, Graduate School of Business Administration, New York, N.Y., professor of management, 1963-73; Hofstra University, professor of management, and dean, 1973—. Visiting faculty member at Columbia University and New York University. Lecturer to business and non-profit organizations on decision making, supervision, and career planning. Member of board of directors of Superior Surgical Manufacturing Company, Inc. Management consultant to Dun & Bradstreet, Goodbody & Co., U.S. Department of Army, Western Electric Co., Prentice-Hall, Inc., Cornell University, and others. *Military service:* U.S. Navy, 1945-46.

MEMBER: Academy of Management (member of board of governors, 1968-70), Society for the Advancement of Management, Eastern Academy of Management (president, 1969-70), Middle Atlantic Association of Colleges of Business Administration (first vice-president, 1975-76), Phi Beta Kappa, Mu Gamma Tau, Omicron Chi Epsilon, Pi Delta Epsilon, Beta Gamma Sigma.

WRITINGS: American Business Dictionary, Philosophical Library, 1957; (editor) A. M. Sullivan, *Human Values in Management,* Dun & Bradstreet, 1968; (editor with E. K. Warren) *The Progress of Management: Process, Behavior, and Operations Research,* Prentice-Hall, 1968, 2nd edition (with Warren) published as *The Progress of Management:*

Process and Behavior in a Changing Environment, 1972; (with Edward Tomeski) *People-Oriented Computer Systems,* Van Nostrand, 1975. Contributor of chapters to books; also contributor of articles and book reviews to professional journals. Member of editorial board of *Academy of Management Journal,* 1970-73.

WORK IN PROGRESS: Managing Managers in American Subsidiaries and German Companies; Executive Recruitment, Selection, Training, Compensation, and Evaluation.

* * *

LEA, David A(lexander) M(aclure) 1934-

PERSONAL: Born July 25, 1934, in Adelaide, South Australia; son of Richard Henry (an engineer) and Lucinda (Cockburn) Lea; married Beverley Cilento, January 4, 1958; children: Mary Anne, Peter, James. *Education:* University of Adelaide, B.A. (first class honors), 1958; Australian National University, Ph.D., 1964. *Religion:* None. *Office:* Geography Department, University of New England, Armidale, New South Wales, Australia.

CAREER: King's College, Adelaide, South Australia, teacher, 1958-61; Australian National University, Canberra, research scholar, 1961-64; Monash University, Melbourne, Victoria, Australia, lecturer in geography, 1964-68; University of Papua New Guinea, Port Moresby, 1968-73, began as senior lecturer, became professor of geography; University of New England, Armidale, Australia, professor of geography, 1974—. Visiting professor at McGill University, 1967-68. *Member:* Institute of Australian Geographers.

WRITINGS: (With Donald D. Harris) *A Regional Geography of South Australia,* Whitcombe & Tombs, 1961, 4th edition, 1975; (with P. G. Irwin) *New Guinea: The Territory and Its People,* Oxford University Press, 1967, 2nd edition, 1971; (with R. G. Ward) *An Atlas of Papua New Guinea,* Collins, 1971.

* * *

LEACH, John Robert 1922-

PERSONAL: Born September 23, 1922, in Selinsgrove, Pa.; son of Clayton Earle (a banker) and Blanche (Attinger) Leach; married Elizabeth Anne Miller, June 7, 1947; children: John Miller. *Education:* Susquehanna University, B.S., 1947; Columbia University, M.A., 1949, Ed.D., 1953. *Religion:* Lutheran. *Home:* 34 College Dr., Jersey City, N.J. 07305. *Office:* Department of Music, Jersey City State College, Jersey City, N.J. 07305.

CAREER: Public school music teacher in Troy, Pa., 1947-49; Susquehanna University, Selinsgrove, Pa., instructor, 1950-53, assistant professor, 1953-57, associate professor, 1957-59; Augustana College, Rock Island, Ill., assistant professor, 1959-62, associate professor, 1962-65; Jersey City State College, Jersey City, N.J., associate professor, 1965-68, professor of music, 1968—. Conductor of college bands, college choir, and church choirs; church organist. Member of board of trustees, Upsala College, 1970—. *Military service:* U.S. Army, 1943-45. *Member:* Music Educators National Conference, American Association of University Professors, New Jersey Music Educators Association.

WRITINGS: Functional Piano for the Teacher, Prentice-Hall, 1968.

LEADER, Ninon 1933-

PERSONAL: Born September 3, 1933, in Budapest, Hungary; daughter of Imre Nemenyi; married Elliot Leader (a professor of theoretical physics), 1961; children: Imre-Bennett, Darian. *Education:* University of Eotvos Lorand, M.A., 1955; Cambridge University, Ph.D., 1961. *Office:* 40 Menelik Rd., London NW2, England.

CAREER: University of California, Berkeley, lecturer in Hungarian, 1963-65; Cambridge University, Clare Hall, Cambridge, England, fellow, 1966-1969; executive editor, *International Journal of Psycho-Analysis* and *International Review of Psycho-Analysis,* 1974—.

WRITINGS: Hungarian Classical Ballads, Cambridge University Press, 1967.

WORK IN PROGRESS: Endre Ady, a selection of one hundred Hungarian poems in a bilingual edition with notes, for Cambridge University Press.

* * *

LEAF, Russell C(harles) 1935-

PERSONAL: Born November 1, 1935, in Chicago, Ill.; son of Norman (a mailman) and Dora (Robok) Leaf; married Susan Ruth Peskin (a psychologist), June 3, 1961; children: Daniel, Sarah, Jonathan. *Education:* University of Chicago, A.B., 1958; Brown University, Sc.M., 1960; University of Pennsylvania, Ph.D., 1965. *Office:* Department of Psychology, Rutgers University, 88 College Ave., New Brunswick, N.J. 08903.

CAREER: Squibb Institute for Medical Research, New Brunswick, N.J., senior research psychopharmacologist, 1963-66; Wesleyan University, Middletown, Conn., assistant professor of psychology, 1966-67, and biology, beginning 1967; currently a faculty member of the psychology department at Rutgers University, New Brunswick, N.J. Consultant in psychopharmacology to Squibb Institute for Medical Research, 1966—, and Shulton, Inc., 1967—. Certified psychologist, State of Connecticut. *Member:* American Psychological Association, Behavior Pharmacology Society, American Association for the Advancement of Science (fellow), American Association of University Professors, New York Academy of Sciences, Eastern Psychological Association, Sigma Xi.

WRITINGS: (Editor with Richard C. DeBold and Frank Barron) *LSD, Man and Society,* Wesleyan University Press, 1967; (with Bernard Palmer and DeBold) *Danny Orlis and Trouble on the Circle R Ranch,* Moody, 1968. Contributor to proceedings of scientific societies, and about twenty-five articles to scientific journals.

WORK IN PROGRESS: Directing research project on "Drugs and Learning" sponsored by U.S. Public Health Service.†

* * *

LEAKE, Jane Acomb 1928-

PERSONAL: Surname is pronounced Leek; born August 12, 1928, in Cincinnati, Ohio; daughter of Laurence Everett (a building estimator) and Ruth (Landwehr) Acomb; married Lowell Leake, Jr. (a professor of mathematics), September 5, 1959; children: Katherine Jane, Lowell Gregory. *Education:* University of Cincinnati, A.B. (with high honors), 1950, M.A., 1952; University of Wisconsin, Ph.D., 1963. *Home:* 334 Witthorne Dr., Cincinnati, Ohio 45215. *Office:* University of Cincinnati, Cincinnati, Ohio 45221.

CAREER: Walnut Hills High School, Cincinnati, Ohio, teacher of English and French, 1952-55; University of Cincinnati, Cincinnati, Ohio, instructor in literature, 1961-64, assistant professor, 1965-69, associate professor, 1969-73, professor of history, 1973—, chairperson of department of history, philosophy, and political science, 1970—. *Member:* Mediaeval Academy of America, American Association of University Professors, American Historical Association, American Civil Liberties Union, Common Cause, National Organization for Women (treasurer, 1968-69), Phi Beta Kappa. *Awards, honors:* Named Outstanding Educator of America, 1971.

WRITINGS: The Geats of Beowulf: A Study in the Geographical Mythology of the Middle Ages, University of Wisconsin Press, 1967; (contributor) David Herlihy, Vsevelod Slessarev, and Robert S. Liopez, editors, *Economy, Society and Government in Medieval Italy; Essays in Honor of Robert L. Reynolds,* Kent State University Press, 1969. Contributor to *Modern Language Quarterly.*

WORK IN PROGRESS: Editing, at the request of the family, the late Robert L. Reynolds' unpublished and incomplete papers concerned with Anglo-Saxon literature and history.

SIDELIGHTS: Jane Leake is competent for research purposes in Latin, Old Norse, Old and Middle English, German, French, Spanish, and the Scandinavian languages.

* * *

LEATHERMAN, LeRoy 1922-

PERSONAL: Born February 10, 1922, in Alexandria, La.; son of LeRoy Sessums (a salesman) and Mary Aline (Dugger) Leatherman. *Education:* Attended Vanderbilt University, 1939-41, Kenyon College, 1941-42, and University of Illinois, 1943-44; Southern Methodist University, B.A., 1948. *Home:* 112 Pinckney St., Boston, Mass. 02114.

CAREER: Dallas Public Library, Dallas, Tex., director of films and recordings department, 1949-53; Martha Graham School and Dance Co., New York City, director and personnel manager, 1953-60; International Film Foundation, New York City, producer and writer, 1962-63; Martha Graham Center, New York City, executive director, beginning 1966; Boston University, Boston, Mass., assistant dean of School for the Arts, 1972-74, associate vice-president for government and university relations, 1974-76. Fellow of L'Abbaye de Royaumont and La Messeuguiere, Alpes Maritime. *Military service:* U.S. Army Air Forces, Intelligence, 1942-46. *Awards, honors: Sewanee Review* fellowship, 1957-58; MacDowell Colony fellowship; Huntington Hartford Foundation fellowship.

WRITINGS: The Caged Birds (novel), Harcourt, 1950; *The Other Side of the Tree,* Harcourt, 1954; (with Heinz Westman) *The Springs of Creativity,* Atheneum, 1961; (author of text) *Martha Graham: Portrait of the Lady as an Artist,* photographs by Martha Swope, Knopf, 1966. Author of film scripts, including "A Dancer's World," "Yugoslavia," "Turkey," and "The Ancient Egyptian." Contributor of short stories and critical essays to *Sewanee Review.*

SIDELIGHTS: Leatherman contributed the text to accompany the almost two hundred photographs taken by Martha Swope for *Martha Graham: Portrait of an Artist.* Oleg Kerensky calls this tribute to the "high priestess" of modern dance "an admirable complement to her performance, . . . both as a reminder for her existing admirers and as an introduction for new ones." According to a *New Statesman* critic, Leatherman "writes very well about what interests him: Martha Graham's personality, her methods of work, her use of props and costumes, her leading dancers and so on." LeRoy Leatherman speaks French and German. He has often traveled in Europe, and he lived in southern France from 1960 to 1961. He has also spent six months traveling in the Orient and the Near East.

BIOGRAPHICAL/CRITICAL SOURCES: New Statesman, March 10, 1967; *Listener*, April 6, 1967.

*　　*　　*

LEAVENWORTH, James Lynn 1915-

PERSONAL: Born December 6, 1915, in Detroit, Mich.; son of James D. (a laborer) and Grace (Biery) Leavenworth; married Marie Bunt (a high school reading specialist), April, 1944; children: Nancy Joan, Deborah Ann, Mary Elizabeth, James Thomas. *Education:* Chaffee Junior College, student, 1935-36; University of Redlands, A.B. (with high honors), 1940; Berkeley Baptist Divinity School, B.D. (with distinction), 1943; Yale University, Ph.D., 1950. *Home:* 15 Willow Lane, Collegeville, Pa. 19426. *Office:* Reach Associates, Inc., 601 Burton Rd., Oreland, Pa.

CAREER: Baptist clergyman; pastor in Niantic, Conn., 1943-45, in Manchester, N.H., 1945-51; American Baptist Board of Education, Valley Forge, Pa., director of department of theological education, 1951-75; Reach Associates, Inc., Oreland, Pa., president and staff director, 1975—. Adjunct professor, San Francisco Theological Seminary. Education consultant, Kanto Gakuin University, Yokohama, Japan. Trustee of Morehouse College, Spellman College, Interdenominational Center, Andover Newton Theological School, Berkeley Baptist Divinity School, Colgate Rochester Divinity School.

WRITINGS: (Editor) *Great Themes in Theology*, Judson, 1958; (contributor) William Wolf, editor, *Protestant Churches and Reform Today*, Seabury, 1964; (with Takaaki Aikawa) *The Mind of Japan*, Judson, 1967. Contributor to religious journals.

WORK IN PROGRESS: Theological Ground, a study in theological presuppositions; *Education for All*, a study of community education in Atlantic City, N.J.

*　　*　　*

LEAVIS, F(rank) R(aymond) 1895-

PERSONAL: Born July 14, 1895, in Cambridge, England; son of Harry Leavis; married Queenie Dorothy Roth (also an author), 1929; children: two sons, one daughter. *Education:* Emmanuel College, Cambridge, history tripos and English tripos. *Home:* 12 Bulstrode Gardens, Cambridge, England.

CAREER: Founder, and editor of *Scrutiny* (a quarterly review), 1932-53; Cambridge University, Downing College, Cambridge, England, fellow, 1936-62, university reader in English, 1959-62, honorary fellow, 1962-64; University of York, Heslington, York, England, honorary visiting professor of English, 1965; University of Wales, Cathays Park, Cardiff, Cheltenham Lecturer, 1968, visiting professor, 1969; University of Bristol, Bristol, England, Churchill Professor of English, 1970. *Member:* American Academy of Arts and Sciences (honorary member). *Awards, honors:* Litt.D. from University of Leeds, 1965, and University of York, 1967; LL.D., University of Aberdeen, 1970.

WRITINGS: New Bearings in English Poetry: A Study of the Contemporary Situation, Chatto & Windus, 1932, new edition, George W. Stewart, 1950; *For Continuity*, Minority Press, 1933, reprinted, Books for Libraries, 1968; *How to Teach Reading: A Primer for Ezra Pound*, Minority Press, 1932, reprinted, Folcroft, 1969; (with Denys Thompson) *Culture and Environment: The Training of Critical Awareness*, Chatto & Windus, 1933, reprinted, Barnes & Noble, 1962; (editor) *Towards Standards of Criticism: Selections from "The Calendar of Modern Letters," 1925-27*, Lawrence & Wishart, 1933, reprinted, Folcroft, 1969; (editor and author of introduction) *Determinations: Critical Essays*, Chatto & Windus, 1934, Folcroft, 1969; *Revaluation: Tradition and Development in English Poetry*, Chatto & Windus, 1936, Norton, 1963; *Education and the University: A Sketch for an 'English School,'* Chatto & Windus, 1943, new edition, 1961, reprinted, Books for Libraries, 1972; *The Great Tradition: George Eliot, Henry James, and Joseph Conrad*, George W. Stewart, 1948, new edition, Chatto & Windus, 1962, New York University Press, 1963.

(Editor and author of introduction) John Stuart Mill, *On Bentham and Coleridge*, Chatto & Windus, 1950, George W. Stewart, 1951; *The Common Pursuit*, Chatto & Windus, 1952, New York University Press, 1964; *D. H. Lawrence, Novelist*, Chatto & Windus, 1955, Knopf, 1956; (author of retrospect) *Scrutiny*, Volumes I-XX reissued in one set, Cambridge University Press, 1963; *"Anna Karenina," and Other Essays*, Chatto & Windus, 1967, Pantheon, 1968; (editor) *A Selection from "Scrutiny,"* two volumes, Cambridge University Press, 1968; (with wife, Queenie Dorothy Leavis) *Lectures in America*, Pantheon, 1969; *English Literature in Our Time and the University*, Chatto & Windus, 1969; (with Queenie Dorothy Leavis) *Dickens: The Novelist*, Chatto & Windus, 1970, Pantheon, 1971; *Nor Shall My Sword: Discourses on Pluralism, Compassion, and Social Hope*, Barnes & Noble, 1972; *Letters in Criticism*, edited and introduced by John Tasker, Chatto & Windus, 1974; *The Living Principle*, Oxford University Press, 1975. Also author of pamphlets on Gerald Manley Hopkins, D. H. Lawrence, and C. P. Snow.

SIDELIGHTS: Dr. Leavis resigned from his position at Cambridge after a controversy surrounding the selection of a person of opposing views as a fellow in English. He wrote of his quarterly and its influence on the literary world: "In the strength of the essential Cambridge which it consciously and explicitly represented, *Scrutiny* not only survived the hostility of the institutional academic powers; it became—who now questions it?—the clear triumphant justification to the world of Cambridge as a human centre. In Cambridge it was the vitalizing force that gave the English School its reputation and influence, and its readers in the world at large, small as the subscribing public was, formed an incomparably influential community. . . . It established a new critical idiom and a new conception of the nature of critical thought."

Alan Lelchuk estimated in his review of *"Anna Karenina," and Other Essays:* "Leavis cares for literature and for standards—and in an age when most literary criticism consists of a pedestrian professionalism and when literary standards are too frequently abandoned for this cause or that promotion, Leavis is a welcome reminder that literary criticism can be a serious discipline." Edward Thomas wrote of Leavis: "His lack of style is as bad in its way as the self-conscious style of the belletrists. Leavis does love great literature, and this comes out in his always relevant and sensitive choice of quotation, yet the very contrast between the language of creative literature and his own critical language is to me symptomatic of a wrong-headed if honourable approach.''

BIOGRAPHICAL/CRITICAL SOURCES—Books: C. D. Narasimhaiah and others, editors, F. R. Leavis: Some Aspects of His Work, Rao & Raghauan, 1963; D. K. Cornelius and Edwin S. Vincent, Cultures in Conflict: Perspectives on the Snow-Leavis Controversy, Scott, Foresman, 1964; D. F. McKenzie and M. P. Allum, F. R. Leavis: A Check List, 1924-1964, Chatto & Windus, 1966; D. J. Enright, Conspirators and Poets, Dufour, 1966.

Articles: New York Herald Tribune Book Review, July 15, 1956; Saturday Review, May 18, 1963; Christian Science Monitor, December 3, 1964, January 22, 1968, June 12, 1969; New York Times, March 31, 1965; Listener, November 30, 1967; Times Literary Supplement, November 30, 1967, July 25, 1968, April 23, 1970; New Statesman, December 8, 1967, January 31, 1969; Books and Bookmen, January, 1968; London Magazine, March, 1968, April, 1969; Spectator, April 12, 1968; New Republic, June 15, 1968, May 22, 1971; Commentary, July, 1968; Books Abroad, summer, 1968, summer, 1969, winter, 1970; New Leader, August 26, 1968; Nation, September 9, 1968, June 9, 1969; New York Review of Books, September 26, 1968; Commonweal, October 25, 1968; Canadian Forum, October, 1968; Antioch Review, Volume XXVIII, number 4, 1968-69; New Yorker, June 28, 1969; Book World, August 10, 1969; Observer Review, January 4, 1970.†

*   *   *

LeBAR, Lois E.   1907-

PERSONAL: Born October 28, 1907, in Olean, N.Y.; daughter of Roscoe Garfield (a merchant) and Alta Isabel (Hathaway) LeBar. Education: Geneseo Normal and Training School (now State University of New York College at Geneseo), Teaching Certificate, 1928; Moody Bible Institute, student, 1933-35; Roosevelt University, B.A., 1943; Wheaton College, Wheaton, Ill., M.A., 1945; New York University, Ph.D., 1951. Religion: Baptist. Home: 703 Howard St., Wheaton, Ill. 60187. Office: Department of Christian Education, Wheaton College, Wheaton, Ill. 60187.

CAREER: Elementary teacher in Perry, N.Y., 1928-33; Moody Bible Institute, Chicago, Ill., teacher of Christian education of children, 1935-41; Wheaton College, Wheaton, Ill., 1949—, began as instructor, professor of Christian education, 1960—, chairman of graduate department, 1953—; currently affiliated with Christian College of South Africa, Salisbury, Rhodesia. Member of Research Commission of National Sunday School Association. Awards, honors: Named with sister, Mary LeBar, as alumnae of the year, Moody Bible Institute, 1959.

WRITINGS: Children in the Bible School, Revell, 1952; Education That Is Christian, Revell, 1958; (contributor) J. R. Hakes, editor, An Introduction to Evangelical Christian Education, Moody, 1964; Focus on People in Church Education, Revell, 1968; Family Devotions with School-Age Children, Revell, 1973. Writer of primary Sunday school lessons and vacation Bible school lessons for Scripture Press, 1936-69.

BIOGRAPHICAL/CRITICAL SOURCES: Kendig Cully, The Search for a Christian Education—Since 1940, Westminster, 1965.

LECHT, Charles Philip   1933-

PERSONAL: Born August 5, 1933, in Providence, R.I.; son of Morris and Lillian (Goldman) Lecht; married Maureen Kelly; children: Eric, Margaret, Nancy, Jonathan. Education: University of Seattle, B.S., 1957; Purdue University, M.S., 1958. Home: Stiles Lane, Greenwich, Conn. 06830. Office: Advanced Computer Techniques Corp., 437 Madison Ave., New York, N.Y.

CAREER: Advanced Computer Techniques Corp., New York, N.Y., president, 1962—. Lecturer on philosophical topics, automation, and management. Military service: U.S. Army, 1960-62; became first lieutenant. Member: Association for Computing Machinery, Mathematical Association of America.

WRITINGS: The Programmer's Fortran, McGraw, 1966; The Programmer's Algol, McGraw, 1967; The Management of Computer Programming Projects, American Management Association, 1967; The Programmer's PL/1, McGraw, 1968. Contributor to Architectural Record, Journal of Engineering Mechanics, Data Processing Digest, and other periodicals.

*   *   *

LECKIE, William H.   1915-

PERSONAL: Born October 18, 1915, in Runge, Tex.; son of Frank N. (an engineer) and Bettie (Stewart) Leckie; married Glorietta Hoffman, November 2, 1942; children: William H., Jr., Bettie Sue. Education: Texas College of Arts and Industries (now Texas A & I University), B.A., 1947, M.A., 1948; University of Oklahoma, Ph.D., 1953. Politics: Democrat. Religion: Episcopalian. Home: 5849 Tetherwood Dr., Toledo, Ohio. Office: Department of History, University of Toledo, Toledo, Ohio 43606.

CAREER: Texas College of Arts and Industries (now Texas A & I University), Kingsville, assistant professor, 1950-53, associate professor, 1953-56, professor of history and chairman of department, 1956-63; University of Toledo, Toledo, Ohio, professor of history and dean of Graduate School, 1963—, vice-president of academic affairs, 1969—. Military service: U.S. Army Air Forces, 1942-46; became master sergeant. Member: American Historical Association, American Association of University Professors, Organization of American Historians, Western Historical Association, Southwestern Social Science Association, Phi Kappa Phi. Awards, honors: Texas A & I University faculty research grant, 1960-61, faculty research fellow, 1968-69; University of Tennessee, summer faculty fellow, 1966; Henry E. Huntington Library summer fellow.

WRITINGS: The Military Conquest of the Southern Plains, University of Oklahoma Press, 1963; The Buffalo Soldiers, University of Oklahoma Press, 1967. Contributor to history and sociology journals.

*   *   *

LEE, Charlotte I(rene)   1909-

PERSONAL: Born August 13, 1909, in Denver, Colo.; daughter of James Terrence and Bertha (Parker) Lee. Education: Municipal University of Wichita (now Wichita State University), A.B., 1930, M.A., 1932; Royal Academy of Dramatic Art, London, England, student, 1939; Northwestern University, Ph.D., 1945. Address: Box 1763, Taos, N.M. 87571.

CAREER: Monte Cassino, Tulsa, Okla., instructor in speech, 1932-36; St. Mary-of-the-Woods College, St. Mary-of-the-Woods, Ind., instructor in speech, 1936-40; William Woods College, Fulton, Mo., chairman of department of speech, 1940-41; Northwestern University, School of Speech, Evanston, Ill., instructor, 1945-48, assistant professor, 1948-53, associate professor, 1953-60, professor of interpretation, 1960-75, professor emeritus, 1975—. Conductor of interpretation workshops and clinics in United States and Canada; has appeared on national television network programs, including "Modern Poetry Series."

MEMBER: Speech Association of America (past member of executive council), Catholic Homiletic Society (associate), Central States Speech Association (vice-president, 1965-66; president, 1967-69), Illinois Speech Association (first vice-president, 1964-65; president, 1965-66), Zeta Phi Eta. *Awards, honors:* Edgar Lee Masters Memorial Award of Society of Midland Authors, 1966; Zeta Phi Eta Award for outstanding contribution to field of speech, 1967-68; New York Speech Association and Illinois Speech and Theatre Association citations, both 1974, for distinguished contributions; Northwestern University Alumni distinguished service award, 1974.

WRITINGS: Oral Interpretation, Houghton, 1952, 4th edition, 1970; (contributor) C. C. Cunningham, *Making Words Come Alive,* W. C. Brown, 1962; (with Karl Robinson) *Speech in Action,* Scott, Foresman, 1966; (co-author) *Speaking of . . . Communication, Interpretation, Theatre,* Scott, Foresman, 1974; *Oral Reading of Scripture,* Houghton, 1974. Author of *Two Choric Dramas for Christmas,* Baker Plays, and a booklet on speech for *Compton Encyclopedia.* Miss Lee was one of the readers on "Voices of Literature," recorded by DePaul University, and also for Dartmouth Recording Project.

WORK IN PROGRESS: The fifth edition of *Oral Interpretation,* for Houghton.

*   *   *

LEE, Irvin H. 1932-

PERSONAL: Born May 6, 1932, in Baltimore, Md.; son of Thomas Ovelton (a contractor) and Emily (Dabney) Lee; married Jacqueline Noullaud, December 17, 1955; children: John Hubert, Patricia Louise. *Education:* Morgan State College, student, 1951-52; Strayer College, student. *Politics:* Democrat. *Religion:* Protestant. *Home:* 2605 Hamlin St. N.E., Washington, D.C. 20018.

CAREER: U.S. Air Force, career service as information superintendent (writer and public relations), served as television writer and producer in Vietnam; currently stationed in Washington, D.C. *Member:* Vietnamese-American Association (Saigon), Authors Guild, Portland Press Club (Portland, Ore.). *Awards, honors—*Military: Air Force Commendation Medal with two oak leaf clusters; Joint Service Commendation Medal.

WRITINGS: Negro Medal of Honor Men, Dodd, 1967, revised edition, 1969; (editor) Kenneth Katsaris, *Evidence and Procedure in the Administration of Justice,* Wiley, 1975. Writer and producer of television shows for American Forces Vietnam Network. Regular contributor to *Airman;* also contributor to popular magazines, including *U.S. Lady, Popular Mechanics, Link,* and *Negro Digest.* Editor of military newspapers, *Bacalan Beacon* (Bordeaux, France), 1953-56, *Scope* (Condon, Ore.), 1956-57, *Skylark* (Spokane, Wash.), 1957-58, and *Afterburner* (Portland, Ore.), 1958-60.

WORK IN PROGRESS: A book on humanitarian aspects of the Vietnam conflict, tentatively entitled *Vietnam: The Other War,* for Dodd; a book on the nature of the Viet Cong, tentatively entitled *Nature of the Enemy,* a study of Vietnamese culture for a half-hour television production and series of five-minute programs.

SIDELIGHTS: Irvin Lee has traveled throughout Europe and Asia to gather material for publication in military and civilian newspapers and magazines. Lee is competent in French. *Avocational interests:* Cooking, horticulture, studying the character traits of people in various countries.

*   *   *

LEE, R(oy) Alton 1931-

PERSONAL: Born May 24, 1931, in White City, Kan.; son of Ralph A. (a farmer) and Alice (Butts) Lee; married Marilyn J. Kurzava, October 19, 1963; children: Michael Alton (deceased), Edward Alan, Deborah Ann. *Education:* Kansas State Teachers College, B.S., 1955, M.S., 1958; University of Oklahoma, Ph.D., 1962. *Politics:* Democrat. *Religion:* Roman Catholic. *Home:* 976 Crestview, Vermillion, S.D. 57069. *Office:* Department of History, University of South Dakota, Vermillion, S.D. 57069.

CAREER: Central State College (now University), Edmond, Okla., 1961-66, began as assistant professor, became associate professor of history; University of South Dakota, Vermillion, associate professor, 1966-70, professor of history, 1970—, chairman of department, 1970-73. *Member:* Organization of American Historians, Phi Alpha Theta. *Awards, honors:* Harry S Truman Library research grant, 1961.

WRITINGS: Truman and Taft-Hartley: A Question of Mandate, University of Kentucky Press, 1966; *A History of Regulatory Taxation,* University Press of Kentucky, 1973. Contributor to historical journals.

WORK IN PROGRESS: Dwight D. Eisenhower: Soldier and Statesman, for Barron's.

*   *   *

LEEDHAM, John 1912-

PERSONAL: Born February 27, 1912, in England; son of Samuel John and Lousa Stella Leedham; married Marion Armstrong, May 22, 1937. *Education:* Wimpole Park, Teacher's Certificate, 1948; Loughborough College of Education, Diploma in Physical Education, 1949, Diploma in Educational Psychology, 1952; University of Leicester, M.A. in Ed., 1955; University of Nottingham, Ph.D., 1969. *Politics:* Liberal. *Religion:* Church of England. *Home:* 48 Swithland Lane, Rothley, Leicestershire, England. *Office:* Department of Educational Technology, Loughborough College of Education, Loughborough, England.

CAREER: South Wigston High School, teacher, 1949-54, headmaster, 1958-62; Bagworth County School, headmaster, 1954-58; Leicester University, Leicester, England, research fellow, 1962-65; Loughborough College of Education, Loughborough, England, principal research lecturer and head of department of educational technology, 1965—. *Military service:* Royal Air Force, 1940-45; received Africa Star. *Member:* Association of Teachers in Departments of Education, Association for Programmed Learning and Educational Technology (chairman), Royal Life Saving Association (examiner). *Awards, honors:* Ministry research award in programmed learning; Rank Organisation award in research; Commander, Order of British Empire, for services to education, 1975.

WRITINGS: The Air We Breathe, Longmans, Green, 1965; (with E. Crouch) Initial Teaching Alphabet: Teachers Manual, Pitman, 1965; (editor with others) Aspects of Educational Technology, nine volumes, Pitman, 1965-75; Programmed Learning in the Schools, Longmans, Green, 1966; Programmed Maths, Longmans, Green, 1966; The Reading Master Scheme, The Rank Organisation, 1966; (with D. V. Parker) Area and Volume, Longmans, Green, 1966; (with Anne Kind and R. W. Kind) Sex Instruction (includes Babies and Families, You Begin Life, You Grow Up, Sex and Your Responsibility, and Contraception), Longmans, Green, 1968; Live Safely with Fire, Longmans, Green, 1969; First Look at Educational Technology, Pitman, 1973; Reading Routes, Longman, 1974. Contributor to Programmed Learning Journal, Educational Research, Times Educational Supplement, and Visual Education.

WORK IN PROGRESS: "Patient-Doctor Counselling Enquiry Information Systems," for a British television station.

* * *

LEEDY, Jack J. 1921-

PERSONAL: Born April 30, 1921, in Pittsburgh, Pa.; son of David Lipschutz (a physician) and Estelle (Brown) Leedy; married Norma Milman, July 17, 1960; children: Ronna, David Michael, Sondra Hope, Cheryl, Janet. Education: University of Pittsburgh, B.S., 1941, M.D., 1944. Office: 799 Broadway, New York, N.Y. 10003.

CAREER: Cumberland Hospital Division of the Brooklyn-Cumberland Medical Center, Brooklyn, N.Y., associate attending psychiatrist, 1957-68; private practice as psychiatrist, New York, N.Y., 1957—. Co-therapist of poetry therapy group, Project Teen Aid, Office of Economic Opportunity, Brooklyn, 1966-67. Military service: U.S. Army, 1943-44. U.S. Army Reserve, 1944-45. Member: American Medical Association, American Psychiatric Association, state and county medical societies; Robert Louis Stevenson Society (founder and president).

WRITINGS: (Editor) Poetry Therapy: The Use of Poetry in the Treatment of Emotional Disorders, Lippincott, 1969; Poetry the Healer, Lippincott, 1973; Poetry the Mind Mender, Lippincott, 1976.

WORK IN PROGRESS: Adventures in Robert Louis Stevenson's Brain.

SIDELIGHTS: Leedy's books advance the notion that poetry therapy may help the mentally ill, particularly "hopeless" schizophrenics, neurotics, retardates, and personality disorders, after all other approaches have failed. Leedy envisions the birth of a new profession, that of poetry therapist, for non-medical persons trained in English or psychology, and suggests that a master's degree might be made available in this form of therapy.

BIOGRAPHICAL/CRITICAL SOURCES: Psychiatric Opinion, April, 1966; Wall Street Journal, March 13, 1975.

* * *

LEES, Gene 1928-

PERSONAL: Born February 8, 1928, in Hamilton, Ontario, Canada; son of Harold (a musician, later a construction engineer) and Dorothy (Flatman) Lees; married Carmen Lister, 1951; married second wife, Micheline A. Ducreux, July, 1955; children: (second marriage) Philippe.

Education: Ontario College of Art, Toronto, student for one year. Home: 5825 Donna Ave., Tarzana, Calif. 91356.

CAREER: Reporter for Canadian newspapers, 1948-55, first for Hamilton Spectator, later for Toronto Telegram and Montreal Star; classical music critic, and film and drama editor for Louisville Times, Louisville, Ky., 1955-58; studied the performing arts in Europe under Reid fellowship, 1958-59; editor of Down Beat (jazz magazine), Chicago, Ill., 1959-61; contributing editor, Hi Fi/Stereo Review, New York, N.Y., 1962-65; columnist for High Fidelity, 1965—. Lyricist, composer, and collaborator with other composers on songs; toured Latin America as manager of jazz sextet under the auspices of U.S. Department of State, 1962; thirty songs with his lyrics were released in a Richmond Organization portfolio, 1968, among them "Waltz for Debby," "Song of the Jet," "Paris Is at Her Best in May," and "Someone to Light up My Life." Radio and television writer and performer for the Canadian Broadcasting Corp. and various independent Canadian radio stations. Member: Composers, Authors, and Publishers Association of Canada.

WRITINGS: And Sleep Until Noon (novel), Simon & Schuster, 1966. Contributor of articles and short stories to the New York Times, Los Angeles Times, Saturday Review, and other periodicals in the United States, Canada, and Europe.

WORK IN PROGRESS: A Broadway musical; film scripts.

SIDELIGHTS: Lees told CA: "Consider myself primarily a lyricist and composer, with songs recorded by Tony Bennett, Frank Sinatra, et al. Have collaborated with such composers as Charles Aznavour of France, Antonio Carlos Jobim of Brazil, and Lalo Schifrin of Argentina. My songs are my primary source of income." Lees helped to introduce the bossa nova in America, and has translated the Portuguese lyrics of many Brazilian songs into English. In 1976 Lees collaborated with Roger Kellaway on the musical score for the film "The Mouse and His Child."

BIOGRAPHICAL/CRITICAL SOURCES: BMI (publication of Broadcast Music, Inc.), November, 1967.

* * *

LEFCOE, George 1938-

PERSONAL: Born February 18, 1938, in Jersey City, N.J.; son of Maurice and Edythe (Sperber) Lefcoe. Education: Dartmouth College, A.B., 1959; Yale University, LL.B., 1962. Office: Law Center, University of Southern California, Los Angeles, Calif. 90007.

CAREER: University of Southern California, Law Center, Los Angeles, assistant professor, 1962-64, associate professor, 1964-66, professor, 1966; Yale University Law School, New Haven, Conn., associate professor of law, 1967-70; University of Southern California, Law Center, professor of law, 1970—. Visiting scholar in Rio de Janeiro to study legal education and the financing of land development in Brazil, summer, 1967. Visiting professor of law, Yale University, 1966, and Boston University, fall, 1974-76.

WRITINGS: Land Development Law, Bobbs, 1966. Contributor to Yale Law Journal, Land Economics, Southern California Law Review, Urban Lawyer, and Stanford Law Review.

* * *

LEFEBVRE d'ARGENCE, Rene-Yvon 1928-

PERSONAL: Born August 21, 1928, in Plouescat, France;

raised in France, Syria, and Vietnam; son of Marc (a general and a mayor) and Andree (Thierry) Lefebvre d'Argence; married Ritva Pelanne, November 2, 1955; children: Chantal, Yann, Luc. *Education:* Sorbonne, University of Paris, Licence es Lettres, 1952; additional study at Ecole Libre des Sciences Politiques, Ecole Nationale des Langues Orientales, and Pembroke College, Cambridge. *Home:* 16 Midhill, Mill Valley, Calif. *Office:* Avery Brundage Collection, Asian Art Museum of San Francisco, Golden Gate Park, San Francisco, Calif. 94118.

CAREER: L'Ecole Francaise d'Extreme-Orient, Vietnam, museum director, 1954-56; Cernuschi Museum, Paris, France, curator, 1956-59; French Government scholar in Taiwan, 1959-61; University of California, Berkeley, professor of Asian art history, 1962-65; De Young Museum, San Francisco, Calif., director of Avery Brundage Foundation, 1964-69; Asian Art Museum of San Francisco, San Francisco, Calif., director and chief curator, 1969—. President, Ecole Francaise, San Francisco. *Military service:* Served with the Free French Army in Indo-China during World War II; received Medaille de la Reconnaissance Francaise.

WRITINGS: Les Ceramiques a base chocolatee, Ecole Francaise d'Extreme-Orient, 1958; *Ancient Chinese Bronzes from the Avery Brundage Collection,* De Young Museum, 1966; *Chinese Ceramics in the Avery Brundage Collection,* De Young Museum, 1967; *Chinese Treasures from the Avery Brundage Collection,* Asia Society, 1968; *Collection Avery Brundage,* [Mexico], 1968; *Chinese Jades in the Avery Brundage Collection,* Center of Asian Art and Culture, 1972; *The Hans Collection of Oriental Art* [San Francisco], 1973; *Chinese, Korean and Japanese Sculpture in the Avery Brundage Collection,* Kodansha, 1975. Contributor to journals in France, Asia, and United States.

WORK IN PROGRESS: Three books, *Atlas of Lin-an Fu: Capital of Sung China, Oriental Art Collections in the San Francisco Bay Area,* and *Ancient Chinese Bronzes in the Avery Brundage Collection,* Volume I.

SIDELIGHTS: Rene-Yvon Lefebvre d'Argence speaks Chinese and Finnish and has a working knowledge of Vietnamese, Japanese, Russian, and Spanish.

*   *   *

LeFEVRE, Perry D(eyo)   1921-

PERSONAL: Born July 12, 1921, in Kingston, N.Y.; son of Johannes and Faye (McFerran) LeFevre; married Carol Baumann, September 14, 1946; children: Susan, Judith, Peter. *Education:* Harvard University, A.B., 1943; Chicago Theological Seminary, B.D., 1946; University of Chicago, Ph.D., 1951. *Home:* 1376 East 58th St., Chicago, Ill., 60637. *Office:* Chicago Theological Seminary, 5757 University Ave., Chicago, Ill. 60637.

CAREER: Clergyman of United Church of Christ. Franklin and Marshall College, Lancaster, Pa., instructor in religion, 1948-49; Knox College, Galesburg, Ill., assistant professor, 1949-51, associate professor of religion, 1951-53; University of Chicago, Chicago, Ill., assistant professor, 1953-57, associate professor of theology and education, 1957-61; Chicago Theological Seminary, Chicago, dean and professor of theology, 1961—. *Member:* Society for Religion in Higher Education, Phi Beta Kappa.

WRITINGS: The Prayers of Kierkegaard, University of Chicago Press, 1956; *The Christian Teacher,* Abingdon, 1958; *Understandings of Man,* Westminster, 1966; *Man:*

Six Modern Interpretations, Geneva Press, 1968; (editor and contributor) *Philosophical Resources for Christian Thought,* Abingdon, 1968; (editor) *Conflict in a Voluntary Institution: A Case Study of a Classic Suburban Church Fight,* Exploration Press, 1975. Editor, *Chicago Theological Seminary Register.*

WORK IN PROGRESS: Interrelationship, theology and the social sciences; theology and the change process.

*   *   *

LEGMAN, G(ershon)   1917-
(Roger-Maxe de La Glannege)

PERSONAL: Name originally George Alexander Legman; born November 2, 1917, in Scranton, Pa.; son of Emil Mendel (a butcher) and Julia (Friedman) Legman; married Beverley Keith, 1943 (deceased); married Christine Conrad (marriage annulled); married Judith Evans (a children's librarian), October 29, 1966; children: (with Sima Colcher) Ariela Colcher-Legman; (third marriage) David Guy, Rafael, Sara Felicity. *Education:* Educated privately. *Politics:* Marxist. *Religion:* Jewish. *Home:* La Cle des Champs, Valbonne (Alpes-Maritimes), France (his home is a ruined installation of the Knights Templar, which he is attempting to restore). *Office:* "Just go down the road past where the pavement ends: it's the little shack with the white fence marked 'L'Atelier.'"

CAREER: Professional writer, 1935—. Has worked as a writer for the theater, as a medical researcher for Dr. Robert L. Dickinson, head of the National Committee on Maternal Health, Planned Parenthood program, and as a bibliographer for the Kinsey Institute; editor of *Neurotica* (a lay psychiatric journal), 1948-51; moved to France in 1953 as a result of harrassment by the U.S. Post Office in connection with his book, *Love & Death;* writer in residence at University of California, La Jolla, 1964-65; member of board of directors, Maledicta, Inc. (international organization for the study of verbal aggression).

WRITINGS: (Under pseudonym Roger-Maxe de La Glannege, an anagram of his original name) *Oragenitalism,* Part 1, J. R. Brussel (New York), 1940; *Love & Death: A Study in Censorhip,* Breaking Point, 1949; (editor) *The Limerick: 1700 Examples, With Notes,* Les Hautes Etudes (Paris), 1953; (editor) *The Compleat "Neurotica," 1948-1951,* Hacker Art Books, 1963; *The Horn Book: Studies in Erotic Folklore,* University Books, 1964; *The Guilt of the Templars,* Basic Books, 1966; *The Fake Revolt,* Breaking Point, 1967; *Rationale of the Dirty Joke,* First Series, Grove, 1968; *No Laughing Matter: Rationale of the Dirty Joke,* Second Series, Breaking Point, 1975. Has edited and translated other works, including *Ubu Roi* (cycle of plays), by Alfred Jarry, and Robert Burns' *Merry Muses of Caledonia* (from the re-discovered Cunningham manuscript). Editor, *Kryptadia: The Journal of Erotic Folklore,* 1968—.

WORK IN PROGRESS: The Ballad: Unexpurgated Folksongs, American and British; second series of *The Horn Book;* a *non*-dictionary study of modern sexual slang, tentatively entitled *A Word for It!;* a volume of essays on the bibliographical history of erotic literature.

SIDELIGHTS: In what has been called "heaven-storming prose," Legman writes to vindicate "the profound *morality* of the sexual impulse." John Clellon Holmes explains: "Appalled by the discovery that the increasing violence and sadism of American culture was the direct result of our society's relentless suppression of sex, the stand he took . . . was summed up in these words: 'Murder having replaced sex in the popular arts, the glorification of one requires the degradation of the other . . . so that we are faced in our culture by the insurmountable schizophrenic contradiction that sex, which is legal in fact, is a crime on paper, while murder—a crime in fact—is, on paper, the best-seller of all time. . . .'' In a letter to *CA*, Legman asks: ''Can anyone explain this double-standard before it blows up the world?''

Legman's work has been banned and then pirated and plagiarized; his intentions have been misrepresented, his personal life limned in outrageous untruths. Legman decided, finally, to ''resist and correct the romantic buncombe'' and to tell it like it is. ''I am telling the truth here for the first complete time,'' he told *CA*, ''including even my sources and inspirations! I can't do better than that.'' He writes: ''1) I consider sexual love the central mystery and central reality of life. (Havelock Ellis.) 2) I am opposed to the use of hallucinating drugs (all) in any continuous fashion. 3) My main amateur interest is the music of Mozart. I consider so-called 'rock & roll' and *contactless-* dance music to be nothing but Hitler's 'Totalitarian-musik' revived. Beware! 4) My style was formed on the influences of three stylists, from whom the modern headlong style of [Louis-Ferdinand] Celine and Henry Miller is derived in fiction: namely, Diderot's *Rameau's Nephew*, and the historical works of Jules Michelet (especially *The Sorceress*), and Carlyle. 5) I believe in a personal and intense style, and in making *value judgements*. This is unfashionable now, but is the only responsible position. 6) I am interested only in folklore and social criticism, and deal with fiction and 'literature' only from the social-critical point of view. Folklore is living. Fiction and 'literature' are dead.''

Legman has collected one of the finest private libraries on the subjects of folklore and erotic literature. His collections, he says, will eventually go to the British Museum, the Bibliotheque Nationale, and the Kinsey Institute. He was also largely responsible for the new Western interest in Japanese origami, through an international exhibition he gave in 1955, at the Museum of Modern Art, Amsterdam, later brought to America.

BIOGRAPHICAL/CRITICAL SOURCES: Contact, July, 1963; *Evergreen,* December, 1966; *Oui,* March, 1975.

*   *   *

Le GUIN, Ursula K(roeber) 1929-

PERSONAL: Born October 21, 1929, in Berkeley, Calif.; daughter of Alfred L. (an anthropologist) and Theodora (Kracaw) Kroeber; married Charles A. Le Guin (a historian), December 25, 1953; children: Elisabeth, Caroline, Theodore. *Education:* Radcliffe College, B.A., 1951; Columbia University, M.A., 1952. *Home:* 3321 Northwest Thurman St., Portland, Ore. *Agent:* Virginia Kidd, Box 278, Milford, Pa. 18337.

CAREER: Writer of science fiction and fantasy. *Member:* Science Fiction Writers of America. *Awards, honors: Boston Globe*—Horn Book Award, 1969, for *A Wizard of Earthsea;* Hugo Award, 1969, for *The Left Hand of Darkness;* Nebula Award, 1969, for *The Left Hand of Darkness,* and 1975, for *The Dispossessed;* National Book Award, 1973, for *The Farthest Shore.*

WRITINGS: Rocannon's World, Ace Books, 1964; *Planet of Exile,* Ace Books, 1966; *City of Illusions,* Ace Books, 1967; *A Wizard of Earthsea,* Parnassus, 1968; *The Left Hand of Darkness,* Ace Books, 1969; *The Lathe of Heaven,* Scribner, 1970; *The Tombs of Atuan,* Atheneum,

1971; *The Farthest Shore,* Atheneum, 1972; *From Elfland to Poughkeepsie* (essay), Pendragon, 1973; *The Dispossessed,* Harper, 1974; *Wild Angels* (poetry), Capra, 1975; *The Wind's Twelve Quarters* (short stories), Harper, 1975.

*   *   *

LEHAN, Richard (D'Aubin Daniel) 1930-

PERSONAL: Born December 23, 1930, in Brockton, Mass.; son of Ralph Anthony (a broker) and Mildred (Desmond) Lehan; married Ann Evans (a teacher), June 11, 1960. *Education:* Stonehill College, B.A., 1952; Boston College, M.A., 1954; University of Wisconsin, Ph.D., 1959. *Office:* Department of English, University of California, Los Angeles, Calif. 90024.

CAREER: University of Texas, Austin, instructor, 1958-61, assistant professor of American literature, 1961-62; University of California, Los Angeles, assistant professor, 1962-66, associate professor, 1966-69, professor of American literature, 1969—. *Member:* Modern Language Association of America. *Awards, honors:* Bromberg Award for excellence in teaching, University of Texas, 1961; University of California, Los Angeles, Alumni Award for Distinguished Teaching, 1970.

WRITINGS: (Contributor) *Six Contemporary Novels,* University of Texas Press, 1962; (contributor) Joseph J. Waldmeir, editor, *Recent American Fiction,* Houghton, 1963; (contributor) *The Modern American Novel: Essays in Criticism,* Random House, 1966; *F. Scott Fitzgerald and the Craft of Fiction,* Southern Illinois University Press, 1966; *Theodore Dreiser: His Work and His Novels,* Southern Illinois University Press, 1969; *A Dangerous Crossing: Literary Existentialism and the Modern American Novel,* Southern Illinois University Press, 1973. Contributor of articles to yearbooks and learned journals, and about fifty reviews to newspapers and journals.

WORK IN PROGRESS: Studying trends in the development of the novel.

*   *   *

LEHANE, Brendan 1936-

PERSONAL: Born May 17, 1936, in London, England; son of Christopher (a teacher) and Honor (Millar) Lehane. *Education:* Attended Eton College, 1949-54, and King's College, Cambridge, 1957-60. *Home:* Hey Farm Cottage, Winsham, Chard, Somersetshire, England.

CAREER: Formerly a private tutor; *About Town,* London, England, features editor, 1961-62; Rupert Hart-Davis Ltd. (publishers), London, assistant editor, 1962; writer. *Military service:* British Army, National Service, 1955-57; became second lieutenant. *Awards, honors:* Arts Council Award, 1967, for *The Quest of Three Abbots.*

WRITINGS: Natural History, M. Joseph, 1967; *The Quest of Three Abbots,* Viking, 1968; *The Compleat Flea,* Viking, 1969; *The Companion Guide to Ireland,* Collins, 1972. Contributor to *Weekend Telegraph, Sunday Times,* and *Woman's Own.*

WORK IN PROGRESS: A novel; *The Companion Guide to Wessex.*

AVOCATIONAL INTERESTS: Ireland and travel (has been in most countries of Europe, around Africa, and parts of the Middle East, with brief visits in United States, Canada, and the Bahamas).

LEHMAN, Anita Jacobs 1920-

PERSONAL: Surname is pronounced *Lee*-man; born April 9, 1920, in New York, N.Y.; daughter of Samuel M. and Mollie (Greenberg) Jacobs; married J. H. Lehman (an engineer), March 14, 1943 (died, 1970); married Marshall L. Carter (a physician); children: (first marriage) Michael Lehman Cowan, Laurie H. *Education:* New York University, student, 1937-38; University of California, Los Angeles, B.A., 1954, M.A., 1959; Stanford University, Pupil Personnel Credential, 1965. *Office:* College of San Mateo, San Mateo, Calif. 94402.

CAREER: Public relations copywriter in New York, Boston, and San Francisco, 1938-48; Beverly Hills (Calif.) High School, English teacher, 1955-60; American River Junior College, Sacramento, Calif., instructor in English, 1960-63; College of San Mateo, San Mateo, Calif., instructor in English, 1963—.

WRITINGS—All with Paul Carter Holmes: *Keys to Understanding: Receiving and Sending the Essay,* Harper, 1968, 2nd edition, 1973; *Keys to Understanding: Receiving and Sending the Poem,* Harper, 1969; *Keys to Understanding: Receiving and Sending the Drama,* Harper, 1970; *Parade of Lines,* Canfield Press, 1971.

WORK IN PROGRESS: Studies on poetry, drama, the short story.

* * *

LEHMAN, Warren (Winfred, Jr.) 1930-

PERSONAL: Born July 18, 1930, in Chicago, Ill.; son of Warren Winfred (an electrical engineer) and Lillian (Ryan) Lehman; married Mary Wooster, July 28, 1951; children: Rachel Hagar, Jocelyn Diane, Charles Wooster, Benjamin Franklin, Naomi, Sebastian Joseph, Jared Septimus (deceased), Asaph Octavius. *Education:* University of Chicago, A.B., 1950, J.D., 1964. *Home:* 625 Walton Place, Madison, Wisc. 53704. *Office:* University of Wisconsin, Madison, Wisc. 53706.

CAREER: Prior to 1956 worked at a variety of jobs, including railroad brakeman, apprentice machinist, inspector, and independent contractor installing storm windows and awnings; Chicago Commission on Human Relations, Chicago, Ill., human relations officer, 1956-60; Western Design Division of U.S. Industries, Santa Barbara, Calif., writer and editor, 1960-61; Chicago Urban League, Chicago, housing specialist, 1961-63; University of Chicago Law School, Chicago, Bigelow teaching fellow, 1964-65; Washington University School of Law, St. Louis, Mo., assistant dean, 1965-67, assistant professor, 1965-68, associate professor of law, 1968-69; University of Wisconsin—Madison, professor of law, 1969—. *Member:* Order of the Coif.

WRITINGS: Practical Law: A Course in Everyday Contracts, Doubleday, 1961; *Parliamentary Procedure,* Doubleday, 1962; (with Dallin Oaks) *A Criminal Justice System and the Indigent,* University of Chicago Press, 1968. Contributor to law journals and newspapers.

WORK IN PROGRESS: Form and Meaning of Beowulf; a study on the early history of the trademark.

* * *

LEMMON, Sarah McCulloh 1914-

PERSONAL: Born October 24, 1914, in Davidsonville, Md.; daughter of William Presstman (an engineer) and Ann (Williams) Lemmon. *Education:* Madison College, Harri-

sonburg, Va., B.S., 1934; Columbia University, M.A., 1936; University of North Carolina, Ph.D., 1952. *Politics:* Democrat. *Religion:* Episcopalian. *Home:* 917 Brookwood Dr., Raleigh, N.C. 27607. *Office:* Meredith College, Raleigh, N.C. 27611.

CAREER: High school history teacher, Annapolis, Md., 1936-40; Oldfields School, Glencoe, Md., academic principal, 1940-43; LaGrange College, LaGrange, Ga., associate professor of history, 1943-47; Meredith College, Raleigh, N.C., assistant professor, 1947-56, associate professor, 1956-63, professor of history, 1963—, chairman of department, 1962—. *Member:* Society of American Historians, National Society of Colonial Dames of America (North Carolina), Historical Society of North Carolina, Delta Kappa Gamma, Phi Alpha Theta.

WRITINGS: (Contributor) *Essays in Southern History,* University of North Carolina Press, 1957; *North Carolina's Role in World War II,* North Carolina Department of Archives and History, 1964; *North Carolina's Role in the First World War,* North Carolina Department of Archives and History, 1967; *Parson Pettigrew of the "Old Church,"* University of North Carolina Press, 1970; *North Carolina and the War of 1812,* North Carolina Department of Archives and History, 1971; (editor) *The Pettigrew Papers,* Volume I: *1685-1818,* North Carolina Department of Archives, 1971; *Frustrated Patriots,* University of North Carolina Press, 1973. Contributor of articles and reviews to history journals. Member of editorial board, *North Carolina Historical Review,* 1960-70.

WORK IN PROGRESS: Editing Volume II of *The Pettigrew Papers, 1819-1848;* a biography of Nathaniel Macon; a social history of Raleigh, N.C., 1865-1914.

SIDELIGHTS: Sarah Lemmon has traveled to Egypt, Lebanon, Jordan, Syria, Israel, Turkey, Crete, and in Europe, gathering material for slide lectures on places of historical interest. *Avocational interests:* Miss Lemmon sings as a mezzo-soprano soloist in a church choir and plays the piano; she enjoys amateur theatricals and writing poetry.

* * *

LENEHAN, William T. 1930-

PERSONAL: Born May 25, 1930, in Winnsboro, Tex.; son of William A. and Syble (Thurman) Lenehan; married Angelena Frensley, August 25, 1962; children: Roma Eileen. *Education:* University of Oklahoma, B.A., 1955, Ph.D., 1963. *Home:* 3526 Tally Ho Lane, Madison, Wis. 53705. *Office:* University of Wisconsin, Madison, Wis. 53706.

CAREER: University of Wisconsin—Madison, 1962—, began as associate professor, currently professor of English. *Military service:* U.S. Air Force, 1951-53. *Member:* Modern Language Association of America, National Council of Teachers of English, American Association of University Professors.

WRITINGS: (Compiler with Wilma Ebbitt) *The Writer's Reader,* Scott, Foresman, 1968.

WORK IN PROGRESS: Editing Washington Irving's *The Alhambra.*

* * *

LENT, Blair 1930-
(Ernest Small)

PERSONAL: Born January 22, 1930, in Boston, Mass.; son of Stanley Blair (an electrical engineer) and Hazel

(Small) Lent. *Education:* Boston Museum School, graduate (with honors), 1953; studied art in Switzerland and Italy, 1953-54. *Home and studio:* 10 Dana St., Cambridge, Mass.

CAREER: Container Corp. of America, Medford, Mass., assistant art director, 1954-56; Bresnick Advertising Co., Boston, Mass., creative designer, 1957-61; professional artist and author and illustrator of children's books. Work has been exhibited at Boston Arts Festival, 1953, 1955-57, Boston Printmaker's Show, 1955-61, 1963, Institute of Contemporary Art, 1955, American Institute of Graphic Arts shows, 1964, 1967, Illustrations for Children, University Art Gallery, Albany, N.Y., 1972, and Contemporary American Illustrators of Children's Books, Rutgers University, 1974-75; had one-man shows of silk screen prints and oils in Provincetown, Mass., 1961, and collage and oils in New York City, 1962; also one-man show, The Work of Blair Lent for Picture Books, Wiggin Gallery, Boston, 1970. *Military service:* U.S. Army Reserve Engineers.

AWARDS, HONORS: Cummings Memorial traveling scholarship of Boston Museum of Fine Arts, 1953-54, and the Museum's Clarissa Barlett traveling scholarship, 1967-68; *Pistachio* and *The Wave* were included on American Institute of Graphic Arts list of best children's books, 1963-64, and *John Tabor's Ride* and *Baba Yaga*, 1965-66, *From King Boggen's Hall to Nothing-at All* and *Why the Sun and the Moon Live in the Sky*, 1967-68, and *The Funny Little Woman*, 1974-75; *Baba Yaga* was an honor book at *New York Herald Tribune's* Children's Book Festival, 1966; included on the *New York Times* list of the year's best juveniles are: *Baba Yaga, John Tabor's Ride*, and *Why the Sun and the Moon Live in the Sky*, 1966, *The Little Match Girl*, 1968, and *The Funny Little Woman*, 1972; *The Wave* received second prize (silver medal) for illustration and design at Bienal Internacional do Livro e Arte Grafica, San Paulo, Brazil, 1965; runner-up for Caldecott Medal, 1965, for *The Wave*, 1969, for *Why the Sun and the Moon Live in the Sky*, and 1971, for *The Angry Moon;* won Caldecott Medal, 1973, for *The Funny Little Woman*.

WRITINGS—Self-illustrated: *Pistachio* (Junior Literary Guild selection), Little, Brown, 1963; *John Tabor's Ride*, Little, Brown, 1966; (pseudonym, Ernest Small, used for author's credit; illustrations by Blair Lent) *Baba Yaga*, Houghton, 1966; (compiler) *From King Boggen's Hall to Nothing-at-All* (poetry), Little, Brown, 1967; *Sunflower*, Houghton, 1976; *Elephant*, Dutton, in press.

Illustrator: *The Wave* (adapted by Margaret Hodges from Lafcadio Hearn), Houghton, 1964; Olga Economakis, *Oasis of the Stars*, Coward, 1965; Arlene Mosel, *Tikki Tikki Tembo*, Holt, 1968; Elphinstone Dayrell, *Why the Sun and the Moon Live in the Sky*, Houghton, 1968; Hans Christian Andersen, *The Little Match Girl*, Houghton, 1968; William Sleator, *The Angry Moon*, Little, Brown, 1970; Arlene Mosel, *The Funny Little Woman*, Dutton, 1972; Kornei Chukovsky, *The Telephone*, Seymour Lawrence, 1976; Aileen Fisher, *I Stood Upon a Mountain*, Crowell, 1976. Contributor to *Horn Book* and *Publisher's Weekly*. Cover designs have appeared on *Atlantic* and *Boston Magazine*. Adapted Elphinstone Dayrell's *Why the Sun and the Moon Live in the Sky* into animated film, 1970, distributed by A.C.I. Films.

SIDELIGHTS: Blair Lent used his second Boston Museum scholarship for six months travel in Russia, 1968. He states: "I sketched the old, but rapidly modernizing cities and villages, and studied local folklore. I have always been fascinated with the vast plains, the birch forest, and the wooden villages of Russia."

Lent is currently building himself a house and studio on his land in northeast Connecticut. He speaks Spanish and fair Italian and Russian.

BIOGRAPHICAL/CRITICAL SOURCES: Francis Brow, *Collage*, Pitman, 1963; Lee Bennet Hopkins, *Books Are by People*, Citation Press, 1969; *Horn Book*, August, 1973.

*   *   *

LENTZ, Perry   1943-

PERSONAL: Born March 27, 1943, in Anniston, Ala.; son of Lucian Boyd (a sales executive) and Carleton (Sterne) Lentz; married Jane Anderson, July 10, 1965; children: Catherine Robinson, Emily Anderson. *Education:* Kenyon College, A.B., 1964; Vanderbilt University, M.A., 1966, Ph.D., 1970. *Home address:* Box 575, Gambier, Ohio 43022. *Agent:* Diarmuid Russell, Russell & Volkening, Inc., 551 Fifth Ave., New York, N.Y. 10017. *Office:* Department of English, Kenyon College, Gambier, Ohio 43022.

CAREER: Vanderbilt University, Nashville, Tenn., teaching fellow, 1964-69; Kenyon College, Gambier, Ohio, assistant professor, 1969-73, associate professor of English, 1973—.

WRITINGS: The Falling Hills (historical novel), Scribner, 1967; *It Must Be Now the Kingdom Coming: An Historical Romance*, Crown, 1972.

SIDELIGHTS: A *Time* reviewer called Perry Lentz's *The Falling Hills* "a first novel of remarkable merit," and Charles Dollen says that it "introduces an exciting new talent on the American literary scene." Written originally as an honors project at Kenyon College, the book tells the story of the Fort Pillow massacre, a little-known Civil War episode in which Confederate conscriptees attacked and destroyed a Union fort that was manned by Negroes and ineffective "Tennessee hillmen." Lentz was able to explore the topical problems of war and roots of the civil rights struggle after studying eyewitness reports of the incident preserved in the National Archives. He managed to tell a story so believable that a *Time* reviewer attributes to his writing "much of the visceral realism that characterized MacKinlay Kantor's *Andersonville*." Although Martin Levin says that "there is a remoteness about the author's rhetoric that makes one feel he is viewing the action through binoculars," most critics have commented on the explicitness of his prose. According to Dollen, Lentz "has a little of the over-earnestness of the young writer. . . . He has blended a novel from stock ingredients, but he has added a new dimension—reality. He takes away the glamor of military life and the glory of battle and shows them for the de-humanizing things they are."

Lentz told *CA:* "My primary desire has been, and remains, to be an effective teacher. Writing is of the moment something of an avocation."

BIOGRAPHICAL/CRITICAL SOURCES: Best Sellers, May 1, 1967; *Time*, May 12, 1967; *New York Times Book Review*, June 18, 1967; *American Scholar*, autumn, 1967.

*   *   *

LEONARD, Calista V(erne)   1919-

PERSONAL: Born August 18, 1919, in Los Angeles, Calif.; daughter of Roy J. (a miner) and Anna H. (an artist; maiden name, Harris) Wright; married Ernest B. Leonard (a real estate salesman), July 5, 1937; children: Ernest J., Jon N., Leo V. *Education:* University of Arizona, B.A.,

1957, M.A., 1958; University of Southern California, Ph.D., 1964. *Home:* 1017 Second St., Santa Monica, Calif. 90403.

CAREER: U.S. Veterans Administration Center, West Los Angeles, Calif., operations research assistant in central research unit, 1959-62, psychology trainee, 1962-63; University of California, Los Angeles, psychology intern in Neuropsychiatric Institute, 1963-64; Marion Davies Children's Clinic, Los Angeles, Calif., staff psychologist, 1965; University of California, Los Angeles, medical psychologist in Neuropsychiatric Institute and assistant professor in department of psychiatry, 1965-73, staff psychologist, 1973—. Licensed psychologist, California, 1964. *Member:* American Psychological Association, Association of Academic Women, Western Psychological Association, California State Psychological Association, Phi Beta Kappa, Phi Kappa Phi.

WRITINGS: (Contributor) N. L. Farberow, E. S. Shneidman, editors, *The Cry for Help*, McGraw, 1961; *Understanding and Preventing Suicide*, C. C Thomas, 1967. Contributor to health and medical publications.

WORK IN PROGRESS: Remediation of impulse problems in adults and children; child-rearing patterns which lead to potential for suicide; understanding and preventing suicidal behavior; biofeedback and autogenic training.

* * *

LEONARD, George E(dward) 1931-

PERSONAL: Born November 12, 1931, in Pittsfield, Mass.; son of Harry Peter and Helen Leonard; married Helen Tevnan, November 12, 1960; children: Melissa, Christa. *Education:* Massachusetts State College (now University of Massachusetts—Amherst), B.S., 1953; Columbia University, M.A., 1954, Ed.D., 1962. *Office:* 325 Education, Wayne State University, Detroit, Mich. 48202.

CAREER: Long Island (N.Y.) Division of Guidance, counselor, 1954-60; Long Island University, Brooklyn, N.Y., assistant professor, 1960-62; Kent State University, Kent, Ohio, assistant professor, 1962-63; Wayne State University, Detroit, Mich., associate professor, 1963-70, professor of education, 1970—. *Member:* American Psychological Association, American Personnel and Guidance Association, Phi Delta Kappa, Kappa Delta Phi. *Awards, honors:* LL.D., Clarke College, 1970.

WRITINGS: Developmental Career Guidance, Wayne State University Press, 1966; *The Elementary School Counselor*, Wayne State University Press, 1967, 2nd revised edition (with William H. Von Hoose and Mildred Peters), 1970; *How to Face Future Success*, Wayne State University Press, 1968; (with John J. Pietrofesa and Van Hoose) *The Authentic Counselor*, Rand McNally, 1971.†

* * *

LEON-PORTILLA, Miguel 1926-

PERSONAL: Born February 22, 1926, in Mexico City, Mexico; son of Miguel Leon-Ortiz and Luisa Portilla; married Ascension Hennandez Trivino (a historian), May 2, 1965. *Education:* Loyola University, Los Angeles, Calif., B.A., 1948, M.A., 1952; National University of Mexico, Ph.D., 1956. *Home:* Alberto Zamora 103, Coyoscan, Mexico City, District Federal 21, Mexico.

CAREER: Mexico City College (now University of the Americas), Mexico City, Mexico, professor of ancient Mexican history, 1954-57; National University of Mexico, Mexico City, professor of ancient Mexican history, 1957—, director of Institute of Historical Research, 1963—. Inter-American Indian Institute, Mexico City, secretary general, 1955-60, director, 1960-66. Lecturer at universities in United States, Israel, and Europe; distinguished lecturer at the seventy-fourth meeting of the American Anthropological Association, 1974. Member of council, Institute of Different Civilizations, Brussels, 1959—; member of Royal Spanish Academy of History; secretary general of thirty-fifth International Congress of Americanists, 1962. *Member:* Royal Spanish Academy of the Language, Societe des Americanistes de Paris. *Awards, honors:* Prize Elias Sourazky, bestowed by Mexican Secretary of Education, 1966; Guggenheim fellowship, 1970.

WRITINGS: La Filosofia Nahuatl: Estudiada en sus Fuentes, Inter-American Indian Institute, 1956, 3rd edition, National University of Mexico, 1966, published as *Aztec Thought and Culture: A Study of the Ancient Nahuatl Mind,* University of Oklahoma Press, 1963; *La Vision de los Vencidos,* National University of Mexico, 1959, 3rd edition, 1963, published as *The Broken Spears: Aztec Account of the Conquest of Mexico,* Beacon Press, 1962; *Los Antiguos Mexicanos a traves se sus Cronicas y Cantares,* Fondo de Cultura Economica (Mexico), 1961, 2nd edition, 1967, published as *The Ancient Mexicans,* Rutgers University Press, 1968; *Literaturas Precolombinas de Mexico,* Editorial Pormaca, 1964, published as *Pre-Columbian Literature of Mexico,* University of Oklahoma Press, 1967; *Trece Poestas del mundo Azteca,* Universidad Nacional de Mexico, 1968.

Nezahualcoyotl, poesia y pensamiento, Gobierno del Estado de Mexico, 1972; *The Voyages of Captain Francisco de Ortega to California,* Dawson's Book Shop, 1973; *Religion de los Nicaraos,* Universidad Nacional de Mexico, 1973. Articles and essays have been published in *Evergreen Review, Current Anthropology, Americas, America Indigena,* and other journals and magazines in Mexico, United States, Belgium, and France.

WORK IN PROGRESS: A book on the lives and works of thirty Indian chroniclers and historians of the sixteenth-century in Mexico.

SIDELIGHTS: Leon-Portilla writes that his "main concern has been to present in a humanistic way the rich heritage of the history, art, and literature of ancient Mexico." *La Filosofia Nahuatl* was published in Moscow in 1961, and *La Vision de los Vencidos* has appeared in German, French, and Italian. Leon-Portilla is fluent in English, French, German, Italian, and Aztec; his travels cover most countries of the Americas, and many in Europe and the Far East.

BIOGRAPHICAL/CRITICAL SOURCES: American Indigena, October, 1966.

* * *

LERBINGER, Otto 1925-

PERSONAL: Born February 23, 1925, in Dingolfing, Germany; son of Franz X. and Johanna (Kuffner) Lerbinger; married J. Elizabeth Thomson, June 14, 1952; children: Jan, Susan. *Education:* Brooklyn College (now of the City University of New York), B.S., 1948; Massachusetts Institute of Technology, Ph.D., 1954. *Office:* Boston University, Boston, Mass. 02215.

CAREER: Boston University, Boston, Mass., assistant professor, 1954-59, associate professor, 1959-62, professor of public relations and head of department, 1963—. Director of research development, Ruder & Finn, Inc. *Military service:* U.S. Army, 1943-46; became staff sergeant. *Member:* American Economic Association, American Sociological Association, American Association for Public Opinion Research, Association for Education in Journalism, Public Relations Society of America.

WRITINGS: (Editor with Albert J. Sullivan) *Information, Influence, and Communication,* Basic Books, 1965; *Designs for Persuasive Communication,* Prentice-Hall, 1972; (with Nathaniel H. Sperber) *Key to the Executive Head,* Addison-Wesley, 1975. Contributor of articles and reviews to journals.

WORK IN PROGRESS: Public Management and Communications.

AVOCATIONAL INTERESTS: Travel.

* * *

LERNER, Robert E. 1940-

PERSONAL: Born February 8, 1940, in New York, N.Y.; son of Oscar (a pharmacist) and Helene (Heyman) Lerner; married Erdmut Krumnack, October 25, 1963; children: Dietlind. *Education:* University of Chicago, A.B., 1960; Princeton University, M.A., 1962, Ph.D., 1964. *Politics:* Independent. *Office:* Department of History, Northwestern University, Evanston, Ill. 60201.

CAREER: Princeton University, Princeton, N.J., instructor in history, 1963-64; Western Reserve University (now Case Western Reserve University), Cleveland, Ohio, assistant professor of history, 1964-67; Northwestern University, Evanston, Ill., assistant professor, 1967-71, associate professor of history, 1971—. *Member:* American Historical Association, Mediaeval Academy of America. *Awards, honors:* Woodrow Wilson fellow, 1960-61; Germanistic Society of America fellow, 1962-63; Fulbright research fellow, 1967-68; National Endowment for the Humanities research fellow, 1972-73.

WRITINGS: The Age of Adversity: The Fourteenth Century, Cornell University Press, 1968; *The Heresy of the Free Spirit,* University of California Press, 1972; (contributor) R. L. DeMolen, editor, *One Thousand Years: Western Europe in the Middle Ages,* Houghton, 1974. Contributor to *Deutsches Archiv, Speculum, Analecta Cisterciensia, Church History, French Historical Studies* and *Modern Philology.*

WORK IN PROGRESS: A study of prophecy in the Middle Ages.

SIDELIGHTS: Robert Lerner reads French, German, Latin, some Italian and Dutch. *Avocational interests:* Music, European culture.

* * *

LEUTHOLD, David Allen 1932-

PERSONAL: Born November 20, 1932, in Billings, Mont.; son of John Henry (a rancher) and Grace (Martin) Leuthold; married Carolyn Varitz, March 23, 1957; children: Janet Elaine, John Anton. *Education:* University of Montana, B.A., 1954, M.A., 1960; University of California, Berkeley, Ph.D., 1965. *Home:* 1501 Ross St., Columbia, Mo. 65201. *Office:* Department of Political Science, University of Missouri, Columbia, Mo. 65201.

CAREER: University of Missouri, Columbia, assistant professor, 1963-68, associate professor of political science,

1968—, director of public opinion survey unit, 1968-73. Visiting professor, University of Michigan, 1967-68. Technical consultant on reapportionment, Missouri State Legislature, 1965. *Military service:* U.S. Marine Corps, 1955-58; became lieutenant. *Member:* American Political Science Association, Missouri Political Science Association (secretary-treasurer, 1964-67).

WRITINGS: California Politics and Problems, 1900-1963: A Selective Bibliography, Institute of Governmental Studies, University of California, 1965; *The Missouri Legislature: A Preliminary Profile,* University of Missouri Research Center, 1967; *Electioneering in a Democracy: Campaigns for Congress,* Wiley, 1968; (contributor) Samuel C. Patterson, editor, *Midwest Legislative Politics,* Institute of Public Affairs, University of Iowa, 1968; *The Effects of Legislative Reapportionment in Missouri,* School of Business and Public Administration, University of Missouri, 1971.

WORK IN PROGRESS: Studies of legislative committee assignments, the effect of editorial endorsements in election campaigns, and the 1974 Democratic midterm conference.

* * *

LEVANTROSSER, William F(rederick) 1925-

PERSONAL: Surname is pronounced *Lev*-un-trosser; born May 31, 1925, in Detroit, Mich.; son of Frederick Rudolph and Grace (Schroeder) Levantrosser; married Verna Belle Edgeler, January 27, 1949; children: Susan, Nancy, Carol, Linda. *Education:* University of Michigan, A.B., 1950, A.M. (education), 1951; Rutgers University, A.M. (political science), 1964, Ph.D., 1965; Ohio State University, postdoctoral fellow, 1965-66. *Politics:* Democrat. *Religion:* "No preference." *Home:* 104 Winifred Dr., North Merrick, N.Y. 11566. *Office:* Department of Political Science, Hofstra University, Hempstead, N.Y. 11550.

CAREER: Dearborn (Mich.) Board of Education, high school teacher of social studies, 1953-61; instructor in political science at Henry Ford Community College, Dearborn, 1966-67; Hofstra University, Hempstead, N.Y., associate professor of political science, 1967—. *Military service:* U.S. Army, 1943-46, 1951-53. U.S. Army Active Reserve, 1953-75, retired as colonel. *Member:* American Political Science Association, Civil Affairs Association, Reserve Officers Association, Phi Delta Kappa, Pi Sigma Alpha. *Awards, honors:* Fellow of Mershon Center for Education in National Security at Ohio State University, 1965-66.

WRITINGS: Congress and the Citizen-Soldier, Ohio State University Press, 1967. Also author of *Defense Manpower,* 1967. Contributor to *Military Affairs* and *American Political Science Review.*

WORK IN PROGRESS: Studies on national security and the role of the military in politics.

AVOCATIONAL INTERESTS: Golf, tennis, running and sport parachuting.

* * *

LEVIN, Ira 1929-

PERSONAL: Born August 27, 1929, in New York, N.Y.; son of Charles (a toy importer) and Beatrice (Schlansky) Levin; married Gabrielle Aronsohn, August 20, 1960 (divorced, January, 1968); children: Adam, Jared, Nicholas. *Education:* Drake University, student, 1946-48; New York University, A.B., 1950. *Residence:* New York, N.Y. *Agent:* Harold Ober Associates, 40 East 49th St., New York, N.Y. 10017.

CAREER: Novelist and playwright. *Military service:* U.S. Army, Signal Corps, 1953-55. *Member:* Dramatists Guild, Authors Guild, American Society of Composers, Authors and Publishers. *Awards, honors:* Edgar Allan Poe Award of Mystery Writers of America, 1953, for *A Kiss Before Dying.*

WRITINGS—Novels: *A Kiss before Dying,* Simon & Schuster, 1953; *Rosemary's Baby,* Random House, 1967; *This Perfect Day* (Literary Guild selection), Random House, 1970; *The Stepford Wives,* Random House, 1972; *The Boys from Brazil,* Random House, 1976.

Plays: *No Time for Sergeants* (adaptation of novel by Mac Hyman; first produced on Broadway at Alvin Theatre, October 20, 1955, produced on the West End at Her Majesty's Theatre, August 23, 1956), Random House, 1956; *Interlock* (first produced on Broadway at ANTA Theatre, February 6, 1958), Dramatists Play Service, 1958; *Critic's Choice* (first produced on Broadway at Ethel Barrymore Theatre, February 14, 1960, produced in London, 1961), Random House, 1961; *General Seeger* (first produced on Broadway at Lyceum Theatre, February 28, 1962), Dramatists Play Service, 1962; "Drat! The Cat," with music by Milton Schafer, first produced on Broadway at Martin Beck Theatre, October 10, 1965; "Dr. Cook's Garden," first produced on Broadway at Belasco Theatre, September 26, 1967; *Veronica's Room* (first produced on Broadway, 1973), Random House, 1974.

Screenplays: "No Time for Sergeants," Warner Bros., 1958; "Critic's Choice," Warner Bros., 1963; "Rosemary's Baby," Paramount, 1968.

Author of television plays for NBC-TV "Clock" and "Lights Out" series, including "The Old Woman," 1950, and for ABC-TV "U.S. Steel Hour," including "The Notebook Warrior," 1954, and "No Time for Sergeants," 1955.

SIDELIGHTS: "To be truly frightening, horror must be logically consistent, and . . . nothing is more scarifying than horror that proceeds directly from the familiar." These, Bruce Cook feels, are the most important aspects of the horror story. Levin has had success with his first two novels, nearly fifteen years apart, which are both horror stories, yet otherwise dissimilar. *A Kiss Before Dying,* the first novel, involves murder. Drexel Drake calls it a "remarkably constructed story depicting an inconceivably vicious character in episodes of chilling horror." Levin, Anthony Boucher says, has "a great talent for pure novel writing—full bodied characterization, subtle psychological exploration, vivid evocation of locale—with strict technical whodunit tricks as dazzling as anything ever brought off. . . . Here is not merely an extraordinary first but an extraordinary suspense novel by the highest professional standards."

Rosemary's Baby, Levin's second novel, is a horror story of a completely different color. Haskel Frankel calls it "the best chiller to come down the gooseflesh trail in many a moonless night, . . . a tale that sneaks up on the reader like some deadly smog to insidiously envelop him before he is fully aware of it." The book deals with witchcraft and diabolism, and the instruments of evil are a young couple living in a fashionably old New York apartment building. Cook feels that the power of the book is "in the perversion of a most commonplace condition, pregnancy, and the ruthless twisting of a marriage to evil ends." Thomas J. Fleming says: "Mr. Levin's suspense is beautifully intertwined with everyday incidents; the delicate line between belief and disbelief is faultlessly drawn." As a contrast to the fantasy element in the story, all the "background details [are] as factual as possible," Levin told *Publishers' Weekly.* He drew on his experiences of living with his wife in an apartment in New York "that had a laundry room kind of like the one in the book. I would never let my wife go down there alone." S. K. Oberbeck writes that "Levin's black-bordered *Ladies' Home Journal* -style horror tale is not without its charms, but today's willowy women in their Rudi Gernreich dresses and yellow hip huggers somehow don't seem to blend convincingly with spell-casting witches and warlocks." This is what Cook is referring to in his two necessary ingredients for the witches spell. Rosemary and Guy are sophisticated young New Yorkers, and things like that just don't happen to such people in such a place. "With the meticulousness of a ghoul in a catacomb," *Time* says, Levin "establishes his heroine Rosemary as a lapsed Catholic. . . . One by one, untoward events happen. . . . Dark signs and other-worldly hints occur; black candles, 'tannis root' or Devil's Fungus, missing articles of clothing." She becomes convinced that she is living next to a coven of witches and that they are casting some kind of spell intended for her expected baby. "The plot hinges on whether Rosemary's fear is real or a fantasy twist brought on by her turning from the faith. . . . Its real horror," Cook writes, "is the betrayal of Rosemary by her husband." Fleming says of the ending: "He has maintained his mastery of the form until we reach his denouement. Up to this point we are with him entirely, admiring his skill and simultaneously searching out possible, probable and improbable explanations of how he is going to extricate his heroine. Here, unfortunately, he pulls a switcheroo which sends us tumbling from sophistication to Dracula. Our thoroughly modern suspense story ends as just another Gothic tale." Cook, however, does not think that this is just another Gothic tale. He feels that the value of the book resides in the fact that it shows "what an immense potential for terror there is when the supernatural impinges upon the commonplace."

Levin's third and fourth novels move into the realm of science fiction. Leo Harris describes *This Perfect Day* as "a study of today in terms of tomorrow" in which, as F. J. Brown explains, "everybody on earth is controlled in every thought, word and action by a gigantic computer known as UniComp." Although Fleming notes that the novel "lacks the nice inner tension 'Rosemary's Baby' automatically possessed with its eerie juxtaposition of past and present" and introduces instead "a dull world" lacking in "political intelligence and scientific imagination," Brown feels that "in this brave new world, Mr. Levin has retained the old-fashioned virtue of writing well and has produced a worthy successor to *Rosemary's Baby.*" The use of technology similarly plays a part in *The Stepford Wives,* in which housewives are murdered and replaced by robots. In this novel, notes Webster Schott, Levin "casts a spell" and the book "becomes believable through emotional transfer."

A Kiss Before Dying was filmed by United Artists in 1956. Roman Polanski's adaptation of *Rosemary's Baby* for Paramount, in 1968, has been called by Cook "true to the book not only in its particulars but in its spirit. Mr. Polanski's direct camera style was the visual equivalent of Mr. Levin's equally direct prose. . . . His use of color added to the awful verisimilitude of the film." "Dr. Cook's Garden" was filmed by American Broadcasting Co. in 1970. *The Stepford Wives* was released by Columbia in 1975.

BIOGRAPHICAL/CRITICAL SOURCES: New York Times, October 25, 1963; Chicago Sunday Tribune, October 25, 1963; New York Times Book Review, April, 1967; Newsweek, April 17, 1967; Publishers' Weekly, May 22, 1967; Times Literary Supplement, June 1, 1967; National Observer, June 12, 1967, February 24, 1969; Time, June 23, 1967; Punch, April 15, 1970; Books, June, 1970; Saturday Review, October 7, 1972; Carolyn Riley, editor, Contemporary Literary Criticism, Gale, Volume III, 1975, Volume VI, 1976.

*　*　*

LEVINE, A(aron) L(awrence)　1925-

PERSONAL: Born July 26, 1925, in Edmonton, Alberta, Canada; son of William (a raw fur merchant) and Angela (Ludan) Levine; married Fay Nagler, August 29, 1951; children: Andrew, Hollie–Ann, Corey, Meredith. Education: University of Alberta, B.A., 1949; University of Toronto, M.A., 1950; London School of Economics and Political Science, Ph.D., 1954. Home: 641 Loyalist Ct., Fredericton, New Brunswick, Canada.

CAREER: Province of Ontario, Department of Economics, Toronto, director of natural resource economic section, 1955-56; University of New Brunswick, Fredericton, 1956—, began as assistant professor, professor of economics, 1967—. Member: Canadian Political Science Association (member of executive council, 1965-67), Canadian Economic Association (member of executive council, 1967-68), American Economic Association, Royal Economic Society and Economic History Society (both United Kingdom); Economic History Association (United States). Awards, honors: Nuffield fellowship, 1962-63; Canada Council senior fellowship, 1967-68.

WRITINGS: Industrial Retardation in Britain, 1880-1914, Basic Books, 1967. Contributor to Population Studies, Canadian Froum, and Journal of Economic Literature.

WORK IN PROGRESS: Research in the economic theory of the business firm and the theory of economic planning; studies on classical and welfare economics.

*　*　*

LEVINE, Edward M(onroe)　1924-

PERSONAL: Born June 2, 1924, in New Castle, Pa.; son of Abe (a merchant) and Daisy (Rosenblum) Levine. Education: University of Pittsburgh, B.A., 1948; University of Chicago, M.A., 1955, Ph.D., 1958. Home: 828 Oakton 1-C, Evanston, Ill. 60202. Office: Department of Sociology, Loyola University, Chicago, Ill. 60626.

CAREER: Purdue University, Lafayette, Ind., assistant professor of political science, 1957-61; Illinois Institute of Technology, Chicago, 1961-68, began as assistant professor, became associate professor of political science, acting chairman of department, 1967-68, director of Metropolitan Studies Center, 1962-64; Loyola University, Chicago, professor of sociology, 1968—. Member of research committee, Chicago Commission on Human Relations; consultant to Community Renewal Foundation, 1963-66. Military service: U.S. Army Air Forces, 1943-46; became sergeant. Member: Evanston Mental Health Association.

WRITINGS: The Irish and Irish Politicians, University of Notre Dame Press, 1966. Contributor to Israel Annals of Psychiatry and Related Disciplines, Journal of Social Psychology, Urban Life and Culture, Mental Hygiene, and other journals.

WORK IN PROGRESS: Sexual Deviance: The Threat to Psychoanalysis; Psychogenic and Other Causes of Hyperactivity in White Middle Class Children; The Aggressive and Libidinal Drives and Their Relationship to the Ego: A Bio-Psycho-Social Developmental Model; The Role Degradation of Transsexuals by Other Sexual Deviants.

*　*　*

LEVINE, George R.　1929-

PERSONAL: Born August 5, 1929, in Boston, Mass.; son of Jacob and Rose L. (Margolis) Levine; married Joan Adler (a social service administrator), June 8, 1958; children: David A., Michael B. Education: Tufts College (now University), B.A., 1951; Columbia University, M.A., 1952, Ph.D., 1961. Home: 45 Woodbridge Ave., Buffalo, N.Y. 14214. Office: Department of English, State University of New York, Buffalo, N.Y. 14214.

CAREER: Northwestern University, Evanston, Ill., instructor in English, 1959-63; State University of New York at Buffalo, assistant professor, 1963-66, associate professor, 1966-70, professor of English, 1970—, provost of faculty of Arts and Letters, 1975. Military service: U.S. Army, Signal Corps, 1952-54. Member: Modern Language Association of America, American Association of University Professors. Awards, honors: State University of New York Research Foundation research grants, 1966, 1967.

WRITINGS: (With B. Tauss, J. Rankin, and F. Wassell) Readings in American English, Prentice-Hall, 1959; Henry Fielding and the Dry Mock, Mouton & Co., 1967. Contributor to journals.

WORK IN PROGRESS: Essays on Alexander Pope and Jonathan Swift; study of the problems in teaching lyric poetry.

*　*　*

LeVINE, Robert A(lan)　1932-

PERSONAL: Born March 27, 1932, in New York, N.Y.; son of Aaron and Emily (Fried) LeVine; married, 1953. Education: University of Chicago, B.A., 1951, M.A., 1953; Harvard University, Ph.D., 1958. Home: 4907 South Dorchester Ave., Chicago, Ill. 60615. Office: Committee on Human Development, University of Chicago, Chicago, Ill. 60637.

CAREER: Northwestern University, Evanston, Ill., instructor, 1958-59, assistant professor of anthropology and political science, 1959-60; University of Chicago, Chicago, Ill., assistant professor, 1960-63, associate professor, 1963-67, professor of human development and anthropology, 1967—, chairman of committee on African studies, 1964-65. Research training candidate, Chicago Institute for Psychoanalysis, 1964-68; member of mental health small grant committee, National Institute of Mental Health, 1966-68. Member: American Anthropological Association (fellow), African Studies Association (fellow), Phi Beta Kappa, Sigma Xi. Awards, honors: Ford Foundation fellow in Africa, 1955-57; Foundations Fund for Research in Psychiatry fellow, 1962-65; National Institute of Mental Health research career development award, 1962-67, 1967-72, research scientist award, 1973—.

WRITINGS: (With E. H. Strangman and L. H. Unterberger) Dreams and Deeds: Achievement in Nigeria, University of Chicago Press, 1966; (with B. B. LeVine) Nyansongo: A Gusii Community in Kenya, Wiley, 1966; (with D. T. Campbell) Ethnocentrism, Wiley, 1972; Culture,

Behavior, and Personality, Aldine, 1973; (editor) *Culture and Personality: Contemporary Readings,* Aldine, 1974.

Contributor: *Markets in Africa,* edited by P. J. Bohannon, Northwestern University Press, 1962; *Six Cultures: Studies of Child Rearing,* edited by Beatrice Whiting, Wiley, 1963; *Old Societies and New States,* edited by Clifford Geertz, Free Press of Glencoe, 1963; *Witchcraft and Sorcery in East Africa,* edited by John Middleton and E. H. Winter, Routledge & Kegan Paul, 1963; *Concepts of Personality,* edited by J. M. Wepman and R. W. Heine, Aldine, 1963; *The Family Estate in Africa,* edited by R. F. Gray and P. H. Gulliver, Boston University Press, 1964; *International Behavior: A Social Psychological Analysis,* edited by H. C. Kelman, Holt, 1965; *Social Structure and the Family: Generational Relations,* edited by Ethel Shanas and G. F. Streib, Prentice-Hall, 1965; *The Study of College Peer Groups,* edited by T. M. Newcomb, Aldine, 1966; *The Study of Early Man,* American Anthropological Association, 1966; *The City in Modern Africa,* edited by H. M. Miner, Praeger, 1967; *The Handbook of Socialization Theory and Research,* edited by D. Goslin, Rand-McNally, 1968; *The Handbook of Method in Cultural Anthropology,* edited by R. Cohen and R. Naroll, Natural History Press, 1968. Contributor to *Africa, Man, Bulletin of the Menninger Clinic,* and other journals.

* * *

LEVINE, Robert M. 1941-

PERSONAL: Born March 26, 1941, in New York, N.Y. *Education:* Colgate University, B.A., 1962; Princeton University, M.A., 1966, Ph.D., 1967. *Office:* Department of History, State University of New York, Stony Brook, N.Y. 11794.

CAREER: State University of New York at Stony Brook, assistant professor, 1966-71, associate professor of history, 1971—. Chairman of committee on Brazilian studies, Conference on Latin American History, 1970-71, and Latin American Seminar, Columbia University, 1972-73; senior Fulbright-Hays lecturer in Brazil, 1973. *Member:* American Historical Association, Latin American Studies Association, Association of Brazilianists, Conference on Latin American History, Phi Beta Kappa.

WRITINGS: Brazil: Field Guide to Research in the Social Sciences, Institute of Latin American Studies, Columbia University, 1967; *The Vargas Regime,* Columbia University Press, 1970. Also author of other publications on Brazilian political history.

WORK IN PROGRESS: Research on Brazilian regionalism, and race relations; a social history of Latin America.

* * *

LEVINSON, Harold M(yer) 1919-

PERSONAL: Born January 9, 1919, in Dorchester, Mass.; son of David B. (a clothier) and Rose (Tuck) Levinson; married Lois Shapiro (a social worker), August 26, 1945; children: Janet, Marsha, Judith. *Education:* University of Michigan, A.B., 1941, M.B.A., 1942, Ph.D., 1950. *Home:* 1127 Clair Circle, Ann Arbor, Mich. 48103. *Office:* Department of Economics, A2, University of Michigan, Ann Arbor, Mich. 48104.

CAREER: U.S. Office of Price Administration, price analyst, 1943-45; University of Michigan, Ann Arbor, instructor, 1947-50, assistant professor, 1950-55, associate professor, 1955-59, professor of economics, 1959—. Research

associate, Institute of Industrial Relations, University of California, Berkeley, 1960-61; academic visitor, London School of Economics and Political Science, 1969-70; adjunct scholar, American Enterprise Institute, 1973—. Senior economist, Study of Employment, Growth, and Price Levels, U.S. Congress Joint Economic Committee, 1959-60; project director, Ford Foundation Study of Union-Management Policies of Adjustment to Technological Change in Transportation Industries, 1964-67. *Member:* American Economic Association, Industrial Relations Research Association. *Awards, honors:* Ford Foundation faculty research fellow, 1956-57.

WRITINGS: Unionism, Wage Trends, and Income Distribution, 1914-47, Bureau of Business Research, University of Michigan, 1951; (co-author) *Labor Relations and Productivity in the Building Trades,* Bureau of Industrial Relations, University of Michigan, 1956; (contributor) *Staff Report on Employment, Growth and Price Levels,* U.S. Government Printing Office, 1959; *Postwar Movement of Prices and Wages in Manufacturing Industries,* U.S. Government Printing Office, 1960; *Collective Bargaining in Steel: Pattern Setter or Pattern Follower?,* University of Michigan-Wayne State University Institute of Industrial Relations, 1962; *Determining Forces in Collective Wage Bargaining,* Wiley, 1966; *Collective Bargaining and Technological Change in American Transportation,* Transportation Center, Northwestern University, 1971; *Collective Bargaining by British Local Authority Employees,* University of Michigan-Wayne State University Institute of Industrial Relations, 1971; *Collective Bargaining by Public Employees in Sweden,* University of Michigan-Wayne State University Institute of Industrial Relations, 1971; *Economic Impact of an Imposed Truck-Rail Operation,* U.S. Department of Transportation, 1975.

WORK IN PROGRESS: Current collective bargaining development in trucking industry; impact of collective bargaining on wages of public sector employees; long run trends in public versus private sector wages in England, Sweden, and the United States.

* * *

LEWALD, H(erald) Ernest 1922-

PERSONAL: Born October 31, 1922, in Koenigsberg, Germany; son of Leo H. (a dentist) and Hetty (Thiel) Lewald; married Louise Marie Shillock (a mathematics instructor), 1949 (divorced, 1973); children: Eric L., Karen L. *Education:* Roosevelt University, student, 1948-50; University of Minnesota, B.A., 1951, M.A., 1955, Ph.D., 1960; Free University of Berlin, graduate study, 1953. *Home:* 4200 Valencia Rd., Knoxville, Tenn. 37919. *Office:* University of Tennessee, Knoxville, Tenn. 37916.

CAREER: Georgia Institute of Technology, Atlanta, instructor in Spanish and German, 1954-57; Carleton College, Northfield, Minn., assistant professor of Spanish and German, 1958-62; associate professor of Spanish at California State College (now California State University), Fullerton, 1962-63, Purdue University, Lafayette, Ind., 1963, and Carleton College, 1963-66; University of Tennessee, Knoxville, professor of Romance languages, 1966—. Adviser for cultural material, American Book Co.

MEMBER: Modern Language Association of America, American Association of Teachers of Spanish and Portuguese, American Association of University Professors, Association for Latin American Studies, South Atlantic Modern Language Association, Phi Beta Kappa, Lambda

Alpha Psi. *Awards, honors:* Fulbright fellowship to Venezuela, 1957; Lilly Foundation grant to Spain, 1959; Organization of American States fellowship to Argentina, 1965, 1968, and 1974; American Council of Learned Societies fellowship to Argentina, 1973.

WRITINGS: (Editor) *Antologia de veinte poetas postmodernistas latinoamericanos,* Instituto Amigos del Libro Argentino (Buenos Aires), 1967; *Buenos Aires, retrato de una sociedad hispanica a traves de su literatura,* Houghton, 1968; (editor) *Argentina: analisis y autoanalisis* (essays), Sudamericana, 1969; (with George E. Smith) *Escritores Platenses,* Houghton, 1971; (editor) *The Cry of Home: Cultural Nationalism and the Modern Writer,* University of Tennessee Press, 1972; *Latinoamerica: sus culturas y sociedades,* McGraw, 1973; *Eduardo Mallea,* Twayne, 1976. Regular contributor to *Books Abroad, Sur, Carleton Miscellany, Revista Iberoamericana, Hispania,* and other journals. Associate editor, *Hispania,* 1969—.

* * *

LEWIS, George Q. 1916-

PERSONAL: Born July 11, 1916, in New York, N.Y.; son of Samuel (a merchant) and Min (Brechner) Lewis; married Ruth Sudler (an advertising copywriter), December 27, 1942. *Education:* University of Alabama, student, 1934. *Politics:* "Humorism." *Home:* 74 Pullman Ave., Elberon, N.J. 07740.

CAREER: Comedy writer; consultant, promoter, publicist, and self-styled humor merchant; instructor at gagwriters' workshops. Member of faculty New School for Social Research, 1972—. Founder of Humor Societies of America; director of Humor Exchange Network. *Member:* National Association of Gagwriters (director). *Awards, honors:* Named Resident Humorist of Long Branch, N.J.

WRITINGS: (With Mark Wachs) *Best Jokes of All Time and How to Tell Them,* Hawthorn, 1966; *Dictionary of Boners and Bloopers,* Scholastic Book Services, 1967. Also author of a series, "Great Gags Galore," John Rain Associates, 1968. Writer of column and articles for Humor Exchange Network.

WORK IN PROGRESS: Giant Book of Happiness.

* * *

LEWIS, Gordon R(ussell) 1926-

PERSONAL: Born November 21, 1926, in Johnson City, N.Y.; son of Frederick C. and Florence E. (Winn) Lewis; married Doris Jane Berlin (a consultant to Scripture Press), June 19, 1948; children: Nancy, Cynthia, Scott. *Education:* Gordon College, A.B., 1948; Faith Theological Seminary, B.Th., 1951; Syracuse University, A.M., 1953, Ph.D., 1959. *Politics:* Republican. *Home:* 1556 South Depew St., Denver, Colo. 80226.

CAREER: Baptist Bible Seminary, Johnson City, N.Y., instructor, 1951-53, professor of apologetics, 1954-58; Conservative Baptist Theological Seminary, Denver, Colo., associate professor, 1958-61, professor of systematic theology and Christian philosophy, 1962—. *Member:* American Philosophical Association (Western division), American Academy of Religion, Evangelical Theological Society, Theta Beta Phi.

WRITINGS: Confronting the Cults, Presbyterian & Reformed, 1966; *Decide for Yourself: A Theological Workbook,* Inter-Varsity Press, 1970; *Judge for Yourself: A Workbook on Contemporary Challenges to Christian Faith,* Inter-Varsity Press, 1974; *What Everyone Should Know about Transcendental Meditation,* Regal Books (Glendale, Calif.), 1975; *Systems of Christian Apologetics,* Moody, 1976. Contributor to religious publications, including *Christianity Today, Foundations,* and *His.*

* * *

LEWIS, Jean 1924-

PERSONAL: Born June 2, 1924, in Shanghai, China, of American parents; daughter of David and Nettie Craig (Lambuth) Lewis. *Education:* Tutored at home. *Politics:* Republican. *Religion:* Protestant. *Home:* 321 Avenue C, New York, N.Y. 10009.

CAREER: Actress and singer in radio, television, and theater, mainly in New York City, 1940-53; program director of American Theatre Wing's Hospital Committee, New York City, 1947-51; executive director of Volunteer Service Photographers, New York City, 1953—. Writer of sales promotion and continuity for women's television shows; author of children's books.

WRITINGS—Juvenile: Pebbles Flintstone, Artists & Writers Press, 1963; *Bamm-Bamm and Pebbles Flintstone,* Artists & Writers Press, 1963; *Touche Turtle and the Fire Dog,* Whitman Publishing, 1963; *The Flintstones at the Circus,* Whitman Publishing, 1963; *The Flintstones Meet the Gruesomes,* Golden Press, 1965; *Boo Boo Bear and the V.I.V.,* Whitman Publishing, 1965; *The Flintstones' Picnic Panic,* Whitman Publishing, 1965; (contributor) *Golden Prize, and Other Stories about Horses,* Whitman Publishing, 1965, revised edition, 1972; *Hoppity Hooper versus Skippity Snooper,* Whitman Publishing, 1966; *Alvin and the Chipmunks and the Deep Sea Blues,* Whitman Publishing, 1966; *The Road Runner and the Bird Watchers,* Whitman Publishing, 1968; *Frankenstein, Jr. and the Devilish Double,* Whitman Publishing, 1968; *Tom & Jerry Scairdy Cat,* Whitman Publishing, 1969; *Tom & Jerry Under the Big Top,* Whitman Publishing, 1969; *Gumby and Pokey to the Rescue,* Western Publishing, 1969.

H. R. Pufnstuf, Western Publishing, 1970; *Jane and the Mandarin's Secret,* Hawthorn, 1970; *Wacky Witch and the Royal Birthday,* Western Publishing, 1971; *Hot Dog,* Grosset & Dunlap, 1971; *Dr. Leo's Pet Patients,* American Heritage Press, 1971; *Kathi and Hash San and the Case of Measles,* Rand, McNally, 1972; *Wacky Witch and the Mystery of the King's Gold,* Western Publishing, 1973; *Lassie and the Busy Morning,* Western Publishing, 1973; *Nancy and Sluggo and the Big Surprise,* Western Publishing, 1974; *Scooby Doo and the Pirate Treasure,* Western Publishing, 1974; *The Sleeping Tree Mystery,* Rand, McNally, 1975; *Bullwinkle's Casserole,* Western Publishing, in press; *Bugs Bunny and Too Many Carrots,* Western Publishing, in press; *Scooby Doo and the Haunted Dog House,* Rand McNally, in press; *Hong Kong Phooey and the Fortune Cookie Caper,* Rand McNally, in press; *Scooby Doo and the Mystery Monster,* Rand McNally, in press.

Adapter: *Swiss Family Robinson,* Artists & Writers Press, 1961; *The Tortoise and the Hare,* Whitman Publishing, 1963; *The Jungle Book,* Golden Press, 1967; *Old Yeller,* Golden Press, 1968; *The Absent-Minded Professor,* Golden Press, 1968; *Chitty Chitty Bang Bang,* Golden Press, 1968.

WORK IN PROGRESS: Miss Prunella and the Pirates; Nellie Bly, juvenile biography of America's first girl reporter; *I Remember Amah,* memoirs of childhood in China; *The Kyoto Cat,* an original story written in the style of a

Japanese fairy tale; *The Gift*, fantasy set in China; *Journey with Genaro; The Temple Summer; The Gingerbread House Mystery.*

SIDELIGHTS: Jean Lewis told *CA*: "Very fond of all animals, particularly cats of which I have two in residence."

* * *

LIDA, Denah (Levy)   1923-

PERSONAL: Born September 9, 1923, in New York, N.Y.; daughter of Haim David (a businessman) and Ephthimia (Semos) Levy; married Raimundo Lida (a professor), December 23, 1955. *Education:* Hunter College (now Hunter College of the City University of New York), B.A., 1943; Columbia University, M.A., 1944; National University of Mexico, Ph.D., 1952. *Home:* 19 Chauncy St., Cambridge, Mass. 02138. *Office:* Brandeis University, South St., Waltham, Mass. 02154.

CAREER: Teacher in New York City public high schools, 1944-45; Office of Inter-American Affairs, New York City, interpreter, 1944-46; Smith College, Northampton, Mass., instructor, 1945-50, assistant professor of Spanish, 1950-53, director of Smith College Junior Year in Mexico, 1951-52; Sweet Briar College, Sweet Briar, Va., assistant professor of modern languages, 1954-55; Brandeis University, Waltham, Mass., instructor, 1955-57, assistant professor, 1957-62, associate professor, 1962-67, professor of Spanish, 1967—, chairwoman, department of Romance languages and comparative literature, 1964-66, 1974—. Visiting summer lecturer at University of Southern California, 1947, and Middlebury College, 1955; visiting lecturer, Harvard University, 1959; associate scholar, Radcliffe College Institute for Independent Study, 1961-62; visiting professor, Harvard University, summer, 1971. *Member:* Modern Language Association of America, Renaissance Society of America, International Association of Hispanists.

WRITINGS: (Editor and author of introduction and notes) Benito Perez Galdos, *El Amigo Manso,* Oxford University Press, 1963. Contributor of articles and reviews to journals. Literary consultant for "El espanol por el mundo," produced by Encyclopaedia Britannica Films.

WORK IN PROGRESS: *Realism and Creativity in Benito Perez Galdos.*

* * *

LIDDERDALE, Halliday Adair   1917-

PERSONAL: Born June 18, 1917, in London, England; son of William Kennedey and Norah Beatrice (Roberts) Lidderdale; married Mary Hero Koumlidou, January 14, 1960; children: Norah Tatiana, Demetrius Andrew. *Education:* Magdalen College, Oxford, B.A., 1940, M.A., 1961. *Politics:* "Anti-authoritarian and anti-racialist." *Religion:* None. *Home:* 8 Court Oak Rd., Harborne, Birmingham, England. *Office:* The British Council, 120 Colmore Row, Birmingham 3, England.

CAREER: British Council, officer, 1946—, served in Baghdad, 1946-48, Athens, 1948-52, Salonica, 1952-56, Lagos and Port Harcourt, Nigeria, 1956-64, and in Birmingham, England, 1964—. *Military service:* British Army, 1940-45; served as captain. *Member:* Travellers Club (London), Edgbaston Golf Club.

WRITINGS: (Editor and translator) *Makriyannis: The Memoirs of General Makriyannis, 1797-1864,* Oxford University Press, 1966.

WORK IN PROGRESS: A study of Greek folk poetry.

AVOCATIONAL INTERESTS: Some sports, most arts, and food and drink.††

* * *

LIDTKE, Vernon L.   1930-

PERSONAL: Born May 4, 1930, in Avon, S.D.; son of Albert (a farmer) and Aganeta (Boese) Lidtke; married Doris Keefe (an assistant professor of mathematics), April 21, 1951. *Education:* University of Oregon, B.A., 1952, M.A. (honors), 1955; University of California, Berkeley, Ph.D., 1962. *Home:* 4806 Wilmslow Rd., Baltimore, Md. 21210. *Office:* Department of History, Johns Hopkins University, Baltimore, Md. 21218.

CAREER: Michigan State University, East Lansing, assistant professor, 1962-66, associate professor of modern European history, 1966-68; Johns Hopkins University, Baltimore, Md., visiting associate professor, 1968, associate professor, 1968-73, professor of history, 1973—, chairman of department, 1975—. Fellow, Davis Center for Historical Studies, Princeton University, 1974-75. *Member:* American Historical Association, American Association of University Professors, Conference Group on Central European History. *Awards, honors:* Fulbright faculty research grant, 1967; Younger Scholar Award, National Endowment for the Humanities, 1969-70.

WRITINGS: *The Outlawed Party: Social Democracy in Germany, 1878-1890,* Princeton University Press, 1966. Contributor of articles and reviews to historical journals. Member of editorial board, *Journal of Modern History,* 1973—.

WORK IN PROGRESS: A book on German working-class culture in an era of industrialization; studies in German popular culture, especially political and social protest songs and literature.

SIDELIGHTS: Vernon Lidtke speaks German, and reads French and Dutch. He has lived in Amsterdam, Munich, Cologne, and Berlin.

* * *

LIEBERMAN, Jethro K(oller)   1943-

PERSONAL: Born October 23, 1943, in Washington, D.C.; son of J. Ben (a communications consultant and author) and Elizabeth (Koller) Lieberman; married Susan Eileen Vucker (a teacher), August 14, 1966; children: Jessica Dumes, Seth Koller. *Education:* Yale University, B.A., 1964; Harvard University, J.D., 1967. *Home:* 215 Villard Ave., Hastings-on-Hudson, N.Y. 10706. *Agent:* Georges Borchardt, 145 East 52nd St., New York, N.Y. 10022.

CAREER: Admitted to the Bar of New York State, District of Columbia, and Supreme Court of the United States; U.S. Senate, Washington, D.C., intern on staff of Senator William Proxmire (Democrat-Wisconson), 1965; *Business Week,* New York City, staff writer, specializing in law, 1967-68; Arent, Fox, Kintner, Plotkin & Kahn, Washington, D.C., associate, 1971-72; Stein & Day Publishers, New York City, vice-president and general counsel, 1972-73; *Business Week,* legal affairs editor, 1973—. Guest lecturer, Yale University, 1975. *Military service:* U.S. Naval Reserve, Judge Advocate General's Corps, 1968-71; became lieutenant. *Member:* American Bar Association, Harvard Club (New York City), Elihu Society, Pi Sigma Alpha.

WRITINGS: Court in Session, Sterling, 1966; Understanding Our Constitution, Walker & Co., 1967; Are Americans Extinct?, Walker & Co., 1968; The Tyranny of the Experts, Walker & Co., 1970; How the Government Breaks the Law, Stein & Day, 1972; The Complete CB Handbook, Avon, 1976; Milestones! 200 Years of American Law, West Publishing, 1976; (contributor) Ralph Nader and Mark Green, editors, Verdicts on Lawyers, Crowell, 1976.

WORK IN PROGRESS: The Limits of the Public and the Private, for Oxford University Press; Crisis at the Bar, for Norton.

*   *   *

LIEN, Arnold J. 1920-

PERSONAL: Surname is pronounced Lean; born December 2, 1920, in Whitewater, Wis.; son of Lien O. (a contractor) and Julia (Sahlie) Lien; married Harriet Stevens (a free-lance copy editor); children: Toby, David, Richard. Education: Stout State University, B.S., 1942; University of Wisconsin, M.Ph., 1947, Ph.D., 1952. Religion: Lutheran. Home: 424 South Pleasant St., Whitewater, Wis. 53190. Office: University of Wisconsin, Whitewater, Wis. 53190.

CAREER: University of Wisconsin—Whitewater, dean of men and director of student personnel, 1948-56, chairman of department of education, 1956-60, dean of School of Graduate Studies, 1960-65, professor of education, 1965—, assistant to the president, 1965-73. Member, Whitewater City Zoning Commission, 1958-60; Whitewater Board of Education, member, 1960-65, 1972-75, president, 1963-65. Military service: U.S. Navy, 1942-46; became ensign. Member: National Education Association, American Educational Research Association, National Measurement Council on Education, Wisconsin Educational Association, Phi Delta Kappa.

WRITINGS: Measurement and Evaluation of Learning, W. C. Brown, 1967, 3rd edition, 1976; A Student Exercise Manual for the Measurement and Evaluation of Learning, W. C. Brown, 1973. Also co-author of Statistics for the Classroom Teacher, 1969. Contributor to education journals.

AVOCATIONAL INTERESTS: Reading; playing golf, volleyball, and badminton; watching football, basketball, baseball, and hockey.

*   *   *

LIGUORI, Frank E. 1917-

PERSONAL: Born February 2, 1917, in McKees Rocks, Pa.; son of James Vincent (a contractor) and Catherine (Pesce) Liguori; married Cecilia Rasdorf (a part-time teacher), August 9, 1958; children: James Edward, Ann Marie, Jean Louise, Daniel David. Education: University of Pittsburgh, B.S., 1938, M.Ed., 1941, Ph.D., 1955; graduate study at Indiana University and Columbia University. Religion: Roman Catholic. Office: Cuyahoga Community College, Parma, Ohio 44130.

CAREER: University of Pittsburgh, Pittsburgh, Pa., instructor in business education, 1941-42, 1946-48; University of Cincinnati, Cincinnati, Ohio, professor of business education, 1948-67; Cuyahoga Community College, Parma, Ohio, dean of business and technologies, 1968—. Military service: U.S. Naval Reserve, 1942-46. Member: Delta Pi Epsilon (past president, Delta chapter), Phi Delta Kappa, Kappa Delta Pi, Delta Delta Lambda.

WRITINGS: Basic Typewriting Operations: Principles and Problems, South-Western Publishing, 1965.

*   *   *

LIJPHART, Arend 1935-

PERSONAL: Surname rhymes with Capehart; born August 17, 1935, in Apeldoorn, Netherlands; son of Anthonius (a corporation executive) and Mathilde T. (d'Angremond) Lijphart; married Eva Tamm, August 10, 1959; children: Antony Sune, Anna Margaretha. Education: Principia College, B.A., 1958; Yale University, M.A., 1959, Ph.D., 1963. Office: Department of Political Science, University of California, Berkeley, Calif. 94720.

CAREER: Elmira College, Elmira, N.Y., instructor in political science, 1961-63; University of California, Berkeley, assistant professor of political science, 1963-68, associate professor, 1968—. Member: American Political Science Association, American Association of University Professors, International Political Science Association.

WRITINGS: The Trauma of Decolonization: The Dutch and West New Guinea, Yale University Press, 1966; (editor) World Politics: The Writings of Theorists and Practitioners, Classical and Modern, Allyn & Bacon, 1966, 2nd edition, 1971; The Politics of Accommodation: Pluralism and Democracy in the Netherlands, University of California Press, 1968, revised edition, 1976; Politics in Europe: Comparisons and Interpretations, Prentice-Hall, 1969. Contributor to journals of United States and abroad.

WORK IN PROGRESS: A book, tentatively entitled Can Democracy Survive?: Toward a Theory of Stable Democracy.†

*   *   *

LILLARD, Richard G(ordon) 1909-

PERSONAL: Born June 3, 1909, in Los Angeles, Calif.; son of Jeremiah Beverley (an educator) and Helen (Hoose) Lillard; married second wife, Louise Davis (a high school teacher), August 27, 1949; children: (first marriage) Sonia Lee; (second marriage) Monique Claire. Education: Sacramento Junior College (now Sacramento City College), student, 1926-28; Stanford University, B.A., 1930; University of Montana, M.A., 1931; Harvard University, graduate student, 1934-35; University of Iowa, Ph.D., 1943. Politics: Democrat. Religion: None. Home: 1629 Sunset Plaza Dr., Los Angeles, Calif. 90069. Office: California State University, Los Angeles, Calif. 90032.

CAREER: High school teacher in Wyoming and California, 1931-33; Los Angeles City College, Los Angeles, Calif., instructor in English, 1933-34, 1935-42; Indiana University, Bloomington, instructor, 1943-45, assistant professor of English, 1945-47; University of California, Los Angeles, assistant professor of English, 1947-49; Los Angeles City College, faculty member, 1949-65, associate professor of English, 1962-65; California State University, Los Angeles, professor of English and American studies, 1965—. Fulbright lecturer on American civilization and literature, University of Grenoble and University of Aix-Marseille, 1957-58. Lecturer on books, censorship, public planning, and environmental problems.

MEMBER: Modern Language Association of America, P.E.N., American Studies Association, American Civil Liberties Union, Western History Association, Sierra Club, California Tomorrow. Awards, honors: Guggenheim fellowship, 1945-46; Silver Medal of Commonwealth Club of California, 1948, for *The Great Forest;* Fund for the Advancement of Education fellowship, 1954-55.

WRITINGS: (With Otis W. Coan) *America in Fiction,* Stanford University Press, 1941, 5th edition, Pacific Books, 1967; *Desert Challenge: An Interpretation of Nevada,* Knopf, 1942; *The Great Forest,* Knopf, 1947; *American Life in Autobiography,* Stanford University Press, 1956; *Eden in Jeopardy: Man's Prodigal Meddling with His Environment—The Southern California Experience,* Knopf, 1966; (with Elna Bakker) *The Great Southwest,* American West, 1972; (with Mary V. Hood) *Hank Monk and Horace Greeley,* Wilmac Press, 1973. Writer of column, "About Nature," for *West Ways* (magazine). Contributor of articles and reviews to *Saturday Review, Esquire, Pacific Spectator,* and other magazines and journals. Editorial assistant, *Mississippi Valley Historical Review,* 1942-43.

WORK IN PROGRESS: Revisions of *American Life in Autobiography,* and *America in Fiction;* a book on the natural history of the Santa Monica Mountains.

SIDELIGHTS: Lillard told *CA* that he is "an amateur gardener, a semi-professional ecologist, and a professional conservationist."

* * *

LINDAUER, John Howard 1937-

PERSONAL: Born November 20, 1937, in Montclair, N.J.; son of John Howard (an engineer-inventor) and Louise (Platts) Lindauer; married Jacqueline Shelly (an author), September, 1960; children: Susan, John. *Education:* Arizona State University, B.S., 1960; Oklahoma State University, Ph.D., 1964. *Home:* 1108 Main, Murray, Ky. *Office:* Murray State University, Murray, Ky.

CAREER: Occidental College, Los Angeles, Calif., assistant professor of economics, 1964-66; Claremont Men's College, Claremont, Calif., associate professor, 1966-67, professor of economics, 1967-74; Murray State University, Murray, Ky., dean, 1974—. Fulbright professor in India, 1972, and at University of Sussex, 1972-73. Consultant to various corporations. *Military service:* U.S. Army, 1954-57. *Member:* American Economic Association, Airplane Owners and Pilots Association, GASP (Group against Smog Pollution; co-founder and vice-chairman).

WRITINGS: Macroeconomics, Wiley, 1968, 3rd edition, 1976; (editor) *Macroeconomic Readings,* Free Press, 1968; (with Sarjit Singh) *Land Taxation and Economic Development,* Kalyani Publishing, 1976; *Principles of Economics,* Saunders, 1976. Contributor to *National Tax Journal, Industrial and Labor Relations Review, Indian Economic Journal,* and other professional journals.

WORK IN PROGRESS: Volume II of *Land Taxation and Economic Development;* a new edition of *Principles of Economics;* a study of government prices as the cause of inflation.

* * *

LINDE, Gunnel 1924-

PERSONAL: Born October 14, 1924, in Stockholm, Sweden; daughter of Gunnar E. and Liv (Nordenstrom) Af Geijerstam; married Einar Linde (a television producer), January 6, 1949; children: Liv, Vysse Gunnel, Sunniva (all daughters). *Education:* Attended Anders Beckmans Reklamskola, Stockholm, 1943-44, and Stockholms Konstskola, 1953. *Home:* Grindavagen 9, Waxholm, Sweden. *Office:* Sveriges Radio, Oxenstiernsgatan 2, Stockholm, Sweden.

CAREER: Journalist with newspapers in Katrineholm, Linkoping, Halsingborg, Sweden, 1945-47, and with Roster i Radio, Stockholm, Sweden, 1948-49; Sveriges Radio, Stockholm, producer of radio programs for children, 1957-63, and television programs for children, 1964—. *Member:* Sveriges Ungdomsforfattares Forening, Samfundet Visans Vanner, Stim Foreningen TV-Producenterna, Stockholms Ostra Zontaklubb. *Awards, honors:* Diploma of Merit (as runner-up), International Hans Christian Andersen Award, 1964, for *Till aventys i Skorstensgrand;* Nils Holgersson Award, 1965, for *The White Stone,* which was also chosen by the American Library Association as one of the notable children's books of 1966; Club 100 prize, and *Expressen* (newspaper) prize, 1974, both for the best family television program of the year, "The White Stone."

WRITINGS—All published by Albert Bonniers, except as noted: *Osynliga klubben och honshusbaten,* 1958; *Tacka vet jag Skorstensgrand,* 1959, translation by Lise Soemme McKinnon published as *Chimney Top Lane,* Harcourt, 1965; *Lurituri,* 1959; *Osynliga klubben och kungliga spoket,* 1960, translation by Anne Parker published as *The Invisible League and the Royal Ghost,* Harcourt, 1970; *Lurituri reser bort,* 1961; *Till aventyrs i Skorstensgrand,* 1962; *Froken Ensam Hemma aker gungstol,* 1963; *Den vita stenen,* 1964, translation by Richard Winston and Clara Winston published as *The White Stone,* Harcourt, 1966; *Med Lill-Klas i Kappsacken,* 1965, translation by Parker published as *Pony Surprise,* Harcourt, 1968; *Den olydiga ballongen,* 1966; *I Eviga skogen,* International Book Production, 1966; *I Evasjams land,* 1967; *Evasjam och Nalle,* 1968; *Evasjam och Lua,* 1968; *Pellepennan och suddagumman,* Sveriges Radios Foerlag, 1968; *Pellepennan och suddagumman och kluddabarnen,* Sveriges Radios Foerlag, 1969; *Loejliga familjerna,* 1971; *Jag aer en varulvsunge,* 1972; *Om man misstaenker barnmisshandel-vad goer man?,* Almaenna Barnhuset, 1975.

Radio scripts include features for adults and children, dramatizations, and serials; television writing (more than 65 programs) has been mainly for children or families; also has eight recordings issued by Decca, Barben, Warner Bros., and others, 1958-65; wrote an opera, "Frooken Ensam Hemma," for the Royal Swedish Opera, 1969-70.

WORK IN PROGRESS: Two books for Albert Bonniers; a television film, "Hands Up."

SIDELIGHTS: In addition to the English translations, some of Linde's books have been published in Danish, Finnish, Norwegian, German, Polish, Yugoslavian, Dutch, and Japanese.

* * *

LINDEMAN, Jack 1924-

PERSONAL: Born December 31, 1924, in Philadelphia, Pa.; son of Samuel David and Elsie (Teitlebaum) Lindeman. *Education:* Attended University of Pennsylvania, 1949; West Chester State College, B.S., 1949; graduate study at University of Mississippi, 1949-50, and Villanova University, 1972. *Politics:* Independent. *Home:* 133 South Franklin St., Fleetwood, Pa. 19522.

CAREER: Teacher in adult education, Henry George School of Social Science, 1951-56, and for Philadelphia (Pa.) Board of Education, 1960-64; editor of *Whetstone* (a literary quarterly), 1955-61; American Preparatory School, Philadelphia, Pa., teacher of history and English, 1956-63; Middletown High School, Middletown, Del., English teacher, 1963; member of faculty of African Center of Lincoln University, Lincoln University, Pa., 1963-64, and Temple University, Philadelphia, 1964-65; The Grier School, Tyrone, Pa., English teacher, 1967-68; Kutztown State College, Kutztown, Pa., member of faculty, 1969—. Frequent lectures and readings given at various Pennsylvania schools, colleges, and universities. *Military service:* U.S. Army, 1943-46; received three battle stars.

WRITINGS: Twenty-One Poems, Atlantis Editions, 1963; *The Conflict of Convictions,* Chilton, 1968. Poems represented in many anthologies, including *Poets of Today, Best Poems of 1966, Where Is Vietnam?,* and *The Writing on the Wall.* About 300 poems have been published in numerous periodicals and newspapers, including *Beloit Poetry Journal, Poetry, Harper's Bazaar, Commonweal, Prairie Schooner, New York Times, Outposts* (London), *Literary Review, New York Herald Tribune, Nation, Southwest Review,* and *New World Writing;* critical articles have appeared in *American Rationalist, Modern Age, Literary Review, Poetry,* and other periodicals.

WORK IN PROGRESS: Journal, a book about life on a small Pennsylvania farm; two books of poems.

SIDELIGHTS: Partially deaf as a result of a World War II injury, Lindeman lived on a small Pennsylvania farm for sixteen years. He has been a student of history "since the first grade," but did not begin writing poetry until the age of twenty-five.

* * *

LINDSAY, Catherine Brown 1928-

PERSONAL: Born March 24, 1928, in St. Paul, Minn.; daughter of Ernest C. and Marguerite (Countryman) Brown; married Kenneth C. Lindsay III, February 7, 1943 (divorced October, 1947); married Edgar Landon Ziegler (divorced). *Education:* University of Minnesota, B.A., 1947, M.A., 1948; further graduate study at New York University and Columbia University. *Politics:* Right-wing Republican. *Religion:* None. *Home:* The Tucson Inn, Drachman Blvd., Tucson, Ariz. 85705.

CAREER: Instructor in English at University of Colorado, Boulder, 1949-51, Vassar College, Poughkeepsie, N.Y., 1951-53, New York University, Washington Square College, New York City, 1954-57, and San Francisco State College (now San Francisco State University), San Francisco, Calif., 1959-60; Scholastic Magazines, New York City, fiction editor, 1960-62; Indiana University, Northwest Campus, Gary, instructor in English at evening classes, 1964-66; Rock Valley College, Rockford, Ill., assistant professor of English, 1967-70. Writer, *Encyclopaedia Britannica,* Chicago, Ill., 1964-65. *Awards, honors:* MacDowell Colony, 1953 and 1971, Yaddo, and Huntington Hartford Foundation, 1956.

WRITINGS: The Country of the Young (novel), Reynal & Hitchcock, 1946; *How to Teach Your Students to Write,* Funk, 1967; *School and Community,* Pergamon, 1970. Short stories have been published in *Co-Ed, American Girl,* and *Practical English,* and about twenty travel articles have appeared in *Co-ed.*

SIDELIGHTS: Catherine Lindsay has traveled in most countries of western Europe, throughout the United States, and in Mexico and Panama.†

* * *

LINDSAY, Cressida 1934-

PERSONAL: Born October 22, 1934, in London, England;

daughter of Philip Lindsay (an author); married Michael Millett (an electronics engineer; separated); children: Amanda Fung, Simon Millett, Dylan Hyatt, Aaron Lindsay, Sophie Hammerton. *Education:* Educated at a convent high school. *Politics:* Anarchist. *Religion:* Christian Spiritualist. *Home:* Old Rectory Farm, Scoulton, Norwich NOR21X, Norfolk, England.

CAREER: Worked in London, England, in a handbag factory, as a junk store owner in Portobello Rd., and as a library assistant, petrol pump assistant, and book shop assistant; writer. *Awards, honors:* Gemini Trust award, 1964; Arts Council grant, 1967.

WRITINGS—Novels: No Wonderland, Anthony Blond, 1960; *Father's Gone to War and Mother's Gone to Pieces,* Anthony Blond, 1963; *No John No,* Anthony Blond, 1966, C. N. Potter, 1967; *Fathers and Lovers,* Anthony Blond, 1969, C. N. Potter, 1970. Contributor of articles and poetry to *Nova, Woman's Own,* and other periodicals.

WORK IN PROGRESS: A novel about country life.

SIDELIGHTS: Adrian Mitchell writes: "[*No, John, No*] succeeds because [Miss Lindsay's] people, especially her women, are drawn with an accurate sympathy.... I believe that Miss Lindsay's vision is, at its best, remarkably clear. She has found her own voice and her own subject.... Her book aches with a valuable compassion."

BIOGRAPHICAL/CRITICAL SOURCES: New York Times Book Review, June 11, 1967.

* * *

LINDSAY, Thomas Fanshawe 1910-

PERSONAL: Born Feburary 1, 1910, in Bhagalpur, India; son of Harry Fanshawe (a British Government official) and Kathleen (an American; maiden name, Huntington) Lindsay. *Education:* Attended Corpus Christi College, Oxford, 1928-32. *Religion:* Roman Catholic. *Home:* Flat Number 1, Buckingham Ct., Buckingham Gate, London S.W.1, England. *Office: Daily Telegraph,* Fleet St., London E.C.4, England.

CAREER: News Chronicle, London, England, reporter and book reviewer, 1932-36; *Tablet,* London, assistant editor, 1936-38; British Council, London, assistant director, 1938-46; Conservative Central Office, London, deputy director of information services, 1947-50; *Daily Telegraph,* London, leader writer and front page parliamentary writer, 1955-66, assistant editor, 1966—. Attached to personal staff of Winston Churchill during 1950 general election. Committee member of Parliamentary Press Gallery, 1956—, and chairman, 1965. *Member:* Oxford and Cambridge Club (London).

WRITINGS: (Translator) Roland Dalbiez, *Psychoanalytical Method and the Doctrine of Freud,* Longmans, Green, 1941; *The Holy Rule for Laymen: A Commentary on the Benedictine Rule,* Burns & Oates, 1947; (editor) *Dictionary of the English and Italian Languages, English-Italian and Italian-English,* Harper, 1948; *Saint Benedict: His Life and Work,* Burns & Oates, 1949, Macmillan, 1950; (translator) Cardinal Giacomo Lercaro, *Methods of Mental Prayer,* Newman Press, 1957; *Parliament from the Press Gallery,* Macmillan, 1967; (with M. Harrington) *The Conservative Party, 1918-1970,* Macmillan, 1974. Editor, *Isis* (Oxford University), 1931-32.

* * *

LINDSTROM, Thais (Stakhy) 1917-

PERSONAL: Born September 1, 1917; daughter of Stakhy

Conrad (a lawyer) and Hope (Kadykova) Lindstrom. *Education:* Hunter College (now Hunter College of the City University of New York), B.A., 1936; University of California, Los Angeles, M.A., 1948; Sorbonne, University of Paris, Ph.D., 1951. *Politics:* Registered Democrat. *Religion:* Russian Orthodox. *Office:* Department of Comparative Literature, Scripps College, Claremont, Calif. 91711.

CAREER: Manhattanville College of the Sacred Heart (now Manhattanville College), Purchase, N.Y., instructor in Russian language and literature, 1952-54; Queens College (now Queens College of the City University of New York), Flushing, N.Y., visiting lecturer in French literature, 1954-55; University of Montana, Missoula, assistant professor of Russian and French language and literature, 1955-57; Western (now Case Western) Reserve University, Cleveland, Ohio, assistant professor of comparative literature and Russian, 1957-60; Sarah Lawrence College, Bronxville, N.Y., professor of Russian, 1960-71; Scripps College, Claremont, Calif., professor of comparative literature, 1971—. Acting director, Fondations des Etats Unis, Paris, France, summers, 1952, 1953. Has appeared regularly on radio and television programs in the field of Russian literature. *Member:* Institut d'Etudes Slaves (Paris), American Association of Teachers of Slavic and East European Languages, Modern Language Association of America, P.E.N.

WRITINGS: Tolstoi en France, Institut d'Etudes Slaves, 1952; *Manual of Beginning Russian,* American Book Co., 1959; *A Concise History of Russian Literature,* New York University Press, Volume I, 1966; *Nikolai Gogol,* Twayne, 1972. Contributor of articles and reviews to *Saturday Review, Theatre Annual,* and other journals.

WORK IN PROGRESS: Volume II of *A Concise History of Russian Literature.*

*   *   *

LING, Dwight L(eroy)   1923-

PERSONAL: Born October 9, 1923, in Johnstown, Pa.; son of Leroy V. and Nellie (Cypher) Ling; married Phyllis May Cooper, June 8, 1946; children: Douglas, Gregory, Angela. *Education:* Pennsylvania State University, B.A., 1948, M.A., 1949; University of Illinois, Ph.D., 1955. *Politics:* Democrat. *Religion:* Methodist. *Home:* 1791 Winchester Dr., Winter Park, Fla. *Office:* Rollins College, Winter Park, Fla. 32789.

CAREER: Centre College of Kentucky, Danville, assistant professor of history, 1949-52; DePauw University, Greencastle, Ind., instructor, 1955-56, assistant professor, 1956-59, associate professor, 1959-65, professor of history and assistant dean, 1965-72; Rollins College, Winter Park, Fla., provost, 1972—. Fulbright lectureship and research grant in the Netherlands, 1976. *Military service:* U.S. Army, 1943-46. *Member:* American Historical Association, Middle East Institute, Middle East Studies Association, American Association of University Administrators.

WRITINGS: Tunisia from Protectorate to Republic, Indiana University Press, 1967. Contributor of articles and reviews to historical journals.

WORK IN PROGRESS: A comparative history of Tunisia and Morocco.

SIDELIGHTS: Ling traveled and studied in Tunisia, 1963, 1967, and 1970.

*   *   *

LING, Trevor   1920-

PERSONAL: Born February 17, 1920, in London, England; son of Albert Oswald and Emma Frances (Meachen) Ling; married Mary Evelyn Inkster (a primary school teacher), August 6, 1949; children: Elspeth Mary, Stephanie Ruth Margaret, Catherine Judith Rosmarie. *Education:* Oxford University, B.A., 1949, M.A., 1953, B.D., 1957; University of London, Ph.D., 1960. *Politics:* Socialist. *Religion:* Church of England. *Office:* University of Manchester, Manchester M13 9PL, England.

CAREER: Baptist minister in England, 1949-59; University of Nottingham, Nottingham, England, university lecturer, 1951-53; University of Rangoon, Rangoon, Burma, chaplain and lecturer, 1960-62; University of Leeds, Leeds, England, lecturer, 1963-66, senior lecturer, 1967-70, professor of comparative religion, 1970-73; University of Manchester, Manchester, England, professor of comparative religion, 1973—. Conducted research in Thailand and Ceylon, 1968. *Military service:* British Army, 1939-46; became warrant officer; received Burma Star. *Member:* International Association for the History of Religion, International Union for the Scientific Study of Population, Royal Asiatic Society, Royal Society for India, Pakistan, and Ceylon, British Sociological Association. *Awards, honors:* B.S. Law Prize for Pali Buddhist studies, School of Oriental and African Studies, University of London, 1961.

WRITINGS: The Significance of Satan, S.P.C.K., 1961; *Buddhism and the Mythology of Evil,* Allen & Unwin, 1962; *Prophetic Religion,* St. Martin's, 1966; *Buddha, Marx, and God,* St. Martin's, 1966; *History of Religion East and West,* St. Martin's, 1968; *The Buddha: Buddhist Civilization in India and Ceylon,* Maurice Temple Smith, 1973.

WORK IN PROGRESS: Buddhism in Southeast Asia: A Short History, for Cambridge University Press.

SIDELIGHTS: Ling is competent in Latin, Greek, Sanskrit, Pali, French, Urdu, and Bengali.

*   *   *

LINNER, Birgitta   1920-

PERSONAL: Born October 25, 1920, in Ystad, Sweden; daughter of Harald E. (a Lutheran minister) and Berta (Cedergren) Erici; married Sven G. Linner (a professor), January 10, 1948. *Education:* University of Lund, law degree, 1946; Stockholm University, diploma in group psychotherapy. *Religion:* Lutheran. *Home:* Svartmunkegraend 2A, SF-20100 Turku-Aabo, Finland.

CAREER: Stockholm Municipal Family Counceling Bureau, Stockholm, Sweden, marriage counselor, 1951-75, family life education consultant, 1969-75; writer and lecturer on sex roles and sex education, currently in Finland. Former instructor in family life education, School of Home Economics, Uppsala, Sweden. Member of planning committee, Scandinavian Seminar on Family Life Education (sponsored by United Nations Food and Agricultural Organization), 1961; member of Royal Commission on Fackskolan (a new type of secondary school), 1962-63.

WRITINGS: Giftastankar: En Bok om kaerlek och aektenskap, Liber, 1959; (with Kerstin Alfven, Miriam Israel, and Barbro Westholm) *Familjekunskap,* Liber, 1962; (with Westholm) *Familj och Samlevnad,* Liber, 1967, revised edition, 1975, teacher's guide, 1971; (with Richard J. Litell) *Sex and Society in Sweden* (photographs by Lennart Nilsson), Pantheon, 1967, revised edition, Harper, 1972; *The Sexual Revolution in Sweden,* UNESCO, 1968; *What Does Equality between the Sexes Imply?,* AMS Press for American Orthopsychiatric Association, 1972; (contributor) *Sexual Development and Behavior*, Dorsey, 1973. Also author of a sex education package, with Barbra Westholm, and of textbooks in Swedish for teen-agers and young adults, dealing with family sociology and law, sexual relations, psychological adjustments, and other topics.

WORK IN PROGRESS: An article on law the status of women in Sweden.

SIDELIGHTS: Mrs. Linner has made a number of prolonged visits in the United States with her husband, who taught at Harvard University, 1948-49, University of Wisconsin, 1963-64, University of Illinois, 1964-65, and University of Indiana, summer, 1967. In 1965 she was invited by Senator Ernest Gruening to testify on Swedish family planning before the Senate Operations Subcommittee on Foreign Aid Expenditures; earlier that year she presented a paper, "Sexual Morality and Sexual Reality: The Scandinavian Approach," at the annual meeting of the American Orthopsychiatric Association in New York. A Swedish edition of *Sex and Society in Sweden* followed the American publication; other editions have been published in Japan, Mexico, France, Germany, and England.

* * *

LIPMAN, Aaron 1925-

PERSONAL: Born March 2, 1925, in New York, N.Y.; son of Jacob (a businessman) and Esther (Chernikovsky) Lipman; married Zelda Berezow (a college instructor), June 7, 1947; children: Joan Marcie, Robert Dean, Nancy Lee. *Education:* City University of New York, B.S.S., 1947; Columbia University, M.A., 1952; National University of Colombia, Ph.D., 1963. *Religion:* Jewish. *Home:* 8798 Southwest 84th St., Miami, Fla. 33143. *Office:* University of Miami, Coral Gables, Fla. 33124.

CAREER: University of Miami, Coral Gables, Fla., instructor in sociology, 1949-51; City University of New York, New York, N.Y., lecturer in sociology, 1951-53; University of Miami, assistant professor, 1953-64, associate professor, 1964-68, professor of sociology, 1968—. Field representative, National Opinion Research Center; research consultant, United Nations Commission Economique pour l'Amerique Latine; director of research projects under grants from U.S. Department of Health, Education, and Welfare, National Institute for Mental Health, and National Science Foundation. Member of board of directors, Jewish Family Service, 1959; trustee, Florida Council on Aging, 1966—. *Military service:* U.S. Army, 1943-46; received Bronze Star and Purple Heart. *Member:* American Sociological Association, Gerontological Society, Southern Sociological Association. *Awards, honors:* Fulbright grants, 1961, 1962, 1966, for study in Colombia, Argentina, and Portugal.

WRITINGS: (With Havens and Rogers) *Medicion en Sociologia*, Tercer Mundo, 1965; *El Empresario Bogotano*, Tercer Mundo, 1966; *The Colombian Entrepreneur in Bogota*, University of Miami Press, 1967. Contributor to sociological journals.

WORK IN PROGRESS: Aging in Portugal.

* * *

LIPMAN, David 1931-

PERSONAL: Born February 13, 1931, in Springfield, Mo.; son of Benjamin (a grocer) and Rose (Mack) Lipman; married Marilyn Lee Vittert, December 10, 1961; children:

Gay Ilene, Benjamin Alan. *Education:* University of Missouri, B.J., 1953. *Religion:* Jewish. *Home:* 1 Saint Alfred Rd., St. Louis, Mo. 63132. *Office: St. Louis Post-Dispatch,* 900 North 12th Blvd., St. Louis, Mo. 63101. *Agent:* McIntosh & Otis, Inc., 475 Fifth Ave., New York, N.Y. 10017.

CAREER: Post-Tribune, Jefferson City, Mo., sports editor, 1953; Springfield Newspapers, Inc., Springfield, Mo., reporter and sportswriter, 1953-54, 1956-57; *Kansas City Star,* Kansas City, Mo., 1957-60, began as reporter, became copy editor; *St. Louis Post-Dispatch,* St. Louis, Mo., assistant sports editor, 1960-68, news editor, 1968-71, senior assistant managing editor, 1971—. *Military service:* U.S. Air Force, 1954-56; became first lieutenant. *Member:* Football Writers Association of America (member of board of directors), Baseball Writers Association of America, Society of Professional Journalists (president, St. Louis chapter), Sigma Delta Chi.

WRITINGS: Maybe I'll Pitch Forever: The Autobiography of LeRoy (Satchel) Paige as Told to David Lipman, Doubleday, 1962; *Mr. Baseball: The Story of Branch Rickey,* Putnam, 1966; *Ken Boyer,* Putnam, 1967; *Joe Namath,* Putnam, 1968; (co-author) *The Speed King: The Story of Bob Hayes,* Putnam, 1971; (co-author) *Bob Gibson: Pitching Ace,* Putnam, 1973.

WORK IN PROGRESS: A biography of quarterback Jim Hart, for Putnam; *Basketball's Greatest Upsets,* for Garrard.

AVOCATIONAL INTERESTS: Hunting.

* * *

LIPMAN, Jean 1909-

PERSONAL: Born August 31, 1909, in New York, N.Y.; married Howard Lipman; children: Peter. *Education:* Wellesley College, B.A.; New York University, M.A. *Residence:* Wilton, Conn. *Office:* Whitney Museum of American Art, New York, N.Y. 10021.

CAREER: Art in America (magazine), New York City, associate editor, 1938-40, editor, 1941-71; Whitney Museum of American Art, New York City, editor, 1971—.

WRITINGS: American Primitive Painting, Oxford University Press, 1942; *American Folk Art in Wood, Metal and Stone,* Pantheon, 1948; (with Alice Winchester) *Primitive Painters in America,* Dodd, 1950; (with Eve Meulendyke) *American Folk Decoration,* Oxford University Press, 1951; (with Mary Black) *American Folk Painting,* C. N. Potter, 1967; *Rufus Porter, Yankee Pioneer,* C. N. Potter, 1968; (co-editor) *Calder's Circus,* Dutton, 1972; *Rediscovery: Jurgan Frederick Huge,* Archives of American Art, 1974; (with Winchester) *The Flowering of American Folk Art,* Viking, 1974; *Provocative Parallels,* Dutton, 1975; (with Helen Franc) *Bright Stars,* Dutton, 1976; *Calder's Universe,* Viking, 1976. Contributor to art journals and national magazines.

* * *

LISON-TOLOSANA, Carmelo 1929-

PERSONAL: Born November 19, 1929, in Puebla de Alfinden, Spain; son of Blas and Maria (Tolosana) Lison-Huget; married Julia Cecile Houssemayne Donald, September 15, 1962. *Education:* Attended University of Zaragoza and University of London; Oxford University, D.Phil., 1963. *Religion:* Roman Catholic. *Office:* Facultad de Politicas y Sociologia, Avda, Puerta de Hierro, Madrid 3, Spain.

CAREER: Director of investigation, Instituto de la Opinion Publica, Madrid, Spain; assistant professor of sociology, University of Madrid, Madrid; currently professor of social anthropology, Universidad Complutense, Madrid. Visiting lecturer, University of Sussex, 1967; visiting professor, State University, Campinas, Brazil, 1972.

WRITINGS: Belmonte de los Caballeros (sociological study), Oxford University Press, 1966; Antropologia social en Espana, Siglo Veintiuno de Espane Editores, 1971; Antropologia cultural de Galicia, Siglo Veintiuno de Espane Editores, 1971; Ensayos de Antropologia social, Ayuso, 1973; Perfiles simbolico morales de la culture Gallego, Akal, 1974.

WORK IN PROGRESS: Another volume of aspects of Galician culture.

AVOCATIONAL INTERESTS: Travel, art, and music.

*   *   *

LISS, Sheldon B. 1936-

PERSONAL: Born November 3, 1936, in Philadelphia, Pa.; son of Jackson B. (a dentist) and Mae (Allen) Liss; married Peggy Kass, August 13, 1971; children: (former marriage) Steven Elliott, Jacqueline Cay. Education: American University, A.B., 1958, Ph.D., 1964; Duquesne University, M.A., 1962. Home: 134 North Revere Rd., Akron, Ohio 44313. Office: Department of History, University of Akron, Akron, Ohio 44325.

CAREER: Executive in private business, 1959-61; Indiana State University, Terre Haute, assistant professor of history and chairman of Latin American Studies, 1964-66; University of Notre Dame, Notre Dame, Ind., visiting professor of history, 1966-67; University of Akron, Akron, Ohio, associate professor, 1967-69, professor of history, 1969—. Peace Corps lecturer in Bolivia, 1966; member of Committee on Mexican Studies and Committee on Gran Colombian Studies. Member: American Historical Association, American Political Science Association, Conference on Latin American History, Latin American Studies Association, American Association of University Professors, Pan American Institute of Geography and History, Society for the History of American Foreign Relations, Ohio Academy of History, Phi Alpha Theta.

WRITINGS: A Century of Disagreement: The Chamizal Conflict, 1864-1964, University Press of Washington, D.C., 1965; The Canal: Aspects of United States-Panamanian Relations, University of Notre Dame Press, 1967; (co-editor) Man, State, and Society in Latin American History, Praeger, 1972. Editorial consultant, Latin American Institute.

WORK IN PROGRESS: Venezuela in Inter-American Relations: A History of Diplomacy and Foreign Policy; A History of Socialist Thought in Latin America, expected completion in 1978.

SIDELIGHTS: Liss speaks Spanish, and reads Portuguese and French.

*   *   *

LITTLE, Ian M(alcolm) D(avid) 1918-

PERSONAL: Born December 18, 1918, in Rugby, England; son of Malcolm Orme (a soldier) and Iris (Brassey) Little; married Doreen Hennessey, April 17, 1946; children: Cosmo M. J., Virginia H. Education: Attended Eton College; New College, Oxford, M.A. (first class honors),

1947; Nuffield College, Oxford, Ph.D., 1949. Home: Cete House, Badger Lane, Hinksey Hill, Oxford, England. Office: Nuffield College, Oxford University, Oxford, England.

CAREER: Oxford University, Oxford, England, fellow at All Souls College, 1948-50, Trinity College, 1950-52, and Nuffield College, 1952—, professor of economics of underdeveloped countries, 1971—. Deputy director, Economic Section of the British Treasury, 1953-55; member of India Project, Center for International Studies, Massachusetts Institute of Technology, 1958-59, 1965; vice-president, Development Center, Organization for Economic Co-operation and Development, Paris, France, 1965-67; board member, British Airports Authority, 1969-74; director, General Funds Investment Trust, 1974—. Military service: Royal Air Force, World War II; became squadron leader; received Air Force Cross.

WRITINGS: A Critique of Welfare Economics, Oxford University Press, 1950, 2nd edition, 1957; The Price of Fuel, Oxford University Press, 1953; (with P. N. Rosenstein-Rodan) Nuclear Power and Italy's Energy Position, National Planning Association (Washington, D.C.), 1957; (with R. Evely) Concentration in British Industry, Cambridge University Press, 1960; Aid to Africa, Pergamon, 1964; (with J. M. Clifford) International Aid, Allen & Unwin, 1965; (with A. C. Rayner) Higgledy-Piggledy Growth Again, Basil Blackwell, 1965; (with J. A. Miorlees) Project Appraisal and Planning for Developing Countries, Heinemann, 1974; (with J. S. Flemming) Why We Need a Wealth Tax, Methuen, 1974. Co-author of Manual of Industrial Project Analysis, 1969. Contributor to economics journals.

*   *   *

LITTLE, (Flora) Jean 1932-

PERSONAL: Born January 2, 1932, in Formosa; daughter of John Llewellyn (a physician and surgeon) and Flora (a physician; maiden name, Gauld) Little. Education: Victoria College, University of Toronto, B.A., 1955. Religion: Christian. Home: 198 Glasgow St. N., Guelph, Ontario, Canada N1H 4X2.

CAREER: Teacher of children with motor handicaps for several years before she started to write full time. Summer camp director and leader of church youth groups. Member: Authors League of America, Council for Exceptional Children, Canadian Authors Association, United Church Women. Awards, honors: Canadian Children's Book Award (joint award of American and Canadian branches of Little, Brown & Co.), 1961, for Mine for Keeps; Vicky Metcalf Award, Canadian Authors Association, 1974, for body of work inspirational to Canadian boys and girls.

WRITINGS: Mine for Keeps, Little, Brown, 1962; Home from Far, Little, Brown, 1965; Spring Begins in March, Little, Brown, 1966; When the Pie Was Opened (poetry), Little, Brown, 1968; Take Wing, Little, Brown, 1968; One to Grow On, Little, Brown, 1969; Look through My Window, Harper, 1970; Kate, Harper, 1971; From Anna, Harper, 1972; Stand in the Wind, Harper, 1975. Contributor to Horn Book, Canadian Library Journal, and Canadian Author and Bookman.

SIDELIGHTS: Miss Little told CA: "Travel when I can. Have very limited vision; was blind at birth, improved somewhat, but had to have one eye removed five years ago. I design and hook rugs, make speeches, get involved, like life." Miss Little lived in Japan, 1972-75, "for the adventure," where she worked on a book, and attended a Japanese language school.

BIOGRAPHICAL/CRITICAL SOURCES: Young Readers' Review, December, 1966, April 1968, October, 1968.

*　　*　　*

LITTLEDALE, Freya (Lota)

PERSONAL: Born in New York, N.Y.; daughter of David Milton (a pianist) and Dorothy (a teacher; maiden name, Passloff) Brown; married Harold Aylmer Littledale (an editor and author); children: Glenn David. *Education:* Ithaca College, B.S.; New York University, graduate study. *Home:* 305 East 86th St., New York, N.Y. 10028. *Agent:* Curtis Brown Ltd., 60 East 56th St., New York, N.Y. 10022.

CAREER: English teacher in Willsboro (N.Y.) public schools, 1952-53; *South Shore Record* (weekly newspaper), Woodmere, N.Y., editor, 1953-55; Maco Magazine Corp., New York City, associate editor, 1960-61; Rutledge Books and Ridge Press, New York City, associate editor, 1961-62; Parents' Magazine Press, New York City, juvenile book editor, 1962-65; free-lance writer and editor, 1965—.

WRITINGS: (Editor) *Grimms' Fairy Tales,* Parents' Magazine Press, 1964; (editor) *Fairy Tales by Hans Christian Andersen,* Parents' Magazine Press, 1964; (editor) *A Treasure Chest of Poetry,* Parents' Magazine Press, 1964; (editor) *Andersen's Fairy Tales,* Scholastic Book Services, 1966; (editor) *Thirteen Ghostly Tales,* Scholastic Book Services, 1966; *The Magic Fish,* Scholastic Book Services, 1967; (with husband, Harold Littledale) *Timothy's Forest,* Lion Press, 1969; (editor) *Ghosts and Spirits of Many Lands,* Doubleday, 1970; *King Fox and Other Old Tales,* Doubleday, 1971; (editor) *Stories of Ghosts, Witches, and Demons,* Scholastic Book Services, 1972; (editor) *Strange Tales from Many Lands,* Doubleday, 1975; *The Elves and the Shoemaker,* Scholastic Book Services, 1975. Also author of three plays for very young children, "Stop that Pancake!," "The King and Queen who Wouldn't Speak," and "The Giant's Garden," included in a Scholastic Book Services collection, 1975. Contributor to elementary school instructional materials for Silver Burdett, and to Rand McNally's "Look and Do" series. Contributor to *Humpty Dumpty.*

*　　*　　*

LITTLETON, C(ovington) Scott 1933-

PERSONAL: Born July 1, 1933, in Los Angeles, Calif.; son of Covington Scott (an investigator and writer) and Adeline (Hotchkiss) Littleton; married Mary Ann Wuest, August 26, 1961; children: Leslie Ann, Cynthia Ellen. *Education:* El Camino College, student, 1952-54; University of California, Los Angeles, A.B. (with highest honors), 1957, M.A., 1962, Ph.D., 1965. *Home:* 1600 La Loma Rd., Pasadena, Calif. 91105. *Office:* Occidental College, 1600 Campus Rd., Los Angeles, Calif. 90041.

CAREER: University of California, Los Angeles, research assistant in folklore center, 1961-62; Occidental College, Los Angeles, Calif., assistant professor, 1962-68, associate professor of anthropology, 1968—, chairman, department of sociology and anthropology, 1967-72, 1974—. Instructor, University of California Extension, 1960-62, 1964—. Consultant, Pasadena Research Institute. *Military service:* U.S. Army, 1950-52. *Member:* American Anthropological Association (fellow), American Folklore Society, International Society for Folklore and Ethnology, American Association of University Professors, Southwestern Anthropological Association, Philological Association of the Pacific Coast, California Folklore Society, Southern California Academy of Sciences, Phi Beta Kappa, Sigma Xi. *Awards, honors:* American Council of Learned Societies grant, 1972.

WRITINGS: The New Comparative Mythology: An Anthropological Assessment of the Theories of Georges Dumezil, University of California Press, 1966, revised edition, 1973; (contributor) George Cardona, H. M. Hoenigswald, and Alfred Senn, editors, *Indo-European and Indo-Europeans,* University of Pennsylvania Press, 1970; (contributor) Jaan Puhvel, editor, *Myth and Law among the Indo-Europeans,* University of California Press, 1970; (editor with Gerald James Larson and Puhvel) *Myth in Indo-European Antiquity,* University of California Press, 1974; (author of introduction) Georges Dumezil, *Gods of the Ancient Norsemen,* University of California Press, 1974. Contributor to folklore and anthropology journals.

WORK IN PROGRESS: A general text in anthropological mythology, *Mythology: An Anthropological Perspective,* a study of interrelationships among language, myth, and ideology, of further applications of the theories developed by Georges Dumezil and Claude Levi-Strauss, of Indo-European origins and the character of Proto-Indo-European culture, and of the relationship between myth and natural catastrophe.

SIDELIGHTS: C. Scott Littleton is competent in French and German, reads Greek and Latin, and has some reading competence in Spanish and Italian.

*　　*　　*

LIU, James T(zu) C(hien) 1919-
(Tzu-chien Liu)

PERSONAL: Chinese name is Tzu-chien Liu, the surname pronounced Lew; born December 19, 1919, in Shanghai, China; son of S. S. (a businessman) and Y. T. (Lin) Liu; married Hui-chen Wang, July 1, 1945; children: Karen. *Education:* Tsinghua University, student, 1936-37; Yenching University, A.B., 1941; University of Washington, Seattle, graduate study, 1947-48; University of Pittsburgh, Ph.D., 1950. *Office:* Department of East Asian Studies, Princeton University, Princeton, N.J. 08540.

CAREER: China University, Peking, lecturer, 1944-45; Yenching University, Peking, China, instructor in history and Chinese literature, 1945-46; International Tribunal, Tokyo, Japan, consultant, 1946-47; Yale University, New Haven, Conn., instructor in political science, 1950-51; University of Pittsburgh, Pittsburgh, Pa., assistant professor, 1952-54, associate professor of history, 1954-60; Stanford University, Stanford, Calif., associate professor of history, 1960-65; Princeton University, Princeton, N.J., professor of East Asian studies and history, 1965—. *Member:* American Historical Association, American Oriental Society, Association for Asian Studies (member of board of directors, 1963-66). *Awards, honors:* Rockefeller Foundation fellow, 1950-51; Fund for the Advancement of Education fellow, 1955-56; Fulbright research fellow, 1963-64; National Endowment for the Humanities grant, 1973-74.

WRITINGS: (Contributor) J. K. Fairbank, editor, *Chinese Thought and Institutions,* University of Chicago Press, 1957; (contributor) D. S. Nivison and A. F. Wright, editors, *Confucianism in Action,* Stanford University Press, 1959; *Reform in Sung China,* Harvard University Press,

1959; *Ou-yang Hsiu: An Eleventh Century Neo-Confucianist,* Stanford University Press, 1967; (editor with P. J. Golas and author of introduction) *Change in Sung China: Innovation or Renovation?,* Heath, 1969; (editor with W. M. Tu) *Traditional China,* Prentice-Hall, 1970; (editor) *Political Institutions in Traditional China: Major Issues,* Wiley, 1974. Contributor to *Encyclopaedia Britannica, Encyclopedia Americana,* and to history journals. Member of editorial board, *Journal of Asian Studies,* 1962-65.

WORK IN PROGRESS: Research on Chinese bureaucratic administration.

AVOCATIONAL INTERESTS: Chinese calligraphy.

* * *

LIU, William T(homas) 1930-

PERSONAL: Born May 6, 1930, in Nanking, China; U.S. citizen; married, 1955; children: three. *Education:* Fu Jen University, student, 1947-48; College of St. Thomas, B.A., 1951; University of Notre Dame, M.A., 1952; Florida State University, Ph.D., 1958; University of Chicago, postdoctoral study, 1961-63. *Office:* Department of Sociology and Anthropology, University of Notre Dame, Notre Dame, Ind. 46556.

CAREER: Catholic Charities, New York, N.Y., social caseworker, 1952-53; Nazareth College, Louisville, Ky., instructor in sociology, 1953-56; Florida State University, Tallahassee, teaching assistant, 1956-58; University of Portland, Portland, Ore., instructor, 1958-59, assistant professor, 1959-61; University of Notre Dame, Notre Dame, Ind., associate professor, 1962-66, professor of sociology, 1966—, director of social science research and training laboratory, 1965-70, director of Institute for the Study of Population and Social Change, 1965—. Consultant, National Institute of Child Health and Human Development, 1970—; chairman of social advisory committee, member of executive committee, and member of board, Planned Parenthood/World Population Federation, 1971—; member of board of directors, National Family Planning Program, 1971—.

MEMBER: American Sociological Association (fellow), American Association for the Advancement of Science, American Association of Teachers of Chinese Language and Culture, National Council on Family Relations, Population Association of America, Chinese Academy for Advancement of Science, American Association of University Professors, Southern Sociological Society, Ohio Valley Sociological Society, Alpha Kappa Delta. *Awards, honors:* Social Science Research Council-American Council of Learned Societies grant, 1962—.

WRITINGS: Social Psychology (in Chinese), Kuo-ming Press, 1957; (editor) *Chinese Society under Communism,* Wiley, 1967; (editor) *Family and Fertility,* University of Notre Dame Press, 1967; (contributor) John Kosa, editor, *Immigrant Scholars in America,* College and University Press, 1967; (with N. J. Pallone) *Catholics U.S.A.: Perspectives on Social Change,* Wiley, 1970; (with May L. Liu) *The Essence of Chinese Cuisine,* Aurora, 1970; (editor with Martha Stuart) *The Emerging Woman: The Impact of Family Planning,* Little, Brown, 1970. Contributor of some twenty-five articles to sociology journals. Guest editor, *American Catholic Sociological Review,* spring, 1963, and *Journal of Marriage and the Family,* April, 1968.†

LOBKOWICZ, Nicholas 1931-

PERSONAL: Last syllable of surname rhymes with "blitz"; born July 9, 1931, in Prague, Czechoslovakia; son of Jan (a landowner) and Maria (Czernin) Lobkowicz; married Josephine Waldburg-Zeil, August 22, 1953; children: John, Eric, Franz, Monika, Joseph, Miriam. *Education:* Kollegium Maria Hilf, Schwyz, Switzerland, B.A., 1950; University of Erlangen, graduate study, 1950; University of Fribourg, Ph.D., 1958. *Politics:* None. *Religion:* Roman Catholic. *Home:* Westpreussenstrasse 7, 8 Munich 81, West Germany. *Office:* Geschwister-Schull-Institut fuer Politische Wissenschaft, Ludwigstrasse 10, 8 Munich 22, West Germany.

CAREER: University of Notre Dame, Notre Dame, Ind., associate professor of philosophy, 1960-67; University of Munich, Munich, Germany, professor of political philosophy, 1967-70, dean of School of Arts and Letters, 1971, university rector, 1971—. Member of board of directors, Federal Institute for International and East European Studies, 1972—. *Member:* Association for Symbolic Logic, Association for the Advancement of Slavic Studies, Deutsche Osteuropagesellschaft. *Awards, honors:* National Endowment for the Humanities senior fellowship to complete second volume of *Theory and Practice,* 1967-68.

WRITINGS: Das Widerspruchsprinzip in der neueren sowjetischen Philosophie, D. Reidel (Dordrecht, Holland), 1959; *Marxismus-Leninismus in der CSR: Die tschechoslowakische Philosophie seit 1945,* D. Reidel, 1961; (contributor) E. McMullin, editor, *The Concept of Matter,* University of Notre Dame Press, 1963; *Theory and Practice,* Volume I: *From Aristotle to Marx,* University of Notre Dame Press, 1967; (editor and contributor) *Marx and the Western World,* University of Notre Dame Press, 1967; (contributor and editor for philosophy) *Sowjetsystem und demokratische Gesellschaft* (title means "The Soviet System and Democratic Society"), Volume I, Herder (Freiburg, Germany), 1967; (contributor) J. Gebhardt, editor, *Die Revolution des Geistes,* Paul List (Munich), 1968; (editor and contributor) *Philosophie und Ideologie,* three volumes, Herder, 1973; (contributor) W. Dallmayr, editor, *Materialien 2u Habermas' "Erkenntnis und Interesse,"* Suhrkamp (Frankfurt), 1974; (contributor) H. Dahm, editor, *Die Technik der Macht,* Walter-Verlag (Olten, Switzerland), 1974; (contributor) H. Laufer, editor, *Freicheit und Gleichheit,* C. H. Beck (Munich), 1974. Contributor to journals in America, Germany, Switzerland, Italy, and Austria. Co-editor of *Studies in Soviet Thought* (Holland), and *Zeitschrift fuer Politik* (Germany).

WORK IN PROGRESS: Analytical Ethics and *Models of Political Theory,* both for Karl Alber.

* * *

LOCKWOOD, Douglas (Wright) 1918-

PERSONAL: Born July 9, 1918, in Natimuk, Victoria, Australia; son of Alfred Wright (a publisher) and Ida (Klowss) Lockwood; married Ruth Hay, October 4, 1941; children: Kim (son), Dale (daughter). *Education:* Attended public school in Natimuk, Australia. *Office address:* G.P.O. Box 751 F, Melbourne, Australia.

CAREER: Herald, Melbourne, Australia, resident correspondent in Northern Territory, 1941—. War correspondent in Borneo, Java, 1944. *Military service:* Australian Army, World War II; became warrant officer. *Member:* Australian Society of Authors (Northern Territory regional vice-president, 1965-68). *Awards, honors: London Evening*

News literary award, 1957, for "The World's Strangest Story"; Walkley Award, 1958, for best piece of newspaper reporting in Australia; *Adelaide Advertiser* book award, 1962, for *I, the Aboriginal.*

WRITINGS: Crocodiles and Other People, Cassell, 1958; *Fair Dinkum,* Cassell, 1959; (with Nancy Polishuk) *Life on the Daly River,* R. Hale, 1961, published as *Four Against the River,* Dutton, 1962; *I, the Aboriginal,* Rigby, 1962; (with Bill Harney) *The Shady Tree,* Rigby, 1963; *We, the Aborigines,* Cassell, 1963; *Up the Track,* Rigby, 1964; *The Lizard Eaters,* Cassell, 1964; (with Doris Blackwell) *Alice on the Line,* Rigby, 1965; *Australia's Pearl Harbour,* Cassell, 1966; *The Front Door: Darwin,* Rigby, 1968; *Northern Territory Sketchbook,* Rigby, 1968.

*   *   *

LOEB, Marshall Robert 1929-

PERSONAL: Born May 30, 1929, in Chicago, Ill.; son of Monroe H. (a house wrecker) and Henrietta (Benjamin) Loeb; married Elizabeth Peggy Loewe, August 14, 1954; children: Michael, Margaret. *Education:* University of Missouri, B.J., 1950; University of Goettingen, graduate study, 1950-51. *Politics:* Independent. *Religion:* Jewish. *Home:* 31 Montrose Rd., Scarsdale, N.Y. 10583. *Office: Time,* Time & Life Building, New York, N.Y. 10020. *Agent:* Littauer & Wilkinson, 500 Fifth Ave., New York, N.Y. 10036.

CAREER: Columnist for several community newspapers, Chicago, Ill., 1944-51; *Columbia Missourian,* Columbia, Mo., reporter, 1948-50; Fridtjof Nansen International Student House, Goettingen, Germany, assistant to director, 1950-51; United Press, staff correspondent in Frankfurt, Germany, 1952-54; *St. Louis Globe Democrat,* St. Louis, Mo., reporter, 1955-56; *Time,* New York, N.Y., contributing editor, 1956-61, associate editor, 1961-65, senior editor, 1965—. Senior writer and editor on issues and policy staff, United Democrats for Humphrey, 1968. Frequent guest lecturer at numerous universities, including Yale University, Harvard University, Dartmouth College, University of Missouri, and University of Texas at Arlington. Associate fellow, Yale University's Berkeley College. *Member:* Overseas Press Club, Kappa Tau Alpha, Omicron Delta Kappa. *Awards, honors:* University of Missouri Award for excellence in financial reporting, 1966, for *Time* cover story on John Maynard Keynes; Fairchild Award for article in *Time* on flight safety; John Hancock Award and Carl M. Loeb Award for best economic story of the year in general magazines, 1974, for *Time* cover story on King Faisal and oil power.

WRITINGS: (With William Safire) *Plunging into Politics,* McKay, 1964. Author and editor of articles, essays, and cover stories in *Time;* contributor to *Reader's Digest, Panorama,* and other periodicals.

*   *   *

LOEHLIN, John C(linton) 1926-

PERSONAL: Born January 13, 1926, in Ferozepore, India; U.S. citizen; son of Clinton Herbert and Eunice (Cleland) Loehlin (missionaries); married Marjorie Leafdale, January 2, 1962; children: Jennifer, James. *Education:* Attended College of Wooster, 1943-44, and Baldwin-Wallace College, 1944-45; Harvard University, A.B., 1947; University of California, Berkeley, Ph.D., 1957. *Home:* 304 Almarion, Austin, Tex. 78746. *Office:* Psychology Department, University of Texas, Austin, Tex. 78712.

CAREER: McCann-Erickson, Inc. (advertising), Cleveland, Ohio, researcher, 1947-49; University of Nebraska, Lincoln, instructor, 1957-60, assistant professor of psychology, 1960-64; University of Texas, Austin, associate professor of psychology, 1964-69, of computer science, 1966-69, professor of psychology and computer science, 1969—. Fellow, Center for Advanced Study in the Behavioral Sciences, 1971-72. *Military service:* U.S. Naval Reserve, active duty, 1944-46, 1951-53; became lieutenant. *Member:* American Psychological Association, Society for the Study of Social Biology, Behavioral Genetics Association, Society for Multivariate Experimental Psychology, Sigma Xi.

WRITINGS: Computer Models of Personality, Random House, 1968; (with G. Lindzey and J. N. Spuhler) *Race Differences in Intelligence,* W. H. Freeman, 1975; (with R. C. Nichols) *Heritability of Personality, Ability, and Interests,* University of Texas Press, 1976.

Contributor: S. S. Tomkins and S. Messick, editors, *Computer Simulation of Personality,* Wiley, 1963; S. G. Vandenberg, editor, *Methods and Goals in Human Behavior Genetics,* Academic Press, 1965; Vandenberg, editor, *Progress in Human Behavior Genetics,* Johns Hopkins Press, 1968; D. N. Walcher and D. L. Peters, editors, *Early Childhood,* Academic Press, 1971; H. Guetzkow, P. Kotler, and R. L. Schultz, editors, *Simulation in Social and Administrative Science,* Prentice-Hall, 1972. Contributor to professional journals.

WORK IN PROGRESS: Studies in human behavior genetics.

*   *   *

LOETHER, Herman J(ohn) 1930-

PERSONAL: Born February 27, 1930, in Pittsburgh, Pa.; son of Herman Carl (a construction superintendent) and Evelyn (Hester) Loether; married Carolyn Louise Jackson (a teacher), June 15, 1957; children: Christopher Paul. *Education:* Los Angeles State College (now California State University, Los Angeles), B.A., 1951; University of Washington, Seattle, M.A., 1953, Ph.D., 1955. *Home:* 6564 Monero Dr., Rancho Palos Verdes, Calif. 90274.

CAREER: California State University, Los Angeles, 1957-67, began as assistant professor, became professor of sociology; California State College, Dominguez Hills, professor of sociology, 1967—. Principal investigator, Portals Research, 1964-66. *Military service:* U.S. Navy, 1955-57. *Member:* American Sociological Association, American Statistical Association, American Association of University Professors, Pacific Sociological Association, Alpha Kappa Delta, Phi Kappa Phi. *Awards, honors:* National Science Foundation faculty fellowship, 1964-66.

WRITINGS—All published by Allyn & Bacon, except as noted: *Problems of Aging: Sociological and Social Psychological Perspectives,* Dickenson, 1967, 2nd edition, 1975; (with Donald G. McTavish) *Descriptive Statistics for Sociologists,* 1974; (with McTavish) *Inferential Statistics for Sociologists,* 1974; (with McTavish) *A Student Handbook of Research Methods,* 1976; (with McTavish) *Statistical Analysis in Sociology,* 1976.

WORK IN PROGRESS: With Sharon Raphael, *Social Gerontology,* for Dickenson.

*   *   *

LOEWE, Ralph E. 1923-

PERSONAL: Surname rhymes with "crow"; born July 26,

1923, in Cleveland, Ohio; married; wife's name, Bessie C.; children: Deborah, Ronald. *Education:* Ohio University, B.A., 1947; Columbia University, M.A., 1950. *Office:* Cuyahoga Community College, Cleveland, Ohio 44115.

CAREER: Cleveland (Ohio) public schools, teacher and chairman of English department, 1951-60, 1961-63; American Greetings Corp., Cleveland, Ohio, humor editor, 1960-61; Cuyahoga Community College, Cleveland, Ohio, associate professor, 1964-69, professor of English, 1969—, department head, 1971-72. *Military service:* U.S. Army, three years. *Member:* National Council of Teachers of English, Modern Language Association of America, American Association of University Professors.

WRITINGS: The Practical Writer, Harcourt, 1968; *The Writing Clinic,* Prentice-Hall, 1972. With Morton Shanberg, author of a one-hour play, "A Killing at Bentley Station," produced by Canadian Broadcasting Corporation and British Broadcasting Corporation; author of local radio programs. Contributor to *Saturday Review, Writer's Digest, Editor and Publisher, Storycraft,* and other publications.

WORK IN PROGRESS: A novel about Warren Hastings of India; a satire on contemporary morals; a novel about teaching in the fifties.

AVOCATIONAL INTERESTS: Theater, archeology, gardening, travel, camping, swimming.

* * *

LOEWENBERG, Gerhard 1928-

PERSONAL: Born October 2, 1928, in Berlin, Germany; son of Walter (a physician) and Anne-Marie (Cassirer) Loewenberg; married Ina Perlstein, August 22, 1950; children: Deborah, Michael. *Education:* Cornell University, A.B., 1949, A.M., 1950, Ph.D., 1955. *Religion:* Jewish. *Home:* 6 Brickwood Knoll, Iowa City, Iowa 52240. *Office:* Department of Political Science, University of Iowa, Iowa City, Iowa 52242.

CAREER: Mount Holyoke College, South Hadley, Mass., instructor, 1953-56, assistant professor, 1956-62, associate professor, 1962-68, professor of political science, 1968-69, chairman of department, 1963-69, acting academic dean, 1968-69; University of Iowa, Iowa City, professor of political science, 1970—. Visiting lecturer at Smith College, 1956, and Columbia University, 1966-67; visiting associate professor at University of California, Los Angeles, 1966, and Cornell University, 1968. *Member:* American Political Science Association, American Association of University Professors, Midwest Political Science Association, Phi Beta Kappa. *Awards, honors:* Fulbright grant for research in Germany, 1956-57; Rockefeller grant, 1961-62; Social Science Research Council fellowship, 1964-65; Guggenheim fellowship, 1969-70; National Science Foundation grants, 1971-72, 1975-77.

WRITINGS: Parliament in the German Political System, Cornell University Press, 1967; (contributor) Henry Steele Commager and others, editors, *Festschrift for Karl Loewenstein,* J. C. B. Mohr, 1971; *Parliament: Change or Decline?,* Aldine-Atherton, 1971; (contributor) Samuel C. Patterson and John C. Wahlke, editors, *Comparative Legislative Behavior: Frontiers of Research,* Wiley, 1972; (contributor) Allan Kornberg, editor, *Legislatures in Comparative Perspective,* McKay, 1973. Contributor to *American Political Science Review, Journal of Politics,* and *Polity, British Journal of Political Science, Legislative Studies Quarterly,* and other professional journals.

WORK IN PROGRESS: A comparative study of the influence of parliamentary institutions on the stability of political systems.

AVOCATIONAL INTERESTS: Music, hiking, bicycling.

* * *

LOFTAS, Tony 1940-

PERSONAL: Born April 18, 1940, in Derby, England; son of Arthur (an engineer) and Nellie (Hayes) Loftas; married Marian Jenner (a teacher), April 17, 1965. *Education:* Queen Mary College, London, B.Sc., 1961; Grey College, University of Durham, Dip.Ed., 1962.

CAREER: University of London Press, London, England, assistant editor (science), 1962-63; *Discovery* (journal of science), London, assistant editor, 1963-64, editor, 1964-66; *World Medicine,* London, managing editor, 1966-67; *Science Journal,* London, life science editor, 1967—. Science correspondent, *Illustrated London News,* 1967—; consultant on science publishing. *Member:* Institute of Biology, Association of British Science Writers, International Science Writers Association, National Union of Journalists, British Press Club.

WRITINGS: Wealth from the Oceans, Phoenix House, 1967; (editor with P. Gwynne) *Advances in Materials Science,* University of London Press, 1967; *The Last Resource,* Hamish Hamilton, 1969, revised edition published as *The Last Resource: Man's Exploitation of the Oceans,* Regnery, 1970; (editor) *The Atlas of the Earth,* forward by Sir Julian Huxley, Mitchell Beazley, 1972. Contributor to *New Scientist, World Medicine,* and other journals.

WORK IN PROGRESS: Long-range project is writing children's stories, in addition to books on marine sciences and technology.†

* * *

LOGAN, Virgil G(lenn) 1904-

PERSONAL: Born June 21, 1904, in Rochester, Ind.; son of Clinton (a farmer) and Ella (Dunlap) Logan; married Lillian M. Stern (a professor), September 30, 1946. *Education:* Western Michigan University, B.A., 1928; University of Alabama, M.A., 1941; University of Wisconsin, Ph.D., 1951. *Politics:* Independent. *Religion:* Seventh-day Adventist. *Home:* 602 15th St., Brandon, Manitoba, Canada.

CAREER: High school teacher in Michigan, 1928-36, and principal of an academy in Tennessee, 1939-40; U.S. War Department, Washington, D.C., personnel specialist, 1942-47; Union College, Lincoln, Neb., assistant professor, 1948-50, professor of speech and chairman of department, 1950-54; University of Evansville, Evansville, Ind., professor of speech, 1954-62, chairman of department, 1957-62; Findlay College, Findlay, Ohio, professor of speech and chairman of department, 1962-65; Brandon University, Brandon, Manitoba, professor of education, 1965—. Visiting professor, University of Prince Edward Island, 1974.

MEMBER: Canadian Speech Association (founding president, 1967-68), Speech Association of America, Association for Supervision and Curriculum Development, National Council of Teachers of English, International Reading Association, American Educational Theatre Association, Adult Education Association of the U.S.A., Canadian Speech and Hearing Association, International Platform Association, International Institute of Arts and Letters (fellow), American Academy of Political and Social Science, National Council for Social Studies, World

Council for Curriculum and Instruction (charter member), Canadian Council of Teachers of English, Canadian Association of Professors of Education, Western States Speech Association, Central States Speech Association.

WRITINGS—All with wife, Lillian M. Logan: *Teaching the Elementary School Child,* Houghton, 1961; *A Dynamic Approach to Language Arts,* McGraw (Canada), 1967; *Design for Creative Teaching,* McGraw, 1971; *Creative Communication: Teaching the Language,* McGraw, 1972; *Educating Young Children,* McGraw, 1974. Contributor to *Speech Teacher* and *Journal of Educational Research.*

WORK IN PROGRESS: Teaching Reading: A Global Concern, for Gage.

* * *

LOMAS, Peter 1923-

PERSONAL: Born February 27, 1923, in Stockport, England; son of Harold (a cotton manufacturer) and Augusta (Hinds) Lomas; married Diana Gough, February 27, 1953; children: Sally, Jonathan, Timothy. *Education:* University of Manchester, M.B. and Ch.B., 1945; Institute of Psychoanalysis, London, England, associate member, 1959, member, 1963. *Home:* Lynwood, June Lane, Midhurst, Sussex, England.

CAREER: Manchester Royal Infirmary, Manchester, England, senior house surgeon, 1946; in general practice in Stockport, England, 1947-53; Cassel Hospital, Richmond, England, junior medical officer in psychiatry, 1953-58; in private practice as psychoanalyst, London, England, 1959-60. Child psychiatrist, Mitcham Child Guidance Clinic, Surrey, England. *Member:* Royal College of Psychologists.

WRITINGS: (Contributor) J. O. Wisdom and H. H. Wolff, editors, *The Role of Psychosomatic Disorder in Adult Life,* Pergamon, 1965; (contributor) Charles Rycroft, editor, *Psychoanalysis Observed,* Constable, 1966; (editor) *The Predicament of the Family,* Hogarth, 1967; *True and False Experience,* Allen Lane, 1973, Toplinger, 1974. Contributor to professional journals.

* * *

LONG, M(olly) 1916-

PERSONAL: Born February 18, 1916, in London, England; daughter of Robert and Susan (Box) Jackson; married Leonard Long (a company director), February 5, 1944. *Education:* Bedford College, London, B.A. (honors), 1938; Institute of Education, London, Teaching Certificate (with distinction), 1939, M.A., 1950. *Home:* 14 Cromer Villas Rd., Southfields, London S.W. 18, England.

CAREER: Kendrick Girls' School, Reading, Berkshire, England, assistant mistress, 1939-43; Beckenham County School, Beckenham, Kent, senior mistress, 1943-46; University of London, Institute of Education, London, England, senior lecturer in methods of teaching geography, 1946—. Chief examiner in geography, British Civil Service, 1955-60; teacher, University of Ghana, 1964, University of British Columbia, 1967. *Member:* Geographical Association (president, 1971), Royal Geographical Society (fellow), British Association for the Advancement of Science.

WRITINGS: (With R. C. Honeybone) *World Geography,* Heinemann, 1962; (editor) *Handbook for Geography Teachers,* Methuen, 1964; (with B. S. Roberson) *Teaching Geography,* Heinemann, 1966; (with Roberson) *World Problems,* English Universities Press, 1969. Contributor to *Geography.*

WORK IN PROGRESS: A book.

* * *

LONGLAND, Jean R(ogers) 1913-

PERSONAL: Born January 11, 1913, in Boston, Mass.; daughter of John Alan and Grace Lucie (Lamb) Longland. *Education:* Wheaton College, Norton, Mass., A.B., 1935; Simmons College, S.B., 1936; additional study at Columbia University, and New York University. *Home:* 490 West End Ave., New York, N.Y. 10024. *Office:* Hispanic Society of America, 613 West 155th St., New York, N.Y. 10032.

CAREER: Hispanic Society of America, New York, N.Y., cataloguer, 1936-46, assistant curator of Portuguese books, 1946-53, curator of the library, 1953—. Cooper Hill Writers Conference, guest lecturer, 1969, member of the faculty, 1970; guest lecturer, City University of New York, 1973. *Member:* American Translators Association, American Association of Teachers of Spanish and Portuguese, Latin American Studies Association, Special Libraries Association, Hispanic Society of America, P.E.N., Authors Guild, Poetry Society of America, American Portuguese Society, Phi Lambda Beta (charter member), Wheaton Club of New York (past vice-president). *Awards, honors:* Second prize for translation, *Poet Lore,* 1970, for poems by Fernando Pessoa; Portugal Prize, International Poetry Association and Portuguese government, 1973; membership medal, Hispanic Society of America, 1974.

WRITINGS: (Editor and translator) *Selections from Contemporary Portuguese Poetry,* Harvey House, 1966. Translator of poetry for other anthologies and for journals. Contributor of articles to professional journals.

WORK IN PROGRESS: Translations of selected poems by Egito Goncalves.

SIDELIGHTS: Longland has travelled extensively in Spain, Portugal, and France.

* * *

LONGSWORTH, Robert M. 1937-

PERSONAL: Born February 15, 1937, in Canton, Ohio; son of Robert H. (an educator) and Margaret (Morrow) Longsworth; married Carol Herndon, August 16, 1958; children: Eric David, Margaret, Ann. *Education:* Duke University, A.B., 1958; Harvard University, M.A., 1960, Ph.D., 1965. *Office:* Oberlin College, Oberlin, Ohio 44074.

CAREER: Oberlin College, Oberlin, Ohio, assistant professor, 1964-70, associate professor of English, 1970—, acting dean, 1974-75, dean, 1975—. President, Citizens' Scholarship Foundation of Oberlin, 1967-68. *Member:* Modern Language Association of America, Mediaeval Academy of America, Society for Religion in Higher Education, Cornish Archaeological Society.

WRITINGS: The Cornish Ordinalia: Religion and Dramaturgy, Harvard University Press, 1967; *Introduction to Drama,* Pendulum Press, 1972.

WORK IN PROGRESS: A study of comic romances in Middle English.

* * *

LONGWORTH, Philip 1933-

PERSONAL: Born February 17, 1933, in London, England; son of Leon (a businessman) and Cecilia (Blank) Longworth; married Ruth Bernstein (a civil servant), July

15, 1959. *Education:* Balliol College, Oxford, B.A., 1956, M.A., 1960. *Politics:* "Vary according to the particular issue." *Religion:* Jewish. *Home:* 38 Canonbury Park N., London N. 1, England.

CAREER: Central Asian Research Centre, London, England, researcher, 1962-65; Commonwealth War Graves Commission, London, historian, 1965-67; University of Birmingham, Birmingham, England, special lecturer in history, 1967-68; University of London, London, England, School of Slavonic and East European Studies, visiting fellow, 1973-74. Scholar-in-residence, Rockefeller Study Center, 1974. *Military service:* British Army, 1951-53. *Awards, honors:* Social Science Research Council grant for social and economic history, 1973.

WRITINGS: *Lermontov's 'A Hero of Our Time,'* New English Library, 1962, New American Library, 1964; *The Art of Victory,* Constable, 1964, Holt, 1966; *The Unending Vigil: A History of the Commonwealth War Graves Commission, 1917-1967,* Constable, 1967; *The Cossacks,* Constable, 1969, Holt, 1970; *The Three Empresses: Catherine I, Anne and Elizabeth of Russia,* Constable, 1972, Holt, 1973; *The Rise and Fall of Venice,* Canstable, 1974; (contributor) H. A. Landsberger, editor, *Rural Protest,* Macmillan, 1975. Contributor to *Encyclopaedia Britannica, Past and Present, Russia* (Milan), *Slavonic and East European Review, Race,* and other journals.

AVOCATIONAL INTERESTS: Music, walking, and theatre.

* * *

LONSDALE, Richard E. 1926-

PERSONAL: Born November 27, 1926, in Stockton, Calif.; son of Elmer (a pattern shop foreman) and Dorothy (Dulfer) Lonsdale; married Joan Spencer, August 26, 1951 (divorced); married second wife, Mildred Jordan, August 26, 1955; children: (second marriage) Alison. *Education:* University of California, Los Angeles, A.B., 1949, M.A., 1953; Syracuse University, Ph.D., 1960. *Home:* 5951 Garfield St., Lincoln, Neb. 68506. *Office:* University of Nebraska, Lincoln, Neb. 68588.

CAREER: Geographer, Central Intelligence Agency, 1953-57; State University of New York at Binghamton, assistant professor of geography, 1960-62; University of North Carolina, Chapel Hill, associate professor of geography, 1962-70; University of Nebraska, Lincoln, professor of geography and chairman of department, 1971—. Consultant to Battelle Memorial Institute, 1968-69, and to Research Triangle Institute, 1969-70. *Military service:* U.S. Army, 1944-46. *Member:* Association of American Geographers, American Association for the Advancement of Slavic Studies. *Awards, honors:* Ford Foundation fellow, 1959-60.

WRITINGS: (Director and chief cartographer) *Atlas of North Carolina,* University of North Carolina Press, 1967; *North Carolina Report,* First Union National Bank (Charlotte, N.C.), 1967; (editor) *Economic Atlas of Nebraska,* University of Nebraska Press, in press. Editor, *Southeastern Geographer,* 1966-71.

WORK IN PROGRESS: Studies of rural or small-town industrialization in the South, the Midwest, Australia, and the Soviet Union.

SIDELIGHTS: Richard Lonsdale has made two visits to the Lenin Library in Moscow and two trips to Australia to study industrial location.

LOOMIS, Charles P(rice) 1905-

PERSONAL: Born October 26, 1905, in Broomfield, Colo.; son of George A. (a farmer) and Sarah (Price) Loomis; married Nellie Holmes, 1936; married Zona Kemp (a sociologist and librarian), May 20, 1950; children: Elizabeth Ann, Laura Sarah, Vera Virginia. *Education:* New Mexico State University, B.S., 1928; North Carolina State College, M.S., 1929; Harvard University, Ph.D., 1933. *Home:* 4362 Fiesta Lane, Houston, Tex. *Office:* Department of Sociology, University of Houston, Houston, Tex.

CAREER: U.S. Department of Agriculture, Washington, D.C., agriculture economist, 1934-38, senior social scientist, 1938-43, chief of Division of Extension and Training, Office of Foreign Agriculture Relations, 1943-44; Michigan State University, East Lansing, head of sociology department, 1944-57, research professor of sociology, 1957-71, professor emeritus, 1971—, named distinguished professor, 1967; University of Houston, Houston, Tex., M. D. Anderson Professor of Sociology, 1971—. Chairman of Mission to Andean Countries, United Nations Refugee Organization, 1946; member of Study Committee for Research Projects, U.S. Public Health Service, 1958-62; member of board of directors, National Training Laboratory, 1960-61; Ford Foundation program specialist in India, 1964-65.

MEMBER: American Sociological Association (member of council, 1960-64, president, 1966-67; representative to U.S. National Commission for UNESCO), Rural Sociological Society (president, 1948), Society for Applied Anthropology (president, 1948), Michigan Academy of Sciences (vice-president, 1962), Phi Kappa Phi. *Awards, honors:* Fellow of Social Science Research Council at University of Heidelberg and University of Koenigsberg, 1933-34.

WRITINGS: (Translator) Ferdinand Tonnies, *Fundamental Concepts of Sociology,* American Book Co., 1940; *Studies of Rural Social Organization in the United States, Latin America and Germany,* Edwards Brothers, 1945; *Studies in Applied and Theoretical Social Science at Michigan State College,* Michigan State College Press, 1950; (with J. Allan Beegle) *Rural Social Systems* (text in rural sociology and anthropology), Prentice-Hall, 1950; (editor with O. E. Leonard) *Readings in Latin American Social Organizations and Institutions,* Michigan State College Press, 1953; (editor with Julio O. Morales, Roy A. Clifford, and Leonard) *Turrialba: Social Systems and the Introduction of Change,* Free Press of Glencoe, 1953; *Rural Social Systems and Adult Education,* Michigan State College Press, 1953; (with Beegle) *Rural Sociology: The Strategy of Change,* Prentice-Hall, 1957; (editor and translator) Ferdinand Tonnies, *Community and Society,* Michigan State University Press, 1957; *Social Systems: Essays on Their Persistence and Change,* Van Nostrand, 1960; (with wife, Zona K. Loomis) *Modern Social Theories,* Van Nostrand, 1961, 2nd edition, 1965; (with Z. K. Loomis and J. E. Gullahorn) *Linkages of Mexico and the United States,* Michigan Agricultural Experiment Station, 1966; *Change in Rural India as Related to Social Power and Sex of Adults,* Indian National Institute of Community Development, 1967; (with Beegle) *The Strategy of Rural Change,* Schekman, 1975; (translator with Engeborg Paulus) Ferdinand Tonnies, *Karl Marx: His Life and Teaching,* Michigan State University Press, 1975.

Author or co-author of six studies on standards of living in rural settlement and reclamation areas, published by U.S. Department of Agriculture, 1935-40. Contributor to sociology journals. Associate editor, *Journal of Sociometry,* 1940-41; editor, *Rural Sociology,* 1942-43.

WORK IN PROGRESS: A study of interaction between citizens of the United States, Canada, and Mexico; a study of factors facilitating or hindering transition from traditional to modern organization in India.

*   *   *

LOOS, Anita   1893-

PERSONAL: Born April 26, 1893, in Sissons (now Mt. Shasta), Calif.; daughter of Richard Beers (a producer and newspaper editor) and Minnie Ellen (Smith) Loos; married Frank Pallma, Jr., June, 1915 (marriage annulled one day later); married John Emerson (an actor, director, and playwright). Education: Attended high school in San Francisco, Calif.

CAREER: Formerly an actress and writer; currently a full-time screenwriter, playwright, and director. Member: Dramatists Guild.

WRITINGS: Gentlemen Prefer Blondes: The Illuminating Diary of a Professional Lady (stories; see also, Plays, below), Boni & Liveright, 1926; But Gentlemen Marry Brunettes (stories), Boni & Liveright, 1928; A Mouse is Born, Doubleday, 1951; No Mother to Guide Her, McGraw, 1961; A Girl Like I (autobiography), Viking, 1966; (author of foreword) Dody Goodman, Women, Women, Women, Dutton, 1966; (translator from the French and adaptor) Jean Canolle, The King's Mare, Evans Brothers, 1967; (with Helen Hayes) Twice Over Lightly, Harcourt, 1972; Kiss Hollywood Goodby (autobiographical), Viking, 1974. Also author, with husband, John Emerson, of Breaking Into the Movies (nonfiction).

Plays: "The Whole Town's Talking," first produced in New York at Bijou Theater, August 29, 1923; "The Fall of Eve," first produced on Broadway at Booth Theater, August 31, 1925; "Gentlemen Prefer Blondes," first produced in New York at Times Square Theater, September 28, 1926, musical version, for which Miss Loos and Joseph Fields wrote the book, first produced on Broadway at Ziegfeld Theater, December 8, 1949; (author and director with husband, John Emerson) "The Social Register," first produced in New York at Fulton Theater, November 9, 1931; Happy Birthday (first produced on Broadway at Broadhurst Theater, October 31, 1946), French, 1948; Gigi (dramatization of the novel by Colette; first produced in New York at Fulton Theater, November 24, 1951), Random House, 1952, revised edition, 1956; "Cheri" (dramatization of Cheri and The End of Cheri, two novels by Colette), first produced on Broadway at Morosco Theater, October 12, 1959. Also author, with John Emerson, of the play "Information Please" (see also, Screenplays, below).

Musicals; author of book: "The Amazing Adele" (based on a play by Pierre Barrillet and Jean-Pierre Gredy), first produced in Philadelphia at Shubert Theater, December 26, 1955; "Gogo Loves You," first produced at Theatre de Lys, October 9, 1964; "Something about Anne" (based on "The King's Mare," a play by Jean Canolle), first produced in London, November, 1966.

Screenplays: "The New York Hat," Biograph, 1912; "The Widow's Kids," Biograph, 1913; "Oh, Sammy!," Biograph, 1913; "Pa Says," Biograph, 1913; "The Power of the Camera," Biograph, 1913; "The Suicide Pact," Biograph, 1913; "The Wedding Gown," Biograph, 1913; "Bink's Vacation," Biograph, 1913; "A Cure for Suffragettes," Biograph, 1913; "A Fallen Hero," Biograph, 1913; "The Hicksville Epicure," Biograph, 1913; "Highbrow Love," Biograph, 1913; "His Hoodoo," Biograph, 1913;

"A Horse on Bill," Biograph, 1913; "The Lady in Black," Biograph, 1913; "False Colors," Paramount, 1914; "When the Roads Part," Biograph, 1914; "Billy's Rival," American Film, 1914; "A Bunch of Flowers," Biograph, 1914; "Gentlemen or Thief," Biograph, 1914; "Manhattan Madness," Fine Arts-Triangle, 1916; "The Wild Girl of the Sierras," Fine Arts-Triangle, 1916; "Little Liar," Triangle, 1916; "The Half Breed," Triangle, 1916; "American Aristocracy," Triangle, 1916; (with John Emerson) "His Picture in the Papers," Triangle, 1916; "Wild and Woolly," Artcraft, 1917; "Reaching for the Moon," Artcraft, 1917; (with Emerson) "Down to Earth," Artcraft, 1917; "In Again-Out Again," Artcraft, 1917; "Under the Top," Famous Players, 1918; (with Emerson) "Come On In," Famous Players, 1918; (with Emerson) "Good-Bye, Bill," Paramount, 1918; (with Emerson) "Hit-the-Trail Holiday," Famous Players, 1918; (with Emerson) "Let's Get a Divorce," Famous Players, 1918; (with Emerson) "Oh, You Women!," Famous Players, 1919; (with Emerson) "A Temperamental Wife," (based on their play, "Information Please"), First National, 1919; (with Emerson) "The Virtuous Vamp," First National, 1919; (with Emerson) "Getting Mary Married," Select, 1919; (with Emerson) "The Isle of Conquest," Select, 1919.

(With Emerson) "The Love Expert," First National, 1920; (with Emerson) "In Search of a Sinner" (adaptation of a story by Charlotte Thompson), First National, 1920; (with Emerson) "Woman's Place," First National, 1921; (with Emerson) "The Perfect Woman," First National, 1921; "The Branded Woman" (adaptation of the play, "Branded," by Oliver D. Bailey), First National, 1921; (with Emerson) "Dangerous Business," First National, 1921; (with Emerson) "Mama's Affair," First National, 1921; "Hold Your Man," Universal, 1921; (with Emerson) "Polly of the Follies," First National, 1922; (with Emerson) "Red Hot Romance," First National, 1922; "The Americano," Tri-Stone, 1923; "The Social Secretary," Tri-Stone, 1924; (with Emerson) "Three Miles Out," Kenma, 1924; (with Emerson) "Learning to Love," First National, 1925; (with Emerson) "The Whole Town's Talking," Universal, 1926; "Stranded," Sterling Pictures, 1927.

(With Emerson) "The Struggle," United Artists, 1931; "Ex-Bad Boy" (adaptation of "The Whole Town's Talking"), Universal, 1931; "Down to Earth," Twentieth Century Fox, 1932; "Blondie of the Follies," Metro-Goldwyn-Mayer, 1932; "The Barbarian," Metro-Goldwyn-Mayer, 1932; "Midnight Mary," Metro-Goldwyn-Mayer, 1933; "Red-Headed Woman" (adaptation of the novel by Katherine Brush), Metro-Goldwyn-Mayer, 1933; (with Emerson) "The Girl from Missouri," Metro-Goldwyn-Mayer, 1934; "Biography of a Bachelor Girl," Metro-Goldwyn-Mayer, 1934; (with Frances Marion and H. W. Hanemann) "Riffraff," Metro-Goldwyn-Mayer, 1936; "San Francisco," Metro-Goldwyn-Mayer, 1936; (with Robert Hopkins) "Saratoga," Metro-Goldwyn-Mayer, 1937; "Mama Steps Out," Metro-Goldwyn-Mayer, 1937; (with Jane Murfin) "The Women" (adaptation of the play by Clare Booth), Loew's, 1939; "Susan and God," Loew's, 1940; "Blossoms in the Dust," Loew's, 1941; (with Edwin Justus Mayer and Leon Gordon) "They Met in Bombay," Loew's, 1941; (with S. K. Lauren) "When Ladies Meet," Loew's, 1941; "I Married an Angel," Loew's, 1942; "Gentlemen Prefer Blondes," Twentieth Century-Fox, 1953; "Gentlemen Marry Brunettes," United Artists, 1955.

Other screenplays include: "How the Day Was Saved"; "A Girl Like Mother"; "His Hated Rival"; "Saved by the Soup"; "Nellie, the Female Villain"; "The Deacon's Whiskers"; "Only a Fireman's Bride."

WORK IN PROGRESS: Souvenirs of Anita Loos, a book about her experiences in Hollywood, New York, and Europe, for Grosset.

SIDELIGHTS: Interest in that mysterious "blonde syndrome" (blondes are dumb but, necessarily, have more fun) could well have gotten its biggest push with *Gentlemen Prefer Blondes,* wherein Anita Loos created Lorelei Lee, played on the stage by Carol Channing and on the screen by Marilyn Monroe. Miss Loos, who calls herself the oldest writer in motion pictures (she produced her first scenario at twelve), created the blonde heroine to typify what to her was the "nation's lowest possible mentality." In *A Girl Like I,* Miss Loos referred to George Santayana who, when asked to name the best philosophical work by an American, replied with a grin, "*Gentlemen Prefer Blondes.*" H. L. Mencken once said to her: "Young woman, do you realize you are the first American writer to ever make fun of sex?"

In *A Mouse is Born* she depicted a type of Lorelei Lee in Hollywood. "Miss Loos' long service in Hollywood vineyards highly qualifies her for the deft and hilarious satire she has written," wrote Richard Maney. "As Effie naively sets down her reactions, we get a sly and acid picture of the lunacies of those who puff and plot in the vicinity of Hollywood and Vine." Miss Loos continued her satirical look at Hollywood in *No Mother to Guide Her,* where Viola Lake is the beautiful actress addicted to "headache pills." Miss Loos "specializes in composite caricatures, and with those broadstrokes she has drawn a gay canvas of the follies, the extravagances, and the exaggerations of filmland," said Seymour Korman. Above all, though often looking at life through dark glasses, Miss Loos maintains her sense of humor. Edith Hamilton once pointed out that "she knows how to laugh, and that knowledge is the very best preservative there is against losing the true perspective."

BIOGRAPHICAL/CRITICAL SOURCES: New York Times Book Review, May 6, 1951; *Chicago Sunday Tribune,* August 2, 1961; *Times Literary Supplement,* February 23, 1967.†

* * *

LOREE, Kate (Lambie) 1920-

PERSONAL: Born June 7, 1920, in Bronxville, N.Y.; daughter of William S. and Ruth (Wallace) Lambie; married Robert F. Loree, Jr. (vice-president of a bank), January 30, 1942; children: Wendy Alix (Mrs. Ronald Wood), Bonnie Ghislaine. *Education:* Miss Master's School, graduate (with honor), 1939; further study at Columbia University and dramatic school. *Politics:* Republican. *Religion:* Episcopalian. *Home:* 24 Maple Ave., Rye, N.Y. 10580.

CAREER: Christ's Church, Rye, N.Y., director of Christian education, 1951-1958; Mayor's Committee for the Handicapped, Rye, chairman, 1961—.

WRITINGS: Pails and Snails (juvenile), Harvey House, 1967. Compiler of a pamphlet, *Living with M.S.,* 1972; also author, with other multiple sclerosis patients, of *The Challenge of Multiple Sclerosis,* 1972. Contributor to *Good Housekeeping* and *International Journal of Religious Education.*

WORK IN PROGRESS: Shocker, a children's book.

SIDELIGHTS: Mrs. Loree writes: "Feel that my own history of illness will somehow be used to help others to maintain their ability [she still walks, more than twenty years after a diagnosis of multiple sclerosis]. This is a longtime project . . . material torn from the experience of my own memory, the children's stories dance from my heart and will wait."

BIOGRAPHICAL/CRITICAL SOURCES: Rye Chronicle, December 16, 1966.

* * *

LOTT, Davis Newton 1913-

PERSONAL: Born May 8, 1913, in San Antonio, Tex.; son of James Newton (a builder) and Sissilla (Davis) Lott; married Arlene Marion Peterson, November 1, 1942; children: Vicki Arlene (Mrs. Jon Arnett), Christy Sue, Laurie Ann. *Education:* Northwestern University, B.S., 1935; University of California, Los Angeles, graduate study. *Politics:* Republican. *Religion:* Lutheran. *Home:* 13222-B Admiral Ave., Marina del Ray, Calif. 90291.

CAREER: Worked in business offices of *Better Homes and Gardens,* Des Moines, Iowa, 1935-36, and Abbott Laboratories, North Chicago, Ill., 1936-37; copywriter with Erwin Wasey Ltd., Chicago, 1937-38, and J. Walter Thompson, Chicago, 1938-39; owner and president of Lott Advertising Agency, Los Angeles, Calif., 1939-41, 1946—; also owner of Lott Publishing Co., Inc. and Western Publications, Santa Monica, Calif., and publisher of *American Buyers' Review* and *American Carwash Review. Military service:* U.S. Naval Reserve, active duty, 1941-46, 1951-52; retired as commander, 1975; during World War II created emergency shiphandling schools for the Navy. *Member:* Los Angeles Library Association (director and membership chairman), Phi Delta Theta.

WRITINGS: Rules of the Road, Illustrated, F. J. Drake, 1942; *Handbook of the Nautical Road,* F. J. Drake, 1943; *Emergency Shiphandling Manual,* U.S. Navy, 1943; *Collision Prevention,* Van Nostrand, 1947; *Dodge City Justice,* Whitman, 1957; *The Inaugural Addresses of the American Presidents,* Holt, 1964; *The Presidents Speak,* Holt, 1965. Also author of *Mystery of Midnight Springs,* and *Treasure-trail.*

WORK IN PROGRESS: They Fathered Freedom and *Meet the Freedom Signers,* both about the signers of the Declaration of Independence, Articles of Confederation, Constitution, and Bill of Rights; *Meet the Astronauts,* a book containing biographical sketches of all seventy-three astronauts; *A Pictorial Digest of the Presidential Elections and Inaugurations.*

* * *

LOUCHHEIM, Kathleen 1903-
(Katie Louchheim)

PERSONAL: Surname is pronounced Lock-hime; born December 28, 1903, in New York, N.Y.; daughter of Leonard B. and Adele (Joseph) Scofield; married Walter C. Louchheim, Jr. (a private investment counselor and vice-chairman of the National Capital Planning Commission), June 25, 1926; children: Mary S. (Mrs. Jerome Lieberthal), Judith Helen (Mrs. Paul Sitton). *Education:* Attended Columbia University, 1926-27. *Home:* 2824 O St. N.W., Washington, D.C. 20007; also maintains a summer house in Chatham, Mass.

CAREER: United Nations Relief and Rehabilitation Administration, New York, N.Y., assistant to director of public information, 1942-46, on special assignment to displaced persons camps in Germany, 1945; Democratic National Committee, Washington, D.C., director of women's activities, 1953-60, vice-chairman, 1956-60; U.S. Department of State, Washington, D.C., special assistant and consultant on women's activities, 1961-62, first woman appointed a deputy assistant secretary of state, 1962, and deputy assistant secretary of state for public affairs, 1962-63, for Community Advisory Services, 1963-66, and for educational and cultural affairs, 1966-68; U.S. ambassador to UNESCO, 1968-69. Member, Defense Advisory Committee on Women in the Armed Forces, 1955-62. Chairman of board of trustees, Federal Woman's Award, 1962-68; member of national advisory board, Arthur and Elizabeth Schlesinger Library of Radcliffe College, 1964—; member, First Lady's Committee for a More Beautiful National Capital, 1965-68; member of board of governors, American National Red Cross, 1966—.

MEMBER: Women's National Press Club (Washington). *Awards, honors:* Litt.D., Drexel Institute of Technology (now Drexel University), 1964; D.H.L., Franklin Pierce College, 1965.

WRITINGS—All under name Katie Louchheim: *With or Without Roses* (poems), Doubleday, 1966; *By the Political Sea,* Doubleday, 1970. Contributor of poetry and articles to magazines and newspapers including *Washington Post, Atlantic Monthly,* and *New Yorker.*

BIOGRAPHICAL/CRITICAL SOURCES: New York Times, October 5, 1966.

* * *

LOVESTRAND, Harold 1925-

PERSONAL: Born September 17, 1925, in Brooklyn, N.Y.; son of Louis B. (a carpenter) and Olga (Eriksen) Lovestrand; married Muriel Lang; children: H. Timothy, Andrea, Joan, Daniel, Steven, Joel. *Education:* Bob Jones University, B.A., 1949; also studied at Moody Bible Institute and Wheaton College, Wheaton, Ill. *Religion:* Baptist. *Office:* First Baptist Church, Spencer, Iowa 53101.

CAREER: Affiliated with Evangelical Alliance Mission (interdenominational), 1952-70, instructor at Bible Institute, Manokwari, West Irian, Indonesia, 1958-63; currently pastor of First Baptist Church, Spencer, Iowa. *Military service:* U.S. Army, 1943-46; served in Italy and Austria.

WRITINGS: Hostage in Djakarta, Moody, 1967.

WORK IN PROGRESS: A book of short stories based on experiences, stories, and observations while a missionary in Indonesia.

* * *

LOWE, Donald M. 1928-

PERSONAL: Born December 27, 1928, in Shanghai, China; son of C. H. and Sien-ung (Nieh) Lowe; married Mei Lee (a biochemist), June 20, 1954 (separated); children: Lisa, Lydia. *Education:* Yale University, B.A., 1950; University of Chicago, M.A., 1951; University of California, Berkeley, Ph.D., 1963. *Office:* Department of History, San Francisco State University, 1600 Holloway Ave., San Francisco, Calif. 94132.

CAREER: U.S. Joint Publications Research Service, New York, N.Y., editor, 1957-58; Hofstra University, Hempstead, N.Y., lecturer in history, 1958; Duquesne Univer-

sity, Pittsburgh, Pa., assistant professor of history, 1958-63; University of California, Riverside, assistant professor of history, 1963-68; San Francisco State University, San Francisco, Calif., associate professor, 1968-72, professor of history, 1972—. *Member:* American Historical Association, Association for Asian Studies, American Civil Liberties Union. *Awards, honors:* Ford Foundation fellowship, 1955-57; Fulbright-Hays grant, 1965; Social Science Research Council grant, 1966-67.

WRITINGS: The Function of "China" in Marx, Lenin, and Mao, University of California Press, 1966.

WORK IN PROGRESS: A study of the relation between history and phenomenology.†

* * *

LOWER, J(oseph) Arthur 1907-

PERSONAL: Surname rhymes with "tower"; born April 20, 1907, in Montreal, Quebec, Canada; son of Joseph F. (a machinist) and Edith (Greaves) Lower; married Thelma Reid (an author), July 23, 1937; children: Philip, Malcolm. *Education:* Attended Vancouver Normal School, 1927; University of British Columbia, B.A. and M.A., 1939; University of Washington, Seattle, graduate student, 1942. *Home:* 4040 West 35th Ave., Vancouver, British Columbia, Canada V6N 3P3.

CAREER: University Hill Secondary School, Vancouver, British Columbia, 1936-71, vice-principal and head of social studies department, 1956-71; Vancouver School Board, Vancouver, executive assistant, 1971-72; Vancouver Community Services, Vancouver, head teacher, 1975—. *Member:* British Columbia Historical Association (past council member), Vancouver Historical Society (past president), Topics of the Day Club. *Awards, honors:* Centennial Medal of Canada for service to the community and writing, 1967.

WRITINGS: Canada: An Outline History, Ryerson, 1966, revised edition, 1973, published as *Canadian History at a Glance,* Barnes & Noble, 1967; *Today's World,* McClelland & Stewart, 1966; (with M. E. Cottingham) *Renaissance to Revolution,* McClelland & Stewart, 1968; *Self-Government in the Commonwealth,* McClelland & Stewart, 1968; *Nationalism to Internationalism,* McClelland & Stewart, 1969; *Parliaments and Congress,* McClelland & Stewart, 1971; *Selections from Hansard,* McClelland & Stewart, 1971; *Canada on the Pacific Rim,* McGraw (Canada), 1975. Contributor to history and education journals.

AVOCATIONAL INTERESTS: Public speaking, gardening, fishing for salmon ("very elusive!") on the British Columbian coast.

* * *

LOWRY, Thomas P. 1932-

PERSONAL: Born November 24, 1932, in Sacramento, Calif.; son of Richard Sims (a maritime executive) and Margaret (Power) Lowry; married second wife, Frances Smith, February 14, 1960; married Thea Snyder, November 26, 1968; children: Margot, Shawn, Richard. *Education:* Stanford University, A.B., 1954, M.D., 1957. *Politics:* Democrat. *Religion:* None. *Home:* 3 Holly Lane, Woodacre, Calif. 94973. *Office:* 1100 Sir Francis Drake Blvd., Kentfield, Calif. 94904.

CAREER: California Department of Corrections, San Quentin, prison psychiatrist, 1963-65; private practice of psychiatry, Kentfield, Calif., 1963-69, 1973—; Ross General Hospital, Ross, Calif., former director of psychiatric services; New Mexico State Hospital, Las Vegas, N.M., director, 1969-71; Desert Retreat Psychiatric Hospital, Las Vegas, Nev., director, 1971-72; Masters and Johnson Clinic, St. Louis, Mo., research associate, 1972-73. *Military service:* U.S. Air Force, Medical Corps, 1961-63; became captain. *Member:* American Psychiatric Association, American Association of Marriage and Family Counselors.

WRITINGS: (Editor and contributor) *Hyperventilation and Hysteria,* C. C Thomas, 1967; *Camping Therapy,* C. C Thomas, 1974; *The Clitoris,* Warren Green, 1976. Contributor of articles to medical journals.

WORK IN PROGRESS: The Classic Clitoris, a study in the history of anatomy.

AVOCATIONAL INTERESTS: Certified scuba diver; student sailplane pilot.

* * *

LUBIN, Bernard 1923-

PERSONAL: Born October 15, 1923, in Washington, D.C.; son of Israel Harry (a businessman) and Anna (Cohen) Lubin; married Alice Weisbord, August 8, 1958. *Education:* George Washington University, B.A., 1952, M.A., 1953; Pennsylvania State University, Ph.D., 1958. *Office:* Department of Psychology, University of Houston, Houston, Tex. 77004.

CAREER: U.S. Merchant Marine, 1943-48; St. Elizabeth's Hospital, Washington, D.C., intern, 1952-53; also intern at Roanoke V.A. Hospital, 1954, Wilkes-Barre V.A. Hospital, 1955; University of Wisconsin, Madison, postdoctoral fellow in psychology at University Hospital, 1957-58; Indiana University, School of Medicine, Indianapolis, instructor in clinical psychology and chief psychologist to adult psychiatric and consultation services, 1958-62, assistant professor, 1962-64, associate professor of clinical psychology, 1964-67; Indiana Department of Mental Health, Indianapolis, director of psychological services, 1962-64, director of research and training, 1964-67; director of Division of Psychology, Mental Health Center, Kansas City, and professor at University of Missouri School of Medicine, 1967-74; University of Houston, Houston, Tex., professor of psychology and director of clinical training program, 1974—. Diplomate of American Board of Examiners in Professional Psychology, and American Board of Examiners in Psychological Hypnosis. President, Midwest Group for Human Resources, 1966-69; president-elect, Indiana Public Health Foundation, 1967-68.

MEMBER: American Psychological Association (fellow), National Training Laboratories (fellow), American Association for the Advancement of Science (fellow), Association for the Advancement of Mental Health Research and Education (secretary, 1962-67), Indiana Psychological Association (president, 1967-68).

WRITINGS: (Contributor) *Readings in Counseling and Guidance,* Macmillan, 1965; (with wife, Alice W. Lubin) *Group Psychotherapy: A Bibliography of the Literature from 1956 through 1964,* Michigan State University Press, 1966; (editor with E. E. Levitt) *The Clinical Psychologist: Background, Roles, and Functions,* Aldine, 1967; (with Levitt) *Depression: Concepts, Controversies and Some New Facts,* Springer Publishing, 1975; (contributor) *Clinical Methods in Psychology,* Wiley, in press. Has published two psychological tests. Contributor of more than seventy articles and reviews to professional journals.

LUBOVE, Roy 1934-

PERSONAL: Born September 3, 1934, in New York, N.Y.; son of Harry and Esther (Siroty) Lubove; married Carole Lynne Gollance (a weaver), June 22, 1958; children: Seth Harris, Rebecca Elizabeth. *Education:* Columbia University, B.A., 1956; Cornell University, Ph.D., 1960. *Office:* School of Social Work, University of Pittsburgh, Pittsburgh, Pa. 15260.

CAREER: Harvard University, Cambridge, Mass., instructor in history, 1960-63; University of Pittsburgh, Pittsburgh, Pa., assistant professor, 1963-66, associate professor, 1966-69, professor of social welfare and history, 1969—.

WRITINGS: The Progressives and the Slums, University of Pittsburgh Press, 1962; *Community Planning in the 1920's,* University of Pittsburg Press, 1963; *The Professional Altruist,* Harvard University Press, 1965; *The Struggle for Social Security: 1900-1935,* Harvard University Press, 1968; *Twentieth-Century Pittsburgh: Government, Business and Environmental Change,* Wiley, 1969.

* * *

LUCAS, J(ohn) R(andolph) 1929-

PERSONAL: Born June 18, 1929, in London, England; son of Egbert de Grey (a clergyman) and Joan Mary (Randolph) Lucas; married Helen Morar Portal, June 17, 1961; children: Edward de Grey, Helen Mary, Richard Henry, Deborah Joan. *Education:* Balliol College, Oxford, B.A. (first class honours), 1951. *Religion:* Church of England. *Home:* Lambrook House, South Petherton, Somerset, England. *Office:* Merton College, Oxford University, Oxford, England.

CAREER: Fellow of Merton College, Oxford University, Oxford, England, 1953-56, and Corpus Christi College, Cambridge University, Cambridge, England, 1956-59; Princeton University, Princeton, N.J., Proctor visiting fellow, 1957-58; University of Leeds, Leeds, England, Leverhulme fellow in philosophy of science, 1959-60; Oxford University, Merton College, fellow, 1960—. Gifford lecturer, University of Edinburgh, 1971-73. Oxford Consumer Group, chairman, 1961-63, 1966-67, vice-chairman, 1963-66. *Awards, honors:* John Locke Prize, Oxford University, 1952.

WRITINGS: The Principles of Politics, Clarendon Press, 1966; *The Concept of Probability,* Clarendon Press, 1970; *The Freedom of the Will,* Clarendon Press, 1970; (with A.J.P. Kenny, H. C. Longuet-Higgins, and C. H. Waddington) *The Nature of Mind,* University of Edinburgh Press, 1972; (with Kenny, Longuet-Higgins, and Waddington) *The Development of Mind,* University of Edinburgh Press, 1973; *A Treatise on Time and Space,* Methuen, 1973; *Democracy and Participation,* Penguin, 1976; *Essays on Freedom and Grace,* S.P.C.K., 1976.

Contributor: R. J. Butler, editor, *Analytical Philosophy,* Barnes & Noble, 1962; Kenneth M. Sayre and Frederick J. Crosson, editors, *Modeling of Mind,* University of Notre Dame Press, 1964; Alan R. Anderson, editor, *Minds and Machines,* Prentice-Hall, 1964; R. S. Summers, *Essays in Legal Philosophy,* Oxford University Press, 1968; Hugo A. Bedan, editor, *Justice and Equality,* Prentice-Hall, 1971; Richard E. Flathman, editor, *Concepts in Social and Political Philosophy,* Macmillan, 1973; Bryan R. Wilson, editor, *Education, Equality and Society,* Allen & Unwin, 1975; J. Rachels, editor, *Moral Problems,* Harper, 1975.

WORK IN PROGRESS: Three books, *An Introduction to the Philosophy of Mathematics, The Principles of Natural Knowledge,* and *The Nature of Justice.*

BIOGRAPHICAL/CRITICAL SOURCES: Yale Review, autumn, 1967.

* * *

LUCKOCK, Elizabeth   1914-

PERSONAL: Born May 7, 1914, in Chatham, Kent, England; daughter of F. Gore (a brigadier general) and Ethel Marian (Maitland) Anley; married Peter Luckock (a lieutenant colonel, British Army, retired; currently in civil service), February 3, 1940; children: Angela Susan, Geoffrey Peter, Robert James. *Education:* Attended Pensionnat Flosissant, Lausanne, Switzerland, 1930-31, and St. James Secretarial College, London, England, 1931-32. *Politics:* Conservative. *Religion:* Church of England. *Home:* Metford Mill, Cattistock, Dorsetshire, England.

CAREER: Held various secretarial positions, including secretary to director of Telecommunications, Addis Ababa, Ethiopia, 1953-57. *Member:* Conservative Association.

WRITINGS: William the Conqueror, Wheaton & Co., 1964, Putnam, 1966; *The Reign of the Conqueror,* Wheaton & Co., 1968; (with Caroline Gundry) *Simon de Montfort: Reformer and Rebel,* Wheaton & Co., 1969. Contributor of travel articles and animal stories to *Lady* and other magazines.

WORK IN PROGRESS: Historical and literary research for children's books; a children's edition of stories from the chronicles of Froissart.†

* * *

LUDLOW, Howard T(homas)   1921-

PERSONAL: Born September 7, 1921, in New York, N.Y.; son of Howard C. (in banking) and Irene E. (Mulvey) Ludlow; married Catherine E. Packard (a high school teacher), June 28, 1952; children: Maureen, Howard, Francis. *Education:* Fordham University, B.S., 1947, M.A., 1949, Ph.D., 1955. *Politics:* Democrat. *Religion:* Roman Catholic. *Home:* 22 Martha Blvd., Parlin, N.J. 08859. *Office:* Seton Hall University, South Orange, N.J. 07079.

CAREER: Seton Hall University, South Orange, N.J., instructor in economics, 1949-53, assistant professor of management, 1954-55, associate professor, 1956-58, professor of industrial relations and chairman of department, 1958—. Visiting professor, Georgetown University, 1964. Public member, New Jersey Minimum Wage Board, 1955; vice-chairman, New Jersey State Board of Mediation, 1956-70; Sayreville (N.J.) Industrial Commission, 1968. *Military service:* U.S. Army, 1942-43. *Member:* Association of Labor Mediation Agencies (president, 1967), Association for Social Economics, American Arbitration Association, Industrial Relations Research Association.

WRITINGS: Business Management, Monarch Books, 1965; *Labor Economics,* Monarch Books, 1966. Contributor to *America* and to professional journals.

WORK IN PROGRESS: Labor Mediation.

* * *

LUDOVICI, Laurence J(ames)   1910-

PERSONAL: Given name originally Lorenz; surname is pronounced Ludo-vee-si; born September 19, 1910, in Colombo, Ceylon; son of James (superintendent of Ceylon police) and Marion Zoe (de Hoedt) Ludovici; married Maria Niedermayer-Schehr, January 10, 1935; children: Raymonde. *Education:* Educated privately and at Oxford University. *Politics:* Liberal. *Religion:* Presbyterian. *Agent:* Harold Ober Associates, Inc., 40 East 49th St., New York, N.Y. 10017. *Home and office:* 751B Finchley Rd., London N.W.11, England; and 6 Avenue Mon Repos, Lausanne, Switzerland.

CAREER: Worked as an editor in London, England, for Jarrolds Publishers, 1934-36, and Methuen & Co., 1936-38; became editorial director at Andrew Dakers Ltd., London, England, 1938-54; full-time professional writer, 1954—. Curator of the Conan Doyle Foundation in Switzerland, 1967-68. Broadcaster. *Military service:* Royal Air Force, 1940-46; became a squadron leader; Royal Air Force Reserve, 1946-50. *Awards, honors:* Junior Book Award of Boys' Clubs of America, 1966, for *The Origins of Language.*

WRITINGS: Fleming: Discoverer of Penicillin, Andrew Dakers, 1952, Indiana University Press, 1955; (translator) Emond Vermeil, *The German Scene (Social-Political-Cultural): 1890 to Present Day,* Harrap, 1956; *The Challenging Sky: The Life of Sir Alliot Verdon-Roe,* Jenkins, 1956; (editor) *Nobel Prize Winners,* Arco, 1956; *Tomorrow Sometimes Comes: Ten Years against Tyranny,* Odhams, 1958; *The World of the Infinitely Small: Explorations through the Microscope,* Phoenix House, 1958; *The World of the Microscope,* Putnam, 1959.

Seeing Near and Seeing Far: The Story of Microscopes and Telescopes, Putnam, 1960; *Great Moments in Medicine,* Roy, 1961; *Cone of Oblivion: A Vendetta in Science,* Parrish, 1961, published as *The Discovery of Anaesthesia,* Crowell, 1962; *The Itch for Play: Gamblers and Gambling in High Life and Low Life,* Jarrolds, 1962; *Links of Life: The Story of Heredity,* Putnam, 1962; *The Great Tree of Life: Paleontology, the Natural History of Living Creatures,* Putnam, 1963. *The Chain of Life: The Story of Heredity,* Phoenix House, 1963; *Origins of Language,* Putnam, 1965; *The Final Inequality: A Critical Assessment of Woman's Role in Society,* Norton, 1965, revised edition, Tower, 1971.

WORK IN PROGRESS: The Final Syllables; The Beautifier.

AVOCATIONAL INTERESTS: Archaeology, music, the arts generally.

* * *

LUKE, Mary M.   1919-

PERSONAL: Born March 24, 1919, in Pittsfield, Mass.; daughter of John Frisbie and Hazel (Fish) Munger; married David L. Luke (divorced); children: Melinda Carey. *Education:* Berkshire Business College, graduate, 1938. *Politics:* Republican. *Religion:* Episcopalian. *Agent:* Claire Smith, c/o Harold Ober Associates, 40 East 49th St., New York, N.Y. 10017. *Home and office:* 51 Tackora Trail, Ridgefield, Conn. 06877.

CAREER: Worked for advertising, oil, and tool firms in New York, N.Y., and then for a documentary film company during World War II; RKO Pictures, Hollywood, Calif., secretary to treasurer of the company, 1943-44; Hunt Stromberg Productions, Hollywood, employee in story and publicity departments, 1944. *Member:* Ridgefield Library and Historical Association (former treasurer), Silver Spring Country Club.

WRITINGS—All published by Coward: *Catherine, the Queen,* 1967; *A Crown for Elizabeth,* 1970; *Gloriana: The Years of Elizabeth,* 1973.

WORK IN PROGRESS: A novel.

SIDELIGHTS: Mrs. Luke told *CA:* "I am interested in gardening, have a greenhouse which takes more time than it should, a teen-ager, two dachshunds and two cats, a large house and no help, which shows where my extra (?) time goes."

* * *

LUNDAHL, Gene 1933-

PERSONAL: Born May 27, 1933, in Sioux City, Iowa; son of Lester Eric (a realtor) and Helen (Baumgart) Lundahl; married Akiko Terashima (a dietician), April 28, 1958; children: Eric, Lesley. *Education:* University of Iowa, B.A., 1956, M.A., 1960; University of Denver, Ph.D., 1966. *Politics:* Conservative: *Religion:* Anglo-Catholic. *Office:* Department of English, University of Denver, Denver, Colo.

CAREER: University of Denver, Denver, Colo., instructor in English, 1965—. *Member:* Modern Language Association of America.

WRITINGS: *Jargon's Journey,* Verb, 1966.

WORK IN PROGRESS: *The Hospital That Laughed,* a collection of short stories; *The Crater,* a novella.

AVOCATIONAL INTERESTS: Poetry and fiction in the comic genres; Latin and Italian poetry translations.††

* * *

LUNDEN, Walter A(lbin) 1899-

PERSONAL: Born March 27, 1899, in Spencerbrook, Minn.; son of Andrew and Lydia (Griep) Lunden; married Lillian M. Chack, June 25, 1924. *Education:* Gustavus Adolphus College, B.A. (cum laude), 1922; University of Minnesota, M.A., 1929; Harvard University, Ph.D., 1934. *Politics:* Republican. *Religion:* Lutheran. *Home:* 711 Beach Ave., Ames, Iowa 50010. *Office:* 104 East Hall, Iowa State University, Ames, Iowa 50010.

CAREER: University of Pittsburgh, Pittsburgh, Pa., assistant professor of sociology, 1930-43; Iowa State University, Ames, professor of sociology, 1947—. Chairman, Governor's Committee on Penal Affairs for Iowa, 1957—. *Military service:* U.S. Aviation Service, 1918. U.S. Army, 1943-47; prison officer; served in Europe; became major. *Member:* American Sociological Society (fellow), American Society of Criminology (fellow), American Association for the Advancement of Science (fellow), American Legion, Lions Club.

WRITINGS: (With P. A. Sorokin) *Power and Morality,* Sargent, 1959; *Statistics on Delinquents and Delinquency,* C. C Thomas, 1964; *The Prison Warden and Custodial Staff,* C. C Thomas, 1965; *Crimes and Criminals,* Iowa State University Press, 1967; *The Murder Cycle,* Art Press, 1972. Also author of *War and Delinquency,* Art Press.

WORK IN PROGRESS: *Crimes in Japan, 1940-64; The Suicide Cycle, 1900-72.*

* * *

LUPOFF, Richard A(llen) 1935-
(Dick Lupoff)

PERSONAL: Born February 21, 1935, in Brooklyn, N.Y.; son of Sol J. (an accountant) and Sylvia (Feldman) Lupoff; married Patricia Loring, August 27, 1958; children: Kenneth, Katherine, Thomas. *Education:* University of Miami, Coral Gables, Fla., B.A., 1956. *Politics:* None. *Religion:* Jewish. *Home:* 3208 Claremont Ave., Berkeley, Calif. 94705. *Agent:* Henry Morrison, Inc., 58 West Tenth St., New York, N.Y. 10011.

CAREER: Remington Rand Univac, New York City, technical writer, 1958-63; International Business Machines Corp., New York City and Poughkeepsie, N.Y., writer and director of technical films, 1963-70. *Military service:* U.S. Army, 1956-58; became first lieutenant. *Member:* Science Fiction Writers of America. *Awards, honors:* Hugo Award at World Science Fiction Convention, 1963, for editing the best "amateur" critical science fiction magazine, *Xero,* 1962.

WRITINGS: *Edgar Rice Burroughs: Master of Adventure,* Canaveral, 1965, revised edition, Ace Books, 1974; *One Million Centuries* (novel), Lancer Books, 1967; (editor with Don Thompson) *All in Color for a Dime,* Arlington House, 1969; *Scared Locomotive Flies* (novel), Ballantine, 1971; (editor with Thompson) *The Comic-Book Book,* Arlington House, 1973; *Into the Aether* (novel), Dell, 1974; *The Triune Man* (novel), Berkeley Publishing, in press; *Lisa Lane* (juvenile novel), Bobbs-Merrill, in press; *Fool's Hill* (novel), Dell, in press; *Barsoom: Edgar Rice Burroughs and the Martian Vision* (nonfiction), Mirage Press, in press. Editor of five volumes of previously unpublished miscellaneous writings of Edgar Rice Burroughs, 1963-64. Writer of radio scripts; contributor of short stories and articles to newspapers and magazines.

WORK IN PROGRESS: Two novels, *New Alabama Blues,* for Dell, and *Demons,* for Harper.

* * *

LURIE, Richard G. 1919-

PERSONAL: Born April 4, 1919, in Boston, Mass.; son of Abraham and Fania Lurie; married Sanna Klaveness, July, 1959 (divorced). *Education:* Harvard University, A.B., 1941. *Office:* 230 East 15th St., New York, N.Y. 10003.

CAREER: Johnston International Publishing Corp., New York City, 1947-63; *American Exporter,* New York City, editor and publisher, 1956; *Worldwide Planning,* Stamford, Conn., editor, 1967-73. U.S. Department of Commerce, former member of World Trade Advisory Committee, and member of trade missions to Italy, 1956, and France, 1957. Marketing consultant; speaker before business groups in North America, Europe, and the Far East. *Member:* World Trade Writers Association (former president), National Press Club, Overseas Press Club, Harvard Club, The Players, Society of Travel Writers.

WRITINGS: *Passports and Profits,* Doubleday, 1965. Contributor to *Venture, Life International, Iron Age, Clipper, Printers' Ink, Duns Review, Medical World News, Business Week Letter,* and other periodicals.

SIDELIGHTS: Travels have taken Lurie to more than sixty countries.

* * *

LYNN, Robert Wood 1925-

PERSONAL: Born April 3, 1925, in Wheatland, Wyo.; married Katharine Wuerth, March 8, 1952; children: Thomas Taylor, Janet Macgregor, Elizabeth Mitchell, Sarah McKee. *Education:* Princeton University, B.A.

(magna cum laude), 1948; Yale University, B.D., 1952; Union Theological Seminary, New York, N.Y., Th.D., 1962. *Office:* Lilly Endowment, Inc., 2801 North Meridian St., Indianapolis, Ind. 46208.

CAREER: Presbyterian clergyman, ordained in 1952; assistant minister, Montview Boulevard Presbyterian Church, 1952-54, 1956-59; Union Theological Seminary, New York, N.Y., assistant professor, 1959-60, Auburn assistant professor of practical theology, 1960-62, associate professor, 1962-65, Auburn Professor of Religious Education and Church and Community, 1965-75, dean of Auburn program, 1960-75; Lilly Endowment, Inc., Indianapolis, Ind., senior program officer, 1975—. Chairman of committee on church and public education, United Presbyterian Church of United States, Board of Christian Education. *Military service:* U.S. Army, 1943-45. *Member:* American Society of Church History, Conference on Science, Philosophy and Religion. *Awards, honors:* Woodrow Wilson fellowship.

WRITINGS: Protestant Strategies in Education, Association Press, 1965; (with Elliott Wright) *The Big Little School,* Harper, 1971.

Contributor: John L. Casteel, editor, *Spiritual Renewal through Personal Groups,* Association Press, 1957; Earl Jabay, editor, *The Search for Identity,* Zondervan, 1967; M. J. Taylor, editor, *Introduction to Christian Education,* Abingdon, 1966. Contributor to religious and educational journals.

* * *

LYONS, Enid (Muriel) 1897-

PERSONAL: Born July 9, 1897, in Duck River (now Leesville), Tasmania, Australia; daughter of William Charles (a sawmill worker) and Eliza (Tagget) Burnell; married Joseph Aloysius Lyons (Prime Minister of Australia, 1932-39), April 28, 1915 (died, 1939); children: Gerald Desmond, Sheila Mary (Mrs. William J. Lacey), Enid Veronica (Mrs. Maurice Austin), Kathleen Patricia (Mrs. G. Edward Gordon), Moira Rose (Mrs. Frank J. Brady), Kevin Orchard, Garnet (deceased), Brendan Aloysius, Barry Joseph, Rosemary Josephine (Mrs. Francis C. McGrath), Peter Julian, Janice Mary (Mrs. Douglas Wotton). *Education:* Educated at a small country school in Tasmania, 1904-11, and then at Teachers' Training College, Hobart, Tasmania, 1912-13. *Politics:* Liberal. *Religion:* Roman Catholic. *Home and office:* Home Hill, Middle Rd., Devonport, Tasmania 7310, Australia.

CAREER: Stood for the Tasmanian Parliament in 1925 at the urging of her husband, who had fostered legislation enabling women to become members, but lost by sixty votes; became first woman to sit on the federal executive of Australian Labour Party, 1926; during her husband's years as Australian Prime Minister (1932-39), she accompanied him on campaign tours and made her own speaking tours in his behalf; after her husband's death, she withdrew to the old family home in Devonport to devote her time to eleven surviving children (one son had died in infancy); she returned to political life during the war to become the first woman member of the Australian House of Representatives, 1943-51, and the first woman to hold ministerial rank in the Australian Parliament (as vice-president of the Executive Council), 1949-51, resigning both posts because of ill health; took on less arduous post as member of governing board of Australian Broadcasting Commission, 1951-62, resigning from the board to live quietly in Devonport. Syndicated columnist for *Melbourne Sun, Adelaide Advertiser,* and *Brisbane Courier Mail,* 1951-55. Former vice-president of Australian Liberal Party. Vice-president, Australian Elizabethan National Theatre, 1954; international vice-president, St. Joan's Internation Social and Political Alliance.

AWARDS, HONORS: Dame Grand Cross of Order of the British Empire (equivalent of knighthood), 1937; honorary fellowship of College of Nursing, Australia, 1950; Australian Mother of the Year, 1950, an honor conferred by American Committee on Motherhood; freedom award of city of Devonport, 1951.

WRITINGS: So We Take Comfort (autobiography), Heinemann, 1965; *The Old Haggis,* Heinemann, 1969; *Among the Carrion Crows,* Rigby, 1972. Also author of *My Life Story,* 1949. Contributor to magazines and newspapers.

WORK IN PROGRESS: The House on the Hill.

SIDELIGHTS: So We Take Comfort is a record of Dame Enid Lyons' marriage (at seventeen) to the man twice her age who became Australia's Prime Minister. Her purpose in writing the book and its sequels, she said, was "broadly historical: to provide a record of the times in which I have lived, the events, and the notable persons with whom I came in contact." With the Prime Minister, she attended the Silver Jubilee of King George V and Queen Mary in London, 1935; on their visit to Washington that same year they were guests of President and Mrs. Roosevelt. She accompanied her husband to London again in 1937 for the coronation of King George VI, and returned alone in 1953, as Dame Grand Cross of the British Empire, for the coronation of Queen Elizabeth II.

Of all that has been written about her, the notable Australian woman cherishes most an essay, "My Favorite Person," by one of her forty-eight grandchildren, which took first prize in an inter-school competition in Tasmania. The twelve-year-old essayist portrayed her "nan" as a slight, white-haired woman, full of understanding, and possessed of a fantastic memory, "determination and drive . . . an expert upholsterer," wall-paperer, artist, and flower arranger, who "can do any manner of things with a hammer and nails," and then close her day by playing the piano for a family songfest.

* * *

LYS, Daniel 1924-

PERSONAL: Surname is pronounced Lees; born December 10, 1924, in Dourgne, France; son of Rene (a manufacturer) and Angele (Peyre) Lys; married Jeanine Grellier, July 26, 1947; children: David, Marjolaine, Christophe. *Education:* College de Revel, B.S., 1943; University of Montpellier, Licence de Philosophie, 1946; Faculte Libre de Theologie Protestante, B.D., 1948, Ph.D., 1960. *Home:* 67 Avenue de Villeneuve–Angouleme, 34-Montpellier, France. *Office:* Faculte de Theologie Protestante, 13 Rue Louis-Perrier, 34-Montpellier, France.

CAREER: Clergyman of Reformed Church of France; College Cevenol, Le Chambon-sur-Lignon, Haute-Loire, France, professor of philosophy, 1948-51; pastor of Reformed Church, Le Chambon-sur-Lignon, 1951-61; Faculte de Theologie Protestante, Montpellier, France, professor of Hebrew and Old Testament, 1958-59; Chicago Theological Seminary, Chicago, Ill., professor of Hebrew and Old Testament, 1961-65; Faculte de Theologie Protestante, professor of Hebrew and Old Testament, 1965—. *Awards, honors:* Ph.D., University of Montpellier, 1973.

WRITINGS: (Contributor) J. J. von Allmen, editor, *Vocabulaire Biblique,* Delachaux & Niestle, 1954, 3rd edition, 1964, published as *Vocabulary of the Bible,* with an introduction by H. H. Rowley, Lutterworth Press, 1958; *Nephesh: Histoire de l'ame dans la revelation d'Israel,* Presses Universitaires de France, 1959; (editor) *Maqqel Shaqedh: Hommage a Wilhelm Vischer,* Causse-Graille-Castelnau, 1960; *Ruach: Le Souffle dans l'Ancien Testament,* Presses Universitaires de France, 1962; *The Meaning of the Old Testament: An Essay on Hermeneutics* (translation of *A la recherche d'une methode pour l'exegese de l'ancien testament*), Abingdon, 1967; *La Chair dans l'Ancien Testament: Basar,* Editions Universitaires, 1967; *Le Plus beau chant de la creation: Commentaire du Cantique des Cantiques,* Editions du Cerf, 1968; *Comprends-tu ce que tu lis?: Initiation au sens de l'Ancien Testament,* Editions du Cerf, 1972. Contributor to theological journals.

WORK IN PROGRESS: A commentary on *Ecclesiastes.*

AVOCATIONAL INTERESTS: Fishing, gardening, reading, music, choir-directing.

BIOGRAPHICAL/CRITICAL SOURCES: Contemporary Currents of French Theological Thought, Union Theological Seminary (Richmond, Va.), 1965.

* * *

MABEY, Richard (Thomas)   1941-

PERSONAL: Born February 20, 1941, in Berkhamsted, England; son of Thomas Gustavus (a bank official) and Nelly (Moore) Mabey. *Education:* St. Catherine's College, Oxford, B.A. (honors), 1963. *Politics:* "Radical; a non-joiner, but with strong left-wing and libertarian leanings." *Religion:* None. *Home:* 78 High St., Southwold, Suffolk, England. *Agent:* Richard Simon, 32 College Cross, London N.1, England.

CAREER: Dacorum College of Further Education, Hemel Hempstead, Hertfordshire, England, lecturer in social studies, 1963-65; Penguin Books Ltd., Education Division, Harmondsworth, Middlesex, England, senior editor, 1966-73; free-lance editor, 1973—. Member of Kenneth Allsop Memorial Trust and Council of the Hertfordshire and Middlesex Trust for Nature Conservation. *Member:* British Film Institute, Society for Education in Film and Television.

WRITINGS: (Editor) *Class: A Symposium,* Anthony Blond, 1967, Dufour, 1969; *Behind the Scene,* Penguin, 1968; *The Pop Process,* Hutchinson, 1969; *Food for Free,* Collins, 1972; *Children in Primary School,* Penguin, 1972; *The Unofficial Countryside,* Collins, 1973; *The Roadside Wildlife Book,* David & Charles, 1974; *The Pollution Handbook,* Penguin, 1974. Contributor to *Countryman, Nova, Illustrated London News, Peace News,* and others.

WORK IN PROGRESS: A number of books on the social history of plants and wildlife; editing an edition of Gilbert White's *Natural History of Selborne,* for Penguin.

* * *

MACAULAY, Neill (Webster, Jr.)   1935-

PERSONAL: Born April 10, 1935, near Columbia, S.C.; son of Neill Webster (a dentist) and Eliza (Barron) Macaulay; married Nancy Copenhaver, August 15, 1958; children: Charles Stuart, Robert Bruce, James Douglas. *Education:* The Citadel, A.B., 1956; University of South Carolina, M.A., 1962; University of Texas, Ph.D., 1965. *Office:* Department of History, University of Florida, Gainesville, Fla. 32611.

CAREER: Planter-exporter (winter vegetables), Pinar del Rio Province, Cuba, 1959-60; free-lance journalist, Miami, Fla., and North Woodstock, N.H., 1960; University of Florida, Gainesville, assistant professor, 1964-69, associate professor, 1969-75, professor of history, 1975—. *Military service:* U.S. Army, 1956-58; became first lieutenant. Cuban Rebel Army, first lieutenant, 1958-59. *Member:* Phi Beta Kappa. *Awards, honors:* Ford Foundation postdoctoral fellowship to Brazil, 1965-66; National Endowment for the Humanities fellowship, 1972-73.

WRITINGS: (Contributor) N. L. Benson, editor, *Mexico and the Spanish Cortes, 1810-1822: Eight Essays,* University of Texas Press, 1966; *The Sandino Affair,* Quadrangle, 1967; *A Rebel in Cuba,* Quadrangle, 1970; *The Prestes Column,* F. Watts, 1974. Contributor to *Men, Bohemia Libre,* and historical and military journals.

WORK IN PROGRESS: Research for a biography of Dom Pedro I, Emperor of Brazil.

* * *

MacDONALD, William L.   1921-

PERSONAL: Born July 12, 1921, in Putnam, Conn.; son of William L. and Susan E. (Elrod) MacDonald; married Dale Ely, 1953; children: two. *Education:* Harvard University, A.B., 1949, A.M., 1953, Ph.D., 1956. *Office:* Department of Art, Smith College, Northampton, Mass. 01060.

CAREER: Boston Architectural Center, Boston, Mass., lecturer in history of architecture, 1950-54; Wheaton College, Norton, Mass., instructor in classics, 1953-54; American Academy in Rome, Rome, Italy, fellow, 1954-56; Yale University, New Haven, Conn., instructor, 1956-59, assistant professor, 1959-63, associate professor of history of art, 1963-65; Smith College, Northampton, Mass., professor of art, 1965—, A. P. Brown Professor, 1974—. *Military service:* U.S. Army Air Forces, 1942-45; became first lieutenant. *Member:* Archaeological Institute of America, Society for Libyan Studies (London), Society of Architectural Historians, Society for the Promotion of Roman Studies (England), American Association of Architectural Bibliographers. *Awards, honors:* Grants from American Philosophical Society, 1959, American Council of Learned Societies, 1963, William Emerson Fund, and Bryant Foundation; Morse fellow, Yale University, 1962-63.

WRITINGS: Early Christian and Byzantine Architecture, Braziller, 1962; *The Architecture of the Roman Empire,* Yale Univeristy Press, 1965; *The Pantheon: Design, Meaning, and Progeny,* Harvard University Press, in press. Also author of *Northampton Massachusetts Architecture and Buildings,* 1975.

* * *

MACFARLANE, Leslie John   1924-

PERSONAL: Born August 22, 1924, in London, England; son of Charles John (a suitcase maker) and Ethel (Vere) Macfarlane; married Marion Sargent (an historian), April 1, 1950; children: Helen, Colin Andrew, Catherine. *Education:* London School of Economics and Political Science, B.Sc., 1954, Ph.D. (external), 1960. *Politics:* Communist Party member, 1942-48; now Socialist. *Religion:* Atheist. *Home:* 14 Crick Rd., Oxford, England. *Office:* St. John's College, Oxford University, Oxford, England.

CAREER: London County Council, London, England, clerical officer, 1941-47, administrative officer, 1947-57; College of Commerce, Birmingham, England, lecturer in politics, 1957-63; Oxford University, Oxford, England, tutor in politics, Ruskin College, 1963-69, tutor in politics and university lecturer, St. John's College, 1969—. *Military service:* British Army, 1943-44. *Member:* Association of University Teachers, Political Studies Association. *Awards, honors:* M.A., Oxford University, 1969.

WRITINGS: British Politics 1918-1964, Pergamon, 1965; *The British Communist Party: Its Origin and Development Until 1929,* MacGibbon & Kee, 1966; *Modern Political Theory,* Thomas Nelson, 1970, Harper, 1973; *Political Disobedience,* Macmillan, 1971; *Violence and the State,* Thomas Nelson, 1974; *Issues in British Politics since 1945,* Longman, 1975; (contributor) B. Parekh, editor, *The Concept of Socialism,* Croom Helm, 1975; (contributor) Ted Honderich, editor, *Social Ends and Political Means,* Routledge & Kegan Paul, 1976. Contributor to journals in Britain and the United States.

WORK IN PROGRESS: Obeying the State, for Thomas Nelson.

SIDELIGHTS: Macfarlane stated: "The most important turning points in my life were joining the Communist Party when I was seventeen and leaving it during the height of post-war Stalinism.... This has been the root of my interest in problems of political dissent and civil disobedience and my distaste for all brands of political extremism."

*   *   *

MacFARQUHAR, Roderick   1930-

PERSONAL: Surname is pronounced MacFarker; born December 2, 1930, in Lahore, Pakistan; son of Alexander (a United Nations official) and Berenice (Whitburn) Mac-Farquhar; married Emily Cohen (a journalist), December 23, 1964. *Education:* Keble College, Oxford, B.A., 1953; Harvard University, A.M., 1955. *Politics:* British Labour Party. *Home:* 187 Queen's Gate, London S.W. 7, England.

CAREER: Daily Telegraph, London, England, Chinese and Asian specialist, 1955-61; *China Quarterly,* London, editor, 1959-68; Oxford University, St. Antony's College, Oxford, England, associate fellow, 1965-68; Columbia University, New York, N.Y., senior research associate, 1969; Royal Institute of International Affairs, London, research fellow, 1971-74; British Parliament, elected member representing division of Belper, 1974—. Commentator, British Broadcasting Corp., 1963-64, 1972-74. *Military service:* British Army, Royal Tank Regiment, 1949-50; became second lieutenant. *Member:* Royal Institute of International Affairs, National Union of Journalists. *Awards, honors:* Rockefeller Foundation grant, 1962; Ford Foundation grant, 1968-69.

WRITINGS: The Hundred Flowers Campaign and the Chinese Intellectuals, Praeger, 1960; (with G. F. Hudson and Richard Lowenthal) *The Sino-Soviet Dispute,* Praeger, 1961; (editor) *China Under Mao,* M.I.T. Press, 1966; *Sino-American Relations, 1969-71,* Praeger, 1972; *The Forbidden City,* Newsweek, 1972; *The Origins of the Cultural Revolution: Contradictions Among the People,* Volume I, Columbia University Press, 1974. Contributor to *New Statesman, Foreign Affairs, World Today, Pacific Affairs, Problems of Communism,* and *Atlantic Monthly.* Member of editorial board, *New Statesman,* 1965-70.

WORK IN PROGRESS: Current Chinese politics.

SIDELIGHTS: MacFarquhar has traveled in Asia, Europe, Soviet Union, United States, Middle East, and West Africa. He has varying degrees of competence in French, Chinese, and other languages.

MacGUIGAN, Mark R(udolph)   1931-

PERSONAL: Born February 17, 1931, in Charlottetown, Prince Edward Island, Canada; son of Mark R. (a judge of Supreme Court of Prince Edward Island) and Agnes V. (Trainor) MacGuigan; married Maryellen Symons (a professor of philosophy), June 17, 1961; children: Ellen Frances, Mark R., Thomas James. *Education:* St. Dunstan's University, B.A., 1951; University of Toronto, M.A., 1953, Ph.D., 1957; Osgoode Hall Law School, Toronto, Barrister-at-Law, 1958; Columbia University, LL.M., 1959, J.S.D., 1961. *Politics:* Liberal. *Religion:* Roman Catholic. *Home:* 2020 Willistead Cres., Windsor, Ontario, Canada.

CAREER: University of Windsor, Windsor, Ontario, former dean and member of the faculty of law; member of Parliament of Windsor, 1968—.

WRITINGS: Cases and Materials on Creditors' Rights, University of Toronto Press, 1962, 2nd edition, 1967; (editor) *Jurisprudence: Readings and Cases,* University of Toronto Press, 1963, 2nd edition, 1966.

*   *   *

MACHOL, Libby   1916-
(Libby MacCall)

PERSONAL: Surname is pronounced May-call; born October 24, 1916, in Cincinnati, Ohio; daughter of Sidney (a dentist) and Selma (a radio actress) Rauh; married Richard Machol (a magazine editor), November 23, 1939; children: Patrica (Mrs. Barton Dominus), Jill (Mrs. Richard Rubinstein). *Education:* Radcliffe College, B.A., 1937. *Religion:* Unitarian Universalist. *Home:* 520 Palmer Ave., Teaneck, N.J. 07666. *Agent:* Oliver G. Swan, Julian Bach Literary Agency, Inc., 18 East 48th St., New York, N.Y. 10017.

CAREER: Active in American Field Service international scholarship program for high school students and in the Quakers' Southern Negro Student Project. Member of executive board, Bergen County Fair Housing Council; president of Teaneck chapter of American Field Service, 1962-65; vice-chairman, Teaneck Communtiy Scholarship Fund.

WRITINGS: Gianna, Beacon, 1967; (with Irving M. Levitas) *You Can Beat the Odds on a Heart Attack,* Bobbs-Merrill, 1975. Under pseudonym Libby MacCall, contributor of detective fiction to *Ellery Queen's Mystery Magazine, Alfred Hitchcock Mystery Magazine,* and *Saint Mystery Magazine.* Editor of the house organ of the Bergen County Fair Housing Council.

WORK IN PROGRESS: A medical biography.

*   *   *

MACK, James D(ecker)   1916-

PERSONAL: Born March 13, 1916, in Bethlehem, Pa.; son of Elmer L. and Lillie (Weiss) Mack; married Helen Standing, June 5, 1941; children: Margaret E., Helen P. *Education:* Lehigh University, B.A., 1938, M.A., 1949. *Religion:* Presbyterian. *Home:* 3675 Township Line Rd., Bethlehem, Pa. 18017. *Office:* Library, Lehigh University, Bethlehem, Pa. 18015.

CAREER: Bethlehem Steel Corp., Bethlehem, Pa., credit clerk, 1939-42; Lehigh University, Bethlehem, Pa., assistant to librarian, 1946-47, assistant librarian, 1947-48, acting librarian, 1948-50, librarian, 1950-69, director of libraries, 1969—. *Military service:* U.S. Navy, 1942-46; became lieutenant. *Member:* Council of National Library Associations (chairman, 1961-62), International Association of Technological University Libraries (president, 1966-69; director, 1969—), American Library Association, American Documentation Institute, American Historical Association, Royal Australian Historical Society, Sigma Xi. *Awards, honors:* American Philosophical Society grant, 1960.

WRITINGS: Matthew Flinders, 1774-1814, Thomas Nelson, 1966. Contributor of articles to professional journals. Editor, *American Documentation,* 1962-63.

AVOCATIONAL INTERESTS: Reading, primarily non-fiction.†

* * *

MacKENZIE, David 1927-

PERSONAL: Born June 10, 1927, in Rochester, N.Y.; son of Hugh (a professor) and Ruth (Walcott) MacKenzie; married Patricia Williams, August 8, 1953; children: Bruce Edward, Bryan James, Brendan Hugh. *Education:* University of Rochester, A.B., 1950; Columbia University, A.M. and Certificate of Russian Institute, 1953, Ph.D., 1962; University of Moscow, research, 1958-59. *Home:* 1000 Fairmont St., Greensboro, N.C. 27401. *Office:* Department of History, University of North Carolina, Greensboro, N.C. 27412.

CAREER: U.S. Merchant Marine Academy, Kings Point, N.Y., assistant professor of Russian language and world history, 1953-58; Princeton University, Princeton, N.J., lecturer in history, 1959-61; Wells College, Aurora, N.Y., assistant professor, 1961-64, associate professor of history, 1965-68; University of North Carolina, Greensboro, professor of history, 1969—. Cornell University, visiting assistant professor, 1962. Tutor in Russian and German. *Military service:* U.S. Army, 1945-47. *Member:* American Historical Association, American Association for the Advancement of Slavic Studies, Southern Conference on Slavic Studies, Phi Beta Kappa. *Awards, honors:* Ford Foundation fellowship for travel in Austria and Yugoslavia, 1955-56; grants from Inter-University Committee on Travel Grants, 1958-59, 1966, American Philosophical Society, 1964, 1967, 1969, and American Council of Learned Societies, 1965-66.

WRITINGS: The Serbs and Russian Pan-Slavism, 1875-1878, Cornell University Press, 1967; *The Lion of Tashkent: The Career of General M. C. Chernizev,* University of Georgia Press, 1974. Contributor to *Russian Review, Canadian Slavic Studies, Journal of Modern History* and *Slavic Review.*

WORK IN PROGRESS: A History of Russia, a textbook; *The Serbian National Movement, 1804-1918.*

SIDELIGHTS: MacKenzie is fluent in German and Russian; able to use French and Serbo-Croatian readily in research.

* * *

MacKENZIE, Norman H(ugh) 1915-

PERSONAL: Born March 8, 1915, in Salisbury, Rhodesia; son of Thomas Hugh (a business manager) and Ruth (Huskisson) MacKenzie; married Rita Hofmann, August 14, 1948; children: Catherine, Ronald. *Education:* Rhodes University, B.A. and M.A., 1936; University of London, Ph.D., 1940. *Religion:* United Church. *Home:* 416 Windward Pl., Kingston, Ontario, Canada. *Office:* Department of English, Queen's University, Kingston, Ontario, Canada.

CAREER: University of Melbourne, Victoria, Australia, lecturer in English, 1946-48; University of Natal, Durban, South Africa, senior lecturer in English, 1949-55; University College of Rhodesia, Salisbury, professor and chairman of English, 1955-65; Laurentian University, Sudbury, Ontario, professor of English and chairman of department, 1965-66; Queen's University, Kingston, Ontario, professor of English, 1966—, director of graduate studies in English, 1966-73, chairman, Council for Graduate Studies and Research, 1971-73. *Military service:* Hong Kong Volunteer Defence Corps, Coastal Defence, 1941-46; prisoner of war in Hong Kong and near Hiroshima, Japan, 1941-45. *Member:* Modern Language Association of America, English Association, International Association of Professors of English, Canadian Association for Irish Studies (member of executive board, 1972—), Hopkins Society (London; president, 1972—).

WRITINGS: South African Travel Literature in the Seventeenth Century, South African Archives, 1955; *Sir Thomas Herbert of Tintern,* University of London Institute of Historical Research, 1956; *The Outlook for English in Central Africa,* Oxford University Press, 1960; (editor with W. H. Gardner) *The Poems of Gerard Manley Hopkins,* 4th edition, Oxford University Press, 1967; *Hopkins,* Oliver & Boyd, 1968; (editor) *Poems by Gerard Manley Hopkins,* Folio Society (London), 1974.

Contributor: *Testing the English Proficiency of Foreign Students,* University of Washington Press, 1961; *English Studies Today,* third series, University of Edinburgh Press, 1964; A. Pollard, editor, *History of Literature in the English Language,* Volume VI: *The Victorians,* Sphere Books, 1970; P. O'Flaherty, editor, *Festschrift for Ronald Seary,* Memorial University (Canada), 1975; E. Domville, editor, *Editing Texts: 1880-1920,* [New York], 1975.

WORK IN PROGRESS: The Poetical Works of Gerard Manley Hopkins, Oxford English Texts Edition; *Reader's Guide to Hopkins,* for Thames & Hudson.

AVOCATIONAL INTERESTS: Music, art, theater, travel.

* * *

MACKLER, Bernard 1934-

PERSONAL: Born July 2, 1934, in New York, N.Y.; son of Max (a fur worker) and Rachel (Polisher) Mackler; married Jeannie C. Baubion; children: Bradley, Laurence. *Education:* Queens College (now Queens College of the City University of New York), B.A., 1956; City College (now City College of the City University of New York), M.S., 1958; University of Kansas, Ph.D., 1963; Alfred Adler Institute, New York, N.Y., Certification in Psychotherapy, 1966. *Home:* 5 Lenox Pl., Scarsdale, N.Y. 10583.

CAREER: Columbia University, Teacher's College, New York City, assistant professor, 1963-67, associate professor, 1967-68, adjunct associate professor of education, 1968-73, research associate of Institute for Urban Studies, 1963-65, associate professor of urban affairs, 1968-69; psychologist in private practice, 1964—; Hunter College of the City University of New York, New York City, associate professor of special education, 1970-74. Faculty member, Alfred Adler Institute, 1965—; assistant director and research psychologist, Center for Urban Education, 1966-68; visiting assistant professor, University of Kansas Medical Center, summer, 1965; visiting associate professor, Hebrew Union Theological Seminary, 1971. Member, Institute for Religious Studies, Jewish Theological Seminary, 1966—;

Kenneth Clark fellow, Metropolitan Applied Research Center, 1974—. Conducted weekly radio series, "How They Grow," and "Topic Teens," WABC, 1963-67. Consultant to numerous medical, civic, and industrial organizations. Member of Fair Housing Group in Scarsdale, 1968—, Community Service Society, 1968-70, and of board of advisors, Community School, 1970—. *Awards, honors:* Research grants from Columbia University, 1963, Department of Health, Education, and Welfare, 1964-67, Sloan Foundation, 1970-71, Phillips Foundation, 1971-72, and Klingenstein Foundations, 1973-74; Educational Press Association prize, 1969, for distinguished educational journalism.

WRITINGS: (Editor with Robert A. Dentler and M. Ellen Warshauer) *The Urban R's: Race Relations as the Problem in Urban Education,* Praeger, 1967; *Philippe Pinel: Unchainer of the Insane* (juvenile), F. Watts, 1968.

Contributor: C. Deck, editor, *Guidelines for Guidance,* W. C. Brown, 1966; I. Wolf, editor, *Current Research in General Psychology,* Prentice-Hall, 1966; J. F. Magary and Janet Bower, editors, *Education and Guidance of Disadvantaged Children and Youth,* Pitman, 1966; Burton Black, editor, *The Establishment and the Disestablished,* Prentice-Hall, 1967; Peter Hiatt and Henry Denn, editors, *Public Library Service for the Functionally Illiterate: A Survey of Practice,* American Library Association, 1967; B. L. Kintz and J. Bruning, editors, *Readings in Introductory Psychology,* Scott, Foresman, 1969; Clarence H. Faust and Jessica Feingold, editors, *Approaches to Education for Character,* Columbia University Press, 1969; R. Maidment and E. Hurwitz, editors, *Criticism, Conflict and Change,* Dodd, 1969; Annette Rubinstein, editor, *Schools against Children,* Monthly Review Press, 1970; A. H. Passow, editor, *Teaching the Disadvantaged Learner,* Teachers College Press, 1972. Author of monographs; contributor of articles and reviews to professional journals. Consulting editor, *Individual Psychology,* 1966—.

*   *   *

MACK SMITH, Denis   1920-

PERSONAL: Born March 3, 1920, in London, England; son of Wilfrid and Alti (Gauntlett) Mack Smith; married Catharine Stephenson, March 18, 1963; children: Sophie, Jacintha. *Education:* Cambridge University, M.A., 1948; Oxford University, M.A., 1961. *Politics:* "Floating voter, inclined to the Left." *Home:* White Lodge, Osler Rd., Headington, Oxford, England. *Office:* All Souls College, Oxford University, Oxford, England.

CAREER: Cambridge University, Cambridge, England, senior lecturer in history, 1953-61, fellow of Peterhouse, 1946-61; Oxford University, All Souls College, Oxford, England, senior research fellow, 1962—, dean of visiting fellows, 1971—.

WRITINGS: Cavour and Garibaldi, 1860, Cambridge University Press, 1954; *Garibaldi: A Great Life in Brief,* Knopf, 1956; (with D. C. Watt) *British Interests in the Middle East,* Oxford University Press, 1958; *Italy: A Modern History,* University of Michigan Press, 1959, enlarged edition, 1969; *Medieval Sicily,* Chatto & Windus, 1968; *Modern Sicily,* Chatto & Windus, 1968; *The Making of Italy, 1796-1870,* Harper, 1968; *Da Cavour a Mussolini,* Bonanno, 1968; *Storia d'Italia dal 1861 al 1958, con documenti e testimonianze,* two volumes, Edizioni Labor (Milan), 1968; (editor) *Garibaldi,* Prentice-Hall, 1968; *Victor Emanuel: Cavour and the Risorgimento,* Oxford

University Press, 1971. Also editor of *Nelson History of England,* and G. La Farina's *Scritti Politici,* 1972.

WORK IN PROGRESS: Italian fascism.

SIDELIGHTS: Mack Smith visits Italy at least three times a year; he also has done research in the archives of Spain, France, Germany, and Austria. All of his books have been translated into Italian. The Italian translation of *Italy: A Modern History* has gone through eight hardback printings.

*   *   *

MacLEOD, Charlotte (Matilda Hughes)   1922-
(Matilda Hughes)

PERSONAL: Surname is pronounced MacLoud; born November 12, 1922, in Bath, New Brunswick, Canada; daughter of Edward Philips and Mabel Maude (Hayward) MacLeod. *Education:* Attended public schools in Weymouth, Mass.; attended School of Practical Art (now the Art Institute of Boston), and holds a diploma from Hampton-Marcuse School of Graphology. *Politics:* "Mostly Democrat." *Home:* 177 Plympton Rd., Seedbury, Mass. 01776. *Agent:* Collins-Knowlton-Wing, Inc., 60 East 56th St., New York, N.Y. 10022. *Office:* 1127 Park Square Building, 31 St. James Ave., Boston, Mass. 02116.

CAREER: N. H. Miller & Co., Inc. (advertising), Boston, Mass., 1952—, copy chief, and member of corporation. Writer of fiction and painter, exhibiting in oils. *Member:* Mystery Writers of America.

WRITINGS: Mystery of the White Knight, Bouregy, 1964; *Next Door to Danger,* Bouregy, 1965; *The Fat Lady's Ghost,* Weybright, 1968; *Mouse's Vineyard,* Weybright, 1968; *Ask Me No Questions,* Macrae, 1971; *Brass Pounder,* Little, Brown, 1971; *Astrology for Skeptics,* Macmillan, 1972.

Under name Matilda Hughes: *The Food of Love,* Bouregy, 1965; *Headlines for Caroline,* Bouregy, 1967.

Contributor to *Murder in Mind* (anthology of Mystery Writers of America), edited by Lawrence Treat, Dutton, 1967. Contributor of some fifteen stories and articles, some self-illustrated, to *Good Housekeeping, Yankee, Edgar Wallace Mystery Magazine, Criminologist,* and *Cricket.*

*   *   *

MACMILLAN, C(harles) J(ames) B(arr)   1935-

PERSONAL: Born April 30, 1935, in Auburn, N.Y.; son of John Walker (an industrial psychologist) and Margaret (Barr) Macmillan; married Joan Tyler Reinberg, June 15, 1958; children: Ann, Tyler. *Education:* Cornell University, B.A., 1957, Ph.D., 1965; Colgate University, M.A., 1959. *Home:* 2316 Armistead Rd., Tallahassee, Fla. 32303. *Office:* College of Education, Florida State University, Tallahassee, Fla. 32306.

CAREER: University of California, Los Angeles, acting assistant professor of philosophy of education, 1962-64; Temple University, Philadelphia, Pa., assistant professor, 1964-68, associate professor of philosophy of education, 1968-70; Florida State University, Tallahassee, associate professor of philosophy of education and chairman of department, 1970—. *Member:* Philosophy of Education Society, Middle Atlantic States Philosophy of Education Society, Phi Delta Kappa, Phi Kappa Phi.

WRITINGS: (Junior editor with B. Paul Komisar) *Psychological Concepts in Education,* Rand McNally, 1967; (senior editor with Thomas W. Nelson) *Concepts of Teach-*

ing, Rand McNally, 1969. Contributor to professional journals.

WORK IN PROGRESS: Research on psychological concepts and theories in education.

AVOCATIONAL INTERESTS: Sailing.

* * *

MacMULLEN, Ramsay 1928-

PERSONAL: Born March 3, 1928, in New York, N.Y.; son of Charles William (an architect and engineer) and Margaret (Richmond) MacMullen; married Edith Merriman Nye, August 7, 1954; children: John, Priscilla, William, Lucinda. *Education:* Harvard University, A.B., 1950, A.M., 1953, Ph.D., 1957; University of St. Andrews, Scotland, graduate study, 1950-51. *Home:* 25 Long Hill Rd., Clinton, Conn. 06413. *Office:* Department of History, Yale University, New Haven, Conn. 06520.

CAREER: University of Oregon, Eugene, instructor, 1956-58, assistant professor of history, 1958-61; Brandeis University, Waltham, Mass., associate professor, 1961-66, professor of history, 1966-67, chairman of classics department, 1965-66; Yale University, New Haven, Conn., professor of classics and history, 1967—, chairman of history department, 1970-72. *Member:* American Philological Association, Society for Promotion of Roman Studies (life member), American Historical Association. *Awards, honors:* Fulbright Research fellowship to Italy, 1960-61; Guggenheim fellowship, 1964; Porter Prize, College Art Association, 1964; Princeton Institute for Advanced Study fellowship, 1964-65; National Endowment for the Humanities senior fellowship, 1974-75.

WRITINGS: Soldier and Civilian in the Later Roman Empire, Harvard University Press, 1963; *Enemies of the Roman Order,* Harvard University Press, 1966; *Constantine,* Dial, 1969; *Roman Social Relations, 50 B.C. to A.D. 284,* Yale University Press, 1974. Contributor of articles to about fifteen learned journals.

BIOGRAPHICAL/CRITICAL SOURCES: Yale Review, autumn, 1967.†

* * *

MACNAMARA, John 1929-

PERSONAL: Born November 9, 1929, in Kilmallock, County Limerick, Ireland; son of Trevor Francis (a physician) and Hannah (O'Leary) Macnamara. *Education:* Attended Castleknock College, 1942-47; University College, Dublin, B.A., 1951, Diploma in Education, 1957; University of Edinburgh, M.Ed., 1959, Ph.D., 1963. *Home:* Douglas Hall, McGill University, Montreal, Quebec, Canada. *Office:* Department of Psychology, McGill University, Montreal, Quebec, Canada.

CAREER: Castleknock College, Dublin, Ireland, teacher of Irish language, 1955-58; St. Patrick's College, Dublin, lecturer in educational psychology, 1960-68, research officer at Educational Research Centre, 1968-69; McGill University, Montreal, Quebec, associate professor, 1969-75, professor of psychology, 1975—. Visiting scholar in psychology, McGill University, 1966-67. *Member:* British Psychological Association, Canadian Psychological Association, American Psychological Association.

WRITINGS: Bilingualism and Primary Education, Edinburgh University Press, 1966; (with George Madaus) *Public Examinations: A Study of the Irish Leaving Certifi-*

cate, Educational Research Centre, St. Patrick's College, 1970. Editor of special issue of *Journal of Social Issues,* April, 1967, on problems in bilingualism.

WORK IN PROGRESS: Research in language and thought, language switching in bilinguals, the problem of meaning, and language learning in infants.

SIDELIGHTS: John Macnamara told *CA* that his main interest is the question "What sort of beast is man who can learn and use a language?" His second interest is "to help language teachers and language students with their work." He is competent in French and Latin.

* * *

MacRAE, Duncan (Jr.) 1921-

PERSONAL: Born September 30, 1921, in Glen Ridge, N.J.; son of Duncan (a chemist) and Rebecca (Kyle) MacRae; married Edith Krugelis (a professor of anatomy), June 24, 1950; children: Amy. *Education:* Johns Hopkins University, A.B., 1942; Harvard University, A.M., 1943, Ph.D., 1950. *Home:* 737 Gimghoul Rd., Chapel Hill, N.C. 27514. *Office:* Department of Political Science, University of North Carolina, Chapel Hill, N.C. 27514.

CAREER: Massachusetts Institute of Technology, Cambridge, staff member of radiation laboratory, 1943-46; Princeton University, Princeton, N.J., instructor, 1949-50, lecturer in sociology, 1950-51; Harvard University, Cambridge, research associate, 1951-53; University of California, Berkeley, assistant professor of sociology, 1953-57; University of Chicago, Chicago, Ill., assistant professor, 1957-62, associate professor, 1962-64, professor of political science and sociology, 1964-72; University of North Carolina at Chapel Hill, William Rand, Jr. Professor of Political Science and Sociology, 1972—. President of Policy Studies Organization, 1974-75.

MEMBER: American Political Science Association, American Sociological Association, American Economic Association, American Association for the Advancement of Science. *Awards, honors:* Fulbright fellow in Paris, 1956-57; Woodrow Wilson Prize, American Political Science Association, 1968.

WRITINGS: (Editor with I. A. Greenwood and J. V. Holdam) *Electronic Instruments,* McGraw, 1948; *Dimensions of Congressional Voting,* University of California Press, 1958; *Parliament, Parties, and Society in France, 1946-1958,* St. Martin's, 1967; *Issues and Parties in Legislative Voting: Methods of Statistical Analysis,* Harper, 1970; *The Social Function of Social Science,* Yale University Press, in press. Contributor to professional journals. Member of editorial board, *Social Forces.*

* * *

MADDEN, William A. 1923-

PERSONAL: Born October 8, 1923, in Cincinnati, Ohio; son of Harold Daniel and Camille (Peurrung) Madden; married Carol Remington, 1947; children: Mary, Benedict, Jane Kristine, Victoria, Pauline. *Education:* University of Notre Dame, A.B., 1947; Xavier University, Cincinnati, Ohio, M.A., 1950; University of Michigan, Ph.D., 1955. *Office:* Department of English, University of Minnesota, Minneapolis, Minn. 55455.

CAREER: Indiana University, Bloomington, instructor, 1955-58, assistant professor, 1958-62, associate professor, 1962-66, professor of English, 1966-69, dean of freshmen, 1967-69; University of Minnesota, Minneapolis, professor of English, 1969—. Visiting summer professor at Columbia University, 1964. Manuscript reader for PMLA, and for Holt, Rinehart & Winston, Indiana University Press, W. W. Norton & Co., and other publishers. City councilman, Bloomington, 1968-69. *Military service:* U.S. Naval Reserve, 1943-46. *Member:* Modern Language Association of America, National Council of Teachers of English, American Association of University Professors, American Civil Liberties Union.

WRITINGS: (Co-editor and contributor) *1859: Entering an Age of Crisis,* Indiana University Press, 1959; *Matthew Arnold: A Study of the Aesthetic Temperment in Victorian England,* Indiana University Press, 1967; (contributor) George Panichas, editor, *Mansions of the Spirit,* Hawthorn, 1967; (editor with George Levine, and contributor) *The Art of Victorian Prose,* Oxford University Press, 1968. Contributor to *Thought, Mediaeval Studies, Review of Politics,* and other journals. Co-founder and co-editor, *Victorian Studies,* 1957-69.

* * *

MADDOX, Marion Errol 1910-

PERSONAL: Born April 12, 1910, in Fulton, Mo.; son of Oren Aubrey and Florence Estelle (Conger) Maddox; married Alma Ferne Rose, April 12, 1932. *Education:* Northeast Missouri State Teachers College (now Northeast Missouri State University), B.S.E., 1938; University of Missouri, M.Ed., 1947, D.Ed., 1951. *Politics:* Democrat. *Religion:* Baptist. *Home:* 460 Oliver, Fayetteville, Ark. 72701. *Office:* Graduate Education Building, Room 102, University of Arkansas, Fayetteville, Ark. 72701.

CAREER: Teacher in rural schools of Missouri, 1929-36; Fulton (Mo.) public schools, elementary school principal, 1936-44, teacher of industrial arts, 1944-47; Fulton High School, Moberly, Mo., local director of trades and industries, 1948-51; University of Arkansas, Fayetteville, assistant professor, 1951-55, associate professor, 1955-58, professor of industrial education, 1958—. *Member:* National Education Association, American Vocational Association (life member), American Industrial Arts Association, National Association of Industrial Teacher Educators, Arkansas Education Association, Arkansas Vocational Association, Phi Delta Kappa, Kappa Delta Pi.

WRITINGS: (With Lavon B. Smith) *Elements of American Industry,* McKnight, 1966; (with others) *Exploring Careers in Industry,* McKnight, 1975. Contributor to journals in his field.

* * *

MADISON, Arnold 1937-

PERSONAL: Born November 28, 1937, in Bayport, N.Y.; son of Arnold Alfred (a lithographer) and Jeanette (Tonder) Madison. *Education:* State University of New York College at Plattsburgh, B.Sc., 1958. *Home:* R.D. 3, Swart Hill Rd., Amsterdam, N.Y. 12010.

CAREER: Public school teacher in Bethpage, N.Y., 1958-68; State University of New York at Albany, instructor, 1975-76; writer for young people. Actor at Wingspread Summer Theatre, Colon, Mich., 1957, and director of community theater productions. Instructor at St. Davids Writer's Conference, 1969, 1970, 1975. *Member:* Mystery Writers of America, Authors League of America, Society of Children's Book Writers, Aircraft Owners and Pilots Association. *Awards, honors: Danger Beats the Drum* was runner-up for Edgar Allan Poe (Edgar) Award of Mystery Writers of America as best juvenile mystery of 1966.

WRITINGS: Danger Beats the Drum (juvenile mystery), Holt, 1966; *Think Wild!,* Holt, 1968; *The Secret of the Carved Whale Bone* (juvenile mystery), McKay, 1969; *Vandalism: The Not So Senseless Crime* (nonfiction), Seabury, 1970; *Drugs and You* (nonfiction), Messner, 1971; *Fast Break to Danger,* Pyramid Publications, 1973; *Vigilantism in America,* Seabury, 1973; *Treasure Hunting,* Hawthorn, 1974; *Smoking and You,* Messner, 1975; *American Globol Diplomacy,* Watts, 1976. More than fifty series and stories to periodicals.

WORK IN PROGRESS: Carry Nation, a young adult biography.

SIDELIGHTS: Arnold Madison told *CA* that "theme is just as necessary to a mystery as to a straight novel. By choosing your characters and setting, you make a statement. Many juvenile mysteries are thin, mere fluff, because their only purpose is pure entertainment. My theme for *Danger Beats the Drum* was how hate can destroy you if you let it. In *The Secret of the Carved Whale Bone,* I wanted to say to the reader that we should open ourselves to progress and be prepared to capitalize on the positive aspects of change and combat the negative results. Although they are cloaked as mysteries, I think they are stated as validly as they would have been in an ordinary novel."

BIOGRAPHICAL/CRITICAL SOURCES: Writer, August, 1972.

* * *

MADSEN, David Lawrence 1929-

PERSONAL: Born April 28, 1929, in Fargo, N.D.; son of Harold S. and Hazel (Pool) Madsen; married Lois Fox, October 3, 1953; children: Andrew, Sarah, Tom. *Education:* University of North Dakota, Ph.B., 1951; University of Chicago, A.M., 1954, Ph.D., 1961. *Home:* 5012 Northeast 41st, Seattle, Wash. *Office:* Department of Education, University of Washington, Seattle, Wash. 98105.

CAREER: University of Chicago, Chicago, Ill., assistant registrar and later registrar, 1954-58, research associate, 1960-62; North Central Association, Chicago, associate secretary, Commission on Colleges and Universities, 1960-62; University of Washington, Seattle, assistant professor, 1962-65, associate professor of higher education, 1965-69; University of Michigan, Ann Arbor, professor of education, 1969-71; University of Washington, professor of education, 1971—. Summer lecturer at Columbia University, 1965. Postdoctoral fellow in educational research, U.S. Office of Education, University of California, Berkeley, 1967-68. *Military service:* U.S. Army, 1951-53; became lieutenant.

MEMBER: History of Education Society (director), American Association for Higher Education, American Educational Research Association, American Historical Association, Organization of American Historians, American Association of University Professors, American Association for the Advancement of Science, Phi Delta Kappa.

WRITINGS: The National University: Enduring Dream of the USA, Wayne State University Press, 1966; *Early National Education: 1776-1830,* Wiley, 1974. Contributor of articles and reviews to education journals.

WORK IN PROGRESS: A history of the American university in the twentieth century.

MAEHL, William Henry, Jr. 1930-

PERSONAL: Surname pronounced "male"; born June 13, 1930, in Chicago Heights, Ill.; son of William Henry and Marvel (Carlson) Maehl; married Audrey Mae Ellsworth, August 25, 1962; children: Christine Amanda. *Education:* University of Minnesota, B.A., 1950, M.A., 1951; King's College, Durham, graduate study, 1955-56; University of Chicago, Ph.D., 1957. *Home:* 2601 Meadowbrook Dr., Norman, Okla. 73069. *Office:* 455 West Lindsey St., Rm. 406, University of Oklahoma, Norman, Okla. 73069.

CAREER: Assistant professor of history at Montclair State College, Upper Montclair, N.J., 1957-58, and Washington College, Chestertown, Md., 1958-59; University of Oklahoma, Norman, assistant professor, 1959-64, associate professor, 1964-70, professor of history, 1970—. Leverhulme visiting research fellow, King's College, University of Durham, 1961-62; visiting fellow, Wolfson College, Oxford University, 1975. *Military service:* U.S. Army, 1953-55. *Member:* American Historical Association, Royal Historical Society (England; fellow), Economic History Society, Historical Association (England), Society for the Study of Labour History, Conference on British Studies. *Awards, honors:* Fulbright scholar at Durham, England, 1955-56; American Philosophical Society grant, 1962, 1967-68, 1971.

WRITINGS: The Reform Bill of 1832, Holt, 1967. Contributor to professional journals.

WORK IN PROGRESS: Chartism in Northeastern England.

*   *   *

MAGDOL, Edward 1918-

PERSONAL: Born September 14, 1918, in Brooklyn, N.Y.; married Miriam Sper; children: one son, one daughter. *Education:* University of Michigan, B.A., 1939; Columbia University, M.A., 1949; University of Rochester, Ph.D., 1971. *Home:* 28 Leroy St., Potsdam, N.Y. 13676. *Office:* Department of History, State University of New York College, Potsdam, N.Y. 13676.

CAREER: Viking Press, New York City, copy editor, 1946-48; high school teacher, New York City, 1949-52; free-lance copy editor and proofreader, 1952-56; *New York Times,* New York City, proofreader, 1958-59; Credit Union National Association, Madison, Wis., editor and feature writer for credit union publications, 1959-68, editor, *Everybody's Money* (magazine), 1964-68; State University of New York College at Potsdam, assistant professor, 1971-74, associate professor of history and chairman of department, 1974—. *Military service:* U.S. Naval Reserve, active duty, 1942-45; became ensign.

WRITINGS: Owen Lovejoy: Abolitionist in Congress, Rutgers University Press, 1967; (with John R. Prindle, Paul Butler, and Jerome Belanger) *It's Not Just Money,* Credit Union National Association International, 1967; *Land the Freedman's Community,* Greenwood Press, 1976.

WORK IN PROGRESS: A collection of the speeches of Thaddeus Stevens; social composition of the American antislavery movement.

*   *   *

MAGUIRE, John David 1932-

PERSONAL: Born August 7, 1932, in Montgomery, Ala.; son of John Henry (a clergyman) and Clyde (Merrill) Maguire; married Lillian Louise Parrish, August 29, 1953; children: Catherine Merrill, Mary Elizabeth, Anne King. *Education:* Washington and Lee University, A.B., (magna cum laude), 1953; University of Edinburgh, graduate study, 1953-54; Yale University, B.D. (summa cum laude), 1956, Ph.D., 1960; postdoctoral research at Yale University and University of Tuebingen, 1964-65, and at University of California, Berkeley, 1968-69. *Politics:* Democrat. *Home:* 223 Store Hill Rd., Old Westbury, N.Y. 11568. *Office:* Office of the President, State University of New York College at Old Westbury, Old Westbury, N.Y.

CAREER: Baptist clergyman. Washington and Lee University, Lexington, Va., acting chaplain, 1952-53; International Student Center of New Haven, Inc., New Haven, Conn., acting director, 1956-58; Yale Divinity School, New Haven, assistant instructor in systematic theology, 1958-59; Wesleyan University, Middletown, Conn., assistant professor, 1960-66, associate professor of religion, 1966-70, associate provost, 1967-68; State University of New York College at Old Westbury, president, 1970—. Visiting lecturer at Pacific School of Religion, 1968-69. Executive secretary of Special Committee on Liberal Studies, Association of American Colleges; member of Connecticut Advisory Committee to U.S. Commission on Civil Rights, 1961-67; consultant, Connecticut Race and Religion Action Commission, 1964—; member of Connecticut board of governors, Americans for Democratic Action, 1966—; president of board, Middlesex County Legal Assistance Association, 1966—; participant, White House Conference on Civil Rights, 1966; permanent trustee and director, Martin Luther King Center for Social Change, Atlanta, Ga., 1968—; vice-president of board of directors, Nassau County Health and Welfare Council, 1971—; member of council of presidents, State University of New York; trustee, Nassau Higher Education Consortium.

MEMBER: American Academy of Religion, Society for Values in Higher Education (fellow; president of board of directors, 1974—), National Association for the Advancement of Colored People (member of executive committee, Middletown branch), Society of Religion in Higher Education (member of board of directors, 1967—), Phi Beta Kappa, Omicron Delta Kappa. *Awards, honors:* Fulbright scholarship to Scotland, 1953-54; Julia A. Archibald High Scholarship award, Yale Divinity School, 1956; Day fellowship, Yale Graduate School, 1956-57; Kent fellowship, 1957-60; Howard Foundation fellowship for postdoctoral study, and Fulbright travel grant to Germany, 1964-65; E. Harris Harbison Award for distinguished teaching, Danforth Foundation, 1968.

WRITINGS: The Dance of the Pilgrim: A Christian Style of Life for Today (collection of lectures), Association Press, 1967. Author of book-length report, "Family Relocation under Urban Renewal in Connecticut." Contributor to various journals, including a number of articles in *Christianity and Crisis,* relating theology to contemporary issues. Member of editorial board, *Christianity and Crisis;* member of editorial advisory committee, Association Press.

SIDELIGHTS: An original "freedom rider," Maguire was imprisoned briefly in 1961 in his native city, Montgomery, Ala., for challenging segregated terminal facilities.

*   *   *

MAHER, Ramona 1934-
(Agatha Mayer)

PERSONAL: Surname is pronounced May-er; born October 25, 1934, in Phoenix, Ariz.; daughter of Raymond E.

(a meteorologist and writer) and Josephine (Allen) Maher; married A. Roberto Martinez (a clinical psychologist), February 11, 1955 (divorced, 1957); married Tim Weeks (a newspaper reporter), June 16, 1960 (divorced, 1972); children: (first marriage) Ramon Esteban. *Education:* Texas Christian University, B.A., 1954; additional study at University of New Mexico, 1954-62 (intermittently), and University of Washington, Seattle, 1964-66, and Arizona State University, 1968-69. *Politics:* Democrat. *Religion:* Methodist. *Home:* 326 West Dobbins Rd., Phoenix, Ariz. 85401. *Office:* Arizona Education Association, 2102 West Indian School Rd., Phoenix, Ariz. 85041.

CAREER: Fort Worth Youth Employment Service, Fort Worth, Tex., director, 1951-54; University of New Mexico Press, Albuquerque, editor, 1955, 1956-61; Kirtland Air Force Base, Shock Tube Facility, Albuquerque, technical editor, 1961-62; University of Alaska, College, assistant to academic vice-president, 1962-63; University of Washington Press, Seattle, managing editor, 1963-67; Arizona Historical Foundation, Tempe, editor, 1968-69; Arizona Education Association, Phoenix, editor, 1970—. Founder with Joy Harvey, Baleen Press (private publishing house). Poetry readings at colleges, universities, and conferences. *Member:* Authors Guild, Mystery Writers of America. *Awards, honors:* First prize in *Seventeen* Short Story Contest, 1954; runner-up in Samuel French Playwriting Contest, 1954, for *When the Fire Dies;* guest editor, *Mademoiselle,* 1954; *The Abracadabra Mystery* was winner of *Calling All Girls* Prize Competition (also sponsored by Dodd, Mead), 1961; Spur Award of Western Writers of America for best western juvenile, 1961, for *Their Shining Hour;* National Endowment for the Arts grant, 1969, and creative writing fellowship, 1974-75.

WRITINGS: When the Fire Dies (play), Samuel French, 1954; *Their Shining Hour* (juvenile western), Day, 1960; *The Abracadabra Mystery,* Dodd, 1961; *A Dime for Romance,* Day, 1963; (under pseudonym Agatha Mayer) *Secret of the Dark Stranger,* Dell, 1964; (with husband, Tim Weeks) *Ice Island,* Day, 1965; *Secret of the Sundial,* Dodd, 1967; *Shifting Sands: The Story of Dunes,* Day, 1968; *Mystery of the Stolen Fish Pond,* Dodd, 1969; *The Blind Boy and the Loon, and Other Eskimo Myths,* Day, 1970; (contributor) *A Part of Space: Ten Texas Writers,* Texas Christian University Press, 1969; *Secret of Grasshopper Hill,* Dodd, 1971; *About Armadillos and Others* (poems), Baleen Press, 1972; *Lincoln County Poems,* Konocti, 1973; *The Glory Horse,* Coward, 1974; (contributor) Gary Elder, editor, *The Far Side of the Storm,* San Marcos Press, 1975; *When Windwagon Smith Came to Westport,* Coward, in press.

Poems represented in several anthologies, including *American Literary Anthology No. 2,* Random House, 1969, *From the Belly of the Shark,* Doubleday, 1973, and *For Neruda, For Chile,* edited by Walter Lowenfels, Beacon Press, 1974. Also author of play, "Princess Scribble-Scrawl," distributed by National Association of Junior Leagues, and of plays produced by Dallas Little Theatre, Texas Christian University Players, and Columbia University. Author of monthly review column on juvenile books, *Arizona Republic,* 1959-61. Contributor of numerous poems, reviews, and juvenile stories to journals, magazines, and newspapers. Co-founder and editor, *Inscape,* 1957-59, 1969-72; book review editor, *New Mexico Quarterly,* 1959-61.

WORK IN PROGRESS: A collection of new poems, for Baleen Press.

MAHER, Trafford P(atrick)   1914-

PERSONAL: Born March 17, 1914, in Platte Center, Neb.; son of Thomas M. (a barber) and Edna P. (Smith) Maher. *Education:* Creighton University, student, 1930-32; St. Louis University, A.B., 1935, A.M., 1938; University of Minnesota, graduate study, 1949; Catholic University of America, Ph.D., 1952. *Home:* 221 North Grand Blvd., St. Louis, Mo. 63103.

CAREER: Entered Roman Catholic order, Society of Jesus (Jesuits), 1932, and was ordained a priest, 1946. Teacher at Catholic high schools in Prairie du Chien, Wis., Denver, Colo., 1939-42, and Omaha, Neb., 1942-43; Catholic University of America, Washington, D.C., faculty member, 1943-57; St. Louis University, St. Louis, Mo., professor, 1957—, and director of department of education. Lecturer in America and many countries abroad. Chairman, Missouri State Commission on Human Rights, 1958-61, Missouri State Advisory Committee of U.S. Commission on Civil Rights.

WRITINGS: Counseling Therapy for Teenagers, Catholic University Press, 1952; *Lest We Build on Sand,* Catholic Hospital Association, 1962; *Self—A Measureless Sea,* Catholic Hospital Association, 1966. Also editor of *A Study and Program for the Education of the Culturally Disadvantaged,* three volumes, Pageant-Poseidon. Contributor to a variety of professional journals.

WORK IN PROGRESS: Human Relations and Civil Rights in the '70's.

*   *   *

MAHESHWARI, Shriram   1931-

PERSONAL: Born November 27, 1931, in India; son of Muniraj Maheshwari; married on May 30, 1955, wife's name, Bimla; children: Manjula (daughter), Rajiv (son), Sanjiv (son), Anjula (daughter), Manish (son). *Education:* D.A.V. College, Kanpur, India, B.A., M.A. (economics), M.A. (political science); University of Delhi, Ph.D., 1965; University of Pennsylvania, M.G.A., 1964. *Religion:* Hinduism. *Office:* Indian Institute of Public Administration, New Delhi, India.

CAREER: Agra University, Agra, India, lecturer, 1955-61; University of Delhi, Indian School of Public Administration, New Delhi, reader in public administration, 1965-73; Indian Institute of Public Administration, New Delhi, professor of political science and public administration, 1973—. *Member:* Indian Public Administration Association (secretary-cum-treasurer).

WRITINGS: (With A. Avasthi) *Public Administration,* Lakshmi Narain Agarwal, 1962, 7th edition, 1974; *The General Election in India,* Chaitanya Publishing House, 1963; *Indian Administration,* Orient Longman, 1968, 2nd edition, 1974; *The Evolution of Indian Administration,* Lakshmi Narain Agarwal, 1970; *Local Government in India,* Orient Longman, 1971; *Government through Consultation,* Indian Institute of Public Administration, 1972; *The Administrative Reforms Commission,* Lakshmi Narain Agarwal, 1972; (editor) *The Study of Public Administration,* Lakshmi Narain Agarwal, 1974.

WORK IN PROGRESS: President's Rule in India, for Macmillan.

*   *   *

MAHRER, Alvin R(aymond)   1927-

PERSONAL: Born November 26, 1927, in Cleveland,

Ohio; son of Edward A. and Fay (Marks) Mahrer; first married in 1952; married second wife, Maya Bargar, April, 1967; children: (first marriage) Rachel, Jonathan, Michael, David. *Education:* Ohio State University, Ph.D., 1954. *Office:* Psychology Department, Miami University, Oxford, Ohio 45056.

CAREER: Fitzsimons Army Hospital, Denver, Colo., assistant chief psychologist, 1954-57; U.S. Veterans Administration Hospital, Denver, Colo., assistant chief psychologist, 1957-59, director of psychological training and laboratory of psychopathology, 1959-67; Miami University, Oxford, Ohio, professor of psychology and director of clinical psychology program, 1967—. Clinical psychologist, University Park Psychological Center (Denver), 1956-67. *Member:* American Psychological Association. *Awards, honors:* Bell Award, 1959.

WRITINGS: The Goals of Psychotherapy, Appleton, 1967; *Personality Classification: New Approaches,* Dorsey, 1968, published as *New Approaches to Personality Classification,* Columbia University Press, 1970; (editor with Leonard Pearson) *Creative Developments in Psychotherapy,* Aronson, 1973. Contributor to scientific journals.†

* * *

MAIER, Joseph (Ben) 1911-

PERSONAL: Born January 24, 1911, in Leipzig, Germany; son of Reuben (a clergyman) and Sophie (Safran) Maier; married Alice Heumann (an administrative assistant), July 14, 1937; children: Doris Helen (Mrs. Boris W. Vallejo). *Education:* University of Leipzig, A.B., 1933; Columbia University, A.M., 1934, Ph.D., 1939. *Home:* 991 Grace Ter., Teaneck, N.J. 07666. *Office:* Department of Sociology, Rutgers University, Newark, N.J. 07102.

CAREER: Aufbau (German-English newspaper), New York City, assistant editor, 1940-43; U.S. Office of War Information, propaganda analyst in New York City, and London, England, 1943-45; Office of U.S. Chief of Counsel, Germany, analyst in Interrogation Division, 1945-46; Schocken Books, Inc., New York City, assistant editor, 1946-47; Rutgers University, New Brunswick, N.J., faculty, 1947—, began as assistant professor, professor of sociology at Newark Campus, 1959—. Visiting lecturer at New York University, 1947; Fulbright professor at University of Frankfurt, 1957-58; visiting summer professor at Columbia University, 1957, 1960. *Member:* American Sociological Association, Academy of Political Science, American Academy of Political and Social Science, Latin American Studies Association.

WRITINGS: On Hegel's Critique of Kant, Columbia University Press, 1939; (with H. Infield) *Cooperative Group Living,* Henry Koosis, 1948; (with Jay Rumney) *Sociology: The Science of Society,* Schuman, 1953; (with R. W. Weatherhead) *Politics of Change in Latin America,* Praeger, 1964; (editor with Weatherhead) Frank Tannembaum, *The Future of Democracy in Latin America,* Knopf, 1975. Weekly columnist, *Aufbau.*

WORK IN PROGRESS: The Latin American University.

SIDELIGHTS: Joseph Maier is fluent in German, French, and Spanish, and has some competence in the classical languages.

* * *

MAJOR, Clarence 1936-

PERSONAL: Born December 31, 1936, in Atlanta, Ga.;

son of Clarence and Inez (Huff) Major; married Joyce Sparrow, 1958 (divorced, 1964). *Education:* Study at Art Institute of Chicago, 1953, Armed Forces Institute, 1956, and New School for Social Research, 1972. *Home:* 535 East 12th St., New York, N.Y. *Agent:* Howard Moorepark, 444 East 82nd St., New York, N.Y. 10028.

CAREER: Essayist, short story writer, novelist, poet, research analyst, editor, and anthologist. Harlem Education Program, New York City, instructor in Writers Workshop, 1967; Young Men's Christian Association, New York City, drawing instructor at Upper Manhattan Branch, 1967; Columbia University, Teachers College, New York City, instructor in Teachers and Writers Collaborative Program, 1967-68. Research analyst for Simulmatics Corp., New York City, 1967; consultant to Pennsylvania Advancement School, 1967-68; newspaper reporter, 1968. Guest lecturer in creative writing and literature, and visiting writer at colleges, universities, libraries, and other institutions. *Military service:* U.S. Air Force, 1954-57; served as record specialist. *Member:* Authors Guild, Authors League. *Awards, honors:* National Council on the Arts prize, Association of American University Presses, 1970; Creative Artists Public Service grant, Cultural Foundation of New York, 1971.

WRITINGS—All poetry, except as noted: *Love Poems of a Black Man,* Coercion, 1964; *Human Juices,* Coercion, 1965; (editor and author of introduction) *The New Black Poetry,* International Publications, 1969; *All-Night Visitors* (novel), Olympia, 1969; *Dictionary of American Slang* (nonfiction), International Publications, 1970 (published in England as *Black Slang,* Routledge & Kegan Paul, 1971); *Swallow the Lake,* Wesleyan University Press, 1970; *Symptoms and Madness,* Corinth Books, 1971; *Private Line,* Paul Breman, 1971; *No* (novel), Emerson Hall, 1972; *The Cotton Club,* Broadside Press, 1972; *The Syncopated Cakewalk,* Barlenmir, 1972; *Slaveship and Relationship* (nonfiction), Emerson Hall, 1973. Also author of a television script, "Africa Speaks to New York," 1970.

Work has appeared in anthologies including *19 Necromancers from Now* (fiction), Doubleday, 1970, *Black on Black* (fiction), Bantam, 1972, *Penguin Book of Black Verse* (poetry), Penguin, 1972, *Black Spirits* (poetry), Random House, 1972, *Studies in Black American Fiction* (nonfiction), Larrimer, 1973, and *From the Belly of the Shark* (nonfiction), Random House, 1973. Contributor of fiction, nonfiction, and poetry to periodicals. Editor, *Coercion Review,* 1958-65; associate editor, *Proof,* 1960, *Caw!,* 1967-68, and *Journal of Black Poetry,* 1967-70; corresponding editor, *Dues,* 1972—.

BIOGRAPHICAL/CRITICAL SOURCES: Ole, November, 1965; *Muhammad Speaks,* November 18, 1966; *National Guardian,* March 17, 1967; *Motive,* May, 1967; Carolyn Riley, editor, *Contemporary Literary Criticism,* Volume III, Gale, 1975.

* * *

MALL, E. Jane 1920-

PERSONAL: Born July 14, 1920, in Chicago, Ill.; daughter of John R. and Lucille (Warren) Rugaber; married Carlton H. Mall (a Lutheran clergyman), April 8, 1950 (deceased); adopted children: Mike, John, Marie, Carlton, Heide. *Education:* Attended Wartburg College, Waverly, Iowa. *Religion:* Lutheran. *Home:* 932 South Monroe, Hinsdale, Ill. 60521.

CAREER: Lutheran Children's Home, Waverly, Iowa, housemother, 1948-49; San Antonio Council for Retarded

Children, San Antonio, Tex., former publicity chairman; currently administrative assistant, Illinois Presbyterian Church, Western Springs, Ill. *Military service:* U.S. Coast Guard Women's Auxiliary (SPARS), World War II.

WRITINGS: Kitty, My Rib, Concordia, 1959; *P.S., I Love You,* Concordia, 1961; *My Flickering Torch,* Concordia, 1968; *Love in Action,* Concordia, 1971; *How Am I Doing, God?,* Concordia, 1973; (contributor) *Disciplines of 1975,* Upper Room, 1975. Also author of *Advent: A Calendar of Devotions,* Abingdon, 1972-75. Contributor to church magazines and papers.

WORK IN PROGRESS: A Mother's Gifts, a book of praise and inspiration, for Abingdon.

SIDELIGHTS: Jane Mall lived in Germany for three years when husband was stationed there as a U.S. Army chaplain. They adopted five German children.

* * *

MALLEN, Bruce E. 1937-

PERSONAL: Born September 4, 1937, in Montreal, Quebec, Canada; son of Mitchell (a retailer) and Mary (Epstein) Mallen; married Marcia Abramson (a registered nurse), December 12, 1965; children: Howard, Jay, Reesa. *Education:* Sir George Williams University (now Concordia University), B.Comm. and B.A., 1958; Columbia University, M.S., 1959; University of Michigan, M.B.A., 1960; New York University, Ph.D., 1963. *Home:* 3475 Mountain Ave., Apt. 1510, Montreal, Quebec, Canada. *Office:* Commerce Faculty, Sir George Williams Campus, Concordia University, Montreal, Quebec, Canada.

CAREER: P. S. Ross & Partners (management consultants), Montreal, Quebec, senior marketing consultant, 1962-64; Bruce Mallen & Associates Inc. (marketing consultants), Montreal, president, 1964—; Concordia University, Sir George Williams Campus, Montreal, lecturer, 1964-65, associate professor, 1965-67, professor of marketing and chairman of department, 1967-71, chairman of graduate studies in business, 1968—, acting dean, faculty of commerce and administration, 1970-71. Part-time lecturer, McGill University. Consultant to Consulate General of Japan in Montreal and Canadian Council of Resource Ministers. *Member:* American Marketing Association (president, Montreal chapter, 1969-70; international director, 1970-71), Association of Industrial Advertisers (past president), Canadian Economic Association, Montreal Economic Association, Advertising and Sales Executive Club of Montreal (director), Sales and Marketing Executives of Montreal (past director).

WRITINGS: (With M. Kelly) *The Role of Sales Management in Modern Marketing,* Canadian Manufacturers Association, 1963; (editor with I. A. Litvak) *Marketing: Canada,* McGraw, 1964, 2nd edition, 1968; (editor) *The Marketing Channel,* Wiley, 1967; (editor with Litvak) *Annotated Bibliography on Marketing in Canada,* American Marketing Association, 1967; (with R. Rotenberg) *The Costs and Benefits of Evening Shopping to the Canadian Economy,* National Retailers' Institute, 1969; *Marketing in the Canadian Environment,* Prentice-Hall, 1973.

Contributor: B. Israelsson and C. Roos, editors, *Marketing Guide: Canada,* General Export Association of Sweden, 1970; V. P. Buell, editor, *Handbook of Modern Marketing,* McGraw, 1970; D. Leighton and D. Thompson, editors, *Canadian Marketing: Problems and Prospects,* Wiley, 1973; *Modern Marketing,* Random House, 1975. Contrib-

utor to marketing and management journals. Past editor, *Canadian Marketer* (journal of Federation of Canadian Marketing); member of editorial board, *Journal of Marketing* (American Marketing Association), and *Journal of Physical Distribution* (United Kingdom).

WORK IN PROGRESS: Principles of Marketing Channels; a basic marketing text, with V. Kirpalani, for Prentice-Hall.

SIDELIGHTS: Mallen told *CA* that he is a "capitalist at heart," with ownership and control interest in various companies. He is competent in French. *Avocational interests:* Reading philosophy and history, skiing, handball.

* * *

MALLOUGH, Don 1914-

PERSONAL: Surname rhymes with "hello"; born May 26, 1914, in Wimbledon, N.D.; son of Malcolm S. (a businessman) and Helen (Geiser) Mallough; married Darlene Dixon, November 9, 1931; children: Donald Dixon, Monte Kim. *Education:* Studied at Los Angeles Baptist Theological Seminary. *Politics:* Republican.

CAREER: Clergyman, Assemblies of God. Headquarters, Assemblies of God, Springfield, Mo., editor of *Christ's Ambassadors Guide,* 1950-54, *Team,* 1954-59, and *Pulpit,* 1958-60, associate editor of *Pentecostal Evangel,* 1960; Faith Tabernacle, Tulsa, Okla., pastor, 1960-67; Bethel Assembly of God, Fremont, Calif., pastor, 1967—.

WRITINGS: Stop the Merry-go-Round!, Baker Book, 1964; *If I Were God,* Baker Book, 1967; *Crowded Detours,* Baker Book, 1970; *Grassroots Evangelism,* Baker Book, 1971.†

* * *

MALONEY, George A(nthony) 1924-

PERSONAL: Born October 29, 1924, in Green Bay, Wis.; son of George John (a paper-mill manager) and Catherine (Karbowski) Maloney. *Education:* Attended University of Wisconsin, 1942-43; St. Louis University, B.A., 1948, Ph.L., 1951; Gregorian University, S.T.L., 1958; Pontifical Oriental Institute, Doctor of Oriental Ecclesiastical Sciences (summa cum laude), 1962; additional study at Fordham University. *Home and office:* John XXIII Institute for Eastern Christian Studies, Fordham University, Bronx, N.Y. 10458.

CAREER: Roman Catholic priest of Jesuit order (S.J.), ordained in Russian Byzantine rite, 1957; studied Russian and worked among Russian emigres in Salzburg, Munich, and Paris during the summers of his school years in Rome, and has since traveled extensively in Russia, Greece, Egypt, and the Near East to meet Eastern Christian groups; Fordham University, John XXIII Institute for Eastern Christian Studies, Bronx, N.Y., associate professor of theology, 1963—, founder and director of Institute (master's study program). Visiting professor of theology, University of San Francisco, 1968. Member, Episcopal Commission on Ecumenism.

WRITINGS: (Editor and contributor) *The Byzantine Christian Heritage,* Fordham University Press, 1966; *The Cosmic Christ: From Paul to Teilhard,* Sheed, 1968; *Russian Hesychasm,* Mouton & Co., 1972; *The Breath of the Mystic,* Dimension Books, 1973; *Man: The Divine Icon,* Dove, 1972; *Listen Prophets,* Dimension Books, 1975; *The Mystic of Fire and Light,* Dimension Books, 1975; *History of Byzantine: Slav Orthodox Theology from 1453 to the*

Present, Nordland, 1975. Contributor to encyclopedias and to *America, Catholic World,* and other journals. Editor, *Diakonia* (ecumenical journal); consulting editor, *New Catholic Encyclopedia,* 1964-65.

WORK IN PROGRESS: A translation of the hymns of St. Symeon the New Theologian; *The Inward Stillness,* a book on prayer.

SIDELIGHTS: Father Maloney speaks seven languages, including Russian and Greek, and reads many others. *Avocational interests:* Swimming and the Green Bay Packers football team.

*   *   *

MALRAUX, (Georges-) Andre   1901-
(Colonel Berger)

PERSONAL: Born November 3, 1901, in Paris, France; son of Fernand-Georges (a businessman, from a seafaring family) and Berthe (Lamy) Malraux; married Clara Goldschmidt (an author), October 26, 1921 (divorced, 1930's); married Josette Clotis (a writer; killed in a rail accident during World War II); married Marie-Madeleine Lioux (a concert pianist; widow of his half-brother, Roland), March, 1948; children: (first marriage) Florence; (second marriage) Gautier and Vincent (both killed in an automobile accident, 1961); Alain (stepson). *Education:* Attended Lycee Condorcet, and Ecole des Langues Orientales, where he developed his interest in archaeology and oriental art. *Address:* 2, rue d'Estienne d'Orves, Verrieres-le-Buisson, 91370, France.

CAREER: After leaving school worked for the bookseller, Rene-Louis Doyon, and in the art department of the publisher, Kra, in Paris, France; in 1923, left, with wife, Clara Goldschmidt Malraux, for Indochina on an archaeological expedition sponsored by the French Government; was imprisoned on a charge of taking ancient sculptures, which were regarded as official property by the colonial regime; his wife returned to France in 1924 to organize a petition of writers (including Andre Gide), which led to his release; returned to France, but set off again for Indochina two months later; collaborated in Saigon with the nationalist "Jeune-Annam" movement on the newspaper, *L'Indochine* (later became *L'Indochine enchainee*); joined the Kuomintang in Indochina and Canton; returned to France in 1927; in 1928, became art editor at the publishing firm, Gallimard, for whom he has continued to work—in between numerous archaeological expeditions, and other activities—both as literary editor, and director of the series, "La Galerie de la Pleiade." Devoted the Prix Goncourt money to a trip in search of the lost city of the Queen of Sheba, in Southern Arabia; spoke at the 1934 Writers' Congress in Moscow (where he was listed as a "Marxist humanist"), and at the June, 1935 Congress of Writers in Defence of Culture, Paris; was involved in the activities of anti-Fascist organizations, including the "Comite mondial antifasciste," and "La Ligue internationale contre l'anti-semitisme." Became Minister of Information in de Gaulle's government, November, 1945-46; was Minister of Culture in the de Gaulle cabinet, 1958-69. *Wartime activity:* In 1936, organized the foreign division of the Republican air-force in the Spanish Civil War; at the outbreak of World War II he joined the French Army; was wounded, imprisoned, then escaped; after further wounds and imprisonment, organized the Resistance in southwest France, heading the Alsace-Lorraine brigade in 1945, under the pseudonym, "Colonel Berger." *Awards, honors*—Military: Officier de la Legion d'honneur,

Compagnon de la Liberation, Medaille de la Resistance, Croix de guerre (1939-45), Distinguished Service Order. Civilian: Prix Goncourt, 1933, for *La Condition humaine;* Prix Louis-Delluc, 1945, for the film *L'Espoir;* Prix Nehru, 1974, for promoting international understanding.

WRITINGS—Fiction: *Lunes en papier* (fantastic tale; also see below), Simon, 1921; *La Tentation de l'Occident* (philosophical tale; also see below), Grasset, 1926, reprinted, Les Bibliophiles comtois, 1962, translation and introduction by Robert Hollander published as *The Temptation of the West,* Vintage Books, 1961; *Les Conquerants* (novel; also see below), Grasset, 1928, revised, "definitive" edition (contains a "postface" by Malraux consisting of his March 5, 1948 speech in defense of Gaullism), 1949, reprinted, Gallimard, 1967, translation by Winifred Stephen Whale published as *The Conquerors,* Harcourt, 1929, revised edition (with "postface" translated by Jacques Le Clerq), Beacon Press, 1956; *Royaume faufelu* (fantastic tale; also see below), Gallimard, 1928; *La Voie royale* (novel; also see below), Grasset, 1930, reprinted, 1968, translation by Stuart Gilbert published as *The Royal Way,* Smith & Haus, 1935; *La Condition humaine* (novel; also see below), Gallimard, 1933, revised edition, 1946, translation by Haakon M. Chevalier published as *Man's Fate,* Smith & Haus, 1934, reprinted, Random House, 1968, translation by Alistair Macdonald published as *Man's Estate,* Methuen, 1934, published as *Man's Estate,* 1948, reprinted, Hamish Hamilton, 1968; *Le Temps du mepris* (novel), Gallimard, 1935, translation by Chevalier, with a forward by Waldo Frank, published as *Days of Wrath,* Random House, 1936 (published in England as *Days of Contempt,* Gollancz, 1936); *L'Espoir* (novel; also see below); Gallimard, 1937, reprinted, 1974; translation by Gilbert and Macdonald published as *Man's Hope,* Random House, 1938, reprinted, 1968 (published in England as *Days of Hope,* Routledge & Kegan Paul, 1938); *La Lutte avec l'ange* (philosophical novel; part of a larger project, the rest of which was destroyed by the Gestapo), Editions du Haut Pays, 1943, published as *Les Noyers de l'Altenburg,* Gallimard, 1948, translation by A. W. Fielding published as *The Walnut Trees of Altenburg,* John Lehmann, 1952.

Art criticism: *Esquisse d'une psychologie du cinema,* Gallimard, 1946; *La Psychologie de l'art,* Skira, Volume I: *Le Musee imaginaire,* 1947, Volume II: *La Creation artisque,* 1948, Volume III: *La Monnaie de l'absolu,* 1949, translation by Stuart Gilbert published as *The Psychology of Art,* Pantheon, Volume I: *Museum without Walls,* 1949, Volume II: *The Creative Act,* 1950, Volume III: *The Twilight of the Absolute,* 1951, revised and enlarged French edition published as *Les Voix du silence* (contains an additional section, "Les Metamorphoses d'Apollon"), Galerie de la Pleiade, Gallimard, 1951, translation by Gilbert published as *The Voices of Silence,* Doubleday, 1953, Volume I: *Museum without Walls,* Volume II: *The Metamorphoses of Apollo,* Volume III: *The Creative Process,* Volume IV: *The Aftermath of the Absolute; Saturne,* Skira, 1949, translation by C. W. Chilton published as *Saturn: An Essay on Goya,* Phaidon, 1957; *Le Musee imaginaire de la sculpture mondiale,* Volume I, Gallimard, 1952, Volume II published as *Des bas-reliefs aux grottes sacree,* Gallimard, 1954, Volume III published as *Le Monde chretien,* 1954; *Le Metamorphose des dieux* (philosophy and religion in art), Gallimard, Volume I: *Le Surnaturel,* 1957, translation by Gilbert published as *The Metamorphosis of the Gods,* Doubleday, 1960, Volume II: *L'Ireel,* 1974, Volume III: *L'Intemporal,* 1976.

Political writings and official speeches: (In dialogue with James Burnham) *The Case for De Gaulle,* Random House, 1949; *Brasilia, la capitale de l'espoir* (French text followed by Spanish and English translations), Presidencia de Republica, Servico de Documentacao, 1959; *Discours, 1958-1965,* Action Etudiante Gaullistes, 1966; *Oraisons funebres,* Gallimard, 1971; *Paroles et ecrits politiques, 1947-1972,* Plon, 1973.

Author of prefaces, including: D. H. Lawrence, *L'Amant de Lady Chatterley,* translated by Roger Cornaz, Gallimard, 1932, preface published as "Preface to *Lady Chatterley's Lover,*" in *Yale French Studies,* Number 11, 1953; William Faulkner, *Sanctuaire,* translated by R. M. Raimbault and Henri Delgove, Gallimard, 1933, preface published as "Preface to Faulkner's *Sanctuary,*" in *Yale French Studies,* Number 10, 1952; Andree Viollis, *Indochine S.O.S.,* Gallimard, 1935; *Goya: Dissins du Musee du Prado,* Skira, 1947; Manes Sperber, *Q'une larme dans l'ocean,* translated by author and Blanche Gidon, Calmann-Levy, 1952; *Tout Vermeer de Delft,* Gallimard, 1952; *Tout l'oeuvre peint de Leonard de Vinci,* Gallimard, 1952; General P. E. Jacquot, *Essai de strategie occidentale,* Gallimard, 1953; Albert Olivier, *Saint-Just et la force des choses* (also see below), Gallimard, 1954; Izis Bidermanas, *Israel,* Clairefontaine, 1955; Andre Parrot, *Sumer,* Gallimard, 1960; *Le Triangle noir* (contains prefaces on Laclos, Goya, and Saint-Just), Gallimard, 1970; Pierre Bockel, *L'Enfant du rire,* Grasset, 1973; Maria Van Ryssellberghe, *Les Cahiers de la petite dame, 1918-1929,* Gallimard, 1973; Georges Bernanos, *Journal d'un cure de campagne,* Plon, 1974; *Correspondance Romain Rolland-Jean Guehenno,* Albin Michel, 1975.

Other: *Les Chenes qu'on abat . . .,* Gallimard, 1970, translation by Irene Clephane published as *Fallen Oaks: Conversation with De Gaulle,* Hamish Hamilton, 1972, published as *Felled Oaks: Conversation with De Gaulle,* revised by Linda Asher, Holt, 1972; *Roi, je t'attends a Babylone,* Skira, 1973; *La Tete d'obsidienne,* Gallimard, 1974; *Lazare,* Gallimard, 1974.

Autobiography: *Le Miroir des limbes,* Gallimard, Volume I: *Antimemoires,* 1967, translation by Terrence Kilmartin published as *Anti-memoirs,* Holt, 1968, Volume II: *La Corde et le souris,* 1975.

Omnibus volumes: *Oeuvres completes,* Skira, 1945; *Scenes choisies,* Gallimard, 1946; *Romans* (contains *Les Conquerants, La Conditions humaine,* and *L'Espoir*), Gallimard, 1947, reprinted, 1969; *Lectures choisies,* edited by Anne Prioleau Jones, Macmillan, 1965; *Oeuvres* (contains *Lunes en papier, Tentation de l'Occident, Les Conquerants, Royaume farfelu, La Voie royale, La Condition humaine, L'Espoir,* and *Antimemoires*), four volumes, Gallimard, 1970.

General editor, *The Arts of Mankind,* 1960—. Contributor to *Action, L'Intransigeant, Commune, Les Conferences de l'Unesco, Liberte de l'esprit, Carrefour, Europe, Nouvelle Revue Francaise, L'Express,* and many other journals and publications.

SIDELIGHTS: W. M. Frohock writes: "For Americans, Malraux has the special interest of being what America rarely produces, an artist who is also an intellectual."

All of Malraux's major novels are strongly biographical—though not personal. Gaetan Picon suggests that "the events which provided the material for the work are directly lived through, but remain external. The encounter between Malraux and History becomes the history of Mal-

raux himself." His experience in Indochina, writes the *Times Saturday Review,* "turned Malraux from a dilettante into a revolutionary." Donald Schier continues: "*L'Espoir* makes it plain that by 1938 Malraux was finding it impossible to identify himself with the Communist Party, although he continued to share, rather suspiciously, in its struggle against Fascism. . . . [In *Les Conquerants,* the] forcing of other people into paths they would not otherwise have taken (. . . not by party discipline but by individual leadership) is the real justification for the hero's existence. . . . Malraux sees himself as a hero." With respect to General de Gaulle, the *Times Saturday Review* comments how "Malraux has come to regard him not as a politician but as a 'mythe vivant.'"

In an interview with Roger Stephane, Malraux noted: "I couldn't say that man is what he does, because, to the question, what is man? I would apply that we are the first civilization which says it doesn't know. . . . We are the only civilization in which man has no purpose. Not that he cannot have one, but that we are still trying to find out what it is. All other civilizations have rested in the end on religion." In an age without faith, he accords a supreme role to the artist: "Art lives because its function is to let men escape from their human condition, not by means of evasion, but through a possession. All art is a way of possessing destiny."

Malraux has been described in the *Times Saturday Review* as "a slight, intense hollow-eyed man, a chain-smoker who looks like a character from a Malraux novel." Janet Flanner writes: "No other French writer is so rapid, compulsive, fascinating and rewarding a monologist. . . . As he walks, words and ideas rush from his brain and out of his mouth in extemporaneous creation, as though they were long quotations from books he had not yet written. . . ." Flanner continues: "He could work at his publishing job by day, and at his writing more than half the night at home. . . . It was in these circumstances that he wrote *La Condition humaine.*"

It is well known that Malraux is not prepared to discuss his personal life with the public. Flanner reports that, "if a question of a biographical nature is inadvertently asked in an interview, Malraux will reply by saying 'Vie Privee' and nothing more. In his own view, which is aloof, his *vie publique* lies in his books." His autobiography reveals the same attitude towards what he calls "confessions": "What interests me in a man is the human condition . . . and some features which express less an individual character, than a particular relationship with the world. . . . I call this book *Antimemoires* because it replies to questions that memoirs do not put, and does not answer those they do." David Caute notes: "These *Antimemoires* break away entirely from the traditional biography or memoir form. Not only is orthodox chronology rejected: there is in addition no attempt to provide a factually coherent outline of the author's life." Schier adds: The various sections of the *Antimemoires* bear the titles of his books but he does not discuss them. Rather the *Antimemoires* provide variations on the novelistic themes: individual action versus party discipline, terrorism as a political technique, art as a surrogate for religion, *fraternite verile.*" Malraux told Stephane: "My problem is this: what answer can life give to the basic question posed by death? This question was always subordinate in great religious cultures which preceded our culture. My intention is to answer it in a fundamental way. This has been made easier for me because my memoirs don't follow a chronological sequence.... Up to a point, we can say that memoirs are essentially novels about the education of the author's personality. But I am concerned with something different, and I have taken another title because of that."

As de Gaulle's minister of culture, Malraux is probably best known for organizing the cleaning of Paris buildings, creating what is alluded to in the *Times Saturday Review* as "Paris blanchi." In the same article, it is reported that *Antimemoires* sold a quarter of a million copies in the first two months of publication.

There are a number of recordings of Malraux's work, including a reading by Malraux himself from *Les Voix du silence,* in the series "Auteurs du 20e Siecle," Philips. A film scenario of *L'Espoir* was made in Barcelona in 1938.

BIOGRAPHICAL/CRITICAL SOURCES—Books: W. M. Frohock, *Andre Malraux and the Tragic Imagination,* Stanford University Press, 1952, revised edition, with new preface, 1967; Gaetan Picon, *Malraux par lui-meme* (with annotations by Malraux), Editions du Seuil, 1953; Janet Flanner, *Men and Monuments,* Harper, 1957; Geoffrey Hartman, *Andre Malraux,* Hillary, 1960; *The Novelist as Philosopher,* edited by John Cruickshank, Oxford University Press, 1962; Charles D. Blend, *Andre Malraux: Tragic Humanist,* Ohio State University Press, 1963; Clara Malraux, *Le Bruit de nos pas,* Grasset, Volume I: *Apprendre a vivre,* 1963, Volume II: *Nos vingt ans,* 1966, translation by Patrick O'Brian published in a single volume as *Memoirs,* Bodley Head, 1967; R. W. B. Lewis, editor, *Malraux: A Collection of Critical Essays,* Prentice-Hall, 1964; Walter G. Langlois, *The Indochina Adventure,* Praeger, 1966; Andre Malraux, *Antimemoires,* Gallimard, 1967; Denis Boak, *Andre Malraux,* Oxford University Press, 1968; P.S.R. Payne, *A Portrait of Andre Malraux,* Prentice-Hall, 1970; Carolyn Riley, editor, *Contemporary Literary Criticism,* Gale, Volume I, 1973, Volume IV, 1975; T. J. Kline, *Andre Malraux and the Metamorphosis of Death,* Columbia University Press, 1973; Jean Lacouture, *Andre Malraux,* Editions du Seuil, 1973, translation by Alan Sheridan published under same title, Pantheon, 1975; Guy Suares, *Malraux, Past, Present, Future,* translated by Derek Coltman, Little, Brown, 1974; C. J. Greshoff, *An Introduction to the Novels of Andre Malraux,* Balkema, 1976.

Articles: *Esprit* (nearly entire issue devoted to Malraux), October, 1948; *Modern Language Quarterly,* June, 1953; *Burlington Magazine,* December, 1954; *University of Kansas City Review,* Volume XXVIII, number 1, 1961; *Observer Weekend Review,* April 5, 1964; *Times Literary Supplement,* November 26, 1964; *Le Nouvel Observateur,* September 11, 1967; *Encounter* (interview), Volume XXX, number 1, 1967; *Times Saturday Review,* November 18, 1967; *Listener,* January 25, 1968, October 31, 1968; *Carleton Miscelany,* winter, 1969; *Melanges-Malraux-Miscellany,* 1969—.†

*   *   *

MALY, Eugene H.   1920-

PERSONAL: Born September 6, 1920, in Cincinnati, Ohio; son of Robert John and Florence (Bill) Maly. *Education:* Athenaeum of Ohio, A.B., 1941, graduate study, 1941-43; Angelicum University, Rome, S.T.D., 1948; Pontifical Biblical Institute, Rome, S.S.D., 1959; additional study at University of Cincinnati, 1944-45, and Hebrew Union College, Cincinnati, 1945-46. *Home and office:* Mount St.

Mary's of the West, Athenaeum of Ohio, 5440 Moeller Ave., Norwood, Ohio 45212.

CAREER: Roman Catholic priest. Athenaeum of Ohio, Mount St. Mary's of the West, Norwood, instructor, 1950-55, assistant professor, 1955-59, associate professor, 1959-60, professor of Sacred Scripture, 1960—. Lecturer at institutions, workshops, and institutes. *Member:* Catholic Biblical Association of America (president, 1962-63), Society of Biblical Literature, National Association of Professors of Hebrew.

WRITINGS: The Epistles of Saints James, Jude, Peter, Liturgical Press, 1960; *The Book of Wisdom* (commentary), Paulist Press, 1962; *The World of David and Solomon,* Prentice-Hall, 1966; *Prophets of Salvation,* Herder & Herder, 1967; (contributor) R. E. Brown and others, editors, *The Jerome Biblical Commentary,* Prentice-Hall, 1968; *The First Book of Samuel* [and] *The Second Book of Samuel,* Liturgical Press, 1970; *Sin: Biblical Perspectives,* Pflaum/Standard, 1973. Contributor to religious and theological journals. Chairman of editorial board, *The Bible Today,* 1962—.

SIDELIGHTS: Father Maly speaks French, German, Italian, Spanish, Latin, Greek, and Hebrew.

*   *   *

MANARIN, Louis H(enry)   1932-

PERSONAL: Born April 1, 1932, in Washington, D.C.; son of Louis and Mary (Urbanek) Manarin; married Jo Ann Matheny, March 22, 1957; children: Louis Timothy, Amy Marie. *Education:* Valley Forge Military Junior College, A.A., 1953; Western Maryland College, B.A., 1955; Duke University, M.A., 1957, Ph.D., 1965. *Religion:* Baptist. *Home:* 8304 Whistler Rd., Richmond, Va. 23227.

CAREER: Virginia Civil War Centennial Commission, Richmond, editor-historian, 1959-61; North Carolina Confederate Centennial Commission, Raleigh, editor, 1961-66; National Archives and Record Service, Washington, D.C., archivist, 1966-67; North Carolina Department of Archives and History, Raleigh, editor, 1967-70; Virginia State Library, Richmond, state archivist, 1970—. Professional lecturer, American University, 1966-68; instructor, North Carolina State University at Raleigh, 1968-70. *Military service:* U.S. Army, Finance Corps, 1957; became second lieutenant.

MEMBER: American Historical Association, Company of Military Historians (fellow), American Military Institute (secretary, 1968), American Records Management Association, Society of American Archivists, Southern Historical Association, Virginia Historical Society, Virginia Genealogical Society (president, 1973-74), Virginia History Federation (treasurer, 1972—), Virginia Microfilm Association, North Carolina Literary and Historical Association, Richmond Civil War Round Table. *Awards, honors:* D.Litt., Western Maryland College, 1974.

WRITINGS: (Editor with Clifford Dowdey) *The Wartime Papers of R. E. Lee,* Little, Brown, 1961; (with Richard Iobst) *The Bloody Sixth,* North Carolina Confederate Centennial Commission, 1965; *North Carolina Troops, 1861-1865,* North Carolina Department of Archives, Volume I: *Artillery,* 1966, Volume II: *Cavalry,* 1968, Volume III: *Infantry,* 1971; (editor) *Richmond at War,* University of North Carolina Press, 1966; *Richmond, 1865-1975: A Pictorial History,* Tom Hale, 1974. Also author of *Richmond Occupied,* 1965, and *Richmond Volunteers,* 1971, for Richmond Civil War Centennial Committee. Editor of the Richmond Civil War Centennial Committee, 1962-66; assistant editor, *Military Affairs* (quarterly publication of American Military Institute), 1965-68; member of editorial board, Virginia Independence Bicentennial Commission.

WORK IN PROGRESS: Research on Robert E. Lee and his strategy, as well as other aspects of Civil War and Virginia history; new volumes of *North Carolina Troops, 1861-1865.*

* * *

MANIS, Melvin 1931-

PERSONAL: Born February 18, 1931, in New York, N.Y.; son of Alex (a contractor) and Hanna (Oyle) Manis; married Jean Denby, 1954; children: Peter, David. *Education:* Franklin and Marshall College, B.A., 1951; University of Illinois, Ph.D., 1954. *Politics:* Democrat. *Religion:* Jewish. *Home:* 20 Harvard Pl., Ann Arbor, Mich. 48103. *Office:* Department of Psychology, University of Michigan, Ann Arbor, Mich. 48104.

CAREER: University of Pittsburgh, Pittsburgh, Pa., instructor in psychology, 1956-58; U.S. Veterans Administration Hospital, Ann Arbor, Mich., chief of psychological research, 1958—; University of Michigan, Ann Arbor, lecturer, 1958-61, associate professor, 1961-66, professor of psychology, 1966—. Fulbright lecturer at University of Ghent, Ghent, Belgium, 1966-67. *Military service:* U.S. Public Health Service, commissioned officer (clinical psychologist), 1954-56. *Member:* American Psychological Association (fellow), American Association of University Professors, Eastern Psychological Association, Midwestern Psychological Association, Phi Beta Kappa, Sigma Xi. *Awards, honors:* U.S. Public Health Service fellowships, 1953-54, 1956-58.

WRITINGS: Cognitive Processes, Wadsworth, 1966; *Introduction to Cognitive Psychology,* Brooks/Cole, 1971. Contributor and consulting editor, *Journal of Abnormal and Social Psychology* and *Personality and Social Psychology;* contributor to other psychology journals.

WORK IN PROGRESS: Thinking and Communication; research in communication.

* * *

MANKEKAR, D. R. 1910-

PERSONAL: Born August 7, 1910, in Mangalore, India; son of Ganpat Rao (an accountant) and Subadraibai Mankekar; married Kamla Chopra (a journalist), September 4, 1958; children: Aruna, Ajit, Urmila, Purnima. *Education:* Educated at Government College, Mangalore, India. *Religion:* Hindu. *Home:* 64F Sujan Singh Park, New Delhi, India 110003.

CAREER: Political reporter in India, 1932-58, political columnist, 1951-65, 1967—; *Times of India,* New Delhi, editor, 1950-58; *Indian Express,* New Delhi and, later, Bombay, India, editor, 1958-65; *Times of India,* editor, 1967-69; Times of India Group of Newspapers, Bombay, general manager, 1969-70. War correspondent on Burma front, Reuters News Agency, 1943-45; director of public relations, with assimilated rank of brigadier, Armed Forces, India, 1948-50. President, All-India Newspaper Editors Conference, 1968-70. *Member:* Indian Council of World Affairs, Press Club of India (New Delhi; president, 1969-70).

WRITINGS: The House that Jinnah Built, Padma Publications, 1945; *The Goa Action,* Popular Book Depot, 1962; *Lal Bahadur Shastri—A Political Biography,* Manaktala & Sons, 1964; *The Red Riddle of Kerala,* Manaktala & Sons, 1965; *Twenty-two Fateful Days,* Manaktala & Sons, 1966, revised edition with two added chapters, 1967; *On the Slippery Slope in Nagaland,* Manaktala & Sons, 1967; *The Guilty Men of 1962,* P. Tnlsi Shah, 1968; *Sir Homi Mody: A Biography,* Popular Prakashan, 1968; *No, My Son, Never!* (novel), Atmaram & Sons, 1969; *Pak Colonialism in East Bengal,* Somaya Publications, 1970; *Pakistan Cut to Size,* Indian Book Co., 1970; *The Press under Pressure,* Indian Book Co., 1972; *Accession to Extinction,* Vikas Publishing, 1973; *A Revolution of Rising Frustrations,* Vikas Publishing, 1974; *The Mewar Saga,* Vikas Publishing, 1976.

SIDELIGHTS: Mankekar's biography of Prime Minister Lal Bahadur Shastri sold over ten thousand copies, was reissued as a paperback, and translated into Marathi; *Twenty-Two Fateful Days,* a book on the armed conflict between India and Pakistan in 1965, established a record in Indian publishing with sales of fifteen thousand.

Mankekar has traveled in the United States, Europe, China, Russia, the United Arab Republic, and southeast Asia.

* * *

MARCUS, Edward 1918-

PERSONAL: Born April 29, 1918, in Brooklyn, N.Y.; son of Herman and Rose (Marayna) Marcus; married Mildred Rendl (an economist), 1956. *Education:* Harvard University, B.S., 1939, M.B.A., 1941; King's College, Cambridge, graduate study, 1946-47; Princeton University, Ph.D., 1950. *Religion:* None. *Office:* Brooklyn College of the City University of New York, Brooklyn, N.Y. 11210.

CAREER: Federal Reserve Board, Washington, D.C., economist in division of international finance, 1950-52; Brooklyn College of the City University of New York, Brooklyn, N.Y., 1952—, began as assistant professor, professor of economics, 1961—, chairman of department of economics, 1966—. Visiting professor at New York University, 1960-61, at Maxwell Center, Syracuse, N.Y., 1961. Consultant to Ira Haupt & Co., 1955-58. *Military service:* U.S. Army, 1941-42. U.S. Coast Guard Reserve, active duty, 1942-46; became commander. *Member:* American Economic Association, American Finance Association, African Studies Association, Society for International Development, American Association of University Professors, Canadian Political Science Association, Royal Economic Society, Metropolitan Economics Association (New York; president, 1966-67), Phi Beta Kappa. *Awards, honors:* Merrill Foundation grant, 1953.

WRITINGS: Canada and the International Business Cycle, Bookman Associates, 1954; (with wife, Mildred Rendl Marcus) *Investment and Development Possibilities in Tropical Africa,* Bookman Associates, 1960; (with M. R. Marcus) *International Trade and Finance,* Pitman, 1965; (with M. R. Marcus) *Monetary and Banking Theory,* Pitman, 1965; (with M. R. Marcus) *Economic Progress and the Developing World,* Scott, Foresman, 1971. Contributor to professional journals.

SIDELIGHTS: Marcus is competent in French, Swedish, and German.

MARCUS, Jacob Rader 1896-

PERSONAL: Born March 5, 1896, in Connellsville, Pa.; son of Aaron (a merchant) and Jennie (Rader) Marcus; married Antoinette Brody, December 30, 1925 (deceased); children: Merle Judith (deceased). Education: University of Cincinnati, A.B., 1917; Hebrew Union College, Cincinnati, Ohio, Rabbi, 1920; University of Kiel, graduate study, 1923; University of Berlin, Ph.D., 1925. Home: 401 McAlpin Ave., Cincinnati, Ohio 45220. Office: Hebrew Union College, Clifton Ave., Cincinnati, Ohio 45220.

CAREER: Hebrew Union College—Jewish Institute of Religion, Cincinnati, Ohio, instructor in Bible and rabbinics, 1920-26, assistant professor of Jewish history, 1926-29, associate professor, 1929-34, professor, 1934-46, Adolph S. Ochs Professor of American Jewish History, 1946-65, Milton and Hattie Kutz Distinguished Service Professor of American Jewish History, 1965—, director of American Jewish Archives, 1947—, director of American Jewish Periodical Center, 1956—. Trustee, Jewish Publication Society. Military service: U.S. Army, Infantry, 1917-19; became second lieutenant.

MEMBER: Jewish Academy of Arts and Sciences, American Academy for Jewish Research, American Jewish Historical Society (president, 1956-59), Central Conference of American Rabbis (president, 1949-50), B'nai B'rith. Awards, honors: LL.D. from University of Cincinnati, 1950, and Dropsie College, 1955; Frank L. Weil Award of National Jewish Welfare Board, 1955; Lee M. Friedman Medal for distinguished service in history, 1961.

WRITINGS: The Rise and Destiny of the German Jew, Sinai Press, 1934; Index to Jewish Festschriften, Hebrew Union College Press, 1937; The Jew in the Medieval World: A Source Book, Union of American Hebrew Congregations, 1938; Communal Sick-Care in the German Ghetto, Hebrew Union College Press, 1947; Early American Jewry, Jewish Publication Society, Volume I, 1951, Volume II, 1953; (editor) Memoirs of American Jews, 1775-1865, Jewish Publication Society, Volumes I and II, 1955, Volume III, 1956; (editor) American Jewish Documents, Eighteenth Century, University Publishers, 1959.

On Love, Marriage, Children . . . and Death, Too, Society of Jewish Bibliophiles, 1966; Studies in American Jewish History, Hebrew Union College Press, 1969; The Colonial American Jew, 1492-1776, Wayne State University Press, 1970; The Handsome Young Priest in the Black Gown, Hebrew Union College Press, 1970; An Index to Scientific Articles on American Jewish History, Ktav, 1971.

BIOGRAPHICAL/CRITICAL SOURCES: Stanley F. Chyet, Biography in Essays in American Jewish History, American Jewish Archives, 1958.

*   *   *

MARDER, Daniel 1923-

PERSONAL: Born July 10, 1923, in Chicago, Ill.; son of Harry S. (a businessman) and Bertha (Isler) Marder; married Barbara Lee Humphrey, March, 1954; children: Kathleen, Mary, Daniel. Education: Attended Wilson Junior College, Chicago, Ill., 1941-42; Roosevelt University, B.A., 1948; University of Iowa, M.F.A., 1950; University of Pittsburgh, Ph.D., 1961. Politics: Independent. Religion: Independent. Home: 2649 South Birmingham Pl., Tulsa, Okla. 74114. Office: Department of English, University of Tulsa, Tulsa, Okla. 74104.

CAREER: Technical editor, New York, N.Y., 1951-53;

correspondent for Time-Life, Inc., and editor of Spanish American Courier, Madrid, Spain, 1953-54; Carnegie Institute of Technology (now Carnegie-Mellon University), Pittsburgh, Pa., editor of news service, 1954-56; University of Pittsburgh, Pittsburgh, assistant professor of English, 1956-62; Bell Telephone of Pennsylvania, Pittsburgh, assistant to vice-president, 1962; Pennsylvania State University, University Park, associate professor of English, 1962-68; Slippery Rock State College, Slippery Rock, Pa., professor of English and chairman of department, 1968-70; University of Tulsa, Tulsa, Okla., professor of English and chairman of department, 1970—. Fulbright professor, University of Skopije (Yugoslavia), 1966-67. Consultant, Ballistics Research Laboratories. Military service: U.S. Army Air Forces, 1943-46; received Presidential Citation, Air Medal, and Chinese Order of Flying Cloud. Member: National Association of Science Writers, Modern Language Association of America, National Council of Teachers of English.

WRITINGS: Craft of Technical Writing, Macmillan, 1960; Hugh Henry Brackenridge, Twayne, 1967; College English, International Correspondence Schools, 1969; (editor and author of introduction) A Brackenridge Reader, University of Pittsburgh Press, 1970; (editor) Hugh Henry Brackenridge, Incidents of Insurrection, College & University Press, 1972.

WORK IN PROGRESS: A memoir of Yugoslavia; a novel on Benedict Arnold.

*   *   *

MARGOLIUS, Sidney 1911-

PERSONAL: Born May 3, 1911, in Perth Amboy, N.J.; son of Max (a businessman) and Helen (Senier) Margolius; married Esther Papert, November 14, 1942; children: Richard. Education: Rutgers University, Litt.B., 1934. Home: 74 Davis Rd., Port Washington, N.Y.

CAREER: Worked for United Press, New York City, 1934-35; Market Observer, New York City, editor, 1936-37; Retailing, New York City, associate editor, 1937-40; PM, New York City, consumer editor, 1940-42, 1945-48; full-time free-lance writer, 1948—. Member of President's Consumer Advisory Council; director of Metropolitan New York Consumer Council; member of New York State Consumer Advisory Committee, and Nassau County, N.Y., Consumer Advisory Council. Consultant to International Cooperation Administration, and to U.S. Government. Military service: U.S. Army, 1942-45.

WRITINGS: How to Buy More for Your Money, Modern Age Books, 1942, revised edition published as The Consumer's Guide to Better Buying, Doubleday, 1947; Your Guide to Financial Security, New American Library, 1955; Better Homes and Gardens Money Management for Your Family, Meredith, 1962; Planning for College, Avon, 1965; How to Make the Most of Your Money, Appleton, 1966; The Innocent Consumer vs. The Exploiters, Trident, 1967; Adulthood for Beginners, Macmillan, 1968; The Great American Food Hoax, Walker & Co., 1971; The Innocent Investor and the Shaky Ground Floor, Trident, 1971; Health Foods: Facts and Fakes, Walker & Co., 1973. Writer of eight public affairs pamphlets. Contributor of about 350 articles to magazines.

SIDELIGHTS: The Consumer's Guide to Better Buying is used as a college and high school textbook, and has had a total sale of 700,000 copies.

BIOGRAPHICAL/CRITICAL SOURCES: Harper's, November, 1967; Book World, December 17, 1967; New York Times Book Review, December 31, 1967; Christian Science Monitor, January 15, 1968.

* * *

MARINACCI, Barbara 1933-

PERSONAL: Surname is pronounced Mar-ee-notch-ee, the first syllable to rhyme with "far"; born September 19, 1933, in San Jose, Calif.; daughter of Karl W. (an importer and writer) and Eleanor (Williams) Kamb; married Rudy Marinacci (an art director), August 30, 1958; children: Michael, Christopher, Ellen. Education: Attended Reed College, 1950-52, Stanford University, 1952, and University of California, Berkeley, 1953. Politics: Democrat. Religion: Unitarian Universalist. Home: 234 Twelfth St., Santa Monica, Calif. 90402.

CAREER: Dodd, Mead & Co., New York, N.Y., an editor, working in fiction and nonfiction, 1955-60; founder and editorial consultant, Bookwrights/West (editorial consultation service), 1975—.

WRITINGS: Leading Ladies (collection of biographies of famous actresses), Dodd, 1961; They Came from Italy (collection of biographies of Italian-Americans in various fields), Dodd, 1967; O Wondrous Singer: An Introduction to Walt Whitman, Dodd, 1970.

WORK IN PROGRESS: A biography of nineteenth-century radical orator Wendell Phillips, tentatively entitled, Eloquent Agitator, for Houghton; a collection of biographics of American botanists, Plants and People, for Dodd.

* * *

MARKS, Norton E(lliott) 1932-

PERSONAL: Born April 7, 1932, in Omaha, Neb.; son of Harry D. and Harriett (Rothholtz) Marks; married Gloria S. Ginsberg, December 24, 1950; children: Shelly Helene, Sanford J. Education: University of Omaha, B.S., 1960; Indiana University, M.B.A., 1961; University of Washington, Seattle, D.B.A., 1965. Home: 11528 Old Hammond Hwy., Baton Rouge, La. Office: Department of Marketing, Louisiana State University, Baton Rouge, La. 70803.

CAREER: Union Pacific Railroad Co., Omaha, Neb., depreciation accountant, 1951-53; Fels and Co., Omaha, Neb., salesman, 1953-54; National Biscuit Co., Omaha, Neb., government and district representative, 1954-59; University of Omaha, Omaha, Neb., veteran's administrator, 1959-60; Seattle University, Seattle, Wash., assistant professor, 1963-64; University of Texas at Austin, assistant professor, 1964-67; University of Notre Dame, Notre Dame, Ind., associate professor of marketing, 1967-71; Louisiana State University, Baton Rouge, professor of marketing and chairman of department, 1971—. Partner, Andersen, Dommermuth, Marks, Associates (consultants); senior partner, Coriden, Dow, Kennedy, and Marks (consultants). Military service: U.S. Navy, 1950-54. Member: American Marketing Association, American Association of University Professors, Southern Marketing Association, Tri-States Marketing Association, Beta Gamma Sigma, South Bend Chamber of Commerce. Awards, honors: Ford Foundation fellowship, 1964.

WRITINGS: (With Robert M. Taylor) Physical Distribution and Marketing Logistics: An Annotated Bibliography, American Marketing Association, 1966; (with Lyndon Taylor) CPM/PERT, University of Texas Press, 1966, revised edition, 1967; (with Taylor) Marketing Logistics, Wiley, 1967; (with Richard A. Scott) Marketing and Its Environment, Wadsworth, 1968; Vending Machines: Introduction and Innovation, University of Texas at Austin, 1969; (editor with R. Rodnight) Research Methods in Neurochemistry, Plenum, 1972; Marketing: An Environmental Study, McGraw, 1972. Contributor to marketing journals.†

* * *

MARLOWE, Alan Stephen 1937-

PERSONAL: Born June 18, 1937; son of J. H. (a farmer) and Beatrice (Bassin) Marlowe; married Heather Hewitt, June 4, 1960 (divorced); married Diane di Prima (a poet and editor), November 30, 1962; children: (second marriage) Alexander H., Tara Johanna. Education: Attended Columbia University for three years. Politics: Natural Anarchist. Religion: Buddhist.

CAREER: Actor with the American Shakespeare Festival, and other companies, 1959-62; director of New York Poets Theatre-American Theatre for Poets, Inc., 1962-65; Poets Press Inc., New York, N.Y., editor and production editor, 1965—. Also, lecturer on Eastern religions, schools of Hinduism, and Buddhism; free-lance designer of book-covers, 1965—.

WRITINGS: (Translator) Jean Genet, Le Condemne a Morte, Poets Press, 1965; (editor and author of introduction) Diane di Prima, Earthsong, Poets Press, 1967; For a Growing Community, privately printed in Ceylon, 1967; John's Book, Poets Press, 1968. Regular contributor to Floating Bear.

WORK IN PROGRESS: Easy Over; Survival Essays; Praises, a book of poems; preparing "a practical text describing the basic rituals and practices of various Hindu and Buddhist schools"; research in Eastern religious philosophies, and iconography, including photographic studies of Hindu temples.

SIDELIGHTS: Marlowe has trained in Yoga for over six years in the United States, Ceylon, India, and Nepal. Another of his interests is photography, particularly portraits of American poets.††

* * *

MARNELL, William H. 1907-

PERSONAL: Born May 22, 1907, in Charlestown, Mass.; son of William H. (an educational supervisor) and Mary V. (Mahoney) Marnell; married Clare L. Martell (a former teacher), August 6, 1958. Education: Boston College, A.B., 1927; Harvard University, A.M., 1929, Ph.D., 1938. Politics: Independent. Religion: Roman Catholic. Home: 7 Cutter Lane, West Yarmouth, Mass. 02673.

CAREER: Boston Traveler, Boston, Mass., chief editorial writer, 1941-50; State College at Boston (now Boston State College), Boston, professor of English, 1950, chairman of department, 1957-1970. Director of Harvard Federal Savings Association, 1950-62. Member: Modern Language Association of America, College English Association, New England Classical Association, Clover Club (president, 1962).

WRITINGS: The First Amendment, Doubleday, 1964; Man-Made Morals, Doubleday, 1966; The Good Life of Western Man, Herder & Herder, 1971; Once Upon a Store, Herder & Herder, 1971; The Right to Know, Seabury, 1973; Vacation Yesterdays of New England, Seabury, 1975. Contributor of chapter on civil disobedience to Yearbook of Institute of Church and State, 1968.

SIDELIGHTS: William Marnell told *CA:* "I now punctuate writing with travel rather than with teaching. The ratio is a month in Europe to each six months at the typewriter."

* * *

MARSHALL, Hubert (Ray) 1920-

PERSONAL: Born January 16, 1920, in Chicago, Ill.; son of Harold L. (a publisher) and Lora (Roberts) Marshall; married Rachelle Lubar, June 21, 1947; children: Nancy, Jonathan. *Education:* Antioch College, A.B., 1947; University of North Carolina, Ph.D., 1950. *Home:* 611 Alvarado Row, Stanford, Calif. 94305. *Office:* Department of Political Science, Stanford University, Stanford, Calif. 94305.

CAREER: University of Florida, Gainesville, assistant professor of political science, 1950-52; U.S. Department of Interior, Office of the Secretary, Washington, D.C., program staff, 1952-53; Stanford University, Stanford, Calif., assistant professor, 1953-57, associate professor, 1957-65, professor of political science, 1965—. *Member:* American Political Science Association, American Society for Public Administration, Western Political Science Association.

WRITINGS: (Contributor) Ian Burton and Robert Kates, editors, *Readings in Resource Management and Conservation,* University of Chicago Press, 1965; (contributor) Allen Kneese and Stephen Smith, editors, *Water Research,* Johns Hopkins Press, 1966; (with Betty Zisk) *The Federal-State Struggle for Offshore Oil,* Bobbs-Merrill, 1966; (contributor) John B. Bunzel, editor, *Issues of American Public Policy,* Prentice-Hall, 1968; (contributor) C. S. Wallia, *Towards Century Twenty-One: Technology, Society and Human Values,* Basic Books, 1970.

WORK IN PROGRESS: Public accountability of the federal bureaucracy in its use of new decision-making techniques.

* * *

MARSHALL, Shirley E(velyn) 1925-

PERSONAL: Born April 27, 1925, in Brooklyn, N.Y.; daughter of Lawrence Roland and Jean (Corin) Repp; married William H. Marshall (a professor of English), August 20, 1949 (deceased); children: Judith, Susan, Barbara (deceased). *Education:* Beaver College, B.A., 1947. *Politics:* Liberal Democrat. *Religion:* Episcopalian. *Home:* 707 East Franklin St., Chapel Hill, N.C. 27514.

CAREER: Teacher in secondary schools, 1947-50. Research assistant and editorial assistant for *Theatre Annual,* 1947-51, *Annals of Mathematical Statistics, Annals of Probability,* and *Annals of Statistics,* 1969-75. Member of Chapel Hill Board of Aldermen, 1972—, Research Triangle Planning Commission, 1972-73, and Joint Regional Forum for North Carolina League of Municipalities, 1973—. Member of Policy Council of the North Carolina Women's Political Caucus.

WRITINGS: (Editor) *A Young American's Treasury of English Poetry,* Washington Square Press, 1967.

* * *

MARTIN, F(rancis) X(avier) 1922-

PERSONAL: Born October 2, 1922, in County Kerry, Ireland; son of Conor John (a medical doctor) and Catherine (Fitzmaurice) Martin. *Education:* Augustinian College, Dublin, Ireland, L.Ph., 1944; Gregorian University, Rome, Italy, B.D., 1951; University College of Dublin, National University of Ireland, M.A., 1952; Peterhouse, Cambridge, Ph.D., 1959. *Home:* Augustinian House of Studies, Dublin 14, Ireland. *Office:* Department of Medieval History, University College, National University of Ireland, Dublin 4, Ireland.

CAREER: Entered Augustinian Order, 1941, ordained Roman Catholic priest, 1952; National University of Ireland, University College of Dublin, Dublin, lecturer in history, 1959-62, professor of medieval history, 1962—. Visiting professor, Latrobe University, Melbourne, 1972—. Difinitor, Anglo-Irish Augustinian Province. Member of Irish Manuscripts Commission, 1963—. Trustee of National Library of Ireland, 1971—. *Member:* Royal Irish Academy, University Club (Dublin).

WRITINGS: The Irish Augustinians in Rome, edited by J. F. Madden, [Rome], 1956; (editor with J. A. Watt and J. B. Morrall, and contributor), *Medieval Studies Presented to Aubrey Gwynn, S.J.,* Three Candles, 1961; *Friar Nugent: A Study of Francis Lavalin Nugent (1569-1635), Agent of the Counter-Reformation,* Methuen, 1962; (editor) *The Irish Volunteers, 1913-15: Recollections and Documents,* Duffy, 1963; (contributor) Isidorus a Villapadierna, editor, *Miscellanea Melchor de Pobladura,* [Rome], 1964; (editor) *The Howth Gun-Running, 1914: Recollections and Documents,* Browne & Nolan, 1964; (contributor) Desmond Williams, editor, *The Irish Struggle, 1916-1926,* Routledge & Kegan Paul, 1966; (editor and contributor) *1916 and University College, Dublin,* Browne & Nolan, 1966; (editor with T. W. Moody, and contributor) *The Course of Irish History,* Mercier Press, 1967; (editor and contributor) *Leaders and Men of the Easter Rising: Dublin 1916,* Cornell University Press, 1967; (contributor) *Miscellanea Historiae Ecclesiasticae,* Volume II, [Louvain], 1967; *1916: Myth, Fact, and Mystery,* Studia Hibernica, 1968. (Editor with F. J. Byrne and contributor) *The Scholar Revolutionary: Eoin MacNeill, 1867-1945,* Irish University Press, 1973; (contributor) E. Kamenka, editor, *Nationalism: The Nature and Evolution of an Idea,* Australian National University Press, 1973; (contributor) B. O'Farrell, editor, *The Irish Parliamentary Tradition,* Gill & Macmillan, 1973; (contributor) C. Mayer and W. Eckermann, editors, *Scientia Augustiniana,* Augustinus-Verlag, 1975; (editor) M. J. Morrin, *John Waldby, c. 1315-c. 1372: Augustinian Preacher and Writer,* Augustinian Historical Institute, 1975; (editor with others) *History of Ireland,* nine volumes, Clarendon Press, 1976—.

Contributor to *International Bibliography of Historical Sciences, New Catholic Encyclopedia, Dictionnaire de Spiritualite;* contributor of articles on Medieval, Renaissance, Counter-Reformation, and modern Irish history to journals. General editor, Dublin Historical Association's "Medieval Series" (booklets). Co-editor, Telefis Eireann "Course of Irish History" programs, 1966; consulting editor, Telefis Eireann series of sixteen talks on the Anglo-Norman invasion of Ireland, 1969.

WORK IN PROGRESS: A biography of Giles of Viterbo, 1469-1532; a history of medieval Ireland, 1000-1600; editing, with A. B. Scott, *The Conquest of Ireland by Gerald of Wales, 1146-1223.*

* * *

MARTINSON, William D. 1924-

PERSONAL: Born May 15, 1924, in Olivia, Minn.; son of Albert William and Genevieve (Dean) Martinson; married

Lois J. Strommen, August 26, 1946; children: Julie Marie. *Education:* St. Cloud State College, B.A., 1949; University of Minnesota, M.A., 1950; Indiana University, Ed.D., 1955. *Religion:* Methodist. *Home:* 5189 Hitching Post Rd., Kalamazoo, Mich. 49001. *Office:* Department of Counseling and Personnel, Western Michigan University, Kalamazoo, Mich. 49008.

CAREER: Sears Roebuck Co., Yankton, S.D., assistant manager, 1948-49; Ball State Teachers College (now Ball State University), Muncie, Ind., instructor in education, 1950-53, acting dean of students, 1953-54; Indiana University, Bloomington, instructor, 1955-56, assistant professor of education and director of counseling, 1956-59; Ministry of Education, Bangkok, Thailand, visiting professor of education and consultant to colleges, 1959-61; Indiana University, associate professor, 1961-63, professor of education and director of counseling, 1963-70; Western Michigan University, Kalamazoo, professor of counseling and personnel, and head of department, 1970—. Visiting summer professor at North Texas State University, 1963, 1964. *Military service:* U.S. Navy, 1943-46.

MEMBER: American Psychological Association, American Personnel and Guidance Association (life member), American College Personnel Association (national executive council member), National Vocational Guidance Association, Association for Counselor Education and Supervision, Indiana College Personnel Association (past president), Phi Delta Kappa. *Awards, honors:* Research grant for work in Sierra Leone, 1965.

WRITINGS: (With James Coleman and Frieda Libaw) *Success in College,* Scott, Foresman, 1959, revised edition, 1967; *Education and Vocational Planning,* Scott, Foresman, 1959, revised edition, 1967; (with Robert Shaffer) *Student Personnel in Higher Education,* Center for Applied Research in Education, 1966; (contributor) Maurice Seay, editor, *Community Education,* Pendell, 1974. Also author of books, booklets, and articles, including *Guidance Services for Thailand,* translated by Thailand educators for publication in Thai, and written monographs published by United Presbyterian Church in the U.S.A., 1963-64; author of "Exploring the World of Work," 1967, and "Planning Beyond High School", 1970, series of long-playing records and tapes, published by H. W. Wilson. Contributor to education journals.

* * *

MARTYN, Kenneth A(lfred) 1926-

PERSONAL: Born July 23, 1926, in Windsor, Ontario, Canada; U.S. citizen; married, 1947; children: four. *Education:* Wayne State University, B.S., 1948; Stanford University, M.A., 1950, Ed.D., 1957. *Office:* American Learning Corp, 15562 Graham St., Huntington Beach, Calif. 92649.

CAREER: Junior high school teacher in Sunnyside, Wash., 1948-51; Palo Alto (Calif.) public schools, elementary teacher, 1950-51, elementary principal, 1951-55, director of personnel, research, and the gifted child program, 1955-57; California State University, Los Angeles, associate dean of instruction curriculum, 1957-58, dean of instruction, 1958-62, professor of special education, 1962—, acting vice-president, 1962-63, vice-president for academic affairs, 1966-70, director of Center for Studies in Special Education, 1970—; American Learning Corp, Huntington Beach, Calif., president, 1970—. Visiting lecturer or professor at other colleges in the West. Consultant to California Coordinating Council for Higher Education, 1965-66, Governor's

Commission on the Los Angeles Riots (McCone Commission), 1965-67, and President's Commission on Civil Disorders, 1967. *Member:* National Education Association, Omicron Delta Kappa.

WRITINGS: (With Robert Shutes) *Meeting Individual Differences: The Gifted Child,* National Press Books, 1955; *Education Study: A Report to the Governor's Commission on the Los Angeles Riots,* State of California, 1965, progress reports, 1966 and 1967; *Increasing Opportunities in Higher Education for Disadvantaged Students,* California Coordinating Council for Higher Education, 1966; (with Edward O. Guerrant) *Toward a More Perfect Union: A Book of Readings in American History for Academically Talented Junior High Students,* Heath, 1967; *Increasing Opportunities for Disadvantaged Students,* State of California, 1967. Contributor to education journals.†

* * *

MARTZ, William J. 1928-

PERSONAL: Born December 5, 1928, in Yonkers, N.Y.; son of Maurice H. and Mary (Hazel) Martz; married Nedra Dee Linville, June 20, 1953. *Education:* University of Rochester, B.A., 1950; Northwestern University, M.A., 1951; Yale University, Ph.D., 1957. *Office:* Department of English, Ripon College, Ripon, Wis. 54971.

CAREER: Middlebury College, Middlebury, Vt., instructor in English, 1955-58; Ripon College, Ripon, Wis., assistant professor, 1958-63, associate professor, 1963-65, professor of English, 1966—. *Member:* Modern Language Association of America, Midwest Modern Language Association.

WRITINGS—All published by Scott, Foresman, except as indicated: (Compiler) *Beginnings in Poetry,* 1965, 2nd edition, 1973; *The Distinctive Voice,* 1966; *The Achievement of Theodore Roethke,* 1966; *The Achievement of Robert Lowell,* 1966; *Shakespeare's Universe of Comedy,* David Lewis, 1971. General editor, "Modern Poets" series, for Scott, Foresman.

* * *

MARX, Wesley 1934-

PERSONAL: Born November 2, 1934, in Los Angeles, Calif.; son of Edward Howard (a business executive) and Kathleen (Woods) Marx; married Judith Mell, August 25, 1962; children: Christopher, Heather, Tyler. *Education:* Stanford University, B.A., 1956. *Home and office:* 18051 Butler, Irvine, Calif. 92664.

CAREER: Independent-Star News, Pasadena, Calif., reporter, 1960-61; free-lance writer, 1961—. Contributing editor, *Los Angeles Magazine,* 1961-64. Editorial consultant, General Dynamics, 1964; correspondent, *National Observer,* Los Angeles, 1965-66. Lecturer of marine affairs at universities including Louisiana State University, Notre Dame University, Oregon Institution of Marine Biology, Iowa State University, and California State University, Fullerton. Member of advisory board of Fund for the Environment, 1970—, and of California's Attorney General's Environmental Task Force. Consultant on marine elements to California Costal Zone Conservation Commission (south coast), 1974. *Military service:* U.S. Marine Corps, 1956-59; became first lieutenant. *Member:* American Civil Liberties Union, Friends of the University of California at Irvine Library, Pi Sigma Alpha. *Awards, honors:* Orange County Authors Award from University of California at Irvine

Friends of the Library, 1967, and James D. Phelan Award, 1968, both for *The Frail Ocean*.

WRITINGS: The Frail Ocean, Coward, 1967; *Man and His Environment: Waste*, Harper, 1971; *Oilspill*, Sierra Club, 1971; *The Protected Ocean*, Coward, 1972; *The Pacific Shore*, Dutton, 1974; *In Disaster's Way*, Coward, 1976. Articles reprinted in other volumes, mainly in urban readings. Contributor to *Atlantic Monthly, American Heritage, Nation, Audubon, Smithsonian, Bulletin of Atomic Scientists, UNESCO Courier, Maclean's Magazine*, and other periodicals and newspapers.

WORK IN PROGRESS: Writing on ocean conservation and ocean politics at the national and international level, including pollution, military exploitation, fishery management, and sea-bed habitation.

SIDELIGHTS: Marx accompanied a Scripps Institute expedition to whale breeding grounds in Baja, California, which led to an article in the *Atlantic Monthly*, "An Eviction of Whales," and also to his first book and a continuing interest in the ocean. He has since participated, as an observer, in a two-month oceanographic cruise to the eastern tropical Pacific sponsored by the U.S. Bureau of Commercial Fisheries. *The Frail Ocean* documents damage to beaches, estuaries, and the open sea by pollution, and urbanization, a subject on which he has testified before government bodies. He believes the issue of international cooperation in ocean management will determine whether or not nations can coexist peacefully on this planet.

Marx also told *CA* that he and his wife have participated in citizens' legal suits on local housing needs and on blocking conversion of Upper Newport Bay in southern California "into a luxury residential marina with peek-a-boo public access. The Bay will now be managed as a state wildlife reserve."

AVOCATIONAL INTERESTS: Photography, ocean body-surfing, and scuba diving in kelp sea forests off California.

* * *

MASEY, Mary Lou(ise) 1932-

PERSONAL: Born April 8, 1932, in Philadelphia, Pa.; daughter of William James (a professor of anatomy) and Ruth Virginia (Busse) Leach; married Jack Masey (a foreign service officer, U.S. Information Agency), December 27, 1959. *Education:* Ohio State University, B.A., 1954; additional study at University of Brussels, 1954-55, Columbia University, 1956-59, and George Washington University, 1962. *Home:* 2716 North St. N.W., Washington, D.C. 20007. *Office:* Dumbarton Oaks, 1703 32nd St. N.W., Washington, D.C. 20007.

CAREER: Writer for chidlren. Guide at two U.S. exhibitions in Soviet Union, the National Exhibition in Moscow, 1959, and the Graphic Arts-USA (exhibit of U.S. Information Agency) in Leningrad, Moscow, Alma-Ata, and Yerevan, 1963-64; currently secretary to the faculty, Dumbarton Oaks, Washington, D.C. Trustee, Harvard University, and Center for Byzantine Studies, Washington, D.C., 1971—. *Awards, honors:* Fulbright scholar at University of Brussels, 1954-55.

WRITINGS—Children's books: Branislav the Dragon (Junior Literary Guild selection), McKay, 1967; *Stories of the Steppes: Kazakh Folk Tales* (Junior Literary Guild selection), McKay, 1968; *The Picture Story of the Soviet Union*, McKay, 1971; *Teddy and the Moon*, Harvey House, 1972.†

MASLOWSKI, Stanley 1937-

PERSONAL: Born January 31, 1937, in Minneapolis, Minn.; son of Frank M. (a factory worker) and Mary (Kronior) Maslowski. *Education:* St. Paul Seminary, St. Paul, Minn., B.A., 1961, M.A., 1963. *Home and office:* Nativity of Mary Catholic Church, 9900 Lyndale Ave. S., Bloomington, Minn. 55420.

CAREER: Roman Catholic priest. Assistant pastor of churches in New Prague, Minn., 1963-65, and Bloomington, Minn., 1965—.

WRITINGS: What's the Good Word?, Bruce, 1967.

WORK IN PROGRESS: God Speaks Today, a book of contemporary homilies.††

* * *

MASON, David E(rnest) 1928-

PERSONAL: Born January 3, 1928, in Natchitoches, La.; son of Charles Culberson (an oil executive) and Marjorie (O'Bannon) Mason; married Betty D. Oxford, August 11, 1950 (divorced); married Alberta Martin (an art gallery director), July 2, 1964; children: (first marriage) David Ernest, Paul Alexander. *Education:* Louisiana State University, B.A., 1949; Southern Baptist Theological Seminary, B.D., 1952, M.Div., 1952; University of Corpus Christi, D.D., 1958; Syracuse University, M.A. (journalism), 1964. *Home:* 527 St. Philip, New Orleans, La. 70116. *Office:* 330 St. Charles Ave., New Orleans, La. 70130.

CAREER: Ordained to ministry of Baptist Church, 1950; pastor in Jefferson, Ga., 1953-55, Jonesboro, La., 1955-60, Alice, Tex., 1960-62; Laubach Literacy, Inc., Syracuse, N.Y., associate director, 1963-66, executive director, 1967-68; Supportive Services, Inc., New York, N.Y., chairman, 1969-72; Greater New Orleans Federation of Churches, executive director, 1972—. Director of Manpower Education Corp., 1968-69. Chairman of Wingspread Conference (association of international voluntary agencies). Vice-chairman of board of trustees, Zephyr Baptist Encampment. *Military service:* U.S. Army, Field Artillery, 1949; became second lieutenant. *Member:* Society for International Development, Association for Education in Journalism, American Management Association, Religious Public Relations Council, Baptist Writers Association, Fellowship of Religious Journalists (president, 1963-64), Southern Baptist Theological Seminary Alumni Association (president, 1957-58).

WRITINGS: Now Then . . ., Broadman, 1957; *The Charley Matthews Story*, Convention Press, 1958; *Eight Steps Toward Maturity*, Convention Press, 1962; *Apostle to the Illiterates*, Zondervan, 1966; *Frank C. Laubach —Teacher of Millions*, Denison, 1967; *Reaching the Silent Billion*, Zondervan, 1967; *The Compulsive Christian*, Zondervan, 1969. Also author of *The Vacant Hearted*, 1963. Contributor of about three hundred articles to religious and scholarly journals.

WORK IN PROGRESS: A manual on managing non-profit organizations.

SIDELIGHTS: David Mason has visited more than 70 of the nations where Laubach Literacy has done work in 313 languages. He pilots his own plane and hunts big game.

* * *

MASSEY, Reginald 1932-

PERSONAL: Born November 23, 1932, in Lahore, Punjab,

India (now in West Pakistan); son of J. M. (a government official) and Mary (Massey) Massey; married Jamila Chohan (a writer and actress), December 6, 1961; children: Marcus Iqbal Ravi. *Education:* University of the Punjab, B.A., 1956; Agra University, M.A., 1959. *Politics:* Liberal internationalist. *Religion:* "Humanist with Christian background." *Home:* 11 Mycenae Rd., Blackheath, London S.E. 3, England. *Agent:* Christopher Busby Ltd., 44 Great Russell St., London W.C. 1, England.

CAREER: Lecturer in literature at St. John's College, Agra, India, and Government College, Bilaspur, India, 1959-61; writer and journalist in India, then France, and now England, 1961—. *Member:* Society of Authors, Royal Society of Arts (fellow).

WRITINGS: (With S. P. Ranchan) *The Splintered Mirror,* P. R. Macmillan, 1960; (with Rina Singha) *Indian Dances,* Faber, 1967; (with wife, Jamila Massey) *The Immigrants,* InterCulture Associates, 1973; (with J. Massey) *The Music of India,* forward by Ravi Shankar, Kahn & Averill, 1975. Poetry anthologized in *Commonwealth Poems of Today,* J. Murray, and *Anthology of Commonwealth Verse,* Blackie & Son. Author of television scripts. Contributor to journals and newspapers.

WORK IN PROGRESS: A critical analysis with provisional title *Anatomy of India;* two filmscripts.

SIDELIGHTS: Reginald Massey speaks French, Hindustani, and Punjabi.

*   *   *

MASSIALAS, Byron G.   1929-

PERSONAL: Born November 1, 1929, in Athens, Greece; son of George and Helen (Hidiroglou) Massialas; married Sara Spentzos, June 9, 1957; children: George, James. *Education:* Greek Classical Gymnasium, diploma, 1948; Butler University, B.A. (cum laude), 1957; Indiana University, M.A., 1958, Ph.D., 1961. *Religion:* Greek Orthodox. *Home:* 2402 Killarney Way, Tallahassee, Fla. 32303. *Office:* Department of Education, Florida State University, Tallahassee, Fla. 32306.

CAREER: Indiana University, University High School, Bloomington, instructor in social studies, 1959-61; University of Chicago, Chicago, Ill., assistant professor of education, 1961-65; University of Michigan, Ann Arbor, associate professor of education and director of research training program in social science education, 1965-70; Florida State University, Tallahassee, professor of education, 1970—. *Member:* American Educational Research Association, American Political Science Association, American Association for the Advancement of Science, National Council for the Social Studies (chairman of international relations committee, 1966-67), Comparative Education Society, American Academy of Political and Social Science, Middle East Institute, Modern Greek Studies Association.

WRITINGS: (Editor and contributor) *The Indiana Experiments in Inquiry,* School of Education, Indiana University, 1963; (editor with A. M. Kazamias) *Crucial Issues in the Teaching of Social Studies,* Prentice-Hall, 1964; (with Kazamias) *Tradition and Change in Education,* Prentice-Hall, 1965; (editor with F. R. Smith) *New Challenges in the Social Studies,* Wadsworth, 1965; (with C. B. Cox) *Inquiry in Social Studies,* McGraw, 1966; (with Jack Zevin) *Creative Encounters in the Classroom,* Wiley, 1967; (editor with Cox) *Social Studies in the United States: A Critical Appraisal,* Harcourt, 1967; (editor) *Education and the*

Political System, Addison-Wesley, 1969; (with Nancy Sprague and Joseph Hurst) *Political Youth, Traditional Schools,* Prentice-Hall, 1972; *Social Issues Through Inquiry,* Prentice-Hall, 1975. Editor, Addison-Wesley's "Social and Behavioral Foundations of Education" series. Author of monographs; contributor to education journals.

WORK IN PROGRESS: Research on the school as a political laboratory; *A Project in Multicultural Learning: Greek-American Contributions to American Society.*

SIDELIGHTS: Byron Massialas speaks modern Greek, Serbian, and French.

*   *   *

MASTERS, Roger D(avis)   1933-

PERSONAL: Born June 8, 1933, in Boston, Mass.; son of Maurice (a travel agent) and S. Grace (Davis) Masters; married Judith Rubin (a social worker), June 6, 1956; children: Seth J., William A., Katherine R. *Education:* Harvard University, A.B. (summa cum laude), 1955; University of Chicago, M.A., 1958, Ph.D., 1961; Institut d'Etudes Politiques, auditor, 1958-59. *Office:* Department of Government, Dartmouth College, Hanover, N.H. 07355.

CAREER: Yale University, New Haven, Conn., instructor, 1961-62, assistant professor of political science, 1962-67; Dartmouth College, Hanover, N.H., associate professor, 1967-73, professor of government, 1973—. *Military service:* U.S. Army, 1955-57. *Member:* American Association for the Advancement of Science, Institute of Society, Ethics, and the Life Sciences (fellow, 1974), American Association of University Professors, American Political Science Association, Phi Beta Kappa. *Awards, honors:* Fulbright fellowship to France, 1958-59; Social Science Research Council fellowship, 1964-65; Guggenheim fellowship, 1967-68.

WRITINGS: (Editor and translator with wife, Judith R. Masters) *Rousseau's First and Second Discourses,* St. Martin's, 1964; *The Nation is Burdened: American Foreign Policy in a Changing World,* Knopf, 1967; *The Political Philosophy of Rousseau,* Princeton University Press, 1968. Chairman of editorial board of "Biology and Social Life" section, *Social Science Information.*

WORK IN PROGRESS: Study of the implications of recent research in ethology and sociobiology for political theory; analysis of the structure of political philosophy.

*   *   *

MASTERS, William H(owell)   1915-

PERSONAL: Born December 27, 1915, in Cleveland, Ohio; son of Francis Wynne and Estabrooks (Taylor) Masters; married Elisabeth Ellis, June 13, 1942 (divorced, 1970); married Virginia E. Johnson, January 7, 1971; children: (first marriage) Sarah Worthington, William Howell III. *Education:* Hamilton College, B.S., 1938; University of Rochester School of Medicine and Dentistry, M.D., 1943. *Politics:* Independent. *Religion:* Episcopalian. *Office:* Reproductive Biology Research Foundation, 4910 Forest Park Blvd., St. Louis, Mo. 63108.

CAREER: Licensed to practice medicine in Ohio, 1943, and Missouri, 1944; certified by American Board of Obstetrics and Gynecology, 1951. Washington University School of Medicine, St. Louis, Mo., instructor, 1947-49, assistant professor, 1949-51, associate professor of obstetrics and gynecology, 1951-63, director of Division of Reproductive Biology, 1960-63, associate professor of clinical obstetrics and gynecology, 1964-69, professor of clinical obstetrics and gynecology, 1969—; Reproductive Biology Research Foundation, St. Louis, director, 1964—. Associate obstetrician and gynecologist to St. Louis Maternity Hospital, Barnes Hospital, and Washington University Clinics; associate gynecologist to St. Louis Children's Hospital; consulting gynecologist to St. Louis City Infirmary and Salem (Ill.) Memorial Hospital. Member of board of directors of Family and Children's Service, Planned Parenthood Association, and Health and Welfare Council, all St. Louis. *Military service:* U.S. Navy, 1942-43; became lieutenant junior grade.

MEMBER: American Medical Association, Gerontological Society, American Fertility Society, Society for Study of Reproduction, International Society for Research in the Biology of Reproduction, International Fertility Association, Endocrine Society, American College of Obstetrics and Gynecology, Society for the Scientific Study of Sex, American Geriatrics Society, American Society of Cytology, Pan American Cancer Cytology Society, Pan-American Medical Association, Comprehensive Medical Society, Comprehensive Health Education, American Association for the Advancement of Science, Missouri State Medical Association, St. Louis Medical Society, New York Academy of Sciences, Eastern Missouri Psychiatric Society (honorary member), Alpha Omega Alpha, Alpha Sigma Lambda, Sigma Xi, Alpha Delta Phi, Bridle Spur Hunt Club, Racquet Club, St. Louis Club. *Awards, honors:* Paul H. Hoch Award of American Psychopathological Association, 1971; SIECUS Citation Award, 1972; Sc.D., Hamilton College, 1973.

WRITINGS—With Virginia E. Johnson: *Human Sexual Response*, Little, Brown, 1966; *Human Sexual Inadequacy*, Little, Brown, 1970; *The Pleasure Bond*, Little, Brown, 1975.

Contributor: *Sex in Our Culture*, Emerson, 1955; *Hormones and the Aging Process*, Academic Press, 1956; H. F. Conn, editor, *Current Therapy*, Saunders, 1958; C. G. Vedder, editor, *Problems of the Middle-Aged*, C. C Thomas, 1965.

Contributor with V. E. Johnson: G. W. Winokur, editor, *Determinants of Human Sexual Behavior*, C. C Thomas, 1963; C. W. Lloyd, editor, *Human Reproduction and Sexual Behavior*, Lea & Febiger, 1964; J. Money, editor, *Sex Research: New Developments*, Holt, 1965; F. A. Beach, editor, *Sex and Behavior*, Wiley, 1965; M. Diamond, editor, *Perspectives in Reproduction and Sexual Behavior*, Indiana University Press, 1968; M. Stuart, Editor, *The Emerging Woman: The Impact of Family Planning*, Little, Brown, 1970; H. S. Kaplan and C. J. Sager, editors, *Progress in Group and Family Therapy*, Brunner, 1972; J. Zubin and J. Money, editors, *Contemporary Sexual Behavior: Critical Issues in the 1970's*, Johns Hopkins Press, 1973; M. S. Calderone, editor, *Sexuality and Human Values*, Association Press, 1974. Also contributor of articles to medical journals.

SIDELIGHTS: The *New York Times* described Dr. William H. Masters as having "all the respectability of a banker ... The scientist who has performed some of the most radical daring research into human behavior is a church-going Episcopalian, ... and a man who describes himself as 'a little on the conservative side.'" Nevertheless, when questioned about the importance of sex education being taught in schools, Dr. Masters replied: "It should be taught in the church and in the school as well. I don't think you can teach it any one place and do it well.... The point is that parents can and should demonstrate to children the importance of an effective and outgoing sexual relationship."

The problems of sexual dysfunction and unhealthy attitudes towards sex are discussed in *Human Sexual Inadequacy*. Alan F. Guttmacher calls it "a powerful document in demonstrating the urgent necessity of sex education for youths as well as adults. Human sexual dysfunction has many causes, almost all psychological; most of these are preventable in an intelligent society concerned with humanizing its sex standards and practices. Masters and Johnson show that the most difficult and baneful sexual influence to be neutralized is religious dogmatism; ..." Martin Roth points out that a weakness of their study is that "their judgment appears to be coloured by that wishful kind of illusion according to which if only an adequate effort were mounted there would be a remedy for all forms of disturbed and maladaptive human conduct, no matter how complex, old and baffling, not in 20 years or a century but now."

Reviewing *Human Sexual Response*, Marion K. Sanders states: "Although their book is confined to stark physiological facts, they are well aware that human sexuality cannot be considered apart from its psychological and social implications. Over the years they have themselves worked closely with social agencies and with juvenile courts; they are compassionate people much more concerned with the human tragedies that result from distorted sexual concepts than with the mechanics of sex."

BIOGRAPHICAL/CRITICAL SOURCES: New Statesman, May 6, 1966; *New York Times Book Review*, May 29, 1966, July 12, 1970; *Book Week*, July 17, 1966; *Scientific American*, August, 1966; Ruth Brecher and Edward Brecher, editors, *An Analysis of "Human Sexual Response,"* Little, Brown, 1966; *Playboy* (interview), May, 1968; *Harpers*, May, 1968, August, 1970; *Newsweek*, June 10, 1968, May 4, 1970, August 24, 1970, February 22, 1971; *New York Times*, April 27, 1970; *Time*, May 25, 1970; *Listener*, June 18, 1970.

* * *

MATHESON, William H(oward) 1929-

PERSONAL: Born July 21, 1929, in Flint, Mich.; son of Howard and Helena (Matheson) Dolan. *Education:* University of Michigan, B.A., 1951, M.A., 1952, Ph.D., 1962. *Home:* 300 South Sappington Rd., Oakland, Mo. 63122. *Office:* Committee on Comparative Literature, Washington University, St. Louis, Mo. 63130.

CAREER: Instructor in French at Yale University, New Haven, Conn., 1953-58, and University of Michigan, Ann Arbor, 1958-59; Tufts University, Medford, Mass., instructor, 1959-62, assistant professor of French, 1962-64; Brandeis University, Waltham, Mass., assistant professor, 1964-66, associate professor of French, 1966-72; Washington University, St. Louis, Mo., professor of comparative literature and chairman of committee on comparative literature, 1972—. *Member:* Modern Language Association of America, Paul Claudel Society, Phi Beta Kappa, Delta Chi.

WRITINGS: Claudel and Aeschylus, University of Michigan Press, 1965; (translator and editor with Carl A. P. Ruck) *Selected Odes of Pindar*, University of Michigan Press, 1968.

WORK IN PROGRESS: European and Asian pastoral; nineteenth- and twentieth-century Japanese poetry under the impact of European poetry; an annotated edition of Claudel's *Soulier de satin;* translations from Maurice Sceve, and contemporary Japanese poetry.

*   *   *

MATHEWS, Harry   1930-

PERSONAL: Born February 14, 1930, in New York, N.Y. *Education:* Studied music at Princeton and Harvard Universities, and at L'Ecole Normale de Musique in Paris. *Home:* 35 Rue de Varenne, Paris, France 75007. *Agent:* Maxine Groffsky, 104 Greenwich Ave., New York, N.Y. 10014.

CAREER: Poet, novelist, and translator. Has lived abroad since 1952.

WRITINGS: The Conversions (novel), Random House, 1962; *Tlooth* (novel), Paris Review-Doubleday, 1966; *The Planisphere* (poetry), Burning Deck, 1974; *The Sinking of the Odradek Stadium and Other Novels,* Harper, 1975. Editor, with John Ashbery, Kenneth Koch, and James Schuyler, of *Locus Solus,* 1960-62. His poems have appeared in *Art and Literature, Hudson Review, Lugano Review, Paris Review, Quarterly Review of Literature,* and other publications.

SIDELIGHTS: Mathews' books may at first seem to be composed of popular "black humor" and absurdity, and have consequently left certain Establishment critics bewildered. Mathews, however, is a member of no particular avant garde group but rather, as a *Times Literary Supplement* reviewer notes, "a delightful original." His novels are games and riddles. In *The Conversions,* writes the *Times Literary Supplement,* "the anonymous narrator, in order to inherit [an] enormous fortune . . . has first to be the possessor of a ritual golden adze, and second to provide answers to three riddles: 'When was a stone not a king?' 'What was La Messe de Sire Fadevant?' and 'Who shaved the Old Man's Beard?'" And *Tlooth* is compounded of "faked documents, diagrams and word puzzles," writes Peter Buitenhuis. Yet there is always simplicity within these complexities of plot. As Ron Padgett writes concerning *Tlooth,* "actually [the plot] goes along with you as you read—it is, in fact, embarrassingly simple; as the dust jacket says, 'the picaresque account of a bizarre quest for revenge.' . . . The story quickly sweeps us into a fantastic horde of details which assume an importance as great as the characters and story, and one is pleasantly overwhelmed, or frightened, or vexed, or bored. All these are possible at once." The *Tri-Quarterly* reviewer adds: "[*Tlooth*'s] ingenious plot is that of travelogue-adventure in which all places are very much the same, even if they are called Afghanistan, Russia, India, Morocco; and in this respect, *Tlooth* very much descends from Apollinaire's *Zone* (1913) with its unbounded sense of literary space and the higher-nonsense fiction of Lewis Carroll and especially, the Frenchman Raymond Roussel." The difference between *Tlooth* and those contemporary novels that it seems to resemble is that *Tlooth* "is a *realized* example of absurd fiction, where the pointlessness of surface event fuses with the theme of underlying absurdity. Unlike previous American forays into the form . . . *Tlooth* has a neatness and brevity that is positively European (perhaps reflecting Mathews' own expatriate status); but it is precisely this difference in degree of elaboration that, to my mind, separates the major American works in the form from the minor."

Padgett further believes that "it would be unjust to describe *Tlooth* as experimental because Mathews has not only broken new ground, he's pieced it back together, and done so professionally. His writing has none of the rawness associated with experimental work, though it is often surprising and cruel. And as 'black humor,' it's a refreshing alternative" to the usual fare "because it's free of the hateful, if affectionate, irony that spoils that other kind of work for me. . . . But perhaps the most curious thing about *Tlooth* is that the nearer it comes to our earth, the nearer it approaches a convenient idea of reality, the more stupendous and terrifying it becomes." Roderick Cook also believes that, although the details rendered are "sometimes very savage and scabrous, . . . the book has nothing to do with modish sick humor." He considers the book to be, "for all its incidental excesses, fantasy, pure and simple." Mathews writes "almost soberly," Padgett adds, "so that when you tune in to the book's humor, it's so funny you think you must have made a mistake. Mathews' style is absolutely suave and debonnaire, . . . so between the style and the surface topic there festers a sort of groomed, fiendish hilarity."

Mathews' control of language and imagination is continually praised. While his method of telling a story is "quite sober, and the language plain, what actually happens is totally bizarre and wonderful," writes Cook. "The descriptions that are blandly handed to you show an imagination and an ingenuity that are often just astonishing." The *Times Literary Supplement* writer saw nothing "plain" about Mathews' language in *The Conversions:* "[The book] is fertile in linguistic skylarkings and fantastic invention. It is as exhilarating to read as a fireworks set-piece is to watch. . . . There is a genuine and delightful vein of poetry and small, ancient-marinerish spurts of entrancing ballad narrative." And, in *Tlooth,* according to Padgett, "there's another whole sense going on behind his words, a sort of phantom story. . . . Reading certain passages in *Tlooth* is like riding a bumper car through a dictionary whose definitions are askew," reminding some critics of Joyce's word frollicking. But, Padgett notes, "Mathews' use of language . . . couldn't be further from Joyce: instead of millions of colored lights whizzing past, the words in *Tlooth* tend to curl up at the edges and pop off the page. So in many ways the language becomes a mystery story in itself, in which the reader is the detective and sometimes the victim. . . . In the novel the title word is 'spoken' by a heaving mass of swamp mud. That's what happens to you when you read *Tlooth,* you are transformed into a horrible bog," and therein entertained.

BIOGRAPHICAL/CRITICAL SOURCES: Times Literary Supplement, September 14, 1962; *Nation,* September 29, 1962; *New Leader,* October 14, 1963; *New York Times Book Review,* October 30, 1966; *Harper's,* November, 1966; *Saturday Review,* November 12, 1966; *Village Voice,* January 26, 1967; *Tri-Quarterly,* winter, 1967; *New York Times,* May 18, 1975; Carolyn Riley, editor, *Contemporary Literary Criticism,* Volume VI, Gale, 1976.

*   *   *

MATHEWS, Jane DeHart   1936-

PERSONAL: Born December 31, 1936, in Asheville, N.C.; daughter of Horace M. (a businessman) and R. (Sherron) DeHart; married Donald G. Mathews (a professor of history), August 22, 1959. *Education:* Duke University, B.A., 1958, M.A., 1961, Ph.D., 1966. *Home:* Grey Bluff Trail, Box 1156, Chapel Hill, N.C.

CAREER: Educational Testing Service, Princeton, N.J.,

staff member of Test Development Division, 1962-64; Rutgers University, New Brunswick, N.J., instructor, 1964-66; assistant professor of history, 1966-68; director of research project, "Government Support of the Arts," for the Rockefeller Foundation, 1968-69; University of North Carolina, Greensboro, lecturer, 1970-71, associate professor of history, 1971—, lecturer in American Studies at Chapel Hill, 1970-71. *Member:* American Studies Association, American Historical Association, Organization of American Historians, Southern Historical Association.

WRITINGS: The Federal Theatre, 1935-1939: Plays, Relief, and Politics, Princeton University Press, 1967.

WORK IN PROGRESS: A study of Black involvement in the New Deal cultural projects, *Public Patronage and Black Culture.*

SIDELIGHTS: "Who now remembers the Federal Theatre of 1935-39?," Harold Clurman asks in his review of Mrs. Mathews' book. It was an exciting though not long-lived project and Clurman says that she has written "an objective but happily not entirely dispassionate book about it." John Rees Moore says that she "does not attempt to assess the aesthetic value of the project, [but] she makes abundantly clear that there is no easy distinction between propaganda and art, and no necessary conflict between documentary realism and imaginative staging." Thomas F. Marshall points out that "her material is a virtual mine of social and political information, and she catches skilfully the feeling of these last years of the Great Depression."

BIOGRAPHICAL/CRITICAL SOURCES: Nation, January 8, 1968; *South Atlantic Quarterly,* summer, 1968; *Kenyon Review,* Volume XXX, number 3, 1968.

* * *

MATILAL, Bimal Krishna 1935-

PERSONAL: Born June 1, 1935, in Calcutta, India; son of Hara Krishna and Parimal (Chakravorty) Matilal; married Karabi Chatterjee, May 8, 1958; children: Tamal, Anvita. *Education:* Calcutta University, B.A. (honors), 1954, M.A., 1956; Harvard University, A.M., 1963, Ph.D., 1965. *Religion:* Hinduism. *Office:* Department of Sanskrit and Indian Studies, University of Toronto, Toronto, Ontario, Canada.

CAREER: Government Sanskrit College, Calcutta, India, lecturer in Sanskrit literature, 1957-62; University of Toronto, Toronto, Ontario, assistant professor, 1965-67, associate professor, 1967-71, professor of Indian philosophy, 1971—. Visiting associate professor, University of Pennsylvania, 1969-70; visiting senior fellow, University of London, 1971-72; Shastri senior fellow, Shastri Indo-Canadian Institute, 1973. Delegate, Third International Congress for Logic, Methodology and Philosophy of Science, Amsterdam, 1967. *Member:* American Oriental Society, International Congress of Orientalists, Society for Asian and Comparative Philosophy (vice-president, 1973—), Asiatic Society (Calcutta). *Awards, honors:* University of Toronto overseas research fellowship.

WRITINGS: The Navya-Nyaya Doctrine of Negation, Harvard University Press, 1968; *Epistemology, Logic and Grammar in Indian Philosophical Analysis,* Mouton & Co. (Holland), 1971. Author of a radio play for All India Radio, 1961. Contributor to journals in Europe, Hawaii, and India. Founder, and editor, *Journal of Indian Philosophy,* 1970—.

WORK IN PROGRESS: With G. Bhattacharya, *A Dictionary of Indian Philosophical Terms; Myth and Mysticism: A Study of Modern Gurus and Ancient Indian Religions.*

BIOGRAPHICAL/CRITICAL SOURCES: The Contribution of Canadian Universities to an Understanding of Asia and Africa: A Bibliographical Directory of Scholars, 2nd edition, Canadian National Commission for UNESCO, 1967.

* * *

MATTHEWS, Desmond S. 1922-

PERSONAL: Born December 16, 1922, in Washington, D.C.; son of Richard Daniel (a postal employee) and Mary Matilda (Brennan) Matthews. *Education:* Educated at Georgetown University, Woodstock College, and at St. Mary's College, Kurseong, West Bengal, India; received B.A., 1948, M.A., 1950. *Home:* St. Joseph's College, Philadelphia, Pa. 19131.

CAREER: Roman Catholic priest of Society of Jesus (Jesuits), ordained in Kurseong, India, 1953; went to India in 1948, taught English and Hindi for two years, and then did missionary work, 1950-63, spending four years in the Himalayas and six among aboriginal tribes in the jungle; member of Jesuit mission and retreat band based in Philadelphia, Pa., 1963—, conductor of retreats in Canada, Europe, Southeast Asia, and the South Pacific. Part-time auxilary chaplain, U.S. Air Force.

WRITINGS: The Joyful Kingdom of Raj Anandpur, Maryknoll Publications, 1967. Contributor of articles, short stories, and essays to *America, Jesuit Missions,* and other Catholic journals.

WORK IN PROGRESS: Research on India, Ireland, and theological subjects.

SIDELIGHTS: Father Matthews speaks Hindustani, Sadani, and Mundari fluently, and is competent in French, Spanish, Latin, Greek. He traveled throughout India and through most of Burma during fifteen years in the Orient, and also has traveled in Europe, the Caribbean, Labrador, and Newfoundland (for the Air Force).

* * *

MATTHEWS, Elmora Messer 1925-

PERSONAL: Born August 15, 1925, in Temple, Tex.; daughter of Neal Edward (a plumber) and Esther (Partin) Messer; married George McAfee Matthews (a Methodist minister), October 24, 1944; children: Neal, Cort, Bruce. *Education:* North Texas State College (now North Texas State University), B.A., 1943; George Peabody College for Teachers, M.A., 1959; Vanderbilt University, Ph.D., 1964. *Religion:* Methodist. *Home address:* Route 3, Box 90, Georgetown, Tex. 78626.

CAREER: University of Texas, Austin, instructor in sociology, 1963-66. *Member:* American Sociological Association.

WRITINGS: Neighbor and Kin: Life in a Tennessee Ridge Community, Vanderbilt University Press, 1966.

AVOCATIONAL INTERESTS: Farm work, animals (Arabian horses and bloodhounds), music.

* * *

MATTHEWS, Joan E(thel) 1914-

PERSONAL: Born May 24, 1914, in Westcliff-on-Sea, Essex, England; daughter of Henry Theodore (headmaster of a school) and Ethel (Wren) Matthews. *Education:* University of Birmingham, Social Studies Diploma, 1935; London School of Economics and Political Science, B.Sc.,

1953; Western Reserve University (now Case Western Reserve University), special student at School of Applied Social Sciences, 1958. *Politics:* "In the main, a Labour Party supporter in general philosophy." *Religion:* Christian. *Home:* 1 Lobbs Wood Close, Humberstone, Leicestershire LE5 IDH, England. *Office:* National College for Training Youth Leaders, Humberstone Dr., Leicestershire LE5 ORG, England.

CAREER: Social worker in settlements, hospitals, and with youth groups in England, 1935-45, 1947-49, and at a displaced persons camp in Germany, 1945-47; University of Wales, University College of Swansea, Swansea, tutor in social administration and social work practice, 1953-61; National College for Training Youth Leaders, Leicestershire, England, principal lecturer in social studies and social group work, 1961—. Member of committee inquiring into the relationship of the Youth Service to the adult community, Youth Service Development Council. *Member:* British Sociological Association, Association of Social Workers, Association of Social Work Teachers.

WRITINGS: Working with Youth Groups, University of London Press, 1966, 2nd revised edition (with J. McAlistair Brew) published as *Youth and Youth Groups,* Faber, 1968; *Professional Training for Youth Work: Educational Methods at the National College for the Training of Youth Leaders, 1961-1970,* Youth Service Information Centre, 1972. Occasional contributor to *Case Conference, Youth Review, New Society,* and other journals.

AVOCATIONAL INTERESTS: Good company, travel abroad, holidays by the warm sea, music, painting.†

*   *   *

MATTHEWS, Stanley G(oodwin)   1924-
(Mark Goodwin)

PERSONAL: Born July 11, 1924, in Capreol, Ontario, Canada; came to United States, 1952; son of Stephen Archibald and Beatrice (Woolfrey) Matthews; married Edith Joan Lord (a teacher), July 24, 1943; children: Douglas Lord, Lois Elizabeth Ann (Mrs. Richard L. Douglass). *Education:* Sir George Williams University, B.A., 1947; Colgate Rochester Divinity School, B.D., 1953; Syracuse University, graduate study, 1953-54. *Politics:* Democratic. *Home:* Brinton Lake Club, Thornton, Pa. 19373.

CAREER: Part-time reporter for *Montreal Gazette* and *Montreal Daily Star,* Montreal, Quebec, during student days; copy editor on *Democrat & Chronicle,* Rochester, N.Y., 1946-48; education and religion reporter and columnist, "The Church Today," in *Montreal Daily Star,* 1948-52; ordained to ministry of United Presbyterian Church in the U.S.A., 1953; pastor in McGraw, N.Y., and copy editor on *Post-Standard,* Syracuse, N.Y., 1953-54; Ohio Council of Churches, Columbus, director of public relations, 1955-56; Religion In American Life, Inc., New York City, director of public relations, 1956-60; George Williams College, Chicago, Ill., director of information, 1961-64; United Presbyterian Church in the U.S.A., New York City, assistant director of information, Fifty Million Fund, 1964-66; Elwyn Institute, Elwyn, Pa., director of development, 1966-68; Publitex International Corp., New York City, president, 1968-70; Matthews Co., Thornton, Pa., president, 1969—; Corporate Marketing Services, Inc., Thornton, president, 1970—. Minister, and member of Presbytery of the Palisades. *Member:* Religious Public Relations Council (chairman of national awards committee, 1957-59; president of New York chapter, 1960), National Society of Fund Raisers, National School Public Relations Association, Delaware Valley Hospital Public Relations Association, Philadelphia Public Relations Association.

WRITINGS: The Night Pastors, Hawthorn, 1967; *Tested Methods in Fund Raising,* Publitex International Corp., 1969; (under pseudonym Mark Goodwin) *The Stripping of Appalachia,* Center for Science in the Public Interest, 1972. Contributor to *Canadian Business, Weedend* (Canada), Presbyterian periodicals, and newspapers, and to *Montreal Standard* under pseudonym Mark Goodwin. Correspondent, Religious News Service, 1945-60. Managing editor, *Northern Messenger* (Montreal), 1948-50, and *Christian Endeavor World* (Columbus), 1956; editor, *Protestant Church Life* (Montreal), 1949-50, Postgrad Association of Alumni, Sir George Williams University, 1950-52, and *Ohio Christian News,* 1955-56.

WORK IN PROGRESS: Three novels, *This Mortal Frame, Gaya,* and *The Extremist.*

AVOCATIONAL INTERESTS: Electronics, carpentry, photography.†

*   *   *

MAUREEN, Sister Mary   1924-

PERSONAL: Born August 6, 1924, in Portland, Me. *Education:* Notre Dame College, Baltimore, Md., B.A., 1950; Marquette University, graduate study, summer, 1950; Catholic University of America, graduate study, 1968—. *Politics:* Democrat. *Home:* 62 Newton St., Waltham, Mass. 02154.

CAREER: Roman Catholic nun. Missionary-teacher in Samoan Islands, for seven years; currently a clinical social worker.

WRITINGS: A Sense of Mission: Your Calling as a Nun, Rosen, 1967. Contributor of essays and articles to *Marist,* and of poetry to other magazines. Associate editor, *Marist.*

*   *   *

MAURER, Armand A(ugustine)   1915-

PERSONAL: Born January 21, 1915, in Rochester, N.Y.; son of Armand Augustine (an accountant) and Louise (Ribson) Maurer. *Education:* University of Toronto, B.A., 1938, M.A., 1943, Ph.D., 1947; Pontifical Institute of Mediaeval Studies, M.S.L., 1945. *Home:* 59 Queens Park Crescent, Toronto, Ontario, Canada.

CAREER: Ordained Roman Catholic priest of Congregation of St. Basil, 1945; University of Toronto, Toronto, Ontario, lecturer, 1946-55, assistant professor, 1955-58, professor of philosophy, 1962—; Pontifical Institute of Mediaeval Studies, Toronto, assistant professor, 1949-53, professor of philosophy, 1953—, religious superior, 1960-67. *Member:* Royal Society of Canada (fellow), Metaphysical Society of America, American Catholic Philosophical Association, Canadian Philosophical Association, Society pour l'Etude de la Philosophie Medieval. *Awards, honors:* Guggenheim fellowship, 1945-55.

WRITINGS: (Editor and translator) St. Thomas Aquinas, *On Being and Essence,* Institute of Mediaeval Studies, 1949; (editor and translator) Aquinas, *The Division and Methods of the Sciences,* Institute of Mediaeval Studies, 1953, 3rd edition, 1963; *Mediaeval Philosophy,* Random House, 1962; (with E. Gilson and T. Langan) *Recent Philosophy,* Random House, 1966; (translator) Master Eckhart, *Parisian Questions and Prologues,* Institute of Mediaeval Studies, 1975. Contributor to *Mediaeval Studies.*

MAVRODES, George I(on) 1926-

PERSONAL: Born November 23, 1926, in Albuquerque, N.M.; son of Tasso (a laborer) and Kathryne (Dardis) Mavrodes. *Education:* Attended University of New Mexico, 1941-42, New Mexico State University, 1942-43; Oregon State College (now Oregon State University), B.S., 1945; Western Baptist Theological Seminary, B.D., 1953; University of Oregon, M.A., 1960; University of Michigan, Ph.D., 1961. *Religion:* Christian. *Office:* Department of Philosophy, University of Michigan, Ann Arbor, Mich. 48104.

CAREER: Princeton University, Princeton, N.J., instructor in philosophy, 1961-62; University of Michigan, Ann Arbor, assistant professor, 1962-67, associate professor, 1967-73, professor of philosophy, 1973—. *Military service:* U.S. Navy, 1945-46. *Member:* American Philosophical Association, Mind Association.

WRITINGS: (Editor with Stuart C. Hackett) *Problems and Perspectives in the Philosophy of Religion,* Allyn & Bacon, 1967; *The Rationality of Belief in God,* Prentice-Hall, 1970; *Belief in God,* Random House, 1970. Contributor to philosophy and theology journals.

WORK IN PROGRESS: A book on the epistemology of religion.

AVOCATIONAL INTERESTS: Photography, hiking and camping.

*   *   *

MAYER, Thomas 1927-

PERSONAL: Born January 18, 1927, in Vienna, Austria; son of Felix (a businessman) and Helen (Pollatschek) Mayer; married Dorothy Harmison, April 7, 1963. *Education:* Queens College (now Queens College of the City University of New York), B.A., 1948; Columbia University, M.A., 1949, Ph.D., 1953. *Politics:* Democratic. *Home:* 3054 Buena Vista Way, Berkeley, Calif. 94708. *Office:* Department of Economics, University of California, Davis, Calif. 95616.

CAREER: U.S. Government, Washington, D.C., economist with Treasury Department, 1951-52, Office of Price Stabilization, 1952, and Department of Interior, 1953; West Virginia University, Morgantown, visiting assistant professor of economics, 1953-54, research associate, 1956; University of Notre Dame, Notre Dame, Ind., assistant professor of finance, 1954-56; Michigan State University, East Lansing, 1956-61, began as assistant professor, became professor of economics; University of California, Davis, professor of economics, 1962—, visiting associate professor at Berkeley, 1962-63. *Military service:* U.S. Army, 1945-46. *Member:* American Economic Association, Royal Economic Society (Britain), Econometric Society, Western Economic Association, American Finance Association.

WRITINGS: Consumer Loans of West Virginia Banks, Bureau of Business Research, West Virginia University, 1957; *Monetary Policy in the United States,* Random House, 1968; *Elements of Monetary Policy,* Random House, 1968; *Permanent Income, Wealth and Consumption,* University of California Press, 1971; (with D. C. Rowan) *Intermediate Macroeconomics,* Norton, 1972.

Contributor: *Private Financial Institutions,* Prentice-Hall, 1964; M. Mueller, editor, *Readings in Macroeconomics,* Holt, 1966; R. Thorn, editor, *Contemporary Monetary Theory and Policy,* Random House, 1966. Contributor of about thirty articles to economic and banking journals. Member of editorial board, *Journal of Economic Literature,* and *Journal of Monetary Economics.*

WORK IN PROGRESS: A monetary economics text; an article on credit allocations.

*   *   *

MAYOR, Stephen (Harold) 1927-

PERSONAL: Born July 24, 1927, in Manchester, England; son of Frank (an accountant) and Lucy (Cowan) Mayor; married Janet Newton (a teacher), July 25, 1953; children: Philip, Caroline, Eleanor, Paul. *Education:* University of Manchester, B.A., 1948, M.A., 1951, B.D., 1953, Ph.D., 1960; Oxford University, M.A., 1964. *Politics:* Labour Party. *Home:* 17 Norham Rd., Oxford, England. *Office:* Mansfield College, Oxford University, Oxford, England.

CAREER: Congregational minister in Chester, England, 1954-58, in Liverpool, England, 1958-64; Oxford University, Mansfield College, Oxford, England, Leverhulme research fellow, 1964—. Exchange minister in Ravena, N.Y., summer, 1967. *Military service:* Royal Air Force, 1948-50; became sergeant.

WRITINGS: Cheshire Congregationalism: A Brief History, Cheshire Congregational Union, 1956; *Problem-Books of the Old Testament,* Independent Press, 1961; *The Churches and the Labour Movement,* Independent Press, 1967; *The Lord's Supper in Early English Dissent,* Epworth Press, 1972. Contributor to religious journals.†

*   *   *

MAZRUI, Ali A(l'Amin) 1933-

PERSONAL: Surname is accented on the second syllable; born February 24, 1933, in Mombasa, Kenya; son of Al'Amin Ali (a judge, Islamic law) and Safia (Suleiman) Mazrui; married Molly Vickerman (a teacher), October 27, 1962; children: Jamal, Al'Amin Ali, Kim Abubakar (all sons). *Education:* University of Manchester, B.A. (with distinction), 1960; Columbia University, M.A., 1961; Oxford University, D.Phil., 1966. *Religion:* Islam. *Home:* 1517 Wells St., Ann Arbor, Mich. 48104. *Office:* Department of Political Science, 5601 Haven Hall, University of Michigan, Ann Arbor, Mich. 48109.

CAREER: University of East Africa, Makerere University College, Kampala, Uganda, lecturer, 1963-65, professor and head of political science, 1965-69, dean of Faculty of Social Sciences, 1967-73; University of Michigan, Ann Arbor, professor of political science, 1973—, member of faculty of Center for Afro-American and African Studies, 1976—. Visiting professor, University of Chicago, 1965; visiting research scholar, University of California, Los Angeles, summer, 1965; research associate, Center for International Affairs, Harvard University, 1965-66; visiting professor, Northwestern University, 1969, and University of Denver, 1969; Commonwealth visiting professor at University of London and University of Manchester, 1971; Dyason lecturer, Australian Institute of International Affairs, 1972. Guest lecturer in more than twenty countries since 1964, including United States, Canada, India, Sweden, England, Iraq, Australia, Singapore, and many countries in his home continent of Africa. Associate political analyst for British Broadcasting Corp., 1962-65, and Radio Uganda, 1964-65; special correspondent for Radio Tanzania, 1964-65. *Member:* International Political Science Association (member of executive committee, 1967-76; vice-president, 1970-73), International Sociological Association (steering committee member, military sociology, 1967-74), International Congress of Africanists (vice-president, 1967-73), International African Institute (member of executive committee, 1968—), African Association of Political Science (member of executive committee, 1973-76), World Order Models Project (director of African section, 1968—). *Awards, honors:* Rockefeller Foundation fellowship in United States, 1960-61, and research grant, 1965-66; National Unity Book prize, Northwestern University, 1969; Center for Advanced Study in Behavioral Sciences fellowship, Stanford University, 1972-74; Hoover Institution on War, Revolution, and Peace fellowship, Stanford University, 1973-74; International Development Research Center research grant, 1975.

WRITINGS: Towards a Pax Africana, University of Chicago Press, 1967; *The Anglo-African Commonwealth,* Pergamon, 1967; *On Heroes and Uhuru-Worship,* Longmans, Green, 1967; *Ancient Greece in African Political Thought* (an inaugural lecture), East African Publishing House, 1967; *Violence and Thought: Essays on Social Tensions in Africa,* Humanities, 1969; (editor with Robert I. Rothberg) *Protest and Power in Black Africa,* Oxford University Press, 1970; *The Trial of Christopher Okigbo* (novel), Heinemann, 1971, Third Press, 1972; *Cultural Engineering and Nation-Building in East Africa,* Northwestern University Press, 1972; (with Hasu H. Patel) *Africa in World Affairs: The Next Thirty Years,* Third Press, 1973; *World Culture and the Black Experience,* University of Washington Press, 1974; *Who Are the Afro-Saxons?: The Political Sociology of the English Language,* Mouton & Co., 1975; *Soldiers and Kinsmen in Uganda: The Making of a Military Ethnocracy,* Sage, 1975; *A World Federation of Cultures: An African Perspective,* Free Press, 1976.

Contributor of articles to *International Affairs* (London), *American Political Science Review, Africa Quarterly* (New Delhi), *Ethics* (Chicago), and some twenty other journals in Africa, Europe, United States, and Asia; also has published some poetry, short stories, and literary criticism. Associate editor, *Transition,* 1965-73; member of editorial board, *Encyclopaedia Africana,* 1964—, *Makerere Journal,* 1964-67, *Journal of African and Asian Studies,* 1966—, *Mawazo,* 1967-73, *Comparative Political Studies,* 1967—, and *East African Law Journal,* 1967—.

WORK IN PROGRESS: Political Deviancy and the Politics of Social Deviancy; Africa, the Black Diaspora and the Third World in International Politics.

*   *   *

MBITI, John S(amuel) 1931-

PERSONAL: Born November 30, 1931, in Kitui, Kenya; married Verena Siegenthaler (a social worker and teacher), May 15, 1965; children: Samuel Kyeni, Maria Mwende, Esther Mwikali, Anna Kavata. *Education:* Makerere University College, University of East Africa (now Makerere University), B.A., 1953; Barrington College, A.B., 1956, Th.B., 1957; Cambridge University, Ph.D., 1963. *Home address:* P.O. Box 80, Kitui, Kenya, East Africa. *Office:* Ecumenical Institute, CH 1298 Celigny, Switzerland.

CAREER: Anglican priest. Teacher Training College, Kangundo, Kenya, teacher, 1957-59; Selly Oak Colleges, Birmingham, England, visiting William Paton Lecturer, 1959-60; St. Michael's Church, St. Albans, England, curate, 1963-64; Makerere University, Kampala, Uganda, 1964-74, began as lecturer in New Testament and African

religions and philosophy, became professor of theology and comparative religion, and head of department; Ecumenical Institute Bossey, Geneva, Switzerland, director, 1974—. Visiting lecturer, University of Hamburg, 1966-67; Harry Emerson Fosdick Visiting Professor, Union Theological Seminary, New York, N.Y., 1972-73. *Member:* Studiorum Novi Testamenti Societas. *Awards, honors:* L.H.D., Barrington College, 1973.

WRITINGS: Mutunga na Ngewa Yake, Thomas Nelson, 1954; (translator into Kikamba) *Treasure Island,* East African Literature Bureau, 1954; *English-Kamba Vocabulary,* East African Literature Bureau, 1959; (editor) *Akamba Stories* (collection of folktales), Oxford University Press, 1966; *African Religions and Philosophy,* Praeger, 1969; *Poems of Nature and Faith,* East African Publishing House, 1969; *Concepts of God in Africa,* Praeger, 1970; *New Testament Eschatology in an African Background: A Study of the Encounter between New Testament Theology and African Traditional Concepts,* Oxford University Press, 1971; *The Crisis of Mission in Africa,* Uganda Church Press (Kampala), 1971; *The Voice of Nine Bible Trees,* Uganda Church Press, 1973; *Love and Marriage in Africa,* Longman, 1973; *Death and the Hereafter in the Light of Christianity and African Religion,* Makerere University Printery, 1974; *Introduction to African Religion,* Praeger, 1975; *The Prayers of African Religion,* S.P.C.K., 1975, Orbis, 1976. Contributor of poems and articles to anthologies and periodicals in Europe, Africa, India, Japan, and the United States.

SIDELIGHTS: John S. Mbiti speaks Kikamba, Swahili, Gikuyu, French, and German. He reads New Testament Greek and a little Old Testament Hebrew.

*   *   *

McALEER, John J(oseph) 1923-

PERSONAL: Born August 29, 1923, in Cambridge, Mass.; son of Stephen Ambrose (a lawyer) and Helen Louise (Collins) McAleer; married Ruth Ann Delaney, December 28, 1957; children: Mary Alycia, Saragh Delaney, Seana Caithlin, John Joseph, Jr., Paul Bernard, Andrew Stephen Charles. *Education:* Boston College, A.B., 1947, M.A., 1949; Harvard University, Ph.D., 1955. *Politics:* Democrat. *Religion:* Roman Catholic. *Home:* 121 Follen Rd., Lexington, Mass. 02173. *Agent:* Ann Elmo Agency, Inc., 52 Vanderbilt Ave., New York, N.Y. 10017. *Office:* 435 Carney Faculty Center, Boston College, Chestnut Hill, Mass. 02167.

CAREER: Boston College, Chestnut Hill, Mass., instructor, 1948-50; Boston College, instructor, 1955-56, assistant professor, 1956-62, associate professor, 1962-65, professor of English, 1965—. *Boston Globe,* daily feature writer, 1959—. *Military service:* U.S. Army, 1943-46; served in North Africa and China-Burma-India theater; became sergeant. *Member:* Modern Language Association of America, National Council of Teachers of English, Thoreau Society, American Association of University Professors. *Awards, honors:* Harvard Prize Foundation fellow, 1952-53; Dexter traveling fellow (Harvard University) in Europe, 1954; faculty fellow, Boston College, 1964-65; Catholic Press Association Award for best critical article, 1969.

WRITINGS: Ballads and Songs Loyal to the Hanoverian Succession, University of California Press, 1962; (contributor) Warren Walker, *Leatherstocking and the Critics,* Scott, Foresman, 1965; *Theodore Dreiser: An Introduction and Interpretation,* Holt, 1968; *Artist and Citizen Thoreau,*

American Transcendental Society, 1971; (editor) *Theodore Dreiser's Notes on Life,* University of Alabama Press, 1974; *The Matter of the Red Man in American Literature,* American Transcendental Society, 1975; *An American Original: Rex Stout, Creator of Nero Wolfe* (biography), Little, Brown, 1976.

Contributor to *The New Catholic Encyclopedia;* a score of poems and short stories have appeared in literary magazines, and articles in about thirty periodicals, including *Insula* (Madrid), *English Studies* (Amsterdam), *Modern Drama, Kiyo* (Japan), *Month* (London), *Walt Whitman Review,* and *Texas Studies in Literature and Language.* Member of reviewing staff, *Thought, America, Best Sellers, Books Abroad, Drama Survey, Literature East and West,* and *Boston Globe.* Contributing editor, *Best Sellers,* 1967—; associate editor of *Dreiser Newsletter* and *Shakespeare Newsletter.*

SIDELIGHTS: McAleer is competent in French, German, Latin, and Urdu.

* * *

McAULEY, James J. 1936-

PERSONAL: Born January 8, 1936, in Dublin, Ireland; son of James Noel (an airline pilot) and Maureen (McCarthy) McAuley; married Almut Nierentz, 1968; children: (previous marriage) James Michael, Anthony Joseph, Kevin Barry; (second marriage) Owen, Rory Garth. *Education:* University College of Dublin, National University of Ireland, B.A. (with honors), 1962; University of Arkansas, M.F.A., 1971. *Home:* 624 Lincoln, Cheney, Wash. 99004. *Office:* Department of English, Eastern Washington State College, Cheney, Wash.

CAREER: Electricity Supply Board, Dublin, Ireland, clerical officer, 1954-59, editorial work, 1959-66. *Kilkenny Magazine,* Kilkenny, Ireland, art critic, 1960-66; *Hibernia National Review,* Dublin, arts consultant, 1964-66; *Irish Times,* Dublin, book reviewer, 1964-66; Municipal Gallery of Modern Art, Dublin, lecturer in contemporary art, 1965-66; Lycoming College, Williamsport, Pa., assistant professor of English, 1968-70; Eastern Washington State College, Cheney, Wash., assistant professor, 1970-73, associate professor of English, 1973—, and director of creative writing program. Visiting lecturer, University of Victoria, 1975. *Member:* College English Association. *Awards, honors:* National Endowment for the Arts fellowship, 1972.

WRITINGS: Observations (poetry), Mount Salus Press, 1960; *A New Address* (poetry), Dufour, 1965; "The Revolution" (verse satire), produced at Lantern Theatre, Dublin, and Lyric Theatre, Belfast, 1966; *Draft Balance Sheet* (poetry), Oxford University Press, 1970; *After the Blizzard,* University of Missouri Press, 1975. Poetry has also been published in *Crazy Horse, Malahat Review, Poetry Northwest, Penguin Anthology of Irish Verse, Faber Anthology of Irish Verse,* other anthologies and periodicals. Associate editor, *Poetry Ireland,* 1962-66.

WORK IN PROGRESS: A novel, *Once Removed;* two long verse works.

* * *

McCALL, George J(ohn) 1939-

PERSONAL: Born April 11, 1939, in Monterey Park, Calif.; son of Weldon George (a truck driver) and Nina Faye (Callahan) McCall; married Michal Moses (a sociologist), June 8, 1964; children: Sarah Jane. *Education;* University of Iowa, B.A., 1961; Indiana University, graduate study, summer, 1961; Harvard University, M.A., 1963, Ph.D., 1965. *Politics:* Democrat. *Religion:* Unitarian Universalist. *Home:* 8250 Glen Echo Dr., St. Louis, Mo. 63121. *Office:* Department of Sociology, University of Missouri, St. Louis, Mo. 63121.

CAREER: Iowa City Press-Citizen, Iowa City, Iowa, sportswriter, 1957-60; University of Iowa, Iowa City, instructor in sociology, 1963-64; University of Illinois, Urbana, instructor, 1964-65, assistant professor, 1965-67, associate professor, 1967-68, Chicago Circle campus, associate professor, 1967-70, professor of sociology, 1970-72; University of Missouri—St. Louis, professor of sociology, 1972—, chairman of department, 1972-74. Visiting lecturer, University of Wisconsin—Madison, 1972. *Member:* American Sociological Association, Society for the Study of Social Problems, Midwest Sociological Society, Phi Beta Kappa, Alpha Delta Sigma. *Awards, honors:* Woodrow Wilson fellowship; National Science Foundation fellowship; National Institute of Mental Health, Visiting Scientist Award.

WRITINGS: (With J. L. Simmons) *Identities and Interactions,* Free Press, 1966; (with Simmons) *Issues in Participant Observation,* Addison-Wesley, 1969; (editor) *Social Relationships,* Aldine, 1970; *Observing the Law: Applications of Field Methods to the Study of the Criminal Justice System,* National Institute of Mental Health, 1975.

Contributor: H. S. Becker, editor, *The Other Side,* Free Press of Glencoe, 1964; L. A. Dexter, D. M. White, editors, *People, Society, and Mass Communications,* Free Press of Glencoe, 1964; G. P. Stone, H. A. Farberman, editors, *Social Psychology Through Symbolic Interaction,* Ginn, 1970; *Society Today,* CRM Books, 1971; K. Thompson, J. Tunstall, editors, *Sociological Perspectives,* Penguin, 1971; J. M. Henslin, editor, *Down to Earth Sociology,* Free Press, 1972; T. L. Huston, editor, *Foundations of Interpersonal Attraction,* Academic Press, 1974. Contributor to professional journals.

WORK IN PROGRESS: Social Psychology, completion expected in 1978.

SIDELIGHTS: McCall has some knowledge of Russian, Finnish, German, and Spanish. *Avocational interests:* Animal behavior (especially wolves and primates), folklore (Negro blues, Russian, Finnish), neuropsychology, ecology, sports, camping, and fishing.

* * *

McCARTHY, Dennis John 1924-

PERSONAL: Born October 14, 1924, in Chicago, Ill.; son of Dennis Francis (a businessman) and Kathryn (Kreutzer) McCarthy. *Education:* St. Louis University, A.M., 1951; Institut Catholique de Paris, S.T.D., 1962; Pontifical Biblical Institute, Rome, Italy, S.S.L., 1963. *Office:* Pontifical Biblical Institute, Via della Pilotta 25, 00187 Rome, Italy.

CAREER: Roman Catholic priest of Jesuit order (S.J.). St. Louis University, Divinity School, St. Louis, Mo., assistant professor, 1963-66, associate professor of Biblical language and literature and departmental chairman, 1966-69; Pontifical Biblical Institute, Rome, Italy, Ordinary professor of Old Testament Exegesis, 1969—.

WRITINGS: Treaty and Covenant, Pontifical Biblical Institute (Rome), 1963; (editor) *Modern Biblical Studies,* Bruce, 1967; *Kings and Prophets,* Bruce, 1968; *Old Testament Covenant,* John Knox, 1972.

McCLELLAN, James (Paul) 1937-

PERSONAL: Born June 26, 1937, in Erie, Pa.; son of James C. (a forester) and Florence S. (Turner) McClellan; married Mary J. Guy (a teacher), August 29, 1959; children: Graham Eliot, Susannah Swift. *Education:* University of Virginia, student, 1955-57, Ph.D., 1964; University of Alabama, B.A., 1960; *Religion:* Episcopalian. *Home:* 8611 Crestview Dr., Fairfax, Va. 22030. *Office:* Dirksen Senate Office Building, Washington, D.C. 20510.

CAREER: University of Alabama, Tuscaloosa, assistant professor of political science, 1964-65; Emory University, Atlanta, Ga., assistant professor of political science, 1965-69; Hampden-Sydney College, Hampden-Sydney, Va., associate professor of government, 1969-74; legislative assistant to U.S. Senator Jesse Helms, 1974—. *Military service:* U.S. Marine Corps Reserve, 1958-64. *Member:* American Political Science Association, Organization of American Historians, Southern Political Science Association, Philadelphia Society.

WRITINGS: (With Russell Kirk) *The Political Principles of Robert A. Taft,* Fleet, 1967; *Joseph Story and the American Constitution,* University of Oklahoma Press, 1971.

WORK IN PROGRESS: The Reform and Reorganization of Congress, 1946-1975.

SIDELIGHTS: McClellan and his co-author, Russell Kirk, in *The Political Principles of Robert A. Taft* present, as Felix Morley says, "a framework around which any definitive life story of the Senator—none that is adequate has yet appeared—will have to be built." He feels that the study is objective, unsentimental, and unbiased. M. Stanton Evans points out that Kirk and McClellan "demonstrate that even in a time of drift and compromise (perhaps especially in such a time), integrity retains its luster."

BIOGRAPHICAL/CRITICAL SOURCES: National Review, April 9, 1968; *University Bookman,* summer, 1968.

*   *   *

McCLELLAND, Lucille Hudlin 1920-

PERSONAL: Born May 31, 1920; daughter of Edward W. and Myrtle (Johnson) Hudlin; married Norman Ross (deceased); married Charles McClelland, July 11, 1964; children: (first marriage) Norman, Margaret, Myrtle, Vicki, Anthony, Lorna. *Education:* Lincoln School for Nursing, Bronx, N.Y., R.N., 1944; Washington University, St. Louis, Mo., B.S., 1959; St. Louis University, M.S.N.E., 1961, Ph.D., 1967. *Religion:* Roman Catholic. *Home:* 27 Windermere Pl., St. Louis, Mo. *Office:* Southern Illinois University, Edwardsville, Ill.

CAREER: Bellevue Hospital, New York, N.Y., ward instructor, 1942-45; Board of Education, East St. Louis, Ill., instructor in practical nursing, 1956-59; St. Mary's Hospital, East St. Louis, clinical instructor, 1956-59; Jacksonville State Hospital, Jacksonville, Ill., nursing administration, 1963-64; St. Louis University, St. Louis, Mo., lecturer in department of education, 1966-67; Southern Illinois University, Edwardsville, associate professor, 1967, dean of School of Nursing, 1968-75, educational consultant and counselor, 1976—. Psychiatric nurse consultant to Illinois Department of Mental Health, 1963-64, and State Psychiatric Institute, Chicago, Ill., 1964-66. *Member:* St. Louis Council on Human Relations. *Member:* American Nurses Association, National League for Nursing, American Association of University Professors, American Association of University Women, Illinois Nursing Association.

WRITINGS: Textbook for Psychiatric Technicians, Mosby, 1967, 2nd edition, 1971. Author of film script, "The Remotivation Technique," Illinois State Department of Mental Health Film Library, 1963. Contributor to *Journal of Personality and Social Psychology.*

*   *   *

McCLURE, Michael 1932-

PERSONAL: Born October 20, 1932, in Marysville, Kan.; wife's name, Joanna; children: daughter. *Home:* 264 Downey St., San Francisco, Calif. 94117.

CAREER: Was a falcon trainer and a teacher of English and drama; currently writer-in-residence, American Conservatory Theatre, San Francisco, Calif. *Awards, honors:* Two Obie Awards, for "The Beard"; National Endowment for the Arts grants, 1967, 1974-75; Guggenheim fellow, 1974; Magic Theater Drama award, 1974; Rockefeller fellowship for theater, 1975.

WRITINGS: Meat Science Essays, City Lights, 1963, revised edition, Dave Hazelwood, 1967; (with Frank Reynolds) *Freewheelin' Frank, Secretary of the Angels* (about the Hell's Angels), Grove, 1967; *Little Odes, Poems, and a Play, The Raptors,* Black Sparrow Press, 1969; *The Mad Club* (novel), Bantam, 1970; *The Adept* (novel), Delacorte, 1971; *Gargoyle Cartoons* (plays; contains "The Shell," "The Pansey," "The Meatball," "The Bow," "Spider Rabbit," "Apple Glove," "The Sail," "The Dear," "The Authentic Radio Life of Bruce Conner and Snoutburbler," "The Feather," "The Cherub"), Delacorte, 1971; *The Mammals* (plays; contains "The Blossom," "The Feast," "Pillow") Cranium Press, 1972; "Wolf Net" (booklength essay) published in *Io,* spring, 1974.

Poetry: *Passage,* Jargon Society, 1956; *Peyote Poem* (broadside), Semina, 1958; *For Artaud,* Totem Press, 1959; *Hymns to St. Geryon, and Other Poems,* Auerhahn, 1959; *Dark Brown,* Auerhahn, 1961; *The New Book: A Book of Torture,* Grove, 1961; *Ghost Tantras,* privately printed, 1964; *Two for Bruce Conner,* Oyez, 1964; *Love Lion, Lioness* (poem poster), Oyez, 1964; *Double Murder! Vahrooooooohr!,* Semina, 1964; *Thirteen Mad Sonnets,* [Milan, Italy], 1965; *Poisoned Wheat,* Oyez, 1965; *Unto Caesar,* Dave Haselwood, 1965; *Dream Table,* Dave Haselwood, 1965; (with Bruce Connor) *(The Mandala Book),* Dave Haselwood, 1966; *Hail Thee Who Play: A Poem,* Black Sparrow Press, 1968; *Love Lion Book,* Four Seasons Foundation, 1968; *The Sermons of Jean Harlow and the Curses of Billy the Kid,* Four Seasons Foundation, 1969; *The Surge: A Poem,* Frontier Press (Columbus, Ohio), 1969; *Lion Fight,* Pierrepont Press, 1969; *Star,* Grove, 1970; *99 Theses,* Tansy Press, 1972; *The Book of Joanna,* Sandollar Press, 1973; *Rare Angel,* Black Sparrow Press, 1974; *September Blackberries,* New Directions, 1974; *Solstice Blossom,* Arif, 1974.

Plays: "The Feast" (first produced in San Francisco at Batman Gallery, December 22, 1960), published in *The Mammals,* Cranium Press, 1972; "The Growl" (first produced in Berkeley at Magic Theater, 1970), published in *Evergreen Review,* April-May, 1964; *The Beard* (first produced in San Francisco at The Committee, August, 1965; produced Off-Broadway at Evergreen Theater, October 16, 1967; produced on West End at Royal Court Theatre, 1968), Oyez, 1965, revised edition, Grove, 1967; *The Blossom; or Billy the Kid* (first produced in New York at American Theatre for Poets, 1964), Great Lakes Books,

1967, published in *The Mammals,* Cranium Press, 1972; *The Shell* (first produced with other plays under program title "The Brutal Brontosaurus," in San Francisco at Magic Theater, 1970), Cape Goliard, 1968, published in *Gargoyle Cartoons,* Delacorte, 1972.

The Cherub (first produced in Berkeley at Magic Theater, 1969; produced with other plays under program title "Gargoyle Cartoons," in Philadelphia at Open Theatre, 1970), Black Sparrow Press, 1970, published in *Gargoyle Cartoons,* Delacorte, 1971; "The Pansey" (first produced with other plays under program title "The Charbroiled Chinchilla," in Berkeley at Magic Theater, 1969; produced in London, 1972), published in *Gargoyle Cartoons,* Delacorte, 1971; "The Meatball" (first produced with other plays under program title "The Brutal Brontosauris," in San Francisco at Magic Theater, 1970; produced under program title "Gargoyle Cartoons," in Philadelphia at Open Theatre, 1970; produced in London, 1971), published in *Gargoyle Cartoons,* Delacorte, 1971; "Spider Rabbit" (first produced with other plays under program title "The Charbroiled Chinchilla," in Berkeley at Magic Theater, 1969; produced under program title "The Brutal Brontosauris," in San Francisco at Magic Theater, 1970; produced under program title "Gargoyle Cartoons," in Philadelphia at Open Theatre, 1970; produced in London, 1971), published in *Gargoyle Cartoons,* Delacorte, 1971; "Apple Glove" (first produced with other plays under program title "The Brutal Brontosauris," in San Francisco at Magic Theater, 1970), published in *Gargoyle Cartoons,* Delacorte, 1971; "The Authentic Radio Life of Bruce Conner and Snoutburbler" (first produced with other plays under program title "The Brutal Brontosauris," in San Francisco at Magic Theater, 1970; produced as "The River, or the Authentic Radio Life of Bruce Conner and Snoutburbler," under program title "Gargoyle Cartoons," in Philadelphia at Open Theatre, 1970), published in *Gargoyle Cartoons,* Delacorte, 1971; "The Bow" (produced with other plays under program title "Gargoyle Cartoons," in Philadelphia at Open Theatre, 1970), published in *Gargoyle Cartoons,* Delacorte, 1971; "The Sail," published in *Gargoyle Cartoons,* Delacorte, 1971; "The Dear," published in *Gargoyle Cartoons,* Delacorte, 1971; "The Feather" (first produced with other plays under program title "Polymorphous Pirates," in Berkeley at Magic Theater, 1972), published in *Gargoyle Cartoons,* Delacorte, 1971.

"Pillow" (first produced in New York at Poets Theatre, 1961), published in *The Mammals,* Cranium Press, 1972; "The Pussy," first produced with other plays under program title "Polymorphous Pirates," in Berkeley at Magic Theater, 1972, produced with "The Button," and "Chekov's Grandmother," in New York, 1973; "The Button," first produced with other plays under program title "Polymorphous Pirates," in Berkeley at Magic Theater, 1972, produced with "The Pussy" and "Chekov's Grandmother," in New York, 1973; "Chekov's Grandmother; or, The Sugar Wolves," produced with "The Pussy," and "The Button," in New York, 1973; "McClure on Toast," first produced in Los Angeles at Company Theater, 1973; "Music Piece" (radio play; produced on KPFA, 1974), produced in Berkeley at Magic Theater, 1974; "The Derby" (musical), first produced in Los Angeles at Company Theater, 1974; "Gorf" (musical; first produced in San Francisco at Magic Theater, 1974), published in *Coevolution Quarterly,* 1974; "One Acts by Michael McClure," produced in New York at Theatre Genesis, 1974.

Omnibus plays: "The Charbroiled Chinchilla" (includes "The Pansy," "The Meatball," "Spider Rabbit"), produced in Berkeley at Magic Theater, 1969; "The Brutal Brontosauris" (includes "Spider Rabbit," "The Meatball," "The Shell," "Apple Glove," "The Authentic Radio Life of Bruce Conner and Snoutburbler"), produced in San Francisco at Magic Theater, 1970; "Gargoyle Cartoons" (includes "The Bow," "Spider Rabbit," "The River, or The Secret Radio Life of Bruce Conner and Snoutburbler," "The Cherub," "The Meatball"), produced in Philadelphia at Open Theatre, 1970; "Polymorphous Pirates" (includes "The Pussy," "The Button," "The Feather"), produced in Berkeley at Magic Theater, 1972.

Contributor: Daisy Aldan, editor, *A New Folder; Americans: Poems and Drawings,* Folder Editions, 1959; Elias Wilentz, editor, *The Beat Scene,* Corinth, 1960; Lawrence Ferlinghetti, editor, *Beatitude Anthology,* City Lights, 1960; Donald M. Allen, editor, *The New American Poetry, 1945-1960,* Grove, 1960; Reidar Ekner, editor, *Helgon & Hetsporrar,* Raben & Sjogren (Stockholm), 1960; Gregory Corso and Walter Hollerer, editors, *Junge Amerikanische Lyrik,* Carl Hanser, 1961; Lyle E. Linville, editor, *Tiger,* Linville-Hansen Associates, 1961; (foreword) Charles Olson, *Maximus from Dogtown—1,* Auerhahn, 1961; Gene Baro, editor, *"Beat" Poets,* Vista, 1961; Thomas Parkinson, editor, *A Casebook on the Beat,* Crowell, 1961; Fernanda Pivano, editor, *Poesi degli Ultimi Americani,* Feltrinelli, 1964; Walter Lowenfels, editor, *Poets of Today,* International Publishers, 1964; Don Allen and W. Tallman, editors, *The Poetics of the New American Poetry,* Grove, 1964; Jean-Jacques Lebel, translator, *La Poesie de la beat generation,* Denoel, 1965; Paris Leary and Robert Kelly, editors, *A Controversy of Poets,* Anchor, 1965; David Meltzer, editor, *The San Francisco Poets,* Ballantine, 1971. Also author of a documentary television play, "The Maze," 1967. Contributor to *Poetry, Semina Two, Life, Chicago Review, Black Mountain Review, Jabberwock, Beatitude, Yugen, Big Table, Kulchur, Nation, City Lights Journal, Imago, Rolling Stone,* and other publications. Editor with James Harmon, *Ark II/Moby I* (magazine), 1957; editor with Lawrence Ferlinghetti and David Meltzer, *Journal for the Protection of All Beings,* 1961.

SIDELIGHTS: McClure's poetry and prose, says a *Times Literary Supplement* reviewer, "is one of the more remarkable achievements in recent American literature, a record of a man's attempt to find the terms he needs for a vital balance, for some kind of homeostasis of body and psyche. He closes the Cartesian gap with his own term for body-and-mind, 'spiritmeat'.... And it is the poetry which demonstrates McClure's self-reliant therapy, his coming to terms with a developing self without benefit of any philosophical or religious ideology. His poems concern the nature of identity and the ways in which an economy of the self can be maintained as a balance between the extremes of loss of self—either psychotic abandon or total absorption into society.... McClure wishes to affirm a positive, earned acceptance of existence in the world."

According to David Kherdian, McClure's best performances are often those in which he "yields to a creative urge, and in the mysterious process of creation produces a work of which the eventual meanings can only be half-known to the artist." McClure himself says: "I write and make no/or few changes. The prime purpose of my writing is liberation. (Self-liberation first & hopefully that of the reader.) The Bulk and its senses must be freed! A poem is as much of me as an arm. Measure, line, etc., is interior and takes an outward shape, is not pre-destined or logical but immediate. I no longer have interest in the esthetic rationales of verse." Robert Peters writes: "The reader is to re-experience the excitement McClure felt at writing the poems. The energy [of the poems] is as important as any direct statement the reader might receive of the traditional sort. McClure fractures the expected and the preconditioned poetic response." The poems in *Hymns to St. Geryon*, McClure adds, "allow for abstractions, boredom, retractions, contradictions. I am free in the forcing of what I am doing to make mistakes. I take in the language, act, object, morphology and I try to uncover all my feelings. There is my will in actions forcing the objects 'chairs of my life' into the abstractions of the long poems. . . . There is no logic but sequence of feelings," he says. "My viewpoint is ego-centric. Self-dramatization is part of a means to belief and Spirit. . . . If Olson's is poetry of the intellect and physiology, I want a writing of the Emotions, intellect and physiology. The direct emotional statement from the body. . . ." The *Times Literary Supplement* writes that "the resulting poem is like an accumulation of gestures which emerge as a single action; an action painting works similarly, as a work without a logically predetermined conclusion or destination." Steve Sanfield notes: "The poems [in *September Blackberries*] are liberating, but McClure gives no guidelines or solutions for being free. He seems to feel there are no solutions, that life itself is the solution, and that being open to the limitless potential of our own meat is freedom."

Spiritmeat is the means to the attainment of pleasure: "I am difficult," says McClure, "but I will return you to the loveliness of your senses." Kherdian explains McClure's desire to create a new romantic, namely *mammal:* "For McClure the old notion of *man* is no longer pleasing. The sensory images of his poetry concern the creatures with which he aligns himself because of their 'warm-bloodedness': the falcon, eagle, and gyrfalcon; and the warm-tempered salmon and kraken. To become, he feels, we must dare to become: man is not a cool cat, he is a warm-blooded . . . ape-mammal-bird-beast-fish. . . . For McClure there can be no distinction between the man and the writer—one being condemned to serve the other—nor can there be a differentiation between the mind and the body; for if the mind is in error it will be reflected by a gesture of the body. The poise he is concerned with in the stance he strikes is determined by the position and balance of the mind: a man's walk being determined by the movement of his thought." According to McClure, the beast-man must growl and proclaim, "We are something like gods. We *are* Truth." And the growls must be heard: "[My poetry has] got to be read out loud or listened to," says McClure, "not read silently. What I'm trying to prove is that poetry's a muscular thing. It comes from out of the silence inside. It doesn't communicate unless you feel it." Mick McAllister writes: "If we sound out the poem, we approach closer to the reality of it. If we listen to it, however, we are retreating again from the participatory environment which is the total translation of the poem."

McClure's forms are often experimental; they are "liable to be a brief metaphysics of freedom, apprehending shape and sequence without the obvious logic of forms," says the *Times Literary Supplement.* "Sometimes they are dull because they dramatize a self repetitiously stumbling, reiterating capitals with shrill largeness, swearing until the expletives are simply spiritual lockjaw. . . . [But] poetry of therapeutic confession is always liable to risk unformed

looseness which, while healthily refusing betrayal by custom, becomes a field of violent energy in a state of hysteria." Robert J. Griffin comments: "Visually his poems stand somewhere between ordinary and shaped poetry. In addition to all caps, he favors a great variety of line lengths, and ruled lines across the page (occasionally lines of close-set dashes) that work like white space italicized. . . . Though the shapes have no overt pictoral reference, visuality clearly matters—the palpable assurance of method in the madness." The *Times Literary Supplement* writer notes that "McClure's main procedure is to let the poem move forwards on a central axis which graphically stabilizes the pain and the inquiry of the action. . . . Robert Creeley calls McClure's kind of formal intensity 'the stress complex in a given unit,' and, writing of Pollock, McClure himself speaks of 'the cloud of our gestures—/—the smoke we make with our arms.' He is conscious, like the painters he admires, of the heroism involved in the liberty of working, in any art, without preconceived, pre-accepted forms. . . . His own poetic structures demand the reader's continuous participation in the dynamic energy and alertness. . . ."

McClure gained a certain degree of notoriety with his play, *The Beard.* The Los Angeles cast was arrested nightly. (The judge finally ruled that nobody had been obscene.) McClure believes, however, that the play has been abused, not because of its alleged obscenities but because it regards us all as divine. Michael Smith, however, thinks the problem is more prosaic: "The audience, accustomed to plays being mostly all alike, has some trouble with *The Beard.* If they think it's poetry they think they should take it seriously. As drama it's thin sludge. And it isn't pornographic despite [its] being saturated in sex and graphic to the point of literalness at the climax."

A play, for McClure, is "a poem with meat on the stage with lights." *The Beard,* with its two protagonists, Billy the Kid and Jean Harlow, is anti-dramatic. Gene Youngblood calls it "a poetic illustration of a premise rather than a telling of a plot." Harold Clurman believes that it is "not a play to like or to dislike. To challenge it as a matter of taste would be absurd. It is a phenomenon to be understood. It has its own completeness, not simply as a text but as a performance." The two American mythological figures have been stripped down to masculine-feminine images. Moreover, "Billy's like a falcon," says McClure, "a strong, beautiful character, and a killer. And Harlow's like a rat, only not the kind of rat you find in the city. A rat in its natural habitat, which is very beautiful—fields and woods." Clurman, who considers *The Beard* "inconsequential as art," commends the play as "a mockery of sex, a 'milestone' on the road to nonentity. We need not despise it. It shows us that our myths . . . are in the process of dissolution. . . . *The Beard* is a caricature of sex as the saving remnant of our personal lives. To realize this is to comprehend much else about our day." Other critics praised the play as an artistic event solely on the basis of its language, which, as Smith notes, is "raunchy and unflinchingly direct, rich in four-letter words as words, shamelessly self-romanticizing, unillusioned, spare, . . . witty rather than clever, and profoundly silly without being camp. . . . The real action is in the words, the patterns and developments of the words, the music of the words. . . . The words dance." The play, says *Newsweek,* is "funny, fast and authentically outrageous." The language is "without question the 'filthiest' ever heard on a commercial stage in the English speaking nations." But, adds the reviewer, "the proper reaction is neither shock nor a bland pretense of not being shocked. . . . McClure raises profanity to a comic passion, the passion of a fiery but inarticulate [Harlow], . . . McClure has written a brilliant little monster of a play." "McClure seems to me to be one of the best playwriting minds now working in America," according to Arthur Sainer who continues: "I thought 'The Beard' was a small masterpiece. Perhaps not so small. The 'Gargoyle Cartoons' don't make it in the same way, but the evening is at least erratically brilliant and sometimes a little awful but never dull, never irrelevant."

McClure has said that he is "close" to D. H. Lawrence and Melville, and, unlike so many experimental poets, he dislikes Ezra Pound and William Carlos Williams. The *Times Literary Supplement* noted that McClure's experiments have "carried him pretty far in . . . honesty and loneliness. His talent is for thoroughgoing risky poems of bodymind which have a mysterious health inside their often maniacal but always serious breaking down of limits and search for freedom. He is a writer who takes his place with a number of American anti-authoritarians reacting to the threats of organized passive formality."

McClure has recorded for "San Francisco Poets," Evergreen Records, 1957. He and his wife, Joanna, made a color videotape for the *September Blackberries* poems for KQED-TV, 1973. A film of scenes from the production of "The Blossom" was made by George Herms.

BIOGRAPHICAL/CRITICAL SOURCES: Donald M. Allen, editor, *The New American Poetry, 1945-1960*, Grove, 1960; *Times Literary Supplement*, March 25, 1965; Paris Leary and Robert Kelly, editors, *A Controversy of Poets*, Anchor, 1965; David Kherdian, *Six Poets of the San Francisco Renaissance*, Giligia Press, 1967; *Books*, September, 1967, October, 1967; *Village Voice*, October 5, 1967, November 2, 1967, November 16, 1967, January 22, 1970; *Newsweek*, November 6, 1967; *Nation*, November 13, 1967, July 20, 1970; *Christian Century*, January 17, 1968; *Los Angeles Free Press*, February 2, 1968; *Show*, May, 1970; *Margins*, Number 18, 1975; Carolyn Riley, editor, *Contemporary Literary Criticism*, Volume VI, Gale, 1976.

* * *

McCONNELL, Jon Patrick 1928-

PERSONAL: Born November 18, 1928, in Champaign, Ill.; son of Everett Jacob (a realtor) and Ruth (Franklin) McConnell; married Beverly Brown (a consultant with Office of Economic Opportunity), October 6, 1952. *Education:* Millikin University, B.S., 1950; Willamette University, J.D., 1956. *Politics:* Democrat. *Home:* 425 Northeast Maple, Pullman, Wash. 99163.

CAREER: Washington State University, Pullman, instructor, 1957-61, assistant professor, 1961-67, associate professor, 1967-72, professor of business law, 1972—. Justice of the peace and city police judge, Pullman, 1963-66. *Military service:* U.S. Navy, 1952-54. *Member:* American Bar Association, American Business Law Association, Washington Bar Association.

WRITINGS: Law and Business: Patterns and Issues, Macmillan, 1966; (with Lothar A. Kreck) *Hospitality Management: Avoiding Legal Pitfalls,* Cahners, 1975.

WORK IN PROGRESS: Law of Innkeepers, for Cahners.

* * *

McCORD, James I(ley) 1919-

PERSONAL: Born November 24, 1919, in Rusk, Tex.; son of Marshal Edward and Jimmie Oleta (Decherd) McCord; married Hazel Thompson, August 29, 1939; children: Vincent, Alison (Mrs. James Zimmerman), Marcia. *Education:* Austin College, B.A., 1938; Union Theological Seminary, Richmond, Va., theological student, 1938-39; Austin Presbyterian Theological Seminary, B.D., 1942; University of Texas, M.A., 1942; further study at Harvard University, 1942-43, and University of Edinburgh, 1950-51. *Home:* 86 Mercer St., Princeton, N.J. 08540. *Office:* Princeton Theological Seminary, Princeton, N.J. 08540.

CAREER: Clergyman of United Presbyterian Church. University of Texas, Austin, instructor, 1940-42; Austin Presbyterian Theological Seminary, Austin, Tex., adjunct professor, 1944-45, dean and professor of systematic theology, 1945-59; Princeton Theological Seminary, Princeton, N.J., president and professor of systematic theology, 1959—. World Presbyterian Alliance, chairman of North American council, 1958-60, secretary, 1959—; North American secretary and chairman of department of theology, World Alliance of Reformed Churches; chairman of department on faith and order, National Council of Churches; chairman of council on theological education, United Presbyterian Church, 1964-67. *Member:* Century Association. *Awards, honors:* Honorary degrees from Austin College, 1949, University of Geneva, 1958, Maryville College and Davidson College, 1959, Princeton University, 1960, Lafayette College and Ursinus College, 1962, Victoria University (Toronto), 1963, and other institutions.

WRITINGS—Editor: (With T.H.L. Parker) *Service in Christ: Essays Presented to Karl Barth on His 80th Birthday,* Eerdmans, 1967; (with Paul C. Empie) *Marburg Revisited,* Augsburg, 1967. Editor, *Supplementa Calviniana;* chairman of editorial council, *Theology Today.*

* * *

McCORMICK, Sister Rose M(atthew) 1914-
(Mary McCormick)

PERSONAL: Born December 10, 1914, in Caledonia, Minn.; daughter of Matthew (a farmer) and Rose (McDonald) McCormick. *Education:* La Crosse State Teachers' College, Elementary Teacher's Certificate, 1933; Maryknoll Teachers' College (now Mary Rogers College), Maryknoll, N.Y., B.Ed., 1948. *Home:* Sisters' Motherhouse, Maryknoll, N.Y. 10545.

CAREER: Elementary teacher in Caledonia, Minn., 1933-35; entered order of Maryknoll Sisters (missionaries), 1935; teacher in Malabon, Rizal, Philippines, 1938-41; taken Japanese prisoner in the Philippines, 1941, and interned until rescue by U.S. forces and guerillas, February 23, 1945; teacher among minority groups in New York, St. Louis, Tucson, and San Juan Capistrano, 1946-58; Confraternity of Christian Doctrine, trainer of teachers of religion, Stockton, Calif., 1958-63; Maryknoll Publications, Maryknoll, N.Y., member of editorial staff, 1963-70; teacher of English, missioned to Kyoto, Japan, 1970-75. National Council of Churches of Christ, member of commission for children, department of education for mission.

WRITINGS: Parents' Guide to Religious Education, Bruce, 1965; *The Global Mission of God's People,* Maryknoll Publications, 1967; *Happenings in the Philippines,* Maryknoll Publications, 1969; *Hello Japan,* Chuo Tosho Publications (Japan), 1974; *Hello America,* Chuo Tosho Publications, 1975. Creator of a series of four religious drawing books for children, Maryknoll Publications, 1968. Scriptwriter for weekly television program, "Let's Talk

About God,'' WNBC, New York, 1965-66, and for series of filmstrips with eight records, ''The Sacraments: Signs of Love,'' Eye Gate Productions, 1968.

* * *

McCREADY, Warren T(homas) 1915-
(Machiavelli)

PERSONAL: Surname rhymes with ''speedy''; born February 8, 1915, in New York, N.Y.; son of Thomas Burns (an office worker) and Louise (Rudolph) McCready. *Education:* University of Chicago, M.A., 1949, Ph.D., 1961. *Office:* Department of Hispanic Studies, University of Toronto, Toronto, Ontario, Canada M5S 1A1.

CAREER: Worked as a seaman out of New York and Philadelphia, 1933-40, an elevator operator, 1940, and a clerk for a freight-forwarding firm, 1945-46; Indiana University, Gary Campus, lecturer in Spanish, 1950-53; Queen's University, Kingston, Ontario, research assistant and lecturer, 1954-56; University of Toronto, Toronto, Ontario, lecturer, 1956-60, assistant professor, 1960-64, associate professor, 1964-69, professor of Spanish, 1969—. *Military service:* U.S. Army Air Forces, 1940-45; became sergeant. *Member:* International Association of Hispanists, Modern Humanities Research Association, Canadian Association of Hispanists, American Association of Teachers of Spanish and Portuguese, American Cryptogram Association (president, 1962-63).

WRITINGS: (With J. A. Molinaro) *Angelica y Medoro, zarzuela inedita de Jose de Canizares, con su loa y entremes,* Quaderni Ibero-Americani (Turin), 1958; *La heraldica en las obras de Lope de Vega y sus contemporaneos,* privately printed, 1962; *Bibliografia tematica de estudios sobre el teatro espanol antiguo,* University of Toronto Press, 1966; (editor) Lope de Vega, *El mejor mozo de Espana,* Anaya (Salamanca), 1967; (author of bibliographical supplement) J.P.W. Crawford, *Spanish Drama before Lope de Vega* (reprint of 1937 edition), University of Pennsylvania Press, 1967. Joint author of current bibliography in *BCom* and *Studies in Philology,* 1960-66. Contributor to *Renaissance and Reformation* and to language journals; also contributor to *Cryptogram* (journal of American Cryptogram Association), under pseudonym Machiavelli. Editor, *Bulletin of the Comediantes,* 1967-72.

WORK IN PROGRESS: Supplement to *Bibliografia tematica de estudios sobre el teatro espanol antiguo;* a book on birth dates.

SIDELIGHTS: McCready hoboed around America for ten months during the Depression and ranged around the world as a seaman, shipping through the Panama Canal fourteen times. ''But,'' he adds, ''the best thing that ever happened to me was the G.I. Bill of Rights for World War II veterans.'' Boyhood hobbies of reading, working with codes and ciphers, and delving into other forms of public and private communication, have evolved into his current pastimes—reading elementary grammars in Welsh, Icelandic, Malay, and other neglected languages, books on archaeological linguistics, and detective novels, and work in cryptanalysis.

* * *

McCUEN, John J(oachim) 1926-

PERSONAL: Born March 30, 1926, in Washington, D.C.; son of Joseph Raymond (a lawyer and politician) and Josephine (Joachim) McCuen; married Gloria Joyce Seidel,

June 16, 1949; children: John Joachim, Jr., Les Seidel. *Education:* U.S. Military Academy, B.S., 1948; Columbia University, M.I.A., 1961; also graduate of U.S. Army Command and General Staff College, 1958-59, and Army War College, 1967-68. *Religion:* Christian Scientist.

CAREER: U.S. Army, regular officer, 1948—, with current rank of lieutenant colonel; served at posts in United States and Germany, 1949-57; armor adviser to Third Royal Thai Army, Utaradit, Thailand, 1957-58; general staff officer in Washington, D.C., and Heidelberg, Germany, 1961-66; commander of Third Squadron, Eight Cavalry Regiment, Mannheim, Germany, 1966-67. *Awards, honors*—Military: Army Commendation Medal with oak leaf cluster.

WRITINGS: The Art of Counter-Revolutionary War: The Strategy of Counter-Insurgency, Faber, 1966, Stackpole, 1967.

WORK IN PROGRESS: Further research on strategy and tactics of counter-insurgency and insurgency, for articles and a second book.††

* * *

McCULLOUGH, W(illiam) Stewart 1902-

PERSONAL: Surname is pronounced Ma-*Cull*-a; born May 12, 1902, in Toronto, Ontario, Canada; son of William (a printer) and Margaret (Graham) McCullough; married Eleanor Slater, September 2, 1931 (died January, 1953); married Dorothy Madgett (a physiotherapist), February 25, 1956; children: (first marriage) Sheila (Mrs. Douglas Browne), Roger, Nora (Mrs. Russell Gibson). *Education:* University of Toronto, B.A., 1924, M.A., 1925, Ph.D., 1949; Knox College, Toronto, Diploma in Theology, 1927; Harvard University, graduate student, 1929-30; Victoria University, Toronto, B.D., 1945. *Home:* 131 Heath St. E., Toronto, Ontario, Canada M4T 1S6. *Office:* University of Toronto, Toronto, Ontario, Canada M5S 1A1.

CAREER: Clergyman of United Church of Canada, ordained in 1927; University of Toronto, University College, Toronto, Ontario, lecturer, 1930-39, assistant professor, 1939-44, associate professor, 1944-52, professor of Near Eastern studies, 1952-70, professor emeritus, 1970—. *Member:* Society of Biblical Literature, American Oriental Society, American Schools of Oriental Research, American Academy of Religion.

WRITINGS: (Contributor) *The Interpreter's Bible,* Volume IV, Abingdon, 1955; (editor) *The Seed of Wisdom,* University of Toronto Press, 1964; *Jewish and Mandaean Incantation Bowls in the Royal Ontario Museum,* University of Toronto Press, 1967; *The History and Literature of the Palestinian Jews from Cyrus to Herod, 550 B.C. to 4 B.C.,* University of Toronto Press, 1975.

* * *

McDANIEL, David (Edward) 1939-
(Ted Johnstone)

PERSONAL: Born June 16, 1939, in Toledo, Ohio; son of Calvin Dale (a teacher) and Margaret (Allis) McDaniel; married Joyce Potter (a computer programmer), December 21, 1963. *Education:* Pasadena City College, A.A., 1960; San Diego State College (now San Diego State University), B.S., 1963; University of California, Los Angeles, graduate student, 1963-64. *Politics:* ''Rational Anarchist.'' *Religion:* ''Scientologist.''

CAREER: KEBS (FM and television station), San Diego,

Calif., classical and pop disc jockey, and television actor and director, 1961-63; writer. Free-lance still and motion picture photographer. *Member:* Baker Street Irregulars, Los Angeles Science Fantasy Society (past director and secretary), Spectator Amateur Press Society (vice-president, 1959—), Fellowship of the Ring (founder).

WRITINGS—All published by Ace Books: *The Dagger Affair*, 1965; *The Vampire Affair*, 1966; *The Monster Wheel Affair*, 1967; *The Rainbow Affair*, 1967; *The Utopia Affair*, 1968; *The Hollow Crown Affair*, 1968. Publisher, *MEST*, and other magazines. Columnist, *Ground Zero, Psi-Phi, Shaggy;* former editor, *I Palantir*.

WORK IN PROGRESS: Television and film scripts; a satire on Hollywood.

SIDELIGHTS: McDaniel has crossed the United States twenty or more times, "hitch-hiking with guitar on my back, or in a jet.... I've lived in a strange city on fifty cents a day," he told *CA*, "and hated every minute of it. Know a lot of brilliant people and steal their thrown-away ideas and copy their characters for my stories; one of these days they'll get organized and take over the world."††

* * *

McDOLE, Carol 1936-
(Carol Farley)

PERSONAL: Born December 20, 1936, in Ludington, Mich.; daughter of Floyd and Thressa Moreen (Radtke) McDole; married Dennis Scott Farley (a lieutenant colonel in U.S. Army), June 21, 1956; children: Denise, Elise, Roderick, Jeannette. *Education:* Western Michigan University, teacher's certificate, 1956; further study at Michigan University, 1968-69. *Address:* (Permanent) 605 East Melendy St., Ludington, Mich. 49431; (current) 7306 Austin St., Annandale, Va. 22003.

CAREER: Elementary teacher in Michigan public schools, 1957; Michigan State University, East Lansing, secretarial work, 1958. *Awards, honors:* Franklin Watts Mystery Medal for *Mystery of the Fog Man*, 1966.

WRITINGS—All under name Carol Farley, except as noted; all published by F. Watts, except as noted: (Under name Carol McDole) *Yekapo of Zopo Land*, Row, Peterson, 1958; *Mystery of the Fog Man*, 1966; *Mystery in the Ravine*, 1967; *Sergeant Finney's Family*, 1969; *The Bunch on Mckellahan Street*, 1971; *The Most Important Thing in the World*, 1974; *The Garden is Doing Fine* (Junior Guild selection), 1975.

WORK IN PROGRESS: A collection of short stories told by an old man reminiscing about his childhood.

* * *

McDONNELL, Virginia B(leecker) 1917-
(Jinny McDonnell; Jean Kirby, a house name)

PERSONAL: Born November 24, 1917; daughter of J. Barclay (a real estate broker) and Helen Borden (Farley) Bleecker; married John H. McDonnell (a utility employee and free-lance writer); children: Gordon R. *Education:* Samaritan Hospital School of Nursing, Troy, N.Y., R.N.; also studied at Russell Sage College. *Religion:* Episcopalian. *Home:* 79 Hudson Park Rd., New Rochelle, N.Y. *Agent:* Elyse Sommer, Inc., Box E, 962 Allen Lane, Woodmere, N.Y. 11598.

CAREER: Surgical nurse in New York City during World War II; Gore Mountain Ski School, North Creek, N.Y.,

former director with husband; *Knickerbocker News,* Albany, N.Y., sports columnist, 1956-58; Free and Accepted Masons, New York City, assistant to director of publications, 1957; *Standard Star* (daily newspaper), New Rochelle, N.Y., reporter, feature writer, and columnist, 1958-62; *Daily Argus,* Mount Vernon, N.Y., women's news editor, 1963; free-lance writer, 1963—. Did art work and sweater designs for *Vogue* over a period of several years, and also designed sportswear for White Stag and other manufacturers. *Member:* Authors League of America.

WRITINGS: Your Future in Nursing, Richards Rosen, 1963; *The Nurse with the Silver Skates,* Ace Books, 1964; *West Point Nurse,* Macfadden, 1965; *Annapolis Nurse,* Macfadden, 1965; (under pseudonym Jean Kirby) *Olympic Duty,* Whitman Publishing, 1965; (under pseudonym Jean Kirby) *Tracy's Little People,* Whitman Publishing, 1965; *Dee O'Hara, Astronauts' Nurse,* Thomas Nelson, 1965; *Dixie Cline, Animal Doctor,* Thomas Nelson, 1966; *The Ski Trail Mystery,* Macrae, 1966; *Foster Pups,* Thomas Nelson, 1966; *Aerospace Nurse,* Messner, 1966; *County Agent,* Messner, 1968; *The Irish Helped Build America,* Messner, 1969; *Storm Over Garnet,* Golden Press, 1969; *Careers in Hotel Management,* Messner, 1971; *Miscalculated Risk,* Western Publishing, 1972; *Silent Partner,* Western Publishing, 1972; *The Deep Six,* Western Publishing, 1973; *The Long Shot,* Western Publishing, 1974; *The Accident,* Western Publishing, 1975. Author of more than three hundred articles and short stories published in magazines and newspapers, some under name Jinny McDonnell.

WORK IN PROGRESS: Rebels in White, a novel, for Doubleday.

SIDELIGHTS: Virginia McDonnell won a house, completely furnished, in 1948, for a jingle entered in a national contest sponsored by *Photoplay.* When she and her son were recovering from polio, Mrs. McDonnell took up skiing and became an instructor. Other hobbies include boating, swimming, reading, knitting, sewing, and gardening.

* * *

McDONOUGH, Thomas E(dmund) 1929-

PERSONAL: Born June 1, 1929, in Brooklyn, N.Y.; son of Stephen Francis and Marcella Alice (Gill) McDonough; married Pamela Ann Wells, November 17, 1956; children: Kevin P., Joan Aileen, Thomas Peter. *Education:* St. John's University, Jamaica, N.Y., B.S. in Ed., 1952, doctoral fellow, 1967—; Hofstra University, M.S. in Ed., 1955. *Religion:* Roman Catholic.

CAREER: High school English teacher in Amityville, N.Y., 1954-57, and West Islip, N.Y., 1957-60; Brentwood (N.Y.) public schools, high school guidance counselor, 1960-64, vocational coordinator for school system, 1964-67. *Military service:* U.S. Army, Signal Corps, 1952-54. *Member:* American Personnel and Guidance Association, New York State Personnel and Guidance Association, West Suffolk Guidance Association, Phi Delta Kappa.

WRITINGS: Your Future as a Guidance Counselor, Richards Rosen, 1966. Contributor to *New York Herald Tribune* and to education journals.

WORK IN PROGRESS: Doctoral dissertation.††

* * *

McEACHERN, Theodore 1928-
PERSONAL: Born April 25, 1928, in Great Falls, S.C.;

son of Furman Edward (a merchant) and Sara (Bye) McEachern; married Woodley Shingler, November 19, 1954; children: Kathryn, Edward, Kirk, Bruce. *Education:* University of South Carolina, A.B., 1949; Emory University, B.D., 1952. *Politics:* None. *Home:* 4804 Merril Lane, Nashville, Tenn. 37211. *Office:* 1808 West End Ave., Nashville, Tenn. 37203.

CAREER: Methodist clergyman. Has served a mountain circuit, and as a campus minister; associate pastor in Charleston, S.C., 1952-53; pastor in Columbia, S.C., 1954; The Methodist Church, Board of Education, Nashville, Tenn., director of youth work in South Carolina Conference, 1954-59; Methodist director of International Christian Youth Exchange, 1958-68; director, Services to Inner City Personnel, 1965-68; Association for Christian Training and Service, Nashville, staff member, 1968—. Chairman of Commission of Ecumenical Voluntary Service, National Council of Churches of Christ in the U.S.A.; participant in ecumenical conferences in Europe and North America.

WRITINGS: Being There for Others, Abingdon, 1967. Contributor to Methodist publications.

WORK IN PROGRESS: Christian Education for Secular Man; Youth Exchange in a Hungry World.††

*   *   *

McEWAN, Keith 1926-

PERSONAL: Born May 17, 1926, in Melborne, Australia; son of John (a tailor) and Emma (Zimmerman) McEwan; married June Whitfeld (a nursing sister), March 1956; children: Robyn, Lewis, Dawn, Paul. *Education:* Attended a state school until fourteen. *Politics:* Democratic Socialist. *Religion:* Atheist. *Home:* 147 Ferguson St., Williamstown, Victoria, Australia.

CAREER: Variously employed as waterside worker, truck driver, cleaner, clerk, and ambulance officer; former painter and docker, Ports and Harbours Department, Williamstown, Victoria, Australia; currently studying to become a teacher of Australian history and social studies.

WRITINGS: Once a Jolly Comrade, Jacaranda Press, 1966.

WORK IN PROGRESS: Once a Jolly Wharfie.††

*   *   *

McFARLAND, Walter B. 1908-

PERSONAL: Born June 19, 1908, in Silver City, N.M.; son of Walter B. (a teacher) and Minnie (Gough) McFarland; married Elizabeth W. Breid, June 28, 1941. *Education:* University of Kansas, A.B., 1930; Stanford University, M.B.A., 1932, Ph.D., 1938. *Home:* 1573 Yio Romero, Alamo, Calif. 94507.

CAREER: University of New Mexico, Albuquerque, instructor in business, 1932-36; Yale University, New Haven, Conn., instructor in accounting, 1938-41; Arthur Andersen & Co., New York City, staff member, 1941-42; McGill University, Montreal, Quebec, associate professor of accounting, 1945-46; National Association of Accountants, New York City, research director, 1946-70; California State University, Hayward, lecturer in accounting, 1970-73. *Member:* National Association of Accountants, American Accounting Association.

WRITINGS: (Co-author) *Cost Accounting,* Ronald, 1953; *Concepts for Management Accounting,* National Association of Accountants, 1966; (with Morton Backer) *External*

Reporting for Segments of a Business, National Association of Accountants, 1968; *Manpower Cost and Performance Management,* National Association of Accountants, 1976.

AVOCATIONAL INTERESTS: Horticulture, travel.

*   *   *

McGEE, T(erence) G(ary) 1936-

PERSONAL: Born January 5, 1936, in Cambridge, New Zealand; son of Barnard James McGee; married Joan Shirley Blanchard, May, 1963; children: Tyler (son). *Education:* University of Auckland, student, 1954-56; Victoria University of Wellington, B.A., 1959, M.A. (first class honors), 1960. *Religion:* None. *Office:* Department of Geography, University of Wellington, Box 196, Wellington C.1, New Zealand.

CAREER: University of Wellington, Wellington, New Zealand, assistant lecturer in geography 1960; University of Malaya, Kuala Lumpur, lecturer in geography, 1961-64; University of Wellington, lecturer in geography, 1965—. Field researcher in Malaysia.

WRITINGS: (Contributor) Wang Gungwu, editor, *Malaysia—A Survey,* Praeger, 1964; *The Southeast Asian City: A Social Geography of the Primate Cities of Southeast Asia,* Praeger, 1967; (with D. W. McTaggart) *Petaling Jaya: A Socio-Economic Survey of a New Town in Selangor, Malaysia,* Department of Geography, University of Wellington, 1967; (contributor) John Forster, editor, *Social Process in New Zealand,* Longman, Paul, 1969; *The Urbanization Process in the Third World: Explorations in Search of a Theory,* Bell, 1971. Contributor to *Pacific Viewpoint* and geography journals.

WORK IN PROGRESS: The Malay World: A Cultural Geography of Malaysia, Indonesia, and the Philippines (tentative title), after further research and travel in the region; specific studies of out-migration in the Malay world, and field work.†

*   *   *

McGOVERN, John P(hillip) 1921-

PERSONAL: Born June 2, 1921, in Washington, D.C.; son of Francis X. (a physician) and Lottie Marie (Brown) McGovern; married Kathrine Dunbar Galbreath, December 20, 1961. *Education:* Duke University, B.S., 1943, M.D., 1945; postdoctoral study in London and Paris, 1949-50. *Office:* McGovern Allergy Clinic, 6969 Brompton Rd., Houston, Tex. 77025.

CAREER: New Haven General Hospital, New Haven, Conn., intern, 1945-46; Duke Hospital, Durham, N.C., resident, 1948-49; Children's Hospital, Washington, D.C., chief resident, 1950, chief of out-patient department, 1951-53; George Washington University School of Medicine, Washington, D.C., assistant professor of pediatrics, 1951-54; Tulane University of Louisiana, New Orleans, associate professor of pediatrics and allergy, 1954-56; McGovern Allergy Clinic, Houston, Tex., director, 1956—; Baylor University, College of Medicine, Houston, Tex., clinical allergy professor in departments of pediatrics and microbiology, 1956—; University of Texas, Graduate School of Biomedical Sciences, Houston, 1963—, began as clinical professor of allergy, currently professor of history of medicine and chairman of department. Distinguished adjunct professor, Kent State University. Diplomate, American Board of Pediatrics. Chairman of the board,

Texas Allergy Research Foundation; regional consultant to Childhood Asthma Research Institute and Hospital, National Medical Advisory Council of Asthmatic Children's Foundation, and Sahuaro School Foundation for Asthmatic Children, Tucson. *Military service:* U.S. Army, Medical Corps, 1946-48; became captain.

MEMBER: American Medical Association, American College of Allergists (fellow; president, 1968), American Association of Certified Allergists (president, 1972), American School Health Association, American Osler Society (president, 1973), American Academy of Allergy (fellow), American Academy of Pediatrics (fellow), American Association for the Study of Headache (president, 1963-64), Academy of Psychosomatic Medicine, American College of Chest Physicians (president of Texas chapter), American Medical Writers' Association, Southern Medical Association, Texas Medical Association, Sigma Xi, Pi Sigma, Pi Kappa Alpha. *Awards, honors:* Borden Award for Research, 1945; Markle scholar in medical science, 1950-55; Smith-Reed-Russell Medal, George Washington University School of Medicine, 1951; Bela Schick Memorial Gold Medal, American College of Allergists, 1969; Clemens von Pirquet Award, Georgetown University of School of Medicine, 1975. Sc.D. from Ricker College, 1971, and University of Nebraska, 1973; LL.D., Union College, 1972; Litt.D., Kent State University, 1973; D.P.M., Illinois College of Pediatric Medicine, 1975.

WRITINGS—All published by C. C Thomas, except as noted: (With William Mandel) *Bibliography on Sarcoidosis, 1878-1963,* National Library of Medicine, 1964; (with James Knight) *Allergy and Human Emotions,* 1967; (with G. T. Stewart) *Penicillin Allergy: Clinical and Immunological Aspects,* 1970; (editor) O. Swineford, Jr., *Asthma and Hay Fever,* 1971; (with C. R. Burns) *Humanism in Medicine,* 1974; (editor with G. Knotts) *School Health Problems,* 1975; (editor with others) *Drugs, Medicines, and Other Agents,* Kent State University Press, 1975; (editor with J. Arena and others) *Davison Memorial Addresses,* University of Texas Press, in press; (editor with M. H. Smolensky and A. Reinberg) *Chronobiology in Allergy and Immunology,* in press; (editor with E. F. Nations and C. G. Roland) *An Annotated Checklist of Osleriana,* Kent State University Press, in press.

Contributor: Frederic Speer, editor, *The Allergic Child,* Hoeber, 1963; *Brennemann's Practice of Pediatrics,* Volume II, Harper, 1968; *William Osler: The Continuing Education,* 1970; *Allergy of the Nervous System,* 1970; *Allergy and Immunology in Children,* 1973; *Biorhythms and Human Reproduction,* Wiley, 1974. Contributor to *Current Therapy,* and other professional journals.

Editor, "American Lecture Series in Allergy and Immunology," C. C Thomas, 1964—; contributing editor, *Review of Allergy,* 1959-65; associate editor of *Journal of Asthma Research,* 1963—, and *Annals of Allergy,* 1965—; advisory editor, *Psychosomatics,* 1962—; member of editorial board of *Chronic Disease Management,* 1967—, *Consultant,* 1970—, *Emergency Medicine,* 1971—, *Journal of School Health,* 1973—, and *Geriatrics,* 1974—.

WORK IN PROGRESS: With M. H. Smolensky and A. Reinberg, *Advances in Asthma and Allergy,* for Fisons Corp.; editing with J. Arena, *Davison Biography.*

McGOWEN, Thomas 1927-
(Tom McGowen)

PERSONAL: Born May 6, 1927, in Evanston, Ill.; son of William Robert (a salesman) and Helene (Nelson) McGowen; married Loretta Swok; children: Alan, Gayle, Maureen, Kathleen. *Education:* Studied at Roosevelt University, 1947, 1948, and American Academy of Art, 1948-49. *Politics:* "Ultra-liberal." *Religion:* Atheist. *Home:* 4449 North Oriole Blvd., Norridge, Ill. 60656.

CAREER: Sidney Clayton & Associates (advertising), Chicago, Ill., production manager, 1949-53; Justrite Manufacturing Co., Chicago, advertising manager, 1953-54; National Safety Council, Chicago, sales promotion director, 1954-59; Hensley Co. (advertising), Chicago, creative director, 1959-69; Field Enterprises Educational Corp. (publishers), Chicago, senior editor, 1969—. *Military service:* U.S. Navy, hospital corpsman, World War II. *Member:* Children's Reading Round Table, Die Schlachtenbummler (group of military history buffs).

WRITINGS—Juveniles; under name Tom McGowen: (Self-illustrated) *The Only Glupmaker in the U.S. Navy,* Albert Whitman, 1966; *The Apple Strudel Soldier,* Follett, 1968; *Dragon Stew,* Follett, 1969; *Last Voyage of the Unlucky Katie Marie,* Whitman, 1969; *The Biggest Toot in Toozelburg,* Reilly & Lee, 1970; *Hammet and the Highlanders,* Follett, 1970; *Sir MacHinery,* Follett, 1970; *The Fearless Fossil Hunters,* Whitman, 1971; *Album of Dinosaurs,* Rand McNally, 1972; *Album of Prehistoric Animals,* Rand McNally, 1974; *Odyssey from River Bend,* Little, Brown, 1975; *Album of Prehistoric Man,* Rand McNally, 1975; *The Spirit of the Wild,* Little, Brown, 1976.

*   *   *

McGREGOR, Craig 1933-

PERSONAL: Born October 12, 1933, in Jamberoo, Australia; son of Alister Stephen Charles (a clerk) and Jean (Craig) McGregor; married Jane Watson, June 10, 1962; children: Robert, Kate, Sarah Alison. *Education:* University of Sydney, B.A., 1955. *Home and office:* 19 Queen St., Woollahra, Sydney, Australia. *Agent:* Innes Rose, John Farquharson Ltd., 15 Red Lion Sq., London WC1R 4QW, England.

CAREER: Journalist in Syndey, Australia, 1950-58; journalist and teacher, London, England, 1958-62, journalist and film and jazz critic, Sydney, Australia, 1962—. Broadcaster of political commentary. *Member:* Australian Society of Authors, Australian Journalists' Association, Campaign for Nuclear Disarmament. *Awards, honors:* Commonwealth Literary Fund fellowship, 1966.

WRITINGS: (With Midget Farrelly) *This Surfing Life,* Rigby, 1965, published as *The Surfing Life,* Arco, 1967, also published as *How to Surf; Profile of Australia,* Hodder & Stoughton, 1966, Regnery, 1967, revised edition, Penguin, 1968; *People, Politics and Pop: Australians in the 'Sixties* (essays, reviews, articles, short stories), Ure Smith, 1967; (editor with David Beal) *Life in Australia* (photographs and text), Southern Cross International, 1967; (with Helmut Gritscher) *The High Country* (photographs and text), Angus & Robertson, 1967; (with others) *In the Making,* Nelson, 1970; *Don't Talk to Me about Love,* Penguin, 1973; *Bob Dylan: A Retrospective,* Angus & Robertson, 1974; *Great Barrier Reef,* Time-Life International, 1974. Story anthologized in *Pick of Today's Short Stories,* Putnam, 1962. Contributor of short stories to periodicals in Britain, Europe, and Australia.

WORK IN PROGRESS: A novel.

SIDELIGHTS: McGregor told *CA* that he has a "sociological bias." According to a *Times Literary Supplement* critic, McGregor is a "portraitist, with the appearance and attitudes of people at large and young people in particular. . . . He writes more vividly and with the breathlessness of a guide who is not only bent on covering more ground than anyone else, but who is convinced it is well worth covering."

AVOCATIONAL INTERESTS: Popular culture, jazz, folk music, and the cinema.

BIOGRAPHICAL/CRITICAL SOURCES: Times Literary Supplement, March 30, 1967.†

* * *

McGUIGAN, Dorothy Gies 1914-

PERSONAL: Surname is pronounced McKwigen; born November 12, 1914, in Ann Arbor, Mich.; daughter of Charles George (a businessman) and Jane (Sturman) Gies; married Bernard Joseph McGuigan, August 3, 1946 (deceased); children: Michael John, Cathleen Mary. *Education:* University of Michigan, A.B., 1936; Columbia University, M.A., 1939; King's College, London, graduate study, 1937-38. *Politics:* Democrat. *Religion:* Episcopalian. *Home:* 470 Rock Creek Dr., Ann Arbor, Mich. 48114. *Office:* Center for Continuing Education of Women, University of Michigan, Ann Arbor, Mich.

CAREER: Macmillan Co. (publishers), New York, N.Y., member of sales promotion staff, 1938-41; free-lance writer in Mexico City, Mexico, 1943-44; American Red Cross, staff assistant in England and Germany, 1944-46; *Stars and Stripes,* feature writer in Germany, 1946-48; University of Michigan, Ann Arbor, School of Business Administration, instructor in English, 1956-58, 1963-66, Center for Continuing Education of Women, program associate, 1970—, lecturer in English, 1974—. *Member:* Phi Beta Kappa, Mortarboard, Womens Research Club of the University of Michigan. *Awards, honors:* Five Avery and Jule Hopwood Awards at University of Michigan, 1934-36, for poetry, essay, and novel.

WRITINGS: The Habsburgs, Doubleday, 1966; *A Dangerous Experiment,* Center for Continuing Education of Women, University of Michigan, 1970; (editor) *A Sampler of Women's Studies,* University of Michigan, 1973; (editor) *New Research on Women,* University of Michigan, 1974; *Metternich and the Duchess,* Doubleday, 1975.

WORK IN PROGRESS: A biography of Aphra Behn; a study on women in the literary trades in early modern England.

SIDELIGHTS: Dorothy McGuigan lived in Europe from 1944 to 1953; she speaks French and German.

* * *

McGUIRE, James Dean 1936-

PERSONAL: Born September 27, 1936, in Greene County, Tenn.; son of Dean Smith (a farmer) and Jean (Park) McGuire; married Maribeth Smith (a teacher), December 28, 1962; children: Kathleen Park, John Timothy. *Education:* Bethel College, McKenzie, Tenn., B.A., 1958; Cumberland Presbyterian Theological Seminary, B.D., 1961. *Home:* 201 Alderman Dr., Greeneville, Tenn. 37743.

CAREER: Presbyterian clergyman. Cumberland Presbyterian Board of Publications and Christian Education,

Memphis, Tenn., various positions, 1961-64, general editor, 1964-74; Cumberland Presbyterian Church, Greeneville, Tenn., pastor, 1974—.

WRITINGS: Becoming Myself, illustrated by H. McClure, and *Teacher's Guide,* John Knox, 1967. Writer of church school materials.

* * *

McHUGH, P(atrick) J(oseph) 1922-

PERSONAL: Born May 7, 1922, in Cliffoney, County Sligo, Ireland; son of Patrick and Delia (Conway) McHugh. *Education:* Studied at Summerhill College, Sligo, Ireland, 1935-40, St. Columban's Seminary, Navan, Ireland, 1940-46, and St. John's Seminary, Camarillo, Calif., 1949-50. *Home address:* 1447 Engracia Ave., Box 479, Torrance, Calif. 90508.

CAREER: Roman Catholic priest, serving in parish and other assignments, 1950—.

WRITINGS: Living the Christian Life, Bruce, 1967; *Christian Marriage for Moderns,* Catholic Information Society, 1969. Author of nine pamphlets, mainly published by Paulist Press. Contributor to *Emmanuel, Homiletic and Pastoral Review, Priest Magazine,* and *Spiritual Life.*

WORK IN PROGRESS: Christian Marriage: A Program for a Parish, for Daughters of St. Paul.

* * *

McINERNY, Ralph 1929-
(Harry Austin, Ernan Mackey)

PERSONAL: Born February 24, 1929, in Minneapolis, Minn.; son of Austin Clifford (a mechanical engineer) and Vivian (Rush) McInerny; married Constance Terrill Kunert, January 3, 1953; children: Cathleen, Mary, Anne, David, Elizabeth, Daniel. *Education:* St. Paul Seminary, St. Paul, Minn., B.A., 1951; University of Minnesota, M.A., 1952; Laval University, Ph.D. (summa cum laude), 1954. *Politics:* "Uncomfortable conservative." *Religion:* Roman Catholic. *Home:* 2158 Portage Ave., South Bend, Ind. *Agent:* Theron Raines, Raines & Raines, 244 Madison Ave., New York, N.Y. 10016. *Office address:* Box 495, University of Notre Dame, Notre Dame, Ind. 46556.

CAREER: Creighton University, Omaha, Neb., instructor in philosophy, 1954-55; University of Notre Dame, Notre Dame, Ind., assistant professor, 1955-59, associate professor of philosophy, 1959—. *Military service:* U.S. Marine Corps, 1946-47. *Member:* American Catholic Philosophical Association (council, 1966—), American Philosophical Association, Metaphysical Society of America, Soren Kierkegaard Society, Writers Guild. *Awards, honors:* Fulbright research grant, Belgium, 1959-60.

WRITINGS: The Logic of Analogy: An Interpretation of St. Thomas, Nijhoff, 1961; *History of Western Philosophy,* Volume I, Regnery, 1963; *Thomism in an Age of Renewal,* Doubleday, 1966; *Jolly Rogerson* (novel), Doubleday, 1967; *Studies in Analogy,* Nijhoff, 1968; *From the Beginnings of Philosophy to Plotinus,* University of Notre Dame Press, 1969; *A Narrow Time,* Doubleday, 1969; *Philosophy from Augustine to Ockham,* University of Notre Dame Press, 1970; *The Priest,* Harper, 1973; *Gate of Heaven,* Harper, 1975. Contributor of scholarly articles to professional journals and symposia, and short stories and novellas to magazines; some magazine fiction has been published under the pseudonyms Harry Austin and Ernan Mackey. Editor, *New Scholasticism,* 1966—.

WORK IN PROGRESS: St. Thomas Aquinas, a volume in Twayne World Authors Series; *Rogerson Agonistes,* a novel.

SIDELIGHTS: McInerny told *CA:* "Early literary aspirations set aside, teleologically, to concentrate on academic career. Returned to fiction in 1963, publishing initially under pseudonyms, then employing my own name.... Have no wish to be a philosophical novelist or an artistic philosopher but intend to keep the two interests distinct. Dislike literary criticism intensely, despise book reviews and, of course, read both avidly. My literary heroes are legion."

* * *

McINTYRE, Kenneth E. 1918-

PERSONAL: Born May 8, 1918, in Wolbach, Neb.; son of Morris and Anna Elizabeth (Gerlach) McIntyre; married Eleanor McNeel, June 9, 1940; children: Mary Jean (Mrs. Jay C. Davis), Douglas, Robert. *Education:* Hastings College, Hastings, Neb., A.B., 1940; University of Nebraska, M.A., 1943, Ph.D., 1948. *Religion:* Methodist. *Home:* 4017 Greenhill Pl., Austin, Tex. 78759. *Office:* University of Texas, Austin, Tex. 78712.

CAREER: High school teacher of English and history in Nebraska, 1940-43; superintendent of schools, St. Paul, Neb., 1943-45; University of South Dakota, Vermillion, assistant professor 1945-48, associate professor of education, 1948-51; University of Tennessee, Knoxville, associate professor of education, 1951-52; University of Texas, Austin, associate professor, 1952-57, professor of educational administration, 1957—. *Member:* American Association of School Administrators, Phi Delta Kappa.

WRITINGS: Selection and On-the-Job Training of School Principals, University of Texas Press, 1960; (with Ben M. Harris and E. W. Bessent) *In-Service Education: Materials for Laboratory Sessions,* Prentice-Hall, 1968.

WORK IN PROGRESS: Research on selection of school administrators and on training programs for school administrators.

* * *

McINTYRE, W(illiam) David 1932-

PERSONAL: Born September 4, 1932, in Hucknall, England; son of John (a clergyman) and Alice Muriel (Stallard) McIntyre; married Marion Jean Hillyard, December 14, 1957; children: John Jefferson, Benjamin James, Ruth Margaret, Marcus Edwin. *Education:* Peterhouse, Cambridge, B.A., 1955, M.A., 1959; University of Washington, Seattle, M.A., 1956; School of Oriental and African Studies, London, Ph.D., 1959. *Politics:* "Floating voter." *Religion:* Congregationalist. *Home:* 331 Greers Rd., Christchurch, New Zealand. *Office:* University of Canterbury, Private Bag, Christchurch, New Zealand.

CAREER: University of Nottingham, Nottingham, England, assistant lecturer, 1959-61, lecturer in history, 1961-65; University of Canterbury, Christchurch, New Zealand, professor of history, 1966—. Occasional broadcaster and commentator on defense and foreign policy issues. Member of advisory committee, Historical Publications Branch, New Zealand Department of Internal Affairs, 1967—; member of executive committee, Paton Theological College, Nottingham, 1963-66; member of board of managers, St. Paul's-Trinity-Pacific Presbyterian Church. *Military service:* British Army, Royal Corps of Signals, 1950-52; became second lieutenant. Territorial Army, 1952-60; became lieutenant.

MEMBER: New Zealand Institute of International Affairs (vice-chairman, Christchurch branch, 1967-70), Canterbury Historical Association (president, 1967).

WRITINGS: Colonies into Commonwealth, Blandford, 1966, 3rd edition, 1974, Walker, 1968; *The Imperial Frontier in the Tropics, 1865-75,* St. Martins, 1967; *Britain, New Zealand and the Security of Southeast Asia in the 1970's,* New Zealand Institute of International Affairs, 1969; *Neutralism, Non-Alignment and New Zealand,* University of New Zealand Press, 1969; *Britain and the Commonwealth since 1907,* Heinemann, 1970; (with W. J. Gardner) *Speeches and Documents on New Zealand History,* Clarendon Press, 1971; *The Commonwealth of Nations, 1869-1971: Origins and Impact,* University of Minnesota Press, in press.

Contributor: Wang Gungwu, editor, *Malaysia—A Survey,* Pall Mall, 1964; *Australia, New Zealand, and the South Pacific: A Handbook,* Blond, 1970; J. Jensen, editor, *The European Experience,* A. H. & A. W. Reed, Volume I, 1970, Volume IV, 1971; K. Keith, editor, *Defence Perspectives,* Price, Milburn, 1972; Mary Boyd, editor, *Pacific Horizons,* Price, Milburn, 1972; *The Commonwealth: Its Past, Present and Future,* New Zealand Institute of International Affairs, 1973. Contributor to historical and American studies journals. Area organizer for the South Pacific, *Historical Abstracts,* 1966—.

WORK IN PROGRESS: An edition of the journal of Henry Sewell, premier of New Zealand; books on the Singapore Naval Base and New Zealand's defence policy between the wars.

AVOCATIONAL INTERESTS: Architectural history, photographing buildings and cities; reading detective stories.

* * *

McKAY, Ernest A. 1918-

PERSONAL: Born October 26, 1918, in Brooklyn, N.Y.; son of Ernest A. (a business executive) and Edna (Acker) McKay; married Ellen French, September 20, 1947; children: Donald, Elizabeth, Jean, David, Richard, John, Stephen. *Education:* Colgate University, A.B., 1939; City University of New York, M.A., 1963; New York University, Ph.D., 1969. *Politics:* Independent Republican. *Religion:* Presbyterian. *Residence:* Lloyd Harbor, N.Y. *Office:* Mobil Oil Corp., 150 East 42nd St., New York, N.Y.

CAREER: Mobil Oil Corp., New York, N.Y., 1939—, wholesale programs manager, 1966—. Consulting editor for Macmillan Co. *Military service:* U.S. Naval Reserve; active duty, 1942-46, 1951-53; became lieutenant commander. *Member:* American Historical Association.

WRITINGS: (Author and editor) *The Macmillan Job Guide to American Corporations,* Macmillan, 1967; *Henry Wilson, Practical Radical,* Kennikat, 1971. Contributor to magazines and journals, including *New England Quarterly, Mid-America, Personnel Journal,* and *Banking.*

WORK IN PROGRESS: Contributing to *Dictionary of Modern British Radicals.*

* * *

McKEACHIE, Wilbert J(ames) 1921-

PERSONAL: Born August 24, 1921, in Clarkston, Mich.;

son of Bert A. (a teacher) and Edith (Welberry) Mc-Keachie; married Virginia Mack, October 30, 1942; children: Linda, Karen. *Education:* Michigan State Normal College (now Michigan State University), B.A., 1942; University of Michigan, M.A., 1946, Ph.D., 1949. *Politics:* Independent. *Religion:* American Baptist. *Home:* 4660 Joy Rd., R.R. 1, Dexter, Mich. 48130. *Office:* Department of Psychology, University of Michigan, 529 Thompson St., Ann Arbor, Mich. 48104.

CAREER: University of Michigan, Ann Arbor, instructor, 1948-50, assistant professor, 1950-55, associate professor, 1955-58, professor of psychology, 1959—, chairman of department, 1961—. Consultant, U.S. Office of Education, 1964. *Military service:* U.S. Naval Reserve, 1942-46; became lieutenant. *Member:* American Psychological Association (board member, 1964-67; president, division on teaching of psychology), American Association for the Advancement of Science, American Civil Liberties Union, National Association for the Advancement of Colored People, Sigma Xi. *Awards, honors:* LL.D., Eastern Michigan University, 1957; Sc.D. from Northwestern University, 1973, and Dennison University, 1975.

WRITINGS: (With J. E. Milholland) *Undergraduate Curricula in Psychology,* Scott, Foresman, 1961; *Teaching Tips: A Guidebook for the Beginning College Teacher,* Wahr, 1965; (with Charlotte Doyle) *Psychology,* Addison-Wesley, 1966, 2nd edition, 1970.

WORK IN PROGRESS: Research on effective college teaching and on teachers' responses to hostility.

AVOCATIONAL INTERESTS: Music (sings in choir and has composed anthems and songs), athletics, including softball (has pitched more than twenty-five no-hit softball games).

*　*　*

McKENNA, Sister Margaret Mary 1930-
(Sister Mary Lawrence McKenna)

PERSONAL: Born May 26, 1930, in Teaneck, N.J.; daughter of Walter F. (a labor union leader) and Stella (Schnell) McKenna. *Education:* Chestnut Hill College, A.B., 1955; University of Notre Dame, M.A., 1961; Ecole Biblique, Jerusalem, diploma, 1970; University of Pennsylvania, doctoral candidate, 1971—. *Home:* 438 East Walnut Lane, Philadelphia, Pa. 19144.

CAREER: Roman Catholic religious, member of Medical Mission Sisters. Medical Mission Sisters Novitiate, Philadelphia, Pa., teacher of Scripture and theology, 1955-67, postulant mistress, 1966-67; La Salle College, Philadelphia, professor of theology, 1970-75. Member of Pennsylvania Governor's Commission on the Status of Women, 1965-66; vice-president of Germantown settlement. *Member:* College Theology Society, Catholic Biblical Association.

WRITINGS—Under name Sister Mary Lawrence McKenna: *Women of the Church: Role and Renewal,* foreword by Jean Danielou, Kenedy, 1967; (with Sisters Mary Pierre, Mary Richard, and Miriam Theresa) *If it Matters,* Medical Mission Sisters, 1967. *Medical Missionary,* co-editor and art director, 1955-65, member of editorial board, 1964-66.

SIDELIGHTS: Sister Margaret McKenna travelled around the world in preparation for *If it Matters,* visiting Ghana, Uganda, East and West Pakistan, India, and Vietnam, in particular. Languages include Latin, Greek, German (all reading ability only), as well as French and Hebrew

(reading and speaking). She is especially interested in change in the Church and religious life, the status of women, art, and new forms of community and urban ministry.

*　*　*

McKENZIE, Barbara 1934-

PERSONAL: Born July 22, 1934, in Mount Vernon, N.Y.; daughter of Leslie and Euphemia (Anderson) McKenzie. *Education:* Rockford College, student, 1952-55; University of Miami, Coral Gables, B.A., 1956, M.A., 1958; Florida State University, Ph.D., 1963. *Home:* 60 Springdale St., Athens, Ga. 30601. *Office:* University of Georgia, Athens, Ga. 30601.

CAREER: Instructor in English at University of Miami, Coral Gables, Fla., 1958-59, Dade County Junior College (now Miami-Dade Junior College), Miami, Fla., 1960-61, and in Florida State University Extension Program at the Strategic Air Command Base, Homestead, 1963-64; Drew University, Madison, N.J., assistant professor of English, 1964-68; University of Georgia, Athens, assistant professor, 1968-72, associate professor of radio-TV-film, 1972—.

WRITINGS: Mary McCarthy, Twayne, 1966; (editor) *The Process of Fiction: Contemporary Stories and Criticisms,* Harcourt, 1969, revised edition, 1974; *Flannery O'Connor's Georgia* (book of photographs), University of Georgia Press, 1976.

WORK IN PROGRESS: An Anthology of Short Fiction, for Harcourt.

*　*　*

McKITRICK, Eric Louis 1919-

PERSONAL: Born July 5, 1919, in Battle Creek, Mich.; son of Fred L. (a railroad executive) and Colleen (Hodges) McKitrick; married Edyth Carol Stevenson (a teacher), December 26, 1946; children: Frederick Louis, Enid Lael, Charles Keith, Mary Caroline. *Education:* Hillsdale College, student, 1940-41; Columbia University, B.S., 1949, M.A., 1951, Ph.D., 1959. *Office:* Department of History, Columbia University, New York, N.Y. 10027.

CAREER: Columbia University, New York, N.Y., lecturer in American history, 1952-54; assistant professor of history at University of Chicago, Chicago, Ill., 1955-59, and Douglas College of Rutgers University, New Brunswick, N.J., 1959-60; Columbia University, associate professor, 1960-65, professor of history, 1965—. *Military service:* U.S. Army, 1941-45. *Awards, honors:* John H. Dunning Prize of American Historical Association, 1960, for *Andrew Johnson and Reconstruction.*

WRITINGS: Andrew Johnson and Reconstruction, University of Chicago Press, 1960; *Slavery Defended: The Views of the Old South,* Prentice-Hall, 1963; (contributor) William N. Chambers and W. Dean Burnham, editors, *The American Party Systems: Aspects of Party Development,* Oxford University Press, 1967; (editor) *Andrew Johnson: A Profile,* Hill & Wang, 1969; (editor with Stanley Elkins) *The Hofstadter Aegis: A Memorial,* Knopf, 1974. Contributor to professional journals.

WORK IN PROGRESS: The Age of Washington and Jefferson, with Stanley Elkins, for Oxford University Press.

*　*　*

McKNIGHT, Edgar V(ernon) 1931-

PERSONAL: Born November 21, 1931, in Wilson, S.C.;

son of William G. and Carrie Belle (DeMars) McKnight; married Shirley Robinson, June 4, 1955; children: Deborah Lynn, Edgar Vernon, Jr. *Education:* College of Charleston, B.S., 1953; Southern Baptist Theological Seminary, B.D., 1956, Th.D., 1960. *Home:* 201 Alpine Way, Greenville, S.C. 29609. *Office:* Furman University, Greenville, S.C. 29613.

CAREER: An ordained Baptist minister, serving churches in Kentucky and South Carolina; Chowan College, Murfreesboro, N.C., chaplain 1960-63; Furman University, Greenville, S.C., assistant professor, 1963-67, associate professor, 1967-74, professor of religion, 1974—. *Member:* Society of Biblical Literature, American Academy of Religion, American Schools of Oriental Research, American Association of University Professors, Torch Club.

WRITINGS: (With Oscar Creech) *A History of Chowan College,* Chowan College, 1964; *Opening the Bible: A Guide to Understanding the Scriptures,* Broadman, 1967; *What Is Form Criticism?,* Fortress, 1969; (with Robert W. Crapps and David A. Smith) *Introduction to the New Testament,* Ronald, 1969. Contributor to professional, college, and church periodicals.

WORK IN PROGRESS: Relation of generative-structural models of language and literature to New Testament hermeneutics.

* * *

McLEAN, Ruari 1917-

PERSONAL: Born June 10, 1917, in Minnigaff, Scotland; son of John Thompson (a civil servant) and Mary (Ireland) McLean; married Antonia Maxwell Carlisle (a history teacher), January 24, 1945; children: David, Andrew, Catriona. *Education:* Attended Eastbourne College, Sussex, England, 1931-35. *Home:* Broomrigg, Dollar, Scotland FK14 7PT. *Office:* Ruari McLean Associates Ltd., The Studios, Broomrigg, Dollar, Scotland FK14 7PT.

CAREER: Rainbird, McLean Ltd. (book design and production), London, England, founder and director, 1953-58; *Motif,* London, founder and editor, 1958-67; typographic designer in free-lance practice, 1958—. Tutor in typography, Royal College of Art, School of Graphic Design, London, 1951-53. Honorary typographical adviser to H.M. Stationery Office, 1966—. *Military service:* Royal Navy, 1940-45; became lieutenant, Royal Naval Volunteer Reserve; received Distinguished Service Cross and Croix de Guerre. *Member:* Society of Industrial Artists and Designers (London; fellow), American Institute of Graphic Arts, New Club (Edinburgh).

WRITINGS: George Cruikshank, Art & Technics, 1948; *Modern Book Design from William Morris to the Present Day,* Faber, 1958; *Joan Hassall,* Oxford University Press, 1960; *Victorian Book Design and Colour Printing,* Faber, 1963, 2nd revised edition, University of California Press, 1972; (translator) Jan Tschichold, *Asymmetric Typography,* Reinhold, 1967; (editor) *The Reminiscences of Edmund Evans,* Oxford University Press, 1967; *Magazine Design,* Oxford University Press, 1969; *Victorian Publishers' Bookbindings in Cloth and Leather,* University of California Press, 1974; *Jan Tschichold: Typographer,* David R. Godine, 1975. Art editor and contributor, *Connoisseur.*

WORK IN PROGRESS: Joseph Cundall: Victorian Publisher.

McMAHON, Edwin M(ansfield) 1930-

PERSONAL: Born May 28, 1930, in Sonora, Calif.; son of Edwin Fremont (a cattleman) and Anna Mae (Bromley) McMahon. *Education:* University of Santa Clara, B.S., 1952, M.A. (theology), 1966; University of San Francisco, graduate student, 1953; Gonzaga University, M.Ed., 1958; University of Ottawa, Ph.D., 1973. *Home address:* Greeley Rt., Box 3A, Coulterville, Calif. 95311.

CAREER: Roman Catholic priest, ordained, 1965. St. Ignatius High School, San Francisco, Calif., head counselor, 1960-61; Alma College, Los Gatos, Calif., instructor in religious psychology, and member of theological faculty for religious, 1963-66; St. Paul University, Ottawa, Ontario, instructor in religious psychology, and member of theology faculty, beginning 1967; University of Ottawa, Ottawa, Ontario, faculty member of department of religious studies, 1970—; member of field faculty, Humanistic Psychology Institute, San Francisco, Calif. Guest lecturer at various colleges and universities.

WRITINGS: (With Peter A. Campbell) *Becoming a Person in the Whole Christ,* Sheed, 1967; *The "In-Between": Evolution in Christian Faith,* Sheed, 1969; (with Campbell) *Please Touch,* Sheed, 1969.

WORK IN PROGRESS: A synthesis between humanistic psychology, psychic research and religion; a reinterpretation of Christianity in the light of human evolution.

AVOCATIONAL INTERESTS: Music, sculpting, fishing, and organic gardening.

* * *

McNAIR, Philip Murray Jourdan 1924-

PERSONAL: Born February 22, 1924, in Tiverton, Devonshire, England; son of Donald and Janie Grace (Jourdan) McNair; married May Aitken, February 3, 1948; children: Philippa Jane Anastasia Hamilton. *Education:* Oxford University, B.A., M.A., 1948, D.Phil., 1962; Cambridge University, Ph.D., 1963. *Religion:* Christian. *Home:* The Elms, 33 Edgbaston Park Rd., Birmingham B15 2RS, England. *Office:* University of Birmingham, Birmingham, England.

CAREER: Cambridge University, Cambridge, England, university lecturer in Italian, 1963-74, dean of Darwin College, 1965-69, fellow, 1965-74; University of Birmingham, Birmingham, England, Serena Professor of Italian and head of Italian department, 1974—. Visiting professor, University of California, Berkeley, 1970. *Military service:* British Army, 1942-48, in both noncommissioned and commissioned ranks.

WRITINGS: (Co-author) *The Mind of Dante,* edited by Uberto Limentani, Cambridge University Press, 1965; *Peter Martyr in Italy,* Oxford University Press, 1967. Contributor to *Encyclopaedia Britannica, Cassell's Encyclopaedia of Literature,* and to periodicals, including *History, Italian Studies, Listener,* and *Bibliotheque d'Humanisme et Renaissance.*

* * *

McNALLY, Robert E(dward) 1917-

PERSONAL: Born December 24, 1917, in New York, N.Y.; son of Louis J. and Margaret C. (Dolan) McNally. *Education:* Georgetown University, A.B., 1942; Woodstock College, S.T.L., 1950; Catholic University of America, M.A., 1952; University of Munich, Dr.Phil. (summa cum laude), 1957. *Home and office:* Fordham University, Bronx, N.Y. 10458.

CAREER: Roman Catholic priest of Society of Jesus (Jesuits). Woodstock College, Woodstock, Md., professor of church history, 1957-66; Fordham University, Bronx, N.Y., professor of historical theology, 1966—. Guest professor, Georgetown University, 1958-59, George Washington University, 1961-62; professor of Catholic studies, Brown University, 1965-66. *Member:* Mediaeval Academy of America, American Catholic Historical Association, Society of Church History. *Awards, honors:* D.H.L., Salve Regina College; American Council of Learned Societies grant-in-aid.

WRITINGS: Der irische Liber de Numeris: Eine Quellenanalyse des pseudo-Isidorischen Liber de Numeris, [Munich], 1957; *The Bible in the Early Middle Ages,* Newman, 1959; *The Reform of the Church,* Herder & Herder, 1963; *The Unreformed Church,* Sheed, 1965; (editor and contributor) *Old Ireland,* Gill & Son, 1965; *Scriptores Hiberniae Minores Corpus Christianorum,* [Turnhout, Belgium], 1973.

Contributor: *Isidoriana,* [Leon, Spain], 1961; *Reformers in Profile,* Fortress Press, 1967; R. A. Schroth, editor, *Jesuit Spirit in a Time of Change,* Newman, 1968. Contributor to *Encyclopaedia Britannica, Catholic Encyclopedia for School and Home,* and *Encyclopedia International;* also contributor of more than thirty articles to theology journals and religion periodicals.

WORK IN PROGRESS: A history of the Bible in the Middle Ages.

*   *   *

McNAMARA, Eugene (Joseph)   1930-

PERSONAL: Born March 18, 1930, in Oak Park, Ill.; son of Martin Joseph (an office worker) and Anna (Ryan) McNamara; married Margaret Lindstrom, July 19, 1952; children: Michael, Mary, David, Brian, Christopher. *Education:* DePaul University, B.A., 1953, M.A., 1955; Northwestern University, Ph.D., 1964. *Politics:* New Democratic Party. *Religion:* Roman Catholic. *Home:* 166 Randolph Pl., Windsor, Ontario, Canada.

CAREER: Fenwick High School, Oak Park, Ill., English teacher, 1953-55; University of Illinois, Chicago, instructor in English, 1955-59; University of Windsor, Windsor, Ontario, associate professor of English, 1959—, director of graduate program in creative writing, 1967—. *Member:* National Council of Teachers of English, Canadian Association of American Studies, Canadian Association of University Teachers of English, League of Canadian Poets.

WRITINGS: Discovery: Voyage of Exploration (twenty-four scripts of radio talks given over the Canadian Broadcasting Corp.), Assumption University Press, 1962; *For the Mean Time* (poetry), Gryphon Press (Windsor), 1965; (editor) *The Interior Landscape: The Literary Criticism of Marshall McLuhan, 1934-1962,* McGraw, 1969; *Outerings* (poetry), Delta Canada, 1970; *Love Scene* (poetry), Hellric House, 1970; *Dillinger Poems,* Black Moss Press, 1971; *Hard Words* (poetry), Fiddlehead, 1972; *Passages and Other Poems,* Sono Nis Press, 1972; *Diving for the Body* (poetry), Borealis Press, 1974; *In Transit* (poetry), Pennyworth Press, 1975. Also author of a teleplay, "The Stranger," with James Hurley, for American ABC-TV series "Johnny Ringo." Contributor of poems, articles, and short stories to anthologies, and to periodicals including: *Amer-*

ica, Critic, Western Humanities Review, Midwestern University Quarterly, Vagabond, Films in Review, Canadian Forum, and *Texas Quarterly.* Editor, *University of Windsor Review,* 1966—.

WORK IN PROGRESS: Short stories; a collection of poems, *Screens.*

SIDELIGHTS: McNamara writes to *CA:* "Poetry is a profession. It is what I profess. It in-forms all that I do otherwise—teach, write criticism, talk on radio, go to conferences. It is what I stand for." And, he adds, "I give forms to loss, grief, etc. I impose order on the chaos, the scattered pieces of my divided self." McNamara concludes: "The poem is a tightrope between the canyon of the trivial (uttering) and the abyss of the ego (self-celebration as an end in itself). A poet must of all men be reverent of others, otherwise he will use them as things in his self-dramatization. It's all been said: trees, rocks, clouds, autumn, women, God, horses, loss of youth, hair, love, hate, rage, lust, and politics. Ordinary must . . . be made fresh."

McNamara feels he was influenced by Thomas Wolfe, Walt Whitman, William Carlos Williams, Robinson Jeffers, and is interested in contemporary American literature.

*   *   *

McQUEEN, William A.   1926-

PERSONAL: Born June 13, 1926, in Greenville, Ala.; son of William Ashley (a farmer) and Erlyne (Turner) McQueen; married Ida Glynn Killough, December 28, 1952; children: Anne, Ellen, Ashley. *Education:* Vanderbilt University, B.A. (magna cum laude), 1949; University of New Mexico, M.A., 1952; University of Illinois, Ph.D., 1962. *Politics:* Democrat. *Home address:* Route 1, Box 8, Chapel Hill, N.C. 27514. *Office:* 520 Greenlaw Hall, University of North Carolina, Chapel Hill, N.C. 27514.

CAREER: University of North Carolina, Chapel Hill, associate professor of English, 1962—. *Military service:* U.S. Army Air Forces, 1945-46. *Member:* Milton Society of America, South Atlantic Modern Language Association, Southeastern Renaissance Conference, Phi Beta Kappa.

WRITINGS: (With Kiffin A. Rockwell) *The Latin Poetry of Andrew Marvell,* University of North Carolina Studies in Comparative Literature, 1964; *A Short Guide to English Composition,* Wadsworth, 1967, 2nd edition, 1971.

WORK IN PROGRESS: Two books, *Milton's Narrative Art* and *Milton: A Selective Bibliography.*

*   *   *

MEASHAM, D(onald) C.   1932-

PERSONAL: Born January 19, 1932, in Birmingham, England. *Education:* University of Birmingham, B.A. (honors), 1953, Certificate in Education, 1954; University of Nottingham, M.Phil., 1971. *Office:* Matlock College of Education, Matlock, Derbyshire, England.

CAREER: Teacher of English and other subjects in secondary schools, 1956-63; Matlock College of Education, Matlock, England, lecturer in English, beginning 1963, head of English department, 1969—. *Military service:* Royal Army Education Corps, national service, 1954-56.

WRITINGS: (Compiler) *Leaving: An Anthology for the Last Year at School,* Hutchinson Educational, 1965; *English Now and Then,* Cambridge University Press, 1965; (editor) *Fourteen: Autobiography of an Age Group,* Cambridge University Press, 1965; (editor) *Larger Than Life,*

Hutchinson Educational, 1966; (editor) *The Personal Element,* Hutchinson Educational, 1969. Contributor of poetry and reviews to *Tribune.*

WORK IN PROGRESS: A novel; research on the novel.

* * *

MEDNICK, Murray 1939-

PERSONAL: Born August 24, 1939, in Brooklyn, N.Y.; son of Sol Joseph and Betty (Greenstein) Mednick. *Education:* Attended Brooklyn College (now of the City University of New York), 1957-61. *Home:* 2417 Magnolia Ave., LaVerne, Calif. 91750. *Agent:* Toby Cole, Actors and Authors Agency, 234 West 44th St., New York, N.Y. 10036.

CAREER: Musician, song-writer, actor. Theater Genesis, New York City, co-artistic director, 1970-74; vice-president, New York Theater Strategy. Playwright in residence, Florida State University, 1972; visiting playwright, State University of New York at Buffalo, 1973; visiting faculty member, California State University, Long Beach, 1975. *Member:* Dramatist's Guild, Writers Guild, National Society for Literature and the Arts. *Awards, honors:* National Council for the Arts poetry award, 1968; Obie award for distinguished playwriting, 1970, for *The Deer Kill;* Rockefeller Foundation grant, 1968, 1972; Guggenheim Foundation grant, 1973; Creative Artist's Public Service grant, to the State University of New York at Buffalo, 1973.

WRITINGS—Plays: "Sand" (first produced in New York at Theater Genesis, March 26, 1967), published in *The New Underground Theater,* Bantam, 1968; *The Hawk: An Improvisational Play* (first produced at Theater Genesis, April 18, 1968; published in *The Off-Off Broadway Book,* edited by Bruce Mailman and Albert Poland, Bobbs-Merrill, 1973), Bobbs-Merrill, 1968; "Willie the Germ" (first produced at Theater Genesis, 1968), published in *More from Off-Off Broadway,* Bobbs-Merrill, 1972; *The Hunter* (first produced at Theater Genesis, 1968), Bobbs-Merrill, 1969; "The Shadow Ripens," first produced in San Diego at Theater Five, 1969, produced in New York City at Theater Genesis, 1970; *The Deer Kill* (first produced at Theater Genesis, 1970), Bobbs-Merrill, 1971; "Cartoon," first produced at Theater Genesis, 1972; "Are You Lookin'?," first produced at Theater Genesis, 1973; "The Black Hole in Space," first produced Off-Broadway at Gate Theatre, June, 1975; "Taxes," first produced Off-Broadway at St. Clement's Church, 1976. Also did adaptation of "Orestes," produced in Los Angeles at The Mark Taper Forum, 1974.

Television plays: "Iowa," commissioned September, 1974, produced by KCET-28; "The Waiter," commissioned July, 1975, produced by KCET-28.

Contributor of poems to *Spero, Transatlantic Review, Maps, Down Here, Genre of Silence, Poggamoggan, Evergreen Review, For Now,* and *The Great Society.*

WORK IN PROGRESS: Two books of poems; a novel, *Ringaleevio;* an untitled film; two plays, tentatively entitled *Visual Arts* and *Nickels.*

SIDELIGHTS: Michael Smith says: "*The Hawk* is a daring experiment that succeeded, and the most important single achievement of Theatre Genesis." The reason that *The Hawk* is such a great achievement is not so much because of its content, which is completely modern, or because of its form, which "is strange but not obstructive," but because it is a breakthrough in the "rigid separation of author, director, [and] actors. . . . Mednick provided a bare scenario to start, and from that the group communally made

The Hawk. The actors' involvement in creating their roles helps to explain the special quality of the acting, which approaches documentary realism within the form; it also lets them improvise in performance: the work goes on. Mednick's effort, I'd guess, shows in the nearly faultless tone of the language, despite its range; in the avoidance or reanimation of cliche, the direct, honest precision of what is told; and in the freedom of imagination behind the play's richness and density." Smith criticizes *The Hawk* because he believes that it "goes too far in pursuit of meanings and wanders into a house of mirrors, leaving those living dying women to choose significances they alone could yield. . . . *The Hawk* is too strong a play to explain itself, and it isn't convincing when it does." However, he concludes that, though "emphasis, balance, [and] proportion are off here and there, . . . the troubles are minor and curable."

BIOGRAPHICAL/CRITICAL SOURCES: Village Voice, October 26, 1967.

* * *

MEIGS, Walter B(erkeley) 1912-

PERSONAL: Born October 29, 1912, in Kansas City, Mo.; son of James B. (a contractor) and Alma (Jones) Meigs; married Helen Finley (a real estate broker), April 4, 1936; children: Berkeley Meigs Constable, Robert Finley. *Education:* University of Kansas, B.S., 1935, M.B.A., 1938; Harvard University, 1938-39; University of Southern California, Ph.D., 1944. *Office:* University of Southern California, Los Angeles, Calif. 90007.

CAREER: University of Southern California, Los Angeles, associate professor, 1945-50, professor of accounting, 1950—, head of department, 1953-63. Professor of finance and control, Instituto Post-Universitario per lo Studio dell'Organizzazion Aziendale, Turin, Italy, 1958. Certified public accountant in California; commissioner of certified public accountant examinations, California State Board of Accountancy. *Member:* American Institute of Certified Public Accountants, Phi Beta Kappa, Beta Alpha Psi, Kappa Sigma.

WRITINGS: Principles of Auditing, Irwin, 1953, 5th edition (with E. John Larsen and Robert F. Meigs), 1973; (with Charles E. Johnson) *Accounting,* McGraw, 1962, 2nd edition published as *Accounting: The Basis for Business Decisions,* 1967, 3rd edition (with A. N. Mosich), 1972; (with Johnson and Thomas F. Keller) *Intermediate Accounting,* McGraw, 1963, 3rd edition, 1974; (with Johnson and Keller) *Advanced Accounting,* McGraw, 1966; (with Johnson and Mosich) *Financial Accounting,* McGraw, 1970, 2nd edition, 1975; (with others) *Modern Advanced Accounting,* McGraw, 1975. Contributor to *Handbook of Auditing Methods* and to journals in his field. Editor of professional examinations department, *Accounting Review;* editor of current reading department, *Management Services.*

* * *

MEISNER, Maurice 1931-

PERSONAL: Born November 17, 1931, in Detroit, Mich.; married Lorraine Faxon (a geneticist), February, 1952; children: Jeffrey, William, Anne. *Education:* University of Chicago, M.A., 1955, Ph.D., 1962. *Office:* Department of History, University of Wisconsin, Madison, Wis. 53706.

CAREER: Harvard University, Cambridge, Mass., postdoctoral research fellow, 1962-63; University of Virginia,

Charlottesville, assistant professor, 1963-66, associate professor of history, 1966-68; University of Wisconsin-Madison, associate professor, 1968-70, professor of history, 1970—. Fellow, Center for Advanced Study in the Behavioral Sciences, 1966-67. *Member:* American Historical Association, Association for Asian Studies.

WRITINGS: Li Ta-chao and the Origins of Chinese Marxism, Harvard University Press, 1967; *The Mozartian Historian,* University of California Press, 1975; *The Chinese People's Republic, 1949-74: An Interpretive History of the First Twenty Years,* Macmillan, 1975. Contributor of articles on Chinese Communism to scholarly journals and books.

WORK IN PROGRESS: The Social and Intellectual Sources of Maoist Utopianism: A Comparative Analysis; Marxism in China: Essays on the History of Maoism.

*   *   *

MELTON, Julius W(emyss), Jr. 1933-

PERSONAL: Born September 25, 1933, in Jackson, Miss.; son of Julius W. (an accountant) and Jane (Williams) Melton; married Ann Kennedy, June 10, 1959; children: Mary Cambria, Catherine Ann, William Dudley. *Education:* Mississippi College, B.A., 1955; Union Theological Seminary in Virginia, B.D., 1958, Th.M., 1959; University of Geneva, 1959-60; Princeton University, A.M., 1962, Ph.D., 1966. *Home:* 822 Concord Rd., Davidson, N.C. 28036. *Office:* Davidson College, Davidson, N.C. 28036.

CAREER: Clergyman of Presbyterian Church. Union Theological Seminary in Virginia, Richmond, instructor in New Testament Greek, 1958-59; Southwestern at Memphis, Memphis, Tenn., assistant professor, 1963-66, associate professor of religion and assistant to president, 1967-70, vice-president for student affairs, 1970-72, director of deferred gifts, 1972-73; Davidson College, Davidson, N.C., director of planned giving, 1973—. Lecturer in humanities, Memphis Academy of Arts, 1964-67. *Member:* American Society of Church History, American Association of University Professors.

WRITINGS: Presbyterian Worship in America: Changing Patterns Since 1787, John Knox, 1967.

*   *   *

MELTZER, Bernard N(athan) 1916-

PERSONAL: Born October 17, 1916, in New York, N.Y.; son of Philip (a fur cleaner and dyer) and Anna (Kemper) Meltzer; married Ida Wasserman, June 11, 1944; children: Iris Jean, William Jay. *Education:* Wayne State University, B.A., 1943, M.A., 1944; University of Chicago, Ph.D., 1948. *Home:* 318 East Cherry St., Mount Pleasant, Mich. 48858. *Office:* Department of Sociology, Central Michigan University, Mount Pleasant, Mich. 48858.

CAREER: University of Chicago, Chicago, Ill., instructor and research associate, 1948-49; McGill University, Montreal, Quebec, assistant professor of sociology, 1949-51; Central Michigan University, Mount Pleasant, associate professor, 1951-55, professor of sociology, 1955—, chairman of department, 1959—. Summer lecturer at Wayne State University, 1945, and McMaster University, 1960. Chairman of Isabella County (Mich.) Civil Rights Committee, 1959. *Member:* American Sociological Association (fellow), American Academy of Political and Social Science, Society for the Study of Social Problems, American Association of University Professors, Ohio Valley

Sociological Society, Michigan Sociological Association (president, 1961-62). *Awards, honors:* Canadian Social Science Research Council grant, 1950; Michigan Academy of Arts, Sciences, and Letters citation and medal, 1969.

WRITINGS: (With P. Smith and H. Doby) *Education in Society: Readings,* Crowell, 1958; (editor with J. Manis) *Symbolic Interaction: A Reader in Social Psychology,* Allyn & Bacon, 1967, 2nd edition, 1972; (with J. Petras and L. Reynolds) *Symbolic Interaction: Genesis, Varieties, and Criticism,* Routledge & Kegan Paul, 1975. Contributor to professional journals.

AVOCATIONAL INTERESTS: Chess.

*   *   *

MELTZER, Morton F. 1930-

PERSONAL: Born April 15, 1930, in New Bedford, Mass.; son of Eli Newton (a businessman) and Bessie Estelle (Mackler) Meltzer. *Education:* Boston University, B.S. (summa cum laude), 1957; Rollins College, M.B.A., 1964. *Home:* 2722 Paseo St., Suite A, Orlando, Fla. 32805. *Office:* Martin Marietta Corp., P.O. Box 5837, Orlando, Fla. 32805.

CAREER: Technical writer for a U.S. Government agency, Joliet, Ill., 1957-58; Raytheon Corp., Bedford, Mass., technical editor, 1958-59; Martin Marietta Corp., Oralndo, Fla., manager of Technical Information Center, 1959—. Professor, Crummer School of Finance and Business Administration, Rollins College; adjunct professor in business communication and public relations, Florida Technological University. Conductor of seminars and workshops in business communication. President, International Galleries, Inc. *Military service:* U.S. Army, 1953-55. *Member:* American Society for Information Science, American Library Association, Special Libraries Association, International Communication Association, American Business Communication Association, International Society for General Semantics, Sigma Delta Chi, Kappa Tau Alpha. *Awards, honors:* George Washington Honor Medal from Freedoms Foundation, 1954.

WRITINGS: The Information Center: Management's Hidden Asset, American Management Association, 1967; *The Information Imperative,* American Management Association, 1971.

WORK IN PROGRESS: Manuscript on management communications in business and industry.

AVOCATIONAL INTERESTS: Photographing tribal life in the jungles of the world.

*   *   *

MELTZOFF, Julian 1921-

PERSONAL: Born February 16, 1921, in New York, N.Y.; son of Nathan G. (a minister) and Sadie L. (Marcus) Meltzoff; married Judith Ann Novikoff (a school psychologist), September 29, 1947; children: Andrew N., Nancy J. *Education:* City College (now City College of the City University of New York), B.S., 1941; University of Nancy, graduate study, 1945; University of Pittsburgh, M.Litt., 1946; University of Pennsylvania, Ph.D., 1950. *Home:* 9303 Shore Rd., Brooklyn, N.Y. 11209.

CAREER: Certified psychologist, New York State. New York University, New York, N.Y., assistant in testing and advisement unit, 1946; U.S. Veterans Administration, assistant chief psychologist in Mental Hygiene Clinic, Regional Office, Philadelphia, Pa., 1950-53, chief psychologist at Veterans Administration Hospital, Philadelphia, 1953-54, and chief of Psychology Division, Veterans Administration Outpatient Clinic, Brooklyn, N.Y., 1954—. *Military service:* U.S. Army, 1942-46; became staff sergeant. *Member:* American Psychological Association (fellow), Eastern Psychological Association, New Jersey Psychological Association.

WRITINGS: (Contributor) M. H. Sherman, editor, *A Rorschach Reader,* International Universities Press, 1960; (contributor) B. I. Murstein, editor, *Handbook of Projective Tests,* Basic Books, 1965; (with Richard L. Blumenthal) *The Day Treatment Center: Principles, Application and Evaluation,* C. C Thomas, 1966; (with Melvin Kornreich) *Research in Psychotherapy,* Atherton, 1970; (contributor) A. E. Bergin and H. H. Strupp, editors, *Changing Frontiers in Science of Psychology,* Aldine-Atherton, 1972; (contributor) *Readings in Psychology Today,* 3rd edition (Meltzoff not associated with previous editions), CRM Books, 1974. Contributor to psychology journals.

* * *

MENARD, Orville D. 1933-

PERSONAL: Born April 4, 1933, in Omaha, Neb.; son of Orville Edward and Myrtle (Weander) Menard; married E. Darlene Book, April 9, 1954. *Education:* University of Omaha, B.A., 1955; University of Nebraska, M.A., 1961, Ph.D., 1964. *Politics:* Democrat. *Home:* 5605 North 80th St., Omaha, Neb. 68134. *Office:* University of Nebraska, Omaha, Neb. 68101.

CAREER: Texas College of Arts and Industries (now Texas Arts and Industries University), Kingsville, instructor in political science, 1963-64; University of Nebraska at Omaha, 1964—, began as associate professor, became professor of political science. Visiting summer professor, Colorado State College (now Northern Colorado University), 1966. *Military service:* U.S. Air Force, stationed in France, 1956-58; became first lieutenant. U.S. Air Force Reserve, 1958-67; became captain. *Member:* American Political Science Association. *Awards, honors:* U.S. Department of State senior faculty fellow, 1967; American Philosophical Society grant, 1971.

WRITINGS: The Army and the Fifth Republic, University of Nebraska Press, 1967. Contributor to *Military Affairs* and *Midwest Quarterly.*

WORK IN PROGRESS: Research on political parties and modernization in France, and on the political history of Omaha, Neb.

* * *

MENASHE, Louis 1935-

PERSONAL: Surname is pronounced Men-*ash*-ee; born December 10, 1935; son of David and Bertha (Molho) Menashe; married Sheila Schreiber (a social worker), June 8, 1958; children: Claudia Lisa. *Education:* City College (now City College of the City University of New York), B.A., 1959; New York University, M.A., 1963, Ph.D., 1966. *Home:* 575 Sixth St., Brooklyn, N.Y. 11215. *Office:* Polytechnic Institute of New York, Brooklyn, N.Y. 11201.

CAREER: Worked in field of educational tape and phonograph recordings, 1955-60; Polytechnic Institute of New York, Brooklyn, assistant professor, 1965-68, associate professor of history, 1968—. Public affairs broadcaster, 1972-74. *Member:* American Historical Association, Amer-

ican Association for the Advancement of Slavic Studies, American Association of University Professors, Phi Beta Kappa. *Awards, honors:* National Endowment for the Humanities fellow, 1970; American Council of Learned Societies fellow, 1972.

WRITINGS: (Editor with Ronald Radosh) *Teach-Ins, U.S.A.: Reports, Documents, Opinions,* Praeger, 1967. Contributor of articles and reviews to *Comparative Studies in Society and History, Russian Review, Science and Society, Nation, Ramparts, Socialist Revolution,* and *Liberation.*

WORK IN PROGRESS: Studies in Pre-Revolutionary Russian Social History; Profiles in the Soviet Experience.

SIDELIGHTS: Louis Menashe is fluent in Spanish, Russian, and French. He told *CA:* "I am most interested in seeing at first hand the revolutionary transformation of backward societies—for example, the USSR and Cuba."

* * *

MENCHIN, Robert S(tanley) 1923-

PERSONAL: Born October 31, 1923, in Kingston, N.Y.; son of Abraham H. and Gertrude (Gorlin) Menchin; married Marylin Barsky, December 26, 1950; children: Jonathan, Scott. *Education:* New York University, B.A., 1948. *Office:* Roberts: Menchin & Meyer, Inc., 1 New York Plaza, New York, N.Y. 10004.

CAREER: Robert S. Menchin & Co. (advertising and public relations), New York City, president, 1966-71; Wall Street Marketing Communications, New York City, president, 1967-71; Roberts: Menchin & Meyer, Inc., New York City, executive vice-president, 1972—. *Military service:* U.S. Army, 1942-45; became sergeant major; received Asiatic-Pacific Service Medal.

WRITINGS: The Last Caprice (nonfiction), Simon & Schuster, 1964.

WORK IN PROGRESS: A nonfiction book, *Second Chance.*†

* * *

MENDEL, Werner M(ax) 1927-

PERSONAL: Born June 11, 1927; son of Herbert I. (an attorney) and Edith (Frankel) Mendel; married Lori Bard; children: Carl, Dirk. *Education:* University of California, Los Angeles, B.A., 1948; Stanford University, M.A., 1949, M.D., 1953; Southern California Psychoanalytic Institute, graduate, 1964. *Office:* School of Medicine, University of Southern California, 1934 Hospital Pl., Los Angeles, Calif. 90033.

CAREER: Psychiatrist, certified by American Board of Psychiatry and Neurology, 1959. Menninger School of Psychiatry, Topeka, Kan., fellow, 1955-57; Metropolitan State Hospital, Norwalk, Calif., staff psychiatrist and director of pilot rehabilitation project for chronic schizophrenics, 1957-58, director of outpatient services, 1958-60; University of Southern California, School of Medicine, Los Angeles, clinical instructor, 1958-60, assistant professor, 1960-64, associate professor, 1964-67, professor of psychiatry, 1967—; Los Angeles County General Hospital, Psychiatric Division, Los Angeles, member of attending staff, 1960—, clinical director of Adult Inpatient Services, 1965-67. Instructor, Southern California Psychoanalytic Institute, 1965—. Consultant to California State Department of Mental Hygiene, 1960—, and to mental health committee of

American Academy of General Practice, 1963-66. Special project director, Basic Books, Inc., 1966-69.

MEMBER: American Medical Association, American Psychiatric Association (fellow), American Association of Medical Colleges, American Psychoanalytic Association, California Medical Association (secretary of section on psychiatry and neurology, 1964-66, and chairman, 1966-67), Southern California Psychoanalytic Institute, Southern California Psychiatric Society, Southern California Institute of Psychoanalysis, Los Angeles County Medical Association.

WRITINGS: (Co-translator of section) *Existence,* Basic Books, 1958; (with G. Green) *Therapeutic Management of Psychological Illness: The Theory and Practice of Supportive Care,* Basic Books, 1967; (editor with P. Solomon, and contributor) *The Psychiatric Consultation,* Grune, 1968; (contributor) *Comprehensive Mental Health,* University of Wisconsin Press, 1968; (editor) *A Celebration of Laughter,* Mara Books, 1970; (with Arthur Burton and others) *Schizophrenia as a Life Style,* Springer Publishing, 1974; (contributor) *Twelve Therapists: How They Live and Actualize Themselves,* Jossey-Bass, 1974; *Supportive Care: Theory and Technique,* Mara Books, 1975. Contributor to *Current Psychiatric Therapies,* 1964, 1966, 1974, and of about sixty articles to medical journals. Editor-in-chief, Mara Books; member of advisory board, *International Encyclopaedia of Neurology, Psychiatry, Psychoanalysis, and Psychology;* member of book review staff, *American Journal of Psychotherapy.*

WORK IN PROGRESS: Schizophrenia, for Spectrum.

*   *   *

MENDLOVITZ, Saul H.   1925-

PERSONAL: Born February 16, 1925; wife's name, Roberta; children: five. *Education:* Syracuse University, B.A., 1947; University of Chicago, M.A., 1951, J.D., 1953. *Office:* Institute for World Order, Inc., 1140 Avenue of the Americas, New York, N.Y. 10036; and Rutgers University, New Brunswick, N.J. 08903.

CAREER: Admitted to Illinois Bar, 1954; University of Chicago Law School, Chicago, Ill., research associate, 1954-56; Rutgers University, New Brunswick, N.J., assistant professor, 1956-58, associate professor, 1959-61, professor of law, 1961—. Harvard University, visiting scholar, 1958-59, consultant to Social Studies Project, 1964; research associate, Princeton University, Center of International Studies, 1966-67; senior fellow, New York University, Center for International Studies, 1967-68. World Law Fund, consultant, 1962—, director of World Order Models Project, 1966—, president of Institute for World Order, 1974—. *Military service:* U.S. Army, 1943-45. *Member:* American Society of International Law (member of executive council, 1966-69). *Awards, honors:* Ford fellowships, 1954-56, 1958-59.

WRITINGS: (Editor) *Legal and Political Problems of World Order,* World Law Fund, 1962; (with Richard A. Falk) *Strategy of World Order,* Volume I: *Toward a Theory of War Prevention,* Volume II: *International Law,* Volume III: *United Nations,* Volume IV: *Disarmament and Economic Development,* all World Law Fund, 1966, Volume V: *Regional Politics and World Order,* W. H. Freeman, 1973; (editor) *On the Creation of a Just World Order,* Free Press, 1975. Also editor of World Order Models Project series "Preferred Worlds for the 1990's", 1966—.

Contributor: Marshall Sklare, editor, *The Jews: Social Patterns of an American Group,* Free Press of Glencoe, 1958; Roland J. Stanger, editor, *West Berlin: The Legal Context,* Mershon Center, Ohio State University, 1966; Richard S. Miller and Stanger, editors, *Essays on Expropriations,* Mershon Center, Ohio State University, 1967. Contributor to journals. Editor, *Correspondent,* 1965.

WORK IN PROGRESS: The U.N. and a Just World Order.

SIDELIGHTS: The series of books entitled *The Strategy of World Order* is the project of the World Law Fund to promote the study of war prevention in the classroom. Their use is being introduced experimentally into traditionally taught courses, in order to promote war prevention as a new academic discipline. Robert E. Riggs, reviewing the first four volumes, says: "The individual selections in the volumes, with some exceptions, are of high quality, and they are tied together in a coherent framework by the editors' thoughtful notes. The emphasis varies from one article to another, but the total impact is to play up the inability of present international institutions to cope with the threat of thermonuclear war and to stress the urgency of transforming the system into something more closely approximating world government."

BIOGRAPHICAL/CRITICAL SOURCES: Books, spring, 1967.

*   *   *

MENNING, J(ack) H(arwood)   1915-

PERSONAL: Born October 2, 1915, in Hondo, Tex.; son of William George and Mary Lillian (Whaley) Menning; married Dorothy Ellen Colby (a reading specialist), March 6, 1943; children: Whitney Harwood (daughter), Colby Harwood (son). *Education:* University of Texas, B.S., 1936, M.B.A., 1940; University of Illinois, graduate study, 1940-42. *Religion:* Episcopalian. *Home:* 46 Guilds Woods, Tuscaloosa, Ala. 35401. *Office:* Box J., University of Alabama in Tuscaloosa, University, Ala. 35486.

CAREER: Texas Lutheran College, Seguin, instructor in business administration, 1936-38; University of Illinois, Urbana, instructor in business English, 1945-46; Northwestern University, Evanston, Ill., instructor in business writing, 1946-47; University of Texas, Austin, assistant professor of business writing, 1947-48; University of Alabama in Tuscaloosa, School of Commerce and Business Administration, University, associate professor, 1948-53, professor of marketing in charge of business writing, 1953—. *Military service:* U.S. Naval Reserve, active duty, 1942-46; became lieutenant. *Member:* American Business Writing Association (president, 1950-52), American Association of University Professors, Beta Gamma Sigma, Alpha Kappa Psi.

WRITINGS: (With C. W. Wilkinson and C. R. Anderson) *Writing for Business,* Irwin, 1951, 3rd edition, 1961; *Writing Business Letters,* Irwin, 1955, revised edition, 1959; (with Wilkinson) *Communicating Through Letters and Reports,* Irwin, 1963, 5th edition, 1972.†

*   *   *

MERRILL, Edward C(lifton), Jr.   1920-

PERSONAL: Born January 29, 1920, in Asheville, N.C.; son of Edward Clifton and Alice (Tiddy) Merrill; married Frances Bonkemeyer, June 2, 1946; children: Susan, Nancy, Ned, Ann. *Education:* University of North Carolina, A.B., 1942; University of Tennessee, M.S., 1948; George Peabody College for Teachers, Ph.D., 1953. *Office:* Office of the President, Gallaudet College, Washington, D.C. 20002.

CAREER: Asheville-Biltmore College (now University of North Carolina at Asheville), instructor, 1946-47; high school teacher and assistant principal, Asheville, 1948-51; George Peabody College for Teachers, Nashville, Tenn., instructor in education, 1953-55; Auburn University, Auburn, Ala., associate professor of education, 1955-57; University of Rochester, Rochester, N.Y., professor of education and associate dean of graduate studies, 1957-60; University of North Carolina at Chapel Hill, professor of education, 1960-61; University of Tennessee at Knoxville, dean of College of Education, 1961-69; Gallaudet College, Washington, D.C., president, 1969—. *Member:* American Association of School Administrators, American Association of Colleges for Teacher Education (liaison representative for Tennessee), Associated Organizations for Teacher Education (chairman of advisory council), Southern Association of Colleges and Schools (chairman of committee on publications).

WRITINGS: (Co-author) *Community Leadership for Public Education,* Prentice-Hall, 1955; (editor) *Better Teaching in School Administration,* Southern States Cooperative Program in Educational Administration, 1955; (contributor) R. T. Gregg and R. F. Campbell, editors, *Administrative Behavior in Education,* Harper, 1957; *How Teachers View School Administration,* New York State Council for Administrative Leadership, 1959; (co-author) *School Administration in Newly Reorganized Districts,* American Association of School Administrators, 1965; *Professional Student Teaching Programs,* Interstate, 1967; (with Lee Katz and Steve L. Mathis III) *The Deaf Child in the Public Schools,* Interstate, 1974. Contributor to education journals.

*   *   *

MERRILL, Walter M. 1915-

PERSONAL: Born May 26, 1915, in Evanston, Ill.; son of Frank E. (a realtor) and Eunice (McIntosh) Merrill; married Anna Montgomery, July 29, 1939; married second wife, Adeline Godfrey, May 13, 1959; married third wife, Rhona H. Brockett, April 17, 1976; children: (first marriage) Scott M.; (second marriage) Adeline B., Margaret B. *Education:* Northwestern University, B.S.L., 1937; Harvard University, A.M., 1941, Ph.D., 1946. *Home:* 222 South Van Pelt St., Philadelphia, Pa. 19103. *Office:* Department of Humanities and Communications, Drexel University, Philadelphia, Pa. 19104.

CAREER: Loomis School, Windsor, Conn., English master, 1942-43; instructor in English at Amherst College, Amherst, Mass., 1943-45, Temple University, Philadelphia, Pa., 1945, Swarthmore College, Swarthmore, Pa., 1945-47, and Northwestern University, Evanston, Ill., 1947-53; Bowdoin College, Brunswick, Me., assistant professor of seventeenth-century English literature, 1953-54; Essex Institute, Salem, Mass., director, 1954-59; Wichita State University, Wichita, Kan., professor of English and chairman of department, 1959-69; Drexel University, Philadelphia, professor of English, 1969—, chairman of department of literature and languages, 1969-71. Artist, exhibiting paintings at shows in Boston, Philadelphia, Chicago, and Wichita areas. Member of board of directors, Wichita Community Theatre, 1959-66, Foundation of Wichita Art

Museum, 1960-65, Wichita Public Library, 1964-65, and Wichita Art Museum, 1965-69 (and treasurer, 1968-69).

MEMBER: Modern Language Association of America, Colonial Society of Massachusetts, Essex Institute. *Awards, honors:* American Council of Learned Societies fellowship, 1951-53; additional grants from American Council of Learned Societies, Northwestern University, Wichita State University, American Philosophical Society, Drexel University, and National Endowment for the Humanities.

WRITINGS: From Statesman to Philosopher: A Study of Bolingbroke's Deism, Philosophical Library, 1949; *Behold Me Once More* (journals of James H. Garrison), Houghton, 1954; *Against Wind and Tide: A Biography of William Lloyd Garrison,* Harvard University Press, 1963; (editor) *The Letters of William Lloyd Garrison,* Harvard University Press, Volume I: *I Will Be Heard,* 1971, Volume III: *No Union with Slaveholders,* 1973. Contributor to *Encyclopaedia Britannica;* also contributor of book reviews and articles to professional journals.

AVOCATIONAL INTERESTS: Comparative arts, especially film as an art form.

*   *   *

MERTON, Stephen 1912-

PERSONAL: Born November 26, 1912, in New York, N.Y.; son of Leslie R. (a civil engineer) and Fanny (Schor) Merton. *Education:* Columbia University, B.A., 1933, M.A., 1935, Ph.D., 1948. *Home:* 22101 Erwin St., Woodland Hills, Calif. 91364. *Office:* City College of the City University of New York, New York, N.Y. 10033.

CAREER: Instructor in English at State University of New York College at Albany, 1938-39, and Colorado College, Colorado Springs, 1939-42; Mary Baldwin College, Staunton, Va., associate professor of English, 1942-43; College of William and Mary, Williamsburg, Va., assistant professor of English, 1943-46; Cornell University, Ithaca, N.Y., instructor in English, 1946-50; City College of the City University of New York, New York, N.Y., professor, 1950—. *Member:* Modern Language Association of America. *Awards, honors:* American Philosophical Society grant, 1963; Fulbright grant, 1966, for research in Taiwan.

WRITINGS: Science and Imagination in Sir Thomas Browne, King's Crown Press, 1949; *Skyscrapers and Pyramids,* American University at Cairo, 1958; *William Hale White (Mark Rutherford),* Twayne, 1967.

WORK IN PROGRESS: A book on science, religion, and poetry.

*   *   *

MERTZ, Barbara (Gross) 1927-
(Barbara Michaels, Elizabeth Peters)

PERSONAL: Born September 29, 1927, in Canton, Ill.; daughter of Earl D. (a printer) and Grace (Tregellas) Gross; children: Elizabeth Ellen, Peter William. *Education:* University of Chicago, Ph.B., 1947, M.A., 1950, Ph.D., 1952. *Agent:* Raines & Raines, 224 Madison Ave., New York, N.Y. 10016.

CAREER: Historian and author. *Member:* Egypt Exploration Society, American Research Council in Egypt.

WRITINGS: Temples, Tombs, and Hieroglyphs: The Story of Egyptology, Coward, 1964; *Red Land, Black Land: The World of the Ancient Egyptians,* Coward, 1966;

(with Richard R. Mertz) *Two Thousand Years in Rome*, Coward, 1968.

Under pseudonym Barbara Michaels: *The Master of Blacktower*, Appleton, 1966; *Sons of the Wolf*, Meredith Press, 1967; *Ammie, Come Home*, Meredith Press, 1968; *Prince of Darkness*, Meredith Press, 1969; *Dark on the Other Side*, Dodd, 1970; *Crying Child*, Dodd, 1971; *Greygallows*, Dodd, 1972; *Witch*, Dodd, 1973; *House of Many Shadows*, Dodd, 1974.

Under pseudonym Elizabeth Peters: *The Jackal's Head*, Meredith Press, 1968; *The Camelot Caper*, Meredith Press, 1969; *The Dead Sea Ciper*, Dodd, 1970; *The Night of 400 Rabbits*, Dodd, 1971; *The Seventh Sinner*, Dodd, 1972; *Borrower of the Night*, Dodd, 1973; *The Murders of Richard III*, Dodd, 1974; *Crocodile on the Sandbank*, Dodd, 1975.

WORK IN PROGRESS: Under pseudonym Barbara Michaels, *Patriot's Dream;* under pseudonym Elizabeth Peters, *Ghost in Green Velvet.*

SIDELIGHTS: Barbara Mertz resided in Germany for two years, and two years in Rome. She speaks and reads Italian and German, and reads French. *Avocational interests:* Reading, needlework, music, cats, football.

* * *

MERTZ, Richard R(olland) 1927-

PERSONAL: Born November 11, 1927, in Wabash, Ind.; son of Rolland H. and Neva Maude (Anderson) Mertz; married Barbara Gross (a writer), June 18, 1950 (divorced, 1970); children: Elizabeth Ellen, Peter William. *Education:* Attended Purdue University, 1944-45; University of Chicago, Ph.B., 1946, S.B., 1948, A.M., 1953; George Washington University, Ph.D., 1963. *Politics:* Independent. *Agent:* Raines & Raines, 475 Fifth Ave., New York, N.Y. 10017.

CAREER: U.S. Department of the Army, Washington, D.C., research analyst, 1952-54, 1955-59, senior research analyst, 1959-62; senior operations research analyst, 1962-63; University of Virginia, Charlottesville, assistant professor of European history, 1963-64; writer and researcher in Rome, Italy, 1964-67; American University, Washington, D.C., assistant professor of European history, 1967-68; University of Geneva, Geneva, Switzerland, research professor, 1968-71; writer. Research associate, Smithsonian Institution, 1969-71. *Military service:* U.S. Army Air Forces, 1946-47. *Member:* American Historical Association, Conference on Central European Studies, Society for Italian Historical Studies, American Association of University Professors. *Awards, honors:* Research fellowships.

WRITINGS: (With Barbara G. Mertz) *Two Thousand Years in Rome*, Coward, 1968. Contributor of articles and reviews to professional journals.

SIDELIGHTS: Mertz is competent in French, German, Italian, Greek, Latin, Coptic, Persian, Pashtu, Demotic, and old, middle, and late Egyptian.

BIOGRAPHICAL/CRITICAL SOURCES: Washington Sunday Star, March 24, 1968.†

* * *

MESSINGER, C. F. 1913-

PERSONAL: Born January 21, 1913, in Allentown, Pa.; son of Melvin A. (a machinist) and Sallie (Diehl) Messinger; married Margaret Nicholls (a teacher), November 26, 1938; children: David, Paul, Diane, *Education:* Gettysburg College, A.B., 1938; Western Reserve University (now Case Western Reserve University), M.A., 1956.

CAREER: Boy Scouts of America, district executive in Jackson, Tenn., 1941-42, and Columbia, Tenn., 1942-45; Philco, Inc., Belvidere, N.J., personnel manager, 1945-47; program or education director at Presbyterian churches in Indianapolis, Ind., 1947-53, and Lakewood, Ohio, 1953-58; United Presbyterian Church in the U.S.A., Board of Christian Education, Philadelphia, Pa., secretary of junior high program, 1958—. Chairman, National Protestant Committee on Scouting; director, Protestant Relationship Service, Boy Scouts of America, beginning 1968.

WRITINGS: (With W. H. Merriam) *Cues for Church Camping*, Geneva Press, 1962; (with W. H. Merriam and Gail Ulrich) *Seeking Meaning with Junior Highs in Camp*, Geneva Press, 1966. Contributor to various denominational publications.††

* * *

MESSNER, Stephen Dale 1936-

PERSONAL: Born October 6, 1936, in Elkhart, Ind.; son of Dale Francis and Dorothy (Havlish) Messner; married Susan Ida Bailey, August 9, 1958; children: Stephanie Sue, Pamela Ann. *Education:* Indiana University, B.S., 1961, M.B.A., 1962, D.B.A., 1966. *Home:* Baxter Road, Storrs, Conn. 06268. *Office:* School of Business Administration, University of Connecticut, Storrs, Conn. 06268.

CAREER: Indiana University, School of Business, Bloomington, faculty research associate, 1965-66; University of Connecticut, School of Business Administration, Storrs, assistant professor of finance and real estate and assistant director of Center for Real Estate and Urban Economic Studies, 1966—. *Military service:* U.S. Air Force, 1954-58; became sergeant. *Member:* American Finance Association, American Real Estate and Urban Economics Association (president, 1974), American Economic Association, Regional Science Association, Beta Gamma Sigma (president of Connecticut chapter), Alpha Kappa Psi.

WRITINGS: A Benefit-Cost Analysis of Urban Redevelopment, Bureau of Business Research, Indiana University, 1967; (editor) *Minority Groups and Housing: A Selected Bibliography, 1950-1967*, Center for Real Estate and Urban Economic Studies, University of Connecticut, 1968; (with W. N. Kinnard, Jr.) *Effective Business Relocation*, Heath Lexington, 1970; (with Kinnard) *Industrial Real Estate*, Society of Industrial Realtors, 1971; (with B. N. Boyce) *Management of an Appraisal Firm*, Society of Real Estate Appraisers, 1972; (with I. Schreibel and V. L. Lyon) *Marketing Investment Real Estate*, Realtors National Marketing Institute, 1975.

WORK IN PROGRESS: Two research projects.

* * *

METCALF, Lawrence E(ugene) 1915-

PERSONAL: Born September 30, 1915, in Dennison, Ohio; son of George Madison (a clerk) and Oma (Cotter) Metcalf; married Barbara M. Stanberry, August 22, 1951; children: Janet, Alan, Andrew. *Education:* Ohio State University, B.Sc.Ed., 1940, M.A., 1945, Ph.D., 1948. *Home:* 1501 Western Ave., Champaign, Ill. 61820. *Office:* University of Illinois, Urbana, Ill. 61801.

CAREER: Goddard College, Plainfield, Vt., instructor, 1946-47; University of Georgia, Athens, associate professor of curriculum and evaluation, 1947-49; University of Illinois, Urbana, assistant professor, 1949-54, associate professor, 1954-61, professor of social studies, 1961—.

WRITINGS: (With M. P. Hunt) *Teaching High School Social Studies*, Harper, 1955, revised edition, 1968; (editor with John J. Deboer and Walter F. Kaulfers) *Readings in Secondary Education*, Allyn & Bacon, 1966; (editor) *Values Education: Rationale, Strategies and Procedures*, National Council for Social Studies, 1971. Contributor to educational journals.

* * *

METZ, Donald L(ehman) 1935-

PERSONAL: Born July 2, 1935, in Chambersburg, Pa.; son of Abram Lehman (a plant guard) and Mary (Diffenderfer) Metz; married Mary Coale Haywood (a sociologist), July 31, 1965. *Education:* Pennsylvania State University, B.A., 1957; Harvard University, S.T.B., 1960; University of California, Berkeley, M.A., 1965, Ph.D., 1971. *Politics:* Democrat. *Home:* 2952 North Stowell Ave., Milwaukee, Wis. 53211.

CAREER: Research assistant at Mount Zion Hospital and Medical Center, San Francisco, Calif., 1962-63, and Survey Research Center, University of California, Berkeley, 1964; Bureau of Community Research, Berkeley, Calif., research associate, 1964-65; Earlham College, Richmond, Ind., assistant professor of sociology, 1969-75; Marquette University, Milwaukee, Wis., assistant professor of sociology, 1975—. Member of Strategy (guiding board of interdenominational campus ministry), Berkeley, Calif. *Member:* American Sociological Association, Society for the Scientific Study of Religion, Religious Research Association, Society for Religion in Higher Education, Harvard Divinity School Alumni Association (advisory council member, 1966-68).

WRITINGS: New Congregations: Security and Mission in Conflict, Westminster, 1967. Contributor of poetry to *Christian Century* and Humanity.

WORK IN PROGRESS: Research on emergency medical care systems and on the effects social science knowledge has on individuals' commitment to societal values.

* * *

METZGER, Michael M(oses) 1935-

PERSONAL: Born June 2, 1935, in Frankfurt am Main, Germany; son of Ernst Ludwig (a physician) and Ilse (Loeffler) Metzger; married Erika Alma Hirt (an associate professor of German), August 30, 1958. *Education:* Columbia University, B.A., 1956; Free University of Berlin, graduate study, 1956-57; Cornell University, Ph.D., 1963. *Office:* Department of German and Slavic Languages, State University of New York, Buffalo, N.Y. 14261.

CAREER: University of Illinois, Urbana, instructor in German, 1961-63; State University of New York at Buffalo, assistant professor, 1963-67, associate professor, 1967-71, professor of German, 1971—. *Member:* Modern Language Association of America, American Association of Teachers of German, American Association of University Professors. *Awards, honors:* Summer research fellowship, State University of New York, 1966, 1968.

WRITINGS: Lessing and the Language of Comedy, Mouton & Co., 1966; (with wife, Erika A. Metzger) *Clara und Robert Schumann*, Houghton, 1967; (with E. A. Metzger) *Paul Klee*, Houghton, 1967; (with Gerard F.

Schmidt) *Der Hofmeister und die Gouvernante*, de Gruyter (Berlin), 1969; (with E. A. Metzger) *Stefan George*, Twayne, 1972; (editor with E. A. Metzger) Aegidius Albertinus, *Institutions Vitae Aulicae oder Hofschul*, Lang (Bern, Switzerland), 1975.

WORK IN PROGRESS: In collaboration with Erika A. Metzger, editing volumes five through seven of *Hofmannswalden-Anthologie*, for Max Niermezer, Tuebingen.

* * *

METZNER, Seymour 1924-

PERSONAL: Born October 29, 1924, in New York, N.Y.; son of Harry (an accountant) and Roslyn (Storper) Metzner. *Education:* Fordham University, B.S.Ed. (cum laude), 1949; Tufts University, Ed.M., 1950; University of Miami, Coral Gables, Fla., Ed.D., 1965. *Office:* Department of Education, California State University, Northridge, 18111 Nordhoff St., Northridge, Calif. 91324.

CAREER: Elementary teacher in Lemon Grove, Calif., 1953-62; Boston University, Boston, Mass., assistant professor of education, 1964-67; City College of the City University of New York, New York, N.Y., assistant professor of education, 1967-70; California State University, Northridge, assistant professor of education, 1970—. Planning consultant, Ford Foundation Two Bridges Model School District Project, 1967-68; test consultant, New York City Board of Examiners, 1968—. *Military service:* U.S. Army, 1942-46; became sergeant. *Member:* American Educational Research Association, International Reading Association, Association for Supervision and Curriculum Development, National Education Association, American Association of University Professors. *Awards, honors: American History in Juvenile Books* was included on American Library Association's list of outstanding reference books of 1966.

WRITINGS: American History in Juvenile Books, H. W. Wilson, 1966; *One-Minute Game Guide*, Fearon, 1968; *Seventy-Seven Games for Reading*, Fearon, 1973; *World History in Juvenile Books*, H. W. Wilson, 1973. Contributor to education journals.

WORK IN PROGRESS: Chalkdust and Children: The American Teacher in Fact and Fancy.†

* * *

MEYENDORFF, John 1926-

PERSONAL: Born February 17, 1926, in Neuilly-sur-Seine, France; son of Theophile (a painter) and Catherine (Schidlovsky) Meyendorff; married Marie Mojaysky, January 26, 1950; children: Paul, Serge, Elizabeth, Ann. *Education:* University of Paris, B.Ph., B.D., and Licencie es-Lettres, 1948, Diplome d'etudes superieres, 1949, Diplome de l'Ecole Pratique des Hautes Etudes, 1954, Docteur es-Lettres, 1958. *Office:* St. Vladimir's Orthodox Theological Seminary, Crestwood, Tuckahoe, N.Y. 10707.

CAREER: Priest of Eastern Orthodox Church. Orthodox Theological Institute, Paris, France, 1950-59, began as lecturer, became assistant professor of church history; St. Vladimir's Orthodox Theological Seminary, Crestwood, N.Y., professor of church history and patristics and editor of *St. Vladimir's Seminary Quarterly*, 1959—. Lecturer in Byzantine theology, Dumbarton Oaks Research Library and Collection, Harvard University, 1959-67; adjunct professor in department of religion, Columbia University, 1962—; professor of Byzantine history, Fordham University, 1967—. Chairman of Faith and Order Commission,

World Council of Churches. *Awards, honors:* LL.D., University of Notre Dame, 1966.

WRITINGS: Introduction a l'etude de Gregoire Palamas, Editions du Seuil, 1959, translation by George Lawrence published as *A Study of Gregory Palamas,* Faith Press, 1964; *St. Gregoire Palamas et la mystique orthodoxe,* Editions du Seuil, 1959, translation published as *St. Gregory Palamas and Orthodox Spirituality,* St. Vladimir's Seminary Press, 1974; (translator from the Greek, and author of commentary and critical notes) Gregorius Palamas, *Defense des saints hesychastes,* two volumes, [Louvian], 1959; *L'Eglise Orthodoxe hier et aujourd'hui,* Editions du Seuil, 1960, 2nd edition, 1969, translation by John Chapin published as *The Orthodox Church: Its Past and its Role in the World Today,* Pantheon, 1962, revised edition with additions by Meyendorff, Darton, Longman, & Todd, 1962; *Orthodoxie et catholicite,* Editions du Seuil, 1965, translation published as *Orthodoxy and Catholicity,* Sheed, 1966; *Le Christ dans la theologie byzantine,* Editions du Cerf, 1969, translation published as *Christ in Eastern Christian Thought,* Corpus Books, 1969; *Marriage: An Orthodox Perspective,* St. Vladimar's Seminary Press, 1970; (editor with Joseph McLelland) *The New Man: An Orthodox and Reformed Dialogue,* Agora Books, 1973; *Byzantine Theology,* Fordham University Press, 1974. Also author of *Byzantine Views of Islam.*

WORK IN PROGRESS: Byzantium and Russia in the Fourteenth Century.

SIDELIGHTS: The Orthodox Church has also been published in Italian, Spanish, Dutch, and German editions.

*   *   *

MEYER, Donald (Burton)   1923-

PERSONAL: Born October 29, 1923, in Lincoln, Neb.; son of Clifford C. (in publishing) and Maude (Myers) Meyer; married Genevieve Rogge, June 5, 1954; married second wife, Jean Shepherd Berwick (an illustrator), July 1, 1965; children: (second marriage) William; (step-children) Rebecca, Sarah, Jeffrey, Rachel. *Education:* Attended Deep Springs College, 1940-41; University of Chicago, B.A., 1947; Harvard University, M.A., 1948, Ph.D., 1953. *Politics:* Democrat. *Religion:* None. *Home:* Norwich Rd., East Haddam, Conn. *Office:* Wesleyan University, Middletown, Conn. 06457.

CAREER: Harvard University, Cambridge, Mass., instructor in history, 1953-55; University of California, Los Angeles, assistant professor, 1955-60, associate professor, 1960-65, professor of American intellectual and social history, 1965-67; Wesleyan University, Middletown, Conn., professor of history, 1967—, and director of American studies. *Military service:* U.S. Army, 1943-46. *Member:* American Historical Association, American Studies Association, Organization of American Historians. *Awards, honors:* Social Science Research Council faculty research grants, 1958, 1962; Guggenheim fellowship, 1966.

WRITINGS: The Protestant Search for Political Realism, University of California Press, 1960; *The Positive Thinkers,* Doubleday, 1965.

*   *   *

MEYER, Herman   1911-

PERSONAL: Born June 8, 1911, in Amsterdam, Netherlands; son of Herman and Elisabeth M. (Otten) Meyer; married Renske M. G. Harmsen, October 7, 1939; chil-

dren: Gerritt Jan, Anna Elisabeth (Mrs. Bert Jan Vermeer), Wouter Joris. *Education:* University of Amsterdam, doctorate, 1943. *Home:* Keizer Karelweg 343, Amstelveen, Netherlands. *Office:* Duits Seminarie, Spui 21, Amsterdam, Netherlands.

CAREER: University of Amsterdam, Amsterdam, Netherlands, professor of German literature, 1947—. Visiting professor, Yale University, 1955, University of Bonn, 1961, University of Pittsburgh, 1964, Princeton University, 1967, Harvard University, 1969. *Member:* P.E.N. Club (Netherlands), Royal Netherlands Academy of Arts and Sciences, Modern Language Association of America (honorary member), Akademie der Wissenschaften zu Goettingen (corresponding member), Deutsche Akademie fuer Sprache and Dichtung, Dutch-German Society (president, 1953—), International Society for Germanic Studies (president, 1960-65; honorary president, 1970—), Maatschappij der Mederlandse Letterkunde. *Awards, honors:* Great Cross of Merit of the German Federal Republic; Golden Goethe Medallion of the Goethe Institut; prize of Germanic Studies Abroad, Deutsche Akademie fuer Sprache und Dichtung, 1974.

WRITINGS: Der Typus des Donderlings in der deutschen Literatur, H. J. Paris (Amsterdam), 1943; *De Levensavond als Litterair Motief,* J. M. Meulenhoff (Amsterdam), 1947; *Das Zitat in der Erzaehlkunst,* Metzler (Stuttgart), 1961, translation by Theodor Ziolkowski and Yetta Ziolkowski published as *The Poetics of Quotation in the European Novel,* Princeton University Press, 1968; *Rilke and Visual Art* (in Japanese), [Tokyo], 1961; *Zarte Empirie* (collected essays), Metzler, 1963; *Der Sonderling in der deutschen Dichtung,* Hanser (Munich), 1963; *Wesenzulge des humoristischen Romans,* Angelsachsen-Verlag (Bremen), 1966; *Diese sehr ernsten Scherze: Eine Studie zu Faust II,* Stiehm (Heidelberg), 1970; *Natuerlicher Enthusiasmus: Das Morgenlaendische in Goethes "Novelle,"* Stiehm, 1973. Editor of *Euphorion,* and *Duitse Kroniek.*

WORK IN PROGRESS: Work on the history of literary motifs; work on the craft of fiction, poetics of verse, and the relationship between literature and the visual arts.

*   *   *

MEYER, Michael A.   1937-

PERSONAL: Born November 15, 1937, in Berlin, Germany; brought to United States in 1941; son of Charles M. (an electrical contractor) and Susanne (Frey) Meyer; married Margaret Jane Mayer, June 25, 1961; children: Daniel Alexander, Jonathan Eugene, Rebecca Ellen. *Education:* Hebrew University of Jerusalem, student, 1956-57; University of California, Los Angeles, B.A., 1959; Hebrew Union College—Jewish Institute of Religion, Los Angeles, B.H.L., 1960; Hebrew Union College—Jewish Institute of Religion, Cincinnati, Ph.D., 1964. *Office:* Hebrew Union College—Jewish Institute of Religion, Cincinnati, Ohio 45220.

CAREER: Hebrew Union College—Jewish Institute of Religion, Los Angeles, Calif., assistant professor of Jewish history, 1964-67; Hebrew Union College—Jewish Institute of Religion, Cincinnati, Ohio, assistant professor, 1967-68, associate professor, 1968-72, professor of Jewish history, 1972—. Visiting assistant professor of Jewish history, University of California, Los Angeles, 1965-67; visiting senior lecturer, University of Haifa, 1970-71, Ben-Gurion University, 1971-72. *Member:* American Historical Association, Central Conference of American Rabbis, American

Academy for Jewish Research, Association for Jewish Studies (vice-president), Historical Society of Israel, Phi Beta Kappa.

WRITINGS: The Origins of the Modern Jews: Jewish Identity and European Culture in Germany, 1749-1824, Wayne State University Press, 1967; Ideas of Jewish History, Behrman, 1974. Contributor to Leo Baeck Institute Year Book, and to Jewish and historical journals.

WORK IN PROGRESS: Further research in German Jewish history and on the history of the Jewish Reform movement.

* * *

MEYER, Michael C. 1935-

PERSONAL: Born September 6, 1935, in Albuquerque, N.M.; son of Jack and Ethel (Lubin) Meyer; married Goldalee Kochman, September 7, 1958; children: Scott Randall, Debra Ann, Sharon Leslie. Education: University of New Mexico, B.A., 1957, M.A., 1961, Ph.D., 1963; also studied at National University of Mexico, 1954, 1956, University of Wisconsin, 1957, and Mexico City College, 1957-58. Home: 5400 North Suncrest Pl., Tucson, Ariz. 85718. Office: Department of History, University of Arizona, Tucson, Ariz. 85721.

CAREER: University of Nebraska, Lincoln, assistant professor, 1963-67, associate professor of history, 1967-72; University of Arizona, Tucson, professor and director of Latin America Center, 1973—. Coordinator of Latin American area studies at Peace Corps Training Center, University of New Mexico, summers, 1963, 1965, 1966. Military service: U.S. Army, 1958-60; served in Japan. Member: American Historical Association, Organization of American Historians, Latin American Studies Association.

WRITINGS: Mexican Rebel: Pascual Orozco and the Mexican Revolution, University of Nebraska Press, 1967; (with David Trask and Roger Trask) A Bibliography of United States-Latin American Relations Since 1810, University of Nebraska Press, 1968; Huerta: A Political Portrait, University of Nebraska Press, 1972; (with Richard E. Greenleaf) Research in Mexican History, University of Nebraska Press, 1973. Contributor to professional journals. Managing editor of Hispanic American Historical Review. Contributor to professional journals.

WORK IN PROGRESS: The Terrazas Family, completion expected in 1977; research in Mexican and U.S. archives.

SIDELIGHTS: Michael Meyer is fluent in Spanish and Portuguese and has fair competence in French and German.

* * *

MEYEROWITZ, Patricia 1933-

PERSONAL: Born March 29, 1933, in London, England; daughter of Jack (a businessman) and Bella (Apple) Marks; married Jacob Meyerowitz (an electronic music composer), October 27, 1957. Education: Attended technical college and secretarial college in London, England, 1949-51, and art college, 1959-60. Home: 12 West 17th St., New York, N.Y. 10011.

CAREER: Artist, doing sculpture and jewelry. Work has been exhibited in London, New York, and Washington, D.C., galleries, including one-woman show at Hartley gallery, New York, 1973.

WRITINGS: Jewelry and Sculpture through Unit Construction, Reinhold, 1967; (editor) Gertrude Stein: Writings and Lectures, 1909-1945 (anthology), P. Owen, 1967, Penguin, 1971; (author of preface and introduction) Gertrude Stein, How to Write, Dover, 1975. Contributor to commemorative anthology on Gertrude Stein, The Widening Circle, edited by William D. Baker.

* * *

MEYERS, Susan 1942-

PERSONAL: Born November 5, 1942, in Brooklyn, N.Y.; daughter of Palmer (a writer) and Helvia (Ostman) Thompson; married former spouse, Stephen A. Meyers, October 6, 1961; children: Jessica Lauren. Education: University of California, Berkeley, A.B., 1965. Home: 2031 Bentley Ave., Los Angeles, Calif. 90025.

MEMBER: Writer's Guild, Society of Children's Book Writers, California Writer's Guild, Southern California Council on Literature for Children and Young People. Awards, honors: Melissa Finds a Mystery was winner of Dodd, Mead's Calling All Girls Prize Competition in mystery category, 1966; Gravel Awards certificate of merit, American Bar Association, 1973, for article "Legal Supermarkets."

WRITINGS: Melissa Finds a Mystery, Dodd, 1966; The Cabin on the Fjord, Doubleday, 1968; The Mysterious Bender Bones, Doubleday, 1970. Author of script for television series "Good Times," CBS-TV.

WORK IN PROGRESS: Margaret Bourke-White: A Different Life, a biography, for Harper.

* * *

MICKIEWICZ, Ellen Propper 1938-

PERSONAL: Surname is pronounced Mits-Keh-vich; born November 6, 1938, in Hartford, Conn.; daughter of George K. and Rebecca (Adler) Propper; married Denis Mickiewicz (an associate professor at Michigan State University), June 2, 1963. Education: Wellesley College, B.A., 1960; Yale University, M.A., 1961, Ph.D., 1965. Home: 361 Southlawn Ave., East Lansing, Mich. 48823. Office: Department of Political Science, Michigan State University, East Lansing, Mich. 48824.

CAREER: Yale University, New Haven, Conn., lecturer in political science, 1965-67; Michigan State University, East Lansing, assistant professor, 1967-69, associate professor, 1969-73, professor of political science, 1973—. Founder and first chairman of the board of directors, Opera Guild of Greater Lansing. Member: American Political Science Association, American Association for the Advancement of Slavic Studies.

WRITINGS: Soviet Political Schools, Yale University Press, 1967; (editor and contributor) Handbook of Soviet Social Science Data, Free Press, 1973.

WORK IN PROGRESS: The Ladder of Power: Recruitment and Mobility in the Communist Party of the Soviet Union.

* * *

MILBURN, Josephine F(ishel) 1928-

PERSONAL: Born April 26, 1928, in Lynchburg, Va.; daughter of Sol Buxton and Mary Virginia (Robinson) Fishel; married Ronald Milburn, May 7, 1955; children: Rosemary, Jeffrey. Education: Lynchburg College, student, 1944-46; University of North Carolina, B.A., 1948; Louisiana State University, M.A., 1949; Duke University, Ph.D., 1956. *Home:* 115 Bowen St., Providence, R.I. 09206. *Office:* Department of Political Science, University of Rhode Island, Kingston, R.I. 02881.

CAREER: Chicago City Junior College, Wilson Branch, Chicago, Ill., instructor, 1956-57; Simmons College, Boston, Mass., instructor, 1957-61, assistant professor, 1961-66, associate professor of government, 1966-70; University of Rhode Island, Kingston, associate professor, 1970—. Lecturer at Northeastern University, 1961-62, Brandeis University, 1963-64; visiting fellow, Australian National University, 1975. Consultant, Office of High Speed Ground Transportation; public member of advisory committee, Commonwealth (Massachusetts) Service Corps, 1964-70. Member of national screening committee, Institute of International Education, 1960-66. Director, Seminar for Women in Politics, Simmons College, 1968-69.

MEMBER: International Political Science Association, American Political Science Association, Conference on British Studies, African Studies Association (fellow), Africa Studies Association (Great Britain), American Association of University Professors, American Association of University Women. *Awards, honors:* Fulbright scholarship for study in New Zealand, 1954-55, 1974-75; fellowship of Commonwealth Studies Center at Duke University for study in Australia, South Africa, and England, 1955; faculty fellow, National Center for Education in Politics, 1964-65; National Science Foundation and American Philosophical Society grants for research in England and Ghana, 1965-66.

WRITINGS: Governments in the Commonwealth, Harper, 1965; *Women as Citizens,* Sage, 1975. Contributor to professional journals.

WORK IN PROGRESS: British Business Independence in Ghana; Strategies for Community Development.

* * *

MILD, Warren (Paul) 1922-

PERSONAL: Born March 22, 1922, in Minneapolis, Minn.; son of Lawrence Albert (a bus driver) and Clara (Kumm) Mild; married Phyllis Jensen (an orders processor), August 21, 1943; children: David, Samuel Joanne. *Education:* University of Minnesota, B.A., 1946, M.A., 1947, Ph.D., 1950. *Politics:* Democrat. *Religion:* American Baptist. *Home:* 1001 Wentz Rd., Blue Bell, Pa. 19422.

CAREER: Bethel College, St. Paul, Minn., instructor in English, 1948-50; University of Redlands, Redlands, Calif., instructor, 1950-51, assistant professor, 1951-55, associate professor of English, 1955-58, director of admissions, 1951-54; American Baptist Convention, Board of Education and Publications, Valley Forge, Pa., director of collegiate education, 1958-65; Ellen Cushing Junior College, Bryn Mawr, Pa., president, 1966-74; full-time writer, 1975—. Member of board of governors, Radnor Scholarship Committee, 1967-68. *Military service:* U.S. Army, 1942-46; became staff sergeant. *Awards, honors:* Ford Foundation fellowship, 1954-55.

WRITINGS: What Do the Lions Eat When Daniel's Out to Lunch? (drama), Judson, 1964; *Strangers Outside the Feast* (drama), Friendship, 1966; *Fractured Questions,* Judson, 1966; *The Drop-Ins,* Judson, 1968. Also made a recording, "Look Back and Dream."

WORK IN PROGRESS: Audiovisual scripts.

MILES, Herbert J(ackson) 1907-

PERSONAL: Born July 7, 1907, in Clarence, Mo.; son of Joseph Edward (a farmer) and Sarah Ellen (Stanley) Miles; married Dorothy Elizabeth Wilson (an assistant professor of music), May 22, 1932; children: Stanley Wilson. *Education:* Westminster College, Fulton, Mo., A.B., 1932, Southwestern Baptist Theological Seminary, Th.M., 1935; Baylor University, M.A., 1949; University of Missouri, Ph.D., 1953. *Politics:* Republican. *Home:* 713 Branner Ave., Jefferson City, Tenn. 37760. *Office:* Department of Sociology, Carson-Newman College, Jefferson City, Tenn. 37760.

CAREER: Ordained to ministry of Baptist Church, 1930; marriage and family life consultant. Pastor in Mabank, Tex., 1932-36, Macon, Mo., 1936-38, West Frankfort, Ill., 1938-43, and Springfield, Mo., 1944-47; Baylor University, Waco, Tex., instructor in sociology and philosophy, 1948-49; Oklahoma Baptist University, Shawnee, instructor in sociology, 1949-53; Carson-Newman College, Jefferson City, Tenn., professor of sociology, 1953-72, professor emeritus, 1972—, chairman of department, beginning, 1955, Russell Bradley Jones lecturer in Christianity, 1966. Lyceum lecturer, Morristown College, 1967; president of Baptist Conference, 1945-46. *Member:* American Association of Marriage and Family Counselors, American Association of Sex Educators and Counselors, Southern Sociological Society, Alpha Kappa Delta.

WRITINGS: Movies and Morals, Zondervan, 1947; *Sexual Happiness in Marriage: A Christian Interpretation of Sexual Adjustment in Marriage,* Zondervan, 1967; (contributor) J. Allan Peterson, compiler, *The Marriage Affair,* Tyndale, 1971; *Sexual Understanding Before Marriage,* Zondervan, 1972; *The Dating Game,* Zondervan, 1975. Also author of *The Cost of Formal Weddings,* 1959, *Marriage Ceremony Trends,* 1963, *Honeymoon Trends,* 1966. Contributor to *Family Life, Midwest Sociologist,* and Baptist journals.

WORK IN PROGRESS: Two books, *The Case for Premarriage Chastity* and *The Way of a Man with a Maid;* research on patterns of masturbation among boys in a church-related college.†

* * *

MILES, O. Thomas 1923-

PERSONAL: Born January 16, 1923, in Baltimore, Md.; son of Oscar T. (in transportation) and Myrtle E. (Seidel) Miles; married Sue M. McCrary, June 7, 1948; children: Sally Lou, Kathleen Virginia. *Education:* Muskingum College, B.A., 1948; Princeton Theological Seminary, B.D., 1951; graduate study at University of Maryland, 1958-62, and San Francisco Theological Seminary, 1963—.

CAREER: Clergyman of United Presbyterian Church; minister in Levittown, N.Y., 1951-57, and Washington, D.C., 1957-65; Central United Presbyterian Church, Buffalo, N.Y., minister, 1965—. *Military service:* U.S. Army, Medical Administrative Corps, 1943-46; became first lieutenant.

WRITINGS: Dialogues with God, Eerdmans, 1966; *Crisis and Creed,* Eerdmans, 1968. Contributor to religious and philosophical periodicals.

WORK IN PROGRESS: A book of essays based on the writings of Rudolph Bultmann.††

MILIC, Louis T(onko) 1922-

PERSONAL: Born September 5, 1922, in Split, Yugoslavia; became a U.S. citizen; son of Tonko Lujo (an engineer) and Helene (Gross) Milic; married Jan Louise Lundgren, November 20, 1970. *Education:* Columbia University, A.B., 1948, M.A., 1950, Ph.D., 1963. *Politics:* Independent liberal. *Home:* 1 Bratenahl Pl., Cleveland, Ohio 44108. *Office:* Department of English, Cleveland State University, Cleveland, Ohio 44115.

CAREER: Montana State College (now University), Bozeman, instructor in English, 1952-54; Columbia University, New York, N.Y., instructor in English at School of General Studies, 1958-63, and assistant professor, 1963-67, associate professor of English at Teachers College, 1967-69; Cleveland State University, Cleveland, Ohio, professor of English and chairman of department, 1969—. *Military service:* U.S. Army Air Forces, 1943-46. *Member:* Modern Language Association of America, Association for Machine Translation and Computational Linguistics. *Awards, honors:* American Council of Learned Societies fellow, 1966-67.

WRITINGS: A Quantitative Approach to the Style of Jonathan Swift, Mouton & Co., 1967, Humanities, 1968; *An Analytical Bibliography of Style and Stylistics,* Free Press, 1967; *Stylists on Style: A Handbook with Passages for Analysis,* Scribner, 1969; (editor) *Studies in Eighteenth-Century Culture,* Press of Case Western Reserve University, 1971; (with William S. Chisholm) *The English Language: Form and Use,* McKay, 1974. Editor, "New Humanistic Research" series, for Teachers College Press. Contributor to periodicals. Review editor, *Computers and the Humanities,* 1966-71; corresponding editor, *Eighteenth-Century Life,* 1974—.

WORK IN PROGRESS: An introductory textbook, *Basic Stylistics; The Augustan Prose Sample,* for Teachers College Press; research in eighteenth-century prose style, especially Richard Steele; creation of a computer package for stylistic analysis, AUTOSTYL.

*   *   *

MILLER, Calvin 1936-

PERSONAL: Born August 28, 1936, in Enid, Okla.; son of David Franklin and Ethel (Kent) Miller; married Barbara Joyce Harman; children: Melanie Dawn, Timothy Grant. *Education:* Oklahoma Baptist University, B.S., 1958; Midwestern Baptist Theological Seminary, B.D., 1961, D.Min. 1975. *Politics:* Republican. *Home:* 11929 Woolworth, Omaha, Neb. 68144.

CAREER: Clergyman of Southern Baptist Convention, 1961—; minister in Plattsmouth, Neb., 1961-66; Westside Baptist Church, Omaha, Neb., minister, 1966—.

WRITINGS: Once Upon a Tree ..., Baker Book, 1967; *Poems of Protest and Faith,* Baker Book, 1968; *Pulpit and Program: Sixteen Days on the Church Calendar,* Baker Book, 1968; *Burning Bushes and Moonwalks,* Word Books, 1971; *A Thirst for Meaning,* Zondervan, 1973, 2nd edition, 1976; *That Elusive Thing Called Joy,* Zondervan, 1975; *The Singer,* Inter-Varsity Press, 1975. Contributor of articles to *Christianity Today, HIS, Baptist Student, Baptist Program,* and other religious periodicals.

WORK IN PROGRESS: The Song, for Inter-Varsity Press.

MILLER, Cecilia Parsons 1909-

PERSONAL: Born July 15, 1909, in Mansfield, Ohio; daughter of Walbridge and Katherine Hooker (Whiteman) Parsons; married H. Lionel Miller (a writer), May 13, 1934; children: Thomas Kenyon, Daniel Benjamin, Damaris Ray (Mrs. Roger E. Milo), Elisabeth Walbridge (Mrs. Wayne R. Thompson). *Education:* Hillsdale College, B.A., 1932. *Religion:* Protestant. *Home:* 264 Walton St., Lemoyne, Pa. 17043.

CAREER: Writer, chiefly of poetry. Arts Festival of Greater Harrisburg, member of executive committee, 1966—, vice-president, 1972-73, president, 1973-74; secretary, Harrisburg Arts Council, 1970-71, 1972, and Harrisburg Manuscript Club. President, Presbyterian Interracial Fellowship of Great Harrisburg, 1968-70. *Member:* National Federation of State Poetry Societies (president, 1959-60; member of advisory board), Pennsylvania Poetry Society (president, 1957-61), Chi Omega Alumnae. *Awards, honors:* Over twenty awards for poetry, including Carl Sandburg Award from North Carolina Poetry Society, 1971, first place award from National Federation of State Poetry Societies, 1974, and Ogden Nash Award, 1974.

WRITINGS—Poetry: Not Less Content, Keystone Press, 1960; *Peculiar Honors,* Keystone Press, 1962; *To March to Terrible Music* (poems), South & West, 1967; *Stand at the Edge,* South & West, 1970. Also author of "Space Where Once a Husband Stood," 1972, for Mrs. Coretta Scott King. Work represented in many anthologies, including *La Poesie Contemporaine aux Etats-Unis,* La Revue Moderne, 1962, *Commemorative Anthology: John F. Kennedy,* Swordsman Publishing, 1964, *Kentucky Harvest,* D. Brandenburg, 1968. Also represented in anthologies prepared by American Poetry League, National Federation of State Poetry Societies, and Pennsylvania Poetry Society. Editor of Pennsylvania Poetry Society *Newsletter,* 1956—, and annual *Prize Poems,* 1958-70; National Federation of State Poetry Societies *Newsletter,* editor, 1963-66, 1968, member of editorial staff of anthology, 1965-67.

WORK IN PROGRESS: Three poetry manuscripts; four novels.

AVOCATIONAL INTERESTS: Environmental concerns, horticulture, collecting ("amateur status"), ten grandchildren, and pets.

*   *   *

MILLER, Clarence J(ohn) 1916-

PERSONAL: Born November 8, 1916, in Plainfield, Iowa; son of Orrin W. (a farmer) and Bessie (Hinckley) Miller; married Phyllis Atzenhoffer, July 29, 1951; children: Arthur W., Leonard D., Kenneth C. *Education:* Iowa State University of Science and Technology, B.S., 1940; University of Connecticut, M.S., 1942; Harvard University, Ph.D., 1955. *Religion:* Unitarian Universalist. *Office:* Regional Advisor, Economic Commission for Africa, United Nations, Addis Ababa, Ethiopia.

CAREER: University of Nebraska, Lincoln, assistant professor, 1950-56, associate professor of agricultural marketing, 1956-65; Stanford Research Institute, Menlo Park, Calif., senior economist, 1966-74; United Nations Economic Commission for Africa, Addis Ababa, Ethiopia, regional advisor, 1974—. Economic advisor, United Nations Food and Agriculture Organization, Caracas, Venezuela, 1956; chief of party of Agency for International Development contract, Weitz-Hettelsater Engineers, Inc., Rio De

Janeiro, Brazil, 1962-63. *Member:* American Agricultural Economics Association, American Association for the United Nations, American Association for the Advancement of Science, American Marketing Association, American Economic Association, American Association of University Professors.

WRITINGS: (Editor) *Marketing and Economic Development: Readings in Agribusiness Research,* University of Nebraska Press, 1967.

SIDELIGHTS: Miller has traveled in most countries of Latin America.

* * *

MILLER, D(ean) A(rthur) 1931-

PERSONAL: Born July 29, 1931, in Chicago, Ill.; son of Donald Braud and Bessie (Garrison) Miller; married Elizabeth Walter, January 16, 1955; married second wife, Mona Schekter, June 24, 1966; children: (first marriage) Douglas, Kenneth; (second marriage) Scott, Eric. *Education:* Northwestern University, B.S., 1953; Columbia University, M.A., 1958; Rutgers University, Ph.D., 1963. *Politics:* Democratic. *Home:* 16 Lynwood Dr., Rochester, N.Y. 14618. *Office:* Department of History, University of Rochester, Rochester, N.Y. 14627.

CAREER: University of Rochester, Rochester, N.Y., assistant professor, 1963-68, associate professor, 1968-72, professor of history, 1972—. *Military service:* U.S. Army, 1955-58.

WRITINGS: The Byzantine Tradition, Harper, 1966; *Imperial Constantinople,* Wiley, 1969. Contributor to *Jahrbucher fuer Geschichte Osteuropas, Byzantinoslavice, Greek Orthodox Review, Annales, E.S.C.,* and *Byzantion;* contributor of reviews to *American Historical Review, Slavic Review,* and *Social Studies.*

WORK IN PROGRESS: Research on urban formation; work on the typologies of kingship and aristocracy.

SIDELIGHTS: Miller is competent in Russian, German, French, Greek, and Latin. *Avocational interests:* Literature and archaeology.

* * *

MILLER, David Louis 1903-

PERSONAL: Born May 6, 1903, in Lyndon, Kan.; son of Otto William and Lucy (Plettner) Miller; married Mary Evelyn Harsh, September 9, 1929; children: Reese Plettner. *Education:* College of Emporia, B.A., 1927; University of Chicago, Ph.D., 1932. *Religion:* Protestant. *Home:* 1413 Ethridge Ave., Austin, Tex. 78703. *Office:* Department of Philosophy, University of Texas, Austin, Tex. 78712.

CAREER: University of Texas at Austin, instructor, 1934, assistant professor, 1935-39, associate professor, 1939-45, professor of philosophy, 1945—, chairman of department, 1940-44, 1949-59. Visiting professor at University of Hamberg, 1960, Kansas State University, 1967, and University of Miami, 1970. Director, Research Analysis Corp., McLean, Va., 1963. *Member:* American Philosophical Association, Philosophy of Science Association, American Association of University Professors, Southwestern Philosophical Society (president, 1947). *Awards, honors:* Texas Institute of Letters award for the book (by a Texan) making the most significant contribution to knowledge in 1959, for *Modern Science and Human Freedom;* Alexander von Humbolt Award, West German government, 1969.

WRITINGS: (With G. V. Gentry) *The Philosophy of A. N. Whitehead,* Burgess, 1938; *Modern Science and Human Freedom,* University of Texas Press, 1959; *Individualism: Personal Achievement and the Open Society,* University of Texas Press, 1967; *George Herbert Mead: Self, Language and the World,* University of Texas Press, 1973. Contributor of about fifty articles to philosophy journals.

* * *

MILLER, Douglas T(aylor) 1937-

PERSONAL: Born May 27, 1937, in Orange, N.J.; son of Harold Elwell (an executive) and Nancy (Taylor) Miller; married Sheila Conboy, August 24, 1963 (divorced, 1975); children: Arden, Gilman. *Education:* Colby College, B.A., 1958; Columbia University, M.A., 1959; Michigan State University, Ph.D., 1965. *Home:* 2621 Dobie Rd., Mason, Mich. 48854. *Office:* Department of History, Michigan State University, East Lansing, Mich. 48823.

CAREER: University of Maine, Orono, instructor, 1963-65, assistant professor of history, 1965-66; Michigan State University, East Lansing, assistant professor, 1966-68, associate professor of history, 1968—. *Member:* American Historical Association, Organization of American Historians, American Studies Association, Popular Culture Association.

WRITINGS: Jacksonian Aristocracy: Class and Democracy in New York, 1830-1860, Oxford University Press, 1967; *The Birth of Modern America, 1820-1850,* Pegasus, 1970; (editor) *The Nature of Jacksonian America,* Wiley, 1972; *Then Was the Future: The North in the Age of Jackson, 1815-1850,* Knopf, 1973; (with Marion Nowak) *The Fifties: A Social and Cultural History,* Doubleday, 1976. Contributor to *Encyclopedia of American History, Encyclopedia of American Biography,* and journals including *American Quarterly, Educational Theory, New York History,* and *Journal of Popular Culture.*

WORK IN PROGRESS: Work on a social and cultural history of America's recent past.

* * *

MILLER, Ella May 1915-

PERSONAL: Born May 22, 1915, in Harper, Kan.; daughter of Reuben M. (a farmer and preacher) and Lucinda Ella (Neuhauser) Weaver; married Samuel E. Miller (a clergyman and professor of Spanish), June 10, 1941; children: Samuel Ernest, John David, Martin Robert, Jeanne Susan. *Education:* Goshen College, B.A. and Th.B., 1941. *Home:* 1312 College Ave., Harrisonburg, Va. 22801. *Office:* Mennonite Broadcasts, Inc., 1111 North Main, Harrisonburg, Va. 22801.

CAREER: Mennonite missionary to Argentina, 1941-52; Mennonite Broadcasts, Inc., Harrisonburg, Va., conductor of homemakers program, "Heart to Heart," 1958—. *Member:* American Mothers Committee, Inc. (Virginia chapter).

WRITINGS: Ella May's Favorite Recipes, Mennonite Broadcasts, 1965; *I Am a Woman,* Moody, 1967; *A Woman in Her Home,* Moody, 1968; *Hints for Homemakers,* Herald, 1973; *Happiness Is Homemaking,* Moody, 1974; *The Joy of Housekeeping,* Revell, 1975. Her radio messages have been printed in leaflet form. Contributor to Mennonite periodicals.

BIOGRAPHICAL/CRITICAL SOURCES: Under the Southern Cross, Mennonite Publishing House, 1943; *The*

Touch of God, Herald, 1965; *God Healed Me,* Herald, 1974.

*   *   *

MILLER, James G(rier)   1916-

PERSONAL: Born July 17, 1916, in Pittsburgh, Pa.; son of Earl Dalton (a clergyman) and Mary Rebekah (Grier) Miller; married Jessie Louise Luthi, September 3, 1938; children: John Grier, Thomas Christian. *Education:* Student at Columbia Bible College, Columbia, S.C., University of South Carolina, 1933-34, and University of Michigan, 1934-35; Harvard University, A.B. (summa cum laude), 1937, A.M., 1938, M.D. (cum laude), 1942, Ph.D., 1943. *Home:* 8911 Shelbyville Rd., Louisville, Ky. 40222. *Office:* President, University of Louisville, Louisville, Ky. 40208.

CAREER: Harvard University, Cambridge, Mass., junior fellow, Society of Fellows, 1938-44; Massachusetts General Hospital, Boston, intern, 1942-43, resident in psychiatry, 1943-44; U.S. Veterans Administration, Washington, D.C., chief of clinical psychology section, 1946-47; University of Chicago, Chicago, Ill., professor in department of medicine, division of psychiatry, 1948-51, professor of psychology and chairman of department, 1948-55; University of Michigan, Ann Arbor, professor of psychiatry and director of Mental Health Research Institute, 1955-67, professor of psychology, 1958-67; Cleveland State University, Cleveland, Ohio, professor of psychology, 1967-71, vice-president for academic affairs, 1967-70, provost, 1970-71; University of Louisville, Louisville, Ky., vice-president of academic educational development, 1971—, president of university, 1973—. Visiting lecturer, Johns Hopkins University School of Medicine, 1971-73. Interuniversity Communications Council (EDUCOM), Pittsburgh, Pa., executive director and secretary, 1964-66, vice-president and principal scientist, 1966-70, trustee, 1970—. Diplomate in clinical psychology, American Board of Examiners in Professional Psychology, 1952—; diplomate in psychiatry, American Board of Examiners in Neurology and Psychiatry, 1953—. Consultant to U.S. Army, 1949-52, 1954-56, U.S. Public Health Service, 1962-63, National Society for Medical Research, 1962—, U.S. Arms Control and Disarmament Agency, 1963-64, United Cerebral Palsy Foundation, 1963-65, Educational Testing Service, 1967—, National Advisory Council on Vocational Rehabilitation, 1967—. *Military service:* U.S. Army, Medical Corps, 1944-46; chief of Office of Strategic Services assessment staff, 1945-46; became captain.

MEMBER: American College of Neuropsychopharmacology (charter fellow), American College of Clinical Pharmacology and Chemotherapy (charter fellow), American College of Psychiatry (charter fellow), American Association for the Advancement of Science (fellow), American Psychiatric Association (fellow), American Psychological Association (fellow; member of council, 1952-55; president, division of clinical psychology, 1958-59), Academy of Psychoanalysis (scientific associate member), American Society for Cybernetics (charter member), Association of American Medical Colleges, American Psychopathological Association, Group for the Advancement of Psychiatry, Operations Research Society, Society for General Systems Research, Society for the History of Technology, Institute of Management Sciences, Phi Beta Kappa, Sigma Xi, Phi Sigma.

WRITINGS: *Unconsciousness,* Wiley, 1942; (with others) *Assessment of Men,* Rinehart, 1948; (editor) *Experiments in Social Process,* McGraw, 1950; (editor and contributor) *The Pharmacology and Clinical Usefulness of Carisoprodol,* Wayne State University Press, 1959; (editor with L. Uhr and contributor) *Drugs and Behavior,* Wiley, 1960; (with George W. Brown and Thomas A. Keenan) *EDUNET Report of the Summer Study on Information Networks,* Wiley, 1967; (with Ralph Waldo Gerard) *Computers and Education,* McGraw, 1967; *Living Systems,* McGraw, 1976.

Contributor: W. Dennis, editor, *Current Trends in Social Psychology,* University of Pittsburgh Press, 1949; M. R. Harrower, editor, *Recent Advances in Diagnostic Psychological Testing,* C. C Thomas, 1950; R. Blake and G. V. Ramsey, editors, *Perception: An Approach to Personality,* Ronald, 1951; L. D. White, editor, *The State of the Social Sciences,* University of Chicago Press, 1955; J. H. Masserman and J. L. Moreno, editors, *Progress in Psychotherapy II,* Grune, 1957; *Research Frontiers I: Industry and the Human Being in an Automized World,* University of Michigan Press, 1957; *Science and Psychoanalysis I,* Grune, 1958; B. M. Bass and I. A. Berg, editors, *Objective Approaches to Personality Assessment,* Van Nostrand, 1959; S. M. Farber and R.H.L. Wilson, editors, *Men and Civilization: Control of the Mind,* McGraw, 1961; W. S. Fields and W. Abbott, editors, *Information Storage and Neural Control,* C. C Thomas, 1962; M. C. Yovits, G. T. Jacobi, and G. D. Goldstein, editors, *Self-Organizing Systems,* Spartan, 1962; R. W. Waggoner and D. J. Carek, editors, *International Psychiatry Clinics: Communication in Clinical Practice,* Little, Brown, 1964; David McK. Rioch and Edwin A. Weinstein, editors, *Disorders of Communication,* Williams & Wilkins, 1964; G. H. Grosser, H. Wechsler, and M. Greenblatt, editors, *The Threat of Impending Disaster,* M.I.T. Press, 1965; Masserman, editor, *Science and Psychoanalysis, VIII,* Grune, 1965.

Contributor to *Encyclopaedia Britannica, American Peoples Encyclopedia,* and more than seventy articles to science, psychology, and education journals. Member of editorial board, *Annual Review of Psychology,* 1948-52, *Progress in Clinical Psychology,* 1963—, and *Handbook of Clinical Psychology,* 1964; *Behavioral Science,* member of editorial board, 1955—, editor, 1964—.

WORK IN PROGRESS: Use of modern technologies and their implementation in higher education; research on information processing.

*   *   *

MILLER, Kenneth E(ugene)   1926-

PERSONAL: Born July 6, 1926, in Chapman, Kan.; son of Glenn Harold (an insurance claims adjuster) and Helen (Halbert) Miller; married Marilyn Marks, June 6, 1951; children: Susan and Lisa (twins). *Education:* University of Kansas A.B., 1949, M.A., 1951; Johns Hopkins University, Ph.D., 1955; University of Copenhagen, research scholar, 1962-63. *Home:* 178 Grove Ter., Livingston, N.J. 07039. *Office:* Rutgers University, 103 Washington St., Newark, N.J. 07102.

CAREER: Instructor in political science at Newark Campus, Rutgers University, Newark, N.J., 1955-56, and Hunter College (now Hunter College of the City University of New York), New York, N.Y., 1956-57; Rutgers University, Newark Campus, assistant professor, 1957-62, associate professor, 1962-67, professor of political science, 1967—, chairman of department, Newark College of Arts and Sciences, 1962-69, associate director of graduate studies, Newark Campus, 1969—. *Military service:* U.S. Army, 1945-46. *Member:* American Political Science Association, American Association of University Professors, American Scandanavian Foundation, Phi Beta Kappa. *Awards, honors:* Fulbright senior research scholar in Denmark, 1962-63.

WRITINGS: Socialism and Foreign Policy, Nijhoff, 1967; *Government and Politics in Denmark,* Houghton, 1968; *Power and the People,* Goodyear Publishing, 1973. Contributor to *Journal of Politics, Journal of the History of Ideas, American-Scandinavian Review,* and *Parliamentary Affairs.*

WORK IN PROGRESS: Research on minority and coalition governments in Britain, Canada, and Scandinavia.

SIDELIGHTS: Kenneth Miller is competent in French, Danish, Swedish, and Norwegian.

*   *   *

MILLER, Lillian B(eresnack) 1923-

PERSONAL: Born February 15, 1923, in Boston, Mass.; daughter of Samuel M. and Ida Frances (Curland) Beresnack; married Nathan Miller (a professor of history), November 3, 1948; children: Hannah E. Lieberman, Joel A., Rebecca S. *Education:* Radcliffe College, A.B. (magna cum laude), 1943; Columbia University, A.M., 1948, Ph.D., 1962. *Office:* National Portrait Gallery, Smithsonian Institution, Washington, D.C. 20560.

CAREER: Bard College, Annandale-on-Hudson, N.Y., instructor in literature, 1946-49; University of Wisconsin-Milwaukee, instructor, 1961-62, lecturer, 1962-67, associate professor of history, 1967-71; Smithsonian Institution, National Portrait Gallery, Washington, D.C., historian, 1971-74, historian of American culture, 1974—. Commissioner, Commission on Artistic Properties for the State of Maryland, 1973—. *Member:* American Historical Association, Organization of American Historians, Eighteenth-Century Studies Association, Authors Guild, Society for Art, Religion, and Culture, Phi Beta Kappa.

WRITINGS: Patrons and Patriotism: The Encouragement of the Fine Arts in the United States, 1790-1860, University of Chicago Press, 1966; *"If Elected ..." Unsuccessful Candidates for the Presidency, 1796-1968,* Smithsonian Institution Press, 1972; *The Lazzaroni: Science and Scientists in Mid-19th Century America,* Smithsonian Institution Press, 1972; *In the Minds and Hearts of the People: Prologue to the American Revolution, 1760-1774,* New York Graphic Society, 1974; *The Dye Is Now Cast: The Road to American Independence, 1774-1776,* Smithsonian Institution Press, 1975. Also editor of the Charles Willson Peale papers for the National Portrait Gallery. Contributor to *American Magazine of Art,* and historical journals.

WORK IN PROGRESS: The Fine Arts in American Civilization, a volume in *Chicago History of American Civilization; The Dynamics of Urban Cultural Change and Institutional Development.*

*   *   *

MILLER, Linda B. 1937-

PERSONAL: Born August 7, 1937, in Manchester, N.H.; daughter of Louis (a property manager) and Helene (Chase) Miller. *Education:* Radcliffe College, A.B. (cum laude), 1959; Columbia University, M.A., 1961, Ph.D., 1965. *Home:* 695 North River Rd., Manchester, N.H. 03104.

Office: 234 Green Hall, Wellesley College, Wellesley, Mass. 02181.

CAREER: Researcher and writer with United Nations Secretariat, 1959, and Foreign Policy Association, 1960-61, both New York City; Barnard College, New York City, assistant professor of political science, 1964-67; Princeton University, Princeton, N.J., research associate, 1966-67; Harvard University, Cambridge, Mass., research associate, Center for International Affairs, 1967-71, lecturer, department of government, 1968-69; Wellesley College, Wellesley, Mass., associate professor, 1969-75, professor of political science, 1975—. *Member:* American Political Science Association, International Institute for Strategic Studies, American Professors for Peace in the Middle East, American Association of University Professors.

WRITINGS: World Order and Local Disorder: The United Nations and Internal Conflicts, Princeton University Press, 1967; (editor and co-author) *Dynamics of World Politics: Studies in the Resolution of Conflict,* Prentice-Hall, 1968; *Cyprus: The Law and Politics of Civil Strife,* Center for International Affairs, Harvard University, 1968; (co-author) *Internal War and International Systems,* Center for International Affairs, Harvard University, 1969. Also author of *The Limits of Alliance: America, Europe and the Middle East,* for Hebrew University, 1974. Contributor to history journals.

*   *   *

MILLER, Paul R(ichard) 1929-

PERSONAL: Born August 28, 1929, in Indianapolis, Ind.; son of Arval H. and Mabel (Teegarden) Miller. *Education:* DePauw University, B.A., 1951; Northwestern University, M.D., 1954. *Politics:* Independent. *Religion:* Agnostic. *Office:* School of Medical Science, Anderson Building, University of Nevada, Reno, Nev. 89507.

CAREER: U.S. Public Health Service, assistant surgeon, 1955-57; Northwestern University Medical School, Chicago, Ill., assistant professor of psychiatry, 1960-69; University of California, Davis, associate professor of psychiatry, 1969-73; University of Nevada, School of Medical Science, Reno, professor and director of Division of Behavioral Sciences, 1973—. *Member:* American Psychiatric Association, American Association for the Advancement of Science, Screenwriters Guild of America.

WRITINGS: Sense and Symbol: A Textbook of Human Behavioral Science, Harper, 1967; *SAID Textbook of Psychopathology,* Rocom, 1976. Also author of "Vincent: Genius, Madness, and Society," CBS-TV special, 1976. Contributor to professional journals.

WORK IN PROGRESS: Work on dreaming; medical education; Paul Klee, and bioethics.

*   *   *

MILLER, Richard S(herwin) 1930-

PERSONAL: Born December 11, 1930, in Boston, Mass.; son of Max (an executive) and Mollie (Kruger) Miller; married Doris Sheila Lunchick, May 24, 1956; children: Andrew, Matthew. *Education:* Boston University, B.S., 1951, LL.B., 1956; Yale University, LL.M., 1959. *Office:* School of Law, University of Hawaii, 1390 Lower Campus Rd., Honolulu, Hawaii 96822.

CAREER: Admitted to Massachusetts Bar, 1956; private practice as partner in law firm, Boston, Mass., 1956-58; Wayne State University, School of Law, Detroit, Mich., associate professor, later professor of law, 1959-65; Ohio State University, College of Law, Columbus, professor of law, 1965-73; University of Hawaii, School of Law, Honolulu, professor of law, 1973—. *Military service:* U.S. Air Force, 1951-53; became lieutenant. *Member:* American Civil Liberties Union, Society of American Law Teachers.

WRITINGS: (Editor with Roland Stranger) *Essays on Expropriation,* Ohio State University Press, 1967; *Courts and the Law: An Introduction to Our Legal System,* Xerox Education Publications, 1971. Contributor to law journals and *World Politics.* Editor-in-chief, *Boston University Law Review,* 1955-56.

WORK IN PROGRESS: Research in the law of torts and no-fault insurance; children's books.

* * *

MILLETT, Allan R(eed) 1937-

PERSONAL: Surname rhymes with "Gillette"; born October 22, 1937, in New York, N.Y.; son of John David (an educator) and Catherine (Letsinger) Millett; married Sarah J. Tyler, April 15, 1960; children: Michael, Douglas, *Education:* DePauw University, B.A., 1959; Ohio State University, M.A., 1963, Ph.D., 1966. *Politics:* Independent. *Religion:* Methodist. *Home:* 1810 Elmwood Ave., Columbus, Ohio 43212. *Office:* Mershon Center, 199 West Tenth Ave., Columbus, Ohio 43201.

CAREER: University of Missouri-Columbia, assistant professor of U.S. military history, 1966-69; Ohio State University, Columbus, associate professor, 1969-74, professor of history, and Mershon Professor of national security studies, 1974—. *Military service:* U.S. Marine Corps, active duty, 1959-62, organized reserve, 1963—; current rank, major. *Member:* American Historical Association, American Military Institute, Marine Corps Association, Organization of American Historians, International Studies Association, American Commission on Military History, Phi Beta Kappa.

WRITINGS: The Politics of Intervention: The Military Occupation of Cuba, 1906-1909, Ohio State University Press, 1968; *The General: Robert L. Bullard and Officership in the U.S. Army, 1881-1925* (biography), Greenwood Press, 1975. Contributor of essays, articles, and bibliography on military studies to books and journals.

WORK IN PROGRESS: An institutional history of the U.S. Marine Corps.

* * *

MILLON, Robert Paul 1932-

PERSONAL: Born May 17, 1932, in Englewood, N.J.; son of Henry Francis (a draftsman) and Louise (Sevent) Millon; married Violeta Zapien (a medical doctor), March 20, 1963; children: Anthony Paul. *Education:* University of Miami, Coral Gables, Fla., B.A. (magna cum laude), 1953; Tulane University of Louisiana, M.A., 1957; University of Texas, graduate student, 1957; University of North Carolina, Ph.D., 1963. *Politics:* Socialist ("not member of any political party"). *Religion:* None. *Home:* Coahuila 5-2, Mexico 7, Federal District, Mexico.

CAREER: Connell and Rader Associates (engineering), Miami, Fla., rodman, then instrumentman on survey crew, 1953-54; J. B. Ford Co. (land surveying), Miami, Fla., instrumentman on survey crew, 1958-59; Rooney Co. (building contractors), Miami, Fla., instrumentman, then party chief on survey crew, 1959-60; full-time writer.

Commissioned by Chamber of Deputies of Mexico's National Congress to write two historical studies, 1965-66. *Military service:* U.S. Naval Reserve, 1949-54.

WRITINGS: Vicente Lombardo Toledano; Biografia Intelectual de un Marxista Mexicano, Libreria Madero, 1964; *Mexican Marxist: Vicente Lombardo Toledano,* University of North Carolina Press, 1966; *Sapata: The ideology of a Peasant Revolutionary,* International Publishers, 1969.

WORK IN PROGRESS: The Hacienda System as a Factor Limiting Economic Development in Mexico, 1876-1910; Left-Wing Infantilism in Mexico.

AVOCATIONAL INTERESTS: Hiking, hunting, football.††

* * *

MILLS, Theodore M(ason) 1920-

PERSONAL: Born May 6, 1920, in Fairfield, Ind.; son of Charles S. (a teacher) and Pearl (Mason) Mills; married Mary Jane Seaman, June 21, 1947; children: Duncan Kimball, Peter Benjamin, Sarah Jane. *Education:* Guilford College, A.B., 1941; Haverford College, M.A., 1942; Harvard University, Ph.D., 1952. *Office:* State University of New York at Buffalo, Buffalo, N.Y. 14214.

CAREER: Served with Friends ambulance unit in China, 1942-45; Harvard University, Cambridge, Mass., lecturer, 1952-55, assistant professor of sociology and of general education, 1956-60; Yale University, New Haven, Conn., associate professor of sociology and director of interaction laboratory, 1960-68; State University of New York at Buffalo, professor of sociology and chairman of department, 1968-72, director of Center for the Study of Human Groups, 1971—. Fulbright visiting lecturer and researcher in Norway, 1955-56; visiting professor, University of Oslo, 1973-74. *Member:* American Sociological Association (fellow), American Anthropological Association, American Psychological Association, Eastern Sociological Association. *Awards, honors:* Social Science Research Council fellow, 1951-52; Center for Advanced Study in the Behavioral Sciences fellow, 1964-65.

WRITINGS: (Co-author) *Group Structure and the Newcomer,* University of Oslo Press, 1957; *Group Transformation: An Analysis of a Learning Group,* Prentice-Hall, 1964; *The Sociology of Small Groups,* Prentice-Hall, 1967; (with Stan Rosenberg) *Readings in the Sociology of Small Groups,* Prentice-Hall, 1970.

Contributor: Dorwin Cartwright and Alvin Zander, editors, *Group Dynamics,* Row, Peterson & Co., 1953; S. Lipset and N. Smelser, editors, *Sociology: The Progress of a Decade,* Prentice-Hall, 1961; B. H. Stoodley, editor, *Society and Self,* Free Press of Glencoe, 1962; W. G. Bennis, E. H. Schein, D. E. Berlew, and F. I. Steele, editors, *Interpersonal Dynamics,* Dorsey, 1964; Lewis A. Coser, editor, *Georg Simmel,* Prentice-Hall, 1965; W. E. Moore and R. M. Cook, editors, *Readings on Social Change,* Prentice-Hall, 1967; Talcott Parsons, editor, *A Review of Modern American Sociology,* Voice of America Broadcasts. Contributor to *Human Relations, Social Problems, American Sociological Review, American Journal of Sociology,* and other journals in his field.

WORK IN PROGRESS: Authority Relations and Group Change: An Experimental Study of Long-Term Groups.

* * *

MILNE, (William) Gordon 1921-

PERSONAL: Born March 17, 1921, in Haverhill, Mass.;

son of Morton Russell (a banker) and Lulu (Smith) Milne. *Education:* Brown University, A.B., 1941, A.M., 1947; Harvard University, Ph.D., 1951. *Religion:* Protestant. *Home:* 501 Green Bay Rd., Lake Bluff, Ill. 60044. *Office:* Lake Forest College, Lake Forest, Ill. 60045.

CAREER: Instructor in English at University of Kansas City, Kansas City, Mo., 1947-48, at Tufts University, Medford, Mass., and at Massachusetts Institute of Technology, Cambridge, 1951; Lake Forest College, Lake Forest, Ill., assistant professor, 1951-53, associate professor, 1953-58, professor of English, 1958—, chairman of department, 1966—. Fulbright professor, University of Wurzburg, 1958-59. *Military service:* U.S. Naval Reserve, 1942-46; became lieutenant commander. *Member:* Modern Language Association of America, American Association of University Professors, Phi Beta Kappa.

WRITINGS: George William Curtis and the Genteel Tradition, Indiana University Press, 1956; *The American Political Novel,* University of Oklahoma Press, 1966. Contributor to literary and historical journals.

WORK IN PROGRESS: The American Novel of Manners.

AVOCATIONAL INTERESTS: Travel, sports, naval matters.

* * *

MILNER, Esther 1918-

PERSONAL: Born March 23, 1918, in Vegreville, Alberta, Canada. *Education:* Queen's University at Kingston, B.A., 1943; University of Minnesota, M.A., 1944; University of Chicago, Ph.D., 1949. *Religion:* Humanist. *Home:* Craryville R.D., N.Y. 12521. *Office:* Brooklyn College of the City University of New York, Brooklyn, N.Y. 11210.

CAREER: Canadian Department of National Defence, Ottawa, Ontario, civilian technician, 1944-46; George Williams College, Chicago, Ill., instructor, 1948; Science Research Associates and Center for Intergroup Education, Chicago, Ill., editor, 1948-49; Atlanta University, Atlanta, Ga., 1949-52, began as assistant professor, became associate professor of human development; Brooklyn College (now Brooklyn College of the City University of New York), Brooklyn, N.Y., assistant professor of developmental psychology, 1952-57; University of Alberta, Edmonton, assistant professor of psychology, 1957-60; Brooklyn College of the City University of New York, School of Education, assistant professor, 1960-65, associate professor, 1965-71, professor of developmental psychology, 1971—. Visiting fellow, University of Aberdeen, 1965-66; resource consultant, Briarcliff College, 1967-68. *Member:* American Psychological Association (fellow), American Association of University Professors, Society for Social Responsibility in Science, New York Academy of Sciences.

WRITINGS: The Failure of Success: The American Crisis in Values, Exposition Press, 1959, revised edition published as *The Failure of Success: The Middle-Class Crisis,* Warren Green, 1968; *Human Neural and Behavioral Development: A Relational Inquiry,* C. C Thomas, 1967; (contributor) Robert Theobald, editor, *Dialogue on Women,* Bobbs-Merrill, 1967; (contributor) H. Whitaker and H. A. Whitaker, editors, *Current Trends in Neurolinguistics,* Academic Press, in press. Contributor to *Annals* of the New York Academy of Science, 1970, and to professional journals.

WORK IN PROGRESS: A chapter to be included in *Les Femmes dan la societe et les roles des sexes,* edited by Andree Michel, for Presses Universitaires de France.

* * *

MILOSH, Joseph E(dmund) 1936-

PERSONAL: Born December 28, 1936, in Blue Island, Ill.; son of Joseph E. (a printer) and Mary (Spyrnal) Milosh; married Sylvia Viscardi, September 8, 1958; children: Michelle, Margaret Ann. *Education:* St. Edward's University, B.A., 1958; University of Fribourg, student, 1956-57; University of Illinois, M.A., 1960, Ph.D., 1963. *Home:* 123 Ilehamwood, DeKalb, Ill. 60115. *Office:* Department of English, Northern Illinois University, DeKalb, Ill. 60115.

CAREER: University of Wisconsin-Madison, instructor, 1963-65, assistant professor, 1965-66, associate professor of English, 1966-70; Northern Illinois University, DeKalb, professor of English, 1970—, coordinator of English education, 1972—, director of freshman English, 1975—. Consultant, National Humanities Series, National Endowment for the Humanities, 1973. *Member:* Modern Language Association of America, National Council of Teachers of English, Mediaeval Academy of America. *Awards, honors:* University of Illinois research fellowship at British Museum, 1960; University of Wisconsin-Madison research grants, 1964, 1967; Kiekhofer Teaching Award, University of Wisconsin, 1966; American Council of Learned Societies study fellowship, 1968-69.

WRITINGS: The Scale of Perfection and the English Mystical Tradition, University of Wisconsin Press, 1966; *Teaching the History of the English Language in the Secondary Classroom,* National Council of Teachers of English, 1972.

WORK IN PROGRESS: A theory of medieval humor; learning processes in the English language arts.

SIDELIGHTS: Milosh is interested in the sound popularization of materials concerning the English language.

* * *

MINSHULL, Roger (Michael) 1935-

PERSONAL: Born June 7, 1935, in Macclesfield, Cheshire, England; son of Eric (a tailor) and Florence (Kirkham) Minshull; married, 1968. *Education:* St. Catherine's College, Oxford, M.A., 1959. *Politics:* "Pragmatic." *Religion:* Agnostic. *Home:* 2 Arlington Ct., Washingborough, Lincolnshire, England.

CAREER: Rishworth School, Halifax, Yorkshire, England, geography assistant, 1959-62; Broughton High School, Salford, Lancashire, England, head of geography department, 1962-66; Levenshulme High School, Manchester, Lancashire, head of geography department, 1966-68; Bishop Grosseteste College, Lincolnshire, England, lecturer in geography, 1968—. Panel member for Certificate of Secondary Education syllabus and teaching materials, Macmillan Co. *Military service:* Territorial Army, lieutenant, 1959—.

WRITINGS: Regional Geography: Theory and Practice, Hutchinson, 1967; *Human Geography from the Air,* Macmillan, 1968; *Landforms from the Air,* Macmillan, 1969.

The Changing Nature of Geography, Hutchinson, 1970; *Settlements from the Air,* Macmillan, 1971; (co-author) *Simulation Games in Geography,* Macmillan, 1972; (co-author) *Correlation Techniques in Geography,* Philip,

1972; (co-author) *Networks in Geography,* Philip, 1973; *Sampling Techniques in Geography,* Philip, 1975; *Introduction to Models in Geography,* Longman, 1975; *Geographical Games,* Nelson, in press; *Geographical Assignments,* Philip, in press. Contributor to magazines, including *Pathe Gazette, Amateur Cine World, Meccano, Classroom Geographer,* and *Journal of American Studies.*

WORK IN PROGRESS: A paper on the ordinance of 1785.

* * *

MINSKY, Marvin (Lee) 1927-

PERSONAL: Born August 9, 1927, in New York, N.Y.; married Gloria Rudisch (a doctor), 1953; children: Margaret, Henry, Juliana. *Education:* Harvard University, B.A. 1950; Princeton University, Ph.D., 1954. *Office:* Department of Electrical Engineering, Massachusetts Institute of Technology, 77 Massachusetts Ave., Cambridge, Mass. 02139.

CAREER: Tufts University, Medford, Mass., research associate, 1953-54; Harvard University, Cambridge, Mass., Society of Fellows, 1954-57; Massachusetts Institute of Technology, Cambridge, staff of Lincoln Laboratory, 1957-58, assistant professor, 1958-61, associate professor, 1961-63, professor of mathematics, 1963-64, professor of electrical engineering, 1964—. Consultant to RAND Corp., Xerox Corp., and other firms. *Military service:* U.S. Navy, 1944-45. *Member:* American Academy of Arts and Sciences (fellow), Institute of Electronics and Electronic Engineers (fellow), National Academy of Sciences, New York Academy of Sciences (fellow).

WRITINGS: Computation: Finite and Infinite Machines, Prentice-Hall, 1967; (editor) *Semantic Information Processing,* M.I.T. Press, 1968; (with Seymour Papert) *Perceptrons,* M.I.T. Press, 1969.

* * *

MINTURN, Leigh 1928-

PERSONAL: Surname rhymes with "intern"; born July 1, 1928, in Chicago, Ill.; daughter of Harold Disney and Emma (Hamsher) Minturn. *Education:* Mount Holyoke College, B.A., 1949; Radcliffe College, M.A., 1950, Ph.D., 1953. *Politics:* Independent. *Home:* 2227 Canyon Blvd., Boulder, Colo. 80302. *Office:* Department of Psychology, University of Colorado, Boulder, Colo. 80302.

CAREER: Ford Foundation research fellow, 1952-58; Cortland State Teachers College (now State University of New York College at Cortland), assistant professor of psychology, 1957-58; University of Illinois, Urbana, lecturer, 1958-61, assistant professor, 1961-63, associate professor of psychology, 1963-67; University of Colorado, Boulder, professor of psychology, 1967—. *Member:* Phi Beta Kappa.

WRITINGS: (With William Lambert) *Mothers of Six Cultures,* Wiley, 1963; (contributor) *Six Cultures: Studies in Child Rearing,* Wiley, 1963; (with John Whiting, I. L. Child, and W. W. Lambert) *Field Guide for a Study of Socialization,* Wiley, 1966; (contributor) N. Kretchmer and D. N. Walcher, editors, *Environmental Influences on Genetic Expression,* U.S. Government Printing Office, 1969. Contributor to psychology journals.

WORK IN PROGRESS: A cross-cultural study of children's judgments of justice; a study of sex roles in contemporary American communes; a study of changes in the status of Rajput women in a north Indian village from 1955 to 1975.

SIDELIGHTS: Minturn has done research in several countries. She lived in Greece for four months while doing research. During the winter of 1974-75 she re-studied Rajput families in an Indian village.

* * *

MISCH, Robert J(ay) 1905-

PERSONAL: Born November 19, 1905, in New York, N.Y.; son of Moses (in real estate) and Jennie (Reshower) Misch; married Janet Wolff (in public relations), June 23, 1928; children: Mary Janet, Katherine Wolff. *Education:* Columbia University, student, 1921-22; Dartmouth College, B.S. (magna cum laude), 1925. *Politics:* Independent. *Home and office:* 251 West 71st St., New York, N.Y. 10023.

CAREER: Albert Frank & Co. (advertising agency), New York City, 1926-38, became copy chief; Al Paul Lefton Co., Inc. (advertising agency), New York City, vice-president, 1938-64; Albert Frank-Guenther Law (advertising agency), New York City, vice-president, 1964-65; writer, lecturer, and consultant on wine and food. *Military service:* New York State Guard; became second lieutenant. *Member:* United World Federalists, Overseas Press Club, Confrerie des Chevaliers du Tastevin, Dutch Treat Club. *Awards, honors:* Medaille Agricole des Vins de France; L'Ordre Merite Agricole.

WRITINGS—All published by Doubleday, except as indicated: *At Daddy's Office* (juvenile), Knopf, 1953; *Robert J. Misch's Foreign Dining Dictionary,* 1960; *Quick Guide to Wine: A Compact Primer,* 1966, revised edition, 1975; *Quick Guide to the World's Most Famous Recipes,* 1969; *Quick Guide to Spirits,* 1972; *Quick Guide to Cheese,* 1973; *Official Guide to Spirits,* 1974; (editor) Patrick G. Duffy, *The Official Mixer's Manual,* revised edition, 1975. Contributor to various periodicals, including *Esquire, Carte Blanche, Cosmopolitan, Gentlemen's Quarterly,* and *Harper's Bazaar.* Writer of column, "Eat, Drink and Be Merry," for North American Newspaper Alliance-United Features, Inc.

WORK IN PROGRESS: An autobiographical novel; a book on the wines of the Americas; articles.

* * *

MISNER, Arthur J(ack) 1921-

PERSONAL: Born July 14, 1921, in Los Angeles, Calif.; son of Arthur J. and Echo J. Misner; married LaVerne Wilson, September 12, 1952; children: Gaile, Lee. *Education:* University of California, Berkeley, B.A., 1942, M.A., 1948, Ph.D., 1954. *Politics:* Democrat. *Home:* 1144 South Monterey St., Alhambra, Calif. 91801.

CAREER: University of California, Berkeley, administration analyst, 1950-52, lecturer, 1952-53, public administration analyst, 1954-55; California State University at Los Angeles, 1955—, started as assistant professor, professor of government, 1962—. President, GORMAC (consultants in government). *Military service:* U.S. Navy, 1942-46; became lieutenant. U.S. Naval Reserve, 1946—; now lieutenant commander. *Member:* American Society for Public Administration, Public Personnel Association, American Association of University Professors, Western Governmental Research Association.

WRITINGS: (With Earl C. Segrest) *Impact of Federal Grants in Aid on California,* Bureau of Public Administration, University of California, 1954; (with E. P. Dvorin)

Introduction to California Government, Addison-Wesley, 1966, 2nd edition, 1969; (editor with Dvorin) *California Politics and Policies*, Addison-Wesley, 1966; (with Dvorin) *Government in American Society* (textbook), Addison-Wesley, 1968, 2nd edition, 1973; (editor with Dvorin) *Government in American Society: A Reader*, Addison-Wesley, 1968; (with Dvorin) *Governments within the States*, Addison-Wesley, 1971.

* * *

MITCHELL, Edward B. 1937-

PERSONAL: Born January 28, 1937, in Aurora, Ill.; son of Edward Cecil (an insurance agent) and Jessie (Wren) Mitchell; married Kay Paul, August 23, 1958; children: Douglas, Samantha. *Education:* Beloit College, B.A., 1959; University of Connecticut, Ph.D., 1963. *Home address:* Route 4, Athens, Ohio 45701. *Office:* Department of English, Ohio University, Athens, Ohio 45701.

CAREER: St. Cloud State College, St. Cloud, Minn., assistant professor of American literature, 1963-65; Ohio University, Athens, assistant professor, 1965-68, associate professor, 1968-73, professor of American literature, 1973—. *Member:* Modern Language Association of America, Popular Culture Association. *Awards, honors:* Baker Awards Committee research grant, Ohio University.

WRITINGS: (Editor with Rainer Schulte) *Continental Short Stories: The Modern Tradition*, Norton, 1968; (compiler with William Holmes) *Nineteenth-Century American Short Stories*, Scott, Foresman, 1970; *Henry Miller: Three Decades of Criticism*, New York University Press, 1971; (editor with Schulte) *International Short Stories*, Norton, in press. Contributor of articles and reviews to journals in his field.

AVOCATIONAL INTERESTS: His farm near Athens, and horseback riding.

* * *

MITCHELL, Richard H(anks) 1931-

PERSONAL: Born April 16, 1931, in Jacksonville, Ill.; son of Charles G. and Blanche (Hanks) Mitchell; married Yoshiko Usuda, December 19, 1960. *Education:* University of Wisconsin, B.S., 1957, M.S., 1958, Ph.D., 1963; additional graduate study at University of Michigan, 1957. *Office:* University of Missouri, St. Louis, Mo. 63121.

CAREER: University of Maryland, Far East Division, lecturer in Japanese history, 1963-66, lecturer, 1967-1968; State University of New York College at New Paltz, associate professor of Japanese history, 1966-67; University of Nebraska, Lincoln, visiting associate professor of Japanese history, 1968-69; University of Rochester, Rochester, N.Y., visiting associate professor of Japanese history, 1969-70; University of Missouri at St. Louis, associate professor of Japanese history, 1970—. Member, Columbia Seminar on Modern East Asia: Japan, and Midwest Japan Seminar. *Military service:* U.S. Army, 1951-54; became sergeant; received Purple Heart.

MEMBER: Association for Asian Studies, International House of Japan, Toho Gakkai (Tokyo). *Awards, honors:* American Philosophical Society grants, 1967, 1970; State University of New York faculty fellowship, 1967; State of New York Education Department research grant, 1967; University of Maryland, Far East Division research award, 1968; University of Missouri at St. Louis summer research grants, 1972, 1974.

WRITINGS: The Korean Minority in Japan, University of California Press, 1967; *Thought Control in Prewar Japan*, Cornell University Press, in press. Contributor to professional journals.

WORK IN PROGRESS: Social Control in Prewar Japan.

AVOCATIONAL INTERESTS: Archaeology, especially the Japanese Jomon period.

* * *

MOAK, Lennox L. 1912-

PERSONAL: Surname rhymes with "poke"; born December 14, 1912; son of Jefferson Monroe (a carpenter) and Lillian (Laird) Moak; married Helen Ross (a part-time writer), July 28, 1938; children: Lynn Martin, Sandra Lee, Marcie Helen, Jefferson Monroe II. *Education:* Southwest Texas State College (now Southwest Texas State University), B.A., 1932; University of Texas, M.A., 1940; University of Pennsylvania, graduate study, 1949-50. *Politics:* Nonpartisan. *Religion:* Baptist. *Home:* 115 West Mermaid Lane, Philadelphia, Pa. 19118. *Office:* 1420 Municipal Services Bldg., Philadelphia, Pa. 19107.

CAREER: Teacher in Port Arthur, Tex., 1934-38; Bureau of Governmental Research, New Orleans, La., assistant director, later director, 1938-49; Bureau of Municipal Research, Philadelphia, Pa., director, 1949-51; City of Philadelphia, director of finance, 1952-54; Pennsylvania Economy League, Philadelphia, director, 1954-72; City of Philadelphia, director of finance, 1972—. Lecturer at Tulane University of Louisiana, 1942-49, and University of Pennsylvania, 1953-55, 1963—. Consultant to governmental bodies in United States and abroad. *Member:* American Society for Public Administration, Governmental Research Association (president, 1964-66), Municipal Finance Officers Association of United States and Canada (vice-president, 1975-76).

WRITINGS: (With Frank Cowan, Jr.) *A Manual of Practice for Administration of Local Sales and Use Taxes*, Municipal Finance Officers Association, 1961; (with Kathryn Killian) *A Manual of Suggested Practice for the Preparation, Consideration, and Execution of Operating Budgets in Local Governments*, Municipal Finance Officers Association, 1964; (with Killian) *A Manual of Suggested Practice of the Preparation and Adoption of Capital Programs and Capital Budgets by Local Governments*, Municipal Finance Officers Association, 1964; (with Kathryn G. Gordon) *A Manual for Budgeting for Smaller Governmental Units*, Municipal Finance Officers Association, 1965; *Administration of Local Government Debt*, Municipal Finance Officers Association, 1970; (with Albert M. Hillhouse) *Concepts and Practices in Local Government Finance*, Municipal Finance Officers Association, 1975. Author of several book-length survey reports published by Municipal Finance Officers Association; also author or collaborator on about 250 research reports on local government subjects in Louisiana and Pennsylvania.

AVOCATIONAL INTERESTS: Genealogy, and improvement of mental health facilities for youngsters.

* * *

MOCK, Edward J(oseph) 1934-

PERSONAL: Born January 28, 1934, in Wilkes-Barre, Pa.; son of Joseph A. (a salesman) and Margaret (Heffernan) Mock; married Patricia Ann Lotter, June 21, 1958; children: Mary Kathryn, Daniel Joseph, Peter John. *Educa-*

tion: King's College, Wilkes-Barre, Pa., B.Sc. (cum laude), 1955; Marquette University, M.B.A., 1957; Ohio State University, Ph.D., 1964. *Politics:* Republican. *Religion:* Roman Catholic. *Office:* 11115 Corobon Lane, Great Falls, Va. 22066.

CAREER: Pennsylvania State University, University Park, associate professor of financial management, 1962-65; University of Southern California, Los Angeles, visiting associate professor of finance, 1965-67; George Washington University, Washington, D.C., professor of finance, 1967-68; with the Susquehanna Corp., Alexandria, Va., 1968; vice-president, Peoples Drug, 1969-73; Pepco, Fairfield, Conn., vice-president, 1973-75; Fin-Econ, Great Falls, Va., president, 1975—. *Military service:* U.S. Army, Finance Corps, instructor at Army Finance School, 1957-60; became first lieutenant. *Member:* American Finance Association.

WRITINGS: Short Problems in Business Finance and Financial Management, International Textbook, 1964; (editor) *Readings in Financial Management,* International Textbook, 1964; (editor) *Readings in International Business,* International Textbook, 1965; *Financial Decision Making,* International Textbook, 1967; *Basic Financial Management: Text and Cases,* International Textbook, 1968; (with Donald H. Shuckett) *Financing for Growth,* American Management Association, 1971; (with Shuckett) *Decision Strategies in Financial Management,* American Management Association, 1973. Editor, "Financial Management" Series, International Textbook and "Money and Banking" Series. Contributor to banking, finance, and management journals.

* * *

MODRAS, Ronald E(dward) 1937-

PERSONAL: Born August 23, 1937, in Detroit, Mich.; son of Edward and Anne (Adamowicz) Modras. *Education:* St. Mary's College, Orchard Lake, Mich., B.A., 1959; Catholic University of America, S.T.B., 1963; University of Tuebingen, Ph.D., 1972. *Home:* 20955 Whitlock Dr., Dearborn Heights, Mich. *Office:* St. John's Seminary, Plymouth, Mich. 48170.

CAREER: Roman Catholic priest, Archdiocese of Detroit, 1963—; parish priest, Detroit, Mich., 1963-67; Institute for Continuing Education, Detroit, professor of ecumenical studies, 1966-68; Marygrove College, Detroit, chaplain, 1967-68; Pius XII Institute for Religious Education, Detroit, visiting professor, 1969-71; St. John's Provincial Seminary, Plymouth, Mich., assistant professor of systematic theology, 1972—. Adjunct professor at University of Detroit, 1972—, Madonna College, 1974—, and St. Mary's College, 1974—. Vice-chairman, Detroit Archdiocesan Commission for Ecumenical Affairs, 1966-68; chairman, National Workshop for Christian Unity, 1968. *Member:* Catholic Society of America.

WRITINGS: Paths to Unity, Sheed, 1968; *Tillich's Theology of the Church,* Wayne State University Press, 1976. Contributor to periodicals, including *America, Columbia,* and *Homiletic and Pastoral Review.* Editor-in-chief of printed media for Archdiocese of Detroit Synod, 1968, including fifty-four pamphlets.

WORK IN PROGRESS: Historical research into the subject of the ecclesiology of Paul Tillich.

SIDELIGHTS: Father Modras is competent in Latin, Polish, German, French and Italian.

MOELLER, Helen 1921-

PERSONAL: Born October 13, 1921, in Oelwein, Iowa; daughter of James T. and Alice (Barker) Maillie; married Lester Moeller (a building contractor and farmer) June 19, 1943; children: James, Jeanne (Mrs. Dennis Muchow), Larry, Patricia, JoAnne, Barbara. *Education:* Grinnell College, student, 1939-40. *Residence:* Stanley, Iowa.

CAREER: Secretary at Rath Packing Co., Waterloo, Iowa, 1941-42, Glenn L. Martin Co., Omaha, Neb., 1942-43, Lutheran Mutual Life Insurance Co., Waverly, Iowa, and then Texas State Department of Agriculture, College Station, 1943; sales clerk in Oelwein, Iowa, 1964-65; Zion American Lutheran Church, Oelwein, Iowa, church office secretary, 1965—. *Member:* National League of American Pen Women (Waterloo-Cedar Rapids branch).

WRITINGS: Tornado, Revell, 1967.

AVOCATIONAL INTERESTS: Knitting, reading, music, people.

* * *

MOHLER, James A. 1923-

PERSONAL: Born July 22, 1923, in Toledo, Ohio; son of Edward Francis (a teacher and writer) and Gertrude (Aylward) Mohler. *Education:* Xavier University, Cincinnati, Ohio, Litt.B., 1946; Bellarmine School of Theology, Ph.L., 1949, S.T.L., 1956; Loyola University, Chicago, Ill., M.S.I.R., 1960; University of Ottawa, Ph.D., 1964, S.T.D., 1965. *Home and office:* John Carroll University, University Heights, Cleveland, Ohio 44118.

CAREER: Entered Society of Jesus, 1942, ordained to Roman Catholic priesthood, 1955. St. Ignatius High School, Chicago, Ill., teacher of religion, mathematics, economics, and Latin, 1949-52; Jesuit Indian Mission, Sault Ste. Marie, Mich., teacher, 1954-56; John Carroll University, Cleveland, Ohio, instructor, 1960-65, assistant professor, 1965-69, associate professor, 1969-74, professor of religious studies, 1974—. Visiting scholar, Union Theological Seminary (N.Y.), 1966. *Member:* Catholic Theological Society of America, American Academy of Religion, College Theology Society, American Association of University Professors, Association for Asian Studies.

WRITINGS: Man Needs God, John Carroll University Press, 1966; (with others) *Speaking of God,* edited by D. Dirscherl, Bruce Publishing, 1967; *The Beginning of Eternal Life: The Dynamic Faith of Thomas Aquinas, Origins and Interpretation,* Philosophical Library, 1968; *Dimensions of Faith, Yesterday and Today,* Loyola University Press, 1969; *The Origin and Evolution of the Priesthood,* Alba, 1970; *The Heresy of Monasticism: The Christian Monks, Types and Anti-Types,* Alba, 1971; *The School of Jesus,* Alba, 1973; *Cosmos, Man, God, Messiah,* John Carroll University Press, 1973; *Dimensions of Love: East and West,* Doubleday, 1975. Contributor to religious journals.

WORK IN PROGRESS: Dualism: Problem of Evil Yesterday and Today.

SIDELIGHTS: Father Mohler is competent in Latin, Greek, French, Italian, and German. He spent 1968 abroad, doing research in Switzerland, France, Italy, and Israel. In 1972 and 1974 he traveled and studied in Japan, China and India.

MOIR, Alfred 1924-

PERSONAL: Surname is pronounced Moy-er; born April 14, 1924, in Minneapolis, Minn.; son of William Wilmerding (a physician) and Blanche (Kummer) Moir. *Education:* Harvard University, A.B., 1948, M.A., 1949, Ph.D., 1953; University of Rome, graduate study, 1950-52. *Home:* 1375 Plaza de Sonadores, Santa Barbara, Calif. 93108. *Office:* University of California, Santa Barbara, Calif. 93106.

CAREER: Harvard University, Harvard College, Cambridge, Mass., proctor, 1949-50; Tulane University of Louisiana, Newcomb College, New Orleans, instructor, 1952-54, assistant professor, 1954-59, associate professor of art history, 1959-63; University of California, Santa Barbara, associate professor, 1963-65, professor of art history, 1965—, chairman of department, 1963-69. Consultant, Isaac Delgado Museum of Art, New Orleans, 1954-57. Art historian in residence, American Academy in Rome, 1969-70. *Military service:* U.S. Army, 1943-46; became master sergeant. *Member:* College Art Association, Society of Architectural Historians, Mediaeval Academy of America, Renaissance Society of America, Southern California Art Historians. *Awards, honors:* Fulbright fellow in Italy, 1950-51.

WRITINGS: (Contributor) *Art in Italy, 1600-1700,* Detroit Institute of Arts, 1965; *The Italian Followers of Caravaggio,* Harvard University Press, 1967; (editor) *Seventeenth-Century Italian Drawings from the Collection of Janos Scholz,* University of California, 1973; *Caravaggio and His Copyists,* College Art Association of America, 1975. Contributor to art journals.

*   *   *

MOLUMBY, Lawrence E. 1932-

PERSONAL: Surname is pronounced Mo-*lum*-bee; born December 18, 1932, in Madison, S.D.; son of Lawrence and Dorothy (Cole) Molumby; married Patricia Ann Corcoran, May, 1969; children: Sarah. *Education:* St. Charles College, student, 1950-52; Catholic University of America, B.A., 1954, M.A., 1955, S.T.L., 1959, M.L.S., 1975; Gregorian University, Rome, Italy, J.C.L., 1966; additional graduate study at University of Notre Dame, 1957, and Richmond Professional Institute, 1960-62. *Office:* 901 G St. N.W., Washington, D.C. 20001.

CAREER: Former Roman Catholic priest. St. John's Seminary, Richmond, Va., librarian, 1960-64; Diocese of Richmond, Va., vice-chancellor, 1966-68; District of Columbia Public Library, Washington, D.C., coordinator of community services, 1969—. Former elected member of Richmond Diocesan Council of Priests. Treasurer, Hope Housing, Inc. (non-profit), 1968; chairman of librarians' committee, Metropolitan Washington Council of Governments, 1973-74; member of board of directors, Friendship House, 1976. *Member:* American Library Association, Smithsonian Associates, National Trust for Historic Preservation, District of Columbia Library Association (member of board of directors, 1976—).

WRITINGS: (Editor with William Jerry Boney) *The New Day: Catholic Theologians of the Renewal,* John Knox, 1968; (contributor) *Cable Handbook,* Communication Service Corp., 1975. Contributing editor, *Cable Libraries.*

*   *   *

MONK, Robert C(larence) 1930-

PERSONAL: Born July 7, 1930, in Holly Grove, Ark.; son of Olin C. (a carpenter) and Mary (Clay) Monk; married Carolyn Parker, August 31, 1952; children: Robbi Lynn, Ellen Marian. *Education:* Texas Technological College (now Texas Tech University), B.A., 1951; Southern Methodist University, B.D., 1954; Princeton University, M.A., 1960, Ph.D., 1963. *Politics:* Democrat. *Home:* 1609 Vegas, Abilene, Tex. 79605. *Office:* McMurry College, Abilene, Tex. 79605.

CAREER: Ordained minister of Northwest Texas Conference of the Methodist Church. Texas A & M University, College Station, director of Wesley Foundation, 1954-58; Texas Methodist Student Movement, Austin, associate director, 1961-64; McMurry College, Abilene, Tex., professor of religion, 1964—. *Member:* American Society of Church History, American Academy of Religion, American Association of University Professors.

WRITINGS: John Wesley: His Puritan Heritage, Abingdon, 1966; (co-author) *Exploring Religious Meaning,* Prentice-Hall, 1974.

WORK IN PROGRESS: Readings in American Methodism.

*   *   *

MONOD, Sylvere 1921-

PERSONAL: Final letter of surname is silent; born October 9, 1921, in Cannes, France; son of Samuel William (a typographer using the pseudonym Maximilien Vox) and Liane (Poulain) Monod; married Annie Digeon, November 10, 1943; children: Isabelle, France, Joelle, Emmanuelle, Pascal. *Education:* Sorbonne, University of Paris, Licence d'Anglais, 1941, Agregation, 1943, Doctorat, 1952. *Religion:* Roman Catholic. *Home:* 18 Boulevard Saint Germain, Paris 5, France. *Office:* Institut d'Anglais, 5 rue de l'Ecole de Medecine, Paris 6, France.

CAREER: Teacher of English at Lycee Corneille, Rouen, France, 1943-45, and Lycee Michelet, Paris, France, 1946-48; University of Caen, Caen, France, lecturer, 1949-54, professor of English and chairman of department, 1955-64; Sorbonne, University of Paris, Paris, professor of English, 1964—. Lecturer in Great Britain, Belgium, Germany, Tunisia, Canada, and United States. Adviser, Sweet Briar (College) Junior Year in France. *Member:* International Association of University Professors of English, Societe des Anglicistes (secretary, 1960-63; vice-president, 1963-67), Dickens Fellowship (vice-president, 1966—), Dickens Society.

WRITINGS: Dickens Romancier (in French), Hachette, 1953, revised edition translated by the author published as *Dickens the Novelist,* University of Oklahoma Press, 1968; *Charles Dickens* (critical study and anthology; in French), Seghers, 1959; (with G. H. Ford, Edgar Johnson, and J. Hillis Miller) *Dickens Criticism: A Symposium,* Charles Dickens Reference Center (Boston), 1962; (editor with G. H. Ford) Dickens, *Hard Times* (critical edition), Norton, 1966; *Histoire de la litterature Anglaise: De Victoria a Elisabeth II,* A. Colin (Paris), 1970; (with Jean Dulck) *Histoire du roman anglais,* Seghers, 1976.

Translator into French, and author of introductory or critical notes in most editions: Charles Dickens, *Contes de Noel,* two volumes, Union Bibliophile de France, 1946, 1947; Dickens, *David Copperfield,* Classiques Garnier, 1956; Dickens, *Oliver Twist,* Classiques Garnier, 1957; Shakespeare, *Henry V* (bilingual edition), Club Francais du Livre, 1958; Dickens, *Pickwick,* Pleiade, 1958; Dickens,

Les Grandes esperances, Classiques Garnier, 1960; Dickens, *Barnabe Rudge,* Pleiade, 1963; Emily Bronte, *Hurlemont (Wuthering Heights),* Classiques Garnier, 1963; Charlotte Bronte, *Jane Eyre,* Classiques Garnier, 1966; Edward Lear, *Limericks,* Aubier, 1974.

WORK IN PROGRESS: A critical edition of Dickens' *Bleak House,* with G. H. Ford, for Norton; translations of Dickens' *Christmas Stories* and *Bleak House,* for Pleiade.

*   *   *

MONSMAN, Gerald Cornelius 1940-

PERSONAL: Born March 3, 1940, in Baltimore, Md.; son of Gerald (a lawyer) and Diana (DeKryger) Monsman; married Nancy Weaver, March 25, 1972. *Education:* Calvin College, student, 1957-59; Johns Hopkins University, B.A., 1961, M.A., 1963, Ph.D., 1965. *Religion:* Presbyterian. *Office:* Department of English, Duke University, Durham, N.C. 27706.

CAREER: Duke University, Durham, N.C., assistant professor, 1965-70, associate professor of English, 1970—. *Member:* Modern Language Association of America, American Association of University Professors, Phi Beta Kappa. *Awards, honors:* Research faculty fellowship, Duke University, 1967, 1970; Blackwood Prize, 1967, 1969, for the most outstanding short story.

WRITINGS: Pater's Portraits: Mythic Patterns in the Fiction of Walter Pater, Johns Hopkins Press, 1967. Contributor to *Blackwood's Magazine, South Atlantic Quarterly, University of Toronto Quarterly,* and *Victorian Newsletter.*

WORK IN PROGRESS: A critical biography of Walter Pater; a critical/analytical study of Gerard Manley Hopkins; a collection of four short stories, tentatively entitled *Light and Darkness.*

*   *   *

MONSOUR, Sally A. 1929-

PERSONAL: Born May 24, 1929, in Valentine, Neb.; daughter of James (a hotel owner) and Minnie (Ferris) Monsour. *Education:* College of New Rochelle, student, 1946-47; Manhattanville College of the Sacred Heart (now Manhattanville College), B.Mus., 1950; Columbia University, M.A., 1952; University of Michigan, Ed.D., 1960. *Religion:* Roman Catholic. *Office:* Georgia State University, Atlanta, Ga. 30303.

CAREER: St. Walburga's Academy, New York, N.Y., piano instructor, 1950-51; Rollins College, Winter Park, Fla., instructor in piano and music education, and director of glee club, 1951-53; Winter Park (Fla.) public schools, teacher of speech and vocal music in secondary schools, 1953-54; Ann Arbor (Mich.) public schools, part-time teacher of vocal music, 1954-58; University of Michigan, Ann Arbor, part-time instructor in music education, 1954-59; University of Colorado, Boulder, 1959-70, began as assistant professor, became professor of music; Georgia State University, Atlanta, professor of music, 1970—. Director of music workshops, National Music Camp, Interlochen, Mich., summers, 1959-70; director of short-term music courses, Extension Division, University of Colorado, summers, 1967-70; visiting lecturer at Eastman School of Music, Catholic University of America, Ohio University, and other universities and colleges. Consultant, Julliard Repertory Project, 1964-68. Member of performing arts panel, Georgia Council for the Arts, 1975—.

MEMBER: Music Teachers National Association, College Music Society (member-at-large of executive board, 1974—), Music Educators National Conference, American Association of University Professors, Pi Kappa Lambda, Delta Kappa Gamma. *Awards, honors:* University of Colorado, research grant from Council on Research and Creative work, 1962, and faculty fellowship for research on certain aspects of Arabic music for children, 1965-66; research grant, Georgia State University, 1971.

WRITINGS: (Contributor) *Music Activities in the Elementary School,* Catholic University of America Press, 1957; (contributor) *Art for Christian Living,* Catholic University of America Press, 1958; (contributor) *Music Skills,* Catholic University of America Press, 1958; (with Mary Jarman Nelson) *Play! A Piano Method for Older Beginners,* Edward B. Marks Music Corp., 1963; (with Margaret Perry) *A Junior High School Music Handbook,* Prentice-Hall, 1963, 2nd edition, 1970; (with Cohen and Lindell) *Rhythm in Music and Dance for Children,* Wadsworth, 1966; *Folk Songs of the Arab World,* Bowmar, 1970; "New Dimensions in Music Series," Books 3-6, American Book Co., 1970; (with Lois Rhea) *Part-Songs from the Middle East,* Mark Foster Publishing, 1970; (with John Batcheller) *Music in Recreation and Leisure,* W. C. Brown, 1972; *Music in Open Education,* Center for Applied Research in Education, 1974; (editor) *Nine Classroom Enrichment Books,* Center for Applied Research in Education, 1974-75. With Cecil Effinger, librettist for the children's opera, "Pandora's Box," G. Schirmer, 1962; editorial consultant for English translation of Jorgen Jersild's *Rhymelaere* and *Melodiaesning,* G. Schirmer, 1962. Columnist, "Keyboard Experience," in *Michigan Music Educator,* 1959-60; contributor of articles and reviews to other journals in her field.

*   *   *

MONTER, E. William 1936-

PERSONAL: Born September 22, 1936, in Cincinnati, Ohio; son of E. William (a printer) and Florence (Stoecklin) Monter; married Barbara S. Heldt (an assistant professor of Russian literature), June 19, 1963. *Education:* Wabash College, B.A., 1958; Princeton University, M.A., 1960, Ph.D., 1963. *Religion:* None. *Office:* Department of History, Northwestern University, Evanston, Ill. 60201.

CAREER: Denison University, Granville, Ohio, instructor in history, 1961-63; Northwestern University, Evanston, Ill., assistant professor, 1963-66, associate professor, 1966-72, professor of history, 1972—. *Member:* American Historical Association, American Society for Reformation Research, Societe d'Histoire et d'Archeologie de Geneve.

WRITINGS: Studies in Genevan Government 1536-1605, Droz, 1964; *Calvin's Geneva,* Wiley, 1967; (editor) *European Witchcraft,* Wiley, 1969; *Witchcraft in France and Switzerland: The Borderlands during the Reformation,* Cornell University Press, 1976.

SIDELIGHTS: E. William Monter has spent about two years in Europe, mostly in Geneva. He speaks French fluently and reads German and Italian.

*   *   *

MONTGOMERY, Constance Cappel 1936-

PERSONAL: Born June 22, 1936, in Dayton, Ohio; daughter of Adam Denison and Louise (Henry) Cappel; married Raymond A. Montgomery, Jr., June 16, 1962; children: Raymond A. III, Anson Cappel. *Education:* Sarah Lawrence College, B.A., 1959; Columbia University,

M.A., 1961. *Home address:* Box 333, Waitsfield, Vt. 05673. *Agent:* Oscar Collier, Seligmann & Collier, 280 Madison Ave., New York, N.Y. 10016.

CAREER: Newsweek, New York City, reporter, and editor of company magazine, 1961-62; Fleet Publishing Corp., New York City, associate editor, 1963-64; *Vogue,* New York City, researcher and writer, 1964-66; Waitsfield Summer School, Waitsfield, Vt., founder (with husband), and teacher, 1966-69; Pine Manor Junior College, Chestnut Hill, Mass., associate professor, 1968-71; Vermont Crossroads Press, Waitsfield, president, 1973—; Goddard College, Plainfield, professor, 1975—. *Member:* Authors League of America, Writers Guild of America, American Association of University Professors. *Awards, honors:* McDowell Colony fellowship, 1972, 1974.

WRITINGS: Hemingway in Michigan, Fleet, 1966; *Vermont School Bus Ride,* Vermont Crossroads Press, 1974; (with husband, Raymond A. Montgomery, Jr.) *Vermont Farm and the Sun,* Vermont Crossroads Press, 1975; (with R. A. Montgomery) *Vermont Roadbuilder,* Vermont Crossroads Press, 1975. Columnist for *Park East,* 1963-65.

WORK IN PROGRESS: A novel; poetry.

AVOCATIONAL INTERESTS: The outdoors.

*   *   *

MONTGOMERY, John Warwick 1931-

PERSONAL: Born October 18, 1931, in Warsaw, N.Y.; son of Maurice Warwick (owner of a retail feed company) and Harriet (Smith) Montgomery; married Joyce Ann Bailer; children: Elizabeth Ann, David Warwick, Catherine Ann. *Education:* Cornell University, A.B. (with distinction), 1952; University of California, Berkeley, B.L.S., 1954, M.A., 1958; Wittenberg University, B.D., 1958, S.T.M., 1960; University of Chicago, Ph.D., 1962; University of Strasbourg, Docteur de l'Universite, mention Theologie Protestante (Th.D.), 1964; LaSalle Extension University, LL.B., 1976; additional study at Columbia University, University of Southern California, University of San Diego, Catholique's Institute on International and Comparative Law, and Chicago Lutheran School of Theology. *Politics:* Independent. *Home:* 2530 Shadow Ridge Lane, Orange, Calif. 92667; and 1, rue de Palerme, 67000 Strasbourg, France (May to September). *Office address:* Melodyland Christian Center, P.O. Box 6000, Anaheim, Calif. 92806.

CAREER: University of California Library, Berkeley, librarian in general reference service, 1954-55; Wittenberg University and Hamma Divinity School, Springfield, Ohio, instructor in Biblical Hebrew, Hellenistic Greek, and Medieval Latin, 1956-59; ordained minister of Lutheran Church in America, 1958, transferred to Lutheran Church-Missouri Synod, 1965; University of Chicago, Chicago, Ill., head librarian of Swift Library of Divinity and Philosophy, and member of federated theological faculty, 1959-60; Waterloo Lutheran University, University College, Waterloo, Ontario, associate professor of history and chairman of department, 1960-64; Trinity Evangelical Divinity School, Deerfield, Ill., professor of church history, 1964-74, chairman of Division of Church History and History of Christian Thought, 1965-74; director of European Program at University of Strasbourg, Strasbourg, France, 1967-74; International School of Law, Washington, D.C., professor of law and theology, 1974-75; Melodyland Christian Center, Anaheim, Calif., professor-at-large, 1976—. Theological consultant, Christian Legal Society, 1975—. Visiting professor at Lutheran seminaries and De Paul University (Catholic); lecturer in United States, Germany, Canada, and Switzerland.

MEMBER: Medical Library Association (diplomate), American Scientific Affiliation (fellow), American Historical Association, World Association of Law (founding member), Societe des Arts (Strasbourg), Chaine des Rotisseurs (chevalier; Paris), Academie Gastronomique Brillat-Savarin (Paris), Lutheran Academy for Scholarship, New York C. S. Lewis Society, Evangelical Theological Society, Society for Reformation Research, American Theological Library Association, Creation Research Society, Tolkien Society, Phi Beta Kappa, Phi Kappa Phi, Beta Phi Mu. *Awards, honors:* Postdoctoral senior research fellowship, Canada Council, 1963; faculty fellowship, American Association of Theological Schools, 1967; John Warwick Montgomery manuscript collection established at Syracuse University Library, 1970.

WRITINGS: The Writing of Research Papers in Theology, University of Chicago Divinity School, 1959; *A Union List of Serial Publications in Chicago-Area Protestant Theological Libraries,* University of Chicago Divinity School Library, 1960; *The Shape of the Past: An Introduction to Philosophical Historiography,* Edwards Brothers, 1962, revised edition, Bethany Fellowship, 1975; *The 'Is God Dead?' Controversy,* Zondervan, 1966; (with Thomas J. J. Altizer) *The Altizer-Montgomery Dialogue: A Chapter in the God is Dead Controversy,* Inter-Varsity Press, 1967; *Crisis in Lutheran Theology* (essays), Baker Books, Volume I, 1967, (editor) Volume II, 1967, 2nd edition, Bethany Fellowship, 1973; *Es confiable el Christianismo?,* Casa Bautista, 1968; *Where is History Going?,* Zondervan, 1969; *Ecumenicity, Evangelicals, and Rome* (essays), Zondervan, 1969.

History and Christianity, Inter-Varsity Press, 1970; *The Suicide of Christian Theology,* Bethany Fellowship, 1970; *In Defense of Martin Luther* (essays), Northwestern Publishing, 1970; *Damned through the Church,* Bethany Fellowship, Volume I, 1970, (editor) Volume II, 1970; *Computers, Cultural Change, and the Christ,* Christian Research Institute, 1970; *The Quest for Noah's Ark,* Bethany Fellowship, 1972, 2nd edition, Pyramid, 1974; (with Joseph Fletcher) *Debate on Situation Ethics,* Bethany Fellowship, 1972; *La Mort de Dieu,* Oberlin (Strasbourg), 1972; *Principalities and Powers: The World of the Occult,* Bethany Fellowship, 1973, 2nd edition, Pyramid, 1975; *Cross and Crucible: Johann Valentin Andreae, 1586-1654,* Nijhoff, 1973; *Verdammt durch die Kirche?,* [Austria], 1973; *How Do We Know There Is a God? and Other Questions,* Bethany Fellowship, 1974; *Como Sabemos Que Hay un Dios?,* Editorial Betania (Puerto Rico), 1975; *The Law above the Law,* Bethany Fellowship, 1975; *The Shaping of America,* Bethany Fellowship, 1976.

Editor; all published by Bethany Fellowship, except as noted: (And translator) *A Seventeenth-Century View of European Libraries,* University of California Press, 1962; (and translator) *Chytraeus on Sacrifice: A Reformation Treatise in Biblical Theology,* Concordia, 1962; *Christianity for the Toughminded,* 1973; *International Scholars Directory,* International Scholarly Publishers, 1973, Marquis, 1975; *Myth, Allegory and Gospel,* 1974; *The Inerrant Word of God,* 1974; *Jurisprudence: A Book of Readings,* International Scholarly Publishers, 1974; *Demon Possession,* 1975. General editor, "Evangelical Perspectives" series, seven volumes, Lippincott, 1970-72.

Contributor: Harvey Warner, editor, *Why—in the World*, Word Books, 1965; Carl F. H. Henry, editor, *Jesus of Nazareth: Saviour and Lord*, Eerdmans, 1966; Merrill C. Tenney, *The Living Word of Revelation*, Zondervan, 1967; Bernard Murchland, editor, *The Meaning of the Death of God: Protestant, Jewish, and Catholic Scholars Explore Atheistic Theology*, Random House, 1967; Ronald H. Nash, editor, *The Philosophy of Gordon Clark*, Presbyterian & Reformed, 1968; Robert Campbell, editor, *Spectrum of Protestant Beliefs*, Bruce Books, 1968; Spitzer and Saylor, editors, *Birth Control and the Christian*, Tyndale, 1969; Geehan, editor, *Jerusalem and Athens: Cornelius Van Til* (a festschrift), Presbyterian & Reformed, 1971; Seth Erlandsson, editor, *Ditt ord aer Sanning: En hanbok om Bibeln, tillaegnad David Hedegaard*, Stiftelsen Biblicum (Uppsala), 1971.

Member of panel on the Bible and the new morality in Educational Communication Association's film series, "God and Man in the Twentieth Century." Editor-at-large and regular contributor, in rotation with six other theologians, to "Current Religious Thought" section of *Christianity Today;* contributor to other theology, history, library, and denominational journals in America and abroad.

WORK IN PROGRESS: A translation-edition of H. G. Masius' *Defense de la religion lutherienne (1699);* a Protestant travel guide to Europe, in collaboration with wife; a work on the era of classical Lutheran orthodoxy (sixteenth and seventeenth centuries); a theological, medical, legal treatment of the abortion question with refutation of the Roe versus Wade opinion; a comprehensive book on Christian apologetics; and *Tractatus Logico-Theologicus*, an apologetic for the Christian faith, modeled on Wittgenstein's *Tractatus Logico-Philosophicus*.

SIDELIGHTS: "My world-view was hammered out at University; there I became a Christian. . . . Like the late C. S. Lewis (one of my greatest heroes), I was literally dragged kicking and screaming into the Kingdom by the weight of evidence for Christian truth." *Avocational interests:* Travel, music, gastronomy and vinology, antique Citroen autos (owns a 1925 C-3, a 1926 B-14, and a 1954 11-B tration avant), book collecting (Latin theological works of the sixteenth and seventeenth centuries, cuisine, modern philosophy, history of occultism, historical bibliography, myths and legends).

* * *

MOODY, Jess C. 1925-

PERSONAL: Born August 19, 1925, in Paducah, Tex.; married Doris Cummins; children: Patrick Jess, Martha Kit. *Education:* Baylor University, B.A., 1951; Southern Baptist Theological Seminary, B.D., 1955. *Home:* 4515 South Flagler, West Palm Beach, Fla. 33405. *Office:* First Baptist Church, 1101 South Flagler Dr., West Palm Beach, Fla. 33401.

CAREER: Clergyman of Southern Baptist Church. Evangelist, 1950-56; pastor in Owensboro, Ky., 1956-61; First Baptist Church, West Palm Beach, Fla., senior minister, 1961—; president, Palm Beach Atlantic College, West Palm Beach, Fla., and at Southern Baptist Pastor's Conference, 1964-65. Guest preacher in United States and Europe. *Member:* International Platform Association, Navy League, Society of Four Arts. *Awards, honors:* D.D., Campbellsville Baptist College.

WRITINGS: Don't Miss It if You Can!, Word Books, 1965; *You Can't Lose for Winning*, Zondervan, 1967; *A

Drink at Joel's Place, Word Books, 1967. Contributor to religious periodicals. Publisher, *Shield*, 1947-50.

* * *

MOORE, Basil John 1933-

PERSONAL: Born June 6, 1933, in Toronto, Ontario, Canada; son of Philip J. (a machinist) and Beryl (Christian) Moore; divorced; children: Robin, Martin. *Education:* University of Toronto, B.A., 1955; Johns Hopkins University, Ph.D., 1958. *Home:* Maple Shade Rd., Middletown, Conn. 06457. *Office:* Wesleyan University, Middletown, Conn. 06457.

CAREER: Wesleyan University, Middletown, Conn., assistant professor, 1958-64, associate professor, 1964-71, professor of economics, 1971—. Consultant, Agency for International Development, and U.S. Bureau of the Budget. *Member:* American Economic Association, Econometric Society, Canadian Economic Association, Royal Economic Society, American Finance Association.

WRITINGS: An Introduction to the Theory of Finance: Asset Holder Behavior Under Uncertainty, Free Press, 1967; *An Introduction to Modern Economic Theory*, Free Press, 1973. Contributor to economic journals.

WORK IN PROGRESS: Financial behavior and financial markets in economic growth and development.

AVOCATIONAL INTERESTS: Skiing, mountain climbing, tennis.

* * *

MOORE, G(ranville) Alexander, Jr. 1937-

PERSONAL: Born October 8, 1937, in Manila, Philippine Islands; son of Granville Alexander (a rear admiral, U.S. Navy) and Emily (Woodward) Moore. *Education:* Harvard University, B.A., 1958; Columbia University, M.A., 1963, Ph.D., 1966. *Politics:* Democrat. *Home:* 2065 Northwest Eleventh Rd., Gainesville, Fla. 32605. *Office:* Center for Latin American Studies, University of Florida, Gainesville, Fla. 32611.

CAREER: Emory University, Atlanta, Ga., assistant professor of anthropology and teacher education, 1965-69; University of Florida, Gainesville, associate professor of anthropology, 1969—, acting chairman of department, 1970-71. *Member:* American Anthropological Association (fellow), American Ethnological Society, Society for Applied Anthropology, Southern Anthropology Society.

WRITINGS: Realities of the Urban Classroom: Observations in Elementary Schools, Praeger, 1967; *Life Cycles in Atchalan: The Diverse Careers of Certain Guatemalans*, Teachers College Press, 1973.

WORK IN PROGRESS: Mirror for Guatemala: Cultural Horizons and Political Arenas in a Developing Nation; Cultural Anthropology, for Harper.

* * *

MOORE, Gene D. 1919-

PERSONAL: Born June 7, 1919, in Vaughn, Mont.; son of William A. and Rose (McAuley) Moore; married Wilma M. Shore, January 24, 1920. *Agent:* Martha Johnson, 2805 O St. N.W., Washington, D.C. 20007.

CAREER: U.S. Army, entered as draftee, 1941, retired as colonel, 1968; self-employed as communications consultant, 1968—, currently under contract to Philco-Ford Corp.

WRITINGS: The Killing at Ngo Tho (novel), Norton, 1967.

WORK IN PROGRESS: A novel based on a U.S. military-civilian intrusion into the culture of Thailand; several other novels.

SIDELIGHTS: "What the author tells is a truly exciting story that . . . helps to suspend judgment about Vietnam itself," writes Herbert Mitgang in his review of *The Killing at Ngo Tho.* "Mr. Moore modestly writes a story about a small action in a northern province that rings with authenticity," Mitgang adds that "the author's inside military knowledge gives his book its rare quality. . . . Seldom have novels been written with such intimate knowledge of high-level American army men."

BIOGRAPHICAL/CRITICAL SOURCES: New York Times Book Review, July 9, 1967.††

* * *

MOORE, John Hebron 1920-

PERSONAL: Born February 26, 1920, in Greenville, Miss.; son of John Pressley (an accountant) and Cora (Hebron) Moore; married Margaret DesChamps (a professor of history), December 21, 1955; children: John Hebron, Jr. *Education:* Mississippi State University, B.S., 1946; University of Mississippi, M.A., 1951; Emory University, Ph.D., 1955. *Office:* Department of History, Florida State University, Tallahassee, Fla. 32306.

CAREER: Emory University, Atlanta, Ga., instructor in history, 1954-55; Delta State College, Cleveland, Miss., assistant professor of history, 1955-56; University of Mississippi, University, assistant professor, 1956-57, associate professor, 1957-62, professor of history, 1962-69, chairman of department, 1966-69; Florida State University, Tallahassee, professor of history, 1970—, chairman of department, 1975—. *Military service:* U.S. Army Air Forces, 1941-45; became first lieutenant; received Air Medal with oak leaf cluster. *Member:* Organization of American Historians, Agricultural History Society, Forest History Society, Southern Historical Association, Mississippi Historical Society. *Awards, honors:* American Council of Learned Societies fellowship to study the industrial revolution in the antebellum cotton kingdom, 1965-66.

WRITINGS: Agriculture in Antebellum Mississippi, Bookman Associates, 1958; *Andrew Brown and Cypress Lumbering in the Old Southwest,* Louisiana State University Press, 1967; (with wife, Margaret D. Moore) *Mississippi: A Students' Guide to Localized History,* Teachers College, Columbia University, 1967. Editor, *Journal of Mississippi History,* 1956-60.

WORK IN PROGRESS: A history of antebellum Mississippi; continuing research in the industrial history of the Old South, with two books expected to result.

* * *

MOORE, Sebastian 1917-

PERSONAL: Born December 21, 1917, in Madras, India; son of Pierce Langrishe (in Indian civil service) and Muriel (Strange) Moore. *Education:* Christ's College, Cambridge, M.A. (honors), 1945; Sant' Anselmo, Rome, Italy, D.D., 1951. *Politics:* "Romantically Left." *Home:* Downside Abbey, Bath, England. *Agent:* A. M. Heath & Co. Ltd., 35 Dover St., London 41X 4EB, England.

CAREER: Roman Catholic priest of Benedictine order (O.S.B.). Entered Downside Benedictine community in 1938; professor of dogma and English literature at Downside, Bath, England, 1951-59; St. Mary's Parish, Liverpool, England, assistant priest, 1960-67, parish priest, 1967—. *Military service:* Royal Navy, 1935-36.

WRITINGS: God Is a New Language, Darton, Longman & Todd, 1967, Paulist Press & Newman, 1968; *No Exit,* Paulist Press & Newman, 1968; (with Kevin MacGuire) *The Experience of Prayer,* Darton, Longman & Todd, 1969; *The Dreamer and Not the Dream,* Darton, Longman & Todd, 1971. Contributor to symposia published by Darton, Longman & Todd. Former editor, *Downside Review.*

AVOCATIONAL INTERESTS: Playing piano, reading historical novels of the Oldenburg type, and science fiction; "a special interest in Albigensians and their beautiful country."†

* * *

MOORE, T(om) Inglis 1901-

PERSONAL: Born September 28, 1901, in Camden, New South Wales, Australia; son of John Edward (a grazier) and Elizabeth (Inglis) Moore; married Peace Flavelle Little, July 27, 1927; children: Pacita Mary Inglis (Mrs. Ivan Gabriel Alexander). *Education:* St. Paul's College, University of Sydney, B.A., 1923; Queen's College, Oxford, B.A., 1926, M.A., 1931. *Religion:* Church of England. *Home:* 79 Dominion Circuit, Deakin, Canberra, Australian Capital Territory 2600, Australia.

CAREER: Instructor in English at Phillips Academy, Andover, Mass., 1926-27, and University of Iowa, Iowa City, 1927-28; University of the Philippines, Manila, associate professor of English, 1928-31; *Sydney Morning Herald,* Sydney, Australia, leader-writer on editorial staff, 1934-40; Australian National University, Camberra, senior lecturer in Pacific studies, 1945-56, senior lecturer in Australian literature, 1956-59, associate professor of Australian literature, 1959-66. Visiting professor of Australian literature, lecturing at seven Canadian universities under auspices of Canadian Humanities Research Association, 1963. Member and acting chairman, Commonwealth Literary Fund Advisory Board, 1945—. *Military service:* Australian Imperial Forces, gunner, 1940-41; deputy assistant director of Army Education Service, 1941-45; major.

MEMBER: Fellowship of Australian Writers (president of Sydney branch, 1935-36; president of Canberra branch, 1953-55; Commonwealth chairman, 1955), Australian Society of Authors (council member), Australian Institute of International Affairs (president of Canberra branch, 1949-51), Australian Institute of Political Science, Australian English Association, International P.E.N. (Sydney branch), University Club (Sydney), University House and University Staff Centre (Canberra). *Awards, honors:* Officer, Order of the British Empire, 1957, for distinguished services to Australian literature.

WRITINGS: The Half Way Sun: A Tale of the Philippine Islands (novel), Angus & Robertson, 1935; (editor with William Moore) *Best Australian One-Act Plays,* Angus & Robertson, 1937; *Adagio in Blue* (poems), Angus & Robertson, 1938; *Emu Parade: Poems from Camp,* Angus & Robertson, 1941; (editor) *Six Australian Poets.* Robertson & Mullins, 1942; *We're Going Through* (radio play in verse), Angus & Robertson, 1945; (editor) *Australia Writes: An Anthology,* F. W. Cheshire, 1953; *Bayonet and Grass* (poems), Angus & Robertson, 1957; (editor) *Henry Kendall,* Angus & Robertson, 1957.

(Editor) *A Book of Australia* (national anthology), Collins, 1961; (editor with Douglas Stewart) *Poetry in Australia,* two volumes, Angus & Robertson, 1964, University of California Press, 1965; (with Dymphna Cusack and Barrie Ovenden) *Mary Gilmore,* Australasian Book Society, 1965; *Rolf Boldrewood,* Oxford University Press, 1968; *Social Patterns in Australian Literature,* University of California Press, 1971; (compiler) *From the Ballads to Brennan,* Angus & Robertson, 1971. Play, "Love's Revenge," anthologized in *Philippine Plays,* 1930, and reprinted in *Six Philippine Plays,* 1957.

AVOCATIONAL INTERESTS: Gardening, especially growing, exhibiting, and breeding roses (has also taken prizes in Canberra shows for iris, camellias, and daffodils).

BIOGRAPHICAL/CRITICAL SOURCES: Meanjin Quarterly, Number 2, 1967.†

*   *   *

MOORHEAD, Max L(eon)   1914-

PERSONAL: Born December 28, 1914, in Grand Junction, Colo.; son of Joseph Edgar (an advertising manager) and Edith (Lillie) Moorhead; married Amy Allen, May 18, 1940. *Education:* Northwestern State College, Alva, Okla., student, 1933-36; University of Oklahoma, B.A., 1937, M.A., 1938; University of California, Berkeley, Ph.D., 1942. *Home:* 1228 Caddell Lane, Norman, Okla. 73069. *Office:* Department of History, University of Oklahoma, Norman, Okla. 73069.

CAREER: Henry J. Kaiser Shipyard, Richmond, Calif., shipfitter, 1942-45; University of Oklahoma, Norman, assistant professor, 1945-51, associate professor, 1951-56, professor, 1956-66, David Ross Boyd Professor of History, 1966-75, professor emeritus, 1975—, chairman of department, 1958-62. Visiting professor, University of Texas, 1962-63; visiting summer professor, University of Colorado, 1966. *Member:* Conference on Latin American History, Organization of American Historians, Western History Association, Phi Beta Kappa.

WRITINGS: (Editor) Josiah Gregg, *Commerce of the Prairies,* University of Oklahoma Press, 1954; *New Mexico's Royal Road,* University of Oklahoma Press, 1958; *Apache Frontier,* University of Oklahoma Press, 1968; *The Presidio,* University of Oklahoma Press, 1975. Contributor to *Encyclopaedia Britannica, Britannica Yearbook,* and to historical journals.

*   *   *

MORGAN, Darold H.   1924-

PERSONAL: Born August 5, 1924, in Coffeyville, Kan.; son of Elmer E. (a railroad employee) and Sara (Froman) Morgan; married Elizabeth Johnson, June 20, 1947; children: Tim, Marshall, Julie. *Education:* Hardin-Simmons University, A.B., 1944; Southwestern Baptist Theological Seminary, Th.M., 1947, Th.D., 1953. *Home:* 202 North Waterview, Richardson, Tex. 75080.

CAREER: Baptist minister. Pastor of churches in Bonham, Tex., 1950-53, Sulpher Springs, Tex., 1953-58, Sherman, Tex., 1958-62, and Birmingham, Ala., 1962-66; Cliff Temple Baptist Church, Dallas, Tex., pastor, 1966-71; president and chief executive officer, Southern Baptist Convention Annuity Board, 1971—. Vice-president, Baptist General Convention of Texas. Trustee, Judson College, Hardin-Simmons University. Member of development board, Bishop College; member, Dallas County Community Action Committee. *Member:* Rotary Club.

WRITINGS: Patterns for the Pilgrimage, Abingdon, 1966.

*   *   *

MORGAN, Geoffrey   1916-

PERSONAL: Born October 13, 1916, in Essex, England; son of Robert (an employee of Bank of England) and Eleanor (Kine) Morgan; wife deceased. *Education:* Attended Clark's Commercial College and The Polytechnic, London, England. *Home:* Bildeston, Suffolk, England. *Agent:* Curtis Brown Ltd., 1 Craven Hill, London W2 3EW, England; John Cushman Associates Inc., 25 West 43rd St., New York, N.Y. 10036.

CAREER: As a young man, worked for various newspapers in London as a reporter; after the war worked six months as a part-time public relations consultant. Full-time professional writer. *Military service:* Royal Air Force, 1941-46. *Member:* Society of Authors, Royal Yachting Association, Press Club, and Wig and Pen Club (all London), Royal Harwich Yacht Club.

WRITINGS: Murderer's Moon, Jenkins, 1942; *No Crest for the Wicked,* Forbes Robertson, 1952; (editor with Michael Hastings) *Guide to English Inns,* Elek, c.1952; *Heavenly Body,* Forbes Robertson, 1953; *Cameras on the Conways,* Lutterworth, 1954; *Conways Ahoy,* Lutterworth, 1955; *Small Boat Sailing,* W. & G. Foyle, 1961; *Tea with Mr. Timothy,* Parrish, 1964, Little, Brown, 1966; *Run for Cover,* Parrish, 1964; (with Pamela Tucker) *The Yachtsman's Pocket Book,* Parrish, 1965; *The Small Wish,* Parrish, 1965; *A Small Piece of Paradise,* Collins, 1967, Knopf, 1968; *A Touch of Magic,* Collins, 1968; *A Window of Sky,* Collins, 1969.

(With Wieslaw Lasocki) *Soldier Bear,* Collins, 1970; *The View from Prospect,* Collins, 1972; *Boy Dominic,* Fontana, 1974; *Summer of the Seals,* Collins, 1975; *Mrs. Mallory,* Collins, in press. Has also adapted many of his books and other scripts for British Broadcasting Corp. Contributor of short stories, and articles on sailing to women's magazines.

SIDELIGHTS: Morgan told *CA* that there is "too much sex, sadism and violence in so many books of today," and that "there is a place for the book that tells a story with simplicity, with feeling, about ordinary people in interesting and sometimes extraordinary circumstances, without resort to microscopic details of their sex lives." Many of Morgan's books have been serialized in magazines.

AVOCATIONAL INTERESTS: Sailing and golf.

BIOGRAPHICAL/CRITICAL SOURCES: Trade News, November, 1964.

*   *   *

MORGAN, James N(ewton)   1918-

PERSONAL: Born March 1, 1918, in Corydon, Ind.; son of John J. B. (a psychologist) and Rose Ann (Davis) Morgan; married Gladys Lucille Hassler, May 12, 1945; children: Kenneth, Timothy, John, Janet. *Education:* Northwestern University, A.B., 1939; Harvard University, M.A., 1941, Ph.D., 1947. *Politics:* Independent. *Religion:* Methodist. *Home:* 1217 Bydding Rd., Ann Arbor, Mich. 48103. *Office:* University of Michigan, Ann Arbor, Mich. 48106.

CAREER: Brown University, Providence, R.I., assistant professor of economics, 1947-49; University of Michigan, Ann Arbor, Carnegie fellow, 1949-51, assistant program director, Survey Research Center, 1951-55, program director, 1955—, associate professor, 1954-57, professor of economics, 1958—. Fellow, Center for Advanced Study in the Behavioral Sciences, Stanford, Calif., 1955-56. Member of board of directors, Social Science Research Council, 1969-74, and Consumers Union, 1974—; chairman, Behavioral Science Division, National Research Council, 1970-73. *Member:* American Economic Association, American Statistical Association (fellow), National Academy of Sciences, Econometric Society.

WRITINGS: Consumer Economics, Prentice-Hall, 1954; (with David, Cohen and Brazer) *Income and Welfare in the U.S.,* McGraw, 1962; (co-author) *The Detection of Interaction Effects,* Survey Research Center, University of Michigan, 1964; (with Barlow and Brazer) *Economic Behavior of the Affluent,* Brookings Institution, 1966; (with others) *Productive Americans,* Survey Research Center, University of Michigan, 1966.

WORK IN PROGRESS: Research into early retirement, dynamics of consumer debt, dynamics of individual economic improvement or failure, and philanthropy.

* * *

MORGULAS, Jerrold 1934-

PERSONAL: Born April 5, 1934, in New York, N.Y.; son of David (an attorney) and Elsie (Feldman) Morgulas; married Susan H. Spies (a teacher), September 11, 1966. *Education:* Yale University, B.A., 1955, LL.B., 1959. *Politics:* Independent. *Religion:* Jewish. *Home:* 207 East 74th St., New York, N.Y. 10021. *Agent:* Candida Donadio, 111 West 57th St., New York, N.Y. 10019. *Office:* M. Carl Levine, Morgulas & Foreman, Esqs., 708 Third Ave., New York, N.Y.

CAREER: M. Carl Levine, Morgulas & Foreman, Esqs. (attorneys), New York, N.Y., partner. *Military service:* U.S. Army, 1957. U.S. Army Reserve, 1957-62; became captain. *Member:* Bar of the City of New York (associate), Yale Club (New York).

WRITINGS: The Accused, Doubleday, 1967; *The Siege,* Holt, 1972.

WORK IN PROGRESS: Two novels, *Victories and Defeats,* and *Peretz.*

AVOCATIONAL INTERESTS: Painting, sculpture, music (especially opera).

* * *

MORIARTY, Alice Marie Ewell 1917-

PERSONAL: Born September 17, 1917, in Fulton, N.Y.; daughter of Mark Dee (a civil engineer) and Eudora (Johnson) Ewell; married Francis M. Moriarty (chief psychologist at Topeka Veterans Administration Hospital), January 30, 1943; children: Anne (Mrs. Thomas Rodriguez), Mark. *Education:* Smith College, B.A., 1938; Columbia University, M.A., 1940; Purdue University, Ph.D., 1942. *Politics:* Democrat. *Religion:* Presbyterian. *Home:* 5001 Cedar Crest Rd., Topeka, Kan. 66606.

CAREER: Connecticut Bureau of Mental Hygiene, Hartford, clinical psychologist, 1942-43; Connecticut Division of Rehabilitation, Hartford, clinical psychologist, 1944-45; Vocational Counseling Service, New Haven, Conn., counselor, 1947-48; Menninger Foundation, Topeka, Kan., research psychologist, 1952-75, consultant in child psychiatric training, 1967-75. Consultant to Topeka State Hospital and Topeka City-County Health Department, 1968. *Member:*

American Psychological Association, Kansas Psychological Association, Topeka Psychological Association (chairman, 1967-68).

WRITINGS: (With Clyde Rousey) *Diagnostic Implications of Speech Sounds,* C. C Thomas, 1965; *Constancy and IQ Change,* C. C Thomas, 1966; (with Riley Gardner) *Personality Development at Preadolescence,* University of Washington Press, 1968; (with Povl W. Toussieng) *Adolescent Coping,* Grune, 1976; (with Lois B. Murphy) *Vulnerability, Coping, and Growth: From Infancy to Adolescence,* Yale University Press, 1976. Contributor to professional journals.

* * *

MORRESSY, John 1930-

PERSONAL: Born December 8, 1930, in Brooklyn, N.Y.; son of John Emmett and Jeanette (Geraghty) Morressy; married Barbara Turner, August 11, 1956. *Education:* St. John's University, Jamaica, N.Y., B.A., 1953; New York University, M.A., 1961. *Residence:* East Sullivan, N.H. *Agent:* James Oliver Brown, James Brown Associates, 22 East 60th St., New York, N.Y. 10022. *Office:* Department of English, Franklin Pierce College, Rindge, N.H. 03461.

CAREER: Teacher, intermittently, 1956-63; St. John's University, Jamaica, N.Y., instructor in English, 1963-66; Monmouth College, West Long Branch, N.J., assistant professor of English, 1966-67; Franklin Pierce College, Rindge, N.H., 1968—, began as associate professor and chairman of English department, currently professor of English. *Military service:* U.S. Army, 1953-55. *Member:* Authors Guild of America.

WRITINGS: The Blackboard Cavalier (novel), Doubleday, 1966; *The Addison Tradition* (novel), Doubleday, 1968; *Starbrat* (novel), Walker & Co., 1972; *Nail Down the Stars* (novel), Walker & Co., 1973; *The Humans of Ziax II* (juvenile), Walker & Co., 1974; *A Long Communion* (novel), Walker & Co., 1974; *Under a Calculating Star* (novel), Doubleday, 1975; *The Windows of Forever* (juvenile), Walker & Co., 1975; *A Law for the Stars,* Laser Books, in press. Contributor of short stories, light verse, essays, and poetry to magazines ranging from *Esquire* to *Spirit.*

WORK IN PROGRESS: A contemporary novel about death.

SIDELIGHTS: Morressy told *CA:* "I write for two main reasons: the fun of fooling with the English language, and the warm sense of achievement at pointing out to the world that the emperor has nothing on (even though the world prefers not to listen). To put it simply, I like what I'm doing." In his novel *The Addison Tradition,* writes a *Best Sellers* reviewer, Morressy has "captured the symptoms and disease of the American college." Morressy's use of "light but pointed sarcasm is . . . satisfyingly accurate," according to a *Christian Science Monitor* reviewer.

BIOGRAPHICAL/CRITICAL SOURCES: Times Literary Supplement, February 2, 1967; *New York Times Book Review,* July 28, 1968; *Best Sellers,* August 15, 1968; *Christian Science Monitor,* August 29, 1968; *Choice,* November, 1968; *Virginia Quarterly Review,* winter, 1969.

* * *

MORRIS, Christopher 1938-

PERSONAL: Born March 28, 1938, in Luton, England; son of Francis Leslie Ashton (an estate agent) and Ethel

Mary (McDonald) Morris; married Georgina Reda Whitehead, March 31, 1962. *Education:* Luton College of Technology, Journalist's Diploma, 1958. *Politics:* Conservative. *Religion:* Church of England. *Home:* 31, Beaumont Ave., St. Albans, Hertsfordshire, AL1 4TL, England.

CAREER: Daily Sketch, London, England, reporter, 1959-62; director and owner of British European News Agency, Madrid, Spain; Madrid correspondent for *Daily Express,* London, Independent Television News, London, 1962-67, *Daily Mail,* London, and British Broadcasting Corp., London, 1967-72; British Broadcasting Corp., London, radio and television news reporter, 1972—. *Member:* Press Club and Pathfinder Club (both London).

WRITINGS: The Day They Lost the H-Bomb, Coward, 1966 (published in England as *The Big Catch,* Angley, 1966).

WORK IN PROGRESS: Books on his journalistic experiences and on Spain.

SIDELIGHTS: The Day They Lost the H-Bomb, the first-published of several books on the H-bomb mishap in Spain, was written in a month; it has appeared in Spanish and Japanese translations.

* * *

MORRIS, Dan (H.) 1912-

PERSONAL: Born March 25, 1912, in Newark, N.J.; son of Joseph and Lena (Yellin) Morris, married Inez Lillie (an author), November 28, 1948; children: Susan Lillie, David Jay. *Education:* Attended college, one year. *Politics:* "Highly independent Democrat." *Home:* 82 Wisconsin St., Long Beach, N.Y. 11561. *Agent:* McIntosh & Otis, Inc., 18 East 41st St., New York, N.Y. 10017.

CAREER: Roamed, and "worked as cowpuncher, cook, and gold miner in the Mojave Desert, dynamiter in Bermuda, and concrete man in Greenland; later was a newspaperman on papers "big and small, from San Francisco to New York, as reporter, editor, columnist, editorial writer, copy reader, makeup man, rewrite man, golf editor, and labor editor." Former on-the-air correspondent for Canadian Broadcasting Corp. Charter member of Long Beach Commission on Human Relations; past president of Long Beach Civic Association. *Military service:* U.S. Navy, Seabees, 1943-45. *Member:* Overseas Press Club, Writers Guild of America (East), San Francisco Press Club, New York Newspaper Guild.

WRITINGS: A Family Guide to Saltwater Fishing, Collier, 1962; *The Savor of the Sea,* Macmillan, 1966; (with Jack Sterling) *The Sterling Cookbook,* Funk, 1969; (with Mike Douglas) *The Mike Douglas Cookbook,* Funk, 1969; (with wife, Inez Morris) *The Pennysaver Cookbook,* Funk, 1969; (with Arthur Lem) *The Hong Kong Cookbook,* Funk, 1970; (with Norman Strung) *Family Fun On and Around the Water,* Cowles, 1970; (with Strung) *The Fisherman's Almanac,* Macmillan, 1970; (with I. Morris) *The Complete Outdoor Cookbook,* Hawthorn, 1970; (with I. Morris) *The Complete Fish Cookbook,* Bobbs-Merrill, 1972; (with I. Morris) *The Weekend Camper,* Bobbs-Merrill, 1973; (with I. Morris) *Who Was Who in American Politics,* Hawthorn, 1974; (with I. Morris) *Money Saver Cookbook for Nourishing and Mouthwatering Meals,* C. R. Gibson, 1975; (with I. Morris) *Camping by Boat: Powerboat, Sailboat, Canoe, Raft,* Bobbs-Merrill, 1975. Writer for radio, including National Broadcasting Co.'s "Monitor." Contributor to magazines.

SIDELIGHTS: Dan Morris told *CA:* "My credo is simple: I write anything for which I am paid, and which I would permit my children to read. That, I believe, is the best form of censorship. As for my interests, they're widely varied because my kind of writing makes it so."†

* * *

MORRIS, Jerrold 1911-

PERSONAL: Born January 22, 1911, in London, England; son of John (a hat manufacturer) and Hilda (Erb) Morris; married Vivian Fay, October 13, 1944; children: John. *Education:* Attended Ashton Preparatory School, Kent, England, and The Polytechnic, London, England; took extension courses in art history at University of London. *Home:* 235 St. Clair Ave. W., Toronto, Ontario, Canada. *Office:* Jerrold Morris Gallery, 15 Prince Arthur Ave., Toronto, Ontario, Canada.

CAREER: Acton Educational Committee, Acton, England, school liaison officer, 1932-34; school art teacher in England, 1932-34; Van Enden Gold Mines, Dutch Guiana, surveyor, 1935-39; Vancouver Art Gallery, Vancouver, British Columbia, curator, 1948-56; San Francisco Museum of Art, San Francisco, Calif., chief curator, 1956-57; Laing Galleries, Toronto, Ontario, manager, 1958-62; Jerrold Morris Gallery, Toronto, Ontario, managing director, 1962—. *Military service:* Royal Canadian Air Force, 1940-46; became squadron leader; received Distinguished Flying Cross and bar. *Member:* Association of Art Museum Directors, Western Association of Art Museum Directors (president, 1935-55).

WRITINGS: On the Enjoyment of Modern Art, McClelland & Stewart, 1965, New York Graphic Society, 1968; *The Nude in Canadian Painting,* New Press (Toronto), 1972; *Canadian Artists and Airmen, 1940-45,* Morris Gallery (Toronto), 1974.

* * *

MORRIS, Richard K(nowles) 1915-

PERSONAL: Born November 16, 1915, in Somerville, Mass.; son of Clifford R. and Mae (Norton) Morris; married Anne Louise Smith (a teacher), July 1, 1946. *Education:* Trinity College, Hartford, Conn., A.B., 1940; Yale University, M.A., 1949, Ph.D., 1951. *Home:* 120 Cherry Hill Dr., Newington, Conn. 06111. *Office:* Department of Education, Trinity College, Hartford, Conn. 06106.

CAREER: Loomis School, Windsor, Conn., master, 1942-44; teacher in Deep River, Conn., then in Chester, Conn., 1945-47; Connecticut Education Association, research and field work, 1947-49; Trinity College, Hartford, Conn., instructor in anthropology and education, 1951-53, assistant professor, 1953-58, associate professor, 1958-66, professor of education, 1967-75, professor emeritus, 1975—, chairman of education department, 1972-75. Summer lecturer, Johns Hopkins University, 1957, 1959. *Member:* National Education Association (life member), Philosophy of Education Society (fellow), American Association of University Professors, Connecticut Education Association (honorary life member), Pi Gamma Mu. *Awards, honors:* Fulbright research scholar in India, 1961.

WRITINGS: John P. Holland: Inventor of the Modern Submarine, U.S. Naval Institute, 1966. Editor and contributor, *Of Man, Animals and Morals,* 1976; also contributor to *Proceedings* of U.S. Naval Institute and professional journals.

WORK IN PROGRESS: A biography, *Captain Extraordinary.*

AVOCATIONAL INTERESTS: Astronomy, sailing, and oil painting.

* * *

MORRIS-JONES, W(yndraeth) H(umphreys) 1918-

PERSONAL: Born August 1, 1918, in Carmarthen, South Wales; son of William James and Annie Mary (Morris) Jones; married Graziella Genre, 1953; children: two daughters, one son. *Education:* London School of Economics and Political Science, B.Sc., (Econ., honors), 1938; Christ's College, Cambridge, research scholar, 1940. *Home:* 95 Ridgway, London S.W. 19, England. *Office:* Institute of Commonwealth Studies, University of London, 27 Russell Sq., London W.C.1, England.

CAREER: University of London, London School of Economics and Political Science, London, England, lecturer in political science, 1946-55; University of Durham, Durham, England, professor of political theory and institutions, 1955-65; University of London, Institute of Commonwealth Studies, director, 1966—. Constitutional advisor to Viceroy of India, 1947. Visiting professor at Indian School of International Studies, New Delhi, 1960, University of Chicago, 1962, and University of California, Berkeley, 1964-65. *Military service:* Indian Army, 1941-46; became lieutenant-colonel. *Member:* Political Studies Association of the United Kingdom. *Awards, honors:* Rockefeller traveling fellow, 1954, 1960, 1966-67.

WRITINGS: Parliament in India, Longmans, Green, 1957; *Government and Politics of India,* Hutchinson, 1964, Doubleday, 1967, 2nd edition, Hutchinson, 1967. Contributor to political science journals.

WORK IN PROGRESS: Research on the Indian Congress Party.

AVOCATIONAL INTERESTS: Motoring, gardening, walking, tennis, music.

* * *

MORSE, J(osiah) Mitchell 1912-

PERSONAL: Born January 14, 1912, in Columbia, S.C.; son of Josiah (a professor) and Etta (Ferguson) Morse; married Frances Belkin, June 30, 1936; children: Jonathan, Carolyn. *Education:* University of South Carolina, A.B., 1932, M.A., 1933; Pennsylvania State University, Ph.D., 1952. *Home:* 115 Morris Rd., Ambler, Pa. 19002. *Office:* Department of English, Temple University, Philadelphia, Pa. 19122.

CAREER: Columbia Record, Columbia, S.C., reporter, 1934; *American Banker,* New York City, news editor, 1935-42; *Nation,* New York City, assistant editor, 1943-45; Free Press of India, New York City, United Nations correspondent, 1945-47; Pennsylvania State University, University Park, instructor, 1948-56, assistant professor, 1956-60, associate professor, 1960-63, professor of English, 1963-67; Temple University, Philadelphia, Pa., professor of English, 1967—. Fulbright lecturer in France, 1964-65. *Member:* Modern Language Association of America, American Comparative Literature Association, International Comparative Literature Association, International Federation for Modern Languages and Literatures, College English Association, National Council of Teachers of English, American Association of University Professors.

WRITINGS: The Sympathetic Alien: James Joyce and Catholicism, New York University Press, 1959; *Matters of Style,* Bobbs-Merrill, 1967; *The Irrelevant English Teacher,* Temple University Press, 1972. Articles have appeared in *New Republic, Hudson Review, Yale Review, Nation, Antioch Review,* and numerous other professional journals. Book review editor, *Journal of General Education,* 1960-67; member of editorial advisory committee, *PMLA,* 1970-74.

* * *

MOSCOW, Warren 1908-

PERSONAL: Born March 15, 1908, in Brooklyn, N.Y.; son of Jacob H. (an insurance salesman) and Stella (Klaas) Moscow; married Ester Loeb, 1934 (divorced, 1944); married Jean Shalen (a teacher), January 10, 1946; children: (first marriage) Judith (Mrs. John P. Heimann); (second marriage) John Warren and Katherine Alexis (twins). *Education:* Attended Columbia University, 1925-26, and Brooklyn Law School, 1926-27. *Politics:* Democrat. *Religion:* None. *Home:* 924 West End Ave., New York, N.Y. 10025; RD 1, Putnam Valley, N.Y. 10579. *Agent:* Paul R. Reynolds, Inc., 12 East 41st St., New York, N.Y. 10017.

CAREER: Reporter on *Brooklyn Daily Citizen,* Brooklyn, N.Y., 1926-28, and *New York American,* New York City, 1928-30; *New York Times,* New York City, political reporter, 1930-52, chief Albany correspondent, 1938-44, war correspondent in the Pacific, 1945; City of New York, Manhattan commissioner of borough works, 1952-53, assistant to the mayor, 1954-55, executive director of New York Housing Authority, 1955-57, executive assistant to the mayor, 1958-61, consultant on intergovernmental affairs, 1962-63; *New York Law Journal,* New York City, editor-in-chief, 1963-66. Director of Public Service Awards Program, Fund for the City of New York, 1973—. *Member:* New York State Legislative Correspondents Association (life; president, 1942), Society of Silurians.

WRITINGS: Politics in the Empire State, Knopf, 1948; *What Have You Done for Me Lately?: The Ins and Outs of New York Politics,* Prentice-Hall, 1966; *Roosevelt and Willkie,* Prentice-Hall, 1968; *The Last of the Big Time Bosses: The Life and Times of Carmine De Sapio,* Stein & Day, 1971. Contributor of articles to various publications.

SIDELIGHTS: Reviewing Moscow's *What Have You Done for Me Lately?,* Eugene H. Nickerson writes: "I commend it highly as a thoroughly interesting and entertaining account of modern New York City politics.... The author offers numerous object lessons but offers no solutions.... [He] does reveal here a profound appreciation for those problems and for the impact of political personalities upon them."

Moscow's book, *Roosevelt and Willkie* is an examination of the 1940 election and campaign "with impartiality and some fresh digging," which Mitchel Levitas calls "an engrossing account." Pennsylvania Senator Hugh Scott praised this as an "interesting and accurate narrative."

BIOGRAPHICAL/CRITICAL SOURCES: New Yorker, June 10, 1967; *New York Times Book Review,* June 25, 1967, August 18, 1968; *Commonweal,* December 15, 1967; *America,* September 7, 1968; *Book World,* September 8, 1968.

* * *

MOSELEY, Virginia D(ouglas) 1917-

PERSONAL: Born January 31, 1917, in Gainesville, Tex.;

daughter of Edward Hilary (a minister) and Leslie (Jones) Moseley. *Education:* University of Oklahoma, B.A., 1938, M.A., 1948; Columbia University, Ph.D., 1958. *Politics:* Independent. *Religion:* Presbyterian. *Residence:* Ottawa, Ontario, Canada. *Office:* Department of English, University of Ottawa, Ottawa, Ontario, Canada K1G 0E8.

CAREER: High school and junior college instructor in English, Gainesville, Tex., 1938-44; Southeastern State College, Durant, Okla., assistant professor of English, 1947-55; Northern Illinois University, DeKalb, assistant professor, 1955-59, associate professor, 1959-63, professor of English, 1963-67; Texas Woman's University, Denton, professor of English, 1967-69; University of Ottawa, Ottawa, Ontario, professor of English, 1969—. Visiting summer professor, University of Waterloo, Waterloo, Ontario, 1966. Church organist in Gainesville, Tex., 1938-44. *Military service:* U.S. Navy Reserve (WAVES), 1944-47; became lieutenant senior grade. *Member:* Modern Language Association of America, American Committee on Irish Studies, James Joyce Foundation, Canadian Association of University Professors, Delta Kappa Gamma, Kappa Delta Pi, Pi Zeta Kappa.

WRITINGS: (Translator with J. Suhadolc) *Those Americans* (Russian travelogue), Regnery, 1962; *Joyce and the Bible,* Northern Illinois University Press, 1967; (contributor) *Ulysses: Cinquante Ans Apres,* Marcel Didier, 1974. Contributor to *James Joyce Quarterly, Modern Drama,* and other professional journals.

WORK IN PROGRESS: A series of articles which are exegeses of the short stories in Joyce's *Dubliners.*

* * *

MOTHNER, Ira S. 1932-

PERSONAL: Born April 29, 1932, in Brooklyn, N.Y.; son of Gus (a merchant) and Jeanette (Sanders) Mothner; married Patricia Tait (a teacher), June 5, 1960; children: Joshua, Jonathan. *Education:* University of Missouri, B.J., 1953; Sorbonne, University of Paris, graduate study, 1956-57. *Politics:* "Erratic." *Religion:* Jewish. *Home:* 515 West End Ave., New York, N.Y. 10024.

CAREER: Look, New York, N.Y., member of staff, beginning 1957, senior editor, beginning 1960, wrote mainly on public affairs and social problems.

WRITINGS: Man of Action (biography of Theodore Roosevelt for teen-agers), Platt, 1966; *Woodrow Wilson, Champion of Peace,* F. Watts, 1969.

WORK IN PROGRESS: A novel for Watts.

* * *

MOULTON, Eugene R(ussell) 1916-

PERSONAL: Born March 18, 1916, in Mogadore, Ohio; son of Leon R. and Della (Meadows) Moulton; married Lillian Foote, May 10, 1941; children: Jeanne Rae, Joanne Mae, Russell Eugene, Jaime Patrick. *Education:* Kent State University, student, 1940-41; Western Reserve University (now Case Western Reserve University), B.A., 1947, M.A., 1948, Ph.D., 1953. *Politics:* Democrat. *Religion:* Protestant. *Home:* 1144 Henry Rd., Billings, Mont. 59102. *Office:* Eastern Montana College, Billings, Mont. 59102.

CAREER: Porcelain Steel Co., Cleveland, Ohio, personnel manager, 1944-46; Carroll College, Waukesha, Wis., associate professor of speech and chairman of department, 1949-52; University of Redlands, Redlands, Calif., professor of speech and chairman of department, 1952-68; Madison College, Harrisonburg, Va., professor of speech and chairman of department of speech and drama, 1968-70; Eastern Montana College, Billings, chairman of division of humanities, 1970-75 and department of speech communication and theatre arts, 1975—. Consultant on creativity, California State Department of Education; member of summer faculty, State University of New York at Buffalo. Member of leadership council, National Creative Education Foundation. Consultant, Lockheed Propulsion Co.; member of speaker's bureau, National Association of Manufacturers. *Military Service:* U.S. Army Air Forces, pilot, 1941-44. *Member:* Speech Association of America, American Forensic Association, Western Speech Association, Pacific Forensic Association (executive secretary, 1962-65), Pi Kappa Delta (province governor, 1954-58).

WRITINGS: Newton D. Baker, Western Reserve University Press, 1954; *Fundamentals of Speech,* Nichols Publishing, 1958, revised edition, 1963; *Dynamics of Debate,* Harcourt, 1966; *The New Interpersonal Communication: Ideas, Their Origination, Organization, and Presentation,* Burgess, 1975. Other writings include "Three Billion Dollar Computer Between Your Ears" (taped lecture), McGraw, 1967. Contributor to speech journals.

WORK IN PROGRESS: Public Speaking: A Creative Act, for Kendall/Hunt.

* * *

MOULTON, J(ames) L(ouis) 1906-

PERSONAL: Born June 3, 1906, in Pembroke Dock, Wales; son of John Davis (a captain, Royal Navy) and Beatrice (Cox) Moulton; married Barbara Aline Coode, June 19, 1937; children: Caroline Louise, Robert Darnell. *Education:* Attended public schools in England. *Home:* Fairmile, Woodham Rd., Woking, Surrey, England. *Agent:* John Farquharson Ltd., 15 Red Lion Sq., London, W.C.1, England.

CAREER: Regular officer in Royal Marines, 1924-61, retired as major general, 1961. Pilot with Fleet Air Arm, 1930-35; General Staff officer, and then commanding officer of Commando units in northwest Europe during World War II; commanding officer of Commando School, 1947-49, and of 3rd Commando Brigade in Middle East, 1952-54; promoted to major general, 1954; chief of Amphibious Warfare, 1957-61. Royal United Service Institution, vice-chairman, 1965-67, chairman, 1967-69. *Awards, honors:* Distinguished Service Order, 1944; Officer, Order of the British Empire, 1950; Companion of the Bath, 1956.

WRITINGS: Haste to the Battle, Cassell, 1963; *Defence in a Changing World,* Eyre & Spottiswoode, 1964; *The Norwegian Campaign of 1940,* Eyre & Spottiswoode, 1966, published as *A Study of Warfare in Three Dimensions,* Ohio University Press, 1967; *British Maritime Strategy in the 1970's,* Royal United Service Institute for Defence Studies, 1969; *The Royal Marines,* Leo Cooper, 1972. *Brassey's Annual,* naval editor, 1964-68, chief editor, 1969-73; defense correspondent, *Glasgow Herald,* 1966-67.

WORK IN PROGRESS: A book on the opening of the Scheldt in autumn, 1944.

* * *

MOUNT, (William Robert) Ferdinand 1939-

PERSONAL: Born July 2, 1939, in London, England; son

of Robert Francis and Lady Julia (Pakenham) Mount. *Education:* Attended Eton College and University of Vienna; Christ Church, Oxford, B.A. (first class honors), 1961. *Politics:* Conservative. *Religion:* Anglican. *Home:* 17 Ripplevale Grove, London N. 1, England. *Office:* Associated Newspapers, London E.C. 4, England; *National Review*, 150 East 35th St., New York, N.Y. 10016.

CAREER: Sunday Telegraph, London, England, editorial assistant, 1961; Conservative Party, London, officer in research department, and secretary to Parliamentary committees on health, social security, and Home Office affairs, 1962-65, assistant, Selwyn Lloyd inquiry into Conservative Party organization, 1964-65; *Daily Sketch*, London, leader writer and columnist, 1965-67; *National Review*, New York, N.Y., an editor, 1967; *Daily Mail*, London, chief leader writer, 1968-73; freelance journalist and novelist, 1973—.

WRITINGS: Very Like a Whale (novel), Weybright & Talley, 1967; *The Theatre of Politics*, Schocken, 1973; *The Man Who Rode Ampersand* (novel), Chatto & Windus, 1975. Contributor to periodicals and newspapers.

AVOCATIONAL INTERESTS: "Innumerable."

* * *

MOYNIHAN, William T. 1927-

PERSONAL: Born June 23, 1927, in Haverhill, Mass.; son of Richard Hull and Harriet (Trumbull) Moynihan; married Ruth Mackenzie Barnes, January 23, 1953; children: Robert, Elaine, Edward, Neil, Susan, Richard, Benjamin. *Education:* St. Bonaventure University, B.A., 1952; University of Connecticut, M.A., 1957; Brown University, Ph.D., 1961. *Home:* Farrell Rd., Storrs, Conn.

CAREER: University of Connecticut, Storrs, 1956-59, 1961—, began as instructor, professor of English, 1966—. *Military service:* U.S. Marine Corps, 1945-49.

WRITINGS: Using Prose, Dodd, 1961, revised edition, 1966; *Reading, Writing and Rewriting*, Lippincott, 1964, revised edition, 1968; (editor) James Joyce, *The Dead*, Allyn & Bacon, 1965; *The Craft and Art of Dylan Thomas*, Cornell University Press, 1966; (editor) *Essays Today*, Harcourt, number 6, 1967, number 7, 1972.

* * *

MUCHA, Jiri 1915-

PERSONAL: Born March 12, 1915, in Prague, Czechoslovakia; son of Alphonse Maria (an art noveau artist) and Maria (Chytilova) Mucha; married Vitezslava Kapralova (a composer), April 26, 1940; married second wife, Geraldine Thomson (also a composer), July 5, 1941; children: (second marriage) John. *Education:* Charles University, medical and literature studies, 1934-39. *Religion:* Protestant. *Home:* Hradcanske namesti 6, Prague 1, Czechoslovakia. *Agent:* Dilia, Vysehradska 28, Prague 2, Czechoslovakia; and A. P. Watt & Son, 26 Bedford Row, London W.C.1, England.

CAREER: Brought up in Prague, Paris, and New York; joined Czech Division of French Army, 1939, was evacuated to Britain in 1940, and served as flight lieutenant in Royal Air Force, 1943-45; during later years of the war also was correspondent for British Broadcasting Corp. in North Africa, Middle East, Southeast Asia, and Northwestern Europe; writer in Prague, Czechoslovakia, 1946-51; arrested for alleged espionage and imprisoned, 1951-54; writer and translator in Prague, 1954—. *Member:* P.E.N., Czechoslovak Writers Union, Garrick Club (London). *Awards,*

honors: Order of Merit; Mlada Fronta Award, 1966, for *Cerny a bily New York;* Memorial Medal, 1968; Ph.D., Dundee University, 1969.

WRITINGS: Most (title means "The Bridge"), Lofox, 1943; *The Problems of Lieutenant Knap* (short stories), Hogarth Press, 1945; *Ohen proti ohni* (war diary; title means "Fire Braves Fire"), Sfinx, 1947; *Sklenena Stena* (title means "The Glass Wall"), Prace, 1948; *Valka pokracuje* (title means "The War Continues"), Knihovna Lidovych Novin, 1949; *Spalena Setba*, Melantrich, 1948, translation published as *The Scorched Crop*, Hogarth Press, 1949; *Cim zraje cas* (title means "Maturing and Time"), Ceskoslovensky Spisovatel, 1958.

Provdepodobna tvar (novel; title means "Probable Face"), Ceskoslovensky Spisovatel, 1963; *Cerny a bily New York* (title means "Black and White New York"), Mlada Fronta, 1965; *Alphonse Mucha: His Life and Art*, Heinemann, 1966; *Alphonse Mucha: The Master of Art Nouveau*, Hamlyn, 1966; *Living and Partly Living* (prison diary), translated from the original Czech by Ewald Osers, Hogarth Press, 1967, McGraw, 1968; *Studene Slunce*, Ceskoslovensky Spisovatel, 1968; *Kankan se svatozari* (title means "Cancan with a Halo"), Obelisk, 1968; (with Marina Henderson and Aaron Scharf) *Mucha*, Academy Editions, 1971; (with Henderson) *The Graphic Works of Alphonse Mucha*, Academy Editions, 1973.

Plays produced: "Zlaty vek," 1948; "Broucci ve fraku," 1960; "Tanec mezi stiny," 1966. Filmscripts include "Roztrzka," "Povoden," "Prvna a posledni," "Vanice," "Kral kralu," "Kohout plasi smrt," "39 in the Shade," and "Prazske noci."

Books; translator into Czech; all published by Statni Nakladatelstvi Krasne Literatury: Jack Lindsay, *The Betrayed Spring*, 1956; Norman Mailer, *The Naked and the Dead*, 1957; Sinclair Lewis, *The Man Who Knew Coolidge*, 1957; Kingsley Amis, *Lucky Jim*, 1959.

Plays; translator into Czech: Edward Albee, *The Zoo Story;* Samuel Beckett, *Happy Days;* William Gibson, *Two for the Seesaw;* Frank Gillroy, *Who Will Save the Ploughboy;* Doris Lessing, *Play with a Tiger;* Brendan Behan, *The Hostage;* Keith Waterhouse and Willis Hall, *Billy Liar, The Long and the Short and the Tall;* Arnold Wesker, *Roots* (Orbis, 1961), and *Kitchen;* Monty Norman, Julian More, and David Heneker, *Irma La Douce;* Wolf Mankowitz, Julian More, David Heneker, and Monty Norman, *Expresso Bongo;* Wolf Mankowitz and Monty Norman, *Belle or Ballad of Dr. Crippen;* Wolf Mankowitz, Monty Norman, and David Heneker, *Make Me an Offer;* John Osborne and Anthony Creighton, *Epitaph for George Dillon;* Peter Shaffer, *The Private Eye, Royal Hunt of the Sun;* Noel Coward, *Nude with Violin;* Patrick Hamilton, *Gas Light;* Monty Norman and Julian More, *The Perils of Scobie Prilt;* Arthur Miller, *A Memory of Two Mondays;* Shelagh Delaney, *Taste of Honey;* Robert Bolt, *A Man for All Seasons* (Orbis, 1963); Peter Ustinov, *Photo Finish, Half Way Up the Tree*, and *The Unknown Soldier and His Wife*.

Regular contributor to *Nation;* also contributor to *New York Review of Books*.

SIDELIGHTS: Mucha was one of a group of young writers who helped launch *Daylight* in London in the early days of World War II, and contributed to John Lehmann's *New Writing*. He was sentenced to prison in Czechoslovakia for espionage for a term of six years in 1951. He served half of the sentence, and wrote *Living and Partly*

Living, a record of thought and events of this time. The book was written underground with pencil stubs by the light of a lamp that he had to dig up and then bury again every day. In 1968 he took active part in the Czechoslovak events as a regular contributor to the weekly *Literarni Listy.*

BIOGRAPHICAL/CRITICAL SOURCES: Observer Reviews April 23, 1967; *Canadian Forum,* August, 1968; *New York Times,* February 16, 1969.

* * *

MULLIGAN, Hugh A. 1925-

PERSONAL: Born March 23, 1925; son of John J. and Jeanette (Wilton) Mulligan; married Brigid Murphy, January 14, 1948. *Education:* Cathedral College, Brooklyn, N.Y., student, 1942-44; Marlboro College, B.A. (summa cum laude), 1948; Harvard University, M.A. (English literature), 1950; Boston University, M.S. (journalism), 1950. *Religion:* Roman Catholic. *Home:* 19 Campbell Ct., Queens Gate Gardens, London S.W. 7, England. *Office:* Associated Press, 83 Farringdon St., London E.C. 4, England.

CAREER: Associated Press, special correspondent, 1951—; has traveled in and reported from 104 countries on all continents; coverage has included such major news events as the missile shots, President Kennedy's trip to Ireland and his assassination and funeral, national political conventions, the Vietnam War, 1965-72, the Arab-Israel Wars of 1967 and 1973, the Cyprus conflict, and President Nixon's 1972 trip to China. *Military service:* U.S. Army Infantry, World War II; served in European theater. *Member:* Overseas Press Club (board of governors). *Awards, honors:* Short story awards from *Tomorrow,* 1948, and *Ellery Queen's Mystery Magazine,* 1949; American Newspaper Publishers Association Gold Medal, 1951; Headliners Award, 1963, 1967; Overseas Press Club award for best foreign reporting, 1967; Sigma Delta Chi award for best foreign reporting, 1971; Associated Press Managing Editors Best Reporting award, 1972; D.Hu.L., Marlboro College, 1973.

WRITINGS: (Contributor) H. Hoke, editor, *The Family Book of Humor,* Hanover House, 1957; (with Saul Pett, Sid Moody, and Tom Henshaw) *The Torch Is Passed: The Associated Press Story of the Death of a President,* Associated Press, 1964; (editor) *The World in 1964* (news yearbook), Associated Press, 1964; *No Place to Die: The Agony of Vietnam,* Morrow, 1967; (with John Barbour, Jules Loh, and Moody) *Lightning Out of Israel,* Prentice-Hall, 1967; (contributor) D. Brown, editor, *How I Got That Story* (anthology), Dutton, 1967.

* * *

MUNDEL, Marvin E(verett) 1916-

PERSONAL: Born April 20, 1916, in New York, N.Y.; son of Maxwell Herbert and Aimee (Baer) Mundel; married second wife, Takako Sawayama, September 13, 1961; children: Peter, Anne. *Education:* New York University, B.S. in M.E., 1936; University of Iowa, M.S., 1938, Ph.D., 1939. *Home and office:* 821 Loxford Ter., Silver Spring, Md. 20901.

CAREER: Research and industrial engineer, 1939-40; Bradley University, Peoria, Ill., assistant professor of general engineering, 1940-42; Purdue University, Lafayette, Ind., assistant professor, 1942-48, associate professor, 1948-50, professor of industrial engineering and chairman of

department, 1950-52; U.S. Army Ordnance Corps, Rock Island, Ill., director of U.S. Army Management Engineering Training Center, 1952-53; M. E. Mundel & Associates (industrial engineering consultants), Silver Spring, Md., president, 1953-63; U.S. Bureau of the Budget, Washington, D.C., principal staff officer for industrial engineering and work measurement, 1963-65; M. E. Mundel & Associates, president, 1965—. Visiting professor of industrial engineering at University of Birmingham, Birmingham, England, 1950-51, and Keio University, Tokyo, Japan, 1960-63.

MEMBER: American Institute of Industrial Engineers (president of Milwaukee chapter, 1954-55; Midwest vice-president, 1955-56; director of Government Division, 1965—), Sigma Xi, Tau Beta Pi, Iota Alpha. *Awards, honors:* Gilbreth Medal from Society for Advancement of Management; centennial award, New York University.

WRITINGS: Systematic Motion and Time Study, Prentice-Hall, 1947; *Motion and Time Study Principles and Practice,* Prentice-Hall, 1950, 3rd edition, 1960; *A Conceptual Framework for the Management Sciences,* McGraw, 1967; *Measuring and Enhancing Productivity in Service and Government Organizations,* Asian Productivity Organization, 1975. Contributor of about one hundred articles to technical journals.

* * *

MUNN, H. Warner 1903-

PERSONAL: Born November 5, 1903, in Athol, Mass.; son of Edward Emerson (a painter) and Jessica (Lemon) Munn; married Malvena Bodway, January 14, 1930; children: John Warner, James Edward, Gerald Douglas, Robin Shawn. *Education:* Attended public schools in Athol, Mass. *Politics:* Democrat. *Religion:* Lutheran. *Home:* 5019 North Vassault, Tacoma, Wash. 98407.

CAREER: Intermittently employed as ice cream, bakery, and Fuller Brush salesman, truck driver, deck hand, brakeman for New York Central Railroad, tool maker and foundry man for L. S. Starrett Co., Athol, Mass., and assistant manager of F. W. Woolworth store, Athol, Mass.; Buffelen Woodworking Co., Tacoma, Wash., rip saw operator and planer, beginning 1958; currently office manager, Stoker-Lad Heating Co., Tacoma. Free-lance writer. *Wartime service:* Massachusetts State Guard, 1940-42. *Member:* Tacoma Writers Club.

WRITINGS—Novels: The Werewolf of Ponkert, Grandon, 1958; *The King of the World's Edge,* Ace Books, 1966; *The Ship from Atlantis,* Ace Books, 1967; *Christmas Comes to the Little House,* Almar Press, 1974; *Merlin's Ring,* Ballantine, 1974; *Banner of Joan,* Grandon, 1975; *Tales of the Werewolf Clan,* Bob Weinberg, 1975. Also author of *The Affair of the Cuckolded Warlock,* 1975, and *Lost Legion.* Short stories included in *By Daylight Only,* Selwyn & Blount, 1928, and *More Macabre,* Ace Books, 1961. Stories and novelettes published in *Weird Tales* and *Unknown,* and some verse in newspapers and amateur magazines. Editor, *Newsletter* of Tacoma Writers Club, 1966, 1967-68.

WORK IN PROGRESS: Two novels, *The Time Knacker* and *Land of the Dark Sun;* a book of short stories tentatively entitled *The Melldrum Box.*

SIDELIGHTS: Munn states "I like to take an obscure fact as a foundation and base upon it fantastic situations and plots." *Avocational interests:* Witchcraft and demonology, folklore, curiosa of all kinds, autobiographies, poetry, ancient history.

* * *

MUNTER, Robert (L.) 1926-

PERSONAL: Born May 4, 1926, in Tacoma, Wash.; son of Delno Liverne (a mechanic) and Evelyn Lorraine (Marshall) Munter; married Marion Irene Gettmann, November 7, 1928; children: Llewelyn Keith, Gavan Rhys. *Education:* University of Washington, Seattle, B.A., 1951, M.A., 1956; Cambridge University, Ph.D., 1961. *Politics:* Democrat. *Religion:* None. *Home:* 5491 Baja Dr., San Diego, Calif. 92115. *Office:* Department of History, San Diego State University, San Diego, Calif. 92115.

CAREER: U.S. Civil Service, education adviser in England, 1954-62; University of Washington, Seattle, assistant professor of history, 1963-64; San Diego State University, San Diego, Calif., assistant professor, 1964-67, associate professor, 1967-70, professor of history, 1970—. *Military service:* U.S. Navy, 1944-46, *Member:* American Historical Association, Phi Alpha Theta.

WRITINGS: Hand-list of Irish Newspapers 1685-1750, Cambridge University Press, 1960; *History of the Irish Newspaper 1685-1760,* Cambridge University Press, 1967.

WORK IN PROGRESS: Englishmen Abroad in the 17th Century, a book on travel accounts of various classes of Englishmen.†

* * *

MURPHY, Brian (Michael) 1931-

PERSONAL: Born January 29, 1931, in Boston, England; son of John and Mona (Stewart) Murphy; married Josephine Pritchet (a social worker), May 2, 1959; children: Justin Sawdon Stewart, Olivia Sophie Stewart, Caspar James Stewart. *Education:* Attended Royal Military Academy, Sandhurst, 1950-52. *Religion:* Church of England. *Home:* 51 Rodenhurst Rd., London S.W. 4, England. *Agent:* Anthony Sheil Associates Ltd., 52 Floral St., Covent Garden, London WC2E 9DA, England. *Office:* I.C.T. House, Putney, London S.W. 15, England.

CAREER: British Army, Infantry, 1949-64, leaving service with rank of captain; International Computers and Tabulators Ltd., London, England, controller strategic liaison, 1964—. Director of Personal Advice Ltd. and Tarrant, Murphy and Associates Ltd. *Member:* International Federation for Information Processing (chairman of public information committee, 1966-68), British Computer Society.

WRITINGS: (Editor) *The Computer in Society,* Anthony Blond, 1967; *Management Accounting,* St. Paul's House, 1970; *Computers in Your Life,* Hutchinson, 1971; *A History of the British Economy, 1086-1970,* Longman, 1973; *How Not to Do Your Duty,* Abson Books, 1973; *The Business of Spying,* Milton House Books, 1973. Contributor to *Financial Times, New Scientist, Computer Weekly, Data Processing.*

AVOCATIONAL INTERESTS: Wine, food, travel.

BIOGRAPHICAL/CRITICAL SOURCES: Financial Times, March 16, 1965.†

* * *

MURPHY, George G(regory) S(tanislaus) 1924-

PERSONAL: Born June 9, 1924, in Bristol, England; son of John Joseph (a wheelwright) and Martha Alice (Foster)

Murphy; married Joan Morgan, April, 1950; married second wife, Joanne Mary Johnson, July 20, 1963; children: (first marriage) Gregory Jon, Russell Maynard; (second marriage) Holly Gaylan, Patrick Quillon. *Education:* University of Bristol, B.A. (honors), 1950; University of Washington, Seattle, Ph.D., 1957. *Politics:* Democrat. *Religion:* Church of England. *Home:* 2034 Thayer Ave., Westwood, Los Angeles, Calif. 90025. *Office:* Department of Economics, University of California, Los Angeles, Calif. 90024.

CAREER: Assistant professor of economics at University of Washington, Seattle, 1956-59, and Stanford University, Stanford, Calif., 1959-61; University of California, Los Angeles, associate professor of economics, 1961—. Fulbright lecturer, University of Essex, 1966-67. Consultant, U.S. Department of Defense, 1966-68, 1974-76. Manager of Net Assessment Programs, General Electric Company Center for Advanced Studies. *Military service:* British Army, Gloucestershire Regiment, medic, 1942-47.

WRITINGS: Soviet Mongolia, University of California Press, 1966.

WORK IN PROGRESS: With M. M. Stoddard and W. T. Lee, *Giants in Darkness: A Glimpse at the Strategic Balance.*

AVOCATIONAL INTERESTS: Sailing.

* * *

MURPHY, Shirley Rousseau 1928-

PERSONAL: Born May 20, 1928, in Oakland, Calif.; daughter of Otto Francis (a trainer of horses) and Helen (an artist; maiden name, Hoffman) Rousseau; married Patrick J. Murphy (a U.S. probation officer), August 5, 1951. *Education:* California School of Fine Arts (now San Francisco Art Institute), A.A., 1951.

CAREER: Sam Kweller, Designer, Los Angeles, Calif., packaging designer, 1952-53; Bullock's Department Store, Los Angeles, Calif., interior decorator, 1953-55; San Bernardino Valley College, San Bernardino, Calif., teacher of mosaics, 1958-61; Canal Zone Library-Museum, Canal Zone, documents assistant, 1964-67; painter and sculptor. Had a dual showing with her mother, Helen Rousseau, at Instituto Panameno de Arte, 1964, and eight one-woman shows in California, 1957-63; paintings, drawings, and sculpture also exhibited at group and juried shows in California, Arizona, and Nevada, and traveling exhibits. *Member:* California Water Color Society, San Francisco Art Institute, San Francisco Women Artists, Marin Society of Artists. *Awards, honors:* Seven awards for sculpture and five for paintings at San Francisco Museum and other exhibitions, 1956-62.

WRITINGS: White Ghost Summer, Viking, 1967; *The Sand Ponies,* Viking, 1967; *Elmos Doolan and the Search for the Golden Mouse,* Viking, 1970; (with husband, Patrick J. Murphy) *Carlos Charles,* Viking, 1971; *Poor Jenny Bright as Penny,* Viking, 1974; *The Grass Tower,* Atheneum, 1976.

WORK IN PROGRESS: A novella, *The Diamond Cup;* a juvenile fantasy, *The Ring of Fire.*

SIDELIGHTS: Shirley Rousseau Murphy spent her childhood riding and showing horses, and lived in the Canal Zone.

BIOGRAPHICAL/CRITICAL SOURCES: H. Rasmusen and A. Grant, *Sculpture from Junk,* Reinhold, 1967.

MURRAY, Dorothy Garst 1915-

PERSONAL: Born September 10, 1915, in Roanoke County, Va.; daughter of Levi and Marjorie (John) Garst; married Max Andrew Murray (a co-owner of family orchard and cattle-raising business), February 6, 1936; children: Anne (Mrs. Robert C. Reid), Max Andrew II, Stephen, Elaine. *Education:* Attended public schools in Roanoke County, Va., and took several extension courses from University of Virginia. *Politics:* "Born and bred in Democratic Party, but a stubborn independent Democrat". *Religion:* Church of the Brethren. *Home address:* R.F.D. 1, Box 672, Roanoke, Va. 24019.

CAREER: Volunteer worker for the mentally retarded since early 1950's. Roanoke Council for Retarded Children, charter member, 1951, and board member; Virginia Association for Retarded Children, charter member, 1952, and president, 1957-59; National Association for Retarded Children, vice-president for Southeast region, 1964-66, chairman of national committee on residential care, 1959-63, chairman of national historical committee, 1967—. Member of Virginia committee for 1960, White House Conference on Children and Youth, and Virginia legislative advisory committee to study services and needs of the mentally retarded, 1962-66; member of executive committee, Virginia Mental Health Study Commission, 1963-65. Church organist for seventeen years. *Awards, honors:* Merit Award for Public Service, Virginia Polytechnic Institute, 1963 (two merit awards are made annually in lieu of honorary degrees).

WRITINGS: This Is Stevie's Story, Brethren Press, 1956, enlarged and revised edition, Abingdon, 1967. Also author of brochures. Contributor to journals and newspapers, including *American Journal on Mental Deficiency, Pastoral Psychology, Mental Health in Virginia,* and *New England Journal of Medicine.*

WORK IN PROGRESS: A history of the National Association for Retarded Children.

AVOCATIONAL INTERESTS: Attending concerts; sewing, needlepoint, and leathercraft; camping, swimming, and horseback riding; reading.

* * *

MURRAY, Les(lie) A(llan) 1938-

PERSONAL: Born in Nabiac, New South Wales, Australia; son of Cecil Allan (a dairy farmer) and Miriam Pauline (Arnall) Murray; married Valerie Gina Maria Morelli (a high school teacher), 1962; children: Christina Miriam, Daniel Allan, Clare Luisa. *Education:* University of Sydney, student, 1957-60, 1962. *Politics:* "Nationalist, anti-colonial, Boeotian as opposed to Athenian, fiercely egalitarian and anti-elitist." *Religion:* Catholic by conversion. *Home:* Bunyah, via Krambach, 2429, New South Wales, Australia.

CAREER: Australian National University, Institute of Advanced Studies, Canberra, translator of scholarly and technical material from western European languages, 1963-67; research in folklore, history, and language in Great Britain, 1967-68. Consultant translator to Australian Government departments, including Royal Military College, Duntroon, and other bodies. Has given poetry readings, lectures, talks in theaters, schools, and universities in Australia and Britain. *Military service:* Royal Australian Naval Reserve, 1960-61. *Member:* Australian Society of Authors, Australian Translators' Association, An Comunn Gaid-healach (Gaelic Society of Scotland). *Awards, honors:* Joint winner of Grace Leven Prize for best book of verse published in Australia in 1965, for *The Ilex Tree.*

WRITINGS: (With Geoffrey J. Lehmann) *The Ilex Tree* (poetry), Australian National University Press, 1965; (translator from the German) Troubetzkoy, *An Introduction to the Techniques of Phonological Description,* Nijhoff, 1967; *The Weatherboard Cathedral* (poetry), Angus & Robertson, 1969; *Poems Against Economics,* Angus & Robertson, 1972; *Lunch and Counter Lunch* (poetry), Angus & Robertson, 1974; *The Vernacular Republic* (poetry), Angus & Robertson, 1975. Poetry included in a number of anthologies. Contributor to Australian Broadcasting Commission programs, and to magazines and newspapers, including *Meanjin, Quadrant,* and *Poetry Australia.* Former co-editor of *Arna and Hermes* at University of Sydney, and former literary editor of *Honi Soit,* the university newspaper; acting editor of *Poetry Australia,* 1973—.

SIDELIGHTS: Murray told *CA* that he has a "vital interest in giving utterance and form to hitherto unexpressed elements of Australian mind and character. Somewhat vain about technical skill. Fear destruction of Nature. Seek post-Galileo universes. Chief sources of inspiration: Australian landscape, folklore, history, war, technology, deserts also important." Interests apart from poetry (his "passion, vocation") include geography, regional studies, landscape, farming, mythology, animals, plants, fine machinery, tall tales, and driving through beautiful country.

* * *

MURRAY, Roger N(icholas) 1932-

PERSONAL: Born June 26, 1932, in Fargo, N.D.; son of Byron Dow (a professor) and Nona (Pence) Murray; married Elaine Erkkila, June 29, 1956; children: Joseph Nicholas, Paula Kay, Jennifer Louise. *Education:* Moorhead State College, B.A., 1954, B.S., 1958; Stanford University, M.A., 1958; University of Iowa, Ph.D., 1965. *Politics:* Pacifist ("being opposed to all wars but wars of resistance"). *Office:* English Department, Arizona State University, Tempe, Ariz. 85281.

CAREER: High school English teacher in Audubon, Minn., 1954-55; University of Colorado, Boulder, instructor in English, 1958-61; Wisconsin State University, Eau Claire, assistant professor of English, 1965-68; Arizona State University, Tempe, assistant professor, 1968-70, associate professor of English, 1971—. Visiting professor, University of Minnesota, 1970-71. *Member:* Modern Language Association of America, National Council of Teachers of English.

WRITINGS: Wordsworth's Style: Figures and Themes in the "Lyrical Ballads" of 1800, University of Nebraska Press, 1967. Contributor to literary journals.

WORK IN PROGRESS: Romantic literary style.

AVOCATIONAL INTERESTS: Painting, conservation, translating poems from French.

* * *

MUSCATINE, Charles 1920-

PERSONAL: Last syllable of surname is pronounced "teen"; born December 28, 1920, in Brooklyn, N.Y.; married Doris Corn; children: Jeffrey, Alison. *Education:* Yale University, B.A. (honors in English with exceptional distinction), 1941, M.A., 1942, Ph.D., 1948. *Home:* 2812 Buena Vista Way, Berkeley, Calif. 94708.

CAREER: University of California, Berkeley, lecturer, 1948, instructor, 1948-49, assistant professor, 1949-55, associate professor, 1955-60, professor of English, 1960—, assistant dean, College of Letters and Science, 1956-60, director, Collegiate Seminar Program, 1974—. Visiting professor at Wesleyan University, Middletown, Conn., 1951-53, and University of Washington, Seattle, summer, 1961. Military service: U.S. Naval Reserve, active duty, 1942-45; became lieutenant; received Navy Commendation Ribbon. Member: Modern Language Association of America, American Academy of Arts and Sciences (fellow), Mediaeval Academy of America, American Civil Liberties Union, Phi Beta Kappa. Awards, honors: American Council of Learned Societies and Fulbright research fellowships in Italy, 1958-59; Guggenheim fellowship and Fulbright research fellowship in France, 1962-63; National Humanities Foundation senior fellowship, 1968-69.

WRITINGS: Chaucer and the French Tradition: A Study in Style and Meaning, University of California Press, 1957; The Book of Geoffrey Chaucer, Book Club of California, 1963; (editor with Marlene Griffith) The Borzoi College Reader, Knopf, 1966, 2nd revised edition, 1976; (contributor) D. S. Brewer, editor, Chaucer and Chaucerians, Thomas Nelson, 1966; (editor and co-author) Education at Berkeley: Report of the Select Committee on Education, University of California Press, 1967; Poetry and Crisis in the Age of Chaucer, University of Notre Dame Press, 1972; (editor with Griffith) First Person Singular, Knopf, 1973. Contributor of articles and reviews to learned journals.

Parts of Chaucer and the French Tradition have been reprinted in: R. Schoeck and J. Taylor, editors, Chaucer Criticism: The Canterbury Tales, Notre Dame Books, 1961; C. Owen, editor, Discussions of the Canterbury Tales, Heath, 1961; J. R. Kreuzer and Lee Cogan, editors, Modern Writings on Major English Authors, Bobbs-Merrill, 1963.

*   *   *

MUSSOFF, Lenore   1927-

PERSONAL: Born February 25, 1927, in Masontown, Pa.; daughter of Theodore (a salesman) and Daisy (Molans) Pinsker; married Sam Mussoff (owner of a shoe store), August 29, 1948; children: Teddy, Ann, Jody. Education: University of Pittsburgh, B.A., 1949, M.Ed., 1961, further graduate study, 1962-65.

CAREER: Allderdice High School, Pittsburgh, Pa., teacher of drama, speech, and advanced placement English, 1959—. Reader, College Entrance Examination Board, Princeton, N.J., 1967. Member: National Council of Teachers of English, Pi Lambda Theta, Mortar Board.

WRITINGS: Ivanhoe—Book Notes, Barnes & Noble, 1966; A Tale of Two Cities—Book Notes, Barnes & Noble, 1966; Oliver Twist—Book Notes, Barnes & Noble, 1967. Wrote preface for Scholastic Book Services edition of A Tale of Two Cities, 1962; co-author of drama curriculum for Pittsburgh Public Schools, 1967; author of "Advanced Placement English Examination," 1968.††

*   *   *

MUSTE, John M(artin)   1927-

PERSONAL: Surname rhymes with "dusty"; born January 21, 1927, in Mount Kisco, N.Y.; son of Abraham John (a minister) and Anna (Huizenga) Muste; married Jean

Sherman, August 26, 1950; children: Peter J., Christopher P. Education: Brown University, A.B., 1949; Miami University, Oxford, Ohio, M.A., 1953; University of Wisconsin, Ph.D., 1960. Politics: Independent. Office: Department of English, Ohio State University, 164 West 17th Ave., Columbus, Ohio 43210.

CAREER: Ohio State University, Columbus, instructor, 1958-62, assistant professor, 1962-67, associate professor, 1967-71, professor of English, 1971—, vice-chairman of department, 1972—. Military service: U.S. Navy, 1944-46. Member: Modern Language Association of America, American Association of University Professors. Awards, honors: American Council of learned Societies grant-in-aid, 1961.

WRITINGS: Say That We Saw Spain Die, University of Washington Press, 1966. Member of editorial board, Ohio State University Press, 1972—.†

*   *   *

MUZUMDAR, Ammu Menon   1919-

PERSONAL: Born July 30, 1919, in Kavasseri, Kerala, India; daughter of Raghava Menon (a farmer); married Haridas T. Muzumdar, June 1, 1960. Education: Annamalai University, B.A. (first class honors), 1940; University of Chicago, M.A., 1950; Columbia University, Doctor of Social Welfare, 1960. Religion: Hinduism. Office: Department of Sociology, University of Arkansas, Little Rock, Ark. 72209.

CAREER: Avvai Home and Orphanage, Madras, India, superintendent, 1943-45; Central College for Women, Nagpur, India, lecturer in economics, 1945-48; M.S. University of Baroda, Baroda, India, senior lecturer, Faculty of Social Work, 1950-57, dean of Faculty of Social Work and professor, 1960-63; University of Arkansas, Pine Bluff, professor of social sciences and social work, 1963-67; member-at-large, U.S. Committee on International Social Work, National Council on Social Welfare, 1969-73; University of Arkansas, Little Rock, professor of social work in the Graduate School of Social Work, 1973—. Head of mental hygiene and psychiatric clinic, S.S. General Hospital, Baroda, 1960-63; head of Fatehgunj Social Welfare Center, 1960-63. Member of social welfare advisory board, Indian Ministry of Education, 1961—; Association of Schools of Social Work in India, vice-president, 1960-63, chairman of accreditation commission, 1962-63; Indian Conference of Social Work, honorary general secretary of Baroda district branch, 1960-63, member of central executive committee, 1961—. Lecturer, workshop chairman, and radio speaker.

MEMBER: National Association of Social Workers, American Sociological Association (associate member), Southwestern Social Science Association. Awards, honors: Awarded the Lady Meherbai D. Tata scholarship (for women for study abroad), 1948-50, in all-India competition; P.E.O. International Peace Scholarship for Women, 1957-59; Asia Foundation grant, 1959-60.

WRITINGS: Social Welfare in India: Mahatma Gandhi's Contributions, Asia Publishing House, 1964. Contributor to journals in United States and India.†

*   *   *

MYERS, L(ouis) M(cCorry)   1901-

PERSONAL: Born November 16, 1901, in Jackson, Tenn.; son of John Caldwell and Alice O'Neil (McCorry) Myers; married Cornelia Pipes, December 13, 1930; children: John

Martin. *Education:* St. Stephen's College (now Bard College), B.A., 1925; Columbia University, M.A., 1929; University of California, Ph.D., 1935. *Home:* 306 East 15th St., Tempe, Ariz. 85281. *Office:* Arizona State University, Tempe, Ariz. 82581.

CAREER: Instructor in French at University of Oregon, Eugene, 1929-32, and in English at Western Washington State College, Bellingham, 1935-36, and University of Idaho, Moscow, 1936-37; Arizona State University, Tempe, professor of English, 1937-72, professor emeritus, 1972—, head of department, 1937-57, head of Division of Language and Literature, 1957-62. *Military service:* U.S. Army, 1942-46; served in North Africa and Italy; became lieutenant colonel; received Legion of Merit. *Member:* Modern Language Association of America, National Council of Teachers of English, Conference on College Composition and Communication, American Association of University Professors, Phi Beta Kappa.

WRITINGS: American English, Prentice-Hall, 1952; *Guide to American English,* Prentice-Hall, 1955, 5th edition (with Gene Montague), 1972; *The Roots of Modern English,* Little, Brown, 1966; (with Richard L. Hoffman) *Companion to "The Roots of Modern English,"* Little, Brown, 1972. Contributor to journals in his field.

* * *

NABOKOV, Peter (Francis) 1940-

PERSONAL: Born October 11, 1940, in Auburn, N.Y.; son of Nicolas (a writer and composer) and Constance (Holladay) Nabokov. *Education:* Attended St. Johns College; Columbia University, B.S., 1965; Goddard College, M.S., 1973. *Office:* Human Resources Research Organization, 27857 Berwick Dr., Carmel, Calif. 93921.

CAREER: After a long stay in Mexico when he was fifteen Nabokov worked on Navaho, Sioux, and Crow reservations in Montana, 1962, and later sailed with the Merchant Marine; *New Mexican,* Santa Fe, N.M., staff reporter, 1967-68; Monterey Peninsula College, Monterey, Calif., instructor in American Indian studies, 1970-73; Human Resources Research Organization, Carmel, Calif., research associate, 1972—. Research associate, Museum of American Indian, Heye Foundation, 1963-75. *Member:* Society for the Prevention of Cruelty to Children. *Awards, honors:* Albuquerque Press Club awards, two first prizes, and New Mexico Press Association, first prize in editorial writing; all 1967.

WRITINGS: Two Leggings: The Making of a Crow Warrior, Crowell, 1967; *Tijerina and the Courthouse Raid,* University of New Mexico Press, 1970, revised edition, Ramparts, 1971.

WORK IN PROGRESS: Native Testimony: An Anthology of Indian/White Relations, for Crowell; *A Crow Miscellany; George Washington Carver,* a juvenile biography.

SIDELIGHTS: Nabokov has traveled the Western Hemisphere from the Amazon River to the coast of Nova Scotia.

BIOGRAPHICAL/CRITICAL SOURCES: Saturday Review, September 9, 1967; *New York Times Book Review,* September 10, 1967; *New York Review of Books,* December 18, 1969; *Washington Post,* January 14, 1970.

* * *

NADDOR, Eliezer 1920-

PERSONAL: Surname originally Nussdorf; born September 23, 1920, in Jerusalem, Israel; son of Solomon Z. and Cyla (Schiffman) Nussdorf; married Sedelle L. Moss, June 20, 1954; children: Daniel S., David J., Rachel D. *Education:* Israel Institute of Technology (Ha-Technion), B.S., 1951, C.E., 1952; Columbia University, M.S., 1953; Case Institute of Technology (now Case Western Reserve University), Ph.D., 1957. *Religion:* Jewish. *Home:* 7907 Knollwood Rd., Baltimore, Md. 21204.

CAREER: Public Works Department, Palestine, assistant quantity surveyor, 1940-42; Case Institute of Technology (now Case Western Reserve University), Cleveland, Ohio, research assistant and instructor, 1953-56; Johns Hopkins University, Baltimore, Md., 1956—, began as assistant professor, professor of operations research, 1964—. Consultant to General Motors Corp., Bell Telephone Laboratories, and General Electric Co. Trustee of Baltimore Hebrew College. *Member:* Operations Research Society of America, Institute of Management Science, American Institute of Industrial Engineers, American Statistical Association, Mathematical Association of America, Association for Computing Machinery, American Association of University Professors.

WRITINGS: Inventory Systems, Wiley, 1966. Contributor of chapters to other books, and papers on operations research, inventory systems, and theory of games.

* * *

NAIK, Madhukar Krishna 1926-

PERSONAL: Surname rhymes with "like"; born January 7, 1926, in Karad, Maharashtra State, India; son of Krishna Pandurang (a revenue inspector) and Indira (Valvade) Naik; married Shakuntala Deekshit, May 1, 1953; children: one. *Education:* Bombay University, B.A. (honors), 1946, M.A., 1948; Karnatak University, Ph.D., 1956; University of Pennsylvania, A.M., 1962. *Religion:* Hindu. *Office:* Karnatak University, Dharwar-3, Mysore, India.

CAREER: Bombay Government Educational Service, lecturer in English, 1948-57; Karnatak University, Dharwar, India, reader, 1957-67, professor of English and chairman of department, 1967—. *Member:* Modern Language Association of America, Indian Association for English Studies, American Studies Research Centre.

WRITINGS: Jivan-Venu (poetry), Abhinav Prakashan, 1953; *William Somerset Maugham,* University of Oklahoma Press, 1966; (author of introduction) *The Autocrat of the Breakfast Table,* Eurasia Publishing, 1967; (editor) *Critical Essays on Indian Writing in English,* Karnatak University, 1968, revised and enlarged edition, 1972; (editor) *Indian Response to Poetry in English* (essays), Macmillan, 1970; (editor) *The Image of India in Western Creative Writing,* Macmillan, 1971; (editor) *Indian Studies in American Fiction,* Macmillan, 1972; *Raja Rao,* Twayne, 1972; *Mulk Raj Anand,* Humanities, 1973. Contributor to *Books Abroad, Literary Criterion, Shakespeare Quarterly,* and journals in India.

WORK IN PROGRESS: A Critical Study of R. K. Narayan; editing *Indian Drama in English.*

* * *

NAIRN, Ronald C(harles) 1922-

PERSONAL: Born November 15, 1922, in Drumcullion, Northern Ireland; now U.S. citizen; son of William John (a rancher) and Alice (Fitzpatrick) Nairn; married Mona Brown, February 19, 1948; children: Susan Elizabeth, Belinda Catherine. *Education:* University of Canterbury, B.A., 1950; Yale University, M.A., 1962, Ph.D., 1963; also attended Royal Air Force Staff College. *Politics:* Republican. *Religion:* Church of England. *Home:* 8616 East Devonshire Ave., Scottsdale, Ariz. 85251.

CAREER: Royal Air Force, pilot, 1941-59, retiring as wing commander; Southeast Asia Treaty Organization, military planner in Thailand, 1956-60; Yale University, New Haven, Conn., research fellow, 1963; University of California, Santa Barbara, professor of political science, 1963-65; Prescott College, Prescott, Ariz., president, 1965-71; chairman of the board, Prescott Corp., 1971-73; president, Schole Center for the Future, 1973—. Consultant to RAND Corp., 1964—, Institute for Defense Analysis, 1966—. *Awards, honors*—Military: Distinguished Flying Medal; Air Force Cross.

WRITINGS: Revolution in World Politics, Wiley, 1963; *International Aid to Thailand: The New Colonialism?,* Yale University Press, 1966.

WORK IN PROGRESS: The Uncertain Saviors: A Study on Spiritual and Secular Missionaries in Southeast Asia.

SIDELIGHTS: Nairn reads, writes, and speaks Thai.†

* * *

NAKAMURA, James I. 1919-

PERSONAL: Born March 16, 1919, in Toppenish, Wash.; son of Ichihei and Suya (Hirayama) Nakamura; married Tetsuko Fujii (an administrative assistant), December 17, 1944; children: Richard Ken, Leonard Isamu. *Education:* Santa Maria Junior College (now Allan Hancock College), A.A., 1939; Columbia University, B.S., 1952, Ph.D., 1964. *Home:* 35 Claremont Ave., New York, N.Y. 10027. *Office:* 916 SIA, Columbia University, New York, N.Y. 10027.

CAREER: Civilian with Department of the Army, 1948-50; lecturer at Columbia University, New York, N.Y., 1956-57, and City College of New York (now City College of the City University of New York), 1957-59; Adelphi College (now Adelphi University), Garden City, N.Y., instructor in economics, 1959-62; Hunter College of the City University of New York, lecturer, 1962-64; Columbia University, assistant professor, 1964-68, associate professor of economics, 1968—, chairman of Seminar on Modern Japan, 1966-67. Co-sponsor, Japanese Economic Seminar (East Coast); member, Japan Economic Research Center, Tokyo. *Military service:* U.S. Army, 1945-48; became first lieutenant. *Member:* American Economic Association, Association for Asian Studies, Phi Beta Kappa. *Awards, honors:* Ford Foundation fellow, 1952-55, 1962-63.

WRITINGS: (Contributor) William W. Lockwood, editor, *The State and Economic Enterprise in Japan,* Princeton University Press, 1965; *Agricultural Production and the Economic Development of Japan,* Princeton University Press, 1966; (contributor) Bernard S. Silberman and Harry D. Harootunian, editors, *Japan in Crisis: Essays in Taisho Democracy,* Princeton University Press, 1974. Contributor to journals in his field.

WORK IN PROGRESS: The role of the alternate attendance system in Tokugawa economic development; an economic history of modern Japan.

SIDELIGHTS: James Nakamura has made six trips to Japan, and three to Southeast Asia.

NAPIER, Priscilla 1908-
(Penelope Hunt, Eve Stewart)

PERSONAL: Born October 5, 1908, in Oxford, England; daughter of Sir William (financial adviser to Egyptian Government) and Alethea (Slessor) Hayter; married Trevylyan Napier (a commander in Royal Navy), August 8, 1931 (died, 1940); children: Miles, Lavinia (Mrs. Alastair Robinson), Anne (Mrs. Archie Hamilton). *Education:* Lady Margaret Hall, Oxford, B.A. (second class honors in history), 1929. *Politics:* Conservative. *Religion:* Church of England. *Home:* Rockingham Castle, Market Harborough, Leicestershire, England. *Agent:* Diana Crawfurd, Curtis Brown, Ltd., 1 Craven Hill, W.2 3E.W., England.

CAREER: Writer. Governor, Tavistock Grammar School; member, Devon County Divisional Executive for Education.

WRITINGS: (Under pseudonym Eve Stewart) *Sheet Anchor* (verse), Sidgwick & Jackson, 1943; *A Late Beginner,* M. Joseph, 1966; (co-translator) *The Art of Prayer,* Faber, 1966; *The Sword Dance: Lady Sarah Lennox and the Napiers,* M. Joseph, 1971; *A Difficult Country: Napiers in Scotland,* M. Joseph, 1972; *Revolution and the Napier Brothers,* M. Joseph, 1973. Contributor to *Punch* under pseudonym Penelope Hunt.

WORK IN PROGRESS: More books on the history of the Napier family including, *Raven Castle* for Chatto & Windus, *Confidence, A Summer Landscape,* and *A Good Fellow.*

* * *

NAPJUS, Alice James 1913-
(James Napjus)

PERSONAL: Surname is pronounced Nap-yus; born August 8, 1913, in Great Falls, Mont., daughter of Alfred Thomas (a rancher) and Eva (Nolan) James; married Thys George Napjus (owner-operator of a greenhouse), June 26, 1937; children: George Alfred, Chris Nolan. *Education:* University of Washington, Seattle, B.A. in Ed., 1956, M.A., 1965. *Politics:* Democrat. *Religion:* Methodist. *Home:* 257 South 168, Seattle, Wash. 98148.

CAREER: Primary teacher in Seattle, Wash., 1950-63; Pacific Lutheran University, Tacoma, Wash., assistant professor, 1963-72, associate professor of education, professor emerita, 1975—. *Member:* National Council of Teachers of English, National Education Association, International Reading Association, Association for Student Teaching.

WRITINGS: The Magic Chair, and Other Stories, Vantage, 1957; (under pseudonym James Napjus) *Trouble on the Infield,* Van Nostrand, 1967; *Freddie Found a Frog,* Van Nostrand, 1969.

WORK IN PROGRESS: A non-fiction series of early Montana; two girls' stories.

* * *

NARVESON, Jan F(redric) 1936-

PERSONAL: Born June 15, 1936, in Erskine, Minn.; son of Carl Robert and Sophie (Krbechek) Narveson; children: Kaja Lee. *Education:* University of Chicago, B.A., 1955, B.A., 1956; Harvard University, M.A., 1957, Ph.D., 1961; Oxford University, graduate student, 1959-60. *Politics:* "Leftish." *Religion:* None. *Home:* 57 Young St. W., Waterloo, Ontario, Canada. *Office:* Department of Philosophy, University of Waterloo, Waterloo, Ontario, Canada.

CAREER: University of New Hampshire, Durham, instructor, 1961-62, assistant professor of philosophy, 1962-63; University of Waterloo, Waterloo, Ontario, assistant professor, 1963-66, associate professor of philosophy, 1966—. Founder and president, Kitchener-Waterloo Chamber Music Society. Member: American Philosophical Association, Canadian Philosophical Association, American Civil Liberties Union, Canadian Civil Liberties Union, Americans for Democratic Action, Phi Beta Kappa. Awards, honors: Woodrow Wilson fellow, 1956-57; Frank Knox Memorial fellow at Oxford University, 1959-60.

WRITINGS: Morality and Utility, Johns Hopkins Press, 1967; Thinking About Ethics, University of Waterloo Press, 1968. Also author of Thinking About Politics, 1969. Contributor to Ethics, Analysis, Mind, Canadian Journal of Philosophy, and other journals in United States, Canada, England and Australia.

AVOCATIONAL INTERESTS: "Major passion for music and audio equipment; minor passion for photography and motor cars."

*   *   *

NASH, Gerald D(avid)   1928-

PERSONAL: Born July 16, 1928, in Berlin, Germany; now U.S. citizen; son of Alfred B. (a businessman) and Alice (Kantorowicz) Nash; married Marie Norris, August 19, 1967. Education: New York University, B.A., 1950; Columbia University, M.A., 1952; University of California, Berkeley, Ph.D., 1957. Religion: Jewish. Home: 9124 Princess Jeanne N.E., Albuquerque, N.M. 87112. Office: Department of History, University of New Mexico, Albuquerque, N.M. 87106.

CAREER: Stanford University, Stanford, Calif., instructor in history, 1957-58, visiting assistant professor, 1959-60; Northern Illinois University, De Kalb, assistant professor, 1958-59; Harvard University, Cambridge, Mass., research fellow at Center for the Study of Liberty, 1960-61; University of New Mexico, Albuquerque, assistant professor, 1961-63, associate professor, 1963-68, professor of history, 1968—, chairman of department, 1974—. Visiting summer professor at University of California, Berkeley, 1959, and University of California, Davis, 1961; visiting summer lecturer at University of Maryland, 1962; visiting associate professor at New York University, 1965-66. Member of advisory board and director, Lincoln Educational Foundation. Member: American Historical Association, Business History Society, Agricultural History Society, Economic History Association, Organization of American Historians (chairman of membership committee, 1968-70), Western History Association, Phi Beta Kappa. Awards, honors: Newberry Library fellow, 1959.

WRITINGS: State Government and Economic Development, Institute of Governmental Studies, University of California, 1964; (editor) Issues in American Economic History: Selected Readings, Heath, 1964, 2nd edition, Heath Lexington, 1971; (editor) Franklin Delano Roosevelt, Prentice-Hall, 1967; (editor) Gifford Pinchot: The Fight for Conservation, University of Washington Press, 1967; U.S. Oil Policy, 1890-1964: Business and Government in 20th Century America, University of Pittsburgh Press, 1968; The Great Tradition: A Short History of 20th Century America, Allyn & Bacon, 1971; The American West in the 20th Century: A Short History of an Urban Oasis, Prentice-Hall, 1973; (with others) Herbert Hoover and the Crisis of American Liberalism, Scheckman, 1973;

(editor) Government and Economy in America since 1860, Greenwood Press, 1976.

Editor, The Historian, 1974—. Member of board of editors, Business History Review, 1964-68, New Mexico Historical Review, 1964—, Journal of American History, 1971-74, and Western Historical Quarterly, 1971—.

WORK IN PROGRESS: The New Deal and Organizational Revolution for St. Martin's.

*   *   *

NASH, Jay Robert   1937-

PERSONAL: Born November 26, 1937, in Indianapolis, Ind.; son of Jay Robert (a writer) and Jerrie Lynn (Kosur) Nash; married Janice P. Schwartz (a teacher), 1962; children: Lee Travis, Andrea. Education: Educated in Europe, B.A., 1958. Agent: Henry Morrison, 58 West 10th St., New York, N.Y. 10011. Office address: P.O. Box 4327, Chicago, Ill. 60680.

CAREER: Milwaukee Literary Times, Milwaukee, Wis., editor, 1960-62; Antioch News, Antioch, Ill., editor, 1961-62; Literary Times, Chicago, Ill., editor and publisher, 1961-70; American Trade Magazines, Chicago, editor, 1962-66; ChicagoLand and FM Guide, Chicago, editor, 1967-70; full-time writer. Founder of Beethoven Memorial Foundation and of Chicago Poets and Writers Foundation. Military service: Was in Intelligence Service. Member: Authors Guild.

WRITINGS—All nonfiction, except as noted: Lost Natives & Expatriates (poetry chapbook), Hors Commerce Press, 1965; (with Ron Offen) Dillinger: Dead or Alive?, Regnery, 1970; Hoover and His FBI, Nelson-Hall, 1972; Bloodletters and Badmen: A Narrative Encyclopedia of American Criminals from the Pilgrims to the Present, M. Evans, 1973; On All Fronts (fiction), December Press, 1974; Hustlers and Con Men: An Anecdotal History of the Confidence Man and His Games, M. Evans, 1976; Darkest Hours: A Narrative Encyclopedia of World-Wide Disasters from Ancient Times to the Present, Nelson-Hall, 1976.

WORK IN PROGRESS: Sins of the Cities, a social history of scandalous manners, morals and mania in America, for Dial; four additional books.

*   *   *

NASH, Nancy   1943-

PERSONAL: Born May 7, 1943, in Kansas City, Mo.; daughter of John E. (a professional golfer) and Margaret (Mills) Nash. Education: "Little formal education." Politics: None. Religion: None. Residence: Hong Kong.

CAREER: Worked in Germany, 1962-63; held various jobs in the United States, 1964-65, including swimming pool attendant at St. Andrews Golf and Country Club, Kansas City, Kan., and leasing agent for an apartment complex in Kansas; spent four months in Japan in 1965, working for two months as a proofreader for an American Company in Tokyo; area director of public relations, East Asia Hilton International, 1967-72. Member: Foreign Correspondents Club (Hong Kong; associate member).

WRITINGS—Author and illustrator: A Pet for Kei-Chan, Tuttle, 1966.

WORK IN PROGRESS: Writing and illustrating two more children's books, one set in Thailand and one in Hong Kong.

SIDELIGHTS: Nancy Nash told CA: "Motivation for

travel and living abroad: curiosity. Motivation for book: needed some money for travel." She speaks and reads German. *Avocational interests:* Sketching, reading, dice, studying Chinese.

* * *

NASR, Seyyed Hossein 1933-

PERSONAL: Surname is pronounced as one syllable, the last two letters slurred; born April 7, 1933, in Tehran, Iran; son of Valiallah (an educator) and Ashraf (Kia) Nasr; married Sussan Danechvary, November 21, 1958. *Education:* Massachusetts Institute of Technology, B.S., 1954; Harvard University, Ph.D., 1958. *Religion:* Muslim. *Home:* Pahlavi Ave., 25 Farkhar St. (Shemiran, Amaniyah), Tehran, Iran. *Office:* Aryamehr University, Eisenhower Ave., Tehran, Iran.

CAREER: University of Tehran, Faculty of Letters, Tehran, Iran, professor of the history of science and philosophy, 1958-72, dean, 1968-72; Aryamehr University, Tehran, chancellor, 1972—. Visiting professor, Harvard University, 1962, 1965; Aga Khan Professor of Islamic Studies, American University of Beirut, 1964-65. Chairman of governing board, Regional Cooperation for Development Institute (Iran, Pakistan, Turkey). *Member:* International Congress of Orientalists, Congress of Iranologists, Congress of Mediaeval Philosophy, International Institute of Philosophy, Imperial Iranian Academy of Philosophy (director, 1974—), Sigma Xi, Harvard/M.I.T. Association of Tehran (president). *Awards, honors:* Royal Book Award of Iran for Persian edition of *Concepts of Nature in Islamic Thought During the Fourth Century.*

WRITINGS: (Editor, and author of introduction and notes) Sadr al-Din Shirazi, *Risalah-i se asl* ("title means "The Three Principles"), University of Tehran Press, 1961; *Hirmis wa niwishtihay-i hirmisi* (title means "Hermes and Hermetic Writings in the Islamic World"), University of Tehran Press, 1961; *Nazar-i mutafakkiran-i islami dar barih-i tabiat* (title means "Concepts of Nature in Islamic Thought during the Fourth Century"), University of Tehran Press, 1962; *Three Muslim Sages: Avicenna, Suhrawardi, Ibn Arabi,* Harvard University Press, 1964; *An Introduction to Islamic Cosmological Doctrines: Conceptions of Nature and Methods Used for Its Study by the Ikhwan al-Safa, al-Biruni, and Ibn Sina,* Belknap Press, 1964; (with H. Corbin) *Histoire de la philosophie islamique,* Gallimard, 1964; *Ideals and Realities of Islam,* Allen & Unwin, 1966, Praeger, 1967; *Islamic Studies: Essays on Law and Society, the Science, and Philosophy and Sufism,* Librairie du Liban, 1967; *Encounter of Man and Nature,* Allen & Unwin, 1968; *Science and Civilization in Islam,* Harvard University Press, 1968.

Ma'arif-i islami dar jahan-i mu'asir (title means "The Islamic Intellectual Heritage in the Contemporary World"), Shirkat-i jihi (Tehran), 1970, 2nd edition, 1974; (editor) *Historical Atlas of Iran,* University of Tehran Press, 1971; *Sufi Essays,* Allen & Unwin, 1972, State University of New York Press, 1973; (editor with M. Mohaghegh, and author of introduction) Abu Rayhan Biruri and Ibn Sina, *Al-As'ilah wa'l-ajwibah* (title means "Questions and Answers"), High Council of Culture and the Arts (Tehran), 1973; *Al-Biruni: An Annotated Bibliography,* High Council of Culture and the Arts, 1973; *Jalal al-Din Rumi: Supreme Persian Poet and Sage,* High Council of Culture and the Arts, 1974; (translator and editor) Allamah Tabatabai, *Shi'ite Islam,* State University of New York Press, 1975;

Islam and the Plight of Modern Man, Longman, in press; *Islamic Science: An Illustrated Study,* Luzac, in press. Contributor of numerous articles in French, English, Persian, and Arabic to professional journals.

WORK IN PROGRESS: An Annotated Bibliography of Islamic Science, and *The Transcendent Theosophy of Sadr al-Din,* both for Imperial Iranian Academy of Philosophy.

SIDELIGHTS: Nasr is competent in French and German in addition to Persian, Arabic, and English; he has some knowledge of Italian and the classical languages. *Avocational interests:* Traditional and sacred art.

* * *

NATHANSON, Leonard 1933-

PERSONAL: Born September 22, 1933, in Brooklyn, N.Y.; son of Morris (a salesman) and Lena (Kelman) Nathanson. *Education:* Brooklyn College (now Brooklyn College of the City University of New York), B.A., 1954; Duke University, M.A., 1955; University of Wisconsin, Ph.D., 1959. *Politics:* Democrat. *Religion:* Jewish. *Home:* 4200 Harding Rd., Nashville, Tenn. 37205. *Office:* Department of English, Vanderbilt University, Nashville, Tenn. 37203.

CAREER: Northwestern University, Evanston, Ill., instructor in English, 1959-60; University of Cincinnati, Cincinnati, Ohio, assistant professor of English, 1960-66; Vanderbilt University, Nashville, Tenn., associate professor of English, 1966—. *Member:* Modern Language Association of America, Renaissance Society of America, Milton Society of America, American Association of University Professors, South Atlantic Modern Language Association, Midwest Modern Language Association, Phi Beta Kappa. *Awards, honors:* Research grants from Taft Memorial Fund, 1962, and Vanderbilt University Research Council, 1967, 1968.

WRITINGS: The Strategy of Truth: A Study of Sir Thomas Browne, University of Chicago Press, 1967; (editor and author of notes) William Shakespeare, *The Tempest,* W. C. Brown, 1969. Contributor of articles and reviews to *Library, Shakespeare Studies, Explicator,* and other professional journals.

WORK IN PROGRESS: A Milton Encyclopedia, for Bucknell University Press.

SIDELIGHTS: Leonard Nathanson speaks French and reads Latin, German, and Italian. *Avocational interests:* Studying and collecting of modern art; the cinema, music.

BIOGRAPHICAL/CRITICAL SOURCES: Criticism, Volume X, number 2, 1968.

* * *

NAUMANN, Anthony 1921-

PERSONAL: Surname is pronounced Now-man; born August 24, 1921, in London, England; son of Frank Charles Gordon (a businessman) and Constance Margery (Wallich) Naumann; married Felicity Gwyn Sterling, January 10, 1944 (divorced); children: Carola Gwyn, Diana Frances. *Education:* Educated in England.

CAREER: St. Peter's School, Seaford, Sussex, England, master, 1939; Naumann, Gepp & Co. Ltd., London, England, director, beginning 1948. *Military service:* British Army, 1939-42; became lieutenant; blinded in action in Tunisia, 1942. *Member:* P.E.N. Club, Royal Society of Literature.

WRITINGS—Poetry: *Flame in the Dark*, Collins, 1962; *If I May Share*, Collins, 1964; *Now Has My Summer*, Collins, 1966; (with Guy Cooper and Julian Nangle) *Poems*, Words Press, 1970. Poetry has been published in a number of magazines in Britain, United States, and Canada. Former editor, *Envoi* (poetry magazine).

WORK IN PROGRESS: Against a Rainy Day, a collection of poems; fiction.†

* * *

NAVASKY, Victor S. 1932-
(William Randolph Hirsch, a joint pseudonym)

PERSONAL: Born July 5, 1932, in New York, N.Y.; son of Macy and Esther (Goldberg) Navasky; married Anne Strongin, March 27, 1966; children: Bruno, Miri. *Education:* Swarthmore College, B.A. (magna cum laude), 1954; Yale University, LL.B., 1959. *Politics:* Democratic. *Religion:* Jewish. *Home:* 33 West 67th St., New York, N.Y. 10023.

CAREER: State of Michigan, Lansing, special assistant to the Governor, 1959-60; *Monocle* (humor magazine), New York City, editor and publisher, 1961-70; *New York Times Magazine*, New York City, editor, 1970-72. Adjunct associate professor, New York University, 1972-73. Consultant, U.S. Civil Rights Commission, 1961. *Military service:* U.S. Army, 1954-56. *Member:* Phi Beta Kappa.

WRITINGS: (With Marvin Kitman and Richard Lingeman, under joint pseudonym William Randolph Hirsch) *The Red Chinese Air Force Exercise, Diet, and Sex Book*, Stein & Day, 1967; *Kennedy Justice*, Atheneum, 1971. Contributor of articles and reviews to professional journals. Contributing editor, *Antioch Review*.

WORK IN PROGRESS: A book about congressional investigations into the communications industry in the fifties.

SIDELIGHTS: Kennedy Justice, explained a *New York Times* reviewer, "is a sophisticated, refined and, to a non-legal mind, exhaustive study of Robert F. Kennedy as Attorney General of the United States. . . . It's a concentrated course in the way the Department of Justice is organized and functions; a classic example of the clash between an inventive, open, concerned and engaged arm of the Government and a settled, stolid, monolithic bureaucracy; a case history of the opposition of idealism and expediency. It will define the word law in ways most laymen have not thought of. It tells how things get done and do not get done in government. It recreates on a believable plane the mystique and attraction of Robert Kennedy. Reading this book may not make you a better man, but it will surely make you a wiser one."

BIOGRAPHICAL/CRITICAL SOURCES: New York Times, October 8, 1971.

* * *

NAVONE, John J(oseph) 1930-

PERSONAL: Surname is pronounced Na-*vone;* born October 19, 1930, in Seattle, Wash.; son of James and Juliet (Micheli) Navone. *Education:* Gonzaga University, M.Phil., 1956; St. Mary's University, Halifax, Nova Scotia, S.T.M., 1963; Gregorian University, Th.D., 1965. *Home and office:* Gregorian University, Piazza della Pilotta 4, Rome 00187, Italy.

CAREER: Entered Society of Jesus in 1949, ordained priest, 1962; Seattle Preparatory School, Seattle, Wash.,

teacher, 1956-59; Gregorian University, Rome, Italy, assistant professor of theology, 1967—, also director of the university publication, *The Gregorian University Newsletter.* Teaches summer school, Seattle University, annually.

WRITINGS: History and Faith in the Thought of Alan Richardson, S.C.M. Press, 1966; *Personal Witness: A Biblical Spirituality*, Sheed, 1967; *Themes of St. Luke*, Gregorian University Press, 1970; (contributor) *Foundations of Theology*, Macmillan, 1972; *Everyman's Odyssey: Seven Plays Seen as Modern Myths about Man's Quest for Personal Integrity*, Seattle University Press, 1974; *A Theology of Failure*, Paulist Press, 1974. Contributor to *America, Commonweal, Catholic World, Scottish Journal of Theology, Faith and Freedom* (Oxford), and other periodicals.

WORK IN PROGRESS: Patterns of Religious Experience.

SIDELIGHTS: Navone is competent in Italian, French, German, Spanish, Latin, Portuguese and Greek. *Avocational interests:* Drama, films, literature, music, art, European history, sociology, international relations, geopolitics, communications.

* * *

NAYLOR, Harriet H. 1915-

PERSONAL: Born December 4, 1915, in White Plains, N.Y.; daughter of Arthur Leslie and Henrietta (Bedford) Core; married George Naylor (a professor), July 31, 1939 (deceased); children: Margery Bedford (Mrs. Peter van Inwagen), Elizabeth Beekman, George Dustin. *Education:* Columbia University, A.B., 1937, graduate study in social work, 1937-39, M.A., 1963. *Politics:* Independent. *Religion:* Congregational. *Home address:* Route 9G, Rhinebeck, N.Y., 12572; and 2701 16th St. S., Arlington, Va. 22204.

CAREER: United Charities and Housekeeping Service, Chicago, Ill., staff member, 1939-40; Girl Scouts of the U.S.A., New York City, training adviser, personnel department, 1960-62; Young Women's Christian Association of the U.S.A. (YWCA), New York City, training consultant, Bureau of Personnel and Training, 1962-66; director of volunteer services, New York State Department of Mental Hygiene, 1967-71; National Center for Voluntary Action, Washington, D.C., consultant, 1970, regional director, 1971, director of education and training, 1971-74; U.S. Department of Health, Education, and Welfare, Washington, D.C., director of volunteer development, 1974—. Instructor, Virginia Commonwealth University, 1973-74. Volunteer worker in various organizations for more than twenty-five years; member of board, Planned Parenthood League of Albany and Albany YWCA. *Member:* Adult Education Association of the U.S.A., American Association of University Women, American Association of Volunteer Administrators, National School Volunteer Program, American Society for Directors of Volunteer Services.

WRITINGS: Volunteers Today: Finding, Training and Working with Them, Association Press, 1967; (contributor) *Social Work Practice*, Columbia University Press, 1969; (contributor) J. C. Cull and R. E. Hardy, editors, *Volunteerism: An Emerging Profession*, C. C Thomas, 1973. Contributor of articles on development through education to *Girl Scout Leader, Adult Leadership*, and other journals.

SIDELIGHTS: Harriet Naylor lived in Greece, Indonesia, Thailand, and East Pakistan, where her husband served with United Nations.

NAYLOR, Phyllis (Reynolds) 1933-

PERSONAL: Born January 4, 1933, in Anderson, Ind.; daughter of Eugene S. and Lura (Schield) Reynolds; married Rex V. Naylor (a speech pathologist), May 26, 1960; children: Alan Jeffrey, Michael Scott. *Education:* Joliet Junior College, Diploma, 1953; American University, B.A., 1963. *Politics:* Independent. *Religion:* Unitarian Universalist. *Home:* 9910 Holmhurst Rd., Bethesda, Md. 20034.

CAREER: Elementary teacher in Hazelcrest, Ill., 1956; Montgomery County Education Association, Rockville, Md., assistant executive secretary, 1958-59; National Education Association, Washington, D.C., editorial assistant with *NEA Journal*, 1959-60; full-time writer, 1960—. Active in civil rights and peace organizations. *Member:* Authors Guild of America, Children's Book Guild (Washington, D.C.).

WRITINGS: Grasshoppers in the Soup, Fortress, 1965; *The Galloping Goat*, Abingdon, 1965; *The New Schoolmaster*, Silver Burdett, 1967; *A New Year's Surprise*, Silver Burdett, 1967; *Jennifer Jean, the Cross-Eyed Queen*, Lerner, 1967; *Knee Deep in Ice Cream*, Fortress, 1967; *To Shake a Shadow*, Abingdon, 1967; *What the Gulls Were Singing*, Follett, 1967; *When Rivers Meet*, Friendship, 1968; *The Dark Side of the Moon*, Fortress, 1969; *Private I*, Fortress, 1969; *To Make a Wee Moon*, Follett, 1969; *Meet Murdock*, Follett, 1969.

Making It Happen, Follett, 1970; *Ships in the Night*, Fortress, 1970; *Wrestle the Mountain*, Follett, 1971; *No Easy Circle*, Follett, 1972; *How to Find Your Wonderful Someone*, Fortress, 1972; *To Walk the Sky Path*, Follett, 1973; *An Amish Family*, J. Philip O'Hara, 1974; *Witch's Sister*, Atheneum, 1975; *Walking through the Dark*, Atheneum, 1976; *Getting Along in Your Family*, Abingdon, in press. Contributor of short stories and articles to juvenile and adult periodicals.

*   *   *

NEAL, Bruce W(alter) 1931-

PERSONAL: Born January 27, 1931, in Belleville, Ontario, Canada; son of Walter John (a railway sectionman) and Harriett (Hammersley) Neal; married Barbara Fennell, August 29, 1953; children: Susan, Janice, Jeffrey, Sharon, Jennifer. *Education:* McMaster University, B.A., 1951, B.D., 1954; graduate study at University of Chicago Divinity School, 1954-56, and University of Toronto, 1971—. *Home:* 121 Hillhurst Blvd., Toronto, Ontario, Canada.

CAREER: Baptist clergyman. Associate secretary for youth, Baptist Convention of Ontario and Quebec, Board of Religious Education, 1956-61; Yorkminster Park Baptist Church, Toronto, Ontario, minister of Christian education, 1961-65; James Street Baptist Church, Hamilton, Ontario, minister, 1965-72; Walmer Road Baptist Church, Toronto, senior minister, 1972—. Member of youth committee, Baptist World Alliance, 1956-64; member of Council of Baptist Federation, 1973—. Member of senate, McMaster Divinity College, 1966-75.

WRITINGS: The Table Is for Eating, Abingdon, 1966; *Bite a Blue Apple*, Abingdon, 1972. Contributor to *Canadian Baptist* and other journals.

*   *   *

NEHRT, Lee Charles 1926-

PERSONAL: Surname is pronounced Nairt; born September 12, 1926, in Baldwin, Ill.; son of Martin William (a blacksmith) and Amanda (Tillock) Nehrt; married Ardith Saltzman (an actress and writer), March 26, 1952; children: Chadwick, Philip, Dana. *Education:* U.S. Coast Guard Academy, B.S., 1949; Institute d'Etudes Politiques, University of Paris, graduate study, 1953-55; Columbia University, M.B.A., 1956, Ph.D., 1962. *Politics:* Independent. *Religion:* None. *Home:* 1000 South Woodlawn, Wichita, Kan. 67218.

CAREER: U.S. Coast Guard, 1945-53; leaving service as lieutenant; North American Aviation, Canoga Park, Calif., foreign operations supervisor, 1956-60; Indiana University, Bloomington, assistant professor, 1962-65, associate professor, 1967-69, professor of international business, 1969-74. Ford Foundation adviser to Tunisian Minister of Planning, Tunis, 1965-67; consultant to United Nations and World Bank. *Member:* Academy of Education in International Business (national president, 1973-75), Society for International Development (member of council, representing North America).

WRITINGS: (With Stefan Robock) *Education for International Business*, Bureau of Business Research, Indiana University, 1963; *Pre-Investment Study of the Sheet Glass Industry*, World Bank, 1964; *International Marketing of Nuclear Power Plants*, Indiana University Press, 1965; *Financing Capital Equipment Exports*, International Textbook, 1966; (editor) *International Finance for Multinational Business*, International Textbook, 1967, 2nd edition, 1972; (with Richard Wright and Frederick Truitt) *International Business Research: Past, Present and Future*, Bureau of Business Research, Indiana University, 1969; *The Political Climate for Private Investment in North Africa*, Praeger, 1970; (with Ali El Salmi) *Managerial Policy and Strategy for the Arab World* (published in Arabic), Dor El Moaref (Cairo), 1973; (with Gono Evans and Lamp Li) *Managerial Policy, Strategy and Planning for South-East Asia*, Chinese University of Hong Kong Press, 1974. Contributor to *Encyclopedia Americana*.

AVOCATIONAL INTERESTS: Squash; mountain climbing (ascents include Mount Kilimanjaro, Mount Fuji, and the Matterhorn).

*   *   *

NELSON, Elof G. 1924-

PERSONAL: Born April 11, 1924, in Minneapolis, Minn.; son of John (a builder) and Ruth (Lind) Nelson; married Marette Johnson; children: Susan, Janice, Carol, Peter, Ann. *Education:* Gustavus Adolphus College, B.A., 1948; University of Minnesota, graduate student, 1949-50; Luther Theological Seminary, B.D., 1953; Andover Newton Theological School, D.Min., 1958; attended San Francisco Theological School, 1973. *Home:* 2805 Scott Ave. N., Minneapolis, Minn. 55422.

CAREER: Lutheran clergyman. Fairview Hospitals, Minneapolis, Minn., clergyman and psychologist, 1958-71; University of Minnesota, Medical School, Minneapolis, assistant professor, 1973—. Member of board, Minnesota State Mental Health Society. *Military service:* U.S. Navy, 1943-46. *Member:* American Association of Marriage Counselors, American Association of Pastoral Counselors, Society of Teachers of Family Medicine, Society for Scientific Study of Religion, Minnesota Council on Family Relations (member of board).

WRITINGS: Your Life Together, John Knox, 1967; *Prime Time: A Guide for Parents*, Minnesota Jaycees, 1972. Contributor to medical journals.

WORK IN PROGRESS: Living Married in the Middle Years.

AVOCATIONAL INTERESTS: Music, skiing.

* * *

NESS, John H., Jr. 1919-

PERSONAL: Born September 29, 1919, in Hagerstown, Md.; son of John H. (a minister) and Myra (Kiracofe) Ness; married Lucille Hull, February 26, 1944 (divorced); married Naomi Grieve, December 14, 1973; children: (first marriage) John Howard, Harry Albert, June Lucille. Education: Lebanon Valley College, A.B., 1940; University of Pennsylvania, M.A., 1942; Bonebrake Theological Seminary (now United Theological Seminary), B.D., 1945; further study at Divinity School of the Protestant Episcopal Church, Philadelphia, Pa., 1940-42, American University, 1964, and University of Denver, 1967. Politics: Independent. Home: 29 Lake Shore Dr., Lake Junaluska, N.C. 28745.

CAREER: Ordained clergyman in Evangelical United Brethren Church (now United Methodist Church); pastor of Evangelical United Brethren churches in York Haven, Pa., 1944-48, Frederick, Md., 1948-53, Mont Alto, Pa., 1953-55 and Manchester, Pa., 1955-58; archivist, Historical Society of Evangelical United Brethren Church, 1958-68; executive secretary, Commission on Archives and History of United Methodist Church, 1968—. Evangelical United Brethren Church, former historian for Pennsylvania Conference, trustee of Historical Society. Member: American Theological Library Association, International Society of Archivists, American Association of State and Local History, World Methodist Historical Society, Ohio Historical Society, Baltimore Conference Historical Society (life member), Free and Accepted Masons. Awards, honors: L.H.D., Lebanon Valley College, 1964.

WRITINGS: The Evangelical United Brethren Church, Department of Christian Education, Evangelical United Brethren Church, 1955; Home Study for Christian Service (guide and workbook), Department of Christian Education, Evangelical United Brethren Church, 1960; One Hundred Fifty Years, Board of Publication, Evangelical United Brethren Church, 1966. Evangelical United Brethren editor, Encyclopedia of World Methodism. Contributor to church publications. Editor, Methodist History, and News Bulletin (World Methodist Historical Society).

* * *

NEU, Charles E. 1936-

PERSONAL: Born April 10, 1936, in Carroll, Iowa; son of Arthur N. (a lawyer) and Martha (Frandsen) Neu; married Deborah Dunning (director of Providence Preservation Society), September 2, 1961; children: Hilary Adams, Douglas Bancroft. Education: Northwestern University, B.A. (with highest distinction), 1958; Harvard University, Ph.D., 1964. Home: 17 Halsey St., Providence, R.I. 02902. Office: Department of History, Brown University, Providence, R.I. 02912.

CAREER: Rice University, Houston, Tex., assistant professor, 1963-68, associate professor of history, 1968-72; Brown University, Providence, R.I., associate professor of history, 1970—. Fellow, Charles Warren Center for Studies in American History. Member: American Historical Association, Organization of American Historians. Awards, honors: Woodrow Wilson fellowship; Younger Scholar fellowship, National Humanities Endowment; Council of Learned Societies fellowship.

WRITINGS: An Uncertain Friendship: Theodore Roosevelt and Japan, 1906-09, Harvard University Press, 1967; The Troubled Encounter: The United States and Japan, Wiley, 1975.

WORK IN PROGRESS: Edward M. House: A Biography, completion expected in 1979.

* * *

NEUVILLE, H(enry) Richmond, Jr. 1937-

PERSONAL: Born February 24, 1937, in New York, N.Y.; son of H. Richmond (an accountant) and Mary (White) Neuville; married Kathleen M. Field, May 29, 1965; children: Anne Elisabeth, Henry Richmond. Education: St. John's University, Jamaica, N.Y., B.A., 1958; Columbia University, M.A., 1964; New York University, Ph.D., 1968. Politics: Independent. Religion: Protestant. Office: Publications and Graphic Arts Branch, Computer Applications Support and Development Office, Kittery, Me.

CAREER: Fairleigh Dickinson University, Teaneck, N.J., instructor in English, 1964-68; Queens College (now Queens College of the City University of New York), Flushing, N.Y., assistant professor of comparative literature, beginning 1968; former member of English department, Nasson College, Springvale, Me.; partner, Neuville Studios (art and photography), 1972—; Computer Applications Support and Development Office, Kittery, Me., head of publications and graphic arts, 1975—. Part-time art instructor. Military service: U.S. Navy, 1958-63; became lieutenant. Member: Renaissance Society of America, Dante Society of America, Modern Language Association of America, American Comparative Literature Association, New York University Colloquium for Comparative Literature (secretary, 1967—), Associazione Internazionale per gli studi della lingua e Letterature Italiana. Awards, honors: Woodrow Wilson fellow, 1963-64.

WRITINGS—Study guides: The Poems of Dylan Thomas, Monarch Books, 1964; Dostoyevsky, The Brothers Karamazov, Monarch Books, 1964; European Literature: Medieval to Neoclassicism, Monarch Books, 1964; Spencer, The Faerie Queene, Barrister Publishing, 1966; Dante, The Divine Comedy, Barrister Publishing, 1966.

WORK IN PROGRESS: The Scepter and the Soul: The Nature and Education of a Prince in Renaissance Literature.

SIDELIGHTS: Neuville is competent in French, Italian, Latin, Classical Greek, Spanish, and German.

* * *

NEVILLE, Jill 1932-

PERSONAL: Born May 29, 1932; daughter of Clive Henry (a businessman) and Betty (MacKnight) Neville; married Peter Duval Smith, August 14, 1959 (divorced; died in Saigon, 1966); children: Judith. Education: Educated in Australia. Politics: Left. Religion: None. Agent: Curtis Brown Ltd., 1 Craven Hill, London, W2 3EW, England.

CAREER: Copywriter for various agencies, London, England, 1953—. Writer.

WRITINGS: Fall Girl (novel), Weidenfeld & Nicolson, 1966; The Girl Who Played Gooseberry (novel), Weidenfeld & Nicolson, 1968; The Love Germ (novel), Weidenfeld

& Nicolson, 1969; *The Living Daylights: A Novel,* Weidenfeld & Nicolson, 1974. Contributor of articles and poetry to periodicals.

WORK IN PROGRESS: A novel, *Lady Lazarus.*

AVOCATIONAL INTERESTS: French culture and language, social work with children.†

* * *

NEWCOMB, Robert N(orman) 1925-

PERSONAL: Born June 19, 1925, in Minneapolis, Minn.; son of Frank Akhurst (vice-president of an insurance company) and Gayle Anita (Norman) Newcomb; married Ruth Elaine Hoffman, February 14, 1945; children: Richard H., John Robert, Bruce William; adopted children: (each corresponding in age to a natural son) Russell, Patrick, Michael. *Education:* Ohio State University, B.A., 1949; MacPhail College of Music, M.S.M., 1951. *Politics:* Independent. *Religion:* Episcopalian.

CAREER: Minister of music in a number of churches throughout the country, 1951-59; Newcomb Organizer, Inc., Clearwater, Fla., president, 1960. *Military service:* U.S. Marine Corps, 1943-46; became sergeant.

WRITINGS: Newcomb Organ Method, Newcomb Organizer, 1961; *Momma and Me Plus Three,* Fell, 1967.

WORK IN PROGRESS: Mayonnaisse in Her Hair, a sequel to *Momma and Me Plus Three;* research for a second book, *Hyprocrisy in Our Churches.*††

* * *

NEWFIELD, Jack 1939-

PERSONAL: Born February 18, 1939, in New York, N.Y. *Education:* Hunter College (now Hunter College of the City University of New York), B.A., 1961. *Politics:* Radical Democrat. *Religion:* Jewish. *Home:* 30 West Ninth St., New York, N.Y. *Agent:* Lynn Nesbitt, Time & Life Building, Rockefeller Center, New York, N.Y. 10020. *Office: Village Voice,* 80 University Place, New York, N.Y. 10003.

CAREER: Village Voice, New York, N.Y., currently assistant editor. *Member:* Southern Christian Leadership Conference.

WRITINGS: A Prophetic Minority, introduction by Michael Harrington, New American Library, 1966 (published in England as *A Prophetic Minority: The American Left,* Anthony Blond, 1967); (contributor) *Animal Ranch: The Great American Fable,* Parallax, 1966; *Robert Kennedy: A Memoir,* Dutton, 1969; *Bread and Roses Too,* Dutton, 1971; (with Jeff Greenfield) *A Populist Manifesto: The Making of a New Majority,* Praeger, 1972; *Cruel and Unusual Justice,* Holt, 1974. Contributor to *Playboy, Nation, Partisan Review, Evergreen Review,* and *New York Times Book Review.*

SIDELIGHTS: Newfield stated: "The writers who have influenced me most are Murray Kempton in terms of style, and Albert Camus in terms of ideas. As for viewpoint, I would list my participation in the movement against the Vietnam War."

BIOGRAPHICAL/CRITICAL SOURCES: New Leader, May 26, 1969; *Village Voice,* June 5, 1969.†

* * *

NEWHOUSE, Neville H. 1919-

PERSONAL: Born March 31, 1919, in Birkenhead, Cheshire, England; son of M. Curzon and Margaret A. (Hiatt) Newhouse; married Irene Jackson, December 6, 1941; children: Celia M., Ruth E. *Education:* University of Liverpool, B.A. (honors), 1940, M.A., 1949. *Religion:* Quaker. *Home and office:* 32, Park Ave., Wrexham, Clwyd, Wales.

CAREER: Bradford Grammar School, Bradford, Yorkshire, England, assistant master, 1950-59; Friends School, Lisburn, County Antrim, Northern Ireland, headmaster, 1961-70; Grove Park School, Wrexham, Wales, headmaster, 1970—. *Wartime service:* Friends Ambulance Unit. *Member:* Rotary Club.

WRITINGS: Joseph Conrad, Evans Brothers, 1967. Also author of *The History of Friends School, Lisburn,* 1974.

WORK IN PROGRESS: A history of eighteenth-century Irish Quakers.

* * *

NEWLOVE, John 1938-

PERSONAL: Born June 13, 1938, in Regina, Saskatchewan, Canada; son of Thomas Harold (a lawyer) and Mary Constant (Monteith) Newlove; married Susan Mary Phillips (a teacher), August 9, 1966; stepchildren: Jeremy Charles Gilbert, Tamsin Elizabeth Gilbert. *Education:* Attended school in Saskatchewan, Canada. *Home:* 666 Woodbine Ave., Toronto, Ontario, Canada.

CAREER: Poet. *Awards, honors:* Koerner Foundation award, 1964; Canada Council grant, 1965, 1967; Governor General's award for poetry, 1972.

WRITINGS: Grave Sirs, privately printed by R. Reid and T. Tanabe (Vancouver), 1962; *Elephants Mothers and Others,* Periwinkle Press, 1963; *Moving in Alone,* Contact Press (Toronto), 1965; *Notebook Pages,* Charles Pachter (Toronto), 1966; *What They Say,* Weed/Flower Press, 1967; *Black Night Widow,* McClelland & Stewart, 1968; *The Cave,* McClelland & Stewart, 1970; *Lies,* McClelland & Stewart, 1972.

WORK IN PROGRESS: A book of poems.

SIDELIGHTS: "Newlove is a lyric poet; emotion colours his experiences and the emotion for the most part is real and deep," Robert Gills comments. *Black Night Widow* includes "black irony, black comedy, black pathos and a black near despair." Although Newlove carries "the sense of what's past and passing and the existential death, his own and others," through his poems, Gills also finds him "on the whole remarkably free from bitterness. . . . Love is a primary value to him."

BIOGRAPHICAL/CRITICAL SOURCES: Canadian Forum, May, 1968; *Fiddlehead,* summer, 1968.

* * *

NEWLYN, Walter T(essier) 1915-

PERSONAL: Born July 26, 1915, in London, England; son of Walter (an engineer) and Maude (Jenkins) Newlyn; married Doreen Harrington, July 26, 1951; children: Sarah, Lucy, Gill, Kate. *Education:* University of London, Diploma in Economics (with distinction), 1939, B.Sc., London School of Economics and Political Science, 1948. *Home:* 61 Grove Lane, Leeds 6, England.

CAREER: John Darling Ltd. (grain merchants), London, England, junior clerk, 1936-39, chartering broker, 1939; University of Leeds, Leeds, England, lecturer, 1949-56, senior lecturer in economics, 1956—, professor of development economics, 1967—. Research fellow, West African

Institute of Social and Economic Research, 1953-54; Government of Uganda, full-time economic adviser, 1956-59, and consultant at other periods; Ford Foundation visiting professor, University of Buenos Aires, 1962; director of economic research, East African Institute of Social Research, 1965-67; director of Bank of Uganda, 1966-67; consultant, Government of Bechuanaland, 1966. *Military service:* Royal Corps of Signals, 1939-45; served in India; became major and staff officer, Combined Operations. *Awards, honors:* Houblon-Norman Fund grant for research in Africa, 1951.

WRITINGS: (Contributor) R. S. Sayers, editor, *Banking in the British Commonwealth,* Oxford University Press, 1952; (with D. C. Rowan) *Money and Banking in British Colonial Africa,* Oxford University Press, 1954; (with U. K. Hicks and others) *Federalism and Economic Growth* (a symposium), Oxford University Press, 1961; *Theory of Money,* Oxford University Press, 1962, 2nd edition, 1971; *Money in an Africal Context,* Oxford University Press, 1966; *Finance for Development,* East African Publishing House, 1968. Also co-author of *Symposium on Cost of Operating Agricultural Machinery in Tropical Africa,* published by the British Colonial Office. Contributor of articles to professional journals.

WORK IN PROGRESS: Financing Economic Development, for Oxford University Press.

AVOCATIONAL INTERESTS: Drama.

*   *   *

NEWMAN, Charles 1938-

PERSONAL: Born May 27, 1938, in St. Louis, Mo.; son of Charles Hamilton and June (Toney) Newman; married Ibolya Zoldi (a ballet teacher), May 2, 1965. *Education:* Yale University, B.A. (summa cum laude), 1960; Balliol College, Oxford, study in philosophy, 1960-61. *Home:* 209 Woodbine, Wilmette, Ill. *Agent:* Perry Knowlton, Curtis Brown Ltd., 60 East 56th St., New York, N.Y. 10022.

CAREER: Administrative assistant to Congressman Sidney R. Yates (Democrat-Illinois), 1962-63; Northwestern University, Evanston, Ill., instructor, 1963-65, assistant professor, 1965-68, associate professor, 1968-73, professor of English, 1973-75; Johns Hopkins University, Baltimore, Md., professor and chairman, The Writing Seminars, 1975—. Director, National Foundation for the Arts, Coordinating Council of Literary Magazines, 1968-74; consultant, Illinois Arts Council. *Military service:* U.S. Air Force Reserve. *Member:* Phi Beta Kappa. *Awards, honors:* Bellamy Prize for scholarship, 1960; Woodrow Wilson fellowship, 1960-61; Fulbright grant, 1961-62; Rockefeller grant, 1967-68; Breadloaf fellowship, 1969; National Endowment Creative Writing fellowship, 1973; distinguished service awards from Midland Authors Society, and Friends of Literature, both 1973; Ingram Merrill grant for creative writing, 1974; Guggenheim fellowship, 1974-75; Zabel Prize for Innovative Writing, National Institute of Arts and Letters, 1975.

WRITINGS: New Axis (novel), Houghton, 1966; (contributor) Richard Kostelanetz, editor, *The Young American Writers,* Funk & Wagnalls, 1968; (editor with George Gomori) *New Writing From East Europe,* Quadrangle, 1968; (author of introduction) E. M. Cioran, *The Fall into Time,* Quadrangle, 1969; (editor) *The Art of Sylvia Plath* (casebook of criticism, bibliography, and uncollected work), Indiana University Press, 1970; (editor with William Henkin) *New American Writers under Thirty,* Indiana

University Press, 1970; (editor with Alfred Appel, Jr.), *Nabokov: Criticism and Reminiscences, Translations and Tributes,* Northwestern University Press, 1970; *The Promisekeeper* (novel), Simon & Schuster, 1971; (editor with George Abbott White) *Literature in Revolution,* Holt, 1972; (editor with Mary Kinzie) *Prose for Borges,* Northwestern University Press, 1972; *A Child's History of America: Some Ribs and Riffs for the Sixties* (nonfiction), Swallow Press, 1973. Short fiction anthologized in *The Young American Writers, Scenes from American Life,* and *Best American Short Stories of 1971.* Contributor of criticism and fiction to literary reviews, and book reviews to *Chicago Tribune.* Former editor, *Criterion* (Yale University literary magazine); *Tri-Quarterly* (Northwestern University magazine), founder, editor, 1964-75, consulting editor, 1975—.

WORK IN PROGRESS: 4 Novellas, for Swallow Press; a novel, *Both Ways;* collection of essays, *Deflections;* collection of stories, *Love Affairs.*

BIOGRAPHICAL/CRITICAL SOURCES: Chicago Tribune, July 31, 1966; Carolyn Riley, editor, *Contemporary Literary Criticism,* Volume II, Gale, 1974.

*   *   *

NEWMAN, Jon O(rmond) 1932-

PERSONAL: Born May 2, 1932, in New York, N.Y.; son of Harold W., Jr. (a lawyer and author) and Estelle L. (Ormond) Newman; married Martha Silberman, June 19, 1953; children: Leigh, Scott, David. *Education:* Princeton University, A.B. (magna cum laude), 1953; Yale University, LL.B., 1956. *Home:* 20 Brookside Blvd., West Hartford, Conn. 06107.

CAREER: Admitted to Connecticut and District of Columbia Bars, 1957; senior law clerk to Chief Justice Earl Warren, Supreme Court of the United States, Washington, D.C., 1957-58; partner in law firm of Ritter, Satter & Newman, Hartford, Conn., 1958-60; executive assistant to U.S. Secretary of Health, Education and Welfare, Washington, D.C., 1961-62; administrative assistant to U.S. Senator Abraham Ribicoff (Connecticut), Washington, D.C., 1963-64; U.S. attorney in Conn., 1964-69; attorney in private law practice, 1969-71; U.S. district judge, District of Connecticut, 1972—. Counsel to majority, Connecticut General Assembly, 1959; special counsel to the governor of Connecticut, 1959-61. Chairman of board of regents, University of Hartford. *Member:* American Judicature Society, Connecticut Bar Association.

WRITINGS: (With Abraham Ribicoff) *Politics: The American Way,* introductions by former Vice-President Hubert Humphrey and President Richard M. Nixon, Allyn & Bacon, 1967.

*   *   *

NGUYEN-Dinh-Hoa 1924-

PERSONAL: Born January 17, 1924, in Hanoi, Vietnam; son of Nguyen-Dinh-Nhan (a government clerk) and Hoang-Thi-Heo; married Tran-Thi-Mit (a language teacher); children: Patricia, Cynthia, Deborah, Gregory. *Education:* University of Hanoi, law student, 1944-45, 1947-48; Union College, Schenectady, N.Y., B.A., 1950; New York University, M.A., 1952, Ph.D., 1956; additional summer study at Georgetown University Institute of Linguistics and Languages, 1954. *Politics:* "Nationalist, pro-Western." *Religion:* "Confucianist, Buddhist." *Home:* 1605 Taylor

Dr., Carbondale, Ill. 62901. *Office:* Department of Linguistics, Southern Illinois University, Carbondale, Ill. 62901.

CAREER: Columbia University, New York, N.Y., lecturer in Vietnamese, 1953-56; instructor in Vietnamese, U.S. Department of Defense, 1954-57; University of Saigon, Faculty of Letters, Saigon, Vietnam, professor of linguistics and English and chairman of English department, 1957-66; Ministry of Education, Saigon, director of cultural affairs, 1962-66; Embassy of Vietnam, Washington, D.C., counselor for cultural affairs, 1966-69; Southern Illinois University, Carbondale, professor of linguistics and foreign languages and literatures, and director of Center for Vietnamese Studies, 1969—. Secretary general, Vietnam National Commission for UNESCO, 1962-66. Visiting professor at University of Washington, Seattle, 1965-66, and University of Hawaii, summer, 1966.

MEMBER: Linguistic Society of America, Linguistic Circle of New York, Linguistic Circle of Saigon (charter member), Vietnamese-American Association (Saigon; chairman of board of directors), American University Alumni Association of Vietnam (charter member; first president), American Oriental Society, Association for Asian Studies, American Council on the Teaching of Foreign Languages, American Council of Teachers of Uncommonly-taught Asian Languages, Teachers of English to Speakers of Other Languages (TESOL). *Awards, honors:* American Council of Learned Societies grant, 1954.

WRITINGS: Newspaper Vietnamese, National Security Agency (Washington), 1955, published as *Read Vietnamese,* Tuttle, 1966; *Quoc-ngu: The Modern Writing System in Vietnam,* [Washington], 1955; *Vietnamese-English Vocabulary,* National Security Agency, Office of Training (Washington), 1955; *Speak Vietnamese,* [Saigon], 1957, revised edition, Tuttle, 1966; *Vietnamese Phrase Book,* Vietnamese-American Association, 1959, 2nd edition, 1961, 3rd edition published as *Say It in Vietnamese,* [Saigon], 1963, published as *Easy Vietnamese,* Tuttle, 1966; *Vietnamese-English Dictionary,* Binh-Minh (Saigon), 1959, Tuttle, 1966, revised and enlarged edition published as *Vietnamese-English Student Dictionary,* Southern Illinois University Press, 1971.

The Vietnamese Language, Department of National Education (Saigon), 1960; *English Phrase Book for Vietnamese,* U.S. Information Service (Saigon), 1962, published as *English Phrase Book for Vietnamese Speakers,* Tuttle, 1976; *Higher Education in the Republic of Vietnam* (pamphlet), Department of National Education, Directorate of Cultural Affairs (Saigon), 1963; "High School English" series, Vietnam Ministry of Education, Book I, 1963, Book II, 1964.

Colloquial Vietnamese, Southern Illinois University Press, 1971; (with Nguyen-ngoc-Bich, William Negherbon, and Vo-Dich) *Some Aspects of Vietnamese Culture: Four Lectures,* Southern Illinois University, Center for Vietnamese Studies, 1972; *Vietnamese Phrase Book,* Tuttle, 1976; *Beginning English for Vietnamese Speakers, Hoc tieng Anh, Cap I,* Tuttle, 1976; *Intermediate English for Vietnamese Speakers, Hoc tieng Anh, Cap II,* Tuttle, 1976. Also author of *Verbal and Non-Verbal Patterns of Respect-Behavior in Vietnamese Society,* 1956, and *Reading List on Vietnamese Language and Writing,* 1962. Contributor to *Word, Asian Culture, Journal of the American Oriental Society, Language Learning, Lingua,* and other journals. Editor, *Van-hoa Nguyet-san,* 1962-66.

WORK IN PROGRESS: Review Grammar of Vietnamese; An Introduction to Traditional Vietnamese Culture; A Bibliography of Vietnamese Linguistics; A Wingding Autobiography; English-Vietnamese Student Dictionary, for Southern Illinois University.

*   *   *

NICOL, Jean 1919-

PERSONAL: Born March 23, 1919, in London, England; daughter of Frank Claud and Dora (Mackenzie) Nicol; married Derek Tangye (an author), February 20, 1943. *Education:* Attended schools in Kent, England. *Politics:* Conservative. *Religion:* Church of England. *Home:* Dorminack, St. Buryan, near Penzance, Cornwall, England.

CAREER: Press relations officer for Savoy Hotel Ltd., London, England, 1940-50; along with her own writing, illustrator of several hardcover editions and all the paperback editions of her husband's books.

WRITINGS: Meet Me at the Savoy, Museum Press, 1952, reissued in an omnibus edition together with Eric Linklater's *The House of Gair,* Odhams, 1954; *Hotel Regina* (novel), M. Joseph, 1967; *Home is the Hotel,* M. Joseph, 1976. Contributor to *Gourmet* (magazine).

Illustrator; all by husband, Derek Tangye: *A Gull on the Roof,* M. Joseph, 1961, Coward, 1962; *A Cat in the Window,* M. Joseph, 1962; *A Drake at the Door,* M. Joseph, 1963; *A Donkey in the Meadow,* M. Joseph, 1965; *Lama,* M. Joseph, 1966; *The Way to Minack,* M. Joseph, 1968; *A Cornish Summer,* M. Joseph, 1970; *Cottage on a Cliff,* M. Joseph, 1972; *A Cat Affair,* M. Joseph, 1974.

BIOGRAPHICAL/CRITICAL SOURCES: Stanley Jackson, *The Savoy,* 1964.

*   *   *

NIEHOFF, Arthur H. 1921-

PERSONAL: Born December 30, 1921, in Indianapolis, Ind.; son of Bernard H. and Marie (Schneider) Niehoff; married Juanita Hobbs, January 17, 1946 (divorced, 1971); children: Justin D. *Education:* Butler University, student, 1940-41; Indiana University, B.A., 1949; Columbia University, Ph.D., 1957. *Home:* 1009 Ashland Ave., Santa Monica, Calif. *Office:* Department of Anthropology, California State University, Los Angeles, Calif. 90032.

CAREER: Milwaukee (Wis.) Public Museum, assistant curator of anthropology, 1951-59; U.S. Department of State, Agency for International Development (AID), adviser on community development in Laos, 1959-61; University of Wisconsin-Milwaukee, assistant professor of anthropology, 1962-63; George Washington University, Human Resources Research Office, Alexandria, Va., senior scientist in anthropology, 1963-68; California State University, Los Angeles, professor of anthropology, 1968—, chairman of department, 1969—. Project leader in research on diffusion of innovations, Nigeria, 1966; has done other field work in India, Thailand, Trinidad, Peru, and Costa Rica. *Military service:* U.S. Army Air Forces, 1941-45. *Member:* American Anthropological Association (fellow), Society for Applied Anthropology, Society for International Development. *Awards, honors:* Lapham Research Medal, 1959, for discovery of a new insect, *Trobocarus niehoffi.*

WRITINGS: Factory Workers in India, Milwaukee Public Museum, 1959; (with Juanita Niehoff) *East Indians in the West Indies,* Milwaukee Public Museum, 1960; (with Conrad Arensberg) *Cultural Reality and Technical*

Change, U.S. Department of State, 1963; (editor) *Casebook of Social Change,* Aldine, 1966; *Introducing Social Change,* Aldine, 1968. Also author of *Planned Change in Agrarian Countries,* 1969. Contributor of more than sixty articles to *Applied Anthropology, International Development Review,* and popular periodicals.

WORK IN PROGRESS: Research on the process of induced social change; analysis of social change in developing countries.

SIDELIGHTS: Arthur Niehoff is fluent in French and Spanish, and speaks some Lao and Hindustani.

*   *   *

NILAND, Powell 1919-

PERSONAL: Born November 6, 1919, in Scranton, Pa.; son of James T. and Elsie (Powell) Niland; married Juel Christine Dasenburg, July 14, 1945; children: Susan, Judith. *Education:* University of Scranton, B.S., 1942; Harvard University, M.B.A., 1948, D.C.S., 1953. *Home:* 6843 Pershing Ave., St. Louis, Mo. 63130. *Office:* Prince Hall, Washington University, St. Louis, Mo. 63130.

CAREER: Harvard University, School of Business Administration, Boston, Mass., instructor, 1949-51, assistant professor, 1951-57; Washington University, St. Louis, Mo., associate professor, 1957-58, professor of management, 1958—. Visiting professor, L'Institut pour l'Etude des Methodes de Direction de l'Entreprise, Lausanne, 1962-63. Consultant to U.S. Army Command Management School, 1956-57, and U.S. Department of State, 1965, 1966. Land Clearance Authority for Urban Renewal, University City, Mo., commissioner, 1967-74, chairman, 1974—. Director, Cummins Mid-America, Inc. *Military service:* U.S. Naval Reserve, Supply Corps, active duty, 1942-45; became lieutenant. *Member:* Academy of Management (fellow), Operations Research Society of America, Institute of Management Sciences, American Institute of Decision Sciences.

WRITINGS: Management Problems in the Acquisition of Special Automatic Equipment, Division of Research, Harvard Business School, 1961; *The Role of River Sites in the Industrial Development of the St. Louis Region,* Graduate School of Business Administration, Washington University, 1961; (with Elmer P. Lotshaw) *The Role of Water Resources in the Industrial Development of the St. Louis Region,* Graduate School of Business Administration, Washington University, 1961; (with C. William Emory) *Making Management Decisions,* Houghton, 1968; *Production Planning, Scheduling and Inventory Control,* Macmillan, 1970. Contributor to management journals; author of more than seventy cases, mainly in the production area. Member of editorial board, *Journal of the Academy of Management,* 1966—.

*   *   *

NININGER, H(arvey) H(arlow) 1887-

PERSONAL: Born January 17, 1887, in Conway Springs, Kan.; son of James Buchanan (a farmer) and Mary Ann (Bower) Nininger; married Addie N. Delp, June 5, 1914; children: Robert D., Doris Elaine Nininger Banks, Margaret Ann Nininger Huss. *Education:* Northwestern State College, Alva, Okla., student, 1907-09; McPherson College, B.S., 1914, D.Sc., 1937; Pomona College, M.S., 1917; University of California, Berkeley, graduate study, summers, 1915-18. *Politics:* Independent. *Home address:* P.O. Box 420, Sedona, Ariz. 86336.

CAREER: Began teaching in rural schools, 1909; Northwestern State College, Alva, Okla., substitute professor of biology, 1912-13; La Verne College, La Verne, Calif., professor of biology, 1914-18; U.S. Bureau of Entomology, special field agent in food conservation program, 1918-19; Southwestern College, Winfield, Kan., professor of biology, 1919-20; McPherson College, McPherson, Kan., professor of zoology and botany, 1920-30; founder of Nininger Laboratory for Research on Meteorites, Denver, Colo., 1930, and director through successive changes in the name of the institution to American Meteorite Laboratory, 1937-46, and American Meteorite Museum, 1946-60; sold the collection in 1960 to National Science Foundation and British Museum of Natural History. Curator of meteorites, Colorado Museum of Natural History, 1930-46; former instructor in meteoritics at University of Denver. *Member:* American Association for the Advancement of Science (fellow), Geological Society of America, Astronomical Society, Meteoritical Society (co-founder; fellow; president, 1937-41), Kansas Academy of Science (fellow; president, 1924-25). *Awards, honors:* Leonard Medal of Meteoritical Society; L.L.D., Arizona State University, 1961.

WRITINGS: A Field Guide to Birds of Central Kansas (pamphlet), 1927; *Our Stone-Pelted Planet,* Houghton, 1933; *A Comet Strikes the Earth,* Desert Magazine Press, 1942, reprinted, American Meteorite Laboratory, 1969; *Chips from the Moon,* Desert Magazine Press, 1942; *The Nininger Collection of Meteorites,* American Meteorite Museum, 1950; *Out of the Sky,* University of Denver Press, 1951; *Arizona's Meteorite Crater,* American Meteorite Museum, 1956; *Ask a Question About Meteorites,* American Meteorite Museum, 1962; *The Published Papers of Harvey Harlow Nininger: Biology and Meteoritics,* edited by George A. Boyd, Arizona State University, 1971; *Find a Falling Star* (autobiography), Eriksson, 1972; *A Photographic Study of Meteorites,* three volumes, Arizona State University, in press. Contributor to *Sky and Telescope, Popular Astronomy, Science,* and other journals and magazines.

SIDELIGHTS: Nininger told *CA:* "Developed successful method of discovering meteorites and, during the 1930's and the 1940's, was credited with making half of the meteorite discoveries in the entire world [two hundred different falls]. By 1960 had accumulated the greatest collection of meteorites ever made by planned search." Nininger made an expedition to Australia, 1958-59, and studied meteorite collections in Europe, 1960.

BIOGRAPHICAL/CRITICAL SOURCES: Harvey H. Nininger, *Find a Falling Star,* Eriksson, 1972.

*   *   *

NISH, Ian Hill 1926-

PERSONAL: Born June 3, 1926, in Edinburgh, Scotland; son of David C. and Marion (Hill) Nish; married Rona Speirs, 1965; children: two daughters. *Education:* University of Edinburgh, M.A., 1951; University of London, M.A., 1958, Ph.D., 1961. *Office:* London School of Economics and Political Science, University of London, London W.C. 2, England.

CAREER: University of Sydney, Sydney, New South Wales, Australia, lecturer in history, 1958-62; University of London, London School of Economics and Political Science, London, England, lecturer in international history, 1962—. *Military service:* British Army, 1944-48; became captain.

WRITINGS: The Anglo-Japanese Alliance: The Diplomacy of Two Island Empires 1894-1907, Oxford University Press, 1966; *The Story of Japan,* Faber, 1968; *Alliance in Decline: A Study in Anglo-Japanese Relations, 1908-23,* Athlone Press, 1972.

* * *

NIST, John (Albert) 1925-

PERSONAL: Born November 27, 1925, in Chicago, Ill.; son of Albert Charles (a livestock buyer) and Margaret T. (Rice) Nist; married Joan Irene Stidham, June 17, 1950 (divorced September 26, 1971); married Maria Grazia Cimmino, December 16, 1971; children: Brian Thomas, Brice Robert, Brent Philip, Blair William, Chiara Ann. *Education:* DePauw University, A.B., 1949; Indiana University, M.A., 1950, Ph.D., 1952. *Politics:* Democrat/Independent. *Religion:* Roman Catholic. *Home:* 1034 Rudd Ave., Auburn, Ala. 36830. *Office:* Department of English, Auburn University, Auburn, Ala. 36830.

CAREER: Eastern Michigan University, Ypsilanti, assistant professor, 1952-55, associate professor of English, 1955-61; University of Brazil, Rio de Janeiro, research fellow, 1961-62; University of Arizona, Tucson, visiting professor of English, 1962-63; Austin College, Sherman, Tex., Shoap Professor of English and chairman of department, 1963-66; Auburn University, Auburn, Ala., professor of English, 1966—. Fulbright lecturer, University of Sao Paulo, 1958-59, and University of Rome, 1970-71. Linguistics consultant, Alabama Department of Education, 1967—. *Military service:* U.S. Naval Reserve, active duty, 1944-46; received two battle stars.

MEMBER: Modern Language Association of America, National Council of Teachers of English, Conference on College Composition and Communication, Linguistics Society of America. *Awards, honors:* Social Science Research Council fellowship to Brazil, 1961-62; Machado de Assis Medal, Brazilian Academy of Letters, 1964.

WRITINGS: The Structure and Texture of "Beowulf," University of Sao Paulo, 1959; *Fui Crucificado,* Editora Anhambi (Sao Paulo), 1960; (editor and translator) *Modern Brazilian Poetry,* Indiana University Press, 1962; (editor) Carlos Drummond de Andrade, *In the Middle of the Road,* University of Arizona Press, 1965; *A Structural History of English,* St. Martin's, 1966; *The Modernist Movement in Brazil: A Literary Study,* University of Texas Press, 1967; *Speaking into Writing: A Guide to English Composition,* St. Martin's, 1969; (editor) *Style in English,* Bobbs-Merrill, 1969; *Handicapped English: The Language of the Socially Disadvantaged,* C. C Thomas, 1974. Contributor to *Encyclopedia of Education,* 1971; also contributor of more than two hundred articles, essays, poems, and reviews to a score of journals in America, Latin America, and Europe.

WORK IN PROGRESS: Literary Creativity, a study of man's creative use of language from the level of phonology to that of style and esthetic value; *The Fantasy (S)expert,* a novel; poems, and lyrics for music.

SIDELIGHTS: John Nist told *CA:* "Motivated by the two central attributes of all esthetic activity: the drive for permanence and the desire to achieve an infinite reiterability. Major frustration is that I have not been able to locate a publisher for five books of my own belles-lettres prose. Too much of American publishing is dominated by the narrow and parochial tastes of New York City." He is competent in Greek, Latin, Portuguese, Spanish, French, German, and Old and Middle English. *Avocational interests:* Travel, hiking, swimming, and experimenting with words.

* * *

NIVEN, Laurence Van Cott 1938- (Larry Niven)

PERSONAL: Born April 30, 1938, in Los Angeles, Calif.; son of Waldemar Van Cott (a lawyer) and Lucy (Doheny) Niven. *Education:* California Institute of Technology, student, 1956-58; Washburn University of Topeka, A.B., 1962; University of California, Los Angeles, graduate study, 1962-63. *Home and office:* 3961 Vanalden, Tarzana, Calif.

CAREER: Full-time writer, mainly for magazines. *Member:* Science Fiction Writers of America. *Awards, honors:* Hugo Award, 1966, for short story, *Neutron Star,* 1970, for novel *Ringworld,* and 1971, for short story *Inconstant Moon;* Nebula Award, 1970, for *Ringworld.*

WRITINGS—Under name Larry Niven; all published by Ballantine, except as indicated: *World of Ptavvs* (novel), 1966; *Gift from Earth,* 1968; *Neutron Star,* 1968; *The Shape of Space,* 1969; *Ringworld,* 1970; (with David Gerrold) *The Flying Sorcerers,* 1971; *Protector,* 1973; *The Flight of the Horse,* 1973; *A Hole in Space,* 1974; (with Jerry Pournelle) *A Mote in God's Eye,* Simon & Schuster, 1974; *Tales of Known Space,* 1975. Also author of short stories published in magazines and included in anthologies.

WORK IN PROGRESS: A novel, *The House Divided; Lucifer's Hammer,* with Jerry Pournelle.

* * *

NOEL, John V(avasour), Jr. 1912-

PERSONAL: Born June 2, 1912, in Lima, Peru; son of John Vavasour (a publisher and journalist) and Eda (Andersen) Noel; married Mary Hess, June 28, 1938: children: Carol, John III, Joyeux. *Education:* College of Charleston, student, 1930-32; U.S. Naval Academy, B.S., 1936; Stanford University, M.A., 1948. *Politics:* Liberal. *Religion:* Episcopalian. *Home:* 38 rue de l'Yvette, Paris 16e, France.

CAREER: U.S. Navy, regular officer, 1936-65, retiring as captain. During World War II had two destroyer commands at sea; postwar assignments included Assistant Chief of Naval Personnel for Special Projects, Washington, D.C., 1955-58, aide to Assistant Secretary of Navy, 1959-61, command of missile cruiser, USS *Springfield* in the Mediterranean, 1961-62, and naval attache and attache for air to France, 1962-65.

MEMBER: Tennis Club of Paris, New York Yacht Club, Travellers Club, Cercle Militaire, Golf Club Saint Cloud, Golf Club of Soto Grande, International Lawn Tennis Clubs of U.S.A. and France. *Awards, honors*—Military: Bronze Star; two commendation ribbons; commander, Legion de Merite (France).

WRITINGS: Division Officers Guide, U.S. Naval Institute, 1952, 6th edition, 1972; (editor) *Naval Terms Dictionary,* Van Nostrand, 1952, 3rd edition (with Edward L. Beach), U.S. Naval Institute, 1971; (reviser) Russell Willson, *Watch Officers Guide: A Handbook for All Deck Watch Officers,* U.S. Naval Institute, 1953, 10th edition, 1971; (with E. R. King) *Ship Handling,* Van Nostrand, 1954; (editor) *Bluejackets Manual,* U.S. Naval Institute, 1955; (editor) *Knight's Modern Seamanship,* Van Nostrand, 1960—. Contributor to proceedings, yearbooks, and other Naval publications. Assistant editor, *U.S. Naval Institute Proceedings*, 1951-53.†

* * *

NOLEN, Claude H. 1921-

PERSONAL: Born July 10, 1921, in Memphis, Tenn.; son of Ernest L. (a merchant) and Margaret (Smith) Nolen; married Jeanne Chappuis, June 7, 1947; children: Cosette, Andree, Denise, Adrienne, Claude H., Jr., Lisa. *Education:* Memphis State University, B.S., 1948; Louisiana State University, M.A., 1949; University of Texas, Ph.D., 1963. *Politics:* Democrat. *Religion:* Catholic. *Office:* Department of History, St. Edward's University, Austin, Tex. 78704.

CAREER: St. Edward's University, Austin, Tex., professor of history, 1956—. *Military service:* U.S. Army Air Forces, 1942-45. *Member:* Organization of American Historians, American Association of University Professors, Southern Historical Association.

WRITINGS: The Negro's Image in the South: The Anatomy of White Supremacy, University of Kentucky Press, 1967.

* * *

NOONAN, Michael John 1921-

PERSONAL: Born September 19, 1921, in Christchurch, New Zealand; son of John Patrick and Eileen (Moloney) Noonan. *Education:* Attended University of Sydney, 1947-50. *Home:* 231 Park West, Marble Arch, London, W.2 2QL, England.

CAREER: Author. *Military service:* Australian Imperial Forces, New Guinea Force, 1941-45; became lieutenant. *Member:* Authors Guild of America, Society of Authors (Great Britain), Writers' Guild, Australian Society of Authors, Society of Australian Writers (England). *Awards, honors:* First prize, Writer's Playhouse (Australia), for "The Man Who Changed the Wind"; fourth prize in *Sydney Morning Herald* novel competition for script, "Tower of Babel"; honorable mention, Miles Franklin Novel Award, for *The December Boys;* first prize, Venice Film Festival, 1954, for "Down in the Forest."

WRITINGS: In the Land of the Talking Trees, Angus & Robertson, 1946; *The Golden Forest*, Angus & Robertson, 1947; *The Patchwork Hero*, John Day, 1958; *Flying Doctor*, John Day, 1961; *Flying Doctor on the Great Barrier Reef*, Hodder & Stoughton, 1962; *Flying Doctor and the Secret of the Pearls*, Hodder & Stoughton, 1962; *The December Boys*, Heinemann, 1963; *Flying Doctor Shadows the Mob*, Hodder & Stoughton, 1964; *Flying Doctor Hits the Headlines*, Hodder & Stoughton, 1965; *Air Taxi*, Brockhampton Press, 1967, Meredith Press, 1968; *Flying Doctor under the Desert*, Brockhampton Press, 1967; *The Pink Beach*, R. Hale, 1969; *The Sun Is God*, Barrie & Jenkins, 1973, Delacorte, 1974.

Films: "The Fifth Wheel" (adaptation of an Israeli novel); "The December Boys" (adaptation of his own novel); "Down in the Forest." Also author of documentary films.

Television: Originator of "Flying Doctor" and "Riptide" series; plays include "The Angry Flower," "Boy on the Telephone," "The Music Upstairs," "The Violent Stranger," and "The Winds of Green Monday." Also author of radio serials, series, and plays.

WORK IN PROGRESS: Chains of Dust, a novel set in inland Australia; *The Invincible Mr. Az*, a children's book set in England; a feature film adaptation of *The Sun Is God;* a television series based on *The Patchwork Hero.*

SIDELIGHTS: Flying Doctor, the book that launched a series of similarly titled novels, was published in England, the United States, Switzerland, Brazil, Germany, Netherlands, Poland, and Belgium. Six of Noonan's other books have been translated into German.

* * *

NORMAN, Alexander Vesey Bethune 1930-
(Vesey Norman)

PERSONAL: Born February 10, 1930, in Delhi, India; son of Alexander Maximilian Bethune (a lieutenant colonel in the British Army) and Shiela Maude (Maxwell) Norman; married Catherine Margaret Barne (a researcher), December 10, 1954; children: Andrew Fion Bethune. *Education:* University of London, B.A., 1958. *Home:* 19 Highgate High St., London N.6, England. *Office:* Wallace Collection, Manchester Sq., London, W1M 6BN, England.

CAREER: Scottish United Services Museum, Edinburgh, assistant curator, 1957-63; Wallace Collection (museum of fine and applied arts), London, England, assistant to director, 1963—. Honorary curator of armoury at Abbotsford. *Military service:* British Army, Scottish Horse Royal Armoured Corps, 1951-55; became second lieutenant. *Member:* Society of Antiquaries of Scotland (fellow), Society of Antiquaries of London (fellow), Museums Association, Arms and Armour Society, Society for Army Historical Research, Meyrick Society.

WRITINGS: (Under name Vesey Norman) *Arms and Armour*, Weidenfeld & Nicolson, 1964, published as *Arms and Armor*, Putnam, 1966; (with Don Pottinger) *Warrior to Soldier, 449 to 1660: A Brief Introduction to the History of English Warfare*, Weidenfeld & Nicolson, 1966, published as *A History of War and Weapons, 449 to 1660: English Warfare from the Anglo-Saxons to Cromwell*, Crowell, 1966; (under name Vesey Norman) *The Medieval Soldier*, Crowell, 1971; *Arms and Armour in the Royal Scottish Museum*, H.M.S.O., 1972.

WORK IN PROGRESS: A book on rapiers and small swords, for Jenkins.

SIDELIGHTS: Arms and Armor has also been published in German and French.

* * *

NORRIS, Theo L. 1926-

PERSONAL: Born September 3, 1926, in Miakka, Fla.; daughter of Edmond Sylvester and Margaret (Johns) Chancey; married Floyd O. Norris (a laundryman), April 17, 1943; children: Cheryl (Mrs. Kenneth T. Wheless), Donald, Kenneth. *Education:* Attended high school in Hardee County, Fla. *Religion:* Seventh-day Adventist.

CAREER: Azusa Valley Sanitarium, Azusa, Calif., second cook, 1965—.

WRITINGS: Cookie: A Puppy's Tale, Southern Publishing, 1967. Short stories for children published in Seventh-day Adventist church papers; one story anthologized in church school reader.

WORK IN PROGRESS: Research for a book on Colonel Hunter, founder of Nevada, Missouri, and missionary to the Indians in Oklahoma Territory.††

NORWOOD, Victor G(eorge) C(harles) 1920-
(Coy Banton, Shane V. Baxter, Jim Bowie, Clay Brand, Walt Cody, Shayne Colter, Wes Corteen, Clint Dangerfield, Johnny Dark, Vince Destry, Doone Fargo, Wade Fisher, G. Gearing-Thomas, Mark Hampton, Hank Janson, Nat Karta, Whip McCord, Brett Rand, Brad Regan, Shane Russell, Mark Shane, Rhondo Shane, Dillon Strange, Jim Tressidy, Paul Tyrone, Portman Willard)

PERSONAL: Born March 21, 1920, in Lincolnshire, England; son of Elmer William (a lieutenant colonel, British Army) and Alice (Austen) Norwood; married Elizabeth McKie (who acts as her husband's private secretary), October 31, 1947; children: Russell Paul, Shane Victor. *Education:* Left school at fourteen; later completed studies (via correspondence) for a diploma from Bennett's College, Sheffield, England. *Politics:* Conservative. *Religion:* None. *Home:* 194 West Common Lane, Westcliff, Scunthorpe, South Humberside, England.

CAREER: Earlier occupations included bank guard, heavyweight boxer and wrestler, singer, head croupier at a gambling establishment, gold and diamond prospector, and private detective; professional writer, 1950—. *Wartime service:* British Merchant Marine, anti-aircraft gunner with Atlantic and Malta convoys, 1939-44; three times mined or torpedoed (seventeen wounds); received Special Marine War Medal and bar, and Italy, Africa, Pacific, and Atlantic stars. *Member:* Royal Society of Literature, Society of Authors, North Lincolnshire Writers' Circle and Association (chairman), Conservative Club (Scunthorpe, Lincolnshire), World Wide Club (London). *Awards, honors:* Cambridge University literary award, 1976.

WRITINGS—Nonfiction: *Man Alone,* T. V. Broadman, 1956; *A Handful of Diamonds,* T. V. Broadman, 1960; *Drums along the Amazon,* R. Hale, 1964; *Jungle Life of Guiana,* R. Hale, 1964; *The Long Haul,* R. Hale, 1967; *Australian Adventure,* M. Joseph, 1975; *Jungle Treasure,* Angus & Robertson, 1975; *Campfire Tales,* Millington Publishers, 1976; *Biography of an Adventurer,* Millington Publishers, 1976.

Fiction; all published by R. Hale, except as noted: *The Untamed,* Scion, 1951; *The Skull of Kanaima,* Scion, 1951; *The Temple of the Dead,* Scion, 1951; *The Caves of Death,* Scion, 1951; (under pseudonym Johnny Dark) *Snake Walk,* Arthur Barker, 1951; (under pseudonym Nat Karta) *Brother Rat,* Arthur Barker, 1952; *Cry of the Beast,* Scion, 1952; (under pseudonym Brad Regan) *Raw Deal for Dames,* Arthur Barker, 1952; (under pseudonym Mark Hampton) *Killer Take All,* Arthur Barker, 1953; (under pseudonym Mark Shane) *Crossfire,* Arthur Barker, 1953; *Boothill Trail,* Arthur Barker, 1954; *Gun Trail to Glory,* Arthur Barker, 1954; *Chango,* Arthur Barker, 1955; *Vengeance Valley,* Arthur Barker, 1955.

The Hellbender, 1963, published as *Rails to Thunderhead,* Arcadia House, 1965; (under pseudonym Wade Fisher) *Ranger Gun-law,* 1963; (under pseudonym Jim Tressidy) *Hard Hombre,* 1964; *Journey of Fear,* 1965; (under pseudonym Rhondo Shane) *Lawman's Code,* 1965; (under pseudonym Coy Banton) *Blood on the Sage,* 1966; *Gunsmoke Justice,* 1966; (under pseudonym Doone Fargo) *Death Valley,* 1966; *Killer's Code,* 1966; (under pseudonym Whip McCord) *Hellfire Range,* 1966; (under pseudonym Wes Corteen) *Gun Chore,* 1966; (under pseudonym Shane Colter) *Halfway to Hell,* 1966.

The Loser, Greenleaf Classics, 1974; *Black Orchids for Ophelia,* Greenleaf Classics, 1974; *The Flame and the Flesh,* Greenleaf Classics, 1974; *River of the Damned,* Dobson, 1975; *The Terror,* Dobson, 1975; *The Alien,* Dobson, 1975; *The Primitives,* Futura, 1975; *The Professional,* Arthur Barker, 1976; *The Dark Star,* Millington Publishers, 1976.

Under pseudonym Shane V. Baxter: *Shadow of a Gunhawk,* R. Hale, 1966; *The Texan,* R. Hale, 1967, Lenox Hill, 1974.

Under pseudonym Clay Brand: *Colt Courage,* R. Hale, 1965; *Powdersmoke,* R. Hale, 1966; *Lattimer's Last Ride,* R. Hale, 1967.

Under pseudonym Walt Cody: *Reap the Wild Wind,* R. Hale, 1966. Also author of *Black Day at Eagle Rock,* 1968, and *Gunsmoke Justice.*

Under pseudonym Vince Destry: *Trail's End,* R. Hale, 1965; *The Glory Trail,* R. Hale, 1967; *A Badge and a Gun,* R. Hale, 1970, Lenox Hill, 1975.

Under pseudonym Hank Janson; all published by Roberts & Vinter: *Sensuality, Top Ten, Playgirl, Raw Deal, Blood Bath,* and *Go with a Jerk,* 1963-65.

Under pseudonym Shane Russell: *The Bounty Trail,* R. Hale, 1963; *Gun Trail and Boot Hill,* R. Hale, 1963; *The Lobo Breed,* R. Hale, 1965.

Also author of: *Hell's Wenches,* 1963; (under pseudonym Clint Dangerfield) *Crossfire,* 1965; (under pseudonym Brett Rand) *Code of the Lawless,* 1967; (under pseudonym Rondo Shane) *The Gun Hellion,* 1967; *The Long Way Home,* 1967; *Valley of the Damned,* 1968; *Island of Creeping Death; Night of the Black Horror.*

Also author of sixteen books under the pseudonym Jim Bowie: *Raw Deal, Scarred Leather, Apache Kid, Apache Gold, Red Hellions, The Drifter, Five-point Law, Trigger Music, Gunshot Grief, Paydirt, Gunflash, Showdown, Renegade Ranger, Call of the Owlhoot, Boothill Gold,* and *Boothill for Badmen.*

Author of three television scripts for British Broadcasting Corp., "Two for the Reaper," "The Dark Years," and "Ricochet"; author of two film scenarios for Zenith Film Productions, "Night of the Black Horror," and "The Earth Is Dark."

Author of about ninety paperback novels under his own name and various pseudonyms published between 1950 and 1960 by Scion, Comyns, Merit Books, Roberts & Vinter, and Brown-Watson. Contributor of over 250 articles and short stories to periodicals including *Vimenn* (Norway), *Reader's Digest, National Geographic, Industrial Diamond Review, Gems & Minerals, Angling Fisherman,* and *Argosy;* contributor of political and sporting articles to periodicals under the pseudonym G. Gearing-Thomas; contributor of articles on gems, travel, prospecting, and mining to periodicals under pseudonyms Paul Tyrone, Dillon Strange, and Portman Willard.

SIDELIGHTS: Norwood told *CA:* "I have travelled the world since I was 16. I have been diamond and gold mining in Brazil, Africa, and Guyana, and have organized and led seven expeditions through little-known areas of the Amazon jungles. . . . I was at one time an amateur champion prizefighter, and am now a keen student of karate, a powerful swimmer, a saltwater angling enthusiast, and my hobbies include archery, rifle and pistol shooting. . . . In my youth I won numerous cups for physique and strength, can still draw and shoot a pistol faster than most men, and have hunted moderately big game in Africa, India, and the U.S.A. with bow and arrow. . . .

"I enjoy writing, and would not wish to do anything else for a living. I did train for opera singing but could not afford to live in London and continue training . . . and the loss of two fingers during one of my Brazilian expeditions put an end to any prospect of taking up wrestling again.

"I consider *Jungle Life of Guiana* to be the best non-fiction book I have so far written. . . . Until recently I wrote a novel *every month* for Robert Hale. . . . I now have other outlets for fiction, and find time to churn out two travel books a year and sundry poems, articles, and short stories."

Norwood also collects coins and stamps, is interested in photography (he illustrates his travel books with his own photographs), and has a "unique library of color travel movies compiled personally during travels abroad." He speaks Spanish, German, Italian, and French "well enough to make myself understood," and has a "fringe grasp" of some of the American Indian dialects. He has made several appearances on television in Britain, Australia, and the United States.

*   *   *

NOURSE, Robert Eric Martin   1938-

PERSONAL: Born August 20, 1938, in Vancouver, British Columbia, Canada; son of Reginald Eric (a military officer) and Rita (Wiggins) Nourse; married Jennifer Louise Wilcox, 1970; children: Robert Edwin Christopher, David Wilcox, Michael Eric, Amelia Louise. *Education:* Carleton University, Certificate in Engineering, 1957; Queen's University at Kingston, B.Sc., 1959; University of Western Ontario, M.B.A., 1964; Harvard University, D.B.A., 1967. *Home:* 1102 The Parkway, London, Ontario, Canada N6A 2X3. *Office:* School of Business Administration, University of Western Ontario, London, Ontario, Canada.

CAREER: University of Western Ontario, School of Business Administration, London, 1967—, currently professor of business administration. *Military service:* Canadian Army, 1959-62; became captain. *Member:* Association of Professional Engineers of Ontario, American Marketing Association.

WRITINGS: (With Robert D. Buzzell) *Product Innovation in Food Processing, 1954-1964,* Division of Research, Harvard Business School, 1967; (with Buzzell, John Matthews, and Theodore Levitt) *Marketing: A Contemporary Analysis,* 2nd edition, McGraw, 1972; (with others) *Canadian Problems in Marketing,* McGraw-Hill Ryerson, 1972. Contributor to business journals.

*   *   *

NUTTALL, A(nthony) D(avid)   1937-

PERSONAL: Born April 25, 1937, in Hereford, England; son of Kenneth (a schoolmaster) and Hilda (Addison) Nuttall; married Mary Donagh, July 1, 1960; children: William James, Mary Addison. *Education:* Merton College, Oxford, B.A., 1959, M.A., 1962, B.Litt., 1963. *Politics:* None. *Religion:* None. *Home:* 35 Kensington Pl., Brighton, Sussex, England. *Office:* Arts Building, University of Sussex, Falmer, near Brighton, Sussex, England.

CAREER: Oxford University, Oxford, England, did research and teaching, 1959-62; University of Sussex, Brighton, England, member of faculty, 1963—.

WRITINGS: William Shakespeare: The Winter's Tale, Edward Arnold, 1966; *Two Concepts of Allegory: A Study of Shakespeare's "The Tempest" and the Logic of Allegorical Expression,* Barnes & Noble, 1967; (editor with D. Bush) John Milton, *Minor Poems,* Macmillan, 1972; *A Common Sky: Philosophy and the Literary Imagination,* University of California Press, 1974. Contributor to *Critical Quarterly, Review of English Studies,* and other publications.

WORK IN PROGRESS: A book on Virgil and Shakespeare.

SIDELIGHTS: A. D. Nuttall told *CA:* "The only language I speak easily is English, but I enjoy reading Latin verse (especially Horace). Am interested primarily in the connection between the study of literature and the study of philosophy. Have in addition a less articulate passion for the art and architecture of Italy."

BIOGRAPHICAL/CRITICAL SOURCES: Criticism, winter, 1969.

*   *   *

NYBERG, Kathleen Neill   1919-

PERSONAL: Born December 20, 1919, in Minneapolis, Minn.; daughter of Royal Delbert (a businessman) and Maybelle (Russell) Neill; married Dennis Fred Nyberg (a Methodist minister), July 10, 1941; children: Dennison Peer, Eric Neill. *Education:* Hamline University, student, 1938-41. *Politics:* Liberal. *Religion:* Protestant.

CAREER: Private secretary to church official in Minneapolis, Minn., 1937-38, and to executive secretary of New Haven (Conn.) Council of Churches, 1942-43; writer.

WRITINGS: The Care and Feeding of Ministers, Abingdon, 1961; *The New Eve,* Abingdon, 1967. Columnist, *Seminary Quarterly;* contributor to other religious periodicals.

WORK IN PROGRESS: Meditations While Meddling and Muddling (working title); research for a novel set in America in the late 1930's.††

*   *   *

OAKLEY, Stewart P(hilip)   1931-

PERSONAL: Born April 21, 1931, in Kenton, Middlesex, England; son of Frederick Heywood (a bank official) and Violet Elsie (White) Oakley; married Helen Condon, September 1, 1957; children: Karin Frances, Robin Charlotte, Tanya Gwyneth. *Education:* Lincoln College, Oxford, B.A., 1952, Dip.Ed., 1953, M.A., 1956; London School of Economics and Political Science, Ph.D., 1961. *Office:* School of European Studies, University of East Anglia, Norwich NOR 88C, England.

CAREER: Highgate (Junior) School, London, England, assistant housemaster, 1953-55; Bec School, Tooting, London, assistant master, 1955-57; Institute of Historical Research, London, fellow, 1958-59; University of Exeter, Exeter, England, tutor in history, 1959-60; University of Edinburgh, Edinburgh, Scotland, assistant lecturer, 1960-62, lecturer in modern European history, 1962-69; University of East Anglia, School of European Studies, Norwich, England, lecturer, 1969-73, senior lecturer, 1973—. Visiting associate professor, University of Minnesota, Minneapolis, 1966-67. *Member:* Historical Association of Great Britain, Association of University Teachers.

WRITINGS: The Story of Sweden, Faber, 1966, 2nd edition, 1969, published as *A Short History of Sweden,* Praeger, 1966; *The Story of Denmark,* Faber, 1972, published as *A Short History of Denmark,* Praeger, 1972.

WORK IN PROGRESS: A biography of Gustavus III of Sweden.

AVOCATIONAL INTERESTS: All aspects of Scandinavian life; music (especially eighteenth and twentieth century).†

* * *

O'BRIEN, Darcy 1939-

PERSONAL: Born July 16, 1939, in Los Angeles, Calif.; son of George J. (a film actor) and Margaret (Churchill) O'Brien; married Ruth Ellen Berke, August 26, 1961; children: Molly. *Education:* Princeton University, A.B., 1961; University of California, Berkeley, M.A., 1963, Ph.D., 1965; Pembroke College, Cambridge, graduate study, 1963-64. *Politics:* Independent. *Religion:* None. *Office:* Department of English, Pomona College, Claremont, Calif. 91711.

CAREER: Pomona College, Claremont, Calif., instructor, 1965-66, assistant professor, 1966-70, associate professor of English, 1970—. Resident fellow in Irish literature, Center for Advanced Study, 1969-70. *Member:* Modern Language Association of America, American Association of University Professors. *Awards, honors:* Woodrow Wilson and Fulbright fellowships.

WRITINGS: The Conscience of James Joyce, Princeton University Press, 1968; *W. R. Rodgers,* Bucknell University Press, 1971; *Patrick Kavanagh,* Bucknell University Press, 1975. Contributor to *Modern Fiction Studies.*

WORK IN PROGRESS: A novel, as yet untitled; *Ireland and Her Writers Today.*†

* * *

O'BRIEN, Patrick 1932-

PERSONAL: Born August 12, 1932, in London, England; son of William Patrick (a personnel manager) and Elizabeth (Stockhausen) O'Brien; married Cassy Cobham, April 15, 1959; children: Karen, Helen, Stephen. *Education:* London School of Economics and Political Science, B.Sc., 1958; Nuffield College, Oxford, D.Phil., 1960. *Politics:* Labour Party. *Religion:* Roman Catholic. *Home:* The Granary, Wellington St, Thame, Oxford, England. *Office:* St. Antony's College, Oxford University, Oxford, England.

CAREER: University of London, School of Oriental and African Studies, London, England, lecturer, 1960-67, reader in economics, 1968-70; Oxford University, Oxford, England, fellow of St. Antony's College and university lecturer in economic history, 1970—. *Military service:* British Army, 1948-50; became sergeant. *Member:* Royal Institute of International Affairs, Association of University Teachers, Economic History Association.

WRITINGS: The Revolution in Egypt's Economic System, Oxford University Press, 1966; (contributor) P. M. Holt, editor, *Political and Social Change in Modern Egypt,* Oxford Univeristy Press, 1968; (contributor) M.A. Cook, editor, *Studies in the Economic History of the Middle East from the Rise of Islam to the Present Day,* Oxford University Press, 1970; *Economic Growth in Britain and France from the Revolution to the Great War,* Allen & Unwin, in press; *The New Economic History of Railways,* Macmillan, in press. Contributor to journals.

WORK IN PROGRESS: English Public Finance, 1793-1815.

SIDELIGHTS: Patrick O'Brien reads French and Arabic. *Avocational interests:* English literature, films, theater, politics.

* * *

O'BRIEN, Sister Mary Celine 1922-

PERSONAL: Born June 2, 1922, in Troy, N.Y.; daughter of Arthur Edmund (a fireman) and Margaret (Collins) O'Brien. *Education:* College of St. Rose, B.E., 1952; State University of New York at Albany, M.S.L.S., 1962. *Politics:* Bipartisan. *Home:* 37 Johnston Ave., Cohoes, N.Y. 12047.

CAREER: Roman Catholic nun, member of Sisters of Mercy; teacher at parochial schools in Albany, Ilion, and Watervliet, N.Y., 1947-58; St. Bernard Academy, Cohoes, N.Y., librarian and teacher, beginning 1958. *Member:* Catholic Library Association, New York State Library Association.

WRITINGS: I Charge Each of You (biography of Dr. Dooley), Holy Cross Publications, 1966. Contributor of book reviews to *Response* (magazine).

WORK IN PROGRESS: A biography of Senator Robert F. Kennedy, for young people.

AVOCATIONAL INTERESTS: The theater, music, cooking.††

* * *

O'CONNOR, A(nthony) M(ichael) 1939-

PERSONAL: Born June 5, 1939, in London, England; son of John Louis and Marjorie (Atkinson) O'Connor; married Angela Mary Templeman, January 1, 1964; children: one son, one daughter. *Education:* Cambridge University, B.A., 1960, Ph.D., 1963. *Office:* Department of Geography, University College, University of London, London WC1E 6BT, England.

CAREER: Makerere University College, Kampala, Uganda, lecturer in geography, 1963-67; University of London, University College, London, England, lecturer in geography, 1967—. University of Ibadan, Ibadan, Nigeria, visiting lecturer, 1967, visiting senior lecturer, 1972-73. *Member:* Institute of British Geographers, Uganda Geographical Association (treasurer, 1965-67).

WRITINGS: Railways and Development in Uganda, Oxford University Press, 1965; *An Economic Geography of East Africa,* Praeger, 1966, 2nd edition, Bell, 1971; *The Geography of Tropical African Development,* Pergamon, 1971. Contributor to *Atlas of Uganda,* and to journals in his field. Editor, *East African Geographical Review,* 1966-67.

WORK IN PROGRESS: Gathering material for *Transport in Tropical Africa* and *Urban Development in East Africa.*†

* * *

O'CONNOR, Francis V(alentine) 1937-

PERSONAL: Born February 14, 1937, in Brooklyn, N.Y.; son of Frank J. (a bank clerk) and Blanche V. (Whalen) O'Connor. *Education:* Manhattan College, B.A., 1959; Johns Hopkins University, M.A., 1960, Ph.D., 1965. *Home:* 250 East 73rd St., Apt. 11C, New York, N.Y. 10021.

CAREER: University of Maryland, College Park, assistant professor of art history, 1964-70; Smithsonian Institution, National Collection of Fine Arts, Washington, D.C., senior visiting research associate, 1970-72. Assistant professor of art history, Evening College of Johns Hopkins University, 1966-67. Lecturer on twentieth-century American art throughout United States. *Member:* College Art Association, American Studies Association, American Society of Aesthetics, Authors Guild, Society for the Arts, Religion and Contemporary Culture (member of board of directors). *Awards, honors:* National Endowment for the Arts grant, 1967-68.

WRITINGS: Federal Art Patronage: 1933-1943, University of Maryland Art Gallery, 1966; *Jackson Pollock,* Museum of Modern Art (New York), 1967; *Federal Support for the Visual Arts: The New Deal and Now,* New York Graphic Society, 1969; (editor) *The New Deal Art Projects: An Anthology of Memoirs,* Smithsonian Institution Press, 1972; (editor) *Art for the Millions: Essays from the 1930s by Artists and Administrators of the WPA Federal Art Project,* New York Graphic Society, 1973. Contributor of articles to *Encyclopaedia Britannica, Cultural Affairs, Art Forum,* and *American Art Journal.*

WORK IN PROGRESS: A critical biography of the painter Jackson Pollock; a study of the dynamics of the creative and patronage process; editing a catalogue on Jackson Pollock's work, for Yale University Press.

SIDELIGHTS: Francis O'Connor has some competence in French, German, and Latin. He also writes poetry.

* * *

O'DONOGHUE, Joseph 1931-

PERSONAL: Born October 27, 1931; son of Mortimer P. (a policeman) and Catherine (Lynch) O'Donoghue. *Education:* Attended Catholic University of America.

CAREER: Roman Catholic priest.

WRITINGS: Elections in the Church, Helicon, 1966.

AVOCATIONAL INTERESTS: Flying (licensed pilot).

BIOGRAPHICAL/CRITICAL SOURCES: Commonweal, May 5, 1967.††

* * *

OFFER, Daniel 1929-

PERSONAL: Born December 24, 1929, in Berlin, Germany; son of Walter Hirsch (a physician) and Ilse (Meyer) Offer; married Judith Lynn Baskin (a research assistant), July 2, 1961; children: Raphael, Tamar. *Education:* University of Rochester, B.A., 1953; University of Chicago, M.D., 1957. *Religion:* Jewish. *Home:* 739 Walden Rd., Winnetka, Ill. 60093. *Office:* Michael Reese Hospital, 2959 South Ellis Ave., Chicago, Ill. 60616.

CAREER: University of Illinois Research and Educational Hospital, Urbana, Ill., intern, 1958; Michael Reese Hospital and Medical Center, Institute for Psychosomatic and Psychiatric Research and Training, Chicago, Ill., resident, 1961-64, associate director, 1964-74, co-chairman of Psychiatric Institute, 1974—. Consultant for Illinois Department of Mental Health. *Military service:* Israeli Army, 1948-50. *Member:* American Society for Adolescent Psychiatry (president, 1972-73), Illinois Psychiatric Society (chairman of membership committee, 1965-66), Chicago Society for Adolescent Psychiatry (secretary-treasurer, 1964-67; president, 1968-69), Institute of Medicine (fellow). *Awards, honors:* Center for Advanced Study of Education fellow.

WRITINGS: (With M. Sabshin) *Normality: Theoretical and Clinical Concepts of Mental Health,* Basic Books, 1966; (with Sabshin) *The Psychological World of the Teen-*

ager: A Study of Normal Adolescent Boys, Basic Books, 1969; (editor with J. F. Masterson) *Teaching and Learning Adolescent Psychiatry,* C. C Thomas, 1971; (editor with D. X. Freedman) *Modern Psychiatry and Clinical Research: Essays in Honor of Roy R. Grinker, Sr.,* Basic Books, 1972; (with wife, Judith Offer) *From Teenage to Young Manhood,* Basic Books, 1975. Editor-in-chief, *Journal of Youth and Adolescence.*

AVOCATIONAL INTERESTS: Music.

* * *

O'FLAHERTY, James C(arneal) 1914-

PERSONAL: Born April 28, 1914, in Henrico County, Va.; son of Daniel Cullers (an attorney) and Grace Virginia (Carneal) O'Flaherty; married Lucy Maupin Ribble (a portrait artist), February 4, 1936; children: James Daniel. *Education:* Student at College of William and Mary, 1933-36, University of Heidelberg, 1935, 1936, and Southern Baptist Theological Seminary, 1937-38; Georgetown College, B.A., 1939; University of Kentucky, M.A., 1941; University of Chicago, Ph.D., 1950. *Politics:* Democratic. *Home:* 2164 Faculty Dr., Winston-Salem, N.C. 27106. *Office:* Wake Forest University, Winston-Salem, N.C. 27109.

CAREER: Ordained Baptist minister, 1939; served as student pastor in Kentucky, 1939-42, and Chicago, Ill., 1942-47. Georgetown College, Georgetown, Ky., instructor in social sciences, 1939-41; high school teacher in Pleasureville, Ky., 1941-42; Wake Forest University, Winston-Salem, N.C., instructor, 1947-51, assistant professor, 1951-53, associate professor, 1953-58, professor of German, 1958—, chairman of department, 1961—, chairman of Institute of Literature, 1963-67. Chairman of advisory committee for postdoctoral Fulbright grants in German, committee on International Exchange of Persons, 1962-63. Member of academic advisory board, Schiller College, Wuerttemberg, Germany, 1965-66.

MEMBER: American Association of Teachers of German (president of North Carolina chapter, 1965-66), Phi Beta Kappa (honorary), Theta Delta Chi, Omicron Delta Kappa (honorary). *Awards, honors:* American Philosophical Society research grant to Germany, 1958; Fulbright grant to Germany, 1960-61.

WRITINGS: Unity and Language: A Study in the Philosophy of J. G. Hamann, University of North Carolina Press, 1952; *Socratic Form: A Study in Hamann's 'Socratic Memorabilia,'* Johns Hopkins Press, 1967; (contributor) Siegfried Mews, editor, *Studies in German Literature of the Nineteenth and Twentieth Centuries,* University of North Carolina Press, 1970; (contributor) R. B. Palmer and R. Hamerton-Kelly, editors, *Philomathes: Essays in the Humanities in Memory of Philip Merlan,* [The Hague], 1971; (co-author) *Raabe's "Else von der Tanne": A Translation and Commentary,* University of Alabama Press, 1972; (senior editor and contributor) *Studies in Nietzsche and the Classical Tradition,* University of North Carolina Press, 1975. Contributor to learned journals. Editor, *Hamann News-Letter,* 1953-55, 1962-63.

WORK IN PROGRESS: Introduction to Hamann's Life and Work, for Twayne's "World Authors' Series."

SIDELIGHTS: James O'Flaherty was attracted in his youth by what appeared to be "the greater idealism of German culture as opposed to the materialism and pragmatism of the Anglo-American tradition." As one still addicted to German literature, philosophy, and music, he says that he has "agonized a great deal about the paradox of the people who could produce Bach and Hitler, the *Kindergarten* and Buchenwald. My publications reflect to some extent my effort to resolve this paradox."

* * *

O'GORMAN, Gerald 1916-

PERSONAL: Born October 22, 1916, in London, England; married Joan Jennings; children: David, Anthony, Josephine. *Education:* University of London, M.R.C.S. and L.R.C.P., 1940; also D.P.M., 1946, M.R.C.P., 1948. *Home:* The Square House, Peppard, Oxford, England.

CAREER: Borocourt Hospital, Reading, England, consultant psychiatrist and physician-superintendent, beginning 1950. Consultant psychiatrist at Royal Berkshire Hospital, Reading, Smith's Hospital, Henley on Thames, England, and at Radcliffe Infirmary, Oxford, England; medical superintendent, Warneford Hospital, Oxford. *Military service:* Royal Army Medical Corps, 1941-46; became major. *Member:* Royal Society of Medicine (fellow), Royal College of Physicians, Royal College of Surgeons, Medico-Psychological Association.

WRITINGS: (Contributor) Howels, editor, *Modern Perspectives in Child Psychiatry,* Oliver & Boyd, 1965; *The Nature of Childhood Autism,* Appleton, 1967, 2nd edition, 1970; (editor) *Modern Trends in Mental Health and Subnormality,* Volume I, Butterworth, 1967, Appleton, 1968.

WORK IN PROGRESS: Investigations in psychodynamics of severe psychiatric disorders in children and young people.†

* * *

OKNER, Benjamin A. 1936-

PERSONAL: Born August 24, 1936, in Chicago, Ill.; son of Hyman and Sylvia (Chertob) Okner. *Education:* Illinois Institute of Technology, B.S., 1957; University of Michigan, M.A., 1960, Ph.D., 1965. *Home:* 1761 R St. N.W., Washington, D.C. 20009.

CAREER: U.S. Treasury Department, Washington, D.C., fiscal economist, Office of Tax Analysis, 1961-63; Brookings Institution, Washington, D.C., research associate, 1964; Council of Economic Advisers, Washington, D.C., staff economist, 1965-66; Ohio State University, Columbus, assistant professor of finance, 1966-68; Brookings Institution, senior fellow, 1968-75; Congressional Budget Office, Washington, D.C., deputy assistant director, 1975—.

WRITINGS: Income Distribution and the Federal Income Tax, Institute of Public Administration, University of Michigan, 1966 (with J. A. Pechman) *Who Bears the Tax Burden?* Brookings Institution, 1974; (contributor) Roger G. Noll, editor, *Government and the Sports Business,* Brookings Institution, 1974.

* * *

OLBY, Robert C(ecil) 1933-

PERSONAL: Born October 4, 1933, in Beckenham, Kent, England; son of Cecil A. (a builder's merchant) and Nesta (Paul) Olby; married Judy Potter (a teacher), September 1, 1962; children: Alastair, Louise, Natasha. *Education:* Imperial College of Science and Technology, London, B.Sc., 1955; Oxford University, D.Phil., 1962. *Home:* Beaconstones, Langbar, North Yorkshire, England. *Office:* Division of the History and Philosophy of Science, University of Leeds, Leeds LS2 9JT, England.

CAREER: Oxford University, Oxford, England, librarian at Botany School, 1962-69; University of Leeds, Leeds, England, lecturer in philosophy, 1969-75, reader in history of science, 1975—, acting head of Division of History and Philosophy of Science, 1974—.

WRITINGS: Origins of Mendelism, Constable, 1966; *Charles Darwin* (biography), Oxford University Press, 1967; *The Path to the Double Helix,* Macmillan (London), 1974, University of Washington Press, 1975.

WORK IN PROGRESS: Further research into the history of genetics.

* * *

OLIVA, Leo E. 1937-

PERSONAL: Born November 5, 1937, in Woodston, Kan.; son of E. I. (a farmer) and Lela (Miller) Oliva; married Marlene Causey, August 31, 1958 (divorced, 1975); children: Eric, Stephanie, Rex. *Education:* Fort Hays Kansas State College, A.B., 1959; University of Denver, M.A., 1960, Ph.D., 1964. *Address:* Box 113, Hays, Kan. 67601.

CAREER: Texas Wesleyan College, Fort Worth, assistant professor of history, 1962-64; Fort Hays Kansas State College, Hays, assistant professor, 1964-67, associate professor, 1967-69, professor of history, 1969—, acting chairman of department, 1966-67, chairman of department, 1967—. Partner in operation of wheat and maize farm in Kansas. *Member:* Organization of American Historians, Western Social Science Association, Kansas State Historical Society, Kansas Corral of the Westerners (sheriff, 1972), Phi Kappa Phi, Phi Alpha Theta, Pi Gamma Mu.

WRITINGS: Soldiers on the Santa Fe Trail, University of Oklahoma Press, 1967. Contributor of articles on western history and book reviews to magazines and journals.

WORK IN PROGRESS: Editing Philip St. George Cooke's *Scenes and Adventures in the Army (1857);* a military history of the Smoky Hill Trail; a study of the Indian in American literature; histories of Kansas frontier forts.

* * *

OLIVER, Mary 1935-

PERSONAL: Born September 10, 1935, in Cleveland, Ohio; daughter of Edward William (a teacher) and Helen M. (Vlasak) Oliver. *Education:* Attended Ohio State University for one year; also spent one year at Vassar College. *Home address:* Box 338, Provincetown, Mass. 02657.

CAREER: Worked at "Steepletop," the estate of Edna St. Vincent Millay, as secretary to the poet's sister, Norma Millay. Chairman of writing department at Fine Arts Work Center, Provinceton, Mass., 1972-73. *Member:* Poetry Society of America. *Awards, honors:* Poetry Society of America, first prize, 1962, for poem "No Voyage," Devil's Advocate Award, 1968, for poem "Christmas, 1966," Shelley Memorial Award, 1970, Alice Fay di Castagnola Award, 1973; National Endowment for the Arts fellow, 1972-73.

WRITINGS: No Voyage, and Other Poems, Dent, 1963, new edition, with nineteen additional poems, Houghton, 1965; *The River Styx, Ohio, and Other Poems,* Harcourt, 1972. Contributor of poetry to periodicals in England and the United States.

SIDELIGHTS: No Voyage, and Other Poems is "the work of a superlative craftsman who has genuine poetic sensibility," writes J. Bryan Hainsworth. He praises Miss

Oliver's appreciation for man's place in nature and says that she "has a great deal to offer anyone who has a capacity for being proud to be alive." Carl Johnson observes: "In the moderation of her stanzas there is residual strength and in her simplicity the discretion of a mature mind." Her poems are "made quietly moving by the specificity of a language demandingly her own," according to Philip Booth.

BIOGRAPHICAL/CRITICAL SOURCES: New Statesman, September 27, 1963; *Commonweal,* March 19, 1965; *Christian Science Monitor,* April 15, 1965; *Minnesota Review,* May-July, 1965; *Virginia Quarterly Review,* summer, 1965; *New York Times Book Review,* November 21, 1965.

* * *

OLLESTAD, Norman (Tennyson) 1935-

PERSONAL: Surname is pronounced Owl-stad; born September 7, 1935, in Los Angeles, Calif.; son of Norman Tennyson (a telephone company employee) and Oral (Pennington) Ollestad; married Dori Carlson, July 28, 1963 (divorced, 1973); children: Norman III. *Education:* University of California, Los Angeles, B.A., 1957, LL.B., 1960. *Politics:* Democrat. *Home:* 3731 South Topanga Canyon, Malibu, Calif. 90265.

CAREER: Actor in motion pictures and television, 1943-60; Federal Bureau of Investigation, Miami, Fla., special agent, 1960-61; assistant U.S. attorney, Los Angeles, Calif., 1961-63; attorney in private practice, Santa Monica, Calif., 1963—. Special hearing officer, U.S. Department of Justice, 1966—. Member of University of California's Project India team, touring India and Indian universities under U.S. Department of State sponsorship, 1967. *Member:* California Bar Association, Los Angeles Bar Association, Santa Monica Bar Association.

WRITINGS: Inside the FBI, Lyle Stuart, 1967.

WORK IN PROGRESS: Outside the FBI.

SIDELIGHTS: Ollestad's *Inside the FBI,* which gives an unflattering picture of J. Edgar Hoover and Federal Bureau of Investigation training, brought about his expulsion from the Society of Former Special Agents of the FBI. The *New York Times* said that the society's executive committee expelled Ollestad for writing a book "detrimental to the good name or best interests of the society."

BIOGRAPHICAL/CRITICAL SOURCES: New York Times, August 1, 1967.

* * *

OLM, Kenneth W(illiam) 1924-

PERSONAL: Born February 5, 1924, in Green Bay, Wis.; son of Erwin Louis and Edith (Hinkel) Olm; married Jane Gray, February 7, 1948 (divorced, 1973); children: Kenneth W., Jr., David L., Robert L., Fred J. *Education:* Lawrence University, student, 1941-43; Pomona College, B.A., 1947; University of New Mexico, M.A., 1948; University of Texas, Ph.D., 1958. *Politics:* Republican (liberal). *Religion:* Episcopalian. *Home:* 4606 Shoal Creek Blvd., Austin, Tex. 78756.

CAREER: University of Texas, El Paso, instructor in economics and business administration, 1948-53; University of Texas, Austin, lecturer, 1953-55, assistant professor, 1955-60, associate professor of management, 1960—. Visiting professor, University of New Mexico, 1966-67. Self-employed business consultant. Member of board of directors,

Citizens National Bank of Austin; chairman of board of University Cooperative Society, Austin. *Military service:* U.S. Army Air Forces, 1943. *Member:* Academy of Management (member of national board of governors and president of Southwest division, 1965-66), American Institute of Industrial Engineers, Southwest Social Science Association, Southern Economic Association. *Awards, honors:* Ford Foundation fellowship to Harvard Business School, 1960.

WRITINGS: (With Francis J. Bridges) *Business Policy: Cases, Incidents and Readings,* Allyn & Bacon, 1966; (with Bridges and J. A. Barnhill) *Management Decisions and Organizational Policy: Text, Cases and Incidents,* Allyn & Bacon, 1971. Contributor to professional journals. Associate editor, *Quarterly* of Southwest Social Science Association.

WORK IN PROGRESS: A text on small business management, completion expected in 1976; revision of *Management Decisions and Organizational Policy.*

* * *

OLSON, Mildred Thompson 1922-

PERSONAL: Born January 14, 1922, in Colman, S.D.; daughter of Martin (a farmer) and Margretha (Christensen) Thompson; married Wayne E. Olson (a minister and teacher), June 18, 1944; children: Ronnalee Gayle, David Wayne, Rebecca Gay, Ronda Lynn. *Education:* Attended Columbia Union College, Takoma Park, Md., 1941-42, 1953-54, Union College, Lincoln, Neb., 1942-43, and University of Missouri, 1972-73. *Religion:* Seventh-day Adventist. *Address:* Sunnydale Academy, Centralia, Mo. 65240.

CAREER: With her husband, was a Seventh-day Adventist missionary in the Middle East for seventeen years; elementary teacher in Beirut, Lebanon, 1954-57, 1959-60, 1962-64, and in Baghdad, Iraq, 1957-59; H.M.S. Richards School, Loveland, Colo., elementary teacher, 1965-71; Sunnydale Academy, Centralia, Mo., teacher of journalism, and librarian, 1971-76.

WRITINGS: Diamondola, Review & Herald, 1966.

WORK IN PROGRESS: A sequel to *Diamondola,* tentatively entitled *Diamondola and Aram;* a children's book on poodles.

SIDELIGHTS: The Olsons and their two older children speak Arabic, and can manage some German, Danish, and Italian. They have driven through Europe from the Middle East several times, were caught in the 1958-59 revolution in Iraq, and were shot at by bandits in southeast Iran in 1964.

* * *

OLSON, Paul R(ichard) 1925-

PERSONAL: Born November 2, 1925, in Rockford, Ill.; son of Oscar Wilhelm (a laborer) and Jenny (Taube) Olson; married Phyllis Edwards (a musician), January 10, 1953; children: Thomas, John, Carl, Andrew. *Education:* University of Illinois, A.B., 1950; Harvard University, Ph.D., 1959. *Politics:* Liberal Democrat. *Office:* Department of Romance Languages, Johns Hopkins University, Baltimore, Md. 21218.

CAREER: Dartmouth College, Hanover, N.H., instructor, 1956-59, assistant professor of Spanish, 1959-61; Johns Hopkins University, Baltimore, Md., assistant professor, 1961-63, associate professor, 1963-68, professor of Spanish, 1968—. *Member:* Modern Language Association of America, Asociacion Internacional de Hispanistas, American Association of Teachers of Spanish and Portuguese. *Awards, honors:* Guggenheim fellowship, 1964-65.

WRITINGS: Circle of Paradox: Time and Essence in the Poetry of Juan Ramon Jimenez, Johns Hopkins Press, 1967. Contributor to language journals.

WORK IN PROGRESS: Research on the novels of Miguel de Unamuno.

* * *

O'NEILL, Charles Edwards 1927-

PERSONAL: Born November 16, 1927, in New Orleans, La.; son of John Henry (a public health engineer) and Albion (Edwards) O'Neill. *Education:* Spring Hill College, A.B., 1950; Institut St.-Louis, Chantilly, France, S.T.L., 1958; Gregorian University, Rome, Italy, Ph.D., 1963. *Office:* Loyola University, New Orleans, La. 70118.

CAREER: Ordained Roman Catholic priest, 1957, member of Society of Jesus (Jesuits). Instructor in history at Jesuit High School, New Orleans, La., 1951-54, Loyola University, New Orleans, 1961-62, and St. Charles College, Grand Coteau, La., 1964; Loyola University, New Orleans, assistant professor, 1965-67, associate professor, 1967-71, professor of history, 1971—. *Member:* Organization of American Historians, American Catholic Historical Association, Louisiana Historical Association, Delta Epsilon Sigma, Alpha Pi Omicron. *Awards, honors:* Chevalier des Palmes Academiques, 1968; award of merit, Outstanding Educators of America, 1970.

WRITINGS: Church and State in French Colonial Louisiana, Yale University Press, 1966; (editor with E. J. Burrus, J. de la Pena, and M. T. Garcia) *Catalogo de documentos sobre la epoca espanola de Luisiana, Seccion de Gobierno del Archivo General de Indias,* Loyola University (New Orleans) and Spanish Archives, 1968; (contributor) *Sacrae Congregationist de Propaganda Fide Memorial Rerum 1622-1972,* Freiburg, Volume I, 1972, Volume II, 1974; (author of foreword) Rodolphe L. Desdunes, *Our People and Our History,* translated by D. O. McCants, Louisiana State University Press, 1973; (contributor) *Spain and the Mississippi Valley,* University of Illinois Press, 1974. Contributor to *Dictionary of Canadian Biography;* also contributor to *Louisiana History* and *America.* Contributor of book reviews to magazines and history journals.

WORK IN PROGRESS: Research on colonial Mississippi Valley missions, and on French culture in Louisiana.

SIDELIGHTS: Charles O'Neill speaks French and Italian, reads Greek, German, and Portuguese.

* * *

O'NEILL, John Joseph 1920-

PERSONAL: Born December 6, 1920, in De Pere, Wis.; son of John J. (a physician) and Elizabeth (Murray) O'Neill; married Dorothy Arnold, December 28, 1943; children: Katherine, Thomas, John, Philip. *Education:* Wisconsin State College—Oshkash, student, 1938-41; Ohio State University, B.S. in Ed., 1947, Ph.D., 1951. *Politics:* Democrat. *Religion:* Roman Catholic. *Home:* 1113 West Church, Champaign, Ill. 61820. *Office:* Speech and Hearing Clinic, University of Illinois, 505 East Green, Champaign, Ill. 61820.

CAREER: Ohio State University, Columbus, instructor, 1949-51, assistant professor, 1951-56, associate professor of

speech and hearing, 1956-59, also assistant professor in School of Medicine, 1955-59; University of Illinois, Urbana, professor of speech and hearing science, 1959—, acting head of department, 1968-69, head of department, 1973—. Research associate, U.S. Naval School of Aviation Medicine, summers, 1953, 1954. Consultant to North American Aviation, 1957-59, and U.S. Air Force School of Aviation Medicine, 1960-62. President of American Board of Examiners in Speech Pathology and Audiology, 1967-68. *Military service:* U.S. Army, Infantry, 1942-45; became sergeant; received Bronze star, with oak-leaf cluster, and Purple Heart. *Member:* American Speech and Hearing Association (fellow; president, 1969), Academy of Rehabilitative Audiology (president, 1969), Acoustical Society of America, American Psychological Association, Illinois Speech and Hearing Association (vice-president, 1960).

WRITINGS: (With H. J. Oyer) *Visual Communication for Hard of Hearing,* Prentice-Hall, 1961; *The Hard of Hearing,* Prentice-Hall, 1964; (with H. J. Oyer) *Applied Audiometry,* Dodd, 1966; (contributor) J. Jerger, editor, *Modern Developments in Audiology,* 2nd edition (O'Neill not associated with earlier edition), 1973; (contributor) S. Singh, editor, *Measurement Procedures in Speech, Hearing and Language,* University Park Press, 1975. Contributor to medical and speech journals.

AVOCATIONAL INTERESTS: Model railroading, collecting jazz records.

* * *

O'NEILL, Patrick Geoffrey 1924-

PERSONAL: Born August 9, 1924, in London, England. *Education:* School of Oriental and African Studies, University of London, B.A., 1949, Ph.D., 1957.

CAREER: University of London, School of Oriental and African Studies, London, England, lecturer, 1949-67, professor of Japanese, 1968.

WRITINGS: A Guide to No, Hinoki Shoten (Tokyo), 1954; *Early No Drama,* Lund, Humphries, 1958; (with S. Yanada) *An Introduction to Written Japanese,* English Universities Press, 1963; *A Programmed Course on Respect Language in Modern Japanese,* English Universities Press, 1966; *Japanese Kana Workbook,* Kodansha International (Tokyo), 1967; *A Programmed Introduction to Literary-Style Japanese,* University of London, 1968; *Japanese Names,* Weatherhill, 1972; *Essential Kanji,* Weatherhill, 1973.

WORK IN PROGRESS: Modern Japanese Plays, a book of translations; the writings of Zeami on No drama.

* * *

O'NEILL, William L. 1935-

PERSONAL: Born April 18, 1935, in Big Rapids, Mich.; son of John Patrick (an oil and gas contractor) and Helen (Marsh) O'Neill; married E. Carol Knollmueller, August 20, 1960; children: Cassandra Leigh, Catherine Lorraine. *Education:* University of Michigan, A.B., 1957; University of California, Berkeley, M.A., 1958, Ph.D., 1963. *Home:* 21 Olden Rd., Edison, N.J. *Office:* Department of History, Rutgers University, New Brunswick, N.J.

CAREER: University of Pittsburgh, Pittsburgh, Pa., visiting assistant professor of history, 1963-64; University of Colorado, Boulder, assistant professor of history, 1964-66; University of Wisconsin-Madison, assistant professor, 1966-69, associate professor of history, 1969-71; Rutgers

University, New Brunswick, N.J., professor of history, 1971—. Visiting associate professor, University of Pennsylvania, 1969-71. *Military service:* U.S. Army Reserve, 1960-66 (six months active duty). *Member:* American Historical Association, Organization of American Historians, American Studies Association, Phi Beta Kappa.

WRITINGS: Divorce in the Progressive Era, Yale University Press, 1967; *Everyone Was Brave: The Rise and Fall of Feminism in America,* Quadrangle, 1969; *The Woman Movement: Feminism in the United States and England,* Barnes & Noble, 1969; *Coming Apart: An Informal History of America in the 1960's,* Quadrangle, 1971; (co-author) *Looking Backward: A Re-introduction to American History,* McGraw, 1974; *The Progressive Years: America Comes of Age,* Dodd, 1975.

Editor: *Echoes of Revolt: The Masses 1911 to 1917,* Quadrangle, 1966; *American Society since Nineteen Forty-Five,* Quadrangle, 1969; *Women at Work,* Quadrangle, 1972; *The American Sexual Dilemma,* Holt, 1972; *Insights and Parallels: Problems and Issues in American Social History,* Burgess, 1973. Contributor to professional journals.

* * *

OPDAHL, Richard D(ean) 1924-

PERSONAL: Born February 26, 1924, in Lake Mills, Iowa; son of Joseph Engvald and Selma (Rholl) Opdahl; married Helen Joyce Bennington, June 15, 1957; children: Steven, David. *Education:* Attended University of Oregon, 1943-44; Harvard University, A.B., 1948; University of California, Los Angeles, graduate study, 1948-49; Long Beach State College (now California State University, Long Beach), M.A., 1951. *Politics:* Democrat. *Religion:* Lutheran. *Home:* 4181 Morning Star Dr., Huntington Beach, Calif. 92647.

CAREER: Long Beach (Calif.) Unified School District, teacher of English and social studies, 1951-61; Long Beach City College, Long Beach, Calif., member of faculty, 1961—. *Military service:* U.S. Army Air Forces, 1943-46; became sergeant. *Member:* California Teachers Association. *Awards, honors:* Architectural awards, for house built in 1957, from American Institute of Architects, *Sunset* (magazine), and City of Los Angeles.

WRITINGS: Pattern and Purpose: A Handbook of Grammar, Usage, and Style, Dickenson, 1967; (editor) *Illusion and Reality: An Introduction to the Short Story,* Dickenson, 1968.

* * *

OPLER, Marvin K(aufmann) 1914-

PERSONAL: Born June 13, 1914, in Buffalo, N.Y.; son of Arthur (a businessman) and Fanny (Coleman-Haas) Opler; married Charlotte Fox (a student counselor and vocational specialist), December 30, 1935; children: Ruth Opler Perry, Lewis Alan. *Education:* Attended University of Buffalo, 1931-33; University of Michigan, A.B., 1935; Columbia University, Ph.D., 1938. *Home:* 61 Heritage Road E., Buffalo, N.Y. 14221. *Office:* Department of Anthropology, State University of New York at Buffalo, Buffalo, N.Y. 14226.

CAREER: Reed College, Portland, Ore., chairman of department of anthropology and sociology, 1938-43; U.S. Department of the Interior, Washington, D.C., chief of community analysis section, War Relocation Authority, 1943-45; Occidental College, Los Angeles, Calif., professor of anthropology and sociology, 1946-47; Stanford University, Stanford, Calif., associate professor of anthropology, 1948-50; Harvard University, Cambridge, Mass., associate professor of anthropology and social relations, 1950-52; Cornell University Medical College, New York, N.Y., professor of anthropology and social psychiatry, and principal investigator for midtown Manhattan mental health research study, 1952-58; State University of New York at Buffalo, professor of social psychiatry in School of Medicine, and professor of sociology and anthropology in Graduate School, 1958—, chairman of anthropology department, 1969-72. Co-founder and lecturer, Institute of Psychoanalysis, Los Angeles, 1946-48; visiting professor at William Alanson White Foundation, 1957-59, New School for Social Research, 1957-58, Tulane University of Louisiana, University of Hawaii, and other universities.

MEMBER: International Association of Social Psychiatry (organizing member), American Anthropological Association (fellow), American Sociological Association, Academy of Psychoanalysis, Northeastern Anthropological Association (first president, 1965-66), Sigma Xi. *Awards, honors:* Social Science Research Council fellowship and award, 1946, 1949; Wenner-Gren Foundation for Anthropological Research grants.

WRITINGS: Culture, Psychiatry and Human Values, C. C Thomas, 1956; (co-author) *Symposium on Preventive and Social Psychiatry,* Walter Reed Institute of Research, 1958; (editor and co-author) *Culture and Mental Health,* Macmillan, 1959; (with L. Srole, T. Sanger, S. Michael, and T.A.C. Rennie) *Mental Health in the Metropolis: The Midtown Manhattan Study,* McGraw, 1962; *Culture and Social Psychiatry,* Atherton, 1967; (with E. Spicer and K. Luamala) *Impounded People,* University of Arizona Press, 1969; (contributor) *Modern Perspectives in International Child Psychiatry,* Oliver & Boyd, 1969; (contributor) *North American Indians in Historical Perspective,* Random House, 1971. Contributor to professional journals. Associate editor, *International Journal of Social Psychiatry,* 1957-58, editor, 1958—; associate editor of *American Anthropologist,* 1962-65, and *Psychosomatics.*

WORK IN PROGRESS: Studies in transcultural and community psychiatry, the evolution of culture, and the evolution of behavioral pathology.

* * *

OPPENHEIM, Joanne 1934-

PERSONAL: Born May 11, 1934, in Middletown, N.Y.; daughter of Abe P. (an electrical engineer) and Helen (Jassem) Fleischer; married Stephen Oppenheim (a lawyer), June 27, 1954; children: James, Anthony, Stephanie. *Education:* Attended University of Miami, 1951-52, and Sarah Lawrence College, 1952-54; Sarah Lawrence College, B.A., 1960. *Home:* Sackett Lake Rd., Box 29, Monticello, N.Y.

CAREER: Teacher in primary grades, Monticello, N.Y., 1960—. Member of Writer's Laboratory, Bank Street College, 1962—. *Awards, honors:* Outstanding Teachers of America award, 1973.

WRITINGS: Have You Seen Trees? W. R. Scott, 1967; *Have You Seen Birds?* W. R. Scott, 1968; (with G. Nook) *Have You Seen Roads?* W. R. Scott, 1969; *Have You Seen Boats?* W. R. Scott, 1971; *On the Other Side of the River,* F. Watts, 1972; *Have You Seen Houses?* W. R. Scott, 1973. Contributor to "Bank Street Readers", Macmillan, 1965.

WORK IN PROGRESS: Have You Seen Clothes?

* * *

OPPENHEIMER, Paul 1939-

PERSONAL: Born May 1, 1939, in New York, N.Y. *Education:* Princeton University, B.A., 1961; Columbia University, M.A., 1962, Ph.D., 1969.

CAREER: Has worked as an ice cream salesman, a printer's devil, and an editor in two publishing houses; Hunter College of the City University of New York, New York City, lecturer in English, 1964-67; City College of the City University of New York, New York City, lecturer, 1967-68, assistant professor, 1970-74, associate professor of English, 1974—. Alfred Hadder fellow, Princeton University, 1969. *Awards, honors:* Academy of American Poets Prize, Princeton University, 1961, 1962.

WRITINGS: Before a Battle, and Other Poems, Harcourt, 1967; (translator and author of introduction and critical appendix) *A Pleasant Vintage of Till Eulenspiegel,* Wesleyan University Press, 1972.

WORK IN PROGRESS: A novel, *The Garden of Deathly Delights; After Various Killings and Other Poems.*

SIDELIGHTS: Oppenheimer writes to *CA:* "My professional passions are twofold: to study medieval literature, in its various languages; and to create modern literature, in poems and plays. The ideal which guides these passions may be found in the foreword to my first book, *Before a Battle.* The battle is to rescue life from abstraction. We are before the battle because, whenever we win it, we discover that we've won it for a moment only and that the battle must be fought again." Phillip Booth notes that Oppenheimer's "title poem is fine, and tellingly promises the poems he has yet to write." Thomas Lask writes: "The work of Paul Oppenheimer is . . . contemplative. He likes to frame the occasion, abstract it from time and place and ponder over it. The reader is always aware of a mind hovering over the material. He is, also, a true child of his times. Madness, betrayal, murder are intrinsic in the themes he is celebrating. The bone is never far below the flesh."

Oppenheimer is fluent in German and Italian and has good knowledge of Latin, Spanish, Dutch, Anglo-Saxon, and French.

BIOGRAPHICAL/CRITICAL SOURCES: New York Times, September 9, 1967; *Christian Science Monitor,* November 9, 1967; *New Yorker,* December, 1972.

* * *

OPTON, Edward M., Jr. 1936-

PERSONAL: Born June 12, 1936, in New York, N.Y.; son of Edward M. and Carolyn (Brown) Opton; married, March 23, 1963. *Education:* Yale University, B.A., 1957; Duke University, Ph.D., 1964. *Office:* The Wright Institute, 2728 Durant Ave., Berkeley, Calif. 94704.

CAREER: North Carolina College at Durham (now North Carolina Central University), visiting instructor in psychology, 1962-63; University of California, Berkeley, assistant research psychologist, 1963-66, associate research psychologist and lecturer, 1966-69; The Wright Institute, Berkeley, senior research psychologist and associate dean of Graduate School, 1969—. Lecturer in psychology, San Francisco State College (now California State University, San Francisco), 1965. *Member:* American Psychological Association, Society for Psychophysiological Research.

WRITINGS: (Contributor) C. D. Spielberger, editor, *Anxiety and Behavior,* Academic Press, 1966; (editor with R. S. Lazarus) *Personality* (readings), Penguin, 1967; (contributor) *Advances in Psychological Assessment,* Science and Behavior Books, 1968. Contributor to *Psychosomatic Medicine, Journal of Gerontology, Psychophysiology,* and other journals.

* * *

O'QUINN, Garland 1935-

PERSONAL: Born July 1, 1935, in Fort Worth, Tex.; son of Garland D. and Mona (Murray) O'Quinn; married Josie Lu Bird (a nurse), May 13, 1961; children: Danny, Lanita. *Education:* U.S. Military Academy, B.S., 1958; Southern Illinois University, M.S., 1963; Pennsylvania State University, Ph.D., 1971. *Home:* 3614 Quiette Dr., Austin, Tex. 78754. *Office:* University of Texas, Austin, Tex.

CAREER: U.S. Army, regular officer, 1958-61, serving as instructor in physical education and assistant gymnastic coach at U.S. Military Academy, West Point, N.Y., 1959-61; Eastern New Mexico University, Portales, instructor in physical education and gymnastic coach, 1963-67; University of Texas at Austin, assistant professor of health and physical education, 1971—. Director of gymnastic program, Portales (N.M.) Recreation Department, 1963-67. Member of U.S. Olympic gymnastic team, Rome, Italy, 1960, and Pan-American gymnastic team, Sao Paulo, Brazil, 1963; participated in U.S. cultural exchange trips to Middle East and Russia, 1961. *Member:* American Association for Health, Physical Education and Recreation. *Awards, honors:* Amateur Athletic Union national side horse champion, 1960; Pan-American side horse champion, 1963.

WRITINGS: Gymnastics for Elementary School Children, W. C. Brown, 1967. Also author of *Developmental Gymnastics: Tumbling Table,* and *Developmental Gymnastics: Tumbling Mats,* both 1973 for Physical Fun Products.

WORK IN PROGRESS: Gymnastics for Physical Education Majors.

* * *

ORTH, Ralph H(arry) 1930-

PERSONAL: Born October 5, 1930, in New York, N.Y.; son of August (a cabinetmaker) and Anna (Brett) Orth; married Audrey Arnold, December 17, 1955 (separated, 1973); children: Steven, Carol, Thomas. *Education:* Queens College (now Queens College of the City University of New York), B.A., 1956; University of Rochester, Ph.D., 1960. *Home:* 30A University Heights, Burlington, Vt. 05401. *Office:* Department of English, University of Vermont, Burlington, Vt. 05401.

CAREER: University of Vermont, Burlington, instructor, 1959-61, assistant professor, 1961-66, associate professor, 1966-70, professor of English, 1970—. *Military service:* U.S. Army, 1951-53. *Member:* Modern Language Association of America, American Association of University Professors.

WRITINGS: (Editor) *The Journals and Miscellaneous Notebooks of Ralph Waldo Emerson,* Harvard University Press, Volume VI, 1966, Volume IX (with Alfred R. Ferguson), 1971, Volume XIII (with Ferguson), 1976; (contributor) J. Albert Robbins, editor, *American Literary Scholarship, 1972,* Duke University Press, 1974. Contributor of articles on American literature to scholarly journals. Member of editorial board, *Journals and Miscellaneous*

Writings of Ralph Waldo Emerson, and *Works of Ralph Waldo Emerson;* Vermont co-ordinator, *American Literary Manuscripts.*

AVOCATIONAL INTERESTS: Outdoors activities, including hiking, biking, boating, and camping.

* * *

OSBORN, Arthur W(alter) 1891-

PERSONAL: Born March 10, 1891, in London, England; son of Walter Osborn; married Mary E. Wilkinson, December 4, 1936 (died, 1971); married Margaret Horgan, 1973. *Education:* Educated privately in England. *Home:* 11 Glen Shian Lane, Mt. Eliza, Victoria, Australia 3930.

CAREER: Representative of British firm in Dutch East Indies, 1913-14; executive of British firm in Australia, 1920-54; writer. *Military service:* British Army, Royal Field Artillery, 1914-18; received Military Cross and was mentioned twice in dispatches. *Member:* English Society for Psychical Research.

WRITINGS: Occultism, Christian Science and Healing, Ruskin (Australia), 1926; *The Superphysical: A Review of the Evidence for Continued Existence, Reincarnation, and Mystical States of Consciousness,* Nicholson & Watson, 1937, reprinted, Barnes & Noble, 1974; *The Expansion of Awareness: One Man's Search for Meaning in Living,* Omega Press, 1955, Theosophical Publishing, 1961; *The Axis and the Rim: The Quest for Reality in a Modern Setting,* Vincent Stuart, 1963, Theosophical Publishing, 1967; *The Future Is Now: The Significance of Precognition,* University Books, 1961; *The Meaning of Personal Existence in the Light of Paranormal Phenomena: The Doctrine of Reincarnation and Mystical States of Consciousness,* Sidgwick & Jackson, 1966, Theosophical Publishing, 1967; *The Expansion of Awareness,* Theosophical Publishing, 1967; *The Cosmic Womb: An Interpretation of Man's Relationship to the Infinite,* Theosophical Publishing, 1969; *What Am I Living For?,* Turnstone Press, 1974. Contributor of articles to various journals.

WORK IN PROGRESS: The Mystic and the Worldling.

SIDELIGHTS: Osborn told *CA:* "Am in sympathy with many religious attitudes but do not belong to any religion, sect, or society. The search for truth has been my governing motivation and this has caused me to explore widely." Osborn has traveled in the United States, Canada, Europe, Southeast Asia, and India. Translations of several of his books have been published in South America and Italy.

BIOGRAPHICAL/CRITICAL SOURCES: Books and Bookmen, March, 1968.

* * *

OSBORN, Robert T(appan) 1926-

PERSONAL: Born June 23, 1926, in Seattle, Wash.; son of George Roger (a businessman) and Helen (Bushee) Osborn; married Dorothy Jean Hurley (a librarian), December 21, 1951; children: Christopher Robert, Jeffrey Tappan, Douglas Hurley. *Education:* Attended University of Washington, 1943-44; University of California, Los Angeles, A.B., 1946; Garrett Theological Seminary, B.D., 1950; University of Zurich, graduate study, 1950-51; Drew University, Ph.D., 1955. *Politics:* Independent. *Home:* 2732 McDowell St., Durham, N.C. 27705.

CAREER: Duke University, Durham, N.C., instructor,

1954-63, associate professor of religion, 1963—. Fulbright grant, University of Tubingen, 1968-69. ·*Military service:* U.S. Navy, 1943-46; became lieutenant junior grade. *Member:* American Academy of Religion (regional president, 1973-74), Omicron Delta Kappa, Durham Toastmasters.

WRITINGS: Freedom in Modern Theology, Westminster, 1967. Contributor to *Christian Century, Canadian Journal of Theology,* and other journals in his field.

AVOCATIONAL INTERESTS: Sailing.

* * *

OSBORNE, Chester G. 1915-

PERSONAL: Born September 18, 1915, in Portsmouth, N.H.; son of James Chester (a pianist and composer) and Viola (also a musician; maiden name, Cofman) Osborne; married Mary Rooney, April 26, 1943; children: Maureen (Mrs. Frank Pagano), Patricia (Mrs. Donald Feiler), Virginia (Mrs. Mark Mesiano), James, Kevin. *Education:* New England Conservatory of Music, Mus.B., 1937; Northwestern University, Mus.M., 1950. *Home address:* Box 517, Center Moriches, Long Island, N.Y. 11934.

CAREER: Boston Symphony Orchestra, and other orchestras, Boston, Mass., trumpeter, 1935-38; Center Moriches High School, Center Moriches, N.Y., member of faculty, 1938—. Writer of children's books. Curator of manuscripts, Manor of St. George (public museum), Mastic, N.Y. Founder of Center Moriches Music Award Association. *Military service:* U.S. Army, 1942-46; became staff sergeant. *Member:* Music Educators National Conference (life member), New York State Teachers Association, New York State School Music Association (adjudicator). *Awards, honors:* Gold Medal, Boys' Clubs of America, for *The First Lake Dwellers.*

WRITINGS: The First Bow and Arrow, Follett, 1951; *The First Puppy,* Follett, 1953; *The First Lake Dwellers,* Follett, 1956; *The First Wheel,* Follett, 1959; *The Wind and the Fire,* Prentice-Hall, 1959; *The Silver Anchor,* Follett, 1967. Contributor to *Encyclopedia Americana;* contributor of articles on regional history, stories, and plays to *Children's Playmate, Instructor, Junior Natural History,* and other periodicals. Contributing editor, *Long Island Forum.*

Musical compositions: "Treasure Island" (overture for band), Mills Music; "British Eighth" (march), National Educational Music Publishers; "I See the Moon" and "Dumb, Dumb, Dumb" (two songs), Elkan-Vogel, 1973; "Connemara Sketches" (for band), William Allen Music, 1975; "Solos and Ensembles for Snare Drum," Elkan-Vogel, 1976.

WORK IN PROGRESS: A novel, tentatively entitled, *The White Tree.*

BIOGRAPHICAL/CRITICAL SOURCES: New York Sunday News, October 4, 1964.

* * *

OSBORNE, G(erald) S(tanley) 1926-

PERSONAL: Born January 29, 1926, in Birmingham, England; son of Joseph Liggins (a lawyer) and Phoebe (Hiatt) Osborne; married Frances Slicher, April 19, 1949; children: Nicholas John, Hugh Robert, Sarah Frances. *Education:* Cambridge University, M.A., 1947; University of London, LL.B., 1952. *Home:* 7 Bayview Rd., Aberdeen, Scotland. *Office:* Aberdeen College of Education, Aberdeen, Scotland.

CAREER: Teacher in England, 1947-49; Ministry of Education, London, England, assistant principal, 1949-50; Commonwealth Relations Office, London, assistant principal, 1950-51; Cornwall County Council, Truro, England, administrative assistant, 1951-53; Derbyshire County Council, Matlock, England, assistant director of education, 1953-61; Aberdeen College of Education, Aberdeen, Scotland, vice-principal, beginning 1961.

WRITINGS: Scottish and English Schools, Longmans, Green, 1966, University of Pittsburgh Press, 1967; Change in Scottish Education, Humanities, 1968.

WORK IN PROGRESS: Secondary Education in Transition, a study of comprehensive reorganization in Scotland, 1968-1975.††

*   *   *

OSBORNE, Leone Neal   1914-

PERSONAL: Born September 25, 1914, in Toledo, Ore.; daughter of Frederick Miles and Virginia (Daniel) Neal; married William Lloyd Osborne (a retired colonel, U.S. Army), January 25, 1941; children: Patricia Diane, Jeanette. Education: Took creative writing courses at University of California, Los Angeles, 1942-43, and American University, 1949-50. Politics: Republican. Religion: Protestant. Home: 1084 Presidio Rd., Pebble Beach, Calif. 93953.

WRITINGS: Than Hoa of Viet-Nam (juvenile), McGraw, 1966.

WORK IN PROGRESS: The White Elephant of Angkor Wat; and Valley of the Blue Sheep.

SIDELIGHTS: As an Army wife, Leone Osborne traveled extensively in the Far East and Europe. Avocational interests: Painting.

*   *   *

OSBORNE, Richard Horsley   1925-

PERSONAL: Born April 25, 1925, in Etwall, Derbyshire, England. Education: University of London, B.Sc., 1950, Ph.D., 1954. Office: Department of Geography, University of Nottingham, Nottingham, England.

CAREER: University of Nottingham, Nottingham, England, member of department of geography.

WRITINGS: East-Central Europe: A Geographical Introduction to Seven Socialist States, Chatto & Windus, 1967.

*   *   *

OSMOND, Humphrey (Fortescue)   1917-

PERSONAL: Born July 1, 1917, in Surrey, England; son of George William Forbes (a captain, Royal Navy) and Dorothy (Gray) Osmond; married Amy Edith Roffey, November 12, 1947; children: Helen Lavinia, Euphemia Janet, Julian Fortescue. Education: Studies at Haileybury and Imperial Service College, then at Guy's Hospital Medical School, University of London, 1936-42; qualified for M.R.C.S. and L.R.C.P., 1949; also holds Diploma of Psychological Medicine. Politics: "Labour Party supporter (England)." Religion: Anglican. Address: Bureau of Research in Neurology and Psychiatry, New Jersey Neurological and Psychiatric Institute, Box 1000, Princeton, N.J. 08540.

CAREER: St. Georges Hospital, London, England, first assistant, 1948-51; Saskatchewan Hospital, Department of Psychiatry, Weyburn, Saskatchewan, clinical director, 1951-53, physician superintendent and director of research,

1958-61; New Jersey Neurological and Psychiatric Institute, Princeton, N.J., director of Bureau of Research in Neurology and Psychiatry, 1963—. Lecturer on schizophrenia at universities and hospitals in United States and Canada. Consultant to National Institute of Mental Health, Bethesda, Md.; consultant, especially on the socio-architecture of mental hospitals, to provincial governments of Saskatchewan and Ontario, and states of Massachusetts, Pennsylvania, New York, and New Jersey. Member of board of directors, American Schizophrenia Foundation. Military service: Royal Navy, 1942-47; became surgeon lieutenant.

MEMBER: Collegium Internationale Neuro-Psychopharmacologicum (founder member; fellow), World Academy of Arts and Sciences, American Psychiatric Association, Royal Medico-Psychological Association, Royal College of Physicians of London.

WRITINGS: (With Abram Hoffer) The Chemical Basis of Clinical Psychiatry, C. C Thomas, 1961; (with Hoffer) How to Live with Schizophrenia, University Books, 1966, revised edition, 1974; (with Hoffer) The Hallucinogens, Academic Press, 1967; (with Hoffer) New Hope for Alcoholics, University Books, 1968; (editor with Bernard Aaronson) Psychedelics: The Uses and Implications of Hallucinogenic Drugs, Anchor Books, 1970; (editor with Henri Yaker and Frances Cheek) The Future of Time: Man's Temporal Environment, Doubleday, 1971; (with Miriam Siegler) Models of Madness, Models of Medicine, Macmillan, 1974. Writer of about one hundred papers on clinical psychiatry and allied subjects.

WORK IN PROGRESS: With A. Moneim El-Meligi, Mr. Wilkins Changes Worlds, an experiential study of recovery from schizophrenia.

SIDELIGHTS: "While my central interest is the study of psychiatry with particular emphasis on schizophrenia," Osmond says, "this has led me to enquire into the umwelt or experiential world, first of mentally ill people and more recently of mentally well people. This interest was initiated from letters written between my old friend Aldous Huxley and myself, combined with my collaboration with Abram Hoffer.... Now engaged [with others] in developing a new human typology."†

*   *   *

OSTROM, Alan (Baer)   1925-

PERSONAL: Born March 2, 1925, in New York, N.Y.; son of Albert Jean (a merchant) and Josephine (Gold) Ostrom; married Sonya Sokoloff (a sculptor), June 23, 1946 (separated, 1975); children: Andrew, Lisa. Education: Bard College, B.A., 1948; Columbia University, M.A., 1950, Ph.D., 1959. Politics: Registered Liberal ("not very active; often perverse"). Religion: None. Residence: Crompond, N.Y., 19517. Office: Department of English, Brooklyn College of the City University of New York, Brooklyn, N.Y.

CAREER: Ohio State University, Columbus, assistant instructor in English, 1952-55; Stevens Institute of Technology, Hoboken, N.J., instructor in humanities, 1959-61; Brooklyn College of the City University of New York, Brooklyn, N.Y., assistant professor, 1961-73, associate professor of English, 1973—, instructor in photography. Professional photographer. Military service: U.S. Navy, 1943-46. Awards, honors: Choice book award, 1967, for The Poetic World of William Carlos Williams.

WRITINGS: The Poetic World of William Carlos Wil-

liams, Southern Illinois University Press, 1966. Contributor of poetry to *Quarterly Review of Literature, Centennial Review,* and other periodicals.

WORK IN PROGRESS: Poems; an article on naturalism in *Native Son* and *An American Tragedy;* a book on the relationships between verbal and visual imagery from 1900-1925.

SIDELIGHTS: Ostrom told *CA:* "Started out to be a chemist, but found I liked the real world of words better than the half-world of mathematics. . . . Much stimulated by a few teachers—[including] Mark Van Doren, Lionel Trilling, Moses Hadas at Columbia. Can't remember *what* they said, but their humanity and commitment caught me up." *Avocational interests:* Horticulture, sculpture and painting (as a viewer); driving sports cars, tennis, girl-watching.

* * *

OTT, Attiat F(arag) 1935-

PERSONAL: Born June 18, 1935, in Cairo, Egypt; daughter of Abdalla (a college professor) and Amina (Ahmed) Farag; married David J. Ott (a college professor), July 2, 1964. *Education:* Attended Lycee Francaise d'Egypt, 1947-52; University of Cairo, B.A. (with honors), 1956; University of Michigan, Ph.D., 1962. *Home:* 262 Salisbury St., Worcester, Mass. 01609.

CAREER: Southern Methodist University, Dallas, Tex., assistant professor, 1962-65, associate professor of economics, 1965-69; Clark University, Worcester, Mass., professor of economics, 1969—. Research associate (nonresident), Brookings Institution, 1964—; adjunct scholar, American Enterprise Institute for Public Policy Research, 1972—. *Member:* Econometric Society.

WRITINGS: (Contributor) G. C. Murphy, editor, *Money in the International Order,* Southern Methodist University Press, 1964; (with husband, David J. Ott) *Federal Budget Policy,* Brookings Institution, 1965, revised edition, 1969; (with D. Ott and J. Yoo) *Macroeconomic Theory,* McGraw, 1975; (with D. Ott) *The 1976 Budget: Short-Run Stabilization Policy and the Long-Run Budget Outlook,* American Enterprise Institute for Public Policy Research, 1975. Contributor to *Journal of Finance, Economica Internazionale, Inter-American Affairs,* and *Quarterly Journal of Economics.*

AVOCATIONAL INTERESTS: Flying (holds private pilot's license).

* * *

OTTEN, Anna

PERSONAL: Born in Czechoslovakia; daughter of Carlo (a chemical engineer) and Emma Kutschig de Cejkovac; married Klaus W. Otten (an electronics engineer). *Education:* Waterloo College, Ontario, B.A., 1953; University of Western Ontario, M.A., 1954, Ph.D., 1958; studied one semester each at the Sorbonne and University of Barcelona, 1960. *Home:* 1925 Trebein Rd., Xenia, Ohio 45385.

CAREER: Antioch College, Yellow Springs, Ohio, assistant professor, 1956-62, associate professor, 1962-70, professor of French and German, 1970—, chairman of department of foreign languages, 1962-64, 1967-70, 1975-76. *Member:* Modern Language Association of America, Intercultural Association of Southwestern Ohio (president, 1966-74).

WRITINGS: (Collaborator) Harry Steinhauer, *Deutsche*

Kultur, Oxford University Press, 1961; (editor) *Mensch und Zeit,* Appleton, 1966, handbook with exercises and tapes, 1967; (editor) P. Hirche, *Naehe des Todes;* Odyssey, 1966; (editor) H. Boell, *Die Spurlosen,* Odyssey, 1967; (editor) L. Ahlsen, *Philemon und Baukis,* Odyssey, 1967; (editor) *Voix et Silences,* Appleton, 1968; (editor) *Meistererzaehlungen,* Appleton, 1969; *Hesse Companion,* Suhrkamp Verlag, 1970; (editor) *Borchert Lesebuch,* Holt, 1972. Author of radio play, "Les Singes au bois sacre." Contributor of reviews to language journals and *Books Abroad.*

WORK IN PROGRESS: Articles about Ionesco, Hesse, and others; interdependence of contemporary developments in German, French, and Spanish literature; a study of machine-aided methods of language teaching; women's studies.

SIDELIGHTS: Mrs. Otten told *CA:* "My career started when I talked to the other little fellow playing in the same sand box. Ever since, I have been trying to communicate with other people, disregarding national, religious, and political barriers. Teaching, studies, writing, and travel have only been a extension of the dialogue that started in the sand box." She is competent in Czech, Spanish, and Latin, and has traveled extensively in Europe, South America, North Africa, the Middle East, Southeast Asia, and Australia.

* * *

OTTERBEIN, Keith Frederick 1936-

PERSONAL: Born May 24, 1936, in Warren, Pa.; married; one child. *Education:* Pennsylvania State University, B.A., 1958; University of Pennsylvania, A.M., 1960; University of Pittsburgh, Ph.D., 1963. *Home:* 50 Jordan Rd., Williamsville, N.Y. 14221. *Office:* State University of New York, Buffalo, N.Y. 14214.

CAREER: American University, Washington, D.C., assistant professor of research, 1963-64; University of Kansas, Lawrence, assistant professor of anthropology, 1964-66; State University of New York at Buffalo, assistant professor, 1966-67, associate professor, 1967-71, professor of anthropology, 1971—, director of graduate studies in anthropology, 1968-69, 1971. Summer field work in the Bahama Islands, 1959, 1961, 1964, and in Nigeria, 1965; winter and spring field work in the Bahama Islands, 1968, 1973, 1975. *Member:* American Anthropological Association (fellow), Society for Applied Anthropology (fellow), Current Anthropology (associate), Society for Cross-Cultural Research, American Sociological Association.

WRITINGS: (Contributor) Paul Bohannan, editor, *Law and Warfare,* Doubleday, 1964; *The Andros Islanders: A Study of Family Organization in the Bahamas,* University of Kansas Press, 1966; *The Evolution of War: A Cross-Cultural Study,* Human Relations Area File Press, 1970; *Comparative Cultural Analysis: An Introduction to Anthropology,* Holt, 1972; *Changing House Types in Long Bay Cays: The Evolution of Folk Housing in an Out-Island Bahamian Community,* Human Relations Area File Press, 1975. Contributor to professional journals.

* * *

OWEN, Thomas Richard 1918-

PERSONAL: Born July 27, 1918, in Aberdare, Glamorganshire, Wales; son of Thomas (a miner) and Margaret Mary (Evans) Owen; married Mary Gwen Davies, April 6, 1942;

children: Lynwen (Mrs. David Nicholas Evans). *Education:* University College of Swansea, Wales, B.Sc., 1939, M.Sc., 1941. *Home:* 14 Wimmerfield Crescent, Killay, Swansea, Glamorganshire, Wales. *Office:* Department of Geology, University College of Swansea, University of Wales, Swansea, Wales.

CAREER: University of Wales, University College of Swansea, Swansea, lecturer, 1947-58, senior lecturer in geology, 1958—, reader in geology, beginning 1974. Geology curator, Swansea Museum. *Military service:* Royal Air Force, 1943-46; became flight lieutenant. *Member:* Geological Society (London; fellow), Geologists Association (former chairman of South Wales branch).

WRITINGS: (With J.G.C. Anderson) *The Structure of the British Isles,* Pergamon, 1968; *Geology Explained in South Wales,* David & Charles, 1973; (contributor) Alan E. Nairn and Francis G. Stehli, editors, *The North Atlantic,* Plenum, 1974. Writer with R. Bradshaw of a thirteen-week television series, "The Changing Earth."

WORK IN PROGRESS: Collaborating with F.H.T. Rhodes on a world stratigraphy textbook; *The Geological Evolution of the British Isles,* for Pergamon.

AVOCATIONAL INTERESTS: Photography, jazz, painting.

* * *

PAARLBERG, Don 1911-

PERSONAL: Born June 20, 1911, in Oak Glen, Ill.; son of Henry Peter (a farmer) and Grace (Int-Hout) Paarlberg; married Eva Louisa Robertson, June 23, 1940; children: Don, Jr., Robert Lynn. *Education:* Purdue University, B.S., 1940; Cornell University, M.S., 1943; Ph.D., 1946. *Politics:* Republican. *Religion:* Protestant. *Home:* 2440 Virginia Ave. N.W., Washington, D.C. 20037.

CAREER: Purdue University, Lafayette, Ind., assistant professor, 1946-47, associate professor, 1948-51, professor of agricultural economics, 1952-53; U.S. Government, Washington, D.C., assistant to Secretary of Agriculture, 1953-57, assistant Secretary of Agriculture, 1957-58, special assistant to the President, 1958-61, coordinator of Food For Peace, 1960-61; Purdue University, Hillenbrand Professor of Agricultural Economics, 1961-69; U.S. Department of Agriculture, Washington, D.C., director of agricultural economics, 1969—. Consultant to Committee for Economic Development, 1961-62, and to Ford Foundation, 1962. *Member:* American Farm Economic Association (secretary-treasurer, 1951-52), Sigma Xi.

WRITINGS: (With F. A. Pearson) *Food,* Knopf, 1944; *American Farm Policy,* Wiley, 1964; *The Great Myths of Economics,* New American Library, 1968.

SIDELIGHTS: Don Paarlberg has visited approximately thirty nations, and has done consulting work abroad for the federal government and private foundations.

* * *

PACIFICO, Carl 1921-

PERSONAL: Born September 12, 1921; son of Joseph (an auto dealer) and Josephine (Di Blasio) Pacifico; married Mary Milano, September 9, 1944; children: Mary Ann, Joseph, Carl. *Education:* Drexel Institute of Technology, B.S. (chemical engineering), 1943. *Home:* 5121 West Penfield Rd., Columbia, Md. 21045.

CAREER: Alcolac Chemicals Corp., Baltimore, Md., ex-

ecutive vice-president, 1954-66; affiliated with Management Supplements, Inc. (management consultants), Columbia, Md., 1966—. Director of Ventron Corp., Beverly, Mass. and Balchem Corp., Slate Hill, N.Y. *Military service:* U.S. Army Air Forces, 1944-46; became second lieutenant. *Member:* American Chemical Society, Commercial Chemical Development Association, Chemical Market Research Association, Chemists Club (New York).

WRITINGS: Exploring Life's Secrets, Arco, 1958; *Creative Thinking in Practice,* Noyes Development Corp., 1966; *Effective Profit Techniques for Managers,* Prentice-Hall, 1968. Also author of *Thinking on Thinking,* 1974.

* * *

PADDEN, R(obert) C(harles) 1922-

PERSONAL: Born September 14, 1922, in St. Paul, Minn.; son of Thomas Joseph (in insurance business) and Florence (Westervelt) Padden; married Adele Lorraine Ludwig (a registered nurse), May 15, 1952; children: Penelope Victoria, Lorraine Adele. *Education:* University of Michigan, student, 1950; University of California, Santa Barbara, B.A., 1952; Duke University, graduate study, 1952; University of California, Berkeley, M.A., 1954, Ph.D., 1959. *Home:* 9 Payne Rd., Barrington, R.I. 02806.

CAREER: University of California, Berkeley, lecturer in speech, 1957-58, assistant professor of modern history, 1958-64; St. Norbert College, West De Pere, Wis., member of history department, 1964-69; Brown University, Providence, R.I., professor of history, 1969—. *Military service:* U.S. Naval Reserve, active duty, 1942-45. *Member:* American Historical Association, Latin American Studies Association, American Society for Ethnohistory.

WRITINGS: The Hummingbird and the Hawk: Conquest and Sovereignty in the Valley of Mexico, 1503-1541, Ohio State University Press, 1967; (contributor) Patricia J. Lyon, editor, *Native South Americans: Ethnology of the Least Known Continent,* Little, Brown, 1974; (editor) *Tales of Potosi,* Brown University Press, 1975. Contributor to *American Historical Review, Reviews in European History, The Americas,* and *Southwestern Journal of Anthropology.*

WORK IN PROGRESS: The Feathered Cross: Ways of Life and Religion in Mexico in the Sixteenth Century, a sequel to *The Hummingbird and the Hawk;* research in Mesoamerican ethnohistory.

SIDELIGHTS: R. C. Padden reads Spanish, Portuguese, Italian, German, French. *Avocational interests:* Fly fishing.

* * *

PADDOCK, William (Carson) 1921-

PERSONAL: Born September 23, 1921, in Minneapolis, Minn.; son of Paul Ezekiel and Sarah (Lee) Paddock; married Elizabeth Mills; children: Paul Mills, Ann Elizabeth. *Education:* Iowa State University of Science and Technology, B.S., 1943; Cornell University, Ph.D., 1950. *Religion:* Presbyterian. *Home address:* Box 593259, Miami, Fla. 33159. *Agent:* Paul R. Reynolds, Inc., 12 East 41 St., New York, N.Y. 10017.

CAREER: Pennsylvania State University, University Park, assistant professor, 1950-52; Iowa State University of Science and Technology, Ames, professor and director of Iowa State-Guatemala Tropical Research Center, Antigua, Guatemala, 1952-55; U.S. International Cooperation Administration, agronomist, Guatemala City, Guatemala, 1955-57; Panamerican School of Agriculture, Tegucigalpa, Honduras, director, 1957-62; National Academy of Sciences, Washington, D.C., head of Latin American affairs, 1962-65; consultant in tropical agricultural development, 1965—. Director, Time Insurance Co., Milwaukee, Wis. *Military service:* U.S. Marine Corps, 1943-46; became first lieutenant. *Member:* American Association for the Advancement of Science, American Phytopathological Society, New York Academy of Sciences, Iowa Academy of Sciences (fellow), Sigma Xi, Phi Kappa Phi, Phi Epsilon Phi.

WRITINGS: (With brother, Paul Paddock) *Hungry Nations,* Little, Brown, 1964; (with P. Paddock) *Famine, 1975—America's Decision: Who Will Survive?,* Little, Brown, 1967; (with wife, Elizabeth M. Paddock) *We Don't Know How,* Iowa State University Press, 1973. Contributor to scientific journals and the popular press.

SIDELIGHTS: William Paddock has traveled extensively studying rural conditions in Latin America and the Middle East. Much of the travel has been by horse and dugout canoe, or by piloting a private plane. See also listing for PADDOCK, Paul (Ezekiel, Jr.).

* * *

PAGE, Curtis C(arling) 1914-

PERSONAL: Born December 21, 1914, in Roxbury, Mass.; son of Harold Poore (a Young Men's Christian Association secretary) and Mabel Frances (Carling) Page; married Annette Sailor, May 30, 1952 (divorced June, 1968); married Theodora Menges (an artist), August 21, 1970; children: two sons, three daughters. *Education:* Yale University, B.A. (with exceptional distinction), 1937, Ph.D., 1947, fellow at School of Drama, 1954-55. *Politics:* Democrat. "I am aggressively, a 'dove.'" *Religion:* Unitarian Universalist. *Home:* 517 43rd St., Des Moines, Iowa 50312. *Office:* Drake University, Des Moines, Iowa 50311.

CAREER: Lafayette College, Easton, Pa., instructor in English, 1941-43; University of Chattanooga, Chattanooga, Tenn., assistant professor of English, 1946-49; Drake University, Des Moines, Iowa, associate professor, 1949-55, professor of English, 1955—, chairman of freshman English program, 1959-67, assistant provost, 1967-69, associate provost, 1969, coordinator of humanities program, 1973—. Peace Corps consultant in Puerto Rico, 1965-66; member of board and chairman of speakers bureau, Iowa Peace Corps Support Organization, 1963-69. President of Drama Workshop of Des Moines, 1958-60, and Des Moines Community Playhouse, 1962-70; member of executive committee, Iowa Arts Council, 1966-68; founder and former president of Mid-Iowa Arts Association. Moderator and producer of various series for commercial and educational television in Iowa. *Military service:* U.S. Coast Guard Reserve, 1942-52; active duty, primarily in North Atlantic, 1942-46; became lieutenant junior grade.

MEMBER: Modern Language Association of America, National Council of Teachers of English, American Association of University Professors, American Association for the United Nations (member of Iowa Board, 1955-60), Omicron Delta Kappa, Phi Eta Sigma, Theta Alpha Phi. *Awards, honors:* Des Moines Public Schools Distinguished Award, 1954; Fund for the Advancement of Education faculty fellowship, 1954-55.

WRITINGS: Drama: Synge's "Riders to the Sea," Ginn, 1966. Contributor of book reviews to *Saturday Review.*

WORK IN PROGRESS: A novel; a critical biography of Stephen Phillips.

* * *

PAGE, William Roberts 1904-

PERSONAL: Born September 27, 1904, in Portland, Dorsetshire, England; son of John (a Methodist clergyman) and Bessie (Roberts) Page; married Dorothy Finch, 1930. *Education:* The Polytechnic, London, England, B.Sc. (second class honors), 1954. *Home:* 74 Antrim Mansions, Antrim Rd., London N.W. 3, England.

CAREER: North London College of Further Education, London, England, teacher of English and social studies, 1948-63, head of department of general education, 1963-68. Former lecturer on current problems, Young Women's Christian Association.

WRITINGS: English Out at Work, Dent, 1960; *Arithmetic Out at Work,* Books I and II, Dent, 1962; *Introducing the Younger Woman,* Cambridge University Press, 1965; *More English Out at Work,* Dent, 1966; *Economics at Work,* Cassell, 1968; *Calculations for Distribution and Commerce,* Longman, 1971; *Government and Politics at Work in Britain,* Longman, 1974.

WORK IN PROGRESS: An introductory book on sociology and politics for further education students.

AVOCATIONAL INTERESTS: Keeping the garden at an old people's home run by a local voluntary committee.

* * *

PAGET, Julian 1921-

PERSONAL: Born July 11, 1921, in London, England; son of Bernard Charles (a soldier) and Winnie Paget; married Diana Frances Farmer, December 3, 1954; children: Olivia Jane, Henry James. *Education:* Christ Church, Oxford, M.A., 1940. *Religion:* Church of England. *Home:* 4 Trevor St., London, S.W. 7, England.

CAREER: British Army, officer in Coldstream Guards, 1940-68, leaving service as lieutenant colonel; World War II assignments were in United Kingdom and continental Europe; adjutant of Coldstream Guards battalion in Palestine, 1945-49; liaison officer stationed at Pentagon, Washington, D.C., 1951-53; commanding officer of Coldstream Guards battalion in Kenya, 1960-63; assigned to Defence Secretariat in Aden, 1965. Full-time writer, 1968—. *Member:* Guards Club.

WRITINGS: Counter-Insurgency Operations, Walker & Co., 1967 (published in England as *Counter-Insurgency Campaigning*); *Last Post: Aden, 1964-67,* Faber, 1969; *The Story of the Guards,* Osprey Publishing, 1976. Regular contributor to British military publications.

SIDELIGHTS: Julian Paget is competent in French and German. *Avocational interests:* Travel, fishing, shooting, photography.

BIOGRAPHICAL/CRITICAL SOURCES: Times Literary Supplement, June 8, 1967.

* * *

PALLONE, Nathaniel John 1935-

PERSONAL: Born October 30, 1935, in Chicago, Ill.; son of Louis Thomas (an engineer) and Adeline (Tenkach) Pallone; married Nicolina Tiranno, June 30, 1956; children: Angela Terese, Andrea Marie. *Education:* Catholic University of America, A.B., 1957, A.M., 1960; New York

University, Ph.D., 1963. *Religion:* "Reluctant Catholic." *Home:* 64 Johnson St., Highland Park, N.J. 08904.

CAREER: Silver Spring (Md.) schools, teacher, 1957-60; St. Francis College, Brooklyn, N.Y., psychologist, 1960-63; University of Notre Dame, Notre Dame, Ind., assistant professor, 1963-66; New York University, New York, N.Y., associate professor, 1966-67, professor of counseling psychology and chairman of department, 1968-72; University of Hartford, West Hartford, Conn., associate dean, 1972-73; Rutgers University, New Brunswick, N.J., professor of education and psychology and dean of University College, 1973—. Licensed psychologist, New Jersey. Private practice in counseling and psychotherapy, 1973—. *Military service:* U.S. Army, during the 1950's; became technical sergeant. U.S. Air Force Reserve member until 1960. *Member:* American Psychological Association (fellow), American Personnel and Guidance Association, American Association of University Professors, Phi Beta Kappa.

WRITINGS: (With J. M. Lee) *Guidance and Counseling in Schools: Foundations and Processes,* McGraw, 1966; (editor with Lee) *Readings in Guidance and Counseling,* Sheed, 1966; (editor) *Readings for Catholic Counselors,* National Catholic Guidance Conference, 1966; (with G. H. Moreau) *Guidelines for Guidance,* National Catholic Education Association, 1968; (with W. H. Liu) *Catholic/USA: Perspectives on Social Change,* Wiley, 1970. Contributor of more than ninety articles to professional journals. Guidance columnist, *Brooklyn Tablet,* 1961-63; editor, National Catholic Guidance Conference *Journal,* 1963-68; editor, *New York State Personnel and Guidance Journal,* 1970-72.

WORK IN PROGRESS: Patterns of Ego Integration: Counseling and Psychotherapy.

* * *

PALMER, David 1928-

PERSONAL: Born November 24, 1928, in Detroit, Mich.; son of Walter Samuel (a businessman) and Elizabeth Ruth (Besancon) Palmer; married Charlene Goldenberg (a poet and painter), June 16, 1951; children: Stephen David, Charna Ruth, Nicholas Alan, Renee Elizabeth. *Education:* Pasadena City College, A.A., 1949; University of California, Los Angeles, B.A., 1951, graduate study in English, 1951-52, M.L.S., 1961. *Politics:* Independent. *Religion:* Episcopalian.

CAREER: Royal-Globe Insurance Group, Oakland, Calif., claims representative, 1956-59; University of California Press, Berkeley, public information writer, 1959-60; Humboldt State College (now California State University, Humboldt), Arcata, Calif., reference librarian, 1961-64; Rockford College, Rockford, Ill., library director, beginning 1964. Has given poetry readings at colleges and universities, Berkeley Town Hall Theatre, Chicago Art Institute, and on radio and television. *Military service:* U.S. Army, 1953-55. *Member:* American Library Association, American Association of University Professors, Illinois Library Association.

WRITINGS: Quickly, Over the Wall (poetry and paintings), Wake-Brook, 1966.

Editor with Malcolm Bradbury; all published by Crane, Russak: *Metaphysical Poetry,* 1970; *Contemporary Criticism,* 1971; *Victorian Poetry,* 1972; *The American Novel and the 1920's,* 1972; *Medieval Drama,* 1973; *Shakespearian Comedy,* 1973. Contributor of poetry to magazines and journals, including *Beloit Poetry Journal, Contact,*

Dalhousie Review, Kayak, Poet and Critic, Quixote; also contributor of reviews to *Library Journal,* 1962—. Formerly an editor, *Beloit Poetry Journal.*

WORK IN PROGRESS: A second book of poetry.

AVOCATIONAL INTERESTS: Conversation, reading, music, painting, hiking, camping, tennis, swimming.†

* * *

PALMER, Edgar Z(avitz) 1898-

PERSONAL: Born April 10, 1898, in Chester, Pa.; son of Charles (a lawyer) and Arletta (Cutler) Palmer; married Opal Yarbrough, September 8, 1924; children: Camilla (Mrs. Louis Hanson), Boyd Z., Charles P. *Education:* Swarthmore College, A.B., 1919; University of Wisconsin, Ph.D., 1928. *Politics:* Democrat. *Religion:* Society of Friends. *Home:* 2415 Winthrop Rd., Lincoln, Neb. 68502.

CAREER: American Friends Service Committee, relief worker in France, 1919-20; Ogden College, Bowling Green, Ky., instructor in social studies, 1920-23; University of Kentucky, Lexington, 1927-46, began as assistant professor, became professor of economics; University of Nebraska, Lincoln, professor of statistics and director of Bureau of Business Research, 1946-63, professor emeritus, 1963—; Ataturk University, Erzurum, Turkey, head of economics and business department, 1963-65; Robert College, Istanbul, Turkey, director of economic research, 1965-66. Part-time director of research, Kentucky Unemployment Compensation, 1937-41; part-time director of statistical research, Kentucky Department of Revenue, 1943-45; research associate, University of Wisconsin Bureau of Business Research and Service, 1945-46; consultant, University of Nebraska Bureau of Business Research, 1974—. Missouri Valley Friends Conference, presiding clerk, 1962. *Member:* Phi Beta Kappa, Beta Gamma Sigma.

WRITINGS: Actuarial Recommendations Relative to Teachers Retirement Legislation for Kentucky, Kentucky Education Association, 1938; *Indexes of Employment and Payrolls in Kentucky,* Kentucky Unemployment Compensation Commission, 1939; *Survey of Employment by Counties,* Kentucky Unemployment Compensation Commission, 1939; *Kentucky Incomes: A Statistical Study of Tax Returns,* Kentucky Department of Revenue, 1944; (contributor) *Inheritance and Estate Taxes in Kentucky,* Kentucky Department of Revenue, 1947; *The Prewar Industrial Pattern of Wisconsin,* University of Wisconsin Press, 1947; *Indicators of Current Business Conditions in Wisconsin,* University of Wisconsin Press, 1947; *Nebraska Business Handbook,* University of Nebraska Press, 1949; *Some Economic Problems of Clay Center, Nebraska,* University of Nebraska Press, 1949; (with Alfred F. Dombrowski) *The Alfalfa Dehydration Industry in Nebraska,* University of Nebraska Press, 1949.

(With Leonard Tobkin) *Types of Business in Nebraska Towns,* University of Nebraska Press, 1954; *Statistical Abstract of Nebraska Business,* University of Nebraska Press, 1957; (with Gerald E. Thompson, Moon H. Kang, and William H. Strawn) *The Community Economic Base and Multiplier,* University of Nebraska Press, 1958; (with David J. Thomas and Robert S. Polkinghorn) *City and Regional Wage Comparisons,* University of Nebraska Press, 1960; *Estimating the Number of Business Establishments in Nebraska,* University of Nebraska Press, 1963; (with Francis X. Murray) *The Omaha Real Estate Market, 1950-1960,* University of Nebraska Press, 1963; *The Meaning and Measurement of the National Income,* University of Nebraska Press, 1966; *Agriculture in Turkey: Long-Term Projections of Supply and Demand,* Robert College (Turkey), 1966; *The Plummers of Harmony Grove,* Friends United Press, 1974.

"The Four Corners: A Play for Quaker Young People," produced in Lincoln, Neb., 1967. Contributor to professional journals. Member of board of editors, *Southern Economic Journal,* 1940-41; editor, *Business in Nebraska,* 1946-63.

*   *   *

PALMER, Eve   1916-

PERSONAL: Born February 20, 1916, in Karoo Desert of Cape Province, South Africa; daughter of Clifford George (a rancher) and Kate (Uhlig) Palmer; married Geoffrey Jenkins (a writer), March 17, 1950; children: David. *Education:* University College, London, Diploma in Journalism, 1937. *Home:* 108 Albert St., Waterkloof, Pretoria, South Africa.

MEMBER: Royal Society of South Africa, National Veld Trust, Botanical Society of South Africa, Wild Life Society, Royal Horitcultural Society, Rose Society.

WRITINGS: Trees of South Africa (text edition), Balkema, 1961, new edition, three volumes, published as *Trees of Southern Africa,* 1972; *The Plains of Camdeboo* (autobiographical), Viking, 1966; *Field Guide to Southern African Trees,* Collins & World, 1976. Former editor, National Veld Trust.

WORK IN PROGRESS: Companion to South Africa, with Geoffrey Jenkins, for Collins & World.

SIDELIGHTS: Eve Palmer's *The Plains of Camdeboo* is an account of her life at Cranemere, the Palmer family's vast ranch in a South African desert, and the struggle to tame the land. Her interests embrace conservation of soil, animals, and plants in Africa.

*   *   *

PALMER, Helen H.   1911-

PERSONAL: Born June 19, 1911, in New Orleans, La.; daughter of Christian (an electrical engineer) and Petra (Olsen) Hanssen; married Arthur Macdonald Palmer (a real estate broker), June 19, 1934; children: Patricia Jean (Mrs. Wade Noland Thomas). *Education:* Louisiana State University, B.A., 1956, M.A., 1960, M.S.L.S., 1961. *Politics:* Democrat. *Religion:* Presbyterian. *Home:* 3753 Hyacinth Ave., Baton Rouge, La. 70808. *Office:* Louisiana State University Library, Baton Rouge, La. 70803.

CAREER: Louisiana State University Library, Baton Rouge, associate librarian in humanities division, 1961-73, librarian and head of science division, 1973—. *Member:* American Library Association, American Association of University Women, Louisiana Library Association, Phi Kappa Phi, Phi Lambda Pi, Baton Rouge Library Club.

WRITINGS: (Compiler with Anne Jane Dyson) *American Drama Criticism: Interpretations, 1890-1965 inclusive, of American Drama since the First Play Produced in America,* Shoe String, 1967, *Supplement 1,* 1970; (compiler with Dyson) *European Drama Criticism,* Shoe String, 1968, *Supplement 1,* 1970, *Supplement 2,* 1974; *English Novel Explication,* Shoe String, 1973.

AVOCATIONAL INTERESTS: Little theater, Baton Rouge Symphony, travel.

PALMER, Henry R(obinson), Jr.   1911-

PERSONAL: Born June 16, 1911, in Stonington, Conn.; son of Henry Robinson and Rieta Woodruff (Babcock) Palmer; married Katharine Cheney Farley, September 23, 1939; children: Benjamin Woodruff, Leigh Farley, Rieta Babcock (Mrs. Howard G. Park), Henry Robinson, III. *Education:* Brown University, B.S., 1936. *Religion:* Protestant. *Home:* 182 Water St., Stonington, Conn. 06378.

CAREER: Stonington Boat Works, Inc., Stonington, Conn., president, 1936-63; Palmer Service, Inc., Stonington, Conn., president, 1963—. Consultant to Marine Historical Association, Mystic, Conn.; consultant, under International Executive Service Corps, to Taiwan Yacht Industries, 1967.

WRITINGS: This Was Air Travel, Superior, 1956; *The Story of the Schneider Trophy Race,* Superior, 1962; *The Seaplanes,* Morgan Aviation Books, 1965; *Remarkable Flying Machines,* Superior, 1972.

*   *   *

PANGLAYKIM, J. (Pangestu)   1922-

PERSONAL: Born March 24, 1922, in Bandung, Indonesia; son of Lielie and Piepje (Tan) Pang; married Evy Njoginghwa, October, 1950; children: Tikky, Pingky, Mary. *Education:* University of Indonesia, B.B.A., 1952, B.Econ., 1954, Drs. (Economics), 1954, Ph.D., 1963; additional graduate study at University of California, Berkeley, 1960-61, and Columbia University, 1963. *Religion:* Roman Catholic. *Office:* c/o Australian National University, Economics P.S., Box 4, Canberra, Australia.

CAREER: In private import/export, banking, and insurance businesses, 1937-55; University of Indonesia, Faculty of Economics and Business Administration, Djakarta, faculty member, 1955-66, associate professor and director of Institute of Management, 1963-66; Australian National University, Canberra, senior research fellow in economics department, School of Pacific Studies, 1966—. Consultant to government agencies and private business and industry; adviser, Indonesian Trade Delegation to Republic of China, Taiwan, 1967. *Member:* Indonesia Society of Economists, Australian Society of Economists.

WRITINGS—In English: State Trading Corporations in Indonesia, University of Indonesia Press, 1963; (contributor) L. A. Mears, editor, *Economics Papers,* Research Institute of Social and Economics Research, University of Indonesia, 1963; *Problems of Credits and Small Industry,* Institute of Social and Economics Research, University of Indonesia, 1963; (with H. W. Arndt) *The Indonesian Economy—Facing a New Era?,* Rotterdam University Press, 1966; (with K. D. Thomas) *Indonesian Exports: Performance and Prospects, 1950-1970,* Rotterdam University Press, 1967; (with Thomas) *Indonesia Facing a New Era: Development Administration,* Committee on Economic Development (Melbourne), 1968; (with I. Palmers) *State Trading Corporation in Developing Countries, with Special Reference to Indonesia,* Rotterdam University Press, 1969.

In Indonesian: *Struktur Management dan Organisasi dalam beberapa Negara Sosialis* (title means "Management and Organizational Structure in Some Selected Socialist Countries"), 2nd edition, P. T. Pembangunan (Djakarta), 1964; *Suatu Pangantar Marketing* (title means "Introduction to Marketing"), 4th edition, P. T. Pembangunan, 1968; *Suatu Pengantar Management* (title means "Introduction to Management"), 4th edition, P. T. Pembangunan, 1968; *Persoalan masa kini, Perusahaan-Perusahaan Multinasional*, Yayasan Proklamasi, Centre for Strategic and International Studies, 1974.

Contributor to *Asian Textiles, World Politics* (Princeton University), *Maandschrift Economie* (Netherlands), *Developing Economies* (Tokyo), and other journals.

WORK IN PROGRESS: ASEAN Economic Cooperation: Prospects and Possibilities; case studies in Indonesian entrepreneurial history.

SIDELIGHTS: Panglaykim is competent in Dutch, German, Bahasa Indonesia, Bahasa Sunda, and Malay.†

* * *

PAPE, Donna (Lugg)   1930-
(D. L. Pape)

PERSONAL: Surname is pronounced Poppy; born June 21, 1930, in Sheboygan, Wis.; daughter of Arthur Phillip and Ruth (Fenninger) Lugg; married William Pape (a carpet mechanic), June 16, 1951; children: Diane Ruth, Janice Lynn, Jean Carol. *Home:* 1734 South 15th St., Sheboygan, Wis. 53081.

CAREER: Free-lance writer, 1960—; photo-journalist, 1960-64; writes verse for various greeting card companies. *Member:* National Writers Club, Author's Guild, Wisconsin Regional Writers' Association, Sheboygan County Writers' Club. *Awards, honors:* First Prize in Wisconsin Regional Writers' Association juvenile writing contest, 1965.

WRITINGS—All published by Whitman Publishing, except as noted: *The Best Surpise of All*, 1961; *Splish, Splash, Splush*, 1962; *Tony Zebra and the Lost Zoo*, 1963; *I Play in the Snow*, 1967; *Mary Lou, The Kangaroo*, E. M. Hale, 1967; *The Seal Who Wanted to Ski*, E. M. Hale, 1967; *Bumper Bear's Bus*, 1968; *Catch That Fish*, L. W. Singer, 1969.

All published by Garrard, except as noted: *Leo Lion Looks at Books*, 1972; *Mrs. Twitter, The Sitter*, 1972; *Mr. Mogg in the Log*, 1972; *Count on Leo Lion*, 1973; *The Kangaroo Who Leaped in Her Sleep*, 1973; *Handy Hands*, Standard Publishing, 1973; *A Special Way to Travel*, Standard Publishing, 1973; *Big Words for Little People*, Standard Publishing, 1973; *A Gerbil for a Friend*, Prentice-Hall, 1973; (with Jan Pape and Jeanette Grote) *Puzzles and Silly Riddles*, Scholastic Book Service, 1973; *A Bone for Breakfast*, 1974; *Promises Are Special Words*, Moody, 1974; *A Very Special Birthday*, Moody, 1975; (with John McInnes) *Taffy Finds a Halloween Witch*, 1975; (with McInnes) *The Big White Thing*, 1975; (with Grote) *Pack of Puzzles*, Scholastic Book Service, 1975. Also author of *Puzzling Pastimes*, 1973, and *Packet of Puzzles*, with Grote, 1973.

"Pape Series of Speech Improvement and Reading," published by Oddo; all 1965: *The Three Thinkers of Thay-lee; Profesor Fred and the Fid-Fuddlephone; Scientist Sam; King Robert, the Resting Ruler; Liz Dearly's Silly Glasses; Shoemaker Fooze.* Contributor to speech therapy workbooks produced by Word-Making Productions; writer of stories for Whithaven Game Co. (a speech therapy game publisher). Contributor to *Humpty Dumpty, Jack and Jill, Highlights, Our Little Messenger, Junior World*, and other publications.

WORK IN PROGRESS: Whoever Heard of a Lost Policeman? for Whitman Publishing.

AVOCATIONAL INTERESTS: Music and art.

PAPIER, Judith Barnard   1932-

PERSONAL: Born February 17, 1932, in Denver, Colo.; daughter of Harry (an author) and Ruth (Eisenstat) Barnard; married Jerre Papier (an electronics engineer), December 20, 1953; children: Cynthia, Andrew. *Education:* Attended Antioch College, 1949-50, Ohio State University, 1950-53, and Northwestern University, 1961-62. *Religion:* Jewish. *Residence:* Wilmette, Ill.

CAREER: Writer and editor. Wilmette Community Concert Association, Wilmette, Ill., vice-president, 1964-67.

WRITINGS: (Co-author) *Beyond the Americas* (series), Scott, Foresman, 1962-63; *The Past and Present of Solomon Sorge*, Houghton, 1967. Book editor, *Chicago Sentinal*.

WORK IN PROGRESS: A novel and short stories.

AVOCATIONAL INTERESTS: Reading biography, history, and studies of society; rug making, cooking, sewing, and political activity.†

* * *

PAPPWORTH, M(aurice) H(enry)   1910-

PERSONAL: Born January, 1910, in Liverpool, England; children: Joanna, Dinah, Sara. *Education:* University of Liverpool, M.B. and Ch.B., 1932, M.R.C.P., 1936, M.D., 1937. *Religion:* Jewish. *Home:* Vale Lodge, Vale of Health, Hampstead, London N.W.3, England. *Office:* 66 Harley St., London, W.1., England.

CAREER: University of Liverpool, Liverpool, England, member of professorial unit, department of medicine, 1935-39; currently a consultant physician. *Military service:* Royal Army Medical Corps, 1941-46; served in North Africa, Italy, Greece, and India; became lieutenant colonel. *Member:* Royal Society of Medicine (London; fellow).

WRITINGS: Primer of Medicine, Butterworth & Co., 1960, 3rd edition, 1969; *Human Guinea Pigs*, Routledge & Kegan Paul, 1967, Beacon, 1968; *Passing Medical Examinations*, Butterworth & Co., 1975. Contributor to medical journals.

SIDELIGHTS: Human Guinea Pigs is an outgrowth of Pappworth's crusade against irresponsible medical experimentation on humans. Although Dr. Louis Lasagna calls it an "indignant little book" and a "diatribe and polemic instead of a sober appraisal," Dr. Michael Halberstam says: "Too often . . . research physicians lose sight of the particular patient, seeing him only as a set of initials in a case report to be presented in a year or two. No physician who reads this book will ever make that mistake again and we shall all be the better for it."

BIOGRAPHICAL/CRITICAL SOURCES: Washington Post, February 27, 1968; *New York Times Book Review*, July 14, 1968; *Nation*, January 27, 1969.

* * *

PAREEK, Udai (Narain)   1925-

PERSONAL: Born January 21, 1925, in Jaipur, India; son of Vijailal and Gaindi Pareek; married Rama Sharma, May 13, 1945; children: Sushama, Surabhi, Anagat. *Education:* St. John's College, Agra, India, B.A., 1944; Teachers Training College, Ajmer, India, B.T., 1945; Calcutta University, M.A., 1950; Agra University, M.A., 1952; University of Delhi, Ph.D., 1956. *Home:* Mohalla Madara, Chaukri Topkhana Desh, Jaipur, India. *Office:* Indian Institute of Management, Ahmedabad 380015, India.

CAREER: Teachers Training School, Jaipur, India, teacher of psychology, 1945-48; Teachers Training College, Bikaner, India, lecturer in psychology, 1953-54; Delhi School of Social Work, Delhi, India, lecturer in psychology, 1954-55; National Institute of Basic Education, New Delhi, India, psychologist, 1956-62; Indian Agricultural Research Institute, New Delhi, psychologist, 1962-66; University of North Carolina, Chapel Hill, visiting associate professor of psychology, 1966-68; National Institute of Health Administration and Education, New Delhi, professor of social sciences, 1968-70; University of Udaipur, Udaipur, India, director, School of Basic Sciences and Humanities, and dean, faculty of social sciences, 1970-73; Indian Institute of Management, Ahmedabad, India, professor of organisational behaviour, 1973—. Director of extension education, Small Industry Extension Training Institute, Hyderabad, India, 1964-66. *Member:* Indian Psychological Association, American Psychological Association, American Sociological Association, Psychometric Society, Society for the Psychological Study of Social Issues, National Training Laboratories (fellow), Madras Psychological Association, Andhra Pradesh Psychological Association (president, 1964-66).

WRITINGS: Developmental Patterns in Reaction to Frustration, Asia Publishing House (Bombay), 1964; (with S. R. Mittal) *A Guide to the Literature of Research Methodology in Behavioural Sciences,* Behavioural Sciences Centre (Delhi), 1965; (editor) *Studies in Rural Leadership,* Behavioural Sciences Centre, 1966; *Behavioural Science Research in India; A Directory, 1925-1965,* Acharan Sahkar, 1966; *A Guide to Indian Behavioural Science Periodicals,* Behavioural Sciences Centre, 1966; (with Rolf P. Lynton) *Training for Development,* Irwin, 1967; (with S. R. Devi and Saul Rosenzweig) *Manual of the Indian Adaptation of the Adult Form of the Rosenzweig P. F. Study,* Roopa Psychological Corp., 1968; (with Willis H. Griffin) *The Process of Planned Change in Education,* Somaiya, 1969.

Foreign Behavioural Research on India: A Directory of Research and Researchers, Acharan Sahkar, 1970; *Poverty and Motivation: Figure and Ground, Psychological Factors in Poverty,* Markham, 1970; (with T. V. Rao) *A Status Study on Population Research in India,* Volume I, McGraw, 1974; (with Rao) *Handbook of Psychological and Social Instruments,* Samashti, 1974; (with Y. P. Singh and D. R. Arora) *Diffusion of an Interdiscipline,* Bookhive, 1974; (with Rao) *From Conformity to Creativity: A New Approach to Teacher Training,* Samashti, 1976; (with Ravi Matthai and Rao) *Decision Making for Institution Building,* Samashti, 1976.

Contributor to professional journals. Editor, *Indian Behavioural Sciences Abstracts;* co-editor, *Manas;* member of editorial board, *Behavioural Science and Community Development, Cross-cultural Social Psychology Newsletter;* former editor, *Education and Psychology;* former collaborating editor, *Indian Journal of Psychology;* former co-editor, *Director of Indian Psychologists.*

WORK IN PROGRESS: Writing articles on educational activities for *Handbook of Organisational Design;* research on organisation development, institution building, and styles of Indian management.

* * *

PARK, Clara Claiborne 1923-

PERSONAL: Born August 19, 1923, in Tarrytown, N.Y.; daughter of Robert Watson and Virginia (McKenney) Claiborne; married David Park (a professor of physics), August 18, 1945; children: Katharine, Rachel, Paul, Jessica. *Education:* Radcliffe College, A.B., 1944; University of Michigan, M.A., 1948. *Politics:* Liberal Democrat. *Office:* English Department, Berkshire Community College, Second St., Pittsfield, Mass. 01201.

CAREER: Berkshire Community College, Pittsfield, Mass., member of English faculty, 1960—. *Member:* National Society for Autistic Children, Common Cause, Phi Beta Kappa. *Awards, honors:* Award from League School for Seriously Disturbed Children, 1967, and National Association for Mental Health award, 1969, both for *The Siege.*

WRITINGS: The Siege, Harcourt, 1967; (with Leon N. Shapiro) *You Are Not Alone: A Guide for Families of the Mentally Ill,* Little, Brown, 1976. Writer of columns for *Berkshire Eagle;* contributor to *Massachusetts Review, Book World,* and *American Scholar.*

SIDELIGHTS: As the mother of an autistic child, Mrs. Park has struggled to bring the child into the world of natural society and emotions from the shut-off otherworld she seems determined to maintain. *The Siege* is about this struggle. Reviewing the book, Robert Coles, a research psychiatrist, says: "She has written a book people like me should *study,* not applaud in arrogant generosity. She is an exceedingly rare and courageous woman, who willingly confronts the obvious, everyday mysteries and frustrations of a disease—if that is the word—we know precious little about. And she does something more: she confronts us with herself, with the dignity that one woman has preserved in the face of the rude, self-important, simple-minded elements in the medical and particularly the psychiatric profession."

BIOGRAPHICAL/CRITICAL SOURCES: Book World, December 17, 1967.

* * *

PARK, Joe 1913-

PERSONAL: Born January 15, 1913, in Evansville, Ind.; son of Joseph (a farmer) and Florence (Whitehead) Park; married Bertha Florence Born, May 4, 1935; children: Joe Charles, Diane Born. *Education:* Evansville College (now University of Evansville), B.S., 1937; University of Michigan, M.A., 1939, Ph.D., 1944. *Politics:* Democrat. *Religion:* None. *Home:* Route 1, Princeton, Wisc. 54968. *Office:* School of Education, Northwestern University, Evanston, Ill. 60201.

CAREER: Northwestern University, Evanston, Ill., assistant professor, 1944-49, associate professor, 1949-54, professor of education, 1954—.

WRITINGS: (Editor) *Selected Readings in the Philosophy of Education,* Macmillan, 1958, 4th edition, 1974; *Bertrand Russell in Education,* Ohio State University Press, 1963; *Rise of American Education: An Annotated Bibliography,* Northwestern University Press, 1965.

WORK IN PROGRESS: A history of Northwestern University School of Education.

* * *

PARKER, Alexander A(ugustine) 1908-

PERSONAL: Born February 28, 1908, in Montevideo, Uruguay; son of Arthur (a diplomat) and Laura (Bustamante) Parker; married Frances Ludwig, October 6, 1941; children: Bernard, Emily (Mrs. Ian Hampton), Catherine,

Joseph. *Education:* Cambridge University, B.A., 1930, M.A., 1933. *Religion:* Roman Catholic. *Home:* 1802 Basin Ledge, Austin, Tex. 78746. *Office:* Department of Spanish and Portuguese, Batts Hall 112, University of Texas, Austin, Tex. 78712.

CAREER: Cambridge University, Gonville and Caius College, Cambridge, England, fellow, 1933-39; University of Aberdeen, Aberdeen, Scotland, lecturer in Spanish and head of department, 1939-49, reader in Spanish, 1949-53; University of London, King's College, London, England, Cervantes Professor of Spanish, 1953-63; University of Edinburgh, Edinburgh, Scotland, professor of Hispanic studies, 1968-69; University of Texas at Austin, professor of Spanish literature, 1970—. Visiting professor at University of the West Indies, 1961, University of Pittsburgh, 1964, 1968, 1969-70, and New York University, 1966; lecturer elsewhere in United States.

MEMBER: Association of Hispanists of Great Britain (president, 1957-59), Royal Spanish Academy (corresponding member), Seville Academy of Letters (corresponding member), Hispanic Society of America (corresponding member), Council for Advanced Scientific Research (Madrid; honorary counciller), Modern Humanities Research Association (United States). *Awards, honors:* Knight Commander of Order of Isabella the Catholic (Spain), 1956; D.Litt., Cambridge University, 1969, University of Durham, 1975.

WRITINGS: The Allegorical Drama of Calderon, Dolphin Book Co., 1943; (editor, and author of introduction and notes) Calderon, *No hay mas Fortuna que Dios,* Manchester University Press, 1947; *Literature and the Delinquent: The Picaresque Novel in Spain and Europe 1599-1753,* Edinburgh University Press, 1957, translation by the author published as *Los Picaros en la literature,* Editorial Gredos, 1976. Also author of *The Spanish Drama from Lope de Vega to Calderon,* 1976. General editor, "Edinburgh Bilingual Library of European Literature," 1967—. Contributor to professional journals.

WORK IN PROGRESS: A bilingual edition, with introduction and notes, of Gongora's *Polifemo; The Theory of Love in Spanish Literature, 1500-1700; The Mind and Art of Calderon;* editing, with Melreena McKendrick, Calderon's *El Magico Prodigiosa.*

SIDELIGHTS: In addition to Spanish, he is competent in Latin, French, German, Italian, and Portuguese. *Avocational interests:* Art, lepidoptera, and horticulture (especially growing irises and lilies).

BIOGRAPHICAL/CRITICAL SOURCES: Boletin de Filologia Espanola, Number 5, November, 1958.

*   *   *

PARKER, Dorothy Mills

PERSONAL: Born in Jacksonville, Fla.; daughter of George Wiley and Lidie V. (Clark) Mills; married Robert Wallace Parker (divorced). *Education:* Attended Florida State University and studied journalism at American University. *Politics:* Democrat. *Religion:* Episcopalian.

CAREER: St. Columba's Episcopal Church, Washington, D.C., parish and press secretary, 1959—. *American Church News,* Washington correspondent, 1958—. Member, Episcopal Diocese of Washington, Department of Information, 1965-66. *Member:* National Society of Colonial Dames of America, National Cathedral Association, English-Speaking Union, Washington Cathedral Choral Society (member of board of directors and press officer), Junior League of Washington (former member board of directors).

WRITINGS: (Compiler and editor) *Lee Chronicle: Studies of the Early Generations of the Lees of Virginia,* New York University Press, 1957. Regular contributor to *Cathedral Age* and other Episcopal publications; columnist, *Georgetowner,* 1956-57; contributor to *Washington Evening Star* and other newspapers.

WORK IN PROGRESS: Tracts, stories, and articles for Episcopal publications.

AVOCATIONAL INTERESTS: Music (especially Renaissance and Baroque), heraldry, illuminated manuscripts, antiques, English history.†

*   *   *

PARKER, Francis H(oward) 1920-

PERSONAL: Born June 23, 1920, in Kuala Lumpur, Malaya; son of Walter Guy (a minister) and Alma E. (Shell) Parker; married Audrey Janell Schriber, December 15, 1945; children: Cynthia Ann, Brian Gareth, Valerie Gail, Diana Leigh. *Education:* Evansville College (now University of Evansville), B.A., 1941; Indiana University, M.A., 1947; Harvard University, Ph.D., 1949. *Home:* R.R. 1, North Vassalboro, Me. 04962.

CAREER: Haverford College, Haverford, Pa., assistant professor, 1949-54, associate professor, 1954-61, professor of philosophy, 1961-66, chairman of department, 1963-66; Purdue University, Lafayette, Ind., professor of philosophy and head of department, 1966-71; Colby College, Waterville, Me., Charles A. Dana Professor of Philosophy and chairman of department, 1971—. Lecturer at Institute of Humanistic Studies, University of Pennsylvania, 1956-60; visiting associate professor, Indiana University, 1961; Fulbright research professor, University of Athens, Greece, 1962-63; Fulbright inter-country lecturer, Hebrew University of Jerusalem, 1963; visiting lecturer, Bryn Mawr College, 1965-66. *Military service:* U.S. Army Air Forces, 1942-46; became captain; received air medal.

MEMBER: American Philosophical Association (executive committee on Eastern division, 1961-64); Metaphysical Society of America (secretary-treasurer, 1959-62; president, 1964-65), Association for Realistic Philosophy (president, 1959-61), Society for Phenomenology and Existential Philosophy, Society for Religion in Higher Education, Phi Beta Kappa, Pi Gamma Mu, Fullerton Club (president, 1958-59). *Awards, honors:* American Council of Learned Societies fellowship, 1962-63.

WRITINGS: (With Henry B. Veatch) *Logic as a Human Instrument,* Harper, 1959; *The Story of Western Philosophy,* Indiana University Press, 1967; *Reason and Faith Revisited,* Marquette University Press, 1971.

Contributor: John Wilde, editor, *The Return to Reason: Essays in Realistic Philosophy,* Regnery, 1953; R. Houde, J. Mullally, editors, *The Philosophy of Knowledge,* Lippincott, 1960; Alvin Planlinga, editor, *Faith and Philosophy,* Eerdmans, 1964; Edward D. Simmons, editor, *Essays on Knowledge and Methodology,* Ken Cook, 1965; J. Clayton Feaver, William Horosz, editors, *Religion in Philosophical and Cultural Perspective,* Van Nostrand, 1967. Contributor to *Twentieth Century Encyclopedia of Religious Knowledge, Collier's Encyclopedia,* and professional journals.

WORK IN PROGRESS: A book on theory of knowledge.

SIDELIGHTS: Parker reads French, German, Latin, and Ancient Greek.

*   *   *

PARKER, Harold T(albot)   1907-

PERSONAL: Born December 26, 1907, in Cincinnati, Ohio; son of Chester Samuel (a college professor) and Lucile (Jones) Parker. Education: University of Chicago, Ph.B., 1928, Ph.D., 1934; Cornell University, graduate study, 1929-30. Home: 1005 Demerius St., Durham, N.C. 27701. Office: Department of History, Duke University, Durham, N.C. 27706.

CAREER: Duke University, Durham, N.C., instructor, 1939-42, assistant professor, 1946-51, associate professor, 1951-57, professor of modern European history, 1957—. Military service: U.S. Army Air Forces, 1942-45; became staff sergeant. Member: American Historical Association, Society for French Historical Studies (president, 1957-58).

WRITINGS: The Cult of Antiquity and the French Revolutionaries, University of Chicago Press, 1937; Three Napoleonic Battles, Duke University Press, 1943; (editor with Theodore Ropp) Historical Synopsis of the World Today, Duke University Press, 1946; (editor with Richard Herr) Ideas in History, Duke University Press, 1965; (with Marvin Brown) Major Themes in Modern European History, Moore Publishing, 1974.

WORK IN PROGRESS: The French Central Government and French Industry: An Administrative History, 1781-1818; A Visual History of Europe.

*   *   *

PARMET, Herbert S.   1929-

PERSONAL: Surname is accented on second syllable; born September 28, 1929, in New York, N.Y.; son of Isaac and Fanny (Scharf) Parmet; married Joan Kronish (a public school teacher), September 12, 1948; children: Wendy Ellen. Education: State University of New York College at Oswego, B.A., 1951; Queens College (now of the City University of New York), M.A., 1957; Columbia University, further study, 1957-62. Politics: Independent Democrat. Home: 18-40 211th St., Bayside, N.Y. 11360.

CAREER: Teacher in North Babylon, N.Y., 1951-54; Mineola High School, Mineola, N.Y., teacher, 1954-68, chairman of department of social studies, 1961-68; Queensborough Community College, Bayside, N.Y., assistant professor, 1968-73, associate professor of history, 1973—. Part-time instructor, Fairleigh Dickinson University, 1958-64. Military service: U.S. Army, 1952-54. Member: Academy of Political Science.

WRITINGS: (With Marie B. Hecht) Aaron Burr: Portrait of an Ambitious Man, Macmillan, 1967; (with Hecht) Never Again: A President Runs for a Third Term, Macmillan, 1968; (contributor) James Moran, editor, Our Presidents, Macmillan, 1969; Eisenhower and the American Crusades, Macmillan, 1972; (contributor) Frank Merli and Theodore Wilson, editors, Makers of American Diplomacy, Scribner, 1974; (contributor) Philip Dolce, George Skau, editors, The Presidency, Scribner, 1976; The Democratic Umbrella: The Years After FDR, Macmillan, 1976. Contributor to New York Times Book Review, Chicago Tribune, and New York Historical Society Quarterly.

*   *   *

PARNES, Sidney J.   1922-

PERSONAL: Born January 5, 1922, in Pittsburgh, Pa.; son of Joseph (a merchant) and Bess (Treelisky) Parnes; married Beatrice Frommer, May 30, 1946; children: Robert, Susan. Education: University of Pittsburgh, B.S., 1946, M.Ed., 1950, Ph.D., 1954. Home: 160 Monroe Dr., Buffalo, N.Y. 14221. Office: Department of Creative Studies, State University of New York College, 1300 Elmwood, Buffalo, N.Y. 14222.

CAREER: Kaufmann's Department Store, Pittsburgh, Pa., training supervisor, 1946-50; University of Pittsburgh, Pittsburgh, Pa., assistant professor, 1950-56; State University of New York College at Buffalo, director of creative education, 1956-67, professor of creative studies, 1967—. Creative Education Foundation, president. Military service: U.S. Army, Signal Corps, 1943-45. Member: National Society for the Study of Communication, American Society for Training and Development.

WRITINGS: (With Harold F. Harding) A Source Book for Creative Thinking, Scribner, 1962; Creative Behavior Guidebook and Workbook, Scribner, 1967; Creativity, Unlocking Human Potential, DOK Publishers, 1972; (with Ruth B. Noller) Toward Supersanity: Channeled Freedom, DOK Publishers, 1973; Aha! Insights into Creative Behavior, DOK Publishers, 1975.

WORK IN PROGRESS: The nurture of creative behavior.

*   *   *

PARRINDER, E(dward) Geoffrey   1910-

PERSONAL: Born April 30, 1910, in London, England; son of William Patrick (a glove agent) and Florence (Bellamy) Parrinder; married Mary Burt, July 25, 1936; children: Catharine (Mrs. David Boston), Philip, Stephen. Education: Attended University of Montpellier, 1932-33; Richmond College, London, B.A., 1938, B.D., 1940; University of London, Ph.D., 1946, D.D., 1952. Politics: "Non-party." Home: 31 Charterhouse Rd., Orpington, Kent, England. Office: King's College, University of London, Strand, London W.C. 2, England.

CAREER: Methodist clergyman. Teacher in Dahomey, Ivory Coast, Nigeria, Africa, 1933-58; University of London, King's College, London, England, reader, 1958-70, professor of comparative study of religions, 1970—, dean of faculty of theology, 1972-74. Wilde lecturer in natural and comparative religion, Oxford University, 1966-69. Member: International Association for the History of Religions (president of British branch, 1972—), Royal Asiatic Society, London Society for Study of Religion.

WRITINGS: West African Religion, Epworth, 1949, 2nd edition, 1961; West African Psychology, Lutterworth, 1951; Religion in an African City, Oxford University Press, 1953; African Traditional Religion, Hutchinson, 1954, 3rd edition, S.P.C.K., 1974; Introduction to Asian Religions, S.P.C.K., 1957; Witchcraft, Penguin, 1958, 2nd edition, Faber, 1962; Worship in the World's Religions, Association Press, 1961, 2nd edition, Sheldon, 1975; Upanishads, Gita and Bible, Faber, 1962, 2nd edition, 1975, Association Press, 1963; Comparative Religion, Allen & Unwin, 1962, Macmillan, 1963; What World Religions Teach, Harrap, 1963, 2nd edition, 1968; Witchcraft European and African, Barnes & Noble, 1963; Jesus in the Qur'an, Barnes & Noble, 1963; The World's Living Religions, Pan Books, 1964, published as Faiths of Mankind, Crowell, 1965, revised edition published in England as Handbook of Living Religions, Arthur Barker, 1967; Christian Debate: Light from the East, Gollancz, 1964, Doubleday, 1966; African Mythology, Paul Hamlyn, 1968; Religion in Africa, Penguin, 1969.

Avatar and Incarnation: The Wilde Lectures in Natural and Comparative Religion at the University of Oxford, Barnes & Noble, 1970; *Dictionary of Non-Christian Religions,* Westminister, 1971; (editor) *Man and His Gods,* Hamlyn, 1971; *The Indestructible Soul,* Allen & Unwin, 1973; *The Bhagarad Gita: A Verse Translation,* Sheldon, 1974, Dutton, 1975; *The Wisdom of the Forest,* Sheldon, 1975. Contributor to *Reader's Digest, London Quarterly, Man, Africa,* and other publications. Member of editorial board, *Religious Studies,* and *Journal of Religion in Africa.*

WORK IN PROGRESS: Mysticism in the World's Religions, for Sheldon.

* * *

PARSONS, William Edward, Jr. 1936-

PERSONAL: Born April 16, 1936, in Lynn, Mass.; son of William Edward (a steamfitter) and Marylyn G. (Bishop) Parsons; married Constance M. Latham (a registered nurse), August 2, 1964; children: Beth Ann, Debra Lynn, Michael William. *Education:* Duke University, B.A., 1958; Drew Theological School, B.D., 1961; Andover Newton Theological School, S.T.M., 1970, currently doctoral candidate. *Office:* U.S. Naval Submarine Base, New London, Groton, Conn. 06340.

CAREER: Methodist clergyman. U.S. Navy, chaplain, 1961—, currently stationed at Submarine Base, Groton, Conn.

WRITINGS: Meditations for Servicemen, Abingdon, 1967; *Silly Putty and Other Children's Sermons,* Abingdon, 1973.

WORK IN PROGRESS: Counseling Insights: A Practical Application of the Counseling Theories of C. G. Jung, William Glasser, and Eric Berne.

* * *

PASCAL, Paul 1925-

PERSONAL: Born March 26, 1925, in New York, N.Y.; son of Benjamin (a musician) and Lillian (Simpson) Pascal; married Naomi Brenner (an editor), June 27, 1948; children: David, Janet. *Education:* University of Vermont, A.B., 1948; American Academy, Rome, Italy, graduate study, 1950-52; University of North Carolina, Ph.D., 1953. *Office:* Classics Department, University of Washington, Seattle, Wash. 98105.

CAREER: University of Washington, Seattle, assistant professor, 1953-63, associate professor, 1963-74, professor of classics, 1974—. *Military service:* U.S. Army, 1943-45; became sergeant. *Member:* American Philological Association.

WRITINGS: (Translator with J. K. Sowards) *The Julius Exclusus of Erasmus,* Indiana University Press, 1968.

* * *

PATERSON, Katherine (Womeldorf) 1932-

PERSONAL: Born October 31, 1932, in Tsing-Tsiang pu, China; daughter of George Raymond (a clergyman) and Mary (Goetchius) Womeldorf; married John Barstow Paterson (a clergyman), July 14, 1962; children: Elizabeth Polin, John Barstow, Jr., David Lord, Mary Katherine. *Education:* King College, A.B., 1954; Presbyterian School of Christian Education, M.A., 1957; Union Theological Seminary, New York, N.Y., M.R.E., 1962. *Politics:* Democrat. *Religion:* United Presbyterian Church. *Home:* 514 Albany Ave., Takoma Park, Md. 20012.

CAREER: Public school teacher in Lovettsville, Va., 1954-55; Presbyterian Church in the United States, Board of World Missions, Nashville, Tenn., missionary in Japan, 1957-62; Pennington School for Boys, Pennington, N.J., teacher of sacred studies and English, 1963-65.

WRITINGS: Who Am I?, John Knox, 1968; *To Make Men Free,* John Knox, 1973; *Justice for All People,* Friendship, 1973; *The Sign of the Chrysanthemum,* Crowell, 1973; *Of Nightingales that Weep,* Crowell, 1974; *The Master Puppeteer,* Crowell, 1976. Contributor to journals.

WORK IN PROGRESS: A book tentatively entitled *Bridge to Terabithia.*

* * *

PATTEN, Thomas H., Jr. 1929-

PERSONAL: Born March 24, 1929, in Cambridge, Mass.; son of Thomas H. and Lydia (Lindgren) Patten; married; wife's name Julie; children: Laurie, Rhonda. *Education:* Brown University, A.B., 1953; Cornell University, M.S., 1955, Ph.D., 1959. *Office:* School of Labor and Industrial Relations, 409 South Kedzie Hall, Michigan State University, East Lansing, Mich. 48823.

CAREER: Ford Motor Co., various executive positions in training and personnel, 1957-65; University of Detroit, Detroit, Mich., professor of management and sociology in College of Commerce and Finance and College of Arts and Sciences, 1965-67; Michigan State University, East Lansing, professor of industrial relations and associate director, School of Labor and Industrial Relations, 1967—. *Military service:* U.S. Marine Corps, 1946-48; served in China. *Member:* American Sociological Association (fellow), Industrial Relations Research Association, American Compensation Association, American Society for Training and Development, International Personnel Management Association, Phi Beta Kappa, Phi Kappa Phi.

WRITINGS: The Foreman: Forgotten Man of Management, American Management Association, 1968; *Manpower Planning and the Development of Human Resources,* Wiley, 1971; *Organization Development: Emerging Dimensions and Concepts,* American Society for Training and Development, 1973; *Pay: Employee Compensation and Incentive Plans,* Free Press, in press; *Organizational Development Through Teambuilding,* Wiley, in press. Writer of articles and reviews concerning personnel management, labor relations, and industrial sociology.

* * *

PATTERSON, C(ecil) H(olden) 1912-

PERSONAL: Born June 22, 1912, in Lynn, Mass.; son of Cecil Edwin and Emma (Banks) Patterson; married Frances Spano, July 4, 1942 (deceased); children: Joseph, Francine, Jenifer (Mrs. Andrew Cohen), Christopher, Thomas, Mary, Charles. *Education:* University of Chicago, B.A., 1938; University of Minnesota, M.A., 1945, Ph.D., 1955. *Home:* 603 West Main, Urbana, Ill. 61801. *Office:* University of Illinois, Urbana, Ill. 61801.

CAREER: Antioch College, Yellow Springs, Ohio, assistant psychologist at Fels Research Institute, 1939-41; U.S. Veterans Administration, clinical psychologist at Veterans Administration Hospital, Canadaigua, N.Y., 1946-47, counseling psychologist at Veterans Administration Regional Office, St. Paul, Minn., 1947-56; University of Illinois, College of Education, Urbana, associate professor, 1956-60, professor of educational psychology, 1960—. *Mili-*

tary service: U.S. Army Air Forces, 1942-46. Member: American Psychological Association (fellow), American Personnel and Guidance Association.

WRITINGS: The Wechsler-Bellevue Scales: A Guide for Counselors, C. C Thomas, 1953; Counseling the Emotionally Disturbed, Harper, 1958; Counseling and Psychotherapy: Theory and Practice, Harper, 1959; (editor) Readings in Rehabilitation Counseling, Stipes, 1960, revised edition, 1971; Counseling and Guidance Services in Schools: A First Course, Harper, 1962, revised edition, 1971; Theories of Counseling and Psychotherapy, Harper, 1966, 2nd edition, 1973; (editor) The Counselor in the School: Selected Readings, McGraw, 1967; Humanistic Education, Prentice-Hall, 1973; Relationship Counseling and Psychotherapy, Harper, 1974.

Contributor: H. Borow, editor, Man in a World of Work, Houghton, 1964; J. C. Gowan and G. D. Demos, editors, Guidance of Exceptional Children, McKay, 1965; Counseling and Psychotherapy: An Overview, McGraw, 1967. Contributor of more than 150 articles to counseling, rehabilitation, and psychology journals, a number of them reprinted in books.

* * *

PATTERSON, James (Tyler) 1935-

PERSONAL: Born February 12, 1935, in Bridgeport, Conn.; son of James (a lawyer and politician) and Sarah (Sands) Patterson; married Nancy Weeks, June 15, 1962; children: Stephen, Marjorie. Education: Williams College, B.A., 1957; Harvard University, M.A., 1961, Ph.D., 1964. Office: History Department, Brown University, Providence, R.I. 02906.

CAREER: Newspaper reporter for two years, and high school teacher for one; Indiana University, Bloomington, assistant professor, 1964-67, associate professor, 1967-70, professor of history, 1970-72; Brown University, Providence, R.I., professor of history, 1972—. Military service: U.S. Army Reserve, 1957-62; active duty, 1957. Member: American Historical Association, Organization of American Historians, Phi Beta Kappa. Awards, honors: Annual manuscript award of the Organization of American Historians, 1966, for Congressional Conservatism and the New Deal; Guggenheim fellowship, 1968-69; National Endowment for the Humanities fellowship, 1969-70.

WRITINGS: Congressional Conservatism and the New Deal: The Formation of the Conservative Coalition in Congress, 1933-1939, University of Kentucky Press, 1967; The New Deal and the States: Federalism in Transition, Princeton University Press, 1969; Mr. Republican: A Biography of Robert A. Taft, Houghton, 1972; Paths to the Present, Burgess, 1975. Contributor to history journals including American History Review, Journal of American History, Journal of Politics, and Historian.

SIDELIGHTS: Patterson has "fair" competence in speaking and reading German; has lived in England and Germany. Avocational interests: Modern literature, sports, politics, travel, and music.

* * *

PATTILLO, Manning M., Jr. 1919-

PERSONAL: Born October 11, 1919, in Charlottesville, Va.; son of Manning M. and Margaret (Camblos) Pattillo; married Martha Aileen Crawford, June 8, 1946; children: Manning M. III, Martha, John. Education: Johns Hopkins

University, student, 1937-38; University of the South, B.A., 1941; University of Chicago, A.M., 1947, Ph.D., 1949. Religion: Episcopalian. Home: 1571 Windsor Parkway, Northeast, Atlanta, Ga. 30319. Office: Oglethorpe University, 4484 Peachtree Rd., Northeast, Atlanta, Ga. 30319.

CAREER: University of Chicago, Chicago, Ill., 1949-56, began as instructor, became associate professor of higher education; Lilly Endowment (philanthropic foundation), Indianapolis, Ind., associate director, 1956-60, executive director for education, 1960-62; Danforth Foundation (philanthropic foundation), St. Louis, Mo., 1962-67, began as associate director, became vice-president; Foundation Library Center (research and information agency for organized philanthropy), New York City, president, 1967-72; University of Rochester, Rochester, N.Y., director of special projects, 1972-75; Oglethorpe University, Atlanta, Ga., president, 1975—. Consultant to colleges, universities, and foundations, 1962—. Active in college accrediting program for North Central Association of Colleges and Secondary Schools, 1949-56. Member: Higher Education Colloquium (steering committee, 1964—), Missouri Historical Society, Phi Beta Kappa, Century Association (New York City), University Club (St. Louis). Awards, honors: LL.D., LeMoyne College and St. John's University; L.H.D. from University of Detroit, College of New Rochelle, and Park College; Litt.D., St. Norbert College.

WRITINGS—With Donald M. Mackenzie: Eight Hundred Colleges Face the Future, Danforth Foundation, 1964; Church-Sponsored Higher Education in the United States, American Council on Education, 1966. Contributor to Liberal Education, College Management, Foundation News, and other professional journals.

WORK IN PROGRESS: Continuing research in the problems and management of philanthropic foundations and the role and financial support of higher education.

* * *

PAULSEN, F(rank) Robert 1922-

PERSONAL: Born 1922, in Logan, Utah; son of Frank and Ella (Ownby) Paulsen; married Marye Lucile Harris, July 31, 1942; married Lydia Ransier Lowry, November 1, 1969; children: (first marriage) Robert Keith. Education: Utah State University, B.S., 1947; University of Utah, M.S., 1949, Ed.D., 1956; postdoctoral study at University of Oregon, 1958, and University of Michigan, 1959-60. Office: College of Education, University of Arizona, Tucson, Ariz. 85721.

CAREER: High school principal, Mount Emmons, Utah, 1948-51; superintendent of schools, Cokeville, Wyo., 1951-55; University of Utah, Salt Lake City, 1955-61, began as assistant professor, became associate professor of education; University of Connecticut, Storrs, professor of education and dean of School of Education, 1961-64; University of Arizona, Tucson, dean of College of Education, 1964—. Vice-president and chairman of board, Southwestern Cooperative Educational Laboratory, 1966—; chairman, State Advisory Committee for Administrator Certification in Connecticut, 1962-64; member, Arizona Advisory Committee on Certification and Teacher Education, 1964—; trustee, Joint Council on Economic Education, 1962-65; member of board of directors, American Journal of Nursing, 1966—. Military service: U.S. Army, 1942-45; served in Southwest Pacific theatre.

MEMBER: American Academy of Political Science,

American Association for the Advancement of Science, American Association of School Administrators, American Educational Research Association, Association for Higher Education, National Education Association, National League for Nursing, Utah Academy of Letters, Arts, and Sciences (honorary), Pi Sigma Alpha, Pi Gamma Mu, Phi Delta Kappa, Kappa Delta Pi, Rotary Club. *Awards, honors:* Postdoctoral fellowships from Kellogg Foundation, 1958, and Carnegie Foundation, 1959-60.

WRITINGS: The Administration of Public Education in Utah, University of Utah Press, 1958; (contributor) Donald E. Tope, editor, *A Forward Look: The Preparation of School Administrators, 1970,* University of Oregon Press, 1960; (contributor) *Administrative Relationships,* Prentice-Hall, 1960; (editor and contributor) *Contemporary Issues in American Education,* University of Arizona Press, 1967; *American Education: Challenges and Images,* University of Arizona Press, 1967; (editor and contributor) *Higher Education: Dimensions and Directions,* University of Arizona Press, 1970. Contributor to *Nursing Outlook, Social Work,* and education journals.

* * *

PAULSON, Belden 1927-

PERSONAL: Born June 29, 1927; son of Henry Thomas (a lawyer) and Evelina (Belden) Paulson; married Louise Hill, January 9, 1954; children: Eric, Steven. *Education:* Oberlin College, B.A., 1950; University of Chicago, M.A., 1955, Ph.D., 1962. *Religion:* Congregationalist. *Home:* 2602 East Newberry, Milwaukee, Wis. 53211. *Office:* University of Wisconsin-Milwaukee, Milwaukee, Wis. 53201.

CAREER: Co-founder and director of slum settlement center, Casa Mia, in Naples, Italy, 1950-53, and of pilot refugee project for establishing refugees in a newly founded community on Sardinia, Italy, 1957-59; United Nations High Commissioner for Refugees, special consultant, Rome, Italy, 1960-61; University of Wisconsin-Milwaukee, assistant professor, 1962-67, associate professor, 1968-70, professor in political science department and at University Extension, 1971—, specializing in politics of developing areas and urban politics. Chairman, program for quality education. *Military service:* U.S. Navy, 1945-46.

MEMBER: American Political Science Association, Society for International Development, Adult Education Association of the U.S.A., American Association of University Professors, Latin American Studies Association, American Association for the Advancement of Science. *Awards, honors:* Subject of network television show "This is Your Life," National Broadcasting Co., March, 1958; award for best case study at Adult Education Association annual conference, 1966. Research awards from Agency for International Development, University of Wisconsin Graduate School, and Social Science Research Council, for work in Italy, 1964, 1973, 1974, and Brazil, 1963, 1967-68.

WRITINGS: (Co-author) *Area Handbook on Jammu and Kashmir State,* edited by Robert I. Crane, Human Relations Area File Press, 1956; *Local Political Patterns in Northeast Brazil: A Community Case Study,* Land Tenure Center, 1964; *The Searchers: Conflict and Communism in an Italian Town,* Quadrangle, 1966. Contributor to political science, adult education, and community development journals.

WORK IN PROGRESS: Research on refugee communities and on a small village in southern Italy; research on urban politics.

SIDELIGHTS: Paulson is active in developing university-related programs in Milwaukee's inner city. He is fluent in Italian, and can communicate in Portuguese. *Avocational interests:* "Weekend farmer."

BIOGRAPHICAL/CRITICAL SOURCES: Kubly, *American in Italy,* Simon & Schuster, 1955.

* * *

PAVEL, Frances 1907-

PERSONAL: Born February 26, 1907, in Bethlehem, Pa.; daughter of Johann and Cecilia (Svantner) Kvacky; married Otto J. Pavel, February 16, 1945. *Education:* West Chester State Teachers College (now West Chester State College), B.S. in Ed., 1935; Columbia University, M.A. in Ed., 1941; other graduate courses at University of California, Los Angeles, and California State College at Los Angeles. *Home:* 4913 Alhama Dr., Woodland Hills, Calif. 91364.

CAREER: Southampton (Pa.) public schools, elementary teacher and principal, 1935-40; Mansfield State Teachers College (now Mansfield State College), Mansfield, Pa., demonstration teacher in laboratory school, 1941-42; Inglewood (Calif.) public schools, elementary teacher, 1944-49, principal, 1949-63. Editor and consultant, Silver Burdett Co., 1942-44.

WRITINGS: Archelon and the Sea Dragon, Children's Press, 1975.

"Read It Myself" series; adaptations; all published by Holt: *The Wolf and the Seven Little Kids,* 1961; *The Ugly Duckling,* 1961; *The Elves and the Shoemaker,* 1961; *Rumpelstilskin,* 1961; *Hansel and Gretel,* 1961; *Goldilocks and the Three Bears,* 1962; *Little Red Riding Hood,* 1962; *Jack and the Beanstalk,* 1962; *Peter and the Wolf,* 1962; *The Frog Prince,* 1962; *Snow White and the Seven Dwarfs,* 1962; *The Golden Goose,* 1962.

WORK IN PROGRESS: Additional adaptations for "Read It Myself" series, including *Little Red Riding Hood, The Wolf and the Seven Little Kids,* and *Peter and the Wolf,* for Franska Publishing; further research and writing about prehistoric sea creatures.

* * *

PAVENSTEDT, Eleanor 1903-

PERSONAL: Born March 16, 1903, in New York, N.Y.; daughter of Edmund William and Elizabeth C. (Probst) Pavenstedt. *Education:* Medical student at University of Geneva, 1922-25, 1926-28, and University of Zurich, 1925-26; University of Geneva, M.D., 1929. *Politics:* Democrat. *Religion:* None. *Home:* 3049 Main Rd., Tiverton, R.I. 02878. *Office:* Tufts-Columbia Point Health Center, 300 Mount Vernon St., Dorchester, Mass. 02125.

CAREER: Massachusetts General Hospital, Boston, assistant child psychiatrist, 1934-37; James Jackson Putnam Children's Center, Roxbury, Mass., senior psychiatrist, 1942-54; Boston University School of Medicine, Boston, Mass., assistant professor, 1954-58, associate professor, 1958-59, professor of child psychiatry, 1959—; Tufts-Columbia Point Health Center, Dorchester, Mass., staff child psychiatrist, 1966—. Training analyst, Boston Psychoanalytical Society and Institute, 1950—. Lecturer, Tufts Medical School, 1965—. *Member:* American Orthopsychiatric Association (fellow; member of board of directors, 1966—), American Academy of Child Psychiatry (fellow; member of council, 1957-62), American Psychoanalytic Association (member of board on professional standards, 1954-56).

Awards, honors: Commonwealth Fund grant to study early child-rearing and mother-child relationship in Japan, 1963-64.

WRITINGS: (Editor with Lucie Jessner) *Dynamic Psychopathology,* Grune, 1959; (editor and contributor) *The Drifters: Children of Disorganized Lower Class Families,* Little, Brown, 1967; (with Viola W. Bernard) *Crisis of Family Disorganization: Programs to Soften Their Impact on Children,* Behavioral Publications, 1971. Contributor to professional journals.†

* * *

PAWLIKOWSKI, John 1940-

PERSONAL: Surname is pronounced Paw-lee-*cow*-ski; born November 2, 1940, in Chicago, Ill.; son of Thaddeus John (a cork molder) and Anna (Mizera) Pawlikowski. *Education:* Studied at Mount St. Philip, Milwaukee, Wis., 1958-60, and Servite Priory, Benburb, Northern Ireland, 1960-62; Loyola University, Chicago, Ill., A.B., 1963, graduate study, 1963-66; also studied at Stonebridge Priory, Lake Bluff, Ill., 1963-66, College of Jewish Studies, Chicago, Ill., 1965 (diploma, 1967), and University of Wisconsin, 1965-67; St. Mary of the Lake Seminary, Mundelein, Ill., S.T.B., 1967; University of Chicago, Ph.D., 1970. *Politics:* "Generally Democratic." *Home:* 1420 East 49th St., Chicago, Ill. 60615. *Office:* Catholic Theological Union, 5401 South Cornell Ave., Chicago, Ill. 60615.

CAREER: Ordained Roman Catholic priest of Servite Fathers (O.S.M.), 1967; University of Chicago, Chicago, Ill., chaplain's assistant at Calvert House (Newman Club), 1967—; Catholic Theological Union, Chicago, assistant professor of ethics, 1968—, acting president. Seminarian-Lay Apostolate Conference, executive chairman, 1964-65, member of executive committee, 1965-66; member of advisory committee, Secretariat for Catholic-Jewish Relations, National Conference of Catholic Bishops, 1971-73; chairman of National Council of Churches' Faith and Order Study Commission on Israel, 1972-73, and Chicago Institute for Inter-religious Research, 1973; fellow, International Institute of Community Service, 1975; also affiliated with Anti-Defamation League of B'nai B'rith, Inter-Seminary Movement, and Southern Christian Leadership Conference. *Member:* American Society of Christian Ethics, Catholic Theological Society of America, American Academy of Religion. *Awards, honors:* Fellowship to Institute of Jewish Studies, Wheeling College; Men of Achievement Award, 1973; Inter-faith Award, American Jewish Committee, 1973; Founder's Citation, National Catholic Conference for Interracial Justice.

WRITINGS: Epistle Homilies, Bruce Publishing, 1966; (contributor) Walter Wagoner, *The Seminary,* Sheed, 1966; *Catechetics and Prejudice,* Paulist/Newman, 1973; (contributor) Michael Zeik and Martin Siegel, editors, *Root and Branch,* Roth, 1973; (contributor) Robert Heyer, editor, *Jewish/Christian Relations,* Paulist/Newman, 1975. Also author of *Proposals for Church-Sponsored New Housing,* 1971. Contributor to journals, including *Furrow, Today, Journal of Ecumenical Studies, Cross Currents, Journal of Religion,* and *Ecumenist.*

WORK IN PROGRESS: Books on theological foundations of social ethics and on Christ and the Jewish-Christian dialogue.

SIDELIGHTS: Father Pawlikowski speaks Polish and some German, modern Hebrew, and French; he reads Latin, French, German, Hebrew (Biblical and modern), and Greek (classical and modern).

PEACH, William Nelson 1912-

PERSONAL: Born October 21, 1912, in Granite, Md.; son of Frank and Mary Anna (Nelson) Peach; married Dorothy Jean Housman, September 1, 1939; children: Dorothy Jean, James Thomas, Joseph William. *Education:* Loyola College, Baltimore, Md., A.B., 1935; Johns Hopkins University, Ph.D., 1939. *Home:* 523 Chautauqua, Norman, Okla. 73069. *Office:* University of Oklahoma, Norman, Okla. 73069.

CAREER: University of Texas, Austin, instructor in economics, 1938-42; Federal Reserve Bank, Dallas, Tex., assistant manager of research and statistics department, 1942-44; University of Texas, assistant professor of economics, 1946-47; University of Syracuse, Syracuse, N.Y., associate professor of economics, 1947-49; University of Oklahoma, Norman, professor of economics, 1949-65, research professor of economics, 1965—. Visiting professor at North Texas State University and College of William and Mary, Norfolk Division. Consultant to University of Pennsylvania-University of Karachi project in Pakistan, 1956-58, to Select Committee on Small Business, U.S. House of Representatives, 1960, to International Cooperation Administration in Sierra Leone and Yemen, 1960, and to Agency for International Development in Washington, D.C., 1961-62, and Brazil, 1964. *Military service:* U.S. Navy, 1944-46.

MEMBER: American Economic Association, American Society for Public Administration, Regional Science Association, Southern Economic Association, Southwestern Social Science Association, Midwest Economic Association, Beta Gamma Sigma, Delta Sigma Pi.

WRITINGS: The Security Affiliates of National Banks, Johns Hopkins Press, 1941; (with Walter Krause) *Basic Data of the American Economy,* Irwin, 1948, 4th edition, 1955; *Principles of Economics,* Irwin, 1955, 3rd edition, 1965; (with George W. Rucker and M. Uzair) *Basic Data of the Economy of Pakistan,* Oxford University Press, 1959; (with Richard W. Poole and James E. Tarver) *County Building Block Data for Regional Analysis: Oklahoma,* Research Foundation, Oklahoma State University, 1965; (with Richard W. Poole, James E. Tarver, Larkin B. Warner, and Lee B. Zink) *Source Notes and Explanations to County Building Block Data for Regional Analysis, Arkansas, Iowa, Kansas, Missouri, Nebraska and Oklahoma,* Research Foundation, Oklahoma State University, 1965; (with Richard W. Poole) *Human and Material Resources of Bryan County, a Profile for Growth and Development,* and sixteen other similarly titled volumes on various Oklahoma counties, Technology Use Studies Center, Southeastern State College, 1965; (reviser with J. A. Constantin) E. W. Zimmerman, *World Resources and Industries,* Harper, 1972; *The Energy Outlook for the 1980's,* U.S. Government Printing Office, 1973. Also author of *A Handbook on the Investment of Reserve Funds,* with Clay L. Cochran and Robert I. Kabat, 1955.

Contributor: Lawrence S. Ritter, editor, *Money and Economic Activity,* Houghton, 1952; Mazafer Sherif and M. O. Wilson, editors, *Emerging Problems in Social Psychology,* University Book Exchange, University of Oklahoma, 1957; Norman W. Brown, editor, *India, Pakistan, Ceylon,* revised edition, University of Pennsylvania Press, 1964. Contributor to *Encyclopedia Americana,* and to journals, including *Rural Electrification, Sooner Magazine,* and *Pakistan Economic Journal.*

PEACOCK, L(elon) J(ames) 1928-

PERSONAL: Born May 25, 1928, in Brevard, N.C.; son of L. J. and Dorothy (Barrett) Peacock; married Marian Davis, June 8, 1945; children: Lynn Barrett, Janice Davis, Timothy Lee. *Education:* Attended Emory University, 1945-47; Berea College, A.B., 1950; University of Kentucky, M.S., 1952, Ph.D., 1956. *Office:* Department of Psychology, University of Georgia, Athens, Ga.

CAREER: U.S. Army Medical Research Laboratory, Fort Knox, Ky., psychophysiologist, 1954-56; Yerkes Laboratories of Primate Biology, Inc., Orange Park, Fla., research associate, 1956-58, acting director, 1958-59; University of Georgia, Athens, assistant professor, 1959-62, associate professor, 1963, professor of psychology, 1966—. *Member:* American Psychological Association, American Association for the Advancement of Science, Society for Neurosciences, Society for Psychophysiological Research, Psychometric Society, International Primatological Society, Southern Society for Philosophy and Psychology, Sigma Xi, Phi Kappa Phi.

WRITINGS: (With R. V. Heckel) *Textbook of General Psychology,* Mosby, 1966. Author or co-author of research reports published by Army Medical Research Laboratory. Contributor to *Nature, Science,* and psychology journals.

* * *

PEARSALL, Ronald 1927-

PERSONAL: Surname is pronounced *Peer*-sall; born October 20, 1927, in Birmingham, England; son of Joseph (an engineer) and Elsie Caroline (Rawlins) Pearsall. *Education:* Studied art, 1950-52, and attended Birmingham College of Art, 1952-54. *Politics:* Conservative. *Religion:* Church of England. *Home:* Ashbrook Park, 9 Upper Church St., St. Leonards on Sea, Sussex, England.

CAREER: Traveled about England, 1954-61, working variously as bank clerk, cinema manager, wine waiter, dance hall musician, private detective, composer, and at other short-term jobs in twenty cities; full-time writer, 1961—. Lecturer in Sweden for British Council, 1964. *Military service:* British Army, Royal Corps of Signals, 1945-48. *Member:* Society for Psychical Research, London Library.

WRITINGS: Scarlet Mask (spy thriller), Lloyd Cole, 1941; *Is That My Hook in Your Ear?,* Stanley Paul, 1966; *Worm in the Bud,* Macmillan, 1969; *The Table Rappers,* St. Martin's, 1972; *Victorian Sheet Music Covers,* Gale, 1972; *Victorian Popular Music,* Gale, 1972; *Collecting Mechanical Antiques,* Arco, 1973; *Edwardian Life and Leisure,* St. Martin's, 1973; *Collecting Scientific Instruments,* Arco, 1974; *Inside the Antique Trade,* Reid & Son, 1974; *Edwardian Popular Music,* David & Charles, 1975; *Night's Black Angels: The Forms and Faces of Victorian Cruelty,* McKay, 1975. Contributor to *Punch, Quarterly Review, Motoring, Homes and Gardens, Field History Today, Books & Bookmen, Ideal Home, Music Review,* and other periodicals in Britain, United States, Canada, and Australia.

SIDELIGHTS: Scarlet Mask, a paperback, was published when Pearsall was fourteen ("the firm decamped without paying me any royalties"). The magazines for which Pearsall has since written range from *Choir* to *Romance, Industrial Safety* to *Animals,* and *Gamekeeper* to *Lady.*

BIOGRAPHICAL/CRITICAL SOURCES: Home and Gardens, August, 1964.

PEDEN, William (Harwood) 1913-

PERSONAL: Born March 22, 1913, in New York, N.Y.; son of Horatio H. and Catherine (Hanna) Peden; married second wife, Margaret Sayers (a professor of Spanish), September 18, 1965; children: (first marriage) Eliza Margaret (Mrs. Carl Mitchell), Sally Munroe; stepchildren: Kerry, Kyle. *Education:* University of Virginia, B.S., 1934, M.S., 1936, Ph.D., 1942. *Politics:* Democrat. *Religion:* Episcopalian. *Home:* 408 Tilly, Columbia, Mo. 65201. *Office:* Arts and Science 227, University of Missouri, Columbia, Mo. 65201.

CAREER: University of Maryland, College Park, instructor, 1938-42, assistant professor of English, 1942-44; University of Virginia, Charlottesville, faculty member of Extension Division, U.S. Armed Forces Institute, 1944-46; University of Missouri, Columbia, associate professor, 1946-50, professor of English, 1950—, writing program director, 1946—, director of university press, 1958-62, member of editorial board of university press, 1962—. Visiting professor, University of New Mexico, 1955-56, University of Maryland, 1971. Lecturer at writers' conferences; member of advisory committee, Scholastic Creative Writing Awards, 1960—; member of executive board, Associated Writing Programs, 1971—. *Awards, honors:* Guggenheim fellowship, 1961-62; Thomas Jefferson Award, McConnell Foundation, 1972.

WRITINGS: Some Aspects of Jefferson Bibliography, Washington and Lee University Press, 1940; (editor with Adrienne Koch) *Life and Selected Writings of Thomas Jefferson,* Modern Library, 1944; (author of introduction) *Thomas Jefferson's 1828 Catalogue of the Library of the University of Virginia,* University Press of Virginia, 1945; (editor with Koch) *Selected Writings of John and John Quincy Adams,* Knopf, 1946; (editor and author of introduction and notes) Increase Mather, *Testimony Against Prophane Customs,* University Press of Virginia, 1953; (editor and author of introduction and notes) Thomas Jefferson, *Notes on the State of Virginia,* University of North Carolina Press, 1954.

(Author of introduction) *Modern Short Stories from Story Magazine,* Grosset, 1960; (editor) *Twenty-Nine Stories,* Houghton, 1960, 2nd edition, 1967; *The American Short Story: Front Line in the National Defense of Literature,* Houghton, 1964; (author of introduction) *Stories by Jean Stafford, John Cheever, Daniel Fuchs, William Maxwell,* Noonday Press, 1966; (author of introduction) *The Golden Shore: Great Short Stories for Young Readers,* Platt, 1967; *Night in Funland, and Other Stories,* Louisiana State University Press, 1968; *Short Fiction: Shape and Substance,* Houghton, 1971; *New Writing from South Carolina,* University of South Carolina Press, 1971; (with George Garrett) *Twilight at Monticello* (novel), Houghton, 1973; *The American Short Story: Continuity and Change,* Houghton, 1975. Contributor of stories and reviews to *New York Times Book Review, Saturday Review, Virginia Quarterly,* and other periodicals. Former book review editor, *Missourian;* editor, *Story,* 1959-62; member of editorial committee, *Studies in Short Fiction,* 1963—.

WORK IN PROGRESS: A novel; short stories; a "personal" biographical study of Thomas Jefferson.

* * *

PELLOWSKI, Anne 1933-

PERSONAL: Born June 28, 1933, in Pine Creek, Wis.; daughter of Alexander (a farmer) and Anna (Dorava) Pellowski. *Education:* College of St. Teresa, B.A., 1955; Columbia University, M.S.L.S. (with honors), 1959; additional graduate study at University of Minnesota, summer, 1955, University of Munich, 1955-56, and New School for Social Research, 1965. *Religion:* Roman Catholic. *Office:* U.S. Committee for UNICEF, 331 East 38th St., New York, N.Y. 10016.

CAREER: College of St. Teresa, Winona, Minn., instructor in English, 1956-57; Winona Public Library, Winona, children's librarian, 1957; New York Public Library, New York City, children's librarian, 1957-59, researcher, 1960-65, senior children's librarian, 1961-62, assistant storytelling and group work specialist, Office of Children's Services, 1963-65; University of Maryland, Overseas Branch, Munich, Germany, instructor in English, 1959-60; U.S. Committee for UNICEF, New York City, director of Information Center on Children's Cultures, 1967—. Adjunct lecturer, University of Maryland, 1965-66; summer lecturer at University of Wisconsin, 1966, and Columbia University, 1967. United States representative at numerous international conferences, including International Film Festival, Moscow, 1973, and conference on film production and distribution of films for young people, Teheran, 1974. *Member:* American Library Association. *Awards, honors:* Fulbright fellow in Germany, 1955-56.

WRITINGS: The World of Children's Literature, Bowker, 1968; (author of introduction) Isabelle Jan, *On Children's Literature,* Schocken, 1974. Records stories for children under CMS label. Contributor to library journals.

SIDELIGHTS: Anne Pellowski was a researcher on children's literature at International Youth Library, Munich, 1955-56, 1959-60, 1966, at International Board on Books for Young People, Vienna, summer, 1963, and at U.S. Library of Congress, 1965-66. She is competent in German, French, Spanish, and Polish, and can work in several other languages.

*　　*　　*

PEPPER, Curtis G.   1920-
(Curtis Bill Pepper)

PERSONAL: Born August 30, 1920, in Huntington, W.Va.; son of Curtis Gordon and Edwina (Sheppard) Pepper; married Beverly Stoll (a sculptor), November 11, 1950; children: Jorie (daughter), John. *Education:* Attended University of Illinois, 1936-38. *Politics:* Democrat. *Home and office:* Torre Olivola, Torre Gentile di Todi (PG), Italy. *Agent:* Julian Bach, Jr., 3 East 48th St., New York, N.Y. 10017.

CAREER: Free-lance writer for television and films, 1949-55; United Press, bureau correspondent, Rome, Italy, 1955-57; Columbia Broadcasting System, bureau correspondent, Rome, Italy, 1957-58; *Newsweek,* bureau chief, Rome, Italy, 1958-68, covering Spain, Italy, Greece, and Middle East; free-lance writer, 1968—. *Military service:* U.S. Army, Military Intelligence, World War II; became major; received Bronze Star for service in Italy.

WRITINGS: The Pope's Back Yard (illustrated with photographs by the author), Farrar, Straus, 1966; (contributor) *Fighting Hero of Israel* (anthology), edited by Harold Ribalow, Signet, 1967; (contributor) *Under Fire* (anthology), edited by Donald Pope, Norton, 1968; *An Artist and the Pope,* Grosset, 1968; (with Christian Barnard) *One Life* (Barnard's autobiography), Macmillan, 1969.

WORK IN PROGRESS: A novel, tentatively entitled *Marco.*

BIOGRAPHICAL/CRITICAL SOURCES: John Bainbridge, *The Expatriots; Life,* October 11, 1969.

*　　*　　*

PEREYRA, Lillian A(nita)   1920-

PERSONAL: Surname is pronounced Pere-*air*-a; born May 9, 1920, in San Francisco, Calif. *Education:* Mount St. Mary's College, Los Angeles, Calif., A.B., 1953; Fordham University, M.A., 1955; University of California, Los Angeles, Ph.D., 1962. *Office:* University of Portland, 5000 North Willamette Blvd., Portland, Ore. 97203.

CAREER: St. Mary's College, Los Angeles, Calif., teacher, 1955-58; Mount St. Mary's College, Los Angeles, instructor in history, 1961-63; University of Portland, Portland, Ore., assistant professor, 1963-67, associate professor, 1967-71, professor of history, 1971—. *Military service:* U.S. Navy, Women's Reserve (WAVES), 1944-46. *Member:* Organization of American Historians, American Association of University Professors. *Awards, honors:* National Endowment for the Humanities senior fellowship, 1971.

WRITINGS: James Lusk Alcorn: Persistent Whig, Louisiana State University Press, 1966. Contributor to *Encyclopedia of World Biography,* 1974, and *Encyclopedia of Southern History.*

WORK IN PROGRESS: Those Gentlemen in Politics: An Account of the Southern Whigs.

*　　*　　*

PERKINS, Edward A., Jr.   1928-

PERSONAL: Born September 23, 1928, in Portland, Ore.; son of Edward A. and Blanche (Burkland) Perkins; married Marilyn Apted (a secretary), January 28, 1955; children: Michael E., Jeffrey C., Robert H., Deana M. *Education:* University of Washington, Seattle, B.A., 1953; Stanford University, M.A., 1956; Oregon State University, Ed.D., 1963. *Home address:* Route 2, Box 556, Pullman, Wash. 99163. *Office:* College of Economics and Business, Washington State University, Pullman, Wash. 99163.

CAREER: High school teacher in Seattle, Wash., 1953-56, in Burlingame, Calif., 1956-58; Oregon State University, Corvallis, instructor, 1958-61; Washington State University, Pullman, assistant professor, 1961-64, associate professor, 1964-69, professor of office administration and business education, 1969—, director, Office Occupations Research and Development Project, 1965-68, chairman of department of office administration, 1972—. Visiting summer professor, Utah State University, 1962, 1965. *Military service:* U.S. Air Force, 1946-49; became sergeant. U.S. Air Force Reserve, 1953—; currently captain. *Member:* National Business Education Association, Western Business Education Association (executive board; historian, 1966-67), Washington State Business Education Association (president, 1966), Eastern Washington Business Education Association (president, 1965-66), Phi Delta Kappa, Kappa Delta Pi.

WRITINGS: (With C. E. Reigel) *Executive Typewriting,* Gregg, 1966; (with Reigel and T. Lockwood) *Practice for Professional Typing,* Gregg, 1968. Also author of *Typing for the Air Force* and "Mimeograph Textbook Curriculum" series, both 1971, and "Fluid Instruction" series and *Reprographics in Business Education,* both 1972. Contributor to business education journals.

AVOCATIONAL INTERESTS: Sports, youth development programs.†

PERRY, Lloyd M(erle)   1916-

PERSONAL: Surname originally Perrigo; born May 24, 1916, in Hodgdon, Me.; son of Percy (a storekeeper) and Medston (Smith) Perrigo; married Elva Wilson, June 19, 1943; children: Rixson Merle, Gregg Chandler, Cynthia Jean. Education: Gordon College, A.B., 1939, B.D., 1943; Columbia University, M.A., 1946; Northern Baptist Theological Seminary, Th.D., 1948; Northwestern University, Ph.D., 1961. Home: 6380 Orchard Valley Dr., Gurnee, Ill. 60031. Office: Trinity Evangelical Divinity School, 2045 Half Day Rd., Deerfield, Ill. 60015.

CAREER: Pastor of Baptist churches in Hampton, N.H., 1940-43, and Brooklyn, N.Y., 1943-46; Aurora College, Aurora, Ill., associate professor of speech, 1946-47; Northern Baptist Seminary, Chicago, Ill., professor of public speaking, 1947-51; Gordon Divinity School, Beverly Farms, Mass., professor of practical theology, 1951-62; Central Baptist Church, Indianapolis, Ind., pastor, 1962-64; Trinity Evangelical Divinity School, Deerfield, Ill., professor of speech and homiletics and chairman of department, 1964—. Pastor of Baptist churches in Wheaton, Ill., 1949-51, Beverly, Mass., 1953-55, and Everett, Mass., 1958-59. Member: American Speech and Hearing Association, Association of Seminary Professors in the Practical Fields, National Association of Teachers of Speech, Phi Alpha Chi, Kappa Delta Pi.

WRITINGS: (With Faris D. Whitesell) Variety in Your Preaching, Revell, 1954; How to Study Your Bible, introduction by Billy Graham, Revell, 1957; (with Edward John Lias) A Manual of Pastoral Problems and Procedures, Baker Book, 1960; Trends and Emphasis in the Philosophy, Materials, and Methodology of American Protestant Homiletical Education as Established by a Study of Selected Trade and Textbooks Published between 1834 and 1954, Northwestern University Press, 1961; A Manual for Biblical Preaching, Baker Book, 1965; (with Robert D. Culver) How to Search the Scriptures, Baker Book, 1967; (contributor) Ralph G. Turnbull, editor, Baker's Dictionary of Practical Theology, Baker Book, 1967; (contributor) Roy C. Irving and Roy B. Zuck, editors, Youth and the Church, Moody, 1968; Biblical Sermon Guide, Baker Book, 1970; Biblical Preaching for Today's World, Moody, 1973; (co-author) Biblical Preaching: Learning to Present God's Message, Moody, 1975; Getting the Church on Target, Moody, 1976; (co-author) Counseling through Bible Preaching, Moody, in press.

*   *   *

PERVIN, Lawrence A.   1936-

PERSONAL: Born August 3, 1936, in Brooklyn, N.Y.; son of Murray (a businessman) and Mary (Reuthen) Pervin; married Barbara Zucker, June 21, 1958; children: David Joshua, Levi Jonathan. Education: Queens College (now Queens College of the City University of New York), B.A., 1957; Harvard University, Ph.D., 1962. Office: Livingston College, Rutgers University, New Brunswick, N.J. 08903.

CAREER: Princeton University, Princeton, N.J., lecturer, 1962-64, assistant professor of psychology, 1964-68; Rutgers University, Livingston College, New Brunswick, N.J., associate professor and associate dean, 1968-71, professor of psychology, 1971—. Member: American Psychological Association, American College Health Association, Phi Beta Kappa.

WRITINGS: (With L. E. Reik and W. Dalrymple) The College Dropout and the Utilization of Talent, Princeton University Press, 1966; Personality: Theory and Assessment, Wiley, 1970, 2nd edition, 1975.

WORK IN PROGRESS: Research on person–situation interaction.

*   *   *

PESEK, Boris P(eter)   1926-

PERSONAL: Born September 21, 1926, in Most, Czechoslovakia; son of Karel (a clerk) and Anna (Vondrakova) Pesek; married Milena Lambertova, October 28, 1948. Education: Attended Charles University, 1945-48; Coe College, B.A., 1952; University of Chicago, M.A., 1953, Ph.D., 1956. Religion: Roman Catholic. Home: 12928 North Colony Dr., Mequon, Wis. 53092. Office: Department of Economics, University of Wisconsin-Milwaukee, Milwaukee, Wis. 53201.

CAREER: Johns Hopkins University, Baltimore, Md., fellow in economics, 1956-57; Michigan State University, East Lansing, assistant professor, 1957-60, associate professor, 1960-62, professor of economics, 1962-67; University of Wisconsin-Milwaukee, professor of economics, 1967—. Member: American Economic Association, Econometric Society.

WRITINGS: Gross National Product of Czechoslovakia, 1945-1956, University of Chicago Press, 1965; (with T. R. Saving) Money, Wealth, and Economic Theory, Macmillan, 1967; Foundations of Money and Banking, Macmillan, 1968. Contributor to economic journals.

AVOCATIONAL INTERESTS: Gothic architecture, chess.

*   *   *

PETERFREUND, Sheldon P(aul)   1917-

PERSONAL: Born December 3, 1917, in Camden, N.J.; son of Otto (a storekeeper) and Sarah (Groag) Peterfreund; married Josephine Rogowicz (a teacher), 1949. Education: Harvard University, B.S., 1939; University of Chicago, M.A., 1940; University of Pennsylvania, Ph.D., 1948. Home: 20 Erregger Ter., Syracuse, N.Y. 13224. Office: Philosophy Department, Syracuse University, Syracuse, N.Y. 13210.

CAREER: Suffolk University, Boston, Mass., assistant professor of philosophy, 1948-49; Syracuse University, Syracuse, N.Y., assistant professor, 1949-55, associate professor, 1955-65, professor of philosophy, 1965—. Military service: U.S. Army Air Forces, 1942-45; became captain; received Air Medal and Presidential Citation. Member: American Philosophical Association, American Association of University Professors.

WRITINGS: (With others) Great Tradition in Ethics, American Book Co., 1953, 3rd edition, in press; An Introduction to American Philosophy, Odyssey, 1959; (with A. Denise) Contemporary Philosophy and Its Origins, Van Nostrand, 1967.

*   *   *

PETERS, Donald L.   1925-
(Leslie Peters)

PERSONAL: Born August 17, 1925, in Lincoln, Neb.; son of Leslie (an engineer) and Blanche (Perry) Peters; married Kristina Hansen, August 27, 1948; children: Scott H., John S. Education: Montana State University, B.S., 1953,

M.Ed., 1955; further graduate study at University of California, Berkeley, 1958, University of Montana, 1959, 1960, and periodically at Eastern Montana College. *Home:* 139 Birchwood Dr., Billings, Mont. 59102. *Office:* Will James Junior High School, Billings, Mont. 59102.

CAREER: Professional photographer in San Francisco, Calif., four years; Roundup (Mont.) public schools, teacher and counselor, 1954-56; Billings (Mont.) public schools, junior high and high school counselor, 1956—. Chairman, Billings Mayor's Committee for Youth, three years. *Military service:* U.S. Army, Paratroops, 1943-46. *Member:* American School Counselor Association (member of board of governors, 1967-72; national president, 1970-71), National Education Association (life member), American Personnel and Guidance Association (life member), Montana Personnel and Guidance Association (past president), Montana Education Association (life member), Phi Kappa Phi. *Awards, honors:* Silver Beaver Award of Boy Scouts of America; Alumni Outstanding Achievement Award, Montana State University.

WRITINGS: For Thinking Teens, Richards Rosen, 1967; *Homeroom Guidance Activities,* Richards Rosen, 1967; *Stories for Thinking Teens,* Richards Rosen, 1968; *For the Time of Your Life,* Richards Rosen, 1975. Writes teenage fiction for magazines under pseudonym Leslie Peters; stories and articles have appeared in *McCall's, Good Housekeeping, Women's Day, Family Circle, Scouting, Boys' Life, American Girl, West* and other periodicals; also contributor to professional journals.

* * *

PETERS, R(ichard) S(tanley) 1919-

PERSONAL: Born October 31, 1919, in Missouri, Uttar Pradesh, India; son of Charles Robert (a member of the Indian Police) and Mabel Georgina Peters; married Margaret Lee Duncan; children: Julia, David, Alison. *Education:* Queen's College, Oxford, B.A. (war degree), 1942; Birkbeck College, London, B.A., 1946, Ph.D., 1949. *Home:* Bridge End Orchard, Saffron Walden, Essex, England. *Office:* Institute of Education, University of London, Malet St., London W.C. 1, England.

CAREER: War service with Friends' Ambulance Unit and Friends' Relief Service, East London, England, 1940-44; Sidcot School, Somersetshire, England, classics master, 1944-46; University of London, London, part-time lecturer, Birkbeck College, 1946-49, full-time lecturer in philosophy and psychology, Birkbeck College, 1949-58, reader in philosophy, Birkbeck College, 1958-62, professor of philosophy of education, Institute of Education, 1962—. Part-time lecturer in ethics and methods of social sciences, London School of Economics and Political Science, University of London, 1952-54; visiting professor, Harvard University, Graduate School of Education, 1961. *Member:* Philosophy of Education Society (Great Britain), Association of University Teachers, Aristotelian Society, National Academy of Education (United States).

WRITINGS: Hobbes, Penguin, 1956, 2nd edition, 1967; *The Concept of Motivation,* Allen & Unwin, 1958, 2nd edition, 1960; (with S. I. Benn) *Social Principles and the Democratic State,* Allen & Unwin, 1959, 2nd edition, 1961; *Authority, Responsibility and Education* (broadcast talks), Allen & Unwin, 1960, revised edition, 1973; *Ethics and Education,* Allen & Unwin, 1966; (with P. H. Hirst) *The Logic of Education,* Routledge & Kegan Paul, 1970; *Reason, Morality and Religion,* Friends Home Service Committee, 1972; *Reason and Compassion,* Routledge & Kegan Paul, 1973; *Psychology and Ethical Development,* Allen & Unwin, 1974.

Editor: George S. Brett, *History of Psychology,* Macmillan, 1953, 2nd edition, Massachusetts Institute of Technology, 1962; *The Concept of Education,* Routledge & Kegan Paul, 1967; *Perspectives on Plowden,* Routledge & Kegan Paul, 1969; (with M. Cranston) *Hobbes and Rousseau: A Collection of Critical Essays,* Doubleday, 1972; (with P. H. Hirst and R. F. Dearden) *Education and the Development of Reason,* Routledge & Kegan Paul, 1972; *Philosophy of Education,* Oxford University Press, 1973; *The Role of the Head,* Routledge & Kegan Paul, 1975; *Nature and Conduct,* Macmillan, 1975. Contributor to *Collier's Encyclopedia, Concise Encyclopaedia of Philosophy and Philosophers,* and to periodicals and newspapers, including *New Scientist, Economist, Listener, Nation, Commentary, Contemporary Psychology,* and philosophy journals.

AVOCATIONAL INTERESTS: Golf.

* * *

PETERSEN, William J. 1929-

PERSONAL: Born August 19, 1929, in Chicago, Ill.; son of Elmer N. (a farmer) and Edna (McAlpine) Petersen; married Ardythe Ekdahl (a teacher), December 20, 1952; children: Kenneth, Randall, Kathryn. *Education:* Wheaton College, Wheaton, Ill., B.A., 1950. *Religion:* Baptist. *Home:* 613 Clearview Ave., Woodbury Heights, N.J. 08097. *Office: Eternity,* 1716 Spruce St., Philadelphia, Pa. 19103.

CAREER: Chain o' Lakes Guide (weekly newspaper), Waupaca, Wis., editor, 1949; *Gideon* (magazine), Chicago, Ill., assistant editor, 1950-51; *Fort Sheridan Tower,* Fort Sheridan, Ill., editor, 1952-53; *Christian Life* (magazine), Chicago, Ill., editorial director, 1953-57; *Eternity* (magazine), Philadelphia, Pa., executive editor, 1957-75, editor, 1975—. *Member:* Evangelical Press Association (past director). *Military service:* U.S. Army, 1951-53.

WRITINGS: Another Hand on Mine, McGraw, 1967; *Astrology and the Bible,* Victor, 1972; *Those Curious New Cults,* Keats Publishing, 1973; *What You Should Know about Gambling,* Keats Publishing, 1974; *How to be a Saint while Lying Flat on Your Back* Zondervan, 1974; *Two Stars for God,* Warner Paperback, 1974. Contributor to a number of religious periodicals.

WORK IN PROGRESS: The Last Days of Man, for Warner Paperback.

SIDELIGHTS: Petersen did research in Congo, Uganda, and Kenya in connection with his book, *Another Hand on Mine.*

* * *

PETERSON, Ottis 1907-

PERSONAL: Born July 12, 1907, in Preston, Idaho; son of Peter Powell (a professor) and Hazel (Parkinson) Peterson; married Jean Rawlins, August 20, 1930 (divorced, 1973); married Audrey M. Bennett, March 3, 1973; children: (first marriage) Patricia Jean (Mrs. R. W. Strazza), Sue (Mrs. G. A. Huguely), Mary Lou (Mrs. L. F. Johnson). *Education:* Attended Utah State University, 1928-29. *Religion:* Mormon. *Home:* 2908 Alamo Rd., Boise, Idaho 83704.

CAREER: Worked as reporter and managing editor, *Herald Journal,* Logan, Utah; reporter and city editor,

Tribune, Salt Lake City, Utah; head of regional office, Office of War Information; director of relocation for postwar return of Japanese from relocation centers; U.S. Bureau of Reclamation, Washington, D.C., assistant to commissioner, 1954-73; free–lance writer and public relations consultant, 1973—. Washington correspondent for *Arizona Republic* and *Portland Oregonian.*

WRITINGS: Water, Garrard, 1966; *Your Future in Engineering Careers,* Richards Rosen, 1975. Contributor to newspapers and magazines. Ghost writer of articles, papers, and speeches on water published under names of various government heads and congressmen.

SIDELIGHTS: Peterson told *CA:* "Interest in water and natural resources stems from early residence in dry country of Utah and membership in Mormon Church, which from early settlement has pioneered in careful management and use of natural resources."

* * *

PETERSON, Walter Scott   1944-

PERSONAL: Born September 5, 1944, in Newton, Kan.; son of Walter Frank (a railroad engineer) and Elizabeth E. (Wiebe) Peterson; married Jean Louise Murray (a social worker), December 16, 1967; children: James Scott, Bethany Rose. *Education:* Yale University, B.A. (summa cum laude), 1966, M.D., 1971. *Home:* 224 Lanyon Dr., Cheshire, Conn. 06410. *Office:* Waterbury Medical Arts Building, Suite 201, 134 Grandview Ave., Waterbury, Conn. 06708.

CAREER: Waterbury Hospital, Waterbury, Conn., intern, 1971-72; Yale-New Haven Hospital, New Haven, Conn., resident in ophthalmology, 1972-74, chief resident, 1974; private practice of ophthalmology, 1974—. On attending staffs of Waterbury, St. Mary's, Yale-New Haven, and West Haven Veteran's Administration Hospitals; member, clinical faculty of ophthalmology, Yale University, School of Medicine. Diplomate, National Board of Medical Examiners, 1972. *Member:* American Medical Association, American College of Surgeons (candidate group), Association for Research in Vision and Ophthalmology, Connecticut State Medical Society, New Haven County Medical Association, Phi Beta Kappa.

WRITINGS: An Approach to "Paterson," Yale University Press, 1967. Contributor to professional journals.

WORK IN PROGRESS: Meter in William Carlos William's poetry; psychological/literary theories of creativity; experimental and clinical research on glaucoma and retinal disease.

BIOGRAPHICAL/CRITICAL SOURCES: Criticism, fall, 1968.

* * *

PETRIE, Asenath   1914-

PERSONAL: Born November 29, 1914, in London, England; married, 1938; children: one son. *Education:* University College and Institute of Psychiatry, University of London, B.Sc., 1936, Ph.D., 1953. *Address:* (Permanent) 30, Hurley St., Belmont, Mass.; (temporary) 3 Degania St., Jerusalem, Israel.

CAREER: Mill Hill Emergency and Maudsley Hospitals, London, England, research psychologist, 1944-47; St. George's and Atkinson Morley Hospitals, London, England, research and clinical psychologist, 1947-51; University of Pennsylvania, Philadelphia, research associate, 1951-52, senior research associate of Institute of Psychiatry, 1953-57; Harvard Medical School, Boston, Mass., research associate, department of surgery, 1957-70; Hadassah Medical Organization, Israel, consultant, 1973—. University of London, lecturer, 1946-47, honorary lecturer at Institute of Psychiatry, 1954-56; associate in research, Beth Israel Hospital, Boston, Mass., 1958—. Consultant, National Institutes of Health, 1965-67; consultant to Hospital Lariboisiere, Paris, France, 1950-56, and University of Pittsburgh School of Public Health, 1965—.

MEMBER: American Psychological Association, British Psychological Association, World Federation for Mental Health. *Awards, honors:* Rockefeller fellow, 1943-47; Fulbright traveling fellow, 1951-52; Lasker Foundation grant, 1957; Foundation Fund for Research in Psychiatry research fellow, 1957-58.

WRITINGS: Personality and the Frontal Lobes, Blakiston, 1952; *Individuality in Pain and Suffering,* University of Chicago Press, 1967. Contributor to professional journals.

WORK IN PROGRESS: Research on pain, suffering, and sensibility.

* * *

PETRIE, Mildred McClary   1912-
(Mildred McClary Tymeson)

PERSONAL: Born September 26, 1912, in South Stukely, Quebec, Canada; daughter of Rodney H. (a contractor) and Sayde M. (Lanphear) McClary; married Ralph A. Tymeson, October 20, 1935; married George W. Petrie III (a college professor), January 1, 1967. *Education:* Atlantic Union College, A.B., 1933; Boston University, A.M., 1947; other courses at Harvard University. *Politics:* Republican. *Religion:* Protestant. *Home:* 4573 Northlake Dr., Sarasota, Fla. 33580; and 1170 Mt. Mary Dr., Green Bay, Wis. 54302.

CAREER: Writer. Choir director in Holden, Mass., 1940-55. *Member:* National League of American Pen Women (branch president, Worcester, Mass., 1964-66), Authors League of America, Worcester County Musical Association.

WRITINGS—All under name Mildred McClary Tymeson: American Authors, Review & Herald, 1940; *Centennial History of City of Worcester,* Commonwealth Press, for City of Worcester, 1948; *The Norton Story,* Commonwealth Press, for Norton Co., 1953; *Men of Metal,* Commonwealth Press, 1954; *Worcester Bankbook,* Davis Advertising, 1954, revised edition, 1966; *Rural Retrospect,* Commonwealth Press, 1956; *The Wyman-Gordon Way,* Commonwealth Press, 1957; *The Book of Quaboag,* Quaboag Historical Society, 1960; *As Far West as the Sunset,* Davis Advertising, 1962; *Two Towers: The Story of Worcester Tech,* Barre Publishers, 1965; *Paul Revere,* Worcester Art Museum, 1965; *But One Lamp: Story of the Massachusetts Dental Society,* Commonwealth Press, for Massachusetts Dental Society, 1965; (with Katharine Knowles) *The Lancastrian Towns,* Barre Publishers, for Town of Lancaster, 1967. Author of movie script, "Old as the Hills," 1960. Contributor of articles to *New England Galaxy* and *Swedish Pioneer Historical Quarterly.*

* * *

PETRIE, Sidney   1923-

PERSONAL: Born October 28, 1923, in London, England;

son of Jack and Fanny Petrie; wife's name, Iris. *Education:* Educated in London, England. *Religion:* Jewish. *Agent:* Curtis Brown Ltd., 60 East 56th St., New York, N.Y. 10022. *Office:* 1 Barstow Rd., Great Neck, N.Y. 11021.

CAREER: Hypnologist in private practice, 1957—; New York Institute of Hypnotherapy, Great Neck, founder and director, 1969—. Television appearances include "David Susskind Show," WNBC-TV, and documentary, "Eye on New York," WCBS-TV. *Member:* International Association of Hypnologists, Association to Advance Ethical Hypnosis.

WRITINGS—With Robert B. Stone, except as noted; all published by Parker Publishing, except as noted: *How to Reduce and Control Your Weight through Self Hypnotism,* Prentice-Hall, 1965; *Martinis and Whipped Cream,* 1966; *How to Strengthen Your Life through Mental Isometrics,* 1967; *What Modern Hypnotism Can Do for You,* Hawthorn, 1968; *The Truth about Hypnotism,* Frewin Publishers, 1969; *The Lazy Lady's Easy Diet: A Fast-action Plan to Lose Weight Quickly for Sustained Slenderness and Youthful Attractiveness,* 1969.

The Miracle Diet for Fast Weight Loss, 1970; *Hypno-cybernetics: Helping Yourself to a Rich, New Life,* 1973; *Fat Destroyer Food: The Magic Metabolizer Diet,* 1974; (with Frank Samuel Caprio) *How to Heighten Your Sexual Pleasure through Simple Mental Stimulation,* Galahad Books, 1974; *Hypno-dietetics: The New No-Willpower Way to Speedy, Permanent Weight Control,* Peter H. Wyden, 1975. Contributor to *Pageant* and *Show.*†

* * *

PETROV, Victor P. 1907-

PERSONAL: Born March 22, 1907, in Harbin, China; naturalized U.S. citizen; son of Porfiry Nicholas (a priest of Russian Orthodox Church) and Catherine (Ryazanov) Petrov; married Elizabeth Onufrieff (a reference librarian), February 6, 1942; stepchildren: Tatiana B. Tontarski. *Education:* Institute of Jurisprudence, Harbin, China, student, 1925-29; American University, B.S., 1951, M.A., 1952, Ph.D., 1954. *Religion:* Russian Orthodox. *Home:* 8919 Battery Rd., Alexandria, Va. 22308.

CAREER: U.S. Navy School of Oriental Languages, Boulder, Colo., instructor, 1945-46; U.S. Naval Language School, Washington, D.C., assistant professor, 1946-50, associate professor, 1950-57, professor of languages and geography, 1957-63; Defense Language Institute, Washington, D.C., professor of languages and geography, 1963-65; Shippensburg State College, Shippensburg, Pa., professor of geography, 1965-67; National Science Foundation, Washington, D.C., assistant program director, foreign science information program, 1967-70; California State University, Los Angeles, professor of geography, 1970-74. Professorial lecturer in geography, George Washington University, 1962-65; visiting professor, University of Victoria. *Member:* Association of American Geographers, Association for Asian Studies, American Association of Teachers of Slavic and East European Languages, American Association of University Professors, American Geographic Society, Royal Canadian Geographical Society.

WRITINGS: Albazinians in China, Kamkin, 1956; *Geography of the Soviet Union,* Kamkin, Part IV-B: *Electric Power,* 1959, Part IV: *Soviet Industry,* 1960, Part IV-A: *Energy Resources,* 1962, Part I: *Physical Features,* 1964, Part II: *Geographic Zone,* 1964, Part III: *Population,* 1964, Part V: *Transportation,* 1967; *100th Anniversary of the Arrival of Russian Naval Squadrons to America,* Kamkin, 1963; *China: Emerging World Power,* Van Nostrand, 1967, 2nd edition, in press; *History of Russina Ecclesiastical Mission in China,* Kamkin, 1968; *Mongolia: A Profile,* Praeger, 1970.

In Russian: *Pod Amerikanskim Flagom* (title means "Under American Flag"), Malyk & Kamkin (Shanghai), 1933; *Lola* (novel), Malyk & Kamkin, 1934; *V Manchzhurii* (title means "In Manchuria"), Slovo (Shanghai), 1937; *Saga Forta Ross* (title means "Saga of Fort Ross"), Kamkin (Washington, D.C.), Book I: *Printsessa Elena* (title means "Princess Elena"), 1961, Book II: *Konets Mechtam* (title means "End of Dreams"), 1963; *Kitayskie Rasskazy* (title means "Chinese Stories"), Kamkin, 1962. Also author of *Kolumby Rossiyskie* (title means "Russian Columbuses"), 1971, and *Kamerge Dvora* (title means "Grand Chamberlain of the Court"), 1973.

Contributor of about fifty articles on geography of the Soviet Union and China, and on astrogeography to professional journals. Contributing editor, *Dictionary of Political Science,* 1964.

WORK IN PROGRESS: A chapter, "Mining and Industry," for *Changing Communist China,* edited by Chiao-min Hsieh.

SIDELIGHTS: Petrov is competent in German in addition to Russian and Chinese; he gets along rather well in several other Slavic languages.

* * *

PETROV, Vladimir 1915-

PERSONAL: Surname is pronounced Pea-trawf; born November 15, 1915, in Odessa, Russia; came to United States in 1944; son of Nicholas and Anna (Litvinsky) Petrov; married Mirtala Kardinalovska (a sculptor and poet), December, 1948; married second wife, Jean Anne MacNab, July 2, 1955; children: (first marriage) George; (second marriage) Susanne, Elizabeth Jean, Vladimir John, Alexander Richard, Anne Marie, Kathrine Jane, Andrei, Carol Larissa. *Education:* Student at Civil Engineering School, Moscow, 1930-33, and Industrial Engineering Institute, Leningrad, 1934-35; Yale University, M.A., Ph.D., 1965. *Politics:* Republican ("since 1952"). *Religion:* Russian Orthodox. *Home:* 4215 Knowles Ave., Kensington, Md. 20795. *Office:* George Washington University, Washington, D.C. 20052.

CAREER: Yale University, New Haven, Conn., lecturer in Russian, intermittently, 1947-65; George Washington University, Washington, D.C., 1965—, began as associate professor, became professor of international affairs. Writer, lecturer, and consultant.

WRITINGS: Soviet Gold, Farrar, Straus, 1949; *My Retreat from Russia,* Yale University Press, 1950; *What China Policy?,* Shoe String, 1961; *Money and Conquest,* Johns Hopkins Press, 1966; *June 21, 1941: Soviet Historians and the German Invasion,* University of South Carolina Press, 1968; *A Study in Diplomacy: The Story of Arthur Bliss Lane,* Regnery, 1971; *Escape from the Future,* Indiana University Press, 1973; *U.S.-Soviet Detente: Past and Future,* American Enterprise Institute for Public Policy Research, 1975; (editor) O. Borisov and B. Koloskov, *Soviet-Chinese Relations, 1945-1970,* Indiana University Press, 1975.

Contributor: W. Gurian, editor, *Soviet Imperialism,* University of Notre Dame Press, 1951; Robert Strausz-Hupe and others, *Protracted Conflict,* Harper, 1959; Strausz-Hupe and others, *A Forward Strategy for America,* Harper, 1961; William R. Kintner and Joseph Z. Kornfeder, *The New Frontier of War,* Regnery, 1962.

Translator into Russian; all published by Chekhov Publishing: E. Franklin Frazier, *The Negro in the United States,* 1953; Frederick Lewis Allen, *The Big Change,* 1954; John Gunther, *Inside U.S.A.,* 1954; Edward Bok, *The Americanization of Edward Bok,* 1955; Winston Churchill, *The Second World War,* Volume IV: *The Hinge of Fate,* Volume V: *Closing the Ring,* 1955. Editor of Russian translation of Warren Commission Report, 1964-65.

Contributor of about four hundred articles to Russian-language periodicals, 1948-62, and other articles to *Life, Reader's Digest, Orbis, Plain Talk, Problems of Communism,* and other journals. Three short stories, originally published in *This Week,* have been reprinted in various magazines in America and abroad; also has done reviews for *American Mercury, Modern Age, Slavic Review,* and other journals.

SIDELIGHTS: Vladimir Petrov's first two books are autobiographical, based in part on his six years in a Siberian concentration camp. Petrov notes that his view of human society is "sceptical-to-pessimistic." He speaks Italian and German. *Avocational interests:* Badminton, swimming, and travel ("until the family became too unmanageable in size").

* * *

PETTY, Walter T. 1918-

PERSONAL: Born June 18, 1918, in St. Paul, Kan.; married Dorothy C. Hart, July 30, 1940; children: Walter T., Jr., Roy A., Claire. *Education:* Central Missouri State College (now University), A.B., B.S., and B.S. in Ed., 1940; University of Iowa, M.A., 1950, Ph.D., 1955; additional graduate study at Washington University, St. Louis, Mo., 1945, and Drake University, 1951. *Home:* 655 Mill St., Williamsville, N.Y. 14221. *Office:* State University of New York, Buffalo, N.Y. 14214.

CAREER: Teaching principal in Blairstown, Mo., 1940-42; Atlas Powder Co., chemist, 1942-44; teacher in Webster Groves, Mo., 1945-46; principal of high school in Leon, Iowa, 1946-48; superintendent of schools, Decatur County, Iowa, 1948-53; Sacramento State College (now California State University, Sacramento), professor of education, 1955-66, chairman of department of elementary education, 1958-61; State University of New York at Buffalo, professor of education, 1966—, chairman of department, 1975—, acting provost, faculty of educational studies, 1975—. *Military service:* U.S. Army, Infantry, 1944-45. *Member:* National Council of Teachers of English, National Conference on Research in English (president, 1969), International Reading Association, American Educational Research Association, National Education Association (life member), New York State English Council, Phi Delta Kappa.

WRITINGS: (Editor) *Meeting Individual Needs through Reading,* Sacramento State College Press, 1958; (with Harry A. Greene) *Developing Language Skills in the Elementary Schools,* Allyn & Bacon, 1959, 5th edition, 1975; *Improving Your Spelling Program,* Chandler Publishing, 1959.

The Language Arts in the Elementary School, Center for Applied Research in Education (New York), 1962; (with Gus Plessas) "You Can Spell," series of thirty books for grades one-eight, with teachers' manuals and workbooks, Allyn & Bacon, 1964-65; (with Mary Bowen) *Slithery Snakes and Other Aids to Children's Writing,* Appleton, 1967; (with Paul Herold and Earline Stoll) *Research in the Teaching of Vocabulary,* National Council of Teachers of English, 1967; (editor) *Issues and Problems in the English Language Arts: A Book of Readings,* Allyn & Bacon, 1967; (with wife, Dorothy C. Petty, and Marjorie Becking) *Experiences in Language,* Allyn & Bacon, 1973, 2nd edition, 1976.

WORK IN PROGRESS: Research in spelling and children's writing.

* * *

PETULLA, Joseph M. 1932-

PERSONAL: Born September 29, 1932, in Oil City, Pa.; son of Louis (a shoe repairer) and Jennie (Ruby) Petulla. *Education:* St. Bonaventure University, B.A., 1954; University of Notre Dame, M.A., 1959; Graduate Theological Union, Berkeley, Calif., Ph.D., 1971. *Politics:* Democrat. *Home:* 1230 Coluso Ave., Berkeley, Calif. 94707. *Office:* Laney College, Oakland, Calif. 94606.

CAREER: Roman Catholic priest. Cathedral Prep School, Erie, Pa., director of religion department, 1958-65; Gannon College, Erie, Pa., instructor in theology, 1965-67; Allegheny College, Meadville, Pa., chaplain for Roman Catholic students, 1967-68; Laney College, Oakland, Calif., instructor in urban studies, 1971-72, lecturer in conservation and resource studies, 1972—. Secretary, Greater Erie Ecumenical Commission, 1965-67; member of board of directors, Erie Neighborhood Action Committee, 1965-67.

WRITINGS: (With William Reedy) *The Friendship of Christ,* Sadlier, 1967; *Faith on Monday* (textbook), Sadlier, 1968; *All Over the World,* Sadlier, 1968; *Where Is Your Brother* (adult education), Sadlier, 1969; (contributor) *Where Do We Go from Here?* (adult education), Sadlier, 1969; *Christian Political Theology: A Marxian Guide,* Orbis, 1972; *Natural Resources in the United States: A History of Their Exploitation and Conservation,* Boyd & Fraser, in press. Contributor to *America, Nation, Cross Currents,* and other periodicals.

WORK IN PROGRESS: Studies in environmental philosophy; history writing and research.

* * *

PFALTZGRAFF, Robert L., Jr. 1934-

PERSONAL: Born June 1, 1934, in Philadelphia, Pa.; son of Robert L. and Mary (Warriner) Pfaltzgraff; married Diane A. Kressler (an associate professor of political science), May 20, 1967. *Education:* Swarthmore College, B.A., 1956; University of Pennsylvania, M.B.A., 1958, M.A., 1959, Ph.D., 1964. *Home:* 663 Wallace Dr., Strafford, Pa. 19087. *Office:* Foreign Policy Research Institute, 3508 Market St., Philadelphia, Pa. 19104.

CAREER: University of Pennsylvania, Philadelphia, research assistant, 1959-63, assistant professor of political science, 1964-71, Foreign Policy Research Institute, research associate, 1964-71, deputy director, 1971-73, director, 1973—. George C. Marshall Professor, College of Europe, 1971-72; associate professor, Tufts University, 1971—. Member of committee on problems of developed countries, U.S. Department of State, Policy Planning Council. *Member:* American Political Science Association, Academy of Political Science, American Academy of Political and Social Science, Institute for Strategic Studies (London), Pennsylvania Political Science Association, Pi Gamma Mu. *Awards, honors:* Guggenheim fellowship, 1968-69.

WRITINGS: (Contributor) *Building the Atlantic World,* Harper, 1963; *Britain Faces Europe: 1957-67,* University of Pennsylvania Press, 1969; *The Atlantic Community: A Complex Imbalance,* Van Nostrand, 1969; (editor) *Politics and the International System,* Lippincott, 1969, 2nd edition, 1972.

(Co-author) *Contending Theories of International Relations,* Lippincott, 1971; (co-editor and contributor) *SALT: Implications for Arms Control in the 1970's,* University of Pittsburgh Press, 1973; (co-editor and contributor) *The Superpowers in a Multinuclear World,* Heath, 1974; (editor) *Contrasting Approaches to Strategic Arms Control,* Heath, 1974; (co-editor and contributor) *New Technologies and Non-Nuclear Conflict: The Others Arms Race,* Heath, 1975. Contributor to *American Behavioral Scientist, Journal of Common Market Studies, New Republic, European Review, New York Times,* and other periodicals. Editor, *Orbis,* 1973—.

WORK IN PROGRESS: Bibliographic Survey of International Relations; National Perspectives on the Changing Global System and the Role of Power; The Impact of Resource Issues on U.S. Alliance Systems; The European-American Relationship in the Late 1970's.

* * *

PHELAN, John Leddy   1924-

PERSONAL: Born July 19, 1924, in Fall River, Mass.; son of Joseph P. (a manufacturer) and Rose (Dunn) Phelan. *Education:* Harvard University, A.B., 1947; University of California, Berkeley, M.A., 1948, Ph.D., 1951. *Politics:* Democrat. *Home:* 5457 Lake Mendota Dr., Madison, Wis. *Office:* History Department, University of Wisconsin, Madison, Wis. 53706.

CAREER: University of Wisconsin—Milwaukee, lecturer, 1956, assistant professor, 1956-58, associate professor of history, 1958-60; University of Wisconsin—Madison, associate professor, 1960-64, professor of history, 1964—. Member of executive council, Milwaukee County Council of Democratic Party, 1958-60. *Member:* American Historical Association, Academy of American Franciscan History. *Awards, honors:* Fulbright scholar in France, 1951-52; Newberry Library fellow, 1953-55; Guggenheim fellow, 1960-61.

WRITINGS: The Millennial Kingdom of the Franciscans in the New World: A Study of the Writings of Geronimo de Mendieta, 1525-1604, University of California Press, 1956; *The Hispanization of the Philippines: Spanish Aims and Filipino Responses, 1565-1700,* University of Wisconsin Press, 1959; *The Kingdom of Quito in the Seventeenth Century: Bureaucratic Politics in the Spanish Empire,* University of Wisconsin Press, 1968. Contributor of a dozen articles on the Spanish Empire and modern Latin America to journals.

WORK IN PROGRESS: Reform, Revolt, and Revolution in the Spanish Empire, 1590-1800.

BIOGRAPHICAL/CRITICAL SOURCES: South Atlantic Quarterly, winter, 1969.

* * *

PHILLIPS, Stella   1927-

PERSONAL: Born December 26, 1927, in Plymouth, Devonshire, England; daughter of George (a chief petty officer, Royal Navy) and Edith Mary (Robb) Temp; married Victor Leonard Phillips (a civil servant with Board of Trade), December 10, 1953; children: S. John Victor, D. Amanda Clare. *Education:* University of Birmingham, Associateship of Library Association, 1952. *Religion:* Church of England. *Home:* 33 Bishopton Ave., Stockton, Cleveland, England. *Agent:* D. C. Benson and Campbell Thomson Ltd., Clifford's Inn, Fleet St., London E.C. 4, England.

CAREER: Shropshire County Library, Shropshire, England, library assistant, 1944-53; Walker Technical College, Wellington, Shropshire, England, librarian, 1960-63. *Member:* Library Association.

WRITINGS—Detective stories; all published by R. Hale: *Down to Death,* 1967; *The Hidden Wrath,* 1968; *Death in Arcady,* 1969; *Death Makes the Scene,* 1970; *Death in Sheep's Clothing,* 1971; *Yet She Must Die,* 1973; *Dear Brother, Here Departed,* 1975. Contributor of stories to periodicals.

* * *

PHYTHIAN, B(rian) A(rthur)   1932-

PERSONAL: First syllable of surname is pronounced as "fith"; born May 15, 1932, in St. Helens, Lancashire, England; son of Arthur and May (Nuttall) Phythian. *Education:* University of Manchester, B.A. (first class honors), M.A., 1954; Wadham College, Oxford, B.Litt., 1956. *Home:* 24 Brackley Rd., Beckenham, Kent, England. *Office:* Langley Park Boys' School, Beckenham, Kent, England.

CAREER: Manchester Grammar School, Manchester, England, senior English master, 1959-70; Langley Boys' School, Beckenham, Kent, England, headmaster, 1970—. Resident tutor, Manchester University Student Village, 1964-68; chairman of Manchester Youth and Community Service, 1965-70, and Manchester University Theatre Association. *Military service:* Royal Air Force, 1956-58; became flying officer. *Member:* National Association of Headmasters.

WRITINGS: R. B. Sheridan, Basil Blackwell, 1965; *The Manchester Grammar School, 1515-1965,* Manchester University Press, 1965; (with G. P. Fox) *Starting-Points,* English Universities Press, 1967; *Considering Poetry,* English Universities Press, 1970; *Concise Dictionary of English Idiom,* English Universities Press, 1974; (editor) *Henry V,* Macmillan, 1976; *Concise Dictionary of English Slang,* Hodder & Stoughton, 1976. Contributor to education journals.

AVOCATIONAL INTERESTS: Music, football, travel.

* * *

PIAGET, Jean   1896-

PERSONAL: Surname pronounced pee-ah-jhay; born August 9, 1896, in Neuchatel, Switzerland; son of Arthur (a professor and author of works on the Middle Ages); married; children: Jacqueline, Lucienne, Laurent. *Education:* Studied at Universitat Zurich, Universite de Paris, and Universite de Neuchatel; received doctorate in natural sciences from Universite de Neuchatel, 1918; from 1919-21 studied in Paris with Theodore Simon (co-author of the Binet-Simon intelligence tests). *Address:* Pinchat, c/o Carouge, Geneve, Switzerland. *Office:* Faculte de Psychologie, Universite de Geneve, Geneve, Switzerland.

CAREER: Worked with Institut Jean Jacques Rousseau, Geneve, Switzerland (now Institut des Sciences de l'Education, an institute of the Universite de Geneve for the scientific study of the child and the training of teachers), 1921-33, co-director, 1933—; Universite de Neuchatel, Neuchatel, Switzerland, professor of philosophy, 1925-29; Universite de Geneve, Geneve, professor of child psychology and the history of scientific thought, 1929-71, honorary professor, 1971—; International Bureau of Education, Geneve, director, 1929-67; Universite de Lausanne, Lausanne, Switzerland, professor of general psychology, 1937-51; University of Paris, Sorbonne, Paris, France, professor of psychology, 1952-63. Established, with the help of the Rockefeller Foundation, and is director of, the International Center of Genetic Epistemology, Geneva, 1955—.

MEMBER: Academie dei Lincei, Academie des Sciences de Bucarest, New York Academy of Science, Boston Academy of Arts and Sciences, Academie des Sciences et Lettres de Montpellier, Academie Royale de Belgique, Academie Internationale de Philosophie des Sciences, Institut Internationale de Philosophie, Union Internationale de Psychologie Scientifique, Association de Psychologie Scientifique de Langue Francaise, Societe Suisse de Logique et de Philosophie des Sciences, Societe de Psychologie de Espagne, Society Suisse de Psychologie, Societe Neuchateloise des Sciences Naturelles, Federacion Columbiana de Psicologia. *Awards, honors:* Recipient of awards from over thirty colleges and universities throughout the world, including Harvard University, 1936, University of Paris, Sorbonne, 1946, University of Oslo, 1960, Cambridge University, 1960, University of Moscow, 1966, and Yale University, 1970; other awards include, Prix de la Ville de Geneve, 1963, American Research Association award, 1967, American Psychological Association award, 1969, Prix Foneme, 1970, and Prix de l'Institut de la Vie, 1973.

WRITINGS: Le Langage et la pensee chez l'enfant, Delachaux & Niestle, 1923, 7th edition, 1968, translation by Marjorie Worden published as *The Language and Thought of the Child,* Harcourt, 1926, 3rd edition, revised, Humanities, 1959; (with others) *Le Jugement et le raisonnement chez l'enfant,* Delachaux & Niestle, 1924, 5th edition, 1963, translation by Worden published as *The Judgment and Reasoning in the Child,* Harcourt, 1928, published as *The Judgment and Reason in the Child,* 1929, reprinted, Littlefield, 1959; *Le Representation du monde chez l'enfant,* Delachaux & Niestle, 1926, translation by Jean Tomlinson and Andrew Tomlinson published as *The Child's Conception of the World,* Harcourt, 1929, reprinted, Littlefield, 1967; *La Causalite physique chez l'enfant,* Delachaux & Niestle, 1927, translation by Marjorie Worden Gabain published as *The Child's Conception of Physical Causality,* Harcourt, 1930.

Le Jugement moral chez l'enfant, Presses universitaire de France, 1932, 4th edition, 1973, translation by Gabain published as *The Moral Judgment of the Child,* Harcourt, 1932, reprinted Free Press of Glencoe, 1966; *La Naissance de l'intelligence chez l'enfant,* Delachaux & Niestle, 1936, 5th edition, 1966, translation by Margaret Cook published as *The Origins of Intelligence in Children,* International Universities Press, 1952, published as *The Origin of Intelligence in the Child,* Routledge & Kegan Paul, 1953, Norton, 1963; *La Construction du reel chez l'enfant,* Delachaux & Niestle, 1937, 3rd edition, 1963, translation by Cook published as *Child's Construction of Reality,* Routledge & Kegan Paul, 1953, published as *The Construction of Reality in the Child,* Basic Books, 1954.

(With Barbel Inhelder) *Le Developpement des quantites chez l'enfant: Conservation et Atomisme,* Delachaux & Niestle, 1940, 2nd edition, augmented, 1962, translation by Arnold J. Pomerans published as *The Child's Construction of Quantities: Conservation and Atomism,* Routledge & Kegan Paul, 1974; (with Alina Szeminska) *La Genese du nombre chez l'enfant,* Delachaux & Niestle, 1941, 3rd edition, 1964, translation by C. Gattegno and F. M. Hodgson published as *The Child's Conception of Number,* Routledge & Kegan Paul, 1952, Norton, 1965; *Classes, relations et nombres: Essai sur les groupements de la logistique et sur la reversibilite de la pensee,* Vrin, 1942; (with Marc Lambercier, Ernest Boesch and Barbara von Albertini) *Introduction a l'etude des perceptions chez l'enfant et analyse d'une illusion relative a la perception visuelle de cercles concentriques,* Delachaux & Niestle, 1942; (with Lambercier) *La Comparaison visuelle des hateurs a distances variables dans la plan fronto-parallele,* Delachaux & Niestle, 1943; (with others) *Essai d'interpretation probabliste de la loi de Weber et de celles des concentrations relatives,* Delachaux & Niestle, 1945; *La Formation du symbole chez l'enfant: Imitation jeu et reve, image et representation,* Delachaux & Niestle, 1945, 2nd edition, 1959, translation by Gattegno and Hodgson published as *Play, Dreams, and Imitation in Childhood,* Norton, 1951.

(With Inhelder) *Experiences sur la construction projective de la ligne droite chez les enfants de 2 a 8 ans,* Delachaux & Niestle, 1946; (with others) *Les Notions de mouvement et de vitesse chez l'enfant,* Presses universitaires de France, 1946, translation by G. E. T. Holloway and M. J. Mackenzie published as *The Child's Conception of Movement and Speed,* Basic Books, 1970; (with Esther Bussmann, Edith Meyer, Vroni Richi, and Myriam van Remoortel) *Le Developpement de la notion de temps chez l'enfant,* Presses universitaires de France, 1946, 2nd edition, 1973, translation by Pomerans published as *The Child's Conception of Time,* Routledge & Kegan Paul, 1969, Basic Books, 1970; *Etude sur la psychologie d'Edouard Claparede,* Delachaux & Niestle, 1946; *La Psychologie de l'intelligence,* Colin, 1947, translation by M. Piercy and D. E. Berlyne published as *The Psychology of Intelligence,* Routledge & Kegan Paul, 1950, Littlefield, 1960; (with Inhelder) *La Representation de l'espace chez l'enfant,* Presses universitaire de France, 1948, translation by F. J. Langdon and J. L. Lunzer published as *The Child's Conception of Space,* Humanities, 1956; (with Inhelder and Szeminska) *La Geometrie sponanee de l'enfant,* Presses universitaires de France, 1948, 2nd edition, 1973, translation by E. A. Lunzer published as *The Child's Conception of Geometry,* Basic Books, 1960; *Le Droit a l'education dans le monde actuel,* U.N.E.S.C.O., 1949; (with M. Boscher) *L'Initiation au calcul: Enfants de 4 a 7 ans,* Bourrelier, 1949; *Traite de logique: Essai de logistique operatoire,* Colin, 1949, 2nd edition published as *Essai de logique operatoire,* Dunod, 1972.

Introduction a l'espitemologie genetique, three volumes, Presses universitaires de France, 1950, 2nd edition, 1973; (with Inhelder) *La Genese de l'idee de hasard chez l'enfant,* Presses universitaires de France, 1951, translation by Lowell Leake, Paul Burrell, and Harold Fishbein published as *The Origin of the Idea of Chance in Children,* Norton, 1975; *Essai sur les transformations des operations logiques: Les 256 operations ternaires de la logique bivalente des propositions,* Presses universitaires de France,

1952; *Logic and Psychology,* translation by Wolfe Mays and F. Whitehead, Manchester University Press, 1953, Basic Books, 1957; *Les Relations entre l'affectivite et l'intelligence dans le developpement mental de l'enfant,* Centre de Documentation Universitaire, 1954; (with others) *L'Enseignement des mathematiques,* Delachaux & Niestle, 1955; (with Inhelder) *De la logique de l'enfant a logique de l'adolescent,* Presses universitaires de France, 1955, translation by Anne Parson and Stanley Milgrom published as *The Growth of Logical Thinking from Childhood to Adolescence: An Essay on the Construction of Formal Operational Structures,* Basic Books, 1958; (editor) *Etudes d'epistemologie genetique,* Presses universitaires de France, 1957; (with Inhelder) *Le genese des structures logique elementaire,* Delachaux & Niestle, 1959, translation by Lunzer and D. Papert published as *The Early Growth of Logic in the Child,* Harper, 1964.

Les Mecanismes perceptifs, Presses universitaires de France, 1961, translation by G. N. Seagrim published as *The Mechanism of Perception,* Basic Books, 1969; *Comments on Vygotsky's Critical Remarks Concerning "The Language and Thought of the Child," and "Judgment and Reasoning in the Child,"* translated by Parson, M.I.T. Press, 1961; (with Evert W. Beth) *Epistemologie mathematique et psychologie: Essai sur les relations entre la logique formelle et la pensee reele,* Presses universitaires de France, 1961, translation published as *Mathematical Epistemology and Psychology,* Gordon & Beech, 1966; (with Inhelder) *Le Developpement des quantites physiques chez l'enfant,* Delachaux & Niestle, 1962; (with Paul Fraisse and Maurice Reuchlin) *Histoire et methode,* Presses universitaires de France, 1963, 3rd edition, 1970, translation by Judith Chambers published as *History and Method,* Basic Books, 1968; (editor with Fraisse) *Traite de psychologie experimentale,* Presses universitaires de France, 1963, 3rd edition, 1970, translation published as *Experimental Psychology: Its Scope and Method,* Basic Books, 1968; (with Fraisse, Elaine Vurpillot, and Robert Frances) *La Perception,* Presses universitaires de France, 1963; *Six etudes de psychologie,* Gonthier, 1964, translation by Anita Tenzer and David Elkind published as *Six Psychological Studies,* Random House, 1967.

(Editor with Maurice Patronnier de Gandillac) *Entretiens sur les notions de genese et de structure,* Mouton, 1965; *Etudes sociologiques,* Librarie Droz, 1965; *Sagesse et illusions de la philosophie,* Presses universitaires de France, 1965, 3rd edition, 1972, translation by Wolfe Mays published as *Insights and Illusions of Philosophy,* World Publishing, 1971; (with Inhelder) *L'Image mentale chez l'enfant,* Presses universitaires de France, 1966, translation by P. A. Chilton published as *Mental Imagery in the Child: A Study of the Development of Imaginal Representation,* Basic Books, 1971; (with Inhelder) *La Psychologie de l'enfant,* Presses universitaires de France, 1966, 6th edition, 1975, translation by Helen Weaver published as *The Psychology of the Child,* Basic Books, 1969; *Biologie et connaissance,* Gallimard, 1966, translation by Beatrix Walsh published as *Biology and Knowledge,* University of Chicago Press, 1971; (editor) *Logique et connaissance scientifique,* Gallimard, 1967; *On the Development of Memory and Identity,* translated by Eleanor Duckworth, Barre, 1968; *Le Structuralisme,* Presses universitaires de France, 1968, 6th edition, 1974, translation by Chaninah Maschler published as *Structuralism,* Basic Books, 1970; *Epistemologie et psychologie de l'identite,* Presses universitaires de France, 1968; (with others) *Epistemologie et psychologie*

de la fonction, Presses universitaires de France, 1968; (with Inhelder) *Memoire et intelligence,* Presses universitaires de France, 1968, translation by Arnold J. Pomerans published as *Memory and Intelligence,* Basic Books, 1973.

Epistemologie des science de l'homme, Gallimard, 1970; *L'Epistemologie genetique,* Presses universitaires de France, 1970, translation by Eleanor Duckworth published as *Genetic Epistemology,* Columbia University Press, 1970, translation by Wolfe Mays published as *The Principles of Genetic Epistemology,* Basic Books, 1972; (with R. Garcia) *Les Explications causales,* Presses universitaires de France, 1971, translation by Donald Miles and Marguerite Miles published as *Understanding Causality,* Norton, 1974; (with others) *Les Theories de la causalite,* Presses universitaires de France, 1971; (with J. Bliss) *Les Direction des mobiles lors de chocs et de poussees,* Presses universitaires de France, 1972; (with Bliss) *La Transmission des mouvements,* Presses universitaires de France, 1972; *Ou va education,* Denoel/Gonthier, 1973, translation by George-Anne Roberts published as *To Understand Is to Invest: The Future of Education,* Grossman, 1973; *La Formation de la notion de force,* Presses universitaires de France, 1973; (with A. Blanchet) *La Prise de conscience,* Presses universitaires de France, 1974; (with C. Bonnet) *Researches sur la contradiction,* two volumes, Presses universitaires de France, 1974; (with M. Amann) *Reussir et comprendre,* Presses universitaires de France, 1974.

Contributor: *Troisieme cours pour le personnel enseignant,* Bureau International d'Education, 1930; *Quatrieme cours pour le personnel enseignant,* Bureau International d'Education, 1931; C. Murchison, editor, *Handbook of Child Psychology,* Clark University Press, 1931; *Le Self-Government a l'ecole,* Bureau International d'Education, 1934; *Le Travail par equipes a l'ecole,* Bureau International d'Education, 1935; *U.N.E.S.C.O., Freedom and Culture,* Columbia University Press, 1951; (author of introduction) *Conference internationale de l'instruction publique,* [Geneva], 1951; E. G. Boring and others, *History of Psychology in Autobiography,* Volume IV, Clark University Press, 1952; Swanson, Newcomb, and Hartley, editors, *Readings in Social Psychology,* Holt, 1952; (author of introduction) R. Girod, *Attitudes collectives et relations humaines,* Presses universitaires de France, 1952; H. E. Abramson, *Conference on Problems of Consciousness,* Josiah Macy Foundation, 1954; P. Osterrieth and others, *Le Probleme des stades en psychologie de l'enfant,* Presses universitaires de France, 1955; P. H. Hock and J. Zubin, editors, *Psychopathology of Childhood,* Grune & Stratton, 1955; J. de Ajuriaguerra and others, *Aktuelle Problem der Gestalttheorie,* Hans Huber, 1955; J. Tanner and Inhelder, editors, *Discussions on Child Development,* Volumes I-IV, Tavistock, 1956, International Universities Press, 1958; (author of introduction) Jan Comenius, *Pages Choisies,* U.N.E.S.C.O., 1957, also published as *Selections,* U.N.E.S.C.O. (Paris), 1957; D. Katz, *Handbuch der Psychologie,* 2nd edition, Benno Schwabe, 1959.

(Author of introduction) M. Margot, *L'Ecole operante,* Delachaux & Niestle, 1960; (author of introduction) M. Nassefat, *Etude quantitative sur l'evolution des operations intellectuals,* Delachaux & Niestle, 1963; (author of introduction) Elaine Vurpillot, *L'Organisation perceptive,* Vrin, 1963; (author of introduction) Inhelder, *Le Diagnostic du raisonnement chez les debiles mentaux,* 2nd edition, Delachaux & Niestle, 1963; (author of introduction) John H. Flavell, *The Developmental Psychology of Jean Piaget,* Van Nostrand, 1963; Richard E. Ripple and Verne N.

Rockcastle, editors, *Piaget Rediscovered,* Cornell University School of Education, 1964; (author of introduction) T. Gouin Decarie, *Intelligence and Affectivity in Early Childhood,* translated by Elisabeth Brandt and Lewis Brandt, International Universities Press, 1965; (author of introduction) Millie Almy and others, *Young Children's Thinking: Studies of Some Aspects of Piaget's Theory,* Teacher's College Press, 1966; (author of introduction) *Dictionnaire d'epistemologie genetique,* Presses universitaires de France, 1966; Marcia W. Piers, editor, *Play and Development: A Symposium,* Norton, 1972. Contributor to *Proceedings of the International Congresses of Psychology;* Harvard Tercentenary Conference. Co-editor of *Revue Suisse de Psychologie* and *Archives de Psychologie.* Contributor to *Mind, British Journal of Psychology, Initiation au Calcul, Scientific American, Enfance, British Journal of Educational Psychology, Revue Suisse Psychologie, Synthese, Methados, Diogene Traite de Psychologie Experimentale, Etudes d'Epistemologie Genetique, Journal de Psychologie Normale et Pathologique, Archives de Psychologie* (Geneve), *American Journal of Mental Deficiency, Acta Psychologica, Annee Psychologique,* and other periodicals.

SIDELIGHTS: "For Piaget, the crucial question in the study of the growing child is how he adjusts himself to the world in which he lives," Frank A. Jennings writes. David Elkind finds that "Piaget's genius for empathy with children, together with true intellectual genius [have] made him the outstanding child psychologist in the world today and one destined to stand beside Freud with respect to his contributions to psychology, education, and related disciplines." Though it has been said of Piaget that "he is by vocation a sociologist, by avocation an epistemologist, and by method a logician," Jennings states that Piaget "tells his listeners and readers that he is not an educator [but] . . . a psychologist with an interdisciplinary bent, . . . an investigator using the tools of the related fields of biology, psychology, and logic to explore the genesis of intelligence in the human young. All his long life he has drawn upon these fields to conduct research and to build his theories of the development of intelligence in children. . . ." Ironically, those who know Piaget best realize that only within the past decade have his writings come to be fully appreciated in America. (Much of his writing has not been translated into English.) Elkind admits that "American psychology and education were simply not ready for Piaget until the fifties. Now the ideas that Piaget has been advocating for more than 30 years are regarded as exceedingly innovative and even as avant garde. The chief outcome of his theory of intellectual development, Eleanor Duckworth states, is "a plea that children be allowed to do their own learning." As a boy, Piaget was most interested in zoology (the results of his studies on snails and mussels were published in *Revue de Zoologie* while he was still in high school). Brought up in a strictly religious home, he became increasingly confused to discover that the biologist view of human nature ran contrary to the doctrines taught at home. (The emotional crisis resulted in his writing a philosophical novel.) With this problem still in his mind together with his belief that every level from the cell to society could be understood only in terms of "totalities" or "structures of the whole," Piaget enrolled in the psychological laboratory at Zurich. Here he attended the lectures of Carl Gustav, Jung, studied under Lippe, and read Bergson, William James, and Hebert Spencer; each have a great influence on him. It was after he was asked to standardize some rea-

soning tests that Piaget decided, according to Burt, that what was needed was not to "calculate percentages and age norms, but instead to examine the actual way in which a child reached his own conclusions, particularly when those conclusions were wrong."

Piaget was most concerned with the questions—"How does the growing child adjust himself to the world in which he lives?" and "How are we to account for the constant recurrence of what to the rational adult seem as gross instances of maladjustment [in the child]?" Burt notes that Piaget "started as others had done, by keeping careful records of what young children of different ages actually said or did. His conclusions were embodied in a succession of suggestive books and papers on a child's 'language and thought,' 'judgment and reasoning,' and 'conception of reality.'" It is difficult for Piaget to say when particular ideas came to him. Roughly, however, during what may be termed a first period, 1922-29, "Piaget explored the extent and depth of children's spontaneous ideas about the physical world and about their own mental processes." It was during this time that Piaget worked out the ingenious techniques aimed at revealing the processes by which a child reaches a reply to a test question. This semi-clinical interview procedure has become a trademark of Piagetian research and investigation. His approach to observing, recording, and understanding the way a child thinks is, Frank G. Jennings states, "to get inside of the child's mind and see the world through the child's eyes." Piaget would "learn to make a good shot at marbles, how to make bad ones; and even how to cheat." He avoided imposing his adult preconceptions on the childish and prelogical world. Concerning his *methode clinique* Piaget writes: "I engage my subject in conversations patterned after psychiatric questioning, with the aim of discovering something about the reasoning underlying their right but especially their wrong answers." Out of this method, according to J. McVicker Hunt, "came the well-known distinctions between egocentric and social language, between prelogical thinking and reasoning, and between animistic and symbolic forms of thinking." Piaget found, for example, that "children not only reasoned differently from adults, but also that they had quite different world-views, literally different philosophies." He saw that, "many youngsters . . . believe that the sun and moon follow them when they are out for a walk," and "in the child's view, objects like stones and clouds are imbued with motives, intentions and feelings," Elkind states. Also, Piaget concluded that it is because children believe that everything has a purpose that they ask the often unanswerable "why" questions. Piaget found, too, that because of the "young child's inability to put himself in another person's position and take that person's point of view, two nursery school children will often speak *at* rather than *to* one another and frequently will chatter on about two quite different and unrelated topics."

In 1929, Piaget traced the origins of the child's spontaneous mental growth to the behavior of infants. He reported the observations he made of his own three children in *The Origins of Intelligence in Children, The Construction of Reality in the Child,* and *Play, Dreams and Imitation in Childhood,* and, according to Elkind, these are now considered classics in the field and have been one of the major forces behind the growth of research activity in the area of infant behavior. "The first two volumes deal with the [sensory-motor] phase of development, i.e., with the development of motor functions and the acquisition of increasing skill in the manipulation of objects, while the third deals with the transition from [sensory-motor] intelligence to early symbolic activity as a substitute for motor action," Peter H. Wolff explains. Wolff adds that Piaget adapted his clinical method to the nonverbal child by substituting games for conversations as experimental procedures, although he still allowed the child's spontaneous play to determine what games were played. He made daily observations of the children and recorded their spontaneous behavior." Such observations led to what Piaget termed the *conservation of the object.* Wolff explains that, "during the early phase of . . . coordination, the child will touch an object as soon as, but only when, he sees his own hand and the desired object in the same visual field, and that seeing only the desired object will be an insufficient stimulus to cause the child to grasp it." This helps to explain the pleasure infants take in the game of peek-a-boo. When the object is not seen, Piaget found the object does not exist for the child.

During Piaget's third and major phase, beginning in 1940, he studied the development of mental abilities of children and adolescents which enable them to construct a world view like the reality recognised by adults. At this time Piaget made discoveries most relevant for education. He also continued his valuable contributions to the fields of psychology and sociology. *Introduction a l'epistemologie genetique* incorporates the work of thirty-two years of empirical observation in genetic epistemology or the formulation of the biological explanation of knowledge. In *Etudes Sociologiques,* "Piaget is especially concerned with the relation of sociological to psychological explanations," Peter L. Berger states. During the last thirty years, Piaget's investigations have attempted to show how the child copes with change while he is receiving a static education. This "research has demonstrated that the mind operates not as a passive mirror but rather as an active artist," Elkind believes. Piaget discovered that much of our knowledge about reality comes by the force of our own logic. One of the major discoveries during Piaget's third period is the importance of reason in the child's spontaneous construction of the world. As far as education is concerned, Miss Duckworth states that "Piaget is not saying that intellectual development proceeds at its own pace no matter what you try to do. He is saying that what schools usually try to do is ineffectual. You cannot further understanding in a child simply by talking to him. Good pedagogy must involve presenting the child with situations in which he himself experiments, in the broadest sense of that term—trying things out to see what happens, manipulating things, manipulating symbols, posing questions and seeking his own answers, reconciling what he finds one time with what he finds at another, comparing his findings with those of other children. Beyond this general implication, Piaget does not claim to be an educator."

Actually, then, Piaget's discoveries have centered around four main stages of development in the growth of the human being. According to Piaget, "the first is a sensory-motor, preverbal stage lasting approximately the first 18 months of life. During this stage is developed the practical knowledge. . . . For an infant, during the first months, an object has no permanence. . . . In a second stage, we have pre-operational representation—the beginning of language, of the symbolic function, and therefore of thought, or representation. . . . In a third stage, the first operations appear, but I call these concrete operations because they operate on objects, and not yet on verbally expressed hypotheses. For example, there are the operations of classification, ordering, the construction of the idea of number, spatial and temporal operations, and all the fundamental operations of elementary logic of classes and relations, of elementary mathematics, of elementary geometry and even of elementary physics. Finally, in the fourth stage, these operations are surpassed as the child reaches the level of what I call formal or hypothetic-deductive operations; that is, he can now reason on hypotheses, and not only on objects. He constructs new operations, operations of propositional logic, and not simply the operations of classes, relations, and numbers." Piaget would like educational systems to realize the limits of children's understanding at certain ages and plan to an extent what is to be taught within these limits. For example, in the past the age of 6 to 7 was considered as *the age of reason.* It was assumed that the child's reasoning abilities were the same as the adolescent's or adult's. However, Piaget has shown that the elementary school child's reasoning ability is limited in a very important respect—he can reason about things but not about verbal propositions. Elkind believes that "attention to the research on children's thinking carried out during Piaget's third period might have helped to avoid some of the difficulties of the 'New Math' program."

"Piaget has devoted 40 years at the University of Geneva to the study of human development [and] to the study of the origin and growth of human knowing," Jerome S. Bruner notes in reference to Piaget's recent collection of essays entitled *Six Psychological Studies.* Yet, despite the magnitude of Piaget's work, he still remains annoyed by pomp and shuns the spotlight except when it concerns the developmental psychology of children. It seems that he always has a twinkle in his eye and most always wears a navy blue beret, smokes a meerschaum pipe, and rides a bicycle. Each summer, as soon as classes are over, he gathers up the research findings of his assistants, departs to solitary residence in the Alps, and walks, meditates, and writes and writes. But, back at school, he continues to teach his young student experimenters to "ask questions without suggesting the answers and to test, by counter-suggestion, the strength of the child's conviction." Though many of his studies have been repeated under more rigorous conditions (Piaget does not use computers) by other investigators, the results have been remarkably consistent with Piaget's. Now a new intelligence scale is being attempted on the basis of the Piaget tests. It seems that all lives, those of children and their parents, will be affected by Piaget's work. As Bruner states: "Piaget has made us realize that the infant, like the adult, is constantly and effectively involved in an effort to bring order and logic and meaning into experience." "In an age of moon shots and automation," Elkind concludes, "the remarkable discoveries of Jean Piaget are evidence that in the realm of scientific achievement, technological sophistication is still no substitute for creative genius."

BIOGRAPHICAL/CRITICAL SOURCES—Magazines: *Times Educational Supplement,* December 6, 1957; *American Sociological Review,* February, 1966; *Saturday Review,* May 20, 1967; *New York Times Book Review,* February 11, 1968; *Education Digest,* March, 1968; *Commonweal,* April 5, 1968; *New York Times Magazine,* May 26, 1968.

Books: Peter H. Wolff, *The Developmental Psychologies of Jean Piaget and Psychoanalysis,* International Universities Press, 1960; William Kessen and Clementina Kuhlman, *Thought in the Young Child: Report with Particular Attention to the Work of Piaget,* Child Development Publications, 1960; Jerome S. Bruner, *The Process of Education,* Harvard University Press, 1960; J. McVicker Hunt, *Intelli-*

gence and Experience, Ronald, 1961; John H. Flavell, *The Developmental Psychology of Jean Piaget* (foreword by Piaget), Van Nostrand, 1963; Richard E. Ripple and Verne N. Rockcastle, editors, *Piaget Rediscovered,* Cornell University School of Education, 1964; Molly Brearly and Elizabeth Hitchfield, *A Teacher's Guide to Reading Piaget,* Routledge & Kegan Paul, 1966; Henry Maier, *Three Theories of Child Development,* Harper, 1965; Bruner, *Towards a Theory of Instruction,* Harvard University Press, 1966; G. E. T. Holloway, *An Introduction to The Child's Conception of Geometry,* Routledge & Kegan Paul, 1967; David Elkind and John Flavell, editors, *Studies in Cognitive Development: Essays in Honor of Jean Piaget,* Oxford University Press, 1969; Richard I. Evans, *Jean Piaget: The Man and His Ideas,* translated by Eleanor Duckworth, Dutton, 1973.

*   *   *

PIAN, Rulan Chao   1922-

PERSONAL: Born April 20, 1922, in Cambridge, Mass.; daughter of Yuen-ren (a university professor) and Buwei (Yang) Chao; married Theodore H. H. Pian (a professor), October 3, 1945; children: Canta Chao-po (daughter). *Education:* Radcliffe College, B.A., 1944, M.A., 1946, Ph.D., 1960. *Home:* 14 Brattle Circle, Cambridge, Mass. 02138. *Office:* Department of Far Eastern Languages, Harvard University, Cambridge, Mass. 02138.

CAREER: Harvard University, Cambridge, Mass., lecturer in department of Far Eastern languages, 1961-74, professor of Far Eastern language, civilization, and music, 1974—, master of South House, 1975—. Visiting professor, Chung Chi College, Hong Kong, 1975; lecturer on Chinese music at colleges and universities in the United States, Europe, and the Far East. Choral conductor in the Chinese community of Boston, intermittently, 1943-68, adviser, 1968—. *Member:* Society for Ethnomusicology (member of council, 1968-71), Chinese Language Teacher's Association (member of executive board, 1965-67). *Awards, honors:* Fulbright-Hayes grant for research in Taiwan, summer, 1964; American Council of Learned Societies grants, 1965-66, 1972; Otto Kinkeldy Award, American Musicological Society, 1968, for *Sonq Dynasty Musical Sources and Their Interpretation.*

WRITINGS: Syllabus for Mandarin Primer, Harvard University Press, 1961; *Sonq Dynasty Musical Sources and Their Interpretation,* Harvard University Press, 1967; (contributor) Jose Maceda, editor, *The Musics of Asia,* National Music Council of the Philippines, 1971; (contributor) Lawrence Berman, editor, *Words and Music: The Scholar's View,* Music Department, Harvard University; (contributor) J. I. Crump and W. P. Malm, editors, *Chinese and Japanese Music Drama,* University of Michigan Press, 1975. Contributor to *The Harvard Dictionary of Music,* 1969, and *Groves Dictionary of Music and Musicians;* contributor of articles to music journals.

WORK IN PROGRESS: A translation, *My Life as a Drum Singer;* translating, transcribing, and annotating a set of four Peking Operas.

*   *   *

PICKARD, Dorothea Wilgus   1902-

PERSONAL: Born February 27, 1902, in Platteville, Wis.; daughter of James Alva (a college professor) and Flavia (McGurer) Wilgus; married Samuel Nelson Pickard (a banker), September 1, 1924 (deceased); children: James

Curtis; twins, Julia (Mrs. John Francis Shaw) and Judith (Mrs. Willard Robinson Yeakel, Jr.); Thomas Nelson, Samuel Wilgus. *Education:* University of Wisconsin, B.A., 1924; studied several summers at Christian Writer's Conference, Green Lake, Wis. *Politics:* Republican. *Religion:* Presbyterian. *Home:* 1010 East Forest Ave., Neenah, Wis. 54956.

CAREER: Free-lance writer. Member of board of visitors, University of Wisconsin, four years; trustee, Ripon College. *Member:* American Association of University Women, Church Women United, Women's Tuesday Club, and various civic organizations in Neenah.

WRITINGS: Mom, Remember?, privately printed, 1953; *And One to Grow On* (juvenile), Bethany Press, 1967; *Call Me Sam,* Wisconsin House, 1972. Author of church dramatic programs; contributor of short stories, articles, and meditations to religious periodicals.

WORK IN PROGRESS: A personal journal.

*   *   *

PICKERING, R(obert) E(aston)   1934-

PERSONAL: Born February 12, 1934, in Carlisle, England; son of Edward (a cashier) and Janet (Easton) Pickering. *Education:* Queen's College, Oxford, B.A., 1958. *Home:* 07150 Lagorce, France. *Agent:* A. M. Heath & Co. Ltd., 40-42 William IV St., London, WC2N 4DD, England.

CAREER: International Atomic Energy Agency, Vienna, Austria, translator, 1959-60; free-lance translator, mainly for United Nations, 1960—. *Military service:* Royal Navy, 1952-54; became sub-lieutenant. *Member:* International Association of Conference Translators (vice-president, 1966-68, 1974-75).

WRITINGS—Fiction: *Himself Again,* Gollancz, 1966, published as *The Uncommitted Man,* Farrar, Straus, 1967; *In Transit,* Constable, 1968.

WORK IN PROGRESS: Revising old manuscripts; writing another novel.

SIDELIGHTS: Pickering does his writing in a "ruined" house he owns in the south of France ("when not earning my living by translating"). He is fluent in French and Russian, and is competent in German and Spanish. He is interested in African art and literature, and has traveled widely all over the African continent.

*   *   *

PIERCE, James Smith   1930-

PERSONAL: Born April 26, 1930, in Brooklyn, N.Y.; son of Edward Lloyd (a banker) and Florence (Young) Pierce; married Alice Kathleen Farrant, June 16, 1957 (divorced); married Deborah Frederick, March 2, 1974; children: (first marriage) Christopher Dion, David Elliott. *Education:* Oberlin College, B.A., 1952; graduate study at University of Wisconsin, summer, 1952, and Columbia University, 1956; Harvard University, Ph.D., 1962. *Office:* Department of Art, University of Kentucky, Lexington, Ky. 40506.

CAREER: Case Western Reserve University, Cleveland, Ohio, 1959-69, began as instructor, associate professor of art history, 1966-69; University of Kentucky, Lexington, professor of art history, 1969—, chairman of department, 1969-73, director, Center for Contemporary Art, 1970-71. Visiting summer professor, Dartmouth College, 1969, 1972.

Military service: U.S. Army, 1952-54. *Member:* College Art Association, Society of Architectural Historians. *Awards, honors:* Bacon art fellowship, Harvard University, 1958-59, for travel in Europe; America the Beautiful Fund grant, 1972, for photographic survey of ancient earthworks of the Ohio valley; National Endowment for the Humanities award, 1976, for study of twentieth-century American environmental folk sculpture.

WRITINGS: From Abacus to Zeus: A Handbook of Art History, Prentice-Hall, 1968; *Paul Klee and Primitive Art,* Garland Publishing, 1975. Contributor to *Encyclopaedia Britannica,* and to *Journal of Typographic Research, Studies in Medieval Culture, Art Journal,* and other periodicals.

WORK IN PROGRESS: Popular Art and Design.

* * *

PIERCY, Marge 1936-

PERSONAL: Born March 31, 1936, in Detroit, Mich.; daughter of Robert and Bert (Bunnin) Piercy. *Education:* University of Michigan, A.B., 1957; Northwestern University, M.A., 1958. *Politics:* Feminist Party. *Home address:* Box 943, Wellfleet, Mass. 02667. *Agent:* Lois Wallace, Wallace, Aitken and Shiel Inc., 118 E. 61st St., New York, N.Y. 10021.

CAREER: Writer. Gives readings of her own poetry. *Awards, honors:* Avery and Jule Hopwood Award of University of Michigan for poetry and fiction (minor award) and for poetry (major award); literature award, Governor's Commission on the Status of Women (Massachusetts); Borestone Mountain Poetry Award (twice); Orion Scott Award in Humanities.

WRITINGS—Poetry: Breaking Camp, Wesleyan University Press, 1968; *Hard Loving,* Wesleyan University Press, 1969; (with Bob Hershon, Emmet Jarrett, and Dick Lourie) *4-Telling,* Crossing Press, 1971; *To Be of Use,* Doubleday, 1973; *Living in the Open,* Knopf, 1976.

Fiction: *Going Down Fast,* Trident, 1969; *Dance the Eagle to Sleep,* Doubleday, 1971; *Small Changes,* Doubleday, 1973; *Woman of the Edge of Time,* Knopf, 1976. Work represented in over thirty anthologies, including *Best Poems of 1967, New Women, The Fact of Fiction,* and *Psyche: The Feminine Poetic Consciousness.* Contributor of poetry, fiction, essays, and reviews to periodicals.

SIDELIGHTS: "It takes courage to break camp," writes Richard M. Elman, and "Marge Piercy's are courageous poems.... As the pun [that is the title of Miss Piercy's book] implies, not only must one make a hopeful new departure, but one must also put a finish to easy cool, the cynical, the modish, to believe anew in language as thought and feeling, in metaphor as possibility. Breaking camp, in short, affirms poetry and, by extension, life." Jane Colville Betts adds that Miss Piercy's poems "form a kind of definition of love. It is a love which seeks unity of self but knows ambivalence in everything, which has suffered all manner of inconvenience but revels in comfort, which can both make use of convention and transcend it.... Love pays attention to the things it loves," writes Miss Betts, and "Marge Piercy has the eye of a poet."

Elman speaks also of the wide range and varied means of her poems, "poems about love, trust, comradeship; celebrations of animals, objects as parts of the real world she inhabits; they are in short and long lines, free and regular meters, using internal rhymes, or no rhymes at all. Where others seem intolerant, she is compassionate. Where others give way to fashionable despair, she hopes by doing and observing." In other words, Piercy, as the *Time* reviewer concludes, "proves that modern poetry can be both compassionate and perceptive, well-structured and inventive."

Speaking of her 1971 collection, *Hard Loving,* Stephen Dobyns notes that "she sees the world and life as generally antihuman, but instead of giving into it, she expresses anger and indignation, throws small but very pointed stones.... Most of Piercy's [protest poems] succeed because they also deal with the causes within us. But in her world there is little chance of winning, and, even if we do win, we will very likely destroy ourselves later. This wouldn't have much effect on Piercy, however, for she would be happy in Valhalla.... Piercy is still one of the best poets I've seen."

BIOGRAPHICAL/CRITICAL SOURCES: Time, January 24, 1968; *Virginia Quarterly Review,* summer, 1968; *Minnesota Review,* Volume 9, number 1, 1969; *Commonweal,* March 28, 1969; *Poetry,* March, 1971; Carolyn Riley, editor, *Contemporary Literary Criticism,* Gale, Volume III, 1975, Volume VI, 1976.

* * *

PIERS, Maria W(eigl) 1911-

PERSONAL: Born May 17, 1911, in Vienna, Austria; came to America in 1939, naturalized in 1944; daughter of Karl (a musicologist) and Elsa (Pazeller) Weigl; married Gerhart Piers (a psychiatrist), July 15, 1938; children: Margaret Maria, Matthew Jakob. *Education:* University of Vienna, Ph.D., 1939; additional study at Northwestern University, 1942, and Chicago Institute of Psychoanalysis. *Religion:* Unitarian Universalist. *Home:* 5811 Dorchester Ave., Chicago, Ill. 60637.

CAREER: Department of Public Welfare, Vienna, Austria, staff member, 1934-38; social worker with Illinois Society for Mental Health, 1940-42, and Association for Family Living, 1941-50; professor at Chicago Medical School, Chicago, Ill., 1949-52, and Chicago Institute of Psychoanalysis, 1959-62; University of Chicago, Chicago, lecturer in psychology and psychiatry, 1962-68; Loyola University, Chicago, dean of Institute for Early Education, 1967—. Member of Advisory Committee for Family Viewing, of board of directors, American Parents Committee, Inc., and of board of advisors, Social Change Advocates. Regular television appearances include "Children Growing," "About People," and "Growing Up with Children" series; conducted radio program, "Childbearing," 1973. Member of board of advisors, Chicago Children's Museum. *Member:* Orthopsychiatric Association, Royal Society of Health, Psychoanalytic Child Care Alumni Association, Chicago Psychoanalytic Association. *Awards, honors:* Immigrant Service League award, 1966; Myrtle Wreath Award, Hadassah, 1971; Young Women's Christian Association leadership award, 1972; Operation Push award, 1975, for achievements in the field of education.

WRITINGS: Growing Up with Children, Quadrangle, 1967; (with Robert Coles) *The Wages of Neglect,* Quadrangle, 1969; (editor) *Play and Development,* Norton, 1972. Also author of *How to Work with Parents,* 1952. Scriptwriter for four national educational television series, including "Children Growing" and "About People." Contributor of over thirty-five articles to professional journals. Advisory editor, Parents' Magazine Enterprises, and Parents' Magazine Films.

WORK IN PROGRESS: A book on infanticide, tentatively entitled, *Those Who Kill Their Children,* for Norton.

BIOGRAPHICAL/CRITICAL SOURCES: Laura Fermi, *Illustrious Immigrants,* University of Chicago Press, 1968.

*   *   *

PIERSON, Robert H. 1911-

PERSONAL: Born January 3, 1911, in Brooklyn, Iowa; son of Will Grant (a bank president) and Mabel Mary Pierson; married Dollis Mae Smith, September 2, 1931; children: Robert G., John Duane. *Education:* Studied for ministry at Southern Missionary College. *Home:* 7777 Maple Ave., Apt. 701, Takoma Park, Md. 20012. *Office:* General Conference of Seventh-day Adventists, 6840 Eastern Ave. N.W., Washington, D.C. 20012.

CAREER: Seventh-day Adventist Church, clergyman, 1933—. Pastor, 1933-35; lay activities secretary in India, 1935-42; pastor in Takoma Park, Md., and evangelist in New York, N.Y., 1942-44; president of British West Indies and Caribbean Unions, 1945-50, of Southern Asia Division, Poona, India, 1950-54, of Kentucky-Tennessee and Texas Conferences, 1954-58, of Trans-Africa Division, Salisbury, Rhodesia, 1958-66; president of General Conference of Seventh-day Adventists, Washington, D.C., 1966—. *Awards, honors:* D.D., Andrews University.

WRITINGS: The Road to Happiness, Voice of Prophecy, 1948; *Wonderful Jesus,* Voice of Prophecy, 1948; (with J. O. Emmerson) *Paddles Over the Kamarang,* Pacific Press Publishing Association, 1953; *The Secret of Happiness,* Southern Publishing, 1958; *Give Us This Day,* Review & Herald, 1959; *501 Illustrations,* Southern Publishing, 1965; *What Shall I Speak About?,* Pacific Press Publishing Association, 1966; *So You Want to Be a Leader,* Pacific Press Publishing Association, 1966; (with G. S. Stevenson) *Final Countdown,* Pacific Press Publishing Association, 1966; *Faith on Tiptoe,* Southern Publishing, 1967; *Though the Winds Blow,* Southern Publishing, 1968; *Heart to Heart,* Review & Herald, 1970; (with L. B. Reynolds) *Bible Answers to Today's Questions,* Southern Publishing, 1973; *Faith Triumphant,* Review & Herald, 1974; *We Still Believe,* Review & Herald, 1975. Contributor of over one thousand articles to religious journals.

*   *   *

PINTNER, Walter McKenzie 1931-

PERSONAL: Born June 19, 1931, in Yonkers, N.Y.; son of Rudolf (a professor) and Margaret (Anderson) Pintner; married Mary M. Miller, June 22, 1958 (deceased); married Sara H. Pedersen, 1970; children: (first marriage) Anne McKenzie, Robert Miller. *Education:* University of Chicago, A.B., 1951, M.A., 1957; University of Leningrad, graduate student, 1959-60; Harvard University, M.A., 1955, Ph.D., 1962. *Politics:* Democrat. *Religion:* None. *Home:* 630 Snyder Hill Rd., Ithaca, N.Y. 14850. *Office:* Department of History, Cornell University, Ithaca, N.Y. 14850.

CAREER: U.S. Department of State, Washington, D.C., intelligence research analyst, 1956-58; Princeton University, Princeton, N.J., instructor in history, 1961-62; Cornell University, Ithaca, N.Y., assistant professor, 1962-68, associate professor of history, 1968—. *Member:* American Historical Association, American Association for the Advancement of Slavic Studies, Wilderness Society, Sierra Club.

WRITINGS: Russian Economic Policy under Nicholas I,

Cornell University Press, 1967. Contributor to *Slavic Review.*

WORK IN PROGRESS: A monograph, *The Emergence of the Modern Russian Bureaucracy.*

*   *   *

PIPES, Richard (Edgar) 1923-

PERSONAL: Born July 11, 1923, in Cieszyn, Poland; came to America in 1940, naturalized in 1943; son of Mark and Sophia (Haskelberg) Pipes; married Irene Eugenia Roth, September 1, 1946; children: Daniel, Steven. *Education:* Attended Muskingum College, 1940-43; Cornell University, A.B., 1945; Harvard University, Ph.D., 1950. *Home:* 17 Berkeley St., Cambridge, Mass. 02138.

CAREER: Harvard University, Cambridge, Mass., instructor in history and literature, 1950-53, tutor, 1953-58, associate professor, 1958-63, professor, 1963-75, Frank J. Baird, Jr. Professor of History, 1975—, Russian Research Center, research associate, 1953-62, associate director, 1962-64, director, 1968-73. Visiting associate professor, University of California, Berkeley, 1956; senior research consultant, Stanford Research Institute, Center for Strategic Studies, 1973—. *Military service:* U.S. Army, 1943-46. *Member:* American Academy of Arts and Sciences (fellow). *Awards, honors:* Guggenheim fellowship, 1956-57, 1965-66; Rockefeller Foundation fellowship, 1961-62; American Council of Learned Societies fellowship, 1965.

WRITINGS: Formation of the Soviet Union: Communism and Nationalism, 1917-1923, Harvard University Press, 1954, revised edition, 1964; *Karamzin's Memoir on Ancient and Modern Russia,* Harvard University Press, 1959; *Social Democracy and the St. Petersburg Labor Movement, 1885-1897,* Harvard University Press, 1963; (editor with John Fine) *Of Giles Fletcher's Russe Commonwealth,* Harvard University Press, 1966; (editor) *Revolutionary Russia,* Harvard University Press, 1968; (co-author) *Western Civilization,* Harper, 1968; *Struve, Liberal on the Left,* Harvard University Press, 1970; *Europe since 1815,* Harper, 1970; *Russia under the Old Regime,* Scribner, 1975. Also editor of *The Collected Works of Peter B. Struve,* fifteen volumes, 1970.

WORK IN PROGRESS: Volume II of the biography of Peter B. Struve.

BIOGRAPHICAL/CRITICAL SOURCES: New York Times Book Review, April 21, 1968.

*   *   *

PITCAIRN, Leonora 1912-

PERSONAL: Born March 11, 1912, in Angus, Scotland; daughter of Peter (a headmaster) and Helen Scott (Liddell) Grant; married Guy Pitcairn, December 14, 1937 (deceased); children: James Ian, Richard Guy. *Education:* Norland Training College, nursing studies, 1930-32. *Religion:* Church of England. *Home:* 17 The Close, Salisbury, Wiltshire, England. *Office:* National Association for Maternal and Child Welfare, London, England.

CAREER: Nurse; volunteer worker in Africa teaching child care, 1937-47; lecturer in nursery training colleges, 1947-51; associated with National Association for Maternal and Child Welfare, London, England, 1951—, first as examination marker, then as teacher and lecturer on parent education. Free-lance writer. Consultant to *Domestic Science* (magazine).

WRITINGS: The Healthy Baby, Longmans, Green, 1951; *Young Student's Book of Child Care*, Cambridge University Press, 1963, 3rd edition, 1973; *Modern Baby Sitting: A Short Handbook*, National Association for Maternal and Child Welfare, 1964; *Group Discussions*, National Association for Maternal and Child Welfare, 1967; *Parents of the Future*, Cambridge University Press, 1968. Writer of leaflets and bulletins on child care and parent education. Contributor of articles on travel and children to magazines, including *She, Lady, Housewife, Mother and Baby, Woman's Realm*.

WORK IN PROGRESS: Colin, a novel based on family stories; other novels.

SIDELIGHTS: Lenora Pitcairn has travelled in Europe, the Soviet Union, United States, Canada, and Africa to study parent education and to gather material for articles.†

* * *

PITCHER, George (Willard) 1925-

PERSONAL: Born May 19, 1925, in Newark, N.J.; son of Edward Arthur (an engineer) and Mary (Porter) Pitcher. *Education:* U.S. Naval Academy, B.S. (electrical engineering), 1946; Harvard University, M.A., 1954, Ph.D., 1957. *Politics:* Independent. *Religion:* None. *Home:* 18 College Rd. W., Princeton, N.J. 08540. *Office:* 111-1879 Hall, Princeton University, Princeton, N.J. 08540.

CAREER: U.S. Navy, midshipman, 1943-46, officer aboard destroyers with Atlantic fleet, 1946-49, 1951-53, in ranks from ensign to lieutenant; Princeton University, Princeton, N.J., instructor, 1956-60, assistant professor, 1960-63, associate professor, 1963-70, professor of philosophy, 1970—. *Member:* American Philosophical Association. *Awards, honors:* Guggenheim fellowship, 1965-66.

WRITINGS: The Philosophy of Wittgenstein, Prentice-Hall, 1964; (editor) *Truth*, Prentice-Hall, 1964; (editor) Wittgenstein, *The Philosophical Investigations: A Collection of Critical Essays*, Doubleday, 1967; (editor with O. P. Word) *Ryle: A Collection of Critical Essays*, Doubleday, 1970; *A Theory of Perception*, Princeton University Press, 1971.

WORK IN PROGRESS: A book on George Berkeley.

AVOCATIONAL INTERESTS: Classical music, tennis, squash racquets.

* * *

PLANTINGA, Alvin C. 1932-

PERSONAL: Born November 15, 1932, in Ann Arbor, Mich.; son of Cornelius A. (a professor) and Lettie (Bossenbroeck) Plantinga; married Kathleen De Boer, June 16, 1955; children: Carl, Jane, Harry, Ann. *Education:* Calvin College, A.B., 1954; University of Michigan, A.M., 1955; Yale University, Ph.D., 1958. *Religion:* Protestant. *Home:* 2200 Heather St. S.E., Grand Rapids, Mich. 49506. *Office:* Calvin College, Grand Rapids, Mich. 49506.

CAREER: Yale University, New Haven, Conn., instructor in philosophy, 1957-58; Wayne State University, Detroit, Mich., instructor, 1958-60, assistant professor, 1960-62, associate professor of philosophy, 1962-63; Calvin College, Grand Rapids, Mich., associate professor, 1963-64, professor of philosophy, 1965—. Visiting lecturer at University of Illinois, 1960, and Harvard University, 1964-65; visiting professor at University of Michigan, 1967, and University of California, Los Angeles, 1972; fellow, Center for Ad-

vanced Study in the Behavioral Sciences, 1968-69; adjunct professor, University of Notre Dame, 1974; visiting fellow, Balliol College, Oxford University, 1975-76. *Member:* American Philosophical Association, American Academy of Arts and Sciences. *Awards, honors:* Woodrow Wilson fellowship, 1954-55; E. Harris Harbison Award for distinguished teaching, 1968; Guggenheim fellowship, 1971-72; National Endowment for the Humanities fellowship, 1975-76.

WRITINGS: (Editor) *Faith and Philosophy*, Eerdmans, 1964; (editor) *The Ontological Argument*, Doubleday, 1965; (contributor) Max Black, editor, *Philosophy in America*, Cornell University Press, 1965; *God and Other Minds: A Study of the Rational Justification of Belief in God*, Cornell University Press, 1967; *The Nature of Necessity*, Oxford University Press, 1974; *God, Freedom and Evil*, Harper, 1974. Contributor to philosophy and metaphysics journals.

WORK IN PROGRESS: Philosophy of religion, of mind, and of science; semantics of modal logic.

AVOCATIONAL INTERESTS: Mountain climbing and hiking, mainly in the Cascades of Washington State and the Grand Tetons of Wyoming.

* * *

PLANTINGA, Leon B(rooks) 1935-

PERSONAL: Born March 25, 1935, in Ann Arbor, Mich.; son of Cornelius A. (a professor) and Lettie (Bossenbroeck) Plantinga; married Carol J. Cevaal, June 7, 1958; children: Amy, Victor, Andrew. *Education:* Calvin College, B.A., 1957; Michigan State University, M.Mus., 1959; Yale University, Ph.D., 1963. *Politics:* Independent. *Religion:* Protestant. *Home:* 164 Woodlawn St., Hamden, Conn. 06517. *Office:* Music Department, Yale University, New Haven, Conn. 06520.

CAREER: Yale University, New Haven, Conn., instructor, 1963-65, assistant professor, 1965-72, associate professor, 1972-74, professor of history of music, 1974—. Pianist and harpsichordist. Consultant to Keyboard Publications. *Member:* International Musicological Society, American Musicological Society (member of board of directors). *Awards, honors:* Alexander von Humboldt-Stiftung grant for research in Germany, 1966-67; Guggenheim fellowship, 1971-72.

WRITINGS: Schumann as Critic, Yale University Press, 1967; *Muzio Clementi: His Life and Music*, Oxford University Press, 1976. Contributor of articles and reviews to *Yale French Studies, Musical Quarterly*, and other music journals.

WORK IN PROGRESS: An Introduction to Romantic Music, for Norton.

SIDELIGHTS: Plantinga is competent in German, French, Italian, Latin.

BIOGRAPHICAL/CRITICAL SOURCES: Times Literary Supplement, January 18, 1968.

* * *

PLASTARAS, James C(onstantine) 1931-

PERSONAL: Surname is accented on second syllable; born August 19, 1931, in Brooklyn, N.Y.; son of James C. (a research engineer) and Alice (Boudreau) Plastaras. *Education:* St. Joseph's College, Princeton, N.J., student, 1949-51; Mary Immaculate Seminary, B.A., 1959; Catholic

University of America, M.A., 1962; State University of Fribourg. S.T.L., 1963; Pontifical Biblical Institute, Rome, Italy, S.S.L., 1964. *Politics:* Independent.

CAREER: Roman Catholic priest; Seminary of Our Lady of Angels, Niagara Falls, N.Y., later Albany, N.Y., instructor in sacred music, 1959-61, assistant professor of sacred scripture, beginning 1964.

WRITINGS: The God of Exodus, Bruce, 1966; *Creation and Covenant,* Bruce, 1968; *Witness of John: A Study of Johannine,* Bruce, 1971. Author of pamphlets; contributor to religious journals.

SIDELIGHTS: Plastaras is competent in French, German, Hebrew, and Greek.†

*   *   *

PLATT, Charles 1944-

PERSONAL: Born October 25, 1944, in Hertfordshire, England; son of Maurice and Marjorie (Hubbard) Platt. *Education:* Attended Cambridge University, one year, and London College of Printing, two years. *Politics:* Left wing. *Religion:* Agnostic. *Home and office:* 45 Colville Gardens, London W.11, England. *Agent:* Scott Meredith Literary Agency, Inc., 845 Third Ave., New York, N.Y. 10022.

CAREER: New Worlds (monthly magazine of science and speculative fiction), London, England, designer and production assistant, 1966—. Free-lance photographer and designer of book jackets. Clive Bingley Ltd. (publishers), personal assistant, 1967.

WRITINGS: Garbage World, Berkley Books, 1967; *The Gas,* Ophelia Press, 1970; *City Dwellers,* Sidgwick & Jackson, 1970; *Planet of the Voles: A Science Fiction Novel,* Putnam, 1971; (editor with Michael Moorcock) *New Worlds No. Five,* Avon, 1974; (editor with Hilary Bailey) *New Worlds No. Six,* Avon, 1975. Regular contributor of short stories to *New Worlds.*

AVOCATIONAL INTERESTS: Photography, music.†

*   *   *

PLIMPTON, George (Ames) 1927-

PERSONAL: Born March 18, 1927, in New York, N.Y.; son of Francis T. P. (a lawyer and former U.S. deputy representative to the United Nations) and Pauline (Ames) Plimpton; married Freddy Medora Espy (a photography studio assistant), March 28, 1968; children: Medora Ames. *Education:* Harvard University, B.A., 1950; King's College, Cambridge, B.A., 1952, M.A., 1954. *Politics:* Democrat. *Religion:* Unitarian Universalist. *Home:* 541 East 72nd St., New York, N.Y. *Agent:* Russell & Volkening, 551 Fifth Ave., New York, N.Y. 10017. *Office:* Paris Review, Inc., 45-39 171st Pl., Flushing, N.Y. 11358.

CAREER: Editor of *The Lampoon* while at Harvard. Principal editor of *Paris Review,* 1953—, publisher, with Doubleday & Co., of Paris Review Editions (books), 1965—. Instructor at Barnard College, 1956-58; associate editor, *Horizon,* 1959-61; contributing editor, *Sports Illustrated,* 1967. Chief editor of annual anthology of work from literary magazines, for the National Foundation on the Arts and Humanities; adviser on John F. Kennedy Oral History Project. *Military service:* U.S. Army, 1945-48; became second lieutenant. *Member:* Century Association; Brook, Piping Rock, and Raquet and Tennis Clubs; Travellers Club (Paris). *Awards, honors:* Associate fellow, Trumbull College, Yale University, 1967; distinguished achievement award, University of Southern California, 1967; D.H.L., Franklin Pierce College, 1968.

WRITINGS: The Rabbit's Umbrella (juvenile), Viking, 1955; (editor) *Writers at Work: The Paris Review Interviews,* Viking, Volume I, 1957, Volume II, 1963, Volume III, 1967, Volume IV, 1974; *Out of My League* (experiences with baseball), Harper, 1961; *Paper Lion* (experiences with football), Harper, 1966; *The Bogey Man* (experiences with golf), Harper, 1968; (editor with Peter Ardery) *The American Literary Anthology,* Number 1, Farrar, Straus, 1968, Number 2, Random House, 1969, Number 3, Viking, 1970; (editor) Jean Stein, *American Journey: The Times of Robert Kennedy* (interviews), Harcourt, 1970; (with Alex Karras and John Gordy) *Mad Ducks and Bears,* Random House, 1973; *One for the Record: The Inside Story of Hank Aaron's Chase for the Home-Run Record,* Harper, 1974. Also author, with William Kronick, of television scripts for ABC-TV, "Plimpton! Shoot-Out at Rio Lobo," 1970, "Plimpton! Did You Hear the One About . . .?," 1971, "Plimpton! The Great Quarterback Sneak," 1971, and "Plimpton! Adventure in Africa," 1972.

WORK IN PROGRESS: A book on boxing and Muhammed Ali; a book on tennis; *The American Literary Anthology,* Number 4; a one-film anthology of the best work of Andy Warhol; a book on his experiences with the New York Philharmonic; possible plans include a minor role with the Metropolitan Opera and playing hockey with the Boston Bruins or the Philadelphia Flyers.

SIDELIGHTS: The "career" cited above does not do justice to the life of this professional amateur, a man who, as Eliot Fremont-Smith notes, has two careers, "that of a skillful and dedicated promoter of the best in literature and the literary life; and that of a reporter on, and representative for the rest of us to, the professional careers of others, mostly in sports." The same man who edits a successful literary quarterly and knows numerous people, literary and otherwise, has also fought in a bullfight staged by Ernest Hemingway in 1954; fought three rounds with the then light heavyweight champion, Archie Moore, in 1959; lost a tennis match, 6-0, to Pancho Gonzales; engaged in a swimming meet against Don Schollander; played a rubber of bridge with Oswald Jacoby as his partner; pitched to eight players in a post-season All-Star game at Yankee Stadium (see *Out of My League*); joined the Detroit Lions, 1963, as a third-string rookie quarterback and, after training, played one exhibition game in Pontiac, Michigan, where he lost 29 yards in five plays (see *Paper Lion*); played golf in three pro-am tournaments (see *The Bogey Man*); sat in as a percussionist with the New York Philharmonic Orchestra for one month in 1967, toured with the orchestra in Canada, then appeared with it on television on the "Bell Telephone Hour," February 2, 1968; conducted Cincinnati Symphony Orchestra, 1971; made his film acting debut as one of the Bedouin extras in "Lawrence of Arabia," Columbia, 1962, had a small part in "The Detective," Twentieth Century-Fox, 1968, played the mayor in Norman Mailer's film, "Beyond the Law," 1968, portrayed Bill Ford in "Paper Lion," United Artists, 1968, while Alan Alda appeared as the celluloid Plimpton, and played a "bad guy" who is shot by John Wayne in the Western "Rio Lobo," 1970. His role in "Rio Lobo" was the subject of "Plimpton! Shoot-Out at Rio Lobo," ABC-TV, 1970, and some of Plimpton's other participatory adventures were similarly recounted in television specials. His stint as a trapeze artist, lion-tamer, and clown for the Clyde Beatty-Cole Brothers Circus was portrayed in "Plimpton! The Man on the Flying Trapeze,"

ABC-TV, 1970; his stand-up comedy act in Las Vegas was presented on "Plimpton! Did You Hear the One About . . .?," ABC-TV, 1971; his return to the football field as a quarterback for the Baltimore Colts (see *Mad Ducks and Bears*) in a game against the Detroit Lions was depicted in "Plimpton! The Great Quarterback Sneak," ABC-TV, 1971; his Kenyan safari to photograph the world's largest elephant was described in "Plimpton! Adventure in Africa," ABC-TV, 1972.

As Donald Jackson good-naturedly complains, Plimpton "has a genius for ubiquity. His name appears in the public prints with the regularity of a leader of a great power, or at least a middle-sized power. A reasonably informed citizen can scarcely make it through a day, it seems, without encountering a new nugget of Plimptonia . . . Plimpton was photographed wrestling with Sirhan Sirhan after Robert Kennedy was shot in Los Angeles. Plimpton was in the Bahamas for the opening of a new casino, in Africa searching for big game. His articles are running in *Sports Illustrated,* his new book is touted in the Sunday book review supplement. I half expected him to appear on all three networks some time the morning after the election to concede (or accept) the Presidency. I find myself looking carefully at newspaper photographs of great events, wondering which role Plimpton has."

He is, as many note, everyman's Walter Mitty, actually managing to do what others only dream of doing. And, "in a country where masculine maturity generally comes with the realization that one will never live to pitch in a World Series game," writes Joseph Epstein, "—and for most of us this realization arrives, I suspect, only on our deathbeds—Mr. Plimpton has hit a best-seller formula." Plimpton doesn't compete to win, but rather to experience at first hand what it feels like to actually be a participant. Bud Shrake, an editor of *Sports Illustrated,* believes that, "if George ever concentrated on one thing, God knows what he could do." But this is not his ambition; rather, as one friend noted, it is "to know everyone of his time who is famous, interesting or talented, and to be wherever they are. Like Oscar Wilde, he wants to make a work of art out of his life." Such a life engenders feelings of envy, even from the successful. Another close friend, the late Robert Kennedy, once said: "If I wanted to be President, which of course I don't, I'd still *rather* be George Plimpton."

"There are people who would perhaps call me a dilettante," says Plimpton, "because it looks as though I'm having too much fun. I have never been convinced there's anything inherently wrong in having fun. You can still be totally committed to what you're doing." He later expanded and qualified this notion: "People think that what I do is all fun and games—and very glamorous. But I assure you it isn't. There is almost no pleasure in the actual moments of participation, because I invariably fail. The one thing that you learn is that professionals are tuned to a terribly high degree of excellence, and there is no conceivable chance that an amateur can reach that, unless by the most outrageous stroke of luck." Gerald Clarke similarly notes that Plimpton "always loses but, in a larger sense, he always wins, proving that even in an age of constricting specialization a man can do almost anything he sets his mind to, if only for a moment. It is Plimpton's triumph that he has restored the word amateur—which today is so often a synonym for bungler—to its original and true connotation: someone who takes up an art or craft not for gain but for love."

"I'm a writer, not an athlete," Plimpton says. He is, explains John Hattman, "a literary artist who has chosen sports as his medium." Brian Glanville writes, concerning *Paper Lion:* "It is certainly to Mr. Plimpton's credit that he should have undertaken his task without a vestige of patronage, as 'one of the boys'; so much so that the footballers came gladly to accept him as one of themselves, wanted him to play in the public exhibition match against the Cleveland Browns, despite the management; repeatedly ask him back to training camp, even use him to represent them at player-drafts. But Mr. Plimpton is *not* one of the boys. . . . He is a sophisticated literary gentleman with a boyish passion for sport, and the two qualities are constantly, in this book, pulling him in two different directions. . . . At his best," Glanville adds, "there is no more satisfying sports writer in America than Mr. Plimpton, precisely because he is, first of all, a writer." Indeed, Jerzy Kosinski reports that to the current college generation Plimpton "is their ultimate vision of the writer. To them he comes closest to the American conception of what a writer ought to be—that he should not just live off the imagination like Proust, but should recreate an ideal search for experience."

Plimpton's books are consistently praised. John K. Hutchens called *Out of My League* "a baseball book such as no one else ever wrote, and one of the best ever," and Hemingway believed it to be "beautifully observed and incredibly conceived. . . . It is the dark side of the moon of Walter Mitty." His books are works of literature, demonstrations "of how well Mr. Plimpton can write," says Glanville, "how impressively he uses simile and metaphor, especially in passages like the one which describes the crowd's invasion of the field at Yankee Stadium." When *Paper Lion* was published, Myron Cope called it "possibly the most arresting and delightful narrative in all of sports literature." And Owen Jenkins noted: "What Plimpton listens for and captures is the talk of the players and coaches that reveals character and intelligence. *Paper Lion* has some of the best monologue (by Night Train Lane) and dialogue I have read in years. The talkers emerge as men who are epic in language as well as deed. . . ." In his book on golf he again treats the psychology of the sport, adding stories, legends, and general trivia. In his review of *The Bogey Man* Fremont-Smith might well be summarizing all of Plimpton's chronicles when he writes: "[Plimpton] conveys a tremendous sense of empathy which comes from his putting himself through the paces of a pro, so that he feels and gets to know intimately the emotions of the sport—despair, self-consciousness, suspense, boredom, yearning, panic and, every once in a while, exultation." And a *New Yorker* reviewer cites *Mad Ducks and Bears* as a continued reminder that "Plimpton, the professional amateur, the dashing public hero, is first and best of all a writer."

BIOGRAPHICAL/CRITICAL SOURCES: New York Herald Tribune, April 21, 1961; Gay Talese, *The Overreachers,* Harper, 1965; *Book Week,* October 23, 1966; *New York Post,* November 9, 1966; *New York Times Magazine,* January 8, 1967; *Carleton Miscellany,* spring, 1967; *Time,* April 7, 1967, November 8, 1968, September 21, 1970; *Life,* June 30, 1967, November 15, 1968, November 29, 1968; *Commentary,* October, 1967; *Book World,* March 17, 1968; *New York Times,* November 4, 1968, July 26, 1970; *Newsweek,* November 11, 1968; *Atlantic,* December, 1968; *National Observer,* December 2, 1968; *Best Sellers,* December 1, 1969; *Washington Post,* May 27, 1970; *New Yorker,* December 6, 1971.

PLOSSL, George W.   1918-

PERSONAL: Surname rhymes with docile; born July 3, 1918, in Brooklyn, N.Y.; son of George Wilfred and Irene Margaret Plossl; married Marion Louise Hagen, May 24, 1941; children: Keith R. *Education:* Columbia University, A.B., 1939, B.S. in M.E., 1940, M.S. in M.E., 1942. *Home:* 103 Willowick Dr., Decatur, Ga. 30038. *Office address:* P.O. Box 32490, Decatur, Ga. 30032.

CAREER: Registered professional engineer in Massachusetts; held a variety of staff positions from mechanical engineer to assistant to works manager in several Standard Oil Co. affiliates in New Jersey, 1946-62; Stanley Works, New Britain, Conn., materials manager for Stanley Tool Division, 1962-64, plant manager of Stanley Strapping Systems Division, 1964-68; G. W. Plossl & Co. (management education and counseling firm), president, 1968. Teacher of college courses in production control and industrial management. *Military service:* U.S. Naval Reserve, active duty, 1942-46; became lieutenant. *Member:* International Materials Management Society, American Institute of Industrial Engineers, American Production and Inventory Control Society (national advisory planning council member), Society for Advancement of Management.

WRITINGS: (With O. W. Wight) *Production and Inventory Control: Principles and Techniques,* Prentice-Hall, 1967; (chapter editor) *Production and Inventory Control Handbook,* McGraw, 1970; *Manufacturing Control: The Last Frontier for Profit,* Reston, 1973; (with H. F. Mather) *The Master Production Schedule: Managements' Handle on the Business,* G. W. Plossl & Co., 1975. Also editor of 3rd edition of *APICS Bibliography.*

WORK IN PROGRESS: With W. E. Welch, *Inventory Control: The Role of Top Management,* for Reston.

*   *   *

PLOTNICOV, Leonard   1930-

PERSONAL: Born December 5, 1930, in New York, N.Y.; son of Benny and Gloria (Bernstein) Plotnicov. *Education:* Cooper Union, Diploma in Art, 1953; Brooklyn College (now Brooklyn College of the City University of New York), B.A., 1954; University of California, Berkeley, Ph.D., 1964. *Home:* 6620 Kinsman Rd., Pittsburgh, Pa. 15217. *Office:* Department of Anthropology, University of Pittsburgh, Pittsburgh, Pa. 15260.

CAREER: University of Pittsburgh, Pittsburgh, Pa., instructor, 1963-64, assistant professor, 1964-67, associate professor, 1967-69, professor of anthropology, 1970—. *Member:* American Anthropological Association, African Studies Association, International African Institute.

WRITINGS: Strangers to the City, University of Pittsburgh Press, 1967; (editor with Arthur Tuden) *Essays in Comparative Social Stratification,* University of Pittsburgh Press, 1969; (editor with Tuden) *Social Stratification in Africa,* Free Press, 1970. Associate editor, *Ethnology.*

WORK IN PROGRESS: Research on modernization, social stratification, and urbanization.

*   *   *

PLOWDEN, Gene   1906-

PERSONAL: Born February 1, 1906, in Jordan, S.C.; son of Robert (a farmer) and Grace (Keels) Plowden; married Elsie Witt, April 16, 1926; married Doris Friedman (a rate analyst), July 31, 1950; children: (first marriage) Grace Je-

nelle (Mrs. Gerald F. Jones). *Education:* Clemson Agricultural College (now Clemson University), B.S. in Agricultural Education, 1924. *Politics:* Democrat. *Religion:* Methodist. *Home:* 720 Southwest 20th Rd., Miami, Fla. 33219.

CAREER: Newspaper reporter in Charleston and Summerville, S.C., 1924; seaman in Merchant Marine, 1924-25; *Sebring American,* Sebring, Fla., city editor, 1925; *Florida Advocate,* Wauchula, Fla., associate editor, 1926-34; *Sarasota Daily Tribune,* Sarasota, Fla., sports editor, 1934-38; reporter, United Press, 1938-41; *Tampa Tribune,* Tampa, Fla., staff writer, 1941-42; Associated Press, Miami, Fla., staff writer, 1946-69. *Military service:* U.S. Navy, 1943-45. *Member:* American Newspaper Guild, National Turf Writers Association, Circus Fans of America, Circus Historical Society, Circus Model Builders, Kiwanis, Sigma Delta Chi.

WRITINGS: History of Hardee County, Florida Advocate, 1929; *Those Amazing Ringlings and Their Circus,* Caxton, 1967; *Merle Evans: Maestro of the Circus,* Seemann, 1971; *Gargantua: Circus Star of the Century,* Seemann, 1972; (with Chuck Tilley) *This Is Horse Racing,* Seemann, 1974; (with Joe Hirsch) *In the Winner's Circle,* Mason-Lipscomb, 1974; *Singing Wheels and Circus Wagons,* Caxton, 1976. Contributor to *American Motorist, Master Detective, Outdoor Life, Motor Age, American Weekly, Turf & Sport Digest,* and other magazines.

WORK IN PROGRESS: Journey to Washington, an autobiography; *Biography of Juan Ortiz,* the only non-Indian in Florida between the De Narvaez and De Soto expeditions.

*   *   *

PLUMMER, Catharine   1922-

PERSONAL: Born September 6, 1922, in New York, N.Y.; daughter of Edmund J. (a podiatrist) and Rose Mary (Gunkel) Plummer; married Walter Cordier Welsh (an advertising executive), January 5, 1952; children: William Gardner, Jeffry Plummer; stepchildren: Penny Anne, Pamela Jane. *Education:* Simmons College, student, 1939-40; University of California, workshop courses in writing. *Politics:* Independent. *Religion:* Roman Catholic. *Home and office:* 151 Kimberlin Heights Dr., Oakland, Calif. 94619. *Agent:* Harold Ober Associates, 40 East 49th St., New York, N.Y. 10017.

CAREER: General Electric Co., Pittsfield, Mass., editor, 1943-52. *Member:* Authors Anonymous (San Francisco). *Awards, honors:* Received state awards for distinguished industrial journalism, 1946, 1947, and awards from International Council of Industrial Editors, 1948, 1950.

WRITINGS: The Rose on the Summit, Putnam, 1951; *All about Brother Bird,* Doubleday, 1966.

WORK IN PROGRESS: Going Home, a novel about the effect of an elderly grandmother on a family; short stories; *Drop by Drop,* a novel about a late nineteenth-century bishop; *Seneschal,* a novel about the gradual disintegration of a marriage.

AVOCATIONAL INTERESTS: Painting, growing roses; people watching.

BIOGRAPHICAL/CRITICAL SOURCES: American Girl, April, 1948.

*   *   *

PLUTCHIK, Robert   1927-

PERSONAL: Born October 21, 1927, in Brooklyn, N.Y.; son of Leon (in clothing industry) and Libby (Solow) Plutchik; married Anita Freyberg, July 1, 1962; children: Lisa Robin, Lori Jill, Roy Elliot. *Education:* City College (now City College of the City University of New York), B.S. (physics), 1949; Columbia University, M.A., 1950, Ph.D. (psychology), 1952. *Home:* 1131 North Ave., New Rochelle, N.Y. 10804. *Office:* Department of Psychology, Albert Einstein College of Medicine, Bronx, N.Y. 10461.

CAREER: Hofstra University, Hempstead, Long Island, N.Y., associate professor of psychology, 1951-67; Columbia University, College of Physicians and Surgeons, New York, N.Y., associate research scientist, department of psychiatry, 1967-68; Bronx State Hospital, Bronx, N.Y., director of evaluation research program, 1968-71; Albert Einstein College of Medicine, Bronx, director of clinical research unit, department of psychiatry, 1971—. Special fellow, National Institute of Mental Health, Bethesda, Md., 1961-63. *Member:* American Psychological Association (fellow), Sigma Xi.

WRITINGS: (With R. W. Hoffmann) *Small Group Discussion in Orientation and Teaching,* Putnam, 1959; *The Emotions: Facts, Theories and a New Model,* Random House, 1962; *Foundations of Experimental Research,* Harper, 1968, 2nd edition, 1974. Poetry included in *National Poetry Anthology.* Contributor to psychology journals.

WORK IN PROGRESS: The Nature of Emotion in Man and Animal, for Harper.

AVOCATIONAL INTERESTS: Sculpturing in stone and wood.

* * *

PLYMELL, Charles 1935-

PERSONAL: Born April 26, 1935, in Holcomb, Kan.; son of Fred Douglass and Audrey (Sipe) Plymell; married Pamela Beach, September 3, 1966. *Education:* Johns Hopkins University, M.A., 1970. *Politics:* None. *Religion:* None. *Home address:* Box 64, Cherry Valley, N.Y. 13320.

WRITINGS: (Editor) Roxie Powell, *Dreams of Straw,* privately printed, 1963; *Apocalypse Rose,* introduction by Allen Ginsberg, D. Haselwood, 1966; *Neon Poems,* Atom Mind Publications, 1970; *The Last of the Moccasins,* City Lights, 1971; *Over the Stage of Kansas,* Telephone Books, 1972; *Trashing of America,* Kulchur Foundations, 1975; *Blue Orchid Numero Uno,* Telephone Books, 1975.

WORK IN PROGRESS: Preparing a book of poetry for Grove Press.

SIDELIGHTS: Plymell told *CA:* "My work is a sublimation or refinement of the basic con or the basic criminal impulse. Its motivation is money and fame."

* * *

PODHRADSKY, Gerhard 1929-

PERSONAL: Born November 10, 1929, in Bregenz, Austria; son of Anton (a tradesman) and Katharina (Trappel) Podhradsky. *Education:* Attended University of Innsbruck, 1950-1955. *Home:* Pfarrhaus, A-6832, Roethis, Austria.

CAREER: Ordained Roman Catholic priest, 1955; parish priest at Lustenau and then at Feldkirch-Altenstadt, Austria, 1955-61; Catholic Charities, Feldkirch, Austria, director, 1961-1972; parish priest at Roethis, Austria, 1967—, dean, 1974—.

WRITINGS: Das Wort vom neuen Leben, Herder, (Vienna), 1959; *Lexikon der Liturgie; ein Ueberblick fuer die Praxis,* Tyrolia-Verlag, 1964, translation by Ronald Walls and Michael Barry, edited by Lancelot Sheppard, published as *New Dictionary of the Liturgy,* Alba, 1967. Contributor to religious publications.

SIDELIGHTS: Lexikon der Liturgie has been translated into Italian and Dutch, in addition to English.

* * *

POGANY, Andras H(enrik) 1919-

PERSONAL: Born June 26, 1919, in Budapest, Hungary; son of Pal Antal (a mechanical engineer) and Gizella (Hoffmann) Pogany; married Hortenzia Lers (a librarian), June 20, 1942; children: Aniko (Mrs. Joseph DePierro), Ildiko (Mrs. Alexander DeAngelis), Andras, Jr., Csaba-Antal, Orsolya, Balazs. *Education:* Pazmany University, Dr.Jur., 1942; Southern Connecticut State College, M.L.S., 1959. *Religion:* Roman Catholic. *Home:* 201 Raymond Ave., South Orange, N.J. 07079. *Office:* Seton Hall University, South Orange, N.J. 07079.

CAREER: Attorney-at-law and member of the bar in Budapest, Hungary, 1946-56; Yale University, New Haven, Conn., assistant bibliographer, 1959-60; Seton Hall University, South Orange, N.J., assistant chief reference librarian, 1960-63, associate university librarian with rank of associate professor, 1963-70, with rank of professor, 1970—. National president, Hungarian Freedom Fighters' Federation, U.S.A., 1966-73; president, World Federation of Hungarian Freedom Fighters, 1973—. Member of board, Federation of Free Hungarian Jurists. Commissioner, Bicentennial Celebrations Commission, New Jersey, 1972—. *Member:* American Academy of Political and Social Science, Catholic Library Association. *Awards, honors:* Golden key of city of Rochester, N.Y., 1966.

WRITINGS: Bela Estvan, a Hungarian Cavalry Colonel in the Confederate Army, Kossuth Foundation, 1962; *A City in the Darkness,* A.-H. Literary Guild (Gainesville, Fla.), 1966; (with wife, Hortenzia Pogany) *Political Science and International Relations: A Recommended List of Books,* Scarecrow, 1967. Author of regular column of political comment appearing in five English-Hungarian newspapers in United States and Canada.

WORK IN PROGRESS: A book, *In God We Trust....*

SIDELIGHTS: Andras Pogany wrote: "I am a dedicated enemy of all forms of totalitarianism, Nazism and Communism alike, and lecture extensively all over the country to keep my fellow-Americans cognizant of the dangers we are facing today...." Pogany fled Hungary after the uprising of 1956. He speaks French, and has a working knowledge of German and Latin. *Avocational interests:* Travel, especially camping with his family.

* * *

POGANY, Hortenzia Lers

PERSONAL: Born in Budapest, Hungary; daughter of Baron Vilmos (Hungarian undersecretary of state) and Elvira Reischl (von Szoreny) Lers; married Andras H. Pogany (an associate university librarian, Seton Hall University), June 20, 1942; children: Aniko (Mrs. Joseph DePierro), Ildiko (Mrs. Alexander DeAngelis), Andras, Jr., Csaba-Antal, Orsolya, Balazs. *Education:* Pazmany University, M.A., 1942; Rutgers University, M.L.S., 1965. *Religion:* Roman Catholic. *Home:* 201 Raymond Ave., South Orange, N.J. 07079. *Office:* Seton Hall University, South Orange, N.J. 07079.

CAREER: High school teacher of Latin in Budapest, Hungary, 1943-44; Hungarian National Archives, Budapest, researcher in department of mediaeval diplomas, 1951-54; Albertus Magnus College, New Haven, Conn., assistant librarian, 1958-60; Seton Hall University, South Orange, N.J., cataloger, 1960-66, chief catalog librarian, 1966—. *Member:* American Classical League, Catholic Library Association, New Jersey Library Association.

WRITINGS: (With husband, Andras H. Pogany) *Political Science and International Relations: A List of Recommended Books,* Scarecrow, 1967.

* * *

POLENBERG, Richard 1937-

PERSONAL: Born July 21, 1937, in New York, N.Y.; son of Morris (in advertising) and Leah (Lieber) Polenberg; married Marcia Weiss, July 12, 1959; children: Lisa, Amy, Michael. *Education:* Brooklyn College (now Brooklyn College of the City University of New York), B.A., 1958; Columbia University, M.A., 1959, Ph.D., 1964. *Office:* Department of History, Cornell University, Ithaca, N.Y. 14850.

CAREER: Brooklyn College (now Brooklyn College of the City University of New York), Brooklyn, N.Y., instructor, 1964-65, assistant professor, 1965-66; Cornell University, Ithaca, N.Y., assistant professor, 1966-67, associate professor, 1967-70, professor of history, 1970—. *Member:* American Historical Association, Organization of American Historians.

WRITINGS: Reorganizing Roosevelt's Government: The Controversy over Executive Reorganization, 1936-39, Harvard University Press, 1966; (editor) *America at War: The Homefront, 1941-1945,* Prentice-Hall, 1968; *War and Society: The United States, 1941-1945,* Lippincott, 1972; (editor) *Radicalism and Reform in the New Deal,* Addison-Wesley, 1972; (co-author) *The American Century: A History of the United States since the 1890's,* Wiley, 1975. Contributor to historical journals.

* * *

POLI, Bernard 1929-

PERSONAL: Born July 16, 1929, in Algiers, Algeria; son of Charles Michel and Yvonne (Besson) Poli; married Michele Perney, July 16, 1957; children: Frederic. *Education:* Sorbonne, University of Paris, Licence es Lettres, 1950, Diplome d'Etudes Superieures, 1952, Agregation d'Anglais, 1953, Doctorat es Lettres, 1965; Yale University, M.A., 1952. *Home:* Rosedale Ave., Ottawa, Ontario, Canada. *Office:* French Embassy, 42 Sussex Dr., Ottawa, Ontario, Canada.

CAREER: Lycee d'Alger, teacher of English, 1955-57; Wellesley College, Wellesley, Mass., lecturer in French, 1957-59; Sorbonne, University of Paris, Paris, France, assistant professor, 1959-62; University of California, Berkeley, Harkness fellow, 1962-64; University of Montpellier, Montpellier, France, associate professor, 1964-65; Sorbonne, University of Paris, and Ecole Normale Superieure, Paris, professor of American literature, 1965-70; University of Tunis, Tunisia, visiting professor, 1970-72; French Embassy, Ottawa, Ontario, cultural counsellor, 1972—. Director, College Franco-Britannique, Cite Universitaire Internationale, 1966-70. *Military service:* French Army, served as interpreter; became first lieutenant. *Member:* Societe des Anglicistes de l'Enseignment Superieur, European

Association for American Studies, French Association for American Studies.

WRITINGS: Mark Twain, Ecrivain de l'Ouest, Presses Universitaires de France, 1965; *Ford Madox Ford and the "Transatlantic Review,"* Syracuse University Press, 1967; *Le Roman Americain, 1865-1917,* Colin, 1972. Contributor to *Etudes Anglaises* and *Modern Language Review.*

* * *

POLISHOOK, Irwin H. 1935-

PERSONAL: Born March 5, 1935, in New York, N.Y.; son of Harry and Frieda (Rosenberg) Polishook; married Sheila Stern (a college professor), December 29, 1957. *Education:* Brooklyn College (now Brooklyn College of the City University of New York), B.A., 1956; Brown University, M.A., 1958; Northwestern University, Ph.D., 1961. *Home:* 302 West Englewood Ave., Teaneck, N.J. 07666. *Office:* Herbert H. Lehman College of the City University of New York, New York, N.Y. 10468.

CAREER: Herbert H. Lehman College of the City University of New York, New York, N.Y., instructor, 1961-64, assistant professor, 1965-67, associate professor, 1968-70, professor of history, 1971—, department chairman, 1968-70. Visiting professor, Northwestern University, 1967. Member of Columbia University Seminar on Early American History and Culture. *Member:* American Historical Association, American Association of University Professors, Organization of American Historians. *Awards, honors:* American Association for State and Local History grant, 1962; Social Science Research Council fellowship.

WRITINGS: Roger Williams, John Cotton, and Religious Freedom: A Controversy in New and Old England, Prentice-Hall, 1967; *Rhode Island and the Union, 1774-1790,* Northwestern University Press, 1969; (editor with Jacob Judd) *Aspects of Early New York Politics and Society,* Sleepy Hollow Restorations, 1975. Contributor of articles and reviews to journals.

WORK IN PROGRESS: A book on the period of the Confederation, 1781-1789; research on church and state in early American history.

* * *

POLITE, Carlene Hatcher 1932-

PERSONAL: Born August 28, 1932, in Detroit, Mich.; daughter of John and Lillian (Cook) Hatcher (both international representatives of the UAW-CIO); divorced; children: Glynda, Lila. *Education:* Attended public schools in Detroit, Mich. *Home:* 21 rue de Dantzig, Paris 13, France.

CAREER: Former professional dancer and teacher of dancing (Martha Graham technique), and organizer of political action-education activities; currently a full-time writer. Elected member of Michigan Democratic State Central Committee, 1962-63; coordinator of Detroit Council for Human Rights, 1963. Active in Vanguard Playhouse, Detroit, 1960-62. *Member:* National Foundation on the Arts and Humanities.

WRITINGS: The Flagellants (novel), Editions Julliard, 1966, Farrar, Straus, 1967; *Sister X and the Victims of Foul Play...,* Farrar, Straus, 1975. Contributor to *Mademoiselle.*

WORK IN PROGRESS: Two more books; literary and political articles for American magazines.

BIOGRAPHICAL/CRITICAL SOURCES: Punch, March 13, 1968.†

POLLITT, Jerome J(ordan) 1934-

PERSONAL: Born November 26, 1934, in Fair Lawn, N.J.; son of John K. (a businessman) and Doris (Jordan) Pollitt. *Education:* Yale University, B.A., 1957; Columbia University, Ph.D., 1963. *Home:* 49 Vantage Rd., Hamden, Conn. 06514. *Office:* Classics Department, Phelps Hall, Yale University, New Haven, Conn. 06520.

CAREER: Yale University, New Haven, Conn., assistant professor of classical art and archaeology, 1962-68, associate professor, 1969-73, professor of classical archaeology and history of art, 1973—. *Military service:* U.S. Army Reserve, 1958-64. *Member:* Archaeological Institute of America, College Art Association.

WRITINGS: The Art of Greece: 1400-1431 B.C., Prentice-Hall, 1965; *The Art of Rome: c. 753 B.C.-337 A.D.,* Prentice-Hall, 1966; *Art and Experience in Classical Greece,* Cambridge University Press, 1974; *The Ancient View of Greek Art,* Yale University Press, 1974. Contributor to professional journals. Editor, *American Journal of Archaeology,* 1974—.

WORK IN PROGRESS: A book on ancient art criticism; a book on classical Greek art.

*   *   *

POMRENKE, Norman E. 1930-

PERSONAL: Born July 20, 1930, in Trenton, Mich.; son of Louis F. and Mary (Terteling) Pomrenke; married Carol Arlene Cogswell, October 2, 1954; children: Lou, Russ, Louise. *Education:* Compton Junior College, A.A., 1956; Michigan State University, B.S., 1958; Florida State University, M.S., 1964. *Office:* Police Department, Baltimore, Md.

CAREER: Former member of police department, Oakland, Calif.; Florida State University, Tallahassee, professor of criminology, 1962-65; University of North Carolina, Chapel Hill, professor of government and law, 1965-67; Baltimore Police Department, Baltimore, Md., director of education and training, 1967—. Consultant, President's Commission on Law and Order. *Military service:* U.S. Air Force, 1951-55; became staff sergeant. *Member:* International Association of Chiefs of Police, International Association of Police Professors, American Association of University Professors.

WRITINGS: (Editor) *Proceedings of Southern Institute for Law Enforcement,* University of North Carolina Press, 1963; (editor) *Police Community Relations,* University of North Carolina Press, 1966; *Law Enforcement Manual: Rules and Regulations,* University of North Carolina Press, 1967; *A Preliminary Study to Determine Law Enforcement Command Personnel Totals and Present Police Management Training Facilities,* Institute of Government, University of North Carolina, 1967.

WORK IN PROGRESS: Special Problems in Police Administration.†

*   *   *

PONTNEY, Jack A(rthur) 1931-

PERSONAL: Born May 8, 1931, in Ann Arbor, Mich.; son of Arthur James and Anna (Higgins) Pontney; married Joan Ann Gregson (a teacher), August 10, 1961. *Education:* University of Redlands, B.A., 1953; Northwestern University, M.A., 1956, Ph.D., 1963. *Home:* 1232 Frances Ave., Fullerton, Calif. 92631. *Office:* California State University, Fullerton, Calif. 92631.

CAREER: University of Southern California, Los Angeles, instructor in economics, 1957-61; California State University, Fullerton, professor of economics, 1961—. Private practice as economic consultant. *Member:* American Economic Association, Economic History Association, American Association of University Professors, Western Economic Association.

WRITINGS: (With Shih-yen Wu) *An Introduction to Modern Demand Theory,* Random House, 1967. Also co-author of *Introductory Economics,* 1970.

*   *   *

POOLE, Josephine 1933-

PERSONAL: Born February 12, 1933, in London, England; daughter of Charles Graham (a managing director of engineering firm) and Astrid (an artist; maiden name, Walford) Cumpston; married Timothy Ruscombe Poole (a driving instructor), July 14, 1956; married second husband, Vincent J. H. Helyar (a farmer), August 29, 1975; children: (first marriage) Theodora Mary, Emily Josephine, Katherine Virginia, Isabel Beatrice; (second marriage) Charlotte Mary, Vincent Graham. *Education:* Attended schools in Cumberland and London, England. *Religion:* Roman Catholic. *Home:* Poundisford Lodge, Poundisford, Taunton, Somersetshire, England. *Agent:* A. P. Watt & Son, 26-28 Bedford Row, London WC1R 4HL, England.

CAREER: Employed as solicitors' secretary, 1950-54; British Broadcasting Corp., London, England, secretary in features department, 1954-56; free-lance writer.

WRITINGS—All juvenile books, except where indicated: *A Dream in the House,* Hutchinson, 1961; *Moon Eyes,* Hutchinson, 1965, Little, Brown, 1967; *The Lilywhite Boys,* Hart-Davis, 1968; *Catch As Catch Can,* Hutchinson, 1969, Harper, 1970; *Yokeham* (adult novel), J. Murray, 1970; *The Visitor,* Harper, 1972 (published in England as *Billy Buck,* Hutchinson, 1972).

AVOCATIONAL INTERESTS: Traveling, history, arts in general.

*   *   *

POOVEY, W(illiam) A(rthur) 1913-

PERSONAL: Born September 20, 1913, in Baltimore, Md.; son of William Arthur (a Lutheran minister) and Opal (Holland) Poovey; married Mary Virginia Smith, June 29, 1940. *Education:* Capital University, B.A., 1934; Evangelical Lutheran Seminary (now Evangelical Lutheran Theological Seminary), graduate, 1939; Northwestern University, M.A., 1939; further study at Union Theological Seminary, New York, N.Y., 1957-58, and New College, University of Edinburgh, 1967; Wartburg College, D.D., 1972; St. Mary's College, University of St. Andrews, further study, 1973. *Home:* 2130 Coates St., Dubuque, Iowa 52001. *Office:* Wartburg Theological Seminary, Dubuque, Iowa 52001.

CAREER: Capital University, Columbus, Ohio, instructor in speech, 1934-39. American Lutheran Church, clergyman, 1939—; parish minister in Monterey Park, Calif., 1939-45, San Antonio, Tex., 1945-53, and Memphis, Tenn., 1953-57; Wartburg Theological Seminary, Dubuque, Iowa, professor of preaching, 1958—. American Lutheran Church, chairman of Commission of Research and Social Action, 1962-72, secretary of Board of Pensions, 1972—.

WRITINGS—All published by Augsburg, except as indicated: (With Nellie Marsh) *Hymn Dramatizations,* Standard Publishing, 1942; *Questions That Trouble Christians*, Wartburg Press, 1946; *Problems That Plague the Saints*, Wartburg Press, 1950; *No Hands But Ours*, Wartburg Press, 1952; *Your Neighbors' Faith*, 1961; *And Pilate Asked*, 1965; *Cross Words*, 1968; *Lenten Chancel Dramas*, 1968; *What Did Jesus Do?*, 1969; *Mustard Seeds and Wineskins*, 1972; *Let Us Adore Him*, 1972; *Signs of His Coming*, 1973; *Stand Still and Move Ahead*, 1973; *Six Faces of Lent*, 1974; *Banquets and Beggars*, 1974; *The Power of the Kingdom*, 1974; *Celebrate with Drama*, 1975; *The Days before Christmas*, 1975.

AVOCATIONAL INTERESTS: The literature, geography, and history of the British Isles.

*   *   *

POPOV, Haralan Ivanov   1907-

PERSONAL: Born March 7, 1907, in Krasno Gradishte, Bulgaria; son of Ivan Poptchernev and Desha (Vitcheva) Tchernia; married Ruth Pernevi, October 16, 1937; children: Paul, Rhoda (Mrs. Juhany Linna). *Education:* Studies at Bible institutes in Danzig, 1931-32, 1934-35, and London, 1936-37. *Home address:* Box 303, Glendale, Calif. 91209. *Office:* Evangelism to Communist Lands, Inc., Glendale, Calif.

CAREER: Evangelical minister. Board member of council of all evangelical churches in Bulgaria, until 1948; imprisoned by Bulgarian communists, 1948-61; currently president of Evangelism to Communist Lands, Inc., Glendale, Calif. Bible printer for communist lands; radio broadcaster; lecturer.

WRITINGS: I Was a Communist Prisoner, Zondervan, 1966; *Tortured for His Faith*, Zondervan, 1970.

*   *   *

PORTER, Bern(ard Harden)   1911-

PERSONAL: Born February 14, 1911, in Porter Settlement, Me.; son of Lewis Harden and Etta Flora (Rogers) Porter; married Helen Elaine Hendren (a poet), 1946 (divorced, 1947); married Margaret Eudine Preston (an author), August 27, 1955 (died, 1975). *Education:* Colby College, Sc.B., 1932; Brown University, Sc.M., 1933; special courses at DaVinci School, 1937, Convair School, 1957, University of Maine, 1960, and Federal School, 1963. *Politics:* Republican. *Religion:* Methodist. *Agent:* William Rutledge, 5228 Irvine Ave., North Hollywood, Calif. *Office:* 22 Salmond Rd., Belfast, Me. 04915.

CAREER: Physicist with Acheson Colloids Corp., 1935-40, with Manhattan District Engineers, 1940-45; Bern Porter Books (publishers), Belfast, Me., president, 1942—. Chairman of the board, Bern Porter, Inc. Artist and illustrator, whose work has been shown in New York, San Francisco, Japan, and Tasmania. Director of Contemporary Gallery, 1947-50, West Coast Design Guild, 1947-50, Fund for Contemporary Expression, 1947-50. Chairman of the board, Institute of Advanced Thinking, 1959—. *Member:* Society for International Development, International Poetry Society (fellow), International Platform Association, Technical Publishing Society (fellow), American Astronautical Society (associate fellow), Society of Technical Writers and Publishers, American Physical Society, Institute of Radio Engineers, American Rocket Society, American Society of Emeriti, National Society of Programmed Instruction, Phi Beta Kappa, Sigma Xi, Kappa Phi Kappa, Chi Gamma Sigma, Xi Epsilon Mu, Fenway Club (Boston), Algonquin Club. *Awards, honors:* Sc.D., Institute of Advanced Thinking, 1959.

WRITINGS—All published by Bern Porter, except as indicated: *Colloidal Graphite: Its Properties and Applications*, Acheson, 1939; *Map of Physics*, Cenco, 1939; *Map of Chemistry*, University of Pennsylvania, 1941; (self-illustrated) *Doldrums*, Al Press, 1941; *Me*, 1943; *Henry Miller Bibliography*, 1943, revised edition, 1969; *Map of Joyceana*, Circle Editions, 1946; *Art Techniques*, Gillick Press, 1947; *The Union of Science and Art*, Greenwood Press, 1948; *Schillerhaus: 1947-1950*, 1955; *Drawings: 1954-1955*, 1956; *Commentary on the Relationship of Art and Science*, Stanford University, 1956; *Rocket Data Book*, Convair, 1956; *Dictionary of Rocket Terminology*, Convair, 1956; *The Works of H. L. Mencken: A Bibliography*, 1957; *Drawings: 1955-1956*, 1959.

F. Scott Fitzgerald: A Bibliography, 1960; *The Waste-Maker, 1926-1961*, 1961; *Scandinavian Summer*, 1961; *Circle: Reproductions of Art Work, 1944-1947*, Circle Editions, 1963; *Reporting and Preventive Maintenance Forms for the 465L Program*, Federal Electric Corp., 1963; *Charcoal Drawings, 1935-1937*, 1963; *I've Left* (essays), Marathon Press, 1963, 2nd edition, 1969; *Assorted Art, 1928-1963*, 1963; *Applicable 465L Publications*, Federal Electric Corp., 1963; *Day Notes for Mother*, 1964; *Native Alphabet*, 1964; *Scigraffiti*, 1964; *AL0110*, 1964; *What Henry Miller Said and Why It Is Important* (booklet), D. Turrell, 1964, 2nd edition, Bern Porter Books, 1969; *Dynamic Test Vehicle Instrumentation and Data System Criteria*, Boeing, 1965; *Dynamic Test Vehicle Data Reduction and Correlation Requirements*, Boeing, 1965; *The First Publication of F. Scott Fitzgerald* (booklet), Quality Books, 1965; *Dynamic Test Program Requirements*, Boeing, 1965; *Mathematics for Electronics*, Prentice-Hall, 1965; *Art Productions: 1928-1965*, D. Turrell, 1965; *Captive Firing of Flight Stage Reliability Study*, Boeing, 1966; *System Methodologies and Their Utilization*, Boeing, 1966; *Moscow*, 1966; *Founds*, Contemporary, 1966; *Cut Leaves*, 1966; *The Box*, 1968; *Knox County, Maine*, 1969; *Dieresis*, 1969; *Artifacts*, 1969; *scda 19*, 1969.

Oraison funebres de Bossuet, 1970; *OEye*, 1970; *Reminiscences, 1927-1970*, 1970; *PER Book*, 1970; *Enry One*, 1970; *Enry 2-5*, 1970; *ULA*, 1971; *Assorted Cuts, 1965-1970*, five volumes, 1971; *b.p.*, 1971; *HEXA 914*, 1971; *Found Poems*, Something Else Press, 1972; *The Waste-Maker, 1926-1961*, Abyss Publications, 1972; *The 14th of February*, 1972; *Trattoria Due Fermi*, 1973; *Hand Fashioned Chocolates*, 1974; *The Manhattan Telephone Book*, Abyss Publication, 1975; *Selected Founds*, Croissant Pamphlet No. 2, 1975; *Run-On*, 1975; *Where To Go/What To Do/When in New York/Week of June 22, 1972*, 1975.

Editor: Henry Miller, *The Plight of the Creative Artist in the U.S.A.*, 1944; Miller, *Henry Miller Miscellanea*, 1945; Miller, *Echolalia*, 1946; *Seashore Brochures*, Christian F. Ver Becke, 1947; *Robert Carleton Brown*, 1956; Harry Kiakis, *The Watts Towers*, 1959; Kiakis, *Venice: Beatnik Capitol*, 1961; Diter Rot, *Cutcards*, 1963; Ray Johnson, *A Book About Death*, 1963; Jack Roth, *The Exciting, Igniting World of Art*, 1964; William B. Faulkner, Jr., *Man*, 1965; *Bay-Area Creators: 1945-1965*, 1965; *B.P. at Schillerhaus*, 1966; *Harry Bowden: His Studio and Work*, 1966; *Wernher von Braun: A Bibliography and Selected Papers*, 1966; *Art Scrapbook*, 1967; *Art Prints*, 1967; *Selected Articles by R. Buckminster Fuller*, 1968; *The Private Papers of Wilhelm Reich, 1942-1954*, 1969; Philip Lloyd Ely, *Bernard Langlais*, 1969; *Contemporary Italian Poets*, 1973; *Ves-*

tigia: Notes on the Life and Work of Janelle Viglini, 1975, *The Viglini Letters,* two volumes, 1975.

Editor and illustrator: Miller, *Semblance of a Devoted Past,* 1944; *The Happy Rock,* 1945; John Hoffman, *Journey to the End,* 1956; William B. Faulkner, Jr., *Henry: An Anthology by World Poets,* 1970.

Illustrator of more than twenty books, including: A. L. Blackwood, *General Physics Text,* 1943; Leonard Wolfe, *Hamadryad Hunted,* 1947; Antoine Artaud, *Judgement,* 1955; Dick Higgins, *What Are Legends,* 1960; Stephen Berry Kimble, *Henry Miller,* 1965; Michael Fraenkel, *Genesis,* 1970; James Joyce, *Poems Pennyeach,* 1970; James Scheville, *Breakout,* 1974. Also illustrator for more than ten magazines and newspapers, 1926-75.

Editor of magazines including: *Colby White Mule,* 1929-32; *The Leaves Fall,* 1942-45; *Circle,* 1944-45; *Broadside,* 1954-56.

Also author of many booklets and pamphlets on art, technology, and literature.

WORK IN PROGRESS: Resume of Physics, three volumes; *The Book of Dos; Here Comes Everybody's Don't Book; The Book of Death; Holy Smokes and Gee Whizzes.*

SIDELIGHTS: Bern Porter writes: "Travels in remote areas like Newfoundland, Tasmania, Russia, Venezuela, with extended living periods among cultures like the Laplanders, Ulithians, Guamanians, Balinese, and others, force me into a continuing search for ways the science of physics can promote a better life. My experiences with the development of the A-bomb and later pilgrimage to Hiroshima have already given rise to many creative forms like sciarch, sciart, et. al., discussed in my biographical work, *I've Left.* I enjoy a large correspondence with creative workers from all over the world. Current interests are centered on techniques and procedures for programed instruction, learning 'by machine' and experiments in visual expression of language structure. Plan additional and prolonged travels."

BIOGRAPHICAL/CRITICAL SOURCES: James Erwin Schevill, *The Roaring Market and the Silent Tomb* (biography), Abbey Press, 1957.

*   *   *

PORTER, Charles A(llan)   1932-

PERSONAL: Born May 31, 1932, in Chicago, Ill.; son of Charles Augustin (a minister) and Emma C. (Fliege) Porter; married Elizabeth Anne Robinson (a teacher of French), November 24, 1956. *Education:* North Park Junior College, student, 1949-51; Northwestern University, B.S., 1953, M.A., 1954; Yale University, Ph.D., 1962. *Politics:* Democrat. *Religion:* None. *Home:* 188 Bishop St., New Haven, Conn. 06511. *Office:* 320 W. L. Harkness Hall, Yale University, New Haven, Conn. 06520.

CAREER: Yale University, New Haven, Conn., instructor, 1960-64, assistant professor, 1964-67, associate professor, 1967-75, professor of French, 1975—; director of Summer Language Institute, 1971. Lecturer, University of Lyon, 1955-56. *Member:* Modern Language Association of America, American Association of Teachers of French. *Awards, honors:* Fulbright fellowship to Universities of Aix-Marseille and Lyon, 1954-56; American Council of Learned Societies grant, 1970-71.

WRITINGS: Restif's Novels; or, An Autobiography in Search of an Author, Yale University Press, 1967.

WORK IN PROGRESS: A monograph on Chateaubriand's imagination.

*   *   *

PORTER, Edward A.   1936-

PERSONAL: Born November 14, 1936, in Baltimore, Md.; son of Howard Franklin, Jr. (a sheetmetal worker) and Ida (Shoemaker) Porter; married Nancy A. Wehner, October 13, 1956; children: Kathryn A., Edward A., Jr. *Education:* University of Maryland, Fire Service Extension, fireman's basic training, 1954, advanced training, 1955, officer training, 1957-58; Baltimore County Police Academy, student, 1959. *Home:* 8204 Dorset Ave., Baltimore, Md. 21237.

CAREER: Baltimore County Police Bureau, Baltimore, Md., 1958—, currently lieutenant. Ordained to Methodist Ministry, 1973; currently assistant pastor, Armistead Gardens Evangelical Methodist Church, Baltimore, Md. *Military service:* Maryland National Guard, Medical Service; became sergeant. *Member:* National Police Officers Association of America, National Rifle Association of America.

WRITINGS: (With Richard D. Fitch) *Accidental or Incendiary,* C. C Thomas, 1968.

WORK IN PROGRESS: Research for book on a policeman's view of true cases.

*   *   *

PORTER, John   1919-

PERSONAL: Born May 4, 1919, in New York, N.Y.; son of Hugh Thomas (an executive) and Edith (Haskin) Porter. *Education:* Studied at Columbia University. *Politics:* Democrat. *Religion:* Buddhist. *Home and office:* Route 112, Lime Rock, Conn. 06039. *Agent:* International Creative Management, 40 West 57th St., New York, N.Y. 10019.

CAREER: National Broadcasting Co., New York, N.Y., director of advertising, 1950-62; Simon's Rock College, Great Barrington, Mass., director of public relations, 1968-75; free-lance writer. *Military service:* U.S. Army Air Forces, pilot, 1942-44; became warrant officer. *Member:* Sports Car Club of America, Wilderness Society.

WRITINGS: Winterkill (novel), Bodley Head, 1967; *All About Beer,* Doubleday, 1975. Contributor of short stories and articles to *Cosmopolitan, Mademoiselle, Esquire, Playboy, Gentleman's Quarterly,* and *King* (England).

WORK IN PROGRESS: Athana, a novel.

AVOCATIONAL INTERESTS: Flying (holds commercial pilot's license), sports car racing (has won several championships).

*   *   *

PORTER, Lyman W(illiam)   1930-

PERSONAL: Born March 19, 1930, in Lafayette, Ind.; son of Charles L. and Mary A. (Stouffer) Porter; married Meredith A. Moeller, April 6, 1958; children: Anne, William. *Education:* Northwestern University, B.S., 1952; Yale University, Ph.D., 1956. *Home:* 2639 Bamboo St., Newport Beach, Calif. 92660. *Office:* Graduate School of Administration, University of California, Irvine, Calif. 92717.

CAREER: University of California, Berkeley, instructor, 1956-58, assistant professor, 1958-63, associate professor of psychology, 1963-67; University of California, Irvine, professor of administration and psychology, 1967—, dean of graduate school of administration. *Member:* American Psychological Association (fellow; president, division of industrial and organizational psychology, 1975-76), Academy of Management (fellow; president, 1973-74), American Association of University Professors, Phi Beta Kappa, Sigma Xi. *Awards, honors:* Ford Foundation faculty research fellow, 1959-60.

WRITINGS: (With Mason Haire and Edwin E. Ghiselli) *Managerial Thinking: An International Study,* Wiley, 1966; (with Edward E. Lawler) *Managerial Attitudes and Performance,* Irwin, 1968; (with Lawler and J. Richard Hackman) *Behavior in Organizations,* McGraw, 1975; (with Richard Steers) *Motivation and Work Behavior,* McGraw, 1975.

* * *

PORTERFIELD, Bruce 1925-

PERSONAL: Born December 31, 1925, in Lansing, Mich.; son of Glenn Edwin (vice-president of an insurance company) and Reba (Cook) Porterfield; married Edith Olson (a missionary), December 31, 1944; children: Brian, Connie, Gwendolyn, Julie, Richard. *Education:* Studied at New Tribes Mission, 1944-46. *Politics:* Republican. *Home:* New Tribes Mission, Woodworth, Wis. 53194.

CAREER: Baptist missionary in Bolivia, 1949-66; New Tribes Mission, Woodworth, Wis., general representative in United States, 1968—. For many years was the Bolivian government representative for the New Tribes Mission in Bolivia, taught and evangelized among savage Indian tribes, made expeditions beyond civilization in the jungles of Bolivia and Brazil, and worked on several Indian languages. *Military service:* U.S. Navy, Seabees, 1943.

WRITINGS: Commandos for Christ, Harper, 1963; *Jungle Fire,* Zondervan, 1966; *Twice Burned,* Brown Gold Publications, New Tribes Mission, 1969.

* * *

PORTISCH, Hugo 1927-

PERSONAL: Born February 19, 1927, in Bratislava (Pressburg), Czechoslovakia; son of Emil (a journalist) and Hedwig (Kundiger) Portisch; married Gertrude Reich (a writer), May 12, 1949; children: Edgar. *Education:* University of Vienna, student, 1945-51, Ph.D., 1951; University of Missouri, graduate study in journalism, 1950. *Home:* Goelsdorfgasse 2, A-1010 Vienna, Austria. *Agent:* Collins-Knowlton-Wing, Inc., 60 East 56th St., New York, N.Y. 10022. *Office:* Kurier, Lindengasse 52, A-1070 Vienna, Austria.

CAREER: Journalist and television commentator. Austrian Information Service, assistant director, New York, N.Y., 1953-55; Austrian Broadcasting System, Vienna, commentator, 1955—, panelist, 1956—. Editor-in-chief, *Kurier,* Vienna, Austria, 1958-67; television commentator in Vienna, 1958—, and Munich, 1960-68. Chairman of board, Austria Press Agency, 1959-61. *Member:* Press Club Concordia (Vienna). *Awards, honors:* Karl Renner Prize, 1966, for outstanding reportage; Golden Camera, for outstanding television achievements.

WRITINGS: So sah ich Sowjetunion, Afrika, Sudamerika, Kremayr, Scheriau, 1964; *Augenzeuge der Weltpolitik,* Sudwestverlag, 1964; *So sah ich China,* Kremayr, Scheriau, 1965, translation by Heinz Von Koschembahr published as *Red China Today,* Quadrangle, 1966; *Eye-Witness in Viet Nam,* Bodley Head, 1967; *So sah ich Siberien,* Kremayr, Scheriau, 1967; *Friede durch Angst,* Molden, 1970; *L'arsenal atomique americain,* Fayard, 1971; *I Saw*

Siberia, Harrap, 1972; *Die deutsche Konfrontation,* Molden, 1974. Contributor to *Saturday Review* and the Austrian press.

SIDELIGHTS: Coverage abroad includes all U.S. presidential campaigns since 1952, and many international conferences. Hugo Portisch traveled on fact-finding tours to Far and Middle East, 1958, Soviet Union and Africa, 1962, Latin America, including Cuba, 1963, China, 1964, Vietnam, Formosa, and Australia, 1965, Siberia, 1967, Czechoslovakia, 1968, and East and West Germany, 1973.

BIOGRAPHICAL/CRITICAL SOURCES: U.S. News and World Report, September 12, 1966.

* * *

POST, Felix 1913-

PERSONAL: Born July 25, 1913, in Berlin, Germany; son of Paul (an art historian) and Clarissa (Daus) Post; married second wife, Kathleen Jane Britten, June 26, 1962; children: (first marriage) Anthony Julian, Deborah Elizabeth. *Education:* University of London, M.B. and B.S., 1939, M.D., 1961. *Politics:* Liberal. *Religion:* Lutheran. *Office:* Bethlem Royal and Maudsley Hospital, London S.E. 5, England.

CAREER: Training posts at hospitals in London, England, and Edinburgh, Scotland; Bethlem Royal and Maudsley Hospital, London, England, consultant psychiatrist, 1947—. *Military service:* British Army, Medical Corps, 1946-47; became major. *Member:* Royal Society of Medicine, Royal College of Psychiatrists (fellow), Royal College of Physicians (fellow).

WRITINGS: The Significance of Affective Symptoms in Old Age, Oxford University Press, 1962; *The Clinical Psychiatry of Late Life,* Pergamon, 1964; *Persistent Persecutory States of the Elderly,* Pergamon, 1966.

WORK IN PROGRESS: Continuing clinical research in psychiatry of old age.

AVOCATIONAL INTERESTS: Gardening and travel.

* * *

POTTER, J(im) 1922-

PERSONAL: Born September 8, 1922, in Huddersfield, England; married Joyce Barbara Smith, September 2, 1944; children: Stephanie Barbara, Caroline Margaret. *Education:* University of Manchester, B.A. (first class honors in history), 1947, M.A., 1949. *Home:* 11 The Chestnuts, Walton on Thames, Surrey, England. *Office:* London School of Economics and Political Science, University of London, Aldwych, London W.C.2, England.

CAREER: Research student in Sweden, 1949-50; University of London, London School of Economics and Political Science, London, England, reader in economic history, with special reference to the United States, 1951—. Visiting professor at Yale University, 1952-53, University of North Carolina, 1958-59, Indiana University, 1965, and University of Kansas, 1968; also visiting summer professor at University of British Columbia and State University of New York at Buffalo. Member of committee of management, Institute of United States Studies, London, England; member of the Marshall Aid Commemoration Commission. *Military service:* Royal Air Force, 1942-46; became flight lieutenant. *Member:* British Association for American Studies, Economic History Society (United Kingdom), Economic History Association (United States), European Association for American Studies.

WRITINGS: (Translator from the Swedish) E. Lundberg, *Business Cycles and Economic Policy in Sweden,* Harvard University Press, 1957; (translator from the Swedish) O. Gasslander, *History of Stockholm's Enskilda Bank to 1914,* Stockholm, 1962; *The American Economy between the World Wars,* Macmillan, 1974.

Contributor: H. C. Allen and C. P. Hill, editors, *British Essays in American History,* St. Martin's, 1957; L. S. Pressnell, editor, *Studies in the Industrial Revolution,* Oxford University Press, 1960; D. V. Glass and D.E.C. Eversley, editors, *Essays in Historical Demography,* Aldine, 1965; R. M. Robertson and J. L. Pate, editors, *Readings in United States Economic and Business History,* Houghton, 1966; A. N. J. den Hollander and S. Skard, editors, *American Civilisation: An Introduction,* Longmans, Green, 1968; Richard Rose, *Lessons from America,* Macmillan, 1974. Contributor to professional journals. Consulting English editor, *Scandinavian Economic History Review,* 1953-62.

WORK IN PROGRESS: *A History of the Population of America, 1607 to the Present.*

* * *

POTVIN, Raymond H(erve) 1924-

PERSONAL: Born October 28, 1924, in Southbridge, Mass.; son of Cleophas R. and Eva (Beauvais) Potvin. *Education:* Assumption College, Worcester, Mass., B.A., 1944; University of Montreal, S.T.B., 1948; Catholic University of America, Ph.D., 1958; Princeton University, postdoctoral study, 1965-66. *Home:* 620 Michigan Ave. N.E., Washington, D.C. 20017. *Office:* Catholic University of America, Washington, D.C. 20017.

CAREER: Roman Catholic priest. Assistant pastor in Springfield, Mass., 1948-53; Catholic University of America, Washington, D.C., lecturer, 1956-57, instructor, 1958-59, assistant professor, 1960-63, associate professor, 1963-67, professor of sociology, 1967—. Lecturer, Georgetown University, 1961. *Member:* American Sociological Association (fellow), American Academy of Political and Social Science, Population Association of America. *Awards, honors:* Fellowship to Princeton University, 1965-66.

WRITINGS: *Belgian Enterprise Councils,* Catholic University of America Press, 1958; (with C. Westoff) *College Women and Fertility Values,* Princeton University Press, 1967; (with A. Suziedelis) *Seminarians of the Sixties,* Cara Press, 1969; (with Suziedelis) *Vocational Challenge and Seminary Response,* Cara Press, 1971. Contributor to *American Sociological Review, Sociological Analysis, Social Forces,* and *Journal of Marriage and Family.*

* * *

POULIN, A(lfred A.), Jr. 1938-

PERSONAL: Born March 14, 1938, in Lisbon, Me.; son of Alfred A. (a laborer) and Alice (Michaud) Poulin; married Basilike H. Parkas; children: Daphne. *Education:* St. Francis College, Biddeford, Me., B.A., 1960; Loyola University, Chicago, Ill., M.A., 1962; University of Iowa, M.F.A., 1968. *Home:* 610 Ellis Dr., Brockport, N.Y. 14420. *Office:* Department of English, State University of New York College at Brockport, Brockport, N.Y. 14420.

CAREER: St. Francis College, Biddeford, Me., instructor, 1962-64; University of Maryland, European Division, Heidelberg, Germany, instructor, 1965; University of New Hampshire, Durham, instructor, 1965-66; St. Francis College, Biddeford, Me., assistant professor of English, 1968-71, chairman of humanities department, 1969-71, assistant to president, 1971; State University of New York College at Brockport, assistant professor of English, 1971—. Communications consultant on Columbia Point Health Project, Tufts University. *Awards, honors:* Danforth associate, 1970-74.

WRITINGS: (Editor with David DeTurk, and contributor) *The American Folk Scene: Dimensions of the Folksong Revival,* Dell, 1967; (editor) *Contemporary American Poetry,* Houghton, 1971, 2nd edition, 1975; (editor) *Making in All Its Forms: Contemporary American Poetics and Criticism,* Dutton, 1972; *In Advent: Poems,* Dutton, 1972. Also translator of *The Poems of Anne Hebert,* Cummington Press. Contributor of poetry to *Atlantic Monthly, Ante, Bitterroot, Choice, North American Review, Chicago Review, Commonweal, Kenyon Review, New American Review,* and other journals.

WORK IN PROGRESS: Editing a small anthology of Georgian poetry, a collection of manuscripts and statements by contemporary American and British poets, and an anthology of contemporary American poetry.

SIDELIGHTS: Poulin told *CA:* "For good or ill, I have chosen not to be exclusively a poet. I have not isolated my work as a poet from my interest in the popular arts, especially songwriting, from my critical interest in the poetry and criticism of others, from the challenge of editing, or from my activities as a teacher. I am convinced that each of these feeds on the other, is strengthened by such interchange. Besides, a man—at least this man—survives on a number of levels, each with its own stress of energy and identity." He is fluent in French.†

* * *

POWELL, Lawrence Clark 1906-

PERSONAL: Born September 3, 1906, in Washington, D.C.; son of G. Harold and Gertrude (Clark) Powell; married Fay Ellen Shoemaker, March 26, 1934; children: Norman Jerrold, Wilkie Haines. *Education:* Occidental College, B.A., 1928; University of Dijon, Ph.D., 1932; University of California, Berkeley, certificate of librarianship, 1937. *Politics:* Democrat. *Religion:* Quaker. *Home:* 6288 North Campbell Ave., Tucson, Ariz. 85718.

CAREER: Occidental College, Los Angeles, Calif., teaching assistant in English, 1929; Vroman's Bookstore, Pasadena, Calif., shipping clerk, 1929-30; worked for rare book stores in Los Angeles and for Western Publishers, 1934-36; University of California Press, Berkeley, editorial assistant, 1936-37; Los Angeles (Calif.) Public Library, employed in order department and associated with various branches, 1937-38; University of California Library, Los Angeles, junior assistant in acquisitions department, 1938-43, chief librarian, 1944-61, director of William Andrews Clark Memorial Library, 1944-66; University of California, School of Library Service, Los Angeles, professor and dean, 1960-66; full-time writer, 1966—; University of Arizona, Tucson, professor-in-residence, 1971—. Conductor of workshops for U.S. Air Force librarians, Tokyo, 1960, 1966. Randolph G. Adams Memorial Lecturer at University of Michigan, 1953; University of Tennessee Library lecturer, and visiting professor at Columbia University, 1954; Trumbull Lecturer at Yale University, 1960; fellow, Center for Advanced Studies, Wesleyan University, 1968; visiting professor, Simmons College, 1968.

MEMBER: American Library Association, Bibliographical

Society of America (president, 1954-56), California Library Association (president, 1950), California Historical Society (fellow), Phi Beta Kappa, Phi Gamma Delta, Zamorano Club, Rounce Club, and Coffin Club (all Los Angeles); Grolier Club (New York City). *Awards, honors:* Guggenheim fellow in Great Britain, 1950-51, 1967; Litt.D., Occidental College, 1955, Juniata College, 1963; Clarence Day Award, 1960; L.H.D., Carnegie Institute of Technology, 1961; Doctor of Humanities, University of Arizona, 1971.

WRITINGS: An Introduction to Robinson Jeffers, Imprimerie Bernigaud & Privat (Dijon), 1932, 2nd edition published as *Robinson Jeffers: The Man and His Work,* Primavera Press, 1934, 3rd edition, San Pasquale Press, 1940; *Philosopher Pickett: The Life and Writings of Charles Edward Pickett,* University of California Press, 1942; *Islands of Books* (essays), Ritchie, 1951; *Land of Fiction* (bibliographical essay), Dawson's Book Shop, 1952; *The Alchemy of Books, and Other Essays and Addresses on Books and Writers,* Ritchie, 1954; (editor) *Libraries in the Southwest,* University of California Library, Los Angeles, 1955; *Books: West, Southwest* (essays), Ritchie, 1957; (reviser) Phil Townsend Hanna, *Libros Californianos; or, Five Feet of California Books,* Zeitlin & Ver Brugge, 1958; *A Passion for Books,* World Publishing, 1959.

Books in My Baggage: Adventures in Reading and Collecting, World Publishing, 1960; *Southwestern Book Trails: A Reader's Guide to the Heartland of New Mexico and Arizona,* Horn & Wallace, 1963; *The Little Package: Pages on Literature and Landscape from a Traveling Bookman's Life,* World Publishing, 1964; (compiler) Walt Whitman, *Leaves of Grass,* Crowell, 1964; *Bookman's Progress: Selected Writings,* Ritchie, 1968; *Fortune and Friendship: An Autobiography,* Bowker, 1968; *California Classics: The Creative Literature of the Golden State,* Ritchie, 1971; *Southwest Classics: The Creative Literature of the Arid Land,* Ritchie, 1974; *Arizona: A Bicentennial History,* Norton, 1976. Also author of monographs, occasional papers, and pamphlets on authors, books and book publishing, libraries, and regional literature.

Author of forewords and introductions for more than forty books, including: William Everson, *San Joaquin,* Ritchie, 1939; Lawrence Durrell, *A Landmark Gone,* [Los Angeles], 1949; *The Intimate Henry Miller,* Signet, 1959; Theodore Roosevelt, *The Rough Riders,* New American Library, 1961; George Wickes, editor, *Henry Miller and the Critics,* Southern Illinois University Press, 1963; *The Raymond Chandler Omnibus,* Knopf, 1964; Frances Clark Sayers, *Summoned by Books,* Viking, 1965; *Come Hither! Papers on Children's Literature and Librarianship,* Yeasayers Press, 1966.

Contributor of articles on books, librarianship and western history to a number of publications, including *Antiquarian Bookman, Arizona Highways, Library Journal, New York Times Book Review, Saturday Review, Westways,* and other library journals, scholarly quarterlies, and literary and book-collecting reviews.

AVOCATIONAL INTERESTS: Reading, book-collecting, music.

BIOGRAPHICAL/CRITICAL SOURCES: Gertrude Clark Powell, *The Quiet Side of Europe,* [Los Angeles], 1959; Betty Rosenberg, *Checklist of the Published Writings of Lawrence Clark Powell,* School of Library Service, University of California, 1966; *New York Times Book Review,* August 18, 1968; *American Literature,* November, 1971.

POWELL, Marvin 1924-

PERSONAL: Born May 5, 1924, in Syracuse, N.Y.; son of William and Gussie (Chainov) Powell; married Rita Cohen, June 17, 1951; children: Jeffrey Arnold, Linda Beth, Laura Wendy. *Education:* Syracuse University, A.B., 1947, M.S. in Ed., 1949, Ph.D., 1952. *Home:* 417 Fairmont Dr., De Kalb, Ill. 60115. *Office:* Northern Illinois University, De Kalb, Ill. 60115.

CAREER: Western Reserve University (now Case Western Reserve University), Cleveland, Ohio, assistant professor of educational psychology, 1952-61, acting director of vocational counseling services, 1953-55; Willoughby-Eastlake Schools, Willoughby, Ohio, director of psychological services, guidance, and research, 1956-61; Northern Illinois University, De Kalb, professor of educational psychology, 1961—. Consultant, State of Illinois Mental Health Program; president, Foundation for Individualized Evaluation and Research, Inc., 1972—. *Military service:* U.S. Army Air Forces, 1943-46. *Member:* American Psychological Association (fellow), American Association for the Advancement of Science (fellow), Society for Research in Child Development, American Educational Research Association, Sigma Xi, Phi Delta Kappa, B'nai B'rith (president of Kishwaukee lodge, 1966-67).

WRITINGS: Psychology of Adolescence, Bobbs-Merrill, 1963; (editor with I. Frank) *Psychosomatic Ailments in Childhood and Adolescence,* C. C Thomas, 1967; *Youth: Critical Issues,* C. E. Merrill, 1973. Contributor of more than thirty articles to psychology and education journals.

WORK IN PROGRESS: Two books, *Introduction to Educational Psychology* and *Teachers' Attitudes.*

*   *   *

POWELL, Milton Bryan 1934-

PERSONAL: Born April 5, 1934, in Jacksonville, Ill.; son of Cedric Milton (a clergyman) and Esther (Stewart) Powell; married Sue Ann Knox, June 14, 1957; children: Catherine, Julie, Gregory, Adrienne. *Education:* Cornell College, Mount Vernon, Iowa, B.A., 1958; University of Iowa, M.A., 1960, Ph.D., 1963. *Home:* 412 Marshall, East Lansing, Mich. 48823. *Office:* Justin Morrill College, Michigan State University, East Lansing, Mich. 48824.

CAREER: Michigan State University, East Lansing, assistant professor, department of American thought and language, 1963-68, Justin Morrill College, associate professor, 1968-72, professor of history, 1972—, director of studies in history, 1968—. *Military service:* U.S. Army, Airborne, 1954-56. *Member:* American Historical Association, American Studies Association, Organization of American Historians.

WRITINGS: (Editor) *The Voluntary Church: American Religious Life, 1740-1860, Seen Through the Eyes of European Visitors,* Macmillan, 1967.

*   *   *

POWERS, Richard M. Gorman 1921-

PERSONAL: Born February 24, 1921, in Chicago, Ill.; son of Thomas and Marcella (Gorman) Powers; married Evelyn Schaeffer, September 23, 1943 (deceased); children: Richard, Elizabeth Terence, Sarah Kathleen, Ann Marie. *Education:* Attended Loyola University, Chicago, Ill., University of Illinois and New School for Social Research. *Politics:* Independent Democrat. *Religion:* Roman Catholic. *Residence:* Ridgefield, Conn.

CAREER: Commercial illustrator and painter. Illustrator of children's books for Viking Press, McGraw-Hill Book Co., Doubleday & Co., and other publishers; also has done illustrations for magazines, including *Life, Reporter,* and *Saturday Evening Post. Military service:* U.S. Army, Signal Corps, 1942-46; became sergeant. *Member:* IDL (professional club in Jamaica, West Indies), Society of Illustrators.

WRITINGS—Self-illustrated: Doubledecker, Coward, 1955; *The Cave-dwellers,* Coward, 1962. Cartoon and text feature, "Powers," published in *Berkshire Eagle,* Pittsfield, Mass., 1964-66. Author and illustrator of articles in *High Fidelity.*

Illustrator: *The Byzantines,* World, 1959; *Migichi,* Crowell, 1966; *Storm Along,* Holt, 1967; Barbara Ritchie, *The Ghost That Haunted the House That Culpepper Built,* Viking, 1968.

WORK IN PROGRESS: A novel, *McTarzan Day at the V.D. Clinic;* a long poem, "Father Lennie Lovebomb Lives."

BIOGRAPHICAL/CRITICAL SOURCES: American Artist, January, 1960.††

* * *

POWLEDGE, Fred 1935-

PERSONAL: Born February 23, 1935, in Nash County, N.C.; son of Arlius Raymond (an auditor) and Pauline (Stearns) Powledge; married Tabitha Morrison, December 21, 1957; children: Pauline Stearns. *Education:* University of North Carolina, B.A., 1957; Columbia University, Russell Sage fellow, 1966-67. *Home and office:* 271 Degraw St., Brooklyn, N.Y. 11231. *Agent:* Joan Raines, 475 Fifth Ave., New York, N.Y. 10017.

CAREER: Associated Press, editor-writer in New Haven, Conn., 1958-60; *Atlanta Journal,* Atlanta, Ga., reporter, 1960-63; *New York Times,* New York, N.Y., reporter, 1963-66; free-lance writer, 1966—. Lecturer, New School for Social Research, New York, N.Y., 1968-69. *Military service:* U.S. Army Reserve, 1957-63.

WRITINGS: Black-Power—White Resistance: Notes on the New Civil War, World Publishing, 1967; *To Change a Child,* Quadrangle, 1968; *Model City, A Test of American Liberalism: One Town's Efforts to Rebuild Itself,* Simon & Schuster, 1970; *Mud Show: A Circus Season,* Harcourt, 1975. Contributor to periodicals including, *New Yorker, Esquire, Playboy,* and *New Republic.*

WORK IN PROGRESS: Research and writing on urban problems, race relations, social revolution, and the environment; an autobiographical book.

SIDELIGHTS: Interest in race relations and social upheaval stems, Powledge says, from being a white Southerner exposed both to the ideas of democracy and to racism. *Avocational interests:* Restoring a hundred year-old house in Brooklyn, and a 250 year-old house in Newport, R.I.; backpacking.

BIOGRAPHICAL/CRITICAL SOURCES: New York Review, February 29, 1968.

* * *

POWRIE, Peter James 1927-

PERSONAL: Surname rhymes with dowry; born September 29, 1927, in London, England; son of James Peter (headmaster of a school) and Margaret (Gardner) Powrie; married Colette Marie Grangier (a teacher), April 10, 1950; children: Philip Peter, Francoise Monique, Mark Peter. *Education:* King's College, London, B.A. (first class honors in geography), Diploma in Education, Associateship. *Home:* 1 Voltaire Court, Ennerdale Rd., Kew, Surrey, England; and Ave. Charles de Thiennes 72, 1200 Bruxelles, Belgium. *Office:* Commission of the European Communities DG VII B4, 120 Rue de la LO1, 1049 Bruxelles, Belgium.

CAREER: Ealing Grammar School for Boys, London, England, teacher and careers master, 1949-59; British European Airways, Ruislip, Middlesex, England, training and education superintendent, 1959-64; British Transport Docks Board, London, England, staff member, 1965-66; National Ports Council, London, England, staff member, 1966-74; Commission of the European Communities, Bruxelles, Belgium, directorate-general for transport, 1974—.

WRITINGS: (With A. J. Mansfield and K. E. Williams) *North West Europe,* Harrap, 1959, 6th edition, 1971; (with Mansfield and Williams) *France and Benelux,* Harrap, 1972; (with Mansfield and M. V. Urwin) *Problem Maps: Western Europe and the British Isles,* Harrap, 1974.

AVOCATIONAL INTERESTS: Camping and caravanning in the United Kingdom and abroad.

* * *

PRALL, Stuart E(dward) 1929-

PERSONAL: Born June 2, 1929, in Saginaw, Mich.; son of Edward E. (an engineer) and Maryan (Green) Prall; married Naomi Shafer, January 20, 1958; children: Julie, David. *Education:* Michigan State University, B.A., 1951; University of Rhode Island, M.A., 1953; University of Manchester, Manchester, England, graduate study, 1953-54; Columbia University, Ph.D., 1960. *Politics:* Democrat. *Home:* 1479 Court Pl., Hewlett, N.Y. 11557.

CAREER: Queens College of the City of New York (now Queens College of the City University of New York), Flushing, N.Y., lecturer in history, 1955-58; Newark State College, Union, N.J., assistant professor of history, 1958-60; Queens College of the City University of New York, instructor, 1960-63, assistant professor, 1964-66, associate professor, 1967-71, professor of history, 1972—. *Member:* American Historical Association, Irish American Cultural Institute, American Society for Legal History, Conference on British Studies (treasurer). *Awards, honors:* Fulbright scholarship in England, 1953-54.

WRITINGS: The Agitation for Law Reform during the Puritan Revolution, 1640-60, Nijhoff, 1966; *The Puritan Revolution: A Documentary History,* Anchor Books, 1968; *The Bloodless Revolution: England, 1688,* Anchor Books, 1972. Contributor to *American Journal of Legal History.*

WORK IN PROGRESS: The Earls of Clanricard in the sixteenth and seventeenth centuries.

* * *

PRESLEY, James (Wright) 1930-

PERSONAL: Born January 13, 1930, in Nash, Tex.; son of James Alex (a Civil Service employee) and Opal (Wright) Presley; married Fran Burton, January 13, 1962; children: John Francis, Ann Burton. *Education:* East Texas State University, B.A., 1950; University of Texas, M.A., 1955, graduate study towards Ph.D., 1956-58; University of the Americas, graduate study, 1955. *Residence:* Texarkana, Tex. *Agent:* Blanche C. Gregory, Inc., 2 Tudor City Pl., New York, N.Y. 10017.

CAREER: Newspaperman, working as reporter in Texarkana, Tex., 1947-49, Shreveport, La., 1958-59, and as copy editor in Amarillo, Tex., 1956, and San Antonio, Tex., 1959-61; free-lance writer, 1961—. Consultant, Red River Regional Council on Alcoholism, 1975—. *Military service:* U.S. Air Force, 1950-53; became staff sergeant. *Member:* American Medical Writers Association, Texas State Historical Association, Phi Alpha Theta. *Awards, honors:* Anson Jones Award, Texas Medical Association, 1971, for excellence in medical writing.

WRITINGS: (With John T. Scopes) *Center of the Storm: Memoirs of John T. Scopes,* Holt, 1967; (with Joe D. Nichols, M.D.) *Please, Doctor, Do Something!,* Natural Food Associates, 1972; (with John M. Ellis, M.D.) *Vitamin B6: The Doctor's Report,* Harper, 1973; (with Gerald W. Getty) *Public Defender,* Grosset & Dunlap, 1974; (with John C. McCamy, M.D.) *Human Life Styling: Keeping Whole in the Twentieth Century,* Harper, 1975. Contributor to magazines, supplements such as *New York Times Magazine,* and to scholarly journals, including *Southwest Review, Southwestern Historical Quarterly,* and *The Americas.* Contributing editor, *Texas Observer,* 1964—.

WORK IN PROGRESS: A history of Texas oil and oilmen, for Putnam; a book on children's nutrition with Hugh Powers, M.D., for Crowell.

SIDELIGHTS: James Presley told *CA:* "My major areas of interest are in medicine/health and general nonfiction. The greatest issue in the world today is health—ecological and individual." He has lived in Mexico and knows Spanish.

* * *

PRESTON, Lee E. 1930-

PERSONAL: Born July 28, 1930, in Dallas, Tex.; son of Lee E. and Cecil (Degan) Preston; married Patricia Leahy, January 27, 1958; children: Katherine, James, Mary Jane. *Education:* Vanderbilt University, B.A., 1951; Harvard University, M.A., 1953, Ph.D., 1958. *Home:* 25 Eltham Dr., Buffalo, N.Y. 14226. *Office:* Department of Environmental Analysis and Policy, State University of New York at Buffalo, Buffalo, N.Y. 14214.

CAREER: University of California, Berkeley, assistant professor, 1958-62, associate professor, 1962-66, professor of business administration, 1966-69, associate dean, School of Business Administration, 1967-69; State University of New York at Buffalo, Melvn H. Baker Professor of American Enterprise and chairman of department of environmental analysis and policy, 1969—, director, Center for Policy Studies, 1973—. Member of White House Task Force on Anti-Trust Policy, 1967-68. Consultant to various government agencies, private firms, law firms, and public bodies. *Military service:* U.S. Army, 1954-56. *Member:* American Economic Association, American Marketing Association. *Awards, honors:* Western Farm Economics Association annual research award, 1961, 1966.

WRITINGS: (With James S. Duesenberry) *Cases and Problems in Economics,* Prentice-Hall, 1960; *Exploration for Non-Ferrous Metals: An Economic Analysis,* Resources for the Future, Inc., 1960; (editor) *Managing the Independent Business,* Prentice-Hall, 1962; *Profits, Competition and Rules of Thumb in Retail Food Pricing,* Institute of Business and Economic Research, University of California, 1963; (with others) *Competition and Price Behavior in the British Columbia Petroleum Industry,* Stanford Research Institute, 1964; (with Norman R. Collins)

Studies in a Simulated Market, Institute of Business and Economic Research, University of California, 1966; (with Paul E. Nelson) *Price Merchandising in Food Retailing: A Case Study,* Institute of Business and Economic Research, University of California, 1966; (editor) *Social Issues in Marketing,* Scott, Foresman, 1968; (with Collins) *Concentration and Price-Cost Margins in Manufacturing Industries,* University of California Press, 1968; *Consumer Good Marketing in a Developing Economy: The Case of Greece,* Center for Economic Research and Planning (Athens), 1968; *Markets and Marketing: An Orientation,* Scott, Foresman, 1970; *Trade Patterns in the Middle East,* American Enterprise Institute, 1970; *The Industry and Enterprise Structure of the U.S. Economy,* General Learning Press, 1971; (with James E. Post) *Private Management and Public Policy,* Prentice-Hall, 1975.

Contributor: C. J. Friedich and J. K. Galbraith, editors, *Public Policy,* Harvard University Graduate School of Public Administration, 1954; Moyer and Hollander, editors, *Markets and Marketing in Developing Economies,* Irwin, 1968; J. F. Weston, editor, *Public Policy toward Mergers,* Goodyear Publishing, 1969; Louis P. Bucklin, editor, *Vertical Marketing Systems,* Scott, Foresman, 1970; J. Fred Weston and Stanley I. Ornstein, editors, *The Impact of Large Firms on the U.S. Economy,* Heath, 1973; Fred C. Allvine, editor, *Public Policy and Marketing Practices,* American Marketing Association, 1973; J. W. McGuire, editor, *Contemporary Management: Issues and Viewpoints,* Prentice-Hall, in press, Contributor of articles, research reports, and reviews to journals in his field.

Member of editorial review board: *Journal of Industrial Economics, Industrial Organization Review, Academy of Management Journal,* and *Journal of Reprints for Antitrust Law and Economics.*

* * *

PRESTWICH, Menna 1917-

PERSONAL: Born February 12, 1917, in Swansea, Wales; daughter of William (a schoolmaster) and Olive (Morris) Roberts; married John Prestwich (a fellow and tutor, Queen's College, Oxford University), August 18, 1938; children: Michael Charles. *Education:* Lady Margaret Hall, Oxford University, B.A. (first class honors), 1938, M.A., 1944. *Religion:* None. *Home:* 18 Dunstan Rd., Old Headington, Oxford, England. *Office:* St. Hilda's College, Oxford University, Oxford, England.

CAREER: Oxford University, Oxford, England, fellow and tutor in modern history, St. Hilda's College, 1947—, university lecturer in history, 1956—. *Member:* Royal Historical Society (fellow).

WRITINGS: (Contributor) J. W. Wallace, editor, *France: Government and Society,* Methuen, 1959; *Cranfield: Politics and Profits under the Early Stuarts,* Clarendon Press, 1966; (contributor) H. R. Trever-Roper, editor, *The Age of Expansion, 1559-1660,* Thames & Hudson, 1968; (contributor) A. F. R. Smith, editor, *The Reign of James VI and I,* Macmillan, 1973.

WORK IN PROGRESS: War and Society in France in the Seventeenth Century, for Faber.

BIOGRAPHICAL/CRITICAL SOURCES: Times Literary Supplement, March 9, 1967; *Listener,* March 23, 1967.

PRICE, Alfred 1936-

PERSONAL: Born August 3, 1936, in Cheam, Surrey, England; son of Lewis (a building contractor) and Augustine (Gefall) Price; married Jane Beaven, March 14, 1964; children: Fiona, Clare. *Education:* Educated at schools in Surrey, England. *Religion:* Church of England. *Address:* c/o Campbell Thomson & McLaughlin Ltd., 31 Newington Green, London N16 9PU, England.

CAREER: Royal Air Force, 1952-74, specialized in electronic warfare, aircraft weaponry, and modern air fighting tactics. *Member:* Royal Historical Society (fellow). *Awards, honors:* L. G. Groves Memorial Prize for aircraft safety, 1963.

WRITINGS: Instruments of Darkness: The Struggle for Radar Supremacy, Kimber & Co., 1967; *German Air Force Bombers of World War II,* Volume I, Doubleday, 1968, Volume II, Hylton-Lacey, 1969; *Luftwaffe: Birth, Life, and Death of an Air Force,* MacDonald & Co., 1970; *Aircraft Versus Submarine,* U.S. Naval Institute, 1974; *Battle over the Reich,* Scribner, 1974; *Spitfire at War,* Ian Allan, 1975; *World War II Fighter Conflict,* MacDonald & Co., 1975. Contributor to *War Monthly.*

WORK IN PROGRESS: An operational history of the German Focke Wulf 190 fighter; collecting material for a long detailed operational history of the Luftwaffe, 1939 to 1945.

SIDELIGHTS: Price told *CA:* "[I am] in the pleasant position of doing [my] one-time hobby as a full-time job. Now [my] greatest problem, in so far as it is a problem, is to find a new hobby absorbing enough to take [my] mind off [my] work for just a few hours each week."

* * *

PRICE, Cecil (John Layton) 1915-

PERSONAL: Born June 14, 1915, in Swansea, Wales; son of Thomas John (a grocer) and Muriel Ernestine (Thornhill) Price; married Ceinwen Daniel Lloyd, August 19, 1940. *Education:* University College of Swansea, Wales, B.A. (honors), 1937, Diploma in Education, 1938, M.A., 1939, Ph.D., 1954. *Home:* 86 Glanbrydan Ave., Swansea, Wales. *Office:* Department of English, University College of Swansea, University of Wales, Singleton Park, Swansea SA2 8PP, Wales.

CAREER: University of Wales, Cardiff, fellow, 1947-49, University College of Wales at Aberystwyth, lecturer, 1949-59, senior lecturer in English, 1959-61, University College of Swansea, professor of English and chairman of department, 1961—, dean, Faculty of Arts, 1971-73. Visiting professor, University of New Brunswick, summer, 1972. *Member:* Bibliographical Society, Royal Institution of South Wales (member of council). *Awards, honors:* Fellow at Folger Shakespeare Library, Washington, D.C., 1960, 1964, 1970, and Humanities Centre of the Australian National University, 1975; grants from British Academy, Leverhulme Trust, Huntington Library, and Newberry Library.

WRITINGS: The English Theatre in Wales in the Eighteenth and Early Nineteenth Centuries, University of Wales Press, 1948; *Cold Caleb: A Life of Ford Grey, First Earl of Tankerville, 1655-1701,* Melrose, 1956; (editor) Richard Brinsley Sheridan, *Letters,* three volumes, Oxford University Press, 1966; *Theatre in the Age of Garrick,* Basil Blackwell, 1973; (editor) Richard Brinsley Sheridan, *Dramatic Works,* two volumes, Oxford University Press, 1973; (editor) Richard Brinsley Sheridan, *Plays,* Oxford University Press, 1975. Contributor to professional journals. Member of editorial advisory board, *Theatre Notebook.*

WORK IN PROGRESS: Drama and Society in the Eighteenth Century, for Clarendon Press; a selection of uncollected letters by Philip Dormer Stanhope, fourth earl of Chesterfield.

* * *

PRICE, Daniel O('Haver) 1918-

PERSONAL: Born September 12, 1918, in Palatka, Fla.; son of Charles Henry and Lillian (O'Haver) Price; married Doris Carter, June 23, 1945; children: Philip Carter, Karen Louise, Gary David. *Education:* Florida Southern College, B.S., 1939; University of North Carolina, M.A., 1942, Ph.D., 1948. *Politics:* Democrat. *Office:* 306 Garrison Hall, University of Texas, Austin, Tex. 78712.

CAREER: University of North Carolina, Chapel Hill, lecturer, 1947-48, associate professor, 1948-51, professor of sociology and research professor at Institute for Research in Social Science, 1951-66, director of the Institute, 1957-66; University of Texas at Austin, professor of sociology, 1966—. Visiting lecturer, Harvard University, 1950; visiting professor, Massachusetts Institute of Technology, 1957; fellow, Center for Advanced Study in the Behavioral Sciences, Stanford, Calif., 1963-64. Consultant to U.S. Bureau of the Budget, Census Bureau, Social Security Administration, and TRACOR, Inc. *Military service:* U.S. Naval Reserve, 1942—; active duty, 1942-45; became captain (retired).

MEMBER: American Sociological Association (chairman of methodology section, 1960-61 and 1968; chairman of committee on committees, 1968), American Statistical Association (fellow), Population Association of America (second vice-president, 1967-68), American Association for the Advancement of Science, Sociological Research Association, International Union for the Scientific Study of Population, Southern Sociological Society.

WRITINGS: (With Margaret Jarman Hagood) *Statistics for Sociologists,* Holt, 1952; (with M. Elaine Burgess) *An American Dependency Challenge,* American Public Welfare Association, 1962; (editor) *The 99th Hour,* University of North Carolina Press, 1967; *Changing Characteristics of the Negro Population,* U.S. Government Printing Office, 1969; (with Melanie M. Sikes) *Rural-Urban Migration Research in the United States: Annotated Bibliography and Synthesis,* U.S. Government Printing Office, 1975. Contributor to *Encyclopaedia Britannica,* and sociology, statistical and demography journals. Associate editor, *Social Forces,* 1947-66, and *American Sociological Review,* 1952-55.

WORK IN PROGRESS: Research on the Negro population.

* * *

PRICE, Glenn W(arren) 1918-

PERSONAL: Born October 16, 1918, in Libertyville, Iowa; son of John Henry (a clergyman) and Sadie (Burger) Price; married Marcia Louise Vaniman (a teacher of the multi-handicapped), August 30, 1940; children: Laura Nancy (Mrs. Daniel P. Sullivan), Christopher Muir. *Education:* La Verne College, A.B., 1940; American University, graduate student, 1940-42; University of Southern California, A.M., 1950, Ph.D., 1954. *Politics:* "Actively independent." *Religion:* "Actively Independent." *Office:* History Department, California State College, Sonoma, Rohnert Park, Calif. 94928.

CAREER: California State Park System, Los Angeles, curator and historian, 1948-58; University of the Pacific, Stockton, Calif., 1958-67, began as assistant professor, became associate professor of history; California State College, Sonoma, Rohnert Park, associate professor, 1967-71, professor of history and chairman of department, 1971—. *Member:* American Historical Association, Organization of American Historians, American Association of University Professors, American Civil Liberties Union (chapter board member), American Association for the United Nations (chapter board member).

WRITINGS: Origins of the War with Mexico: The Polk-Stockton Intrigue, University of Texas Press, 1967. Associate editor, *Pacific Historian,* 1959-65; editor, *Far-Westerner,* 1960-61.

WORK IN PROGRESS: A book on U.S. foreign relations from the War of 1812 to the Civil War; a biography of Commodore Robert Field Stockton.

SIDELIGHTS: Price told *CA,* "More interested in what is called, without much precision, 'cultural history,' than in political." *Avocational interests:* Conservation, backpacking in the Sierra Nevadas.†

* * *

PRICE, Kingsley Blake 1917-

PERSONAL: Born August 24, 1917, in Salem, Ind.; son of James Allan and Hildred Louella (Blake) Price. *Education:* University of California, Berkeley, A.B., 1938, M.A., 1942, Ph.D., 1946. *Office:* Department of Philosophy, Johns Hopkins University, Baltimore, Md. 21218.

CAREER: University of California, Berkeley, lecturer in philosophy, 1946-47; assistant professor of philosophy at University of Nevada, Reno, 1947-48, Sarah Lawrence College, Bronxville, N.Y., 1948-51, and University of Washington, Seattle, 1951-53; Johns Hopkins University, Baltimore, Md., assistant professor, 1953-57, associate professor, 1957-63, professor of philosophy and education, 1963—. Visiting summer associate professor at Stanford University, 1959, and Ohio State University, 1962; visiting summer professor at University of California, Berkeley, 1964, 1968, and University of California, Davis, 1968, 1969; visiting professor, Stanford University, 1971-72. *Member:* American Philosophical Association, Philosophy of Education Society, American Society for Aesthetics (president, 1973-74; member of executive board, 1974-75), American Association of University Professors.

WRITINGS: Education and Philosophical Thought, Allyn & Bacon, 1962, expanded and revised edition, 1967. Contributor to *Encyclopedia Americana* and *Encyclopedia of Philosophy;* also contributor to professional journals.

WORK IN PROGRESS: Aesthetic Experience: An Essay on Knowing and Appreciation; two other books, *Philosophical Foundations of Education* and *Introduction to Philosophy.*

* * *

PRIDHAM, Radost 1922-

PERSONAL: Born February 5, 1922, in Washington, D.C.; daughter of Jordan (a journalist) and Nella (a jour-

nalist; maiden name, Taneva) Slivopolsky-Pilgrim; married J. E. Pridham (an army oficer), June 7, 1948. *Education:* Educated in Sofia, Bulgaria. *Religion:* Church of England. *Home:* 54 Elm Park House, London S.W. 10, England. *Office:* Bulgarian Section, British Broadcasting Corp., Bush House, Strand, London, WC2B 4PH, England.

CAREER: Editor of *Home and World,* Sofia, Bulgaria, 1942-43, and contributor to other women's magazines in Bulgaria; British Broadcasting Crop., London, England, radio broadcaster and translator in Bulgarian section, 1964—; writer and translator. *Member:* Society of Authors, Radiowriters Association, Translators Association, and Children's Writers (all Great Britain).

WRITINGS: (Compiler and adapter) *A Gift from the Heart: Folk Talks from Bulgaria,* Methuen, 1966, World Publishing, 1967; (editor) *The Peach Thief* (anthology of Bulgarian short stories), Cassell, 1968; (translator) Blaga Dimitrova, *Journey to Oneself,* Cassell, 1969. Contributor to *Guardian, Times* (London), *Observer, Lady,* and other periodicals and newspapers.

WORK IN PROGRESS: A biography, *Dr. H. Sandwith.*

* * *

PRIESTLEY, F(rancis) E(thelbert) L(ouis) 1905-

PERSONAL: Born March 12, 1905, in Banbury, England; son of George Ernest, and Catherine (Roberts) Priestley; married Carman Dixon Craig, August 2, 1933; children: Christopher. *Education:* University of Alberta, B.A., 1930, M.A., 1932; University of Toronto, Ph.D., 1940. *Home:* 269 Woburn Ave., Toronto, Ontario, Canada MSM 1L1.

CAREER: University of Alberta, lecturer in English at Edmonton Campus, 1931-32, and Calgary Campus, 1934-37; University of British Columbia, Vancouver, assistant professor of English, 1940-44; University of Toronto, Toronto, Ontario, 1944-72, began as assistant professor, professor of English, 1955-72. *Member:* International Association of Professors of English, Humanities Association of Canada (president, 1962-64), Royal Society of Canada (fellow), Royal Society of Literature (United Kingdom; fellow). *Awards, honors:* Nuffield fellowship, 1949-50; D.Litt., Mount Allison University, 1964, University of Alberta, 1973, University of Western Ontario, 1973.

WRITINGS: (Editor) William Godwin, *Political Justice* (critical edition), three volumes, University of Toronto Press, 1946; (with Harcourt Brown, David Hawkins, and Karl Deutsch) *Science and the Creative Spirit,* edited by Brown, University of Toronto Press, 1958; (general editor) *Representative Poetry,* three volumes, University of Toronto Press, 1962-63; (general editor) *The Collected Works of J. S. Mill,* University of Toronto Press, 1963-70; *The Humanities in Canada,* University of Toronto Press, 1964; *Language and Structure in Tennyson's Poetry,* Deutsch, 1973. Contributor to scholarly journals. Special editor, *Canadian Dictionary,* McClelland & Stewart, 1962. Member of board of editors, *Journal of the History of Ideas.*

WORK IN PROGRESS: Essays on the poetry of Tennyson and Browning and eighteenth-century thought; a book on Browning for Deutsch's Language Library.

SIDELIGHTS: Priestley told *CA:* "[My] main pleasure in writing is in trying to achieve complete clarity of exposition with a degree of concise elegance, a task made interesting by its difficulty." *Avocational interests:* Photography, jazz.

PRINCE, Carl E. 1934-

PERSONAL: Born December 8, 1934, in Newark, N.J.; son of Phillip G. (a businessman) and Anne (Silver) Prince; married Sue Grill, June 14, 1959; children: Elizabeth, Jonathan. *Education:* Rutgers University, B.A., 1956, M.A., 1958, Ph.D., 1963. *Politics:* Democrat. *Home:* 356 Gregory Ave., West Orange, N.J. 07052. *Office:* Department of History, New York University, 19 University Pl., New York, N.Y. 10003.

CAREER: Fairleigh Dickinson University, Madison, N.J., instructor in history, 1960-63; Rutgers University, visiting assistant professor of history at New Brunswick and Newark campuses, 1962-66; Seton Hall University, South Orange, N.J., assistant professor, 1963-66, associate professor of history, 1966-68; New York University, associate professor, 1968-75, professor of history, 1975—, acting chairman of department of history, Washington Square College, 1971-72. Member of advisory historical committee, New Jersey Tercentenary Commission, 1963-64. Chairman of Linden (N.J.) chapter, Independent Voters for Johnson, 1964; trustee, Bet Yeled Hebrew Folk School. *Member:* American Historical Association, Organization of American Historians, Institute of Early American History and Culture, American Association for State and Local History, American Association of University Professors, New Jersey Historical Society. *Awards, honors:* Frank Weil Institute fellowship, 1965; National Endowment for the Humanities, younger scholar fellowship, 1968-69.

WRITINGS: Middlebrook: American Eagle's Nest, Somerset Press, 1958; *New Jersey's Jeffersonian Republicans,* Institute of Early American History and University of North Carolina Press, 1967. Contributor to regional history journals. Editor of the papers of William Livingston at New York University, 1975—.

WORK IN PROGRESS: Six volumes of the papers of William Livingston, for the New Jersey Historical Commission.

*   *   *

PRITCHARD, J(ohn) Harris 1923-

PERSONAL: Born May 6, 1923, in Portland, Ore.; son of Natcher William (a merchant) and Ella (LaGasa) Pritchard; married Joann Elliott (a musician), February 19, 1954; married second wife, Louise Smith (a public relations interviewer), November 15, 1966; children: (first marriage) Blair Kendall, Rawn Kenley. *Education:* University of California, B.A., 1949; Washington and Lee University, student, 1943; University of Vienna, graduate study in economics, 1950. *Politics:* Republican. *Religion:* Unitarian Universalist.

CAREER: Adverti-Shows of California (organizational fund raising presentations), Los Angeles, owner and producer, 1950-53; co-owner of Aircraft Sales & Service Co. and publisher of *Western Aircraft Dealers Association Monthly,* San Francisco, Calif., 1954-58; Jones, Brakeley & Rockwell, Inc. (industrial public relations), New York, N.Y., programs creation, beginning 1959. Fund raising consultant to church, community, military, and charity organizations, beginning 1952. *Military service:* U.S. Army, 1942-46, 1949-51; became captain; received Bronze Star, European Campaign Ribbon with three battle stars, Purple Heart with oak leaf cluster.

WRITINGS: September 23: A Lesson for Today, A.J.L. Publishing, 1966; *Complete Fund-Earning Guide,* A.J.L.

Publishing, 1967. Contributor of about fifty feature articles annually to industrial, business, and aviation periodicals.

WORK IN PROGRESS: The Spurious, a work of fiction based on true experiences.

AVOCATIONAL INTERESTS: Private and business flying, photography.††

*   *   *

PROKOP, Phyllis Stillwell 1922-

PERSONAL: Born December 5, 1922, in Weleetka, Okla.; daughter of Albert and Dora (Woodward) Stillwell; married Charles L. Prokop (a technical adviser for Exxon), June 5, 1944; children: Charles Kent, Bert Kimball. *Education:* University of Oklahoma, B.A., 1944; University of Houston, M.A., 1972. *Residence:* Houston, Tex.

CAREER: Former high school teacher.

WRITINGS: Conversations with Giants, Concordia, 1964; *Conversations with Prophets,* Concordia, 1966; *Sunday Dinner Cookbook,* Broadman, 1969; *Heavenscope,* Broadman, 1975.

WORK IN PROGRESS: A biographical novel about King Hezekiah of Judah.

*   *   *

PROUDFOOT, J(ohn) J(ames) 1918-

PERSONAL: Born May 17, 1918, in London, England; son of Thomas (a company director) and Winifred (Braid) Proudfoot. *Education:* Educated at schools in London, England, and City of London College; Advertising Association, diploma, 1934. *Politics:* Conservative. *Religion:* Church of England. *Home:* 37 Rosary Gardens, London S.W. 7, England.

CAREER: Samson Clark Ltd., London, England, media assistant, 1934-35; Saward Baker & Co. Ltd., London, market research assistant, 1935-39; Mather & Crowther Ltd., London, account executive, 1946-53; Attwood Statistics Ltd., London and Rotterdam, director, 1954-63; freelance marketing consultant, 1963—. *Military service:* British Army, 1939-46; served with General Staff, Allied Forces Headquarters, Italy; became major. *Member:* Institute of Practitioners in Advertising, Advertising Association, Market Research Society, European Society for Opinion Surveys and Market Research.

WRITINGS: A Marketing Plan for the New Europe, Hutchinson, 1966. Contributor to advertising and marketing journals.

AVOCATIONAL INTERESTS: Travel, paintings, antiques, gardening.

*   *   *

PRUITT, William O(badiah), Jr. 1922-

PERSONAL: Born September 1, 1922, in Easton, Md.; son of William Obadiah and Janye (Garlington) Pruitt; married Erna Nauert, February 5, 1951; children: Cheryl Ann, Charles Robert. *Education:* University of Maryland, B.A., 1947; University of Michigan, M.A., 1948, Ph.D., 1952. *Religion:* Evolutionary Humanism. *Office:* Department of Zoology, University of Manitoba, Winnipeg, Manitoba, Canada R3T 2N2.

CAREER: Rocky Mountain Biological Laboratory, Gothic, Colo., staff, 1952; Arctic Aeromedical Laboratory, Fairbanks, Alaska, research biologist, 1953-56; Canadian

Wildlife Service, contract biologist, 1957-58; University of Alaska, College, associate professor of biology, 1959-62; University of Oklahoma, Norman, visiting professor, 1963-65; Memorial University of Newfoundland, St. John's, associate professor of biology, 1965-69; University of Manitoba, Winnipeg, professor of zoology, 1969—. *Military service:* U.S. Army, 1943-46. *Member:* Arctic Institute of North America (fellow), American Society of Mammalogists, Ecological Society of America, Canadian Society of Zoologists, Sigma Xi, Phi Sigma.

WRITINGS: (Translator from the Russian, with William Prychodko) A. N. Formozov, *Snow Cover as an Environmental Factor and Its Role in the Ecology of Mammals and Birds,* Boreal Institute, University of Alberta, 1964; (contributor) N. J. Wilimovsky and John N. Wolfe, editors, *Environment of the Cape Thompson Region, Alaska,* Division of Technical Information, United States Atomic Energy Commission, 1966; *Animals of the North,* illustrated by William D. Berry, Harper, 1967. Writer of miscellaneous scientific reports for government agencies and laboratories. Contributor of articles and reviews to professional journals; also contributor to popular periodicals, including *Audubon, Harper's, Scientific American, Atlantic, Naturalist, Holiday, Beaver* and *Nature Canada.*

WORK IN PROGRESS: Research on cyclic fluctuations of small mammals and on adaptations of mammals to boreal environments; "Boreal Ecology" in "Studies in Biology" series for Edward Arnold (London).

*   *   *

PRUYSER, Paul W(illem)   1916-

PERSONAL: Born May 28, 1916, in Amsterdam, Netherlands; son of Herman J. and Elizabeth (van Dingstee) Pruyser; married Jansje M. Fontijn, April 17, 1946; children: Henriette, Herman, Pauline. *Education:* University of Amsterdam, candidate in psychology, 1948; Boston University, Ph.D., 1953. *Religion:* Presbyterian. *Home:* 3337 Northwest 35th St., Topeka, Kan. 66618. *Office address:* Menninger Foundation, P.O. Box 829, Topeka, Kan. 66601.

CAREER: Staff clinical psychologist at National Veterans Epilepsy Center, 1950-54, and Topeka State Hospital, Topeka, Kan., 1954-55; Menninger Foundation, Topeka, staff clinical psychologist, 1956-62, associate director of department of education, 1961-62, director of department of education, 1962-71, Henry March Pfeiffer Professor, 1972—; Kansas Neurological Institute, Topeka, chairman of committee on research and education, 1960—. Lecturer in psychology, McCormick Theological Seminary, Chicago, Ill., 1959—; professorial lecturer in pastoral psychology, St. Louis University, School of Divinity, 1964—; Lyman Beecher Lecturer, Yale Divinity School, 1968. *Military service:* Netherlands Army, 1939-40.

MEMBER: American Psychological Association, American Association for the Advancement of Science, Association of American Medical Colleges, American Association on Mental Deficiency, Society for the Scientific Study of Religion (member of council, 1963-65; vice-president, 1964-65; president, 1974-75), Kansas Psychological Association.

WRITINGS: (Author of foreword) Sigurd D. Peterson, *Retarded Children: God's Children,* Westminster, 1960; (author of foreword) H. Faber, *Pastoral Care and Clinical Training in America,* Van Loghem Slaterus (Netherlands), 1961; (with Karl A. Menninger and M. Mayman) *A Manual for Psychiatric Case Study,* 2nd edition, Grune, 1962; (with

Menninger and Mayman) *The Vital Balance,* Viking, 1963; (member of editorial committee) *A Psychiatrist for a Troubled World: Selected Papers of William C. Menninger, M.D.,* edited by B. H. Hall, Viking, 1967; *A Dynamic Psychology of Religion,* Harper, 1968; *Between Belief and Unbelief,* Harper, 1974.

Contributor: S. Doniger, editor, *Know Thyself,* Association Press, 1962; Karl Menninger and S. Hiltner, editors, *Constructive Aspects of Anxiety,* Abingdon, 1963; Robert Dentler, editor, *Major American Social Problems,* Rand McNally, 1967; James W. Lapsley, editor, *The Concept of Willing,* Abingdon, 1967; Joseph Havens, editor, *Psychology and Religion: A Contemporary Dialogue,* Van Nostrand, 1968. Contributor to *Encyclopedia of Mental Health,* F. Watts, 1963, and to medical, pastoral psychology, and other journals. Member of editorial board, *Bulletin of Menninger Clinic,* 1958—, and *Journal for the Scientific Study of Religion,* 1961-66; member of editorial advisory board, *Pastoral Psychology,* 1967—.

SIDELIGHTS: "With some qualifications one could say that Paul Pruyser's is the most significant single work in the field of psychology of religion since the classic study of William James," says William A. Sadler, Jr. reviewing *A Dynamic Psychology of Religion.* Pruyer's approach, according to Sadler, "asks not which religious factors are most significant, but rather, which data of experience have religious significance," and he "views religion more in terms of psychic functions than as a special kind of experience. . . ."

BIOGRAPHICAL/CRITICAL SOURCES: Pastoral Psychology, Number 121, 1962; *Christian Century,* September 25, 1968.

*   *   *

PRYBYLA, Jan S(tanislaw)   1927-

PERSONAL: Born October 21, 1927, in Katowice, Poland; son of Wiktor P. (a lawyer) and Anna (Hager) Prybyla; married Jacqueline Meyer, November 29, 1958, *Education:* University College of Cork, National University of Ireland, B.C., 1949, M.E.S., 1950, Ph.D., 1953; University of Strasbourg, Diploma in Higher European Studies, 1953. *Home:* 534 Ridge Ave., State College, Pa. 16801. *Office:* N. Burrowes Building, Pennsylvania State University, University Park, Pa. 16802.

CAREER: Free Europe University in Exile France, assistant to president, 1953-58; Pennsylvania State University, University Park, assistant professor, 1958-62, associate professor, 1962-65, professor of economics, 1965—. *Member:* American Economic Association, Association for Comparative Economics, Freedom House. *Awards, honors:* Liberal arts scholar, Pennsylvania State University, 1965; Linback Award for excellence in teaching, 1971.

WRITINGS: (With Elton Atwater and Kent Forster) *World Tensions: Conflict and Accommodation,* Appleton, 1967, 2nd edition, 1972; (editor with Harry G. Shaffer) *From Underdevelopment to Affluence: Western, Soviet and Chinese Views,* Appleton, 1968; (editor) *Comparative Economic Systems: Text and Readings,* Appleton, 1969; *The Political Economy of Communist China,* International Textbook, 1970; *The Chinese Economy: Problems and Policies,* Norton, 1975. Contributor to professional journals.

*   *   *

PSATHAS, George   1929-

PERSONAL: Surname is pronounced *Sath*-us; born February 22, 1929, in New Haven, Conn.; son of Milton Emanuel and Melpa (Joannides) Psathas; married Irma Mary Amatruda (a teacher), February 5, 1951; children: Christine, David, Anthony. *Education:* Yale University, B.A. (with honors), 1950, Ph.D., 1956; University of Michigan, M.A., 1951; additional graduate study at Oxford University, summer, 1950, Harvard University, 1961-62, and National Training Laboratories, Bethel, Me., summer, 1962. *Office:* Department of Sociology, Boston University, Boston, Mass. 02215.

CAREER: Indiana University, Bloomington, instructor, 1955-59, assistant professor, sociology department, 1959-63; Washington University, St. Louis, Mo., research associate of Social Science Institute, 1963-68, associate professor of sociology in nursing, 1963-64, adjunct associate professor, department of sociology-anthropology, 1963-65, associate professor, 1965-68; Boston University, Boston, Mass., professor of sociology, 1968—, director, Center for Applied Social Science, 1970-73. *Member:* American Sociological Association (fellow), American Psychological Association, American Association of University Professors, Midwest Group for Human Resources (founding member; member of board of trustees, 1967-69), Eastern Sociological Society. *Awards, honors:* National Institute of Mental Health research grants, 1958—, and postdoctoral fellowship, 1961-62; National Science Foundation research grant, 1960-62; Grant fellow, 1963.

WRITINGS: The Student Nurse and the Diploma School of Nursing, Springer Publishing, 1968; *Phenomenological Sociology,* Wiley, 1973.

Contributor: R. Mack, editor, *Race, Class, and Power,* American Book Co., 1963; J. Levy and R. H. Hunter, editors, *Dialogues: Behavioral Science Research,* Western Interstate Commission for Higher Education, 1963; G. E. Stollak, B. G. Guerney, and M. A. Rothburg, editors, *Psychotherapy Research: Selected Readings,* Rand McNally, 1966; P. J. Stone and others, editors, *The General Inquirer: A Computer Approach to Content Analysis,* M.I.T. Press, 1966; M. Reda, editor, *Systems and Processes,* College & Universities Press, 1968; R. Ravalko, editor, *Sociological Perspectives on Occupations,* F. T. Peacock, 1972; J. Manis and B. Meltzer, editors, *Symbolic Interaction,* Allyn & Bacon, 1972; R. Zaner and D. Ihde, editors, *Interdisciplinary Phenomenology,* Nijhoff, 1975. Contributor of about twenty-five articles to professional journals.

WORK IN PROGRESS: Studies of blindness, mobility, and mapping.

* * *

PUCCIANI, Oreste F(rancesco) 1916-

PERSONAL: Born April 7, 1916, in Cleveland, Ohio; son of Ettore (a candy manufacturer) and Eugenie (Williams) Pucciani. *Education:* Western (now Case Western) Reserve University, B.A., 1939; Harvard University, M.A., 1940, Ph.D., 1943. *Home:* 2192 Beech Knoll Rd., Los Angeles, Calif. 90046. *Office:* French Department, University of California, Los Angeles, Calif. 90024.

CAREER: Harvard University, Cambridge, Mass., instructor in Romance languages, 1943-46, 1947-48, Sheldon traveling fellow in France and Italy, 1946-47; University of California, Los Angeles, assistant professor, 1948-54, associate professor, 1954-60, professor of French, 1960—, chairman of department, 1961-66, affiliated professor, Graduate School of Education, 1973—. *Member:* American Association of Teachers of French, Modern Language

Association of America, American Council of Teachers of Foreign Languages, American Society of the French Legion of Honor, American Association of University Professors, Phi Beta Kappa. *Awards, honors:* Knight's Cross of the French Legion of Honor.

WRITINGS: The French Theater Since 1930, Ginn, 1954; (translator) Racine, *Phaedra,* Appleton, 1961; (contributor) *Sartre: A Collection of Essays,* Prentice-Hall, 1962; (with J. Hamel) *Langue et Langage,* with teacher's manual, Holt, 1967, revised edition, 1974; (contributor) *Theatre of the Double: Genet-Ionesco,* Bantam, 1969; (author of forward) L. A. Belkind, editor, *Jean-Paul Sartre: Sartre and Existentialism in English,* Kent State University Press, 1970; (translator) Oskar Panizza, *The Council of Love,* Viking, 1973; (contributor) *The Philosophy of Sartre,* University of Southern Illinois Press, in press. Contributor of a short story to *Things with Claws,* Ballantine, 1961; contributor to *Historire de la Philosophie* and *Encyclopedie de la Pleiade.*

WORK IN PROGRESS: Langue et Culture, with J. Hamel.

SIDELIGHTS: Pucciani is competent in Italian, German, Latin, and Spanish.

* * *

PUGH, J(ohn) W(ilbur) 1912-

PERSONAL: Born November 27, 1912, in Reedley, Calif.; son of John William (an optometrist) and Dollie (Reed) Pugh; married Dorothy Eileen Coleman, July 3, 1937; children: John W. *Education:* Attended University of California, Berkeley, 1930-33, Stanford University, 1943-44, University of Santa Clara, 1944, and Sacramento State College (now California State University, Sacramento), 1963; received certificate of American Institute of Banking, 1943. *Religion:* Protestant. *Home:* 3820 San Juan Ave., Fair Oaks, Calif. 95628.

CAREER: Managed service station in San Jose, Calif., 1933-35; employed by Bank of America in various California communities, 1935-43, became assistant cashier; Joshua Hendy Iron Works, Sunnyvale, Calif., cost accountant, 1943-45; Placer County Bank, Auburn, Calif., assistant cashier, 1945-50; Crocker-Citizens National Bank, Fair Oaks, Calif., assistant vice-president and manager, 1950-73; instructor at Anthony Schools (Calif.), 1973—. Evening instructor in real estate appraising and finance, and member of college advisory council, American River Junior College, 1954—. Past president of both Fair Oaks Chamber of Commerce and Business Association. *Member:* American Institute of Banking, Association for Bank Audit, Control and Operation (president of Central Valley conference, 1954), International Platform Association, California Bankers Association (president of Group 1, 1958), California Writers Club, Fair Oaks Rotary Club (president, 1964-65), Masons.

WRITINGS: (With William Hippaka) *California Real Estate Finance,* Prentice-Hall, 1966, revised edition, 1973; *Real Estate Finance Outlook,* McGraw, 1966; *The Effect of Government Borrowing on Real Estate Finance,* American River Press, 1967.

WORK IN PROGRESS: California history of the mid-nineteenth century.

AVOCATIONAL INTERESTS: Color photography.

PURVES, Alan C(arroll) 1931-

PERSONAL: Born December 14, 1931, in Philadelphia, Pa.; son of Edmund Randolph and Mary Carroll (Spencer) Purves; married Anita Woodruff Parker, June 18, 1960 (died, 1975); children: William C., Theodore R. *Education:* Harvard University, A.B., 1953; Columbia University, M.A., 1956, Ph.D., 1960. *Office:* Department of Secondary Education, University of Illinois, Urbana, Ill. 61801.

CAREER: Hofstra University, Hempstead, N.Y., lecturer in English, 1956-58; Columbia College, New York City, instructor in English, 1958-61; Barnard College, New York City, assistant professor of English, 1961-65; Educational Testing Service, Princeton, N.J., associate examiner, 1965-68; University of Illinois, Urbana, associate professor, 1968-70, professor of English, 1970-73, professor of English education, 1973—. *Military service:* U.S. Army, 1953-55. *Member:* Modern Language Association of America, National Council of Teachers of English, National Conference on Research in English, American Educational Research Association.

WRITINGS: (Editor) Theodore Spencer, *Selected Essays,* Rutgers University Press, 1967; (with Victoria Rippere) *Elements of Writing about a Literary Work,* National Council of Teachers of English, 1968; (with Richard Beach) *Literature and the Reader,* National Council of Teachers of English, 1972; *How Porcupines Make Love: Notes on a Response-Centered Curriculum,* Wiley, 1972; (editor) *Responding,* eighteen volumes, Ginn, 1973; *Literature Education in Ten Countries,* Wiley, 1973; (editor with Daniel U. Levine) *Education Policy and International Assessment,* McCutchan, 1975. Contributor to professional journals. Associate editor, *Odyssey Review,* 1961-64; editor, *Research in the Teaching of English,* 1973—.

WORK IN PROGRESS: A book on children's literature.

* * *

PYE, Lucian W(ilmot) 1921-

PERSONAL: Born October 21, 1921, in Shansi Province, China; son of Watts Orson and Gertrude (Chaney) Pye; married Mary Toombs Waddill, December 24, 1944; children: Evelyn Kathleen, Lucian Christopher, Virginia Chaney. *Education:* Carleton College, B.A., 1943; Yale University, M.A., 1949, Ph.D., 1951. *Home:* 72 Fletcher Rd., Belmont, Mass. 02178. *Office:* Department of Political Science, Massachusetts Institute of Technology, Cambridge, Mass. 02139.

CAREER: Washington University, St. Louis, Mo., 1949-51, began as instructor, became assistant professor of political science; Yale University, New Haven, Conn., research associate in international relations, 1951-52; Princeton University, Princeton, N.J., research associate, Center for International Studies, 1952-56; Massachusetts Institute of Technology, Cambridge, assistant professor, 1956-57, associate professor, 1957-60, professor of political science, 1960—, senior staff member, Center for International Studies, 1956—. Visiting lecturer, Columbia University, 1956; visiting associate professor, Yale University, 1959-60. Trustee of Asia Society, Asia Foundation, Council on Foreign Relations, Inc., and East-West Center. *Military service:* U.S. Marine Corps, 1943-46; became first lieutenant. *Member:* American Political Science Association, Association for Asian Studies.

WRITINGS: Guerrilla Communism in Malaya, Princeton University Press, 1956; *Politics, Personality and Nation-Building: Burma's Search for Identity,* Yale University Press, 1962; (editor) *Communications and Political Development,* Princeton University Press, 1963; (editor with Sidney Verba, and contributor) *Political Culture and Political Development,* Princeton University Press, 1965; *Aspects of Political Development,* Little, Brown, 1966; *Southeast Asia's Political Systems,* Prentice-Hall, 1967; *The Spirit of Chinese Politics: A Psychocultural Study of the Authority Crisis in Political Development,* M.I.T. Press, 1968; *Warlord Politics,* Praeger, 1971; *China: An Introduction,* Little, Brown, 1972; (editor) *Political Science and Area Studies,* Indiana University Press, 1975; *Mao Tse-tung: The Man in the Leader,* Basic Books, 1976.

Contributor: *Nationalism and Progress in Free Asia,* edited by P. W. Thayer, Johns Hopkins Press, 1956; *The Politics of the Developing Areas,* edited by G. A. Almond and J. S. Coleman, Princeton University Press, 1960; *The Emerging Nations,* edited by M. F. Millikan and D.L.M. Blackmer, Little, Brown, 1961; *Political Decision-Makers,* edited by D. Marvick, Free Press of Glencoe, 1961; *The Role of the Military in Underdeveloped Countries,* edited by J. J. Johnson, Princeton University Press, 1962; *The New Nations: The Problem of Political Development,* edited by Lucy Mair, University of Chicago Press, 1963; *Federalism in the Commonwealth,* edited by William S. Livingston, Cassell, 1963; *Studying Politics Abroad,* edited by R. E. Ward, Little, Brown, 1964; *The Internal War,* edited by H. Eckstein, Macmillan, 1964; *World Pressures on American Foreign Policies,* edited by M. O. Irish, Prentice-Hall, 1964; *Foreign Policy in the Sixties,* edited by R. Hilsman and R. C. Good, Johns Hopkins Press, 1965; *Political Parties and Political Development,* edited by J. LaPalombara and M. Weiner, Princeton University Press, 1966; *Modernization: The Dynamics of Growth,* edited by M. Weiner, Basic Books, 1966; *Communication and Change in the Developing Countries,* edited by D. Lerner and W. Schramm, East-West Publications, 1966; *Contemporary Political Science,* edited by Ithiel de Sola Pool, McGraw, 1967; *Post-Primary Education and Political and Economic Development,* edited by Don C. Piper and Taylor Cole, Duke University Press, 1969; *China: Management of a Revolutionary Society,* edited by John M. H. Lindbeck, University of Washington Press, 1971; *Ethnicity: Theory and Experience,* edited by Nathan Glazer and Daniel P. Moynihan, Harvard University Press, 1975.

* * *

QUALE, G(ladys) Robina 1931-

PERSONAL: Born January 10, 1931, in Manistee, Mich.; daughter of Leslie Alexander (in real estate and insurance) and Gladys (Dyer) Quale. *Education:* University of Michigan, B.A., 1952, M.A., 1953, Ph.D., 1957. *Religion:* Episcopalian. *Office:* Albion College, Albion, Mich. 49224.

CAREER: Albion College, Albion, Mich., instructor, 1957-60, assistant professor, 1960-65, associate professor of history, 1965—. *Member:* American Historical Association, American Academy of Political and Social Science, Association for Asian Studies, Middle East Studies Association, American Association of University Professors. *Awards, honors:* Carnegie grant, 1961-62; Great Lakes Colleges Association fellowship, 1966-67.

WRITINGS: Eastern Civilizations, Appleton, 1966, 2nd edition, Prentice-Hall, 1975.

WORK IN PROGRESS: Chronology of the Latter Ch'ing Period.

QUAYLE, Eric 1921-

PERSONAL: Born November 14, 1921, in Bootle, Lancashire, England; son of Alfred Henry (a company director) and Amy (Flannagan) Quayle; married Jean Elizabeth Thorne, January 4, 1947; children: Davina, Christine, Quinton. Education: Attended commercial school in Birmingham, England. Politics: "Left of Center." Religion: None. Home: Carn Cobba, Zennor, St. Ives, Cornwall, England.

CAREER: Newburys Ltd. (furnishing specialists), Aston, Birmingham, England, director, 1945—. Consultant on old books and bibliography, British Broadcasting Corporation. Member: Society of Authors.

WRITINGS: Ballantyne the Brave: A Victorian Writer and His Family (biography), Dufour Editions, 1967; A Bibliography of R. M. Ballantyne: A Bibliography of First Editions, Dawsons of Pall Mall, 1968; The Ruin of Sir Walter Scott, Hart-Davis, 1968, C. N. Potter, 1969; The Collector's Book of Books, C. N. Potter, 1971; The Collector's Book of Children's Books, Studio Vista, 1971, C. N. Potter, 1972; The Collector's Book of Detective Fiction, Studio Vista, 1972; The Collector's Book of Boys' Stories, Studio Vista, 1973; Old Cook Books: An Illustrated History, Studio Vista, 1976.

SIDELIGHTS: Eric Quayle is a book collector, especially of the Victorian period and first editions of English literature. He has an extensive library of English literature, and one of the largest collections of early children's books in private hands.

BIOGRAPHICAL/CRITICAL SOURCES: Birmingham Post & Mail Year Book, 1967.

*　　*　　*

QUEEN, Stuart Alfred 1890-

PERSONAL: Born February 26, 1890, in Fredonia, Kan.; son of Charles N. (a clergyman) and Nettie A. (Swigart) Queen; married Alice Hamilton, April 17, 1918 (deceased); married Charlotte Barr, June 4, 1927 (deceased); children: (first marriage) Stuart, Jr.; (second marriage) Margaret Ellen. Education: Pomona College, A.B., 1910; University of Chicago, A.M., 1913, Ph.D., 1919. Politics: Democrat. Religion: Unitarian.

CAREER: California State Board of Charities and Corrections, San Francisco, secretary, 1913-17; director, Texas School of Civics and Philanthropy, 1917-18; University of Illinois, Urbana, instructor in sociology, 1919; Goucher College, Baltimore, Md., associate professor of social technology, 1919-20; Simmons College, Boston, Mass., professor of social economy and director of School of Social Work, 1920-22; University of Kansas, Lawrence, professor of sociology, 1922-30; Community Fund and Council of Social Agencies, Detroit, Mich., associate secretary, 1930-32; Washington University, St. Louis, Mo., professor of sociology, 1932-58; University of Arizona, Tucson, professor of sociology, 1961-67. Visiting professor at Wichita State University, 1958-60, and Southern Illinois University, 1960-61. Member: American Sociological Association (president, 1941), Sociological Research Association, American Association of University Professors, Midwest Sociological Society, Pacific Sociological Association.

WRITINGS: The Passing of the County Jail, G. Banta, 1920; Social Work in the Light of History, Lippincott, 1922; (with Delbert M. Mann) Social Pathology, Crowell, 1925; (with Amos G. Warner and Ernest B. Harper) American Charities and Social Work, Crowell, 1930; (with Walter B. Bodenhafer and Harper) Social Organization and Disorganization, Crowell, 1935; (with F. Stuart Chapin) Research Memorandum on Social Work in the Depression, Social Science Research Council, 1937, reprinted, Arno, 1972; (with Lewis F. Thomas) The City, McGraw, 1939; (with Jeanette R. Gruener) Social Pathology: Obstacles to Social Participation, Crowell, 1940; (with John B. Adams) The Family in Various Cultures, Lippincott, 1952, 2nd edition (with Robert W. Habenstein and Adams), 1961, 3rd edition (with Habenstein), 1967, 4th edition, 1974; (with David B. Carpenter) The American City, McGraw, 1953, reprinted, Greenwood Press, 1972; (with William N. Chambers and Charles M. Winston) The American Social System: Social Control, Personal Choice and Public Decision, Houghton, 1956. Contributor of more than thirty articles to professional journals.

AVOCATIONAL INTERESTS: Mountain climbing and hiking (president of Southern Arizona Hiking Club, 1965-66).†

*　　*　　*

QUICK, Annabelle 1922-
(Annabelle MacMillan)

PERSONAL: Born October 16, 1922, in Greeley, Colo.; daughter of Alfred Karl (owner of a farm implement store) and Marie (Frater) Johnson; married Donald W. MacMillan, March 28, 1949 (divorced, 1951); married John W. Quick (owner of a dry cleaning business), November 24, 1962. Education: Colorado State College (now University), A.B., 1943; further study at School of Sacred Music, Union Theological Seminary, New York, N.Y., 1945, 1946, and University of Uppsala, 1950-52. Politics: Republican. Religion: Episcopalian. Home: 96 Fifth Ave., New York, N.Y. 10016.

CAREER: Macmillan Co., New York City, editorial trainee, 1945-48; Denver (Colo.) public schools, music teacher, 1948-49; Silver Burdett Co., New York City, assistant music editor, 1949-50; A/B Max Sievert, Sundbyberg, Sweden, export secretary, 1950-52; Modern Language Association of America, New York City, convention and exhibit manager, 1952-73; Special Libraries Association, New York City, conference and exhibit coordinator, 1974-75. Translator; reader of children's books in Swedish, Danish, Norwegian, and German for various American publishers; editor, transcriber, and arranger of musical compositions. Member: American Society of Association Executives, National Association of Exhibition Managers, New York Society of Association Executives.

WRITINGS—Translator from the Swedish under name Annabelle MacMillan; all published by Harcourt, except as noted: Karin Anckarsvard, The Mysterious Schoolmaster, 1959; Anckarsvard, The Robber Ghost, 1961; Sven Gillsater, Pia's Journey to the Holy Land, 1961; Anckarsvard, Rider by Night, 1962; Laszlo Hamori, Dangerous Journey, 1962; Ralph Herrmanns, Lee Lan Flies the Dragon Kite, 1962; Anckarsvard, Aunt Vinnie's Invasion, 1962; Anckarsvard, Madcap Mystery, 1962; Jeanna Oterdahl, April Adventure, 1962; Ann Mari Falk, Who is Erika?, 1963; Anna Lisa Warnlof, The Boy Upstairs, 1963; Kerstin Thorvall, Girl in April, 1963; Anckarsvard, Springtime for Eve, 1963; Oterdahl, Tina and the Latchkey Child, 1963; Hamori, Flight to the Promised Land, 1963; Warnlof, Fredrika's Children, 1964; Falk, A Place of Her Own, 1964; Herrmanns, The Car Named Julia, 1964; Hans Peterson, Lise-

lott and the Quiffin, Coward, 1964; Kai Soderhjelm, *Free Ticket to Adventure,* 1964; Anckarsvard, *Aunt Vinnie's Victorious,* 1964; Herrmanns, *Children of the North Pole,* 1964; Oterdahl, *Island Summer,* 1964; Nan Inger, *Katie and Nan,* 1965; Anckarsvard, *Doctor's Boy,* 1965; Hamori, *Adventure in Bangkok,* 1966; Anckarsvard, *The Riddle of the Ring,* 1966; Edor Burman, *Three Wolverines of Rushing Valley,* Dutton, 1966; Inger, *Katie and Nan Go to Sea,* 1966; Barbro Lindgren, *Hilding's Summer,* Macmillan, 1967; Ulla Sundin-Wickman, *Andreas in King's Park,* 1967; Anckarsvard, *Struggle at Soltuna,* 1968; Anna Wahlenberg, *The Diamond Bird,* Doubleday, 1968; Stina Hammar, *Two in the Family,* Doubleday, 1970. Has also published a number of musical arrangements.

SIDELIGHTS: Annabelle Quick is fluent in Danish and Norwegian and competent in German, Italian, and Spanish. *Avocational interests:* Handcrafts, gourmet cooking.

* * *

QUIERY, William H. 1926-

PERSONAL: Born December 12, 1926, in Detroit, Mich.; son of Thomas H. and Margaret (Bartlett) Quiery. *Education:* St. Louis University, A.B., 1952, M.A., 1953, Ph.L., 1954, Th.B., 1960. *Agent:* Curtis Brown Ltd., 60 East 56th St., New York, N.Y. *Office:* Newman Bookstore, 3329 Eighth St. N.E., Washington, D.C. 20017.

CAREER: Roman Catholic priest, 1960-69. Member of editorial staff of *America,* 1961-62, and *Catholic Mind,* 1961-62; Sogang College, Seoul, Korea, associate professor of English, 1963-66; Jesuit Writers Service (literary service for Jesuit order), New York City, director, 1967-69; Billy Budd Films, New York City, vice-president, producer and writer, 1968-72; Newman Bookstore, Washington, D.C., manager, 1972—. *Military service:* U.S. Navy, World War II. *Member:* Authors Guild, American Library Association, American Guild of Authors and Composers.

WRITINGS: Facing God, Sheed, 1967; *A Missionary Handbook of Social Doctrines and Practice,* St. Paul Publications, 1968; *Hyphenated Priests,* Corpus, 1969.

In Korean: *Chun Hyang Song,* libretto and piano score published separately, Asia Foundation and Sogang College (Seoul), 1965; *Twoebi-topwi Chum* (dance drama; title means "The Miracle of the Compost Pile"), Asia Foundation (Seoul), 1966.

Film scripts, all produced by Billy Budd Films: "To Be A Woman," 1969; "To Be A Man," 1970; "To Be in Love," 1970; "Me and the Monsters," 1971; "The Boo-Boo Monster Enters a Beauty Contest," 1972.

Author of pamphlets published by Divine Word Publications and Committee for the Development of Socio-Economic Life in Asia (SELA). Contributor of articles, poetry, and short stories to Catholic periodicals, and other magazines.

* * *

QUINN, R(obert) M(acLean) 1920-

PERSONAL: Born October 28, 1920, in Chicago, Ill.; son of Robert John (a businessman) and Mathilda (Jansen) Quinn; married Jacqueline Strawn, August 25, 1945; children: Georgianna MacLean Quinn May. *Education:* Yale University, student, 1939-42; University of Arizona, B.A., 1945; Johns Hopkins University, Ph.D., 1957. *Office:* University of Arizona, Tucson, Ariz. 85721.

CAREER: University of Arizona, Tucson, instructor, 1945-50, assistant professor, 1950-57, associate professor, 1957-62, professor of art history, 1962—. Professor of art and adviser to students, Guadalajara Summer School, Guadalajara, Mexico, 1960—. Past president, Tucson Art Center. *Member:* American Council of Learned Societies, American Association of University Professors, Phi Beta Kappa, Phi Kappa Phi. *Awards, honors:* Kress Foundation travel grants to Spain in 1959, 1962.

WRITINGS: Fernando Gallego and the Retablo of Ciudad Rodrigo, University of Arizona Press, 1962. Author of introduction to catalogue for Tucson Art Center's exhibition on Spanish colonial style.

Film scripts; all produced by University of Arizona Radio-Television Bureau, distributed by Contemporary Films: "The Kress Collection," "Yankee Painter," "A Masterpiece of Spanish Painting," "American Realists," "The Clowns Never Laugh," "Cajititlan."

WORK IN PROGRESS: Colonial Art and Architecture in Mexico, for University of Arizona Press; a history of Hispano-Flemish painting.

SIDELIGHTS: Quinn's travel has been concentrated in Spain and Mexico. He speaks Spanish and German, and reads French, Italian, Dutch, Danish, and Catalan.

* * *

QUINN, Vincent 1926-

PERSONAL: Born November 24, 1926, in New York, N.Y.; son of John (a stone-molder) and Florence (Schoberl) Quinn; married Esther Casier (a college teacher and author), June 18, 1951; children: Stephen, Thomas. *Education:* Columbia University, A.B., 1948, M.A., 1950, Ph.D., 1959. *Office:* Department of English, Brooklyn College of the City University of New York, Brooklyn, N.Y. 11210.

CAREER: Iona College, New Rochelle, N.Y., instructor, 1950-54, assistant professor of English, 1954-59; Brooklyn College of the City University of New York, Brooklyn, N.Y., instructor, 1959-63, assistant professor, 1964-68, associate professor, 1969-72, professor of English, 1973—, chairman of department, 1967-70. *Military service:* U.S. Army, Counter-Intelligence Corps, 1945-47. *Member:* Modern Language Association of America.

WRITINGS: Hart Crane, Twayne, 1963; *Hilda Doolittle (H. D.),* Twayne, 1967.

* * *

QUINTON, Anthony Meredith 1925-

PERSONAL: Born March 25, 1925, in Gillingham, Kent, England; son of Richard Frith (a surgeon-captain, Royal Navy) and G. L. (Jones) Quinton; married Marcelle Wegier, August 2, 1952; children: Joanna, Edward. *Education:* Christ Church, Oxford, M.A. (first class honors), 1948. *Politics:* Conservative. *Religion:* None. *Home:* Savile House, Mansfield Rd., Oxford, England. *Office:* New College, Oxford University, Oxford, England.

CAREER: Oxford University, Oxford, England, fellow of All Souls College, 1949-55, university lecturer in philosophy, 1950—, fellow and tutor of New College, 1955—. Visiting professor at Swarthmore College, 1959-60, and Stanford University, 1964. *Military service:* Royal Air Force, 1943-46; became flying officer. *Member:* Mind Association, Aristotelian Society (president, 1975-76).

WRITINGS: (Contributor) J. R. Smythies, editor, *Brain and Mind*, Routledge & Kegan Paul, 1965; (contributor) I. T. Ramsey, editor, *Biology and Personality*, Basil Blackwell, 1965; (contributor) B. Williams and A. Montefiore, editors, *British Analytical Philosophy*, Routledge & Kegan Paul, 1966; (editor and author of introduction) *Political Philosophy*, Oxford University Press, 1967; *The Nature of Things*, Routledge & Kegan Paul, 1973; *Utilitarian Ethics*, Macmillan, 1973; (translator with H. Sholinowski) K. Ajdukiewics, *Problems and Theories of Philosophy*, Cambridge University Press, 1973. Regular contributor to *Times Literary Supplement, New York Review of Books;* contributor to philosophy journals.

WORK IN PROGRESS: A general history of philosophy in one large volume, for Oxford University Press.

* * *

QUIRIN, G(eorge) David 1931-

PERSONAL: Born March 29, 1931, in Calgary, Alberta, Canada; son of George Edward and Helen (Welsh) Quirin; married Jean McNamee, March 2, 1957; children: John Jacob, Kathleen Ann, James Joseph. *Education:* University of Alberta, B.A., 1952, M.A., 1958; Princeton University, A.M., 1960, Ph.D., 1961. *Home:* 173 Inglewood Dr., Toronto, Ontario, Canada. *Office:* School of Business, University of Toronto, Toronto, Ontario, Canada.

CAREER: Imperial Oil Limited, Calgary, Alberta, various positions, 1952-56; Hubert Harries & Associates, Calgary, economist, 1956-58; Canadian Government, Department of Northern Affairs and National Resources, Ottawa, Ontario, economic consultant, 1960-61; University of British Columbia, Vancouver, associate professor of finance, 1961-66; University of Toronto, School of Business, Toronto, Ontario, associate professor, 1966-68, professor of economics and statistics, 1969—. Visiting professor at University of Malaya, 1963, and University of Singapore, 1963-64. Research director, Royal Commission on Automobile Insurance, Victoria, 1966-68.

WRITINGS: *The Economics of Oil and Gas Exploration in Northern Canada*, Queen's Printer, 1962; *The Capital Expenditure Decision*, Irwin, 1967. Also author of monographs for University of Toronto.

* * *

RABB, Theodore K. 1937-

PERSONAL: Born March 5, 1937, in Teplice-Sanov, Czechoslovakia; son of Oskar Kwasnik (an author) and Rose (Oliner) Rabinowicz; married Tamar M. Janowsky, June 7, 1959; children: Susannah Lynette, Jonathan Richard, Jeremy David. *Education:* Queen's College, Oxford, B.A., 1958, M.A., 1962; Princeton University, A.M., 1960, Ph.D., 1961. *Office:* Department of History, Princeton University, Princeton, N.J. 08540.

CAREER: Stanford University, Stanford, Calif., instructor in history, 1961-62; Northwestern University, Evanston, Ill., instructor in history, 1962-63; Harvard University, Cambridge, Mass., assistant professor of history, 1963-67; Princeton University, Princeton, N.J., associate professor of history, 1967—. *Member:* American Historical Association, Conference on British Studies, Renaissance Society of America, Society for the History of Discoveries, Royal Historical Society (fellow), Historical Association (England), Hakluyt Society (England). *Awards, honors:* Fellowships from Guggenheim Foundation, American Philo-

sophical Society, Social Science Research Council, and Folger Shakespeare Library.

WRITINGS: (Editor) *The Thirty Years' War: Problems of Motive, Extent, and Effect*, Heath, 1964, 2nd edition, 1972; *Enterprise and Empire: Merchant and Gentry Investment in the Expansion of England, 1575-1930*, Harvard University Press, 1967; (editor with J. E. Seigel) *Action and Conviction in Early Modern Europe: Essays in Memory of E. H. Harbison*, Princeton University Press, 1969; (with M. Chambers, D. Herlihy, and R. Grew) *The Western Experience*, Knopf, 1974; *The Struggle for Stability in Early Modern Europe*, Oxford University Press, 1975. General editor, Heath's "Civilization and Society" series. Contributor to historical journals. Editor, *Journal of Interdisciplinary History*.

WORK IN PROGRESS: A biography of Sir Edwin Sandys; an edition of *Das Standebuch*.

AVOCATIONAL INTERESTS: Chess, music.

* * *

RABINOVITZ, Rubin 1938-

PERSONAL: Born July 18, 1938, in New York, N.Y.; son of Samuel M. and Esther Rabinovitz. *Education:* Rutgers University, B.A., 1959; Columbia University, M.A., 1961, Ph.D., 1966. *Religion:* Jewish. *Home:* 3938 Wonderland Hill Ave., Boulder, Colo. 80302. *Office:* Department of English, University of Colorado, Boulder, Colo. 80309.

CAREER: Columbia University, New York, N.Y., instructor, 1966-68, assistant professor of English, 1968-74; University of Colorado, Boulder, associate professor of English, 1974—. *Member:* Modern Language Association of America. *Awards, honors:* National Endowment for the Humanities, fellowship; Woodrow Wilson fellowship.

WRITINGS: *The Reaction Against Experiment in the English Novel, 1950-60*, Columbia University Press, 1967; *Iris Murdoch*, Columbia University Press, 1968; (contributor) James Brophy and Raymond Porter, editors, *Aspects of Irish Literature: Essays in Honor of William York Tindall*, Iona College Press, 1972. Contributor of book reviews to *New York Times Book Review, New York*, and *Modern Fiction Studies;* contributor of articles to *Reader's Adviser* and *Twentieth-Century Literature*.

WORK IN PROGRESS: A book on the fiction of Samuel Beckett, completion expected in 1977.

* * *

RABINOWITCH, Alexander 1934-

PERSONAL: Surname is pronounced Ra-*bin*-o-witch; born August 30, 1934, in London, England; son of Eugene (a biophysicist) and Anna (Morosoff) Rabinowitch; married Janet Bernstein (an editor at Indiana University Press), February 18, 1962; children: Ellen, Michael. *Education:* Knox College, B.A., 1956; University of Chicago, M.A., 1961; Moscow State University, graduate study, 1963-64; Indiana University, Ph.D., 1965. *Home:* 3635 Bainbridge Dr., Bloomington, Ind. 47401. *Office:* Department of History, Indiana University, Bloomington, Ind. 47401.

CAREER: University of Southern California, Los Angeles, assistant professor of history, 1965-67; Indiana University, Bloomington, assistant professor, 1968-69, associate professor, 1969-76, professor of history, 1976—, director of Russian and East European Institute, 1976—. Member, Institute for Advanced Study, School of Historical Studies,

Princeton University, 1973-74. *Military service:* U.S. Army, 1957-59; became first lieutenant. *Member:* American Historical Association, American Association for the Advancement of Slavic Studies, American Association of University Professors. *Awards, honors:* Research grant, Indiana University International Affairs Center, summer, 1966; National Endowment for the Humanities fellow, 1967-68; American Council of Learned Societies postdoctoral fellowship, 1970-71; International Research and Exchanges Board, Senior Scholars' Exchange Program, exchange senior scholar to Moscow State University, 1970-71; Institute for Advanced Study, National Endowment for the Humanities grant, 1973-74.

WRITINGS: Prelude to Revolution: The Petrograd Bolsheviks and the July 1917 Uprising, Indiana University Press, 1968; (co-editor and contributor) *Revolution and Politics in Russia,* Indiana University Press, 1972; *The Bolsheviks Come to Power: The Revolution of 1917 in Petrograd,* Norton, 1976. Contributor of reviews to professional journals.

WORK IN PROGRESS: A book, tentatively titled *Petrograd under Bolshevik Rule: October, 1917-1921.*

* * *

RACHLEFF, Owen S. 1934-

PERSONAL: Surname is pronounced *Rack*-leff; born July 16, 1934, in New York, N.Y.; son of Harold Kirman (a banker) and Theresa (Friedman) Rachleff. *Education:* Columbia University, B.F.A., 1956; University of London, M.A., 1958. *Politics:* Unaffiliated. *Religion:* Hebrew. *Agent:* Curtis Brown Ltd., 575 Madison Ave., New York, N.Y. 10022.

CAREER: World House Galleries, New York City, director, archaeological art, 1960-62; Harry N. Abrams, Inc. (publisher), New York City, author-in-residence, 1963-67; American Heritage Publishing Co., New York City, staff writer and editor, 1967-68; teacher at New School for Social Research, beginning 1968; New York University, New York City, assistant professor of humanities, 1969—; Hofstra University, assistant professor, 1972—. Free-lance author, 1968—; actor Off-Broadway since 1975, appearing in productions including "The Crucible," "Importance of Being Earnest," and "Major Barbara." *Member:* City Club of New York, *Awards, honors:* MacDowell Colony fellowships, 1960, 1965.

WRITINGS: Rembrandt's Life of Christ, Abradale Press, 1966; *Young Israel: A History of the Modern Nations,* Lion Press, 1968; *Great Bible Stories and Master Paintings: A Complete Narration of the Old and New Testaments,* Abrams, 1968; *An Illustrated Treasury of Bible Stories,* Abradale Press, 1970; *The Occult Conceit: A New Look at Astrology, Witchcraft and Sorcery,* Cowles Book Co., 1971; *The Magic of Love,* Gibson, 1972; *Sky Diamonds: The New Astrology,* illustrations by Robert Rappaport, Hawthorn, 1973; *The Secrets of Superstitions: How They Help, How They Hurt,* Doubleday, 1976.

Plays: "Cain," produced in Florida, 1965; "Javelin," produced Off-Broadway, 1966; "From the Classifieds," produced Off-Broadway, 1970.

WORK IN PROGRESS: Counterspells, a study of protective magic; *Exploring the Bible with Your Child,* a guide.

* * *

RADCLIFF, Peter (Edward, Jr.) 1932-

PERSONAL: Born April 29, 1932, in Istanbul, Turkey; son of Peter Edward (a minister) and Ruth (Allison) Radcliff; married Diana March (a teacher), August 25, 1956; children: Peter, Sharon, Daniel. *Education:* Oberlin College, B.A., 1954; University of Washington, Seattle, M.A., 1956, Ph.D., 1958. *Home:* 811 Castro St., San Francisco, Calif. *Office:* Department of Philosophy, San Francisco State University, San Francisco, Calif. 94132.

CAREER: Instructor in philosophy at Oberlin College, Oberlin, Ohio, 1958-59, and University of California, Riverside, 1959-60; University of Alberta, Edmonton, assistant professor of philosophy, 1960-63; San Francisco State University, San Francisco, Calif., faculty member, 1963-66, associate professor, 1966-72, professor of philosophy, 1972—. *Member:* American Philosophical Association, American Federation of Teachers. *Awards, honors:* Woodrow Wilson fellowship, 1954-55.

WRITINGS: (Editor) *The Limits of Liberty: Studies of Mills on Liberty,* Wadsworth, 1966.

* * *

RADER, Benjamin G(ene) 1935-

PERSONAL: Born August 25, 1935, in Delaware, Mo.; son of Lowell Leslie (an electrician) and Lydia (Eddings) Rader; married Barbara Koch, June 10, 1961; children: Anne Elizabeth, Stephen Lowell. *Education:* Southwest Missouri State College (now University), A.B., 1958; Oklahoma State University, M.A., 1959; University of Maryland, Ph.D., 1964. *Home:* 3100 South 31st St., Lincoln, Neb. 68508. *Office:* University of Nebraska, Lincoln, Neb. 68508.

CAREER: Oklahoma State University, Stillwater, instructor in history, 1961; University of Montana, Missoula, assistant professor of history, 1962-67; University of Nebraska, Lincoln, associate professor, 1967-72, professor of history, 1972—. *Awards, honors:* Honorable mention, Frederick Jackson Turner Award of Organization of American Historians, for *The Academic Mind and Reform.*

WRITINGS: The Academic Mind and Reform, University of Kentucky Press, 1966. Contributor to professional journals.

WORK IN PROGRESS: Politics of urban reform.

* * *

RAE, Wesley D(ennis) 1932-

PERSONAL: Born August 12, 1932, in Minnewaukan, N.D.; son of Jesse V. (a farmer) and Agnes (Olson) Rae; married Bette J. Johnson, October 17, 1958; children: Amy Irene, Jonathan Goodfellow. *Education:* North Dakota State University, Fargo, B.S., 1954; University of Wisconsin, M.S., 1957, Ph.D., 1961. *Home:* 1500 Apple Ridge Trail, Flint, Mich. 48507.

CAREER: Syracuse University, Utica College, Utica, N.Y., assistant professor, 1961-66, associate professor of English, 1966-69; University of Michigan–Flint, associate professor, 1969-72, professor of English and chairman of department, 1972-74, dean of College of Arts and Sciences, 1974-75. *Military service:* U.S. Army, 1954-56. *Member:* Modern Language Association of America, American Association of University Professors (vice-president, New York State Conference, 1968-69).

WRITINGS: Thomas Lodge, Twayne, 1967.

WORK IN PROGRESS: A critical edition, *Complete Poetry of Thomas Lodge.*

RAHTJEN, Bruce D(onald) 1933-

PERSONAL: Surname is pronounced *Rah* -jen; born May 14, 1933, in Rochester, N.Y.; son of Donald F. (a clergyman) and Anne (Miller) Rahtjen; married Jeanne Hamilton, June 5, 1954 (divorced, 1973); married Irma McCormac Evans, July 23, 1973; children: (first marriage) Donald Bruce, Nancy Jeanne, James Robert. *Education:* University of Rochester, A.B. (cum laude), 1955; Colgate Rochester Divinity School, B.D., 1958; Drew University, Ph.D., 1964. *Politics:* Democrat. *Home:* 1019 West 70th St., Kansas City, Mo. 64113. *Office:* Department of Biblical Theology, St. Paul School of Theology, 5123 Truman Rd., Kansas City, Mo. 64127.

CAREER: Methodist minister. Pastor of churches in New York and New Jersey, 1954-60; Colgate Rochester Divinity School, Rochester, N.Y., instructor in Bible, 1960-62; St. Paul School of Theology, Kansas City, Mo., assistant professor, 1962-67, associate professor, 1967-73, professor of Biblical theology, 1973—. Archaeological research in Israel, one season. Member of board of directors, Greater Kansas City Memorial Society. *Member:* Society of Biblical Literature, American Academy of Religion, Phi Beta Kappa.

WRITINGS: Scripture and Social Action, Abingdon, 1966; *Biblical Truth and Modern Man,* Abingdon, 1968. Contributor to religious and archaeological journals and Methodist publications; regular reviewer for *Kansas City Star.*

WORK IN PROGRESS: Research in relationship between Biblical theology and social ethics; workbook on "experimental theology"; a book of musings on theology and psychology from an existentialist perspective.

AVOCATIONAL INTERESTS: Camping, fishing, and gardening.

* * *

RAJSKI, Raymond B. 1917-

PERSONAL: Surname is pronounced Ray-ski; born August 26, 1917, in Chicago, Ill.; son of Stanley and Catherine (Lacki) Rajski; married Erma J. Giebel, February 14, 1942; children: Douglas Scott, Betsy Rae, Patti Rae. *Education:* Attended Northwestern University, 1938-41, and Georgetown University School of Foreign Service. *Politics:* Republican ("with reservations"). *Religion:* Protestant. *Home:* 1753 Whitcomb Ave., Des Plaines, Ill. 60018.

CAREER: U.S. Air Force, fighter pilot, operations, intelligence, and executive officer, 1941-53, with disability retirement in rank of captain; editorial cartoonist, 1955—, working for newspapers in Salt Lake City, Utah, Spokane, Wash., and Chicago and Des Plaines, Ill., and for U.S. Air Force News Service. *Member:* Association of American Editorial Cartoonists, Air Force Association, Disabled American Veterans. *Awards, honors*—Military: Air Medal with cluster. Other: Nominated five times for Pulitzer Prize in journalism, once for Pulitzer Prize in letters; fourteen Freedoms Foundation awards for editorial cartoons.

WRITINGS: (Editor) *A Nation Grieved: The John F. Kennedy Assassination in Editorial Cartoons,* Tuttle, 1967.

WORK IN PROGRESS: Historical documentary on presidential assassinations; political cartoons.

BIOGRAPHICAL/CRITICAL SOURCES: John Chase, *Today's Cartoon,* Hauser Press, 1962; *Chicago Daily News,* October 10, 1967, November 16, 1967.

RAKOSI, Carl 1903-
(Callman Rawley)

PERSONAL: Writes under original name, but did social work under legally adopted name of Callman Rawley; born November 6, 1903, in Berlin, Germany; came to United States in 1910; son of Hungarian nationals, Leopold and Flora (Steiner) Rakosi; married Leah Jaffe, May 6, 1939; children: Barbara, George. *Education:* University of Wisconsin, B.A., 1924, M.A., 1926; University of Pennsylvania, Master of Social Work, 1940. *Religion:* Jewish. *Home:* 4451 South Colfax Ave., Minneapolis, Minn. 55409.

CAREER: University of Texas, Austin, instructor, 1928-29; Cook County Bureau of Public Welfare, Chicago, Ill., social worker, 1932-33; Federal Transient Bureau, New Orleans, La., supervisor, 1933-34; Tulane University of Louisiana, Graduate School of Social Work, New Orleans, field work supervisor, 1934-35; Jewish Family Welfare Society, Brooklyn, N.Y., caseworker, 1935-40; Jewish Social Service Bureau, St. Louis, Mo., case supervisor, 1940-43; assistant director of Jewish Children's Bureau and Bellefaire (residential treatment center for disturbed children), both Cleveland, Ohio, 1943-45; Jewish Family and Children's Service, Minneapolis, Minn., executive director, 1945-68. Private practice in psychotherapy and marriage counseling, 1958-68. Resident writer, Yaddo, Saratoga Springs, N.Y., 1968-75; writer-in-residence, University of Wisconsin, 1969-70; member of faculty, National Poetry Festival, 1973; visiting poet, Michigan State University, 1974.

MEMBER: National Association of Social Workers (president of South Minnesota chapter, 1959-61), National Conference of Jewish Communal Service (vice-president, 1957-58), Family Service Association of America (chairman of Midwest regional committee, 1961-64; chairman of committee on long-range planning, 1964-66). *Awards, honors:* National Endowment for the Arts award, 1969, fellowship, 1972.

WRITINGS: Selected Poems, New Directions, 1941; *Amulet,* New Directions, 1967; *Two Poems,* Modern Editions Press, 1971; *Ere-Voice,* New Directions, 1971; *Ex Cranium, Night,* Black Sparrow Press, 1975.

Work anthologized in: *Objectivists Anthology,* edited by Louis Zukofsky; *America, a Prophesy,* edited by Rothenberg and Quasha; *The American Literary Anthology,* no. 3, edited by Louis Simpson; *Poems One Line and Longer,* edited by William Cole; *Heartland II,* edited by Lucien Stryk; *Inside Outer Space,* edited by Robert Vas Dias; *The American Caravan,* edited by Van Vyck Brooks; *Modern Things,* edited by Parker Tyler. Contributor of poetry to *Paris Review, Quarterly Review of Literature, Poetry, Massachusetts Review, Transition, Exile,* and other journals.

SIDELIGHTS: Rakosi told *CA:* "Between the years 1939 and 1965 I wrote no poetry. Was stimulated to write again by the interest of Andrew Crozier, a young British poet. *Amulet* represents my current work and revisions of earlier poems." Rakosi was a member of the Objectivists Group of poets. He stopped writing, Jim Harrison says, because he felt that "his intensely individual lyricism was irrelevant and impossible to continue." He devoted his time to his social work and his family. Harrison feels that Rakosi's social concerns are direct and evident; there is a total concern for the 'here and now,' a sense too that poetry as an art can be but one of the sacraments replacing none of the others." Rakosi's poetry is "humane, attentive to the ordinary until the ordinary ceases to be so." The poems, Harrison feels, "are 'made things' and throughout the book we sense the intelligence that directed the craft." Stanley Cooperman notes that "what Rakosi has, delightfully, is an ability to translate emotion into objects, tastes, smells: and these, in turn, are completely familiar—except that the familiarity occurs in unexpected juxtapositions of sound and theme ... the reader is almost surprised to find himself moving from a homely, apparently naive, sometimes even domestic landscape into a mind that is neither naive nor domestic.... Rakosi's work is at once irreverent and serious; highly intellectual and simplistic." Both Harrison and Cooperman feel that many of Rakosi's poems are worthy of inclusion in anthologies. Harrison says further, "Rakosi is a maker, not a bearer, and should be read and saluted by those who care for the life of the poet."

BIOGRAPHICAL/CRITICAL SOURCES: New York Times Book Review, January 28, 1968; *Prairie Schooner,* fall, 1968; *Contemporary Literature,* spring, 1969; *Iowa Review,* winter, 1971; *Margins,* February, 1975; *Preview,* June, 1975.

* * *

RAMSEY, G(ordon) C(lark) 1941-

PERSONAL: Born May 28, 1941, in Hartford, Conn.; son of Clark McNary and Virginia A. (Childs) Ramsey. *Education:* Yale University, B.A., 1963; private organ and choral studies. *Politics:* Republican. *Religion:* Episcopalian. *Residence:* West Haven, Conn. *Office:* 901-A Yale Station, New Haven, Conn.

CAREER: Worcester Academy, Worcester, Mass., instructor in English, assistant to the headmaster, and alumni director, 1963-69, director of glee club, 1964-65; Yale Alumni Fund, New Haven, Conn., secretary of the board, 1969-71; Association of Yale Alumni, New Haven, assistant executive director, 1972—. Historian, Yale Alumni Fund, 1973—. Technical expert for 1938 Chevrolet, Vintage Chevrolet Club of America. *Member:* American Guild of Organists (executive committee, Worcester chapter, 1964-67). *Awards, honors:* Research grant from Dodd, Mead & Co., for work in Great Britain on Agatha Christie book.

WRITINGS: Agatha Christie, Mistress of Mystery, Dodd, 1967. Contributor to *HiFi Stereo Review, New York Herald Tribune,* and *New York Times.* Record critic, *American Organist,* 1966-68; editor, "The Stovebolts" newsletter for Southern New England Region, Vintage Chevrolet Club of America, 1975—.

* * *

RAMUNDO, Bernard A. 1925-

PERSONAL: Born June 12, 1925, in New York, N.Y.; son of Domenick J. and Marie C. (Spaziante) Ramundo; married Jane M. McDermott (a public health nurse), May 30, 1947; married second wife, Ellen E. Manescalchi (a U.S. Army nurse), February 2, 1962; children: (first marriage) Karen, Marie, Kevin James, Keith Domenick. *Education:* City College (now of the City University of New York), A.B., 1947; Columbia University, LL.B., 1949, M.A., 1957, Certificate of Russian Institute, 1958; American University, Ph.D., 1966. *Religion:* Roman Catholic. *Home:* 7908 Rocton Ave., Chevy Chase, Md. 20015. *Office:* Office of International Programs, Department of Transportation, Washington, D.C. 20950.

CAREER: U.S. Army, 1943-46, 1950-72; became colonel in Judge Advocate General's Corps, stationed in Washington, D.C. Currently member of staff, Office of International Programs, Department of Transportation, Washington, D.C. Associate professorial lecturer in law, George Washington University, 1963—. *Awards, honors*—Military: Legion of Merit; Commendation Medal with oak leaf cluster. *Member:* American Bar Association.

WRITINGS: The (Soviet) Socialist Theory of International Law (monograph), Institute for Sino-Soviet Studies, George Washington University, 1964; (contributor) Arthur Larson, C. Wilfred Jenks, and others, editors, *Sovereignty within Law,* Oceana, 1965; *Peaceful Coexistence: International Law in the Building of Communism,* Johns Hopkins Press, 1967; *Leninism: Rationale of Party Dictatorship,* American Bar Foundation, 1970; *The Soviet Legal System: A Primer,* American Bar Foundation, 1971, revised edition, 1974. Contributor to *Journal of Legal Education, Journal of Law and Economic Development, Army Information, American Journal of International Law* and various law reviews.

WORK IN PROGRESS: A primer on negotiation concepts and techniques.

SIDELIGHTS: Bernard Ramundo is fluent in Russian; also speaks Italian and Spanish.

* * *

RAND, Earl (James) 1933-

PERSONAL: Born August 5, 1933, in Bakersfield, Calif.; son of Roy Chester (a businessman) and Myrtle (Gooch) Rand; married Jane Warner, December 29, 1956 (divorced, 1974); children: David Thoreau, Robert Frost. *Education:* University of California, Los Angeles, B.A., 1954; University of Texas, M.A., 1961, Ph.D., 1966. *Home:* 176 G St., Brawley, Calif. 92227. *Office:* Department of English, University of California, Los Angeles, Calif. 90024.

CAREER: Linguistic specialist at University of Texas, Austin, and adviser to Republic of China Ministry of Education on Taiwan English teachers retraining, 1962-65; University of California, Los Angeles, associate professor of English as a second language and of Chinese linguistics, 1966—. U.S. Department of Interior, Bureau of Indian Affairs, consultant, 1967-68; Government of India, adviser to Indian Institute of Technology, 1968-70. Director, summer English language program, University of Zaire, Democratic Republic of the Congo, 1974. *Member:* Linguistic Society of America, American Association of Teachers of Chinese Language and Culture, Teachers of English to Speakers of Other Languages, Linguistic Circle of New York.

WRITINGS: Oral Approach Drills, Taiwan Provincial Normal University, 1964; (with Charles T. C. Tang) *Oral Approach Drill Pictures,* Taiwan Provincial Normal University, 1965; *The Syntax of Mandarin Interrogatives,* University of California Press, 1969; *Constructing Dialogs,* Holt, 1969; *Constructing Sentences,* Holt, 1969; *Drills on the English Verb Auxiliary,* Holt, 1970. Editor, "Linguistic Approach to English" series, ten books, Taiwan Provincial Normal University, 1964-65.

WORK IN PROGRESS: An Introduction to Research and Statistics in Second-Language Teaching.

* * *

RAND, Paul 1914-

PERSONAL: Born August 15, 1914, in Brooklyn, N.Y.;

children: Catherine. *Education:* Pratt Institute, graduate, 1932; studied at Parsons School of Design, 1932, and Art Student's League of New York, 1934. *Home and studio:* Goodhill Rd., Weston, Conn. 06880.

CAREER: Designer, typographer, painter, and teacher, Studio of George Switzer, New York City, apprentice, 1932-35; *Esquire,* New York City, art director, 1936-41; Cooper Union, Laboratory School of Design, New York City, instructor in graphic design, 1938-42; Pratt Institute, Brooklyn, N.Y., instructor in postgraduate course, 1946; Yale University, School of Art and Architecture, New Haven, Conn., professor of graphic design, 1956—. Honorary professor, Tama University, Tokyo, Japan, 1958. Design consultant to IBM, Westinghouse, and other corporations. Former member, Fulbright scholarship jury; visitor at Museum School, Boston Museum of Fine Arts; member of art education advisory board, New York University. Work exhibited in United States, Europe, Japan, and Russia.

MEMBER: Industrial Designers Society of America, Alliance Graphique International (Paris), Royal Society of Arts (London; Benjamin Franklin fellow). *Awards, honors:* Citation, Philadelphia College of Art, 1962; American Institute of Graphic Arts Gold Medal, 1966; Hall of Fame, New York Art Director's Club, 1972; named honorary member, Royal Designer for Industry, London, 1973; other awards from *Financial World* for best design and typography of annual reports, Museum of Modern Art for fabrics design, *New York Times* jury for children's book illustrations, and Society of Typographic Arts for trademarks.

WRITINGS: Thoughts on Design, Wittenborn, 1946; *The Trademarks of Paul Rand,* Wittenborn, 1960; (contributor) *Education of Vision,* Braziller, 1965. Contributor of articles on design, advertising, and typography to periodicals.

Illustrator: *I Know a Lot of Things,* Harcourt, 1956; *Sparkle Sparkle Spin,* Harcourt, 1957; *Little 1,* Harcourt, 1962; *Listen, Listen,* Harcourt, 1970.

BIOGRAPHICAL/CRITICAL SOURCES: Yusaku Kamekura, *Paul Rand: His Work from 1946-58,* Knopf, 1958.

* * *

RANDALL, Lilian M. C. 1931-

PERSONAL: Born February 1, 1931, in Berlin, Germany; daughter of Frederick H. (a history professor) and Elisabeth (Ziegler) Cramer; married Richard H. Randall, Jr. (director of Walters Art Gallery), April 11, 1953; children: Christopher, Julia, Katherine. *Education:* Mount Holyoke College, B.A., 1950; Radcliffe College, M.A., 1951, Ph.D., 1955. *Residence:* Baltimore, Md.

CAREER: Radcliffe Institute for Independent Study, Cambridge, Mass., associate scholar, 1961-63; Johns Hopkins University, Baltimore, Md., visiting lecturer in medieval art, 1965, 1968; assistant director, Maryland Arts Council, 1971-72; curator of manuscripts, Walters Art Gallery, 1974—. *Member:* Mediaeval Academy of America, College Art Association, Phi Beta Kappa. *Awards, honors:* Arthur Kingsley Porter Prize for best article published in *Art Bulletin,* 1957, for "Exempla and Their Influence on Gothics Marginal Illunination."

WRITINGS: Images in the Margins of Gothic Manuscripts, University of California Press, 1966; (co-editor and contributor) *Gathering in Honor of Dorothy E. Miner,* [Baltimore, Md.], 1973; (editor) *Paris for Sale: The Diary of George A. Lucas (1824-1909),* two volumes, Princeton University Press, 1976. Contributor to *Art Bulletin, Speculum, Apollo,* and other art journals.

* * *

RANSFORD, Oliver 1914-

PERSONAL: Born April 25, 1914, in Bradford, England; son of Thomas Oliver (a minister of religion) and Mabel Louise (Thomas) Ransford; married Doris Irene Gallaway, July 19, 1939; children: Andrew, Carol, Charlotte. *Education:* University of London and Middlesex Hospital, M.D., F.F.A.R.C.S. (fellow of Faculty of Anaesthetists, Royal College of Surgeons), and Diploma in Anaesthesia, 1936. *Home:* 8 Herman Rd., Bulawayo, Rhodesia. *Agent:* David Higham, David Higham Associates Ltd., 76 Dean St., London W.1, England. *Office address:* P.O. Box 1451, Bulawayo, Rhodesia.

CAREER: In private practice as consultant anesthetist, Bulawayo, Rhodesia, 1947—. Consultant anesthetist to Rhodesia Railways, Rhodesia Defence Forces; honorary consultant anesthetist to Bulawayo Group of Hospitals. *Military service:* British Army, Medical Corps, 1939-45; became major. *Member:* Rhodesian Medical Association (president, Mababeland branch), Bulawayo Club.

WRITINGS: Livingstone's Lake: The Drama of Nyasa, Africa's Inland Sea, Crowell, 1966; *The Battle of Majuba Hill,* Crowell, 1967; *Bulawayo: Historic Background of Rhodesia,* Balkema, 1968; *The Rulers of Rhodesia from Earliest Times to the Referendum,* Murray, 1968; *The Battle of Spion Kop,* Murray, 1969; *The Slave Trade: The Story of Transatlantic Slavery,* Murray, 1971; *Rhodesian Tapestry,* Books of Rhodesia, 1971; *The Great Trek,* Murray, 1972; (with T. W. Baxtee) *Livingstone in Africa,* J. Cape, 1972. Contributor to journals.

WORK IN PROGRESS: A biography of David Livingstone.

AVOCATIONAL INTERESTS: Historical and archaeological research in South and Central Africa.

* * *

RAPHAEL, Rick 1919-

PERSONAL: Born February 20, 1919; son of Louis N. and Viola (Felix) Raphael; married June 5, 1941; first wife's name, Dolores; married second wife, Elizabeth Van Schaick (an educational specialist), July 1, 1958; children: Patricia (Mrs. Thomas Thruston), Christopher, Melanie (Mrs. Frederick Swensen), Karen, Teresa, Stephanie. *Education:* Attended Boise Junior College, University of New Mexico, and Colorado State University. *Politics:* Democrat. *Religion:* Episcopalian.

CAREER: U.S. Army, active duty, 1936-45, and reserve service, until 1965, retiring as captain; intermittently political reporter, science writer, managing editor, and news editor of daily newspapers, 1945-58; *Idaho Daily Statesman,* Boise, copy editor, 1958-59; KBOI-TV and Radio, Boise, assistant news director and political editor, 1959-65; press and legislative aide to U.S. Senator Frank Church (Democrat-Idaho), Washington, D.C., beginning 1965.

MEMBER: Nuclear Energy Writers Association, Episcopal Society for Cultural and Racial Unity, Idaho State Society (secretary, 1966), Boise World Affairs Association (vice-president, 1963-65), Sigma Delta Chi, U.S. Senate Press Secretaries, U.S. Senate Staff Club. *Awards, honors—Military:* Bronze Star with V cluster; Purple Heart with oak leaf cluster; battle stars for service in European theater. Civilian: New Mexico Press Association Award, 1957; Idaho Press Association awards, 1963, 1964; Radio-Television News Directors Award for nation's leading film documentary on water pollution, 1963.

WRITINGS: The Thirst Quenchers, Gollancz, 1965; *Code Three,* Simon & Schuster, 1966. Numerous novelettes and short stories have been published in *Astounding, Analog,* and *Fantastic,* some of them anthologized in *Prelude to Analog,* Doubleday, 1962, and *Analog 2,* Doubleday, 1966.

WORK IN PROGRESS: A political novel; a science fiction novel; several short fiction pieces.

SIDELIGHTS: Raphael told *CA:* "My major premise in science fiction writing has been that while technology changes, human reactions and emotions do not. People will vary in future years from today's patterns only to the degree that environment modulates their emotions." *Avocational interests:* Sailing.††

* * *

RAPSON, Richard L(awrence) 1937-

PERSONAL: Born March 8, 1937, in New York, N.Y.; son of Louis (a businessman) and Grace (Levenkind) Rapson; married Susan Burns (a teacher), March 29, 1975; children: (previous marriage) Kim Elizabeth, Jason Alan. *Education:* Amherst College, B.A., 1958; Columbia University, Ph.D., 1966. *Home:* 282 Makaweli Pl., Honolulu, Hawaii 90825. *Office:* Department of History, University of Hawaii, Honolulu, Hawaii 96822.

CAREER: Amherst College, Amherst, Mass., instructor in American studies, 1960-61; Stanford University, Stanford, Calif., instructor in history, 1961-65; University of California, Santa Barbara, assistant professor of history, 1965-66; University of Hawaii, Honolulu, assistant professor, 1966-68, associate professor, 1968-71, professor of history, 1971—. Visiting professor, Stanford University, 1973-74; academic dean, coordinator of American Heritage Program, and visiting professor, Chapman College's World Campus Afloat, U.S. Bicentennial Voyage, 1976. *Member:* American Historical Association, Organization of American Historians (regional membership director, 1968-70), Phi Beta Kappa. *Awards, honors:* Woodrow Wilson fellowship; Social Science Research Council grant; Danforth Foundation teacher's grant.

WRITINGS: (Editor) *Individualism and Conformity in the American Character,* Heath, 1967; (contributor) Alan Hodge, editor, *Varieties of Travel,* Oliver & Boyd, 1967; *Britons View America: Travel Commentary, 1860-1935,* University of Washington Press, 1971; (editor) *Cult of Youth in Middle Class America,* Heath, 1971; (editor) *Major Interpretations of the American Past,* Appleton, 1971. General editor, "The Literature of History" series, four volumes, Appleton, 1971. Contributor to professional journals.

WORK IN PROGRESS: The Pursuit of Meaning: America, 1600-2000.

* * *

RASKIN, Ellen 1928-

PERSONAL: Born March 13, 1928, in Milwaukee, Wis.; daughter of Sol and Margaret (Goldfisch) Raskin; married present husband, Dennis Flanagan (editor of *Scientific American*), August 1, 1960; children: (first marriage) Susan Beth Kuhlman. *Education:* University of Wisconsin, student, 1945-49. *Home:* 12 Gay St., New York, N.Y. 10014.

CAREER: Commercial illustrator and designer, New York, N.Y., 1950—, designing more than one thousand book jackets and doing both magazine and advertising illustrations; author and illustrator of picture books, 1966—. *Awards, honors:* New York Herald Tribune Children's Book Week Award (best picture book), 1966, for *Nothing Ever Happens on My Block; Songs of Innocence* was included in American Institute of Graphic Arts exhibit of 50 best books of the year, 1966; *Spectacles* was named one of the best-illustrated children's books by *New York Times Book Review,* 1968; Boston Globe-Horn Book, 1973 Honor Book, for *Who, Said Sue, Said Whoo?;* Newbery Honor Book, 1975, for *Figgs & Phantoms.*

WRITINGS—All self-illustrated: *Nothing Ever Happens on My Block,* Atheneum, 1966; (set William Blake's poems to music for voice and piano, and designed and illustrated book) *Songs of Innocence,* two volumes, Doubleday, 1966; *Silly Songs and Sad,* Crowell, 1967; *Spectacles,* Atheneum, 1968; *Ghost in a Four-Room Apartment,* Atheneum, 1969; *And It Rained,* Atheneum, 1969

A & The, Atheneum, 1970; *The World's Greatest Freak Show,* Atheneum, 1971; *Franklin Stein,* Atheneum, 1972; *Who, Said Sue, Said Whoo?,* Atheneum, 1973; *Moe Q. McGlutch, He Smokes Too Much,* Parents' Magazine Press, 1973; *Moose, Goose and Little Nobody,* Parents' Magazine Press, 1974; *Twenty-two, Twenty-three,* Atheneum, 1976.

Illustrator: Dylan Thomas, *A Child's Christmas in Wales,* New Directions, 1959; Molly Cone, *The Jewish Sabbath,* Crowell, 1966; Susan Bartlett, *Books,* Holt, 1968; Suzanne Stark Morrow, *Inatuk's Friend,* Little, Brown, 1968; B. K. Weiss, *A Paper Zoo,* Macmillan, 1968; Rebecca Caudill, *Come Along!,* Holt, 1969; Christina Rossetti, *Goblin Market,* Dutton, 1970.

Novels: *The Mysterious Disappearance of Leon (I Mean Noel),* Dutton, 1971; *Figgs & Phantoms,* Dutton, 1974; *The Tattooed Potato and Other Clues,* Dutton, 1975.

AVOCATIONAL INTERESTS: Book collecting, gardening.

BIOGRAPHICAL/CRITICAL SOURCES: Ann Block and Carolyn Riley, editors, *Children's Literature Review,* Volume I, Gale, 1976.

* * *

RATCLIFFE, James M(axwell) 1925-

PERSONAL: Born May 26, 1925, in Kewanee, Ill.; son of James Maxwell (a businessman) and Madeleine (Hoffrichter) Ratcliffe; married Hildegund Weide, August 24, 1969; children: James Maxwell III. *Education:* University of Chicago, A.B., 1946, J.D., 1950. *Politics:* Republican. *Home:* 5536 Dorchester Ave., Chicago, Ill. 60637. *Office:* 2223 King Dr., Chicago, Ill. 60616.

CAREER: Admitted to Illinois Bar, 1950; Illinois Committee for Constitutional Revision, Chicago, field secretary, 1950; University of Chicago, Chicago, Ill., field secretary, 1951-53, assistant dean of Law School, 1953-68; R. R. Donnelley & Sons Co., Chicago, director of public affairs, 1968—. Member of advisory committee, Institute on Continuing Education of Illinois Bar; vice-chairman, Chicago Great Books Council, 1956-58; vice-president and director, Printing Industries of America; director, Associated Employers of Illinois; president, Chicago Public Affairs Group. *Military service:* U.S. Army Air Forces, 1943-46; became staff sergeant. U.S. Air Force Reserve, 1951-57;

became captain. *Member:* American Bar Association, Chicago Bar Association, Beta Theta Phi, Quadrangle Club, University Club, Economic Club, Executives Club.

WRITINGS: (Editor) *The Good Samaritan and the Law,* Doubleday, 1966.

* * *

RATHBONE, Robert Reynolds 1916-

PERSONAL: Born January 24, 1916, in Exeter, N.H.; son of James Colburn (an insurance salesman) and Lillian (Reynolds) Rathbone; married Harriett Durkee, August 30, 1941; children: Anne Lincoln. *Education:* Middlebury College, A.B., 1939; Harvard University, A.M., 1947. *Home:* 7 Durham Dr., Lynnfield, Mass. 01940. *Office:* Department of English, Massachusetts Institute of Technology, Cambridge, Mass. 02139.

CAREER: Swampscott High School, Swampscott, Mass., teacher of English, 1947-49; technical writer and editor, "Project Whirlwind," 1949-52; technical writer and editor, Lincoln Laboratory, 1952-54; Massachusetts Institute of Technology, Cambridge, assistant professor, 1954-59, associate professor, 1959-69, professor of English, 1969—. Teacher of industrial courses in writing and editing. *Military service:* U.S. Naval Reserve, World War II; became lieutenant. *Member:* Society of Technical Writers and Publishers (senior member), Audubon Society of New Hampshire (trustee).

WRITINGS: (With J. B. Stone) *A Writer's Guide for Engineers and Scientists,* Prentice-Hall, 1962; (with Rosenstein and Schneerer) *Engineering Communications,* Prentice-Hall, 1964; *Communicating Technical Information,* Addison-Wesley, 1966, revised edition, 1972; (with others) *Write, Write, Write!,* Haden, 1976. Contributor of ten articles on computer equipment to *Radio-Electronic Engineering,* 1951-52; contributor of numerous articles on writing and the teaching of writing.

AVOCATIONAL INTERESTS: Conservation, fishing, oil painting.

* * *

RATNER, Leonard G(ilbert) 1916-

PERSONAL: Born July 30, 1916, in Minneapolis, Minn.; married Ingeborg Hecht, February 11, 1944; children: Karen, Miriam. *Education:* University of California, Los Angeles, B.Ed., 1937; University of California, Berkeley, M.A., 1939, Ph.D., 1947. *Office:* Stanford University, Stanford, Calif. 94305.

CAREER: University of California, Berkeley, lecturer in music, 1944-47; Stanford University, Stanford, Calif., 1947—, began as instructor, professor of music, 1957—. Composer. *Member:* American Musicological Society (council member). *Awards, honors:* Ford Foundation faculty fellowship, 1955-56; Guggenheim fellowship, 1962-63.

WRITINGS: Music: The Listener's Art, McGraw, 1957, 2nd edition, 1966; *Harmony, Structure and Style,* McGraw, 1962. Also author of papers on music presented at musical societies.

WORK IN PROGRESS: A book, tentatively entitled *The Classic Style: A Musical Language.*

* * *

RATNER, Sidney 1908-

PERSONAL: Born June 18, 1908, in New York, N.Y.; son of Israel (a businessman) and Olga (Handman) Ratner; married Louise M. Rosenblatt (a professor of English education), June 16, 1932; children: Jonathan B. *Education:* City College (now of the City University of New York), B.A., 1930; Columbia University, M.A., 1931, Ph.D., 1942. *Home:* 11 Cleveland Lane, Princeton, N.J. 08540. *Office:* Rutgers University, New Brunswick, N.J. 08540.

CAREER: Instructor at Sarah Lawrence College, Bronxville, N.Y., 1938-39, and Cooper Union, New York, N.Y., 1938-41; U.S. Government, Washington, D.C., economist, Board of Economic Warfare, 1942-43, senior economist, Foreign Economic Administration, 1944-45, principal economist, Planning Division, Office of Foreign Liquidation, U.S. Department of State, 1946; Rutgers University, New Brunswick, N.J., assistant professor, 1946-47, associate professor, 1948-57, professor of history, 1958—. Member, Institute for Advanced Study, Princeton, N.J., 1956-57. Lecturer at American Studies Seminar, Kyoto, Japan, summer, 1964, and at universities in Lagos and Nigeria, spring, 1967. Chairman of Conference on Methods in Philosophy and the Sciences, 1950-51, and John Dewey Centennial Executive Committee, 1959; member of American Association for the Advancement of Science jury awarding social science prize, 1953-55.

MEMBER: American Economic Association, American Historical Association, Economic History Association, Econometric Society, Economic History Society (Britain). *Awards, honors:* Social Science Research Council grant, 1957.

WRITINGS: (Co-author) *John Dewey, Philosopher of Science and Freedom,* Dial, 1950; (co-author) *Vision and Action,* Rutgers University Press, 1953; (co-author) *Life, Language, Law,* Antioch Press, 1957; (co-author) *Philosophy and History,* New York University Press, 1963; (editor with J. Altman and J. Wheeler) *John Dewey and Arthur F. Bentley: A Philosophical Correspondence,* Rutgers University Press, 1964; *Taxation and Democracy in America,* Wiley, 1968; (author of introduction and editor with Peter Asch) A. F. Bentley, *Makers, Users, and Masters,* Syracuse University Press, 1969; *The Tariff History in America,* Van Nostrand, 1972. Contributor to economic and political science journals.

WORK IN PROGRESS: American Economic Growth and Welfare; a book on the economic history of World War II, *Patterns of War Economy.*

AVOCATIONAL INTERESTS: Literature, music, the theater, dancing, swimming, tennis.

* * *

RAUCH, Irmengard 1933-

PERSONAL: Born April 17, 1933, in Dayton, Ohio; daughter of Konrad (an electronics research engineer) and Elsa (Knott) Rauch; married Gerald F. Carr (a professor); children: Christopher, Gregory. *Education:* University of Dayton, B.S., 1955; Ohio State University, M.A., 1957; University of Michigan, Ph.D., 1962; also studied at National University of Mexico and University of Munich. *Office:* University of Illinois, Urbana, Ill. 61801.

CAREER: University of Wisconsin—Madison, 1962-66, began as instructor, became assistant professor of Germanic linguistics; University of Pittsburgh, Pittsburgh, Pa., associate professor of Germanic linguistics, 1966-68; University of Illinois, Urbana, associate professor, 1968-72, professor of Germanic linguistics, 1972—. *Member:* American Association of Teachers of German, Linguistic Society of America, Modern Language Association of America, Societas Linguistica Europaea, International Linguistic Association, International Phonetics Association, American Association for the Advancement of Science, Alpha Sigma Tau, Delta Phi Alpha. *Awards, honors:* Fulbright fellow in Munich, Germany, 1957-58; University of Wisconsin research grant, 1966; National Science Foundation and Linguistic Society of America travel grant, 1972.

WRITINGS: The Old High German Dipthongization, Mouton & Co., 1967; (editor with C. T. Scott) *Approaches in Linguistic Methodology,* University of Wisconsin Press, 1967; (editor with J. Eichhoff) *Der Heliand,* Wissenschaftliche Buchgesellschaft, 1973; (editor with Gerald F. Carr) *Linguistic Method: The Herbert Penzl Festschrift,* Peter de Ridder Press, in press. Contributor to *Linguistics, Monatshefte, Lingua, Indogermanische,* and other journals.

WORK IN PROGRESS: Several books in linguistics.

SIDELIGHTS: Irmengard Rauch is competent in several modern European and classical languages.

*   *   *

RAWLEY, James A. 1916-

PERSONAL: Born November 9, 1916, in Terre Haute, Ind.; son of Frank S. (a lawyer) and Annie B. (Vanes) Rawley; married Ann F. Keyser, April 7, 1945; children: John, James. *Education:* University of Michigan, A.B. (with honors), 1938, A.M., 1939; Columbia University, Ph.D., 1949. *Politics:* Democrat. *Religion:* Episcopalian. *Home:* 2300 Bretigne Dr., Lincoln, Neb. 68512. *Office:* Department of History, University of Nebraska, Lincoln, Neb. 68508.

CAREER: Instructor in history at New York University, New York City, 1946-51, and Hunter College (now Hunter College of the City University of New York), New York City, 1951-53; Sweet Briar College, Sweet Briar, Va., associate professor, 1953-58, professor of history, 1958-66, chairman of department, 1953-57, chairman of Division of Social Studies, 1961-64; University of Nebraska, Lincoln, professor of history and chairman of department, 1966-67, 1973—. Lecturer, Columbia University, 1946-48; summer visiting professor, University of Virginia, 1962. Researcher in Anglo-American cultural relations, London, England, 1959-60, and 1968; researcher and writer, Charlottesville, Va., 1963-64. *Military service:* U.S. Army, 1942-46; became first lieutenant. *Member:* American Historical Association, Royal Historical Society (fellow), Organization of American Historians, Academy of Political Science, Southern Historical Association.

WRITINGS: Edwin D. Morgan, 1811-1883, Columbia University Press, 1955; (contributor) Donald Sheehan and Harold C. Syrett, editors, *Essays in Historiography,* Columbia University Press, 1960; *The American Civil War History: An English View,* University Press of Virginia, 1965; *Turning Points of the Civil War,* University of Nebraska Press, 1966; *Race and Politics: Bleeding Kansas and the Coming of the Civil War,* Lippincott, 1969; *Lincoln and Civil War Politics,* Holt, 1969; *The Politics of Union,* Dryden Press, 1974. Contributor to historical journals.

WORK IN PROGRESS: The Atlantic Slave Trade, for Batsford.

RAY, Sibnarayan 1921-

PERSONAL: Born January 20, 1921, in Calcutta, India; son of Upendra Nath (a professor) and Rajkumari (Mitra) Ray; married Gita Ray (a free-lance writer), May 10, 1951; children: Amitabha, Maitreyi. *Education:* Calcutta University, B.A. (honors), 1940, M.A., 1942; additional graduate study at University of London and University of Chicago, 1957-58. *Politics:* Democrat. *Religion:* Humanist. *Home:* 14 Fuller St., Bulleen, Victoria 3105, Australia. *Office:* University of Melbourne, Parkville, Victoria 3052, Australia.

CAREER: Calcutta University, City College, Calcutta, India, lecturer in English, 1945-55; Asian Trade Union College, Calcutta, professor of politics, 1952-55; Bombay University, Bombay, India, professor of English, 1960-63; University of Melbourne, Parkville, Victoria, Australia, reader and head of Indian studies, 1963—. Director, Renaissance Publishers, Calcutta, 1949—. Member, International Committee on Modernization in Asia, Korea University, Seoul, 1965—. Member, Bengali Literary Academy of Chittagong University, 1975—. *Member:* Institute of Historical Studies (fellow), South Asian Studies Association of Australia and New Zealand (life member), Indian Renaissance Institute (honorary secretary, 1960-65), International Humanist and Ethical Union (member of board of directors, 1960-68), Australia-India Society of Victoria (president, 1965-68). *Awards, honors:* Rockefeller Foundation fellow, 1956-58; M.A., University of Melbourne.

WRITINGS: Radicalism, Renaissance Publishers, 1946; (with Ellen Roy) *In Man's Own Image,* Renaissance Publishers, 1948; *Explorations,* Renaissance Publishers, 1956; *Sahityachinta* (in Bengali), Mitralaya, 1957; (editor and author of introduction) *Vietnam Seen Between East and West,* Praeger, 1966; (editor, author of introduction, and contributor) *Gandhi India and the World,* Temple University Press, 1970; (editor) *Asia, 1971,* Quadrant, 1971; *Kavir Nirvasan* (in Bengali), Prakashbhavan, 1973; *Autumnal Equinox,* Writers Workshop, 1973; (with Marian Maddern) *I Have Seen Bengals Face,* Editions Indian, 1974; (editor) *Vak,* Writers Workshop, 1975. Also author of a collection of poems and six volumes of essays, published in Bengali.

Contributor: Leopold Labedz, editor, *Revisionism: Essays on the History of Marxist Ideas,* Praeger, 1962; E. P. Whittemore, editor, *Socialism: The First Hundred Years,* Centre for Labour and Social Studies (Rome), 1964; S. P. Ailyar, R. Srinivasan, editors, *Studies in Indian Democracy,* Allied, 1965; Sang-Eun Lee, editor, *Problems of Modernization in Asia,* Korea University (Seoul), 1966; A. Bose, editor, *Calcutta Essays on Shakespeare,* Calcutta University, 1966; *Australia, a Part of Asia?: A Symposium,* University of New South Wales, 1968.

M. Govindan, editor, *Poetry and Renaissance,* Sameeksha, 1974; B. N. Pande, editor, *The Spirit of India,* Igas, 1975; Wang Gungwu, editor, *Self and Biography,* Sydney University Press, 1976. Contributor to *Quest, Quadrant, Hemisphere,* and other publications. Honorary editor, *Radical Humanist* (Calcutta), 1954-66.

WORK IN PROGRESS: Asia, Modernization and the West; The Vertical Individual in the Bengal Renaissance; M. N. Roy: Portrait of a Revolutionary; The Muslim Intelligentsia of Bangladesh.

AVOCATIONAL INTERESTS: Painting, music, theater.

RAYNER, Claire 1931-
(Sheila Brandon, Berry Chetwynd, Ann Lynton, Ruth Martin, Isobel Saxe)

PERSONAL: Born January 22, 1931; married Desmond Rayner (works in advertising), June 23, 1957; children: Amanda, Adam, Jason. *Home:* 7, Pasture Rd., North Wembley, Middlesex, England. *Agent:* Michael Horniman, A. P. Watt & Son, 26/28 Bedford Row, London WC1R 4HL, England.

CAREER: Until 1960, worked in London as a state registered nurse; now full-time writer. Presents regular television family advice show, "Pebble Mill," for British Broadcasting Corp.

*WRITINGS—*Nonfiction: *Mothers and Midwives,* Allen & Unwin, 1962; *What Happens in the Hospital,* Hart-Davis, 1963; *The Calendar of Childhood: A Guide for All Mothers,* Elbury Press, 1964; *Your Baby,* Hamlyn, 1965; *Careers with Children,* R. Hale, 1966; *Housework the Easy Way,* Corgi, 1967; *The House on the Fen,* Corgi, 1967; *Shall I Be a Nurse?,* Wheaton, 1967; *Home Nursing and Family Health,* Transworld, 1967; *101 Facts an Expectant Mother Should Know,* Dickens Press, 1967; *For Children: Equipping a Home for a Growing Family,* Macdonald, for Council of Industrial Design, 1967; *Essentials of Outpatient Nursing,* Arlington Books, 1967; *101 Facts of Practical Baby Care,* Dickens Press, 1967; *A Parent's Guide to Sex Education,* Corgi, 1968, Dolphin Books, 1969; *People in Love: A Modern Guide to Sex in Marriage,* Hamlyn, 1968, revised edition published as *About Sex,* Fontana Books, 1972; *Womens' Medical Dictionary,* Corgi, 1971; *When to Call the Doctor: What to Do Whilst Waiting,* Corgi, 1972; *The Shy Person's Book,* Wolfe, 1973, McKay, 1974; *Childcare Made Simple,* W. H. Allen, 1973; *Where Do I Come From?,* Arlington Books, 1975.

Fiction: *Shilling a Pound Pears,* Hart-Davis, 1964; *Starch of Aprons,* R. Hale, 1967, published as *The Hive,* Corgi, 1968; *Lady Mislaid,* Corgi, 1968; *Death on the Table,* Corgi, 1969; *The Meddlers,* Simon & Schuster, 1970; *A Time to Heal,* Simon & Schuster, 1972; *The Burning Summer,* Allison & Busby, 1972; *The Performers,* Cassell, Volume I: *Gower Street,* 1973, Simon & Schuster, 1973, Volume II: *The Haymarket,* 1974, Simon & Schuster, 1974, Volume III: *Paddington Green,* 1975, Volume IV: *Soho Square,* 1976.

Fiction under pseudonym Sheila Brandon; all published by Corgi: *The Final Year,* 1962; *Cottage Hospital,* 1963; *Children's Ward,* 1964; *The Lonely One,* 1965; *The House on the Fen,* 1967; *The Doctors of Downlands,* 1968; *The Private Wing,* 1971; *Nurse in the Sun,* 1972.

Under pseudonym Lynn Lynton: *Mothercraft,* Corgi, 1967.

Under pseudonym Isobel Saxe: *Desperate Remedies,* Corgi, 1968.

Woman's Own, regular columnist under house pseudonym Ruth Martin, nine years, under name Claire Rayner, 1975—; regular columnist of "Problem Page" for *Petticoat,* and *Sun.* Contributor to magazines and newspapers.

WORK IN PROGRESS: Further volumes of *The Performers*.

* * *

RAYNER, E(dgar) G(eoffrey) 1927-
PERSONAL: Born January 2, 1927, in Great Britain; son of Thomas (a miner) and Jane (Wragg) Rayner; married Pamela Wood, December 23, 1954; children: Christian, Felix, Polly. *Education:* Queens' College, Cambridge, B.A., 1948. *Home:* 324 Victoria Park Rd., Leicestershire, England.

CAREER: Schoolmaster in England, 1949—, currently at Wyggeston Boys' School, Leicester, England. Chief examiner in specified history level, University of London Examining Board, 1970—. *Member:* Historical Association.

WRITINGS: (With N. C. Dexter) *Liberal Studies: An Outline Course,* two volumes, Pergamon, 1964; (with Dexter) *Guide to Contemporary Politics,* Pergamon, 1966; (with R. F. Stapley and J. B. Watson) *New Objective Tests in Twentieth-Century History,* University of London Press, 1974.

WORK IN PROGRESS: Two books on English and European history, 1760-1848 and 1848-1914; a collection of document-based questions on twentieth-century history.

AVOCATIONAL INTERESTS: Politics, drama.

* * *

RE, Edward D(omenic) 1920-
PERSONAL: Born October 14, 1920, in Santa Marina, Italy; U.S. citizen, brought to United States in 1928; son of Anthony and Marina (Maetta) Re; married Margaret Ann Corcoran (an attorney), June 3, 1950; children: Mary Ann, Anthony John, Marina, Edward, Victor, Margaret, Matthew, Joseph, Mary Elizabeth, Mary Joan, Mary Ellen, Nancy Madeline. *Education:* St. John's University, B.S. (cum laude), 1941, LL.B. (summa cum laude), 1943; New York University, J.S.D., 1950. *Religion:* Roman Catholic. *Home:* 184 Beach, 143rd St., Neponsit, N.Y. 11694. *Office:* U.S. Customs Court, 1 Federal Plaza, New York, N.Y. 10007.

CAREER: Pratt Institute, Brooklyn, N.Y., instructor in legal aspects of engineering, 1947-48; St. John's University, School of Law, Brooklyn, N.Y., instructor, 1947-49, assistant professor, 1949-50, associate professor, 1950-51, professor, 1951-61, adjunct professor of law, 1969—; Foreign Claims Settlement Commission of the United States, Washington, D.C., chairman, 1961-68; Assistant Secretary of State for Educational and Cultural Affairs, Washington, D.C., 1968-69; U.S. Customs Court, New York, N.Y., judge, 1969—. Visiting professor, Georgetown University, School of Law, 1962-67. Board of Higher Education of the City of New York, member, 1958-69, member emeritus, 1969—. *Military service:* U.S. Army Air Forces, 1943-47. U.S. Air Force Reserve, Judge Advocate General's Department, retired as colonel; received Air Force Commendation Medal, 1961.

MEMBER: American Bar Association (chairman, international and comparative law section, 1965-67), American Society of International Law, Consular Law Society, Judge Advocate's Association, Foreign Law Association (president, 1971-73), Federal Bar Council (president, 1973-74), American Law Institute, American Arbitration Association, National Panel of Arbitrators, National Catholic Educational Association, Reserve Officers Association, New York State Bar Association. *Awards, honors:* Honorary doctorate, University of Aquila, Italy, 1960; Interfaith Award, Morgenstern Foundation, 1961; LL.D. from St. Mary's College (Notre Dame, Ind.), 1968, St. John's University, 1968, and Maryville College (St. Louis, Mo.), 1969; other awards from educational, cultural, religious, and civic organizations.

WRITINGS: Foreign Confiscations in Anglo-American Law, Oceana, 1951; Brief Writing and Oral Argument, Oceana, 1951, 4th edition, 1974; (with Lester B. Orfield) Cases and Materials on International Law, Bobbs-Merrill, 1955, revised edition, 1965; Selected Essays on Equity, Oceana, 1955; (contributor) Grindel, editor, Concept of Freedom, Regnery, 1955; (contributor) Le Regime matrimonial dans les legislations contemporaines, Institut de Droit Compare de l'Universite de Paris, 1957; (with Zechariah Chafee, Jr.) Cases and Materials on Equity, Foundation Press, 1958, 5th edition, 1967; (contributor) International Arbitration: Liber Amicorum for Martin Domke, Nijhoff, 1967; Cases and Materials on Equity and Equitable Remedies, Foundation Press, 1975. Contributor of numerous articles and reviews to legal journals.

*   *   *

READ, Elfreida   1920-

PERSONAL: Born October 2, 1920, in Vladivostok, Russia; daughter of Albert (an accountant) and Maria (Yacub) Ennock; married George J. Read (a business executive), July 10, 1941; children: Jeananne Patricia, Philip Kendall. Education: Attended Shanghai Public School for Girls, 1927-36. Religion: Unitarian. Home: 2686 West King Edward Ave., Vancouver, British Columbia, Canada V6L 1T6.

MEMBER: Western Canadian Writers Club. Awards, honors: Arts Club top poetry award for British Columbia poetry, 1965; second prize in International Co-operation Year playwriting contest, 1965; first prize for short story for children in national Canadian Centennial contest, 1966.

WRITINGS:—All juveniles: The Dragon and the Jadestone, Hutchinson, 1958; The Magic of Light, Hutchinson, 1959; The Enchanted Egg, Hutchinson, 1963, published as The Magical Egg, Lippincott, 1965; The Spell of Chuchuchan, Hutchinson, 1966, World Publishing, 1967; Magic for Granny, Burns & MacEachern, 1967; Twin Rivers, Burns & MacEachern, 1968; No One Need Ever Know, Ginn, 1971; Brothers By Choice (Junior Literary Guild "Book of the Month"), Farrar, Straus, 1974. Also author of poetry, adult plays, and plays for children.

WORK IN PROGRESS: An adult novel.

*   *   *

READ, Piers Paul   1941-

PERSONAL: Born March 7, 1941, in Beaconsfield, England; son of Herbert (a poet) and Margaret (Ludwig) Read; married Emily Boothby, July 28, 1967. Education: St. John's College, Cambridge, B.A., 1961, M.A., 1962. Religion: Roman Catholic. Home: Old Byland, Yorkshire, England. Agent: Deborah Rogers Ltd., 29 Goodge St., London W1P 1FP, England.

CAREER: Times Literary Supplement, London, England, sub-editor, 1964-65; novelist. Awards, honors: Ford Foundation fellow in Berlin, 1963-64; Harkness fellow in New York and Lexington, Mass., 1967-68.

WRITINGS: Game in Heaven with Tussy Marx, Weidenfeld & Nicolson, 1966, McGraw, 1967; The Junkers, Secker & Warburg, 1968, Knopf, 1969; Monk Dawson, Lippincott, 1970; The Professor's Daughter, Lippincott, 1971; The Upstart, Lippincott, 1973; Alive: The Story of the Andes Survivors, Lippincott, 1974. Author of a television play, "Coincidence," produced by British Broadcasting Corp.

SIDELIGHTS: Read's stay in Germany provided him with the backroom for The Junkers. David Williams says it is a novel of "very high quality indeed." He handles the material "with a sure and satisfying sense of form." Martin Seymour-Smith calls the book "cool and clever."

Read has traveled in the Far East, Indochina, Africa, and Europe; he lived in Munich and Berlin over a two-year period.

BIOGRAPHICAL/CRITICAL SOURCES: Spectator, June 21, 1968; Punch, July 17, 1968, January 1, 1969; Carolyn Riley, editor, Contemporary Literary Criticism, Volume IV, 1975.

*   *   *

READE, B(rian) Edmund   1913-

PERSONAL: Born January 13, 1913, in Torquay, England; son of Thomas Glover (an art master) and Susan (King) Reade; married Margaret Ware, April 21, 1941; children: Alban. Education: King's College, Cambridge, B.A., 1934, M.A., 1938. Home: 6 Abingdon Villas, London W.8, England.

CAREER: Victoria and Albert Museum, London, England, assistant keeper, department of engraving, illustration, and design, 1936-58, deputy keeper, department of prints and drawings, 1958-73. Organizer of Alphonse Mucha Exhibit at Victoria and Albert Museum, 1963, and Aubrey Beardsley Exhibit in London, 1966, New York, 1967, and Los Angeles, 1967-68.

WRITINGS: Edward Lear's Parrots, Duckworth, 1949; The Dominance of Spain, Harrap, 1951; Regency Antiques, Batsford, 1953; Art Noveau and Alphonse Mucha, H.M.S.O., 1963, 2nd edition, 1967; Aubrey Beardsley, H.M.S.O., 1966, 2nd edition, 1969, also published as Beardsley, Studio Vista, 1967, Viking, 1969; Ballet Designs and Illustrations, H.M.S.O., 1967; (editor and author of introduction) Sexual Heretics: Male Homosexuality in English Literature from 1850 to 1900, Routledge & Kegan Paul, 1970, Coward, 1971; Eye of a Needle (poems), D'Arch Smith, 1971; Louis Wain, H.M.S.O., 1972. Did catalogues raisonnes for Lear Exhibit in London, 1958, and for Beardsley shows in London, 1966, and New York, 1967. Contributor to art journals in England.

*   *   *

READER, Desmond H.   1920-

PERSONAL: Born June 20, 1920, in London, England; son of Harold Norton (an army major) and Sarah (Wasserfall) Reader; married Dolores Stella Nita (a part-time scriptwriter), October 25, 1950; children: Nicholas, William, Howard, James. Education: Educated in Egypt and Mauritius, 1925-37; Cambridge University, B.A. (honors), 1948, M.A. and Ph.D., 1953. Politics: Progressive Party (South Africa). Religion: Protestant. Home: 3 Kilkenny Rd., Parkview, Johannesburg, South Africa. Office: South African National Institute for Personnel Research, P.O. Box 10319, Johannesburg, South Africa.

CAREER: Has taught in universities; South African National Institute for Personnel Research (psychological, sociological, and industrial research), Johannesburg, chief research officer, beginning 1958. Part-time internship at Tara Mental Hospital, Johannesburg. Member of national executive and council, South African Institute of Race Relations, and chairman of Southern Transvaal region; member of executive board, South Africa National Council on Alcoholism. *Member:* Royal Anthropological Institute of Great Britain and Northern Ireland (fellow), Association of Social Anthropologists of the Commonwealth, South African Psychological Association.

WRITINGS: (Contributor) *The Baumannville Community,* University of Natal, 1955; *The Black Man's Portion: History, Demography and Living Conditions in the Native Locations of East London, Cape Province,* Oxford University Press, 1961; *Zulu Tribe in Transition: The Makhanya of Southern Natal,* Manchester University Press, 1966; *Alcoholism and Excessive Drinking: A Sociological Review,* National Institute for Personnel Research (Johannesburg), 1967; *Drinking Patterns in Rhodesia: Highfield African Township Salisbury,* Institute for Social Research, University of Rhodesia, 1971. Contributor to professional journals.

WORK IN PROGRESS: A further book on Zulu religion and magic; a new thematic apperception test for South African Bantu; a criteria for the distinction rural/urban in African urbanization; sensitivity training as a small-group technique in South Africa.†

* * *

REASKE, Christopher R(ussell) 1941-

PERSONA: Born October 14, 1941, in Montclair, N.J.; son of Herbert Edward (a professor) and Alice (Russell) Reaske; married Mary Katharine Arny, June 29, 1963; children: Suzanne Travis, Katharine Russell. *Education:* Yale University, A.B. (cum laude), 1963; Harvard University, A.M., 1964, Ph.D., 1968. *Home:* 1503 East Park Pl., Ann Arbor, Mich. *Office:* Department of English, University of Michigan, Ann Arbor, Mich. 48104.

CAREER: University of Michigan, Ann Arbor, assistant professor of English, 1968—.

WRITINGS: How to Analyze Poetry, Monarch Books, 1966; *Shakespeare's Othello,* Barrister Publishing Co., 1966; *How to Analyze Drama,* Monarch Books, 1966; (editor) *Seven Essayists: Varieties of Excellence in English Prose,* Scott, Foresman, 1969; *The College Writer's Guide to the Study of Literature,* Random House, 1970; (editor and author of introduction with Robert F. Willson, Jr.) *Student Voices on Political Action, Culture, and the University,* Random House, 1971; (with wife, Mary Traves Arny) *Ecology: A Writer's Handbook,* Random House, 1972; (compiler with John Ray Knott) *Mirrors: An Introduction to Literature,* Canfield Press, 1972, 2nd edition, 1975. Contributor of poetry to *Yale Literary Magazine.*

WORK IN PROGRESS: Style and Rhetoric; poems.†

* * *

REBUFFAT, Gaston 1921-

PERSONAL: Born May 7, 1921, in Marseille, France; son of Marius and Rose (Durbec) Rebuffat; married Francoise Darde; children: Frederique, Joel, France. *Home:* La Dy, Chamonix, Haute-Savoie, France.

CAREER: Mountain-climbing guide, photographer, director of mountain-climbing movies, and author.

WRITINGS: (With Gabriel M. Ollive) *Calanques,* Arthaud, 1949; *Etoiles et tempetes: Six faces nord,* Arthaud, 1954, translation by Wilfrid Noyce and Sir John Hunt published as *Starlight and Storm: The Ascent of Six Great North Faces of the Alps,* Dent, 1956, Dutton, 1957; *Du Mont Blanc a l'Himalaya,* Arthaud, 1955, translation by

Geoffrey Sutton published as *Mont Blanc to Everest,* Studio Publications, and Crowell, 1956; *Neige et Roc,* Hachette, 1959, translation by Eleanor Brockett published as *On Snow and Rock,* Oxford University Press, 1963, new French edition published as *Glace, Neige et Roc,* Hatchett, 1969, translation by Patrick Evans published as *On Ice, Rock and Snow,* Oxford University Press, 1971.

(With Pierre Tairraz) *Entre terre et ciel,* Arthaud, 1962 (based on a film of the same title), translation by Eleanor Brockett published as *Between Heaven and Earth,* Oxford University Press, 1965; *Mont-Blanc: Jardin ferrique,* Hachette, 1962; *Un Guide Raconte,* Hachette, 1964; *Cervin cime exemplaire,* [France], translation by Eleanor Brockett published as *Men and the Matterhorn,* Oxford University Press, 1967; *Le Massif du Mont Blanc: Les 100 plus belles courses,* Denoel, 1973, translation by Jane Taylor and Colin Taylor published as *The Mont Blanc Massif: The 100 Fine Routes,* Oxford University Press, 1975; *Le Massif des Ecrins: Le 100 plus belles courses et randonnees,* Denoel, 1974; *Les Horizon Gagnes,* Denoel, 1975 (based on a film of the same title). Also author of *A la Rencontre du soleil,* 1971. Contributor to *Le Monde.*

* * *

RECK, Rima Drell 1933-

PERSONAL: Born September 29, 1933, in New York, N.Y.; daughter of Jacob and Liza (Maizenberg) Drell; married Andrew J. Reck (a professor of philosophy), August 30, 1956. *Education:* Brandeis University, B.A. (summa cum laude), 1954; graduate study at University of Caen and Sorbonne, University of Paris, 1954-55; Yale University, Ph.D., 1960. *Office:* Department of Foreign Languages, Louisiana State University, New Orleans, La. 70122.

CAREER: Tulane University of Louisiana, New Orleans, instructor in French, 1958-61; Louisiana State University in New Orleans, assistant professor, 1961-64, associate professor of French and comparative literature, 1964-68, professor of comparative literature, 1968—. *Member:* Modern Language Association of America, American Association of Teachers of French, Societe des Professeurs Francais en Amerique, American Association of University Professors, South Central Modern Language Association, Phi Beta Kappa. *Awards, honors:* Fulbright fellowship, 1954-55; American Philosophical Society grants, 1962, 1964; Louisiana State University Research Council grant, 1964; American Council of Learned Societies grants, 1968, 1970; Guggenheim fellow, 1972-73.

WRITINGS: (With others) *Studies in Comparative Literature,* Louisiana State University Press, 1962; (with others) *Bernanos, Confrontations,* Minard (Paris), 1966; (editor) *Explorations of Literature,* Louisiana State University Press, 1966; *Literature and Responsibility: The French Novelist in the Twentieth Century,* Louisiana State University Press, 1969; (contributor) *The Cry of Home,* University of Texas, 1972. Contributor to *Encyclopedia of World Literature in the Twentieth Century,* Ungar; also contributor of articles, translations from the French, and reviews to journals, including *Modern Drama, Yale French Studies,* and *Books Abroad.* Assistant editor, *Southern Review,* 1963-64, associate editor, beginning 1964.

SIDELIGHTS: Rima Reck is fluent in French and Italian, and reads German. *Avocational interests:* Music, sewing, travel.†

REDDAWAY, Peter (Brian) 1939-

PERSONAL: Born September 18, 1939, in Cambridge, England; son of W. B. (an economist) and Barbara (Bennett) Reddaway; married Kathleen Tietgens, 1972. *Education:* Cambridge University, B.A., 1962, M.A., 1965; graduate study at Harvard University, 1962-63, University of Moscow, 1963-64, and London School of Economics and Political Science, 1964-65. *Religion:* Church of England. *Agent:* Patrick Seale, 2 Motcomb St., Belgrave Sq., London, SW1, England. *Office:* London School of Economics and Political Science, University of London, Houghton St., London W.C.2, England.

CAREER: University of London, London School of Economics and Political Science, London, England, lecturer, 1965-72, senior lecturer in political science with special reference to Russia, 1972—. Free-lance broadcaster for British Broadcasting Corp. and other stations. Adviser, Amnesty International. *Member:* American Association for the Advancement of Slavic Studies, National Association for Soviet and East European Studies (Britain), Great Britain-U.S.S.R. Association, Centre for the Study of Religion and Communism (Britain), Writers and Scholars Educational Trust (Britain).

WRITINGS: (Editor with Leonard Schapiro, and contributor) *Lenin: The Man, the Theorist, the Leader—A Reappraisal,* Pall Mall, 1967; (contributor) W. C. Fletcher, A. Strover, editors, *Religion and the Search for New Ideals in the USSR,* Praeger, 1967; (editor) *Soviet Short Stories,* Volume II, Penguin, 1968; (contributor) *USSR: Dibattito nella Communita Cristiana,* Jaca Book (Milan), 1968; (contributor) Christopher Hill, editor, *Rights and Wrongs: Some Essays on Human Rights,* Penguin, 1969; (editor) *Uncensored Russia: The Human Rights Movements in the Soviet Union,* McGraw, 1972. Contributor to *Soviet Studies, Survey, Problems of Communism, New Statesman, Spectator, Economist, Frontier,* and to newspapers in England.

WORK IN PROGRESS: A study of the Soviet labor camp system since the mid 1950's.

SIDELIGHTS: Reddaway is fluent in Russian and French, and competent in German. *Avocational interests:* Singing, theater-going, the arts, sports, walking.

BIOGRAPHICAL/CRITICAL SOURCES: New York Times Book Review, January 7, 1968.

* * *

REDDING, Robert Hull 1919-

PERSONAL: Born December 3, 1919, in Los Angeles, Calif.; married Grace Feeney, July 14, 1956. *Education:* Graduate of Fairbanks (Alaska) High School. *Home address:* P.O. Box 546, Valdez, Alaska 99686.

CAREER: Resident of Alaska for forty-seven years, living in every geographical section, and working at a wide variety of jobs. *Military service:* U.S. Army Air Forces, 1942-46; became sergeant. *Member:* Pioneers of Alaska. *Awards, honors:* First prize for nonfiction, League of Alaska Writers, 1965; prizes in poetry, juvenile writing, and fiction, League of Alaska Writers, 1966.

WRITINGS—All juveniles: *Aluk: An Alaskan Caribou,* Doubleday, 1967; *Mara: An Alaskan Weasel,* Doubleday, 1968; *North to the Wilderness: The Story of an Alaskan Boy,* Doubleday, 1970. Stories, articles, and poems have been published in youth magazines and some adult periodicals; publications also include a series of essays on Alaska in the 1930's.

WORK IN PROGRESS: More juveniles with an Alaskan background; books about animals.

* * *

REDEKOP, John Harold 1932-

PERSONAL: Born November 29, 1932, in Herbert, Saskatchewan, Canada; son of Jacob Frank (a teacher) and Agnes (Wiebe) Redekop; married Doris Nikkel, August 21, 1956; children: Wendy, Gary, Heather, Bonnie. *Education:* University of British Columbia, B.A., 1954, B.Ed., 1958; University of Heidelberg, graduate study, 1955-56; University of California, Berkeley, M.A., 1961; University of Washington, Seattle, Ph.D., 1965. *Religion:* Mennonite Brethren. *Home:* 298 Ferndale Place, Waterloo, Ontario, Canada N2J 3X9. *Office:* Political Science Department, Wilfrid Laurier University, Waterloo, Ontario, Canada.

CAREER: Langley (British Columbia) School District, high school teacher, 1956-60; Pacific College, Fresno, Calif., assistant professor, 1964-66, associate professor of political science, 1966-68; Wilfrid Laurier University, Waterloo, Ontario, professor of political science, 1968—. *Member:* Canadian Political Science Association.

WRITINGS: The American Far Right: A Case Study of Billy James Hargis and Christian Crusade, Eerdmans, 1967; *The Star Spangled Beaver: Twenty-four Canadians Look South,* Peter Martin Associates, 1972; *Making Political Decisions,* Herald Press, 1972; *Labor Problems in Christian Perspective,* Eerdmans, 1972. Contriutor to religious journals; regular columnist, *Mennonite Brethren Herald.*

WORK IN PROGRESS: Political Socialization, a study of Canada's daily papers; *Interpretations of Canadian Politics.*

* * *

REDFERN, W(alter) D(avid) 1936-

PERSONAL: Born February 22, 1936, in Liverpool, England; son of Walter Barton and Charlotte (Jones) Redfern; married Angela Kirkup (a schoolteacher), March 30, 1963. *Education:* Cambridge University, B.A., 1957, M.A. and Ph.D., 1960. *Home:* 18 Northcourt Ave., Reading, Berkshire, England. *Office:* Faculty of Letters, University of Reading, Reading, Berkshire, England.

CAREER: University of Reading, Reading, Berkshire, England, lecturer in department of French studies, 1960-72, reader, 1972—.

WRITINGS: The Private World of Jean Giono, Blackwell, 1967; (contributor) J. Flower, editor, *France Today,* Methuen, 1971, 2nd edition, 1973; (author of introduction) Jules Valles, *Le Bachelier,* University of London Press, 1972; *Paul Nizan,* Princeton University Press, 1972.

WORK IN PROGRESS: A study of Georges Darien.

AVOCATIONAL INTERESTS: Sports, cinema, music, reading.

* * *

REED, Ishmael 1938-

PERSONAL: Born February 22, 1938, in Chattanooga, Tenn.; son of Bennie (an auto worker) and Thelma (Coleman) Reed; married Priscilla Rose, September 1960 (separated, 1963); children: Timothy Brett (daughter). *Education:* State University of New York at Buffalo, student, 1956-60. *Politics:* Independent. *Agent:* James Seligmann, Inc., 280 Madison Ave., New York, N.Y. 10016.

CAREER: Writer. Co-founder of the *East Village Other* and *Advance* (Newark community newspaper), 1965; editorial director, Yardbird Publishing Co., Inc., 1971; director, Reed, Cannon & Johnson Communications Co., 1973. Guest lecturer, University of California, Berkeley, 1968, 1969, 1974, and 1976; lecturer, University of Washington, Seattle, 1969-70; visiting professor of modern literature series, State University of New York at Buffalo, summer, 1975. Member of board of directors, Coordinating Council of Literary Magazines. *Awards, honors:* Nominated for Pulitzer Prize in poetry, 1973; National Institute of Arts and Letters award, for best non-commercial novel of 1974; National Endowment fellowship for creative writing, 1974; Guggenheim Memorial Foundation award for fiction, 1975.

WRITINGS: The Free-Lance Pallbearers (novel), Doubleday, 1967; (contributor) Walter Lowenfels, editor, *Where Is Vietnam?: American Poets Respond*, Anchor Books, 1967; *Yellow Back Radio Broke-Down*, Doubleday, 1969; (editor) *19 Necromancers from Now*, Doubleday, 1970; *Mumbo Jumbo*, Doubleday, 1972; *Conjure* (poetry), University of Massachusetts Press, 1972; *Chattanooga* (poetry), Random House, 1973; *The Last Days of Louisiana Red*, Random House, 1974; *Secretary to the Spirits* (poetry), Nok Publishers, 1975; *Flight to Canada*, Random House, 1976.

Contributor of articles and reviews to *New York Times, Los Angeles Times, Washington Post, San Francisco Chronicle, Black World, Ramparts,* and *Arts Magazine;* also contributor to *Poets of Today, Liberator,* and *Umbra.*

WORK IN PROGRESS: A film script, "Black Halloween."

SIDELIGHTS: Martin Tucker says of Reed and *The Free-Lance Pallbearers:* "Ishmael Reed can hardly be called a camp follower. His novel inverts conventional attitudes for sustained comic effect; his feints are brilliant and his punches swift.... However, he is prone to rely on the in-joke and to join in a growing army of writers who 'grotest' too much." Sara Blackburn finds the book quite timely.

In an interview with John O'Brien, Ishmael Reed when asked about the novel-is-dead idea, stated: "The novel-is-dead idea is probably something created by businessmen who are more interested in pushing books that sell, books about how to do things or how to diet. Storytelling will always exist.... You'll get more independent publishing companies, more controlled by artists and writers. Small publishers. Literature will be kept alive and will endure."

BIOGRAPHICAL/CRITICAL SOURCES: Commonweal, January 26, 1968; *Nation,* February 5, 1968; Joe David Bellamy, editor, *The New Fiction: Interviews with Innovative American Writers,* University of Illinois Press, 1974; Carolyn Riley, editor, *Contemporary Literary Criticism,* Volume II, 1974, Volume III, 1975, Volume V, 1976, Volume VI, 1976.

* * *

REEVES, Bruce Douglas 1941-

PERSONAL: Born August 27, 1941, in Salt Lake City, Utah; son of Paul Sylvester (a tilesetter) Florence (Hyler) Reeves; married Sherrill McPhee (a children's librarian), September 29, 1964; children: Simone Patricia. *Education:* Attended San Jose State College (now University), 1959-61, and University of California, 1963-64. *Politics:* Stevensonian Democrat. *Religion:* Agnostic. *Residence:* Berkeley, Calif. *Agent:* Scott Meredith Literary Agency, Inc., 845 Third Ave., New York, N.Y. 10022.

CAREER: "Have worked in several different libraries, but never on a career basis. Have always considered myself a writer, even during the years before I sold anything. Was employed longest at the San Jose Public Library, San Jose, Calif., and the Bancroft Library, University of California, Berkeley. Am also a serious painter, working primarily in oils and watercolor, as well as in ink and pastel. Specialize in portraits and what might be called psychological paintings (always of human beings)." *Member:* California Writer's Club (1966-67).

WRITINGS: The Night Action (novel), New American Library, 1966. Also author of *Man on Fire* (novel), 1971. Has also written television plays for San Francisco Screen Artists Repertory Company, 1973-74. Contributor to *Playboy* and other periodicals.

WORK IN PROGRESS: Carry Me Along, a novel; *North Beach,* a book of short stories; *The Movie Freak,* a novel; *The Househusband,* a novel; critical essays for *The Masterplots,* new edition, for Salem Press.

AVOCATIONAL INTERESTS: Collecting art, including works by Picasso, Grosz, Dali, and Charlot; travel.

* * *

REGER, Roger 1933-

PERSONAL: Born February 26, 1933, in North Dakota; son of Arthur W. (a laborer) and Hilda (Hohbein) Reger; married Janice Bakke (a registered nurse), February 8, 1960 (divorced, 1971); children: John, Jane, Karl. *Education:* University of Texas, B.A., 1957, M.A., 1958; Eastern Michigan University, M.A.Ed., 1962; University of Michigan, Ph.D., 1974. *Politics:* Democrat. *Religion:* Unitarian Universalist. *Home:* 98 Wesley Ave., Buffalo, N.Y. 14214. *Office:* Board of Cooperative Educational Services, 455 Cayuga Rd., Buffalo, N.Y. 14225.

CAREER: Wayne County Training School, Northville, Mich., clinical psychologist, 1960-63; Wayne (Mich.) community schools, school psychologist, 1963-65; Board of Cooperative Educational Services, Buffalo, N.Y., director of special educational services, 1965—. *Military service:* U.S. Navy, 1951-54. *Member:* American Psychological Association, Society for Research in Child Development, American Educational Research Association, American Association for the Advancement of Science, Council for Exceptional Children.

WRITINGS: School Psychology, C. C Thomas, 1965; (with Wendy Schroeder and Kathie Uschold) *Special Education: Children with Learning Problems,* Oxford University Press, 1968; *Preschool Programming of Children with Disabilities,* C. C Thomas, 1970.

* * *

REICHARD, Robert S. 1923-

PERSONAL: Born May 10, 1923, in New York, N.Y.; son of Theodore (a sales manager) and Etta (Sahr) Reichard; married Hazel Warmflash, July 22, 1957; children: Alison, Peter. *Education:* City College (now City College of the City University of New York), B.B.A., 1943; New York University, graduate study, 1948-54. *Home:* 4555 Henry Hudson Pkwy., New York, N.Y. 10471.

CAREER: Institute of World Affairs, New York City, research statistician, 1946-50; Prentice-Hall, Inc., New York City, economics editor, 1950-56; Curtiss-Wright, Woodridge, N.J., economic analyst, 1956-57; McGraw-Hill Book Co., New York City, economics editor, 1957-72; economics and price editor, Technical Publishing, 1972—. Advisor to Bureau of Labor Statistics. Also instructor in college economics in evening classes. *Military service:* U.S. Army, 1940-43. *Member:* American Economic Association, American Marketing Association, American Statistical Association.

WRITINGS: Practical Techniques of Sales Forecasting, McGraw, 1966; *The Numbers Game,* McGraw, 1972; *The Figure Finaglers,* McGraw, 1974. Contributor to professional journals.

* * *

REID, Mildred I. 1908-

PERSONAL: Born April 29, 1908, in Boston, Mass.; daughter of Julius (an artist) and Harriet (Fest) Weinzerl; married C. Allan Reid, 1928 (died November, 1958); children: Robert Allan. *Education:* Columbia University, student, 1926-28. *Religion:* Protestant. *Home:* Writers' Colony, Penacook Rd., Contoocook, N.H. 03229; and 917 Bucida Rd., Delray Beach, Fla. 33444 (winter).

CAREER: Professional dancer, 1918-25; professional singer, 1918-41; began literary criticism service for writers, 1947, operating a summer colony at Contoocook, N.H., 1947—, and counseling writers by correspondence and in classes conducted (at various times) in Chicago, Boston, and Florida. Professional lecturer in United States and Canada. *Member:* National League of American Pen Women. *Awards, honors:* Monthly Krock's Award, The Manuscriptors Club, 1956, for *The Devil's Handmaidens.*

WRITINGS: Writers: Here's How!, House of Little Books, 1940, revised edition, Burkehaven, 1974; *Writers: Let's Plot!,* Humphries, 1943, revised edition, Burkehaven, 1974; *Writers: Help Yourselves!,* Wilcox & Follett, 1944; *Writers: Make It Sell!,* Wilcox & Follett, 1944, revised edition, Burkehaven, 1975; (with Delmar E. Bordeaux) *Writers: Try Short Shorts,* Bellevue Books, 1947; *Writers: Learn to Earn!,* Humphries, 1948; *The Devil's Handmaidens* (novel), Humphries, 1951; *Writers: Why Stop Now!,* Burkehaven, 1962, revised edition, 1974; *Over Fool's Hill* (novel), Humphries, 1964. Also writer of radio scripts, short stories, articles, plays, and poems.

* * *

REINEMER, Vic 1923-

PERSONAL: Born June 7, 1923, near Circle, Mont.; son of Henry R. (a farmer) and Ida (Steiner) Reinemer; married Lois Grindy, June 23, 1951; children: Eric Paul, Michael Mark, Steven John, Jonathan Peter. *Education:* Attended Shrivenham University; University of Montana, B.A., 1948; graduate study at the Sorbonne, Paris, and George Washington University. *Politics:* Democrat. *Religion:* Methodist. *Residence:* Falls Church, Va. *Agent:* Marie Rodell—Frances Collin Literary Agency, 141 East 55th St., New York, N.Y. 10022. *Office:* 161 Russell, Senate Office Building, Washington, D.C.

CAREER: Western Livestock Reporter (magazine), Billings, Mont., field representative; *Freedom and Union* (magazine), Washington, D.C., assistant to editor, 1950-51; *Charlotte News,* Charlotte, N.C., associate editor, 1951-55; U.S. Senate Staff, Washington, D.C., executive secretary, 1955-73; Senate Subcommittee on Reports, Accounting, and Management, staff director, 1973—. Visiting lecturer, University of Montana, fall, 1960. Chairman, Fairfax County Housing Committee, 1962; commissioner, Fairfax

County Consumer Protection Commission, 1973—; member of board of directors, Wesley Housing Development Corp., 1974—. *Military service:* U.S. Army Air Forces, pilot, 1942-45; became first lieutenant; received Air Medal and four oak leaf clusters and Presidential Unit Citation (twice). *Awards, honors:* Sidney Hillman Award for editorials on civil rights and civil liberties, 1954; Western States Water and Power Conference, George Norris Award, 1972.

WRITINGS: (With Lee Metcalf) *Overcharge,* McKay, 1967. Contributor to *New York Times Magazine, Progressive, New Republic,* and *Nation.*

* * *

REINING, Conrad C(opeland) 1918-

PERSONAL: Surname is pronounced *Rye*-ning; born January 17, 1918, in Copley, Ohio; son of Henry (a restaurant owner) and Elizabeth (Schilling) Reining; married Priscilla Alden Copeland (an anthropologist), June 26, 1944; children: Robert Cushman, Anne Elizabeth, Conrad Copeland Schilling. *Education:* University of Akron, B.A., 1940; University of Chicago, graduate study, 1940-42; Oxford University, B.Litt., 1952, D.Phil., 1959. *Politics:* Democratic. *Religion:* Episcopalian. *Home:* 3601 Rittenhouse St. Northwest, Washington, D.C. 20015. *Office:* Catholic University of America, Washington, D.C. 20064.

CAREER: University of Minnesota, Minneapolis, assistant professor of anthropology, 1956-59; American University, Washington, D.C., associate research professor in Foreign Areas Studies Division, 1959-60; U.S. Library of Congress, Washington, D.C., head of African Section, 1960-66; Catholic University of America, Washington, D.C., professor of anthropology, 1966—. *Military service:* U.S. Army, 1942-46; became major; received battle stars for combat duty in Mediterranean and European theaters. *Member:* American Anthropological Association (fellow; secretary, 1968-70), African Studies Association (fellow; member, board of directors, 1967-70), American Association for the Advancement of Science (fellow), American Ethnological Society (fellow), Society for Applied Anthropology (fellow), East African Academy of Science, Royal Anthropological Institute (Great Britain; fellow), Washington Anthropological Society (vice-president, 1966-68; president, 1968-70).

WRITINGS: (Co-author) *Area Handbook for Germany,* U.S. Government Printing Office, for Foreign Areas Studies Division, American University, 1961; (editor) *A List of American Doctoral Dissertations on Africa,* U.S. Government Printing Office, for Library of Congress, 1962; (editor with Walter W. Deshler) *Agricultural Development Schemes in Sub-Saharan Africa: A Bibliography,* U.S. Government Printing Office, for Library of Congress, 1963; *The Zande Scheme: An Anthropological Case Study of Economic Development in Africa,* Northwestern University Press, 1966. Contributor to *American Anthropologist.*

WORK IN PROGRESS: A history of the idea of practical use of anthropology in the British Empire; reports on one year's field research in rural Hungary; a study on historical demographic ethnology of German speakers in Hungary.

AVOCATIONAL INTERESTS: Electronics, woodworking, photography.

* * *

REISMAN, John M(ark) 1930-

PERSONAL: Born May 22, 1930, in Perth Amboy, N.J.;

son of Harry (a plumber) and Frieda (Feuerman) Reisman; married Margo Sue Jacobson, June 19, 1955; children: Hope, David, Carl, Andrew. *Education:* Rutgers University, B.S., 1952; Michigan State University, M.A., 1955, Ph.D., 1958. *Home:* 730 Milburn St., Evanston, Ill. 60201. *Office:* Department of Psychology, De Paul University, Chicago, Ill. 60614.

CAREER: Children's Memorial Hospital, Chicago, Ill., staff psychologist, 1958-59; Northwestern University Medical School, Chicago, instructor in psychology, 1958-59; Rochester Mental Health Center, Rochester, N.Y., chief psychologist, children and youth division, 1959-69; Memphis State University, Memphis, Tenn., professor of psychology and director of psychology clinic, 1969-75; De Paul University, Chicago, professor of psychology and director of clinical training, 1975—. Clinical associate, University of Rochester; consultant, Hillside Children's Center. *Military service:* U.S. Navy, 1952-54; became lieutenant junior grade. *Member:* American Psychological Association.

WRITINGS: The Development of Clinical Psychology, Appleton, 1966; *Toward the Intergration of Psychotherapy,* Wiley, 1971; *Principles of Psychotherapy with Children,* Wiley, 1973; *The History of Clinical Psychology,* Irvington, 1976. Contributor to professional journals.

WORK IN PROGRESS: The Anatomy of Friendship, completion expected, 1980.

*   *   *

REISS, Albert J(ohn), Jr. 1922-

PERSONAL: Born December 9, 1922, in Cascade, Wis.; son of Albert John and Erma Amanda (Schueler) Reiss; married Emma Lucille Hutto, June, 1953; children: Peter C., Paul Wetherington, Amy. *Education:* Marquette University, Ph.B., 1944; University of Chicago, M.A., 1948, Ph.D., 1949. *Home:* 45 Center Rd., Woodbridge, Conn. 06525. *Office:* Department of Sociology, Yale University, New Haven, Conn. 06520.

CAREER: Illinois Board of Public Welfare Commissioners, Springfield, social research analyst, 1946-47; University of Chicago, Chicago, Ill., instructor, 1947-49, assistant professor, 1949-52, associate director of Chicago Community Inventory, 1947-52; Vanderbilt University, Nashville, Tenn., associate professor, 1952-54, professor of sociology, 1954-58, chairman of department of sociology and anthropology, 1952-58; University of Iowa, Iowa City, professor of sociology, 1958-60, chairman of department of sociology and anthropology, 1959-60, director of Iowa Urban Community Research Center, 1958-60; University of Wisconsin, Madison, professor of sociology and director of Wisconsin Survey Research Laboratory, 1960-61; University of Michigan, Ann Arbor, professor of sociology, 1961-70, chairman of department, 1964-70, director of Center for Research on Social Organization, 1961-70; Yale University, New Haven, Conn., professor of sociology and of Institute for Social and Policy Studies, and lecturer in law, 1970—, chairman of sociology department, 1972—. Member of Mental Health Small Grants Committee, National Institutes of Health, 1960-64; member of advisory panel for sociology and social psychology, National Science Foundation, 1963-65; member of behavioral sciences panel to Wooldridge Committee, Executive Office of the President, Office of Science and Technology, 1964; consultant to President's Commission on Law Enforcement and Administration of Justice, 1966-67, and National Advisory Commission on Civil Disorders, 1967-68; member, National

Advisory Committee on Juvenile Justice and Delinquency Prevention, 1975—. *Military service:* U.S. Army Air Forces, 1943-44.

MEMBER: American Sociological Association (fellow; member of council, 1962-65; member of executive committee, 1963-65), American Association for the Advancement of Science (fellow), Society for the Study of Social Problems (member of council, 1965-67; vice-president, 1966-67; president, 1969), American Statistical Association, Law and Society Association, International Society of Criminology (associate member), International Association of Chiefs of Police (associate member), Ohio Valley Sociological Association (president, 1966). *Awards, honors:* Bicentennial Medal, Columbia University; M.A. (privatim), Yale University, 1970.

WRITINGS: (Editor) *Selected Readings in Social Pathology,* University of Chicago Bookstore, 1947; (with E. W. Burgess, Louis Wirth, and Don T. Blackiston) *Survey of the Chicago Crime Commission,* Chicago Crime Commission, 1948.

(Editor with Paul K. Hatt) *Reader in Urban Sociology,* Free Press of Glencoe, 1951, revised edition published as *Cities and Society: A Reader in Urban Sociology,* 1957; *Patterns of Occupation Mobility for Workers in Four Cities,* Chicago Community Inventory Publications, 1953; *A Review and Evaluation of Research on the Community: A Memorandum to the Committee on Social Behavior,* Social Science Research Council, 1954; (with Jay W. Artis and Albert L. Rhodes) *Population Handbook: Nashville,* Institute of Research and Training in the Social Sciences, Vanderbilt University, 1955; (with Otis Dudley Duncan) *Social Characteristics of Urban and Rural Communities,* Wiley, 1956; (editor with Elizabeth Wirth Marvick) *Community Life and Social Policy: Selected Papers By Louis Wirth,* University of Chicago Press, 1956; *A Socio-Psychological Study of Conforming and Deviating Behavior Among Adolescents,* University of Iowa Press, 1959.

Occupations and Social Status, Free Press of Glencoe, 1961; (editor and author of introduction) *Louis Wirth on Cities and Social Life,* University of Chicago Press, 1964; (editor and author of introduction) *Schools in a Changing Society,* Free Press, 1965; (with Rosemary Sarri and Robert Vinter) *Treating Youthful Offenders in the Community,* Correctional Research Associates, 1966; *Studies in Crime and Law Enforcement in Major Metropolitan Areas, Field Studies III,* two volumes, U.S. Government Printing Office, 1967; (editor) *Cooley and Sociological Analysis,* University of Michigan Press, 1968; *The Police and the Public,* Yale University Press, 1971.

Contributor: R. M. Fisher, editor, *The Metropolis in Modern Life,* Doubleday, 1955; *Juvenile Delinquency and Education,* U.S. Government Printing Office, 1956; Hans Zetterberg, editor, *Sociology in the United States of America,* UNESCO, 1956; William Dobriner, editor, *The Suburban Community,* Putnam, 1958; Hendrick M. Ruitenbeck, *The Problem of Homosexuality in Modern Society,* Dutton, 1963; Ruth S. Caven, editor, *Readings in Juvenile Delinquency,* Lippincott, 1964; Howard S. Becker, editor, *The Other Side: Perspectives on Deviance,* Free Press of Glencoe, 1964; Rose Giallombardo, editor, *Juvenile Delinquency,* Wiley, 1966; David J. Burdua, editor, *The Police: Six Sociological Essays,* Wiley, 1967; John Gagnon and William Simon, editors, *Sexual Deviance,* Harper, 1967; Howard S. Becker and others, editors, *Institutions and the Person,* Aldine, 1968; Barbara McLennan, editor, *Crime in*

Urban Society, Dunellen, 1970; Herbert Costner, editor, *Sociological Methodology,* Jossey-Bass, 1971; Angus Campbell and Philip Converse, editors, *The Human Meaning of Social Change,* Russell Sage, 1972; Daniel Glaser, editor, *Handbook of Criminology,* Rand McNally, 1974; N. J. Demerath, III and others, editors, *Social Policy and Sociology,* Academic Press, 1975; A. Wallace Sinarko and L. Broedburg, editors, *Perspectives on Attitude Assessment: Surveys and their Alternatives,* Smithsonian Institution Press, 1975.

Author or editor of various other survey reports. Editor, ''Arnold and Caroline Rose Monograph'' series of the American Sociological Association, 1968-71. Contributor to *The Municipal Yearbook,* 1957, *Britannica Book of the Year,* 1959, *Encyclopaedia Britannica,* 1959, *A Dictionary of the Social Sciences,* Free Press of Glencoe, 1964, *Worterbuch der Soziologie,* 1965, *The New Catholic Encyclopedia,* 1967, and to sociology, law, and education journals. Book review editor, *Journal of Marriage and Family Living,* 1949-52; associate editor, *American Journal of Sociology,* 1950-52, 1961-64, *Social Problems,* 1961-64, and *Social Forces,* 1974-77; sociology editor, *Encyclopedia of Social Sciences,* 1961-67.

* * *

REISS, Edmund (Allen) 1934-

PERSONAL: Surname is pronounced Rees; born October 12, 1934, in Brooklyn, N.Y.; son of Edmund Lewis (an executive with Standard Oil of New Jersey) and Mabel (Curfman) Reiss; married Dorothy Kauffman, August 20, 1955; married second wife, Louise Horner, July 17, 1964; children: (first marriage) Kathryn Lynn, Geoffrey Scott. *Education:* Pennsylvania State University, B.A., 1955, M.A., 1956; Harvard University, Ph.D., 1960. *Office:* Department of English, Duke University, Durham, N.C. 27706.

CAREER: Suffolk University, Boston, Mass., instructor in English, 1957-60; Western Reserve University (now Case Western Reserve University), Cleveland, Ohio, assistant professor, 1960-63, associate professor of English, 1963-64; Pennsylvania State University, University Park, associate professor of English, 1964-67; Duke University, Durham, N.C., professor of English, 1967—. Visiting professor, Harvard University, summers, 1969, 1970, and 1973, Columbia University, 1973. *Member:* International Association of University Professors of English, International Arthurian Society, Modern Language Association of America, Mediaeval Academy of America, Modern Humanities Research Association, American Comparative Literature Association, Dante Society of America, National Council of Teachers of English. *Awards, honors:* American Philosophical Society fellow, 1962, grant, 1970; American Council of Learned Societies grant, 1963; Huntington Library fellowship, 1965.

WRITINGS: (Editor and author of foreword) Mark Twain, *The Mysterious Stranger, and Other Stories,* New American Library, 1962; (editor and author of afterword) Mark Twain, *A Connecticut Yankee in King Arthur's Court,* New American Library, 1963; *Sir Thomas Malory,* Twayne, 1966; *Elements of Literary Analysis,* World Publishing, 1967.

The Art of the Middle English Lyric: Essays in Criticism, University of Georgia Press, 1972; (contributor) *Chaucer the Love Poet,* University of Georgia Press, 1973. Contributor to literary journals. Bibliographer and Medieval Latin

section head, *International Bibliography of the Modern Language Association;* co-editor, *Chaucer Review;* associate editor, *Journal of Medieval and Renaissance Studies,* 1970—.

WORK IN PROGRESS: Editing *The Art of Geoffrey Chaucer: A Collaborative Study,* for Duke University Press; co-editing *The Complete Poetry of John Skelton,* for Clarendon Press, and *A Concordance to the Poetry of John Skelton; William Dunbar,* for Twayne; and *Themes and Patterns in the Canterbury Tales.*†

* * *

RENAN, Sheldon (Jackson) 1941-

PERSONAL: Born June 29, 1941, in Portland, Ore.; son of George Donald (owner of a food distributing firm) and Louise (Esterly) Renan; married Barbara Stross (an educational consultant), March 14, 1966; children: George. *Education:* Yale University, B.A., 1963.

CAREER: Free-lance writer, and copywriter for advertising agencies prior to 1968; University of California Art Museum, Berkeley, director of film programs, 1968-70, director of Pacific Film Archive, 1971-74; television producer, Renan Productions, 1975; currently producer for Public Broadcasting Service. Member of junior council, Museum of Modern Art, New York, N.Y., 1965-66.

WRITINGS: An Introduction to the American Underground Film, Dutton, 1967 (published in England as *The Underground Film: An Introduction to Its Development in America,* Studio Vista, 1969).

Television scripts: (With Edwin O. Reischaver and Donald Richie, and producer) ''The Japanese Film'' series, Public Television Service, 1975; (and producer) ''The International Animation Festival'' series, Public Television Service, 1975. Has written some film scripts for commercial shorts, and film criticism. Contributor of short stories to literary magazines, and articles to *Film Culture, Art Voices, San Francisco Magazine,* and other periodicals.

SIDELIGHTS: Nicholas Gosling welcomes *An Introduction to the Underground Film,* saying it ''is nearly as important for its mere existence as for its content. An understanding of Underground Cinema's true aims and achievements is hard to come by with so few facts available. A serious book on the subject is therefore to be rejoiced over.''

Renan has lived in Japan for twelve months over a six year period.

BIOGRAPHICAL/CRITICAL SOURCES: Observer Review, July 7, 1968.

* * *

RENKEN, Aleda 1907-

PERSONAL: Born June 21, 1907, in Jefferson City, Mo.; daughter of John L. and Lilly (Kaeppel) Beck; married C. J. Renken (a Civil Service employee), June 14, 1931; children: John, Elizabeth (Mrs. Terrance Boone), Tim, Anne (Mrs. Anthony Marshall), Steve. *Education:* Attended Warrensburg Teachers College, University of Missouri, and Lincoln University, Jefferson City, Mo. *Religion:* Lutheran. *Home:* Route 2, Holts Summit, Mo.

CAREER: Department of Conservation, Jefferson City, Mo., circulation manager, *Conservationist,* beginning 1953; currently free-lance writer. *Member:* Jefferson City Writers Guild. *Awards, honors:* Writer of the Year award from Missouri State Writer's Guild.

WRITINGS—Juvenile; all published by Concordia, except as indicated: *Kathy*, F. Watts, 1967; *Never the Same Again*, Westminster, 1971; *Jeff and the Bad Guy*, 1973; *Picked on Pat*, 1973; *Rough Rapids Ahead*, 1974; *The Two Christmases*, 1974; *Adventure on Padre Island*, 1975; *Mystery of Cottage Cove*, 1975. Contributor of articles and short stories to *Conservationist*, *Wee Wisdom*, and *Cresset*.

WORK IN PROGRESS: Two young adult novels, *One Last Time to Suck Your Thumb* and *Dig from the Minute*; an adult novel, not yet titled.

AVOCATIONAL INTERESTS: Fishing, hiking, oil painting, and bowling.

*   *   *

RENSHAW, Patrick (Richard George) 1936-

PERSONAL: Born February 26, 1936, in London, England; son of George Albert (a journalist) and Winifred Norah (Thorpe) Renshaw; married Mary Davies (a teacher and lecturer), August 29, 1959; children: Patrick Donovan Maynard, David George Caradoc, Rebecca, John Howell Richard. *Education:* Studied at Jesus College, Oxford, 1956-59, Queen's College, Oxford, 1959-60, and Northwestern University, 1960-61. *Politics:* Labour Party. *Religion:* Agnostic. *Residence:* Sheffield, England. *Agent:* Curtis Brown Group Ltd., 1 Craven Hill, London, W2 3EW, England. *Office:* Department of History, Sheffield University, Sheffield, England.

CAREER: Bedfordshire Times, Bedfordshire, England, reporter, 1961-62; *Oxford Mail and Times*, Oxford, England, reporter and sub-editor, 1962-68; Sheffield University, Sheffield, England, lecturer in modern history, 1968—. Visiting lecturer, Syracuse University, 1971-72. *Military service:* Royal Air Force, 1954-56. *Member:* National Union of Journalists (branch treasurer, 1965-66), British Association for American Studies, Society for the Study of Labour History, Oxford Union Society.

WRITINGS: The Wobblies: The Story of Syndicalism in the United States, Doubleday, 1967; *The General Strike*, Methuen, 1975; *Nine Days in May*, Methuen, 1975, published as *Nine Days That Shook Britain*, Doubleday, 1976. Contributor to *History Today, Guardian, Sunday Times* (London), *Times Literary Supplement, Journal of American Studies*, and other periodicals.

WORK IN PROGRESS: A book-length study of the race relations in urban America, 1890-1940.

SIDELIGHTS: Some of Renshaw's writings have been translated into Italian and Japanese.

*   *   *

RESCHER, Nicholas 1928-

PERSONAL: Born July 15, 1928, in Germany; naturalized U.S. citizen in 1944; son of Erwin Hans (an attorney) and Meta (Landau) Rescher; first married in 1951; married second wife, Dorothy Henle, February 10, 1968; children: two sons, one daughter. *Education:* Queens College (now Queens College of the City University of New York), B.S., 1949; Princeton University, M.A., 1950, Ph.D., 1951. *Home:* 1200 Sheridan Ave., Pittsburgh, Pa. 15206. *Office:* Department of Philosophy, University of Pittsburgh, Pittsburgh, Pa. 15260.

CAREER: Princeton University, Princeton, N.J., instructor in philosophy, 1951-52; RAND Corp., Santa Monica, Calif., research mathematician, 1954-57; Lehigh University, Bethlehem, Pa., associate professor of philosophy, 1957-61; University of Pittsburgh, Pittsburgh, Pa., professor of philosophy, 1961-70, university professor, 1970—. *Military service:* U.S. Marine Corps, 1952-54. *Member:* Royal Asiatic Society of Great Britain and Ireland (fellow), International Union of History and Philosophy of Science (secretary general, 1970-75), Sigma Xi. *Awards, honors:* Ford Foundation fellow, 1959-60; L.H.D., Loyola University (Chicago), 1970; Guggenheim fellow, 1971-72.

WRITINGS: (With Olaf Helmer-Hirschberg) *On the Epistemology of the Inexact Sciences*, RAND Corporation, 1960; *Al-Farabi: An Annotated Bibliography*, University of Pittsburgh Press, 1962; *Al-Farabi's Short Commentary on Aristotle's Prior Analytics*, University of Pittsburgh Press, 1963; *The Development of Arabic Logic*, University of Pittsburgh Press, 1964; *Studies in the History of Arabic Logic*, University of Pittsburgh Press, 1964; *Introduction to Logic*, St. Martin's, 1964; *Hypothetical Reasoning*, North-Holland Publishing, 1964; *Al-Kindi: An Annotated Bibliography*, University of Pittsburgh Press, 1964; *Logic of Commands*, Dover, 1966; *Temporal Modalities in Arabic Logic*, Humanities, 1966; (editor) *Galen and the Syllogism*, University of Pittsburgh Press, 1966; *The Philosophy of Leibniz*, Prentice-Hall, 1967; (editor) *The Logic of Decision and Action* (essays), University of Pittsburgh Press, 1967; *Distributive Justice*, Bobbs-Merrill, 1967; *Studies in Arabic Philosophy*, University of Pittsburgh Press, 1968; *Topics in Philosophical Logic*, Reidel, 1968; *Essays in Philosophical Analysis*, University of Pittsburgh Press, 1969; *Many-Valued Logic*, McGraw, 1969; *Introduction to Value Theory*, Prentice-Hall, 1969; (editor with Kurt Baier) *Values and the Future*, Free Press, 1969.

Scientific Explanation, Free Press, 1970; (editor and contributor) *Essays in Honor of Carl G. Hempel*, Reidel, 1970; (with Michael E. Marmura) *The Refutation by Alexander of Aphrodisias of Galen's Treatise on the First Mover*, Central Institute of Islamic Research, 1970; (with Alastair Urquhart) *Temporal Logic*, Springer-Verlag, 1971; *Welfare: The Social Issues in Philosophical Perspective*, University of Pittsburgh Press, 1972; *The Coherence Theory of Truth*, Clarendon Press, 1973; *The Primacy of Practice*, Basil Blackwell, 1973; *Studies in Modal Logic*, Basil Blackwell, 1974.

AVOCATIONAL INTERESTS: The study of history and biography.

*   *   *

RESNICK, Marvin D. 1933-

PERSONAL: Born February 19, 1933, in New York, N.Y.; son of Arthur (a manufacturer) and Leah (Cantor) Resnick. *Education:* Attended St. Lawrence University, 1951-52; New York University, B.A., 1954, M.A., 1966; graduate courses at Columbia University, Hunter College of the City University of New York, and City College of the City University of New York. *Home:* 520 East 84th St., New York City 10028. *Office:* State University of New York, Farmingdale, Long Island, N.Y.

CAREER: Yonkers Herald-Statesman, Yonkers, N.Y., reporter, 1956-58; *Roll Call* (newspaper), Washington, D.C., assistant editor, 1959-60; administrative assistant to Congressman George M. Rhodes, Washington, D.C., 1960; free-lance writer for magazines and newspapers, Washington, D.C., 1960-63; New York (N.Y.) public schools, teacher of English, 1963-66; State University of

New York at Farmingdale, 1966—, began as assistant professor, became associate professor of English. Lecturer, Queens College of the City University of New York, School of General Studies, 1967-70. *Military service:* U.S. Army, information specialist, 1954-56.

WRITINGS: (Editor and author of critical notes) George Eliot, *Silas Marner,* Barnes & Noble, 1966; *The Black Beret: A Biography of Che Guevara,* Ballantine, 1970. Also author of a play, "In the Name of America," read at the Actor's Studio, 1974. Contributor to *Think, New Republic, Challenge,* and various trade and government publications; free-lance writer for North American Newspaper Alliance Feature Syndicate, and contributor of features to metropolitan dailies in New York, Atlanta, Washington, D.C., Boston, Detroit, and other cities.

WORK IN PROGRESS: Creative Composition at the Two-year College Level, a textbook for Harper; three novels and screenplays, *Snows, The Last Guerrilla,* and *Adventures in the C.I.A.*

*   *   *

RESNIK, H(arvey) L(ewis) P(aul)   1930-

PERSONAL: Born April 6, 1930, in Buffalo, N.Y.; son of Samuel and Celia (Greenberg) Resnik; married Audrey Ruth Frey (a psychiatric nurse), August 30, 1964; children: Rebecca Gabrielle, Henry Seth Maccabee, Jessica Ruth. *Education:* University of Buffalo (now State University of New York at Buffalo), B.A. (magna cum laude), 1951; Columbia University, M.D., 1955; Philadelphia Psychoanalytic Institute, Certificate in Psychoanalysis, 1967. *Office:* George Washington University, School of Medicine, Washington, D.C.

CAREER: Philadelphia General Hospital, Philadelphia, Pa., intern, 1955-56, resident in surgery, 1956-57; Jackson Memorial Hospital, Miami, Fla., resident in psychiatry, 1959-61; University of Pennsylvania, School of Medicine, Philadelphia, fellow in psychiatry, 1961-62, instructor in psychiatry, 1962-67; State University of New York at Buffalo, associate professor of psychiatry, 1967-68, professor of psychiatry and deputy chairman of department, 1968-70; George Washington University, School of Medicine, Washington, D.C., clinical professor of psychiatry, 1969—; Johns Hopkins University, School of Medicine, Baltimore, Md., lecturer in psychiatry, 1969—. Director of emergency psychiatric services, Philadelphia General Hospital, 1966-67; E. J. Meyer Memorial Hospital, Buffalo, clinical director of psychiatry, 1967-68, director of psychiatry, 1968-69. National Institute of Mental Health, consultant on scientific study of suicide, 1967-68, chief of Center for Studies of Suicide Prevention, 1969-73, chief of Mental Health Emergencies Section, 1973-75. *Military service:* U.S. Air Force, Medical Corps, 1957-59; served in France, Turkey, and Lebanon; became captain. U.S. Naval Reserve, Medical Reserve, 1972—; present rank, captain.

MEMBER: American Medical Association, American Psychiatric Association, American Association of Marriage Counselors, Philadelphia Psychoanalytic Society. *Awards, honors:* Charles W. Burr Research Award, Philadelphia General Hospital, 1957; sustained superior performance award, National Institute of Mental Health, 1974.

WRITINGS: (Contributor) H. L. Silverman, editor, *Marital Counseling: Psychology, Ideology, Science,* C. C Thomas, 1967; (editor and contributor) *Suicidal Behaviors: Diagnosis and Management,* Little, Brown, 1968; (contributor) M. Ortega and E. S. Shneidman, editors, *On Death and Dying,* Little, Brown, 1969; (editor with M. E. Wolfgang, and contributor), *Treatment of the Sexual Offender,* Little, Brown, 1972; *Sexual Behavior: Social, Clinical and Legal Aspects,* Little, Brown, 1972; (with Harvey Ruben and Diane D. Ruben) *Emergency Psychiatric Care,* Charles Press, 1975. Contributor of articles on sexual offenders, suicide, and community anti-suicide organization to medical publications.

WORK IN PROGRESS: With H. L. Parad, *Emergency Mental Health and Disaster Aid.*

*   *   *

REUL, R(ose) Myrtle   1919-

PERSONAL: Born July 3, 1919, in Dooley, Mont.; daughter of Z. John (a photographer and rancher) and Victoria (Robinson) Crouse; married Paul A. Reul (an insurance salesman), December 24, 1937; children: M. Santa Marie (Mrs. Richard Schoof), Pauline C. (Mrs. William L. Holland). *Education:* Jackson County Community College, A.A., 1946; Albion College, B.A., 1947; Michigan State University, M.A., 1952, M.S.W., 1953, Ed.D., 1957, postdoctoral study, 1959. *Politics:* Republican. *Religion:* Baptist. *Home:* 204 Riverside Dr., Athens, Ga. 30601. *Office:* Affirmative Action Office, University of Georgia, Athens, Ga. 30601.

CAREER: Public school teacher in Michigan, 1947-51; Family Service Agency, Jackson, Mich., caseworker, 1951-52; Michigan Children's Aid Society, Lansing, supervisor, 1952-54; Michigan State University, East Lansing, field instructor, 1953-54, instructor in School of Social Work, 1954-57, coordinator of visiting teacher program, 1955-67, assistant professor, 1957-63, associate professor in School of Social Work, 1963-67; University of Georgia, Athens, professor in School of Social Work, 1968—, associate dean, 1971-74, university Affirmative Action officer, 1974—. Board member of Michigan Child Study Clubs, 1955-61, and Michigan Family Relations Council, 1958-66; member of day care committee, Michigan Youth Commission, 1960-66; technical consultant to Michigan Department of Health Agricultural Labor Camp Advisory Committee, 1965—; member of Division on the Family, Michigan Human Resources Council, 1965-68; chairperson, Council of Social Work Education Commission on the role and status of women in social work education, 1972—. *Member:* National Association of Social Workers, National Conference on Social Welfare, International Social Science Honor Society, Council on Social Work Education, National Family Relations Council, Academy of Certified Social Workers, Delta Tau Kappa. *Awards, honors:* L.H.D., Albion College, 1967.

WRITINGS: Parents Plus, Michigan Children's Aid Society, 1952; *A Survey of the State-wide Michigan Children's Aid Society,* Michigan United Fund, 1956; *A Practical Approach to Marriage,* Michigan State University Press, 1965; *Chartbook for Parents Through the Seas of Adolescence,* Vantage, 1965; *Where Hannibal Led Us,* Vantage, 1967.

(Contributor) Joseph W. Eaton, editor, *Migration and Social Welfare,* National Association of Social Workers, 1971; (contributor) Frank M. Loewenbery and Ralph Dalgoff, editors, *The Practice of Social Intervention: Roles, Goals and Strategies,* F. T. Peacock, 1972; *The Migration Episode and Its Consequences,* Center for Rural Manpower and Public Affairs, Michigan State University, 1972; *Mobility: An Old Science with a New Cast,* Center for

Rural Manpower and Public Affairs, Michigan State University, 1974; *Territorial Boundaries of Rural Poverty: A Profile in Exploitation*, Michigan State University, Cooperative Extension Service, 1974. Contributor to *Michigan State University Magazine, Michigan State Economic Record, Y.W.C.A. Magazine, School Food Service Journal*, and other professional journals.

* * *

REUTER, Carol (Joan) 1931-

PERSONAL: Born June 7, 1931, in Newark, N.J.; daughter of Clarence J. (a dentist) and Sabina (Zorn) Feinberg; married Peter J. Reuter (an engineer), October 21, 1956; children: Susan Deborah. *Education:* Smith College, A.B., 1952. *Home:* 1 Pool Dr., Roslyn, N.Y. 11576.

CAREER: Free-lance writer, editor, and copywriter for several New York publishers. *Member:* Phi Beta Kappa.

WRITINGS—Teen novels: (With Jean Fiedler) *The Last Year*, McKay, 1962; *The Secret of the Sea Rocks*, McKay, 1967; (with Susan Freelund) *The Roll 'em Cookbook: The Art of Filling and Saucing Gourmet Food*, Sea Cliff Press, 1974.

WORK IN PROGRESS: Another mystery/romance for young people, this one with a Cretan archaeological background.

AVOCATIONAL INTERESTS: Archaeology, playing guitar with a folk-singing group.†

* * *

REUTER, Frank T. 1926-

PERSONAL: Born March 18, 1926, in Kankakee, Ill.; son of Frank T. (a contractor) and Evelyn (Scott) Reuter; married Kathleen Pester, June 16, 1951; children: Mark, Stephen, Christopher, Ann, Katherine. *Education:* University of Illinois, B.S. in Journalism, 1950, M.A., 1959, Ph.D., 1960. *Religion:* Roman Catholic. *Home:* 3617 Winifred Dr., Fort Worth, Tex. 76133. *Office:* Texas Christian University, Fort Worth, Tex. 76129.

CAREER: Henry Reuter & Sons, Kankakee, Ill., sales engineer, 1950-56; West Liberty State College, West Liberty, W.Va., instructor, 1960-62; Texas Christian University, Fort Worth, assistant professor, 1962-66, associate professor, 1966-71, professor of history, 1971—, dean of Graduate School, 1970-75. *Military service:* U.S. Navy, 1944-46. *Member:* American Historical Association, Organization of American Historians, Society of Historians of American Foreign Relations, Phi Alpha Theta.

WRITINGS: West Liberty State College: The First 125 Years, privately printed, 1963; *Catholic Influence on American Colonial Policies, 1898-1904*, University of Texas Press, 1967.

WORK IN PROGRESS: The United States as an Emerging Nation.

* * *

REYNOLDS, Clark Winton 1934-

PERSONAL: Born March 13, 1934, in Chicago, Ill.; son of Lee Davis and Lilla (Hall) Reynolds; married Dorothy Floris, February 21, 1959; children: Rebecca Lynn, Clark Winton III, Matthew Lee. *Education:* Claremont Men's College, A.B. (magna cum laude), 1956; graduate study at Massachusetts Institute of Technology, 1956-57, 1958, and Harvard Divinity School, 1957-58; University of California,

Berkeley, M.A., 1961, Ph.D., 1962. *Office:* Food Research Institute, Stanford University, Stanford, Calif. 94305.

CAREER: Occidental College, Los Angeles, Calif., assistant professor of economics, 1961-62; Yale University, New Haven, Conn., assistant professor, 1962-66, associate professor of economics, 1966-67; Stanford University, Food Research Institute, Stanford, Calif., associate professor, 1967-72, professor of economics, 1972—. Visiting professor, College of Mexico, 1964, and summer, 1965; visiting lecturer, Stockholm School of Economics, 1968; visiting fellow, St. Anthony's College, Oxford University, 1975. Member of Rockefeller Commission to Latin America, 1969; consultant, Brookings Institution, 1976—.

WRITINGS: (With M. Mamalakis) *Essays on the Chilean Economy*, Irwin, 1965; (with Donald Nichols) *Principles of Economics*, Holt, 1970; *The Mexican Economy: Twentieth-Century Structure and Growth*, Yale University Press, 1972. Contributor to professional journals.

WORK IN PROGRESS: Flow of funds analysis and financial structure development in Brazil, Colombia, Costa Rica, and Jamaica; a study of employment and poverty in the Central American Common Market.

* * *

REYNOLDS, Lloyd George 1910-

PERSONAL: Born December 22, 1910, in Wainwright, Alberta, Canada; came to United States in 1934, naturalized in 1940; son of George Franklin and Dorothy (Carl) Reynolds; married Mary Trackett (a political scientist), June 12, 1937; children: Anne Frances (Mrs. James F. Skinner), Priscilla (Mrs. Kermit Roosevelt, Jr.), Bruce Lloyd. *Education:* University of Alberta, B.A., 1931; McGill University, M.A., 1934; Harvard University, Ph.D., 1936. *Politics:* Democrat. *Religion:* Episcopalian. *Home:* 75 Old Hartford Turnpike, Hamden, Conn. 06517. *Office:* Department of Economics, Yale University, New Haven, Conn. 06511.

CAREER: Harvard University, Cambridge, Mass., instructor in economics, 1936-39; Johns Hopkins University, Baltimore, Md., assistant professor, 1939-41, associate professor of political economy, 1941-45; Yale University, New Haven, Conn., associate professor, 1945-47, professor, 1947-52, Sterling Professor of Economics, 1952—, head of department of economics, 1951-59, director of Economic Growth Center, 1960—. Director, National Bureau of Economic Research, New York, N.Y., 1958—. Regional price director, U.S. Office of Price Administration, 1941-42; co-chairman of Appeals Committee, National War Labor Board, 1943-45; consultant, U.S. Bureau of the Budget, 1945-47, Social Science Research Center, University of Puerto Rico, 1951-54; director of Program in Economic Development and Administration, Ford Foundation, 1955-57. Research secretary, Committee on Employment, Social Science Research Council, 1955-57. Research director, Labor and National Defense Study, Twentieth Century Fund.

MEMBER: American Economic Association (member of executive committee, 1952-55; vice-president, 1959), Industrial Relations Research Association (president, 1955), American Academy of Arts and Sciences (fellow), American Academy of Political Science, Century Association (New York), Cosmos Club (Washington, D.C.). *Awards, honors:* Rockefeller Foundation traveling fellowship, 1951; Guggenheim fellowship, 1954-55, 1967; LL.D., University of Alberta, 1958; Ford Foundation faculty research fellowship, 1959-60.

WRITINGS: *The British Immigrant in Canada*, Oxford University Press, 1935; *The Control of Competition in Canada*, Harvard University Press, 1940; *Labor and National Defense*, Twentieth Century Fund, 1941; *Trade Union Publications*, three volumes, Johns Hopkins Press, 1944; *Labor Economics and Labor Relations*, Prentice-Hall, 1946, 6th edition, 1974; *The Structure of Labor Markets*, Harper, 1951; (with C. Taft) *The Evolution of Wage Structure*, Yale University Press, 1956; *Economics: A General Introduction*, Irwin, 1963, 4th edition, 1973; (with P. Gregory) *Industrialization in Puerto Rico*, Prentice-Hall, 1965; (with Nicholas A.Michas) *Programmed Learning Aid for Principles of Economics: Macro*, Learning Systems Co., 1971; (with Michas) *Programmed Learning Aid for Principles of Economics: Micro*, Learning Systems Co., 1971; *The Three Worlds of Economics*, Yale University Press, 1971; (editor with George D. Green and Darrell R. Lewis) *Current Issues of Economic Policy*, Irwin, 1973; (with Dennis Starleaf) *Macroeconomics: Analysis and Policy*, Irwin, 1973; *Microeconomics: Analysis and Policy*, Irwin, 1973; (compiler with Stanley H. Masters and Collette Moser) *Readings in Labor Economics and Labor Relations*, Prentice-Hall, 1974. Contributor to journals in his field. Member of board of editors, *American Economic Review*, 1951-53.

WORK IN PROGRESS: Essays in economic development.

SIDELIGHTS: Lloyd Reynolds traveled widely in central and east Africa as leader of a four-man research team for the Carnegie Foundation in 1952. *Avocational interests:* Mountaineering.†

* * *

RHODE, Eric 1934-

PERSONAL: Born May 10, 1934, in Genoa, Italy; son of Allan H. (a businessman) and Helen J. (Davidson) Rhode; married Maria Halpern; children: David. *Education:* Educated at Fettes College, Edinburgh, Scotland, and St. Edmund Hall, Oxford. *Home:* 50 Gordon Pl., London W. 8, England. *Agent:* A. D. Peters, 10 Buckingham St., Adelphi, London W.C. 2, England.

CAREER: Child psychotherapist, journalist and broadcaster, London, England.

WRITINGS: *Tower of Babel: Speculations on the Cinema*, Weidenfeld & Nicolson, 1966, Chilton, 1967; *A History of the Cinema: From Its Origin to 1970*, Hill & Wang, 1976. Author of radio play, "The Pagoda Fugue," and scripts for British Broadcasting Corp. Contributor to *New Statesman, Encounter, Listener, Times Literary Supplement*, and other periodicals.

AVOCATIONAL INTERESTS: Particularly interested in the visual arts.†

* * *

RHODES, Albert 1916-

PERSONAL: Born May 10, 1916, in Sheffield, Yorkshire, England; son of Ernest (a blacksmith and farrier) and Annie (Cartwright) Rhodes; married Eileen Evelyn Collins, July 29, 1939; children: Peter, Jennifer. *Education:* Attended Chesterfield Technical College, 1930-34. *Politics:* Liberal. *Religion:* Church of England. *Home and office:* 8 High Trees Walk, Ferndown, Dorsetshire, England. *Agent:* John Farquharson Ltd., 15 Red Lion Sq., London W.C.1, England.

CAREER: Novelist. *Military service:* British Army, 1939-45; became sergeant.

WRITINGS—Novels: *Butter on Sunday*, Dobson, 1964; *A Summer of Yesterday*, Dobson, 1967; *Calico Bloomers*, Dobson, 1968. Also author of radio and stage plays.

WORK IN PROGRESS: *Shout into the Wind; Derbyshire Lead Mining;* television scripts.

SIDELIGHTS: *Butter on Sunday* was adapted for a trilogy of one-hour plays aired by British Broadcasting Corp. Rhodes was forty-eight when his first book was published; says he is a compulsive writer, getting up at six o'clock to write for an hour daily before going to his business.

* * *

RHYMER, Joseph 1927-

PERSONAL: Born September 23, 1927, in Birmingham, England; son of Frank Joseph (a printer) and Kate Rose (Slater) Rhymer. *Education:* University of Leeds, B.A. (honors in philosophy), 1952; University of Edinburgh, M.Th., 1975. *Religion:* Roman Catholic. *Home:* 13/1 Whistlefield Ct., 2 Canniesburn Rd., Bearsden, Glasgow, G61 1PX, Scotland. *Agent:* David Bolt, Bolt and Watson Ltd., 8 Storey's Gate, London S.W.1, England. *Office:* Notre Dame College, Bearsden, Glasgow, Scotland.

CAREER: Community of the Resurrection, Mirfield, England, member, 1952-63, with ordination as Anglican priest, 1956; left Anglican order and was received into Catholic Church, 1963; Codrington College, Barbados, West Indies, vice-principal, 1957-63; Moor Park School, Ludlow, Shropshire, England, deputy headmaster, 1964-66; Christ's College, Liverpool, England, senior lecturer in theology, 1966-68; Notre Dame College, Liverpool, senior lecturer in theology, 1968-75; Notre Dame College, Bearsden, Glasgow, Scotland, lecturer in religious education, 1975—. Editorial consultant, Darton, Longman & Todd Ltd. *Military service:* Royal Navy, 1945-48. *Member:* Aristotelian Society, Society for Old Testament Study, Catholic Biblical Association.

WRITINGS: *Way Through the Old Testament*, Sheed, Volume III: *The Prophets and the Law*, 1964, Volume I: *The Beginnings of a People*, 1966, Volume II: *The Covenant and the Kingdom*, 1968, Volume IV: *The Babylonian Experience*, 1971, Volume V: *The People of the Messiah*, 1972; *The Good News: St. Mark's Insight*, Darton, Longman & Todd, 1965; (editor) H. Gaubert, *The Bible in History*, six volumes, Darton, Longman & Todd, 1968-72; *The Old Testament*, Darton, Longman & Todd, 1969; (editor) *The Christian Priesthood*, Darton, Longman & Todd, 1970; (with A. Bullan) *Companion to the Good News*, Collins, 1971; (editor) *The Bible Is for All*, Collins, 1973; *Good News in Romans*, Collins, 1974; *The Bible in Order*, Doubleday, 1975.

Contributor: L. Bright, editor, *The People of God*, Sheed, 1965; Bright, editor, *Theology in Modern Education*, Darton, Longman & Todd, 1965; Bright and S. Clements, editors, *The Committed Church*, Darton, Longman & Todd, 1966; Bright, editor, *Prophets*, Sheed, 1971.

WORK IN PROGRESS: *Atlas of the Bible; Companion to the Old Testament;* research in the sociology of religious education.

* * *

RIBMAN, Ronald (Burt) 1932-

PERSONAL: Born May 28, 1932, in New York, N.Y.; son

of Samuel M. (a lawyer) and Rosa (Lerner) Ribman; married Alice Rosen (a nurse), August 27, 1967; children: James, Elana. *Education:* Attended Brooklyn College (now Brooklyn College of the City University of New York), 1950-51; University of Pittsburgh, B.B.A., 1954, M.Litt., 1958, Ph.D., 1962. *Home:* 50 West 96th St., New York, N.Y. 10025. *Agent:* Flora Roberts, 116 East 59th St., New York, N.Y. 10022.

CAREER: Otterbein College, Westerville, Ohio, assistant professor of English, 1962-63; full-time writer, 1963—. Rockefeller Playwright-in-residence, Public Theater, 1975. *Military service:* U.S. Army, 1954-56. *Awards, honors:* Obie Award, 1965-66, for the best play Off-Broadway, "Journey of the Fifth Horse"; Rockefeller Foundation grants, 1966, 1968; "The Final War of Olly Winter" was nominated for Emmy Award of American Academy of Television Arts and Sciences, 1967; Guggenheim Foundation grant, 1970; National Foundation of the Arts fellow, 1973; Straw Hat award, 1973, for best new play, "The Poison Tree."

WRITINGS—All stage plays, except as noted: *Harry, Noon and Night* (produced Off-Broadway at American Place Theatre, 1965), published as *Harry, Noon and Night* [and] *The Journey of the Fifth Horse* (also see below), Little, Brown, 1967; *The Journey of the Fifth Horse* (produced Off-Broadway at American Place Theatre, April 21, 1966; new adaptation produced by Canadian Broadcasting Co., 1969), published as *Harry, Noon and Night* [and] *The Journey of the Fifth Horse*, Little, Brown, 1967; "The Ceremony of Innocence," produced Off-Broadway at American Place Theatre, December 14, 1967, new adaptation produced by Granada Television, London, 1974; "The Final War of Olly Winter" (television play; produced by Columbia Broadcasting System, 1967), published in *Great Television Plays*, edited by William I. Kaufman, Dell, 1969; "Passing through from Exotic Places" (contains three one-act plays, "The Son Who Hunted Tigers in Jakarta," "Sunstroke," "The Burial of Esposito" [also see below]), produced Off-Broadway at Sheridan Square Theater, December 7, 1969; (with William Gunn) "The Angel Levine" (screenplay; based on a story by Bernard Malamud), United Artists, 1969; "The Burial of Esposito," published in *The Best Short Plays 1971*, edited by Stanley Richards, Chilton, 1971; "Fingernails Blue as Flowers" (one-act play; produced Off-Broadway at American Place Theatre, 1971), published in *The American Place Theatre: Plays*, edited by Richard Schotter, Dell, 1973; "A Break in the Skin," produced in New Haven, Conn. at Yale University Repertory Theater, October, 1972. Also author of "The Poison Tree," scheduled for production on Broadway.

WORK IN PROGRESS: A new play, "Pleasure Dome."

SIDELIGHTS: Mary Otis Hivnor, who calls *The Journey of the Fifth Horse* "different, irreverent and refreshing," notes that the play "occurs 100 years ago, in Russia, with princes, samovars, old nurses, and things which for us are romantically remote." The play is actually based in part on the Turgenev novelette *Diary of a Superfluous Man* and Hivnor writes that Ribman has used the characters and appointments of the novelette "as some painters use classical paintings, as a foil, something to struggle with and comment on by elaboration or variation. But it remains an exercise, a tour de force; there is no attempt at contemporaneity." A *Variety* reviewer writes that "The Ceremony of Innocence" "represents the work of a promising playwright with a flair for words, stage craftmanship and the

creation of roles good actors can effectively embroider." Reviewing "A Break in the Skin," Mel Gussow notes that "the play has an undeniable theatricality and, often, a fanciful humor."

In an interview with John Gruen, Ribman comments: "My plays are about words. . . . The trouble is that in this age people go to *see* a play. . . . If you're too visual you can't focus attention on what you want to say." Ribman continues, "You write a play with the intention that it's not only going to have meaning for a month or a year, but that it's going to have meaning for a much longer time—maybe for all time."

National Educational Television produced, on "NET Playhouse," "The Journey of the Fifth Horse," 1966, 1968, and 1969, and "The Ceremony of Innocence," 1970.

BIOGRAPHICAL/CRITICAL SOURCES: Nation, January 15, 1968; *Kenyon Review,* Volume XXX, number 2, 1968; *New York Times,* June 7, 1970, October 20, 1972; *Variety,* June 22, 1970.

* * *

RICE, Berkeley 1937-

PERSONAL: Born January 29, 1937, in Hyannis, Mass.; son of Jackson M. Rice (a physician). *Education:* Amherst College, B.A., 1959; Sorbonne, University of Paris, graduate study, 1959-60; Columbia University, M.A., 1961. *Residence:* North Tarrytown, N.Y. *Office:* Psychology Today, 1 Park Ave., New York, N.Y. 10016.

CAREER: Look Magazine, New York City, assistant editor, 1963-64; *Newsweek,* correspondent in West Africa, 1964-65; free-lance writer, 1965-72; *Psychology Today,* New York City, senior editor, 1973—.

WRITINGS: Enter Gambia: The Birth of an Improbable Nation, Houghton, 1967; *The Other End of the Leash,* Little, Brown, 1968; *The C-SA Scandal,* Houghton, 1971.

* * *

RICE, Elizabeth 1913-

PERSONAL: Born May 28, 1913, in Marshall, Tex.; daughter of Eddie (a railroad agent) and Willie (Burns) Rice; married Emmett Lynn Bauknight (an attorney), November 23, 1938 (deceased); children: Stella Lynn. *Education:* Sophie Newcomb College, student, 1930-31; University of Texas, B.S. in Arch., 1936. *Religion:* Episcopalian. *Home:* 1305 Alta Vista, Austin, Tex. 78704.

CAREER: Illustrator of children's books. *Member:* Alpha Alpha Gamma (national president, 1947-48).

WRITINGS—Self-illustrated: *I'm Alvin,* Steck, 1967; *Benje: The Squirrel Who Lost His Tail,* Childrens Press, 1969; *Jacki,* Childrens Press, 1969; *Henry and Benjamin,* Steck, 1970; *Yippi,* Steck, 1971; *Who-oo-oo,* Steck, 1973.

Illustrator: Dorothy Bracken, *Rodeo,* Steck, 1949; Esther Buffler, *Mary,* Steck, 1949; Buffler, *Rodrigo and Rosalita,* Steck, 1949; Washington Irving, *Rip Van Winkle* [and] *The Legend of the Sleepy Hollow,* adapted by R. A. Pulliam and O. N. Darby, Steck, 1949; Robert Louis Stevenson, *Kidnapped,* adapted by Pulliam and Darby, Steck, 1949; Adda Mai Sharp, *Where Is Cubby Bear?,* Steck, 1950; Sharp, *Daffy,* Steck, 1950; Sharp, *Gee Whillikins,* Steck, 1950; Sharp, *Secret Places,* Steck, 1955; Sharp and Epsie Young, *Gordo and the Hidden Treasure,* Steck, 1955; Sharp and Young, *Heart of the Wind,* Steck, 1955; Sharp and Young, *Chichi's Magic,* Steck, 1955; Anne Welsh

Guy, *Book of Tails,* Steck, 1957; Katharine Jones Carter, *Willie Waddle,* Steck, 1959; Guy, *Book of Tongues,* Steck, 1960; Sharp, "The Woodland Frolic Series," seven books, Steck, 1965; Ruth Van Ness, *Puddle Duck,* Steck, 1966; Solveig Paulson Russell, *If You Were a Cat,* Childrens Press, 1967; Nina Shackelford, *When Birds Migrate,* Steck, 1968; Mary Bruce, *The Bear Who Lost His Hair,* Steck, 1968; Marilyn Leitner Reiss, *Thackery Turtle,* Steck, 1969. Also illustrator of *Happy Longlegs,* Steck; *A Texas History,* Steck; "The Wonder Book Series," four books, Steck.

AVOCATIONAL INTERESTS: Landscape and western painting, gardening, summers in Mexico.

*   *   *

RICH, John Martin 1931-

PERSONAL: Born December 14, 1931, in Tuscaloosa, Ala.; son of Emanuel M. (a jeweler) and Bertha (Rose) Rich. *Education:* University of Alabama, B.A., 1954, M.A., 1955; Ohio State University, Ph.D., 1958. *Office:* 528 Education Building, University of Texas, Austin, Tex. 78712.

CAREER: University of Tennessee at Martin, assistant professor of education, 1958-60; State University of New York College at Oneonta, associate professor of education, 1960-61; Iowa State University of Science and Technology, Ames, assistant professor, later associate professor of education, 1961-66; University of Kentucky, Lexington, associate professor of education, 1966-69; University of Texas, Austin, professor of education and chairman of department of cultural foundations of education, 1969—. Visiting summer professor at Indiana University, 1963, University of Illinois, 1965, Nevada Southern University, 1966, and University of Washington, 1969. *Member:* Philosophy of Education Society (archivist, 1964—; member of executive board, 1967-68; secretary-treasurer, 1968-70), American Education Studies Association (member of executive council, 1972-74; president, 1975-76), North Central Philosophy of Education Society (secretary-treasurer, 1964-65; president, 1966-67), Ohio Valley Philosophy of Education Society (president, 1966-67).

WRITINGS: (Editor) *Readings in the Philosophy of Education,* Wadsworth, 1966, 2nd edition, 1972; *Education and Human Values,* Addison-Wesley, 1968; *Chief Seattle's Unanswered Challenge,* Ye Galleon, 1970; *Humanistic Foundations of Education,* Charles A. Jones Publishing, 1971; (editor) *Conflict and Decision: Analyzing Educational Issues,* Harper, 1972; *New Directions in Educational Policy,* Professional Educators Publications, 1974; *Challenge and Response: Education in American Culture,* Wiley, 1974; *Innovations in Education: Reformers and Their Critics,* Allyn & Bacon, 1975. Contributor to education journals.

*   *   *

RICHARDS, Audrey I(sabel) 1899-

PERSONAL: Born July 8, 1899, in London, England; daughter of Henry Erle (a lawyer) and Isabel (Butler) Richards. *Education:* Newnham College, Cambridge, M.A., 1922; London School of Economics and Political Science, Ph.D., 1929. *Religion:* Church of England. *Home:* Crawley Cottage, Elmdon, Saffron Walden, Essex, England.

CAREER: University of London, London School of Economics and Political Science, London, England, lecturer in social anthropology, 1931-33, 1935-37; University of the Witwatersrand, Johannesburg, South Africa, lecturer in social anthropology, 1938-40; British Colonial Office, London, staff member, 1940-44; University of London, reader in social anthropology, 1946-50; Makerere University College, Kampala, Uganda, director of East African Institute of Social Research, 1950-56; Cambridge University, Cambridge, England, fellow of Newnham College, 1956-67, Smuts Reader in Anthropology, 1961-67, honorary fellow of Newnham College, 1967—; director, Centre of African Studies, 1964-66. Did anthropological field work in Northern Rhodesia, 1930-31, 1933-34, 1957, in Northern Transvaal, 1939-40, in Uganda, 1950-55. Director of Anglia Television Co., 1958—. Secretary of Colonial Research Committee, 1944-47; Colonial Social Science Research Council, secretary, 1944-50, member, 1956-62.

MEMBER: Royal Anthropological Institute (president, 1960-62), African Studies Association (United Kingdom; president, 1963-66), Association of Social Anthropologists, Royal Commonwealth Society. *Awards, honors:* Wellcome Medal for applied anthropology; Rivers Memorial Medal for field work; Commander, Order of the British Empire, 1955.

WRITINGS: Hunger and Work in a Savage Tribe: A Functional Study of Nutrition Among the Southern Bantu, Routledge & Sons, 1932, World Publishing, 1964; *Land, Labour and Diet in Northern Rhodesia: An Economic Study of the Bemba Tribe,* Oxford University Press, for International Institution of African Languages and Cultures, 1939, 2nd edition, 1962; *Bemba Marriage and Present Economic Conditions,* Rhodes-Livingstone Institute, 1940; (editor) *Economic Development and Tribal Change: A Study of Immigrant Labour in Buganda,* Heffer, for East African Institute of Social Research, 1952, revised edition, Oxford University Press, 1975; *Chisungu: A Girl's Initiation Ceremony Among the Bemba of Northern Rhodesia,* Grove, 1956; (editor) *East African Chiefs: A Study of Political Development in Some Uganda and Tanganyika Tribes,* Praeger, 1960; *The Changing Structure of a Ganda Village: Kisoz, 1892-1952,* East African Publishing House (Nairobi), 1966; *The Multicultural States of East Africa,* McGill-Queens University Press, 1969; (editor with Adam Kuper) *Councils in Action,* Cambridge University Press, 1971; (editor with Ford Sturrock and Jean M. Fortt) *Subsistence to Commercial Farming in Present-Day Buganda: An Economic and Anthropological Survey,* Cambridge University Press, 1973.

WORK IN PROGRESS: Study of social mechanisms of pre-literate peoples; ritual of the Bemba.

SIDELIGHTS: Audrey Richards is competent in French, German, Luganda, Chiemba. *Avocational interests:* Walking, gardening.

BIOGRAPHICAL/CRITICAL SOURCES: Jean Sybil La Fontaine, editor, *The Interpretation of Ritual: Essays in Honour of A. I. Richards,* Tavistock Publications, 1972.†

*   *   *

RICHARDS, Max D(eVoe) 1923-

PERSONAL: Born May 23, 1923, in Nova, Ohio; son of Paul Leroy (an insurance agent) and Dorothy (Daniels) Richards; married Winona Marie Patersen, March 3, 1950 (divorced); children: Cassandra, Elizabeth. *Education:* Attended Miami University, Oxford, Ohio, 1941-43; Harvard University, M.B.A., 1947; University of Illinois, Ph.D., 1955. *Home:* 625 East Waring Ave., State College,

Pa. 16801. *Office:* 101 Business Administration, Pennsylvania State University, University Park, Pa. 16802.

CAREER: University of Illinois, Urbana, instructor in management, 1949-54; University of Wichita, Wichita, Kan., 1954-56, began as assistant professor, became associate professor of management and head of department; Pennsylvania State University, College of Business Administration, University Park, associate professor, 1956-65, professor of management, 1965—, chairman of department, 1965-67, assistant dean of graduate programs, 1967—. Consultant to U.S. Air Force and to aerospace firms. *Military service:* U.S. Naval Reserve, active duty, 1943-46; became lieutenant junior grade. *Member:* Institute of Management Sciences, Academy of Management (secretary-treasurer, 1963-65; vice-president, 1966; president, 1967), Beta Gamma Sigma, Sigma Iota Epsilon, Order of Artus. *Awards, honors:* Ford Foundation fellowship, 1965-66.

WRITINGS: (With W. A. Nielander) *Readings in Management,* South-Western Publishing, 1958, 3rd edition, 1969; (with R. Carzo) *Mathematics in Collegiate Business Schools,* South-Western Publishing, 1963; (with P. Greenlaw) *Management Decision Making,* Irwin, 1966, revised edition published as *Management Decisions and Behavior,* 1972. Contributor to *Advanced Management, Manager's Key, Journal of Applied Psychology, Decision Sciences,* and *Academy of Management Journal.*

WORK IN PROGRESS: Research on organization structure and strategy as related to managerial capabilities and environmental attitudes.

* * *

RICHARDS, R(onald) C(harles) W(illiam) 1923-
(K. Allen Saddler)

PERSONAL: Born April 15, 1923, in England; son of Charles James (a shopkeeper) and Alice (Bloomfield) Richards; married Doris Edmondson, September 9, 1945; children: Richard Samuel. *Education:* Attended elementary school in South London, England. *Politics:* Labour. *Religion:* Agnostic. *Home:* 6 South St., Totnes, Devonshire TQ9 5DZ, England. *Agent:* John Hayes, 32 The Drive, Morden, Surrey, England.

CAREER: Former printer in London, England; full-time writer, journalist, and theatre reviewer for *Guardian,* and *Plays & Players. Member:* National Union of Journalists, Writers' Guild.

WRITINGS—Under pseudonym K. Allen Saddler: *The Great Brain Robbery,* Elek, 1965; *Gilt Edge,* Elek, 1966; *Talking Turkey,* M. Joseph, 1968. Author of radio plays for British Broadcasting Corp., including "The Penstone Commune," 1973, "Willie Banks and the Technological Revolution," 1973, "Who Needs Money?," 1974, "The Road," 1974, "Noises Off," 1976, and "Them," 1976. Contributor to *Sunday Times* (London).

SIDELIGHTS: Richards told *CA:* "Aim at general amusement of the reader. Do not let grammar, logic or spelling hinder me in this aim. Use the framework of the thriller as it is the simplest method whereby I can air my prejudices."

* * *

RICHARDSON, James L(ongden) 1933-

PERSONAL: Born December 1, 1933, in Childers, Queensland, Australia; son of Charles Longden (an agricultural scientist) and Helen Mary (Mallam) Richardson. *Education:* University of Sydney, B.A. (honors), 1954; Magdalen College, Oxford, B.A. (honors), 1958; Nuffield College, Oxford, student in politics, 1958-61. *Office:* Department of Political Science, SGS, Australian National University, Canberra, Australian Capital Territory, Australia.

CAREER: Harvard University, Cambridge, Mass., research associate, Center for International Affairs, 1961-63; Oxford University, Balliol College, Oxford, England, research fellow in international relations, 1963-65; United Kingdom Foreign Office, Arms Control and Disarmament Research Unit, researcher, 1965-66; University of Sydney, Sydney, New South Wales, Australia, lecturer, 1967-73, associate professor of government, 1973-75; Australian National University, Canberra, professor of political science, 1975—. *Member:* Australian Institute of International Affairs, International Institute for Strategic Studies (London), Australian Political Science Association.

WRITINGS: Germany and the Atlantic Alliance: The Interaction of Strategy and Politics, Harvard University Press, 1966.

Contributor: H. G. Gelber, editor, *Problems of Australian Defence,* Oxford University Press, 1970; C. Holbraad, editor, *Super Powers and World Order,* Australian National University Press, 1971; Bruce Brown, editor, *Asia and the Pacific in the 1970's,* Australian National University Press, 1971; G. Greenwood and N. Harper, editors, *Australia in World Affairs, 1966-1970,* Australian Institute of International Affairs, 1974; R. J. O'Neill, editor, *The Strategic Nuclear Balance: An Australian Perspective,* Strategic and Defence Studies Centre, Australian National University, 1975. Contributor of articles and reviews to journals.

WORK IN PROGRESS: Research in international crises, international relations theory, and the relationship between peaceful and military nuclear programs.

* * *

RICHARDSON, (Stewart) Lee (Jr.) 1940-

PERSONAL: Born July 8, 1940, in Washington, D.C.; son of Stewart Lee (an auditor) and Margaret (Strachan) Richardson; married Doralee Forsythe, December 23, 1960; children: Lee-Ellen, Stewart III, Lauren. *Education:* University of Richmond, B.S. in B.A., 1962; Emory University, M.B.A., 1963; University of Colorado, D.B.A., 1966. *Religion:* Southern Baptist. *Home:* 814 Kenilworth Pkwy., Baton Rouge, La. 70808. *Office:* Department of Marketing, Louisiana State University, Baton Rouge, La. 70803.

CAREER: Louisiana State University, Baton Rouge, assistant professor of marketing, 1966—, chairman of department, 1975—. Director, Consumer Education and Finance, White House Office of Consumer Affairs, 1972-73, Office of Consumer Affairs, Federal Energy Administration, 1973-74. Management consultant. *Member:* American Marketing Association, Beta Gamma Sigma, Sigma Iota Epsilon.

WRITINGS: (Editor with H. A. Wolf) *Readings in Finance,* Appleton, 1966; (editor with P. R. Cateora) *Readings in Marketing: The Qualitative and Quantitative Areas,* Appleton, 1967; (editor) *Dimensions of Communication,* Appleton, 1969; (with S. Brown) *Problems of Low Income Consumers,* Louisiana State University, 1973; (contributor) M. Unger and Wolf, editors, *Personal Finance,* 3rd edition, Allyn & Bacon, 1974; (contributor) *1973 Yearbook of Agriculture,* U.S. Department of Agriculture, 1974; (contributor) P. Sethi, editor, *The Unstable Ground,* Melville Publishing, 1974; (contributor) T. Garman and S. Eckert, editors, *The Consumer's World,* McGraw, 1974.

WORK IN PROGRESS: Research on consumerism and U.S. energy policy.

* * *

RICHARDSON, S(tanley) D(ennis) 1925-

PERSONAL: Born March 28, 1925, in Spalding, England; son of George Edward and Eunice (Mountford) Richardson; married Janet Jezzard (a medical doctor), September 13, 1957; children: Kaitrin, Martin. *Education:* Oxford University, M.A., 1950, B.Sc., 1952, D.Phil., 1955. *Home:* 26 Lewis Rd., Rotorua, New Zealand. *Office address:* P.O. Box 2057, Rotorua, New Zealand.

CAREER: University of Aberdeen, Aberdeen, Scotland, lecturer, 1954-61; New Zealand Forest Service, director of research, 1961-66; University College of North Wales, Bangor, professor of forestry, 1966-74; independent consultant, 1974—. *Military service:* Royal Marines, 1942-46; became captain.

WRITINGS: Forestry in Communist China, Johns Hopkins Press, 1966. Contributor of more than eighty articles to popular and professional journals.

WORK IN PROGRESS: World forestry; diseconomies of scale.

AVOCATIONAL INTERESTS: Campanology (the study of bells).

* * *

RICHARDSON, William John 1920-

PERSONAL: Born November 2, 1920, in Brooklyn, N.Y.; son of Frederick E. and Mary (Oliver) Richardson. *Education:* College of the Holy Cross, A.B., 1941; University of Louvain, Ph.D., 1960, maitre agrege, 1962; William Alanson White Institute, diploma in psychoanalysis, 1975. *Home and office:* Fordham University, Bronx, N.Y. 10458.

CAREER: Roman Catholic priest of Society of Jesus (Jesuits). LeMoyne College, Syracuse, N.Y., instructor in English and philosophy, 1947-50; St. Peter's College, Jersey City, N.J., assistant professor of philosophy, 1960-63; Fordham University, Bronx, N.Y., associate professor, 1963-74, professor of philosophy, 1974—; Austen Riggs Center, Inc., Stockbridge, Mass., director of research, 1975—. *Member:* Metaphysical Society of America, Society for Phenomenology and Existential Philosophy, Association for Existential Psychology and Psychiatry (member of executive council), American Catholic Philosophical Association. *Awards, honors:* Bollingen fellow, 1962-63; Cardinal Mercier Prize in philosophy, 1965.

WRITINGS: Heidegger: Through Phenomenology to Thought, Nijoff, 1963, 3rd edition, 1975. Contributor of articles on Heidegger to *Thought, Philosophisches Jahrbuch, Theological Studies,* and other journals.

WORK IN PROGRESS: Ontology of Language.

* * *

RICHMAN, Barry M. 1936-

PERSONAL: Born March 18, 1936, in Montreal, Quebec, Canada; son of Edward and Belle (Cohen) Richman; married Vivian Freedman, June 5, 1960; children: Viana, Stuart. *Education:* McGill University, B.Comm., 1958; Columbia University, M.S., 1959, Ph.D., 1962. *Home:* 20755 Seaboard Rd., Malibu, Calif. 90265. *Office:* University of California, Los Angeles, Calif. 90024.

CAREER: University of California, Los Angeles, assistant professor, 1962-64, associate professor, 1965-66, professor of management and international business, 1967—. *Member:* American Economic Association, International Academy of Management (fellow), American Sociological Association. *Awards, honors:* Various research fellowships and grants, including a Ford Foundation grant, 1966-69.

WRITINGS: Soviet Management, with Significant American Comparisons, Prentice-Hall, 1965; (with Richard N. Farmer) *Comparative Management and Economic Progress,* Irwin, 1965; (with Farmer) *International Business,* Irwin, 1966; (with Farmer) *Incidents in Applying Management Theory,* Wadsworth, 1966; *Management Development and Education in the Soviet Union,* Bureau of Business and Economic Research, Michigan State University, 1967; *A Firsthand Study of Industrial Management in Communist China,* Graduate School of Business Administration, University of California, Los Angeles, 1967; *Industrial Society in Communist China,* Random House, 1969; (with Melvyn Copen) *International Management and Economic Development,* McGraw, 1972; (with Farmer) *Leadership Goals and Power in Higher Education,* Jossey-Bass, 1974; (with Farmer) *Management and Organizations,* Random House, 1975. Contributor of articles on management and economic development in the Soviet Union, India, and Communist China to journals.

* * *

RICHMOND, Anthony H(enry) 1925-

PERSONAL: Born June 8, 1925, in Ilford, England; married Freda Williams, March 29, 1952; children: Glenys Catriona. *Education:* University of London, B.Sc., 1949, Ph.D., 1965; University of Liverpool, M.A., 1950. *Religion:* Quaker. *Office:* Department of Sociology, York University, Downsview, Ontario, Canada.

CAREER: University of Edinburgh, Edinburgh, Scotland, lecturer, 1952-63; Bristol College of Science and Technology, Bristol, England, reader, 1963-65; York University, Downsview, Ontario, professor of sociology, 1965—. Consulting editor in sociology, Pergamon Press. *Wartime service:* Served in Friends Ambulance Unit, World War II. *Member:* British Sociological Association, Canadian Association of Sociology and Anthropology, American Sociological Association, International Union for the Scientific Study of Population.

WRITINGS: Colour Prejudice in Britain, Routledge & Kegan Paul, 1954; *The Colour Problem,* Penguin, 1955, revised edition, 1961; *Post-War Immigrants in Canada,* University of Toronto Press, 1967; *Readings in Race and Ethnic Relations,* Pergamon, 1972; *Ethnic Residential Segregation in Metropolitan Toronto,* Institute for Behavioral Research, 1972; *Migration and Race Relations in an English City,* Oxford University Press, 1973. Contributor to professional journals in United States, Britain, and Canada.

WORK IN PROGRESS: A multivariate model of immigrant adaptation; a comparative study of immigrants in Canada and Australia.

* * *

RICHMOND, Leigh (Tucker) 1911-

PERSONAL: Born April 21, 1911, in Troy, Pa.; daughter of Royal K. (an Episcopal clergyman) and Juliet (Luttrell) Tucker; married Walter F. Richmond (a research physicist); children: Tuc, Leigh, Scott (daughters). *Office address:* The Centric Foundation, Inc., P.O. Box 1117, Merritt Island, Fla. 32952.

CAREER: Research anthropologist and writer; formerly associated with Richmond Research, Claremont, N.H.; currently secretary-treasurer, The Centric Foundation, Inc., Merritt Island, Fla.

WRITINGS—All with husband, Walt Richmond; all published by Ace Books: The Lost Millenium, 1967; Shock Wave, 1967; Phoenix Ship, 1969; Gallagher's Glacier, 1970; Positive Charge, 1970; Challenge the Hellmaker, 1976. Contributor of short stories to science fiction magazines, including Analog.

WORK IN PROGRESS: Co-developer with husband, Walt Richmond, of centric analysis, the mathematics of trigonometry applied to relativity.

* * *

RICHMOND, Robert P. 1914-

PERSONAL: Born December 14, 1914, in Jersey City, N.J.; son of Ralph P. (an osteopath) and Rebecca (Holtz) Richmond; married Frances Chaffee (a school librarian); children: Robert C., Carol L., Marion H. Education: Attended public schools in East Orange, N.J. Politics: "Sometime Republican." Religion: Protestant.

CAREER: U.S. Veterans Administration Center, White River Junction, Vt., employee in payroll department, 1947-72. Military service: U.S. Army, 1943-46; served in European theater. Member: New Hampshire Historical Society, Hanover Historical Society.

WRITINGS: The Day the Indians Came, Van Nostrand, 1966; Powder for Bunker Hill, Macrae Smith, 1968; Powder Alarm 1774, Auerbach, 1971. Author of story "Escape on Ice Skates," originally published in Boys' Life.

SIDELIGHTS: Richmond told CA: "[I] believe young people need historical perspective in order to better understand their society. I stress the dignity of the individual, and his duty to stand for the right as he sees it."†

* * *

RICHMOND, Walt(er F.) 1922-

PERSONAL: Born December 5, 1922, in Memphis, Tenn.; son of Walter and Jessie (Forbes) Richmond; married Leigh Tucker (a research anthropologist); children: Scott (daughter). Office address: The Centric Foundation, Inc., P.O. Box 1117, Merritt Island, Fla. 32952.

CAREER: Research physicist and writer; formerly senior partner, Richmond Research, Claremont, N.H.; currently president, The Centric Foundation, Merritt Island, Fla.

WRITINGS—All with wife, Leigh Richmond; all published by Ace Books: The Lost Millenium, 1967; Shock Wave, 1967; Phoenix Ship, 1969; Gallagher's Glacier, 1970; Positive Charge, 1970; Challenge the Hellmaker, 1976. Contributor of short stories to science ficiton magazines, including Analog.

WORK IN PROGRESS: Co-developer with wife, Leigh Richmond, of centric analysis, the mathematics of trigonometry applied to field theory and relativity.

* * *

RICKEY, Mary Ellen 1929-

PERSONAL: Born January 11, 1929, in Baton Rouge, La.; daughter of Frank Atkinson (a professor) and Mary Ellen (Patterson) Rickey. Education: Louisiana State University, B.A., 1949; Duke University, M.A., 1950; Johns Hopkins University, graduate study, 1952-53; University of Florida,

Ph.D., 1955. Politics: Democrat. Religion: Episcopalian. Home: 2140 Baringer Ave., Louisville, Ky. 40204. Office: Department of English, University of Louisville, Louisville, Ky. 40208.

CAREER: Louisiana State University, Baton Rouge, instructor in English, 1950-52; University of Kentucky, Lexington, 1955-68, began as instructor, became professor of English; University of Louisville, Louisville, Ky., professor of English, 1968—. Member: Modern Language Association of America, Southern Renaissance Conference, Phi Beta Kappa.

WRITINGS: Rhyme and Meaning in Richard Crashaw, University of Kentucky Press, 1961; Utmost Art: Complexity in the Poetry of George Herbert, University of Kentucky Press, 1966.

WORK IN PROGRESS: A monograph on Shakespeare and Rabelais; study of seventeenth-century conceptions of relationship of body and soul.

* * *

RICKS, David F(rank) 1927-

PERSONAL: Born March 30, 1927, in Wilson, Wyo.; son of David and Eva (Little) Ricks; married Annie (Endicott) Russell, April 18, 1949; children: David, Margaret, Richard, Thomas, Ann, Sarah. Education: University of Chicago, B.A., 1948, Ph.D., 1956. Politics: Democrat. Religion: Unitarian Universalist. Home: 15 Rectory Lane, Scarsdale, N.Y. Office: Department of Psychology, City College of the City University of New York, New York, N.Y. 10033.

CAREER: Harvard University, Cambridge, Mass., research associate in department of social relations, 1956-60; Brandeis University, Waltham, Mass., assistant professor of psychology, 1960-64; Columbia University, Teachers Collge, New York City, 1964-72, professor of psychology, 1966-72; City College of the City University of New York, New York City, professor of psychology, 1972—. Member of board, Westchester Association for Mental Health. Military service: U.S. Navy, 1945-46. Member: American Psychological Association, New York Psychological Association, Phi Beta Kappa, Sigma Xi. Awards, honors: U.S. Public Health Service fellow, Judge Baker Guidance Center, 1955-56.

WRITINGS: Mood and Personality, Holt, 1966; (editor with Merrill Roff) Life History Research in Psychopathology, University of Minnesota Press, Volume I, 1970, Volume III (with Alexander Thomas), 1974. Contributor to Harvard Review, and psychology and medical journals.

WORK IN PROGRESS: A book with Abraham Wandersman and Paul Poppen, integrating current work in humanistic and behavioral approaches to psychotherapy; a textbook of psychopathology through the life span.

* * *

RIDDLEBERGER, Patrick Williams 1915-

PERSONAL: Born October 6, 1915, in Woodstock, Va.; son of Frank Belew (a salesman) and Anna (Williams) Riddleberger; divorced; children: Anne (Mrs. Francis Luzzatto), Patrick (deceased). Education: Virginia Military Institute, A.B., 1939; University of California, Berkeley, M.A., 1949, Ph.D., 1953. Home: 14 Brookside Court, Edwardsville, Ill. 62025. Office: History Department, Southern Illinois University, Edwardsville, Ill. 62025.

CAREER: U.S. Army, 1939-46, became captain; University of Maryland, College Park, instructor, later assistant professor of history, 1953-60; Southern Illinois University, Edwardsville Campus, associate professor, 1960-66, professor of history, 1966—. Director (as visiting Fulbright scholar), American Studies Research Centre, Hyderabad, India, 1964-65.

WRITINGS: George Washington Julian, Radical Republican: A Study in Nineteenth-Century Politics and Reform, Indiana Historical Bureau, 1966. Contributor to professional journals.

WORK IN PROGRESS: 1866: The Critical Year Revisited.

* * *

RIEMER, Neal 1922-

PERSONAL: Born August 25, 1922, in Freehold, N.J.; son of Elick Jacob and Elizabeth (Krupnick) Riemer; married Ruby Riemer, September 15, 1946; children: David Raphael, Jeremiah Michael, Seth Daniel. *Education:* Clark University, B.A. (with high honors), 1943; Harvard University, M.A., 1947, Ph.D., 1949. *Home:* Village Rd., Green Village, N.J. 07935. *Office:* Department of Political Philosophy, Drew University, Madison, N.J. 07940.

CAREER: Harvard University, Cambridge, Mass., teaching fellow, 1947-48; Pennsylvania State University, University Park, instructor, 1948-50, assistant professor, 1950-54, associate professor, 1954-59, professor of political science, 1959-64; University of Wisconsin, Milwaukee, professor of political science, 1964-72, associate dean, College of Liberal Arts, 1969-71; Drew University, Madison, N.J., Andrew W. Mellon Professor of Political Philosophy, 1972—. Fulbright professor of American studies, University of Innsbruck, 1961-62. *Military service:* U.S. Army Air Forces, 1943-45. *Member:* American Political Science Association, American Civil Liberties Union. *Awards, honors:* Rockefeller fellowship, 1958-59; University of Wisconsin, Milwaukee, outstanding professor award, 1967-68.

WRITINGS: Problems of American Government, McGraw, 1952; *World Affairs: Problems and Prospects,* Appleton, 1958; *A Modern Democratic Theory for America* (monograph), Pennsylvania State University Institute of Public Administration, 1960; *The Revival of Democratic Theory,* Appleton, 1962; (co-author) *Americana-Austriaca,* Braumuller, Volume I, 1966, Volume II, 1970; *The Representative: Trustee? Delegate? Partisan? Politico?,* Heath, 1967; *The Democratic Experiment,* Van Nostrand, 1967; *James Madison,* Washington Square Press, 1968. General editor, "Problems in Political Science" series, Heath.

WORK IN PROGRESS: Prophetic Politics.

AVOCATIONAL INTERESTS: Travel.

* * *

RIENOW, Robert 1909-

PERSONAL: Surname is pronounced Reno; born December 4, 1909, in Grafton, Wis.; son of Charles (a printer) and Agatha (Jaeger) Rienow; married Leona Train (a writer), April 8, 1931. *Education:* Carthage College, A.B., 1930; Columbia University, M.A., 1933, Ph.D., 1937; Ohio State University, graduate study, 1934-35. *Politics:* Democrat. *Religion:* Protestant. *Home:* Hollyhock Hollow Farm, R.D. 2, Selkirk, N.Y. 12158. *Agent:* Oliver Swan, Julian Bach Literary Agency, 18 East 48th St., New York, N.Y. 10017. *Office:* Graduate School of Public Affairs, State University of New York, Albany, N.Y. 12203.

CAREER: School principal in Sussex, Wis., 1931-32; Union College (now Union College and University), Schenectady, N.Y., instructor in political science, 1934-35; State University of New York at Albany, instructor, 1936-39, assistant professor, 1939-43, professor of political science, Graduate School of Public Affairs, 1947—. State University of New York, extension instructor at School of Industrial and Labor Relations at Cornell University, 1946—, member of publications committee, 1966—. Consultant to New York Department of Education and U.S. Treasury Department. *Military service:* U.S. Army, Infantry, 1943-46; became first lieutenant. New York National Guard, beginning 1947; retired as brigadier general.

MEMBER: American Political Science Association, American Association of University Professors, Environmental Defense Fund (member of advisory council), Wilderness Society, National Grange, National Parks Association, Nature Conservancy (chairman, Eastern New York chapter, 1955—; member of national board of governors, 1956-62, 1964-70), Defenders of Wildlife (member of national board of trustees, 1959-75), New York State Political Science Association (president, 1955-56), State University Faculties Association, University Club of Albany, Masons, Sierra Club (member of advisory council, Atlantic chapter, 1965—). *Awards, honors:* George Washington Honor Medal, Freedoms Foundation, 1956; Litt.D., Carthage College, 1963, and Ripon College, 1970.

WRITINGS: Nationality of a Merchant Vessel, Columbia University Press, 1937; *Calling All Citizens* (high school text), Houghton, 1943, 3rd edition, 1952; *Introduction to Government* (college text), Knopf, 1952, 3rd edition, 1964; *American Problems Today,* Heath, 1953, 3rd edition, 1964; *New York State and Local Government,* New York State Education Department, 1954, 2nd edition, 1958; *American Government in Today's World,* Heath, 1956, 4th edition, 1966; (with wife, Leona T. Rienow) *Our New Life with the Atom,* Crowell, 1959; *Contemporary International Politics,* Crowell, 1961; *The Citizen and His Government,* Houghton, 1963; *Our Changing Social Order,* Heath, 1964; (with Leona T. Rienow) *Of Snuff, Sin, and the Senate,* Follett, 1965; (with Leona T. Rienow) *The Lonely Quest: The Evolution of Presidential Leadership,* Follett, 1966; (with Leona T. Rienow) *Moment in the Sun: A Report on the Deteriorating Quality of the American Environment,* Dial, 1967; *Vistas on the 1967 Constitutional Convention,* New York State Education Department, 1967; *Man against His Environment,* Ballantine, 1970.

Author of pamphlets on government and conservation, including U.S. Information Services publication, "Calling All Citizens," published in four Asiatic languages. Contributor to *Compton's Encyclopedia, World Book Encyclopedia,* and *Book of Knowledge;* also contributor of articles, some co-authored with wife, to *Saturday Review, Harper's, Coronet, Pageant, New York Times Magazine, This Week,* and professional journals.

WORK IN PROGRESS: A book, tentatively titled *The New Star in the Sky,* an analysis of the impact of INTELSAT on world order; other writing on conservation, public affairs, and manpower problems.

SIDELIGHTS: Robert Rienow lives on, and protects, about 140 acres of woodland, which has been restored to a flourishing state. He is interested in organic gardening.

* * *

RIESELBACH, Leroy N(ewman) 1934-

PERSONAL: Born July 11, 1934, in Milwaukee, Wis.; son

of L. LeRoy (a lawyer) and Lillian (Newman) Rieselbach; married Helen Funk, June 29, 1957; children: Erik, Kurt, Alice, Karen. *Education:* Harvard University, A.B., 1956; Yale University, M.A., 1958, Ph.D., 1964. *Home:* 108 Glenwood E., Bloomington, Ind. 47401. *Office:* Department of Political Science, Indiana University, Bloomington, Ind. 47401.

CAREER: Indiana University, Bloomington, lecturer, 1964, assistant professor, 1964-66, associate professor, 1966-70, professor of government, 1970—, chairman of department of political science, 1971—. Postdoctoral fellow, Mental Health Research Institute, University of Michigan, Ann Arbor, 1964-65; research associate, Center for International Affairs, Harvard University, 1969. *Member:* American Political Science Association, Midwest Political Science Association.

WRITINGS: The Roots of Isolationism, Bobbs-Merrill, 1967; (editor with George I. Balch) *Psychology and Politics: An Introductory Reader,* Holt, 1969; (editor) *The Congressional System: Notes and Readings,* Duxbury, 1970; (contributor) Michael Haas and Henry Kariel, editors, *Approaches to the Study of Political Science,* Chandler, 1970; (contributor) Oliver Walter, editor, *Political Scientists at Work,* Duxbury, 1971; *Congressional Politics,* McGraw, 1973; (editor) *People vs. Government: Essays on Institutional Responsiveness,* Indiana University Press, 1975; *Congressional Reform in the Seventies,* General Learning Press, 1976. Contributor of articles and reviews to professional journals.

WORK IN PROGRESS: Co-author of *Political Behavior in America,* for Wiley.

* * *

RIESMAN, Evelyn Thompson 1912-

PERSONAL: Born February 14, 1912, in Brookline, Mass.; daughter of Maurice de Kay (an electro-chemist) and Lilian (Hastings) Thompson; married David Riesman (a university professor), July 15, 1936; children: Paul, Jennie, Lucy (Mrs. Michael Oelbaum), Michael. *Education:* Sorbonne, University of Paris, student for one year; Bryn Mawr College, B.A., 1935. *Home:* 49 Linnaean St., Cambridge, Mass. 02138.

WRITINGS: (With husband, David Riesman) *Conversations in Japan,* Basic Books, 1967; (contributor) Herbert Bergman, editor, *Cinema and Literature,* Bobbs-Merrill, 1975. Contributor of stories and articles to *Twice a Year, Antioch Review, Southwest Review,* and other periodicals.

WORK IN PROGRESS: Novella, *The Garden Party.*

SIDELIGHTS: Evelyn Riesman told *CA:* "In my writing I try to express something about the quality of feminine sensibility and experience." Mrs. Riesman travels with her husband when he lectures, attends conferences, or is on sabbatical. She has lived for several months in Japan and England. *Avocational interests:* Modern painting, film, French contemporary writers, playing music and tennis.

* * *

RILEY-SMITH, Jonathan (Simon Christopher) 1938-

PERSONAL: Born June 27, 1938, in Harrogate, Yorkshire, England; son of William Henry Douglas (chairman of a brewery) and Elspeth Agnes Mary (Craik Henderson) Riley-Smith; married Marie-Louise Jeannetta Field, July, 1968. *Education:* Cambridge University, B.A. (honors),

1960, M.A. and Ph.D., 1964. *Politics:* Conservative. *Religion:* Roman Catholic. *Home:* 53 Hartington Grove, Cambridge, England. *Office:* Queen's College, Cambridge University, Cambridge, England.

CAREER: University of St. Andrews, St. Andrews, Scotland, assistant lecturer in mediaeval history, 1964-65, lecturer, 1966-72; University of Cambridge, Cambridge, England, assistant lecturer, 1972-75, lecturer in medieval history, 1975—, fellow of Queen's College and director of studies in history, 1972—.

WRITINGS: The Knights of St. John in Jerusalem and Cyprus c. 1050-1310, Macmillan, 1967; (editor with Ursula Lyons and contributor) Ibn al-Furat, *Ayyubids, Mamlukes and Crusaders,* Heffer, 1971; *The Feudal Nobility and the Kingdom of Jerusalem, 1174-1277,* Macmillan, 1973.

WORK IN PROGRESS: An introduction to the history of the crusades.

* * *

RIMA, I(ngrid) H(ahne) 1925-

PERSONAL: Surname is pronounced *Rye*-ma; born March 13, 1925, in Germany; naturalized U.S. citizen; daughter of Max F. and Hertha (Grunsfeld) Hahne; married Philip W. Rima (an engineer), June 23, 1956; children: David, Eric. *Education:* Hunter College (now Hunter College of the City University of New York), B.A., 1945; University of Pennsylvania, M.A., 1946, Ph.D., 1952. *Home:* 7402 Mountain Ave., Philadelphia, Pa. *Office:* Temple University, Philadelphia, Pa. 19122.

CAREER: Temple University, Philadelphia, Pa., instructor, 1946-51, assistant professor, 1951-60, associate professor, 1960-65, professor of economics, 1965—, chairman of department, 1968—. Visiting professor, University of Pennsylvania, summers, 1972 and 1973. Consultant, International Business Machines Corp. *Member:* American Economic Association, Phi Beta Kappa.

WRITINGS: Development of Economic Analysis, Irwin, 1967, revised edition, 1972; (editor) *A Forum on Systems Management,* Bureau of Economic and Business Research, Temple University, 1969; (editor) *Readings in the History of Economic Theory,* Holt, 1970. Also contributor to *Introduction to Modern Economics.*

WORK IN PROGRESS: James Mill and classical economics; application of marginal analysis to resource allocation in complex hardware systems.†

* * *

RINGOLD, May Spencer 1914-

PERSONAL: Born May 1, 1914, in Winona, Miss.; daughter of Thomas Harrison (an advertising salesman) and Mary (Beard) Spencer; divorced; children: May Spencer Ringold, Marcus Ringold. *Education:* Mississippi State College for Women, B.A., 1936; University of Mississippi, M.A., 1950, Emory University, Ph.D., 1956. *Politics:* Democrat. *Religion:* Methodist.

CAREER: Assistant professor of history at Georgia State College (now Georgia State University), Atlanta, 1956-57, and Oglethorpe University, Atlanta, Ga., 1956-58; Clemson University, Clemson, S.C., assistant professor, 1958-61, associate professor of history, 1961-67; Mississippi State College for Women, Columbus, professor of history, beginning 1967.

WRITINGS: The Role of the State Legislature in the Con-

federacy, University of Georgia Press, 1967. Contributor to history journals.

WORK IN PROGRESS: Editing Gourdin-Young family papers, 1850-1876.††

* * *

RINGWALD, Donald C(harles) 1917-

PERSONAL: Born April 3, 1917, in Kingston, N.Y.; son of Charles Adam and Cornelia (Davis) Ringwald. *Education:* Educated in public schools of New York State. *Address:* P.O. Box 7015, Capitol Station Annex, Albany, N.Y. 12225.

CAREER: Served in deck and purser's departments on Hudson River steam vessels, 1936-41; with U.S. Veterans Administration, 1946, 1948-74, became financial manager. *Military service:* U.S. Army, 1941-46; became captain. *Member:* Steamship Historical Society of America (director, 1959-65, 1971—; president, 1973), Steamer Alexander Hamilton Society (trustee, 1974—; vice-president, 1974—), Sons and Daughters of Pioneer Rivermen, World Ship Society, Great Lakes Historical Society, Great Lakes Maritime Institute, Canal Society of New York State, Marine Historical Society of Detroit.

WRITINGS: Hudson River Day Line, Howell-North, 1965; *Day Line Memories* (booklet), Hudson River Day Line Railroad Alumni Association, 1971; *The Mary Powell,* Howell-North, 1972. Contributor to newspapers and magazines, including *American Neptune, Marine News, Ships and the Sea,* and *Telescope.* Editor, *Steamboat Bill* (journal of Steamship Historical Society of America), 1955-60, editor-in-chief, 1961-66.

WORK IN PROGRESS: Research and writing on the history of Hudson River steam navigation.

* * *

RINVOLUCRI, Mario (Francesco Giuseppe) 1940-

PERSONAL: Surname is pronounced Rin-*vo*-luke-ree; born June 9, 1940, in Cardiff, Wales; son of Giuseppe and Mina (Moore) Rinvolucri; married Sophie Laure Gabrielle Leyris; children: Lola-Agnes, Martin. *Education:* Queen's College, Oxford, B.A., 1961. *Politics:* Labour Party. *Religion:* Agnostic ("ex-Roman Catholic"). *Home:* 33 Kinnaird Way, Cambridge, England.

CAREER: Journalist with Reuters (news agency), London, England, 1961-62; magazine correspondent in Athens, Greece, 1962-65, and part-time teacher of English in Athens, 1963-64; teacher of English in Cambridge, England, 1966-67; free-lance writer, 1967-69.

WRITINGS: Anatomy of a Church: Greek Orthodoxy Today, Burns & Oates, 1966; (translator) Sotiris Spatharis, *Behind the White Screen,* London Magazine Editions, 1967. Also author of *Hitch-Hiking,* 1975. Contributor to *Tablet, Month, Guardian,* and other publications.

WORK IN PROGRESS: A book for the teaching of advanced oral English and a book on the use of sketch and mime for teaching English to foreigners, both with James Dixey; collecting tapes, slides, and film of Greek shadow theatre, for Weidner Library, Harvard University.

* * *

RINZLER, Alan 1938-

PERSONAL: Born October 26, 1938, in New York, N.Y.; son of Harvey (a doctor) and Evelyn (Rothman) Rinzler; married Marilyn Gross, January 28, 1962; children: Jonathan, Peter. *Education:* Harvard University, B.A., 1960. *Religion:* Jewish. *Office:* Macmillan Publishing Co., Inc., 866 Third Ave., New York, N.Y. 10022.

CAREER: Macmillan Publishing Co., Inc., New York, N.Y., senior editor, beginning 1965.

WRITINGS: (Editor) *The New York Spy,* David White, 1967; (with Max Wolff) *The Educational Park: A Guide to Its Implementation,* Center for Urban Education, New York, 1970; (editor) *Manifesto Addressed to the President of the United States From the Youth of America,* Macmillan, 1970.†

* * *

RISELEY, Jerry B(urr, Jr.) 1920-
(Galdo Monk)

PERSONAL: First syllable of surname rhymes with "wise"; born March 17, 1920, in Stockton, Kan.; son of Jerry Burr (an attorney) and Esta Ella (Scott) Riseley; married Eunice Olive Smith, July 31, 1943; children: Valrie Lillian, Stephanie Ann, Gheri-Llynn, Melanie Ann, Christopher Scott. *Education:* Attended Kansas State University, 1937-38, and Fort Hays Kansas State College; University of Kansas, B.S., 1941; University of Southern California, J.D., 1948. *Politics:* Democrat. *Religion:* Protestant. *Address:* 117 North Ash St., Stockton, Kan. 67669.

CAREER: Admitted to California State Bar, 1948; attorney practicing in Los Angeles, Calif., 1948-68. Justice of the peace of Stockton (Kan.) Township, 1969. Judge advocate, California department of Disabled American Veterans. *Military service:* U.S. Army, Infantry, parachutist and combat infantryman, 1941-45; became first lieutenant. *Member:* Disabled Officers Association (member of national executive committee, 1950-60), Pacific Coast Society for Legal History (public relations chairman).

WRITINGS: Where Sex is Illegal, Brandon House, 1967; *Henry Miller's "Tropic" Trial,* Authentic Research Press, 1969. Also author of *Sex, Doctors, and Lawyers,* and *Sex, Teachers and Psychiatrists and the Life and Virtue of Joseph Scott,* both by Brandon House. Regular columnist, *Los Angeles Daily Journal,* 1964-67, with some columns published under pseudonym Galdo Monk. Editor-in-chief, *Valley Bar Bulletin* and *Valley Bar Journal,* 1957-58.

WORK IN PROGRESS: A book on George R. Houston, the mystic millionaire, titled *Tomorrow the Water; The Susie Flock Story;* a book on mythical Zorbo and its mythical lawyers; a research project on public records; a textbook on junior college education.††

* * *

RITCHEY, John A(rthur) 1919-

PERSONAL: Born November 13, 1919, in Camden, Ind.; son of Arthur (an engineer) and Mabelle (Gronninger) Ritchey; married Frances Curtis, June 8, 1941; children: Diane (Mrs. David McMullen), Robin (Mrs. Peter Huebner). *Education:* Purdue University, B.S.E.E., 1941; Massachusetts Institute of Technology, M.S., 1946; University of Chicago, Ph.D., 1958. *Home:* 320 North 16th Ave., Bozeman, Mont. 59715. *Office:* Department of Industrial Engineering/Computer Science, Montana State University, Bozeman, Mont. 59715.

CAREER: Revere Copper & Brass, Chicago, Ill., personnel assistant, 1941-42; Proctor & Gamble, Cincinnati, Ohio, production supervisor, 1946-52; Purdue University,

Lafayette, Ind., assistant professor, 1952-55, associate professor, 1955-59, professor of industrial engineering, 1959-68; Stanford Research Institute, Menlo Park, Calif., operations analyst, 1968-70; Montana State University, Bozeman, professor of industrial engineering and chairman of department, 1970—. Participant in Ford Foundation industrial development project in Egypt, 1965-66. *Military service:* U.S. Navy, 1942-46; became lieutenant. *Member:* American Society for Engineering Education, American Institute of Industrial Engineers, Sigma Xi.

WRITINGS: (With H. T. Amrine and O. S. Hulley) *Manufacturing Organization and Management,* Prentice-Hall, 1957, 3rd edition, 1975. Editor, "Classics in Industrial Engineering," Prairie Publishers (Lafayette).

*   *   *

RITCHIE, Paul 1923-

PERSONAL: Born August 14, 1923, in Sydney, Australia; son of Percy William (an architect) and Elsie May (Fraser) Ritchie; married Diana Maxine Haas, June 10, 1963; children: Portia Innes. *Education:* Studied art at East Sydney Technical College, 1946-49. *Politics:* "Bystander." *Religion:* Agnostic. *Home:* Sta. Eulalia del Rio, Ibiza, Spain. *Agent:* A. M. Heath & Co. Ltd., 35 Dover St., London W1X 4EB, England.

CAREER: Painter prior to 1960, with side jobs as market researcher, surveyor's chainman, and day laborer in Australia, 1947-52, and as salesman, holiday season Santa Claus, social worker, and farmer while living in England, Germany, and Spain, 1952-60; writer, 1960—. Although Ritchie uses the past tense in connection with his work as an artist, his paintings have been exhibited in Sydney, London, Stockholm, Hildesheim, and Barcelona. *Military service:* Australian Army, 1942-46; served in Southwest Pacific. *Awards, honors:* British Arts Council prose bursary, 1968-69.

WRITINGS: The Unlucky Seed, Cassell, 1962; *The Protagonist,* Calder & Boyars, 1967; *Saint Honey* (three-act play), Calder & Boyars, 1967; *Confessions of a People Lover,* Calder & Boyars, 1968; *David, Are You There?* (play), Calder & Boyars, 1968; *Australia,* Macmillan, 1968; *Pitfall,* Milton House, 1973.

WORK IN PROGRESS: The Last Victorian.

*   *   *

RITSCHL, Dietrich 1929-

PERSONAL: Born January 17, 1929, in Basel, Switzerland; son of Hans and Gertrud (Stoerring) Ritschl; married Rosemarie Courvoisier, April 18, 1952; children: Christian, Lucas, Stephan, Johannes. *Education:* Studied at University of Tuebingen, University of Basel, and University of Bern, 1945-50; University of Edinburgh, Ph.D., 1957. *Home:* 4418 Reigoldswil, BL, Switzerland. *Office:* Department of Theology, University of Mainz, Mainz, West Germany.

CAREER: Ordained to Presbyterian ministry, 1950; assistant minister in Zyfen, Switzerland, 1950-52; minister in Scotland, 1952-58, in Wimberly, Tex., 1958-62; Austin Presbyterian Seminary, Austin, Tex., guest professor, 1958-60, associate professor of history of dogma and New Testament, 1960-63; Pittsburgh Theological Seminary, Pittsburgh, Pa., professor of history of doctrine and systematic theology, 1963-69; Union Theological Seminary, New York, N.Y., Harry Emerson Fosdick Professor,

1969-70; University of Mainz, Mainz, West Germany, professor of systematic theology, 1970—. Guest lecturer at Presbyterian College, Montreal, Quebec, 1957, at Episcopal Seminary of the Southwest, Austin, Tex., 1959-61; member of United Theological Faculty in Melbourne, Australia, and guest professor at Knox College, Dunedin, New Zealand, 1970, 1972, 1974. Special lecturer and minister in Hungary, Czechoslovakia, Russia, India, and Mexico.

WRITINGS: Vom Leben in der Kirche, [Neukirchen], 1957, translation published as *Christ Our Life,* Oliver & Boyd, 1960; *Die Homiletische Funktion der Geminde,* EvZ (Zurich), 1960; *A Theology of Proclamation,* John Knox, 1960; *The Faith and Mission of the Church,* S.C.M. Press, 1961; *Nur Menschen,* Kathe Vogt Verlag (Berlin), 1962; *Athanasius,* [Zurich], 1963; *Memory and Hope: An Inquiry into the Presence of Christ,* Macmillan, 1967. Contributor to theology journals in Switzerland, Germany, Britain, Hungary, and the United States.

*   *   *

RITTER, Lawrence S. 1922-

PERSONAL: Born May 23, 1922, in New York, N.Y.; son of Irving (a teacher) and Bella (Gerwitz) Ritter; divorced; children: Stephen. *Education:* Indiana University, B.A., 1942; University of Wisconsin, M.A., 1948, Ph.D., 1951. *Home:* 270 West End Ave., New York, N.Y. 10023. *Office:* Graduate School of Business Administration, New York University, New York, N.Y. 10006.

CAREER: Michigan State University, East Lansing, instructor, 1949-50, assistant professor of economics, 1951-55; Federal Reserve Bank of New York, New York City, economist, 1955-60; New York University, Graduate School of Business Administration, New York City, professor of finance, 1960—, chairman of department, 1962—. Visiting associate professor, Yale University, 1960. Consultant to United States Treasury, Board of Governors of Federal Reserve System, American Bankers Association, Association of Reserve City Bankers, and Federal Deposit Insurance Corp. *Military service:* U.S. Navy, 1941-45; became lieutenant junior grade. *Member:* American Economic Association, American Finance Association (president, 1970), Royal Economic Society, Authors Guild. *Awards, honors:* Lindback Foundation Award for Distinguished Teaching at New York University, 1963.

WRITINGS: Money and Economic Activity, Houghton, 1952, 3rd edition, 1967; *The Glory of Their Times: The Story of the Early Days of Baseball,* Macmillan, 1966; (with William L. Silber) *Money,* Basic Books, 1970, 3rd edition, in press; (with Silber) *Principles of Money, Banking, and Financial Markets,* Basic Books, 1974, 2nd edition, in press. Editor, *Journal of Finance,* 1964-66. Contributor to economics journals.

*   *   *

RITZ, Joseph P. 1929-

PERSONAL: Born November 6, 1929, in Chicago, Ill.; married Ann M. Girard, July 26, 1958; children: Joanne, Michael, Robert, Jonathan, Margaret. *Education:* Seattle University, student, 1951-52; Marquette University, B.S. in Journalism, 1955; Fordham University, graduate student, 1960-61. *Religion:* Roman Catholic. *Home:* 6301 Smith Rd., Hamburg, N.Y. 14075.

CAREER: Reporter for newspapers in Gloversville, N.Y., 1955-57, and New Haven, Conn., 1957-59; Fordham University, Bronx, N.Y., assistant news director, 1959-61; *Newburgh Evening News,* Newburgh, N.Y., reporter, 1961-64; *Buffalo Courier-Express,* Buffalo, N.Y., reporter, 1964—. *Military service:* U.S. Army, 1948-51. *Member:* American Newspaper Guild (former vice-president, Empire State council; currently president, Buffalo chapter). *Awards, honors:* American Political Science Association Award for excellence in reporting public affairs, 1967; Page One Award, Buffalo Newspaper Guild, 1967, 1969, 1971.

WRITINGS: The Despised Poor: Newburgh's War on Welfare, Beacon, 1966. Contributor to several national magazines.

WORK IN PROGRESS: A biography of Millard Fillmore.

*   *   *

RIVES, Stanley G(ene)   1930-

PERSONAL: Born September 27, 1930, in Decatur, Ill.; son of James and Frances Bunker (Haverfield) Rives; married Sandra Belt, December 28, 1957; children: Jacqueline, Joseph. *Education:* Northwestern University, student, 1948-49, Ph.D., 1963; Illinois State University, B.S., 1952, M.S., 1955. *Home:* 402 Marian, Normal, Ill. 61761. *Office:* Office of Undergraduate Instruction, Illinois State University, Normal, Ill. 61761.

CAREER: Instructor in speech at West Virginia University, Morgantown, 1955-56, and Northwestern University, Evanston, Ill., 1956-58; Illinois State University, Normal, assistant professor, 1958-63, associate professor, 1963-67, professor of information science, 1967—, dean of Undergraduate Instruction, 1972—. Visiting professor, University of Hawaii, Honolulu, 1963-64. Member of board of directors, National Debate Tournament. *Military service:* U.S. Army, 1952-54. *Member:* Speech Association of America (member of legislative assembly, 1966-70), American Forensic Association, American Association for Higher Education, American Association of University Professors, Central States Speech Association, Midwest Forensic Association (president, 1961-63), Illinois Speech and Theatre Association.

WRITINGS: (With Donald Klopf) *Individual Speaking Contests: Preparation for Participation,* Burgess, 1967; (with Gene A. Budig) *Academic Quicksand: Some Trends and Issues in Higher Education,* Professional Educators Publications, 1973. Contributor to *Journal of the American Forensic Association.*

*   *   *

RIVET, A(lbert) L(ionel) F(rederick)   1915-

PERSONAL: Surname is pronounced Reev-ay; born November 30, 1915, in England; son of Albert Robert and Rose (Bulow) Rivet; married Audrey Catherine Webb, April 8, 1947; children: Peter Leo, Anne Catherine. *Education:* Oriel College, Oxford, B.A., 1938, M.A., 1947. *Politics:* Socialist. *Religion:* Church of England. *Office:* Department of Classics, University of Keele, Keele, Staffordshire, England.

CAREER: Teacher in Hitchin, England, 1938-39; Civil Defence worker in London, England, 1939-40; bookseller in Cambridge, Norwich, and then Crowborough, England, 1946-51; Ordnance Survey Department, London, and Edinburgh, Scotland, assistant archaeology officer, 1951-64; University of Keele, Keele, Staffordshire, England, lecturer, 1964-67, reader in Romano-British studies, 1967-74, professor of Roman provincial studies, 1974—. Member of

executive committee and Faculty of Archaeology, History and Letters, British School at Rome. *Military service:* British Army, Royal Artillery and Royal Signals, 1940-46; became major.

MEMBER: Royal Archaeological Institute (member of council, 1955-59, 1963-67), Society of Antiquaries (London), Society of Antiquaries of Scotland (member of council, 1960-64), Society for the Promotion of Roman Studies (member of council, 1967-75), German Archaeological Institute (honorary corresponding fellow).

WRITINGS: (Contributor) P. Corder, editor, *Romano-British Villas,* Council for British Archaeology, 1955; (compiler) *Ordnance Survey Map of Roman Britain,* 3rd edition, Ordnance Survey, 1956; *Town and Country in Roman Britain,* Hutchinson, 1958, revised edition, 1964; (contributor) S. S. Frere, editor, *Problems of the Iron Age in Southern Britain,* Institute of Archaeology (London), 1960; (compiler) *Ordnance Survey Map of Southern Britain in the Iron Age,* Ordnance Survey, 1962; (editor) *The Iron Age in Northern Britain,* Edinburgh University Press, 1966; (contributor) J. S. Walker, editor, *The Civitas Capitals of Roman Britain,* Leicester University Press, 1966; (editor and contributor) *The Roman Villa in Britain,* Praeger, 1969.

(Contributor) M. Jesson and D. Hill, editors, *The Iron Age and Its Hill-Forts,* [Southampton], 1971; (contributor) R. Chevallier, editor, *Litterature Greco-Romaine et geographie historique,* [Paris], 1974. Contributor to *Oxford Classical Dictionary,* and *Princeton Dictionary of Classical Archaeology.* Writer of reviews on the subject of Roman Britain. Editor, *Proceedings* of the Society of Antiquaries of Scotland, 1961-64.

WORK IN PROGRESS: Gallia Narbonensis, for Routledge & Kegan Paul; with Colin C. Smith, *The Place-names of Roman Britain,* for Batsford.

*   *   *

ROBBINS, S(allie) A(nn)   1940-

PERSONAL: Born March 21, 1940, in Washington, D.C.; married Sabin Robbins IV (executive director of Friends of the National Zoo), June 29, 1962; children: Sabin V., William Galt. *Education:* Attended Holton-Arms School, Washington, D.C., and Mary Washington College. *Residence:* Washington, D.C. *Address:* c/o Bantam Books, Inc., 666 Fifth Ave., New York, N.Y. 10019.

CAREER: Member of board of directors, Junior League of Washington, 1967-68, and Holton-Arms School, 1968-75.

WRITINGS: See America Free, Bantam, 1967; *See Canada Free,* Bantam, 1968.

*   *   *

ROBERTS, (Edward) Adam   1940-

PERSONAL: Born August 29, 1940, in Penrith, England; son of Michael (a teacher and writer) and Janet (a writer; maiden name, Adam-Smith) Roberts; married Frances Dunn, September 16, 1966; children: one son, one daughter. *Education:* Magdalen College, Oxford, B.A., 1962; London School of Economics and Political Science, studies in international relations, 1965-68. *Office:* London School of Economics and Political Science, University of London, Houghton St., Aldwych WC2A 2AE, England.

CAREER: Peace News (weekly), London, England, assistant editor, 1962-65; University of London, London School of Economics and Political Science, London, lecturer in international relations, 1968—. *Member:* Institute for Strategic Studies, Royal Institute of International Affairs (associate member).

WRITINGS: (Editor) *The Strategy of Civilian Defence: Non-Violent Resistance to Aggression,* Faber, 1967, published as *Civilian Resistance as a National Defense,* Stackpole, 1968; (with Philip Windsor) *Czechoslovakia 1968: Reform, Repression and Resistance,* Columbia University Press, 1969. Contributor to newspapers and journals, including *New Society, World Today, Survival;* also contributor to British Broadcasting Corp.

SIDELIGHTS: Roberts told *CA:* "Although not a pacifist, I have been concerned with the development of the concept of national defense by non-violent resistance. I have also made a number of detailed studies of particular countries which have been involved in conflict in this century, including Algeria and Vietnam." He speaks French, and some German.†

* * *

ROBERTS, C(atherine) 1917-

PERSONAL: Born August 19, 1917, in Oakland, Calif.; daughter of Edward Earl and Vida (Collins) Roberts; married Richard Stanley Wrey Thorne (director of an industrial biological laboratory in Copenhagen), April 12, 1952. *Education:* University of California, Berkeley, A.B., 1938, Ph.D., 1943. *Home:* Lyngbakkevej 12, 2840 Holte, Denmark.

CAREER: Carlsberg Laboratorium, Copenhagen, Denmark, microbiologist, 1946-61. *Awards, honors:* American Association of University Women fellowship for study in Denmark, 1946; Emil Christian Hansen Silver Medal (Copenhagen), 1948, for work on yeast microbiology.

WRITINGS: The Scientific Conscience, Braziller, 1967; *The Three Faces of Humanism,* Gryphon, 1975. Writer of a number of scientific papers on the yeast fungi, 1948-61.

WORK IN PROGRESS: Science, Animals, and Evolution.

* * *

ROBERTS, (Ray) Clayton 1923-

PERSONAL: Born November 10, 1923, in Changsha, China; son of Ray Clayton (a Young Men's Christian Association secretary) and Eva (Rewalt) Roberts; married Margaret Anne Vail, August 23, 1952. *Education:* Whitman College, student, 1941-43, 1946; University of Washington, Seattle, B.A., 1947, M.A., 1948; University of Glasgow, graduate study, 1949-50; Cornell University, Ph.D., 1952. *Politics:* Democrat. *Religion:* Agnostic. *Home:* 284 Blenheim Rd., Columbus, Ohio 43214. *Office:* Department of History, Ohio State University, Columbus, Ohio 43210.

CAREER: Ohio State University, Columbus, instructor, 1952-56, assistant professor, 1956-61, associate professor, 1961-66, professor of history, 1966—.

WRITINGS: The Growth of Responsible Government in Stuart England, Cambridge University Press, 1966. Contributor to *Huntington Library Quarterly, Yale Law Journal,* and history journals.

WORK IN PROGRESS: Schemes and Undertakings: A Study of Politics and Power in Stuart England.

ROBERTS, Edgar V. 1928-

PERSONAL: Born October 20, 1928, in Minneapolis, Minn.; son of Edgar V. (a janitor) and Svea Elizabeth (Swenson) Roberts; married Nanette Marion McNiff, December 18, 1954; children: Jonathan, David, April. *Education:* University of Minnesota, B.A. (summa cum laude), 1951, M.A., 1952, Ph.D., 1960. *Politics:* "Independent-Democrat-Liberal." *Home:* 113 Glendale Rd., Scarsdale, N.Y. 10583. *Office:* Herbert H. Lehman College of the City University of New York, Bronx, N.Y. 10468.

CAREER: University of Minnesota, Minneapolis, instructor in English literature, 1952-57; Wayne State University, Detroit, Mich., instructor in English literature, 1957-61; Herbert H. Lehman College of the City University of New York, Bronx, N.Y., instructor, 1961-64, assistant professor, 1965-69, associate professor, 1969-74, professor of English literature, 1974—. *Military service:* U.S. Army, 1946-47. *Member:* Modern Language Association of America, Society for Theatre Research, American Association of University Professors, East African Wildlife Society, Audubon Society, Wilderness Society, Sierra Club.

WRITINGS: Writing Themes About Literature, Prentice-Hall, 1964, 3rd edition, 1973; (contributor of music) Henry Fielding, *The Author's Farce,* edited by Charles B. Woods and Curt A. Zimansky, University of Nebraska Press, 1966; (editor) Henry Fielding, *The Grub-Street Opera,* University of Nebraska Press, 1968; (editor) John Gay, *The Beggar's Opera* (text edition), University of Nebraska Press, 1969; *A Practical College Rhetoric: Writing Themes and Tests,* Winthrop Publishing, 1975. Contributor of articles and reviews to drama, speech, and library journals.

WORK IN PROGRESS: Editing the plays of Henry Fielding, for Wesleyan University Press and Oxford University Press.

AVOCATIONAL INTERESTS: Singing (bass-baritone solo voice; sang with Sir Thomas Beecham's Choral Society, 1955); jogging.

* * *

ROBERTS, Edward B(aer) 1935-

PERSONAL: Born November 18, 1935, in Chelsea, Mass.; son of Nathan (a retailer) and Edna (Podradchik) Roberts; married Nancy Helen Rosenthal, June 14, 1959; children: Valerie Jo, Mitchell Jonathan, Andrea Lynne. *Education:* Massachusetts Institute of Technology, S.B. and S.M. in E.E., 1958; S.M. (industrial management), 1960, Ph.D., 1962. *Politics:* Republican. *Religion:* Judaism. *Home:* 17 Fellsmere Rd., Newton, Mass. 02159. *Office:* Alfred P. Sloan School of Management, Massachusetts Institute of Technology, 50 Memorial Dr., Cambridge, Mass. 02139.

CAREER: Massachusetts Institute of Technology, Alfred P. Sloan School of Management, Cambridge, instructor, 1960-61, assistant professor, 1961-65, associate professor, 1965-70, professor of management, 1970—, David Sarnoff Professor of Management of Technology, 1974—, associate director of M.I.T. Research Program on the Management of Science and Technology, 1963-73, chairman of M.I.T. Technology and Health Management Group, 1974—. President, Pugh-Roberts Associates, Inc., Cambridge, 1963—. Consultant to National Aeronautics and Space Administration, 1961, RAND Corp., 1963-69, and the President's Council for Management Improvement, 1972-73. Member, Air Force Scientific Advisory Board, 1967-70, and Department of Commerce Technical Advisory Board, 1967-72.

Member of Massachusetts Institute of Technology Alumni Council, 1957—. *Member:* Institute of Management Sciences (member of national council, 1967-69), American Association for the Advancement of Science, American Economic Association, Institute of Electrical and Electronics Engineers, Sigma Xi, Tau Beta Pi, Eta Kappa Nu, Tau Kappa Alpha, Alpha Epsilon Pi. *Awards, honors:* American Marketing Association 1966 award as government/defense/space marketing man of the year, for writings on research and development marketing.

WRITINGS: (Contributor) *Problems in Industrial Dynamics,* M.I.T. Press, 1963; *The Dynamics of Research and Development,* Harper, 1964; (co-author) *Systems Simulation for Regional Analysis,* M.I.T. Press, 1968; (co-author) *Persistent Poppy: A Computer-Aided Search for Heroin Policy,* Ballinger, 1975. Contributor to engineering, technology, and management journals. Associate editor, *Management Science Bulletin,* 1964-67; *I.E.E.E. Transactions on Engineering Management,* special issue editor, 1967, member of editorial advisory board, 1967—; member of editorial advisory board, *Industrial Marketing Management,* 1975—.

WORK IN PROGRESS: Research on systems analysis, research and development management, the formation and growth of new enterprise, and health care management; co-author of *The Dynamics of Human Service Delivery.*

* * *

ROBERTS, Edwin A(lbert), Jr. 1932-

PERSONAL: Born November 14, 1932, in Weehawken, N.J.; son of Edwin Albert (an artist) and Agnes (Seuferling) Roberts; married Barbara Collins, June 14, 1958; children: Elizabeth Adams, Leslie Carol, Amy Barbara, Jacqueline Harding. *Education:* Student at College of William and Mary, 1952-53, and New York University, 1955-58. *Politics:* Independent. *Religion:* Roman Catholic. *Home:* 4740 Powder House Dr., Rockville, Md. 20853.

CAREER: Dow Jones & Co., Inc., editorial writer for *Wall Street Journal,* New York, N.Y., 1957-63; *National Observer,* news editor, 1963-69, columnist, 1969—. *Member:* International Oceanographic Foundation, White House Correspondents Association. *Awards, honors:* Pulitzer Prize, 1974, for distinguished commentary.

WRITINGS—All published by Dow Jones: *Latin America,* 1964; *The Stock Market,* 1965; *America Outdoors,* 1966; *The Smut Rakers,* 1966; *Russia Today,* 1967; (editor) *The Busy Rich,* 1967.

WORK IN PROGRESS: Research in oceanography and Soviet politics.

SIDELIGHTS: Roberts is "a generalist-journalist by vocation, a deep-sea fisherman by avocation." He writes: "Increasingly disturbed by government intrusion into lives of individuals, and costly and ineffectual character of that intrusion."

* * *

ROBERTSON, Charles L(angner) 1927-

PERSONAL: Born July 30, 1927, in Milan, Italy; U.S. citizen; son of Charles D. (a businessman) and Gladys (Langner) Robertson; married Janet Pope, March 18, 1950 (deceased); married Angelika Pohl Huber, March 19, 1970; children: Katherine, Jennifer, Heidi, Christina. *Education:* Northwestern University, B.S. and M.A., 1950; University of Strasbourg, further graduate study, 1950-51; Princeton

University, M.A., 1952, Ph.D., 1959. *Home:* 71 Dryad's Green, Northampton, Mass. 01060. *Office:* Smith College, Northampton, Mass. 01060.

CAREER: Princeton University, Princeton, N.J., instructor in politics, 1952-54; Smith College, Northampton, Mass., instructor, 1954-59, assistant professor, 1959-62, associate professor, 1962-68, professor of government, 1968—, director of Smith College Junior Year in Geneva, Switzerland, 1964-66, 1971-72. Lecturer, Amherst College, 1970-71; occasional guest lecturer, University of Massachusetts. *Military service:* U.S. Army, 1945-47; became sergeant. *Member:* American Political Science Association, International Studies Association, Phi Beta Kappa.

WRITINGS: *The Emergency Oil Lift to Europe in the Suez Crisis,* Bobbs-Merrill, 1965; *International Politics Since World War II: A Short History,* Wiley, 1966, 2nd edition, 1975.

WORK IN PROGRESS: *The Politics of International Economic Relations.*

* * *

ROBILLIARD, Eileen Dorothy 1921-

PERSONAL: Surname is pronounced Ro-*billy*-erd; born July 21, 1921, in Abbottabad, North West Frontier Province, India; daughter of Alfred Gordon (a captain, Royal Irish Regiment) and Irene Grace (de Putron) Connors; children: St. John Anthony. *Education:* Educated in Guernsey, Channel Islands, and at King's College, London. *Home:* 6 Fulton Terrace, Le Foulon, St. Peter Port, Guernsey, Channel Islands.

CAREER: Has worked as civil servant for British Admiralty Office, school teacher, free-lance journalist, character actress in provincial repertory, and in social welfare; as musician has combined variously the occupations of choir mistress and choral conductor, lecturer, school music teacher, private and class teacher of piano, and composer of piano and vocal music. *Member:* Music Teachers Association, Guernsey Music Society (past president).

WRITINGS: *The Persistent Pianist,* Oxford University Press, 1967.

* * *

ROBIN, Richard S(hale) 1926-

PERSONAL: Born April 18, 1926, in Stamford, Conn.; son of Edwin Joseph (a businessman) and Eva (Effron) Robin; married Joann Cohan, January 29, 1961; children: David Seth, Deborah Elizabeth. *Education:* Harvard University, B.A., 1948, Ph.D., 1958. *Home:* 78 Woodbridge St., South Hadley, Mass. 01075. *Office:* Department of Philosophy, Mount Holyoke College, South Hadley, Mass. 01075.

CAREER: University of Connecticut, Storrs, instructor in philosophy, 1958-62; Mount Holyoke College, South Hadley, Mass., assistant professor, 1962-66, associate professor, 1966-71, professor of philosophy, 1971—. Member of graduate faculty, University of Massachusetts, 1963—. Danforth Foundation associate, 1967—. *Member:* American Philosophical Association, Society for the Advancement of American Philosophy (member of executive circle, 1973-75), American Association of University Professors, Charles S. Peirce Society (president, 1965-67). *Awards, honors:* Harvard University philosophy department grant, 1961-62; Henry P. Kendall Foundation grant, 1962.

WRITINGS: (Editor with Edward C. Moore, and contributor) *Studies in the Philosophy of Charles Sanders Peirce,* second series, University of Massachusetts Press, 1964; *Annotated Catalogue of the Papers of Charles S. Peirce,* University of Massachusetts Press, 1967. Editor, *Transactions of the Charles S. Peirce Society,* 1971—.

* * *

ROBINS, Lee N(elken) 1922-

PERSONAL: Born August 29, 1922, in New Orleans, La.; daughter of Abraham and Leona (Reiman) Nelken; married Eli Robins (a physician), February 22, 1946; children: Paul, James, Thomas, Nicholas. *Education:* Radcliffe College, B.A., 1942, M.A., 1943, Ph.D., 1951. *Home:* 1 Forest Ridge, Clayton, Mo. 63105. *Office:* Washington University Medical School, 4940 Audubon, St. Louis, Mo. 63110.

CAREER: Washington University, Medical School, St. Louis, Mo., research assistant in department of psychiatry and neurology, 1954-58, research instructor, 1958-59, research assistant professor, 1959-62, research associate professor, 1962-66, research professor of sociology, 1966-68, professor of sociology in psychiatry, 1968—. *Member:* American Sociological Association (fellow), Society for the Study of Social Problems, American Public Health Association, Society for Life History Research in Psychopathology, American Psychopathological Association, International Sociological Association, American Association for Psychiatry, Midwest Sociological Society.

WRITINGS: Deviant Children Grown Up, Williams & Wilkins, 1966. Also author of two monographs, *A Follow-Up of Vietnam Drug Users,* 1973, and *The Vietnam Drug User Returns,* 1974, both for Special Action Office.

WORK IN PROGRESS: A book with working title, *Growing Up Black in a White City,* about the childhood variables predicting the adult outcome of Negro boys.

* * *

ROBINSON, A(ntony) M(eredith) Lewin 1916-

PERSONAL: Born October 11, 1916, in Swindon, England; son of William Edward (a clergyman) and Margaret (Ostler) Robinson; married Helen Margaret Austin, October 21, 1944; children: Andrew, Dorothea, David. *Education:* Rhodes University, B.A., 1937; University of London, Diploma in Librarianship, 1939; University of Cape Town, Ph.D., 1961. *Home:* 136 Camp Ground Rd., Newlands, Cape Town, South Africa. *Office:* South African Library, Cape Town, South Africa.

CAREER: University of Natal Library, Durban, South Africa, assistant, 1940-43; University of Cape Town, Cape Town, South Africa, assistant, 1943-45; South African Library, Cape Town, deputy librarian, 1945-61, director, 1961—. Lecturer in bibliography, University of Cape Town, School of Librarianship; member, National Library Advisory Council, 1972—. Member of council, Cape Tercentenary Foundation, 1961—. *Member:* Library Association (Great Britain; fellow), South African Library Association (honorary secretary, 1946-48), English Association (vice-president, 1974—), Rotary Club (Cape Town; chairman of youth service committee, 1966-67; president, 1970-71). *Awards, honors:* Carnegie grants for travel in Europe, 1951, and United States, 1965.

WRITINGS: Catalogue of Theses and Dissertations Accepted by South African Universities, 1918-41, privately printed, 1943; *William McDougall, M.B., D.Sc., F.R.S.: A Bibliography,* Duke University Press, 1943; *Bibliography of African Bibliographies,* South African Library, 1950, 3rd edition, 1960; *None Daring to Make Us Afraid: English Periodical Literature in the Cape Colony, 1824-1835,* Maskew Miller, 1962; *Systematic Bibliography,* Clive Bingley, 1965, 3rd edition, 1971; (editor) *Thomas Pringle's Narrative of a Residence in South Africa, 1934,* C. Struik, 1967; (editor) *The Letters of Lady Anne Barnard to Henry Dundas, 1793-1803,* A. A. Balkerna, 1973; (co-editor) *Francois Le Vaillant: Traveller in South Africa and his Collection of 165 Water-color Paintings,* Library of Parliament, 1973. General editor, "Grey Bibliographies" series. Contributor to *Encyclopaedia of Southern Africa, Dictionary of South African Biography,* and library journals. Editor, *Quarterly Bulletin* (publication of the South African Library).

WORK IN PROGRESS: Editing the South African journal of Stanley Leighton, M.P., 1889; a catalogue of early printed books to 1550 in South African collections.

* * *

ROBINSON, Donald W(ittmer) 1911-

PERSONAL: Born July 4, 1911, in Williamsport, Pa.; son of Francis Martin (an officer, U.S. Navy) and Anna (Laedlein) Robinson; married Esther Louise Stanbro, December 14, 1950. *Education:* Harvard University, A.B., 1932; University of Pennsylvania, Ph.D., 1944. *Politics:* Independent. *Religion:* Unitarian Universalist. *Office:* Special Publications, Phi Delta Kappa, Eighth and Union, Bloomington, Ind. 47401.

CAREER: Taught American history at high schools in Upper Darby, Pa., Brookline, Mass., and Berkeley, Calif., 1936-46; University of Tampa, Tampa, Fla., professor of education, 1946-48; assistant to president, Colorado Women's College, 1948-49; University of Mississippi, University, associate professor of education, 1949-51; California College of Arts and Crafts, Oakland, executive dean, 1951-55; teacher of social studies and head of department, Sequoia Union School District, Calif., 1956-62; Phi Delta Kappa (international education fraternity), Bloomington, Ind., associate editor and director of special publications, beginning 1962; National Association of Secondary School Principals, Washington, D.C., staff member, beginning 1968. Project director, National Council of Social Studies, 1965-66; member of National Curriculum Committee, Unitarian-Universalist Association, 1972—. Consultant, U.S. Office of Education. *Member:* Phi Delta Kappa.

WRITINGS: (With Harold Oyer, Daniel Roselle, and Elmer Pflieger) *Promising Practices in Civic Education,* National Council for the Social Studies, 1967; (editor) *As Others See Us: An International View of American History,* Houghton, 1969; (editor) *Verdict on America: Readings From Textbooks of Other Countries,* Houghton, 1974. Columnist, writing "Scraps from a Teacher's Notebook" for *Phi Delta Kappan.* Contributor to *Saturday Review* and education journals.

WORK IN PROGRESS: Editing *Fifty Years of the "Kappan,"* an anthology.†

* * *

ROBINSON, Philip 1926-

PERSONAL: Born December 10, 1926; son of Frederick John (in insurance) and Lucy (Bedford) Robinson; married Patricia Tryphena Chew, August 31, 1957. *Education:* Corpus Christi College, Cambridge, B.A. (honors in classics), 1948. *Politics:* "Centrist." *Home:* 154 Hersham Rd., Walton on Thames, Surrey, England. *Office:* International Computers Ltd., Lovelace Rd., Brockhall, Berkshire, England.

CAREER: Produce exporter in Bombay, Calcutta, and other cities in India, 1950-58; International Computers Ltd., Berkshire, England, programmer, compiler designer, and computer language specialist, 1962—. *Member:* British Computer Society, British Astronomical Association, British Interplanetary Society.

WRITINGS: The Pakistani Agent (fiction), Hart-Davis, 1965; *Masque of a Savage Mandarin* (fiction), Macdonald & Co., 1969; (editor with others) *Executive Programs and Operating Systems* (nonfiction), Macdonald & Co., 1970; (co-author) *Computers* (nonfiction), Collier–Macmillan, 1971; *Computer Programming*, Collier–Macmillan, 1972; *Advanced Cobol: ANS 76,* Macdonald & Co., 1976. Contributor to periodicals.

WORK IN PROGRESS: Seven textbooks covering teaching English as a second language, import/export, insurance, computer applications, and English for business careers; two novels.

SIDELIGHTS: Robinson's chief interests are India and space travel. He lists his "likes" as American science fiction, tennis, bridge, and golf, the plays of Pinter and Ionesco, hot climates, sea voyages, anything alcoholic except aniseed derivatives, almost any kind of music, old buildings (but not ruins), anything exotic, surrealist, or fantastic, the countryside (below 6,000 feet). His "dislikes" include cults and catchwords, pop art, other people's motor cars, air travel, big businessmen, Brecht, the English sky for eight months of the year, and politicians. Robinson told *CA* that he writes specialist computer texts to improve his professional reputation, English-language texts to make money, and fiction to please himself.

*   *   *

ROBINSON, Virgil E.   1908-

PERSONAL: Born January 9, 1908, in St. Helena, Calif.; son of Dores Eugene and Ella May (White) Robinson; married Alta Ruby Ellegard, August 17, 1930; children: Donald Eugene, Marvin James, Jennifer Dawn. *Education:* Pacific Union College, B.A., 1934; Seventh-day Adventist Theological Seminary, M.A., 1947. *Religion:* Seventh-day Adventist. *Office address:* Solusi College, Private Bag T 5399, Bulawayo, Rhodesia, Africa.

CAREER: Malamulo Mission Training School, Malawi, Africa, normal director, 1936-45; Kamagambo Training School, Kenya, Africa, principal, 1947-53; Helderberg College, Sometwet West, Cape, South Africa, teacher of history, 1955-61; Home Study Institute (correspondence school), Takoma Park, Md., senior editor, beginning 1962; currently affiliated with Solusi College, Bulawayo, Rhodesia. *Member:* Christian Writers' Association (Takoma Park; president, 1965).

WRITINGS: Those Adventurous Years, Southern Publishing, 1959; *Cabin Boy to Advent Crusader,* Southern Publishing, 1961; *Restless Missionary,* Review & Herald, 1963; *Ye Shall Reap,* Southern Publishing, 1964; *Only in Africa,* Review & Herald, 1965; *The Judsons of Burma,* Review & Herald, 1966; *Brave Men to the Battle,* Pacific Press Publishing Association, 1967; *Luther the Leader,* Review & Herald, 1967; *Desert Track and Jungle Trail,* Pacific Press Publishing Association, 1969; *Magnificent Missionary: The*

Story of Dwight L. Moody, Southern Publishing, 1969; *A Flame for God,* Review & Herald, 1975; *William Booth and His Army,* Pacific Press Publishing Association, 1976; *James White,* Review & Herald, 1976. Editor, *Malamulo Tidings,* 1937-45.

WORK IN PROGRESS: A History of Solusi College; Son of New Hampshire, a biography of D. E. Robinson; *Third Angel over Africa.*

SIDELIGHTS: Robinson first went to Africa as a boy of thirteen and he lived there until nineteen; his residence on that continent totals almost thirty years. *Avocational interests:* Camping, mountain climbing, gardening.

*   *   *

ROBINSON, W(illiam) R(onald)   1927-

PERSONAL: Born October 21, 1927, in Steubenville, Ohio; son of Jacob Lederer (a carpenter) and Ethel (McGuire) Robinson; married Mina Shumway, June 10, 1952; children: Monica, Christopher, Teresa, Keenan. *Education:* Attended University of Kentucky, 1948-50; Ohio State University, B.A., 1952, M.A., 1956, Ph.D., 1962. *Home:* 2125 Northwest Seventh Lane, Gainesville, Fla. 32601. *Office:* English Department, University of Florida, Gainesville, Fla. 32601.

CAREER: University of Virginia, Charlottesville, instructor, 1962-64, assistant professor of American literature, 1964-67; University of Florida, Gainesville, associate professor, 1967-71, professor of American and contemporary literature, 1971—. *Military service:* U.S. Army, 1946-47. *Member:* Society for the Study of Criteria.

WRITINGS: Edwin Arlington Robinson: A Poetry of the Act, Western Reserve University Press, 1967; (editor and contributor) *Man and the Movies,* Louisiana State University Press, 1967. Contributor to *Shenandoah, Southern Humanities Review, Georgia Review, Film Journal,* and other periodicals.

WORK IN PROGRESS: Books on the movies, Ernest Hemingway's *A Farewell to Arms,* and Edwin Arlington Robinson's poetry of life.

*   *   *

ROBITSCHER, Jonas B(ondi, Jr.)   1920-

PERSONAL: Born October 28, 1920, in New York, N.Y.; son of Jonas Bondi and Elsa (Eisinger) Robitscher; married Jean Begeman, June 1, 1950; children: Jan, Christine, John. *Education:* Brown University, A.B., 1942; George Washington University, J.D., 1948, M.D., 1955. *Politics:* Democrat. *Home:* 779 Clifton Rd. N.E., Atlanta, Ga. 30307. *Office:* School of Law, Emory University, Atlanta, Ga. 30322.

CAREER: Wall Street Journal, New York, N.Y., Washington Bureau reporter, 1944-46; Covington, Burling, Rublee, Acheson & Shorb, Washington, D.C., law clerk, 1946-48; admitted to District of Columbia Bar, 1948; U.S. Federal Trade Commission, Washington, D.C., attorney, 1948-51; George Washington University Hospital, Washington, D.C., intern, 1955-56; Institute of the Pennsylvania Hospital, Philadelphia, resident in psychiatry, 1956-59; private practice of psychiatry, Bryn Mawr, Pa., 1959-72; Emory University, Atlanta, Ga., Henry R. Luce Professor of Law and the Behavioral Sciences, 1972—. Graduate, Philadelphia Association for Psychoanalysis; lecturer in law, Villanova University, 1965-72; director, National Institute of Mental Health program, Social Legal Uses of Forensic

Psychiatry, University of Pennsylvania, 1969-72. *Member:* American Medical Association, American Psychiatric Association, Georgia Psychiatric Society, Atlanta Psychoanalytic Society, Phi Beta Kappa, Alpha Omega Alpha.

WRITINGS: Pursuit of Agreement: Psychiatry and the Law, Lippincott, 1966; (editor and contributor) *Eugenic Sterilization,* C. C Thomas, 1974. Contributor to medical and legal journals.

* * *

ROCK, Irvin 1922-

PERSONAL: Born July 7, 1922, in New York, N.Y.; son of Daniel J. (a lawyer) and Lilian (Weinberger) Rock; married Romola Hardy, October 25, 1945; married second wife, Sylvia Shilling, July 24, 1963; children: (first marriage) Peter, Alice; (second marriage) Lisa, David. *Education:* City College (now City College of the City University of New York), B.S., 1947, M.A., 1948; New School for Social Research, Ph.D. (summa cum laude), 1952. *Home address:* R.D. 1, Box 760, Newton, N.J. 07860. *Office:* Institute for Cognitive Studies, Rutgers University, Newark, N.J. 07102.

CAREER: Licensed psychologist, New York State. New School for Social Research, New York City, lecturer, 1952-53, assistant professor, 1953-56, associate professor of psychology, 1956-59; Yeshiva University, Ferkauf Graduate School, New York City, associate professor, 1959-61, professor of experimental and clinical psychology, 1962-67, chairman of department, 1959-61; Rutgers University, Institute of Cognitive Studies, Newark, N.J., professor of psychology, 1967—. Visiting professor, Swarthmore College, 1963; visiting scholar, Cambridge University, 1973. *Military service:* U.S. Army, 1943-45; served in European theater; received three battle stars. *Member:* American Psychological Association (fellow), American Association for the Advancement of Science (fellow), Psychonomic Society, Eastern Psychological Association. *Awards, honors:* Grants from U.S. Public Health Service, 1950-62, and National Science Foundation, 1963-67; research scientist award, 1968.

WRITINGS: (Contributor) *Festschrift for Gardner Murphy,* Harper, 1960; (contributor) Jordan Scher, editor, *Theories of the Mind,* Free Press of Glencoe, 1962; (contributor) C. Scheerer, editor, *Cognition: Theory, Research, Promise,* Harper, 1964; *The Nature of Perceptual Adaptation,* Basic Books, 1966; (contributor) D. Hamburg, K. Pribram, and A. Stunkard, editors, *Perception and Its Disorders,* Williams & Wilkins, 1970; (contributor) A. Gilgen, editor, *Contemporary Scientific Psychology,* Academic Press, 1970; *Orientation and Form,* Academic Press, 1973; *An Introduction to Perception,* Macmillan, 1975. Contributor to *Encyclopedia Americana,* 1970. Contributor of fifty articles to scientific journals. Consultant, *Scientific American,* 1959—; member of advisory board, *Vision Research.*

WORK IN PROGRESS: An article to be included in *Cognitive Processes,* edited by William Epstein, for Wiley; editing the sensation and perception section of *International Encyclopedia of Neurology, Psychiatry, Psychoanalysis, and Psychology;* research on form and space perception.

* * *

ROCKWELL, Anne F. 1934-

PERSONAL: Born February 8, 1934, in Memphis, Tenn.; daughter of Emerson (an advertising executive) and Sabina (Fromhold) Foote; married Harlow Rockwell (a free-lance artist, designer, and illustrator), March 16, 1955; children: Hannah, Elizabeth, Oliver Penn. *Education:* Studied at Sculpture Center, New York City, three years, and Pratt Graphic Arts Center, one year. *Politics:* Liberal Democrat. *Religion:* Episcopalian. *Home:* 4 Raymond St., Old Greenwich, Conn. 06870.

CAREER: Silver Burdett Publishers, Morristown, N.J., member of production department, 1952; Young and Rubicam (advertising), art-buying secretary, 1953; Goldwater Memorial Hospital, New York, N.Y., assistant recreation leader, 1954-56; author and illustrator of children's books. *Member:* Authors Guild.

WRITINGS—Juvenile; all self-illustrated: *Paul and Arthur Search for the Egg,* Doubleday, 1964; *Gypsy Girl's Best Shoes,* Parents' Magazine Press, 1966; *Sally's Caterpillar,* Parents' Magazine Press, 1966; *Filippo's Dome: Brunelleschi and the Cathedral of Florence,* Atheneum, 1967; *The Stolen Necklace: A Picture Story from India,* World Publishing, 1968; *Glass, Stones and Crown: The Abbe Sugar and the Building of St. Denis,* Atheneum, 1968; *The Good Llama,* World Publishing, 1968; *Temple on the Hill: The Building of the Parthenon,* Atheneum, 1969; *The Wonderful Eggs of Furicchia: A Picture Story from Italy,* World Publishing, 1969.

When the Drum Sang: An African Folktale, Parents' Magazine Press, 1970; *The Dancing Stars: An Iroquois Legend,* Crowell, 1971; *The Monkey's Whiskers: A Brazilian Folktale,* Parents' Magazine Press, 1971; *Paintbrush and Peacepipe: The Story of George Catlin,* Atheneum, 1971; *Tuhurahura,* Parents' Magazine Press, 1971; *What Bobolino Knew,* McCall Publishing, 1971; *Paul and Arthur and the Little Explorer,* Parents' Magazine Press, 1972; *The Awful Mess,* Parents' Magazine Press, 1973; *The Boy Who Drew Sheep,* Atheneum, 1973; *Games (and How to Play Them),* Crowell, 1973; *The Wolf Who Had a Wonderful Dream: A French Folktale,* Crowell, 1973; *Befana: A Christmas Story,* Atheneum, 1974; *Gift for a Gift,* Parents' Magazine Press, 1974; *The Gollywhopper Egg,* Macmillan, 1974; *The Story Snail,* Macmillan, 1974; *The Three Bears and Fifteen Other Stories,* Crowell, 1975; *Big Boss,* Macmillan, 1975; *Poor Goose,* Crowell, 1976; *No More Work,* Greenwillow Books, 1976.

With husband, Harlow Rockwell: *Olly's Polliwogs,* Doubleday, 1970; *Molly's Woodland Garden,* Doubleday, 1971; *The Toolbox,* Macmillan, 1971; *Machines,* Macmillan, 1972; *Thruway,* Macmillan, 1972; *Toad,* Doubleday, 1972; *Head to Toe,* Doubleday, 1973.

Illustrator: Marjorie Hopkins, *The Three Visitors,* Parents' Magazine Press, 1967; Jane Yolen, *The Ministrel and the Mountain,* World Publishing, 1967; Lillian Bason, *Eric and the Little Canal Boat,* Parents' Magazine Press, 1967; Hopkins, *The Glass Valentine,* Parents' Magazine press, 1968; (and compiler) *Savez-vous planter les choux? and Other French Songs,* World Publishing, 1969; Paul Showers, *What Happens to a Hamburger,* Crowell, 1970; Kathryn Hitte, *Mexicali Soup,* Parents' Magazine Press, 1970; Joseph Jacobs, *Munacher and Manacher: A Irish Story,* Crowell, 1970; Ann (Lane) Petry, *Legends of the Saints,* Crowell, 1970; Jacobs, *Master of all Masters,* Grosset & Dunlap, 1972; Hopkins, *A Gift for Tolum,* Parents' Magazine Press, 1972; Walter Dean Myers, *The Dancers,* Parents' Magazine Press, 1972; Barbara Brenner, *Cunningham's Rooster,* Parents' Magazine Press, 1975.

WORK IN PROGRESS: Research for a book on the rebuilding of Athens after the Persian Wars, for children nine to twelve.

BIOGRAPHICAL/CRITICAL SOURCES: Bookworld, May 5, 1968, November 9, 1969; New York Times Book Review, June 9, 1968, October 27, 1968; Children's Book World, November 3, 1968; Books and Bookmen, May, 1969; Young Readers Review, May, 1969; Saturday Review, February 21, 1970.†

*　　*　　*

RODRIGUEZ-ALCALA, Hugo   1917-

PERSONAL: Born November 25, 1917, in Paraguay; married Sally Jean Stover, October 6, 1960; children: Ramiro Antonio, Marina Renee, Kimberly, Christopher Jose. Education: University of Asuncion, J.D., 1943; University of Wisconsin, Ph.D., 1963. Religion: Roman Catholic. Home: 3827 Gates Pl., Riverside, Calif. 92504. Office: Department of Spanish, University of California, Riverside, Calif. 92502.

CAREER: University of California, Riverside, professor of Spanish and chairman of department. Military service: Paraguayan Army, 1934-35. Member: Modern Language Association of America, International Association of Hispanists, Institute of Latin-American Literature, Paraguayan Academy of the Language. Awards, honors: First prize, Paraguayan Ministry of Education, for Horas liricas, 1939.

WRITINGS: La Danza de la Muerte, [Asuncion], 1937; Estampas de la guerra, Editorial Zampiropolos, 1939; Horas liricas (poems), Imprenta Nacional, 1939.

Francisco Romera: Vida y Obra, Columbia University Press, 1951; (with Everett W. Hesse) Cinco yanquis en Espana, Ronald, 1955; (contributor) La Cultura y la literatura iberoamericana, Ediciones de Andrea, 1957; Korn, Romero, Guiraldes, Unamuno, Ortega, Ediciones de Andrea, 1958; Mision y pensamiento de Francisco Romero, National University of Mexico Press, 1959.

Abril que cruza el mundo (poetry), Editorial Estaciones, 1960; Ensayos de norte a sur, University of Washington Press, 1960; (contributor) Homenaje a Alejandro Korn (1860-1960), Universidad Nacional de la Plata, 1960; (with William Wilson) Por Tierras de sol y de espanol, Ronald, 1963; (with wife, Sally Rodriguez-Alcala) Un pais hispanico visto por dentro, Prentice-Hall, 1965; El arte de Juan Rulfo, Instituto Nacional de Bellas Artes, 1965; (editor with S. Rodriguez-Alcala) Cuentos nuevos del sur, Prentice-Hall, 1967; Literatura paraquaya, Centro Editor de America Latina, 1968; Historia de la literatura paraguaya, Ediciones de Andrea, 1970; Palabras de los dias: Poemas, Facultad de Humanidades y Educacion, Universidad del Zulia, 1972; Narrativa hispanoamericana, Editorial Gredos, 1973.

Contributor of about one hundred articles, translations, short stories, poems, and reviews to yearbooks, journals, and newspapers in North and South America, Mexico, and Europe; articles include a series of twenty-two about Brazil published in El Pais, 1940.

WORK IN PROGRESS: Roa Bastos and His "Visionary" Art, studies in Latin-American fiction; a collection of his own poetry; a book of short narratives.

*　　*　　*

RODRIGUEZ-ALCALA, Sally   1938-

PERSONAL: Born September 20, 1938, in Seattle, Wash.;

daughter of Charles Freeman (a salesman) and H. Elizabeth (Stanley) Stover; married Hugo Rodriguez-Alcala (a professor), October 6, 1960; children: Ramiro Antonio, Marina Renee, Kimberly, Christopher Jose. Education: Attended Whitworth College, 1956-57, 1958; University of Washington, Seattle, B.A., 1961. Home: 3827 Gates Pl., Riverside, Calif. 92504.

WRITINGS—With husband, Hugo Rodriguez-Alcala: Un pais hispanico visto por dentro, Prentice-Hall, 1965; (editor) Cuentos nuevos del sur, Prentice-Hall, 1967.

SIDELIGHTS: Sally Rodriguez-Alcala spent six months traveling in South America with her husband, 1961, primarily in Paraguay, Argentina, and Brazil, and lived in Mexico City, Mexico for two years, 1972-74.

*　　*　　*

ROE, W(illiam) G(ordon)   1932-

PERSONAL: Born January 5, 1932, in Bournemouth, England; son of William Henry (a hotel worker) and Dorothy Myrtle (Hayman) Roe; married Mary Primrose Andreen, June 27, 1953; children: Helen Mary Gabrielle, William Patrick Logan, Rachel Caroline Jane, Michael Christopher Giles. Education: Jesus College, Oxford, B.A., 1953, M.A., 1957, D.Phil., 1962; St. Stephen's House, Oxford, Diploma in Theology (with distinction), 1957. Politics: Uncommitted. Home and office: St. Oswald's Vicarrage, Church St., Durham, England.

CAREER: Clergyman of Church of England; curate in Bournemouth, England, 1958-61; St. Michael's Church, Abingdon, Berkshire, England, priest in charge, 1961-69; St. Chad's College, Durham, England, vice-principal, 1969-74; St. Oswald's Church, Durham, vicar, 1974—. Chairman, Abingdon and District Council of Churches, 1965-67; rural dean of Durham, 1974—. Military service: British Army, 1953-55; became sergeant.

WRITINGS: Lamennais and England: The Reception of Lamennais's Religious Ideas in England in the Nineteenth Century, Oxford University Press, 1966.

WORK IN PROGRESS: Nineteenth-Century Spirituality; Religion and Social Problems.

*　　*　　*

ROGERS, Alan   1933-

PERSONAL: Born February 25, 1933, in Wallington, Surrey, England; son of E. W. (a local preacher) and Edith (Cuthbert) Rogers; married Marjorie Dawe (a musician), August 1, 1958; children: Malcolm D., Katherine Hilary. Education: University of Nottingham, B.A., 1954, M.A., 1956, Certificate of Education, 1957, Ph.D., 1966. Religion: Church of England. Office: University of Nottingham, Nottingham, England.

CAREER: School teacher and part-time university teacher, 1957-59; University of Nottingham, Department of Adult Education, Nottingham, England, lecturer, 1959-65; senior lecturer in history, 1965—. Member, European Architectural Heritage Year Educational Panel. Member: Royal Historical Society (fellow), Society of Antiquaries (fellow).

WRITINGS: (Editor) The Making of Stamford, Leicester University Press, 1965; History of Lincolnshire, Darwin Finlayson, 1970; Medieval Buildings of Stamford, Department of Adult Education, University of Nottingham, 1970; This Was Their World, B.B.C. Publications, 1972; Religious Foundations of Medieval Stamford, Department of

Adult Education, University of Nottingham, 1974. Contributor to historical journals. Editor, *Bulletin of Local History, East Midlands Region; Landscapes and Documents.*

WORK IN PROGRESS: A book on medieval Stamford; *Projects in Local History,* for David & Charles.

* * *

ROGERS, Katharine M(unzer) 1932-

PERSONAL: Born June 6, 1932, in New York, N.Y.; daughter of Martin (a business executive) and Jean (a psychiatrist; maiden name, Thompson) Munzer; married Kenneth C. Rogers (a college president), August 4, 1956; children: Margaret, Christopher, Thomas. *Education:* Barnard College, B.A. (summa cum laude), 1952; Columbia University, Ph.D., 1957. *Politics:* Liberal. *Home:* Hoxie House, Stevens Institute of Technology, Hoboken, N.J. 07030. *Office:* Brooklyn College of the City University of New York, Brooklyn, N.Y. 11210.

CAREER: Instructor in English at Skidmore College, Saratoga Springs, N.Y., 1954-55, and Cornell University, Ithaca, N.Y., 1955-57; Brooklyn College of the City University of New York, Brooklyn, N.Y., instructor, 1958-64, assistant professor, 1965-70, associate professor, 1971-73, professor of English, 1974—, member of doctoral faculty, 1972—. *Member:* Modern Language Association, National Organization for Women, Phi Beta Kappa. *Awards, honors:* Fulbright fellow at Newnham College, Cambridge, 1952-53.

WRITINGS: The Troublesome Helpmate: A History of Misogyny in Literature, Washington University Press, 1966; *William Wycherley,* Twayne, 1972. Contributor of scholarly articles to professional journals.

WORK IN PROGRESS: A book on women in eighteenth-century England.

SIDELIGHTS: Katharine Rogers told *CA:* "My intense concern with the status of women (spurred by some deplorable experiences in my professional life—e.g., being deprived of academic tenure with each pregnancy) provided a driving motive for writing my first book."

* * *

ROGERS, Raymond A(rthur) 1911-

PERSONAL: Born January 29, 1911, in Fort Collins, Colo.; son of Clark (a farmer) and Ida (Morrish) Rogers; married Dorothy Conroe, May 31, 1936; children: Jean (Mrs. James E. Hall). *Education:* Colorado State University, Fort Collins, B.S., 1933; Colorado State College (now University of Northern Colorado), M.A., 1940. *Home:* 818 West Valley View Dr., Fullerton, Calif. 92635. *Office:* Union Oil Research Center, Brea, Calif. 92621.

CAREER: Teacher of science at Ault (Colo.) High School, 1934-37, and at Erie (Colo.) High School, 1937-39; Union Oil Co. of California, Brea, chemist, 1940-47, supervisor of training, 1947-49, research chemist, 1949-51, personnel supervisor, 1951-53, senior research chemist, 1953-66, technical editor, 1966—. *Member:* Society for Technical Communication.

WRITINGS: (Contributor) S. I. Hayakawa, editor, *Language, Meaning, and Maturity,* Harper, 1954; *Coming Into Existence,* World Publishing, 1967; *How to Report Research and Development Findings to Management,* Pilot Books, 1973. Contributor to *ETC: A Review of General Semantics.*

ROGNESS, Alvin N. 1906-

PERSONAL: Born May 16, 1906, in Astoria, S.D.; son of I. A. and Mina (Engelstad) Rogness; married Nora M. Preus, June 30, 1934; children: Michael, Stephen, Paul, Martha (Mrs. Wayne D. Vetter), Peter, Andrew. *Education:* Augustana College, Sioux Falls, S.D., B.A., 1927; Luther Theological Seminary, B.Th., 1932; University of Minnesota, graduate study, 1932-34. *Home:* 1555 Branston, St. Paul, Minn. 55108.

CAREER: Ordained to Lutheran ministry, 1934; pastor in Duluth, Minn., 1934-37, Ames, Iowa, 1937-42, Mason City, Iowa, 1942-51, Sioux Falls, S.D., 1951-54; Luther Theological Seminary, St. Paul, Minn., president, 1954-74. Member of Board of Christian Education, Evangelical Lutheran Church, 1950-60; delegate to World Council of Churches for American Lutheran Church, New Delhi, India, 1961. Trustee, St. Olaf College. *Awards, honors:* D.D., Pacific Lutheran University, 1949.

WRITINGS—All published by Augsburg, except as noted: *On the Way,* 1943; *If God Were King,* 1948; *The Age and You,* 1949; *Who Shall be God?,* 1954; *His Increasing Church,* 1957; *Why Bother with God?,* Thomas Nelson, 1965; *Captured by Mystery,* 1966; *Forgiveness and Confession: Keys to Renewal,* 1970; *The Wonder of Being Loved: Messages for Lent and Every Season,* 1972; *Appointment with Death,* Thomas Nelson, 1972; *The Jesus Life: A Guide for Young Christians,* 1973; *The Touch of His Love: Devotions for Every Season,* 1973; *Signs of Hope in the Thunder of Spring,* 1973; *Bridges to Hope,* 1975. Contributor to *Lutheran Standard* and theological journals.†

* * *

ROHRER, Wayne C(urry) 1920-

PERSONAL: Born December 30, 1920, in Milwaukee, Wis.; son of George Ernest (a golf professional) and Leone (Pastorino) Rohrer; married Rea Lou Matson, 1947; children: Robin (daughter), Christopher, Benjamin, Amy. *Education:* Texas A&M University, B.S., 1946, M.S., 1948; Michigan State University, Ph.D., 1955. *Politics:* Democrat. *Religion:* Congregational. *Home:* 1819 Leavenworth, Manhattan, Kan. 66502.

CAREER: Texas A&M University, College Station, assistant professor of sociology and research assistant, 1947-49; Michigan State University, East Lansing, research assistant, 1949-52; University of Maryland, College Park, 1952-59, began as assistant professor, became associate professor of sociology; Kansas State University, Manhattan, professor of sociology, 1959—. Member, Manhattan Human Relations Board, 1964-67. *Military service:* U.S. Army Air Forces, 1942-46; became captain (brevet major). *Member:* Midwest Sociological Society.

WRITINGS: (Senior author, with Louis H. Douglas) *The Agrarian Transition in America: Dualism and Change,* Bobbs-Merrill, 1969; *Black Profiles of White Americans,* F. A. Davis, 1970. Contributor to sociology journals.

WORK IN PROGRESS: Research in social change.

* * *

ROLO, Paul Jacques Victor 1917-

PERSONAL: Surname rhymes with "polo"; born November 6, 1917, in Alexandria, Egypt; son of Max Jacques and Yvonne (Harari) Rolo; married Rosemary Ann Carless, March 22, 1952; children: Janc, Hugh. *Education:* Balliol College, Oxford, B.A. (first class honors), 1938.

Home: Barlaston Lea, Barlaston, Staffordshire, England. *Office:* Department of History, University of Keele, Keele, Staffordshire, England.

CAREER: Oxford University, Balliol College, Oxford, England, lecturer in history and politics, 1946-49; University of Keele, Keele, England, lecturer in history and politics, 1951-61, senior lecturer, 1961-71, professor of history, 1971—, deputy vice-chancellor, 1974-77. *Military service:* British Army, 1940-46; became major. *Member:* Trentham Gold Club (Staffordshire).

WRITINGS: George Canning, Macmillan, 1965; *Entente Cordiale,* Macmillan, 1969.

* * *

ROMANELL, Patrick 1912-

PERSONAL: Surname originally Romanelli; born October 2, 1912, in Bari, Italy; son of Joseph Romanelli; married Edna Pellegrino, June 25, 1939. *Education:* Brooklyn College (now Brooklyn College of the City University of New York), B.A. (magna cum laude), 1934; Columbia University, M.A., 1936, Ph.D., 1937. *Home:* 6767 Fiesta Dr., El Paso, Tex. 79912. *Office:* University of Texas at El Paso, Tex. 79999.

CAREER: Instructor in philosophy at Brooklyn College (now Brooklyn College of the City University of New York), Brooklyn, N.Y., 1936-41, and Barnard College, New York, N.Y., 1941; University of Panama, Panama City, professor of philosophy, 1941-44; Wells College, Aurora, N.Y., associate professor of philosophy and chairman of department, 1946-52; University of Texas, Medical Branch, Galveston, professor of medical philosophy, 1953-62; University of Oklahoma, Norman, professor of philosophy in the university and professor of medical philosophy, Medical Center, 1962-65; University of Texas at El Paso, H. Y. Benedict Professor of Philosophy, 1965—. Fulbright professor, University of Turin, 1952-53; Smith-Mundt Professor, University of Ecuador, 1956. U.S. Department of State specialist in Central and South America, 1961. Vice-president, IVth National Congress of Philosophy, Brazil, 1962.

MEMBER: American Philosophical Association, American Association for the History of Medicine, American Association of University Professors, Southwestern Philosophical Society (president, 1961), Brazilian Institute of Philosophy, Latin American Studies Association. *Awards, honors:* Cutting and Carnegie fellow in Mexico, 1945-46; American Philosophical Society grantee in England and Netherlands, 1957; U.S. Public Health Service grantee in England, Netherlands, Greece, Italy, and France, 1960-63.

WRITINGS: The Philosophy of Giovanni Gentile, Vanni, 1938; *Croce versus Gentile,* Vanni, 1946; (with others) *Homenaje a Antonio Caso,* Editorial Stylo (Mexico City), 1947; (with Chauncey D. Leake) *Can We Agree?,* University of Texas Press, 1950; (editor) *John Locke: A Letter Concerning Toleration,* Liberal Arts Press, 1950, 2nd edition, 1955; *Making of the Mexican Mind,* University of Nebraska Press, 1952; *Verso un Naturalismo Critico,* Taylor Editore (Turin), 1953; *Toward a Critical Naturalism,* Macmillan, 1958; (editor and translator) *Benedetto Croce: Guide to Aesthetics,* Bobbs-Merrill, 1965; *Para um Naturalismo Dialectico,* Editorial Presenca (Lisbon), 1967; (with others) *Religion in Philosophical and Cultural Perspective,* Van Nostrand, 1967; *Il Naturalismo Critico,* Taylor Editore, 1969; (with others) *Mexican Education in Cultural Perspective,* College of Education, University of Arizona, 1971; (with others) *Humanistic Perspectives in Medical Ethics,* Prometheus Books, 1972.

Contributor to philosophy and other professional journals in United States and abroad, and to *Pan American, Scientific Monthly, Science, Forum, Journal of the History of Ideas, Bulletin of the History of Medicine, Latin American Research Review,* and others. Member of editorial board, *Encyclopedia of Philosophy,* 1962-66; book editor, *Journal of Philosophy,* 1939-51.

WORK IN PROGRESS: John Locke's Medical Philosophy; and *Culture and Nature,* an expansion of *Toward a Critical Naturalism,* which the author considers his major philosophical work to date.

BIOGRAPHICAL/CRITICAL SOURCES: Giovanni De Crescenzo, *Naturalismo e Ipotesi Metafisica,* Edizioni Scientifiche Italiane (Naples), 1962; *Op. cit.* (journal), Number 2, 1965; *Rivista Brasileira de Filosofia,* Volume XV, number 60, 1965; Jude P. Dougherty, editor, *Approaches to Morality,* Harcourt, 1966; Giovanni De Crescenzo, *Patrick Romanell e L'odierno Naturalismo Statunitense,* La Nuova Italia (Florence), 1966, 2nd edition, 1969.

* * *

ROMANUS, Charles Franklin 1915-

PERSONAL: Born July 6, 1915, in Decatur, Ill.; son of Charles Henry (a railroader) and Lulu Lucille (Crail) Romanus; married Annie Julia Armstrong (a teacher of Latin), August 12, 1940; children: Kathleen L., Charles Franklin, Jr., Charlene Ann. *Education:* Blackburn Junior College, student, 1932-34; Illinois State University, B.Ed., 1936; University of Illinois, A.M., 1937; Louisiana State University, graduate study, 1938-41. *Religion:* Protestant. *Home:* 9022 Leesburg Pike, McLean, Va. 22101. *Office:* Office, Chief of Military History, Washington, D.C. 20315.

CAREER: High school teacher, 1940-43; active duty in U.S. Army, 1943-46, and U.S. Army Reserve, 1949-68, retiring as lieutenant colonel; assigned to Office of Chief of Military History, Washington, D.C., as chief of Organizational History Branch, 1956-62, chief of General Reference Branch, 1962-67, historian, 1967-68; historian (as civilian) in Office of Chief of Military History, 1968—.

WRITINGS—All published by U.S. Army, except as indicated: (With Riley Sunderland) *Stilwell's Mission to China,* 1953; (with Sunderland) *Stilwell's Command Problems,* 1956; (with Sunderland) *Time Runs Out in China-Burma-India,* 1959; (with William R. Ross) *Quartermaster Corps in the ETO,* 1962; (with Sunderland) *Stilwell's Personal File: China, Burma, India, 1942-44,* Scholarly Resources, in press.

WORK IN PROGRESS: Another volume for "U.S. Army in World War II Series," *The Riviera to the Rhine.*

* * *

ROOD, Ronald (N.) 1920-

PERSONAL: Surname rhymes with "food"; born July 7, 1920, in Torrington, Conn.; son of Nellis Frost (a life insurance underwriter) and Bessie (Chamberlain) Rood; married Margaret Bruce (a teacher), December 21, 1942; children: Janice, Thomas Elliot, Alison, Roger Warren. *Education:* University of Connecticut, B.S., 1941, M.S., 1949. *Home and office address:* R.R. 1, Box 131, Lincoln, Vt. 05443.

CAREER: Long Island Agricultural and Technical Institute, Farmingdale, N.Y., instructor in biology, 1949-53;

Grolier Enterprises, New York, N.Y., research editor, 1954-64; Middlebury College, Middlebury, Vt., instructor in biology, 1956-58; full-time writer. Church choir director. *Military service:* U.S. Army Air Forces, fighter pilot, World War II; received Air Medal. *Member:* Forest and Field, League of Vermont Writers (president, 1965-67, 1975), American Forestry Association, National Wildlife Federation, Outdoor Writers Association of America, Vermont Natural Resources Council.

WRITINGS: The How and Why Wonder Book of Insects, Grosset, 1960; *The How and Why Wonder Book of Ants and Bees,* Grosset, 1962; *Land Alive: The World of Nature at One Family's Door,* Stephen Greene Press, 1962; *The How and Why Wonder Book of Butterflies and Moths,* Grosset, 1963; *The Loon in My Bathtub,* Stephen Greene Press, 1964; *The Sea and Its Wonderful Creatures,* Whitman Publishing, 1965; *Bees, Bugs and Beetles: The Arrow Book of Insects,* Four Winds, 1965; *Hundred Acre Welcome: The Story of a Chincoteague Pony,* Stephen Greene Press, 1967; *Vermont Life Book of Nature,* Stephen Greene Press, 1967; *How Do You Spank a Porcupine?,* Trident, 1969; *Animal Champions,* Grosset, 1969; *Answers About Insects,* Grosset, 1969; *Animals Nobody Loves,* Stephen Greene Press, 1971; *Who Wakes the Groundhog?,* Norton, 1973; *May I Keep This Clam Mother? It Followed Me Home,* Simon & Schuster, 1973. Contributor to *Reader's Digest, Coronet, Audubon Magazine, Christian Herald, New York Times, Pageant, Vermont Life,* and other periodicals.

SIDELIGHTS: As a boy of seven, Rood wrote to Thornton Burgess with a question about a baby turtle; he received such a detailed and friendly answer that he decided he wanted to emulate the nature writer.

*   *   *

ROONEY, David Douglas   1924-

PERSONAL: Born May 17, 1924, in London, England; son of Douglas and Violet (Broadbridge) Rooney; married E. Muriel Coutts, August 18, 1948; children: Kathryn, Keith. *Education:* Oxford University, M.A., B.Litt. *Religion:* Church of England. *Home:* 81 Wimblington Rd., March, Cambridgeshire, England.

CAREER: Campbell College, Belfast, Northern Ireland, senior history master, 1954-60; Royal Military Academy, Sandhurst, England, senior lecturer, 1960-64; King's School (operated by British Families Education Service for children of British military and other services in Germany), Gutersloh, Germany, headmaster, 1964-72; Neale Wade School, March, Cambridgeshire, England, headmaster, 1972—. *Military service:* British Army, 1944-47; served in India and West Africa; became staff captain.

WRITINGS: (With E. Halladay) *Building of Modern Africa,* Harrap, 1965, 2nd edition, 1967; *The Story of the Commonwealth,* Pergamon, 1967; *Stilwell,* Ballantine, 1971.

AVOCATIONAL INTERESTS: Tennis, swimming, squash, and refereeing rugby.

*   *   *

RORTY, Richard M(cKay)   1931-

PERSONAL: Born October 4, 1931, in New York, N.Y.; son of James (a writer) and Winifred (Raushenbush) Rorty; married Amelie Oksenberg (a college teacher), June 15, 1954; children: Jay. *Education:* University of Chicago,

B.A., 1949, M.A., 1952; Yale University, Ph.D., 1956. *Politics:* Democrat. *Religion:* None. *Office:* Department of Philosophy, Princeton University, Princeton, N.J. 08540.

CAREER: Yale University, New Haven, Conn., instructor in philosophy, 1955-56; Wellesley College, Wellesley, Mass., instructor, 1958-60, assistant professor of philosophy, 1960-61; Princeton University, Princeton, N.J., assistant professor, 1961-65, associate professor, 1965-70, professor of philosophy, 1970—. *Military service:* U.S. Army, 1957-58. *Member:* American Philosophical Association (member of executive committee, Eastern division), Metaphysical Society of America. *Awards, honors:* American Council of Learned Societies fellow, 1969-70; Guggenheim fellow, 1973-74.

WRITINGS: (Editor) *The Linguistic Turn: Recent Essays in Philosophical Method,* University of Chicago Press, 1967; (editor) *Exegesis and Argument,* Van Gorcum, 1973. Contributor to anthologies and philosophical journals.

*   *   *

ROSE, Richard   1933-

PERSONAL: Born April 9, 1933, in St. Louis, Mo.; son of Charles I. (a merchant) and Mary (Conely) Rose; married Rosemary J. Kenny, April 14, 1956; children: Clare, Charles, Lincoln. *Education:* Johns Hopkins University, B.A., 1953; London School of Economics and Political Science, graduate study, 1953-54; Oxford University, D.Phil., 1959, postdoctoral study, 1959-60. *Politics:* "Border-state democrat." *Religion:* Lapsed Southern Presbyterian. *Home:* 1 East Abercromby St., Helensburgh, Dunbartonshire, Scotland. *Office:* Politics Department, University of Strathclyde, Glasgow C.1, Scotland.

CAREER: St. Louis Post-Dispatch, St. Louis, Mo., reporter, 1955-57; University of Manchester, Manchester, England, lecturer in politics, 1961-66; University of Strathclyde, Glasgow, Scotland, professor of politics, 1966—. Member of United States-United Kingdom Fulbright Educational Commission, 1971—. *Member:* International Political Science Association, International Sociological Association, American Political Science Association, Political Studies Association (England), Scottish Political Studies Association (president), American Civil Liberties Union, Phi Beta Kappa.

WRITINGS: (With D. E. Butler) *The British General Election of 1959,* St. Martin's, 1960; (with Mark Abrams) *Must Labour Lose?,* Penguin, 1960; *Politics in England,* Little, Brown, 1964, 2nd edition, 1974; (editor) *Studies in British Politics,* St. Martin's, 1966; *Influencing Voters,* St. Martin's, 1967; (editor) *Policy-Making in Britain,* Free Press, 1969; *People in Politics,* Basic Books, 1970; *Governing Without Consensus: An Irish Perspective,* Faber, 1971; *The Problem of Party Government,* Free Press, 1974; (with T. Mackie) *International Almanac of Electoral History,* Free Press, 1974; (editor) *Electoral Behavior,* Free Press, 1974; (editor) *Lessons from America,* Wiley, 1974; (editor) *Management of Urban Change,* Sage, 1974. Election correspondent, *Times* (London), 1964. Contributor to *Times* (London), *New Society,* and academic journals in Great Britain and America.

WORK IN PROGRESS: The Presidency and the Executive Branch; comparative parity of policy studies.

AVOCATIONAL INTERESTS: Architecture, music, travel.

ROSEBERRY, Cecil R. 1902-

PERSONAL: Born Cecil R. Rosenberry, October 7, 1902, in Red House, N.Y.; son of James F. (a railroad station agent) and Alice (Swanson) Rosenberry; married Mary Frawley, 1925; children: Richard, Robert. *Education:* Cornell University, B.A., 1926. *Politics:* Republican. *Religion:* Protestant ("no church"). *Home:* 14 Warren St., Albany, N.Y. 12203. *Office:* State Education Department, Albany, N.Y. 12224.

CAREER: Reporter for *Ithaca Journal,* Ithaca, N.Y., 1923-29, and *Rochester Times-Union,* Rochester, N.Y., 1929-31; *Ithaca Journal,* assistant editor, 1931-36; *Albany Knickerbocker-News,* Albany, N.Y., columnist and critic, 1936-42; *Buffalo Evening News,* Buffalo, N.Y., reporter and critic, 1946; *Albany Times-Union,* Albany, columnist, critic, and feature writer, 1948-61; consultant in various research-writing projects for New York State, principally in Education Department, 1961—. *Military service:* U.S. Naval Reserve, Intelligence, 1942-45; served as lieutenant. *Member:* Adirondack Mountain Club, Savage Club of Ithaca.

WRITINGS: Before Cayuga, Board of Education, Ithaca, N.Y., 1950; *Capitol Story,* State of New York, 1964; *Steamboats and Steamboat Men,* Putnam, 1966; *The Challenging Skies,* Doubleday, 1966; *A History of the New York State Library,* New York State Education Department, 1970; *Glenn Curtiss: Pioneer of Flight,* Doubleday, 1972. Contributor to *Saturday Evening Post, American Mercury, Coronet,* and other magazines.

WORK IN PROGRESS: From Niagara to Montauk: Scenic Treasures of New York State, in collaboration with the New York State Geological Survey.

SIDELIGHTS: Cecil Roseberry has flown with the U.S. Air Force in the Arctic for magazine material—to Thule and into the Greenland Ice Cap, to Point Barrow in Alaska, and on missions near the North Pole; he also has flown north of the Arctic Circle in Norway, for material on the Royal Norwegian Air Force and to Air Force bases in Germany and France. *Avocational interests:* Mountain climbing and camping in the Adirondacks; music.

*   *   *

ROSEN, Edward 1906-

PERSONAL: Born December 12, 1906, in New York, N.Y.; son of Max (a salesman) and Rose (Steckels) Rosen; married Sally Fairchild, June 9, 1959; children: Carla Jeannette. *Education:* City College (now City College of the City University of New York), B.A., 1926; Columbia University, M.A., 1929, Ph.D., 1939. *Home:* 315 Riverside Dr., New York, N.Y. 10025. *Office:* Graduate School and University Center of the City University of New York, 33 West 42nd St., New York, N.Y. 10036.

CAREER: Graduate School and University Center of the City University of New York, New York, N.Y., faculty, 1926—, began as instructor, professor of history of science, 1959—. Visiting professor at Massachusetts Institute of Technology, 1957-58, and Indiana University, 1963-64. *Military service:* U.S. Army Air Forces, 1943-45. *Member:* Phi Beta Kappa, Phi Alpha Theta. *Awards, honors:* Guggenheim fellow, 1940-41, 1945-46; Fund for the Advancement of Education (Ford Foundation) fellow, 1951-52; National Science Foundation research grant, 1962-63.

WRITINGS: Three Copernican Treatises, Columbia University Press, 1939, 3rd edition, Octagon, 1971; *The Naming of the Telescope,* Abelard, 1947; (translator) Vasco Ronchi, *Optics, the Science of Vision,* New York University Press, 1957; (translator and editor) *Kepler's Conversation with Galileo's Sidereal Messenger,* Johnson Reprint, 1965; (translator and author of commentary) Johann Kepler, *Somnium,* University of Wisconsin Press, 1967; *Introductions a l'astronomie de Copernic,* Blanchard, 1975. Contributor to learned journals.

*   *   *

ROSENBAUM, Eileen 1936-

PERSONAL: Born January 11, 1936, in Tarentum, Pa.; daughter of Saul (a retail store owner) and Rose (Shure) Landay; married Alan H. Rosenbaum (in printing production), June 10, 1956; children: Steven, Roger. *Education:* Moravian Seminary for Women, student, 1949-53; Carnegie Institute of Technology (now Carnegie-Mellon University), B.S., 1957. *Politics:* "Feminist." *Religion:* Jewish. *Home:* 498 Union Ave., Westbury, N.Y. 11590.

CAREER: Psychological Corp., New York City, statistician, 1958-59; Chester Gore Co., Inc. (advertising agency), New York City, assistant to the president, 1959-62.

WRITINGS: Two for Trouble, Doubleday, 1967; *The Kidnapers Upstairs,* Doubleday, 1968; *A Different Kind of Birthday,* Doubleday, 1969; *Ronnie,* Parents' Magazine Press, 1969; *Black Film Stars,* Drake, 1974.

*   *   *

ROSENBAUM, Peter S. 1940-

PERSONAL: Born March 26, 1940; son of LeRoy S. and Phoebe (Weiss) Rosenbaum; married Joan Grossman, July 15, 1962. *Education:* Wesleyan University, Middletown, Conn., B.A., 1962; Massachusetts Institute of Technology, Ph.D., 1965. *Office address:* Teachers College, Columbia University, Box 77, New York, N.Y. 10027.

CAREER: International Business Machines Corp., Research Division, Yorktown Heights, N.Y., manager of language learning group, 1965-69; Columbia University, Teachers College, New York, N.Y., associate professor of linguistics and education, 1969—. *Member:* Linguistic Society of America, Association for Computing Machinery, National Council of Teachers of English (member of committee on research, 1970—), Association for Machine Translation and Computational Linguistics, Linguistic Circle of New York, Phi Beta Kappa, Phi Delta Kappa. *Awards, honors:* Woodrow Wilson fellowship.

WRITINGS: The Grammar of English Predicate Complement Constructions, M.I.T. Press, 1967; (with Roderick A. Jacobs) *Grammar I* [and] *Grammar II,* Ginn, 1967; (with others) "Ginn Language and Composition Series," Ginn, 1968; (with Jacobs) *English Transformational Grammar,* Blaisdell, 1968; (compiler with Jacobs) *Readings in English Transformational Grammar,* Ginn, 1970; (with Jacobs) *Transformations, Style, and Meaning,* Xerox College Publishing, 1971; *Peer-Mediated Instruction,* Teachers College Press, 1973. Writer of articles and scientific reports.†

*   *   *

ROSENBAUM, Walter A(nthony) 1937-

PERSONAL: Born October 20, 1937, in Pittsburgh, Pa.; son of Walter and Julia (Luther) Rosenbaum; married Jean Annette Camfield, July 9, 1960; children: Brian Anthony, Douglas Michael. *Education:* University of Redlands, B.A. (magna cum laude), 1959; Princeton University, M.A.,

1962, Ph.D., 1964. *Politics:* Democratic. *Religion:* Presbyterian. *Home:* 2629 Northwest Tenth Ave., Gainesville, Fla. 32603. *Office:* Department of Political Science, University of Florida, Gainesville, Fla. 32603.

CAREER: University of Florida, Gainesville, assistant professor, 1962-68, associate professor, 1968-75; professor of political science, 1975—. Policy formulation officer, U.S. Environmental Protection Agency, 1974-75. *Member:* American Political Science Association, Southern Political Science Association, Pi Sigma Alpha, Pi Gamma Mu, Omicron Delta Kappa, Pi Kappa Delta. *Awards, honors:* Woodrow Wilson fellowship, 1959; Danforth Associates award, 1967; National Science Foundation summer fellowship, 1967.

WRITINGS: (With Edward C. Dreyer) *Political Opinion and Electoral Behavior,* Wadsworth, 1966, 3rd edition, Duxbury, 1975; (with John S. Spanier and William Burris) *Analysing American Politics,* Duxbury, 1972; *Politics of Environmental Concern,* Praeger, 1973; *Political Culture and Public Opinion,* Praeger, 1974; (with Gladys M. Kammerer) *Against Long Odds: The Theory and Practice of Successful Government Consolidation,* Sage, 1975.

WORK IN PROGRESS: A study of public openion and its effect upon political power in the United States.

*   *   *

ROSENBERG, Harold   1906-

PERSONAL: Born February 2, 1906, in New York, N.Y.; son of Abraham and Fanny (Edelman) Rosenberg; married May Natalie Tabak (a writer), March 13, 1932; children: Patia Myra. *Education:* LL.B., 1927. *Home:* 30 Neck Path Springs, East Hampton, N.Y. 11937. *Office: New Yorker* Magazine, 25 West 43rd St., New York, N.Y. 10036.

CAREER: Writer and lecturer; former national art editor of American Guide Series; director of Longview Foundation, 1944—; professor, art department and committee on social thought, University of Chicago, 1966—; art critic, *New Yorker* (magazine), 1967—. Lecturer, New School of Social Research, 1953-54; Regents Lecturer, University of California, Berkeley, 1962; lecturer, Christian Gauss Seminars in Criticism, Princeton University, 1963; visiting professor, Southern Illinois University, 1965. Consultant to U.S. Treasury, 1944-46, and Advertising Council, 1946-74. Member of advertising council, Smithsonian Institution; commissioner, National Collection of Fine Arts. *Member:* International Society of Art Critics, American Academy of Arts and Sciences. *Awards, honors:* Frank Jewett Mather Award of College Art Association of America, 1964; D.Litt., Lake Forest (Ill.) College, 1968; D.F.A., Maryland Institute of College Art, 1971.

WRITINGS: Trance above the Streets (poems), Gotham Bookmart, 1943; (translator) Henri de Kerillis, *I Accuse deGaulle,* Harcourt, 1946; (author of introduction) Aaron Siskind, *Photographs,* Horizon Press, 1959; *The Tradition of the New* (essays), Horizon Press, 1959, 2nd edition, 1960; *Arshile Gorky: The Man, the Time, the Idea,* Horizon Press, 1962; *The Anxious Object: Art Today and Its Audience,* Horizon Press, 1964; *Artworks and Packages,* Horizon Press, 1968; *Act and the Actor: Making the Self,* World Publishing, 1970; *The De-Definition of Art: Action Art to Pop to Earthworks,* Horizon Press, 1972; *Barnett Newman: Broken Obelisk and Other Sculptures,* University of Washington Press, 1972; *Discovering the Present: Three Decades in Art, Culture, and Politics,* University of Chicago Press, 1973; *De Kooning,* Abrams, 1974; *Art on

the Edge, Macmillan, 1975. Contributor to literary and art periodicals and popular magazines since the 1930's, with poems and articles in *Partisan Review, Poetry, New Yorker, Vogue, Esquire, New York Times Book Review, Art in America, Kenyon Review, Temps Modernes,* and other American and French publications.

SIDELIGHTS: Alfred Kazin writes: ". . . the great joy of Harold Rosenberg's *Act and the Actor: Making the Self* is that this critic writes in order to think things out, thinks for the pleasure of thinking (thinking is constantly illustrated here as a life-style)—yet advances the thesis that we are nothing but what we do." Reviewing *The De-Definition of Art,* Bill Marvel states: "One reads an art critic for his point of view, for an angle on what's going on that is different from one's own and, hopefully more enlightened. With Harold Rosenberg, whose critical services to art go back to the days of 'action painting' and before, one gets considerably more than an angle. One gets a sense of conscience, a conviction that art does matter, and because it matters there are moral issues involved."

BIOGRAPHICAL/CRITICAL SOURCES: Nation, November 17, 1969; *Books,* April, 1970; *Canadian Forum,* March, 1971; *New Yorker,* April 3, 1971; *Vogue,* May, 1971; *New York Times,* April 20, 1972; *National Observer,* July 8, 1972.

*   *   *

ROSENBERG, Jerry M.   1935-

PERSONAL: Born February 5, 1935, in New York, N.Y.; son of Frank (a businessman) and Esther (Gardner) Rosenberg; married Ellen Young, September 11, 1960; children: Lauren Monica, Elizabeth. *Education:* City College (now City College of the City University of New York), B.S., 1956; Ohio State University, M.A., 1957; Sorbonne, University of Paris, Certificate, 1958; New York University, Ph.D., 1962. *Religion:* Hebrew. *Home:* 515 Tulfan Ter., New York, N.Y. 10463. *Office:* Polytechnic Institute of Brooklyn, Brooklyn, N.Y. 11201.

CAREER: Government Bureau of Automation, Paris, France, research psychologist, 1957-58; State University of New York, School of Industrial and Labor Relations at Cornell University, Ithaca, assistant professor, 1961-64; Columbia University, New York, N.Y., assistant professor, 1964-68; Polytechnic Institute of Brooklyn, Brooklyn, N.Y., professor of management and chairman of department, 1974—. Lecturer, Institute of Productivity, Tel-Aviv, summer, 1962; visiting professor, University of British Columbia, summer, 1967. Former conference director, American Foundation on Automation and Employment. Former member of New York Mayor's Committee on Youth and Work and of National Conference of Christians and Jews advisory committee for labor, management, and public interest. *Member:* American Psychological Association, Industrial Relations Research Association, Columbia Seminar on Technology and Social Change. *Awards, honors:* Fulbright and French government grants.

WRITINGS: Automation, Manpower and Education, Random House, 1966; *New Conceptions of Vocational-Technical Education,* Teachers College, Columbia University, 1967; *The Death of Privacy,* Random House, 1969; *The Computer Prophets,* Macmillan, 1969.

AVOCATIONAL INTERESTS: Tennis, travel, collecting autographed documents and maps.

ROSENBERG, Jessie 1941-

PERSONAL: Born November 1, 1941, in Greenville, Miss.; daughter of Marvin (a department store manager) and Jane (Baker) Rosenberg. *Education:* University of North Carolina at Greensboro, B.A., 1963, M.F.A., 1968; Tulane University of Louisiana, graduate study, 1963-67. *Religion:* Jewish. *Agent:* Lynn Nesbit, International Creative Management, 40 West 57th St., New York, N.Y. 10019.

WRITINGS: Sudina (novel), Dutton, 1967. Poetry anthologized in *New Campus Writing, 1966,* and published in *Atlantic* and *Greensboro Review.*††

* * *

ROSENBERG, Shirley Sirota 1925-

PERSONAL: Born June 30, 1925, in New York, N.Y.; daughter of Charles and Donia (Rudoy) Sirota; married Jerome David Rosenberg (a physicist), August 27, 1947; children: Jonathan, Hindy. *Education:* Brooklyn College (now Brooklyn College of the City University of New York), B.A., 1946. *Home:* 116 East 4th St. S.E., Washington, D.C.

CAREER: Brooklyn Examiner, Brooklyn, N.Y., managing editor, 1946-49; *Washington Ledger,* Washington, D.C., manager editor, 1953-55; Washington reporter, *Parent's Magazine,* 1967-70; Smithsonian Institution, Washington, D.C., editor, 1972—; free-lance writer. Consultant to Children's Bureau, U.S. Department of Health, 1967, Office of Deputy Assistant Secretary for Population and Family Planning, 1967-68, and National Institute on Alcohol Abuse and Alcoholism, 1971-72.

WRITINGS: (With Frances G. Conn) *The First Oil Rush,* Duell, Sloan & Pearce, 1967. Regular contributor to *Friends, Look, Kiwanis, Family Weekly, Washington Star, Washington Post,* and to other magazines and newspapers. Editor, *Alcohol and Health,* 1971.

* * *

ROSENBERGER, Harleigh M. 1913-

PERSONAL: Born December 11, 1913, in Dublin, Pa.; son of Allen M. (a laborer) and Ella (Mood) Rosenberger; married Dorothy Swartley; children: Harleigh, Jr., James Robert, Marcia Lynne. *Education:* Bluffton College, B.A. (with honors), 1940; Colgate Rochester Divinity School, B.D., 1942. *Politics:* Republican. *Home:* 1973 75th Ave. N., St. Petersburg, Fla. 33702.

CAREER: Pastor of Baptist churches in Fairport, N.Y., 1941-45, Lockport, N.Y., 1945-54, Denver, Colo., 1954-59, and Detroit, Mich., 1959-65; Irondequoit United Church of Christ, Rochester, N.Y., pastor, beginning, 1965; senior minister, First Congregational Church, St. Petersberg, Fla. President, American Baptist Convention Ministers, 1964; member of board of managers, Rochester Council of Churches. *Awards, honors:* Community Service Award, Detroit, 1964.

WRITINGS: Thoughts Along the Road, Judson, 1966.

* * *

ROSENBURG, John M. 1918-

PERSONAL: Born June 2, 1918, in Mountain Home, Pa.; son of Henry H. and Naomie (Frezatt) Rosenburg; married Ursula Donohue (a nurse), October 8, 1939; children: Gerarda (Mrs. Edward Wahlers), Henrietta, John. *Education:* Ithaca College, B.S., 1943. *Politics:* Democrat. *Religion:* Roman Catholic. *Home:* 1 Warrior Rd., R.D. 2, Malvern, Pa. *Agent:* Barbara Rhodes Literary Agency, 60 Sutton Pl. S., New York, N.Y. 10022.

CAREER: United Press International, New York City, correspondent, 1944-51; American Telephone & Telegraph Co., New York City, public relations staff, 1951-62; Bell Telephone Co. of Pennsylvania, Philadelphia, public relations manager, 1962—. Lecturer on writing and public relations at colleges. *Member:* Overseas Press Club of America, Pittsburgh Press Club. *Awards, honors:* Boys' Club of America Junior Book Award for best-liked book, 1963, for *The Story of Baseball.*

WRITINGS: Baseball for Boys, Oceana, 1960; *Basic Basketball,* Oceana, 1962; *The Story of Baseball,* Random House, 1962; *Your Bird Dog and You,* A. S. Barnes, 1976.

WORK IN PROGRESS: Two plays, "The Hero League" and "The Househusband"; two books, *The Washingtons, The Drummer and the General.*

AVOCATIONAL INTERESTS: Horses, hunting, and hunting dogs.

* * *

ROSENFIELD, John M(ax) 1924-

PERSONAL: Born October 9, 1924, in Dallas, Tex.; son of John M. and Claire (Burger) Rosenfield; married Ella Ruth Hopper, 1948; children: Sarah Ann, Paul Thomas. *Education:* University of Texas, student, 1941-43; University of California, Berkeley, B.A., 1945; Southern Methodist University, B.F.A., 1947; University of Iowa, M.F.A., 1949; Harvard University, Ph.D., 1959. *Home:* 75 Coolidge Rd., Arlington, Mass. 02174. *Office:* Fogg Art Museum, Harvard University, Cambridge, Mass. 02138.

CAREER: University of Iowa, Iowa City, instructor in history of art, 1949-50, 1952-54; University of California, Los Angeles, assistant professor of history of art, 1957-60; Harvard University, Cambridge, Mass., research fellow, 1960-65, associate professor of fine arts, 1965-68, professor of history of art, 1968—, chairman of department of fine arts, 1972—. Lecturer at University of Maryland, 1960-62, and Northeastern University, 1964-67. *Military service:* U.S. Army, 1943-46, 1950-51; served in Southeast Asia during World War II; became technical sergeant. *Member:* College Art Association, Association for Asian Studies, Association for Oriental Studies. *Awards, honors:* American Council of Learned Societies grant for research in Japan, 1962-64; Harvard University traveling fellowship in Asia and Middle East, 1967.

WRITINGS: The Dynastic Arts of the Kushans, University of California Press, 1966; (translator) S. Noma, *Arts of Japan, Ancient and Medieval,* Kodansha (Tokyo), 1966; *Japanese Arts of the Heian Period,* Asia Society (New York), 1967; (editor with shujiro Shimada) *Traditions of Japanese Art: Selections from the Kimiki and John Powers Collection,* Fogg Art Museum, Harvard University, 1970; (editor with Fumiko E. and Edwin A. Cranston) *The Courtly Tradition in Japanese Art and Literature: Selections from Hofer and Hyde,* Fogg Art Museum, Harvard University, 1973.

WORK IN PROGRESS: The history of Asian art, especially Buddhist.†

* * *

ROSENSAFT, Menachem Z. 1948-

PERSONAL: Born May 1, 1948, in Bergen Belsen, Germany; son of Josef (in real estate) and Hadassah Rosensaft; married Jean Bloch, January 13, 1974. *Education:* Attended schools in Switzerland and New York; Johns Hopkins University, B.A., M.A., 1971; Columbia University, M.A., 1975. *Politics:* Democrat. *Religion:* Jewish. *Home:* 179 East 70th St., New York, N.Y. 10021. *Office:* City College of the City University of New York, New York, N.Y. 10033.

CAREER: City College of the City University of New York, New York, N.Y., lecturer in Jewish studies, 1972—. *Member:* Phi Beta Kappa. *Awards, honors:* Over-to-youth literary award of *Jewish Chronicle* (London), 1967, for article, "The Tragedy of Victory."

WRITINGS: Moshe Sharett, Statesman of Israel, Shengold, 1966; *Fragments, Past and Future* (poetry), Shengold, 1968; *Not Backward to Belligerency,* Yoseloff, 1969. Contributor to Jewish publications. Editor, *Bergen Belsen Youth Magazine,* 1965. Member of editorial advisory board, *Jewish Quarterly* (London), 1971-72.

WORK IN PROGRESS: A book about Austrian antisemitism.

SIDELIGHTS: In addition to German, Rosensaft speaks and writes French and Yiddish fluently; he has a working knowledge of Italian, Spanish, and Hebrew.

* * *

ROSENTHAL, A(braham) M(ichael) 1922-

PERSONAL: Born May 2, 1922, in Sault Ste. Marie, Ontario, Canada; came to United States in 1926, naturalized in 1951; son of Harry and Sarah Marie Rosenthal; married Ann Marie Burke, March 12, 1949; children: Jonathan Harry, Daniel Michael, Andrew Mark. *Education:* City College (now City College of the City University of New York), B.S., 1944. *Home:* 262 Central Park West, New York, N.Y. *Office: New York Times,* 229 West 43rd St., New York, N.Y. 10036.

CAREER: New York Times, New York, N.Y., staff member, 1944—, United Nations correspondent, 1946-54, foreign correspondent in India, 1954-58, Warsaw, Poland, 1958-59, Geneva, Switzerland, 1960-61, Tokyo, Japan, 1961-63, metropolitan editor, 1963-67, assistant managing editor, 1967—. *Member:* Council on Foreign Relations, Overseas Press Club, Players. *Awards, honors:* Overseas Press Club citation for work in India, 1956, for work in Poland, 1960, and for magazine writing, 1965; Pulitzer Prize for international reporting, 1960; Page One Award of New York Newspaper Guild, 1960, 1965; George Polk Memorial Award, 1960, 1965; LL.D., City College of the City University of New York, 1974; Honor Award of the Association of Indians in America, 1974, for contribution to arts and letters and to better understanding between the peoples of India and the United States.

WRITINGS: Thirty-eight Witnesses, McGraw, 1964; (editor with Arthur Gelb) *The Night the Lights Went Out,* Signet Books, 1965; (editor with Gelb) *The Pope's Journey,* Bantam, 1965; (with Gelb) *One More Victim,* New American Library, 1967. Contributor to *New York Times Magazine, Saturday Evening Post, Collier's,* and *Foreign Affairs.*

* * *

ROSENTHAL, Albert H(arold) 1914-

PERSONAL: Born November 26, 1914, in Denver, Colo.; son of Max (an electrical contractor) and Anna M. (Schatz) Rosenthal. *Education:* University of Denver, B.A., 1936; University of Minnesota, M.A., 1938; Harvard University, Ph.D., 1949. *Home:* 6303 Indian School Rd. N.E., Apt. 607, Albuquerque, N.M. 87110. *Office:* University of New Mexico, Albuquerque, N.M. 87106.

CAREER: Federal Security Agency, Washington, D.C., personnel officer, 1941-42; U.S. Department of State, Washington, D.C., assistant director, UNESCO Relations Staff, 1946-49; University of Denver, Denver, Colo., professor of public administration and director, School of Public Administration, 1949-51; U.S. Department of Health, Education, and Welfare, regional director (Rocky Mountain region), Denver, 1951-64; University of Minnesota, Minneapolis, professor of public administration, 1965-67; University of New Mexico, Albuquerque, professor of political science and director of advanced program in public science policy administration, 1967—. United Nations advisor in public administration to Ireland, 1963-64. U.S. Government work includes summer posts with Bureau of the Budget, 1965, Department of Commerce, 1966, and at Manned Spacecraft Center, National Aeronautics and Space Administration, 1967. Head of Office of Public Understanding of Science, National Science Foundation, 1970-71. *Military service:* U.S. Navy, 1942-46; received Navy Citation.

MEMBER: American Society for Public Administration (council member, 1961—), American Academy of Political and Social Science, American Political Science Association, Phi Beta Kappa. *Awards, honors:* Rockefeller Public Service Award, 1957; Denver Federal Business Association Award, 1958; Phi Beta Kappa Alumni Award, 1962; New Mexico Distinguished Public Service Award, 1970.

WRITINGS: Administrative Problems of UNESCO, U.S. Department of State, 1948; *The Social Programs of Sweden: A Search for Security in a Free Society,* University of Minnesota Press, 1967; (editor) *Public Science Policy and Administration,* University of New Mexico Press, 1973; (co-editor) *Fish and Wildlife Resources Evaluation,* U.S. Government Printing Office, 1975. Member of board of editors, *Public Administration Review.*

* * *

ROSEVEAR, John 1936-
(Jim Circus)

PERSONAL: Surname is two syllables; born April 11, 1936, in West Branch, Mich.; son of John Oscar (a postman) and Lois (Bourassa) Rosevear; married Lee Lundberg, August 16, 1958 (divorced); married Merrill Crockett, December 24, 1964 (divorced); children: (second marriage) Jessica Mary, Matthew Alexander. *Education:* Attended Michigan State University, 1954-55. *Home address:* Box 1074, Detroit, Michigan 48231.

CAREER: He has held over a hundred different jobs in the past decade. Presently, an itinerant house painter. *Military service:* U.S. Marine Corps, 1955-58.

WRITINGS: Pot: A Handbook of Marihuana, University Books, 1967. Contributor to *East Village Other, A Way Out,* and *Los Angeles Free Press.*

SIDELIGHTS: Rosevear tells *CA:* "I am a dope fiend." The most interesting thing about his book, *Pot,* according to David Sanford, is that "Mr. Rosevear spent seven months in prison for his researches in home-growing marijuana." Clara Lucioli explains: "The author argues that the drug is harmless; that truth could dispel its mystery; that laws against sale should be repealed, and that the taxing of this non-addictive drug as is done with the more harmful and potentially addictive alcohol and tobacco would destroy its present bootlegging and criminal associations. . . . [He] makes a plea for some research and 'a thorough examination of the present situation.'"

BIOGRAPHICAL/CRITICAL SOURCES: New York Times Book Review, October 22, 1967.

* * *

ROSNOW, Ralph L. 1936-

PERSONAL: Born January 10, 1936, in Baltimore, Md.; son of Irvin (a merchant) and Rebecca (Faber) Rosnow; married Marion Medinger. *Education:* University of Maryland, B.S., 1957; George Washington University, M.A., 1958; American University, Ph.D., 1962. *Office:* Psychology Department, Temple University, Philadelphia, Pa. 19122.

CAREER: Bureau of Social Science Research, Washington, D.C., research psychologist, 1963; Boston University, Communication Research Division, Boston, Mass., assistant professor, 1963-67; Temple University, Philadelphia, Pa., associate professor, 1967-70, professor of psychology, 1970—. Academic visitor in social psychology, London School of Economics and Political Science, University of London, 1973; visiting professor of psychology, Harvard University, spring, 1974. *Military service:* U.S. Army Reserve, Medical Specialist Corps, 1958-66; became first lieutenant. *Member:* American Association for the Advancement of Science (fellow), American Psychological Association (fellow), Society of Experimental Social Psychology.

WRITINGS: (Editor with E. J. Robinson) *Experiments in Persuasion,* Academic Press, 1967; (contributor) *Psychological Foundations of Attitudes,* Academic Press, 1968; (editor with Robert Rosenthal) *Artifact in Behavioral Research,* Academic Press, 1969; (co-author with J. A. Cheyne, K. Craik, B. Kleinmuntz, Rosenthal, and R. Walters) *New Directions in Psychology IV,* Holt, 1970; (with R. E. Lana) *Introduction to Contemporary Psychology,* Holt, 1972; (editor with Lana) *Readings in Contemporary Psychology,* Holt, 1972; (with Rosenthal) *The Volunteer Subject,* Wiley-Interscience, 1975; (with Rosenthal) *Primer of Methods for the Behavioral Sciences,* Wiley, 1975. Contributor to *The Encyclopedia of Education,* 1971.

WORK IN PROGRESS: Advisory editor of "Reconstruction of Society" series, for Oxford University Press.

* * *

ROSS, Angus 1911-

PERSONAL: Born July 19, 1911, in Herbert, Otago, New Zealand; son of John Alexander (a farmer) and Janet (Gibson) Ross; married R.M.E. McKenzie, May 27, 1937 (deceased); married second wife, M. C. Garrett, November 11, 1950; children: (first marriage) Bruce Jerome. *Education:* University of Otago, B.A., 1932, M.A. (first class honors), 1933; King's College, Cambridge, Ph.D., 1949; St. John's College, Cambridge, research study, 1962. *Politics:* Independent. *Religion:* Presbyterian. *Home:* 134 Cannington Rd., Dunedin, New Zealand. *Office:* Department of History, University of Otago, Dunedin, New Zealand.

CAREER: University of Otago, Dunedin, New Zealand, lecturer, later senior lecturer, 1936-56, reader, 1956-64, professor of history, 1964—, dean of Faculty of Arts and Mu-

sic, 1959-61. Chairman of Otago Regional Committee, New Zealand National Historic Places Trust. Otago Museum, member of management committee, 1951-56, and trust board, 1959-61; member of board of governors, Otago High School, 1952-54. Member of New Zealand University grants committee, 1967-74. New Zealand delegate to Commonwealth Relations Conference, New Delhi, India, 1965. *Military service:* New Zealand Army, 2nd Division, 1940-45; battalion commander in Otago and Southland Regiment, 1951-53; became honorary colonel, 1964; received Military Cross and bar Aristion Andrias (Greek), efficiency decoration, and was mentioned in dispatches.

MEMBER: Royal Society of New Zealand, Royal Institute of International Affairs (branch chairman; national vice-president), Royal Commonwealth Society, English Historical Association, Dunedin Club. *Awards, honors:* Walter Frewen Lord Prize of Royal Commonwealth Society, 1936; Bowen and Arnold Atkinson prizeman, University of New Zealand; Smuts Commonwealth fellowship, University of Cambridge, 1970-71.

WRITINGS: (Contributor) J. D. Freeman and W. R. Geddes, editors, *Anthropology in the South Seas,* Thomas Avery & Sons, Ltd., 1959; *23 Battalion,* War History Branch, Department of Internal Affairs, New Zealand, 1959; *New Zealand Aspirations in the Pacific in the Nineteenth Century,* Clarendon Press, 1964; *New Zealand in the Pacific World,* New Zealand National Party, 1965; *The New Zealander at War,* New Zealand Publishing Society, 1966; (contributor and editor) *New Zealand's Record in the Pacific Islands in the Twentieth Century,* Longmans, Green, 1969; (contributor) G. A. Woud and P. S. O'Connor, editors, *W. P. Morrell: A Tribute,* University of Otago Press, 1973; (contributor) *The Commonwealth: Its Past, Present and Future,* New Zealand Institute of International Affairs, 1973.

WORK IN PROGRESS: A study of New Zealand's relations with the United Kingdom in the inter-war years.

* * *

ROSS, James F(rancis) 1931-

PERSONAL: Born October 8, 1931, in Providence, R.I.; married Kathleen M. Fallon, 1956; children: four. *Education:* Catholic University of America, A.B., 1953, A.M., 1954; Brown University, Ph.D., 1958; University of Pennsylvania, J.D., 1975. *Home:* 4807 Springfield Ave., Philadephia, Pa. 19143. *Office:* Department of Philosophy, University of Pennsylvania, Philadelphia, Pa. 19104.

CAREER: Providence (R.I.) Redevelopment Agency, staff consultant, 1957-60; University of Michigan, Ann Arbor, instructor in philosophy, 1959-61; University of Pennsylvania, Philadelphia, assistant professor, 1962-65, associate professor, 1965-68, professor of philosophy, 1968—, chairman of department, 1965-70; admitted to Pennsylvania Bar, 1975. Visiting lecturer, Johns Hopkins University, 1964. Member of Institute for Advanced Study, Princeton, N.J., 1975-76. *Member:* American Philosophical Association, American Theological Society, Society for Religion in Higher Education. *Awards, honors:* Christian R. and Mary F. Lindback Foundation Award for distinguished teaching, University of Pennsylvania; award for distinguished scholarship, Catholic University of America, 1972; National Endowment for the Humanities fellowship, 1975-76.

WRITINGS: (Translator) Paul Grenet, *Le Thomism,* Harper, 1967; *Introduction to the Philosophy of Religion,* Macmillan, 1967; *Philosophical Theology,* Bobbs-Merrill,

1967; (editor) *Studies in Medieval Philosophy,* Greenwood Press, 1971.

WORK IN PROGRESS: A New Theory of Analogy; Individual Rights and the Public Interest, a philosophical analysis of problems of Constitutional law.

* * *

ROSS, Nathaniel 1904-

PERSONAL: Born June 11, 1904, in New York, N.Y.; son of Harris and Sarah (Lazarus) Ross; married Barbara Munder, December 19, 1929; married Edith Wilsker Friedmann (a clinical psychologist), September 7, 1963; children: (first marriage) Judith (Mrs. Alan Edward Schoening), John, *Education:* Columbia University, B.A., 1924, M.D., 1929; New York Psychoanalytic Institute, certificate of graduation, 1941. *Politics:* Liberal Democrat. *Religion:* None. *Home and office:* 830 Park Ave., New York, N.Y. 10021.

CAREER: Licensed to practice medicine in New York and Connecticut; certified by American Board of Psychiatry and Neurology, 1942. Bellevue Hospital, New York City, intern, 1929-30; Bellevue Psychiatric Hospital, New York City, assistant psychiatrist, 1930-31, senior psychiatrist, 1931-40; private practice, New York City, 1931—; New York University, College of Medicine, New York City, instructor, 1931-36, assistant clinical professor, 1936-41, associate clinical professor, 1952-55; Court of General Sessions, New York City, psychiatrist, 1932-33, research psychiatrist, Committee for the Study of Suicide, 1937-40, associate visiting psychiatrist, 1952-55; associate attending psychiatrist, Beth Israel Hospital, 1942-44; attending psychiatrist, Hillside Hospital, 1946-48; instructor in psychoanalytic psychopathology, 1946-48; teaching associate and associate attending psychoanalyst, Clinic for Training and Research, Columbia University, 1948-52; State University of New York, Downstate Medical Center, Brooklyn, training analyst, Division of Psychoanalytic Education, 1955—, associate clinical professor, later clinical professor of psychiatry, 1955—; Kings County, N.Y., associate attending psychiatrist, 1955—.

MEMBER: American Medical Association, American Psychiatric Association (life fellow), American Psychoanalytic Association (life member), International Psycho-Analytical Association, Royal Society of Medicine (London), New York Psychoanalytic Society, Psychoanalytic Association of New York (former chairman of clinic admissions committee, student loan fund committee, training analysts, selection committee, curriculum committee, 1956-65; alternate representative to board on professional standards, 1961-65), New York Society for Clinical Psychiatry, New York Academy of Medicine.

WRITINGS: (With John Frosch) *Annual Survey of Psychoanalysis,* ten volumes, International Universities Press, 1950-69; (contributor) H. A. Abramson, editor, *The Psychiatric and Somatic Treatment of Bronchial Asthma,* Williams & Wilkins, 1951; (contributor) *The American Handbook of Psychology,* McGraw, 1965; (contributor) *Psychoanalytic Techniques: A Handbook for the Psychoanalytic Practitioner,* Basic Books, 1967; (contributor) B. E. Moore and B. D. Fine, editors, *A Glossary of Psychoanalytic Terms and Concepts,* American Psychoanalytic Association, 1967, 2nd edition, 1968; (contributor) *Mental Disorders in Childhood and Adolescence,* Van Nostrand, 1972; (contributor) B. Wolman, editor, *Dictionary of Behavioral Science,* Van Nostrand, 1973; (author of foreword) Gertrude Blanck and Rubin Blanck, *Ego Psy-*

chology: Theory and Therapy, Columbia University Press, 1974. Contributor of articles and reviews to professional journals. Associate editor, *Journal of the American Psychoanalytic Association,* 1953-72.

WORK IN PROGRESS: With his wife, Edith W. Ross, *The Nature of Human Love;* a book on psychoanalysis and moral and ethical values; a revision of psychoanalytic theory in the light of the latest findings in neurophysiology, computer operation, and information theory, in collaboration with others; correlating material concerning a revision of classic psychoanalytic theory on psychosexuality.

* * *

ROSS, Raymond S(amuel) 1925-

PERSONAL: Born April 14, 1925, in Milwaukee, Wis.; son of Samuel and Agnes (Thorkildsen) Ross; married Jean Joy Reichmann, June 19, 1948; children: Mark, Scott. *Education:* University of Illinois, student, 1943; Marquette University, Ph.B., 1949, M.A., 1950; Purdue University, Ph.D., 1954. *Home:* 1714 Norfolk Dr., Birmingham, Mich. 48009. *Office:* Department of Speech Communication and Theatre, Wayne State University, Detroit, Mich. 48202.

CAREER: Marquette University, Milwaukee, Wis., instructor, 1950-51; Ohio State University, Columbus, 1954-58, began as instructor, became assistant professor of speech; Wayne State University, Detroit, Mich., 1958—, began as assistant professor, professor of speech, 1965—. Coordinator, University of Michigan-Wayne State University Institute of Industrial Relations, 1959—. *Military service:* U.S. Army, 1943-45. *Member:* International Communication Association, American Psychological Association, American Speech and Hearing Association, Speech Communication Association. *Awards, honors:* Foundation for Economic Education (U.S. Steel Corp.) postdoctoral fellowship, 1955; distinguished alumni award of Marquette University School of Speech, 1963.

WRITINGS: (Co-author) *The Air Force Staff Officer,* U.S. Government Printing Office, 1961; *Speech Communication Fundamentals and Practice,* Prentice-Hall, 1965, 3rd edition, 1974; (contributor) *The Communicative Arts and Sciences of Speech,* C. E. Merrill, 1967; *Persuasion: Communication and Interpersonal Relations,* Prentice-Hall, 1974. Associate editor, *Speech Monographs.*

WORK IN PROGRESS: A fourth edition of *Speech Communication,* and co-authoring *Human Communication: An Introduction High School Students,* both for Prentice-Hall.

* * *

ROSS, Russell M. 1921-

PERSONAL: Born June 2, 1921, in Washington, Iowa; son of Harold Ellis (an educator) and Lucille (Dorris) Ross; married Shirley Jackson, June 1, 1944; children: Sherly L., Julie R. *Education:* University of Iowa, B.A., 1942, M.A., 1946, Ph.D., 1948; Harvard University, Certificate in Business Administration, 1945. *Politics:* Republican. *Religion:* Presbyterian. *Home:* 315 Highland Dr., Iowa City, Iowa 52240. *Office:* Department of Political Science, University of Iowa, Iowa City, Iowa 52240.

CAREER: University of Iowa, Iowa City, instructor, 1946-48, assistant professor, 1948-52, associate professor, 1952-60, research professor, 1963-64, professor of political science, 1965—, chairman of department, 1970-73. Summer visiting professor at San Jose State College (now University), 1950, 1952. Mayor of University Heights, Iowa, 1954-60; executive assistant to Governor of Iowa, Des Moines, 1960-62; chairman of Johnson County Metropolitan Planning Commission, 1964-65. *Military service:* U.S. Naval Reserve, 1942-45; became lieutenant; received Presidential Citation. *Member:* International City Managers Association, American Political Science Association, American Society for Public Administration, American Association of University Professors, Phi Beta Kappa, Pi Sigma Alpha, Phi Kappa Alpha.

WRITINGS: Government and Administration of Iowa, Crowell, 1957; (with others) *Urban Responses to Agricultural Change,* University of Iowa Press, 1961; (with others) *Approaches to the Study of Urbanization,* University of Kansas Press, 1964; (with K. F. Millsap) *State and Local Government and Administration,* Ronald, 1966; *Iowa's Unified Court System,* University of Iowa Press, 1974. Also author of monographs, *Handbook for Iowa Councilmen,* 1950, and *The 53rd Iowa Legislative Assembly,* 1954. Contributor to public management and political science journals.

WORK IN PROGRESS: The Commission System of Urban Government.

*   *   *

ROSTVOLD, Gerhard N(orman) 1919-

PERSONAL: Born October 15, 1919, in Nashwauk, Minn.; son of Arndt A. (an iron miner) and Olive M. (Ness) Rostvold; married Virginia Fay Faubion, February 3, 1945; children: Roger Mark, Laura Ann, Christine Marie, Ellen Alicia. *Education:* Stanford University, B.A. (with great distinction), 1948, M.A., 1949, Ph.D., 1955. *Home:* 1045 Yale Ave., Claremont, Calif. 91711. *Office:* Urbanomics Research Associates, 401 Harvard, Claremont, Calif. 91711.

CAREER: Licensed public accountant in California. Stanford University, Stanford, Calif., instructor in economics, 1949-51; U.S. Office of Price Stabilization, Spokane, Wash., price economist, 1951-52; Pomona College, Claremont, Calif., member of faculty, 1952-66, Stedman-Sumner Professor of Economics, 1961-66, chairman of department, 1961-62; Urbanomics Research Associates, Claremont, Calif., owner and consulting economist, 1966—. Chairman, California State Advisory Board on Public Lands, 1971-74, and National Advisory Board on Public Lands. Member of national and California advisory boards, U.S. Bureau of Land Management; member of advisory committee, Invest-In-America Council; member, California Statewide Social Science Study Commission. Director, Los Angeles Regional Plan Association, 1967—. Trustee, California Council of Economic Education; member of board of trustees, Sutro Mortgage Investment Trust. Consulting economist to corporations, law firms, and public agencies. *Military service:* U.S. Army Air Forces, 1942-45. *Member:* American Economic Association, National Tax Association, Western Economic Association, (president, 1966-67), Lambda Alpha. *Awards, honors:* Wig Distinguished Professor Award, Pomona College, 1962; National Science Foundation fellow, Stanford University, 1965-66; Department of the Interior Conservation award, 1975.

WRITINGS: (With others) *California Local Finance,* Stanford University Press, 1960; *Southern California Metropolis–1980,* Southern California Research Council, 1960; *Financing California Government,* Dickenson, 1967. Contributor of articles and reviews to economics journals.

WORK IN PROGRESS: Economics for the Age of Policy: The Economics of Energy; The Economics of the Environment; The Economics of the Public Utility Enterprise.

*   *   *

ROTE, Kyle 1928-

PERSONAL: Born October 27, 1928, in San Antonio, Tex.; son of Jack Tobin and Emma Bell (Owens) Rote; married Sharon Kay Ritchie (a television speaker), August 2, 1965; children: Christopher, Gary, Kyle. *Education:* Attended Vanderbilt University, and Southern Methodist University, 1947-51.

CAREER: Sportscaster; former professional football player. WNEW-Radio, New York City, director of sports and community relations, beginning 1960. National sports director, National Foundation for Neuromuscular Disease, and Society for the Prevention of Juvenile Delinquency. *Awards, honors:* Inducted into National Football Foundation Hall of Fame, 1964.

WRITINGS: Pro Football for the Fan, Doubleday, 1964; *The Language of Pro Football,* Random House, 1966.†

*   *   *

ROTH, Arnold 1929-

PERSONAL: Born February 25, 1929, in Philadelphia, Pa.; son of Louis (a salesman) and Rose (Paris) Roth; married Caroline Wingfield, October 26, 1952; children: Charles Perino, Adam Wingfield. *Education:* Philadelphia Museum College of Art, student, 1946-48. *Residence:* Princeton, N.J.

CAREER: Free-lance cartoonist and illustrator.

WRITINGS—Self-illustrated: *Pick a Peck of Puzzles,* Norton, 1966; *Crazy Book of Science,* Grosset, 1971; *A Comick Book of Sports,* Scribner, 1974; *A Comick Book of Pets,* Scribner, 1976.

Illustrator: *Grimm's Fairy Tales,* Macmillan, 1963; Clifton Fadiman, *Wally the Word Worm,* Macmillan, 1963; Bennett Cerf, *Houseful of Laughter,* Random House, 1963; Jane Yolen, *The Witch Who Wasn't,* Macmillan, 1964; Richardson, Smith, and Weiss, *Six in a Mix,* Harper, 1965; Joseph Rosner, *The Hater's Handbook,* Delacorte, 1965; Holiday Magazine, *Choosing and Enjoying Wine,* Curtis, 1965; Julius Schwartz, *Go On Wheels,* McGraw, 1966; *Kids' Letters to the FBI,* Prentice-Hall, 1966; F. D. Roosevelt and others, *The President's Mystery Plot,* Prentice-Hall, 1967; Donald Pearce, *In the President's and My Opinion,* Prentice-Hall, 1967; Samuel Blum, *What Every Nice Boy Knew about Sex,* Geis, 1967; Jane Yolen, *Isabel's Noel,* Funk, 1967; Brock Brower, *The Inchworm War and the Butterfly Peace,* Doubleday, 1970; Ralph Schoenstein, *Little Spiro,* Morrow, 1971; Schoenstein, *I Hear America Mating,* St. Martin's, 1972. Contributor of illustrations to magazines, including *Punch, Holiday, Saturday Evening Post, Playboy, Look, Life, Sports Illustrated, Esquire, Show Business Illustrated.*

AVOCATIONAL INTERESTS: Playing saxophone ("quite loudly").

BIOGRAPHICAL/CRITICAL SOURCES: Punch, August 31, 1966.

*   *   *

ROTH, Audrey J. 1927-

PERSONAL: Born February 4, 1927, in Newark, N.J.;

daughter of Eugene (a sales manager) and Ida (Kaufman) Dynner; married Raymond N. Roth, June 26, 1949; children: Sharon Lee, David Michael. *Education:* Ohio State University, B.A., 1946, M.A., 1947. *Residence:* Miami, Fla. *Office:* Department of English, Miami-Dade Community College, Miami, Fla.

CAREER: Former advertising copywriter in Ohio, teacher of English and advertising at Youngstown University, Youngstown, Ohio, and teacher of humanities at University of Miami, Coral Gables, Fla.; Miami-Dade Community College, Miami, Fla., associate professor of English, 1962—. *Member:* Conference on College Composition and Communication (secretary, executive committee, 1969-73), National Council of Teachers of English, College English Association (member of board of directors), National Academy of Television Arts and Sciences, Miami Film Teacher's Association (president).

WRITINGS: (Editor with Thelma Altshuler and Martha McDonough) *Prose as Experience,* Houghton, 1965; *The Research Paper: Form and Content,* Wadsworth, 1966, 2nd edition, 1971; (editor with Altshuler) *Writing Step by Step,* Houghton, 1969; *Success: A Search for Values,* Holt, 1969; (co-editor) *Alienation and Belonging: A Search for Values,* Holt, 1970; (editor) *Personal Identity: A Search for Values,* Holt, 1971; (with Oliver Camacho) *Words People Use,* Winthrop Publishing, 1972. Contributor of articles to professional journals. Columnist, *Optometric Weekly.*

WORK IN PROGRESS: Two books, tentatively entitled, *Weaving Compositions,* and *Writing about Oneself,* completion expected, 1976.

* * *

ROTH, Jack J(oseph) 1920-

PERSONAL: Born December 17, 1920, in Poland; son of Max and Dinah (Kraus) Roth. *Education:* University of Chicago, B.A., 1942, Ph.D., 1955; Institute of Political Studies, University of Paris, graduate study, 1949-50. *Home:* 24301 Bryden Rd., Beachwood, Ohio 44122. *Office:* Department of History, Case Western Reserve University, Cleveland, Ohio 44106.

CAREER: Roosevelt University, Chicago, Ill., 1951-68, began as assistant professor, professor of history, 1963-68, chairman of department, 1960-68; Case Western Reserve University, Cleveland, Ohio, professor of history, 1968—, chairman of department, 1968-73. Visiting associate professor, University of Chicago, 1962; visiting professor, University of Wisconsin, 1964-65. *Military service:* U.S. Army, 1942-46. *Member:* American Historical Association. *Awards, honors:* American Philosophical Society grant, 1963.

WRITINGS: (Co-translator) Georges Sorel, *Reflections on Violence,* Free Press of Glencoe, 1951; (editor) *World War I: Turning Point in Modern History,* Knopf, 1967. Contributor to history journals in United States, France, and Germany.

* * *

ROTH, Julius A(lfred) 1924-

PERSONAL: Born July 19, 1924, in Haledon, N.J.; son of Jacob John and Lidia (Meier) Roth; married Jessica Bell, November 5, 1949; children: Steven, Timothy, Amy. *Education:* Paterson State College (now William Paterson College of New Jersey), student, 1942-44; University of Chicago, A.M., 1950, Ph.D., 1954. *Politics:* "?". *Religion:*

None. *Office:* Department of Sociology, University of California, Davis, Calif. 95616.

CAREER: University of Chicago, Chicago, Ill., research associate, Industrial Relations Center, 1954, and Committee for Human Development, 1955-59; Community Studies, Kansas City, Mo., research associate, 1959-60; Columbia University, New York, N.Y., research scientist and project director, Research Center, New York School for Social Work, 1960-64; Boston University, Boston, Mass., associate professor of sociology, 1964-66; University of California, Davis, professor of sociology, 1966—. Visiting appointments to University of New South Wales, 1969, University of Aberdeen, and University of Wales, 1971-72, Institute of Preventive Medicine, Leiden, and Institute of Social Medicine, Hanover, 1974, and University of Copenhagen, 1975. *Member:* American Sociological Association, American Anthropological Association, American Psychological Association, American Association for the Advancement of Science, Society for the Study of Social Problems, American Association of University Professors.

WRITINGS: Timetables: Structuring the Passage of Time in Hospital Treatment and Other Careers, Bobbs-Merrill, 1963; (with Elizabeth M. Eddy as junior author) *Rehabilitation for the Unwanted,* Atherton, 1967. Contributor to *Review of General Semantics, Midwest Sociologist,* and other professional journals.

WORK IN PROGRESS: Study of professionalism, evaluation in higher education.

* * *

ROTH, Mary Jane

PERSONAL: Born in Chicago, Ill.; daughter of Frederick Edgar (a civil engineer) and Ethel M. (Godman) Morrow; married Lloyd J. Roth (a professor at University of Chicago), December 22, 1938; children: Dennis Morrow, Marc Tobin, Keven Simone (daughter). *Education:* Northwestern University, B.S., 1935; graduate study at Columbia University, 1944, and University of Iowa, 1946; Rosary College, River Forest, Ill., M.A. in Library Science, 1968. *Religion:* Protestant. *Home:* 155 Warwick St., Park Forest, Ill. 60466.

CAREER: Worked as professional actress in radio, summer stock, and vaudeville (a straight woman for Edgar Bergen and Edmund Lowe), with appearances on "First Nighter," "Wayside Theatre," and in many soap operas, and played platform dates with costumed monodramas and play readings; taught creative dramatics at Loofburrow School, Oak Park, Ill., and privately; directed plays for Recreation Department, Park Forest, Ill., and taught there and in Community Children's Theatre; developed and directed a reader's theater for schools; puppeteer; conducts puppet workshops for adults and children; lecturer. Currently children's librarian, Park Forest (Ill.) Public Library. *Member:* American Library Association, American Educational Theatre Association (regional governor, Children's Theatre Conference), Illinois Library Association, Zeta Phi Eta, Gamma Phi Beta.

WRITINGS: The Pretender Princess, Morrow, 1967; *His Majesty, the Frog,* Morrow, 1971.

WORK IN PROGRESS: Fiction books for children; a novel for teenagers.

ROTHENBERG, Gunther Eric 1923-

PERSONAL: Born July 11, 1923, in Berlin, Germany; son of Erich and Charlotte (Cohen) Rothenberg; married, 1952 (divorced, 1967); married, 1969. *Education:* University of Illinois, B.A., 1954, Ph.D., 1958; University of Chicago, M.A., 1956. *Home:* 210 East Lutz Ave., Lafayette, Ind. 47906. *Office:* Department of History, Purdue University, Lafayette, Ind. 47907.

CAREER: Served in British Army, 1941-46, and U.S. Air Force, 1949-55; Illinois State University, Normal, instructor in history, 1958; Southern Illinois University, Carbondale, assistant professor of modern European history, 1958-62; University of New Mexico, Albuquerque, associate professor, 1962-68, professor of military history, 1968-73; Purdue University, Lafayette, Ind., professor of military history, 1973—. Associate, Historical Evaluation and Research Organization (HERO), Washington, D.C. Member, United States Commission on Military History. *Member:* American Historical Association, Company of Military Collectors and Historians, American Military Institute, American Association for the Advancement of Slavic Studies. *Awards, honors:* American Philosophical Society grants, 1959, 1965, 1969, 1975; American Council of Learned Societies grant, 1962; Guggenheim fellowshiip, 1962-63.

WRITINGS: The Austrian Military Border in Croatia: 1522-1747, University of Illinois Press, 1960; *The Military Border in Croatia: 1740-1881,* University of Chicago Press, 1966; *The Army of Francis Joseph,* Purdue University Press, 1975. Contributor to historical journals. Member of editorial board of *Military Affairs,* 1973-75, and *Austrian History Yearbook,* 1973-76.

WORK IN PROGRESS: The Art of War in the Age of Napoleon.

* * *

ROTHWELL, Kenneth J(ames) 1925-

PERSONAL: Born October 13, 1925, in Perth, Australia; son of Horace P. and Violet (Hoddinott) Rothwell; married Alida Eidner, October 17, 1952; children: Kylie, Karin, Andrew Carlson. *Education:* University of Western Australia, B.A., 1949, M.A., 1954; University of Stockholm, graduate study, 1952; Harvard University, Ph.D., 1960. *Home address:* Box 124, Durham, N.H. 03824. *Office:* Department of Economics, University of New Hampshire, Durham, N.H. 03824.

CAREER: Reserve Bank of Australia, economic assistant, 1946-55; Harvard University, Cambridge, Mass., research associate, 1955-57; Bucknell University, Lewisburg, Pa., assistant professor of economics, 1957-60; Dartmouth College, Hanover, N.H., assistant professor, 1961-63; University of New Hampshire, Durham, associate professor, 1963-67, professor of economics, 1967—, dean of School of Business and Economics, 1966-67. Visiting professor, Institute of Social Studies, The Hague, and University of Stockholm, 1971-72. Affiliated with United Nations Missions to Indonesia, Ethiopia, and Iran, 1974-75. Consultant to Pan American Union, Academy for Interscience Methodology, and United Nations Center for Development, Planning, Programs, and Policy. *Military service:* Royal Australian Air Force, 1943-45; became flight lieutenant. *Member:* American Economic Association, Society for International Development, Latin American Studies Association.

WRITINGS: (With M. O. Clement and R. D. Pfister)

Theoretical Issues in International Economics, Houghton, 1967; *New England-Japan Commercial and Educational Exchanges,* New England Center, 1972; *Administrative Issues of Developing Economies,* Heath, 1972; *The New Political Economy in the Pacific,* Ballinger, 1975. Contributor to professional journals and magazines.

WORK IN PROGRESS: Studies in comparative economics, finance and administration.

* * *

ROVER, Constance (Mary) 1910-

PERSONAL: Born December 15, 1910, in Cockermouth, Cumberland, England; daughter of William George and Caroline (Wheeler) Skerry; married Frederick Herbert Rover (a former solicitor), April 22, 1944; children: Helen Judith (Mrs. Brian Self). *Education:* University of London, B.Sc., 1948, M.Sc., 1961, Ph.D., 1966. *Home:* 2 Oaks View, Hythe, Kent, England. *Agent:* Curtis Brown Ltd., 1 Craven Hill, London W2 3EW England.

CAREER: Free-lance lecturer, 1948-57; Polytechnic of North London, London, England, 1957-71, began as lecturer, became principal lecturer in government and deputy head of department of government and law; development of "woman studies" in southeast Kent, 1971—. *Member:* International Alliance of Women, National Women's Citizens' Association, Suffragette Fellowship, Fawcett Society.

WRITINGS: The Punch Book of Women's Rights, Hutchinson, 1967, A. S. Barnes, 1969; *Women's Suffrage and Party Politics in Britain, 1866-1914,* Routledge & Kegan Paul, 1967; *Love, Morals, and the Feminists,* Routledge & Kegan Paul, 1970. Contributor of short articles and reviews to periodicals.

WORK IN PROGRESS: Continuing research in the women's emancipation movement in Britain and America.

* * *

ROWE, A(lbert) W(ard) 1915-

PERSONAL: Born July 1, 1915, in St. Ives, Cornwall, England; son of Anthony (a harbor master) and Margaret (Ninnes) Rowe; married Joan Whipp, January 24, 1945; children: Gillian, Janet, Isabel. *Education:* University of London, B.A. (honors in English), M.Phil., L.R.A.M., Teachers Certificate, and Diploma in Education. *Home:* 57A Pearson Park, Hull, Yorkshire, England.

CAREER: Formerly, lecturer at a training college, and headmaster at David Lister Comprehensive School, Hull, Yorkshire, England. Radio and television broadcaster. *Military service:* Royal Air Force, 1939-45.

WRITINGS: (With Gareth Walters) *Harmonica and Recorder Teacher's Manual,* with pupils' primary and secondary books, Hohner, 1958; *The Education of the Average Child,* Harrap, 1959; (with Walters) "Worcester" series (graded part pieces for harmonica and recorder), two books, Hohner, 1959; *The New Hohner Melodica Tutor,* Hohner, 1961; "English Through Experience" series, five books (Books I-IV with Peter Emmens), Blond Educational, 1963-67, revised edition, 1975; *Desk Book of Plain English,* Basil Blackwell, 1965; (contributor) Brian Jackson, editor, *English Versus Examinations,* Chatto & Windus, 1965; (editor) *People Like Us: Short Stores for Secondary Schools,* Faber, 1965; (editor) "Active Anthologies" series, five books, Blond Educational, 1967-69; *Language for Living,* Basil Blackwell, 1967; *The School as a Guidance*

Community, Pearson Press, 1971; *Making the Present: A Social and Economic History of Britain, 1918-72*, Hutchinson, 1975. Writer of booklets and pamphlets, some for use in primary schools. Contributor of articles and reviews to professional journals.

WORK IN PROGRESS: Two books, *Changing a School* and *Educating Ordinary Children;* a two-book anthology of prose and verse for primary schools; research into attitudes of secondary school pupils towards school and life.

AVOCATIONAL INTERESTS: Sports, especially rugby football; travel in Europe and America; reading, especially poetry and novels; music (plays clarinet and harmonica).†

*   *   *

ROWLAND, D(onald) S(ydney) 1928-

(Annette Adams, Jack Bassett, Hazel Baxter, Karla Benton, Helen Berry, Lewis Brant, Alison Bray, William Brayce, Fenton Brockley, Oliver Bronson, Chuck Buchanan, Rod Caley, Roger Carlton, Janita Cleve, Sharon Court, Vera Craig, Wesley Craille, John Dryden, Freda Fenton, Charles Field, Graham Garner, Burt Kroll, Helen Langley, Henry Lansing, Harvey Lant, Irene Lynn, Hank Madison, Chuck Mason, Stuart McHugh, G. J. Morgan, Edna Murray, Lorna Page, Olive Patterson, Alvin Porter, Alex Random, W. J. Rimmer, Donna Rix, Matt Rockwell, Charles Roscoe, Minerva Rossetti, Norford Scott, Valerie Scott, Bart Segundo, Frank Shaul, Clinton Spurr, Roland Starr, J. D. Stevens, Mark Suffling, Kay Talbot, Will Travers, Sarah Vine, Elaine Vinson, Rick Walters, Neil Webb)

PERSONAL: Born September 23, 1928, in Great Yarmouth, Norfolk, England; son of Arthur (a carpenter) and Beatrice (Rix) Rowland; married Jessie Robinson, June 24, 1950; children: Donna Janita, Donald Arthur, Janita Ellen. *Education:* Left school at the age of twelve. *Politics:* "Non-political." *Religion:* Church of England. *Home:* 1 Quay Angel, Gorleston-on-Sea, Great Yarmouth, Norfolk NR31 6TJ, England. *Agent:* Michael Bakewell and Associates Ltd., 118 Tottenham Court Rd., London W1P 9HL, England.

CAREER: Entered British Army at seventeen and served 1945-50, became acting sergeant; between 1950 and 1953 worked at various jobs, including fish curing and exporting, fruit canning, and construction; film projectionist, 1953-57; senior clerk and local government officer (entertainments), 1957-63; full-time writer of action novels, 1964—. *Member:* Society of Authors, Western Writers of America.

WRITINGS—Under name D. S. Rowland: *The Battle Done*, Wright & Brown, 1958; *Drygulch Valley*, Wright & Brown, 1961; *Gunsmoke Pay-Off*, Wright & Brown, 1961; *Vengeance for Water Valley*, Wright & Brown, 1961; *Showdown at Singing Springs*, Wright & Brown, 1962; *12 Platoon*, Wright & Brown, 1962; *Both Feet in Hell*, Wright & Brown, 1962; *Murder Range*, Wright & Brown, 1962; *Not for Glory*, Combat Library, 1962; *Rough Justice*, R. Hale, 1963, published as *Bullets at Dry Creek*, Arcadia House, 1965; *The Long Trail*, R. Hale, 1963, published as *Law of the Holster*, Arcadia House, 1967; *Lonely Star*, R. Hale, 1964, Arcadia House, 1965; *Empty Saddles*, R. Hale, 1964; *Crossfire*, R. Hale, 1966; *Gun Rogues*, R. Hale, 1967, Arcadia House, 1969; *Depot in Space* (science-fiction), Gresham, 1973; *Master of Space* (science-fiction), R.

Hale, 1974; *Space Venturer* (science-fiction), R. Hale, in press; *Nightmare Planet* (science-fiction), R. Hale, in press.

Western novels; under pseudonym Jack Bassett: *Shooting Trouble*, Gresham, 1966; *Forked Trail*, Gresham, 1966; *No Quarter*, Gresham, 1966; *Gunsmoke Creek*, Gresham, 1967; *Saddle Scum*, R. Hale, 1967; *Big Tracks*, R. Hale, 1968.

Under pseudonym Lewis Brant; all published by R. Hale, except as noted: *Dark Prairie*, 1964; *Hard to Kill*, 1965; *Bitter Round-Up*, 1966; *Gunhand*, 1966; *Gunshot Pay-Off*, 1966; *The Backshooter*, 1967; *Gun Trail*, 1967; *Blood in the Dust*, Arcadia House, 1967; *Gringo Basin*, Lenox Hill, 1973; *Gunslick*, 1975; *Shale Creek Showdown*, in press.

Under pseudonym William Brayce: *Range Hog*, Gresham, 1966.

Under pseudonym Oliver Bronson: *Raw Deal*, Gresham, 1965; *Cattleman's Creed*, Gresham, 1966.

Under pseudonym Chuck Buchanan: *Brave Star*, Gresham, 1966.

Under pseudonym Rod Caley: *Lonesome Valley*, Gresham, 1966.

Under pseudonym Wesley Craille: *Hell-Bent*, Gresham, 1966.

Under pseudonym John Dryden; all published by R. Hale: *Quick on the Draw*, 1965; *Wide-Loop Range*, 1965; *Hard Ridden*, 1966; *Killer Streak*, 1973; *Range Rights*, 1973; *The Wideloopers*, 1974; *Crooked Brand*, 1974.

Under pseudonym Charles Field; all published by R. Hale: *Kingdom of Grass*, 1964; *Saddle Tramp*, 1965; *Star Brand Killer*, 1965; *Trail End*, 1966.

Under pseudonym Burt Kroll; all published by R. Hale, except as noted: *Water Rights*, Gresham, 1966; *Greenhorn Gun*, Gresham, 1966; *Hungry Guns*, Gresham, 1967; *Coyote Trail*, 1968; *Snake Breed*, Gresham, 1968; *Gunsmoke Showdown*, 1972; *Shoot on Sight*, 1973; *Mocking Bird Creek*, 1973; *Broken Down Cowboy*, 1974; *Lone-Wolf Lawman*, 1974.

Under pseudonym Henry Lansing: *Bleak Range*, Gresham, 1966.

Under pseudonym Harvey Lant; all published by R. Hale, except as noted: *Range Fury*, Gresham, 1966; *High, Wide and Handsome*, Gresham, 1966; *Bad Medicine*, Gresham, 1967; *Gun Rage*, 1967; *Slaughter Trail*, 1969; *Pistol Range*, 1973; *Fighting Marshall*, 1973; *Gun Hell*, 1973; *Angry Guns*, 1974; *Range Grab*, 1974.

Under pseudonym Hank Madison; all published by R. Hale, except as noted: *Riding High*, Gresham, 1966; *Wanted Dead or Alive*, Gresham, 1966; *Gunsmoke Legacy*, 1967; *Fighting Mad*, 1967; *Killer in the County*, 1967; *Arizona Pay-off*, 1972; *Man from Texas*, 1973; *The Straight Shooter*, 1973; *Desperate Gun*, 1974; *Frontier Law*, in press.

Under pseudonym Chuck Mason; all published by R. Hale, except as noted: *Back Trail*, Gresham, 1966; *Gunman Notorious*, Gresham, 1966; *The Law Dealer*, Gresham, 1966; *Ride Hard Shoot Fast*, Gresham, 1967; *Hell Branded*, 1967; *Gunlightning*, 1967; *Under Cover Law*, Gresham, 1968; *Hell Star*, 1972; *Gun for Hire*, 1972; *Hangrope Fever*, 1973; *Quick Triggers*, 1973; *Gun Trap*, 1974; *Fast Draw Law*, 1974; *Backlash*, 1974; *Killer Brand*, 1975; *Death in Oak Ridge*, in press.

Under pseudonym Stuart McHugh; all published by Gresham: *Gun Shy*, 1966; *Prairie Wolf*, 1966; *Riding for a Fall*, 1967; *Running Wild*, 1967.

Under pseudonym G. J. Morgan; all published by Futura, except as noted: *Border Fury*, 1975; *Trail of Death*, 1975; *Hell on Wheels*, 1975; *Hell on Wheels*, Milton House, 1975; *Steel Tracks-Iron Men*, in press; *The Rail Rogues*, in press.

Under pseudonym Alvin Porter: *The Corpse Maker*, Gresham, 1966; *Bitter Feud*, Gresham, 1967; *Crooked Spurs*, Gresham, 1967; *Riding Through*, R. Hale, 1967.

Under pseudonym W. J. Rimmer: *The Sidewinders*, Gresham, 1966.

Under pseudonym Matt Rockwell: *Trigger Help*, Gresham, 1966.

Under pseudonym Charles Roscoe; all published by R. Hale: *Gunsmoke Law*, 1964; *Cattleman's Country*, 1965; *Gunswift Justice*, 1965; *Draw or Die*, 1966.

Under pseudonym Norford Scott; all published by R. Hale: *Roughshod*, 1965; *Tight Rein*, 1966; *Whiphand*, 1966; *Vengeance of the Diamond M.*, 1967; *Kicking Horse Valley*, 1967; *Saddled for Hell*, 1967; *Terror Law*, 1969.

Under pseudonym Bart Segundo: *Boss of Bender County*, R. Hale, 1964.

Under pseudonym Frank Shaul: *Black Sundown*, R. Hale, 1964; *Saddle Pard*, R. Hale, 1966; *Lawman Courageous*, R. Hale, 1968.

Under pseudonym Clinton Spurr; all published by R. Hale: *Vengeance Gun*, 1964; *The Hell Raisers*, 1965; *Trail Fever*, 1965; *Short Rope*, 1966; *Shoot and Run*, 1967; *Killer Brand*, 1967; *Gun Fever*, 1967; *Death Wore Spurs*, 1969; *Trigger Fever*, 1972; *Wyoming Wild*, 1973; *The Loner*, 1973; *The Ambusher*, 1973; *Close Call,*, 1974; *Running Iron*, 1974; *Hell Tracks*, in press.

Under pseudonym J. D. Stevens; all published by R. Hale: *Bitter Valley*, 1964; *Twisted Trail*, 1965; *Shoot First*, 1965; *Heartbreak Range*, 1966.

Under pseudonym Will Travers; all published by R. Hale: *Rogue Rancher*, 1964; *Gun Crazy*, 1965; *Gold Fever*, 1966; *Showdown*, 1966.

Under pseudonym Rick Walters: *Gunsmoke Pass*, Gresham, 1966; *Wild Bunch*, Gresham, 1966.

Under pseudonym Neil Webb; all published by R. Hale: *Danger Trail*, 1964; *Rope Branded*, 1965; *Thunder Canyon*, 1965; *Trigger Law*, 1966; *High Stakes*, 1966; *Big Saddle*, 1966; *Bullet Proof*, 1973; *Bleak Valley*, 1973; *Guns of Hate*, 1973; *Gun Wolves*, 1974; *Killer Law*, 1974; *Hostile Range*, in press.

Romantic novels; under pseudonym Annette Adams: *Island of Decision*, Gresham, 1968; *Doctor of the Heart*, Gresham, 1968; *The Heart Healer*, Gresham, 1968.

Under pseudonym Hazel Baxter; all published by Gresham: *Locum in Love*, 1968; *Surgeon's Help*, 1968; *Helicopter Nurse*, 1968; *Doctor in Doubt*, 1969; *Night Sister*, 1969; *Doctor's Endeavour*, 1970.

Under pseudonym Karla Benton; all published by R. Hale: *Romantic Island*, 1971; *Nurse on Loan*, 1971; *Nurse Abroad*, 1972; *Carefree Doctor*, 1973; *Nurse in Love*, 1973.

Under pseudonym Helen Berry; all published by Gresham: *Highland Love*, 1968; *Doctor Needs a Wife*, 1968; *Occupation: Nurse*, 1968; *Highland Nurse*, 1969; *Wayward Nurse*, 1969; *Winged Nurse*, 1970.

Under pseudonym Alison Bray; all published by Gresham: *Prescription for Love*, 1968; *Doctor's Destiny*, 1968; *Surgeon's Honour*, 1968; *Doctor's Legacy*, 1968; *Prescription for Nurse*, 1969; *Hospital Sister*, 1969; *Nurse at Crag House*, 1970; *Poor Little Rich Nurse*, 1970.

Under pseudonym Janita Cleve; all published by R. Hale: *African Love Song*, 1971; *For Love or Money*, 1971; *Love Thy Neighbor*, 1971; *Nurse at Pinewood*, 1972; *Resident Nurse*, 1973.

Under pseudonym Sharon Court; all published by R. Hale: *Daughter of Destiny*, 1971; *Pathway to Love*, 1971; *Surgical Nurse*, 1972; *Nurse in Need*, 1972; *Dutiful Nurse*, 1972.

Under pseudonym Vera Craig; all published by R. Hale, except as noted: *Part Time Nurse*, 1969, published as *Now and Forever*, Dell, 1973; *Enchanted Nurse*, 1969, published as *Land of Enchantment*, Dell, 1974; *Nurse in Jeopardy*, 1969, published as *Path of Peril*, Dell, 1974; *Unselfish Nurse*, 1970, published as *The Love Barrier*, Dell, 1974; *Case Nurse*, 1970, published as *Glen Hall*, Dell, 1972.

Under pseudonym Freda Fenton; all published by Gresham: *The Nurse Inherits*, 1968; *Nurse Hopeful*, 1968; *Doctor Abroad*, 1969; *Doctor's Inheritance*, 1969; *District Nurse*, 1969; *Impulsive Nurse*, 1970.

Under pseudonym Helen Langley: *Where the Heart Lies*, Gresham, 1968.

Under pseudonym Irene Lynn; all published by Gresham: *Romantic Doctor*, 1968; *Tropical Nurse*, 1969; *Doctor Duty*, 1970; *Doctor in Bondage*, 1970.

Under pseudonym Edna Murray; all published by Gresham: *Patient Lover*, 1968; *Love Thy Doctor*, 1968; *Married to Medicine*, 1968; *Emergency Nurse*, 1968; *Ward Sister*, 1968; *Loving Nurse*, 1969; *Island Nurse*, 1970; *Faithful Nurse*, 1970; *Cruise Nurse*, 1970; *Nurse in Danger*, 1970.

Under pseudonym Lorna Page; all published by Gresham: *Love is a Doctor*, 1968; *Doctor of Decision*, 1968; *Temporary Nurse*, 1969; *The Nurse Investigates*, 1969; *Fortunate Nurse*, 1970; *Doctor's Prescription*, 1970.

Under pseudonym Olive Patterson; all published by Gresham: *Mystery Clinic*, 1968; *Runaway Doctor*, 1968; *Nurse Errant*, 1969; *Temptation Doctor*, 1970.

Under pseudonym Donna Rix; all published by R. Hale: *Doctor of the Isles*, 1971; *Conflict of Love*, 1971; *Career Nurse*, 1972; *Nurse in Clover*, 1973; *Heart of a Nurse*, 1973; *Nurse Courageous*, 1973.

Under pseudonym Minerva Rosetti; all published by Lenox Hill: *Heiress to Crag Castle*, 1973; *Mansion to Menace*, 1974; *Sinister House*, in press.

Under pseudonym Valerie Scott; all published by R. Hale: *Ski Lift to Love*, 1971; *Race to Love*, 1971; *Doctor in Her Life*, 1972; *Mysterious Nurse*, 1973; *Secretive Nurse*, 1973; *Dedicated Nurse*, 1974.

Under pseudonym Kay Talbot; all published by Gresham: *Her Favourite Doctor*, 1968; *Doctor's Slave*, 1968; *Hospital Romance*, 1969; *Dental Nurse*, 1969; *Country Doctor*, 1969; *Passionate Nurse*, 1970; *Heartbreak Nurse*, 1970.

Under pseudonym Sarah Vine: *Overseas Nurse*, Wright & Brown, 1969.

Under pseudonym Elaine Vinson; all published by R. Hale: *Lover's Quest*, 1971; *Enchanted Isle*, 1971; *Island of Desire*, 1972; *Nurse on Skis*, 1972; *Doubtful Nurse*, 1973.

Science Fiction novels; all published by R. Hale, except as noted; under pseudonym Fenton Brockley: *Star Quest,* 1974.

Under pseudonym Roger Carlton: *Beyond Tomorrow,* 1975; *Star Arrow,* 1975.

Under pseudonym Graham Garner: *Space Probe,* 1974; *Starfall Muta,* 1975; *Rifts of Time,* in press.

Under pseudonym Alex Random: *Star Cluster Seven,* 1974; *Dark Constellation,* 1975; *Cradle of Stars,* 1975.

Under pseudonym Roland Starr: *Operation Omina,* Lenox Hill, 1970; *Omina Uncharted,* 1974; *Time Factor,* 1975; *Return from Omina,* in press.

Under pseudonym Mark Suffling: *Project Oceanus,* 1975; *Space Crusader,* 1975; *Spaceway to Danger,* in press.

*   *   *

ROY, Gregor 1929-

PERSONAL: Born March 7, 1929, in Scotland; son of Alfred Leith (a laborer) and Mary Graham (Schofield) Roy; married Patricia Allen, August 5, 1962 (divorced). *Education:* University of Glasgow, M.A., 1951. *Politics:* Scottish Nationalist. *Religion:* Calvinist. *Home:* 1654 Third Ave., New York, N.Y. 10028.

CAREER: Lecturer and writer, Warwickshire, England, 1951-57; hotel manager in Bermuda, 1957-58; teacher in Connecticut, 1958-59; ski lodge manager in Stowe, Vt., 1959-60; teacher in New York, N.Y., 1960-62. Editorial consultant to publishing companies. *Military service:* British Army, served in Korea with Black Watch Regiment; became lieutenant. *Awards, honors:* Religious Arts Festival Poetry Award, 1962; American Heritage Award, 1974.

WRITINGS: (Translator) Francois Derry, *Our Unknown Earth,* Stein & Day, 1968; (translator) Jean-Marie Paupert, *Politics of the Gospel,* Holt, 1969. Also author of six study guides, published by Monarch, 1964-66. Contributor of articles, essays, and fiction to magazines, including *Nation, Commonweal, Cross Currents, America,* and *Mademoiselle.*

WORK IN PROGRESS: A novel, *Stranger in the Land; Collected Poems.*

SIDELIGHTS: Roy told *CA* that "like Camus, I believe we are in desperate need of a Renaissance, and I believe that literature and the arts must play a decisive role in effecting this."

*   *   *

ROYCE, R(ussell) Joseph 1921-

PERSONAL: Born August 19, 1921, in New York, N.Y.; son of Alfred and Clara (Andersen) Royce; married Lee Summerlin, April 3, 1944; children: Christopher, Janet. *Education:* City College (now City College of the City University of New York), student, 1937-38; Denison University, A.B., 1941; Ohio State University, graduate study, 1941-42; University of Chicago, Ph.D., 1951. *Office:* Center for Advanced Study in Theoretical Psychology, University of Alberta, Edmonton, Alberta, Canada T6G 2E9.

CAREER: Drake University, Des Moines, Iowa, assistant professor of psychology, 1949-51; University of Redlands, Redlands, Calif., 1951-60, began as assistant professor, became associate professor of psychology; University of Alberta, Edmonton, professor of psychology and head of department, 1960-67, founder and director of Center for Advanced Study in Theoretical Psychology, 1967—. Visiting professor, University of Hawaii, summer, 1964. Lecturer at national and international societies and universities in North America, Europe, United Kingdom, and Australia. Statistical consultant, U.S. Air Force. *Military service:* U.S. Army Air Forces, 1942-46; became first lieutenant.

MEMBER: American Psychological Association, Society for Multivariate Experimental Psychology, Behavior Genetics Association, Canadian Psychological Association, Institute on Religion in an Age of Science (member of board of advisors), Western Psychological Association, California State Psychological Association, Alberta Psychological Association, Sigma Xi. *Awards, honors:* Ford Foundation faculty fellow, 1955-60; Canada Council senior research fellow in Europe, 1965-66; grants from National Institute of Mental Health, American Academy of Arts and Sciences, National Research Council (Canada), and other institutions and foundations.

WRITINGS: The Encapsulated Man: An Interdisciplinary Essay on the Search for Meaning, Van Nostrand, 1964; (editor and contributor) *Psychology and the Symbol: An Interdisciplinary Symposium,* Random House, 1965; (editor and contributor) *Toward Unification of Psychology,* University of Toronto Press, 1970; (editor with W. W. Rozeboom) *The Psychology of Knowing,* Gordon & Breach, 1972; (editor and contributor) *Multivariate Analysis and Psychological Theory,* Academic Press, 1973.

Contributor: R. S. Daniel, editor, *Contemporary Readings in General Psychology,* Houghton, 1959, 2nd edition, 1965; W. A. Fullager, H. G. Lewis, and C. F. Cumber, editors, *Readings for Educational Psychology,* 2nd edition (Royce not associated with 1st edition), Crowell, 1964; J. P. Guilford, editor, *Fields of Psychology,* 3rd edition (Royce not associated with previous editions), Van Nostrand, 1966; R. B. Cattell, editor, *Handbook of Multivariate Experimental Psychology,* McNally & Loftin, 1966; D. N. Jackson and S. Messick, editors, *Problems in Human Assessment,* McGraw, 1967; J.F.T. Bugental, editor, *Challenges of Humanistic Psychology,* McGraw, 1967; Joseph Havens, editor, *Psychology and Religion,* Van Nostrand, 1968; M. Manosevitz, G. Lindzey, and D. D. Theissen, editors, *Behavioral Genetics: Method and Research,* Appleton, 1969; V. S. Sexton and H. Misiak, editors, *Historical Perspectives in Psychology: Readings,* Brooks-Cole, 1971; B. B. Wolman, editor, *Handbook of Psychology,* Prentice-Hall, 1973; E. C. Carterette and M. P. Friedman, editors, *Handbook of Perception,* Volume I: *Historical and Philosophical Roots to Perception,* Academic Press, 1974; M. T. Holmes and W. Poley, editors, *Current Problems in Animal Behavior Genetics,* Pavlov Institute of Physiology (Leningrad), 1975; A. Debons and W. Cameron, editors, *NATO Conference on Information Sciences,* International Publishing (Netherlands), 1975; W. J. Arnold, editor, *Nebraska Symposium on the Conceptual Foundations of Theory and Methods in Psychology,* University of Nebraska Press, 1975. Also contributor to *Extra-Terrestrial Intelligence: The Biocosmic Community,* edited by J. Christian.

Contributor of more than 100 articles and reviews to professional journals. Associate editor, *Multivariate Behavioral Research,* 1965-74, *Psychological Record,* 1965-75, *Perspectives: A Journal of General and Liberal Studies,* 1969—, *Journal of Psycholinguistic Research,* 1970—; editor, *Newsletter of the Philosophical Psychology Division of the American Psychological Association,* 1965-69.

WORK IN PROGRESS: Four books, including a *Multi-Factor Theory of Individuality,* with Allan Buss; a play, "You're Ill Sam Gill, Take a Pill."

AVOCATIONAL INTERESTS: Sports (currently skiing and golfing), aficionado of bullfighting, chess, and theatre.

BIOGRAPHICAL/CRITICAL SOURCES: T. S. Krawiec, *The Psychologist,* Volume III, Ohio University Press, 1975

* * *

ROYSTER, Vermont (Connecticut) 1914-

PERSONAL: Born April 30, 1914, in Raleigh, N.C.; son of Wilbur High and Olivette (Broadway) Royster; married Frances Claypoole, June 5, 1937; children: Frances Claypoole, Sara Eleanor. *Education:* University of North Carolina, A.B., 1935. *Politics:* "No party affiliation." *Religion:* Episcopalian. *Home:* 903 Arrowhead Rd., Chapel Hill, N.C. 27514. *Office:* University of North Carolina, Chapel Hill, N.C. 27514.

CAREER: New York (N.Y.) City News Bureau, reporter, 1935-36; *Wall Street Journal,* New York, N.Y., Washington correspondent, 1936-40, 1945-46, chief of Washington Bureau, 1946-49, associate editor, 1949-58, editor, 1958-71; Dow Jones & Co., Inc., New York, N.Y., vice-president and member of executive committee, 1960-71; University of North Carolina, Chapel Hill, William Rand Kenan Professor of Journalism and Public Affairs, 1971—. Phi Beta Kappa Visiting Scholar, 1976-77. Trustee of Webb School, Bellbuckle, Tenn., 1955-60, and St. Augustine's College; member of selection committee, Morehead Fellowships, 1966; member of advisory board, Pulitzer Prizes, 1967. Presidential appointee, National Historical Publications and Records Commission, 1973—. *Military service:* U.S. Naval Reserve, active duty, 1940-45; became lieutenant commander. *Member:* American Society of Newspaper Editors (president, 1965-66), National Conference of Editorial Writers (chairman, 1957), National Press Club, Overseas Press Club, Phi Beta Kappa, Sigma Delta Chi (fellow). *Awards, honors:* Pulitzer Prize for editorial writing, 1953; Sigma Delta Chi Medal for distinguished service in journalism, 1958; LL.D., University of North Carolina, 1959; Litt.D., Temple University, 1964; William Allen White Award, University of Kansas, 1971; Loeb Memorial Award, University of California, Los Angeles, 1975.

WRITINGS: (Co-author) *Main Street and Beyond,* Doubleday, 1959; *Journey through the Soviet Union,* Dow Jones, 1962; *A Pride of Prejudices,* Knopf, 1967; *The American Press and the Revolutionary Tradition,* American Enterprise Institute, 1974; (contributor) Andrew Scott and Earle Wallace, editors, *Politics U.S.A.,* Macmillan, 1974; (contributor) *America's Continuing Revolution,* Doubleday, 1975. Contributor to *Saturday Evening Post, Reader's Digest, Collier's,* and other periodicals. Regular columnist, "Thinking Things Over," in *Wall Street Journal.*

WORK IN PROGRESS: Origins of Freedom of Speech and of Press, 1665-1770.

SIDELIGHTS: Vermont Royster was named for his grandfather, whose father had endowed all of *his* children with names of states. He received the Pulitzer Prize in 1953 for the bulk of his writings, not for the usual single editorial. He has written on politics, economics, foreign af-fairs, books, music, theater, and considers himself a nineteenth-century liberal. He has traveled "everywhere but Red China."

BIOGRAPHICAL/CRITICAL SOURCES: Vermont Royster, *A Pride of Prejudices,* Knopf, 1967.

* * *

RUBENSTEIN, Richard L(owell) 1924-

PERSONAL: Born January 8, 1924, in New York, N.Y.; son of Jesse George (an industrial engineer) and Sara (Fine) Rubenstein; married Ellen van der Veen, April 3, 1947 (divorced, 1963); married Betty Rogers Alschuler, August 21, 1966; children: (first marriage) Aaron, Hannah, Jeremy, Nathaniel (deceased). *Education:* University of Cincinnati, A.B., 1946; Jewish Theological Seminary, M.H.L., ordained Rabbi, 1952; Harvard University, S.T.M., 1955, Ph.D., 1960. *Politics:* Democrat. *Home:* 3046 Cloudland Dr., Tallahassee, Fla. 32306. *Agent:* George Borchardt, 145 East 52nd St., New York, N.Y. 10022. *Office:* Department of Religion, Florida State University, Tallahassee, Fla.

CAREER: Temple Beth Emunah, Brockton, Mass., rabbi, 1952-54; Temple Israel, Natick, Mass., rabbi, 1954-56; Harvard University, Cambridge, Mass., interim director of B'nai B'rith Hillel Foundation, 1956-58; University of Pittsburgh and Carnegie Institute of Technology, Pittsburgh, Pa., director of B'nai B'rith Hillel Foundation and chaplain to Jewish students, 1958-70; Florida State University, Tallahassee, professor of religion and director, Center for the Study of Southern Culture and Religion, 1970—. Charles E. Merrill adjunct professor in humanities, University of Pittsburgh, 1964-70; member of graduate faculty and academic advisory council, Jewish Teachers' Seminary of New York. Lecturer at U.S. and Canadian universities, at Albert Schweitzer College, Switzerland, 1963, University of Edinburgh, 1964, Catholic University of Lublin and other Catholic institutions in Poland, 1965, at University of Mainz, University of Bonn, and University of Heidelberg, 1972. John Phillips fellow, Phillips Exeter Academy, 1970; fellow, National Humanities Institute, Yale University, 1976-77. *Member:* Rabbinical Assembly of America, American Academy of Religion, Society for the Scientific Study of Religion, Society for the Arts, Religion, and Contemporary Culture (fellow), Society for Religion and Higher Education (fellow), Springtime Tallahassee.

WRITINGS: After Auschwitz: Radical Theology and Contemporary Judaism, Bobbs-Merrill, 1966; *The Religious Imagination,* Bobbs-Merrill, 1967; *Morality and Eros,* McGraw, 1970; *My Brother Paul,* Harper, 1972; *Power Struggle,* Scribner, 1974; *The Cunning of History,* Harper, 1975. Contributor of numerous articles and reviews to journals and to magazines, including *Cross Currents, Psychoanalytic Review, Playboy, Christian Century, Commonweal, Psychology Today,* and *New York Times.*

WORK IN PROGRESS: A book on Jesus; a book on political theory.

* * *

RUBENSTEIN, (Clarence) Robert 1926-

PERSONAL: Born July 4, 1926, in San Francisco, Calif.; son of Louis and Frances (Berman) Rubenstein; married Anne Magrath, March 29, 1949; children: Catherine, Dirk, Jeffrey, Matthew. *Education:* Stanford University, A.B., 1947; Stanford University Medical School, M.D., 1952;

Western New England Institute for Psychoanalysis, graduate, 1960. *Home:* 25 Beach Rd., Belvedere, Calif. 94920. *Office:* Department of Psychiatry, Mount Zion Hospital, 1600 Divisadero St., San Francisco, Calif. 94115.

CAREER: San Francisco Hospital, San Francisco, Calif., intern, 1951-52; Yale University, Medical School, New Haven, Conn., resident in department of psychiatry, 1952-55, instructor, 1955-58, assistant professor, 1958-59, assistant clinical professor, 1959-65, associate clinical professor of psychiatry, 1965-73, Yale Psychiatric Institute, assistant director, 1957-61, consulting supervisor, 1961-66, co-director, 1966-73, fellow of Ezra Stiles College, 1964-73; Mount Zion Hospital, San Francisco, director of inpatient services, 1973-75, director of psychiatric services, 1975—. Attending psychiatrist, Yale-New Haven Hospital, 1955-73. Member of scholars study committee, Center for Research and Education in American Liberties, Columbia University, 1966-70; faculty member, San Francisco Psychoanalytic Institute, 1973—; counsellor, Policy Sciences Center, 1974—. Consultant to organizations including Connecticut Juvenile Courts and Veterans Administration Hospital, West Haven, and to the New Haven anti-poverty program, 1964-73. Trustee of Western New England Institute for Psychoanalysis, 1966-70, and Putney School, 1971—; member of board of directors, Westside Community Health Center, 1973—. *Military service:* U.S. Army, 1945-46.

MEMBER: American Psychoanalytic Association (fellow), American Psychiatric Association (president of New Haven-Middlesex chapter, 1964-65), Conference on Science, Philosophy and Religion (fellow), Western New England Psychoanalytic Society, Connecticut State Medical Society, Sigma Xi. *Awards, honors:* National Institute of Mental Health career teacher grantee, 1957-59.

WRITINGS: (Contributor) *American Handbook of Psychiatry,* Basic Books, 1959; (with Harold D. Lasswell) *The Sharing of Power in a Psychiatric Hospital,* Yale University Press, 1966; (contributor) C. Faust and J. Feingold, editors, *Education for Character: Strategies for Change in Higher Education,* Harper, 1969; (contributor) A. Rogow, editor, *Politics, Personality, and Social Science in the Twentieth Century,* University of Chicago Press, 1969. Contributor to *Political Science Annual,* Volume I, Bobbs-Merrill, 1966, and medical journals.

WORK IN PROGRESS: With Harold D. Lasswell, *The Future of Psychiatry,* a study of the psychology of political participation and the therapeutic process; *The Psychotherapeutic Treatment of the Psychoses.*

*   *   *

RUE, John E.   1924-

PERSONAL: Born April 5, 1924, in Mapleton, Minn.; son of Peter (a farmer) and Ruth Harriet (Healy) Rue; married Sally Rochlin, June 9, 1957; children: Ruth Rachel, David Rochlin. *Education:* University of Minnesota, B.A., 1944, M.A., 1953, Ph.D., 1963. *Religion:* Society of Friends. *Office:* Department of Political Science, Oakland University, Rochester, Mich. 48063.

CAREER: Served with Society of Friends Ambulance and Service units in North China, 1946-51; Reed College, Portland, Ore., instructor in political science, 1958-60; San Fernando Valley State College (now California State University, Northridge), assistant professor of political science, 1961-64; Stanford University, Stanford, Calif., visiting assistant professor, 1964-65, visiting associate professor of

political science, and research fellow at Hoover Institution on War, Revolution, and Peace, 1965-66, research associate at Hoover Institution, 1966-67; Oakland University, Rochester, Mich., associate professor, 1967-72, professor of political science and Chinese studies, 1972—. *Awards, honors:* Grant from Social Science Research Council Joint Committee on Contemporary China, 1966-67.

WRITINGS: Mao Tse-tung in Opposition, 1927-35, Stanford University Press, 1966; (contributor) *Mao Tse-toung* (in French), l'Editions L'Herne (Paris), 1972; (contributor with Dennis J. Doolin) *World Communism: A Handbook,* Hoover Institution Press, 1973. Contributor to *Art International* (Lugano), and *Friend's Journal.*

WORK IN PROGRESS: Mao Tse-tung: The Road to Power.

*   *   *

RUECKERT, William H(owe)   1926-

PERSONAL: Surname is pronounced Rick-ert; born November 4, 1926, in Cleveland, Ohio; son of Frederic (an engineer) and Elizabeth (Howe) Rueckert; married Betty Ehlers (a teacher), January 30, 1954; children: Theron Kincaid, Quentin Howe, Jordan Frederic Burke, Morgan Paul. *Education:* Williams College, B.A., 1950; University of Michigan, M.A., 1951, Ph.D., 1956. *Home:* 16 Landing Rd. S., Rochester, N.Y. 14610. *Office:* English Department, State University of New York College at Geneseo, Geneseo, N.Y.

CAREER: Instructor in English at Russell Sage College, Troy, N.Y., 1954-56, and Oberlin College, Oberlin, Ohio, 1956-57; University of Illinois, Urbana, 1957-65, began as instructor, became associate professor of English; University of Rochester, Rochester, N.Y., associate professor, 1965-67, professor of English, 1967-75; State University of New York College at Geneseo, professor of English and chairman of department, 1975—. *Military service:* U.S. Navy, 1945-46. *Member:* Modern Language Association of America.

WRITINGS: Kenneth Burke and the Drama of Human Relations, University of Minnesota Press, 1963; *Glenway Westcott,* Twayne, 1965; (editor) *Critical Responses to Kenneth Burke: 1924-1966* (essays), University of Minnesota Press, 1969. Also writer of reviews and essays.

WORK IN PROGRESS: Faulkner from Within: Destructive and Generative Being in the Novels of William Faulkner; Walt Whitman and America.

AVOCATIONAL INTERESTS: Ecology, sailing.

*   *   *

RUGOFF, Milton   1913-

PERSONAL: Surname is pronounced *Rue*-goff; born March 6, 1913, in New York, N.Y.; married Helen Birkenbaum. *Education:* Columbia University, B.A., 1933, M.A., 1934, Ph.D., 1940. *Home:* 18 Ox Ridge Rd., Elmsford, N.Y. 10523. *Office:* Chanticleer Press, 424 Madison Ave., New York, N.Y. 10017.

CAREER: Alfred A. Knopf, Inc. (publishers), New York City, associate editor, 1943-47; *The Magazine '47,* New York City, associate editor, 1947-48; Chanticleer Press, New York City, editor and vice-president, 1948—. *Military service:* U.S. Army, 1943-46; became sergeant. *Member:* Authors Guild, Hakluyt Society, American Folklore Society.

WRITINGS: Donne's Imagery: A Study in Creative Sources, [New York], 1939, reprinted, Russell, 1961; (editor) *A Harvest of World Folk Tales,* Viking, 1949; (editor) *The Great Travelers,* two volumes, Simon & Schuster, 1960; *Marco Polo's Adventures in China,* American Heritage Press, 1962; (editor) *Travels of Marco Polo,* New American Library, 1962; (editor) *Bligh's Mutiny on the H.M.S. Bounty,* New American Library, 1962; *Prudery and Passion: Sexuality in Victorian America,* Putnam, 1971; (editor) *The Britannica Encyclopedia of American Art,* Simon & Schuster, 1973; (editor) *The Wild Places: A Photographic Celebration of Unspoiled America,* Harper, 1973.

WORK IN PROGRESS: A book on the Beecher family, expected completion in 1977.

SIDELIGHTS: Rugoff has remained especially interested in the fields of folklore, social history, natural history, and art, as evidenced in his books. Each study seems to fill a gap so often found in these areas. *A Harvest of World Folk Tales* includes about two hundred folk tales collected from nineteen different sections of the world. Indeed, the stories "offer rich stuff for speculation when we are in a philosophic mood," Marion Lowenthal points out. *The Great Travelers* includes a collection of first-hand narratives of wayfarers, wanderers, and explorers in all parts of the world, from 450 B.C. to the present. This source is an excellent "family book" the *Kirkus Service* believes, as it includes, Martin Levin explains, photographs, prints, and skillful editing, making it "a beautifully orchestrated symposium." *The Britannica Encyclopedia of American Art,* containing both biographical and critical information, "lends itself as well to an evening of casual browsing as it does to more serious use as a reference source," according to James Auer.

BIOGRAPHICAL/CRITICAL SOURCES: New York Herald Tribune Book Review, December 14, 1949; *Kirkus Service,* September 15, 1960; *New York Times Book Review,* December 4, 1960; *Milwaukee Journal,* November 11, 1973.

* * *

RULAND, Richard (Eugene) 1932-

PERSONAL: Born May 1, 1932, in Detroit, Mich.; son of Eugene John and Irene (Janette) Ruland; married Barbara Nolan, December 15, 1973. *Education:* University of Western Ontario, A.B., 1953; University of Detroit, A.M., 1955; University of Michigan, Ph.D., 1960. *Office:* Department of English, Washington University, St. Louis, Mo. 63130.

CAREER: Yale University, New Haven, Conn., instructor, 1960-64, assistant professor of English and American studies, 1964-68, director of undergraduate studies in American studies, 1963-64; Washington University, St. Louis, Mo., visiting associate professor, 1967-68, associate professor, 1968-69, professor of American literature, 1969—, chairman of department, 1969-73. Visiting Bruern Professor of American Literature, University of Leeds, Leeds, England, 1964-65; visiting Fulbright professor of American literature, University of Groningen, The Netherlands, 1975. *Member:* Modern Language Association of America, American Studies Association, Association of Departments of English (member of executive committee, 1972-74; president, 1974). *Awards, honors:* Morse fellow, Yale University, 1966-67.

WRITINGS: The Rediscovery of American Literature:

Premises of Critical Taste, 1900-1940, Harvard University Press, 1967; (editor) *Walden: Twentieth-Century Interpretations,* Prentice-Hall, 1968; (editor) *Theories of American Literature,* Dutton, Volume I: *The Nature Muse,* 1972, revised edition, 1976, Volume II: *A Storied Land,* 1976; *America in Modern European Literature: From Image to Metaphor,* New York University Press, 1976. Contributor of articles to professional journals, *New York Times;* and contributor of reviews to *Yale Review, South Atlantic Quarterly,* and *Journal of the University Film Producers Association.*

* * *

RUMSEY, Marian (Barritt) 1928-

PERSONAL: Born May 18, 1928, in Nebraska City, Neb.; daughter of John L. (a medical doctor) and Sara (Thomas) Barritt; married William J. Rumsey, August 31, 1948; children: William, Thomas. *Education:* San Diego State College (now San Diego State University), student, 1945-46. *Home address:* Box 341381, c/o Yacht Flyaway, Coral Gables, Fla. 33134.

WRITINGS—All published by Morrow: *Seal of Frog Island,* 1960; *Shipwreck Bay,* 1966; *High Country Adventure,* 1967; *The Beaver of Weeping Water,* 1968; *Devil's Doorstep,* 1966; *Danger on Shadow Mountain,* 1970; *Lost in the Desert,* 1971; *Lion on the Run,* 1973.

* * *

RUSSELL, Andy 1915-

PERSONAL: Born December 8, 1915, in Lethbridge, Alberta, Canada; son of Harold George (a rancher) and Lorenda Scarlett (McTavish) Russell; married Anna Kathleen Riggall; children: Richard Herbert, Charles Andrew, Harold John, Gordon Riggall, Lorenda Anne. *Education:* Educated at public schools in Alberta, Canada. *Home address:* Box 68, Waterton Lakes Park, Alberta, Canada T0K 2M0.

CAREER: Rancher, veteran outdoorsman, photographer, and professional guide and lecturer; has also instructed shooting classes, filmed motion picture material on assignment, filmed television features, and appeared in television films; free-lance writer for magazines, 1945—. *Member:* Authors Guild, National Rifle Association.

WRITINGS: (Illustrated with own photographs) *Grizzly Country,* Knopf, 1967; *Trails of a Wilderness Wanderer,* Knopf, 1971; *Horns in the High Country,* Knopf, 1973; *The High West,* Viking, 1974; *The Rockies,* Hurtig Publishers, 1975. Contributor of more than seventy stories and articles to national magazines.

WORK IN PROGRESS: A feature-length film of an environmental nature concerned with the Yukon Territory; another book.

* * *

RUSSETT, Cynthia Eagle 1937-

PERSONAL: Born February 1, 1937, in Pittsburgh, Pa.; daughter of Jacob Eugene (a ceramic engineer) and Julia (O'Brien) Eagle; married Bruce Martin Russett (a professor at Yale University), June 18, 1960; children: Margaret Ellen, Mark David, Lucia Elizabeth, Daniel Alden. *Education:* Trinity College, Washington, D.C., A.B., 1958; Yale University, M.A., 1959, Ph.D., 1964. *Home:* 70 Martin Ter., Hamden, Conn. 06517.

CAREER: Yale University, New Haven, Conn., part-time lecturer in American history, 1964—.

WRITINGS: The Concept of Equilibrium in American Social Thought, Yale University Press, 1966; *Darwin in America: The Intellectual Response, 1865-1912,* W. H. Freeman, 1976.

WORK IN PROGRESS: A study of scientific and social scientific theories of gender differences in the Anglo-American intellectual community after 1870.

* * *

RUTZ, Viola Larkin   1932-

PERSONAL: Born March 14, 1932, in New York, N.Y.; married Harold Rutz (a professor), June 26, 1954. *Education:* Concordia College (now Concordia Teachers College), River Forest, Ill., B.S. in Ed.

CAREER: Elementary school teacher.

WRITINGS: Little Tree and His Wish, Concordia, 1966.

WORK IN PROGRESS: Children's books.

* * *

RYALS, Clyde de L(oache)   1928-

PERSONAL: Born December 19, 1928, in Atlanta, Ga.; son of Chester A. and Ruth (de Loache) Ryals; married Hildegard Thun Scheffey Ellerkmann, September 4, 1971. *Education:* Emory University, A.B., 1947, M.A., 1949; University of Pennsylvania, Ph.D., 1957. *Politics:* Democrat. *Religion:* Episcopalian. *Home:* 1620 University Dr., Durham, N.C. 22707. *Office:* 319 Allen Building, Duke University, Durham, N.C. 27706.

CAREER: University of Maryland, College Park, instructor in English, 1956-57; University of Pennsylvania, Philadelphia, instructor, 1957-60, assistant professor, 1960-64, associate professor, 1964-69, professor of English, 1969-73, graduate chairman, 1969-72; Duke University, Durham, N.C., professor of English, 1973—. Member of executive council, Episcopal Diocese of Pennsylvania, 1963-67. *Awards, honors:* Guggenheim fellow, 1972-73.

WRITINGS: Theme and Symbol in Tennyson's Poetry to 1850, University of Pennsylvania Press, 1964; (editor) Tennyson, *Poems, Chiefly Lyrical,* University of Pennsylvania Press, 1966; *From the Great Deep,* Ohio University Press, 1967; (editor) Mrs. Humphrey Ward, *Robert Elsmere,* University of Nebraska Press, 1967; (editor) *Nineteenth-Century Literary Perspectives,* Duke University Press, 1974; *Browning's Later Poetry, 1871-1889,* Cornell University Press, 1975.

* * *

RYCROFT, Charles (Frederick)   1914-

PERSONAL: Born September 9, 1914, in Basingstoke, England; son of Sir Richard and Emily (Lowry-Corry) Rycroft; married Chloe Majolier (a physician), 1946 (divorced, 1962); children: Julia, Catherine, Francis. *Education:* Trinity College, Cambridge, B.A. (first class honors), 1936; University College, London, M.B., 1945, B.S., 1945. *Home:* 97 Greenhill, Hampstead, London N.W. 3, England. *Agent:* A. D. Peters, 10 Buckingham St., London W.C. 2, England. *Office:* 18 Wimpole St., London W.1, England.

CAREER: House physician at Maudsley Hospital, London, England, 1946; psychotherapist and psychoanalyst in private practice, London, 1948—. Part-time consultant in psychotherapy to Tavistock Clinic, London, 1956-68. *Member:* British Psycho-Analytical Society (librarian, 1950-56; scientific secretary, 1956-58), British Psychological Society.

WRITINGS: (Editor) *Psychoanalysis Observed,* Coward, 1967; (contributor) James Mitchell, editor, *The God I Want,* Constable, 1967; *Anxiety and Neurosis,* Penguin, 1968; *Imagination and Reality,* Hogarth, 1968; *Critical Dictionary of Psychoanalysis,* Basic Books, 1969; *Reich,* Viking, 1971. Contributor of reviews to *Observer, New Society, New York Review of Books.* Assistant editor, *International Journal of Psycho-Analysis,* 1955-58.

* * *

RYDER, A(rthur) J(ohn)   1913-

PERSONAL: Born April 17, 1913, in Leeds, England; son of Charles Foster (a farmer) and Mabel Elizabeth (Sims) Ryder; married Krystyna K. Rajcher, April 9, 1946. *Education:* Oriel College, Oxford, B.A. (honors), 1934; London School of Economics and Political Science, Ph.D., 1958. *Politics:* Conservative. *Religion:* Church of England. *Home:* 74 Clifton Hill, London N.W. 8, England. *Office:* St. David's University College, Lampeter, Wales.

CAREER: British Council, staff lecturer in English and history in Middle East, 1939-45; Control Commission for Germany, education officer, 1946-56; Conservative Party, London, England, research officer, 1958-62; St. David's University College, Lampeter, Wales, lecturer, 1962-69, senior lecturer in history, 1969—. Lay reader in Church of England. *Member:* Association of University Teachers.

WRITINGS: The German Revolution of 1918, Cambridge University Press, 1967; *Twentieth-Century Germany: From Bismarck to Brandt,* Macmillan, 1973. Writer of pamphlet on German Revolution for Historical Association, 1959. Contributor to *History* (London) and *Trivium* (Lampeter).

AVOCATIONAL INTERESTS: Literature, travel, antiques.

* * *

RYDER, Meyer S.   1909-

PERSONAL: Born August 3, 1909, in Chicago, Ill.; son of Samuel and Rose (Rothman) Ryder; married Cecilie Sagstad, April 10, 1959; children: Michael. *Education:* University of Chicago, Ph.B., 1930; Marshall Law School, LL.B., 1935. *Home:* 2000 Longshore Dr., Ann Arbor, Mich. 48105. *Office:* Graduate School of Business Administration, University of Michigan, Ann Arbor, Mich. 48104.

CAREER: Regional director, National Labor Relations Board, 1942-48; member of general council, International Association of Machinists, 1948-50; public member, U.S. Wage Stabilization Board, 1951-53; University of Michigan, Graduate School of Business, Ann Arbor, professor of industrial relations, 1953—. Visiting professor at Netherlands School of Economics, 1967, and Tuskegee Institute, 1969. Member of Michigan, Illinois, and U.S. Supreme Court Bars; professional arbitrator of labor disputes. *Member:* National Academy of Arbitrators (board of governors), Industrial Relations Research Association, American Arbitration Association. *Awards, honors:* National Labor Relations Board award for service, 1944.

WRITINGS: (With R. S. Smith) *The University's Role in Labor Relations,* University of Michigan Press, 1956; (with Rehmus and Cohen) *Management Preparation for Collec-*

tive Bargaining, Dow, 1966; Managing Industrial Conflict in Holland at the Plant Level, Graduate School of Business Administration, University of Michigan, 1970. Contributor to legal, business, and labor relations journals.

WORK IN PROGRESS: A comparative study of labor-disputes handling procedures in United States and Britain; comparative labor relations systems, United States and Britain.†

*   *   *

SACHS, Albert Louis   1935-
   (Albie Sachs)

PERSONAL: Born January 30, 1935, in Johannesburg, South Africa; son of E. S. (a trade unionist) and Ray (Ginsburg) Sachs; married Stephanie Kemp (a physiotherapist), September 30, 1966. Education: University of Cape Town, B.A., 1953, LL.B., 1956; University of Sussex, graduate study. Politics: Anti-apartheid. Agent: Hope Leresche & Steele, 11 Jubilee Pl., Chelsea, London SW3 3TE, England.

CAREER: Attorney, with practice in Cape Town, South Africa, 1957-66; arrested for anti-apartheid activities, October, 1963, and held without charge in solitary confinement for six months; went into self-imposed exile in England, 1966. Part-time writer and legal adviser for a radical weekly journal, 1956-63; speaker on South African political and legal subjects.

WRITINGS—All under name Albie Sachs: The Jail Diary of Albie Sachs, Harvill, 1966, McGraw, 1967, published as Jail Diary, Sphere Books, 1969; Stephanie on Trial, Harvill, 1968; South Africa: The Violence of Apartheid, Christian Action Publications, 1969, 2nd edition, 1970; Justice in South Africa, University of California Press, 1973. Contributor of feature stories on Pondoland, Basutoland, and Swaziland to a Cape Town newspaper.

SIDELIGHTS: Albert Sachs writes "Since student days my major passion has been trying to combat racial contempt; my major joy—some personal association with the emancipation of the Afro-Asian world. Feel wretched that many of my friends are in prison for life and that many fine South Africans will die before South Africa is freed. . . ."

David Lytton of Statesman wrote that an important feature of The Jail Diary of Albie Sachs ". . . was the compassion Mr. Sachs felt towards his captors and the efforts he made to convince them that their prisoners were persons, not abstract enemies of officialdom." Lytton also reviewed Stephanie on Trial saying, "The experience is placed in a perspective where personal suffering seems reduced to a philosophic concept. He writes with the fastidousness of the judicial mind. Clarity is the predominant quality of the style as compassion is of the content. He draws the characters of this barely credible story vividly and always with the effort to disclose or discover the humanity, even in those who would appear to have lost that quality." A Punch reviewer called Stephanie on Trial "one of the most complete indictments of the South African Government that I have yet come across." Avocational interests: Sleeping late, reading, listening to music, mountain climbing, walking tours.

BIOGRAPHICAL/CRITICAL SOURCES: Statesman, October 11, 1968; Punch, October 30, 1968; Atlantic, April, 1967; New Yorker, July 1, 1967.†

SACK, John   1930-

PERSONAL: Born March 24, 1930, in New York, N.Y.; son of John Jacob (a clerk) and Tracy (Levy) Sack. Education: Harvard University, A.B., 1951; Columbia University, graduate study, 1963-64. Office: Esquire, 488 Madison Ave., New York, N.Y. 10022.

CAREER: United Press, correspondent in Japan and Korea, 1953-54, and Albany, N.Y., 1954-55; Columbia Broadcasting System, New York City, documentary writer and producer, 1961-66; Esquire, New York City, correspondent in Vietnam, 1966-67, contributing editor, 1967—. Military service: U.S. Army, 1951-53; served in Korea. Member: P.E.N.

WRITINGS: The Butcher, Rinehart, 1952; From Here to Shimbashi, Harper, 1955; Report From Practically Nowhere, Harper, 1959; M, New American Library, 1967; (with William Lewis Calley) Lieutenant Calley: His Own Story as Told to John Sack, Viking, 1971 (published in England as Body Count: Lieutenant Calley's Story as Told to John Sack, Hutchinson, 1971); The Man-Eating Machine, Farrar, Straus, 1973. Writer of television documentaries. Contributor to magazines, including Harper's, Atlantic Monthly, Holiday, Town and Country, Playboy, Eros, New Yorker.

SIDELIGHTS: Leonard Kriegel believes that M "is one of the finest examples of what has come to be called the 'documentary novel.' Sack manages to make M Company both vivid and human. . . ." Although Neil Sheehan writes that "while [M is] a fine and often powerful book, [it] also suffers to some extent from the stark simplicity of its viewpoint," Elizabeth Pond believes that the book's strength lies in its concern with specifics, with single details, and in its avoidance of generalization. "One is tempted," Miss Pond writes, "to say this book is funny, lunatic, savage, compassionate, moral, real, important. But it's not the sort of book that takes kindly to adjectives." Kriegel concludes: "Sack's approach is essentially the approach of the impressionistic prose poet; he has gone to school with James Agee and made very good use of what he has learned. . . . He has written a superb book."

BIOGRAPHICAL/CRITICAL SOURCES: Book Week, March 12, 1967; Christian Science Monitor, April 6, 1967; New York Times Book Review, May 14, 1967; Nation, October 23, 1967.

*   *   *

SACKMAN, Harold   1927-

PERSONAL: Born May 11, 1927, in New York, N.Y.; son of Louis and Lena Sackman; married Kathleen Kiviat, 1951; children: Jeffrey, Sharon, Amy. Education: City College (now City College of the City University of New York), B.S., 1948; Columbia University, M.A., 1949; Fordham University, Ph.D., 1953. Home: 13609 Bayliss Rd., Los Angeles, Calif. 90049. Office: Rand Corp., 1700 Main St., Santa Monica, Calif.

CAREER: Fordham University, Bronx, N.Y., research assistant working on Air Force projects, 1950-53; Psychological Research Associates, Washington, D.C., research assistant, 1952-53; Rand Corp., Santa Monica, Calif., social scientist in Systems Research Laboratory, 1953-54; System Development Corp. (independent nonprofit organization supported by U.S. Government and foundations), Santa Monica, supervisor of problem design group in air defense program, 1954-58, scientist working on SAGE computer program, 1959-63, senior human factors scientist, 1964-66, senior research scientist, 1968-70; University of Southern California, Social Science Research Institute, Los Angeles, Calif., project manager, 1970-71; Kansas State University, Manhattan, professor of computer science and chairman of department, 1971-72; Rand Corp., senior psychologist, 1972—. Lecturer, University of California, Los Angeles, 1968-71. *Military service:* U.S. Naval Reserve, active duty as electronics technician, 1945-46. *Member:* American Psychological Association (associate member), American Association for the Advancement of Science, Association for Computing Machinery, Phi Beta Kappa.

WRITINGS: Computers, System Science, and Evolving Society, Wiley, 1967; (contributor) Perry E. Rosove, editor, *Developing Computer-Based Information Systems,* Wiley, 1967; (contributor) K. deGreene, editor, *Systems Psychology,* McGraw, 1970; (contributor) George F. Weinwurm, editor, *On the Management of Computer Programming,* Auerbach, 1970; (editor with Norman Nie, and contributor) *The Information Utility and Social Choice,* AFIPS Press, 1970; *Man-Computer Problem Solving,* Mason & Lipscomb, 1970; *Mass Information Utilities and Social Excellence,* Mason & Lipscomb, 1971; (contributor) Alan F. Westin, editor, *Information Technology in a Democracy,* Harvard University Press, 1971; (editor with R. L. Citrenbaum, and contributor) *Online Planning,* Prentice-Hall, 1972; (editor with H. Borko, and contributor) *Computers and the Problems of Society,* AFIPS Press, 1972; (editor with B. Boehm, and contributor) *Planning Community Information Utilities,* AFIPS Press, 1972; (editor with E. Mumford, and contributor) *Human Choice and Computers,* North Holland Publishing, 1975; *Delphi Critique: Expert Opinion, Forecasting, and Group Process,* Heath, 1975. Writer of classified and other reports for U.S. Air Force, Social Science Research Institute and other organizations, and papers on man-computer communications and system test and evaluation for professional journals.

* * *

SAGAR, Keith (Milsom) 1934-

PERSONAL: Born June 14, 1934, in Bradford, Yorkshire, England; son of Harry Heald and Emily (Milsom) Sagar. *Education:* King's College, Cambridge, B.A., 1955, M.A., 1957; University of Leeds, Ph.D., 1962. *Politics:* Socialist. *Religion:* None. *Home:* 1 The Green, Osbaldeston, Nr. Blackburn, Lancashire, England.

CAREER: University of Leeds, Extra-Mural Department, Leeds, England, administrative assistant, 1957-59; Workers' Educational Association, tutor-organizer, Northeast Derbyshire, England, 1959-63; University of Manchester, Extra-Mural Department, Manchester, England, staff tutor, 1963-74, senior staff tutor in literature, 1974—. *Military service:* British Army, National Service, 1956. *Member:* Association of Tutors in Adult Education.

WRITINGS: The Art of D. H. Lawrence, Cambridge University Press, 1966; (contributor) *Criticism in Action,* Longmans, Green, 1969; *Hamlet,* Basil Blackwell, 1969; (editor) D. H. Lawrence, *The Mortal Coil and Other Stories,* Penguin, 1971; (editor) D. H. Lawrence, *The Princess and Other Stories,* Penguin, 1971; (editor) *Selected Poems of D. H. Lawrence,* Penguin, 1972; *Ted Hughes,* Longman, 1972; *The Art of Ted Hughes,* Cambridge University Press, 1975; (contributor) *The Art of Emily Bronte,* Vision Press, 1976. Contributor to *D. H. Lawrence Review,*

Sunday Times (London), *Guardian, Twentieth Century,* and other periodicals.

WORK IN PROGRESS: D. H. Lawrence: Life into Art; editing volume VII of *The Letters of D. H. Lawrence,* for Cambridge University Press, completion expected, 1980.

SIDELIGHTS: Sagar has travelled in the United States, Italy, and places associated with D. H. Lawrence. *Avocational interests:* The theater, music (listening), photography, keeping marine tropical fishes and other exotic creatures, tennis (playing), football (watching), and walking.

* * *

SAHAKIAN, Mabel Lewis 1921-

PERSONAL: Surname is pronounced Saw-*hawk*-yawn; born March 2, 1921, in West Newton, Pa.; daughter of Paul Tyson (an accountant) and Blanch (d'Happart) Lewis; married William S. Sahakian (a professor and author), 1945; children: James William, Richard Lewis, Barbara Jacquelyn, Paula Leslie. *Education:* West Virginia University, student, 1939-40; Gordon College, B.A., 1944; Boston University, M.Div., 1947, additional study, 1947-49. *Politics:* Independent. *Home:* 49 Eisenhower Circle, Wellesley, Mass. 02181.

CAREER: Minister of United Church of Christ (Congregational), 1953—; associate pastor in Dedham, Mass., 1953-55, Chelsea, Mass., 1955-58, and Bedford, Mass., 1958-60; Northeastern University, Boston, Mass., lecturer, 1961-71, senior lecturer in philosophy, 1971—. Interim minister at Congregational churches in Milton, Mass., 1966-67, Braintree, Mass., 1968-69, and Norwood, Mass., 1972-73. *Member:* American Philosophical Association, Children of the American Revolution (chairman of public relations), Daughters of the American Revolution (chapter regent member, 1964-67), Boston Authors Club, Boston Business and Professional Women's Club, Boston Museum of Fine Arts, Alpha Phi. *Awards, honors:* D.Sc., Curry College, 1957.

WRITINGS—With husband, William S. Sahakian: *Realms of Philosophy,* Schenkman, 1965, revised edition, 1974; *Ideas of the Great Philosophers,* Barnes & Noble, 1966; *Rousseau as Educator,* Twayne, 1974; *John Locke,* Twayne, 1974; *Plato,* Twayne, 1976. Contributor to periodicals.

* * *

SAID, Edward W. 1935-

PERSONAL: Born November 1, 1935, in Jerusalem, Palestine; son of William A. (a businessman) and Hilda (Musa) Said; married Mariann Cortas, December 15, 1970; children: Wadie, Najla. *Education:* Princeton University, A.B., 1957; Harvard University, A.M., 1960, Ph.D., 1964. *Home:* 90 Morningside Dr., New York, N.Y. 10027. *Office:* Columbia University, New York, N.Y. 10027.

CAREER: Harvard University, Cambridge, Mass., tutor in history and literature, 1961-63; Columbia University, New York, N.Y., instructor, 1963-65, assistant professor, 1965-68, associate professor of English, 1968-70, professor of English and comparative literature, 1970—. Fellow, Center for Advanced Study (on leave from Columbia), University of Illinois, 1967-68; visiting professor of comparative literature, Harvard University, 1974; fellow, Center for Advanced Study in the Behavioral Sciences, Stanford University, 1975-76. *Member:* American Association of University Professors, Phi Beta Kappa, Princeton Club of

New York, Men's Faculty Club (Columbia University). *Awards, honors:* Woodrow Wilson fellowship; Guggenheim fellow, 1972-73.

WRITINGS: Joseph Conrad and the Fiction of Autobiography, Harvard University Press, 1966; *Beginnings: Intention and Method,* Basic Books, 1975. Contributor of articles and reviews to *Kenyon Review, Nation, Book Week, Partisan Review,* and other periodicals.

WORK IN PROGRESS: Literary history; contemporary Arabic literature and politics; theory of interpretation and criticism.

SIDELIGHTS: Edward Said is competent in French, Latin, Italian, and Spanish; and he knows German and Arabic. *Avocational interests:* Modern philosophy (Continental in particular), music (the piano).

*   *   *

ST. JOHN, Wylly Folk 1908-
(Eleanor Fox, Eve Larson, Katherine Pierce, Mary Keith Vincent, Michael Williams)

PERSONAL: Born October 20, 1908, near Ehrhardt, S.C.; daughter of William Obed (an insurance man) and Annie Claire (Mattox) Folk; married Thomas F. St. John (advertising manager of a weekly newspaper), January 1, 1930; children: Anne Folk (Mrs. Neil D. Pratt). *Education:* University of Georgia, A.B. (journalism), 1930. *Politics:* "Vote for the man, not the party." *Religion:* "No current affiliation. Have strong religious beliefs but they are not denominational." *Home:* 198 Dogwood Ave. N.E., Social Circle, Ga. 30279. *Agent:* Lurton Blassingame, 60 East 42nd St., New York, N.Y. 10017.

CAREER: Atlanta Journal and Constitution Magazine, Atlanta, Ga., staff writer, 1941-54, 1962-75. *Member:* Authors Guild, Mystery Writers of America, National Society of Literature and the Arts, Atlanta Press Club, Plot Club (Atlanta), Phi Beta Kappa, Theta Sigma Phi, Phi Kappa Phi. *Awards, honors:* Georgia Author of the Year in fiction, 1968, 1973; Brenda Award, 1970, for outstanding contributions to journalism; Mystery Writers of America special awards for *Uncle Robert's Secret,* 1973, and *The Secret of the Seven Crows,* 1974.

WRITINGS—All published by Viking: *The Secrets of Hidden Creek* (juvenile), 1966; *The Secrets of the Pirate Inn,* 1968; *The Christmas Tree Mystery,* 1969; *The Mystery of the Gingerbread House,* 1969; *The Mystery of the Other Girl,* 1971; *Uncle Robert's Secret,* 1972; *The Secret of the Seven Crows,* 1973; *The Mystery Book Mystery,* in press. Author of five book-length novels published in *Redbook;* contributor of stories and articles to magazines, including *Glamour, Toronto Star Weekly, Liberty, Family Circle, American,* and *American Weekly.*

WORK IN PROGRESS: The Mystery of Gryphon Rock.

SIDELIGHTS: St. John used her three grandchildren as central characters in *The Secrets of Hidden Creek* and her nieces and nephews in *The Secrets of the Pirate Inn* and subsequent juvenile books. All prior stories and articles (more than a thousand) had been for adults. *Avocational interests:* Reading; gardening, especially growing roses and herbs; travelling.

*   *   *

SALAZAR, Fred A. 1942-

PERSONAL: Born April 26, 1942, in Caracas, Venezuela; son of Carlos F. (an attorney and politician) and Rosemarie (Fernandes) Salazar. *Education:* Educated at Coindre Hall, Huntington, N.Y., New York Military Academy, and Mount St. Benedict Abbey, Trinidad, British West Indies. *Religion:* Roman Catholic. *Agent:* Oliver Swan, Julian Bach Literary Agency, 3 East 48th St., New York, N.Y. 10017.

CAREER: Amazonas, Inc., Westport, Conn., former president; Royal Rorima, Inc., New York, N.Y., vice-president, beginning 1967; Djuka Enterprises, Inc. (art importers), Richmond Hill, N.Y., president, beginning 1968. Consultant on Latin American affairs. *Member:* New York Zoological Society.

WRITINGS: (With Jack Herschlag) *The Innocent Assassins,* Dutton, 1967. Contributor to periodicals.

WORK IN PROGRESS: Three books, *Tropical Hoboes, Overland to Wai Wai,* and *Juka.*

SIDELIGHTS: The Innocent Assassins is Salazar's journal of exploration in Amazon jungle country and his encounter there with Stone-Age Indians.

BIOGRAPHICAL/CRITICAL SOURCES: Christian Science Monitor, March 8, 1967.††

*   *   *

SALE, Roger 1932-

PERSONAL: Born August 19, 1932, in New Haven, Conn.; son of William M., Jr. (a teacher) and Helen (Stearns) Sale; married Dorothy Young, July 16, 1955; children: Timothy, Margaret. *Education:* Swarthmore College, B.A., 1953; Cornell University, M.A., 1954, Ph.D., 1957. *Politics:* Democrat. *Religion:* Presbyterian. *Home:* 3511 East Schubert Pl., Seattle, Wash. 98122. *Office:* Department of English, University of Washington, Seattle, Wash. 98105.

CAREER: Amherst College, Amherst, Mass., instructor, 1957-60, assistant professor of English, 1960-62; University of Washington, Seattle, 1962—, began as assistant professor, professor of English, 1970—. Former director of Upward Bound Project. Visiting summer professor, Cornell University, 1965.

WRITINGS: (Editor and author of introduction) *Discussions of the Novel,* Heath, 1960; (contributor) Paul J. Alpers, editor, *Elizabethan Poetry: Modern Essays in Criticism,* Oxford University Press, 1967; *Reading Spenser: An Introduction to the Faerie Queene,* Random House, 1968; *On Writing,* Random House, 1970; *Modern Heroism,* University of California Press, 1973. Contributor of about twenty articles and one hundred reviews to *Argus, Hudson Review, New Republic, Antioch Review, Seattle Post Intelligencer,* and other publications.

WORK IN PROGRESS: A History of Seattle.

*   *   *

SALEM, James M. 1937-

PERSONAL: Born November 15, 1937, in Portage, Wis.; son of Carleton A. and Blanche (Cross) Salem; married Donna McLernon, December 27, 1958; children: Timothy, Betsy, Jennifer, Jon. *Education:* Wisconsin State University-LaCrosse, B.S., 1961; Kent State University, graduate study, 1961-62; Louisiana State University, Ph.D., 1965. *Politics:* Liberal. *Religion:* Humanist. *Home:* 50 Southmont Dr., Tuscaloosa, Ala. 35401. *Office:* American Studies Program, University of Alabama, University, Ala. 35486.

CAREER: Kent State University, Kent, Ohio, assistant professor of English, 1965-67; University of Alabama, University, assistant professor, 1967-68, associate professor of English, 1968-74, professor of American studies, 1974—, director of American Studies Program, 1968—. Consultant in American literature to Scarecrow Press, Inc. Military service: U.S. Army, active duty, 1956. U.S. Army Reserve, 1959-64. Member: American Studies Association, Popular Culture Association.

WRITINGS: "A Guide to Critical Reviews" series, published by Scarecrow, Part I: American Drama from O'Neill to Albee, 1966, 2nd edition, 1973, Part II: The Musical from Rodgers and Hart to Lerner and Loewe, 1967, 2nd edition, 1975, Part III: British and Continental Drama from Ibsen to Pinter, 1968, Part IV: The Screenplay, two volumes, 1971; Drury's Guide to Best Plays, revised 2nd edition, Scarecrow, 1969; A New Generation of Essays, W. C. Brown, 1972. Writer of one-act plays for school and children's theaters, published by Dramatic Publishing. Contributor to Serif, Renascence, Shaw Review, Nutshell, Graduate, and other periodicals.

WORK IN PROGRESS: People Culture, a book on popular culture; a new edition of A New Generation of Essays; a revised edition of British and Continental Drama from Ibsen to Pinter; several nonfiction pieces.

SIDELIGHTS: Salem undertook "A Guide to Critical Reviews" because no reference book existed to help him run down reviews of American plays for his doctoral dissertation; he started the volume on American drama as soon as he received his Ph.D., and says that the "other parts grew out of that book's popularity."

*   *   *

SALLAWAY, George H(enry) 1930-

PERSONAL: Born May 31, 1930, in Scarsdale, N.Y.; son of George Henry (an advertising man with Hearst magazines) and Louise (Giblin) Sallaway. Education: St. Thomas Seminary, Denver, Colo., B.A., 1951; North American College, Pontifical Gregorian University, Rome, Italy, S.T.B., 1953, S.T.L., 1955. Home: 1122 Colorado St., Austin, Tex. 78701. Office: 2704 Rio Grande 9, Austin, Tex. 78705.

CAREER: Roman Catholic priest; pastor in diocese of Amarillo, Tex., beginning 1955; Texas Conference of Churches, Austin, associate executive director, 1969—. Chaplain, and lecturer on Sacred Scripture and dogmatic theology at Texas Technological College (now Texas Tech University), Lubbock, 1956-59, and West Texas State University, Canyon, beginning 1962; consultant, Texas Catholic Conference, 1963—; administrator, South West Training Labs, 1969—, and Texas Consultation on Religion and Education, 1971. Panelist on local weekly inter-faith television programs. Member: John Henry Cardinal Newman Honorary Society (fellow), Canyon Pastors Association.

WRITINGS: Follow Me: Be Human, Helicon, 1966. Contributor to Ave Maria, Lamp, Eucharist, Sign, and National Catholic Reporter.

WORK IN PROGRESS: My Nights With Myself, a book of personal reflections on the priesthood (not autobiographical but first-person singular, existential reflections), for Helicon.

AVOCATIONAL INTERESTS: Skiing.†

SALSBURY, Stephen 1931-

PERSONAL: Born October 12, 1931, in Oakland, Calif.; son of Ralph Thomas (a mining engineer) and Roma E. (Connor) Salsbury. Education: Occidental College, A.B., 1953; Harvard University, A.M., 1957, Ph.D., 1961. Home: 23 Carriage Lane, Newark, Del. 19711. Office: Department of History, University of Delaware, Newark, Del. 19711.

CAREER: Harvard University, Graduate School of Business Administration, Boston, Mass., research associate, 1961-62; University of Delaware, Newark, assistant professor, 1963-68, associate professor, 1968-70, professor of history, 1970—, chairman of department, 1974—. Visiting assistant professor of history, Johns Hopkins University, 1967-68. Military service: U.S. Air Force, 1955-57, 1962-63; became first lieutenant; received Commendation Medal for service in Turkey, 1963. Member: American Historical Association, Organization of American Historians, Economic History Association, Agricultural History Society, Railway and Locomotive Historical Society, Historical Society of Delaware.

WRITINGS: The State, the Investor, and the Railroad, Harvard University Press, 1967; (with Alfred D. Chandler, Jr.) Pierre S. duPont and the Making of the Modern Corporation, Harper, 1971; Essays on the History of the American West, Dryden, 1975.

WORK IN PROGRESS: An Economic Analysis of American Transportation Policy, 1800-1960.

AVOCATIONAL INTERESTS: Railroads; Australian history, natural resources, and flora (has traveled widely in Australia).

*   *   *

SAMFORD, Doris E. 1923-

PERSONAL: Born September 3, 1923, in Johnstonville, Ill.; daughter of Leonard F. and Mabel (Pedicord) Samford; married John Post, April 14, 1946 (divorced). Education: Eastern Illinois State Teachers College (now Eastern Illinois University), A.A., 1942; University of Denver, A.B., 1953, M.A., 1960. Politics: Republican. Religion: Episcopalian. Home: 4960 West Oregon Pl., Denver, Colo. 80219. Office: Denver Public Schools, 414 14th St., Denver, Colo. 80201.

CAREER: Teacher in rural schools, 1942-43, 1948-49; U.S. Civil Service, secretary to provost marshal, Okinawa, 1949-50; Denver (Colo.) public schools, librarian, 1953—, Program for Pupil Assistance teacher. Former elementary school teacher. Military service: Women's Army Corps (WACS), 1943-45; received Southwest Pacific ribbon with battle star and Philippine Liberation ribbon with battle star. Member: National Education Association, Colorado Education Association, Colorado Association of School Librarians, Colorado Library Association, American Legion, Women's Army Corps-Veterans Association, Women's Overseas Service League, Denver Classroom Teachers Association.

WRITINGS: Ruffles and Drums, Pruett, 1967.

WORK IN PROGRESS: A children's book based on summers spent with a grandmother.

AVOCATIONAL INTERESTS: Fishing, photography, reading (especially on the Civil War and pioneer America), visiting museums from coast to coast, camping (also has a Colorado mountain cabin), playing chess and an auto-harp, swimming, collecting music-boxes, restoring antique furniture.

* * *

SAMMONS, Jeffrey L(eonard) 1936-

PERSONAL: Born November 9, 1936, in Cleveland, Ohio; son of Harold Leonard (a school official) and Therese (Herrmann) Sammons; married Kathryn J. Stella, June 28, 1958; married second wife, Christa Smith, October 20, 1967; children: (first marriage) Rebecca Kathryn; (second marriage) Charles Leonard, Harold Hawthorne, Benjamin Gardner. *Education:* Yale University, B.A., 1958, Ph.D., 1962. *Office:* German Department, Yale University, New Haven, Conn. 06520.

CAREER: Brown University, Providence, R.I., instructor, 1961-62, assistant professor of German, 1963-64; Yale University, New Haven, Conn., assistant professor, 1964-67, associate professor, 1967-69, professor of German, 1969—, chairman of Department of Germanic Languages and Literatures, 1969—. Visiting professor, University of California, Santa Cruz, 1971. *Member:* Modern Language Association of America, American Association of Teachers of German, American Association of University Professors, Heinrich-Heine-Gesellschaft, Lessing Society. *Awards, honors:* Guggenheim fellow, 1972-73.

WRITINGS: The Nachtwachen von Bonaventura: A Structural Analysis, Mouton & Co., 1965; (translator) Peter Demetz, *Marx, Engels, and the Poets,* University of Chicago Press, 1967; *Angelus Silesius,* Twayne, 1967; *Heine: Selections,* Prentice-Hall, 1969; *Heinrich Heine: The Elusive Poet,* Yale University Press, 1969; *Six Essays on the Young German Novel,* University of North Carolina Press, 1972, 2nd edition, 1975. Contributor to professional journals.

WORK IN PROGRESS: Literary Sociology and Practical Criticism: An Inquiry.

* * *

SAMPEDRO, Jose Luis 1917-

PERSONAL: Born February 1, 1917, in Barcelona, Spain; son of Luis and Matilde (Saez) Sampedro; married Isabel Pellicer, July 10, 1944; children: Isabel. *Education:* University of Madrid, Dr.Econ. (highest honors), 1950. *Home:* Marques de Urquijo, 11, Madrid 8, Spain. *Office:* Direccion General de Aduanas, Calle Guzman el Bueno 137, Madrid 3, Spain.

CAREER: Spanish Ministry of Finance, Madrid, civil officer, 1935-48; University of Madrid, Faculty of Political and Economic Sciences, Madrid, Spain, assistant lecturer, 1949-55, professor of economic structure, 1955-72; Direccion General de Aduanas, Madrid, Spain, head of technical cabinet, 1972—. Adviser to Spanish Ministry of Commerce, 1951-57, and Ministry of Finance, 1957-62; representative of Ministry of Finance at Organisation Europeenne de Cooperation Economique-Organisation de Cooperation et de Developpement Economiques in Paris, 1958-62. *Military service:* Spanish Army, 1936-39. *Member:* Colegio Nacional de Economistas, Sociedad de Autores de Espana. *Awards, honors:* Calderon de la Barca (national prize for Spanish playwrights), 1950.

WRITINGS: Congreso en Estocolmo (novel), Aguilar, 1952; *Principios Practicos de Localizacion Industrial,* Aguilar, 1952; *Efectos de la Unidad Economica Europea,* Espasa-Calpe, 1957; *Realidad Economica y Analisis Estructural,* Aguilar, 1958; *El Futuro Europeo de Espana,* Espasa-Calpe, 1960; *El Rio que nos Lleva* (novel), Aguilar, 1961; *Perfiles Economicos de las Regiones Espanolas,* Sociedad de Estudios y Publicationes del Banco Urquijo, 1964; *Las Fuerzas Economicas de Nuestro Tiempo,* Guadarrama, 1967, translation by S. E. Nodder published as *Decisive Forces in World Economics,* McGraw, 1967; *El Caballo Desnudo* (novel), Planeta, 1970.

Three-act plays: "La Paloma de Carton," 1950; "Un Sitio para Vivir," 1956.

WORK IN PROGRESS: A novel, *October, October* (proposed title); research on economic structuralism applied to development theory.

SIDELIGHTS: "Main interest is *understanding life,*" Sampedro wrote, "and expressing my insights about [it]. Main pleasure is to try to reconcile several ways for this understanding: (a) a logical and scientific way (hence my interest in formal structuralism as a general theory); (b) intuitive and artistic visions (hence my literary work; science is not enough); (c) even comprehensive, quasi-physical attempts to wholeness in an 'Oriental Wisdom' style (very much interested by Tao, I-Ching Book, and dialectics). I am a NIP (non-important person)." Sampedro speaks or reads six languages, including English and German.

* * *

SAMPSON, Robert C. 1909-

PERSONAL: Born February 1, 1909, in Stoughton, Wis.; son of Andrew and Elsie (Carnell) Sampson; married Lucille Jolliffe. *Education:* University of Wisconsin, B.A., 1934, M.A., 1941. *Office:* Sampson Associates, Inc., 1585 Hickory, Winnetka, Ill. 60093.

CAREER: U.S. Bureau of the Budget, Washington, D.C., personnel director, 1942-47; Chesapeake & Ohio Railway, Cleveland, Ohio, director of staff services, 1947-55; Boating Industry Association, Chicago, Ill., director of manufacturing services, 1955-61; Sampson Associates (management counselors), Winnetka, Ill., president, 1961—. Visiting professor of behavioral sciences management, Lake Forest College; conductor of management development conferences on subjects drawn from the behavioral sciences.

WRITINGS: The Staff Role in Management—Its Creative Uses, Harper, 1955; *Managing the Managers: A Realistic Approach to Applying the Behavioral Sciences,* McGraw, 1965; (contributor) *Handbook of Business Administration,* McGraw, 1967; (contributor) *For Executives Only,* Dartnell, 1967; *How to Survive the Business Rat Race,* McGraw, 1970. Contributor to *Harvard Business Review, Factory,* and other management journals. Publisher and editor, *Management Translator.*

WORK IN PROGRESS: People Problems and Problem People: How to Cope with Them in the Work World, for McGraw; *Office Administrator's Employee Counseling Manual: Non-directive First-Aid Counseling,* for Dartnell.

* * *

SAMUELS, Warren J. 1933-

PERSONAL: Born September 14, 1933, in New York, N.Y.; son of Emanuel Abraham (a contractor) and Lillian (Glazer) Samuels; married Sylvia Joan Strake; children: Kathy Joan, Susan Jill. *Education:* University of Miami, Coral Gables, Fla., B.B.A., 1954; University of Wisconsin,

M.S., 1955, Ph.D., 1957. *Office:* Department of Economics, Michigan State University, East Lansing, Mich. 48824.

CAREER: Assistant professor of economics at University of Missouri, Columbia, 1957-58, and Georgia State College (now Georgia State University), Atlanta, 1958-59; University of Miami, Coral Gables, Fla., assistant professor, 1959-62, associate professor of economics, 1962-68; Michigan State University, East Lansing, professor of economics, 1968—. Consultant in public finance and public utilities fields. *Member:* American Economic Association, National Tax Association, Association for Comparative Economics, Law and Society Association, Association for Evolutionary Economics, American Association of University Professors, Western Economic Association.

WRITINGS: The Classical Theory of Economic Policy, World Publishing, 1966; *Pareto on Policy,* Elsevier, 1974. Contributor to *Land Economics, Indian Economic Journal,* and other economics and public utilities journals. Editor, *Journal of Economic Issues.*

WORK IN PROGRESS: The theory of property rights; institutional economics; aspects of history of economic thought.

*　*　*

SANDERS, James A(lvin)　1927-

PERSONAL: Born November 28, 1927, in Memphis, Tenn.; son of Robert Erastus (a railroad engineer) and Sue (Black) Sanders; married Dora Geil Cargille (a dance instructor and musician), June 30, 1951; children: Robin David. *Education:* Vanderbilt University, B.A. (magna cum laude), 1948, B.D. (with honors), 1951; Theologie Protestante de Paris, theological study, 1950-51; Hebrew Union College, Ph.D., 1955. *Home:* 99 Claremont Ave., New York, N.Y. 10027. *Office:* Union Theological Seminary, New York, N.Y.

CAREER: Ordained Presbyterian minister, Cincinnati, Ohio, 1955. Vanderbilt University, Nashville, Tenn., instructor in French, 1948-49; Colgate Rochester Divinity School, Rochester, N.Y., assistant professor, 1954-57, associate professor, 1957-60, Joseph B. Hoyt Professor of Old Testament, 1960-65; Union Theological Seminary, New York, N.Y., professor of Old Testament, 1965-70, Auburn Professor of Biblical Studies, 1970—. American Schools of Oriental Research, Jerusalem, Jordan, annual professor, 1961-62, associate trustee, 1963-66, member of committee on Dead Sea Scrolls, 1963—. *Member:* Society of Biblical Literature (associate-in-council, 1963—), American Academy of Religion, American Schools of Oriental Research Alumni Association (president, 1964), Phi Beta Kappa. *Awards, honors:* Fulbright grant, 1950-51; Rockefeller Foundation fellow, 1953-54; Guggenheim fellowship, 1961-62, 1972-73; Litt.D., Acadia University, 1973; D.D., University of Glasgow, 1975.

WRITINGS: Suffering as Divine Discipline, Colgate Rochester Divinity School Press, 1955; *The Old Testament in the Cross,* Harper, 1961; *The Psalms Scroll of Qumran Cave 11,* Clarendon Press, 1965; *The Dead Sea Psalms Scroll,* Cornell University Press, 1967; *Torah and Canon,* Fortress, 1972. Contributor to *The Interpreter's Dictionary of the Bible, Harper's Dictionary of Biblical Biography, Encyclopedia Americana, American Peoples Encyclopedia.* Also contributor to theological and other learned journals in United States, England, France, Israel, and Germany. Member of editorial board, *Journal of Biblical Literature, Interpretation,* and *Journal of the Study of Judaism.*

SANDERS, Ronald　1932-

PERSONAL: Born July 7, 1932, in Union City, N.J.; son of George Harry (a musician) and Rose (Rachlin) Sanders; married Beverly Gingold (a teacher), March 19, 1967. *Education:* Kenyon College, B.A., 1954; Columbia University, M.A., 1957. *Politics:* Social Democrat (non-party). *Religion:* Jewish. *Home and office:* 49 West 12th St., New York, N.Y. 10011. *Agent:* George Borchardt, Inc., 145 East 52nd St., New York, N.Y. 10022.

CAREER: Queens College (now Queens College of the City University of New York), Flushing, N.Y., lecturer in history, 1958-65; *Midstream,* New York, N.Y., associate editor, 1965-73, editor, 1973-75. Free-lance lecturer. *Military service:* U.S. Army, 1953-55. *Member:* Phi Beta Kappa. *Awards, honors:* Fulbright fellowship to France, 1960-61; B'nai B'rith book award, 1970.

WRITINGS: (Editor with Albert Fried) *Socialist Thought,* Anchor Books, 1964; *Israel: The View From Masada,* Harper, 1966; *The Downtown Jews: Portrait of an Immigrant Generation,* Harper, 1969; (contributor) Werner Keller, editor, *Diaspora,* Harcourt, 1969; (contributor) Irving Howe and Carl Gershman, editors, *Israel, the Arabs and the Middle East,* Bantam, 1972; *Reflections on a Teapot,* Harper, 1973; (contributor) Douglas Villiers, editor, *Next Year in Jerusalem,* Viking, 1975. Contributor to opinion periodicals, including *Commentary, New Republic, Nation, New Leader.*

WORK IN PROGRESS: The New World of Shem, Ham and Japheth, for Little, Brown.

SIDELIGHTS: Ronald Sanders speaks French, speaks and reads Hebrew, reads Spanish, Portuguese, Latin, Yiddish, and German, and is learning Russian for planned writings. He did research in Israel, 1963-64, and again in 1966.

*　*　*

SANDERS, Thomas E.　1926-

PERSONAL: Cherokee name, Nippawanock (Dawn Star); adopted name, Narragansett-Wampanoag; surname legally Sanders; born April 30, 1926, in Picher, Okla.; son of John Allen and Grace (Layne) McAlister; married Louise Halley Foreshaw, May 11, 1947 (divorced). *Education:* Studied at Northeastern Oklahoma Agricultural and Mechanical College, 1943-44, University of Oklahoma, 1946-48, and Mississippi College, 1948-49; University of Denver, B.A., 1950, M.A., 1951; further graduate study at University of Colorado, University of Missouri, and Barry College. *Home:* 12110 Lake Carroll Dr., Tampa, Fla. 33618. *Office:* Department of English, University of Southern Florida, Tampa, Fla. 33620.

CAREER: Kansas City (Mo.) Public Library, librarian, 1952-54; public school teacher in Kansas City, Mo., 1954-60, and Miami, Fla., 1960-62; Miami-Dade Junior College, Miami, Fla., teacher of English and creative writing, 1962-68; University of Southern Florida, Tampa, associate professor of English, 1968—. Consultant, New Tomaguog Memorial Indian Museum, Hope Valley, R.I., 1969. *Military service:* U.S. Army, 1944-46. *Member:* National Council of Teachers of English, National Education Association, Conference on College Composition and Communication, National Congress of American Indians, Missouri Historical Society, Florida Education Association. *Awards, honors:* McAnally Medal for creative research, University of Missouri, 1952.

WRITINGS: The Discovery of Poetry, Scott, Foresman,

1967; *The Discovery of Fiction,* Scott, Foresman, 1967; *The Discovery of Drama,* Scott, Foresman, 1968; (with Franklin D. Hester) *The Now Reader,* Scott, Foresman, 1969; *Currents: Concerns and Composition,* Glencoe Press, 1971; *Speculations: An Introduction to Literature through Fantasy and Science,* Glencoe Press, 1973; (with Walter W. Peck) *Literature of the American Indian,* Glencoe Press, 1973, abridged edition, 1976; *A Dictionary of Literary Terms and Movements,* Glencoe Press, 1976. Writer of monographs, *The Magazine in America,* and *Missouri, Mother of Authors,* Kansas City Public Library, 1954. Also writer of television script, "You and Shakespeare," produced in Kansas City, Mo., 1954. Contributor of poetry and short stories to *Glass Hill, Foothills, Western Humanities Review, Epos,* and other periodicals.

SIDELIGHTS: Thomas Sanders told *CA:* "Hart Crane is my academic interest. Suppose I'm a frustrated creator because I lack the ability of great writers. As a result, want to make sure others share my enthusiasm for them. Teaching and writing about writing seems to satisfy that need. They make me feel valuable—which is, I think, why writers write."

* * *

SANDERSON, Jayne 1943-

PERSONAL: Born March 6, 1943, in Brisbane, Australia; daughter of Charles Haddan and Lillian (Wilson) Spurgin; married Colin Sanderson (working in science), January 11, 1965; children: Zoe Beth. *Education:* Studied art two years at Brisbane Technical College. *Office:* 26 Olive Rd., Cricklewood, London NW2, England.

CAREER: Book designer and illustrator in Australia, 1964-67; free-lance designer in England, 1968—; currently designing and screen printing wallpapers and fabrics, under trade name Jayne Mairi Designs. *Awards, honors:* Design Centre award for British book design, 1971, for jacket design for *The Beginnings of Industrial Britain.*

WRITINGS: (Co-editor) *Under Twenty-Five* (anthology of writing and illustrating by young Australians), Jacaranda, 1966; (illustrator) "Digger" series for Endeavor Books, Jacaranda, 1967. Also designer of book jacket for S. D. Chapman and J. D. Chambers, *The Beginnings of Industrial Britain,* University Tutorial Press, 1971; illustrator and designer of catalogue, "Agar Aids for Electron Microscopy."

* * *

SANDISON, Alan 1932-

PERSONAL: Born November 13, 1932, in Aberdeenshire, Scotland; son of William Alexander and Bella Jane (Meston) Sandison. *Education:* University of Aberdeen, M.A. (first class honors in English language and literature), 1958; Peterhouse College, Cambridge, Ph.D., 1963. *Politics:* Radical. *Office:* Department of English Studies, University of Strathclyde, Livingstone Tower, 26 Richmond St., Glasgow G1 1XH, Scotland.

CAREER: University of Exeter, Exeter, England, lecturer in English, 1963-71; University of Durham, Durham, England, lecturer, 1971-74; University of Strathclyde, Glasgow, Scotland, professor of English studies, 1974—. *Military service:* British Army, National Service, 1951-53.

WRITINGS: (Contributor) Andrew Rutherford, editor, *Kipling's Mind and Art* (symposium), Oliver & Boyd, 1964; *The Wheel of Empire,* Macmillan, 1967; *The Last Man in Europe: An Essay on George Orwell,* Macmillan, 1974.

AVOCATIONAL INTERESTS: Theatre.

* * *

SANDS, Edith Sylvia (Abeloff) 1912-

PERSONAL: Born February 15, 1912, in Brooklyn, N.Y.; daughter of Louis and Jennie (Goldstein) Abeloff; married Abraham M. Sands (an ophthalmologist), June 5, 1932; children: Stephanie Lou (Mrs. P. M. Fersko), John Eliot. *Education:* Adelphi University, B.A., 1932, City College (now City College of the City University of New York), M.B.A. (with honors), 1956; New York University, Ph.D. (with distinction), 1961. *Home:* 874 Carroll St., Brooklyn, N.Y. 11215. *Office:* Department of Business Finance, Long Island University, Brooklyn, N.Y. 11201.

CAREER: Long Island University, Brooklyn, N.Y., assistant professor, 1961-65, associate professor, 1965-69, professor of business finance, 1969—, chairman of department, 1962-72. Consultant to Management Publications Division, U.S. Small Business Administration, and to Bank of Bombay, India. Volunteer worker and officer in various community health, educational, and cultural organizations. *Member:* American Economic Association, American Finance Association, Financial Management Association, American Management Association, National Association of Business Economists, Academy of Management, New York Society of Security Analysts, Money Marketeers of New York City, Beta Gamma Sigma (member of national executive committee, 1971-76). *Awards, honors:* Achievement award of Baruch School Alumni of City College, 1968.

WRITINGS: How to Select Executive Personnel, Reinhold, 1963. Contributor to *Encyclopedia of Management,* Reinhold, 1972. Also contributor of articles and reviews to professional journals. Editor of *Tape* (publication of Long Island University), 1966-71.

* * *

SANGSTER, Jimmy 1927-

PERSONAL: Born December 2, 1927, in North Wales; son of Dudley (in real estate) and Ruth (Bowlden) Sangster; married Sandra Schwartz (an interior designer); children: Mark James. *Education:* Educated in Wales; left school at fifteen to start work in the film industry. *Politics:* "Middle." *Agent:* Shapiro Lichtman, 9200 Sunset Blvd., Los Angeles, Calif. 90210. *Office:* 1 Carlton Tower Pl., Sloane St., London S.W.1, England; 1590 Lindacrest Dr., Beverly Hills, Calif. 90210.

CAREER: Free-lance assistant film director, 1948-50; free-lance film production manager, 1950-55; free-lance writer and film producer, 1957—. *Military service:* Royal Air Force, 1945-48. *Member:* Screen Writers Guild of Great Britain (member of council, 1963-64), Association of Cine and Allied Technicians (London), Directors Guild of America, Writers Guild of America (West).

WRITINGS—Novels: Private I, Norton, 1967; *Foreign Exchange,* Norton, 1968; *Touchfeather,* Norton, 1968; *Touchfeather Too,* Norton, 1970; *Your Friendly Neighborhood Death Pedlar,* Dodd, 1971.

Film scripts: "The Criminal" (original screenplay); "The Mummy"; "Deadlier than the Male" (original screenplay), for Universal Pictures; "Maniac" (original screenplay), for Columbia Pictures; "Scream of Fear" (original screenplay), for Columbia Pictures; "The Nanny," for Twentieth Century-Fox; "The Anniversary," for Twentieth Century-

Fox; "Fear in the Night," for Hammer Films; three Frankenstein films; three Dracula films; and about thirty other screen plays.

Television scripts: "Motive for Murder" (six-part serial); "The Assassins" (six-part serial); "The Big Deal" (ninety-minute live play); "I Can Destroy the Sun" (ninety-minute live play); "A Taste of Evil"; and others. Script consultant, CBS-TV, 1972, D'Antoni Weitz, 1975.

* * *

SAPORTA, Marc(el) 1923-

PERSONAL: Born March 20, 1923, in Constantinople, Turkey; son of Jacques (a banker) and Simone (Namias) Saporta; married Denise Kleman, June 2, 1948; children: Karine, Rose-Noelle. *Education:* Sorbonne, Universite de Paris, B.A. and M.A.; Facultad de Derecho, Madrid, LL.D.

CAREER: Worked for UNESCO, Paris, France, 1948-53; journalist for several newspapers and magazines, and editor of *Informations & Documents* (periodical), Paris, France, 1954—. *Military service:* French Army, 1947; became under-lieutenant.

WRITINGS—Under name Marc Saporta, except as noted: (Under name Marcel Saporta) *La Conference intergouvernementale de Geneve, 18 aout-6 septembre, 1952, et La Convention universelle du droit d'auteur de l'U.N.E.S.C.O., 6 septembre, 1952,* Editions Internationales, 1952; (under name Marcel Saporta, editor with Jacques Lacombe) *Les Lois de l'air,* Editions Internationales, 1953; *Le Furet* (novel), Editions du Seuil, 1959; *La Quete* (novel), Editions du Seuil, 1961; *La Distribution* (novel), Gallimard, 1961; *Composition no. 1* (novel), Editions du Seuil, 1962, translation by Richard Howard published as *Composition no. 1,* Simon & Schuster, 1963; *Les Invites* (novel), Editions du Seuil, 1964; (translator) Ernest Hemmingway, *Paris est une fete,* Gallimard, 1964; (with Georges Soria) *Le Grand defi: Encyclopedie comparee USA-URSS,* Laffont, 1967; *Histoire du roman americain,* Seghers, 1970; *La vie quotidienne contemporaine aux U.S.A.,* Hatchette, 1972. Also translator of Jack Kerouac, *The Dharma Bums.* Contributor to French radio programs (ORTF), and to *L'Express, Quinzaine Litteraire,* and other publications.

SIDELIGHTS: Saporta is known in America for his *Composition no. 1,* a "novel" of some 200 unbound, boxed pages which one shuffles like a deck of cards before proceeding to read. John Simon dismissed the novel as a gimmick, and added: "One sheet of a quasi-introduction . . . tells us most of the plot, which is cheating. . . . [Yet] without this subterfuge the whole box would be utterly incomprehensible. . . . The sheets of *Composition no. 1* are neither art nor science nor life. . . . It is impossible to find and follow relationships in them, and without interrelation there is no art, no science, no life." Each page of this novel is self-contained to some degree and narrates an entire incident, although certain characters recur on other pages. Benjamin DeMott calls it hokum, but he allows that it is, in the final analysis, amusing. "Every page in the box," he writes "must be suitable, obviously, for a conclusion, as well as for a beginning or a middle." And that all of them *are* suitable is a triumph of literary skill, as well as what DeMott calls "a sharp dig at several contemporary fictional conventions. . . . The box, seen as anything except a parody, does amount to another cardboard coffin for the corpse of the novel."

BIOGRAPHICAL/CRITICAL SOURCES: Book Week, November 24, 1963; *Harper's,* February, 1964; Sharon Spencer, *Space, Time and Structure in the Modern Novel,* New York University Press, 1971; Leon Roudiez, *French Fiction Today,* Rutgers University Press, 1972.

* * *

SARGENT, Robert 1933-

PERSONAL: Born March 26, 1933, in Northfield, Vt.; son of Robert Samuel and Hildred (Norman) Sargent. *Education:* Educated in Vermont public schools and at Vermont College, Montpelier.

CAREER: Artist, writer, and producer of television programs and films. Lived in Europe, 1956-65, designing book jackets for Scandinavian publishers, and producing children's television programs for National Broadcasting Co. *Military service:* U.S. Army, Special Services.

WRITINGS—All self-illustrated: *The Restless Rabbit,* McGraw, 1966; *A Trick on a Lion,* McGraw, 1966; *The Alligator's Problem,* Scribner, 1966; *A Bug of Some Importance,* Scribner, 1967; *The Small Seabird,* Scribner, 1967; *The Adventurous Moth,* Simon & Schuster, 1968; *Six Magical Folk Tales,* Lancelot Press, 1968; *Ten Fairy Tales,* Simon & Schuster, 1968; *Everything is Difficult at First,* Scribner, 1968; (adaptor) *Peter and the Wolf,* Lancelot Press, 1969; *The Princess' Party,* Putnam, 1969; *What Is Beautiful?,* Lancelot Press, 1969; *The Hungry Elephant,* Lancelot Press, 1969; *Dogs Are Friends to Owls, and Cats Aren't,* Lancelot Press, 1969. Writer of scripts for documentary films; contributor to literary journals.

SIDELIGHTS: Robert Sargent's books are aimed to show "people at the rich old age of wonder that life is a fairy tale." He speaks German, French, Italian, and Finnish. *Avocational interests:* Travel, music.†

* * *

SARNAT, Marshall 1929-

PERSONAL: Surname originally Sarnatzky; born August 1, 1929, in Chicago, Ill.; son of Maurice (a pharmacist) and Dena (Lew) Sarnatzky; married Carmela Shainker (a botanist), January 17, 1956; children: Don, Iddo, Tamar. *Education:* Hebrew University of Jerusalem, B.A., 1955; Northwestern University, M.B.A., 1957, Ph.D., 1965. *Religion:* Jewish. *Home:* Nayot 34, Jerusalem, Israel. *Office:* School of Business, Hebrew University, Jerusalem, Israel.

CAREER: Hebrew University of Jerusalem, Jerusalem, Israel, instructor, 1959-65, school of business administration, lecturer, 1965-67, senior lecturer, 1967-72, associate professor of finance, 1972—, director of Institute of Business Research, 1973—. Visiting professor, New York University, 1967-68, University of California, Berkeley, 1973, University of Toronto, 1973. Director, Israel Financial Research Institute, 1964—; member, National Council for Insurance, 1965—. *Member:* American Economic Association, European Economic Association, American Finance Association, Beta Gamma Sigma. *Awards, honors:* International Institute of Management research fellow, Berlin, 1975.

WRITINGS: The Development of Securities Market in Israel, J. C. B. Mohr, 1966; *Saving and Investment through Retirement Funds in Israel,* Maurice Falk Institute, 1966; (with H. Levy) *Investment and Portfolio Analysis,* Wiley, 1972; (co-author) *Corporate Investment and Financing Decisions,* Wiley, 1976. Contributor to financial and economic journals.

WORK IN PROGRESS: Decision-making under uncertainty; co-author of *The Bank and the Economy: 75 Years of Bank Levmi Le'yisrael;* capital markets and economic growth.

*   *   *

SAROYAN, Aram   1943-

PERSONAL: Born September 25, 1943; son of William (the writer) and Carol (Marcus) Saroyan; married Gailyn McClanahan, October 9, 1968; children: three. *Education:* Attended the University of Chicago, New York University, and Columbia University. *Residence:* Bolinas, Calif.

CAREER: Writer. Publisher and editor of *Lines* (magazine), 1964-65.

WRITINGS: (With Jenni Caldwell and Richard Kolmar) *Poems,* Acadia, 1963; *In* (poetry), Bear Press (LaGrande, Ore.), 1965; *Works* (24 poems), Lines (New York), 1966; *Poems,* Lines (Cambridge, Mass.), 1967; *Aram Saroyan,* Random House, 1968; *Pages,* Random House, 1969.

Words and Photographs, Big Table Publishing, 1970; *Cloth: An Electric Novel,* Big Table Publishing, 1971; *The Rest,* Telegraph Books, 1971; *Poems,* Telegraph Books, 1972; *The Street: An Autobiographical Novel,* Bookstore Press, 1974; *O My Generation,* Blackberry Books, 1976; (with wife Gailyn Saroyan) *How to Start a Family and Not Go Permanently Crazy: A Young Parent's Companion,* Blackberry Books, in press. Contributor of poetry and prose to *New York Times Sunday Magazine, New York Times Book Review, Village Voice, Nation, Rolling Stone, Paris Review,* and *Poetry.*

SIDELIGHTS: Saroyan "credits his typewriter with exerting a great influence on his one-word (or one-letter) poems, which are visual and verbal puns," Howard Junker writes. "If it were another typeface, I'd write subtly different poems," Saroyan told Junker. "And when a ribbon gets dull, my poems I'm sure change." Indeed, according to Robert Vas Dias, "the text of Aram Saroyan's book of concrete poetry, *Works,* is printed in red IBM type, a fact that is significant (as what isn't?) to this form."

BIOGRAPHICAL/CRITICAL SOURCES: Poetry, June, 1967; *Newsweek,* April 22, 1968.

*   *   *

SARRIS, Andrew   1928-

PERSONAL: Born October 31, 1928, in Brooklyn, N.Y.; son of George Andrew (in real estate) and Themis (Katavolos) Sarris; married Molly Haskell (a writer), May 31, 1969. *Education:* Columbia College, A.B., 1951. *Politics:* Democratic. *Religion:* Greek Orthodox. *Home:* 19 East 88th St., New York, N.Y. 10028.

CAREER: 20th Century-Fox, New York City, reader and scriptwriter, 1955-65; *Village Voice,* New York City, film critic, 1960—; *Cahiers du Cinema* (English edition), New York City, editor in chief, 1965-67; School of Visual Arts, New York City, instructor in screen writing, 1966-68; New York University, New York City, assistant professor of cinema, 1967-69; Columbia University, New York City, associate professor of cinema, 1969—. Member, Program Committee, New York Film Festival at the Lincoln Center. *Military service:* U.S. Army Signal Corps, 1952-54. *Member:* National Society of Film Critics (chairman), New York Film Critics Circle, American Society of Cinematologists. *Awards, honors:* Guggenheim fellowship, 1968.

WRITINGS: The Films of Josef von Sternberg, Museum of Modern Art, 1966; (editor) *Interviews with Film Directors,* Bobbs-Merrill, 1967; (editor) *The Film,* Bobbs-Merrill, 1968; *The American Cinema: Directors and Directions,* Dutton, 1968; (editor) *Film 68/69,* Simon & Schuster, 1969; *Confessions of a Cultist: On the Cinema, 1955-1969,* Simon & Schuster, 1970; *The Primal Screen: Essays on Film and Related Subjects,* Simon & Schuster, 1973; *John Ford,* British Film Institute, 1975.

WORK IN PROGRESS: The American Sound Film, for Oxford University Press; *Cinema: Politics Versus Aesthetics,* for Columbia University Press.

BIOGRAPHICAL/CRITICAL SOURCES: Commonweal, April 25, 1971.

*   *   *

SAUL, Leon J(oseph)   1901-

PERSONAL: Born April 26, 1901, in New York, N.Y.; son of Mark (a businessman) and Florence (Brackman) Saul; married Rose C. Schulz, December 16, 1934; children: Susan Ellen (Mrs. Richard L. Spencer), Margaret Ann (Mrs. Carl Sweatman), Catherine Mary (Mrs. Blair E. McNeill). *Education:* Columbia University, B.A., 1921, M.A., 1923; University College, London, further graduate study, 1923-24; Harvard University, M.D., 1928. *Religion:* Quaker. *Home:* 275 Highland Ave., Media, Pa.

CAREER: Commonwealth Fund research fellow at Harvard Medical School and Boston Psychopathic Hospital, both Boston, Mass., 1929-32; Chicago Institute for Psychoanalysis, Chicago, Ill., staff member, 1932-42; Philadelphia Psychoanalytic Institute, Philadelphia, Pa., instructor and training analyst, 1946-70, analyst emeritus, 1970—; private practice of psychiatry, Philadelphia, 1946—; University of Pennsylvania Medical School and Hospital, Philadelphia, professor of clinical psychiatry, 1948-60, professor of psychiatry, 1960-69, professor emeritus, 1969—. Psychiatric consultant, Swarthmore College, 1947-71, psychiatrist emeritus, 1971—. *Military service:* U.S. Naval Reserve, active duty, 1942-46; became commander.

MEMBER: American Psychiatric Society, American Psychoanalytic Association, American Psychosomatic Society (past president), American Medical Association, American Academy of Psychoanalysis, American College of Psychoanalysts (founding fellow), American College of Psychiatrists (emeritus fellow).

WRITINGS: Emotional Maturity, Lippincott, 1947, 3rd edition, 1971; *Bases of Human Behavior,* Lippincott, 1951; *The Hostile Mind,* Random House, 1956; *Technic and Practice of Psychoanalysis,* Lippincott, 1958; *Fidelity and Infidelity and What Makes or Breaks a Marriage,* Lippincott, 1967; (with H. Parens) *Dependence in Man,* International Universities Press, 1971; *Psychodynamically Based Psychotherapy,* Science House, 1972; *Psychodynamics of Hostility,* Jason Aronson, 1976; *Childhood Emotional Patterns,* Van Nostrand, in press. Contributor of more than 175 articles to professional journals. Contributing editor, *Psychoanalytic Forum;* member of editorial board, *International Journal of Psychoanalytic Psychotherapy.*

WORK IN PROGRESS: The Maturing of Corey Jones.

SIDELIGHTS: After three decades of psychiatric practice, Saul considers man's hostility to man as humanity's sole basic problem. Other views: "Power does not corrupt everyone—not an Augustus, a Washington, a Jefferson, a Churchill. There are men of good will and men of evil; what makes one or the other is not heredity at all. It is how they were reared. . . . Like our pets, we each reflect how we were treated in earliest childhood. . . . Wars begin in the mind of a child in reaction to abuse.''

* * *

SAVARY, Louis M(ichael) 1936-

PERSONAL: First syllable of surname rhymes with "pave"; born January 17, 1936, in Scranton, Pa.; son of Louis Michael and Margaret (Nagy) Savary. *Education:* Fordham University, A.B., 1960; Woodstock College, Ph.L., 1961, S.T.L., 1968; Catholic University of America, M.A., 1963, Ph.D., 1965, S.T.D., 1970. *Home:* 5704 Roland Ave., Baltimore, Md. 21210. *Office:* Just for You Books, 623 Brielle Ave., Brielle, N.J. 08730.

CAREER: Roman Catholic priest, member of Society of Jesus (Jesuits); Collins Associates, New York, N.Y., writer and senior editor, 1967-74; affiliated with Just for You Books, Brielle, N.J., 1974—. *Member:* Mathematical Association of America, American Statistical Association, American Society of Composers, Authors and Publishers (ASCAP), Institute for Consciousness and Music.

WRITINGS: Man: His World and His Work, Paulist Press, 1967; *The Kingdom of Downtown: Finding Teenagers in Their Music,* Paulist Press, 1967; (co-author) *Christian Awareness,* four volumes, Christian Brothers Publications, 1968; (co-author) *Listen to Love,* Regina Press, 1968; (co-author) *Patterns of Promise,* St. Mary's College Press, 1968; (co-author) *Living with Christ,* with teacher's guides, four volumes, St. Mary's College Press, 1968-69; (with Adrianne Blue) *Faces of Freedom,* St. Mary's College Press, 1969; (with Blue) *Horizons of Hope,* St. Mary's College Press, 1969; (with Maureen P. Collins) *Ritual and Life,* St. Mary's College Press, 1970; (with Collins) *Shaping of a Self,* St. Mary's College Press, 1970; (co-author) *Teaching your Child about God,* St. Mary's College Press, 1970; (with Thomas J. O'Connor) *Finding Each Other,* Paulist/Newman, 1971; (with O'Connor) *Finding God,* Paulist/Newman, 1971; *Getting High Naturally,* Association Press, 1971; *Love and Hate in America Today,* Association Press, 1971; *Popular Song and Youth Today,* Association Press, 1971; *Touch with Love,* Association Press, 1971; *Cycles,* three volumes, Regina Press, 1971-73.

One Life Together: A Celebration of Love in Marriage, Regina Press, 1972; *A Time for Salvation,* Regina Press, 1972; *Jesus: The Face of Man,* Harper, 1972; (with Marianne S. Andersen) *Passages: A Guide for Pilgrims of the Mind,* Harper, 1972; (with Helen L. Bonny) *Music and Your Mind: Listening with a New Consciousness,* Harper, 1973; *Psychological Themes in the Golden Epistle of William of Saint Thierry,* University of Salzburg, 1973; (with Shirley Linde) *The Sleep Book,* Harper, 1974; (with Muriel James) *The Power at the Bottom of the Well: Transactional Analysis and Religious Experience,* Harper, 1974; *Integrating Values: Theory and Exercises for Clarifying and Integrating Religious Values,* Pflaum/Standard, 1974; (with Helen Bonny) *ASC and Music Experience: A Guide for Facilitators and Leaders,* ICM Press, 1974; *Creativity and Children: Stimulating Imaginative Responses to Music,* ICM Press, 1974; *Who Has Seen the Wind?: The Holy Spirit in the Church and the World,* Regina Press, 1975; (with Muriel James) *The Third Self of Friendship,* Harper, 1975; (with Mary Paolini and George Lane) *Interpersonal Communication: A Worktext for Self-Understanding and Growth in Personal Relations,* Loyola University Press, 1975.

Editor: (With Thomas J. O'Connor) *The Heart Has Its Seasons,* Regina Press, 1971; (with Paul Carrico) *Contemporary Film and the New Generation,* Association Press, 1971; (with Maureen P. Collins) *Peace, War and Youth,* Association Press, 1971; (with Thomas P. Collins) *A People of Compassion: The Concerns of Edward Kennedy,* Regina Press, 1972; (with Mary Paolini) *Moments with God: A Book of Prayers for Children,* Regina Press, 1975.

Filmstrip texts; all produced by Thomas S. Klise, except as noted: "Images of Christ," 1971; "Images of Revelation," 1971; "Images of Love," 1971; "Images of the Future," 1971; "Images of the New Man," 1972; "A Time to Grow," Sisters of the Good Shepherd, 1972; "Social Studies," W. H. Sadlier, 1972-73; "Religious Awareness" series, 1973; "A Call to Consecration," Sisters of the Good Shepherd, 1973.

Author of two recordings for the Institute for Consciousness and Music, "Creative Listening: Music and Imagination Experiences for Children," and, with M. Trinitas Bochini, "A New Way to Music: Altered States of Consciousness and Music." Co-author of *Religious Awareness Teaching Program,* with teacher's guide and parent/teacher guide, 6 volumes, St. Mary's College Press, 1970; also author of four booklets for Just for You Books, including *Getting to Know You: A Funbook for Families,* 1974, and *Side by Side: Another Funbook for Couples,* 1975. Contributor to *Religious Book Guide* and *Review for Religious.*

* * *

SAVELLE, Max(well) 1896-

PERSONAL: Born January 8, 1896, in Mobile, Ala.; son of Myles Hicks (a contractor) and Rosabel (Pooley) Savelle; married second wife, Jean Reeda Happ, March 18, 1950; children: (first marriage) David; (second marriage) Michele Anne, Jon Marc. *Education:* Columbia University, A.B., 1924, M.A., 1926, Ph.D., 1932. *Home:* 4545 55th Ave. N.E., Seattle, Wash. 98105.

CAREER: Columbia University, New York, N.Y., instructor in history, 1926-32; Stanford University, Stanford, Calif., assistant professor, 1932-35, associate professor, 1935-41, professor of history, 1941-47; University of Washington, Seattle, professor of history, 1947-67, professor emeritus, 1967—. Fulbright lecturer, University of Madrid, 1960-61; Rockefeller lecturer, University of Chile, 1963; U.S. Department of State lecturer in Australia, 1966. *Military service:* U.S. Navy, 1918-19. *Member:* American Historical Association (member of council, 1948-52; president of Pacific Coast branch, 1956), Organization of American Historians, American Antiquarian Society. *Awards, honors:* Cutting traveling fellow in Europe, 1930-31; Social Science Research Council traveling fellow, 1938-39; Fulbright scholar in France, 1950.

WRITINGS: George Morgan: Colony Builder, University of California Press, 1932; *The Diplomatic History of the Canadian Boundary 1749-63,* Yale University Press, 1940; *Foundations of American Civilization: A History of Colonial America,* Holt, 1942, revised edition published as *A History of Colonial America,* revised by Robert Middlekauff, 1964; *Seeds of Liberty,* University of Washington Press, 1948; *This Is My America,* Stanford University Press, 1948; *The United States: Colonial Period,* Pan American Institute of Geography and History, 1953; (with T. McDowell) *Short History of American Civilization,* Holt, 1957; (co-editor) *A Workbook to Accompany "A History of World Civilization,"* Holt, 1957; (general editor with others, and contributor) *A History of World Civilization,* two volumes, Holt, 1957; *The Colonial Period in the History of the New World,* [Mexico], 1962; *Colonial Origins of American Thought,* Van Nostrand, 1964; *Is Liberalism Dead?,* University of Washington Press, 1967; (with Margaret Anne Fisher) *The Origins of American Diplomacy: The International History of Angloamerica 1492-1763,* Macmillan, 1967; *Empires to Nations: Expansion in America, 1713-1824,* University of Minnesota Press, 1974.

Contributor: R. B. Morris, editor, *The Era of the American Revolution,* Columbia University Press, 1939; Arthur Link and Richard Leopold, editors, *Problems in American History,* Prentice-Hall, 1952, revised edition, 1957. Also contributor to professional journals.

* * *

SAVETH, Edward N(orman) 1915-

PERSONAL: Born February 16, 1915, in New York, N.Y.; son of Isidor and Eva Saveth; children: Henry. *Education:* City College (now City College of the City University of New York), B.S.S., 1935; Columbia University, M.A., 1937, Ph.D., 1947. *Home:* 110 Riverside Dr., New York, N.Y.

CAREER: New Mexico Highlands University, Las Vegas, associate professor of history, 1948; New School for Social Research, New York, N.Y., professor of history, Graduate Faculty, 1959-64; Fulbright professor of American intellectual history, Kyoto University, 1964-65; currently Distinguished Professor, State University of New York at Fredonia. Lecturer for U.S. Information Service in Japan and Nepal. *Member:* American Historical Association, American Studies Association. *Awards, honors:* American Philosophical Society grant, 1961.

WRITINGS: American Historians and European Immigrants, 1875-1925, Columbia University Press, 1948; *Understanding the American Past,* Little, Brown, 1954; (contributor) D. Sheehan and H. C. Syrett, editors, *Essays in American Historiography in Honor of Allan Nevins,* Columbia University Press, 1960; *Henry Adams,* Twayne, 1963; *American History and the Social Sciences,* Free Press of Glencoe, 1964. Revisions editor for items on American history and civilization, *Encyclopedia Americana.* Contributor to *World Book Encyclopedia, Commentary, Diogenes, Fortune, New York Times Book Review, Survey,* and other journals.

WORK IN PROGRESS: A textbook centered on the social science approach to American history; collecting materials on American historical interpretation for a short book, and on the history of the American family and American intellectual history; *The American Patrician.*

SIDELIGHTS: Understanding the American Past was published in Chinese translation in Taiwan, 1957, and several of his articles have been translated into Japanese and other languages.

* * *

SAVILLE, Lloyd (Blackstone) 1913-

PERSONAL: Born October 13, 1913, in New York, N.Y.; married Eugenia Turk Curtis, July 13, 1932; children: Curtis Lloyd, Lynn Adele. *Education:* University of Pennsylvania, A.B., 1935; Columbia University, A.M., 1936, Ph.D., 1950. *Home:* 1103 Anderson St., Durham, N.C. 27705. *Office:* Department of Economics and Business Administration, Duke University, Durham, N.C. 27706.

CAREER: Employed in process control operations by Standard Oil Co. of New Jersey, 1933-42; U.S. Office of Price Administration, Washington, D.C., economist, 1942-43, 1945-46; Duke University, Durham, N.C., assistant professor, 1946-51, associate professor, 1951-57, professor of economics, 1957—. Fulbright lecturer at University of Turin, 1959-60, and American Cultural Center in Paris, summer, 1960. *Military service:* U.S. Navy, 1943-45; served on destroyer in the Pacific theater; became lieutenant. *Member:* American Economic Association, Economic History Association, American Statistical Association, American Association of University Professors, Southern Economics Association. *Awards, honors:* Fund for the Advancement of Education faculty fellow in Rome, 1954-55; Guggenheim fellow, 1959; Ford Foundation faculty research fellow, 1962-63; Duke University endowment grant, 1965-66.

WRITINGS: (Contributor) *Employment, Income, and Retirement Problems of the Aged,* Duke University Press, 1963; *Regional Economic Development in Italy,* Duke University Press, 1967. Contributor of articles to economics journals in the United States and Europe.

WORK IN PROGRESS: Tuscan Economic Development in the High Middle Ages.

* * *

SAVITZ, Leonard D. 1926-

PERSONAL: Born June 7, 1926, in Philadelphia, Pa.; son of Harry (a clerk) and Minnie (Aaronson) Savitz; married Faye Weiss, June 25, 1961; children: Steven M., Jonathan L., Ruth L. *Education:* Temple University, B.S., 1949, M.S., 1950; University of Pennsylvania, Ph.D., 1960. *Politics:* Democrat. *Religion:* Jewish. *Home:* 615 Anthony Rd., Elkins Park, Pa. 19117. *Office:* Temple University, Philadelphia, Pa. 19122.

CAREER: Temple University, Philadelphia, Pa., instructor, 1955-60, assistant professor, 1960-68, professor of sociology, 1968—. *Military service:* U.S. Army, 1944-46. *Member:* American Sociological Association, American Society of Criminology, Society for the Study of Social Problems.

WRITINGS: (With N. Johnston and M. Wolfgang) *Sociology of Crime and Delinquency,* Wiley, 1964; (with Johnston and Wolfgang) *Sociology of Punishment and Correction,* Wiley, 1964; *Dilemmas in Criminology,* McGraw, 1967. Also author of *The Socialization of Police,* 1970, and *City Life and Delinquency,* 1973.

WORK IN PROGRESS: The Fear of Rape; criminal urbanization Philadelphia and Dade County, Florida; the scaled seriousness of drug offenses.

* * *

SAX, Gilbert 1930-

PERSONAL: Born July 13, 1930, in New York, N.Y.; son of William and Belle (Wolfe) Sax; married Lois Johnson; children: (previous marriage) Laurie, Kathy, Karen; stepchildren: Debra, Jennifer. *Education:* University of California, Los Angeles, B.A., 1953, M.A., 1956, Ph.D., 1958. *Home:* 3733 47th Place N.E., Seattle, Wash. 98105. *Office:* Department of Educational Psychology, University of Washington, Seattle, Wash. 98195.

CAREER: High school teacher of the mentally retarded and teacher of adult education, Los Angeles, Calif., 1954-56; University of Hawaii, Honolulu, assistant professor,

1958-62, associate professor and chairman of department of educational psychology, 1962-66; University of Washington, Seattle, professor of educational psychology, 1966-69, professor of education and psychology, 1969—. Certified psychologist, California State Board of Medical Examiners; licensed psychologist, Washington State, 1968; member, State Board of Psychological Examiners, 1972-73. Visiting summer professor at University of Southern California, 1959, University of Wisconsin, 1962. Chairman of test selection committee, Hawaii Department of Education, 1959-66; member, Hawaii State Advisory Committee on Mental Retardation, 1960-61.

MEMBER: American Psychological Association (fellow), National Education Association, American Educational Research Association, National Society for the Study of Education, American Association of University Professors, Phi Delta Kappa, Alpha Mu Gamma, Sigma Xi.

WRITINGS: Construction and Analysis of Educational and Psychological Tests, privately printed, 1962, revised edition, 1968; Empirical Foundations of Educational Research, Prentice-Hall, 1968; Principles of Educational Measurement and Evaluation, Wadsworth, 1974; Study Guide for Principles of Educational Measurement and Evaluation, Wadsworth, 1974; Instructor's Manual to Accompany Principles of Educational Measurement and Evaluation, Wadsworth, 1974. Contributor of about twenty-five articles and reviews to Encyclopedia of Educational Research and professional journals.

WORK IN PROGRESS: A text on educational and psychological tests, for Wadsworth.

* * *

SCANZONI, John H. 1935-

PERSONAL: Born March 25, 1935, in Chicago, Ill.; son of Victor and Ida Scanzoni; married Letha Dawson (a freelance writer), July 7, 1956; children: Stephen, David. Education: Wheaton College, Wheaton, Ill., A.B., 1958; University of Oregon, Ph.D., 1964. Politics: Independent. Religion: Presbyterian. Home: 2115 Wimbleton La., Bloomington, Ind. 47401. Office: Department of Sociology, Indiana University, Bloomington, Ind. 47401.

CAREER: Indiana University, Bloomington, assistant professor, 1964-68, associate professor, 1968-72, professor of sociology, 1972—. Member: American Sociological Association, National Council on Family Relations, Ohio Valley Sociological Society.

WRITINGS: (Editor) Readings in Social Problems: Sociology and Social Issues, Allyn & Bacon, 1967; Opportunity and the Family, Free Press, 1970; The Black Family in Modern Society, Allyn & Bacon, 1971; Sexual Bargaining: Power Politics in American Marriage, Prentice-Hall, 1972; Sex Roles, Life-Styles and Childbearing, Free Press, 1975; (with wife, Letha Scanzoni) Men, Women and Change, McGraw, 1976. Contributor to professional journals.

* * *

SCHAFER, Grant C. 1926-

PERSONAL: Born June 16, 1926; son of Charles J. (a farmer) and Christina (Dietrich) Schafer; married Joy F. Steuck, December 24, 1951; children: Tove. Education: Jamestown College, Jamestown, N.D., A.B., 1949; University of Denver, M.B.A., 1950. Home address: Box 1B, Guffey, Colo. 80820. Office: Department of Accounting, University of Denver, Denver, Colo. 80210.

CAREER: Certified public accountant. Von Tobel & Carr (certified public accountants), Denver, Colo., staff accountant, 1949-51; Fargo Foundry Co., Fargo, N.D., controller, 1951-52; W. L. Clasquin & Co., Denver, senior accountant, 1952-53; C. M. & W. Drilling Co., Denver, chief accountant, 1953-54; University of Denver, Denver, professor of accounting, 1954—. President and director of Guffey Books, Inc. Military service: U.S. Navy, 1944-46. Member: American Institute of Certified Public Accountants, American Accounting Association, American Taxation Association, Colorado Society of Certified Public Accountants, Beta Gamma Sigma.

WRITINGS: Elements of Federal Taxation, C. E. Merrill, 1961; Elements of Income Taxation, Raceview Publishing, 1964, 5th edition, 1968; Elements of Income Tax, Irwin, 1971; Elements of Income Tax—Individual, Guffey Books, 1973, 3rd edition, 1976.

* * *

SCHECHTER, William 1934-
(Chester Williams)

PERSONAL: Born January 31, 1934, in Vienna, Austria; son of Harry and Regina (Schild) Schechter; married Lucille Hartfuer (director of special sales for Harper's Bazaar), October 21, 1963; stepchildren: Christine, Alan. Education: Ohio State University, B.A., 1955. Politics: Democrat. Religion: Jewish. Residence: Lake Hill, N.Y. 12448.

CAREER: Chicago Tribune, sports correspondent in Columbus, Ohio, 1953-55; Columbus Citizen, Columbus, Ohio, reporter, 1955; Printers' Ink, New York City, associate editor, 1959-62; director of public relations for State Comptroller Arthur Levitt, Albany, N.Y., 1963-66, and Democratic State Committee, New York City, 1966; New York State Senate Minority, Albany, information director, 1967; Sperry & Hutchinson Co., New York City, manager of financial relations, 1967-72; director of public relations, Texstar Corp., 1973—. Candidate for Congress, New York twenty-seventh district, 1974. Professional staff adviser to Robert F. Kennedy for U.S. Senate campaign, 1964, and presidential campaign, 1968, to Frank O'Connor for New York governor's campaign, 1966, and to Nathan Straus for congressional campaign, 1968. Military service: U.S. Air Force, 1955-58; became first lieutenant. Member: American Civil Liberties Union, Authors Guild, B'nai B'rith.

WRITINGS: Countdown '68: Profiles for the Presidency, Fleet Press, 1967; History of Negro Humor in America, Fleet Press, 1969; (under pseudonym Chester Williams) Gable, Fleet Press, 1971.

AVOCATIONAL INTERESTS: Skiing, tennis, squash, horseback riding, swimming.

* * *

SCHECTER, Jerrold L. 1932-

PERSONAL: Born November 27, 1932, in New York, N.Y.; married Leona Protas, June, 1954; children: Evelind, Steven, Kate, Doveen, Barnet. Education: University of Wisconsin, B.A., 1953; Harvard University, graduate study, 1963-64. Office: 888 16th St. N.W., Washington, D.C. 20006.

CAREER: Wall Street Journal, New York City, staff correspondent, 1957-58; Time, New York City, contributing editor, 1958-60; Time-Life News Service, staff member of China Southeast Asia Bureau, Hong Kong, 1960-63, bureau chief in Tokyo, Japan, 1964-68, bureau chief in Moscow, Soviet Union, 1968-71; *Time,* New York City, White House correspondent in Washington, D.C., 1971-72, diplomatic editor, 1973—. *Military service:* U.S. Navy, 1953-57.

WRITINGS: The New Face of Buddha: Buddhism and Political Power in Southeast Asia, Coward, 1967; (author of introduction) *Krushchev Remembers: The Last Testament,* Little, Brown, 1974; (with wife, Leona Schecter, and children) *An American Family in Moscow,* Little, Brown, 1975.

BIOGRAPHICAL/CRITICAL SOURCES: New York Times Book Review, May 21, 1967; *Time,* June 16, 1967; *Virginia Quarterly Review,* autumn, 1967.

* * *

SCHENK, H(ans) G(eorg)   1912-

PERSONAL: Born April 6, 1912, in Prague, Czechoslovakia; son of Ferdinand (a university professor) and Ilse (Hofgraeff) Schenk; married Joyce Marjorie Hazell (a teacher), April 12, 1944; children: Graham. *Education:* German University, Prague, Doctor of Law, 1935; Oxford University, D.Phil., 1944, M.A., 1946. *Politics:* Liberal. *Religion:* Roman Catholic. *Home:* 4 Capel Close, Oxford, England. *Agent:* David Higham Associates Ltd., 76 Dean St., Soho, London W1V 6AH, England. *Office:* Wolfson College, Oxford University, Oxford, England.

CAREER: Germany University, Prague, Czechoslovakia, first assistant, Institute of Political Science, 1935-38; Ministry of Social Welfare, Prague, Czechoslovakia, civil service post, 1938-39; emigrated to England, 1939; Oxford University, Oxford, England, university lecturer in European social history, 1946—, fellow at Wolfson College, 1966—. *Member:* Royal Historical Society (fellow).

WRITINGS: The Aftermath of the Napoleonic Wars, Routledge & Kegan Paul, 1947, Fertig, 1967; (contributor) A. Goodwin, editor, *The European Nobility in the Eighteenth Century,* A. & C. Black, 1953, revised edition, Torchbooks, 1967; *The Mind of the European Romantics,* Constable, 1966, Anchor Books, 1969; (contributor) C. W. Crawley, editor, *New Cambridge Modern History,* Volume IX, Cambridge University Press, 1966.

WORK IN PROGRESS: European cultural history since 1900.

SIDELIGHTS: The Mind of the European Romantics has been translated into German, Dutch, and Japanese. *Avocational interests:* Chess, music; mountain walking in the Alps, Pyrenees, English Lake district, and Ireland.

* * *

SCHISGAL, Murray (Joseph)   1926-

PERSONAL: Born November 25, 1926, in Brooklyn, N.Y.; son of Abraham (a tailor) and Irene (Sperling) Schisgal; married Reene Schapiro, June 29, 1958; children: Jane, Zachary. *Education:* Quit high school in 1943 to join the Navy but earned diploma later in night school; attended Brooklyn Conservatory of Music and Long Island University; Brooklyn Law School, LL.B., 1953, New School for Social Research, B.A., 1959. *Home:* 275 Central Park West, New York, N.Y. 10024.

CAREER: Worked at odd jobs to support his studies and writing, including pin-setter in a bowling alley, hand-trucker in the garment district, dress racker at Klein's Department Store, and saxophone and clarinet player in a small band, all in New York, 1947-50; practised law in New York, 1953-55; James Fenimore Cooper Junior High School, East Harlem, N.Y., English teacher, 1955-60; full-time writer, 1960—. Lecturer and instructor in playwriting at colleges and universities. *Military service:* U.S. Navy, 1944-46; became radioman, third class. *Awards, honors:* Vernon Rice Award, Outer Circle Award, and *Saturday Review* Critics Poll award, all 1963, for *The Tiger.*

WRITINGS—Plays: *The Typists* [and] *The Tiger* (one-acts; "The Tiger" first produced, under the title "The Postman," with "The Typists" and "A Simple Kind of Love Story" [also see below], in London at British Drama League Theatre, December 11, 1960; both produced Off-Broadway at Orpheum Theatre, February, 1963), introduction by Schisgal, Coward, 1963; *Luv* (first produced in London at London Arts Theatre, April 18, 1963, produced on Broadway at Booth Theatre, November 11, 1964), introduction by Walter Kerr and an interview with Schisgal by Ira Peck, Coward, 1963; *Fragments, Windows and Other Plays* (contains "Windows," first produced in Los Angeles, 1965; "Reverberations," "The Old Jew," and "Fragments," first produced in Stockbridge, Mass. at Berkshire Playhouse, August, 1967; "Reverberations" produced as "The Basement," with "Fragments," under program title "Fragments," Off-Broadway at Cherry Lane Theatre, October, 1967; "Memorial Day," first produced in Baltimore, 1968), Coward, 1965; *Jimmy Shine* (two-act; produced on Broadway at Brooks Atkinson Theatre, December 5, 1968), Atheneum, 1969; *Ducks and Lovers* (first produced in London at London Arts Theatre, October 19, 1961), Dramatists Play Service, 1972; "The Chinese" (first produced in Paris, 1968; produced, with "Dr. Fish" [also see below], on Broadway at Ethel Barrymore Theatre, March 10, 1970), published in *Best Short Plays of the World Theatre, 1968-1973,* Crown, 1973; *All American Millionaire* (produced on Broadway, 1974), Dramatists Play Service, 1974; *All Over Town* (produced on Broadway, 1974), Dramatists Play Service, 1975.

Unpublished plays: "A Simple Kind of Love Story," first produced in London, with "The Postman" and "The Typists," at British Drama League Theatre, December 11, 1970; "Knit One, Purl Two," first produced in Boston at Poets Theatre, March 27, 1963; "Doctor Fish," first produced, with "The Chinese," on Broadway at Ethel Barrymore Theatre, March 10, 1970.

Other: (Co-adaptor) "Ducks and Lovers" (screenplay; based on play of same title), Association of British Pictures, 1962; "The Love Song of Barney Kempenski" (television play), produced by American Broadcasting Companies, September 14, 1966; "The Tiger Makes Out" (screenplay; adaptation of "The Tiger"), Columbia Pictures, 1967.

SIDELIGHTS: "I am going to write 900 words on why I like Murray Schisgal," wrote Walter Kerr. "I like Murray Schisgal because he is one step ahead of the avant-garde.... If the avant-garde, up to now, has successfully exploded the bright balloons of cheap optimism, Mr. Schisgal is ready to put a pin to the soapy bubbles of cheap pessimism.... [He] doesn't necessarily deny that things are tough all over; he just sees how preposterous it is that we should take such *pleasure* in painting clouds black.... Mr. Schisgal's knife—a very funny one, glinting brightly as it digs—is out for people who wear black on black while lovingly congratulating themselves upon the profundity of their losses."

Critics don't always agree that Schisgal writes good plays. Robert Graham Kemper, for instance, writes: "Murray Schisgal had a big, funny idea, so big that, without doing any more thinking, he made two funny plays out of it." Commenting on "Fragments," Kemper continues: "It is a funny concept, and one that is theatrically inventive and psychologically sound. But cash-paying customers expect more for their money than a concept. They want characters, plot and dialogue. One has the feeling that it was only out of a sense of duty that Mr. Schisgal went ahead with characters, plot and dialogue." Jack Kroll came away from "Fragments" with the opposite point of view. "Schisgal gives the impression," he wrote, "... of a writer fabricating 'ideas' to make plays that have the haberdashery, but not the guts, of the advanced art that he has his eye on." Edith Oliver writes: "There are a number of hints here and there, that this play is an early effort of Mr. Schisgal's; too many lines are high-flown or obvious, and too many attempts at humor misfire. Nevertheless, I'm for any author who tries to use comedy as a means of getting at something serious, so I'm for Mr. Schisgal, win or lose."

Several critics caustically attributed the impressive success of *Luv* to Mike Nichols' direction of the play, saying that Schisgal's script by itself was sketchy and inadequate. Schisgal, however, in an interview with Ira Peck, indicated that his theme had been carefully developed from a well-defined notion. "The emotion of love," he told Peck, "has been perverted and misused to such an extent that it can only be defined by using another word which comes closer to what we experience, to what we think, and how we behave. It can be l-u-v, l-o-v, or x-y-z, but it certainly can't be a word that has been abused as much as l-o-v-e. L-u-v is the perversion of l-o-v-e.... We use it as a repository for insincerity, for physical desire, and perhaps primarily for money, ... the cheap movies, the cheap books, and the cheap slap-dash psychological tripe that is continually being drummed into our heads.... Love has become a commodity rather than an emotion." John Simon writes: "What this is, of course, is not devastating social satire, still less avant-garde theatre; it is plain and simple burlesque or vaudeville.... One of the troubles is that Schisgal is not quite up to what he is trying to poke fun at.... Whoever likes his Beckett in Bobby-sox, his Ionesco on a bagel with lox, may relish this occasionally funny and largely insipid lampoon." Simon continues: "The playwright scatters his shots in all directions, in an attempt to puncture whatever he can hit, without committing himself to any point of view. And that, in anything but a piece of unpretentious zaniness, is immoral."

Commenting on "The Chinese" and "Dr. Fish," Alan Bruce notes that "behind the laughs that undeniably fill Murray Schisgal's latest comedies a nagging disappointment persists. The material is still unsatisfactorily skimpy and appears to be put together with a dangerous disregard for its relationship to human truths." A *National Observer* reviewer writes, however, that "for that matter, you wouldn't swear that Mr. Schisgal's ["The Chinese"] isn't saying something profound about brotherhood."

Frederick Lumley believes that Schisgal's theatre "is like a puppet one where the characters act out different changes of fortune, exchange roles and become the mouthpiece of their author's type of ventriloquistic wit." But Haskel Frankel, who has experienced the "laughter that leaves a bitter aftertaste," cites with admiration "that special half-cracked dialog that is a Schisgal specialty. The talk is interesting, often funny, and always revealing." *Luv* was filmed by Columbia Pictures, 1967.

BIOGRAPHICAL/CRITICAL SOURCES: New York Herald Tribune Magazine, November 8, 1964; *New York Times,* November 22, 1964; *Hudson Review,* spring, 1965; *Village Voice,* September 7, 1967, October 12, 1967; *Time,* October 6, 1967; *National Observer,* October 9, 1967, March 16, 1970; *New Yorker,* October 14, 1967; *Newsweek,* October 16, 1967; *Nation,* October 23, 1967; *Washington Post,* December 27, 1967; Frederick Lumley, *New Trends in 20th Century Drama,* Oxford University Press, 1967; *Christian Century,* January 3, 1968; *Christian Science Monitor,* March 16, 1970; Carolyn Riley, editor, *Contemporary Literary Criticism,* Volume VI, Gale, 1976.

* * *

SCHLAPBACH-OBERHANSLI, Trudi 1944-
(Trudi Oberhansli)

PERSONAL: Born February 11, 1944, in Kreuzlingen, Switzerland; daughter of Ernst and Anna (Schmitz) Oberhansli; married, 1969; children: two daughters. *Education:* Attended Textile and Fashion School in St. Gallen, Switzerland, for one year, served apprenticeship as textile designer for two and one-half years, and studied in Paris for six months. *Religion:* Protestant. *Home:* Finkenhubelweg 6, 3012 Bern, Switzerland.

CAREER: Free-lance artist, illustrator, and designer of greeting cards and textiles; presently with A. Boss & Co. (greeting card publishers), Bern, Switzerland. *Awards, honors:* Swiss Federal drawing competition scholarship, 1966, 1969.

WRITINGS—Under name Trudi Oberhansli; all self-illustrated picture books: *Schlaf, Kindlein, Schlaf,* Artemis Verlag (Zurich), 1967, translation published as *Sleep, Baby Sleep,* Atheneum, 1967; *Der Mausball,* Artemis Verlag, 1968, translation published as *The Mouseball,* Atheneum, 1969.

* * *

SCHLATTER, Richard 1912-

PERSONAL: Born March 3, 1912, in Fostoria, Ohio; son of Daniel and Bessie (Bulger) Schlatter; married Suzanna Wynmalen, December 21, 1940; children: Daniel David, Heidi Suzanne. *Education:* Harvard University, A.B., 1934; Oxford University, B.Litt., 1936, D.Phil., 1938. *Home:* 180 College Ave., New Brunswick, N.J. *Office:* Provost, Rutgers University, New Brunswick, N.J. 08903.

CAREER: Harvard University, Cambridge, Mass., assistant professor and tutor in history at Harvard College, 1937-46, senior tutor at Adams House, 1942-46; Rutgers University, New Brunswick, N.J., professor of history, 1946—, chairman of department, 1955-60, executive director of Research Council, 1961-62, vice-president and provost of university, 1962—. Lecturer, Salzburg Seminar in American Studies, summer, 1947; Fulbright professor, University of Liverpool, 1950-51; visiting professor and director of Ford Foundation project in the humanities, Princeton University, 1959-63. Member of Fulbright Selection Committee, 1952, and Woodrow Wilson Foundation Selection Committee, 1961-62; trustee of Solebury School, 1958-64, and Midland School, 1965—.

MEMBER: American Historical Association, Phi Beta Kappa; Century Association and Harvard Club (both New York). *Awards, honors:* Rhodes scholar, 1934-37; Ford

Foundation fellow, 1954-55; Humanities Council senior fellow, 1959.

WRITINGS: The Social Ideas of Religious Leaders, 1660-88, Oxford University Press, 1940, Octagon, 1968; (editor and author of introduction) Joseph Morgan, *The History of the Kingdom of Basaruah,* Harvard University Press, 1946; *Private Property: The History of an Idea,* Rutgers University Press, 1951; (editor and author of introduction) *Puritan Politics: The Political Writings of Richard Baxter,* Rutgers University Press, 1957; (contributor) John Higham, editor, *The Reconstruction of American History,* Harper, 1962; (general editor) *Humanistic Scholarship in America: The Princeton Studies,* fifteen volumes, Prentice-Hall, 1963-68; *Hobbes's Thucydides,* Rutgers University Press, 1975. Contributor of articles and reviews to historical journals.

WORK IN PROGRESS: A biography of Oliver Cromwell; a study of Richard Baxter and the Puritan mind in the seventeenth century.

*   *   *

SCHLOAT, G. Warren, Jr.   1914-

PERSONAL: Born July 15, 1914, in Mexico, Mo.; son of G. Warren (a builder) and Bessie (Thompson) Schloat; married Virginia Wilson, February 13, 1937; children: G. Warren III, Anson Wilson. *Education:* Otis Art Institute, Los Angeles, Calif., student, 1935-37. *Home:* 17361 Regalo Lane, San Diego, Calif. 92128. *Office:* Sunburst Communications, Inc., 39 Washington Ave., Pleasantville, N.Y. 10570.

CAREER: Walt Disney Productions, Burbank, Calif., animator and story director, 1939-45; Compton Advertising, Inc., New York, N.Y., vice-president and creative director, 1955-62; Warren Schloat Productions, Inc. (publishers of audiovisual materials for schools; now a subsidiary of Prentice-Hall, Inc.), Pleasantville, N.Y., president, 1962-72; Sunburst Communications, Inc., Pleasantville, N.Y., chairman of the board, 1972—.

*WRITINGS—*All photographic picture books; all published by Scribner: *What Shall I Do?,* 1949; *Adventures of a Letter,* 1949; *Playtime for You,* 1950; *Milk for You,* 1951; *The Wonderful Egg,* 1952; *Your Wonderful Teeth,* 1954; *The Magic of Water,* 1955; *Andy's Wonderful Telescope,* 1958.

All published by Knopf: *The Haunted Forest,* 1961; *Duee, a Boy of Liberia,* 1962; *Kwaku, A Boy of Ghana,* 1962; *Prapan, A Boy of Thailand,* 1963; *Naim, A Boy of Turkey,* 1963; *Johnnyshah, A Boy of Iran,* 1963; *Uttam, A Boy of India,* 1963; *Fay Gow, A Boy of Hong Kong,* 1964; *Junichi, A Boy of Japan,* 1964; *Conchita and Juan, A Girl and Boy of Mexico,* 1964; *Maria and Ramon, A Girl and Boy of Puerto Rico,* 1966; *Fernando and Marta, A Boy and Girl of Spain,* 1970.

SIDELIGHTS: Schloat has traveled in Africa, Europe, and Asia, photographing material and gathering stories for his books, which are used in many school systems throughout America.

*   *   *

SCHMITZ, Michael J.   1934-

PERSONAL: Born March 31, 1934, in Milwaukee, Wis.; son of Joseph A. and Gladys (Pedersen) Schmitz; married, June 2, 1956; wife's name Jeanne E.; children: Joseph A. II, Susan M. *Education:* University of Wisconsin, B.S.,

1956; Rutgers University, graduate student, 1965; University of Wisconsin-Milwaukee, M.B.A., 1967. *Politics:* Republican. *Religion:* Roman Catholic. *Home:* 7721 North Links Way, Milwaukee, Wis. 53217. *Office:* First Wisconsin National Bank, 777 East Wisconsin Ave., Milwaukee, Wis. 53202.

CAREER: First Wisconsin National Bank, Milwaukee, 1958—, currently first vice-president. Director, Bel Canto Chorus, Milwaukee Red Cross. *Military service:* U.S. Army, intelligence officer, 1956-58. *Member:* American Institute of Banking, Kiwanis Club.

WRITINGS: Branch Bank Organization, Bankers, 1966.

*   *   *

SCHNELLE, Kenneth E(dward)   1914-

PERSONAL: Born August 8, 1914, in New Haven, Conn.; son of Charles J. and Chrystella (Glynn) Schnelle; married Louise Rindelaub; children: Timothy J., Susan L. *Education:* University of Connecticut, student, 1932-34; Yale University, B.A., 1937, M.A., 1941; Harvard University, graduate study, 1937-38; University of Minnesota, M.A., 1950, Ph.D., 1952. *Home address:* R.D. 1, Edinboro, Pa. 16412. *Office:* Department of Economics, Edinboro State College, Edinboro, Pa. 16412.

CAREER: Held U.S. Civil Service posts in Japan as director of civilian personnel, 8th Army Headquarters, 1946-47, and chief of municipal branch, Government Section, Supreme Commander of the Allied Powers in Japan, 1947-48; private practice as psychologist, Reno, Nev., 1948-49; University of Oklahoma, Norman, assistant professor, 1952-54; private practice as business consultant, Oklahoma City, Okla., 1954-56; Michigan Technological University, Houghton, professor of business administration, 1956-69; American University, Cairo, Egypt, professor of economics, 1969-70; St. Francis College, Loretto, Pa., professor of industrial relations, 1970-71; Edinboro State College, Edinboro, Pa., professor of economics, 1971—. Councilman, City of Hancock. *Military service:* U.S. Army Reserve, 1937—. with active duty, 1941-46; received Bronze Star; retired as colonel. *Member:* American Economic Association, Lions Club.

WRITINGS: Case Analysis and Business Problem Solving, McGraw, 1967.

WORK IN PROGRESS: Research Methods in Business and Economics; Human Relations in Industry.

*   *   *

SCHOEN, Barbara   1924-

PERSONAL: Surname rhymes with "phone"; born July 4, 1924, in New York, N.Y.; daughter of Howard Canning (a physician) and Caroline (Colgate) Taylor; married Donald Robert Schoen (vice-president of Cresap, McCormick & Paget), November 9, 1946; children: Robert Taylor, John Wakeman, Claire Colgate, Susan Bayard. *Education:* Bryn Mawr College, A.B., 1946; Boston University, M.A., 1949. *Politics:* Independent. *Religion:* Protestant. *Residence:* Bronxville, N.Y.

CAREER: Harvard University Medical School, Boston, Mass., technician in biophysical laboratory, 1947-48; State University of New York College at Purchase, assistant professor of language arts, 1971—.

WRITINGS: A Place and a Time (novel for young adults), Crowell, 1967; *A Spark of Joy,* Crowell, 1969. Short stories have appeared in *Seventeen.*

WORK IN PROGRESS: A work of non-fiction.

AVOCATIONAL INTERESTS: Raising orchids and other tropical plants, sailing, skin diving, and shelling.

* * *

SCHOFIELD, B(rian) B(etham) 1895-

PERSONAL: Born October 11, 1895, in Alderly Edge, Cheshire, England; son of Thomas Dodgshon (a merchant) and Margaret Annie (Bradley) Schofield; married Doris Sibyl Ambrose, 1922 (divorced, 1941); married Norah Kathleen Handley, 1941 (died, 1946); married Grace Mildred Seale, August 17, 1946; children: (first marriage) two sons; (third marriage) two daughters. *Education:* Educated at Royal Naval Colleges at Osborne and Dartmouth, England, 1908-12. *Religion:* Church of England. *Home and office:* Holme, Lower Shiplake, Henley-on-Thames, England.

CAREER: Royal Navy, 1913-50, rising from midshipman to rear-admiral, 1947, and retiring as vice-admiral, 1950. Naval attache at The Hague and Brussels, 1939-40; commanded "H.M.S. King George V," 1945-46; chief of staff to the admiral, British Joint Services Mission in Washington, D.C., 1948-50. *Member:* Royal United Service Institution, U.S. Naval Institute, Military Commentators (London). *Awards, honors*—Military: Commander, Order of the British Empire, 1943; Companion of the Bath, 1949; Legion of Honor (United States); King George VI Coronation Medal; mentioned in dispatches for action in World War II.

WRITINGS: The Royal Navy Today, Oxford University Press, 1960; *The Russian Convoys,* Batsford, 1964; *British Sea Power,* Batsford, 1967; (with L. F. Martyn) *The Rescue Ships,* James Blackwood, 1968; *The Loss of the Bismarck,* Ian Allen, 1972; *The Attack on Taranto,* Ian Allen, 1973; *Operation Neptune,* Ian Allen, 1974. Contributor to Purnell's *History of World War II,* and to military periodicals, including *U.S. Naval Review* and *Proceedings* of U.S. Naval Institute.

WORK IN PROGRESS: The Arctic Convoys.

* * *

SCHOONHOVEN, Calvin R(obert) 1931-

PERSONAL: First syllable of surname rhymes with "loan"; born November 22, 1931, in Racine, Wis.; son of Roy (a printer) and Angeline (Wessels) Schoonhoven; married Arlen Stoesz, August 18, 1956; children: Randall, Richard. *Education:* Wheaton College, Wheaton, Ill., B.A., 1955, graduate study, 1955-56; Fuller Theological Seminary, B.D., 1958; University of Basel, D.Theol. (insigni cum laude), 1961. *Home:* 1030 Topeka, Pasadena, Calif. 91104. *Office:* Fuller Theological Seminary, 135 North Oakland, Pasadena, Calif. 91101.

CAREER: Ordained to Baptist ministry, 1960; Fuller Theological Seminary, Pasadena, Calif., visiting lecturer in systematic theology, 1962-63, assistant professor, 1963-66, associate professor of biblical interpretation, 1966—, director of library, 1963—. *Member:* American Theological Library Association.

WRITINGS: The Wrath of Heaven, Eerdmans, 1966.

WORK IN PROGRESS: Research in the field of myth and Sacred Scripture.†

SCHRADER, George A(lfred), Jr. 1917-

PERSONAL: Born May 30, 1917, in English, Ind.; son of George A. (an insurance man) and Elizabeth W. (Weatley) Schrader; married Katharine Jones, May 29, 1941; married second wife, Norma Rogers (a librarian), January 28, 1967; children: (first marriage) George A. III, Ann. *Education:* Park College, B.A., 1939; Yale University, B.D., 1942, Ph.D., 1945; postdoctoral study at University of Heidelberg, 1952-53, and University of Munich, 1957-58. *Politics:* Democrat. *Office:* Department of Philosophy, Yale University, New Haven, Conn. 06520.

CAREER: Trinity University, San Antonio, Tex., instructor, 1944-45, assistant professor of philosophy, 1945-47; Colgate University, Hamilton, N.Y., instructor in philosophy, 1947-48; Yale University, New Haven, Conn., assistant professor, 1949-55, associate professor, 1955-63, professor of philosophy, 1963—, chairman of department, 1964-70, master of Bramford College, 1959-66. Member, board of directors of New Haven Redevelopment Agency, 1963-67, and of Day Prospect Hill School. *Member:* American Philosophical Association, Metaphysical Society of America, Society for Phenomenology and Existential Philosophy, Society for Religion in Higher Education, Kantgesellschaft, American Association of University Professors. *Awards, honors:* Morse fellowship at Yale University, 1950-53; Billings Memorial Citation, 1951; Fulbright research fellowhip, 1957-58.

WRITINGS: (Editor and contributor) *Existential Philosophers: Kierkegaard to Merieau-Ponty,* McGraw, 1967.

Contributor: C. W. Hendel, editor, *The Philosophy of Kant and Our Modern World,* Liberal Arts Press, 1957; Paul Ramsey, editor, *Faith and Ethics,* Harper, 1957; *Nomos,* Volume III, Liberal Arts Press, 1960; *The Library of Living Theology,* Volume III, Macmillan, 1962; Eduard D. Simmons, editor, *Essays on Knowledge and Methodology,* Cook Publishing, 1965; James Edie, editor *An Invitation to Phenomenology,* Quadrangle, 1965. Contributor to *Philosophy* (England), *Kanstudien* (Germany), *Revista di Filosofia* (Italy), *Yale Scientific Magazine,* and philosophy journals in United States. Member of editorial board, *Journal of Existentialism.*

WORK IN PROGRESS: A book on ethics and existence; a second book, on personal knowledge and ethical action.††

* * *

SCHREITER, Rick 1936-

PERSONAL: Born February 16, 1936, in Boston, Mass.; son of Ehrich E. M. (in industrial sales) and Grace A. (Sullivan) Schreiter. *Education:* Harvard University, student, 1953-54; Rhode Island School of Design, B.F.A., 1958.

CAREER: Graphic artist, primarily working as book illustrator.

WRITINGS: (Juvenile; self-illustrated) *The Delicious Plums of King Oscar the Bad,* Quist, 1967. Also author and illustrator of *The Modest Adventures of Barnaby Dob.*

Illustrator: Hans Christian Anderson, *Great Claus and Little Claus,* Grove, 1968; Anderson, *What the Good Man Does Is Always Right,* Dial, 1968; *The Derby Ram: A Ballad,* Doubleday, 1970.†

* * *

SCHRIRE, Theodore 1906-

PERSONAL: Surname rhymes with "clearer"; born November 6, 1906, in Capetown, South Africa; son of Max (a company director) and Rebecca (Mauerberger) Schrire; married Sylvia Sohn; children: Tamar (Mrs. Mervyn Smith), Carmel (Mrs. W. L. Steiger), Sharon (Mrs. David Godfrey), Gail (Mrs. Michael Flesch). *Education:* University of Capetown, M.A., 1926, M.B. and Ch.B., 1930. *Religion:* Jewish. *Home:* 17 Rugby Rd., Capetown, South Africa.

CAREER: University of Capetown, Capetown, South Africa, senior lecturer, department of surgery, 1950-67; Groote Schuur Hospital, Capetown, South Africa, head of casualty department, 1959-74. *Member:* Royal College of Surgeons (fellow), Medical Association of South Africa, American College of Chest Physicians (fellow), Royal Society of South Africa (fellow), South African Archeological Society (member of council). *Awards, honors:* Hamilton Maynard Medal of Medical Association of South Africa.

WRITINGS: Emergencies, C. C Thomas, 1962; *Hebrew Amulets: Their Interpretation and Decipherment,* Routledge & Kegan Paul, 1966; *Surgical Emergencies,* Heinemann, 1972. Associate editor, *South African Archeological Bulletin.*

*   *   *

SCHROEDER, David   1924-

PERSONAL: Surname is pronounced *Shray*-dur; born September 20, 1924, in Halbstadt, Manitoba, Canada; son of Henry H. (a farmer) and Maria (Kehler) Schroeder; married Mildred Alice Bartel (a nurse), June 25, 1949; children: Dorothy Marie, Lynette Ruth, Allan David. *Education:* Mennonite Brethren Bible College, Th.B., 1949; Bethel College, Newton, Kan., A.B., 1951; Bethany Theological Seminary, Chicago, Ill., B.D., 1956; University of Hamburg, Theol.D., 1959. *Home:* 745 Coventry Rd., Winnipeg 20, Manitoba, Canada.

CAREER: Mennonite minister. Pastor in Winnipeg, Manitoba, 1951-54; Canadian Mennonite Bible College, Winnipeg, Manitoba, associate professor of Bible and ethics, 1959—. Chairman of Winnipeg Board of Education, Conference of Mennonites in Canada, 1960-66; member, Canadian Mennonite Publishing Association, 1960-68; member of board, Mennonite Biblical Seminary, 1961—; guest professor, Mennonite Biblical Seminary, Elkhart, Ind., 1974-75.

WRITINGS: Learning to Know the Bible, Faith & Life, 1965. Contributor to supplementary volume of *The Interpreters Bible Dictionary.*

WORK IN PROGRESS: Studies on higher education and on New Testament ethics.

*   *   *

SCHROETER, James   1927-

PERSONAL: Born June 29, 1927, in Hammond, Ind.; son of Robert R. (a salesman) and Mathilda (Dobson) Schroeter; married Joan Gitzel (a professor), September 3, 1950; children: Judith Helen, Joseph Henry. *Education:* University of Chicago, B.A., 1950, M.A., 1952, Ph.D., 1959. *Politics:* Democrat ("and/or independent"). *Home:* Av. du Temple 21 b, Lausanne 1012, Switzerland. *Office:* Faculty of Letters, University of Lausanne, 1005 Lausanne, Switzerland.

CAREER: University of Nebraska, Lincoln, instructor in English, 1952-53; University of Chicago, Chicago, Ill., lecturer in English and humanities, 1953-61; Temple Univer-

sity, Philadelphia, Pa., assistant professor of English, 1961-62; Illinois Institute of Technology, Chicago, associate professor, 1962-68, professor of English, 1968-74; visiting professor at University of Lausanne, Lausanne, Switzerland, 1974—, and University of Basel, Basel, Switzerland, 1975—. Visiting professor, University of Nebraska, summer, 1962; Fulbright professor in France, 1968-69. *Military service:* U.S. Army Air Forces, 1945-46. *Member:* Modern Language Association of America, National Council of Teachers of English, American Association of University Professors, Swiss Association of University Teachers.

WRITINGS: Willa Cather and Her Critics, Cornell University Press, 1967. Contributor to *A Mirror for Greek Tragedy,* edited by Albert Cook; also contributor to journals, including *Yale Review, Southern Review, PMLA,* and *American Literature.*

*   *   *

SCHULTE, Rainer

PERSONAL: Born in Simmern, Germany. *Education:* University of Mainz, student, 1956-58, 1960-62, M.A., 1962; Dickinson College, student, 1958-59; University of Michigan, Ph.D., 1965. *Home:* 605 West Lamar, McKinney, Tex. 75069. *Office address:* University of Texas at Dallas, Box 688, Richardson, Tex. 75080.

CAREER: Ohio University, Athens, 1965-75, began as assistant professor, became professor of English and director of comparative literature; University of Texas at Dallas, professor of comparative literature, 1975—.

WRITINGS: (Editor with Edward Mitchell) *Continental Short Stories: The Modern Tradition,* Norton, 1968; *The Suicide at the Piano* (poetry), Kanchenjunga Press, 1969; (editor with Quincy Troupe) *Giant Talk: An Anthology of Third World Writing,* Random House, 1975. Also author of play "Needle off Center: A Multi-Media Show," 1971. Contributor of poetry, essays, book reviews, fiction, and criticism to journals in his field. Editor-in-chief, *Mundus Artium: A Journal of International Literature and the Arts.*

WORK IN PROGRESS: The Sacred Present: An Introduction to Modern International Poetry.

*   *   *

SCHULTZ, Barbara   1923-

PERSONAL: Born March 7, 1923, in Newport, R.I.; daughter of Joseph B. (a house painter) and Flora M. (Smith) Weatherly; married Ray Schultz (an artist), September 20, 1947, in Paris, France. *Education:* Formal education ended with grade school diploma at Brooklyn Thoracic Hospital, where she was a tuberculosis patient; later took courses in French, oil painting, Egyptian hieroglyphics, and English composition. *Politics:* Independent. *Home:* 1046 Lafayette St., Cape May City, N.J. 08204.

CAREER: Various jobs prior to 1963, including mother's helper for five children, proofreader for a New York engineering firm, clerical work at Brooklyn Polytechnic Institute, and secretary for an optometrist.

WRITINGS: The Secret of the Pharaohs (juvenile mystery), Bobbs-Merrill, 1966; *The House on Pinto's Island* (juvenile mystery), Bobbs-Merrill, 1968.

WORK IN PROGRESS: An adult mystery, *Gift-Wrapped for Murder;* a juvenile mystery, *The Secret of the Madonna.*

SIDELIGHTS: Barbara Schultz "started writing as a

child, when illness and erratic home life encouraged introspection and solitude." She lived in Paris for six months after her marriage, and then briefly in Lausanne, Switzerland.

* * *

SCHULTZ, Harry D. 1923-

PERSONAL: Born September 11, 1923; son of Harry J. (owner of a drug store chain) and Theresa (Stachowiak) Schultz; married Gladys Irene Roosevelt, 1947 (divorced, 1952); married Dawn Courtman (an economist), August 24, 1963 (divorced, 1971). *Education:* Los Angeles City College, student, 1941-43. *Politics:* Republican. *Religion:* Protestant. *Home address:* P.O. Box 5414, Amsterdam, Netherlands. *Office address:* P.O. Box 2523, Lausanne 1002, Switzerland.

CAREER: Owner and publisher, at various times, of thirteen newspapers in Palm Springs, North Hollywood, Lake Arrowhead, San Bernardino, and other California locations, 1946-57; stockbroker, 1959-60; stock market trader in Europe, 1960-64; publisher of weekly "International Harry Schultz Letter," 1964—, currently with offices in England, Canada, the Netherlands, Germany, and Switzerland. Financial adviser (at $1,250 an hour); organizer of international monetary seminars in New York and Los Angeles, 1967, London, 1968, Montreal, 1971, and Bermuda, 1973. Defeated Republican candidate for California State Assembly, 1948. President of San Bernardino County Newspaper Publishers Association, 1956-57, and International Investment Letters Association, 1973-76. *Military service:* U.S. Army Air Forces, 1943-46. *Member:* National Press Club (Washington, D.C.). *Awards, honors:* Nominated for Pulitzer Prize in editorial writing, 1964, for editorial campaign conducted by *Palm Springs Limelight News.*

WRITINGS: Bear Markets—How to Survive and Make Money in Them, Prentice-Hall, 1964; (with Samson Coslow) *A Treasury of Wall Street Wisdom,* Investors' Press, 1966; *Handbook for Understanding Swiss Banks,* Public Press, 1967; *The International Monetary Muddle,* La Jolla Rancho Press, 1969; (co-author) *The Dollar Devaluation: Mechanics and Timing,* Financial & Economic Research Corp., 1971; *What the Prudent Investor Should Know about Switzerland and Foreign Money Havens,* Arlington House, 1971; *Panics and Crashes: How You Can Make Money out of Them,* Arlington House, 1972; *You and Gold,* Financial & Economic Research Corp., 1973; *Inflation and Inflation Hedges,* Financial & Economic Research Corp., revised edition, 1974; *Financial Tactics and Terms for the Sophisticated International Investor,* Harper, 1974; (with James E. Sinclair) *How the Experts Buy and Sell Gold Bullion, Stocks and Coins,* Arlington House, 1975. Also author of *How to Keep Your Money and Freedom.*

WORK IN PROGRESS: An autobiography; *Happiness Is a Warm HSL,* a collection of cartoons from "International Harry Schultz Letter."

SIDELIGHTS: Although based in Europe, Schultz travels constantly, writing from every continent.

BIOGRAPHICAL/CRITICAL SOURCES: Barron's, October 23, 1967, November 27, 1967; *News of the World,* March 17, 1968.

* * *

SCHWARTZ, Elkanah 1937-

PERSONAL: Born March 15, 1937, in New York, N.Y.; son of Ben and Blanche (Saltz) Schwartz. *Education:* Brooklyn College (now Brooklyn College of the City University of New York), B.A., 1957; Rabbinical Academy, Rabbi, 1962; also studied at a seminary in Israel, 1957-58, and took graduate courses at New York University, 1957-67. *Home:* 350 Empire Blvd., Brooklyn, N.Y. 11225. *Office:* Union of Orthodox Jewish Congregations of America, 116 East 27th St., New York, N.Y. 10016.

CAREER: Union of Orthodox Jewish Congregations of America, New York, N.Y., former assistant editor of *Jewish Life,* currently public affairs director.

WRITINGS: American Life: Shtetl Style, Jonathan David, 1967.

* * *

SCHWARTZ, Louis B. 1913-

PERSONAL: Born February 22, 1913, in Philadelphia, Pa.; married; children: two. *Education:* University of Pennsylvania, B.S., 1932, LL.B., 1935. *Home:* 510 Woodland Ter., Philadelphia, Pa. 19104. *Office:* University of Pennsylvania Law School, 3400 Chestnut St., Philadelphia, Pa. 19104.

CAREER: U.S. Securities and Exchange Commission, Washington, D.C., attorney, 1935-39; U.S. Department of Justice, Washington, D.C., chief of general crimes and special projects section, 1939-43, chief of decree section, Antitrust Division, 1945-46; University of Pennsylvania, Philadelphia, member of Law School faculty, 1946—, Benjamin Franklin Professor, 1964—. Visiting professor at Cambridge University, Harvard University, Columbia University, University of California, and Salzburg Seminar in American Studies; lecturer in Britain, France, the Scandinavian countries, and India. Served on U.S. interdepartmental committees on war crimes and status-of-forces treaties; member of Attorney General's National Committee to Study the Antitrust Laws, 1954-55; director of National Commission on Reform of Federal Criminal Laws, 1967-71. *Military service:* U.S. Naval Reserve, active duty, 1944-45; became lieutenant junior grade.

MEMBER: American Law Institute, American Bar Association, National Legal Aid and Defender Association, Americans for Democratic Action (national board member), American Civil Liberties Union, Pennsylvania Bar Association, Philadelphia Bar (member of executive committee), Order of the Coif, Beta Gamma Sigma.

WRITINGS: Free Enterprise and Economic Organization: Legal and Related Materials, Foundation Press, 1952, 4th edition, 1972; (editor) *Crime and the American Penal System,* American Academy of Political and Social Science, 1962; *Law Enforcement Handbook for Police,* West Publishing, 1971. Contributor to law journals.

* * *

SCHWARTZ, Mildred A(nne) 1932-

PERSONAL: Born November 17, 1932, in Toronto, Ontario, Canada; daughter of Max and Rebecca (Silverberg) Schwartz. *Education:* University of Toronto, B.A., 1954, M.A., 1956; Columbia University, Ph.D., 1965. *Religion:* Jewish. *Home:* 1450 East 55th Pl., Apt. 818S, Chicago, Ill. 60637. *Office:* University of Illinois at Chicago Circle, Chicago, Ill. 60680.

CAREER: Held research jobs prior to 1962; University of Calgary, Calgary, Alberta, assistant professor of sociology, 1962-64; University of Chicago, Chicago, Ill., research associate, 1964-66; University of Illinois at Chicago Circle, associate professor, 1966-69, professor of sociology, 1969—. Visiting professor, Harvard University, 1973. *Member:* American Sociological Association, American Political Science Association, Canadian Sociology and Anthropology Association, Association for Canadian Studies in the United States, International Studies Association, Canadian Political Science Association.

WRITINGS: Public Opinion and Canadian Identity, University of California Press, 1967; (with F. C. Engelmann) *Political Parties and the Canadian Social Structure,* Prentice-Hall, 1967; *Trends in White Attitudes toward Negroes,* National Opinion Research Center, 1967; *Politics and Territory,* McGill-Queen's University Press, 1974; (with Engelmann) *Canadian Political Parties: Origin, Character, Impact,* Prentice-Hall, 1975.

Contributor: B. Blishen, editor, *Canadian Society,* Macmillan, 1961, 2nd edition, 1964; John Meisel, editor, *Papers on the 1962 Election,* University of Toronto Press, 1964; H. Vollmer and D. L. Mills, editors, *Professionalization,* Prentice-Hall, 1966; Richard Preston, editor, *The Influence of the United States on Canadian Development,* Duke University Press, 1972; Richard Rose, editor, *Electoral Behavior,* Free Press, 1974; Dennis Forcese and Stephen Richer, editors, *Issues in Canadian Society: Introduction to Sociology,* Prentice-Hall, 1975.

WORK IN PROGRESS: Politics, Stratification, Inequality; The Canadian Voter; Responses to Threats to Legitimacy; continuing work with F. C. Engelmann on Austrian politics.

*　　*　　*

SCOGGINS, James (Lawrence) 1934-

PERSONAL: Born January 1, 1934, in Chattanooga, Tenn.; son of Lawrence and Mildred (Wallace) Scoggins; married Anna Scrudder, September 8, 1957; children: Anna Ruth, Dana Elizabeth, Michael Lawrence. *Education:* University of Georgia, student, 1951-52; University of Chattanooga, A.B., 1958; Johns Hopkins University, M.A., 1959; University of Illinois, Ph.D., 1963. *Politics:* Democrat (liberal). *Office:* Department of English, University of Minnesota, Minneapolis, Minn. 55455.

CAREER: University of Illinois, Urbana, instructor in English, 1963; University of Minnesota, Minneapolis, assistant professor, 1963-66, associate professor, 1966-71, professor of English, 1971—, associate director of Minnesota Orientation Center, 1967. Fulbright lecturer, Charles University, Prague, Czechoslovakia, 1970-71; lecturer, Rydal Mt. Summer School, 1971. *Military service:* U.S. Air Force, 1952-56. *Member:* Modern Language Association of America, American Association of University Professors, Keats-Shelley Association of America, Charles Lamb Society.

WRITINGS: Imagination and Fancy: Complementary Modes in the Poetry of Wordsworth, University of Nebraska Press, 1967. Contributor to professional journals.

WORK IN PROGRESS: Research on the Romantic essay.†

*　　*　　*

SCOTSON, John L(loyd) 1928-

PERSONAL: Born November 16, 1928, in Rochdale, Lancashire, England; son of James (an engineer) and Edna (Lloyd) Scotson; married Margaret Naylor, July 31, 1954; children: Timothy John, Andrew Mark. *Education:* University of Leicester, B.Sc., 1952, M.A., 1962. *Religion:* Nonconformist (member of Knighton Evangelical Free Church). *Home:* 5 Asquith Blvd., Leicester, Leicestershire, England. *Office:* Loughborough Technical College, Loughborough, Leicestershire, England.

CAREER: Teacher in secondary schools and research in community relationships, 1954-62; Loughborough Technical College, Loughborough, Leicestershire, England, senior lecturer, 1962—. Probation volunteer. *Military service:* Royal Air Force, 1952-54; flying officer. *Member:* Association of Teachers in Technical Institutes, Prison Visitors Association.

WRITINGS: (With N. Elias) *The Established and the Outsiders,* Cass & Co., 1965; *Introducing Society,* Routledge & Kegan Paul, 1975.

*　　*　　*

SCOTT, Amoret (Scudamore) 1930-

PERSONAL: Born March 27, 1930, in Vancouver, British Columbia, Canada; married Christopher Scott (a writer), April 2, 1956. *Home:* Miltons, Stratfield Saye, Reading, England. *Agent:* Irene Josephy, 35 Craven St., Strand, London, WC2N 5NG, England.

CAREER: Collector of antiques; arranger of collections and exhibitions of antiques for various firms and for television; author with husband of books on antique collecting. *Member:* Royal Commonwealth Society, Royal United Service Institution, Ephemera Society (founder member and membership secretary), Parrot Society (founder member).

WRITINGS—All with husband, Christopher Scott, except as indicated: The A-Z of Antique Collecting, Parrish, 1963; *Collecting Bygones,* McKay, 1964; *Dummy Board Figures,* Golden Head Press, 1966; *Tobacco and the Collector,* Parrish, 1966; *Collecting,* M. Joseph, 1967; *Antiques as an Investment,* Oldbourne, 1967; (with Roy Curtis) *Passport to the Portobello,* Macdonald, 1968; *Discovering Staffordshire Figures,* Shire Publications, 1969; *Discovering Smoking Antiques,* Shire Publications, 1970; *Treasures in Your Attic,* Kaye & Ward, 1971; *Discovering Stately Homes,* Shire Publications, 1973; *Wellington,* Shire Publications, 1973. Regular contributor to *Saturday Book;* also contributor to *Country Life, Antique Collector, Antiques* (United States), and other magazines and newspapers.

SIDELIGHTS: Amoret Scott speaks French and German; has traveled throughout Europe, going further afield each year. *Avocational interests:* Parrots in art and history (has extensive collection of material on parrots, dating back to the eleventh century) and the live birds as well; eighteenth and nineteenth-century paper ephemera.

*　　*　　*

SCOTT, Ann Herbert 1926-

PERSONAL: Born November 19, 1926, in Germantown, Philadelphia, Pa.; daughter of Henry Laux and Gladys (Howe) Herbert; married William Taussig Scott (a professor of physics), September 29, 1961; children: Peter Herbert, Katherine Howe. *Education:* University of Pennsylvania, B.A., 1948, graduate student, 1948-49; Yale University, M.A., 1958. *Politics:* Democrat. *Religion:* Society of Friends. *Home and office:* 570 Cranleigh Dr., Reno, Nev. 89502.

CAREER: Rider College, Trenton, N.J., teacher of English, 1949-50; New Haven State Teachers College (now Southern Connecticut State College), New Haven, part-time teacher of English, 1956-58; Wider City Parish, New Haven, coordinator of volunteer work, 1958-61. Member of Reno area committee, American Friends Service Committee, Northern California Office, 1966—. *Member:* League of Women Voters, National Association for the Advancement of Colored People, Phi Beta Kappa, Mortar Board, Sphinx and Key.

WRITINGS: Big Cowboy Western, Lothrop, 1965; *Let's Catch a Monster,* Lothrop, 1967; *Sam,* McGraw, 1967; *Not Just One,* Lothrop, 1968; *Census, U.S.A.: Fact Finding for the American People, 1790-1970,* Seabury, 1968; *On Mother's Lap,* McGraw, 1972.

SIDELIGHTS: Ann Scott's first two books evolved from her work in a housing-project neighborhood in New Haven; *Census, U.S.A.* is a study of American census-taking.

* * *

SCOTT, Arthur L(incoln) 1914-

PERSONAL: Born May 31, 1914, in Kew Gardens, Long Island, N.Y.; son of George T. (a religious administrator) and Ruth (Cowing) Scott; married Frances Elizabeth Costello, December 28, 1940; children: Patricia Anne (Mrs. Robert E. Behal), Lawrence T., Elizabeth L. *Education:* Princeton University, B.A., 1937; University of Michigan, M.A., 1940, Ph.D., 1948; also studied summers at Harvard University, 1936, 1937, and Stanford University, 1940. *Politics:* Republican. *Religion:* Episcopalian. *Home:* 891 Harbor View Pl., San Diego, Calif. 92106.

CAREER: Alborz College, Teheran, Iran, instructor in English, 1937-39; University of Illinois, Urbana, instructor, 1947-54, assistant professor, 1954-62, associate professor of American literature, 1962-70. *Military service:* U.S. Naval Reserve, active duty, 1943-46; became lieutenant junior grade. *Member:* Modern Language Association of America, National Council of Teachers of English, American Studies Association, Kiwanis Club.

WRITINGS: (Editor) *Mark Twain, Selected Criticism,* Southern Methodist University Press, 1955, revised edition, 1967; *On the Poetry of Mark Twain,* University of Illinois Press, 1966; *Mark Twain at Large,* Regnery, 1969. Contributor to *Dalhousie Review, PMLA, American Literature, Prairie Schooner,* and other literary and professional journals.

AVOCATIONAL INTERESTS: Travel (has visited every corner of the earth, including Australasia, 1968), sports, social and religious work.

* * *

SCOTT, Charles T. 1932-

PERSONAL: Born October 21, 1932, in New York, N.Y.; son of Charles T. (in advertising) and Elizabeth (Flanagan) Scott; married Anne Mulgrew, June 1, 1957; children: Robert, Michael, Elisabeth, Sheila. *Education:* St. John's University, Jamaica, N.Y., B.A., 1954; New York University, M.A., 1958; University of Texas, Ph.D., 1963. *Religion:* Roman Catholic. *Home:* 4737 Lafayette Dr., Madison, Wis. 53705. *Office:* Department of English, University of Wisconsin, Madison, Wis. 53706.

CAREER: Columbia University, Teachers College Project in Afghanistan, instructor in English, 1958-60; University of Wisconsin—Madison, assistant professor, 1963-65, associate professor, 1965-68, professor of English, 1968—,

chairman of English department, 1970-74, director of program in English for foreign students, 1963—. English-language tutor to Crown Prince Akihito and Crown Princess Michiko, and consultant to English Language Education Council, Tokyo, and Japan Society, Inc., 1965-66. Member of English-teaching advisory panel, U.S. Information Agency. *Military service:* U.S. Army, 1954-56. *Member:* Linguistic Society of America, National Council of Teachers of English, Teachers of English to Speakers of Other Languages, Linguistic Circle of New York.

WRITINGS: Persian and Arabic Riddles: A Language-Centered Approach to Genre Definition, Research Center in Anthropology, Folklore, and Linguistics, Indiana University, 1965; *Preliminaries to English Teaching,* English Language Education Council (Tokyo), 1966; (editor with Irmengard Rauch) *Approaches in Linguistic Methodology,* University of Wisconsin Press, 1966; (editor with Jon L. Erickson) *Readings for the History of the English Language,* Allyn & Bacon, 1968.

WORK IN PROGRESS: Introduction to English Phonology.

* * *

SCOTT, Christopher 1930-

PERSONAL: Born March 6, 1930, in Canterbury, England; married Amoret Scudamore (a writer on antiques and collecting), April 2, 1956. *Education:* Attended Royal Military Academy, Sandhurst, 1948-50. *Politics:* "Mild Conservative." *Religion:* Church of England. *Home:* Miltons, Stratfield Saye, Reading, England. *Agent:* Irene Josephy, 35 Craven St., Strand, London, WC2N 5NG, England. *Office:* Estate Office, Stratfield Saye, Reading, England.

CAREER: British Army, regular officer in Royal Artillery and Army Air Corps, 1950-56; currently chief agent to Duke of Wellington, Reading, England. Antique collector, and author with wife of books on antique collecting. *Member:* Royal Forestry Society, Royal Institution of Chartered Surveyors, Southern Sports Council, Southern Arts Association.

WRITINGS—With wife, Amoret Scott: *The A-Z of Antique Collecting,* Parrish, 1963; *Collecting Bygones,* McKay, 1964; *Dummy Board Figures,* Golden Head Press, 1966; *Tobacco and the Collector,* Parrish, 1966; *Collecting,* M. Joseph, 1967; *Antiques as an Investment,* Oldbourne, 1967; *Discovering Staffordshire Figures,* Shire Publications, 1969; *Discovering Smoking Antiques,* Shire Publications, 1970; *Treasures in Your Attic,* Kaye & Ward, 1971; *Discovering Stately Homes,* Shire Publications, 1973; *Wellington,* Shire Publications, 1973. Regular contributor to *Saturday Book;* also contributor to *Times* (London), *Country Life, Antiques* (United States), *Antique Collecting* (England), and other journals. Joint editor, *Proof* (magazine), 1965-67.

AVOCATIONAL INTERESTS: Photography, travel, flying.

* * *

SCOTT, George Walton 1921-

PERSONAL: Born June 2, 1921; son of Philip Dennis (a doctor) and Marguerite (Walton) Scott; married Maritta Tornelund, February 16, 1958; children: Philip Walton, Thomas Walton. *Education:* King's College, London, B.A. (honors), 1947. *Politics:* "Belong to no party." *Religion:*

Church of England. *Home:* 8 Cedars Rd., London S.W.13, England. *Office:* School of Broadcasting, British Broadcasting Corp., 3 Portland Pl., London WIA 1AA, England.

CAREER: The Polytechnic, London, England, lecturer in English, 1947-52; Swedish Educational Authorities, Stockholm, lecturer in English, 1952-57; Swedish Broadcasting Corp., Stockholm, radio producer, 1957-62; British Broadcasting Corp., London, radio producer, then head of Spanish and Portuguese section in external broadcasting department, 1962-72, chief assistant, School of Broadcasting, 1972—. *Military service:* British Army, World War II; received five decorations.

WRITINGS: Shamrock, Leek, and Thistle, Radio Sweden, 1961; *The Swedes: A Jigsaw Puzzle,* Sidgwick & Jackson, 1967; *Robert Hessick,* St. Martin's, 1972; (with Jane O'Neill and Peter Matthews) "Vinegar and Brown Paper" (a musical), first produced on the West End at The Haymarket Theatre, May 11, 1976.

WORK IN PROGRESS: A biography of Tobias Smollett.

SIDELIGHTS: George Scott is fluent in French and Spanish in addition to Swedish, and knows some German. *Avocational interests:* Travel, antiques, painting.

*   *   *

SCOTT, Lloyd F.   1926-

PERSONAL: Born May 26, 1926, in Prescott, Ariz.; son of Edwin H. (a businessman) and Cora (Matthes) Scott; married Ann F. Burling, April 5, 1952; children: Lloyd Gordon, Sally Ann, Susan Frances. *Education:* University of California, A.B., 1950, M.A., 1952, Ph.D., 1955. *Home:* 445 Nora Ct., Walnut Creek, Calif. *Office:* Department of Education, University of California, Berkeley, Calif. 94720.

CAREER: University of California, Berkeley, 1957—, began as assistant professor, professor of education, 1967—, and coordinator of laboratory schools. *Military service:* U.S. Naval Reserve, active duty, 1944-46; served in Battle of Leyte Gulf; received Presidential Unit Citation. *Member:* National Council of Teachers of Mathematics, American Educational Research Association, California Teachers Association, California Teachers of Mathematics.

WRITINGS: Trends in Elementary School Mathematics, Rand McNally, 1966; (with John U. Michaelis and Ruth H. Grossman) *New Designs for the Elementary School Curriculum,* McGraw, 1967, 2nd edition published as *New Designs for Elementary Curriculum and Instruction,* 1975; (with A. K. Ruddell) *Ginn Elementary Mathematics,* Ginn, 1968; (with W. E. Lamon) *Learning and the Nature of Mathematics,* SRA, 1970; (with others) *Ginn Mathematics: An Applied Approach,* Ginn, 1974. Contributor to educational journals.

WORK IN PROGRESS: Research in mathematics learning and elementary mathematics.

*   *   *

SCOTT, Peter Dale   1929-
(Adam Greene, John Sproston)

PERSONAL: Born January 11, 1929, in Montreal, Quebec, Canada; son of Francis Reginald (a professor and poet) and Marian Mildred (Dale) Scott; married Mary Elizabeth Marshall (a psychiatric social worker), June 16, 1956; children: Catherine Dale, Thomas, John Daniel. *Education:* McGill University, B.A., 1949, Ph.D., 1955; graduate study at Institut d'Etudes Politiques, University of Paris, 1950, and

University College, Oxford, 1950-52. *Home:* 2823 Ashby Ave., Berkeley, Calif. 94705. *Office:* English Department, University of California, Berkeley, Calif. 94720.

CAREER: Sedbergh School, Montebello, Quebec, teacher, 1952-53; McGill University, Montreal, Quebec, lecturer in political science, 1955-56; Canadian Foreign Service, posts in Ottawa, with United Nations, and in Warsaw, Poland, 1957-61; University of California, Berkeley, assistant professor of speech, 1961-66, assistant professor of English, 1966-68, associate professor, 1968—. *Member:* Foisard Society.

WRITINGS: Poems, Fantasy Press, 1953; (with others) *Education at Berkeley,* University of California Press, 1966; (with Franz Schurmann and Reginald Zelnik) *The Politics of Escalation in Vietnam,* Beacon Press, 1966; (translator with Czeslaw Milosz) Zbigniew Herbert, *Selected Poems,* Penguin, 1968; *The War Conspiracy,* Bobbs-Merrill, 1972; (contributor) Mark Selden, editor, *Remaking Asia,* Pantheon, 1974; (contributor) Steve Weissman, editor, *Big Brother and the Holding Company,* Ramparts, 1975. Also contributor to *Pentagon Papers,* Volume V, edited by N. Chomsky and H. Zinn, 1973. Contributor of poems, translations of poetry, and articles to journals and periodicals.

WORK IN PROGRESS: Dark-Age Pastoral, a scholarly study; translations of Virgil's *Eclogues;* a book-length study on covert U.S. political forces and events.

*   *   *

SCOTT, William G(eorge)   1926-

PERSONAL: Born October 19, 1926, in Chicago, Ill.; son of George E. (an architect) and Esther (Mooney) Scott; married Julia Eigelsbach, September 3, 1955; children: Therese, William, Gerard, Andrea, Mary. *Education:* DePaul University, A.B., 1950; Loyola University, Chicago, Ill., M.S.I.R., 1952; Indiana University, D.B.A., 1957. *Office:* Department of Management, University of Washington, Seattle, Wash. 98105.

CAREER: Loyola University, Chicago, Ill., instructor in labor relations, 1952-53; Indiana University, Bloomington, lecturer in management, 1954-56; Georgia State College (now University), Atlanta, associate professor of management, 1956-59; DePaul University, Chicago, associate professor, 1959-62, professor of management, 1962-66, chairman of department, 1959-62; University of Washington, Seattle, professor of management, 1966—. Consultant to U.S. Internal Revenue Service and to Field Educational Enterprises. *Military service:* U.S. Army, Medical Corps, 1946-47. *Member:* Academy of Management.

WRITINGS: Human Relations in Management, Irwin, 1962; *Social Ethic in Management Literature,* Georgia State College, 1959; (editor with Keith Davis) *Readings in Human Relations,* McGraw, 1963, 3rd edition published as *Human Relations and Organizational Behavior: Readings and Comments,* 1969; *Management of Conflict,* Irwin, 1965; *Organization Theory: A Structural and Behavioral Analysis,* Irwin, 1967, revised edition, 1972; (compiler) *Organization Concepts and Analysis,* Dickenson, 1969; (with Theo Haimann) *Management in the Modern Organization,* Houghton, 1970, 2nd edition, 1974; (compiler with James E. Curtis) *Social Stratification: Canada,* Prentice-Hall, 1973; (compiler with Patrick E. Connor and Haimann) *Dimensions in Modern Management,* Houghton, 1974. Associate editor, *Academy of Management Journal.*†

SCOTT, Winfield H(arker) 1932-

PERSONAL: Born March 27, 1932, in Tamaqua, Pa. *Education:* Pennsylvania State University, B.S., 1954, M.S., 1955, Ph.D., 1958. *Home:* 2514 Mill Rd. N.W., Washington, D.C. 20007.

CAREER: U.S. Public Health Service Hospital, Fort Worth, Tex.,psychologist, 1957-59; University of Maryland, School of Medicine, Baltimore, 1959-67, became associate professor of medical psychology; National Institute of Mental Health, Bethesda, Md., chief of clinical psychology, Adult Psychiatry Branch, beginning 1967; currently associated with Washington School of Psychology, Washington, D.C.

WRITINGS: (With Benjamin Pope) *Psychological Diagnosis in Clinical Practice,* Oxford University Press, 1967.†

* * *

SCRIABINE, Helen (Gorstrine) 1906-

PERSONAL: Born February 13, 1906, in Dvinsk, Russia; came to United States in 1950, naturalized in 1955; daughter of Aleksander and Nadeschda (Taznanskaja) Gorstrine; children: Alexander Scriabine. *Education:* Technirum, Russia, B.A., 1923; University of Leningrad, M.A. (with honor), 1941; Syracuse University, Ph.D., 1962. *Home:* 28 West Park Rd., Iowa City, Iowa 52240. *Office:* Department of Russian Language and Literature, University of Iowa, Iowa City, Iowa 52240.

CAREER: Teacher in Soviet Union before coming to America; Air Force Language School, Syracuse, N.Y., deputy chief instructor in Russian, 1950-53; University of Iowa, Iowa City, assistant professor, 1960-66, professor of Russian language and literature, 1966—. Summer teaching at Columbia University, 1962, Middlebury College, 1964, and Institute of Soviet Study, Munich, Germany, 1966-71. *Member:* Modern Language Association of America.

WRITINGS: Les Faux Dieux: Essai sur l'humour, Michel Zostchenko et Marcel Ayme, two volumes, Mercure de France, 1963; (with Koschenova) *History of Russian Literature,* Lucas Brothers, 1963; (editor) *Pushkin Stories, Lermontov Stories, Checkov Stories,* Lucas Brothers, 1964; *V Blokade,* Bashkiezev (Munich), 1964, translation by Norman Luxenburg published as *Siege and Survival: The Odyssey of a Leningrader,* Southern Illinois University Press, 1971; (editor) *Short Stories by Pushkin, Lermontov and Dostoevsky,* Harper, 1965; *Leningrader Tagebuch: Aufzeichnungen aus d. Kreigsjahren, 1941-1945,* Biederstein-Verlag, 1972. Contributor to Russian journals and to *Books Abroad.*

WORK IN PROGRESS: A book on the development of Russian humor; Part II of *History of Russian Literature.*

AVOCATIONAL INTERESTS: Travel.†

* * *

SCRIVEN, Michael (John) 1928-

PERSONAL: Born March 28, 1928, in Beaulieu, Hampshire, England; son of Victor Reginald and Hilda (Grice) Scriven; married Mary Anne Warren, 1970. *Education:* University of Melbourne, B.A., 1948, M.A., 1950; Oxford University, D.Phil., 1956. *Politics:* Independent. *Religion:* Atheist. *Home:* 1384 Queens Rd., Berkeley, Calif. 94708. *Office:* Department of Philosophy, University of California, Berkeley, Calif. 94720.

CAREER: University of Minnesota, Minneapolis, instructor in philosophy, 1952-55, research associate in philosophy of science, 1955-56; Swarthmore College, Swarthmore, Pa., assistant professor of philosophy, 1956-60; Indiana University, Bloomington, professor of the history and philosophy of science, 1960-66; University of California, Berkeley, professor of philosophy, 1966—. Fellow, Center for Advanced Study in the Behavioral Sciences, 1962-63; Alfred North Whitehead Fellow, Harvard University, 1970-71. Summer teaching at New School for Social Research, 1959, and Wesleyan University, 1961, 1962. *Member:* American Philosophical Association, Mind Association, Parapsychological Association.

WRITINGS: (Editor with Herbert Feigl) *Foundations of Science and the Concepts of Psychology and Psychoanalysis,* University of Minnesota Press, 1956; *Applied Logic,* Behavioral Research Laboratories, 1964; *Primary Philosophy,* McGraw, 1966; (editor with W. J. Moore and Eugene P. Wigner) *Symmetries and Reflections,* Indiana University Press, 1967. Also author of *Evaluation,* 1974. Contributor of more than 150 articles and reviews to journals.

WORK IN PROGRESS: The Theory and Practice of Evaluation, for Edge Press; *Scientific Philosophy of Science,* for Wadsworth.

AVOCATIONAL INTERESTS: Range from parapsychology through sports cars to social reform.

* * *

SCUORZO, Herbert E(rnest) 1928-

PERSONAL: Surname is pronounced Skoo-or-zo; born November 8, 1928, in Newark, N.J.; son of Ernest (an attorney) and Carrie (Belott) Scuorzo; married Loretta M. Weber, July 2, 1955; children: Linda, Mark, Karen, Janet. *Education:* Seton Hall University, student, 1948-50, M.A., 1955, law student, 1955-57, postdoctoral study, 1966-67; Montclair State College, A.B., 1951; New York University, Ed.D., 1961. *Religion:* Byzantine Catholic. *Home:* 114 Milton Pl., South Orange, N.J. 07079.

CAREER: WSOU-FM, South Orange, N.J., broadcast engineer, 1949-50; Newark (N.J.) public schools, teacher, 1953-62, vice-principal, 1962-64, principal, 1964-74; currently dean of instruction at Essex County College, Newark, N.J. Instructor in audiovisual education at New York University, 1961, and Newark State College, 1962; instructor in educational media at Seton Hall University, 1966—. Ralston Purina Co., adviser on Education Through Pets Program, 1961-65, and Pets and People Program, 1962-65. *Military service:* U.S. Navy, 1946-48. U.S. Naval Reserve, electronics instructor, 1949-51. U.S. Air Force, training officer, 1951-52. U.S. Air Force Reserve, beginning 1953; retired as major. *Member:* National Education Association (life member), New Jersey Education Association, New Jersey Audio Visual Education Association (president, 1967-69), New Jersey Audio Visual Council, Newark Public School Principals Association (legislative chairman, 1966-70).

WRITINGS: The Practical Audio Visual Handbook for Teachers, Parker Publishing, 1967. Audiovisual columnist for *Grade Teacher,* 1961-67; contributor to other educational publications. Editor, *New Jersey Audio Visual News,* 1965—.

WORK IN PROGRESS: A novel based on inner city schools, their teachers, and students.

SEABERG, Stanley 1929-

PERSONAL: Born August 7, 1929, in Los Angeles, Calif.; son of William (a motel operator) and Evelyn (Olney) Seaberg; married Imogene Bieberdorf (a secretary), August 23, 1952; children: Sylvia, Sonja. *Education:* Southern California College, B.A., 1952; San Francisco State College (now University), M.A., 1958; Yale University, graduate study, 1963-64. *Home:* 20153 Somerset Dr., Cupertino, Calif. 95129.

CAREER: Teacher in secondary schools in Fontana, Calif., 1957-59, Cupertino, Calif., 1959-63, Sunnyvale, Calif., 1964-66; Henry M. Gunn Senior High School, Palo Alto, Calif., teacher of history, 1966—. *Military service:* U.S. Army, 1954-56. *Member:* American Historical Association, American Studies Association, American Federation of Teachers, Society for the Comparative Study of Society and History, National Council for the Social Studies, California State Council for the Social Studies. *Awards, honors:* General Electric fellowship in economics, 1962; research grant, American Federation of Teachers, 1966; Fulbright fellowship, 1972.

WRITINGS: The Pioneer Versus the Wilderness: Did the Frontier Create the American?, Scholastic Book Services, 1966; *The American Experience,* Addison-Wesley, 1970; *The Negro in America,* two volumes, Scholastic Book Services, 1970; *The Comparative Approach to American History,* Foreign Policy Association, 1972. Also author of *The Challenges of Automation: Can Man Control the Machine?* Contributor to education journals.

AVOCATIONAL INTERESTS: Gardening, camping, hiking.

* * *

SEED, Jenny 1930-

PERSONAL: Born May 18, 1930, in Cape Town, South Africa; daughter of Ivan Washington (a draftsman) and Bessie (Dickerson) Booysen; married Edward Robert Seed (a railway employee), October 30, 1953; children: Anne, Dick, Alan, Robbie. *Education:* Educated in Cape Town, South Africa. *Home:* 10 Pioneer Crescent, Northdene, Queensburgh, Natal, South Africa.

CAREER: Draftsman in Roads Department and Town Planning Department, Pietarmaritzburg, South Africa, before marriage; free-lance writer, mainly for children.

WRITINGS—All published by Hamish Hamilton, except as noted: *The Dancing Mule,* Thomas Nelson, 1964; *The Always-late Train,* Nasionale Boekhandel, 1965; *Small House, Big Garden,* 1965; *Peter the Gardener,* 1966; *Tombi's Song,* 1966, Rand McNally, 1968; *To the Rescue,* 1966; *Stop Those Children,* 1966; *Timothy and Tinker,* 1967; *The Red Dust Soldiers,* Heinemann, 1968; *The River Man,* 1968; *The Voice of the Great Elephant,* 1968, Pantheon, 1969; *Kulumi the Brave,* 1970; *The Prince of the Bay,* 1970; *The Great Thirst,* 1971; *The Broken Spear,* 1972; *The Bushman's Dream,* 1974; *The Sky Green Lizard,* 1973.

WORK IN PROGRESS: Research in South African history.

SIDELIGHTS: Seed told *CA:* "When my children were young, I wrote fantasy to entertain them. Most of the stories were published and a couple grew into little novels. Now that they are older, hearing their homework gives me other ideas—for historical settings." *The Red Dust Soldiers* and *The Canvas City* are the first of the historical novels for young people. Her children's stories have been republished and broadcast in Canada, England, Rhodesia, New Zealand, and Australia.

* * *

SEEGERS, Kathleen Walker 1915-

PERSONAL: Born December 12, 1915, in Keokuk, Iowa; daughter of Henry S. (a lawyer) and Edith (O'Harra) Walker; married Scott Seegers (a writer for *Reader's Digest*), November 24, 1960. *Education:* University of Iowa, student, 1933-36; George Washington University, B.A., 1937. *Home and office:* 626 Boyle Lane, McLean, Va. 22101.

CAREER: Foreign Policy Association, Washington, D.C., assistant editor, 1937-41; *Inter-American* (magazine), Washington, D.C., associate editor, 1941-47; Pan American Union (now Organization of American States), Washington, D.C., editor of *Americas* (magazine), 1949-60. *Member:* Women's National Press Club, Delta Gamma.

WRITINGS: Alliance for Progress, the Challenge of the Western Hemisphere, Coward, 1964; *Brazil, Awakening Giant,* Thomas Nelson, 1967. Adapter of eight books, distributed abroad by U.S. Information Agency to foreigners studying English.

* * *

SEEMAN, Bernard 1911-

PERSONAL: Born October 19, 1911, in New York, N.Y.; son of William J. (a manufacturing jeweler) and Lena (Kerner) Seeman; married Geraldine Adele Micallef, January 19, 1932. *Education:* City College (now City College of the City University of New York), student, three years. *Home:* 372 Central Parkway, New York, N.Y. 10025. *Agent:* Evelyn Singer Agency, Inc., Box 163, Briarcliff Manor, N.Y. 10510. *Office:* Science & Medicine Publishing Co., 515 Madison Ave., New York, N.Y. 10022.

CAREER: Magazine writer and editor. Free-lance writer for *Ken,* 1938-39; Far East correspondent for *Friday,* 1939-40; Latin American correspondent for *Click,* 1941; Far East correspondent for *Readers' Scope* and other publications, 1945; associate editor in New York City, of *Magazine Digest,* 1946-49, and *People Today,* 1950-52; editor of *Show,* New York City, 1952-56; editor and vice-president of *Internist Observer,* New York City, 1963-75; executive vice-president, Science & Medicine Publishing Co., 1975—. Special consultant on Japan, U.S. Office of War Information, 1944. *Member:* Federation of American Scientists, American Association for the Advancement of Science, Academy of Political Science, National Academy of Recording Arts and Sciences, National Association of Science Writers, Authors Guild, International Platform Association. *Awards, honors:* Howard W. Blakeslee Award of American Heart Association, 1962, for *The River of Life.*

WRITINGS: Enemy Japan, U.S. Office of War Information, 1942; (with Lawrence A. Salisbury) *Cross Currents in the Philippines,* Institute of Pacific Relations, 1946; (with Henry Dolger) *How to Live with Diabetes,* Norton, 1958, 2nd edition, 1965; *The River of Life,* Norton, 1961; *Man Against Pain,* Chilton, 1962; *The Story of Electricity and Magnetism,* Harvey House, 1967; *Your Sight,* Little, Brown, 1968. Contributor to *Saturday Evening Post, Coronet, Pageant, This Week, Holiday, Negro Digest,* and other periodicals.

WORK IN PROGRESS: A collection of poems, some previously published and others unpublished.

AVOCATIONAL INTERESTS: Photography (does some for magazines and record albums), astrophotography.

* * *

SEFTON, James E(dward) 1939-

PERSONAL: Born July 29, 1939, in San Francisco, Calif.; son of Edward and Kathryn (Shiell) Sefton. *Education:* University of California, Los Angeles, A.B., 1961, Ph.D., 1965. *Politics:* Moderate Republican. *Religion:* Presbyterian. *Office:* Department of History, California State University, 18111 Nordhoff St., Northridge, Calif. 91324.

CAREER: California State University, Northridge, instructor, 1965-66, assistant professor, 1966-69, associate professor, 1969-73, professor of history, 1973—. Manuscript reader for University of California Press, Louisiana State University Press, Houghton Mifflin & Co., and Dryden Press. *Member:* American Historical Association, Organization of American Historians, Southern Historical Association, Civil War Round Table, Phi Alpha Theta, Phi Sigma Kappa (faculty adviser).

WRITINGS: The United States Army and Reconstruction, 1865-1877, Louisiana State University Press, 1967; (contributor) William Kramer, editor, *The American West and the Religious Experience,* Los Angeles, 1974. Contributor of articles and reviews to *Civil War History, Military Affairs, Louisiana History, History: Reviews of New Books, Arizona and the West,* and other periodicals.

WORK IN PROGRESS: Research for book on Reconstruction.

AVOCATIONAL INTERESTS: Hand bookbinding and restoration, railroads, photography; Scottish, Irish, and American folk music; intercollegiate athletics, numismatics.

* * *

SEGAL, Ronald (Michael) 1932-

PERSONAL: Born July 14, 1932, in Cape Town, South Africa; son of Leon (managing director) and Mary (Charney) Segal; married Susan Wolff, July 17, 1962; children: Oliver, Miriam, Emily. *Education:* University of Cape Town, B.A., 1951; Trinity College, Cambridge, B.A. (honors), 1954; University of Virginia, Francis duPont fellow, 1955-56. *Home:* The Old Manor House, Manor Rd., Walton-on-Thames, Surrey, England.

CAREER: National Union of South African Students, director of faculty and cultural studies, 1951-52; *Africa South: An International Journal* (quarterly), Cape Town, South Africa, founder, 1956, publisher and editor, 1956-60; went into exile in England where he published and edited *Africa South in Exile,* 1960-61; Penguin Books Ltd., London, England, general editor of "Penguin African Library," 1961—. Convenor at International Conference on Economic Sanctions against South Africa, London, 1964, and International Conference on South West Africa, Oxford, England, 1966.

WRITINGS: The Tokolosh (novel), Sheed, 1960; *Political Africa: A Who's Who of Personalities and Parties,* George Stevens, 1961; *African Profiles,* Penguin, 1962; *Into Exile,* McGraw, 1963; *The Anguish of India,* Stein & Day, 1965 (published in England as *The Crisis of India,* J. Cape, 1965); *The Race War: The World-Wide Clash of White and Non-White,* J. Cape, 1966, Viking, 1967; (editor with Ruth First) *South-West Africa: Travesty of Trust,* Deutsch, 1967; *America's Receding Future,* Weidenfeld & Nicolson, 1968, published as *Americans: A Conflict of Creed and Reality,* Viking, 1969; *The Struggle against History,* Weidenfeld & Nicolson, 1971, Bantam, 1973; *Whose Jerusalem? The Conflicts of Israel,* Bantam, 1973; *The Decline and Fall of the American Dollar,* Bantam, 1974.

WORK IN PROGRESS: A biography of Leon Trotsky, for Harcourt.

SIDELIGHTS: Ronald Segal was banned from all gatherings in South Africa because of anti-government politics in 1959, and went into exile in England.

* * *

SEGEL, Harold B(ernard) 1930-

PERSONAL: Born September 13, 1930, in Boston, Mass.; son of Abraham Barney (a publisher) and Florence (Aleshnick) Segel. *Education:* Boston College, B.S., 1951; Harvard University, Ph.D., 1955. *Politics:* Independent. *Religion:* Jewish. *Office:* 1233 International Affairs Bldg., Columbia University, New York, N.Y. 10027.

CAREER: University of Florida, Gainesville, assistant professor of Slavic languages and literatures, 1955-59; Columbia University, New York, N.Y., assistant professor, 1959-62, associate professor, 1962-69, professor of Slavic literatures, 1969—. Visiting professor, University of Stockholm, fall, 1972. *Member:* American Association for the Advancement of Slavic Studies, American Society for Eighteenth-Century Studies, Polish Institute. *Awards, honors:* Fulbright-Hayes and American Council of Learned Societies fellowships.

WRITINGS: (Compiler, and author of book-length introduction) *The Literature of Eighteenth Century Russia: A History and Anthology,* two volumes, Dutton, 1967; (translator) *The Major Comedies of Alexander Fredro,* Princeton University Press, 1969; *The Trilogy of Alexander Sukhovo-Kobylin,* Dutton, 1969; *The Baroque Poem,* Dutton, 1974; *Twentieth-Century Russian Drama,* Dutton, in press. Contributor to *New Leader, Polish Review, Slavic Review,* and other journals.

WORK IN PROGRESS: Polish Romantic Drama, for Cornell University Press.

* * *

SEIGNOLLE, Claude 1917-

PERSONAL: Born June 25, 1917, in Perigueux, France. *Education:* Educated at Lyceum Lakanal, Sceaut, France. *Religion:* Roman Catholic. *Home:* 5, Avenue de Robinson, F 92290, Chatenay-Malabry, France. *Agent:* A. van Hageland, Agence Litteraire, 10 Blutsdelle, Alsemberg, Belgium.

CAREER: Writer and folklorist. *Military service:* French Army, Artillery, World War II; taken prisoner of war. *Member:* Societe Prehistorique Francaise (life member).

WRITINGS: Le folklore du Hurepoix, G. P. Maisonneuve, 1937; *En Sologne (enquete folklorique),* G. P. Maisonneuve, 1945; *Les fouilles de Chatenay et Robinson,* G. P. Maisonneuve, 1945; *Le rond des sorciers,* Editions des Guatre-Vents, 1945; *Contes populaires de Guyenne,* G. P. Maisonneuve, 1946; *D'un frontstalag a Londres; recit,* Editions PERFRAC, 1946.

La malvenue, roman fantastique, G. P. Maisonneuve, 1952; *Le bahut noir,* Le Terrain vague, 1958; *Le diable en sabots,* Le Terrain vague, 1959; *Le rond des sorciers. Version definitive,* Le Terrain vague, 1959; *Le Diable dans la tradition populaire,* Besson et Chantemerle, 1959.

Le folklore de Languedoc, Besson et Chantemerle, 1960; *Le galoup,* E.P.M., 1960; *Le chupador,* E.P.M., 1960; *Un homme nu,* E.P.M., 1961; *Un corbeau de toutes couleurs,* Denoel, 1962; *Lithos et moi,* Le Terrain vague, 1962; *Les maledictions,* G. P. Maisonneuve et Larose, 1963, translation by Bernard Wall published as *The Accursed: Two Diabolical Tales,* with lyric introduction by Lawrence Durrell, Coward, 1967; *La folklore de la Provence,* G. P. Maisonneuve et Larose, 1963; *Les evangiles du diable selon la croyance populaire,* G. P. Maisonneuve et Larose, 1964; *La Malvenue et autres recits diaboliques,* Marabout Geant, 1965; *La nuit des Halles; contes fantastiques,* G. P. Maisonneuve et Larose, 1965. Work anthologized in collections in France and abroad.

WORK IN PROGRESS: Other fantasy-novels and stories.

SIDELIGHTS: Claude Seignolle's writings have been translated into Dutch, German, Spanish, and Swedish.

BIOGRAPHICAL/CRITICAL SOURCES: Bernard Planque, *Un Aventurier de l'Insolite: Claude Seignolle,* P. Fanlac, 1960; A. Durand-Tullou, *Du Chien au Loup-Garou dans l'oeuvre de Claude Seignolle,* G. P. Maisonneuve, 1961; *Au Pays du Fantastique de Claude Seignolle,* Virton, 1966.

* * *

SEILER, John A(ndrew) 1927-

PERSONAL: First syllable of surname rhymes with "eye"; born March 23, 1927, in Boston, Mass.; son of Andrew Sebastian (a businessman) and Elva (Shaleen) Seiler; married Catherine Walker, June 17, 1950; children: Marcia, Matthew Reed. *Education:* Harvard University, A.B., 1951, M.B.A., 1953, D.B.A., 1957, M.Arch., 1974. *Politics:* Democrat. *Religion:* Unitarian Universalist. *Home:* 87 Lincoln Rd., Wayland, Mass. 01778.

CAREER: Harvard University, Cambridge, Mass., Graduate School of Business Administration, instructor, 1956-57, assistant professor, 1957-63, associate professor of business administration, 1963-70, administrative director, master of business administration program, 1968-70; director, Development Sciences, Inc., 1970—. Trustee, Williston Academy, 1966; vice-president, Peter McLaughlin Associates, 1974—. Lecturer, Graduate School of Design, Harvard University, 1974—. *Military service:* U.S. Army Air Forces, 1945-47.

WRITINGS: (With R. R. Lawrence) *Organizational Behavior and Administration,* Irwin, 1965; *Systems Analysis in Organizational Behavior,* Irwin, 1967; (contributor) *The Changing College Classroom,* Jossey-Bass, 1969; (with J. McKenney and W. MacFarlan) *The Management Game-Simulated Decision Making,* Macmillan, 1970. Contributor to professional journals, including *Harvard Business Review* and *Behavioral Science.*

WORK IN PROGRESS: Co-editing *International Encyclopedia of Architecture, Engineering and Urban Planning,* for Garland Press.

* * *

SELORMEY, Francis 1927-

PERSONAL: Born April 15, 1927, in Dzelukofe, Ghana; son of Felix Nani (a teacher) and Patience (Kulewoshie) Selormey; married Cordelia Amegayibor (a teacher), April 25, 1953; children: Cyrilla Mabel, Gertrude Felicia, Caspar Felix, Melchior Christian, Frances Kathleen, Gilbert Kofi, Kwesi. *Education:* St. Augustine's Training College, Cape

Coast, Ghana, Teachers' Certificate A, 1946; Achimota College, Physical Education Certificate, 1951; College of Technology, Kumasi, Physical Education Certificate, 1954. *Religion:* Roman Catholic. *Residence:* Accra, Ghana.

CAREER: Primary and middle school teacher in Ghana schools, 1947-50, 1951-53; Teacher Training College, Hohoe, Ghana, tutor in physical education and health science, 1955-60; Central Organisation of Sport, Ho, Cape Coast, Ghana, senior regional sports organizer, 1961-65; Ghana Film Industry Corp., Accra, script writer, 1965-68; director of sports for Ghana, 1968-72; Loyalty Group of Companies (textile firm), Accra, deputy managing director, 1972—. Quiz master on weekly program, "Treble Chance," for Ghana Television, 1966—.

WRITINGS: The Narrow Path, Praeger, 1966. Author of short stories and news commentaries for Ghana Broadcasting.

WORK IN PROGRESS: The Path Widens, a sequel to his first book (the story of an African childhood); *The Wickedness of God,* with the theme that God is wicked to have allowed man to fall into sin and to suffer; a collection of free verse, tentatively entitled *The Voice of a Ghanaian.*

SIDELIGHTS: Selormey told *CA:* "Books should be written perpetuating the good in the past, for use in the future, to contrast the deteriorating state of the present.... The carefree attitude of parents towards the growth of children today, particularly in Ghana, led me to write *The Narrow Path.*"

* * *

SEMMLER, Clement (William) 1914-

PERSONAL: Born December 23, 1914, in Mercunda, South Australia; son of John Frederick and Marie (Kleinig) Semmler; married Catherine Wilson, December 20, 1974; children: (former marriage) Jacqueline, Peter. *Education:* University of Adelaide, B.A., 1936, M.A., 1938. *Home:* 11/10 Elgin St., Woolwich, Sydney, New South Wales 2110, Australia. *Office:* Australian Broadcasting Commission, 145 Elizabeth St., Sydney, New South Wales 2000, Australia.

CAREER: Australian Broadcasting Commission, Sydney, New South Wales, supervisor of youth education for South Australia, 1942-46, assistant director of variety, 1947-48, assistant controller of programs, 1948-60, assistant general manager for programs, 1960-64, deputy general manager, 1965—. Member of Library Council of New South Wales, and Advisory Committee on the Humanities, National Library of Australia Council; member of advisory committee, Flinders University of South Australia Drama Centre; chairman of advisory committee, Board of Advanced Education, and of education committee, Alexander Mackie College of Advanced Education. *Member:* University Club (Sydney). *Awards, honors:* D.Litt., University of New England, 1968; Officer, Order of the British Empire, 1970, for services to Australian literature.

WRITINGS: For the Uncanny Man: Essays on James Joyce and Others, F. W. Cheshire, 1963; (editor with Derek Whitelock) *Literary Australia,* F. W. Cheshire, 1965; *Barcroft Boake—Poet of the Stockwhip,* Oxford University Press, 1965; *A. B. "Banjo" Paterson,* Oxford University Press, 1965; (editor and author of introduction) *Stories of the Riverina,* Angus & Robertson, 1965; *Kenneth Slessor,* Longmans, Green and British Council, 1966; (editor) *Coast to Coast, 1965-1966* (Australian short stories),

Angus & Robertson, 1966; *The Banjo of the Bush*, Lansdowne Press, 1966; (editor and author of introduction) *Twentieth Century Australian Literary Criticism*, Oxford University Press, 1967; *A. B. Paterson—Great Australian*, Oxford University Press, 1967; (editor with A. B. Paterson and author of introduction) *The World of Banjo Paterson*, Angus & Robertson, 1967; *The Art of Brian James and Other Essays on Australian Literature*, University of Queensland Press, 1972; *Douglas Stewart*, Twayne, 1974; (contributor) G. Dutton, editor, *Australian Literature*, Penguin, 1976. Contributor to literary journals. Literary reviewer, *Sydney Morning Herald;* editorial consultant, *Poetry Australia*.

WORK IN PROGRESS: History of Australian Broadcasting, completion expected in 1977.

AVOCATIONAL INTERESTS: Jazz music (regarded as Australian authority on jazz), golf, gardening.

* * *

SETON-WATSON, Christopher 1918-

PERSONAL: Born August 6, 1918, in London, England; son of Robert William (a professor) and Marion (Stack) Seton-Watson. *Education:* Attended New College, Oxford, 1937-39. *Home and office:* Oriel College, Oxford, England.

CAREER: Oxford University, Oxford, England, fellow of Oriel College, 1946—, lecturer in politics, 1950—. Chairman of United Kingdom council, World University Service, 1964—. *Military service:* British Army, Royal Horse Artillery, 1939-45; became major; received Military Cross, 1941, and bar, 1945.

WRITINGS: Italy from Liberalism to Fascism, 1870-1925, Methuen, 1967, Barnes & Noble, 1968; (contributor) S. J. Woolf, editor, *European Fascism*, Weidenfeld & Nicolson, 1968.

WORK IN PROGRESS: The Making of the New Europe, 1906-1920, with Hugh Seton-Watson; research in twentieth-century European history and international relations, with special reference to Italy.

SIDELIGHTS: A reviewer of *Italy from Liberalism to Fascism* in the *Observer Review* calls the book "impressive in the sanity of its judgments and the clarity of its narrative." Denis Mack Smith says that Seton-Watson "has written a thorough and even meticulous political history with plentiful footnotes and a useful bibliography. . . . Not even in Italian does there exist a comparable survey which covers the years 1870-1925 in such detail."

BIOGRAPHICAL/CRITICAL SOURCES: Observer Review, December 10, 1967; *New York Review of Books*, October 24, 1968.

* * *

SEVERIN, (Giles) Timothy 1940-

PERSONAL: Born September 25, 1940, in Jorhat, Assam, India; son of Maurice Rimington Watkins (a tea planter) and Inge Severin; married Dorothy Sherman (a lecturer in Spanish, Westfield College, London), March 24, 1966; children: Ida. *Education:* Oxford University, B.A., 1962, M.A. and B.Litt., 1968. *Home:* 16 Thanet St., London, WC1, England. *Agent:* Julian Bach, Jr., 3 East 48th St., New York, N.Y. 10017.

CAREER: Writer on the history of travel and exploration. In 1961 led the Oxford Marco Polo route project, to trace Polo's route as far as the border of China. *Member:* Royal Geographical Society, Hakluyt Society.

WRITINGS: Tracking Marco Polo, Routledge & Kegan Paul, 1964; *Explorers of the Mississippi*, Routledge & Kegan Paul, 1967, Knopf, 1968; *The Golden Antilles*, Knopf, 1970; *The African Adventure*, Dutton, 1973; *The Horizon Book of Vanishing Primitive Man*, American Heritage Press, 1973 (published in England as *Vanishing Primitive Man*, Thames & Hudson, 1973); *The Oriental Adventure*, Little, Brown, 1976. Contributor to *Geographical Magazine, American Heritage*, and *Horizon*.

WORK IN PROGRESS: An account of the Brendan Voyage during which Severin will follow the path of medieval Irish monks across the North Atlantic in a 36-foot leather boat (curragh).

SIDELIGHTS: Eugene D. Schmiel comments on *The Golden Antilles:* "Using internal and external criticism to separate fact from fancy, Severin has . . . written a factual account of voyages to and lives in the Antilles. Pretension, bombast, personal glorification, and outright lying have been pruned, accurate historical reporting (and a colorful style) have been substituted, and the result is an extremely useful and, in some ways, important, book. It will be able to be used in the future as a fine introduction to this era."

BIOGRAPHICAL/CRITICAL SOURCES: Best Sellers, October 1, 1970.

* * *

SEWARD, John Neil 1924-
(Jack Seward)

PERSONAL: Born October 11, 1924, in Houston, Tex.; son of John Neil and LaNelle (Denny) Seward; married Jean Aiko Morimoto, January 14, 1963; children: John Neil III, William Kenneth. *Education:* University of Oklahoma, student, 1941-43; University of Michigan, A.B., 1945; University of Hawaii, graduate study, 1950-51. *Religion:* Protestant. *Home:* Route One, Celeste, Tex. 75423.

CAREER: U.S. Civil Censorship Detachment, Osaka, Japan, censor, 1947-49; Pan-Pacific Trading Co., Tokyo, Japan, branch manager, 1950; U.S. Central Intelligence Agency, stationed in Far East, 1951-56; Yashica Camera Co., Tokyo, export sales manager, 1957-60; Sunbeam Corp., Tokyo, Far East representative, 1960-66; full-time writer, 1966-70; Far East representative, Scholastic Magazines, Inc., 1970-72; University of Texas at Dallas, professor of Japanese, 1973-75; director of international operations, Ecology and Environment, Inc., 1975—. *Military service:* U.S. Army, 1943-47; became second lieutenant.

WRITINGS—Under name Jack Seward: *Cave of the Chinese Skeletons*, Tuttle, 1964; *Japan Guide*, American-Oriental Associates (Hong Kong), 1964; *Hara-Kiri: Japanese Ritual Suicide*, Tuttle, 1967; *Japanese in Action*, Weatherhill, 1968; *The Frogman Assassination*, Tower, 1968; *The Eurasian Virgins*, Tower, 1968; *Assignment: Find Cherry*, Tower, 1969; *The Chinese Pleasure Girl*, Tower, 1969.

The Diplomat, Lotus Press, 1971; *The Japanese*, Morrow, 1972; *More About the Japanese*, Lotus Press, 1972; *The Darned Nuisances*, Lotus Press, 1972; *Tekisasu no Koinobori* (in Japanese), Shin-Takeuchi Shoten, 1974.

WORK IN PROGRESS: Three books, *The Americans and Their Japan Experience, Rape of Maiden, Slaughter of Priest*, and *A Ray of Truth*.

* * *

SEWELL, J. Leslie 1923-

PERSONAL: Born November 1, 1923, in Gretna, Scotland. *Education:* Educated in England. *Home:* 27 Linden Mansions, Hornsey Lane, Highgate, London, England.

CAREER: Young & Rubicam (advertising), London, England, marketing executive, 1957-59; Radar Pubblicita (advertising), Milan, Italy, marketing manager, 1959-61; marketing consultant, London, England, 1962—. Course director, College of the Institute of Marketing; lecturer in marketing, market research and advertising. *Member:* Marketing Society.

WRITINGS: Marketing and Market Assessment, Routledge & Kegan Paul, 1966. Contributor to *Business, Direttore Commerciale, Commentary,* and *Asset Journal.*

WORK IN PROGRESS: A book on the use of consultants by business firms; a guide to the operation of small businesses.

AVOCATIONAL INTERESTS: Chess.

*   *   *

SEWELL, W. R. Derrick   1931-

PERSONAL: Born February 9, 1931, in Rock Ferry, England; son of Wilfred (a company director) and Winifred (Bott) Sewell; married Elizabeth F. Kilgour, May 13, 1961; children: Kirsty, Wendy Anne, Robert. *Education:* University of London, B.Sc. (honors in economics), 1954; University of Washington, Seattle, M.A., 1956, Ph.D., 1964; Ecole Normale de Chartres, summer study, 1950-53. *Home:* 3926 Woodhaven Ter., Victoria, British Columbia, Canada. *Office:* University of Victoria, Victoria, British Columbia, Canada.

CAREER: British Columbia Bureau of Economics and Statistics, Victoria, research assistant, 1956-57; Canada Department of Northern Affairs and National Resources, Water Resource Branch, Vancouver, British Columbia, economist, 1957-63; University of Chicago, Chicago, Ill., assistant professor of economics and geography, 1964-66; University of Victoria, Victoria, British Columbia, associate professor, 1966-68, professor of geography and economics, 1969—. Honorary sessional lecturer on resource economics, University of British Columbia, 1961-62; visiting professor at Utah State University, summer, 1965, University of North Carolina, spring, 1968, University of Hawaii, spring, 1971, and University of Edinburgh, spring, 1972, spring, 1973. Consultant to United Nations, U.S. Special Commission on Weather Modification, Association of American Geographers, and governmental agencies in United States and Canada; organizer of conferences and symposia on environmental control and resources in both countries.

MEMBER: Association of American Geographers, Canadian Association of Geographers, Institute of Public Administration of Canada, Canadian Economics Association, Regional Science Association, Institute of British Geographers, Western Regional Science Association. *Awards, honors:* Research grants from National Science Foundation and Resources for the Future, 1965, Canadian Department of Environmental Research, 1967-75, and Canadian Council, 1968, 1973, 1975.

WRITINGS: Water Management and Floods in the Fraser River Basin, Department of Geography, University of Chicago, 1965; (editor and contributor) *Human Dimensions of Weather Modification,* Department of Geography, University of Chicago, 1966; (editor and contributor) *The Human Use of Atmospheric Resources,* National Science Foundation, 1968; (co-editor and contributor) *Forecasting*

the Demands for Water, Queen's Printer, 1969; (co-author) *Water Resources Research in Canada: Social Science Needs and Priorities,* Queen's Printer, 1969; (co-author) *Recreational Fishing Evaluation,* Queen's Printer, 1970; (co-editor and contributor) *The Geographer and Society,* Department of Geography, University of Victoria, 1970; (co-editor and contributor) *Resources, Recreation, and Research,* Department of Geography, University of Victoria, 1970; (co-editor and contributor) *Perceptions and Attitudes in Resources Management,* Information Canada, 1971; (editor and contributor) *Modifying the Weather: A Social Assessment,* Department of Geography, University of Victoria, 1973; (editor and contributor) *Environmental Quality,* Sage Publications, 1974.

Contributor: J. G. Jensen, editor, *Spatial Organization of Land Uses,* Oregon State University Press, 1964; Robert M. Brown, editor, *Man Versus Environment,* National Sanitation Foundation, 1966; R. Flaegle, editor, *Weather Modification: Science and Public Policy,* University of Washington Press, 1968; George S. Thompkins, editor, *Geographical Perspectives,* Tantalus Press, 1968; R. J. Chorley, editor, *Water, Earth and Man,* Methuen, 1969; Maynard M. Bufschmidt, editor, *Regional Planning: Challenge and Prospects,* Praeger, 1969; W. J. Maunder and H. D. Foster, editors, *Pollution,* University of Victoria Press, 1969; F. M. Leversedge, editor, *Priorities in Water Management,* Department of Geography, University of Victoria, 1973; J. T. Coppock and C. B. Wilson, editors, *Environmental Quality,* Scottish Academic Press, 1974; Ian Appleton, editor, *Leisure Research and Policy,* Scottish Academic Press, 1974.

Contributor to *Annals,* Association of American Geographers, 1960, 1964, and to proceedings; contributor of articles and reviews to geography, conservation, economics, and business journals. Member of editorial board, American Geophysical Union, 1969—, *Environment and Behaviour,* 1969—, and *Natural Resources Journal,* 1972—.

*   *   *

SEYMOUR, Stephan A(ndrew)   1920-

PERSONAL: Born October 4, 1920, in New York, N.Y.; children: Diana (Mrs. Mort Hedson), Stephanie, Ronald. *Education:* Franklin and Marshall College, B.S., 1941; California College of Medicine, M.D., 1947. *Home:* 6844 Sepulveda, Van Nuys, Calif. *Agent:* Bertha Klausner, International Literary Agency, 71 Park Ave., New York, N.Y. 10016.

CAREER: Seymour Hospital, Long Beach, Calif., director, 1952-60; Seymour Hospital, Los Angeles, Calif., director, 1960-64; physician with Ross-Loos Medical Group, Los Angeles, Calif., 1964—. Former member of U.S. Olympic team, and holder of American javelin record three years; holder of marathon indoor run championship (238 miles), 1965, and other marathon running and swimming titles. Lecturer on radio and television. President of Magnolia Little Theatre. *Military service:* U.S. Army, Medical Corps. *Member:* American Medical Association, California Medical Association, Los Angeles Athletic Club, Beverly Hills Club. *Awards, honors:* Helms awards as most inspirational U.S. athlete, 1956, and for contribution to sports.

WRITINGS: How to Improve Your Thinking and Solve Your Problems, Fell, 1965. Contributor to magazines and newspapers.

WORK IN PROGRESS: A dictionary on communication.††

SHAO, Stephen P(inyee) 1924-

PERSONAL: Born January 24, 1924, in I-hsing, Kiangsu, China; came to United States in 1948, naturalized in 1956; son of Chu Tang (an educator) and Shawyuen (Wang) Shao; married Betty Lucille Outen, June 18, 1953 (deceased); married Priscilla Griffin, September 1, 1969; children: (first marriage) Stephen Pinyee, Jr., Dale Hilton, Lawrence Peter, Alan Terence; (second marriage) Patricia Sue, Christian Lynn, Aron Eastwood. Education: National Hunan University of China, B.B.A., 1946; Baylor University, M.A., 1949; University of Texas, Ph.D., 1956. Religion: Baptist. Home: 5161 Lake Shore Rd., Virginia Beach, Va. 23455. Office: Old Dominion University, Hampton Blvd., Norfolk, Va. 23508.

CAREER: Board for Texas State Hospitals and Special Schools, Austin, chief accountant, 1952-54; Bluefield College, Bluefield, Va., head of department of business administration, 1954-56; Old Dominion University, Norfolk, Va., assistant professor, 1956-57, associate professor, 1957-58, professor of management and statistics, 1958-70, professor of quantitative sciences and chairman of business and economics department, 1971—. Lecturer at a group of universities in Taiwan and Hong Kong, summer, 1961. Senior statistics consultant, Norfolk Naval Supply Center, 1962-68. Member: American Statistical Association, American Economic Association, American Accounting Association, American Institute for Decision Sciences, Southern Management Association, Alpha Kappa Psi.

WRITINGS: Mathematics of Finance, South-Western, 1962, 2nd edition published as Mathematics for Management and Finance, with Basic and Modern Algebra, 1969, 3rd edition, 1976; Statistics for Business and Economics, C. E. Merrill, 1967, 3rd edition, 1976; Workbook for Statistics, C. E. Merrill, 1973; Mathematics and Quantitative Methods for Business and Economics, South-Western, 1976.

WORK IN PROGRESS: Basic Statistics for Business and Economics.

AVOCATIONAL INTERESTS: Swimming, fishing, tennis.

*   *   *

SHARP, Dorothea Elizabeth

PERSONAL: Born in London, England. Education: University of Toronto, B.A. and M.A.; Oxford University, D.Phil. Address: c/o Westminster Bank, 214 Holborn, London W.C. 1, England.

CAREER: Taught at Oxford University, Oxford, England; formerly senior lecturer in philosophy and history of political ideas at University of London, London, England; currently writer. Member: Society of Authors.

WRITINGS: Franciscan Philosophy at Oxford in the Thirteenth Century, Oxford University Press, 1930, Russell, 1964. Contributor to Revue Neoscolastique, Archives d'Histoire Doctrinele du Moyen Age, and New Scholasticism.

WORK IN PROGRESS: Marsilius of Padua.

*   *   *

SHARP, Margery 1905-

PERSONAL: Born 1905; daughter of J. H. Sharp; married Geoffrey L. Castle (a major in the Royal Army), 1938. Education: Bedford College, London, B.A. (French hon-

ours). Address: c/o The Westminster Bank Ltd., St. James Square, London S.W. 1, England. Agent: Blanche C. Gregory, Inc., 2 Tudor City Place, New York, N.Y. 10017.

CAREER: Worked for the Armed Forces Education Program during World War II. Full-time professional writer.

WRITINGS—All published by Little, Brown, except as noted: Rhododendron Pie, Appleton, 1930; Fanfare for Tin Trumpets, Barker, 1932, Putnam, 1933; The Nymph and the Nobleman, Barker, 1932; Flowering Thorn, Putnam, 1934; Sophie Cassmajor, Putnam, 1934; Four Gardens, Putnam, 1935; The Nutmeg Tree, 1937; Harlequin House, 1939; Stone of Chastity, 1940; Three Companion Pieces (contains The Nymph and the Nobleman, Sophie Cassmajor, and The Tigress on the Hearth), 1941; Lady in Waiting (play based on The Nutmeg Tree), Samuel French, 1941; Cluny Brown, 1944; Britannia Mews, 1946; Foolish Gentlewoman, 1948.

Lise Lillywhite, 1951; The Gipsy in the Parlour, 1954; The Tigress on the Hearth, Collins, 1955; Eye of Love, 1957; Rescuers, 1959; Melisande, 1960; Something Light, Collins, 1960, 1961; Martha in Paris, Collins, 1962, 1963; Martha, Eric and George, 1964; Lost at the Fair, 1965; The Sun in Scorpio, 1965; In Pious Memory, 1967; Rosa, 1970; The Innocents, 1972; The Lost Chapel Picnic (short stories), 1973; The Faithful Servants, 1975.

Juveniles: Miss Bianca, 1962; The Turret, 1963; Miss Bianca in the Salt Mines, 1966; Miss Bianca in the Orient, 1970; Miss Bianca in the Antarctic, 1971; Miss Bianca and the Bridesmaid, 1972.

Plays: "Meeting at Night," 1934; "The Foolish Gentlewoman," 1949; "The Birdcage Room" for television, 1954.

Contributor to Encyclopaedia Britannica; frequent contributor to magazines in England and United States including Woman's Home Companion, Harper's Bazaar, Saturday Evening Post, Strand, Fiction Parade, Punch, and Collier's.

SIDELIGHTS: Miss Sharp is known for her dry humor and ease at farcical writing. Her heroines are usually wonderfully zany—the most successful being Julia Packett, an endearing lady of easy virtue, in The Nutmeg Tree, and Cluny Brown, a parlor maid with an affinity for plumbing. In Pious Memory, concerns a sweet-natured English lady who begins to suspect that the husband she has recently buried might have been the wrong man. Although the New Yorker felt that it all ended as "something complicated and clever that does not quite come off," Martin Levin found the novel one of her "most effervescent. . . . There is hardly a wasted word in this astringent little farce." The Christian Science Monitor reviewer wrote: "Miss Sharp's wit . . . usually manages to keep this bubble of an entertainment from drifting over the edge into black humor."

Cluny Brown was made into a motion picture by Twentieth Century-Fox, 1946; The Nutmeg Tree was filmed under the title, "Julia Misbehaves" by M-G-M, 1948; Britannia Mews was filmed under the title "The Forbidden Street" by Twentieth Century-Fox, 1949; the 1962 Columbia film "The Notorious Landlady" was based on her short story "The Tenant."

AVOCATIONAL INTERESTS: Gardening and painting.

BIOGRAPHICAL/CRITICAL SOURCES: New York Times Book Review, April, 1967; Christian Science Monitor, May 4, 1967; New Yorker, June 22, 1967; National Review, June 27, 1967.

SHAULL, (Millard) Richard 1919-

PERSONAL: Born November 24, 1919, in Felton, Pa.; son of Millard (a welfare worker) and Anna (Brenneman) Shaull; married Mildred Miller (a teacher), May 17, 1941; children: Madelyn, Wendy. *Education:* Elizabethtown College, B.A., 1938; Princeton Theological Seminary, Th.B., 1941, Th.D., 1959. *Politics:* Democrat. *Home:* 17 Alexander St., Princeton, N.J. 08540. *Office:* Princeton Theological Seminary, Princeton, N.J. 08540.

CAREER: Presbyterian missionary in Colombia, South America, 1942-50; Campinas Theological Seminary, Campinas, Brazil, professor of church history, 1952-59; Mackenzie Institute, Sao Paulo, Brazil, vice-president, 1960-62; Princeton Theological Seminary, Princeton, N.J., professor of ecumenics, 1962—. Brazilian Student Christian Movement, general secretary, 1956-58, and participant in World Student Christian Federation programs and consultations in Japan, Korea, India, Germany, France, and throughout Latin America. Chairman of board of directors, North American Congress on Latin America, 1966—; chairman, World Student Christian Federation, 1968-73. *Awards, honors:* Guggenheim fellowship for study of Latin American political ideologies, 1965.

WRITINGS: Encounter with Revolution, Association Press, 1955; (with Carl Oglesby) *Containment and Change,* Macmillan, 1967; *Befreiung durch veraenderung,* Kaiser, 1970.

WORK IN PROGRESS: A theological and historical study of modern social revolutions, for John Knox.

* * *

SHAW, Alan George Lewers 1916-

PERSONAL: Born February 3, 1916, in Melbourne, Victoria, Australia; son of George (a solicitor) and Ethel (Lewers) Shaw; married Peggy Perrins, May 21, 1956. *Education:* University of Melbourne, B.A. (honors), 1938; Oxford University, B.A., 1940, M.A., 1944. *Home:* 197 Domain Rd., South Yarra, Victoria, Australia. *Office:* Monash University, Clayton, Victoria, Australia.

CAREER: Wartime posts with Australian Department of Information, 1940-41, Department of the Army, 1941-42, and Department of Rural Reconstruction, 1943-44; University of Melbourne, Melbourne, Victoria, Australia, lecturer in history, 1941-50, dean of Trinity College, 1946-50; University of Sydney, Sydney, New South Wales, Australia, senior lecturer in history, 1952-64, subwarden of St. Paul's College, 1953-56; Monash University, Melbourne, Victoria, Australia, professor of history, 1964—.

MEMBER: Australian Academy of the Humanities (fellow), Australian Academy of the Social Sciences (fellow), Royal Australian Historical Society (councillor, 1954-64), Australian Institute of International Affairs (councillor, 1946-50), New South Wales History Teachers Association (president, 1959; councillor, 1959-63), Royal Historical Society of Victoria (councillor, 1965—). *Awards, honors:* Co-recipient of Harbison-Higinbotham Prize, University of Melbourne, 1945, for *The Australian Coal Industry;* Nuffield traveling scholarship, 1950-51; Smuts visiting fellow at Cambridge University, 1967.

WRITINGS: (With G. R. Bruns) *The Australian Coal Industry,* Melbourne University Press, 1944; *Economic Development of Australia,* Longmans, Green, 1944, 4th revised edition, 1966; *The Story of Australia,* Faber, 1955, 4th revised edition, 1973; *Modern World History,* F. W.

Cheshire, 1959; *Convicts and the Colonies,* Faber, 1966, new edition, 1971; (editor) *Great Britain and the Colonies,* Methuen, 1970; (editor) John West, *History of Tasmania,* Angus & Robertson, 1972. Contributor to journals in Australia. Editor, *Journal of Royal Australian Historical Society,* 1956-64.

AVOCATIONAL INTERESTS: Golf, bridge.

* * *

SHAW, Charles R. 1921-

PERSONAL: Born February 28, 1921, in Indianapolis, Ind.; son of Thomas O. (a merchant) and Hilda (Rodenbeck) Shaw; married Margery Schlamp, May 31, 1942 (divorced); children: Barbara Rae. *Education:* Attended Hanover College, 1938-41; New York University, M.D., 1946. *Office:* M. D. Anderson Hospital, University of Texas, Houston, Tex.

CAREER: Certified psychiatrist. Hawthorn Center, Northville, Mich., staff psychiatrist, 1956-67; University of Texas, M. D. Anderson Hospital, Houston, 1967—, began as associate professor, currently professor of biology. *Military service:* U.S. Army, 1943-45. U.S. Air Force, 1951-53; became captain. *Member:* American Psychiatric Association, Genetics Society of America, American Society of Human Genetics.

WRITINGS: The Psychiatric Disorders of Childhood, Appleton, 1966, 2nd edition, 1971; *When Your Child Needs Help,* Morrow, 1972; *When You Need Help with Cancer,* Morrow, 1974. Editor, *Biochemical Genetics.*

WORK IN PROGRESS: An autobiographical novel, *Cancer Breakthrough.*

SIDELIGHTS: Shaw told *CA:* "Writing is strictly a sideline as I'm busy and active in cancer research. Moved into this field about 1962, a defector from psychiatry. My novel is a personal account of a successful effort in cancer research, with emphasis on personalities and the effects of success and failure in research." *Avocational interests:* Flying airplanes.

* * *

SHAW, Edward P(ease) 1911-

PERSONAL: Born December 18, 1911, in Lowell, Mass.; son of Paul Hervey (an industrial engineer) and Ruth (Pease) Shaw; married Eleanor Snell, December 26, 1936; children: Dana Paul, Susan Barbara. *Education:* Harvard University, A.B. (magna cum laude), 1933, A.M., 1934, Ph.D., 1937. *Home:* 9 Country Club Cir., Kennebunk, Me. 04043.

CAREER: University of Illinois, Urbana, instructor in French, 1938-42; Miami University, Oxford, Ohio, associate professor of Romance languages, 1946-47; State University of New York at Albany, professor of French language and literature, 1947-73, professor emeritus, 1973—, chairman of Division of Humanities, 1965-68. *Military service:* U.S. Army Air Forces, 1942-46; became major; received Bronze Star and Army Commendation Medal.

MEMBER: Modern Language Association of America, American Association of Teachers of French, American Association of University Professors, Federation of Modern Language Teachers of New York. *Awards, honors:* Sheldon traveling fellow, Harvard University, 1937-38; State University of New York Research Foundation grants, 1955-56, 1961; Danforth Foundation grant, 1962; Palmes Academiques, chevalier, 1962, officier, 1973.

WRITINGS: Jacques Cazotte (1719-1792), Harvard University Press, 1942; (editor with C. W. Colman) Maurois, *La Machine a lire les pensees* (college edition), Crowell, 1944; *The Case of the Abbe de Moncrif*, Bookman Associates, 1953; (with D. L. Demorest) *French Civilization through Fiction*, Ginn, 1956; *Francois-Augustin Paradis de Moncrif (1687-1770)*, Bookman Associates, 1958; (with J. T. Fotos) *Dix Contes*, Macmillan, 1961; *Problems and Policies of Malesherbes as "Directeur de la Librairie" in France (1750-1763)*, Antioch Press, for Research Foundation of State University of New York, 1966; (with A. Rogers) *Selected Literary References in the Manuscript Journal (1750-1969) of Joseph D'Hemery*, State University of New York Press, 1972. Contributor to language journals.

* * *

SHAW, John Bennett 1913-

PERSONAL: Born October 10, 1913, in Tulsa, Okla.; son of Earl A. (a businessman) and Helen (Bennett) Shaw; married Margaret Fitzgerald, June 9, 1938 (died, 1969); married Dorothy Rowe; children: Margaret Helen (Mrs. John Bricke), Patrick Bennett, Catherine Mary, Mary Elizabeth, Barbara Louise. *Education:* University of Notre Dame, A.B. (cum laude), 1937; Columbia University, graduate work, 1937-38; University of Tulsa, M.A. in literature, 1940. *Politics:* Democrat. *Religion:* Roman Catholic. *Home:* 1917 Fort Union Dr., Santa Fe, N.M. 87501.

CAREER: Bennett Drilling Co., Tulsa, Okla., secretary-manager, 1938-59; University of Tulsa, Tulsa, instructor in literature, 1939-40; Tulsa Book and Record Shop, Tulsa, owner-manager, 1942-54; Fitzgerald Funeral Service, Tulsa, funeral director, 1956-70; Catholic Center, Tulsa, director (lay), 1966-70; lecturer on Sherlock Holmes throughout the United States and abroad. Twice chairman, Friends of the Tulsa Public Library, 1957-70; administrative chairman, Tulsa City County Library System, 1961-67; chairman of Oklahoma Council on Libraries, 1964-66, University of Notre Dame Library Council, 1964-70, and Oklahoma State Department of Libraries, 1966-70; board member, St. John's Hospital School of Nursing, 1962-70. Has worked with National Board of Christian Family Movement and Young Christian Students. *Member:* Baker Street Irregulars, American Library Trustees Association (secretary, 1968), Southwestern Library Association (second vice-president), Oklahoma Library Association (chairman, trustee division), Equestrian Order of Holy Sepulchre of Jerusalem (knight commander). *Awards, honors:* Citizen's Recognition Award, Oklahoma Library Association, 1965; Citation of Merit, American Library Association, 1968.

WRITINGS: (Editor) *The Whole Art of Detection*, Black Cat Press, 1968; (contributor) *Baker Street and Beyond*, Bobbs-Merrill, 1976. Has written several privately printed pamphlets of "Sherlockian interest" and contributes to *Baker Street Journal* and *Sherlock Holmes Journal* (London).

WORK IN PROGRESS: Several articles, booklets, and quizzes concerning Sherlock Holmes, especially treatment of death in the canon.

SIDELIGHTS: Shaw's personal library totals 20,000 volumes which are gradually being placed in university libraries. Shaw told *CA* that his personal collection of Sherlock Holmes alone numbers about eight thousand items and is considered the "largest Holmes collection in [the] world." A member of the Baker Street Irregulars, he believes that Sir Arthur Conan Doyle was but an agent, and that the stories were actually written by Dr. John H. Watson. Shaw was invited into the society because of his exhaustive bibliography of Sherlock Holmes material.

BIOGRAPHICAL/CRITICAL SOURCES: Tulsalite, May 16, 1966.

* * *

SHAW, Marvin E(vert) 1919-

PERSONAL: Born August 15, 1919, in Bellefont, Ark.; son of Carl Easer (a farmer) and Eula (Brown) Shaw; married Lilly May Street (a school administrator), June 9, 1947; children: Michael David. *Education:* Arkansas College, Batesville, A.B., 1947; University of Arkansas, M.A., 1949; University of Wisconsin, Ph.D., 1953. *Politics:* Democrat. *Home:* 2815 Northwest 28th Pl., Gainesville, Fla. 32605. *Office:* Department of Psychology, University of Florida, Gainesville, Fla. 32601.

CAREER: Johns Hopkins University, Baltimore, Md., research associate, 1953-55, assistant professor of psychology, 1955-56; Massachusetts Institute of Technology, Cambridge, associate professor of psychology, 1956-59; University of Florida, Gainesville, associate professor, 1959-62, professor of psychology, 1962—. Consultant to Towle Silversmiths, 1957-59, Dewy and Almy Chemical Co., 1957-58, and Nestle Co., 1958-59. *Military service:* U.S. Army Air Forces, 1942-45; became first lieutenant; received Air Medal with three oak-leaf clusters and Distinguished Flying Cross. *Member:* American Psychological Association (fellow; chairman of Division 8 membership committee, 1963-66), Psychonomic Society, Society of Experimental Social Psychology, Eastern Psychological Association, Sigma Xi, Gainesville Torch Club.

WRITINGS: (Contributor) D. Wilner, editor, *Decisions, Values, and Groups*, Pergamon, 1960; (contributor) L. Berkowitz, editor, *Advances in Experimental Social Psychology*, Academic Press, 1964; (contributor) J. Sikowski, editor, *Experimental Methods and Instrumentation in Psychology*, McGraw, 1966; (with J. M. Wright) *Scales for the Measurement of Attitudes*, McGraw, 1967; (with Philip Costanzo) *Theories of Social Psychology*, McGraw, 1970; *Group Dynamics: The Psychology of Small Group Behavior*, McGraw, 1971. Contributor to a dozen professional journals. Consulting editor, *Journal of Personality and Social Psychology*, *Journal of Personality*, and *Memory and Cognition*.

WORK IN PROGRESS: A revision of *Group Dynamics*.

* * *

SHEA, John S. 1933-

PERSONAL: Born July 18, 1933, in New York, N.Y.; son of John S. and Marie (Russell) Shea; married Marion Smith, June 23, 1962; children: Stuart, John, Thomas. *Education:* Iona College, A.B., 1954; Marquette University, A.M., 1956; University of Minnesota, Ph.D., 1967. *Politics:* Independent liberal. *Religion:* Roman Catholic. *Home:* 2106 Noyes St., Evanston, Ill. 60201. *Office:* Department of English, Loyola University of Chicago, Chicago, Ill. 60626.

CAREER: University of Minnesota, Minneapolis, instructor in English, 1958-64; Washington University, St. Louis, Mo., instructor, 1964-67, assistant professor of English, 1967-69; Loyola University of Chicago, Chicago, Ill., assistant professor, 1969-72, associate professor of English, 1972—, assistant chairman of department, 1973—. Reader,

College Entrance Examination Board, 1965-74. *Military service:* U.S. Army, 1956-58. *Member:* National Council of Teachers of English, Conference on College Composition and Communication, Greater St. Louis Council of Teachers of English (member of executive committee, 1965-68). *Awards, honors:* Danforth Foundation teacher grant, 1962-64; Mellon Foundation grant, 1975.

WRITINGS: (With M. Steinmann, R. D. McClure, and N. P. Barker) *Themes and Exercises,* 4th edition, University of Minnesota Press, 1960, 6th edition, 1962; (editor) Bernard Mandeville, *Aesop Dress'd,* Augustan Reprint Society, 1966; (editor with H. Anderson) *Studies in Criticism and Aesthetics, 1660-1800,* University of Minnesota Press, 1967. Editor, *Restoration and Eighteenth Century Theatre Research,* 1972—.

WORK IN PROGRESS: Research on Dryden and eighteenth-century English literature.

AVOCATIONAL INTERESTS: Sports, music, politics.

*   *   *

SHEEHAN, Susan

PERSONAL: Born in Vienna, Austria; married Neil Sheehan (a reporter for *New York Times*), March 30, 1965; children: Maria Gregory, Catherine Fair. *Education:* Wellesley College, B.A., 1958. *Home:* 4505 Klingle St. N.W., Washington, D.C. 20016. *Agent:* Robert Lescher, 155 East 71st St., New York, N.Y. 10021. *Office: New Yorker,* 25 West 43rd St., New York, N.Y. 10036.

CAREER: New Yorker, New York, N.Y., staff writer, 1962—. *Awards, honors:* Guggenheim fellow, 1975-76.

WRITINGS: Ten Vietnamese (collection of sketches), Knopf, 1967. Contributor of articles to magazines.

WORK IN PROGRESS: A biography of Alfred Knopf, for Houghton.

SIDELIGHTS: Mrs. Sheehan noted in her introduction to *Ten Vietnamese* that journalists tend to concentrate on Viet Nam's "leaders and would-be leaders" to the neglect of "the 95% that don't count." With her husband, she spent about a year in Viet Nam and interviewed representatives of that 95%, including a peasant, a landlord, a politician, an orphan, a Buddhist monk, a South Vietnamese soldier, a Viet Cong, and a North Vietnamese prisoner. Gavin Young was critical of Mrs. Sheehan's selection, especially of the absence of Vietnamese who objected to America's presence. Despite this, he felt it was "one of the most revealing books yet written about Viet Nam.... Susan Sheehan brings back into focus some of those brave little people for whose welfare, after all, Americans claim to be fighting."

Sheehan is competent in French, German, and Spanish.

AVOCATIONAL INTERESTS: Crime and law.

BIOGRAPHICAL/CRITICAL SOURCES: Christian Century, March 8, 1967; *Best Sellers,* March 15, 1967; *Christian Science Monitor,* March 22, 1967; *Book Week,* March 26, 1967; *New York Times Book Review,* April, 1967; *New Yorker,* April 1, 1967.

*   *   *

SHELL, Virginia Law   1923-
(Virginia W. Law)

PERSONAL: Born July 4, 1923, in Dothan, Ala.; daughter of Clinton (a state employee) and Margaret (Stokes) Wil-

liams; married Burleigh A. Law (a missionary; killed in the Congo by rebel soldiers, August 4, 1964); married Donald L. Shell, 1973; children: (first marriage) David, Paul, Margaret Ann. *Education:* Attended Asbury College; Florida State University, A.B., 1962; Scarritt College for Christian Workers, M.A., 1966. *Home:* 7902 Van Gogh Ct., Potomac, Md. 20854.

CAREER: Methodist missionary in the Congo, 1950-64, working as a teacher, using French language, at Wembo Nyama mission station while husband directed building of Lambuth Hospital, 1950-58, and assisting husband in opening new mission services (school, churches, and medical aid), in Lomela, 1958-64; director of marriage enrichment, United Methodist Board of Discipleship, 1969-75. Lecturer on the Congo; leader of retreat groups.

WRITINGS—Under name Virginia W. Law: *Appointment Congo,* Rand McNally, 1966; *As Far As I Can Step,* Word Books, 1971. Contributor to Methodist publications.

SIDELIGHTS: Virginia Shell has traveled in eighteen countries of Europe and Africa. She is competent in French and the native dialect, Otetela.

*   *   *

SHELLEY, Bruce   1927-

PERSONAL: Born December 20, 1927, in Owensboro, Ky.; son of Leroy and Mabel (Travers) Shelley; married Mary Elizabeth Harrington, August 1, 1952; children: Marshall, David, Karen. *Education:* Columbia Bible College, Columbia, S.C., B.A., 1952; Fuller Theological Seminary, M.Div., 1955; University of Iowa, Ph.D., 1957; Harvard University, postdoctoral study, 1967. *Home:* 3041 South Wolff, Denver, Colo. 80236.

CAREER: Baptist clergyman. Conservative Baptist Theological Seminary, Denver, Colo., assistant professor, 1957-59, associate professor, 1959-63, professor of church history, 1963—. *Military service:* U.S. Army, 1946-48; became sergeant. *Member:* American Society of Church History, Evangelical Theological Society, Conference on Faith and History.

WRITINGS: Conservative Baptists: A Story of 20th Century Dissent, Conservative Baptist Seminary, 1960; *By What Authority?,* Eerdmans, 1965; *Evangelicalism in America,* Eerdmans, 1967; *The Cross and Flame,* Eerdmans, 1967; *Let's Face It,* Moody, 1968; (editor) Earl S. Kalland and others, *A Call to Christian Character: Toward a Recovery of Biblical Piety,* Zondervan, 1970; *A History of Conservative Baptists,* Conservative Baptist Seminary Press, 1971. Contributor to *Encyclopedia of Southern Baptists,* 1971, *The New International Dictionary of the Christian Church,* 1974, and *Encyclopedia Americana,* 1974. Contributing editor, *United Evangelical Action.*

WORK IN PROGRESS: The History of American Evangelicalism.

*   *   *

SHENK, Wilbert R.   1935-

PERSONAL: Born January 16, 1935, in Sheridan, Ore.; son of Kenneth M. and Frances (Kilmer) Shenk; married Juanita Brenneman, October 10, 1957; children: Suzanne, Maria, Thomas. *Education:* Attended Hesston College, 1951-53; Goshen College, B.A., 1955; University of Oregon, M.A., 1963; attended University of Aberdeen, 1973-75. *Religion:* Mennonite. *Home:* 1801 Frances Ave., Elkhart, Ind. 46514.

CAREER: Mennonite Central Committee, Akron, Pa., field director in Indonesia, 1955-59, assistant director of overseas services, 1963-65; Mennonite Board of Missions, Elkhart, Ind., secretary for overseas missions, 1965—.

WRITINGS: (Editor) *A Kingdom of Priests: The Church in New Nations,* Herald Press, 1967; *The Challenge of Church Growth,* Institute of Mennonite Studies, 1973; (compiler) *Bibliography of Henry Venn's Writings,* Institute of Mennonite Studies, 1975. Occasional contributor to denominational periodicals.

SIDELIGHTS: Shenk travels frequently in the course of his work, particularly to Asia, Africa, Middle East, and Europe. He speaks, reads, and writes Indonesian fluently.

* * *

SHEPARD, Elaine (Elizabeth) 1923-

PERSONAL: Born April 2, 1923, in Olney, Ill.; daughter of Thomas J. (a sculptor) and Bernice (Shadle) Shepard; married George F. Hartman (a retired colonel, U.S. Air Force), October 1, 1943 (divorced, 1958). *Education:* Attended McKendree College, one year. *Politics:* Independent. *Religion:* Methodist. *Home:* 12 East 62nd St., New York, N.Y. 10021. *Agent:* Paul Reynolds Literary Agency, 12 East 41st St., New York, N.Y. 10017.

CAREER: Author, lecturer, reporter, actress. Only woman reporter accredited to all three of President Eisenhower's major world tours in the Middle East, Far East, and South America; accredited to President Nixon's 1972 visit to Austria, Poland, Iran, and the Soviet Union; combat correspondent in Vietnam for Mutual Broadcasting System. Has filed reports from over seventy countries and interviewed scores of heads of state, including King Faisal of Saudi Arabia, Khrushchev, Nehru, Castro, and Chou En-lai. Moderator on two television programs in Washington, D.C. *Member:* Overseas Press Club of America, American Federation of Television and Radio Artists, Screen Actors Guild, Actors' Equity Association. *Awards, honors:* Two citations from 145th Aviation Battalion for participation in night helicopter assault missions in Vietnam.

WRITINGS: Forgive Us Our Press Passes, Prentice-Hall, 1962; *The Doom Pussy,* Trident, 1967. Contributor to numerous periodicals including *McCall's, Better Homes & Gardens, Pageant,* and *Parade.*

WORK IN PROGRESS: Silent Dice, a narrative of experiences in Middle East oil countries; *Lady Sun,* the story of outstanding women of achievement in Iran; *In A Frail Canoe,* a novel incorporating experiences as the only woman reporter to have sailed with both Sixth and Seventh Fleets.

SIDELIGHTS: J. D. Kirwan, who calls *The Doom Pussy* an "outstanding book about the Vietnamese War," writes: "Miss Shepard has conveyed both the spirit of the war and the *esprit* of the warriors. . . . It is the account of a sensitive and perceptive reporter, telling not only how it is, but *why* it is. The book should be required reading for doves as well as hawks, although the former run the risk of having their preconceived pinfeathers ruffled by reality."

BIOGRAPHICAL/CRITICAL SOURCES: National Review, March 21, 1967.

* * *

SHEPARD, Paul Howe 1925-

PERSONAL: Born July 12, 1925, in Kansas City, Mo.; son of Paul Howe (a horticulturist) and Clara (Grigsby) Shepard; married Melba Wheatcroft, July 13, 1950; married second wife, June Smith (a geneticist and teacher), March 21, 1965; children: (first marriage) Kenton Howe, Margaret Elizabeth, Jane. *Education:* University of Missouri, A.B., 1949; Yale University, M.S., 1952, Ph.D., 1954. *Home:* 5241 Palmer Canyon Rd., Claremont, Calif. 91711; and Ashfield Rd., Williamsburg, Mass. 01096. *Office:* Pitzer College, Claremont, Calif. 91711.

CAREER: Field secretary, Conservation Federation of Missouri, 1949-50; Knox College, Galesburg, Ill., 1954-64, began as instructor, became associate professor of biology and director of Green Oaks; Smith College, Northampton, Mass., lecturer in zoology, 1965-70; Dartmouth College, Hanover, N.H., professor of environmental perception, 1971-73; Claremont Colleges, Claremont Graduate School and Pitzer College, Claremont, Calif., Avery Professor of Natural Philosophy and Human Ecology, 1973—. *Military service:* U.S. Army, 1943-46; served in European theater; became sergeant. *Awards, honors:* Fulbright research scholar in New Zealand, 1961; Guggenheim fellowship in writing, 1968-69.

WRITINGS: Man in the Landscape, Knopf, 1967; (editor with Daniel McKinley) *The Subversive Science: Essays Towards an Ecology of Man,* Houghton, 1969; (editor with McKinley) *Environ/mental: Essays on the Planet as a Home,* Houghton, 1971; *The Tender Carnivore and the Sacred Game,* Scribner, 1973. Regular contributor to *Landscape;* also contributor to *BioScience, Perspectives in Biology and Medicine,* and *School Science and Mathematics.*

WORK IN PROGRESS: Thinking Animals, a book about animals as an instrument of thought in the evolution of the human mind.

* * *

SHEPHERD, James L(eftwich) III 1921-

PERSONAL: Born November 20, 1921, in Houston, Tex.; son of James Leftwich, Jr. (a lawyer) and Marguerite (Street) Shepherd; married Patricia Drake, September 10, 1953 (died, 1972). *Education:* Rice Institute (now Rice University), A.B., 1943, M.A., 1947; Institut de Phonetique, University of Paris, certificat, 1948; University of Paris, Docteur (lettres), 1953. *Religion:* Presbyterian. *Home:* 209 Castle Ave., Waco, Tex. 76710. *Office:* Baylor University, Waco, Tex. 76703.

CAREER: Baylor University, Waco, Tex., instructor, 1948-50, assistant professor, 1953-57, associate professor, 1957-63, professor of French, 1963-73, professor of Italian, 1974—. *Military service:* U.S. Army, 1943-46. *Member:* American Association of Teachers of French, Modern Language Association of America, American Association of University Professors, American Association of Teachers of Italian, South Central Modern Language Association.

WRITINGS—Editor, and translator from the French: Frederic Leclerc, *Texas and Its Revolution,* Anson Jones, 1950; Eugene Maissin, *The French in Mexico and Texas (1838-1839),* Anson Jones, 1961; Frederic Gaillardet, *Sketches of Early Texas and Louisiana,* University of Texas Press, 1966. Translator of *New York to Patagonia,* by Daniel Barbey and Henri Boucher, published serially in *Realites* (English edition), 1951; contributor to professional journals. Associate editor, *South Central Bulletin,* 1960-64.

WORK IN PROGRESS: Research on the Champ d'Asile,

a Napoleonic veterans' colony near the present Liberty, Tex., with a possible translation of a French work on this subject; a translation of the sonnets of Vittorio Alfieri.

* * *

SHEPPARD, Francis Henry Wollaston 1921-

PERSONAL: Born September 10, 1921, in England; son of Leslie Alfred (deputy keeper of printed books, British Museum) and Dorothy (Ewbank) Sheppard; married Pamela Gordon Davies, 1949 (died, 1954); married Elizabeth Fleur Lees, 1957; children: one son, two daughters. *Education:* King's College, Cambridge, B.A. (honors in history), 1945; University of London, Ph.D., 1953. *Home:* 55 New St., Henley on Thames, Oxford, England. *Office:* Greater London Council, County Hall, London S.E.1, England.

CAREER: London Museum, London, England, assistant keeper, 1949-53; London County Council, London, general editor of "Survey of London," 1954—. Mayor, Henley on Thames, 1970; president, Henley Symphony Orchestra, 1973—. *Member:* Society of Antiquaries of London (fellow), Royal Historical Society (fellow). *Awards, honors:* Alice Davis Hitchcock Medallion, Society of Architectural Historians of Great Britain, 1964, for two volumes of "Survey of London."

WRITINGS: Local Government in St. Marylebone, 1688-1835, Athlone Press, 1958; *London, 1808-1870: The Internal Wen,* University of California Press, 1971. General editor, "Survey of London" series, Volumes XXVI-XXXVII, Athlone Press, 1956-1973.

WORK IN PROGRESS: Brakspear's Brewery: Henley on Thames, 1779-1979.

AVOCATIONAL INTERESTS: Music, European unity.

* * *

SHERIDAN, James E(dward) 1922-

PERSONAL: Born July 15, 1922, in Wilmington, Del.; son of Philip Lambert and Iva Alverna (Green) Sheridan; married Sonia Landy (an artist), September 27, 1947; children: Jamy. *Education:* University of Illinois, B.S., 1949, M.A., 1950; Columbia University, graduate study, 1947-48; University of California, Berkeley, Ph.D., 1961. *Residence:* Evanston, Ill. *Office:* Department of History, Northwestern University, Evanston, Ill. 60201.

CAREER: Stanford University, Stanford, Calif., lecturer in modern Chinese history, 1960; Northwestern University, Evanston, Ill., instructor, 1961-62, assistant professor, 1962-64, associate professor, 1964-68, professor of Far Eastern history, 1968—, chairman of history department, 1969-74. *Military service:* U.S. Navy, 1941-45; became ensign. *Member:* American Historical Association, Association for Asian Studies. *Awards, honors:* Fulbright fellowship to France, 1950-51; Ford Foundation fellowships, 1956-57, 1958-59, 1959-60; Social Science Research Council-American Council of Learned Societies fellowships, 1966-67, 1971-72.

WRITINGS: Chinese Warlord: The Career of Feng Yu-hsiang, Stanford University Press, 1966; *China in Disintegration: The Republican Era in Chinese History, 1912-1949,* Free Press, 1975.

SIDELIGHTS: Sheridan traveled in Taiwan, Japan, and Hong Kong, 1957-60, and again in 1966-67. He is competent in Russian, French, and Chinese.

SHERIDAN, L(ionel) A(stor) 1927-
(Lee Ang Shoy)

PERSONAL: Born July 21, 1927, in Croydon, England; son of Stanley Frederick (a businessman) and Anne (Quednau) Sheridan; married Margaret Helen Beghin, June 1, 1948; children: Peter Louis. *Education:* University of London, LL.B., 1947; Lincoln's Inn, Barrister-at-Law, 1948; Queen's University of Belfast, Ph.D., 1953. *Religion:* None. *Home:* Cherry Trees, St. Nicholas, South Glamorgan, Wales. *Office:* University College, Cardiff, Wales.

CAREER: Queen's University of Belfast, Belfast, Northern Ireland, lecturer in law, 1949-56; University of Malaya, Singapore, professor of law, 1956-63; Queen's University of Belfast, Belfast, professor of comparative law, 1963-71; University College, Cardiff, Wales, professor of law, 1971—. *Member:* Society of Public Teachers of Law, Association of University Teachers. *Awards, honors:* LL.D., University of Singapore, 1963, and University of London, 1969.

WRITINGS: Fraud in Equity, Pitman, 1957; (with B. T. Tan) *Elementary Law,* Donald Moore (Singapore), 1957; (with V. T. H. Delany) *The Cy-Pres Doctrine,* Sweet & Maxwell, 1959, supplement, 1961; *The Federation of Malaya Constitution,* University of Malaya Law Review, 1961, 2nd edition (with H. E. Groves) published as *The Constitution of Malaysia,* Oceana, 1967; (editor and contributor) *Malaya, Singapore, the Borneo Territories: The Development of Their Laws and Constitutions,* Stevens & Sons, 1961; *Constitutional Protection: Expropriation and Restrictions on Property Rights,* Oceana, 1963; (with G. W. Keeton) *Equity,* Pitman, 1969, supplement, 1974; (editor and contributor) *Survey of the Land Law of Northern Ireland,* H. M. S. O., 1971; (with Keeton) *The Modern Law of Charities,* 2nd edition, Northern Ireland Legal Quarterly, 1971, supplement, 1975; (with Keeton) *A Casebook on Equity and Trusts,* 2nd edition, Professional Books, 1974; *Rights in Security,* McDonald & Evans, 1974; (with Keeton) *The Law of Trusts,* 10th edition, Professional Books, 1974.

Author of Irish supplements: Keeton, *An Introduction to Equity,* 3rd edition, Pitman, 1952, 5th edition, 1961; C. Sweet, *Real Property,* 3rd edition, Butterworth & Co., 1956; Keeton, *Law of Trusts,* 7th edition, Pitman, 1957, 9th edition, 1968.

Contributor: *The United Kingdom: The Development of Its Laws and Constitution,* Stevens & Sons, 1955; *A Bibliographical Guide to United Kingdom Law,* Institute of Advanced Legal Studies, 1956, 2nd edition, 1973; *Studies in Law,* Asia Publishing House (Bombay), 1961; *Report of the Regional Conference on Legal Education, Singapore, 1962,* Faculty of Law, University of Singapore, 1964; *Die moderne Demokratie und ihr Recht,* J. C. B. Mohr, 1966; *Law, Justice and Equity,* Pitman, 1967.

Contributor to *Yearbook of World Affairs,* and to more than twenty-five journals in England, Canada, Ireland, Malaya, Australia, Germany, India, and United States. Editor, *University of Malaya Law Review,* 1959-60, *Irish Jurist,* 1964, and *Northern Ireland Legal Quarterly,* 1964-65.

* * *

SHERMAN, (Marcus) Harvey 1917-

PERSONAL: Born June 9, 1917, in Pittsburgh, Pa.; son of Samuel (a merchant) and Ella (Grossman) Sherman; married Evelyn Gurkoff, June 25, 1950; children: Daniel, Joshua. *Education:* Los Angeles Junior College (now Los Angeles City College), A.A., 1937; University of California, Berkeley, A.B. (with highest honors), 1938, M.A., 1939; University of Chicago, graduate study, 1939-41. *Home:* 399 Murray Ave., Englewood, N.J. 07631. *Office:* Port Authority of New York and New Jersey, 1 World Trade Center, New York, N.Y. 10048.

CAREER: U.S. Bureau of the Budget, Washington, D.C., organization and methods analyst, Administrative Management Division, 1946-48, staff assistant to the director, 1948-49, budget and planning officer, 1949-51; U.S. Technical Cooperation Administration, Washington, D.C., director of public administration staff, 1951-53; U.S. Foreign Operations Administration, Washington, D.C., public administration advisor for the Near East, Africa, and South Asia, 1953-55; Port Authority of New York and New Jersey, New York, N.Y., director of organization and procedures department, 1955-73, director of management services, 1973—, acting personnel director, 1964-65, acting director of terminals, 1970-71. Instructor, Department of Agriculture Graduate School, 1949-51; visiting lecturer, Syracuse University, 1951, 1956; instructor in government, City College (now City College of the City University of New York), 1957-59; member of advisory committee, Business School, Manhattan College, 1958—; president, International Study and Research Institute, 1963—; chairman of advisory board for graduate program in public administration, Nova University, 1973—. Member of advisory board, Committee on Government Improvement; consultant, National Aeronautics and Space Administration, 1968—. *Military service:* U.S. Army, 1941-46; became captain.

MEMBER: American Society for Public Administration (president of New York metropolitan chapter, 1958-59; national president, 1964-65), National Academy of Public Administration, Association of Internal Management Consultants, American Political Science Association, American Association for the United Nations (chapter vice-president, 1962-63), Urban League (member of board of directors, Bergen county chapter, 1963-64), Conference on the Public Service, Organization Development Council, Phi Beta Kappa. *Awards, honors:* McKinsey Foundation Award and Organization Development Council Award, both for *It All Depends: A Pragmatic Approach to Organization.*

WRITINGS: It All Depends: A Pragmatic Approach to Organization (Executive Book Club selection), University of Alabama Press, 1966. Contributor of articles in the field of management and public administration to professional journals.

*　　*　　*

SHERRILL, Robert G(lenn) 1925-

PERSONAL: Born December 24, 1925, in Frogtown, Ga.; son of Cliff (a newspaper reporter) and Susan (McGinley) Sherrill; married Mary Bergeson (a musician). *Education:* George Pepperdine College (now Pepperdine University), B.A., 1949; University of Texas, M.A., 1956. *Politics:* "Independent radical." *Home:* 617 North Carolina Ave. S.E., Washington, D.C. 20003.

CAREER: Variety of newspaper jobs prior to 1954; instructor in English at Texas A&M University, College Station, 1956-57, and University of Missouri, Columbia, 1958-59; *Texas Observer,* Austin, associate editor, 1960-63; *Miami Herald,* Miami, Fla., chief of capitol bureau, Tallahassee, 1963-65; *Nation,* New York, N.Y., Washington

editor, 1965—. *Wartime service:* U.S. Merchant Marine, engineer, World War II. *Awards, honors:* Rockefeller fellow, 1957.

WRITINGS: (With others) *Retrospect and Prospect,* Syracuse University Press, 1956; *The Accidental President,* Grossman, 1967; *Gothic Politics in the Deep South: Stars of the New Confederacy,* Grossman, 1968, revised edition, Ballantine, 1969; (with H. Ernst) *The Drugstore Liberal,* Grossman, 1968; *Military Justice Is to Justice as Military Music Is to Music,* Harper, 1970, revised edition, 1971; *Why They Call It Politics: A Guide to America's Government,* Harcourt, 1972, 2nd edition, 1974; *The Saturday Night Special, and Other Guns with which Americans Won the West, Protected Bootleg Franchises, Slew Wildlife, Robbed Countless Banks, Shot Husbands Purposely and by Mistake, and Killed Presidents,* Charterhouse, 1973; *The Last Kennedy,* Dial, 1976. Contributor to *Harper's, New York Times Magazine, Playboy,* and *Esquire.*

*　　*　　*

SHERRIN, Ned 1931-

PERSONAL: Born February 18, 1931, in Low Ham, Somersetshire, England; son of Thomas Adam (a farmer) and Dorothy (Drewett) Sherrin. *Education:* Exeter College, Oxford, M.A., 1954; Gray's Inn, Barrister-at-Law, 1955. *Home:* 19 Wellington Sq., London SW3 4NJ, England. *Agent:* Margaret Ramsay, 14A Goodwin's Ct., London WC2N 4LL, England.

CAREER: Former television producer-director in England for Associated Television and British Broadcasting Corp., and creator of television program, "That Was the Week That Was" (popular satire); film producer, Columbia Pictures, London, England, 1966-68; free-lance producer and writer, 1969—. Director of musical play, "Come Spy with Me," Whitehall Theatre, London, 1966-67. *Military service:* Royal Corps of Signals, 1949-51; became lieutenant. *Awards, honors:* Awards of Guild of Television Producers and Directors, 1963, 1964, 1966.

WRITINGS—All with Caryl Brahms, except as indicated: *Cindy-Ella or I Gotta Shoe,* W. H. Allen, 1962; (editor with David Frost) *That Was the Week That Was,* W. H. Allen, 1963; *Rappel, 1910,* W. H. Allen, 1964; *Benbow Was His Name,* Hutchinson, 1967; "Sing a Rude Song" (play), produced on West End at Garrick Theatre, 1971; "Fish Out of Water" (play; adaptation of George Feydeau's *Le Main Passe*), produced in London at Greenwich Theatre, July 1, 1971; *Ooh! La-la!* (based on a play by Feydeau), W. H. Allen, 1973; "Liberty Ranch" (play), produced in London at Greenwich Theatre, 1973; *After You Mr. Feydeau,* W. H. Allen, 1974. With Caryl Brahms, has written plays for radio, television, and stage, including "Little Beggars," "Shut Up and Sing," "Take a Sapphire," "No Bed for Bacon," "Cindy-Ella," "The Spoils," "Nicholas Nickelby," and many song lyrics.

*　　*　　*

SHERWOOD, William Robert 1929-

PERSONAL: Born July 23, 1929, in York Harbor, Me.; son of William R. and Dora (Siegel) Sherwood; married Marcia Anne Bozzo, June 9, 1967 (separated, 1975); children: Seth N. *Education:* Harvard University, B.A., 1951, M.A., 1956; Columbia University, Ph.D., 1964. *Office:* Department of English, Reed College, Portland, Ore. 97202.

CAREER: Vassar College, Poughkeepsie, N.Y., assistant professor of English, 1960-67; Herbert H. Lehman College of the City University of New York, Bronx, N.Y., assistant professor, 1967-69, associate professor of English, 1969-73; Vassar College, associate professor of English and humanities, 1973-75; Reed College, Portland, Ore., associate professor of English and humanities, 1975—. *Military service:* U.S. Army, 1954-56. *Member:* Modern Language Association of America, American Association of University Professors. *Awards, honors:* Fulbright scholar in Norway, 1951-52.

WRITINGS: (Editor with Lynn C. Bartlett) *The English Novel: Background Readings,* Lippincott, 1967; *Circumference and Circumstance: Stages in the Mind and Art of Emily Dickinson,* Columbia University Press, 1968.

* * *

SHINER, Larry (Ernest) 1934-

PERSONAL: Born May 6, 1934, in Oklahoma City, Okla.; son of Ernest A. (an insurance man) and Nelda (Dountain) Shiner; married Billie Sue Braddy, August 25, 1955; children: Laurence, Suzanna, Eduardo. *Education:* Oberlin College, student, 1952-55; Northwestern University, B.A., 1956; Drew University, B.D., 1959; University of Strasbourg, Docteur es Sciences Religieuses, 1961. *Home:* 905 South Glenwood, Springfield, Ill. *Office:* Sangamon State University, Springfield, Ill. 62703.

CAREER: University of Tampa, Tampa, Fla., assistant professor of philosophy, 1961; Cornell College, Mount Vernon, Iowa, associate professor of religion, 1962-71; Sangamon State University, Springfield, Ill., associate professor of philosophy, 1971-74, acting dean of humanities, 1974-75, dean of academic programs, 1975—. *Member:* American Philosophical Association, Society for Phenomenology and Existential Philosophy. *Awards, honors:* William S. Pilling traveling fellowship, 1959-60; Society of Religious Higher Education cross-disciplinary fellow, 1967-68.

WRITINGS: The Secularization of History: An Introduction to the Theology of Friedrich Gogarten, Abingdon, 1966. Contributor of articles to professional journals. Editor of special issue (on American social thought and action) of *Christianisme Social.*

WORK IN PROGRESS: Problem of historical method; phenomenology and social science methodology.

* * *

SHOBEN, Edward Joseph, Jr. 1918-

PERSONAL: Born October 3, 1918, in Oberlin, Ohio; son of Edward Joseph (a railroad passenger agent) and Clara (Wharton) Shoben; married Anne Smith, April 4, 1942 (separated, 1967); children: Edward Joseph III. *Education:* University of Southern California, A.B. (cum laude), 1939, M.A., 1945, Ph.D., 1947. *Politics:* Independent. *Religion:* Episcopalian.

CAREER: Psychological Guidance Center, Los Angeles, Calif., counselor and psychometrist, 1945-46; University of Iowa, Iowa City, assistant professor of psychology, 1947-50, director of student counseling office, 1949-50; Columbia University, Teachers College, New York, N.Y., associate professor, 1950-56, professor of psychology and education, 1956-65, director of Office of College Relations, 1964-65; University of Cincinnati, Cincinnati, Ohio, professor of higher education and psychology and director of Center for Research and Training in Higher Education, 1965-66;

American Council on Education, Washington, D.C., director of Commission on Academic Affairs, 1966-69; Evergreen State College, Olympia, Wash., executive vice president, beginning 1969. Certified in clinical psychology, American Board of Examiners in Professional Psychology, 1955. Chairman of subcommittee on psychology, Quartermaster Research and Development Board, National Research Council-National Academy of Sciences, 1959-66; chairman of Task Force on Adolescents and Youth, Joint Commission on the Mental Health of Children, 1967-68; member of joint committee on the preparation of college teachers, Council of Graduate Schools, Association of American Colleges, 1965-66. Consultant to Veterans Administration, 1951-66, Basic Books, Inc., 1952-61, and Scott, Foresman & Co., 1964-67.

MEMBER: American Psychological Association (fellow; president of division of counseling psychology, 1958-59, division on the teaching of psychology, 1959-61, division of esthetics, 1961-62, and division of philosophical psychology, 1963-64), American Association for Humanistic Psychology (president, 1964-65), American Association for the Advancement of Science (fellow), New York Academy of Sciences (fellow), American Sociological Association, American Society for Aesthetics, National Council of Teachers of English, Education Writers Association, American Educational Research Association, Philosophy of Education Society, Sigma Xi, Psi Chi, Alpha Kappa Delta, Epsilon Phi, Phi Delta Kappa.

WRITINGS: (With L. F. Shaffer) *The Psychology of Adjustment,* 2nd edition (not associated with 1st edition), Houghton, 1956; (editor with Floyd L. Ruch) *Perspectives in Psychology,* Scott, Foresman, 1964; (with J. L. Fine and James Malfetti) *The Development of a Criterion for Driver Behavior,* Teachers College, Columbia University, 1965; (with Fine and Malfetti) *Manual for the Columbia Driver Judgment Test,* Teachers College, Columbia University, 1965; (editor with Ohmer Milton) *Learning and the Professors,* Ohio University Press, 1968.

Contributor: F. L. Ruch, *Psychology and Life,* 3rd edition, Scott, Foresman, 1948; *Psychotherapy: Theory and Research,* edited by O. H. Mowrer, Ronald, 1953; *An Introduction to Clinical Psychology,* revised edition, edited by L. A. Pennington and I. Berg, Ronald, 1954; *Counseling and General Education,* edited by Melvene Hardee, World Book Co., 1955; *Alcoholism as a Medical Problem,* edited by H. D. Kruse, Paul Hoeber, 1956; *Education as a Discipline,* edited by K. Davis and J. Kuethe, University of Wisconsin Press, 1963; *A Reassessment of the Curriculum,* edited by D. Huebner, Teachers College, Columbia University, 1964; *Revolution in Counseling,* edited by J. Krumboltz, Houghton, 1966; *Morality and Mental Health,* edited by O. H. Mowrer, Rand McNally, 1967; *Issues in Higher Education 1967,* Association for Higher Education, 1967; *Improving College Teaching,* edited by C.B.T. Lee, American Council of Education, 1967.

Contributor of about seventy articles to *American Family, Antioch Review, Mademoiselle,* and psychology, education, and guidance journals. Editor, *Teachers College Record,* 1960-65, and *Educational Record,* 1966—; associate editor, *Journal of Abnormal and Social Psychology,* 1955-61, and *Psychological Record,* 1965—; member of publications board, American Psychological Association, 1951-54; member of editorial board, *British Journal of Social and Clinical Psychology,* 1962-67.

WORK IN PROGRESS: Current concerns include contemporary student movements in the United States, the dynamics of American youth culture, the relationship between our educational system and our national concern with mental health, and the potentialities of the humanities for education in a scientific age.

SIDELIGHTS: Shoben told *CA:* "An unreconstructed Anglophile, I'm fond of all of Britain. . . . Moderately fluent in Spanish, can stumble about in Italian, crawl in German, and inch along in French. My principal suffering stems from being a comfortable antique whose arteries don't seem to harden and an unapologetic academic who longs for the academy to play a more vigorous social role. . . . Suspect Shakespeare of being more instructive than either Freud or Skinner."†

*   *   *

SHOVER, John L.   1927-

PERSONAL: Born July 15, 1927, in Delaware, Ohio; son of Walter S. (a salesman) and Alice (Yeager) Shover; married Doortje Karreman, October 6, 1973. *Education:* Ohio Wesleyan University, A.B., 1949; Ohio State University, M.A., 1952, Ph.D., 1957. *Office:* Department of History, University of Pennsylvania, Philadelphia, Pa. 19174.

CAREER: Instructor in history at Ohio State University, Columbus, 1955-56, and DePauw University, Greencastle, Ind., 1956-58; San Francisco State College (now University), San Francisco, Calif., 1958-68, began as assistant professor, became professor of history; University of Pennsylvania, Philadelphia, 1968—, began as associate professor, professor of history, 1976—. Fulbright lecturer in political science, University of Sind, Hyderabad, West Pakistan, 1962-63; Fulbright lecturer in history, Leningrad State University, U.S.S.R., 1974. *Military service:* U.S. Naval Reserve, 1945-56. *Member:* American Historical Association, Organization of American Historians, Social Science History Association, Agricultural History Society.

WRITINGS: Cornbelt Rebellion: The Farmers' Holiday Association, University of Illinois Press, 1965; (with Michael P. Rogin) *Political Change in California,* Greenwood Press, 1970; (editor) *Politics of the Nineteen Twenties,* Xerox College Publishing, 1970. Contributor to *Agricultural History, Journal of American History,* and *American Quarterly.*

WORK IN PROGRESS: First Majority, Last Minority: The Transformation of Rural Life in America.

*   *   *

SHOWALTER, Jean B(reckinridge)

PERSONAL: Born in Roanoke, Va.; daughter of English (an attorney) and Jean (Staples) Showalter; married John O. Strom-Olsen. *Education:* Wellesley College, B.A., 1963. *Religion:* Episcopalian. *Residence:* Montreal, Quebec, Canada.

CAREER: Doubleday & Co., Inc., New York, N.Y., associate editor of children's books, 1966-68.

WRITINGS—Juvenile books: *Around the Corner,* Doubleday, 1966; *The Donkey Ride,* Doubleday, 1967.

AVOCATIONAL INTERESTS: History.

*   *   *

SHRIVER, George H(ite), Jr.   1931-

PERSONAL: Born October 26, 1931, in Jacksonville, Fla.; son of George Hite and Hazel (Riggle) Shriver; married

Donna Newcomer (a piano teacher), August 16, 1953; children: Rebecca, Bonnie, Laurie, David. *Education:* Stetson University, A.B. (magna cum laude), 1953; Southeastern Baptist Theological Seminary, B.D., 1956; Duke University, Ph.D. (politics and religion), 1961. *Home:* 120 Lee St., Statesboro, Ga. 30458. *Office:* Georgia Southern College, Statesboro, Ga. 30458.

CAREER: Camp Ridgecrest for Boys, Ridgecrest, N.C., camp pastor, 1956-58; Duke University, Durham, N.C., instructor in religion, 1958-59; Southeastern Baptist Theological Seminary, Wake Forest, N.C., instructor, 1959-61, assistant professor, 1961-65, associate professor of church history, 1965-73; Georgia Southern College, Statesboro, associate professor of history, 1973—. Visiting professor of religion, Meredith College, 1966-67; visiting professor of church history, Duke University, 1970-71. Consultant to Abingdon Press, University of North Carolina Press, and religious journals.

MEMBER: American Society of Church History, American Historical Association, American Academy of Religion, American Association of University Professors, Baptists for Unity, North Carolina Teachers of Religion (president, 1971). *Awards, honors:* American Association of Theological Schools fellow and Swiss-American exchange scholar, in Switzerland, 1965-66.

WRITINGS: (Editor) *American Religious Heretics,* Abingdon, 1966; (translator) Georges Crespy, *From Science to Theology,* Abingdon, 1968; (translator) R. Stouffer, *The Humanness of John Calvin,* Abingdon, 1971; (editor) *Contemporary Reflections on the Medieval Christian Tradition,* Duke University Press, 1974. Contributor of articles and reviews to journals.

WORK IN PROGRESS: Research in world views on religious liberty and in church renewal; research on Mercersburg Theology, with emphasis on Philip Schaff.

SIDELIGHTS: George Shriver speaks French and reads French, German, Spanish, Greek, Hebrew, and Latin. *Avocational interests:* Hiking, tennis, playing autoharp.

*   *   *

SHRYOCK, (Edwin) Harold   1906-

PERSONAL: Born April 14, 1906, in Seattle, Wash.; son of Alfred Quimby (a physician) and Stella (Tefft) Shryock; married Daisy May Bagwell (a registered nurse), April 30, 1929; children: Patricia Helen (Mrs. G. Carleton Wallace), Edwin F. *Education:* Pacific Union College, B.S., 1930; Loma Linda University, M.D., 1934; University of Southern California, M.A., 1939. *Religion:* Seventh-day Adventist. *Home:* 11593 Acacia St., Box 638, Loma Linda, Calif. 92354.

CAREER: Pacific Union College, Angwin, Calif., instructor in chemistry, 1930-31; Loma Linda University, School of Medicine, Loma Linda, Calif., instructor, 1934-39, assistant professor, 1939-45, associate professor, 1945-57, professor of anatomy and chairman of department, 1957-75, associate dean, 1950-51, dean, 1951-54. Personal counselor. *Member:* American Association of Anatomists, American Association for the Advancement of Science, Sigma Xi, Alpha Omega Alpha.

WRITINGS: Happiness for Husbands and Wives, Review & Herald, 1949; *Happiness and Health,* Pacific Press Publishing, 1950; *On Becoming a Man,* Review & Herald, 1951; *On Becoming a Woman,* Review & Herald, 1951; *Highways to Health,* Review & Herald, 1953; *Living,* Pacific Press Publishing, 1958; *Mind if I Smoke?*, Pacific Press Publishing, 1959; *On Being Sweethearts*, Review & Herald, 1966; *On Being Married Soon*, Review & Herald, 1968; *You and Your Health*, Pacific Press Publishing, 1970. Contributor of about a dozen articles to medical journals.

* * *

SHUGRUE, Michael F(rancis) 1934-

PERSONAL: Born July 28, 1934, in Chicago, Ill.; son of Frank R. and Helen (Conter) Shugrue. *Education:* University of Nebraska, A.B., 1956; Duke University, M.A., 1957, Ph.D., 1960. *Home:* 100 Bleecker St., Apt. 24A, New York, N.Y. 10012.

CAREER: University of Illinois, Urbana, instructor in English, 1960-62; University of Nebraska, Lincoln, assistant professor of English and assistant to chancellor, 1962-63; University of Illinois, assistant professor of English, 1963-65; Modern Language Association of America, New York City, director of English programs and coordinator of Association of Departments of English, 1965-73; City University of New York, professor of English and director of academic development at City College, New York City, 1973-74, professor of English and dean of Richmond College, Staten Island, N.Y., 1974—. Adjunct professor of English, New York University, 1965-71. *Member:* Modern Language Association of America, National Council of Teachers of English.

WRITINGS: (Editor with W. H. McBurney) Marivaux, *The Virtuous Orphan*, Southern Illinois University Press, 1965; (editor) Farquhar, *The Recruiting Officer*, University of Nebraska Press, 1966; *How the New English Will Help Your Child*, Association Press, 1966; (editor) *Selected Prose and Poetry of Daniel Defoe*, Holt, 1968; *English in a Decade of Change*, Pegasus, 1969; (editor with Harry Finestone) *Prospects for the 70's*, Modern Language Association of America, 1973; (editor with Carolina Shrodes and Finestone) *The Conscious Reader*, Macmillan, 1974. General editor, "Foundations of the Novel: Representative Early Eighteenth-Century Fiction" series, seventy-one volumes, Garland Publishing, 1972-73. Contributor to scholarly and professional journals.

* * *

SHULMAN, Morton 1925-

PERSONAL: Born April 2, 1925, in Toronto, Ontario, Canada; son of David and Nettie (Wintrope) Shulman; married Gloria Bossin, May 30, 1950; children: Dianne, Geoffrey. *Education:* University of Toronto, M.D., 1948. *Politics:* New Democratic Party. *Religion:* Jewish. *Home:* 66 Russell Hill Rd., Toronto, Ontario, Canada. *Office:* 378 Roncesvalles Ave., Toronto, Ontario, Canada.

CAREER: General practitioner of medicine, Toronto, Ontario, 1948-63, and former chief coroner of Toronto, 1963-67; member of Provincial Parliament of Ontario, 1967—.

WRITINGS: Anyone Can Make a Million, McGraw, 1967, revised edition, Stein & Day, 1973; *The Billion Dollar Windfall*, Morrow, 1969. Also author of weekly column for *Toronto Sun*.

WORK IN PROGRESS: An Amateur Tinkers with Organized Crime.

SIDELIGHTS: Written in a few weeks, *Anyone Can Make a Million* took only a few more weeks after publication to reach the top of the best seller list and settle there for a long stay. The title come-on and tempting green-back book jacket undoubtedly contributed to its success, but however presumptuous the title seems, there is a basis for Shulman's boast: he himself became a millionaire by investing shrewdly. Using his own experience, he has written a manual with advice concerning what V. G. Vartan calls, "the potentials and pitfalls of the securities market." Of course, as John Brooks says "anyone who can make a million will probably do so, in the market or some other way; the rest of us never will."

Shulman's writing skill has also been appreciated. In fact, Brooks finds the book "too entertaining to be saddled by such a preposterous title." Although his former position as chief coroner of Toronto may make him an unlikely investment counselor, Shulman does use "scalpel-sharp prose," according to Vartan. *Time* reports that despite the active sales of the book, there has been "no noticeable influence on activity [in those markets Shulman recommends]." J. B. Woy says: "Perhaps Dr. Shulman made a million by methods described in this volume, but it is ridiculous to suggest that anyone can do it."

SIDELIGHTS: Morton Shulman has traveled widely through Russia, China, Nepal, India, Outer Mongolia, and Europe; he sails every winter in the Caribbean or the Mediterranean.

BIOGRAPHICAL/CRITICAL SOURCES: Harper's, August, 1967; *New York Times Book Review*, August 6, 1967; *Time*, August 18, 1967.

* * *

SHULMAN, Sandra (Dawn) 1944-

PERSONAL: Born December 15, 1944, in London, England; daughter of Alfred (a textile merchant) and Gladys (Davis) Shulman; married David Montague (a lawyer), 1972. *Education:* St. Godrics College, diploma, 1962. *Politics:* Socialist. *Religion:* "Jewish/Agnostic." *Home and office:* 98 Dudley Ct., Upper Berkeley St., London W1, England. *Agent:* Bolt & Watson, 8 Storey's Gate, London SW1, England; and George Borchardt, Inc., 145 East 52 St., New York, N.Y. 10022.

CAREER: Longacre Press, London, England, secretary and personal assistant to fiction editor of children's magazines, 1962-63; free-lance journalist and film researcher.

WRITINGS—All published by Paperback Library, except where indicated: *The Menacing Darkness*, 1966; *Castlecliffe*, 1967; *The Bride of Devil's Leap*, 1968; *The Daughters of Astaroth*, 1968; *The Lady of Arlac*, 1969; *The Prisoner of Garve*, 1970; *The Temptress*, 1971; *Francesca: The Florentine*, Morrow, 1973; *Madonna of the Shadows*, New English Library, 1973; *Guide to Drugs*, Davis-Poynter, 1975; *Encyclopedia of Astrology*, Hamlyn, 1976. Contributor of children's serials and short stories to periodicals.

WORK IN PROGRESS: Death Masque, a thriller; *The Feminine Principle*, a medical and social history; and a renaissance novel for Davis-Poynter.

SIDELIGHTS: Sandra Shulman speaks French, Italian, Greek, and German. She has traveled extensively in South America and Europe. *Avocational interests:* Comparative religion, occult subjects and European history, and medical history.

* * *

SIBLEY, Marilyn McAdams 1923-

PERSONAL: Born September 30, 1923, in Bedias, Tex.;

daughter of Horace A. (a rancher) and Nevada (Stuart) McAdams; married J. Dale Sibley (an insurance agent), June 24, 1944; children: David McAdams, Stuart Dale, Mark McAdams. *Education:* Sam Houston State College (now University), B.A., 1943; University of Houston, M.A., 1961; Rice University, Ph.D., 1965. *Religion:* Baptist. *Home:* 702 Bison, Houston, Tex. 77024.

CAREER: University of Houston, Houston, Tex., instructor in history, 1961-62; Houston Baptist University, Houston, professor of history and chairman of department of history and political science, 1966—. Visiting professor, University of Texas at Austin, 1973. Director, Horace A. McAdams Ranch, Inc., Huntsville, Tex. *Member:* American Historical Association, Organization of American Historians, Southern Historical Association, Southwestern Historical Association, East Texas Historical Association. *Awards, honors:* Summerfield G. Roberts Award of the Sons of the Republic of Texas, 1967, for *Travelers in Texas, 1761-1860.*

WRITINGS: Travelers in Texas, 1761-1860, University of Texas Press, 1967; *The Port of Houston: A History,* University of Texas Press, 1968; *George W. Brackenridge: Maverick Philanthropist,* University of Texas Press, 1973. Contributor of gardening articles to *Better Homes and Gardens, Flower and Garden,* and *Organic Gardening,* and articles on Texas history to regional journals. Editorial assistant, *Journal of Southern History,* 1964-65.

WORK IN PROGRESS: In the Eyes of Strangers: Texas, 1861-1960.

AVOCATIONAL INTERESTS: All growing things, especially the wild flowers and native trees of Texas.

* * *

SICHEL, Werner 1934-

PERSONAL: Born September 23, 1934, in Munich, Germany; son of Joseph and Lily (Greenwood) Sichel; married Beatrice Bonne, February 22, 1959; children: Lawrence, Linda. *Education:* New York University, B.S., 1956; Northwestern University, M.A., 1960, Ph.D., 1964. *Home:* 5046 Merryview Dr., Kalamazoo, Mich. 49008. *Office:* Department of Economics, Western Michigan University, Kalamazoo, Mich. 49001.

CAREER: Lake Forest College, Lake Forest, Ill., instructor, 1959-62; Roosevelt University, Chicago, Ill., assistant professor, 1959-60; Western Michigan University, Kalamazoo, instructor, 1960-64, assistant professor, 1964-66, associate professor, 1966-72, professor of economics, 1972—. Fulbright-Hays senior lecturer, University of Belgrade, 1968-69. *Member:* American Economic Association.

WRITINGS: (Editor) *Industrial Organization and Public Policy: Selected Readings,* Houghton, 1967; (editor) *Antitrust Policy and Economic Welfare,* Bureau of Business Research, University of Michigan, 1970; (with Peter Eckstein) *Basic Economic Concepts: An Aid to the Study of Economic Problems,* Rand McNally, Volume I: *Microeconomics,* 1974, Volume II: *Macroeconomics,* 1974; (editor with Thomas G. Gies) *Public Utility Regulation: Change and Scope,* Heath, 1975; (editor) *The Economic Effects of Multinational Corporations,* Bureau of Business Research, University of Michigan, 1975. Contributor of articles to journals including *Journal of Risk and Insurance,* and *Journal of Economic Issues.*

SIDOWSKI, Joseph B(oleslaus) 1925-

PERSONAL: Born June 25, 1925, in Wilmington, Del. *Education:* Pomona College, B.A., 1952; University of Wisconsin, M.A., 1954, Ph.D., 1956. *Home:* 12710 52nd St., Tampa, Fla. 33617. *Office:* University of South Florida, Tampa, Fla. 33620.

CAREER: San Diego State College (now University), San Diego, Calif., 1956-68, began as instructor, professor of psychology, 1961-68; University of South Florida, faculty member, 1969—. Visiting scientist at University of Wisconsin, Regional Primate Research Center, 1968-69. *Military service:* U.S. Army, 1942-45. *Member:* International Primatological Society, American Psychological Association (fellow), Psychonomic Society, American Association for the Advancement of Science, Sigma Xi. *Awards, honors:* National Institute of Mental Health special postdoctoral fellow at University of California, Los Angeles, Brain Research Institute, 1963.

WRITINGS: Experimental Methods and Instrumentation in Psychology, McGraw, 1966. Contributor to professional journals. Editor, *Journal of Behavioral Research Methods and Instrumentation,* 1968—, and of special issues, *American Psychologist,* 1969, 1975.

WORK IN PROGRESS: Research in experimental psychology, learning, and instrumentation.

* * *

SIEBERT, Fred(rick) Seaton 1901-

PERSONAL: Born December 13, 1901, in Tower, Minn.; son of Frank F. and Sarah (Paine) Siebert; married Eleanor Barkman, July 13, 1931; children: Mary Elise, Andrew W. *Education:* University of Wisconsin, A.B., 1923; University of Illinois, J.D., 1929. *Home:* 2463 Shawnee, Okemos, Mich. *Office:* Michigan State University, East Lansing, Mich.

CAREER: Duluth Herald, Duluth, Minn., reporter, 1923-24; *Chicago Herald-Examiner,* Chicago, Ill., copy desk, 1924; University of Illinois, Urbana, instructor, 1929-37, assistant professor of journalism, 1937-40; Northwestern University, Evanston, Ill., professor of journalism, 1940-41; University of Illinois, director of School of Journalism and Communications, 1941-57; Michigan State University, East Lansing, director of Division of Mass Communications and School of Journalism, 1957-60, dean of College of Communication Arts, 1960-67, professor of journalism, 1967—. Admitted to Illinois Bar, 1929; legal counsel to press associations. *Member:* Association for Education in Journalism (president, 1960), Sigma Delta Chi, Kappa Tau Alpha, Alpha Delta Sigma. *Awards, honors:* Illinois Press Association Medal, 1938; University of Missouri School of Journalism medal.

WRITINGS: Copyreading: A Collection of Laboratory Exercises, 1930, 2nd edition, T. Nelson, 1933; *The Rights and Privileges of the Press,* Appleton, 1934; *Freedom of the Press in England, 1476-1776,* University of Illinois Press, 1952; (with Theodore Peterson and Wilbur Schramm) *Four Theories of the Press,* University of Illinois Press, 1956; *The Mass Media in a Free Society,* New York University, 1956; *A Study of Master's Degree Programs in Journalism,* American Council on Education for Journalism, 1963; *Report on Copyrights, Clearances and Rights of Teachers in the New Educational Media,* American Council on Education, 1963. Member of editorial board, *Journalism Quarterly.*

WORK IN PROGRESS: Broadcast Program Regulation.

SIEGEL, Irving H(erbert) 1914-

PERSONAL: Born February 1, 1914, in New York, N.Y.; son of David and Rebecca (Horowitz) Siegel; married Adelaide Simons (an information specialist), January 2, 1937; children: Judith Adrian, Ruth Elise. *Education:* City College (now City College of the City University of New York), B.S., 1934; New York University, M.A., 1935; Columbia University, Ph.D., 1951. *Politics:* Independent ("very"). *Religion:* Jewish (unorthodox). *Home:* 8312 Bryant Dr., Bethesda, Md. 20034. *Office:* U.S. Department of Commerce, Washington, D.C. 20230.

CAREER: U.S. Bureau of Labor Statistics, Washington, D.C., assistant chief, Productivity Division, 1941-43; U.S. Veterans Administration, Washington, D.C., chief economist, 1945-49; Johns Hopkins University, Baltimore, Md., director of Soviet Productivity Study, Operations Research Office, and university lecturer in political economy, 1949-51; Twentieth Century Fund, Washington, D.C., director of American Technology Study, 1951-53; U.S. Council of Economic Advisers, Washington, D.C., senior staff economist, 1953-60, consultant, 1960-61; Research Analysis Corp., McLean, Va., chief of Economics Division, 1960-63, member of research council, 1963-65; W. E. Upjohn Institute for Employment Research, Washington, D.C., economist, 1965-70; U.S. Department of Commerce, Washington, D.C., economic adviser, 1972—. Consultant to Patent, Trademark, and Copyright Research Institute of George Washington University, 1955-72, International Business Machines, 1957-65, and American Chemical Society, 1970-73. *Military service:* U.S. Army, 1943-44.

MEMBER: American Statistical Association (fellow), American Economic Association, Econometric Society, Operations Research Society of America, American Association for the Advancement of Science (fellow), Washington Statistical Society (vice-president, 1948-49), New York Academy of Sciences (fellow), Phi Beta Kappa.

WRITINGS: (With H. Magdoff and M. B. Davis) *Production Employment and Productivity in Fifty-nine Manufacturing Industries, 1919-36,* three volumes, U.S. Works Progress Administration, 1939; *Concepts and Measurement of Production and Productivity,* U.S. Bureau of Labor Statistics, 1952; *Soviet Labor Productivity,* Johns Hopkins Operations Research Office, 1952; *Strengthening Washington's Technical-Resource Base,* Research Analysis Corp., 1963; (co-editor and contributor) *Dimensions of Manpower Policy: Programs and Research,* Johns Hopkins Press, 1966; (editor and contributor) *Manpower Tomorrow: Prospects and Priorities,* Kelley, 1967; *Aggregation and Averaging,* Upjohn, 1968; (contributor) *Chemistry in the Economy,* American Chemical Society, 1973. Contributor of scores of articles to professional and technical journals. Member of editorial board, *Idea.*

WORK IN PROGRESS: Books and papers on economic measurement, production and productivity concepts, technological change and its implications for society, statistical methods, patents, competition, and profits.

SIDELIGHTS: Siegel's reflections on factual writing: "Remember, in your kindly evening thoughts, the old guy, maid, or mom who counseled you that every paragraph should have a topic sentence. This precept would not make, and could destroy, a Shakespeare (who also would not heed); but it could also improve the output of most of us, who are required merely to tell others what we have in mind. To tell others, we must first find out; and here the topic sentence exerts its discipline, serving as a true instrument of creative research in self-discovery."

SILBERG, Richard 1942-

PERSONAL: Born March 14, 1942, in New York, N.Y.; son of Alexander (a theatrical agent) and Helene (Karp) Silberg. *Education:* Harvard University, A.B., 1963. *Religion:* Jewish.

CAREER: Actor in Harvard productions, in summer stock, and with Poet's Theatre, Caravan Theatre, and other groups, appeared in OM Theatre Workshop's "Riot."

WRITINGS: The Devolution of the People, Harcourt, 1967.

WORK IN PROGRESS: A book, tentatively entitled *Symbolic Organization: The Opening of the Third Eye.*††

*   *   *

SILBEY, Joel H. 1933-

PERSONAL: Born August 16, 1933, in Brooklyn, N.Y.; son of Sidney R. (a businessman) and Estelle (Mintzer) Silbey; married Rosemary Johnson, August 13, 1959; children: Victoria, David. *Education:* Brooklyn College (now Brooklyn College of the City University of New York), B.A., 1955; University of Iowa, M.A., 1956, Ph.D., 1963. *Home:* 105 Judd Falls Rd., Ithaca, N.Y. 14850. *Office:* History Department, McGraw Hall, Cornell University, Ithaca, N.Y. 14853.

CAREER: Assistant professor of history at San Francisco State College (now University), San Francisco, Calif., 1960-64, University of Pittsburgh, Pittsburgh, Pa., 1964-65, and University of Maryland, College Park, 1965-66; Cornell University, Ithaca, N.Y., associate professor, 1966-68, professor of history, 1968—. *Member:* American Historical Association, Organization of American Historians, Social Science History Association, Southern Historical Association.

WRITINGS: The Shrine of Party, University of Pittsburgh Press, 1967; *The Transformation of American Politics, 1840-1860,* Prentice-Hall, 1967; (co-editor) *Voters, Parties and Elections,* Xerox College Publishing, 1972; (co-editor) *American Political Behavior,* Harper, 1974; (contributor) Arthur S. Link, editor, *Critical American Elections,* American Philosophical Society, 1973. Contributor of articles and book reviews to professional journals.

WORK IN PROGRESS: A study of the democratic party, 1860-1870; public opinion and the coming of the Civil War; co-authoring, *A History of American Electoral Behavior.*

*   *   *

SILVER, Harold 1928-

PERSONAL: Born October 25, 1928, in Hull, Yorkshire, England; son of Samuel (a furrier) and Esther (Harris) Silver; married Pamela Cutler; children: Claire, Vicki. *Education:* Jesus College, Cambridge, M.A., 1952; University of Hull, M.Ed., 1956. *Politics:* Socialist. *Religion:* None. *Home:* 138 New Park Rd., London, England. *Office:* Chelsea College, University of London, Manresa Rd., London S.W.3, England.

CAREER: Hull College of Commerce, Hull, England, assistant lecturer in English and modern languages, 1956-58; Huddersfield College of Technology, Huddersfield, England, lecturer in English, 1958-60; University of London, Chelsea College, London, England, senior lecturer, 1961-71, reader, 1972-73, professor of education, 1974—. Has served as interpreter and translator for United Nations,

International Telecommunications Union, and other organizations. *Military service:* British Army, Service Corps, 1947-49. *Member:* Association of University Teachers (president of Chelsea branch, 1965-67), Society for Research into Higher Education (secretary of London area, 1965-67), History of Education Society, Society for the Study of Labour History.

WRITINGS: (Translator from the Russian) Marshal V. I. Chuikov, *The Beginning of the Road,* MacGibbon & Kee, 1963, published as *The Battle for Stalingrad,* Holt, 1964; *The Concept of Popular Education,* MacGibbon & Kee, 1965; *Robert Owen on Education,* Cambridge University Press, 1969; (with S. J. Teague) *History of British Universities, 1800-1969, Excluding Oxford and Cambridge,* Society for Research into Higher Education, 1970; *Modern English Society,* Methuen, 1970; *Equal Opportunity in Education,* Methuen, 1973; *A Social History of Education in England,* Methuen, 1973; *The Education of the Poor,* Routledge & Kegan Paul, 1973; *English Education and the Radicals, 1780-1850,* Routledge & Kegan Paul, 1974. Contributor of articles and reviews to education and social history journals. Editor, *Concern,* 1950-52.

WORK IN PROGRESS: A study of British and American nineteenth-century education and social science; co-authoring a book, *Education as Action.*

SIDELIGHTS: Harold Silver speaks French, Russian, and German. *Avocational interests:* Music.

* * *

SILVER, Nathan 1936-

PERSONAL: Born March 11, 1936, in New York, N.Y.; son of Isaac (an architect) and Libby (Nachimowsky) Silver; married Caroline Green (a writer), May 26, 1961 (divorced); married Helen McNeil (a university lecturer); children: Liberty, Gabriel. *Education:* Cooper Union Art School, student, 1952-55; Columbia University, B.Arch., 1958; Cambidge University, M.A., 1966. *Home:* 6 Westchester House, Seymour St., London W2 2JJ, England. *Agent:* Harold Matson Co., Inc., 22 East 40th St., New York, N.Y. 10016. *Office:* Feilder & Mawson Architects, 88 Seymour St., London W2 2JJ, England.

CAREER: Registered architect, New York State. Columbia University, School of Architecture, New York, N.Y., assistant professor of architecture, 1961-64; Cambridge University, School of Architecture, Cambridge, England, lecturer in architecture, 1964-68; architect, Partner, Silver, Penney, 1967-68, Nathan Silver, London, England, 1969-72, Feilder & Mawson Architects, London, 1973—. *Military service:* Army National Guard. *Member:* Royal Institute of British Architects, National Council of Architectural Registration Boards, Savile Club. *Awards, honors:* Guggenheim fellowship, 1968; certificate of merit, Municipal Art Society, 1968; National Book Award Nomination from National Book Committee, 1968, for *Lost New York;* National Endowment for the Arts grant, 1970.

WRITINGS: Lost New York, Houghton, 1967; (with Charles Jencks) *Adhocism: The Case for Improvisation,* Doubleday, 1973. Contributor to *New Statesman,* and architectural journals. Architectural critic, *New Statesman.*

WORK IN PROGRESS: Architecture without Buildings: Yurts, Zomes and Other Domes, an anthology.

BIOGRAPHICAL/CRITICAL SOURCES: New York Times, September 29, 1967.

SILVER, Samuel M. 1912-

PERSONAL: Born June 7, 1912, in Wilmington, Del.; son of Adolph D. (a tailor) and Adela (Hacker) Silver; married Elaine Shapiro, February 8, 1954; children: Leon, Joshua, Barry, Noah, Daniel. *Education:* University of Delaware, B.A., 1933; Hebrew Union College—Jewish Institute of Religion, Rabbi and M.H.L., 1940. *Politics:* Independent. *Home:* 53 Nutmeg Lane, Stamford, Conn. 06905.

CAREER: Rabbi. University of Maryland, College Park, director of Hillel Foundation, 1940-42; assistant rabbi of congregation in Cleveland, Ohio, 1946-52; Union of American Hebrew Congregations, New York, N.Y., editor of *American Judaism,* 1952-59; Temple Sinai, Stamford, Conn., rabbi, 1959—. *Military service:* U.S. Army, chaplain, 1942-46; served in Hawaii and Philippines. *Member:* Central Conference of American Rabbis, Association of Jewish Chaplains (president, 1963-64).

WRITINGS: How to Enjoy This Moment, Trident, 1967; (editor) *The Quotable American Rabbis,* Droke, 1967; (with Libbie L. Braverman) *The Six Day Warriors,* Bloch, 1969; *Explaining Judaism to Jews and Christians,* privately printed, 1971, Arco, 1973. Also author of *When You Talk English You're Often Speaking Hebrew,* 1974. Writer of weekly column, "Silver Linings," for Seven Arts Feature Syndicate of the Jewish Telegraphic Agency.

* * *

SILVERA, Alain 1930-

PERSONAL: Born September 19, 1930, in Alexandria, Egypt; son of Sylvain (a judge) and Vera (Miloslavsky) Silvera; married Dolores Dibblee, July 30, 1955; children: David. *Education:* Cornell University, A.B., 1952; Harvard University, A.M., 1953, Ph.D., 1962; Ecole Normale Superieure, Paris, France, graduate study, 1956-57. *Home:* 225 North Merion Ave., Bryn Mawr, Pa. 19010. *Office:* History Department, Bryn Mawr College, Bryn Mawr, Pa. 19010.

CAREER: Bryn Mawr College, Bryn Mawr, Pa., assistant professor, 1961-68, associate professor, 1968-72, professor of history, 1973—. Fulbright lecturer, University of Lille, 1966-67, 1968-69. *Military service:* U.S. Army, 1954-56; served in Verdun, France; became sergeant. *Member:* American Historical Association, Society for French Historical Studies, Societe d' Histoire moderne et contemporaine (Paris), American Association for Middle East Studies. *Awards, honors:* Research fellowship in Paris, 1959-61; American Association for Middle East Studies research fellowship in Cairo and Jerusalem, 1963; Fulbright grants to France, 1966-67, 1968-69; American Council of Learned Societies fellowship, 1974-75.

WRITINGS: Daniel Halevy and His Times, Cornell University Press, 1966; *The End of the Notables,* Wesleyan University Press, 1974. Contributor of articles and reviews to professional journals, including *Journal of Modern History, Mid-East, Choice.*

WORK IN PROGRESS: A history of Ecole Normale Superieure; a history of the Eastern question in the nineteenth century.

SIDELIGHTS: Silvera is fluent in French, and competent in Arabic. He has traveled extensively in Europe, Balkans, Near East, and North Africa.

* * *

SILVERMAN, Hillel E. 1924-

PERSONAL: Born February 24, 1924, in Hartford, Conn.;

son of Morris (a rabbi) and Althea (an author; maiden name, Osber) Silverman; married Devora Halaban, January 8, 1950; children: Gail, Sharon, Jonathan. *Education:* Yale University, B.A. (with highest honors), 1944; Hebrew University of Jerusalem, graduate study, 1947; Jewish Theological Seminary of America, Rabbi and M.A., 1949, Ph.D., 1951. *Office:* Sinai Temple, 10400 Wilshire Blvd., Los Angeles, Calif. 90024.

CAREER: Congregation Shearith Israel, Dallas, Tex., rabbi, 1954-64; Sinai Temple, Los Angeles, Calif., rabbi, 1964—. Member of national board of directors of rabbinical advisory council, United Jewish Appeal, and national cabinet, Rabbinical Assembly of America; past regional president, Zionist Organization of America; member of board of a number of Los Angeles civic, religious, and philanthropic organizations, including Community Relations Council and Jewish Family Service. *Military service:* U.S. Navy, Chaplain Corps, 1951-54; served overseas in Mediterranean theater. U.S. Naval Reserve, 1954—; now commander. *Member:* Jewish Historical Society (member of board of directors).

WRITINGS: (With father, Morris Silverman) *Selihot Prayers for Forgiveness,* Prayer Book Press, 1954; (with M. Silverman) *Prayer Book for Summer Camps,* Prayer Book Press, 1954; (with M. Silverman) *Tishah B'av Eve Service,* Prayer Book Press, 1955; *Judaism Looks at Life,* Jonathan David, 1967; *Judaism Meets the Challenge,* Jonathan David, 1973; *From Week to Week,* Hartmore, 1975. Sermons anthologized in *Best Sermons of 1961, Best Sermons of 1963,* and *Best Sermons of 1967.* Contributor to magazines and journals, including *Jewish Spectator, Jewish Digest,* and *Congress Weekly.*

*   *   *

SILVERSTONE, Paul H. 1931-

PERSONAL: Born June 8, 1931, in London, England; son of Arthur and Pearl (Finkelstein) Silverstone. *Education:* Yale University, A.B., 1953; Harvard University, LL.B., 1956. *Home:* 330 West 58th St., New York, N.Y. 10019. *Office:* Overland Overseas Tours Inc., 501 Fifth Ave., New York, N.Y. 10017.

CAREER: Attorney, New York, N.Y., 1958; Travel Near & Far, Inc., New York, N.Y., secretary-treasurer, 1965-70; currently partner, Lewin & Silverstone (attorneys). Secretary-treasurer, Dearing House for Stamps and Coins Inc. *Military service:* U.S. Army, 1956-58. *Member:* World Ship Society, U.S. Naval Institute (associate), Belgian Nautical Research Association, Naval Records Club, Yale Club of New York City, Collector's Club (New York).

WRITINGS: U.S. Warships of World War II, Doubleday, 1966; *U.S. Warships of World War I,* Doubleday, 1970; (with Jon L. Allen) *Stamp Collector's Guide to Europe,* Arco, 1974. Contributing editor, *Warship International.*

WORK IN PROGRESS: Encyclopedia of Modern Naval History.

*   *   *

SIMMEL, Marianne L(enore) 1923-

PERSONAL: Born January 3, 1923, in Jena, Germany. *Education:* Smith College, A.B., 1943; Harvard University, A.M., 1945, Ph.D., 1949. *Office:* Department of Psychology, Brandeis University, Waltham, Mass. 02154.

CAREER: Instructor in psychology at Cambridge Junior College, Cambridge, Mass., 1945-46, and Hofstra University, Hempstead, N.Y., 1946-48; Wellesley College, Wellesley, Mass., visiting lecturer, 1948-49; University of Illinois, College of Medicine, Chicago, 1950-58, began as instructor, became clinical associate professor of psychology; Illinois State Psychopathic Institute, Chicago, head of psychological laboratory, 1952-58, assistant director of Institute, 1952-55; Duke University Medical School, Durham, N.C., visiting lecturer in medical psychology, 1958-59; Brandeis University, Waltham, Mass., research associate, 1959-61; New School for Social Research, New York City, associate professor of psychology, 1961-63; Brandeis University, 1963—, began as associate professor, currently professor of psychology. Special research fellow, U.S. Public Health Service, National Institute of Mental Health, 1959-61, 1969-70; research associate in neurology, Mount Sinai Hospital, New York City, 1961-70. Assistant psychologist, Massachusetts General Hospital, 1959-61, 1963-72. Diplomate in clinical psychology, American Board of Examiners in Professional Psychology; certified psychologist in New York and Massachusetts.

MEMBER: American Psychological Association (fellow), Psychonomic Society, American Association of University Professors, American Society for Aesthetics, Eastern Psychological Association, Massachusetts Psychological Association, Phi Beta Kappa, Sigma Xi. *Awards, honors:* Research award, American Rehabilitation Counseling Association, 1964.

WRITINGS: (Contributor) P. Hock and J. Zubin, editors, *Psychopathology of Childhood,* Grune, 1955; (contributor) M. Baldwin and P. Bailey, editors, *Temporal Lobe Epilepsy,* C. C Thomas, 1958; (editor) *The Reach of Mind: Essays in Memory of Kurt Goldstein,* Springer, 1967. Contributor to *International Encyclopedia of the Social Sciences;* contributor of about thirty translations, research papers, and articles to *American Journal of Psychology, Journal of Neurology, Neurosurgery and Psychiatry, Child Development,* and other medical and psychology journals.

WORK IN PROGRESS: A book on sensory phantoms; research on sensory mechanisms and the cognitive processes in general.

*   *   *

SIMMONDS, George W. 1929-

PERSONAL: Born January 20, 1929, in Halle, Germany; son of Arthur and Hilde (Heinemann) Simmonds; married Florence A. Fagioli, September 5, 1951; children: Katherine Ann, David George. *Education:* Yale University, B.A., 1950; Columbia University, M.A. and Certificate of Russian Institute, 1952, Ph.D., 1964. *Office:* Department of History, University of Detroit, Detroit, Mich. 48221.

CAREER: U.S. Department of State, U.S. Information Service, New York City, Soviet area information and editorial specialist, 1950-52; Columbia University, Russian Institute, New York City, supervisor of U.S. Air Force Russian Area Training Program, 1954-55, 1956-57; Carleton College, Northfield, Minn., instructor in history, 1957-60; Elmira College, Elmira, N.Y., 1960-67, began as assistant professor, became associate professor of history, co-director and founder of Russian Studies Program, 1965-67; Wayne State University, Detroit, Mich., associate professor of history, 1967-70; University of Detroit, Detroit, associate professor of history and chairman, Russian and East European Studies Program, 1970—. *Military service:* U.S. Army, 1952-54; instructor and intelligence analyst, Psychological Warfare Center, 1953-54; became sergeant.

Member: American Historical Association, American Association for the Advancement of Slavic Studies, New York State Conference of European Historians. *Awards, honors:* Ford Foundation fellow, 1955-56; co-recipient of Catherine McGraw Rock Award, Elmira College, for outstanding contribution to teaching and curriculum, 1962; grant from Research Fund of College Center of Associated Colleges of Finger Lakes, for research in Moscow and Leningrad, 1964.

WRITINGS: (Editor and author of introduction) *Soviet Leaders: Biographies of 42 Prominent Figures in Government, Science, and the Arts,* Crowell, 1967. Reviewer for *Slavic Review, Choice, Library Journal,* and *Journal of Modern History.*

WORK IN PROGRESS: A book on the politics of the Russian conservative gentry during the period 1906-1916; first scholarly English-language edition of the memoirs of D. N. Shipov.

* * *

SIMMONS, Billy 1931-

PERSONAL: Born September 23, 1931, in Leesville, La.; son of James E. (a college professor) and Frances (Hamilton) Simmons; married Florence Abernathy, December 20, 1955; children: Charissa, Craig. *Education:* Mississippi College, Clinton, B.A. (magna cum laude), 1956; New Orleans Baptist Theological Seminary, B.D., 1959, Th.D., 1962. *Home:* 802 Alpine, Marshall, Tex. 75670. *Office:* East Texas Baptist College, Marshall, Tex. 75670.

CAREER: Clergyman, Southern Baptist Convention. Pastor in Woodville, Tex., 1962-67; Central Baptist Church, Carthage, Tex., pastor, 1967-68; East Texas Baptist College, Marshall, professor of religion and chairman of department, 1968—, trustee. Member, Panola County Youth Welfare Council. *Military service:* U.S. Air Force, 1951-54; became staff sergeant. *Member:* Rotary Club.

WRITINGS: A Functioning Faith, Word Books, 1967; *Resplendent Themes: Meditations on the Christian Life,* Crescendo Book, 1971; *Galatians: Magna Charta of Christian Liberty,* Crescendo Book, 1972; (contributor) *The Teacher's Bible Commentary,* Broadman, 1972. Contributor of articles and curriculum materials for Southern Baptist Sunday School Board to *Context, Adult Life and Work Annaul, Collegiate Teacher,* and other publications.

SIDELIGHTS: Simmons is competent in German and New Testament Greek; he has limited competence in Hebrew. *Avocational interests:* Fishing, hunting, and most other sports.

* * *

SIMMONS, J(oseph) Edgar (Jr.) 1921-

PERSONAL: Born May 28, 1921, in Natchez, Miss.; son of Joseph Edgar and Hazel Dorothy (Clark) Simmons; married Kathleen Floyd, January 28, 1954; children: Joseph Edgar III, Edward Floyd. *Education:* Attended Copiah-Lincoln Junior College, 1939-41; Columbia University, B.S., 1947, M.A., 1948; Sorbonne, University of Paris, studied modern literature, 1953-54. *Home:* 633 Lexington Ave., Jackson, Miss.

CAREER: DePauw University, Greencastle, Ind., instructor of English, 1948-50; *The Irish Press,* Dublin, Ireland, columnist, 1954-55; College of William and Mary, Williamsburg, Va., assistant professor of English, 1955-57; *New Orleans Times Picayune,* New Orleans, La., editorial writer, 1956 (summer); *Natchez Times,* Natchez, Miss., columnist, telegraph editor, editor, and managing editor, 1957-59; Southern Illinois University, Carbondale, lecturer in English, 1963-64; Mississippi College, Clinton, assistant professor of English, 1964-66; University of Texas at El Paso, assistant professor (creative writing), beginning 1966; currently free-lance writer. Member, board of directors, Hinds County (Miss.) Mental Health Association. *Military service:* U.S. Army Air Forces, 1942-45. *Member:* Mississippi Poetry Society (vice-president, 1963-66), American Society for Aesthetics, Modern Language Association. *Awards, honors:* Bellamann Award for Poetry, 1964; Texas Institute of Letters award, 1968, for *Driving to Biloxi.*

WRITINGS: Pocahantas, and Other Poems, Virginia Gazette, 1957; *Driving to Biloxi* (poetry), Louisiana State University Press, 1968.

Contributor: *New Directions in Prose and Poetry,* edited by James Laughlin, New Directions, 1966; *Southern Writing in the Sixties,* edited by J. W. Corrington and M. Williams, Louisiana State University Press, 1967; *Red Clay Reader 4,* edited by C. Whisnant, Southern Review, 1967; *The Honey and the Gall* (poems of married life), edited by Chad Walsh, Macmillan, 1967; *Poems Southwest,* edited by A. Wilber Stevens, Prescott College Press, 1968; *New Directions,* Volume 20, 1968; *Doors Into Poetry,* edited by Chad Walsh, Prentice-Hall, 1969; *New Southern Poets,* edited by Guy Owen, University of North Carolina Press, 1975.

Also contributor to *Yale Review, Nation, New Republic, Harvard Advocate, Harper's, New York Times, New York Times Book Review, Commonweal, Prairie Schooner, Sage, Janus, New York Herald Tribune,* and other periodicals.

WORK IN PROGRESS: Poetry; an interpretation of Aristotle's *Imitation;* "expansions on Carl Jung's synchronicity principle"; *The New American Composition,* an experimental freshman English textbook, for Lippincott.

SIDELIGHTS: Simmons' three year sojourn in Europe included visits to "the homes and the haunts of the poets" in England and Ireland. The following individuals have most influenced his life and poetry: Carl Jung (in particular, his principle of "individuation"), John Crowe Ransom, Alfred North Whitehead, Paul Valery, Ortega y Gasset, the existentialists, the moderns in aesthetics, Ernst Cassirer, Jacques Maritain, Erich Neumann, Wallace Stevens, and James Dickey.

* * *

SIMMS, Peter (F. J.) 1925-

PERSONAL: Born May 25, 1925, in Orpington, Kent, England; son of Francis Henry (an Anglican priest) and Margaret Annie (Rae) Simms; married Sao Sanda of Yawnghwe, September, 1954. *Education:* Jesus College, Cambridge, M.A. (honors), 1949, graduate study in Sanskrit, 1952-53. *Permanent address:* United Oxford and Cambridge University Club, 71 Pall Mall, London S.W.1, England. *Agent:* A. M. Heath & Co. Ltd., 40-42 William IV St., London WC2N 4DD, England.

CAREER: Svenskahandelshogskolan, Helsinki, Finland, lecturer, 1949-50; free-lance writer in Paris, France, 1950-51; Prasarnmitr Teachers' Training College, Bangkok, Thailand, lecturer, 1953-54; free-lance writer in Laos, and on trip by car from London, England, to Rangoon, Burma, 1954-57; editor in Rangoon, Burma, 1957-59, and lecturer at

University of Rangoon, 1959-61; correspondent in Laos for *Time* (magazine), *New York Times,* and *Observer* (London), 1961-62; free-lance journalist in British Guiana, Laos, and elsewhere in Southeast Asia for *Time* and newspapers, 1962—. *Military service:* British Army, 1943-47; posted to India, 1945.

WRITINGS: Treasures of a Kingdom, Oxford University Press, 1958; *The Irrawady,* Oxford University Press, 1962; *Trouble in Guyana,* Allen & Unwin, 1966.

WORK IN PROGRESS: A book tentatively entitled *Drug Traffic,* for Oxford University Press.

*   *   *

SIMON, John (Ivan)   1925-

PERSONAL: Born May 12, 1925, in Subotica, Yugoslavia; son of Joseph (a businessman) and Margaret (Reves) Simon. *Education:* Harvard University, A.B., 1946, A.M., 1948, Ph.D., 1959. *Politics:* "None, except when a man like Eugene McCarthy comes along; then all out for him." *Religion:* None. *Home:* 200 East 36th St., New York, N.Y. 10016. *Agent:* Lois Wallace, Wallace, Aitken & Sheil, Inc., 118 East 61st St., New York, N.Y. 10021.

CAREER: Harvard University, Boston, Mass., teaching fellow in English and humanities, 1950-53; University of Washington, Seattle, instructor in humanities and comparative literature, 1953-54; Massachusetts Institute of Technology, Cambridge, instructor in humanities, 1954-55; Bard College, Annandale-on-Hudson, N.Y., assistant professor of literature, 1957-59; Mid-Century Book Society, New York City, associate editor, 1959-61; *Hudson Review,* New York City, theatre critic, 1960—; *New Leader,* New York City, film critic, 1963-73; "Crofts Classics," Appleton-Century-Crofts, New York City, general editor, 1966-75; *Commonweal,* New York City, theatre critic, 1967-68; *New York* Magazine, New York City, drama critic, 1968-75, film critic, 1975—; *Esquire,* New York City, film critic, 1973-75. *Military service:* U.S. Army Air Forces, 1944-45. *Member:* P.E.N. *Awards, honors:* Fulbright fellowship; Rockefeller travel grant; George Polk Memorial Award for film criticism, 1968; George Jean Nathan Award in Dramatic Criticism, 1969-70.

WRITINGS: Acid Test, introduction by Dwight Macdonald, Stein & Day, 1963; *Private Screenings: Views of the Cinema of the Sixties,* Macmillan, 1967; (editor with R. Schickel) *Film, '67-'68,* Simon & Schuster, 1968; *Fourteen for Now,* Harper, 1969; *Movies into Film,* Dial, 1971; *Ingmar Bergman Directs,* Harcourt, 1972; *Uneasy Stages: A Chronicle of the New York Theatre, 1963-1973,* Random House, 1976; *Singularities: Essays on the Theatre, 1964-1974,* Random House, 1976.

SIDELIGHTS: Both *Acid Test* and *Private Screenings: Views of the Cinema of the Sixties* are collections of Simon's critical reviews. *Acid Test* includes essays on films, books, theater, fine arts, poetry, critics. Simon's movie reviews written between 1963 and 1966 appear in *Private Screenings.* The pieces in *Acid Test* (originally appearing in *Arts, Horizon, New Republic, New York Times,* among others) show "wit and verbal energy, a love of literature and the arts, lots of information, strongly defined tastes, and a conviction that aesthetics and morality are not unconnected," Emile Capouya states. R. K. Burns finds that "some of the essays are sweeping and speculative; others detailed and analytical. When discussing drama and cinema, [the author] is expert; when fiction, poetry, and art are his subjects, he is more courageous, opinionated, and interesting."

In his review of *Private Screenings,* Vern Bailey writes that "the cinema's new wave of prestige has brought with it a new kind of film critic." However, Bailey admits that Simon "believes not more than half-dozen great films have been made, though he defends twelve personal favorites." In view of Simon's reviews included in *Private Screenings,* Andrew Sinclair observes two sides of Simon: "The good John Simon has claims to be the best film critic now writing on either side of the Atlantic. He is learned, dedicated, witty and determined to raise the level of the cinema by the quality of his criticism. Yet the moment that the good John Simon has his readers in a state of stimulated gratitude, the bad John Simon leaps onto the page in an explosion of squibs and graffiti. Like Marlow's Faustus, he exchanges the search after truth and enlightenment for the puerile satisfaction of lighting bangers under the tails of the great. Inside the good John Simon, the imp is always larking about. . . . He calls criticism the poetry of life. Its function is to punish bad art and to comprehend good art. His morality as a critic should be 'a relevance to human life, an elegance of spirit, a generosity and adventuresomeness of outlook, and above all, a concept or intimation of what the ideal solution to an artistic problem would be.'. . . John Simon changes from the good critic to the bad chucker of *merde* at the least suspicion that an alternative version of what is good cinema can exist. He is as absolute and arrogant in his judgments as any dictator of culture, a rigidity that is his great strength and weakness."

However, Joseph Papp feels much more negatively about Simon's approach; specifically: "John Simon's put-down of *The Wars of the Roses* . . . through petty fault-finding and bitchy nit-picking is his stock in trade. . . . John Simon, it appears, came to the play with his familiar aberration: an abhorrence for the 'imperfect.' Well concealed under his trained intellectual cool, his deadly feelers sought out the vulnerable areas and hammered away at them with all the cunning cruelty Mr. Simon has developed over the years. In the process, unfortunately, this critic missed the real experience, the spirit of the piece, the stuff which we know of as drama, all of which surpasses the minutiae of 'defects.'"

Simon, though, has something of his own to say about critics and criticism and the problems that lie therein: "True artistic talents is a marvelously unimpeachable thing, which not even some of the self-destructive things theater people do—far more deleterious than the most ill-considered review—can obliterate. But 'personal attacks'—what are these personal attacks? Does anyone really want criticism to be impersonal? Written by a computer? Yes, of course, among the unenlightened, we still hear the old toothless saw 'objective criticism,' debunked though the notion has been by every critic worth his salt and pepper. Geometry, perhaps, can be objective and impersonal: so can xerography; but criticism? It is one of the most personal, most subjective arts—just like the arts of acting, directing, or playwriting. Like them, it may fail to persuade; or sway only in a demagogic, public-besotting manner. But if a critic can play upon the public's vices to the point of making some vicious, undeserved attack stick, is that his fault only, or is the public just as guilty? And is the reviewer who likes everything *less* personal than he who carps? Is the man who gushes about Sandy Dennis or the genius of Neil Simon, being impersonal, objective? The real danger, as I see it, is the pursuit of an impossible impersonality."

BIOGRAPHICAL/CRITICAL SOURCES: Newsweek,

July 8, 1963; *Saturday Review,* September 14, 1963; *Reporter,* December 14, 1967; *Kenyon Review,* Issue number 2, 1968; *New York Times Book Review,* January 14, 1968; *Carleton Miscellany,* spring, 1968; *Commonweal,* April 12, 1968; *Variety,* October 22, 1969, June 13, 1973; *New York Times,* December 31, 1969; *New York,* August 10, 1970; *Nation,* March 1, 1971.

*   *   *

SIMON, (Marvin) Neil 1927-

PERSONAL: Born July 4, 1927, in Bronx, N.Y.; son of Irving (a garment salesman) and Mamie Simon; married Joan Baim (a dancer), September 30, 1953 (died, 1973); married Marsha Mason (an actress), 1973; children: (first marriage) Ellen, Nancy. *Education:* Attended New York University, 1946, and University of Denver. *Residence:* Los Angeles, Calif.

CAREER: Warner Brothers, Inc., New York City, mailroom clerk, 1946; Columbia Broadcasting System, New York City, comedy writer, with his brother Danny, for Goodman Ace; comedy writer, with his brother Danny, for "The Phil Silvers Arrow Show," NBC-TV, 1948, "The Tallulah Bankhead Show," NBC-TV, 1951, "The Sid Caeser Show," NBC-TV, 1956-57, "The Phil Silvers Show," CBS-TV, 1958-59, "The Garry Moore Show," CBS-TV, 1959-60, briefly for "The Jackie Gleason Show" and "The Red Buttons Show," both CBS-TV, and for NBC-TV specials. Playwright. Owner of Eugene O'Neill Theatre, New York City. *Military service:* U.S. Army Air Force Reserve, sports editor of *Rev-Meter,* the Lowry Field (Colorado) base newspaper, 1946. *Member:* Dramatists Guild, Writers Guild of America. *Awards, honors:* Academy of Television Arts and Sciences (Emmy) award, 1957, for "The Sid Caesar Show," and 1959, for "Sergeant Bilko" ("The Phil Silvers Show"); Antoinette Perry (Tony) award nomination, 1963, for the book (dialogue) for musical "Little Me," 1963, for *Barefoot in the Park,* 1968, for *Plaza Suite,* 1969, for the book for musical *Promises, Promises,* 1970, for *Last of the Red Hot Lovers,* 1972, for *The Prisoner of Second Avenue;* Writers Guild nomination for best screenplay, 1967, for "Barefoot in the Park"; *Evening Standard* award, 1967; Sam S. Shubert Foundation award, 1968; Academy of Motion Picture Arts and Sciences (Oscar) nomination for best screenplay, 1968, for "The Odd Couple"; Writers Guild Award for best screenplay, 1969, for "The Odd Couple," 1971, for "The Out-of-Towners."

WRITINGS—Plays: (With brother, Danny Simon) *Come Blow Your Horn* (first produced in New Hope, Pa., at Bucks County Playhouse, August, 1960; produced on Broadway at Brooks Atkinson Theatre, February 22, 1961; produced on the West End at Prince of Wales Theatre, February 17, 1962), Doubleday, 1963; *Barefoot in the Park* (first produced, under title "Nobody Loves Me," in New Hope, Pa., at Bucks County Playhouse, 1962; produced, under title *Barefoot in the Park,* on Broadway at Biltmore Theatre, October 23, 1963; produced on the West End, 1965), Random House, 1964; *The Odd Couple* (first produced on Broadway at Plymouth Theatre, March 10, 1965; produced on the West End at Queen's Theatre, October 12, 1966), Random House, 1966; *Sweet Charity* (musical; based on screenplay "Nights of Cabiria" by Federico Fellini; music and lyrics by Cy Coleman and Dorothy Fields; first produced on Broadway at Palace Theatre, January 29, 1966; produced on the West End at Prince of Wales Theatre, October 11, 1967), Random House, 1966; *Star-*

Spangled Girl (first produced on Broadway at Plymouth Theatre, December 21, 1966), Random House, 1967; *Plaza Suite* (three one-acts entitled "Visitor from Hollywood," "Visitor from Mamaroneck," "Visitor from Forest Hills"; first produced on Broadway at Plymouth Theatre, February 14, 1968; produced on the West End at Lyric Theatre, February 18, 1969), Random House, 1969; *Promises, Promises* (musical; based on screenplay "The Apartment" by Billy Wilder and I.A.L. Diamond; music by Burt Bacharach; lyrics by Hal David; first produced on Broadway at Shubert Theatre, December 1, 1968; produced on the West End at Prince of Wales Theatre, October 2, 1969), Random House, 1969.

The Last of the Red Hot Lovers (three-act comedy; first produced in New Haven at Shubert Theatre, November 26, 1969; produced on Broadway at Eugene O'Neill Theatre, December 28, 1969), Random House, 1970; *The Gingerbread Lady* (originally titled "It Only Hurts When I Laugh"; first produced in New Haven at Shubert Theatre, November 4, 1970; produced on Broadway at Plymouth Theatre, December 13, 1970), Random House, 1971; *The Prisoner of Second Avenue* (first produced in New Haven at Shubert Theatre, October 12, 1971; produced on Broadway at Eugene O'Neill Theatre, November 11, 1971), Random House, 1972; *The Sunshine Boys* (first produced in New Haven at Shubert Theatre, November 21, 1972; produced on Broadway at Broadhurst Theatre, December 20, 1972), Random House, 1973; *The Good Doctor* (comedy with music; adapted and suggested from stories by Anton Chekhov; music by Peter Link; lyrics by Neil Simon; first produced on Broadway at Eugene O'Neill Theatre, November 27, 1973), Random House, 1974; *God's Favorite* (first produced on Broadway at Eugene O'Neill Theatre, December 11, 1974), Random House, 1975.

Omnibus collection: *The Comedy of Neil Simon* (contains: *Come Blow Your Horn, Barefoot in the Park, The Odd Couple, Star-Spangled Girl, Promises, Promises, Plaza Suite, The Last of the Red Hot Lovers*), Random House, 1971.

Unpublished plays: (Contributor of sketches) "Tamiment Revue," Tamiment, Pa., 1952-53; (contributor of sketches, with Danny Simon) "Catch a Star!" (musical revue), first produced on Broadway at Plymouth Theatre, November 6, 1955; (contributor of sketches, with Danny Simon) "New Faces of 1956," first produced on Broadway at Ethel Barrymore Theatre, June 14, 1956; (adapter) "Little Me" (musical; based on the novel by Patrick Dennis), music by Cy Coleman, first produced on Broadway at Lunt-Fontanne Theatre, November 17, 1962, produced on the West End at Cambridge Theatre, November 18, 1964; (contributor of sketch) "Broadway Revue" (satirical musical revue), first produced in New York City at Karmit Bloomgarden Theatre, November, 1968; "The Trouble with People" (five sketches), NBC-TV special, November 12, 1972; (editor of book for musical) "Seesaw" (based on William Gibson's "Two for the Seesaw," 1958), first produced on Broadway, April 11, 1973; "California Suite" (four vignettes), first produced in Los Angeles, April, 1976.

Plays published only: (With William Friedberg) *Adventures of Marco Polo: A Musical Fantasy* (music by Clay Warnick and Mel Pahl), Samuel French, 1959; (adapter with Friedberg) *Heidi* (based on the novel by Johanna Spyri; music by Warnick), Samuel French, 1959.

Screenplays: "After the Fox," United Artists, 1966;

"Barefoot in the Park," Paramount, 1967; "The Odd Couple," Paramount, 1968; "The Out-of-Towners" (expanded first act omitted from play *Plaza Suite*), Paramount, 1970; "Plaza Suite," Paramount, 1971; "The Last of the Red Hot Lovers," Paramount, 1972; "The Heartbreak Kid" (based on short story by Bruce Jay Friedman), Twentieth Century-Fox, 1972; "The Sunshine Boys," Columbia, 1974; "Murder by Death," Columbia, 1976. Also screenwriter of "Bogart Slept Here," a project Warner Brothers abandoned.

SIDELIGHTS: "When I was a kid," said Neil Simon, "I climbed up on a stone ledge to watch an outdoor movie of Charlie Chaplin. I laughed so hard I fell off, cut my head open and was taken to the doctor, bleeding and laughing. I was constantly being dragged out of the movies for laughing too loud. . . . my idea of the ultimate achievement in a comedy is to make a whole audience fall onto the floor, writhing and laughing so hard that some of them pass out." According to one *Life* reporter, Simon has, in a sense, reached his goal. "At *The Odd Couple* at least two people a week do—literally—fall out of their seats laughing." Similarly, *Time* began a review of *Barefoot in the Park* by stating that, "if the theater housing this comedy has an empty seat for the next couple of years, it will simply mean that someone has fallen out of it. *Barefoot* is detonatingly funny."

Tom Prideaux has noted that Simon's gags, unlike those which might be expected from a former television writer, "are not isolated jokes meant for standup comics. Instead of being sprayed out to be funny and forgotten, they are used to build up character." "One important thing I've learned about comedy," Simon has said, "is to make your characters likeable even when you're exposing their worst faults." Prideaux considered this to be the secret of Simon's success. "Audiences identify . . . with [Simon's] people and feel that they too are being liked and forgiven."

Neil Simon has a great deal to say about people, their lives and situations. He explained: "I just finished reading this biography of Chekhov, which I loved. He talked about his life's work. . . . 'Trying to show people how absurdly they live their lives.' That's what I'm trying to do. I do it through the medium of comedy, but I don't do it just to get a laugh from the audience. I also show them how absurdly we live our lives. To me, that is the point I try to make in all of my work." Simon takes his characters and situations from people he knows, things he's seen. It makes the theatricality of it all the more real. For example, Danny Simon told how *The Odd Couple* came into being: "You know *The Odd Couple* was born of my desire to write a play about my own divorce—but I couldn't find anything funny about it. This fellow Roy Gerber and I were living together, and one time I burnt a dinner and the next morning Roy said to me, 'That was a great dinner last night. What are we going to have tonight for dinner?' And I answered him like a wife: 'What are we going to have tonight? Crap we're going to have. That's all I'm good for? To slave over a hot stove for you all day long? Do I ever get out to see a show once? Do you ever take me to meet your friends?'

"And then Roy dug the bit I was doing and he said, 'Do you ever kiss me when I walk in the door? Do you ever hold my hand once in a while? Do you ever call the office to see if I'm all right?' Then I thought, 'Oh, my God, that's it. That's the play I've been looking for for two years—the story about two divorced men living together and the same problems they each had with their wives repeat with each other.'

"I wrote 14 pages. Doc [Neil Simon's childhood nickname] loved the 14 pages and begged me to write it and begged me to write it. But I needed to make a living doing television during the day. So after a long time, Doc said to me, 'Danny, if you're not going to write it, I'm going to do it.' And I told him to go ahead, there was no sense in wasting the idea. But all he used was the idea."

Neil Simon is original; however, because of his enormous success, both popular and financial, his artistic talents have been continuously questioned. Tom Prideau explained that "Simon's commercial success tends to becloud his status as a writer. If he is so popular, some critics assume, he cannot be much good. Nonsense. Simon is a very good writer—but limited. His comic lines are superbly written; no waste syllables or extra fat smudge their impact. He writes to build character rather than milk laughs, with the result that laughs are a natural accompaniment to the show. It is silly, however, to compare Simon with such masters of comedy as Moliere or Shaw. He has nowhere near their bite or breadth. But on his modest ground he is developing integrity and depth. Simon sticks to what he knows—middle-class family life, Hollywood and Broadway—and his feelings are full of mercy and fun. His greatest handicap may be that he is incorrigibly unpretentious. Taken separately, Simon's talents may not seem sufficient to justify his enormous rewards. But it must be noted that Neil Simon is not only selling entertainment. By making a modern audience feel that its foibles and vices are not too serious because he makes them seem so funny, Simon is also selling a sort of forgiveness: absolution by laughter."

Stanley Kauffmann, however, does not appear to buy what Simon is selling. "I'm not interested in proving that the play [*The Last of the Red Hot Lovers*] is a failure or in predicting that it will close—I don't care if it runs ten years. I'm interested in why the B'nai Broadway Anti-Defamation League, of which the *Times* seems to be president, has rallied to Simon's support.

"The reason isn't obscure. He is, apparently, the last of his breed—the last regular, prolific manufacturer of plays for Broadway. In the high days, Broadway had many people writing regularly for it, at various levels. Numerous playwrights had eight, ten, twelve plays produced during their careers, and there were some astonishing front-runners. . . . He is one of the last who can work comfortably for Broadway . . . and whose future is ordained, almost metaphysically, by his past. He is the sole survivor and must be safeguarded. He's becoming the whooping crane or passenger pigeon of Broadway, and the Department of the Interior, as well as *The New York Times,* may be asked to help preserve him." Simon's success, in Kauffmann's words, is based on and supported merely "by his past."

Simon's "past" involves many hits and many changes. His writing has taken new direction. Simon wants the audience to laugh, but he also wants to be taken seriously. Concerning Simon's direction, Brendan Gill comments: "Since 'Plaza Suite' is a hit, I feel all the more free to express my disappointment in the direction that Mr. Simon's work appears to be taking. A few years back, with 'Barefoot in the Park,' one got the impression that he was experimenting with a new form of comedy—an agreeably disordered form, in which jokes arrived and departed so quietly that they were scarcely to be noticed as jokes and there was room between them for evocations of real life, observed with wit and charm. The carefully carpentered plots and the innumerable mechanical gags that disfigure 'Plaza Suite' strike me as a long step backward. I hope it is not idle to regret that the greater Mr. Simon's success in the world, the fewer the chances he seems willing to take with his considerable talent." Gill seems to be putting Simon's efforts in a closed category as has Harold Clurman. Clurman expressed his view of Simon's success in terms of a Broadway hit formula: "Neil Simon upholds a great tradition: he writes sure-fire comedies for the big audiences everywhere in the United States—our national Broadway. His insights are conventional—they match the audience's preconceptions—and his comedy technique is firmly set in the theatrical line of which he is the one steadily producing heir. His writing covers the structure of his slight plots with a bright patina of canny wisecracks which invariably produce the expected laughs, although one can hardly remember them shortly after they have exploded. The formula is a pillar of show business."

Many critics are not willing to accept Simon's ability to be serious. The stereotype of a Simon hit clouds reactions to what Simon is saying beneath the laughs. Brendan Gill says that Simon "holds 'Last of the Red Hot Lovers' to be something new for him; he calls it a serious comedy, and I fear that he intends to display a still greater degree of seriousness in the future. It is a grave misreading of his gifts, for Mr. Simon's so-called seriousness has a banality of insight not easily to be distinguished from that of soap opera."

Simon has his own feelings on the subject of seriousness and playwriting on the whole. Paul D. Zimmerman writes that "Simon still runs an obstacle course of fear and self-doubt with each new play. 'Every time I start a play, I panic because I feel I don't know how to do it,' he says. 'I keep wishing I had a grownup in the room who would tell me how to begin. I still have all the fears I had in the beginning. I just hide them better now.' He couldn't hide them from Maureen Stapleton, the co-star with George C. Scott of 'Plaza Suite,' who remembers Simon's face before opening night. 'How can I characterize that look?' Stapleton asks. 'It's like the doctor had just told him, "You've got two minutes to live." It's that look of death, and all the playwrights get it.' ... 'Arthur Miller says in his plays "how tragic life is" and thank God for playwrights like him,' says Simon. 'My view is "how sad and funny life is." I can't think of a humorous situation that does not involve some pain. I used to ask, "What is a funny situation?" Now I ask, "What is a sad situation and how can I tell it humorously?"' Simon has no formula for comic success. The closest he can come to describing his comic technique is to say that he places his characters in intolerable situations and under constant pressures. ... 'And I know with each play that if I can only find a more powerful microscope, I can see deeper and find out more. I believe that if I keep on working, I am going to unearth some kind of secret that will make it unnecessary for me to write again. But all I find is clues. And the more of them I find, the more fascinating and frightening life becomes. If I stop writing plays, I've got nothing left to do. It's the only way I have of finding out what life is all about.' So, inside Neil Simon the success, lives a serious playwright struggling to get out. He has lived the American dream and found it puzzling, contradictory and ultimately unsatisfying. And his accomplishments up to now, as he sees them, are mixed and mean little if they are not prologue to more important visions of the human predicament. Laughs only count now as echoes of the truth. 'I just can't go any farther in terms of success,' he says. 'But as a writer, I feel I'm just at the beginning.'''

Clive Barnes is one critic who has not only acknowledged but commended Simon on his "echoes of the truth": "Go to 'Plaza Suite,' forget the laughs and look at the suffering. Neil Simon is the poet of the new compromise; he understands, and sadly forgives, every shabby transaction of the soul. There is more to Mr. Simon than meets the funnybone. It is true—and this is perhaps a present limitation—he plays footsie with the prejudices of his audience, massages their convictions and is occasionally a sucker for the overslick one-liner. But beneath this easy, brilliant professional glaze is something very serious, and very sad." At times, however, Simon is still referred to as a gag writer, but Jack Kroll expresses a different perspective on Simon's comedic finesse and the seriousness therein; again, the "echoes of the truth" are being noted: "In 1968's 'Plaza Suite,' Simon fiddled around unsuccessfully with 'serious' overtones in his palimpsest of gags. In 'Lovers,' the serious comes right out of the funny, and both come right out of Simon's own feeling for people, the times and serious stuff like that. As befits the professional gag writer that he was and in a sense still is, he has always been a 'situation' man, as in 'The Odd Couple,' but for the first time his situation seems less a contrivance than a good comic idea, funny in itself, but also bearing the force of his own attitudes and sensibility.... For the first time I found myself laughing at a Simon play because it seemed to know something about life, not just about the Broadway laugh market." Finally, Simon's efforts are seen as being more than Clurman's impression of the Broadway laugh formula.

Marilyn Stasio also recognizes and supports Simon's serious efforts: "With 'Last of the Red Hot Lovers,' Simon steps distinctly out of polite-comedy circles and into the arena of the black humorists. There is nothing at all funny about the painfully neurotic and really quite profoundly unhappy characters in this play, which is actually about the disintegration of our moral codes and the chaos which such a breakdown has made of our emotional lives. What makes the play so wildly funny is not its author's vision, for Simon's is close to tragedy, but his conceptualization of that vision as high comedy-of-manners. It is neither the personae of the characters nor the situations of their drama which Simon treats humorously, but only the superficial foibles which they have erected as elaborate defenses against their own anxieties." A reviewer from *Time* summarizes the comic-tragedy of Simon's efforts in a review of *The Last of the Red Hot Lovers:* "Behind the laughs lies Simon's most serious play. In some peculiar way, comedy is no laughing matter. It is remarkably moral. It hopes to reform by ridicule. While it may seem like a strange thing to say, the only proper forebear of Neil Simon would be someone like Moliere. This is the kind of playwright who peppers the society's precepts with a stinging humor. In his later plays Simon is saying a dead-serious thing—that the Judeo-Christian ethic as applied to a husband-and-wife relationship is bankrupt. Men and women are supposed to be true to one another until death do them part, but that is not what happens. However, Simon is not sufficiently perceptive or honest when he suggests that adultery is some sort of casual byplay. Adultery is either revenge or renaissance, and it is usually a coroner's report on a marriage. Simon ought to risk more seriousness. The wine of wisdom is in him, and he ought to let it breathe longer between the gags." Whereas some critics feel that Simon should stick to typical Broadway "sitcom," others believe that Simon does have the ability and ought to, at this point, take more chances than he previously had.

In taking further chances, Simon attempted his most serious play, *The Gingerbread Lady*. A *Variety* reviewer comments on the possible future of such serious endeavors: "It will be interesting to see the general reaction to 'The Gingerbread Lady.' Perhaps the same observers who have down-graded Simon as merely a clever writer of frivolous comedies will now criticize him for what they will call a morbid or even maudlin play. Audiences who expect a typical Simon comedy hit may be disturbed and even annoyed at such somber and basically tragic subject matter. It remains to be seen whether the playwright, a master of comedy dialog, dramatic structure and characterization, can have equal success or even reasonable success as a serious dramatist, toward which he has been increasingly pointing in his last few plays. If not, he could possibly follow the example of the late Philip Barry, for instance, who had numerous comedy hits but failed repeatedly at the serious dramas to which he aspired. Whatever its critical and public impact, however, 'The Gingerbread Lady' is an absorbing play and an admirable attempt by a distinguished author." Reviewing "The Trouble with People," an NBC-TV special, John J. O'Connor criticizes not only Simon's serious attempts and possible disasters, but also the varying value of Simon's content: "While hefty chunks of the concoctions have been splendidly funny, the wholes have been curiously unsatisfying. The situations are less sustained than repeated. The three acts of 'The Last of the Red Hot Lovers' offered three variations on a single theme. The first act of 'The Prisoner of Second Avenue' is not quite so funny when it is transferred, almost intact, to the second act. And, at his most consciously serious, in 'The Gingerbread Lady,' Mr. Simon has edged closest to sheer disaster. It would seem, then, that Mr. Simon would be at his most effective in a series of short sketches presented in the medium that nurtured his gift for comedy. Based on last night's special, the answer is sometimes yes, sometimes no." The criticism is based on a comedic viewpoint, again keeping Simon in a category where he is, by other's standards, competing with his own past comedic successes.

In regard to Simon's further, more current achievements, Clive Barnes comments on *The Prisoner of Second Avenue* and Simon's comedic growth: "The initial set-up for the comedy is as brilliant as is Mr. Simon's wont. But more and more Mr. Simon is discovering that where there's a wont there's a way, more and more he is getting into deeper and far funnier communication with his comic muse.... Mr. Simon understands the essential moroseness of comedy. The one-line wisecracks seem a thing of the past—perhaps he grew tired of critics and dinner parties stealing them—and now his humor has a sad air to it, all the more deliciously funny for that undercurrent of discontent.... The play has some lovely touches and many sweetly poised jokes. At times Mr. Simon is as elegant as a matador in the way he teases and plays with dialogue, or else swiftly builds up a situation with the inspired concentration of a man constructing a house of cards. There is a special delight in watching the finesse of his technique." Tom Prideaux also sees the growth in Simon's work and expresses his optimism for the future of Simon's efforts and Broadway: "If an efficient critic tried to sum up what happened to Broadway in 1971, he might simply tell what happened to Neil Simon. For Broadway and Simon are so close that if Simon sneezes Broadway gets a cold, a psychosomatic cold caused by the fear that if Simon sickens, Broadway might die.... In his next play Simon made another stab at unorthodoxy and hit the jackpot with *The Prisoner of Second Avenue*. In this excursion, the world's most successful living playwright exhibits tendencies that Broadway would have found alarming six years ago, namely the avant-garde influence of Eugene Ionesco and Jules Feiffer. Black comedy? Not exactly. But hints of gray. Broadway and Simon are changing their stripes together; the prognosis for their mutation is hopeful."

Following Simon's progress on the Broadway stage, Marilyn Stasio, in her review of *The Sunshine Boys*, contends that Simon's "comic vision" is quite profound: "There are show-biz laughs, nostalgia laughs, New Jersey laughs—laughs for everybody. And because the laughter is grounded in penetrating character study, it always feels warm and rich and gratifying. For there is genuine depth to this comic vision, which is trained on a real relationship between people of substance. And beneath the surface hilarity of their banter and battling is the genuinely affecting theme of two human beings learning to accept old age.... Willie, the partner who stubbornly and sadly clings to old bitternesses, ancient memories, and an independence being cruelly corroded by old age. A beautiful team. A beautiful play."

Putting criticism aside, a *Time* review takes note of Simon's annual gifts to the Broadway stage: "Santa Claus is just an alias for Neil Simon. Every year just before Christmas, he loads up packets of goodies and tosses two unbridled hours of laughter to Broadway audiences. Santa Simon is back again with a cripplingly funny show aptly called *The Sunshine Boys*.... Beneath the bantering foolery, the play is warm, affectionate and touching. None of Simon's comedies has been more intimately written out of love and a bone-deep affinity with the theatrical scene and temperament.... As playgoers, we should return the bows that they take and reserve a special one for the annual bounty of Neil Simon."

One of Simon's more recent gifts to Broadway was a play adaptation of some Checkhov short stories, entitled *The Good Doctor*. Jack Kroll discusses his concern for the attempt and possible repercussions of such an attempt: "Art can be made out of anything. T. S. Eliot called Dryden the great master of hatred and Swift the great master of disgust. Neil Simon's play, *The Good Doctor,* formally anoints its author as the great master of chutzpah. With the sly and sassy bravado which only that pungent Yiddish word can convey, America's most prolific and successful playwright has identified himself with Anton Chekhov. No, no, not Anton Chekhov the fat delicatessen waiter—Anton Chekhov the skinny Russian writer, the great playwright who insisted that his plays were comedies, not tragedies. Simon of course has Chekhov's problem in reverse: certain stuffed shirts and double-domes steadfastly refuse to take Simon's gag-filled plays, with their echoes of vaudeville and television, seriously. Simon is right to be bothered by this, since there is nothing so serious as comedy. The real critical question is not how serious Simon is, but how funny Simon is.... Simon's gambit in this play has a genuinely outrageous charm—he really does raise chutzpah to an esthetic power. When Christopher Plummer comes on in Chekhovian drag—beard, pince-nez, walking stick—chattering with Great Man affability ('What force is it that compels me to write so incessantly? I have no choice. I am a writer'), only a snowman would be unmoved by Simon's obvious cry from the heart, 'Godammit, I'm a writer!' Simon is going to be jumped on and bitten by critics outraged at 'what he has done to Checkhov.' What concerns me is what Chekhov, who can take care of himself, has done to Simon." Simon is still fighting to be taken seriously. He does not want the title of "most successful playwright"; he wants to be recognized as a serious playwright.

God's Favorite, Simon's recent endeavor, was not very well received by Clive Barnes, who writes: "Having set up the situation Mr. Simon starts letting off jokes like firecrackers. Admittedly far, far too many of these jokes are concerned with brand names and television reference. Mr. Simon nowadays appears to believe that you only have to mention names like Lemon Pledge or 'Hollywood Squares' to raise a laugh. Well, with the unsophisticated you can, but this kind of name-dropping is cheap humor, quite unworthy of our finest comic playwright. The rest of the humor is that New York wry on the rocks that Mr. Simon has practically patented for smoothness. At their best, his jokes have a kind of hilariously deadpan ecstasy and, even better, are taken from life. Unfairly enough, whereas this may be Mr. Simon's most imaginative play (Job for laughs does take a bit of imagining), it is not one of his better works. Not only is the opening slow, but also the ending is anticlimactic. If you have exploited tragedy for its humor, how do you get around a happy ending? The holocaust is over, Job is relieved, but the audience has still got to get out of the theater with an ending in its mind. This is a structural problem that is possibly insoluble; certainly Mr. Simon scarcely comes to grips with it." Barnes continues more positively, however, noting Simon's past successes and affirming his belief in Simon's ability: "A Neil Simon comedy is an annual blessing and ritual like Thanksgiving. We have, in the past, had better and, more occasionally, worse, but this will keep things going well enough until next year."

Commenting on Simon's serious endeavors, Mel Brooks (formerly a member of the writing team with Neil and Danny Simon for "The Phil Silvers Show" and others) was quoted by Richard Meryman as having said "Doc is going to have a long, hard road. He's got to get his papers stamped. He doesn't have his credentials and he will not be allowed into Serious Land. I think it is very important that he launch this deeper side of his talent. The best thing Doc could do to make that transition would be to dip his pen in the blood of his heart and write for an off-Broadway 199-seat house a total tragedy. The easiest thing Doc could do is just obliquely to insinuate there's more to life than one laugh after another."

In one sense, Simon has achieved incredible stature, not only as a successful playwright, but also as a talented, brilliant, comic, and serious playwright. Simon, himself, states: "I've gotten the kind of reviews I've always admired. For the first time in my life I've seen the words 'distinguished playwright'—I've seen it in a half-dozen reviews. This is something I've been striving for all my life." However, in another sense, it does not appear that the general public, and critics on the whole, really take into serious consideration what Simon is saying. Kroll notes that "the opening of a Neil Simon comedy has become the greatest display of conditioned reflexes since Pavlov's drooling canines...." The conditioned responses initiated by Simon's past successes make Simon wonder if anyone is really listening to him at all. Simon told Richard Meryman: "You know, all those days when I was saying that I was going to prove I could be a successful playwright—prove it to the world or whoever, maybe my mother or father or just to myself—there was no longer any enjoyment when it came off. It's like the child who calls out, 'Daddy, daddy, watch me. I'm going to dive into the pool.' And daddy watches, but it isn't enough. The child says, 'No, you weren't really watching.'"

Simon's hits-only straight play records include: *Come Blow Your Horn,* 677 performances, 1960-61 season; *Barefoot in the Park,* 1,530 performances, 1963-64 season; and *The Odd Couple,* 964 performances, 1964-65 season.

Movies based on his original plays include: "Come Blow Your Horn," adapted by Norman Lear, Paramount, 1963; "Sweet Charity," Universal, 1969; and "Star-Spangled Girl," Paramount, 1971.

Television series based on Simon's original plays include: "Barefoot in the Park," ABC-TV, 1970-71 season; "The Odd Couple," ABC-TV, beginning fall season, 1970.

BIOGRAPHICAL/CRITICAL SOURCES: Time, November 1, 1963, January 12, 1970, January 15, 1973; *Life,* April 9, 1965, March 6, 1970, May 7, 1971; *Newsweek,* January 2, 1967, February 26, 1968, February 2, 1970, November 23, 1970, December 10, 1973, April 26, 1976; *Nation,* March 4, 1968; *Vogue,* April 1, 1968, October 1, 1968, January 1, 1970; *New York Times,* August 4, 1968, December 3, 1968, December 31, 1969, November 17, 1971, December 9, 1973, December 12, 1974, December 22, 1974; *Playbill,* January, 1969; *Critic's Choice,* December, 1969; *Variety,* December 24, 1969, February 25, 1970, November 4, 1970, September 8, 1971, December 27, 1972; *Cue,* January 3, 1970, January 15, 1972; *Village Voice,* January 8, 1970; *Show Business,* January 10, 1970; *Washington Post,* January 13, 1970, February 9, 1971; *Christian Science Monitor,* January 17, 1970, November 11, 1970; *New York Times Magazine,* March 22, 1970; *New Republic,* January 16, 1971; Danny Simon, "Only the Shadow Knows" (comedy), first produced in New Hope, Pa. at Bucks County Playhouse, September 4, 1971; *TV Guide,* November 4, 1972; Carolyn Riley, editor, *Contemporary Literary Criticism,* Volume VI, Gale, 1976.†

*   *   *

SIMON, Rita James 1931-

PERSONAL: Born November 26, 1931, in Brooklyn, N.Y.; daughter of Abraham (a businessman) and Irene (Waldman) Mintz; married Julian L. Simon (a professor), June 25, 1961; children: David, Judith, Daniel. *Education:* University of Wisconsin, B.A., 1952; Cornell University, graduate student, 1952-54; University of Chicago, Ph.D., 1957. *Religion:* Jewish. *Office:* Department of Sociology, University of Illinois, Urbana, Ill. 61822.

CAREER: University of Chicago, Chicago, Ill., assistant professor, and research associate, Law School, 1959-61; Columbia University School of Social Work, New York, N.Y., research associate, 1961-63; Yale University, New Haven, Conn., university lecturer, 1962-63; University of Illinois, Urbana, associate professor, 1963-68, professor of sociology and law, 1968—. Visiting professor, Hebrew University of Jerusalem, 1974-75. *Member:* American Sociological Association. *Awards, honors:* Guggenheim fellowship, 1966; Ford Foundation fellow, 1971.

WRITINGS: The Jury and the Defense of Insanity, Little, Brown, 1967; (editor) *As We Saw the Thirties,* University of Illinois Press, 1967; (editor) *Readings in the Sociology of Law,* Chandler Publishing, 1968; (with Jeffrey O'Connell) *Payment for Pain and Suffering,* Insurers Press, 1972; *Public Opinion in America, 1936-1970,* Rand-McNally, 1974; *The Jury System,* Sage Publications, Inc., 1975. Also author of monograph, *Women and Crime,* 1975. Contributor to sociology journals.

SIMON, Sidney   1927-

PERSONAL: Born May 29, 1927, in Pittsburgh, Pa.; son of Frank E. and Bessie (Finklestein) Simon; married Marianne Preger, December 21, 1956; children: John, Douglas, Julianna, Matthew. Education: Pennsylvania State University, B.A., 1949, M.Ed., 1952; New York University, Ed.D., 1958. Home: 25 Montague Rd., Leverett, Mass. 01054. Office: College of Education, University of Massachusetts, Amherst, Mass.

CAREER: High school teacher, principally of English, in Bradford, Pa., 1950-52, Baldwin, Long Island, N.Y., 1952-54, and New York, N.Y., 1954-57; assistant professor at Paterson State College (now William Paterson College of New Jersey), Wayne, 1958-59, and Queens College of the City University of New York, Flushing, N.Y., 1959-65; Temple University, College of Education, Philadelphia, Pa., associate professor, 1965-69; University of Massachusetts, College of Education, professor of education, 1969—. Co-director of summer workshops at Princeton University, University of Rochester, and other colleges. Participant, Mississippi Church Rebuilders, 1965, and speaker on behalf of CORE, Freedom Week Rally, and student help projects in slum areas. Military service: U.S. Navy, World War II. Member: Association for Supervision and Curriculum Development, National Education Association, Association for Higher Education, National Council for the Social Studies, American Association of University Professors, John Dewey Society.

WRITINGS: Henry, the Uncatchable Mouse (juvenile), Norton, 1964; The Armadillo without a Shell (juvenile), Norton, 1966; (with Louis E. Raths and Merrill Harmin) Values and Teaching, C. E. Merrill, 1966.

(With Howard Kirschenbaum and Rodney Napier) Wad-ja-get?: The Trading Game in American Education, Hart Publishing, 1971; (with Kirschenbaum and Leland W. Howe) Values Clarification: A Handbook of Practical Strategies for Teachers and Students, Hart Publishing, 1972; (with Harmin and Kirschenbaum) Clarifying Values through Subject Matter: Applications for the Classroom, Winston Press, 1973; (with Robert C. Hawley and David D. Britton) Composition for Personal Growth: Values Clarification through Writing, Hart Publishing, 1973; (compiler with Kirschenbaum) Readings in Values Clarification, Winston Press, 1973; I Am Lovable and Capable: A Modern Allegory on the Classical Put-down, Argus Communications, 1974; Meeting Yourself Halfway: Thirty-one Values Clarification Strategies for Daily Living, Argus Communications, 1974; (editor with Donald A. Read) Humanistic Education Sourcebook, Prentice-Hall, 1975; (with Jay Clark) More Values Clarification: A Guidebook for the Use of Values Clarification in the Classroom, Pennant Press, 1975.

Contributor of chapter to Concern for the Individual in Student Teaching, yearbook of Association for Student Teaching, 1963, and about twenty articles to Harvard Educational Review, Journal of Higher Education, and other journals. Columnist, writing "Visiting Professor of Heresy" for Temple University News.†

*   *   *

SIMONSON, Solomon S.   1914-

PERSONAL: Born April 19, 1914, in Brooklyn, N.Y.; son of Alexander Falk and Rebecca Rachel (Finkelstein) Simonson; married Hana M. Gutwillig, January 27, 1957; children: Charles Gordon, Rose Jeanne, Alexander Falk.

Education: Brooklyn College (now Brooklyn College of the City University of New York), B.A., 1935, M.A., 1939; St. Lawrence University, LL.B., 1938; Northwestern University, Ph.D., 1943. Home: 13 Dalewood Dr., Suffern, N.Y. Office: Office of the Dean, Borough of Manhattan Community College of the City University of New York, New York, N.Y. 10019.

CAREER: Brooklyn College (now Brooklyn College of the City University of New York), Brooklyn, N.Y., instructor in speech, 1935-41; Northwestern University, Evanston, Ill., graduate fellow, 1941-45; State College of Iowa (now University of Northern Iowa), Cedar Falls, assistant professor of English and speech, 1945-46; University of Denver, Denver, Colo., associate professor of speech and law, 1946-49; State University of New York at Fredonia, professor of speech and chairman of department, 1949-59, founder and director of Communications Center; Yeshiva University, New York City, professor of English, speech, and communications, 1959-66, head of doctoral research in communications, 1966-73; Borough of Manhattan Community College of the City University of New York, New York City, dean, 1972—. Consultant to Verrazano College, 1967-72; member of judging committee for Howard W. Blakeslee Award, 1970-73. Member: National Council of Teachers of English, Speech Association of America (past president, New York State branch). Awards, honors: Ford Foundation grant, 1953; best poem award of American Literary Association for "Fascinated Fool."

WRITINGS: Crisis in Television: A Study of the Private Judgment and the Public Interest, Living Books, 1966. Writer of two filmstrips with guides, "Julius Caesar," 1968, and "Hamlet," 1969, both for Popular Science. Contributor to professional and educational journals, including Journal of the History of Ideas, Review of Religion, Studies in the Mass Media, and Philosophy and Phenomenological Research.

WORK IN PROGRESS: Crisis in Education: The New Three Rs: Reasons, Right, and Response.

*   *   *

SIMPSON, Myrtle L(illias)   1931-
(M. L. Emslie)

PERSONAL: Born July 5, 1931, in Great Britain; daughter of Hamish and Kathleen (Calvert) Emslie; married Hugh W. Simpson (a pathologist), March 21, 1959; children: Robin, Bruce, Rona, Rory. Education: Educated in United Kingdom and India. Politics: Tory, "with overtones of Scottish Nationalist." Religion: Presbyterian. Home: 2 Kirklee Ter., Glasgow, Scotland. Agent: Winant Towers Ltd., 14 Clifford's Inn, London EC4A 1DA, England.

CAREER: Mountaineer and explorer; first woman to cross the Greenland ice cap. Trained as a radiographer in Edinburgh, Scotland, qualifying in 1953; went to New Zealand that same year, looking for higher hills to climb than those in the Scottish highlands; moved on to Australia, 1956, and spent two years traveling the continent, working at a variety of jobs "when out of pocket," including pearl diving and cooking for alligator hunters in the Northern Territory; returned to Scotland to help organize the Edinburgh Andean expedition in 1958; climbed the highest mountain in Peru and five other summits over 22,000 feet (married an expedition scientist the following year); member of the Scottish Spitsbergen expedition, 1960, two expeditions to Iceland, 1961 and 1962, and the Scottish Surinam expedition in South America, 1963; with her husband and two other men crossed the Greenland ice cap on skis, 1965; reached most northerly latitude achieved by a woman in 1968, on *Daily Telegraph* North Pole expedition; return to Greenland with British Broadcasting Crop. to film eskimo way of life, 1970-73; member of the British Ladies Himalayan expedition, 1974. Guide on tourist ship, "Lindblad Explorer." Lecturer and broadcaster on expeditions and personal experiences. *Member:* Society of Authors, P.E.N., Scottish Ski Club (president). *Awards, honors: Daily Telegraph* travel award, December 1967, for a Greenland trip the Simpsons made with their children the previous summer; Mungo Park medal for exploration, 1971.

WRITINGS—All published by Gollancz: *Home is a Tent* (autobiographical), 1964; *White Horizons* (autobiographical), 1967; *Due North!*, 1970; *Simpson the Obstratician* (biography), 1972; *Greenland Summer*, 1973. Also author of *Armadillo Stew*.

Under maiden name, M. L. Emslie: "Far and Near Readers" series on travel; published by W. & R. Chambers, 1960: *Journey to Amazon; Black Fellows and Buffaloes; Lapland Journey; Spitsbergen Adventure; Three in the Andes.* Contributor to *National Geographic, Woman's Own, Sunday Express* (London), *She, Guardian,* and other periodicals and newspapers.

WORK IN PROGRESS: A book on Himalayan journey; a biography of Lady Franklin.

SIDELIGHTS: Believers in keeping the family together and exposing children to the simple primitive life, the Simpsons took their firstborn son, Robin, then an infant, on the Spitzbergen expedition, a four-month sojourn six hundred miles from the North Pole. When Bruce was born in 1961 and Rona in 1962, they too accompanied their parents on the 1963 Surinam expedition to South America, living for a time in a Wai Ana Indian village deep in the rain forest. The three children were left behind on the crossing of the Greenland ice cap, but flew to join their parents at Stromfjord and spent the summer living in an Eskimo encampment. Mrs. Simpson is "very involved in ski training of Scottish juniors to competition standard."

BIOGRAPHICAL/CRITICAL SOURCES: Myrtle L. Simpson, *Home is a Tent*, Gollancz, 1964; M. L. Simpson, *White Horizons*, Gollancz, 1967.

* * *

SINAI, I(saac) Robert 1924-

PERSONAL: Born October 10, 1924, in Joniskis, Lithuania; came to United States in 1962, naturalized in 1969; son of Boris and Ella (Zotnick) Sinai; married Anne Witten, August 18, 1946; children: Joshua B. *Education:* Educated in South Africa. *Home:* 21 Grant St., Potsdam, N.Y. 13676. *Office:* State University of New York College at Potsdam, Potsdam, N.Y. 13676.

CAREER: Free-lance journalist in Johannesburg, South Africa, London, England, and Paris, France, 1946-51; Israel Federation of Labor, editor of *Work*, 1952-55, officer in international relations department, 1957-60; Israel Labour Party, representative on secretariat of Asian Socialist Conference, Rangoon, Burma, 1955-57; Israel Foreign Office, information officer, 1962; University of Pennsylvania, Philadelphia, consultant to Foreign Policy Research Institute, 1963; instructor at New School for Social Research, New York City, 1963-66, and New York University, New York City, 1964-66; Long Island University, Brooklyn, N.Y., associate professor of political science and history, 1966-72;

State University of New York College at Potsdam, associate professor of political science, 1973—. Associate, Columbia University Seminar on International Research, 1964-65; guest lecturer at Princeton University, University of Wisconsin, Johns Hopkins University, and Columbia University. *Member:* Authors Guild, American Association of University Professors, American Historical Association, American Political Science Association, Academy of Political Science. *Awards, honors:* Rockefeller Foundation fellow, 1965-66.

WRITINGS: The Challenge of Modernization, Norton, 1964; *In Search of the Modern World*, New American Library, 1967; (editor) *Modernization and the Middle East*, American Academic Association for Peace in the Middle East, 1970; (editor with wife, Anne Sinai) *Israel and the Arabs: Prelude to the Jewish State*, Facts on File, 1972; (contributor) Frank Tachau, editor, *The Developing Nations: What Path to Modernization?*, Dodd, 1972; (contributor) William Appleman Williams, editor, *The Shaping of American Diplomacy*, 2nd edition, Rand McNally, in press. Also author of papers on international relations; contributor to newspapers and periodicals.

WORK IN PROGRESS: Crisis of the Modern World.

* * *

SINGER, Fred J. 1931-

PERSONAL: Born August 8, 1931, in Berlin, Germany; naturalized U.S. citizen, 1962; son of Robert Vilmos and Adele (Ohlson) Singer; married Emmy von Scheven (an instructor), April 4, 1958. *Education:* Educated in Tientsin, China. *Politics:* Independent. *Religion:* "Non-believer." *Home:* 4017 Southwest Fairvale Dr., Portland, Ore. 97221.

CAREER: After leaving China, lived in Thailand, 1947-58; formerly manager, Varityper Corp., San Francisco, Calif.; writer, 1966—.

WRITINGS: Epigrams at Large, Philosophical Library, 1967.

WORK IN PROGRESS: A second book of epigrams.

SIDELIGHTS: Fred Singer speaks Siamese, Russian, and Chinese, in addition to German.

* * *

SINGER, Irving 1925-

PERSONAL: Born December 24, 1925, in New York, N.Y.; son of Isidore (a grocer) and Nettie (Stromer) Singer; married Josephine Fisk, June 10, 1949; children: Anne W., Margaret W., Emily S., Benjamin I. *Education:* Harvard University, A.B. (summa cum laude), 1948, M.A., 1949, Ph.D., 1952; studied at Biarritz American University, 1945-46, Oxford University, 1949-50, University of Paris, 1955-56. *Home:* 352 Marlborough St., Boston, Mass. 02115. *Office:* Department of Philosophy 14N-427, Massachusetts Institute of Technology, Cambridge, Mass. 02115.

CAREER: Cornell University, Ithaca, N.Y., instructor in philosophy, 1953-56; University of Michigan, Ann Arbor, assistant professor of philosophy, 1956-59; Massachusetts Institute of Technology, Cambridge, visiting lecturer, 1958-59, associate professor, 1959-69, professor of philosophy, 1969—. Visiting lecturer at Johns Hopkins University, 1957-58; visiting assistant professor at Harvard University, summer, 1958. *Military service:* U.S. Army, 1944-46.

MEMBER: American Philosophical Association. *Awards, honors:* Postdoctoral Fulbright research scholar, 1955-56;

Bollingen grants-in-aid, 1958, 1959, 1965-66; American Council of Learned Societies grants-in-aid, 1958, 1966-67; *Hudson Review* fellow in criticism, 1958-59; Guggenheim fellow, 1965-66; Bollingen fellow, 1966-67; fellow of the Villa I Tatti, Harvard University Center for Italian Renaissance Studies in Florence, Italy, 1965-67; Rockefeller Foundation grant, 1970-72.

WRITINGS: (Editor and author of introduction) George Santayana, *Essays in Literary Criticism,* Scribner, 1956; *Santayana's Aesthetics,* Harvard University Press, 1957; *The Nature of Love: Plato to Luther,* Random House, 1966; *The Goals of Human Sexuality,* Norton, 1973; (contributor) R. Wertz, editor, *Readings on Ethical and Social Issues in Bio-Medicine,* Prentice-Hall, 1973. Translation of an essay by Jose Ortega y Gasset included in *Hudson Review Anthology,* Vintage, 1962. Articles and reviews have appeared in *Mercure* (Paris), *Tematy* (Poland), *Analysis, Philosophical Review, New York Review of Books, Hudson Review, Journal of Biosocial Science,* and other periodicals.

WORK IN PROGRESS: Sequel to *The Nature of Love.*

*   *   *

SINGH, Lalita Prasad 1936-

PERSONAL: Born March 5, 1936, in Chazipur, Uttar Pradesh, India; son of Jhunni (a teacher) and Motidevi Singh; wife's name, Utimraj; children: Shaila, Asha, Abha, Indu (daughters). *Education:* Allahabad University, B.A., 1955, M.A., 1957; Delhi University, Ph.D., 1962; Australian National University, Ph.D., 1965. *Home:* 12400 Olivier St., Montreal, Quebec, Canada. *Office:* Department of Political Science, Concordia University, Montreal, Quebec, Canada.

CAREER: St. Andrews College, Gorakhpur University, Gorakhpur, India, assistant professor of political science, 1957-58; University of Missouri, Columbia, visiting assistant professor of political science, 1964-65; Pennsylvania State University, University Park, assistant professor of political science, 1965-66; University of Western Ontario, London, assistant professor of political science, 1966-68; Concordia University, Montreal, Quebec, associate professor of political science, 1968—.

WRITINGS: The Colombo Plan: Some Political Aspects, Department of International Relations, Australian National University, 1963, revised edition, 1964; *The Politics of Regional Economic Cooperation in Asia: A Study of Asian International Organizations,* University of Missouri Press, 1966; *The United Nations and Namibia,* East African Publishing House, in press. Contributor of more than twenty-five articles to professional journals.

WORK IN PROGESS: Indonesian Foreign Policy; United Nations and Decolonisation; Indian Foreign Policy.

*   *   *

SINGLETON, John 1930-

PERSONAL: Born August 7, 1930, in Philadelphia, Pa.; son of William Francis (a chemist) and Janet (Anthony) Singleton; married Anne Haase, December 27, 1953; children: Mark, William, Peter. *Education:* Oberlin College, A.B., 1952; Haverford College, M.A., 1953; Stanford University, Ph.D., 1965. *Religion:* Society of Friends (Quaker). *Home:* 7536 Graymore Rd., Pittsburgh, Pa. 15221. *Office:* University of Pittsburgh, IDEP, 165 Mervis Hall, Pittsburgh, Pa. 15260.

CAREER: U.S. Bureau of Indian Affairs, mathematics and science teacher at Fort Totten Indian Reservation in North Dakota, 1953-55; education and training specialist for Truk District, U.S. Trust Territory of the Pacific Islands, 1955-59; Ford Foundation foreign area training fellow in Japan, 1961-63; University of Hawaii, East-West Center, Honolulu, associate director for international development fellowships and seminars, Institute of Advanced Projects, 1963-66; University of Pittsburgh, Pittsburgh, Pa., 1966—, began as associate professor, now professor, with joint appointment between department of anthropology and the international and development education program. *Member:* Society for Applied Anthropology (fellow), Association for Asian Studies, American Anthropological Association (fellow), American Educational Research Association, American Association for the Advancement of Science, Council on Anthropology and Education (former president), Comparative Education Society.

WRITINGS: Nichu: A Japanese School, Holt, 1967; (contributor) Thomas Weaver and others, editors, *To See Ourselves: Anthropology and Modern Social Issues,* Scott, Foresman, 1973; (contributor) Daniel Hughes, Sherwood Lingenfelter, editors, *Political Development in Micronesia,* Ohio State University Press, 1974; (contributor) Philip Foster, James Sheffield, editors, *Education and Rural Development: The World Yearbook of Education,* Evans Brothers, 1974; (contributor) George Spindler, editor, *Education and Culture Process,* Holt, 1974. Contributor to education journals.

WORK IN PROGRESS: Research in Japanese education and multicultural education.

*   *   *

SIONIL JOSE, F(rancisco) 1924-

PERSONAL: Born December 3, 1924, in Rosales, Pangasinan, Philippines; son of Antonio and Sofia (Sionil) Jose; married March 12, 1949; wife's name, Teresita; children: Antonio, Evelina, Brigida, Ephraim, Eugenio, Alejo, Nicanor. *Education:* University of Santo Tomas, Litt.B., 1949. *Religion:* Roman Catholic. *Home:* 53 Jersey St., Project 8, Quezon City, Philippines. *Office:* Solidaridad Publishing House, 531 Padre Faura, Ermita, Manila, Philippines.

CAREER: U.S. Information Service, assistant editor at U.S. Embassy, Manila, Philippines, 1948-49; *Manila Times,* Manila, associate editor of *Sunday Magazine,* 1949-57, managing editor of *Sunday Magazine,* 1957-60, also editor of annual publication, *Progress,* 1958-60; *Asia Magazine,* Hong Kong, managing editor, 1961-62; Colombo Plan Headquarters, Colombo, Ceylon, information officer, 1962-64; Solidaridad Publishing House, Manila, Philippines, publisher, 1965—, publisher and editor of *Solidarity* (monthly magazine on current affairs and the arts), 1966—. Also manager of Solidaridad Bookshop, 1965—, and Solidaridad Galleries, 1967—, both Manila; correspondent for *London Economist,* 1968-69. Lecturer in creative writing and English, Arellano University, 1962; professorial lecturer at graduate school, University of the East, Manila, 1975—. Consultant to Department of Agrarian Reform, 1968—, and to Land Reform Authority, Manila; also consultant to other cultural and land reform conferences in Berlin, Rio de Janeiro, Seoul, Sydney, and Bangkok.

MEMBER: International Association for Culture and Freedom, Association for Asian Studies, Philippine P.E.N. (founder and secretary), Manila Overseas Press Club.

Awards, honors: Smith-Mundt leader grant, U.S. Department of State, 1955; Asia Foundation grant for travel in Middle East and Southeast Asia, 1955, and for travel in United States, South America, and Southeast Asia, 1960; literary awards include three first prizes for magazine writing from Philippine National Press Club, and Palanca Award (first prize), for short story.

WRITINGS: The Chief Mourner (novel), [Manila], 1953; *The Balete Tree,* (novel), [Manila], 1956; *The Pretenders* (novel), Regal Publishing, 1964, (editor) *Asian PEN Anthology,* Taplinger, 1967; *The God Stealer and Other Stories,* R. P. Garcia, 1968. Also editor of *Equinox I* (anthology), 1965. Contributor of short stories to Philippine, Australian, German, Russian, and Malaysian anthologies and journals. Editor, *Comment* (Philippine quarterly), 1956-66.

WORK IN PROGRESS: Two novels about the Filipino in transition; a non-fiction work, *Nationalism and Culture.*

SIDELIGHTS: Most of Sionil Jose's fiction is based on Filipino themes—the Filipino's search for identity, quest for integrity in a corrupt society, and urbanization. He has traveled extensively in South America, Middle East, Europe, and Asia, visiting land reform projects, rural reform institutes, and meeting with specialists in land projects.

BIOGRAPHICAL/CRITICAL SOURCES: Miguel Bernad, *Philippine Studies,* Ateno de Manila University Press, 1967.

* * *

SIPPL, Charles J. 1924-

PERSONAL: Born October 11, 1924, in Wausau, Wis.; son of Charles A. (a grocer) and Susan (Janson) Sippl; married: wife's name, Margaret Ellen; children: Thomas Lee, Charles Paul, Diane Marie, Andrew Donald, Bradley Allan, Roger Jeffry, Christine Louise. *Education:* University of Wisconsin, student, 1942-43, 1946-47, 1960-61, earned B.Sc.; University of Miami, Miami, Fla. M.A., 1962; further study at University of California, Berkeley, 1962-63, and University of California, Los Angeles, 1962-66. *Politics:* Democrat. *Religion:* Roman Catholic.

CAREER: Teacher of business, data processing and related courses at Loyola University of Los Angeles, California State University, Los Angeles, California State University, Northridge, and California State University, Long Beach; University of California, Los Angeles, currently an instructor in Extension Division. *Military service:* U.S. Navy, during World War II, became lieutenant junior grade. *Member:* Association for Computing Machinery, Data Processing Management Association, American Management Association, Alpha Tau Omega.

WRITINGS—Editor: (With Charles P. Sippl) *Computer Dictionary,* Howard W. Sams, 1965, 2nd edition, 1974; (with C. P. Sippl) *Computer Dictionary and Handbook,* Howard W. Sams, 1966, 2nd edition, 1972; (with Larry C. Schmalz and Thomas R. Bailey) *Beginner's Computer Glossary for Managers and Businessmen,* Newport Computer Information, 1972, published as *Beginning Computer Glossary for Businessmen,* Funk, 1973; (with Schmalz) *Computer Glossary for Students and Teachers,* Newport Computer Information, 1972; (with William T. Blessum) *Computer Glossary for Medical and Health Sciences,* Funk, 1973; (with Wen M. Chow) *Computer Glossary for Engineers and Scientists,* Funk, 1973; (with Marshall N. McFie) *Computer Glossary for Accountants and Bankers,* Funk, 1973; *Data Communications Dictionary,* Van Nostrand, 1976. Editor and publisher, *Computer Processing Update* (twice-monthly newsletter).

WORK IN PROGRESS: Computer Appreciation, Applications and Impact, for Prentice-Hall; *Computer Applications for Management Control,* for Howard W. Sams; pamphlets on computer topics for high schools and industry.†

* * *

SISSMAN, L(ouis) E(dward) 1928-

PERSONAL: Born January 1, 1928, in Detroit, Mich.; son of Edward James (an advertising man) and Marie (Anderson) Sissman; married Anne Bierman, November 27, 1958. *Education:* Harvard University, A.B. (cum laude), 1949. *Home:* Prospect Hill, Still River, Mass. 01467.

CAREER: Prentice-Hall, Inc. (publishers), New York City, copy editor, 1950-51; A. S. Wyn, Inc. (publishers), New York City, production manager, 1951-52; John F. Kennedy Campaign Staff, Boston, Mass., campaign aide, 1952; John C. Dowd (advertising), Boston, senior writer, 1953-56; Kenyon & Eckhardt (advertising), Boston, senior writer and superviser, 1956-65, creative vice-president, 1965-72; Quinn & Johnson (advertising), Boston, creative vice-president, 1972—. Semi-professional photographer. Board member, Visiting Nurse Association, Boston, 1963—; creative chairman, United Fund, Boston, 1964. *Member:* New England Poetry Club, St. Botolph Club (Boston). *Awards, honors:* Guggenheim fellowship, 1968; National Institute of Arts and Letters grant, 1968; New England Poetry Society Golden Rose award, 1968.

WRITINGS: Dying: An Introduction (poetry), Little, Brown, 1968; *Scattered Returns,* Little, Brown, 1969; *Pursuit of Honor* (poems), Little, Brown, 1971; *Innocent Bystander: The Scene from the Seventies,* introduction by John Updike, Vanguard, 1975. Contributor of verse to *New Yorker, Atlantic Monthly,* and other magazines. Contributing editor, *Boston Magazine.*

AVOCATIONAL INTERESTS: Motor sports and automotive competition, typography and design, naval and military history, painting, music, railway history, and urban architecture.†

* * *

SITWELL, Sacheverell 1897-

PERSONAL: Born November 15, 1897, in Scarborough, England; son of Sir George Reresby (fourth baronet of the peerage established in 1808) and Lady Ida Sitwell (formerly Lady Ida Emily Augusta Denison); brother of Dame Edith and Sir Osbert Sitwell; married Georgia Doble, 1925; children: two sons. *Education:* Attended Eton College and Balliol College, Oxford. *Address:* Weston Hall, Towcester, Northamptonshire, England.

CAREER: Succeeded to baronetry as sixth baronet, in 1969. Served as justice of the peace, 1943, and as high sheriff of Northamptonshire, 1948-49; among the numerous enterprises he has undertaken was the organization, in 1919, with his brother, Osbert, and others, of the Exhibition of Modern French Art, at the Mansard Gallery at Heal's, described by Roger Fry as "the most representative show of modern French art seen in London for many years"; he also established the Magnasco Society, devoted to the Italian art of the 17th and 18th centuries. *Military service:* Grenadier Guards, World War I. *Member:* Beefsteak Club. *Awards, honors:* Awarded the Freedom of the City of Lima, Peru, 1960.

WRITINGS: All Summer in a Day: An Autobiographical Fantasia, Doran, 1926; (with Osbert Sitwell) *All at Sea: A Social Tragedy in Three Acts for First-Class Passengers Only* (play), Duckworth, 1927, Doubleday, Doran, 1928; *Augustan Books of English Poetry,* Benn, 1928; *Beckford and Beckfordism: An Essay,* Duckworth, 1930; *Far from My Home, Stories: Long and Short,* Duckworth, 1931; *Touching the Orient: Six Sketches,* Duckworth, 1934; *Dance of the Quick and the Dead: An Entertainment of the Imagination,* Faber, 1936, Houghton, 1937; (with Edith Sitwell and Osbert Sitwell) *Trio: Dissertations on Some Aspects of National Genius* (Northcliffe Lectures at the University of London, 1937), Macmillan, 1938, reprinted, Books for Libraries, 1970; *Old Fashioned Flowers,* Scribner, 1939; *Poltergeists: An Introduction and Examination followed by Chosen Instances,* Faber, 1940, University Books, 1959; *Sacred and Profane Love,* Faber, 1940; *The Homing of the Winds, and Other Passages in Prose,* Faber, 1942; *Splendours and Miseries,* Faber, 1943; *The Hunters and the Hunted,* Macmillan, 1947; *Morning, Noon and Night in London,* Macmillan, 1948.

Cupid and Jacaranda, Macmillan, 1952; *Selected Works,* Bobbs-Merrill, 1953; *Truffle Hunt with Sacheverell Sitwell* (essays), R. Hale, 1953; (with Handasyde Buchanan and James Fisher) *Fine Bird Books, 1700-1900,* Van Nostrand, 1953; (with James Russell) *Old Garden Roses,* Rainbird, 1955; (with Wilfrid Blunt) *Great Flower Books, 1700-1900,* edited by Patrick W. Synge, Collins, 1955; *Journey to the Ends of Time* (fantasia on philosophical themes), Volume I: *Lost in the Dark Wood,* Random House, 1959; *For Want of a Golden City* (autobiography), John Day, 1973.

Poetry: *The People's Palace,* Blackwell, 1918; *Doctor Donne and Gargantua: First Canto* (also see below), drawings by Wyndham Lewis, privately printed at Favil Press, 1921, Houghton, 1930; *The Hundred and One Harlequins,* Boni & Liveright, 1922; *Doctor Donne and Gargantua: Canto the Second* (also see below), Favil Press, 1923; *The Parrot,* Poetry Bookshop (London), 1923; *The Thirteenth Caesar, and Other Poems,* Grant Richards, 1924, Doran, 1925; (with Edith Sitwell and Osbert Sitwell) *Poor Young People,* Fleuron, 1925; *Exalt the Eglantine, and Other Poems,* Fleuron, 1926; *Doctor Donne and Gargantua: Canto the Third* (also see below), privately printed at Shakespeare Head Press, 1926; *The Cyder Feast, and Other Poems,* Doran, 1927; *Two Poems, Ten Songs,* Duckworth, 1929; *Doctor Donne and Gargantua: The First Six Cantos,* Houghton, 1930; *Canons of Giant Art: Twenty Torsos in Heroic Landscapes,* Faber, 1933; *Collected Poems,* introductory essay by Edith Sitwell, Duckworth, 1936; *Selected Poems,* preface by Osbert Sitwell, Duckworth, 1948.

To Henry Woodward, Covent Garden, 1972; *Tropicalia,* Ramsay Head Press, 1972; *Agamemnon's Tomb,* Tragara Press, 1972. Also author of *Rosario d'Arabeschi, Basalla and Dionysia, A Triptych of Poems, The Strawberry Feast, Ruralia, To E. S., Variations upon Old Names of Hyacinths, Lily Poems, The Archipelago of Daffodils, A Charivari of Parrots, Flowering Cactus, A Look at Lowerby's English Mushrooms and Fungi, Auricula Theatre, Lyra Varia, The House of the Presbyter, Nigritian, Twelve Summer Poems of 1962, Doctor Donne and Gargantua* (Cantos Seven and Eight), *Badinerie, An Indian Summer, Temple of Segesta, l'Amour au Theatre Italien,* and *A*

Notebook upon My New Poems, all published by Smart, 1972-74.

Travel: *Romanian Journey,* Scribner, 1938; *Mauretania: Warrior, Man and Woman,* Duckworth, 1940; *Valse des Fleurs: A Day in St. Petersburg and a Ball at the Winter Palace,* Faber, 1941; *The Netherlands: A Study of Some Aspects of Art, Costume, and Social Life,* Batsford, 1948, revised edition, Hastings House, 1974; *Spain,* Batsford, 1950, 2nd edition, 1953, Norton, 1962; *Portugal and Madeira,* Batsford, 1954; *Denmark,* Hastings House, 1956; *Arabesque and Honeycomb,* R. Hale, 1957, Random House, 1958; *Malta,* illustrated by Tony Armstrong Jones, Batsford, 1958; *Bridge of the Brocade Sash: Travels and Observations in Japan,* Weidenfeld & Nicolson, 1959, World Publishing, 1970; (with Toni Schneiders) *Austria,* Viking, 1959; *Golden Wall and Mirador: From England to Peru,* World Publishing, 1961; *The Red Chapels of Banteai, and Temples in Cambodia, India, Siam, and Nepal,* Weidenfeld & Nicolson, 1962, published as *Great Temples of the East,* Obolensky, 1963.

History: *Southern Baroque Art: A Study of Painting, Architecture and Music in Italy and Spain of the 17th and 18th Centuries,* Knopf, 1924, 3rd edition, Duckworth, 1930, reprinted, Books for Libraries, 1971; *German Baroque Art,* Duckworth, 1927, Doran, 1928; *The Gothick North: A Study of Medieval Life, Art and Thought,* Houghton, 1929 (published in England as *The Gothick North,* Duckworth, 1929, Volume I: *The Visit of the Gypsies,* Volume II: *These Sad Ruins,* Volume III: *The Fair-Haired Victory*); *Spanish Baroque Art: With Buildings in Portugal, Mexico, and Other Colonies,* Duckworth, 1931, reprinted, Benjamin Blom, 1971; *Mozart,* Appleton, 1932, reprinted, Books for Libraries, 1970; *Liszt,* Houghton, 1934, revised edition, Philosophical Library, 1956; *A Background for Domenico Scarlatti, 1685-1757,* Faber, 1935, reprinted, Greenwood Press, 1970; *Conversation Pieces: A Survey of English Domestic Portraits and Their Painters,* Batsford, 1936, Scribner, 1937; *Narrative Pictures: A Survey of English Genre and Its Painters,* Batsford, 1937, Scribner, 1938, reprinted, Benjamin Blom, 1972; *La Vie Parisienne: A Tribute to Offenbach,* Faber, 1937, Houghton, 1938; *German Baroque Sculpture,* descriptive notes by Nikolaus Peusner, Duckworth, 1938.

Primitive Scenes and Festivals, Faber, 1942; *British Architects and Craftsmen: A Survey of Taste, Design, and Style during Three Centuries, 1600-1830,* Batsford, 1945, 2nd edition, Scribner, 1936, 4th edition, Batsford, 1948, reprinted, Pan Books, 1973; *The Romantic Ballet from Contemporary Prints,* Batsford, 1948; *Theatrical Figures in Porcelain: German 18th Century,* Curtain Press, 1949; *Monks, Nuns and Monasteries,* Holt, 1965; *Baroque and Rococo,* Putnam, 1967 (published in England as *Southern Baroque Revisited,* Weidenfeld & Nicolson, 1967); *Gothic Europe,* Holt, 1969.

Author of introduction: Cyril W. Braumont, *The History of Harlequin,* C. W. Braumont, 1926; (and author of notes) *A Book of Towers, and Other Buildings of Southern Europe,* Random House, 1928; (with wife, Georgia Sitwell) Francis Bamford, editor, *Dear Miss Heber* (eighteenth-century correspondence), Constable, 1936; G. Anthony, *Massine: Camera Studies,* Routledge & Kegan Paul, 1940; *Country House Baroque,* Haywood Hill, 1940; Katherine A. Esdaile, *English Church Monuments (1510-1840),* Batsford, 1946; (and author of notes) John James Audubon, *American Birds,* Batsford, 1949; Tom Clarkson, *The Pavement and the Sky*, Wingate, 1951; *The Book of Wallpaper*, Barker, 1954; *Great Palaces of Europe*, Putnam, 1964.

Editor: John Gould, *Tropical Birds*, Batsford, 1948; (with Roger Madol) Pierre J. Redoute, *Album*, Collins, 1954; *Great Houses of Europe*, Putnam, 1961.

Contributor: R. S. Lambert, editor, *Grand Tour: A Journey in the Tracks of the Age of Aristocracy*, Faber, 1935; *Diversion*, Collins, 1946; *The Bedside Lilliput*, Hulton Press, 1950; John Sutro, editor, *Diversion*, Parrish, 1950; *The Gypsies of Grandad*, Athelnay Books, 1969. Contributor to *Daily Telegraph*, *Sunday Times* (London), *Listener*, *Spectator*, *Encounter*, *Geographical Magazine*, *New York Times Magazine*, *Realities*, and many other newspapers and periodicals.

SIDELIGHTS: Some critics feel that the work of Sacheverell Sitwell has been unjustly neglected, as compared with that of his sister, Edith, and his brother, Osbert. Leonard Clark writes: "[He] lacks much of the religious and mystic passion of his sister, and the wit and nostalgia of his brother, [but] they do not possess to the same extent his purity of utterance or his beautifully woven poetic line."

Sitwell's intellectual and artistic interests developed at an early age. Max Wykes-Joyce admiringly comments: "What schoolboy could now discover, as did he, in a village post-office, a translation of Flaubert's *Salammbo* for sale?—a discovery which, by his own admission, profoundly altered the subsequent development of his imaginative life." He told the *New Yorker:* "I began writing poems when I was seventeen, to please my sister Edith, and she and my brother Osbert both encouraged me." (To this he added: "By the way, it is a mistake to treat us as a circus. We are quite different.")

His first prose work, *Southern Baroque Art*, was published at his own expense. In his interview with the *New Yorker* he said: "I paid fifty pounds to have it brought out. I'm just beginning to make money out of my books." Private means also enabled him to travel, he continued: "Thank goodness I've always had a small income of my own and was able to travel when young. Travel is a great advantage to writers."

Sitwell's books on travel have received high praise; the *Spectator* described *Gothick North* as "an imaginative pilgrimage of an extremely sensitive and independent mind to a number of the less familiar remains of the art and society of the latest centuries of the Middle Ages." But he is less interested in modern civilization. Leonard Clark writes: "Sacheverell Sitwell does not often stoop to gaze upon the drab colours of a mechanical and repetitive age...."

Michael Borrie, writing of *Gothic Europe*, notes: "The range of Sir Sacheverell's visual experience is truly vast, and his enthusiasm and affection for his subject are unbounded. Everything he sees conjures up a host of other images, memories and associations, the harvest of a long lifetime's looking, which pour from his pen in an almost Joycean flood. As with all his books, the result is as much a revelation of himself as of the past he brings to life with such imagination. It is a welcome addition to the long, and one hopes, still lengthening list of his works that have given pleasure to so many." A *Virginia Quarterly Review* writer concurs: "No one writes as imaginatively about architecture as Sacheverell Sitwell. His gatherings-together and his comparisons invariably shed new light on examples one may have thought had been thoroughly explored before."

Many consider him exceptionally gifted in appearance and personality, as well as in writing ability. Sir Osbert gave this glowing portrait of his brother at the age of about twenty-five: "His very handsome head, with hair curling at the sides, and with its cut and contours so Italian in essence, but so northern in colour, translated perfectly the strange power and intensity that have always been his, the generous warmth of his temperament, ... the passion of many kinds that burns in him...."

It was reported in the *New Yorker* that he has "a collection of six thousand records, which he plays on a hand-made gramophone." Sitwell also told his interviewer that he put "Recreations none" on lists for *Who's Who:* "I used to invent flippant entries," he said. "Then I suddenly took on this note of austerity. It shows how serious-minded I am."

A reading by Sacheverell Sitwell of excerpts from *Spain, Mauretania* and *Roumanian Journey* was issued by Columbia Records, 1953.

BIOGRAPHICAL/CRITICAL SOURCES: R. L. Megroz, *The Three Sitwells*, Richard Press, 1927; Sir Osbert Sitwell, *Laughter in the Next Room*, Little, Brown, 1948; *Illustrated London News*, June 26, 1948; *Spectator*, May 5, 1950, July 19, 1969; *New Yorker*, November 8, 1952; Max Wykes-Joyce, *Triad of Genius*, P. Owen, 1953; *Fortnightly Review*, August, 1953; *New York Times Magazine*, August 19, 1962; John Lehmann, *A Nest of Tigers: The Sitwells in Their Time*, Atlantic-Little, Brown, 1968; *New York Times Book Review*, September 22, 1968; *Virginia Quarterly Review*, spring, 1970; Sacheverell Sitwell, *For Want of a Golden City*, John Day, 1973.

* * *

SKIBBE, Eugene M(oritz) 1930-

PERSONAL: Born July 16, 1930, in Minneapolis, Minn.; son of Frank Eugene (a furrier) and Helen (Moritz) Skibbe; married Margaret Froiland (a teacher), August 1, 1953; children: Katharine Ellen, Stephen Luther, Susan Khristine, Jonathan Eliot. *Education:* St. Olaf College, B.A., 1952; Luther Theological Seminary, St. Paul, Minn., B.Th. and C.T., 1956; Ecumenical Institute of World Council of Churches, Geneva, Switzerland, graduate study, 1957; University of Heidelberg, Th.D., 1962. *Home:* 2010 West 49th St., Minneapolis, Minn. 55409. *Office:* Augsburg College, Minneapolis, Minn. 55454.

CAREER: Lutheran minister. Augustana College, Sioux Falls, S.D., instructor in religion, 1958-60; pastor of Lutheran church in Madison, Wis., 1963-64; Augsburg College, Minneapolis, Minn., assistant professor, 1964-68, associate professor, 1968-75, professor of religion, 1975—. Guest instructor at Lutheran Student Center, University of Wisconsin, 1963-64; lecturer in systematic theology, Luther Theological Seminary, St. Paul, Minn. *Member:* American Association of University Professors (chapter president, 1968—), American Academy of Religion. *Awards, honors:* American Lutheran Church future faculty fellowship to Germany, 1961; Institute for World Order grant, 1974.

WRITINGS: Protestant Agreement on the Lord's Supper, Augsburg, 1968. Contributor of articles and translations to journals in United States and Germany.

WORK IN PROGRESS: Studies on developing theology of ecumenical movement and on symbolism in the Lord's Supper; a book on "objectivity in teaching about religion" in public schools.

* * *

SKIDMORE, Thomas E. 1932-

PERSONAL: Born July 22, 1932, in Troy, Ohio; son of

Ernest Anton (a business executive) and Josephine (Hale) Skidmore; married Felicity Hall (a research assistant), August 31, 1957; children: David, James, Robert. *Education:* Denison University, B.A., 1954; Oxford University, B.A., 1956, M.A., 1958; Harvard University, Ph.D., 1961. *Home:* 2025 Chadbourne Ave., Madison, Wis. 53705. *Office:* Department of History, University of Wisconsin, Madison, Wis. 53706.

CAREER: Harvard University, Cambridge, Mass., instructor in history, 1960-61, research fellow in Latin American studies, 1961-64, assistant professor of history, 1964-66; University of Wisconsin—Madison, assistant professor, 1966-67, associate professor, 1967-68, professor of history, 1968—. *Member:* American Historical Association, Latin American Studies Association (president, 1972).

WRITINGS: Politics in Brazil, 1930-1964: An Experiment in Democracy, Oxford University Press, 1967; *Black into White: Race and Nationality in Brazilian Thought,* Oxford University Press, 1974. Contributor to professional journals.

WORK IN PROGRESS: A book tentatively entitled *The United States and Brazil,* for Harvard University Press.

SIDELIGHTS: The *Virginia Quarterly Review* writer said in his review of *Politics in Brazil* that Skidmore "has packed a remarkable amount of information into the pages of his book, which succeeds in coming to grips with the social and economic aspects of Brazil's political problems remarkably well. The author endeavors to bring understanding to the complex and dramatic events which he unfolds and largely succeeds in his efforts. For anyone interested in modern Brazil this book is a must." Skidmore is competent in Portuguese, Spanish, French, and German.

BIOGRAPHICAL/CRITICAL SOURCES: Virginia Quarterly Review, autumn, 1967.

*   *   *

SKLAR, Robert   1936-

PERSONAL: Born December 3, 1936, in New Brunswick, N.J.; son of Leon (a junior high school principal) and Lilyn (Fuchs) Sklar; married Kathryn Kish, November 27, 1958; children: Leonard, Susan. *Education:* Princeton University, A.B., 1958; University of Bonn, graduate study, 1959-60; Harvard University, Ph.D., 1965. *Office:* Department of History, University of Michigan, Ann Arbor, Mich. 48104.

CAREER: Associated Press, Newark, N.J., rewrite desk, 1958-59; *Los Angeles Times,* Los Angeles, Calif., staff writer, 1959; University of Michigan, Ann Arbor, assistant professor, 1965-69, associate professor, 1969-75, professor of history, 1975—. Visiting associate professor, University of Auckland, New Zealand, 1970; Fulbright lecturer, University of Tokyo and Sophia University, Japan, 1971; Distinguished Visiting Professor of American Studies, Bard College, 1976-77. *Awards, honors:* Guggenheim fellow, 1970-71.

WRITINGS: F. Scott Fitzgerald: The Last Laocoon, Oxford University Press, 1967; (contributor) Werner M. Mendel, editor, *A Celebration of Laughter,* Mara Books, 1970; (editor) *The Plastic Age: 1917-1930,* Braziller, 1970; *Movie-Made America: A Cultural History of American Movies,* Random House, 1975; (contributor) Richard Glatzer and John Raeburn, editors, *Frank Capra: The Man and His Films,* University of Michigan Press, 1975. Contributor to *Encyclopaedia Britannica,* and *Dictionary of American Biography;* also contributor of articles, essays, and reviews to periodicals.

*   *   *

SKLARE, Marshall   1921-

PERSONAL: Born October 21, 1921, in Chicago, Ill.; son of Irving (a businessman) and Bee (Lippman) Sklare; married Rose Bernards (an editor), June 8, 1947; children: Daniel, Judith, Joshua. *Education:* Northwestern University, student, 1938-39, 1940-43; University of Chicago, M.A., 1945; Columbia University, Ph.D., 1953. *Religion:* Jewish. *Home:* 12 Nathan Rd., Newton Centre, Mass. 02159. *Office:* Department of Sociology, Brandeis University, Waltham, Mass. 02154.

CAREER: American Jewish Committee, New York City, director, Division of Scientific Research, 1953-66; Yeshiva University, New York City, professor of sociology, 1966-70; Brandeis University, Waltham, Mass., professor of American Jewish studies and sociology, 1970—. Fulbright lecturer, University of Jerusalem, 1965-66.

WRITINGS: Conservative Judaism: An American Religious Movement, Free Press of Glencoe, 1955, revised edition, Schocken, 1972; (with M. Vosk) *The Riverton Study: How Jews Look at Themselves and Their Neighbors,* American Jewish Committee, 1957; (editor) *The Jews: Social Patterns of an American Group,* Free Press of Glencoe, 1958; (with J. Greenblum) *Jewish Identity on the Suburban Frontier: A Study of Group Survival in the Open Society,* Basic Books, 1967; *America's Jews,* Random House, 1971; (editor) *The Jew in American Society,* Behrman, 1974; *The Jewish Community in America,* Behrman, 1974.

WORK IN PROGRESS: A revised edition of *Jewish Identity on the Suburban Frontier.*

*   *   *

SKOLNIKOFF, Eugene B.   1928-

PERSONAL: Born August 29, 1928, in Philadelphia, Pa.; son of Benjamin H. and Betty (Turoff) Skolnikoff; married Winifred Weinstein, September 15, 1957; children: David, Matthew, Jessica. *Education:* Massachusetts Institute of Technology, S.B. and S.M., 1950, Ph.D., 1965; Oxford University, B.A. and M.A., 1952. *Politics:* Democrat. *Religion:* Jewish. *Home:* 3 Chandler St., Lexington, Mass. 02173. *Office:* Building E53-473, Massachusetts Institute of Technology, Cambridge, Mass. 02139.

CAREER: Massachusetts Institute of Technology, Cambridge, administrative staff, 1952-55; Institute for Defense Analyses, Washington, D.C., systems analyst, 1957-58; Office of Special Assistant to the President for Science and Technology, White House, Washington, D.C., staff, 1958-63; Massachusetts Institute of Technology, lecturer and research associate, 1963-66, associate professor, 1966-68, professor of political science, 1968—, chairman of department, 1970-74, director, Center for International Studies, 1972—. Visiting professor, Fletcher School of Law and Diplomacy, Tufts University, 1965-72. Consultant to Department of State, Agency for International Development, Office of Science and Technology, Organization for Economic Co-operation and Development, and Ford Foundation. Holder of patent on hybrid circuits. *Military service:* U.S. Army Security Agency, project engineer, 1955-57. *Member:* American Association for the Advancement of Science (fellow; secretary of social and economic sciences section), American Political Science Association, American Academy of Arts and Sciences (fellow; councilor, 1974—), International Council for Science Policy Studies, International Studies Association, Council on Foreign Relations, Sigma Xi, Tau Beta Pi, Eta Kappa Nu. *Awards, honors:* Rhodes scholar.

WRITINGS: Science, Technology and American Foreign Policy, M.I.T. Press, 1967; *The International Imperatives of Technology,* Institute of International Studies at Berkeley, 1972; (editor with D. A. Kay) *World Eco-Crisis,* University of Wisconsin Press, 1972. Contributor to *Science, World Politics, Technology & Culture,* and other journals. Member of editorial board of *International Organization, Technology Review, Science Studies.*

WORK IN PROGRESS: Research in international politics, implications of space, the technological gap, science and economic development, science policy formation, and environment.

* * *

SKOTHEIM, Robert Allen 1933-

PERSONAL: Born January 31, 1933, in Seattle, Wash.; son of Sivert O. (a teacher) and Marjorie (Allen) Skotheim; married Nadine Vail, June 14, 1953; children: Marjorie Carol, Kris Vail, Julia Alice. *Education:* Princeton University, student, 1951-53; University of Washington, Seattle, A.B., 1955, A.M., 1958, Ph.D., 1962; Harvard University, law student, 1955-56. *Office:* Office of Provost, Hobart and William Smith Colleges, Geneva, N.Y. 14456.

CAREER: University of Washington, Seattle, instructor in history, 1962-63; Wayne State University, Detroit, Mich., assistant professor, 1963-66, associate professor of history (on leave), 1966-67; University of California, Los Angeles, visiting associate professor of history, 1966-67; University of Colorado, Boulder, associate professor, 1967-71, professor of history, 1971-72; Hobart and William Smith Colleges, Geneva, N.Y., provost and dean of faculty, 1972—. *Member:* American Historical Association, American Studies Association, Organization of American Historians. *Awards, honors:* Guggenheim fellowship, 1967-68.

WRITINGS: American Intellectual Histories and Historians, Princeton University Press, 1966; (editor with Lawrence Gelfand) W. Stull Holt, *Historical Scholarship in the United States, and Other Essays,* University of Washington Press, 1967; (editor) *The Historian and the Climate of Opinion,* Addison-Wesley, 1969; *Totalitarianism and American Social Thought,* Holt, 1971; (contributor and author of introduction) Hutchins Hapgood, *A Victorian in the Modern World,* University of Washington Press, 1972; (editor with Michael McGiffert) *American Social Thought: Sources and Interpretation,* two volumes, Addison-Wesley, 1972. Contributor to history and other journals.†

* * *

SLACK, Walter H. 1932-

PERSONAL: Born December 25, 1932, in Joliet, Ill.; son of Walter Lloyd (a truck driver) and Gladys (Harmon) Slack; married Mary Ellen Peterson, August 23, 1959; children: Gregory Winston, Jeffrey Hastings, Carolyn Elizabeth. *Education:* Joliet Junior College, A.A., 1953; University of Illinois, B.A., 1956, M.A., 1959; University of Iowa, Ph.D., 1963. *Politics:* Republican. *Religion:* Protestant. *Home:* 219 Hazelcroft Ave., New Castle, Pa. 16105. *Office:* Westminster College, New Wilmington, Pa. 16142.

CAREER: Joliet Herald-News, Joliet, Ill., news reporter, 1957-59; Westminster College, New Wilmington, Pa., instructor, 1963-65, associate professor of political science, 1965—. *Military service:* U.S. Air Force, 1950-52. *Member:* American Friends of Vietnam.

WRITINGS: The Commonwealth of the Mind, Philosophical Library, 1967.

WORK IN PROGRESS: The Grim Science: The Struggle for Power.

* * *

SLADE, Richard 1910-

PERSONAL: Born July 19, 1910, in England; son of Richard Simon (a chef) and Ellen (Reardon) Slade. *Education:* Weymouth Teacher Training College, Ministry of Education Certificate, 1947.

CAREER: Waiter in Belgium and Austria, 1928-31; Gascoigne Junior School, Barking, Essex, England, teacher, 1948—. Elementary exchange teacher in Los Angeles, Calif., 1965-66. *Military service:* British Army, Royal Corps of Signals, 1941-46; took part in Normandy invasion.

WRITINGS—All published by Faber, except as noted: *You Can Make a String Puppet,* 1957; *Clever Hands,* 1959; *Your Book of Heraldry,* 1960; *Masks and How to Make Them,* 1964; *Take an Egg Box,* 1965; *Your Book of Modeling,* 1967, published as *Modeling in Clay, Plaster and Papier-mache,* Lothrop, 1968; *Toys from Balsa,* 1968; *Tissue Paper Craft,* 1968; *Patterns in Space,* 1969; *Geometrical Patterns,* 1970; *Paper Aeroplanes: How to Make Aeroplanes from Paper,* 1970, St. Martin's, 1971; *Carton Craft,* 1972, S. G. Phillips, 1972; *Take a Tin Can,* 1973. Contributor to *Art Craft and Education;* also contributor of travel articles to *Lady,* and articles on photography and motorcycling to British national magazines.

WORK IN PROGRESS: Other books on handicraft.

SIDELIGHTS: Richard Slade has covered most of Europe by motorcycle during school holidays, and has traveled in Russia, Palestine, Egypt, Japan, India, Hawaii, Central America, and most of North America. He told *CA:* "I look upon art and crafts for children as means rather than ends, as method rather than subject. I see the use of the hand as promoting the development of thought. . . ."†

* * *

SLATER, Philip E(lliot) 1927-

PERSONAL: Born May 15, 1927, in Riverton, N.J.; son of John Elliot (a consulting engineer) and Pauline (Holman) Slater. *Education:* Harvard University, A.B., 1950, Ph.D., 1955. *Office:* Greenhouse, Inc., 12 Essex St., Cambridge, Mass. 02138.

CAREER: Harvard University, Cambridge, Mass., lecturer in sociology, 1958-61; Brandeis University, Waltham, Mass., 1961-71, began as assistant professor, professor of sociology, 1968-71; currently associated with Greenhouse, Inc., Cambridge, Mass.

WRITINGS: Microcosm, Wiley, 1966; (with Warren G. Bennis) *The Temporary Society,* Harper, 1968; *The Glory of Hera: Greek Mythology and the Greek Family,* Beacon Press, 1968; *The Pursuit of Loneliness: American Culture at the Breaking Point,* Beacon Press, 1970; *Earthwalk,* Anchor, 1973. Contributor to *Harvard Business Review, Mercurio,* and sociology and medical journals.

SLATER, Ralph P(hipps) 1915-

PERSONAL: Born December 19, 1915, in Hobart, Okla.; son of Charles Elmer (a farmer) and Ada (Phipps) Slater. *Education:* Student at Oklahoma State University of Agriculture and Applied Science, 1934-37, and University of Oklahoma, 1938; Colorado College, B.A., 1959. *Politics:* Republican. *Religion:* Protestant.

CAREER: U.S. Army Air Forces and U.S. Air Force, flying officer, 1941-63, with overseas assignments including three years in U.S. Air Attache Office in Belgrade, Yugoslavia; retired as lieutenant colonel and command pilot. Ralph Phipps Slater Communications (public relations and writing), Arlington, Va., self-employed, beginning 1963. *Member:* Aviation/Space Writers Association, National Aviation Club, National Press Club.

WRITINGS: The Sword and the Plow: The Role of the American Military in Contemporary Society, Praeger, 1968. Writer of Washington column for *Flying,* 1964.††

* * *

SLAVITT, David R. 1935-
(Henry Sutton)

PERSONAL: Born March 23, 1935, in White Plains, N.Y.; son of Samuel Saul (a lawyer) and Adele (Rytman) Slavitt; married Lynn Meyer, August 27, 1956; children: Evan Meyer, Sarah Rebecca, Joshua Rytman. *Education:* Yale University, A.B. (magna cum laude), 1956; Columbia University, M.A., 1957. *Politics:* Independent. *Religion:* Jewish. *Agent:* William Morris Agency, 1350 Avenue of the Americas, New York, N.Y. 10019.

CAREER: Georgia Institute of Technology, Atlanta, instructor in English, 1957-58; *Newsweek,* New York, N.Y., 1958-65, started as mailroom clerk, became book and film critic and associate editor; was also a book reviewer for *New York Herald Tribune.*

WRITINGS: Suits for the Dead (poetry), Scribner, 1961; *The Carnivore* (poetry), University of North Carolina Press, 1965; *Rochelle; or Virtue Rewarded* (novel), Chapman & Hall, 1966, Delacorte, 1967; (contributor) G. Garrett, editor, *The Girl in the Black Raincoat,* Duell, Sloan & Pearce, 1966; (contributor) W. R. Robinson, editor, *Man and the Movies,* Louisiana State University Press, 1967; *Fell Free* (novel), Delacorte, 1968; *Day Sailing and Other Poems* (poetry), University of North Carolina Press, 1969; *Anagrams* (novel), Hodder & Stoughton, 1970, Doubleday, 1971; (translator) Virgil, *The Eclogues of Virgil,* Doubleday, 1971; *Child's Play* (poetry), Louisiana State University Press, 1972; *ABCD* (novel), Doubleday, 1972; (translator) Virgil, *The Eclogues and the Georgics of Virgil,* Doubleday, 1972; *The Outer Mongolian* (novel), Doubleday, 1973; (contributor) Garrett, editor, *The Writer's Voice,* Morrow, 1973; *Vital Signs: New and Selected Poems,* Doubleday, 1975; *The Killing of the King* (novel), Doubleday, 1975.

Under pseudonym Henry Sutton; all novels: *The Exhibitionist,* Geis, 1967; *The Voyeur,* Geis, 1968; *Vector,* Geis, 1970; *The Liberated,* Doubleday, 1973. Contributor to *Kenyon Review, Sewanee Review, Yale Review, New Republic, Esquire,* and other periodicals.

SIDELIGHTS: The publication of *The Exhibitionist* created a good deal of ambiguity around the character and intentions of David Slavitt. Critics could not decide whether they should dismiss him, as the *National Observer* did, as "a brilliant, extraordinarily articulate, and clever young man who has produced a trashy book," or guardedly praise him, in the manner of Paul O'Neil, for presenting us with "a kind of moral-social riddle [rather] than a publishing 'event'; [*The Exhibitionist*] indicts as well as mirrors the times and does so for the same reason that makes it deserving of attention—because of the sardonic and baffling way it reflects its author's ego, ambitions and assessment of his literary era." One of Slavitt's own rationalizations runs thus: "If you want to produce a best-seller you can only appeal to some kind of external reality. If you criticize *The Exhibitionist,* you are really criticizing 10, 15, or 20 million people; if the bulk of Americans hadn't felt that a book like this was okay, I wouldn't have written it."

When Bennett Cerf, Groucho Marx, Esquire, Inc., and others read the galley proofs, they surrendered their interest in Bernard Geis Associates. After publication, Malcolm Muggeridge dismissed the story as standard pornography. Eliot Fremont-Smith concluded that the novel lacks the enthusiasms to be truly pornographic. It was Robert Brown who explained the popular success of *The Exhibitionist:* "One simply likes to read dirty books. And this, although it everywhere provokes laughter and nowhere lust, is certainly a dirty book." Slavitt claims that he is glad he wrote the novel and feels no guilt, believing that "commercial success is nothing to be ashamed of" and rebuking those who still believe that "any novelist who sells more than 5,000 copies of anything in hardback is an object of suspicion, envy, and contempt." In an article for the *Kenyon Review* he explained what he believes to be the difference between "serious" and "popular" writers. "The serious ones," he says, "work themselves up into believing their foolishness. The popular writers know what they are doing, and treat the myths with some civilized distance. These myths are the remnants of coherence and life in the novel. The general public ... still shares, across the board, an interest in these few formulas. The best-seller list is an embarrassment, but can be instructive too, for it shows over and over again how hoi polloi will forgive even intelligence and elegance (just as the more sophisticated readers will overlook the rough-hewn characters of some of the more vulgar writers) if only these formulations are in evidence and alive."

Slavitt was writing for the *New York Herald Tribune* when Bernard Geis saw one of his reviews and approached him with an impressive offer of money and fame. Slavitt quickly learned the formula and contrived the racy scenes, says O'Neil, "amid 'whoops of laughter,' as a dialogue between Slavitt and his wife, who—after picking a suitable aberration from a copy of Krafft-Ebing—would invent conversation for the characters involved and recite it into a tape recorder." Reviewing his own novel for the *Kenyon Review,* Slavitt writes that "given its peculiar and piquant genre, *The Exhibitionist* is rather a good book." "I write for the money," he admits, "and spend like a poet—which very few poets are able to do. The independence this anomalous career affords me is entirely welcome, and even instructive. It is a great joy to bomb into a college under my real name, read poems, and then, at the inevitable party afterward, admit to writing best-sellers under another name. The reactions are poignantly diverting. There is either disbelief, or envy, or belligerence, or, most usually, all three—which, like a thick combination sandwich, is truly delicious."

A *Newsweek* reviewer comments, however, that "inside that fat, prosperous Henry Sutton lives a slim Slavitt struggling to get out. This Slavitt is a serious novelist and poet.... 'I'm the only writer I know who has a high-brow publisher, a middle-brow publisher and a low-brow publisher,' [Slavitt] says." Commenting on Slavitt's *The Carnivore*, the *Chicago Review* writes: The long [poem], "Elegy for Walter Stone" is a real achievement and that rare thing, an addition to a genre which has engaged some of the greatest poets of the language. Time will tell if this poem will join those, but meanwhile it seems the most likely candidate.... [These poems are] all handled with ease, intelligence, humor and compassion."

Slavitt says that he knew as a child that he would become a writer—"if I were a religious fanatic, I could say I had seen signs and wonders." O'Neil calls him a man who "has a caustic humor, uses obscure literary references and foreign phraseology incessantly in conversational infighting, indulges in long, severe silences, strikes shamelessly pedantic poses, ... and can create unease, doubt and even alarm in those upon whom he utilizes the complete arsenal." His personality is too complex to be explained with facility. "His rationalization of *The Exhibitionist* and getting-rich-quick," adds O'Neil, "duplicates both the tone and vehemence with which he explained his earlier decision to abandon journalism for poetry and poverty. But one is forced to guess that he was really talking about something else both times—about ends rather than means, about some compulsive need for the spotlight, for fame, for applause, for expansion of a painfully constricted ego—and believes every word with which he has justified these wildly conflicting attitudes."

Film rights to *The Exhibitionist* and *Rochelle* have been sold.

BIOGRAPHICAL/CRITICAL SOURCES: Chicago Review, Volume XVIII, number 1, 1965; *Book Week*, August 15, 1965; *New Statesman*, July 15, 1966; *Times Literary Supplement*, August 11, 1966; *New York Times*, September 9, 1967, November 3, 1967; *New York Times Book Review*, September 17, 1967; *Book World*, October 29, 1967; *National Observer*, October 30, 1967; *Kenyon Review*, Volume XXX, number 1, 1968; *Life*, January 26, 1968; *Esquire*, March, 1968; *Newsweek*, February 17, 1969; Carolyn Riley, editor, *Contemporary Literary Criticism*, Volume V, Gale, 1976.

* * *

SLOANE, Leonard 1932-

PERSONAL: Born January 26, 1932, in New York, N.Y.; son of Herman (an advertising executive) and Betty (Levine) Sloane; married Annette Weber, July 11, 1954; children: Elliot B., Steven A. *Education:* Queens College (now Queens College of the City University of New York), B.A., 1952; Columbia University, M.S., 1953. *Home:* 68-24 Juno St., Forest Hills, N.Y. 11375. *Agent:* Julian Bach Literary Agency, 3 East 48th St., New York, N.Y. 10017. *Office: New York Times,* 229 West 43rd St., New York, N.Y. 10036.

CAREER: Wall Street Journal, New York City, staff reporter, 1956-57; *Purchasing Magazine,* New York City, business editor, 1957-62; *New York Times,* New York City, business-financial reporter, 1963—. *Military service:* U.S. Navy, 1953-56; became lieutenant. *Member:* New York Financial Writers Association (president, 1970-71), Deadline Club of Society of Professional Journalists (member of executive council, 1974—).

WRITINGS: (With Tom Mahoney) *The Great Merchants,* Harper, 1966, revised edition, 1974. Contributor to *Cosmo-*

politan, Saturday Review, New York, Ladies Home Journal, and *True.*

* * *

SLOCUM, Walter L(ucius) 1910-

PERSONAL: Born June 28, 1910, in Glenham, S.D.; son of Edward C. and Julianna (Sannes) Slocum; married Esther L. Clark, June 4, 1935; children: Richard, Clark, Irene. *Education:* South Dakota State University, B.S., 1933; University of Wisconsin, Ph.D., 1940. *Religion:* Methodist. *Home:* Northwest 1470 Orion Dr., Pullman, Wash. 99163. *Office:* Washington State University, Pullman, Wash. 99163.

CAREER: South Dakota State University, Brookings, assistant professor, 1940-42, associate professor of sociology, 1942-43; U.S. Department of Agriculture, War Food Administration, Washington, D.C., statistician, 1943-44; U.S. Veterans Administration, Washington, D.C., assistant chief of Research Division, Vocational Education, 1947-51, chief, 1951; Washington State University, Pullman, professor of rural sociology and chairman of department, 1951-75, professor emeritus, 1975—. University of Punjab, Lahore, India, professor of sociology, 1958-60; visiting professor at Garrett Theological Seminary, summer, 1963, Texas A & M University, 1964, and Oklahoma State University, 1967. Consultant to U.S. Department of Agriculture, 1958-61, 1965, and Office of Economic Opportunity, San Francisco, 1966-67. Member of board, Wesley Foundation, 1960-66. *Military service:* U.S. Naval Reserve, active duty, 1944-46; became lieutenant.

MEMBER: American Sociological Association, Rural Sociological Society, Pacific Sociological Association.

WRITINGS: Agricultural Sociology, Harper, 1962; *Occupational Careers,* Aldine, 1966, 2nd edition, 1974. Other publications (articles and Agriculture Experiment Station bulletins) total almost ninety.

WORK IN PROGRESS: A book on the sociology of retirement including an appraisal of retirement communities.

AVOCATIONAL INTERESTS: Hunting and fishing.

* * *

SLUCKIN, W(ladyslaw) 1919-

PERSONAL: Born March 20, 1919, in Warsaw, Poland; married Alice Klaus (a psychiatric social worker), 1942; children: Timothy Jan, Andrew Martin. *Education:* University of London, B.Sc. (engineering), 1942, B.Sc. (psychology), 1950, Ph.D., 1955. *Office:* Department of Psychology, University of Leicester, Leicester, England.

CAREER: University of Durham, Durham, England, research assistant, 1951-53, lecturer in psychology, 1953-60; University of Leicester, Leicester, England, lecturer, 1960-62, reader, 1962-65, professor of psychology, 1965—, head of department, 1973—.

WRITINGS: Principles of Alternating Currents, Cleaver-Hume, 1951, 2nd enlarged edition (with J. R. Greener), 1959; (with T. G. Connolly) *An Introduction to Statistics for the Social Sciences,* Cleaver-Hume, 1953, enlarged edition, 1958; *Minds and Machines,* Penguin, 1954, revised and enlarged edition, 1960; *Imprinting and Early Learning,* Methuen, 1964, Aldine, 1965, revised edition, 1972; *The Impressionable Age,* Leicester University Press, 1967; *Early Learning in Man and Animal,* Allen & Unwin 1970, Schenkman, 1972.

SIDELIGHTS: Sluckin's *Minds and Machines* has been translated into Spanish, Polish, Italian, and Portuguese; his *Imprinting and Early Learning* has been translated into Spanish and Portuguese, and *Early Learning in Man and Animal* translated into Dutch.

* * *

SMITH, Arthur C. 1916-

PERSONAL: Born December 4, 1916, in Los Banos, Calif.; son of Archibald C. (a banker) and Pearl (Horn) Smith; married Eileen Barbara Murray, December 20, 1947; children: Linda Barbara, Terrence Murray. *Education:* San Jose State College (now San Jose State University), A.B. (magna cum laude), 1939; graduate study at University of California, Berkeley, 1939, and Stanford University, 1940; Cornell University, Ph.D., 1951. *Religion:* Protestant. *Home:* 687 Woodland Ave., Hayward, Calif. 94541. *Office:* Department of Biological Sciences, California State University, 25800 Hillary St., Hayward, Calif. 94542.

CAREER: High school teacher in Daly City, Calif., 1940-42; Rockefeller Foundation Mexican Agricultural Program, assistant staff entomologist in Mexico, 1948-49; California State Department of Health, Bureau of Vector Control, area representative, 1952-53, technical consultant on fly control, 1953-60; California State University, Hayward, professor of biological science, 1959—, chairman of department, 1963-69, instructor in photography, 1960—. Consultant to Office of Solid Waste Management, Environmental Protection Agency, 1967-72; member of board of directors, California Natural Areas Coordinating Council, 1968—. Consultant to other government agencies, and member of advisory committees for museums and parks. *Military service:* U.S. Army Air Forces, 1942-46; became first lieutenant. *Member:* Association for the Education of Teachers in Science (president, 1966-67), Nature Conservancy (trustee, Northern California chapter, 1965-67), Sigma Xi. *Awards, honors:* Rockefeller Foundation fellowship in Mexico, 1948-49.

WRITINGS: *Introduction to the Natural History of the San Francisco Bay Region,* University of California Press, 1959; *Western Butterflies,* Lane, 1961; (with Edmund C. Jaeger) *Introduction to the Natural History of Southern California,* University of California Press, 1966.

General editor, "California Natural History Guides," 1955—, with forty books published to date, and thirty additional titles planned. Contributor of more than eight hundred reviews and articles on science and natural history to magazines and newspapers; also contributor of more than one thousand photographs. Nature editor, *Pacific Discovery,* 1959-62.

WORK IN PROGRESS: With J. W. Tilden, *A Field Guide to Western Butterflies,* for Houghton; with Steve Grillos, *Weeds of California;* additional titles in "California Natural History Guides" series, including *Introduction to the Insects of California, Rare and Endangered Plants and Animals of California,* and *Survival in the Sierra Madre.*

AVOCATIONAL INTERESTS: Collecting insects, reptiles, wild flowers, rocks, minerals, and fossils; mountain climbing, hiking, and camping.

* * *

SMITH, C(lifford) T(horpe) 1924-

PERSONAL: Born July 11, 1924, in Johannesburg, South Africa; son of Joseph William and Caroline (Thorpe) Smith; married Susan Margaret Machin (a teacher), August 10, 1949 (died, 1973); children: two sons, one daughter. *Education:* St. Catharine's College, Cambridge, B.A., 1946, M.A., 1949. *Religion:* Church of England. *Office:* Centre for Latin American Studies, University of Liverpool, Liverpool L69 3BX, England.

CAREER: University of Leicester, Leicester, England, assistant lecturer in department of geography, 1949-51; Cambridge University, Cambridge, England, lecturer in geography, 1951-70, fellow of St. John's College, 1960-70, and tutor, 1963-70; University of Liverpool, Liverpool, England, professor of Latin American geography and director of Centre for Latin American Studies, 1970—. *Member:* Royal Geographical Society (fellow), Institute of British Geographers, Society for Latin American Studies, Economic History Society, Liverpool University Association of University Teachers, Peruvian Society. *Awards, honors:* Murchison grant, Royal Geographical Society, 1968.

WRITINGS: (With J. M. Lambert and others) *The Making of the Norfolk Broads,* Royal Geographical Society, 1961; *An Historical Geography of Western Europe Before 1800,* Longmans, Green, 1967; (co-editor and contributor) *Latin America: Geographical Perspective,* Methuen, 1971. Writer of articles and papers for *Geographical Journal* and other periodicals.

WORK IN PROGRESS: *Man and Land in the Peruvian Andes;* articles on Peru and the Andes.

* * *

SMITH, Clodus R(ay) 1928-

PERSONAL: Born May 15, 1928, in Blanchard, Okla.; son of William Thomas (a farmer) and Rachel (Hale) Smith; married Pauline Chaat, June 25, 1950; children: Martha Lynn, William Paul, Paula Diane. *Education:* Cameron State Agricultural College, A.A., 1948; Oklahoma State University of Agriculture and Applied Science, B.S., 1950, M.S., 1955; Cornell University, Ed.D., 1960. *Religion:* Methodist. *Home:* 3174 Onaway Rd., Shaker Hts., Ohio 44120. *Office:* Cleveland State University, Cleveland, Ohio 44115.

CAREER: Teacher of agriculture at high schools in Oklahoma, 1949-52, and Texas, 1952-57; University of Maryland, College Park, assistant professor, 1959-61, associate professor of agriculture and extension education, 1962-73, director of summer school, 1963-72, administrative dean of summer programs, 1972-73; Cleveland State University, Cleveland, Ohio, special assistant to the president, 1973-74, vice-president for university relations, 1974—. Consultant to industrial, and other educational and government groups; director of interdisciplinary approach to leadership development, U.S. Office of Education Leadership Development Seminar series. *Member:* American Association of Teacher Educators in Agriculture (regional vice-president, 1962-66), National Association of College and University Summer Sessions (founder; president, 1964-65), Phi Kappa Phi (secretary, 1966-67; president, 1968-69), Phi Delta Kappa, Lions Club, Masons. *Awards honors:* Danforth faculty fellow, 1962; research award, National Project on Agricultural Communications.

WRITINGS: (With Lloyd Partain and James Champlin) *Rural Recreation for Profit,* Interstate, 1966; *Planning and Paying for College,* Crowell-Collier, 1968. Contributor to educational and agricultural journals. Editor, *Maryland*

Vocational Agricultural News and *Collegiate Reporter*, 1960-63.

AVOCATIONAL INTERESTS: Hunting and fishing.

* * *

SMITH, Cornelius C. 1913-

PERSONAL: Born July 18, 1913, at Fort Huachuca, Ariz.; son of Cornelius C. (a colonel, U.S. Army, and writer about the American Southwest) and Kathleen (Crowley) Smith; married Grace Mantel, July 18, 1944. *Education:* University of Southern California, B.A., 1937; Claremont Graduate School, M.A., 1953, Ph.D., 1955. *Politics:* Republican. *Religion:* Episcopalian. *Home:* 5218 Old Mill Rd., Riverside, Calif. 92504.

CAREER: U.S. Marine Corps, officer, 1937-46, retired as lieutenant colonel; U.S. Marine Corps Reserve, retired as colonel. H. O. Ruhnau, Riverside, Calif., designer, 1947-48; Arabian-American Oil Co., Dhahran, Saudi Arabia, architectural engineer, 1948-49; Scripps Institution of Oceanography, La Jolla, Calif., museum curator, 1950-52; U.S. Strategic Air Command, 15th Air Force, March Air Force Base, Calif., chief of historical division (as civilian), 1955-66. Painter and sculptor, with work exhibited at one-man shows in California, Arizona, Texas, and Montana, and included in U.S. Department of State traveling exhibit sent to Europe, Asia, and South America. *Member:* Society for the Preservation and Encouragement of Barber Shop Quartet Singing in America (president, Riverside chapter). *Awards, honors*—Military: Legion of Merit and Bronze Star for service in Pacific theater. Other: Winner of $6,500 on Groucho Marx's "You Bet Your Life" show, 1952 (the winnings paid the way to his master's degree and doctorate).

WRITINGS: William Sanders Oury: History-Maker of the Southwest, University of Arizona Press, 1967; *Emilio Kosterlitzsky: Eagle of Sonora and the Southwest Border,* Arthur H. Clark, 1970; *"Corney,"* Presidid Press, 1976; *A Southwestern Vocabulary,* University of Arizona Press, 1976; *Tanque Verde Ranch,* University of Arizona Press, in press; *Old Arizonians,* Arthur H. Clark, in press. Contributor of articles, usually self-illustrated, to periodicals, including *Desert, Montana, Arizona Highways,* and *Ford Times.*

WORK IN PROGRESS: Parade of Fools.

BIOGRAPHICAL/CRITICAL SOURCES: Montana, autumn, 1962.

* * *

SMITH, Dorothy Stafford 1905-
(Sarah Stafford Smith)

PERSONAL: Born February 3, 1905, in Hove, Sussex, England; daughter of William (a chief constable) and Mary Jeffares (Cunningham) Stafford; married Percy Heber Smith, March 13, 1943 (deceased). *Education:* Avery Hill Training College, Teacher's Certificate, 1926; University of London, Certificate in French, 1929; Certificate from Sorbonne, University of Paris, 1938. *Home:* 18 The Hermitage, Lewisham Hill, London S.E. 13, England.

CAREER: Teacher of English, French, and general elementary subjects in London, England and Alton, Hampshire, England, 1926-59; teacher of English in Rome, Italy, 1959-64, and London, 1964-66; currently full-time writer. *Member:* Amnesty International.

WRITINGS—Under pseudonym Sarah Stafford Smith: *The Ink-bottle Club* (juvenile), F. Watts, 1967; *The Ink-bottle Club Abroad,* F. Watts, 1969; *The Imperceptible Gate* (poetry), Outposts Publications, 1970; (contributor) Noel Streatfield, *Summer Holiday Book,* Dent, 1973; (contributor) Geraldine Calca Cash, editor, *Keats Prize Poems: An Anthology of Poetry,* London Literary Editions, 1973. Contributor of short stories and poems to *Courier, Outposts, Poetry of Today,* and other periodicals.

* * *

SMITH, Duane A(llan) 1937-

PERSONAL: Born April 20, 1937, in San Diego, Calif.; son of Stanley W. (a dentist) and Ila (Bark) Smith; married Gay Woodruff, August 20, 1960; children: Laralee Ellen. *Education:* University of Colorado, B.A., 1959, M.A., 1961, Ph.D., 1964. *Home:* 2911 Cedar Ave., Durango, Colo. 81301. *Office:* Fort Lewis College, Durango, Colo. 81301.

CAREER: Fort Lewis College, Durango, Colo., assistant professor, 1964-67, associate professor, 1967-72, professor of history, 1972—. *Member:* Organization of American Historians, North American Society for Sport History, Western History Association, Colorado Historical Society, Montana Historical Society, Phi Alpha Theta. *Awards, honors:* Huntington Library research grants, 1968 and 1973; Hafen Award, 1971, for an outstanding magazine article; American Association for State and Local History Certificate of Commendation, for *Horace Tabor.*

WRITINGS: Rocky Mountain Mining Camps: The Urban Frontier, Indiana University Press, 1967; (with M. Benson and C. Ubbelohde) *A Colorado History,* Pruett, 1972; *Horace Tabor: His Life and the Legend,* Colorado Associated University Press, 1973; *Silver Saga: The Story of Caribou, Colorado,* Pruett, 1974.

WORK IN PROGRESS: An urban-mining study of the San Juan mountain region of Colorado.

SIDELIGHTS: Smith told *CA:* "Probably the most important motivation for research on mining camps was the desire to uncover a more realistic and honest history as opposed to much of the literature which passes for the true history of the mining frontier."

AVOCATIONAL INTERESTS: Fishing and other sports, and conservation.

* * *

SMITH, Elbert B(enjamin) 1920-

PERSONAL: Born May 1, 1920, in Benham, Ky.; son of Elbert Benjamin (a businessman and farmer) and Gladys (Huffaker) Smith; married Jean Smith (an elementary teacher), 1944; children: Randall, Stephen, Amy, Scott, Robert. *Education:* Maryville College, A.B. (cum laude), 1940; University of Chicago, A.M., 1947, Ph.D., 1949. *Politics:* Democrat. *Religion:* Presbyterian. *Office:* Department of History, University of Maryland, College Park, Md. 20742.

CAREER: Youngstown University, Youngstown, Ohio, associate professor of history, 1949-57; Iowa State University of Science and Technology, Ames, associate professor, 1957-63, professor of history, 1963-67; University of Wisconsin—Madison, visiting professor of history, 1967-68; University of Maryland, College Park, professor of history, 1968—. Fulbright professor at University of Tokyo and Ochanomizu Women's University, Tokyo, Japan, 1954-55.

Democratic candidate from Iowa for U.S. Senate, 1962, 1966; campaign manager in Iowa for President Johnson, 1964. *Military service:* U.S. Navy, 1942-46; became lieutenant junior grade. *Member:* American Historical Association, Organization of American Historians, American Association of University Professors, American Association for the United Nations.

WRITINGS: Magnificent Missourian: The Life of Thomas Hart Benton, Lippincott, 1958; *The Death of Slavery: The United States 1837-65,* University of Chicago Press, 1967; *The Presidency of James Buchanan,* University Press of Kansas, 1975. Contributor to *Encyclopaedia Britannica* and *Collier's Encyclopedia;* also contributor to *American Heritage, Japan Quarterly, Midwest Quarterly,* and other journals.

WORK IN PROGRESS: A biography of Francis P. Blair; *Reflections on the American Experience.*

BIOGRAPHICAL/CRITICAL SOURCES: South Atlantic Quarterly, summer, 1968.

* * *

SMITH, Eugene L(ewis) 1912-

PERSONAL: Born April 13, 1912, in Rockwell City, Iowa; son of Roy Leslie and Lois Lulu (Lewis) Smith; married Idalene Gulledge, July 12, 1939; children: Lu Ann (Mrs. William Polk), Rosemary. *Education:* Willamette University, A.B., 1934; Drew University, B.D., 1937; New York University, Ph.D., 1944. *Home:* 190 Diamond Spring Rd., Denville, N.J. 07834.

CAREER: Ordained to Methodist ministry, 1940; pastor in Roselle, N.J., 1938-44, Jersey City, N.J., 1944-47, and Brooklyn, N.Y., 1947-49; The Methodist Church, New York City, general secretary of Division of World Mission, 1949-64, president of Council of Secretaries, 1964; World Council of Churches, New York City, executive secretary, 1964-73; Denville United Methodist Community Church, Denville, N.J., pastor, 1973—. Lecturer at Southern Methodist University, Ohio Wesleyan University, Union Theological Seminary in the Philippines, and other universities and theological schools. Vice-president, National Council of Churches, 1954-57; member of board of directors, Union Theological Seminary, New York City. *Member:* Phi Delta Kappa, Rotary Club of Upper Manhattan. *Awards, honors:* D.D. from Willamette University, 1956, and Payne Theological Seminary; Litt.D., American University, 1957; LL.D., Loyola University, 1971; L.H.D., MacMurray College.

WRITINGS: The Power Within Us, Abingdon, 1948; *They Gird the Earth for Christ,* Abingdon, 1952; *God's Mission—and Ours,* Cokesbury, 1961; *Mandate for Mission,* Friendship, 1968. Contributor of articles to publications of different faiths.

SIDELIGHTS: Many of Eugene Lewis' articles have been published in Swedish, German, French, Spanish, and Japanese.

* * *

SMITH, Gaddis 1932-

PERSONAL: Born December 9, 1932, in Newark, N.J.; son of George D. (a banker) and Elizabeth (Heller) Smith; married Barclay Manierre, June 7, 1951; children: Tarrant Putnam, Edgar Heller. *Education:* Yale University, B.A., 1954, M.A., 1958, Ph.D., 1961. *Politics:* Democrat. *Home:* 201 Bishop St., New Haven, Conn. 06511. *Office:* Depart-

ment of History, Yale University, New Haven, Conn. 06520.

CAREER: Duke University, Durham, N.C., instructor in history, 1958-61; Yale University, New Haven, Conn., assistant professor, 1961-64, associate professor of history, 1964—, director of graduate studies, 1967—. *Member:* American Historical Association, Organization of American Historians, Council on Foreign Relations, Canadian Historical Association.

WRITINGS: Britain's Clandestine Submarines, 1914-15, Yale University Press, 1964; *American Diplomacy during the Second World War,* Wiley, 1965; *Dean Acheson,* Cooper Square, 1972.

WORK IN PROGRESS: A survey of American maritime history.

* * *

SMITH, Genevieve Love 1917-

PERSONAL: Born December 10, 1917, in Brookville, Pa.; daughter of Herbert A. (a jeweler) and Grace (Markel) Love; married second husband, John J. Smith (a chemist), December 20, 1962. *Education:* Chatham College, B.A., 1939; Marine Biological Laboratory, Woods Hole, Mass., summer student, 1938, 1939; Duquesne University, M.Ed., 1965. *Religion:* Presbyterian. *Residence:* Deming, N.M.

CAREER: Merck Institute in Biological Research, Rahway, N.J., nutritional researcher, 1941-42; Presbyterian University Hospital, School of Nursing, Pittsburgh, Pa., instructor in basic sciences, 1943; University of Pittsburgh, School of Nursing, Pittsburgh, instructor in anatomy and physiology, 1944; Pennsylvania State University Extension, Dubois, instructor in zoology, 1951-52; Business Training College, Pittsburgh, instructor in medical terminology and anatomy and researcher in programed instruction, 1959-61; Point Park College, Pittsburgh, assistant professor of medical terminology and anatomy, working in the development of programed instruction, 1961-66, assistant professor involved in programed instruction, beginning 1966. *Member:* National Society for Programmed Instruction, American Educational Research Association, Pennsylvania Academy of Science.

WRITINGS: (With Phyllis E. Davis) *Medical Terminology* (programed text), Wiley, 1963, 2nd edition, 1967; *Spelling By Principles* (programed text), Appleton, 1966.

AVOCATIONAL INTERESTS: Colour photography; nature study, especially birds and wild flowers; music, art, orchid culture, and bridge.

* * *

SMITH, Hallett (Darius) 1907-

PERSONAL: Born August 15, 1907, in Chattanooga, Tenn.; son of Charles Wilson and Elizabeth (Atkinson) Smith; married Mary Elizabeth Earl, December 30, 1931; children: Diana Russell (Mrs. David Gordon), Hallett Earl. *Education:* University of Colorado, B.A., 1928; Yale University, Ph.D., 1934. *Politics:* Democrat. *Home:* 1455 South Marengo, Pasadena, Calif. 91106. *Office:* Huntington Library, San Marino, Calif. 91108.

CAREER: Williams College, Williamstown, Mass., instructor, 1931-36, assistant professor, 1937-40, associate professor, 1940-45, professor of English, 1946-49; California Institute of Technology, Pasadena, professor of English and chairman of Division of Humanities and Social Sciences, 1949-70; Huntington Library, San Marino, Calif., senior research associate, 1970—. Member of advisory committee, Guggenheim Foundation. *Member:* Modern Language Association of America, American Academy of Arts and Sciences (fellow), Phi Beta Kappa (senator-at-large, 1961—). *Awards, honors:* Guggenheim fellow, 1947-48; Poetry Chap-Book Award of Poetry Society of America, 1953, for *Elizabethan Poetry;* L.H.D., University of Colorado, 1968.

WRITINGS: (Editor with Roy Lamson) *The Golden Hind,* Norton, 1942, revised edition, 1956; (editor with Lamson) *The Critical Reader,* Norton, 1949, 2nd edition, 1962; *Elizabethan Poetry,* Harvard University Press, 1952; (contributor) Meyer H. Abrams, editor, *The Norton Anthology of English Literature,* Norton, 1962, 3rd edition, 1974; (editor) *Twentieth Century Interpretations of "The Tempest,"* Prentice-Hall, 1969; *Shakespeare's Romances: A Study of Some Ways of the Imagination,* Henry E. Huntington, 1972; (contributor) G. Blakemore Evans, editor, *Riverside Shakespeare,* two volumes, Houghton, 1974. Member of editorial committee, *PMLA* and *HLQ.*

*   *   *

SMITH, Iain Crichton   1928-

PERSONAL: Born January 1, 1928, on Isle of Lewis, Scotland; son of John (a sailor) and Christina (Campbell) Smith. *Education:* University of Aberdeen, M.A. (honors), 1950. *Politics:* Socialist. *Home:* 42 Combie St., Oban, Argyll, Scotland.

CAREER: Teacher of English, Clydebank High School, Scotland, 1952-55, and Oban High School, Oban, Argyll, Scotland, 1955—. *Military service:* British Army, Education Corps, 1950-52; became sergeant. *Member:* Educational Institute of Scotland.

WRITINGS: The Long River (poems), Macdonald (Edinburgh), 1955; *Thistles and Roses* (poems), Eyre & Spottiswoode, 1961; *The Law and the Grace* (poems), Eyre & Spottiswoode, 1965; *The Golden Lyric* (pamphlet; essay on the poetry of Hugh MacDiarmid), 1967; *Consider the Lilies* (novel), Gollancz, 1968, published as *The Alien Light,* Houghton, 1969; *The Last Summer,* Gollancz, 1969; *Survival Without Error,* Gollancz, 1970; *My Last Duchess* (novel), Gollancz, 1971; *The Beach and the Kid* (short stories), Gollancz, 1973. Contributor to periodicals and newspapers, including *New Statesman, Listener, Times Literary Supplement,* and *Spectator.*

BIOGRAPHICAL/CRITICAL SOURCES: Times Literary Supplement, October 14, 1965; *Listener,* March 7, 1968.

*   *   *

SMITH, James A.   1914-

PERSONAL: Born April 23, 1914, in Utica, N.Y.; son of Ambrose William (a bus driver) and Lillian (Platt) Smith; married Dorothy Beekman, April 12, 1941; children: Susan Anne, Patricia Lee. *Education:* Albany State Teachers College (now State University of New York at Albany), B.S., 1937; Syracuse University, M.S.Ed., 1949, Ed.D., 1955. *Politics:* Republican. *Religion:* Presbyterian. *Home:* Sleepy Hollow, Route 3, Oswego, N.Y. 13126.

CAREER: Teacher in rural elementary school, Millers Mills, N.Y., 1933-36; teaching principal in Bethlehem Center, N.Y., 1936-41, then in Slingerlands, N.Y., 1941-44; State University of New York College at Oneonta, demon-

stration teacher, 1946-48; Syracuse University, Syracuse, N.Y., demonstration teacher, 1946-48, director of demonstration school, 1948-58, director of teacher preparation in early childhood and elementary education, 1948-65; State University of New York College at Oswego, professor of education, beginning 1965. Visiting professor at Northwestern University, 1956, and University of Southern California, 1958, 1962. President of board of directors, New York State Council for Children, 1958-59. *Military service:* U.S. Marine Corps, 1944-46. *Member:* Phi Delta Kappa.

WRITINGS: I Play (social studies text), L. W. Singer, 1957; *I Know People,* L. W. Singer, 1957; *I Live with Others,* L. W. Singer, 1957; *I Have Friends,* L. W. Singer, 1957; (with Don Donley, Robert Lovette, and David Van Dyck) *Independent Activities,* State University of New York (Albany), 1958; (with George Kopp and Clarence Hunnicutt) *A Survey of the Instructional Program in the Elementary Schools,* Bureau of School Service, Syracuse University, 1959.

(With A. Patterson, F. Patterson, C. W. Hunnicutt, and J. Grambs) *This Is Our Land,* with *Teacher's Manual,* L. W. Singer, 1963; (with A. Patterson, F. Patterson, C. W. Hunnicutt, and J. Grambs) *Man Changes His World,* with *Teacher's Manual,* L. W. Singer, 1963; (with Thomas Clayton) *A Survey of the Lake Placid School System,* Bureau of School Service, Syracuse University, 1963; *Creativity: Its Nature and Nurture,* Syracuse University Press, 1964; *Setting Conditions for Creative Teaching in the Elementary School,* Allyn & Bacon, 1966; *The Lake Placid Report: Elementary Schools,* Bureau of Social Services, Syracuse University, 1967; *Creative Teaching of the Creative Arts in the Elementary School,* Allyn & Bacon, 1967; *Creative Teaching of Reading and Literature in the Elementary School,* Allyn & Bacon, 1967; *Creative Teaching of the Language Arts in the Elementary School,* Allyn & Bacon, 1967, 2nd edition, 1973; *Creative Teaching of the Social Studies in the Elementary School,* Allyn & Bacon, 1967; (with Alvin M. Wescott) *Creative Teaching of Mathematics in the Elementary School,* Allyn & Bacon, 1967.

Adventures in Communication: Language Arts Method, Allyn & Bacon, 1972; (with Dorothy Hickok) *Creative Teaching of Music in the Elementary School,* Allyn & Bacon, 1974; (with John E. Ritson) *Creative Teaching of Art in the Elementary School,* Allyn & Bacon, 1975; *Creative Teaching of Reading in the Elementary School,* Allyn & Bacon, 1975; *Creative Teaching of Children's Literature,* Allyn & Bacon, 1976; (with Dorothy Park) *Word Music and Word Magic,* Allyn & Bacon, 1976; *Organizing the Classroom for Teaching the Language Arts,* F. T. Peacock, 1976. Contributor of over 150 articles and reviews to education journals. Adult book editor, *Childhood Education,* 1959-62; editor, *Oswego Axle* (Rotary magazine), 1971-73.

WORK IN PROGRESS: Creative Teaching of Social Studies.

*   *   *

SMITH, James Roy   1920-

PERSONAL: Born June 8, 1920, in Cradock, Va.; son of Clayton Alexander and Dorothy (Creadle) Smith; married Bonnie Joanne Holley, June 14, 1948; children: Anne Holley, Martha Kay, Janet Claire. *Education:* Randolph-Macon College, B.A., 1943; University of Richmond, M.A., 1948; Garrett Theological Seminary, B.D., 1949. *Home:* 1109 Anesbury Ct., Alexandria, Va. 22308.

CAREER: Methodist clergyman. Minister in Richmond, Va., 1940-44, 1948-53, and Hopewell, Va., 1953-57; Mount Olivet Methodist Church, Arlington, Va., minister, 1957-73; United Methodist Church, Roanoke, Va., district superintendent, 1973-76; Aldersgate United Methodist Church, Alexandria, Va., minister, 1976—. The Methodist Church, member of General Board of Evangelism and General Board of Christian Social Concerns; president, Virginia Conference Board of Evangelism. Member of board, Ludhiana Christian Medical College, India, and Crippled Children's Foundation, Arlington. Military service: U.S. Army Reserve, Chaplains Corps, 1944-72; with active duty, 1944-48; graduate of Command and General Staff College and Industrial College; retired as colonel. Member: Military Chaplains Association of the U.S.A. (president, 1970-72), General Commission on Chaplains (board member), Foundation for Religious Action in the Social and Civil Order (board member). Awards, honors: Freedoms Foundation awards, 1961, 1963, 1964, 1968, 1970, and 1972, for sermons and addresses; D.D., Southwestern College, Winfield, Kan., 1965.

WRITINGS: God Still Speaks in the Space Age, Beacon Press, 1967; His Finest Week, Upper Room, 1971. Contributor to national magazines and denominational publications.

*   *   *

SMITH, Lavon B(enson)   1921-

PERSONAL: Born May 31, 1921, in Winslow, Ark.; son of Paul B. (a teacher) and Ethel (Hight) Smith; married Mary Neeley, March 27, 1942; children: Jerry, Dwight, Mary Lavon (Mrs. Gary Hungate). Education: University of Arkansas, B.A., 1950, M.A., 1963. Religion: Methodist. Residence: Fayetteville, Ark.

CAREER: Hackett (Ark.) public schools, science teacher, 1950-51; Camp Chaffee, Fort Smith, Ark., arts and crafts instructor, 1951-53; Fayetteville (Ark.) public schools, junior high school teacher of industrial arts, 1953-65. Director of children's arts and crafts program in Fayetteville, Ark. Military service: U.S. Army, 1944-46; became staff sergeant. Member: National Education Association, American Vocational Education Association, Arkansas Education Association, Arkansas Industrial Education Association.

WRITINGS: Fundamentals of Leather Carving, Tandy Leather Co., 1955; (with Marion E. Maddox) Elements of American Industry, McKnight & McKnight Publishing, 1966; (with Wilbur R. Miller) Exploring Careers in Industry, 2nd edition, McKnight Publishing, 1975.†

*   *   *

SMITH, Michael (Townsend)   1935-

PERSONAL: Born October 5, 1935, in Kansas City, Mo.; son of Lewis Motter (a merchant) and Dorothy Jane (Pew) Smith. Education: Yale University, student, 1953-56. Agent: Sterling Lord Agency, 660 Madison Ave., New York, N.Y. 10021. Office: Bobbs-Merrill Co. Inc., 4 West 58th St., New York, N.Y. 10019.

CAREER: Village Voice (newspaper), New York City, theatre critic, 1959-71, associate editor, 1962-65, Obie award judge, 1962-68, 1972—; Bobbs-Merrill Co. Inc., New York City, director of Theatre Genesis, 1971—. Manager and co-director, Sundance Festival Theatre, Upper Black Eddy, Pa., 1968; producer and co-director, Caffe Cino

(cafe theatre), New York City, 1968. Director of plays including (all produced in New York City, except as noted): "I Like It," 1963; Gertrude Stein, "Three Sisters Who Are Not Sisters," 1964; Sam Shepard, "Icarus' Mother," 1965; Soren Agenoux, "Charles Dickens' 'Christmas Carol,'" 1967; "Vorspeil nach Marienstein," 1967; H. M. Kontoukas, "With Creatures Make My Way," 1967; Ronald Tavel, "The Life of Juanita Castro," Denver, 1968; Maria Irene Fornes, "Dr. Kheal," Denver, 1968; Emanuel Peluso, "Hurricane of the Eye," 1969; "Captain Jack's Revenge," 1970; "Peas," Denver, 1971; Jean-Claude van Itallie, "Eat Cake," Denver, 1971; "Country Music," 1971; Tavel, "Bigfoot," 1972; Fornes, "Tango Palace," 1973. Instructor at New School for Social Research, New York City, 1964-65, Project Radius, Dalton, Ga., 1972, and Hunter College of the City University of New York, 1972. Member: Drama Desk. Awards, honors: Brandeis University creative arts citation, 1965; Village Voice Off-Broadway (Obie) award, 1972, for direction of "Country Music."

WRITINGS: (Editor with Nick Orzel, and author of introduction) Eight Plays from Off-Off Broadway, Bobbs-Merrill, 1966; Theatre Trip, Bobbs-Merrill, 1968; (editor) The Best of Off-Off Broadway, Dutton, 1969; Theatre Journal, Winter 1967, University of Missouri Press, 1968; More Plays from Off-Off Broadway, Bobbs-Merrill, 1972.

Plays: "I Like It" (first produced in New York City, 1963), published in Kulchur, 1963; "The Next Thing" (first produced in New York City, 1966), published in The Best of Off-Off Broadway, edited by the author, Dutton, 1969; (with Johnny Dodd and Remy Charlip) "More! More! I Want More!," first produced in New York City, 1966; (with Dodd and Ondine) "Vorspiel nach Marienstein," first produced in New York City, 1967; "Captain Jack's Revenge" (first produced Off-Off Broadway at Cafe La Mama, March, 1970, produced on the West End at Royal Court Theatre, January 22, 1971), published in New American Plays 4, edited by William M. Hoffman, Hill & Wang, 1971; "A Dog's Love" (opera; music by John Herbert McDowell), first produced in New York City, 1971; "Tony," first produced in New York City, 1971; "Peas," first produced in Denver, 1971; "Country Music" (first produced in New York City, 1971), published in The Off-Off Broadway Book, edited by Albert Poland and Bruce Mailman, Bobbs-Merrill, 1972; "Double Solitaire," first produced in Denver, 1973; "Prussian Suite," first produced in New York City, 1974.

Also author of "The Dinner Show" (play), 1974, and "Point Blank" (play). Occasional contributor to New York Times, Drama Review, Plays and Players (London), and other periodicals.

SIDELIGHTS: Michael Smith wrote CA: "I wanted to be a writer because I wanted a writer's life: to be able to work anywhere, to play and work in the same gesture, to travel, to be able to use many interests, to live on the freedom of imagination. It doesn't work out that way all the time—I've been feeling stuck in a rut like anybody else—but I've been having an interesting and varied experience, and the future keeps opening. I am happier living in nature, but circumstances have kept most of my writing career in New York City, where I'm part of a theatrical community that is sometimes warmly supportive, sometimes restrictive, rarely (any more) challenging or inspiring. I've supported myself mainly by journalism, and my 'own' writing has often been slighted; my city life leaves me no time for any writing except criticism and prose like this, and I go to the country to write anything else. I've had quite a number of plays produced, but not in a context of commercial or popular success. I've written two novels which haven't been published; I want to write another but I feel rather discouraged. Criticism is what I get the most reinforcement for, because it's useful to other people, but it's the least satisfying writing for me. The main theme of my writing is individual consciousness in the context of the family and of historical circumstance.

"My major area of interest as a critic has been contemporary experimental theatre, originally from a more or less literary point of view . . . more recently from the vantage of a theatre worker (I have worked extensively in stage lighting and production and have directed some score of plays by myself and other contemporary dramatists). A major part of my life is music: I play the harpsichord, piano, recorders, and the occasional drum. For the past several years I have concentrated on the music of J. S. Bach, but lately I'm also playing French and Italian Baroque music. I built my harpsichord (from a kit) and also built myself a small house in the Berkshires.

"My most recent play is about the youth of Frederick the Great, and I played contemporary semi-improvised music with a band in the performances, as well as directing, designing, and producing the play.

"As a theatre critic, I have been going to the theatre several times a week for 15 years. Lately I'm disinclined to see theatre: I feel sated with entertainment. I went often to Europe in the '60s seeing theatre everywhere I went. I spent two months in India and Southeast Asia in 1970 seeing traditional theatre. Unfortunately, since you ask, I am competent in no languages but English."

* * *

SMITH, Nila Banton

PERSONAL: Born in Altona, Mich.; daughter of George Addison (an auctioneer) and Ella (Banton) Smith. *Education:* University of Chicago, B.A., 1928; Columbia University, M.A., 1929, Ph.D., 1932. *Politics:* Republican. *Religion:* Methodist. *Home and office:* 10787 Wilshire Blvd., Los Angeles, Calif. 90024.

CAREER: Detroit (Mich.) public schools, teacher, 1926-30, supervisor of reading, 1930-32; Greensboro College, Greensboro, N.C., head of department of education, 1932-33; Whittier College, Whittier, Calif., dean of School of Education, 1933-37; Indiana University, Bloomington, associate professor of education, 1937-39; University of Southern California, Los Angeles, professor of education and director of Reading Institute, 1948-63; Glassboro State College, Glassboro, N.J., Distinguished Service Professor of Education, 1964-68; University of Southern California, Los Angeles, Distinguished Service Professor of Education, 1968-74. Summer lecturer at University of Hawaii, University of Puerto Rico, University of Arizona, University of Chicago, and University of Michigan. Lecturer on reading in United States and abroad.

MEMBER: International Reading Association (past president), National Society for the Study of Education, National Education Association, National Council of Teachers of English, National Conference of Research in English, American Educational Research Association, American Association of School Administrators, Association for Supervision and Curriculum Development, Phi Beta Kappa, Pi Lambda Theta, Kappa Delta Pi, Delta Kappa Gamma, Delta Phi Upsilon (honorary member).

Awards, honors: Citation of Merit from International Reading Association for work in reading instruction field; Distinguished Service Award from Los Angeles Reading Association; Nila Banton Smith Reading Council named in her honor, 1969; Nila Banton Smith Historical Collection in Reading established in her honor, 1970.

WRITINGS: One Hundred Ways of Teaching Silent Reading, World, 1925; (with Grace Storm) *Reading Activities in Primary Grades,* Ginn, 1930; *A Historical Analysis of American Reading Instruction,* Silver Burdett, 1934, published as *American Reading Instruction: Its Development and Its Significance in Gaining a Perspective on Current Practices in Reading,* 1934, revised edition, International Reading Association, 1965; *Adventures in Teacher Education,* Stewart, 1937; (with Stephen F. Bayne) *Frontiers Old and New,* Silver Burdett, 1947 (originally published as Book 5 of "The Unit-Activity Reading" series, below); (with Bayne) *Distant Doorways,* Silver Burdett, 1948 (originally published as Book 4 of "The Unit-Activity Reading" series, below); (with Bayne) *On the Long Road,* Silver Burdett, 1948 (originally published as Book 6 of "The Unit-Activity Reading" series, below).

(Editor) H.L.J. Carter and D. J. McGinnis, *Effective Reading for College Students,* Dryden, 1957; *Read Faster and Get More from Your Reading,* Prentice-Hall, 1958, published as *Faster Reading Made Easy,* Popular Library, 1963; (with others) *Graded Selections for Informal Reading Diagnosis, Grades 1 through 3,* New York University Press, 1959; *Graded Selections for Informal Reading Diagnosis, Grades 4 through 6,* New York University Press, 1963; *Reading Instruction for Today's Children,* Prentice-Hall, 1963; (editor with others) *Challenges in Reading,* Bobbs-Merrill, 1965; (editor with others) *Voyages in Reading,* Bobbs-Merrill, 1965; (compiler with others) *Riches in Reading,* Bobbs-Merrill, 1967; (with Ruth Strickland) *Some Approaches to Reading,* edited by Sylvia Sunderlin, Association for Childhood Education International, 1969; (editor) *Current Issues in Reading,* International Reading Association, 1969; (editor) *Reading Methods and Teacher Improvement,* International Reading Association, 1971.

Series: (With Stuart A. Courtis) "Picture-Story Reading Lessons," World, 1924-27, teacher's manual, 1924, revised edition, 1926; (with others) "The Unit-Activity Reading," Silver Burdett, Pre-primer, Primer, and Books 1-3, 1935, revised editions, 1940, additional Primer and Books 2-3, 1938-39, Books 4-6, 1940; "Learning to Read," six books, Silver Burdett, 1945, teacher's edition with guides, 1945; (with Vivian L. Teubner) "Read and Do" (to accompany "Learning to Read"), five books, Silver Burdett, 1945; "Be a Better Reader," Prentice-Hall, Books 1-7 (secondary grades), 1959-61, Books 1-4, 3rd editions, 1969, Books 1-2, special editions, 1971, Book 6, 2nd edition, 1973, Foundations A, B, C (elementary grades), 1968-69; (editor and compiler with Hazel C. Hart and Clare R. Baker) "Best of Children's Literature," six books, Bobbs-Merrill, 1960-66.

Also author of numerous booklets on reading. Contributor of more than 200 articles to professional journals.

WORK IN PROGRESS: Revising Foundations A, B, C of "Be a Better Reader" series, and *Reading Instruction for Today's Children.*

* * *

SMITH, Norris Kelly 1917-

PERSONAL: Born October 5, 1917, in Little Rock, Ark.; son of Hay Watson (a clergyman) and Jessie Alice (Rose)

Smith; married Mary Davis, August 14, 1941. *Education:* Columbia University, A.B., 1939, A.M., 1949, Ph.D., 1961. *Religion:* Presbyterian. *Home:* 6975 Cornell Ave., University City, Mo. 63130. *Office:* Washington University, Box 1189, St. Louis, Mo. 63130.

CAREER: Instructor at Columbia College, Columbia University, New York City, 1947-52, and Hunter College (now Hunter College of the City University of New York), New York City, 1952-56; Washington University, St. Louis, Mo., 1956—, professor of art history, 1963—, acting chairman of department of art and archaeology, 1963-67. *Military service:* U.S. Army Air Forces, 1943-45; became staff sergeant.

WRITINGS: Frank Lloyd Wright: A Study in Architectural Content, Prentice-Hall, 1966; *Medieval Art: An Introduction to the Art and Architecture of Europe, A.D. 300—A.D. 1300,* W. C. Brown, 1967; *On Art and Architecture in the Modern World,* American Life Foundation, 1971.

WORK IN PROGRESS: A book on perspective, tentatively entitled *Perspective in Another Perspective.*

* * *

SMITH, Richard N. 1937-

PERSONAL: Born March 6, 1937, in Somerville, Mass.; son of Earle H. (a lawyer) and Alice (Sullivan) Smith. *Education:* Harvard University, A.B. and A.M., 1960. *Agent:* Theron Raines, 244 Madison Ave., New York, N.Y. 10016.

CAREER: N. W. Ayer & Sons, New York, N.Y., public relations, beginning 1965. Director, Irish International Bank. *Military service:* U.S. Coast Guard Reserve, 1960—; now lieutenant. *Member:* Mystery Writers of America.

WRITINGS: Death Be Nimble, New American Library, 1967.

WORK IN PROGRESS: A biography of Jonathan Wild, English criminal and detective.††

* * *

SMITH, Sally Liberman 1929-

PERSONAL: Born May 7, 1929, in New York, N.Y.; daughter of I. (a businessman) and Bertha B. Liberman; married Robert Solwin Smith, March 12, 1953 (divorced); children: Randall Alan, Nicholas Lee, Gary Gordon. *Education:* Bennington College, B.A., 1950; New York University, M.A., 1955. *Politics:* Democrat. *Home:* 3216 Cleveland Ave. N.W., Washington, D.C. 20008. *Office:* 1809 Phelps Pl. N.W., Washington, D.C.

CAREER: Free-lance writer in field of social and psychological problems and elementary education. Founder and director of the Laboratory School of Kingsbury Center, Washington, D.C., 1967—. Designer of experimental projects, using the arts as the route to teaching elementary school children, including the Potomac summer project, 1966, and the Friends-Morgan Project, 1967; writer and producer of films documenting work at the Laboratory School. Member of board, National Child Research Center, 1964-67. *Member:* Pan Pacific Southeast Asia Women's Group (program chairman, 1963-65). *Awards, honors:* Named one of ten outstanding young women of the year, *Mademoiselle* (magazine), 1955, for work in mental health field.

WRITINGS: A Child's Guide to a Parent's Mind, Schu-

man, 1951; *Nobody Said It's Easy,* Macmillan, 1965. Author of pamphlets and a number of magazine articles.

WORK IN PROGRESS: A book on educating children with learning disabilities.

SIDELIGHTS: Sally Liberman Smith has lived in Paris and Geneva, and has traveled in Europe, the Middle East, and Asia. She speaks some French. *Avocational interests:* Theater, dance, and world affairs.

* * *

SMITH, Warren Sylvester 1912-

PERSONAL: Born March 11, 1912, in Bangor, Pa; son of Warren Sylvester (a grocer) and Sybilla (Steinmetz) Smith; married Mae Wilson (an editor), July 4, 1943; children: Paula (Mrs. John Dunning), Rodney, Selden. *Education:* Muhlenberg College, B.A., 1933; University of Iowa, M.A., 1937. *Religion:* Society of Friends. *Home address:* Box 66, Lemont, Pa. 16851. *Office:* 127 Arts Bldg., Pennsylvania State University, University Park, Pa. 16801

CAREER: High school English and drama instructor, Bangor, Pa., 1933-42; Pennsylvania State University, University Park, 1946—, began as instructor, professor of theatre arts, 1955-66, director of general education in the arts and assistant director of Institute for Arts and Humanistic Studies, 1966-69, director and professor of general education in the arts, 1969—, managing director of Mateer Playhouse, summers, 1958-60. Guest director and instructor, University of Miami, summer, 1950; summer co-director of work camps, American Friends Service Committee, 1953-55. *Military service:* U.S. Army, 1942-46. *Member:* American Educational Theatre Association, American National Theatre and Academy, Association for General and Liberal Studies, American Association of University Professors. *Awards, honors:* American Council of Learned Societies grants-in-aid for study in England, 1965, and Europe, 1972.

WRITINGS: (With W. H. Walters) *Attending the Play* (study guide for adult education), Center for Continuing Liberal Education, Pennsylvania State University, 1959; (editor and author of introduction) George Bernard Shaw, *The Religious Speeches of Bernard Shaw,* Pennsylvania State University Press, 1963; (editor and author of introduction) *Shaw on Religion,* Dodd, 1967; *The London Heretics, 1870-1914,* Constable, 1967, Dodd, 1968; (editor and author of introduction) Shaw, *Plays,* Norton, 1970. Author of a series of nine articles, "The Victorian Heretics of London," published in *Christian Century,* 1963; contributor of articles to other periodicals, including *Nation, Quaker History, Cosmopolitan, Players,* and *Pulpit.* Member of board of editors, *Shaw Review.*

WORK IN PROGRESS: Responding to the Arts, for Holt.

* * *

SMITHERMAN, P(hillip) H(enry) 1910-

PERSONAL: Born March 27, 1910, in London, England; son of Henry (a tutor) and Frances (Holder) Smitherman; married Rosemary Wright, November 24, 1945; children: Robin, Rowena, Lavinia, Victoria. *Education:* Attended New College, Oxford, 1929-32. *Politics:* Conservative. *Religion:* Church of England. *Home:* Northacre, Godalming, Surrey, England.

CAREER: British Army, 1932-59, serving as regimental officer, Royal Signals, 1932-52, and staff officer, War Office, London, 1952-59, retired as colonel, 1959.

WRITINGS—All published by Evelyn: *Cavalry Uniforms of the British Army,* 1961; *Uniforms of the Scottish Regiments,* 1962; *Infantry Uniforms of the British Army,* Volume I, 1963, Volume II, 1965, Volume III, 1970; *Uniforms of the Royal Artillery,* 1965; *Uniforms of the Yeomanry Regiments,* 1967.

* * *

SMITHIES, Richard H(ugo) R(ipman) 1936-

PERSONAL: Born June 19, 1936, in Canberra, Australia; son of Arthur and Katharine (Ripman) Smithies; married Maura Cavanagh, December 22, 1963; children: Susannah Cassandra, Padraic Arthur. *Education:* Harvard University, B.A., 1957, Ll.B., 1960. *Agent:* Harold Matson Co., 22 East 40th St., New York, N.Y. 10016.

CAREER: Harvard University, Cambridge, Mass., instructor; Kramer, Marx, Greenlee & Backus, New York City, junior associate attorney, 1961-64. Producer and director, "The Poker Session," New York City; director, New Theatre Workshop, New York City, Orleans Arena Theatre, Orleans, Mass., and Circle Theatre, Providence, R.I. Lead actor, Orleans Arena Theatre, summer, 1968.

WRITINGS: An Academic Question, Horizon, 1965; *Disposing Mind,* Horizon, 1966; *The Shoplifter,* Horizon, 1968; *Death Takes a Gamble,* New American Library, 1968; *Death Gets an A,* New American Library, 1968; (with wife, Maura Cavanagh) *The Yeggs and the Yahbuts,* Random House, 1969; (with Cavanagh) *The Tease,* New American Library, 1975.

Plays: (With Maura Cavanagh) "The Wizard and the Phoenix" (juvenile); "The Swineherd" (juvenile); (with Cavanagh) "Where It's At" (musical revue), produced Off-Broadway, spring, 1969.

SIDELIGHTS: Smithies used recollections from his seven years at Harvard as faculty child, undergraduate, law student, and instructor to write his Columbia University/Greenwich Village centered mystery, *An Academic Question.* Smithies feels that "people become more vivid in the context of violence and emotional strain." Therefore, this novel is complicated by murder, dope-pushing, and blackmail. Smithies later used his impressions of Connecticut for a "clever tale of threats and theft and murder," in *The Shoplifter,* the *New Yorker* reviewer explains. Thomas Lask adds that "Smithies, who wrote an entrancing whodunit in *Disposing Mind,* has done it again in *The Shoplifter.* He has marked out a territory for himself that includes a section of Connecticut inhabited by a cultivated, station-wagon contingent conscious mainly of family, money and business standing. They are literate, interested in the proper things, make superb gossips and possess their own quota of the corrupt and homicidal."

BIOGRAPHICAL/CRITICAL SOURCES: New York Times Book Review, July 7, 1968; *New Yorker,* July 13, 1968.†

* * *

SMOUT, T(homas) C(hristopher) 1933-

PERSONAL: Born December 19, 1933, in Birmingham, England; son of Arthur J. G. (a company director) and A. Hilda (Follows) Smout; married Anne-Marie Schoening, August 15, 1959; children: Pernille Anne, Andrew Michael Christian. *Education:* Clare College, Cambridge, M.A., 1957, Ph.D., 1960. *Office:* University of Edinburgh, Edinburgh, Scotland.

CAREER: University of Edinburgh, Edinburgh, Scotland, assistant, 1959-61, lecturer, 1962-66, reader, 1966-71, professor of economic history, 1971—.

WRITINGS: Scottish Trade on the Eve of Union, 1660-1707, Oliver & Boyd, 1963; *A History of the Scottish People, 1560-1830,* Collins, 1969, Scribner, 1970.

WORK IN PROGRESS: A book on nineteenth-century Scotland; a socio-economic atlas of early Victorian Scotland; with others, a book on Scottish historical demography, 1615-1939.

AVOCATIONAL INTERESTS: Bird-watching, walking, admiring towns.

* * *

SMUCKER, Leonard 1928-

PERSONAL: Born April 3, 1928, in Smithville, Ohio; son of J. N. (a minister) and Mary (Lantz) Smucker; married Lois Rich, June 17, 1951; children: Steven, Stuart, Stanford, Sterling. *Education:* Bluffton College, A.B., 1950; Bethany Theological Seminary, Chicago, Ill., B.D., 1955; University of Southern California, Ph.D., 1959. *Home:* 2600 Oaklawn Ave., Elkhart, Ind. 46514. *Office:* Oaklawn Psychiatric Center, Elkhart, Ind. 46514.

CAREER: Los Angeles County (Calif.) Office of Counselor and Mental Health, deputy counselor, 1958; Goshen College, Goshen, Ind., instructor in psychology, 1960; Beatty Memorial Hospital, Westville, Ind., staff psychologist, 1960-63; Oaklawn Psychiatric Center, Elkhart, Ind., clinical psychologist, 1963—. *Member:* American Psychological Association, American Academy of Psychotherapists, American Association of Marriage Counselors, American Association for Humanistic Psychology.

WRITINGS: Spring: A Therapeutic Relationship, Herald, 1967.

AVOCATIONAL INTERESTS: Woodcarving, playing guitar, unicycling, growing bonsai.†

* * *

SNEED, Joseph Tyree 1920-

PERSONAL: Born July 21, 1920, in Calvert, Tex.; son of Harold Marvin and Cara (Weber) Sneed; married Madelon Juergens, March 15, 1944; children: Clara Hall, Cara Carleton, Joseph Tyree IV. *Education:* Southwestern University, Georgetown, Tex., B.B.A., 1941; University of Texas, LL.B., 1947; Harvard University, S.J.D., 1958. *Politics:* Republican. *Religion:* Episcopalian. *Home:* 2672 Filbert, San Francisco, Calif. 94123. *Office address:* Ninth Circuit, Court of Appeals, P.O. Box 547, San Francisco, Calif. 94101.

CAREER: Member of Texas, New York, and North Carolina State Bars; University of Texas, Main University (now University of Texas at Austin), School of Law, assistant professor, 1947-51, associate professor, 1951-54, professor of law, 1954-57; Cornell University, School of Law, Ithaca, N.Y., professor of law, 1957-62; Stanford University, School of Law, Stanford, Calif., professor of law, 1962-71; Duke University, School of Law, Durham, N.C., professor of law and dean, 1971-73; deputy attorney general, U.S. Department of Justice, 1973; U.S. Court of Appeals, Ninth Circuit, San Francisco, Calif., judge, 1973—. President, Association of American Law Schools, 1968; trustee of College Retirement Equities Fund and Teachers Insurance and Annuity Association of America, 1967-71;

member of advisory committee, National Institute of Law Enforcement and Criminal Justice, 1974—. Member of board of visitors, Law School, Hastings College, 1974-75. *Military service:* U.S. Army Air Forces, 1942-46; became sergeant. *Member:* American Bar Association, American Law Institute, American Judicature Society, Federal Bar Association, International Fiscal Association, Harvard Club (San Francisco). *Awards, honors:* LL.D., Southwestern University, 1968.

WRITINGS: Configurations of Gross Income, Ohio State University Press, 1967.

*   *   *

SNODGRASS, A(nthony) M(cElrea)   1934-

PERSONAL: Born July 7, 1934; son of William McElrea (an army officer) and Kathleen (Owen) Snodgrass; married Ann E. Vaughan, November 7, 1959; children: Nell, Rachel, Elspeth. *Education:* Worcester College, Oxford, B.A., 1959, M.A. and D.Phil., 1963. *Politics:* Labour Party. *Home:* 1 Dunbar's Close, Canongate, Edinburgh EH8 8BW, Scotland. *Office:* Department of Archaeology, University of Edinburgh, 19 George Sq., Edinburgh EH8 9JZ, Scotland.

CAREER: University of Edinburgh, Edinburgh, Scotland, lecturer, 1961-69, reader, 1969-75, professor of classical archaeology, 1975—. Member, Midlothian Valuation Appeal Committee, 1966—. *Military service:* Royal Air Force, 1953-55; served in Iraq; became flying officer. *Member:* Hellenic Society (member of council, 1964-67, 1973—), Roman Society.

WRITINGS: Early Greek Armour and Weapons, Edinburgh University Press, 1964; *Arms and Armour of the Greeks,* Cornell University Press, 1967; *The Dark Age of Greece,* Edinburgh University Press, 1971. Contributor to classical journals.

SIDELIGHTS: Snodgrass is fluent in French and Italian, and is competent in German, modern Greek, and Turkish.

*   *   *

SNORTUM, Niel K(lendenon)   1928-

PERSONAL: Born January 3, 1928, in Bemidji, Minn.; son of Selmer I. and Elizabeth (Mott) Snortum; married Elizabeth Clare, August 5, 1951; children: Knute Jonathan, Lisa Karen. *Education:* Grinnell College, B.A., 1950; Stanford University, Ph.D., 1955. *Office:* Department of English, San Francisco State University, San Francisco, Calif. 94132.

CAREER: Stanford University, Stanford, Calif., acting instructor in English, 1952-55; University of Michigan, Ann Arbor, instructor, 1955-57, assistant professor of English, 1957-61; San Francisco State University, San Francisco, Calif., associate professor, 1961-66, professor of English, 1966—. Lecturer on American folklore and study of language to clubs and civic groups, 1954—, and on the American West and folklore for educational television, 1959-61. Worked as a wrangler and trail guide in the Sierra foothills, summers, 1950-55; folksinger and sailing-master at a Lake Michigan resort, summers, 1955-61. *Military service:* U.S. Army, 1946-47; became staff sergeant. *Member:* National Council of Teachers of English, Conference on College Composition and Communication, American Folklore Society.

WRITINGS: Contemporary Rhetoric, Prentice-Hall, 1967; (with Daniel Knapp) *The Sounds of Chaucer's English,*

National Council of Teachers of English, 1967; (contributor) *Harper Studies in Language and Literature,* Harper, 1974. Contributor to professional journals.

WORK IN PROGRESS: An anthology of medieval English literature; a study of interview techniques and their applicability to composition teaching.

*   *   *

SNOW, Peter G(ordon)   1933-

PERSONAL: Born July 3, 1933, in Boulder, Colo.; son of Carl Wilson (a chemical engineer) and Gladys (Gordon) Snow; married Jean Ann Howell, December 26, 1958; children: Steven Gregory. *Education:* Attended University of Colorado, 1951-52, Frank Phillips Junior College, 1953, Morris Harvey College, 1957; Texas Technological College (now Texas Tech University), B.A., 1958, M.A., 1960; University of Virginia, Ph.D., 1963. *Home:* 84 Olive Ct., Iowa City, Iowa 52240. *Office:* Department of Political Science, University of Iowa, Iowa City, Iowa 52240.

CAREER: University of Iowa, Iowa City, assistant professor, 1962-66, associate professor, 1966-70, professor of political science, 1970—. *Military service:* U.S. Army, Infantry, 1953-55; became sergeant. *Member:* American Political Science Association, Latin American Studies Association, Midwest Conference of Political Scientists.

WRITINGS: Argentine Radicalism: The History and Doctrine of the Radical Civic Union, University of Iowa Press, 1965; (contributor) Robert D. Tomasek, editor, *Latin American Politics,* Anchor Books, 1966; (editor) *Government and Politics in Latin America: A Reader,* Holt, 1967; (contributor) Ben Burnett and Kenneth Johnson, editors, *Political Forces in Latin America,* Wadsworth, 1968; *Political Forces in Argentina,* Allyn & Bacon, 1971; *El Radicalismo Chileno,* Editorial Francisco de Aguirre, 1972. Contributor to *American Political Science Review, Midwest Journal of Political Science, American Behavioral Scientist, Cinencias Politicas Sociales, Revista Espanola de Opinion Publica, Jahrbuch des Oeffentlichen Rechts,* and other journals.

WORK IN PROGRESS: The Rutinization of Charisma: A Study of Juan Peron and Peronism.

SIDELIGHTS: Snow spent 1966-67, 1972, and part of 1975 in Argentina.

*   *   *

SNOW, Roslyn   1936-

PERSONAL: Born July 28, 1936, in Chicago, Ill; daughter of David (a lawyer) and Regina (Kohn) Snow. *Education:* University of Illinois, A.B., 1958, A.M., 1959. *Politics:* Democrat. *Religion:* Jewish. *Office:* Department of English, Orange Coast College, Costa Mesa, Calif. 92626.

CAREER: Orange Coast College, Costa Mesa, Calif., associate professor of English, 1962—.

WRITINGS: (With Jacob Fuchs) *Man: Alternatives of Experience,* Wadsworth, 1967.

WORK IN PROGRESS: Spelling by Sound, a slide and sound programmed spelling course for college students.

*   *   *

SOBEL, Lester A(lbert)   1919-

PERSONAL: Born October 3, 1919, in New York, N.Y.; son of David (a baker) and Ray Dorothy (Mendelson) Sobel; married Eileen Lucille Helfer, May 3, 1953; children: Martha Lorraine, Sharon Ruth, Jonathan William. *Education:* City College (now City College of the City University of New York), B.B.A., 1942. *Religion:* Jewish. *Home:* 226 Porterfield Pl., Freeport, N.Y. 11520. *Office:* Facts on File, Inc., 119 West 57th St., New York, N.Y. 10019.

CAREER: Facts on File, Inc., New York, N.Y., editor and writer, 1946—, editor-in-chief, 1960-70, vice-president, 1964—. Editor-in-chief of *News Year* (reference annual), 1960-63, *News Dictionary* (reference annual), 1964-73, and "Interim History" (book series), 1964-73. *Military service:* U.S. Army, 1942-44; became sergeant; received Bronze Star Medal.

WRITINGS—All published by Facts on File: *National Issues,* 1956; (editor) *Space: From Sputnik to Gemini,* 1965; (editor) *South Vietnam: U.S. Communist Confrontation in Southeast Asia,* Volume I, 1966, Volume II, 1969; (editor) *Civil Rights 1960-66,* 1967; (editor) *Russia's Rulers: The Khrushchev Period,* 1971; (editor) *Inflation and the Nixon Administration,* Volume I, 1974, Volume II, 1975; (editor) *Israel and the Arabs: The October 1973 War,* 1974; (editor) *Money and Politics,* 1974; (editor) *Energy Crisis,* Volume I, 1974, Volume II, 1975; (editor) *Chile and Allende,* 1974; (editor) *Political Terrorism,* 1975; (editor) *Presidential Succession,* 1975; (editor) *Kissinger and Detente,* 1975; (editor) *Argentina and Peron,* 1975; (editor) *World Food Crisis,* 1975.

WORK IN PROGRESS: Collecting material for books on urban problems, the attack on privacy, and the arms race.

* * *

SOHL, Frederic J(ohn) 1916-

PERSONAL: Surname rhymes with "pole"; born March 5, 1916, in Brooklyn, N.Y.; son of Frederick Martin (a grocer) and Anna (Koster) Sohl; married Mildred Mantay (an assistant librarian), January 7, 1940; children: Kathryn, Frederic M. *Education:* New York University, B.S., 1951. *Politics:* Independent. *Home:* 223-08 Murdock Ave., Queens Village, N.Y. 11429.

CAREER: Federal Bureau of Investigation, Washington, D.C., fingerprint classifier, 1939-41; Reliable Stores Corp., Washington, D.C., assistant credit manager, 1941-43; Pullman Co., New York City and Chicago, Ill., pullman conductor, 1943-44; Title Guarantee & Trust Co., New York City, credit man, 1946-48; Underwriters Trust Co., New York City, manager of credit department, 1948-53, assistant secretary, 1953-62, vice-president and loan officer, 1962-74. *Military service:* U.S. Army, 1944-46; served in Burma and China; became staff sergeant; received Bronze Star Medal.

WRITINGS: His Majesty's Wonderful Nose, Reilly & Lee, 1967.

WORK IN PROGRESS: Short stories of ancient China.

SIDELIGHTS: Several decades passed between the writing of *His Majesty's Wonderful Nose* and it's publication; Sohl wrote the story while on Army duty in China in World War II, to tell his children when he returned home. While his daughter was attending the University of Chicago, she mentioned the tale to a juvenile author, Jean Kellogg, who passed it on to a publisher.

* * *

SOLBERG, S(ammy) E(dward) 1930-

PERSONAL: Born December 6, 1930, in Fertile, Minn.; son of Samuel Donald (an engineer and farmer) and Clara (Reseland) Solberg; married Joan Todd, October 21, 1956; children: Stacey Gawain, Gwynth Undine, Samuel Kristan, Heatherann, Todd Lachlan. *Education:* Western Montana College, B.S., 1951; University of Washington, M.A., 1960, Ph.D., 1972; Yonsei University, Seoul, Korea, graduate study, 1960-64. *Residence:* Seattle, Wash. *Office:* University of Washington, Seattle, Wash. 98105.

CAREER: Writer on Korean literature, life, and arts, and translator from Korean; instructor in English at University of Maryland, Far East Division, and Yonsei University, Seoul, Korea, 1961-64; University of Washington, Seattle, assistant to the director, Institute for Comparative and Foreign Area Studies, 1973, lecturer in Asian-American studies, 1975—. *Military service:* U.S. Army, 1953-55; became sergeant. *Member:* American Comparative Literature Association, International Comparative Literature Association. *Awards, honors:* National Endowment for the Humanities fellowship, 1973-74.

WRITINGS: The Land and People of Korea, Lippincott, 1966, revised edititon, 1974; (compiler and translator) *Anthology of Korean Literature,* University of Washington Press, in press. Also compiler and translator of "Selections from Korean Literature," for Far Eastern and Russian Institute, University of Washington, 1965. Translations of poems, essays, short stories, songs, and plays have appeared in *Korea Through Her Arts* (Seoul), and *East-West Review,* and articles and reviews in *Hyondai munhak* (Korea), *Comment* (Manila), *Korean Affairs,* and various other literary and professional journals in Korea, 1962—.

WORK IN PROGRESS: Revising translations and critical commentary on the poetry of Han Yong-un; editing an edition of poetry by Carlos Bulosan with historical and critical analysis.

SIDELIGHTS: Solberg told *CA:* "Major interests are de-urbanization and natural silence (something no sound-proofing can give)."

* * *

SOLBRIG, Otto T(homas) 1930-

PERSONAL: Born December 21, 1930, in Buenos Aires, Argentina; son of Hans Joajim (a businessman) and Rose Mabel (Muggleworth) Solbrig; married Roberta Mae Chittum, August 4, 1956 (divorced, 1969); married Dorothy Jane Crosswhite, June 21, 1969; children: (first marriage) Hans Joseph, Heide Frances. *Education:* Attended Universidad Nacional de La Plata, 1950-54; University of California, Berkeley, Ph.D., 1959. *Politics:* Democrat. *Home:* 16 Pleasant View Rd., Arlington, Mass. 02174. *Office:* Department of Biology, Harvard University, Cambridge, Mass. 02138.

CAREER: Harvard University, Cambridge, Mass., curator of botany, 1959-66; University of Michigan, Ann Arbor, associate professor, 1966-68, professor of botany, 1968-69; Harvard University, professor of biology, 1969—. Member of several botanical expeditions to South America. *Member:* International Association of Plant Biosystematists (secretary general), Botanical Society of America, American Association for the Advancement of Science, Genetical Society of America, Society for the Study of Evolution (secretary), American Academy of Arts and Sciences (fellow), American Society of Naturalists, American Society of Plant Taxonomists, Phi Beta Kappa, Sigma Xi. *Awards, honors:* Cooley Award for research paper, 1962; M.A., Harvard University, 1969.

WRITINGS: Evolution and Systematics, Macmillan, 1966; *Plant Biosystematics,* Macmillan, 1969; *Evolution of Sex in Plants,* Harvard University Press, 1976. Contributor to *Biosystematic Literature Review,* International Association of Plant Taxonomy; contributor of more than ninty articles on plant genetics and evolution to journals.

WORK IN PROGRESS: Population Biology; research in plant genetics and evolution.

AVOCATIONAL INTERESTS: Reading history, sailing.

*   *   *

SOLOMON, Carl   1928-

PERSONAL: Born March 30, 1928, in New York, N.Y.; son of Morris Hamilton (a salesman) and Ann (Shipman) Solomon; married Olive Blake, 1950. *Education:* Courses at City College (now City College of the City University of New York), 1943-48, and Brooklyn College (now Brooklyn College of the City University of New York), 1948-50; also studied at Sorbonne, University of Paris, 1947, and New School for Social Research, 1965. *Politics:* Democratic. *Religion:* Jewish. *Home:* 3120 Wilkinson Ave., Bronx, N.Y.

CAREER: Merchant seaman, 1945-49, shipping as messman to Europe, West Indies, Canada, and American ports; publisher's reader, New York, N.Y., 1950—, with Ace Books, Inc., 1950-68; bookseller, 1968—.

WRITINGS: Mishaps, Perhaps, City Lights, 1966; *More Mishaps,* City Lights, 1968. Book reviewer for *New Leader.*

SIDELIGHTS: Solomon told *CA:* "Write when I feel I have something to say. Would never have been published if I hadn't met Allen Ginsberg in a mental hospital in 1949."

BIOGRAPHICAL/CRITICAL SOURCES: Spectrum, winter, 1960.

*   *   *

SOLOMON, Irving I.   1922-

PERSONAL: Born March 5, 1922, in New York, N.Y.; son of Max and Helen Solomon; married Frieda Ruffman; children: Maxinne, Stephanie, Charisse, Marc. *Education:* City College (now City College of the City University of New York), B.A., 1942; George Washington University, graduate study. *Religion:* Hebrew. *Home:* 20 Central Park Rd., Plainview, Long Island, N.Y. 11803. *Office:* National Retail Merchants Association, 100 West 31st St., New York, N.Y. 10001.

CAREER: Has worked as market and system engineer for International Business Machine and president and owner of National Cybernetics Corp.; former manager of Eastern District, Ernst & Ernst, New York City; currently vice-president and general manager, National Retail Merchants Association, Information Systems Division, New York City; New York University, New York City, associate professor of computer science, 1959—. *Member:* American Mathematical Society, Systems and Procedures Association (president), Association de Cybernetique (U.S. representative, 1959—), National Retail Merchants Association (program chairman, 1964-68), Retail Research Association (program chairman, 1960—), Data Processing Management Association (vice-president, 1960-64), American Management Association.

WRITINGS: (With L. Weingart) *Management Uses of the Computer,* Harper, 1966; *Feasibility,* Thompson Publica-

tions, 1970. Contributor to journals. Editor, *Data Processing Management Association Journal* and *Systems and Procedures Association Newsletter.*

WORK IN PROGRESS: A textbook on accounting systems.

*   *   *

SOLOMON, Ruth (Freeman)   1908-

PERSONAL: Born April 21, 1908, in Kiev, Russia; daughter of Harry von Glasman and Jenny (Packer) Freeman; married Joseph C. Solomon (a physician), March 21, 1930; children: George Freeman, Daniel Freeman. *Education:* Syracuse University, A.B. (summa cum laude), 1929; University of Vienna, graduate study, 1930. *Home:* 34 25th Ave., San Francisco, Calif. 94121.

MEMBER: Phi Beta Kappa.

WRITINGS—All novels: *The Candlesticks and the Cross,* Putnam, 1967; *The Eagle and the Dove,* Putnam, 1971; *The Ultimate Triumph,* Putnam, 1974; *The Wolf and the Leopard,* Putnam, 1976.

WORK IN PROGRESS: Two novels.

BIOGRAPHICAL/CRITICAL SOURCES: San Francisco Chronicle, April 11, 1967; *Courier,* spring, 1967; *San Francisco Examiner,* July 26, 1967, August 6, 1967; *Indianapolis News,* August 26, 1967; *Detroit News,* November 14, 1967; *Chicago Tribune,* December 14, 1967.

*   *   *

SORELL, Walter   1905-

PERSONAL: Born May 2, 1905, in Vienna, Austria; came to United States in 1939, naturalized in 1945; son of Alexander and Caroline (Bodascher) Sorell; married Gertrude Sorell Eisenstein (a designer), January 11, 1938. *Education:* Attended University of Vienna; Columbia University, M.F.A., 1955. *Home:* 25 West 64th St., New York, N.Y. 10023.

CAREER: Information specialist, U.S. Information Agency, writing for *America Illustrated, Span,* and Voice of America, 1950-66; New School for Social Research, New York City, lecturer in dramatic literature, 1957—; Columbia University, New York City, associate in music, 1958—. Lecturer at Cornell University, College of Wooster, University of North Carolina, and other schools.

WRITINGS: (Editor and contributor) *The Dance Has Many Faces,* World Publishing, 1951, revised edition, Columbia University Press, 1966; *The Story of the Human Hand,* Bobbs-Merrill, 1967; *The Dance through the Ages,* Grosset, 1967; *Hanya Holm* (biography), Wesleyan University Press, 1969; *The Duality of Vision,* Bobbs-Merrill, 1969; *The Dancer's Image: Points and Counterpoints,* Columbia University Press, 1971; *Facets of Comedy,* Grosset, 1972; *The Swiss: A Cultural Panorama of Switzerland,* Bobbs-Merrill, 1972; *The Other Face: The Mask in the Arts,* Bobbs-Merrill, 1974; *The Mary Wigman Book,* Wesleyan University Press, 1975; *Three Women,* Bobbs-Merrill, 1975.

Translator: (With Denver Lindley) Erich Maria Remarque, *Arch of Triumph,* Appleton, 1945; William Herzog, *From Dreyfus to Petain,* Creative Age Press, 1948; *Goethe's World* (anthology), New Directions, 1949; Herman Hesse, *Steppenwolf,* Random House, 1963; Mary Wigman, *The Language of Dance,* Wesleyan University Press, 1966; Johannes Urzidil, *Prague,* Scherpe Verlag, 1966.

Plays: "Isadora Duncan" (verse), produced by National Broadcasting Co., 1955; "Everyman Today," produced by Union Theological Seminary and Phoenix Theatre, 1958; "Between Now and Then" produced in Germany, 1959; "Resurrection After Cocktail Time," tryout in Westport, Conn., 1959; "The Flowering of a Barren Fig Tree," tryout by American Place Theatre, 1965; "Olivia and a Dream" (comedy), optioned by Renaissance Theatre, Berlin; "Cain and Evil." Also writer of television plays for National Broadcasting Co. and Columbia Broadcasting System.

Contributor to *Collier's Encyclopedia;* also contributor of fiction, articles, reviews, poetry, and translations to periodicals, including *Saturday Review, Vogue, Horizon, Esquire, Opera News, Tomorrow, Shakespeare Quarterly.* Editor, *Dance Observer,* 1959-64; contributing editor, *Dance News,* 1970—; drama editor, *Cresset;* member of advisory board, *Dance Scope.*

* * *

SORENSEN, Thomas C. 1926-

PERSONAL: Born March 31, 1926, in Lincoln, Neb.; son of Christian A. (an attorney) and Annis (Chaikin) Sorensen; brother of Theodore Sorensen; married Mary Jane Barstler, July 5, 1947; children: Ann Christine, Alan Thomas, Jens Christian. *Education:* University of Nebraska, B.A., 1947. *Politics:* Democrat. *Home:* 250 Beverly Rd., Scarsdale, N.Y. 10583.

CAREER: Financial executive. With U.S. Information Agency, Washington, D.C. and overseas, 1951-61, deputy director, 1961-65; University of California, Berkeley, Calif., vice-president, 1966-68; Leasco Corp., New York City, vice-president, 1969-70; Sartorious and Co., New York City, partner, 1971-74; general partner, Advest Co., and president, Advest International, New York City, 1973—. Member of board of directors of Hyde Park Bank, Pennsylvania Mutual Fund, and Public Media Inc. *Awards, honors:* Arthur S. Flemming Award as "One of the Ten Outstanding Young Men in the Federal Service," 1962.

WRITINGS: The Word War: The Story of American Propaganda, foreword by Robert F. Kennedy, Harper, 1968. Contributor to *Jefferson Encyclopedia,* World, 1968; regular contributor, *The Sorensen Report,* 1974—.

SIDELIGHTS: Sorensen has written a book which "will go a long way toward clarifying America's image abroad," writes Joseph Menez. Sorensen, Menez adds, believes "on the one hand, that ideas are weapons and that American ideas ought to get a decent hearing; and on the other, that America's credibility must be based on truthfulness." Says former head of the Voice of America, John Chancellor, "we have clearly come a long way in the craft of international persuasion and public relations, and Sorensen's book is a workmanlike chronicle of that development."

AVOCATIONAL INTERESTS: Politics.

BIOGRAPHICAL/CRITICAL SOURCES: Book World, June 16, 1968; *Best Sellers,* July 1, 1968.

* * *

SORENSON, Herbert 1898-

PERSONAL: Born April 12, 1898, in Dawson, Minn.; married Mabel Ahlquist (a researcher); children: Barbara (Mrs. J. F. Hulka). *Education:* St. Cloud State College, student, 1919-20; University of Minnesota, B.S., 1924, M.A., 1925, Ph.D., 1928. *Politics:* Independent. *Home and office:* 12405 North 28th St., Tampa, Fla. 33612.

CAREER: Teacher and principal in Minnesota, 1916-18; superintendent of schools and high school teacher in Sherman, S.D., 1920-22; Northwestern University, Evanston, Ill., statistician, 1924-25; University of Minnesota, Minneapolis, faculty, 1928-37, began as instructor, became associate professor; Duluth State Teachers College (now University of Minnesota, Duluth), president, 1938-46; Griffenhagen & Associates, Chicago, Ill., staff, 1946-47; University of Kentucky, Lexington, professor, 1947-50, distinguished professor of educational psychology, 1950-67; University of South Florida, Tampa, professor of educational psychology, 1967-70; writer of textbooks, 1970—. Visiting professor, University of Oslo, 1950-51. *Military service:* U.S. Navy, 1918. U.S. Coast Guard Reserve; became lieutenant. *Member:* Sigma Xi. *Awards, honors:* $10,000 Carnegie grant to study adult abilities, 1934.

WRITINGS: Statistics for Students of Psychology in Education, McGraw, 1936; *Adult Abilities in Extension Classes,* University of Minnesota Press, 1938; *Adult Abilities,* University of Minnesota Press, 1940; *Psychology in Education,* McGraw, 1940, 4th edition, 1964; (with Marguerite Malm) *Psychology for Living,* McGraw, 1948, 3rd edition (with Malm and Garlie A. Forehand), 1971; *Fundamentals of Statistics,* Vantage, 1961. Author of workbooks and of twelve booklets on motivation and guidance.

WORK IN PROGRESS: Psychology for Parents, completion expected in 1976.

* * *

SOURS, John Appling 1931-

PERSONAL: Born January 28, 1931, in Chicago, Ill.; son of William J. (a businessman) and Olive (Appling) Sours; married Angela Dinah Mathews; children: Christopher, Caroline, Jane. *Education:* Yale University, A.B., 1953; Cornell University Medical College, M.D., 1957; Columbia Psychoanalytic Clinic, Certificate in Psychoanalytic Medicine, 1967. *Home:* 120 West 88th St., New York, N.Y. 10028. *Office:* The Adams, Suite 207, 6 East 86th St., New York, N.Y. 10028.

CAREER: Columbia University, College of Physicians and Surgeons, New York, N.Y., clinical assistant professor of psychiatry, 1967—, training and supervising psychoanalyst, 1975—. In active practice of general and child psychiatry and psychoanalysis; assistant attending psychiatrist at New York State Psychiatric Institute, Vanderbilt Clinic, and Columbia Presbyterian Medical Center; associate attending psychiatrist, St. Luke's Hospital, 1971—. *Military service:* U.S. Naval Reserve, Medical Corps, staff psychiatrist at Naval Aerospace Center, Pensacola, Fla., 1961-63; became lieutenant commander. *Member:* American Psychiatric Association (fellow), American College of Physicians (fellow), Association for Psychoanalytic Medicine, International Association for Child Psychiatry and Psychology, American Psychoanalytic Association, American Academy of Child Psychiatry, Royal College of Psychiatrists, Association for Child Psychoanalysis, Association for Applied Analysis, New York Psychiatric Society. *Awards, honors:* Fulbright scholar in London, England, 1958-59; National Institute of Mental Health career teacher grant, 1965-67.

WRITINGS: (With J. D. Goodman) *The Child Mental Status Examination,* Basic Books, 1967; (contributor) Lebovici and Caplan, editors, *Changing Concepts in Adolescence,* Basic Books, 1967; (contributor) S. Aniti, editor, *American Handbook of Psychiatry,* Volume I, Basic Books, 1974. Contributor of about forty papers in neurology and psychiatry to journals.

WORK IN PROGRESS: Studies in techniques of psychoanalysis and psychotherapy.

*   *   *

SPAIN, Rufus B(uin) 1923-

PERSONAL: Born January 29, 1923, in Gordo, Ala; son of John Ellis (a railroad engineer) and Nona (Cameron) Spain; married Elizabeth Finch, November 22, 1945 (deceased); married Carol Hanna, December 20, 1958; children: (first marriage) Elizabeth, John; (second marriage) Julia, David. Education: Clarke Memorial Junior College, diploma, 1942; Mississippi College, B.A., 1947; Vanderbilt University, M.A., 1948, Ph.D., 1961. Politics: Democrat. Religion: Baptist. Home: 2218 Carolinda Dr., Waco, Tex. 76710. Office: Department of History, Baylor University, Waco, Tex. 76703.

CAREER: Cumberland University, Lebanon, Tenn., assistant professor of history, 1948-50; Baylor University, Waco, Tex., assistant professor, 1957-62, associate professor, 1962-66, professor of history, 1966—. Military service: U.S. Army, Infantry, 1943-46, 1951-53; served in Europe, 1943-45, and 1952-53; became first lieutenant. Member: American Historical Association, Organization of American Historians, American Association of University Professors, Southern Historical Association, Southern Baptist Historical Society.

WRITINGS: At Ease in Zion: A Social History of Southern Baptists, 1865-1900, Vanderbilt University Press, 1967. Contributor to Encyclopedia of the South, and Tennessee Historical Quarterly.

WORK IN PROGRESS: Baptist in American Culture.

*   *   *

SPALTER, Max 1929-

PERSONAL: Born July 27, 1929, in Luneberg, Germany; son of Isaac and Sara (Stern) Spalter; married Dorothy Rosenoff (a teacher), March, 1959; children: Susan. Education: City College (now City College of the City University of New York), B.A. (cum laude), 1950; Columbia University, M.A. (with honors), 1958, Ph.D., 1965. Home: 40-25 Hampton St., Elmhurst, N.Y. 11373. Office: Staten Island Community College, Staten Island, N.Y. 10301.

CAREER: State University of New York College at Fredonia, instructor in English, 1962-63; Yeshiva University, Stern College for Women, New York City, instructor in English, 1963-64; Columbia University, New York City, instructor in English, 1963-68; Staten Island Community College, Staten Island, N.Y., professor of English, 1968—. Awards, honors: Council for Research in the Humanities grant for research, 1966; City University of New York research awards and faculty grants, 1970, 1971.

WRITINGS: Brecht's Tradition, Johns Hopkins Press, 1967. Contributor to Educational Theatre Journal.

*   *   *

SPANOS, William V(aios) 1925-

PERSONAL: Born January 1, 1925, in Newport, N.H.; son of Vaios and Mary (Stassos) Spanos; married Margaret Prince (a college instructor), June 10, 1954; children: Maria, Stephania, Aristides. Education: Wesleyan University, Middletown, Conn., A.B., 1950; Columbia University, M.A., 1954; University of Wisconsin, Ph.D., 1964. Home: 43 Matthew St., Binghamton, N.Y. Office: State University of New York, Binghamton, N.Y. 13901.

CAREER: Mount Hermon School, Mount Hermon, Mass., teacher of English, 1951-53; Encyclopedia Americana, editor and writer, 1953-55; University of Kentucky, Lexington, instructor in English, 1960-62; Knox College, Galesburg, Ill., assistant professor of English, 1962-66; State University of New York at Binghamton, 1966—, began as assistant professor, became professor of English. Fulbright professor, National University of Athens, 1969-70. Military service: U.S. Army, Infantry, 1943-45; received European Theater Medal with two battle stars, Combat Infantry Badge, Purple Heart. Member: Modern Language Association of America, American Association of University Professors, Phi Beta Kappa.

WRITINGS: (Editor) A Casebook on Existentialism, Crowell, 1966; The Christian Tradition in Modern British Verse Drama: The Poetics of Sacramental Time, Rutgers University Press, 1967; (editor) A Casebook on Existentialism 2, Crowell, 1976. Contributor of articles, reviews, and monographs to scholarly journals. Founder and co-editor, boundary 2: A Journal of Postmodern Literature, 1972—.

WORK IN PROGRESS: Icon and Time: Towards a Postmodern Hermeneutics; a book on postmodern literature; a book of dialogues with contemporary American poets.

*   *   *

SPARKS, Bertel M(ilas) 1918-

PERSONAL: Born March 12, 1918, in McKee, Ky.; son of Levi (a farmer) and Lula (Gabbard) Sparks; married Martha Evans, August 20, 1952. Education: Eastern Kentucky University, B.S., 1938; University of Kentucky, LL.B., 1948; University of Michigan, LL.M., 1949, S.J.D., 1955. Politics: Republican. Religion: Presbyterian. Home: 1707 Woodburn Rd., Durham, N.C. 27705. Office: School of Law, Duke University, Durham, N.C. 27706.

CAREER: High school teacher in Evarts, Ky., 1938-40, and Parrott, Ky., 1940-41; New York University, School of Law, New York, N.Y., instructor, 1949-50, assistant professor, 1950-52, associate professor, 1952-54, professor of law, 1954-67; Duke University, School of Law, Durham, N.C., professor of law, 1967—. Visiting professor at University of Michigan, summer, 1956, University of Kentucky, summer, 1957, and Duke University, 1966-67. Fifth Avenue Presbyterian Church, deacon, 1954-56, ruling elder, 1957-67; ruling elder, Trinity Avenue Presbyterian Church, 1967—. Military service: U.S. Army, special agent, Counterintelligence Corps, 1941-45; became first lieutenant; received Bronze Star Medal. Member: American Bar Association.

WRITINGS: Contracts to Make Wills, New York University Press, 1956; Cases on Trusts and Estates, Callaghan & Co., 1965. Contributor to popular and professional periodicals.

SIDELIGHTS: Sparks' special interest as a legal scholar concerns the rules of social policy involved in the transmittal of wealth from one generation to another.

*   *   *

SPARKS, Merrill 1922-

PERSONAL: Born October 5, 1922, in Mount Etna, Iowa; son of David G. and Ollie (Hickman) Sparks. Education: Attended University of Besancon, 1945; University of Southern California, B.A., 1948; also studied at University of Iowa, 1948-51, and Columbia University, 1951-52. Politics: Independent. Residence: Mount Etna, Iowa.

CAREER: Professional pianist and entertainer in Los Angeles, Calif., the Midwest, and Florida, 1953—. *Military service:* U.S. Army, Infantry, 1942-46; served in Italy. *Member:* American Guild of Authors and Composers, Authors Guild, Modern Poetry Association, American Federation of Musicians. *Awards, honors:* Co-recipient with Vernon Duke, Cross of Merit, Order of St. Brigida (Rome), 1966, for "Anima Eroica" cantata; co-recipient with Vladimir Markov, P.E.N. Translation Award, 1968, for *Modern Russian Poetry.*

WRITINGS: (Editor and translator with Vladimir Markov) *Modern Russian Poetry,* MacGibbon & Kee, 1966, Bobbs-Merrill, 1967. Author of text for chamber cantata, "Anima Eroica," with music by Vernon Duke, 1966. Poems published in American literary magazines.

WORK IN PROGRESS: Writing poems; translations of Russian and Spanish poetry; an opera libretto.

SIDELIGHTS: Timothy Binyon says of *Modern Russian Poetry:* "The translators have set themselves a superhuman task and it is amazing how much has been accomplished: the versions can scarcely ever be faulted as far as sense is concerned, and they preserve to a remarkable degree the metres and rhyme schemes of the originals." Markov contributed the "sense" to the translations, while Sparks made the sense into poetry with "respect and a sense of fascination with the original," according to a *London Times* critic. Speaking of poetry, Sparks told *CA:* "My life is poetry. And for me, poetry is a difficult trip toward light. It is more than a tiresome parade of trivia or the easy evoking abstractions. Since the poet conveys an insight of an impression by words, he *must* use them. The physical world impinges upon us. And because we are sensuous, we should praise that world. But the flame's image persists after the flame is extinguished. And its physical appearance and energy is transformed. We, too, burn, and change. Great poetry considers these continuing, subtle shifts and brings us to a larger illumination."

BIOGRAPHICAL/CRITICAL SOURCES: *London Times,* January, 1967; *New Statesman,* January 13, 1967; *Times Literary Supplement,* June 1, 1967; *Detroit News,* August 12, 1967.

* * *

SPEAR, Allan Henry 1937-

PERSONAL: Born June 24, 1937, in Michigan City, Ind.; son of Irving S. (a salesman) and Esther (Lieber) Spear. *Education:* Oberlin College, B.A., 1958; Yale University, M.A., 1960, Ph.D., 1965. *Home:* 2204 Seabury Ave., Minneapolis, Minn. 55406. *Office:* Department of History, University of Minnesota, Minneapolis, Minn. 55455.

CAREER: University of Minnesota, Minneapolis, lecturer, 1964-65, assistant professor, 1965-67, associate professor of history, 1967—. Minnesota state senator, 1973—. *Member:* Organization of American Historians. *Awards, honors:* National Endowment for the Humanities grant, 1967-68.

WRITINGS: *Black Chicago: The Making of a Negro Ghetto, 1890-1920,* University of Chicago Press, 1967; (contributor) N. Huggins, M. Kilson, and D. Fox, editors, *Key Issues in the Afro-American Experience,* Harcourt, 1971. Contributor to historical journals.

* * *

SPEIER, Hans 1905-

PERSONAL: Surname rhymes with "buyer"; born February 3, 1905, in Berlin, Germany; came to United States in 1933, naturalized in 1940; son of Adolf and Anna (Person) Speier; married Lisa Griesbach, August 30, 1929; married second wife, Margit Leipnik, February 18, 1967; children: (first marriage) Sybil D. (Mrs. Harvey Barten), Steven W. *Education:* Attended University of Berlin, 1923-25; University of Heidelberg, Ph.D., 1928. *Home:* 167 Concord Ave., Hartsdale, N.Y. 10530.

CAREER: Ullstein Publishing House, Berlin, Germany, book editor, 1929-31; Deutsche Hochschule fuer Politick, Berlin, lecturer in political sociology, 1931-33; New School for Social Research, Graduate Faculty, New York, N.Y., professor of sociology, 1933-42; Federal Communications Commission, Washington, D.C., section chief and later acting chief of Foreign Broadcast Intelligence Service, 1942-44; U.S. Office of War Information, Washington, D.C., adviser to chief of Overseas Branch, 1944-45; U.S. Department of State, Washington, D.C., associate (acting) chief of Occupied Areas Division, 1945-47; New School for Social Research, Graduate Faculty, professor of sociology, 1947; RAND Corp., Santa Monica, Calif., head of Social Science Division, 1948-60, member of Research Council, 1961-69, chairman of Research Council, 1961-62; University of Massachusetts, Amherst, Robert M. MacIver Professor of Sociology and Political Science, 1969-73. Visiting professor at University of Illinois, 1936, and University of Michigan, summer, 1941. Member of U.S. Air Force Scientific Advisory Board, 1948-51; consultant to U.S. Department of State, 1947-51, Research and Development Board, 1948-51, Ford Foundation, 1951, and U.S. Scientific Advisory Board, 1958-62.

MEMBER: American Academy of Arts and Sciences (fellow), World Academy of Art and Science (fellow), American Sociological Association, Deutsche Gesellschaft fuer Soziologie (honorary member). *Awards, honors:* Fellow, Center for Advanced Study in the Behavioral Sciences, 1956-57; senior fellow, Council of Foreign Relations (New York), 1964.

WRITINGS: (Editor with Alfred Kahler and co-author) *War in Our Time,* Norton, 1939; *The Salaried Employee in German Society,* Volume I, Works Progress Administration and Department of Social Sciences, Columbia University, 1939; (editor) Emil Lederer, *State of the Masses,* Norton, 1940; (with Ernst Kris) *German Radio Propaganda,* Oxford University Press, 1944; *Social Order and the Risks of War,* George Stewart, 1952; *German Rearmament and Atomic War,* Row, Peterson & Co., 1957; (editor with W. P. Davison) *West German Leadership and Foreign Policy,* Row, Peterson & Co., 1957; *Divided Berlin: The Anatomy of Soviet Political Blackmail,* Praeger, 1961; (translator and author of introduction) Grimmelshausen, *Courage, The Adventuress [and] The False Messiah,* Princeton University Press, 1964; *Force and Folly: Essays on Foreign Affairs and the History of Ideas,* M.I.T. Press, 1968; *Witz und Politik: Essay ueber die Macht und das Lachen,* Edition Interfrom AG, 1975.

Contributor: *Makers of Modern Strategy,* edited by Edward Mead Earle, Princeton University Press, 1943; (with Margaret Otis) *Radio Research 1942-1943,* edited by Paul F. Lazarsfeld and Frank Stanton, Duell, Sloan, & Pearce, 1944; *An Introduction to the History of Ideas,* edited by Harry Elmer Barnes, University of Chicago Press, 1947; *Continuities in Social Research,* edited by Paul F. Lazarsfeld and Robert K. Merton, Free Press, 1950; *Public Opinion and Communication,* edited by Bernard Berelson and Morris Janowitz, Free Press, 1950; *Propaganda in War* and Crisis, edited by Daniel Lerner, George W. Stewart, 1951; The Process and Effects of Mass Communications, edited by Wilbur Schramm, University of Illinois Press, 1954; Psychological Aspects of Global Conflict, Industrial College of the Armed Forces, 1955; American Foreign Policy, edited by Harold K. Jacobson, Random House, 1960; Ancients and Moderns: Essays in the History of Political Philosophy in Honor of Leo Strauss, edited by J. Cropsey, Basic Books, 1964; The Arts in Society, edited by R. N. Wilson, Prentice-Hall, 1964; Historia y Elementos de la Sociologie del Concimiento, edited by I. L. Horowitz, Volume I, University of Buenos Aires Press, 1964; Krieg und Frieden im industriellen Zeitalter, edited by Uwe Nerlich and C. Bertelsmann, [Gutersloh], 1966; Congratulatio fuer Joseph C. Witsch, Kiepenheuer & Witsch, 1966; The United States and the Atlantic Community, edited by James R. Roach, University of Texas Press, 1967; Der Friede im nuklearen Zeitalter, edited by Oskar Schatz, Manz Verlag, 1970. Contributor of articles to American, British, and German journals.

WORK IN PROGRESS: Communication and Propaganda in World History, three volumes, for University of Hawaii Press; editing Die Angestellten in der Weimarer Republik.

SIDELIGHTS: Divided Berlin: The Anatomy of Soviet Political Blackmail was translated for German, Japanese, and Spanish editions.

*   *   *

SPENCE, Jonathan D(ermot) 1936-

PERSONAL: Born August 11, 1936, in England; son of Dermot Gordon Chesson and Muriel (Crailsham) Spence; married Helen Alexander, September 15, 1962; children: Colin Chesson, Ian Alexander. Education: Cambridge University, B.A., 1959; Yale University, Ph.D., 1965. Office: Yale University, New Haven, Conn. 06520.

CAREER: Yale University, New Haven, Conn., 1965—, began as assistant professor, professor of Chinese history, 1971—. Military service: British Army, 1954-56; became first lieutenant.

WRITINGS: Ts'ao Yin and the K'ang-hsi Emperor: Bondservant and Master, Yale University Press, 1966; To Change China: Western Advisers to China, 1620-1960, Little, Brown, 1969 (published in England as The China Helpers: Western Advisers to China, 1620-1960, Bodley Head, 1969); Emperor of China: Self-Portrait of K'ang-Hsi, Knopf, 1974.

WORK IN PROGRESS: Studies in Chinese local and medical history.

SIDELIGHTS: Lawrence H. Battistini identifies Spence's central theme in The China Helpers as depicting "the failure of the advisers to remake China in a Western image and the ability of China to profit from their expertise while at the same time . . . being able to remain essentially Chinese." Battistini continues: "Spence writes with mastery of biographical detail, a good grasp of Chinese history and a deep understanding of and sympathy for the Chinese. . . . Among the many merits of Spence's work is its complete detachment from any form of ethnocentrism." The New York Times Book Review adds, "It is serious historical entertainment at its best."

Spence is competent in French, German, Spanish, and Chinese.

BIOGRAPHICAL/CRITICAL SOURCES: New York Times Book Review, July 16, 1969; Yale Review, autumn, 1969.

*   *   *

SPENCER, Colin 1933-

PERSONAL: Born July 17, 1933, in London, England; son of Harry (a master builder) and Gypsy (Heath) Spencer; married Gillian Chapman (an archaeologist), October 2, 1959. Education: Studied at Brighton Art College. Politics: Socialist. Religion: Humanist. Home: 44, Lonsdale Sq., London, N.I., England. Agent: John Cushman Associates, Inc., 24 West 43rd St., New York, N.Y. 10036.

CAREER: Full-time writer and painter. Paintings exhibited in Cambridge and London. Military service: British Army, Royal Army Medical Corps, 1950-52. Member: Writer's Guild of Great Britain.

WRITINGS—Novels: An Absurd Affair, Longmans, Green, 1961; Anarchists in Love (Book I of Quartet), Eyre & Spottiswoode, 1963, published as The Anarchy of Love, Weybright, 1967; Poppy, Mandragora and the New Sex, Anthony Blond, 1966; Asylum, Anthony Blond, 1966; The Tyranny of Love (Book II of Quartet), Weybright, 1967; Lovers in War (Book III of Quartet), Anthony Blond, 1970; Panic, Secker & Warburg, 1971; How the Greeks Kidnapped Mrs. Nixon, Quartet Books, 1974.

Plays: "The Ballad of the False Barman" (musical; music by Clifton Parker), first produced in London at Hampstead Theatre Club, 1966; "Spitting Image" (first produced in London at Hampstead Theatre Club, 1968; produced on West End at Duke of York's Theatre, 1968; adapted for American stage by Donald Driver and produced Off-Broadway at Theatre de Lys, February 19, 1969), published in Plays and Players, September, 1968; "The Trail of St. George," first produced at Soho Theatre, March 8, 1972; "The Sphinx Mother," first produced in Salzburg, Austria, 1972; "Why Mrs. Newstadter Always Loses," first produced in London, 1972; "Summer at Camber—39," first produced in London, 1973.

Contributor to London, Transatlantic Review, and other periodicals.

WORK IN PROGRESS: Book IV of Quartet, The Victims of Love; a documentary for television on vandalism.

SIDELIGHTS: Yorick Blumenfeld commenting on The Anarchy of Love and The Tyranny of Love writes: "Spencer is at his best when verbalizing emotions, when dissecting the inner recesses of the soul." Guy Davenport notes that the two novels are "vividly drawn, wonderfully heard, and quite powerfully written. . . . England has many writers more polished than Mr. Spencer, but none quite so wildly energetic in his passion for reality."

In an interview by Peter Burton, Spencer comments that in the play "Spitting Image," he "wanted the audience to be in tears at the end of Act One and roaring with laughter at the end of the play. I achieved this with some London audiences but in New York the play was staged in one act and had lost all the gentleness and reality." Spencer continues, "being a painter the visual side is very strong and I get especial pleasure out of linking dialogue to mental pictures."

BIOGRAPHICAL/CRITICAL SOURCES: National Review, November 5, 1968; Washington Post, December 24, 1968; Transatlantic Review, spring, 1970.

SPENCER, Margaret 1916-

PERSONAL: Born August 26, 1916, in Armadale, Victoria, Australia; daughter of John Howard Lidgett (a public health physician) and Gladys Maeva (Walpole) Cumpston; married Terence Edward Thornton Spencer (a medical practitioner), December 13, 1941. Education: University of Sydney, M.Sc., 1939. Home: 1 George St., Tenterfield, New South Wales, Australia. Agent: Laurence Pollinger Ltd., 18 Maddox St., Mayfair, London W1R 0EU, England.

CAREER: University of Sydney, Sydney, New South Wales, Australia, researcher in entomology as Linnean Macleay Fellow, 1939-40; University of New England, Armidale, New South Wales, Australia, lecturer in zoology, 1940-45; University of Sydney, tutor in zoology, Commonwealth Reconstruction Training Scheme, 1946-48, teaching fellow in zoology, 1949-50; Papua New Guinea, Department of Public Health, entomologist engaged in anopheline mosquito investigation, 1954-61, 1971, 1974, and 1975. Member: Australian Entomological Society, Australian and New Zealand Association for Advancement of Science, Queensland Entomological Society, Australian Society of Authors, Linnean Society of New South Wales, Quota International (president, Tenterfield club, 1968).

WRITINGS: Doctor's Wife in New Guinea, Angus & Robertson, 1959; Doctor's Wife in Papua, R. Hale, 1964; Doctor's Wife in Rabaul, R. Hale, 1967. Contributor of articles to popular periodicals, and papers to scientific journals.

WORK IN PROGRESS: A book for the general reader on actual investigations on malaria-carrying mosquitoes in Papua New Guinea; biographical writing.

SIDELIGHTS: Margaret Spencer's initial stimulus to write, she says, came with the discovery that "Australians generally knew very little about the country [Papua New Guinea] or people for whom they held responsibility under United Nations trusteeship—or if they did, they had no awareness of the indigenes as people, human beings, with the same fears, loves, hates, joys as themselves, only translated by a different setting."

* * *

SPERGEL, Irving A. 1924-

PERSONAL: Surname is pronounced Spur-gull; born January 17, 1924, in New York, N.Y.; son of Julius and Frieda (Mann) Spergel; married Bertha Jampel (a reading specialist), September 1, 1949; children: Barry, Mark, Daniel. Education: City College (now City College of the City University of New York), B.S.S., 1946; Columbia University, M.A., 1947, D.S.W., 1960; University of Illinois, M.S.W., 1952. Religion: Hebrew. Home: 5729 South Maryland, Chicago, Ill. 60637. Office: School of Social Service Administration, University of Chicago, 969 East 60th St., Chicago, Ill. 60637.

CAREER: New York City Youth Board, New York City, street gang worker, supervisor, consultant, 1950, 1952-54, 1958-60; Lenox Hill Neighborhood Association, New York City, director of street gang project, 1954-57; New York University, School of Social Work, New York City, lecturer in social research, 1959-60; Columbia University, New York City, research associate, 1960; University of Chicago, School of Social Service Administration, Chicago, Ill., professor, 1960—. United Nations advisor to Hong Kong for youth work, 1970-71. Military service: U.S.

Army, 1943-46. Member: National Association of Social Workers, Council on Social Work Education.

WRITINGS: Racketville, Slumtown, Haulburg, University of Chicago Press, 1964; Street Gang Work, Addison-Wesley, 1966; Community Problem Solving: The Delinquency Example, University of Chicago Press, 1969; (editor) Community Organization: Studies in Constraint, Sage, 1972; Planning for Youth Development, United Nations, 1973; Community Structure and Deviance, University of Chicago Press, in press.

WORK IN PROGRESS: A history of community organization practice in the United States.

AVOCATIONAL INTERESTS: Handball, swimming, jogging.

* * *

SPIEGELMAN, Judith M.

PERSONAL: Born in New York, N.Y.; daughter of William Z. (a journalist and public relations director) and Dora (Moreiss) Spiegelman. Education: Brooklyn College (now Brooklyn College of the City University of New York), B.A. (cum laude), 1951; Harvard University, M.Ed., 1956. Home: 310 East 74th St., New York, N.Y. 10021.

CAREER: Former editorial researcher for Newsweek and Woman's Day, and staff writer for Scholastic Magazines, all New York City; United Nations Children's Fund, New York City, staff writer and press liaison, 1964—. Substitute elementary teacher, New York City schools. Member: Authors Guild, Forum of Writers for Young People (vice-president), Foreign Press Association.

WRITINGS—All juveniles: Let's Go to the Battle of Gettysburg, Putnam, 1965; UNICEF's Festival Book, U.S. Committee for UNICEF, 1966; With Washington at Valley Forge, Putnam, 1967; Ali of Turkey, Messner, 1969; (with Jack Ling) Two Brothers of Peru, Messner, 1969; Shaer of Afghanistan, Messner, 1969; Dayapala of Ceylon, Messner, 1970; Galong, River Boy of Thailand, Messner, 1970; Ketut, Boy Woodcarver of Bali, Messner, 1971. Contributor to Cosmopolitan, Seventeen, and Scholastic Teacher.

AVOCATIONAL INTERESTS: Foreign travel, world customs, art, religion, history, photography.

* * *

SPIELBERGER, Walter Jakob 1925-

PERSONAL: Born January 31, 1925, in Regensburg, Germany; son of Joseph (a clerk) and Ursula (Windl) Spielberger; married Jacquelyn E. Farber; children: Beatrice. Education: University of Berlin at Charlottenburg, Bachelor of Science in Mechanical Engineering, 1944. Religion: Catholic. Home: Trieblach 9, A-9210 Poertsdrach a.W., Munich, West Germany. Office: Krauss-Maffei AG, Munich, West Germany.

CAREER: Reynold C. Johnson Co. (Volkswagen-Porsche distributor), Burlingame, Calif., general service manager, beginning 1955; currently project representative, MBT Leopard two. Military service: German Army, 1943-45; became captain. Member: Society of Automotive Engineers, Sports Car Club of America, Verband Deutscher Ingenieure. Awards, honors: Various awards from both Volkswagen and Porsche.

WRITINGS: Die deutschen Panzer III und IV, [Lehmann], 1967; (with F. Wiener) Sturmartillerie: From Assult Guns to Hunting Panther, two volumes, Aero, 1968;

Strassenpanzer: Armor in Russia, Aero, 1968; (with Uwe Feist) *Halbketten Fahrzenge: Armor in the Western Desert,* Aero, 1968; (with Feist) *Panzerkampfwagen IV,* John W. Caler, 1968; (with Feist) *Armor on the Eastern Front,* Aero, 1968; (with Feist) *Militarfahrzeuge: German Softskinned Vehicles of World War Two,* Aero, 1970; *Der mittlere Kampfpanzer Leopard und seine Abarten,* Motorbuch, 1974. Also author of numerous other articles on German armor. Contributor to *Truppendienst, Feldgrau,* and other magazines.

WORK IN PROGRESS: Several publications on German armor.

SIDELIGHTS: Spielberger has one of the largest, privately owned collections of German armor. He speaks French and English in addition to his native German.

* * *

SPILLER, Earl A(lexander), Jr. 1934-

PERSONAL: Born August 15, 1934, in Buffalo, N.Y.; son of Earl Alexander and Helen (Hanford) Spiller; married Elinor Agnes Harper, June 9, 1956; children: Linda Jane, Barbara Jo. *Education:* Ohio Wesleyan University, B.A., 1956; University of Michigan, M.B.A., 1957, Ph.D., 1960. *Politics:* Republican. *Religion:* Protestant. *Home:* 1326 Lockett Lane, Kirkwood, Mo. 63122. *Office:* Department of Accounting, Washington University, St. Louis, Mo. 63130.

CAREER: University of Michigan, Ann Arbor, instructor in accounting, 1959-60; Washington University, St. Louis, Mo., assistant professor, 1960-64, associate professor, 1964-69, professor of accounting, 1969—. Auditor, Arthur Anderson & Co., 1967-68. *Member:* American Accounting Association, National Association of Accountants, American Institute of Certified Public Accountants, American Economic Association, Phi Beta Kappa, Beta Gamma Sigma, Omicron Delta Kappa, Delta Sigma Rho.

WRITINGS: (Contributor) Joseph W. Towle, editor, *Ethics and Standards in American Business,* Houghton, 1963; *Financial Accounting: Basic Concepts,* Irwin, 1966, 2nd revised edition, 1976. Contributor to accounting journals.

* * *

SPINDLER, George Dearborn 1920-

PERSONAL: Born February 28, 1920, in Stevens Point, Wis.; son of Frank Nicholas (a college professor) and Winifred (Hatch) Spindler; married Louise Schaubel (a research assistant and lecturer in anthropology), May 29, 1942; children: Sue Carol (Mrs. H. Lloyd Walker). *Education:* Central State Teachers College (now Wisconsin State University-Stevens Point), B.S., 1940; University of Wisconsin, M.A., 1947; University of California, Los Angeles, Ph.D., 1952. *Office:* Department of Anthropology, Stanford University, Stanford, Calif. 94305.

CAREER: Stanford University, Stanford, Calif., assistant professor, 1952-55, associate professor, 1955-60, professor of anthropology, 1960—. Burton Lecturer, Harvard University, 1957; Edith P. Merritt Lecturer, San Francisco State College (now San Francisco State University), 1969. Advisory editor, Holt, Rinehart & Winston, 1966—. *Military service:* U.S. Army, Intelligence, 1942-45; became first lieutenant. *Member:* American Anthropological Association (fellow), Southwestern Anthropological Society (president, 1962-63). *Awards, honors:* Fellow, Center for Ad-

vanced Study in the Behavioral Sciences, 1956-57; distinguished alumni award, Wisconsin State University, 1972.

WRITINGS: (Editor and contributor) *Education and Anthropology,* Stanford University Press, 1955; *Menomini Acculturation,* University of California Press, 1955; *Transmission of American Culture,* Harvard University Press, 1959; (editor and contributor) *Education and Culture,* Holt, 1963; (with wife, Louise Spindler, and Alan Beals) *Culture in Process,* Holt, 1966, revised edition, 1973.

Being an Anthropologist, Holt, 1970; (with Louise Spindler) *Dreamers Without Power: The Menomini Indians,* Holt, 1971; *Bungbach: Urbanization and Identity in a German Village,* Holt, 1973; (editor and contributor) *Education and Cultural Process: Toward an Anthropology of Education,* Holt, 1974; *The Making of Psychological Anthropology,* Holt, 1976. Editor, *American Anthropologist,* 1962-66. Editor with Louise Spindler: *Case Studies in Cultural Anthropology,* Holt, 1960—; *Methods in Cultural Anthropology,* Holt, 1965—; *Case Studies in Education and Culture,* Holt, 1966—; *Basic Anthropology Units,* Holt, 1974—.

* * *

SPINELLI, Altiero 1907-

PERSONAL: Born August 31, 1907, in Rome, Italy; married Ursula Hirschmann, 1945; children: six. *Education:* Attended Law Faculty at the University of Rome until time of arrest. *Politics:* European Federalist. *Religion:* None. *Home:* V 12, Av. Boileau, 1040 Brussels, Belgium. *Office:* 200 Rue de la Loi, 1040 Brussels, Belgium.

CAREER: Political prisoner in Italy because of anti-Fascist activity, 1927-43; member of Italian Resistance, 1943-45; European Federalist Movement, general secretary, 1948-62; Johns Hopkins University, School for Advanced International Studies, Bologna, Italy, visiting professor, 1962-66; Istituto Affari Internazionali, Rome, Italy, founder and director, 1966-70; member of the Commission of the European Economic Community, 1970—.

WRITINGS: Dagli Stati Sovrani agli Stati Uniti d'Europa, La Nuova Italia (Florence), 1950; *L'Europa non cade del cielo,* Il Mulino (Bologna), 1960; *Tedeschi al bivio,* Opere Nuove (Rome), 1960; *Rapporto sull' Europa,* Communita (Milan), 1965; *The Eurocrats,* translation by C. Grove Haines, Johns Hopkins Press, 1966; *Il Lungo monologo* (autobiographical essay), Atheneum (Rome), 1967; *The European Adventure,* Charles Knight Press (London), 1972.

WORK IN PROGRESS: Activity in the Commission of the European Community.

* * *

SPIVACK, Charlotte K(esler) 1926-

PERSONAL: Born July 23, 1926, in Schoharie, N.Y.; daughter of William L. and Laura (Snyder) Roscoe; married Edwin L. Kesler, November 11, 1948; married second husband, Bernard Spivack (a professor of English), October 17, 1956; children: (second marriage) Carla Naomi, Loren Adlai. *Education:* New York College for Teachers (now State University of New York at Albany), B.A., 1947; Cornell University, M.A., 1948; University of Missouri, Ph.D., 1954. *Home:* 209 Alpine Dr., Amherst, Mass. 01002. *Office:* English Department, University of Massachusetts, Amherst, Mass. 01002.

CAREER: University of Missouri, Columbia, instructor in

English, 1952-54; College of William and Mary, Richmond, Va., assistant professor of English, 1954-56; Fisk University, Nashville, Tenn., began as assistant professor, became associate professor of English, 1956-64; University of Massachusetts, Amherst, associate professor, 1964-71, professor of English, 1971—. *Member:* Modern Language Association of America, Renaissance Society of America, Dante Society. *Awards, honors:* American Association of University Women national fellowship.

WRITINGS: (With William Bracy) *Early English Drama,* American R.D.M., 1966; *George Chapman,* Twayne, 1967. Contributor to literary journals.

WORK IN PROGRESS: Books on Henry Medwall, first English playwright, and on Jacobean drama, tentitively entitled *Jacobean Drama: The Frame of Things Disjoint;* research on the Renaissance, especially drama.

AVOCATIONAL INTERESTS: Music.

* * *

SPOCK, Benjamin (McLane) 1903-

PERSONAL: Born May 2, 1903, in New Haven, Conn.; son of Benjamin Ives and Mildred Louise (Stoughton) Spock; married Jane Davenport Cheney, June 25, 1927; children: Michael, John Cheney. *Education:* Yale University, B.A., 1925; Yale Medical School, student, 1925-27; Columbia University, College of Physicians and Surgeons, M.D., 1929. *Office:* 538 Madison Ave., New York, N.Y. 10022.

CAREER: Presbyterian Hospital, New York City, intern in medicine, 1929-31; New York Nursery and Child's Hospital, service in pediatrics, 1931-32; New York Hospital, service in psychiatry, 1932-33, assistant attending pediatrician, 1933-47; practice in pediatrics, New York City, 1933-44 and 1946-47; Cornell University, Medical College, New York City, instructor in pediatrics, 1933-47; New York City Health Department, consultant in pediatric psychiatry, 1942-47; Mayo Clinic, Rochester, Minn., consultant in psychiatry, 1947-51; Mayo Foundation for Medical Education and Research, Rochester, associate professor of psychiatry, 1947-51; University of Pittsburgh, Pittsburgh, Pa., professor of child development, 1951-55; Western Reserve University (now Case Western Reserve University), Cleveland, Ohio, professor of child development, 1955-67. *Military service:* United States Naval Reserve, lieutenant commander, Medical Corps, 1944-46. *Member:* National Committee for a Sane Nuclear Policy (SANE), National Conference for a New Politics (NCNP; member of executive board, 1967—). *Awards, honors:* Family Life Book Award, 1963, for *Problems of Parents;* Thomas Paine Award, National Emergency Civil Liberties Committee, 1968. Honorary degrees from University of Durham, Yale University, and other universities.

WRITINGS: The Common Sense Book of Baby and Child Care, Duell, Sloan & Pearce, 1946, published as *The Pocket Book of Baby and Child Care,* Pocket Books, 1949, 2nd edition published as *Baby and Child Care,* 1957, 4th edition, 1976; (with John Reinhart) *A Baby's First Year,* Duell, Sloan, Pearce, 1955; (with Miriam F. Lowenberg) *Feeding Your Baby and Child,* Duell, Sloan, Pearce, 1955; *Dr. Spock Talks with Mothers: Growth and Guidance,* Houghton, 1961; *On Being a Parent . . . of a Handicapped Child,* National Society for Crippled Children and Adults (Chicago), 1961; *Problems of Parents,* Houghton, 1962; *Prejudice in Children: A Conversation with Dr. Spock,* Anti-Defamation League of B'nai B'rith (New York), 1963;

(with M. O. Lerrigo) *Caring for Your Disabled Child,* Macmillan, 1965; (with Mitchell Zimmerman) *Dr. Spock of Vietnam,* Dell, 1968; *Decent and Indecent: Our Personal and Political Behavior,* McCalls Publishing, 1970; *A Teenager's Guide to Life and Love,* Simon & Schuster, 1970; *Raising Children in a Difficult Time,* Norton, 1974.

SIDELIGHTS: Twenty-eight million copies of Dr. Spock's *Baby and Child Care* have been sold since its first printing in 1946. It has been published in some thirty languages, including Catalan, Russian, and Urdu. *Baby and Child Care* has changed with the times. According to a *Parade* reviewer, the latest edition ". . . contains a section on working mothers, pays more attention to male participation in child-rearing, avoids sexual stereo-typing, even updates baby formulas." A *Washington Post* columnist agrees: "Spock has changed—somewhat. . . . He plans to keep recommending that infants receive constant parental care, but will no longer specify which parent should curtail his career to supply it. . . . He'll continue to state that sexual identity is necessary to mental health, but no longer suggest that it be re-enforced through the selection of toys and clothes." Spock is, however, angered and appalled at the growing attitude that childraising is burdensome and unfulfilling work. He told a *New York Times* reporter, "If our society can get it through its noodle that rearing children is exciting and creative work, we'll have accomplished something useful."

With regard to childrearing, many people blame Spock for the restlessness and rebellion in today's youth. *Newsweek* states: "It has been commonplace during the past couple of decades to speak of our children as the Spock Generation. . . . what we really seem to say when we speak of the Spock Generation is that America's children have been nurtured indulgently and permissively." A three-year study of 1,000 students at the University of California, Berkeley and San Francisco State University was conducted by psychologists M. Brewster Smith, Norma Haan and Jeanne H. Block to test the relationship of parental guidance to social involvement and unrest. Many of the students involved in the study had been jailed for participation in demonstrations. According to *Newsweek* the psychologists found that those students actively involved in demonstrations "described their parents as being more permissive and less authoritarian than did the other, uninvolved students. These parents had a close relationship with their children and avoided imposing flat prohibitions and arbitrary punishments on them." Then the psychologists ". . . concluded—quite approvingly—'that the emergence of a dedicated spontaneous generation concerned with humanitarian values and personal authenticity is a triumph of Spockian philosophy.'"

Spock himself was involved in demonstrations against the Vietnam War and was indicted by a Federal Grand Jury on January 5, 1968, for conspiring to counsel American youths to avoid the draft. He was later acquitted on appeal of his case. When questioned about his involvement, Spock said, "What is the use of physicians like myself trying to help parents to bring up children, healthy and happy, to have them killed in such numbers for a cause that is ignoble."

Reviewing *Decent and Indecent,* a *Time* reporter wrote: "Spock's most useful perception, perhaps, is his understanding that man in the 20th century has indulged in such an orgy of self-depreciation that he grows violent in self-revulsion. There is, mourns Spock, 'an unprecedented loss of belief in man's worthiness.' Art becomes grotesquerie, music a concert where the players splinter their instruments in a convulsion that suggests strychnine poisoning. 'This represents emotional regression all the way back to the one-to-two-year-old level,' Spock writes briskly, 'when the child in a spell of anger wants to antagonize and mess and destroy on a titanic scale.' What troubles the doctor is that such impulses escape the nursery; fathers and mothers, artists, politicians, scientists and generals—all of them go around breaking things. Medicine cannot cope with civilization as tantrum.''

BIOGRAPHICAL/CRITICAL SOURCES: Nation, March 11, 1968, October 13, 1969; *Village Voice,* April 25, 1968; *Life,* May 17, 1968, September 12, 1969; *Harper's,* May, 1968; *National Observer,* June 17, 1968, July 2, 1968; *Newsweek,* September 23, 1968, September 15, 1969, February 2, 1970; *New York Times,* December 14, 1968, August 6, 1969, January 28, 1970, November 3, 1970; Jessica Mitford, *The Trial of Dr. Spock,* Knopf, 1969; *New York Times Book Review,* February 16, 1969, March 15, 1970; *Esquire,* February, 1969, May, 1970; *Christian Century,* October 22, 1969; *New Republic,* February 7, 1970; *Time,* February 16, 1970, November 16, 1970; *L'Express,* September, 1970; *Best Sellers,* January 15, 1971; *Detroit News,* October 3, 1971; *Washington Post,* September 24, 1971, December 4, 1971; *Parade,* March 14, 1976.

*   *   *

SPOONER, John D.   1937-
(Brutus)

PERSONAL: Born July 25, 1937, in Boston, Mass.; son of Herbert M. (a stockbroker) and Helen (Fine) Spooner; married Susan Farnsworth (a model), June 25, 1966; children: Scott, Nicholas Monroe, Amanda Davis. *Education:* Harvard University, A.B., 1959. *Home:* 22 Newton St., Weston, Mass. 02193. *Agent:* International Creative Management, 40 West 57th St., New York, N.Y. 10019. *Office:* Shearson, Hayden, Stone, Inc., 28 State St., Boston, Mass. 02109.

CAREER: H. Hentz & Co. (stockbrokers), Boston, Mass., office manager, beginning 1961; currently vice-president of Shearson, Hayden, Stone, Inc. (stockbrokers), Boston, Mass. *Military service:* U.S. Army Reserve, 1957-65. *Member:* Authors Guild, Owl Club, Hasty Pudding Institute of 1770, Harvard Club of Boston, Belmont Country Club.

WRITINGS—All published by Little, Brown: *The Pheasant-Lined Vest of Charlie Freeman,* 1967; *Three Cheers for War in General,* 1968; (under pseudonym Brutus) *Confessions of a Stockbroker,* 1971; *Class,* 1973; *King of Terrors,* 1975. Contributor to *Writer, Cad, Atlantic, Cosmopolitan,* and *Town and Country.* Contributing editor, *Boston Magazine.*

WORK IN PROGRESS: An original screenplay about prohibition; a sequel to *Confessions of a Stockbroker.*

BIOGRAPHICAL/CRITICAL SOURCES: Best Sellers, April 15, 1968.

*   *   *

SPORES, Ronald   1931-

PERSONAL: Born January 25, 1931, in Eugene, Ore.; son of Marvin C. (a farmer) and Marie (Norwood) Spores; married Marianne Scholes, April 1, 1959; children: Tani-Lisa France, Ronald Jonathan Santiago. *Education:* University of Oregon, B.S., 1953; University of the Americas, Mexico City, M.A., 1960; Harvard University, A.M., Ph.D., 1964. *Home:* 4205 Wallace Lane, Nashville, Tenn. 37215. *Office:*

Department of Anthropology, Vanderbilt University, Nashville, Tenn. 37203.

CAREER: Vanderbilt University, Nashville, Tenn., assistant professor, 1964-73, professor of anthropology and program director, 1973—. *Military service:* U.S. Army. *Member:* American Anthropological Association (fellow), Royal Anthropological Society.

WRITINGS: The Mixtec Kings and Their People, University of Oklahoma Press, 1967. Contributor to *Handbook of Middle American Indians, American Anthropologist* and *Southwestern Journal of Anthropology.*

WORK IN PROGRESS: A Comparative Study of Ancient Mexican Kingdoms; Intergroup Conflict in the Mixteca.

*   *   *

SPREIREGEN, Paul D.   1931-

PERSONAL: Born December 12, 1931, in Boston, Mass.; son of Jacob H. and Janet E. (Zisman) Spreiregen; married Rose Helene Bester, 1961. *Education:* Massachusetts Institute of Technology, B.Arch., 1954; Fulbright student in Italy, 1954-55. *Home:* 2215 Observatory St. N.W., Washington, D.C. 20007.

CAREER: Architect and city planner, practicing in Milan, Italy, 1954, Stockholm, Sweden, 1956, New York, N.Y., 1957, Boston, Mass., 1958-59, San Francisco, Calif., 1960, and Washington, D.C., 1961—. Lecturer throughout United States. Visiting critic in architecture, Yale University, Catholic University, Harvard University, University of Tennessee, and University of Pennsylvania. Advisor to the Ford Foundation sponsored Study of the Profession of Landscape Architects, 1969-72. Broadcaster of weekly radio program on architecture and planning for National Public Radio, entitled ''Places for People,'' 1972—. *Member:* American Institute of Architects (director of urban programs, 1962-66), National Endowment for the Arts (program director, 1966-70). *Awards, honors:* Arnold W. Brunner grant-in-aid, 1965; American Institute of Architects grant, 1967; president's award, American Society of Landscape Architects, 1968.

WRITINGS: Urban Design: The Architecture of Towns and Cities, McGraw, 1965; (editor and author of preface) *The Modern Metropolis: Collected Essays of Hans Blumenfeld,* M.I.T. Press, 1966; (editor and author of introduction) *On the Art of Designing Cities: Collected Essays of Elbert Peets,* M.I.T. Press, 1968; (with Heikki von Hertzen) *Building a New Town: Finland's Garden City, Tapiola,* M.I.T. Press, 1971, revised edition, 1973. Contributor to magazines and professional journals.

*   *   *

SPRINGER, E(ustace) Laurence   1903-

PERSONAL: Born November 9, 1903, in Fort Washington, Md.; son of Ruter William (a lawyer and professor of religion) and Gertrude (Lynch) Springer; married Elizabeth Randolph Ballard, July 25, 1940 (died May 18, 1971); married Virginia Lindsley Loomis, October 9, 1975; children (first marriage) Elizabeth Randolph. *Education:* Attended Dickinson College, 1920-21; Princeton University, B.A., 1924; University of Buffalo, M.A., 1928. *Religion:* Protestant. *Politics:* Independent. *Home:* 2112 Caminito Circulo Sur, La Jolla, Calif. 92037.

CAREER: Nichols School, Buffalo, N.Y., instructor in history, 1924-30; Troy Country Day School, Troy, N.Y., headmaster, 1930-35; Montgomery School, Wynnewood,

Pa., associate headmaster, 1935-36; Pingry School, Elizabeth, N.J., headmaster, 1936-61; free-lance school consultant (on a national basis), La Jolla, Calif. 1961—; senior partner, Educational Partners (consultants), 1975—. Member of College Entrance Examination Board, 1944-61; consultant in survey of American-sponsored schools in South America for U.S. Department of State, 1964. Trustee of La Jolla Country Day School and Musical Arts Society of La Jolla. *Member:* Princeton Club (New York), San Diego Yacht Club, La Jolla Beach and Tennis Club. *Awards, honors:* Litt.D., Princeton University, 1959.

WRITINGS: (Co-editor) *Handbook for Independent School Operation,* Van Nostrand, 1961; (with Francis Parkman) *The Independent School Trustee,* National Association of Independent Schools, 1964, 3rd edition, 1974; *Independent School Administration,* Harper, 1967. Contributor to *Atlantic Monthly, Yachting.*

AVOCATIONAL INTERESTS: Sailing, music, travel.

* * *

SPRINGER, Marilyn Harris 1931-
(Marilyn Harris)

PERSONAL: Born June 4, 1931, in Oklahoma City, Okla.; daughter of John P. (an oil man) and Dora (Veal) Harris; married Edgar V. Springer, Jr. (a professor), February 21, 1953; children: John P., Karen Louise. *Education:* Cottey College, student, 1949-51; University of Oklahoma, B.A., 1953, M.A., 1955. *Politics:* Independent. *Home:* 1846 Rolling Hills, Norman, Okla. 73069.

CAREER: Writer.

WRITINGS—Under name Marilyn Harris: *King's Ex* (short stories), Doubleday, 1967; *In the Midst of Earth* (novel), Doubleday, 1969; *The Peppersalt Land,* Four Winds Press, 1970; *The Runaway's Diary,* Four Winds Press, 1971; *Hatter Fox,* Random House, 1973; *The Conjures,* Random House, 1974; *Bledding Sorrow,* Putnam, 1976. Stories anthologized in *Prize Stories: The O. Henry Awards,* 1968, and published in *Red Clay Reader, Malahat Review, Trace,* and *London Weekend Telegraph.*

WORK IN PROGRESS: A Child Is Burning, a novel; *The Doorknob Man,* a collection of short stories.†

* * *

SPRUG, Joseph W(illiam) 1922-

PERSONAL: Born April 9, 1922, in Fort Smith, Ark.; son of Urban Louis (an artist) and Anna (Timmermann) Sprug; married Mary Joan Storm, June 15, 1957; children: Barbara, Stephen, Thomas, David, Margaret, Katherine. *Education:* St. Meinrad College, B.A., 1946; Catholic University of America, B.S.L.S., 1947, M.A., 1949. *Politics:* Independent. *Religion:* Roman Catholic. *Home:* 403 Riley Rd., Austin, Tex. 78746. *Office:* St. Edward's University Library, Austin, Tex. 78704.

CAREER: Catholic University of America, Washington, D.C., cataloger, 1947-51, head cataloger, 1951-52; Catholic Library Association, Washington, D.C., editor and indexer, 1952-61; Fresno County (Calif.) Library, head of technical processes, 1961-62; St. Vincent College, Latrobe, Pa., head of technical processes, 1962-64; Loretto Heights College, Denver, Colo., director of library, 1964-71; curator of Gimble Aeronautical History Collection, Air Force Academy, 1971-73; St. Edward's University, Austin, Tex., chief librarian, 1973—. *Member:* Society of Indexers, Catholic Library Association (executive council member, 1959-61), Beta Phi Mu.

WRITINGS: (Editor) *Catholic Periodical Index,* Catholic Library Association, annually, 1952-61; *Index to Orate Fratres-Worship,* Liturgical Press, 1957; (compiler) *Guide to Catholic Literature,* Catholic Library Association, 1960; (compiler) *Catholic Supplement to Wilson Standard Catalog for High School Libraries,* H. W. Wilson, 1965-67; *An Index to G. K. Chesterton,* Catholic University of America Press, 1966; *Index to the Twentieth Century Encyclopedia of Catholicism,* two volumes, Hawthorn, 1971; (co-author) *Time Research: 1172 Studies,* Scarecrow, 1974; *Index to American Reference Books Annual 1970-74,* Libraries Unlimited, 1974. Compiler of other indexes, and book reviewer for journals.

WORK IN PROGRESS: An index to C. S. Lewis.

* * *

STABB, Martin S(anford) 1928-

PERSONAL: Born April 5, 1928, in New York, N.Y.; son of Saul (a merchant) and Rose (Falk) Stabb; married Gloria Lipstein, June 19, 1949; children: David, Sally, Jonathan. *Education:* Rutgers University, B.A., 1949; University of California, Los Angeles, M.A., 1953, Ph.D., 1956. *Politics:* Independent. *Home:* 1351 Penrose Circle, State College, Pa. 16801. *Office:* Department of Spanish, Italian, and Portuguese, Pennsylvania State University, University Park, Pa. 16802.

CAREER: Colgate University, Hamilton, N.Y., instructor in Romance languages, 1953-55; University of Missouri, Columbia, instructor, 1955-56, assistant professor, 1956-59, associate professor, 1959-64, professor of Spanish and chairman of department of Romance languages, 1964-68; Pennsylvania State University, University Park, professor of Spanish and chairman of department of Spanish, Italian, and Portuguese, 1970—. Visiting professor, University of Wyoming, summer, 1967. *Member:* Modern Language Association of America, American Association of Teachers of Spanish and Portuguese, Instituto Internacional de Literatura Iberoamericana, Phi Beta Kappa. *Awards, honors:* American Philosophical Society grant, 1962; Social Science Research Council grant, 1968.

WRITINGS: In Quest of Identity: Patterns in the Spanish American Essay of Ideas, University of North Carolina Press, 1967; *Jorge Luis Borges,* Twayne, 1970. Contributor to language journals.

WORK IN PROGRESS: A book on the sociology of Spanish American literature; further research on the essay in Spanish American literature, contemporary Argentine letters, and the history of ideas in Spanish America.

SIDELIGHTS: In 1968 and 1969, Stabb travelled in South America, doing research concentrated in Buenos Aires. *Avocational interests:* Fly fishing, reading science fiction, and travel.

* * *

STACKHOUSE, Max L. 1935-

PERSONAL: Born July 29, 1935; married; wife's name Norma Jean (a piano teacher at New England Conservatory of Music); children: Dale, David, Sara. *Education:* DePauw University, B.A. (with honors), 1957; Netherlands Opleidings Institut, graduate study, 1957-58; Harvard University, B.D., 1961, Ph.D., 1965. *Home:* 68 Chester St., Newton Highlands, Mass. 02161. *Office:* Andover Newton Theological School, Newton Centre, Mass. 02159.

CAREER: Ordained minister of United Church of Christ,

1963; Harvard University, Divinity School, Cambridge, Mass., lecturer in ethics, 1964-66; Andover Newton Theological School, Newton Centre, Mass., assistant professor, 1966-69, associate professor, 1969-73, professor of Christian social ethics, and chairman of department of religion and society, 1973—. Visiting lecturer at Boston College, Bucknell University, Ohio Wesleyan University, United Theological College (Bangalore, India), and other colleges and theological schools. Mead-Swing Lectureship, Oberlin College, 1975. *Member:* American Academy of Religion, Society for Religion in Higher Education, Societe Europein de Culture, American Society of Christian Ethics, Society for the Scientific Study of Religion, Civil Liberties Union of Massachusetts. *Awards, honors:* Danforth summer fellowship, 1965, 1975.

WRITINGS: (Editor and author of introduction) Walter Rauschenbusch, *The Righteousness of the Kingdom,* Abingdon, 1968; (editor and co-author of introduction) *The Death of Dialogue and Beyond,* Friendship, 1969; *The Ethics of Necropolis,* Beacon Press, 1971; (editor and author of introduction) James Luther Adams, *On Being Human—Religiously,* Beacon Press, 1976.

Contributor: Marty and Peerman, editors, *New Theology, No. 4,* Macmillan, 1966; D. B. Robertson, editor, *Voluntary Association,* John Knox, 1966; Theodore Sizer, editor, *Religion and Public Education,* Houghton, 1967; Donald Cutler, editor, *The World Yearbook of Religion: The Religious Situation,* volume 1, Beacon Press, 1969. Contributor to *Christian Century, Commonweal, Zygon, Comprendre, Journal for the Scientific Study of Religion, Religion and Society* (India), *Worldview, Christianity and Crisis,* and other journals. Member of editorial board, *Journal of Current Social Issues.*

WORK IN PROGRESS: A study of Hinduism and society compared to the West; a systematic study of religion and society as a foundation for social ethics.

AVOCATIONAL INTERESTS: Sports and music.

* * *

STACKHOUSE, Reginald 1925-

PERSONAL: Born April 30, 1925, in Toronto, Ontario, Canada; son of Edward Ingram and Emma (McNeill) Stackhouse; married Margaret Allman, June 2, 1951; children: Mary, Elizabeth, Ruth, John. *Education:* University of Toronto, B.A., 1946, M.A., 1951; Wycliffe College, L.Th., 1950, B.D., 1954; Yale University, Ph.D., 1962. *Politics:* Progressive Conservative. *Home:* 30 Earl Rd., Scarborough, Ontario, Canada. *Office:* Wycliffe College, Toronto, Ontario, Canada.

CAREER: Clergyman, Church of England. Rector of churches in Islington, Ontario, 1950-56, and Toronto, Ontario, 1956-60; Wycliffe College, Toronto, Ontario, professor of philosophical theology, 1962—, principal, 1975—. Vice-chairman, Scarborough Board of Education, 1967; chairman of board of governors, Centennial College, Scarborough, 1966-68. Member of Twenty-ninth Parliament of Canada.

WRITINGS: Christianity and Politics, English Universities Press, 1966. Columnist, *Canadian Churchman.*

* * *

STADLER, Karl R(udolph) 1913-

PERSONAL: Born October 8, 1913, in Vienna, Austria. *Education:* Studied at University of Vienna, 1931-38; University of Bristol, B.A., 1940; University of London, M.A., 1952; University of Nottingham, Ph.D., 1970. *Office:* Department of History, University of Linz, 4045 Linz, Austria.

CAREER: University of Nottingham, Nottinghamshire, England, senior lecturer in history, 1946-68; University of Linz, Linz, Austria, chair of modern history, 1968—.

WRITINGS: Adult Education and European Co-operation, Sijthof (Leiden), 1958; (with M. Szecsi) *Die NS-Justiz in Osterreich und ihre Opfer,* Herold (Vienna), 1962; *Osterreich 1938-45 im Spiegel der NS-Akten,* Herold, 1966; *The Birth of the Austrian Republic 1918-1921,* Sijthof, 1966; *Hypothek auf die Zukunft,* Europa, 1968; *Austria,* Benn, 1971; *Opfer verlorener Zeiten,* Europa, 1972; (with I. Kykal) *Richard Bernaschek: Odyssee eines Rebellen,* Europa, 1976.

WORK IN PROGRESS: Studies in the First Austrian Republic; Fascism, Communism; history of the labor movement.

* * *

STAFFORD-CLARK, David 1916-

PERSONAL: Born March 17, 1916, in Bromley, Kent, England; son of Francis and Cordelia (Stephens) Stafford-Clark; married Dorothy Oldfield Stewart (a part-time professional assistant to husband), December 16, 1941; children: Maxwell, Priscylla Stafford-Clark Russo, Jonathan, Nigel. *Education:* University of London, M.B., B.S., M.R.C.S., L.R.C.P., 1939, M.D., 1947, D.P.M., 1948. *Politics:* Liberal. *Religion:* "Unorthodox Christian." *Home:* Villa Belinda Kantara, P.O. Yeni Iskele, North Kibris, via Mersin 10, Turkey. *Agent:* Curtis Brown Group Ltd., 1 Craven Hill, London W2 3EW, England. *Office:* York Clinic, 117 Borough High St., London S.E. 1, England.

CAREER: Held training appointments at Maudsley Hospital, London, England, and then was resident at Massachusetts General Hospital, Boston, Mass., 1949; University of Reading, Reading, England, lecturer in psychology, 1950-54; Guy's Hospital, consultant physician in psychological medicine, 1950-74, physician in charge, department of psychological medicine, 1954-74, director of York Clinic, 1954-74, first chairman, division of psychiatry, 1973; also consultant physician to Institute of Psychiatry, University of London, and to Bethlehem Royal and Maudsley Hospitals. Visiting professor at Johns Hopkins University, 1962; visiting lecturer at Oxford University, Cambridge University, University of London, Harvard University, Yale University, Stanford University, and other universities in United States, Scotland, and Ireland. Consultant to Royal College of Music, National Association for Mental Health, and Canadian Mental Health Association; consultant-adviser on medical aspects of productions to Hammer Films and University International, including John Huston's "Freud"; adviser and director of medical programs on television and radio, including British Broadcasting Corp. "Lifeline" series. *Military service:* Royal Air Force Volunteer Reserve, medical parachutist, 1939-45; became squadron leader; mentioned in dispatches twice.

MEMBER: Royal College of Physicians (fellow), Royal Society of Medicine (fellow), Royal Society of Arts (fellow), New York Academy of Sciences, Royal Medico-Legal Society (member of council). *Awards, honors:* Silver Medal of Royal Society of Arts, 1959; literary prizes, including Gate Prize for Poetry, and three film awards.

WRITINGS: *Autumn Shadow* (poetry), Blackwell, 1941; *Sounds in the Sky* (poetry), Blackwell, 1944; *Psychiatry Today,* Pelican, 1952; *Mental Health for Red Cross Workers,* British Red Cross Society, 1958; *Psychiatry for Students,* Allen & Unwin, 1964, 4th edition, 1974; *What Freud Really Said,* Macdonald & Co., 1965; (author of foreword) Gillian Freeman, *The Undergrowth of Literature,* Thomas Nelson, 1967; *Five Questions in Search of an Answer: Religion and Life, Some Inescapable Contradictions,* Thomas Nelson, 1970.

Contributor: G. Allen Birch, editor, *Emergencies in Medical Practices,* Livingstone (Edinburgh), 1948, 3rd edition, 1952; *Case Histories in Psychosomatic Medicine,* Norton, 1952; H. Gardiner-Hill, editor, *Compendium of Emergencies,* 2nd edition, Butterworth, 1956; *Taylor's Medical Jurisprudence,* 11th edition, J. & A. Churchill, 1956, 12th edition, 1965; *Schizophrenia: Somatic Aspects,* Pergamon, 1957; *Frontiers in General Hospital Psychiatry,* International Universities Press, 1961; *A Short Textbook of Medicine,* English Universities Press, 1963; *The Pathology and Treatment of Sexual Deviation,* Oxford University Press, 1964.

Contributor to *Treasures of the British Museum,* 1971, and *Encyclopaedia Britannica,* 1974; also contributor of sections to other medical books, and to medical and science journals. Television writing includes more than two hundred performed scripts.

WORK IN PROGRESS: *The Myth of Harley; Soldier Without a Rifle,* the first novel of a trilogy.

SIDELIGHTS: Stafford-Clark told *CA:* "Present personal interests apart from professional work include the acceptance of a multi-racial society as an important goal of humanity, and the lowering of barriers of thought and communication between human beings all over the world." *Avocational interests:* Travel, reading, making and watching films, theatre.

* * *

STAGG, Paul L. 1914-

PERSONAL: Born February 24, 1914, in Eunice, La.; married Mathilde Persinger, October 17, 1939; children: Brenda, Margaret Jane. *Education:* Louisiana College, B.A., 1936; Southern Baptist Theological Seminary, Th.M., 1939; further study at Union Theological Seminary, New York, N.Y., and Columbia University.

CAREER: Baptist clergyman, with pastorate in Front Royal, Va., 1947-59; American Baptist Home Mission Societies, Division of Evangelism, Valley Forge, Pa., administrative associate, beginning 1959. Participant in move to desegregate public schools in Virginia during 1950's, in the freedom movement of the early 1960's, in marches (including Selma and Birmingham), and in many demonstrations for fair housing in Philadelphia; jailed in North Carolina in segregation protest. Chairman, Upper Marion Fair Housing Council, King of Prussia, Pa.; member of board, Delaware Valley Fair Housing Council. *Awards, honors:* Distinguished Service Award of Junior Chamber of Commerce.

WRITINGS: *The Converted Church: From Escape to Engagement,* Judson, 1967; *Preaching in a New Age,* American Baptist Home Mission Societies, 1968.††

* * *

STAHLECKER, Lotar V(ictor) 1915-

PERSONAL: Born April 27, 1915, in Delmont, S.D.; son

of Gottlieb F. (a lumber dealer) and Maria (Joachim) Stahlecker; married Luanna Hall (a librarian), November 19, 1945. *Education:* Attended Southern State College (now University of South Dakota at Springfield), 1936-38, and University of Michigan, summers, 1939, 1948; University of Iowa, B.A., 1947, M.A., 1948, Ph.D., 1950. *Home:* 409 Burr Oak Dr., Kent, Ohio 44240. *Office:* Kent State University, Kent, Ohio 44240.

CAREER: Teacher in South Dakota, 1938-41, and at Perkins Hospital School, Iowa City, Iowa, 1947-49; Kent State University, Kent, Ohio, 1950—, began as assistant professor, professor of special education, 1963—. Fulbright lecturer in special education, Jyvaskyla, Finland, 1960-61. Member of national education committee, Boy Scouts of America, 1964—. *Military service:* U.S. Army, 1942-45; became staff sergeant. *Member:* International Reading Association, American Association on Mental Deficiency, Council for Exceptional Children, National Society for the Study of Education, Ohio Association for Gifted Children, Association of Ohio Teachers for Slow Learners, Kappa Delta Pi, Phi Delta Kappa, Mu Iota Sigma.

WRITINGS: (Contributor) *Educating Tomorrow's Leaders,* Ohio State Department of Education, 1961; (editor) *Occupational Information for the Mentally Retarded: Selected Readings,* C. C Thomas, 1967. Creator of fourteen video tapes for classroom teaching of exceptional children. Contributor to essay collections; also contributor to educational periodicals.

WORK IN PROGRESS: *Working With Parents; Prescriptive Teaching for the Mentally Retarded.*

AVOCATIONAL INTERESTS: Travel (Mexico, Europe, Canada, Russia, British Isles).††

* * *

STANGE, G(eorge) Robert 1919-

PERSONAL: Born September 28, 1919, in Chicago, Ill.; son of George (an insurance broker) and Dagmar (Ruus) Stange; married Alida Butler, April 13, 1963; children: Maren, Margit, Eric. *Education:* Harvard University, S.B., 1941, Ph.D., 1949. *Politics:* Independent. *Home:* 69 Chestnut St., Boston, Mass. 02108. *Office:* Department of English, Tufts University, Medford, Mass. 02155.

CAREER: Little, Brown and Co., Boston, Mass., assistant editor, 1946-47; Bennington College, Bennington, Vt., member of literature faculty, 1949-51; University of Minnesota, Minneapolis, assistant professor, 1951-55, associate professor, 1955-60, professor of English, 1960-67; Tufts University, Medford, Mass., professor of English, 1967—. Associate faculty member, Cambridge University, 1955-56; visiting professor, University of Chicago, 1960-61. *Military service:* U.S. Navy, 1943-46; became lieutenant. *Awards, honors:* Fund for Advancement of Education faculty fellowship, 1955-56; Guggenheim fellowship, 1961-62.

WRITINGS: (Editor) *Poetry of Coleridge,* Dell, 1959; (with W. E. Houghton) *Victorian Poetry and Poetics,* Houghton, 1959, 2nd edition, 1968; (editor) Thackeray, *Henry Esmond,* Holt, 1962; *Matthew Arnold: The Poet as Humanist,* Princeton University Press, 1967; (editor) *The Cambridge Editions of Tennyson and of Browning,* Houghton, 1974.

WORK IN PROGRESS: *The Anti-Natural Tradition.*

* * *

STANKEVICH, Boris 1928-

PERSONAL: Born August 19, 1928, in Los Angeles,

Calif., son of Vacheslav and Virginia (Henderson) Stankevich; married Patricia Holton, June 8, 1962; children: Dimitri (adopted). *Education:* California State College (now University) at Los Angeles, B.A., 1962. *Politics:* Democrat. *Religion:* Protestant.

CAREER: Progress-Bulletin, Pomona, Calif., copy editor, beginning 1952. *Military service:* U.S. Marine Corps, 1946-48.

WRITINGS: Two Green Bars (juvenile), Harcourt, 1967.

WORK IN PROGRESS: A second juvenile book.††

*   *   *

STANLEY, John   1940-

PERSONAL: Born February 20, 1940, in Santa Maria, Calif.; son of Myron Gilbert (a layer of hardwood floors) and Frances (Hartman) Stanley; married Erica Jones, June 15, 1962; children: Russ Maurus. *Education:* Napa Junior College, student, 1958-59; San Francisco State College (now San Francisco State University), B.A., 1962. *Politics:* "Democratic leanings." *Home:* 1082 Grand Teton Dr., Pacifica, Calif. 94044. *Agent:* Mel Bloom Agency, Beverly Hills, Calif.

CAREER: Worked for two papers in Napa, Calif., 1959-60; *San Francisco Chronicle,* San Francisco, Calif., 1960—, began as copy boy, then feature and news review writer, staff reviewer of science fiction, fantasy, and horror books for Sunday edition, currently associate editor of *Sunday Datebook.* Writer, director, and producer of motion pictures.

WRITINGS: (With Mal Whyte) *The Great Comics Game,* Price, 1966; (with Whyte) *The Monster Movie Game,* Troubador, 1974; *World War III* (novel), Avon, 1976; (with Kenn Davis) *The Dark Side* (private eye novel), Avon, 1976. Author of screenplay, "Nightmare in Blood," World Wide Films, 1976. Also author of hundreds of profiles on movie and television personages.

WORK IN PROGRESS: The Playpen: A World War III Fable; The Buff's Guide to Fantastic Film Viewing; Hit Sniper; Pentagon Bacillus; A World War III Caper.

AVOCATIONAL INTERESTS: Collecting science fiction, fantasy, horror and psychic phenomena books, old comic books, pulp magazines, and old magazines in general, radio shows from the forties and fifties.

*   *   *

STANLEY, Julian C(ecil)   1918-

PERSONAL: Born July 9, 1918, in Macon, Ga.; son of Julian C. (a real estate broker) and Ethel (Cheney) Stanley; married Rose Sanders (a part-time child psychologist and textbook author), August 18, 1946; children: Susan R. *Education:* Georgia Southern College, B.S., 1937; Harvard University, Ed.M., 1946, Ed.D., 1950. *Politics:* Democrat. *Office:* Department of Psychology, Johns Hopkins University, Baltimore, Md. 21218.

CAREER: High school teacher of science and mathematics in Atlanta, Ga., 1937-42; Newton Junior College, Newton, Mass., instructor in psychology, 1946-48; Harvard University, Cambridge, Mass., instructor in education, 1948-49; George Peabody College for Teachers, Nashville, Tenn., associate professor of educational psychology, 1949-53; University of Wisconsin, Madison, associate professor, later professor of education, 1953-62, professor of educational psychology, 1962-67, director of laboratory of experi-

mental design, 1961-67; Johns Hopkins University, Baltimore, Md., professor of education and psychology, 1967-71, professor of psychology, 1971—. Fulbright-Hays art lecturer in New Zealand and Australia, 1974. Member of advisory council, Cooperative Research Branch, U.S. Office of Education, 1962-64; College Entrance Examination Board, member of committee of examiners for Aptitude Test, 1961-65, chairman of committee, 1965-68. *Military service:* U.S. Army Air Forces, 1942-46; became staff sergeant.

MEMBER: American Educational Research Association (president, 1966-67), American Psychological Association (fellow; president of division of educational psychology, 1965-66; president of division of evaluation and measurement, 1972-73), National Council on Measurement in Education (president, 1963-64), American Association for the Advancement of Science (fellow), Psychometric Society (director, 1962-65), American Statistical Association (fellow), Institute of Mathematical Statistics, Tennessee Psychological Association (president, 1951). *Awards, honors:* Social Science Research Council fellow at University of Michigan, 1955; Rockefeller Foundation postdoctoral fellow in statistics at University of Chicago, 1955-56; Fulbright research scholar in educational psychology at University of Louvain, 1958-59; National Institute of Mental Health special postdoctoral fellow, 1965-67; fellow, Center for Advanced Study in the Behavioral Sciences, 1965-67.

WRITINGS: Measurement in Today's Schools, 3rd edition (first two editions by Ross), and *Workbook,* Prentice-Hall, 1954, 4th edition, 1964; (with Donald T. Campbell) *Experimental and Quasi-Experimental Designs for Research,* Rand McNally, 1966; (editor and contributor) *Improving Experimental Design and Statistical Analysis,* Rand McNally, 1967; (with Gene V. Glass) *Statistical Methods in Education and Psychology,* Prentice-Hall, 1970; (with Kenneth D. Hopkins) *Measurement and Evaluation in Education and Psychology,* Prentice-Hall, 1972; (editor with Glenn H. Bratht and Kenneth D. Hopkins) *Perspectives in Educational and Psychological Measurement,* Prentice-Hall, 1972; (editor) *Preschool Programs for the Disadvantaged,* Johns Hopkins University Press, 1972; (editor and contributor) *Compensatory Education for Children, Ages 2 to 8,* Johns Hopkins University Press, 1973; (editor and contributor with David P. Keating and Lynn H. Fox) *Mathematical Talent: Discovery, Description, and Development,* Johns Hopkins University Press, 1974. Also author of *Proceedings of the Terman Memorial Symposium on Intellectual Talent,* symposium held at Johns Hopkins University, 1975; co-author of two project reports for U.S. Office of Education, 1962.

Contributor: Frederick C. Gruber, editor, *Partners in Education,* University of Pennsylvania Press, 1958; Raymond O. Collier, Jr. and Stanley M. Elam, editors, *Research Design and Analysis,* Phi Delta Kappa, 1961; Jerome M. Seidman, editor, *Educating for Mental Health,* Crowell, 1963; N. L. Gage, editor, *Handbook of Research on Teaching,* Rand McNally, 1963; Ellis B. Page, editor, *Readings for Educational Psychology,* Harcourt, 1964; Egon Guba and Elam, editors, *The Training and Nurture of Educational Researchers,* Phi Delta Kappa, 1965; Keating, editor, *Intellectual Talent: Research and Development,* Johns Hopkins University Press, 1976. Contributor of lesser sections to other books and symposia, to the *International Encyclopedia of the Social Sciences,* and more than 200 articles, abstracts, and reviews to psychology and education journals.

STARBUCK, George (Edwin) 1931-

PERSONAL: Born June 15, 1931, in Columbus, Ohio; son of George W. (a professor) and Margaret Beiswanger; name legally changed to Starbuck; married Janice King, April 25, 1955; married second wife, Judith Luraschi (an artist), July 28, 1962; married third wife, Kathryn Dermand, May 18, 1968; children: (first marriage) Margaret Mary, Stephen George, John Edward; (second marriage) Anthony Luigi, Joshua Beiswanger. *Education:* Attended California Institute of Technology, 1947-49, University of California, 1950-51, University of Chicago, 1954-57, and Harvard University, 1957-58. *Politics:* "Pinko; that is, domestically a libertarian meliorist; in foreign policy, close to AFSC." *Religion:* "One of my major interests." *Office:* Boston University, Boston, Mass. 02215.

CAREER: Houghton Mifflin Co., Boston, Mass., editor in trade department, 1958-61; American Academy in Rome, Italy, fellow, 1961-63; State University of New York at Buffalo, librarian and lecturer, 1963-64; University of Iowa, Writers Workshop, Iowa City, associate professor, 1964-67, director, 1967-70; Boston University, Boston, Mass., professor, 1971—. *Military service:* U.S. Army, 1952-54; served as corporal in Military Police Corps. *Member:* P.E.N. *Awards, honors:* Prix de Rome of American Academy of Arts and Letters; Guggenheim fellowship; Yale Series of Younger Poets Award; and several other literary awards.

WRITINGS: Bone Thoughts (poetry), Yale University Press, 1960; *White Paper* (poetry), Little, Brown, 1966; *Elegy in a Country Church Yard,* Pym-Randall, 1975. His poems have appeared in *New Yorker, Harper's, Atlantic, Poetry, New Republic, Saturday Review, Noble Savage, Yale Review,* and other publications.

WORK IN PROGRESS: A long study of metaphor; a fourth collection of poems.

SIDELIGHTS: Starbuck's songs of protest are usually concerned with love, war, and the spiritual temper of the times. John Holmes believes that "there hasn't been as much word-excitement . . . for years," as one finds in *Bone Thoughts.* Harvey Shapiro points out that Starbuck's work is attractive because of its "witty, improvisational surface, slangy and familiar address, brilliant aural quality . . .," and adds that Starbuck may become a "spokesman for the bright, unhappy young men. . . ."

Thomas Gunn, on the other hand, believes that Starbuck "is not even very elegant," but, Louise Bogan writes, his daring satire "sets him off from the poets of generalized rebellion."

After reading *Bone Thoughts,* Holmes hoped for other books in the same vein; R. F. Cayton finds that, in *White Paper,* the verse again stings with parody. Although Robert D. Spector wasn't sure of Starbuck's sincerity in *Bone Thoughts,* he rates the poems in *White Paper,* which range "from parody to elegy to sonnets, and even acrostic exercises," as "generally superior examples of their kind." In particular, Spector writes, when Starbuck juxtaposes McNamara's political language and a Quaker's self-immolation by burning, or wryly offers an academician's praise for this nation's demonstration of humanity by halting its bombing for "five whole days," we sense this poet's genuine commitment.

Starbuck reads French, speaks Italian, and "covets" Chinese.

BIOGRAPHICAL/CRITICAL SOURCES: New Yorker, March 26, 1960; *Yale Review,* June, 1960; *New York Herald Tribune Book Review,* June 12, 1960; *New York Times Book Review,* October 23, 1960; *Saturday Review,* February 11, 1967.

* * *

STARK, Werner 1909-

PERSONAL: Born December 2, 1909, in Marienbad, Czechoslovakia; son of Adolf (a physician) and Jenny (Schneider) Stark; married Kate Franck, August 14, 1934. *Education:* Attended London School of Economics and Political Science, 1930-31, and University of Geneva, 1933; University of Hamburg, Dr.rer.pol., 1934; University of Prague, Dr.jur., 1936. *Office:* Institut fuer Soziologie, Sigmund-Haffner-Gasse 18/IV, A 5020 Salzburg, Austria.

CAREER: Prague School of Political Science, Prague, Czechoslovakia, lecturer in social legislation, 1937-39; Cambridge University, Cambridge, England, guest lecturer in economics, 1941-42; University of Edinburgh, Edinburgh, Scotland, lecturer in social theory, 1945-51; University of Manchester, Manchester, England, reader in history of economics, 1951-63; Fordham University, New York, N.Y., professor of sociology, 1963-75; University of Salzburg, Salzburg, Austria, honorary professor, 1974—. Visiting professor, Purdue University, 1960-61. *Military service:* British Army, Intelligence Corps, 1944-45; became sergeant. *Member:* American Sociological Association, American Association for the Sociology of Religion. *Awards, honors:* M.A., University of Edinburgh, 1947.

WRITINGS: Ursprung und Aufstieg des landwirtschaftlichen Grossbetriebs in den bohmischen Landern, Verlag Rudolf M. Rohrer, 1934; *Sozialpolitik,* Verlag Rudolf M. Rohrer, 1936; *The Ideal Foundations of Economic Thought: Three Essays on the Philosophy of Economics,* Kegan Paul, Trench, Trubner & Co., 1943; *The History of Economics in Its Relation to Social Development,* Kegan Paul, Trench, Trubner & Co., 1944; *America: Ideal and Reality; The United States of 1776 in Contemporary European Philosophy,* Kegan Paul, Trench, Trubner & Co., 1947; (editor) Jeremy Bentham, *Economic Writings,* three volumes, Allen & Unwin, 1952-54; *The Sociology of Knowledge: An Essay in Aid of a Deeper Understanding of the History of Ideas,* Free Press of Glencoe, 1958, German translation by Stark published as *Die Wissenssoziologie: Ein beitrag sum tieferen verstaendnis des geisteslebens.* F. Enke, 1960; *Social Theory and Christian Thought: A Study of Some Points of Contact,* Routledge & Kegan Paul, 1959; *Montesquieu: A Pioneer of the Sociology of Knowledge,* Routledge & Kegan Paul, 1960; *The Fundamental Forms of Social Thought,* Routledge & Kegan Paul, 1962, Fordham University Press, 1963; *The Sociology of Religion: A Study of Christendom,* Fordham University Press, Volume I: *Established Religion,* 1966, Volume II: *Sectarian Religion,* 1967, Volume III: *The Universal Church,* 1967, Volume IV: *Types of Religious Man,* 1970, Volume V: *Types of Religious Culture,* 1972. Editor, "Rare Masterpieces of Philosophy and Science," for Routledge & Kegan Paul. Contributor to journals.

WORK IN PROGRESS: The Social Bond, Volume I: *The Phylogenesis of Sociality,* Volume II: *The Ontogenesis of Sociality,* for Fordham University Press.

SIDELIGHTS: Werner Stark is competent in German, Latin, French, and has some familiarity with Italian. All but one of the books published in the period 1943-58 have been translated into other languages. *The History of Eco-*

nomics and *The Sociology of Knowledge* have appeared in Italian, Japanese, German, and Spanish. *Avocational interests:* Travel.

BIOGRAPHICAL/CRITICAL SOURCES: Times Literary Supplement, March 23, 1967; Madeline H. Engel, editor, *The Sociological Writings of Werner Stark: A Bibliography and Selected Annotations,* privately printed, 1975.

*   *   *

STARR, Roger 1918-

PERSONAL: Born April 16, 1918, in New York, N.Y.; son of Frederick and Lillie (Bernhard) Starr; married Manya (Fifi) Garbat (a screen and television writer), December 2, 1945; children: Adam, Barnaby. *Education:* Yale University, B.A., 1939. *Politics:* Democrat. *Religion:* Jewish (Reform). *Home:* 45 East 82nd St., New York, N.Y. 10028. *Agent:* Julian S. Bach, Jr., 3 East 48th St., New York, N.Y. 10017. *Office:* Housing and Development Administration, 100 Gold St., New York, N.Y. 10038.

CAREER: Frederick Starr Contracting Co., New York City, president, 1945-73; Citizens' Housing and Planning Council of New York, Inc., New York City, executive director, 1958-73; Housing and Development Administration, New York City, administrator and commissioner, 1974—. Lecturer, Pratt Institute, 1960—, New School for Social Research, 1964—; adjunct professor, City College of the City University of New York, 1970—. Member of board of directors, American Society of Planning Officials, National Housing Conference and United Neighborhood Houses of New York; chairman, Rent Guidelines Board, 1969-73. *Military service:* U.S. Army, Office of Strategic Services, 1943-45; served in Burma and China; became first lieutenant.

WRITINGS: The Living End, Coward, 1966; *Urban Choices,* Penguin, 1968; *Housing and the Money Market,* Basic Books, 1975. Contributor of articles on housing and related subjects to *Horizon, Journal of Housing, Fordham Law Review, New Leader, Village Voice, Public Interest, Commentary, New York Times Sunday Magazine, American Heritage, New York Affairs, New Republic, New York,* and *National Review.*

*   *   *

STEARNS, Peter N. 1936-

PERSONAL: Born March 3, 1936, in London, England; son of Raymond Phineas (a teacher) and Elizabeth (Scott) Stearns; children: Duncan Scott, Deborah Clark. *Education:* Harvard University, A.B., 1957, A.M., 1959, Ph.D., 1963. *Home:* 1081 Shady Ave., Pittsburgh, Pa. 15232. *Office:* Carnegie-Mellon University, Schenley Park, Pittsburgh, Pa. 15213.

CAREER: University of Chicago, Chicago, Ill., instructor, 1962-63, assistant professor, 1963-66, associate professor of history, 1966-68; Rutgers University, New Brunswick, N.J., professor of history, 1968-74, chairman of department, 1969-74; Carnegie-Mellon University, Pittsburgh, Pa., Heinz Professor of History, 1974—. *Member:* American Historical Association, Society for French Historical Studies, Societe d'Histoire Moderne, Phi Beta Kappa. *Awards, honors:* Koren Prize of Society for French Historical Studies, 1966, for article in *American Historical Review;* Newcomen Prize of Newcomen Society, 1966, for article in *Business History Review;* Guggenheim fellowship, 1973-74.

WRITINGS: European Society in Upheaval, Macmillan, 1967, revised edition, 1975; *Priest and Revolutionary,* Harper, 1967; (editor) *A Century for Debate,* Dodd, 1969; *Modern Europe 1789-1914,* Scott, Foresman, 1969; *Workers and Protest,* Peacock, 1971; *Revolutionary Syndicalism and French Labor,* Rutgers University Press, 1971; (editor) *Impact of Industrialization,* Prentice-Hall, 1972; *European Experience since 1815,* Harcourt, 1973; (editor) *Other Side of Western Civilization,* Harcourt, 1973; *1848: The Revolutionary Tide in Europe,* Norton, 1974; (editor) *Workers and the Industrial Revolution,* Transaction, 1974; *Lives of Labor: Work in Mature Industrial Societies,* Holmes, 1975; *The Face of Europe,* Forum, 1975; *Old Age in Modern History: The Case of France,* Croom, Helm Publishers, 1976. Editor of *Comparative Studies in Social History,* Croom Helm Publishers. Contributor to historical journals. Managing editor, *Journal of Social History;* consulting editor in European history, Forum Press, 1972—.

*   *   *

STEGNER, Page 1937-

PERSONAL: Born January 31, 1937, in Salt Lake City, Utah; son of Wallace (a novelist and critic) and Mary (Page) Stegner; married Marion Mackenzie, June 20, 1959; children: Wallace Page, Rachel. *Education:* Stanford University, A.B. and M.A., Ph.D., 1965. *Office:* Crown College, University of California, Santa Cruz, Calif.

CAREER: Ohio State University, Columbus, assistant professor of English, 1965-67; University of California, Crown College, Santa Cruz, 1968—, currently associate professor.

WRITINGS: Escape Into Aesthetics: The Art of Vladimir Nabokov, Dial, 1966; *The Edge* (novel), Dial, 1968; (compiler and author of introduction) *Nabokov's Congeries,* Viking, 1968; (editor) *The Portable Nabokov,* Viking, 1969; (editor) *Introduction to Fiction,* Scott, Foresman, 1969; *Hawks and Harriers* (novel), Dial, 1971.

WORK IN PROGRESS: A novel entitled *Confessions of an Onanist;* a collection of stories entitled *California of the Mind.*

*   *   *

STEIN, Charles S. 1940-

PERSONAL: Born April 22, 1940, in New York, N.Y. *Education:* City College (now City College of the City University of New York), B.B.A., 1961; New York University, M.B.A., 1962.

CAREER: Now in professional sales administration with Bristol-Myers, New York, N.Y.

WRITINGS: (With E. M. Mazze and H. Madeheim) *Readings in Organization and Management,* Holt, 1964; (with Mazze and Madeheim) *Articles and Essays in International Business,* Holt, 1965.††

*   *   *

STEIN, Peter (Gonville) 1926-

PERSONAL: Born May 29, 1926, in Liverpool, England; son of Walter O. (a solicitor) and Effie (Walker) Stein; married Janet Chamberlain (a research biochemist), July 22, 1953; children: Barbara J., Penelope E., Dorothy C. *Education:* Gonville and Caius College, Cambridge, B.A., 1949, LL.B., 1950, M.A., 1951; University of Pavia, graduate study, 1951-52; University of Aberdeen, Ph.D., 1955. *Religion:* Church of England. *Office:* Queens' College, Cambridge University, Cambridge, England.

CAREER: Admitted a solicitor of Supreme Court in England, 1951; University of Nottingham, Nottinghamshire, England, assistant lecturer in law, 1952-53; University of Aberdeen, Aberdeen, Scotland, lecturer in jurisprudence, 1953-56, professor of jurisprudence, 1956-68, dean of Faculty of Law, 1961-64; Cambridge University, Queens' College, Cambridge, England, Regius Professor of Civil Law, 1968—. Visiting professor at University of Virginia and University of Colorado, 1965-66, University of Witwatersrand, South Africa, 1970, and University of Louisiana, 1974; guest lecturer at other universities in America, Austria, Belgium, France, Germany, Italy, Netherlands, Czechoslovakia, and Poland. Member of scientific council, Max Planck Institute for European Legal History, Frankfurt, Germany. Military service: Royal Naval Volunteer Reserve, 1944-47; became sub-lieutenant.

WRITINGS: Fault in the Formation of Contract in Roman Law and Scots Law, Oliver & Boyd, 1958; (editor) Buckland, Textbook of Roman Law, 3rd edition, Cambridge University Press, 1963; Regulae Iuris: From Juristic Rules to Legal Maxims, Edinburgh University Press, 1966; (with John Shand) Legal Values in Western Society, Edinburgh University Press, 1974; (editor with R. L. Meck and D. D. Raphael) Adam Smith's Lectures on Jurisprudence, Oxford University Press, 1976. Contributor of articles, mainly on Roman law and legal history, to law journals in United States and Europe.

*   *   *

STEINBERG, Jonathan   1934-

PERSONAL: Born March 8, 1934, in New York, N.Y.; son of Milton (a rabbi) and Edith (Alpert) Steinberg; married Jill Meier, November 13, 1960; children: Matthew David, Daniel Andrew, Peter James. Education: Harvard University, B.A. (magna cum laude), 1955; Cambridge University, M.A., 1963, Ph.D., 1965. Politics: Democrat (United States); Liberal (United Kingdom). Religion: Jewish. Home: 57 Moorfield Rd., Duxford, Cambridge, England. Office: Trinity Hall, Cambridge University, Cambridge, England.

CAREER: In investment banking business in Hamburg, London, and New York, 1958-61; Cambridge University, Cambridge, England, research fellow of Christ's College, 1963-66, official fellow and director of studies in history at Trinity Hall, 1966—, university lecturer, 1966—. Visiting lecturer, Harvard University, 1968-69. Military service: U.S. Army; Medical Service, 1955-57. Member: American Historical Association, Royal Historical Society (fellow), Navy Records Society (member of executive committee, 1965—), Phi Beta Kappa. Awards, honors: Woodrow Wilson fellowship, 1957-58.

WRITINGS: (Translator) M. Boveri, Treason in the 20th Century, Putnam, 1961; (translator) F. Heer, The Intellectual History of Europe, Weidenfeld & Nicolson, 1966; Yesterday's Deterrent: Tirpitz and the Birth of the German Battle Fleet, Macmillan, 1966. Also author of Inside Switzerland, 1976.

WORK IN PROGRESS: Comparisons between the fascist seizure of power in Italy and the National Socialist seizure of power in Germany.

*   *   *

STEINKRAUS, Warren E(dward)   1922-

PERSONAL: Born February 14, 1922, in Boston, Mass.; son of John Herman (a clergyman) and Florence (Rabe) Steinkraus; married Barbara Morris, July 15, 1948; children: Elizabeth Joy. Education: Baldwin-Wallace College, A.B., 1943; Boston University, S.T.B. (magna cum laude), 1946, Ph.D., 1952; also studied at University of Iowa, Harvard University, and Fitzwilliam College, Cambridge, 1970. Politics: Democrat. Religion: Methodist. Home: 89 Sheldon Ave., Oswego, N.Y. 13126. Office: Department of Philosophy, State University of New York College at Oswego, Oswego, N.Y. 13126.

CAREER: Emerson College, Boston, Mass., part-time instructor in English literature, 1946-49; Cornell College, Mount Vernon, Iowa, instructor in philosophy, 1949-50; DePauw University, Greencastle, Ind., assistant professor of philosophy, 1950-56; Iowa Wesleyan College, Mount Pleasant, associate professor of philosophy, 1956-59; Union College, Barbourville, Ky., professor of philosophy, 1959-64; State University of New York College at Oswego, professor of philosophy, 1964—, acting chairman of department, 1968-69, faculty exchange scholar, 1975—. Member of Indiana State Board, American Civil Liberties Union, 1954-56. Member: American Philosophical Association, Metaphysical Society of America, American Society for Aesthetics, Hegel Society of America (vice-president, 1969-70). Awards, honors: Jacob Sleeper Fellow, Boston University, 1946-47; New York State Research Foundation, study grants, 1965-67, 1969-70; summer faculty fellowship, 1966, 1967; American Council of Learned Societies travel grant to Interamerican Congress of Philosophy, Brasilia, Brazil, 1972; National Endowment for the Humanities, Council for Philosophical Studies visiting scholar, Millsaps College, 1971, 1972; Doctor of Humane Letters, Baldwin-Wallace College, 1975.

WRITINGS: (Editor and contributor) New Studies in Berkeley's Philosophy, Holt, 1966; (with G. R. Malkani) Discussion on Law of Karma, Indian Institute of Philosophy, 1966; (contributor) Paul Edwards, editor, The Encyclopedia of Philosophy, Macmillan, 1967; (contributor) R. Ginsberg, editor, The Critique of War, Regnery, 1969; (contributor) Christensen, editor, Hegel and the Philosophy of Religion, Nijhoff, 1970; (editor and contributor) New Studies in Hegel's Philosophy, Holt, 1971; (editor and contributor) Philosophy of Art, Benziger, 1974; (contributor) E. Freeman, editor, The Abdication of Philosophy, Open Court, 1975; (editor with Robert N. Beck) Studies in Personalism: Selected Writings of Edgar Sheffield Brightman, Claude Stark, 1975. Contributor to philosophy journals. Music editor, Motive, 1943-46; editor, Philosophical Forum, 1947; editorial consultant, Kraus Reprints, 1967-69; literature editor, Idealistic Studies (journal), 1974—.

WORK IN PROGRESS: Co-editing the Proceedings of the Hegel Society of America; idealism, east and west, its history and social implications; an essay, "God for the Outward Bound," for James Christian's volume, Biocosmos: Philosophical Reflections on the Implications of Extraterrestrial Life.

AVOCATIONAL INTERESTS: Music (Steinkraus is an amateur musician), model railroads, languages, gardening.

*   *   *

STEINMETZ, Lawrence L(eo)   1938-

PERSONAL: Born September 26, 1938, in Newburg, Mo.; son of Leo Ewald (a photogrammetric engineer) and Sadie (Kriete) Steinmetz; married Sally Wismer, December 27, 1958; children: Susan Diane, James Bradley, Marcy Marie.

Education: University of Missouri, B.S., 1959, M.S., 1960; University of Michigan, Ph.D., 1964. *Politics:* Republican. *Home:* 245 Fair Place, Boulder, Colo. 80302. *Office:* Department of Management, University of Colorado, Boulder, Colo. 80302; and High Yield Management, Inc., 2305 Broadway, Boulder, Colo. 80302.

CAREER: The Kroger Company, Little Rock, Ark., management training, 1959-61; Henry Ford Community College, Dearborn, Mich., lecturer, 1961-63; University of Colorado, Boulder, assistant professor, 1964-66, associate professor, 1966-69, professor of management, 1969—, head of Management and Organization Division, 1971-74. President, High Yield Management, Inc., 1968—. Consultant to IBM, TRW, General Dynamics, Management Health & Development Corp., Beverly Hills, Calif., and other corporations. Member of water board, Wagoner Water District, Boulder, Colo. *Military service:* U.S. Army, 1960-61; became first lieutenant. *Member:* Academy of Management, American Marketing Association, Colorado Society of Personnel Administrators, Sigma Iota Epsilon, Beta Gamma Sigma, Delta Sigma Pi.

WRITINGS: Grass Roots Approach to Industrial Peace, Bureau of Industrial Relations, University of Michigan, 1966; (with A. Dale Allen and Robert J. Johnson) *Labor Law,* Media Masters, 1967; (with others) *Managing the Small Business,* Irwin, 1968; *Managing the Marginal and Unsatisfactory Performer,* Addison-Wesley, 1969; *Interviewing Skills for Supervisors,* Addison-Wesley, 1971; *First Line Management,* Business Publications, 1975; *Art and Skill of Delegation,* Addison-Wesley, 1976. Contributing editor, *Personnel Management Abstracts.*

*   *   *

STEMBER, Charles Herbert 1916-

PERSONAL: Born December 7, 1916, in Brooklyn, N.Y.; son of Maxwell M. (an accountant) and Etta (Tuch) Stember; married Barbara Durant, October 7, 1940; married second wife, Sue Cohen (a singer), November 26, 1958; children: Emily Maxine, Nicholas Samuel. *Education:* University of Wisconsin, B.S., 1941; Columbia University, Ph.D., 1955. *Home:* 8 Honey Brook Dr., Princeton, N.J. 08540. *Office:* Department of Economics, Rutgers University, New Brunswick, N.J. 08903.

CAREER: National Opinion Research Center, New York, N.Y., study director, 1947-52; Pennsylvania State University, State College, associate professor of home economics, 1955-56; University of Chicago, Chicago, Ill., associate professor of social psychology, 1957-58; Rutgers University, New Brunswick, N.J., professor of sociology, 1958—. Consultant, American Jewish Committee. Vice-president, Strykers Bay Neighborhood Council, 1964-65. *Military service:* U.S. Army, 1943-46; became sergeant. *Member:* American Sociological Association, American Association of University Professors, Eastern Sociological Association.

WRITINGS: (With Hyman and others) *Interviewing in Social Research,* University of Chicago Press, 1954; *Education and Attitude Change,* Institute of Human Relations Press, 1961; (with others) *Jews in the Mind of America,* Basic Books, 1966. Contributor to *Journal of Social Issues, Urban Review, Medical Aspects of Human Sexuality,* and *Public Opinion Quarterly.*

WORK IN PROGRESS: The Sexual Factor in Racial Hostility; the social psychology of dress and adornment.

BIOGRAPHICAL/CRITICAL SOURCES: New York Post, June 13, 1961.

STEPHAN, Leslie (Bates) 1933-

PERSONAL: Surname is pronounced Stefan; born May 1, 1933, in Boston, Mass.; daughter of Leslie Marriner (a dentist) and Ann (Gustafson) Bates; married Richard Allen Stephan (a consultant), January 22, 1955; children: John Eric, Johanna, Anne Christina, Mark David, Martin Jonathan, Maria Alvina. *Education:* Attended Skidmore College, 1951-52, Simmons College, 1952-54; Radcliffe College, B.A. (cum laude), 1957. *Home:* 93 North Main St., Topsfield, Mass. 01983. *Agent:* Oliver G. Swan, Julian Bach Literary Agency, 18 East 48th St., New York, N.Y. 10017.

CAREER: Director of nursery school in Harrison, N.Y., 1958-59.

WRITINGS: A Dam for Nothing, Viking, 1966.

WORK IN PROGRESS: Another novel.

SIDELIGHTS: Leslie Stephan lived in Iraq, 1955, in Switzerland, 1960-63, in Mexico, 1966-67, in Algeria, 1968. She speaks German, French, and some Spanish. *Avocational interests:* Reading, gardening, swimming, walking, and listening to music.

*   *   *

STEPHENS, Donald G. 1931-

PERSONAL: Born October 25, 1931, in Yorkton, Saskatchewan, Canada; son of C. B. and Rowena (Kinney) Stephens; married Dor-Lou Jones, May 23, 1959; children: Hilary, Lindsay. *Education:* University of New Brunswick, B.A., 1954, M.A., 1955; University of Edinburgh, Ph.D., 1958. *Religion:* Anglican. *Home:* 1711 Drummond Dr., Vancouver, British Columbia, Canada. *Office:* Department of English, University of British Columbia, Vancouver, British Columbia, Canada.

CAREER: University of British Columbia, Vancouver, lecturer, 1955-56, 1958, associate professor of English, 1964—. *Member:* Modern Language Association of America, Humanities Association, Association of Canadian University Teachers of English.

WRITINGS: Bliss Carman, Twayne, 1966; *Contemporary Voices,* Prentice-Hall, 1972; *Prairies,* University of British Columbia Press, 1974. Associate editor, *Canadian Literature* (quarterly).

WORK IN PROGRESS: A study of Canadian poetry and early prose.

*   *   *

STEPHENS, Edward Carl 1924-

PERSONAL: Born July 27, 1924, in Los Angeles, Calif.; son of Carl Edward and Helen (Kerner) Stephens; married Florence Burn, January 20, 1962; children: Edward Carl, Jr., Sarah, Matthew. *Education:* Occidental College, A.B., 1947; Northwestern University, M.S., 1955. *Home:* 1635 Hinman Ave., Evanston, Ill. 60201. *Agent:* Brandt & Brandt, 101 Park Ave., New York, N.Y. 10017. *Office:* Fisk Hall, Northwestern University, Evanston, Ill. 60201.

CAREER: Dancer-Fitzgerald-Sample, Inc., New York, N.Y., account executive, 1955-63; Northwestern University, School of Journalism, Evanston, Ill., assistant professor, 1963, associate professor of advertising, 1965—. Author. *Military service:* U.S. Navy, destroyer officer, 1943-46, submarine officer, 1950-53; received Purple Heart. U.S. Naval Reserve, now captain. *Member:* Association for Education in Journalism, American Academy of Advertising, American Association of University Professors, Authors Guild of the Authors League of America, Navy League, Naval Institute.

WRITINGS—All published by Doubleday, except as noted: *A Twist of Lemon*, 1958; *Submarines* (juvenile nonfiction), Golden Press, 1959; *One More Summer*, 1960; *Blow Negative!*, 1962; *Roman Joy*, 1965; *A Turn in the Dark Wood*, 1967; *The Submariner*, 1973.

SIDELIGHTS: Reviewing *A Turn in the Dark Wood*, Martin Levin says: "Mr. Stephens is a witty, inventive writer, and his story of an updated Babbitt's decline, fall and rise has a high quota of truly comic interludes.

A reviewer for the *New York Times Book Review* writes of *The Submariner:* "Mr. Stephens mingles farce and melodrama to produce a nautical spellbinder. The writing is well above the action-novel level and the course is tricky and paradoxical."

BIOGRAPHICAL/CRITICAL SOURCES: Best Sellers, December 1, 1967; *New York Times Book Review,* December 17, 1967.

*   *   *

STEPHENS, Wade C. 1932-

PERSONAL: Born November 27, 1932, in Pittsfield, Mass.; son of John U. (a clergyman) and Louise (Koons) Stephens; married Jean R. Samuels, June 18, 1954; children: Carol, David, Elizabeth. *Education:* Princeton University, A.B., 1954, Ph.D., 1957; Cornell University, M.A., 1955. *Religion:* Presbyterian. *Home:* Humphreys Dr., Lawrenceville, N.J. 08648.

CAREER: Lawrenceville School (preparatory school), Lawrenceville, N.J., chairman of classics department, 1957-74, chairman of language department, 1974—. Latin Advanced Placement Committee for the College Board, member, 1962-68, chairman, 1964-68. *Member:* American Philological Association, Phi Beta Kappa, Lake Placid Club.

WRITINGS: (With Emilio Springhetti) *Lingua Latina Viva, Book II,* McGraw, 1967; *The Spirit of the Classical World,* Putnam, 1967. Author of articles on classical subjects.

*   *   *

STERLING, Chandler W(infield) 1911-

PERSONAL: Born January 28, 1911, in Dixon, Ill.; son of Robert Winfield and Mary (Chandler) Sterling; married Catherine Ricker, June 17, 1935; children: Mary, Margaret (Mrs. James Moore), Kathy (Mrs. Michael Clark), Ann (Mrs. Donald Crouse), Beth, Sarah, Jonathan, Julia. *Education:* Northwestern University, B.A., 1932; Seabury-Western Theological Seminary, ministerial study, 1938. *Residence:* Souderton, Pa. *Agent:* Oscar Collier, 280 Madison Ave., New York, N.Y. 10017.

CAREER: Ordained priest of Protestant Episcopal Church, 1938; served parishes in Wilmette, Ill., Oak Park, Ill., Milwaukee, Wis., Freeport, Ill., Elmhurst, Ill., and then Chadron, Neb., 1938-56; Episcopal bishop of Montana, 1956-68; assistant to Bishop of Pennsylvania, 1968-71; Good Shepherd Episcopal Church, Hilltown, Pa., rector, 1971-73; Lindisfarne Association, Southampton, N.Y., lecturing resident fellow, 1973-75. Preaching and teaching missioner; public lecturer, 1968. *Member:* American Church Union (president, 1965-70). *Awards, honors:* D.D. Seabury-Western Theological Seminary, 1957.

WRITINGS: Little Malice in Blunderland, Morehouse, 1965; *Arrogance of Piety,* Morehouse, 1969; *The Holroyd Papers,* Bartholomew House, 1970; *The Eighth Square,* Trinity Press, 1970; *The Icehouse Gang,* Scribner, 1972; *Beyond This Land of Whoa,* Pilgrim Publications, 1973; *The Door of Perception,* Pilgrim Publications, 1974; *The Witnesses,* Regnery, 1975. Contributor to church publications.

*   *   *

STERN, J(oseph) P(eter)

PERSONAL: Born in Prague, Czechoslovakia. *Office:* Department of German, University of London, London, England.

CAREER: Cambridge University, Cambridge, England, formerly fellow and tutor of St. John's College; currently professor of German and head of department, University of London, London, England.

WRITINGS: Ernst Juenger, a Writer of Our Time, Yale University Press, 1952; *G. C. Lichtenberg: A Doctrine of Scattered Occasions,* Indiana University Press, 1959; *Re-Interpretations: Seven Studies in Nineteenth-Century German Literature,* Basic Books, 1964; *Idylls and Realities: Studies in Nineteenth-Century German Literature,* Ungar, 1972; *On Realism,* Routledge & Kegan Paul, 1973; *Hitler: The Fuehrer and the People,* Fontana, 1975.

*   *   *

STERN, James 1904-

PERSONAL: Born December 26, 1904, in County Meath, Ireland; son of Henry J. J. and Constance (Watt) Stern; married Tania Kurella, November 9, 1935. *Education:* Attended Eton College, 1918-1923. *Agent:* Elaine Green Ltd., 31, Newington Green, London N. 16, England.

CAREER: Writer. *Member:* Royal Society of Literature (fellow). *Awards, honors:* National Institute of Arts and Letters grant, 1949; Arts Council of Great Britain, first award for the short story, 1966.

WRITINGS: The Heartless Land, Macmillan, 1932; *Something Wrong* (collection of twelve short stories), Secker & Warburg, 1938; *The Hidden Damage,* Harcourt, 1947; *The Man Who Was Loved,* Harcourt, 1951; (translator from the German) *Anonymous, A Woman in Berlin,* Harcourt, 1954; (editor and translator) *Grimm's Fairy Tales* (complete edition), Routledge & Kegan Paul, 1959; *The Stories of James Stern,* Harcourt, 1969; (translator with Elisabeth Duckworth) Franz Kafka, *Letters to F. B.,* Schocken, 1973; (contributor) Stephen Spender, editor, *W. H. Auden: A Tribute,* Macmillan, 1975.

Also translated from the German works by Bertolt Brecht, Hermann Broch, Thomas Mann, Sigmund Freud, Hugo von Hofmannsthal, and Stefan Zweig, many in collaboration with his wife. Contributor of articles and book reviews to the *New York Times, Nation, New Republic,* and *Partisan Review.*

SIDELIGHTS: Paul Bailey, in his review of *The Stories of James Stern,* notes that Stern's work contains "marvelous passages, descriptions of landscapes and animals that are sometimes worthy of Lawrence." Not only are the climates of Africa and Ireland (the principle settings of the stories) "skillfully differentiated," but, Bailey adds, "Stern is gifted in other ways, too. . . ." For example, he records "upper-class chat with a positively gleeful accuracy. . . ."

BIOGRAPHICAL/CRITICAL SOURCES: Listener, March 7, 1968; Observer Review, March 17, 1968; London Magazine, April 1968.

* * *

STERN, Robert M. 1927-

PERSONAL: Born August 26, 1927, in Boston, Mass.; son of Barnett S. (a wholesale meat dealer) and Rose (Cohen) Stern; married Lucetta P. Smith (a clinical psychologist), December 26, 1953; children: Everett John, Caroline Jo. Education: University of California, Berkeley, B.S., 1948; University of Chicago, M.B.A., 1952; Columbia University, Ph.D., 1958. Home: 612 Oswego, Ann Arbor, Mich. 48104. Office: Department of Economics, University of Michigan, Ann Arbor, Mich. 48104.

CAREER: Union College, Schenectady, N.Y., instructor in economics, 1953-54; Columbia University, New York, N.Y., assistant professor of economics, 1959-61; University of Michigan, Ann Arbor, assistant professor, 1961-63, associate professor, 1963-66, professor of economics, 1966—. Consultant, United Nations Conference on Trade and Development, 1966. Member: American Economic Association, Royal Economic Society, Phi Beta Kappa. Awards, honors: Fulbright fellow to the Netherlands, 1958-59; Ford Foundation faculty research fellow, 1964-65.

WRITINGS: (Editor with Gottfried Haberler) Equilibrium and Growth in the World Economy: Economic Essays by Ragnar Nurkse, Harvard University Press, 1961; Foreign Trade and Economic Growth in Italy, Praeger, 1967; (with Edward E. Leamer) Quantitative International Economics, Allyn & Bacon, 1970; The Balance of Payments: Theory and Economic Policy, Aldine, 1973; (with J. Francis and B. Schumacher) Price Elasticities in International Trade, Macmillan, 1976. Contributor of more than twenty articles and reviews to professional journals.

WORK IN PROGRESS: Tariffs and Employment; Macroeconomic Interdependence under Floating Exchange Rates.

* * *

STERNLIEB, George 1928-

PERSONAL: Born August 16, 1928, in New York, N.Y.; son of Bernard J. and Golda (Mayer) Sternlieb; married Phyllis Fox (a mathematician), April 23, 1958; children: David, Benjamin. Education: Brooklyn College (now Brooklyn College of the City University of New York), B.A., 1950; Harvard University, M.B.A., 1953, D.B.A., 1962; postdoctoral study at Harvard University and Columbia University. Home: 66 Old Short Hills Rd., Short Hills, N.J. Office: Rutgers University, Center for Urban Policy Research, New Brunswick, N.J. 08903.

CAREER: Bloomingdale's, New York, N.Y., merchandising executive, 1953-58; Harvard University, School of Business Administration, Boston, Mass., research associate, 1958-59; Adams Associates (business consultants), Bedford, Mass., co-founder and treasurer, 1959-66; Rutgers University, Graduate School of Business Administration, Newark Campus, Newark, N.J., associate professor, 1962-65, professor of marketing, 1965-68, New Brunswick Campus, New Brunswick, N.J., professor of urban and regional planning, 1968—, director, Center for Urban Policy Research, 1969—. Member of federal, state, and local urban development and planning committees. Consultant to Boston Redevelopment Authority and Westinghouse Advance Systems.

WRITINGS: The Future of the Downtown Department Store, Harvard University Press, 1962; Garden Apartment Houses: A Municipal Cost-Revenue Analysis, Bureau of Economic Research, Rutgers University, 1964; The Tenement Landlord, Urban Studies Center, Rutgers University, 1966; (co-author) Social Needs and Social Resources—Newark: 1967, Research Center, Rutgers Center, Rutgers University, 1967; Newark, New Jersey: Population and Labor Force, Institute of Management Labor Relations, Rutgers University, 1967; (co-author) Leisure Market Studies, two volumes, Urban Studies Center, Rutgers University, 1967; The Urban Housing Dilemma, New York City Housing Development Administration and Rutgers University, 1970; (co-author) Housing in an Affluent Suburb: Princeton, New Jersey, Transaction Books, 1971; (with Patrick Beaton) The Zone of Emergence, Transaction Books, 1972; (co-author) New York City: Housing and People, New York City Housing Development Administration, 1973; (with Bernard P. Indik) The Ecology of Welfare, Transaction Books, 1973; (co-author) Housing Development and Municipal Costs, Center for Urban Policy Research, Rutgers University, 1973; (with Lynne B. Sagalyn) Zoning and Housing Costs: The Impact of Land Use Controls on Housing Price, Center for Urban Policy Research, Rutgers University, 1973; (with Robert W. Burchell) Residential Abandonment: The Tenement Landlord Revisited, Center for Urban Policy Research, Rutgers University, 1973.

Contributor: The Impact of Sales Taxes as a Function of Family Income, Graduate School of Business Administration, Rutgers University, 1965; Some Aspects of the Abandoned House Problem, Department of Housing and Urban Development, 1970; Society, Transaction Books, 1972. Contributor to planning, business, and marketing journals.

* * *

STEVENS, Edwin L. 1913-

PERSONAL: Born November 21, 1913, in Delhi, N.Y.; son of Edwin Logan (a jeweler) and Flora (Lockwood) Stevens; married Lucille V. Morehouse (a classification analyst for U.S. Department of Agriculture), August 11, 1961. Education: Rutgers University, A.B., 1936; Columbia University, M.A., 1944, and additional study towards doctorate. Politics: Independent. Religion: Episcopalian. Home: 3122 Legation St. N.W., Washington, D.C. 20015. Office: Speech Department, George Washington University, Washington, D.C. 20052.

CAREER: Rutgers University, New Brunswick, N.J., assistant purchasing agent, 1936-40, instructor in speech, 1940-42; Columbia University, New York, N.Y., instructor in speech, 1942-43; George Washington University, Washington, D.C., assistant professor, 1947-50, associate professor, 1950-61, professor of speech, 1961—. Consultant in speech to National War College, 1947-56, Industrial College of the Armed Forces, 1948—, Foreign Service Institute, 1948-66, Walter Reed Army Institute of Research, 1954—; also consultant to other government agencies and to private industry. Military service: U.S. Army, Signal Corps, 1943-46; became first lieutenant.

MEMBER: Speech Association of America, Phi Beta Kappa, Phi Delta Kappa, Omicron Delta Kappa, Tau Kappa Alpha. Awards, honors: U.S. Department of the Army Patriotic Civilian Service Award, 1964.

WRITINGS: (With Richard C. Reager and Ernest MacMahon) Speech Is Easy, Rutgers University Press, 1942;

(with Reager and Norman P. Crawford) *You Can Talk Well*, Rutgers University Press, 1960, revised edition, 1963.

* * *

STEVENS, Norma Young 1927-

PERSONAL: Born October 23, 1927, in Canton, Ga.; daughter of Sherman Taylor (a cotton buyer) and Cora Lee (Stephens) Young; married Howard Lamar Stevens (a missionary teacher), September 6, 1949; children: Catherine Lynn, Karen Leigh, Kristen Leslie. *Education:* University of Georgia, B.F.A. (landscape architecture), 1949, Ed.D., 1970; New Orleans Baptist Theological Seminary, M.R.E., 1956, graduate study, 1956-58. *Politics:* Democrat. *Religion:* Baptist. *Home:* (Permanent address) 109 Elder Rd., Athens, Ga.; (current address) 2103 Hampton Ave., Nashville, Tenn. 37215.

CAREER: Landscape architect, Nashville, Tenn., 1950-54; teacher of art and English, Torreon, Coahuila, Mexico, 1963-74, also helping in design of church buildings and student centers, with Department of Testing and Counseling, 1970-74; Belmont College, Nashville, teacher, 1974—.

WRITINGS: Go Out with Joy, Broadman, 1966; (contributor) Bill Cannon, editor, *Everyday, Five Minutes with God,* Broadman, 1969. Author of plays, programs, and articles in Spanish for use by the Baptist Church in Latin America.

* * *

STEVENS, R(obert B.) 1933-

PERSONAL: Born June 8, 1933, in Leicester, England; son of John Skevington and Enid Dorothy (Bocking) Stevens; married Rosemary Anne Wallace (a professor), January 30, 1961; children: Carey Thomasine, Richard Nathaniel. *Education:* Keble College, Oxford, B.A., 1955, B.C.L., 1956, M.A., 1958; Yale University, LL.M., 1958. *Home:* 19 Edgehill Rd., New Haven, Conn. 06511.

CAREER: Yale University, New Haven, Conn., assistant professor, 1959-61, associate professor, 1961-65, professor of law, 1965—. Consultant to United Nations and Agency for International Development.

WRITINGS: (With B. S. Yamey) *The Restrictive Practices Court: A Study of the Judicial Process and Economic Policy,* Weidenfeld & Nicolson, 1965; (with B. Abel-Smith) *Lawyers and the Courts: A Sociological Study of the English Legal System, 1750-1965,* Harvard University Press, 1967; (with Abel-Smith) *In Search of Justice: Society and the Legal System,* Penguin, 1969; (editor) *Income Security,* McGraw, 1970; (with wife, Rosemary Stevens) *Welfare Medicine in America,* Free Press, 1974.

WORK IN PROGRESS: A history of the House of Lords as a judicial body; the rise of American lawyers and legal education.

* * *

STEVENS, Richard P. 1931-

PERSONAL: Born June 16, 1931, in New Castle, Pa.; son of George W. and Marie (Connor) Stevens. *Education:* University of Notre Dame, B.A., 1954; Georgetown University, M.A., 1958, Ph.D., 1960. *Religion:* Roman Catholic. *Home address:* Box 329A, R.D. 1, Oxford, Pa. *Office:* Lincoln University, Lincoln University, Pa. 19352.

CAREER: King's College, Wilkes-Barre, Pa., assistant professor of history and political science, 1958-61; Pius XII University College, Roma, Lesotho, Southern Africa, chairman of political science department, 1962-63; Lincoln University, Lincoln University, Pa., associate professor, 1964-68, professor of political science, 1968—, director of African Student Center, 1964-66, acting director of African Language and Area Center, 1966-67, chairman of political science department, 1967. Visiting fellow, Princeton University, 1968; visiting professor, University of Kuwait, spring, 1973, and University of Khartoum, 1974-76. *Member:* African Studies Association (fellow), Middle East Studies Association, American Committee on Africa (board), African Bureau (London). *Awards, honors:* Fulbright scholar, in Egypt, 1965; Fulbright teaching fellow, University of Khartoum, 1975-76.

WRITINGS: American Zionism and U.S. Foreign Policy, 1942-47, Pageant, 1962; *Lesotho, Botswana and Swaziland: The Former High Commission Territories in Southern Africa,* Praeger, 1967. Also author of *Palestine before the Mandate.* Contributor to *Encyclopaedia Britannica, Encyclopedia Americana, Collier's Encyclopedia, Grolier's Encyclopedia,* and *Book of Nations;* contributor to journals.

SIDELIGHTS: Stevens has traveled extensively in Mexico, West Indies, Africa, and the Middle East, studying "those cultural aspects promoting or inhibiting political modernization as well as racism in international affairs."

* * *

STEVENS, Shane 1941-

PERSONAL: Born October 8, 1941, in New York, N.Y. *Education:* Columbia University, M.A., 1961. *Politics:* "Participatory anarchist." *Agent:* Lynn Nesbit, International Creative Management, 40 West 57th St., New York, N.Y. 10019.

CAREER: Stevens calls his vocation "traveler," having traveled to Mexico, South America, Cuba, Asia, and Africa; about the rest he adds: "I am very secretive."

WRITINGS: Go Down Dead (novel), Morrow, 1967; *Way Uptown in Another World* (novel), Putnam, 1971; *Dead City* (novel), Holt, 1973; *Rat Pack* (novel), Seabury, 1974. Also author of screenplay "The Me Nobody Knows," 1975. Contributor to *Saturday Review, Village Voice, Evergreen,* and other periodicals.

WORK IN PROGRESS: Two novels of courage and decay tentatively entitled *The Saturday Crowd* and *The Good Guys Only Win in the Movies.*

SIDELIGHTS: One of the most authentic books about Harlem, *Go Down Dead,* was written by a young white man who, according to James R. Frakes, makes prominent Negro writers seem prissy. Written from the point of view of a 16-year old Negro, the book depicts a Harlem "you've never seen before," says Frakes, adding: "Dante had the same kind of trouble overcoming incredulity in his mapping of the Inferno.... To pick at the flaws in Stevens' book—the inconsistency of the speaking voice, the blobs of fake philosophizing, the focus-blurring digressions—seems irrelevant in the presence of its doomsday revelations. What this novel shouts is that 'you'd better believe it!'"

Publishers' Weekly called it "an angry and ruthlessly honest novel.... The writing is brutal and uncompromising, the situations are harsh and authentic, and the result is a tragic and important book." It is a book from the depths, written in a voice "not completely strangled by despair," writes Frakes, "a voice that can pitch itself both above and below a sustained, wordless scream.

In this century such voices, though not common, have been heard: Gorki, Wright, Dahlberg, Genet. Now, at least in terms of expressing the inexpressible, of giving dramatic shape to a writhing mass of underground raw material, Shane Stevens swells the furious chorus." Stevens himself adds: "The time of the novel is now, the place is here, and the mood is bitter despair and murderous hatred. It is written exactly as it is being lived, written in the language of the people who live it. There are no artful barriers to protect the reader from direct involvement in the action. Let the reader beware! What is happening to the book's people is happening to *him*." The book, nevertheless, is "also a story told by a storyteller," he says, "for that's what novels are really all about." He began the novel in Harlem in 1959, "kept at it across the wasteland of San Francisco and on into desolate Mexico, finally finishing it in a . . . burst of love in mother New York, 1966. It's a supremely personal vision, a private nightmare that exploded in my brain and forged onto my consciousness a style suited to the vision." Stevens writes: "I am a novelist: that's my punishment for living. . . . I am a writer, always, now and forever; nothing I would do could shatter the significance of that. Whatever I have done in my life, I have done with that in mind. The details are of no consequence. . . ." *Avocational interests:* Motorcycling and scuba diving.

BIOGRAPHICAL/CRITICAL SOURCES: Publishers' Weekly, October 31, 1966; *New York Times Book Review,* January 29, 1967; *Time,* February 24, 1967; *Village Voice,* August 24, 1967.

*   *   *

STEVENS, William 1925-

PERSONAL: Born September 22, 1925, in Flushing, N.Y.; son of Walter E. and Viola (Needham) Stevens; married Ann P. Thompson, November 29, 1949; children: Holly, Marc, Heidi, Grant, Lise. *Education:* "Negligible." *Home:* 3688 Latimore, Shaker Heights, Ohio 44122. *Agent:* Roberta Pryor, International Creative Management, 40 West 57th St., New York, N.Y. 10018.

CAREER: Industrial purchasing agent for some years before he gave up business in 1964 to move to Martha's Vineyard and "settle down to serious writing"; worked part-time in a bank on the island while writing *The Peddler*. *Military service:* U.S. Army Air Forces, 1943-45.

WRITINGS: The Peddler, Little, Brown, 1966; *The Gunner,* Atheneum, 1968; *The Cannibal Isle,* Little, Brown, 1970; *The Best of Our Time,* Random House, 1973. Editor, *Editur International,* 1973-75.

WORK IN PROGRESS: A novel on Spain.

SIDELIGHTS: William Stevens comments on his writing career thus far: "Great American Dream realized at 39; quit work and took wife and five children to Martha's Vineyard. Went broke, became an underprivileged family." The Stevens family lived in Spain, 1970-75. Stevens' book *The Gunner* was sold to Universal for filming.

*   *   *

STEWART, D(avid) H(ugh) 1926-

PERSONAL: Born August 12, 1926, in Fort Wayne, Ind.; son of Carey Hugh (a Young Men's Christian Association secretary) and Priscilla (Stauffer) Stewart; married Diane Silva (a secretary), July 25, 1949; children: Marc Silva, Christopher David. *Education:* University of Michigan,

A.B., 1947, A.M., 1949, Ph.D., 1959; Columbia University, Certificate of Russian Institute and A.M., 1954. *Home:* 2304 Bristol, Bryan, Tex. 77801. *Office:* Department of English, Texas A&M University, College Station, Tex. 77843.

CAREER: Instructor in English at Valparaiso University, Valparaiso, Ind., 1949-50, and University of Oregon, Eugene, 1950-52; University of Michigan, Ann Arbor, instructor in Russian, 1955-56; assistant professor of English at Eastern Michigan University, Ypsilanti, 1957-59, and University of Alberta, Edmonton, 1959-60; University of Michigan, associate professor of English, 1960-67; Idaho State University, Pocatello, professor of English and chairman of department, 1968-72; Pennsylvania State University, University Park, Pa., professor of English and chairman of department, 1972-75; Texas A&M University, College Station, professor of English and chairman of department, 1975—. *Military service:* U.S. Navy, 1944-46. *Member:* Modern Language Association of America, National Council of Teachers of English, American Association of University Professors, Phi Kappa Phi. *Awards, honors:* Horace Rackham research grant for travel and study in the Soviet Union, 1966.

WRITINGS: (Contributor) Utley, Bloom, and Kinney, editors, *Bear, Man, and God,* Random House, 1964; *Mikhail Sholokhov: A Critical Introduction,* University of Michigan Press, 1967; *The Wiley Reader: Designs for Writing,* Wiley, 1976. Contributor to "A Check List of Explication" in *Explicator,* annually, 1960-74; contributor of articles and reviews to *Queen's Quarterly, American Slavic and East European Review,* and other journals.

*   *   *

STEWART, Sheila 1928-

PERSONAL: Born January 6, 1928, in Devonshire, England; father unknown, and mother disappeared after her birth; married Eric Stewart (an antique dealer), April 16, 1952; children: Sarah, Timothy, Mathew. *Education:* First ward of Waifs and Strays (Church of England Children's Society) to attend grammar school; continued on to Bishop Otter Teacher Training College, 1946-48. *Politics:* Conservative. *Religion:* Church of England. *Home:* Combe Rising, Ascott, near Shipston-on-Stour, Warwickshire, England.

CAREER: Taught for four years before her marriage, and has operated a nursery school; currently runs a village club for senior citizens. Speaker on Victorian glass, country anecdotes, at various clubs, dinners, and institutions. *Awards, honors:* Best Radio Feature Script Award, Writer's Guild of Great Britain, 1974.

WRITINGS: A Home from Home (autobiography), Longmans, Green, 1967; *Country Kate,* Roundwood Publishers, 1971; *Country Courtship,* Roundwood Publishers, 1976. Radio plays for British Broadcasting Corporation include "No Business Like Show Business," 1970, "Country Kate," 1974, and "The Taxman Cometh," 1975. Contributor to *Canadian Boy.*

SIDELIGHTS: Sheila Stewart told *CA:* "[I am] interested in the welfare of children, particularly children in orphanages and institutions. Spent all my own childhood in a Home, and I have dealt with many unwanted children. Therefore interested in legal abortion, birth control, and education (though not necessarily in that order)."

BIOGRAPHICAL/CRITICAL SOURCES: Times Lit-

erary Supplement, May 25, 1967; *New Statesman*, May 26, 1967; *Books and Bookmen*, August, 1967.

* * *

STINNETT, Ronald F. 1929-

PERSONAL: Surname accented on second syllable; born October 16, 1929, in Cleveland, Tenn.; son of Owen Earnest and Lillian (McNeely) Stinnett; married Betty Burleson, June 9, 1956; children: Barbara Dean, Debora Jean, Ronald F., Jr., Sean Lee. *Education:* State University of New York at Cortland, B.S., 1952; University of Minnesota, M.A., 1956, Ph.D., 1961. *Politics:* Democrat. *Religion:* Baptist.

CAREER: Junior college teacher in Cazenovia, N.Y., 1953-55, and high school teacher in Middletown, N.Y., 1956-57; Minnesota Citizens for Kennedy-Johnson, executive director, 1960; campaign director for mayoral candidate, Minneapolis, Minn., 1961, 1963; Minnesota Gubernatorial Recount, statistical director, 1962-63; Democratic Senatorial Campaign Committee, Washington, D.C., research director, 1963-65; Office of the Vice-President, Washington, D.C., assistant to vice-president, 1965-67; Publicom, Inc., Washington, D.C., president, 1967-68; The Washington Group, Inc., Washington, D.C., president, beginning 1968. Lecturer, Robert Taft Institute of Government, 1965-66. President, International Energy Markets, Ltd. *Member:* American Academy of Political and Social Science, American Political Science Association, Speech Association of America, Kappa Delta Pi, Phi Delta Kappa.

WRITINGS: Recount, National Document Publishers, 1964; *Democrats, Dinners, Dollars,* Iowa State University Press, 1967; (contributor) *Dictionary of American History,* Scribner, 1973.

WORK IN PROGRESS: A book on national politics, *Campaigns and Elections.*†

* * *

STOCK, Ernest 1924-

PERSONAL: Born August 6, 1924, in Frankfurt, Germany; came to United States in 1940; son of Leo (a businessman) and Julie (Marx) Stock; married Bracha Heiblum, February 11, 1961; children: Adlai J. *Education:* City College (now City College of the City University of New York), student, 1942-43; Princeton University, A.B., 1948; Columbia University, M.S., 1949, M.A., 1958, Ph.D., 1963. *Religion:* Jewish. *Home:* Nayot 6, Jerusalem, Israel. *Office:* Hiatt Institute, Brandeis University, 6 Maneh St., Jerusalem, Israel.

CAREER: Foreign editor of *Jerusalem Post,* Jerusalem, Israel, and Jerusalem correspondent for United Press, 1949-50; B'nai B'rith Hillel Foundations, New York City, assistant to national director, 1951-52; Ford Foundation, New York City, research fellow in Middle East, 1952-53; Council of Jewish Federations and Welfare Funds, New York City, consultant on overseas studies, 1954-61; Jewish Agency for Israel, Inc., New York City, representative in Israel, 1961-65; Brandeis University, Jacob Hiatt Institute, Jerusalem, Israel, director, 1966—. *Military service:* U.S. Army, 1943-46; served in Europe; became staff sergeant; received battle star. *Member:* American Political Science Association, Phi Beta Kappa, Princeton Club (New York).

WRITINGS: (Contributor) *Commentary on the American Scene,* Knopf, 1953; *Israel on the Road to Sinai,* Cornell University Press, 1967; *From Conflict to Understanding: Jews and Arabs in Israel,* American Jewish Committee, Institute of Human Relations, 1968. Contributor to *Reporter, Commentary, Foreign Policy Bulletin, Midstream, Political Science Quarterly, Forum, Middle Eastern Studies, Jewish Journal of Sociology, Encyclopedia Judaica,* and *American Jewish Year Book.*

WORK IN PROGRESS: A book, *Israel: The Limits of the Dream.*

* * *

STOCKWELL, Edward G(rant) 1933-

PERSONAL: Born June 11, 1933, in Newburyport, Mass.; son of Frank Whitten (a physician) and Margaret (Winters) Stockwell; married Janet Wiranis, August 18, 1956; children: Edward, Jr., Christopher, Susie. *Education:* Harvard University, A.B., 1955; University of Connecticut, M.A., 1957; Brown University, Ph.D., 1960. *Politics:* Independent. *Religion:* Unitarian Universalist. *Home:* 1203 Brownwood, Bowling Green, Ohio 43402. *Office:* Department of Sociology, Bowling Green State University, Bowling Green, Ohio 43403.

CAREER: University of Connecticut, Storrs, professor of rural sociology, 1961-72; Bowling Green State University, Bowling Green, Ohio, professor of sociology, 1972—. *Member:* American Sociological Society, American Statistical Association, Rural Sociological Society, Population Association of America, International Union for the Scientific Study of Population, Eastern Sociological Society.

WRITINGS: Population and People, Quadrangle, 1968.

* * *

STOFF, Sheldon (Ptaschevitch) 1930-

PERSONAL: Born March 28, 1930, in Brooklyn, N.Y.; son of Morris and Celia (Lanz) Stoff; married Lorraine Marshak, February 28, 1930; children: Jesse Andrew, Joshua Jordan. *Education:* State University of New York College at Farmingdale, A.A., 1953; Cornell University, B.S. and M.S., 1960, Ed.D., 1964. *Office:* Department of Education, Adelphi University, Garden City, N.Y. 11530.

CAREER: Adelphi University, Garden City, N.Y., instructor in philosophy of education, 1964-66; Queens College (now Queens College of the City University of New York), Flushing, N.Y., assistant professor of philosophy of education, 1966-72; Adelphi University, chairman of department of education, 1972—, director, Center for Humanistic Education and Research, 1973—. Waldorf Institute, philosophy consultant, 1966—, coordinator, graduate summer session, 1968—. *Military service:* U.S. Navy, 1951-52; received Korean Medal. *Member:* Middle Atlantic States Philosophy of Education Society, National Conference of Christians and Jews, Phi Delta Kappa.

WRITINGS: The Two-Way Street: Guideposts to Peaceful School Integration, David Stewart, 1967; (with H. Schwartzberg) *The Human Encounter: Readings in Education,* Harper, 1969, 2nd edition, 1973.

* * *

STOIANOVICH, Traian 1921-

PERSONAL: Born July 20, 1921, in Grajesnica, Yugoslavia; son of Vasil and Menka (Naum) Stoianovich; married Marcelle Caffe (an artist), December 14, 1945; children: Christian, Diana. *Education:* University of Rochester, B.A., 1942; New York University, M.A., 1949; University of Paris, Doctorat Universite, 1952. *Home:* 60 Rector St., Metuchen, N.J. 08840. *Office:* Department of History, Rutgers University, New Brunswick, N.J. 08903.

CAREER: New York University, New York, N.Y., instructor in history, 1952-55; Rutgers University, New Brunswick, N.J., instructor, 1955-57, assistant professor, 1957-60, associate professor, 1961-67, professor of history, 1967—. Visiting assistant professor at University of California, Berkeley, summer, 1960, and Stanford University, 1960-61; visiting associate professor at New York University, summer, 1963, 1966-67; visiting professor at Sir George Williams University, summer, 1969. *Military service:* U.S. Army, Intelligence, 1942-45; became master sergeant. *Member:* American Historical Association, American Association of University Professors. *Awards, honors:* American Philosophical Society research fellow in Paris and Belgrade, 1958; Fulbright research fellow in Salonika, 1958-59.

WRITINGS: A Study in Balkan Civilization, Knopf, 1967; *French Historical Method: The "Annales" Paradigm,* Cornell University Press, 1976. Contributor to *Journal of Economic History, Slavic Review,* and other professional journals.

WORK IN PROGRESS: The Balkan city; Balkan society and economy, 1500 to the present; millenarian movements in the Balkans; the family in Europe and the Balkans; European society and economy.

SIDELIGHTS: Stoianovich is competent in French, German, Russian, Serbo-Croatian, and Bulgarian.

*   *   *

STOKER, Alan 1930-
(Alan Evans)

PERSONAL: Born October 2, 1930, in Sunderland, County Durham, England; son of Robert and Edith (Milne) Stoker; married Irene Evans, April 30, 1960; children: Neil Douglas, John Robert. *Education:* Attended schools in Sunderland, England, 1935-47. *Home:* 9 Dale Rd., Walton on Thames, Surrey, England. *Agent:* Murray Pollinger, 11 Long Acre, London WCZE 9LH, England.

CAREER: Civil servant in England, 1951—, currently as an executive officer. *Military service:* British Army, Royal Artillery, 1949-51. Army Reserve, now sergeant.

WRITINGS—Under pseudonym Alan Evans: *The End of the Running,* Cassell, 1966; *Mantrap,* Cassell, 1967; *Bannon,* Cassell, 1968; *Vicious Circle,* R. Hale, 1970; *The Big Deal,* R. Hale, 1971; *Running Scared,* Hodder Publications, 1975.

WORK IN PROGRESS: Kidnap, a childrens' thriller; an adventure novel.

AVOCATIONAL INTERESTS: Rugby football, beer, smoking ("hate gardening and any kind of work about the house").

*   *   *

STOLPER, Wolfgang F(riedrich) 1912-

PERSONAL: Born May 13, 1912, in Vienna, Austria; son of Gustav (a writer) and Paula (Deutsch) Stolper; married Martha Voegeli, August 11, 1938; children: Thomas Eliot, Matthew Wolfgang. *Education:* Studied at University of Berlin, 1930-31, University of Bonn, 1931-33, and University of Zurich, 1933-34; Harvard University, M.A., 1935, Ph.D., 1938. *Home:* Department of Economics, University of Michigan, Ann Arbor, Mich. 48104.

CAREER: Harvard University, Cambridge, Mass., instructor and tutor, 1936-41; Swarthmore College, Swarthmore, Pa., assistant professor, 1941-48, associate professor of economics, 1948-49; University of Michigan, Ann Arbor, associate professor, 1949-54, professor of economics, 1954—. Civilian research analyst, U.S. Strategic Bombing Survey, World War II. Lecturer at University of Heidelberg, 1948, and Massachusetts Institute of Technology, 1955-56; Fulbright professor, 1966; guest professor in Zurich, Switzerland, summers, 1969—. Chief of various missions abroad for United Nations, Agency for International Development, and International Bank for Reconstruction and Development (World Bank); consultant to Ford Foundation, UNESCO, and United Nations Economic Commission for Africa. *Member:* American Economic Association, Nigerian Economic Association. *Awards, honors:* Guggenheim fellow, 1947-48.

WRITINGS: (Translator with William H. Woglom) August Losch, *Economics of Location,* Yale University Press, 1954; *Structure of the East German Economy,* Harvard University Press, 1960; *Germany Between East and West,* National Planning Association, 1960; *Planning Without Facts,* Harvard University Press, 1966. Co-author of National Development Plan for Nigeria, 1962-68, and of other economic reports to United Nations, World Bank, and foreign governments. Contributor to learned journals.

WORK IN PROGRESS: Economic development problems.

AVOCATIONAL INTERESTS: Playing in chamber music groups.

*   *   *

STONE, Philip James III 1936-

PERSONAL: Born October 6, 1936, in Chicago, Ill.; son of Philip James, Jr. and Alice (Peterson) Stone. *Education:* University of Chicago, A.B., 1956; Harvard University, Ph.D., 1960. *Office:* Department of Social Relations, William James Hall 1250, Harvard University, Cambridge, Mass. 02138.

CAREER: National Institutes of Health, Bethesda, Md., psychologist in adult psychiatry branch, 1958-60; Harvard University, Cambridge, Mass., lecturer and research associate, department of social relations, 1960-67; Center for Advanced Study in the Behavioral Sciences, Stanford, Calif., fellow, 1967-69; Harvard University, Cambridge, Mass., associate professor, 1968, professor of social relations, 1969—.

WRITINGS: (With D. C. Dunphy, M. S. Smith, and D. M. Ogilvie) *The General Inquirer: A Computer Approach to Content Analysis,* M.I.T. Press, 1966; (with E. B. Hunt and J. Marin) *Experiments in Induction,* Academic Press, 1966; *User's Manual for the General Inquirer,* M.I.T. Press, 1969; (with G. Gerbner and others) *Analysis of Communication Content,* Wiley, 1969; (with A. Szalai and others) *The Use of Time,* Mouton & Co., 1972; (with E. Kelly) *Computer Recognition of English Word Senses,* North Holland Publishing, 1975. Contributor to journals.

WORK IN PROGRESS: A book on data structures in social sciences.

*   *   *

STONE, Wilfred (Healey) 1917-

PERSONAL: Born August 18, 1917, in Springfield, Mass.; son of Lester Lyman (a farmer and businessman) and Clara

(Gilbreth) Stone; married Cary Lee Laird (a psychiatric social worker), December 30, 1954; children: Gregory Ingram, Miriam Lee. *Education:* University of Minnesota, B.A., 1941, M.A., 1946; Harvard University, Ph.D., 1950. *Politics:* Democrat. *Home:* 830 Escondido Rd., Stanford, Calif. 94305. *Office:* Department of English, Stanford University, Stanford, Calif. 94305.

CAREER: Instructor, University of Minnesota, Minneapolis, 1946, Harvard University, summer, 1950; Stanford University, Stanford, Calif., instructor, later assistant professor, 1950-57, associate professor, 1957-63, professor of English literature, 1963—. Visiting summer professor, University of Vermont, 1954. *Military service:* U.S. Navy, Naval Aviation, 1942-45; became lieutenant. *Member:* Modern Language Association of America, American Association of University Professors. *Awards, honors:* Grants from Ford Foundation, 1953-54, Guggenheim Foundation, 1957-58, 1968, and American Council of Learned Societies, 1967; Dinkelspiel Award of Stanford University, 1962, for service to undergraduate education; Christian Gauss Award ($1,000) of Phi Beta Kappa Senate for best book of literary criticism, 1966, for *The Cave and the Mountain;* Commonwealth Club of California gold medal, 1966.

WRITINGS: Religion and Art of William Hale White ("Mark Rutherford"), Stanford University Press, 1954; (editor with Robert Hoopes) *Form and Thought in Prose,* Ronald, 1954; *The Cave and the Mountain: A Study of E. M. Forster,* Stanford University Press, 1966; (with J. G. Bell) *Prose Style: A Handbook for Writers,* McGraw, 1968, 3rd edition, 1975; (editor with Nancy Packer and Hoopes) *The Short Story: An Introduction,* McGraw, 1976.

WORK IN PROGRESS: Art and Money, a critical study.

SIDELIGHTS: Stanley Weintraub believes the *The Cave and the Mountain* is "the best of the many studies of E. M. Forster (Lionel Trilling's famous one not excepted)." Weintraub states that "it is rich with biographical and background data, eschews the sentimental platitudes chronic in Forster criticism, and provides tough-minded appraisals not only of Forster's novels and other works but of why the dean of English novelists withdrew from fiction-writing so early in his career." Andrew Wright agrees that Stone's book "is going to be a necessary adjunct to all Forster studies in [the] future, and a desideratum for all mere readers of Forster's novels."

Wright compliments Stone on his exhaustive research; "there aren't enough critics who are willing to go to the trouble Stone has gone to," he writes. He notes that Stone has read all of Forster's own works, including early essays which were published "in extremely fugitive circumstances"; he has read the writers whom Forster admired, talked and corresponded with Forster, and "tracked down biographical references to Forster in many out-of-the-way sources." Accordingly, Wright believes that the biographical section is "first-class."

BIOGRAPHICAL/CRITICAL SOURCES: Kenyon Review, June, 1966; *Books Abroad,* autumn, 1967.

* * *

STOREY, R(obin) L(indsay) 1927-

PERSONAL: Born July 25, 1927, in Newcastle upon Tyne, England; son of George Frederick and Jean Wright (Brough) Storey; married Sheila Bredon Challenger, June 16, 1956; children: Hugh James, Rachel Alison. *Education:* New College, Oxford, B.A., 1951, M.A., 1955; University

of Durham, Ph.D., 1954. *Home:* 19 Elm Ave., Beeston, Nottinghamshire, England. *Office:* History Department, University of Nottingham, Nottinghamshire, England.

CAREER: Public Record Office, London, England, assistant keeper, 1953-62; University of Nottingham, Nottinghamshire, England, lecturer, 1962-64, senior lecturer, 1964-66, reader in history, 1966-73, professor of English history, 1973—. *Member:* Royal Historical Society (fellow), Canterbury and York Society (honorary treasurer, 1958-65; member of council, 1965-68; honorary general editor, 1968—), Thornton Society of Nottinghamshire (honorary general editor of Record Section, 1966—).

WRITINGS: The Register of Thomas Langley, Volumes I-VI, Surtees Society, 1956-70; *Thomas Langley and the Bishopric of Durham,* S.P.C.K., 1961; *The End of the House of Lancaster,* Barrie & Rockliff, 1966, Stein & Day, 1967; *The Reign of Henry VII,* Blandford, 1968; *Chronology of the Medieval World 800-1491,* Barrie & Jenkins, 1973. Contributor of articles and reviews to history journals.

WORK IN PROGRESS: History of pre-Reformation church in England.

* * *

STORROW, H(ugh) A(lan) 1926-

PERSONAL: Born January 13, 1926, in Long Beach, Calif.; son of Joseph Henry (an accountant) and Iva (Strader) Storrow; married Ruth Ann Maggard, August 15, 1953; children: Joel Leslie, Alan Bruce, Richard French. *Education:* University of Southern California, A.B. (magna cum laude), 1946, M.D., 1950. *Politics:* Republican. *Religion:* Methodist. *Home:* 3050 Kirklevington Dr. #102, Lexington, Ky. 40502. *Office:* Department of Psychiatry, University of Kentucky Medical Center, Lexington, Ky. 40506.

CAREER: Licensed to practice medicine in California, 1950, Kentucky, 1960, and Minnesota, 1966; certified by American Board of Psychiatry and Neurology, 1955. Intern at U.S. Public Health Service Hospital, Baltimore, Md., 1949-50; resident or staff psychiatrist at hospitals in Maryland, Kentucky, Kansas, and California, 1950-55; Yale University, School of Medicine, New Haven, Conn., instructor in psychiatry, 1955-56; University of California, Los Angeles, School of Medicine, assistant professor of psychiatry, 1956-60, Medical Center, attending in psychiatry, 1957-60; University of Kentucky, School of Medicine, Lexington, associate professor of psychiatry, 1960-65, associate physician in department of psychiatry at university hospital, 1962-65; U.S. Public Health Service Hospital and U.S. Veterans Administration Hospital, Lexington, attending in psychiatry, 1960-65; University of Minnesota, Minneapolis, professor of psychiatry at School of Medicine and university hospitals, 1965-66; University of Kentucky, professor of psychiatry at School of Medicine and senior psychiatrist at university hospital, 1966—. Teaching consultant in psychiatry, School of Nursing, University of California Medical Center, 1957-60. *Military service:* U.S. Naval Reserve, 1943-46.

MEMBER: American Medical Association, American Psychiatric Association (fellow), Southern Psychiatric Association, Kentucky Psychiatric Association (president, 1974-76), Fayette County Medical Society, Phi Beta Kappa.

WRITINGS: (Contributor) A. S. Levy and A. L. Lincoln,

editors, *Methods and Standards of Client Evaluation,* Bureau of Rehabilitation Services, Kentucky Department of Education, 1961; (contributor) Riessman, Cohen, and Pearl, editors, *Mental Health of the Poor,* Free Press of Glencoe, 1965; (contributor) J. H. Masserman, editor, *Current Psychiatric Therapies,* Volume V, Grune, 1965; *Introduction to Scientific Psychiatry: A Behavioristic Approach to Diagnosis and Treatment,* Appleton, 1967; *Outline of Clinical Psychiatry,* Appleton, 1969. Contributor of about twenty-five articles and chapters to professional journals and books.

WORK IN PROGRESS: Problem-centered psychotherapy articles dealing with behavior modification, critical incident technique, and the use of the semantic differential to measure student attitudes toward psychiatry.

* * *

STORY, G(eorge) M(orley) 1927-

PERSONAL: Born October 13, 1927, in St. John's, Newfoundland; son of George Errington (an accountant) and Dorothy Katherine (White) Story. *Education:* Memorial University of Newfoundland, student, 1946-48; McGill University, B.A. (honors in English), 1950; Oxford University, D.Phil., 1954. *Politics:* Liberal Conservative. *Religion:* Methodist. *Home:* 335 Southside Rd., St. John's, Newfoundland, Canada.

CAREER: Memorial University of Newfoundland, St. John's, assistant professor, 1954-58, associate professor, 1959-63, professor of English, 1964—. Public orator, 1960—. *Member:* Bibliographical Society of Great Britain. *Awards, honors:* Rhodes scholarship, 1951-53.

WRITINGS: (With E. R. Seary) *Reading English,* Macmillan, 1958, revised edition published as *The Study of English,* St. Martin's, 1960; (editor with Helen Gardner) *The Sonnets of William Alabaster,* Oxford University Press, 1959; (editor) *Lancelot Andrewes: Sermons,* Clarendon Press, 1967; (with Seary and W. J. Kirwin) *The Avalon Peninsula of Newfoundland: An Ethno-linguistic Study,* National Museum of Canada, 1967; (editor with Herbert Halpert) *Christmas Mumming in Newfoundland: Essays in Anthropology, Folklore and History,* University of Toronto Press, 1969.

WORK IN PROGRESS: A Newfoundland dialect dictionary; a dictionary of Newfoundland proverbs; textual criticism and bibliography; a study of Tudor literature and Renaissance humanism (especially Erasmus).

AVOCATIONAL INTERESTS: Collecting rare books, especially European humanist works; travel and gardening.

* * *

STRACKBEIN, O(scar) R(obert) 1900-

PERSONAL: Born January 23, 1900, in Doss, Tex.; son of William Christian (a rancher) and Anna (Knopp) Strackbein; married Martha Arnold, 1936 (died April, 1958); married Anne Griffin, December 31, 1959; children (first marriage) Susie Rosalie (Mrs. Charles H. Thomas), William Christian. *Education:* University of Texas, B.A., 1920, M.B.A., 1922. *Home:* 3505 North Abingdon St., Arlington, Va. 22207. *Office:* 815 15th St. N.W., Washington, D.C. 20005.

CAREER: Washington and Lee University, Lexington, Va., assistant professor, 1922-24; assistant trade commissioner for U.S. Department of Commerce in Havana, Cuba, and Caracas, Venezuela, 1924-30; special expert, U.S. Tariff Commission, 1931-33; American Federation of Labor Unions, Washington, D.C., economist, 1933-37; U.S. Department of Labor, Washington, D.C., member of public contract board, 1937-41; Wallace Clark & Co., New York City, senior staff engineer, 1941-45; Parker & Strackbein (management engineers), New York City, partner, 1945-50; Nation-Wide Committee on Import-Export Policy (formerly National Labor Management Council on Foreign Trade Policy), Washington, D.C., founder, chairman, 1950-69, president, 1969—. Director, Applied Polytechnic Research Corp. *Military service:* U.S. Naval Reserve Force, 1918. *Member:* National Press Club, Phi Beta Kappa.

WRITINGS: The Prevailing Minimum Wage Standard, Graphic Arts Press, 1939; *American Enterprise and Foreign Trade,* Public Affairs Press, 1965; *Philosophy of Self-Management,* Fell, 1967; *The Anatomy of Civilization,* Fell, 1969; *Permissiveness,* Vantage, 1970. Contributor to journals.

AVOCATIONAL INTERESTS: Philosophy, psychology, gardening, and amateur ornithology.

* * *

STRAND, Mark 1934-

PERSONAL: Born April 11, 1934, in Summerside, Prince Edward Island, Canada; son of Robert Joseph and Sonia (Apter) Strand; married Antonia Ratensky, September 14, 1961 (divorced, 1974); children: Jessica. *Education:* Antioch College, B.A., 1957; Yale University, B.F.A., 1959; State University of Iowa, M.A., 1962. *Home:* 169 West 21st St., New York, N.Y. 10011.

CAREER: University of Iowa, Iowa City, instructor in English, 1962-65; University of Brazil, Rio de Janeiro, Fulbright lecturer, 1965-66; Mount Holyoke College, South Hadley, Mass., assistant professor, 1967; visiting professor at University of Washington, Seattle, 1968, 1970, Columbia University, New York, N.Y., 1969, and Yale University, New Haven, Conn., 1969-70; Brooklyn College of the City University of New York, associate professor, 1970-72; Princeton University, Princeton, N.J., Bain-Swiggett Lecturer, 1973—. Hurst Professor of Poetry, Brandeis University, Waltham, Mass. *Awards, honors:* Fulbright scholarship for study in Italy, 1960-61; Ingram Merrill fellowship, 1966; National Council for the Humanities grant, 1967-68; Rockefeller fellowship, 1968-69; Edgar Allan Poe award, 1974; National Institute of Arts and Letters award, 1975; Guggenheim fellowship, 1975-76.

WRITINGS: Sleeping with One Eye Open (poems), Stone Wall Press, 1964; *Reasons for Moving* (poems), Atheneum, 1968; (editor) *The Contemporary American Poets,* New American Library, 1968; *Darker* (poems), Atheneum, 1970; (editor) *New Poetry of Mexico* (anthology), Dutton, 1970; (translator) *18 Poems from the Quechua,* Halty Ferguson, 1971; (translator and editor) Rafael Alberti, *The Owl's Insomnia,* Atheneum, 1973; *The Sargeantville Notebook* (poems), Burning Deck, 1974; *The Story of Our Lives* (poems), Atheneum, 1973; (editor with Charles Simic) *Another Republic: Seventeen European and South American Writers,* Ecco Press, 1976.

WORK IN PROGRESS: More poems; translations of Carlos Drummond de Andrade.

SIDELIGHTS: The *Virginia Quarterly Review* writes of *Reasons for Moving:* "Mr. Strand is highly successful in erasing the boundary between dreams and reality. The resulting sensation is frightening, but refreshing." Donald

Sheehan notes that the "poems become parables—brief tales which are fully lucid in their own terms and yet utterly beyond explanation in any other.... Each image in the sequence follows from and prepares for another. The poem thus has an Aristotelean logic.... This logical order rests, though, on an absolutely illogical premise." A few of the poems demonstrate "a kind of elegantly flawless art," according to Laurence Lieberman, "that bespeaks a perfect tuning of the instrument."

In *Darker,* "Strand has found his own precarious voice," writes the *Antioch Review,* "and we must rejoice to accept this important collection by a major poet of our days."

Strand told *CA* that translating "is not an activity I enjoy, but rather a discipline I find instructive. I travel when I can."

BIOGRAPHICAL/CRITICAL SOURCES: Yale Review, autumn, 1968; *Contemporary Literature,* Volume X, number 2, 1969; *Virginia Quarterly Review,* summer, 1969; *Antioch Review,* fall/winter, 1970-71; Carolyn Riley, editor, *Contemporary Literary Criticism,* Volume VI, Gale, 1976.

*   *   *

STRAUS, Murray A(rnold)   1926-

PERSONAL: Born June 18, 1926, in New York, N.Y.; son of Samuel (a wholesaler) and Kathleen (Miller) Straus; married Jacqueline Harris (a craft store proprietor), February 28, 1948; children: Carol Marie, John Samuel. *Education:* University of Wisconsin, B.A., 1948, M.S., 1949, Ph.D., 1956. *Politics:* Left-wing Democrat. *Religion:* Unitarian Universalist. *Home:* R.F.D. 1, Durham, N.H. *Office:* University of New Hampshire, Durham, N.H. 03824.

CAREER: University of Ceylon, Colombo, lecturer in sociology, 1949-52; Washington State University, Pullman, assistant professor of sociology, 1954-57; University of Wisconsin—Madison, assistant professor of sociology, 1957-59; Cornell University, Ithaca, N.Y., associate professor of family sociology, 1959-61; University of Minnesota, Minneapolis, professor of sociology, College of Liberal Arts, 1961-68, chairman of Division of Family Social Science, School of Home Economics, 1961-64; University of New Hampshire, Durham, professor of sociology, 1968—. Visiting professor, University of York, England, 1974, and University of Massachusetts, 1975. Member of advisory panel on marriage and divorce statistics, National Office of Vital Statistics, 1963-65; National Council on Family Relations, member of board of directors, 1963-70, president, 1972-73; Groves Conference on the Family, member of board of directors, 1968-70, chairman, 1968; member of advisory panel on social problems research, National Institute of Mental Health, 1972-76. *Military service:* U.S. Army, 1944-46.

MEMBER: International Sociological Association, International Society for Research on Aggression, American Sociological Association (secretary-treasurer, methodology section, 1966-69; council, family section, 1967-70), Rural Sociological Society, Society for Applied Anthropology, Society for the Study of Social Problems, Association for Asian Studies, Indian Sociological Society, Royal Asiatic Society (Ceylon branch), American Association for the Advancement of Science, American Association of University Professors, Midwest Sociological Society. *Awards, honors:* Fulbright research scholar at University of Bombay, 1964-65.

WRITINGS: (With Joel I. Nelson) *Sociological Analysis:*
An Empirical Approach Through Replication, Harper, 1968; (editor) *Family Analysis: Readings and Replications of Selected Studies,* Rand McNally, 1969; *Family Measurement Techniques,* University of Minnesota Press, 1969; (co-editor) *Family Problem Solving,* Dryden, 1971; (co-editor) *Violence in the Family,* Dodd, 1974.

Contributor: Neil J. Smelser, William T. Smelser, editors, *Personality and Social Systems,* Wiley, 1963; Marvin B. Sussman, editor, *Sourcebook in Marriage and the Family,* Houghton, 1968. Contributor to other symposia and *Collier's Encyclopedia Yearbook;* writer of a number of Agricultural Experiment Station bulletins in Washington State and Wisconsin. Co-compiler of index to *Marriage and Family Living,* Volumes I-XXIV, published as separate issue by National Council on Family Relations, September, 1963; about sixty articles have appeared in professional journals. Assistant editor, *Sociological Abstracts,* 1957-59; editor, "Articles in Brief," *Marriage and Family Living,* 1960—; founding editor, *Teaching Sociology,* 1973—. Member of publications committee, Midwest Sociological Society, 1962-64; member of publications board, National Council on Family Relations, 1966-69, and chairman of board, 1967-68.

WORK IN PROGRESS: Class and Family in Three Societies: A Study in Bombay, Minneapolis and San Juan.

AVOCATIONAL INTERESTS: Sailing, skiing, photography, travel.

*   *   *

STRENG, Frederick J.   1933-

PERSONAL: Born September 30, 1933, in Seguin, Tex.; son of Adolph Carl (a teacher) and Elizabeth (Hein) Streng; married Ruth Helen Billnitzer, June 6, 1955; children: Elizabeth Ann, Mark Andrew. *Education:* Texas Lutheran College, B.A., 1955; Southern Methodist University, M.A., 1956; Wartburg Theological Seminary, further study, 1956-57; University of Chicago, B.D., 1960, Ph.D., 1963; Benares Hindu University, graduate study, 1961-62. *Politics:* Independent. *Religion:* "Liberal Christian." *Office:* Southern Methodist University, Dallas, Tex. 75222.

CAREER: University of Dubuque, Dubuque, Iowa, instructor in English, 1957; University of Southern California, Los Angeles, assistant professor of history of religions, 1963-66; Southern Methodist University, Dallas, associate professor of history of religions, 1966-73, professor of religion, 1974—. Carnegie Fellow in the Civilization of India, University of Chicago, 1962-63; visiting associate professor, University of California, Berkeley, spring, 1973; visiting professor, Divinity School, Harvard University, fall, 1973. *Member:* American Academy of Religion, American Society for the Study of Religion, Association for Asian Studies, American Oriental Society, American Association of University Professors, Society for Religion in Higher Education. *Awards, honors:* Fulbright grant to India, 1961-62.

WRITINGS: Emptiness: A Study in Religious Meaning, Abingdon, 1967; *Understanding Religious Man,* Dickenson, 1969; (editor with others) *Ways of Being Religious: Readings for a New Approach to Religion,* Prentice-Hall, 1973. Contributor to professional journals.

WORK IN PROGRESS: Editing "Religious Life of Man," a series of paperbacks for college students on the major world religions; research in Buddhist "perfection of wisdom" literature; development of a method for studying religion combining elements of "structuralism" and phenomenology; research in the significance of the history of religions for Christian theology.

AVOCATIONAL INTERESTS: Music, the plastic arts, creative literature, and photography.

* * *

STRICKLAND, Arvarh E(unice) 1930-

PERSONAL: Born July 6, 1930, in Hattiesburg, Miss.; son of Eunice (a plasterer) and Clotiel (Marshall) Strickland; married Willie Pearl Elmore (a teacher), June 17, 1951; children: Duane Arvarh, Bruce Elmore. *Education:* Tougaloo College, A.B. (summa cum laude), 1951; University of Illinois, M.A., 1953, Ph.D., 1962. *Politics:* Democrat. *Relgiion:* Methodist. *Home:* 4100 Defoe Dr., Columbia, Mo. 65201. *Office:* Department of History, University of Missouri, Columbia, Mo. 65201.

CAREER: High school teacher in Hattiesburg, Miss., 1951-52; Tuskegee Institute, Tuskegee, Ala., instructor in history, 1955-56; high school principal in Camden, Miss., 1956-57; supervisor of Madison County (Miss.) Negro schools, 1957-59; Chicago State College (now University), Chicago, Ill., assistant professor, 1962-65, associate professor, 1965-68, professor of American history, 1968-69; University of Missouri, Columbia, professor of history, 1969—, special assistant to the chancellor, winter, 1972. Visiting lecturer, University of Illinois, summer, 1967. *Military service:* U.S. Army, 1953-55. U.S. Army Reserve, 1955-61. *Member:* American Historical Association, Organization of American Historians, American Association of University Professors, National Association for the Advancement of Colored People, Association for the Study of Afro-American Life and History, Southern Historical Association, Illinois State Historical Society, Chicago Historical Society, Chicago Urban League, Alpha Phi Alpha. *Awards, honors:* Woodrow Wilson fellow, 1959.

WRITINGS: *History of the Chicago Urban League,* University of Illinois Press, 1966; (with Jerome Reich and Edward Biller) *Building the United States,* Harcourt, 1971; (with Reich) *The Black American Experience,* Harcourt, 1974. Contributor to history journals.

WORK IN PROGRESS: *History of Illinois, 1930-1968.*

* * *

STRICKLAND, Rennard (James) 1940-

PERSONAL: Born September 26, 1940, in St. Louis, Mo.; son of R. J. (a businessman) and Adell G. (director of senior citizen programs) Strickland. *Education:* Northeastern State College, Tahlequah, Okla., B.A., 1962; University of Virginia, J.D., 1965, S.J.D., 1970; University of Arkansas, M.A., 1966. *Office:* School of Law, University of Tulsa, Tulsa, Okla. 74104.

CAREER: University of Arkansas, Fayetteville, assistant professor and coordinator of basic speech, 1966-69; University of West Florida, Pensacola, assistant professor, 1970-71; St. Mary's University of San Antonio, San Antonio, Tex., associate professor, 1971-72; University of Tulsa, Tulsa, Okla., associate professor, 1972-74, professor of law, 1975, acting dean of law, 1974; University of Washington, Seattle, associate professor of law, 1975-76; University of Tulsa, John W. Shleppey Research Professor of Law, 1976—. Fellow of Doris Duke Foundation, 1970-73, and American Bar Foundation; Sylvan Lange Distinguished Visiting Professor, St. Mary's University, summer, 1972;

member of Prelaw Committee, Law School Admissions Council, 1974-76; visiting professor, University of New Mexico, summer, 1975. Director, Indian Heritage Association, 1966—; visitor, Indian Law Center, 1974-75.

MEMBER: American Society of Legal History, American Judicaire Society, Communications Association of America, Seldon Society, Phi Alpha Delta, Phi Delta Phi, Pi Kappa Delta, Delta Sigma Rho, Tau Kappa Alpha, Alpha Chi. *Awards, honors:* American Council of Learned Societies fellow, 1972.

WRITINGS: (With Donal Stanton and Jimmie N. Rogers) *Sourcebook on Labor Management Relations,* Debate Sourcebook, 1965; (with Stanton) *Sourcebook on Economic-Military Assistance,* Debate Sourcebook, 1966; (with Jack Gregory) *Sourcebook on Criminal Investigation,* Debate Sourcebook, 1967; *Sam Houston with the Cherokees, 1829-1833,* University of Texas Press, 1967; (editor with Gregory) *Starr's History of the Cherokees,* Indian Heritage Association, 1967; (with Gregory) *Sourcebook on the Draft,* Debate Sourcebook, 1968; (with Gregory) *Cherokee Spirit Tales,* Indian Heritage Association, 1969.

(With Gregory) *Sourcebook on Environmental Policy,* Debate Sourcebook, 1970; (editor with Richard Johannesen and Ralph Eubanks) *Language Is Sermonic: Richard M. Weaver on the Nature of Rhetoric,* Louisiana State University Press, 1970; (with Gregory) *Sourcebook on Judicial Reform,* Debate Sourcebook, 1971; (with Gregory) *Creek-Seminole Spirit Tales,* Indian Heritage Association, 1971; (editor with Gregory) *Hell on the Border: He Hanged Eighty-eight Men,* Indian Heritage Association, 1972; (with Gregory) *Choctaw Spirit Tales,* Indian Heritage Association, 1973; (with Gregory) *American Indian Spirit Tales,* Indian Heritage Association, 1973; *How to Get into Law School,* Hawthorn, 1974; *Fire and the Spirits: Cherokee Law from Clan to Court,* University of Oklahoma Press, 1975; *Teachers on Trail: A Legal Primer for the Classroom Teachers,* Hawthorn, 1976. Also author, with Earl B. Pierce, of *The Cherokee People,* 1973. Contributor to proceedings, and to professional journals.

WORK IN PROGRESS: *American Indian Law and Policy,* with Fred Ragsdale; *Careers in Law; 1976-1977 Prelaw Handbook; Law at the Dawn,* with Garrick Bailey; *The Creek Way: Law in an Indian Confederacy; Before the Trail of Tears: The Cherokee Removal Debate,* with William Strickland; *Communications in a Changing Society,* with Jack Gregory; a book with Gregory, tentatively entitled *American Indian Women;* editing *Federal Handbook of Indian Law.*

* * *

STROH, Thomas F. 1924-

PERSONAL: Born November 2, 1924, in Freeport, N.Y.; son of August F. (a certified public accountant) and Florence Stroh; married Audrey Merrit, September 19, 1946. *Education:* Colgate University, B.A., 1948; Columbia University, M.A., 1963, professional diploma, 1965, Ed.D., 1968. *Home:* 507 Northwest 87th Ave., Miami, Fla. 33172.

CAREER: Dun & Bradstreet, New York City, reporter, 1948-52; Shaw Walker, New York City, salesman, 1952-57; sales manager, 1957-64; West Virginia Pulp & Paper Co., New York City, supervisor of marketing training, 1964-66; private business education consultant, 1966—; Florida Atlantic University, Boca Raton, member of Department of Marketing faculty, 1968—. Editor and trustee, Intercollegiate Video Clearing House, 1974—. *Military service:* U.S.

Marine Corps, 1942-46; participated in three invasions; wounded twice. *Member:* Phi Kappa Psi, Delta Pi Epsilon. *Awards, honors:* Landis Annual Film Competition first prize, Industrial Management Society, 1974, for "Eastern Air Lines Marketing Case History."

WRITINGS: Salesmanship: Personal Communication and Persuasian in Marketing, Irwin, 1966; *Techniques of Practical Selling,* Dow Jones-Irwin, 1966; *The Uses of Video Tape in Training and Development,* American Management Association, 1969; *Managing the New Generation in Business,* McGraw, 1972; *Training and Developing the Professional Salesman,* American Management Association, 1973; *Effective Psychology for Sales Managers,* Prentice-Hall, 1974; *The Purchasing Guide to the Naked Salesman,* Cahners, 1975. Author and producer of eleven educational films for Florida Atlantic University, including "Eastern Air Lines Marketing Case History," 1974, and "Styles of Leadership," 1975.

WORK IN PROGRESS: Sales Management: People and Functions, for McGraw.

*   *   *

STRONG, Leah A(udrey) 1922-

PERSONAL: Born March 14, 1922, in Buffalo, N.Y.; daughter of Robert Leroy and Dorothy (Kennedy) Strong. *Education:* Allegheny College, A.B., 1943; Cornell University, A.M., 1944; Syracuse University, Ph.D., 1953. *Home:* 1173 Forest Hill Rd., Macon, Ga. 31204. *Office:* Wesleyan College, Macon, Ga. 31201.

CAREER: Syracuse University, Syracuse, N.Y., instructor in English, 1947-52; Cedar Crest College, Allentown, Pa., assistant professor of English, 1953-61; Wesleyan College, Macon, Ga., professor of American studies, 1961—. *Member:* American Studies Association, Modern Language Association of America, American Association of University Professors, Southeastern American Studies Association (secretary-treasurer, 1972—), South Atlantic Modern Language Association, Southern Humanities Conference (chairman, 1974-75).

WRITINGS: Joseph Hopkins Twichell: Mark Twain's Friend and Pastor, University of Georgia Press, 1966. Contributor to *Pacific Northwest Quarterly, Mississippi Quarterly,* and other periodicals.

WORK IN PROGRESS: Research on Mark Twain and Charles Dudley Warner.

*   *   *

SUGARMAN, Daniel A(rthur) 1931-

PERSONAL: Born March 16, 1931, in New York, N.Y.; son of Louis (a musician) and Sue (Newman) Sugarman; married Barbara Levine (a psychologist), February 22, 1959; children: Jeremy, Rhona, Amy. *Education:* New York University, B.A., 1952; Columbia University, M.A., 1953, Ph.D., 1957. *Politics:* Independent. *Religion:* Jewish. *Home:* 275 Springfield Ave., Paramus, N.J. 07652. *Agent:* Curtis Brown Ltd., 60 East 56th St., New York, N.Y. 10022. *Office:* 681 Broadway, Paterson, N.J.

CAREER: Psychologist at Veterans Administration Hospital, Montrose, N.Y., 1953-57, for West Milford (N.J.) public schools, 1955-57, and Wayne (N.J.) public schools, 1957-62; psychologist in private practice, Paterson, N.J., 1959—; William Paterson College of New Jersey, Wayne, associate professor of education, 1961—. Consultant, St. Mary's Hospital, Passaic, N.J., 1958—. *Member:* Amer-

ican Psychological Association, American Academy of Psychotherapy, New Jersey Psychological Association.

WRITINGS: (With Rolaine Hochstein) *Seven Stories for Growth,* Pitman, 1965; (with Hochstein) *Seventeen Guide to Knowing Yourself,* Macmillan, 1967; (with Lucy Freeman) *Search for Serenity,* Macmillan, 1970; (with Hochstein) *The Seventeen Guide to You and Other People,* Macmillan, 1972. Contributor to magazines, including *Reader's Digest* and *Seventeen.*

AVOCATIONAL INTERESTS: Travel, skiing, tennis.

*   *   *

SUGARMAN, Tracy 1921-

PERSONAL: Born November 14, 1921, in Syracuse, N.Y.; son of David (a lawyer) and Golda (Sophian) Sugarman: married June Feldman (a worker in inter-group relations), September 24, 1943; children: Richard Steven, Laurie Ellen. *Education:* Syracuse University, B.F.A., 1943. *Politics:* Democrat. *Religion:* Jewish. *Home:* 9 Old Hill Rd., Westport, Conn. *Agent:* Monica McCall, Inc., 667 Madison Ave., New York, N.Y. 10021. *Office:* Rediscovery Productions, Inc., 2 Halfmile Common, Westport, Conn. 06880.

CAREER: Free-lance illustrator, 1945-69, work appeared in many national magazines, including *Ladies' Home Journal, McCall's, Esquire,* and *Saturday Evening Post;* also illustrator for William Morrow and Co., Simon and Schuster, Doubleday & Co., and other publishing houses, pictorial reportage for American industry and governmental agencies; Rediscovery Productions, Inc. (educational documentary film producers), Westport, Conn., co-founder, writer, and producer, 1969—. Vice-chairman, Fairfield County Democratic Council. *Military service:* U.S. Navy, 1943-45; smallboat officer in Normany Invasion; became lieutenant junior grade. *Member:* Society of Illustrators, American Association for the United Nations (past president, Westport chapter), Westport Artists Association (past president).

WRITINGS: Stranger at the Gates, Hill & Wang, 1966. Also author of six documentary films for CBS-TV, including "How Beautiful on the Mountains." Contributor of articles to *American Artist, Vista Volunteer,* and U.S. Information Agency publication.

SIDELIGHTS: Sugarman participated in the Mississippi Summer Project in 1964, and has since been "deeply involved" in the civil rights movement as a lecturer and worker. This involvement is shared with his wife and children; all have been working with civil rights groups.

*   *   *

SUH, Dae-Sook 1931-

PERSONAL: Born November 22, 1931, in Hoeryong, Korea; son of Ch'ang-hi (a minister) and Chong-hi (Paik) Suh; married Yun-ok Park (a chemist), October 29, 1960; children: Maurice Min-ho, Kevin Min-kul. *Education:* Texas Christian University, B.A., 1956; Indiana University, M.A., 1958; Columbia University, Ph.D., 1964. *Home:* 7122 Niumalu Loop, Honolulu, Hawaii 96825. *Office:* Department of Political Science, University of Hawaii, Honolulu, Hawaii 96822.

CAREER: Columbia University, New York, N.Y., research associate of East Asian Institute, 1964-65, 1968-69; University of Houston, Houston, Tex., 1965-70, began as assistant professor, became associate professor of political science; University of Hawaii, Honolulu, senior fellow of East-West Center, 1971, professor of political science, 1972—, director, Center for Korean Studies, 1973—. *Member:* American Political Science Association, Association for Asian Studies.

WRITINGS: Korean Communist Movement, 1918-1948, Princeton University Press, 1967; (contributor) R. F. Staar, editor, *Communist Ruled States,* University of South Carolina Press, 1968; (contributor) Collier and Glaser, editors, *The Conditions for Peace in Europe,* Public Affairs Press, 1969; *Documents of Korean Communism, 1918-49,* Princeton University Press, 1970; (contributor) T. T. Hammond, editor, *The Anatomy of Communist Takeover,* Yale University Press, 1975; (editor) *Political Leadership in Korea,* University of Washington Press, 1976.

WORK IN PROGRESS: The Workers' Party of Korea, 1945-75.

SIDELIGHTS: Suh is competent in Chinese, Japanese, Russian, and French.

*   *   *

SULEIMAN, Michael W(adie)   1934-

PERSONAL: Born February 26, 1934, in Tiberias, Palestine; son of Wadie Michael and Jameeleh (Ailabouny) Suleiman; married Penelope Ann Powers (a bacteriologist), August 31, 1963; children: Suad Michelle, Gibran Michael. *Education:* Bradley University, B.A., 1960; University of Wisconsin, M.S., 1962, Ph.D., 1965. *Home:* 427 Wickham Rd., Manhattan, Kan. 66502. *Office:* Department of Political Science, Kansas State University, Manhattan, Kan. 66506.

CAREER: Kansas State University, Manhattan, assistant professor, 1965-68, associate professor, 1968-72, professor of political science, 1972—, head of department, 1975—. Member of Midwest Conference of Political Scientists, and American Research Center in Egypt. *Member:* American Political Science Association, Middle East Institute, Middle East Studies Association of North America. *Awards, honors:* Ford Foundation fellowship, 1969-70; American Research Center in Egypt fellowship, 1972-73.

WRITINGS: Political Parties in Lebanon: The Challenge of a Fragmented Political Culture, Cornell University Press, 1967; (contributor) Elaine C. Hagopian and Ann Paden, editors, *The Arab-Americans: Studies in Assimilation,* Medina University Press, 1969; (contributor) T. Y. Ismael, editor, *Governments and Politics of the Contemporary Middle East,* Dorsey, 1970; (contributor) Ibrahim Abu-Lughod, editor, *The Arab-Israeli Confrontation of June, 1967: An Arab Perspective,* Northwestern University Press, 1970; (contributor) Michael H. Prosser, editor, *Intercommunication Among Nations and Peoples,* Harper, 1973. Also author of *Guide to a Correspondence Course in International Relations,* 1966. Contributor to political science journals.

WORK IN PROGRESS: Research on political socialization in the Arab world, a study of values and the process of inculcation of values in the young.

SIDELIGHTS: Suleiman did research in Lebanon, as Vilas traveling fellow from University of Wisconsin, 1963-64, and spent summer of 1965 in Geneva under United Nations internship program.

*   *   *

SULLENS, Idelle   1921-

PERSONAL: Born June 28, 1921, in Prairie City, Ore.; daughter of Russell H. and Madeleine (Barlow) Sullens. *Education:* Northwestern School of Commerce, Portland, Ore., secretarial certificate, 1939; Stanford University, A.B. (with distinction), 1943, Ph.D., 1959; University of Washington, Seattle, M.A., 1950. *Home address:* Box 4418, Carmel, Calif. 93921. *Office:* Monterey Peninsula College, Monterey, Calif. 93940.

CAREER: Employed in various business positions, 1939-41; U.S. Naval Reserve, active duty, 1944-49, 1950-54, leaving service as commander in Supply Corps; Monterey Peninsula College, Monterey, Calif., instructor in English and humanities, 1958—, head of department, 1968-69. *Member:* Early English Text Society, Modern Language Association of America, National Council of Teachers of English, American Association of University Women, California Teachers Association.

WRITINGS: Principles of Grammar, Prentice-Hall, 1966; (editor with Edith Karas and Raymond Fabrizio) *The Inquiring Reader,* Health, 1967, 2nd edition, 1974; *The Whole Idea Catalog,* Random House, 1971; (with others) *Gentrain: An Interdisciplinary Approach to the Humanities,* National Endowment for the Humanities, 1974.

WORK IN PROGRESS: An anthology of readings, tentatively entitled *Literature: The Western Tradition,* four volumes; *The Works of Robert Mannyng of Brunne: 1303-1338;* a volume of personal verse to be issued privately.

*   *   *

SULLIVAN, Clara K(atherine)   1915-

PERSONAL: Born April 4, 1915, in Brooklyn, N.Y.; daughter of Harry (an insurance executive) and Marie (Graber) Freedberg; married John Paul Sullivan (an insurance broker), February 7, 1948. *Education:* Mount Holyoke College, B.A., 1936; Columbia University, M.A., 1943, Ph.D., 1959. *Home:* 336 Pensacola Rd., Venice, Fla. 33595. *Office:* Theodore W. Barber, Attorney, 307 West Venice Ave., Venice, Fla. 33595.

CAREER: Chase National Bank, New York City, research assistant, 1943-48; private research in public finance, Boston, Mass., 1948-58; Harvard University Law School, Cambridge, Mass., economist, International Program in Taxation, 1959-64; Columbia University, New York City, senior economist, International Economic Integration Program, 1963-64; private economic research, Boston, 1964-67; Houghton Mifflin Co., Boston, economics editor, 1967-69; free-lance editor, 1969—; Theodore W. Barber (attorney), Venice, Fla., office manager, 1969—. *Member:* American Economic Association, Taxation with Representation, Venice Taxpayers' League.

WRITINGS: The Search for Tax Principles in the European Economic Community, Harvard Law School, 1963; *The Tax on Value Added,* Columbia University Press, 1965; (contributor) Carl S. Shoup, editor, *Fiscal Harmonization in Common Markets,* Columbia University Press, 1967.

*   *   *

SULLIVAN, John L.   1908-

PERSONAL: Born December 12, 1908, son of John L. and Catherine (McNellis) Sullivan; married Jean Masten (a clerk-stenographer), March 17, 1942; children: John, Gregory, Laurie Jean. *Education:* Virginia Junior College, Virginia, Minn., A.A., 1928; College of St. Thomas, LL.B., 1933; University of California, Los Angeles, Class A Vocational Educational Credential, 1966. *Religion:* Roman Catholic. *Home:* 1402 Spruce St., South Pasadena, Calif. 91030.

CAREER: Federal Bureau of Investigation, Los Angeles, Calif., special agent, 1941-62; Pasadena City College, Pasadena, Calif., assistant professor and coordinator of police science, 1963-64. South Pasadena, Calif., city councilman, 1966-72, 1974-78, mayor, 1972-74. *Member:* Society of Former Special Agents of the F.B.I., California State Police Officers' Association, Los Angeles County Peace Officer's Association (life member), Loyal Order of the Moose.

WRITINGS: Introduction to Police Science, McGraw, 1966, 2nd edition, 1971.

*   *   *

SUMMERFIELD, John D(udley)   1927-
(Jack D. Summerfield)

PERSONAL: Born August 16, 1927, in Dallas, Tex.; son of Edward C. (a salesman) and Deyo (Hayden) Summerfield; married Preshia Chauncey, September 7, 1957; children: Edward Ford, Jenna Lynn. *Education:* University of Texas, B.F.A., 1949, M.A., 1954; also studied at Columbia University, 1959-60, and took advanced management course at Harvard University, 1961. *Politics:* Independent Democrat. *Religion:* "Interdenominational Protestant." *Home:* 9271 Virginian Lane, LaMesa, Calif. 92041. *Office:* KPBS Stations, San Diego State University, San Diego, Calif.

CAREER: WGBH, Boston, Mass., FM manager, 1950-52 and 1956-59; Riverside Radio WRVR (FM), New York City, general manager, 1960-68; consultant, Ford Foundation, 1968-69; New School for Social Research, New York City, director of urban reporting project, 1969-70; Corporation for Public Broadcasting, New York City, project officer, 1970-71; stations KPBS-TV and KPBS-FM, San Diego, Calif., general manager, 1971—. JDS Associates (telecommunications production and consultants), New York City, director, beginning 1964. Broadcaster on radio and television; executive producer, "We Shall Overcome" (civil rights film), Brandon Films. Chairman of Eastern Educational Radio Network, 1962, and National Educational Radio Network, 1963; chairman of national advisory committee, Educational Communications System, 1963-66; member of executive committee, Armstrong Memorial Research Foundation Awards, 1965—. *Military service:* U.S. Navy, 1945-46. U.S. Army, 1952-54; became first lieutenant.

MEMBER: National Association of Educational Broadcasters (vice-chairman of board of directors, 1966), International Radio and Television Society, New York State Educational Radio-Television Association (treasurer and trustee, 1960-63), Overseas Press Club, Sigma Delta Chi, Alpha Epsilon Rho. *Awards, honors:* CBS News and Public Affairs fellowship at Columbia University, 1959-60; under his direction, Riverside Radio WRVR has received seventeen national awards, including Armstrong Foundation Awards, 1964, 1965, 1967, and 1968, George Foster Peabody Award, 1965, and duPont Award, 1966.

WRITINGS—Under name Jack D. Summerfield: (Editor with Lorlyn Thatcher) *The Creative Mind and Method,* University of Texas Press, 1960; (contributor) David Brown and Richard Bruner, editors, *How I Got That Story,* Dutton, 1966. Contributor to educational journals.

WORK IN PROGRESS: The history of educational radio.†

SUNDELL, Roger H(enry)   1936-

PERSONAL: Born May 1, 1936, in Jamestown, N.Y.; son of Arnold C. and Mary (Robertson) Sundell; married Julie Pearce, June 16, 1964 (divorced, 1973). *Education:* Yale University, A.B., 1959; Washington University, St. Louis, Mo., M.A., 1963, Ph.D., 1965. *Office:* Department of English, University of Wisconsin, Milwaukee, Wis. 53201.

CAREER: University of Delaware, Newark, began as instructor, assistant professor of English, 1964-68; University of Wisconsin-Milwaukee, assistant professor, 1968-72, associate professor of English, 1972—, associate chairman of department, 1971-74. *Member:* Modern Language Association of America, Renaissance Society of America, Milton Society of America, American Association of University Professors. *Awards, honors:* Summer faculty fellowship, University of Delaware, 1966.

WRITINGS: (Compiler with R. F. Dietrich) *The Art of Fiction: A Handbook and Anthology,* with instructor's manual, Holt, 1967, 2nd edition, 1974. Contributor of articles to journals. Associate editor, *Seventeenth Century News.*

WORK IN PROGRESS: A series of essays on the narrative method in John Milton's *Paradise Lost* and *Paradise Regained.*

*   *   *

SURACE, Samuel J.   1919-

PERSONAL: Surname is pronounced Sir-*ace;* born January 10, 1919, in East Rochester, N.Y.; son of James and Serina (Speranza) Surace; married Elizabeth M. Hasson (a composer), September 8, 1947. *Education:* Los Angeles City College, A.A., 1949; University of California, Los Angeles, B.A., 1952, M.A., 1954; University of California, Berkeley, Ph.D., 1961. *Home:* 10564 Lauriston Ave., Los Angeles, Calif. 90064. *Office:* Department of Sociology, University of California, Los Angeles, Calif. 90024.

CAREER: University of California, Los Angeles, assistant professor, 1961-68, associate professor of sociology, 1968—. Consultant, U.S. Office of Economic Opportunity. *Member:* American Sociological Association, Pacific Sociological Association, Phi Beta Kappa.

WRITINGS: Ideology, Economic Change and the Working Classes: The Case of Italy, University of California Press, 1966; (co-author) *The Mexican-American People,* Free Press, 1970. Contributor to sociology journals.

WORK IN PROGRESS: Migration and settlement in urban places; social change: studies and theories.

AVOCATIONAL INTERESTS: Music (former professional jazz guitarist), public affairs, art, social history.

*   *   *

SUTHERLAND, Douglas   1919-

PERSONAL: Born November 18, 1919, in Appleby, Westmoreland, England; son of George Gordon and Hope (Paton) Sutherland; married Moyra Fraser (an actress), 1943; married second wife, Susan Justice, 1953; married third wife, Diana Francesca Fendall, 1962; children: (first marriage) Carol; (second marriage) James, Adam; (third marriage) Charles, Joanna. *Education:* Educated in Scotland. *Politics:* None. *Religion:* Presbyterian. *Home:* Rohallian Lodge, Murthly, Perthshire, Scotland. *Agent:* A. M. Heath Ltd., 40-42 William IV St., London WC2N

4DD, England; and Richard Curtis, 156 East 52nd St., New York, N.Y. 10022.

CAREER: Voice and Vision (public relations firm), London, England, managing director, 1950-55; Directors' Wine Club Ltd., London, managing director, 1955-60; author. Director, Aberdeen Stadiums Ltd. *Military service:* British Army, 1939-46; became major; received Military Cross, and was twice mentioned in dispatches.

WRITINGS: Burgess and Maclean, Doubleday, 1963; *The Yellow Earl,* Coward, 1965; *Against the Wind,* Heinemann, 1966; *Royal Homes and Gardens,* Frewin, 1967; *The Landowners,* Anthony Blond, 1968; *Behold! The Hebrides,* Frewin, 1968; *Raise Your Glasses,* Macdonald & Co., 1969; *The Argyll and Sutherland Highlanders,* Cooper, 1969; *The Twilight of the Swans,* New English Library, 1970; *Tried and Valiant,* Cooper, 1971; *How to Be an Englishman,* Frewin, 1972; *Strike!,* Heinemann, 1975. He has also published under undisclosed pseudonyms. Contributing editor, *Exclusive* (magazine).

WORK IN PROGRESS: Rohallian, the biography of a house.

SIDELIGHTS: Sutherland lived one year on an otherwise uninhabited island in the Orkneys. *Avocational interests:* Shooting, fishing, bridge, backgammon.

* * *

SUTHERLAND, John P. 1920-

PERSONAL: Born June 12, 1920; son of Joseph F. (a policeman) and Hazel M. (Hogan) Sutherland; married Virginia C. Shockley, October 19, 1942. *Education:* University of Missouri, B.A., 1947, B.J., 1948. *Religion:* Roman Catholic.

CAREER: Barrick Publishing Co., Kansas City, Mo., assistant editor, 1948-50; *Wall Street Journal,* reporter in Washington, D.C., 1950-52; *U.S. News & World Report,* White House correspondent, Washington, D.C., 1952—. *Military service:* U.S. Army, Field Artillery, 1942-45; served in Aleutian Islands; became lieutenant. *Member:* National Press Club, White House Correspondents Association (president, 1971-72).

WRITINGS: Men of Waterloo, Prentice-Hall, 1966.

SIDELIGHTS: John Sutherland has traveled to sixty-five countries on journalism assignments, which include war coverage in Vietnam.

* * *

SUTTON, Gordon 1910-

PERSONAL: Born January 28, 1910, in England; married Doreen Fowler (an art teacher); children: Ann (Mrs. Ian Fenwick), David, Gillian. *Education:* Attended College of Art, Nottingham, England, 1926-31; College of Art, Birmingham, England, Art Teacher's Diploma, 1933; University of Nottingham, M.Ed., 1958; University of Leicester, Ph.D., 1963. *Religion:* Church of England. *Home:* 21 Wreake Dr., Rearsby, Leicester, England. *Office:* University of Warwick, Warwick, England.

CAREER: City of Leicester College of Education, Scraptoft, Leicester, England, principal lecturer in fine art and head of department, 1949-75, member of board of governors; University of Warwick, Warwick, England, moderator in fine arts and crafts, 1970—. *Military service:* Royal Air Force, 1940-45; became flying officer. *Member:* Association of Teachers in Colleges and Department of Education. *Awards, honors:* Leverhulme research award, 1967.

WRITINGS: Artisan or Artist?, Pergamon, 1967; (contributor) Joan Tooke, editor, *Religious Studies,* Blond Educational, 1972.

WORK IN PROGRESS: The Byzantine Image in English Mediaeval Manuscripts, researched under Leverhulme research award; *A Painter's Book of Colour.*

* * *

SUTTON, Jefferson H. 1913- (Jeff Sutton)

PERSONAL: Born July 25, 1913, in Los Angeles, Calif.; son of Thomas Shelley (an editor) and Sarah Elizabeth (King) Sutton; married Eugenia Geneva Hansen (a teacher), February 1, 1941; children: Chris (son), Gale (daughter). *Education:* San Diego State College (now University), B.A., 1954, M.A., 1956. *Home:* 4325 Beverly Dr., La Mesa, Calif. 92041.

CAREER: International News Photos, photographer with Los Angeles (Calif.) bureau, 1937-40; after the war was employed as newspaper reporter, then as research engineer in human factors engineering with Convair/General Dynamics, and later in editorial public relations; writer and self-employed editorial consultant to aerospace industries, 1960—. *Military service:* U.S. Marine Corps, 1941-45; became technical sergeant.

WRITINGS—All under name Jeff Sutton, except as noted: *First on the Moon,* Ace Books, 1958; *Bombs in Orbit,* Ace Books, 1959; *Spacehive,* Ace Books, 1960; *Apollo at Go,* Putnam, 1963; (under Jefferson Sutton) *The Missile Lords,* Dell, 1964; *The Atom Conspiracy,* Ace Books, 1966; *The River,* Tower, 1966; (with wife, Jean Sutton) *The Beyond,* Putnam, 1967; *Beyond Apollo,* Gollancz, 1967; *H-Bomb over America,* Ace Books, 1967; (with Jean Sutton) *The Programmed Man,* Putnam, 1968; (with Jean Sutton) *The Lord of the Stars,* Putnam, 1969; *Whisper from the Stars,* Dell, 1970; *Alton's Unguessable,* Ace Books, 1970; *Alien from the Stars,* Putnam, 1970; *Boy Who Had the Power,* Putnam, 1971; *Mindblocked Man,* DAW Books, 1972.

WORK IN PROGRESS: Dusk of the Hawk, a political suspence novel.

SIDELIGHTS: Sutton writes to *CA:* "Writing is my hobby, business, pastime, pleasure. My interests are people—all kinds of people, and the settings in which they function. Write as I feel rather than what might be marketable, but usually stay in areas in which I am more knowledgeable—space and astronautics, war, newspaper backgrounds—and in areas of pure imagination; i.e., science fiction. . . . Man as a dramatic animal is especially compelling. . . . Life, wherever and however it occurs, is fascinating."

Sutton has travelled in the Americas, the South Pacific, and the Orient.

AVOCATIONAL INTERESTS: Space, the desert, the tide pools.

BIOGRAPHICAL/CRITICAL SOURCES: Young Readers' Review, March, 1968.

* * *

SUTTOR, T(imothy) L(achian) 1926-

PERSONAL: Surname rhymes with "butter"; born May 11, 1926, in Tamworth, New South Wales, Australia; son of Pearson Lachlan (with Caltex Ltd., Australia) and Joyce (Strang) Suttor; married Patricia Ingham (a librarian), April

23, 1955; children: Carmel, Gregory, Felicity, Edward. *Education:* New England University, Armidale, B.A., 1945; University of Sydney, B.A. (honors), 1946, M.A., 1949; Australian National University, Ph.D., 1960. *Politics:* "Diffuse responsibility and spending power." *Religion:* Roman Catholic. *Home:* 887 Victoria, Windsor, Ontario, Canada. *Office:* Department of Religious Studies, University of Windsor, Windsor, Ontario, Canada.

CAREER: With Order of Preachers (Dominicans), Melbourne, Victoria, Australia, 1949-54; Hardie Rubber Co., Sydney, Australia, accounts clerk, 1955-57; Australian National University, Canberra, Australian Capital Territory, research student and lecturer in modern history, 1957-61, lecturer in ancient history, 1962-64; Dominican Training College, Canberra, lecturer in history of philosophy, 1963-64; University of Toronto, St. Michael's College, Toronto, Ontario, 1964-68, began as assistant professor, became associate professor of theology; University of Windsor, Windsor, Ontario, professor of theology, 1968—. Lecturer in marriage and medical ethics at St. Michael's Hospital Nurses Training School, St. Joseph's Hospital, and Scarboro Regional School of Nursing, 1965—. Interviewer on religious topics, Canadian Broadcasting Commission, 1967. *Member:* Canadian Theological Society, American Catholic Historical Association, Canadian Catholic Historical Association (president, 1970-72), Canadian Society of Church History (president, 1974).

WRITINGS: (Contributor) *Catholics and the Free Society*, F. W. Cheshire, 1961; *Hierarchy and Democracy in Australia*, Melbourne University Press, 1966; (contributor) J. Robinson, editor, *Faith and Reform*, Fordham University Press, 1969; (editor) St. Thomas Aquinas, *Summa Theologiae*, Volume XI, Blackfriars, 1970. Author of scripts for Australian Broadcasting Corp., 1961-63, and of a videotape, "Icon Versus Eros." Contributor to *Twentieth Century* (Melbourne), *Manna, Catholic Mind, Hermes, Canadian Journal of Theology* and other journals.

WORK IN PROGRESS: The Semantics of Christian Humanism; Eros and Dogma, The Face of Wisdom, John's Gospel.

SIDELIGHTS: Suttor told *CA:* "Take my theological thinking more seriously than anyone else does, and enjoy it. . . . Also my concern is with human ecology and the hostility of the modern city to the human psyche, and the effects of this in politics and religion."

*   *   *

SVARTVIK, Jan 1931-

PERSONAL: Born August 18, 1931, in Torsby, Sweden; son of Gustav (a building contractor) and Sigrid (Nilsson) Svartvik; married Gunilla Berner, June 14, 1958; children: Agneta, Jesper, Rikard. *Education:* Attended Duke University, 1951-52; University of Uppsala, M.A., 1955, Ph.D., 1966; University of Durham, graduate study, 1959-60. *Home:* Tumlaregr 7, S-222 51 Lund, Sweden. *Office:* English Department, University of Lund, Helgonabacken 14, S-223 62 Lund, Sweden.

CAREER: University of London, University College, London, England, research assistant, 1961-64, lecturer in English, 1964-65; Gothenburg University, Bothenburg, Sweden, lecturer in English, 1965-66, docent, 1966-70; University of Lund, Lund, Sweden, professor of English, 1970—.

WRITINGS: On Voice in the English Verb, Mouton &

Co., 1966; (with R. Quirk) *Investigating Linguistic Acceptability*, Mouton & Co., 1966; *The Evans Statements: A Case for Forensic Linguistics*, Almqvist & Wiksell, 1968; (with H. Carvell) *Computational Experiments in Grammatical Classification*, Mouton & Co., 1969; (with Quirk, S. Greenbaum, and G. Leech) *A Grammar of Contemporary English*, Longman, 1971; (with Leech) *A Communicative Grammar of English*, Longman, 1975.

BIOGRAPHICAL/CRITICAL SOURCES: Best Sellers, December 1, 1967.

*   *   *

SWADLEY, Elizabeth 1929-

PERSONAL: Born March 4, 1929, in Springfield, Mo.; daughter of John B. (a minister) and Grace (Mizer) Youngblood; married James Paul Swadley (a Baptist pastor); children: John Paul, Mark Lynn, Susan Alice. *Education:* Southwest Baptist College, A.A., 1956. *Religion:* Baptist. *Home:* 720 West LaSalle, Springfield, Mo. 65807.

CAREER: Addressograph-Multigraph Corp., Springfield, Mo., office manager, 1956-62.

WRITINGS: Your Christian Wedding, Broadman, 1966; *Acknowledging My Stewardship*, Convention Press, 1968; *Dinner on the Grounds*, Broadman, 1972; *Christmas at Home*, Broadman, 1975. Also author of curriculum materials for Woman's Missionary Union and Southern Baptist Convention.

*   *   *

SWALLOW, Norman 1921-
(George Leather)

PERSONAL: Born February 17, 1921, in Manchester, England; son of George Herbert (a schoolteacher) and Annie (Leather) Swallow; married Madeline Naylor (a physiotherapist), September 8, 1945. *Education:* Keble College, Oxford, B.A. (second class honors), 1942. *Home and office:* 36 Crooms Hill, London S.E.10, England.

CAREER: British Broadcasting Corp., London, England, writer-producer in radio, 1946-50, and in television, 1950-57, assistant head of films, 1957-60, assistant editor of "Panorama," 1960-63; Denis Mitchell Films Ltd., London, writer-director, 1963-67; executive producer of "Omnibus" (television program), London, 1968-71; British Broadcast Corp., head of arts features, 1971-74; Granada Television Ltd., London, executive producer, 1974—. Member of program working party, TV for Industry Ltd., 1963-64. *Military service:* British Army, 1942-46. *Member:* Society of Film and Television Arts (fellow), Association of Cinematography and Television Technicians, British Film Institute, Society of Authors, Savile Club (London).

WRITINGS: (Contributor) *Working in Television*, Focal Press, 1956; *Factual Television*, Hastings House, 1966; *Eisenstein: A Documentary Portrait*, Allen & Unwin, 1976. Author of more than fifty television scripts, and about the same number for radio. Contributor to *New Statesman* under pseudonym George Leather; also contributor of articles to *Spectator, Times Educational Supplement*, and *New Commonwealth;* at one time wrote short stories and literary criticism for British journals.

WORK IN PROGRESS: A novel; several radio scripts.

SIDELIGHTS: Swallow has traveled in, and written extensively about, the Middle East and parts of Asia.

SWANN, Donald (Ibrahim) 1923-
(Hilda Tablet)

PERSONAL: Born September 30, 1923, in Llanelli, Wales; son of Herbert William (a doctor) and Naguime Sultan (Piszova) Swann; married Janet Mary Oxborrow, August 7, 1955; children: Rachel, Natasha. *Education:* Christ Church, Oxford, M.A. (honors), 1948. *Politics:* Liberal pacifist. *Religion:* "Christian anglican with Quaker leanings." *Home:* 13 Albert Bridge Rd., London S.W.11, England.

CAREER: Songwriter, singer, pianist, and entertainer, 1948—; founder, Albert House Press, 1975. *Wartime service:* Conscientious objector; served with a Quaker ambulance unit for the United Nations Relief and Rehabilitation Administration in Greece and the Middle East for four years during World War II. *Member:* British Musicians Union, Composers' Guild.

WRITINGS: Sing Round the Year (new carols), Bodley Head, 1964, D. White, 1966; *The Space Between the Bars* (a book of reflections), Hodder & Stoughton, 1968, Simon & Schuster, 1969; *The Road Goes Ever On* (song cycle adapted from J.R.R. Tolkien's "The Lord of the Rings" trilogy), Allen & Unwin, 1970; (with Arthur Scholey) *The Song of Caedmon* (narration with song), Bodley Head, 1970; *The Rope of Love* (carol anthology), Bodley Head, 1973; *Swann's Way Out,* Weidenfeld & Nicholson, 1975.

Other: (Contributor) "Penny Plain" (revue), produced in London, 1951; (with Michael Flanders) *Airs on a Shoestring* (revue; first produced in London at Royal Court Theatre, April 22, 1953), Samuel French, 1957; (contributor) "Pay the Piper" (revue), produced in London, 1954; (with Philip Guard) "Wild Thyme" (musical), first produced in London at Duke of York's Theatre, July 4, 1955; (with Flanders) "Fresh Airs" (revue), first produced in London, January, 1956; (composer and performer with Flanders) "At the Drop of a Hat" (two-man entertainment), first produced in London at New Lindsey Theatre, December 31, 1956, (ran for nearly two and a half years), produced at Edinburgh Festival, 1959, first produced in New York at John Golden Theatre, October 8, 1959, toured United States and Canada, 1960-61, toured Great Britain and Ireland, 1961-62; (composer and performer with Flanders) "At the Drop of Another Hat," first produced in London at Haymarket Theatre, October 2, 1963, toured Australia and New Zealand, September-December, 1964; "Perelandra" (musical drama based on the novel by C. S. Lewis), first produced in London at Mermaid Theatre, June 21, 1964, produced in Philadelphia at Haverford College and in New York at Bryn Mawr College, 1970.

In 1955 the British Broadcasting Corp. Third Programme presented "Emily Butter," one of numerous satirical pieces Swann composed for radio under the pseudonym Hilda Tablet, with scripts by the poet Henry Reed; in January, 1959, he composed and performed for television his own musical settings of "Te Deum" and "Venite" under the program title "Meeting Point"; in 1962 he completed "Festival Matins" and "The Story of Bontzye Sheweig," a musical fable, with Leslie Paul; in 1969 he completed *Requiem for the Living,* a choral setting to the words of C. Day Lewis, for Schirmers & Curwens.

With Michael Flanders, he wrote and recorded animal songs and verse entiled "The Bestiary of Flanders and Swann"; he has set to music the poems of John Betjeman and others (four were published by Chappells in 1963, one appears as a carol in "Sing Round the Year"); he has settings of other poets including some in modern Greek, German, and Russian. With Flanders, he recorded both "At the Drop of a Hat" and "At the Drop of Another Hat"; he has also recorded his coral autobiography, "Between the Bars" and a concert-in-search-of-peace, "A Crack in Time"; many of his other compositions have been recorded and published.

SIDELIGHTS: With Sydney Carter, the songwriter and poet of "religious protest," he gives joint lecture-recitals, and appeared in three television programs called "Strike That Rock" filmed in the Holy Land, 1975. Swann's *At the Drop of a Hat* was produced on television for David Suskind's "Festival of the Performing Arts," 1962; "Between the Bars" and "A Crack in Time" were presented in Rome, Belfast, Great Britain, and the Middle East. While in New York with "At the Drop of a Hat," he appeared on Jack Parr, Ed Sullivan, and Dave Garroway shows. His favorite recreation is visiting the launderette.

BIOGRAPHICAL/CRITICAL SOURCES: Best Sellers, December 1, 1967.

* * *

SWARTZ, Marc J(erome) 1931-

PERSONAL: Born October 31, 1931, in Omaha, Neb.; son of Samuel and Esther (Brown) Swartz; married Audrey Rosenbaum (a psychiatric social worker), September, 1952; children: William Forman, Matthew Brown, Robert Weil. *Education:* Washington University, St. Louis, Mo., A.B., 1952, A.M., 1953; Harvard University, Ph.D., 1958. *Home:* 8552 Nottingham, La Jolla, Calif. 92037. *Office:* Department of Anthropology, University of California, San Diego, Calif.

CAREER: University of Massachusetts, Amherst, instructor, 1957-58, assistant professor of anthropology, 1958-59; University of Chicago, Chicago, Ill., assistant professor, 1959-64; Michigan State University, East Lansing, associate professor, 1964-67, professor of anthropology and African studies, 1967-69; University of California, San Diego, professor of anthropology, 1969—, chairman of department, 1971-75. Visiting professor of anthropology, Cornell University, 1967-68. Organizer of conference of local-level politics at Burg Wartenstein, Austria, 1966; field researcher in Micronesia and Africa. *Member:* American Anthropological Association (fellow), American Ethnological Society, African Studies Association of Great Britain. *Awards, honors:* Research grants from National Institute of Mental Health for work with Bena Tribe in Tanzania, 1962-63, 1975, from Social Science Research Council for Micronesia, 1965-66, from African Studies Center, Michigan State University, for Tanzania, 1965, and from Wenner-Gren Foundation for Austria, 1966, and Spain, 1975; Guggenheim fellow, 1975.

WRITINGS: (Editor with V. W. Turner) *Political Anthropology,* Aldine, 1966; (editor) *Local-Level Politics,* Aldine, 1968; (with David K. Jordan) *Anthropology: Perspective on Humanity,* Wiley, 1975. Contributor to journals in his field.

WORK IN PROGRESS: A cross-cultural study of the nuclear family.

* * *

SWEENEY, Charles 1922-
(R.C.H. Sweeney)

PERSONAL: Born June 11, 1922, in Maidenhead, Berkshire, England; son of Charles Johnston Victor (a headmaster) and May Lilias (Inglis) Sweeney; married Celia Rands, November 21, 1959; children: Katharine Helen, Daniel Charles. *Education:* Attended University of Bristol, 1947-48. *Politics:* "Nil." *Religion:* "Nil."

CAREER: British Museum, London, England, employed in entomology department, 1945-47; Pest Control Ltd., seconded to Tanganyika Government as research entomologist in Tanga, 1948-52, seconded to Sudan Government as senior entomologist in Kadugli, Kordofan, 1952-56; Overseas Research Service, United Kingdom, principal scientific officer in Nyasaland, 1956-65, research entomologist in Swaziland, 1965-67. *Military service:* Royal Air Force, 1940-45. *Member:* Royal Entomological Society (fellow), Zoological Society (London; scientific fellow), Institute of Biology.

WRITINGS: Check-List of the Mammals of Nyasaland, Nyasaland Society, 1959; *The Snakes of Nyasaland,* Nyasaland Government and Nyasaland Society, 1962; (under name R.C.H. Sweeney) *The Scurrying Bush,* Pantheon, 1965 (published in England under name Charles Sweeney, Chatto & Windus, 1965); *Animal Life of Malawi,* UNESCO Publications, Volume I, *Invertebrates,* Volume II, *Vertebrates,* 1967; *Grappling with a Griffon,* Pantheon, 1969; *Jebels by Moonlight,* Chatto & Windus, 1969; *Background of Baobabs,* Constable, 1973, published as *Naturalist in the Sudan,* Taplinger, 1974. Contributor of papers on entomological and zoological subjects to specific journals.

WORK IN PROGRESS: African Animals, a guide.

SIDELIGHTS: Sweeney speaks several African languages. *Avocational interests:* Photography, literature, botany, and philosophy.†

*   *   *

SWETS, John A(rthur)   1928-

PERSONAL: Born June 19, 1928, in Grand Rapids, Mich.; son of John A. and Sara Henrietta (Heyns) Swets; married Maxine Ruth Crawford, July 16, 1949; children: Stephen Arthur, Joel Brian. *Education:* University of Michigan, B.A., 1950, M.A., 1953, Ph.D., 1954. *Home:* 35 Myopia Hill Rd., Winchester, Mass. 01890.

CAREER: University of Michigan, Ann Arbor, instructor in psychology, faculty consultant to Electronic Defense Group, and staff member of Annual Linguistic Institute, 1954-56; Massachusetts Institute of Technology, Cambridge, began as assistant professor of psychology, became associate professor and project supervisor in Research Laboratory of Electronics, 1956-63; Bolt Beranek and Newman, Inc., Cambridge, consultant, 1958-63, supervisory scientist, 1962-64, director of Information Sciences Division and vice-president, 1964-69, senior vice-president, 1969-74, director, 1971-74, chief scientist, 1975—. Summer visiting research fellow, Instituut voor Perceptie Onderzoek, Eindhoven, Netherlands, 1958; Regents' professor, University of California, 1969. National Academy of Sciences-National Research Council, member of Committee on Hearing and Bioacoustics, member of Vision Committee.

MEMBER: Acoustical Society of America (fellow), American Association for the Advancement of Science (fellow), American Psychological Association (fellow), Psychonomic Society, Psychometric Society, Eastern Psychological Association, Psychonomic Society, Psychometric Society, Sigma Xi.

WRITINGS: (Editor) *Signal Detection and Recognition by Human Observers,* Wiley, 1964; (with D. M. Green) *Signal Detection Theory and Psychophysics,* Wiley, 1966; (editor with L. L. Elliott) *Psychology and the Handicapped Child,* U.S. Government Printing Office, 1974.

Contributor: B. F. Lomov, editor, *Detection and Recognition of Signals,* Moscow University Press, 1966; R. N. Haber, editor, *Contemporary Theory and Research in Visual Perception,* Holt, 1968; B. Brake, editor, *Sensory Evaluation of Food: Principles and Methods,* Rydbert, 1969; F. Bresson and M. DeMontmollin, editors, *The Simulation of Human Behavior,* Dunod, 1969; T. Saracevic, editor, *Introduction to Information Science,* Bowker, 1970; M. H. Appley, editor, *Adaptation-Level Theory: A Symposium,* Academic Press, 1971; J.A. Jacquez, editor, *Computer Diagnosis and Diagnostic Methods,* C. C Thomas, 1972. Also author of scientific papers and reports for University of Michigan, Massachusetts Institute of Technology, and government scientific groups. Contributor to *Encyclopedia of Science and Technology,* McGraw, 1971; contributor to professional journals.

*   *   *

SYMONDS, (John) Richard (Charters)   1918-

PERSONAL: Born February 10, 1918, in Oxford, England; son of Sir Charles (a neurologist) and Janet (Poulton) Symonds; married Juanita Ellington, October 9, 1948; children: Peter, Jeremy. *Education:* Corpus Christi College, Oxford, M.A., 1939. *Office address:* United Nations, Post Box 863, Tunisia.

CAREER: Government of Bengal, Calcutta, deputy director, Relief and Rehabilitation, 1944-45; United Nations Relief and Rehabilitation Administration, member of mission to Austria, 1946-47; United Nations Technical Assistance Board and Special Fund, resident representative in Ceylon and Yugoslavia, and then regional representative in Europe, East Africa, and Southeast Africa, 1950-65; Oxford University, Institute of Commonwealth Studies, Oxford, England, senior research officer, 1963-65; University of Sussex, Stanmer, Brighton, England, fellow of Institute of Development Studies and professional fellow of the university, 1966-71; United Nations Institute for Training and Research, representative in Europe, 1972-75; United Nations Development Program, resident representative in Tunisia, 1975—.

WRITINGS: The Making of Pakistan, Faber, 1950; *The British and Their Successors–A Study in the Development of the Government Services in the New States,* Northwestern University Press, 1966; *International Targets for Development,* Faber, 1970; (editor with Michael Carder and contributor) *The United Nations and the Popular Question,* McGraw, 1973.

*   *   *

SYRACUSE, Marcella Pfeiffer   1930-
(Marcella Pfeiffer)

PERSONAL: Born March 30, 1930, in New York, N.Y.; daughter of Edward Aloysious (a physician) and Marcella (Charde) Pfeiffer. *Education:* College of New Rochelle, B.A.; Fordham University, M.S. in R.E. *Home:* 1220 Pelham Parkway South, Bronx, N.Y. 10461.

CAREER: Writer. Religious education consultant.

WRITINGS—Under name Marcella Pfeiffer; all published by Sadlier: God Loves Us, 1965; *God's Gifts to Us,* 1965;

In Christ Jesus, 1965; *The Body of Christ,* 1965; *Love the Lord,* 1966; *Alive in Christ,* 1966; *Christ With Us,* 1967; *Take and Eat,* 1971; *Peace I Give You,* 1972.

*   *   *

SYVERUD, Genevieve Wold   1914-

PERSONAL: First syllable of surname rhymes with "leave"; born December 7, 1914, in Kennedy, Minn.; daughter of Thomas O. (a hotel owner) and Emily (Spangrud) Wold; married Alfred E. Syverud (executive director of Lutheran Social Services of Northern California), October 10, 1935; children: Stephen L., Barbara (Mrs. Lee C. Sather). *Education:* St. Olaf College, B.A., 1935; music courses at University of California, Berkeley, 1956, San Francisco State College (now University), 1958, Pacific Lutheran Theological Seminary, 1964, California State College at San Leandro, 1967. *Politics:* Republican. *Home:* 30 Broadview Ter., Orinda, Calif. 94563.

CAREER: Choir director at various churches in Minnesota, Wisconsin, and California; Waldorf College, Forest City, Iowa, assistant dean of women and drama coach, 1944-45; director of music at Lutheran churches in West Allis, Wis., 1951-55, and Berkeley, Calif., 1960-63; Our Savior's Lutheran Church, Lafayette Calif., minister of music, 1963-71; Christ Lutheran church, El Cerrito, Calif., director of interpretive choir, 1971—.

WRITINGS: This is My Song of Songs, Augsburg, 1966. Regular contributor to *Scope* (publication of American Lutheran Church Women).

WORK IN PROGRESS: A compilation of articles on church seasons, hymn study, and prayer; *Did You Miss Us Jesus,* a book on prayer experiences; *The Choir Member Prays,* a book of choir devotionals.

*   *   *

TACHERON, Donald Glen   1928-

PERSONAL: Born march 1, 1928, in Pendleton, Ore.; son of Frank and Mable Tacheron; married, 1955; children: Ben, Kathryn, Leah, Sam. *Education:* University of Oregon, B.S., 1955, graduate study, 1957-59; University of Washington, Seattle, M.A., 1957. *Home:* 5332 Sherrill Ave., Chevy Chase, Md. 20015.

CAREER: Served with U.S. Merchant Marine, 1944-49; *Eugene Register-Guard,* Eugene, Ore., county editor, 1957-61; American Political Science Association, Washington, D.C., congressional fellow, 1961-62, assistant director, 1962-64, associate director 1964-68; Library of Congress, Congressional Research Service, Washington, D.C., senior specialist in American government and chief of government division, 1968, deputy director, 1969-70; U.S. Congress, Joint Committee on Congressional Operations, Washington, D.C., director of research, 1971—. *Military service:* U.S. Army, 1950-52. *Awards, honors:* Public affairs reporting award, American Political Science Association, 1960.

WRITINGS: (With Morris K. Udall) *The Job of the Congressman,* Bobbs-Merrill, 1967, 2nd edition, 1970.

*   *   *

TAFT, Ronald   1920-

PERSONAL: Born June 3, 1920, in Melbourne, Australia; son of Harry (a businessman) and Olga (Mushatsky) Taft; married Ellen Braumann (a stenographer), April 1, 1943;

children: Barbara (Mrs. David Mushin), David, Marcus. *Education:* University of Melbourne, B.A., 1939; Columbia University, M.A., 1941; University of California, Berkeley, Ph.D., 1950. *Religion:* Jewish. *Home:* 5 Charles St., Kew, Victoria, Australia. *Office:* Monash University, Melbourne, Australia.

CAREER: Australian Department of Aircraft Production, Melbourne, industrial psychologist, 1942-44; Australian Institute of Management, Melbourne, personnel advisory officer, 1945-47; University of Western Australia, Nedlands, senior lecturer, 1951-56, reader in psychology, 1957-65; University of Melbourne, Melbourne, reader in psychology, 1966-68; Monash University, Melbourne, professor of social psychology, 1968—. *Member:* Australian Psychological Society (fellow; president, 1962), Academy of Social Sciences in Australia (fellow).

WRITINGS: (With T. R. Sarbin and D. E. Bailey) *Clinical Inference and Cognitive Theory,* Holt, 1960; *From Stranger to Citizen,* Tavistock Publications, 1966. Contributor to professional journals. Editor, *Australian Journal of Psychology,* 1966-70.

WORK IN PROGRESS: Research on assimilation of immigrants, on creativity, and on coping with unfamiliar cultures.

*   *   *

TAGLIABUE, John   1923-

PERSONAL: Born July 1, 1923, in Cantu, Italy; has been a U.S. citizen all his life; son of Battista (a restaurateur) and Adelaide (Boghi) Tagliabue; married Grace Ten Eyck (an art teacher), September 11, 1946; children: Francesca, Diana, *Education:* Columbia University, B.A., 1944, M.A., 1945, additional study, 1947-48. *Home:* 59 Webster St., Lewiston, Me. 04240. *Office:* Department of English, Bates College, Lewiston, Me. 04240.

CAREER: Teacher of American literature at American University of Beirut, Beirut, Lebanon, 1945-46, State College of Washington (now Washington State University), Pullman, 1946-47, Alfred University, Alfred N.Y., 1948-50, and University of Pisa, Pisa, Italy, 1950-52; Bates College, Lewiston, Me., associate professor, 1953-72, professor of English, 1972—. Fulbright lecturer, Tokyo University, 1958-60; Summer lecturer at International Institute of Madrid, 1956, 1957, and at University of Natal, Brazil, 1968. *Member:* Phi Beta Kappa (vice-president at Bates College, 1965—). *Awards, honors:* Fulbright student in comparative literature, 1950-52.

WRITINGS: Poems, 1941-57, preface by Mark Van Doren, Harper, 1959, 2nd edition, 1969; *A Japanese Journal* (poems), Kayak Press, 1966; *The Buddha Uproar* (poems), Kayak Press, 1967, 2nd edition, 1970; (contributor) *Where is Vietnam?* (anthology of poems), edited by Walter Lowenfels, Doubleday, 1967; *The Doorless Door* (poems), Mushinsha Press, 1970; *Poems on the Winters Tale,* Ktaadn Poetry Press, 1973. Author of several plays, including twelve plays for puppets entitled "The Adventures of Mario," performed for college audiences. Contributor of poems and essays to *Atlantic, Chicago Review, Transatlantic Review, Poetry, Saturday Review, Harpers, Epos, Kayak, Literary Review, Literature East and West, Massachusetts Review, Minnesota Review, Motive, Shenandoah, Virginia Quarterly Review,* and other periodicals.

WORK IN PROGRESS: A Shakespeare Notebook; A Greek Cousin; A Japanese Journal Continued; The Italy Poems, 1950-74; Musician's Planetarium.

SIDELIGHTS: Tagliabue told *CA* that he keeps a travel journal, often of poems, related to his travels in Italy, France, Spain, England, Greece, Mexico, Guatemala, and Japan. Donald W. Baker says that the language of Tagliabue's poems "is clear and simple" and that the poems "escape the closest danger of apparent naivete, inanity, [and become] graceful cadences, delicate assertions, or meticulous ironies." Baker continues: "Peacefully, dreamily, the poems [composing *A Japanese Journal*] contemplate people and incidents of Japan, Japanese works of art, and moments of tenuous emotion in the poet. . . . Though it seems to float with clouds and petals through space and light, such poetry does not pretend. It radiates the quiet beauty of an imagination attuned to the world. I have often admired Mr. Tagliabue's accomplished work. Here he has struck a lovely grace note, a precise, tasteful, delicate, often subtly complex book, which I shall keep for a long time." Tagliabue has given poetry readings in Italy, Greece, Spain, Japan, and Brazil. His poems have been recorded for the Library of Congress.

BIOGRAPHICAL/CRITICAL SOURCES: Poetry, December, 1967.

*   *   *

TAIT, Alan A(nderson)   1934-

PERSONAL: Born July 1, 1934, in Edinburgh, Scotland; son of Stanley (a businessman) and Margaret (Anderson) Tait; married Susan Somers, August 2, 1963; children: Anthony. *Education:* University of Edinburgh, M.A., 1957; Trinity College, Dublin, Ph.D., 1966. *Religion:* Protestant. *Home:* Auchengare, Rhu, Dunbartonshire, Scotland. *Office:* Department of Economics, University of Strathclyde, George St., Glasgow, Scotland.

CAREER: University of Dublin, Trinity College, Dublin, Ireland, lecturer in public finance, 1959-68, fellow, 1968, senior tutor, 1969-71; University of Strathclyde, Glasgow, Scotland, Professor of monetary and financial economics, 1971—. Visiting professor, University of Illinois, 1965.

WRITINGS: Survey of the Fertiliser Industry in Ireland, Stationery Office (Ireland), 1963; *Survey of the Chemical Industry in Ireland,* Stationery Office (Ireland), 1964; *The Taxation of Personal Wealth,* University of Illinois Press, 1967; (editor and contributor) *Economic Policy in Ireland,* Institute of Public Administration (Dublin), 1968; (editor and contributor) *Ireland: Some Problems of a Developing Economy,* Gill & Macmillan, 1971; *Value-Added Tax,* McGraw, 1972.

WORK IN PROGRESS: Research in public finance, particularly in the field of value-added taxation and patterns of government expenditure.

AVOCATIONAL INTERESTS: Music, art.

*   *   *

TAKTSIS, Costas   1927-

PERSONAL: First syllable of surname rhymes with "lock"; born October 8, 1927, in Salonika, Greece; son of Gregory C. (a lawyer) and Elli (Zahos) Taktsis. *Education:* University of Athens, law studies. *Politics:* "Sex-Revolutionary." *Religion:* None. *Home:* 27-29 Kleomenous St., Athens T.T. 140, Greece.

CAREER: Writer. *Military service:* Greek Army, 1950-52; became second lieutenant.

WRITINGS: Tpito Stephani (novel), [Athens], 1963,

translation by Leslie Finer published as *The Third Wedding,* Alan Ross, 1967. Short stories and essays have appeared in Greek literary reviews and *London Magazine*.

SIDELIGHTS: Taktsis speaks and writes English and French. He lived in Australia and the United States, and travelled in Europe and Africa.

BIOGRAPHICAL/CRITICAL SOURCES: Observer, March 26, 1967; *Times Literary Supplement,* March 30, 1967; *New Statesman,* March 31, 1967.††

*   *   *

TALBOT, Allan R.   1934-

PERSONAL: Born January 19, 1934, in New York, N.Y.; son of John H. and Ada May (Langdon) Talbot; married Elizabeth Speakman, August 22, 1959; children: Katharine, David. *Education:* Rutgers University, B.A., 1959, M.A., 1960.

CAREER: Administrative assistant to Mayor Richard Lee, New Haven, Conn., 1960-62; New Haven (Conn.) Redevelopment Agency, assistant director, 1962-64; Community Progress, Inc., New Haven, director of administration, 1964-65; Corde Corp. (educational research), Wilton, Conn., executive director, 1966-67; Urban America, Inc., Washington, D.C., director of Urban Policy Center, beginning 1967. Associate fellow, Branford College, Yale University. *Military service:* U.S. Army, 1953-55; became sergeant.

WRITINGS: The Mayor's Game: Richard Lee of New Haven and the Politics of Change, Harper, 1967; *Power along the Hudson: The Storm King Case and the Birth of Enviromentalism,* Dutton, 1972. Contributor of articles to *Harper's.*

AVOCATIONAL INTERESTS: Travel, sailing.†

*   *   *

TALBOT, Norman (Clare)   1936-

PERSONAL: Born September 14, 1936, in Gislingham, Suffolk, England; son of Francis Harold (a farm laborer) and Agnes (Rampley) Talbot; married Jean Margaret Perkins (a part-time lecturer), August 17, 1960; children: Clare Elizabeth, Nicholas John, Ruth Catherine. *Education:* Hatfield College, Durham, B.A. (first class honors), 1959; University of Leeds, Ph.D., 1962; Yale University, postdoctoral study, 1967-68. *Politics:* Pacifist Socialist. *Religion:* Society of Friends. *Home:* 54 Addison Rd., New Lambton, New South Wales, Australia. *Office:* University of Newcastle, New South Wales, Australia.

CAREER: University of Newcastle, New South Wales, Australia, 1963—, began as lecturer, associate professor of English, 1973—. Presented two television series on Shakespeare, Sydney, Australia. *Member:* Australian Universities' Languages and Literature Association, Australian and New Zealand American Studies Association. *Awards, honors:* Gregory Award for poetry, 1965; American Council of Learned Societies fellowship to Yale University, 1967-68.

WRITINGS: The Seafolding of Harri Jones (poetry; pamphlet), Nimrod Publications, 1965; (editor) *XI Hunter Valley Poets plus VII,* privately printed, 1966; *The Major Poems of John Keats* (criticism), University of Sydney Press, 1968; *Poems for a Female Universe,* South Head Press, 1968; *Son of a Female Universe* (poetry), South Head Press, 1971; *The Fishing Boy* (poetry), South Head

Press, 1973; (editor) *Hunter Valley Poets 1973*, Nimrod Publications, 1973; (editor) *IV Hunter Valley Poets*, Nimrod Publications, 1975. Poetry anthologized, published in numerous Australian journals, and in periodicals in England, the United States and Canada; contributor of articles and reviews to *Poetry Australia, Southern Review* (Australia), *Quadrant*, and other journals.

WORK IN PROGRESS: Three books of poetry, *Find the Lady/A Female Universe Rides Again, Overhill Faraway*, and *And Close Your Eyes;* an edition of a William Morris story; a book of innocence and masks in literature; and Australian anthology.

SIDELIGHTS: Talbot told *CA:* "I'm primarily a poet in a world/language which finds poets incomprehensible and at once boring and absurd, . . . a teacher because I like it and because no one will pay me enough for the poems, . . . [and] a critic only when it is necessary, which isn't often. Much of the poetry is elegiac, much of it comic, but whatever the tone the basic orientation is on sex and compassion. . . ."

* * *

TALBOT, Toby 1928-

PERSONAL: Born November 29, 1928, in New York, N.Y.; daughter of Joseph and Bella Tolpen; married Daniel Talbot (a film producer and founder of New Yorker Theatre and New York Films), January 6, 1951; children: Nina, Emily, Sarah. *Education:* Queens College (now Queens College of the City University of New York), B.A., 1949; Brooklyn College (now Brooklyn College of the City University of New York), M.A., 1953; Columbia University, graduate student, 1953-55. *Home:* 180 Riverside Dr., New York, N.Y. 10024. *Agent:* Raines & Raines, 475 Fifth Ave., New York, N.Y. 10017. *Office:* John Jay College of Criminal Justice of the City University of New York, New York, N.Y. 10003.

CAREER: Instructor in Spanish at Syracuse University, Syracuse, N.Y., 1949-50 and Long Island University, Brooklyn, N.Y., 1950-53; Columbia University, Columbia College, New York City, lecturer in Spanish, 1958-65; Long Island University, lecturer in Spanish, 1967-68; John Jay College of Criminal Justice of the City University of New York, New York City, assistant professor of Spanish, 1974—. Lecturer in Latin American film, New School for Social Research, 1974-75.

WRITINGS: (Editor) *The World of the Child*, Doubleday, 1962; *I Am Maria*, Cowles, 1969; *My House Is Your House*, Cowles, 1970; *Count Lucanor's Tales*, Dial, 1970; *Once Upon A Truffle*, Cowles, 1971; *Coplas: Spanish Folk Poems*, Four Winds, 1972; *The Night of the Radishes*, Putnam, 1972; *The Rescue*, Putnam, 1973; *Away Is So Far*, Four Winds, 1974; *Two by Two*, Follett, 1974; *A Bucketful of Moon*, Lothrop, 1975.

Translator: Benito Perez Galdos, *Compassion*, Ungar, 1962; Jose Ortega Y Gasset, *On Love: Aspects of A Single Theme*, Meridian Books, 1966; Ortega Y Gasset, *The Origin of Philosophy*, Norton, 1968; Felix Marti Ibanez, *Ariel*, MD Publications, 1969; Roberto Conde, *The First Stages of Modernization in Latin America*, Harper, 1973. Also author of a documentary film, "Berimbau," 1972. Education editor, *El Diario de Neuva York*, 1951-53.

* * *

TAMUNO, Tekena N. 1932-

PERSONAL: Born January 28, 1932, in Okrika, Nigeria;

son of Mark Tamuno (a tribal chief) and Ransoline I. Igbiri; married Olu G. Tamuno (a librarian), January 5, 1963; children: Ene, Ibirobo, Alali, Boma. *Education:* University College, Ibadan (now University of Ibadan), B.A., 1958; Birkbeck College, University of London, Ph.D., 1962; studied at Columbia University, 1965-66. *Religion:* Christian. *Home:* 18 Sankore Ave., Ibadan, Nigeria. *Office:* Department of History, University of Ibadan, Ibadan, Nigeria.

CAREER: Baptist High School, Port-Harcourt, Nigeria, tutor, 1952-53; Urbobo College, Warri, Nigeria, tutor, 1958-59; University of Ibadan, Ibadan, Nigeria, 1962—, began as senior lecturer in history, professor of history, 1971—, head of history department, 1972—, dean, Faculty of Arts, 1973-75, chairman, committee of deans, 1974-75. *Member:* Historical Society of Nigeria. *Awards, honors:* Rockefeller Foundation fellowship, 1965-66.

WRITINGS: Nigeria and Elective Representation, 1923-1947, Heinemann, 1966; *The Police in Modern Nigeria*, Ibadan University Press, 1970; *The Evolution of the Nigeria State: The Southern Phase, 1898-1914*, Longman, 1972; (editor with J.F.A. Ajayi) *The University of Ibadan, 1948-1973: A History of the First Twenty-five Years*, Ibadan University Press, 1973; *History and History-Makers in Modern Nigeria*, Ibadan University Press, 1973.

AVOCATIONAL INTERESTS: Organ music, fishing.

* * *

TANA, Tomoe (Hayashima) 1913-

PERSONAL: Born April 16, 1913, in Hokkaido, Japan; daughter of Daisen (a minister) and Kiyono (Shimizu) Hayashima; married Daisho Tana (a Buddhist minister), September 17, 1938; children: Yasuto, Shibun, Chinin, Akira (sons). *Education:* Studied at Futaba Junior College, one year, and Foothill College, 1974. *Religion:* Buddhist. *Home:* 4170 Coulombe Dr., Palo Alto, Calif. 94306.

AWARDS, HONORS: Poetry Contest of Palace of Japan award, 1949; first place award, Tanka contest, United States, 1951.

WRITINGS: (With Lucille Nixon) *Sounds From the Unknown*, A. Swallow, 1963. Also author of *One Hundred Poems in America*, for Palo Alto (Calif.) Unified School District, and contributor to *English II* (anthology), Addison-Wesley.

WORK IN PROGRESS: Tomoshibi, a biography of Lucille Nixon and a collection of her works; translating three volumes of husband's Japanese works into English, tentatively entitled *The Sunday School Text*.

BIOGRAPHICAL/CRITICAL SOURCES: Minnesota Review, Volume 5, numbers 3 and 4, index issue, August-October, October-December.

* * *

TANNENBAUM, Robert 1915-

PERSONAL: Born June 29, 1915, in Cripple Creek, Colo.; son of Henry (an accountant) and Nettie (Porges) Tannenbaum; married Edith Lazaroff, February 4, 1945; children: Judith (Mrs. Ronald Press), Deborah Ruth. *Education:* Santa Ana Junior College, A.A., 1935; University of Chicago, A.B., 1937, M.B.A. (with honors), 1938, Ph.D., 1949. *Home:* 12800 Kling St., North Hollywood, Calif. 91604. *Office:* Graduate School of Management, University of California, Los Angeles, Calif. 90024.

CAREER: Certified psychologist, State of California; diplomate, American Board of Professional Psychology. Oklahoma A&M College (now Oklahoma State University of Agriculture and Applied Science), Stillwater, instructor in accounting, 1937-39; University of Chicago, Chicago, Ill., lecturer in business, 1940-42, instructor, 1946-47, assistant professor of industrial relations, 1947-48; University of California, Los Angeles, assistant professor, 1948-51, associate professor, 1951-57, professor of personnel management and industrial relations, 1957-61, professor of industrial relations and behavioral science, 1962-71, professor of development of human systems, 1971—. Institute of Industrial Relations, research economist, 1957-62, research behavioral scientist, 1962-68. Visiting professor of personnel management and human relations, Institute for Post-Graduate Study of Industrial Organization, Turin, Italy, 1958; lecturer at Arbertsgemeinschaft fuer Soziale Betriebagestaltung, Heidelburg, at Centre d'Etudes Industrielles, Geneva, and at British Institute of Management, London, 1958. Director, Organization Renewal Program, Israel, 1969-70; consultant in organizational development to TRW Systems, Aluminum Co. of Canada Ltd., SAGA Food Service, and Procter and Gamble Co. *Military service:* U.S. Navy, 1942-46; became lieutenant; received letter of commendation.

MEMBER: American Sociological Association, American Psychological Association, (fellow), International Association of Applied Behavioral Scientists, Society for the Psychological Study of Social Issues, Los Angeles County Psychological Association, Phi Beta Kappa, Beta Gamma Sigma.

WRITINGS: Cost Under the Unfair Practices Acts, University of Chicago Press, 1939; (with Irving R. Weschler and Fred Massarik) *Leadership and Organization: A Behavioral Science Approach,* McGraw, 1961; (contributor) Harold Koontz, editor, *Toward a Unified Theory of Management,* McGraw, 1964. Author of script for half-hour film in "Management Development Series," produced by University of California Extension Media Center, 1966 and of a tape-cassette presentation, "OD-Other Dimensions: Does This Path Have a Heart," produced by CREDR Corp., 1974. Contributor to professional journals. Member of board of editors, *Journal of Humanistic Psychology* and *Journal of Transpersonal Psychology.*

* * *

TANSELLE, G(eorge) Thomas 1934-

PERSONAL: Surname is pronounced *Tan-* sell; born January 29, 1934, in Lebanon, Ind.; son of K. Edwin (a grocer) and Madge (Miller) Tanselle. *Education:* Yale University, B.A. (magna cum laude), 1955; Northwestern University, M.A., 1956, Ph.D., 1959. *Office:* Department of English, University of Wisconsin, Madison, Wis. 53706.

CAREER: Chicago City Junior College, Chicago, Ill., instructor in English, 1958-60; University of Wisconsin–Madison, instructor, 1960-61, assistant professor, 1961-63, associate professor, 1963-68, professor of English, 1968—. Member of Planning Institute of Commission on English, Ann Arbor, summer, 1961, Center for Editions of American Authors, 1970-73, and Kennedy Center Advisory Committee for Drama for the Bicentennial, 1974-75.

MEMBER: Modern Language Association of America (member of executive committee of bibliographical evidence group, 1974—), Modern Humanities Research Association, National Council of Teachers of English, Printing

Historical Society, Private Libraries Association, Manuscript Society (member of board of directors, 1974—), American Antiquarian Society (member of publications committee, 1972; council member, 1974—), Bibliographical Society of America (member of council, 1970; vice-chairman of publications committee, 1974—), Bibliographical Society (London), Edinburgh Bibliographical Society, Oxford Bibliographical Society, Cambridge Bibliographical Society, Bibliographical Society of the University of Virginia, Grolier Club, Caxton Club, Phi Beta Kappa. *Awards, honors:* Kiekhofer Teaching Award, University of Wisconsin, 1963; Guggenheim fellowship, 1969-70; Jenkins Prize for Bibliography, Union College, 1973; American Council of Learned Societies fellowship, 1973-74.

WRITINGS: Royall Tyler, Harvard University Press, 1967; *Guide to the Study of United States Imprints,* Belknap, 1971. Co-editor, *The Writings of Herman Melville,* fifteen volumes projected, Northwestern University Press and Newberry Library, 1968—. Contributor to scholarly journals, including *Studies in Bibliography, Book Collector, Library, Shakespeare Quarterly, Gutenberg Jahrbuch, Modern Language Review, American Literature,* and *PMLA.* Member of board of editors, *Contemporary Literature,* 1962—, *Abstracts of English Studies,* 1964—, and *Resources for American Literary Study,* 1971—; member of advisory committee for *Papers* of the Bibliographical Society of America, 1967—.

WORK IN PROGRESS: Essays on the theory and techniques of analytical and descriptive bibliography; a descriptive bibliography of Herman Melville; a study of the publishing career of B. W. Huebsch; research in the history of American publishing and printing.

AVOCATIONAL INTERESTS: Collecting books pertaining to the development of literary publishing in the United States; collecting bibliography.

* * *

TAPSELL, R(obert) F(rederick) 1936-

PERSONAL: Born August 3, 1936, in Croydon, England; son of Cecil Albert (an interior decorator) and Hilda (Holdforth) Tapsell; married Shirley Fussell, October 31, 1964; children: John Robert. *Education:* School of Slavonic and East European Studies, London, B.A. (honors in history), 1963. *Politics:* Liberal. *Religion:* None.

CAREER: Scindia Steam Navigation Co. Ltd., London, England, administrative posts, 1952-54, 1957-60; Plunkett Foundation for Agricultural Co-operation, London, research assistant, 1963-64; University of Manchester, Manchester, England, administrative assistant, 1964-66; East Anglia University, Norwich England, senior administrative assistant, 1966-69; University of Essex, Colchester, England, assistant registrar, 1969—. *Military service:* Royal Air Force, junior technician, 1954-56.

WRITINGS: The Year of the Horsetails (novel), Knopf, 1967; *The Unholy Pilgrim* (novel), Knopf, 1968; *Shadow of Wings,* Hutchinson, 1972.

SIDELIGHTS: The Year of the Horsetails was originally conceived as a thesis on Tartar military methods. Tapsell has traveled in most countries of Western Europe, and in the Balkans, Egypt, and Iraq. *Avocational interests:* Military history, genealogy, fencing.†

* * *

TARLING, (Peter) Nicholas 1931-

PERSONAL: Born February 1, 1931, in Iver, England; son

of Ronald William (an accountant) and Doris Neville (Bibbye) Tarling. *Education:* Cambridge University, B.A., 1952, M.A. and Ph.D., 1956. *Religion:* None. *Office:* University of Auckland, Private bag, Auckland, New Zealand.

CAREER: Royal Historical Society, London, England, assistant editor of "Writings on British History, 1901-33," 1956-57; University of Queensland, Brisbane, Australia, lecturer, 1957-61, senior lecturer in history, 1962-65; University of Auckland, Auckland, New Zealand, associate professor, 1965-68, professor of history, 1968—, dean of faculty of arts, 1972-74. Member, Queen Elizabeth II Arts Council of New Zealand, 1975—. *Member:* Royal Asiatic Society (London; fellow), Royal Historical Society (London; fellow), New Zealand Asian Studies Society (president, 1974—), Association of University Teachers of New Zealand (president, 1970-71, 1973-74). *Awards, honors:* Litt.D., Cambridge University, 1974.

WRITINGS: Anglo-Dutch Rivalry in the Malay World, 1780-1824, Cambridge University Press, 1962; *Piracy and Politics in the Malay World,* F. W. Cheshire, 1963; *A Concise History of Southeast Asia,* Praeger, 1966 (published in Australia as *Southeast Asia, Past and Present,* F. W. Cheshire, 1966); (editor) *China and Its Place in the World,* Blackwood & Paul, 1967; *British Policy in the Malay Peninsula and Archipelago, 1824-1871* (originally published as an entire issue of *Journal of Royal Asiatic Society,* Malayan Branch, October, 1957), Oxford University Press, 1969; (editor with J. Ch'en) *Studies in the Social History of China and Southeast Asia,* Cambridge University Press, 1970; *Britain: The Brookes and Brunei,* Oxford University Press, 1971; *Imperial Britain in Southeast Asia,* Oxford University Press, 1975. Contributor of some thirty articles to journals, mainly periodicals concerned with Asia.

WORK IN PROGRESS: A study of British relations with Borneo and the Philippines; a biography of Sir James Brooke; study of British policy in Southeast Asia, 1930-45.

AVOCATIONAL INTERESTS: Amateur dramatics (mostly acting), and listening to music (has large collection of records of the late nineteenth and early twentieth centuries).

*   *   *

TARPEY, Lawrence Xavier   1928-

PERSONAL: Born August 4, 1928, in New Bedford, Mass.; son of Andrew F. and Barbara (Carney) Tarpey; children: Lawrence X., Jr., Matthew, Thaddeus, Dominic, Theresa, Sarah, Trudy. *Education:* University of Notre Dame, A.B., 1953; Indiana University, M.B.A., 1955; Cornell University, Ph.D., 1964. *Home:* 108 Brigadoon Pkwy., Lexington, Ky. *Office:* College of Business and Economics, University of Kentucky, Lexington, Ky. 40506.

CAREER: Delta State College, Cleveland, Miss., instructor in business administration, 1956-57; University of Kentucky, College of Business and Economics, Lexington, assistant professor, 1960-64, associate professor, 1964-66, professor of business administration, 1966—. Dean, Hallie Sellasie University, Addis Ababa, Ethiopia, 1969-70. Member of advisory committee for Graduate Record Examination Advanced Test in Business Administration, Educational Testing Service. Member of Lexington Education Committee and Lexington Committee on Religion and Human Rights. *Military service:* U.S. Army, 1955-56. *Member:* American Marketing Association, American Economic Association, American Association of Univer-

sity Professors (member of executive council, 1967-68), American Civil Liberties Union (president, central Kentucky branch). *Awards, honors:* Ford Foundation faculty summer fellowship, 1964; Gulf Oil faculty research grant, 1965; University of Kentucky faculty research fellowship, 1967.

WRITINGS: (Contributor) Joseph Massie, editor, *Fundamentals of Management,* Prentice-Hall, 1964; (with George Field and John Douglas) *Marketing Management: A Behavioral Systems Approach,* C. E. Merrill, 1966; (with Douglas and Field) *Human Behavior in Marketing,* C. E. Merrill, 1967. Contributor of articles and book reviews to professional journals.

*   *   *

TARRANT, Desmond   1924-

PERSONAL: Born September 17, 1924, in Hampshire, England; son of Richard George and Alice Maud (Pepper) Tarrant; married Doreen Kathleen Mason, December 24, 1947; children: Paul Richardson, Leigh Gawain, Amanda Felicity. *Education:* University of London, B.A. (honors), 1951, M.A., 1956; University of Kentucky, graduate study, 1952; research at University of Pennsylvania, 1958-59. *Home:* 13 Cassel Ave., Branksome Park, Bournemouth, England.

CAREER: Farnborough Technical College, Farnborough, England, lecturer in charge of English until 1968; English teacher at colleges and universities in Britain and the United States. Lecturer, poet, and author. *Military service:* Royal Air Force; became flight lieutenant. *Member:* Society of Authors.

WRITINGS: James Branch Cabell: The Dream and the Reality, University of Oklahoma Press, 1967. Contributor of articles and short stories to periodicals and of articles on evolution to journals in the United Kingdom, United States and India, including *World Union, The Mankind Quarterly* and *God, Death, and Intelligence.* Advisory editor, *Cabellian* (published at University of Cincinnati), 1967.

WORK IN PROGRESS: A novel, *The Night Is Not for Dreaming;* poems.

SIDELIGHTS: Tarrant has traveled extensively in Europe, United States, Africa, and Near East.

*   *   *

TATE, Gary   1930-

PERSONAL: Born August 2, 1930, in Hiawatha, Kan.; son of James Cedric and Beulah (Killian) Tate; married Priscilla Ray Weston, March 9, 1973; children: (previous marriage) Lorraine, Carolyn, *Education:* Baker University, B.A., 1952; University of New Mexico, M.A., 1956, Ph.D., 1958. *Home:* 2624 Boyd, Fort Worth, Tex. 76109. *Office:* English Department, Texas Christian University, Fort Worth, Tex.

CAREER: University of Wyoming, Laramie, instructor in English, 1957-58; Ohio Wesleyan University, Delaware, assistant professor of English, 1958-60; University of Tulsa, Tulsa, Okla.; associate professor of English, 1960-70; Northern Arizona University, Flagstaff, professor of English, 1970-71; Texas Christian University, Fort Worth, Addie Levy Professor of Literature, 1971—.

WRITINGS: (Editor) *Reflections on High School English,* University of Tulsa, 1966; (editor with E.P.J. Corbett) *Teaching Freshman Composition,* Oxford University

Press, 1967; (editor with E. Alworth & D. Hayden) *Classics in Linguistics*, Philosophical Library, 1967; (editor with Corbett), *Teaching High School Composition*, Oxford University Press, 1970; (editor) *From Discovery to Style*, Winthrop Publishing, 1973. Founder and editor, *Freshman English News*, 1971—.

WORK IN PROGRESS: Helping You Write, For Winthrop Publishing; editing *Teaching Composition: Ten Bibliographical Essays*, for Texas Christian University Press.

*   *   *

TATE, George T(homas) 1931-

PERSONAL: Born October 5, 1931; in Hollywood, Ala.; son of Haynes M. (a farmer) and Edith (Machen) Tate; married Vivian Close, February 15, 1958; children: Vivian. *Education:* Vanderbilt University, B.A., 1952; Emory University, M.A., 1954; University of Kentucky, Ph.D., 1957. *Politics:* Democrat. *Religion:* Methodist. *Home:* 1228 Lancaster Dr., Alexandria, La. 71301. *Office:* U.S. Veterans Administration Hospital, Alexandria, La. 71301.

CAREER: State Colony and Training School Pineville, La., psychologist, 1957; Etowah Health Center, Gadsden, Ala., clinical psychologist, 1958; clinical psychologist in private practice, Gadsden, Ala., 1958-59; U.S. Veterans Administration Center, Biloxi, Miss., coordinator of psychological services, 1959-64; U.S. Veterans Administration Hospital, Alexandria, La., chief of psychology service, 1964—. Instructor at University Center, Gadsden, Ala., 1958-59, and University Center, Mary Mitchell High School, Biloxi, Miss., 1961-64. Chairman, Louisiana State Board of Examiners of Psychologists, 1972-73. *Member:* American Psychological Association, Louisiana Psychological Association (member of executive board, 1966), Central Louisiana Psychological Association (president, 1966).

WRITINGS: Strategy of Therapy: Toward the Engineering of Social Growth, Springer, 1967. Contributor to professional journals.

*   *   *

TATE, James 1943-

PERSONAL: Born December 8, 1943, in Kansas City, Mo.; son of Samual Vincent Appleby (a pilot) and Betty Jean Whitsitt. *Education:* Attended University of Missouri, 1963-64; Kansas State College, B.A., 1965; University of Iowa, M.F.A., 1967. *Home:* 950 North Pleasant St., Amherst, Mass. 01002.

CAREER: University of Iowa, Iowa City, instructor in creative writing, 1966-67; University of California, Berkeley, visiting lecturer, 1967-68; Columbia University, New York, N.Y., assistant professor of English, 1969-71; University of Massachusetts, Amherst, associate professor of English, 1971—. Poet-in-residence, Emerson College, 1970-71; consultant, Coordinating Council of Literary Magazines, 1971-74. *Awards, honors:* Yale Series of Younger Poets award, 1966; National Institute of Arts and Letters award for poetry, 1974.

WRITINGS—All poetry, except as noted: *The Lost Pilot*, Yale University Press, 1967; *The Torches*, Unicorn Press, 1968, revised edition, 1971; *Notes of Woe: Poems*, Stone Wall Press, 1968; *Row with Your Hair*, Kayak, 1969; *Shepherds of the Mist*, Black Sparrow Press, 1969; *The Oblivion Ha-Ha*, Little, Brown, 1970; *Wrong Songs*, Halty Ferguson, 1970; *Hints to Pilgrims*, Halty Ferguson, 1971; *Absences*, Little, Brown, 1972; *Hottentot Ossuary* (short prose), Temple Bar Bookstore, 1974. Contributor to *Paris Review, Transatlantic Review, New Yorker, Nation, Atlantic, Poetry, Quarterly Review of Literature, Shenandoah*, and other publications. Poetry editor, *Dickinson Review*, 1967—.

WORK IN PROGRESS: Viper Jazz, a book of poems.

SIDELIGHTS: According to Julian Symons, Tate writes with intelligence, wit, and negligent ease, being "an ironical, original, self-absorbed poet who glances with amusement at love, humanity, himself." The strengths and weaknesses of his poetry, says a *Virginia Quarterly Review* writer, "are characteristic of the poet's generation. Freshness, attractive eccentricity, winning irreverence, and a laudable independence give these poems a flavor quite their own; but," he adds, "most of them lack something vital: a purpose, a sense of direction, a goal."

William H. Pritchard, however, praises Tate's "lively fantasies," and allows that, in "The Lost Pilot," "fancy becomes imagination as the voice speaks beautifully, moving over the lines with inevitable rightness." His sensibility, says Harold Jaffe, sometimes recalls that of Robert Lowell in *Life Studies,* but he notes that Tate's "low-keyed, offhand style is his own and counterpoints forcefully with the feelings of estrangement, anger, and self-abasing humor to be found in a good many of the poems."

His technique is as well his own, "always confident[ly] . . . [choosing] to err on the side of adventure rather than caution," says Jaffe, "and his poems frequently manifest a trust in the unconscious that brings Sylvia Plath to mind. More often than not the effect justifies this trust. . . ." The effect produced is that "of a wayward imagination constantly straining against reason and 'reality,'" says Louis L. Martz, "but resigning itself to the daily world so long as wit is allowed to have its fancy flights within an agreed limit."

In *The Oblivion Ha-Ha*, Tate exhibits "a major talent," according to a *Virginia Quarterly Review* writer who continues: "The poems move freely to surprising and ultimately right conclusions. But the world they investigate is constricted, a world in which every generous gesture, even Tate's own, is suspect."

Tate told *CA:* "As W. C. Williams says, '. . . and I along with the rest, squirting little hoses of objection.' Something like that; a form of protest, as well as celebration. Poets are almost pathologically concerned with good and evil, beauty and ugliness: they do not want to let it pass by, either extreme, unnoticed. I suppose poets have a greater sense of evil than most people; they want to order the world for a moment, freeze it, understand it. And the language, of course, is the music which can make the painful truths palpable. It's fear, it's love, love of intensity, obsession with beauty. . . ."

BIOGRAPHICAL/CRITICAL SOURCES: Nation, April 24, 1967; *Times Literary Supplement*, May 18, 1967; *New Statesman*, June 16, 1967; *Christian Science Monitor*, July 11, 1967; *Yale Review*, summer, 1967; *Hudson Review*, summer, 1967; *Virginia Quarterly Review*, summer, 1967, autumn, 1970; *Carleton Miscellany*, fall, 1967; *Poetry*, February, 1968; Carolyn Riley, editor, *Contemporary Literary Criticism*, Gale, Volume II, 1974, Volume VI, 1976.

TATE, Velma 1913-
(Francine Davenport, Valerie Taylor, Nacella Young)

PERSONAL: Born September 7, 1913, in Aurora, Ill.; daughter of Marshall J. and Elsie (Collins) Young; divorced; children: Marshall John, Jerry Jay, James Richard. *Education:* Attended Blackburn College, 1935-37. *Politics:* "No affiliation." *Religion:* "No affiliation." *Agent:* Eleanor Langdon Associates, 8 West Oak St., Chicago, Ill. 60610.

CAREER: Specialty Salesman Magazine, Chicago, Ill., creator of display advertising, 1959-75. *Member:* American Civil Liberties Union, Women's International League for Peace and Freedom, Mattachine Midwest, Illinois Freedom to Read Committee.

WRITING—Under pseudonym Valerie Taylor, except as indicated: *Hired Girl,* Universal Distributing & Publishing, 1952; *Whisper Their Love,* Crest Books, 1957; *The Girls in 3-B,* Crest Books, 1959; *Stranger on Lesbos,* Crest Books, 1960; *Unlike Others,* Midwood Tower, 1963; *Return to Lesbos,* Midwood Tower, 1963; *A World Without Men,* Midwood Tower, 1963; *Journey to Fulfillment,* Midwood Tower, 1964; (under pseudonym Francine Davenport) *Secret of the Bayou,* Ace Books, 1966. Contributor of poetry, under pseudonym Nacella Young, and articles, fillers, and short stories to popular and religious periodicals, including *Ladies' Home Journal, Christian Century, Prairie Schooner, Canadian Forum,* and *Catholic Home Journal.*

WORK IN PROGRESS: A serious historical novel; a murder mystery.

SIDELIGHTS: Tate's work as Valerie Taylor is banned in South Africa, and, she writes, "as a worker for civil rights, [I] think this is a good place to be banned." She also says: "My lesbian books are not lurid, nor are they meant to be pro-gay propaganda, but true to life." *Secret of the Bayou* has been translated into French and Dutch, and several of the Valerie Taylor books have been published in England. Miss Tate speaks French, German, and Spanish. She lived in the Canary Islands for a time.

*   *   *

TAUBER, Gilbert 1935-

PERSONAL: Born April 20, 1935, in New York, N.Y.; son of Joseph H. and Frances L. Tauber; married Susanne Weil, December 25, 1960; children: Sarah Elizabeth, Katherine Jessica. *Education:* City College (now City College of the City University of New York), B.A., 1956; Hunter College of the City University of New York, graduate study in urban planning, 1974-75. *Home:* 53 Demarest Mill Rd., West Nyack, N.Y. 10994.

CAREER: Dover Publications, Inc. (book publishers), New York City, publicity director, 1958-59; New York Convention and Visitors Bureau, Inc., New York City, assistant promotion director, 1960-65; Hudson River Valley Commission (state agency), Tarrytown, N.Y., information officer, 1965-71; environmental affairs consultant, 1971—. Lecturer in architectural walking-tour program, Museum of the City of New York, 1959-61. Consultant to business firms on New York City landmarks, history, and ethnic groups. *Military service:* U.S. Army, 1956-58; served in Italy.

WRITINGS: (With Samuel Kaplan) *The New York City Handbook,* Doubleday, 1966, revised edition, 1968.

WORK IN PROGRESS: Hudson Valley Tourways, a guide to the Hudson Valley.

SIDELIGHTS: Taber's idea for *The New York City Handbook* grew out of his interest in architecture and landmarks, and experiences "in coping with the nitty-gritty of life in Manhattan."

*   *   *

TAUBER, Kurt P(hilip) 1922-

PERSONAL: Born October 6, 1922, in Vienna, Austria; son of Richard (an industrialist) and Anny (Kohn) Tauber; married Esther M. Moss, April 13, 1944; children: Gwen Michele. *Education:* Harvard University, student, 1940-43, S.B., 1946, A.M., 1948, Ph.D., 1951. *Politics:* "Socialist humanism." *Religion:* None. *Home:* 7 Southworth St., Williamstown, Mass. 01267. *Office:* Department of Political Science, Williams College, Williamstown, Mass. 01267.

CAREER: Field director, Massachusetts Department of Public Health, 1951-52; University of Buffalo (now State University of New York at Buffalo), assistant professor of government, 1953-60; Williams College, Williamstown, Mass., assistant professor, 1960-64, associate professor, 1964-69, professor of political science, 1969—. *Military service:* U.S. Army Air Forces, 1943-46; served in European Theater; became captain. *Member:* Caucus for a New Political Science, American Association of University Professors, American Civil Liberties Union (chairman of Niagara Frontier branch, 1954-55). *Awards, honors:* Fulbright fellow, 1955-56, 1973-74; American Council of Learned Societies fellow, 1964-65; American Philosophical Society fellow, 1964-65; Guggenheim fellow, 1968-69.

WRITINGS: Beyond Eagle and Swastika: German Nationalism Since 1945, two volumes, Wesleyan University Press, 1967. Contributor of articles to *World Politics, Ethics, Political Science Quarterly, New York Times Magazine,* and other periodicals.

WORK IN PROGRESS: German Historiography Since 1945.

SIDELIGHTS: Tauber told *CA:* "A dissatisfied chemistry major in college, a listless U.S. soldier in a God-forsaken airbase in Britain, I received a Christmas package from my wife that contained Sabine's *History of Political Theory.* From then on there was no doubt in my mind that I wanted to spend my life doing political science."

*   *   *

TAUBMAN, William 1941-

PERSONAL: Born November 13, 1941, in New York, N.Y.; son of Howard (critic-at-large, *New York Times*) and Nora (Stern) Taubman; married Jane Andelman (an assistant professor of Russian), 1969; children: Alexander James. *Education:* Harvard University, B.A., 1962; Columbia University, M.A. and Certificate of Russian Institute, 1965, Ph.D., 1969; Moscow State University, exchange student, 1965-66. *Home:* 46 Orchard St., Amherst, Mass. *Office:* Political Science Department, Amherst College, Amherst, Mass. 01002.

CAREER: Amherst College, Amherst, Mass., instructor, 1967-69, assistant professor, 1969-73, associate professor of political science, 1973—. *Member:* American Political Science Association, American Association for the Advancement of Slavic Studies, American Association of University Professors, Council on Foreign Relations. *Awards, honors:* Woodrow Wilson fellowship, 1962; Fulbright Hays fellowship, 1965-66; International Affairs fellowship, Council on Foreign Relations, 1970-71.

WRITINGS: The View from Lenin Hills: Soviet Youth in Ferment, Coward, 1967; *Governing Soviet Cities: Bureaucratic Politics and Urban Development in the USSR,* Praeger, 1973; (editor) *Globalism and Its Cities: The American Foreign Policy Debate of the 1960's,* Heath, 1973.

WORK IN PROGRESS: Explaining and Evaluating the Cold War.

SIDELIGHTS: Taubman's year as an exchange student in Russia is the subject of *The View from Lenin Hills.* Fred M. Hechinger says of this book: "The Taubman view from Lenin Hills is clear, fresh and entertaining. The conclusion that many young Russians are not anti-capitalist in the way many Americans are anti-Communist is shrewdly accurate and worth thinking about." Taubman, fluent in Russian, was one of the interpreters for the Soviet National Basketball Team on its American tour in 1965.

BIOGRAPHICAL/CRITICAL SOURCES: New York Times, January 22, 1968.

* * *

TAVEL, Ronald 1940-

PERSONAL: Surname pronounced Tah-*vel;* born May 17, 1940, in New York, N.Y.; son of George and Florence (Sterns) Tavel. *Education:* Brooklyn College (now Brooklyn College of the City University of New York), B.A.; University of Wyoming, M.A., 1961. *Home:* 438 West Broadway, New York, N.Y. 10012. *Agent:* Helen Merrill, 337 West 22nd St., New York, N.Y. 10011.

CAREER: After leaving college, traveled extensively in Canada, Mexico, France, Spain, and Africa. From December, 1964, to fall, 1966, worked as scenarist for Andy Warhol at Warhol's studio ("the factory") in New York City; founded and named the "Theatre of the Ridiculous" in New York City, 1965; currently lecturer for New York State Council on the Arts. Playwright-in-residence at Play-House of the Ridiculous, 1965-67, Theatre of the Lost Continent, 1971-73, Actor's Studio, 1972, and Yale Divinity School, 1975. Actor in films written by himself for Andy Warhol Films, Inc., and other films, include "Fifty Fantasticks," 1964, "Bitch," 1965, "Jail," 1967, "Suicide Notions: Fire Escape," 1972, and "In Search of the Cobra Jewels," 1972. Advisor to Subplot Theatre (part of American Place Complex); founding member, New York Theatre Strategy.

AWARDS, HONORS: Lyric poetry contest winner, 1955, for the poem, "Virginia Woolf"; Obie Awards, for "Boy on the Straight-Back Chair," 1968-69, and "Bigfoot," 1972-73; grants from American Place Theatre, 1970, Rockefeller Foundation, 1972, Creative Artists Public Service Program, 1972, 1974, Guggenheim Foundation, 1973, and National Endowment for the Arts, 1974-75; New York State Council on the Arts Younger Audience commission, 1975-76.

WRITINGS: Street of Stairs (novel; sections published in *Chicago Review,* Volume XVI, number 4, 1964, Volume XVII, number 1, 1964, Volume XVIII, number 2, 1965, and *Intransit,* 1967), Olympia Press, 1968.

Plays: "Christina's World" (three-act verse play), published in *Chicago Review,* Volume XVI, number 1, 1963; "The Life of Juanita Castro" (one-act; also see below; first produced with "Shower" in New York at Coda Galleries, June 29, 1969; produced with "Shower" Off-Broadway at St. Marks Playhouse, July 29, 1965), published in *Tri-Quarterly,* Number 6, 1966; "Shower" (one-act; first produced with "The Life of Juanita Castro" in New York at Coda Galleries, June 29, 1965; produced with "The Life of Juanita Castro" Off-Broadway at St. Marks Playhouse, July 29, 1965), published in *The Young American Writers,* edited by Richard Kostelanetz, Funk, 1967; "Tarzan of the Flicks," first produced in Plainfield, Vt. at Goddard College, December, 1965; "The Life of Lady Godiva" (one-act; first produced in New York at Play-House of the Ridiculous, April, 1966), published in *The New Underground Theatre,* edited by Robert Shroeder, Bantam, 1968; "Screen Test" (one-act; also see below; first produced with "Indiria Gandhi's Daring Device" in New York at Play-House of the Ridiculous, September 29, 1966; "Indiria Gandhi's Daring Device" (one-act), first produced with "Screen Test" in New York at Play-House of the Ridiculous, September 29, 1966.

"Kitchenette" (one-act; also see below; first produced in New York at Play-House of the Ridiculous, January, 1967), published in *Partisan Review,* spring, 1967; "Gorilla Queen" (full-length; first produced at Judson Poets Theatre, March, 1967; produced Off-Broadway at the Martinique Theatre, April 26, 1967), published in *The Best of Off-Off Broadway,* edited by Michael Smith, Dutton, 1969, published in *The Off-Off Broadway Book: The People, the Plays, the Theatres,* edited by Bruce Mailman and Albert Poland, Bobbs-Merrill, 1972; "Vinyl" (one-act; also see below; first produced at Caffe Cino, October, 1967), published in *Clyde,* Volume XII, number 2, 1966; "Canticle of the Nightingale (one-act musical), first produced in Stockholm, Sweden, 1968, produced in New York at Manhattan Theatre Club, June, 1973; "Cleobis and Bito" (one-act dance-oratorio), first produced in New York at the Extension, March, 1968; "Arenas of the Lutetia" (full-length; first produced in New York at Judson Poets Theatre, November, 1968), published in *Experiments in Prose,* edited by Eugene Wildman, Swallow Press, 1969; "Boy on the Straight-Back Chair" (full-length musical; music by Orville Stoeber), first produced Off-Broadway at American Place Theatre, February 14, 1969.

"Vinyl Visits an FM Station" (one-act; first produced Off-Off Broadway at the Playwrights Unit, May, 1970), published in *Drama Review,* Volume XIV, number 4, 1970; "Bigfoot" (full-length), first produced in New York at Theatre Genesis, November, 1972; "Secrets of the Citizens Correction Committee" (one-act; first produced in New York at Theatre at Saint Clement's, October, 1973), published in *Scripts,* Number 3, January, 1972; "Queen of Greece" (full-length), first produced in New York at Theatre Genesis, November, 1973; "The Last Days of British Honduras," first produced Off-Broadway at New York Shakespeare Festival Public Theatre, October, 1974.

Films; all produced by Andy Warhol Films, Inc.: (Author of scenario) "Harlot," 1964, published in *Film Culture,* spring, 1966; "The Life of Juanita Castro," 1965; (author of scenario) "Philip's Screen Test," 1965 (never released); "Screen Test," 1965; "Kitchen" (film version of his play, "Kitchenette"), 1965; (author of scenario) "Horse," 1965; (author of scenario) "Space," 1965; "Suicide," 1965; (author of scenario) "Withering Heights," 1966; "The Chelsea Girls," 1966; (author of scenario) "Hedy; or, The 14-Year-Old Girl," 1966; "Vinyl," 1967.

Other works: "The Banana Diary" (book-length essay), published in *Film Culture,* spring, 1966; (contributor) Gregory Battock, editor, *The New American Cinema,* Dutton,

1967; "Words for Bryan to Sing and Dance" (poetry), performed by the Marian Sarach Dance Company at Judson Poets Theatre, April, 1971; (author of lyrics) "No More Masterpieces" (record), Mention Records, 1971. Contributor of essays, poetry, and articles to *Writing at Wyoming, Chicago Review, Wormwood, Tri-Quarterly, Aspen, Film Culture, Graffitti, Filmwise,* and other periodicals. Literary advisor, *Scripts,* 1971-72.

WORK IN PROGRESS: A children's play, "The Clown's Tail."

SIDELIGHTS: In 1965 Tavel named a new movement and offered "Shower" (a play which he wrote in 48 hours) as its first representative. He considered christening a Theatre of the Preposterous, but decided that what he really wanted was "the flat and uncagey irrevocability of 'ridiculous'" and the Theatre of the Ridiculous was born. As chief spokesman for the movement, Tavel writes: "If asked what styles or temperaments most directly influence the Theatre of the Ridiculous, I should say Pop, Camp, Psychodelic, and Art Noveau. . . . Theatre of the Ridiculous is a Community of Ourselves taking momentary time to laugh at its position as the ridiculous."

Dan Sullivan writes, "who can object to being put-on when it is done with [such] verve . . .?" Tavel writes: "A genuine work of art will, by necessity, undermine the social structure and the moral cadre on which our existences are postulated. For a real work of art is, by definition, an act of truth, and our social structure is a lie. . . . It is my contention that the Artist has two great competitors and therefore enemies: the religious figure and the political figure. These two propose a static paradise and boundaried limit on man's possibilities—one in heaven, the other on earth. But it is the artist's job to raise man to the level of the contemplation of his possibility of possibilities, a non-action and therefore unlimited state, the artistic state, as it were."

Moreover, one can find in Tavel's comments on "Shower" his recommendations for the direction which the Theatre of the Ridiculous must take. "Shower," he writes, "was dirty like the Mae West I loved for so many years, it was action packed and streamlined for movement, yet totally devoid of character or identity, direction, plot, or subject matter. Each personage parried the others with lightning speed to his own content, but no one ever answered the question posed to him, everyone argued and fought and killed around non-existent objects and indecipherable goals, syllogistic logic reared its weak head only every third dramatic beat, and word and emotive association held the day. A quotidian nothingness had been built over a foundation of subliminal cement."

Tavel believes that his work "seeks an order beyond the trap of words by dispensing with the response and action and idea that words usually dictate" and Peter Michelson believes that he has been successful in this respect. Michelson explains that "the ridiculous goes beyond the absurd by abandoning dialectic altogether as a mode of understanding. Serious form, in the ridiculous, happens only at those epiphanal moments when the images explode their shot. Between times what you get is patter and amusement." Michelson notes that Tavel has borrowed from Oscar Wilde the notion that "nature is understood by the images of it that we construct" which is decadent, he continues, "in that it eschews the reality of dialectical morality and substitutes a reality determined by artistic imagination. The thesis of 'Gorilla Queen,' and that of much pop art, is that our 'heroic' ideals are the Grade B products of Grade B films. Tavel has turned these heroes, heroines, and heroics into moral ironies by reflecting them in the light of their own moral vacuity, *i.e.* their absurdity. Thus decadence becomes a figural representation of the ridiculousness of, for example, sentimentalized virility. . . . The Ridiculous sensibility, then, not only images an outrageous morality, but it also avails us of a decadent metaphysics."

Many critics were quick to deride Tavel's work. Robert Brustein quipped: "['Gorilla Queen'] is a curious combination of nastiness and innocence. What is especially nasty about it is its abortive puns; and it is particularly innocent of talent." But others were able to evaluate "Gorilla Queen," and other Tavel plays, more open-mindedly. Michael Smith writes: "I like [Tavel's] plays. I am mystified by his writing but convinced of its integrity; it really is what it is, whatever it is. Its peculiarities are necessary, even compulsive, not [modish] mannerism, not failed imitation. For all its silliness, his writing is dense, felicitous, energetic, complex, and intelligent; and his theatrical vision is not only outrageous but original."

Dan Sullivan called "Gorilla Queen" "a kind of apotheosis" of camp and Smith said of the play: "It's a camp, it's a trip, it's a nightmare. It's silly, exhausting, fun, disgusting, and disturbing because deep inside it's real. Tavel is really doing something." In his review of "The Life of Lady Godiva," Smith perhaps summarized the reactions of many to Tavel's plays. Smith called "Godiva" "terrifically entertaining" and added that "beyond that, its flavor is inexpressible, almost unspeakable. . . . It is a true novelty among forms." In another review, Smith concluded that Tavel's plays, "—like those of Pinter or H. M. Koutoukas—have a unique personal style, persuasively suggesting an original and self-contained theatrical mind."

The Play-House of the Ridiculous closed in the spring of 1967. "It grew up in a night and disappeared in a night—but," according to Dan Isaac, "not before allowing Ronald Tavel to write a number of plays just the way he wanted to." Julius Novick summarizes the critics' reactions to Tavel's plays: "There are two schools of thought about Ronald Tavel. One school feels that he is something very interesting; the other school walks out on his productions at the first available opportunity and never returns."

A *Newsweek* reviewer notes that although "some critics are put off by his 'camp' ambiance," Tavel may be "the best young playwright around. . . . He is one of the few playwrights who has true instinct for how and when to 'involve' and uninvolve the audience, and his self-parody is not only funny but part of the dramatic pattern." Marilyn Stasio, reviewing "Boy on the Straight-Back Chair," believes that Tavel "has not as yet devised, however, a really satisfactory means of communicating with audiences outside his own admiring cult." Martin Duberman notes that in the play "Tavel trades too long and relies too heavily on word-play. . . . But though *Boy* fails to sustain itself, there can be no doubt that Tavel has a formidable array of talents. With a little more control, a little less self-indulgence, he could well emerge as a major dramatist."

Tavel's plays have been translated into a half-dozen languages and been performed in Japan, Australia, Canada, and much of Europe. Some of his poems were taped for broadcast by WRVR's "Anthology of the Air," 1966.

BIOGRAPHICAL/CRITICAL SOURCES: Village Voice, April 28, 1966, January 12, 1967, March 16, 1967, December 5, 1968, March 6, 1969; *Tri-Quarterly,* Number 6, 1966; *New York Times,* March 20, 1967; *World Journal*

Tribune, March 21, 1967; *Partisan Review*, spring, 1967, fall, 1969; *Wall Street Journal*, April 24, 1967; *Financial Times*, April 25, 1967; *New Republic*, May 6, 1967, September 9, 1967; *Hudson Review*, summer, 1967; *New Statesman*, July 14, 1967; *Drama Review*, Volume XIII, number 1, 1968; *Cue*, March 22, 1969; *Newsweek*, March 24, 1969; Carolyn Riley, editor, *Contemporary Literary Criticism*, Volume VI, Gale, 1976.

*   *   *

TAVES, Isabella 1915-

PERSONAL: Born September 20, 1915, in Lincoln, Neb.; daughter of Cornelius William and Blanche (Roberts) Taves; married Daniel D. Mich, November 4, 1944 (deceased). *Education:* Northwestern University, B.S., 1932. *Home:* 137 East 38th St., New York, N.Y. 10016. *Agent:* Julian Bach, 3 East 48th St., New York, N.Y. 10017.

CAREER: Free-lance magazine writer. *Member:* Authors League of America, Women in Communications, Overseas Press Club of America, Phi Beta Kappa, Alpha Phi. *Awards, honors:* Merit Award, Northwestern University; Headliner Award, Women in Communications, 1974.

WRITINGS: Successful Women, Dutton, 1943; (with Margaret Hubbard Ayer) *The Three Lives of Harriet Hubbard Ayer*, Lippincott, 1953; *The Quick Rich Fox*, Random House, 1960; *I Learned About Women from Them*, McKay, 1963; *Women Alone*, Funk, 1968; *Destiny Times Six*, M. Evans, 1970; *Not Bad for a Girl*, M. Evans, 1972; *Love Must Not Be Wasted*, Crowell, 1974. Author of column, "Women Alone," distributed by Tribune Syndicate. Contributor of articles to *Ladies' Home Journal, Reader's Digest, McCall's, Good Housekeeping*, and other popular periodicals.

SIDELIGHTS: Miss Taves says of *Women Alone:* "I started the book as therapy when I was a widow of seven months after 21 years of marriage. I didn't know the answers to living alone and I wanted to find them." She traveled the country and toured resorts gathering her material.

BIOGRAPHICAL/CRITICAL SOURCES: Washington Post, July 1, 1968.

*   *   *

TAYLOR, Alison 1927-

PERSONAL: Born November 7, 1927, in Coulsdon, Surrey, England; daughter of Graham (a business executive) and Dorothy (Young) Taylor. *Education:* Studied at Guildhall School of Music and Drama, London, England, 1945-48, licentiate of G.S.M., 1947. *Home:* 16 The Willows, Maidenhead Rd., Windsor, Berkshire, England.

CAREER: Free-lance teacher and lecturer in drama, speech, and English, in and around London, England, 1948-61; assistant county youth officer with special responsibility for drama, Middlesex County Council, 1961-64; free-lance writer, lecturer, adjudicator, organizer of projects in connection with Duke of Edinburgh's Award, and examiner of spoken English, 1964-69; free-lance documentary film scriptwriter, 1969—. *Member:* British Drama League.

WRITINGS: The Cinderella of Chulo (play), Samuel French, 1959; (with Marjorie Thomas) *Challenge to Susan*, Parrish, 1965; *The Story of the English Stage*, Pergamon, 1967; *For and Against: A Discussion on the Award Scheme*, Pergamon, 1967; *Off Stage and On*, Pergamon, 1969.

WORK IN PROGRESS: Scriptwriting for sponsored documentary films.

*   *   *

TAYLOR, Benjamin J. 1934-

PERSONAL: Born October 25, 1934, in Clay, Ky.; son of Ernest Roy (a factory worker) and Lottie (Marks) Taylor; married Alcarla Taylor, July 29, 1974; children: (previous marriage) Howard C., Dawn L. *Education:* Oakland City College, Oakland City, Ind., B.S., 1959; Indiana State University, M.A., 1961; Indiana University, Ph.D., 1966. *Politics:* Independent. *Religion:* Baptist. *Home:* 2128 Wilkinson Ct., Norman, Okla. 73069. *Office:* Department of Economics, University of Oklahoma, Norman, Okla. 73069.

CAREER: Oakland City College, Oakland City, Ind., assistant professor of economics, 1961-63; Indiana University, Bloomington, lecturer in economics, 1965-66; Arizona State University, Tempe, assistant professor, 1966-68, associate professor, 1968-70, professor of economics, 1970-71, chairman of department, 1969-71, director of Bureau of Business and Economic Research, 1967-68; University of Oklahoma, Norman, professor of economics, 1971—. *Military service:* U.S. Army, 1954-56. *Member:* American Economic Association, Western Economic Association.

WRITINGS: The Operation of the Taft Hartley Act in Indiana, Indiana University Press, 1967; *Arizona Labor Relations Law*, Arizona State University, 1967; *Labor Relations Law*, Prentice-Hall, 1975. Contributor to *Labor Law Journal* and *Arizona Business Bulletin*.

WORK IN PROGRESS: Writing on Indian manpower problems.

*   *   *

TAYLOR, John 1921-

PERSONAL: Born September 4, 1921, in Glasgow, Scotland; son of John Noel (an advertising executive) and Ellen (Callander) Taylor; married Deirdre Welch. *Education:* Attended Streatham Grammar School. *Politics:* None. *Religion:* Roman Catholic. *Home:* The Mews, Broadwater Ct., Tunbridge Wells, Kent, England. *Office:* Accolade Publications Ltd., 100 Great Portland St., London, W.1, England.

CAREER: The Tailor and Cutter Ltd., London, England, editor of *Tailor and Cutter* (magazine), 1946-69, and *Man about Town* (magazine), 1952-60, also former managing editor of five magazines published for the clothing industry, including *Tailor and Cutter, Manufacturing Clothier, Buttons*, and *Hards Year Book of Clothing Industry;* director of textile business press, Industrial Publishing Co., 1969-71; Accolade Publications Ltd., London, founder and editor, 1971—. Appears monthly on television shows in England. *Military service:* Royal Navy, air gunner and then pilot with Fleet Air Arm, 1940-46; became sub-lieutenant. *Member:* Clothing Institute, London Press Club. *Awards, honors:* Fashion Writer of the Year, British Clothing Institute, 1970.

WRITINGS: It's a Small, Medium and Outsize World (collection of essays), Hugh Evelyn, 1966, World Publishing, 1967; *On Women* (verse), Hobbs, 1969; *The Care and Feeding of Young Ladies*, M. Joseph, 1975. Regular columnist for three London magazines, *Weekend* (weekly column), *Penthouse* (monthly column), and *Punch* (weekly column).

TAYLOR, Theodore 1921-
(T. T. Lang)

PERSONAL: Born June 23, 1921, in Statesville, N.C.; son of Edward Riley (a molder) and Elnora (Langhans) Taylor; married Gweneth Goodwin, October 25, 1946; children: Mark, Wendy, Michael. Education: Attended U.S. Merchant Marine Academy, 1942-43; studied at Columbia University and with American Theatre Wing, 1947-49. Politics: Republican. Religion: Protestant. Home: 675 Diamond St., Laguna Beach, Calif. Agent: Armitage Watkins, A. Watkins, Inc., 77 Park Ave., New York, N.Y. 10016.

CAREER: Sunset News, Bluefield, W. Va., sports editor, 1946-47; director of public relations for New York University, New York, N.Y., 1947-49, and Orlando Sentinel-Star, Orlando, Fla., 1949-50; lieutenant, U.S. Navy, 1950-55; Paramount Pictures Corp., Perlberg-Seaton Productions, Hollywood, Calif. associate producer, 1955-61; Columbia Pictures Industries, Inc., Hollywood, press agent, 1961-64; Twentieth Century-Fox Film Corp., Hollywood, press agent and production coordinator, 1965-69; full-time writer, 1969—. Producer and director of documentary films. Military service: U.S. Merchant Marine, 1942-44; U.S. Navy, 1945-46. Member: Academy of Motion Picture Arts and Sciences, Writers Guild, Authors League of America. Awards, honors: Juvenile Silver Medal, Commonwealth Club of California, Jane Addams Children's Book Award, Lewis Carroll Shelf Award, and Woodward School Award, 1970, all for The Cay.

WRITINGS: The Magnificent Mitscher, Norton, 1955; Fire on the Beaches, Norton, 1957; People Who Make Movies, Doubleday, 1967; The Body Trade, Fawcett, 1968; The Cay (juvenile), Doubleday, 1969; (with Robert Houghton) Special Unit Senator, Random House, 1970; Air Raid–Pearl Harbor (juvenile), Crowell, 1971; The Children's War (juvenile), Doubleday, 1972; Rebellion Town (juvenile), Crowell, 1973; The Maldonado Miracle (juvenile), Doubleday, 1973; (with Kreskin) The Amazing World of Kreskin, Random House, 1974; Teetoncey (juvenile), Doubleday, 1974; Teetoncey and Ben O'Neal, Doubleday, 1975. Author of two screenplays, "Showdown," Universal, 1972, and "Night without End," and of seventeen documentary films. Also author of books under the pseudonym T. T. Lang. Short stories and novelettes have been published in Redbook, Argosy, Saturday Evening Post, and other periodicals.

WORK IN PROGRESS: The Odyssey of Ben O'Neal, for Doubleday; A Shepherd Watches, nonfiction, for Doubleday; a biography of composer Jule Styne, for Random House.

SIDELIGHTS: Taylor has traveled extensively in Europe and the Far East while making documentary films.

* * *

TAYLOR, Thomas 1934-

PERSONAL: Born December 11, 1934, in Fort Leavenworth, Kan.; son of Maxwell Davenport and Lydia (Happer) Taylor. Education: U.S. Military Academy, B.S., 1960; University of California, Berkeley, M.A., 1970, J.D., 1976. Politics: Democrat. Religion: None. Home: 14 Menlo Pl., Berkeley, Calif. 94707. Agent: William Morris Agency, 1350 Avenue of the Americas, New York, N.Y. 10019.

CAREER: U.S. Army, commissioned second lieutenant, 1960, discharged as major, 1968; served overseas in Germany, Greece, Saudi Arabia, Panama, and Vietnam; received Silver Star, Bronze Star with "v" device and oak leaf cluster, Air Medal, Purple Heart, Commendation Medal, and Cross for Gallantry (Vietnam). Awards, honors: Breadloaf fellowship, 1968; Corothers Prize in Literary Composition, University of California, 1969.

WRITINGS: A-18 (war novel), Crown, 1967; A Piece of This Country, Norton, 1970.

WORK IN PROGRESS: P.O.W., a Vietnam war novel; "Patricia Hearst," a Wagnerian rock opera; Grass, a screenplay.

SIDELIGHTS: Taylor told CA: "I feel that eventually movies will be my main medium. What I strive for is to show how the events of the 1970's impressed someone who lived through them. History is accelerating so that to think of a few years past is almost nostalgia."

* * *

TAYLOR, Warren 1903-

PERSONAL: Born July 2, 1903, in Bedford County, Tenn.; son of Sidney Johnston and Margaret Jane (Taylor) Taylor; married Adele Elizabeth Wanner, August 26, 1933; children: Geoffrey Warren, Joseph Ransom, Thomas William, William Dickinson. Education: Vanderbilt University, B.A., 1924, M.A., 1926; University of Chicago, Ph.D., 1937. Religion: Unitarian Universalist. Home: 227 South Professor St., Oberlin, Ohio 44074.

CAREER: Instructor at University of Tennessee, Knoxville, 1926-29, Oberlin College, Oberlin, Ohio, 1930-34, and University of Chicago, Chicago, Ill., 1934-37; Oberlin College, instructor, 1937-41, assistant professor, 1941-47, associate professor, 1947-50, professor of English, 1950-70, professor emeritus, 1970—, head of humanities program, 1947-70; Hiram College, Hiram, Ohio, distinguished professor of humanities, 1970-74. Visiting professor at University of Arkansas, 1953, University of New Mexico, 1955, College of the Pacific, 1959, and other universities and colleges. Member: Modern Language Association of America, Renaissance Society of America, American Association of University Professors (national council member, 1950-53; first vice-president, 1959-60). Awards, honors: Ford Foundation faculty fellowship, 1951-52.

WRITINGS: (Co-author) The Humanities at Oberlin, Oberlin College, 1958; (editor with Donald Hall) Poetry in English, Macmillan, 1963, 2nd edition, 1970; Models for Thinking and Writing, World Publishing, 1966; Tudor Figures of Rhetoric, Language Press, 1972. Contributor to professional journals. Member of editorial board, College English, 1953-55; associate editor, Humanist, 1955-57.

* * *

TEITELBAUM, Harry 1930-

PERSONAL: Born September 23, 1930, in Leipzig, Germany; son of Simon (a furrier) and Rencia (Erdtrachter) Teitelbaum; married Marilyn L. Nober (a teacher), November 7, 1953; children: Mark Steven, David Hal, Deborah Randee. Education: Brooklyn College (now of the City University of New York), B.A., 1952, M.A., 1953; New York University, currently Ph.D. candidate. Residence: Fort Salonga, N.Y.

CAREER: Taught in New York City and with U.S. Air Force schools in Germany; teacher of English at high schools in Elmont, N.Y., 1955-60, and Plainview, N.Y., 1960-66; John F. Kennedy High School, Plainview, teacher of English and head of department, 1966—. Hofstra University, 1958-74, began as adjunct associate professor, became adjunct professor; Suffolk County Community College, member of adjunct faculty, 1975—. *Military service:* U.S. Army, Military Intelligence in Germany, 1953-55. *Member:* National Education Association, National Council of Teachers of English, American Association of University Professors, New York State Teachers Association, New York State English Council, Nassau English Chairmen's Association.

WRITINGS: How to Write Theses, Monarch Press, 1966, revised edition published as *How to Write Theses and Themes*, 1975; *How to Write Book Reports*, Monarch Press, 1975. Author of handbook on research papers for high school students. Contributor to educational journals.

* * *

TENNYSON, G(eorg) B(ernhard) 1930-

PERSONAL: Born July 13, 1930, in Washington, D.C.; son of Georg Bernhard and Emily (Zimmerli) Tennyson; married Elizabeth C. Johnstone, July 13, 1953; children: Noel Emily, Holly Elizabeth. *Education:* George Washington University, A.B., 1953, M.A., 1959; graduate study at Shakespeare Institute, Stratford on Avon, England, summer, 1952, and University of Freiburg, 1953-54; Princeton University, M.A., 1961, Ph.D., 1963. *Religion:* Anglo-Catholic. *Home:* 4963 Densmore Ave., Encino, Calif. 91436. *Office:* Department of English, University of California, Los Angeles, Calif. 90024.

CAREER: Washington Star, Washington, D.C., reporter, 1956-57; National Security Agency, Washington, D.C., classified work, 1957-59; University of North Carolina, Chapel Hill, assistant professor of English, 1962-64; University of California, Los Angeles, assistant professor, 1964-67, associate professor, 1967-71, professor of English, 1971—. *Military service:* U.S. Army, Signal Corps, 1954-56. *Member:* Modern Language Association of America, Philological Association of the Pacific Coast, Victorian Society (London), Carlyle Society (Edinburgh), Conference on Christianity and Literature, Philadelphia Society. *Awards, honors:* Fulbright fellow in Germany, 1953-54; Guggenheim fellow, 1970-71.

WRITINGS: Sartor Called Resartus: The Genesis, Structure, and Style of Thomas Carlyle's First Major Work, Princeton University Press, 1966; *An Introduction to Drama*, Holt, 1967; (contributor) *From the Medieval Epic to the Epic Theatre of Bertolt Brecht*, University of Southern California Press, 1967; (editor) *A Carlyle Reader: Selections From the Writings of Thomas Carlyle*, Random House, 1968; *Carlyle and the Modern World*, Carlyle Society, 1972; (contributor) *Victorian Prose: A Guide to Research*, Modern Language Association of America, 1973; *Carlyle and His Contemporaries*, Duke University Press, 1975; (editor with Edward L. Ericson, Jr.) *Religion and Modern Literature*, Eerdmans, 1975; (with Donald Gray) *Victorian Literature: Poetry*, Macmillan, 1976; *Evolution of Consciousness: Studies in Polarity*, Wesleyan University Press, 1976. Contributor to *Southern Review, Victorian Poetry, Montashefte*, and other journals. *Nineteenth-Century Fiction*, editor, 1971-74, member of advisory board, 1974—; member of advisory board of *Victorian Studies*, 1970-73, and *Occasional Review*, 1974—.

WORK IN PROGRESS: A critical study of Victorian devotional poetry; a subject index to *Nineteenth-Century Fiction, 1945-74*; a study of the works of Owen Barfield.

AVOCATIONAL INTERESTS: Art, architecture, gardening, Confederate history, ecclesiastical history, Christian mysticism.

* * *

TERPSTRA, Vern 1927-

PERSONAL: Born August 20, 1927, in Wayland, Mich.; son of Benjamin and Lucy (Jonker) Terpstra; married Bonnie Lou Fuller, September 18, 1950; children: Benjamin, Mark, Kathryn Ann, James Richard. *Education:* University of Michigan, B.B.A., 1950, M.B.A., 1951, Ph.D., 1965; University of Brussels, graduate study, 1952-53. *Religion:* Presbyterian. *Home:* 750 Lans Way, Ann Arbor, Mich. *Office:* Graduate School of Business, University of Michigan, Ann Arbor, Mich. 48104.

CAREER: Church Missionary Society, director of education for the Congo, and director of a Congo normal school, 1953-61; Marketing Science Institute, Philadelphia, Pa., resident fellow, 1963-64; University of Pennsylvania, Wharton School, Philadelphia, assistant professor of marketing, 1964-66; University of Michigan, Graduate School of Business, Ann Arbor, associate professor, 1966-70, professor of international business, 1970—. Consultant in international studies, Marketing Science Institute, 1964-66; consulting editor on international business, Holt, Rinehart & Winston, 1971—. *Military service:* U.S. Navy, 1945-46. *Member:* American Economic Association, American Marketing Association, Academy of International Business (president, 1971-72).

WRITINGS: (With Liander and Sherbini) *Marketing Development in the European Economic Community*, McGraw, 1964; (editor with Alderson and Shapiro) *Patents and Progress: Sources and Impact of Changing Technology*, Irwin, 1965; (with Sherbini, Yoshino, and Liander) *Comparative Analysis for International Marketing*, Allyn & Bacon, 1967; *American Marketing in the Common Market*, Praeger, 1967; *University Education for International Business*, Academy of International Business, 1969; *International Marketing*, Holt, 1972.

WORK IN PROGRESS: Research in international marketing by multinational firms.

SIDELIGHTS: Terpstra speaks and reads French and Swahili.

* * *

TERRY, Walter 1913-

PERSONAL: Born May 14, 1913, in Brooklyn, N.Y.; son of Walter Matthews and Frances Lindsay (Gray) Terry. *Education:* University of North Carolina, B.A., 1935; studied dance privately (with the view of becoming a critic, not a performer). *Office: Saturday Review*, 488 Madison Ave., New York, N.Y. 10022.

CAREER: Boston Herald, Boston, Mass., dance critic, 1936-39; *New York Herald Tribune*, New York City, dance critic and editor, 1939-42, 1945-66; *World Journal Tribune*, New York City, dance critic and editor, 1966-67; *Saturday Review*, New York City, dance critic and editor, 1967—. Conductor of weekly radio programs, "Invitation to Dance," beginning 1940; lecturer on dance topics throughout United States; dance consultant for national television shows, including "Camera 3," "Frontiers of Faith," and "Eye on New York," Own performances have been limited to dancing with a student company at University of North Carolina and as principal dancer in British production of "Rose Marie" at Royal Opera House in Cairo, 1943. *Military service:* U.S. Army, 1942-45; stationed in Africa and Middle East, 1943-45; became master sergeant.

WRITINGS: (Contributor) *Dance: A Basic Educational Technique,* 1941; *Invitation to Dance,* A. S. Barnes, 1942; *Star Performance: The Story of the World's Great Ballerinas,* Doubleday, 1945; *Ballet in Action,* photographs by Paul Himmel, introduction by George Balanchine, Putnam, 1954; *The Dance in America,* Harper, 1956, revised edition, 1971; *Ballet: A New Guide to the Liveliest Art,* Dell, 1959.

On Pointe! The Story of Dancing and Dancers on Toe, Dodd, 1962; *Isadora Duncan: Her Life, Her Art, Her Legacy,* Dodd, 1963; *The Ballet Companion,* Dodd, 1968; *Ballet: A Pictorial History,* Van Nostrand, 1969; *Miss Ruth: The "More Living Life" of Ruth St. Denis,* Dodd, 1969; *Careers for the Seventies: Dance,* Macmillan, 1971.

Author of scripts for Voice of America and for television shows. Contributor to magazines and newspapers, including *Look, This Week, Kenyon Review, Horizon, Theatre Arts, Pageant, Dance, Ballet Annual, Sunday Times, Dancing Times,* and *Politiken* (Copenhagen). Dance editor, *Encyclopaedia Britannica.*

* * *

TeSELLE, Sallie McFague 1933-

PERSONAL: Born May 25, 1933, in Quincy, Mass.; daughter of Maurice Graeme and Jessie (Reid) McFague; married Eugene A. TeSelle, Jr. (professor), September 12, 1959; children: Elizabeth, John. *Education:* Smith College, B.A., 1955; Yale University, B.D., 1959, Ph.D., 1964. *Politics:* Democrat. *Religion:* Methodist. *Home:* 2007 Linden Ave., Nashville, Tenn. 37212. *Office:* Vanderbilt University, Nashville, Tenn. 37203.

CAREER: Yale University, Divinity School, New Haven, Conn., lecturer in Christianity and contemporary culture, 1963-65; currently associate professor of theology and dean of Divinity School, Vanderbilt University, Nashville, Tenn. *Member:* American Academy of Religion, Society for Religion in Higher Education, Phi Beta Kappa.

WRITINGS: Literature and the Christian Life, Yale University Press, 1966; *Speaking in Parables: A Study in Metaphor and Theology,* Fortress, 1975. Editor, *Soundings: A Journal of Indisciplinary Studies,* 1967-75.

* * *

TETEL, Marcel 1932-

PERSONAL: Born October 11, 1932, in Paris, France; became U.S. citizen; married Joan Lieberman (a teacher), June 16, 1957; children: Jocelyn, Marc. *Education:* University of Chattanooga, B.A., 1954; Emory University, M.A., 1956; University of Florence, graduate study, 1957-58; University of Wisconsin, Ph.D., 1961. *Home address:* Duke Station 4666, Durham, N.C. 27706. *Office:* Department of Romance Languages, Duke University, Durham, N.C. 27706.

CAREER: Duke University, Durham, N.C., instructor, 1960-62, assistant professor, 1962-65, associate professor, 1965-68, professor of Romance languages, 1968—. *Member:* Modern Language Association of America, American Association of Teachers of French, American Association of Teachers of Italian, Renaissance Society of America, Societe des Amis de Rabelais, Societe des Amis

de Montaigne, South Atlantic Modern Language Association, Southeastern Renaissance Conference. *Awards, honors:* Fulbright grants, 1957-58, 1966-67; American Council of Learned Societies grant-in-aid, 1963; Guggenheim fellowship, 1969; American Philosophical Society grant, 1974.

WRITINGS: Etude sur le Comique de Rabelais, Olschki (Florence), 1964; *Rabelais,* Twayne, 1967; *Rabelais et l'Italie,* Olschki, 1969; (editor) Luigi Pirandello, *Enrico IV,* Appleton, 1971; *Marguerite De Navarre's Heptameron: Themes, Language and Structure,* Duke University Press, 1973; *Montaigne,* Twayne, 1974. Editor, *Journal of Medieval and Renaissance Studies,* 1971—.

* * *

THALER, Susan 1939-
(Susan Schlachter)

PERSONAL: Surname pronounced *Thah*-ler; born April 20, 1939, in New York, N.Y.; daughter of Bernard (a businessman) and Helen (Fogel) Schlachter; married Allan Edward Thaler (an architect), August 17, 1964; children: Sebastian, Alexander. *Education:* Studied evenings at Columbia University, 1957-59, and New School for Social Research, 1960-62. *Politics:* Republican. *Religion:* Jewish. *Residence:* Glen Rock, N.J. *Agent:* John Schaffner, 425 East 51st St., New York, N.Y. 10022.

CAREER: American Girl, New York City, assistant to fiction editor, 1960-66; *Ingenue,* New York City, lively arts editor, 1966-67; *American Girl,* fiction editor, 1968-71.

WRITINGS: Rosaria (teen-age novel), McKay, 1967. Also author of a story which originally appeared in *American Girl,* then was anthologized, under name Susan Schlachter, in *American Girl Book of Dog Stories,* Random House, 1966. Short stories also have appeared in *Redbook, Woman's Day, American Girl,* and *Madamoiselle.* Contributor to *Writers Digest.*

WORK IN PROGRESS: An autobiographical teen-age novel.

* * *

THAYNE, Mirla Greenwood 1907-

PERSONAL: Born March 16, 1907, in Union Utah; daughter of Thomas Foster (a farmer and realtor) and Emma (Burgon) Greenwood; married Clifton Earl Thayne (a salesman) June 26, 1929; children: Richard Grant, Gordon Earl, Sharon Renee (Mrs. Glennis T. Bronson), David C. *Education:* Brigham Young University, special student. *Religion:* Church of Jesus Christ of Latter-day Saints. *Home:* 414 North 600 East, Provo, Utah 84601.

CAREER: Composer; lecturer, and entertainer. Teacher of adult education class in creative writing, Provo, Utah, 1963-64, and church school teacher. Lecturer and entertainer, presenting more than a thousand programs of her songs and poems. *Member:* American Society of Composers, Authors and Publishers (ASCAP), International Platform Association, National League of American Pen Women (former branch president), Poetry Society of America, League of Utah Writers (former president of Utah Valley chapter). M.U.S.I.C. (Utah composers' guild). *Awards, honors:* Three first prizes for articles in national contests of National League of American Pen Women; other prizes for stories and articles in League of Utah Writers contests; Eliza R. Snow short story contest, *Deseret News,* first prize; and other prizes.

WRITINGS: *The Little Things* (poetry and prose), Deseret, 1966; *When He Comes Again* (children's book), Deseret, 1973. Ten prayer and special occasion songs have been published as sheet music, and several recorded; the published songs include the widely used "When He Comes Again." Contributor of articles, stories, songs, and poems to periodicals, including *Instructor, Utah Sings, Ideals, Music Ministry, Pen Woman, Era, Improvement,* and *Family Weekly.*

WORK IN PROGRESS: *Let the Valleys Sing,* a book on music; *One Solitary Life,* an adult book; *Awareness, The Divine Gift,* an adult book.

* * *

THIELE, Margaret Rossiter 1901-

PERSONAL: Surname rhymes with "really"; born May 16, 1901, in Battle Creek, Mich.; daughter of Frederick M. (a physician) and Mary (Henry) Rossiter; married J. Henry White; married second husband, Edwin R. Thiele (a professor), July 22, 1962; children: (first marriage) Winifred (Mrs. Adriel Chilson), Daphne (Mrs. Robert Odell), Donald R. (deceased). *Education:* Pacific Union College, B.A., 1921; San Jose State College (now San Jose State University), M.A., 1958. *Politics:* Republican. *Religion:* Seventh-day Adventist. *Home:* 33274 La Colina, Porterville, Calif. 93257.

CAREER: Between 1934-54, toured with former husband, J. Henry White of the White Brothers, who lectured and exhibited "camera paintings" of China; during these coast to coast tours she sometimes lectured on Chinese literature.

WRITINGS: *Whirlwind of the Lord,* Review & Herald, 1954; *By Saddle and Sleigh,* Review & Herald, 1965; *None But the Nightingale: An Introduction to Chinese Literature,* Tuttle, 1967; *A Home for Su Lan,* edited by Richard Utt, Pacific Press, 1971. Also author of *Tonio and Mishi.* Contributor of articles to *Life and Health.*

WORK IN PROGRESS: *Candle in the Night; The New-Fashioned Girl.*

* * *

THIESENHUSEN, William C. 1936-

PERSONAL: Born February 12, 1936, in Waukesha, Wis.; son of Arthur Henry and Myrtle (Honeyager) Thiesenhusen; married Virginia Waring, September 17, 1960; children: James Waring, Kathryn Hague, Gail Ann. *Education:* University of Wisconsin, B.S., 1958, M.S., 1960, Ph.D., 1965; Harvard University, M.P.A., 1962. *Office:* 310 King Hall, University of Wisconsin, Madison, Wis. 53706.

CAREER: University of Wisconsin, assistant professor of agricultural economics at Madison Campus, 1965-68, associate professor of agricultural journalism, 1968-72, and agricultural economics, 1971-72, professor of agricultural economics and agricultural journalism, 1972—, director, Land Tenure Center, 1971—, assistant professor of economics at Milwaukee Campus, 1966-67. *Member:* American Economic Association, American Farm Economic Association, Association for Evolutionary Economics, Latin American Studies Association.

WRITINGS: (Contributor) *Tenencias de la Tierra y Politicas Comparadas,* Book II, Colegio de Postgraduados, Escuela Nacional de Agricultura (Mexico), 1965; *Chile's Experiments in Agrarian Reform,* University of Wisconsin Press, 1966. Contributor to economic journals in the United States, Latin America, and Asia.

WORK IN PROGRESS: Research on land reform and agricultural programs in Latin America.

* * *

THOM, Robert 1929-

PERSONAL: Surname, legally changed when he was seven, is pronounced Tom; born July 2, 1929, in New York, N.Y.; son of Julius (an accountant) and Lily (Pendlebury) Flatow; married Millie Perkins (an actress), December 24, 1964; children: (previous marriage) Kate, Elizabeth; (current marriage) Lille. *Education:* Yale University, B.A., 1951; attended Cambridge University, 1951-52. *Politics:* Democrat, "more or less." *Religion:* "Gone."

CAREER: Writer of motion pictures, teleplays, stage plays, and books. *Awards, honors:* Emmy Award for best dramatic show of 1963, for "The Madman," episode of "The Defenders," CBS-TV.

WRITINGS: *Viaticum* (poetry), Golden Goose Press, 1949; *Children of the Ladybug* (two-act play), Yale University Press, 1956; *The Earthly Paradise,* Trident, 1965; *Wild in the Streets,* Pyramid, 1968. Contributor to *Esquire.*

Screenplays: "All the Fine Young Cannibals," Metro-Goldwyn-Mayer, 1960; "The Subterraneans," Metro-Goldwyn-Mayer, 1960; "Wild in the Streets," American International, 1968; "Angel, Angel, Down We Go," American International, 1969; "Bloody Mama," American International, 1970.

Teleplays: "The Madman," "The Boy Between," "Custody," all for "The Defenders"; "The Legend of Lylah Clare," "Jeremy Rabbitt the Secret Avenger," both for "DuPont Theater"; "Cheer Me On, Dear, No Matter What," for "Mr. Broadway"; "Who's the Fairest One of All?," "August Heat," both for "Great Ghost Stories"; "Buddy," for "For the People"; "Eddie Carew," for "Kraft Theater"; and others.

Stage plays: "Compulsion," "Bicycle Ride to Nevada," "The Minotaur," and "Sundial."

WORK IN PROGRESS: *Sex and Two Singular Minds,* a dialogue with philosopher Paul Weiss; a novel with tentative title, *The Way Up and the Way Down,* about the "secret joys of patricide".

SIDELIGHTS: Thom told *CA:* "Have survived as far East as Turkey—still cannot survive as far west as Los Angeles—but *try* to—intermittently. Motivation: to put down anguish, discover merriment, find an honest man—myself (hopefully) in 20 years; understand drugs, liquor, women, murder, abiding peace, and possibly myself." His play, *Children of the Ladybug,* portrays the results of a marriage without love, which, according to Joseph Langland, provides "the focus for a frank and dramatic auditing and analysis."

BIOGRAPHICAL/CRITICAL SOURCES: *Saturday Review,* January 19, 1957.†

* * *

THOMAS, Audrey (Callahan) 1935-

PERSONAL: Born November 17, 1935, in Binghamton, N.Y.; daughter of Donald Earle (a teacher) and Frances (Corbett) Callahan; married Ian Thomas (a sculptor and art teacher), December 6, 1959 (separated); children: Sarah, Victoria, Claire. *Education:* Smith College, B.A., 1957; University of British Columbia, M.A., 1963, currently doctoral candidate in English. *Home:* 3305 West 11th Ave., Vancouver, British Columbia, Canada.

CAREER: Writer. Member: Writers Union of Canada.

WRITINGS—All novels, except as indicated: Ten Green Bottles (short stories), Bobbs-Merrill, 1967; Mrs. Blood, Bobbs-Merrill, 1970; Munchmeyer and Prospero on the Island, Bobbs-Merrill, 1972; Songs My Mother Taught Me, Bobbs-Merrill, 1973; Blown Figures, Talonbooks (Vancouver), 1974, Knopf, 1975.

WORK IN PROGRESS: A book of short stories, and a radio play.

* * *

THOMAS, Edwin J(ohn) 1927-

PERSONAL: Born November 14, 1927, in Flint, Mich.; married, 1950; wife's name Vivian; children: Melinda Sue, Lisa K. Education: Wayne University (now Wayne State University), A.B. (with high distinction), 1951, M.S.W., 1953; University of Michigan, Ph.D., 1956. Home: 2224 Vinewood Blvd., Ann Arbor, Mich. 48104. Office: School of Social Work, University of Michigan, Ann Arbor, Mich. 48104.

CAREER: University of Michigan, Ann Arbor, research director, Aid to Dependent Children Study, 1956-57, assistant professor, 1956-59, associate professor, 1959-63, professor of social work and psychology, 1963—, head of Human Growth and Behavior Sequence, 1963-73. Visiting professor, University of Bradford. Consultant on behavioral intervention; part-time private practice in behavior therapy. Wayne State University, special lecturer, 1960. Military service: U.S. Army, 1946-48; served with Army of Occupation in Japan. Member: Alpha Kappa Delta. Awards, honors: Fulbright grant, 1967-68.

WRITINGS: (Contributor) L. Kogan, editor, Social Science Theory and Social Work Research, National Association of Social Workers, 1960; (contributor) N. A. Polansky, editor, Social Work Research, University of Chicago Press, 1960; (with Donna L. McLeod) In-Service Training and Reduced Workloads: Experiments in a State Welfare Department, Russell Sage, 1960; (with R. Feldman and Jane Kamm) Concepts of Role Theory: An Introduction Through Programmed Instruction and Programmed Case Analysis, Ann Arbor Publishers, 1964.

(Editor with Bruce J. Biddle) Role Theory: Concepts and Research, Wiley, 1966; (editor) Behavioral Science for Social Workers, Free Press, 1967; (editor) The Socio-Behavioral Approach and Applications to Social Work, Council on Social Work, 1967; (contributor) Edgar F. Borgatta, William W. Lambert, editors, Handbook of Personality Theory and Research, Rand McNally, 1967; (co-author) Behavior Therapy in Psychiatry, American Psychiatric Association, 1973; (editor) Behavior Modification Procedure: A Sourcebook, Aldine, 1974. Contributor to professional journals.

* * *

THOMAS, Estelle Webb 1899-

PERSONAL: Born January 11, 1899, in Woodruff, Ariz.; daughter of Edward Milo and Charlotte (Maxwell) Webb; married James H. Thomas (a former irrigation supervisor for Bureau of Indian Affairs and rancher), April 30, 1917; children: Wayne Russell, Edward Murray, Kathleen (Mrs. Richard E. Cloward). Education: Lived in Mexico as a child, and had two years of tutoring at Jaurez Academy, 1910-12. Politics: Republican. Religion: Church of Jesus Christ of Latter-day Saints. Home address: Box 38, Pinedale, Navajo County, Ariz. 85934. Agent: Ruth Cantor, 156 Fifth Ave., New York, N.Y. 10010.

CAREER: Teacher in Arizona elementary schools, 1914-31, and substitute teacher in Indian schools for several years during World War II; lived on a Navajo reservation in New Mexico, 1936-60, writing most of that time as a "stringer" for Farmington Daily Times and other newspapers in Gallup, N.M., and Holbrook, Ariz. Teacher of social relations, Clay Springs Relief Society, 1960—. President of chapter, American Women's Voluntary Service, Tohatchi, N.M., 1942-44. Member: American Gold Star Mothers, American Defenders of Bataan and Corregidor. Awards, honors: First prize for short story in Latter-day Saints centennial contest, 1947; Eliza Snow Short Story Award, 1947; Clover poetry contest prize, 1972; third prize in list of 100 books published by University Presses, for Gift of Laughter.

WRITINGS—For young people: Billy and the Bar-Bar-A, Caxton, 1955; The Torch Bearer, F. Watts, 1959; Gift of Laughter, Westminster, 1967; End of the Trail (poems), Chiva Publishing, 1974; Life's Willing Servant (biography of Charlotte Maxwell Webb), Graphicopy, 1975. Poems included in a number of anthologies; short stories, articles, poems, and pen-and-ink drawings have appeared in most juvenile periodicals, including Child Life, Story Parade, and Children's Friend.

WORK IN PROGRESS: A novel, Long Dark Road.

* * *

THOMAS, Stanley 1933-
(Steve Wyandotte)

PERSONAL: Born November 3, 1933, in Hythe, Kent, England; son of Ronald Charles (an auto sales manager) and Muriel (Wilson) Thomas; married Hilda Northcott, October 7, 1955 (divorced); children: Kim, Mark, Pamela. Education: Attended primary and secondary schools in Guildford, England. Politics: Liberal. Religion: Agnostic. Office: Supreme Court of Ontario, Court House, Room 405, University Ave., Toronto, Ontario, Canada.

CAREER: Took up bicycle racing after emigrating to Canada in 1949, and won the Maritime five-mile championship, 1950; held a variety of short-term jobs ("six-month average for each"), between 1950 and 1957, jobs ranging from caramel cook in a candy factory to bank clerk; employed in the offices of Supreme Court of Ontario, Toronto, 1957—, began as clerk in the Attorney-General's Department, currently assistant registrar.

WRITINGS: Jehovah's Witnesses and What They Believe, Zondervan, 1967. Author of a story published in Alfred Hitchcock's Mystery Magazine under pseudonym Steve Wyandotte. Contributor of humorous monographs to Toronto Financial News.

WORK IN PROGRESS: A novel, The Soul-Winner, which traces the fall of an evangelist.

SIDELIGHTS: Thomas wrote his book about Jehovah's Witnesses after leaving the Watchtower Society in 1959 to rejoin the Anglican Church. During eight years with Jehovah's Witnesses, Thomas was an area Bible study conductor, public lecturer for the Watchtower Society, and trainer of lecturers.

* * *

THOMPSON, Donnis Stark 1928-

PERSONAL: Born September 28, 1928, in Stockton, Ill.; daughter of Dick (a farmer) and Maybelle (Emory) Stark; married Stanley F. Thompson (a retail lumberman), August

15, 1953; children: Eric (stepson), Tucker (son), Teri (daughter), Tollef and Tok (sons). *Education:* Attended University of Alaska. *Home address:* Timberlost Lake, Box 217, Kenai, Alaska.

CAREER: Served for six years under the Territorial Government as assistant U.S. commissioner in Kenai, Alaska (her husband was then U.S. commissioner); with her husband, currently operates a building materials store in Kenai; in addition, "we fish a commercial fish site, have a homestead, and sell real estate."

WRITINGS: The Loon Lake Mystery: An Alaskan Tale, Criterion, 1966; *Mystery at the Alaska Fish Site,* Criterion, 1967. Contributor of short stories and articles to *Woman's Day, Vogue, Redbook, Maclean's Magazine, Chatelaine, Alaska Sportsman, Catholic Home Messenger, Canadian Home Journal, Pen, Grit,* and *Philadelphia Enquirer.* Regular columnist, *Anchorage Daily Times,* 1954-62.

WORK IN PROGRESS: A book.

SIDELIGHTS: Donnis Thompson was bitten by the Alaska bug when she saw "Spawn of the North" at age eight; she finally traveled to Alaska in 1951, married there, and has been on so many committees and boards in Kenai that she says she could write a book in the length of time it would take to list them.

* * *

THOMPSON, Evelyn Wingo 1921-

PERSONAL: Born April 14, 1921, in Franklin, Ky.; daughter of Charles Russell (a farmer) and Mary (Blewett) Wingo; married Luther Joe Thompson (a minister and writer), August 23, 1945; children: Joseph Mark, Luther Kent. *Education:* Western Kentucky University, A.B., 1944; graduate study at University of Tennessee and Woman's Missionary Training School. *Politics:* Independent. *Religion:* Baptist. *Home:* 8905 Highfield Rd., Richmond, Va. 23229.

WRITINGS: Luther Rice: Believer in Tomorrow, Broadman, 1967.

WORK IN PROGRESS: Biography of early American women.

* * *

THOMPSON, George G(reene) 1914-

PERSONAL: Born March 17, 1914, in Bucklin, Kan.; son of Otie K. and Georgia (Beach) Thompson; married Evelyn W. Schuller, October 25, 1940; children: Kenrick Steven. *Education:* Fort Hays Kansas State College, B.A., 1937, M.S., 1938; University of Iowa, Ph.D., 1941. *Home:* 203 West Southington Ave., Worthington, Ohio 43085. *Office:* Department of Psychology, Ohio State University, Columbus, Ohio 43210.

CAREER: Southern Illinois University, Carbondale, assistant professor of psychology, 1941-42; Syracuse University, Syracuse, N.Y., assistant professor, 1942-46, associate professor, 1946-49, professor of psychology, 1949-59; Ohio State University, Columbus, professor of psychology, 1959—. Harvard University, special research associate, 1943-45. *Member:* American Psychological Association, Society for Research in Child Development, American Educational Research Association, American Association for the Advancement of Science (fellow), Sigma Xi.

WRITINGS: Child Psychology, Houghton, 1952, 2nd edition, 1962; (with R. G. Kuhlen) *Psychological Studies of Human Development,* Appleton, 1952, 3rd edition, 1970; (with E. F. Gardner) *Social Relations and Morale in Small Groups,* Harcourt, 1957; (with Gardner and F. J. DiVesta) *Educational Psychology,* Appleton, 1959, 2nd edition (with DiVesta), published as *Educational Psychology: Instruction and Behavioral Change,* Irvington, 1970; (editor) *Social Development and Personality,* Wiley, 1971. Publications include "The Syracuse Scale of Social Relations," developed with E. F. Gardner; editor of monographs for the Society for Research in Child Development. Contributor to professional journals. Consulting editor, *Journal of Genetic Psychology Monographs,* and *Journal of Psychological Reports.*

* * *

THOMPSON, Luther Joe 1918-

PERSONAL: Born November 9, 1918, in Watertown, Tenn.; son of Eli Wilson and Lucile (Neal) Thompson; married Evelyn Wingo, August 23, 1945; children: Joseph Mark, Luther Kent. *Education:* Cumberland University, student, 1937-39; Carson-Newman College, A.B. (summa cum laude), 1941; Southern Baptist Theological Seminary, M.Th., 1945; University of Edinburgh, Ph.D., 1952. *Office:* First Baptist Church, Monument Ave. and the Blvd., Richmond, Va. 23220.

CAREER: Ordained to the Baptist ministry in Watertown, Tenn; pastor in Selmer, Tenn., 1944-45, Springfield, Tenn., 1945-50, McAlester, Okla., 1950-54, and Jackson, Miss., 1954-60; First Baptist Church, Chattanooga, Tenn., senior minister, 1960-68; First Baptist Church, Richmond, Va., pastor, 1968—. Guest preacher at Baptist assemblies, at Southern Baptist Theological Seminary, and for U.S. Air Force in Far East, 1965. Member of Board of University Associates, University of Richmond, executive committee of Richmond Baptist Association, and long range study committee of Baptist General Association of Virginia; member of board of trustees of Midwestern Baptist Theological Seminary, Blue Mountain College, Golden Gate Baptist Theological Seminary, and Carson-Newman College. *Awards, honors:* George Washington Honor Medal, Freedoms Foundation at Valley Forge, for series of sermons entitled "The Price of Liberty," 1960, and "Faith and Freedom," 1964.

WRITINGS: Monday Morning Religion, Broadman, 1961; *Through Discipline to Joy,* Broadman, 1966.

* * *

THOMPSON, Paul (Richard) 1935-

PERSONAL: Born August 20, 1935, in England; married Thea Vigne; children: Stephen, Sarah. *Education:* Corpus Christi College, Oxford, M.A., 1958; Queen's College, Oxford, D.Phil., 1964. *Home:* Sturricks, Great Bentley, Essex, England. *Office:* University of Essex, Colchester, Essex, England.

CAREER: Oxford University, Queen's College, Oxford, England, junior research fellow, 1961-64; University of Essex, Colchester, England, lecturer, 1964-67, reader in social history, 1967—. *Member:* Victorian Society (conference organizer).

WRITINGS: Architecture: Art or Social Service?, Fabian Society, 1963; (with Peter Kidson and Peter Murray) *A History of English Architecture,* Penguin, 1965; (editor) *Close to the Wind: Memoirs of Admiral Sir William Creswell,* Heinemann, 1965; *Socialists, Liberals, and Labour:*

The Struggle for London, 1885-1914, University of Toronto Press, 1967; *The Work of William Morris,* Viking, 1967; *William Butterfield: Victorian Architect,* M.I.T. Press, 1971; *The Edwardians: The Remaking of British Society,* Indiana University Press, 1975. Editor, Victorian Society Conference Reports, 1963-66, and *Oral History,* 1971—.

* * *

THOMPSON, Wayne N. 1914-

PERSONAL: Born December 22, 1914, in Chicago, Ill.; son of William Irvin (a farmer) and Florence Christine (Hodgson) Thompson; married Lois Laura Lockwood, July 14, 1956. *Education:* Western Illinois University, B.Ed., 1936; Northwestern University, M.A., 1939, Ph.D., 1943; New York University, Diploma in Radio, 1945. *Religion:* Presbyterian. *Home:* 5643 Meadow Lake Lane, Houston, Tex. 77027. *Office:* University of Houston, Houston, Tex. 77004.

CAREER: High school teacher in Illinios and Kentucky, 1936-42; University of Missouri, Columbia, instructor and assistant director of forensics, 1942, assistant professor, 1945-47; American University, Washington, D.C., instructor and director of forensics, 1942-43; Bowling Green State University, Bowling Green, Ohio, assistant professor and director of forensics, 1943-45; University of Illinois, Chicago Division, assistant professor, 1947-51, associate professor, 1951-57, professor of speech, 1957-63, head of department, 1947-63; University of Texas, Austin, professor of speech and education, graduate adviser in speech, 1963-68; University of Houston, Houston, Tex., professor of speech, 1968—. Visiting professor, Auburn University, fall, 1974. *Member:* Speech Communication Association, American Forensic Association, Texas Speech Communication Association, Southern Speech Communication Association (president, 1973-74), Houston Tennis Association, Phi Beta, Pi Kappa Delta (secretary of Illinois province, 1958-59), Delta Sigma Rho, Kappa Delta Pi, Austin Tennis Club (president, 1967).

WRITINGS: (With Seth Fessenden) *Basic Experiences in Speech,* Prentice-Hall, 1951, 2nd edition, 1958; *Fundamentals of Communication,* McGraw, 1957; *Quantitative Research in Public Address and Communication,* Random House, 1967; *Modern Argumentation and Debate,* Harper, 1971; *Aristotle's Deduction and Induction,* Rodopi, 1975; *The Process of Persuasion,* Harper, 1975. Contributor of about fifty articles to journals. Editor, *Journal of Communication,* 1959-61, and *Speech Monographs,* 1963-65.

WORK IN PROGRESS: Responsible Communication.

AVOCATIONAL INTERESTS: Tennis, spectator sports, theater.

* * *

THOMPSON, William Irwin 1938-

PERSONAL: Born July 16, 1938, in Chicago, Ill.; son of Chester Andrew and Lillian (Fahey) Thompson; married Gail Joan Gordon, February 3, 1960; children: Evan Timothy, Hilary Joan. *Education:* Pomona College, B.A., 1962; Cornell University, M.A., 1964, Ph.D., 1966. *Office address:* Lindisfarne Association, P.O. Box 1395, Southampton, N.Y. 11968.

CAREER: Massachusetts Institute of Technology, Cambridge, instructor, 1965-66, assistant professor of humanities, 1966-68; York University, Toronto, Ontario, associate professor, 1968-72, professor of humanities, 1972-73; Lind-

isfarne Association, Southampton, N.Y., founder, and director, 1973—. Visiting professor, Syracuse University, 1973. *Member:* American Committee for Irish Studies, Esalen Institute. *Awards, honors:* Woodrow Wilson fellowship, 1962; Old Dominion fellowship, 1967.

WRITINGS: The Imagination of an Insurrection: Dublin, Easter 1916, Oxford University Press, 1967; *At the Edge of History,* Harper, 1971; *Passages about Earth: An Exploration of the New Planetary Culture,* Harper, 1974. Contributor of articles to *Tulane Drama Review, Sewanee Review, Antioch Review,* and other journals.

AVOCATIONAL INTERESTS: Anthropology, archaeology, and 8mm film-making.

BIOGRAPHICAL/CRITICAL SOURCES: Times Literary Supplement, September 21, 1967; *South Atlantic Quarterly,* summer, 1968; *Time,* April 26, 1971, *Best Sellers,* July 15, 1971.

* * *

THOMSON, F(rancis) P(aul) 1914-

PERSONAL: Born December 17, 1914, in Corstorphine, Scotland; son of William George (a tapestry expert) and Elizabeth Hannah (Tann) Thomson; married Ester Sylvia Nilsson (a Swedish educational psychologist), 1954. *Education:* Studied at Polytechnic School of Engineering, London, 1935-39; attended Acton College of Technology, London, 1939-42, College of Adult Education, Elsinore, Denmark, 1947, and Stockholm University Extra-Mural Department, 1947-49. *Home:* "The Cottage," 39 Church Rd., Watford WD1 3PY, Hertfordshire, England.

CAREER: Chartered engineer; involved in TV and radar research, 1935-42; special operations executive, 1942-44; senior planning engineer in postwar research and reconstruction of communications industry; founder of campaign to reform postal and banking systems, 1947, and worked towards passage of legislative reforms in Parliament in 1965; governor of Watford College of Technology, 1965-68; consultant on post office and bank giro systems, 1968-71; associate consultant (banking and security), Communications & Equipment Consultants, Ltd., 1969—. Advisor on postal giro systems to the Government of India Banking Commission, 1971; member, City & Guilds of London Institute's Advisory Committee on Presentation of Technical Information, 1971—; giro advisor, Post Office User's National Council, 1974.

MEMBER: Institution of Electronic and Radio Engineers, Programmed Learning and Teaching Machine Standards Committee of the British Standards Institution, Management Committee of Verulam Hospitals Group (for diagnosis and treatment of the mentally sub-normal), Kennedy-Galton Research Centre for Mental Subnormality, Special Forces Association Committee (chairman, 1961-62), Anglo-Swedish Society (life member). *Awards, honors:* Officer, Order of the British Empire, 1975.

WRITINGS: Giro Credit Transfer Systems, Pergamon, 1964; *Money in the Computer Age,* Pergamon, 1968; (editor) *Banking Automation,* two volumes, Pergamon, 1971; (editor and revisor with wife, Ester Sylvia Thomson) William George Thomson, *A History of Tapestry,* 3rd edition, E. P. Publishing, 1973. Contributor of papers to various professional journals, including *Police Journal, Journal of Economics Association,* and *Credit.*

WORK IN PROGRESS: A treatise on language laboratories and programmed learning; with S. J. L. Blumlein, *Alan*

Dower Blumblein, 1903-42: Engineer Extraordinary; Security Systems, Essentials and Equipment for Newnes-Butterworth; *Public Services and Reforms We Deserve.*

*   *   *

THOMSON, George H(enry)   1924-

PERSONAL: Born July 22, 1924, in Bluevale, Ontario, Canada; son of George Theodore (a farmer and businessman) and Catherine Jeannette (Brock) Thomson; married Dorothy Frances Hoyt (a librarian), May 14, 1956. *Education:* University of Western Ontario, B.A. (first class honors), 1947; University of Toronto, M.A., 1948, Ph.D., 1951. *Home:* 655 Echo Dr., Ottawa, Ontario, Canada. *Office:* Department of English, University of Ottawa, Ottawa, Ontario, Canada.

CAREER: Mount Allison University, Sackville, New Brunswick, 1953-66, began as lecturer, associate professor of English, 1959-66; Wayne State University, Detroit, Mich., visiting professor of English, 1966-67; researcher in Cambridge, Mass., 1967-69; University of Ottawa, Ottawa, Ontario, professor of English, 1969—. *Member:* American Society for Aesthetics, Association of Canadian Teachers of English, English Association, Modern Language Association of America. *Awards, honors:* Canada Council senior fellowship, 1967-68, to study narrative tragedy.

WRITINGS: The Fiction of E. M. Forster, Wayne State University Press, 1967; (contributor) Oliver Stallybrass, editor, *Aspects of E. M. Forster,* Harcourt, 1969; (editor and author of introduction) E. M. Forster, *Albergo Empedocle and Other Writings,* Liveright, 1971. Contributor of critical articles and reviews to *Dalhousie Review, Wisconsin Studies in Contemporary Literature, Alphabet, Modern Fiction Studies,* and other journals.

WORK IN PROGRESS: A study on narrative theory; a study on the Bloomsbury group.

*   *   *

THORNBURG, Newton K(endall)   1930-

PERSONAL: Born May 13, 1930, in Harvey, Ill.; son of Newton Kendall and Rhea (Mattox) Thornburg; married Karin Larson, September 21, 1953; children: Kristen, Mark, Douglas. *Education:* University of Iowa, B.A., 1951, and further study at Writers Workshop, 1953. *Politics:* "Disaffected liberal." *Religion:* Agnostic. *Home address:* R.F.D., Jane, Mo. *Agent:* Lurton Blassingame, 60 East 42nd St., New York, N.Y. 10017.

CAREER: Advertising copywriter for various agencies, 1960-70; author and rancher, 1970—.

WRITINGS: Gentlemen Born, Fawcett, 1967; *Knockover,* Fawcett, 1968; *To Die in California,* Little, Brown, 1973; *Cutter and Bone,* Little, Brown, 1976.

*   *   *

THORNE, Christopher   1934-

PERSONAL: Born May 17, 1934, in Surrey, England; married; children: two daughters. *Education:* Attended St. Edmund Hall, Oxford, 1955-58. *Office:* University of Sussex, Sussex, England.

CAREER: Charterhouse, Godalming, Surrey, England, senior history master, 1951-56; British Broadcasting Corp., Radio, London, England, head of further education, 1966-68; University of Sussex, Sussex, England, 1968—, began as lecturer, currently reader in international relations. *Military service:* Royal Navy, 1953-55; became lieutenant.

WRITINGS: Ideology and Power, Macmillan, 1965; *Chartism,* Macmillan, 1966; *The Approach of War, 1938-39,* St. Martin's, 1967; *The Limits of Foreign Policy,* Putnam, 1973. Editor, Macmillan's "The Making of the Twentieth Century" series. Contributor to *Orbis.* Reviewer, *Spectator.*

WORK IN PROGRESS: A study of Anglo-American relations and the Far East in World War II.

AVOCATIONAL INTERESTS: Acting, piano, sports (played cricket for England Schools team and for British Navy).

*   *   *

THORP, Edward O.   1932-

PERSONAL: Born August 14, 1932, in Chicago, Ill.; son of Oakley Glenn and Josephine (Gebert) Thorp; married Vivian Sinetar, January 28, 1956; children: Raun, Karen, Jeffrey. *Education:* University of California, Los Angeles, B.A., 1953, M.A., 1955, Ph.D., 1958. *Office:* Department of Mathematics, University of California, Irvine, Calif. 92664.

CAREER: University of California, Los Angeles, instructor in mathematics, 1955-59; Massachusetts Institute of Technology, Cambridge, C.L.E. Moore Instructor, 1959-61; New Mexico State University, University Park, assistant professor, 1961-63, associate professor of mathematics, 1963-65; University of California, Irvine, associate professor, 1965-67, professor of mathematics, 1967—. Chairman of Oakley, Sutton Management Corp., 1972—; vice-president of Oakley, Sutton Securities Corp., 1972—. *Member:* American Mathematical Society, Institute of Mathematical Statistics (fellow), American Statistical Association, American Economic Association, Phi Beta Kappa. *Awards, honors:* Research grants from National Science Foundation, 1962-64, and Office of Scientific Research, U.S. Air Force, 1964-74.

WRITINGS: Beat the Dealer, Random House, 1962, revised edition, 1966; *Elementary Probability,* Wiley, 1966; (with S. Kassouf) *Beat the Market,* Random House, 1967; (contributor) J. Bicksler, editor, *Investment Decision Making,* Heath Lexington, 1975; (contributor) W. Eadington, editors, *Gambling and Society,* C. C Thomas, 1975.

WORK IN PROGRESS: Research in stock market, game theory, probability theory, functional analysis.

SIDELIGHTS: Thorp's public image as a mathematician rests largely on his discovery of a valid method of circumventing gambling odds, a system that he estimates could net him $300,000 a month if casinos at Las Vegas and elsewhere did not interfere. An article in *Life,* "The Professor Who Beats the Bank," credited Thorp with "doing for gambling what Roger Bannister did for the mile," but pointed out that part of his troubles with the gambling dealers stems "from his insistence on letting the world in on his discovery"—both in *Beat the Dealer,* and in a scientific paper on the subject, published prior to the book in *Proceedings of the National Academy of Sciences.*

BIOGRAPHICAL/CRITICAL SOURCES: Sports Illustrated, January 11, 1964; *Life,* March 27, 1964; *Newsweek,* December 18, 1967; *Wall Street Journal,* January 18, 1974, April 22, 1974, September 23, 1974; *Science News,* March 22, 1975.

*   *   *

THORPE, Michael   1932-

PERSONAL: Born September 18, 1932, in Great Yarmouth, Norfolk, England; son of Ernest Gordon (a brewery manager) and Muriel Florence (Bateman) Thorpe; married Pauline Constance Keith, February 11, 1956; married second wife, Elin Elgaard Berg, July, 1971; children: (first marriage) Lucy, Edmund Keith Gordon. *Education:* University College (now University of Leicester), B.A. (honors), 1954; University of Singapore, M.A., 1964. *Politics:* "A personal variety of Socialism." *Address:* P.O. Box 1456, 73 Salem St., Sackville, New Brunswick, Canada. *Office:* Department of English, Mount Allison University, Sackville, New Brunswick, Canada.

CAREER: During his early career taught English at colleges in Turkey and Nigeria; Nanyang University, Singapore, lecturer in English, 1962-64; University of Leiden, Leiden, Netherlands, senior lecturer in English, 1965-70; University of Calgary, Calgary, Alberta, 1970-74, began as associate professor, became professor of English; Mount Allison University, Sackville, New Brunswick, professor of English and head of department, 1974—. *Military service:* British Army, 1955-57; became sergeant. *Member:* English Association.

WRITINGS: (Editor) *Modern Poems,* Oxford University Press, 1963; *Siegfried Sassoon: A Critical Study,* University Press (Leiden) and Oxford University Press (London), 1966, Oxford University Press (New York), 1967; (editor) *Modern Prose,* Oxford University Press, 1968; *By the Niger and Other Poems,* Fortune Press, 1969; *A Choice of Clough's Verse,* Feber, 1969; *Arnold,* Evans Brothers, 1969, Arco, 1971; *The Poetry of Edmund Blunden,* Bridge Books, 1971; *Clough: The Critical Heritage,* Routledge & Kegan Paul, 1972; *Doris Lessing,* Longman, 1973; (editor) Siegfried Sassoon, *Letters to a Critic,* Bridge Books, 1976; *V. S. Naipaul,* Longman, 1976. Contributor of poems and reviews to *Times* (London), and other publications.

WORK IN PROGRESS: Doris Lessing's Africa, for Evans Brothers.

AVOCATIONAL INTERESTS: Travel, reading, walking.

*   *   *

THULSTRUP, Niels 1924-

PERSONAL: Born May 6, 1924, in Aalborg, Denmark. *Education:* University of Copenhagen, Th.M., 1950, D.Th., 1968. *Home:* Sofievej 23, DK 2900, Hellerup, Denmark.

CAREER: University of Copenhagen, Copenhagen, Denmark, assistant professor, 1950-59; Evangelical-Lutheran Church of Denmark, pastor, 1959-68; University of Copenhagen, professor of systematic theology, 1968—. *Member:* Soren Kierkegaard Society (founder, 1948; secretary, 1948-66; vice-president, 1967). *Awards, honors:* Swenson-Kierkegaard Memorial fellowship.

WRITINGS: (Editor) Soren Kierkegaard, *Bidrag til en Bibliografi,* Munksgaard (Copenhagen), 1951; (editor) Kierkegaard, *Philosophisch-Theologische Schriften und Aesthetisch-Philosophische Schriften* (includes *Either-Or* and pseudonymous works), Jakob Hegner (Cologne), Volumes I-IV, 1951-60; *Introduktion til Oversaettelse af Augustin Confessiones,* Haase (Copenhagen), 1952; (editor) Kierkegaard, *Breve og Akstykker vedrorende,* Munksgaard, Volume I, 1953, Volume II, 1954; (editor) Kierkegaard, *Philosophiske Smuler,* Munksgaard, 1955, published as *Philosophical Fragments,* Princeton University Press, 1962; *Introduceret Udgave af: Katalog over Soren Kierkegaard's Bibliotek,* Munksgaard, 1957.

(Editor and author of introduction and notes) Kierkegaard, *Frygt og Baeven,* Gyldendal, 1961; (editor and author of introduction and notes) Kierkegaard, *Afsluttende uvidenskabelig Efterskrift,* Volumes I and II, Gyldendal, 1962; (editor with Howard A. Johnson) *A Kierkegaard Critique,* Harper, 1962; *Kierkegaard's Forhold til Hegel,* Gyldendal, 1967; *Kierkegaard's Verhaeltnis zu Hegel Forschungsgeschichte,* Kohl-Hammer, 1970. Also editor of *Soeren Kierkegaard's Papirer,* Volumes I-XXIII. Editor, *Kierkegaardiana,* Munksgaard, 1955-75. Contributor of articles and reviews to *Theology Today* (Princeton), and to other learned journals in Denmark, Norway, Italy, Switzerland, Japan, Germany, and Belgium.

WORK IN PROGRESS: Editing with Howard V. Hong, *Kierkegaard Encyclopaedi,* Volumes I-XXII, for Rosenkilde og Bagger, and *Soeren Kierkegaard's Collected Works,* Volumes I-XXVI, for Princeton University Press.

*   *   *

THUNA, Leonora 1929-
(Lee Thuna)

PERSONAL: Daughter of Marcus and Bertha (Lester) Thuna. *Education:* Hunter College (now Hunter College of the City University of New York), B.A., 1951. *Politics:* Liberal Democrat. *Religion:* Jewish. *Residence:* New York, N.Y.; and Beverly Hills, Calif. *Agent:* Helen Harvey, 110 West 57th St., New York, N.Y.

CAREER: Norman, Craig & Kummel (advertising agency), New York City, copywriter, 1955-57; Ogilvy & Mather Advertising, New York City, copy group head, 1958-65; full-time playwright, 1965—. *Member:* Dramatists Guild, Writers Guild of America East.

WRITINGS: The Natural Look (comedy; first produced on Broadway at Longacre Theater, March 11, 1967), Samuel French, 1965; "After You, Mr. Hyde" (musical), first produced in East Haddam, Conn., at Goodspeed Opera House, June 24, 1968; "Show Me Where the Good Times Are" (musical), first produced on Broadway at Edison Theatre, March 5, 1970; "Silverplate," first produced in New Fairfield, Conn., at Candlewood Theatre, June, 1971; (with Saint Subber) *The Baby Book,* Price, Stern, 1972; (with Harry Cauley) "Let Me Hear You Smile," first produced on Broadway at Biltmore Theatre, January 16, 1973.

WORK IN PROGRESS: A musical, "The Eleventh."

BIOGRAPHICAL/CRITICAL SOURCES: New York Times, February 4, 1967; *Show Business,* November 2, 1968.

*   *   *

THURBER, Walter A(rthur) 1908-

PERSONAL: Born November 27, 1908, in East Worcester, N.Y.; son of Louis A. (a storekeeper) and Anna (Lape) Thurber; children: David L., Robert N. *Education:* Union College, Schenectady, N.Y., B.S. in E.E., 1933; New York State College for Teachers, Albany (now State University of New York at Albany), M.S., 1938; Cornell University, Ph.D., 1940. *Politics:* Republican. *Religion:* Methodist. *Office:* 101 Sycamore St., Liverpool, N.Y. 13088.

CAREER: Teacher in New York public schools, 1926-29, 1933-38; Cortland State Teachers College (now State University of New York College at Cortland), instructor, 1940-43, assistant professor of physics, physical science, and earth science, 1943-48, professor of science, 1948-59; Syracuse University, Syracuse, N.Y., visiting professor of science education, 1959-64, adjunct professor, 1964-69; Cornell University, Laboratory of Ornithology, Ithica, N.Y., field collaborator, 1970—. Visiting professor, National University of El Salvador, San Salvador, 1973—; with Ministry of Education of El Salvador; advisor to National Park Service of El Salvador. Consultant in science education to New York State Education Department, Florida State Education Department, and Organization of Central American States. President, Cortland (N.Y.) Civic Association for Education, 1950-51. *Member:* American Association for the Advancement of Science (fellow), National Science Teachers Association, New York Academy of Sciences, American Ornithological Union, Wilson Ornithological Society, Cooper Ornithological Society, Sigma Xi, Phi Delta Kappa.

WRITINGS: Exploring Science, Allyn & Bacon, Books 1-6, 1955, 4th edition (with Mary Durkee), 1965, Books 7-9 (with Robert Kilburn), 1965-66; (with A. T. Collette) *Teaching Science in Today's Secondary Schools,* Allyn & Bacon, 1959, 3rd edition, 1968; (with Kilburn) *Exploring Earth Science,* Allyn & Bacon, 1965, 3rd edition (with Kilburn and Peter Howell), 1975; (with Kilburn) *Exploring Life Science,* Allyn & Bacon, 1965, 2nd edition, 1970; (with Kilburn) *Exploring Physical Science,* Allyn & Bacon, 1966, 2nd edition, 1970.

WORK IN PROGRESS: Reproductive biology of green violet-ear hummingbirds, *Calibri Thalassinus,* at Cerro Verde, El Salvador; ornithology of El Salvador.

SIDELIGHTS: Thurber's books have been published in Canada, Great Britain, and Asia. He is presently active in promoting the conservation of plants and animals in El Salvador, Central America. He speaks some Spanish. *Avocational interests:* Nature study, bird watching, mountain climbing, travel.

* * *

THWAITE, M(ary) F. (Austin)

PERSONAL: Born in Birmingham, England; married T.E.S. Thwaite, 1950. *Education:* Educated in England. *Religion:* Unitarian Universalist. *Home:* 16 Brooklands Dr., Goostney, North Crewe, England.

CAREER: County librarian, Hertfordshire, England, 1948-52. Occasional lecturer on history of children's books. *Member:* Library Association (Great Britain; fellow).

WRITINGS: From Primer to Pleasure, Library Association, 1963, 2nd edition, 1972; (author of introductory essay and compiler of bibliography) John Newbery, *A Little Pretty Pocket-Book,* Oxford University Press, 1966, Harcourt, 1967.

WORK IN PROGRESS: Studying seventeenth-century literature; special interest in the life and publishing activities of JohnNewbery (1712-1767).

* * *

TICHY, H(enrietta) J. 1912-

PERSONAL: Surname rhymes with "fishy"; born March 24, 1912, in New York, N.Y.; daughter of Henry Anton (a businessman) and Meta (Homan) Tichy. *Education:* Hunter College (now Hunter College of the City University of New York), B.A., 1932; Columbia University, M.A., 1934; New York University, Ph.D., 1942. *Politics:* Independent. *Religion:* Lutheran. *Home:* Valley Rd., Locust Valley, N.Y. 11560; and 793 Dune Rd., Westhampton

Beach, N.Y. 11978. *Office:* Department of English, Herbert H. Lehman College of the City University of New York, New York, N.Y. 10468.

CAREER: Herbert H. Lehman College of the City University of New York, New York, N.Y., instructor and tutor, 1934-39, 1940-41, instructor, 1941-44, assistant professor, 1944-59, associate professor, 1959-70, professor of English, 1970—. Consultant on technical writing, Smith, Kline & French Laboratories, 1952-64, Exxon Research and Engineering Co., 1952—, Vicks Research Division, 1960—, and International Business Machines Corp., 1965; lecturer and consultant on technical writing and editing.

MEMBER: American Association for the Advancement of Science, Modern Language Association of America, National Council of Teachers of English, Society of Technical Writers and Publishers (national secretary, 1962-63), American Association of University Professors, Society for Technical Communication (fellow), Association of Neighbors and Friends of Hunter College (public relations director, ten years), Hunter College Alumni Association, English Graduate Association of New York University (president 1966-70, 1974). *Awards, honors:* Society for Technical Communication award, 1970, for *The Steps to Effective Writing;* citation from Girl Scout Council of Greater New York, for ten years of service in Training and Education Division.

WRITINGS: The Bible in the Poetry of Pope, New York University Press, 1942; *Biblical Influence in English Literature: A Survey of Studies,* Edwards Brothers, 1953; (editor) *Better Communication,* American Institute of Chemical Engineers, 1953; *Engineers Can Write Better,* American Institute of Chemical Engineers, 1954; *Guide for Writers and Speakers,* American Institute of Chemical Engineers, 1956; (with Kenneth A. Kobe) *Chemical Engineering Reports,* Interscience 1957; *Effective Writing for Engineers, Managers, Scientists,* Wiley, 1966. Author of *The Steps to Effective Writing,* Exxon Research and Engineering Co.; also author of booklets for Girl Scout Council of Greater New York; contributor to anthologies.

WORK IN PROGRESS: Effective Speaking, for Wiley.

* * *

TIGUE, Ethel Erkkila 1918-

PERSONAL: Surname is pronounced like the first syllable of "tiger"; born February 19, 1918, in Virginia, Minn.; daughter of Oscar John and Serafia (Heikkila) Erkkila; married Ralph Tigue (a high school counselor in St. Paul schools), June 30, 1941; children: Randall, Kevin. *Education:* University of Minnesota, Duluth, B.E., 1938, graduate study, 1944-45. *Politics:* Democrat. *Religion:* Unitarian Universalist. *Home:* 1175 Goodrich Ave., St. Paul, Minn. 55105. *Agent:* Celine Brevannes, 28 Bauer Pl., Westport, Conn. 06880.

CAREER: High school teacher in Shakopee, Minn., 1938-41; *Women's News* (weekly paper), Duluth, Minn., city editor, 1940-41; Glass Block Department Store, Duluth, advertising manager, 1941-44; high school teacher and counselor in Burley, Idaho, 1947-51; free-lance advertising layout artist, St. Paul, Minn., 1956-59. Part-time editor for Webb Publishing, and free-lance writer. Teacher of writing at adult education workshops and privately. *Awards, honors:* McKnight Foundation Humanities Award, 1962, unpublished manuscript of novel, "Stranger Come Home."

WRITINGS: (With Ruth Slonim) *Sketchings* (poetry), Interstate, 1938; *Betrayal* (novel), Dodd, 1959; (with Louise Bower) *Secret of Willow Coulee,* Abingdon, 1966; (with Bower) *Packy,* Abingdon, 1967; *Looking Forward to a Career—Writing: Job Opportunities within the Field of Writing,* Dillon, 1970; (with Jane Nugent Green) *You and Your Private I: Personality and the Written Self-Image,* Llewellyn, 1975. Contributor to newspapers and magazines, including *Writer, Writer's Digest, Minneapolis Sunday Tribune, Farmer,* and *St. Paul Pioneer Press.*

BIOGRAPHICAL/CRITICAL SOURCES: St. Paul Pioneer Press Pictorial Magazine, March 15, 1959; *Minnesota Writers,* Denison, 1961; *Suomen Silta* (Helsinki), April, 1966; *St. Paul Dispatch,* November 25, 1966.†

*   *   *

TILLMAN, Rollie, Jr.   1933-

PERSONAL: Born April 11, 1933, in Lake Wales, Fla.; son of Rollie and Louise (Johnson) Tillman; married Mary Windley Dunn, June 22, 1957; children: Mary Windley, Jane Guion, Rollie III. *Education:* University of North Carolina, B.S., 1955; Harvard University, M.B.A., 1957, D.B.A., 1962. *Religion:* Episcopalian. *Home:* 404 Lakeshore Lane, Chapel Hill, N.C. 27514. *Office:* Graduate School of Business, Carroll Hall, University of North Carolina, Chapel Hill, N.C. 27514.

CAREER: University of North Carolina, Graduate School of Business, Chapel Hill, assistant professor, 1961-63, associate professor, 1963-68, professor of business and director of executive program, 1968—. Chairman of board of directors of North Carolina National Bank, Chapel Hill Board, and St. Mary's College. *Member:* American Marketing Association, Southern Marketing Association.

WRITINGS: (With C. A. Kirkpatrick) *Promotion: Persuasive Communication in Marketing,* Irwin, 1968, revised edition, 1972; (with Luther H. Hodges, Jr.) *Text and Cases in Bank Marketing,* Addison-Wesley, 1968. Assistant editor, *Harvard Business Review,* 1958-59.

*   *   *

TIMBERLAKE, Richard Henry, Jr.   1922-

PERSONAL: Born June 24, 1922, in Steubenville, Ohio; son of Richard Henry (a salesman) and Elizabeth (James) Timberlake; married second wife, Hildegard Weber, May 28, 1960; children: (first marriage) Richard III, David, Megan; (second marriage) Christopher, Thomas. *Education:* Kenyon College, A.B., 1946; Columbia University, A.M., 1950; University of Chicago, Ph.D., 1959. *Politics:* Libertarian. *Religion:* Episcopalian. *Home:* 195 Maple Circle, Athens, Ga. 30601. *Office:* University of Georgia, Athens, Ga. 30601.

CAREER: Muhlenberg College, Allentown Pa., instructor in economics, 1948-51; Norwich University, Northfield, Vt., assistant professor of economics, 1953-55; Rensselaer Polytechnic Institute, Troy, N.Y., instructor in economics, 1955-58; Florida State University, Tallahassee, associate professor of economics, 1958-63; University of Georgia, Athens, professor of finance, 1963—. *Military service:* U.S. Army Air Forces, 1943-45; pilot with 8th Air Force; became first lieutenant; received Air Medal with three oak leaves, and Purple Heart with one leaf.

WRITINGS: Money, Banking and Central Banking, Harper, 1965; *Money and Banking,* Wadsworth, 1972. Contributor to professional journals. Member of board of editors, *Southern Economic Journal,* 1963-66.

WORK IN PROGRESS: The Political Economy of Central Banking in the United States before 1914, a book dealing with central banking institutional development in the United States from 1789 to 1914.

*   *   *

TINDALL, Gillian   1938-

PERSONAL: Born May 4, 1938, in London, England; married R. G. Lansdown (a psychologist); children: Harry. *Education:* Oxford University, M.A. (first class honors), 1959. *Politics:* None. *Religion:* None. *Agent:* Curtis Brown Group Ltd., 1 Craven Hill, London W2 3EW, England.

CAREER: Writer.

WRITINGS: No Name in the Street, Cassell, 1959, published as *When We Had Other Names,* Morrow, 1960; *The Water and the Sound,* Cassell, 1961, Morrow, 1962; *The Edge of the Paper,* Cassell, 1963; *The Israeli Twins,* J. Cape, 1963; *A Handbook on Witches,* Arthur Barker, 1965, Atheneum, 1966; *The Youngest,* Secker & Warburg, 1967, Walker & Co., 1968; *Someone Else,* Walker & Co., 1969; *Fly Away Home,* Hodder & Stoughton, 1971; *Dances of Death* (short stories), Walker & Co., 1973; *The Born Exile* (biography), Harcourt, 1974. Regular contributor to *Observer, Guardian,* and *New Statesman.*

SIDELIGHTS: Gillian Tindall is fluent in French; she has lived in France, and traveled in eastern Europe, Israel, and the Soviet Union.

*   *   *

TING, Walasse   1929-

PERSONAL: Born October 13, 1929, in Shanghai, China; son of Ho-Chang (a merchant) and Ying Ting; married Natalie Lipton, June 4, 1962; children: Mia, Jesse. *Education:* Self-educated. *Politics:* None. *Religion:* None. *Home:* 463 West St., New York, N.Y. 10014.

CAREER: Artist and poet, 1953—.

WRITINGS: My Shit & My Love, Galerie Smith (Brussels), 1961; *1 Cent Life* (with lithographs by Rauschenberg, Indiana, Dine, Lichtenstein, and others), Kornfeld & Klipstein (Bern), 1964; *Chinese Moonlight* (translations and recompositions of 63 poems by 33 Chinese poets writing between 340 B.C. and 1523 A.D.), Wittenborn, 1967; *Hot & Sour Soup,* Sam Francis Foundation, 1968; *All in My Head,* Yves Riviere (Paris), 1974; *Red Mouth,* Yves Riviere, 1976. Also author of *Green Banana* (poems), 1971.

SIDELIGHTS: Regarding his public image, Ting told Alexander Keneas: "Newpapers say I'm a wild man, but I don't think so. Maybe because of some poems I write." Keneas writes that Ting's poems, "with a jazzy, staccato rhythm, lament what he believes to be the mind-strangling and stomach-glutting pursuit of the American dream." Ting says simply: "I hungry, I eat. I tired, I sleep. Sometimes I want money—but not to make more money. I want to make another Book."

Ting's nine-pound folio, *1 Cent Life,* was exhibited in New York at the Museum of Modern Art, then throughout the United States and in Europe.

BIOGRAPHICAL/CRITICAL SOURCES: New York Times, November 26, 1967; *New York Times Book Review,* March 11, 1968.

*   *   *

TOEKES, Rudolf L(eslie)   1935-

PERSONAL: Born March 14, 1935, in Budapest, Hungary;

son of Rudolf R. and Elizabeth (Fotter) Toekes; married Mary Phillips, August 29, 1959; children: Anne Elizabeth. *Education:* University of Budapest, law student, 1954-56; Western (now Case Western) Reserve University, B.A., 1959; Columbia University, M.A., 1961, Ph.D., 1965. *Office:* Department of Government, Wesleyan University, Middletown, Conn. 06457.

CAREER: Wesleyan University, Middletown, Conn., assistant professor of government, beginning 1964. *Member:* American Political Science Association, American Association for the Advancement of Slavic Studies.

WRITINGS: Bela Kun and the Hungarian Soviet Republic of 1919, Praeger, for Hoover Institution, 1967.

WORK IN PROGRESS: The Communist Party and the Hungarian Intellectuals 1919-1944.††

*   *   *

TOEPFER, Ray Grant   1923-

PERSONAL: Surname is pronounced *Tep-*fer; born February 26, 1923, in Hays, Kan.; son of Raymond Frederick (a lumberman) and Beth (Graunke) Toepfer; married Edith Dreispiel (a junior high school teacher), June 30, 1946; children: Betty Nora, Marcia Lynn. *Education:* University of Wisconsin, B.A., 1941, M.A., 1943; City University of New York, Ph.D., 1971. *Politics:* Independent. *Religion:* "No preference." *Home:* 2160 Hone Ave., Bronx, N.Y. 10461. *Agent:* Bill Berger Associates, Inc., 444 East 58th St., New York, N.Y. 10021. *Office:* Department of English, Brooklyn College of the City University of New York, Brooklyn, N.Y. 11210.

CAREER: DeFi Manufacturing Co. (stationers), New York, N.Y., 1947-63, became assistant manager; Brooklyn College of the City University of New York, Brooklyn, N.Y., 1964—, began as lecturer, currently assistant professor of English. Writer. *Military service:* U.S. Army, 1943-46; edited army newspaper in Greenland, 1943-44.

WRITINGS: Prelude to Autumn (poems), Craftsman, 1942; *The Scarlet Guidon,* Coward, 1957; *The White Cockade,* Chilton, 1966; *The Witness,* Muller, 1966; *The Second Face of Valor,* Chilton, 1966; *Liberty of Corporal Kincaid,* Chilton, 1968; *Beat of a Distant Drum,* Chilton, 1969; *Endplay,* Fawcett, 1975.

WORK IN PROGRESS: A novel; a suspense novel; a book on writing fiction.

SIDELIGHTS: Toepfer reads Latin, Old English, German, and French—"after a fashion." *Avocational interests:* Swimming, golf, cycling, hiking, woodworking, gardening, puttering with his car, collecting Americana (Civil War buff), flying.

*   *   *

TOLIVER, Harold E(arl)   1932-

PERSONAL: Born February 16, 1932, in McMinnville, Ore.; son of Marion Earl and Mabel (Mallery) Toliver; married Mary J. Bennette, June 20, 1954; children: Brooks Allen, Tricia Lynne. *Education:* University of Oregon, B.A., 1954; Johns Hopkins University, M.A., 1958; University of Washington, Seattle, Ph.D., 1961. *Home:* 1405 Skyline Dr., Laguna Beach, Calif. 92651. *Office:* Department of English and Comparative Literature, University of California, Irvine, Calif. 92664.

CAREER: Ohio State University, Columbus, assistant professor, 1961-63; University of California, Los Angeles, as-

sistant professor, 1964-65; University of California, Irvine, 1965—, began as associate professor, currently professor of English. *Awards, honors:* Guggenheim fellow, 1963-64, 1975-76.

WRITINGS: Marvell's Ironic Vision, Yale University Press, 1965; *Pastoral Forms and Attitudes,* University of California Press, 1971; *Animate Illusions: Explorations of Narrative Structure,* University of Nebraska Press, 1974.

Editor with James Calderwood: *Forms of Poetry,* Prentice-Hall, 1968; *Perspectives on Drama,* Oxford University Press, 1968; *Perspectives on Poetry,* Oxford University Press, 1968; *Perspectives on Fiction,* Oxford University Press, 1968; *Forms of Drama,* Prentice-Hall, 1969; *Essays in Shakespearean Criticism,* Prentice-Hall, 1970; *Forms of Prose Fiction,* Prentice-Hall, 1972; *Forms of Tragedy,* Prentice-Hall, 1972. Contributor to scholarly and critical journals.

WORK IN PROGRESS: Poetry and the Past.

*   *   *

TOMMERAASEN, Miles   1923-

PERSONAL: Surname is pronounced Tom-er-aah-sen; born January 30, 1923, in Sioux Falls, S.D.; son of Cornelius (a pharmacist) and Ester E. (Stonebraker) Tommeraasen; married Marilyn D. Fladmark, November 23, 1945; children: Marsha, Mark, Miles C. *Education:* Morningside College, B.A., 1943; Northwestern University, M.B.A., 1948; University of Nebraska, Ph.D., 1965. *Politics:* Republican. *Religion:* Lutheran. *Home:* 601 Sycamore Dr., Lincoln, Neb. 68510. *Office:* University of Nebraska, Lincoln, Neb. 68508.

CAREER: Arthur Andersen & Co. (public accountants), Chicago, Ill., staff member, 1946-50; Morningside College, Sioux City, Iowa, assistant professor, 1950-51, associate professor, 1952-56, professor of business administration, 1957-64, chairman of department of economics and business administration, 1951-61, dean of men, 1953-60, executive vice-president, 1960-64; University of Nebraska, Lincoln, professor of finance, 1964—, vice-chancellor for business and finance, 1969—. Treasurer, Siouxland Rehabilitation Center, 1963-64; member of board of directors, Lincoln Chamber of Commerce, 1972—, treasurer, 1975. *Member:* American Institute of Certified Public Accountants, American Finance Association, American Accounting Association, Financial Executive Institute, Financial Analysts Society, Nebraska Society of Certified Public Accountants (board, 1967-68), Iowa Society of Certified Public Accountants.

WRITINGS: State Centralized Investment Process: Structure Controls, and Operations, University of Nebraska Press, 1966.

WORK IN PROGRESS: Research in current trends in the administration of state funds, and in maximizing the corporate cash position.

AVOCATIONAL INTERESTS: Travel, golf, home movies.

*   *   *

TOOLE, William Bell III   1930-

PERSONAL: Born September 23, 1930, in Augusta, Ga.; son of William Bell, Jr. (a sales manager) and Mary Anita (Haverstick) Toole; married Katie Durham, June 7, 1955; children: Laurel Anita, William Durham. *Education:* Presbyterian College, B.A., 1954; Vanderbilt University, M.A., 1955, Ph.D., 1963. *Religion:* United Church of Christ. *Home:* 2515 Kenmore Dr., Raleigh, N.C. 27608. *Office:* North Carolina State University, Raleigh, N.C.

CAREER: Presbyterian College, Clinton, S.C., 1955-58, began as instructor, became assistant professor of English; Vanderbilt University, Nashville, Tenn., instructor in English, 1960-63; North Carolina State University at Raleigh, assistant professor, 1963-66, associate professor, 1966-71, professor of English, 1971—, assistant dean 1971-72, associate dean of Liberal Arts, 1972—. *Military service:* U.S. Army, 1948-49. *Member:* Modern Language Association of America, College English Association, South Atlantic Modern Language Association, Southeastern Renaissance Conference.

WRITINGS: Shakespeare's Problem Plays: Studies in Form and Meaning, Mouton & Co., 1966. Contributor of articles on English and American writers to *Chaucer Review, Arlington Quarterly, CEA Critic,* and other journals.

AVOCATIONAL INTERESTS: Tennis.

* * *

TOPPIN, Edgar A(llan) 1928-

PERSONAL: Born January 22, 1928, in New York, N.Y.; son of Vivien Leopold (an elevator operator) and Catherine Maud (Joell) Toppin; married Antoinette L. Lomax (an instructor in education at Virginia State College), April 2, 1953; children: Edgar Allan Jr., Avis Ann Lillian, Antoinette Louise. *Education:* Howard University, B.A., 1949, M.A., 1950; Northwestern University, Ph.D., 1955. *Politics:* Democrat. *Religion:* Episcopalian. *Home:* 20411 Williams St., Ettrick, Va. 23803. *Office:* Department of History, Virginia State College, Petersburg, Va. 23803.

CAREER: Alabama State College (now University), Montgomery, instructor in history, 1954-55; Fayetteville State College (now University), Fayetteville, N.C., chairman of social science, 1955-59; University of Akron, Akron, Ohio, assistant professor, 1959-63, associate professor of history, 1963-64; Virginia State College, Petersburg, professor of history, 1964—. Visiting summer professor at North Carolina College (now North Carolina Central University), 1959, 1963, Western Reserve University (now Case Western Reserve University), 1962, University of Cincinnati, 1964, and San Francisco State College (now University), 1969. Member of board of directors, Fayetteville (N.C.) United Fund, 1958, Akron (Ohio) Community Service Center and Urban League, 1960-63, and Southern Fellowships Fund, 1966—.

MEMBER: American Historical Association, Association for the Study of Negro Life and History (member of executive council, 1962—), Association of Social Science Teachers, Organization of American Historians, Southern Historical Association, Virginia Historical Society, Ohio Historical Society. *Awards, honors:* Old Dominion Foundation grant.

WRITINGS: (With Lavinia Dobler) *Pioneers and Patriots: The Lives of Six Negroes of the Revolutionary Era,* Doubleday, 1965; *A Mark Well Made: The Negro Contribution to American Culture,* Rand McNally, 1967; (with Carol Drisko) *The Unfinished March: The Negro in the United States, Reconstruction to World War I,* Doubleday, 1967; *A Biographical History of Blacks in America since 1958,* McKay, 1971; *The Black American in United States History,* Allyn & Bacon, 1973. Contributor of articles and re-

views to *Phylon, African Forum,* and to historical journals. Member of editorial board, Associated Publishers, 1963—, and board of editors, *Journal of Negro History,* 1963—.

AVOCATIONAL INTERESTS: Spectator sports, chess, bridge, reading Russian novels.

BIOGRAPHICAL/CRITICAL SOURCES: Richmond Afro-American, June 3, 1967.†

* * *

TOWEY, Cyprian 1912-

PERSONAL: First syllable of surname rhymes with "how"; born May 17, 1912, in Stewartville, Minn.; son of Thomas Francis (a farmer) and Ellen (Ellis) Towey. *Education:* Studied at Passionist institutions in Detroit and Chicago, received B.A., 1941; St. Louis University, M.A., 1943; further study at Georgetown University, 1953, University of Michigan, 1955, and American Academy in Rome, 1962. *Politics:* Eclectic. *Home and office:* St. Gabriel Monastery, 1100 North 63rd St., Des Moines, Iowa 50311.

CAREER: Roman Catholic priest of Congregatio Passionis (Passionist). Teacher of Latin language and literature at Catholic high school in St. Louis, Mo., 1943-56, and at a junior college in Warrenton, Mo., 1956-63; Library of Congress, Washington, D.C., research, 1963-64; St. Joseph Retreat House, Owensboro, Ky., director of adult education, 1964-65; St. Gabriel Monastery, Des Moines, Iowa, assistant superior, beginning 1965. Lecturer on foreign language pedagogy at teacher institutes and university summer schools. *Awards, honors:* Fulbright award to American Academy in Rome and Virgilian Summer School at Naples, 1962.

WRITINGS: Sermo Latinus (text), J. W. Edwards, 1962; *Latin Pedagogy,* J. W. Edwards, 1962; (co-author) *Lingua Latina Viva* (text), McGraw, 1966. Contributor to *Latinitas* (Rome), *Vita Latina* (Paris), *Catholic Educator,* and other journals.

SIDELIGHTS: Towey writes to *CA:* "Interest in 'spoken' communication Latin has been prompted by a sociological motive: the urgent need for a precise, simple auxiliary second language for supra-national communication.... This common second language medium has to be non-national, yet broadly rooted in most world cultures, which Latin is, e.g., lexicon of sciences and practical arts." Spent ten months in research at Library of Congress to obtain suitable textual material for a modern Latin series to be titled "Cultura Universalis."

BIOGRAPHICAL/CRITICAL SOURCES: Classical World, January, 1966; *Wanderer,* May 11, 1967.†

* * *

TOWNLEY, Ralph 1923-

PERSONAL: Born October 13, 1923, in Horncastle, England; son of Francis Harry and May (Poucher) Townley; married Jozy Smith, August 20, 1949; children: Christopher Harry, Miranda Jane. *Education:* Attended University of Nottingham; University of London, B.Sc. (honours in economics), 1949, M.Sc., 1951. *Politics:* Liberal. *Religion:* Quaker. *Home:* 40 New Shore Rd., Waterford, Conn. *Office address:* Box 20, Grand Central Station, New York, N.Y. 10017.

CAREER: United Nations, New York, N.Y., official, 1951—, seconded to U.N. Development Program, 1959—.

Visiting lecturer, University of Pittsburgh, 1960; Montague Burton Lecturer, University of Nottingham, 1965; Tobin fellow, Dartmouth College, 1968. President, New York Friends Center, 1959-61; deputy to secretary, General World Population Conference, 1972-75.

WRITINGS: (Co-author) *The Evolution of International Organizations*, edited by D.E.T. Luard, Thames & Hudson, 1966, Praeger, 1967; *United Nations: A View from Within*, Scribner, 1968.

* * *

TOWNSEND, J(ames) Benjamin   1918-

PERSONAL: Born February 17, 1918, in Stillwater, N.Y.; son of Jackson (a manufacturer) and Lula May (Townsend) Townsend; married Jeannette Thankful Rice, September 15, 1945; children: Josephine Rice, Jackson II, Rhys Frederick, Clarissa Rowe. *Education:* Princeton University, A.B., 1940; Harvard University, M.A., 1942; Yale University, Ph.D., 1951. *Home:* 614 West Ferry St., Buffalo, N.Y. 14222. *Office:* Department of English, Annex B, State University of New York at Buffalo, Buffalo, N.Y. 14214.

CAREER: Yale University, New Haven, Conn., instructor in English, 1948-50, 1951-53; University of North Carolina at Greensboro, assistant professor of English, 1953-57; State University of New York at Buffalo, 1957—, began as assistant professor, currently professor of English. Smithsonian Institution, assistant director of National Portrait Gallery, 1967-68. *Military service:* U.S. Army, 1942-45; attached to Office of Strategic Services, 1943-45; became sergeant. *Member:* Modern Language Association of America, American Association of University Professors, Phi Beta Kappa, Princeton Club of New York.

WRITINGS: *John Davidson, Poet of Armageddon*, Yale University Press, 1961; *100*, Albright Knox Art Gallery (Buffalo), 1962; (editor) *This New Man*, with an essay by Oscar Handlin, Smithsonian Institute Press, for National Portrait Gallery, 1968; *Martha Visser't Hooft: Paintings and Drawings, 1950-1973*, Charles Burchfield Center, 1973; *Six Corporate Collectors: Western New York's New Art Patrons*, Charles Burchfield Center, 1975. Art critic for journals.

WORK IN PROGRESS: A selective, annotated bibliography of nineteenth-century American painting for the Archives of American Art, Smithsonian Institution; editing the journals and sketchbooks of Charles Burchfield.

AVOCATIONAL INTERESTS: Travel, art collecting.

* * *

TOYNBEE, Polly (Mary Louisa)   1946-

PERSONAL: Born December 27, 1946, on Isle of Wight; daughter of Philip Theodore (a writer) and Anne (Powell) Toynbee; granddaughter of the historian, Arnold Toynbee. *Education:* Attended St. Anne's College, Oxford. *Politics:* Labour. *Religion:* None. *Home:* 1 Crescent Grove, London S.W. 4, England. *Agent:* A. D. Peters, 10 Buckingham St., London WC2N 6BU, England.

CAREER: Journalist with *Observer*, London, England, 1968-70, *Washington Monthly*, Washington, D.C., 1970-71, and *Observer*, 1971—.

WRITINGS: *Leftovers* (novel), Weidenfeld & Nicolson, 1966; *A Working Life* (social reporting), Hodder & Stoughton, 1970. Contributor to *Washington Post, Cosmopolitan,*

Queen, Observer, Town, New Statesman, Evening Standard, and *Sunday Telegraph.*

WORK IN PROGRESS: A reporting book entitled *Hospital.*

BIOGRAPHICAL/CRITICAL SOURCES: *Nova,* October, 1966; *Privateye,* April, 1967.

* * *

TRABASSO, Tom   1935-

PERSONAL: Born May 25, 1935, in Poughkeepsie, N.Y.; son of Anthony J. and Viola (Opitz) Trabasso; married Susan Schwerdtle, June 28, 1958. *Education:* Union College, Schenectady, N.Y., B.S., 1957; Michigan State University, M.A., 1959, Ph.D., 1961. *Office:* Institute of Child Development, University of Minnesota, Minneapolis, Minn. 55455.

CAREER: University of California, Los Angeles, associate professor of psychology, 1963-69; Princeton University, Princeton, N.J., professor of psychology, 1969-76; University of Minnesota, Institute of Child Development, Minneapolis, professor, 1976—.

WRITINGS: (With Gordon H. Bower) *Attention in Learning: Theory and Research*, Wiley, 1968; (with Deborah Harrison) *Black English: A Seminar*, Lawrence Erlbaum Associates, 1976. Contributor of articles to professional journals.

WORK IN PROGRESS: Research in human cognition, thinking and language comprehension, and cognitive development.

* * *

TRALINS, S. Robert   1926-
(Bob Tralins, Robert S. Tralins; pseudonyms: Ray Z. Bixby, Norman A. King, Keith Miles, Sean O'Shea, Rex O'Toole, C. Sydney, Rex Toole, Ruy Traube)

PERSONAL: Born April 28, 1926; son of Emanuel and Rose (Miller) Tralins; married, September 2, 1945, wife's name, Sonya; children: Myles J., Alan H. *Education:* Attended Eastern College (now University of Baltimore), 1946-48. *Home:* 7941 West Dr., North Bay Village, Fla. 33141.

CAREER: Writer. *Military service:* U.S. Marine Corps Reserve, 1943-45.

WRITINGS—Under real name or form of real name: *How to Be a Power Closer in Selling*, Prentice-Hall, 1960; *Dynamic Selling*, Prentice-Hall, 1961; *Torrid Island*, Novel Books, 1961; *Pleasure Was My Business* (autobiography of Madam Sherry [pseudonym of Ruth Barnes] as told to Tralins), Lyle Stuart, 1961; *Caesar's Bench*, Tuxedo Books, 1961; *Law of Lust*, Tuxedo Books, 1961; *Congo Lust*, Tuxedo Books, 1961; *Naked Hills*, Tuxedo Books, 1961.

Hillbilly Nymph, Tuxedo Books, 1962; *Freak Woman*, Novel Books, 1962; *Nymphokick*, Merit Books, 1962; *Four Queens*, Novel Books, 1962; *Seductress*, Novel Books, 1962; *Female Rapist*, Novel Books, 1962; *Love Goddess*, Novel Books, 1962; *Primitive Orgy*, Novel Books, 1962; *Passion Potion*, Novel Books, 1962; *Hired Nymph*, Novel Books, 1962; *Office Girl*, Novel Books, 1962; *Four Wild Dames*, Novel Books, 1962; *Seduction Salon*, Novel Books, 1962; *International Girl*, Novel Books, 1962; *Barechested Beauty*, Novel Books, 1962; *Smuggler's Mistress*, Novel Books, 1962; *Jazzman in Nudetown*, Bedside Books,

1963; *Orgy of Terror,* Novel Books, 1963; *Freak Lover,* Novel Books, 1963; *Colossal Carnality,* Novel Books, 1963; *Love Experiment,* Novel Books, 1963.

The Ultimate Passion, Novel Books, 1964; *Experiment in Desire,* Novel Books, 1964; *Love Worshiper,* Novel Books, 1964; *Erotic Play,* Novel Books, 1964; *Goddess of Raw Passion,* Novel Books, 1964; *Donna Is Different,* Novel Books, 1964; *The One and Only Jean,* Novel Books, 1964; *Rites of the Half-Women,* Novel Books, 1965; *Squaresville Jag,* Belmont Books, 1965; (with Dr. Michael M. Gilbert) *Twenty-one Abnormal Sex Cases,* Paperback Library, 1965; *They Make Her Beg,* Novel Books, 1965.

Beyond Human Understanding: Strange Events, Ace Books, 1966; *The Miss from S.I.S.,* Belmont Books, 1966; *The Chic Chick Spy,* Belmont Books, 1966; *The Cosmozoids,* Belmont Books, 1966; *The Ring-a-Ding UFO's,* Belmont Books, 1966; *Strange Events Beyond Human Knowledge,* Avon Books, 1967; *Cairo Madam,* Paperback Library, 1968; *Clairvoyant Strangers,* Popular Library, 1968; *Weird People of the Unknown,* Popular Library, 1969; *Children of the Supernatural,* Lancer, 1969; *Fetishism,* Paperback Library, 1969; *Runaway Slave,* Lancer, 1969; *Slave's Revenge,* Lancer, 1969; *Panther John,* Lancer, 1969.

All published by Popular Library, except as noted: *Supernatural Strangers,* 1970; *ESP Forewarnings,* 1970; *Clairvoyant Women,* 1970; *Clairvoyance in Women,* Lancer, 1971; *Supernatural Warnings,* 1972; *Ghoul Lover,* 1973. Author of screenplay "Illegal Tender," 1975; also author of *Song of Africa,* 1968, *Black Brute,* 1969, and *Slave King,* 1970.

Under pseudonym Ray Z. Bixby: *The Rites of Lust,* Softcover Library, 1967.

Under pseudonym Norman A. King: *French Leave,* Midwood, 1967.

Under pseudonym Keith Miles: *Dragon's Teeth,* Popular Library, 1973.

Under pseudonym Sean O'Shea: *Whisper,* Softcover Library, 1965; *What a Way to Go,* Belmont Books, 1966; *Sex Variations in Voyeurism,* Award Books, 1967; *Psychokick,* Lancer Books, 1967; *Operation Boudoir,* Belmont Books, 1967; *Win with Sin,* Belmont Books, 1967; *The Nymph Island Affair,* Belmont Books, 1967; *The Invasion of Nymphs,* Belmont Books, 1967; *Topless Kitties,* Belmont Books, 1968.

Under pseudonym Rex O'Toole: *Cheating and Infidelity in America,* Belmont Books, 1968. Also author of *Remember to Die,* 1967, and *Variations in Exhibitionism,* 1967.

Under pseudonym C. Sydney; all published by Midwood Books: *Lure of Luxury,* 1966; *Trick or Treat,* 1966; *Sin Point,* 1966; *Hideaway Lane,* 1966; *Ripe and Ready,* 1966; *Lost and Found,* 1966; *Executive Wife,* 1967; *Take Me Out in Trade,* 1967.

Under pseudonym Rex Toole: *Soft Sell,* Bee-Line Books, 1967; *Nymphet Syndrome,* Award Books, 1967.

Under pseudonym Ruy Traube: *The Seduction Art,* Belmont Books, 1967; *Uninhibited,* Belmont Books, 1968; *Memoirs of a Beach Boy Lover,* Lancer, 1969.

WORK IN PROGRESS: *Mnemonics* and *Psychiatry and Psychology.*

SIDELIGHTS: Tralins told *CA:* "[I am] reverting to the writing of serious, long length fiction." He adds: "[I have] been moving in this direction for twenty years."

TRAVIS, Walter Earl 1926-

PERSONAL: Born September 7, 1926, in Peekskill, N.Y.; son of Earle Douglas and Mary (Barrette) Travis; married Barbara Begeny (a teacher); children: Mary Beth, Paul, John. *Education:* San Francisco State College (now University), A.B., 1950, M.A., 1955; Columbia University, Ed.D., 1964. *Politics:* Democrat. *Religion:* Catholic. *Home:* 19982 Via Escuela Dr., Saratoga, Calif. 95070. *Office:* DeAnza College, Cupertino, Calif. 95014.

CAREER: Instructor and chairman of social studies department at high schools in Richmond, Calif., 1950-52, and El Cerrito, Calif., 1952-62; Foothill College, Los Altos Hills, Calif., member of history and political science faculty, 1962-68; DeAnza College, Cupertino, Calif., chairman of Social Science Division, 1967—. *Military service:* U.S. Naval Reserve, 1944-46. *Member:* American Historical Association, Organization of American Historians, California Teachers Association, Phi Delta Kappa.

WRITINGS: (Editor) *Congress and the President: Readings in Executive-Legislative Relations,* Teachers College Press, 1967.

* * *

TREFETHEN, James B(yron, Jr.) 1916-

PERSONAL: Surname is accented on second syllable, Tre*feth*-en; born June 3, 1916, in Brockton, Mass.; son of James Byron (a contractor) and Mabel (Churchill) Trefethen; married Julia Edes, August 30, 1941; children: James Edes, Ann Trefethen Kerr, Frances Trefethen Hopkins, Clinton David, Holly Trefethen Snide. *Education:* Northeastern University, B.A., 1940; University of Massachusetts, M.S., 1948. *Home:* 10415 Edgefield Dr., Adelphi, Md. 20783. *Office:* Wildlife Management Institute, 709 Wire Building, Washington, D.C. 20005.

CAREER: Wildlife Management Institute, Washington, D.C., director of publications, 1948—. *Military service:* U.S. Army, 1943-45; served in Normandy and Northern France campaigns. *Member:* International Association of Game, Fish, and Conservation Commissioners, Wildlife Society, National Rifle Association (life member), Outdoor Writers Association of America, Forest History Society, Boone and Crockett Club. *Awards, honors:* Jade of Chiefs Award, Outdoor Writers Association of America, 1975; Conservation Education Award, Wildlife Society, 1976, for *An American Crusade for Wildlife.*

WRITINGS: Crusade for Wildlife, Stackpole, 1961; *Wildlife Management and Conservation,* Heath, 1963; (editor with Leonard Miracle) *Hunters Encyclopedia,* Stackpole, 1966; *Americans and Their Guns,* Stackpole, 1967; (editor with Clarence Cottam) *Whitewings: The Life History, Status, and Management of the White-winged Dove,* Van Nostrand, 1968; *The Wild Sheep in Modern North America,* Winchester Press, 1975; *An American Crusade for Wildlife,* Winchester Press, 1975; *The American Landscape, 1776-1976,* Wildlife Management Institute, 1976. Editor, *Proceedings* of the National Watershed Congress and *Transactions* of the North American Wildlife and Natural Resources Conference, 1952—.

AVOCATIONAL INTERESTS: Outdoor sports, including shooting.

* * *

TREGEAR, Thomas R(efoy) 1897-

PERSONAL: Born June 28, 1897, in Bognor Regis, Sussex, England; son of Thomas (an estate agent) and Elizabeth (Refoy) Tregear; married Norah Walden (a doctor of medicine), August 9, 1921; children: Jean (Mrs. P. Ashman James), Mary, Richard T. *Education:* London School of Economics and Political Science, B.Sc. (honors), 1922, Ph.D., 1934. *Politics:* British Labour Party. *Religion:* Quaker. *Home:* 24A Portland Rd., Oxford, England.

CAREER: Central China University, Wuchang, Hupeh, lecturer, 1923-27, professor of geography, 1946-51; teacher of geography at schools in Malden, Essex, England, 1927-29, and Winscombe, Somersetshire, England, 1929-46; University of Hong Kong, Hong Kong, lecturer in geography, 1952-59; Woodbrooke College, Birmingham, England, warden, 1959-63; tutor and writer. *Military service:* Sussex Yeomanry, 1915-19; became sergeant. *Member:* Geographical Association.

WRITINGS: World Economic Geography Notes (in Chinese), Central China University, 1950; *Land Use Map of Hong Kong and the New Territories,* Macmillan, 1956; *Hong Kong Gazetteer,* Hong Kong University Press, 1958; *Land Use in Hong Kong and the New Territories,* Geographical Publications, 1958; (with L. Berry) *The Development of Hong Kong and Kowloon as Told in Maps,* Macmillan, 1959; *A Geography of China,* University of London, 1965; *Economic Geography of China,* Butterworth & Co., 1970; *The Chinese: How They Live and Work,* Praeger, 1973. Contributor of articles to *Encyclopedia Britannica,* 1974, and to *Collier's Encyclopedia,* 1974.

WORK IN PROGRESS: A new edition of *A Geography of China.*

* * *

TRENT, James W(illiam) 1933-

PERSONAL: Born October 28, 1933, in Los Angeles, Calif.; son of Clark Heath (a hospital purchasing agent) and Loa Blanche (Kern) Trent; married Gretchen Anne Maeshner, April 12, 1958; children: Karl, Julie. *Education:* University of Santa Clara, A.B., 1955; University of California, Berkeley, Ph.D., 1964. *Politics:* Democrat. *Religion:* Roman Catholic. *Office:* Graduate School of Education, 320 Moore Hall, University of California, Los Angeles, Calif. 90024.

CAREER: University of California, Center for Research and Development in Higher Education, Berkeley, administrative assistant, 1960, research psychologist and project director, 1961-68; University of California, Los Angeles, assistant professor, 1968-69, associate professor of higher education, 1969—. University of California Extension instructor in tests and measurements, prior to 1968. Consultant, Higher Education Executive Associates, 1967—. *Member:* American Psychological Association, Society for the Psychological Study of Social Issues, Society for the Scientific Study of Religion, American Educational Research Association.

WRITINGS: (With Jenette Golds) *Catholics in College: Religious Commitment and the Intellectual Life,* University of Chicago Press, 1967; (with Leland L. Medsker) *Beyond High School: A Psychological Study of 10,000 High School Graduates,* Jossey-Bass, 1968; (contributor) *Student Activism and Protest,* Jossey-Bass, 1970; *In and Out of College,* Jossey-Bass, 1971; (contributor) *Handbook of Research on Teaching,* Rand McNally, 1973. Author or co-author of reports on U.S. Office of Education cooperative research projects published by Center for Research and Development in Higher Education and in journals.†

TRICE, Harrison M. 1920-

PERSONAL: Born May 25, 1920, in Amarillo, Tex.; son of John Edward (a realtor) and Ora Mae (Miller) Trice; married Alice Buran (a teacher), March 4, 1944; children: Richard Harrison, Catherine Ann. *Education:* Louisiana State University, B.A., 1945; University of Wisconsin, M.A., 1949, Ph.D., 1955. *Office:* New York State School of Industrial and Labor Relations, Cornell University, Ithaca, N.Y.

CAREER: University of Wisconsin—Madison, instructor in sociology, 1949-55; Cornell University, New York State School of Industrial and Labor Relations, Ithaca, N.Y., assistant professor, 1955-59, associate professor, 1959-67, professor of sociology, 1967—. Research consultant, Christopher D. Smithers Foundation, 1962—. *Member:* American Sociological Association (fellow), Society for the Study of Social Problems (chairman of committee on psychiatric sociology).

WRITINGS: Alcoholism in America, McGraw, 1967; (with Paul M. Roman) *Schizophrenia and the Poor,* New York State School of Industrial and Labor Relations, Cornell University, 1967; (with George Ritzer) *An Occupation in Conflict,* New York State School of Industrial and Labor Relations, Cornell University, 1969; (with James Belasco) *The Assessment of Change Agents in Therapy and Training,* McGraw, 1969; (with Roman) *Spirits and Demons at Work: Alcohol and Other Drugs on the Job,* Cornell University Press, 1972; (editor with Roman) *The Sociology of Psychotherapy,* Jason Aronson, 1974; (editor with Roman) *Explorations in Psychiatric Sociology,* Davis Publications, 1974. Contributor to journals in area of psychiatric sociology.†

* * *

TRIGGER, Bruce G(raham) 1937-

PERSONAL: Born June 18, 1937, in Preston (now Cambridge), Ontario, Canada; son of John Wesley and Gertrude E. (Graham) Trigger; married Barbara Marian Welch, December, 1968; children: Isabel Marian, Rosalyn Theodora. *Education:* University of Toronto, B.A., 1959; Yale University, Ph.D., 1964. *Politics:* Social Democrat. *Religion:* None. *Home:* 3495 rue de la Montagne, Montreal, Quebec, Canada. *Office:* Department of Anthropology, McGill University, Montreal, Quebec, Canada.

CAREER: Chief archaeologist with Pennsylvania-Yale expedition to Egypt, 1962, and Oriental Institute Sudan expedition, 1964; Northwestern University, Evanston, Ill., assistant professor of anthropology, 1963-64; McGill University, Montreal, Quebec, 1964—, began as associate professor, currently professor of anthropology, chairman of department, 1970-75. *Member:* American Anthropological Association (foreign fellow), Royal Anthropological Institute (fellow), Canadian Society for Archaeology Abroad, Sigma Xi.

WRITINGS: History and Settlement in Lower Nubia, Yale University Publications in Anthropology, 1965; *The Late Nubian Settlement at Arminna West,* Publications of the Pennsylvania-Yale Expedition to Egypt, Number 2, 1967; *Beyond History: The Methods of Prehistory,* Holt, 1968; *The Huron: Farmers of the North,* Holt, 1969; *The Meroitic Funerary Inscriptions from Arminna West,* Publications of the Pennsylvania-Yale Expedition to Egypt, Number 4, 1970; (with James F. Pendergast) *Cartier's Hachelaga and the Dawson Site,* McGill-Queen's, 1972. Also author of *The Children of Aataentsic: A History of* the *Huron People to 1660*, 1975, and *Nubia under the Phar-aohs*, 1976.

*   *   *

TRIPP, Paul 1916-

PERSONAL: Born February 20, 1916, in New York, N.Y.; son of Benjamin (a singer and actor) and Esther (Stelzer) Tripp; married Ruth Enders (an actress), August 8, 1943; children: Suzanne (Mrs. Richard Jurmain), David. *Education:* Ctiy College (now City College of the City University of New York), student, 1927-31. *Politics:* Independent. *Home:* 2 Fifth Ave., New York, N.Y. 10011.

CAREER: Editor of *Ridgefield Park Bulletin* (weekly newspaper), Ridgefield Park, N.J., 1946-47; specialist in entertainment for children, 1949—, producing and acting in television series, narrating films, and writing songs. Creator, director, and star of "Mr. I. Magination," 1949-52, and producer and star of "On the Carousel," 1954-59, both CBS-TV series; star of "Birthday House," NBC-TV series, 1963-67; narrator of fourteen films produced by Childhood Productions, Rome, Italy, 1965-68, and star, writer, and lyricist of one, "The Christmas That Almost Wasn't," 1966. President of Fantasy Music Publishing, Inc., New York, N.Y., 1960-63, director, 1960—. Member of New York City Youth Board, 1955-57. *Military service:* U.S. Army, 1942-45; served in China-Burma-India theater; became staff sergeant.

MEMBER: American Society of Composers, Authors and Publishers (ASCAP), National Society of Literature and the Arts, Screen Writers Guild, National Academy of Television Arts and Sciences (member of board of governors, 1958—; trustee, 1960-61), The Players (New York). *Awards, honors:* Look Award, George Foster Peabody Award, and Ohio State Television Award, all for "Mr. I. Magination"; Emmy Award of National Academy of Television Arts and Sciences and four Ohio State Television awards for "On the Carousel"; "Tubby the Tuba," a film short, was nominated for an Oscar by Academy of Motion Picture Arts and Sciences; nominated for Grammy Award, 1966.

WRITINGS: The Strawman Who Smiled by Mistake (illustrated by Wendy Watson), Doubleday, 1967; *The Little Red Flower*, Doubleday, 1968. Collaborated with wife, Ruth Enders Tripp on play "Sackful of Dreams," 1974. Writer of script and lyrics for film, "The Christmas That Almost Wasn't"; has also written more than thirty record albums for children, including "Tubby the Tuba," "Story of Celeste," "Mr. I. Magination," and "Birthday House." He has written and published about 600 songs. Contributor to *Television* (quarterly); columnist, "Don't Kid Me," in *Rockland Independent* (published in Rockland County, N.Y.).

WORK IN PROGRESS: An animated full-length film based on "Tubby the Tuba"; autobiography, tentatively entitled *Audience in a Playpen*.

AVOCATIONAL INTERESTS: Mythology.

*   *   *

TRIPPETT, Frank 1926-
(R. G. O. Swivett)

PERSONAL: Born July 1, 1926, in Columbus, Miss.; son of S. B. and Bess (Leftwich) Trippett; married Betty Timberlake, April 6, 1951; children: John, Bess, Robert, Nan. *Education:* Attended Mississippi College, Duke Univer-

sity, and University of Mississippi, 1944-47. *Home and office:* 4 Stuyvesant Ave., Larchmont, N.Y.

CAREER: Reporter and wire editor in Meridian, Miss., 1948; reporter and photographer in Fredericksburg, Va., 1948-54; *St. Petersburg Times*, St. Petersburg, Fla., state capitol bureau chief, 1955-61; *Newsweek*, New York City, associate editor, national affairs, 1961-68; *Look*, New York City, senior editor, 1968-71; free-lance writer and editor, 1971—.

WRITINGS: The States: United They Fell, World Publishing, 1967; *The First Horseman*, Time-Life, 1974; *Child Ellen*, Prentice-Hall, 1975.

*   *   *

TRITT, Robert E(arl) 1921-

PERSONAL: Born October 9, 1921, in Ordway, Colo.; son of Edward C. and Iris (Jackson) Tritt; married Patricia A. Fleharty, December 20, 1948; children: Roy, Robert, Patrick. *Education:* Colorado College, A.B., 1947; Stanford University, M.B.A., 1949; University of Southern California, D.B.A., 1965. *Politics:* Republican. *Religion:* Catholic. *Office:* University of Georgia, Athens, Ga. 30601.

CAREER: Roy's Markets, Inc., San Diego, Calif., president, 1949-61; University of Southern California, Los Angeles, instructor, 1961-63; University of Georgia, Athens, associate professor of marketing, beginning 1963. *Military service:* U.S. Army, 1942-46; became first lieutenant. *Member:* American Marketing Association, International Executives Association, Southern Marketing Association, Optimist Club.

WRITINGS: Sales Management Organization Game, with player's manual and administrator's manual, Irwin, 1967. Contributor to business journals.††

*   *   *

TROY, Lawrence M. 1928-

PERSONAL: Born August 19, 1928, in Brooklyn, N.Y.; son of Nathan (a businessman) and Ruth (Eisenberg) Troy; married Sylvia Epstein, December 15, 1951; children: Joel. *Education:* New York University, B.A., 1950, J.D., 1953, M.A., 1958. *Politics:* Democrat. *Religion:* Jewish. *Home:* 3210 Brower Ave., Oceanside, N.Y. 11572.

CAREER: Private practice of law, 1953—; Lafayette High School, Brooklyn, N.Y., teacher of social studies, 1956—.

WRITINGS: (With Epstein and Shostak) *Barron's Guide to Law Schools*, Barron's, 1967; (with Epstein and Shostak) *How to Prepare for the Law School Admissions Test*, Barron's, 1967, 2nd edition, 1973.

WORK IN PROGRESS: A third edition of *How to Prepare for the Law School Admissions Test*.

AVOCATIONAL INTERESTS: Collecting books (history and biography) and stamps (American and ships).

*   *   *

TRUBOWITZ, Sidney 1926-

PERSONAL: Born February 4, 1926, in New York, N.Y.; son of Louis (an insurance agent) and Anna (Breslow) Trubowitz; married Naomi Klenetsky, June 17, 1962; children: Lara Andreya, Jason Alexander. *Education:* City College (now City College of the City University of New York), B.S.S., 1948; Columbia University, M.A., 1949, Ed.D., 1966; Queens College (now Queens College of the City University of New York), Professional Diploma in Administration, 1957. *Politics:* "Liberally oriented." *Home:* 1225 Park Ave., New York, N.Y. 10008. *Office:* Department of Education, Queens College of the City University of New York, New York, N.Y. 11367.

CAREER: New York (N.Y.) public schools, principal, beginning 1966; currently associate professor and chairman of department of graduate programs in educational services. *Military service:* U.S. Navy, 1944-46. *Awards, honors:* Education Press Association of America award, 1972, for article "Confessions of a Ghetto Administrator."

WRITINGS: Handbook for Teaching in the Ghetto School, Quadrangle, 1968.

WORK IN PROGRESS: Administration of Open Classroom Schools.

AVOCATIONAL INTERESTS: Tennis, biking, jogging.

*   *   *

TRUMBO, Dalton 1905-
(Sam Jackson, Robert Rich)

PERSONAL: Born December 9, 1905, in Montrose, Colo.; son of Orus Bonham and Maud (Tillery) Trumbo; married Cleo Beth Fincher (a photographer), March 13, 1939; children: Nikola (Mrs. Derrick Taylor), Christopher, Melissa. *Education:* Attended University of Colorado, 1924-25, University of Southern California, 1928-30. *Home:* 8710 St. Ives Dr., Los Angeles, Calif. 90069. *Agent:* Miss Shirley Burke, 370 East 76th St., Suite B-704, New York, N.Y. 10021.

CAREER: Car washer; section hand; worked for nine years as a bread-wrapper and later as an estimator on the night shift for Divis Perfection Bakery, Los Angeles, Calif.; reader at Warner Bros.; managing editor, *The Hollywood Spectator;* founding editor, *The Screenwriter,* 1945; screenwriter since 1936. Served as national chairman of Writers for Roosevelt, 1944. War correspondent, U.S. Army Air Forces, 1945.

MEMBER: Screen Writers Guild of America (director, 1945), Delta Tau Delta, Mulholland Club. *Awards, honors:* National Booksellers Award, 1939, for *Johnny Got His Gun;* Academy Award, 1957, for "The Brave One"; Teachers Union of New York annual award, 1960; Writers Guild Laurel Award, for achievement in screenwriting, 1970; Cannes Film Festival Special Jury Grand Prize, International Critics Prize, Interfilm Jury World Council of Churches Prize, Atlanta Film Festival Golden Dove Peace Prize, and Golden Phoenix for Best of Festival, all 1971, and Belgrade Film Festival, Audience and Director's Award and Japanese International Festival of the Arts Grand Prize, both 1972, all for "Johnny Got His Gun."

WRITINGS: Eclipse (novel), L. Dickson & Thompson (London), 1935; *Washington Jitters* (novel), Knopf, 1936; *Johnny Got His Gun* (novel), Lippincott, 1939, reprinted, Lyle Stuart, 1970; *The Remarkable Andrew* (novel), Lippincott, 1941; *The Biggest Thief in Town* (three-act comedy; produced in New York at Mansfield Theatre, March 30, 1949), Dramatists Play Service, 1949; *Additional Dialogue: Letters of Dalton Trumbo, 1942-1962,* edited by Helen Manfull, M. Evans, 1970; *The Time of the Toad: A Study of Inquisition in America* (includes "The Time of the Toad," "The Devil in the Book," and "Honor Bright and All that Jazz"; also see below) Harper, 1972. Contributor to *North American Review, Forum, Vanity Fair, Saturday Evening Post, Liberty, McCall's, New Masses, Masses and Mainstream, Nation, Theatre Arts,* and *Playboy.*

Pamphlets: *Harry Bridges,* League of American Writers, 1941; *The Time of the Toad: A Study of Inquisition in America,* Hollywood Ten, 1948; *The Devil in the Book,* Emergency Defense Committee, 1956.

Screenplays: "Jealousy," Columbia, 1934; "The Story of Isadore Bernstein," Columbia, 1936; (with Tom Reed) "Love Begins at Twenty," Warner Bros., 1936; "Road Gang," Columbia, 1936; (collaborator) "Devil's Playground," Columbia, 1937; "A Man to Remember" (based on Katharine Haviland-Taylor's short story "Failure"), RKO, 1938; "Fugitives for a Night," RKO, 1938; "Sorority House," RKO, 1939; "Career," RKO, 1939; (with Nathanael West and Jerry Cady) "Five Came Back," RKO, 1939; (with Ernest Pagano) "The Flying Irishman," RKO, 1939; "Heaven with a Barbed Wire Fence," Twentieth Century-Fox, 1939; "Half a Sinner," Universal, 1940; "We Who are Young," Metro-Goldwyn-Mayer, 1940; "Kitty Foyle" (adaptation of the book by Christopher Morley), RKO, 1940; "A Bill of Divorcement," RKO, 1940; "Curtain Call," RKO, 1940; "The Remarkable Andrew," Paramount, 1942; "Tender Comrade," RKO, 1943; "A Man Named Joe," Metro-Goldwyn-Mayer, 1943 (novelization by Randall M. White published as *A Guy Named Joe,* Grosset, 1944); "Thirty Seconds Over Tokyo," Metro-Goldwyn-Mayer, 1944; "Our Vines Have Tender Grapes" (adaption of the book by George Victor Martin), Metro-Goldwyn-Mayer, 1945.

(Under pseudonym Robert Rich) "The Brave One," King Brothers Productions, 1957; "Exodus" (adaption of the book by Leon Uris), United Artists, 1960; "Spartacus" (based on the novel by Howard Fast), Universal, 1960; "The Last Sunset" (based on *Sundown at Crazy Horse* by Howard Rigsby), Universal, 1961; "Lonely are the Brave" (based on *The Brave Cowboy* by Edward Abbey), Universal, 1962; "The Sandpiper," Metro-Goldwyn-Mayer, 1965; "Hawaii" (adaption of the book by James A. Michener), United Artists, 1966; "The Fixer" (adaption of the book by Bernard Malamud), Metro-Goldwyn-Mayer, 1968; "The Horsemen," Columbia, 1971; (and director) "Johnny Got His Gun," Cinemation Industries, 1971; (with Lorenzo Semple, Jr.) "Papillon" (based on the book by Henri Charriere), Metro-Goldwyn-Mayer, 1973. Also author of approximately 34 other filmscripts.

WORK IN PROGRESS: A novel concerning the recollections of a sub-commandant at Auschwitz; a filmscript based on Jorge Amado's *Gabriela, Clove and Cinnamon.*

SIDELIGHTS: Trumbo was a member of the Hollywood Ten who refused to tell the House Committee on Un-American Activities whether he was, or ever had been, a Communist. Because he kept silent he was convicted of contempt of Congress and served a year's sentence at the Federal Correctional Institution in Ashland, Ky. Between 1947 and 1960, Trumbo was anathema to anyone in the movie business. Living in self-exile in Mexico, he began to turn out scripts under various pseudonyms for low-budget films until the 1960's when Trumbo's name appeared as the screenwriter of "Exodus." *Additional Dialogue* contains Trumbo's letters from those blacklisted years. A. D. Murphy wrote of the collection: "His [Trumbo's] letter-writing style is marked by a fine sense of humor, plus the detailed outrage of a wounded Sagittarian, and a pen far more temperate than those of his prosecutors."

Johnny Got His Gun, Trumbo's best-known novel, is a strong and vivid story written in terms of the thoughts of a hospitalized World War I soldier who is without arms, legs, face, sight, or hearing, in other words, a living dead man. Because of his uselessness the protagonist decides to be an educational exhibit. He doesn't think that people would learn much about anatomy from him, "but they would learn all there was to know about war. That would be a great thing, to concentrate war in one stump of a body and to show it to people so they could see the difference between a war that's in newspaper headlines and liberty loan drives and a war that is fought out lonesomely in the mud somewhere, a war between a man and a high explosive shell. . . . He would make an exhibit of himself to show all the little guys what would happen to them . . . and he would have a sign over himself and the sign would say here is war and he would concentrate the whole war into such a small piece of meat and bone and hair that they would never forget it as long as they lived." In reviewing the novel, F. T. Marsh thought it the toughest assignment he had ever had. "It's a terrible story, remorseless, uncompromising. Even for one who believes that everything in life is subject for the novelist, that there should be no limitations of any kind to the honest portrayal of that which is, this book was a shocking and violent experience." Luella Creighton echoed Marsh: "Gruesome physical details are copiously supplied, but one feels not for mere effect. The whole thing seems to be a sincere attempt to describe with fiendish clarity the effect on body and soul of subjection to war." B. R. Redman noted that it is "not merely a powerful anti-war document; it is also a powerful and brilliant work of the imagination. In giving voice to a human experience that has hitherto been voiceless, Mr. Trumbo has written a book that can never be forgotten by anyone who ever reads it."

Trumbo has noted that the book is concerned with the "romantic" wars—a war that began like a "summer festival." World War II, he maintains, was "an entirely different affair." In 1939, *Johnny Got His Gun* was, in effect, a leftist document, but after Pearl Harbor, notes Trumbo, "its subject matter seemed as inappropriate to the times as the [World War I] shriek of bagpipes." It was rumored that the book was suppressed during the war years, but Trumbo received no indication of this. "If, however, it had been banned and I had known about it, I doubt that I should have protested very loudly. There are times when it may be needful for certain private rights to give way to the requirements of a larger public good. I know that's a dangerous thought, and I shouldn't wish to carry it too far, but World War II was *not* a romantic war." As the war continued and *Johnny* went out of print, both the American Civil Liberties Union and right-wing Americans sought to have the book reissued. They wanted Trumbo to be their symbol for peace. "Nothing could have convinced me so quickly that *Johnny* was exactly the sort of book that shouldn't be reprinted until the war was at an end," he said. Speaking of the 1971 movie version of *Johnny Got His Gun* (in which Trumbo made his directing debut) a *Variety* reviewer noted: "'Johnny' was in abeyance for 32 years. It was once produced as a radio broadcast but until now its situation of a hero shut off from all human contact . . . has precluded film production. The present intensification of pacifist sentiment in U.S. and round the world gave rise to the revival of the tome."

Washington Jitters was dramatized by John Boruft and Walter Hart and produced at the Guild Theatre, New York City, May 2, 1938, published by French, 1938. The films "The Kid from Kokomo," Warner Bros., 1939, "The Lone Wolf Strike," Columbia, 1940, "Accent on Love," Twentieth Century-Fox, 1941, and "You Belong to Me," Co-

lumbia, 1941, refilmed as "Emergency Wedding," Columbia, 1950, were based on his stories.

BIOGRAPHICAL/CRITICAL SOURCES: Saturday Review, September 9, 1939; *Books,* September 10, 1939; *New York Times,* September 10, 1939, December 11, 1966, June 4, 1967, October 27, 1970; *Canadian Forum,* December, 1939; Dalton Trumbo, *Johnny Got His Gun,* Bantam, 1967; *Variety,* December 9, 1970, May 12, 1971.†

* * *

TSAMBASSIS, Alexander N(icholas) 1919-

PERSONAL: Surname is pronounced Cham-*bah*-sis; born January 2, 1919, in Aleppo, Syria; son of Nicholas A. (an accountant) and Eupraxia (Sevastou) Tsambassis; married Katharine N. Voulelis, June 26, 1955; children: Nicholas A. *Education:* University of Athens, B.A., 1940; Seabury-Western Theological Seminary, B.D., 1948; Northwestern University, Ph.D., 1957. *Home:* 311 Madison Ave., West Brownsville, Pa. 15417.

CAREER: Greek-American Cultural Institute, director and teacher of English, 1952-53; Ohio Northern University, Ada, assistant professor of philosophy, 1957-60; Marietta College, Marietta, Ohio, assistant professor, 1960-61, associate professor of philosophy, 1961-64; California State College, California, Pa., professor of philosophy, 1964—. Bowling Green State University, visiting professor, 1962-63. *Military service:* Greek Army, 1944-46. *Member:* American Philosophical Association, Metaphysical Society of America, American Society for Aesthetics, British Society of Aesthetics, College Art Association, Society for Ancient Greek Philosophy.

WRITINGS: (Editor) *Human Experience and Its Problems: Introductory Readings in Philosophy,* Wadsworth, 1967. Regular contributor to *Choice;* occasional contributor to philosophy journals.

SIDELIGHTS: Tsambassis is competent in classical and modern Greek, French, Italian, and German. *Avocational interests:* Classical music, ancient Greek culture, art, travel, and photography (has large color slide collection of paintings and sculpture of all periods and regions).

* * *

TSUKAHIRA, Toshio George 1915-

PERSONAL: Born December 22, 1915, in Los Angeles, Calif.; son of Kuhei (a businessman) and Kikue (Akazawa) Tsukahira; married Lilly Yuri Fujioka, April 4, 1942. *Education:* Meiji University, Tokyo, Japan, student, 1933-36; University of California, Los Angeles, A.B., 1939, M.A., 1941; Harvard University, Ph.D., 1951. *Religion:* Protestant Episcopalian. *Office:* U.S. Department of State, Washington, D.C. 20520.

CAREER: Harvard University, Cambridge, Mass., instructor in history, 1951-54; University of California, Berkeley, assistant professor of history, 1954-55; U.S. Department of State, Washington, D.C., foreign service officer, 1955—, with posts in Japan, 1962-68, Thailand, 1968-71, Japan, 1972-75. *Military service:* U.S. Army, 1944-47; became captain. *Member:* Foreign Service Association, Association of Asian Studies.

WRITINGS: Postwar Strategy of the Japanese Communist Party, Center for International Studies, Massachusetts Institute of Technology, 1954; *Feudal Control in Tokugawa Japan: The Sankin Kotai System,* East Asian Research Center, Harvard University, 1966.

WORK IN PROGRESS: History of modernization of Japan.

* * *

TUCKER, James 1929-
(David Craig)

PERSONAL: Born August 15, 1929, in Cardiff, Wales; son of William Arthur (a company director) and Irene (Bushen) Tucker; married Marian Craig, July 17, 1954; children: Patrick, Catherine, Guy, David. Education: University of Wales, B.A., 1951. Home: 5 Cefn Coed Rd., Cardiff, Wales. Agent: Peter Janson-Smith Ltd., 31 Newington Green, London N. 16, England.

CAREER: Western Mail, Cardiff Wales, leader writer, 1954-56; Daily Mirror, London, England, reporter, 1956-58; has held various jobs with newspapers, 1958—. Military service: Royal Air Force, 1951-53; became flying officer. Member: P.E.N.

WRITINGS: Equal Partners (novel), Chapman & Hall, 1960; The Right Hand Man (novel), Four Square Books, 1961; Honourable Estates (nonfiction), Gollancz, 1966; Burster (novel), Gollancz, 1966.

Under pseudonym David Craig; all published by Stein & Day: The Alias Man, 1968; Message Ends, 1969; Young Men May Die, 1970; Contact Lost, 1970; Walk at Night, 1971. Writer of television and radio documentaries. Contributor to Punch, Spectator, New Society, and Sunday Times.

WORK IN PROGRESS: A novel; critical book on Anthony Powell, for Macmillan.

* * *

TUDYMAN, Al 1914-

PERSONAL: Born December 1, 1914, in Illinois; son of William and Anna (Hajek) Tudyman; married Sarah Knepper, March 19, 1948; children: Barbara Ann, William C. Education: Northwestern University, B.S. in Ed., 1938, M.A., 1939; Stanford University, Ed.D., 1948. Home: 4470 Hillsborough Dr., Castro Valley, Calif. 94546. Office: Oakland Public Schools, 1025 Second Ave., Oakland, Calif. 94606.

CAREER: Teacher in Cook County, Ill., 1935-36; Kellogg Foundation, Battle Creek, Mich., counselor, 1936-37; Westchester (Ill.) public schools, teaching principal, 1937-41; Cook County (Ill.) Board of Education, assistant superintendent in charge of special education, 1946-48; Oakland (Calif.) public schools, director of special education, 1948—. Part-time instructor in special education, University of California, Los Angeles, 1950-51, San Francisco State College (now University), Chico State College (now California State University, Chico), and California State University, Hayward. Former president, Society for Crippled Children, Alameda County, Calif. Military service: U.S. Army Air Forces, 1941-45; became lieutenant colonel. U.S. Air Force Reserve, 1945-74. Member: National Council of Administrators of Special Education (president, 1955), Council for Exceptional Children (president of East Bay chapter, 1949; member of national board of governors).

WRITINGS: (Contributor) The Student Teacher in the Elementary Schools, revised edition, Prentice-Hall, 1960; (with Thomas L. McFarland) About Friends, Stanwix, 1963; About Fun and Play, Stanwix, 1963; (with Marvin C. Groelle) About King, Stanwix, 1963; (with Groelle) A Functional Basic Word List for Special Pupils, Stanwix,

1963; (with Groelle) About Mary and Bill, Stanwix, 1963; (with Kent Friel) Enjoy the Seasons, Stanwix, 1963; (with Hannah Lai) About Going Away, Stanwix, 1964; (with Lai) About Things at Home, Stanwix, 1964; (with Lai) Come Along, Stanwix, 1964. Editor, "Pacemaker Books" series, Fearon, 1963-66. Also senior consultant of the "Functional Basic Reading" series, Stanwix. Contributor to magazines.

* * *

TUERCK, David G(eorge) 1941-

PERSONAL: Surname is pronounced Teerk; born February 11, 1941, in Belleville, Ill.; son of George N. (a musician) and Bertha (Brandmeyer) Tuerck; married Gay Herzog, June 2, 1962; children: John. Education: George Washington University, A.B., 1962, A.M., 1964; University of Virginia, Ph.D., 1966. Politics: Republican. Religion: United Church of Christ.

CAREER: University of Illinois at Chicago Circle, Chicago, assistant professor of economics, 1966-70; California State College, Bakersfield, associate professor of economics, beginning 1970. Member: American Economic Association, Southern Economic Association, Omicron Delta Epsilon.

WRITINGS: (With Leland B. Yeager) Trade Policy and the Price System, International Textbook, 1966.

WORK IN PROGRESS: Public finance (some legal aspects) and international economics.

AVOCATIONAL INTERESTS: Music.†

* * *

TUGGY, Joy Turner 1922-

PERSONAL: Born September 20, 1922, in Carupano, Venezuela; daughter of Donald D. (a missionary) and Faith (Hollingsworth) Turner; married Alfred E. Tuggy (a missionary and teacher), June 1, 1946; children: Frieda, John, David, Alfred, Samuel, Dale, Timothy, Janice, Rubylene. Education: Columbia College, Columbia, S.C., B.A., 1943, M.A., 1964; Conservatory of Music, Maracay, Venezuela, Artists' Diploma, 1974. Politics: Republican. Home: Apdo. 475, Maracay, Venezuela.

CAREER: Missionary and teacher with Christian (Evangelical) Church; Orinoco River Mission, South Pasadena, Calif., teacher of Bible, music, and languages at Las Delicias Bible Institute in Venezuela, 1943-58; currently teacher at Seminario Evangelico Asociado and Conservatoria de Musica del Estado Aragua, both Maracay, Venezuela.

WRITINGS: The Missionary Wife and Her Work, Moody, 1966.

WORK IN PROGRESS: A translation into Spanish of an accordion method based on hymns; a course of study (in Spanish) on the Christian home; a programmed course of study in music theory and sight singing.

AVOCATIONAL INTERESTS: Gardening, music, books, stamps, painting, architecture.

* * *

TURK, Laurel H(erbert) 1903-

PERSONAL: Born June 29, 1903, in Hiawatha, Kan.; son of Noah Gleaves (a farmer) and Sarah Frances (Brown) Turk; married Esther Lucille Liebig, June 1, 1927; children: Thomas Liebig, Jane Elizabeth (Mrs. William B. Schlansker). Education: University of Arizona, student, 1920-21; University of Missouri, A.B., 1924; University of Kansas,

M.A., 1926; Stanford University, Ph.D., 1933; Centro de Estudios Historicos, Madrid, Spain, postdoctoral study, 1935. *Politics:* Independent. *Religion:* Episcopalian. *Home:* 209 Hillsdale Ave., Greencastle, Ind. 46135. *Office:* DePauw University, Greencastle, Ind.

CAREER: Acting instructor at Indiana University, Bloomington, 1926-27, and Lehigh University, Bethlehem, Pa., 1927-28; DePauw University, Greencastle, Ind., instructor, 1928-30, assistant professor, 1930-36, associate professor, 1936-40, professor of Romance languages, 1940-68, emeritus professor, 1968—, department head, 1963-68. Instructor at Stanford University, 1931-32; lecturer at English Institute for Peruvian Teachers of English, Cuzco, Peru, 1948. *Member:* American Association of Teachers of Spanish and Portuguese (member of executive council, 1944-46, 1964—; secretary-treasurer, 1951-64), Modern Language Association of America, American Association of University Professors, Rotary (past president of Greencastle club). *Awards, honors:* Encomienda de la Orden del Merito Civil, Spanish Government, 1965.

WRITINGS: (Editor with Agnes M. Brady) *Classical Spanish Readings,* Appleton, 1938; (editor with Brady) *Romantic Spanish Readings,* Appleton, 1939; *Introduction to Spanish,* Heath, 1941; (with Brady) *Spanish Letter Writing,* Heath, 1942; *Spanish Review Grammar and Composition,* Heath, 1943; *Asi se aprende el espanol,* Heath, 1946; *Practical Spanish,* Heath, 1946; (with Edith M. Allen) *El espanol al dia,* Heath, Book I, 1949, 4th edition, 1973, Book II, 1950, 4th edition, 1973, Book III (with Allen and Cesar A. Munoz-Plaza), 1968, revised edition, 1974; (editor with Brady) *Cuentos y comedias de America,* Houghton, 1950; (editor with Brady) *Cuentos y comedias de Espana,* Houghton, 1952; (editor) Lopez Luna, *El gaucho Smith,* Heath, 1952; *Foundation Course in Spanish,* Heath, 1957, 3rd edition (with Aurelio M. Espinosa, Jr.), 1974; *Mastering Spanish,* Heath, 1970, 2nd edition, 1974; (with Espinosa) *Lecturas hispanicas,* Heath, 1972.

SIDELIGHTS: Laurel Turk has traveled in all European and Latin American countries.

* * *

TURLINGTON, Henry E.   1918-

PERSONAL: Born October 25, 1918, in Gainesville, Fla.; son of John Edwin (a professor of agricultural economics) and May (Baldwin) Turlington; married Helen Nobels (executive secretary of Interchurch Council), May 7, 1943; children: John E., Henry, Jr., Lynn, Carol. *Education:* University of Florida, A.B., 1938; Southern Baptist Theological Seminary, Th.M., Th.D., 1945; Princeton Theological Seminary, postdoctoral study, 1956-57. *Home:* 110 Carolina Ave., Chapel Hill, N.C. 27514. *Office:* University Baptist Church, Chapel Hill, N.C.

CAREER: Baptist clergyman. Southern Baptist Theological Seminary, Louisville, Ky., faculty, 1944-47, 1949-58, became associate professor of New Testament interpretation; University of Shanghai, Shanghai, China, professor of philosophy and religion (under auspices of Foreign Mission Board of Southern Baptist Convention), 1947-49; pastor in Delray Beach, Fla., 1958-61; University Baptist Church, Chapel Hill, N.C., pastor, 1961—. Trustee, Meredith College, 1967-71. *Member:* Society of Biblical Literature, Ministerial Association of Chapel Hill.

WRITINGS: Luke's Witness to Jesus, Broadman, 1967; (contributor) Clifton J. Allen, general editor, *The Broadman Bible Commentary,* Volume VIII, Broadman,

1971. Contributor to denominational periodicals. Director, *Biblical Recorder,* 1963-66.

* * *

TURNER, Darwin T(heodore)   1931-

PERSONAL: Born May 7, 1931, in Cincinnati, Ohio; son of Darwin Romanes (a pharmacist) and Laura (Knight) Turner; married Edna Bonner, June 1, 1949 (divorced August, 1961); married Maggie Jean Lewis (a teacher), February 29, 1968; children: Pamela (Mrs. Robert Welch), Darwin Keith, Rachon. *Education:* University of Cincinnati, B.A., 1947, M.A., 1949; University of Chicago, Ph.D., 1956. *Home:* 5 Washington Pl., Iowa City, Iowa 52240. *Office:* University of Iowa, 303 English-Philosophy Bldg., Iowa City, Iowa 52242.

CAREER: Clark College, Atlanta, Ga., instructor in English, 1949-51; Morgan State College, assistant professor of English, 1952-57; Florida A & M University, Tallahassee, professor of English and chairman of department, 1957-59; North Carolina Agricultural and Technical State University, Greensboro, professor of English, 1959-70, chairman of English department, 1959-66, dean of Graduate School, 1966-70; University of Michigan, Ann Arbor, professor of English, 1970-71; University of Iowa, Iowa City, visiting professor, 1971-72, professor of English, 1972—, chairman of Afro-American studies, 1972—. Workshop director, Institute for Teachers of English in Colleges, Indiana University, 1965; visiting professor at University of Wisconsin—Madison, 1969, and University of Hawaii, summer, 1971. Member of Wellesley Conference on Pre-College Programs for Southern Negro Students, 1964, advisory committee to U.S. Office of Education, 1965, and Graduate Record Examination Board, 1970-73. Consultant to National Endowment for the Humanities programs in ethnic studies and humanities, 1973—.

MEMBER: Modern Language Association of America, National Council of Teachers of English (director, 1971—), College Language Association (president, 1963-65), Conference on College Composition and Communication (member of executive committee, 1965-67), College English Association (member of board of directors, 1971-74), Association for the Study of Afro-American Life and History, National Association for the Advancement of Colored People, Midwest Modern Language Association, South Atlantic Modern Language Association, North Carolina-Virginia College English Association, North Carolina Teachers Association, Phi Beta Kappa, Alpha Phi Alpha, Theta Alpha Phi, Lambda Iota Tau. *Awards, honors:* American Council of Learned Societies research grant, 1965; Duke University-University of North Carolina Cooperative Program in Humanities fellowship, 1965-66; Creative Scholarship Award, College Language Association, 1970; Rockefeller Foundation research grant, 1971; Professional Achievement Award, University of Chicago Alumni Association, 1972; Carter G. Woodson Award, 1974; National Endowment for the Humanities grants for work and research in Afro-American studies, 1974-78.

WRITINGS: Katharsis, Wellesley Press, 1964; *Nathaniel Hawthorne's "The Scarlet Letter,"* Dell, 1967; *In a Minor Cord: Three Afro-American Writers and Their Search for Identity,* Southern Illinois University Press, 1971; (co-author) *The Teaching of Literature by Afro-American Writers: Theory and Practice,* National Council of Teachers of English, 1972.

Editor: (With Jean M. Bright) *Images of the Negro in*

America, Heath, 1965; *Black American Literature: Essays,* C. E. Merrill, 1969; *Black American Literature: Fiction,* C. E. Merrill, 1969; *Black American Literature: Poetry,* C. E. Merrill, 1969; (and compiler) *Afro-American Writers,* Appleton, 1970; *Black American Literature: Essays, Poetry, Fiction, Drama,* C. E. Merrill, 1970; (and author of introduction) *Black Drama in America: An Anthology,* Fawcett, 1971; *Voices from the Black Experience: African and Afro-American Literature,* Ginn, 1972; *Responding: Five,* Ginn, 1973; *Selected Writings of Jean Toomer,* Howard University Press, in press.

Author of introduction: Paul Laurence Dunbar, *The Strength of Gideon,* Arno, 1969; Charles W. Chesnutt, *The House behind the Cedars,* Collier, 1969; Paul Laurence Dunbar, *The Sport of the Gods,* Arno, 1969; Zora Neale Hurston, *Mules and Men,* Harper, 1970; Countee Cullen, *Color,* Arno, 1970; Countee Cullen, *One Way to Heaven,* Lorrimer, 1972.

Contributor: R. Hemenway, editor, *The Black Novelist,* C. E. Merrill, 1970; N. Wright, Jr., editor, *What Black Educators Are Saying,* Hawthorn, 1970; (and author of introduction) William Brasmer and Dominick Consolo, editors, *Black Drama: An Anthology,* C. E. Merrill, 1970; A. Gayle, editor, *The Black Aesthetic,* Doubleday, 1971; John Blassingame, editor, *New Perspectives on Black Studies,* University of Illinois Press, 1971; Ruth Miller, editor, *Backgrounds to Black American Literature,* Chandler, 1971; Therman B. O'Daniel, editor, *Langston Hughes, Black Genius: A Critical Evaluation,* Morrow, 1971; Jay Martin, editor, *A Singer in the Dawn: Reinterpretations of Paul Laurence Dunbar,* Dodd, 1975.

Poetry represented in many anthologies, including *A Rock against the Wind,* edited by Lindsay Patterson, Dodd, 1974, and *When the Mode of the Music Changes: A Short Course in Song Lyrics and Poems,* Ginn, 1975.

Contributor to *Encyclopaedia Britannica, Encyclopedia International, Dictionary of American Biography,* and *Contemporary Dramatists.* Also contributor of articles, book reviews, and poetry to English, history, and sociology journals. Advisory editor, *College Language Association Journal,* 1960—, *Bulletin of Black Books,* 1971—, and *Obsidian,* 1974—.

SIDELIGHTS: Darwin Turner told *CA:* "I write poetry to purge myself of particular emotions and ideas. I write articles because I've been asked or because I have something which I believe other people should know or may want to know. No single writer has been a major influence." *Avocational interests:* Chess, bridge.

BIOGRAPHICAL/CRITICAL SOURCES: Cincinnati Post, June 6, 1944, September 25, 1944; *Baltimore Afro-American,* May 10, 1947; *Chicago Defender,* May 24, 1947; *Cincinnati Post and Times Star,* June 12, 1964; *Negro Digest,* January, 1969.

* * *

TURNER, Graham 1932-

PERSONAL: Born September 8, 1932, in Macclesfield, Cheshire, England; son of Fred and Annie Gertrude (Bradbury) Turner; married Jean Staton Forster, July 25, 1962; children: Patrick Henry, Rachel Elizabeth, Hannah Lucy. *Education:* Attended Christ Church, Oxford, 1950-53, and Stanford University, 1953-54. *Religion:* Christian. *Home:* Wootton House, Wootton Boars Hill, Oxford, England. *Agent:* Hilary Rubinstein, A. P. Watt and Son, 26/28 Bedford Row, London WC2, England.

CAREER: Reporter for *The Scotsman,* Edinburgh, Scotland, 1958-61, *Sunday Times,* London, England, 1961-63, and British Broadcasting Corp., London, 1963-65; British Broadcasting Corp., economics correspondent, 1965-70; freelance writer and broadcaster, 1971—. *Military service:* Royal Air Force, 1955-58; served as education officer.

WRITINGS: The Car Makers, Eyre & Spottiswoode, 1963; (with John Pearson) *The Persuasion Industry,* Eyre & Spottiswoode, 1965; *The North Country,* Eyre & Spottiswoode, 1967; *Business in Britain,* Little, Brown, 1969; *The Leyland Papers,* Eyre & Spottiswoode, 1971. Contributor to *Encounter, Observer,* and *Listener.*

WORK IN PROGRESS: A book tentatively entitled *More than Conquerors,* for Harper.

BIOGRAPHICAL/CRITICAL SOURCES: Listener, June 15, 1967; *Times Literary Supplement,* November 2, 1967.

* * *

TURNER, H(arold) W(alter) 1911-

PERSONAL: Born January 13, 1911, in Napier, New Zealand; son of Herbert John (a house-builder) and Charlotte (Noone) Turner; married Maude Yeoman, February 1, 1939; children: Alison (Mrs. Heiko Wassing), David, Helen (Mrs. Christopher John Duncan), Carolyn (Mrs. Peter Andrew Hulm). *Education:* Canterbury University College, B.A., 1933, M.A. (first class honors), 1935; studied at Knox College Theological Hall, 1936-38, and University of Edinburgh, 1938; Melbourne College of Divinity, B.D., 1943, D.D., 1963. *Home:* 12A Don Terrace, Aberdeen, AB2 2UH, Scotland.

CAREER: Presbyterian clergyman. Stuart Residence Halls Council, Dunedin, New Zealand, hall warden, 1942-51; minister of church in Dunedin, New Zealand, 1951-54; Fourah Bay College—The University College of Sierra Leone, Freetown, Sierra Leone, lecturer in theology, 1955-62; University of Nigeria, Nsukka, senior lecturer in religion, 1963-66; University of Leicester, Leicester, England, lecturer in phenomenology and history of religion, 1966-70; Emory University, Atlanta, Ga., professor of world religions, 1970-72; Aberdeen University, Aberdeen, Scotland, 1973—, began as lecturer, currently senior lecturer in religious studies. Thomas Burns Memorial Lecturer, University of Otago, 1976. *Member:* International Association for Mission Studies, African Studies Association (United Kingdom), Deutsche Gesellschaft fuer Missionswissenschaft, International Association for History of Religions (British branch), Society for African Church History. *Awards, honors:* Jordan traveling fellowship in comparative religion, University of London.

WRITINGS: Halls of Residence, New Zealand Council for Educational Research, 1953, Oxford University Press, 1954; *Profile through Preaching,* Edinburgh House Press, 1965; (with Robert C. Mitchell) *A Comprehensive Bibliography of Modern African Religious Movements,* Northwestern University Press, 1967; *History of an African Independent Church,* 2 volumes, Clarendon Press, 1967; *Living Tribal Religions,* Ward Lock Educational, 1971; *From Temple to Meeting House,* Mouton & Co., 1976. Also author of *Rudolf Otto's Idea of the Holy: A Guide for Students,* 1974.

Contributor: H. J. Greschat, and others, editors, *Wort und Religion: Kalima na Dini,* Evangelisches Missions Verlag, 1969; S. C. Neill, and others, editors, *Concise Dictionary of the Christian World Mission,* Abingdon, 1971; W. J.

Hollenweger, editor, *Die Pfingstkirchen,* Evangelisches Verlag, 1971; M. E. Glasswell, E. W. Fashole-Luke, editors, *New Testament Christianity for Africa and the World,* Lutterworth, 1974; B. E. Gates, editor, *Afro-Caribbean Religion,* Ward Lock Educational, 1976. Contributor to *Encyclopaedia Britannica,* 1974; contributor to religious and social science journals.

WORK IN PROGRESS: Garrick Braide: Nigeria's First Prophet; a series, "Bibliographies of New Religious Movements in Primal Societies," for G. K. Hall.

AVOCATIONAL INTERESTS: Carpentry, gardening.

BIOGRAPHICAL/CRITICAL SOURCES: Outlook (Christchurch, New Zealand), August 5, 1967.

* * *

TURNER, W(illiam) Price 1927-
(Bill Turner)

PERSONAL: Born August 14, 1927, in York, England; son of William Bissett (a printer) and Annie (Anderson) Turner; married Anne Hill, July 17, 1950; children: Kenneth Price, Leslie Cummings. *Education:* Attended a senior secondary school in Glasgow, Scotland, one year. *Politics:* None. *Religion:* None. *Home:* 8 Methley Ter., Leeds LS7 3NL, England.

CAREER: British Broadcasting Corp., Glasgow, Scotland, television captions artist, 1958-60; University of Leeds, Leeds, England, Gregory fellow in poetry, 1960-62; *Yorkshire Post,* Leeds, sub-editor, 1962-63; Swarthmore Adult Education Centre, Leeds, tutor in creative writing, 1963-65; full-time writer, 1965—. Fellow in creative writing, Glasgow University, 1973-75. Gives public readings of his poetry (two tapes of readings are in Harvard University's Poetry Room). *Military service:* British Army, Royal Engineers, 1945-47.

WRITINGS: The Rudiment of an Eye (poems), Villiers Publications, 1956; *The Flying Corset* (poems), Villiers Publications, 1962; *Fables from Life* (poems), Northern House, 1966; *Circle of Squares* (novel), Walker & Co., 1969.

Under name Bill Turner: *Bound to Die* (novel), Walker & Co., 1967; *Sex Trap* (novel), Constable, 1968; *Another Little Death* (novel), Walker & Co., 1970; *The Moral Rocking-Horse* (poems), Barrie & Jenkins, 1970; *Hot-Foot* (novel), Constable, 1973.

Librettist for a children's musical play, "Baldy Bane," published in pamphlet form by British Broadcasting Corp.; author of three broadcast plays, "The Lair of the Boneyard Clerk," "The Symbol," and "The Refuge." Crime fiction reviewer for *Yorkshire Post,* 1963-66. Editor, *Poet* (Glasgow), 1951-54.

WORK IN PROGRESS: A new collection of poems, tentatively entitled *Thistledown.*

* * *

TURPIN, James W(esley) 1927-

PERSONAL: Born December 18, 1927, in Ashland, Ky.; son of James W. and Hope (Duke) Turpin; married Donna Wrenn Turner, September 14, 1974; children: (first marriage) Keith, Payton, Scott, Jan; (second marriage) Rabbani Hope. *Education:* Attended Berea College, Cornell University, and Bucknell University; Emory University, M.D., 1955. *Home:* 44 Lindwood Ave., Ardmore, Pa. 19003. *Agent:* Sterling Lord Agency, 75 East 55th St., New York, N.Y. 10022.

CAREER: Physician. Interned at Crawford W. Long Hospital, Atlanta, Ga., 1955-56, and then took residency in general medicine at Sonoma County Hospital, Santa Rosa, Calif., 1956-57; general practice of medicine, Coronado, Calif., 1957-61; founder of Project Concern (providing medical assistance in developing areas of the world), San Diego, Calif., 1961, currently president. Assisted in founding medical clinic in Tijuana, Mexico, 1960; established clinic in Walled City in Kowloon, Hong Kong, 1962, floating clinics in Taumati Typhoon Shelter, Hong Kong, 1963, clinic in squatter area of Chinese refugees in Jordan Valley, Hong Kong, 1964, hospital at DaMpaa, South Vietnam, and mobile village clinics, 1964, and a fourth clinic in Hong Kong, 1966; also instigated village medical assistant program in South Vietnam, training young men of the villages to use basic medicines. *Member:* Venerable Order of St. John's the Divine, Masons, Explorers Club (New York). *Awards, honors:* Named one of ten outstanding young men in America by U.S. Jaycees, 1963; Freedom Leadership Medal of Freedoms Foundation at Valley Forge, 1966; honorary doctorates from George Williams College, 1967 and Berea College, 1969.

WRITINGS: (With Al Hirshbert) *Vietnam Doctor: The Story of "Project Concern,"* McGraw, 1966; (with Hirshbert) *A Faraway Country,* World Publishing, 1971.

* * *

TURTON, Godfrey (Edmund) 1901-

PERSONAL: Born January 4, 1901, in Kildale, Yorkshire, England; son of Robert Bell (a rural landowner) and Marion (Beaumont) Turton; married Elvira Haynes, September 21, 1932; children: Jessica Anne (Mrs. Arnold Grayson), Sarah Marion (Mrs. Terence Marler). *Education:* Balliol College, Oxford, B.A. (first class honors), 1923. *Politics:* "Floating vote." *Religion:* Undenominational. *Home:* 2 Linton Rd., Oxford OX2 6UG, England. *Agent:* Harold Matson Co., Inc., 22 East 40th St., New York, N.Y. 10016.

CAREER: Reporter in Budapest, Hungary, for Az Est newspapers, 1926; film exhibitor in Tahiti and Fiji, 1927; *Truth* (weekly periodical), London, England, lead writer and editorial assistant, 1937-54; Clarendon Press, Oxford, England, staff of *Oxford Latin Dictionary,* 1954-71. Former farmer in Easby, Yorkshire, and Kidlington, Oxfordshire; former owner and manager of Kildale Estate, Yorkshire. Represented Kildale and Easby on Stokesley Rural District Council, 1943-45.

WRITINGS—All novels, except as indicated: *There Was Once a City,* Methuen, 1927; *My Lord of Canterbury,* Doubleday, 1967; *The Emperor Arthur,* Doubleday, 1967; *Builder's of England's Glory* (non-fiction), Doubleday, 1969; *The Devil's Churchyard,* Doubleday, 1970; *The Festival of Flora,* Doubleday, 1972; *The Syrian Princesses,* Cassell, 1974.

* * *

TUTAEV, David 1916-

PERSONAL: Surname is pronounced Tut-a-yev; born October 7, 1916, in Russia; now a British citizen; son of David Christopher (an editor) and Helen Tutaev; married Beryl Carlise Fonseca (divorced); children: David, Christopher, Mary Anne. *Education:* Educated in public schools in England. *Politics:* Labour. *Religion:* Christian. *Agent:* John Farquharson Ltd., 15 Red Lion Sq., London W.C.1, England.

CAREER: Ministry of Information, London, England, specialist in Soviet affairs, 1942-45; Daily Express, London, foreign correspondent, 1945; theater director in England and United States, 1947-52; free-lance scriptwriter and author. Examiner in speech and drama, London Academy of Music and Drama, 1959—; staff member of External Services, British Broadcasting Corp., London, 1962. Member: P.E.N.

WRITINGS: The Soviet Caucasus, Harrap, 1942; (translator) Chekhov, Wife for Sale, J. Calder, 1959; The Consul of Florence (biography), Secker & Warburg, 1966, published as The Man Who Saved Florence, Coward, 1967; The Impossible Takes Longer: Memoirs of Vera Weizmann as Told to David Tutaev, Harper, 1967; (translator and compiler) Anna Alliluyeva and Sergei Alliluyev, The Alliluyev Memoirs, Putnam, 1968; A Comedy But Not Divine, Macdonald & Co., 1971. Author of about twenty scripts produced by British Broadcasting Corp. and foreign radio. Contributor to Everyman's Concise Encyclopaedia of Russia, 1961.

WORK IN PROGRESS: Volume II of A Comedy But Not Divine; a play, "The Coming Trial of Joseph Stalin."

SIDELIGHTS: David Tutaev is competent in Russian and French. He has traveled in the Soviet Union, much of Europe, Israel, and the United States.

BIOGRAPHICAL/CRITICAL SOURCES: New Statesman, October 27, 1967, October 8, 1971; Time, January 5, 1968; Christian Science Monitor, January 25, 1968.

* * *

UCELAY, Margarita 1916-

PERSONAL: Born May 5, 1916, in Madrid, Spain; daughter of Enrique and Pura Ucelay; married Ernesto DaCal, 1936 (divorced, 1965); children: Enrique Ucelay DaCal. Education: Institute Escuela, Madrid, Spain, A.B., 1933; University of Madrid, studied in School of Law, 1933-36; Columbia University, M.A., 1941, Ph.D., 1950. Home: 300 Riverside Dr., New York, N.Y. 10025. Office: Department of Spanish, Barnard College, New York, N.Y. 10027.

CAREER: Vassar College, Poughkeepsie, N.Y., instructor, 1939-41; Hunter College (now Hunter College of the City University of New York), New York City, lecturer, 1942-43; Columbia University, Barnard College, New York City, 1943—, began as lecturer, professor of Spanish literature, 1968—, chairman of department, 1961-65, 1967—. Worked and acted in experimental theater in Madrid, Spain, for almost a decade before coming to the United States, and has been associated with experimental theaters here. Member: Hispanic Institute in the United States.

WRITINGS: "Los espanoles pintados por si mismos": Estudio de un genero costumbrista, El Colegio de Mexico, 1951; (with Ernesto DaCal) Literatura del siglo XX, Dryden Press, 1955, revised edition, Holt, 1968; (with Amelia A. del Rio) Vision de espana, Holt, 1968.

AVOCATIONAL INTERESTS: History of the theater and costuming.

* * *

UEDA, Makoto 1931-

PERSONAL: Born May 20, 1931, in Hyogo-ken, Japan; son of Masao and Chieko (Shindo) Ueda; married Etsuko Hori, July 7, 1962; children: Edward Minoru, Eunice Mika. Education: Kobe University, B.Litt., 1954; University of Nebraska, M.A., 1956; University of Washington, Seattle, Ph.D., 1961. Home: 160 Formway Ct., Los Altos, Calif. Office: Department of Asian Languages, Stanford University, Stanford, Calif.

CAREER: University of Toronto, Toronto, Ontario, lecturer, 1961, assistant professor, 1962-64, associate professor, 1965-67, professor of Japanese, 1968-71; Stanford University, Stanford, Calif., professor of Japanese and comparative literature, 1971—.

WRITINGS: (Translator) The Old Pine Tree, and Other Noh Plays, University of Nebraska Press, 1962; Zeami, Basho, Yeats, Pound: A Study in Japanese and English Poetics, Mouton & Co., 1965; Literary and Art Theories in Japan, Press of Western Reserve University, 1967; Matsuo Basho, Twayne, 1970; (editor) Modern Japanese Haiku: An Anthology, University of Toronto Press, 1976; Modern Japanese Writers and the Nature of Literature, Stanford University Press, 1976.

* * *

ULETT, George A(ndrew) 1918-

PERSONAL: Born January 10, 1918, in Needham, Mass.; son of George Ulett; married Pearl C. Lawrence (a child psychiatrist), September 10, 1942; children: Richard C., Judith Ann, Carol Lynn. Education: Stanford University, B.A., 1940; University of Oregon, M.S., 1943, Ph.D. and M.D., 1944.

CAREER: University of Oregon Medical School Hospitals and Clinics, Portland, rotating intern, 1944-45; Boston City Hospital, Boston, Mass., assistant resident in neurology, 1945-46; Barnes and McMillan Hospitals, St. Louis, Mo., assistant resident, 1948, resident in neuropsychiatry, 1948-49; U.S. Public Health Service, St. Louis, fellow, 1949-50, assistant professor, 1950-53, associate professor, 1953-56, professor of psychiatry, 1956-64; Malcolm Bliss Mental Health Center, St. Louis, medical director, 1956-61; City Hospital Division, St. Louis, director of psychiatric services, 1959-61; State of Missouri, Division of Mental Diseases, acting director, 1961-62, director, 1962—; University of Missouri, School of Medicine, St. Louis, professor of psychiatry, 1964—, chairman of department of psychiatry, Missouri Institute of Psychiatry, St. Louis, 1962—. Certified by American Board of Neurology and Psychiatry, 1950, and American Board of Electroencephalography, 1953. Military service: U.S. Army, Medical Corps, 1946-47; became captain.

MEMBER: American Medical Association, American Psychiatric Association (fellow), American Electroencephalographic Society (past secretary), American Society of Medical Psychiatry (past president), Society of Biological Psychiatry, American Association for the Advancement of Science (fellow), Collegium Internationale Neuro-Psychopharmacologicum, Central Electroencephalographic Society (past president), Mid-Continent Psychiatric Association, Missouri State Medical Association, Sigma Xi. Awards, honors: U.S. Public Health Service postdoctoral fellowship in neuropsychiatry, 1949-50; Missouri Academy of General Practice annual award, 1966, for leadership in improvement of health care.

WRITINGS: (With D. W. Goodrich) A Synopsis of Contemporary Psychiatry, 2nd edition, Mosby, 1960, 5th edition, 1972; A Rorschach Introductory Manual, 3rd edition, Bardgett Publishing Co., 1960; (editor with R. M. Steinhilber) Psychiatric Research in Public Service, American

Psychiatric Association, 1962; (with D. B. Peterson) *Applied Hypnosis and Positive Suggestion,* Mosby, 1965.

Contributor: *Alcoholism: An Interdisciplinary Approach,* C. C Thomas, 1959; *Progress in Neurology and Psychiatry,* Volume 17, Grune, 1962; *Psychosomatic Medicine,* Lea & Febiger, 1962; *Applications of Electroencephalography in Psychiatry, A Symposium,* edited by W. P. Wilson, Duke University Press, 1965.

Author of four pamphlets for U.S. Air Force School of Aviation Medicine, 1952-57, and other medical guides. Contributor to *World Book Encyclopedia;* also contributor of more than eighty articles to *Nursing Outlook, Science, Focus/Midwest,* and medical journals.

WORK IN PROGRESS: With D. Goldman, *Useful Psychiatry for the Internist.*†

*   *   *

ULLMANN, Walter 1910-

PERSONAL: Born November 29, 1910, in Pulkau, Austria; son of Rudolf (a medical practitioner) and Leopoldine (Apfelthaler) Ullmann; married Mary Elizabeth Finnemore Knapp, November 23, 1940; children: Frederick Ralph, Carl Nicholas Tancred. *Education:* Studied at University of Vienna, University of Innsbruck, University of Munich, and Cambridge University; received M.A., Juris Utriusque Doctor, Litterarum Doctor, and Doctor rerum politicarum h.c. *Home:* 128 Queen Edith Way, Cambridge, England. *Office:* Trinity College, Cambridge University, Cambridge, England.

CAREER: University of Vienna, Vienna, Austria, assistant lecturer, 1935-38; Ratcliffe College, Leicester, England, history and modern languages master, 1943-47; University of Leeds, Leeds, England, lecturer in medieval history, 1947-49; Cambridge University, Cambridge, England, university lecturer in medieval history, 1949-57, reader in medieval ecclesiastical institutions, 1957-65, professor of medieval ecclesiastical history, 1965-72, professor of medieval history, 1972—, fellow of Trinity College. Part-time lecturer, British Foreign Office, 1944-46; visiting professor, Johns Hopkins University, 1964-65. *Military service:* British Army, Royal Pioneer Corps and Royal Engineers, 1940-43. *Member:* Royal Historical Society, British Academy (fellow), Henry Bradshaw Society.

WRITINGS: The Medieval Idea of Law, Methuen, 1946; *The Origins of the Great Schism,* Burns & Oates, 1948, revised edition, 1972; *Medieval Papalism,* Methuen, 1949; *The Growth of Papal Government in the Middle Ages,* Methuen, 1955, 4th edition, 1970; *The Medieval Papacy: St. Thomas and Beyond,* Blackfriars Press, 1960; (editor) *Liber regie capelle,* Henry Bradshaw Society, 1961; *Principles of Government and Politics in the Middle Ages,* Methuen, 1961, 3rd edition, 1974; *A History of Political Ideas in the Middle Ages,* Penguin, 1965, revised edition, 1970; *The Individual and Society in the Middle Ages,* Johns Hopkins Press, 1966; *Papst und Koenig,* University of Salzburg Press, 1967; *The Relevance of Medieval Ecclesiastical History,* Cambridge University Press, 1967; *The Carolingian Renaissance and the Idea of Kingship,* Barnes & Noble, 1969; *The Future of Medieval History,* Cambridge University Press, 1973; *A Short History of the Papacy in the Middle Ages,* Methuen, 1972, 2nd edition, 1974; *Law and Politics in the Middle Ages,* Cornell University Press, 1975. Editor of "Cambridge Studies in Medieval Life and Thought." Contributor of articles to learned journals in England and European countries. Advisory editor, *Papste*

und Papsttum; member of editorial board, *Journal of Ecclesiastical History.*

AVOCATIONAL INTERESTS: Music, travel.

*   *   *

ULMER, Melville J(ack) 1911-

PERSONAL: Born May 17, 1911, in New York, N.Y.; son of Saul (a silk manufacturer) and Lillian (Ulmer) Ulmer; married Naomi Zinken (a teacher of biology), June 1, 1937; children: Melville Paul, Stephanie-Marie. *Education:* New York University, B.S., 1937, M.A., 1938; Columbia University, Ph.D., 1948. *Politics:* Liberal. *Home:* 10401 River Rd., Potomac, Md. 20854. *Office:* Department of Economics, University of Maryland, College Park, Md. 20742.

CAREER: New York American, New York, N.Y., reporter, 1930-37; U.S. Bureau of Labor Statistics, Washington, D.C., chief of General Price Research Section, 1940-45; assistant chief of Reports Division, Smaller War Plants Corp., 1945-46; U.S. Department of Commerce, chief of Financial Organization Section, 1946-48; American University, Washington, D.C., lecturer in economics and statistics, 1943-48, adjunct professor, 1948-50, associate professor, 1950-52, professor of economics, 1952-61, chairman of department, 1954-61; University of Maryland, College Park, professor of economics, 1961—. Research associate, National Bureau of Economic Research, 1950-60; Fulbright visiting professor, Netherlands School of Economics, 1958-59, 1965-66. Economic consultant to U.S. Bureau of the Budget, Department of State, General Services Administration, Department of Commerce, Pan-American Union, Government of Canada, and Organization of American States.

MEMBER: American Economic Association, American Statistical Association, Econometric Society, American Association for the Advancement of Science (fellow), Pi Gamma Mu, Artus, Cosmos Club. *Awards, honors:* Free University of Brussels Medal; Merrill Foundation Award in Economics, 1959; Wilton Park Fellowship Award of the British Foreign Office, 1966; National Endowment for the Humanities senior fellow, 1975.

WRITINGS: The Economic Theory of Cost of Living Index Numbers, Columbia University Press, 1949; *Economics: Theory and Practice,* Houghton, 1959, 2nd edition, 1965; *Capital in Transportation, Communication and Public Utilities: Its Formation and Financing,* Princeton University Press, 1960; *Welfare State, U.S.A.: An Exploration In and Beyond the New Economics,* Houghton, 1969. Author of monographs; contributor to *Funk and Wagnalls International Year Book, Jefferson Encyclopaedia,* and economic journals; contributor of reviews and popular articles to magazines and newspapers. Editor, *Survey of Current Business,* 1948-50; contributing editor, *New Republic,* 1970—.

WORK IN PROGRESS: A book on the present state and future prospects of the American economy and the possible contributions of democratic economic planning.

AVOCATIONAL INTERESTS: Politics; horseback riding (has shown horses, hunted, tries to ride daily, and keeps two horses); painting, especially in gauche; instrumental music, particularly piano; sailing.

*   *   *

UNKELBACH, Kurt 1913-

PERSONAL: Born November 21, 1913, in New Britain,

Conn.; son of Max J. (an architect) and Louise (Gunther) Unkelbach; married Evelyn Haskell; children: Evelyn P. and L. Cary (daughters). *Education:* Student at Wesleyan University, Middletown, Conn., 1932-34, and Pasadena Playhouse, 1934-36. *Religion:* Protestant. *Home:* Starks Rd., R.F.D. 3, Winsted, Conn. 06098. *Agent:* Knox Burger, Knox Burger Associates, Ltd., 39½ Washington Square S., New York, N.Y. 10012.

CAREER: Radio writer for various independent stations and networks, 1936-41; account executive with advertising and public relations agencies in New York, N.Y., 1947-64; full-time writer, 1964—. *Military service:* U.S. Army, 1941-46; served in South Pacific; became captain. *Member:* Dramatist Guild of the Authors League of America.

WRITINGS: Love on a Leash, Prentice-Hall, 1964; *The Dog in My Life,* Four Winds, 1966; *The Winning of Westminster,* Prentice-Hall, 1966; *Murphy,* Prentice-Hall, 1967; *Ruffian: International Champion,* Prentice-Hall, 1967; *The Dog Who Never Knew,* Four Winds, 1968; *Both Ends of the Leash,* Prentice-Hall, 1968; *A Cat and His Dogs,* Prentice-Hall, 1969; *Catnip,* Prentice-Hall, 1970; (with wife, Evelyn Unkelbach) *The Pleasures of Dog Ownership,* Prentice-Hall, 1971; *You're a Good Dog, Joe,* Prentice-Hall, 1971; *Albert Payson Terhune: A Centennial Biography,* Charterhouse, 1972; *How to Bring Up Your Pet Dog,* Dodd, 1972; *Those Lovable Retrievers,* McGraw, 1973; *Tiger Up a Tree,* Prentice-Hall, 1973; *How to Make Money in Dogs,* Dodd, 1974; *Uncle Charlie's Poodle,* Dodd, 1975. Ghost writer of other books.

Author of "Straw Hat," play produced on Broadway, 1937, and of 150 radio plays, 1936-41; also wrote scripts for twenty commercial films, 1948-56. Columnist and free-lance contributor to dog magazines, including *Dog World, Dogs in Canada,* and *American Kennel Gazette.* Contributing editor, *Dogs,* 1970—; canine editor, *On the Sound,* 1971-74; pet editor, *American Home,* 1974—.

WORK IN PROGRESS: Winning Ways, for F. Watts; *Beloved Beast,* for Dutton; a novel about feral dogs; a collection of humorous articles about dogs and dog lovers; two ghosting assignments.

SIDELIGHTS: Unkelbach told *CA:* "What I write about reflects ... my lifelong avocations of the dog and cat worlds, animals in general, nature, ornithology, ecology, biology, and fishing. In a sense, these avocations have become vocations, since they provide the fuel for my typewriter." Unkelbach breeds, trains, and exhibits Labrador Retrievers.

* * *

UNWIN, Derick (James) 1931-

PERSONAL: Born November 21, 1931, in Malta; son of Frederick Alexander (a noncommissioned officer, British Navy) and Helen Sophia (Jukes) Unwin; married Geraldine Ann Moore; children: five. *Education:* Attended Dartford Technical College, 1951-53; University of Leeds, B.Sc. (honours), 1956; University of Loughborough, M.A., 1966. *Office:* Education Centre, New University of Ulster, Coleraine, Northern Ireland.

CAREER: North Walsham High School, Norfolk, England, senior physics teacher, 1958-63; University of Loughborough, Loughborough, England, research fellow in programmed learning, 1963-65; Bulmershe College of Education, Reading, England, head of department of educational technology, 1965-68; New University of Ulster, Edu-

cation Centre, Coleraine, Northern Ireland, senior lecturer in new media, 1968—. *Member:* Royal Statistical Society (fellow), Association for Programmed Learning and Educational Technology (vice-president, 1965—), British Computer Society.

WRITINGS: Kinematics, Methuen, 1964; (with John Leedham) *Programmed Learning in the Schools,* Longmans, Green, 1965; *Mass, Weight, and Density,* Methuen, 1966; *Newton's Laws of Motion,* Methuen, 1967; (editor with Leedham) *Aspects of Educational Technology,* Methuen, 1967; (compiler with Frank Atkinson) *The Computer in Education: A Select Bibliography,* United Kingdom Library Association, 1968; (editor) *Media and Methods: Instructional Technology in Higher Education,* McGraw, 1969. Contributor to various education publications. Editor, *Programmed Learning and Educational Technology;* contributing editor, *Educational Technology.*

WORK IN PROGRESS: Research in the design of media systems for teaching and learning; the role of simulation and academic gaming in education; editing *Encyclopaedia of Educational Media, Communication and Technology,* for Macmillan.

AVOCATIONAL INTERESTS: Squash racquets, golf, and gardening.

* * *

UNWIN, Nora S(picer) 1907-

PERSONAL: Born February 22, 1907, in Surbiton, Surrey, England; daughter of George Soundy (a master printer) and Eleanor Mary (Eady) Unwin. *Education:* Studied at Leon Underwood's Studio, 1924-26, and Kingston School of Art, 1926-28; Royal College of Art, Diploma in Design, 1932. *Home:* Old Street Rd., Peterborough, N.H. 03458.

CAREER: Professional artist; author of self-illustrated books for children, 1939—. Painter, book-illustrator, engraver, and part-time teacher in England, 1933-46, and United States, 1946—. Director of art at Tenacre Country Day School, Wellesley, Mass., 1957-59; currently teaching at Sharon Art Center, Sharon, N.H. Had one-woman shows in Boston and eastern United States, 1948-50, 1954-56, 1957, 1960, 1964, 1966-71; work exhibited in Europe, North and South America, Near and Far East, including Royal Academy, Metropolitan Museum of Art, Library of Congress, and New York Public Library. Board member, Boston Printmakers, 1959—, New Hampshire Art Association, 1961, and Sharon Art Centre, 1964-68. Trustee, Zion Research Foundation (Boston), 1958—.

MEMBER: Society of American Graphic Artists, National Academy of Design, Royal Society of Painter-Etchers and Engravers (fellow), New Hampshire Art Association, Boston Print Makers, Printmakers of Albany, Cambridge Art Association, Boston Watercolor Society. *Awards, honors:* Awards, purchase prizes, and honorable mentions from Society of American Graphic Artists, 1951, National Association of Women Artists, 1953, National Academy of Design, 1958, Cambridge Watercolor Society, 1965, Cambridge Art Association, 1967, Boston Print Makers, New Hampshire Art Association, and others.

WRITINGS—Self-illustrated: Round the Year, Chatto & Windus, 1939, Holiday House, 1940; *Lucy and the Little Red Horse,* Delamore, 1942; *Doughnuts for Lin,* Dutton, 1950; *Proud Pumpkin,* Dutton, 1953; *Poquito, the Little Mexican Duck,* McKay, 1959; *Two Too Many,* McKay, 1962; *The Way of the Shepherd,* McGraw, 1963; *Joyful the*

Morning, McKay, 1963; *The Midsummer Witch,* McKay, 1966; *Sinbad, the Cygnet,* John Day, 1970. Illustrator of other books for American and British publishers. Contributor of poetry to periodicals.

WORK IN PROGRESS: A picture book; paintings and prints.

AVOCATIONAL INTERESTS: Music, playing the recorder and piano; needlework, gardening, and travel.

* * *

URDA, Nicholas 1922-

PERSONAL: Born March 10, 1922, in Herrick Center, Pa.; divorced. *Education:* Syracuse University, student, 1940-42; New York University, B.A., 1951. *Politics:* Democrat. *Residence:* Herrick Center, Pa. 18430.

CAREER: Salesman with Saks Fifth Avenue, New York, N.Y., 1945-48, and receiving clerk for a cable company, Passaic, N.J., 1952-60; psychiatric aide at Farview State Hospital, Waymart, Pa., 1960—; owner of small tree farm in Herrick Center, Pa., specializing in growing of premium Christmas trees. *Military service:* U.S. Army Air Forces, 1942-45; combat gunner with 8th Air Force, and survivor of a bomber crash in England, 1945; became staff sergeant; received Air Medal with oak leaf cluster, Purple Heart, and two battle stars. *Member:* American Legion, Herrick Athletic Club.

WRITINGS: Eighty-Eight Best Limericks, Edwards Brothers, 1964; *The Philosophy of Hylozoism,* Edwards Brothers, 1966; *The Blue Eyed Monkey* (poetical discourses), Adams, 1968; *Ontology of the Irrational,* Courier Press. 1974.

WORK IN PROGRESS: A treatise on the criminally insane.

SIDELIGHTS: Nicholas Urda describes himself as, "a moderate in practical affairs and a free thinker in writing." Interests center on ancient history, philosophy, and philology.

* * *

URDANG, Constance (Henriette) 1922-

PERSONAL: Born December 26, 1922, in New York, N.Y.; daughter of Harry Rudman (a teacher) and Annabel (Schafran) Urdang; married Donald Finkel (an author and poet), August 14, 1956; children: Liza, Thomas Noah, Amy Maria. *Education:* Smith College, A.B., 1943; University of Iowa, M.F.A., 1956. *Home:* 6943 Columbia Pl., St. Louis, Mo. 63130. *Agent:* Maxine Groffsky, 104 Greenwich Ave., New York, N.Y. 10011.

CAREER: U.S. Department of the Army, Washington, D.C., military intelligence analyst, 1944-46; National Bellas Hess, Inc., New York City, copy editor, 1947-51; P. F. Collier & Son, New York City, editor, 1952-54; currently free-lance writer and editor. *Awards, honors:* Carleton *Miscellany's* First Centennial Award for prose, for "Natural History" (portion of a novel).

WRITINGS: (Editor with Paul Engle) *Prize Short Stories, 1957: The O. Henry Awards,* Doubleday, 1957; (editor with Engle and Curtis Harnack) *Prize Short Stories, 1959: The O. Henry Awards,* Doubleday, 1959; *Charades and Celebrations* (poems), October House, 1965; *Natural History* (novel), Harper, 1969; *The Picnic in the Cemetery* (poems), Braziller, 1975. Contributor of poetry and prose to many periodicals.

BIOGRAPHICAL/CRITICAL SOURCES: Poetry, April, 1968; *Saturday Review,* July 19, 1969; *New York Times Book Review,* July 20, 1969; *Book World,* August 17, 1969; *Virginia Quarterly Review,* autumn, 1969.

* * *

UTT, Walter C(harles) 1921-

PERSONAL: Born August 27, 1921, in St. Helena, Calif.; son of Charles D. (a college teacher) and Miriam (Clark) Utt; married Martha Rooks (a librarian), June 17, 1943; children: Shirley, Kenneth. *Education:* Pacific Union College, B.A., 1942; University of California, Berkeley, M.A., 1946, Ph.D., 1952. *Home:* 215 Clark Way, Angwin, Calif. 94508. *Office:* Department of History, Pacific Union College, Angwin, Calif. 94508.

CAREER: University of California, Berkeley, lecturer in speech, 1949-51; Pacific Union College, Angwin, Calif., 1951—, began as instructor, professor of history and chairman of history department, 1956—. *Member:* American Historical Association, Societe de l'Histoire des Protestantisme Francais, Phi Beta Kappa.

WRITINGS: The Wrath of the King, Pacific Press Publishing Association, 1966.

WORK IN PROGRESS: Political activity of Huguenot exiles, 1683-1698.

AVOCATIONAL INTERESTS: Military uniforms, French philately.

* * *

UTTLEY, John 1914-

PERSONAL: Born September 12, 1914; son of James Arthur (an engineer) and Alison (a writer for children; maiden name, Taylor) Uttley; married Helen Paine, April 12, 1947. *Education:* St. John's College, Cambridge, M.A. (honors), 1936. *Religion:* Church of England. *Home:* Le Hurel House, Guernsey, Channel Islands.

CAREER: Schoolmaster at St. Lawrence, Ramsgate, Eton, and Stowe, England, 1937-60; director of a property company, 1961—. *Military service:* British Army, Royal Artillery, 1939-45; became captain.

WRITINGS: Story of the Channel Islands, Faber, 1966.

AVOCATIONAL INTERESTS: Boating, gardening, cinematography, and historical sites.††

* * *

VALDES, Donald M(anuel) 1922-

PERSONAL: Born November 20, 1922, in Roselle Park, N.J.; son of Casimiro H. and Edna (Reindel) Valdes; married Johnnie Hardiman, March, 1945; children: Thomas, John, Andrea, Salena. *Education:* University of Maine, student, 1941-42; Montclair State College, B.A., 1948; George Peabody College for Teachers, M.A., 1949; Ohio State University, Ph.D., 1958. *Politics:* Democrat. *Religion:* Presbyterian. *Home:* 15 Sunset Hill, Granville, Ohio 43023. *Office:* Denison University, Granville, Ohio 43023.

CAREER: Denison University, Granville, Ohio, 1953—, currently professor of sociology. *Military service:* U.S. Army Air Forces, 1942-45; pilot; became second lieutenant. *Member:* American Sociological Association, North Central Sociological Society, Ohio Academy of Science, Alpha Kappa Delta, Omega Delta Kappa.

WRITINGS: (With Dwight G. Dean) *Experiments in Soci-*

ology, Appleton, 1963, 3rd edition, Prentice-Hall, 1976; (with Dean) Sociology in Use, Macmillan, 1965.

WORK IN PROGRESS: Work on history of race relations.

AVOCATIONAL INTERESTS: Anthropology.

* * *

VALETTE, Rebecca M(arianne Loose) 1938-

PERSONAL: Born December 21, 1938; daughter of Gerhard (a professor) and Ruth A. (Bischoff) Loose; married Jean-Paul Valette (an author), August 6, 1959; children: Jean-Michel, Nathalie Marie, Pierre Alexis. Education: Mount Holyoke College, B.A. (cum laude), 1959; University of Colorado, Ph.D., 1963. Politics: Democrat. Religion: Roman Catholic. Home: 16 Mt. Alvernia Rd., Chestnut Hill, Mass. 02167. Office: Boston College, Chestnut Hill, Mass. 02167.

CAREER: University of South Florida, Tampa, examiner and instructor in French and German, 1961-63; North Atlantic Treaty Organization Defense College, Paris, France, instructor in English, 1963-64; Wellesley College, Wellesley, Mass., instructor in French, 1964-65; Boston College, Chestnut Hill, Mass., assistant professor, 1965-68, associate professor, 1968-73, professor of French and education, 1973—. Fulbright senior lecturer in West Germany, 1974. Member: American Council on the Teaching of Foreign Languages, Modern Language Association of America, American Association of Teachers of French, American Association of Teachers of German, National Association of Language Laboratory Directors, Teachers of English to Speakers of Other Languages.

WRITINGS: Modern Language Testing, Harcourt, 1967; (with husband, Jean-Paul Valette) Lisons, McGraw, 1967; (editor with Robert Morgenroth) C'est de la Prose, Harcourt, 1968; (editor) Lectures libres, Harcourt, 1969; Arthur de Gobineau and the Short Story, University of North Carolina Press, 1969; Directions in Foreign Language Testing, Modern Language Association of America, 1969; (with Edward D. Allen) Modern Language Classroom Techniques, Harcourt, 1973; (with Renee S. Disnick) Modern Language Performance Objectives and Individualization, Harcourt, 1973; (with Jean-Paul Valette) France: A Cultural Review Grammar, Harcourt, 1973; (with Jean-Paul Valette) French for Mastery 1: Salut, les amis! and French for Mastery 2: Tous Ensemble, Heath, 1975. Contributor to professional journals.

WORK IN PROGRESS: Research into second-language acquisition; essay on women's liberation.

SIDELIGHTS: Rebecca Valette has lived in France for several periods, and in Germany. She has lectured in Yugoslavia, Great Britain, West Germany, France, the Netherlands, and Canada.

* * *

Van ANROOY, Francine 1924-
(Frans van Anrooy)

PERSONAL: Born April 19, 1924, in The Hague, Netherlands; daughter of J. W. H. and A. M. L. (Maronier) Van Anrooy; married K. W. F. Scholten van Aschat (a banker), July 4, 1953; children: Louise, Christiaan, Gys. Education: University of Amsterdam, Master of Law, 1952. Religion: Protestant. Home: Waldeck Pyzmontlaan 20, Amsterdam, Netherlands.

WRITINGS—Under name Frans van Anrooy: Knopedozus (juvenile), Vermande, 1963; The Bird Tree (juvenile), Harcourt, 1967; The Sea Horse (juvenile), Harcourt, 1968; The Lady of the Sea (juvenile), Carolrhoda, 1971.

* * *

VANDERVELDE, Marjorie (Mills) 1908-

PERSONAL: Born September 13, 1908, in LeGrand, Iowa; daughter of E. M. (a doctor of medicine) and Anna (Burgess) Mills; married Andrew Vandervelde, December 31, 1929. Education: Attended Penn (now William Penn) College and Iowa State University.

CAREER: Writer, especially on travel. Has special interest in primitive cultures, and has spent time with the Caribou Eskimos of the Northwest Territories, Cuna Indians of San Blas, Choco Indians of the Darien jungle in Panama and Colombia, and the Havasupai Indians. Member: National Press Women, National Writers Club, Iowa Press Women. Awards, honors: Awards from state groups; National Press Women award, 1975, for Across the Tundra.

WRITINGS: Keep Out of Paradise, Broadman, 1966. Also author of juvenile books, Sam and the Golden People, Could It Be Old Hiari, and Across the Tundra, for Montana Indian Publications. Contributor to national magazines. With her husband, author of regular press feature, "Traveling with Vanderveldes," and regular column, "The World at Our Feet."

WORK IN PROGRESS: Beauty Is—A Ring in Her Nose?

* * *

Van der VEUR, Paul W. 1921-

PERSONAL: Born August 28, 1921, in Medan, Indonesia; son of Wilhelmus Marius (a physician) and Johanna (Guldemond) Van der Veur; married Barbara Walker; children: Ann, Mark, Julia, Paul Roscoe. Education: Swarthmore College, B.A., 1949; University of Minnesota, M.A., 1950; Cornell University, Ph.D., 1955. Office: Department of Government, Ohio University, Athens, Ohio 45701.

CAREER: Yale University, New Haven, Conn., instructor in political science, 1954-56, co-director of Indonesia research project, 1955-56; University of Hawaii, Honolulu, assistant professor, 1956-59, associate professor of political science, 1959-61; Australian National University, Canberra, senior research fellow, 1961-66; Northern Illinois University, De Kalb, professor of political science, 1966-67; Ohio University, Athens, professor of government and director of Southeast Asia program, 1967-73. Military service: Royal Netherlands Indies Army, 1941-47; prisoner of war, 1942-45; became sergeant. Member: Association for Asian Studies, American Political Science Association, Southeast Asia Development Advisory Group, Council on New Guinea Affairs, Papua and New Guinea Historical Society.

WRITINGS: (With Richard J. Coughlin, Stephen W. Reed, and Ed Bruner) Indonesia, three volumes, Human Relations Area File Press, 1956; (editor with David G. Bettison and Colin A. Hughes) The Papua-New Guinea Elections 1964, Australian National University Press, 1965; Search for New Guinea's Boundaries, Australian National University Press, 1966; Documents and Correspondence on New Guinea's Boundaries, Australian National University Press, 1966. Contributor to political science journals and other publications.

WORK IN PROGRESS: A political history of the Eurasians of Indonesia, completion expected in 1978.

van der ZEE, John 1936-

PERSONAL: Born January 30, 1936, in San Francisco, Calif.; son of Herman A. (a judge) and Mary (McGushin) van der Zee; married Diane Hunt, November 28, 1959; children: Peter John. *Education:* Stanford University, A.B., 1957. *Agent:* Lynn Nesbit, International Creative Management, 40 West 57th St., New York, N.Y. 10019.

CAREER: Copywriter with Batten, Barton, Durstine & Osborn, San Francisco, Calif., 1958-61, Benton & Bowles, Inc., New York, N.Y., 1961-62, Fletcher Richards, Calkins & Holden, San Francisco, 1962-63, and Batten, Barton, Durstine & Osborn, 1964-66; McCann-Erickson, Inc., San Francisco, copywriter, 1966—. *Military service:* California National Guard, 1957-61. *Member:* Phi Gamma Delta. *Awards, honors:* James D. Phelan Award for Literature, 1964, for manuscript of novel (unpublished), "The Hand-Picked Man."

WRITINGS: The Plum Explosion, Harcourt, 1967; *Blood Brotherhood,* Harcourt, 1970; (with Hugh Wilkerson) *Life in the Peace Zone: An American Company Town,* Macmillan, 1971; *Canyon: The Story of the Last Rustic Community in Metropolitan America,* Harcourt, 1972; *The Greatest Men's Party on Earth: Inside the Bohemian Grove,* Harcourt, 1974. Contributor to *Ramparts.*

WORK IN PROGRESS: A work of fiction.†

* * *

VANN, Richard T(ilman) 1931-

PERSONAL: Born June 25, 1931, in Belton, Tex.; son of William Harvey and Osee (Maedgen) Vann. *Education:* Southern Methodist University, B.A., 1952; Oxford University, B.A., 1954, M.A., 1958; Harvard University, M.A., 1957, Ph.D., 1959. *Office:* Wesleyan University, Middletown, Conn. 06457.

CAREER: Harvard University, Cambridge, Mass., tutor and instructor in history, 1955-61; Carleton College, Northfield, Minn., assistant professor of history, 1961-64; Wesleyan University, Middletown, Conn., senior tutor, College of Letters, and associate professor of history, 1964-69, professor of history and letters, 1969—. *Awards, honors:* Conference on British Studies Quinquennial Book Prize, 1974.

WRITINGS: (Editor) *Century of Genius: European Thought 1600-1700,* Prentice-Hall, 1967; *The Social Development of English Quakerism, 1655-1755,* Harvard University Press, 1969. Executive editor, *History and Theory,* 1965—.

WORK IN PROGRESS: A Demographic History of the British Quakers.

* * *

Van ORMAN, Richard A(lbert) 1936-

PERSONAL: Born August 16, 1936, in Evansville, Ind.; son of Fred Harold (a hotelman) and Harriett (Hodges) Van Orman; married Bonnie Baker O'Brien, August 17, 1962; children: Wade Hodges, Brenda O'Brien. *Education:* Michigan State University, B.A., 1958, M.A., 1960; Indiana University, Ph.D., 1964. *Politics:* Independent. *Religion:* Episcopalian. *Home:* 229 Beacon Pl., Munster, Ind. 46321. *Office:* Calumet Campus, Purdue University, Hammond, Ind. 46323.

CAREER: Purdue University, Calumet Campus, Hammond, Ind., assistant professor, 1966-71, associate professor of history, 1971—. *Member:* Organization of American Historians, Western History Association, Kansas Historical Society. *Awards, honors:* Newberry Library research award; Huntington Library research grant.

WRITINGS: A Room for the Night: Hotels of the Old West, Indiana University Press, 1966; (contributor) John A. Carroll, editor, *Reflections of Western Historians,* University of Arizona Press, 1969; (with Oscar O. Winther) *A Classified Bibliography of the Periodical Literature of the Trans-Mississippi West, 1957-1967,* Indiana University Press, 1970.

* * *

VAN SLINGERLAND, Peter 1929-

PERSONAL: Born June 21, 1929, in Albany, N.Y.; married Amanda Cushman, July 28, 1960; children: Lucy. *Education:* Attended Harvard University. *Residence:* Patterson, N.Y. *Agent:* James Brown Associates, Inc., 22 East 60th St., New York, N.Y. 10022.

CAREER: Panaria Films, Rome, Italy, writer, 1949-50; *Look,* New York, N.Y., senior editor, 1953-60. *Military service:* U.S. Army, Counterintelligence Corps, special agent, 1951-53. *Awards, honors:* "A Special Announcement" was runner-up for an Emmy Award of Academy of Television Arts and Sciences, 1957.

WRITINGS: Something Terrible Has Happened, Harper, 1966. Television play, "A Special Announcement," produced on "Studio One," 1956.††

* * *

VAN SLYKE, Lyman P(age) 1929-

PERSONAL: Born April 20, 1929, in Duluth, Minn.; son of William Ralph (a mining engineer) and Frances (Baird) Van Slyke; married Barbara Heaps (a social worker), July 11, 1953; children: Peter Baird, John Porter, Elizabeth Munro. *Education:* Carleton College, B.A., 1951; University of California, Berkeley, M.A., 1958, Ph.D., 1964. *Home:* 591 Salvatierra St., Stanford, Calif. 94305. *Office:* Department of History, Stanford University, Stanford, Calif.

CAREER: Stanford University, Stanford, Calif., assistant professor, 1968-68, associate professor of history, 1968—. Director of Inter-University Program for Chinese Language Studies in Taipei, Taiwan, 1964-65. *Military service:* U.S. Navy, 1951-55. U.S. Naval Reserve, 1955-67.

WRITINGS: Enemies and Friends: The United Front in Chinese Communist History, Stanford University Press, 1967; (editor) *The Chinese Communist Movement: A Report of the U.S. War Department,* Stanford University Press, 1968. Author of introductions to three books. Contributor of articles and reviews to journals.

WORK IN PROGRESS: Research on China, 1920-40; a study of the Sino-Japanese war, 1937-1945; explorations in psycho history; chapters for *The Cambridge History of China.*

SIDELIGHTS: Lyman Van Slyke lived in Taiwan for three years, and visited the People's Republic of China in 1975. He is fluent in Chinese.

* * *

Van VOGT, A(lfred) E(lton) 1912-

PERSONAL: Born April 26, 1912, in Manitoba, Canada; son of Henry (an attorney) and Agnes (Buhr) Van Vogt; married Edna Mayne Hull, May 9, 1939 (died January 20,

1975). *Education:* Attended schools in Manitoba; also studied at University of Ottawa and University of California. *Religion:* Rationalist. *Address:* P.O. Box 3065, Los Angeles, Calif. 90028. *Agent:* Forrest J. Ackerman, Ackerman Agency, 2495 Glendower Ave., Los Angeles, Calif. 90027.

CAREER: Professional writer, 1932—, chiefly of science fiction. Western representative of trade papers, MacLean Publishing Co., Toronto, Ontario, 1935-39. First director of Hubbard Dianetic Research Foundation of California, 1950-51. *Member:* International Society for General Semantics, Authors Guild of the Authors League of America, Science Fiction Writers of America, International Dianetic Society (president, 1958—), California Association of Dianetic Auditors (president, 1959—).

WRITINGS—Fiction, except as indicated: *Slan,* Arkham, 1946; *The Book of Ptath,* Fantasy Press, 1947, reissued in paperback as *200 Million A.D.: World of A,* Simon & Schuster, 1948; *Pawns of Null-A* (sequel to *World of A*), Ace Books, c.1949, reissued as *The Players of Null-A,* Berkley Books, 1966.

The Voyage of the Space Beagle, Simon & Schuster, 1950, reissued as *Mission Interplanetary,* Macfadden, 1950; *The House That Stood Still,* Greenberg, 1950, revised edition published as *The Mating Cry,* Galaxy, 1960; *The Weapon Shops of Isher,* Greenberg, 1951; *The Weapon Makers* (sequel to *The Weapon Shops of Isher*), Greenberg, 1952, reissued as *One Against Eternity,* Ace Books, 1954; *Away and Beyond* (collection), Pellegrini & Cudahy, 1952; *Destination: Universe!* (collection), with introduction by the author, Pellegrini & Cudahy, 1952; *The Universe Maker,* Ace Books, 1953; (with wife, E. Mayne Hull) *Planets for Sale,* Fell, 1954; (with Charles Edward Cooke) *The Hypnotism Handbook* (nonfiction), Griffin, 1956; *Empire of the Atom,* Shasta, 1957; *The Mind Cage,* Simon & Schuster, 1957; *Siege of the Unseen,* Ace Books, 1959; *The War against the Rull,* Simon & Schuster, 1959.

The Wizard of Linn (sequel to *Empire of the Atom*), Ace Books, 1962; *The Violent Man,* Farrar, Straus, 1962; *The Beast,* Doubleday, 1963; *Rogue Ship,* Doubleday, 1965; (with E. Mayne Hull) *The Winged Man,* Doubleday, 1966; *A Van Vogt Omnibus,* Sidgwick & Jackson, 1967; *Far-Out Worlds of A. E. Van Vogt,* Ace Books, 1968; *The Silkie,* Ace Books, 1969.

Quest for the Future, Ace Books, 1970; *Children of Tomorrow,* Ace Books, 1970; *The Battle of Forever,* Ace Books, 1971; *More Than Superhuman* (collection), Dell, 1971; *The Proxy Intelligence and Other Mind Benders,* Paperback Library, 1971; *M-33 in Andromeda,* Paperback Library, 1971; *The Darkness on Diamondia,* Ace Books, 1972; *The Book of Van Vogt* (collection), Daw Books, 1972; *Future Glitter,* Ace Books, 1973; *The Money Personality* (nonfiction), Prentice-Hall, 1973; *The Man with a Thousand Names,* Daw Books, 1974; *The Secret Galactics,* Prentice-Hall, 1974; *Reflections of A. E. Van Vogt* (autobiography), Fictioneer Books, 1975.

WORK IN PROGRESS: A science fiction series, *Color of A Woman; To Conquer Kiber,* for Daw Books; *The Anarchistic Colossus,* for Ace Books; *The Galactic Connection,* for Doubleday.

BIOGRAPHICAL/CRITICAL SOURCES: The Oral History Collection of Columbia University, Butler Library, Columbia University, 1964; Sam Moskowitz, *Modern Masterpieces of Science Fiction,* World Publishing, 1965; Carolyn Riley, editor, *Contemporary Literary Criticism,* Volume I, Gale, 1973; *Reflections of A. E. Van Vogt,* Fictioneer Books, 1975.

* * *

VARS, Gordon F(orrest) 1923-

PERSONAL: Born February 10, 1923, in Erie, Pa.; son of Ethan W. and Mildred (Place) Vars; married former spouse Annis Tallentire (a social worker), August 22, 1949; married Alice McVetty, December 21, 1975; children: (prior marriage) Christine Ann, Lynn Burdick. *Education:* Antioch College, A.B., 1948; Ohio State University, M.A., 1949; George Peabody College for Teachers, Ed.D., 1958. *Home:* 986 South Lincoln St., Kent, Ohio 44240. *Office:* 404F Education Building, Kent State University, Kent, Ohio 44242.

CAREER: Teacher at secondary school in Bel Air, Md., 1949-52, and at Demonstration School, George Peabody College for Teachers, Nashville, Tenn., 1952-55; State University of New York College at Plattsburgh, associate professor of education, 1956-60; Cornell University, Ithaca, N.Y., associate professor of education, 1960-66; Kent State University, Kent, Ohio, professor of education, 1966—. *Military service:* U.S. Army, Infantry, 1944-46. *Member:* National Association for Core Curriculum (executive secretary-treasurer, 1959—), Association for Supervision and Curriculum Development, National Middle School Association, National Council of Teachers of English, Phi Delta Kappa, Kappa Delta Pi.

WRITINGS: (With William Van Til and John Lounsbury) *Modern Education for the Junior High School Years,* Bobbs-Merrill, 1961, 2nd edition, 1967; (editor) *Guidelines for Junior High and Middle School Education,* National Association of Secondary-School Principals, 1966; (editor) *Common Learning: Core and Interdisciplinary Team Approaches,* International Textbook, 1969. Contributor to professional yearbooks and journals. Editor, *Core Teacher* (quarterly newsletter of National Association for Core Curriculum).

* * *

VASILIU, Mircea 1920-

PERSONAL: Born July 16, 1920, in Bucharest, Rumania; son of Matei (a lawyer) and Florica (Tantareanu) Vasiliu; married Natalie Maiden, November 25, 1950. *Education:* University of Bucharest, B.A. (law), 1942, M.A., 1943. *Home:* 124 Highland Rd., Glen Cove, N.Y. 11542.

CAREER: Rumanian Diplomatic Corps, attache in Bucharest, 1943-46, third secretary in Washington, D.C., 1946-48; artist and writer. *Military service:* Royal Rumanian Cavalry; became lieutenant.

WRITINGS—Autobiographical: *The Pleasure is Mine,* Harper, 1955; *Which Way to the Melting Pot?,* Doubleday, 1963.

Juveniles, self-illustrated; all published by John Day, except as indicated: *Everything is Somewhere,* 1959; *The Year Goes Round,* 1964; *Hark, the Little Angel,* 1965; *Do You Remember?,* 1966; *The World is Many Things,* 1967; *The Merry Wind,* 1967; *Mortimer, the Friendly Dragon,* 1968; *One Day in the Garden,* 1969; *What's Happening?,* 1969; *The Good Night, Sleep Tight Book,* Golden Press, 1973; *Once Upon a Pirate Ship,* Golden Press, 1974.

Illustrator: Nancy Sherman, *Miss Agatha's Lark,* Bobbs-Merrill, 1968.

VAUGHAN, Sheila Marie 1930-

PERSONAL: Born August 26, 1930, in Pasadena, Calif.; daughter of Raymond Victor (a U.S. Treasury agent) and Mary (Deur) Vaughan. *Education:* Immaculate Heart College, Los Angeles, Calif., B.A., 1957, California Teacher's Credential, 1960, M.A., 1964; graduate study at University of California, Berkeley, 1958, and Oklahoma State University, 1959. *Politics:* Democrat. *Home:* 5515 Franklin Ave., Los Angeles, Calif. 90028.

CAREER: Roman Catholic religious of Sisters of the Immaculate Heart. Elementary teacher, 1950-54; parochial high school science teacher, Long Beach, Calif., 1954-63, chairman of department, 1956-63; Paraclete High School, Los Angeles, Calif., principal, 1963—. Chairman of Curriculum Development Committee for Elementary School Science, Archdiocese of Los Angeles, 1956. *Member:* American Association for the Advancement of Science, National Science Teachers Association, National Association of Biology Teachers, National Association of Secondary School Administrators, California Association of Chemistry Teachers, California Association of Secondary School Administrators.

WRITINGS: Matter, Energy and Living Things (elementary science text), McGraw, 1967. Author of course of study in biology for Los Angeles parochial high schools, 1955, and course of studies in science for diocesan elementary schools, 1956.

AVOCATIONAL INTEREST: Painting, exploring, sports (especially golf and swimming).††

* * *

VAUGHN, Donald E(arl) 1932-

PERSONAL: Born March 28, 1932, in Denton, Tex.; son of Robert Ray and Addie V. (Whitley) Vaughn; married Lottie Sue Martin, August 29, 1953; children: Martin Lee, Donna Sue, Debra Ann, Diana Kay, Erla Joyce. *Education:* North Texas State University, B.B.A., 1953, M.B.A., 1955, Ph.D., 1961. *Religion:* Baptist. *Home:* Route 4, Carbondale, Ill. *Office:* Department of Finance, Southern Illinois University, Carbondale, Ill. 62901.

CAREER: North Texas State University, Denton, part-time instructor in business administration, 1953-54; West Texas State University, Canyon, instructor in finance, 1957-59; University of Texas, Austin, lecturer in business finance, 1959-61; Louisiana State University, Baton Rouge, assistant professor, 1961-64, associate professor, 1964-69, professor of business finance, 1969-70; Southern Illinois University, Carbondale, professor of business finance, 1970—, chairman of department of finance, 1973—. Visiting financial analyst, Federal Power Commission, 1972-73. *Military service:* Texas National Guard, 1951-55. U.S. Army, 1955-57; became sergeant. *Member:* American Finance Association, Southern Economic Association, Southwest Finance Association (vice-president, 1964; president, 1965), Southwestern Social Science Association.

WRITINGS: Credit Union Management, Bureau of Business, Louisiana State University, 1966; (with Richard L. Norgaard) *Cases in Financial Decision Making,* Prentice-Hall, 1967; *Survey of Investments,* Holt, 1967, 2nd edition, 1974; (with Norgaard and Hite Bennett) *Financial Planning and Management,* Goodyear Publishing, 1972. Contributor to business textbooks, and to journals in his field.

WORK IN PROGRESS: Studies in regulated industries; contributor of work to *Wealth Management Handbook,* for McGraw.

AVOCATIONAL INTERESTS: Stock market studies, merger making, and woodwork.

* * *

VAUGHN, Richard C(lements) 1925-

PERSONAL: Born January 17, 1925, in Ionia, Mich.; son of Forrest H. (a designer) and Alice (Haynor) Vaughn; married Frances E. Foreman, March 18, 1947; children: Bonnie, Barbara, Carolyn, Vicki, Elizabeth. *Education:* Michigan State University, B.A., 1948; University of Toledo, M.I.E., 1955. *Home:* 1222 Ridgewood Ave., Ames, Iowa 50010. *Office:* Iowa State University of Science and Technology, Ames, Iowa 50010.

CAREER: Mather Spring Co., Toledo, Ohio, chief industrial engineer, 1955; Ford Motor Co., Monroe, Mich., process engineer, 1955-56; Detroit Harvester, Dura Division, Toledo, methods and process supervisor, 1956-57; University of Florida, Gainesville, assistant professor of industrial engineering, 1957-62; Iowa State University of Science and Technology, Ames, associate professor, 1962-67, professor of industrial engineering, 1968—. Instructor in mathematics at evening session, University of Toledo, 1952-57. *Military service:* U.S. Coast Guard Reserve, active duty, 1942-45. U.S. Naval Reserve, 1946-51. *Member:* American Society for Engineering Education, American Society for Quality Control, American Institute of Industrial Engineers.

WRITINGS: Legal Aspects of Engineering, Prentice-Hall, 1962; *Introduction to Industrial Engineering,* Iowa State University Press, 1967; *Quality Control,* Iowa State University Press, 1974.

WORK IN PROGRESS: Applied Queueing Theory.

* * *

VERDUIN, John R(ichard), Jr. 1931-

PERSONAL: Born July 6, 1931, in Muskegon, Mich.; son of John Richard (a salesman) and Dorothy (Eckman) Verduin; married Janet M. Falk, January 26, 1963; children: John Richard III, Susan E. *Education:* University of Albuquerque, B.S., 1954; Michigan State University, M.A., 1959, Ph.D., 1962. *Home:* 107 North Lark Lane, Carbondale, Ill. 62901. *Office:* Southern Illinois University, Carbondale, Ill. 62901.

CAREER: Public school teacher in Muskegon, Mich., 1954-56, and Greenville, Mich., 1956-59; State University of New York College at Geneseo, assistant professor, 1962-64, associate professor of education, 1964-67; Southern Illinois University, Carbondale, associate professor, 1967-70, professor in department of educational administration and foundations, 1970—, assistant dean, 1967-73. Special consultant to American Association of Colleges for Teacher Education, 1966-67; State of Illinois Gifted Program, member of advisory council, 1968—, chairman, 1973—; member of Teacher Education Committee of Illinois Association of Supervision and Curriculum Development. Member of Carbondale Models Cities Committee, and Goals for Carbondale committee; member and chairman of education commission, First United Methodist Church, Carbondale. *Military service:* U.S. Marine Corps, 1951. *Member:* Association for Supervision and Curriculum Development, American Educational Research Association, Phi Delta Kappa, Kappa Delta Phi.

WRITINGS: Cooperative Curriculum Improvement, Prentice-Hall, 1967; *Conceptual Models in Teacher Educa-*

tion, American Association of Colleges for Teacher Education, 1967; (co-author) *Pre-Student Teaching Laboratory Experiences,* Kendall-Hunt, 1970; (contributor) William Joyce, Robert Oana, and W. Robert Houston, editors, *Elementary Education in the Seventies,* Holt, 1970. Also author of reports on educational research and projects for the State of Illinois; contributor of articles to education journals.

WORK IN PROGRESS: Adult Education Instruction.

AVOCATIONAL INTERESTS: Woodworking, gardening, golfing, and tennis.

* * *

VERGANI, Luisa 1931-

PERSONAL: Born June 21, 1931, in Verona, Italy; daughter of Orfio and Anna Maria (Trestini) Zamboni; married Gian Angelo Vergani (a teacher), November 5, 1960; children: Robert, George, David. *Education:* University of Milan, dottore, 1956. *Home:* 3637 Saddle Dr., Spring Valley, Calif. 92077.

CAREER: University of Colorado, Boulder, associate in Italian, 1962-63; University of San Diego, College for Women, San Diego, Calif., assistant professor of Italian, 1964-69; San Diego State University, San Diego, Calif., 1969—, currently associate professor of Italian. *Member:* American Association of Teachers of Italian, Pacific Coast Philological Association.

WRITINGS: (With husband, Gian Angelo Vergani) *Italiano Moderno,* Pruett, 1966; *The Prince* (study guide), Cliff's Notes, 1967; *Divine Comedy: Inferno Notes* (study guide), Cliff's Notes, 1969. Contributor of articles to journals in her field.

WORK IN PROGRESS: A translation into English of Giovanni Pontano's *Dialogues;* an article on the influence of Ravenna mosaics on Dante.

* * *

VERNON-JACKSON, Hugh (Owen Hardinge) 1925-

PERSONAL: Born February 17, 1925; son of Percy and Frances Raymond (Hardinge) Vernon-Jackson; married Jean Kathleen Hole, April 29, 1961; children: Robert Gerald van Cortlandt, Caroline Frances Herringham, Helena Mary Hardinge. *Education:* University of British Columbia, B.Com., 1946, B.A., 1947; St. John's University, Shanghai, China, graduate study, 1948-49; University of Washington, Seattle, M.A., 1950; University of London, Postgraduate Certificate in Education, 1952; Columbia University, Ed.D., 1968. *Home:* Delawarr House, Lymington, Hampshire, England. *Office:* Canadian International Development Agency, Ottawa, Ontario, Canada.

CAREER: Ministry of Education, Northern Nigeria, senior education officer, 1952-61; Department of Education, West Cameroon, principal of Government Teacher Training College, 1961-62, principal of Cameroon College of Arts and Science, 1962-63; Columbia University, Teachers College, New York, N.Y., Peace Corps training staff, 1963-65; Grenada Teachers College, Grenada, West Indies, principal, 1965-67; Canadian External Aid Office, Education Division, Ottawa, Ontario, unit chief, beginning 1967; Canadian International Development Agency, Ottawa, deputy director of education division, 1968-70; University of Botswana, Lesotho and Swaziland, Botswana Campus, Gaborones, pro vice-chancellor, 1970-73; Canadian International Development Agency, education specialist, 1973—. Con-

sultant on Peace Corps training programs at Ohio University, Athens, 1965, and St. Croix, Virgin Islands, 1965, 1966.

MEMBER: Royal Institute of Public Administration (United Kingdom), African Studies Association (United Kingdom and United States), Canadian Association of African Studies, Canadian Institute of International Affairs, Society for International Development, Canadian Vocational Association, Nigerian Historical Society, International African Institute. *Awards, honors:* Order of Merit, Federal Republic of Cameroon; Northern Nigerian Self-government Medallion.

WRITINGS: West African Folk Tales, two volumes, University of London Press, 1958; *More West African Folk Tales,* two volumes, University of London Press, 1963; (with mother, Frances Vernon-Jackson) *Voice mon Conte,* University of London Press, 1966; *Language, Schools, and Government in Cameroon,* Teachers College, Columbia University, 1967. Contributor to scholarly journals. Editor, *West Cameroon Teachers Journal,* 1962-63.

WORK IN PROGRESS: West Cameroon folk tales.

* * *

VERY, Alice 1894-

PERSONAL: Born February 25, 1894, in Alleghany, Pa.; daughter of Frank W. and Portia (Vickers) Very; married Edmund R. Brown (a publisher), June 22, 1916; children: Rosalyn, Edmund Hosmer, Charlotte (Mrs. Cedric Jackson), Cynthia Brown Kallish, Martha (Mrs. Robert Bragg). *Education:* Wellesley College, A.B., 1916. *Politics:* Progressive. *Religion:* Christian Science. *Home:* 10 Edge Hill Rd., Sharon, Mass. 02067.

CAREER: Editorial work with the Boston publishing firms of Four Seas Co., 1916-30, Bruce Humphries, 1930-63, and Branden Press, Inc., 1963-67.

WRITINGS: The Human Abstract, Humphries, 1936; (with husband, Edmund R. Brown) *How to Use Peat Moss,* Humphries, 1940; *Round-the-Year Plays for Children,* Plays, 1956; (editor) *A Comprehensive Index of Poet Lore,* Branden, 1966; *Write on the Water* (poems), Branden, 1974. Associate editor, *World in Books.*

WORK IN PROGRESS: A book of poems, *Metamorphosis;* a "paraphonic" translation of Heine; a life of Joe Gould; compiling *The Lord's Prayer, with Commentary by the Author,* for Branden; poems, plays, articles, and short stories.

SIDELIGHTS: Alice Very has knowledge of Greek, Latin, French, and German.

* * *

VEYSEY, Laurence R(uss) 1932-

PERSONAL: Surname rhymes with "easy"; born August 12, 1932, in Los Angeles, Calif.; son of W. Robert (a writer) and Dorothy L. (Moore) Veysey; married Sheila Evelyn Ashby, August 31, 1965; children: John. *Education:* Yale University, B.A., 1953; University of Chicago, M.A., 1957; University of California, Berkeley, Ph.D., 1961. *Politics:* Independent. *Religion:* None. *Residence:* Capitola, Calif. *Office:* Adlai E. Stevenson College, University of California, Santa Cruz, Calif. 95060.

CAREER: Harvard University, Cambridge, Mass., instructor in history, social studies, and general education, 1961-64; University of Wisconsin-Madison, assistant professor of history, 1964-66; University of California, Santa Cruz, associate professor, 1966-71, professor of history, 1971—. Charles Warren fellow, Harvard University, 1974-75. *Military service:* U.S. Army, 1953-54. *Member:* American Historical Association, Organization of American Historians, Phi Beta Kappa. *Awards, honors:* American Council of Learned Societies fellowship, 1969-70; National Endowment for the Humanities fellowship, 1974-75.

WRITINGS: The Emergence of the American University, University of Chicago Press, 1965; *Law and Resistance: American Attitudes toward Authority,* Harper, 1970; *The Communal Experience: Anarchist and Mystical Counter-Cultures in America,* Harper, 1973; (contributor) Carl Kaysen, editor, *Content and Context,* McGraw, 1973; (editor) *The Perfectionists: Radical Social Thought in the North, 1815-1860,* Wiley, 1973. Contributor to *American Quarterly, Psychology Today,* and history journals.

WORK IN PROGRESS: A chapter in *The Organization of Knowledge in American Society, 1860-1920,* for Johns Hopkins University Press; research on the academic disciplines in the twentieth century.

*   *   *

VINCENT, Joan 1920-

PERSONAL: Born September 22, 1920, in Cedar Rapids, Iowa; married October 1, 1944 (divorced, 1963); children: Christopher, Frances. *Education:* Studied art at Cleveland College, Art Students League, New York, N.Y., and Greason Studios, Detroit, Mich. *Politics:* Democrat. *Religion:* Unity.

CAREER: Self-described "plunger into many forms of art"; sometime artist, with one-woman show at Gallerie Neut, New York, N.Y., 1945; has done bookkeeping, modeling, and sales work, including four years as head of the record department in a Detroit (Mich.) store; wrote publicity for Detroit chapter, Daughters of the American Revolution, 1952-63, and worked backstage with Harlequins, Inc. (theater), Sandusky, Ohio, 1963-66; meanwhile has written three historical novels and three other books (one published).

WRITINGS: Divorcee, Tower, 1966. Contributor to *Jazz Record* and several other periodicals.

WORK IN PROGRESS: Revision of a book on alcoholism.††

*   *   *

VINE, Paul Ashley Laurence 1927-

PERSONAL: Born December 13, 1927, in England; son of Laurence Arthur (a judge) and Nellie Florence (Ashley) Vine; children: Ashley, Deirdre. *Education:* Lincoln College, Oxford, M.A., 1952. *Politics:* Conservative. *Religion:* Church of England. *Home:* Cliffords Inn, London E.C.4, England.

CAREER: British Insurance Association, London, England, secretariat, 1953-56; affiliated with Automobile Association, 1956-71, and Foreign Office, 1971-73; free-lance writer and broadcaster. *Military service:* British Army, Intelligence Corps, 1946-49; became lieutenant. *Member:* International Athletes Club, Achilles Club, United University Club, Vincents Club.

WRITINGS: London's Lost Route to the Sea, David & Charles, 1965; *London's Lost Route to Basingstoke,* David & Charles, 1969; *The Royal Military Canal,* David &

Charles, 1972. Also author of preface, George Smith, *Our Canal Population,* 1975. Contributor to *Country Life, Oxford, Week-end Telegraph, Sussex County Magazine, Motor Boat,* and *Yachting.*

WORK IN PROGRESS: The Waterways of Sussex; Pleasure Boating in the Victorian Era.

SIDELIGHTS: Vine holds the British 220-yards low hurdles record.

*   *   *

VIVIANO, Benedict T(homas) 1940-

PERSONAL: Given names originally Thomas Michael; Benedict is his monastic name; born January 22, 1940, in St. Louis, Mo.; son of Frank Gaetano and Carmeline (Chiappetta) Viviano. *Education:* Aquinas Institute of Philosophy and Theology (now Aquinas Institute of Theology), B.A., M.A. (philosophy), M.A. (theology); Catholic University of America, graduate study, 1966-67; Harvard University, Ph.D., 1976. *Home:* 2570 Asbury St., Dubuque, Iowa 52001. *Agent:* T. C. Donlan, 1165 East 54th Pl., Chicago, Ill. 60615.

CAREER: Roman Catholic priest, member of Dominican Order. St. Dominic's School, Brookline, Mass., chaplain, 1967-68; American Schools of Oriental Research, Jerusalem, Israel, fellow, 1971-72; Aquinas Institute of Theology, Dubuque, Iowa, assistant professor of New Testament, 1972—.

WRITINGS: (With Edward Zerin) *What Catholics Should Know About Jews,* Priory, 1967. Contributor to *Reality, Listening, Dominicana, Cross and Crown, Revue biblique,* and *Catholic Biblical Quarterly.*

WORK IN PROGRESS: A monograph, tentatively entitled *Study as Worship: Aboth and the New Testament.*

SIDELIGHTS: Father Viviano is competent in Hebrew, Greek, Latin, French, German, Italian, and Aramaic. *Avocational interests:* Music, hiking, singing, history.

*   *   *

VLAHOS, Olivia 1924-

PERSONAL: Surname is pronounced *Vlay*-hose; born January 8, 1924, in Houston, Tex.; daughter of Robert (a salesman) and Sophia (Riesner) Lockart; married John Vlahos (a playwright), June 25, 1947; children: Michael, Melissa, Stephanie. *Education:* Attended Sullins College, 1941; University of Texas, B.F.A., 1945; Sarah Lawrence College, M.A., 1965. *Religion:* Unitarian Universalist. *Home:* 18 Crawford Rd., Westport, Conn. 06880.

CAREER: Norwalk Community College, Norwalk, Conn., 1967—, began as lecturer, currently assistant professor of anthropology.

WRITINGS: Human Beginnings, Viking, 1966; *African Beginnings,* Viking, 1967; *Battle-Ax People: Beginnings of Western Culture,* Viking, 1968; *New World Beginnings,* Viking, 1970; *Far Eastern Beginnings,* Viking, 1976.

*   *   *

VOEGELI, V(ictor) Jacque 1934-

PERSONAL: Surname is pronounced *Vo*-ge-lee; born December 21, 1934, in Jackson, Tenn.; son of Victor Jacque (a railroad roundhouse foreman) and Winnie (Lassiter) Voegeli; married Jean King, October 14, 1956; children: Jay, Charles. *Education:* Murray State College, B.S., 1956; Tulane University of Louisiana, Ph.D., 1965. *Reli-*

gion: Presbyterian. *Office:* Department of History, Vanderbilt University, Nashville, Tenn. 37235.

CAREER: Tulane University of Louisiana, New Orleans, instructor, 1963-65, assistant professor of history, 1965-67; Vanderbilt University, Nashville, Tenn., assistant professor, 1967-69, associate professor, 1969-73, professor of history and chairman of department, 1973—. *Military service:* U.S. Army, 1956-58; became first lieutenant. *Member:* Organization of American Historians, Southern Historical Association.

WRITINGS: Free but Not Equal: The Midwest and the Negro during the Civil War, University of Chicago Press, 1967.

WORK IN PROGRESS: Research in politics and race relations in the Civil War and Reconstruction.

*   *   *

VOLKART, Edmund H(owell) 1919-

PERSONAL: Born November 9, 1919, in Aberdeen, Md.; son of Ernest (a lawyer) and Edna (Ripken) Volkart; married Mary Ellen Drew, June 16, 1949; children: Karen Elaine, Kirsten. *Education:* St. John's College, Annapolis, Md., B.A., 1939; Yale University, M.A., 1942, Ph.D., 1947. *Home:* 750 Ululani St., Kailua, Hawaii 96734. *Office:* Department of Sociology, University of Hawaii, Honolulu, Hawaii.

CAREER: Syracuse University, Syracuse, N.Y., instructor in sociology, 1946-47; Yale University, New Haven, Conn., instructor, 1947-49, assistant professor of sociology, 1949-54; Stanford University, Stanford, Calif., assistant professor, 1954-55, associate professor, 1955-60, professor of sociology, 1960-62, director of program in medicine and behavioral sciences, 1959-62; Oregon State University, Corvallis, dean of Humanities and Social Sciences, 1962-63, dean of faculty, 1963-65; American Sociological Association, Washington, D.C., executive officer, 1965-70; University of Hawaii, Honolulu, professor of sociology, 1970—. Visiting research associate, Graduate School of Education, Harvard University, 1950-52; member of social science subcommittee and policy and planning board, National Institute of Mental Health, 1962-64. *Military service:* U.S. Naval Reserve, 1942-45; became lieutenant; received Legion of Merit. *Member:* American Sociological Association, American Association for the Advancement of Science, Sociological Research Association, Phi Kappa Phi.

WRITINGS: (Editor) *Social Behavior and Personality,* Social Science Research Council, 1951; (editor with W. Richard Scott) *Medical Care,* Wiley, 1966. Contributor to journals. National editor for social psychology, UNESCO Project in Social Sciences, 1957-64.

WORK IN PROGRESS: Writing on censorship, mass communication, and social theory.

AVOCATIONAL INTERESTS: Reading detective stories.

*   *   *

von HILDEBRAND, Alice 1923-

PERSONAL: Born March 11, 1923, in Brussels, Belgium; daughter of Henri and Marthe (van de Vorst) Jourdain; married Dietrich von Hildebrand (a professor emeritus of philosophy at Fordham University), July 16, 1959. *Education:* Manhattanville College, B.A., 1944; Fordham University, M.A., 1946, Ph.D., 1949. *Religion:* Roman Catholic.

Home: 43 Calton Rd., New Rochelle, N.Y. 10804. *Office:* Department of Philosophy, Hunter College of the City University of New York, New York, N.Y.

CAREER: Hunter College of the City University of New York, New York, N.Y., lecturer, 1947-57, instructor, 1957-60, assistant professor, 1960-64, associate professor, 1964-70, professor of philosophy, 1970—. *Awards, honors:* William O'Brien Award, 1963.

WRITINGS: (With husband, Dietrich von Hildebrand) *True Morality and Its Counterfeits,* McKay, 1955; (with D. von Hildebrand) *Graven Images,* McKay, 1957; (with D. von Hildebrand) *The Art of Living,* Franciscan Herald, 1965; (editor) *Greek Culture: The Adventure of the Human Spirit,* Braziller, 1966; *Philosophy of Religion,* Franciscan Herald, 1970; (contributor) *Wahrheit und Wert,* Verlag Josef Habbel, 1970; (contributor) *Rehabilietirung der Philosophie,* Verlag Josef Habbel, 1975.

SIDELIGHTS: Alice von Hildebrand speaks French, German, Italian, and Spanish. *Avocational interests:* Classical music, fine arts.

*   *   *

Von KLEMPERER, Klemens 1916-

PERSONAL: Born November 2, 1916, in Berlin, Germany; son of Herbert (an industrialist) and Frieda (Kuffner) Von Klemperer; married Elizabeth Lee Gallaher (a professor of English); children: Catharine, James. *Education:* Studied at French Gymnasium in Berlin, Germany, and at University of Vienna, 1934-38; Harvard University, M.A., 1940, Ph.D., 1949. *Home:* 23 Washington Ave., Northampton, Mass. 01060. *Office:* Department of History, Smith College, Northampton, Mass. 01060.

CAREER: Smith College, Northampton, Mass., instructor, 1949-50, assistant professor, 1950-56, associate professor, 1956-61, professor, 1961-69, L. Clark Seelye Professor of History, 1969—. Visiting summer professor, Stanford University, 1960; Fulbright professor, University of Bonn, 1963-64; overseas fellow, Churchill College, Cambridge University, 1973-74. *Military service:* U.S. Army, 1943-46; became first lieutenant. *Member:* American Historical Association. *Awards, honors:* Guggenheim fellow in Austria, 1957-58.

WRITINGS: Germany's New Conservatism: Its History and Dilemma in the Twentieth Century, Princeton University Press, 1957; *Mandate for Resistance: The Case of the German Opposition to Hitler,* Smith College Press, 1969; *Ignaz Seipel: A Christian Statesman in a Time of Crisis,* Princeton University Press, 1972. Contributor to professional journals.

WORK IN PROGRESS: A work on the "foreign policy" of the German resistance to Hitler.

*   *   *

VON SALIS, Jean-R. 1901-

PERSONAL: Born December 12, 1901, in Berne, Switzerland; son of Adolf (a physician) and Marie Pauline (Hunerwadel) Von Salis; married Elsie Huber, September 28, 1940; children: Thomas. *Education:* Studied at Universities of Montpellier, Berne, Berlin, and Paris, receiving M.A., University of Berne, and Docteur-es-lettres, University of Paris. *Religion:* Reformed Church. *Home:* Schloss Brunegg, 5505 Brunegg, Switzerland. *Office:* Swiss Institute of Technology, 8006 Zurich, Switzerland.

CAREER: With Syndic de la Presse Etrangere, Paris, France, 1930-35; Swiss Institute of Technology, Zurich, Switzerland, professor of history and political science, 1935-68. Guest professor at University of Vienna, 1947, and University of Lausanne, 1965-66. Member of Swiss National Commission for UNESCO, 1946-64, University Reform Commission in Germany, 1948, and Swiss National Foundation for Scientific Research, 1952-64; chairman of Pro Helvetia Foundation, 1952-64. *Member:* Association of Swiss Writers. *Awards, honors:* Prize Academie Francaise, 1933; honorary Dr. hic., University of Geneva, 1959.

WRITINGS: Sismondi, 1773-1842, two volumes, H. Champion (Paris), 1932, new edition V and S (Geneva), 1973; *Fritz Wotruba,* Amstutz & Herdeg (Zurich), 1948; *Weltgeschichte der Neusten Zeit,* three volumes, Orell Fussli (Zurich), 1951-60; *Im Lauf der Jahre,* Orell Fussli, 1962; *R. M. Rilke: The Years in Switzerland,* University of California Press, 1964; *Weltchronik 1939-45,* Orell Fussli, 1966; *Switzerland and Europe,* Oswald Wolff (London), 1971; *Geschichke und Politik,* Orell Fussli, 1971; *Grewhue berschreitungen,* Orell Fussli, 1975.

AVOCATIONAL INTERESTS: Music (particularly the piano).

* * *

VORSPAN, Albert 1924-

PERSONAL: Born February 12, 1924, in St. Paul, Minn.; son of Ben and Fanny Vorspan; married Shirley Nitchun; children: Charles, Roberta, Kenneth, Deborah. *Education:* New York University, B.A., 1946. *Politics:* Democrat. *Religion:* Jewish. *Home:* 134 Harris Ave., Hewlett, Long Island, N.Y. *Office:* Union of American Hebrew Congregations, 838 Fifth Ave., New York, N.Y. 10021.

CAREER: Union of American Hebrew Congregations, New York, N.Y., director of Commission on Social Action, 1953—. Democratic candidate for Congress from New York's Fifth District, 1968. *Military service:* U.S. Navy, World War II; became lieutenant junior grade.

WRITINGS: (With Eugene J. Lipman) *Justice and Judaism,* Union of American Hebrew Congregations, 1956; *Giants of Justice,* Union of American Hebrew Congregations, 1960; (with Lipman) *A Tale of Ten Cities,* Union of American Hebrew Congregations, 1962; *Jewish Values and Social Crisis: A Casebook for Social Action,* Union of American Hebrew Congregations, 1968; *My Rabbi Doesn't Make House Calls,* Doubleday, 1969; *To Do Justly: A Junior Casebook for Social Action,* Union of American Hebrew Congregations, 1969; *So Your Kids Are Revolting . . .?,* Doubleday, 1970; *Mazel Tov! You're Middle-Aged,* Doubleday, 1974; *I'm Okay, You're a Pain in the Neck,* Doubleday, 1976.

* * *

VOSS, Carl Hermann 1910-

PERSONAL: Born December 8, 1910, in Pittsburgh, Pa.; son of Carl August (a clergyman) and Lucy (Wilms) Voss; married Dorothy Katherine Grote, November 25, 1940 (divorced, 1957); married Phyllis MacKenzie Gierlotka (faculty member of University of Northern Florida), May 9, 1959; children: (first marriage) Carlyn Grote (Mrs. Harold Iuzzolino); stepchildren: Christine Elisabeth Gierlotka. *Education:* University of Pittsburgh, B.A., 1931, Ph.D., 1942; Union Theological Seminary, New York, N.Y., M.Div., 1935; also studied at Yale Divinity School, 1938-

40, International People's College, Elsinore, Denmark, and University of Geneva. *Politics:* Democrat. *Home:* 7783 Point Vincente Ct., Baymeadows, Jacksonville, Fla. 32216. *Office:* Edward Waters College, 1658 Kings Rd., Jacksonville, Fla. 32209.

CAREER: Protestant clergyman. Minister in Raleigh, N.C., 1935-38; Cheshire Academy, Cheshire, Conn., chaplain, 1938-40; Smithfield Congregational Church, Pittsburgh, Pa., 1940-43; executive secretary of Christian Council of Palestine, 1943-46; extension secretary of Church Peace Union (now Council of Religion and International Affairs) and World Alliance for International Friendship through Religion, 1943-49; chairman of executive council, American Christian Palestine Committee, 1946-56; minister of Flatbush Unitarian Church, Brooklyn, N.Y., 1952-56, and New England Congregational Church, Saratoga Springs, N.Y., 1957-64; St. Lawrence University, Canton, N.Y., visiting professor of theology and history of religions, 1964-65; editor, Excalibur Books, 1964—; Brandeis University, Waltham, Mass., Messill research associate, 1965-67; Edward Waters College, Jacksonville, Fla., professor of philosophy and religion and chairman of humanities division, 1973—. Lecturer at New School for Social Research, 1948-56, Skidmore College, 1960-61, 1965-66, and Hebrew University of Jerusalem, 1966, 1973, and 1976; scholar-in-residence, Ecumenical Institute for Advanced Theological Studies, Jerusalem, Israel, 1976.

WRITINGS: Answers on the Palestine Question, American Christian Palestine Committee, 1947, 5th edition published as *The Palestine Problem Today,* Beacon Press, 1953; (editor) *The Universal God* (interfaith anthology), World Publishing, 1953; (with Theodore Huebener) *This Is Israel,* Philosophical Library, 1956; *Rabbi and Minister* (the friendship of Stephen S. Wise and John Haynes Holmes), World Publishing, 1964; *In Search of Meaning: Living Religions of the World,* World Publishing, 1968; (editor) *Stephen S. Wise: Servant of the People* (letters), Jewish Publication Society, 1969; (editor) John Haynes Holmes, *A Summons Unto Men: An Anthology of Writings,* Simon & Schuster, 1971; (compiler) *Quotations of Courage and Vision: A Source Book for Speaking, Writing, and Meditation,* Association Press, 1972. Editor, *World Alliance Newsletter,* 1945-48, and *Land Reborn,* 1949-56.

WORK IN PROGRESS: American Christian Interest in the Holy Land, three volumes; *Theologians I Have Known.*

SIDELIGHTS: Carl Voss has traveled widely in North America, Europe, Africa, and the Middle East, visiting the Middle East area fourteen times in the past thirty years.

* * *

VRBA, Rudolf 1924-

PERSONAL: Born September 11, 1924, in Topolcany, Czechoslovakia; now a British and Canadian citizen; married Gertrude Sidon (a physician), 1949 (divorced, 1956); children: Helena, Zuzana. *Education:* Czech Technical University, Ing. Chem., 1949, Dr. tech. Sc., 1951; Czechoslovak Academy of Science, C.Sc., 1956. *Politics:* Independent. *Office:* Department of Pharmacology, Faculty of Medicine, University of British Columbia, Vancouver 8, British Columbia, Canada.

CAREER: Ministry of Health, Prague, Czechoslovakia, member of scientific staff, Institute of Industrial Hygiene and Occupational Diseases, 1953-58; Ministry of Agriculture, Israel, staff member of Veterinary Institute, 1958-60;

Medical Research Council, Carshalton, England, staff member of Neuropsychiatric Research Unit, 1960-67; University of British Columbia, Vancouver, associate professor of pharmacology, 1967—. Visiting lecturer on pharmacology at Harvard University and Massachusetts General Hospital, 1973-75. *Military service:* Czechoslovak Insurrection Army; received Order of Insurrection, Medal for Bravery, Medal of Czechoslovak Partyzan Honor. *Member:* British Biochemical Society, Biochemical Society of Canada, International Neurochemical Society, Society of Authors (London), Authors Club (London). *Awards, honors:* Rockefeller grant, 1960-62, for research in neurochemistry.

WRITINGS: (Contributor) D. Richter, editor, *Metabolism of the Nervous System,* Pergamon, 1957; (contributor) F. Brucke, editor, *Biochemistry of the Central Nervous System,* Pergamon, 1959; (contributor) J. Folch, editor, *Chemical Pathology of the Nervous System,* Pergamon, 1961; *I Cannot Forgive,* Gibbs & Phillips, 1963, Grove, 1964; *Factory of Death,* Corgi, 1964; (contributor) A. Lajtha, editor, *Protein Metabolism of the Nervous System,* Plenum, 1970. Author, with A. Kleinzeller and J. Malek, of 390-page monograph, "Manometric Methods and Their Application in Biology and Biochemistry," published in *Statni zdravotnicke nakladatelstvi v Praze,* 1954. Contributor of more than fifty research papers, articles, and reviews to scientific journals in fields of biochemistry, neurochemistry, and immunochemistry.

WORK IN PROGRESS: Research in the metabolism of glucose in the brain and other organs; biochemical aspects of cancer; tumor immunology.

SIDELIGHTS: At eighteen Vrba was arrested by the Nazis and held prisoner in the Majdanek and Auschwitz extermination camps, 1942-44. He escaped from Auschwitz in April, 1944, carrying a detailed report on extermination camps and policy, which was delivered to Allen Dulles in Switzerland. Vrba speaks and reads Russian, German, Hungarian, and Polish. *I Cannot Forgive* was also published in Germany.

BIOGRAPHICAL/CRITICAL SOURCES: R. Manvell and H. Fraenkel, *The Incomparable Crime,* Heinemann, 1967; Yuri Suhl, *They Fought Back,* Crown, 1967.

* * *

VREELAND, Jane D. 1915-

PERSONAL: Born August 23, 1915, in Flocktown, N.J.; daughter of George W. and Margaret (Stevens) Vreeland. *Education:* Newark State College, B.S., 1943; Columbia University, M.A., 1947, and additional study. *Home:* 39 Mulberry St., New Paltz, N.Y. 12561. *Office:* State University of New York College at New Paltz, New Paltz, N.Y. 12561.

CAREER: Teacher in Warren and Essex Counties, N.J.; teacher in New Britain, Conn., 1945-48; helping teacher, New Jersey State Department of Education, 1948-51; Lincoln School, Pearl River, N.Y., supervisor, 1956-65, principal, 1965-66; State University of New York College at New Paltz, assistant professor of education, 1966—. Supervisor of student teachers in Gloucester, England, for two months annually, 1973-75. *Member:* Delta Kappa Gamma.

WRITINGS: (With Wann and Conklin) *Learning About Our Country* (elementary textbook), Allyn & Bacon, 1964.

WADDINGTON, Miriam 1917-
(E. B. Merritt)

PERSONAL: Born December 23, 1917, in Winnipeg, Manitoba, Canada; daughter of Isidore (a small manufacturer) and Musha (Dobrushin) Dworkin; married Patrick Donald Waddington, July 5, 1939 (divorced, 1965); children: Marcus Frushard, Jonathan John. *Education:* University of Toronto, B.A., 1939, Diploma in Social Work, 1942; University of Pennsylvania, M.S.W., 1945. *Home:* 32 Yewfield Crescent, Don Mills, Toronto, Ontario, Canada M3B 2Y6. *Office:* Department of English, York University, Toronto, Ontario, Canada.

CAREER: Jewish Child Welfare Bureau, Montreal, Quebec, assistant director, 1945-46; McGill University, School of Social Work, Montreal, field instructor, 1946-49; Montreal Children's Hospital, Montreal, staff member, 1952-54; John Howard Society, Montreal, staff member, 1955-57; Jewish Family Bureau, Montreal, caseworker, 1957-60; North York Family Service, Toronto, Ontario, casework supervisor, 1960-62; York University, Toronto, 1964—, began as assistant professor, currently professor of English and Canadian literature. *Member:* Modern Language Association of America, International P.E.N., Otto Rank Association. *Awards, honors:* Canada Council senior fellowship in creative writing, 1962-63; Canada Council academic grant, 1968-69; Senior Arts fellowship, 1971-72; D.Litt., Lakehead University, 1975.

WRITINGS: Green World, First Statement Press, 1945; *The Second Silence,* Ryerson, 1955; *The Season's Lovers,* Ryerson, 1958; *The Glass Trumpet,* Oxford University Press, 1966; (author of poems accompanying the photographs) *Call Them Canadians,* Queen's Printer, 1968; *Say Yes* (poetry), Oxford University Press, 1969; *A. M. Klein* (criticism), Copp, 1970; *Driving Home: Poems New and Selected,* Oxford University Press, 1972; *The Dream Telescope* (poetry), Routledge & Kegan Paul, 1973; (editor) *John Sutherland: Essays, Controversies, Poems,* New American Library, 1973; (editor) *The Collected Poems of A. M. Klein,* McGraw, 1974. Writer of radio scripts on Chekhov and Poe. Contributor of reviews, stories, and articles to magazines and newspapers, including *Canadian Literature, Tamarack Review, Queen's Quarterly, Canadian Forum.*

WORK IN PROGRESS: The Price of Gold, poems; *Collected Criticism by Miriam Waddington.*

SIDELIGHTS: Miriam Waddington is fluent in Yiddish and reads French, German, and Hebrew.

BIOGRAPHICAL/CRITICAL SOURCES: Poetry, February, 1968.

* * *

WAGATSUMA, Hiroshi 1927-

PERSONAL: Born June 17, 1927, in Tokyo, Japan; son of Sakae (a professor) and Midori (Suzuki) Wagatsuma; married Reiko Ichimura, August 18, 1954; children: Erika, Julia. *Education:* University of Tokyo, Bungakushi (M.A. equivalent), 1953, diploma from Graduate Research Division (Ph.D. equivalent), 1958; University of Michigan, M.A., 1957; Nihon University, Doctor of Letters, 1968. *Permanent address:* 1-17-6 Shakujii, Nerima-ku, Tokyo, Japan. *Current address:* 3168 Dona Sofia Dr., Studio City, Calif. 91604. *Office:* Department of Anthropology, University of California, Los Angeles, Calif. 90024.

CAREER: Konan University, Kobe, Japan, assistant professor of social science, 1958-61; Research and Training Institute for Family Court Research Officers, Tokyo, Japan, lecturer and research associate, 1961-62; University of California, Berkeley, assistant research psychologist, Institute of Human Development, 1962-66; University of Hawaii, Honolulu, research psychologist, Social Science Research Institute, 1966-67; University of Pittsburgh, Pittsburgh, Pa., associate professor, 1967-69, professor of sociology, anthropology, and psychiatry, 1969-74; University of California, Los Angeles, professor of anthropology, 1974—. Marriage counselor, Kobe Family Court, 1960-61; lecturer at Kobe National University, 1960-61, School of Social Welfare, University of California, 1963-65; visiting senior lecturer, Chinese University of Hong Kong, 1969-71. *Member:* American Anthropological Association, Association for Asian Studies, Japan Psychoanalytic Association, Japanese Association of Social Psychology, Japanese Society of Ethnology.

WRITINGS: (With Takao Sofue) *Sekai no Kokumin Sei* (title means "National Characters in the World"), Kodansha, 1959; *Ai no Ninshiki ni Tsuite-Kekkon no Kofuku* (title means "Psychological Analysis of Marital Life"), Kobunsha, 1959.

(Editor) *Ningen no Kodo* (title means "Human Behavior"), Nakayama Shoten, 1960; *Jiga no Shaki Shinri* (title means "Social Psychology of the Self"), Seishin Shobo, 1964; (with George DeVos) *Japan's Invisible Race: Caste in Culture and Personality,* University of California Press, 1966; (with T. Yoneyama) *Henken no Kozo-Nihon-jin no Jinshu Taido* (title means "The Structure of Prejudice: The Racial Attitudes of the Japanese"), Nihon Hoso Shuppan Kyokai, 1967; (with S. Kawaguchi) *California Personality Inventory* (in Japanese), Seishin Shobo, 1968.

(Translator with Yuzuru Sasaki) Harold Isaacs, *Kami no Kora* (title means "Children of God"), Shinehosha, 1970; (translator) Karen Horney, *Gendai no Shinkeisho teki,* Seishin Shobo, 1973; *Hiko Shonen no Jirei Kenkyu* (title means "Case Studies of Juvenile Delinquents"), Seishin Shobo, 1973; (with Hiroko Hara) *Shitsuke* (title means "Child Training"), Kobundo, 1974; (with George DeVos) *Heritage of Endurance,* University of California Press, Volume I: *Cultural Continuities in Urban Japan,* 1976, Volume II: *Family Cohesion vs. Delinquency in Urban Japan,* 1976.

*   *   *

WAGGONER, Hyatt H. 1913-

PERSONAL: Born November 19, 1913, in Pleasant Valley, N.Y.; married Louise Feather, June 26, 1937; children: Veronica (Mrs. Edward D. Johnson), Jane (Mrs. Christopher Lloyd). *Education:* Middlebury College, A.B., 1935; University of Chicago, M.A., 1936; Ohio State University, Ph.D., 1942. *Politics:* "Radical and transcendental." *Religion:* Episcopalian. *Home:* 34 Lincoln Ave., Barrington, R.I. 02806. *Office:* Brown University, Providence, R.I. 02912.

CAREER: University of Omaha, Omaha, Neb., instructor in English, 1939-42; University of Kansas City, Kansas City, Mo., instructor, 1942-44, assistant professor, 1944-47, associate professor, 1947-50, professor of English, 1950-56, chairman of department, 1952-56; Brown University, Providence, R.I., professor of American literature, 1956—, chairman of American civilization program, 1960—. *Member:* Modern Language Association of America, American Studies Association. *Awards, honors:* M.A., Brown University, 1957; Guggenheim fellow, 1963-64.

WRITINGS: (With Fred A. Dudley, Norbert Fuerst, and Francis R. Johnson) *The Relations of Literature and Science: A Selected Bibliography, 1930-1949,* State College of Washington, 1949; *The Heel of Elohim: Science and Values in Modern American Poetry,* University of Oklahoma Press, 1950; (editor) *Nathaniel Hawthorne: Selected Tales and Sketches,* Rinehart, 1950, revised edition, 1962; *Hawthorne: A Critical Study,* Harvard University Press, 1955, revised and enlarged edition, 1963; *William Faulkner: From Jefferson to the World,* University of Kentucky Press, 1959.

Nathaniel Hawthorne, University of Minnesota Press, 1962; (editor) Hawthorne, *The House of the Seven Gables* (with new text based on the manuscript), Houghton, 1964; (editor with George Monteiro) Hawthorne, *The Scarlet Letter* (facsimile text), Chandler Publishing, 1967; *American Poets from the Puritans to the Present,* Houghton, 1968; *Emerson as Poet,* Princeton University Press, 1975.

Contributor: *The Tragic Vision and the Christian Faith,* edited by Nathan Scott, Association Press, 1957; *Interpretations of American Literature,* edited by Charles Feidelson and Paul Brodtkorb, Oxford University Press, 1959; *A Scarlet Letter Handbook,* edited by Seymour L. Gross, Wadsworth, 1960; *The Scarlet Letter: An Annotated Text* [with] *Backgrounds and Sources* [and] *Essays in Criticism,* edited by Edward Sculley Bradley, Richmond Beatty, and E. Hudson Long, Norton, 1962; *A Casebook on the Hawthorne Question,* edited by Agnes Donohue, Crowell, 1962; *Hawthorne Centenary Essays,* edited by R. H. Pearce, Ohio State University Press, 1964; *American Literary Masters,* Holt, 1965.

Hawthorne, edited by A. N. Kaul, Prentice-Hall, 1966; *Faulkner,* edited by Robert Penn Warren, Prentice-Hall, 1966; *Forster,* edited by Malcolm Bradbury, Prentice-Hall, 1966; *Mansions of the Spirit,* edited by George A. Panichas, Hawthorn, 1967; *Twentieth-Century Interpretations of "The Sound and the Fury,"* edited by Michael Cowan, Prentice-Hall, 1968; *Six American Novelists,* edited by Richard Foster, University of Minnesota Press, 1968. Contributor to *American Literary Scholarship: An Annual,* 1963—, and to *Explicator Encyclopedia,* 1966; more than fifty articles and reviews have been published in literary journals.

WORK IN PROGRESS: Further work on Hawthorne and the Hawthorne tradition.

SIDELIGHTS: In *American Poets from the Puritans to the Present,* Waggoner attempts "to discover what is American about our poetry . . . [and] to look at representative poets in terms of their own values," writes a *Virginia Quarterly Review* critic. He adds that "Emerson's essay, 'The Poet,' emerges as the central document and Emerson himself as the central figure in our poetry."

AVOCATIONAL INTERESTS: Walking on the beach in Rhode Island and on the Long Trail in Vermont; gardening; collecting and studying nature books.

BIOGRAPHICAL/CRITICAL SOURCES: Virginia Quarterly Review, spring, 1968; Christian Science Monitor, April 25, 1968; Carleton Miscellany, winter, 1969.

*   *   *

WAGNER, C(harles) Peter 1930-
(Epafrodito, Lewis Graham Underwood)

PERSONAL: Born August 15, 1930, in New York, N.Y.; son of C. Graham (a buyer) and Mary (Lewis) Wagner;

married Doris Mueller (a missionary), October 15, 1950; children: Karen, Ruth, Rebecca. *Education:* Rutgers University, B.S., 1952; Fuller Theological Seminary, B.D., 1955, M.A., 1968; Princeton Theological Seminary, Th.M., 1962; University of Southern California, Ph.D. candidate. *Politics:* Democrat. *Home address:* Box 989, Pasadena, Calif. 91102.

CAREER: Congregational clergyman, 1955—; Instituto Biblico del Oriente, San Jose, Bolivia, director, 1956-61; Instituto Biblico Emaus, Cochabamba, Bolivia, professor and director, 1962-71; Andes Evangelical Mission, Cochabamba, Bolivia, associate director, 1964-71; Fuller Theological Seminary, Pasadena, Calif., professor of church growth and Latin American studies, 1971—; Fuller Evangelistic Association, Pasadena, president for missions and evangelism, 1971—. *Member:* Phi Beta Kappa.

WRITINGS: (With Joseph S. McCullough) *The Condor of the Jungle,* Revell, 1966; *Defeat of the Bird God,* Zondervan, 1967; *Latin American Theology,* Eerdmans, 1969; *The Protestant Movement in Bolivia,* William Carey Library, 1970; (with Ralph Covell) *An Extension Seminary Primer,* William Carey Library, 1971; *A Turned-On Church in an Uptight World,* Zondervan, 1971; *Frontiers in Missionary Strategy,* Moody, 1972; (editor) *Church/Mission Tensions Today,* Moody, 1972; *Look Out! The Pentecostals Are Coming,* Creation House, 1973; *Stop the World, I Want to Get On,* Regal Books, 1974; *Your Church Can Grow: Seven Vital Signs of a Healthy Church,* Regal Books, 1976. Contributor, at times under pseudonym, to religious periodicals. Former editor, *Vision Evangelicax* (Cochabamba), *Pensamiento Cristiano* (Cordova, Argentina), and *Andean Outlook.*

WORK IN PROGRESS: A book on the ethical justification of culturally homogeneous churches in a pluralistic society, entitled *Church Growth This Side of the Melting Pot.*

* * *

WAGNER, Jean Pierre 1919-

PERSONAL: Born October 25, 1919, in Bitche, France; son of Mathieu (a pharmacist) and Marie (Delles) Wagner; married Ghislaine Baillon, September 1, 1942; children: Marie-Odile, Elisabeth. *Education:* Birmingham-Southern College, B.A., 1938; Universite de Strasbourg, licence-es-lettres, 1939, diplome d'etudes superieures, 1939, agregation, 1945; Universite de Paris, doctorat-es-lettres, 1963. *Religion:* Roman Catholic. *Home:* 36 Clos de Franquieres, 38-Biviers, France. *Office:* Faculte des Lettres, 38-Grenoble, France.

CAREER: Ecole Nationale d'Ingenieurs, Strasbourg, France, professor of English, 1945-59; Universite de Grenoble, Grenoble, France, professor of American literature and civilization, 1959—.

WRITINGS: Les Poetes negres des Etats-Unis, Istra, 1963, translation by Kenneth Douglas published as *Black Poets of the United States,* University of Illinois Press, 1973; (editor with Sim Copans) *J'entends l'Amerique qui chante,* Nouveaux Horizons (Paris), 1963; *Runyonese: The Mind and Craft of Damon Runyon,* Stechert-Hafner, 1965.

WORK IN PROGRESS: Research on Negro writers of the United States and Southern writers, especially Flannery O'Connor; also research on American slang and dialects.

SIDELIGHTS: Wagner is fluent in English and German, and has some knowledge of Italian, Spanish, and Russian.

WAGONER, Walter D. 1918-

PERSONAL: Born December 15, 1918, in St. Louis, Mo.; son of Stanley B. and Donelia S. Wagoner; married Mariana Parcells, March 12, 1942; children: Walter, Jr., Lynda (Mrs. Fredric Bogel), Diane. *Education:* Yale University, B.A., 1941, B.D., 1945; University of Chicago Divinity School, graduate study in church history, 1950-52; Princeton Theological Seminary, Th.M., 1958. *Home:* 137 Middlesex Rd., Chestnut Hill, Mass. 02167.

CAREER: Ordained minister of Congregational Christian Church (now United Church of Christ), 1945; Yale University, New Haven, Conn., chaplain, 1946-47; Colby College, Waterville, Me., chaplain and assistant professor, 1947-50; Northwestern University, Evanston, Ill., university chaplain, 1952-55; Fund for Theological Education, Princeton, N.J., executive director, 1955-67; Graduate Theological Union, Berkeley, Calif., associate dean of academic affairs, 1967-68; Boston Theological Institute, Cambridge, Mass., director, 1968—. Lecturer at San Francisco Theological Seminary, Drew University and Boston University, 1964, United Theological Seminary, 1965, and other seminaries. Member of U.S. Conference, Committee on Information and Support, World Council of Churches, 1960—. American secretary of summer session, Mansfield College, Oxford University, 1963—; member of board of advisers, Institute for Educational Planning, Inc., 1966—. *Military service:* U.S. Marine Corps, chaplain, 1945-46. *Member:* National Conference of Fellowship Administrators (co-chairman, 1961-63), Yale Club of Princeton (secretary, 1957-65). *Awards, honors:* Honorary degrees from Pacific School of Religion and McGill University, both 1967, and College of the Holy Cross, 1971.

WRITINGS: (Co-editor and contributor) *Unity in Mid-Career,* Macmillan, 1963; *Bachelor of Divinity,* Association Press, 1963; *The Seminary: Protestant and Catholic,* Sheed, 1966; (co-editor and contributor) *Horizons of Theological Education,* American Association of Theological Schools, 1966; *Bittersweet Grace,* World Publishing, 1967; *Say a Good Word for Jesus,* United Church Press, 1973. Contributor to *Christian Century,* and other religious and educational journals.

* * *

WAHLKE, John C(harles) 1917-

PERSONAL: Born October 29, 1917, in Cincinnati, Ohio; son of Albert B. C. and Clara (Ernst) Wahlke; married Virginia Joan Higgins, December 1, 1943; children: Janet, Dale. *Education:* Harvard University, B.A., 1939, M.A., 1947, Ph.D., 1952. *Home:* 1822 Morningside Dr., Iowa City, Iowa 52240. *Office:* University of Iowa, Iowa City, Iowa 52240.

CAREER: Traffic clerk for industrial firms, 1939-42; Amherst College, Amherst, Mass., instructor, 1944-51, assistant professor of political science, 1951-53; Vanderbilt University, Nashville, Tenn., assistant professor, 1953-55, associate professor, 1955-61, professor of political science, 1961-63; State University of New York at Buffalo, professor of political science, 1963-66, chairman of department, 1965-66; University of Iowa, Iowa City, professor of political science, 1966-71; State University of New York at Sunny Brook, professor of political science, 1971-73; University of Iowa, professor of political science, 1973—. Visiting professor at University of Massachusetts, 1951-52, and University of California, Berkeley, 1958-59. *Military service:* U.S. Army, observation pilot, Field Artillery,

1942-45; became captain; received Air Medal with two oak leaf clusters.

MEMBER: American Political Science Association (member of executive committee, 1964-65; member of council, 1964-66), International Political Science Association, American Association of University Professors, Midwest Conference of Political Scientists, Southern Political Science Association, Phi Beta Kappa. *Awards, honors:* Social Science Research Council faculty grant, 1955.

WRITINGS: (Editor) *The Causes of the American Revolution,* Heath, 1950, 3rd edition, 1973; (editor) *Loyalty in a Democratic State,* Heath, 1952, 3rd edition, 1973; (editor with H. Eulau) *Legislative Behavior,* Free Press of Glencoe, 1959; (with Eulau, W. Buchanan, and L. Ferguson) *The Legislative System,* Wiley, 1962; (co-editor and co-author) *Government and Politics,* Random House, 1966, 2nd edition, 1971; (editor with Bernard E. Brown) *The American Political System,* Dorsey, 1967, revised edition, 1973; (editor with Samuel C. Patterson) *Comparative Legislative Behavior,* Wiley, 1972; (editor) William O. Chittick, *The Analysis of Foreign Policy Outputs,* C. E. Merrill, 1975.

WORK IN PROGRESS: The Modern Theory of Representation, a theory-and-research monograph.

* * *

WAITLEY, Douglas 1927-

PERSONAL: Born November 28, 1927, in Evanston, Ill.; son of Douglas and Marian Waitley; married Mary Avery, April 23, 1960; children: Jeff. *Education:* Northwestern University, B.S., 1949, M.A., 1956. *Home:* 2650 Hillside Lane, Evanston, Ill. 60201. *Office:* Dale's Employment Service, Inc., 1015 Central, Evanston, Ill.

CAREER: Currently president of Dale's Employment Service, Inc., Evanston, Ill. *Military service:* U.S. Navy, 1952-54.

WRITINGS: Portrait of the Midwest, Abelard, 1964; *My Backyard: A Living World of Nature,* David White, 1970; *Roads of Destiny: The Trails that Shaped a Nation,* Luce, 1970; *The War Makers: Twentieth Century Strongmen,* Luce, 1971.

WORK IN PROGRESS: America at War: The Twentieth Century.

* * *

WAKEFIELD, Dan 1932-

PERSONAL: Born May 21, 1932, in Indianapolis, Ind.; son of Ben H. (a pharmacist) and Brucie (Ridge) Wakefield. *Education:* Attended Indiana University, 1950-51; Columbia University, B.A., 1955. *Agent:* Knox Burger, 39½ Washington Square South, New York, N.Y. 10012.

CAREER: Princeton Packet, Princeton, N.J., news editor, 1955; Columbia University, New York City, research assistant to Professor C. Wright Mills, 1955; *Nation,* New York City, staff writer, 1956-59; free-lance writer, 1959—. Staff member, Bread Loaf Writer's Conference, 1964 and 1966; visiting lecturer at University of Massachusetts, 1965-67, University of Illinois, 1968, and University of Iowa, 1972. *Member:* Authors Guild of America, P.E.N., Beacon Hill Civic Association. *Awards, honors:* DeVoto fellowship to Bread Loaf Writers Conference, 1958; Neiman fellowship, Harvard University, 1963-64; Short story prize, National Council of the Arts, 1968; Rockefeller Foundation grant in imaginative writing, 1969; National Book Award nomination, 1970, for *Going All the Way.*

WRITINGS: Island in the City: The World of Spanish Harlem (nonfiction), Houghton, 1959; *Revolt in the South* (nonfiction), Grove, 1961; (editor) *The Addict: An Anthology,* Fawcett, 1963; *Between the Lines* (nonfiction), New American Library, 1967; *Supernation at Peace and War* (nonfiction), Atlantic Monthly Press, 1968; (contributor) Robert Manning and Michael Janeway, editors, *Who We Are: An Atlantic Chronicle of the United States and Vietnam,* Atlantic Monthly Press, 1969; *Going All the Way* (novel; Literary Guild selection), Delacorte, 1970; *Starting Over* (novel; Literary Guild selection), Delacorte, 1973. Short stories included in *Best American Stories of 1966,* and *American Literary Anthology #2;* contributor of numerous articles, essays, reviews, and short stories to *Atlantic, Esquire, Commentary, Playboy,* and other periodicals. Contributing editor, *Atlantic Monthly,* 1969—.

SIDELIGHTS: An *Atlantic* editor once called Wakefield "one of the best of a rare and vanishing breed . . . [and] an independent writer-reporter who finds the delicate balance between head and heart." In his books and numerous published articles, Wakefield has scrutinized his environment in order to "tell it like it is" in what a *Time* reporter calls "less an eyewitness report than a very private vision."

His first book, *Island in the City,* is the story of the world of Spanish Harlem ("one of the world's worst slums") where he lived for six months in "personal immersion in the major experiences of his subjects," according to A. D. Vidich. In his book, says Elihu Katz, "Wakefield . . . tries (and sometimes too hard) to be poetic and to communicate insight into how it feels to be on the night coach from Puerto Rico, at a spiritualist seance, on a drug cure, in a sweatshop. . . . He tries to communicate his sadness over all those who do not understand." Critics speak of his "warmth" as well as his "ability to disturb"; and he has been praised as an "honest and legitimately angry young man." According to Harrison Salisbury, "some of the social workers who devote themselves to the Puerto Ricans and some of the sociologists who have made long and elaborate studies . . . may know Spanish Harlem more comprehensively than Mr. Wakefield. But no one—with the possible exception of Christopher Rand—. . . has captured the spirit of the Puerto Rican in New York so warmly and so sensitively."

In his later books, and particularly in *Supernation at Peace and War,* Wakefield continues to be "an entertaining, often rueful, and revealing guide," according to R. R. Lingeman, as "he conducts us through his journalistic quest." Originally an assignment from the *Atlantic,* Wakefield traveled throughout the United States for four months and his article was published in the March, 1968, issue, with the subtitle, "being certain observations, depositions, testimonies and graffiti gathered on a one-man fact-and-fantasy-finding tour of the most powerful nation in the world." Wakefield adopts what David Cort sees as "a classical satirical tone: . . . an innocent credulous voice producing effects of deadpan irony." He is concerned with the U.S.A. in 1968, "at war with itself and with enemies half way round the world." Concerning these "two wars," Wakefield divides U.S. society into three major attitudinal blocks: "Protest, Patriotism, and Pacification." Florence Casey defines these groups as "divided quite naturally from the several hundred people interviewed: 1. Those who are 'against' (the war, suburban life, black poverty, Mother, and The Way Things Are); 2. Those who were 'for' (the war, suburbia, black impoverishment, Mother, and The Way Things Are); and 3. Those who were uncertain (about some, or all, of the same items)." A *Time* reviewer comments: "The well-fed, worried face of supernation deserves a better effort." Thomas Laske, however, writes: "The scenes in this book may not always be familiar, but the arguments will be. They are part of a continuing dialogue going on all over the country. His book is a handy and inviting way of becoming part of it."

Commenting on Wakefield's journalistic style, Robert Phelps writes: "As one of our very best journalists in the past decade, Dan Wakefield has been conspicuous for two virtues: a novelist's instinct for the right detail . . . and then something even rarer, an intimate, yet never merely egocentric, scale of observation." In a review of Wakefield's first novel, *Going All the Way*, Robert Kirsch notes that the book is "filled with a kind of wry humor and irony which comes not so much from exaggeration as from keen observation of life. . . . But beneath the humor is the sharp sadness of life that is no life at all, bound by bias, crippled by reaction, and which could only bring the desire for flight and escape, for new beginnings." Edgar Z. Friedenberg believes that "although it is not a very good novel, . . . it is nevertheless a very good book. . . . His touch throughout the book is deft and sure, and there is none of the awkwardness of a writer who sets out to do something and fails."

Going All the Way has been published in Britain, Japan, and Italy; *Starting Over* has been published in Finland and Norway.

BIOGRAPHICAL/CRITICAL SOURCES: Kirkus Service, December 1, 1958, April 15, 1968; *Bookmark*, February, 1959; *New York Herald Tribune Book Review*, February 15, 1959; *New York Times Book Review*, February 15, 1959, May 1, 1966, June 8, 1968, August 9, 1970; *Saturday Review*, March 7, 1959; *Booklist*, March 15, 1959; *Christian Century*, March 25, 1959; *Nation*, May 2, 1959, November 11, 1968; *Catholic World*, June, 1959; *American Anthropology*, December, 1959; *American Journal of Sociology*, March, 1960; *America*, May 14, 1966; *National Review*, May 17, 1966, July 30, 1968; *Book Week*, May 22, 1966; *Atlantic*, June, 1966, August, 1970; *Commonweal*, June 10, 1966, June 12, 1968; *Christian Science Monitor*, June 16, 1966, June 13, 1968; *Reporter*, June 16, 1966; *Commentary*, 1966; *Time*, February 23, 1968, June 14, 1968; *Publisher's Weekly*, April 22, 1968; *Washington Post*, August 26, 1970; *New York Review of Books*, November 5, 1970.

* * *

WALIULLAH, Syed 1922-

PERSONAL: Born August 15, 1922, in Noakhali, India (now Pakistan); son of Syed Ahmedullah and N-Nissa Begum; married Anne-Marie Thibaud, September, 1955; children: Simine, Iraj. *Education:* Calcutta University, M.A., 1945. *Religion:* Islam. *Residence:* Paris, France.

CAREER: Writer. *Awards, honors:* Adamjee Prize (Pakistan); other awards from Bengali Academy.

*WRITINGS—*In Bengali, except as noted: *Nayanchara*, Purvasha, 1945; *Lalshalu*, Comrade, 1949, translation by Quaiser Saeed, Anne-Marie Thibaud (Waliullah's wife), Jeffrey Gibian, and Malik Khayyam published as *Tree Without Roots*, Chatto & Windus, 1967; *Bahi Pir*, Bengali Academy, 1955; *Tarangavanga*, Bengali Academy, 1958; *Lal Chadar* (in Urdu), Writers' Guild (Pakistan), 1961; *Chander Amabasya*, Naoroze Kitabistan, 1964; *Suranga*,

Bengali Academy, 1964; *Diu Tira o anyanya galpa*, Naoroze Kitabistan, 1965; *Kando Nadi Kando*, Naoroze Kitabistan, 1968.

SIDELIGHTS: Calling *Tree Without Roots* "an outstanding novel," Edwin Morgan describes it as "a story of unanswered questions about ends and means; a subtle, objective probing of an enigmatic character; a presentation, through economically chosen detail, of a whole traditional way of life which has almost everything to be said against it—except that human beings contrive to live it. . . . The whole book has a distinct, quietly compelling flavour and atmosphere." The tale is of a wandering holy man's attempt to establish religious awareness in a community while gaining security there for himself. His success in both, being based upon an original deceit, turns to tragedy in his uncomforted mind. "Its own merits should give [Waliullah] a wide and enthusiastic following," writes a *Times Literary Supplement* critic. "He has long been honoured in his own country. . . . We should have heard of [him] before now."

AVOCATIONAL INTERESTS: Music (both Oriental and Occidental), and painting, "when mood demands."

BIOGRAPHICAL/CRITICAL SOURCES: New Statesman, March 17, 1967; *Times Literary Supplement*, April 6, 1967.††

* * *

WALKER, Augusta 1914-

PERSONAL: Born April 14, 1914, in Cincinnati, Ohio; daughter of Henry Gage and Leona (Sloane) Walker. *Education:* University of Michigan, B.A. and M.A., 1944. *Home:* 330 West 88th St., New York, N.Y. 10024. *Agent:* Diarmuid Russell, Russell & Volkening, Inc., 551 Fifth Ave., New York, N.Y. 10017.

CAREER: Woman's College of the University of North Carolina (now University of North Carolina at Greensboro), faculty member, 1945-47; Lingnan University, Canton, China, faculty member, 1947-50; Hunter College of the City University of New York, New York, N.Y., teacher in evening program, 1963-65. *Awards, honors:* Partisan Review fellowship, 1957.

WRITINGS: Around a Rusty God (novel), Dial, 1954; *The Eating Valley* (novel), Dial, 1956; *A Midwest Story* (novel), Dial, 1959; *A Back-Fence Story* (novel), Knopf, 1967; (contributor) *A Casebook on Harold Pinter's The Homecoming*, Grove, 1971. Stories anthologized in *Avon Book of Modern Writing*, 1953, and *Prize Stories: The O. Henry Awards*, 1954. Contributor of articles and stories to *Yale Review, Antioch Review, Modern Drama, Partisan Review,* and *Filmwise*.

* * *

WALKER, Franklin (Dickerson) 1900-

PERSONAL: Born November 13, 1900, in Republic, Mich.; son of John Franklin (a professor) and Lillian (Dickerson) Walker; married Dorothy Griffith, 1924; married second wife, Imogene Bishop (a professor), August 15, 1933; children: (first marriage) Franklin Victor; (second marriage) Susan Imogene. *Education:* University of Arizona, student, 1918-20; Oxford University, B.A., 1923, M.A., 1953; University of California, Berkeley, Ph.D., 1932. *Politics:* Democrat. *Home and office:* Mills College, Oakland, Calif. 94613.

CAREER: Francis Parker School, San Diego, Calif., teacher, 1924-26; San Diego State College (now San Diego

State University), San Diego, Calif., 1926-28, 1930-40, began as instructor, became professor of English; University of Oregon, Eugene, professor of English, 1940-43; Mills College, Oakland, Calif., Reinhardt Professor of American Literature, 1946-66, professor emeritus, 1966—. Visiting lecturer, University of Uppsala, 1949-50; visiting professor, University of California, Berkeley, 1966-67. *Military service:* U.S. Army Air Forces, 1943-46; became major. *Member:* American Studies Association, Pacific Coast Philological Association, California Historical Society (honorary fellow), Berkeley Fellows (life member), Phi Beta Kappa, Sigma Chi. *Awards, honors:* Rhodes scholar at Oxford University, 1920-23; Huntington Library fellow, 1952-53; Guggenheim fellow, 1960-61; Henry Raup Wagner Award for distinction in California history, 1972.

WRITINGS: Frank Norris: A Biography, Doubleday, 1932; *San Francisco's Literary Frontier,* Knopf, 1939; *Ambrose Bierce,* Colt Press, 1941; *A Literary History of Southern California,* University of California Press, 1950; *The Seacoast of Bohemia: An Account of Early Carmel,* Book Club of California, 1966; *Jack London and the Klondike,* Henry E. Huntington, 1966; *Irreverent Pilgrims: Melville, Browne, and Mark Twain in the Holy Land,* University of Washington Press, 1974.

Editor: *Prentice Mulford's California Sketches,* Book Club of California, 1935; *The Washoe Giant in San Francisco,* privately printed, 1939; (with G. Ezra Dane) *Mark Twain's Travels with Mr. Brown,* Knopf, 1940; Mary Austin, *Mother of Felipe, and Other Stories,* Book Club of California, 1950; Jack London, *The Call of the Wild, and Other Stories,* New American Library, 1960; Jack London, *The Sea-Wolf, and Selected Stories,* New American Library, 1964. Member of editorial board, *American Literature* (Huntington Library quarterly).

* * *

WALKER, Jeremy D(esmond) B(romhead) 1936-

PERSONAL: Born October 24, 1936, in Mawgan Porth, Cornwall, England; son of James Gerald Bromhead (British Army) and Sylvia Patricia (Pollard-Lowsley) Walker; married Catherine Elizabeth Forster, September 12, 1963; children: Lucy Clare, Adam. *Education:* Trinity College, Oxford, B.A. (honors), 1961, M.A., 1964. *Politics:* "Radical Left Wing." *Religion:* None. *Home:* 456 Pine Ave. W., Apt. 1, Montreal, Quebec, Canada. *Office:* Philosophy Department, Samuel Bronfman Building, McGill University, Montreal, Quebec, Canada.

CAREER: University of Leicester, Leicester, England, assistant lecturer, 1963-65, lecturer in philosophy, 1965-66; McGill University, Montreal, Quebec, assistant professor, 1966-69, associate professor of philosophy, 1969—. Visiting lecturer in philosophy at University of Minnesota, 1968, and Sir George Williams University, 1970-73.

WRITINGS: A Study of Frege, Cornell University Press, 1965; *To Will One Thing,* McGill-Queen's University Press, 1972; *Apocalypse with Figures,* DC Books, 1974. Contributor of reviews to *Philosophical Books,* 1964-66.

WORK IN PROGRESS: The Philosophical and Social Theory of Karl Marx; Existence and Commitment, a study of post-Hegdian philosophy; *Description and Illumination.*

SIDELIGHTS: Walker is competent in ancient Greek, Latin, and French, and has some familiarity with Italian, Spanish, and German. *Avocational interests:* Music—as listener and performer (plays violin, piano, and organ); English literature from Caedmon on, Russian novelists, and Greek and Roman literature, history, and society.

* * *

WALKER, Sydney III 1931-

PERSONAL: Born October 4, 1931, in Chicago, Ill.; son of Charles Edward (a salesman) and Jean (Leistakow) Walker; married Gail Waldron (a physician), December 14, 1963; children: Sydney IV, Sybil Rebbecca, Cleta. *Education:* University of California, Los Angeles, B.A., 1953; University of Southern California, M.S., 1956; University of California, Berkeley, graduate student, 1959-60; Boston University, M.D., 1964. *Politics:* Republican. *Religion:* Episcopalian. *Home:* 6276 Camino de La Costa, La Jolla, Calif. *Office:* Southern California Neuropsychiatric Institute, 6794 La Jolla Blvd., La Jolla, Calif.

CAREER: University of Pittsburgh, Pittsburgh, Pa., teaching fellow, department of psychiatry, 1965-66; former teaching fellow in neurology, University of Southern California, Los Angeles; currently director of Southern California Neuropsychiatric Institute, La Jolla, Calif. *Military service:* U.S. Army, 1953-55; became first lieutenant. *Member:* American Psychiatric Association, Los Angeles Neurological Society. *Awards, honors:* Annual essay award (first prize) of American Therapeutic Society, 1964.

WRITINGS: Psychiatric Signs and Symptoms Due to Medical Problems, C. C Thomas, 1967; *Hyperactivity: A Symptom in Search of a Diagnosis,* Houghton, 1976. Contributor to professional journals.

WORK IN PROGRESS: Neuropsychiatric Evaluation of Children; and *The Neuropsychiatric Evaluation of the Eyewitness.*

* * *

WALKER, Ted 1934-

PERSONAL: Born November 28, 1934, in Lancing, England; son of Edward Joseph (a carpenter) and Winifred (Schofield) Walker; married Lorna Benfell, August 11, 1956; children: Edward, Susan, Margaret, William. *Education:* St. John's College, Cambridge, B.A. (honours), 1956. *Politics:* "Leftish." *Religion:* "Apprehensive agnostic."

CAREER: Poet. High School for Boys, Chichester, Sussex, schoolmaster and teacher of French and Spanish, 1953-67; full-time author and broadcaster, 1967-71; New England College, Arundel, Sussex, poet-in-residence, 1971—. *Member:* Society of Authors, Royal Society of Literature (fellow). *Awards, honors:* Eric Gregory award, 1964, for *Fox on a Barn Door;* Cholmondeley Award, 1966, for *The Solitaries;* Alice Hunt Bartlett Award, 1967, for *The Solitaries;* Major Arts Council of Great Britain award.

WRITINGS—Poetry: Those Other Growths, Northern House, 1964; *Fox on a Barn Door,* J. Cape, 1965, Braziller, 1966; *The Solitaries,* Braziller, 1967; *The Night Bathers,* J. Cape, 1970; *Gloves to the Hangman,* J. Cape, 1973. Regular contributor of poems to *New Yorker;* contributor of short stories to other periodicals. Founding editor, with John Cotton, *Priapus.*

SIDELIGHTS: "Ted Walker is a very good poet indeed," writes Kevin Crossley-Holland. "He has an eagle eye, a musical ear, and an impressive assurance, and he is, praise be, highly accessible. In the span of two small collections, he has clearly defined his area—the phenomena of the natural world, more especially of the shallows, the no-man's land where earth and water meet, and then the points of contact between man and that world. Any poem, virtually any line, is recognisably his.''

Walker himself, according to Philip Legler, defined his thematic concern as a "fear and loss which looks for the beauty that remains among the ruins of lost faith, lost innocence and lost animal strength." Laurence Lieberman, comparing *Fox on a Barn Door* with *The Solitaries,* writes that in the former, the self, for Walker, "exists in a stalemate with its terrors, half-crippled, conditioned to deadening compromises with loss. But in *The Solitaries,* several poems deepen the vision, exploring psychic states in which the solitary human—or animal—soul, pushed or driven to harrowing extremity, finds a haunting beauty in the mere act of survival against powerful odds."

Ian Hamilton, on the other hand, finds Walker's poems somewhat wearisome. He writes: "When [Walker] is not abasing himself before a dead syllabic count, he presses dutiful iambics into tricky rhyme-schemes—but hardly ever does one get the sense of a personal voice in useful conflict with the regulations." David Galler writes: "Quite a few of the poems, though neatly accomplished, leave the reader somewhat short of a sure emotional response."

But Legler believes that Walker's language is the most exciting aspect of his poetry, and Crossley-Holland adds that Walker's poems are "full of movement, delicate, very cool, and alive to the possibilities of language without being intoxicated by it." Legler concludes that "there is a directness and simplicity which mark Ted Walker as one of the best young English poets writing today."

BIOGRAPHICAL/CRITICAL SOURCES: New York Times Book Review, November 20, 1966; *Kenyon Review,* January, 1967; *Poetry,* March, 1967, May, 1967; *Observer,* March 26, 1967; *Books and Bookmen,* May, 1967; *New Statesman,* May 12, 1967; *Yale Review,* winter, 1968.

* * *

WALLACH, Erica 1922-

PERSONAL: Born February 19, 1922, in Schlawe, Germany; now an American citizen; daughter of Willy (a physician) and Maria Therese (Fittica) Glaser; married Robert Wallach (a banker); children: Madeleine, Robert. *Education:* Studied law and languages at University of Geneva (received diploma), and law at University of Frankfurt am Main. *Residence:* Warrenton, Va.

CAREER: Editor of bi-monthly magazine "Vissen und Tat," Frankfurt, Germany, 1946-48; teacher of French and Latin, Warrenton, Va., 1960—.

WRITINGS: Light At Midnight, Doubleday, 1967, German translation by author published as *Licht um Mitternacht,* Piper, 1969.

SIDELIGHTS: Charged with spying for the United States after crossing into East Germany in 1950 to search for her foster parents, Mrs. Wallach spent five years in East German prisons and Russian labor camps north of the Arctic Circle. At one time she was sentenced to execution. After the death of Stalin her case was reopened, she was found innocent, and released. In addition to forced stays behind the Iron Curtain, she also has lived in Spain, France, and Switzerland. Along with her native German, she speaks French, Spanish, and Russian.

BIOGRAPHICAL/CRITICAL SOURCES: "The Erica Wallach Story," Committee on Un-American Activities, U.S. House of Representatives, 1958; Flora Lewis, *The Red Pawn,* Doubleday, 1965; *New York Times Book Review,* June 18, 1967.

WALLERSTEIN, Immanuel 1930-

PERSONAL: Born September 28, 1930, in New York, N.Y.; son of Lazar and Sally (Guensberg) Wallerstein; married Beatrice Morgenstern, May 25, 1964; children: Katharine Ellen. *Education:* Columbia University, A.B., 1951, M.A., 1954, Ph.D., 1959; Oxford University, graduate study, 1955-56. *Religion:* Jewish. *Office address:* McGill University, P.O. Box 6070, Station A, Montreal, Quebec, Canada.

CAREER: Columbia University, New York, N.Y., instructor, 1958-59, assistant professor, 1959-63, associate professor of sociology, 1963-71; McGill University, Montreal, Quebec, professor of sociology, 1971—. President of research commission, Centre Quebecois Internationales, 1973-74. *Military service:* U.S. Army, 1951-53. *Member:* African Studies Association (president, 1972-73), American Sociological Association, International Sociological Association (vice-president, research commission, movements and imperialism, 1973-78).

WRITINGS: Africa: The Politics of Independence, Random House, 1961; *The Road to Independence: Ghana and the Ivory Coast,* Mouton & Co., 1964; (editor) *Social Change: The Colonial Situation,* Wiley, 1966; *Africa: The Politics of Unity,* Random House, 1967; *University in Turmoil: The Politics of Change,* Atheneum, 1969; (editor with Paul Starr) *The University Crisis: A Reader,* two volumes, Random House, 1970; *The Modern World System: Capitalist Agriculture and the Origins of the European World Economy in the Sixteenth Century,* Academic Press, 1974. Contributor to professional journals. Member of editorial board of *African Studies Bulletin,* 1965-69, *Africa Today,* 1968—, *Journal of Comparative and Commonwealth Politics,* 1973—, *American Journal of Sociology,* 1975—, and *Canadian Journal of Sociology,* 1975—.

* * *

WALLOWER, Lucille

PERSONAL: Born in Waynesboro, Pa.; daughter of Roland C. (in advertising) and Nora Grace (Werdebaugh) Wallower. *Education:* Studied at Pennsylvania Museum School of Art and Traphagen School of Fashion. *Home:* 828 Greenwood Ave., Jenkintown, Pa. 19046.

CAREER: Harrisburg Public Library, Harrisburg, Pa., school librarian, 1943-44, assistant children's librarian, 1944-46; fashion artist at Pomeroy's Inc., 1946-49, and at Bowman's, Inc., 1949-52, in Harrisburg; Abington Library, Jenkintown, Pa., children's librarian, 1959-72, librarian, 1972-75; free-lance writer and illustrator, 1975—. Director, Harrisburg Art Association Studio, 1943-48. *Member:* Pennsylvania Library Association, Historical Society of Pennsylvania, Philadelphia Reading Roundtable, Old York Road Historical Society.

WRITINGS—All self-illustrated except as noted: *A Conch Shell for Molly* (Junior Literary Guild selection), McKay, 1940; *Chooky,* McKay, 1942; *The Roll of Drums,* Albert Whitman, 1945; *Your Pennsylvania,* Penns Valley, 1953, 3rd edition, 1964; *The Pennsylvania Primer* (not self-illustrated), Penns Valley, 1954, 4th edition, 1970; *Indians of Pennsylvania,* Penns Valley, 1956, 2nd edition, 1965; *Old Satan,* McKay, 1956; *The Hippity Hopper,* McKay, 1957; *The Morning Star,* McKay, 1957; *All About Pennsylvania,* Penns Valley, 1958.

They Came to Pennsylvania, Penns Valley, 1960; *Your State: Pennsylvania,* Penns Valley, 1962; *Pennsylvania*

A B C, Penns Valley, 1963; *The Lost Prince*, McKay, 1963; *My Book About Abraham Lincoln*, Penns Valley, 1967; *William Penn* (not self-illustrated), Follett, 1968; *Colonial Pennsylvania*, Thomas Nelson, 1969; *The Pennsylvania Dutch* (not self-illustrated), Penns Valley, 1971; *Introduction to Pennsylvania* (not self-illustrated), McRoberts, 1974; *Bicentennial Workshop*, Penns Valley, 1975.

Stories included in *Uncle Sam's Story Book*, McKay, 1944, *Stories from the East and North*, Silver Burdett, 1945, *With New Friends*, Silver Burdett, 1946, and *Shining Hours*, Bobbs-Merrill, 1961.

WORK IN PROGRESS: Illustrating two books.

*   *   *

WALTON, Bryce 1918-

PERSONAL: Born May 31, 1918, in Blythedale, Mo.; son of Paul Dean and Golda (Powers) Walton; married Ruth Arschinov (a photographer), January 1, 1954; children: Krissta Kay. *Education:* Attended Los Angeles Junior College, 1939-41, and California State College at Los Angeles (now California State University, Los Angeles), 1946-47. *Politics:* Democrat. *Religion:* None. *Home:* 8935 Wonderland Ave., Hollywood, Calif. *Agent:* Theron Raines, 475 Fifth Ave., New York, N.Y. 10017.

CAREER: Sailor, migrant farmer, gold miner, railroad section hand, and other employment, 1938-41; free-lance writer, 1945—. Instructor in short story writing, Ann Elwood College, 1946-47. *Military service:* U.S. Navy and U.S. Marine Corps, combat correspondent, 1942-45; received special citation from Admiral Nimitz for coverage of Iwo Jima action. *Awards, honors:* Alfred Hitchcock Best Short Story of the Year Award, 1961; Best Detective Stories of the Year awards from Dutton, 1961, and Dell, 1964.

WRITINGS: Sons of Ocean Deeps, John C. Winston, 1952; *The Long Night*, Falcon Press, 1952; *Cave of Danger*, Crowell, 1967; *Harpoon Gunner*, Crowell, 1968; *Hurricane Reef*, Crowell, 1970; *The Fire Trail*, Crowell, 1974.

Some of the more than 1,000 short stories Walton has published have been anthologized in: *The Earth in Peril*, Ace Books, 1957; *Best Detective Stories of the Year*, Dutton, 1961; *To Be Read Before Midnight*, Random House, 1962; *Hitchcock's Anti-Social Register*, Dell, 1966; *Ellery Queen's 1967 Anthology*, Davis Publications, 1967. Also has written television scripts for "Alfred Hitchcock Presents" series.

WORK IN PROGRESS: A science fiction novel, *The Star Crawlers*.

SIDELIGHTS: Walton told *CA:* "My only motive in writing is to get readers to say, 'I couldn't stop reading it.' Also have things to say, but if they aren't said very entertainingly they won't be read." *Avocational interests:* Reading, skin diving, travel, spelunking, sailing.

*   *   *

WALWORTH, Arthur 1903-

PERSONAL: Born July 9, 1903, in Newton, Mass.; son of Arthur Clarence, Jr. (a civil engineer) and Ruth Richardson (Lippincott) Walworth. *Education:* Yale University, B.A., 1925. *Home:* 155 Elm St., New Haven, Conn. 06508.

CAREER: With educational department of Houghton Mifflin Co., Boston, Mass., 1927-43, and with U.S. Office of War Information, 1943. *Member:* Cosmos Club (Washington, D.C.), Graduate Club (New Haven). *Awards, honors:* Pulitzer Prize in biography, 1958, for *Woodrow Wilson.*

WRITINGS: School Histories at War: A Study of the Treatment of Our Wars in the Secondary School History Books of the United States and Those of Its Former Enemies, Harvard University Press, 1938; *Black Ships Off Japan: The Story of Commodore Perry's Expedition*, Knopf, 1946; *Cape Breton, Isle of Romance*, Longmans, Green, 1948; *The Medomak Way: The Story of the First Fifty Years of an American Summer Camp for Boys*, Bisbee Press, 1953; *Woodrow Wilson*, two volumes, Longmans, Green, 1958, 2nd edition, one volume, Houghton, 1965; *America's Moment, 1918: American Diplomacy at the End of World War I*, Norton, in press.

*   *   *

WANNAN, William Fielding 1915-
(Bill Wannan)

PERSONAL: Born May 28, 1915, in Melbourne, Victoria, Australia; son of William Llewellyn Fearn (a schoolmaster) and Ruby (Bostock) Wannan; married Ora White (a teacher of French and English), November 23, 1943; children: Paula. *Education:* Educated at schools in Melbourne, Australia. *Home:* 23 Malvern Grove, Caulfield 3161, Victoria, Australia.

CAREER: Full-time professional writer, and anthologist of Australian folklore (non-aboriginal). *Military service:* Australian Army, 1942-46; served in South Pacific Theater; became lieutenant. *Member:* Australian Journalists' Association, Australian Society of Authors, Fellowship of Australian Writers.

WRITINGS—All under name Bill Wannan; anthologies compiled, except as noted; all published by Lansdowne, except as noted: *The Corporal's Story* (verse), Bread and Cheese Club (Melbourne), 1943; *The Australian*, Australasian Book Society, 1954, 4th edition, Rigby, 1964; *Tales from Back O'Bourke*, Bronzewing Books, 1957; *Bullockies, Beauts and Bandicoots*, 1960; *A Treasury of Australian Humor*, 2nd edition, Ure Smith, 1965; *Hay, Hell and Booligal*, 1961; *A Treasury of Australian Frontier Tales*, 1961; *Modern Australian Humour*, 1962; *Very Strange Tales: The Turbulent Times of Samuel Marsden* (history), 1962; *A Treasury of Australian Wildlife Stories*, 1963; *A Marcus Clarke Reader*, 1963; *Tell 'em I Died Game* (history of bushranging), 1963; *Australian Pavements*, 1964; *Crooked Mick of the Speewah and Other Tall Tales*, 1965; *Fair Go, Spinner*, 1964; *The Wearing of the Green*, 1965; *The Heather in the South*, 1966; (with Tom Prior and H. Nunn) *Plundering Sons* (pictorial history of Australian bushranging), 1966; *My Kind of Country*, Rigby, 1967; *The Black Stump and Beyond* (selections from three earlier anthologies), Ure Smith, 1967; *Australian Folklore: A Dictionary of Lore, Legends and Popular Allusions*, 1970; *Folk Medicine*, Hill of Content, 1970; *An Australian Book of Days*, Hill of Content, 1970; *Folklore of the Australian Pub*, Macmillan, 1972; *Robust, Ribald, and Rude Verse of Australia*, 1972; *With Malice Aforethought*, 1973; *Dictionary of Australian Humorous Quotations*, Macmillan, 1974; *Legendary Australians*, Rigby, 1974. Author of weekly column on Australian folklore in *Australasian Post*, 1955—.

WORK IN PROGRESS: A collection of Australian folktales and legends.

SIDELIGHTS: J. S. Ryan writes: "One major anthologist upon whose work demand must be made will be Wannan." Of *The Australian*, Ryan writes: "This anthology represents a combing of literary and subliterary sources, yet it reads well and is a world away from the serialized versions in which much of the material was first assembled. It attains a quite remarkable degree of homogeneity and so should attract a wide variety of readers.... Perhaps, however, its great value in this generation will be as a source book for overseas readers whose interest in our emergent literature has been so aroused in the last decade.'' Ryan concludes: ''Wannan's place is alongside Russel Ward as a classifier and collector of the materials which are the mainsprings of the national spirit and of the emerging literature, however, rough so much of it was in the nineteenth century.''

BIOGRAPHICAL/CRITICAL SOURCES: Aumla (journal of the Australasian Universities Language and Literature Association), May, 1965; *Times Literary Supplement,* January 5, 1967.

* * *

WARD, John M(anning) 1919-

PERSONAL: Born July 6, 1919, in Sydney, New South Wales, Australia; son of Alexander Thomson (a sales manager) and Mildred (Davis) Ward; married Patricia Bruce Webb (a teacher-librarian), November 2, 1951; children: Jennifer Bruce, Anne Pamela Bruce. *Education:* University of Sydney, B.A., 1939, M.A., 1945, LL.B., 1946. *Religion:* Presbyterian. *Office:* University of Sydney, Sydney, New South Wales, Australia.

CAREER: University of Sydney, Sydney, New South Wales, Australia, Challis Professor of History, 1949—, chairman of professorial board, 1974-75, of academic board, 1975—. Dominion fellow, St. John's College, Cambridge University, 1951; visiting professor of history, Yale University, 1963; visiting fellow, All Souls College, Oxford University, 1968; Smuts Visiting Fellow, Cambridge University, 1972. Member of Archives Authority of New South Wales, 1961—, and Council of the Library of New South Wales, 1970—. *Member:* Australian Humanities Academy (fellow), Academy of Social Sciences in Australia (fellow).

WRITINGS: (Contributor) C. Harley Grattan, editor, *Australia,* University of California Press, 1946; *British Policy in the South Pacific, 1786-1893,* Australasian Publishing Co., 1948; (contributor) A. H. McDonald, editor, *Trusteeship in the Pacific,* Angus & Robertson, 1950; *Earl Grey and the Australian Colonies,* Melbourne University Press, 1958; (contributor) A. L. McLeod, editor, *The Pattern of Australian Culture,* Cornell University Press, 1963; (contributor) R. W. Winks, editor, *British Commonwealth Historiography,* Duke University Press, 1966; *Empire in the Antipodes,* Edward Arnold, 1966, Norton, 1968; *Changes in Britain, 1919-1957,* Thomas Nelson, 1968; (contributor) D. Dufty and others, editors, *Historians at Work,* Hicks, 1973; *Colonial Self-Government: The British Experience, 1759-1856,* Macmillan, in press.

WORK IN PROGRESS: Studies in Australian Conservatism: James Macarthur.

* * *

WARD, Philip C. 1932-

PERSONAL: Born January 19, 1932, in New York, N.Y.; son of Francis T. (an investment banker) and Alice (Waterman) Ward; married Kathleen Ladd, March 10, 1962; children: Sam, Tony. *Education:* Trinity College, Hartford, Conn., B.A., 1954. *Politics:* Radical. *Religion:* None.

CAREER: College traveler in the Midwest for Harper & Brothers, 1958-59; Morgan Stanley & Co., New York, N.Y., statistician, 1959-60; Little, Brown & Co., Boston, Mass., assistant to advertising manager, 1961-63, library promotion manager, 1964-65, associate juvenile editor, 1966-68, juvenile editor, beginning 1968. Member of board of directors, Children's Book Council. *Military service:* U.S. Air Force, 1954-57; became first lieutenant.

WRITINGS: Tony's Steamer (juvenile), Little, Brown, 1968.

AVOCATIONAL INTERESTS: Ward notes that his interests range from ships and the sea to combating racism.††

* * *

WARD, William G. 1929-

PERSONAL: Born March 4, 1929, in Hanley, Saskatchewan, Canada; married Katharine J. DeFrancois. *Education:* Mankato State College, B.S., 1953, M.S., 1958; additional study at University of Colorado and Syracuse University. *Office:* Southern Illinois University, Edwardsville, Ill. 62025.

CAREER: High school teacher for several years, and former newspaperman, working on *Minneapolis Tribune,* Minneapolis, Minn., and *Mankato Free Press,* Mankato, Minn.; Syracuse University, Syracuse, N.Y., assistant professor of journalism, 1964-66; University of Nevada, Reno, associate professor of journalism, 1966-69; Southern Illinois University, Edwardsville, professor of mass communications and director of journalism, 1969—. *Military service:* U.S. Army, 1951-53; became sergeant. *Awards, honors:* Pioneer of Journalism, National Scholastic Press Association, 1972.

WRITINGS: Reporting and Writing Sports, Columbia Scholastic Press Association, 1965; *The Student Journalist and Creative Writing,* Richards Rosen, 1967; *Newspapering: A Guidebook for Students,* National Scholastic Press Association, 1967; *The Student Journalist and Editorial Leadership,* Richards Rosen, 1968; *The Student Journalist and Designing the Opinion Pages,* Richards Rosen, 1969; *The Student Journalist and Thinking Editorials,* Richards Rosen, 1969; *The Student Journalist and Writing Editorials,* Richards Rosen, 1969; *Common Study Assignments,* Richards Rosen, 1971; *The Student Journalist and Depth Reporting,* Richards Rosen, 1972; *Writing in Journalism,* National Scholastic Press Association, 1972; (editor) *The Student Press,* Richards Rosen, 1972, 1973; *My Kingdom for Just One Strackeljohn,* Richards Rosen, 1973; *The Photographer as Reporter,* National Scholastic Press Association, 1974; *Creative Photojournalism,* Richards Rosen, 1975. Contributor to *Nation, National Observer, Camera 35, Christian Science Monitor, Editor & Publisher,* and *Journalism Quarterly.* Advisory editor and columnist, *Scholastic Editor.*

WORK IN PROGRESS: A book on writing wit and humor; a topical history of journalism; literature of journalism; sports photography.

* * *

WARGO, Dan M. 1920-

PERSONAL: Born October 26, 1920, in Sheppton, Pa.; son of Michael and Anna (Demko) Wargo; married Dorothy Recksiek; children: Diana, David. *Education:* Pennsylvania State University, B.A., 1950, M.A., 1951; additional study at Yeshiva University, Hofstra University,

Adelphi University, New York University, and City College of New York (now City College of the City University of New York). *Religion:* Lutheran. *Home:* 1070 Washington Dr., Centerport, N.Y. 11721.

CAREER: Free-lance writer and television actor in New York City, 1951-53; Curry College, Milton, Mass., teacher of speech, drama, and radio, 1953; teacher of speech and English in public schools in Rye, N.Y., 1953-54, and West Hempstead, N.Y., 1954-57; Mineola High School, Mineola, N.Y., director of dramatics, 1957—; Suffolk County Community College, Selden, N.Y., instructor in speech, 1966—. Managing director of Millville (Pa.) Summer Theatre, 1947-51; currently director of Mineola Community Theatre. *Military service:* U.S. Navy, Seabees, 1943-46; became second class petty officer. *Member:* New York State Speech Association, Long Island Speech Association (past president).

WRITINGS: A Survey of the Public Performance Program in Interpretative Reading in Pennsylvania Colleges and Universities, Pennsylvania State University Press, 1951; (with wife, Dorothy R. Wargo) *Dramatics in the Christian School,* Concordia, 1966. Author of workshop plays. Contributor to *Long Island Press* and reviewer for *Players.*

WORK IN PROGRESS: 99 Situations and How to Use Them, real-life situations to be used in role playing; a collection of audition material.

*   *   *

WARMBRUNN, Werner 1920-

PERSONAL: Born July 3, 1920, in Frankfurt am Main, Germany; now a U.S. citizen; married Ellen Croson, July 29, 1961. *Education:* Cornell University, B.A., 1942; Stanford University, M.A., 1948, Ph.D., 1955. *Home:* 3003 Claremont Heights Dr., Claremont, Calif. 91711. *Office:* Department of History, Pitzer College, Claremont, Calif. 91711.

CAREER: Teacher in Putney, Vt., 1944-47; Peninsula School, Menlo Park, Calif., co-director, 1949-52; Stanford University, International Center, Stanford, Calif., foreign student adviser and director, 1952-64; Pitzer College, Claremont, Calif., associate professor, 1964-66, professor of history, 1966—. *Member:* American Historical Association.

WRITINGS: The Dutch under German Occupation, 1940-45, Stanford University Press, 1963.

WORK IN PROGRESS: Belgium under German Occupation, 1940-44.

*   *   *

WARNER, Gary 1936-

PERSONAL: Born May 27, 1936, in Adrian, Mich.; son of Kenneth E. (a banker) and Ethel Warner; married Joyce M. Snead, January 4, 1957 (divorced); children: Jeff, Wendi, Greg. *Education:* Michigan State University, B.A. (with highest honors), 1958; further courses at several Bible colleges. *Home:* 3623 Gillham Rd., Kansas City, Mo. 64111. *Office:* Fellowship of Christian Athletes, 1125 Grand Ave., Kansas City, Mo. 64106.

CAREER: Adrian Daily Telegram, Adrian, Mich., reporter, 1958-59, sports editor, 1960-65; Michigan Bell Telephone Co., Detroit, Mich., magazine writer, 1959-60; Billy Graham Evangelistic Association, Minneapolis, Minn., writer, 1965-67; Fellowship of Christian Athletes, Kansas

City, Mo., 1967—, currently national director of communication division and editor of *Christian Athlete* (magazine). Lay preacher and speaker to youth groups; basketball official and baseball umpire. *Member:* Evangelical Press Association, Associated Church Press. *Awards, honors:* Associated Press sports writing award.

WRITINGS: (Editor) *Out to Win,* Moody, 1967; *The Home Team Wears White,* Zondervan, 1970; (editor) *A Special Kind of Man,* Creation House, 1973. Writer of film scripts for Fellowship of Christian Athletes, and brochures and devotional booklets. Contributor of articles and stories to general interest magazines. Former editorial associate, *Decision* (magazine).

*   *   *

WARNOCK, G(eoffrey) J(ames) 1923-

PERSONAL: Born August 16, 1923, in Leeds, Yorkshire, England; son of James (a physician) and Kathleen (Hall) Warnock; married Mary Wilson (an educator), July 9, 1949; children: Kathleen, Felix Geoffrey, James Marcus Alexander, Stephana, Grizel Maria. *Education:* New College, Oxford, B.A., 1948, M.A., 1952. *Office:* Office of the Principal, Hertford College, Oxford University, Oxford, England.

CAREER: Oxford University, Oxford, England, Brasenose College, lecturer in philosophy, 1949-50, fellow and tutor in philosophy, 1950-53, Magdalen College, fellow and tutor in philosophy, 1953-71, Hertford College, principal, 1972—. Visiting lecturer at University of Illinois, 1957; visiting professor at Princeton University, 1962, and University of Wisconsin, 1966-67. *Military service:* British Army, Irish Guards, 1942-45; became captain. *Member:* Aristotelian Society.

WRITINGS: Berkeley, Peguin, 1953; *English Philosophy since 1900,* Oxford University Press, 1958, 2nd edition, 1969; (editor) J. L. Austin, *Sense and Sensibilia,* Clarendon Press, 1962; *Contemporary Moral Philosophy,* St. Martin's, 1967; *The Object of Morality,* Methuen, 1971.

*   *   *

WARREN, James E(dward), Jr. 1908-

PERSONAL: Born December 11, 1908, in Atlanta, Ga.; son of James Edward (an attorney) and Jean (Mauck) Warren. *Education:* Emory University, A.B., 1930, M.A.T., 1941; other courses at Georgia State College (now University), Yale University, and Cambridge University. *Politics:* "No party." *Religion:* Methodist. *Home:* 544 Deering Rd. N.W., Atlanta, Ga. 30309.

CAREER: Atlanta (Ga.) public schools, junior high and high school teacher of English, Latin, history, and journalism, 1933-59; Lovett School, Atlanta, Ga., head of English department, 1960-73, poet-in-residence, 1974—. Part-time instructor in English at Georgia Institute of Technology. *Military service:* U.S. Army, 1942-45; became sergeant. *Member:* Poetry Society of America, Georgia Writers Association (trustee), Kappa Phi Kappa. *Awards, honors:* Poetry Society of America Annual Award, 1937; Georgia Writers Association, Literary Achievement Award for Poetry, 1967, for *Selected Poems;* Georgia Association of Independent Schools Excellence in Teaching Award, 1974.

WRITINGS: This Side of Babylon (poetry), Banner Press, 1938; *Against the Furious Men* (poetry), Banner Press, 1946; *The Teacher of English: His Materials and Opportunities,* A. Swallow, 1956; *Selected Poems,* Branden

Press, 1967; *How to Write a Research Paper*, Branden Press, 1972. Also author of *History of the Lovett School*, 1976. Writer of over ten brochures of poetry, privately printed, 1964-74. Work represented in many anthologies, including *Adam among the Television Trees*, compiled by V. R. Mollenkott, Word, Inc., 1971, and *The Diamond Anthology*, edited by Charles Angoff, A. S. Barnes, 1971. Contributor of poetry to *Atlantic Monthly, Sewanee Review, Good Housekeeping, Saturday Review, Prairie Schooner, New York Times*, and other publications in America, Canada, England, Belgium, Japan, France, and Greece; contributor of educational articles and translations of Horace, Catullus, and other classical writers to professional journals.

AVOCATIONAL INTERESTS: Family history.

BIOGRAPHICAL/CRITICAL SOURCES: Georgia Magazine, October-November, 1967.

* * *

WASKIN, Yvonne 1923-

PERSONAL: Born July 12, 1923, in Grand Haven, Mich.; daughter of Jay L. and Bertha (McKissick) Fisher; married Leon S. Waskin, August 20, 1949 (deceased); children: Leon S., Jr., Randolph B. *Education:* Western Michigan University, B.S., 1945; Wayne State University, M.Ed., 1950. *Home:* 5853 Smithfield Ave., East Lansing, Mich. 48823. *Office:* Michigan State University, East Lansing, Mich. 48823.

CAREER: Teacher in Dowagiac, River Rouge, and Lansing (Mich.) public schools, 1945-54; Michigan State University, East Lansing, faculty member, 1954-67, assistant professor of education, 1967—. *Member:* National Council of Teachers of English.

WRITINGS: (With Louise Parrish) *Teacher-Pupil Planning*, Pitman, 1967.

* * *

WASSENBERGH, Henri Abraham 1924-

PERSONAL: Born August 16, 1924, in Hattem, Netherlands; son of Henri Abraham (a prosecutor for the Queen) and Maria Catherine (Jansen) Wassenbergh; married Catherine Elizabeth Giesen, October 30, 1950; children: Robin Evert, Henriette Catherine, Henri Arnoldus. *Education:* University of Amsterdam, law degree, 1947; University of Paris and Institut des Hautes Etudes Internationales, graduate study, 1948-49; University of Leyden, doctor's degree, 1957. *Home:* Mechelsestraat 7, The Hague, Netherlands. *Office:* KLM Royal Dutch Airlines, Schiphol Airport, Netherlands.

CAREER: KLM Royal Dutch Airlines, Schiphol Airport, Netherlands, 1950—, former secretary to the president and member of management staff, then deputy head of foreign relations, 1957-67, head of foreign relations, 1967-71, head of foreign relations and co-operation bureau, 1971—. Member, Airtransport Commission of International Chamber of Commerce, Central Board for Economic Relations, and supervisory board of NLM-Netherlands Airlines. *Military service:* Netherlands Army, Infantry Reserve; present rank major.

WRITINGS: Post-War International Civil Aviation Policy and the Law of the Air, Nijhoff, 1957, 2nd edition, 1962; *Aspects of Air Law and Civil Air Policy in the Seventies*, Nijhoff, 1970. Contributor to law journals and other periodicals.

WASSER, Henry H. 1919-

PERSONAL: Born April 13, 1919, in Pittsburgh, Pa.; son of Nathan (a merchant) and Mollie (Mendelson) Wasser; married Solidelle Fortier, August 20, 1942; children: Frederick Anthony, Felicity Louise. *Education:* Ohio State University, B.A. (cum laude) and M.A., 1940; Columbia University, Ph.D., 1951. *Office:* Richmond College of the City University of New York, Staten Island, N.Y.

CAREER: Instructor at University of Akron, Akron, Ohio, 1943-44, and New York University, New York City, 1945-46; City College of the City University of New York, New York City, instructor, 1946-53, assistant professor, 1953-61, associate professor of English, 1961-66; Richmond College of the City University of New York, Staten Island, N.Y., professor of English and dean of faculty, 1966-73; California State University, Sacramento, professor of English and vice-president for academic affairs, 1973-74; Richmond College of the City University of New York, professor of English, 1974—. Fulbright professor of American literature, University of Salonika, 1955-56; University of Oslo, Fulbright professor of American literature, 1962-64, and director of American Institute, 1963-64; visiting professor, University of Sussex, 1972. Columbia University, seminar associate in American civilization, 1961-69, seminar associate in higher education, 1969—; conductor of seminars on American literature at University of Urbino, University of Ljubljana, and University of Warsaw, 1964, and for teachers in Sweden and Norway; lecturer at universities in England, Sweden, Germany, Poland, 1962-64, and Norway, 1972. Member of advisory board, General Electric "College Bowl" (television quiz), 1960-61.

MEMBER: American Studies Association (member of executive council), Modern Language Association of America, English Graduate Union (Columbia University), English Round Table (New York University), Phi Beta Kappa.

WRITINGS: The Scientific Thought of Henry Adams [Salonika, Greece], 1956; (contributor) *American Studies in Transition*, University of Pennsylvania Press, 1964; (editor with Sigmund Skard, and contributor) *Americana Norvegica: Norwegian Contributions to American Studies*, University of Pennsylvania Press, 1966; (contributor) *U.S.A. in Focus*, Scandinavian University Press (Oslo), 1966. Columnist, *Times Higher Education Supplement* (London), 1973—. Contributor to *Encyclopedia Americana* and *Encyclopedia Americana Annual*, and to professional journals.

* * *

WATKINS, Grace F. 1927-

PERSONAL: Born July 10, 1927, in Akron, Ohio; daughter of Charles and Mildred (Endlich) Farah; married William A. Watkins (a scientist), September 6, 1947; children: Bruce, Sandra, Stephen, James, Laurel. *Education:* Studied at Houghton College, Houghton, N.Y., 1945-47, and Wheaton College, Wheaton, Ill., 1947-48. *Religion:* Protestant. *Home:* 24 Hayway Rd., East Falmouth, Mass. 02536.

WRITINGS: A Certain Radiance, Zondervan, 1966; *Gladness in My Heart*, Zondervan, 1968.

* * *

WATKINS, J(ohn) W(illiam) N(evill) 1924-

PERSONAL: Born July 31, 1924, in Woking, Surrey, England; son of William Hugh (a company director) and Winifred (Jeffries) Watkins; married Millicent Roe (a teacher), April 4, 1952; children: Hugh, Susan, Kate, Julie. *Education:* London School of Economics and Political Science, B.Sc., 1949; Yale University, M.A., 1950. *Home:* 11 Erskine Hill, London N.W. 11, England. *Office:* London School of Economics and Political Science, University of London, London, England.

CAREER: University of London, London School of Economics and Political Science, London, England, assistant lecturer, then lecturer in political science, 1950-57, reader in the history of philosophy, 1957-66, professor of philosophy, 1966—. *Military service:* Royal Navy, 1938-46; became lieutenant; received Distinguished Service Cross. *Member:* British Society for the Philosophy of Science (president, 1972-75).

WRITINGS: Hobbes's System of Ideas, Hutchinson, 1965, Barnes & Noble, 1968.

*   *   *

WATSON, Tom, Jr.   1918-

PERSONAL: Born June 15, 1918, in Tampa, Fla.; son of J. Tom and Mary (Boisseau) Watson; married Lucille Jamison (a concert soprano), December 4, 1961; children: Anne Katheryn, Tom III, Mary Goree, Robert Nelson, Rebecca Dale. *Education:* Studied at University of Florida, 1937-40, and Wheaton College, 1951. *Religion:* Evangelical Christian. *Home:* 3105 Independence Dr., Lakeland, Fla. 33803.

CAREER: Free-lance writer of network daytime serials, 1939-41; *Tampa Morning Tribune,* Tampa, Fla., reporter, 1945-46; Radio Station WSWN, Belle Glade, Fla., owner and manager, 1947-51; missionary to Japan and Korea, 1951-59; Evangelical Alliance Mission, radio and films secretary, 1961-68. Founder of Radio Station HLKX, Inchon, Korea, 1956. Producer of documentary and dramatic films on foreign countries. *Military service:* U.S. Army Air Forces, 1942-45; pilot.

WRITINGS: The Will of My Father, Moody, 1963; *T. J. Bach: A Voice for Missions,* Moody, 1965; *Sex Is a Four-Letter Word,* Creation House, 1971; *How to Be Happy in an Unhappy Situation,* Regal Books, 1975. Contributor to religious periodicals. Editor, *Horizons* (magazine), 1967-69.

*   *   *

WATTENBERG, William W(olff)   1911-

PERSONAL: Born January 5, 1911, in New York, N.Y.; son of Louis (a cotton converter) and Bella (Wolff) Wattenberg; married Jean Arvey (a psychologist), July 25, 1942; children: Franklin A., David A. *Education:* City College (now City College of the City University of New York), B.S., 1930; Columbia University, A.M., 1932, Ph.D., 1936. *Politics:* Democrat. *Religion:* Jewish. *Home:* 5861 Burnhum Rd., Bloomfield Hills, Mich. 48013. *Office:* College of Education, Wayne State University, Detroit, Mich. 48202.

CAREER: Columbia University, Teachers College, New York, N.Y., research associate at Lincoln School, 1930-36; Northwestern University, Evanston, Ill., instructor in educational psychology, 1936-38; Chicago Teachers College (now Chicago State University), Chicago, Ill., faculty member, 1938-46; Wayne State University, Detroit, Mich., professor of educational psychology, 1946—. Associate superintendent, Detroit (Mich.) Board of Education, 1966-68; interim chairman, Monitoring Commission for Detroit School Desegregation Case, 1975—. Treasurer, Student Aid Foundation of Michigan, 1947—. *Military service:* U.S. Army, 1942-45; became major.

MEMBER: American Psychological Association, American Sociological Association, National Society for the Study of Education, American Educational Research Association. *Awards, honors:* Liberty Bell Award of Michigan Bar Association.

WRITINGS: On the Educational Front, Columbia University Press, 1936; (with Fritz Redl) *Mental Hygiene in Teaching,* Harcourt, 1951, 2nd edition, 1959; *The Adolescent Years,* Harcourt, 1955, 2nd edition, 1973; *All Men Are Created Equal,* Wayne State University Press, 1967. Former editor, *Chicago Schools Journal* and *Yearbook* of National Society for the Study of Education.

WORK IN PROGRESS: Self-Preservation.

AVOCATIONAL INTERESTS: Stamp collecting and travel.

*   *   *

WATTERS, (Walter) Pat(terson)   1927-

PERSONAL: Born February 28, 1927, in Spartanburg, S.C.; son of Walter Patterson (an army officer) and Mary (Bookout) Watters; married Cecile Rhinehart, June 6, 1952 (divorced, 1969); married Glenda Herbert Bartley, March 10, 1971; children: (first marriage) Patrick John, Ellen Leslie. *Education:* Emory University, B.A., 1951; University of Iowa, M.A., 1953. *Home:* 553 Greenwood Ave., Atlanta, Ga. 30308.

CAREER: Atlanta Journal, Atlanta, Ga., reporter, 1952-59, city editor, 1959-61, columnist, 1961-63; Southern Regional Council (human relations organization), Atlanta, director of information, 1963-75; free-lance writer, 1975—.

WRITINGS: (With Reese Cleghorn) *Climbing Jacob's Ladder: The Arrival of Negroes in Southern Politics,* Harcourt, 1967; *The South and the Nation,* Pantheon, 1970; *Down to Now: Reflections on the Southern Civil Rights Movement,* Pantheon, 1971; (editor with Stephen Gillers) *Investigating the FBI,* Doubleday, 1973. Contributor of essay to *New American Review #5,* edited by Theodore Soltaroff, New American Library, 1969. Contributor to *New South, New York Times Magazine, Atlanta, Reporter, Dissent, New Republic, Nation.*

WORK IN PROGRESS: The Angry Middle-Aged Men, for Grossman.

SIDELIGHTS: Watters told *CA* that he is "rather deeply committed to writing about the South, its people and problems, out of various motivations, including the belief that most of the crucial concerns of the world today are in sharp psychological focus here."

*   *   *

WATTS, John D. W.   1921-

PERSONAL: Born August 9, 1921, in Laurens, S.C.; son of J. Wash (a missionary and seminary professor) and Mattie Liela (Reid) Watts; married Winifred Williams, August 2, 1946; children: Cheryl, Reid, Linda, James. *Education:* Mississippi College, Clinton, B.A., 1941; Baptist Bible Institute (now New Orleans Baptist Theological Seminary), Th.M., 1944; Southern Baptist Theological Seminary, Th.D., 1948; University of Zurich, postdoctoral study, 1949-52. *Office:* Baptist Theological Seminary, Ruschlikon, Switzerland.

CAREER: Baptist clergyman. Baptist Theological Seminary, Ruschlikon, Switzerland, professor of Old Testament, 1948—, dean, 1957-63, president, 1964-70. Visiting professor at Southern Baptist Theological Seminary, 1970-72, and Serampore College (India), 1972-75. Member of Study Commission on Doctrine, Baptist World Alliance, 1965-70. American television appearances in connection with the work of the Swiss seminary include "Baptist Hour" in December, 1966, and "This Is the Answer," 1967. Member of board of International American School in Zurich, 1964-70, Bangalore Baptist Hospital, 1973-75, and Woodstock School (India), 1974-75. *Military service:* U.S. Naval Reserve, chaplain, 1944-46; became lieutenant. *Member:* Society for Biblical Literature, International Organization of Old Testament Scholars, Society for Old Testament Study (Great Britain), Swiss Theological Society for Biblical Study, Indian Society.

WRITINGS: Vision and Prophecy in the Book of Amos, Eerdmans, 1958; *Lists of Words Occurring Frequently in the Hebrew Bible,* Eerdmans, 1959; *Studying the Book of Amos,* Broadman, 1966; *A Commentary on the Book of Obadiah,* Eerdmans, 1968, 1969; *Basic Patterns in Old Testament Religion,* Vantage, 1971. Contributor to *Broadman Bible Commentary,* 1970-72, and *Cambridge Commentary on the New English Bible,* 1975. Contributor to theological journals in Europe and United States.

* * *

WATTS, Ronald L(ampman) 1929-

PERSONAL: Born March 10, 1929, in Karuizawa, Japan; son of Horace Godfrey (a clergyman) and Ruth (Jenkins) Watts; married Donna Catherine Douglas Paisley (a high school teacher), June 30, 1954. *Education:* University of Toronto, B.A., 1952; Oxford University, B.A., 1955, M.A., 1959, D.Phil., 1962. *Home:* 105 Lower Union St., Kingston, Ontario, Canada. *Office:* Queen's University, Kingston, Ontario, Canada.

CAREER: Queen's University at Kingston, Kingston, Ontario, lecturer in philosophy, 1955-61, assistant professor of political science, 1961-63, associate professor, 1963-65, professor of political science, 1965—, assistant dean, 1964-66, associate dean, 1966-69, dean of arts and science, 1969-74, principal and vice-chancellor, 1974—. *Member:* Canadian Political Science Association, Canadian Association of University Teachers, Canadian Institute of International Affairs, Canadian Humanities Association. *Awards, honors:* Rhodes scholar, 1952; Canada Council senior fellow, 1967-68.

WRITINGS: (Contributor) Ursula K. Hicks and others, editors, *Federalism and Economic Growth in Underdeveloped Countries,* Oxford University Press, 1961; *New Federations: Experiments in the Commonwealth,* Clarendon Press, 1966; *Multicultural Societies and Federalism,* Information Canada, 1970; *Administration in Federal Systems,* Hutchinson Educational, 1970; (contributor) R. M. Burns, editor, *One Country or Two?,* McGill-Queen's University Press, 1971. Contributor to *Public Policy,* and *Queen's Quarterly.*

WORK IN PROGRESS: Research on a theoretical framework for the comparative study of federal systems.

AVOCATIONAL INTERESTS: Sailing (both racing and cruising), aviation history.

* * *

WAUGH, Harry 1904-

PERSONAL: Born June 9, 1904, in Chilwick, England; son of Alexander Adam and Mary Anne (Jennings) Waugh; married Diana Oppenheim, April 30, 1936; married second wife, Prudence D'Arcy Waters, June 4, 1970; children: (second marriage) Jamie and Harriet (twins). *Education:* Attended Cranleigh School, Surrey, England. *Home:* 19 Bolton St., London W1Y 8HD, England. *Office:* 14 Camden Sq., London NW1 9UY, England.

CAREER: Entered wine trade, 1934; joined firm of John Harvey & Sons (wine merchants), London, England, 1945, director, 1952-66; currently wine consultant, Harry Waugh Ltd., London, England. Director, Chateau Latour, Bordeaux, France. Commissioner, Inland Revenue. *Military service:* British Army, Welsh Guards, 1940-45; became captain. *Member:* Les Compagnons du Beaujolais (president and founder of British branch), Brook's Club. *Awards, honors:* Les Amis du Vin (Washington, D.C.) award, 1973.

WRITINGS: Bacchus on the Wing, Wine & Spirits Publications, 1966; *The Changing Face of Wine,* Wine & Spirit Publications, 1968; *Diary of a Winetaster,* Quadrangle, 1972; *Winetaster's Choice,* Quadrangle, 1974. Also author of *Pick of the Bunch,* for Wine & Spirit Publications. Contributor of articles on wine and travel to publications.

SIDELIGHTS: Waugh travels constantly to vineyards in France, and lectures in the United States annually. *Avocational interests:* Collecting Victorian fairings and nineteenth-century oil paintings.

* * *

WEATHERS, Winston 1926-
(Tobias Palmer)

PERSONAL: Born December 25, 1926, in Pawhuska, Okla.; son of Russell O. (a building contractor) and Edith (Casey) Weathers. *Education:* University of Oklahoma, B.A., 1950, M.A., 1951, Ph.D., 1964; Middlebury College, Bread Loaf School of English, graduate study, summer, 1952. *Home:* 100 Center Plaza, Tulsa, Okla. 74119. *Office:* Department of English, University of Tulsa, Tulsa, Okla. 74104.

CAREER: University of Tulsa, Tulsa, Okla., lecturer, 1957-59, instructor, 1959-62, assistant professor, 1962-66, associate professor, 1966-69, professor of English, 1969—. *Member:* Phi Beta Kappa.

WRITINGS: On the Air, Northwestern Press, 1945; *Mysteries for Radio,* Eldridge Entertainment House, 1946; *Adventures in Radio,* Northwestern Press, 1947; *The Big Broadcast,* Northwestern Press, 1948; (with Otis Winchester) *The Strategy of Style,* McGraw, 1967; (with Winchester) *The Prevalent Forms of Prose,* Houghton, 1968; *The Archetype and the Psyche: Essays in World Literature,* University of Tulsa Press, 1968; *Par Lagerkvist,* Eerdmans, 1968; (with Winchester) *Copy and Compose,* Prentice-Hall, 1969; *William Blake's "The Tyger": A Casebook,* C. E. Merrill, 1969; *Messages from the Asylum,* Joseph Nichols, 1970; (with Winchester) *The Attitudes of Rhetoric,* Prentice-Hall, 1970; *Indian and White: Sixteen Eclogues,* University of Nebraska Press, 1970; *The Lonesome Game,* David Lewis, 1970; *The Island,* Joseph Nichols, 1974; (under pseudonym Tobias Palmer) *An Angel in My House,* Ave Maria Press, 1975; *The Creative Spirit,* Joseph Nichols, 1975.

* * *

WEBSTER, Richard A. 1928-

PERSONAL: Born June 13, 1928, New York, N.Y.; son of Morton S. and Ida (Adelberg) Webster; married Brenda

Schwabacher; children: Lisa, Michael, Rebecca. *Education:* Harvard University, B.A., 1950; Columbia University, M.A., 1954, Ph.D., 1959. *Religion:* Judaism. *Office:* History Department, University of California, Berkeley, Calif. 94720.

CAREER: University of California, Berkeley, currently professor of history. *Awards, honors:* Fulbright scholar, 1954-55; American Council of Learned Societies fellow, 1962-63; Guggenheim fellow, 1966-67; National Endowment for the Humanities fellow in Rome, 1973-74.

WRITINGS: The Cross and the Fasces, Stanford University Press, 1960; *L'imperialismo industriale italiano,* translated from the manuscript by Mariangela Chiabrando, Einaudi, 1974, published as *Industrial Imperialism in Italy, 1908-1915,* University of California Press, 1975.

* * *

WEBSTER, Staten Wentford   1928-

PERSONAL: Born February 14, 1928, in Dallas, Tex.; son of Daniel Wentford (an electrician) and Dessie (Hatter) Webster; married second wife, Linda Sonja Shlep (an elementary vice-principal), August 6, 1966; children: (first marriage) Marc, Scot. *Education:* University of California, B.A., 1949, M.A., 1957, Ph.D., 1960. *Politics:* Democrat. *Home:* 536 Santa Fe Ave., Richmond, Calif. *Office:* School of Education, University of California, Berkeley, Calif. 94720.

CAREER: Richmond (Calif.) Union High School District, social studies teacher, 1950-52, 1954-56; University of California, Berkeley, supervisor of teacher education, 1960-67, associate professor, 1967-70, professor of education, 1970—. Associate research director, California Commission on Public School Administration, 1960-62. Consultant, National Teacher Corps. *Military service:* U.S. Army, Signal Corps, 1952-54. *Member:* National Education Association, National Society for the Study of Education, California Teachers Association, Phi Delta Kappa.

WRITINGS: (Editor and contributor) *The Disadvantaged Learner: Knowing, Understanding, Educating,* Chandler Publishing, 1966; *Discipline in the Classroom: Principles and Problems,* Chandler Publishing, 1968; (compiler) *Knowing and Understanding Socially Disadvantaged Ethnic Minority Groups,* Intext Press, 1972; *The Education of Black Americans,* Intext Press, 1974. Contributor to education journals.

WORK IN PROGRESS: Further research on the ethnic anxiety.

AVOCATIONAL INTERESTS: Reading, sports, travel, oil painting, jazz, and sailing.

* * *

WEDEL, Alton F.

PERSONAL: Born in Eau Claire, Wis.; son of Karl (a clergyman) and Elsie (Gueldner) Wedel; married Mildred R. Baumann (a home economist), September 2, 1945; children: Mark, Kathleen, Timothy. *Education:* Concordia College, Milwaukee, Wis., A.B., 1941; Concordia Seminary, St. Louis, Mo., M.Div., 1945, D.D., 1969. *Politics:* Republican. *Home:* 5317 Whiting, Minneapolis, Minn. 55435.

CAREER: Clergyman of Lutheran Church-Missouri Synod. Missionary in Manitoba-Saskatchewan District, Canada, 1945-47; pastor in Bessemer, Mich., 1947-50, Pop-

lar Bluff, Mo., 1950-54, and St. Louis, Mo., 1954-62; Mount Olive Lutheran Church, Minneapolis, Minn., pastor, 1962—. Chairman of Board of Social Ministry, Lutheran Church-Missouri Synod; member of Division of Welfare Services, Lutheran Council; member of board, Evangelical Lutherans in Mission.

WRITINGS: A Cross to Glory, Concordia, 1966; *Chin Up?,* Concordia, 1969. Writer of devotional booklets for Luther Laymen's League, and contributor to denominational periodicals.

* * *

WEDEL, Leonard E.   1909-

PERSONAL: Born March 26, 1909, in Meno, Okla.; son of Jacob Benjamin (a grocer) and Adena (Eck) Wedel; married Juanita Gary; children: Thomas, Dorothy (Mrs. Jones). *Education:* University of Oklahoma, A.B., 1935, M.S., 1937; also studied at George Peabody College for Teachers, 1955-57, and YMCA Law School, 1963-64. *Politics:* Democrat. *Religion:* Baptist. *Home address:* Route 6, Franklin, Tenn. 37064. *Office:* Baptist Sunday School Board, 127 Ninth Ave., N,, Nashville, Tenn. 37203.

CAREER: Elementary and high school teacher in Fairview, Okla., 1932-33, elementary school principal in Newcastle, Okla., 1933-39; business college instructor in Enid, Okla., 1939-41; minister of education at churches in Enid, Okla., 1941-43, and Oklahoma City, Okla., 1943-44; director of personnel, Baptist Sunday School Board, Nashville, Tenn., 1944—. *Member:* American Society of Personnel Administration (director, 1960-65), Administrative Management Society, Protestant Church-Owned Publishers Association (president, 1965), Baptist Public Relations Association, Tennessee Industrial Personnel Conference (president, 1964), Tennessee Credit Union League (director, 1960-66), Middle Tennessee Press Club (president, 1965-67), Nashville Chamber of Commerce, Kiwanis Club.

WRITINGS: Building and Maintaining a Church Staff, Broadman, 1967; *So You Want a Job,* Broadman, 1971. Contributor to church administration journals.

AVOCATIONAL INTERESTS: Operating a small farm.†

* * *

WEEKS, Christopher   1930-

PERSONAL: Born June 5, 1930, in Boston, Mass.; son of Arnold Noble and Alice (Phillips) Weeks; married Anita Susan Hills (a computer systems specialist), January 27, 1968. *Education:* Yale University, B.S., 1952; George Washington University, graduate study, 1955-56; University of Michigan, M.A., 1957; Harvard University, M.P.A., 1963. *Home:* 1916 Lombard St., Philadelphia, Pa. 19146. *Office:* City Development Office, City Hall, Philadelphia, Pa.

CAREER: Franklin Management Corp., Boston, Mass., management assistant, 1954-55; International Cooperation Administration, Washington, D.C., assistant for North African operations, 1957-60; Executive Office of the President, Washington, D.C., senior examiner on foreign aid and international economic policy, Bureau of the Budget, 1960-64, special assistant to Sargent Shriver, director of Office of Economic Opportunity, 1964-66; University City Science Center, Philadelphia, Pa., director of career development office, 1966-68; Philco-Ford Corp., Educational and Technical Services Division, Fort Washington, Pa., manager of advanced programs, 1968-69; vice-president, Gladstone Association, 1969-74; city development coordinator, Philadelphia, 1974—. *Military service:* U.S. Navy, 1952-54; became lieutenant junior grade.

AWARDS, HONORS: Professional achievement award from director of U.S. Bureau of the Budget, 1961; first recipient of Budget Bureau's advanced studies fellowship (one awarded annually), 1962; Claude Moore Fuess Award, Phillips Academy, 1967, for significant public service.

WRITINGS: Job Corps: Dollars and Dropouts, Little, Brown, 1967; *Career Development in Philadelphia Public Schools: A Program Leading Toward Universal Continuing Education,* University City Science Center, 1967.

SIDELIGHTS: Weeks speaks, reads, and writes French fluently, and speaks Spanish and Arabic.

*   *   *

WEEKS, Sheldon G. 1931-

PERSONAL: Born November 18, 1931, in New York, N.Y.; son of Harold Eastman and Virginia (Travell) Weeks; married Sally Shoop, August 18, 1957; married second wife, Margaret Kironde (an artist), January 26, 1964; children: (first marriage) Sara Graham, Abigail E.; (second marriage) Harold Mutambuze, Edisa Mirembe. *Education:* Swarthmore College, A.B., 1954; Putney Graduate School, A.M., 1960; Harvard University, Ed.D., 1968. *Religion:* Society of Friends. *Office:* Educational Research Unit, University of Papua New Guinea, Port Moresby, Papua New Guinea.

CAREER: American Friends Service Committee, New York, N.Y., program and youth secretary, 1955-59; Harvard University, Center for Studies in Education and Development, Cambridge, Mass., instructor, 1965-67, assistant professor of education, 1968-69; Makerere Institute of Social Research, Kampala, Uganda, senior research fellow, 1969-72; University of Dar es Salaam, Dar es Salaam, Tanzania, associate professor of sociology, 1972-74; University of Papua New Guinea, Educational Research Unit, Port Moresby, research professor and director, 1975—. President, Sheffield Projects, Inc. (non-profit organization); trustee, Gandhian Foundation. *Member:* African Studies Association, Comparative Education Association, American Sociological Association, Society for Applied Anthropology.

WRITINGS: Divergence in African Education: The Case of Kenya and Uganda, Teachers College, Columbia University, 1967; (with C. C. Wallace) *Success or Failure in Rural Uganda: A Story of Young People,* Makerere Institute of Social Research Press, 1975. Has done some writing under undisclosed pseudonyms; contributor to professional journals, including *African Review, Taamuli, International Social Science Journal,* and *Journal of Developing Areas.* Contributing editor, *Africa Today,* and editor of special edition, "Education in African Development," February, 1967.

WORK IN PROGRESS: A study of the quality of primary schooling in Papua New Guinea; a report on wastage in tertiary institutions; a study of the vocational activities of tertiary students; a survey of non-formal education in Papua New Guinea; a social history of Sogeri Senior High School.

*   *   *

WEIK, Mary Hays

PERSONAL: Surname rhymes with "like"; born in Greencastle, Ind.; daughter of Jesse W. (a Lincoln biographer) and Allie (Hays) Weik; married Joseph Grifalconi (divorced); children: John, Ann. *Education:* DePauw University, A.B. *Politics:* Independent. *Home:* 166 Second Ave., New York, N.Y. 10003.

CAREER: Former newspaper reporter in Chicago, Ill., and Indianapolis, Ind.; writer for magazines in New York, N.Y., and consultant to social agencies and schools in New York; co-founder and director of Fellowship of World Citizens, Committee to End Radiological Hazards, and People Against The Atom. *Awards, honors: The Jazz Man* was runner-up for John Newbery Medal, American Library Association, 1967.

WRITINGS: Adventure: A Book of Verse; The House at Cherry Hill, Knopf, 1938; *The Jazz Man* (illustrated with woodcuts by her daughter, Ann Grifalconi), Atheneum, 1966; *The Scarlet Thread: A Group of One-Act Plays,* Atheneum, 1968; *A House on Liberty Street,* Atheneum, 1973. Author of "World Community Series" (studies on United Nations reform). Also author of *Atomenergie: Milliardengeschaeft auf buergerrechnung,* with Helga Vowinckel, 1975, and of monographs on atomic pollution of water, vegetation, and air. Poetry has been published in *Harper's,* short stories in various magazines, and articles in *Journal of Human Relations* and other periodicals. Editor of newsletter, "Window On the World."

WORK IN PROGRESS: Tiger, Tiger . . . , a book on the hazards of nuclear power.

SIDELIGHTS: Weik speaks French, German, and a little Italian ("wish I knew ten more [languages]; communication is hard enough between two Americans!"). She spent six years (1956-62) as a non-governmental observer at the United Nations. Weik has made a number of rambling bus trips around the United States, Canada, and Mexico, and traveled ("mostly on second-class trains") in Europe and North Africa. *The Jazz Man* has also been published in Germany and South Africa.

*   *   *

WEIL, Herbert S., Jr. 1933-

PERSONAL: Surname rhymes with "style"; born January 3, 1933, in New Orleans, La.; son of Herbert S. (an attorney) and Virginia (Ullman) Weil; married Judith Richardson (a professor), June 15, 1961; children: Frederick, Leslie Nicol. *Education:* Attended Yale University, 1950-51; Tulane University of Louisiana, B.A., 1954; University of Paris and University of Lille, graduate study, 1954-55; Stanford University, M.A., 1961, Ph.D., 1964. *Home:* 5 Holly Lane, Storrs, Conn. 06268. *Office:* Department of English, University of Connecticut, Storrs, Conn. 06268.

CAREER: University of Connecticut, Storrs, instructor, 1962-64, assistant professor, 1964-68, associate professor of English, 1968—. *Military service:* U.S. Navy, 1955-58; became lieutenant junior grade. *Member:* College English Association (secretary-treasurer, New England branch, 1965-66), American Association of University Professors, Shakespeare Association, American Comparative Literature Association, American Society for Aesthetics, Phi Beta Kappa. *Awards, honors:* Fulbright grant, 1954-55; Woodrow Wilson fellow, 1958-59, 1961-62.

WRITINGS: (Editor with William Moynihan and Donald Lee) *Reading, Writing, and Re-writing,* Lippincott, 1964, revised edition, 1968; *Discussions of Shakespeare's Romantic Comedy,* Heath, 1966. Contributor to "Shakespeare Survey" series, Cambridge University Press, 1969, 1972.

WORK IN PROGRESS: Some Feeling of the Sport: Humor and Irony in Shakespeare's Comedies; Film as Filter: Some Influences of Movie-going upon Reading; That Was in Thy Rage: Characterization by Delayed Effect; Call Me What Instrument You Will: Varieties of Characterization in Novels, Plays, and Films.

*   *   *

WEIL, Irwin 1928-

PERSONAL: Surname rhymes with "style"; born April 16, 1928, in Cincinnati, Ohio; son of Sidney (an insurance broker) and Florence (Levy) Weil; married Vivian Max (a teacher of philosophy), December 27, 1950; children: Martin, Alice, Daniel. Education: University of Chicago, A.B., 1948, M.A., 1951; New School for Social Research, dramatic studies, 1948-59; Harvard University, Ph.D., 1960. Religion: Jewish. Office: Russian Department, Northwestern University, Evanston, Ill. 60201.

CAREER: Theater stage manager at Lake Hopatcong, N.J., 1949; Library of Congress, Washington, D.C., senior social science research analyst, 1951-54; Brandeis University, Waltham, Mass., lecturer, 1958-60, assistant professor of Russian literature, 1960-65; Northwestern University, Evanston, Ill., associate professor, 1966-70, professor of Russian and comparative literature, 1970—. United States exchange professor to University of Moscow and Soviet Academy of Sciences, 1960, 1963, 1968. Member: American Association of Teachers of Slavic and East European Languages (member of executive council), American Association for the Advancement of Slavic Studies (member of board of directors).

WRITINGS: Gorky: Literary Development and Influence on Soviet Intellectual Life, Random House, 1966. Contributor to Saturday Review, Boston Globe, Chicago Tribune, Judaism, and to professional journals.

WORK IN PROGRESS: A work on Tolstoy, his European antecedents, and the Europeans and Americans influenced by him; literary traditions in United States and Russia in a revolutionary environment.

SIDELIGHTS: Weil is competent in Russian, French, German, Polish, Italian, Hebrew, and Yiddish. Avocational interests: Talking about writers of Russian, European, and Biblical literature; classical and folk music, especially Russian and European.†

*   *   *

WEINER, Leonard 1927-

PERSONAL: Born August 19, 1927, in Boston, Mass.; son of Louis (a tailor) and Bessie (Teran) Weiner; married Nancy Gorvine, October, 1953; married second wife, Janet Barker (a research assistant), December 12, 1967; children: (first marriage) Lynne, Eric, Karen. Education: Brandeis University, B.A. (magna cum laude), 1952, Ph.D., 1965; University of Kansas, M.A., 1955.

CAREER: Tufts University, Medford, Mass., instructor in psychology, 1957-59; Boston State Hospital, Psychiatric Home Treatment Service, Boston, Mass., research psychologist, 1959-60, research director, 1960-63; Tufts University, instructor in psychology at Boston School of Occupational Therapy, 1964-68, and clinical instructor in psychiatry (psychology) at School of Medicine, 1966-68; University of Massachusetts, Boston Campus, assistant professor of psychology, 1965-67, director of Upward Bound program, 1966-67; Age Center of New England,

Inc., Boston, executive director, beginning 1968. Private practice as clinical psychologist, beginning 1960. Director of Wellmet Project, Inc., 1960-62, and General Practitioner Psychiatric Consultation Program, 1965-68. Consultant to Educational Projects, Inc., and to U.S. Office of Economic Opportunity, 1966-67. Military service: U.S. Army, 1945-47; became sergeant.

MEMBER: American Psychological Association, International Society for Comprehensive Medicine, American Association for the Advancement of Science, American Academy of Political and Social Science. Awards, honors: Gold Achievement Award for psychiatric home treatment service, American Psychiatric Association, 1964.

WRITINGS: (With Alvin Becker and Tobias T. Friedman) Home Treatment: Spearhead of Community Psychiatry, University of Pittsburgh Press, 1967. Contributor to professional journals.

WORK IN PROGRESS: A study of the relationship between the physician and the psychiatric disciplines.††

*   *   *

WEINSTEIN, Brian 1937-

PERSONAL: Born October 10, 1937, in Jamestown, N.Y. Education: Yale University, B.A., 1959; Harvard University, graduate study, 1959-61, Ph.D., 1963; University of Paris, auditor, 1961-62. Office address: Box 1101, Howard University, Washington, D.C. 20001.

CAREER: Howard University, Washington, D.C., 1966—, currently professor of political science. Member: American Political Science Association, African Studies Association.

WRITINGS: African Schools of Public Administration, Boston University Press, 1965; Gabon: Nation-Building on the Ogooue, M.I.T. Press, 1967; Eboue, Oxford University Press, 1972; Introduction to African Politics, Praeger, 1974.

WORK IN PROGRESS: A book on the politics of language.

*   *   *

WEINSTEIN, James 1926-

PERSONAL: Born July 17, 1926, in New York, N.Y.; son of Joseph and Bobbie (Kaufman) Weinstein; married Anne Farrar (a city planner), June, 1968; children: (prior marriage) Lisa, Joshua David. Education: Cornell University, A.B., 1949; Columbia University, M.A., 1957. Politics: Socialist. Religion: None. Home: 529 Laidley St., San Francisco, Calif. 94131.

CAREER: Historian and editor. Military service: U.S. Navy, 1945-46.

WRITINGS: The Decline of Socialism in America, 1912-1925, Monthly Review, 1967; The Corporate Ideal in the Liberal State, 1900-1918, Beacon Press, 1968; (editor with David W. Eakins) For a New America, Vintage, 1970; Ambiguous Legacy: The Left in American Politics, F. Watts, 1975. Contributor to Nation, Labor History, and other history and political science journals. Editor, Studies on the Left, 1960-67; editor, Socialist Revolution, 1970—.

*   *   *

WEIR, LaVada

PERSONAL: Born in Kansas City, Mo.; foster daughter of Manual P. (a building contractor) and Elsie Nestlerode; married former spouse Fred J. Weir, July 26, 1950; chil-

dren: Lucy, Joan and Tracy (twins). *Education:* University of Kansas, B.A., 1941; University of Southern California, graduate study, 1946-50. *Residence:* Redondo Beach, Calif.
CAREER: Worked as saleswoman, ghost writer of speeches, in restaurants, and with U.S. Navy shipbuilding program in Kansas and Missouri; taught high school English and drama in Kansas, 1943-45, and California, 1945-51. *Member:* P.E.N., Authors Guild, Southern California Writers Guild, Southwest Manuscripters, Southern California Council on Literature for Young People and Children, Surf Writers. *Awards, honors:* Awards for best comedy in Southern California Theatre Tourney and for *Hic Away Henry* in Southern Books Competition.
WRITINGS: (With daughter, Joan Weir) *Hic Away Henry* (juvenile), Steck, 1967; *Little Pup* (juvenile), Steck, 1969; *Howdy!* (juvenile), Steck, 1971; "Laurie Newman Adventure" series; published by Children's Press, all 1974: *Breaking Point; Chaotic Kitchen; Edge of Fear; The Horse-Flambeau; Laurie Loves a Horse; A Long Distance; Men!; The New Girl.* Author of drama reviews and weekly column, "Backstage with LaVada," for *Daily Breeze,* Redondo Beach, Calif., 1956-60.
WORK IN PROGRESS: A new series for young readers, based on the plays of William Shakespeare.

*   *   *

WEISS, Herbert F. 1930-

PERSONAL: Born July 25, 1930, in Vienna, Austria; son of Richard P. (a business executive) and Lisa (Blau) Weiss. *Education:* New York University, B.A., 1952; Columbia University, M.A., 1954, Ph.D., 1965; University of Paris, Certificate, 1956. *Office:* Department of Political Science, Brooklyn College of the City University of New York, Brooklyn, N.Y. 11210.
CAREER: New York University, New York, assistant professor, 1965-67, associate professor of political science, 1967-69; Brooklyn College of the City University of New York, Brooklyn, N.Y., associate professor, 1969-72, professor of political science, 1972—. *Military service:* U.S. Army, 1954-55. *Member:* African Studies Association. *Awards, honors:* The Melville J. Herskovits Prize of the African Studies Association, 1968.
WRITINGS: (Co-editor) *P.S.A.—Documents,* Centre de Recherche et d'Information Socio-Politiques (Brussels), 1963; (author of introduction) B. Verhaegen, *Congo Nineteen Sixty-four: Political Documents of a Developing Nation,* Princeton University Press, 1966; (co-editor) *Congo 1966,* Centre de Recherche et d'Information Socio-Politiques, 1967; *Political Protest in the Congo,* Princeton University Press, 1967.
WORK IN PROGRESS: *Rebellion in the Congo;* a study of Patrice Lumumba's political party; a study of political party mobilization under Mobutu.

*   *   *

WEISSTEIN, Ulrich W(erner) 1925-

PERSONAL: Born November 14, 1925, in Breslau, Germany; son of Rudolf (a lawyer) and Berta (Wende) Weisstein; first married, 1952; married Judith Schroeder, May 9, 1964; children: (first marriage) Cristina, Claudia Cecily; (second marriage) Eric Wolfgang, Anton Edward. *Education:* Studied at University of Frankfurt, 1947-50, 1951-52, University of Iowa, 1950-51; Indiana University, M.A., 1953, Ph.D., 1954. *Home:* 2204 Queens Way, Bloomington, Ind. *Office:* Indiana University, Bloomington, Ind. 47401.

CAREER: Lehigh University, Bethlehem, Pa., instructor, 1954-57, assistant professor of German, 1957-58; Indiana University, Bloomington, assistant professor, 1959-62, associate professor, 1962-67, professor of German and comparative literature, 1967—. Summer professor at Moravian College, 1959, University of Wisconsin, 1966, Middlebury School of German, 1970, and University of Hamburg, 1971. *Member:* Modern Language Association of America, American Comparative Literature Association, International Comparative Literature Association, American Association of Professors of German. *Awards, honors:* Guggenheim fellow, 1974-75.
WRITINGS: Heinrich Mann: Eine historisch-kritische Einfuehrung in sein dichterisches Werk, Max Niemeyer Verlag (Tuebingen), 1962; (translator) Wolfgang Kayser, *The Grotesque in Art and Literature,* Indiana University Press, 1963; *The Essence of Opera,* Free Press of Glencoe, 1964; *Max Frisch,* Twayne, 1967; *Einfuehrung in die Vergleichende Literaturwissenschaft,* Kohlhammer, 1968; (editor) *Expressionism as an International Literary Phenomenon,* [Paris], 1973. Editor of German section, Twayne's "World Authors Series"; editor, *Yearbook of Comparative and General Literature.*

*   *   *

WELBOURN, F(rederick) B(urkewood) 1912-

PERSONAL: Born October 14, 1912, in Rainhill, Lancashire, England; son of Burkewood (an electrical engineer) and Edith Annie (Appleyard) Welbourn; married Hebe Flower Shann (a departmental medical officer), March 16, 1946; children: Peter, Frances, Mary. *Education:* Emmanuel College, Cambridge, B.A., 1934, M.A., 1938; Westcott House, Cambridge, theology studies, 1936-38. *Politics:* "Conservative radical." *Home:* 44 Church Rd., Winterbourn Down, Bristol, England. *Office:* Department of Theology, University of Bristol, Royal Fort, Bristol 8, England.
CAREER: Ordained minister of Church of England. Cambridge University, Cambridge, England, chaplain of several colleges, 1938-43; Student Christian Movement in Schools, London, England, general secretary, 1943-46; Makerere University College, Kampala, Uganda, 1946-64, intermittently chaplain, warden of Mitchell Hall, and senior lecturer in religious studies; University of Bristol, Bristol, England, lecturer in the study of religion, 1966—. *Member:* Royal African Society, International African Institute, Current Anthropology.
WRITINGS: Science and Humanity, S.C.M. Press, 1948; *East African Rebels,* S.C.M. Press, 1961; *East African Christian,* Oxford University Press, 1965; *Religion and Politics in Uganda, 1952-1962,* East African Publishing House, 1965; (with B. A. Ogot) *A Place to Feel at Home,* Oxford University Press, 1966; *Atoms and Ancestors,* Edward Arnold, 1968.
WORK IN PROGRESS: African Religions, with special reference to Buganda; the religious significance of contemporary English social phenomena.

*   *   *

WELCH, Holmes (Hinkley) 1921-

PERSONAL: Born October 22, 1921, in Boston, Mass.; son of E. Sohier (a trustee) and Barbara (Hinkley) Welch; married Marya Wankowicz, 1944 (divorced, 1972); children: Barbara, Marina, Holmes, Nathaniel. *Education:*

Harvard University, B.A., 1942, M.A., 1956. *Home:* Bolton Rd., Harvard, Mass. 01451.

CAREER: U.S. Department of State, Office of European Affairs, Washington, D.C., divisional assistant, 1942-45; First National Bank of Boston, Boston, Mass., trainee, 1945-48; employed in private business, 1948-54; U.S. Department of State, consul in Hong Kong, 1957-61; researcher in Hong Kong on grant from Joint Committee on Contemporary China, 1961-64; Harvard University, Cambridge, Mass., research associate of East Asian Research Center, 1964-72, assistant director of Center for the Study of World Religions, 1967-68. *Member:* Association for Asian Studies, Royal Asiatic Society (Hong Kong).

WRITINGS: Parting of the Way: Lao Tzu and the Taoist Movement, Beacon Press, 1957, revised edition, 1967; *The Practice of Chinese Buddhism, 1900-1950,* Harvard University Press, 1967; (contributor) *China in Perspective,* Wellesley College, 1967; *The Buddhist Revival in China,* Harvard University Press, 1968; *Buddhism under Mao,* Harvard University Press, 1972. Contributor to *Saturday Review, Harper's, New Yorker,* and other journals.

WORK IN PROGRESS: Editing *Some Taoist Studies.*

* * *

WELDON, Fay 1933-

PERSONAL: Born September 22, 1933, in England; daughter of Frank Thornton and Margaret (Jepson) Birkinshaw; married Ron Weldon (an antique dealer); children: Three. *Education:* University of St. Andrews, M.A., 1954. *Home:* 3 Chalcot Crescent, London N.W.1, England. *Agent:* Clive Goodwin, 79 Cromwell Rd., London S.W.7, England.

WRITINGS: The Fat Woman's Joke, MacGibbon & Klee, 1967, published as *And the Wife Ran Away,* McKay, 1968; "Permanence" (one-act comedy), first produced on a bill with eight other one-acts in London at Comedy Theatre, April 9, 1969; *Down Among the Women,* Heinemann, 1971, St. Martin's, 1972; *Female Friends,* St. Martin's, 1975; *Words of Advice* (one-act play), Samuel French, 1975. Also author of one-act play, "Friends." Writer of more than forty television plays for BBC-TV and commercial networks, including "Poor Mother," October 13, 1970, and "Office Party," August 17, 1971, for "Armchair Theatre," and "Your Obedient Servant," for "Upstairs, Downstairs," 1972.

BIOGRAPHICAL/CRITICAL SOURCES: New York Times Book Review, March 3, 1968; *Stage,* January 1, 1970, October 22, 1970, July 19, 1971, August 26, 1971; *Variety,* December 20, 1972; *Time,* February 26, 1973; Carolyn Riley, editor, *Contemporary Literary Criticism,* Volume VI, 1976.

* * *

WELLER, Charles 1911-

PERSONAL: Born December 10, 1911, in Peekskill, N.Y.; son of Charles (in real estate) and Gertrude (Redler) Weller; married Dorothy Campbell, June 26, 1940. *Education:* Johns Hopkins University, A.B., 1933; Long Island College of Medicine (now State University of New York Downstate Medical Center), M.D., 1938. *Politics:* Republican. *Religion:* Presbyterian. *Home:* 5 Kane Ave., Larchmont, N.Y. 10538.

CAREER: Physician in private practice of internal medicine, subspecializing in diabetes, Larchmont, N.Y.,

1940—. President, Health Systems Agency, Westchester County. *Member:* American College of Physicians (fellow), American Society of Internal Medicine (member of board of trustees, 1963—), Society for Advanced Medical Systems (president, 1975), Alliance for Engineering in Medicine and Biology (president, 1976), New York Diabetes Association (member of board of directors, 1963—), New York State Society of Internal Medicine (president, 1963-64), Westchester County Medical Society (trustee), Larchmont Rotary Club (president, 1952).

WRITINGS: (Contributor) *Family Medical Guide,* Meredith, 1964; (with Brian Richard Boylan) *The New Way to Live with Diabetes,* Doubleday, 1966, revised edition, 1976; (with Boylan) *How to Live With Hypoglycemia,* Doubleday, 1968; *The Management of Stable Adult Diabetes,* C. C Thomas, 1969; (contributor) *Current Therapy, 1969,* Saunders, 1969; (editor) *Computer Application in Health Care Delivery,* Symposia Specialists, 1976.

* * *

WELLS, Donald A(rthur) 1917-

PERSONAL: Born April 17, 1917, in St. Paul, Minn.; son of Harry Edward (a businessman) and Madeline H. (Sears) Wells; married June Elizabeth Mickman, September 7, 1940; children: Miriam June, Michael John. *Education:* University of Minnesota, forestry student, 1936-39; Hamline University, B.A., 1940; Boston University, S.T.B., 1943, Ph.D., 1946. *Home:* 169 Paukaa Dr., Hilo, Hawaii 96720. *Office:* University of Hawaii, Box 1357, Hilo, Hawaii 96720.

CAREER: Ordained to Methodist ministry, 1943; pastor in Allston, Mass., 1942-44, and Weston, Mass., 1944-46; Bedford Mental Hospital, Bedford, Mass., therapist, 1945-46; Oregon State University, Corvallis, assistant professor of philosophy, 1946-48; Washington State University, Pullman, assistant professor, 1948-53, associate professor, 1953-57, professor of philosophy, 1957-69, chairman of department, 1948-69; University of Illinois, Chicago, professor of philosophy and chairman of department, 1969-71; University of Hawaii, Hilo, professor of philosophy, 1971—. Counselor for conscientious objectors. *Member:* American Philosophical Association, American Association of University Professors, Northwest Philosophical Association, Conference on the Teaching of Philosophy (Pacific division), American Civil Liberties Union, Fellowship of Reconciliation.

WRITINGS: God, Man and the Thinker: Philosophies of Religion, Random House, 1962; (contributor) Herbert Otto, editor, *Exploration in Human Potentialities,* C. C Thomas, 1966; *The War Myth,* Pegasus, 1967. Contributor to philosophy journals.

* * *

WELLS, Stanley W. 1930-

PERSONAL: Born May 21, 1930, in Hull, England; son of Stanley Cecil and Doris (Atkinson) Wells; married Susan Hill (a novelist), 1975. *Education:* University College, London, B.A., 1951; University of Birmingham, Ph.D., 1961. *Politics:* None. *Home and office:* Shakespeare Institute, Stratford-upon-Avon, England.

CAREER: Shakespeare Institute (affiliate of University of Birmingham), Stratford-upon-Avon, England, fellow, 1961—, reader in English, 1972—, director of Royal Shakespeare Theatre summer school, 1971—, governor of Royal

Shakespeare Theatre, 1974—. Trustee, Shakespeare Birthplace Trust, 1975—. *Member:* Malone Society (member of council), Society for Theatre Research.

WRITINGS: (Editor) *Thomas Nashe: Selected Writings,* Edward Arnold, 1964, Harvard University Press, 1965; (editor) William Shakespeare, *A Midsummer Night's Dream,* Penguin, 1967; (editor) *A Book of Masques in Honour of Allardyce Nicoll,* Cambridge University Press, 1967; (editor) William Shakespeare, *Richard II,* Penguin, 1967; *Shakespeare: A Reading Guide,* Oxford University Press, 1969; *Literature and Drama: With Special Reference to Shakespeare and His Contemporaries,* Routledge & Kegan Paul, 1970; (editor) William Shakespeare, *The Comedy of Errors,* Penguin, 1972; (editor) Charles Jasper Sisson, *Boar's Head Theatre: An Inn-yard Theatre of the Elizabethan Age,* Routledge & Kegan Paul, 1972; (editor) *Select Bibliographical Guides: Shakespeare,* Oxford University Press, 1973. Also editor of *English Drama,* 1975. Contributor of articles and reviews to Shakespeare and English studies journals.

WORK IN PROGRESS: Other writings on Shakespeare and his contemporaries.

* * *

WELLS, Tom H. 1917-

PERSONAL: Born June 3, 1917, in Austin, Tex.; son of Peter Boyd and Eleanor (Henderson) Wells; married Carolyn McConnell, December 28, 1943; children: Lucy, Sarah, Tom, Jr., Christopher, Julia, Peter. *Education:* Attended University of Texas, 1934-35; U.S. Naval Academy, B.S., 1940; Emory University, M.A., 1961, Ph.D., 1963. *Politics:* Republican. *Home:* 607 Williams Ave., Natchitoches, La. 71457. *Office:* Northwestern State College of Louisiana, Natchitoches, La. 71457.

CAREER: U.S. Navy, regular office, 1940-60, serving in World War II, in Korea, and as sub-chief of U.S. Naval Mission to Colombia, 1954-56, retired with rank of commander, 1960; Northwestern State College of Louisiana, Nachitoches, assistant professor, 1963-65, associate professor of history, beginning 1965. *Member:* U.S. Naval Institute, Southern Historical Association, Louisiana Historical Association (member of board of directors, 1967-68), Texas State Historical Association, North Louisiana Historical Association, Natchitoches Audubon Society (president), Natchitoches Chamber of Commerce (director). *Awards, honors*—Military: Bronze Star, Presidential Unit Citation, and sixteen battle stars (twelve in World War II and four in Korean War).

WRITINGS: Commodore Moore and the Texas Navy, University of Texas Press, 1960; *The Slave Ship Wanderer,* University of Georgia Press, 1967; (contributor) Allan Nevins, Charles I. Robertson, and Bell I. Wiley, editors, *Civil War Books: A Critical Bibliography,* Louisiana State University Press, 1967; *The Confederate Navy: A Study in Organization,* University of Atlanta Press, 1971. Weekly columnist, *Natchitoches Times.* Contributor of articles and reviews to historical and other learned journals.

WORK IN PROGRESS: Research on Alexander Gillon of the South Carolinian Navy during the American Revolution, and on the Colonial trading firm of Murphy, Barr, Davenport & Smith, in Spanish Louisiana and Texas.†

WELSCH, Roger L(ee) 1936-
(Robert Wells)

PERSONAL: Born November 6, 1936, in Lincoln, Neb.; son of Christian (a laborer) and Bertha (Flack) Welsch; married Marilyn Henry, August, 1958; children: Chris, Jennifer, Joyce. *Education:* University of Nebraska, B.A., 1958, M.A., 1960; folklore studies at University of Colorado, 1962, and Indiana University, 1963, 1964. *Home:* 541 South 54th, Lincoln, Neb. 68510.

CAREER: Dana College, Blair, Neb., instructor in German, 1960-64; Nebraska Wesleyan University, Lincoln, assistant professor of folklore and German, 1964-73; University of Nebraska, Lincoln, teacher of folklore in Extension Division, 1966—, member of English and anthropology faculties, 1973—. Field operative, Smithsonian Institution, 1974—. Lectures on folklore, and presents programs on folklore and folk music; collections from field investigations on deposit with Archives of Traditional Music, Indiana University. *Member:* American Folklore Society (life member), Nebraska State Historical Society, Association of Living History, Farms and Agricultural Museum (member of board of directors), Phi Sigma Iota, Delta Phi Alpha. *Awards, honors:* President's Award for creative young faculty, Nebraska Wesleyan University, 1967.

WRITINGS: A Treasury of Nebraska Pioneer Folklore, University of Nebraska Press, 1966; *An Outline-Guide to Nebraska Folklore* (syllabus), Extension Division, University of Nebraska, 1966; *Sod Walls: The Story of the Nebraska Sod House,* Purcell Publications, 1967; (translator) Kaarle Krohn, *Folklore Methodology,* University of Texas Press, 1971; *Shingling the Fog and Other Plains Lies,* Swallow Press, 1971; *The Tall-tale Postcard: A Pictorial History,* A. S. Barnes, in press.

Recordings: "Songs for Today," Lutheran Records, 1963; "Sweet Nebraska Land," Folkways, 1965. Contributor to folklore journals and regional magazines, writing regularly for *Abstracts of Folklore Studies,* 1963—.

WORK IN PROGRESS: Books on horse trading, tall tale materials, regional folklore, and folk architecture.

BIOGRAPHICAL/CRITICAL SOURCES: Ray Lawless, *Folksongs and Folksingers,* Duell, 1960.

* * *

WELTGE, Ralph (William) 1930-

PERSONAL: Born August 15, 1930, in Du Quoin, Ill.; son of William Bernard (a clergyman) and Elsie (Niedringhaus) Weltge; married Sigrid Wortmann, September 6, 1961; children: Karen, Kirsten. *Education:* Elmhurst College, B.A., 1952; Eden Theological Seminary, B.D., 1955. *Politics:* Democrat. *Home:* 37 West Southampton Ave., Philadelphia, Pa. 19118. *Office:* 1505 Race St., Philadelphia, Pa. 19102.

CAREER: Clergyman of United Church of Christ. Assistant pastor in Houston, Tex., 1955-57; World Council of Churches, Geneva, Switzerland, staff member of youth department, 1957-62; United Church Board for Homeland Ministries, Philadelphia, Pa., secretary for young adult program, beginning 1962. *Member:* Clergy and Laymen Concerned About Vietnam, Association for the Study of Abortion, Racial Justice Now.

WRITINGS: The Church Swept Out, United Church Press, 1967; (editor) Wardell B. Pomeroy and others, *The Same Sex: An Appraisal of Homosexuality,* Pilgrim Press, 1969.

WORK IN PROGRESS: Studies on the new generation and church renewal.

SIDELIGHTS: Weltge has traveled extensively in Europe, Middle East, and Asia.††

* * *

WENZEL, Siegfried 1928-

PERSONAL: Born August 20, 1928, in Germany; son of Paul (a foundry engineer) and Mary (Schindler) Wenzel; married Elizabeth Brown (a college instructor), December 26, 1958; children: Anne Beatrice, Mary Margaret, Thomas Paul, Elizabeth Jane. *Education:* University of Parana, A.B., 1952, Teacher's Diploma, 1953; Ohio University, M.A., 1956; Ohio State University, Ph.D., 1960. *Religion:* Roman Catholic. *Home:* 337 Dickinson Ave., Swarthmore, Pa. 19081. *Office:* Department of English, University of Pennsylvania, Philadelphia, Pa. 19174.

CAREER: Ohio State University, Columbus, instructor, 1959-60; University of North Carolina, Chapel Hill, instructor, 1960-61, assistant professor, 1962-65, associate professor, 1965-70, professor of English and comparative literature, 1970-75; University of Pennsylvania, Philadelphia, Pa., professor of English, 1975—. *Member:* Modern Language Association of America (section chairman, 1967), Mediaeval Academy of America, Early English Text Society. *Awards, honors:* American Council of Learned Societies fellowship, 1964-65; Guggenheim fellow, 1968-69; National Endowment for the Humanities fellow, 1975-76.

WRITINGS: The Sin of Sloth, University of North Carolina Press, 1967. Contributor of articles to *Traditio, Speculum, Anglia,* and other journals, and reviews to *Journal of English, German Philology, Medium Aerum,* and others.

WORK IN PROGRESS: Verses in Sermons, completion expected in 1977; translating and editing a Latin treatise on "The Virtues"; editing *Fasciculus Morum.*

* * *

WERKMEISTER, W(illiam) H(enry) 1901-

PERSONAL: Born August 10, 1901, in Asendorf, Germany; came to America in 1923, naturalized in 1929; son of Frederic S. and Caroline (Ostwald) Werkmeister; married Lucyle Thomas (a writer), August 11, 1940. *Education:* University of Munster, student, 1920-23; University of Nebraska, Ph.D., 1927. *Home:* 3354 East Lakeshore Dr., Tallahassee, Fla. 32303. *Office:* Department of Philosophy, Florida State University, Tallahassee, Fla. 32306.

CAREER: University of Nebraska, Lincoln, faculty, 1926-53, began as instructor, professor of philosophy, 1945-53, chairman of department, 1947-53; University of Southern California, Los Angeles, professor of philosophy and director of School of Philosophy, 1953-66; Florida State University, Tallahassee, professor of philosophy, 1966-72, professor emeritus, 1972—. Exchange professor, University of Berlin, 1936-37; visiting professor, Harvard University, 1950-51; special lecturer, University of Istanbul, 1956; graduate school lecturership, University of Southern California, 1962. Member of steering committee, East-West Philosophy Conference, 1964. *Member:* American Philosophical Association (president of Pacific division, 1964), Mind Association, American Society for Value Inquiry (past president), Florida Philosophical Association (past president), Phi Beta Kappa.

WRITINGS: A Philosophy of Science, Harper, 1940, reprinted by University of Nebraska Press, 1965; *The Basis*

and Structure of Knowledge, Harper, 1948; *An Introduction to Critical Thinking,* Johnsen, 1948; *A History of Philosophical Ideas in America,* Ronald, 1949; (editor) *Facets of the Renaissance,* University of Southern California Press, 1958; *Outline of a Value Theory: Six Lectures,* University of Istanbul, 1959.

Theories of Ethics, Johnsen, 1961; (editor) *Francis Bacon: His Career and His Thought,* University of Southern California Press, 1962; (editor) Ralph Tyler Flewelling, *The Forest of Yggdrasill,* University of Southern California Press, 1962; *Man and His Values,* University of Nebraska Press, 1967; *Historical Spectrum of Value Theories,* Johnsen, Volume I: *The German Language Group,* 1970, Volume II: *The Anglo-American Group,* 1973; (editor) *Reflections on Kant's Philosophy,* Florida State University, 1975; *Kant: The Architectonic and Development of His Philosophy,* Open Court, 1975.

Contributor: *The Philosophy of Ernst Cassirer,* edited by Paul Athus Schilpp, Library of Living Philosophers, 1949; *Symposium on Social Theory,* edited by Llewellyn Gross, Harper, 1959; *Sinn und Sein,* edited by Richard Wisser, Max Niemeyer Verlag, 1960; *Scientism and Value,* edited by Helmut Schoeck and James W. Wiggins, Van Nostrand, 1960; *Essays in Philosophy,* edited by C. T. K. Chari, Ganesh & Co. (Madras), 1962; *Philosophy and Culture: East and West,* edited by Charles Moore, University of Hawaii Press, 1962; *New Studies in Berkeley's Philosophy,* edited by Warren E. Steinkrau, Holt, 1966; *Mesnchliche Existenz und Moderne Welt,* edited by Richard Schwarz, Walter de Gruyter & Co., 1967. Contributor of over 100 articles to journals. Editor, *Personalist* (quarterly), 1959-66.

WORK IN PROGRESS: Man in Perspective.

* * *

WERNSTEDT, Frederick L(age) 1921-

PERSONAL: Born February 8, 1921, in Portland, Ore.; son of Lage (a forester) and Adele (Wilcox) Wernstedt; married Irene Nita Jolivette (a librarian), August 31, 1948; children: Carolyn Ann, Kris Frederick. *Education:* University of California, Los Angeles, B.A., 1948, Ph.D., 1953; Syracuse University, M.A., 1950. *Home:* 219 Elm St., State College, Pa. 16801.

CAREER: Pennsylvania State University, University Park, assistant professor, 1952-58, associate professor, 1958-67, professor of geography, 1967—. Fulbright professor, University of Malaya, 1968. Has done field work in the Philippines, Thailand, and Malaysia. *Military service:* U.S. Army, 1942-46; became first lieutenant. *Member:* Association of American Geographers, Association for Asian Studies. *Awards, honors:* Fulbright grant to the Philippines, 1951-52.

WRITINGS: (With J. E. Spencer) *The Philippine Island World,* University of California Press, 1967; (with P. D. Simkins) *Philippine Migration: Digos Valley, Davao Province,* Yale University Southeast Asia Program, 1972; *World Climatic Data,* Climatic Data Press, 1972; *Mexico Campground Guide and Trailer Atlas,* Climatic Data Press, 1974. Contributor to *Economic Geography, Journal of Asian Studies, Journal of Tropical Geography,* and others.

* * *

WERR, Donald F. 1920-

PERSONAL: Born March 29, 1920, in Chicago, Ill.; son of

Frank Paul (an optical worker) and Mary (Moore) Werr. *Education:* Studied for priesthood, 1933-47; Our Lady of Angels Seminary, Cleveland, Ohio, A.B., 1944; Catholic University of America, M.A., 1957. *Home and office:* Quincy College, Quincy, Ill. 62301.

CAREER: Roman Catholic priest of Franciscan order (O.F.M.); Quincy College, Quincy, Ill., instructor in theology and residence counselor, 1947-51, chairman of department of theology, 1955—, vice-president for public relations, 1960—. President of Western Illinois Division of Alcoholism Programs, 1964—, and Dowling Foundation for Alcoholism Half Way Houses; member of Christian Heritage Planning Commission, State of Illinois Sequicentennial, 1967. Speaker on weekly radio program, WLS, Chicago, 1962—. *Military service:* U.S. Air Force, chaplain, 1951-55. U.S. Air Force Active Reserve, currently chaplain for Scott Air Force Base, Belleville, Ill. *Member:* Society of Catholic Teachers of Sacred Doctrine, North American Association of Alcoholism Programs, Educational Press Association of America.

WRITINGS: Guide for Christian Marriage, McCutchan, 1966; *Today's World,* McCutchan, 1966. Editor, *Quincy College Alumni Magazine.*

WORK IN PROGRESS: A college text on teaching about alcoholism; research in the "new theology."

* * *

WESLAGER, C(linton) A(lfred) 1909-

PERSONAL: Surname pronounced Wes-law-ger, with a hard "g"; born April 30, 1909, in Pittsburgh, Pa.; son of Fred H. (a contractor) and Alice (Lowe) Weslager; married Ruth Hurst, June 9, 1933; children: Ann (Mrs. George G. Tatnall), Clinton, Jr., Thomas. *Education:* University of Pittsburgh, B.A., 1933. *Home:* Old Public Rd., Hockessin, Del. 19707.

CAREER: Life Savers Corp., Port Chester, N.Y., sales promotion manager, 1933-37; E. I. du Pont de Nemours & Co., Inc., Wilmington, Del., 1937—, sales manager, 1959-66, automotive products marketing manager, 1966-68; Brandywine College, Wilmington, Del., visiting professor, 1968—. Member of faculty of history department, Wesley College, 1964, and University of Delaware, 1965, 1967. Consultant to Smithsonian Institution on log cabins in the Delaware Valley; lecturer to historical, archeological, and other learned societies. President of Richardson Park (Del.) Board of School Trustees, 1953-57. *Member:* Chemical Specialties Manufacturers Association (chairman of automotive division, 1959-60), Eastern States Archeological Federation (president, 1954-58), Archeological Society of Delaware (president, 1942-48, 1950-53). *Awards, honors:* Award of Merit from American Association for State and Local History, 1965, 1968.

WRITINGS: Delaware's Forgotten Folk, University of Pennsylvania Press, 1943; *Delaware's Buried Past,* University of Pennsylvania Press, 1944; *Delaware's Forgotten River,* Hambleton, 1947; (contributor) H. Clay Reed, editor, *Delaware: A History of the First State,* three volumes, Lewis Historical Publishing Co., 1947; *The Nanticoke Indians,* Pennsylvania Historical Commission, 1948; *Brandywine Springs,* Knebels, 1949; *Indian Place-Names in Delaware,* Archeological Society of Delaware, 1950; (contributor) Charles B. Clark, editor, *The Eastern Shore of Maryland and Virginia,* three volumes, Lewis Historical Publishing Co., 1950; *Red Men on the Brandywine,* Knebels, 1953; *The Richardsons of Delaware,* Knebels, 1957.

Dutch Explorers, Traders and Settlers in the Delaware Valley, University of Pennsylvania Press, 1961; *The Garrett Snuff Fortune,* Knebels, 1965; *The English on the Delaware,* Rutgers University Press, 1967; *The Log Cabin in America: From Pioneer Days to the Present,* Rutgers University Press, 1969; *History of the Delaware Indians,* Rutgers University Press, 1972; *Magic Medicines of the Indians,* Middle Atlantic Press, 1973.

Author of six monographs on regional history subjects, 1959-64. Also author of more than one hundred historical essays, papers, and book reviews, published by Columbia University Press, University of Delaware Press, and by historical, archeological, and folklore journals. Editor, *Hole News* (Life Savers Corp.), 1936-37, Archeological Society of Delaware, 1938-53, *F&F Magazine* (Du Pont Co.), 1946-47, and Historic Red Clay Valley, Inc., 1960-66. Contributing editor, *Delaware Today,* 1965.

* * *

WESSER, Robert F. 1933-

PERSONAL: Born February 18, 1933, in Buffalo, N.Y.; son of Michael and Irene C. (Dauscher) Wesser; married Janet L. Newman, December 22, 1956 (divorced, 1968); children: Kathryn J., Robert M. *Education:* University of Buffalo (now State University of New York at Buffalo), B.A. (magna cum laude), 1954, M.A., 1956; University of Rochester, Ph.D., 1961. *Politics:* Democrat. *Home:* Westville Apartments, Slingerlands, N.Y. 12159. *Office:* State University of New York, Albany, N.Y. 12222.

CAREER: State University of New York at Buffalo, assistant professor of American studies, 1959-66, assistant dean, College of Arts and Sciences, 1965-66; State University of New York at Albany, associate professor, 1966-72, professor of history, 1972—. *Member:* American Historical Association, American Studies Association, Organization of American Historians, New York State Historical Association, Phi Beta Kappa.

WRITINGS: Charles Evans Hughes: Politics and Reform in New York, 1905-1910, Cornell University Press, 1967; (contributor) Arthur M. Schlesinger, Jr., and Fred L. Israel, editors, *History of American Presidential Elections, 1789-1968,* Chelsea House, 1971. Contributor to *Journal of American History, Labor History,* and other history journals. Member of editorial board, *New York History.*

* * *

WESSMAN, Alden E(benhart) 1930-

PERSONAL: Born March 3, 1930, in Boston, Mass.; son of Gustaf A. E. (a chemist) and Lillian (Ericson) Wessman; married Iphigenia Jane Scourtis, June 27, 1959; children: Eric, Christopher, Victoria. *Education:* Harvard University, A.B., 1952; Princeton University, Ph.D., 1956. *Home:* 132 Corona Ave., Pelham, N.Y. 10803. *Office:* Psychology Department, City College of the City University of New York, New York, N.Y. 10031.

CAREER: Harvard University, Cambridge, Mass., research associate, laboratory of social relations, 1956-61, lecturer in clinical psychology, 1960-61; Sarah Lawrence College, Bronxville, N.Y., member of psychology faculty, 1961-65; Dartmouth College, Hanover, N.H., research director of Project ABC (program providing disadvantaged boys with scholarships to independent private schools) and adjunct associate professor of psychology, 1965-69; City College of the City University of New York, New York,

N.Y., associate professor of psychology, 1969—. *Member:* American Psychological Association, American Association for the Advancement of Science, Sigma Xi.

WRITINGS: (With David F. Ricks) *Mood and Personality,* Holt, 1966; (with Bernard S. Gorman) *The Personal Experience of Time,* Plenum, in press. Contributor to psychology journals.

WORK IN PROGRESS: Research and writing on moods, emotions, temporal experience, and personality.

* * *

WEST, David (Alexander) 1926-

PERSONAL: Born November 22, 1926, in Aberdeen, Scotland; son of David (a shipwright) and Helen (Ogg) West; married Pamela Frances Murray, July 1, 1953; children: Anne Christina, Catherine Mary, Angus Cromarty, Malcolm David, Andrew Murray. *Education:* University of Aberdeen, M.A. (first class honors in classics), 1948; Cambridge University, B.A. (first class honors), 1951; Oxford University, graduate study. *Politics:* None. *Religion:* None. *Home:* Dukewilly, Hexham, Northumberland, England. *Office:* Department of Classics, University of Newcastle upon Tyne, Newcastle upon Tyne NE1 7RU, England.

CAREER: University of Sheffield, Sheffield, England, assistant lecturer in classics, 1952-55; University of Edinburgh, Edinburgh, Scotland, lecturer in humanity, 1955-69; University of Newcastle upon Tyne, Newcastle upon Tyne, England, professor of Latin, 1969—, dean of faculty of arts, 1976—. *Military service:* Royal Air Force, 1948-49; became sergeant. *Member:* Roman Society, Classical Association.

WRITINGS: Reading Horace, Edinburgh University Press, 1967; *The Imagery and Poetry of Lucretius,* Edinburgh University Press, 1969.

WORK IN PROGRESS: Articles on *The Aeneid.*

SIDELIGHTS: West told *CA* that his "motivation" for writing is his wish "to share the joy I take in Latin poetry and to buy enough food for my children."

* * *

WEST, J(ohn) F(rederick) 1929-

PERSONAL: Born February 6, 1929, in Ashford, Kent, England; son of Frederick (a headmaster) and Lydia Mary (Anstey) West; married Vera Eveline Mackenzie, December 21, 1957; children: Sarah Vivienne, Richard Alexander. *Education:* Queens' College, Cambridge, B.A., 1952, M.A., 1959. *Home:* 86 Walsingham Rd., Woodthorpe, Nottingham NG5 4NR, England.

CAREER: Assistant forest manager with a timber company in North Borneo, 1952-53; commercial assistant with a firm in West Africa, 1953-54; schoolmaster at secondary schools in Coventry and Nottingham, England, 1955-66; Trent Polytechnic, Nottingham, England, lecturer, 1967-69, senior lecturer in liberal studies, 1969—. *Military service:* British Army, 1947-49. *Member:* Viking Society for Northern Research, Foeroya Frodskaparfelag.

WRITINGS: The Great Intellectual Revolution, J. Murray, 1965, Citadel, 1966; (editor) *The Journals of the Stanley Expedition to the Faroe Islands and Iceland in 1789,* Foeroya Frodskaparfelag, Volume I, 1970, Volume II, in press; (translator) Hedin Bru, *The Old Man and his Sons,* Paul Eriksson, 1970; *Faroe: The Emergence of a*

Nation, Paul Eriksson, 1973. Contributor to British, Danish, and Norwegian newspapers and journals.

WORK IN PROGRESS: Continuing work on Faroese history, particularly nineteenth-century administrative documents; translation of a Faroese novel.

SIDELIGHTS: J. F. West is competent in Norwegian, Danish, Swedish, Faroese, French and Malay ("the last two rusty"). *Avocational interests:* Scandinavian culture, mountaineering, music, politics.

* * *

WESTFALL, Richard S(amuel) 1924-

PERSONAL: Born April 22, 1924, in Fort Collins, Colo.; son of Alfred van Rensselaer and Dorothy M. (Towne) Westfall; married Gloria Dunn, August 23, 1952; children: Alfred, Jennifer, Kristin. *Education:* Yale University, B.A., 1948, M.A., 1949, Ph.D., 1955. *Religion:* Presbyterian. *Home:* 2222 Browncliff Rd., Bloomington, Ind. 47401. *Office:* Indiana University, Bloomington, Ind. 47401.

CAREER: California Institute of Technology, Pasadena, instructor in history, 1952-53; University of Iowa, Iowa City, instructor, 1953-55, assistant professor of history, 1955-57; Grinnell College, Grinnell, Iowa, assistant professor, 1957-60, associate professor of history, 1960-63; Indiana University, Bloomington, professor of history of science, 1963—. *Military service:* U.S. Navy, 1944-46. *Member:* American Historical Association, History of Science Society, American Association of University Professors, Sigma Xi. *Awards, honors:* Research grant, National Science Foundation, 1961-62.

WRITINGS: Science and Religion in Seventeenth Century England, Yale University Press, 1958; (contributor) Carlo L. Golino, editor, *Galileo Reappraised,* University of California Press, 1966; (author of introduction) Sir David Brewster, *Memoirs of the Life, Writings, and Discoveries of Sir Isaac Newton,* Johnson Reprint, 1966; (editor with V. E. Thoren) *Steps in the Scientific Tradition: Readings in the History of Science,* Wiley, 1968; (contributor) *The Concept of Order,* University of Washington Press, 1968; (author of introduction) Robert Hooke, *Posthumous Works,* Johnson Reprint, 1969.

The Annus Mirabilis of Sir Isaac Newton, M.I.T. Press, 1970; *Force in Newton's Physics,* MacDonald, 1971; *The Construction of Modern Science,* Wiley, 1971; *Perspectives in the History of Science and Technology,* University of Oklahoma Press, 1971; *Science, Medicine, and Society in the Renaissance,* Science History Publications, 1972; *Experiment and Mysticism in the Scientific Revolution,* Science History Publications, 1975. Contributor to *Encyclopaedia Britannica, New Catholic Encyclopedia* and *Encyclopedia Americana;* contributor to science and history journals.

WORK IN PROGRESS: A biography of Isaac Newton.

* * *

WESTPHAL, Wilma Ross 1907-
(Nancy Richard West)

PERSONAL: Born March 15, 1907, in Howard, Kan.; daughter of John T. (an architect and builder) and Laura (Richard) Ross; married Chester E. Westphal (a Seventh-day Adventist minister), June 24, 1931; children: (twins) Rosilee Mae (Mrs. Royce Williams), Marilee June (Mrs. Lauren Taylor). *Education:* Attended Eugene Business

College, Eugene, Ore., 1926-28, Walla Walla College, 1927-29, University of Panama, 1943-44; private study in interior design and decoration. *Politics:* Republican. *Home:* 527 Viewridge Dr., Angwin, Calif. 94508. *Agent:* Scott Meredith Literary Agency, Inc., 845 Third Ave., New York, N.Y. 10022.

CAREER: Rogue River Academy, Medford, Ore., teacher, 1929-31, 1937-38; Seventh-day Adventist foreign mission work, with husband, in Central and South America, teaching classes in cultural and domestic arts, 1931-45, and also teaching at American school in La Ceiba, Honduras, 1938-40; interior designer, doing homes, churches, medical clinics, hospitals, and other buildings in Washington, D.C., 1946-53, Angwin, Calif., 1953-58, Oakland, Calif., 1958-62, Redding, Calif., 1962-69. Head of department of interior design, Pacific Union College, 1954-61; teacher of interior design, adult education program, Shasta College, 1964; teacher of creative writing, 1968—. *Member:* National Society of Interior Designers (member of board of directors, 1958-59), Western Writer's Association, Women's Improvement Club (board member of Redding chapter, 1964-65, 1967-68), Women's Friendship Club (Redding). *Awards, honors:* Bronze plaque (highest in category) for church exhibits at Sacramento State Fair, 1956-59; honorary doctorate, Hamilton State University, 1973; Placque of Merit, Clover International Poetry Competition, 1974.

WRITINGS: Jeanie, Review & Herald, 1960; *Jeanie Goes to the Mission Field,* Review & Herald, 1966; (translator from the Spanish) *Cell Number 350,* Pacific Press Publishing Association, 1973; (with Ralph Escondon) *Smoke and Ashes,* Dorrance, 1974; *Heratic at Large,* Review & Herald, in press; *Harry Moyle Tippett, Tin Miner's Son,* Review & Herald, in press; *Soldados de la Cruz* (title means "Soldiers of the Cross"), Pacific Press Publishing Association, in press. Author of five book-length serials published in *Youth's Instructor;* occasional columnist writing "Household Hints" for *Review & Herald;* contributor of serials, articles, stories, and poetry to other church and educational periodicals.

WORK IN PROGRESS: A college text on interior design; a book of short, light verse tentatively entitled *Terse Verse or Worse;* a book of more serious poetry, tentatively entitled *At the Foot of the Rainbow;* a third "Jeanie" book; a child's book of verse; and a book entitled *Feathers in the Wind.*

AVOCATIONAL INTERESTS: Travel, color dynamics, architectural types of different countries; painting; collecting art, including artifacts and sculptured pieces from different parts of the world.

* * *

WESTWATER, Sister Agnes Martha 1929-
(Martha Earley)

PERSONAL: Born January 3, 1929, in Boston, Mass.; daughter of Joseph J. (a steel contractor) and Martha (Earley) Westwater. *Education:* St. John's University, Jamaica, N.Y., B.S. (cum laude), 1957, M.A., 1962; Dalhousie University, Ph.D., 1973. *Home:* Mount St. Vincent, Halifax, Nova Scotia, Canada.

CAREER: Roman Catholic nun, member of order of Sisters of Charity; teacher of English in Catholic educational institutions in New York, N.Y., 1950-57, Montreal, Quebec, 1957-62, Arvida, Quebec, 1962-66, and Vancouver, British Columbia, 1966-67; Mount St. Vincent University,

Halifax, Nova Scotia, 1967—, currently assistant professor of English.

WRITINGS: Nothing on Earth, Bruce, 1967; *Walter Bagehot: The Conservatism of a Victorian Liberal,* Dalhousie University Press, 1973. Two short stories under name Martha Earley, included in children's books published by Ginn. Contributor to *Humanities Association Review.*

* * *

WHISNANT, Charleen (Swansea) 1933-

PERSONAL: Born May 27, 1933, in Charlotte, N.C.; daughter of Henry and Elvilee Dixon (Scism) Swanzey; married Murray Whisnant (an architect), August 25, 1956; children: Ena Meredith, Thomas Wolfe. *Education:* Meredith College, B.A., 1954; University of North Carolina, M.A., 1955. *Religion:* Quaker. *Home:* 6366 Sharon Hills Rd., Charlotte, N.C. 28207. *Agent:* Thompson Talent, Yale Pl., Charlotte, N.C.

CAREER: University of North Carolina, Chapel Hill, instructor in English, 1956-57; Queens College, Charlotte, N.C., member of English faculty, 1957-65. Member of board of directors, Friends of Mint Museum of Art. *Member:* American Association of University Women, North Carolina Writers Conference, North Carolina Council on Human Relations, North Carolina Literary and Historical Association.

WRITINGS: (Editor) *Red Clay Reader,* Volumes I-VII, Southern Review, 1964-67; (contributor) *Southern Writing in the Sixties,* Louisiana State University Press, 1967; *Poetry Power,* North Carolina Department of Cultural Resources, 1973; *Word Magic,* Doubleday, 1974. Contributor of poetry to *Prairie Schooner.* Editor, *Carolina Quarterly,* 1957, and *Southern Voices,* 1974—.

WORK IN PROGRESS: Grandpa Pound, a book on Ezra Pound as a teacher and his influence on young writers.

BIOGRAPHICAL/CRITICAL SOURCES: Durham Morning Herald, November 20, 1966; *Saturday Review,* December 24, 1966; *Atlanta Journal,* January 8, 1967; *Greensboro Daily News,* January 8, 1967; *Charlotte Observer,* November 22, 1970; *Chapel Hill Weekly,* May 5, 1974.

* * *

WHITAKER, David 1930-

PERSONAL: Born April 18, 1930, in Knebworth, Hertfordshire, England; son of Richard Archer (an accountant) and Helen (Nicholas) Whitaker; married June Barry (an actress), June 8, 1963. *Education:* Educated privately by tutors. *Politics:* Conservative/Liberal. *Religion:* Protestant. *Home:* 1 Marine Parade, Watsons Bay, 2030, Sidney N.S.W., Australia.

CAREER: Became a writer in England after successful surgery for a bone disease that rendered him an invalid through much of his youth; primarily a writer, beginning 1957. Story consultant, story editor, and contract writer for British Broadcasting Corp. for several years; now freelance writer, with more than 150 television and film credits since 1967. *Member:* Writer's Guild of Great Britain (chairman, 1966-68).

WRITINGS: Doctor Who, Muller, 1964, published as *Doctor Who and the Daleks,* White Lion, 1975; *The Crusaders,* Muller, 1965.

Plays: "A Hand in Marriage"; "The Curse of the Daleks," produced at Wyndhams Theatre, London.

Films: "Subterfuge," produced by International Pictures; "Man on a Tightrope"; and material and/or dialogue for "City Beneath the Sea," "The Invasion of Earth," "Attack on the Iron Coast," and "Submarine X-1."

Television work includes six plays and eleven six-part serials.

WORK IN PROGRESS: Research for a play about man's desire for power over his fellows; the first part of an autobiography, embracing the tremendous changes in the world of entertainment on our daily lives.

SIDELIGHTS: Whitaker told *CA:* "I travel widely in Europe, particularly France and Italy—fascinated by tradition and historic societies influencing each new generation, and the essential differences between this and the developing or newer countries, which approach national and international problems without the pressures of the past dictating or advising their decisions."†

* * *

WHITCOMB, Edgar D(oud)   1918-

PERSONAL: Born November 6, 1918, in Hayden, Ind.; son of John William and Louise (Doud) Whitcomb; married Patricia Louise Dolfuss, May 22, 1952; children: Patricia Louise, Linda Ann, Shelley Jean, Alice Elaine, John Doud. *Education:* Indiana University, LL.B., 1950. *Politics:* Republican. *Religion:* Methodist. *Home:* 636 North Poplar, Seymour, Ind. 47274. *Office:* Suite 3300, Indiana Square, Indianapolis, Ind. 46204.

CAREER: Admitted to State Bar of Indiana, 1952; attorney with practice in Seymour and Indianapolis, Ind., 1952-66, 1973—. Indiana state senator, 1951-54; U.S. Department of Justice, assistant U.S. attorney general for southern district of Indiana, 1955-56; Secretary of State, Indiana, 1966-68; governor of the state of Indiana, 1969-73; president of World Trade Center, Indianapolis, 1973—. Chairman, Great Lakes Commission, 1965-66. *Military service:* U.S. Army Air Forces, 1940-46; became major; received Air Medal with oak-leaf cluster and Presidential Unit Citation with six oak-leaf clusters. U.S. Air Force Reserve, 1946—; now colonel. *Member:* American Bar Association, Phi Delta Phi.

WRITINGS: Escape from Corregidor, Regnery, 1958.

* * *

WHITE, Elmer G.   1926-

PERSONAL: Born February 27, 1926, in Chicago, Ill.; son of Frank M. and Lillian (Roth) White; married Kathleen Connor, August 19, 1950; children: David, Paul, Andrew. *Education:* University of Iowa, B.A., 1950; Northwestern University, M.A., 1962; University of Notre Dame, further graduate study, 1964. *Office:* Pembroke-Country Day School, 5121 State Line Rd., Kansas City, Mo. 64112.

CAREER: Great Lakes Naval Training Center, Electronic Supply Office, Great Lakes, Ill., commodity specialist and editorial assistant, 1950-52; Culver Military Academy, Culver, Ind., 1952-75, began as assistant instructor, master instructor in English, 1968-75; Pembroke-Country Day School, Kansas City, Mo., teacher of English, 1975—. *Military service:* U.S. Army Air Forces, radio operator and gunner, 1944-46; became sergeant. *Member:* National Council of Teachers of English, National Fencing Coaches Association of America, Amateur Fencers League of America, Independent Schools Association of Central States (member of teacher's council), Indiana Council of

Teachers of English (chairman of language committee, 1971-75).

WRITINGS: (With M. L. Brown and E. B. Jenkinson) *Two Approaches to Teaching Syntax,* Indiana University Press, 1966; (with Brown) *A Grammar for English Sentences,* Books 1-2, C. E. Merrill, 1967; *Language: An Approach to Meaning,* C. E. Merrill, 1971.

* * *

WHITE, M(ary) E(llen)   1938-

PERSONAL: Born January 17, 1938, in Syracuse, Kan.; daughter of K. E. (a farmer) and Dorothea (Downer) White. *Education:* Stanford University, B.A., 1959; University of Iowa, M.A., 1961; Ohio State University, Ph.D. candidate, 1961—. *Politics:* "Organized chaos." *Religion:* None. *Agent:* Lynn Nesbit, International Creative Management, 40 West 57th St., New York, N.Y. 10019.

CAREER: York University, Toronto, Ontario, lecturer in philosophy, beginning 1967. *Member:* American Philosophical Association.

WRITINGS: In the Balance (novel), Harper, 1968; *Con,* Harper, 1972. Short stories published in *New Directions Annual 18, Year's Best Science Fiction,* 10th Annual, and *Paris Review.*

WORK IN PROGRESS: A novel, *Logic Book.*

BIOGRAPHICAL/CRITICAL SOURCES: Book World, January 21, 1968; *New Republic,* February 24, 1968; *New York Times Book Review,* March 24, 1968.†

* * *

WHITE, Melvin R(obert)   1911-

PERSONAL: Born January 7, 1911, in Chugwater, Wyo.; son of Robert Reid (a building contractor) and Cecelia Rebecca (Danielson) White. *Education:* University of Iowa, B.A., 1932, M.A., 1933; University of Wisconsin, Ph.D., 1948; postdoctoral study at Columbia University and Television Workshop, 1949, and Institute for Advanced Study in Theatre Arts, 1959-60. *Politics:* Republican. *Religion:* Congregationalist. *Home:* 583 Boulevard Way, Piedmont, Calif. 94610.

CAREER: High school principal in Andrew, Iowa, 1933-34; high school teacher in Galesburg, Ill., 1934-38; Washington State University, Pullman, instructor in radio, 1938-40; Indiana University, Bloomington, assistant professor of speech, 1941-42; University of Wyoming, Laramie, assistant professor of speech and chairman of department, 1946-47; University of Hawaii, Honolulu, associate professor of speech, 1948-51; Brooklyn College of the City University of New York, Brooklyn, N.Y., associate professor of speech and theater, 1952-68, deputy chairman of department, 1965-68; California State College at Hayward (now California State University, Hayward), associate professor of speech and drama, 1968-71; Chaminade College of Honolulu, Honolulu, Hawaii, professor of speech, 1971; University of Hawaii—Hilo College, Hilo, director of theatre, 1972-73; University of Arizona, Tucson, professor of speech communication, 1974; California Polytechnic State University, San Luis Obispo, lecturer in speech, 1974-75. Visiting summer professor at University of Oklahoma, 1949, University of Wisconsin, 1950, University of Arkansas, 1964; exchange professor, University of Hawaii, 1962-63; adjunct professor of speech, Brooklyn College of the City University of New York, summers 1973, 1974. Workshop director of readers theater productions and lecturer throughout United States, and in El Salvador, Guatemala, and Canada. Consultant to Texas Fine Arts Commission; consultant on little theater program, McGraw-Hill Book Co. *Military service:* U.S. Naval Reserve, active duty, 1942-45.

MEMBER: American Educational Theatre Association (executive secretary-treasurer, 1965-66), American National Theatre and Academy (member of board of directors), International Theatre Institute of UNESCO, Speech Association of America, American Community Theatre Association (executive secretary-treasurer, 1965-66), Children's Theatre Conference (executive secretary-treasurer, 1965-66), United States Institute for Theatre Technology (member of board of directors). *Awards, honors:* American Educational Theatre Association Award for outstanding service, 1962; silver trophy presented by Adjutant General, U.S. Army, for contribution to Army theater project, 1967; Gold Masque Award, U.S. Army Southern Command, 1967.

WRITINGS: Radio and Assembly Plays, Northwestern Press (Minneapolis), 1941; *Highlights of History,* Northwestern Press, 1942; (contributor) *Your Speech and Mine,* Lyons & Carnahan, 1945; *Children's Programs for Radio Broadcast,* Northwestern Press, 1948; (with Jean Hinton Bennion) *Mr. Geography,* Northwestern Press, 1948; *Radio Materials for Practice and Broadcast,* Northwestern Press, 1950; *Beginning Radio Production,* Northwestern Press, 1950; *Microphone Technique for Radio Actors,* Northwestern Press, 1950; *Beginning Television Production,* Burgess, 1953; (with Leslie Irene Coger) *Studies in Readers Theatre,* S & F Press, 1963; *The Mikado for Readers' Theatre and Stage,* S & F Press, 1964; *From the Printed Page,* S & F Press, 1965; (with Coger) *Readers Theatre Handbook: A Dramatic Approach to Literature,* Scott, Foresman, 1967, revised edition, 1973; (with Frank Whiting) *Playreaders Repertory: Anthology for an Introduction to Theatre,* Scott, Foresman, 1970.

Editor, *Directory of the American Educational Theatre Association,* 1965. Contributor of more than fifty articles and about twenty reviews to speech and theater journals. *Players,* editor of radio section, 1947-49, associate editor of magazine, 1950-51, editor of makeup department, 1957-61; *Educational Theatre Journal,* special editor, Thomas Wood Stevens Memorial Issue, December, 1951, managing editor and business editor, 1958-61, 1965-67.

WORK IN PROGRESS: With James Carlsen, *Literature on Stage: Readers Theater Anthology.*

* * *

WHITE, Ray Lewis 1941-

PERSONAL: Born August 11, 1941, in Abingdon, Va.; son of Benjamin Wesley (a farmer) and Maude (Patterson) White. *Education:* Emory and Henry College, B.A., 1962; University of Arkansas, M.A., 1963, Ph.D., 1971. *Office:* English Department, Illinois State University, Normal, Ill. 61761.

CAREER: North Carolina State University at Raleigh, instructor, 1965-68; Illinois State University, Normal, assistant professor, 1968-70, associate professor, 1970-73, professor of English, 1973—. *Member:* Modern Language Association of America, American Association of University Professors, Society for the Study of Midwestern Literature, Phi Beta Kappa. *Awards, honors:* Woodrow Wilson fellowship; Newberry Library research awards; National Defense Education Act fellowship.

WRITINGS: The Achievement of Sherwood Anderson, University of North Carolina Press, 1966; (editor) Sherwood Anderson, *Return to Winesburg,* University of North Carolina Press, 1967; *Sherwood Anderson: Country Editor,* University of North Carolina Press, 1967; *Gore Vidal,* Twayne, 1968; *A Story Teller's Story: A Critical Text,* Press of Case Western Reserve University, 1968; (editor) *Sherwood Anderson's Memoirs: A Critical Edition,* University of North Carolina Press, 1969; (editor) S. Anderson, *Tar: A Midwest Childhood,* Press of Case Western Reserve University, 1969; *Checklist of Sherwood Anderson,* C. E. Merrill, 1969; *The Merrill Studies in Winesburg, Ohio,* C. E. Merrill, 1971; *Marching Men,* Press of Case Western Reserve University, 1972; (editor) *Sherwood Anderson—Gertrude Stein: Correspondence and Personal Essays,* University of North Carolina Press, 1972; *Winesburg, Ohio: The Genetic Text,* University of North Carolina Press, 1976; *Sherwood Anderson: A Reference Bibliography,* G. K. Hall, 1976.

* * *

WHITE, Stanhope 1913-
(Sabiad)

PERSONAL: Born July 21, 1913, in Middlesbrough, Yorkshire, England; son of Dyson (a tailor) and Flora (Berry) White; married Margaret Bruce Caddick, January 26, 1940; children: Stanhope Peter, Richard Geoffrey. *Education:* Emmanuel College, Cambridge, B.A. (second class honors), 1934, M.A., 1936. *Politics:* "Floating voter." *Religion:* Atheist. *Home:* 47 Severn Dr., Guisborough, Cleveland, England.

CAREER: Circumnavigated Iceland as deckhand on a trawler when fifteen; in 1934 went to Sinai with the Egyptian Desert Survey, to Iceland as a survey geologist, and to East Africa as surveyor on an expedition; appointed to British Colonial Administrative Service, 1935, and served in Nigeria, 1936-54, with final appointment as director of Department of Trade and Industry; Fisons Fertilizers Ltd., Felixstowe, England, 1954-68, chief safety officer, 1967-68; employed by Imperial Chemical Industries, Wilton, England, 1968-75. *Military service:* Nigeria Regiment, 1939-40. *Member:* Institute of Industrial Safety Officers, Chartered Institute of Secretaries (associate member). *Awards, honors:* Coronation Medal.

WRITINGS: Descent from the Hills, J. Murray, 1963; *Dan Bana,* Cassell, 1966; *Lost Empire on the Nile: H. M. Stanley, Emin Pasha and the Imperialists,* R. Hale, 1969. Author of series of short stories under pen name, Sabiad (Abiad is the Shuwa Arabic for White); contributor of articles to *Journal of Royal Geographical Society, Empire Journal of Experimental Agriculture,* and magazines.

WORK IN PROGRESS: Mysterious Moorlands: The Story of the North Yorkshire Moors.

SIDELIGHTS: Stanhope White speaks Hausa, and knew at various times some Swahili, Tiv, Fulani, and Arabic.

* * *

WHITE, Theodore Edwin 1938-
(Ted White; pseudonyms: Ron Archer and Norman Edwards, the latter a joint pseudonym)

PERSONAL: Born February 4, 1938, in Washington, D.C.; son of Edwin Paul (a photographer) and Dorothea (Belz) White; married Sylvia Dees, November 30, 1958; married second wife, Robin Postal, February 26, 1966 (separated); children: Avielle. *Education:* Attended public schools in Falls Church, Va. *Politics:* "Nominally Democrat; iconoclastic." *Religion:* "Agnostic; personal theism." *Home:* 1014 North Tuckahoe St., Falls Church, Va. 22046. *Agent:* Henry Morrison, Inc., 58 West 10 St., New York, N.Y. 10011.

CAREER: Writer, with a work background of "every job every would-be novelist has held, save that of shoe salesman." Head of foreign department at Scott Meredith Literary Agency, Inc., New York City, 1963; assistant editor of *Magazine of Fantasy and Science Fiction,* New York City, 1963-68; editor of *Amazing Stories* and *Fantastic,* 1968—. Associate editor, Lancer Books, New York City, 1966. Chairman of 25th World Science Fiction Convention. *Member:* Fantasy Amateur Press Association (president, 1957), Washington (D.C.) Science Fiction Association (president, 1955), New York Futurians, New York Fanoclasts (founder), Falls Church Fanoclasts (founder).

WRITINGS—Under name Ted White, except as indicated: (With T. Carr, under joint pseudonym Norman Edwards) *Invasion from 2500,* Monarch Books, 1964; *Android Avenger,* Ace Books, 1965; *Phoenix Prime,* Lancer Books, 1966; *The Sorceress of Qar,* Lancer Books, 1966; *The Jewels of Elsewhen,* Belmont Books, 1967; *Secret of the Marauder Satellite,* Westminster, 1967; (with Dave Van Arnam) *Sideslip,* Pyramid Books, 1968; *Spawn of the Death Machine,* Paperback Library, 1968; *No Time Like Tomorrow,* Crown, 1969; *By Furies Possessed,* Signet, 1970; *Trouble on Project Ceres* (juvenile), Westminster, 1971; *Starwolf,* Lancer Books, 1971; (editor) *The Best from "Amazing Stories,"* Manor, 1973; (editor) *The Best from "Fantastic,"* Manor, 1973. Contributor of articles and stories to *Rogue, Gamma, Startling Mystery, If, Magazine of Fantasy and Science Fiction;* also contributor of record reviews and musical criticism to *Metronome, Jazz Guide, 33 Guide.*

WORK IN PROGRESS: Further books.

*   *   *

WHITE, William   1910-

PERSONAL: Born September 4, 1910, in Paterson, N.J.; son of Noel D. (a chemist) and Beccia (Firkser) White; married Gertrude Mason (a professor of English), June 20, 1951; children: Geoffrey M., Roger W. *Education:* University of Chattanooga, B.A., 1933; University of California, Los Angeles, graduate courses, 1935-40; University of Southern California, M.A., 1937; University of Dijon, further study, 1951; University of London, Ph.D., 1953. *Politics:* Democrat. *Religion:* Methodist. *Home:* 25860 West 14 Mile Rd., Franklin, Mich. 48025. *Office:* Department of Speech Communications, Oakland University, Rochester, Mich. 48063.

CAREER: Whitman College, Walla Walla, Wash., instructor in English, 1941-42; Mary Hardin-Baylor College, Belton, Tex., assistant professor of journalism, 1946-47; Ohio Wesleyan University, Delaware, assistant professor of journalism, 1947; Wayne State University, Detroit, Mich., assistant then associate professor, 1947-60, professor of journalism, 1960-74, adjunct professor of American studies, 1974—, acting chairman of journalism department, 1956-57, 1965-66, chairman of American studies program, 1967-74; Oakland University, Rochester, Mich., professor of speech communications and director of journalism program, 1974—. Visiting professor at University of Southern California, Los Angeles, 1962, Chungang Univer-

sity, Hankuk University, and Soong Sil College, all Seoul, Korea, 1963-64, University of Rhode Island, Kingston, 1966, University of Hawaii, Honolulu, 1969, California State College (now University), Long Beach, 1969. Reporter, columnist, and editor for local newspapers, 1924—. *Military service:* U.S. Army, intelligence service, 1942-45; also associated with several servicemen's newspapers.

MEMBER: American Association of University Professors, Modern Language Association of America, Bibliographical Society of America, American Association for the History of Medicine, Association for Education in Journalism, American Studies Association, Modern Humanities Research Association, Thoreau Society, Whitman Birthplace Association, Private Libraries Association, Michigan Academy of Science, Arts and Letters, Book Club of Detroit, Friends of Detroit Public Library, Sigma Delta Chi, Blue Key, Theta Chi. *Awards, honors:* Foundation for Economic Education fellowship, 1956; Wayne State University research grants, 1957, 1963, 1966; Fulbright fellowship, 1963-64; American Philosophical Society fellowship, 1965; National Endowment for the Humanities grant, 1967-70, 1972.

WRITINGS: A Henry David Thoreau Bibliography, 1908-1937, Faxon, 1939; (editor) A. E. Housman, *Three Comic Poems,* Jake Zeitlin, 1941; *John Donne Since 1900: A Periodical Bibliography,* Faxon, 1942; *D. H. Lawrence: A Checklist, 1931-1950,* Wayne State University Press, 1950; (editor) *This Is Detroit, 1701-1951: 250 Years in Pictures,* Wayne State University Press, 1951; *Sir William Osler: Historian and Literary Essayist,* Wayne State University Press, 1951; *John Ciardi: A Bibliography,* Wayne State University Press, 1959; (editor with H. W. Blodgett) *Walt Whitman: An 1855-56 Notebook,* Southern Illinois University Press, 1959; (editor) *A. E. Housman: A Centennial Memento,* Oriole Press, 1959; (editor) *A. E. Housman to Joseph Ishill: Five Unpublished Letters,* Oriole Press, 1959; *W. D. Snodgrass: A Bibliography,* Wayne State University Press, 1960; *Karl Shapiro: A Bibliography,* Wayne State University Press, 1960; (editor) Walt Whitman, *The People and John Quincy Adams,* Oriole Press, 1961, revised edition, 1962; *Ernest Hemingway: Guide to a Memorial Exhibition,* University of Detroit Library, 1961; (with Zoltan G. Zeke) *George Orwell: A Selected Bibliography,* Boston Linotype Print, 1962; (consulting editor) A. E. Housman, *A Shropshire Lad,* Avon, 1966; *Wilfred Owen (1893-1918): A Bibliography,* Kent State University Press, 1967; (editor) *By-Line: Ernest Hemingway* (Literary Guild selection), Scribner, 1967; *Walt Whitman's Journalism: A Bibliography,* Wayne State University Press, 1968; *Studies in "The Sun Also Rises,"* C. E. Merrill, 1969; *Guide to Ernest Hemingway,* C. E. Merrill, 1969; *Checklist of Ernest Hemingway,* C. E. Merrill, 1970; (editor) *Walt Whitman in Our Time,* Wayne State University Press, 1970; *Edwin Arlington Robinson: A Supplementary Bibliography,* Kent State University Press, 1971; (editor with Roger Asselineau) *Walt Whitman in Europe Today,* Wayne State University Press, 1972; (editor) Ernest Bramah, *Kai Lung: Six,* Non-Profit Press, 1974; *Nathaniel West: A Comprehensive Bibliography,* Kent State University Press, 1975.

Contributor to *The New Cambridge Bibliography of English Literature,* Volume III, 1969, Volume IV, 1972. Editor, *Walt Whitman Review,* 1956—, and *Wayne Journalism Newsletter,* 1956-74; contributing editor, *Annual Bibliography of English Language and Literature,* 1963—; associate editor, *American Book Collector,* 1965—; editorial advisor, *Emily Dickinson Bulletin,* 1971—, and *Hemingway Notes,* 1972-74.

WORK IN PROGRESS: Editing with eight others, *The Collected Writings of Walt Whitman,* for New York University Press; *Ernest Bramah,* for Twayne; a compilation of newspaper and magazine articles by Ernest Hemingway, for Scribner; with others, *American Literary Scholarship,* for Duke University Press; *John P. Marquand: A Bibliography,* for Yale University Library.

BIOGRAPHICAL/CRITICAL SOURCES: Time, May 19, 1967; *Book Week,* May 28, 1967; *New York Times Book Review,* May 28, 1967; *National Observer,* May 29, 1967; *Christian Science Monitor,* June 1, 1967; *New Republic,* June 10, 1967; *Atlantic Monthly,* July, 1967; *Commonweal,* August 11, 1967.

*   *   *

WHITEMAN, Maxwell 1914-

PERSONAL: Born January 17, 1914, in Philadelphia, Pa.; son of Tovia (a rabbi) and Nechama (Millman) Whiteman; married Elizabeth Hartwell Delano, May 8, 1937; children: Bethel (daughter). *Education:* "No formal education." *Religion:* Jewish. *Home:* 414 Westview Rd., Elkins Park, Pa. 19117. *Office:* Union League, 140 South Broad St., Philadelphia, Pa. 19102.

CAREER: Antiquarian bookseller, 1935-53, specializing in social and ethnic history, with emphasis on Negro history and literature; American Jewish Archives, Cincinnati, Ohio, associate director, 1955-58; Dropsie College (now University), Philadelphia, Pa., librarian and lecturer in American Jewish history, 1958-64; Union League of Philadelphia, Philadelphia, historian and archivist, 1964—. Officer, Museum of American Jewish History. Commissioner, Pennsylvania Historical Museum Commission, 1971—. Chairman, Cheltenham Township Historical Commission, 1970—. Member, National Endowment for the Humanities Great Issues Program, 1973—. Consultant, Military Order of the Loyal Legion War Library and Museum. *Member:* Jewish Publication Society of America (publication committee member, 1955—), American Jewish Historical Society (board member, 1956-64), Pennsylvania Geneological Society, John Alden Kindred, Historical Society of Pennsylvania, Philobiblon Club. *Awards, honors:* Awards from American Association for State and Local History, for *Pieces of Paper: Gateway to the Past,* 1967, for *Copper for America: The Hendricks.*

WRITINGS: A Century of Fiction by American Negroes, 1853-1952, Phila Jacobs, 1955; (editor) William W. Brown, *Clotelle: A Tale of the Southern States* (facsimile edition), privately printed, 1955; (with Edwin Wolf II) *A History of the Jews of Philadelphia from Colonial Times to the Age of Jackson,* Jewish Publication Society, 1957; *Mankind and Medicine: History of the Einstein Medical Center of Philadelphia,* Einstein Medical Center, 1966; *Pieces of Paper: Gateway to the Past,* Union League of Philadelphia, 1967; *History of Philadelphia Fellowship Commission,* Philadelphia Fellowship Commission, 1968; *While Lincoln Lay Dying,* Philadelphia Union League, 1968; *Copper for America: The Hendricks Family and a National Industry, 1755-1939,* Rutgers University Press, 1971; *Gentlemen in Crisis: The First Century of the Union League of Philadelphia, 1862-1962,* Union League of Philadelphia, 1975. Contributor to historical journals and Jewish periodicals. Associate editor, *American Jewish Archives.*

WORK IN PROGRESS: Anxious Immigrants: East European Jews in Philadelphia.

SIDELIGHTS: Maxwell Whiteman was the first to teach Negro history in Philadelphia. He is a collector of rare and early American Judaica, and of books on early American economic thought and the Delano family in America.

*   *   *

WHITESON, Leon 1930-

PERSONAL: Born October 19, 1930, in Bulawayo, Southern Rhodesia; son of Charles (a businessman) and Rebecca (Goldman) Whiteson; married Janine Kahn (an artist), March 18, 1950; children: Paul, Karen. *Education:* Attended Milton School, Bulawayo, Rhodesia; University of Capetown, B.Arch., 1953. *Politics:* "Apolitical." *Religion:* Jewish. *Agent:* Jonathan Clowes Ltd., 19 Jeffrey's Pl., London NW1 9PP, England.

CAREER: Registered architect in United Kingdom, working as assistant architect in a variety of offices, 1954-65; full-time writer, beginning 1965.

WRITINGS: Nora Eckdorf (novel), Eyre & Spottiswoode, 1967. Author of television play, "Blood of the Lamb," for British Broadcasting Corp., and of commissioned radio scripts. Contributor of short story to *Transatlantic Review.*

WORK IN PROGRESS: A novel and several plays.

SIDELIGHTS: Nora Eckdorf, writes Kenith Trodd, "is not, as one hyper-enthusiast told me, 'the greatest since Lawrence' but the comparison isn't reckless. The arrogance, control, nerve and talent in this study of a wealthy ageing Jewess hurtling towards madness (her crippling strength mockingly annihilated by the weak males in her circle) show Whiteson beckoning, not absurdly, for huge stature. The writing is shrewd, the impact, perhaps by design, almost repellent." Whiteson speaks Spanish and French.

BIOGRAPHICAL/CRITICAL SOURCES: New Statesman, June 9, 1967.††

*   *   *

WHITLOCK, Glenn E(verett) 1917-

PERSONAL: Born September 1, 1917, in Arroyo Grande, Calif.; son of Edwin Samuel (a merchant) and Annie (Everett) Whitlock; married Louise Fillingim, November 20, 1953 (deceased); married Emalee Rogers (a teacher), April 10, 1965; children: (first marriage) Glenn Elliott, Carole Louise; (second marriage) Elise Babette. *Education:* Occidental College, A.B., 1940, A.M., 1951; McCormick Theological Seminary, B.D., 1944; University of Southern California, Ph.D., 1959. *Politics:* Democrat. *Home:* 30545 Palo Alto Dr., Redlands, Calif. 92373. *Office:* Johnston College, University of Redlands, Redlands, Calif. 92373.

CAREER: Ordained minister of Presbyterian Church, 1944; pastor in Harrisburg, Ill., 1944-46; Westminster Foundation of Southern California, Los Angeles, university pastor, 1946-47, 1953-58; United Presbyterian Church in the U.S.A., Synod of Southern California, Los Angeles, church career counselor, 1959-69; University of Redlands, Johnston College, Redlands, Calif., faculty fellow of humanistic psychology, 1969—. Visiting lecturer, California Baptist Theological Seminary. *Member:* American Association of Pastoral Counselors (fellow), American Psychological Association, Institutes of Religion and Health, Association for Humanistic Psychology.

WRITINGS: From Call to Service: The Making of a Minister, Westminster, 1968; *Preventive Psychology and the*

Church, Westminster, 1973. Contributor to religious and psychology journals.

WORK IN PROGRESS: Understanding and Coping with Human Crises; Confluent Learning in Higher Education.

BIOGRAPHICAL/CRITICAL SOURCES: Pastoral Psychology, February, 1967.

* * *

WHITMAN, Ruth (Bashein) 1922-

PERSONAL: Born May 28, 1922, in New York, N.Y.; daughter of Meyer D. (a lawyer) and Martha (Sherman) Bashein; married Cedric Whitman, October 13, 1941 (divorced, 1958); married Firman Houghton, July 23, 1959 (divorced, 1964); married Morton Sacks (a painter), October 6, 1966; children: (first marriage) Rachel Whitman, Leda Whitman; (second marriage) David Houghton. *Education:* Radcliffe College, B.A. (magna cum laude), 1944. *Politics:* Liberal. *Religion:* "Secular Jewish." *Home:* 70 Williston Rd., Brookline, Mass. 02140. *Office:* Radcliffe College, Cambridge, Mass.

CAREER: Houghton Mifflin Co., Boston, Mass., editorial assistant, 1941-42, educational editor, 1944-45; Harvard University Press, Cambridge, Mass., free-lance editor, 1945-60; *Audience* (magazine), Cambridge, poetry editor, 1958-63; teacher of poetry workshop, Cambridge Center for Adult Education, 1965-68; Radcliffe College, Cambridge, seminar instructor in poetry, 1969—; poet and translator. Member of board of directors, New Poet's Theater, Cambridge, and Cambridge School of Ballet. *Member:* Poetry Society of America (member of executive board, 1962—), New England Poetry Club. *Awards, honors:* Reynolds Lyric Award of Poetry Society of America, 1961; MacDowell Colony fellowships, 1962, 1964, 1972-74; Jennie Tane Award of *Massachusetts Review,* 1962; Alice Fay di Costagnola Award of Poetry Society of America, 1968, for manuscript of *The Marriage Wig;* fellowship to Radcliffe Institute for Independent Study, 1968-69; National Foundation for Jewish Culture grant, 1968.

WRITINGS: Blood and Milk Poems, Clarke & Way, 1963; (co-translator) *Selected Poems of Alain Bosquet,* New Directions, 1963; (co-translator) Isaac Bashevis Singer, *Short Friday,* Farrar, Straus, 1966; (translator and compiler) *An Anthology of Modern Yiddish Poetry* (bilingual edition), October House, 1966; *The Marriage Wig, and Other Poems,* Harcourt, 1968; (editor and translator) *The Selected Poems of Jacob Glatstein,* October House, 1972; *The Passion of Lizzie Borden: New and Selected Poems,* October House, 1973. Also translator of modern French and Greek poetry.

WORK IN PROGRESS: A book-length poem, *Tamsen Donner: The Journal of a Pioneer Woman;* a collection of shorter poems, *In the Country of the Whitethroated Sparrow.*

* * *

WHITNEY, Elizabeth Dalton 1906-

PERSONAL: Born May 24, 1906, in Asheville, N.C.; daughter of George Louis (a contractor) and Mary Rose (Wilson) Dalton; married Lyman Fiske Whitney, March 17, 1931 (died June, 1957); married James Otis Post (president of Post Products Co.), September 17, 1965. *Education:* Studied at University of North Carolina, 1926, Yale Summer School of Alcohol Studies, 1943. *Politics:* Republican. *Religion:* Unitarian Universalist. *Home:* Pill Hill, Duxbury, Mass.

CAREER: Archers Co. (manufacturers of archery equipment), Pinehurst, N.C., executive partner, 1926-31; founder and executive director of Voluntary Health Organization, 1945—. Lecturer at Yale School of Alcohol Studies, 1945-48, and International Congress on Alcoholism, Prague, 1966. Member of Massachusetts State Advisory Council on Alcoholism, 1957-62; chairman of health division, United Community Services fund drive, Boston, 1964. Producer and conductor of weekly radio program, "Alcoholism Is Everybody's Business," WNAC, 1950-68. *Member:* International Council on Alcoholism, National Council on Alcoholism, American Association of Criminology (honorary life member), Duxbury Art Association, Duxbury Yacht Club. *Awards, honors:* Fellowship to Yale Summer School of Alcohol Studies, 1943; citation from Greater Boston Council on Alcoholism.

WRITINGS: The Lonely Sickness, Beacon Press, 1965; *Living with Alcoholism,* Beacon Press, 1968; *World Dialogue on Alcohol and Drug Dependence,* Beacon Press, 1970. Author of booklets and pamphlets published by Greater Boston Council on Alcoholism; former writer of question and answer column on alcoholism in five weekly newspapers in Boston area. Former contributing editor of *Sportswomen,* and columnist for *National Archery Magazine.*

WORK IN PROGRESS: A novel (not about alcoholism), tentatively titled *Luellyn Rumple;* a gourmet cookbook for owners of small boats.

AVOCATIONAL INTERESTS: Art, crafts, sailing, and cuisine.

BIOGRAPHICAL/CRITICAL SOURCES: And Put It on the Front Page Please!, Washburn, 1960; John H. Cutler, *What About Women?,* Washburn, 1961.

* * *

WHITTET, G(eorge) S(orley) 1918-

PERSONAL: Born June 22, 1918, in Scotland; son of George and Elizabeth (Robertson) Whittet; married Pauline Ella Watson, August 9, 1952; children: Susan Fiona, Andrew John. *Education:* Educated in Scotland. *Home:* 2 Harrow Rd., Carshalton, Surrey, England.

CAREER: Studio Magazine, London, England, editor, 1946-64; *Studio International,* London, editor, 1964-65; *Esso Magazine,* London, staff writer, 1966. Art adviser to collectors and publications. *Military service:* British Army, 1939-46; became staff sergeant; mentioned in dispatches. *Member:* International Association of Art Critics.

WRITINGS: Bouquet, Studio Books, 1949; *London,* World Publishing, 1967; *Scotland Explored,* Thames & Hudson, 1969; *Lovers in Art,* Dutton, 1972. Contributor to radio and television; has written as an art critic for periodicals and newspapers in half a dozen countries, including *Art and Artists, Le Monde* (Paris), *Pictures on Exhibit, Graphis, Statesman, Illustrated Weekly of India, D'Ars* (Milan); verse and poetry have been published in *Highway 16 Courier* and *Evening News* (Glasgow), and anthologized in *More Comic and Curious Verse,* Penguin.

WORK IN PROGRESS: A critical autobiography entitled *One-Man View;* stage plays.

SIDELIGHTS: Whittet is mainly concerned with "the human rather than the academic aspect of art, . . . the revelation of the artist's personality and history and through him his society's peculiarities." He says that he loves "to travel and meet new people but am content to be a

Scotsman anywhere. Intelligence in women I regard as the sauce on the steak.''

*   *   *

WHITTINGTON, H(orace) G(reeley) 1929-

PERSONAL: Born January 5, 1929, in Galveston, Tex.; son of Thomas Monroe (manager of a cotton compress) and Hallie Marie (Hobbs) Whittington; married Kathleen Taggett, May 2, 1970; children: Howard Gregory, Leslie Ann, Kirk Monroe, Sara Helen, Amy Kathleen, Michael Thomas. *Education:* Rice University, B.A., 1948; Baylor University, M.D., 1952. *Politics:* Democrat. *Religion:* Unitarian Universalist. *Home:* 2754 South Paris Place, Denver, Colo. 80232.

CAREER: Menninger School of Psychiatry, Topeka, Kan., resident, 1955-58; University of Kansas, Lawrence, director of mental health clinic, Student Health Service, 1958-61; Community Mental Health Services, Topeka, Kan., director, 1962-65; private practice of psychiatry, Denver, Colo., 1965—; Department of Health and Hospitals, Denver, Colo., director of psychiatry, 1965-73; director, Western Institute of Human Resources, 1973-74; senior psychiatric consultant, Furt Logan Mental Health Center, 1974-75; clinical director, Malcolm X Center for Mental Health, 1975—. *Member:* American Psychiatric Association, Sigma Xi, Alpha Omega Alpha.

WRITINGS: Psychiatry on the College Campus, International Universities Press, 1963; *Psychiatry in the American Community,* International Universities Press, 1966; *Development of an Urban Mental Health Center,* C. C Thomas, 1971; *Clinical Practice in Community Mental Health Centers,* International Universities Press, 1973. Contributor to scientific journals.

SIDELIGHTS: Whittington became interested in creative writing while a student at Rice; after short stories and several novels were rejected over an eight-year period, he decided to confine writing to psychiatric endeavors.

*   *   *

WHITTINGTON, Harry 1915-
(Whit Harrison, Kel Holland, Harriet Kathryn Myers, Steve Phillips, Clay Stuart, Hondo Wells, Harry White, Hallam Whitney)

PERSONAL: Born February 4, 1915, in Ocala, Fla.; son of Harry Benjamin and Rosa (Hardee) Whittington; married Kathryn Odom, February 9, 1936; children: Harriet Kathryn Beebe, Howard Hardee. *Education:* Educated in Florida public schools; took extension and night courses in psychology, writing, English, and other subjects at various colleges. *Religion:* Episcopalian. *Address:* P.O. Box 10781, St. Petersburg, Fla. 33733. *Agent:* Mauri Grashin Agency, 8730 Sunset Blvd., Los Angeles, Calif. 90069.

CAREER: Griffith Advertising Agency, St. Petersburg, Fla., copywriter, 1933-35; Capitol Theatre, St. Petersburg, assistant advertising manager, 1935-36; U.S. Post Office, St. Petersburg, clerk, 1936-45; editor of *Labor Advocate* and other periodicals, St. Petersburg, 1938-45; professional writer, 1947—. *Military service:* U.S. Navy, stationed at Pearl Harbor, 1945-46; became petty officer. *Member:* Authors Guild, Western Writers of America, Mystery Writers of America (former member of board).

WRITINGS: Vengeance Valley, Phoenix Books, 1945; *Her Sin,* Phoenix Books, 1946; *The Lady Was a Tramp,* Handi-Books, 1950; *Slay Ride for a Lady,* Handi-Books, 1950; *Call Me Killer,* Graphic Books, 1951; *Murder Is My Mistress,* Graphic Books, 1951; *Mourn the Hangman,* Graphic Books, 1951; *Brass Monkey,* Handi-Books, 1951; *Forever Evil,* Paperback Library, 1951; *Swamp Kill,* Paperback Library, 1951; *Satan's Widow,* Paperback Library, 1951; *Married to Murder,* Paperback Library, 1951; *Fires That Destroy,* Gold Medal Books, 1951; *So Dead My Love,* Ace Books, 1952; *Drawn to Evil,* Ace Books, 1952; *You'll Die Next,* Ace Books, 1953; *Cracker Girl,* Beacon, 1953; *Wild Oats,* Beacon, 1953; *Prime Sucker,* Beacon, 1953; *The Woman Is Mine,* Gold Medal Books, 1953; *Saddle the Storm,* Gold Medal Books, 1954; *Naked Island,* Ace Books, 1954; *Desire in the Dust,* Gold Medal Books, 1955; *One Got Away,* Ace Books, 1955; *A Woman on the Place,* Ace Books, 1955.

Across That River, Ace Books, 1956; *Humming Box,* Ace Books, 1956; *Backwoods Tramp,* Gold Medal Books, 1956; *Brutes in Brass,* Gold Medal Books, 1956; *Saturday Night Town,* Crest Books, 1956; *Mink,* Gallimard (Paris), 1956; *Web of Murder,* Gold Medal Books, 1957; *Strangers on Friday,* Abelard, 1957; *Play for Keeps,* Abelard, 1957; *One Deadly Dawn,* Ace Books, 1957; *Valerie,* Avon, 1957; *Man in the Shadow,* Avon, 1957; *Star Lust,* B & B Library, 1958; *Halfway to Hell,* Avon, 1958; *Vengeance Is the Spur,* Abelard, 1958; *Ticket to Hell,* Gold Medal Books, 1958; *Desert Stake-Out,* Gold Medal Books, 1958; *Heat of Night,* Gold Medal Books, 1958; *Trouble Rides Tall,* Abelard, 1958; *Devil Wears Wings,* Abelard, 1959; *Rebel Woman,* Avon, 1959; *Strange Bargain,* Avon, 1959; *Die, Lover,* Avon, 1959; *Strictly for the Boys,* Stanley Books, 1959.

Nita's Place, Pyramid Books, 1960; *Journey into Violence,* Pyramid Books, 1960; *Guerrilla Girls,* Pyramid Books, 1960; *Night for Screaming,* Ace Books, 1960; *Hell Can Wait,* Gold Medal Books, 1960; *Connolly's Woman,* Gold Medal Books, 1960; *Young Nurses,* Pyramid Books, 1961; *Haven for the Damned,* Gold Medal Books, 1961; *God's Back Was Turned,* Gold Medal Books, 1961; *Searching Rider,* Ace Books, 1961; *A Trap for Sam Dodge,* Ace Books, 1961; *Wild Sky,* Ace Books, 1962; *Cross the Red Creek,* Avon, 1962; *Hot as Fire—Cold as Ice,* Belmont Publishing, 1962; *69 Babylon Park,* Avon, 1963; *Don't Speak to Strange Girls,* Gold Medal Books, 1963; *Drygulch Town,* Ace Books, 1963; *Prairie Raiders,* Ace Books, 1963; *The Fall of the Roman Empire,* Gold Medal Books, 1964; *High Fury,* Ballantine, 1964; *Hangrope Town,* Ballantine, 1964; *Wild Lonesome,* Ballantine, 1965; *Valley of the Savage Men,* Ace Books, 1965; *Doomsday Mission,* Banner Books, 1967; *Doomsday Affair: Man from U.N.C.L.E.,* No. 2, Ace Books, 1967; *Bitter Mission of Captain Burden,* Avon, 1968, published as *Burden's Mission,* 1968; *Treachery Trail,* Whitman, 1968; *Smell of Jasmine,* Avon, 1968; *Desert Stake-Out,* Fawcett, 1968; *Charro,* Fawcett, 1969.

Under pseudonym Whit Harrison; all published by Paperback Library, except as noted: *Body and Passion,* 1951; *Native Girl,* 1952; *Sailors Weekend,* 1952; *Army Girl,* 1952; *Girl on Parole,* 1952; *Rapture Alley,* 1952; *Shanty Road,* 1953; *Strip the Town Naked,* Beacon, 1960; *Any Woman He Wanted,* Beacon, 1960; *A Woman Possessed,* Beacon, 1961.

Under pseudonym Kel Holland: *The Tempted,* Beacon, 1964.

Under pseudonym Harriet Kathryn Myers: *Small Town Nurse,* Ace Books, 1962; *Prodigal Nurse,* Ace Books, 1963.

Under pseudonym Clay Stuart: *His Brother's Wife,* Beacon, 1964.

Under pseudonym Harry White: *Shadow at Noon,* Pyramid Books, 1955.

Under pseudonym Hallam Whitney; all published by Paperback Library, except as noted: *Backwoods Hussy,* 1952; *Shack Road,* 1953; *Sinners Club,* 1953; *City Girl,* 1953; *Backwoods Shack,* 1954; *Wild Seed,* Ace Books, 1955.

Motion pictures: "High Fury," Eroica (Italy); "Desire in the Dust," Twentieth Century-Fox; "The Naked Island," Twentieth Century-Fox; "Black Gold," Warner Brothers; "Trouble Rides Tall," Warner Brothers; "Wyoming Wildcatter," Warner Brothers; "Backwoods Tramp," Battaglia Films (France); "A Ticket to Hell," Avers Film (France); (writer and producer) "Face of the Phantom," Whittington-United Films production, 1961. Television scripts include "Lawman," "The Dakotas," and "The Alaskans."

Contributor to *The Mystery Writers Handbook,* Harper, and *The Quality of Murder,* Dutton. More than one hundred short stories and novelettes, under his own name and pseudonyms (including Hondo Wells and Steve Phillips), have appeared in *Male, Stag, Manhunt, Adam, Detective Tales, Mammoth Western, Dime Detective,* and similar magazines.

SIDELIGHTS: The film "Adios, Gringo" (Trans-Lux, 1968) was based on a novel by Whittington. GMF Picture Corp., filmed Earl Felton's adaptation of *Brutes in Brass,* 1969.

*   *   *

WICKERT, Frederic R(obinson) 1912-

PERSONAL: Born March 9, 1912, in Chicago, Ill.; son of Rudolph and Martha (Kay) Wickert; married Dorothy Dodge (a teacher), May 30, 1940; children: Susan, Melissa. *Education:* University of California, Los Angeles, B.A., 1933; University of Chicago, Ph.D., 1938. *Home:* 638 Baldwin Ct., East Lansing, Mich. 48823. *Office:* Department of Psychology, Olds Hall, Michigan State University, East Lansing, Mich. 48824.

CAREER: Western Electric Co., Hawthorne Station, Ill., personnel investigator, 1936-40; Commonwealth Edison Co., Chicago, Ill., 1940-47, began as employee interviewer, became research psychologist; Michigan State University, East Lansing, associate professor, 1947-58, professor of psychology and business administration, 1958—, chief of inservice training advisory team in Vietnam, 1955-57. Fulbright professor at University of Graz, 1953-54, and University of Toulouse, 1960-61; visiting professor at University of Canterbury, New Zealand, University of Otago, and Monash University, Australia. Team leader in Japan and Korea for Johns Hopkins University Operations Research Office, 1952-53; consultant to governments of Ghana and Nigeria, 1960, and to Peace Corps, 1961-62. *Military service:* Reserve officer, commissioned in U.S. Army Air Corps, 1933, and serving continuously in reserves (air) until 1954, with active duty in U.S. Army Air Forces, 1941-46; became colonel.

MEMBER: International Association of Applied Psychology, American Psychological Association, Society for Applied Anthropology, American Management Association, American Marketing Association, American Society for Training and Development, American Society for Consumer Research, Academy of Management, Midwestern Psychological Association, Phi Beta Kappa, Sigma Xi, Psi Chi, Sigma Iota Epsilon.

WRITINGS: (Editor) *Psychological Research on Problems of Redistribution,* U.S. Superintendent of Documents, 1947; (with G. Grimsley) *Psychological Techniques in Personnel Research,* Michigan State College Press, 1948; (with E. W. Weidner and others) *The International Programs of American Universities,* Institute of Research on International Programs, Michigan State University, 1958; (editor and translator) *Readings in African Psychology from French-Language Sources,* African Studies Center, Michigan State University, 1967; (with D. E. McFarland) *Measuring Executive Effectiveness,* Appleton, 1967; (editor with H. Meltzer) *Humanizing Organizational Behavior,* C. C Thomas, in press. Contributor to professional periodicals.

WORK IN PROGRESS: Psychological theories of promotion and commercial persuasion.

*   *   *

WICKWIRE, Franklin B(acon) 1931-

PERSONAL: Born April 4, 1931, in Madison, Ind.; son of Grant Townsend (a geologist) and Ruth (Bacon) Wickwire; married Mary Botts, June 14, 1957; children: Pamela M., Alan T. *Education:* Hanover College, B.A., 1952; Indiana University, M.A., 1956; Yale University, Ph.D., 1961. *Politics:* Independent. *Religion:* Protestant. *Home:* Amherst Rd., Pelham, Mass. *Office:* University of Massachusetts, Amherst, Mass. 01002.

CAREER: University of Massachusetts, Amherst, instructor, 1959-61, assistant professor, 1961-66, associate professor of British history, 1966—. Consultant to Harvard, Princeton, and Duke University Presses, and to Addison-Wesley Publishing Co. *Military service:* U.S. Army, Artillery, 1952-54; served in Korea; became staff sergeant. *Member:* American Historical Association, Society of American Historians, Conference on British Studies. *Awards, honors:* Fulbright research grant for work at University of London, 1965-66.

WRITINGS: British Subministers and Colonial America, Princeton University Press, 1966; (with wife, Mary B. Wickwire) *Cornwallis: The American Adventure,* Houghton, 1970. Contributor to *William and Mary Quarterly, American Historical Review, Huntington Library Quarterly, Manuscripts,* and *Listener* (London).

*   *   *

WIEGAND, G(uenther) Carl 1906-

PERSONAL: Born May 25, 1906, in Marburg, Germany; son of Friedrich (a professor) and Julie (von Zezschwitz) Wiegand; married present wife, Elizabeth Kankel, March 24, 1968. *Education:* University of New Mexico, B.A., 1944, M.A., 1945; Northwestern University, Ph.D., 1950. *Religion:* Episcopalian. *Home:* 308 Birchlane Dr., Carbondale, Ill. 62901. *Office:* Department of Economics, Southern Illinois University, 207 Birchlane Dr., Carbondale, Ill. 62901.

CAREER: Spent ten years on Wall Street, including four years with Bendix Luitweiler & Co. (members of New York Stock Exchange) as head of research department; Loyola University, Chicago, Ill., assistant professor of economics, 1946-50; University of Mississippi, Oxford, associate professor of economics, 1950-55; University of Illinois, Urbana, visiting professor, 1955-56; Southern Illinois University, Carbondale, professor of economics, 1956-75, professor emeritus, 1975—; currently president of

Thunderbird Travel Inc., and executive vice-president of Committee for Monetary Research and Education. Lecturer at University of Cape Town and at universities in India, Europe, and Southeast Asia. *Member:* American Economic Association, Mont Pelerin Society, Rotary Club.

WRITINGS: A Preface to the Social Sciences, Economic Institute (Chicago), 1949; (co-author) *A Proper Monetary and Banking System for the United States,* edited by Bell and Spahr, Ronald, 1960; *Economics: Its Nature and Importance,* Barron's, 1968, second edition, 1975; (contributor) *Essays by Foreign Economists,* Forum Free Enterprise (Bombay), 1968; (contributor) *Toward Liberty: Essays in Honor of Ludwig von Mises,* Institute of Humane Studies, 1971; (editor and contributor) *Toward a New World Monetary System,* [New York], 1973; (contributor) Senholz, editor, *Gold and Money,* [Westport, Conn.], 1975; (editor) *Inflation and Monetary Crisis,* Public Affairs Press (Washington, D.C.), 1975. Contributor of about three hundred articles to newspapers and periodicals in the United States, Germany, India, South Africa, Argentina, Mexico, Guatemala, and Venezuela.

* * *

WIEMER, Rudolf Otto 1905-

PERSONAL: Born March 24, 1905, in Friedrichroda, Germany; son of Fritz (a teacher) and Elisabeth (Kretzschmar) Wiemer; married Elisabeth Peinemann, October 12, 1932; children: Wolfgang, Reinhart, Uta. *Education:* Attended teacher's training college in Gotha, Germany, 1923-24. *Religion:* Evangelical Lutheran. *Home:* Nussanger 73, 34 Goettingen, West Germany.

CAREER: Teacher in Czechoslovakia, 1924-25, and then successively in Sondershausen, Hachelbich, Frankenhausen, Othfresen, Salzgitter, and Goettingen, Germany, 1925-67. *Military service:* German Army, 1940-45. *Awards, honors:* Sud-Verlag Konstanz Lyric Prize, 1948.

WRITINGS: Die Gitter singen, J. G. Oncken, 1952; *Der Mann am Feuer,* J. G. Oncken, 1953; *Die Strasse, die du wandern musst,* Deutscher Laienspielverlag, 1955; *Die Nacht der Tiere,* Burckhardthaus, 1957; *Der Ort zu unseren Fussen,* Steinkopf, 1958; *Das kleine Rasenstuck,* Steinkopf, 1959.

Pit und die Krippenmanner (juvenile), Steinkopf, 1960, translation published as *Pete and the Manger Men,* Muhlenberg Press, 1962; *Der Verlorene Sohn* (juvenile), Mohn, 1960; *Machet die Tore weit,* Guetersloher Verlagsanstalt Gerd Mohn, 1960; *Jona und der Grosse Fisch,* Mohn, 1960; *Nich Stunde Noch Tag,* Steinkopf, 1961; *Fremde Zimmer,* Steinkopf, 1962; *Ernstfall,* Steinkopf, 1963; *Nele geht nach Bethlehem,* Steinkopf, 1963; *Stier und Taube,* Steinkopf, 1964; *Kalle Schneemann* (juvenile), Steinkopf, 1964; *Joseph und seine Bruder* (juvenile), Mohn, 1964, translation by Paul T. Martinsen published as *Joseph and His Brothers,* Augsburg, 1967; *Die Weisen aus dem Abendland,* Steinkopf, 1965.

Liebes altes Lesebuch, M. von Schroeder, 1966; *Der Gute Rauber Willibald* (juvenile), Steinkopf, 1966, translation by Barbara Kowal Gollob published as *The Good Robber Willibald,* Atheneum, 1968; *Wir Tiere in dem Stalle,* Steinkopf, 1966, translation published as *Animals at the Manger,* Augsburg, 1969; *Helldunkel,* Steinkopf, 1967; *Come Unto Me* (originally published in German), translation by Martinsen, Augsburg, 1968.

Das Pferd, das in die Schule kam (juvenile), Steinkopf, 1970; *Unsereiner* (novel), Steinkopf, 1971; *Beispiele zur deutschen grammatik* (poems), Fietkau, 1971; *Geschichten aus dem Raeuberhut,* Schwann, 1972; *Der Kaiser und Der Kleine Mann* (juvenile), Steinkopf, 1972; *Wortwechsel* (poems), Fietkau, 1973; *Ein Weihnachtsboum fuer Ludmilla Winzig* (juvenile), Arena, 1974; *Selten wie Sommerschnee* (juvenile), Schaffstein, 1974; *Bundes deutsch,* Peter Hammer, 1974; *Wo wir Menschen sind,* Schwann, 1974; *Zwischenfaelle* (novel), Steinkopf, 1975; *Micha moechte gern* (juvenile), Bitter, 1975.

* * *

WIESENTHAL, Simon 1908-

PERSONAL: Born December 31, 1908; son of Asher (a businessman) and Rosa (Rapp) Wiesenthal; married Cyla Muller, September 9, 1939; children: Pauline Rose, Kreisberg Gerard. *Education:* Attended University of Prague, 1929-33; University of Lemberg, Engineer-Architect, 1939. *Religion:* Jewish. *Home:* Mestrozigasse 5, Vienna 19, Austria 1190. *Agent:* Robert Halpern, 225 Broadway, New York, N.Y. 10007.

CAREER: Practicing architect in Lemberg, Poland, 1939-41; arrested in 1941, and spent World War II years in Nazi concentration camps of Janowska, Lwow, Gross-Rosen, Buchenwald, and Mauthausen; set up and directed the Jewish Documentation Center in Linz, Austria, 1947-54, building up a vast network of documents and informants to bring Nazi war criminals to justice; directed a number of Jewish welfare agencies in Linz, 1954-61, before establishing the Jewish Documentation Center in Vienna, Austria. *Member:* Association of Jews Persecuted by the Nazis (president), Union International des Resistant et Deportes (Brussels; past vice-president), Federal Association of Jewish Communities of Austria (past vice-president), B'nai B'rith. *Awards, honors:* Diploma of Honor of International Resistance; Needle of Honour, Austrian Resistance Movement; Diploma of Honour, League of the United Nations; Freedom Medals of Netherlands and Luxembourg; Dr. Hon. Causa, Hebrew Union College.

WRITINGS: KZ Mauthausen (title means "Concentration Camp Mauthausen"), Landes Verlag, 1946; *Grossmufti-Grossagent der Achse* (title means "Head-Mufti, Head-Agent of the Axis"), Ried Verlag, 1947; *Ich jagte Eichman* (title means "I Hunted Eichmann"), Siegberg Mohn Verlag, 1961; (editor) *Verjaehrung?* (title means, "Limitation?"), Europaische Verlagsansertalt, 1965; *The Murderers Among Us: The Wiesenthal Memoirs,* introduction and biographical note by Joseph Wechsberg, McGraw, 1967; *Die sonneblume,* Hoffman & Campe Verlag, 1970, translation by H. A. Piehler published as *The Sunflower,* W. H. Allen, 1970; *Segel der hoffnung: Die geheime mission des Christoph Columbus,* Walter Verlag, 1972, translation by Richard Winston and Clara Winston published as *Sails of Hope: The Secret Mission of Christopher Columbus,* Macmillan, 1973.

WORK IN PROGRESS: The Case of Krystyna Jaworska.

SIDELIGHTS: Wiesenthal's credo is "never forget." He has brought almost one thousand Nazis to trial, tracked Adolf Eichmann to his hideout in Argentina and Stangl, the Treblinka commandant, to Sao Paulo. He believes that Nazi crimes can never be atoned for, nor the murderers all caught, but pursues them so that time will not erase the guilt.

In addition to Polish and German, Wiesenthal is competent in Russian, Yiddish, and English.

WIGGINS, Sam P.   1919-

PERSONAL: Born September 20, 1919, in Salisbury, N.C.; son of James Andrew (a minister) and Mollie (Wilhelm) Wiggins; married Jean Bessent, June 29, 1947; children: Stanley, David, Timothy, Mark. *Education:* Georgia Teachers College (now Georgia Southern College), B.S., 1940; Duke University, M.Ed., 1942; George Peabody College for Teachers, Ph.D., 1952. *Politics:* Independent. *Religion:* Protestant. *Home:* 7858 Normandie, M-3, Middleburg Heights, Ohio 44130.

CAREER: Georgia Southwestern College, Americus, laboratory school teacher-principal, 1940-42; Emory University and Agnes Scott College, Atlanta, Ga., director of student teaching, 1948-53; George Peabody College for Teachers, Nashville, Tenn., professor and administrator, 1953-67; Cleveland State University, Cleveland, Ohio, dean of College of Education, 1967-75. Chief adviser, Korean Teacher Education Project, 1961-62; director, Southern Higher Education Study, 1964-66. Member, Welfare Federation of Greater Cleveland. *Military service:* U.S. Naval Reserve, active duty, 1942-47; four battle stars; retired as commander, 1962. *Member:* National Education Association, American Association of Colleges for Teacher Education (president, 1974-75), Associated Organizations for Teacher Education (chairman of advisory council), Phi Delta Kappa, Kappa Phi Kappa, Pi Gamma Mu.

WRITINGS: The Student Teacher in Action, Allyn & Bacon, 1957; *Successful High School Teaching,* Houghton, 1958; *Southern High Schools and Jobless Youth,* George Peabody College, 1961; *Battlefields in Teacher Education,* George Peabody College, 1964; *The Desegregation Era in Higher Education,* McCutchan, 1966; *Higher Education in the South,* McCutchan, 1966; (co-author) *Differentiated Staffing,* Prentice-Hall, 1972.

*   *   *

WILBURN, Jean Alexander   1915-

PERSONAL: Born March 22, 1915, in Brooklyn, N.Y.; daughter of George Folet (a lawyer) and Ella (Salter) Alexander; married Raymond N. Wilburn, December 31, 1937 (divorced); children: Christopher Alexander. *Education:* University of California, Berkeley, B.A., 1944; Columbia University, M.A., 1963, Ph.D., 1964. *Politics:* Democratic ("usually"). *Religion:* Episcopalian.

CAREER: Buyer and merchandise manager for Bloomingdale's, Franklin Simon, Consolidated Retail Stores, and Newberry's, all New York City; Barnard College, New York City, assistant professor of economics, beginning 1964. *Member:* American Economic Association, Phi Beta Kappa.

WRITINGS: (With Victor R. Fuchs) *Productivity Differences Within the Service Sector,* National Bureau of Economic Research, 1966; *Biddle's Bank: The Crucial Years,* Columbia University Press, 1967.

WORK IN PROGRESS: Research on higher education in the "seven sister" colleges for women.

AVOCATIONAL INTERESTS: Breeding red English cocker spaniels for show quality.

BIOGRAPHICAL/CRITICAL SOURCES: Philadelphia Bulletin, March 23, 1967.††

WILCOX, Collin   1924-
(Carter Wick)

PERSONAL: Born September 21, 1924, in Detroit, Mich.; son of Harlan C. and Lucille (Spangler) Wilcox; married Beverly Buchman, December 23, 1954 (divorced, 1964); children: Christopher, Jeffrey. *Education:* Antioch College, A.B., 1948. *Politics:* Democrat. *Religion:* None. *Home:* 867 Elizabeth, San Francisco, Calif. 94114. *Agent:* Lurton Blassingame, 60 East 42nd St., New York, N.Y. 10017.

CAREER: Began as advertising copywriter in San Francisco, Calif., 1948-50; teacher of art at Town School, San Francisco, 1950-53; partner in Amthor & Co. (furniture store), San Francisco, 1953-55; owner of lamp firm under his own name, San Francisco, 1955-71, designing and manufacturing lamps and other decorative items for the home. *Military service:* U.S. Army, 1943. *Member:* Mystery Writers of America, Sierra Club.

WRITINGS—All published by Random House, except as noted: *The Black Door,* Dodd, 1967; *The Third Figure,* Dodd, 1968; *The Lonely Hunter,* 1969; *The Disappearance,* 1970; *Dead Aim,* 1971; *Hiding Place,* 1972; *Long Way Down,* 1973; *Aftershock,* 1975; (under pseudonym Carter Wick) *The Faceless Man,* Saturday Review Press, 1975; *The Third Victim,* Dell, 1976; *Time Limit,* in press.

WORK IN PROGRESS: Three books, *Silent Witness, Swok In the Sky,* and *Identity Crisis.*

BIOGRAPHICAL/CRITICAL SOURCES: San Francisco Chronicle, May 21, 1967.

*   *   *

WILCOX, Roger P.   1916-

PERSONAL: Born March 26, 1916, in Hopkins, Mich.; son of James H. (a cab driver) and Hazel (Parmelee) Wilcox; married Eva Tullius (a resource teacher), August 26, 1939; children: James R., Kenneth P., David H. *Education:* Michigan State University, A.B., 1938, M.A., 1970; University of Michigan, M.A., 1951. *Politics:* Liberal Republican. *Religion:* Protestant. *Office:* 2954 Helber St., Flint, Mich. 48504.

CAREER: Junior high school teacher in Romulus, Mich., 1939-41; high school teacher in Holly, Mich., 1941-45, in Howell, Mich., 1945-50; Michigan State University, East Lansing, instructor in communication skills, 1950-53; General Motors Institute, Flint, Mich., 1953-76, became professor of communication. Flint Child Guidance Clinic, member of advisory board, 1956-63, vice-president, 1962-63. President, Flint Mental Health Services, 1962-63. Consultant, Great Lakes Marketing Associates, Inc., 1975—. *Member:* International Communication Association, American Business Communication Association, Michigan Speech Association (president, 1949-50; chairman of editorial board, 1965-69).

WRITINGS: An Outline of Parliamentary Procedure, privately printed, 1944; *Oral Reporting in Business and Industry,* Prentice-Hall, 1967. Editor, *International Communication Association Newsletter,* 1970-73.

WORK IN PROGRESS: Communicating on the Job through Writing and Speaking, for Houghton.

*   *   *

WILDERS, John (Simpson)   1927-

PERSONAL: Surname rhymes with "builders"; born July 30, 1927, in Mansfield, England; son of Charles Alban (a civil engineer) and Ida (Simpson) Wilders; married Benedikte Schack, July 24, 1954; children: Sarah Catherine, Thomas Christopher, James Christian. *Education:* St. John's College, Cambridge, B.A., 1940, Ph.D., 1954. *Religion:* Church of England. *Home:* 4 Water Eaton Rd., Oxford University, Oxford, England. *Office:* Worcester College, Oxford, England.

CAREER: Princeton University, Princeton, N.J., Jane Eliza Procter visiting fellow, 1952-53, instructor in English, 1953-54; University of Bristol, Bristol, England, junior fellow, 1954-55, assistant lecturer, 1955-57, lecturer, 1957-67, senior lecturer in English, 1967-68; Oxford University, Worcester College, Oxford, England, tutorial fellow in English, 1968—. Visiting professor, University of California, Santa Barbara, fall, 1975; visiting research fellow, Australian National University, 1976. Royal Shakespeare Theatre, director of Summer School, 1959-68, governor, 1965—, executive council member, 1968—. Actor in radio and television plays, and in Argo Recording Co.'s "Works of Shakespeare"; member of television discussion panel on theological and religious topics. *Military service:* Royal Navy, 1945-47.

WRITINGS: (Editor and author of introduction and commentary) Samuel Butler, *Hudibras,* Oxford University Press, 1967; (editor) *Shakespeare: The Merchant of Venice,* Macmillan (London), 1969. Contributor of articles and reviews to *Cambridge Review, Essays in Criticism, Review of English Studies, Notes and Queries,* and *Western Mail.*

* * *

WILKIE, James W. 1936-

PERSONAL: Born March 10, 1936, in Idaho Falls, Idaho; son of Waldo Wallace (an advertising manager) and Lucile (Likins) Wilkie; married Edna Monzon (a research associate), July 27, 1963; children: Garrick James, Michelle Marie. *Education:* University of Southern California, student, 1954-55; Mexico City College (now University of the Americas), B.A. (magna cum laude), 1958; University of California, Berkeley, M.A., 1959, Ph.D., 1966. *Office:* Department of History, University of California, Los Angeles, Calif. 90024.

CAREER: High school teacher of Spanish, San Diego, Calif., 1959-60; Mexico City College (now University of the Americas), Puebla, Mexico, instructor in history, 1960; Ohio State University, Columbus, assistant professor, 1965-67, associate professor of history, 1967-68; University of California, Los Angeles, associate professor, 1968-71, professor of history, 1971—, director of Latin American Center, 1970—. Director of Latin American Oral History Project, 1963—. *Member:* Conference on Latin American History (chairman, Committee on Historical Statistics, 1974—), Latin American Studies Association, Oral History Association. *Awards, honors:* Modern Foreign Language fellow, 1962-63; Woodrow Harrison Mills traveling fellow, 1963-64; American Council of Learned Societies, Foreign Area fellow, 1964-65, grant, 1971; Bolton Prize, 1967, for *The Mexican Revolution.*

WRITINGS: The Mexican Revolution: Federal Expenditure and Social Change since 1910, University of California Press, 1967; (editor with A. L. Michaels) *Insurgent Mexico,* Simon & Schuster, 1969; *Bolivian Revolution and U.S. Aid since 1952,* Latin American Center, University of California, 1969; (with wife, Edna Monzon de Wilkie) *Mexico Visto en el Siglo XX,* Instituto Mexicano de Investigaciones Economicas, 1969; *Elitelore,* Latin American Cen-

ter, University of California, 1973; *Measuring Land Reform,* Latin American Center, University of California, 1974; (editor with Michael C. Meyer and Edna Monzon de Wilkie) *Contemporary Mexico,* University of California Press, 1975. Contributor to *Journal of Church and State, Journal of Library History, Latin American Research Review,* and *Journal of Latin American Lore.*

AVOCATIONAL INTERESTS: Hiking in the Idaho wilderness area.

* * *

WILKIE, Katharine E(lliott) 1904-

PERSONAL: Born February 6, 1904, in Lexington, Ky.; daughter of J. Milward and Katharine (Crockett) Elliott; married Raymond Abell Wilkie (a hardware salesman), December 29, 1926; children: Raymond Abell, Jr., Milward Elliott. *Education:* University of Kentucky, A.B., 1924, M.A., 1939. *Politics:* Democrat. *Religion:* Protestant. *Home:* 312 Irvine Rd., Lexington, Ky. 40502.

CAREER: Teacher in Kentucky schools, 1925-26, 1951-69, as ninth grade teacher of English at Tates Creek Junior High School, Lexington, 1964-69; author of children's books. Teacher of course in writing children's literature in the Over 57 Writer's Workshop, conducted by University of Kentucky, summers, 1968 and 1970. *Member:* National Education Association, Kentucky Educational Association, Central Kentucky Educational Association, Mortar Board, Theta Sigma Phi, Chi Delta Phi, Kappa Delta Pi.

WRITINGS: Zack Taylor: Young Rough and Ready, Bobbs-Merrill, 1952; *Will Clark: Boy in Buckskins,* Bobbs-Merrill, 1953; *Mary Todd Lincoln: Girl of the Bluegrass,* Bobbs-Merrill, 1954; *George Rogers Clark: Boy of the Old Northwest,* Bobbs-Merrill, 1958; *John Sevier: Son of Tennessee,* Messner, 1958; *Simon Kenton: Young Trail Blazer,* Bobbs-Merrill, 1960; *Daniel Boone: Taming the Wilds,* Garrard, 1960; *Robert Louis Stevenson: Storyteller and Adventurer,* Houghton, 1961; *The Man Who Wouldn't Give Up: Henry Clay,* Messner, 1961; *William Fargo: Boy Mail Carrier,* Bobbs-Merrill, 1962; (with Elizabeth R. Moseley) *Father of the Constitution: James Madison,* Messner, 1963; *Ferdinand Magellan: Noble Captain,* Houghton, 1963; *William Penn: Friend to All,* Garrard, 1964; *Kentucky Government* (published in connection with Ralph W. Steen's *Government by the People*), Steck, 1964, revised edition, 1975; (with Moseley) *Teacher of the Blind: Samuel Gridley Howe,* Messner, 1965; *Maria Mitchell: Stargazer,* Garrard, 1966; (with Moseley) *Kentucky Heritage,* Steck, 1966; *Pocahontas, Indian Princess,* Garrard, 1969; (with Moseley) *Frontier Nurse: Mary Breckenridge,* Messner, 1969; *Clyde Beatty: Boy Animal Trainer,* Bobbs-Merrill, 1968; *Helen Keller: Handicapped Girl,* Bobbs-Merrill, 1969; *Charles Dickens: An Inimitable Boz,* Abelard, 1970.

SIDELIGHTS: Father of the Constitution: James Madison has been translated into Spanish and Portuguese.

* * *

WILKINSON, Winifred 1922-

PERSONAL: Born September 1, 1922, in Atlanta, Ga.; daughter of Boyce Taylor and Ruby (Gaffney) Wilkinson; married George Rowe Hausmann (a Unity minister), December 19, 1965. *Education:* Agnes Scott College, B.A., 1946; Unity Training School, Lee's Summit, Mo., graduate, 1958. *Home:* 11298 Heath Rd., Chesterland, Ohio

44026. *Office:* Unity Center of Cleveland, 5637 Mayfield Rd., Cleveland, Ohio 44124.

CAREER: Ordained Unity minister, 1959; Unity Church, Little Rock, Ark., minister, 1957-58; Unity Center of Cleveland, Cleveland Heights, Ohio, minister, 1958-66, co-minister with husband, 1966—. Association of Unity Churches, member of board of directors, 1965-67; Great Lakes Unity Regional Conference, secretary, 1966-67.

WRITINGS: Focus on Living, Unity Books, 1967; *Miracle Power for Today,* Doubleday, 1969.

SIDELIGHTS: Reverend Wilkinson wrote and presented "Focus on Living," a five-minute week-day radio program heard on WCLV-FM, 1964-68.

* * *

WILLARD, Mildred Wilds 1911-

PERSONAL: Born October 11, 1911, in New Kensington, Pa.; daughter of John Michael (a grocer) and Emma (Miller) Wilds; married Kester T. Willard, October 13, 1934; children: John Michael, Thomas Gordon. *Education:* Allegheny College, student, 1928-30; Northwestern University, A.B., 1932; University of Chicago, graduate courses. *Religion:* Unitarian Universalist. *Home:* 4212 Linden Ave., Western Springs, Ill. 60558. *Agent:* Dorothy Markinko, McIntosh & Otis, Inc., 475 Fifth Ave., New York, N.Y. 10017.

CAREER: High school English teacher in Lancaster, Wis., 1932-34; *Chicago Tribune,* Chicago, Ill., reporter, 1935-43; secondary and elementary teacher in Illinois schools, 1956-62. *Awards, honors:* First prize for short story, Midwest Writers Conference, 1950.

WRITINGS: The Man Who Had to Invent a Flying Bicycle, Stackpole, 1967; *The Magic Candy Mystery,* Transition Press, 1969; *The Cloud Crasher,* Transition Press, 1969; *The Luck of Harry Weaver,* F. Watts, 1971; *The Ice-cream Cone,* Follett, 1973. Contributor of forty short stories to confession and children's magazines; contributor to Childcraft Books and Science Research Associates multi-level reading program.

WORK IN PROGRESS: A children's novel; adult fiction.

* * *

WILLETS, F(rederick) W(illiam) 1930-

PERSONAL: Born August 31, 1930, in Birmingham, England. *Education:* Attended Ruskin College, Oxford. *Residence:* Lives in a small village in Cambridgeshire, England. *Agent:* Curtis Brown Ltd., 1 Craven Hill, London W2 3EW, England.

CAREER: Writer.

WRITINGS: Some Notes from Cunard (poems), Golden Head Press, 1967; *Cunard in the Desert* (experimental prose), Calder & Boyars, 1969.

Radio plays: "Scrap," broadcast by BBC Third Programme, 1967, and by KPFA, Berkeley, Calif., 1969; "The Passing" and "The Pool," both broadcast by BBC Third Programme, 1967; "A Definition of Love," broadcast by BBC Third Programme, 1968; "Transcript," broadcast by WGBH in America, 1968; "The Fold," broadcast in Germany, 1968.††

* * *

WILLEY, Keith (Greville) 1930-

PERSONAL: Born August 14, 1930, in Boonah, Queensland, Australia; son of Greville Maynard (an accountant) and Eileen May (Kuske) Willey; married Elaine Noreen Fitzgerald, April 25, 1953; children: Joanna Lynette, Patricia Mary, Tanya Dale. *Education:* Attended Brisbane Grammar School, 1944-45. *Politics:* None. *Religion:* Roman Catholic. *Office: Sun,* Broadway, Sydney, New South Wales, Australia.

CAREER: Earlier career includes "eighteen years mostly spent as journalist in Australia and New Guinea, also a period as a professional crocodile shooter in the Northern Territory"; *Sun,* Sydney, New South Wales, Australia, feature writer, beginning 1966. *Member:* Australian Journalists' Association, Australian Society of Authors, Journalists Club (Sydney), Brookvale Rugby League Club. *Awards, honors:* Walkley national awards for Australian journalism, 1961, 1962, 1963.

WRITINGS: (With Frank Flynn) *Northern Gateway,* F. P. Leonard, 1963; (with Flynn) *The Living Heart,* F. P. Leonard, 1964; *Eaters of the Lotus,* Jacaranda Press, 1964; *Strange Seeker,* Macmillan, 1965; *Assignment New Guinea,* Jacaranda Press, 1965; *Crocodile Hunt,* Angus & Robertson, 1966; *The Red Centre,* Lansdowne Press, 1967; (with Ian Walsh) *Inside Rugby League,* Horwitz, 1968; (with Flynn) *Northern Frontiers,* F. P. Leonard, 1968; *The First Hundred Years: The Story of Brisbane Grammar School, 1868-1968,* Macmillan, 1968; (with Robin Smith) *New Guinea: A Journey through 10,000 Years,* Lansdowne Press, 1969; *Naked Island and Other South Sea Tales,* Hodder & Stoughton, 1970; *Boss Drover,* Rigby, 1971; *Tales of the Big Country,* R. Hale, 1973; *Queensland in Colour,* Lansdowne Press, 1973. Author of radio scripts; contributor of several hundred articles and short stories to magazines and newspapers.†

* * *

WILLIAMS, Aston R. 1912-

PERSONAL: Born June 16, 1912, in Kimberley, South Africa; son of Peter Fred (a clergyman) and Ethel (Stobart) Williams; married Kathleen Elizabeth Mitchell, July 1, 1957; children: Gavin D., Brian G., Roy T. *Education:* Rhodes University, M.Sc., 1933; University of South Africa, B.A., 1943; University of Natal, B.Ed., 1949, Ph.D., 1963. *Home:* 7 Creer Rd., Westville, Durban, Natal, South Africa. *Office:* Natal College for Advanced Technical Education, Durban, Natal, South Africa.

CAREER: University of Pretoria, Pretoria, Transvaal, South Africa, lecturer in mathematics, 1934; Pretoria Technical High School, Pretoria, lecturer in mathematics, 1935-37, headmaster, 1937-45; Pietermaritzburg Technical College, Pietermaritzburg, Natal, South Africa, principal, 1945-48; Natal College for Advanced Technical Education, Durban, Natal, South Africa, director (principal), beginning 1949. Member of council and senate, University of Natal, beginning 1953. *Member:* Association of Colleges for Advanced Technical Education (secretary, 1945-51; past chairman of executive committee), Association for Higher Education (United States), Royal Society of South Africa, South African Institute of Management (founder member), Rotary International (district governor, 1966-67), Durban Chamber of Commerce (member of council of directors, beginning 1958). *Awards, honors:* U.S. Department of State Leader Program award, 1955; Carnegie Corp. grant, 1960.

WRITINGS: Mathematics I, Van Schaik, 1939; *Mathematics III* (in English and Afrikaans; latter section entitled

Matesis III), Nasionale Pers, 1943; *Mathematics IV* and *Mathematics V,* Nasionale Pers, 1945; *Mathematics for Standards VI and VII,* Van Schaik, 1963; *Mathematics for Advanced Technical Students,* Nasionale Pers, 1967; *General Education in Higher Education,* Teachers College Press, 1968.

WORK IN PROGRESS: Continuing research in general and technical education.

SIDELIGHTS: Williams has visited Britain many times to study general education, and has been in the United States and Canada three times, twice to study education and once as a Rotary governor.††

* * *

WILLIAMS, Edward J(erome) 1935-

PERSONAL: Born March 19, 1935, in Wilkins Township, Pa.; son of Edward Cleveland and Cecilia (Pankowski) Williams; married Grace Calterone, August 6, 1960; children: Nancy Marie, Jean Marie, Ann Marie, Susan Marie. *Education:* Potomac State Jr. College (now Potomac State College of West Virginia University), A.A., 1958; Duquesne University, B.A., 1960, M.A., 1961; Johns Hopkins University, Ph.D., 1966. *Politics:* Democrat. *Religion:* Roman Catholic. *Home:* 1722 South Camino Seco, Tucson, Ariz. 85710. *Office:* Political Science Department, University of Arizona, Tucson, Ariz. 85721.

CAREER: St. Francis College, Fort Wayne, Ind., instructor in political science and history, 1961-62; Marquette University, Milwaukee, Wis., assistant professor of political science, 1965-68; University of Arizona, Tucson, associate professor, 1968-72, professor of political science, 1972—. Visiting professor, University of New Mexico, 1974. Associate editor, Institute of Government Research Publications, University of Arizona, 1973-74. Co-host of weekly political interview radio program, 1972-74; political commentary for weekly public affairs radio program, 1972—. Program director, Center of Christian Democratic Action, 1965. *Military service:* U.S. Army, 82nd Airborne Division, 1954-56. *Member:* American Political Science Association, Latin American Studies Association. *Awards, honors:* Choice Academic Book of the Year, 1967, for *Latin American Christian Democratic Parties.*

WRITINGS: Latin American Christian Democratic Parties, University of Tennessee Press, 1967; *The Political Themes of Inter-American Relations,* Duxbury, 1971; *Latin American Political Thought: A Developmental Perspective* (monograph), Institute of Government Research, University of Arizona, 1974; (with Freeman J. Wright) *Latin American Politics: A Developmental Approach,* Mayfield, 1975. Contributor of articles and book reviews to political and governmental journals.

WORK IN PROGRESS: A study of the domestic and foreign policy implications of the discovery of Mexican oil.

* * *

WILLIAMS, Heathcote 1941-

PERSONAL: Born November 15, 1941, in Helsby, Cheshire, England; son of Heathcote Williams. *Agent:* Emmanuel Wax, ACTAC, 16 Cadogan Lane, London S.W.1, England.

CAREER: Associate editor, *Transatlantic Review,* London, England. *Awards, honors: Evening Standard* Drama Award, and Obie Award, *Village Voice,* both 1970, for *AC/DC;* George Devine Award, 1970; John Whiting Award, 1971.

WRITINGS: The Speakers, Hutchinson, 1964, Grove, 1967; *The Local Stigmatic* (play; first produced in Edinburgh at Traverse Theatre, 1965; produced in London, 1966; produced Off-Broadway at Actors Playhouse, November 3, 1969), published in *Traverse Plays,* edited by Jim Haynes, Penguin, 1966, published as *AC/DC [and] The Local Stigmatic: Two Plays* (also see below), Viking, 1973; *AC/DC* (first produced on West End at Royal Court Theatre, November 11, 1970; produced in Brooklyn by Chelsea Theatre Center at Brooklyn Academy of Music, February 23, 1971), published as *AC/DC [and] The Local Stigmatic: Two Plays,* Viking, 1973. Also author of a screenplay, "Malatesta," 1969. Founding editor, *Suck* (Amsterdam).

SIDELIGHTS: The Speakers, a documentary narrative on the inhabitants of London's Hyde Park, "takes four . . . eccentrics, reports what they say in detail, and follows one of them into his solitary private life," says John Bowen, adding that the book is "immensely readable, immensely sad, immensely convincing. There is no story, no development, but there is the fascination that the speakers themselves exert on their audiences, and the fascination of exploring the oddities of personality." Bowen also notes that Williams "has an acute ear and he has curiosity and compassion. Because his book is concentrated and selective, it gives a stronger sense of the reality of a certain part of Speakers' Corner than an attendance at the Corner itself." S. K. Oberbeck adds: "As the 'speakers' rage and babble through these pages, they imprint an arresting message of the world's madness." Eric Davis, who credits Williams with an important discovery, the "documentary novel freed from Zola," adds, "Williams writes with Blake's etching tool."

In *AC/DC,* according to Marilyn Stasio, "Williams is exploring such issues as the control of man by machine; the evolution of language into both a lethal weapon and a defensive tool; and the concept of ego-destruction . . . as the ultimate peace." Harold Clurman considers it "a play not to be lightly dismissed; at the same time, it is one not readily to be recommended." John Russell Taylor adds: "Certainly taken bit by bit the play is astounding in the virtuosity of its writing, but taken as a whole it has passages of monotony and tedium, which test (and are perhaps design to test?) an audience's patience to the utmost."

BIOGRAPHICAL/CRITICAL SOURCES: Newsweek, February 13, 1967; *New York Times Book Review,* February 26, 1967; *Plays and Players,* January, 1971; *Cue,* March 6, 1971; *Nation,* March 15, 1971.

* * *

WILLIAMS, Margaret (Anne) 1902-

PERSONAL: Born July 15, 1902, in Manchester, Conn.; daughter of Michael (a writer) and Margaret (Olmsted) Williams. *Education:* Manhattanville College, B.A. 1923; Oxford University, B.A., 1935, M.A. (first class honors), 1938.

CAREER: Roman Catholic religious, professed in Society of the Sacred Heart, 1933; Manhattanville College, Purchase, N.Y., professor of English, 1935-69, professor emeritus, 1969—; University of the Sacred Heart, Tokyo, Japan, professor of English, 1969—. *Member:* Mediaeval Academy of America, Modern Language Association of America, English Literary Society of Japan.

WRITINGS: (Editor and translator) *Word-Hoard: Passages from Old English Literature,* Sheed, 1940; *Second*

Sowing, Sheed, 1942; (editor and translator) *Glee-Wood: Passages from Middle English Literature,* Sheed, 1949; *The Sacred Heart in the Life of the Church,* Sheed, 1957; *Saint Madaleine Sophie: Her Life and Letters,* Herder & Herder, 1965; (editor and translator) *The Pearl-Poet: His Complete Works,* Random House, 1967; (translator and author of introduction) *Piers Plowman,* Random House, 1970.

WORK IN PROGRESS: Further research in the field of Middle English literature, especially the works of the Pearl-Poet; the history of the Marina legend; Oriental influences on Middle English.†

*   *   *

WILLIAMS, Raymond (Henry)   1921-

PERSONAL: Born August 31, 1921, in Abergavenny, Wales; son of Henry Joseph and Gwendolen (Bird) Williams; married Joyce Mary Dalling, June 19, 1942; children: Merryn, Ederyn, Gwydion Madawc. *Education:* Trinity College, Cambridge, M.A., 1946. *Politics:* Socialist. *Religion:* None. *Home:* White Cottage, Hardwick, Cambridge, England. *Office:* Jesus College, Cambridge University, Cambridge, England.

CAREER: Oxford University Delegacy for Extra-Mural Studies, Oxford, England, staff tutor in literature, 1946-61; Cambridge University, Jesus College, Cambridge, England, fellow and lecturer in English studies, 1961-67, director of English studies, 1961—, university reader in drama, 1967—. *Military service:* British Army, Guards Armoured Division, 1941-45; became captain.

WRITINGS: Reading and Criticism, Muller, 1950; *Drama from Ibsen to Eliot,* Chatto & Windus, 1952, Columbia University Press, 1954, revised edition, Penguin, 1964, new edition published as *Drama from Ibsen to Brecht,* Chatto & Windus, 1968, Oxford University Press, 1969; *Drama in Performance,* Muller, 1954, 3rd edition, Penguin, 1973; *Culture and Society, 1780-1950,* Chatto & Windus, 1958, Harper, 1966; *Border Country,* Chatto & Windus, 1960, Horizon, 1961; *The Long Revolution,* Chatto & Windus, 1961, Harper, 1966; *Communications,* Penguin, 1961; *Second Generation,* Chatto & Windus, 1964; *Modern Tragedy,* Stanford University Press, 1966.

(Editor) *Pelican Book of Prose,* Volume II: *From 1780 to the Present Day,* Penguin, 1970; *The English Novel from Dickens to Lawrence,* Chatto & Windus, 1970; (editor) *George Orwell,* Viking, 1971; *The Country and the City,* Oxford University Press, 1973; *Television: Technology and Cultural Form,* Fontana Paperbacks, 1973; *Keywords,* Fontana Paperbacks, 1976.

Television plays produced by British Broadcasting Corp.: "Letter from the Country," 1966; "Public Inquiry," 1967. General editor, "New Thinkers' Library," 1961—.

WORK IN PROGRESS: The third novel in his "Border Country" trilogy (*Border Country* and *Second Generation* are the others); television play, "The Volunteer."

AVOCATIONAL INTERESTS: Camping, gardening.

*   *   *

WILLIAMS, Robert Coleman   1940-

PERSONAL: Born January 4, 1940, in Bridgend, Wales; son of Arthur Gustavus Edwin and Annie Gertrude (Hayes) Williams; married former wife Christina Gavrelle Hobhouse, August 30, 1963; married Diana Zillah Temple;

children: Oliver Hobhouse, Hayes Ap Robert. *Education:* Oxford University, B.A., 1962, M.A., 1965. *Politics:* Conservative. *Religion:* Roman Catholic. *Home:* Brynarlais, Llansteffan, Dyfed, Wales. *Office:* Thurman Publishing Ltd., 27 Queen Anne St., London W1M 0DA, England.

CAREER: Cornwall Academy, Great Barrington, Mass., assistant master in English department, 1963-64; College of the Holy Cross, Worcester, Mass., instructor in English and rugby football coach, 1964-66; Trinity College, Carmarthen, Wales, lecturer in English and drama department, 1966-68; managing director of Atlantic & Western Consultants Ltd., 1968—; chairman of Thurman Publishing Ltd. and the Thurman Group of Companies, London, England, 1974—. Free-lance television interviewer and broadcaster, 1959-63; personal economic adviser to Crown Prince Hassan of Jordan and Royal Scientific Society of Jordan, 1972-73. *Military service:* Territorial Army, Welch Regiment; became lieutenant. *Member:* Royal Society of Literature, Early English Text Society, Mediaeval Academy of America, Royal Geographical Society (fellow), Geological Society of London (fellow), British Schools' Exploring Society, Carlton Club.

WRITINGS: Ladycross (poems), Fantasy Press, 1962; (editor) *Concordance to the Collected Poems of Dylan Thomas,* University of Nebraska Press, 1967. Author with wife, Christina Hobhouse, of a television play for British Broadcasting Corp., "Under the Gooseberry Bush," 1967. Contributor of poetry to *Cornhill Magazine, Isis,* and Oxford periodicals, and articles to military journals.

WORK IN PROGRESS: Poetry; plays for stage and television; further studies on the poetry of Dylan Thomas.

SIDELIGHTS: Williams was a survey assistant on an expedition to Labrador in 1958. *Avocational interests:* Fishing and conversation.

*   *   *

WILLIAMSON, Robert C(lifford)   1916-

PERSONAL: Born April 25, 1916, in Los Angeles, Calif.; son of Bert A. (an electrical engineer) and Mary (Kenyon) Williamson; married Virginia Lorenzini, April 11, 1953; children: Lawrence, Eric. *Education:* University of California, Los Angeles, B.A., 1938, M.A., 1940; University of Southern California, Ph.D., 1951. *Home:* Route 4, Bethlehem, Pa. 18015. *Office:* Department of Social Relations, Lehigh University, Bethlehem, Pa. 18015.

CAREER: Los Angeles City College, Los Angeles, Calif., 1946-60, became professor of sociology and psychology; Haverford College, Haverford, Pa., visiting professor of sociology, 1962-63; Lehigh University, Bethlehem, Pa., professor of sociology and chairman of department of social relations, 1963—. Smith-Mundt Professor, National University of El Salvador, 1958; Fulbright professor at National University of Colombia, 1961, and Catholic University, Santiago, Chile, 1967-68. Lecturer and consultant, Peace Corps, 1962-63; chairman of Latin American section, American Friends Service Committee, 1965-67. *Military service:* U.S. Army Air Forces, 1942-45. *Member:* American Sociological Association, American Psychological Association, Sierra Club. *Awards, honors:* Social Science Research Council grant, 1960.

WRITINGS: (With S. S. Sargent) *Social Psychology,* Ronald, 2nd edition (not associated with 1st edition), 1958, 3rd edition, 1966; *Marriage and Family Relations,* Wiley, 1966, 2nd edition, 1972; (with Georgene H. Seward) *Sex*

Roles in Contemporary Society, Random House, 1970. Contributor of over twenty-five articles to professional journals.

SIDELIGHTS: Williamson did research on cross-national attitudes in Germany and Spain, 1965, and India and Japan, 1966; he also has visited the Soviet Union on two of his six trips to Europe, and traveled in Africa, 1953-54. He is fluent in French, German, and Spanish, and has "limited" competency in Italian, Portuguese, and Russian.

* * *

WILLIS, Corinne Denneny
(Patricia Denning)

PERSONAL: Born in Buffalo, N.Y.; daughter of Edward James (a postal supervisor) and Cora (Swartz) Denneny; married Norman Willis (an insurance broker), October 14, 1944; children: Peter Denneny. Education: D'Youville College, B.A.; St. Louis University, M.A.; Genesee State Teachers College, graduate student in library science. Politics: Democrat. Religion: Roman Catholic. Home: 3052 Eggert Rd., Tonawanda, N.Y. 14150. Agent: Muriel Fuller, P.O. Box 193, Grand Central Station, New York, N.Y. 10017.

CAREER: Taught English in senior high schools in Buffalo, N.Y., until 1944; Genesee-Humboldt Junior High School, Buffalo, N.Y., librarian, 1961—.

WRITINGS: The Ivory Cage (Junior Literary Guild selection), McKay, 1966; Boy Minus Girl, McKay, 1967; Tilly, McKay, 1968. Contributor of serials and short stories to American Girl, Twelve/Fifteen, and magazines in Ireland; under pseudonym Patricia Denning, contributor in earlier years of about twenty-five short stories to Catholic World, Extension, and other magazines.

SIDELIGHTS: Willis lived in a small English seaside town with her British-born husband for several years following World War II.

* * *

WILLIS, Stanley E. II 1923-

PERSONAL: Born July 9, 1923, in Hoisington, Kan.; son of Stanley Earl (a Missouri Pacific Railroad executive) and Leota (Brewer) Willis; married Edith Clark Blair, June 23, 1945; children: Alan Matson. Education: Stanford University, B.A., 1944; McGill University, M.D. and C.M., 1948; University of San Diego, J.D., 1968. Politics: Independent. Religion: Episcopalian. Home: 7161 Encelia Dr., La Jolla, Calif. 92037.

CAREER: U.S. Navy, reserve service as ensign while attending medical school, 1943-48, active duty, 1948-57; U.S. Naval Hospital, Bethesda, Md., 1948-50, began as intern, became resident in psychiatry, U.S. Naval Hospital, Oakland, Calif., 1952-55, began as resident, became senior resident in psychiatry, clinical director of West Coast Naval Psychiatric Treatment Center, 1955-56, chief of psychiatry, 1957; resigned from Navy as commander, 1957; psychiatrist in private practice, La Jolla, Calif., 1957—. Adjunct professor of law, University of San Diego, 1968—. Diplomate, American Board of Neurology and Psychiatry, 1955. Member of board of directors, San Diego Light Opera Association and Old Globe Theatre.

MEMBER: American Psychiatric Association (fellow), American Medical Association, American Ontoanalytic Association, California Medical Association, Southern California Psychiatric Society, San Diego Yacht Club.

WRITINGS: (With C. W. Wahl and others) New Dimension in Psychosomatic Medicine, Little, Brown, 1965; (with Wahl and others) Sexual Problems, Free Press, 1967; Understanding and Counseling the Male Homosexual, Little, Brown, 1967. Contributor to medical and legal journals.

WORK IN PROGRESS: Compiling a case book for use in forensic psychiatry classes; research into the psychodynamics of the criminal mind.

AVOCATIONAL INTERESTS: Sailing (owner and skipper of forty-seven foot sloop, Pacifica).

* * *

WILLKENS, William H(enry) R(obert) 1919-

PERSONAL: Born August 5, 1919, in New Britain, Conn.; son of Fred H. (a professor) and Emma (Langefeld) Willkens; married Rose Mary Gardner (a nursing instructor), June 12, 1944; children: David G., Daniel F. Education: University of Pittsburgh, A.B. (cum laude), 1942, M.Ed., 1954, Ph.D., 1958; Colgate Rochester Divinity School, B.D., 1949. Politics: Republican. Home: 109 Farmington Dr., Butler, Pa. 16001. Office: Slippery Rock State College, Slippery Rock, Pa. 16057.

CAREER: Baptist minister. Pastor of Evangelical Reformed Church in Pittsburgh, Pa., 1941-42, and of Baptist churches in Lincoln, N.Y., 1946-50, and Pittsburgh, Pa., 1950-57; Alderson-Broaddus College, Philippi, W.Va., professor of education, 1957-60, academic dean, 1959-60; Crozer Theological Seminary, Chester, Pa., professor of religious education and director of studies, 1960-68; Slippery Rock State College, Slippery Rock, Pa., chairman, student teaching department and professor of education, 1968—, acting dean of School of Arts and Sciences, 1968. North Boro's School of Religious Education, president, 1951-56; West Virginia Inservice Collegiate Training Program, curriculum chairman, 1959-60. Military service: U.S. Naval Reserve, active duty, 1942-45; became lieutenant.

MEMBER: National Education Association, Association of Teacher Educators, Association for Supervision and Curriculum Development, Pennsylvania Association of Teacher Educators, Doctoral Association of Educators (life member), Pennsylvania State Education Association, Phi Delta Kappa, Phi Eta Sigma, Sigma Kappa Phi.

WRITINGS: A Christian Style of Life, Judson, 1966; The Youth Years, Judson, 1967; Man Responds to God, Judson, 1969; (editor and contributor) Guidebook for New Professionals in Education, Kendall/Hunt, 1971, 2nd edition, 1974. Contributor to Westminster Dictionary of Christian Education, 1963, and to Baptist journals and curriculum courses.

AVOCATIONAL INTERESTS: Color photography.

* * *

WILLMOTT, Peter 1923-

PERSONAL: Born September 18, 1923, in Oxford, England; son of Benjamin Merriman (a motor engineer) and Dorothy (Waymouth) Willmott; married Phyllis Noble (an author), July 31, 1948; children: Lewis, Michael. Education: Attended Ruskin College, Oxford, 1948-49; University of London, B.Sc., 1959. Religion: Agnostic. Home: 27 Kingsley Pl., London N.6, England. Office: Institute of Community Studies, 18 Victoria Park Sq., London E.2, England.

CAREER: Automobile engineering apprentice in Luton,

Bedfordshire, England, 1939-44; coal miner in Wales, 1944-45; social welfare worker in London, England, 1945-48; labor union research officer in London, 1949-53; Institute of Community Studies, London, research officer, 1954-56, deputy director, 1956-65, co-director, 1965—. Visiting professor of environmental studies, University College, University of London, 1972—.

WRITINGS: (With Michael Young) *Family and Kinship in East London,* Free Press of Glencoe, 1957; (with Young) *Family and Class in a London Suburb,* Humanities, 1960; *The Evolution of a Community,* Humanities, 1963; *Adolescent Boys of East London,* Humanities, 1966, revised edition, Pelican, 1969; (with Young) *The Symmetrical Family,* Pantheon, 1974.

WORK IN PROGRESS: Social research on urban problems, poverty and social policy.

*   *   *

WILLNER, Ann Ruth   1924-

PERSONAL: Born September 2, 1924, in New York, N.Y.; daughter of Norbert and Bella (Richman) Willner. *Education:* Hunter College (now Hunter College of the City University of New York), B.A., 1945; Yale University, M.A., 1946; University of Chicago, Ph.D., 1961. *Office:* Department of Political Science, University of Kansas, Lawrence, Kan. 66045.

CAREER: Government of Indonesia, Djakarta, adviser on organization and training and small industries, 1952-54; Library of Congress, Washington, D.C., foreign affairs analyst, Legislative Reference Service, 1960-61; University of Chicago, Chicago, Ill., research associate, 1961-62; State University of New York at Binghamton, assistant professor of political science, 1962-63; Princeton University, Center of International Studies, Princeton, N.J., research associate, 1964-69; University of Kansas, Lawrence, professor of political science, 1969—. *Member:* American Political Science Association, Association for Asian Studies. *Awards, honors:* Grants from Phi Beta Kappa, Rockefeller Foundation, and American Council of Learned Societies.

WRITINGS: The Neotraditional Accommodation to Political Independence, Center of International Studies, Princeton University, 1966; *Charismatic Political Leadership—A Theory,* Center of International Studies, Princeton University, 1968. Contributor to *World Politics, New Leader, Asian Survey, Human Organization,* and other academic journals.

WORK IN PROGRESS: A Study of Charismatic Political Leadership.

SIDELIGHTS: Ann Willner has lived and traveled in western Europe, Middle East, Asia, and Australia. She is competent in Indonesian-Malayan and Dutch.

*   *   *

WILLS, A(lfred) J(ohn)   1927-

PERSONAL: Born November 23, 1927, in Wickham, Hampshire, England; son of Gerald Alfred (in Royal Naval Reserve) and Violet (Stubington) Wills. *Education:* Trinity College, Oxford, B.A., 1949; University of London, Post-Graduate Certificate in Education, 1951. *Religion:* Church of England. *Home:* Myrtle Cottage, Stedham, Midhurst, Sussex, England. *Office:* King Edward VI School, Norwich, Norfolk, England.

CAREER: Education officer, Northern Rhodesia Govern-

ment, African Education Department, 1951-58; engaged in teaching and writing, mostly in London, England, 1958-60; North-Western Polytechnic, London, assistant lecturer, 1960-63; King Edward VI School, Norwich, Norfolk, England, assistant history master, 1964—. *Member:* Historical Association, Politics Association, Norfolk Print Club, Climbers Club.

WRITINGS: Notes for Teachers on the History of Some Tribes in Northern Rhodesia, Government Printer (Lusaka), 1958; *Notes for Teachers on "Travels in Northern Rhodesia,"* Oxford University Press (Cape Town), 1958; *An Introduction to the History of Central Africa,* Oxford University Press, 1964, 3rd edition, 1973; (contributor) J. Anene and G. Brown, editors, *Africa in the Nineteenth and Twentieth Centuries,* jointly published by Thomas Nelson and Ibadan University Press, 1965, 2nd edition, 1967; *The Story of Africa,* Holmes & Meier, 1973.

SIDELIGHTS: A. J. Wills told *CA:* "The fact that my father had farmed in Rhodesia in the early 1920's, coupled with my own interest in postwar Africa, helps to account for my original choice of a career. My wish to write on African history has been partly due to first-hand experience of the shortage of textbooks available." On his return to England in 1958, Wills traveled overland by car from Rhodesia, through the Congo and Nigeria, to Algeria. He speaks French. *Avocational interests:* Sketching, music, sailing, hill walking.

*   *   *

WILSON, Carolyn   1938-

PERSONAL: Born February 6, 1938, in Pine Bluff, Ark.; daughter of Byron L. (a photographer) and Virginia Lou (Moore) Wilson; married John G. Schisler (a farmer), January 31, 1959; children: John Byron, Richard Glen. *Education:* Attended Arkansas Agricultural and Mechanical College (now University of Arkansas at Monticello), 1955-56; Hendrix College, B.A., 1958. *Religion:* Methodist.

CAREER: Williamson, Williamson & Ball, Attorneys, Monticello, Ark., secretary, 1958-59; free-lance writer.

WRITINGS: The Scent of Lilacs (mystery), Ace Books, 1966.

WORK IN PROGRESS: The Light on the Mountain, a mystery.

BIOGRAPHICAL/CRITICAL SOURCES: Writers' Digest, November, 1967.††

*   *   *

WILSON, Clifton E.   1919-

PERSONAL: Born July 8, 1919, in White Bird, Idaho; son of Charlie and Edith (Carlson) Wilson; married Geneal Cowan, September 11, 1947. *Education:* Washington State University, student, 1937-39; University of Utah, B.S., 1950, M.A., 1953; University of Minnesota, Ph.D., 1964. *Politics:* Democrat. *Home:* 3331 North Olsen Ave., Tucson, Ariz. 85719. *Office:* Department of Political Science, University of Arizona, Tucson, Ariz. 85721.

CAREER: Associated Press, newsman in Boise, Idaho, 1946-47, and Salt Lake City, Utah, 1947-53; University of Minnesota, Minneapolis, assistant director of World Affairs Program, 1954-56, research fellow and assistant director of Center for International Relations and Area Studies, 1956-60, instructor in political science, 1959-60; University of Montana, Missoula, instructor in political science, 1960-61;

University of Arizona, Tucson, assistant professor, 1961-65, associate professor, 1965-68, professor of political science, 1968—, research specialist at Institute of Government Research, 1962-74, director of Institute, 1971-74. *Military service:* U.S. Marine Corps, 1943-46. *Member:* American Society of International Law, American Political Science Association, International Studies Association, Western Political Science Association, American Association for the United Nations (member of local board of directors).

WRITINGS: Cold War Diplomacy, University of Arizona Press, 1966; *Diplomatic Privileges and Immunities,* University of Arizona Press, 1967; *The United Nations,* Steck, 1968; (contributor) Stuart Nagel, editor, *Environmental Politics,* Praeger, 1974.

WORK IN PROGRESS: United Nations Resolutions and International Law.

* * *

WILSON, D(udley) B(utler)   1923-

PERSONAL: Born January 22, 1923, in Manchester, England; son of Thomas Turnbull (a textile buyer) and Hilda (Butler) Wilson; married Dorothy Jean Parker; children: Penelope Margaret, Alexander Giles, Victoria Tamzin. *Education:* Cambridge University, B.A. (second class honors), 1947; University of Paris, Doctorat de l'Universite, 1952. *Home:* 86 Gilesgate, Durham, England.

CAREER: University of Aberdeen, Aberdeen, Scotland, assistant lecturer, 1950-53; University of Durham, Durham, England, lecturer specializing in poetry of the French Renaissance, 1953-69, reader in French, 1969—. *Military service:* British Army, Queen's Royal Regiment, 1942-44.

WRITINGS: Ronsard, Poet of Nature, Manchester University Press, 1961; *Descriptive Poetry in France from Blason to Baroque,* Manchester University Press, 1967; *French Renaissance Scientific Poetry,* Athlone Press, 1974. Contributor to journals.

WORK IN PROGRESS: Bibliographical work on the continental book 1501-1600; a study of early science and sixteenth-century scientific poetry; a book on science in the poetry of Sieve, Ronsard, and Guy Lefevre de la Bodere, completion expected in 1980.

AVOCATIONAL INTERESTS: Collecting books and old objects; good food and wine.

* * *

WILSON, Harris W(ard)   1919-

PERSONAL: Born September 8, 1919, in Frederick, Okla.; son of John Benjamin (a lawyer) and Anna Wilson; married Bobby Lark Case (a secretary), April 22, 1942; children: Golder North, John Robert. *Education:* University of Missouri, B.S., 1941; University of Chicago, M.A., 1947; University of Illinois, Ph.D., 1953. *Politics:* Democrat. *Religion:* Methodist. *Home:* 1204 South Carle, Urbana, Ill. 61801. *Office:* 100 English Building, University of Illinois, Urbana, Ill. 61801.

CAREER: Alabama Polytechnic Institute (now Auburn University), Auburn, instructor in English, 1947-49; University of Illinois, Urbana, instructor, 1953-55, assistant professor, 1955-57, associate professor, 1957-60, professor of English, 1960—. *Military service:* U.S. Army, 1941-46; became captain; received three battle stars and Air Medal. *Member:* National Council of Teachers of English (direc-

tor), Modern Language Association of America. *Awards, honors:* Guggenheim fellowship, 1961-62.

WRITINGS: (Editor) *Arnold Bennett and H. G. Wells: The Record of a Personal and Literary Friendship,* University of Illinois Press, 1960; (with Louis G. Locke) *University Handbook,* Holt, 1960, 2nd edition, 1966; (with Locke) *University Readings,* Holt, 1961; (editor) *The Wealth of Mr. Waddy: An Unpublished Incomplete Novel by H. G. Wells,* Southern Illinois University Press, 1970. Contributor to professional journals.

WORK IN PROGRESS: Wells and the Fabians, completion expected in 1978.

* * *

WILSON, Jack   1937-

PERSONAL: Born October 2, 1937, in Bally Robert, County Down, Northern Ireland; son of James (a sea captain) and Eileen Florence (Aiken) Wilson; married Vera Munn, October 2, 1963. *Politics:* none. *Religion:* Presbyterian. *Home:* 3 Dunleady Pk., Dundonald, County Down, Northern Ireland. *Office:* W.D.R. & R. T. Taggart, 32 Wellington Pk., Belfast, Northern Ireland.

CAREER: Invalided most of his youth by tuberculosis, Wilson read all of the Hornblower books and aimed for a life at sea; entered the British Merchant Navy as a cadet trainee at sixteen, but was forced out by poor eyesight; primarily a full-time writer in County Down, Northern Ireland, 1954-58, supplementing his income by working as farm laborer; physician's receptionist, 1958-60; librarian for James Munce Partnership (architects), Belfast, Northern Ireland, 1960-72; owner of printing business, 1972-74; technical librarian for W.A.R. & R. T. Taggart (architects), Belfast; novelist. *Member:* Irish P.E.N. (vice-chairman of Belfast center, 1966-68).

WRITINGS—Novels: *The Wild Summer,* Muller, 1963; *Adam Grey,* Muller, 1964, published as *The Night Comer,* Corgi, 1966; *The Tomorrow Country,* Muller, 1967; *Dark Eden,* Muller, 1969. Author of radio play, "A Day Like Tomorrow," 1965, and documentary, "Ring Master," 1966, both produced by British Broadcasting Corp.

WORK IN PROGRESS: Adams Island, a novel set on a fictitious island off the north coast of Ireland.

SIDELIGHTS: "Chiefly interested in rural settings and characters," Wilson writes, "probably because my childhood and youth were spent among the farmlands of County Down. ... The writer I most admire and who may have influenced me more than any other is John Steinbeck. American fiction I find more dramatically aware and alive than the work of most current English novelists."

BIOGRAPHICAL/CRITICAL SOURCES: Books and Bookmen, November, 1967; *Arts Council Review,* 1971; John Wilson Foster, *Forces and Themes in Ulster Fiction,* Macmillan, 1974.

* * *

WILSON, Julia   1927-

PERSONAL: Born April 26, 1927, in Chicago, Ill.; daughter of Isadore (a metal worker) and Fannie (Lenitz) Kowitch; married John Wilson (an associate professor), June 25, 1950; children: Rebecca, Roy, Erica. *Education:* Brooklyn College (now of the City University of New York), B.A., 1948; graduate study at New York University, 1949-50, and Bank Street College of Education, 1961-

62, 1963-64. *Religion:* Hebrew. *Home:* 44 Harris St., Brookline, Mass. 02146.

CAREER: Mexico City College (now University of the Americas), Mexico City, Mexico, instructor in English, 1951-55; Bronx House Nursery and Kindergarten, Bronx, N.Y., teacher and director, 1961-63; teacher in the Bronx, 1963-64.

WRITINGS: Becky, Crowell, 1967.

AVOCATIONAL INTERESTS: Making hooked rugs and jewelry, refurbishing old furniture.

BIOGRAPHICAL/CRITICAL SOURCES: Lee Bennett Hopkins, *Books Are by People,* Citation Press, 1969.

*   *   *

WILSON, Keith   1927-

PERSONAL: Born December 26, 1927, in Clovis, N.M.; son of Earl C. and Marjorie (Edwards) Wilson; married Heloise Brigham, February 15, 1958; children: Kathy, Kristin, Kevin, Kerrin, Roxanne. *Education:* U.S. Naval Academy, B.S., 1950; University of New Mexico, M.A., 1956, additional study through 1958. *Home:* 1500 Locust, Las Cruces, N.M. *Office:* Department of English, New Mexico State University, Las Cruces, N.M. 88001.

CAREER: U.S. Navy, midshipman, 1946-50, officer, 1950-54, leaving the service as lieutenant; Sandia Corp., Albuquerque, N.M., technical writer, 1958-60; University of Arizona, Tucson, instructor in English, 1960-65; New Mexico State University, Las Cruces, assistant professor of English, 1965—. *Awards, honors:* D. H. Lawrence fellowship in writing, 1972; National Endowment for the Arts creative writing fellowship, 1975-76; Fulbright-Hays senior fellowship, 1975-76.

WRITINGS—All poetry: *Sketches for a New Mexico Hill Town,* Prensa de Lagar-Wine Press, 1966; *The Shadow of Our Bones,* Prensa de Lagar-Wine Press, 1968; *The Old Car, and Other Black Poems,* Grande Ronde Press, 1968; (contributor) Ronald Schreiber, editor, *31 New American Poets,* Hill & Wang, 1968; (contributor) Wilbur Stevens, editor, *Poems Southwest,* Prescott College Press, 1968; *Graves Registry, and Other Poems,* Grove, 1969; *Homestead,* Kayak, 1969; *The Old Man and Others,* New Mexico State University, 1971; *Midwatch,* Sumac Press, 1972. Contributor to *Poetry, Descant, New Mexico Quarterly, El Corno Emplumado,* and other periodicals in Mexico, Canada, Japan, Argentina, New Zealand, and the United States.

WORK IN PROGRESS: While Dancing Feet Shatter the Earth, poetry; *Martingale,* a novelette; *Some Faces for America,* one-act plays, poems, short stories.

SIDELIGHTS: Wilson told *CA:* "Primarily I consider myself a poet—I have been heavily influenced by William Carlos Williams, Robert Burns, William Blake, Robert Creeley, Robert Duncan, Charles Olson, and many others. My poems are, in part, descriptions of emotional geography (concerns with the sea, the Southwest, loves and losses, gains)."

Robert Sward believes that "the strongest quality in Keith Wilson's poems (*Sketches for a New Mexico Hill Town*) is the feeling for the landscape of the Southwest, and the sense of a man growing with that landscape. The man's powers are reflected in the light that everywhere surrounds him. Implicit here, too, are the three worlds that make up the Southwest, the Indian, the [white American] and the Mexican, each with its own aura, and each the counterpart of the other. Many of the poems . . . come out of the effort of a man to pass into other areas that are, for him, extensions of his own consciousness."

Wilson reads and writes Spanish and is especially interested in South American poetry.

BIOGRAPHICAL/CRITICAL SOURCES: Grande Rondo Review, Number 6, 1966; *Poetry,* March, 1967; *University of Portland Review,* spring, 1967.

*   *   *

WILSON, Robert M(ills)   1929-

PERSONAL: Born March 20, 1929, in Pittsburgh, Pa.; son of C. B. and Helen (Mills) Wilson; married Barbara Stewart, August 11, 1951; children: Richard, James, Sharon. *Education:* California State College, California, Pa., B.S., 1950; University of Pittsburgh, M.S., 1956, Ed.D., 1960. *Office:* College of Education, University of Maryland, College Park, Md. 20740.

CAREER: Elementary teacher in West Mifflin, Pa., 1954-59; Edinboro State College, Edinboro, Pa., associate professor, 1960-63, professor of education and director of reading clinic, 1963-65; University of Maryland, College Park, associate professor of education and director of reading center, 1965—. *Military service:* U.S. Air Force, 1950-54. *Member:* International Reading Association, National Education Association, National Council of Teachers of English, College Reading Association (chairman of research commission, 1967, and ethics commission, 1968-69), National Conference on Research in English, Maryland State Education Association, Maryland Corrective Remedial Reading Association, Phi Delta Kappa, Phi Sigma Pi.

WRITINGS: Diagnostic and Remedial Reading, C. E. Merrill, 1967; *Programmed Word Attack for Teachers,* C. E. Merrill, 1968; (co-author) *Reading and the Elementary School Child,* Van Nostrand, 1973; (co-author) *Focusing on the Strengths of Children,* Fearon, 1974; (co-author) *Learning Center,* Instructo Corp., 1975. Co-author, "Visual Lingual Reading Program," Tweedy Transparencies, 1967. Contributor to education journals. Editor, *Maryland State Newsletter in Reading;* editor of review section, *Journal of the Reading Specialist,* 1966-68.

WORK IN PROGRESS: Programmed Comprehension for Teachers, for C. E. Merrill.

*   *   *

WINCHESTER, Otis   1933-

PERSONAL: Born May 23, 1933, in Tulsa, Okla.; son of O. Winfred (a certified public accountant) and Elizabeth (Hazleton) Winchester; married Lois Wilson, June 22, 1953; children: William Paul, Bruce Robinson. *Education:* Phillips University, student, 1951-52; University of Tulsa, B.A., 1955, M.A., 1956; University of Colorado, graduate study, 1956; University of Oklahoma, Ph.D., 1962. *Home address:* Route 2, Box 815, Collinsville, Okla. 74021. *Office:* Department of English, University of Tulsa, Tulsa, Okla. 74101.

CAREER: University of Wyoming, Laramie, instructor in speech, 1958-59; University of Tulsa, Tulsa, Okla., 1960—, began as assistant professor, currently professor of English. *Member:* National Council of Teachers of English, Conference on College Composition and Communication.

WRITINGS—All with Winston Weathers: *The Strategy of Style*, McGraw, 1967; *The Prevalent Forms of Prose*, Houghton, 1968; *Copy and Compose*, Prentice-Hall, 1969; *The Attitudes of Rhetoric*, Prentice-Hall, 1970; *The Sound of Your Voice*, Allyn & Bacon, 1972. Also author of short stories, essays, and articles.

WORK IN PROGRESS: Adrienne, a novel.

* * *

WINDER, Mavis Areta 1907-
(Mavis Areta, Mavis Areta Wynder)

PERSONAL: Born September 21, 1907, in Timaru, New Zealand; married James Stanley Winder (a shop manager), February 21, 1935. *Education:* Attended New Zealand primary schools and Ashburton Technical College. *Religion:* Baptist. *Home:* 45 Cholmondeley Ave., Christchurch 2, New Zealand. *Agent:* A. M. Heath & Co. Ltd., 40-42 William IV St., London WC2N 4DD, England; and Brandt & Brandt, 101 Park Ave., New York, N.Y. 10017.

CAREER: Shorthand typist for advertising agency in Christchurch, New Zealand, 1923-35, and for Ministry of Supply during World War II; partner, with husband, 1935—, in grocery business and later in book store; novelist.

WRITINGS—Religious novels under name Mavis Areta Winder: *The Things Temporal*, Victory Press, 1955; *Safer Than a Known Way*, Victory Press, 1956; *The Mysterious Way*, Zomer & Keuning (Netherlands), 1965; *The Lamp in the Window*, Zomer & Keuning, 1967; *Folly Is Joy*, R. Hale, 1973.

Under name Mavis Areta; all published by Wright & Brown: *A Reed Shaken*, 1949; *Badge of Bondage*, 1953; *As We Forgive Them*, 1954; *Nest Among the Stars*, 1956; *Silvers of Silverstream*, 1957; *Faint Is the Bliss*, 1958; *No Easy Path*, 1961; *Memory's Yoke*, 1962; *How Great a Fire*, 1963; *Love Keeps No Score*, 1964.

Under name Mavis Winder: *Shadowed Journey*, Jenkins, 1955; *The Stubble Field*, Jenkins, 1956; *Stranger to Mercy*, Jenkins, 1957; *Render Unto Caesar*, Jenkins, 1957; *The Gulf Between*, Jenkins, 1958; *Vain Is the Glory*, Jenkins, 1959; *Reap the Whirlwind*, Jenkins, 1961; *Scent of the Woods*, R. Hale, 1965; *River in the Valley*, R. Hale, 1965; *The Glitter and the Gold*, R. Hale, 1967; *The Fanned Flame*, R. Hale, 1968.

Under name Mavis Areta Wynder: *Smile at the Storm* (religious novel), Moody, 1967.

SIDELIGHTS: Eleven of Mavis Winder's novels have been translated into Dutch, seven into Norwegian, and several into other languages; they have been serialized in England, Canada, Australia, Norway, Denmark, Belgium, and the Netherlands. In 1962-63, she traveled overseas for a full year, visiting the United States, Canada, and Europe.

* * *

WINDHAM, Joan 1904-

PERSONAL: Born April 13, 1904, in Yorkshire, England; daughter of Ashe (a British Army officer) and Cora Ellen (Middleton) Windham; married O. H. Tidbury (a brigadier in the British Army), May 8, 1959 (died, 1961); married H. D'oyly-Lyle (a major in the British Army), September 24, 1964. *Education:* St. Thomas' Hospital, London, M.C.S.P. (in physiotherapy), 1929, General Nursing Certificate, early 1940's. *Politics:* Conservative. *Religion:* Roman Catholic.

CAREER: Private practice in physiotherapy with own surgery, Berkshire, England, 1930-39, 1947-53; St. Thomas' Hospital, London, general nursing, 1943-46; held various jobs as a schoolmatron or nurse in boarding schools, 1953-58. *Military service:* British Army, 1939-42; served as a Red Cross commandant; was awarded service medals.

WRITINGS—All published by Sheed, except as noted: *Six O'Clock Saints*, 1934, reprinted, 1974; *More Saints for Six O'Clock*, 1935; (translator) Camille Melloy, *The King's Christmas Present*, 1936; *The Adventures of Saint Paul*, 1936; (translator) Camille Melloy, *Heaven on Earth*, 1937; *Saints by Request*, 1937; *Saints Who Spoke English*, 1939, reprinted, 1974; *The New Carol*, 1939; *New Six O'Clock Saints*, 1945; *Sixty Saints for Boys*, 1948; *Here Are Your Saints*, 1948, reprinted, 1972; *Saints Upon a Time*, 1956; *Sixty Saints for Girls*, 1962; *Saints for all Seasons*, 1972; *Sixteen Saints for Six O'Clock*, 1972; *Saints You Have Asked for*, 1974; *Saints Specially for Girls*, 1974; *Saints Specially for Boys*, 1974; *Story Library of the Saints*, Catholic Press, 1974.†

* * *

WINDMILLER, Marshall 1924-

PERSONAL: Born June 29, 1924, in Sacramento, Calif.; son of Louis L. and Gladys (Hook) Windmiller; married Myra Bailey. *Education:* University of the Pacific, B.A., 1948; Sorbonne, University of Paris, graduate study, 1948-49; University of California, Berkeley, M.A., 1954, Ph.D., 1964. *Office:* San Francisco State University, 1600 Holloway, San Francisco, Calif. 94132.

CAREER: San Francisco State University, San Francisco, Calif., assistant professor, 1959-64, associate professor, and director of International Relations Center, 1964-69, professor of international relations, 1969—. Regular foreign affairs commentator on KPFA, Berkeley, and other listener-supported radio stations. *Military service:* U.S. Army, 1943-46; became sergeant. *Member:* International Studies Association, American Political Science Association, American Civil Liberties Union.

WRITINGS: (With Gene D. Overstreet) *Communism in India*, University of California Press, 1959; *Five Years on Free Radio*, TLD Press, 1965; *The Peace Corps and Pax Americana*, Public Affairs Press, 1970. Contributor to newspapers and magazines, including *Nation, Progressive, Canadian Dimension, Ramparts, St. Louis Post-Dispatch, Tribune* (London), *Motive, Nouvelle Democraties*, and *Review of International Affairs* (Belgrade).

* * *

WINES, Roger (Andrew) 1933-

PERSONAL: Born November 29, 1933, in Brooklyn, N.Y.; son of Andrew J. and Katharine (Duffy) Wines; married Peggy Elder (a registered nurse), 1959; children: Mark, John, Steven, Thomas, Katharine. *Education:* Fordham University, A.B., 1954; Columbia University, M.A., 1957, Ph.D., 1961; University of Wuerzburg, graduate study, 1958-59. *Home:* 31 Linden Ave., North Pelham, N.Y. 10803. *Office:* History Department, Fordham University, Bronx, N.Y. 10458.

CAREER: Fordham University, Bronx, N.Y., instructor, 1959-62, assistant professor, 1962-67, associate professor of modern European and German history, 1967—, chairman of history department, 1965-68, director of Bensalem College, 1973-74. *Military service:* U.S. Army, 1954-56;

became first lieutenant. *Member:* American Historical Association, American Catholic Historical Association, American Association of University Professors (member of national council, 1973-76). *Awards, honors:* Fulbright scholar in Germany, 1958-59; American Philosophical Society grant-in-aid, 1965.

WRITINGS: (Editor) *Enlightened Despotism: Reform or Reaction?,* Heath, 1967. Contributor to history journals.

WORK IN PROGRESS: Editing the historical writings of Leopold von Ranke.

*   *   *

WINETROUT, Kenneth 1912-

PERSONAL: Born September 8, 1912, in Galion, Ohio; son of Clarence Arthur (a businessman) and Sylvia (Ricker) Winetrout; married Julia Foster, May 6, 1944; children: Mark, Nancy. *Education:* Cornell University, student, 1930-31; Ohio State University, A.B. (with high honors), 1935, M.A., 1939, Ph.D., 1947. *Politics:* Independent. *Home:* 10 Hickory Lane, Hampden, Mass. 01036. *Office:* Department of Education, American International College, Springfield, Mass. 01109.

CAREER: Teacher in Galion, Ohio, 1936-37, San Sebastian, Puerto Rico, 1938-39, and Xenia, Ohio, 1939-41; Stephens College, Columbia, Mo., instructor in writing and creative writing, 1946-48; American International College, Springfield, Mass., assistant professor, 1948-50, associate professor, 1950-52, professor of education, 1952—, Margaret C. Ellis Professor, 1969—, chairman of department, 1948—. Visiting professor, Smith College, 1970, Mount Holyoke College, 1972-73, 1974-75; visiting summer professor at University of Arkansas, 1953-55, University of Massachusetts, 1958, 1960, University of Connecticut, 1959, Trinity College, 1961, 1968, University of Hartford, 1962, and Washington University, St. Louis, Mo., 1964; visiting lecturer at Wesleyan University, 1965-66. Member of Springfield board, Massachusetts Society for the Prevention of Cruelty to Children, 1954-57, and executive committee, Springfield Citizens Action Commission, 1960-62; trustee, Town of Hampden Library, 1967-70. *Military service:* U.S. Naval Reserve, active duty, 1942-45.

MEMBER: Philosophy of Education Society, International Society for General Semantics, American Association of University Professors, John Dewey Society, New England Philosophy of Education Society (president, 1962-63), Foreign Policy Association of the Connecticut Valley (member of board of directors, 1950-57; president, 1956-57), World Affairs Council of the Connecticut Valley (member of board of directors, 1958—; vice-president, 1962-66), Adult Education Association of Massachusetts (president, 1952-53), Phi Delta Kappa, American Civil Liberties Union. *Awards, honors:* Ford Foundation grant, 1952-53.

WRITINGS: (Contributor) I. L. Horowitz, editor, *The New Sociology,* Oxford University Press, 1964; (co-editor) *An Experimental In-Service Economic Education Course,* Western Massachusetts Economic Education Council, 1966; *F.C.S. Schiller and the Dimensions of Pragmatism,* Ohio State University Press, 1967; (contributor) White and Averson, editors, *Sight, Sound, and Society,* Beacon Press, 1968; *Arnold Toynbee: The Ecumenical Vision,* Twayne, 1975. Contributor to education and other journals.

WORK IN PROGRESS: Editing letters of William Polk.

WINGATE, Isabel B(arnum) 1901-

PERSONAL: Born October 12, 1901, in Danbury, Conn.; daughter of Starr Clifford (a sales representative) and Louise (Lyon) Barnum; married John W. Wingate, June 22, 1925; children: Elaine Louise (Mrs. Elaine W. Conway), John Barnum. *Education:* Radcliffe College, A.B., 1923; New York University, M.S., 1925; Yeshiva University, Ph.D., 1961. *Politics:* Republican. *Religion:* Congregationalist. *Home:* 63 East Ninth St., New York, N.Y. 10003. *Office:* Institute of Retail Management, Tisch Hall, New York University, Washington Sq., New York, N.Y. 10003.

CAREER: New York University, New York, N.Y., instructor, 1926-33, assistant professor and coordinator, 1934-46, associate professor, 1947-61, professor of retailing, 1961-66, professor of retail management, 1966-68, professor emeritus, 1968—. First woman member, New York University Senate, 1949-52; New School for Social Research, Institute for Retired Professionals, member of textile group, 1968—, chairman, 1974—; member, International Fibercare Institute, 1974—. Young Men's Christian Association of Greater New York, member of general assembly, 1953-59, of board of managers of Intercollegiate Branch, 1956-64, and of committee on campus work, 1967-68. *Member:* American Association of Textile Chemists and Colorists, Eta Mu Pi. *Awards, honors:* New York Times Certificate of Achievement for distinguished participation in the distributive program of New York high schools, 1966; New York University Retailing Alumni Achievement Award, 1968.

WRITINGS: Textile Fabrics and Their Selection, Prentice-Hall, 1934, 6th edition, 1970; *Laboratory Swatch Book for Textile Fabrics,* Prentice-Hall, 1937, 6th edition, W. C. Brown, 1970; (co-author) *Know Your Merchandise,* Gregg, 1944, 4th edition, 1975; (editor) *A Dictionary of Textile Terms,* Dan River Mills, Inc., 9th edition, 1964; (editor) *Textile Dictionary,* Fairchild, 5th edition, 1967. Contributor to *Encyclopaedia Britannica,* yearbooks, and education and trade journals.

WORK IN PROGRESS: A 7th edition of *Textile Fabrics and Their Selection.*

AVOCATIONAL INTERESTS: Gardening, fishing, knitting.

*   *   *

WINGO, T(ullius) Lowdon, Jr. 1923-

PERSONAL: Born January 20, 1923, in El Paso, Tex.; son of Tullius Lowdon and Ella Mae (Hill) Wingo; married Josette P. Dermody (a teacher), 1949; children: Anthony K., Laird S. *Education:* University of Chicago, B.A., 1949, M.A., 1950; Harvard University, M.P.A., 1957. *Home:* Hopkinson House, Philadelphia, Pa. 19106. *Office:* Fels Center, B1, University of Pennsylvania, Philadelphia, Pa. 19174.

CAREER: Wingo Insurance Service, El Paso, Tex., partner, 1950-52; City of El Paso, director of planning, 1953-56; Resources for the Future, Inc. (economic research), Washington, D.C., research associate, 1957-68, director of urban and regional studies, 1968-73; University of Pennsylvania, Pittsburgh, chairman of department of city and regional planning, 1973-75, associate dean, School of Public and Urban Policy, 1973—. Consultant to National Capital Transportation Agency, 1962-63, to Organization of American States, 1966, 1967, on project in urban and regional planning in Ljubljana, Yugoslavia, 1967, to Stanford Research Institute project on urban public facilities in India, 1967-68, and to Ford Foundation, 1968. Lecturer at universities, including Northwestern University, University of California, Harvard University, and Cornell University. *Military service:* U.S. Army Air Forces, 1943-46. *Member:* Regional Science Association (council member, 1964-66), Phi Beta Kappa.

WRITINGS: Transportation and Urban Land, Resources for the Future, 1960; (editor) *Cities and Space,* Johns Hopkins Press, 1963; (editor with Harvey S. Perloff) *Issues in Urban Economics,* Johns Hopkins Press, 1968; (with G. Cameron) *Cities, Regions and Public Policy,* Longman, 1973.

Contributor: Joseph J. Spengler, editor, *National Resources and Economic Growth,* Resources for the Future, 1961; *Trends in American Living and Outdoor Recreation,* U.S. Government Printing Office, 1962; Howard W. Ottoson, editor, *Land Use Policy and Problems in the United States,* University of Nebraska Press, 1963; Harvey S. Perloff, editor, *Design for a Worldwide Study of Regional Development,* Resources for the Future, 1966; *Regional Accounting for Policy Decisions,* Resources for the Future, 1966. General series editor, *The Government of Metropolitan Regions,* four volumes, Johns Hopkins Press, 1970-72. Contributor to planning and urban affairs journals.

WORK IN PROGRESS: A book on urban development and developing countries; a volume on the analysis and policy aspects of the quality of life in advanced societies.

*　　*　　*

WINTER, Nathan H.   1926-

PERSONAL: Born March 20, 1926, in New York, N.Y.; son of Sol and Fannie (Sachs) Winter; married Magda Markowitz, February 5, 1948; children: Steven, Elaine, Jonathan. *Education:* New York University, B.A., 1949, M.A., 1955, Ph.D., 1963; Jewish Theological Seminary of America, B.R.E., 1950; Brooklyn Law School, J.D., 1954. *Home:* 46 Burroughs Way, Maplewood, N.J. *Office:* Department of Hebrew Culture and Education, New York University, 735 East Building, New York, N.Y. 10003.

CAREER: Congregation Oheb Shalom, South Orange, N.J., director of education, beginning 1954; Jewish Theological Seminary of America, New York City, lecturer in history, 1963—; New York University, New York City, instructor, 1964-68, associate professor of Hebrew culture and education, 1968—, Judge Abraham Lieberman Professor of Judaic Studies, 1971, chairman of department, 1971—. Lecturer, Institute for Religious and Social Studies, 1966. New Jersey director of education, United Synagogue of America, 1964—. President of Educators Assembly, and member of board of directors. *Military service:* National U.S. Army, 1943-46. *Member:* National Council for Jewish Education (executive board member), American Association for Jewish Education (chairman of personnel committee), Jewish Education Association of Essex County (former chairman of principals' council), Alumni Association of the Teachers Institute of Jewish Theological Seminary (vice-president). *Awards, honors:* Founders Day Award, New York University, 1964.

WRITINGS: Jewish Education in a Pluralist Society, New York University Press, 1966. Contributor to Jewish periodicals. Member of editorial advisory board, *Our Age* (youth magazine).

WINTERS, Bayla   1921-
(Bernice Winters)

PERSONAL: First name originally Bernice; legally changed; born January 4, 1921, in New York, N.Y.; daughter of George (a salesman) and Mary (Lockwood) Mason; married George S. Winters (with U.S. Department of Defense), February 26, 1939; children: Hollace Mason (Mrs. Arnold Jay Michels), Sherrie Marsha (Mrs. John Thomas Hauge). *Education:* Studied at University of Judaism, Los Angeles, 1948-50, and at Los Angeles Valley College, 1963, 1973. *Politics:* Democrat. *Religion:* Jewish. *Home:* 2700 Scott Rd., Burbank, Calif. 91504.

CAREER: Everywoman's Village, Van Nuys, Calif., teacher of writing, 1965-73; University of California, Los Angeles, faculty member, 1972—. Administrative assistant, Outreach Drug Abuse Facility, 1973. Literary consultant; consultant and staff member, Los Angeles Poetry Center. Reader and lecturer on radio and to college groups. *Member:* Centro Studi e Scambi Internazionali (Rome), California Federation of Chaparral Poets, Valley Writers Club (founding member; president, 1965-66). *Awards, honors:* Poetry awards from *Writer's Digest,* 1965, Poetry Society of Virginia, California Federation of Chaparral Poets, *Promethean Lamp,* 1966, and Los Angeles Valley College; Monticello Arkansas Award; National Federation of Poetry Societies award, 1967; Ruth Forbes Sherry Poetry Prize, 1967.

WRITINGS—Under name Bernice Winters: *The Tropic of Mother,* Olivant, 1966; *bitchpoems,* Olivant, 1970. Poems anthologized in *Promethean Lamp, Singing Mariners, Discourses on Poetry, Wings of Pegasus.* Also author and producer of "Janis Joplin and the Folding Co., KPFK-Radio. Editor of three educational record albums. Contributor of poems to magazines and journals in United States and abroad. Editor of poetry column, "Peasant Under Glass," for *Burbank Independent;* West Coast editor, *Goliards.*

WORK IN PROGRESS: Polyester Woman; working on a television presentation.

SIDELIGHTS: Bayla Winters told *CA:* "I try to write a social commentary employing the idiom in the air and on the tongue and trust it has enough validity to endure for tomorrow and be evocative notwithstanding the fact that I am aware my deliberate use of language may 'date' the manuscript. While my first book, *The Tropic of Mother,* represents one voice, I do maintain another, less harsh, less hostile. With these two, I feel I can adequately oscillate in the spectrum of semantics. . . . A poet is/should be a chronicler in his own time and not concern himself [with] 'slanting' for posterity. If the work is vital (honest) *today,* it will endure. . . ." Bayla Winters' poems have been translated into French and Greek.

*　　*　　*

WIRTH, Arthur G.   1919-

PERSONAL: Born August 3, 1919, in Columbus, Ohio; son of Arthur T. (a salesman) and Norma (Wagner) Wirth; married Marian Jenks (a teacher), March 15, 1947. *Education:* Ohio State University, A.B. (summa cum laude), 1940, M.A., 1941, Ph.D., 1949. *Politics:* Democrat. *Religion:* Unitarian Universalist. *Home:* 7443 Cromwell, Clayton, Mo. 63105. *Office:* Graduate Institute of Education, Washington University, St. Louis, Mo. 63130.

CAREER: Ohio State University, Columbus, instructor at

University School, 1946-48, university instructor, 1948-49; Brooklyn College (now Brooklyn College of the City University of New York), Brooklyn, N.Y., teacher, department of education, 1949-61, deputy chairman for teacher education program, Division of Graduate Studies, 1954-58; Washington University, Graduate Institute of Education, St. Louis, Mo., professor of history and philosophy of education, 1961—. Specialist in secondary education, UNESCO Mission in Ecuador, 1951-52. Member of executive board, St. Louis White House Conference on Education, 1962-64. Consultant, Phelps-Stokes Fund Project for Negro Education, North Carolina and Georgia, 1957-58. *Military service:* U.S. Army Air Forces, 1941-45; became first lieutenant; received Distinguished Flying Cross and Air Medal.

MEMBER: Philosophy of Education Society (fellow), John Dewey Society, Comparative Education Society, National Society of College Teachers of Education, History of Education Society, American Association of University Professors, American Civil Liberties Union, Midwest Philosophy of Education Society, Phi Beta Kappa, Tau Kappa Theta.

WRITINGS: (Author of introduction and final chapter) *Organizing the Teaching Profession,* Free Press of Glencoe, 1955; (contributor) Herman A. Estrin and Delmer M. Goode, editors, *College and University Teaching,* W. C. Brown, 1964; *John Dewey as Educator: His Design for Work in Education, 1894-1904,* Wiley, 1966; (contributor) Donald Vandenberg, editor, *Teaching and Learning,* University of Illinois Press, 1970; *Education in the Technological Society,* Intext, 1972; *Public Alternative Schools* (monograph), Ohio State University Press, 1974; (contributor) Ralph Smith, editor, *Regaining Educational Leadership,* Wiley, 1974. Editor, "John Dewey Lecture Series," Harper, 1959-66, and "Monographs in Educational Theory," Ohio State University Press, 1963-66. Contributor of about forty articles to education journals.

*   *   *

WISE, Charles C(onrad), Jr.   1913-

PERSONAL: Born April 1, 1913, in Washington, D.C.; son of Charles Conrad (a police detective) and Lorena May (Sweeney) Wise; married Ruth Miles Baxter (a concert dancer), November 19, 1938; children: Gregory Baxter, Charles Conrad III (deceased), Jenifer. *Education:* George Washington University, J.D., 1936, A.B. (cum laude), 1938; Columbus University, M. Fiscal Admin., 1942; American University, graduate study, 1945-46. *Politics:* None. *Religion:* Methodist. *Home:* Solon-Lair, Cross Keys Penn Laird, Va. 22846. *Office:* Blue Ridge Community College, Weyers Cave, Va. 24486.

CAREER: Admitted to District of Columbia and Federal Bars, 1935; U.S. Government, Washington, D.C., 1933-73, holding civil service posts, including attorney for Railroad Retirement Board, 1939-41, claims attorney with War Department, 1941-43, assistant counsel, Office of General Counsel, Department of the Navy, 1946-47, counsel with Reconstruction Finance Corp., 1947-53, executive secretary of Subversive Activities Control Board, 1953-61, and security adviser to Department of Defense, 1962-73; Blue Ridge Community College, Weyers Cave, Va., lecturer in religion, philosophy, thanatology, and political science, 1973—. Instructor in English at George Washington University, 1960, and American University, 1961. *Military service:* U.S. Navy, 1943-46; became lieutenant. *Member:* Federal Bar Association, Phi Beta Kappa, Delta Theta Phi.

WRITINGS: Windows on the Passion, Abingdon, 1967; *Windows on the Master,* Abingdon, 1968; *Ruth and Naomi,* McClure Press, 1971; (contributor) John White, editor, *What is Meditation?,* Doubleday, 1974.

WORK IN PROGRESS: Windows on the Infinite, a gospel of Jesus Christ for the "New Age" psychically inspired.

AVOCATIONAL INTERESTS: Collecting books and records.

BIOGRAPHICAL/CRITICAL SOURCES: Washington Evening Star, January 7, 1967.

*   *   *

WISE, Raymond L.   1895-

PERSONAL: Born June 24, 1895, in New York, N.Y.; son of Leo (a realtor) and Minerva (Cashman) Wise; married Karena Post, September 1, 1923 (died, 1966); married Eva Jonas, March 1, 1967; children: (first marriage) William, David. *Education:* Columbia University, A.B., 1916, J.D., 1919. *Politics:* Democrat. *Religion:* Jewish. *Home:* 745 North Shore Dr., Miami Beach, Fla. 33141.

CAREER: Admitted to New York Bar, 1919, and Florida Bar, 1952; practicing attorney, 1919—, currently in Florida. Special Assistant to U.S. attorney for Southern District of New York, 1921-22; deputy assistant attorney general, State of New York, 1928-29; city councilman, Surfside, Fla., 1962-64, municipal judge, 1965-67. *Military service:* U.S. Army, Infantry, 1917-18; became first lieutenant. *Member:* Florida Bar Association, Dade County Bar Association (chairman, committee on professional ethics, 1962-66).

WRITINGS: Legal Ethics, Matthew Bender, 1966, 2nd edition, 1970; *Order Please: A Plea for World Order,* Central Book Co., 1970. Also author of *Judicial Ethics,* 1973. Contributor to *Vista, Nation,* and other periodicals. Associate editor, *Columbia Law Review,* 1919.

WORK IN PROGRESS: Code for U.S. Judges.

*   *   *

WISE, S(ydney) F(rancis)   1924-

PERSONAL: Born November 14, 1924, in Toronto, Ontario, Canada; son of Francis Evelyn (a salesman) and Marjorie Louise (Hutton) Wise; married Verna Isobel Mulholland, September 6, 1947; children: John Francis Hutton, Catherine Ellen, Bruce Douglas. *Education:* University of Toronto, B.A. (honors), 1949, B.L.S., 1950; Queen's University at Kingston, M.A., 1953. *Religion:* Anglican. *Home:* 12 Orrin Ave., Ottawa, Ontario, Canada. *Office:* Department of History, Carleton University, Ottawa, Ontario, Canada.

CAREER: Royal Military College of Canada, Kingston, Ontario, lecturer in history, 1950-55; Queen's University at Kingston, Kingston, 1955-66, began as assistant professor, became professor of history; Canadian Forces Headquarters, Directorate of History, Ottawa, Ontario, chief historian, 1966-73; Carleton University, Ottawa, professor of history, 1973—. Social Science Research Council of Canada, vice-president, 1973-74, president, 1974-75. Chairman, Archaeological and Historic Sites Board of Ontario, 1973-75; vice-chairman, Ontario Heritage Foundation, 1975—. *Military service:* Royal Canadian Air Force, pilot, 1943-45.

MEMBER: Canadian Historical Association (executive councillor, 1962-65; vice-president, 1972-73; president,

1973-74), American Historical Association, Ontario Historical Society (vice-president, 1966-68; president, 1968-69).

WRITINGS: (With R. A. Preston and H. M. Werner) *Men in Arms: A History of the Interrelationships of Warfare and Western Society,* Praeger, 1956, 2nd edition, 1963; (with Robert Craig Brown) *Canada Views the United States: Nineteenth-Century Political Attitudes,* University of Washington Press, 1967; (editor) *The Narrative of Sir Francis Bond Head,* McClelland & Stewart, 1968; (with Douglas M. Fisher) *Canada's Sporting Heroes: Their Lives and Times,* General Publishing, 1974.

WORK IN PROGRESS: The first volume of *History of the Royal Canadian Air Force;* co-authoring with R. A. Preston, *The War of 1812.*

*   *   *

WITHROW, Dorothy E.   1910-

PERSONAL: Born June 9, 1910, in Philadelphia, Pa.; daughter of John A. and Edna (Matthews) Withrow. *Education:* University of Pennsylvania, B.S., 1932, M.A., 1942; Columbia University, Ed.D., 1955. *Politics:* Republican ("usually"). *Religion:* Methodist. *Home:* 502 County Line Rd., Huntingdon Valley, Pa. 19006.

CAREER: High school teacher of English in Philadelphia, Pa., 1935-48, and of remedial reading, 1948-57; School District of Philadelphia Reading Clinic, supervisor and psychologist, 1957-69. Supervisor and instructor in High School and College Reading Center, Columbia University, Teachers College, summers, 1951-58. Huntingdon Valley Public Library, member of board of trustees, 1965—, vice-president, 1966-67, president, 1975-76. *Member:* National Retired Teachers Association, American Library Association, American Library Trustees Association, Pennsylvania Education Association, Pennsylvania Library Association, Philadelphia Retired Teachers Association. *Awards, honors:* National founders achievement award, The Questers, 1970.

WRITINGS: (With Ruth Strang and Ethlyne Phelps) *Gateways to Readable Books,* 3rd edition (Miss Withrow was not associated with earlier editions), H. S. Wilson, 1958, 5th edition (with Helen Carey and Bertha Hirzel), 1975. Contributor to educational journals.

AVOCATIONAL INTERESTS: Reading, travel, library work, theater, antiques; collecting fine china, silver; church work, listening to symphonic music, singing, and playing the piano.

*   *   *

WOLFE, Peter   1933-

PERSONAL: Born August 25, 1933, in New York, N.Y.; son of Milton B. (an optician) and Mae (Salius) Wolfe; married Marie Paley, December 22, 1962; children: Philip Graham, John Bennett. *Education:* City College (now City College of the City University of New York), B.A., 1955; Leigh University, M.A., 1957; University of Wisconsin, Ph.D., 1965. *Politics:* Democrat. *Home:* 4444 West Pine, Apt. 422, St. Louis, Mo. 63108. *Office:* Department of English, University of Missouri, St. Louis, Mo. 63121.

CAREER: University of Nebraska, Lincoln, assistant professor of English, 1964-67; University of Missouri, St. Louis, assistant professor, 1967-68, associate professor, 1968-76, professor of English, 1976—. Visiting professor, University of Windsor, summer, 1971, and University of California, Los Angeles, summer, 1975. *Military service:*

U.S. Army, Ordnance Corps, 1957-59. *Member:* Modern Language Association of America (president, Modern Literature Section, 1972, 1976), American Association of University Professors, Kipling Society, James Joyce Society, Arnold Bennett Society. *Awards, honors:* National Endowment for the Humanities, summer fellow, 1974.

WRITINGS: The Disciplined Heart: Iris Murdoch and her Novels, University of Missouri Press, 1966; *Mary Renault,* Twayne, 1969; *Rebecca West: Artist and Thinker,* Southern Illinois University Press, 1971; *Graham Greene: The Entertainer,* Southern Illinois University Press, 1972; *John Fowles: Magus and Moralist,* Bucknell University Press, 1976. Editor, *Virginia Woolf Quarterly.*

WORK IN PROGRESS: Dreamers Who Live Their Dreams: The World of Ross Macdonald, for Bowling Green University Press, and *Jean Rhys,* for Twayne.

AVOCATIONAL INTERESTS: Music, particularly modern jazz; sports, especially hockey and basketball.

*   *   *

WOLFENSTEIN, E. Victor   1940-

PERSONAL: Born July, 1940. *Education:* Columbia University, A.B. (magna cum laude), 1962; Princeton University, M.A., 1964, Ph.D., 1965. *Office:* University of California, Los Angeles, Calif. 90024.

CAREER: University of California, Los Angeles, associate professor of political science.

WRITINGS: The Revolutionary Personality: Lenin, Trotsky, Gandhi, Princeton University Press, 1967; *Personality and Politics,* Dickenson, 1969. Also author of *The Victims of Democracy: Malcolm X and the Black Revolution.*

WORK IN PROGRESS: This Machine Kills Fascists: Woody Guthrie in America, 1912-1952, in collaboration with Judith F. Wolfenstein.

*   *   *

WOLF-PHILLIPS, Leslie   1929-

PERSONAL: Born February 19, 1929, in Worcester, England; son of Walter George (a house painter) and Anne (Wilesmith) Phillips; married Lisa Wolf (a teacher), July 23, 1960; children: Jonathan, Rebekah. *Education:* University of Bristol, Certificate in Education, 1953; University of London, Certificate in Religious Education, 1954; London School of Economics and Political Science, B.Sc. (first class honors), 1958. *Politics:* Labour Party. *Office:* London School of Economics and Political Science, Aldwych, London W.C. 2, England.

CAREER: Worcestershire Education Committee, Worcestershire, England, teacher, 1950-51; London County Council, London, England, teacher, 1954-60; University of London, London School of Economics and Political Science, London, lecturer in political science, 1960—. Examiner in political science to University of London and Local Government Examination Board. Director, International Summer Schools for American Institute for Foreign Study, 1972—. Consultant to National Association of Local Government Officers. *Military service:* Royal Army Educational Corps, instructor and registrar, Command Education Centre, Gibraltar, 1947-49. *Member:* Royal Institute of Public Administration, Hansard Society for Parliamentary Government, Political Studies Association of the United Kingdom, Association of University Teachers. *Awards, honors:* LL.M., University College, University of London, 1970.

WRITINGS: (Editor) *Constitutions of Modern States,* Praeger, 1968; *Comparative Constitutions,* Macmillan, 1972. Contributor to *Political Studies, Parliamentary Affairs, Government and Opposition,* and *Political Quarterly.*

WORK IN PROGRESS: Editing *Dictionary of Comparative Government,* for publication by Scribner in America and Weidenfeld & Nicolson in England.

SIDELIGHTS: Leslie Wolf-Phillips represented Friends World Committee for Consultation at United Nations Organization Seminar on Human Rights in Budapest, 1966. He also has visited Russia, East Germany, and Yugoslavia under Quaker auspices, and the United States.

* * *

WOLPERT, Stanley A(lbert) 1927-

PERSONAL: Born December 23, 1927, in Brooklyn, N.Y.; son of Nathan and Frances (Gittelson) Wolpert; married, 1953; wife's name, Dorothy; children: Daniel, Adam. *Education:* City College (now City College of the City University of New York), B.A., 1953; University of Pennsylvania, A.M., 1955, Ph.D., 1959. *Home:* 811 Thayer Ave., Los Angeles, Calif. 90024. *Office:* History Department, University of California, Los Angeles, Calif. 90024.

CAREER: University of California, Los Angeles, instructor, 1959-60, assistant professor, 1960-63, associate professor, 1963-66, professor of history, 1967—, chairman of department, 1968—. Visiting professor at University of Hawaii, 1960, and University of Pennsylvania, 1961. *Military service:* U.S. Navy, 1945-49; became lieutenant. *Member:* American Historical Association, Association for Asian Studies, Conference on British Studies, American Oriental Society. *Awards, honors:* American Council of Learned Societies-Social Science Research Council fellow, 1961; Watumull Prize ($500) of American Historical Association for best work on the history of India published in the United States, 1963, for *Tilak and Gokhale;* Distinguished Teaching Award, University of California, Los Angeles, 1975.

WRITINGS: Aboard the Flying Swan, Scribner, 1954; *Tilak and Gokhale,* University of California Press, 1962; *Nine Hours to Rama,* Random House, 1962; *India,* Prentice-Hall, 1965; *Morley and India, 1906-1910,* University of California Press, 1967; *The Expedition,* Little, Brown, 1968; *An Error of Judgment,* Little, Brown, 1970; *A History of India,* Oxford University Press, 1976.

SIDELIGHTS: Michael Malloy reports that in preparation for *An Error of Judgment,* Stanley Wolpert "combed 2,317 pages of transcripts and evidence for his facts." Malloy describes Wolpert as "a first-rate storyteller, and from his rich imagination he provides the thoughts and beliefs that must have prompted the testimony of his characters, bringing them out of their dusty pages and into living reality."

BIOGRAPHICAL/CRITICAL SOURCES: New York Times Book Review, February 18, 1968; *National Observer,* May 4, 1970.

* * *

WOLSK, David 1930-

PERSONAL: Born May 29, 1930, in New York, N.Y.; son of Isidore (a lawyer) and Pauline (Pressman) Wolsk; married Ingrid Andersen (a weaver), 1953; children: Nina, Julie. *Education:* Allegheny College, B.A., 1951; Columbia University, graduate student, 1951-54; University of Michi-

gan, Ph.D., 1961. *Politics:* Democrat. *Religion:* Jewish. *Home:* 1097 Matheson Lake Rd., R.R. 6, Victoria, British Columbia, Canada. *Office:* University of Victoria, Victoria, British Columbia, Canada.

CAREER: University of Michigan, Ann Arbor, assistant professor of psychology, 1963-67, research associate at Kresge Hearing Institute, 1963-67; Neurophysiology Institute, Copenhagen, Denmark, staff member, 1967-70; Danish Institute for Educational Research, Copenhagen, member of staff, 1970-74; University of Victoria, Victoria, British Columbia, associate professor of education, 1974—. *Military service:* U.S. Army, 1954-56. *Member:* American Psychological Association.

WRITINGS: (With M. Alpern and M. Lawrence) *Sensory Processes,* Brooks/Cole, 1967; *An Experience-Centered Curriculum,* UNESCO, 1975. Contributor to professional journals.

WORK IN PROGRESS: Curriculum development; educational research.

* * *

WOLTERS, O(liver) W(illiam) 1915-

PERSONAL: Born June 8, 1915, in Reading, England; son of Albert William (a professor) and Gertrude (Lewis) Wolters; married Euteen Khoo, 1955; children: Pamela Gwyneth, Nigel Christopher William. *Education:* Lincoln College, Oxford, B.A. (first class honors in history), 1937; School of Oriental and African Studies, University of London, Ph.D., 1962. *Home:* 112 Comstock Rd., Ithaca, N.Y. *Office:* Cornell University, Ithaca, N.Y. 14850.

CAREER: Malayan Civil Service, 1938-57; University of London, School of Oriental and African Studies, London, England, lecturer, 1957-63; Cornell University, Ithaca, N.Y., professor, 1963—, Goldwin Smith Professor of Southeast Asian History, 1975—, chairman of dpeartment of Asian studies, 1970-72.

WRITINGS: Early Indonesian Commerce, Cornell University Press, 1967; *The Fall of Srivijaya in Malay History,* Cornell University Press, 1970. Contributor to specialist journals on Asian topics.

WORK IN PROGRESS: Medieval Vietnamese History.

* * *

WONNACOTT, Paul 1933-

PERSONAL: Born March 16, 1933, in London, Ontario, Canada; son of Gordon (a teacher) and Muriel (Johnston) Wonnacott; married Donna Cochrane, July 2, 1960; children: David, Ann, Alan, Bruce. *Education:* University of Western Ontario, B.A., 1955; Princeton University, M.A., 1957, Ph.D., 1959. *Office:* University of Maryland, College Park, Md. 20742.

CAREER: Columbia University, New York, N.Y., instructor, 1958-59, assistant professor of economics, 1959-62; Royal Commission on Banking and Finance, Toronto, Ontario, research staff member, 1962; University of Maryland, College Park, associate professor, 1962-67, professor of economics, 1967—. Senior staff member, Council of Economic Advisors, 1968-70; member of board of governors, Federal Reserve Board, 1974-75. *Member:* American Economic Association, Canadian Economics Association.

WRITINGS: The Canadian Dollar, University of Toronto Press, 1960, 2nd edition, 1965; *The Height, Structure, and Significance of Interest Rates,* Queen's Printer (Ottawa),

1962; (with R. J. Wonnacott) *Free Trade between the United States and Canada: The Potential Economic Effects,* Harvard University Press, 1967; *Macroeconomics,* Irwin, 1974. Contributor to journals.

WORK IN PROGRESS: Sectorial Free Trade.

* * *

WOOD, Clement Biddle 1925-

PERSONAL: Born September 3, 1925; son of Clement Biddle and Emily (Philler) Wood; married first wife, 1949; married Jessie Leigh Hunt, July 25, 1964; children (first marriage) Marion, Clement, Willard, Alexander; step-children: Cabell Bruce, Leigh Bruce, Thomas Bruce, James Bruce. *Education:* Harvard University, B.A., 1949; University of Pennsylvania, graduate student, 1950-51. *Home:* 16 Bis rue de l'Abbe de l'Epee, Paris 5e, France. *Agent:* Alain Bernheim, 16 Avenue Hoche, Paris 17e, France.

CAREER: U.S. Information Service, Washington, D.C., propagandist, 1951-53; farmer in Conshohocken, Pa., 1953-59; screenwriter in Paris, France, 1959-65. *Military service:* U.S. Army, Infantry, 1943-46; became second lieutenant. *Member:* Travellers Club (Paris), Knickerbocker Club (New York).

WRITINGS: Welcome to the Club (novel), McGraw, 1966. Story anthologized in *40 Best Stories from Mademoiselle,* Harper, 1960. Films include "The Day and the Hour," "Barbarella" (co-author), "Tales from Poe," and "Welcome to the Club."

WORK IN PROGRESS: A novel, as yet untitled, on the Vietnam War.

SIDELIGHTS: Wood told *CA:* "Travel constantly. Speak French, German, Italian. Like: Children, dogs. Dislike: Reading newspapers, but am nevertheless under a compulsion to write about such charming current problems as Race, War, Bomb."

AVOCATIONAL INTERESTS: Skiing and sailing.††

* * *

WOOD, Mary 1915-

PERSONAL: Born January 19, 1915, in New Orleans, La.; daughter of Edmund Lee (a journalist) and Ida May (Thompson) Hawes; married Charles P. Wood, Jr., January 30, 1934 (divorced); children: Sally (Mrs. Alexander Thomson III). *Education:* Attended Millersburg Female College. *Politics:* Liberal Democrat. *Religion:* Episcopalian. *Home:* 416 Riverside Dr., Covington, Ky.

CAREER: Radio station WLW, Cincinnati, Ohio, scriptwriter, 1939-43; *Cincinnati Post and Times-Star,* Cincinnati, Ohio, columnist, 1943—.

WRITINGS: Just Lucky, I Guess, Doubleday, 1967.

WORK IN PROGRESS: "A book about my nutty mother and her cook, who tried unsuccessfully to make a million dollars overnight in the depth of the Great Depression."

SIDELIGHTS: Mrs. Wood says that she likes "to loaf on Caribbean beaches, go to parties and stay up most of the night telling lies and drinking, and dearly love money which, unfortunately, I have never had enough of. Also love my daughter, my three grandchildren and dogs, in that order. Am also dedicated to keeping myself happy which consumes much of my time."

WOOD, Nancy 1936-

PERSONAL: Born June 20, 1936, in Trenton, N.J.; daughter of Harold William (a businessman) and Eleanor (Green) Clopp; married former husband, Oscar Dull III, 1953, married Myron Gilmore Wood (a photographer), March 1, 1961 (divorced 1969); married Richard Thompson (a surgeon), August 23, 1972; children: Karin Alison, Christopher Keith, Eleanor Kathryn, India Hart. *Education:* Studied at Bucknell University, 1955-56, and University of Colorado Extension, 1958-59. *Politics:* Democrat. *Home:* 825 Paseo, Colorado Springs, Colo. 80907. *Agent:* Marie Rodell-Frances Collin, 141 East 55 St., New York, N.Y. 10022.

CAREER: Writer.

WRITINGS: Clearcut: The Deforestation of America, Sierra Club Books, 1971; *The Last Five Dollar Baby,* Harper, 1972; *In This Proud Land,* New York Graphic Society, 1973; *Many Winters,* drawings by Frank Howell, Doubleday, 1974; *The Kind of Liberty Bend,* Harper, 1976; *The Paper Bag Cowboy,* Harper, 1976; *The Man Who Gave Thunder to the Earth,* Doubleday, 1976.

Author of text; photographs by Myron Wood: *Central City: A Ballad of the West,* Chaparral Press, 1963; *West to Durango,* Chaparral Press, 1964; *Little Wrangler,* Doubleday, 1969; *Colorado: Big Mountain Country,* Doubleday, 1969, revised edition, 1972; *Hollering Sun,* Simon & Schuster, 1972.

WORK IN PROGRESS: Research on the history of the Ute Indians; a feminist novel.

* * *

WOOD, Robert L. 1925-

PERSONAL: Born January 4, 1925, in Springfield, Mo.; son of Russell L. (a shoemaker) and Beulah C. (Willsie) Wood. *Education:* University of Washington, Seattle, B.A. (cum laude), 1950. *Home:* 1614 21st Ave. E., Seattle, Wash. 98102.

CAREER: King County Superior Court, Seattle, Wash., official court reporter, 1951—. *Military service:* U.S. Army, 1943-46. *Awards, honors: Across the Olympic Mountains* was named Northwest Book of the Year by Burien Library Guild, 1967.

WRITINGS: Across the Olympic Mountains: The Press Expedition, 1889-90, Mountaineers, 1967; *Trail Country: Olympic National Park,* Mountaineers, 1968; *Wilderness Trails of Olympic National Park,* Mountaineers, 1970. Editor, *Mountaineer Bulletin,* 1964-65.

WORK IN PROGRESS: A companion volume to *Across the Olympic Mountains,* about military expeditions in the mountains in 1885 and 1890.

* * *

WOODHOUSE, Martin 1932-
(John Charlton)

PERSONAL: Born August 29, 1932, in Romford, Essex, England; son of Robert Arnold (a physician) and Josephine (Fielding) Woodhouse. *Education:* Cambridge University, B.A., 1954, M.A., 1958; St. Mary's Hospital Medical School, London, M.B. and B.Ch., 1957.

CAREER: Earned spending money writing science fiction for American pulp magazines while still at Cambridge University; after completing military service and a year as research scholar with the Medical Research Council Applied

Psychology Unit at Cambridge, England, he returned to writing with a children's television series, a slapstick film series, and as lead writer for four years of "The Avengers," a television series popular in both the United States and Great Britain; tiring of television, he began writing espionage thrillers, published *Tree Frog* in 1966, and early in 1967 went to Hollywood to do the script for the movie version of his book; plans to settle next in Grenada, West Indies. *Military service:* Royal Air Force, pilot officer, 1959-61. *Member:* Institute of Electrical Engineers (medical division).

WRITINGS: Tree Frog, Coward, 1966; *Bush Baby,* Coward, 1968; *Rock Baby,* Heinemann, 1968; *Phil and Me,* Coward, 1970; *Mama Doll,* Coward, 1972; *Blue Bone,* Coward, 1973; (with Robert Ross) *The Medici Guns,* Dutton, 1974. Also author of some science fiction under pseudonym John Charlton.

SIDELIGHTS: Woodhouse went through medical school to please his father, never has practiced, but did do research in neurology and the relationship between computers and human operators.

AVOCATIONAL INTERESTS: Skiing, rock climbing, exploring caves (owns one in Barbados; intends to open a nightclub in it).

BIOGRAPHICAL/CRITICAL SOURCES: New York Times Book Review, January 15, 1967; *Publishers' Weekly,* January 30, 1967.†

* * *

WOODMAN, Harold D. 1928-

PERSONAL: Born April 21, 1928, in Chicago, Ill.; son of Joseph B. and Helen (Sollo) Woodman; married Leonora Becker)a professor), October 3, 1954; children: Allan James, David Edward. *Education:* Roosevelt University, B.A., 1957; University of Chicago, M.A., 1959, Ph.D., 1964. *Home:* 1100 N. Grant St., West Lafayette, Ind. 47906. *Office:* Department of History, Purdue University, Lafayette, Ind. 47907.

CAREER: Roosevelt University, Chicago, Ill., lecturer in American history, 1962-63; University of Missouri, Columbia, assistant professor, 1963-66, associate professor of American history, 1966-69, professor of history, 1969-71; Purdue University, Lafayette, Ind., professor of history, 1971—. *Member:* American Historical Association, Organization of American Historians, Economic History Association, Agricultural History Society, American Association of University Professors, Southern Historical Association. *Awards, honors:* Everett Eugene Edwards Memorial Award of Agricultural History Society, 1962, for "Chicago Businessmen and the 'Granger Laws,'"; Ramsdell Award of Southern Historical Association, 1964, for "The Profitability of Slavery: A Historical Perennial"; Social Science Research Council faculty grant, 1969-70.

WRITINGS: (Editor with Allen F. Davis) *Conflict or Consensus in American History,* Heath, 1966, expanded two-volume edition, 1968, 4th edition, 1976; *Slavery and the Southern Economy,* Harcourt, 1966; *King Cotton and His Retainers,* University of Kentucky Press, 1968; *The Legacy of the American Civil War,* Wiley, 1973. Contributor to professional journals.

WORK IN PROGRESS: A study of interregional trade in the United States during the nineteenth century.

WOODS, Margaret 1921-

PERSONAL: Born October 20, 1921, in Sutton Coldfield, Warwickshire, England; daughter of Harry Gilbert (a company director) and Florence (Hadaway) Robbins; married Phillip Tom Woods (formerly a public servant), June 21, 1941; children: Dickon. *Education:* Attended La Combe, Rolle, Switzerland, 1937-38, and a secretarial college in Birmingham, England, 1938-39. *Politics:* "Left of center." *Religion:* Agnostic. *Home:* Eastwood Oak, Tarrington, Herefordshire, England.

CAREER: Cooper, Dennison & Walkden Ltd. (wholesale stationers), Birmingham, England, shorthand typist, 1939-40. *Military service:* Women's Auxiliary Air Force, 1940-42.

WRITINGS: Dog in a Fair (juvenile), Oliver & Boyd, 1967.

AVOCATIONAL INTERESTS: The countryside and all country matters, cooking, gardening.

* * *

WOODS, Sister Frances Jerome 1913-

PERSONAL: Born January 4, 1913, in Guthrie, Okla.; daughter of Francis Michael (a tailor) and Catherine Ryan (Kennedy) Woods. *Education:* Our Lady of the Lake College, B.A., 1940; Catholic University of America, M.A., 1945, Ph.D., 1949. *Home and office:* Our Lady of the Lake College, 411 Southwest 24th, San Antonio, Tex. 78207.

CAREER: Roman Catholic nun, member of Congregation of Divine Providence. Teacher of history at Catholic high school in Tulsa, Okla., 1942-44; Our Lady of the Lake College, San Antonio, Tex., 1948-67, began as instructor, professor of sociology, 1963-67, vice-president, 1964-67; member, Council of Congregation of Divine Providence, 1967-70; Our Lady of the Lake College, professor of sociology, 1970—. Summer visiting lecturer at Catholic University of America, 1957, University of Western Ontario, 1958, and Fordham University, 1960. Member of board, Family Life Bureau of National Catholic Welfare Conference, 1960-61; Consultant to Hogg Foundation, 1959-61, National Institutes of Health, 1964-67, and to Community Welfare Council and Public Housing Authority, both San Antonio; member of priorities committee, Economic Opportunity Development Corp., 1966.

MEMBER: American Catholic Sociological Association (president, 1961-62), American Sociological Association, American Anthropological Society, Religious Research Association, National Council on Family Relations, Religious Education Association, Society for the Scientific Study of Religion, Southwestern Sociological Society. *Awards, honors:* National Institute of Mental Health grant for research on persistence and change in a marginal group, 1962-65; Social Science Research Council grant for computer simulation of same project, 1965; Piper Professor Award, Piper Foundation, 1973.

WRITINGS: Mexican Ethnic Leadership in San Antonio, Texas, Catholic University Press, 1949; *Cultural Values of American Ethnic Groups,* Harper, 1956; *The American Family System,* Harper, 1959; (with Alice Calverley) *A Community Experiment in Establishing a Senior Center,* Hogg Foundation, University of Texas, 1964; *Introductory Sociology,* Harper, 1966; *Marginality and Identity: A Colored Creole Family through Ten Generations,* Louisiana State University Press, 1972. Contributor to *New Catholic*

Encyclopedia, Social Casework, Exceptional Children, and other sociology journals. Former associate editor, *American Catholic Sociological Review.*

*　*　*

WOODWARD, John (William) 1920-

PERSONAL: Born September 19, 1920, in Derby, England. *Education:* Educated privately. *Home:* Abbots Lodge, 2 Madeley St., Derby, Derbyshire, England; Elm Field, 41 Empress Rd., Derby, Derbyshire, England; and Cedar Cottage, The Village Green, Abbots Bromley, near Rugeley, Staffordshire, England.

CAREER: Rolls-Royce Ltd., Derby, England, librarian, 1946-58, various posts in administration, personnel, employment, and as a welfare officer, 1958-62; Four Names Publishing Co., Derby, chairman, 1952—; poet and playwright. *Member:* Derby and Derbyshire Dumas Association (life president, 1946—), International Writers' Guild (life president, 1952—), Derby International Writers' Guild (life president, 1961—).

WRITINGS: Beyond the Dawn (poems), Peter Ratazzi, 1949; *Prelude. Pebbles in the Pool. Fugue.* (poems), Four Names, 1952; (with David Charles Young) *Jeptha Young, His Life and Works,* Four Names, 1959; (editor) *MSS Anthology,* Derby Writers' Guild, 1958; (editor) *Four Names Anthology,* Four Names, 1956; (editor) *Purrings of Pussycat* (poems), Four Names, 1957-58.

Plays; all published by Four Names, 1952-66, and produced at Derby, Ripley Wirksworth, Naworth Castle, Carlisle, England: "Divorce by Death"; "Cry with the Thunder"; "The Reluctant Dustman"; "A Gift from the Gods"; "Come Back, Peter"; "His Grace, the Dustman"; "A Woman's Place"; "Beyond the Bridge"; "Dilute with Water"; "Tudor England" (pageant).

WORK IN PROGRESS: A poetry collection, *Though Roses Die;* two new plays, "Spare That Tree" and "Winter Sunshine"; a novel, *The Unexpected;* research on Henry VIII and Tudor England.††

*　*　*

WOODWARD, Ralph Lee, Jr. 1934-

PERSONAL: Born December 2, 1934, in New London, Conn.; son of Ralph Lee (a college president) and Beaulah Mae (Suter) Woodward; married Anne Hamilton, July 22, 1956; married second wife, Sue Dawn McGrady, December 30, 1958; children: (second marriage) Mark Lee, Laura Lynn, Matthew McGrady. *Education:* Central College, A.B., 1955; Tulane University of Louisiana, M.A., 1959, Ph.D., 1962; also studied in Mexico, summer, 1954. *Politics:* Democrat. *Religion:* Episcopalian. *Home:* 5750 Norland Ave., New Orleans, La. 70114. *Office:* Department of History, Tulane University, New Orleans, La. 70118.

CAREER: University of Wichita, Wichita, Kan., assistant professor of history, 1961-62; University of Southwestern Louisiana, Lafayette, assistant professor of history, 1962-63; University of North Carolina, Chapel Hill, assistant professor, 1963-67, associate professor of history, 1967-70; Tulane University of Louisiana, New Orleans, professor of history, 1970—, head of department, 1973-75. Fulbright-Hays lecturer at University of Chile and Catholic University of Valparaiso, 1965-66, and National University of Buenos Aires and University of Salvador, 1968. *Military service:* U.S. Marine Corps, 1955-57; became captain.

MEMBER: American Historical Association, Conference on Latin American History, American Association of University Professors, Latin American Studies Association, South Eastern Conference on Latin American Studies (president, 1975-76). *Awards, honors:* Henry L. and Grace Doherty Foundation fellow in Central America, 1960-61; honorable mention, James A. Robertson Memorial Prize of Conference on Latin American History, 1967, for article, "Economic and Social Origins of the Guatemalan Political Parties," 1967; honorable mention, Herbert E. Bolton Memorial Prize of Conference on Latin American History, 1968, for book, *Class Privilege and Economic Development.*

WRITINGS: Class Privilege and Economic Development: The Consulado de Comercio of Guatemala, 1793-1871, University of North Carolina Press, 1966; *Robinson Crusoe's Island: A History of the Juan Fernandez Islands,* University of North Carolina Press, 1969; (editor) *Positivism in Latin America, 1850-1900,* Heath, 1971; (contributor) *Applied Enlightenment: Nineteenth-Century Liberalism,* Middle American Research Institute, Tulane University of Louisiana, 1972; *Central America: A Nation Divided,* Oxford University Press, 1976. Also author of a correspondence course in Latin American history, for University of North Carolina. Contributor to *Inter-American Law Review, Caribbean Studies, Hispanic American Historical Review,* and other journals in his field; abstractor for *Historical Abstracts* and *America: History and Life.* Associate editor, *Revista del Pensamiento Centroamericano,* 1974—.

WORK IN PROGRESS: A History of the Spanish American Merchant Guilds, 1592-1885.

SIDELIGHTS: Ralph Woodward, Jr. speaks Spanish and French. He reads Spanish, French, Portuguese, and Italian.

*　*　*

WOODYARD, David O. 1932-

PERSONAL: Born April 27, 1932, in Oak Park, Ill.; son of Wilfred Cole (a businessman) and Sara (Taylor) Woodyard; married Joanne Adamson, June 18, 1955; children: Sara Jane, Kimberly Ann. *Education:* Denison University, B.A., 1954; Union Theological Seminary, New York, B.D., 1958; Oberlin Graduate School of Theology, S.T.M. (summa cum laude), 1965; Vanderbilt University, D.Min., 1974. *Home:* Mount Parnassus, Granville, Ohio 43023. *Office:* Denison University, Granville, Ohio 43023.

CAREER: Baptist clergyman. Denison University, Granville, Ohio, dean of chapel and assistant professor of religion, 1960—.

WRITINGS—All published by Westminster: *Living Without God—Before God,* 1968; *To Be Human Now,* 1969; *The Opaqueness of God,* 1970; *Beyond Cynicism: The Practice of Hope,* 1972; *Strangers and Exiles: Living by Promises,* 1974. Work has been anthologized in *Best Sermons,* edited by Paul Butler, 1959, 1962, 1967. Contributor to religious periodicals.

*　*　*

WORCESTER, Dean A(mory), Jr. 1918-

PERSONAL: Born May 1, 1918, in Boulder, Colo.; son of Dean Amory (a professor of psychology) and Elsie (Rohwer) Worcester; married Joy Pestal (a teacher), March 27, 1941; children: Jane Worcester Anchan, Jonathan, Mary Worcester Anderson, David, Mark. *Education:* University of Nebraska, B.A., 1939, M.A., 1940; University of Minnesota, Ph.D., 1943. *Politics:* Independent. *Religion:* Liberal Protestant. *Home:* 6550 18th N.E., Seattle, Wash. 98115. *Office:* Department of Economics, University of Washington, Seattle, Wash. 98195.

CAREER: Louisiana State University, Baton Rouge, assistant professor of economics, 1943-45; University of Georgia, Athens, associate professor of marketing, 1945-46; University of Washington, Seattle, assistant professor, 1946-51, associate professor, 1951-66, professor of economics, 1966—, acting chairman of department, 1966. Visiting professor, University of the Philippines, 1967-69. *Member:* American Economic Association, Western Economic Association (vice-president, 1966; president, 1967), Rotary International.

WRITINGS: Fundamentals of Economics, Ronald, 1952; *Monopoly, Big Business and Welfare,* University of Washington Press, 1967; *Beyond Welfare and Full Employment,* Lexington, 1972. Contributor to a number of professional journals.

WORK IN PROGRESS: Functions of the state, especially as related to the interrelations of unemployment, inflation, and tax-supported welfare and other transfer programs in a society primarily oriented to expanding the range of private decision making; altruism as motivation.

* * *

WORLAND, Stephen T. 1923-

PERSONAL: Born February 21, 1923, in Neoga, Ill.; son of James V. and Mary B. (Montgomery) Worland; married Roberta Weeks McCarthy, August 19, 1948; children: Susan, Nancy, Robert, Priscilla, Sally, Stephen, Joy. *Education:* University of Illinois, B.A., 1947, M.A., 1949, Ph.D., 1956. *Office:* University of Notre Dame, Notre Dame, Ind. 46556.

CAREER: Michigan State University, East Lansing, instructor in economics, 1954-58; University of Notre Dame, Notre Dame, Ind., assistant professor, 1958-61, associate professor of economics, 1961—. *Military service:* U.S. Navy, Supply Corps, 1943-46; became ensign. *Member:* American Economic Association, Catholic Economic Association.

WRITINGS: Scholasticism and Welfare Economics, University of Notre Dame Press, 1967.††

* * *

WORTMAN, Max S(idones), Jr. 1932-

PERSONAL: Born December 15, 1932, in Iowa City, Iowa; son of Max Sidones (a purchasing agent) and Pearl (Hansban) Wortman; married Cora Ann Reed, October 3, 1959; children: Kirk Bradley, Sara Elizabeth. *Education:* Iowa State University of Science and Technology, B.S. in C.E., 1956; University of Minnesota, Ph.D., 1962. *Politics:* Republican. *Religion:* Presbyterian. *Home:* 148 Red Gate Lane, Amherst, Mass. 01002. *Office:* University of Massachusetts, Amherst, Mass. 01003.

CAREER: Iowa State University of Science and Technology, Ames, instructor in engineering graphics, 1956-57; University of Minnesota, Minneapolis, instructor in mechanical engineering, 1957-61; University of Iowa, Iowa City, assistant professor, 1961-64, associate professor of industrial relations, 1964-68; University of Massachusetts, Amherst, professor of industrial relations, 1968—. Industrial relations and management consultant. Member of

research advisory group, U.S. Equal Employment Opportunity Commission, 1966; member, Iowa City Civil Service Commission, 1966-68; vice-chairman, Massachusetts State Manpower Planning Council, 1972—. Member of national executive committee, United Campus Christian Fellowship, 1962-64; member of executive committee, Presbyterian Synod of Iowa, 1964-67. Delegate to Iowa State Republican convention, 1962, 1964, 1966, 1968.

MEMBER: Academy of Management (member of board of governors, 1967-68, 1972-73; president of Midwest division, 1967-68), American Economic Association, Industrial Relations Research Association (president of Iowa chapter, 1966-67), International Industrial Relations Association, Public Personnel Association, American Association of University Professors, Institute of Management Sciences, Midwest Business Administration Association (vice-president, beginning 1967), Midwest Case Research Association (committee chairman, beginning 1966), Midwest Economics Association, Alpha Kappa Psi, Beta Gamma Sigma, Iota Rho Chi, Psi Chi, Omicron Delta Epsilon, Sigma Iota Epsilon. *Awards, honors:* Ford Foundation faculty research fellow, 1963-64; research grants from University of Iowa and industry.

WRITINGS: (With C. W. Randle) *Collective Bargaining,* 2nd edition (not associated with 1st edition), Houghton, 1966; *Creative Personnel Management,* Allyn & Bacon, 1967; (compiler) *Critical Issues in Labor,* Macmillan, 1969; (editor with Fred Luthans) *Emerging Concepts in Management,* Macmillan, 1969, 2nd edition, 1975; (with G. C. Witteried) *Labor Relations and Collective Bargaining,* Allyn & Bacon, 1969; (with Richard M. Hodgetts) *Administrative Policy: Text and Cases in the Policy Sciences,* Wiley, 1975. Contributor of more than thirty articles to professional journals. Member of editorial board, *Journal of the Academy of Management.†*

* * *

WORTMAN, Richard 1938-

PERSONAL: Born March 24, 1938, in New York, N.Y.; son of Joseph (an attorney) and Ruth (Nacht) Wortman; married Marlene Stein (a historian), June 14, 1960; children: Leonie. *Education:* Cornell University, B.A., 1958; University of Chicago, M.A., 1960, Ph.D., 1964. *Home:* 1331 East 50th St., Chicago, Ill. 60615. *Office:* Department of History, University of Chicago, Chicago, Ill. 60637.

CAREER: University of Chicago, Chicago, Ill., instructor, 1963-64, assistant professor, 1964-69, associate professor of history, 1969—. Research in Soviet Union, 1967-68, 1971; research associate, Institute for Psycho-Social Studies, 1974-75. *Member:* American Association for the Advancement of Slavic Studies, American Association of University Professors.

WRITINGS: The Crisis of Russian Populism, Cambridge University Press, 1967. Contributor to *Slavic Review, Midway,* and *Canadian-American Slavic Studies.*

WORK IN PROGRESS: The Development of a Russian Legal Consciousness, for University of Chicago Press; research on Russian autocracy.

SIDELIGHTS: In addition to Russian, Richard Wortman is competent in French and German.

* * *

WRAIGHT, A(aron) Joseph 1913-

PERSONAL: Surname rhymes with "fate"; born July 31,

1913, in St. Louis County, Mo.; son of Edward Earl (a tool and die maker) and Sarah Ann (Dowell) Wraight; married Esther Lee Ollis (a receptionist), April 6, 1949. *Education:* Washington University, St. Louis, Mo., A.B., 1939, M.S., 1941; Clark University, Worcester, Mass., Ph.D., 1951. *Religion:* Christian. *Home:* 5431 Connecticut Ave. N.W., Washington, D.C. 20015. *Agent:* Frederick Reinstein, 1010 Vermont Ave. N.W., Washington, D.C. *Office:* U.S. Coast and Geodetic Survey, Washington Science Center, Rockville, Md. 20852.

CAREER: U.S. Coast and Geodetic Survey, Washington, D.C., field geographer, 1942-49, geographer and assistant to the director, 1952-59, chief geographer, 1961—. Edinboro State College, Edinboro, Pa., professor of geography and geology, 1959-60; Anne Arundel Community College, Severna Park, Md., part-time professor of geography, 1962—; Southeastern University, Washington, D.C., chairman of department of physical science, 1966—. Chairman of board, University Press of Washington, 1961-62; chairman of publications, American Congress on Surveying and Mapping, 1962-66.

MEMBER: Association of American Geographers, National Council for Geographic Education, American Name Society, Royal Geographic Society (fellow), Sigma Xi. *Awards, honors:* Meritorious Service Award, U.S. Department of Commerce, 1957; Exceptional Service Award, U.S. Coast and Geodetic Survey, 1957.

WRITINGS: The Field Study of Places, University Press of Washington, 1954; (with Elliot B. Roberts) *U.S. Coast & Geodetic Survey—150 Years,* U.S. Government Printing Office, 1957; *Our Dynamic World,* Chilton, 1966; (with Lewis Heck) *Delaware Place Names,* U.S. Government Printing Office, 1967. Contributor to *Encyclopaedia Britannica* and *Harper's Encyclopedia of Science.* Assistant editor, *Surveying & Mapping,* 1956-62.

WORK IN PROGRESS: External Boundaries of the United States, for Rand McNally; *Ocean Studies for the Young.*

SIDELIGHTS: Aaron Wraight has traveled in North and South America, Europe, Africa, parts of Asia, and Australia, and he participated in exploratory expeditions to the little known highlands of northern South America. Wraight is competent in Spanish and reads French and German. He drew up and donated a master transportation plan for Washington, D.C., 1955, much of which has been put into use.

*   *   *

WREN, Christopher S. 1936-

PERSONAL: Born February 22, 1936, in Hollywood, Calif.; son of Samuel McIndoe (an actor) and Virginia (Sale) Wren; married Jaqueline Marshall Braxton, November 28, 1964; children: Celia Marshall. *Education:* Dartmouth College, B.A., 1957; attended University of Edinburgh, 1957-58; Columbia University, M.S., 1960-61; attended Stanford University, 1967-68. *Religion:* Episcopalian. *Agent:* Sterling Lord, 660 Madison Ave., New York, N.Y. 10021.

CAREER: Look Magazine, New York, N.Y., sports researcher, 1961-62, assistant editor, 1962-64, senior editor, beginning 1964. Has been a reporter in the Soviet Union, Vietnam, Sweden, England, and France. *Military service:* U.S. Army, 1958-60; captain, Special Forces (airborne). *Member:* American Alpine Club, Phi Beta Kappa. *Awards,*

honors: Professional journalism fellowship, Stanford University, 1967-68; Bell Education Awards; special citation from National Conference of Christians and Jews.

WRITINGS: (With Jack Shepherd) *Quotations from Chairman LBJ,* Simon & Schuster, 1968; (with Shepherd) *The Almanack of Poor Richard Nixon,* World, 1968; (with Shepherd) *The Super Summer of Jamie McBride,* Simon & Schuster, 1971; *Winners Got Scars Too: The Life and Legends of Johnny Cash,* Dial, 1971 (published in England as *Johnny Cash: Winners Got Scars Too,* W. H. Allen, 1973).

SIDELIGHTS: Quotations from Chairman LBJ is a little red book parodying the Red Chinese bible, *Quotations from Chairman Mao Tse Tung,* and achieving a clever satire of Johnson and his administration. When its surprise popularity prompted a startled Berkeley bookseller to ask, "Why are the straight people bothering with it?," Christopher Wren replied: "It talks for the silent center." He and Jack Shepherd (both "disillusioned Johnson supporters," according to John Quirk), carefully noted several thousand Johnson remarks on file cards, selected the best, then grouped them under appropriate titles such as "Humility and Self-Criticism," "Piety and Correct Example," and "The Ultimate Reflection" ("I'm the only President you've got"). Inevitably the actual quotes "conceal more than they reveal," says Quirk, and Malcome Muggeridge observes: "The joke falls flat, not because of any failure on the part of the two journalists, . . . but simply because the quotations themselves are too commonplace to be funny." Nevertheless, this book, which Quirk calls the "penultimate anti-book," sold out immediately in bookstores, to become one of the year's most successful books.

Wren is competent in French, Russian, and Mandarin Chinese. He reportedly gave up attempts to translate LBJ into Chinese, because it "loses in translation."

BIOGRAPHICAL/CRITICAL SOURCES: Village Voice, January 4, 1968; *New York Times Book Review,* March 24, 1968; *Commonweal,* June 14, 1968; *Esquire,* June, 1968.†

*   *   *

WRIGHT, Beatrice A(nn) 1917-

PERSONAL: Born December 16, 1917, in New York, N.Y.; daughter of Jerome and Sonia (Gillen) Posner; married M. Erik Wright (a university professor and psychiatrist), September 7, 1940; children: Colleen (Mrs. Kenneth Rand), Erik, Woody. *Education:* Brooklyn College (now Brooklyn College of the City University of New York), B.A., 1938; University of Iowa, M.A., 1940, Ph.D., 1942. *Office:* University of Kansas, Lawrence, Kan. 66044.

CAREER: Swarthmore College, Swarthmore, Pa., instructor in psychology, 1942-43; counselor, U.S. Employment Service, 1944-46; Stanford University, Stanford, Calif., research associate, 1946-48; San Francisco State College (now University), San Francisco, Calif., assistant professor of psychology, 1948-49; employed in parent education programs, California State Board of Education, Adult Education Division, 1950-51; research and writing, 1951-59; University of Western Australia, Perth, visiting lecturer, 1960-61; University of Kansas, Lawrence, research associate in psychology, 1961-62; Menninger Foundation, Topeka, Kan., rehabilitation research and clinical fellowship, 1962-64; University of Kansas, associate professor, 1964-67, professor of psychology, 1967—. Visiting professor at University of Hawaii, summer, 1965, and California State College, Dominquez Hills, 1968-69; distinguished professor, Department of Exceptional Children, University of Southern California, summer, 1967.

MEMBER: American Psychological Association (fellow; president of division on psychological aspects of disability, 1962-63; member of council, 1966—), American Orthopsychiatric Association, Kansas Psychological Association (fellow), Sigma Xi. *Awards, honors:* Research award of division of rehabilitation counseling, American Personnel and Guidance Association, 1959, for co-authored report, "Adjustment to Misfortune"; Child Study Association of America Book Award, 1960, for *Physical Disability: A Psychological Approach;* research grants from National Society for Crippled Children and Adults, Vocational Rehabilitation Administration, and various foundations.

WRITINGS: (With Roger G. Barker, Lee Meyerson, and Mollie R. Gonick) *Adjustment to Physical Handicap and Illness,* Social Science Research Council, 1946, revised edition, 1953; *Psychology and Rehabilitation,* American Psychological Association, 1959; *Physical Disability: A Psychological Approach,* Harper, 1960. Co-author of book-length monograph, "Adjustment to Misfortune: A Problem of Social Psychological Rehabilitation," published in *Artificial Limbs,* 1956. Author of "Disabling Myths About Disability," first published by National Society for Crippled Children and Adults, 1963, and reprinted in two parts in *Accent on Living,* and as a chapter in a Vocational Rehabilitation Administration publication.

Contributor: M. R. Harrower-Erickson and M. E. Steiner, *Large Scale Rorschach Techniques,* C. C Thomas, 1945; Eric Wittkower and R. A. Cleghorn, editors, *Recent Developments in Psychosomatic Medicine,* Lippincott, 1954; B. J. Biddle and E. J. Thomas, editors, *Role Theory,* Wiley, 1966. Contributor to *Exceptional Children, Journal of Abnormal and Social Psychology,* and other professional journals. Editor, *Bulletin* (publication of division on psychological aspects of disability, American Psychological Association), 1956-58.

WORK IN PROGRESS: Studies on hope and expectation.

SIDELIGHTS: Psychology and Rehabilitation was published in Japanese, and there have been Dutch and Polish translations of *Physical Disability.* In lieu of avocational interests, Dr. Wright listed "some major accomplishments of [her] children": Colleen, a Woodrow Wilson fellow and Phi Beta Kappa at Stanford University, 1967; Erik, a National Merit scholar, first-place winner in mathematics at the National Science Fair, 1964, and recipient of Conant Prize, Harvard University, 1965; Woody, a National Merit scholar, and Harvard national scholar, 1966.††

*　　　*　　　*

WRIGHT, (Charles) Conrad 1917-

PERSONAL: Born February 9, 1917, in Cambridge, Mass.; son of Charles Henry Conrad (a teacher) and Elizabeth L. (Woodman) Wright; married Elizabeth Hilgendorff (a librarian), September 4, 1948; children: Conrad E., Nielson, Elizabeth L. *Education:* Harvard University, A.B., 1937, A.M., 1942, Ph.D., 1946. *Religion:* Unitarian Universalist. *Home:* 9 Lowell St., Cambridge, Mass. 02138. *Office:* Divinity School, Harvard University, Cambridge, Mass. 02138.

CAREER: Massachusetts Institute of Technology, Cambridge, instructor, 1946-50, assistant professor of history, 1950-54; Harvard University, Divinity School, Cambridge, Mass., lecturer, 1954-69, professor of American church history, 1969—, registrar, 1955-67. *Member:* American Historical Association, American Society of Church History, Unitarian Historical Society (president, 1962—), Cam-

bridge Historical Society (vice-president, 1965-67). *Awards, honors:* Carnegie Award of American Historical Association, 1954, for *The Beginnings of Unitarianism in America;* L.H.D., Meadville Theological School, 1968.

WRITINGS: (Co-author) *Harvard Divinity School,* Beacon Press, 1954; *The Beginnings of Unitarianism in America,* Beacon Press, 1955; (editor) *Three Prophets of Religious Liberalism,* Beacon Press, 1961; *The Liberal Christians,* Beacon Press, 1970; (editor) *Religion in American Life,* Houghton, 1972; (co-author and editor) *A Stream of Light,* Unitarian Universalist Association, 1975.

WORK IN PROGRESS: American Unitarian history.

*　　　*　　　*

WRIGHT, George B(urton) 1912-

PERSONAL: Born May 3, 1912, in La Crosse, Wis.; son of K. Charles (a railroad employee) and Frances (Tracey) Wright; married Bernice E. Sebald, September 30, 1939; children: Charles E., Cary L. *Education:* University of Wisconsin, Ph.B., 1937. *Religion:* Congregational.

CAREER: Parker Pen Co., Janesville, Wis., sales and marketing assignments, beginning 1937, national sales manager, beginning 1961. Corporate vice-president in charge of marketing, N.M.S. Industries. *Military service:* U.S. Naval Reserve; served in Pacific area during World War II; became lieutenant.

WRITINGS: The Art and Skill of Ingenious Selling, Parker Publishing, 1967; *New Techniques for Effective Sales Management,* Parker Publishing, 1969.††

*　　　*　　　*

WRIGHT, J(ames) Leitch, Jr. 1929-

PERSONAL: Born August 9, 1929, in Ashland, Va.; son of J. Leitch and Frances (Bagley) Wright; married Elizabeth Hatcher, December 20, 1956; children: Marshall Felton, Nancy Mann, Margaret Leitch, Helen Lee, Lucy Langhorne. *Education:* Virginia Military Institute, B.S., 1950; University of Virginia, M.A., 1956, Ph.D., 1958. *Office:* History Department, Florida State University, Tallahassee, Fla. 32306.

CAREER: Virginia Military Institute, Lexington, assistant professor of history, 1958-61; Randolph-Macon College, Ashland, Va., professor of history, 1961-68; Florida State University, Tallahassee, professor of history, 1968—. *Military service:* U.S. Army, 1950-52; became first lieutenant. *Member:* American Historical Association, Organization of American Historians, American Association of University Professors, Southern Historical Association, Florida Historical Association, Florida Anthropological Society. *Awards, honors:* Certificate of commendation, American Association of State and Local History, 1972, for *Anglo-Spanish Rivalry in North America.*

WRITINGS: William Augustus Bowles, Director General of the Creek Nation, University of Georgia Press, 1967; *Anglo-Spanish Rivalry in North America,* University of Georgia Press, 1971; *Britain and the American Frontier, 1783-1815,* University of Georgia Press, 1975; *British St. Augustine* (monograph), Historic St. Augustine Preservation Board, 1975; *Florida in the American Revolution,* University of Florida Press, 1975. Contributor of articles and reviews to professional journals.

WORK IN PROGRESS: Body and Soul: The Southern Indians, 1670-1815.

WRIGHT, William E(dward) 1926-

PERSONAL: Born November 5, 1926, in Fairfield, Ala.; son of Cecil Augustus and Myrtle (Greer) Wright; married Norma Lacy, September 2, 1950; children: Mariellen Lacy. Education: University of Colorado, B.S., 1951, M.A., 1953, Ph.D., 1957; University of Vienna, graduate study, 1954-55. Politics: Democratic Party. Religion: Protestant. Home: 18200 Honeysuckle Lane, Deephaven, Minn. 55391. Office: Department of History, University of Minnesota, Minneapolis, Minn. 55455.

CAREER: University of Minnesota, Minneapolis, instructor, 1957-59, assistant professor, 1959-61, associate professor, 1961-73, professor of history, 1973—. Military service: U.S. Army, 1945-47; became staff sergeant. Member: American Historical Association, American Association for the Advancement of Slavic Studies, American Association of University Professors, Czechoslovak Society of Arts and Sciences in America. Awards, honors: McKnight Foundation Award in the humanities, 1961, for manuscript of Serf, Seigneur, and Sovereign; Fulbright research fellow in Austria, 1962-63; Phi Alpha Theta award, 1968.

WRITINGS: Serf, Seigneur, and Sovereign, University of Minnesota Press, 1966. Associate editor, Journal of Central European Affairs, 1955-56.

WORK IN PROGRESS: A biography of Joseph II, King of Germany and Emperor of the Holy Roman Empire; agrarian history in Austria and Bohemia in the eighteenth century.

*   *   *

WRIGHTSMAN, Lawrence S(amuel), Jr. 1931-

PERSONAL: Born October 31, 1931, in Houston, Tex.; son of Lawrence Samuel (an engineer) and Vivian (Grove) Wrightsman; married Shirley Fish (a researcher), October 21, 1955; children: Allan Jefferson. Education: Southern Methodist University, B.A., 1953, M.A., 1954; University of Minnesota, Ph.D., 1959. Home: 6421 Currywood Dr., Nashville, Tenn. 37205. Office: George Peabody College for Teachers, Nashville, Tenn. 37203.

CAREER: Instructor in psychology at University of Minnesota, Minneapolis, 1955-58, and at Hamline University, St. Paul, Minn., 1956; George Peabody College for Teachers, Nashville, Tenn., assistant professor, 1958-61, associate professor, 1961-66, professor of psychology, 1966—. Visiting associate professor of psychology, University of Hawaii, 1965-66. Member: American Psychological Association, American Association for the Advancement of Science, Society for the Psychological Study of Social Issues.

WRITINGS—All published by Brooks/Cole: (Editor) Contemporary Issues in Social Psychology, 1968, 2nd edition (with J. C. Brigham), 1973; (with F. H. Sanford) Psychology: A Scientific Study of Man, 3rd edition (Wrightsman was not associated with earlier editions), 1970, 4th edition, 1975; (editor with J. O'Connor and N. J. Baker) Cooperation and Competition: Readings in Mixed Motive Games, 1972; Social Psychology in the Seventies, 1972, 2nd edition, 1976; Assumptions About Human Nature: A Social Psychological Analysis, 1974. Contributor to professional journals.

*   *   *

WYLIE, Laurence William 1909-

PERSONAL: Born November 19, 1909, in Indianapolis, Ind.; son of William H. (a minister) and Maude (Stout) Wylie; married Anne Stiles, July 27, 1940; children: Jonathan, David. Education: Institut d'Etudes Politiques, University of Paris, student, 1929-30; Indiana University, A.B., 1931, A.M., 1933; Brown University, Ph.D., 1940. Religion: Quaker. Home: 997 Memorial Dr., Cambridge, Mass. 02138. Office: William James Hall, Harvard University, Cambridge, Mass. 02138.

CAREER: Simons College, Boston, Mass., instructor, 1936-40, assistant professor 1940-43; Haverford College, Haverford, Pa., assistant professor, 1943-48, associate professor, 1948-57, professor, 1957-58, chairman of department of Romance languages, 1948-58; Harvard University, Cambridge, Mass., C. Douglas Dillon Professor of the Civilization of France, 1959—, fellow of Kirkland House, 1960-62, acting master of Quincy House, 1962-63. College Entrance Examination Board, member of French committee, 1951-56, chairman, 1956-58; chairman of French committee, School and College Study, 1952-54 and Conference on French Community Studies, 1956; chairman, Franco-American Commission on Cultural Exchange, 1965-67. Cultural attache, U.S. Embassy, Paris, France, 1965-67. Member of board of directors, Institute for American Universities.

MEMBER: Modern Language Association of America, American Association of Teachers of French (vice-president, 1962-64), American Academy of Arts and Sciences, American Anthropological Association (liaison fellow), Societe d'Ethnographie Francaise, Society for French Historical Studies, Society for Applied Anthropology, Phi Gamma Delta, Automobile Club de France, Signet Club. Awards, honors: Social Science Research Council fellow, 1950-51; Ford Foundation faculty fellow, 1955-56; Guggenheim fellow, 1957-58; honorary doctorate, Universite de Montpellier, 1966; D.H.L., Indiana University, 1967; National Endowment for the Humanities, senior fellow, 1972-73; Camargo fellow, 1972-73.

WRITINGS: Saint-Marc Girardin Bourgeois, Syracuse University Press, 1947; (contributor) Germaine Bree, editor, Culture, Literature, and Articulation, Northeast Conference on the Teaching of Foreign Languages, 1955; Village in the Vaucluse, Harper, 1957 3rd edition, Harvard University Press, 1974; (with Stanley Hoffmann and others) In Search of France, Harvard University Press, 1962; (co-author) Youth: Change and Challenge, Basic Books, 1963; (with others) Deux Villages, Houghton, 1965; (editor) Chanzeaux: A Village in Anjou, Harvard University Press, 1966; (with Armand Begue) Les Francais, Prentice-Hall, 1967; (with Franklin Chu and Mary Terrall) France: The Events of May-June 1968, Council for European Studies, 1973. Associate editor, French Review and Symposium.†

*   *   *

WYNKOOP, William M. 1916-

PERSONAL: Born January 26, 1916, in Montclair, N.J.; son of Carl Burson (in coal business) and Margaret T. (Magee) Wynkoop. Education: Dartmouth College, A.B., 1938; Columbia University, M.A., 1950, Ph.D., 1962. Politics: Liberal. Home: 146 Waverly Pl., New York, N.Y. Office: New Jersey Hall, Hamilton St., Rutgers University, New Brunswick, N.J.

CAREER: Instructor in English at Wayne State University, Detroit, Mich., 1950-52, and Adelphi University, Garden City, N.Y., 1952-59; Rutgers University, New Brunswick, N.J., 1959—, associate professor of English,

1965—. *Military service:* U.S. Army, Medical Corps, 1942-46; became staff sergeant. *Member:* American Association of University Professors, American Civil Liberties Union, War Resisters League, Milton Society of America, Fellowship of Reconciliation, Holland Society of New York.

WRITINGS: Three Children of the Universe: Emerson's View of Shakespeare, Bacon, and Milton, Humanities, 1967.

WORK IN PROGRESS: Compilation of anthology of autobiographical writings by blind authors.

SIDELIGHTS: William Wynkoop has a "fair" knowledge of German, French, Spanish, and Latin.

* * *

WYNNE-TYSON, Esme 1898-
(Amanda, Peter de Morny, Diotima)

PERSONAL: Born June 29, 1898, in London, England; married L. C. Wynne-Tyson (a wing commander, Royal Air Force), June 22, 1918; children: Timothy Jon Lynden. *Education:* Educated at a boarding school in England, by a governess, and at a convent in Belgium. *Religion:* "Philosophy of compassion." *Home:* 9 Park Lane, Selsey, Sussex, England.

CAREER: Child actress on London stage, making first appearance at Haymarket Theatre in "The Blue Bird," and playing the lead in "Where the Rainbow Ends" at the Savoy Theatre in 1911; wrote curtain-raisers in collaboration with Noel Coward; following her marriage, began to write plays and novels, and eventually began a literary collaboration with John Davys Beresford, who shared her interest in metaphysics and in a mutual gospel she later named "philosophy of compassion." *Member:* Society of Authors, London Vegetarian Society. *Awards, honors:* Millenium Guild of New York, special prize ($500) for humanitarian articles, 1957, and M.R.L. Freshel Award ($1,000), 1962, for *The Philosophy of Compassion.*

WRITINGS—Fiction: *Security,* George H. Doran, 1927; *Momus,* Collins, 1928; *Melody,* Collins, 1929; *Incense and Sweet Cane,* Collins, 1930; *Quicksand,* Collins, 1927; (with John Davys Beresford) *Men in the Same Boat,* Hutchinson, 1943; (with Beresford) *The Riddle of the Tower,* Hutchinson, 1944; (with Beresford) *The Gift,* Hutchinson, 1947.

Nonfiction: *Prelude to Peace: The World-Brotherhood Educational Movement,* Daniel, 1936; *The Unity of Being,* Andrew Dakers, 1949; *This Is Life Eternal: The Case for Immortality,* Rider & Co., 1951, Dutton, 1953; (under pseudonym Peter de Morny) *The Best Years of Their Lives,* Centaur Press, 1955; *Mithras, the Fellow in the Cap,* Rider & Co., 1958, 2nd edition, Centaur Press, 1972; *The Philosophy of Compassion: The Return of the Goddess,* Vincent Stuart, 1962; (editor and author of introduction) Porphyrius, *Abstinence from Animal Food,* translation by Thomas Taylor, Centaur Press, 1965. Author of plays; contributor of verse, articles, reviews, and children's stories (under pseudonym Amanda) and philosophical articles (under pseudonym Diotima) to *Contemporary Review, Guardian, Hindustan Times, Health and Life, Humanist, Voice, With Sword and Shield,* and other publications. Editor, *World Forum,* beginning 1961.

WORK IN PROGRESS: Free-lance writing, mainly humanitarian and philosophical.

BIOGRAPHICAL/CRITICAL SOURCES: Esme Wynne-Tyson, *Voice,* March-April-May issue, 1962.†

YABLONSKY, Lewis 1924-

PERSONAL: Born November 23, 1924, in Irvington, N.J.; son of Harry and Fannie Yablonsky; married; children: Mitchel. *Education:* Rutgers University, B.S., 1948; New York University, M.A., 1952, Ph.D., 1957. *Home:* 221 Euclid St., Santa Monica, Calif. 90402. *Office:* Department of Sociology, California State University, Northridge, Calif. 91326.

CAREER: Essex County Youth House, Newark, N.J., supervisor, 1950-51; City College (now City College of the City University of New York), New York City, lecturer in sociology, 1951-56; lecturer at Columbia University, New York City, 1955-57, Harvard University, Cambridge, Mass., 1958, and Smith College, Northampton, Mass., 1959; University of Massachusetts, Amherst, associate professor of sociology, 1958-61; University of California, Los Angeles, associate professor, 1961-63; California State University, Northridge, professor of sociology, 1963—. Director of the crime prevention program, Morningside Heights, Inc., New York City, 1953-57. Consultant to Rockefeller Brothers Organization on Delinquency, 1957, and to Columbia Broadcasting System, 1958. *Military service:* U.S. Navy, 1943-46. *Member:* American Group Psychotherapy Association (president, 1959), American Sociological Association. *Awards, honors:* Society for the Study of Social Problems award, 1959.

WRITINGS: The Violent Gang, Macmillan, 1962; *The Tunnel Back: Synanon,* Macmillan, 1965; *The Hippie Trip,* Pegasus, 1968; *Robopaths: People As Machines,* Penguin, 1972; *Crime and Delinquency,* Rand McNally, 1974; *George Raft,* McGraw, 1974; *Psychodrama,* Basic Books, 1976. Contributor to *Federal Probation* and to *Social Problems* (journal of the Society for the Study of Social Problems).

BIOGRAPHICAL/CRITICAL SOURCES: New Republic, February 13, 1965.

* * *

YAFA, Stephen H. 1941-

PERSONAL: Born May 21, 1941, in Lowell, Mass.; son of Louis A. (a business manager) and Ethel (Pike) Yafa. *Education:* Dartmouth College, A.B., 1963; Carnegie Institute of Technology (now Carnegie-Mellon University), M.F.A., 1965. *Politics:* Independent.

CAREER: Elementary school teacher in Los Angeles, Calif., 1966-68. *Awards, honors:* Writers Guild of America, West, award for best college screenplay, 1964, for manuscript, "Paxton Quigley's Had the Course."

WRITINGS: Paxton Quigley's Had the Course (novel), Lippincott, 1968. Also author of screenplays including "Three in the Attic" (based on the author's novel *Paxton Quigley's Had the Course*), and "Summertree," produced, 1971, by Kirk Douglas. Contributor to *Playboy.*

WORK IN PROGRESS: Hey is for Horses; a book about a Negro child growing up in contemporary America.†

* * *

YANCEY, William L(ayton) 1938-

PERSONAL: Born August 6, 1938, in Chipley, Fla.; son of Malcolm N. (an engineer) and Annie Mae (Mitchell) Yancey; married Martha J. Wood (a sociologist), March 31, 1961. *Education:* Florida State University, B.S., 1961; Washington University, St. Louis, Mo., M.A., 1963,

Ph.D., 1967. *Politics:* Democrat. *Home:* 7208 Lincoln Dr., Philadelphia, Pa. 19119. *Office:* Department of Sociology, Temple University, Philadelphia, Pa.

CAREER: Washington University, St. Louis, Mo., assistant professor of sociology, 1967-68; Vanderbilt University, Nashville, Tenn., assistant professor of sociology, 1968-72; Temple University, Philadelphia, Pa., associate professor of sociology, 1972—. *Military service:* U.S. Army Reserve, 1956-63. *Member:* American Sociological Association, Society for the Study of Social Problems.

WRITINGS: (With Lee Rainwater) *The Moynihan Report and the Politics of Controversy* (including the text of Daniel P. Moynihan's "The Negro Family: The Case for National Action"), M.I.T. Press, 1967. Also author of *Black Families and the White House,* 1966.

WORK IN PROGRESS: Research on adaptations to poverty and on the social and community problems in public housing.†

* * *

YATES, Alfred 1917-

PERSONAL: Born November 17, 1917, in Farnworth, England; son of William Oliver (a cotton-bleacher) and Fanny Yates; married Joan Mary Fellows, September 8, 1943; children: Rosemary Susan, William Stephen. *Education:* University of Sheffield, B.A., 1938, Diploma in Education, 1939; Queen's University of Belfast, B.Ed., 1950.

CAREER: National Foundation for Educational Research in England and Wales, London, England, senior research officer, 1951-59, consultant, 1966—; Oxford University, Oxford, England, senior tutor and lecturer in educational psychology, department of education, beginning 1959; National Foundation for Educational Research, Buckinghamshire, England, director, 1972—. *Military service:* Royal Engineers, 1940-46; became captain. *Member:* British Psychological Society (fellow). *Awards, honors:* M.A., Oxford University, 1960.

WRITINGS: (With A. F. Watts and D. A. Pidgeon) *Secondary School Examinations,* Newnes Educational, 1955; (with Pidgeon) *Admission to Grammar Schools,* Newnes Educational, 1957; (editor) *Grouping in Education,* Wiley, 1966; (editor and author of introduction) *Students from Overseas,* Humanities, 1971; (editor) *Current Problems of Teacher Education,* Unipub, 1971; *The Organization of Schooling: A Study of Educational Grouping Practices,* Routledge & Kegan Paul, 1971; *Role of Research in Educational Change,* Pacific Books, 1971. Contributor to education journals.

WORK IN PROGRESS: With D. A. Pidgeon, *An Introduction to Educational Measurement.*

AVOCATIONAL INTERESTS: Theater; sports, especially association football and cricket; travel in Europe.†

* * *

YATES, J. Michael 1938-

PERSONAL: Born April 10, 1938, in Fulton, Mo.; son of Joel Hume (a U.S. Army Air Forces colonel) and Marjorie Dianne (Carmichael) Yates. *Education:* Attended Westminster College, Fulton, Mo.; University of Kansas City (now University of Missouri at Kansas City), B.A., 1960, M.A., 1961; University of Michigan, graduate study. *Politics:* Nihilist. *Religion:* Nihilist. *Home:* 4565 Church St., Delta, British Columbia, Canada. *Office:* Sono Nis Press, Vancouver, British Columbia, Canada.

CAREER: Did free-lance radio and advertising work while attending school; Public Radio Corporation, Houston, Tex., national creative and promotional director, 1961-62; Ohio University, Athens, instructor in comparative literature, 1964-65; University of Alaska, Fairbanks, special lecturer in literature and creative writing, 1965-66; University of British Columbia, Vancouver, writer-in-residence, 1966-71; Sono Nis Press, Vancouver, president, 1971—. Visiting professor of English and writer-in-residence, University of Arkansas, fall, 1972. Member of editorial board, Prism International Press, 1966-71. Has given readings at colleges and universities in Canada and the United States. *Member:* P.E.N., League of Canadian Poets (former member of executive board), Canadian Writer's Union. *Awards, honors:* University of Kansas City (now University of Missouri at Kansas City) poetry prize, 1960; International Broadcasting Award, 1961, 1962; Major Hopwood Award for poetry, 1964, for drama, 1964; Canada Council grants, 1968, 1969, 1971, Arts Award, 1972, 1974-75; *Far Point* (magazine) contributor's prize, 1970.

WRITINGS—Poetry: *Spiral of Mirrors,* Golden Quill, 1967; *Hunt in an Unmapped Interior and Other Poems,* Golden Quill, 1967; *Canticle for Electronic Music,* Morriss, 1967; (with Bob Flick) *Parallax,* Morriss, 1968; *The Great Bear Lake Meditations,* Oberon Press, 1970; *Selected Poems,* Oberon Press, 1972; *Nothing Speaks for the Blue Moraines,* Sono Nis Press, 1973; *Breath of the Snow Leopard,* Sono Nis Press, 1974; *The Qualicum Physics,* Kanchenjunga Press, 1975.

Stage plays: "Subjunction," produced in Fairbanks, December, 1965; *Night Freight* (produced in Toronto, 1972; also see below), Playwrights Co-op, 1972; *Quarks* (three plays), Playwrights Co-op, 1975.

Radio plays: "The Broadcaster," "Theatre of War," "The Calling," "Night Freight," "The Panel," all 1968.

Screenplay: "The Grand Edit," premiered at University of Alaska Fine Arts Festival, April, 1966.

Other; all published by Sono Nis Press: *Man in the Glass Octopus* (short stories), 1968; (editor with Andreas Schroeder, and contributor) *Contemporary Poetry of British Columbia* (anthology), Volume I, 1970; *The Abstract Beast* (fiction and drama), 1971; (editor with Charles Lillard) *Volvex: Poetry from the Unofficial Languages of Canada in English Translation* (anthology), 1971; (editor) *Contemporary Fiction of British Columbia,* 1971; *Exploding* (novel), 1972; *The Grand Master Cranker of Raccoons: New and Selected Fiction,* 1975.

Work represented in many anthologies, including *Stories from Pacific and Arctic Canada,* Macmillan, 1974, and *Mirrors,* Gage, 1975. Contributor of poetry, fiction, translations, philosophical essays, reviews, and short criticism to numerous journals in Canada, United States, Australia, New Zealand, and Europe. *Prism International,* editor-in-chief, 1966-67, poetry editor, 1967-71; with Andreas Schroeder, founder and editor, *Contemporary Literature in Translation,* 1968-74; general editor, *Campus Canada;* founder and member of editorial board, *Canadian Fiction Magazine.*

WORK IN PROGRESS: Two books of poetry, *The Completely Collapsible Portable Man,* for McClelland & Stewart, and *The Self-Conscious Nothing; Mobile Cages,* a book of observations on life and literature; *Beyond Black and White,* a book of poems and photographs.

SIDELIGHTS: J. Michael Yates wrote to *CA:* "Basically

all my writing centers around the polarities between absolute wilderness and absolute technology. Of History: all human records are of wars. Of my nihilism: I create the world in my incessant creation of worlds." Yates has said that there are no rules or codes; history, myth, and scholarship have only closed doors for him, and he finds his poems are more and more surreal without the "ism" suffix. *Spiral of Mirrors*, his first collection, displays a variety of directions, while *Hunt in an Unmapped Interior* shows "a fondness for metaphors of wilderness, ... movement toward nothingness or a psychic center, fluid relations of dream and real worlds, rejection of the human as a concept. . . ."

Yates adds: "Aside from writing, I fish and ride motorcycles. Usually I spend about a month each year in either Alaska, Northern British Columbia, or the Northwest Territories fishing and making notes."

He also translates from several languages, including German, French, Italian, Anglo-Saxon, Old Irish, and Norwegian.

*   *   *

YODER, Glee   1916-

PERSONAL: Born September 15, 1916, in Elkhart, Iowa; daughter of Earl M. (a salesman) and Mary D. (Mathis) Goughnour; married R. Gordon Yoder (a business administrator), August 20, 1939; children: Marcia (Mrs. Dennis Emmert). *Education:* McPherson College, A.B. (cum laude), 1938. *Religion:* Church of the Brethren. *Home:* 6406 East 15th St., Wichita, Kan. 67206.

CAREER: Elementary teacher in Kansas, 1938-39; Church of the Brethren, McPherson, Kan., children's director for Western region, 1948-53; McPherson College, McPherson, teacher of Christian education, 1951-52, 1953-54; Church of the Brethren, McPherson, administrative assistant for Western region, 1953-64, administrative assistant for district of Kansas, 1964-67; free-lance writer, 1965—. Young and Rubicam, survey interviewer in Nampa, Idaho, 1943, and McPherson, 1953. *Member:* National League of Pen Women, Kansas Authors Club.

WRITINGS: The Church and Infants and Toddlers, Brethren Press, in cooperation with Christian Board of Publication and Warner Press, 1966; *Take It from Here: Suggestions for Creative Activities,* Judson Press, 1973; *Take It From Here, Series Two,* Judson Press, 1975.

Church school curriculum courses; all published by Warner Press, except as indicated: *Who Is God?,* Christian Board of Publication, in cooperation with Brethren and Judson Presses, 1969; *The Christian Faces Life,* 1970; *A World-Wide Fellowship,* 1972; *Found for Life,* 1973; *Christian Sign Language,* 1974. Also author of vacation church school curriculum courses, *All That Is within Me* and *Handle with Care.*

WORK IN PROGRESS: Two church school curriculum courses, *The Ten Commandments,* and *Foundation Series.*

*   *   *

YODER, Norman M.   1915-

PERSONAL: Born January 1, 1915, in Cleveland, Ohio; son of Mahlon O. (a guard) and Anna E. (Kitzel) Yoder; married Lois B. Bennett, June 24, 1943; children: Judith Ann. *Education:* Baldwin-Wallace College, A.B., 1938; Ohio State University, M.A., 1939, Ph.D., 1942. *Religion:* Methodist. *Home:* 301 Breezewood Dr., Bay Village, Ohio 44140. *Office:* Cleveland Society for the Blind, 1909 East 101st St., Cleveland, Ohio 44106.

CAREER: Ohio State University, Columbus, instructor, 1940-42; free-lance writer, 1942-43; Cleveland Graphite Bronze Co., Cleveland, Ohio, labor relations, 1943-44; Ohio Division for the Blind, regional supervisor, 1944-55; Pennsylvania State Commission for the Blind, Harrisburg, vocational rehabilitation consultant, 1955-57, acting director, 1957-59, commissioner, 1959-68; Cleveland Society for the Blind, Cleveland, director of program and staff development, 1968-70, associate executive director of rehabilitation services, 1970—. Lecturer at Pennsylvania State University, University of Pittsburgh, and Southern Illinois University. *Member:* American Association of Workers for the Blind (past president), National Council of State Agencies for the Blind (past president).

WRITINGS—With M. K. Bauman: *Placing the Blind and Visually Handicapped in Professional Occupations,* [Philadelphia], 1962; *Adjustment to Blindness Reviewed,* Payne-Thomas, 1966; *Placing the Blind and Visually Handicapped in Clerical, Service, and Industrial Occupations,* [Philadelphia], 1967. Contributor to journals.

*   *   *

YOUNG, David P(ollock)   1936-

PERSONAL: Born December 14, 1936, in Davenport, Iowa; son of Cecil T. (a businessman) and Mary (Pollock) Young; married Chloe Hamilton (a museum curator), June 17, 1963; children: Newell Hamilton, Margaret Helen. *Education:* Carleton College, A.B., 1958; Yale University, M.A., 1959, Ph.D., 1965. *Home:* 220 Shiperd Circle, Oberlin, Ohio. *Office:* Department of English, Rice Hall, Oberlin College, Oberlin, Ohio 44074.

CAREER: Oberlin College, Oberlin, Ohio, instructor, 1961-65, assistant professor, 1965-69, associate professor, 1969-73, professor of English, 1973—. *Member:* Modern Language Association of America, American Association of University Professors. *Awards, honors:* Tane Prize for Poetry of *Massachusetts Review,* 1965; National Endowment for the Humanities fellowship to England, 1967-68; International Poetry Forum award, 1968.

WRITINGS: Something of Great Constancy: The Art of "A Midsummer Night's Dream," Yale University Press, 1966; *Sweating Out the Winter* (poetry), University of Pittsburgh Press, 1969; *The Heart's Forest: Shakespeare's Pastoral Plays,* Yale University Press, 1972; *Boxcars* (poetry), Ecco Press, 1972; (translator) Rainer M. Rilke, *Duino Elezier,* Barn Dream Press, 1975.

WORK IN PROGRESS: A new collection of poems; a study of Yeats and Stevens.

*   *   *

YOUNG, Jordan Marten   1920-

PERSONAL: Born September 25, 1920, in New York, N.Y.; son of Irving L. and Frieda (Shapiro) Young; married Dionir de Souza Gomes, May 10, 1952; children: Jordan Marten. *Education:* University of California, Berkeley, B.A., 1947, M.A., 1948; Princeton University, Ph.D., 1953. *Home:* 159 Meadowbrook Dr., Princeton, N.J. 08540. *Office:* Pace University, Pace Plaza, New York, N.Y. 10038.

CAREER: Princeton University, Princeton, N.J., instructor, 1950-53; Interamericano (investment banking), Rio de Janeiro, Brazil, staff member, 1953-55; Industrias Consolidadas (industrial chemicals), Caracas, Venezuela, general manager, 1955-56; Pace University, New York, N.Y., associate professor, 1956-65, professor of Brazilian, Latin American, and Caribbean affairs, 1965—. *Military service:* U.S. Army, 1944-46; became sergeant. *Member:* American Historical Association, Overseas Press Club, Princeton Club of New York. *Awards, honors:* Doherty Foundation grant for research in Chile, 1948-49; U.S. Office of Education grant for research in Brazil; Fulbright travel grant to Brazil, 1966-67.

WRITINGS: Brazil: The Revolution of 1930 and the Aftermath, Rutgers University Press, 1967; (contributor) B. Burnett and K. Johnson, editors, *Political Forces in Latin America,* Wadsworth, 1968, 2nd edition, 1970; (contributor) H. Keith and S. Edwards, editors, *Conflict and Continuity in Brazilian Society,* University of South Carolina Press, 1969; (editor) *Brazil, 1954-64: End of a Civilian Cycle,* Facts on File, 1972; (author of introduction) L. Sobel, editor, *Chile and Allende,* Facts on File, 1974. Contributor to *Hispanic American Historical Review* and *Journal of Inter American Studies.*

WORK IN PROGRESS: Brazil, 1964-75, for Facts on File.

SIDELIGHTS: Jordan Young speaks fluent Portuguese, "tolerable" Spanish. He has been involved in Brazilian area studies since 1941 when he went to Brazil as an undergraduate.

* * *

YOUNG, Margaret B(uckner) 1922-

PERSONAL: Born March 20, 1922, in Campbellsville, Ky.; daughter of Frank W. and Eva (Carter) Buckner; married Whitney M. Young, Jr. (an executive director of National Urban League), January 2, 1944 (died March 11, 1971); children: Marcia Elaine Boles, Lauren Lee Young Casteel. *Education:* Kentucky State College (now University), B.A., 1942; University of Minnesota, M.A., 1946; Atlanta University, further graduate study, 1958. *Home:* 330 Oxford Rd., New Rochelle, N.Y. 10804.

CAREER: Instructor at Kentucky State College (now University), Frankfort, 1943, and Atlanta University, Atlanta, Ga., 1958; instructor in education and psychology at Spelman College, Atlanta, Ga., 1958-60. Chairman of board, Whitney M. Young, Jr. Memorial Foundation. Appointed alternate representative of U.S. delegation to United Nations, 1973. Member of board of trustees of Xavier University; member of board of directors of Philip Morris, Inc.; member of the board of directors and board of governors, voluntary public service organizations, councils, and committees. Member of National Committee for the Day Care of Children, 1963-66, and New Rochelle Volunteer Bureau, 1963-67. *Member:* Child Study Association of America (member of board of directors, 1962—).

WRITINGS: The First Book of American Negroes, F. Watts, 1966; *The Picture Life of Martin Luther King,* F. Watts, 1968; *The Picture Life of Ralph J. Bunche,* F. Watts, 1968; *Black American Leaders,* F. Watts, 1969; *The Picture Life of Thurgood Marshall,* F. Watts, 1970. Author of a Public Affairs pamphlet, "How to Bring Up Your Child Without Prejudice." Contributing editor, *Ladies Home Journal,* 1975—.

SIDELIGHTS: Margaret Young wrote that she has "had considerable 'exposure' to the needs and problems of race relations.... Interested in writing in an area which contributes to and strengthens the child's interest in and knowledge of the Negro citizen." She described herself as "crit-

ical but in a truth-seeking way. I sometimes bend over backwards trying to be objective and examining all sides of a question. I don't like generalizing about races, religions, or classes of people."

BIOGRAPHICAL/CRITICAL SOURCES: New York Post, August 8, 1965, and "Closeup," April 4, 1967; Lee Bennett Hopkins, *Books Are By People,* Citation Press, 1969.

* * *

YOUNG, Warren R(ichard) 1926-

PERSONAL: Born April 2, 1926, in Neoga, Ill.; son of Orville E. (a teacher and farmer) and Marie (Buchanan) Young; married Ligia Gaitan, April 30, 1955; children: Gregory Warren, Brandon Richard. *Education:* Purdue University, B.S., 1948. *Politics:* Independent. *Religion:* Protestant. *Home:* 39 North Greenwich Rd., Armonk, N.Y. 10504.

CAREER: Life (magazine), New York, N.Y., reporter, 1948-50, assistant editor, 1950-54, science and medicine editor, 1954-59, staff writer, 1959-66; free-lance writer, Armonk, N.Y., 1966—. Consultant to Kurosawa Productions, Inc., for projected film based on his *Life* article, "The Runaway Train." *Military service:* U.S. Army Air Forces, 1944-45. *Member:* National Press Club, Overseas Press Club, Sigma Delta Chi. *Awards, honors:* Grand prize, shared with photographer Howard Sochurek, in Sherman Fairchild International Air Safety Writing Awards, 1962; citations for reportage from American Medical Association and American Association for the Advancement of Science, 1965; Aviation/Space Writers Association Strebie Award for best aviation writing in any medium, 1968, for "Ten Minutes to Love."

WRITINGS: (Editor of American edition) Wolfgang D. Muller, *Man among the Stars,* Criterion, 1957; (contributor) *Great Readings from Life,* Harper, 1960; (with Joseph R. Hixson) *LSD on Campus,* Dell, 1966; (contributor) *The Healthy Life,* Time-Life, 1966; (editor) *To the Moon,* Time-Life, 1969; (contributor) Leo J. Ryan, editor, *USA/ From Where We Stand,* Fearon, 1970. Contributor to *Book of Knowledge Annual,* Grolier, 1966, *Reader's Digest Bedside Reader,* 1970, and *Reader's Digest 50th Anniversary Treasury,* 1972. Major articles have been published in *McCall's, Smithsonian,* and *Reader's Digest.* Founder and editor, *Purdue Scientist,* 1947.

SIDELIGHTS: Warren Young was the subject of a documentary film by Robert Drew Associates while undergoing "Zero-G" experiments; the film was shown on television, including the "Ed Sullivan Show" and "CBS News" and in theater newsreels.

BIOGRAPHICAL/CRITICAL SOURCES: McCall's, March, 1967.

* * *

YOUNG, William H(enry) 1912-

PERSONAL: Born October 7, 1912, in Coraopolis, Pa.; son of Clarence Albert and Jeanette (Way) Young; married Sara Reish, August 23, 1938; children: Diane Young Grant, Jeffrey, Eleanor. *Education:* University of Pittsburgh, A.B., 1933, M.A., 1937; University of Wisconsin, Ph.D., 1941. *Home:* 2125 Van Hise Ave., Madison, Wis. 53705. *Office:* Department of Political Science, University of Wisconsin, Madison, Wis. 53706.

CAREER: University of Pennsylvania, Philadelphia, instructor, 1941-45, assistant professor of political science, 1946-47; University of Wisconsin—Madison, associate professor, 1947-50, professor of political science, 1950—, chairman of department, 1952-59, assistant to chancellor, 1964—. State of Wisconsin, director of Division Department Research, 1949-50, executive secretary to governor, 1950. Consultant, Ford Foundation; member of political science panel for doctorate fellowships, Woodrow Wilson National Foundation, 1963-67. Member of board, Wisconsin Welfare Council, 1954-57, Oscar Rennebohm Foundation, Inc., 1960—, and United Neighborhood Centers of Dane County. *Military service:* U.S. Army, Adjutant General's Corps, 1944-46; became first lieutenant. *Member:* American Political Science Association, American Society for Public Administration. *Awards, honors:* LL.D., University of Pittsburgh, 1962.

WRITINGS: (Reviser) Frederic A. Ogg and R. Orman Ray, *Introduction to American Government,* 11th edition (not associated with earlier editions), Appleton, 1956, 13th edition, 1966, condensed version published as *Essentials of American Government: The National Government,* Appleton, 1961, revised edition published as *Essentials of American National Government,* 1963, 2nd revised edition, 1969; (reviser) Ogg and Ray, *Essentials of American Government,* 8th edition (not associated with earlier editions), Appleton, 1959, 9th edition, 1964; (reviser) Ogg and Ray, *Essentials of American State and Local Government,* 10th edition (not associated with earlier editions), Appleton, 1969.

* * *

YOUNIE, William John 1932-

PERSONAL: Born July 25, 1932, in Boston, Mass.; son of Edward Theodore (a machinist) and Beatrice (Green) Younie; married Anne Marie Ring, September 8, 1956; children: Anne Elizabeth, John William. *Education:* Massachusetts State College at Boston (now University of Massachusetts, Boston), B.S., 1953; Tufts University, Ed.M., 1954; Columbia University, Ed.D., 1959. *Home:* 307 South Dr., Paramus, N.J. 07652. *Office:* William Paterson College, 300 Pompton Rd., Wayne, N.J. 07470.

CAREER: Southbury Training School, Southbury, Conn., director of education, 1959-64; Columbia University, Teachers College, New York, N.Y., associate professor of education, 1964-70; William Paterson College, Wayne, N.J., professor of special education, 1970—. Adjunct associate professor, Fordham University, 1958-67. Consultant, Elwyn Institute, 1965—; president of New York Federation, Council for Exceptional Children, 1966-67. *Member:* American Association on Mental Deficiency, American Personnel and Guidance Association, National Rehabilitation Association, National Association for Retarded Citizens, American Rehabilitation Counseling Association, Phi Delta Kappa.

WRITINGS: Guidelines for Establishing School-Work Study Programs for Educable Mentally Retarded Youth, Virginia State Department of Education, 1966; (contributor) Jerome Hellmuth, editor, *Educational Therapy,* Special Child, 1966; (contributor) I. Ignacy Goldberg, editor, *A Selected Bibliography in Special Education,* Teachers College, Columbia University, 1967; *Instructional Approaches to Slow Learning,* Teachers College, Columbia University, 1967; (with H. Rusalem) *The World of Rehabilitation,* Day, 1971. Contributor to professional journals.

WORK IN PROGRESS: Several items related to the vo-cational education and rehabilitation of the handicapped, including a book on teaching cooking skills and several booklets on basic community skills for the developmentally disabled.

AVOCATIONAL INTERESTS: Furniture design and construction, photography, railroads, and "breweriana."

* * *

ZABIH, Sepehr 1925-

PERSONAL: Born 1925, in Tehran, Persia (now Iran); naturalized American citizen; married Joan Werner (a psychiatric social worker), June 14, 1959; children: Ramin, Leyla. *Education:* London School of Journalism, diploma, 1954; University of California, B.A., 1957, M.A., 1958, Ph.D., 1963. *Office:* Department of Government, St. Mary's College of California, Moraga, Calif. 74575.

CAREER: Writer in western Europe and Middle East for Iranian publications, 1949-51; correspondent in Iran for *Times* and *Daily Mail,* both London, England, 1950-53; St. Mary's College of California, Moraga, assistant professor of government, 1963-64; Oberlin College, Oberlin, Ohio, assistant professor of government, 1964-65; St. Mary's College of California, assistant professor, 1965-68, associate professor of government, 1968—. University of California, Berkeley, research fellow, Department of Political Science, 1964—, lecturer in Extension Division, 1966—, research scholar, Institute of International Studies, 1973—. Summer instructor or lecturer at U.S. Army Language School, 1958, 1959, and University of Colorado, 1963; guest scholar, Brookings Institution, Washington, D.C., 1969. *Member:* American Political Science Association, Middle East Studies Association of North America, Phi Beta Kappa.

WRITINGS: The Communist Movement in Iran, University of California Press, 1966; (with Chubin Shahram) *The Foreign Relations of Iran: A Small State in a Zone of Great-Power Conflict,* University of California Press, 1975. Did translations into Persian of William Gallagher's *Marxism and the Working Class,* 1945, and Lenin's *On Youth,* 1946, both translations published in Tehran.

WORK IN PROGRESS: Nonalignment within an Alliance: The Case of CENTO.†

* * *

ZACHARY, Hugh 1928-
(Ginny Gorman, Zach Hughes, Peter Kanto, Derral Pilgrim, Olivia Rangely, Marcus van Heller, Elizabeth Zachary)

PERSONAL: Born January 12, 1928, in Holdenville, Okla; son of John F. (a builder) and Ida Louise (Duckworth) Zachary; married Elizabeth Wiggs (an artist), June 20, 1948; children: Whitney Leigh (Mrs. Allen Walters), Leslie Beth (Mrs. Horace Collier). *Education:* University of North Carolina, B.A., 1951. *Politics:* Independent; registered Democrat. *Home:* 7 Pebble Beach Dr., Yaupon Beach, N.C. 28461; and Gorlestow-On-Sea, Norfolk, England. *Agent:* Virginia Kidd, Box 278, Milford, Pa. 18337.

CAREER: Announcer-newsman for numerous radio and television stations throughout the United States, 1948-61; full-time writer. Owner of Gallery Six Kitchens and Interiors, selling and installing kitchen cabinets, and providing interior decorating service; co-owner of Island Florist, Yaupon Beach, N.C. *Military service:* U.S. Army, 1946-48. *Awards, honors:* Nebula Award nomination, Science Fiction Writers of America, for *World Where Sex Was*

Born; Southern Book Award, for *The Beachcomber's Handbook of Seafood Cookery.*

WRITINGS—All novels, except as indicated: *One Day in Hell,* Newstand Library, 1961; *A Feast of Fat Things,* Harris-Wolfe, 1968; *The Beachcomber's Handbook of Seafood Cookery* (nonfiction; Book-of-the-Month Club selection), Blair, 1970; *Gwen, In Green,* Fawcett Gold Medal, 1974; *Wild Card Poker* (nonfiction), Stephen Green Press, 1975. Also author of poetry. Contributor of short stories, articles, poems, and essays to magazines, newspapers and journals.

Under pseudonym Ginny Gorman: *Flames of Joy,* Neva, 1967.

Under pseudonym Zach Hughes: *Book of Rack the Healer,* Award Books, 1973; *Legend of Miaree,* Ballantine, 1974; *Seed of the Gods,* Berkley, 1974; *Tide,* Putnam, 1974; *The Stork,* Berkley, 1975; *The St. Francis Effect,* Berkley, 1976; *Tiger In the Stars,* Halequin, 1976. Also author of screenplay "Tide," for American Broadcasting Co., "Movie of the Week."

Under pseudonym Peter Kanto; all published by Brandon House, except as indicated: *A Man Called Sex,* 1965; *Call Me Gay,* 1965; *Two Way Beach Girl,* 1965; *Too Young to Wait,* 1966; *Bedroom Touchdown,* Playtime, 1966; *Beach Wife,* 1966; *One Lonely Summer,* 1966; *License to Prowl,* 1966; *Gold in Her Eyes,* 1966; *Glamour Boy,* 1966; *Color Her Willing,* 1967; *The Love Standard,* 1967; *Matinee in Three Scenes,* 1967; *The Bedroom Beat,* 1967; *Playboy's Lament,* Corinth, 1967; *The Girl With the Action,* 1967; *Tomcat,* 1967; *The Johnson Girls,* 1967; *The Love Boat,* 1967; *Wallins' Wantons,* Corinth, 1967; *Neighborly Lover,* 1967; *Black and White,* Playtime, 1967; *The Girls Upstairs,* Playtime, 1968; *Suddenly, Wonderfully Gay,* 1968; *Moonlighting Wives,* 1968; *The Sullied Virgin,* Man's Magazine, 1968; *Two Beds for Liz,* 1968; *A Small Slice of War,* Caravelle, 1968; *The Snake Room,* United Graphics, 1968; *Angel Baby,* United Graphics, 1968; *Taste of Evil,* Bee-Line, 1969; *First Experiences,* Bee-Line, 1969; *World Where Sex Was Born,* Olympia, 1969; *Nest of Vixens,* Olympia, 1969; *Back Way In,* Oracle, 1969; *Unnatural Urges,* Olympia, 1969.

The Coupling Game, Olympia, 1970; *Twenty Nights in Eros,* Pendulum, 1970; *Rosy Cheeks,* Bee-Line, 1970; *Naked Joy,* Olympia, 1970; *Green Thumb and Silver Tongue,* Olympia, 1970; *Sexpo, Danish Style,* Olympia, 1970; *Rake's Junction,* Lancer, 1970; *On Campus,* Midwood, 1970; *A Dick for all Seasons,* Olympia, 1970; *Das Grofse Sexpiel,* Olympia Press (Germany), 1970; *Der Sexplanet,* Olympia Press, 1971; *Her Husband's Best Friend,* Greenleaf Books, 1971; *The Sex Experiment at Diddle U.,* Bee-Line, 1971; *Super Sex Stars,* Bee-Line, 1971; *Doing It With Daughter,* Bee-Line, 1972; *Lustful Nights,* Bee-Line, 1972; *Girl In Revolt,* Greenleaf Classics, 1972; *Lay-A-Day,* Bee-Line, 1972; *Try Me!,* Bee-Line, 1973; *Make the Bride Blush,* Bee-Line, 1973. Contributor of short stories to magazines.

Under pseudonym Derral Pilgrim: *Lolila,* Novel Books, 1964; *Lust Addict,* Playtime, 1965; *Battalion Broads,* Playtime, 1965. Contributor of short stories and articles to magazines.

Under pseudonym Olivia Rangely: *The Bashful Lesbian,* Brandon House, 1965.

Under pseudonym Marcus van Heller: *Das Drachennest,* Olympia Press, 1970.

Under pseudonym Elizabeth Zachary; Gothic novels: *The Competition for Alan,* Lancer Books, 1971; *The Legend of the Deadly Doll,* Award Books, 1973.

WORK IN PROGRESS: Writings based on his experiences as a mate on a tugboat working the North Sea oil fields.

SIDELIGHTS: Hugh Zachary told *CA* that he finally "gathered enough courage to leave the time clock and try writing. In the first year I sold $400 worth of writing and doubled it the next year. I bought an old boat and started commercial fishing to supplement my massive writing earnings and began to gather material which appears in almost every book I write. *Tide* . . . could not have been written without my days of spending my time on the ocean trying to catch enough fish to make a house payment."

He also commented: "I'm primarily a fiction writer and I write as I read, eager to see what happens next. I feel that it is the writer's first duty to entertain, to tell a story. I've been called a regional writer simply because my people usually function in a small town setting and because Southport, scene of many of my books, is a picture-book, old-fashioned Southern town with interesting pecularities," *Avocational interests:* Collecting stamps, hunting treasure, boats, and fishing.

*   *   *

ZAGORIA, Donald S. 1928-

PERSONAL: Born August 24, 1928, in Somerville, N.J. *Education:* Rutgers University, B.A., 1948; Columbia University, M.A., 1950, Ph.D., 1963. *Address:* Box 436, Crugers, N.Y. 10521. *Office:* Department of Political Science, Hunter College of the City University of New York, 695 Park Ave., New York, N.Y. 10021.

CAREER: U.S. Government, analyst of Russian and Chinese politics, 1951-61; RAND Corp., member of Social Science Division, 1961-63; Hunter College of the City University of New York, New York, N.Y., associate professor, 1963-67, professor of government, 1967—. Adjunct professor of government, Columbia University, 1963-67; guest lecturer at Army War College and National War College. Chairman of Rural Development Panel, Southeast Asia Development Advisory group (SEADAG), 1973-75. Fellow, Research Institute on International Change, Columbia University. Consultant to Institute of Defense Analyses. *Member:* Council on Foreign Relations, National Committee on U.S.-China Relations. *Awards, honors:* Rockefeller Foundation grant for research in Asia, 1963-64; grant for research in India from Social Science Research Council and Columbia University, 1965; Guggenheim Foundation grant for research in India, 1967-68; Ford Foundation faculty fellowship in political science for study of the sources of peasant radicalism in Asia, 1971-72; Rockefeller Foundation grant for research of the "Four Powers" and the "Two Koreas," 1975-76.

WRITINGS: The Sino-Soviet Conflict, 1956-61, Princeton University Press, 1962, paperback edition with new introduction, Atheneum, 1964; *Vietnam Triangle: Moscow/Peking/Hanoi and the War in Vietnam,* Pegasus, 1968.

Contributor: Laquer and Labedz, editors, *The Future of Communist Society,* Praeger, 1962; *Contemporary Civilization,* Scott, Foresman, 1967; Richard Lowenthal, editor, *Issues of the Future of Asia,* Praeger, 1968; *China in Crisis,* Chicago University Press, 1969; John Lewis, editor, *Peasant Rebellion and Communist Revolution in Asia,*

Stanford University Press, 1974; Charles Gati, editor, *Caging the Bear,* Bobbs-Merrill, 1974; William Barnds, editor, *The Two Koreas in East Asian Affairs,* New York University Press, 1976. Contributor of numerous articles to newspapers, magazines, and professional journals. *Comparative Politics,* member of editorial committee, editor of special issue, April, 1976.

SIDELIGHTS: The Sino-Soviet Conflict, 1956-61, has been translated into Japanese, German, Portuguese, and French.

*   *   *

ZAHNISER, Marvin R(alph)   1934-

PERSONAL: Born June 29, 1934, in New Kensington, Pa.; son of Clarence H. (a professor) and Fannie (Weir) Zahniser; married Adrienne Allen, August 28, 1956; children: Mark Howard, Keith Allen, Craig Alexander. *Education:* Greenville College, A.B., 1956; University of Michigan, M.A., 1957; University of California, Santa Barbara, Ph.D., 1963. *Politics:* Independent. *Religion:* Protestant. *Home:* 1788 Coventry Rd., Columbus, Ohio 43212. *Office:* History Department, Ohio State University, Columbus, Ohio 43210.

CAREER: High school teacher, Oak Lawn, Ill., 1959-60; visiting assistant professor of history at University of Washington, Seattle, 1963-64, and University of Iowa, Iowa City, 1964-65; Ohio State University, Columbus, assistant professor, 1965-67, associate professor, 1967-73, professor of history and chairman of department, 1973—. *Member:* American Historical Association, American Association of University Professors, Organization of American Historians, South Carolina Historical Society, Ohio Academy of History, Alpha Kappa Sigma. *Awards, honors:* Mershon Foundation fellowship, 1965-66.

WRITINGS: Charles Cotesworth Pinckney: Founding Father, University of North Carolina Press, for Institute of Early American History and Culture at Williamsburg, 1967; *Uncertain Friendship: American-French Diplomatic Relations through the Cold War,* Wiley, 1975. Contributor to historical journals.

WORK IN PROGRESS: American Diplomatic Missions That Failed, completion expected in 1978.

AVOCATIONAL INTERESTS: Playing piano, athletics, group singing.

*   *   *

ZAMOYTA, Vincent C.   1921-

PERSONAL: Born December 13, 1921, in Brooklyn, N.Y.; son of Stanislaus William (a machinist) and Apolonia (Lipowski) Zamoyta; married Carolyn Jane Moore, January 15, 1966; children: Ruth Apolonia. *Education:* Catholic University of America, B.A., 1944, Ph.D., 1956; Fordham University, M.A. (philosophy), 1952; St. John's University, Jamaica, N.Y., M.A. (theology), 1962; Seton Hall University, M.A. (education), 1964. *Religion:* Roman Catholic. *Home:* 2 Clearbrook Dr., Smithtown, N.Y. 11787. *Office:* Department of Theology, St. John's University, Jamaica, N.Y.

CAREER: High school teacher of Latin and English, 1944-54; Catholic University of America, Washington, D.C., instructor in philosophy, 1954-62; Seton Hall University, South Orange, N.J., assistant professor of theology, 1962-66; St. John's University, Jamaica, N.Y., associate professor of theology, 1966—. Teacher of religious education,

Notre Dame Pontifical Institute, summers, 1975, 1976. *Member:* National Council of Catholic Men, College Theology Society, Catholic Interracial Council.

WRITINGS: (Compiler) *The Theology of Christ: Sources,* Bruce Publishing, 1967; (contributor) *To Be a Man,* Prentice-Hall, 1969. Contributor to *Catholic World, Catholic Layman.* Member of editorial advisory committee, *Tablet,* 1969—.

WORK IN PROGRESS: A Catholic Bible for Laymen.

*   *   *

ZARNOWITZ, Victor   1919-

PERSONAL: Born November 3, 1919, in Lancut, Poland; naturalized U.S. citizen; son of Leopold (a teacher) and Bertha (Blumenfeld) Zarnowitz; married Lena Engelman, January 12, 1946; children: Steven L., Arthur H. *Education:* University of Cracow, student, 1937-39; University of Heidelberg, A.M., 1949, Ph.D. (summa cum laude), 1951. *Home:* 5752 South Blackstone Ave., Chicago, Ill. 60637. *Office:* Graduate School of Business, University of Chicago, Chicago, Ill. 60637.

CAREER: Tutor, later instructor in economics at University of Heidelberg, Heidelberg, Germany, and University of Mannheim, Graduate School of Business, Mannheim, Germany, 1949-51; National Bureau of Economic Research, Inc., New York, N.Y., member of research staff, 1951-63, director of study of short-term economic forecasting, beginning 1963, senior research staff, 1969—; University of Chicago, Graduate School of Business, Chicago, Ill., associate professor, 1959-64, professor of economics and finance, 1965—. Columbia University, lecturer, 1956-57, 1958-59, visiting professor of economics, 1957-58. U.S. Department of Commerce, director of research project, 1972-75, consultant to Bureau of Economic Analysis, 1976—. *Member:* American Economic Association, American Statistical Association, Econometric Society, Centre for International Research on Economic Tendency Surveys, Chicago Association of Commerce and Industry. *Awards, honors:* Social Science Research Council postdoctoral research fellowship at Harvard University, 1953-54; Ford Foundation faculty research fellowship, 1963-64.

WRITINGS: Die Theorie des Einkommensverteilung (title means "The Theory of Income Distribution"), J. C. B. Mohr, 1951; (contributor) G. H. Moore, editor, *Business Cycle Indicators,* National Bureau of Economic Research, 1961; *Unfilled Orders, Price Changes, and Business Fluctuations,* National Bureau of Economic Research, 1962; *An Appraisal of Short-Term Economic Forecasts,* Columbia University Press for National Bureau of Economic Research, 1967; (editor and co-author) *The Business Cycle Today,* National Bureau of Economic Research, 1972; (contributor) Bert A. Hickman, editor, *Econometric Models of Cyclical Behavior,* National Bureau of Economic Research, 1972; *Orders, Production, and Investment: A Cyclical Behavior,* National Bureau of Economic Research, 1973. Contributor to *International Encyclopedia of Social Sciences,* Macmillan, 1968. Co-editor of *Economic Prospects,* 1971-73, and *Economic Outlook USA,* 1974—. Contributor to professional journals.

WORK IN PROGRESS: A study of cyclical indicators; evaluation of forecasts based on econometric models; international economic indicators.

SIDELIGHTS: Victor Zarnowitz is competent in Russian, and has reading knowledge of French and Hebrew. *Avoca-*

tional interests: Literature, music, travel (Europe and Asia).

* * *

ZAWADSKY, Patience 1927-
(Patience Hartman; Becky Lynne, a pseudonym)

PERSONAL: Surname is pronounced Za-*wad*-sky; born March 30, 1927, in Trenton, N.J.; daughter of William C. and Mabel (Leicht) Hartman; married John P. Zawadsky (chairman of philosophy department at Wisconsin State University-Stevens Point), September 8, 1948; children: John, Paul, Rebecca, Elizabeth. *Education:* Douglass College, Rutgers University, B.A., 1948. *Politics:* Democrat. *Religion:* Catholic. *Home:* 3900 Jordan Lane, Stevens Point, Wis. 54481.

CAREER: WTNJ, Trenton, N.J., writer, producer, and actor for radio series, "Teen-Age," 1943-44; Harvard University, Cambridge, Mass., research assistant and secretary, 1949-51; self-employed editor and researcher, Cambridge, 1951-54; Kilmer Job Corps, Edison, N.J., writing consultant, 1966; Wisconsin State University-Stevens Point, lecturer in English, 1967-72. Free-lance writer for magazines. *Member:* American Association of University Women, Phi Beta Kappa.

WRITINGS: (Co-author) *Datebook of Popularity*, Prentice-Hall, 1960; (co-author) *Are These the Wonderful Years?*, Abbey Press, 1965; *The Mystery of the Old Musket* (juvenile), Putnam, 1968; *Welcome to Longfellow*, Transition, 1969; *Stand-In for Murder*, Transition Publications, 1969; *Demon of Raven's Cliff*, Belmont-Tower, 1971; *The Man in the Long Black Cape*, Scholastic Book Services, 1972; *How Much Is That in Rubles*, University of Wisconsin-Stevens Point, 1973. Also author of radio play, "Christmas Fantasy," 1944.

Musicals: "Heavens to Bacchus," first produced at Douglass College, Rutgers University, 1945; "Navy Blues," first produced at Douglass College, Rutgers University, 1946; "Rest Upon the Wind," first produced at Douglass College, Rutgers University, 1948; "Hey, Mr. Time," first produced by University of Florida Sandspurs, 1949; "Goldilocks and the Three Bears: A Moral Musical," produced, 1973; "The Princess and the Frog," produced 1974; "The Bunny with the Lopsided Ear," produced, 1975.

Contributor of about forty articles and stories to *Teen* under pseudonym Becky Lynne; contributor to *Datebook* under maiden name, Patience Hartman; also contributor of articles and short stories to ten other teen and juvenile magazines. In the adult field, has published verse in *Saturday Evening Post, Life Today, Empire,* and *Laugh Book,* and articles in *Coronet, Discovery, Personal Romances, Chatelaine, Family Digest, Ford Times, Ladies Home Journal,* and a number of other magazines.

* * *

ZEIGERMAN, Gerald 1939-
(Ziggy Gerald)

PERSONAL: Born May 31, 1939, in Philadelphia, Pa.; son of Joseph H. (a physician) and Molly (Blecher) Zeigerman. *Education:* Attended Goddard College, 1957-58, and University of Pennsylvania, 1959-60. *Religion:* Judaism. *Residence:* Philadelphia, Pa. *Agent:* Robert Lescher, 155 East 71st St., New York, N.Y. 10021.

CAREER: Writer. *Awards, honors:* Fellowship to Bread Loaf Writers' Conference, 1967, and to MacDowell Colony, 1968.

WRITINGS: A Rightful Inheritance (novel), Atheneum, 1967. Author of column, under pseudonym Ziggy Gerald, "The TV Watch," in *Film Bulletin* (motion picture trade journal), 1959-60. Contributor of short stories to *Transatlantic Review, Swank, Story,* and *Mademoiselle;* also contributor to *Writer* and *Center City Philadelphian.*

WORK IN PROGRESS: A novel.

* * *

ZEITLIN, Irving M. 1928-

PERSONAL: Born October 19, 1928, in Detroit, Mich.; son of Albert and Rose Zeitlin; married Esther Ann Levine (an artist), August 15, 1950; children: Ruth, Michael, Beth, Jeremy. *Education:* Wayne State University, B.A., 1958, M.A., 1961; Princeton University, M.A., 1963, Ph.D., 1964. *Home:* 439 Sumach St., Toronto, Ontario, Canada. *Office:* Department of Sociology, University of Toronto, Toronto, Ontario, Canada M5S 1A1.

CAREER: Indiana University, Bloomington, assistant professor, 1965-68, associate professor of sociology, 1968-70; Washington University, St. Louis, Mo., professor of sociology, 1970-72, chairman of department, 1971-72; University of Toronto, Toronto, Ontario, professor of sociology and chairman of department, 1972—. *Member:* American Sociological Association, American Association of University Professors. *Awards, honors:* National Science Foundation postdoctoral fellow, 1964-65.

WRITINGS: Marxism: A Re-Examination, Van Nostrand, 1967; *Ideology and the Development of Sociological Theory,* Prentice-Hall, 1968; *Liberty, Equality, and Revolution in Alexis de Tocqueville,* Little, Brown, 1971; *Capitalism and Imperialism: An Introduction to Neo-Marxian Concepts,* Markham, 1972; *Rethinking Sociology: A Critique of Contemporary Theory,* Prentice-Hall, 1973. Contributor of *Journal of World History, Cahiers de l'Isea,* and other journals.

* * *

ZELAZNY, Roger 1937-

PERSONAL: Born May 13, 1937, in Cleveland, Ohio; son of Joseph Frank and Josephine (Sweet) Zelazny; married Judith Callahan, August 20, 1966; children: Devin Joseph. *Education:* Western Reserve University (now Case Western Reserve University), B.A., 1959; Columbia University, M.A., 1962. *Residence:* Santa Fe, New Mexico. *Agent:* Henry Morrison, Inc., 58 West 10th St., New York, N.Y. 10011.

CAREER: U.S. Social Security Administration, claims representative in Cleveland, Ohio, 1962-65, social insurance specialist in Baltimore, Md., 1965-69; currently full-time writer. Speaker and lecturer at many colleges, universities, and writing workshops and conferences. *Military service:* U.S. Army Reserve, 1960-66. *Member:* Science Fiction Writers of America (secretary-treasurer, 1967-68), Authors Guild, Authors League of America. *Awards, honors:* Science Fiction Writers of America Nebula Awards, 1965, for best novella, "He Who Shapes," and best novelette, "The Doors of His Face, the Lamps of His Mouth"; Science Fiction Achievement Award, 1966, for *. . . And Call Me Conrad,* and 1968, for *Lord of Light;* Prix Apollo, 1972, for the French edition of *Isle of the Dead.*

WRITINGS: This Immortal, Ace Books, 1966; *The Dream Master,* Ace Books, 1966; *Four for Tomorrow,* Ace Books, 1967; *Lord of Light,* Doubleday, 1967; (editor)

Nebula Award Stories 3, Doubleday, 1968; *Isle of the Dead*, Ace Books, 1969; *Damnation Alley*, Putnam, 1969; *Creatures of Light and Darkness*, Doubleday, 1969; *Nine Princes in Amber*, Doubleday, 1970; *The Doors of His Face, The Lamps of His Mouth, and Other Stories*, Doubleday, 1971; *Jack of Shadows*, Walker & Co., 1971; *The Guns of Avalon*, Doubleday, 1972; *Today We Choose Faces*, Signet, 1973; *To Die in Italbar*, Doubleday, 1973; *Sign of the Unicorn*, Doubleday, 1975; *Doorways in the Sand*, Harper, 1976; *My Name is Legion*, Ballantine, 1976; *The Hand of Oberon*, Doubleday, 1976. Contributor of more than seventy short stories and articles to science fiction periodicals, including *Amazing Stories, Analog, Galaxy*, and *Worlds of Tomorrow*.

WORK IN PROGRESS: With Philip K. Dick, *Deus Irae*, for Doubleday; *Bridge of Ashes*, for Signet.

SIDELIGHTS: Zelazny did his graduate studies in the area of Elizabethan and Jacobean drama, which, he says, "probably influenced my writing considerably, both thematically and stylistically. Read French and German. Am interested in general science, Oriental culture, poetry, oceanography, religion, dramatic literature, arms and armaments." His work has been published in nine languages, including Greek, Hebrew, and Japanese. The Roger Zelazny Manuscript Collection was established at Syracuse University Library in 1966.

BIOGRAPHICAL/CRITICAL SOURCES: Baltimore Sun, January 29, 1967; *Algol*, Volume XIII, 1968; *Extrapolation: A Journal of Science Fiction and Fantasy*, December, 1973.

*   *   *

ZELLER, Frederick A. 1931-

PERSONAL: Born October 18, 1931, in Perham, Minn.; son of F. A. and Cecille (Lucking) Zeller; married Amy Doyle, June 10, 1954. *Education:* University of North Dakota, B.Sc., 1955, M.A., 1956; Ohio State University, Ph.D., 1963. *Religion:* Roman Catholic. *Home address:* Box 60B, Route 6, Morgantown, W.Va. *Office:* Office of Research and Development, West Virginia University, Morgantown, W.Va. 26506.

CAREER: Ohio State University, Columbus, assistant professor of economics, 1959-65; West Virginia University, Morgantown, 1965—, began as associate professor of economics, currently associate research professor, director of Institute for Labor Studies, 1965-67, director of Office of Research and Development, 1967-71. *Military service:* U.S. Army, Infantry, 1956-58; became first lieutenant. *Member:* American Economics Association, Rural Sociological Society, Industrial Relations Research Association, Elks, Knights of Columbus.

WRITINGS: Fundamentals of Economics, College of Commerce and Administration, Ohio State University, 1964; (with R. Miller and G. Miller) *The Practice of Local Union Leadership*, Ohio State University Press, 1965; (editor with R. Miller) *Manpower Development in Appalachia: An Approach to Unemployment*, Praeger, 1968; *Strengthening Labor's Role in the War on Poverty*, West Virginia University Center for Appalachian Studies and Development, 1968; (with F. Stottlemyer) *Mountain State in Perspective*, Department of Commerce (West Virginia), 1968; (with others) *Manpower Development and Job Training in Appalachian States*, West Virginia University, 1972; (with others) *Approaches to University Extension Work with the Disadvantaged*, West Virginia University,

1972. Also author of other reports on Appalachia published by West Virginia University; author of booklets on careers for U.S. Department of Labor. Contributor of articles to journals.

WORK IN PROGRESS: Utilization of Scientific and Technical Manpower in Coal Mining; Organizational Mobility: Preparation for In-tra Organizational Movement; The General Theory of Economic Production and Addiction to Work.

*   *   *

ZIEL, Ron 1939-

PERSONAL: Born July 17, 1939, in New York, N.Y.; son of Roland Wolfgang (a chemist) and Edith (Kegel) Ziel. *Education:* Pratt Institute, B.F.A., 1961. *Politics:* Conservative Republican. *Religion:* Protestant. *Home address:* Box 433, Montauk Hwy., Bridgehampton, N.Y. 11932.

CAREER: MEA Associates, New York, N.Y., assistant art director, 1963-66; Dan's Papers (publisher), Bridgehampton, N.Y., art director and executive editor, 1967—. Vice-president of public relations, Royal Hudson Co., 1969—. *Military service:* U.S. Army, Signal Corps, 1961-62; became second lieutenant. *Member:* National Railway Historical Society (president, Long Island chapter, 1965-69).

WRITINGS: The Twilight of Steam Locomotives, Grosset, 1963, revised edition, 1970; *The Story of Steamtown and Edaville*, F. Nelson Blout, 1965; *Steel Rails to the Sunrise*, Hawthorn, 1965; (with George H. Foster) *Steam in the Sixties*, Meredith, 1967; (with Foster) *Steel Rails to Victory*, Hawthorn, 1970; (with Michael Eagleson) *Twilight of World Steam*, Grosset, 1973. Also co-author of *Southern Steam Specials*, 1970.

WORK IN PROGRESS: A photo-volume of streamlined steam locomotives; another photo-volume on camelback locomotives, in collaboration with Michael A. Eagleson.

SIDELIGHTS: In the process of pursuing the vanishing steam locomotive, Ziel has traveled in forty-seven states and forty-four countries since 1961. He "deeply regrets not having lived in the era of Lucius Beebe, with whom I carried on extensive correspondence in the years just prior to his death."

BIOGRAPHICAL/CRITICAL SOURCES: Railroad Magazine, June, 1966.

*   *   *

ZIMMER, Paul J. 1934-

PERSONAL: Born September 18, 1934, in Canton, Ohio; son of Jerome F. (a shoe salesman) and Louise (Surmont) Zimmer; married Suzanne Kohlauner, April 4, 1959; children: Erik Jerome, Justine Mary. *Education:* Attended Kent State University, 1952-53, 1956-59. *Politics:* Democrat. *Religion:* None. *Home:* 5515 Hobart St., Pittsburgh, Pa. 15217. *Office:* University of Pittsburgh Press, Pittsburgh, Pa. 15213.

CAREER: Macy's Department Store, San Francisco, Calif., manager of book departments, 1961-63; San Francisco News Co., San Francisco, manager, 1963-64; University of California, Los Angeles, manager of bookstore, 1964-66; University of Pittsburgh Press, Pittsburgh, Pa., assistant director, 1967—. Poet-in-residence, Chico State College (now California State University, Chico), 1970. *Military service:* U.S. Army, 1954-55. *Awards, honors:*

Borestone Mountain Award, 1971; National Endowment for the Arts fellowship, 1974-75.

WRITINGS: The Ribs of Death (poems), October House, 1967; *The Republic of Many Voices* (poems), October House, 1969. Editor, "Pitt Poetry" series, 1967—.

WORK IN PROGRESS: The Zimmer Poems; Earthbound, a book of poems; a novel, *The Commissioner of Paper Sports.*

*   *   *

ZINBARG, Edward D(onald) 1934-

PERSONAL: Born October 24, 1934, in New York, N.Y.; son of Harry and Esther (Cohen) Zinbarg; married Barbara L. Scheffres, December 20, 1956; children: Elizabeth, Allison. *Education:* City College (now City College of the City University of New York), B.B.A., 1954; University of Pennsylvania, M.B.A., 1955; New York University, Ph.D., 1959. *Politics:* Independent. *Religion:* Jewish. *Home:* 5 Hardwell Rd., Shorthills, N.J. 07078. *Office:* Prudential Insurance Co., Newark, N.J. 07101.

CAREER: Fitch Investment Service, security analyst, 1955-56; Morgan Guaranty Trust Co., New York City, assistant to economist, 1956-59; Prudential Insurance Co. of America, Newark, N.J., vice-president, 1960—. Adjunct professor of finance, City College of the City University of New York, New York City, 1958-74. *Member:* American Finance Association, New York Society of Security Analysts, Beta Gamma Sigma.

WRITINGS: (With Jerome B. Cohen and Arthur Zeikel) *Investment Analysis and Portfolio Management,* Irwin, 1967, 3rd edition, in press. Contributor to financial journals.

*   *   *

ZITTA, Victor 1926-

PERSONAL: Born November 5, 1926, in Titel, Yugoslavia; son of Victor (a civil servant) and Clara (Paraker) Zitta; married Dorothea Mateja (a student of languages), April 24, 1954; children: Yvonne, Victor, Peter. *Education:* Studied at Pazmany University, Budapest, Hungary, 1946-47, and University of Salzburg, Salzburg, Austria, 1947-49; Assumption College, Windsor, Ontario, B.A., 1953; University of Michigan, M.A., 1956, Ph.D., 1962. *Politics:* Republican. *Religion:* Jewish. *Home:* 4102 Jefferson St., Hyattsville, Md.

CAREER: Gonzaga University, Spokane, Wash., assistant professor of political science, 1958-60; University of Michigan, Ann Arbor, research assistant at Law School, 1960-61; DePauw University, Greencastle, Ind., visiting lecturer, 1961; Marquette University, Milwaukee, Wis., assistant professor of political science, 1961-65; Hollins College, Roanoke, Va., associate professor of political science, 1965; University of Maryland, College Park, associate professor of political science, 1966-68. Vice-president, Progressive Conservative Association, Windsor, Ontario, 1953-54. *Member:* American Political Science Association, American Association of University Professors, Phi Kappa Phi, Pi Sigma Alpha.

WRITINGS: Georg Lukacs' Marxism: Alienation, Dialectics, Revolution, Nijhoff, 1964, Humanities, 1965. Also author of introduction to a translation of Georg Lukacs' *Revolution and Revelation,* 1975. Editor with J. Dunner, *Dictionary of Political Science* and *Handbook of Historical Concepts.*

WORK IN PROGRESS: Second volume of *Georg Lukacs' Marxism.*

*   *   *

ZOBEL, Hiller B(ellin) 1932-

PERSONAL: Born February 23, 1932; son of Hiller (a chemist) and Harriet (Bellin) Zobel; married Rya W. Featherston, November 23, 1973; children (previous marriage): John H., David H., Elizabeth T., Sarah B. *Education:* Harvard University, A.B., 1953, LL.B., 1959; Oxford University, graduate study, 1956. *Politics:* Democrat. *Religion:* Jewish. *Home:* 294 Jerusaleum Rd., Cohasset, Mass. 02025. *Office:* Boston College Law School, Boston, Mass. 02135.

CAREER: Bingham, Dana & Gould (attorneys), Boston, Mass., associate, 1959-67; Harvard University Law School, Cambridge, Mass., research associate, 1962-63; Boston College Law School, Boston, associate professor of law, 1967—. Partner, Brown, Rudnick, Freed & Gesmer (attorneys), 1972—. *Military service:* U.S. Naval Reserve, active duty, 1953-55. *Member:* Maritime Law Association of the United States, American Antiquarian Society, Society of American Historians, Massachusetts Bar Association, Massachusetts Historical Society, Colonial Society of Massachusetts. *Awards, honors:* Recipient with L. Kinvin Wroth of Littleton-Griswold Prize of American Historical Association, 1966, for *Legal Papers of John Adams.*

WRITINGS: (Editor with L. Kinvin Wroth) *Legal Papers of John Adams,* three volumes, Belknap Press, 1965; *The Boston Massacre,* Norton, 1970. Contributor to law journals.

WORK IN PROGRESS: Admiralty.

*   *   *

ZODHIATES, Spiros 1922-

PERSONAL: Born March 13, 1922, in Cyprus; son of George and Mary (Toutazou) Zodhiates; married Joan Wassell; children: Priscilla, Lois Ann, Philip, Mary Clare. *Education:* Studied in Cairo, Egypt, at Abet School, 1936-41, and American University in Cairo, student, 1941-43, 1945-46; National Bible Institute (now Shelton College), B.Th., 1947; New York University, M.A., 1951. *Politics:* Republican. *Religion:* Baptist. *Home:* 18 Grand Ave., Ridgefield Park, N.J. 07660. *Office:* American Mission to Greeks International, 801 Broad Ave., Ridgefield, N.J. 07657.

CAREER: American Mission to Greeks International (non-profit religious and charitable organization), Ridgefield, N.J., field representative and general secretary, 1946-65, president, 1965—. Broadcasts weekly on "New Testament Light" and daily on "A Look at the Book" radio programs aired in the United States and Canada in both Greek and English; also broadcasts weekly over Radio Ceylon. *Military service:* British Army, 1943-45; served in Middle East. *Awards, honors:* Gold Medal of Greek Red Cross.

WRITINGS: Behavior of Belief, Eerdmans, 1960, 3rd edition, 1966; *Pursuit of Happiness,* Eerdmans, 1966; *Was Christ God?,* Eerdmans, 1966; *To Love is to Live,* Eerdmans, 1967. Author of more than one hundred Bible-study booklets, published by American Mission to Greeks International and its Greek publishing house, O Logos, Athens. Sunday sermons syndicated in 150 Greek newspapers and magazines around the world. Has edited a guide to Modern

Greek pronunciation, and tape-recorded the entire Koine New Testament in Modern Greek pronunciation. Editor-in-chief, *Voice of the Gospel* (magazine), Athens, and *Pulpit Helps* (newspaper).

* * *

ZOLBERG, Aristide R(odolphe) 1931-

PERSONAL: Born June 14, 1931, in Brussels, Belgium; came to United States in 1948, naturalized in 1954; *Education:* Columbia University, A.B., 1953; Boston University, M.A., 1956; University of Chicago, Ph.D., 1961. *Home:* 5726 South Kenwood Ave., Chicago, Ill. 60637. *Office:* Department of Political Science, University of Chicago, Chicago, Ill. 60637.

CAREER: Northwestern University, Evanston, Ill., lecturer in political science, Evening Division, 1961; University of Wisconsin—Madison, assistant professor of political science, 1961-63; University of Chicago, Chicago, Ill., assistant professor, 1963-66, associate professor, 1966-69, professor of political science, 1969—, chairman of department, 1969-72. Visiting professor, Princeton University, 1972-73. Member, Institute for Advanced Study, 1972-73. *Military service:* U.S. Army, 1954-55. *Member:* American Political Science Association, African Studies Association (fellow).

WRITINGS: (Contributor) Helen Kitchen, editor, *The Educated African,* Praeger, 1962; *One Party Government in the Ivory Coast,* Princeton University Press, 1964, revised edition, 1969; (contributor) James S. Coleman and Carl G. Rosberg, Jr., editors, *Political Parties and National Integration in Tropical Africa,* University of California, 1964; (contributor) Rosberg and William H. Friedland, editors, *African Socialism,* Stanford University Press, 1964; *Creating Political Order: The Party-States of West Africa,* Rand McNally, 1966; (contributor) Harry Johnson, editor, *Economic Nationalism in Old and New States,* University of Chicago Press, 1967; (co-editor) *Ghana and the Ivory Coast: Patterns of Modernization,* University of Chicago Press, 1971. Contributor to *Encyclopedia Americana Yearbook,* 1966, 1967, and to professional journals.

* * *

ZOLBROD, Paul G(eyer) 1932-

PERSONAL: Born December 10, 1932, in Pittsburgh, Pa.; son of Herman (a laborer) and Caroline (Engler) Zolbrod. *Education:* University of Pittsburgh, A.B., 1958, M.A., 1964, Ph.D., 1967; graduate study at University of Caen, France, 1958-59, and Brown University, 1959-60. *Politics:* Democrat. *Religion:* Jewish. *Home address:* RD 2, Meadville, Pa. 16335. *Office:* Department of English, Allegheny College, Meadville, Pa. 16335.

CAREER: Driver-salesman for cleaning firm, Pittsburgh, Pa., 1952-53; University of Pittsburgh, instructor in English at Titusville Campus, 1963-64; Allegheny College, Meadville, Pa., associate professor of English, 1964—. Visiting postdoctoral fellow, University of New Mexico, 1971-72. Democratic committeeman, Meadville, Pa. *Military service:* U.S. Army, 1953-55; served in Japan. *Member:* Modern Language Association of America, American Association of University Professors, Phi Beta Kappa. *Awards, honors:* Fulbright fellow at University of Caen, 1958-59.

WRITINGS: (Editor with C. G. Katope) *Beyond Berkeley,* World Publishing, 1966; (with Katope) *The Rhetoric of Revolution,* Macmillan, 1968; (editor with R. C. Tobias) *Shakespeare's Late Plays: Essays in Honor of Charles Crow,* Ohio University Press, 1975. Contributor of essays, articles, and reviews to journals, magazines, and newspapers.

WORK IN PROGRESS: Compiling an English translation of *The Navaho Creation Story;* assembling an oral history of phases of life among the Allegany Senecas.

SIDELIGHTS: Paul Zolbrod speaks French and Navaho, and reads Greek, Old English, and German. *Avocational interests:* Mountain climbing, studying the past, American Indian poetry and culture, and cabinet making.

* * *

ZOTOS, Stephanos

PERSONAL: Born in Constantinople, Turkey, of Greek parentage; son of Xenophon and Julie (Stavros) Zotos; married Chryssoula Theodoratoy; children: Paul. *Education:* Educated in Greece and France. *Religion:* Greek Orthodox. *Home:* 3 Naramanlaki St., Athens, Greece.

CAREER: Embros (daily newspaper), Athens, Greece, foreign editor, 1944-49, and accredited war correspondent during civil war in Greece, 1946-49; foreign correspondent covering United Nations and United States for newspapers and radio stations in Greece, France, and Belgium, 1949-62; *National Herald,* New York City, managing editor, 1955-57; *Helenic Review,* New York City, managing editor, 1959-61; Royal Greek Embassy, Washington, D.C., director of press and information service, 1962-63; Greek Orthodox Church of North and South America, New York City, director of press and information service, beginning 1968. Has been radio commentator and lecturer on world affairs in United States. *Military service:* Greek Army, liaison work with British forces, 1940-41. *Member:* Guild of Greek Journalists, United Nations Correspondents Association (secretary, 1958). *Awards, honors:* Palms of French Academy for *To Taxeidi Sti Gallia.*

WRITINGS: *To Taxeidi Sti Gallia* (title means "The Voyage to France"), Dimitratos (Athens), 1946; *Kynigondas Skies* (short stories; title means "Chasing Shadows"), Dimitratos, 1947; *To Karavani Tis Lypis* (title means "The Caravan of Despair"), Embros (Athens), 1948; *Greece: The Struggle for Freedom,* Crowell, 1967; *The Greeks: The Dilemma of Past and Present,* Funk, 1969. Also author of *H Ameriki Enantion the Amerikis* (title means "America Versus America"). Contributor of articles on a variety of topics to English, French, and Greek magazines and newspapers.

SIDELIGHTS: Stephanos Zotos writes and speaks fluently in French and is competent in German. *Avocational interests:* Bridge (Olympic world champion, 1937-38), tennis (former member of Greek national team).

* * *

ZUBRZYCKI, Jerzy (George) 1920-

PERSONAL: Surname is pronounced Zu-*bry*-ski; born January 12, 1920, in Cracow, Poland; son of Joseph Felix (a geologist) and Zofia (Madeyska) Zubrzycki; married Alexandra Krolikowska, October 23, 1943; children: Thomas, Anna, John, Joanna. *Education:* London School of Economics and Political Science, B.Sc.Econ., 1948, M.Sc.Econ., 1951; Free Polish University Abroad, London, England, Ph.D., 1955. *Religion:* Catholic. *Home:* 68 Schlich St., Canberra, Australian Capital Territory, Australia 2600. *Office:* Australian National University, Canberra, Australian Capital Territory, Australia 2600.

CAREER: British Foreign Office, London, England, principal research officer, 1952-55; Australian National University, Canberra, Australian Capital Territory, fellow in department of demography, 1955-62, professorial fellow in sociology, Institute of Advanced Studies, 1962-70, professor of sociology and head of department, 1970—. Visiting lecturer, University of Texas, 1962; visiting professor, Brown University, 1968-69; visiting research professor, Carleton University, 1973-74. Member of panel of foreign affairs commentators, Australian Broadcasting Commission, 1956—. Fellow, Academy of Social Science in Australia, 1967—. Commonwealth Immigration Advisory Council, member, and chairman of Committee on Social Patterns, 1971-74. *Military service:* British Army, Special Operations, 1940-45; received Order of the British Empire (military). *Member:* International Union for the Scientific Study of Population, American Sociological Association, International Sociological Association (council member, 1966—).

WRITINGS: Polish Immigrants in Britain: A Study of Adjustment, Nijhoff, 1956; *Immigrants in Australia: A Demographic Survey Based upon the 1954 Census,* and *Statistical Supplement,* Melbourne University Press, 1960; *Settlers of the Latrobe Valley: A Sociological Study of Immigrants in the Brown Coal Industry of Australia,* Australian National University Press, 1964; (with Miriam Gilson) *The Foreign-Language Press in Australia: 1848-1964,* Australian National University Press, 1967; (editor) *The Teaching of Sociology in Australia and New Zealand,* F. W. Cheshire, 1970.

Contributor: Brinley Thomas, editor, *The Economics of International Migration,* Macmillan, 1958; L. Henry and W. Winkler, editors, *International Population Conference, Vienna 1959,* International Union for the Scientific Study of Population, 1959; W. D. Borrie and others, editors, *The Cultural Integration of Immigrants,* UNESCO, 1959; *Atlas of Australian Resources,* Department of National Development (Canberra), 1960; C. A. Price, editor, *The Study of Immigrants in Australia,* Australian National University Press, 1960; Allan Stoller, editor, *New Faces,* F. W. Cheshire, 1966. Contributor to professional journals in Europe and Australia. Editor, *Australian and New Zealand Journal of Sociology,* 1964-70.

WORK IN PROGRESS: Research on ethnic minorities and social class in Australia.

155388

Ref. - v.21-24 - Rev.